The **Rough Guide** to

China

written and researched by

David Leffman, Simon Lewis, Mark South and Martin Zatko

www.roughguides.com

Contents

Chinese architecture colour section following p.312

Chinese cuisine colour section following p.600

Chinese festivals colour section following p.792

◀◀ Signs along Nanjing Lu, Shanghai ◀ Yao woman in rice terraces, Guangxi

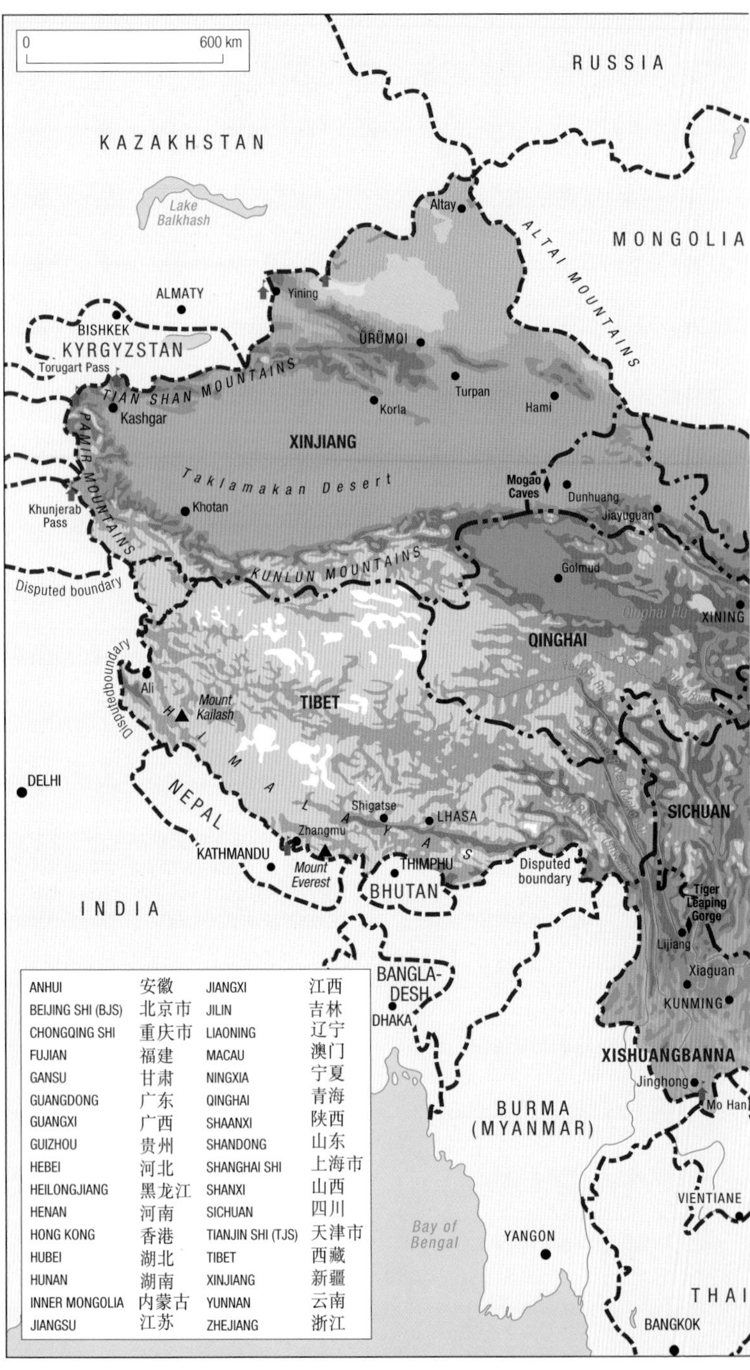

ANHUI	安徽	JIANGXI	江西
BEIJING SHI (BJS)	北京市	JILIN	吉林
CHONGQING SHI	重庆市	LIAONING	辽宁
FUJIAN	福建	MACAU	澳门
GANSU	甘肃	NINGXIA	宁夏
GUANGDONG	广东	QINGHAI	青海
GUANGXI	广西	SHAANXI	陕西
GUIZHOU	贵州	SHANDONG	山东
HEBEI	河北	SHANGHAI SHI	上海市
HEILONGJIANG	黑龙江	SHANXI	山西
HENAN	河南	SICHUAN	四川
HONG KONG	香港	TIANJIN SHI (TJS)	天津市
HUBEI	湖北	TIBET	西藏
HUNAN	湖南	XINJIANG	新疆
INNER MONGOLIA	内蒙古	YUNNAN	云南
JIANGSU	江苏	ZHEJIANG	浙江

N
Lake Baikal
Irkutsk
Ulan Ude
Heihe
Amur River
Manzhouli
Yichun
Qiqihar
HEILONGJIANG
HARBIN
ULAN BATOR
CHANGCHUN
Jilin
Gobi Desert
INNER MONGOLIA
JILIN
Erlianhot
Changbai Shan Nature Reserve
SHENYANG
Jinzhou
LIAONING
NORTH KOREA
SEA OF JAPAN
HEBEI
Chengde
Dandong
Hohhot
Great Wall
Yellow River
BJS
PYONGYANG
Datong
BEIJING
Tangshan
Dalian
Wutai Shan
TJS
TIANJIN
Bay of Bohai
SEOUL
YINCHUAN
TAIYUAN
Yantai
SHIJIAZHUANG
SOUTH KOREA
NINGXIA
SHANXI
Tai Shan
JI'NAN
LANZHOU
Yan'an
Qingdao
YELLOW SEA
SHANDONG
Yuncheng
Anyang
Terracotta Army
GANSU
ZHENGZHOU
JIANGSU
XI'AN
Kaifeng
Xuzhou
Hongze Hu
Jiuzhaigou Scenic Reserve
SHAANXI
Song Shan
JAPAN
Tai Hu
Huai River
HENAN
Songpan
NANJING
Wudang Shan
Xiangfan
HEFEI
PACIFIC OCEAN
Suzhou
SHANGHAI
Wolong Panda Reserve
CHONGQING SHI
HUBEI
ANHUI
Huang Shan
SHANGHAI SHI
Three Gorges Dam
WUHAN
HANGZHOU
Ningbo
CHENGDU
Emei Shan
CHONGQING
Poyang Hu
ZHEJIANG
Leshan
Jingdezhen
Yangzi River
Wulingyuan Scenic Reserve
EAST CHINA SEA
Dongting Hu
NANCHANG
Fanjing Shan
HUNAN
JIANGXI
FUJIAN
CHANGSHA
GUIZHOU
Heng Shan
FUZHOU
GUIYANG
TAIPEI
Guilin
Ganzhou
Liuzhou
Xiamen
Meizhou
Li River
Hong Shui River
TAIWAN
GUANGDONG
YUNNAN
NANNING
GUANGZHOU
Wuzhou
GUANGXI
Zhuhai
Shenzhen
Hekou
Youyi Guan
HONG KONG
MACAU
Beihai
HANOI
SOUTH CHINA SEA
HAIKOU
HAINAN
Wuzhi Shan
LAOS
Sanya
VIETNAM
PHILIPPINES
LAND
MANILA
metres
6000
5000
4000
3000
2000
1000
500
200
0

Introduction to China

You can't ignore China: more than a country, it's a civilization, and one that has continuously recycled itself, not much perturbed by outsiders, for three millenia. Its script reached perfection in the Han dynasty, two thousand years ago, and those stone lions standing sentinel outside sleek new skyscrapers are built to a three-thousand-year-old design. Yet this ancient culture is now undergoing the fastest creative and commercial upheaval the world has ever seen, with Hong Kong-style skylines rearing up across the country. This dizzying modernisation is visible in every aspect of Chinese life, and it is the tension and contrast between wrenching change and continuity that makes modern China such an endlessly fascinating destination.

The first thing that strikes visitors to the country is the extraordinary density of its population. In central and eastern China, villages, towns and cities seem to sprawl endlessly into one another along the grey arteries of busy expressways. These are the Han Chinese heartlands, a world of chopsticks, tea, slippers, grey skies, shadow-boxing, teeming crowds, chaotic train stations, smoky temples, red flags and the smells of soot and frying tofu.

Move west or north away from the major cities, however, and the population thins out as it begins to vary: indeed, large areas of the People's Republic are inhabited not by the "Chinese", but by scores of distinct ethnic minorities, ranging from animist hill tribes to urban Muslims.

▶ Hanging incense spirals, Hong Kong

Here, the landscape begins to dominate: green paddy fields and misty hilltops in the southwest, the scorched, epic vistas of the old Silk Road in the northwest, and the magisterial mountains of Tibet.

While travel around the country itself is the easiest it has ever been, it would be wrong to pretend that it is an entirely simple matter to penetrate modern China. The main tourist highlights – the Great Wall, the Forbidden City, the Terracotta Army and the Yangzi gorges – are relatively few considering the vast size of the country, and much of China's historic architecture has been deliberately destroyed in the rush to modernize. Added to this are the frustrations of travelling in a land where few people speak English, the writing system is alien and foreigners are sometimes viewed as exotic objects of intense curiosity – though overall you'll find that the Chinese, despite a reputation for curtness, are generally hospitable and friendly.

Fact file

- With an **area** of 9.6 million square kilometres, China is the fourth largest country in the world and the most populous nation on earth, with around 1.3 billion people. Of these, 92% are of the **Han** ethnic group, with the remainder comprising about sixty minorities such as Mongols, Uyghurs and Tibetans.
- The main **religions** are Buddhism, Taoism and Christianity, though the country is officially atheist.
- China's longest river is the **Yangzi** (6275km) and the highest peak is **Qomolongma** – Mount Everest (8850m) – on the Nepalese border.
- The **Chinese Communist Party** is the sole political organization, and is divided into Executive, Legislative and Judicial branches. The chief of state (President) and the head of government (Premier) are elected for five-year terms at the National People's Congress.
- After decades of state planning, the **economy** is now mixed, with nationally-owned enterprises on the decline and free-market principles ubiquitous.

Where to go

As China has opened up in recent years, so the emphasis on tourism has changed. Many well-known cities and sights have become so developed that their charm has vanished, while in remoter regions – particularly Tibet, Yunnan and the northwest – previously restricted or "undiscovered" places have become newly accessible. The following outline is a selection of both "classic" China sights and less-known attractions, which should come in handy when planning a schedule.

Inevitably, **Beijing** is on everyone's itinerary, and the Great Wall and the splendour of the Forbidden City are certainly not to be missed; the capital also offers some of the country's best food and nightlife. **Chengde**, too, just north of Beijing, has some stunning imperial buildings, constructed by emperors when this was their favoured retreat for the summer.

South of the capital, the **Yellow River valley** is the cradle of Chinese civilization, where remnants of the dynastic age lie scattered in a unique landscape of loess terraces. The cave temples at **Datong** and **Luoyang** are magnificent, with huge Buddhist sculptures staring out impassively across their now industrialized settings. Of the historic capitals, **Xi'an** is the most obvious destination, where the celebrated Terracotta Army still stands guard over the tomb of Emperor Qin Shi Huang. Other ancient towns include sleepy **Kaifeng** in Henan and **Qufu**, the birthplace of Confucius, in Shandong, both offering architectural treasures and an intimate, human scale that's missing in the large cities. The area is also well supplied with holy mountains, providing both beautiful scenery and a rare continuity with the past: **Tai Shan** is perhaps the grandest and most imperial of the country's pilgrimage sites; **Song Shan** in Henan sees followers of the contemporary kung-fu craze making the trek to the Shaolin Si, where the art originated;

▲ Beijing nightlife in Sanlitun

▲ Lijiang "Old Town", Yunnan

and **Wutai Shan** in Shanxi features some of the best-preserved religious sites in the country.

Dominating China's east coast near the mouth of the Yangzi, **Shanghai** is the mainland's most Westernized city, a booming port where the Art Deco monuments of the old European-built Bund – the riverside business centre – rub shoulders with a hyper-modern metropolis, crowned with two of the world's tallest skyscrapers. It's interesting to contrast Shanghai's cityscape with that of rival business hub **Hong Kong**, off China's south coast. With its colonial heritage and refreshingly cosmopolitan outlook, there's almost

Wildlife

Although China's varied geography and climate have created a wealth of wildlife habitats, the country's vast human population has put pressure on the environment, bringing some high-profile creatures to the edge of extinction. Most famous of these is the giant panda, which survives in pockets of high-altitude bamboo forest across the southwest. A few Siberian tigers haunt the northeastern highlands, while the critically endangered South China tiger numbers just thirty wild individuals. Less well-known rarities include the snub-nosed golden monkey, white-headed langur and Chinese alligator, all of which are possible – with a lot of luck – to see in the wild. Birdlife can be prolific, with freshwater lakes along the Yangzi and in western Guizhou, along with the vast saline Qinghai Lake, providing winter refuge for hosts of migratory wildfowl – including rare Siberian and black-necked cranes.

Emei Shan, Sichuan

nothing Hong Kong cannot offer in the way of tourist facilities, from fine beaches to great eating, drinking and nightlife. Nearby **Macau** is also worth a visit, if not for its casinos then for its Baroque churches and Portuguese cuisine.

In the southwest of the country, Sichuan's **Chengdu** and Yunnan's **Kunming** remain two of China's most interesting and easy-going provincial capitals, and the entire region is, by any standards, exceptionally diverse, with landscapes encompassing everything from snowbound summits and alpine lakes to steamy tropical jungles. The karst (limestone peak) scenery is particularly renowned, especially along the Li River between **Yangshuo** and **Guilin** in Guangxi. In Sichuan, pilgrims flock to see the colossal Great Buddha at **Leshan**, and to ascend the holy mountain of **Emei Shan**; to the east, the city of **Chongqing** marks the start of river trips down the **Yangzi**, Asia's longest river, through the **Three Gorges**. As Yunnan and Guangxi share borders with Vietnam, Laos and Burma, while Sichuan rubs up against Tibet, it's not surprising to find that the region is home to near-extinct wildlife and dozens of ethnic autonomous regions. The attractions of the latter range from the traditional Bai town of **Dali**, the Naxi town of **Lijiang** and the Dai villages of **Xishuangbanna** in Yunnan, to the Khampa heartlands of

Long-horned Miao girls in Sugoa, Guizhou

western Sichuan, the exuberant festivals and textiles of Guizhou's Miao and the wooden architecture of Dong settlements in Guangxi's north.

The huge area of China referred to as the Northwest is where the people thin out and real wilderness begins. Inner Mongolia, just hours from Beijing, is already at the frontiers of Central Asia; here you can follow in the footsteps of Genghis Khan by going horseriding on the endless grasslands of the steppe. To the south and west, the old **Silk Road** heads out of Xi'an right to and through China's western borders, via **Jiayuguan**, terminus of the Great Wall of China, and the lavish Buddhist cave art in the sandy deserts of **Dunhuang**.

West of here lie the mountains and deserts of vast Xinjiang, where China blends into old Turkestan and where simple journeys between towns become modern travel epics. The oasis cities of **Turpan** and **Kashgar**, with their bazaars and Muslim heritage, are the main attractions, though the blue waters of **Tian Chi**, offering alpine scenery in the midst of searing desert, are deservedly popular. Beyond Kashgar, travellers face some of the most adventurous routes of all, over the Khunjerab and Torugut passes to Pakistan and Kyrgyzstan respectively.

Tibet remains an exotic destination, especially if you come across the border from Nepal or brave the long road in from Golmud in Qinghai province. Despite fifty years of Chinese rule, coupled with a mass migration of Han Chinese into the region, the manifestations of Tibetan culture remain intact

Martial Arts

Thousands of martial arts have evolved in China, usually in isolated communities that had to defend themselves, such as Daoist temples and clan villages. All, though, can be classed into two basic types: external, or hard, styles concentrate on building up physical strength to overpower opponents; the trickier but perhaps ultimately more effective, internal, or soft, styles concentrate on developing and focusing the internal energy known as *qi*. Both styles use forms – prearranged sets of movements – to develop the necessary speed, power and timing; as well as kicks, punches and open palm strikes they also incorporate movements inspired by animals.

The most famous external style is Shaolin kung fu, developed in the Shaolin Temple in Henan Province (see p.281) and known for powerful kicks and animal styles – notably eagle, mantis and monkey. The classic Shaolin weapon is the staff and there's even a drunken form, where the practitoner sways and lurches as if inebriated.

But the style that you're most likely to see – it's practised in the open air all over the country – is the internal tai ji quan. The body is held in a state of minimal tension to create the art's characteristic "soft" appearance. Its emphasis on slow movements and increasing *qi* flow means it is excellent for health, and it's a popular workout for the elderly.

▲ Lijiang resident and horse

– the Potala Palace in **Lhasa**, red-robed monks, lines of pilgrims turning prayer wheels, butter sculptures and gory frescoes decorating monastery halls. And Tibet's mountain scenery, which includes **Mount Everest**, is worth the trip in itself, even if opportunities for independent travel are more restricted than elsewhere in China.

When to go

China's **climate** is extremely diverse. The **south** is subtropical, with wet, humid summers (April–Sept), when temperatures can approach 40°C, and a typhoon season on the southeast coast between July and September. Though it is often still hot enough to swim in the sea in December, the short winters (Jan–March), can be surprisingly chilly.

Central China, around Shanghai and the Yangzi River, has brief, cold winters, with temperatures dipping below zero, and long, hot, humid summers. It's no surprise that three Yangzi cities – Chongqing, Wuhan and Nanjing – are proverbially referred to as China's three "furnaces". Rainfall here is high all year round. Farther north, the **Yellow River basin** marks a rough boundary beyond which central heating is fitted as standard in buildings, helping to make the region's harsh winters a little more tolerable. Winter temperatures in Beijing rarely rise above freezing from December to

Chinese script

Chinese characters are simplified images of what they represent, and their origins as pictograms can often still be seen, even though they have become highly abstract today. The earliest-known examples of Chinese writing are predictions that were cut into "oracle bones" over three thousand years ago during the Shang dynasty, though the characters must have been in use long before as these inscriptions already amount to a highly complex writing system. As the characters represent concepts, not sounds, written Chinese cuts through the problem of communication in a country with many different dialects. However, learning characters is a never-ending job – though you only need to recognize a couple of thousand for everyday use. Foreigners learning Mandarin use the modern **pinyin** transliteration system of accented Roman letters – used throughout this book – to help memorize the sounds. For more on language, see p.995.

March, and biting winds off the Mongolian plains add a vicious wind-chill factor. In summer, however, temperatures here can be well over 30°C. In **Inner Mongolia** and **Manchuria**, winters are at least clear and dry, but temperatures remain way below zero, while summers can be uncomfortably warm. **Xinjiang** gets fiercely hot in summer, though without the humidity of the rest of the country, and winters are as bitter as anywhere else in

◀ Potala Palace, Tibet

Urban pollution

A reliance on coal for power and heating, factories spewing untreated waste into the atmosphere, growing numbers of vehicles, and the sheer density of the urban population all conspire to make Chinese cities some of the most **polluted** on earth. Black sludge fills canals and streams; buildings are mired by soot; blue sky is only a memory; the population seem permanently stricken with bronchitis; and acid rain withers plants. In summer, the worst spots are the Yangzi valley "furnaces" of Nanjing, Chongqing and Wuhan; winter in Xi'an, on the other hand, features black snow.

northern China. **Tibet** is ideal in midsummer, when its mountain plateaus are pleasantly warm and dry; in winter, however, temperatures in the capital, Lhasa, frequently fall below freezing.

Overall, the **best time to visit** China is **spring** or **autumn**, when the weather is at its most temperate. In the spring, it's best to start in the south and work north or west as summer approaches; in the autumn, start in the north and work south.

Average temperatures and rainfall

	Jan	Feb	Mar	Apr	May	Jun	Jul	Aug	Sep	Oct	Nov	Dec
Beijing												
Max/min (°C)	1/-10	4/-8	11/-1	21/7	27/13	31/18	31/21	30/20	26/14	20/6	9/-2	3/-8
Max/min (°F)	34/14	39/18	52/30	70/45	81/55	88/64	88/70	86/68	79/57	68/43	48/28	37/18
rainfall (mm)	4	5	8	17	35	78	243	141	58	16	11	3
Chongqing												
Max/min (°C)	9/5	13/7	18/11	23/16	27/19	29/22	34/24	35/25	28/22	22/16	16/12	3/-8
Max/min (°F)	48/41	55/45	64/52	73/61	81/66	84/72	93/75	95/77	82/72	72/61	61/54	37/18
rainfall (mm)	15	20	38	99	142	180	142	122	150	112	48	20
Hong Kong												
Max/min (°C)	18/13	17/13	19/16	24/19	28/23	29/26	31/26	31/26	29/25	27/23	23/18	20/15
Max/min (°F)	64/55	63/55	66/61	75/66	82/73	84/79	88/79	88/79	84/77	81/73	73/64	68/59
rainfall (mm)	33	46	74	137	292	394	381	367	257	114	43	31
Kunming												
Max/min (°C)	20/8	22/9	25/12	28/16	29/18	29/19	28/19	28/19	28/18	24/15	22/12	20/8
Max/min (°F)	68/46	72/48	77/54	82/61	84/64	84/66	82/66	82/66	82/64	75/59	72/54	68/46
rainfall (mm)	8	18	28	41	127	132	196	198	97	51	56	15
Shanghai												
Max/min (°C)	8/1	8/1	13/4	19/10	25/15	28/19	32/23	32/23	28/19	23/14	17/7	12/2
Max/min (°F)	46/34	46/34	55/39	66/50	77/59	82/66	90/73	90/73	82/66	73/57	63/45	54/36
rainfall (mm)	48	58	84	94	94	180	147	142	130	71	51	36

things not to miss

It's not possible to see everything that China has to offer in one trip – and we don't suggest you try. What follows, in no particular order, is a selective taste of the country's highlights: stunning scenery, distinctive cuisine, exuberant festivals and monumental architecture. They're arranged in five colour-coded categories, which you can browse through to find the very best things to see and experience. All highlights have a page reference to take you straight into the guide, where you can find out more.

01 **Li River scenery** Page **642** • Take a boat trip here to admire the weird, contorted peaks of the sort you'll see on Chinese scroll paintings.

02 Birdwatching, Cao Hai Page **678** • Being punted around this shallow lake in search of rare birdlife is a wonderfully restful experience.

03 Mount Everest Page **937** • The sight of the mountain towering above ensures you won't regret the long journey up to Base Camp.

04 The Terracotta Army Page **265** • Near the old capital of Xi'an, these 2200-year-old, life-size soldiers guard the tomb of China's first emperor.

05 Jiayuguan fort Page **837** • A famously lonely outpost overlooking the desert at the western tail of the Great Wall.

06 Sisters' Meal festival Page **673** • Join tens of thousands of locals in Taijiang, Guizhou, as they participate in this annual three-day showcase of ethnic Miao culture.

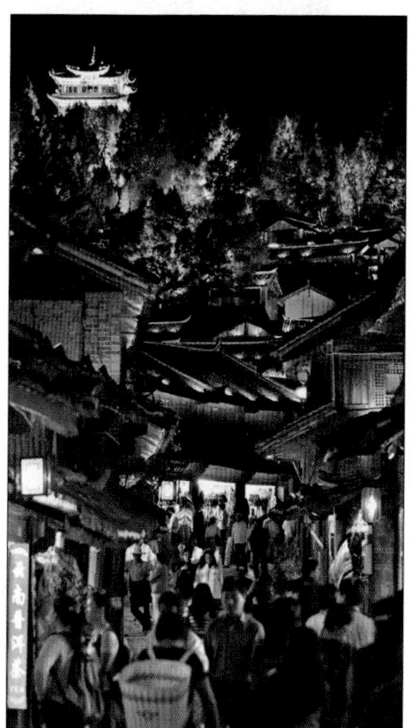

07 Lijiang Page **707** • This ancient Naxi town has been dolled up by the tourist industry into an attractive fairground of cobbled lanes, rustic wooden houses and gurgling streams.

08 The Silk Road Page **806** • Abandoned cities such as Jiaohe hint at the former importance of this ancient trading route.

09 The Yellow River Page **205** • Redistributing billions of tons of soil annually along its 5500km-long flow, this turbulent river is also known as "China's Sorrow" for causing devastating floods.

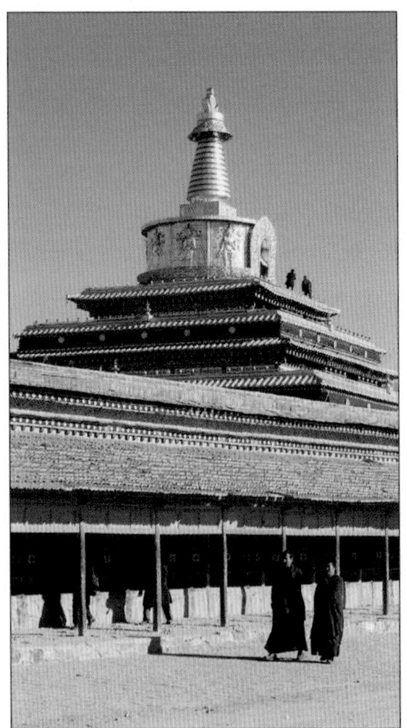

10 Labrang Monastery, Xiahe Page **823** • One of the most important Tibetan Buddhist monasteries, a riot of lavishly decorated halls, butter sculptures and ragged pilgrims.

11 The Jokhang, Lhasa Page **909** • Stuffed with gorgeous statuary and perpetually wreathed in juniper smoke and incense, this is the holiest temple in Tibet.

12 Beijing duck Page **116** • A northern Chinese culinary speciality and absolutely delicious – crisp skin and juicy meat eaten in a pancake.

13 Harbin Ice Festival Page **196** • "Lurid" and "outrageous" don't begin to describe the bizarre sculptures here – everything from life-size ice castles to fantastical snowy tableaux.

14 Confucius Temple Page **310** • This lavish complex in Confucius's home town of Qufu shows the esteem in which China's great sage was held.

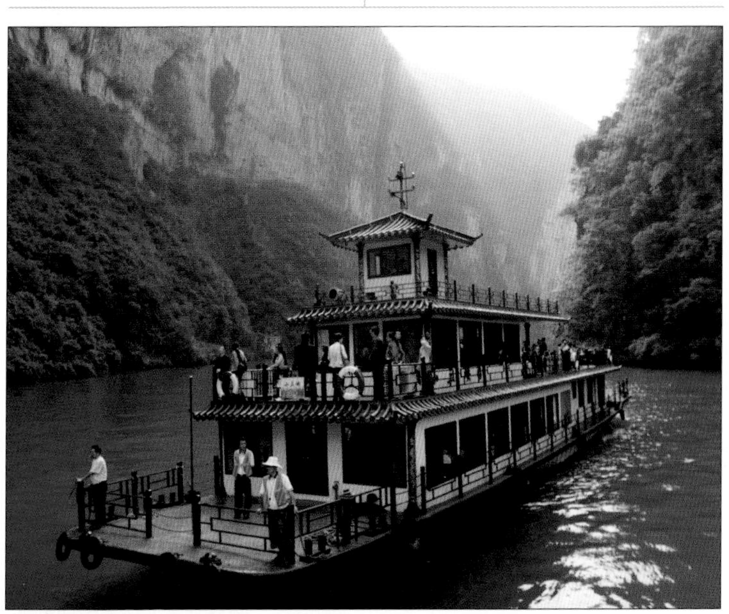

15 A cruise down the Yangzi River Page **784** • Enjoy awesome scenery and a wealth of historic sights along this famed river and its offshoots, such as the Three Little Gorges.

16 The Great Wall Page **132** • Once the division between civilizations, this monumental barrier is still awe-inspiring.

17 Changbai Shan Nature Reserve Page **189** • Well worth a visit – though you'd have to be exceptionally lucky to spot its rare Siberian tigers.

18 Dim sum Page **520** • The classic Cantonese breakfast; there's no better place to try it than Guangzhou.

19 **Chengde** Page **158** • The emperors' former retreat from the heat of summer holds a string of pretty temples.

20 **The Great Buddha (Dafo), Leshan** Page **767** • You'll feel a mere speck as you gaze up at the world's largest carved Buddha.

21 Sichuanese teahouses Page **755** • Relaxed places to gossip, read or socialize for the price of a cup of tea.

22 Meili Xue Shan Page **723** • A wilderness area that offers great hiking, superlative views and a glimpse of the Tibetan world.

23 The Forbidden City Page **94** • Once the centre of the Chinese imperial universe and off limits to the hoi polloi, the emperor's impressive palace complex in Beijing is now open to all.

24 Mogao Caves Page **842** • These thousand-year-old man-made caves on the old Silk Road contain China's most impressive Buddhist heritage.

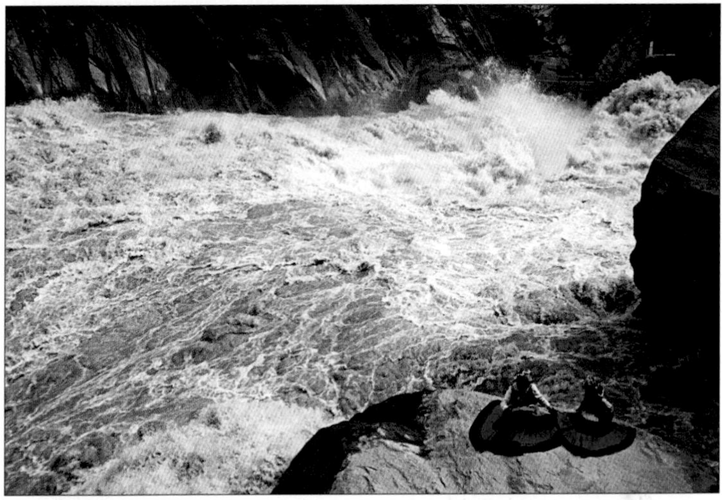

25 Tiger Leaping Gorge Page **717** • One of China's great hikes, along a ridge above a dramatic gorge, with attractive homestays along the way.

26 Hong Kong's skyline Page **592** & **597** • The drive of generations of the former colony's inhabitants is writ large in this electrifying cityscape.

27 Kashgar's Sunday market Page **874** • Crowds from all over Central Asia descend to trade livestock, carpets, knives and clothes at this weekly event, which continues to provide Kashgar's most tantalizing proof of its history as a major stop on the Silk Road.

28 Minority villages, Yunnan Page **696** • Bordering Laos, Burma and Vietnam, Yunnan is home to a range of ethnic groups with very different cultures and lifestyles.

29 The Hanging Temple, Datong Page **236** • Not for the faint-hearted: this rickety wooden temple, housing shrines to China's three main faiths, is suspended on a cliff-face by flimsy-looking scaffolding.

30 Tai Shan Page **301** • The taxing ascent of this holy peak in Shandong is rewarded with some immaculate temples and pavilions.

31 The Bund, Shanghai Page **376** • An elegant parade of colonial architecture, nestling incongruously at the heart of Shanghai's gaudy modernity.

Basics

Basics

Getting there

China's most important long-haul international gateways are Beijing, Hong Kong, Guangzhou and Shanghai, though many other Chinese cities are served by international flights, operated mainly by airlines based in East Asia. There are also well-established overland routes into China – including road and rail links from its Southeast Asian neighbours, as well as the alluring Trans-Siberian Express from Moscow.

Fares to Hong Kong are at their highest during the fortnight before Christmas, the fortnight before Chinese New Year (see p.51) and from mid-June to early October. The cheapest time to fly there is in February (after Chinese New Year), May and November. For Beijing and Shanghai, peak season is generally in the summer. Flying on weekends is slightly more expensive; price ranges quoted below assume midweek travel.

Flights from the UK and Ireland

You can fly **direct** to China from London Heathrow with Air China, Virgin Atlantic, British Airways, China Eastern and Cathay Pacific to either Beijing (10hr), Hong Kong (12hr) or Shanghai (11hr). Other airlines flying via a change of planes in a hub city include Aeroflot, Air France, KLM, Singapore, Swiss and Thai. Flying to China from other UK airports or from the Republic of Ireland involves either catching a connecting flight to London or flying via the airline's hub city.

From the UK, the lowest available **fares** to Beijing or Shanghai start from around £400 in low season, rising to £800 in high season; flights to Hong Kong are slightly cheaper. Less popular airlines such as Air China and Aeroflot offer competitive fares, while British Airways often run special offers or promotions.

Flights from the US and Canada

From North America, there are more flights to **Hong Kong** than to other Chinese destinations, though there's no shortage of flights to Beijing and Shanghai and there are some direct services to Guangzhou. Airlines flying **direct** include Air Canada, Air China, Cathay Pacific, United and China Eastern. You can also choose to fly to a Chinese provincial city – Chinese, Japanese, Korean and Hong Kong airlines offer services to cities throughout China via their respective hubs. It takes around thirteen hours' **flying time** to reach Beijing from the West Coast; add seven hours or more to this if you start from the East Coast (including a stopover on the West Coast en route). New routes over the North Pole shave off a couple of hours flying time; so far, that's Air Canada's Toronto, Air China's New York, United's Chicago and Continental's Newark flights to Beijing.

Round-trip fares to Hong Kong, Beijing and Shanghai are broadly comparable: in low season, expect to pay US$900–1300/CAN$917–1325 from the West Coast (Los Angeles, San Francisco, Vancouver), or US$1100–1400/CAN$1120–1426 from the East Coast (New York, Montréal, Toronto). To get a good fare during high season it's important to buy your ticket as early as possible, in which case you probably won't pay more than US$250/CAN$255 above what you would have paid in low season.

Flights from Australia, New Zealand and South Africa

The closest entry point into China from Australia and New Zealand is Hong Kong, though from Australia it's also possible to fly direct to Guangzhou, Shanghai and Beijing. It's not a problem to fly elsewhere in China from either country if you catch a connecting flight along the way, though this can involve a long layover in the airline's hub city.

From eastern Australia, some of the cheapest fares to Hong Kong (Aus$800–1050) are with Cathay Pacific, China Airlines, EVA Airlines or Singapore Airlines; to Shanghai (Aus$1000–1200) with Royal Brunei, Singapore or Japan Airlines (JAL); to Guangzhou (Aus$1050–1200) with Singapore, Malaysia Airlines, JAL and Air China; and to Beijing (Aus$1000–1200) with Singapore, JAL, Malaysia or China Eastern. Cathay, Qantas, Air China and China Eastern fly direct; other trips require a stopover in the airline's hub city. **From Perth**, fares to the above destinations are Aus$100 or so more expensive.

Flights **from New Zealand** are limited; the only direct flights are the Air New Zealand routes from Auckland to Shanghai and Hong Kong, which cost around NZ$1600–2000, and the Air Singapore, Air New Zealand, and Malaysia Airlines flight to Hong Kong (around NZ$1800).

From South Africa, South African Airlines have direct flights to Hong Kong (14hr), which will cost around US$2500/ZAR17,000 in high season.

Round-the-World flights

If China is only one stop on a much longer journey, you might want to consider buying a **Round-the-World** (**RTW**) ticket (around £1000/US$1800). Some travel agents can sell you an "off-the-shelf" RTW ticket that will have you touching down in about half a dozen cities (Hong Kong is on many itineraries); others will have to assemble one for you, which can be tailored to your needs but is apt to be more expensive.

Airlines, agents and operators

When booking airfares, the cheapest online deals are often with stock operators such as STA, Trailfinders and Flight Centres, though it's always worth checking airline

Six steps to a better kind of travel

At Rough Guides we are passionately committed to travel. We feel strongly that only through travelling do we truly come to understand the world we live in and the people we share it with – plus tourism has brought a great deal of **benefit** to developing economies around the world over the last few decades. But the extraordinary growth in tourism has also damaged some places irreparably, and of course **climate change** is exacerbated by most forms of transport, especially flying. This means that now more than ever it's important to **travel thoughtfully** and **responsibly**, with respect for the cultures you're visiting – not only to derive the most benefit from your trip but also to preserve the best bits of the planet for everyone to enjoy. At Rough Guides we feel there are six main areas in which you can make a difference:

- Consider what you're contributing to the **local economy**, and how much the services you use do the same, whether it's through employing local workers and guides or sourcing locally grown produce and local services.
- Consider the **environment** on holiday as well as at home. Water is scarce in many developing destinations, and the biodiversity of local flora and fauna can be adversely affected by tourism. Try to patronize businesses that take account of this.
- Travel with a purpose, not just to tick off experiences. Consider **spending longer** in a place, and getting to know it and its people.
- Give thought to how often you **fly**. Try to avoid short hops by air and more harmful night flights.
- Consider **alternatives to flying**, travelling instead by bus, train, boat and even by bike or on foot where possible.
- Make your trips "**climate neutral**" via a reputable carbon offset scheme. All Rough Guide flights are offset, and every year we donate money to a variety of charities devoted to combating the effects of climate change.

websites themselves for specials – and, often, a lot more flexibility with refunds and changing dates.

There are some bargains to be had on auction sites, too, if you're prepared to bid keenly – but you usually only find out exact departure times, routes and the like after you've won, so you'll need to be flexible. For advice and recommended auction sites, try Ⓦwww.cheapflightsfinder.com.

Airlines

Aeroflot Ⓦwww.aeroflot.com/cms/en
Air Canada Ⓦwww.aircanada.com
Air China Ⓦwww.airchina.com.cn
Air France Ⓦwww.airfrance.com
Air New Zealand Ⓦwww.airnz.co.nz
Alitalia Ⓦwww.alitalia.com
All Nippon Airways (ANA) Ⓦwww.anaskyweb.com
American Airlines Ⓦwww.aa.com
Asiana Airlines Ⓦwww.flyasiana.com
Austrian Airlines Ⓦwww.aua.com
British Airways Ⓦwww.ba.com
Cathay Pacific Ⓦwww.cathaypacific.com
China Airlines Ⓦwww.china-airlines.com
China Eastern Airlines Ⓦwww.chinaeastern.co.uk
China Southern Airlines Ⓦwww.cs-air.com
Continental Airlines Ⓦwww.continental.com
Delta Ⓦwww.delta.com
Emirates Ⓦwww.emirates.com
EVA Air Ⓦwww.evaair.com
Finnair Ⓦwww.finnair.com
JAL (Japan Airlines) Ⓦwww.jal.com
KLM (Royal Dutch Airlines) Ⓦwww.klm.com
Korean Air Ⓦwww.koreanair.com
Lufthansa Ⓦwww.lufthansa.com
Malaysia Airlines Ⓦwww.malaysiaairlines.com
Malev Hungarian Airlines Ⓦwww.malev.hu
Nepal Airlines Ⓦwww.nepalairlines.com.np
PIA (Pakistan International Airlines) Ⓦwww.piac.com.pk
Qantas Airways Ⓦwww.qantas.com
Qatar Airways Ⓦwww.qatarairways.com
Royal Brunei Ⓦwww.bruneiair.com
Royal Jordanian Ⓦwww.rj.com
SAS (Scandinavian Airlines) Ⓦwww.flysas.com
Singapore Airlines Ⓦwww.singaporeair.com
Swiss Ⓦwww.swiss.com
Thai Airways Ⓦwww.thaiair.com
United Airlines Ⓦwww.united.com
US Airways Ⓦwww.usair.com
Vietnam Airlines Ⓦwww.vietnamairlines.com
Virgin Atlantic Ⓦwww.virgin-atlantic.com

Agents and operators

Absolute Asia US Ⓣ1-800/736-8187, Ⓦwww.absoluteasia.com. Numerous tours of China lasting from between 6 and 16 days, in first-class accommodation, such as the 16-day "Silk Road" tour.
Adventure Center US Ⓣ1-800/228-8747 or 510/654-1879, Ⓦwww.adventure-center.com. Dozens of tours in China and Tibet, from a week-long whizz around the highlights to a month of walking, hiking and biking expeditions.
Adventures Abroad US Ⓣ1-800/665-3998 or 360/775-9926, Ⓦwww.adventures-abroad.com. Small-group specialists with tours through China and Mongolia.
Asian Pacific Adventures US Ⓣ1-800/825-1680 or 818/886-5190, Ⓦwww.asianpacificadventures.com. Numerous tours of China, focusing on southwestern ethnic groups and often-overlooked rural corners.
Backroads US Ⓣ1-800/GO-ACTIVE or 510/527-1555, Ⓦwww.backroads.com. Cycling and hiking between Beijing and Hong Kong.
Birdfinders UK Ⓣ01258/839066, Ⓦwww.birdfinders.co.uk. Several trips per year to find rare and endemic species in mainland China and Tibet.
China Holidays UK Ⓣ020/74872999, Ⓦwww.chinaholidays.co.uk. Aside from mainstream

packages to the Three Gorges, Shanghai and Guilin, they also run a "Taste of China" gastronomic tour sampling food between Beijing and Hong Kong.

CTS Horizons UK ⓣ020/7836 9911, ⓦwww.ctshorizons.com. The China Travel Service's UK branch, offering an extensive range of tours including some cheap off-season hotel-and-flight packages to Beijing, and tailor-made private tours.

Exodus UK ⓣ020/8675 5550, ⓦwww.exodus.co.uk. Offers some interesting and unusual overland itineraries in the wilds of Tibet, Inner Mongolia and the Northwest.

Explore Worldwide UK ⓣ01252/760 000, ⓦwww.explore.co.uk. Big range of small-group tours and treks, including Tibet tours and trips along the Yangzi. Some supplements for single travellers.

Geographic Expeditions US ⓣ1-800/777-8183 or 415/922-0448, ⓦwww.geoex.com. Travel among the ethnic groups of Guizhou, Tibet, Yunnan and western Sichuan as well as more straightforward trips around Shanghai and Beijing.

Intrepid Travel UK ⓣ020/8960 6333, Australia ⓣ1300/360 667 or 03/9473 2626; ⓦwww.intrepidtravel.com. Small-group tours with the emphasis on cross-cultural contact and low-impact tourism; visits some fairly out-of-the-way corners of China.

Imaginative Traveller UK ⓣ020/8742 8612, ⓦwww.imaginative-traveller.com. An emphasis on the unusual, with cycling tours, a panda trek in Sichuan and a Kunming–Kathmandu overland trip.

Mir Corp US ⓣ206/624-7289, ⓦwww.mircorp.com. Specialists in Trans-Siberian rail travel, for small groups as well as individual travellers.

Mountain Travel Sobek US ⓣ1-888/MTSOBEK or 510/687-6235, ⓦwww.mtsobek.com. Adventure tours to Tibet, northern Yunnan and along the Silk Road.

North South Travel UK ⓣ01245/608 291, ⓦwww.northsouthtravel.co.uk. Friendly, competitive travel agency, offering discounted fares worldwide, including to Beijing. Profits are used to support projects in the developing world, especially the promotion of sustainable tourism.

On the Go Tours UK ⓣ020/7371 1113, ⓦwww.onthegotours.com. Runs group and tailor-made tours to China and other destinations.

Pacific Delight Tours US ⓣ1-800/221-7179 or 212/818-1781, ⓦwww.pacificdelighttours.com. City breaks, cruises along the Li and Yangzi rivers, plus a range of tours to Tibet, the Silk Road and western Yunnan.

Regent Holidays UK ⓣ0117/921 1711, ⓦwww.regent-holidays.co.uk. Offers interesting Trans-Siberian packages for individual travellers in either direction and with different possible stopover permutations.

REI Adventures US ⓣ1-800/622-2236, ⓦwww.rei.com/travel. Cycling and hiking tours throughout China.

The Russia Experience UK ⓣ020/8566 8846, ⓦwww.trans-siberian.co.uk. Besides detailing their Trans-Siberian packages, their website is a veritable mine of information about the railway.

STA Travel UK ⓣ0871/2300 040, US ⓣ1-800/781-4040, Australia ⓣ134 782, New Zealand ⓣ0800/474 400, South Africa ⓣ0861/781 781; ⓦwww.statravel.co.uk. Worldwide specialists in independent travel; also student IDs, travel insurance, car rental, rail passes, and more. Good discounts for students and under-26s. China options include tours from 8 to 21 days in length, covering Beijing, Shanghai and the Yangzi and Li rivers, among others.

Sundowners Australia ⓣ03/9672 5300, ⓦwww.sundownersoverland.com. Tours of the Silk Road, plus Trans-Siberian rail bookings.

Trailfinders UK ⓣ0845/058 5858, Ireland ⓣ01/677 7888, Australia ⓣ1300/780 212; ⓦwww.trailfinders.com. One of the best-informed and most efficient agents for independent travellers. Numerous China options on offer.

Travel CUTS Canada ⓣ1-866/246-9762, US ⓣ1-800/592-2887; ⓦwww.travelcuts.com. Canadian youth and student travel firm.

Travel Indochina Australia ⓣ1300/138 755, ⓦwww.travelindochina.com.au. Covers the obvious China sights but goes a bit beyond them, too; also arranges cross-border visas for Thailand, Laos, Vietnam and Cambodia.
Wild China US ⓣ888/902-8808. ⓦwww.wildchina.com. Small group tours to out-of-the-way places, such as minority villages in Guizhou and Yunnan, as well as hiking after pandas in Sichuan.
World Expeditions UK ⓣ020/8870 2600, ⓦwww.worldexpeditions.co.uk; Australia ⓣ1300/720 000, ⓦwww.worldexpeditions.com.au; New Zealand ⓣ0800/350 354, ⓦwww.worldexpeditions.co.nz. Offers cycling and hiking tours in rural areas, including a Great Wall trek.

Overland routes

China has a number of **land borders** open to foreign travellers. When planning your trip, remember that Chinese visas must be used within three months of their date of issue, and so you may have to apply for one en route. Visas are obtainable in the capitals of virtually all European and Asian countries, and are likely to take several days to be issued (see p.59 for embassy addresses). Note that most nationalities can fly to Hong Kong without a visa, and easily pick one up there.

Via Russia and Mongolia

One of the classic overland routes to China is through Russia on the so-called **Trans-Siberian Express**. As a one-off trip, the rail journey is a memorable way to begin or end a stay in China; views of stately birch forests, misty lakes and arid plateaus help time pass much faster than you'd think, and there are frequent stops during which you can wander the station platform, purchasing food and knick-knacks – packages (see p.32) include more lengthy stopovers. The trains are comfortable and clean: second-class compartments contain four berths, while first-class have two and even boast a private shower.

There are actually two rail lines from Moscow to Beijing: the **Trans-Manchurian** (see p.200), which runs almost as far as the Sea of Japan before turning south through Dongbei (Manchuria) to Beijing; and the **Trans-Mongolian** (see p.81), which cuts through Mongolia from Siberia. The Manchurian train takes about six days, the Mongolian train about five. The latter is more popular with foreigners, Trans-Mongolian Chinese Train #4 being the preferred service – a scenic route that rumbles past Lake Baikal and Siberia, the grasslands of Mongolia, and the desert of northwest China, skirting the Great Wall along the way. At the Mongolia/China border, you can watch as the undercarriage is switched to a different gauge. The one drawback of this route is that you will need an additional visa for Mongolia.

Meals are included while the train is in China. In Mongolia, the dining car accepts payment in both Chinese and Mongolian currency; while in Russia, US dollars or Russian roubles can be used. It's worth having small denominations of US dollars as you can change these on the train throughout the journey, or use them to buy food from station vendors along the way – though experiencing the cuisine and people in the dining cars is part of the fun. Bring instant noodles and snacks as a backup and that great long novel you've always wanted to read.

Tickets and packages

Booking tickets needs some advance planning, especially during the popular summer months. Sorting out travel arrangements from abroad is also complex – you'll need transit visas for Russia, as well as for Mongolia if you intend to pass through there, and if you plan on reaching or leaving Moscow by rail via Warsaw, you'll have to get a transit visa for Belarus, too. It's therefore advisable to use an experienced **travel agent** who can organize all tickets, visas and stopovers if required, in advance. Visa processing is an especially helpful time saver, given the queues and paperwork required for visas along the route.

You can cut complications and keep your costs down by using the online ticket booking system offered by **Real Russia** (Ⓦwww.realrussia.co.uk); they mark up prices about 20 percent but do save you a lot of hassle. A second-class Moscow to Beijing ticket booked with them costs around £550 – they will then help you sort out your visas for a small fee (as will all other agencies). They also offer tours: a nine-day tour, including a couple of night's accommodation in Moscow, costs £900 per person, a little less if you book as a group. Another agency offering a wide range of inexpensive tours is **Monkey Business** (Ⓦwww.monkeyshrine.com); a Moscow to Beijing trip, including a couple of nights in a youth hostel, costs around £600 in standard class. Note that tours with Russian agencies offer good value for money; try **All Russia Travel Service** (Ⓦwww.rusrailtravel.ru) or **Ost West** (Ⓦwww.ostwest.com). Tailor-made tours from Western companies will be much more expensive, but offer the minimum hassle: the **Russia Experience** (Ⓦwww.trans-siberian.co.uk) has a good reputation. For details of companies at home which can sort out Trans-Siberian travel, check the lists of specialist travel agents (see p.29). Finally, for detailed, up-to-date information on all ways to get tickets, check Ⓦwww.seat61.com/trans-siberian.htm.

Via the Central Asian republics

From Russia, you can also theoretically reach China through several Central Asian countries, though the obstacles can occasionally be insurmountable; contact the in-country agents listed below, or Trans-Siberian operators listed earlier in this section, for up-to-date practicalities.

The main cities of **Kazakhstan** and **Kyrgyzstan** – Almaty and Bishkek – are both still linked by daily trains to Moscow (3 days), though getting Russian transit visas and booking berths on these trains is not easy. Kyrgyzstan-based **Asia Silk Travel** (Ⓦwww.centralasiatravel.com) or **Kyrgyz Concept** (Ⓦeng.concept.kg) are good sources of background information, including visa requirements, and can make bookings. It is also possible to get into Central Asia via **Turkmenistan**, and thence to the rest of Central Asia, via northeastern Iran or from Azerbaijan across the Caspian Sea, thus bypassing Russia completely. **Ayan Travel** (Ⓦwww.ayan-travel.com), based in the Turkmenistan capital, Ashgabat, are the people to contact for this stage of the journey.

Once in the region, crossing into China from Kazakhstan is straightforward – there are comfortable twice-weekly trains from

Almaty to Ürümqi, which take 35 hours and cost about US$80 for a berth in a four-berth compartment. There are also cheaper, faster, less comfortable buses (US$60; about 24hr). From Bishkek in Kyrgyzstan, Kashgar in the northwestern Chinese province of Xinjiang is only eleven hours' drive away (about US$55), and the two cities are linked by buses in summer months. Foreigners, however, have had difficulties in trying to use these and have usually had to resort to expensive private transport, run by local tour operators, to help them across (see p.854). You may well be expected to bribe the border guards US$20 or so.

From Pakistan and Nepal

The routes across the Himalayas to China are among the toughest in Asia. The first is from Pakistan into Xinjiang province over the **Karakoram Highway**, along one of the branches of the ancient Silk Road. This requires no pre-planning, except for the fact that it is open only from May to October, and closes periodically due to landslides. Check your government's travel advice as the area is home to some fundamentalist militants and **attacks on Westerners** have occurred; at the time of writing it was regarded as very dangerous. The Karakoram Highway actually starts at Rawalpindi (the old city outside the capital Islamabad), and in theory you can get from here to Kashgar in four days on public buses. From Rawalpindi, first take one of the daily minibuses that run the arduous fifteen-hour trip up the Indus gorge to the village of Gilgit, where you'll have to spend a night. From Gilgit, the next destination is the border town of Sust, a five-hour journey. There are a couple of daily buses on this route. Once in Sust, immediately book your ticket to Kashgar for the next morning – it costs 1450 rupees (about US$35). A few travellers have managed to talk their way into being issued a visa at the border, but you're strongly advised to have one already. The route is popular with cyclists, but there's no guarantee that you will be allowed to bike across the border; you'll probably have to load your bike on a bus for this part of the trip. For more on crossing the Chinese border here, see p.882.

Another popular route is **from Nepal into Tibet**, but Nepal's political situation can be volatile, and you should check your government's travel advice on the latest situation – practical details are covered on p.898. It's advisable to arrive in Nepal with a Chinese visa already in your passport, as the Chinese Embassy in Nepal often does not issue visas at all and at the best of times will only issue group visas. The **Tibetan border** is closed to travellers during politically sensitive times, for example after the riots in 2010.

From **India** there are, for political reasons, no border crossings to China. For years, authorities have discussed opening a bus route from Sikkim to Tibet, north from Darjeeling, but despite both sides working on the road, the border remains closed.

From Vietnam

Vietnam has three border crossings with China – **Dong Dang**, 60km northeast of Hanoi; **Lao Cai**, 150km northwest; and the little-used **Mong Cai**, 200km south of Nanning. All three are open daily between 8.30am and 5pm. Officious Chinese customs officials at these crossings occasionally confiscate guidebooks, including this one (see p.59); bury it at the bottom of your bag.

A **direct train** service from Hanoi is advertised as running all the way to **Beijing** (60hr), passing through **Nanning** and **Guilin**. In practice, though, you'll probably have to change trains in Nanning. Similarly, there are daily trains from Hanoi to Lao Cai, eleven hours' away in Vietnam's mountainous and undeveloped northwest (near the pleasant resort of Sa Pa), from where you can cross into Yunnan province at Hekou, and catch regular buses to Kunming. From Mong Cai, there are also regular buses to Nanning.

From Laos and Burma (Myanmar)

Crossing into China **from Laos** also lands you in Yunnan, this time at Bian Mao Zhan in the Xishuangbanna region. Formalities are very relaxed and unlikely to cause any problems, though take some hard cash as you can't change travellers' cheques on the Chinese side. It's 220km on local buses north from here to the regional capital,

Jinghong. Alternatively there are also direct daily buses between Luang Namtha in Laos and Jinghong (8hr).

Entering China **from Burma** (Myanmar) is a possibility, too, with the old Burma Road cutting northeast from Rangoon (Yangon) to Lashio and the crossing at Wanding in Yunnan, just south of Ruili. At present, this border is open only to groups travelling with a tour agency, which will sort out all the necessary paperwork in Yangon. Be aware that border regulations here are subject to change.

Getting around

China's public transport is comprehensive and good value: you can fly to all regional capitals and many cities, the rail network extends to every region, and you can reach China's remotest corners on local buses. Tibet is the one area where there are widespread restrictions on independent travel (see p.898), though a few other localities around the country are officially off-limits to foreigners.

However, getting around such a large, crowded country requires planning, patience and stamina. This is especially true for long-distance journeys, where you'll find travelling in as much comfort as you can afford saves a lot of undue stress. **Tours** are one way of taking the pressure off, and may be the only practical way of getting out to certain sights.

Public holidays – especially the May, October and Spring Festival breaks (see p.51) – are rotten times to travel, as half China is on the move between family and workplace: ticket prices rise (legally, by no more than fifteen percent, though often by up to fifty), bus- and train-station crowds swell insanely, and even flights become scarce.

By rail

China's rail network is vast, efficient and reliable. The country invests billions of yuan annually on the network, considering a healthy transport infrastructure as essential to economic growth – and political cohesion. Recent years have seen some impressive developments: a rail line over the mountains between eastern China and **Tibet** completed in 2005; the country's first ultra-fast **bullet** trains, which began operation in eastern China in 2007; and a new **high-speed network** linking Hong Kong with Beijing and Shanghai, and eastern cities with Lanzhou, Chengdu and Kunming, due for completion around 2013.

Food, though expensive and ordinary, is always available on trains, either from trolleys serving snacks and polystyrene boxes of rice and stir-fries or in a restaurant car. You can also buy snacks from vendors at train stations during the longer station stops.

Timetables and tickets

Booths outside train stations sell national **train timetables** in book form and single sheets covering local services, which are often also printed on the back of city maps. These are all in Chinese only, and can be very complex (even Chinese people have trouble with the books); it's much easier to check **online train schedules** in English at Ⓦwww.travelchinaguide.com/china-trains.

Tickets – always **one-way** – show the date of travel and destination, along with the train number, carriage, and seat or berth number. They become available up to twenty days in advance, though it can be as little as four. **Station ticket offices** are almost all computerized, and while queues can tie you up for an hour or more of jostling, you'll generally get what you're after if you have some flexibility. At the counter, state your

SANYA CHINA
TRAVEL

please request our new brochure • Please request our new brochure •
Bringing Asia Closer
SANYA CHINA
TRAVEL

PATA
Pacific Asia Travel Association

ABTA

6790
ATOL
PROTECTED

destination, the train number if possible, the day you'd like to travel, and the class you want, and have some alternatives handy. If you can't speak Chinese, get someone to write things down for you before setting out, as staff rarely speak English, though you may strike it lucky in big cities. In cities, you'll also find **downtown advance purchase offices**, where you pay a small commission (around ¥5/ticket); it makes sense to try these places first as train stations are often located far from city centres. **Agents**, such as hotel travel services, can also book tickets for a commission of ¥40 or more each. The best way to **book tickets online**, and have them delivered to your hotel door in major Chinese cities, is through Ⓦwww.travelchinaguide.com; you'll pay a surcharge of about 25 percent for this.

If you've bought a ticket but decide not to travel, you can get most of the fare **refunded** by returning the ticket to a ticket office at least two hours before departure. The process is called *tuipiao* (退票, *tuìpiào*) and there's sometimes a window especially for this at stations.

Ticket classes

There are **four ticket classes**: soft sleeper, hard sleeper, soft seat and hard seat, not all necessarily available on each train. **Soft sleeper** (软卧, *ruǎnwò*) costs around the same as flying, and gets you a berth in a four-person compartment with a soft mattress, fan, optional radio and a choice of Western- or Chinese-style toilets. **Hard sleeper** (硬卧, *yìngwò*), about two-thirds the price of *ruǎnwò*, is the best value. Carriages are divided into twenty sets of three-tiered **bunks**; the lowest bunk is the largest, but costs more and gets used as communal seating during the day; the upper bunk is cheapest but headroom is minimal. Each set of six bunks has its own vacuum flask of boiled water (topped up from the urn at the end of each carriage) – bring your own mugs and tea. Every carriage also has a toilet and washbasin, which can become unsavoury. There are fairly spacious **luggage racks**, though make sure you chain your bags securely while you sleep.

In either sleeper class, on boarding the carriage you will have your ticket exchanged for a metal tag by the attendant. The tag is swapped back for your ticket (so you'll be able to get through the barrier at the station) about half an hour before you arrive at your destination, whatever hour of the day or night this happens to be.

Soft seat (软座, *ruǎnzuò*) is widespread on services whose complete route takes less than a day. Seats are around the cost of an express-bus fare, have plenty of legroom and are well padded. More common is **hard seat** (硬座, *yìngzuò*), which costs around half the soft-seat fare but is only recommended for relatively short journeys, as you'll be sitting on a padded three-person bench, with every available bit of floor space crammed with travellers who were unable to book a seat. You'll often be the focus of intense and unabashed speculation from

Sample train fares

The fares below are for one-way travel on express trains. As always in China, the faster services are more expensive.

	Hard seat	Hard sleeper	Soft sleeper
From Beijing			
Guangzhou	¥200	¥550	¥750
Hong Kong	¥215	¥595	¥925
Shanghai	¥135	¥375	¥515
Xi'an	¥140	¥390	¥530
From Xi'an			
Guangzhou	¥220	¥610	¥830
Turpan	¥215	¥585	¥805
Ürümqi	¥225	¥625	¥840

peasants and labourers who can't afford to travel in better style.

Finally, if there's nothing else available, you can buy an **unreserved ticket** (无座, *wúzuò*; literally "no seat"), which lets you board the hard-seat section of the train – though you might have to stand for the entire journey if you can't upgrade on board.

Types of train

The different **types of train** each have their own code on timetables. **High-speed** services include the D-class, which travel up to 250km/hr; followed by Z-, T- and K-class trains, which can still reach 150–200km/hr. These all have modern fittings with text tickers at the carriages' end scrolling through the temperature, arrival time at next station and speed. **No-smoking rules** are often vigorously enforced.

Ordinary trains (普通车, *pǔtōng chē*) have a number only and range from those with clean carriages and able to top 100km/hr, to ancient plodders destined for the scrapheap with cigarette-burned linoleum floors and grimy windows. A few busy, short-haul express services, such as the Shenzhen–Guangzhou train, have **double-decker carriages**.

Boarding the train

Turn up at the station with time to spare before your train leaves. All luggage has to be passed through **x-ray machines** at the station entrance to check for dangerous goods such as firecrackers. You then need to work out which **platform** your train leaves from – most stations have electronic departure boards in Chinese, or you can show your ticket to station staff who will point you in the right direction. Passengers are not allowed onto the platform until the train is in and ready to leave, which can result in some mighty stampedes out of the crowded waiting rooms when the gates open. Carriages are **numbered** on the outside, and your ticket is checked by a guard as you board. Once on the train, you can **upgrade** any ticket at the controller's booth, in the hard-seat carriage next to the restaurant car (usually #8), where you can sign up for beds or seats as they become available.

By bus and minibus

Buses go everywhere that trains go, and well beyond, usually more frequently and occasionally faster. Finding the departure point isn't always easy though; even small places can have **multiple bus stations**, generally located on the side of town in which traffic is heading.

Bus station **timetables** – except electronic ones – can be ignored; ask station staff about schedules and frequencies, though they generally can't speak English. **Tickets** are easy to buy: ticket offices at main stations are often computerized, queues are seldom bad, and – with the exception of backroad routes, which might only run every other day – you don't need to book in advance. In country towns, you sometimes buy tickets on board the bus. **Destinations** are always displayed in Chinese characters on the front of the vehicle. Take some **food** along, although buses usually pull up at inexpensive roadhouses at mealtimes. Only the most upmarket coaches have **toilets**; drivers stop every few hours or if asked to do so by passengers (roadhouse toilets are some of the worst in the country, however).

Downsides to bus travel include drivers who spend the journey chatting on their mobile phone or coast downhill in neutral, with the engine off; and the fact that vehicles are obliged to use the horn before overtaking anything – earplugs are recommended. **Roadworks** are a near-certainty too, as highways are continually being repaired, upgraded or replaced; in 2010, a 100km-long jam on the Tibet–Beijing highway, blamed on roadworks, took nine days to clear.

Types of buses

There are various **types of buses**, though there's not always a choice available for particular routes and if there is, station staff will assume that as a foreigner you'll want the fastest, most comfortable and most expensive service.

Ordinary buses (普通车, *pǔtōng chē*) are cheap and basic, with lightly padded seats; they're never heated or air-conditioned, so dress accordingly. Seats can be cramped and luggage racks tiny; you'll have to put anything bulkier than a satchel on the roof or your lap, or beside the driver. They tend to stop off frequently, so don't count on an average speed of more than 30km/hr.

Express buses (快车, *kuài chē*) are the most expensive and have good legroom, comfy seats that may well recline, air-conditioning and video. Bulky luggage gets locked away in the belly of the bus, a fairly safe option.

Sleeper buses (卧铺车, *wòpù chē*) have cramped, basic bunks instead of seats, minimal luggage space and a poor safety record, and are not recommended if there is any alternative.

The final option is **minibuses** (小车, *xiǎochē*; or 包车, *bāochē*) seating up to twenty people, common on routes of less than 100km or so. They cost a little more than the same journey by ordinary bus, can be extremely cramped, and often circuit the departure point for ages until they have filled up.

By plane

China's **airlines** link all major cities. The main operators are Air China (Ⓦwww.airchina.com.cn), China Southern (Ⓦwww.cs-air.com) and China Eastern (Ⓦwww.ce-air.com), which – along with smaller regional companies – are overseen by the Civil Aviation Administration of China, or **CAAC**. Flying is a luxury worth considering for long distances as prices compare with soft-sleeper train travel; planes are modern and well maintained and service is good.

Buying tickets from local airline offices or hotel desk tour agents is easy, and there seem to be enough flights along popular routes to cope with demand. Agents often give substantial discounts on advertised fares, especially if you book a day or two in advance. Competitive fares are available if you **buy e-tickets online** at Ⓦwww.elong.net or Ⓦenglish.ctrip.com. You'll need to provide a phone number to confirm the booking and to book more than 24 hours in advance if using an overseas credit card.

Timetables are displayed at airline offices and agent desks, and often on the back of city maps; there's a handy **online schedule** at ⓦwww.feeyo.com/enflight.htm. **Fares** are based on one-way travel (so a return ticket is the price of two one-way tickets) and include all **taxes**. As an illustration, from Beijing, expect to pay at least ¥740 to Xi'an; ¥900 to Shanghai; ¥1120 to Chengdu; ¥1230 to Shenzhen; ¥1000 to Kunming; ¥1440 to Ürümqi, and ¥2100 to Hong Kong.

Airlines frequently provide an **airport bus** running to and from the airport. As these can be 30km or more from city centres, it's worth finding out if a bus is available, if not already mentioned in this guide. **Check-in time** for all flights is two hours before departure.

By car

Driving a car across China is an appealing idea, but currently forbidden to foreign tourists (though foreign residents can take a driving test). It is possible, however, to **rent vehicles** for local use in **Beijing**, **Shanghai** and **Hong Kong**, from rental companies at the airports. You need an international driving licence and a credit card to cover the deposit. Special licence plates make these rental vehicles easily identifiable to Chinese police, so don't try taking them beyond the designated boundaries.

Generally, the only option is to rent a **taxi**, **minibus** or Chinese **Jeep**, complete **with driver**. Prices are set by negotiating and average ¥400 a day, and you'll be expected to provide lunch for the driver. It's cheapest to approach drivers directly, though if you can't speak Chinese your accommodation should be able to help, and some tour operators run vehicles, too – and might include the services of an interpreter. In Tibet, renting a Jeep with a driver is pretty much the only way to reach many destinations (see p.900).

The mainland Chinese theoretically **drive on the right** although, like everything in China, road rules seem subject to negotiation and it's common to see vehicles running red lights, using pavements a shortcuts, or simply driving on the left. Drivers use their horns instead of the brake, and lorries and buses plough ahead regardless while smaller vehicles get out of the way. Unsurprisingly perhaps, over 200 people are killed per day in traffic accidents. In Hong Kong, however, they drive on the left and actually take traffic regulations seriously.

By ferry

Though there are few public ferries in China, you can make one of the world's great river journeys down the **Yangzi** between Chongqing and Yichang, via the mighty **Three Gorges** – though the spectacle has been lessened by the construction of the giant Three Gorges Dam. Another favourite is the day-cruise down the **Li River** between Guilin and Yangshuo in southwestern Guangxi province, past a forest of pointy mountains looking just like a Chinese scroll painting. By **sea**, there are **passenger ferries** between Hong Kong and Macau; between Guangxi and Hainan Island; and from ports in Shandong and Shanghai to neighbouring South Korea and Japan.

Conditions on board are greatly variable, but on overnight trips there's always a choice of **classes** – sometimes as many as six – which can range from a bamboo mat on the floor right through to private cabins. Don't expect anything too impressive, however; many mainland services are cramped and overcrowded, and cabins, even in first-class, are grimly functional.

By bicycle

China has the highest number of **bicycles** (自行车, *zìxíngchē*) of any country in the world, with about a quarter of the population owning one, despite a rising trend towards mopeds, motorbikes and cars. Few cities have any hills and some have **bike lanes**, though many of the bigger cities are in the process of banning bicycles from main roads in order to free them up for cars.

Rental shops or booths are common around train stations, where you can rent a set of wheels for ¥5–10 a day. You will need to leave a deposit (¥200–400) and/or some form of ID, and you're fully responsible for anything that happens to the bike while it's in your care, so check brakes, tyre pressure and gears before renting. Most rentals are bog-standard black rattletraps – the really deluxe models feature working bells and brakes. There are **repair shops** all over the place should you need a tyre patched or a chain fixed up (around ¥2). If the bike sustains any serious damage, it's up to the parties involved to sort out responsibility and payment on the spot. Always use a **bicycle chain** or lock – they're available everywhere – and in cities, leave your vehicle in one of the ubiquitous designated **parking areas**, where it will be guarded by an attendant for a few jiao.

An alternative to renting is to **buy a bike**, a sensible option if you're going to be based anywhere for a while. All department stores sell them: a heavy, unsophisticated machine will only set you back about ¥250, whereas a mountain bike will be upwards of ¥500. A **folding bike** (around ¥350) is a great idea, as you can cycle around all day and when you're tired, put it in the boot of a taxi; plus, you can take it from one destination to another on the bus. You can also **bring your own bike** into China; international airlines usually insist that the front wheel is removed, deflated and strapped to the back, and that everything is thoroughly packaged. Inside China, airlines, trains and ferries all charge to carry bikes, and the ticketing and accompanying paperwork can be baffling. Where possible, it's easier to stick to long-distance buses and stow it for free on the roof, no questions asked. Another option is to see China on a **specialized bike tour** such as those offered by Bike China (Ⓦwww.bikechina.com), Bike Asia (Ⓦwww.bikeasia.com) or Cycle China (Ⓦwww.cyclechina.com).

Tours

Local tour operators, who are listed throughout the guide, offer excursions ranging from city coach tours to river cruises and multiday cross-country hikes or horse treks. While you always pay for the privilege, sometimes these tours are good value: travel, accommodation and food – usually plentiful and excellent – are generally included, as might be the services of an interpreter and guide. And in some cases, tours are the most practical (if not the only) way to see something really worthwhile, saving endless bother organizing local transport and accommodation. In general, **foreign-owned operations** tend to give better service – or at least to understand better what Westerners want when they take a tour.

On the downside, there are disreputable operators who'll blatantly overcharge for mediocre services, foist unhelpful guides on you and spend three days on what could better be done in an afternoon. Bear in mind that many Chinese tour guides are badly paid, and supplement their income by taking tourists to souvenir shops where they'll receive commissions. It always pays to make exhaustive **enquiries** about the exact nature of the tour, such as exactly what the price includes and the departure/return times, before handing any money over.

City transport

All Chinese cities have some form of **public transit system**. An increasing number have (or are building) **light-rail systems** and underground **metros**; elsewhere, the **city bus** is the transport focus. These are cheap and run from around 6am to 9pm or later, but – Hong Kong's apart – are usually slow and crowded. Pricier **private minibuses** often run the same routes in similar comfort but at greater speed; they're either numbered or have their destination written up at the front.

Taxis are always available in larger towns and cities; main roads, transit points and tourist hotels are good places to find them. They either cost a fixed rate within certain limits – ¥6 seems normal – or about ¥8 to hire and then ¥1–3 per kilometre. You'll also find (motorized or cycle-) **rickshaws** and **motorbike taxis** outside just about every mainland bus and train station, whose highly erratic rates are set by bargaining beforehand.

Accommodation

Although Chinese hotels are often lacking in character – old family-run institutions of the kind that can be found all over Asia and Europe are rare – there is an increasing range of choice, especially in large cities, where you can find foreigner-friendly hostels, budget business accommodation, upmarket international chains and even trendy boutique-style hotels.

Price is not a good indicator of quality, however, with a good deal of overlap between the various places. The Chinese hospitality industry is on a steep learning curve, so new places are often vastly better than old ones.

Security in accommodation is reasonably good; if you lock things inside your bag before going out, you are unlikely to have problems.

Finding a room

Increasingly, **booking ahead** is a routine procedure. You can book by phone, through the accommodation's own website if there is one, or by using an **accommodation-booking website** such as elong (Ⓦwww.elong.net) or China Trip (Ⓦenglish.ctrip.com), both of which have English-language content and offer massive discounts on selected mid-range to upmarket hotel rates. These two don't require pre-payment for rooms; you simply reserve through the website and pay on arrival. Budget travellers should check out **hostel websites** such as hostel bookers (Ⓦwww.hostelbookers.com), or the hostel organization websites listed on p.45. Sometimes, the local CITS (see p.67) can also wrangle good discounts for you.

For some hotels, however, the concept of booking ahead may be alien, and you won't make much headway without spoken Chinese – though it's a good idea to call (or to ask someone to call for you) to see if vacancies exist before lugging your bag across town. Be aware that even at these places **room rates** displayed at reception are always just the starting point in negotiations. Staff are generally amenable to **bargaining** and it's normal to get thirty percent off the advertised price, even more perhaps in low season or where there's plenty of competition. Always ask to **see the room first**. Rooms usually have either **twin beds** (双人房, *shuāngrén fáng*) or **single beds** (单人房, *dānrén fáng*), which often means "one double bed", rather than a small bed; some places also have triples or even quads.

If you haven't booked ahead, time things so that you reach your destination in broad daylight, then deposit your bag at a left-luggage office at the train or bus station and check out possible accommodation options. New arrivals at city bus and train stations are often besieged by **touts** wanting to lead them to a hotel where they'll receive a commission for bringing guests in; these people are generally OK, but you do need to be very clear about how much you're willing to pay before being dragged all over town.

If you find yourself being turned away by cheaper hotels, they probably haven't obtained **police permission** to take foreigners, and would face substantial fines for doing so. The situation is dependent on the local authorities, and can vary not just from province to province, but also from town to town. Nothing is ever certain in China, however: being able to speak Chinese greatly improves your chances, as does being able to write your name in Chinese on the register (or having it printed out so the receptionist can do this for you) – in which case the authorities need never know that a foreigner stayed.

Checking in and out

Checking in involves filling in a **form** (see Form p.42) giving details of your name, age, date of birth, sex and address, places where you are coming from and going to, how many days you intend staying and your visa and passport numbers. Upmarket hotels have English versions, and might fill them in for you, but hotels unaccustomed to foreigners usually have them in Chinese only, and might never have seen a foreign passport before – which explains why hotel receptionists can panic when they see a foreigner walk in the door. There's an example of this form in English and Chinese below to help smooth difficulties.

You always **pay in advance**, including a **deposit** which may amount to twice the price of the room. Assuming you haven't broken anything – make sure everything works properly when you check in – deposits are refunded; just don't lose the receipt.

In really cheap places, you won't get a **key** from reception; instead, you'll get a piece of paper that you take to the appropriate **floor attendant** who will give you a room card and open the door for you whenever you come in. If your room has a **telephone**, disconnect it to avoid being woken by prostitutes calling up through the night.

Check-out time is noon, though you can ask to keep the room until later for a proportion of the daily rate. Make sure you arrange this **before** check-out time, however, as staff may otherwise refuse to refund room deposits, claiming that you have overstayed. Conversely, if you have to leave very early in the morning (to catch transport, for instance), you may be unable to find staff to refund your deposit, and might also encounter locked front doors or compound gates. This is most of a problem in rural areas, though often the receptionist sleeps behind the desk and can be woken up if you make enough noise.

Hotels

The different Chinese words for hotel are vague indicators of the status of the place. Sure signs of upmarket pretensions are **dajiudian** (大酒店, *dà jiǔdiàn*) which translates as "big wine shop" or, in the countryside, **shan zhuang** (山庄, *shān zhuāng*) or "mountain resort". **Binguan** (宾馆, *bīnguǎn*) and **fandian** (饭店, *fàndiàn*) are more general terms for hotel, covering everything from downmarket lodgings to smart new establishments; reliably basic are **guesthouse** (客栈, *kèzhàn*), **hostel** (招待所, *zhāodàisuǒ*) and **inn** (旅馆, *lǚguǎn*;

临时住宿登记表
REGISTRATION FORM FOR TEMPORARY RESIDENCE
请用正楷填写 Please write in block letters

英文姓 Surname	英文名 First name	性别 Sex
中文姓名 Name in Chinese	国籍 Nationality	出生日期 Date of birth
证件种类 Type of certificate (eg "Passport")	证件号码 Certificate no.	签证种类 Type of visa
签证有效期 Valid date of visa	抵店日期 Date of arrival	离店日期 Date of departure
由何处来 From	交通工具 Carrier	往何处 To
永久地址 Permanent address		停留事由 Object of stay
职业 Occupation		
接待单位 Received by		房号 Room no.

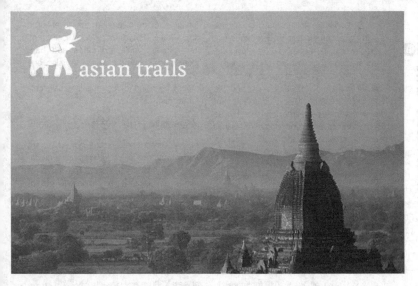

or 旅舍, *lǚshè*). Sometimes you'll simply see a sign for "accommodation" (住宿, *zhùsù*).

Whatever type of hotel you are staying in, there are two things you can rely on: one is a pair of plastic or paper **slippers**, which you use for walking to the bathroom, and the other is a vacuum flask of drinkable **hot water** that can be refilled any time by the floor attendant – though upmarket places tend to provide electric kettles instead. **Breakfast** is sometimes included in the price; nearly all hotels, even fairly grotty ones, will have a restaurant where at least a Chinese breakfast of buns, pickles and congee is served between 7am and 9am.

Upmarket

In the larger cities, you'll find **upmarket** four- or five-star hotels. Conditions in such hotels are comparable to those anywhere in the world, with all the usual **facilities** on offer – such as swimming pools, gyms and business centres – though the finer nuances of service will sometimes be lacking. Prices for standard doubles in these places are upwards of ¥1200 (❾ in this book's price-code scheme), with a fifteen percent **service charge** on top; the use of credit cards is routine. In **Hong Kong** and **Macau**, the top end of the market is similar in character to the mainland, though prices are higher and service more efficient – price codes for these areas are found on p.584.

Even if you cannot afford to stay in the upmarket hotels, they can still be pleasant places to escape from the hubbub, and nobody in China blinks at the sight of a stray foreigner roaming around the foyer of a smart hotel. As well as air-conditioning and clean toilets, you'll find **cafés and bars** (sometimes showing satellite TV), telephone and fax facilities and seven-days-a-week money changing (though this is usually only for guests).

Mid-range

Many Chinese hotels built nowadays are **mid-range**, and every town in China has at least one hotel of this sort. The quality of mid-range places is the hardest to predict from the price: an old hotel with cigarette-burned carpets, leaking bathrooms and grey bedsheets might charge the same as a sparkling new establishment next door; newer places are generally better, as a rule. In remote places, you should get a twin in a mid-range place for ¥150, but expect to pay at least ¥300 in any sizeable city.

There's been a recent explosion in **urban budget hotels** aimed at money-conscious businessmen, which offer small (but not cramped) clean double rooms with showers, phones, TV and internet portals right in city centres. Some places like Kunming, Chengdu and Shanghai have local brands, but nationwide chains include *7 Days Inn* (Ⓦwww.7daysinn.cn), *Home Inn* (Ⓦwww.homeinns.com) and *Motel 168* (Ⓦwww.motel168.com). At around ¥200 a double, they're a very good deal and need to be booked in advance both because of their popularity and because you'll only get the cheapest rooms this way – prices are otherwise fixed. The English-language pages

Accommodation price codes

The accommodation listed in this book has been given one of the following price codes, which represent the price of the cheapest **double room**. In the cheaper hotels that have **dormitories** or that rent out individual beds in small rooms, we give the price of a bed in yuan.

It should generally be noted that in the **off season** – from October to June, excluding holidays such as Christmas and Chinese New Year – prices in tourist hotels are more flexible, and often lower, than during the peak summer months.

Price codes do not take into account the **service charge** of fifteen percent added to bills in all mid-range and upmarket hotels.

❶ ¥80 and under
❷ ¥81–139
❸ ¥140–199
❹ ¥200–299
❺ ¥300–449
❻ ¥450–599
❼ ¥600–799
❽ ¥800–1199
❾ ¥1200 and over

on their websites are not always up-to-date, but staff at reception usually speak a little English if you call ahead.

Cheap hotels

Cheap hotels, with doubles costing less than ¥150, vary in quality from the dilapidated to the perfectly comfortable. In many cities, they're commonly located near the train or bus stations, though they may need persuading to take foreigners. Where they do, you'll notice that the Chinese routinely **rent beds** rather than rooms – doubling up with one or more strangers – as a means of saving money. Foreigners are seldom allowed to share rooms with Chinese people, but if there are three or four foreigners together it's often possible for them to share one big room; otherwise you might have to negotiate a price for the whole room.

Hostels and guesthouses

China has a rapidly expanding network of **youth hostels** (青年旅舍, *qīngnián lǚshè*), many affiliated with the IYHA. Contact details for individual hostels are given through the guide, and **booking ahead** is always advisable. The Chinese youth hostel website isn't always up to speed, and there's sometimes better info and easier booking available through the international IYHA site or Ⓦwww.hostelbookers.com. IYHA members get a small discount, usually ¥10, and you can join at any mainland hostel for ¥60.

Hong Kong, Macau and a few regions of China (mostly in southwestern provinces) also have a number of **privately run guesthouses** in everything from family mansions to Mongolian tents, whose variety comes as a relief after the dullness of mainland accommodation. Prices for double rooms in these guesthouses are generally lower than in hotels.

Youth hostel associations

China

YHA China Ⓦwww.yhachina.com.

International

International Youth Hostel Association (IYHA) Ⓦwww.hihostels.com.

UK and Ireland

Youth Hostel Association (YHA) Ⓣ0800/0191700, Ⓦwww.yha.org.uk.
Scottish Youth Hostel Association Ⓣ01786/891400, Ⓦwww.syha.org.uk.
Irish Youth Hostel Association Ⓣ01/830 4555, Ⓦwww.anoige.ie.
Hostelling International Northern Ireland Ⓣ028/9032 4733, Ⓦwww.hini.org.uk.

US and Canada

Hostelling International-American Youth Hostels Ⓣ301/495-1240, Ⓦwww.hiayh.org.
Hostelling International Canada Ⓣ613/237-7884, Ⓦwww.hihostels.ca.

Australia and New Zealand

Australia Youth Hostels Association Ⓦwww.yha.com.au.
Youth Hostelling Association New Zealand Ⓣ0800/278 299 or 03/379 9970, Ⓦwww.yha.co.nz.

University accommodation

In some cities with limited alternatives, **university accommodation** might be an option, though as youth hostels continue to proliferate and campuses are huge and often far from arrival points or sights, they're not always such a good choice. Once at the campus, you need to locate the accommodation for foreign students or teachers, which will be called something like the "Foreign Experts' Building" (外国专家楼, *wàiguó zhuānjiā lóu*). These act as hotels offering doubles and singles at low-end hotel rates, and you have to fill in all the usual forms.

Camping

Camping is only feasible in Hong Kong – where there are free campsites scattered through the New Territories – and in wilderness areas of Tibet, Sichuan, Yunnan, Qinghai, Xinjiang, Gansu and Inner Mongolia, far away from the prying eyes of thousands of local villagers. Don't bother trying to get permission for it: this is the kind of activity that the Chinese authorities do not have any clear idea about, so if asked they will certainly answer "no".

Food and drink

The Chinese love to eat, and from market-stall buns and soup, right through to the intricate variations of regional cookery, China boasts one of the world's greatest cuisines. Meals are considered social events, and the process is accordingly geared to a group of diners sharing a variety of different dishes with their companions. Fresh ingredients are available from any market stall, though unless you're living long term in the country there are few opportunities to cook for yourself.

Ingredients

In the south, **rice** as grain, noodles, or dumpling wrappers is the staple, replaced in the cooler north by **wheat**, formed into buns or noodles. **Meat** is held to be invigorating and, ideally, forms the backbone of any meal. Pork is the most common meat used, except in areas with a strong Muslim tradition where it's replaced with mutton or beef. **Fowl** is considered especially good during old age or convalescence; most rural people in central and southern China seem to own a couple of chickens, and the countryside is littered with duck and geese farms. **Fish and seafood** are highly regarded and can be expensive – partly because local pollution means that they often have to be imported – as are rarer **game** meats.

Eggs – duck, chicken or quail – are a popular nationwide snack, often flavoured by hard-boiling in a mixture of tea, soy sauce and star anise. There's also the so-called "thousand-year-old" variety, preserved for a few months in ash and straw – they look gruesome, with translucent brown albumen and green yolks, but actually have a delicate, brackish flavour. **Dairy products** serve limited purposes in China. Goat's cheese and yoghurt are eaten in parts of Yunnan and the Northwest, but milk is considered fit only for children and the elderly and is not used in cooking.

For a comprehensive menu reader and useful phrases for ordering food and drink, see p.1006. For more on Chinese food, see the Chinese cuisine colour section.

Vegetables accompany nearly every Chinese meal, used in most cases to balance tastes and textures of meat, but also appearing as dishes in their own right. Though the selection can be very thin in some parts of the country, there's usually a wide range on offer, from leafy greens to water chestnuts, mushrooms, bamboo shoots, seaweed and radish.

Soya beans are ubiquitous in Chinese cooking, being a good source of protein in a country where meat has often been a luxury. The beans themselves are small and green when fresh, and are sometimes eaten this way in the south. They are also salted and used to thicken sauces, fermented to produce **soy sauce**, or boiled and pressed to make white cakes of **tofu** (bean curd). Fresh tofu is flavourless and as soft as custard, though it can be pressed further to create a firmer texture, deep-fried until crisp, or cooked in stock and used as a meat substitute in vegetarian cooking. The skin that forms on top of the liquid while tofu is being made is itself skimmed off, dried, and used as a wrapping for spring rolls and the like.

Seasonal availability is smoothed over by a huge variety of **dried**, **salted** and **pickled vegetables**, meats and seafood, which often characterize local cooking styles. There's also an enormous assortment of regional **fruit**, great to clean the palate or fill a space between meals.

Breakfast, snacks and street food

Breakfast is not a big event by Chinese standards, more something to line the stomach for a few hours. Much of the country is content with a bowl of **zhou** rice porridge (also known as congee) flavoured with pickles and eaten with plain buns, or **doujiang** (sweetened soya milk) accompanied by a fried dough stick. Another favourite is a plain soup with noodles or **wuntun** dumplings and perhaps a little meat. Guangdong and Hong Kong are the exceptions, where the traditional breakfast of **dim sum** (also known as **yum cha**) involves a selection of tiny buns, dumplings and dishes served with tea.

Other **snacks and street food** are served through the day from small, early-opening **stalls** located around markets, train and bus stations. These serve grilled chicken wings; kebabs; spiced noodles; baked yams and potatoes; boiled eggs; various steamed or stewed dishes dished up in earthenware **sandpots**; grilled corn and – in places such as Beijing and Sichuan – countless local treats. Also common are **steamed buns**, which are either stuffed with meat or vegetables (*baozi*) or plain (*mantou*, literally "bald heads"). The buns originated in the north and are especially warming on a winter's day; a sweeter Cantonese variety is stuffed with barbecued pork. Another northern snack now found everywhere is the ravioli-like **jiaozi**, again with a meat or vegetable filling and either fried or steamed; **shuijiao** are boiled *jiaozi* served in soup. Some small restaurants specialize in *jiaozi*, containing a bewildering range of fillings and always sold by weight.

Restaurants and eating out

The cheapest **hole-in-the-wall canteens** are necessarily basic, with simple food costing a few yuan a serve and often much better than you'd expect from the furnishings. Proper **restaurants** are usually bright, busy places whose preferred atmosphere is *renao*, or "hot and noisy", rather than the often quiet norm in the West. Prices at these places obviously vary a lot, but even expensive-looking establishments charge only ¥15–50 for a main dish, and servings tend to be generous. Restaurants are often divided up by floor, with the cheapest, most public area on the ground floor and more expensive, private booths with waitress service upstairs.

While the cheaper places might have long hours, **restaurant opening times** are early and short: breakfast lasts from around 6–9am; lunch 11am–2pm; and dinner from around 5–9pm, after which the staff will be yawning and sweeping the debris off the tables around your ankles.

Ordering and dining

Pointing is all that's required at street stalls and small restaurants, where the ingredients are displayed out front in buckets, bundles and cages; canteens usually have the fare laid out or will have the selection scrawled illegibly on strips of paper or a board hung on the wall. You either tell the cook directly what you want or buy chits from a cashier, which you exchange at the kitchen hatch for your food and sit down at large communal tables or benches.

When you enter a **proper restaurant** you'll be escorted to a chair and promptly given a pot of tea, along with pickles and nuts in upmarket places. The only tableware provided is a spoon, a bowl and a pair of chopsticks. Unless you're in a big tourist destination, **menus** will be Chinese-only and the restaurant staff will probably be unable to speak English, though fortunately there's a growing trend for **photo menus** – in fact, some regional Chinese dishes have such obscure names that even non-local Chinese have to ask what they are. Alternatively, have a look at what other diners are eating – the Chinese are often delighted that a foreigner wants to eat Chinese food, and will indicate the best food on their table.

If this fails, you might be escorted through to the kitchen to make your choice by pointing at the raw ingredients. You need to get the idea across here if you want different items cooked together, otherwise you might end up with separate plates of nuts, meat and vegetables when you thought you'd ordered a single dish of chicken with cashews and green peppers. Note also that unless you're specific about how you want your food prepared, it inevitably arrives stir-fried.

When **ordering**, unless eating a one-dish meal like Beijing duck or a hotpot, try to select items with a **range of tastes and**

textures; it's also usual to include a soup. In cheap places, servings of noodles or rice are huge, but as they are considered basic stomach fillers, quantities decline the more upmarket you go. Note that dishes such as *jiaozi* and some seafood, as well as fresh produce, are **sold by weight**: a *liang* is 50g, a *banjin* 250g, a *jin* 500g, and a *gongjin* 1kg.

Dishes are all **served** at once, placed in the middle of the table for diners to share. With some poultry dishes you can crunch up the smaller bones, but anything else is spat out on to the tablecloth or floor, more or less discreetly depending on the establishment – watch what others are doing. **Soups** tend to be bland and are consumed last (except in the south where they may be served first or as part of the main meal) to wash the meal down, the liquid slurped from a spoon or the bowl once the noodles, vegetables or meat in it have been picked out and eaten. **Desserts** aren't a regular feature in China, though sweet soups and buns are eaten (the latter not confined to main meals) in the south, particularly at festive occasions.

Resting your chopsticks together across the top of your bowl means that you've **finished** eating. After a meal, the Chinese don't hang around to talk over drinks as in the West, but get up straight away and leave. In canteens, you'll **pay** up front, while at restaurants you ask for the bill and pay either the waiter or at the front till. **Tipping** is not expected in mainland China, though in Hong Kong you generally leave around ten percent.

Western and international food

There's a fair amount of **Western and international food** available in China, though supply and quality vary. Hong Kong, Shanghai and Beijing have the best range, with some excellent restaurants covering everything from Russian to Brazilian cuisine, and there are international food restaurants in every Chinese city of any size, with Korean and Japanese the best represented. Elsewhere, upmarket hotels may have Western restaurants, serving expensive but huge **buffet breakfasts** of scrambled egg, bacon, toast, cereal and coffee; and there's a growing number of **cafés** in many cities, especially ones with large foreign expat populations. **Burger**, **fried chicken** and **pizza** places are ubiquitous, including domestic chains such as *Dicos* alongside *McDonald's*, *KFC* and *Pizza Hut*.

Self-catering

Self-catering for tourists is feasible to a point. **Instant noodles** are a favourite travel food with the Chinese, available anywhere – just add boiling water, leave for five minutes, then stir in the flavourings supplied. Fresh **fruit and veg** from markets needs to be washed and peeled before eating raw; you can supplement things with **dried fruit**, **nuts and seeds**, roast and cured meats, biscuits and all manner of snacks. In cities, these things are also sold in more hygienic situations in **supermarkets**; many provincial capitals also have branches of the international chain **Carrefour** (家乐福, *jiālèfú*), where you can find small caches of Western foods.

Drink

Water is easily available in China, but never drink what comes out of the tap. **Boiled water** is always on hand in hotels and trains, either provided in large vacuum flasks or an urn, and you can buy **bottled spring water** at station stalls and supermarkets – read the labels and you'll see some unusual substances (such as radon) listed, which you'd probably want to avoid.

Tea

Tea has been known in China since antiquity and was originally drunk for medicinal reasons. Over the centuries a whole **social culture** has sprung up around this beverage, spawning **teahouses** that once held the same place in Chinese society that the local pub or bar does in the West. Plantations of neat rows of low tea bushes adorn hillsides across southern China, while the brew is enthusiastically consumed from the highlands of Tibet – where it's mixed with barley meal and butter – to every restaurant and household between Hong Kong and Beijing.

Often the first thing you'll be asked in a restaurant is *he shenme cha* – "what sort of tea would you like?" Chinese tea comes in red, green and flower-scented **varieties**, depending on how it's processed; only Hainan produces Indian-style **black** tea. Some regional kinds, such as *pu'er* from Yunnan, Fujian's *tie guanyin*, Zhejiang's *longjing* or Sichuan's *zhuye qing*, are highly sought after; indeed, after locals in Yunnan decided that banks weren't paying enough interest, they started investing in *pu'er* tea stocks, causing prices to soar.

The manner in which it's **served** also varies from place to place: sometimes it comes in huge mugs with a lid, elsewhere in dainty cups served from a miniature pot; there are also formalized **tea rituals** in parts of Fujian and Guangdong. When drinking in company, it's polite to top up others' cups before your own, whenever they become empty; if someone does this for you, lightly tap your first two fingers on the table to show your thanks. If you've had enough, leave your cup full, and in a restaurant take the lid off or turn it over if you want the pot refilled during the meal.

Chinese leaf tea is never drunk with milk or sugar, though recently **Taiwanese bubble tea** – Indian-style tea with milk, sugar and sago balls – has become popular in the south. It's also worth trying some **Muslim** *babao cha* or **Eight Treasures Tea**, which involves dried fruit, nuts, seeds and crystallized sugar heaped into a cup with the remaining space filled with hot water, poured with panache from an immensely long-spouted copper kettle.

Alcohol

The popularity of **beer** in China rivals that of tea, and, for men, is the preferred mealtime beverage (drinking alcohol in public is considered improper for Chinese women, though not for foreigners). The first brewery was set up in the northeastern port of Qingdao by the Germans in the nineteenth century, and now, though the Tsingtao label is widely available, just about every province produces at least one brand of four-percent Pilsner. Sold in litre bottles, it's always drinkable, often pretty good, and is actually cheaper than bottled water. Draught beer is becoming available across the country.

Watch out for the term "**wine**" on English menus, which usually denotes **spirits,** made from rice, sorghum or millet. Serving spirits to guests is a sign of hospitality, and they're always used for toasting at banquets. Again, local home-made varieties can be quite good, while mainstream brands – especially the expensive, nationally famous Moutai and Wuliangye – are pretty vile to the Western palate. **Imported beers and spirits** are sold in large department stores and in city bars, but are always expensive. China does have several commercial **wine labels**, the best of which is Changyu from Yantai in Shandong province, and there are ongoing efforts to launch wine as a stylish niche product, with limited success so far.

Western-style bars are found not only in Hong Kong and Macau, but also in the major mainland cities. These establishments serve both local and imported beers and spirits, and are popular with China's middle class as well as foreigners. Mostly, though, the Chinese drink alcohol only with their meals – all restaurants serve at least local beer and spirits.

Soft drinks

Canned drinks, usually sold unchilled, include various lemonades and colas. **Fruit juices** can be unusual and refreshing, however, flavoured with chunks of lychee, lotus and water chestnuts. **Coffee** is grown and drunk in Yunnan and Hainan, and imported brews are available in cafés; you can buy instant powder in any supermarket. **Milk** is sold in powder form as baby food, and increasingly in bottles for adult consumption as its benefits for invalids and the elderly become accepted wisdom.

The media

Xinhua is the state-run news agency that supplies most of the national print and TV media. All content is Party-controlled and censored, though there is a limited openness about social issues and natural disasters as long as the government is portrayed as successfully combatting the problem. Stories about corrupt local officials, armed confrontations between developers and peasants being forced off their land, or the appalling conditions of coal-mine workers do occasionally get through the net, though both journalists and editors take a risk reporting such things: several doing so have been jailed for "revealing state secrets", or even beaten to death by the thugs they were trying to expose.

Newspapers and magazines

The national **Chinese-language newspaper** is the *People's Daily* (with an online English edition at ⓦenglish.peopledaily.com.cn), though all provincial capitals and many major cities produce their own dailies with a local slant. **Lifestyle magazines** have really taken off in the last few years, and newsagent stalls sag under the weight of publications covering fashion, teens, interior furnishings and countless other subjects.

The only national **English-language newspaper** is the *China Daily* (ⓦwww.chinadaily.com.cn), which is scarce outside big cities. **Hong Kong**'s English-language media includes the locally produced newspapers the *South China Morning Post* and the *Standard*, published alongside Asian editions of *Time*, *Newsweek*, the *Asian Wall Street Journal* and *USA Today*. These have so far remained openly critical of Beijing on occasion, despite the former colony's changeover to Chinese control.

Most big cities, including Beijing, Shanghai, Kunming, Chengdu and Chongqing have free **English-language magazines aimed at expats** containing listings of local venues and events, plus classifieds and feature articles; they're monitored by the authorities, though this doesn't stop them sailing quite close to the wind at times.

Television and radio

Chinese **television** comprises a dozen or so channels run by the state television company, **CCTV**, plus a host of regional stations; not all channels are available across the country. Most of the content comprises news, flirty game shows, travel and wildlife documentaries, soaps and historical dramas, and bizarre song-and-dance extravaganzas featuring performers in fetishistic, tight-fitting military outfits entertaining party officials with rigor-mortis faces. Tune in to **CCTV 1** for news; **CCTV 5** is dedicated to sport; **CCTV 6** shows films (with at least one war feature a day, in which the Japanese are shown getting mightily beaten); **CCTV News** broadcasts an **English-language** mix of news, documentaries and travel shows; and **CCTV 11** concentrates on Chinese opera. The **regional stations** are sometimes more adventurous, with a current trend for frank dating games, which draw much criticism from conservative-minded government factions for the rampant materialism displayed by the contestants.

On the **radio** you're likely to hear the latest soft ballads, or versions of Western pop songs sung in Chinese. For **news from home**, you'll need to bring a **shortwave radio** with you; see the websites of the **BBC World Service** (ⓦwww.bbc.co.uk/worldservice), **Radio Canada** (ⓦwww.rcinet.ca), the **Voice of America** (ⓦwww.voa.gov) and **Radio Australia** (ⓦwww.abc.net.au/ra) for schedules and frequencies.

Festivals

China celebrates many secular and religious festivals, three of which – the Spring Festival (Chinese New Year), the May 1 Labour Day, and National Day on October 1 – involve nationwide holidays. Avoid travel during these times, as the country's transport network becomes severely overloaded.

Most festivals take place according to dates in the **Chinese lunar calendar**, in which the first day of the month is the time when the moon is at its thinnest, with the full moon marking the middle of the month. By the Gregorian calendar used in the West, such festivals fall on a different day every year – check online for the latest dates. Most festivals celebrate the turning of the seasons or auspicious dates, such as the eighth day of the eighth month (eight is a lucky number in China), and are times for gift giving, family reunions, feasting and the setting off of firecrackers. It's always worth visiting temples on festival days, when the air is thick with incense, and people queue up to kowtow to altars and play games that bring good fortune, such as trying to hit the temple bell by throwing coins.

Aside from the following national festivals, China's **ethnic groups** punctuate the year with their own ritual observances, which are described in the relevant chapters of the guide. In Hong Kong, all the national Chinese festivals are celebrated.

A holidays and festivals calendar

January/February Two-week-long **Spring Festival** (see box below). Everything shuts down for a national holiday during the first week.

February **Tiancang Festival** On the twentieth day of the first lunar month, Chinese peasants celebrate Tiancang, or Granary Filling Day, in the hope of ensuring a good harvest later in the year.

March **Guanyin's Birthday** Guanyin, the Bodhisattva of Mercy, and probably China's most popular deity, is celebrated on the nineteenth day of the second lunar month.

April 5 **Qingming Festival** This festival, also referred to as Tomb Sweeping Day, is the time to visit the graves of ancestors and burn ghost money in honour of the departed.

April 13–15 **Dai Water Splashing Festival** Anyone on the streets of Xishuangbanna, in Yunnan province, is fair game for a soaking.

Spring Festival (Chinese New Year)

The **Spring Festival** is two weeks of festivities marking the beginning of the lunar **New Year**, usually in late January or early February. In Chinese astrology, each year is associated with one of twelve animals, and the passing into a new phase is a momentous occasion. The festival sees China at its most colourful, with shops and houses decorated with good-luck messages. The first day of the festival is marked by a family feast at which *jiaozi* (dumplings) are eaten, sometimes with coins hidden inside. To bring luck, people dress in red clothes (red being a lucky colour) and eat fish, since the Chinese script for fish resembles the script for "surplus", something everyone wishes to enjoy during the year. Firecrackers are let off almost constantly to scare ghosts away and, on the fifth day, to honour **Cai Shen**, god of wealth. Another ghost-scaring tradition is the pasting up of images of door gods at the threshold. Outside the home, New Year is celebrated at **temple fairs**, which feature acrobats and clouds of smoke as the Chinese light incense sticks to placate the gods. The celebrations end with the **lantern festival**, when the streets are filled with multi-coloured paper lanterns; many places also have flower festivals and street processions with paper dragons and other animals parading through the town. It's customary at this time to eat *tang yuan*, glutinous rice balls stuffed with sweet sesame paste.

May 1 Labour Day A three-day national holiday when everyone goes on the move.

May 4 Youth Day Commemorating the student demonstrators in Tian'anmen Square in 1919, which gave rise to the Nationalist "May Fourth Movement". It's marked in most cities with flower displays.

June 1 Children's Day Most schools go on field trips, so if you're visiting a popular tourist site, be prepared for mobs of kids in yellow baseball caps.

June/July Dragon-boat Festival On the fifth day of the fifth lunar month, dragon-boat races are held in memory of the poet Qu Yuan, who drowned himself in 280 BC. The traditional food to accompany the celebrations is *zongzi* (lotus-wrapped rice packets). Another three-day public holiday.

August/September Ghost Festival The Chinese equivalent of Halloween, this is a time when ghosts from hell are supposed to walk the earth. It's not celebrated so much as observed; it's regarded as an inauspicious time to travel, move house or get married.

September/October Moon Festival On the fifteenth day of the eighth month of the lunar calendar, the Chinese celebrate what's also known as the Mid-Autumn Festival. Moon cakes, containing a rich filling of sugar, lotus-seed paste and walnut, are eaten, and plenty of spirits consumed. The public get a further three days off.

September/October Double Ninth Festival Nine is a number associated with *yang*, or male energy, and on the ninth day of the ninth lunar month such qualities as assertiveness and strength are celebrated. It's believed to be a good time for the distillation (and consumption) of spirits.

September 28 Confucius Festival The birthday of Confucius is marked by celebrations at all Confucian temples. It's a good time to visit Qufu, in Shandong province, when elaborate ceremonies are held at the temple there.

October 1 National Day Another week-long holiday when everyone has time off to celebrate the founding of the People's Republic. TV is even more dire than usual as it's full of programmes celebrating Party achievements.

December 25 Christmas This is marked as a religious event only by the faithful, but for everyone else it's an excuse for a feast and a party.

Sport and outdoor activities

Since 2008, when China hosted the Olympics, athletic passion has become almost a patriotic duty. But the most visible forms of exercise are fairly timeless; head to any public space in the morning and you'll see citizens going through all sorts of martial-arts routines, playing ping pong and street badminton, even ballroom dancing. Sadly though, facilities for organized sport are fairly limited.

The Chinese are good at "small ball" games such as squash and badminton, and, of course, table tennis, at which they are world champions, but admit room for improvement in the "big ball" games, such as **football**. Nevertheless, Chinese men follow foreign football avidly, with games from the European leagues shown on CCTV5. There's also a national obsession among students for **basketball**, which predates the rise to international fame of NBA star **Yao Ming**, who plies his trade for the Houston Rockets.

If China has an indigenous "sport", however, it's the **martial arts** – not surprising, perhaps, in a country whose history is littered with long periods of civil conflict. Today, there are hundreds of Chinese martial-arts styles, usually taught for exercise rather than for fighting.

As for **outdoor activities**, hiking for its own sake has yet to catch on, though tourists have plenty of opportunities for step-aerobic-type exercise up long, steep staircases ascending China's many **holy mountains**. Snow sports have become popular in Dongbei, which has several **ski resorts**, while the wilds of Yunnan and Sichuan, along with Qinghai and Tibet, are drawing increasing numbers of adventurous young city-born Chinese – always dressed in the latest outdoor gear – to **mountaineering** and four-wheel-drive expeditions.

Culture and etiquette

The Chinese are, on the whole, pragmatic, materialistic and garrulous. Many of the irritations experienced by foreigners – the sniggers and the unhelpful service – can almost invariably be put down to nervousness and the language barrier, rather than hostility. Visitors who speak Chinese will encounter an endless series of delighted and amazed interlocutors wherever they go, invariably asking about their country of origin, their job and the reason they are in China.

If you're **invited** to someone's home, take along a **gift** – a bottle of spirits, some tea or an ornamental trinket are good choices (anything too utilitarian could be considered patronizing) – though your hosts won't impolitely open this in front of you. **Restaurant bills** are not shared out between the guests but instead people will go to great lengths to pay the whole amount themselves. Normally this honour will fall to the person perceived as the most senior, and as a foreigner dining with Chinese you should make some effort to stake your claim, though it is probable that someone else will grab the bill before you do. Attempting to pay a "share" of the bill will embarrass your hosts.

Privacy

The Chinese have almost no concept of **privacy** – even public toilets are built with partitions so low that you can chat with your neighbour while squatting. All leisure activities including visits to natural beauty spots or holy relics are enjoyed in large noisy groups, and the desire of some Western tourists to be "left alone" is variously interpreted by locals as eccentric or arrogant.

Exotic foreigners inevitably become targets for **blatant curiosity**. People stare and point, voices on the street shout out "helloooo" twenty times a day, or – in rural areas – people even run up and jostle for a better look, exclaiming loudly to each other, *laowai, laowai* ("foreigner"). This is not usually intended to be aggressive or insulting, though the cumulative effects of such treatment can be annoying and alienating.

Spitting and smoking

Various other forms of behaviour perceived as antisocial in the West are considered perfectly normal in China. The widespread habit of **spitting**, for example, can be observed in buses, trains, restaurants and even inside people's homes. Outside the company of urban sophisticates, it would not occur to people that there was anything disrespectful in delivering a powerful spit while in conversation with a stranger. **Smoking**, likewise, is almost universal among men, and any attempt to stop others from lighting up is met with incomprehension. As in many countries, handing out cigarettes is a basic way of establishing goodwill, and non-smokers should be apologetic about turning down offered cigarettes.

Clothing

Chinese clothing styles lean towards the casual, though surprisingly for such an apparently conservative-minded country, summertime **skimpy clothing** is common in all urban areas, particularly among women (less so in the countryside). Even in potentially sensitive Muslim areas, many Han Chinese girls insist on wearing miniskirts and see-through blouses. Although Chinese men commonly wear shorts and expose their midriffs in hot weather, Western men who do the same should note that the bizarre sight of hairy flesh in public – chest or legs – will instantly become the focus of giggly gossip. The generally relaxed approach to clothing applies equally when visiting temples, though in **mosques** men and women alike should cover their bodies above the wrists and ankles. As for **beachwear**, bikinis and briefs are in, but nudity has only recently made its debut, on southern Hainan Island (see p.563).

Casual clothing is one thing, but **scruffy clothing** is quite another. If you want to earn the respect of the Chinese – useful for things like getting served in a restaurant or checking into a hotel – you need to make some effort with your appearance. While the average Chinese peasant might reasonably be expected to have wild hair and wear dirty clothes, a rich foreigner doing so will arouse a degree of contempt.

Meeting people

When **meeting people** it's useful to have a name or **business card** to flash around – Chinese with business aspirations hand them out at every opportunity, and are a little crestfallen if you can't produce one in return. It's polite to take the proffered card with both hands and to have a good look at it before putting it away – though not in your back pocket. If you don't speak Chinese but have your name in Chinese printed on them, they also become useful when checking in to hotels that are reluctant to take foreigners, as the staff can then copy your name into the register.

Shaking hands is not a Chinese tradition, though it is fairly common between men. Bodily contact in the form of embraces or back-slapping can be observed between same-sex friends, and these days, in cities, a boy and a girl can walk round arm in arm and even kiss without raising an eyebrow.

Voice levels in China seem to be pitched several decibels louder than in most other countries, though this should not necessarily be interpreted as a sign of belligerence.

Sex and gender issues

Women travellers in China usually find incidence of **sexual harassment** less of a problem than in other Asian countries. Chinese men are, on the whole, deferential and respectful. A more likely complaint is being ignored, as the Chinese will generally assume that any man accompanying a woman will be doing all the talking. Women on their own visiting remote temples or sights need to be on their guard – don't assume that all monks and caretakers have impeccable morals.

Prostitution, though illegal, is everywhere in China. Single foreign men are likely to be approached inside hotels; it's common practice for prostitutes to phone around hotel rooms at all hours of the night. Bear in mind that the consequence of a Westerner being caught with a prostitute may be unpleasant, and that AIDS is on the increase.

Homosexuality is increasingly tolerated by the authorities and people in general, though public displays may get you in trouble outside the more cosmopolitan cities. There are gay bars in most major cities, especially Beijing and Shanghai.

Dating a local won't raise many eyebrows in these relaxed times, though displays of mixed-race public affection certainly will.

Shopping

China is a good place to shop for tourist souvenirs, folk art, clothes, household goods and faked designer labels – but not for real designer brands or electronic goods (including mobile phones), which are all cheaper at home or online. Even small villages have markets, while larger cities will also have big department stores, shopping malls and even international supermarket chains.

Prices in stores are fixed, but **discounts** (折扣, *zhékòu*) are common: they're marked by a number between one and nine and the character "折", indicating the percentage of the original price you have to pay – "8折", for example, means that the item is on sale at eighty percent of its original price. At markets you're expected to **bargain** for goods unless prices are displayed. If you can speak Chinese, hang around for a while to get an idea what others are paying, or just ask at a few stalls selling the same things; Chinese shoppers usually state the price they're willing to pay, rather than beginning low and working up to it after haggling. Don't become obsessed about saving every last yuan; being charged more than locals and getting ripped off from time to time is inevitable.

Souvenirs popular with foreign tourists include "chops" (stone seals with your name engraved in characters on the base); all manner of reproduction antiques, from porcelain to furniture; mementos of Mao and the Cultural Revolution – Little Red Books and cigarette lighters that chime "*The East is Red*"; T-shirts and "old-style" Chinese clothes; scroll paintings; and ethnic jewellery and textiles. Chinese tourists also look for things like local teas, "purple sand" teapots and bright tack. Pretty much the same selection is sold at all tourist sites, irrespective of relevancy. For **real antiques**, you need specialist stores or markets – some are listed in the guide – where anything genuine is meant to be marked with a wax seal and requires an export licence to take out of the country. The Chinese are clued-up, avid collectors and value their culture highly, so don't expect to find any bargains.

Clothes are a very good deal in China, with brand stores such as Giordano, Baleno, Meters/Bonwe and Yishion selling high quality smart-casual wear. Fashion-conscious places such as Shanghai and Hong Kong also have **factory outlet** stores, selling last year's designs at low prices, and all major cities have specialist stores stocking outdoors and hiking gear, though it often looks far better than it turns out to be for the price. **Sizes** bear no relation to what it says on the label, so always try things on before buying them. Silk and other **fabrics** are also good value, if you're into making your own clothes. **Shoes** are inexpensive too, though anything larger than size 8/42 is rare.

All bookstores and many market stalls in China sell **music CDs** of everything from Beijing punk to Beethoven, plus **VCDs** and **DVDs** of domestic and international movies (often subtitled – check on the back). While extremely cheap at ¥5–35, many of these are **pirated** (the discs may be confiscated at customs when you get home). Genuine DVD films may be region-coded for Asia, so check the label and whether your player at home will handle them; there are no such problems with CDs or VCDs.

Hong Kong is the only place with a comprehensive range of **Western goods**; on the mainland, your best bet is to head to provincial capitals, many of which have a branch of **Carrefour** (家乐福, *jiālèfú*) or **Wal-Mart** (沃尔玛, *wòěrmǎ*), where you may find small caches of foreign goodies.

Children

Children in China are, thanks to the one-child policy, usually indulged and pampered, and foreigners travelling with children can expect to receive lots of attention from curious locals – and the occasional admonition that the little one should be wrapped up warmer.

While **formula and nappies** might be available in modern, big city supermarkets, elsewhere you'll need to bring a supply (and any **medication** if required) with you – local kids don't use nappies, just pants with a slit at the back, and when baby wants to go, mummy points him at the gutter. Similarly, changing facilities and baby-minding services are virtually unknown on the mainland outside high-end international hotels.

Hong Kong is the only part of China where children are specifically catered to by attractions such as Ocean World and Disneyland; elsewhere, the way that most Chinese tourist sites are decked up like fairground rides makes them attractive for youngsters in any case. Things to watch for include China's poor levels of **hygiene** (keeping infants' and toddlers' hands clean can be a full-time occupation), spicy or just unusual food, plus the **stress levels** caused by the ambient crowds, pollution and noise found in much of the country – though it often seems to affect parents more than children.

Travel essentials

Costs

China is an **expensive** place to travel compared with the rest of Asia. Though food and transport are good value, accommodation can be expensive for what you get, and **entry fees** for temples, scenic areas and historic monuments are becoming high even on an international scale – so much so that the central government is trying to get local authorities to reduce them (with little effect so far). Actual prices vary considerably between **regions**: Hong Kong and Macau are as costly as Europe or the US; the developed eastern provinces are expensive by Chinese standards; and the further west you go, the more prices fall.

By doing everything cheaply and sticking mostly to the less expensive interior provinces, you can survive on £29/US$45/¥300 a day; travel a bit more widely and in better comfort and you're looking at £58/US$90/¥600 a day; while travelling in style and visiting only key places along the east coast, you could run up daily expenses of £145/US$225/¥1500 and above.

It used to be government policy to **surcharge** foreigners for public transport and admission fees for sights. Though the practice is officially banned, you might still be sold the most expensive option for these things, without being informed of less costly alternatives; take comfort in the fact that Chinese tourists suffer the same treatment. **Discount rates** for pensioners and students are available for many entry fees, however. Students generally need a Chinese student card, though ISIC cards sometimes work; pensioners can often just use their passports to prove they are over 60 (women) or 65 (men).

Crime and personal safety

While the worst that happens to most visitors to China is that they have their pocket picked on a bus or get **scammed** (see below), you do need to take care. Carry passports and money in a concealed money belt, and keep some foreign notes – perhaps around US$200 – separately from the rest of your cash, together with your travellers'-cheque receipts, insurance policy details and photocopies of your passport and visa. Be wary on **buses**, the favoured haunt of **pickpockets**, and **trains**, particularly in hard-seat class and on overnight journeys.

One of the most dangerous things you can do in China is **cross a road**: marked pedestrian crossings might as well not be there for all the attention shown them by motorists; and even when traffic lights flash green to show it's safe to cross, you'll find that vehicles are still permitted to turn in to or out of the road. **Hotel rooms** are on the whole secure, dormitories much less so, though often it's your fellow travellers who are the problem here. Most hotels should have a safe, but it's not unusual for things to go missing from these. Wandering around cities late at night is as bad an idea in China as anywhere else; similarly, walking alone across the countryside is ill-advised, particularly in remote regions. If anyone does try to rob you, run away or, if this isn't possible, stay calm and don't resist.

You may see stress-induced **street confrontations**, though these rarely result in violence, just a lot of shouting. Another irritation, particularly in the southern cities, are gangs of **child beggars**, organized by a nearby adult. They target foreigners and can be very hard to shake off; handing over money usually results in increased harassment.

Emergency numbers

Police ⓣ110
Fire ⓣ119
Ambulance ⓣ120
Though you are generally better off taking a taxi to the nearest hospital than calling for an ambulance.

The police

The **police**, known as the **Public Security Bureau** or **PSB**, are recognizable by their dark blue uniforms and caps, though there are a lot more around than you might at first think, as plenty are undercover. They have much wider powers than most Western police forces, including establishing the guilt of criminals – trials are used only for deciding the sentence of the accused (though this is changing and China now has the beginnings of an independent judiciary). If the culprit is deemed to show proper remorse, this will result in a more lenient sentence.

The PSB also have the job of looking after foreigners, and you'll most likely have to seek them out for **visa extensions**, reporting theft or losses, and obtaining permits for otherwise closed areas of the country (mostly in Tibet). On occasion, they might seek you out; it's common for the

Scams

A good number of professional **con artists** target tourists – especially in places such as Shanghai, Beijing and Guilin – with variations on the following scam. A sweet-looking young couple, a pair of girls, or perhaps a kindly old man, will ask to practise their English or offer to show you round. Having befriended you – which may take hours – they will suggest some refreshment, and lead you to a teahouse, art gallery or restaurant. After eating or drinking, you will be presented with a bill for thousands of yuan, your new "friends" will vanish or pretend to be shocked, and some large gentlemen will appear. It's hard to believe just how convincing these people can be – never eat or drink with a stranger unless you know how much you're expected to pay.

police to call round to your hotel room if you're staying in a remote place – they usually just look at your passport and then move on.

While individual police often go out of their way to help foreigners, the PSB itself has all the problems of any police force in a country where corruption is widespread, and it's best to minimize contact with them.

Offences to avoid

With adjacent opium-growing areas in Burma and Laos, and a major Southeast Asian distribution point in Hong Kong, China has a massive **drug problem**. Heroin use has become fairly widespread in the south, particularly in depressed rural areas, and ecstasy is used in clubs and discos. In the past, the police have turned a blind eye to foreigners with drugs, as long as no Chinese are involved, but you don't want to test this out. In 2010, China **executed** a British national for drug trafficking, and annually holds mass executions of convicted drug offenders on the UN anti-drugs day in June.

Visitors are not likely to be accused of **political crimes**, but foreign residents, including teachers or students, may find themselves expelled from the country for talking about politics or religion. The Chinese they talk to will be treated less leniently. In Tibet, and at sensitive border areas, censorship is taken much more seriously; **photographing** military installations (which can include major road bridges), instances of police brutality or gulags is not a good idea.

Electricity

The electricity supply runs on 220 volts, with the most common type of **plug** a dual flat prong, except in Hong Kong, where they favour the UK-style square triple prong. Adaptors are widely available from neighbourhood hardware stores.

Entry requirements

All foreign nationals require a **visa** to enter mainland China, available worldwide from Chinese embassies and consulates and through specialist tour operators and visa agents, and online. However, they're easiest to obtain in **Hong Kong** – often without the documentation insisted on by overseas agents – if you're planning to come that way (see p.580).

Visas must be used within three months of issue, and **cost** £20–150 depending on the visa type, the length of stay, the number of entries allowed, and your nationality. Your passport must be valid for at least another six months from your planned date of entry into China, and have at least one blank page for visas. You'll be asked your **occupation** – it's not wise to admit to being a journalist, photographer or writer, as you might be called in for an interview. At times of political sensitivity, you may be asked for a copy of any air tickets and hotel bookings in your name. **Don't overstay your visa**: the fine is ¥500 a day, along with the possibility that you may be deported and banned from entering China for five years.

Tourist visas (L) are valid for between one and six months, and can be single- or multiple-entry – though multiple-entry visas usually require you to leave China every thirty days. One- or three-month visas are fairly easy to obtain through embassies or consulates, six-month visas much less so – Hong Kong is probably the only place you're likely to get one, and only if you can prove you've spent time in China previously.

A **business visa** (F) is valid for between three months and two years and can be either multiple- or single-entry. To apply, you'll need an official invitation from a government-recognized Chinese organization, except in Hong Kong, where you can just buy one. **Twelve-month work visas** (Z) again require an invitation, plus a **health certificate**.

Students intending to study in China for less than six months need an invitation or letter of acceptance from a college there and will be given an F visa. If you're intending study for longer than six months, there is an additional form, available from Chinese embassies and online, and you will also need a health certificate; then you'll be issued with an X visa, which allows you to stay and study for up to a year.

You're allowed to **import** into China up to 400 cigarettes and 1.5l of alcohol and up to ¥20,000 cash. Foreign currency in excess of US$5000 or the equivalent must be declared. It's illegal to import **printed or**

filmed matter critical of the country, but this is currently only a problem with Chinese border guards at crossings from Vietnam, who have confiscated guidebooks to China that contain maps showing Taiwan as a separate country (such as this one); keep them buried in the bottom of your bags.

Chinese embassies and consulates

Australia 15 Coronation Drive, Yarralumla, Canberra, ACT 2600 ⓣ02/6273 4780, ⓦau.china-embassy.org/eng.
Canada 515 St Patrick St, Ottawa, Ontario K1N 5H3 ⓣ1-613/789-3434, ⓦca.chineseembassy .org/chn.
Ireland 40 Ailesbury Rd, Dublin 4 ⓣ01/269 1707.
New Zealand 2–6 Glenmore St, Wellington ⓣ04/4721382, ⓦwww.chinaembassy.org.nz.
South Africa 965 Church St, Arcadia, Pretoria ⓣ012/4316500, ⓦwww.chinese-embassy.org.za.
UK 49–51 Portland Place, London W1B 1JL ⓣ020/7299 4049, ⓦwww.chinese-embassy .org.uk.
US 3505 International Place, Washington DC 20008 ⓣ1-202/495-2266, ⓦwww .chinese-embassy.org.

Visa extensions

Visa extensions are handled by the **Public Security Bureau** (**PSB**), so you can apply for one in any reasonably sized town – the department will be called something like "Aliens' Entry Exit Section". The cost, and the amount of hassle you'll have, varies greatly depending on where you are and your nationality. In particular, many places want to see a receipt from your accommodation, proving that you're staying in the town in which you're applying.

A **first extension**, valid for a month, is easy to obtain and costs ¥160 (though US citizens pay more). However, the particular PSB office may decide to levy extra charges on top, or even waive the fee completely. In some small towns, the process takes ten minutes; in cities, it can take up to a week. The worst place to apply is Tibet (you'll be given a week's extension at most); next worst is Beijing and then Shanghai.

A **second or third extension** is harder to get, and impossible if your visa was originally issued in Hong Kong. In major cities, you will probably be turned away, though you'd be unlucky to come away without some kind of extension from PSB offices in small towns. You will be asked your reasons for wanting an extension – simply saying you want to spend more time in this wonderful country usually goes down well, or you could cite illness or transport delays. Don't admit to being low on funds. Fourth or even fifth extensions are possible, but you'll need to foster connections with a PSB office. Ask advice from a local independent travel agent – they often have the right sort of contacts. In Shanghai and Beijing, it is possible to get extra extensions from a visa agent – they advertise in the back of expat magazines.

Health

No vaccinations are required to visit China, except for yellow fever if you're coming from an area where the disease is endemic. It's worth taking a **first-aid kit** with you, particularly if you will be travelling extensively outside the cities, where getting hold of the appropriate medicines might be difficult. Include bandages, plasters, painkillers, oral rehydration solution, medication to counter diarrhoea, vitamin pills and antiseptic cream. A sterile set of hypodermics may be advisable, as re-use of hypodermics does occur in China. Note there is widespread ignorance of sexual health issues, and AIDS and STDs are widespread – always practise **safe sex**.

The most common health hazards in China are the **cold and flu infections** that strike down a large proportion of the population in the winter months. **Diarrhoea** is also common, usually in a mild form while your stomach gets used to unfamiliar food, but also sometimes with a sudden onset accompanied by stomach cramps and vomiting, which indicates **food poisoning**. In both instances, get plenty of rest, drink lots of water, and in serious cases replace lost salts with **oral rehydration solution** (**ORS**); this is especially important with young children. Take a few sachets with you, or make your own by adding half a teaspoon of salt and three of sugar to a litre of cool, previously boiled water. While down with diarrhoea, avoid milk, greasy or spicy foods, coffee and most fruit, in favour of bland foodstuffs such as rice, plain noodles and soup. If symptoms persist, or if you notice blood or mucus in your stools, consult a doctor as you may have **dysentery**.

To avoid stomach complaints, eat at places that look busy and clean and stick to fresh, thoroughly cooked food. Shellfish is a potential hepatitis A risk, and best avoided. Fresh fruit you've peeled yourself is safe; other uncooked foods may have been washed in unclean water. **Don't drink untreated tap water** – boiled or bottled water is widely available.

Hepatitis A is a viral infection spread by contaminated food and water, which causes an inflammation of the liver. The less common **hepatitis B** virus can be passed on through unprotected sexual contact, transfusions of unscreened blood, and dirty needles. Hepatitis symptoms include yellowing of the eyes and skin, preceded by lethargy, fever, and pains in the upper right abdomen.

Typhoid and cholera are spread by contaminated food or water, generally in localized epidemics; both are serious conditions and require immediate medical help. Symptoms of **typhoid** include headaches, high fever and constipation, followed by diarrhoea in the later stages. The disease is infectious. **Cholera** begins with sudden but painless onset of watery diarrhoea, later combined with vomiting, nausea and muscle cramps. Rapid dehydration rather than the infection itself is the main danger, and should be treated with constant oral rehydration solutions.

Summer outbreaks of **malaria** and **dengue fever** occur across southern China, usually in localized areas. Symptoms are similar – severe headaches, joint pains, fever and shaking – though a rash might also appear with dengue. There's no cure for dengue fever, whereas malaria can be prevented and controlled with medication; both require immediate medical attention to ensure that there are no complications. You can minimize your chances of being bitten by mosquitoes in the first place by wearing light-coloured, full-length clothing and insect repellent in the evenings when mosquitoes are active.

In tropical China, the **temperature and humidity** can take a couple of weeks to adjust to. High humidity can cause **heat rashes**, **prickly heat** and **fungal infections**. Prevention and cure are the same: wear loose clothes made of natural fibres, wash frequently and dry-off thoroughly afterwards. Talcum or anti-fungal powder and the use of mild antiseptic soap help, too.

Don't underestimate the strength of the sun in the tropics, desert regions such as Xinjiang or high up on the Tibetan Plateau. Sunscreen is not easily available in China. Signs of **dehydration** and **heatstroke** include a high temperature, lack of sweating, a fast pulse and red skin. Reducing your body temperature with a lukewarm shower will provide initial relief.

Plenty of places in China – Tibet and the north in particular – also get very **cold**. Watch out here for **hypothermia**, where the core body temperature drops to a point that can be fatal. Symptoms are a weak pulse, disorientation, numbness, slurred speech and exhaustion. To prevent the condition, wear lots of layers and a hat, eat plenty of carbohydrates, and stay dry and out of the wind. To treat hypothermia, get the victim into shelter, away from wind and rain, give them hot drinks – but not alcohol – and easily digestible food, and keep them warm. Serious cases require immediate hospitalization.

High altitude, in regions such as Tibet and parts of Xinjiang, Sichuan and Yunnan, prevents the blood from absorbing oxygen efficiently, and can lead to **altitude sickness**, also known as **AMS** (acute mountain sickness). Most people feel some symptoms above 3500m, which include becoming easily exhausted, headaches, shortness of breath, sleeping disorders and nausea; they're intensified if you ascend to altitude rapidly, for instance by flying direct from coastal cities to Lhasa. Relaxing for the first few days, **drinking** plenty of water, and taking painkillers will ease symptoms. Having acclimatized at one altitude you should still ascend slowly, or you can expect the symptoms to return.

If for any reason the body fails to acclimatize to altitude, serious conditions can develop including **pulmonary oedema** (characterized by severe breathing trouble, a cough and frothy white or pink sputum), and **cerebral oedema** (causing severe headaches, loss of balance, other neurological symptoms and eventually coma). The only treatment for these is **rapid descent**: in Tibet, this means flying out to Kathmandu or Chengdu without delay. You also need to see a doctor as soon as possible.

Hospitals, clinics and pharmacies

Medical facilities in China are best in major cities with large expat populations, where there are often high-standard clinics, and the hotels may even have resident doctors. Elsewhere, larger cities and towns have hospitals, and for minor complaints there are plenty of pharmacies that can suggest remedies, though don't expect English to be spoken.

Chinese hospitals use a mix of Western and traditional Chinese medicine approaches, and sometimes charge high prices for simple drugs and use procedures that aren't necessary – they'll put you on a drip just to administer antibiotics – so always ask for a second opinion from a Western-trained doctor if you're worried (your embassy should be able to recommend one if none is suggested in the guide). In an **emergency**, you're better off taking a cab than waiting for an ambulance – it's quicker and will work out much cheaper. There's virtually **no free health care** in China even for its citizens; expect to pay around ¥500 as a consultation **fee**.

Pharmacies are marked by a green cross, and if you can describe your ailment or required medication, you'll find many drugs which would be restricted and expensive in the West are easily available over the counter for very little money. Be wary of **counterfeit drugs**, however; check for spelling mistakes in the packaging or instructions.

Medical resources for travellers

In the UK and Ireland

MASTA (Medical Advisory Service for Travellers Abroad) UK ⓦwww.masta-travel-health.com. Fifty clinics across the UK.

Tropical Medical Bureau Republic of Ireland ⓦwww.tmb.ie.

In the US and Canada

Canadian Society for International Health ⓦwww.csih.org. Extensive list of travel health centres in Canada.

CDC ⓦwww.cdc.gov. Official US government public health agency, with good travel-health information.

International Society for Travel Medicine ⓦwww.istm.org. A full list of clinics worldwide specializing in travel health.

In Australia, New Zealand and South Africa

Netcare Travel Clinics ⓦwww.travelclinic.co.za. Travel clinics in South Africa.

Travellers' Medical & Vaccination Centre ⓦwww.tmvc.com.au. Website lists travellers' medical and vaccination centres throughout Australia and New Zealand.

Insurance

China is a realtively safe place to travel, though traffic accidents, respiratory infections, petty theft and transport delays are all fairly common occurences – meaning that it's sensible to ensure you've arranged some form of **travel insurance** before leaving home.

Internet

Internet bars (网吧, *wǎngbā*) with high-speed connections are everywhere in China, from big cities – where some seat hundreds of people – to rural villages. They're invariably full of network-gaming teenagers, and are usually hidden away off main roads, rarely on ground floors, and only ever signed in Chinese (see characters above). They're generally open 24 hour and **cost** ¥2–5 per hour, though you may have to pay a ¥10 deposit and each bar has its own setup: sometimes you're given a card with a password to use on any available machine, sometimes the staff log you in at a particular terminal. Technically, you are also supposed to show your passport before being allowed near a computer.

All large hotels have **business centres** where you can get online, but this is expensive, especially in the classier places (around ¥30/hr). Better value are the **backpacker hostels**, where getting online costs around ¥5/hr or is free. But the best deal is to tote a **laptop** – cities such as Beijing, Shanghai, Xi'an, Chengdu and Hong Kong have cafés with free **wi-fi**, and many hotels and even youth hostels have ADSL sockets in their rooms.

In an attempt to keep control of news and current affairs, China's internet censors have set up the dryly named "**Great Firewall**" or Net Nanny, which blocks access to any websites deemed undesirable by the state – currently including Twitter, YouTube and Facebook. To get around it, you need to use a **web proxy** or **VPN** (Virtual Private Network) such as WiTopia, Hotspot Shield or UltraSurf, all of which cost a few pounds a month and offer a free limited period trial. Technically this is illegal, but the government pays no attention to foreigners who do this – just about every foreign business in China runs a VPN. For Chinese nationals, it's a different matter, and you will never find a public computer, such as in a hotel or business centre, running one.

Laundry

Big city hotels, and youth hostels all over, offer a **laundry service** for anything between ¥10 and ¥100; alternatively, some hostels have self-service facilities or you can use your room sink (every corner store in China sells **washing powder**). Otherwise, ask at accommodation either for the staff to wash your clothes or for the nearest **laundry**, where they usually charge by dry weight. Laundromats are virtually unknown in China.

Living in China

It is becoming increasingly easy for foreigners to live in China full time, whether as a student, a teacher or for work. Anyone planning to stay more than six months is required to pass a **medical** (from approved clinics) proving that they don't have any venereal disease – if you do have a VD, expect to be deported and your passport endorsed with your ailment.

Many mainland cities – including Beijing, Shanghai, Guangzhou, Kunming and Chengdu – have no restrictions on where foreigners can **reside**, though either you or your landlord must register with the local PSB. **Property rental** is inexpensive if you avoid purpose-built foreign enclaves – two-bedroom flats cost upwards of ¥1500 a month, though ¥10,000 and above is more likely in a city like Shanghai. The easiest way to find accommodation is to go through an **agent**, who will generally charge one month's rent as a fee. There are plenty who advertise in expat magzines and online.

Teaching

There are **schemes** in operation to place **foreign teachers** in Chinese educational institutions – contact your nearest Chinese embassy (see p.59 for addresses) for details. Some employers ask for a TEFL qualification, though a degree, or simply the ability to speak the language as a native, is usually enough.

The standard **teaching salary** for a foreigner is ¥3500 per month for a bachelor's degree, ¥4000 for a master's degree and ¥5000 for a doctorate. This isn't enough to put much away, but you should also get subsidized on-campus accommodation, plus a fare to your home country – one-way for a single semester and a return for a year's work. The workload is usually fourteen hours a week and, if you work a year you get paid through the winter holiday. Most teachers find their students keen, hard-working, curious and obedient, and report that it is the contact with them that makes the experience worthwhile. That said, avoid talking about religion or politics in the classroom as this can get them into trouble. You'll earn more – up to ¥12,000 a month – in a **private school**, though be aware of the risk of being ripped off by a commercial agency (you might be given more classes to teach than you'd signed up for, for example). Check out the institution thoroughly before committing yourself.

Studying

Many universities in China now host substantial populations of **Western students**, especially in Beijing, Shanghai and Xi'an. Indeed, the numbers of foreigners at these places are so large that in some ways you're shielded from much of a "China experience", and you may find smaller centres like Chengdu and Kunming offer both a mellower pace of life and more contact with Chinese outside the campus.

Most foreign students come to China to study **Mandarin**, though there are many additional options available – from martial arts to traditional opera or classical literature – once you break the language barrier. Courses cost from the equivalent of US$2400 a year, or US$800 a semester. Hotel-style campus accommodation costs around US$10 a day; most people move out as soon as they speak enough Chinese to rent a flat.

Your first resource is the nearest Chinese embassy, which can provide a list of contact details for Chinese universities offering the courses you are interested in; most universities also have English-language **websites**. Be aware, however, that promotional material may have little bearing on what is actually provided; though teaching standards are good, university administration departments are often confused or misleading places. Ideally, visit the campus first and be wary of paying course fees up front until you've spoken to a few students.

Working

There is plenty of **work** available for foreigners in mainland Chinese cities, where a whole section of expat society gets by as actors, cocktail barmen, Chinglish correctors, models, freelance writers and so on. To really make any money here, however, you need either to be employed by a foreign company or start your own business.

China's vast markets and WTO membership present a wealth of **commercial opportunities** for foreigners. However, anyone wanting to do business here should do thorough research beforehand. The difficulties are formidable – red tape and shady business practices abound. Remember that the Chinese do business on the basis of mutual trust and pay much less attention to contractual terms or legislation. Copyright and trademark laws are often ignored, and any successful business model will be immediately copied. You'll need to develop your *guanxi* – connections – assidiously, and cultivate the virtues of patience, propriety and bloody-mindedness.

Study and work programmes

AFS Intercultural Programs ⓦ www.afs.org. Intercultural exchange organization whose China offerings include academic and cultural exchanges that are anywhere from one month to a year long.

Council on International Educational Exchange (CIEE) ⓦ www.ciee.org. Leading NGO offering study programs and volunteer projects around the world. China options include: an academic semester or year abroad; a gap year (US students only); summer study; and paid teaching for a semester or year.

Mail

The Chinese mail service is fast and efficient, with letters taking a day to reach destinations in the same city, two or more days to other destinations in China, and up to several weeks to destinations abroad. **Overseas postage rates** are fairly expensive and vary depending on weight, destination and where you are in the country. The International **Express Mail Service** (**EMS**), however, is unreliable, with items often lost in transit or arriving in pieces, despite registered delivery and online tracking. **DHL** (Ⓦwww.dhl.com), available in a few major cities, is a safer bet.

Main post offices are open daily between about 8am and 8pm; smaller offices may keep shorter hours or close at weekends. As well as at post offices, you can post letters in green **postboxes**, though these are rare outside big cities.

To send **parcels**, turn up with the goods you want to send and the staff will sell you a box and pack them in for ¥15 or so. Once packed, but before the parcel is sealed, it must be checked at the customs window and you'll have to complete masses of paperwork, so don't be in a hurry. If you are sending valuable goods bought in China, put the receipt or a photocopy of it in with the parcel, as it may be opened for customs inspection farther down the line.

Poste restante services are available in any city. Mail is kept for several months, and you'll need to present ID when picking it up. Have letters addressed to you c/o Poste Restante, GPO, street, town or city, province. Check under both your surname and given names, as mail can easily be misfiled.

Maps

Street maps are available in China from street kiosks, hotel shops and bookshops for almost every town and city. Most are in Chinese only, showing bus routes, hotels, restaurants and tourist attractions; local bus, train and flight timetables are often printed on the back as well. The same vendors also sell pocket-sized provincial **road atlases**, again in Chinese only.

Some of the major cities and tourist destinations also produce **English-language** maps, available at upmarket hotels, principal tourist sights or tour operators' offices. In Hong Kong and Macau, the local tourist offices provide free maps, which are adequate for most visitors' needs.

Countrywide maps, which you should buy before you leave home, include the excellent 1:4,000,000 map from GeoCenter, which shows relief and useful sections of all neighbouring countries, and the Collins 1:5,000,000 map. One of the best maps of Tibet is *Stanfords Map of South-Central Tibet; Kathmandu–Lhasa Route Map*.

Money

The mainland **Chinese currency** is formally called **yuan** (¥), more colloquially known as **renminbi** (RMB, literally "the people's money") or **kuai**. One yuan breaks down into ten **jiao**, also known as **mao**. **Paper money** was invented in China and is still the main form of exchange, available in ¥100, ¥50, ¥20, ¥10, ¥5 and ¥1 notes, with a similar selection of mao. One mao, five mao, and ¥1 **coins** are increasingly common, though people in rural areas may never have seen them before. China suffers regular outbreaks of **counterfeiting** – everyone checks their change for watermarks, metal threads and the feel of the paper.

The yuan floats within a narrow range set by a basket of currencies, keeping Chinese exports cheap (much to the annoyance of the US). At the time of writing, the **exchange rate** was approximately ¥6.5 to US$1, ¥10.5 to £1, ¥9 to €1, ¥6.5 to CAN$1, ¥6 to A$1, ¥5 to NZ$1 and ¥1 to ZAR1.

Hong Kong's currency is the Hong Kong **dollar** (HK$), divided into one hundred cents, while in **Macau** they use **pataca** (usually written MOP$), in turn broken down into 100 avos. Both currencies are worth slightly less than the yuan, but while Hong Kong dollars are accepted in Macau and southern China's Special Economic Zones and can be exchanged internationally, neither yuan nor pataca is any use outside the mainland or Macau respectively. Tourist hotels in Beijing, Shanghai and Guangzhou also sometimes accept payment in Hong Kong or US dollars.

Banks and ATMs

Banks in major Chinese cities are sometimes open seven days a week, though **foreign exchange** is usually only available Monday to Friday, approximately between 9am and noon and again from 2pm to 5pm. All banks are closed for the first three days of the Chinese New Year, with reduced hours for the following eleven days, and at other holiday times. In Hong Kong, banks are generally open Monday to Friday from 9am to 4.30pm, until 12.30pm on Saturday, while in Macau they close thirty minutes earlier.

Cirrus, Visa and Plus **cards** can be used to make cash withdrawals from **ATMs** operated by the Bank of China, the Industrial and Commercial Bank of China, China Construction Bank and Agricultural Bank of China, as long as they display the relevant logo. In major east coast cities, almost every one of these banks' ATMs will work with foreign cards, but elsewhere it's likely that only the main branch of the Bank of China will have a suitable machine. Note that most ATMs are inside banks or shopping centres, so close when they do, though some are accessible 24 hours a day. The maximum for each withdrawal is ¥2500; your bank back home will charge a **fee** on each withdrawal, either a fixed rate or a percentage of the transaction. Keep your **exchange receipts** and when you leave you can change your yuan into dollars or sterling at any branch of the Bank of China.

Travellers' cheques and foreign currency

Travellers' cheques can be replaced if lost or stolen (keep a list of the serial numbers separate from the cheques) and attract a slightly better rate of exchange than cash. The downsides include having to pay a fee when you buy them, and that they can be cashed only at branches of the Bank of China and at tourist hotels.

It's worth taking along a small quantity of **foreign currency** (US, Canadian or Australian dollars, British pounds or euros) as cash is more widely exchangeable than travellers' cheques. Don't try to change money on the **black market** – you'll almost certainly get ripped off.

Credit cards and wiring money

China is basically a cash economy, and **credit cards**, such as Visa, American Express and MasterCard, are only accepted at big tourist hotels and the fanciest restaurants, and by some tourist-oriented shops; there is usually a four percent handling charge. It's straightforward to obtain cash advances on a Visa card at many Chinese banks (however, the commission is a steep three percent). Visa card holders can also get cash advances using ATM machines bearing the "Plus" logo, and book hotels and the like online.

It's possible to **wire money** to China through Western Union (Ⓦwww.westernunion.cn); funds can be collected from one of their agencies or branches of the Postal Savings Bank of China.

Opening hours

China officially has a **five-day week**, though this only really applies to government offices, which open Monday to Friday approximately 8am to noon and again from 1pm to 5pm. Generalization is difficult, though: post offices open daily, as do many shops, often keeping long, late hours, especially in big cities. Although banks *usually* close on Sundays – or for the whole weekend – even this is not always the case.

Tourist sights open every day, usually between 8am and 5pm and without a lunch break. Most public **parks** open from about 6am. **Museums** tend to have more restricted hours, often closing one day a week. If you arrive at an out-of-the-way place that seems to be closed, however, don't despair – knocking or poking around will often turn up a drowsy doorkeeper. Conversely, you may find other places locked and deserted when they are supposed to be open.

For dates of public holidays, see pp.51–52.

Phones

Everywhere in China has an **area code**, which must be used when phoning from outside that locality; these are given for all telephone numbers throughout the guide. **Local calls** are free from land lines, and **long-distance** China-wide calls are ¥0.3 a minute. International calls cost from ¥3.5 a minute (much cheaper if you use an IP internet phone card – see below).

Card phones, widely available in major cities, are the cheapest way to make domestic long-distance calls (¥0.2 for 3min), and can also be used for international calls (under ¥10 for 3min). They take **IC Cards** (IC 卡, *IC kǎ*) which come in units of ¥20, ¥50 and ¥100. There's a fifty percent discount after 6pm and on weekends. You will be cut off when your card value drops below the amount needed for the next minute. A cheaper option is the **IP card**, which can be

Dialling codes

To **call mainland China** from abroad, dial your international access code (☎00 in the UK and the Republic of Ireland, ☎011 in the US and Canada, ☎0011 in Australia, ☎00 in New Zealand and ☎27 in South Africa), then ☎86 (China's country code), then area code (minus initial zero) followed by the number.

To call **Hong Kong**, dial your international access code followed by ☎852, then the number; and for **Macau**, dial your international access code, then ☎853 and then the number.

Phoning abroad from China

To **call abroad** from mainland China, Hong Kong or Macau, dial ☎00, then the country code (see below), then the area code minus initial zero (if any), followed by the number.

UK ☎44
Ireland ☎353
Australia ☎61
New Zealand ☎64
US & Canada ☎1
South Africa ☎27

used with any phone, and comes in ¥100 units. You dial a local number, then a PIN, then the number you're calling. Rates are as low as ¥2.4 per minute to the US and Canada, ¥3.2 to Europe.

Both IC and IP cards are sold from corner stores, mobile-phone emporiums, and from street hawkers (usually outside the mobile-phone emporiums) all over the country. These cards can only be used in the places you buy them – move to another city and you'll have to buy a new card.

Mobile coverage in China is excellent and comprehensive; they use the GSM system. Assuming your phone is unlocked and compatible, buy a Chinese **SIM card** (SIM卡, *SIM kǎ*) from any China Mobile shop or street kiosk (you will have a new number). SIM cards **cost** upwards of ¥80 depending on how "lucky" the number is – favoured sixes and eights bump up the cost, unlucky fours make it cheaper. They come with ¥50 of time, which you extend with prepaid **top up cards** (充值卡, *chōngzhí kǎ*). Making and receiving domestic calls this way costs ¥0.6 per minute; an international call will cost around ¥8 a minute, though often you can only send texts overseas. The cheapest **mobile phones** to buy will cost around ¥200; make sure the staff change the operating language into English for you.

Photography

Photography is a popular pastime among the Chinese, and all big towns and cities have photo stores selling the latest cameras (especially Hong Kong – see p.616), where you can also download your digital images onto disc for around ¥30, though prints are expensive at ¥1 each. Camera batteries, film and memory cards are fairly easy to obtain in city department stores. **Film processing** is becoming harder to arrange; it's probably best to take it home with you.

Chinese people are often only too pleased to have their picture taken, though many temples **prohibit photography** inside buildings, and you should avoid taking pictures of anything to do with the military, or that could be construed as having strategic value, including ordinary structures such as bridges in sensitive areas along borders, in Tibet, and so fourth.

Time

China occupies a single time zone, eight hours ahead of GMT, thirteen hours ahead of US Eastern Standard Time, sixteen hours ahead of US Pacific Time and two hours behind Australian Eastern Standard Time. There is no daylight saving.

Tourist information

The **internet** is your best source of information before you travel, as Chinese tourist offices overseas mostly sell packages and have little to offer individual travellers. Once you reach the mainland, you'll find the

CITS (China International Travel Service; 中国国际旅行社, *zhōngguó guójì lǚxíngshè*) and alternatives such as the **CTS** (China Travel Service; 中国旅行社, *zhōngguó lǚxíngshè*) everywhere from large cities to obscure hamlets. While they all book flight and train tickets, local tours and accommodation, their value to independent travellers varies from office to office – some are extremely clued-up and helpful, others totally indifferent and uninformed. Don't take it for granted that anyone will speak English at these places. Other sources of information on the ground include accommodation staff or tour desks – especially at youth hostels – and backpacker cafés in destinations such as Dali and Yangshuo that see heavy numbers of foreign tourists.

Cities with large expat populations (including Beijing, Shanghai, Chengdu and Guangzhou) have English-language **magazines** with bar, restaurant and other **listings**. These are usually distributed free in bars and upmarket hotels, and often have accompanying websites, listed throughout the guide.

Hong Kong and Macau both have efficient and helpful tourist information offices, and several free listings magazines; see p.580 and p.622 for more on these.

Chinese tourist offices abroad

Australia and New Zealand ⓦ www.cnto.org.au
Canada ⓦ www.tourismchina.org
UK ⓦ www.cnto.org.uk
US ⓦ www.cnto.org

Government websites

Australian Department of Foreign Affairs ⓦ www.dfat.gov.au, ⓦ www.smartraveller.gov.au
British Foreign & Commonwealth Office ⓦ www.fco.gov.uk
Canadian Department of Foreign Affairs ⓦ www.dfait-maeci.gc.ca
Irish Department of Foreign Affairs ⓦ www.foreignaffairs.gov.ie
New Zealand Ministry of Foreign Affairs ⓦ www.mft.govt.nz
South African Department of Foreign Affairs ⓦ www.dfa.gov.za/consular/travel_advice.htm
US State Department ⓦ www.travel.state.gov

China online

China Backpacker ⓦ chinabackpacker.info. Heaps of trekking information for well-known and very off-the-beaten-path areas of China. Dated in parts but still a great resource.
China Bloglist ⓦ www.chinabloglist.org. Directory with links to over 500 blogs about China, most of whose writers claim unique insights in to the country, its people and culture. Check out the Angry Chinese Blogger.
China Daily ⓦ www.chinadaily.com.cn. The official, state-approved version of the news. Read it and yawn.
China expat ⓦ www.chinaexpat.com. Aimed at foreign residents, but a generally useful English-language resource, with a wide range of China-related articles and plenty of links.
China From Inside ⓦ www.chinafrominside.com. Glimpses into China's traditional martial arts, with dozens of English-language articles and interviews with famous masters.
China Hush ⓦ www.chinahush.com. Translations of what Chinese net forums are saying about popular national press stories – but not the sort of stories that would ever surface in the China Daily.
chinaSMACK ⓦ www.chinasmack.com. Similar to China Hush, but with a definite cruel and trashy tabloid slant. Gives a rare insight into underbelly of contemporary Chinese life.
China Trekking ⓦ www.chinatrekking.com. Inspiring trekking background; plenty of first-hand details you won't find elsewhere.
Danwei ⓦ www.danwei.org. English-language analysis of highbrow and "serious" goings-on in the Chinese media. Thorough and worthy, but could do with an occasional injection of humour.
International Campaign for Tibet ⓦ www.savetibet.org. An authoritative source of current news from Tibet.
Managing the Dragon ⓦ www.managingthedragon.com. Blog commentary on economic subjects from investor-who-lost-millions Jack Perkowski (who has since bounced back).
Middle Kingdom Life ⓦ www.middlekingdomlife.com. Online manual for foreigners planning to live and work in China, providing a sane sketch of the personal and professional difficulties they're likely to face.
Sexy Beijing ⓦ www.sexybeijing.tv. Internet TV series whose Western host talks to young Chinese about mostly gender-related issues. Lighthearted and occasionally insightful.
Travel China ⓦ www.travelchinaguide.com. Unusual in covering obscure places and small-group tours, as well as the normal run of popular sites and booking links.

Youku ⓦ www.youku.com. One of the many YouTube-style clones in China, with a similar range of content (all in Chinese).
Zhongwen ⓦ www.zhongwen.com. A handy online Chinese/English dictionary.

Travellers with disabilities

In **mainland China** the disabled are generally hidden away, so attitudes are not very sympathetic and little special provision is made. As it undergoes an economic boom, much of the country resembles a building site, with intense crowds and traffic, few access ramps and no effort to make public transport accessible. Ribbed paving down every city street is intended to help blind people navigate, but frankly Chinese pavements are unevenly surfaced obstacle courses of trees and power poles, parked vehicles, market stalls and random holes – the last thing anyone designs them for is unobstructed passage. Only a few upmarket international hotel chains, such as *Holiday Inn*, have experience in assisting disabled visitors. The situation **in Hong Kong** is considerably better; check out the Hong Kong Tourist Association website (ⓦ www .discoverhongkong.com) for their extensive Accessible Hong Kong listings.

Given the situation, it may be worth considering an organized tour. Take spares of any specialist clothing or equipment, extra supplies of drugs (carried with you if you fly), and a prescription including the generic name (in English and Chinese characters) in case of emergency. If there's an association representing people with your disability, contact them early on in the planning process.

Guide

Guide

CHAPTER 1

Highlights

* **Forbidden City** Imperial magnificence on a grand scale and the centre of the Chinese universe for six centuries. See p.94
* **Temple of Heaven** This classic Ming-dynasty building, a picture in stone of ancient Chinese cosmogony, is a masterpiece of architecture and landscpae design. See p.99
* **798 Art District** This huge complex of galleries and studios provides the focus for a thriving contemporary arts scene. See p.106
* **Nanluogu Xiang** Artsy alley of laidback cafés, restaurants and bars, at the centre of a charming neighbourhood. See p.110
* **Summer Palace** Escape the city in this serene and elegant park, dotted with imperial architecture. See p.114
* **Hotpot** A northern Chinese classic, a stew of sliced lamb, tofu, cabbage and anything else you fancy boiled up at your table. Specialist restaurants abound, but *Dong Lai Shun Fan Zhuang* is one of the best. See p.118
* **Acrobatics** The style may be vaudeville, but the stunts, performed by some of the world's greatest acrobats, are breathtaking. See p.125
* **The Great Wall** One of the world's most extraordinary engineering achievements, the old boundary between civilizations is China's must-see. See p.132

▲ Entrance to the Forbidden City, Beijing

Beijing and around

The brash modernity of **BEIJING** (北京, *běijīng*; the name means "Northern Capital") comes as a surprise to many visitors. Crisscrossed by freeways, spiked with high-rises, this vivid metropolis is China at its most dynamic. For a thousand years, the drama of China's **imperial history** was played out here, with the emperor sitting enthroned at the centre of the Chinese universe, and though today the city is a very different one, it remains spiritually and politically the heart of the country. Between the swathes of concrete and glass, you'll find some of the lushest temples, and certainly the grandest remnants of the Imperial Age. Unexpectedly, some of the country's most pleasant scenic spots lie within the scope of a day-trip, and, just to the north of the city, one of the world's most famous sights, the long and lonely **Great Wall**, winds between hilltops.

First impressions of Beijing are of an almost inhuman vastness, conveyed by the sprawl of apartment buildings, in which most of the city's population of 22 million are housed, and the eight-lane freeways that slice it up. It's a notion that's reinforced on closer acquaintance, from the magnificent **Forbidden City**, with its stunning wealth of treasures, the concrete desert of **Tian'anmen Square** and the gargantuan buildings of the modern executive around it, to the rank after rank of office complexes that line its mammoth roads. Outside the centre, the scale becomes more manageable, with parks, narrow alleyways and ancient sites such as the **Yonghe Gong**, the **Observatory** and, most magnificent of all, the **Temple of Heaven**, offering respite from the city's oppressive orderliness and rampant reconstruction. In the suburbs beyond, the two **summer palaces** and the **Western Hills** have been favoured retreats since imperial times.

Beijing is an invaders' city, the capital of oppressive foreign dynasties – the Manchu and the Mongols – and of a dynasty with a foreign ideology – the Communists. As such, it has assimilated a lot of outside influence, and today has an international flavour reflecting its position as the capital of a major commercial power. As the front line of China's grapple with **modernity**, it is being ripped up and rebuilt at a furious pace – attested by the cranes that skewer the skyline and the white character

When to visit Beijing

If the Party had any control over it, no doubt Beijing would have the best climate of any Chinese city; as it is, it has one of the worst. The **best time to visit** is in autumn, between September and October, when it's dry and clement. In winter, it gets very cold, down to minus 20°C, and the mean winds that whip off the Mongolian plains feel like they're freezing your ears off. Summer (June–Aug) is muggy and hot, up to 30°C, and the short spring (April & May) is dry but windy.

chai ("demolish") painted on old buildings. Students in the latest fashions while away their time in internet cafés, hip-hop has overtaken the clubs, businessmen are never without their laptops and schoolkids carry mobile phones in their lunchboxes. Rising incomes have led not just to a brash consumer-capitalist society Westerners will feel very familiar with, but also to a revival of older **Chinese culture** – witness the re-emergence of the teahouse as a genteel meeting place and the interest in imperial cuisine. In the evening, you'll see large groups of the older generation performing the *yangkou* (loyalty dance), Chairman Mao's favourite dance universally learned a few decades ago, and in the *hutongs*, the city's twisted grey stone alleyways, men sit with their pet birds and pipes as they always have done.

Beijing is a city that almost everyone enjoys. For new arrivals, it provides a gentle introduction to the country, and for travellers who've been roughing it round rural China, the creature comforts on offer are a delight. But it's essentially a private city, whose surface is difficult to penetrate; sometimes, it seems to have the superficiality of a theme park. Certainly, there is something mundane about the way tourist groups are efficiently shunted around, from hotel to sight and back to hotel, with little contact with everyday reality. To get deeper into the city, wander what's left of the labyrinthine *hutongs*, "fine and numerous as the hairs of a cow" (as one Chinese guidebook puts it), and check out the little antique markets, the residential shopping districts, the smaller, quirkier sights, and the parks, some of

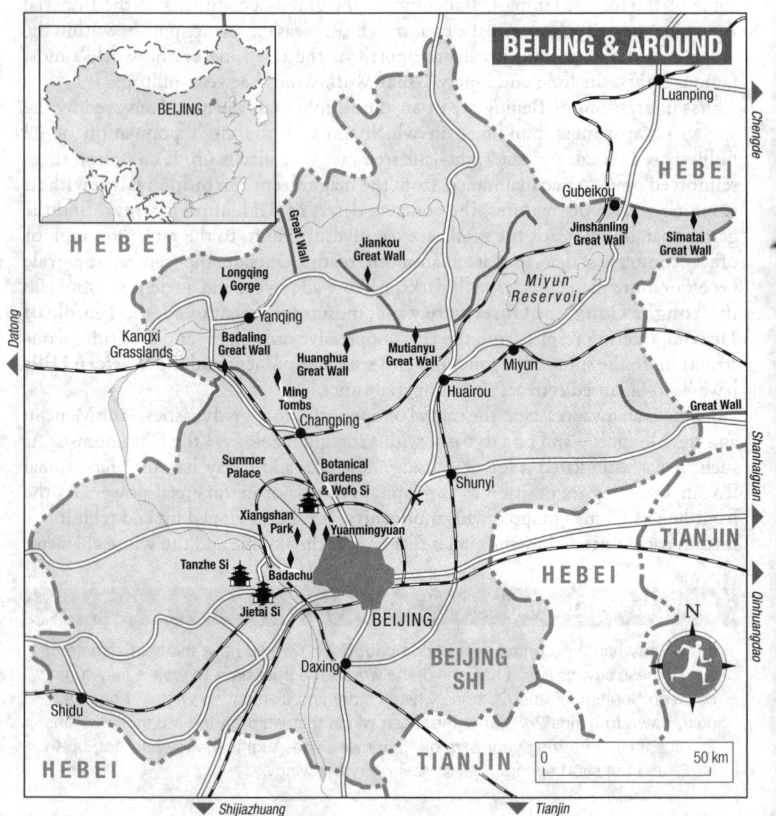

the best in China, where you'll see Beijingers performing *tai ji* and hear birdsong – just – over the hum of traffic. Take advantage, too, of the city's burgeoning nightlife and see just how far the Chinese have gone down the road of what used to be called spiritual pollution.

Getting to Beijing is no problem: it's the centre of China's **transport** network so you'll probably wind up here sooner or later, whether you want to or not, and to avoid the capital seems wilfully perverse. On a purely practical level, it's a good place to stock up on visas for the rest of Asia, and to arrange transport out of the country – most romantically, on the Trans-Siberian or Trans-Mongolian trains. To take in its superb sights requires a week, by which time you may well be ready to move on to China proper; Beijing is a fun place, but make no mistake, it in no way typifies the rest of the nation.

Some history

It was in Tian'anmen, on October 1, 1949, that Chairman Mao Zedong hoisted the red flag to proclaim officially the **foundation of the People's Republic**. He told the crowds that the Chinese had at last stood up, and defined liberation as the final culmination of a 150-year fight against foreign exploitation.

The claim, perhaps, was modest. Beijing's **recorded history** goes back a little over three millennia, to beginnings as a trading centre for Mongols, Koreans and local Chinese tribes. Its predominance, however, dates to the mid-thirteenth century, and the formation of **Mongol China** under Genghis and later **Kublai Khan**. It was Kublai who took control of the city in 1264, and who properly established it as a capital, replacing the earlier power centres of Luoyang and Xi'an. Marco Polo visited him here, working for a while in the city, and was clearly impressed with the level of sophistication; he observed in *The Travels*:

> **So great a number of houses and of people, no man could tell the number I believe there is no place in the world to which so many merchants come, and dearer things, and of greater value and more strange, come into this town from all sides than to any city in the world.**

The **wealth** came from the city's position at the start of the Silk Road, and Polo described "over a thousand carts loaded with silk" arriving "almost each day", ready for the journey west out of China. And it set a precedent in terms of style and grandeur for the Khans, later known as emperors, with Kublai building himself a palace of astonishing proportions, walled on all sides and approached by great marble stairways.

With the accession of the **Ming dynasty**, who defeated the Mongols in 1368, the capital temporarily shifted to present-day Nanjing, but Yongle, the second Ming emperor, returned, building around him prototypes of the city's two greatest **monuments** – the Imperial Palace and Temple of Heaven. It was in Yongle's reign, too, that the basic **city plan** took shape, rigidly symmetrical, extending in squares and rectangles from the palace and inner-city grid to the suburbs, much as it is today.

Subsequent, post-Ming history is dominated by the rise and eventual collapse of the Manchus – the **Qing dynasty**, northerners who ruled China from Beijing from 1644 to the beginning of the twentieth century. The capital was at its most prosperous in the first half of the eighteenth century, the period in which the Qing constructed the legendary **Summer Palace** – the world's most extraordinary royal garden, with two hundred pavilions, temples and palaces, and immense artificial lakes and hills – to the north of the city. With the central Imperial Palace, this was the focus of endowment and the symbol of Chinese wealth and power. However, in 1860, the Opium Wars brought British and French troops to the walls of the capital, and the Summer Palace was first looted and then razed to the ground by the British.

While the imperial court lived apart, within what was essentially a separate walled city, conditions for the civilian population, in the capital's suburbs, were starkly different. Kang Youwei, a Cantonese visiting in 1895, described this dual world:

> **No matter where you look, the place is covered with beggars. The homeless and the old, the crippled and the sick with no one to care for them, fall dead on the roads. This happens every day. And the coaches of the great officials rumble past them continuously.**

The indifference, rooted according to Kang in officials throughout the city, spread from the top down. From 1884, using funds meant for the modernization of the nation's navy, the Empress Dowager Cixi had begun building a new Summer Palace of her own. The empress's project was really the last grand gesture of **imperial architecture** and patronage – and like its model was also badly burned by foreign troops, in another outbreak of the Opium War in 1900. By this time, with successive waves of occupation by foreign troops, the empire and the imperial capital were near collapse. The **Manchus abdicated** in 1911, leaving the Northern Capital to be ruled by warlords. In 1928, it came under the military dictatorship of Chiang Kai-shek's **Guomindang**, being seized by the Japanese in 1939, and at the end of **World War II**, the city was controlled by an alliance of Guomindang troops and American marines.

The **Communists** took Beijing in January 1949, nine months before Chiang Kai-shek's flight to Taiwan assured final victory. The **rebuilding of the capital**, and the erasing of symbols of the previous regimes, was an early priority. The city that Mao Zedong inherited for the Chinese people was in most ways primitive. Imperial laws had banned the building of houses higher than the official buildings and palaces, so virtually nothing was more than one storey high. The roads, although straight and uniform, were narrow and congested, and there was scarcely any industry. The new plans aimed to reverse all but the city's sense of ordered planning, with Tian'anmen Square at its heart – and initially, through the early 1950s, their inspiration was Soviet, with an emphasis on heavy industry and a series of poor-quality high-rise housing programmes.

In the zest to be free from the past and create a modern, people's capital, much of **Old Beijing** was destroyed, or co-opted: the Temple of Cultivated Wisdom became a wire factory and the Temple of the God of Fire produced electric lightbulbs. In the 1940s, there were eight thousand temples and monuments in the city; by the 1960s, there were only around a hundred and fifty. Even the city walls and gates, relics mostly of the Ming era, were pulled down and their place taken by ring roads and avenues.

More destruction was to follow during the **Cultural Revolution**. Under Mao's guidance, Beijing's students organized themselves into a political militia – the **Red Guards**, who were sent out to destroy the Four Olds: old ideas, old culture, old customs and old habits. They attacked anything redolent of capitalism, the West or the Soviet Union; few of the capital's remaining ancient buildings escaped destruction. Things improved with the death of Mao and the accession of pragmatic Deng Xiaoping and his fellow moderates, who embraced capitalism, though not, as shown by the massacre at Tian'anmen Square and the surrounding events of 1989, freedom (see p.92).

In 2008 Beijing succeeded in putting on a spectacular, if politicized, **Olympic Games**. This was the city's grand coming out party, and no expense was spared to show that it, and the country as a whole, could hold its own on the world stage. To prepare for its big moment, the city's infrastructure was vastly upgraded, and the process continues today. In the past few years, six new subway lines have opened, along with a new airport terminal and a light-rail system. Some US$12 billion has been spent on green projects, including a 125-kilometre tree belt around the city to curb the winter sandstorms that rage in from the Gobi desert, the adoption of strict European vehicle-emission standards, and the relocation of polluting factories to the suburbs. Parks and verges have been prettified, fetid canals cleaned, and public facilities are better than anywhere else in China – the public toilets just west of Tian'anmen Square are the most expensive in the country, costing more than a million yuan. Historic sites have been opened, renovated, or, it sometimes appears, invented. With lots of money washing around for prestige projects, and no geographical constraints or old city to preserve, Beijing has become an architect's playground: Paul Andreu's National Centre for the Performing Arts (nicknamed the "Egg") and Rem Koolhaas's double-z shaped CCTV tower ('the Twisted Donut') have joined Herzog and DeMeuron's "Bird's nest" Olympic Stadium as the latest in weird-looking, statement architecture.

The city gleams like never before, but what little character Beijing had is fast disappearing as old city blocks and *hutongs* are demolished. Now, the city's main problems are the pressures of **migration**, pollution and **traffic** – car ownership has rocketed, and the streets are nearing gridlock.

Orientation

There's no doubt that Beijing's initial culture shock owes much to the artificiality of the city's **layout**. The main streets are huge, wide and dead straight, aligned east–west or north–south, and extend in a series of widening rectangles across the whole thirty square kilometres of the inner capital.

The pivot of the ancient city was a north–south road that led from the entrance of the Forbidden City to the city walls. This remains today as **Qianmen Dajie**, though the main axis has shifted to the east–west road that divides Tian'anmen Square and the Forbidden City and, like all major boulevards, changes its name every few kilometres along its length. It's generally referred to as **Chang'an Jie**.

Few traces of the old city remain except in the **street names**, which look bewilderingly complex but are not hard to figure out once you realize that they are compounds of a name, plus a direction – *bei*, *nan*, *xi*, *dong* and *zhong* (north, south, west, east and middle) – and the words for inside and outside – *nei* and *wai* – which indicate the street's position in relation to the old city walls that enclosed the centre. Central streets often also contain the word *men* (gate), which indicates that they once had a gate in the wall along their length.

The **ring roads**, freeways arranged in concentric rectangles centring on the Forbidden City, are rapid-access corridors. The first, running round Tian'anmen Square, is nominal, but the second and third, Erhuan Lu and Sanhuan Lu, are useful, cutting down on journey times but extending the distance travelled and therefore much liked by taxi drivers. The fourth and fifth are too out of the way to be of much interest to visitors. While most of the sights are in the city centre, most of the modern buildings – hotels, restaurants, shopping centres and flashy office blocks – are along the ring roads.

Arrival

The first experience most visitors have of China is the smooth ride along the freeway, lined with hoardings and jammed with cars, that leads from the airport into Beijing. Unless you arrive by train, it's a long way into the centre from either the bus stations or the airport, and even when you get into downtown you're still a good few kilometres from most hotels, which tend to cluster between the second and third ring roads. It's a good idea to hail a **taxi** from the centre to get you to your final destination rather

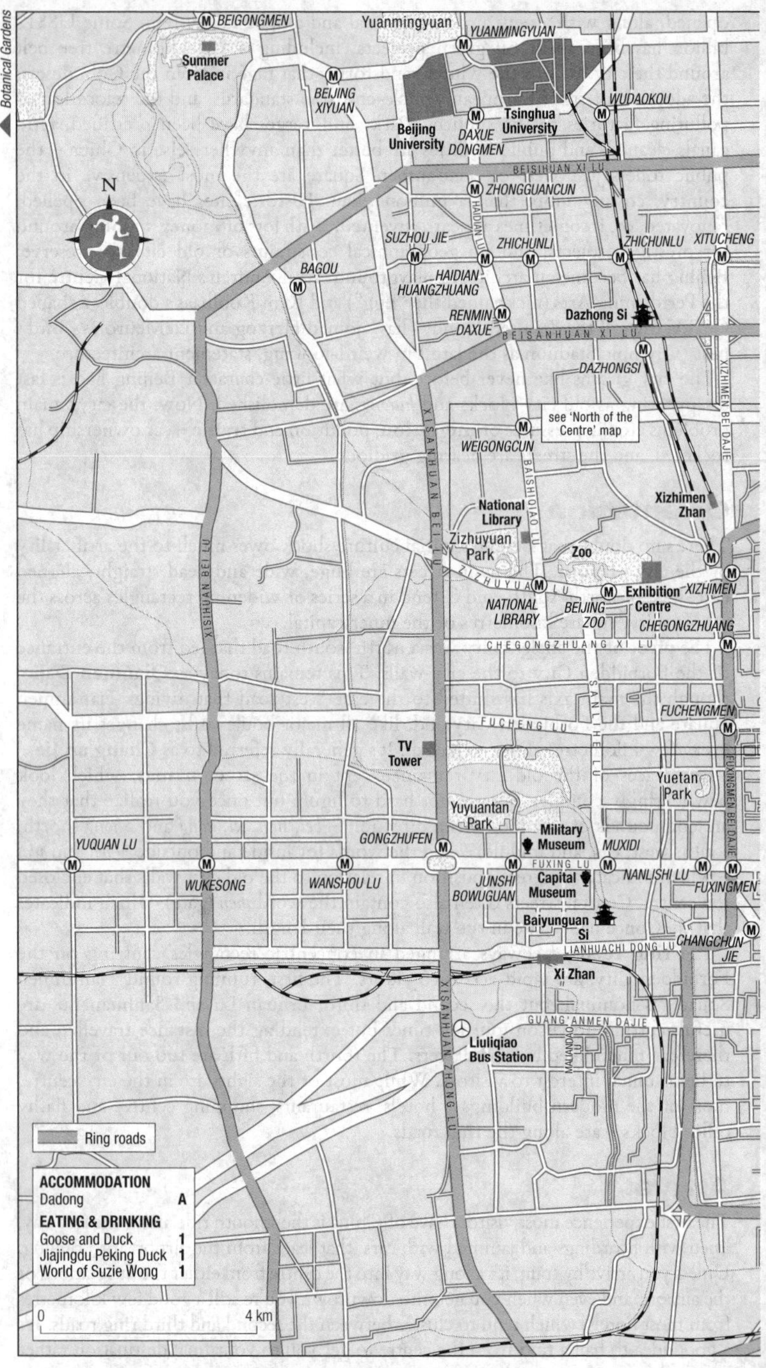

Botanical Gardens
BEIGONGMEN
Yuanmingyuan
YUANMINGYUAN
Summer Palace
BEIJING XIYUAN
WUDAOKOU
Tsinghua University
Beijing University
DAXUE DONGMEN
BEISIHUAN XI LU
ZHONGGUANCUN
HAIDIAN LU
SUZHOU JIE
ZHICHUNLI
ZHICHUNLU
XITUCHENG
BAGOU
HAIDIAN HUANGZHUANG
RENMIN DAXUE
Dazhong Si
BEISANHUAN XI LU
DAZHONGSI
XIZHIMEN BEI DAJIE
see 'North of the Centre' map
WEIGONGCUN
BAISHIQIAO LU
National Library
Xizhimen Zhan
Zizhuyuan Park
Zoo
ZIZHUYUAN LU
Exhibition Centre
XIZHIMEN
NATIONAL LIBRARY
BEIJING ZOO
CHEGONGZHUANG
XISIHUAN BEI LU
XISANHUAN BEI LU
CHEGONGZHUANG XI LU
SANLIHE LU
FUCHENGMEN
FUCHENG LU
TV Tower
Yuetan Park
FUXINGMEN BEI DAJIE
Yuyuantan Park
Military Museum
YUQUAN LU
GONGZHUFEN
MUXIDI
FUXING LU
NANLISHI LU
WUKESONG
WANSHOU LU
JUNSHI BOWUGUAN
Capital Museum
FUXINGMEN
Baiyunguan Si
CHANGCHUN JIE
LIANHUACHI DONG LU
Xi Zhan
XISANHUAN ZHONG LU
GUANG'ANMEN DAJIE
Liuliqiao Bus Station
MALIANDAO LU
Ring roads
ACCOMMODATION
Dadong A
EATING & DRINKING
Goose and Duck 1
Jiajingdu Peking Duck 1
World of Suzie Wong 1
0 4 km

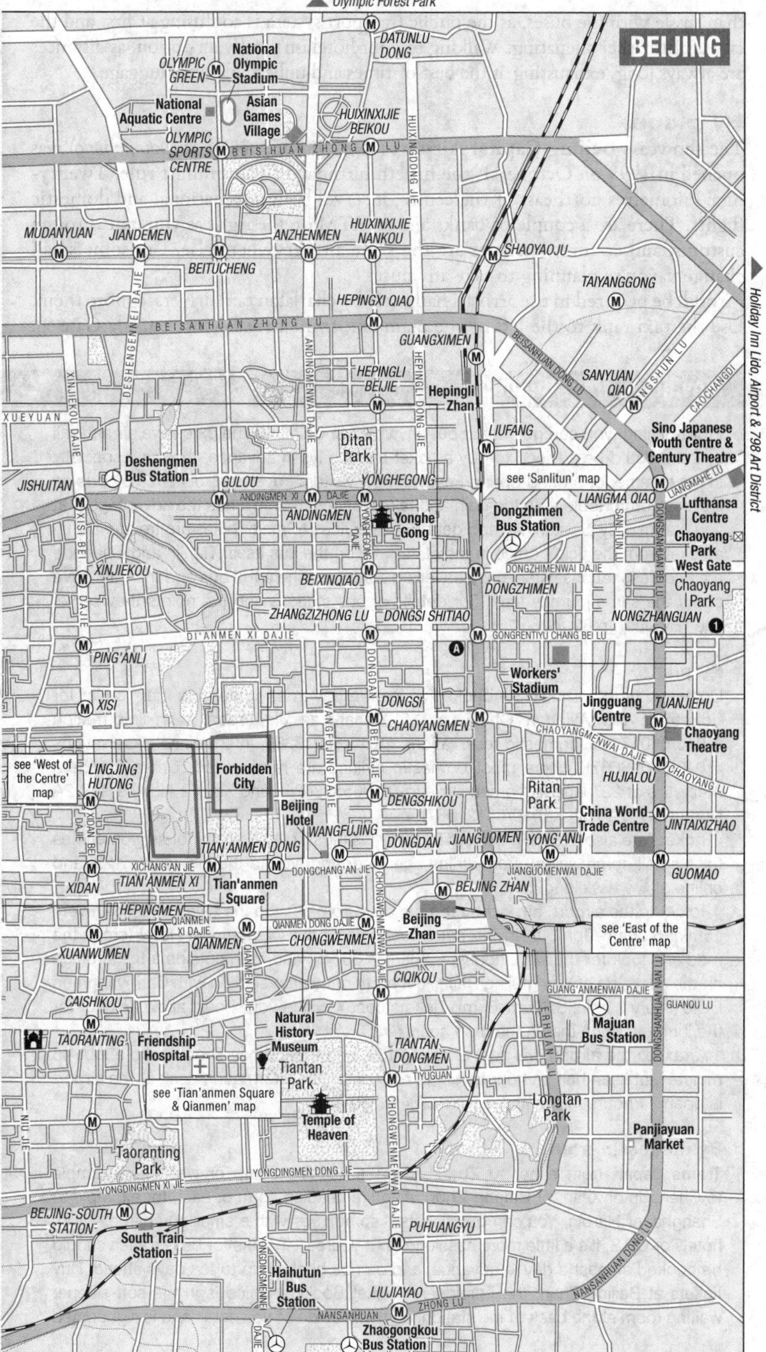
BEIJING
Olympic Forest Park
Holiday Inn Lido, Airport & 798 Art District
National Olympic Stadium
National Aquatic Centre
Asian Games Village
Ditan Park
Yonghe Gong
Dongzhimen Bus Station
Deshengmen Bus Station
Sino Japanese Youth Centre & Century Theatre
Lufthansa Centre
Chaoyang Park West Gate
Chaoyang Park
Workers' Stadium
Jingguang Centre
Chaoyang Theatre
Ritan Park
China World Trade Centre
Forbidden City
Beijing Hotel
Tian'anmen Square
Beijing Zhan
Hepingli Zhan
Majuan Bus Station
Natural History Museum
Friendship Hospital
Tiantan Park
Temple of Heaven
Longtan Park
Panjiayuan Market
Taoranting Park
South Train Station
Haihutun Bus Station
Zhaogongkou Bus Station
see 'Sanlitun' map
see 'West of the Centre' map
see 'East of the Centre' map
see 'Tian'anmen Square & Qianmen' map

than tussle with the buses, as the public transport system is confusing at first and the city layout rather alienating. Walking to your hotel isn't really an option, as distances are always long, exhausting at the best of times and unbearable with luggage.

By plane

The showcase **Beijing Capital Airport** (北京首都机场, *běijīng shǒudū jīchǎng*) was opened in 1999 on October 1, the fiftieth birthday of Communist rule. Twenty-nine kilometres northeast of the centre, it serves both international and domestic flights. There are a couple of banks and an ATM on the right as you exit through customs, and commission rates are the same as everywhere else. Get some small change if you're planning to take any buses.

You'll be pestered in the arrivals hall itself by charlatan taxi drivers; ignore them. Use the taxi rank to the left of the main exit from arrivals (just outside Gate 9).

Moving on from Beijing

From Beijing, you can get just about anywhere in China via the extensive air and rail system. You'd be advised to buy a ticket a few days in advance, though, especially in the summer or around Spring Festival. Few visitors travel long-distance by **bus** as it's less comfortable than the train and takes longer, though it has the advantage that you can usually just turn up and get on, as services to major cities are frequent. Buy a ticket from the ticket office in the station, or on the bus itself. Tianjin and Chengde are two destinations within easy travelling distance, where the bus and the train have about the same journey time. For details of bus stations and the points they serve, see "By bus", p.82.

By plane

Domestic **flights** should be booked at least a day in advance. The main outlet for **tickets** is the Aviation Office, at 15 Xichang'an Jie (open 24hr; information ⓣ010/66017755, domestic reservations ⓣ010/66013336, international reservations ⓣ010/66016667), where most domestic airlines are represented. China Southern Airlines is at 227 Chaoyangmen Dajie (ⓣ010/65533624), and Xinhua Airlines is at 2A Dong Chang'an Jie (ⓣ010/65121587).

Tickets are also available from CITS (see "Listings", p.132), from hotels (sometimes for a small commission), from airline agents dotted around the city (see p.129) and online at ⓦwww.elong.com.

To get to the airport, **airport buses** run daily from outside the Aviation Office (every 15min; 5.30am–9pm), from the northwest side of the *International Hotel* (cross the road and look for the sign; hourly; 6.30am–4.30pm), and from outside a ticket office on the east side of Wangfujing Dajie, just north of the intersection with Chaoyangmen Dajie (every 30min; 5.30am–6pm). Tickets cost ¥16 and you should allow an hour for the journey, twice that in the rush hour.

A **taxi** to the airport will cost around ¥150, and the journey should take about 45 minutes, at least half an hour longer in rush hour. The information desk at the airport is open 24 hours for enquiries (ⓣ010/64563604).

By domestic train

Trains depart from either **Xi Zhan**, if you're heading south or west, for example to Chengdu or Xi'an, or **Beijing Zhan**, if you're heading north or east, for example to Shanghai or Harbin. You can buy tickets – sometimes with a small surcharge – from hotels or CITS; it's a little more hassle to do it yourself. Tickets for busy routes should be booked at least a day in advance, and can be booked up to ten days ahead. Buy tickets at Beijing Zhan; the Foreigners' Ticket Booking Office is in the soft-sleeper waiting room at the back of the station, on the left side as you enter, and is signposted

A trip to the city centre will cost around ¥150, including the ¥10 toll. The most convenient way to get into town on public transport is with the new **light rail** "Airport Express", which runs from terminal 3 and stops at terminal 2 and Sanyuanqiao, then terminates at Dongzhimen (东直门, *dōngzhímén*), where you can transfer to the subway network. The ride takes about twenty minutes and tickets cost ¥25. The trains run every fifteen minutes from 6.30am to 10.30pm. If you want to continue your journey from Dongzhimen by cab, note that cabbies at the Dongzhimen exit commonly gouge new arrivals, so walk a little way and hail a cab from the street.

Comfortable, if cramped, **airport buses** can be found outside Gate 11. Buy tickets (¥16) from the desk directly in front of the exit. They leave regularly on nine routes. The most useful are line 1, which stops at Dongzhimen (for the subway), Dongsishitiao and Yabao Lu and finishes at the Airline Office in Xidan);

in English. It's open daily (5.30am–7.30am, 8am–6.30pm & 7–11pm). There's a timetable in English on the wall; you may be asked to show your passport. At Xi Zhan, the Foreigner's Ticket Booking Office is on the second floor and is open 24 hours. You can also get tickets from outlets: there's one on the first floor in the Wangfujing Department Store at 225 Wangfujing Dajie (daily 9–11am & 1–4pm) and another in the Air China ticket office in the China World Trade Centre at 1 Jianguomenwai Dajie (daily 8am–6pm). For train information (in Chinese only), phone ⓣ010/65129525.

Trans-Siberian and Trans-Mongolian trains

The International Train Booking Office (Mon–Fri 8.30am–noon & 1.30–5pm; ⓣ010/65120507) is the best thing about the *International Hotel* at 9 Jianguomenwai Dajie. Here you can buy **tickets to Moscow and Ulaan Baatur** with the minimum of fuss (they also take internet bookings – ⓦwww.cits.net/travel/reservation/train.jsp – though you have to pay by bank transfer). BTG Travel, on Fuxingmenwai Dajie (see p.132) have a desk for Trans-Siberian tickets that charges about the same.

Out of season, few people make the journey, but in summer there may well not be a seat for weeks. Allow yourself a week or two for dealing with embassy bureaucracy. After putting down a ¥100 deposit on the ticket at the booking office, you'll be issued with a reservation slip. Take this with you to the embassy when you apply for visas and the process should be fairly painless. A Russian transit visa, valid for a week, costs around US$50, with a surcharge for certain nationalities (mostly African and South American). Transit visas for Mongolia are valid for one week and cost US$30; tourist visas valid for a month cost US$40). You can also buy tickets at the Foreigners' Ticket Booking Office in Beijing Zhan (see opposite) though they aren't much good on visa advice.

Chinese train #3, which follows the **Trans-Mongolian route**, leaves every Wednesday from Beijing Zhan and takes five and a half days. A bunk in a second-class cabin with four beds – which is perfectly comfortable – costs around US$600. The Russian train #19, which follows the **Trans-Siberian route**, leaves on Saturdays from Beijing Zhan and takes six days. A Mongolian train leaves for Ulaan Baatur every Tuesday and costs around US$200 for one bed in a four-bed berth.

The **tour company** Monkey Business can organize your trip, though you pay a lot more than the ticket price for the privilege. Their office is in the *Poachers Inn* (43 Beisanlitun Nan, off Sanlitun Bar Street; ⓣ010/65916519; ⓦwww.monkeyshrine.com). A basic second-class ticket costs almost US$850 (excluding visas but including a night in Moscow). Other packages include stopovers in Ulaan Baatur, Lake Baikal and Irkutsk.

line 2, which goes to the far north and west of the city; line 3 to Guomao and Beijing Zhan, and line 4 to Zhongguancun.

By train

Beijing has two main **train stations**. **Beijing Zhan**, the central station (北京站, *běijīng zhàn*), just south of Dongchang'an Jie, is where trains from destinations north and east of Beijing arrive. There are **left-luggage** lockers as well as a main luggage office here (see p.131 for details). Most arrivals will need to head straight to the **bus station**, about 100m east of the station, the **subway stop** at the northwestern edge of the concourse, or to the **taxi rank**, over the road and 50m east. Don't get a cab from the station concourse, as none of the drivers here will use their meters.

Travellers from the south and west of the capital will arrive at the west station, **Xi Zhan** (西站, *xī zhàn*) Asia's largest rail terminal, at the head of the Beijing–Kowloon rail line. The left-luggage office is downstairs (¥15/day; 5am–midnight).

Beijing does have more stations, though you are unlikely to arrive at them unless you have come on a suburban train from, for example, the Great Wall at Badaling or Shidu. Beijing North, also known as **Xizhimen Zhan** (西直门站, *xīzhímén zhàn*), is at the northwestern edge of the second ring road. Beijing South, or **Yongdingmen Zhan** (永定门站, *yǒngdìngmén zhàn*), is where the fast rail link with Tianjin arrives; it's in the south of the city, just inside the third ring road, with a bus station outside. Both are on the subway.

By bus

The **bus system** in Beijing is extensive, but complicated, as there are many terminuses, each one serving buses from only a few destinations. **Dongzhimen** (东直门公共汽车站, *dōngzhímén gōnggòng qìchēzhàn*), on the northeast corner of the second ring road, connected by subway, is the largest bus station and handles services from Shenyang and the rest of Dongbei. **Deshengmen** (德胜门公共汽车站, *déshèngmén gōnggòng qìchēzhàn*), also called Beijiao, the north station serving Chengde and Datong, is just north of the second ring road, on the route of bus #55, which will take you to Xi'anmen Dajie, west of Beihai Park. **Haihutun** (海户屯公共汽车站, *hǎihùtún gōnggòng qìchēzhàn*) in the south, at the intersection of the third ring road, Nansanhuan Zhong Lu, and Yongdingmenei Dajie, is for buses from Tianjin and cities in southern Hebei. **Private minibuses** are more likely to terminate outside one of the two main train stations.

Information and maps

A large fold-out **map** of the city is vital. There is a wide variety available at all transport connections and from street vendors, hotels and bookshops. The best map to look out for, labelled in English and Chinese, and with bus routes, sights and hotels marked, is the *Beijing Tour Map*. Fully comprehensive A-Z map books are available from bookshops and street vendors outside Beijing Zhan subway stop, but only in Chinese.

Warning: scams

Spend any time in tourist areas of the capital and you will inevitably be approached by youths, usually sweet-looking girls, claiming to be art students or asking to practise their English. Their aim is to get you to visit a bogus art gallery or teahouse, and pay ridiculous prices for a few cups of tea or for prints purporting to be paintings. They'll go to astonishing lengths to befriend foreigners.

Beijing Travel Service (BTS) is an official **tourist information service** with a few central offices (see p.132 for details). They're mostly interested in selling tours and handing out leaflets.

There are a number of English-language publications that will help you get the best out of the city. The *China Daily* (¥1), available from the Friendship Store, the Foreign Language Bookstore and the bigger hotels, has a listings section detailing cultural events. *Beijing This Month* covers the same ground, with light features aimed at tourists. Much more useful are the **free magazines** aimed at the large expat community, which contain up-to-date and fairly comprehensive entertainment and restaurant listings. Look for *City Weekend* (Ⓦwww.cityweekend.com.cn/beijing) and *Time Out* (Ⓦwww.timeout.com/cn/en/beijing). Both have listings sections including club nights, art happenings and gigs, with addresses written in pinyin and Chinese; you can pick up copies in most bars and other expat hang-outs. Anyone intending to live here should get hold of the fat *Insiders Guide to Beijing*, published by the Middle Kingdom Press, which includes plenty of information on finding places to live and doing business. It's available in the Friendship Store.

City transport

The scale of the city militates against taking "bus number 11" – Chinese slang for walking – almost anywhere, and most of the main streets are so straight that going

Useful bus routes

Bus routes are indicated by red or blue lines on all good maps; a dot on the line indicates a stop, the tiny characters next to it the stop's name – which you need to know for the conductor to work out your fare. Trying to show the poor man a dot on a map in a swaying, crammed bus is all but impossible; fortunately, the Beijing Tour Map has stops marked in pinyin. The following are some of the most useful services:

Bus #1 and double-decker #1 From Xi Zhan east along the main thoroughfare, Chang'an Jie.

Double-decker #2 From the north end of Qianmen Dajie, north to Dongdan, the Yonghe Gong and the Asian Games Village.

Double-decker #4 From Beijing Zoo to Qianmen via Fuxingmen.

Bus #5 From Deshengmen, on the second ring road in the northwest of the city, south down the west side of the Forbidden City and Tian'anmen to Qianmen Dajie.

Bus #15 From Beijing Zoo down Xidan Dajie past Liulichang, ending at the Tianqiao area just west of Yongdingmennei Dajie, close to Tiantan Park.

Bus #20 From Beijing Zoo to Yongdingmen Zhan, south of Taoranting Park.

Bus #52 From Xi Zhan east to Lianhuachi Qiao, Xidan Dajie and Tian'anmen Square, then east along Chang'an Jie.

Trolleybus #103 From Beijing Zhan, north up the east side of the Forbidden City, west along Fuchengmennei Dajie, then north up Sanlihe Lu to Beijing Zoo.

Trolleybus #104 From Beijing Zhan to Hepingli Zhan in the north of the city, via Wangfujing.

Trolleybus #105 From the northwest corner of Tiantan Park to Xidan Dajie, then west to Beijing Zoo.

Trolleybus #106 From Yongdingmen Zhan to Tiantan Park and Chongwenmen, then up to Dongzhimennei Dajie.

Bus #300 Circles the third ring road.

Bus #332 From Beijing Zoo to Beida (University and the Summer Palace).

Luxury Bus #802 From Xi Zhan to Panjiayuan Market in the southeast.

Luxury Bus #808 From just northwest of Qianmen to the Summer Palace.

by foot soon gets tedious. The **public transport system** is extensive but somewhat oversubscribed; most visitors quickly tire of the heaving buses and take rather more taxis than they'd planned – still, at least they're cheap. **Cycling** is a good alternative, with plenty of rental outlets in the city.

Buses

Even though every one of the city's two-hundred-odd **bus and trolleybus services** runs about once a minute, you'll find getting on or off at busy times hard work (rush hours are 7–9am & 4.30–6pm). The **fare** for ordinary buses is ¥1. There are also five comfortable double-decker bus services, costing ¥2 a trip. **Tourist buses** – which look like ordinary buses but have route numbers written in green – make regular trips (mid-April to mid-Oct) between the city centre and certain out-of-town attractions; useful routes are listed in the text.

Services generally run from 5.30am to 11pm every day, though some are 24-hour. Buses numbered in the 200s only provide night services. All routes are efficiently organized and easy to understand – an important factor, since stops tend to be a good kilometre apart. Buses numbered in the 800s are modern, air-conditioned, and actually quite pleasant, but more expensive, with fares starting at ¥3 and going up to ¥10.

A word of warning – be very wary of **pickpockets** on buses. Skilful thieves target Westerners, and especially backpackers, looking not just for money but also coveted Western passports.

The subway

Clean, efficient and very fast, the **subway** is an appealing alternative to the bus, though it is very crowded during rush hours. Mao Zedong ordered its construction in 1966, and more than 20km were open within three years, but until 1977 it was reserved for the use of senior cadres only, apparently because it was too close to the underground defence network.

The subway operates daily from 5.30am to 11pm, and entrances are marked by a logo of a square inside a "G" shape. **Tickets** cost ¥2 per journey; buy them from the ticket offices at the top of the stairs above the platforms. Anyone staying more than a couple of weeks should consider buying a stored-value swipe card, available from subway stations and valid for bus and subway tickets. The deposit is ¥20, which you receive back when you return it, and you can put as much on it as you like. All stops are marked in pinyin, and announced in English and Chinese over an intercom when the train pulls in.

A **loop line** runs around the city, making useful stops at Beijing Zhan, Jianguomen (under the flyover, close to the Ancient Observatory), Yonghe Gong (50m north of the temple of the same name) and Qianmen, at the northern end of Qianmen Dajie. The **east–west** line runs from the western to the eastern suburbs; useful stops are Junshi Bowugaun (Military Museum), Tian'anmen (west and east) and Wangfujing. There are interchanges at Fuxingmen and Jianguomen. Handy **line 4** runs north–south on the west side of the city, with useful stops at both summer palaces, the zoo, Xidan and Xisi. **Line 5** is north–south on the east side, and connects with the loop line at Yonghe Gong. The other lines are suburban and not likely to be of interest to visitors. A light-rail line runs from Dongzhimen to the airport and there's a dedicated line running between the two big train stations.

Taxis

Taxis cost ¥2 per kilometre, with a minimum fare of ¥10. Using a taxi after 11pm will incur a surcharge of twenty percent. Drivers are generally honest (except the ones who hang around transport links), but if they don't put the meter on, you can

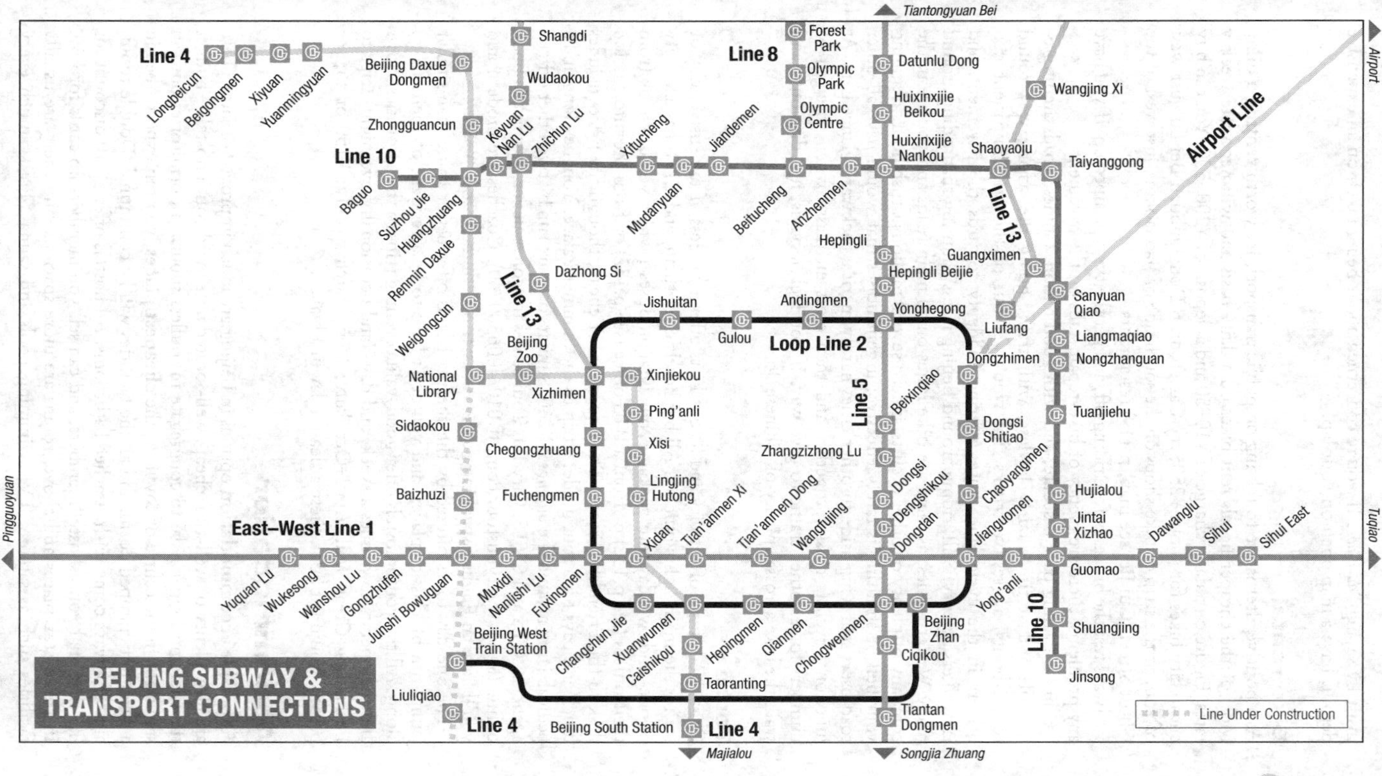

BEIJING SUBWAY & TRANSPORT CONNECTIONS
Line Under Construction
Tiantongyuan Bei
Airport
Tuqiao
Songjia Zhuang
Majialou
Pingguoyuan
Airport Line
Line 4
Line 8
Line 10
Line 13
Loop Line 2
Line 5
East–West Line 1
Longbeicun
Beigongmen
Xiyuan
Yuanmingyuan
Beijing Daxue Dongmen
Zhongguancun
Shangdi
Wudaokou
Keyuan Nan Lu
Zhichun Lu
Baguo
Suzhou Jie
Huangzhuang
Renmin Daxue
Weigongcun
National Library
Sidaokou
Baizhuzi
Xitucheng
Jiandemen
Mudanyuan
Beitucheng
Anzhenmen
Forest Park
Olympic Park
Olympic Centre
Datunlu Dong
Huixinxijie Beikou
Huixinxijie Nankou
Hepingli
Hepingli Beijie
Wangjing Xi
Shaoyaoju
Taiyanggong
Guangximen
Liufang
Sanyuan Qiao
Liangmaqiao
Nongzhanguan
Tuanjiehu
Hujialou
Jintai Xizhao
Guomao
Dawanglu
Sihui
Sihui East
Shuangjing
Jinsong
Dazhong Si
Beijing Zoo
Xizhimen
Jishuitan
Gulou
Andingmen
Yonghegong
Dongzhimen
Xinjiekou
Ping'anli
Xisi
Lingjing Hutong
Chegongzhuang
Fuchengmen
Beixinqiao
Zhangzizhong Lu
Dongsi
Dengshikou
Dongdan
Dongsi Shitiao
Chaoyangmen
Jianguomen
Yong'anli
Xidan
Tian'anmen Xi
Tian'anmen Dong
Wangfujing
Yuquan Lu
Wukesong
Wanshou Lu
Gongzhufen
Junshi Bowuguan
Muxidi
Nanlishi Lu
Fuxingmen
Changchun Jie
Xuanwumen
Caishikou
Hepingmen
Qianmen
Chongwenmen
Beijing Zhan
Ciqikou
Taoranting
Tiantan Dongmen
Beijing West Train Station
Liuliqiao
Beijing South Station

insist by saying "*da biao*". If you're concerned about being taken on an expensive detour, have a map open on your lap.

Bike rental

As a positive alternative to relying on public transport, it's worth **renting a bike**. Most of the cheaper hotels rent bikes on a daily basis and will negotiate weekly rates. Figure on a daily charge of ¥10–50 and a deposit of ¥200–500. You can buy cheap city bikes for about ¥250; try Carrefour, 6 Dongsanhuan Bei Lu, just west of zoo, or the strip of bike shops on the south side of Jiaodaokou, just west of the Ghost Street (Gui Jie; see map, p.119) restaurants.

Always test the brakes before riding off, and get the tyres pumped up. If you have any problems, there are plenty of bike-repair stalls on the pavement.

Chinese cycling pace is sedate, and with good reason. Chinese roads are unpredictable and at times fairly lawless, with traffic going the wrong way round roundabouts, aggressive trucks that won't get out of the way, impatient taxi drivers in the cycle lane, buses veering suddenly towards the pavement, and jaywalkers aplenty. Still, riding around Beijing is less daunting than riding around many Western cities, as there are **bike lanes** on all main roads and you are in the company of plenty of other cyclists, indeed several million at rush hours. Ringing your bell or shouting is rarely effective; urgent noises that would have all other road users scurrying aside in other cities hardly merit a backward glance here. At junctions, cyclists cluster together and then cross en masse when strength of numbers forces other traffic to give way. If you feel nervous, just dismount and walk the bike across – plenty of Chinese do.

Tours

Organized **tours** of the city and its outskirts offer a painless, if expensive, way of seeing the main sights quickly. All big hotels offer them, and CITS has a variety of one- and two-day tour packages, on "Dragon Buses", which you can book from their offices (see p.132) or from a BTS office (see p.132) or from the information desk in the Friendship Store. These tours aren't cheap, though the price includes lunch and pays for a tour guide: a trip to the Summer Palace, Yonghe Gong and a pedicab jaunt around the *hutongs* is ¥260. Similar tours are run by two other official agencies: CTS and CYTS. City Bus Tour scores for convenience, as you can book online (Ⓦwww.citybustour.com, Ⓣ010/4006500760). Coaches are modern and you'll have an English-speaking guide. A day trip with them costs ¥380.

The one-day tours offered by the cheaper hotels offer better value than similar jaunts run by classier places, and you don't have to be a resident of theirs to go along. All the youth hostels offer good-value evening trips to the acrobatics shows and the opera a few times a week, and day- (and occasionally overnight) trips to Jinshanling Great Wall (April–Oct daily; Nov–March weekly; ¥150 or so; see p.135). You must book these at least a day in advance.

Accommodation

Affordable **accommodation** options in Beijing are much improved of late. There are now plenty of well-run, cheap, well-located hotels and youth hostels – budget travellers no longer have to congregate in soulless suburban dormitories but can stay right in the centre of town. At the **cheapest places**, you can expect a bed in a clean but cramped dorm, and all the facilities will be communal. Double rooms almost always come with attached bathrooms. All hostels offer a ¥10 discount for international youth hostel members, and can sell you membership cards for ¥60. In **three-star** places and above, rooms are more spacious, and there are usually facilities such as satellite TV, swimming pools and saunas. Pretty much every hotel has a tour office, a restaurant and a business centre. **Luxury hotels** are of an international standard and are generally foreign-run and -managed, and sometimes offer discounts of up to seventy percent off-season.

Hotels in **Qianmen** are close to the centre in a shabby but vibrant area. Most of the mid-range and high-class hotels are **east of the centre**, strung out along the international shopping streets of Wangfujing and Jianguomen or clustered around subway stations. Further north, the **Sanlitun district** has some good accommodation options for all budgets, with plenty of places to eat and drink nearby. The most charismatic places to stay are those hidden in the *hutongs* **north of the centre** around Houhai and Nanluogu Xiang, close to good eating and nightlife options; there's something here for all budgets. Beijing being the size it is, proximity to a subway station is a big advantage; if the subway is withn reasonable distance, the nearest stop has been noted in the review.

Except at the cheapest places, you should always **haggle** politely for a room – rack rates are only an indication, and hardly anyone pays those any more. You can often get a worthwhile discount if you book online (see p.41) a few days in advance, or try the airport reservations counter when you arrive.

Qianmen

See map, p.91.

Jianguo Qianmen (建国前门饭店, *jiànguó qiánmén fàndiàn*) 175 Yong'an Lu ⓣ010/63016688; Hepingmen subway. Big, popular three-star hotel with its own theatre, which nightly shows a version of Beijing Opera, mostly to visiting tour groups (see p.124). ❻

Leo Hostel (广聚园青年旅舍, *guǎngjùyuán qīngnián lǚshè*) 52 Dazhalan Xi Jie ⓣ010/86608923, ⓦwww.leohostel.com; Qianmen subway. Big, well-run hostel, ten minutes' walk from Tian'anmen Square, with a bar, pool table, DVD lounge and free maps. As it's on the bustling, pedestrianized Dazhalan strip, it's easy to find. A leafy and attractive courtyard helps compensate for rooms that are a bit tatty round the edges. Four-person dorms ¥50 without bathroom, ¥80 with, rooms ❸

Qianmen Youth Hostel (前门客栈, *qiánmén kèzhàn*) 33 Meishi Jie ⓣ010/63132369; Qianmen subway. Well-located in a *hutong* just a couple of minutes' walk from Tian'anmen Square. Communal spaces might be considered poky but rooms, in a nineteenth-century building, looking over a secluded courtyard, have attractive carved wooden balconies outside. Insist on the upper floors, as ground-floor rooms are very dark. If you take a room without a bathroom note that the trip to the outside toilets and showers is a long, chilly one in winter. Some of the cheapest dorms in the city at ¥45 for a four- or six-bed dorm. Rooms without bathroom ❶, with bathroom ❷

East of the centre

See map, p.104.

Beijing (北京饭店, *běijīng fàndiàn*) 33 Dongchag'an Jie ⓣ010/65137766, ⓦwww.chinabeijinghotel.com; Wangfujing subway. The most central hotel, just east of Tian'anmen Square, and one of the most recognizable buildings in Beijing. The view from the top floors of the west wing, over the Forbidden City, is superb. But it's pricey, renovations have expunged the historic feel and service is not up to scratch. ❽

Cote Cour SL 70 Yanyue Hutong, Dongcheng Qu ⓣ010/65128021, ⓦwww.hotelcotecoursl.com; Dengshikou subway. Fourteen-room courtyard-style boutique hotel, in the middle of the city but in a quiet *hutong*. You'll have to reserve in advance. There's no restaurant but free breakfast is served in the lounge. Taxis sometimes won't go down the alley, so you'll have to walk for five minutes after being dropped off – call the hotel before you arrive and they'll arrange a taxi to pick you up. ❽

Holiday Inn Crowne Plaza (国际艺苑皇冠饭店, *guójìyìyuàn huángguān fàndiàn*) 48 Wangfujing Dajie ⓣ010/65133388; Dengshikou subway. Well-established hotel with artsy pretensions (there's an on-site gallery) that's handy for the shops. ❾

Haoyuan (好园宾馆, *hǎoyuán bīnguǎn*) 53 Shijia Hutong ⓣ010/65125557. A sedate little courtyard hotel just half a kilometre from Dengshikou subway stop. Rooms are small, with Ming-style furniture. Head north up Dongdan Bei Dajie and take the last alley to the right before the intersection with Dengshikou Dajie. The hotel is 200m down here on the left, marked by two red lanterns. It's often full, so book ahead. ❼

Jianguo (建国饭店, *jiànguó fàndiàn*) 5 Jianguomenwai Dajie ⓣ010/65002233, ⓦwww.hoteljianguo.com; Yong'an Li subway. Well run and good looking, with many of the rooms arranged around cloistered gardens, this place is deservedly very popular with regular visitors. The restaurant, *Justine's*, has some of the best French food in the city. ❽

Kapok Hotel (木棉花酒店, *mùmiánhuā jiǔdiàn*) 16 Donghuamen Dajie ⓣ010/65259988, ⓦwww.hotelkapok.com; Wangfujing subway. This swish hotel, ten minutes' walk from the Forbidden City has glass walls and a bamboo theme. There aren't too many luxury extras, but overall it's clean, chic, well located, and not too pricey. Staff are friendly but could improve their English skills. ❺

New Otani (长富宫饭店, *chángfúgōng fàndiàn*) 26 Jianguomenwai Dajie ⓣ010/65125555, ⓕ39810; Jianguomen subway. You can get seriously pampered in this five-star, modern, Japanese-run mansion, one of the most luxurious in Beijing, though the fee for the privilege is hefty. ❾

Novotel Xin Qiao (诺富特新桥宾馆, *nuòfùtè xīnqiáo bīnguǎn*) 2 Dong Jiao Min Xiang ⓣ010/65133366, ⓦwww.novotel.com; Chongwenmen subway. A decent chain hotel that's the best within its range if you want comfort, reliability and familiarity. ❺

Peninsula Palace (王府饭店, *wángfǔ fàndiàn*) 8 Jingyu Hutong ⓣ010/65128899, ⓦwww.beijing.peninsula.com; Dengshikou subway. A discreet and well-located upmarket place with a good shopping centre; now regularly voted the city's top place to stay. ❾

Saga Youth Hostel (实佳国际青年旅舍, *shíjiā guójì qīngnián lǚshè*) 9 Shijia Hutong, off Chaoyangmen Nan Xiaojie ⓣ010/65272773. In a quiet *hutong* off a busy street, and just walkable from the main train station. It's signposted off Chaoyangmen Nan Xiao Jie, just beyond the stop for bus #24. The hostel is clean and utilitarian, with a tour office, bike rental, internet access, a kitchen and a washing machine. Unusually, some of the otherwise plain dorms have TVs. Dorm beds ¥60, rooms ❸

St Regis (国际俱乐部饭店, *guójìjùlèbù fàndiàn*) 21 Jianguomenwai Dajie ⓣ010/64606688, ⓕ03299; Jianguomen subway. One of the most expensive hotels in the city. Rooms have a butler thrown in, who'll unpack your suitcase for you. ❾

North of the centre

See map, pp.108–109.

Bamboo Garden (竹园宾馆, *zhúyuán bīnguǎn*) 24 Xiaoshiqiao Hutong ⓣ010/64032229, ⓦwww.bbgh.com.cn; Gulou subway. A quiet, charming courtyard hotel in a *hutong* close to the Drum and Bell towers. Quiet gardens are its best feature. A recent renovation has added to its charm. ❻

Chinese Box Courtyard Hostel (团圆四合院客栈, *tuányuánsìhéyuàn kèzhàn*) 52 Xisi Bei Er Tiao ⓣ010/66186768; Xisi subway. This family-run courtyard hotel, hidden behind a sturdy red door in a *hutong*, is one of the best cheapies, but avoid it if you're averse to cats – there are at least six slinking round. Dorms are on the pricey side but the two rather incongruously luxurious double rooms, featuring huge beds, are excellent value. Free wi-fi, laundry is ¥15, and there's a room to watch DVDs in. A fairly minimal breakfast is included. Dorms ¥80–100, rooms ❺

Courtyard 7 (秦唐府客栈七号院, *qíntángfǔ kèzhàn qīhàoyuàn*) 7 Qian Gulouyuan Lane ⓣ010/64060777; Zhangzizhong Lu subway. Rooms in this courtyard hotel off Nanluogu Xiang might be on the small side, but it more than makes up for it with a peaceful ambience and good location. All the rooms face the courtyard, and are elegantly furnished throughout, with four-poster beds and colourful tiled bathrooms. The *hutong* is pleasant and clean but you won't get a cab to go down it. ❺

Double Happiness (阅微庄四合院宾馆, *yuèwéizhuāng sìhéyuàn bīnguǎn*) 37 Dongsi Sitiao ⓣ010/64007762. This courtyard hotel has larger rooms than most, with wooden floors and the usual traditional Chinese carved and lacquered decor. The courtyards are attractive, with red lanterns and plenty of foliage. It's central, but a couple of hundred metres down a narrow alley that taxis won't travel – still, Dengshikou subway is only a couple of minutes' walk away. A bit chilly in winter. ❺

Downtown Backpackers (东堂青年旅舍, *dōng táng qīng nián lǚ shè*) 85 Nanluogu Xiang ⓣ010/84002429; Beixinqiao subway. Possibly the best backpacker place, with a location on artsy Nanluogu Xiang, Beijing's trendiest *hutong*, that can't be beat; you won't be short of eating and nightlife options. There are a couple of single rooms and doubles, which get rapidly booked up. The plumbing can be a bit noisy in winter. Six-bed dorms ¥60, rooms ❸

Drum Tower Youth Hostel (鼓楼青年旅舍, *gǔ lóu qīng nián lǚshè*) 51 Jiugulou Dajie, ⓣ010/64037702; Gulou subway. A good location, spartan but clean rooms, friendly staff and a mellow rooftop patio make this hostel on a main road worth considering. There's a self-service kitchen and all the facilities you might expect but no free internet (¥8/hr). Dorms ¥50, rooms ❷

Green Tea Hotel (格林豪泰酒店, *gélín háotài jiǔdiàn*) 46 Fangjia Hutong ⓣ010/64032288; Yonghe Gong subway. A typical example of one of the new business hotel chains – efficient, clean, cheap, characterless. But this branch scores for its location at the back of the Fangjia Hutong complex of trendy arts venues, restaurants and bars. ❷

Guxiang 20 (古巷20号商务会, *gŭ xiàng èr shí hào shāng wù huì*) 20 Nanluogu Xiang ⓣ010/64005566; Beixinqiao subway. Well located on trendy Nanluogu Xiang, this swanky new place is done out in opium-den chic. The best doubles have four-poster beds, and there's a tennis court on the roof. It doesn't maintain much presence on the street and looks rather clubby. ❺

Lama Temple Youth Hostel (雍和国际青年旅舍, *yōng hé guó jì qīng nián lǚshè*) 56 Beixinqiao Toutiao ⓣ010/64028663. First *hutong* north of the Dongzhimennei and Yonghegong Dajie intersection, not far from Beixinqiao subway; look for the yellow sign at the *hutong* entrance. Well-located courtyard hostel just south of the Yonghe Gong. Rooms are spacious but dark and there's a large common room with a lively bar. Staff are keen. For meals, it's handy both for Ghost Street and Nanluogu Xiang. Dorms ¥60, rooms ❸

Lüsongyuan (侣松园宾馆, *lǚsōngyuán bīnguăn*) 22 Banchang Hutong ⓣ010/64040436. A slightly old-fashioned courtyard hotel converted from a Qing-dynasty mansion, with elegant rooms and pleasant gardens. It's popular with tour groups, so you'll probably have to book ahead in season (April–Sept). It's well located in an alley off Nanluogu Xiang. Take bus #104 from the station and get off at Beibingmasi bus stop. Walk south for 50m and you'll see a sign in English pointing down an alley to the hotel. ❻

Mao'er Hutong (冒儿胡同客栈, *maòérhútóng kèzhàn*) 28 Mao'er Hutong, off Nanluogu Xiang ⓣ13661219901, ⓦwww.bb-china.com. Intimate courtyard hotel stuffed with chinoiserie. Service is highly personal and the owner is eager to please. Note that the alley is too narrow for taxis, so there's a five-minute walk. The whole place is non-smoking. You'll certainly need to book in advance. ❹

Red Lantern House (红灯笼宾馆, *hóngdēnglóng bīnguăn*) 5 Zhengjue Hutong, Xinjie Kou ⓣ010/63015433; Xinjiekou subway. A converted courtyard house in a quiet *hutong*, close to the Houhai bar area. The courtyard, with its jumble of lanterns and ornaments, is quite something. Offers bike rental, internet and laundry. The alley is east off Xinjie Kou, its entrance marked by a *Dairy Queen*; from Beijing Zhan, take bus #22. Two- to four-bed dorms ¥45–60, rooms ❸, breakfast included.

Sitting on the Walls Courtyard House (城墙客栈, *chéngqiáng kèzhàn*) 57 Nianzi Hutong ⓣ010/64027805. Another converted courtyard house that offers a bit of character, friendly staff, pets and dodgy plumbing. It's very central, just behind the Forbidden City, though not near a subway stop. It's a little tough to find first time, and taxi drivers don't know where it is; you'll have to wend your way through the alleyways, following the signs. Dorms ¥70, rooms ❸

Sleepy Town Inn (丽舍什刹海国际青年旅店, *lì shè shí shà hăi guó jì qīn nián lǚ diàn*) 103 Deshengmennei Dajie ⓣ010/64069954, ⓦwww.sleepyinn.com.cn; Jishuitan subway. Homely place with friendly staff and a great location, beside a canal just off Houhai Lake, but few facilities. Dorms are good value. Four- to eight-bed dorms ¥60, rooms ❸

Sanlitun

See map, p.121.

Great Wall Sheraton (长城饭店, *chángchéng fàndiàn*) 6 Dongsanhuan Bei Lu ⓣ010/65005566, ⓦwww.sheraton.com/beijing; Liangmaqiao subway. A very swish, five-star modern compound out on the third ring road. ❾

Hotel G (极栈酒店, *jízhàn jiŭdiàn*) A7 Workers' Stadium ⓣ010/65523600, ⓦwww.hotel-g.com. At night every window of this slick boutique hotel is lit up a different colour. The nightclubby impression is reinforced inside by sharp lines and subdued lighting; it's aimed squarely at the hip young crowd who like to party in nearby Sanlitun. Rooms are cosy and standards high, making this one of the best in its price range. ❽

Kempinski (凯宾斯基饭店, *kăibīnsījī fàndiàn*) Lufthansa Centre, 50 Liangmaqiao Lu ⓣ010/64653388, ⓦwww.kempinski-beijing.com; Liangmaqiao subway. Off the third ring road on the way to the airport, this five-star place is a little out of the way, though with a huge shopping complex attached and an expat satellite town of bars and restaurants nearby, there's no shortage of diversions on site. ❾

Opposite House (瑜舍, *yúshè*) Building 1, 11 Sanlitun Lu ⓣ010/64176688, ⓦwww.theoppositehouse.com; Nongzhanguan subway. Another trendy hotel, this one decorated with modern Chinese art. Rooms are minimalist chic but comfortable; bathrooms have wooden tubs and waterfall showers. It's just around the corner from Sanlitun, so there's no shortage of restaurants and nightlife in the area – but what there isn't is a subway stop anywhere nearby. There's no sign on the outside, but look for the green building next to the 3.3 Mall. ❾

Zhaolong International Youth Hostel (兆龙青年旅舍, *zhàolóngqīngnián lǚshè*) 2 Gongrentiyuchang Bei Lu ⓣ010/65972299; Nongzhanguan subway. Behind the swanky *Zhaolong Hotel*. Another clean and ably managed hostel, a short stumble from the bars on Sanlitun Lu. Offers free laundry, bike rental and internet access. Dorm beds ¥60–70, rooms ❹

The City

Beijing requires patience and planning to do it justice. Wandering aimlessly around without a destination in mind will rarely be rewarding. The place to start is **Tian'anmen Square**, geographical and psychic centre of the city, where a cluster of important sights can be seen in a day, although the **Forbidden City**, at the north end of the square, deserves a day, or even several, all to itself. **Qianmen**, a noisy market area south of here, is a bit more alive, and ends in style with one of the city's highlights, the **Temple of Heaven** in Tiantan Park. The giant freeway, **Chang'an Jie**, zooming east–west across the city, is a corridor of high-rises with a few museums, shopping centres and even the odd ancient site worth tracking down. **Wangfujing Dajie**, running off Chang'an Jie, is one of the capital's main shopping streets. Scattered in the **north** of the city, a section with a more traditional and human feel, are some magnificent **parks, palaces and temples**, some of them in the *hutongs*; to the east, the **Sanlitun** area is a ghetto of expat services including some good upscale restaurants and plenty of bars. An expedition to the outskirts is amply rewarded by the **Summer Palace**, the best place to get away from it all.

Tian'anmen Square and the Forbidden City

The first stop for any visitor to Beijing is **Tian'anmen Square**. Physically at the city's centre, symbolically it's the heart of China, and the events it has witnessed have shaped the history of the People's Republic from its inception. Chairman Mao lies here in his marble **memorial hall**, with the **Great Hall of the People** to the west and the **Museum of Chinese History** to the east. Monumental architecture that's much, much older lies just to the north – China's Imperial Palace, the **Forbidden City**, now open to all. Paul Andreu's striking dome-shaped **National Centre for the Performing Arts**, just to the west, is a high-visibility example of the city planners' ambitions to create a modern, cosmopolitan world capital – and you can see the designs for plenty more such prestige projects at the **Museum of Urban Planning**, just south of the square.

Tian'anmen Square

Covering more than forty hectares, **Tian'anmen Square** (天安门, *tiānānmén*) must rank as the greatest public square on earth. It's a modern creation, in a city that traditionally had no squares, as classical Chinese town planning did not allow for places where crowds could gather. Tian'anmen only came into being when imperial offices were cleared from either side of the great processional way that led south from the palace to Qianmen and the Temple of Heaven, and the broad east–west thoroughfare, Chang'an Jie, had the walls across its path removed. In the words of one of the architects: "The very map of Beijing was a reflection of the feudal society, it was meant to demonstrate the power of the emperor. We had to transform it, we had to make Beijing into the capital of socialist China." The square was not enlarged to its present size until ten years after the Communist takeover, when the Party ordained the building of ten new Soviet-style official

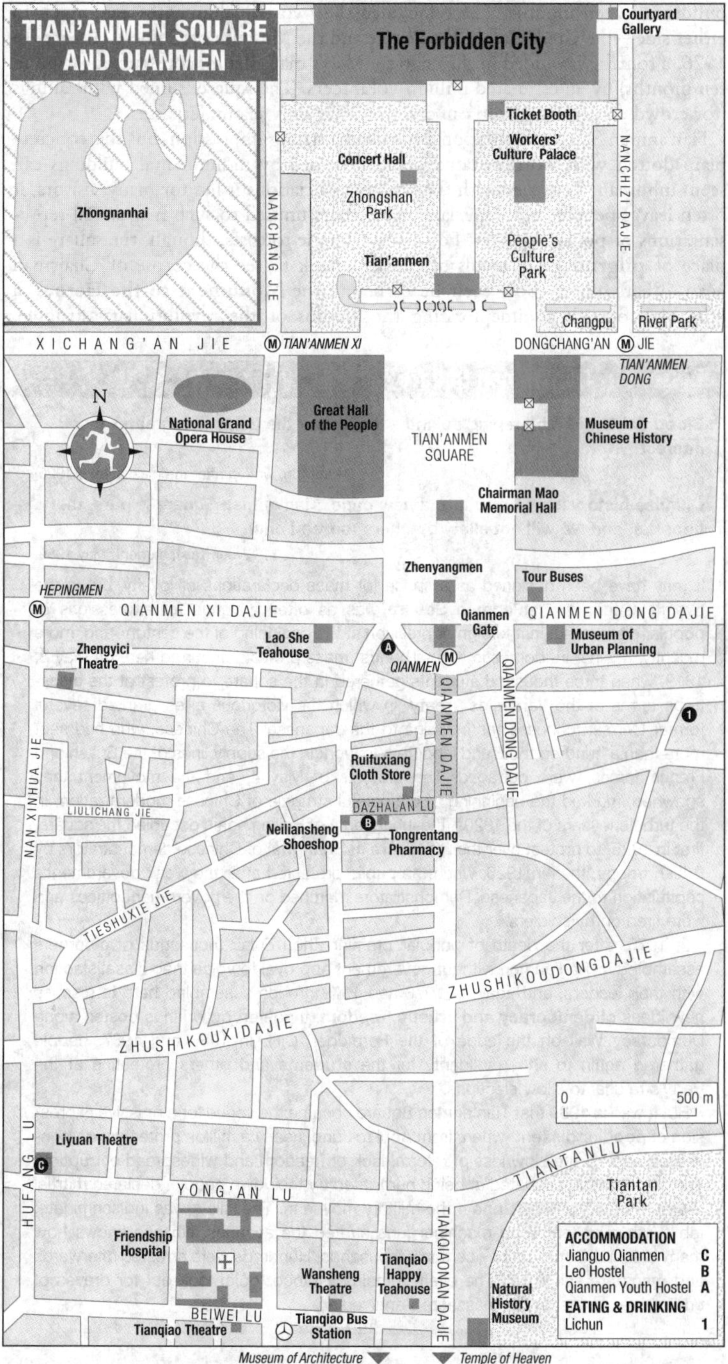
TIAN'ANMEN SQUARE AND QIANMEN
The Forbidden City
Courtyard Gallery
Ticket Booth
Workers' Culture Palace
Concert Hall
Zhongshan Park
Zhongnanhai
NANCHANG JIE
NANCHIZI DAJIE
People's Culture Park
Tian'anmen
Changpu
River Park
XICHANG'AN JIE
TIAN'ANMEN XI
DONGCHANG'AN JIE
TIAN'ANMEN DONG
National Grand Opera House
Great Hall of the People
TIAN'ANMEN SQUARE
Museum of Chinese History
Chairman Mao Memorial Hall
Zhenyangmen
Tour Buses
HEPINGMEN
QIANMEN XI DAJIE
Qianmen Gate
QIANMEN DONG DAJIE
Museum of Urban Planning
Lao She Teahouse
Zhengyici Theatre
QIANMEN
QIANMEN DAJIE
QIANMEN DONG DAJIE
Ruifuxiang Cloth Store
NAN XINHUA JIE
LIULICHANG JIE
DAZHALAN LU
Neiliansheng Shoeshop
Tongrentang Pharmacy
TIESHUXIE JIE
ZHUSHIKOUDONGDAJIE
ZHUSHIKOUXIDAJIE
0
500 m
Liyuan Theatre
TIANTANLU
Tiantan Park
HUFANG LU
YONG'AN LU
Friendship Hospital
Wansheng Theatre
Tianqiao Happy Teahouse
TIANQIAONAN DAJIE
Natural History Museum
BEIWEI LU
Tianqiao Theatre
Tianqiao Bus Station
ACCOMMODATION
Jianguo Qianmen C
Leo Hostel B
Qianmen Youth Hostel A
EATING & DRINKING
Lichun 1
Museum of Architecture
Temple of Heaven

buildings in ten months. These included the two that dominate Tian'anmen to either side – the Great Hall of the People and the Museum of Chinese History. In 1976, a fourth was added in the centre – Mao's mausoleum, constructed (again in ten months) by an estimated million volunteers. The square is lined with railings (for crowd control), and you can enter or leave only via underpasses.

Tian'anmen Square unquestionably makes a strong impression, but this concrete plain dotted with worthy statuary and bounded by monumental buildings can seem inhuman. Together with the bloody associations it has for many visitors, it often leaves people cold, especially Westerners unused to such magisterial representations of political power. For many Chinese tourists, though, the square is a place of **pilgrimage**. Crowds of peasants flock to see the corpse of Chairman Mao, others quietly bow their heads before the **Monument to the Heroes**, a 30m-high obelisk commemorating the victims of the revolutionary struggle.

Dissent in Tian'anmen Square

Blood debts must be repaid in kind – the longer the delay, the greater the interest.

Lu Xun, writing after the massacre of 1926.

Chinese history is about to turn a new page. Tian'anmen Square is ours, the people's, and we will not allow butchers to tread on it.

Wuer Kaixi, student, May 1989.

It may have been designed as a space for mass declarations of loyalty, but in the twentieth century **Tian'anmen Square** was as often a venue for expressions of popular dissent; against foreign oppression at the beginning of the century, and, more recently, against its domestic form. The first mass protests occurred here on May 4, 1919, when three thousand students gathered in the square to protest at the disastrous terms of the **Versailles Treaty**, in which the victorious allies granted several former German concessions in China to the Japanese. The Chinese, who had sent more than a hundred thousand labourers to work in the supply lines of the British and French forces, were outraged. The protests of May 4, and the movement they spawned, marked the beginning of the painful struggle of Chinese modernization. In the turbulent years of the 1920s, the inhabitants of Beijing again occupied the square, first in 1925, to protest over the **massacre in Shanghai** of Chinese demonstrators by British troops, then in 1926, when the public protested after the weak government's capitulation to the Japanese. Demonstrators marched on the government offices and were fired on by soldiers.

In 1976, after the death of popular premier Zhou Enlai, thousands of mourners assembled in Tian'anmen without government approval to voice their dissatisfaction with their leaders, and again in 1978 and 1979 groups assembled here to discuss new ideas of **democracy and artistic freedom**, triggered by writings posted along Democracy Wall on the edge of the Forbidden City. In 1986 and 1987, people gathered again to show solidarity for the **students** and others protesting at the Party's refusal to allow elections.

But it was in **1989** that Tian'anmen Square became the venue for a massive expression of **popular dissent**, when, from April to June, nearly a million protesters demonstrated against the slowness of reform, lack of freedom and widespread corruption. The government, infuriated at being humiliated by their own people, declared martial law on May 20, and on **June 4** the military moved in. The killing was indiscriminate; tanks ran over tents and machine guns strafed the avenues. No one knows how many died in the massacre – certainly thousands. Hundreds were arrested afterwards and many are still in jail. The event remains a taboo topic; look out for droves of undercover police on the massacre's anniversary.

Among the visitors is the occasional monk, and the sight of robed Buddhists standing in front of the uniformed sentries outside the Great Hall of the People makes a striking juxtaposition. At dawn, the flag at the northern end of the square is raised in a military ceremony and lowered again at dusk, which is when most people come to see it, though foreigners complain that the regimentation of the crowds is oppressive and reminds them of school. After dark, the square is at its most appealing and, with its sternness softened by mellow lighting, it becomes the haunt of strolling families and lovers.

For an overview of the square, head to the south gate, **Zhenyangmen** (正阳门, *zhèng yáng mén*; daily 9am–4pm; ¥20), similar to Tian'anmen (the north gate) and 40m high, which gives a good idea of how much more impressive the square would look if Mao's mausoleum hadn't been stuck in the middle of it.

The Museum of Urban Planning

Beijing's newest attraction, just off Qianmen Dong Dajie, is the six-storey, marble-faced **Museum of Urban Planning** (规划博物馆, *guī huà bó wù guǎn*; Tues–Sun 9am–5pm; ¥30). Along with a host of rather banal displays and presentations on Beijing's bright urban future, a fascinating model shows the city as it used to look in imperial times, when every significant building was part of an awesome, grand design. The star attraction, though, is an enormous diorama of Beijing that takes up the entire top floor: it illustrates what the place will look like once it's finished being ripped up and redesigned in 2020. Visitors can wander Gulliver-like around the amazingly detailed mock-up. You might even catch some locals coming to see just what their home is being bulldozed for.

The Chairman Mao Memorial Hall

At the centre of the centre of China lies a corpse that nobody dare remove.

Tiziano Terzani, *Behind the Forbidden Door*

The **Chairman Mao Memorial Hall** (毛主席纪念堂, *máozhǔxí jìniàntáng*; daily 8.30–11am; Oct–April also Mon, Wed & Fri 2–4pm), home to the pickled corpse of the architect of modern China, is an ugly building, looking like a school gym, which contravenes the principles of *feng shui* (geomancy), presumably deliberately, by interrupting the line from the palace to Qianmen and by facing north. Mao himself wanted to be cremated, and the erection of the mausoleum was apparently no more than a power ploy by his would-be successor, Hua Guofeng. In 1980, Deng Xiaoping said it should never have been built, although he wouldn't go so far as to pull it down.

After depositing your bag at the offices on the eastern side, you join the orderly queue of Chinese on the northern side. This advances surprisingly quickly, and takes just a couple of minutes to file through the chambers in silence – photography is banned and the atmosphere reverent – any joking around will cause deep offence. Mao's corpse is draped with a red flag within a crystal coffin. Mechanically raised from a freezer every morning, it looks unreal, like wax or plastic. It is said to have been embalmed with the aid of Vietnamese technicians who had recently worked on Ho Chi Minh (rumour has it that Mao's left ear fell off and had to be stitched back on). Once through the marble halls, you're herded past a splendidly wide array of tacky Chairman Mao souvenirs.

Great Hall of the People and the National Museum

Taking up almost half the west side of the square is the **Great Hall of the People** (人民大会堂, *rénmín dàhuìtáng*; daily 8.30am–3pm; ¥30; buy tickets and leave bags at the office on the south side). This is the venue of the National People's Congress, and hundreds of black limos with tinted windows are parked outside when it's in session. When it isn't, it's open to the public (hours and ticket information above). What you see on the mandatory route is a selection of the 29 reception rooms – all looking like the lobby of a Chinese three-star hotel, with badly fitted red carpet and armchairs lined up against the walls.

That giant building on the east side of the square is the **National Museum of China** (中国历史博物馆, *zhōngguó lìshǐ bówùguǎn*), shut for a massive renovation at the time of writing. When it reopens, it will be interesting to see whether its huge collection of exhibits are still divided up according to a Marxist view of history, into "primitive", "slave", "feudal" and "semi-colonial".

Tian'anmen and towards the Forbidden City

Tian'anmen, the "Gate of Heavenly Peace" (天安门, *tiānānmén*; daily 8am–5pm; ¥15), was once the main entrance to the Forbidden City. The boxy gatehouse is familiar across the world, and occupies an exalted place in Chinese communist iconography, appearing on banknotes, coins, stamps and indeed virtually any piece of state paper you can imagine. As such, it's a prime object of pilgrimage, with many visitors milling around waiting to be photographed in front of the large **portrait of Mao** (one of the very few still on public display), which hangs over the central passageway. From the reviewing platform above, Mao delivered the liberation speech on October 1, 1949, declaring that "the Chinese people have now stood up". For the pricey entrance fee you can climb up to this platform yourself, where security is tight – all visitors have to leave their bags, are frisked and have to go through a metal detector before they can ascend. Inside, the fact that most people cluster around the souvenir stall selling official certificates of their trip reflects the fact that there's not much to look at.

Once through Tian'anmen, you find yourself on a long walkway, with the moated palace complex and massive Wumen gate directly ahead (this is where you buy your ticket to the Forbidden City). The two **parks** on either side, Zhongshan Park (中山公园, *zhōng shān gōng yuán*) and the People's Culture Park (both daily 6am–9pm; Zhongshan Park ¥10), are great places to chill out away from the rigorous formality nearby. On the eastern side, the **Workers' Culture Palace** (劳动人民文化宫, *láo dòng rén mín wén huà gōng*; ¥2) – symbolically named in deference to the fact that only with the Communist takeover in 1949 were ordinary Chinese allowed within this central sector of their city – has a number of modern exhibition halls (sometimes worth checking) and a scattering of original fifteenth-century structures, most of them Ming or Qing ancestral temples. The hall at the back often holds art exhibitions. The western **Zhongshan Park** boasts the remains of the Altar of Land and Grain, a biennial sacrificial site with harvest functions closely related to those of the Temple of Heaven (see p.99).

The Forbidden City

The Gugong (故宫, *gùgōng*), or Imperial Palace, is much better known by its unofficial title, the **Forbidden City**, a reference to its exclusivity. Indeed, for the five centuries of its operation, through the reigns of 24 emperors of the Ming and Qing dynasties, ordinary Chinese were forbidden from even approaching the walls of the palace. The complex, with its maze of eight hundred buildings and reputed nine thousand chambers, was the symbolic and literal heart of the capital, and of the empire, too. From within, the **emperors**, the Sons of Heaven, issued commands with absolute authority to their millions of subjects.

Although the earliest structures on the Forbidden City site began with Kublai Khan during the Mongol dynasty, the **plan** of the palace buildings is essentially Ming. Most date to the fifteenth century and the ambitions of the Emperor Yongle, the monarch responsible for switching the capital back to Beijing in 1403.

The halls were laid out according to geomantic theories – in accordance to the *yin* and *yang*, the balance of negative and positive – and since they stood at the exact centre of Beijing, and Beijing was considered the centre of the universe, the harmony was supreme. The palace complex constantly reiterates such references, alongside personal symbols of imperial power such as the dragon and phoenix (emperor and empress) and the crane and turtle (longevity of reign).

After the Manchu dynasty fell in 1911, the Forbidden City began to fall into disrepair, exacerbated by looting of artefacts and jewels by the Japanese in the 1930s and again by the Nationalists, prior to their flight to Taiwan, in 1949. A programme of **restoration** has been underway for decades, and today the complex is in better shape than it was for most of the last century.

To do it justice, you should plan to spend a day here, though you can wander the complex for a week and keep discovering new aspects. The central halls, with their wealth of imperial pomp, may be the most magnificent buildings, but for many visitors it's the side rooms, with their displays of the more intimate accoutrements of court life, that bring home the realities of life for the inhabitants of this, the most gilded of cages.

Visiting the Forbidden City

The complex is open to visitors daily (April–Sept 8.30am–4.30pm; Oct–March 8.30am–3.30pm; last admission 30min before closing; ¥40 Nov–March, ¥60 April–Oct, including special exhibitions), but note that the entrance is quite a way after Tian'anmen; just keep on past the souvenir stalls till you can't go any further. You have the freedom of most of the hundred-hectare site, though not all of the buildings, which are labelled in English. The ticket has a map on the back, which also shows where the exhibitions are. If you want detailed explanation of everything you see, you can tag on to one of the numerous tour groups or buy one of

Life inside the Forbidden City

The emperors rarely left the Foribidden City – perhaps with good reason. Their lives, right up to the fall of the Manchu in the twentieth century, were governed by an extraordinarily developed taste for luxury and excess. It is estimated that a single meal for a Qing emperor could have fed several thousand of his impoverished peasants, a scale obviously appreciated by the last influential occupant, the Empress Dowager Cixi (see p.115), who herself would commonly order preparation of 108 dishes at a single sitting. Sex, too, provided startling statistics, with the number of Ming-dynasty **concubines** approaching ten thousand. At night, the emperor chose a girl from his harem by picking out a tablet bearing her name from a pile on a silver tray. She would be delivered to the emperor's bedchamber naked but for a yellow cloth wrapped around her, and carried on the back of a servant, since she could barely walk with her bound feet.

The only other men allowed into the palace were **eunuchs**, to ensure the authenticity of the emperor's offspring. In daily contact with the royals, they often rose to considerable power, but this was bought at the expense of their dreadfully low standing outside the confines of the court. Confucianism held that disfiguration of the body impaired the soul, and eunuchs were buried apart from their ancestors in special graveyards outside the city. In the hope that they would still be buried "whole", they kept and carried around their testicles in bags hung on their belts. They were usually recruited from the poorest families – attracted by the rare chance of amassing wealth other than by birth. Eunuchry was finally banned in 1924 and the remaining 1500 eunuchs were expelled from the palace. An observer described them "carrying their belongings in sacks and crying piteously in high-pitched voices".

the many specialist books on sale. The audio tour (¥40), available by the main gate, is also worth considering – though if you do this, it's worth retracing your steps afterwards for an untutored view. Useful **bus routes** serving the Forbidden City are #5 from Qianmen, and #54 from Beijing Zhan, or you could use #1, which passes the complex on its journey along Chang'an Jie. You can get to the back gate, opposite Jingshan Park, on buses #101, #103 or #109. The nearest **subways** are Tian'anmen west and east.

From Wumen to Taiheman

The **Wumen** (Meridian Gate) itself is the largest and grandest of the Forbidden City gates and was reserved for the emperor's sole use. From its vantage point, the Sons of Heaven would announce the new year's calendar to their court and inspect the army in times of war. It was customary for victorious generals returning from battle to present their prisoners here for the emperor to decide their fate. He would be flanked, on all such imperial occasions, by a guard of elephants, the gift of Burmese subjects.

Passing through the Wumen you find yourself in a vast paved court, cut east–west by the **Jinshui He**, the Golden Water Stream, with its five marble bridges, decorated with carved torches, a symbol of masculinity. Beyond is a further ceremonial gate, the **Taihemen**, Gate of Supreme Harmony, its entrance guarded by a magisterial row of lions, and beyond this a still greater courtyard where the principal imperial audiences were held. Within this space the entire court, up to one hundred thousand people, could be accommodated. They would have made their way in through the lesser side gates – military men from the west, civilian officials from the east – and waited in total silence as the emperor ascended his throne. Then, with only the Imperial Guard remaining standing, they kowtowed nine times.

The ceremonial halls

The main **ceremonial halls** stand directly ahead, dominating the court. Raised on a three-tiered marble terrace is the first and most spectacular of the three, the **Taihedian**, Hall of Supreme Harmony. This was used for the most important state occasions, such as the emperor's coronation or birthdays and the nomination of generals at the outset of a campaign, and last saw action in an armistice ceremony in 1918. A marble pavement ramp, intricately carved with dragons and flanked by bronze incense burners, marks the path along which the emperor's chair was carried. His golden dragon throne stands within.

Moving on, you enter the **Zhonghedian**, Hall of Middle Harmony, another throne room, where the emperor performed ceremonies of greeting to foreigners and addressed the imperial offspring (the product of several wives and numerous concubines). The hall was used, too, as a dressing room for the major Taihedian events, and it was here that the emperor examined the seed for each year's crop.

The third of the great halls, the **Baohedian**, Hall of Preserving Harmony, was used for state banquets and imperial examinations, graduates from which were appointed to positions of power in what was the first recognizably bureaucratic civil service. Its galleries, originally treasure houses, display various finds from the site, though the most spectacular, a vast block carved with dragons and clouds, stands at the rear of the hall. This is a Ming creation, reworked in the eighteenth century, and it's among the finest carvings in the palace. It's certainly the largest – a 250-tonne chunk of marble transported here from well outside the city by flooding the roads in winter to form sheets of ice.

The imperial living quarters

To the north, paralleling the structure of the ceremonial halls, are the three principal palaces of the **imperial living quarters**. Again, the first chamber, the

Qianqinggong, Palace of Heavenly Purity, is the most extravagant. It was originally the imperial bedroom – its terrace is surmounted by incense burners in the form of cranes and turtles (symbols of immortality) – though it later became a conventional state room. Beyond, echoing the Zhonghedian in the ceremonial complex, is the **Jiaotaidian**, Hall of Union, the empress's throne room; and finally the **Kunninggong**, Palace of Earthly Tranquillity, where the emperor and empress traditionally spent their wedding night. By law the emperor had to spend the first three nights of his marriage, and the first day of Chinese New Year, with his wife. This last palace is a bizarre building, partitioned in two. On the left is a large sacrificial room with its vats ready to receive offerings (1300 pigs a year under the Ming). The wedding chamber is a small room, off to one side, painted entirely in red, and covered with decorative emblems symbolizing fertility and joy. It was last pressed into operation in 1922 for the child wedding of Pu Yi, the last emperor, who, finding it "like a melted red wax candle", decided that he preferred the Yangxindiang and went back there.

The **Yangxindiang**, or Mind Nurture Palace, is one of a group of palaces to the west where emperors spent most of their time. Several of the palaces retain their furniture from the Manchu times, most of it eighteenth-century; in one, the **Changchungong** (Palace of Eternal Spring), is a series of paintings illustrating the Ming novel, *The Story of the Stone*. To the east is a similarly arranged group of palaces, adapted as **museum galleries** for displays of bronzes, ceramics, paintings, jewellery and Ming and Qing arts and crafts. The atmosphere here is much more intimate, and you can peer into well-appointed chambers full of elegant furniture and ornaments, including English clocks decorated with images of English gentlefolk, which look very odd among the jade trees and ornate fly whisks.

Exhibitions in the Forbidden City

The Forbidden City is increasingly being devoted to museum space – fifty thousand square metres today and, in a few years, four hundred thousand. It's growing into one of the best museums in China, and after appreciating the palace itself, it's worth visiting a second time just to take in the exhibits. There's a strip of exhibition halls on the western side of the complex and a few more in the northeast: all exhibitions are free unless specified otherwise. Check out what's on at Ⓦwww.dpm.com.cn; new exhibitions are opening all the time.

In the western galleries you'll find exhibits detailing aspects of **Qing dynasty life** – insignia, weapons, musical instruments, the life of concubines and so on – but the most gorgeous relics, including exquisite lacquerware and carvings of jade, wood, bamboo and ivory are in the Hall of Treasures at the northern end. The shows in the northeast corner of the palace are mainly of **pottery** and **porcelain**, but check the **painting gallery**, whose show is changed monthly. Just north of this, in the Yangxindiang and Leshoutang, a hall just north of it, is a large show of **jewellery** (¥10). The first hall houses mostly gold, silver and jade tableware and tea and wine utensils. There are also gold chimes, seals, books and a pagoda that was used to store any hair that fell out, on brushing, from the imperial head of Emperor Qianlong's mother. The second hall holds the costumes and utensils the emperor and empress used. Particularly impressive is a huge jade carving illustrating a Taoist immortal taming the waves. It weighs over five tonnes and reputedly took ten years to carve.

The show of **clocks** and **watches** in Fengxiandian, the eastern palace quarters, is a real crowd pleaser (¥10). On display is the result of one Qing emperor's passion for liberally ornamented Baroque timepieces, most of which are English and French, though the rhino-sized water clock by the entrance is Chinese. There's even one with a mechanical scribe that can write eight characters. Some clocks are wound to demonstrate their workings at 11am and 2pm.

Leading you away from the palace chambers – and offering, by this stage, something of a respite – the Kunningmen heads out from the Inner Court to the **Imperial Garden**. There are a couple of cafés here (and toilets) amid a pleasing network of ponds, walkways and pavilions, the classic elements of a Chinese garden. At the centre is the **Qinandian**, Hall of Imperial Peace, dedicated to the Taoist god of fire, Xuan Wu. You can exit here into Jingshan Park (see p.107), which provides an overview of the complex.

South of Tian'anmen

The **Qianmen** area, to the south of Tian'anmen, offers a tempting antidote to the prodigious grandeurs of the Forbidden City – and a quick shift of scale. The lanes and *hutongs* here comprise a **traditional shopping quarter**, full of small, specialist stores, which, to a large extent, remain grouped according to their particular trades – though how much character will survive the present huge demolitions is debatable. Down Qianmen Dajie, once the Imperial Way, now a clogged road clustered with small shops, the **Natural History** and **Architecture** museums are worth a browse, and **Tiantan**, the ravishing Temple of Heaven, perfectly set in one of Beijing's best parks, is an example of imperial architecture at its finest.

Qianmen

The entry to this quarter is marked by the imposing, fifteenth-century, double-arched **Qianmen** gate (前门, *qiánmén*) just south of Tian'anmen Square. Before the city's walls were demolished, this sector controlled the entrance to the inner city from the outer, suburban sector. Shops and places of entertainment were banned from the former in imperial days, and they became concentrated in the Qianmen area.

Qianmen Dajie, the quarter's biggest street, runs immediately south from the gate, and is now a pedestrianized open-air mall with a Chinatown feel to it. Off to either side are trading streets and *hutongs*, with intriguing traditional pharmacies and herbalist shops, dozens of clothes shops, silk traders and an impressive array of side stalls and cake shops selling fresh food and cooked snacks. For a rather sanitized taste of the district's old delights, visit the Lao She Tea House, which puts on daily shows of acrobatics and opera (see p.125).

Dazhalan Lu

Cramped **Dazhalan Lu** (大栅栏, *dàzhàlán*) is the oldest and most interesting of the Qianmen lanes leading west off Qianmen Dajie; the lane's entrance is marked by a white arch on the west side of the road This was once a major theatre street, now it's a hectic, pedestrianized shopping district, with mostly tea shops and clothing stores occupying the genteel old buildings. At no. 24, Tongrengtang (同仁堂, *tóngréntáng*), a famous **traditional Chinese medicine** store, has shelves full of deer horn, bear-heart capsules and the like, and a formidable array of aphrodisiacs. At the end of the street, marked by a scattering of Chinese-only hotels, was the old red-light district, formerly containing more than three hundred brothels. This is one of the last substantial networks of *hutongs* left in the city, and it's certainly worth wandering (or, better, biking) down random alleyways, though expect to get lost – at least, for a while.

Liulichang Jie

Turning north at the western end of Dazhalan, then heading west along a *hutong*, then north and west again, brings you to **Liulichang Jie** (琉璃厂, *liúlíchăng*). Liulichang, whose name literally means "Glaze factory street", after the erstwhile factories here making glazed tiles for the roofs of the Forbidden City, has been rebuilt as a heritage street, using Ming-style architecture; today, it's full of curio stores – remember to bargain hard.

The Temple of Heaven

Set in its own large and tranquil park about 2km south of Tian'anmen along Qianmen Dajie, **Tiantan**, otherwise known as the **Temple of Heaven** (天坛, *tiāntán*; daily 8am–8pm, buildings close at 5pm; ¥35 for a ticket that includes access to all buildings; tickets for just the park: low season ¥10, high season ¥15), is widely regarded as the high point of Ming design. For five centuries it was at the very heart of imperial ceremony and symbolism, and for many modern visitors its architectural unity and beauty remain more appealing – and on a much more accessible scale – than the Forbidden City. There are various **bus routes** to Tiantan: bus #106 runs from Dongzhimen to the north entrance; #17 passes the west gate on its way from Qianmen; and #41 from Chongwenmen stops close to the east gate. You could also just get the subway to Tiantan Dong Men (east gate).

The temple was begun during the reign of Emperor Yongle and completed in 1420. It was conceived as the prime meeting point of Earth and Heaven, and symbols of the two are integral to its plan. Heaven was considered round, and Earth square, thus the round temples and altars stand on square bases, while the whole park has the shape of a semicircle sitting beside a square. The intermediary between Earth and Heaven was, of course, the **Son of Heaven**, the emperor, and the temple was the site of the most important ceremony of the imperial-court calendar, when the emperor prayed for the year's harvests at the **winter solstice**. Purified by three days of fasting, he made his way to the park on the day before the solstice, accompanied by his court in all its magnificence. On arrival, he would meditate in the Imperial Vault, ritually conversing with the gods on the details of government, before spending the night in the Hall of Prayer for Good Harvests. The following day, amid exact and numerological ritual, the emperor performed animal sacrifices before the Throne of Heaven at the Round Altar.

It was forbidden for the commoners of old Beijing to catch a glimpse of the great annual procession to the temple and they were obliged to bolt their windows and remain, in silence, indoors. The Tiantan complex remained sacrosanct until it was thrown open to the people on the first Chinese National Day of the Republic in October 1912. Two years after this, the infamous General Yuan Shikai performed the solstice ceremonies himself, as part of his attempt to be proclaimed emperor. He died before the year was out.

The temple buildings

Although you're more likely to enter the actual park from the north or the west, to properly appreciate the religious ensemble it's best to skirt round to the south entrance, the Zhaohen Gate, from where you can follow the ceremonial route up through the complex. The main pathway from Zhaozhen leads straight to the **Round Altar**, consisting of three marble tiers representing Man, Earth and (at the summit) Heaven. The tiers themselves are composed of blocks in various multiples of nine, which the Chinese saw as cosmologically the most powerful odd number, representing both Heaven and Emperor. The top terrace now stands bare, but the spot at its centre, where the Throne of Heaven was placed, was considered to be the middle of the Middle Kingdom – the very centre of the earth. Various acoustic properties are claimed for the surrounding tiers, and from this point it is said that all sounds are channelled straight upwards. To the east of the fountain, which was reconstructed after fire damage in 1740, are the ruins of a group of buildings used for the preparation of sacrifices.

Directly ahead, the **Imperial Vault of Heaven** is an octagonal structure made entirely of wood, with a dramatic roof of dark blue, glazed tiles. It is preceded by the so-called **Echo Wall**, said to be a perfect whispering gallery, although the unceasing cacophony of tourists trying it out makes it impossible to tell.

The principal temple building – the **Hall of Prayer for Good Harvests**, at the north end of the park – amply justifies all this build-up. It is, quite simply, a wonder. Made entirely of wood, without the aid of a single nail, the circular structure rises from another three-tiered marble terrace to be topped by three blue-tiled roofs of harmonious proportions. Four compass-point pillars support the vault (in representation of the seasons), enclosed in turn by twelve outer pillars (for the months of the year). The dazzling colours of the interior, surrounding the central dragon motif, make the pavilion seem ultramodern; it was, in fact, entirely rebuilt, faithful to the Ming design, after the original was destroyed by lightning in 1889. The official explanation for this appalling omen was that it was divine punishment meted out on a sacrilegious caterpillar, which was on the point of reaching the golden ball on the hall's apex when the lightning struck.

The Natural History and Architecture museums

Two museums are worth combining with a trip to Tiantan. Just north of Tiantan's west gate, the **Natural History Museum** (自然博物馆, *zìrán bówùguǎn*; daily 8.30am–5pm; ¥15) includes a great room of dinosaur skeletons, though the rest of the dusty place can be safely skipped. A short walk to the southwest is the **Museum of Architecture** (古代建筑博物馆, *gǔdài jiànzhú bówùguǎn*; daily 9am–5pm; ¥15). Look for the red arch south off Beiwei Lu; the ticket office is just beyond here and the museum itself is further down the road on the right. This was once the Xiannong Temple, where the emperor ritually ploughed a furrow to ensure a good harvest. You can see the gold-plated plough he used in the Hall of Worship. The Hall of Jupiter has a fantastically ornate ceiling and cutaway models of famous buildings from all over the country. Anyone who has ever wondered how a *dougong* works – those ornate interlocking brackets seen on temples – can satisfy their curiosity here. There's a great model of the city as it appeared in 1949, before the Communists ripped it up.

Niu Jie and the Muslim Quarter

Some 3km southwest of Qianmen, **Niu Jie** (牛街, *niújiē*; Ox Street) is a cramped thoroughfare in the city's **Muslim Quarter**. The street, a *hutong* leading off Guang'anmen Dajie, on the route of bus #6 from the north gate of Tiantan Park, is lined with offal stalls and vendors selling fried dough rings, rice cakes and *shaobang* (muffins). The white hats and the beards worn by the men are what most obviously set these Hui minority people apart from the Han Chinese – there are nearly two hundred thousand of them in the capital. The focus of the street is the **mosque** at its southern end (牛街清真寺, *niújiē qīngzhēnsì*; daily 8am–5pm; ¥10, free for Muslims), an attractive building colourfully decorated in Chinese style with abstract decorations and text in Chinese and Arabic over the doors. You won't be allowed into the main prayer hall if you're not a Muslim, but you can inspect the courtyard, where a copper cauldron, used to cook food for the devotees, sits near the graves of two Persian imams who came here to preach in the thirteenth century.

West of the centre

Heading west from Tian'anmen Square along **Xichang'an Jie**, the giant freeway that runs east–west across the city, you pass a string of grandiose buildings, the headquarters of official and corporate power. Though most of the sites and amenities are elsewhere, western Beijing has enough of interest to kill a day or two. There's a good shopping district, **Xidan**, the **Military Museum** and the **Capital Museum**, and the pleasant **Baiyun Guan** to chill out in.

Zhongnanhai to Xidan

West along Xichang'an Jie, the first major building you pass is, on the left, the new **National Centre for the Performing Arts** (中国国家大剧院, *zhōng guó guó jiā dà jù yuàn*), an undeniably striking contrast to the surrounding, somewhat po-faced, monumentalism. Designed by French architect Paul Andreu and nicknamed, for obvious reasons, the "Egg", the glass-and-titanium dome houses a concert hall, two theatres and a 2500-seat opera house. Visitors enter through a tunnel under the lake outside.

You may not realize it, but on the north side of the road you are passing the **Communist Party Headquarters**, the **Zhongnanhai** (中南海 *zhōngnán hǎi*). Armed sentries stand outside the gates, ensuring that only invited guests actually get inside. This is perhaps the most important and historic building in the country, base since 1949 of the Central Committee and the Central People's Government, and Mao and Zhou Enlai both worked here. Before the Communist takeover it was home to the Empress Dowager Cixi.

Just west, the **Aviation Office**, the place to buy tickets and catch the airport bus, stands on the site of Democracy Wall, and over the road looms **the Beijing Concert Hall**, recessed a little from the street, another uninspiring construction. **Xidan**, the street heading north from the next junction, is worth exploring, at least along its initial few blocks, though not at weekends, when it's heaving with people. This is where the locals shop, and the area is a dense concentration of **department stores**. The choice is less esoteric and the shopping experience less earthy than in Qianmen, but if you want to know what the kids are wearing this season, this is the place to go.

It takes persistence to continue much beyond this point, though you might be spurred on by the sight of the **Parkson Building** (百盛购物中心, *bǎishèng gòuwùzhōngxīn*) on the north side of the next main junction, a shopping centre for seriously rich Chinese. On the fifth floor of the south building is an exhibition hall

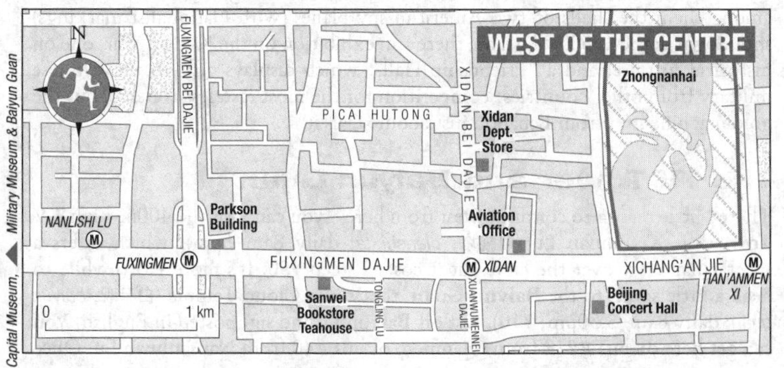

(daily 9.30am–4.30pm; ¥15) with the air of an exclusive private collection, showing "masterpieces" from the craftwork factories across China – similar to the stuff you'll see in the Friendship Store but of much better quality. Though it's all terribly kitsch – a Red Army meeting in ivory, for example – the craftsmanship in evidence is astonishing. If you're peckish, head for the giant food court on the sixth floor.

The Capital and Military museums

A kilometre west of here, on the south side of the street and not far from Muxidi subway stop, the new **Capital Museum** (首都博物馆, *shǒu dū bó wù guān*; Tues–Sun 9am–5pm; free; Ⓦ www.capitalmuseum.org.cn/en) is easy to miss, despite its size – from the outside, it rather resembles the bank headquarters that precede it. Inside, the architecture is much more interesting; a bronze cylinder shoots down through the roof as if from heaven. The layout is simple: exhibition halls concering the city are in the cube, cultural relics in the cylinder. The ground-floor gallery in the **cylinder** holds Ming and Qing paintings, mostly landscapes. The calligraphy upstairs can be safely missed unless you have a special interest, but the bronzes on level three are pretty interesting: a sinister third-century-BC owl-headed dagger, for example, or the strangely modern-looking three-legged cooking vessels decorated with geometrical patterns – which are more than three thousand years old. The display of jade on the fourth floor is definitely worth lingering over; some astonishing workmanship has gone into the buckles, boxes and knick-knacks here, and the white quail-shaped vessels are particularly lovely. The **cube** of exhibition halls on the building's west side can be travelled around rather faster. The bottom level hosts a confusing show on the history of Beijing – there aren't enough English captions to make any sense of the exhibition whatsoever – while the models of historical buildings on next level up can be skipped in favour of the show-stealing Buddhist figurines on the top floor. As well as depictions of serene, long-eared gentlemen, there are some very esoteric Lamaist figures from Tibet; the Goddess Marici, for example, comes with her own pig-drawn chariot, and other fierce deities have lion heads or many arms.

The stern Soviet-looking **Military Museum** on Fuxing Lu (军事博物馆, *jūnshì bówùguǎn*; daily 8am–4.30pm; ¥15) is more exciting than its name suggests; it does its job of impressing you with China's military might and achievements very well. Catch bus #1, which terminates close by, or the subway to Junshi Bowuguan. On entering, you are confronted with giant paintings celebrating martial valour, then an enormous rocket standing proud at the centre of the high main hall. Exhibits stake out the history of the **People's Liberation Army**, with heavy emphasis, inevitably, on the war against the Nationalists and the Japanese. Curiosities include, in the rear courtyard, a somewhat miscellaneous group of old aircraft – among them the shells of two American spy planes (with Nationalist markings) shot down in the 1950s. Upstairs, there's an exhibition on the Korean War, one on historical warfare, and a "Friendship Hall", which displays gifts to the Chinese military from other countries; competition for the most tasteless is fierce, but the gold machine gun from Lebanon just about steals it.

The TV Tower and Baiyun Guan

There's little reason to continue west from here – you can visit the 400m-high **TV Tower** on Xisanhuan Lu (电视塔, *diànshì tǎ*; daily 8am–5pm), which offers a spectacular view over the city, but it costs a steep ¥50. It's more worthwhile to head a little south to the **Baiyun Guan**, the White Cloud Temple (白云观, *báiyún guān*; daily 8am–5.30pm; ¥10), just off Baiyun Lu and signposted in English. You can get here on bus #212 from Qianmen, or bus #40 from Nansanhuan Lu. Once the most influential Taoist centre in the country, the temple has been extensively renovated after a long spell as a military barracks and is now the location for the China Taoism Association. There are thirty resident monks, and it's become a popular place for pilgrims, with a busy, thriving feel to it that is in some ways preferable to the more touristy Lamaist temple, the Yonghe Gong (see p.111). There are three monkeys depicted in relief sculptures around the temple, and it is believed to be lucky to find all three: the first is on the gate, easy to spot as it's been rubbed black, and the other two are in the first courtyard. Though laid out in a similar way to a Buddhist temple, it has a few unusual features, such as the three gateways at the entrance, symbolizing the three worlds of Taoism – Desire, Substance and Emptiness. The attached bookshop has only one text in English, the *Book of Changes*, but plenty of tapes and lucky charms. The place is at its most colourful during the New Year temple fair (see "Festivals", p.51).

East of the centre

As you head east from Tian'anmen Square, you enter the upmarket, commercial eastern side of the city. Here you'll find **Wangfujing**, the oldest shopping street in the city, and still one of the best, though these days the international zone of Jianguomen, further east, is rather more glamorous. It's not all mindless materialism; the **China Art Gallery**, at the north end of Wangfujing, and the **Ancient Observatory** on Jianguomen are welcoming oases of culture. Further north, **Sanlitun** remains a raucous nightlife zone, though it has some civilized parts. It's a long way northeast from here towards the airport, but the **798 Art District**, an abandoned factory complex now full of art galleries, is an intriguing new must-see.

Wangfujing Dajie

Wangfujing Dajie (王府井大街, *wángfŭjĭng dàjiē*; head north from the *Beijing Hotel* on Dongchang'an Jie) is where the capital gets down to the business of **shopping** in earnest. But it does have some decent sights as well, and it's short enough to stroll along its length. For a century the haunt of quality stores, on the western side of the street are plenty of small stores selling clothes. Just before the crossroads with Dong'anmen Dajie is the Foreign Languages Bookstore (see p.127), the largest in China and a good resource for travellers. On the other side of the street, the Sun Dong'an Plaza is a glitzy mall; you're better off going for a snack than to buy any of the very pricey, mostly designer clothes on sale, though the basement stalls are worth a browse if you're after tea or souvenirs. In the evening, check out the street food on sale at the **Dong'anmen Night Market**, which runs west off the northern end of the street (see p.117).

On the eastern side of the street, a number of **hutongs** lead into a quiet area well away from the bustle of the main street. The ten brothers of a Ming-dynasty emperor used to live here, so that he could keep a wary eye on them, and you can still see their palace at the end of Shuaifuyuan *hutong*, now converted into a medical college. Continuing east through the *hutongs*, you'll reach Dongdan Bei Dajie, parallel to Wangfujing, which is rapidly becoming a shopping centre to rival it, full of clothing boutiques.

The China Art Gallery

When you're tired of shopping, head north to the **China Art Gallery** (中国美术馆, *zhōngguó mĕishùguăn*; Tues–Sun 9am–4pm; entrance fee varies ¥2–20), at the top

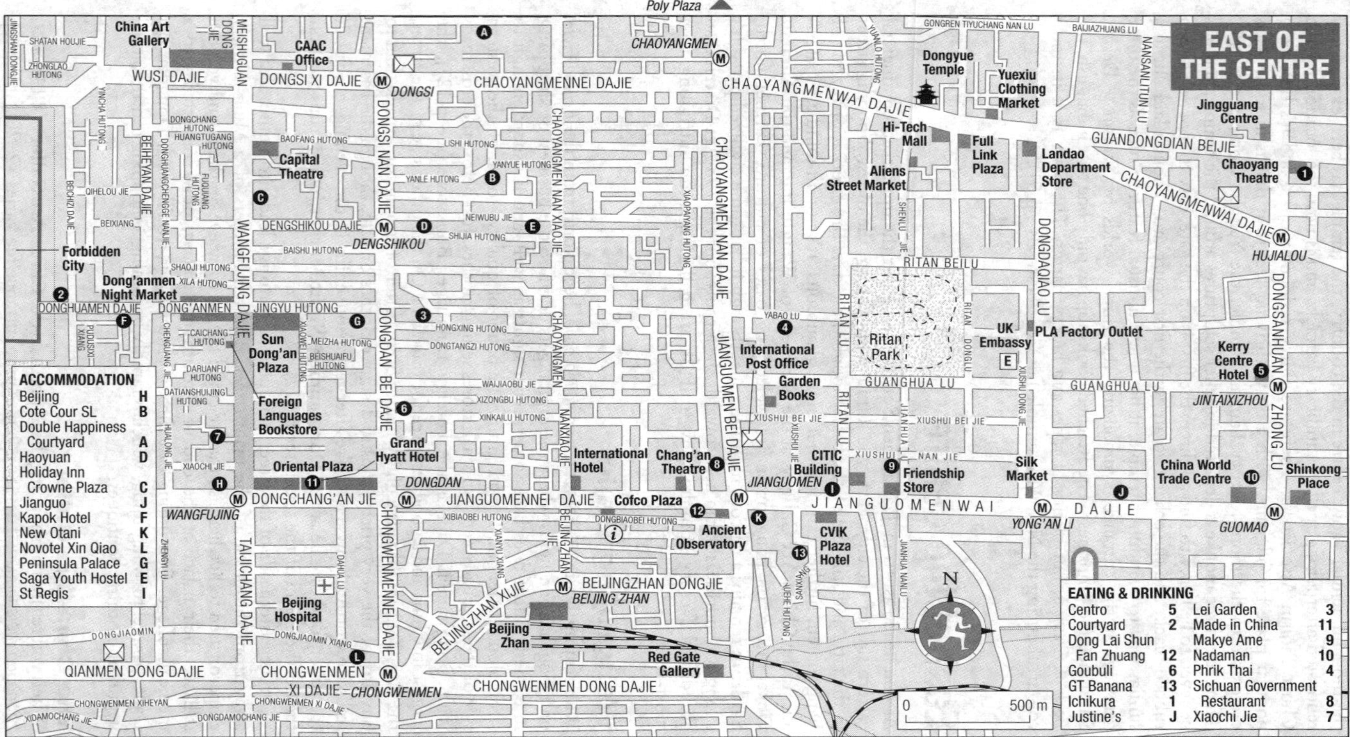
EAST OF THE CENTRE
ACCOMMODATION
Beijing H
Cote Cour SL B
Double Happiness Courtyard A
Haoyuan D
Holiday Inn Crowne Plaza C
Jianguo J
Kapok Hotel F
New Otani K
Novotel Xin Qiao L
Peninsula Palace G
Saga Youth Hostel E
St Regis I
EATING & DRINKING
Centro 5
Courtyard 2
Dong Lai Shun Fan Zhuang 12
Goubuli 6
GT Banana 13
Ichikura 1
Justine's J
Lei Garden 3
Made in China 11
Makye Ame 9
Nadaman 10
Phrik Thai 4
Sichuan Government Restaurant 8
Xiaochi Jie 7
0 500 m
N
Poly Plaza
China Art Gallery
CAAC Office
Capital Theatre
Forbidden City
Dong'anmen Night Market
Sun Dong'an Plaza
Foreign Languages Bookstore
Oriental Plaza
Grand Hyatt Hotel
Beijing Hospital
International Hotel
Chang'an Theatre
Cofco Plaza
Ancient Observatory
Beijing Zhan
Red Gate Gallery
International Post Office
Garden Books
CITIC Building
CVIK Plaza Hotel
Friendship Store
Silk Market
Ritan Park
UK Embassy
PLA Factory Outlet
Aliens Street Market
Hi-Tech Mall
Full Link Plaza
Landao Department Store
Dongyue Temple
Yuexiu Clothing Market
Jingguang Centre
Chaoyang Theatre
Kerry Centre Hotel
China World Trade Centre
Shinkong Place
WUSI DAJIE
DONGSI XI DAJIE
CHAOYANGMENNEI DAJIE
CHAOYANGMENWAI DAJIE
DONGSI NAN DAJIE
CHAOYANGMEN NAN XIAOJIE
CHAOYANGMEN NAN DAJIE
DENGSHIKOU DAJIE
WANGFUJING DAJIE
DONGDAN BEI DAJIE
DONGHUAMEN DAJIE
DONGCHANG'AN JIE
JIANGUOMENNEI DAJIE
JIANGUOMEN BEI DAJIE
JIANGUOMENWAI DAJIE
GUANGHUA LU
RITAN LU
RITAN BEILU
DONGDAQIAO LU
DONGSANHUAN ZHONG LU
GUANDONGDIAN BEIJIE
NANSANLITUN LU
BEIJINGZHAN DONGJIE
BEIJINGZHAN XIJIE
TAIJICHANG DAJIE
CHONGWENMENNEI DAJIE
CHONGWENMEN DONG DAJIE
CHONGWENMEN XI DAJIE
QIANMEN DONG DAJIE
CHAOYANGMEN
DONGSI
DENGSHIKOU
DONGDAN
WANGFUJING
JIANGUOMEN
YONG'AN LI
GUOMAO
JINTAIXIZHOU
HUJIALOU
BEIJING ZHAN
CHONGWENMEN

end of Wangfujing, on the route of bus #2, which runs north–south between Qianmen and Andingmen Dajie; otherwise it's a short walk west from Dongsi subway. A huge and draughty building, it usually holds several shows at once, though there's no permanent collection. Shows in the past have included specialist women's and minority exhibitions, and even a show of Socialist Realist propaganda, put up not to inspire renewed vigour but as a way to consider past follies – revolutionary imagery has long had its day and Chinese painting is enjoying a renaissance. You can see the work of the Bejing art colleges in July, when they hold their degree shows here. Check the listings magazines (see p.50) for what's on.

Jianguomen Dajie

Jianguomen Dajie (建国门大街, *jiànguómén dàjiē*), the strip beyond the second ring road, is Beijing's rich quarter, a ritzy area with an international flavour thanks to its large contingent of foreigners and staff from the weird Jianguomen embassy compound. Eating and staying around here will soon sap most travellers' budgets (first-time tourists can be heard here expressing disappointment that China is as expensive as New York), but the wide variety of shopping offered – good clothes markets, the notorious Silk Market and malls that wouldn't look out of place in Hong Kong – will suit all pockets.

An unexpected survivor marooned amid the high-rises, the **Ancient Observatory** (古观象台, *gǔguānxiàngtái*; Mon–Fri 9–11.30am & 1–4.30pm; ¥10) is a charming surprise, tucked in the southwest corner of the Jianguomen intersection, beside the Jianguomen subway stop. The first observatory on this site was founded under the orders of Kublai Khan, the astronomers' commission being to reform the then faulty calendar. Later it was staffed by Muslim scientists, as medieval Islamic science enjoyed pre-eminence, but, bizarrely, in the early seventeenth century it was placed in the hands of Jesuit Christian missionaries. The Jesuits, a small group led by one Matteo Ricci, arrived in Beijing in 1601 and astonished citizens and the emperor with a series of precise astronomical forecasts. They re-equipped the observatory and remained in charge through to the 1830s. Today, the building is essentially a shell, and the best features of the complex are the **garden**, a placid retreat, and the eight Ming-dynasty **astronomical instruments** sitting on the roof, stunningly sculptural armillary spheres, theodolites and the like. The small attached **museum**, displaying early astronomy-influenced pottery and navigational equipment, is an added bonus.

Turn up Ritan Lu and you'll hit the **Jianguomen Diplomatic Compound**, the first of two embassy complexes (the other is at Sanlitun, well northeast of here), a giant toytown with neat buildings in ordered courtyards and frozen sentries on red and white plinths. **Ritan Park** (日坛公园, *rìtán gōngyuán*) is a five-minute walk from Jianguomen Dajie. It's popular with embassy staff and courting couples, who make use of its numerous secluded nooks. It also hosts a few upscale restaurants.

North of the park you enter the city's Russian zone, where all the shop signs are in the Cyrillic alphabet; to the north, Shenlu Jie is full of fur shops aimed squarely at the Russian moll. The street ends in the giant **Aliens Street Market** (老番街市场, *lǎofānjiē shìchǎng*; 9.30am–6pm), a chaotic mall of gaudy trinkets, fakes and questionable fashion, thronging with Russian tourists and traders.

Back on Jianguomen Dajie, continuing east you'll reach the **Friendship Store**, the Chinese state's idea of a shopping centre, once the only kind allowed, and now overtaken by its commercial competitors. Its top floors are devoted to the usual range of goods – clothes, jewellery and paintings – but its lower floor is of more use, with a foreign exchange (open daily), a supermarket selling plenty of foreign goodies, an information desk where you can pick up the *China Daily* and a bookshop. On the other side of the road, the CVIK Plaza (赛特广场, *sàitè guǎngchǎng*; daily 9am–9pm) is a more modern shopping centre with five floors of clothes and accessories. There's a food court in the basement and a Bank of China on the first floor.

The main reason to continue beyond here is to head for the **Silk Market**, a giant six-storey mall of fake goods (see p.128), just north of Yong'an Li subway stop. From here, it's a dull couple of kilometres to the **China World Trade Centre** just before the intersection with the third ring road. Dedicated consumers who make it here are rewarded with Beijing's most exclusive mall, boasting four gleaming storeys of pricey goods, as well as a basement ice-skating rink. The Wellcome Supermarket here is one of the best in the city, though – unsurprisingly – it's not cheap. The new Shin Kong Plaza next door (新光天地, *xīnguāng tiāndì*) has some of the city's best restaurants (see p.120), as well as a decent basement food court.

Chaoyangmen Dajie and Sanlitun

North of Jianguomen Dajie, the Ming-dynasty **Dongyue Temple** (东岳庙, *dōngyuèmiào*; Tues–Sun 8am–5pm; ¥10), a short walk from Ritan Park or Chaoyangmen subway stop, is an intriguing place. Pass under the Zhandaimen archway and you enter a courtyard holding around thirty annexes, each of which deals with a different aspect of Taoist life, the whole making up a sort of surreal spiritual bureaucracy. There's the "Department of Suppressing Schemes", "Department of Wandering Ghosts", even a "Department for Fifteen Kinds of Violent Death". In each, a statue of Taoist deity Lao Zi holds court over brightly painted figures, many with monstrous animal heads, too many limbs and the like. The temple shop sells red tablets for worshippers to sign and leave outside the annexes as petitions to the spiritual officials. Departments dealing with longevity and wealth are predictably popular, but so, tellingly, is the "Department for Official Morality".

Not far north of here is the **Poly Plaza** (保利大厦, *bǎolì dàshà*), at Dongsi Shitiao subway stop. It's mostly offices, but at the back lies a small **museum** (Mon–Sat 9.30am–4.30pm; ¥50), which, though comparatively pricey, has one of the most select collections of antiquities in the capital. In the Hall of Ancient Bronzes you'll find four of the twelve bronze animals that were looted from the Old Summer Palace (see p.114); all were bought in the west by patriotic businessmen, and their return was much heralded. The second hall displays ancient Buddha statues.

East of here is the **Sanlitun** bar district (三里屯, *sānlǐtún*; see map on p.121). By night, it's raucous and gaudy, but during the day beguilingly civilized, with many small cafés and restaurants that are good for people-watching. As well as drinking, there are plenty of opportunities to eat and shop here.

798 Art District

Although it's out on the way to the airport, the **798 Art District** (798艺术区, *qī jiǔ bā yì shù qū*), a collection of art galleries, boutiques and cafés, is the latest hotspot for the arty crowd; take bus #915, #918 or #934 from Dongzhimen Station, or better, just take a taxi (¥15) as it's not easy to find first time. Originally, it was an electronics factory; when that closed down in the 1990s artists moved in and converted the airy, light and, above all, cheap spaces into studios. As the Chinese art market blossomed, galleries followed, then shops and cafés.

There are exhibition openings every week, and every art form is well represented – though with such a lot of it about, it varies in quality. Many **galleries** close on a Monday. Note that unlike all other Beijing sites, it's actually better on a weekend, when there's a buzz about the place; it can feel dead on a weekday.

The **most interesting galleries** are Galeria Continua, the huge Long March Space, Beijing Commune, Marcella Gallery, the huge Beijing Tokyo Art Projects and White Space (see p.125); but make sure to pop into the impressive new Ullens Centre for Contemporary Art too (see p.126). There are a few decent places to eat; you could try unproven, over-the-top new destination restaurant *Superganbei* but you'd probably be better off at the relaxed *Timezone 8* bookshop-café (see p.128). It wouldn't be worth turning up here just to go shopping, but if you're in the market for a designer dress, try the UCCA shop (see p.126). To arrange a three-hour walking tour of the complex (¥100–300/person) send a request to Ⓔtour798@yahoo.com.cn or call Ⓣ010/13811224385.

North of the centre

The area north of the Forbidden City has a scattered collection of sights, many of them remnants of the imperial past, when this area was the home of princes, dukes and monks. Beyond the imperial parks of **Jingshan** and **Beihai** is the one part of the city that is truly a pleasure to walk around – the well-preserved *hutong* district around **Houhai**. Tucked away here you'll find **Prince Gong's Palace**, **Song Qingling's residence** and the **Bell** and **Drum towers**, all within strolling distance of one another.

A few kilometres east of here, you'll find the appealing **Nanluogu Xiang**, a street where the artsy set hang out, and, right next to the Yonghe Gong subway stop, the **Yonghe Gong** Tibetan lamasery – one of Beijing's most colourful (and popular) attractions. While you're in the vicinity, don't miss the peaceful – and unjustly ignored – **Confucius Temple** and **Ditan Park**, within easy walking distance of one another.

West of this area, you'll find a number of little **museums**; the homes of two twentieth-century cultural icons, **Lu Xun** and **Xu Beihong** now hold exhibitions of their works, while the **Baita Si** functions as a museum of religious relics as well as a place of pilgrimage.

Jingshan and Beihai parks

Jingshan Park (景山公园, *jǐngshān gōngyuán*; daily 6am–9pm; ¥3) is a natural way to round off a trip to the Forbidden City. An artificial mound, it was created by the digging of the palace moat, and served as a windbreak and a barrier to malevolent spirits (believed to emanate from the north) for the imperial quarter of the city. It takes its name, meaning Coal Hill, from a coal store once sited here. Its history, most momentously, includes the suicide of the last Ming emperor, **Chong Zhen**, in 1644, who hanged himself here from a locust tree after rebel troops broke into the imperial city. The spot, on the eastern side of the park, is easy to find as it is signposted everywhere (underneath signs pointing to a children's playground), though the tree that stands here is not the original.

It's the **views** from the top of the hill that make this park such a compelling target: they take in the whole extent of the Forbidden City – giving a revealing perspective – and a fair swathe of the city outside, a deal more attractive than at ground level. To the west is Beihai with its fat snaking lake; in the north, Gulou and Zhonglou (the Drum and Bell towers); and to the northeast, the Yonghe Gong.

Almost half of **Beihai Park** (北海公园, *běihǎi gōngyuán*; daily 6am–8pm; ¥5, buildings ¥20), a few hundred metres west of Jingshan on the route of bus #5 from Qianmen, is water – and a favourite ice-skating spot in the winter months.

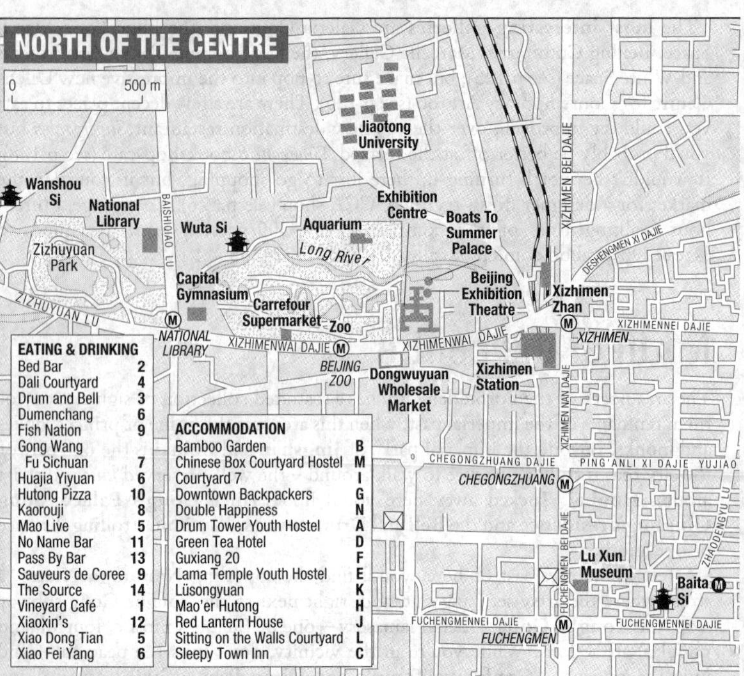

The park was supposedly created by Kublai Khan, long before any of the Forbidden City structures were conceived, and its scale is suitably ambitious: the lake was man-made, an island being created in its midst with the excavated earth. Emperor Qianlong oversaw its landscaping into a classical garden, and Mao's widow, the ill-fated Jiang Qing, was a frequent visitor here. Today, its willows and red-columned galleries make it a grand place to retreat from the city and recharge. Most of the buildings (daily 6am–4pm) lie on the central island, whose summit is marked by a white dagoba, built in the mid-seventeenth century to celebrate a visit by the Dalai Lama, a suitable emblem for a park that contains a curious mixture of religious buildings, storehouses for cultural relics and imperial garden architecture.

Just inside the south gate, the **Round City** encloses a courtyard that holds a jade bowl, said to have belonged to Kublai Khan. The white jade Buddha in the hall behind was a present from Burma. The **island** is accessible by a walkway from here. It's dotted with religious architecture, which you'll come across as you scramble around the rocky paths, including the **Yuegu Lou**, a hall full of steles, and the giant **dagoba** sitting on top with a shrine to the demon-headed, multi-armed Lamaist deity, Yamantaka, nestling inside. There's a boat dock near here, where you can rent rowing **boats**, or you can rent duck-shaped pedal boats from near the south gate – good ways to explore the lake and its banks. On the north side of the lake, the impressive **Nine Dragon Screen**, in good condition, is one of China's largest at 27m long. The Five Dragon Pavilions nearby are supposedly in the shape of a dragon's spine. Over on the other side of the lake, the gardens and rockeries here were popular with Emperor Qianlong, and it's easy to see why – even when the place is crowded at weekends, the atmosphere is tranquil.

The Shicha lake area (Houhai)

The area north of Beihai Park, colloquially known as **Houhai** (后海, *hòuhǎi*), has become a heritage zone, and it's the only part of the city centre where the *hutong* alleyways have been preserved at any scale. The area centres on the three artificial **Shicha lakes**, created during the Yuan dynasty, and the port for a canal network that served the capital. The choked, grey alleys show Beijing's other, private, face; here you'll see cluttered courtyards and converted palaces, and come across small open spaces where old men sit with their pet birds. There are also two giant old buildings, the **Bell** and **Drum towers**, hidden away among the alleys. The area has been prettified, with touristy venues being built and rickshaw tours running from outside the Bell Tower, but it retains its charm, at least for the moment. It's also become one of Beijing's hipper hang-outs, with plenty of bars and restaurants along the lakeside (see p.122). The best way to get around is certainly by **bike**. Traffic is light and you're free to dive into any alley you fancy, though you're almost certain to get lost – in which case, cycle around until you come to one of the lakes, the only big landmarks around. The best point of entry is the *hutong* nearest the northern entrance to Beihai Park – take bus #13 from the Yonghe Gong, or walk from Gulou or Xinjiekou subway stop.

Prince Gong's Palace and around

Residence of the last Qing emperor's father, **Prince Gong's Palace** (恭王府, *gōngwángfǔ*; daily 9am–4.30pm; ¥30) is the best-kept courtyard house in the city. To get here, follow the curving alley north from Beihai Park's north entrance – Qianhai Hu (the southernmost lake) will be on your right – then take the first left, then the first right on to Qianhai Xi Jie. If you're trying to reach the palace directly by bus, you'll have to get off on Dianmen Xi Dajie and walk the same route. The attractive, leafy garden of the palace is split into discreet compounds and imaginatively landscaped. The largest hall hosts irregular performances of **Beijing Opera** – though you'll have to time your arrival with that of the tour groups, at around 11am, 4pm and 7.30pm, to witness these. There are plenty of other **old palaces** in the area, as this was once something of an imperial pleasure ground and home to a number of high officials and distinguished eunuchs. The Palace of Tao Beile, now a school, is just west of here on Liuyin Jie. Doubling back and heading north along the lakeside, you'll come to the humpbacked Yinding Bridge, at the point where the lake is narrowest. Over the bridge is the excellent *Kaorouji* restaurant (see p.119), which boasts good views over the lake. Opposite, you'll find the *Buddha Bar* (among many others), a great place to sit outside with a coffee.

Song Qingling's Former Residence and the Drum and Bell towers

From Yinding Bridge, head north along the lakeside and loop around to the west and you'll reach **Song Qingling's Former Residence** (宋庆龄故居, *sòngqìnglíng gùjū*; Tues–Sun 9am–4pm; ¥20), another Qing mansion, with a delicate, spacious garden. Song Qingling, the wife of Sun Yatsen, commands great respect in China and an exhibition inside details her busy life in a dry, admiring tone. From here, an alley will take you on to Gulou Xi Dajie, a major street, at the eastern end of which squats the **Drum Tower** (鼓楼, *gŭlóu*; daily 9am–4.30pm; ¥20), a fifteenth-century Ming creation. From this vantage point drums were beaten to mark dusk and to call imperial officials to meetings. Every half hour between 10am and noon and from 2 to 4pm a troupe of drummers whacks cheerfully away at the giant drums inside. They're not, to be blunt, very artful, but it's still an impressive sight. The building's twin, the **Bell Tower** (钟楼, *zhōnglóu*; same times and prices), is at the other end of the plaza. Originally Ming, it was destroyed by fire and rebuilt in the eighteenth century. It still has its original bell, which used to be rung at dawn. These towers stand on the city's main north–south axis – head directly south, going round Jingshan Park, and past the Forbidden City, and you'll eventually come to Qianmen Dajie, a route followed by bus #5.

Xu Beihong Museum

Just outside the *hutong* quarter, but easily combined with a visit to Houhai, the **Xu Beihong Museum** (徐悲鸿纪念馆, *xúbēihóng jìniànguǎn*; Tues–Sun 9–11am & 1.30–4.30pm; ¥5) at 53 Xinjiekou Bei Dajie, on the route of bus #22 from Qianmen or #38 from the east end of Fuchingmennei Dajie, and five minutes' walk north of Jishuitan subway stop, is definitely worth the diversion. The son of a wandering portraitist, Xu Beihong (1895–1953) did for Chinese art what his contemporary Lu Xun did for literature. Xu had to look after his whole family from the age of 17 after his father died, and spent much of his early life in semi-destitution before receiving the acclaim he deserved. His extraordinary facility is well in evidence here in seven halls that display a huge collection of his work, including many of the ink paintings of horses he was most famous for, but also oil paintings in a Western style, which he produced when studying in France, and large-scale allegorical images that allude to events in China at the time. However, the images that are easiest to respond to are his delightful sketches and studies, in ink and pencil, often of his son.

Nanluogu Xiang

There aren't, to be frank, too many streets in Beijing that could be called appealing, so north–south *hutong* **Nanluogu Xiang** (南锣鼓巷, *nán luó gŭ xiàng*) is a little oasis.

Dotted with laidback cafés, boutiques and restaurants, it has become a playground for the city's bobos (bourgeois-bohemians). Still, in the alleys around you'll see enough open-air mahjong games, rickety stores and old men sitting out with their caged birds to maintain that ramshackle, backstreet Beijing charm. If there seems to be a surfeit of bright and beautiful young things, that's because of the drama school just around the corner. All in all, it's a great place to idle over a cappuccino; *Xiao Xin's* and the *Pass By Bar* (see p.122) are recommended venues.

Yonghe Gong and around

Though it is a little touristy, the colourful **Yonghe Gong**, Tibetan Lama Temple (雍和宫, *yōngghé gōng*; daily 9am–5pm; ¥25), is well worth a visit; it couldn't be much easier to reach – Yonghe Gong subway stop is right next door. It was built towards the end of the seventeenth century as the residence of Prince Yin Zhen. In 1723, when the prince became the Emperor Yong Zheng and moved into the Forbidden City, the temple was retiled in imperial yellow and restricted thereafter to religious use. It became a lamasery in 1744, housing monks from Tibet and also from Inner Mongolia, over which it had a presiding role, supervising the election of the Mongolian Living Buddha, who was chosen by lot from a gold urn. After the civil war in 1949, the Yonghe Gong was declared a national monument and for thirty years was closed; remarkably, it escaped the ravages of the Cultural Revolution.

Visitors are free to wander through the prayer halls and ornamental gardens, though the experience is largely aesthetic rather than spiritual. As well as the amazing mandalas hanging in side halls, there is some notable statuary. In the Third Hall, the **Pavilion of Eternal Happiness**, are *nandikesvras*, representations of Buddha having sex. Once used to educate the emperors' sons, the statues are now completely covered by drapes. The **Hall of the Wheel of Law**, behind it, has a gilded bronze statue of the founder of the Yellow Hat sect and paintings that depict his life, while the thrones next to it are for the Dalai Lamas when they used to come here to teach. In the last, grandest hall – the **Wanfu Pavilion** – an 18m-high statue of the Maitreya Buddha is made from a single trunk of sandalwood, a gift for Emperor Qianlong from the seventh Dalai Lama. The wood is Tibetan and it took three years to ship it to Beijing.

The lamasery also functions as an active **Tibetan Buddhist centre**, though it's used basically for propaganda purposes, to show China guaranteeing and respecting the religious freedom of minorities. It's questionable how genuine the monks you see wandering around are – at best, they're state-approved.

Confucius Temple and Ditan Park

Opposite the Yonghe Gong, on the west side, is a quiet *hutong* lined with little shops selling religious tapes, incense and images. This street, one of the city's oldest, has been home to scholars since the Yuan dynasty and is lined with *pailous*, decorative arches, which once graced many of Beijing's streets – they were torn down in the 1950s for being a hindrance to traffic. On the right, about 100m down, the **Confucius Temple** (孔庙, *kǒngmiào*; daily 8.30am–5pm; ¥10) is as restrained as the Yonghe Gong is gaudy. One of the best things to do here is sit on a bench in the peaceful courtyard, among ancient, twisted trees, and enjoy the silence.

Returning to the Yonghe Gong and heading north, **Ditan Park** (地坛公园, *dìtán gōngyuán*; daily 6am–9pm; ¥1, buildings ¥5) is just 100m away, more interesting as a place to wander among the trees and spot the odd *tai ji* performance than for its small **museum** (¥5) holding the emperor's sedan chair and the enormous altar at which he performed sacrifices to the earth.

Around Fuchengmennei Dajie

Heading west from the south end of Beihai Park along Wenjin Jie, you'll come to **Fuchengmennei Dajie**, the area's shopping district. A couple of places along here make it worth a nose around on the way to the deservedly popular Summer Palace. Bus #101 from the north exit of the Forbidden City, and #13 from the Yonghe Gong, traverse the street. The **Guangji Si** (广济寺, *guǎngji sì*), headquarters of the China Buddhist Association, is a working Buddhist temple near its eastern end, on the north side of the road, with an important collection of painting and sculpture. There's no entrance fee and visitors are free to look around. Farther west along the street you'll come to a temple on the north side that's been converted into a school – the spirit wall now forms one side of a public lavatory. Beyond this, the massive white dagoba of the **Baita Si** (白塔寺, *báitǎ sì*; Tues–Sun 9am–5pm; ¥20) becomes visible, rising over the rooftops of a labyrinth of *hutongs*; the only access is from Fuchengmennei Dajie. Shaped like an upturned bowl with an ice-cream cone on top, the 35m-high dagoba was built to house relics in the Yuan dynasty and designed by a Nepalese architect. The temple is worth a visit just for the small Buddha statues, mostly Tibetan, housed in one hall. Another hall holds a collection of bronze luohans, including one with a beak, small bronze Buddhas and other, weirder Lamaist figures, together with silk and velvet priestly garments, which were unearthed from under the dagoba in 1978. Just outside the temple there's a tasty pancake stall.

Lu Xun Museum

Continue west and, just before the giant intersection with Fuchengmen Bei Dajie, you'll see Xisantiao Hutong to the north, which leads to the **Lu Xun Museum** (鲁迅博物馆, *lǔxùn bówùguǎn*; Tues–Sun 9am–4pm; ¥10), a large and extensively renovated courtyard house. Lu Xun (1881–1936) is widely accepted as the greatest modern Chinese writer, who gave up a promising career in medicine to write books (see p.991).

A hater of pomposity, he might feel a little uneasy in his house now, where the atmosphere is of uncritical admiration. His possessions have been preserved like relics, incidentally giving a good idea of what Chinese interiors looked like at the beginning of last century, and there's a photo exhibition of his life, lauding his achievements. A bookshop in the eastern building sells English translations of his work, including his most popular book, *The True Story of Ah Q*.

Beijing Zoo

Beijing Zoo (北京动物园, *běijīng dòngwùyuán*; daily 7.30am–5pm; ¥20), on Xizhimenwai Dajie, marks the edge of the inner city. There's a subway stop, Xizhimen, 1km east of the zoo, and a bus terminus just south of it; bus #7, which you can catch from Fuchingmen Dajie, terminates here. Xizhimen Zhan (Beijing North train station) is north of the subway stop. The zoo itself, flanked on either side by the monumental Capital Gymnasium and Soviet-built **Exhibition Centre** (展览馆, *zhǎnlǎn guǎn*), is not a great attraction unless you really need to see a panda. You can join the queues to have your photo taken sitting astride a plastic replica, then push your way through to glimpse the living variety – kept in relatively palatial quarters and highly familiar through ritual diplomatic mating exchanges over the last decades. While the pandas lie on their backs in their luxury pad, waving their legs in the air, other animals, less cute or less endangered, slink, pace or flap around their miserable cells. Much the best part of the rest of the zoo is the **aquarium**, though it's a bit pricey (¥100, children ¥50).

Wuta Si and Wanshou Si

Past the zoo, head north up Baishiqiao Lu, take the first right and follow the canal, and ten minutes' walk will bring you to the **Wuta Si** (五塔寺, *wu5tăsì*; daily 9am–4.30pm; ¥20). The central hall is radically different from any other sacred building you'll see in the capital. Completed in 1424, it's a stone cube decorated on the outside with reliefs of animals, Sanskrit characters and Buddha images – each has a different hand gesture – and is topped with five layered, triangular spires. It's visibly Indian in influence, and is said to be based on a temple in Bodhgaya, where Buddha gained enlightenment. There are 87 steps to the top (¥5), where you can inspect the spire carvings at close quarters – including elephants and Buddhas, and, at the centre of the central spire, a pair of feet. The new halls behind the museum are home to statues of bulbous-eyed camels, docile-looking tigers, puppy-dog lions and the like, all collected from the spirit ways of tombs and long-destroyed temples.

From here it's a half-hour stroll following the river west back to Baishiqiao Lu, through the bamboo groves of **Zizhuyuan Park** (紫竹院公园, *zǐzhúyuàn gōngyuán*), and out of the park's northwest exit to the **Wanshou Si** (万寿寺, *wànshòusì*; daily 9am–4.30pm; ¥20). This Ming temple, a favourite of Cixi's, is now a small museum of ancient art, with five exhibition halls of Ming and Qing relics, mostly ceramics.

The summer palaces and far northwest

In the northwest corner of the city is a cluster of attractions that improve the further out you go. The **Dazhong Si** is worth a poke around on the way to or from more alluring destinations, and the nearby districts of Haidian and Zhongguancun are known for hi-tech shopping and youth culture.

Though it's eclipsed by its newer neighbour, **Yuanmingyuan**, the old Summer Palace, is worth checking out for the sobering history it attests to. Nearby **Yiheyuan**, usually known in English as the Summer Palace, is an excellent place to get away from the city smog – a recommended escape, summer or winter.

Dazhong Si

The **Dazhong Si** (大钟寺, *dàzhōng sì*; Great Bell Temple; Tues–Sun 8am–4.30pm; ¥15) is one of Beijing's most interesting little museums, showcasing several hundred **bronze bells** from temples all over the country. It's stuck out on Beisanhuan Lu, the north section of the third ring road, a long way from the centre; buses #302 and #367 go right past, or you can take the subway to Dazhongsi stop and walk 200m west. The best way to visit is on the way to or from the Summer Palace.

The bells here are considerable works of art, their surfaces enlivened with embossed texts in Chinese and Tibetan, abstract patterns and images of storks and dragons. The odd, scaly, dragon-like creature shown perching on top of each bell is a pulao, a legendary animal supposed to shriek when attacked by a whale (the wooden hammers used to strike the bells are carved to look like whales). The smallest bell here is the size of a goblet; the largest, a Ming creation called the **King of Bells**, is as tall as a two-storey house. Hanging in the back hall, it is, at fifty tonnes, the biggest and oldest surviving bell in the world, and can reputedly be heard up to 40km away. You can climb up to a platform above it to get a closer look at some of the 250,000 Chinese characters on its surface, and join Chinese visitors in trying to throw a coin into the small hole in the top. The method of its construction and the history of Chinese bell-making are explained by displays, with English captions, in side halls. Audio tapes and CDs on sale of the bells in action are more interesting than they might appear: the shape of Chinese bells dampens vibrations, so they only sound for a short time and can be effectively used as instruments.

Haidian

It's not an obvious tourist attraction, but the whole of **Haidian district** (海淀, *hǎidiàn*), northwest of the third ring road, west of the Wudaokou subway stop, bears mentioning: here you'll find the more underground bars and clubs, and on Zhongguangcun Lu (中关村, *zhōngguāncūn*), nicknamed Electronics Street, a hi-tech zone of computer shops. In the north of the area, on the way to the Summer Palace, you'll pass **Beijing University** (or "Beida" as it's known colloquially; 北京大学, *běijīng dàxúe*), China's most prestigious university. Originally established and administered by the Americans at the beginning of the twentieth century, it stood in Jingshan Park and was moved to its present site in 1953. Now busy with new contingents of foreign students from the West, it was half-deserted during the Cultural Revolution when both students and teachers, regarded as suspiciously liberal, were dispersed for "re-education". The pleasant campus, with its old buildings and quiet, well-maintained grounds, makes it nicer than most of the city's parks. A Second university, Tsinghua, is not far from here, to the east, though it's much less attractive. Around the gates of both universities you'll find small, inexpensive **restaurants**, **bars** and **internet cafés** catering for students.

Yuanmingyuan

Beijing's original Summer Palace, the **Yuanmingyuan** (圆明园, *yuánmíng yuán*; daily 9am–6pm; ¥15), is a thirty-minute walk north of Beida, or take the subway to Yuanmingyuan. Built by the Qing emperor Kangxi in the early eighteenth century, the palace, nicknamed "China's Versailles" by Europeans, once boasted the largest royal gardens in the world – with some two hundred pavilions and temples set around a series of lakes and natural springs. Marina Warner recreates the scene in *The Dragon Empress*:

> **Scarlet and golden halls, miradors, follies and gazebos clustered around artificial hills and lakes. Tranquil tracts of water were filled with fan-tailed goldfish with telescopic eyes, and covered with lotus and lily pads; a superabundance of flowering shrubs luxuriated in the gardens; antlered deer wandered through the grounds; ornamental ducks and rare birds nestled on the lakeside.**

Today, however, there is little to hang your imagination upon. In 1860, the entire complex was burnt and destroyed by British and French troops, ordered by the Earl of Elgin to make the imperial court "see reason" during the Opium Wars. There are plenty of signs to remind you of this, making Yuanmingyuan a tiresome monument to contemporary Chinese xenophobia. The park extends over 350 hectares but the only really identifiable ruins are the **Hall of Tranquillity** in the northeastern section. The stone and marble remains of fountains and columns hint at how fascinating the original must once have been, with its marriage of European Rococo decoration and Chinese motifs. The government is jazzing the place up with a programme of restoration and construction, but this remains an attraction wholly eclipsed by the new Summer Palace.

The Summer Palace

Yiheyuan, the **Summer Palace** (颐和园, *yíhéyuán*; daily 8am–7pm, buildings close at 4pm; ¥40), is certainly worth the effort to seek out. This is one of the loveliest spots in Beijing, a vast public park where the latter-day imperial court would

Empress Dowager Cixi

The notorioius Cixi entered the imperial palace at 15 as Emperor Xianfeng's **concubine**, quickly becoming his favourite and bearing him a son. When the emperor died in 1861, she became regent, ruling in place of her infant boy. For the next 25 years, she in effect ruled China, displaying a mastery of intrigue and court politics. When her son died of syphilis, she installed her nephew as puppet regent, imprisoned him, and retained her authority. Her fondness of extravagant gestures (every year she had ten thousand caged birds released on her birthday) drained the state's coffers, and her deeply conservative policies were inappropriate for a time when the nation was calling out for reform.

With foreign powers taking great chunks out of China's borders on and off during the nineteenth century, Cixi was moved to respond in a typically misguided fashion. Impressed by the claims of the xenophobic **Boxer Movement** (whose Chinese title translated as "Righteous and Harmonious Fists"), Cixi let them loose on all the foreigners in China in 1899. The Boxers laid seige to the foreign legation's compound in Beijing for nearly two months before a European expeditionary force arrived and, predictably, slaughtered the agitators. Cixi and the emperor escaped the subsequent rout of the capital by disguising themselves as peasants and fleeing the city. On her return, Cixi clung to power, attempting to delay the inevitable fall of her dynasty. One of her last acts, before she died in 1908, was to arrange for the murder of her puppet regent.

decamp during the hottest months of the year. The site is perfect, surrounded by hills, cooled by the lake (which takes up two-thirds of the park's area) and sheltered by garden landscaping. The impressive temples and pleasure houses are spread out along the lakeside and connected by a suitably majestic gallery.

The quickest route here is to take the subway to Beigongmen stop. There's also an interesting boat service from the back of the Exhibition Centre, which is just east of the zoo (boats leave hourly between 10am and 4pm; ¥40 single, ¥70 return).

There have been summer imperial pavilions at Yiheyuan since the eleventh century, although the present layout is essentially eighteenth-century, created by the Manchu emperor Qianlong. However, the key character associated with the palace is the **Empress Dowager Cixi** (see above) – Yiheyuan was very much her pleasure ground. She rebuilt the palaces in 1888 and determinedly restored them in 1902 after foreign troops had ransacked them. Her ultimate flight of fancy was the construction of a magnificent marble boat from the very funds intended for the Chinese navy. Whether her misappropriations had any real effect on the empire's path is hard to determine, but it certainly speeded the decline, with China suffering heavy naval defeats during the war with Japan. To enjoy the site, however, you need know very little of its history – like Beihai, the park, its lake and pavilions form a startling visual array, like a traditional landscape painting brought to life.

The palaces

The **palaces** are built to the north of the lake, on and around Wanshou Shan (Longevity Hill), and many remain intimately linked with Cixi – anecdotes about whom are staple fare for the numerous guides. Most visitors enter through the **East Gate**, where the buses stop, above which is the main palace compound, including the **Renshoudian** (Hall of Benevolence and Longevity), a majestic hall where the empress and her predecessors gave audience. It contains much of the original nineteenth-century furniture, including an imposing throne. Beyond, to the right, is the **Deheyuan** (Palace of Virtue and Harmony), dominated by a three-storey **theatre**, complete with trap doors for the appearances and disappearances of the actors. Theatre was one of Cixi's main passions and she sometimes took part in performances, dressed as Guanyin, the goddess of mercy. The next major building along the path is the **Yulantang** (Jade Waves Palace). This is where the child emperor Guangxu was kept in captivity for ten years, while Cixi exercised his powers. Just to the west is the dowager's own principal residence, the **Leshoutang** (Hall of Joy and Longevity), which houses Cixi's hardwood throne, and the table where she took her notorious 108-course meals. The chandeliers were China's first electric lights, installed in 1903 and powered by the palace's own generator.

Kunming lake

From here to the northwest corner of the lake runs the **Long Gallery**, the 900m-long covered way, painted with mythological scenes and flanked by various temples and pavilions. It is said that no pair of lovers can walk through without emerging betrothed. Near the west end of the gallery is the infamous **marble boat**, completed by Cixi with purloined naval cash and regarded by her acolytes as a suitably witty and defiant gesture. Close by, and the tourist focus of this site, is a jetty with **rowing boats** for rent (¥30/hour). You can dock again below Wanshou Shan and row out to the two **bridges** – the Jade Belt on the western side and Seventeen Arched on the east. In winter, the Chinese skate on the lake here, an equally spectacular sight, and skates are available for rent.

Eating, drinking, nightlife, entertainment and shopping

You're spoilt for choice when it comes to food in Beijing. Splurging in classy **restaurants** is a great way to spend your evenings, as prices in even the most luxurious places are very competitive and a lot more affordable than their equivalent in the West. Beijing has a great deal of entertainment options, too, with a lively arts scene, and it's well worth seeking them out; remember you won't have much opportunity outside the capital. There is a promising **bar and club scene** worth sampling, if just for the strange cultural juxtapositions it throws up. If you want to check out a Chinese disco or local rock band, this is the place to do it, and again, a night on the town won't break your budget. **Shopping** is another diverting pastime, with the best choice of souvenirs and consumables in the country; in particular, Beijing still has a collection of intriguing little markets offering an appealing and affordable alternative to the new giant malls.

Eating

Nowhere else on the Chinese mainland can compete with the culinary wealth of Beijing: every style of **Chinese food** is available, plus just about any Asian and most world cuisines. Among all this abundance it's sometimes easy to forget that **Beijing** has its own culinary tradition – specialities well worth trying are **Beijing duck** (*Beijing kaoya*) and **Mongolian hotpot**. Beijing duck appears in Chinese restaurants worldwide and consists of small pieces of meat that you dip in plum sauce, then wrap with chopped onions in a pancake. It's very rich and packs a massive cholesterol count. Mongolian hotpot is healthier, a poor man's fondue, involving a large pot of boiling stock into which you dip strips of mutton, cabbage and noodles.

Western food is easy to find in Beijing, though it generally costs a little more than Chinese, and **Japanese** and **Korean** cuisine are also widley available.

Breakfast, snacks and fast food

Many visitors find the Chinese **breakfast** of dumplings and glutinous bland and unappealing, but *jian bing guozi*, the classic Beijing breakfast snack – vegetables wrapped in an omelette wrapped in a pancake – deftly assembled by street vendors in thirty seconds, is definitely worth trying (¥3). For cheap and filling **suppers**, try street food like *huntun*, basically wuntun soup, and *xianr bing* – stuffed pancake – or the diverse varieties of noodles. These days you'll only find street food at the **food markets**, which are at their best in summer (see below).

Every mall and shopping centre has a **food court**, usually in the basement but sometimes on the top floor, which offers inexpensive meals from a variety of outlets. You have to buy a plastic card at a central booth, which is debited at the counter when you order. Good food courts can be found at the Parkson Building on Fuxingmennei Dajie, in the Xidan Department Store, and, on Wangfujing, on the top floor of the Sun Dong'an Plaza and basement of the Oriental Plaza, and at Raffles Mall at Dongzhimen; but the best is the new one in the basement at Shin Kong place in Guomao.

Dong'anmen Night Market (东华门夜市, *dōnghuámén yèshì*) Dong'anmen Dajie, off Wangfujing Dajie; see map, p.104. Stalls set up along the street offering *xiaochi* (literally, "small food") from all over China. Nothing is more than a few yuan, except the odd delicacy such as scorpion on a stick for ¥10.

Goubuli (狗不理, *gǒubùlǐ*) 29 Dazhalan Dajie, 88 Dongdan Bei Dajie. Delicious steamed buns with various fillings (the original fast food) for a few yuan. You can eat them here – the downstairs canteen is cheaper than upstairs – or take away, as most customers do.

Kempi Deli (凯宾斯基饭店, *kǎibīnsījī fàndiàn*) 1F, *Kempinski Hotel*, Lufthansa Centre, 50 Liangmaqiao Lu; see map, p.121. Deserves a mention for producing the city's best bread and pastries. Prices halve after 8pm.

Xiaochi Jie (小吃街, *xiǎochījiē*) Xiagongfu Jie, running west off the southern end of Wangfujing Dajie; see map, p.104. This alley is lined with stalls where pushy vendors sell exotica at fixed prices. It's the perfect place to sample food to freak the folks back home: skewers of fried scorpions, silkworm pupae, crickets and sparrows are all available for less than ¥10 – though none of them, in truth, tastes of much. You can also get good noodles and seafood for a few yuan.

Cafés

As well as the places listed below, note that some **bars** are also great places to linger over a capuccino, notably *Pass By Bar* (see p.122), *Drum and Gong* (see p.122) and *No Name* (see p.122). All those, and the places below, have free wi-fi.

Bookworm (书虫, *shū chóng*) Sanlitun Nan Jie, back of building 4 ⓦwww.beijingbookworm.com; see map, p.121. This bistro-café-lending library raises the tone of the whole area. There's a programme of events and lectures, and a literary festival every March.

Sculpting in Time 7 Weigongcun Lu, outside the southern gate of the Beijing Insititute of Technology. A casual, attractive café with a largely student clientele. Fit in by drinking lattes, browsing the book collection and gazing thoughtfully out of the window. They serve good muffins and pasta dishes here, too.

Starbucks 1F, China World Trade Centre, Jianguomenwai Dajie; COFCO plaza, 8 Jianguomennei Dajie; Chaoyangmenwai Dajie, opposite the Dongyue Temple; Sun Dong'an Plaza (basement) and Oriental Plaza (1F, A07) on Wangfujing Dajie; north side of Xidan Plaza, Xidan. The coffee colonizers have overtaken *McDonald's* as the most potent symbol of Westernization. A medium-sized cup of their caffeinated mud is ¥15.

Timezone 8 4 Jiuxianqiao Lu, 798 Arts District. This fashionable bookshop-cum-café-restaurant is the best pitstop for anyone shlepping round the galleries of 798.

Vineyard Café (葡萄院儿, *pú táo yuàn ér*) 31 Wudaoying Hutong, south of Yonghe Gong Bridge; see map, pp.108–109. Good western wine and food, including pizzas. Cross the second ring road onto Yonghe Gong Dajie and take the first *hutong* on the right. Good brunches; combine with a trip to the Yonghe Gong. Closed Mon.

Xiaoxin's (小新的店, *xiǎo xīn de diàn*) 103 Nanluogu Xiang; see map, pp.108–109. A cosy staple of artsy Nanluogu Xiang with a limited menu but a tasty cheesecake.

Restaurants

All the expensive **hotels** have several well-appointed restaurants, where the atmosphere is sedate but prices are sometimes not as high as you might expect; look out for their special offers, advertised in the city's listings magazines. Local restaurants, though, are cheaper and livelier. Expect to eat earlier than you would in Western cities: lunch is around noon and dinner around 6pm or 7pm. Few places stay open after 11pm. Telephone numbers have been included in the reviews below only for the more expensive and popular restaurants where **reservations** are advisable.

Qianmen

The place listed below is marked on the map on p.91.

Lichun (利群烤鸭店, *lìqún kǎoyādiàn*) 11 Bei Xiang Hutong ⓣ010/67025681. Deep in a *hutong*, this place is tough to find but offers good duck at half the price of the chains (¥80). From Qianmen subway stop, walk east along Qianmen Dong Dajie and take the first right into Zhengyi Lu, and at the end turn right. Then follow the English sign to the "Lijun Roast Duck Restaurant" – left, left and it's on the left. You'll probably have to ask. The restaurant is in a shabby old courtyard house, and it's small, so you'd be wise to reserve beforehand.

East of the centre

Unless otherwise stated, the places listed below are marked on the map on p.104.

Courtyard (四合院, *sìhé yuàn*) 95 Donghuamen Dajie, outside the east gate of the Forbidden City ⓣ010/65268883, ⓦwww.courtyardbeijing.com. This elegant, modish place specializes in fusion cuisine – continental food with a Chinese twist – which will set you back ¥250 or so. There's an art gallery downstairs (see p.126) and a cigar lounge upstairs.

Dong Lai Shun Fan Zhuang (东来顺饭庄, *dōng lái shùn fàn zhuāng*) Xiaoyangmao Jie, just off Jianguomennei Dajie. A great place to sample hotpot; it's inexpensive, with a very good reputation among locals, and an English menu. Stick to the staples – glass noodles, veg, tofu and lots of thinly sliced meat – for a good feed. It's just around the corner from the Ancient Observatory. Around ¥50/person.

Jiajingdu Peking Duck (嘉靖都烤鸭店, *jiā jìng dū kǎo yā diàn*) 8 Hot Spring Chamber, Chaoyang Park West Gate ⓣ010/65918008, ⓦwww.afunti.com.cn; see map, pp.78–79. This place is pure theatre; you sit in what looks like an Imperial hall, and the emperor and his concubines come out to greet you. It might be bizarre but the imperial fantasy is done with admirable thoroughness and the banquets are pretty good – though the duck is the last of many courses, so arrive hungry. Only set meals, starting at ¥200.

Justine's (建国饭店, *jiànguó fàndiàn*) *Jianguo Hotel*, 5 Jianguomenwai Dajie. An elegant French restaurant with a good wine list. Try the lobster soup or grilled lamb. Around ¥150/person.

Lei Garden (利苑酒家, *lìyuàn jiǔjiā*) 3F, Jinbao Tower, 89 Jinbao Jie, Wangfujing, behind the *Regent Hotel* ⓣ010/85221212. This upmarket and well-established Cantonese restaurant has great lunchtime dim sum. Try the crab with egg yolk.

Made in China (北京东方君悦大酒店, *běijīng dōngfāngjūnyuè dàjiǔdiàn*) *Grand Hyatt* hotel, 1 Dong Chang'an Jie, Wangfujing ⓣ010/65109608. Situated in the gleaming new hotel, it's one of the swankiest places in town, with reliably excellent food from the open kitchens. A great place to try Beijing duck, with a date.

Makye Ame (玛吉阿米西藏风情餐吧, *mǎjíāmǐ xīzàngfēngqíng cānbā*) 2F, A1 Xiushui Nan Jie, just behind the Friendship Store. ⓣ010/65069616. Hale and hearty Tibetan food in a cosy atmosphere, rather more upscale than anywhere in Tibet. Try the *tashi delek* (a yak meat lasagne) and wash it down with butter tea. Tibetan singing and dancing on Wed & Fri nights.

Nadaman (北京中国大饭店, *běijīngzhōngguó dàfàndiàn*) 3F, *China World Hotel*, China World Trade Centre ⓣ010/65052266. Discreet, simple and pricey Japanese restaurant with a set menu priced at ¥300/person. Most of the ingredients are flown in from Japan.

Phrik Thai (泰辣椒, *tàilàjiāo*) Gateway Building, 10 Yabao Lu ⓣ010/65925236. Elegant Thai restaurant popular with expats. Try the red curry and chicken satay.

Sichuan Government Restaurant (四川酒楼, *sìchuān jiǔlóu*) Gongyun Tou Tiao, off

Jianguomennei Dajie. A great place for Sichuan food, serving the homesick bureaucrats who work in the same building. Head north up the alley that passes the east side of the Chang'an Theatre and after 200m there's an alley to the right with a public toilet opposite. Fifty metres down the alley a set of green and gold gates on the left marks the entrance to the Sichuan Government Building. Pass through the gates and the restaurant is on the left. There's no English menu, but it's tasty and inexpensive, and very spicy.

North of the centre

The places listed below are marked on the map on pp.108–109.

Dali Courtyard (大理院子, *dàlǐ yuànzi*) 67 Xiaojingchang Hutong, Gulou Dong Dajie ⓣ010/840 41430. This bohemian-looking courtyard restaurant tucked down a *hutong* has no menu – you simply turn up, pay the fixed price (¥100/200/300) then the chef gives you whatever Yunnanese food he feels like cooking. Call to reserve, and ask for a table outside if the weather permits.

Fish Nation (鱼邦, *yú bāng*) 31 Nanluogu Xiang. You wouldn't guess from the decor, but this is an English restaurant, with a surprisingly authentic fish'n'chips for ¥60. Shame about the lacklustre service, but there's a good balcony.

Gong Wang Fu Sichuan Restaurant (恭王府四川饭店, *gōngwángfǔ sìchuān fàndiàn*) 14 Liuyin Jie, just north of Prince Gong's Palace ⓣ010/66156924. Fiery Sichuan food in a lavishly re-created traditional setting with bamboo chairs and a lot of rosewood – but with pop art on the walls. Sees plenty of tourist traffic, so there's an English menu and they'll tone down the spices if asked. Around ¥80/head.

Huajia Yiyuan (花家怡园, *huā jiā yí yuán*) 235 Dongzhimennei Dajie ⓣ010/51283316. This secluded courtyard restaurant, with caged song birds and pleasant outdoor seating, is an excellent place to sample Beijing duck, a bargain at ¥88. It's a few doors east of the *Lama Temple Youth Hostel*.

Hutong Pizza (胡同批萨, *hú tóng pī sà*) 9 Yindingqiao ⓣ010/66175916. A charming little courtyard restaurant serving up good, square pizzas. It's sunk in an alley; go to the *hutong* directly opposite *Kaorouji* and follow the signs.

Kaorouji (烤肉季, *kǎoròují*) 14 Qianhai Dong Yuan ⓣ010/64045921. In the *hutongs* close to the Drum Tower, this Muslim place takes advantage of its great lakeside location with big windows and, in summer, balcony tables. The beef and barbecued lamb dishes are recommended. From the Drum Tower, continue south down Di'anmenwai Dajie, then take the first *hutong* on the right; the restaurant is a short walk down here, just before the lake bridge. Around ¥60/head. Daily 11am–2pm & 5–8.30pm.

Sauveurs de Coree (韩香馆, *hán xiāng guǎn*) 29 Nanluogu Xiang ⓣ010/64016083. If you're new to spicy Korean cuisine, go for one of the set meals at this little Korean bistro, which start at ¥50 for Korean staple *bibimbap*, a mixed claypot. Finish with iced cinnamon tea.

The Source (都江源, *dū jiāng yuán*) 14 Banchang Hutong ⓣ010/64003736, ⓦwww.yanclub.com. Foreigner-friendly Sichuan set-meals, starting at ¥120/person, in a courtyard next to the *Lüsongyuan Hotel*.

Sanlitun

The places listed below are marked on the map on p.121.

Bei (瑜舍, *yúshè*) *Opposite House* hotel, 11 Sanlitun Lu ⓣ010/64105230. Stick with one of the three tasting menus (¥300/400/500, and bizarrely

Ghost Street

Dongzhimennei Dajie, nicknamed **Ghost Street** (Gui Jie; 簋街, *guǐjiē*), is lined with dozens of restaurants, all festooned with red lanterns and neon, to make for a colourful and boisterous scene, especially on weekends. Take the subway to Yonghe Gong and walk south for ten minutes.

Note that staff will likely speak little or no English; though few establishments have an English menu, plenty have a picture menu. Many venues specialize in hotpot and *shuixhuyu* (spicy Sichuan-style fish served in oil on a heated metal tray). You can't go too far wrong just picking somewhere busy, but recommended is famous hotpot brand **Xiao Fei Yang** (小肥羊, *xiǎo féi yáng*; 209 Dongzhimennei Dajie, south side) and duck restaurant **Huajia Yiyuan** (see listing, above). For spicy fish, try **Dumenchang** (独门冲, *dú ménchōng*; 208 Dongzhimennei Dajie, south side). For *malatang*, a dry, spicy hotpot, try **Xiao Dong Tian** (小洞天, *xiǎodòngtiān*; 269 Dongzhimennei Dajie, north side).

named after David Bowie songs), for a range of stylish, tasty north Asian food with a twist; examples include bacon and miso soup and salmon cooked in green tea. Closed Mon.

Bellagio (鹿港小镇, *lùgǎng xiǎozhèn*) Raffles City Shopping Mall, No. 1 Dongzhimen Nan Dajie, ⓣ010/84098075; Shin Kong Place, 87 Jianguo Lu, ⓣ010/65305658. This bright and trendy Taiwanese chain has a good range of Sichuan dishes and Taiwanese specialities such as *migao* – steamed glutinous rice flavoured with shrimp and mushroom, and *caipu dan*, a turnip omlette. It's open till 4am, so good for late night, post-club snacks.

Dadong (大董烤鸭店, *dàdǒng kǎoyādiàn*) 1-2/F, Nanxincang Int'l Building, Á2, Dongsi Shi Tiao, southwest of Dongsi Shitiao Bridge ⓣ010/51690328. This fashionable spot has a good reputation for its crispy skinned, succulent Beijing duck. Don't restrict yourself to the signature dishes though; the rest of the Chinese fare is fine too.

Hai Di Lao (海底捞, *hǎidǐlāo*) Á Baijiazhuang Lu ⓣ010/65950079. This reasonably priced chain is a great place for spicy Sichuan hotpot, with a good choice of broths and a make-your-own-dipping-sauce counter. Order the *la mian* noodles and the chef will come and pull them acrobatically at your table. Good attention to detail; you get a free manicure while you're waiting for a table.

Middle 8th (中8楼, *zhōngbālóu*) Building 8, Sanlitun Dong Lu, the alley running east from 3.3 Mall ⓣ010/64130629. This classy Yunnan restaurant is not as pricey as its frosty modernist decor would have you believe; you can fill up for less than ¥150. Specialities are the mushroom dishes, but the goats' cheese and wild herb salad are also very good. Wash it down with rice wine. There's a selection of fried insects for the adventurous.

Serve the People (为人民服务, *wèirénmín fúwù*) 1 Sanlitun Xiwujie. Trendy Thai restaurant, going for an ironic Soviet look. Thai staples such as green curry and *tom yam* seafood soup are all worth sampling, and you can ask them to tone down the spices if you want.

Three Guizhou Men (三个贵州人, *sāngèguìzhōurén*) 8 Gongti Xilu (behind *Bellagio*) ⓣ010/65518517/9. Hearty Guizhou cusine and stylish decor. Try house specialities rice tofu and vermicelli with pork, but leave some room for the steamed ribs. Note that it's close to Sanlitun and open 24hr, so a good place to sate post-drink peckishness. A meal should come to around ¥150/head.

Drinking, nightlife and entertainment

Beijing has great nightlife, with **clubs** packed nightly, the best DJs flown in from all over the world and all music tastes catered for. The city's **bars** have given a boost to its live **music scene**, providing much-needed venues. Meanwhile, most visitors take in at least a taste of **Beijing Opera** and the excellent Chinese **acrobats** – both of which seem pretty timeless. In contrast, the contemporary theatrical scene is changing fast as home-grown dramatists experiment with foreign forms. **Cinemas** might be full of Hollywood product but there is plenty of opportunity to catch the serious and fairly controversial movies emerging from a new wave of younger film-makers.

Bars

Plenty of **bars** are clustered around **Sanlitun Lu**, also called Jiu Ba Jie (literally, "Bar Street"), all within staggering distance of one another. To get here take any bus east from Dongsi Shitiao subway stop. An alternative bar scene exists around the prettified **Shicha lakes** (known locally as "Houhai") where lounge bars now proliferate the way pondweed once did. There are other small bar scenes nearbly, around the Drum and Bell towers and around Nanluogu Xiang, and in the far northwest of the city at Chaoyang Park West Gate. A Tsingtao beer will generally set you back ¥15 or more. Phone numbers for those bars that have regular live music have been included below. For up-to-the-minute bar reviews, check the expat magazines.

Sanlitun and east of the centre

Just inside the northeast section of the third ring road, this busy area can be reached by taking the subway to Dongsi Shitiao, then bus #113 east; get off at the third stop. The main strip – **Sanlitun Lu** – is sometimes called **Jiuba Jie**. Unless otherwise stated, the places listed below are marked on the map on p.121.

Centro (炫酷酒廊, *xuàn kù jiǔ láng*) 1F, *Kerry Centre Hotel*, 1 Guanghua Lu; see East of the Centre map p.104. Slinky lounge bar whose cocktails will cost the best part of a red bill. Dress up.

Ichikura (一藏酒吧, *yīcáng jiǔbā*) 36 Dong San Huan Bei Lu, on the right side of the Chaoyang Theatre building; see East of the Centre map p.104. This two-storey Japanese whisky bar is as tasteful and understated as the acrobatic shows next door are glitzy and vulgar. A great range of single malts – including superb Japanese varieties – and attention to detail (check out the round ice cubes) make this dark, cosy venue a hidden gem.

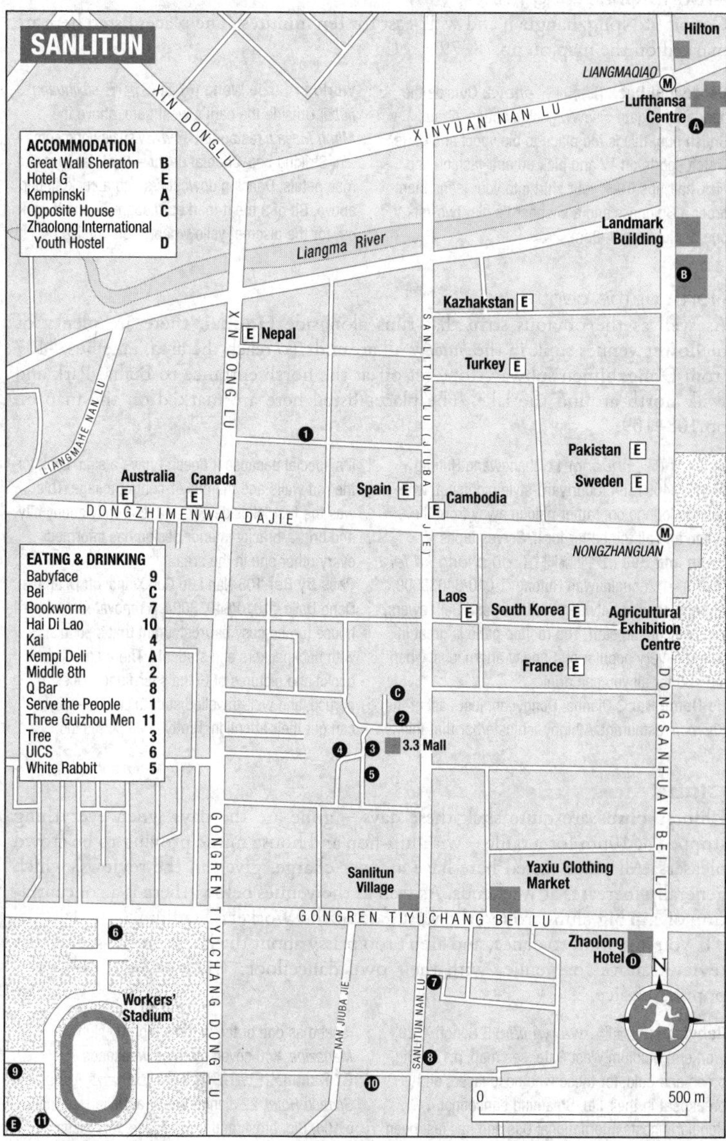

Kai (开吧, *kăi ba*) Sanlitun Bei Jie, behind 3.3 Mall. A raucous little dive bar, popular with foreigners for its ¥10 beers.

Q Bar (Q吧, *Qbā*) 6F, *Eastern Hotel*, corner of Sanlitun Nan Lu and Gongti Nan Lu. Sleek and well-run lounge bar with good cocktails; at its best in summer when drinkers spill out onto the terrace.

Tree (树酒吧, *shù jiŭbā*) 43 Sanlitun Lu, behind 3.3 Mall ⓣ010/64151954, ⓦwww.treebeijing.com. Cosy, relaxed and understated bar, with a decent selection of Belgian white beers and good pizza.

Around Chaoyang Park

Get off at Nongzhanguan and walk east for ten minutes. The places listed here are marked on the map on pp.78–79.

Goose and Duck (鹅和鸭, *éhéyā*) Outside the park's west gate ⓦwww.gdclub.net.cn. A faux British pub, this is the place to play pool and darts, watch sports on TV and pick up anti-fashion and hick-hair tips. Tuck your shirt into your jeans then order a Guinness and a shepherd's pie. Two-for-one drinks from 4–8pm.

World of Suzie Wong (苏西黄酒吧 *sūxīhuáng jiŭbā*) Outside the park's west gate, above the *Mirch Masala* restaurant ⓦwww.suziewong.com.cn. Striking neo-Oriental decor – think lacquer and rose petals. Dancing downstairs and a cocktail bar above. Bit of a meat market, though. To find it, look out for the discreet yellow neon sign outside.

North of the centre

As well as the obvious strip that runs alongside **Houhai**, there are plenty of mellower venues sunk in the *hutongs* all around. To reach the area, take bus #107 from Dongzhimen subway stop, get off at the north entrance to Beihai Park and walk north around the lake. The places listed here are marked on the map on pp.108–109.

Bed Bar (床, *chuáng*) 17 Zhangwang Hutong ⓣ010/84001554. Courtyard-style nightspot, with beds to lounge on, rather hidden away from the action and all the better for it. Serves tapas.

Drum and Bell (鼓钟咖啡馆, *gŭ zhōng kā fēi guăn*) 41 Zhonglouwan Hutong ⓣ010/84033600. A great location between the Drum and Bell towers, with welcoming staff. The rooftop patio is great in summer. Very popular on Sunday afternoons, when it's ¥50 for all you can drink.

No Name Bar 3 Qianhai Dongyuan, just east of the *Kaorouji* restaurant. A hippy-ish café/bar that thinks it's special because it doesn't have a sign. Look for the red walls and the out-of-control foliage. This was the first lakeside bar, and its trendy anonymity and bric-a-bracky interior design has informed every other one in the area.

Pass By Bar 108 Nan Luo Guo Xiang, off Di'anmen Dong Dajie ⓣ010/84038004. A renovated courtyard house turned cosy bar/restaurant that's popular with backpackers and students. There are lots of books and pictures of China's far-flung places to peruse, and well-travelled staff to chat to – if you can get their attention. Pretty good pizzas too.

Clubs

Chinese **clubs** are quite slick these days – gone are the days when everything stopped at 10pm for a raffle – with hip-hop and house music proving to be crowd pleasers. All places listed here have a cover charge, given in the reviews, which generally increases at weekends. As well as the venues below, there is a concentration of hip big clubs around the west gate of the Workers' Stadium.

If you just want to dance, and aren't too prissy about the latest music, see the bar reviews above for venues with their own dancefloor; *World of Suzie Wong* is a popular choice.

Babyface (娃娃脸, *wá wá liăn*) 6 Gongti Xi Lu, Workers' Stadium West Gate; see map, p.121. Big, brash and bold, for those who need lasers and breakbeat in their life. Steaming dancefloor. Regularly hosts international DJs and has just been ranked as one of the world's top fifty clubs by *DJ Magazine*. ¥40 cover, more on weekends.

GT Banana (巴那那俱乐部, *bānànà jùlèbù*) *Scitech Hotel*, 22 Jianguomenwai Dajie; see map, p.104. Big, brash and in your face, this mega club has three sections – techno, funk and chill-out – and features go-go girls, karaoke rooms and an enthusiastic, young clientele. Mon–Thurs & Sun 8.30pm–4am, Fri & Sat 8.30pm–5am. ¥20, weekends ¥40.

Vics (威克斯, *wēikèsī*) Inside the Workers' Stadium's north gate; see map, p.121. The low cover charge and cheapish drinks (bottled beer ¥15) make it popular with students and embassy brats. Women get in free on Wed and get free drinks till midnight. Thurs is ragga/reggae night. Hip-hop, R&B and techno all weekend. Daily 7pm–6am. ¥30 except Thurs, when entry's free.

White Rabbit (大白兔, *dàbáitù*) Tongli Studio, Sanlitun Jie Ⓦwww.whiterabbitclub.blogspot.com, see map, p.121. Underground dive bar run by DJs, with a good sound system that blasts out techno most nights. It's a cut above other clubs, at least musically, and it attracts a crowd more interested in dancing than posing. Open Wed–Sun. No cover

Entertainment and art

There's always a healthy variety of **cultural events** taking place in the city. Check the *China Daily* for listings on officially approved events. For the best rundown of street-level happenings, including gigs, track down a copy of *Time Out*, available at expat bars and restaurants.

Live music

To hear **traditional Chinese music**, visit the concert halls, or the Sanwei Bookstore (see p.125) on a Saturday night. **Western classical music** is popular and can be heard at any of the concert halls. Mainstream Chinese **pop** is hard to avoid, much as you may want to, as it pumps out of shops and restaurants.

Beijing Concert Hall (音乐厅, *yīnyuètīng*) 1 Beixinhua Jie, just off Xichang'an Jie Ⓣ010/66055812; see map, p.101. Sates the considerable appetite in the capital for classical music, with regular concerts by Beijing's resident orchestra, and visiting orchestras from the rest of China and overseas. Ticket prices vary. You can get tickets at the box office or at the CVIK Plaza.

Fobidden City Concert Hall (中山公园音乐厅, *zhōngshāngōngyuán yīnyuètīng*) Zhongshan Park, Xichang'an Jie Ⓣ010/65598285; Ⓦwww.fcchbj.com. A stylish new hall, with performances of Western and Chinese classical music.

Poly Plaza Theatre (保利大厦国际剧院, *bǎolìdàshà guójìjùyuàn*) Poly Plaza, 14 Dongzhimen Nan Dajie Ⓣ010/65001188; Ⓦwww.polytheatre.com; see map, pp.78–79. A gleaming hall that hosts diverse performances of jazz, ballet, classical music, opera and modern dance for the city's cultural elite. Tickets are on the pricey side, usually starting at ¥100.

Workers' Stadium (工人体育场, *gōngrén tǐyùchǎng*) Gongren Tiyuchang Bei Lu, Ⓣ010/65016655; see map, p.121. Giant gigs, mostly featuring Chinese pop stars, though Vanessa Mae and Bjork have also played here.

Beijing rock

Beijing has a vibrant rock scene. Good local bands to look out for are The Retros, Joyside and Queen Sea Big Shark, all of whom sing some songs in English. Most decent bands are on Modern Sky and Badhead records. You can check the scene out at: **Mao Livehouse** (光芒, *guāng máng*; Ⓣ010/64025080, Ⓦwww.maolive.com), 111 Gulou Dong Dajie, at the north end of Nanluogu Xiang; **D22** (Ⓣ010/62653177, Ⓦwww.d22beijing.com), 242 Chengfu Lu – come out of Wudaokou subway stop and walk towards the Beijing University East Gate; and at the tiny **What Bar** (什么酒吧, *shénme jiǔbā*) 72 Beichang Jie, just north of the west gate of the Forbidden City. Tickets at all venues cost around ¥30.

If you're here in May, check out the annual **Midi rock festival** (Ⓦwww.midifestival.com) in Haidian Park, just west of Beijing University campus. Plenty of local talent is on display, though foreign acts are banned. Tickets are ¥100 for the four-day event, ¥50 for one day.

Film

There are plenty of cinemas showing **Chinese films** and dubbed **Western films**, usually action movies. Just twenty Western films are picked by the government for release every year. Despite such restrictions, these days most Beijingers have an impressive knowledge of world cinema, thanks to the prevalence of pirated DVDs.

Some of the largest **screens** in Beijing, showing mainstream Chinese and foreign films, are: the old Dahua Cinema at 82 Dongdan Bei Dajie (大华电影院, *dàhuá diànyǐngyuàn*; Ⓣ010/65274420, Ⓦwww.dhfilm.cn); Star City in the Oriental Plaza Mall (BB65, 1 Dongchang'an Jie; Ⓣ010/85186778, Ⓦwww.xfilmcity.com); the Xin Dong'an Cinema on the fifth floor of the Sun Dong'an Plaza on Wangfujing (Ⓣ010/65281988, Ⓦwww.xfilmcity.com); and the UME Huaxing Cinema (Ⓣ010/62555566) – which has the biggest screen – at 44 Kexueyuan Nan Lu, Haidian, next to the Shuang Yu Shopping Centre, just off the third ring road. Tickets cost ¥50 or more. There are usually two showings of foreign movies, one dubbed into Chinese, the other subtitled; ring to check.

Space for Imagination (Ⓣ010/62791280), at 5 Xi Wang Zhuang Xiao Qu, Haidian, opposite Qinghua University's east gate, is a charming cineastes' bar that shows avant-garde films every Saturday at 7pm. The best **art-film** venue is **Cherry Lane Movies** (Ⓣ010/64042711, Ⓦwww.cherrylanemovies.com.cn), which organizes showing at Yugong Yishan (see p.123). Their screenings, which include obscure and controversial underground Chinese films, usually with English subtitles, take place every Sunday at 8pm (¥50), followed by a discussion, sometimes featuring the director or cast members.

Traditional opera

Beijing Opera (*jīng xì*; see p.977) is the most celebrated of the country's 350 or so regional styles – a unique combination of song, dance, acrobatics and mime, with some similarities to Western pantomime.

Chang'an Theatre (长安大剧场, *chángān dàjùchǎng*) 7 Jianguomennei Dajie Ⓣ010/65101309; see map, p.104. Tickets from ¥40. An hour-long performance with a lot of acrobatics is put on nightly at 7.15pm.

Liyuan Theatre 1F *Jianquo Qianmen* hotel, 175 Yong'an Lu. Nightly performances begin at 7.30pm. There's a ticket office in the front courtyard of the hotel (daily 9–11am, noon–4.45pm & 5.30–8pm). Tickets cost ¥70–180; the more expensive seats are at tables at the front where you can sip tea and nibble pastries during the performance. In season, you'll need to book tickets a day or two in advance. The opera shown is enlivened with some martial arts and slapstick.

National Centre for the Performing Arts (中国国家大剧院, *zhōng guó guó jiā dà jù yuàn*) 2 Xi Chang'an Jie Ⓣ010/66550000, Ⓦwww.chncpa.org. This is that giant egg west of Tian'anmen Square. The opera hall seats over two thousand, with fantastic acoustics and lighting to capture every nuance of the performance. There's an English subititle screen too. You'll likely be in elevated company; Wen Jiabao is a big fan. There is a performance every night at 7.30pm. The box office is open daily from 9.30am or you can ring to reserve. Ticket prices vary, but cost at least ¥150.

Zhengyici Theatre (正义祠剧场, *zhèngyìcí jùchǎng*) 220 Xiheyan Dajie, Qianmen Ⓣ010/63033104; see map, p.91. The only surviving wooden Beijing Opera theatre left, and worth a visit just to check out the architecture. Nightly performances begin at 7.30pm, last two hours and cost ¥150. Dinner – duck, of course – costs an additional ¥110. Check the *China Daily* for listings.

Drama and dance

Spoken drama was only introduced into Chinese theatres in the twentieth century. But the **theatre**, along with most of China's cinemas, was closed down for almost a decade during the Cultural Revolution, during which only eight "socially improving" plays were allowed to be performed. The People's Art Theatre Company reassembled in 1979. As well as drama, good old-fashioned **song-and-dance** extravaganzas are very popular.

Beijing Exhibition Theatre (展览馆, *zhǎnlǎn guǎn*) 135 Xizhimenwai Dajie ⓣ010/68354455, ⓦwww.bjexpo.com; see map, pp.108–109. For the glitzier type of show. Musicals at ¥50–100 a ticket are a lot cheaper than at home.

Capital Theatre (首都剧场, *shǒudū jùchǎng*) 22 Wangfujing Dajie ⓣ010/65253677, ⓦwww.bjry.com; see map, p.104. Home to the People's Art Theatre Company, this is the most prestigious, and largest, theatre. Tickets cost at least ¥60.

Puppet Theatre (中国木偶剧院, *zhōngguó mùǒujùyuàn*) Section 1, Anhua Xi Li, Bei Sanhuan Lu (third ring road), opposite the Sogo Department Store ⓣ010/64254798, ⓦwww.puppetchina.com. Daily shows at 6.30pm for ¥40. The skilled puppeteers here produce shows pitched at a family audience.

Acrobatics and martial arts

Certainly the most accessible and exciting of the traditional Chinese entertainments, **acrobatics** covers anything from gymnastics and animal tricks to magic and juggling. Professional acrobats have existed in China for two thousand years and the tradition continues at the main training school, Wu Qiao in Hebei province, where students begin training at the age of 5. The style may be vaudeville, but performances are spectacular, with truly awe-inspiring feats.

Chaoyang Theatre (朝阳剧场, *cháoyáng jùchǎng*) 36 Dongsanhuan Zhong Lu ⓣ010/65072421; see map, p.104. The easiest place to see a display. Shows are nightly (7.15–8.30pm; ¥180, it can be cheaper if you book through your hotel). There are plenty of souvenir stalls in the lobby – buy after the show rather than in the interval, as prices go down.

Tianqiao Theatre (天桥乐茶园, *tiānqiáolè cháyuán*) 95 Tianqiao Lu Xuanwu, east end of Beiwei Lu ⓣ010/63037449, ⓦwww.tianqiaoacrobatictheater.com; see map, p.91. One of the old staples for acrobatics, in an old-fashioned but newly renovated theatre. Nightly performances begin at 7.15pm. Tickets ¥180.

Wansheng Theatre (万胜剧场, *wànshèng jùchǎng*) 95 Tianqiao Market, Qianmen, ⓣ010/63037449; see map, p.91. Nightly performances begin at 7.15pm and cost ¥100–150.

Teahouse theatres

A few **teahouse theatres**, places to sit and snack and watch performances of Beijing Opera, sedate music and martial arts, have reappeared in the capital.

Lao She Teahouse (老舍茶馆, *lǎoshě cháguǎn*) 3F, Dawancha Building, 3 Qianmen Xi Dajie ⓣ010/63036830, ⓦwww.laosheteahouse.com; see map, p.91. You can watch a variety show of opera, martial arts and acrobatics (¥40–130) here. Performances are at 2.30pm and 7.40pm and last an hour and a half; the afternoon performances are cheaper.

Sanwei Bookstore Teahouse (三味书屋, *sānwèi shūwū*) 60 Fuxingmennei Dajie ⓣ010/66013204, opposite the *Minzu Hotel*; see map, p.101. The haunt of expats and arty Chinese, with performances of light jazz on Fridays and Chinese folk music on Saturdays (8.30–10pm).

Tianqiao Happy Teahouse (天桥乐茶园, *tiānqiáolè cháyuán*) 113 Tianqiao Nan Dajie ⓣ010/63040617. A tourist trap that gives a colourful taste of the surface aspects of Chinese culture (¥180). Even the staff are in costume. Performances at 7pm. Closed Mon.

Contemporary art

Beijing is the centre for the vigorous **Chinese arts scene** and there are plenty of interesting new galleries opening up. The best place to find out about new shows is in the expat magazines. For mainstream art, visit the **China Art Gallery** (see map, p.104 & p.103), but for a taste of the more exciting contemporary scene, put on some black clothes and check out the **798 Art District**, also known as Dashanzi, up towards the airport (see p.106). Some of the most reputable galleries here are the Beijing Commune (ⓣ010/86549428, ⓦwww.beijingcommune.com), White Space (ⓣ010/84562054, ⓦwww.alexanderochs-galleries.de), Beijing Tokyo Art Projects (ⓣ010/84573245, ⓦwww.tokyo-gallery.com) and the huge new Ullens Centre for Contemporary Art (Ⓣ010/64386675, Ⓦwww.ucca.org.cn; ¥15). To find your way around, study the maps dotted around the complex, or head to the Timezone #8 "Bookstore-cafe" (see p.117) and pick up the handy little RedBox art guide (¥10), whose maps show all the good Beijing galleries. Note that just about everywhere is closed on a Monday.

The area is particularly lively during the 798 Art Festival – though the size of the festival, and its dates, and, indeed, whether it happens at all, are dependent on the precarious political climate. It should be scheduled for the autumn.

Courtyard Gallery (四合院画廊, *sìhéyuàn huàláng*) 95 Donghuamen Dajie Ⓣ010/65268882, Ⓦwww.courtyard-gallery.com; see map, p.104. Located in an old courtyard house opposite the east gate of the Forbidden City. There's also a cigar shop and a very classy restaurant here.

The Red Gate Gallery (红门画廊, *hóngmén huàláng*) Dongbianmen Watchtower, Chongwenmen Dajie Ⓣ010/65251005, Ⓦwww.redgategallery.com; see map, p.104. One of the best places to see contemporary art, with a high profile. The gallery is housed in a beautiful restored watchtower.

Wanfung (云峰画廊, *yúnfēng huàláng*) 136 Nanchizi Dajie Ⓣ010/65233320, Ⓦwww.wanfung.com.cn. In the old archive building of the Forbidden City, showing established contemporary artists, sometimes from abroad. Can be chintzy.

Shopping

Beijing has a good reputation for shopping, with the widest choice of anywhere in China. **Clothes** are particularly inexpensive, and are one reason for the city's high number of Russians, as smuggling them across the northern border is a lucrative trade. There's also a wide choice of **antiques and handicrafts**, but don't expect to find any bargains or particularly unusual items as the markets are well picked over. Be aware that just about everything that is passed off as antique is fake. Good souvenir buys include: **art materials**, particularly brushes and blocks of ink; signature **chops** carved with a name; small **jade** items; and handicraft items such as **kites** and painted snuff bottles.

There are four main shopping districts: **Wangfujing**, popular and mainstream; **Xidan**, characterized by giant department stores; **Dongdan**, which mainly sells brand-name clothes; and **Qianmen**, perhaps the area that most rewards idle browsing, with a few oddities among the cheap shoes and clothes stores. In addition, and especially aimed at visitors, **Liulichang** is a good place to get a lot of souvenir buying done quickly. For general goods, check the **department stores**, which sell a little of everything, and provide a good index of current Chinese taste. The Beijing Department Store, on Wangfujing, and the Xidan Department Store on Xidan Dajie are prime examples, or check out the newer Landao Department Store, on Chaoyangmenwai Dajie. The Parkson Building, west of Xidan on Fuxingmen Dajie, is the plushest. Rising living standards for some are reflected in the new giant **malls**, where everything costs as much as it does in the West. Try the Sun Dong'an Plaza, on Wangfujing, Raffles City at Dongzhimen, or the Shin Kong or China World Trade Centre plazas on Jianguomen if you don't get enough of this at home.

Shops are open daily from 8.30am to 8pm (7pm in winter), with large shopping centres staying open till 9pm.

Antiques, souvenirs and carpets

If you're a serious antique hunter, go to Tianjin, where the choice is more eclectic and prices cheaper (see p.144). That said, there's no shortage of **antique stores** and **markets** in Beijing offering opium pipes, jade statues, porcelain Mao figures, mahjong sets and Red Guard alarm clocks. Almost all of the old stuff is fake, though; even copies of Mao's Little Red Book are new, and aged with tea.

Liulichang, south of Hepingmen subway stop, has the densest concentration of curio stores in town, with a huge selection of wares, particularly of art materials, porcelain and snuff boxes, though prices are steep. Chairman Mao's Little Red Book is ubiquitous (and only costs about ¥10), and the most popular memento is a soapstone **seal** for imprinting names in either Chinese characters or Roman letters (starting at around ¥40); to see ancient traditions meeting modern technology, go round the back and watch them laser-cut it. For contemporary curios, try Yandai Xiejie, a *hutong* full of little stores selling souvenir notebooks, matchboxes and the like, at the north end of Houhai Lake.

There are **tea shops** all over the city, including chains such as Zhang Yiyuan (22 Dazhalan, ①010/63034001) and Wu Yutai (44 Dongsi Bei Dajie, ①010/64041928), but for all your tea-related needs, check out Maliandao Lu (马连道茶叶街, *mǎliándào cháyèjiē*), just south of the west train station, which hosts hundreds of tea shops along 2km-long stretch. They all offer free tea tastings, but remember that you're expected to bargain for the actual product. You're spoilt for choice, of course, but check out four-storey Tea City, about halfway down. There's plenty of tea paraphernalia around, which make good gifts – look for porous Yixing ware teapots.

Arts and Crafts Store (工艺美术商店, *gōngyìměishù shāng'diàn*) 293 Wangfujing. A good if predictable selection of expensive objets d'art.

Beijing Curio City (北京古玩城, *běijīng gǔwánchéng*) Dongsanhuan Nan Lu, west of Huawei Bridge. A giant mall of more than 250 stalls. Visit on a Sunday, when other antique traders come and set up in the streets around. The mall includes a section for duty-free shopping; take your passport and a ticket out of the country along and you can buy goods at the same reduced price as at the airport. Daily 9.30am–6.30pm.

Friendship Store (友谊商店, *yǒuyí shāngdiàn*) Jianguomenwai Dajie; see map, p.104. Tourist souvenirs with a wide range of prices, but more expensive than the markets. Large carpet section.

Hongqiao Department Store (红桥百货中心, *hóngqiáo bǎihuò zhōngxīn*) Opposite the northeast corner of Tiantan Park. This giant, cramped and humid store can be wearying but has some good bargains. The top floor sells antiques and curios; one stall is given over solely to Cultural Revolution kitsch. The stalls share space, oddly, with a pearl and jewellery market. The second floor sells clothes and accessories and the first is the place to go for small electronic items, including such novelties as watches that speak the time in Russian when you whistle at them.

Liulichang (琉璃厂, *liúlí chǎng*) East of Qianmen Dajie (see p.91). This has the densest concentration of curio stores, with a great choice, particularly of art materials and chops, though prices are steep.

Panjiayuan Market (潘家园, *pānjiā yuán*) On Panjia Lu, just south of Jinsong Zhong Jie; see map, pp.78–79. Beijing's biggest antique market, well worth browsing around, even if you have no intention to buy, for the sheer range of secondhand goods, sometimes in advanced stages of decay, on sale. Open weekdays, but it's at its biggest and best at weekends from 6am–3pm.

Zhaojia Chaowai Market 43 Huawei Bei Lu, off Dongsanhuan Lu, 100m north of Panjiayuan Junction. 10am–5.30pm. Some carpets and enormous quantities of reproduction traditional Chinese furniture in all sizes and styles, for those whose lives lack lacquer.

Books

Beijing can claim a better range of **English-language literature** than anywhere else in China. If you're starting a trip of any length, stock up here. The expensive hotels all have bookstores with fairly decent collections, though at off-putting prices. You'll also find copies of foreign **newspapers and magazines**, such as *Time* and *Newsweek*, sold for around ¥40.

Foreign Languages Bookstore (外交书店, *wàijiāo shūdiàn*) 235 Wangfujing Dajie; see map, p.104. It might not look like much, but this is the largest foreign-language bookshop in China. Downstairs are textbooks and translations of Chinese classics, and the products of Beijing Foreign Language Press, while the third floor sells pricey imported books, including plenty of modern novels. Mon–Sat 9am–7pm.

Friendship Store (友谊商店, *yǒuyí shāngdiàn*) Jianguomenwai Dajie; see map, p.104. As well as a wide variety of books on all aspects of Chinese culture, the bookshop within the store sells foreign newspapers (¥80), a few days out of date. It's all very expensive, though. Daily 9am–8.30pm.

Garden Books (韬奋西文书局, *tāofènxīwén shūjú*) 44 Guanghua Lu, opposite the Brazilian Embassy Ⓦ www.gardenbooks.cn; see map, p.104. Charming bookstore and expat favourite, with an eclectic selection of imported novels, children's books and cookbooks. Daily 8am–9pm.

Timezone 8 (现代书店, *xiàn dài shū diàn*) 4 Jiuxianqiao Lu, 798 Art District. This chic art bookstore with attached café is the most civilized venue in that bobo playground, the 798 Arts District. Tote an Apple Mac to really fit in. Free wi-fi. Daily 8.30am–9pm.

Clothes

Clothes are a bargain in Beijing; witness all the Russians buying in bulk. The best place to go is **Jianguomen Dajie**, where the Friendship Store and the CVIK Plaza offer something for every budget (see p.105). The Silk Market is a giant six-storey mall for knock-offs of branded clothes. Bear in mind that if you're particularly tall or have large feet, you'll have difficulty finding clothes and shoes to fit you. For Chinese street fashion, head to Xidan, and, for designer creations, to the malls.

Aliens Street Market (老番街, *lǎo fān jiē*) Yabao Lu, south of the Fullink Plaza; see map, p.104. This huge mall is where the Russians come, en masse. There's a vast range of goods, but it's particularly worth picking over for clothes and accessories.

Beijing Silk Shop 5 Zhubaoshi Jie, just west of Qianmen Dajie. Located just inside the first *hutong* to the west as you head south down Qianmen Dajie, this is the best place in Beijing to buy quality silk clothes in Chinese styles, with a wider selection and keener prices than any of the tourist stores. The ground floor sells silk fabrics, while clothes can be bought upstairs.

Dongwuyuan Wholesale Market (动物园服装批发市场, *dòng wù yuán fú zhuāng pī fā shì chǎng*) Xizhimenwai Daijie, south of the zoo; see map, p.108. This giant indoor market is full of stalls selling very cheap clothes, shoes and accessories to locals. You'll have to bargain, and there won't be anything in any large sizes, but it's one of the city's best places to pick up a few cut-price outfits.

Five Colours Earth (五色土, *wǔ sè tǔ*) 10 Dongzhimen Nan Dajie. Interesting and unusual collections, often incorporating fragments of old embroidery, by a talented local designer. Not too expensive either; you can pick up a coat for ¥500.

Mingxing Clothing Store (明星服饰商店, *míngxīngfúshì shāngdiàn*) 133 Wangfujing Dajie. Well-made Chinese-style garments, such as *cheongsams* and *qipaos*.

Neiliansheng Shoeshop (合格证, *hé gé zhèng*) Western end of Dazhalan, Qianmen; see map, p.91. Look for the giant shoe in the window. All manner of handmade flat, slip-on shoes and slippers in traditional designs, starting from ¥100 or so – great gifts.

PLA Official Factory Outlet Dongsanhuan Bei Lu, about 1km north of the China World Trade Centre. As well as military outfits, they stock such oddments as wrist compasses, canteens and police hats. There's also a huge selection of military footwear and chunky fur-lined coats. Bus #300 from Guomao subway stop.

Plastered T-shirts (创可贴T恤, *chuàngkětiē tīxù*) 61 Nanluogu Xiang, Ⓦ www.plasteredtshirts.com. Hipster T-shirts and sweatshirts whose designs reference everyday Beijing life – subway tickets, thermoses and so on. They look a bit naff here but might be considered cool by the time you get them home.

Ruifuxiang Clothes Store 5 Dazhalan, off Qianmen Dajie (see map, p.91); also at 190 Wangfujing Dajie. Silk and cotton fabrics and a good selection of shirts and dresses. Mon–Sat 8.30am–8pm.

Silk Market (秀水街, *xiùshuǐ jīe*) Xiushui Jie, off Jianguomenwai Dajie, very near Yong'anli subway stop; see map, p.104. This huge six-storey mall for tourists has electronics, jewellery and souvenirs, but its main purpose is to profit through flouting international copyright laws, with hundreds of stalls selling fake designer labels. You'll need to bargain hard; you shouldn't pay more than ¥80 for a pair of jeans, or ¥70 for trainers. There are also a few tailors – pick out your material, then bargain, and you can get a suit made in 24hr for ¥800 or so. Vendors are tiresomely pushy.

Yansha Outlets Mall (燕莎奥特莱斯购物中心, *yàn shān ào tè lái sī gòu wù zhōng xīn*) 9 Dongsihuannan Jie, the southern end of the eastern section of the fourth ring road. A huge outlet for genuine designer clothes and bags, all old lines, at discounts of between thirty and fifty percent.

Yaxiu Clothing Market (雅秀市场, *yà xiù shì chǎng*) 58 Gongrentiyuchang Bei Lu. A two-storey mall of stalls selling designer fakes. Like the Silk Market, but a little less busy. The third floor is tailors, and the fourth is souvenirs.

Yuexiu Clothing Market (越秀市场, *yuè xiù shì chǎng*) 99 Chaoyangmennei Dajie. A new market with a little bit of everything and a great deal of fake clothes. Not many foreigners come here as yet, so the prices are a little more competitive, though you'll still have to barter.

Listings

Airline offices The following foreign airlines have offices in Beijing:
Aeroflot, 1F, *Jinglun Hotel*, 3 Jianguomenwai Dajie ⓣ010/65002412; Air Canada, Rm C201, Lufthansa Centre, 50 Lianmaqiao Lu ⓣ010/64682001; Air China, Xidan Aviation Office, 15 Chang'an Xi Lu ⓣ800/8101111; Air France, Room 1606-1611, Building 1, Kuntai International Mansion, 12A Chaowai Dajie ⓣ4008808808; Alitalia, Room 141, *Jianguo Hotel*, 5 Jianguomenwai Dajie ⓣ010/65918468; All Nippon Airways, Fazhan Dasha, Room N200, 5 Dongsanhuan Bei Lu ⓣ010/65909174; Asiana Airlines, 12F, Building A, Jiacheng Plaza, 18 Xiaguangli ⓣ010/64684000; Austrian Airlines, Room 603, Lufthansa Centre, 50 Liangmaqiao Lu ⓣ010/64622161; British Airways, Room 210, SCITECH Tower, 22 Jianguomenwai Dajie ⓣ010/65124070; Canadian Airlines, Room C201, 50 Liangmaqiao Lu ⓣ010/64637901; China Southern Airlines, Building A, AVIC Building, 2 Dongsanhuan Nan Lu ⓣ010/9503333; Continental Airlines, 500 Sunflower Tower, 37 Maizidian Jie ⓣ010/85726686; Dragonair, Rm 1710, Office Tower 1, Henderson Centre,18 Jianguomennei Dajie ⓣ01065182533; Japan Airlines, 1F Changfugong Office Building, 26A Jianguomenwai Dajie ⓣ400/8880808; KLM, 1609-1611 Kuntai International Building, Chaoyangmenwai Dajie ⓣ4008808222; Korean Air, 1602 Hyundai Motor Building, 38 Xiaoyun Lu ⓣ400/6588888; Lufthansa, Rm S101, Lufthansa Centre, 50 Liangmaqiao Lu ⓣ010/64688838; Delta Airlines, 501B, West Wing, China World Trade Centre, 1 Jianguomenwai Dajie ⓣ4008140081; Pakistan Airlines, Room 106A, China World Trade Centre, 1 Jianguomenwai Dajie ⓣ010/65052256; Qantas, Lufthansa Centre, B7-8, 10F, West Tower, LG Twin Tower, B12 Jianguomenwai Dajie ⓣ010/65679006; SAS Scandinavian Airlines, Room 430, Beijing Sunflower Tower, 37 Maizidian Jie ⓣ010/85276100; Shanghai Airlines, Nanzhuyuan Yiqu, Building 3, Beijing Capital International Airport ⓣ010/64569019; Singapore Airlines, Room 801, Tower 2, China World Trade Centre, 1 Jianguomenwai Dajie ⓣ010/65052233; Swissair, Room 612, Scitech Tower, 22 Jianguomenwai Dajie ⓣ010/65123555; Thai International, Rm 303, W3 Tower, Oriental Plaza ⓣ010/85150088; United Airlines, Lufthansa Centre, 50 Liangmaqiao Lu ⓣ010/64631111.

Banks and exchange The Commercial Bank (Mon–Fri 9am–noon & 1–4pm) in the CITIC Building at 19 Jianguomenwai Dajie, next to the Friendship Store, has the widest service, and is the only place that will let you change money into non-Chinese currencies (useful for travellers taking the train to Russia). The main branch of the Bank of China (Mon–Fri 9am–noon & 1.30–5pm) is at 8 Yabuo Lu, off Chaoyangmen Dajie, just north of the International Post Office, but it doesn't do anything the smaller branches won't. You'll find other branches in the CVIK Plaza (Mon–Fri 9am–noon & 1–6.30pm), the China World Trade Centre (Mon–Fri 9am–5pm, Sat 9am–noon), the Sun Dong'an Plaza (Mon–Fri 9.30am–noon & 1.30–5pm) and the Lufthansa Centre (Mon–Fri 9am–noon & 1–4pm). A foreign-exchange office (daily 9am–6.30pm) inside the entrance to the Friendship Store is one of the few places you can change money at the weekend at the standard rate. If you have applied for a visa and only have a photocopy of your passport, some hotels and the Hong Kong and Shanghai Bank in the *Jianguo Hotel* will reluctantly advance cash on travellers' cheques; most banks won't. There are ATM machines in every mall, usually in the basement, and in four- and five-star hotels.

Bike rental Pretty much all the hotels rent bikes, at ¥20–50/day, depending on how classy the hotel is. You can also rent from many places in the *hutongs* around Houhai (see map, p.108). You can buy cheap city bikes for about ¥250; try Carrefour (see p.86) or the strip of bike shops on the south side of Jiaodaokou, just west of the Ghost Street (Gui Jie; see map, p.108) restaurants.

Courier service DHL has a 24hr office at 2 Jiuxian Qiao in the Chaoyang district (ⓣ010/64662211). More convenient are the offices in the *New Otani Hotel* (daily 8am–8pm; ⓣ010/65211309) and at L115, China World Trade Centre (daily 8am–8pm).

Embassies Visa departments usually open for a few hours every weekday morning (phone for exact times and to see what you'll need to take).

Remember that they'll take your passport from you for as long as a week sometimes, and it's very hard to change money without it, so stock up on cash before applying for any visas. You can get passport-size photos from an annexe just inside the front entrance of the Friendship Store. Some embassies require payment in US dollars; you can change travellers' cheques for these at the CITIC Building (see "Banks and exchange" above). Most embassies are either around Sanlitun in the northeast or in Jianguomenwai compound, north of and parallel to Jianguomenwai Dajie: Australia, 21 Dongzhimenwai Dajie, Sanlitun ⓣ010/51404111; Azerbaijan, 7-2-5-1 Tayuan Building ⓣ010/65324614; Canada, 19 Dongzhimenwai Dajie, Sanlitun ⓣ010/51394000; France, 3 Dong San Jie, Sanlitun ⓣ010/85328080; Germany, 17 Dongzhimenwai Dajie, Sanlitun ⓣ010/85329000; India, 1 Ritan Dong Lu, Sanlitun ⓣ010/65321908; Ireland, 3 Ritan Dong Lu, Sanlitun ⓣ010/65322691; Italy, 2 Dong'er Jie, Sanlitun ⓣ01085327600; Japan, 7 Ritan Lu, Jianguomenwai ⓣ010/65322361; Kazakhstan, 9 Dong Liu Jie, Sanlitun ⓣ010/65326183; Kyrgyzstan, 2-4-1 Tayuan Building ⓣ010/65326458; Laos, 11 Dongsi Jie, Sanlitun ⓣ010/65321224; Mongolia, 2 Xiushui Bei Jie, Jianguomenwai ⓣ010/65321203; Myanmar, (Burma) 6 Dongzhimenwai Dajie, Sanlitun ⓣ010/65321425; New Zealand, 1 Ritan Dong'er Jie, Sanlitun ⓣ010/65327000; North Korea, Ritan Bei Lu, Jianguomenwai ⓣ010/65321186; Pakistan, 1 Dongzhimenwai Dajie, Sanlitun ⓣ010/65322660; Russian Federation, 4 Dongzhimen Bei Zhong Jie ⓣ010/65321381; South Africa, 5 Dongzhimenwai Dajie ⓣ010/65320171; South Korea, 20 Dongfang Dong Lu ⓣ010/85310700; Thailand, 40 Guanghua Lu, Jianguomenwai ⓣ010/65321749; visa and consular section Fifteenth floor, Building D, Twin Tower, Jianguomenwai Da Jie ⓣ010/85664469; UK, 11 Guanghua Lu, Jianguomenwai ⓣ010/51924000; visa and consular section at 21F, Kerry Centre, 1 Guanghua Lu ⓣ010/85296600; Ukraine, 11 Dong Lu Jie, Sanlitun ⓣ010/65324014; US, 55 Anjialou (entrance on Tianze Lu), ⓣ010/85313333; visa call centre ⓣ4008872333; Uzbekistan, 7 Beixiao Jie, Sanlitun ⓣ010/65326305; Vietnam, 32 Guanghua Lu, Jianguomenwai ⓣ010/65321155.

Hospitals and clinics Most big hotels have a resident medic. The following two hospitals have foreigners' clinics where some English is spoken: Peking Union Medical College Hospital, 1 Shuaifuyuan, Wangfujing (Mon–Fri 8am–4.30pm; the foreigner unit is south of the inpatient building; ⓣ010/65295284, ⓦwww.pumch.ac.cn); and the Sino Japanese Friendship Hospital, in the northeast of the city just beyond Beisanhuan Dong Lu (daily 8–11.30am & 1–4.30pm with a 24hr emergency unit; ⓣ010/64221122, ⓦwww.zryhyy.com.cn). At each of the above you will have to pay a consultation fee of around ¥200.

For services run by and for foreigners, try the Beijing International SOS Clinic, Suite 105, Kunsha Building, 16 Xin-yuan-li (daily 24hr; ⓣ010/64629112, ⓦwww.internationalsos.com); the International Medical and Dental Centre, S111 Lufthansa Centre, 50 Liangmaqiao Lu (ⓣ010/64651384); the Hong Kong International Clinic, 3F, *Swissôtel Hong Kong Macau Centre*, Dongsi Shitiao Qiao (daily 9am–9pm; ⓣ010/65012288 ext 2346); or the United Family Hospital, the only completely foreign-operated clinic, 2 Jingtai Lu (appointment ⓣ010/59277000, emergency ⓣ010/59277120, ⓦwww.unitedfamilyhospitals.com). Expect to pay at least ¥500 for a consultation.

For emergencies, the AEA International Clinic has English-speaking staff and offers a comprehensive (and expensive) service at 14 Liangmahe Lu, not far from the Lufthansa Centre (clinic ⓣ010/64629112, emergency calls ⓣ010/64629100).

Internet Beijing is one of the few places in China that doesn't abound in internet cafés, thanks to a mass closure a few years ago. Those still open are heavily regulated – you will be asked to show your passport before being allowed near a computer. There's one on Ping'an Dajie, oppsite the entrance to Nanluogu Xiang. All hotels have business centres with internet available, but it can be ridiculously expensive, especially in the classier places. Your best option is to head for a backpacker hotel or hostel, where access is generally free. Most cafés and bars have wi-fi.

Kids There's an amusement park inside Chaoyang Park (daily 8.30am–6pm) with lots of rides – though it's no Disneyland – or they could try ice-skating on the basement level 2 of the China World Trade Centre (Mon, Wed, Fri & Sat 10am–10pm, Tues & Thurs 10am–5.50pm, Sun 10am–8pm; ¥30/hr) – though be aware that Chinese kids are very good. Sights that youngsters might enjoy are the zoo and aquarium (see p.112), pedal boating on Houhai and the Summer Palace, (see p.109 & p.116) the acrobat shows (see p.125) and the Puppet Theatre (see p.125), and the Natural History Museum (see p.100). If you're tired of worrying about them in the traffic, try taking them to pedestrianized Liulichang, the Olympic Green, the 798 Art District, or the parks – Ritan Park has a good playground (see p.105) and Chaoyang Park has boating. Check

Ⓦwww.beijing-kids.com for more suggestions and advice. Note that most Beijing attractions are free for children under 1.2m high.

Language courses You can do short courses (from two weeks to two months) in Mandarin Chinese at Beijing Foreign Studies University, 2 Xi Erhuan Lu ⓣ010/68468167; at the Bridge School in Jianguomenwai Dajie ⓣ010/64940243, which offers evening classes; or the Cultural Mission at 7 Beixiao Jie in Sanlitun ⓣ010/65323005, where most students are diplomats. For courses in Chinese lasting six months to a year, apply to Beijing International School at Anzhenxili, Chaoyang ⓣ010/64433151; Beijing University in Haidian ⓣ010/62751230; or Beijing Normal University, at 19 Xinjiekouwai ⓣ010/62207986. Expect to pay around US$1500 in tuition fees per semester.

Left luggage The main left-luggage office at Beijing Zhan is on the east side of the station (daily 5am–midnight; ¥10/day). There's also a left-luggage office in the foreigners' waiting room, signposted at the back of the station, with lockers for ¥20 (5am–midnight). The left-luggage office at Xi Zhan is downstairs on the left as you enter (5am–midnight; ¥15/day). There are 24hr left luggage offices at each terminal at the airport; follow the signs. Price is dependent on size, but all but the biggest suitcase will cost a reasonable ¥20/day.

Libraries The Beijing National Library (Mon–Fri 8am–5pm; ⓣ010/68415566), 39 Baishiqiao Lu, just north of Zizhuyuan Park, is one of the largest in the world, with more than ten million volumes, including manuscripts from the Dunhuang Caves and a Qing-dynasty encyclopedia. The oldest texts are Shang-dynasty inscriptions on bone. You'll need to join before they let you in. To take books out, you need to be resident in the city, but you can turn up and get a day pass that lets you browse around. An attached small cinema shows Western films in English at weekends; phone for details. The Library of the British Embassy, 4F Landmark Building, 8 Dong Sanhuan Bei Lu, has a wide selection of books and magazines; anyone can wander in and browse.

Mail The International Post Office is on Chaoyangmen Dajie (Mon–Sat 8am–6pm), just north of the intersection with Jianguomen Dajie. This is where poste restante letters (addressed poste restante, GPO, Beijing) end up, dumped in a box; you have to rifle through them all and pay ¥1.5 for the privilege (you'll also need to bring your passport for identification). Letters are only kept for one month, after which the officious staff are quick to send them back. It's also possible to rent a PO box here, and there's a packing service for parcels and a wide variety of stamps on sale. Other convenient post offices are in the basement of the China World Trade Centre; on Xi Chang'an Jie; just east of the Concert Hall; and at the north end of Xidan Dajie. All are open Mon–Sat 9am–7pm. EMS can be sent from any post office.

Pharmacies There are large pharmacies at 136 Wangfujing and 42 Dongdan Bei Dajie, or you could try the famous Tongrentang Medicine Store on Dazhalan (see p.98), which also has a doctor for on-the-spot diagnosis. For imported non-prescription medicines, try Watsons at the *Holiday Inn Lido*, Shoudujichang Lu (daily 9am–9pm), in the northeast of the city, the basment of Raffles Mall, Dongzhimen or at the Full Link Plaza on Chaoyangmenwai Dajie (daily 10am–9pm).

PSB The Foreigners' Police, at 2 Andingmen Dong Dajie (Mon–Fri 8am–noon & 1.30–4pm; ⓣ010/84015292), will give you a first visa extension for a fee of ¥160. It will take them up to a week to do it, so make sure you've got plenty of cash before you go, as you can't change money without your passport. Apply for a second extension and you'll be told to leave the country: don't, just leave Beijing and apply elsewhere. The nearest place with a friendly PSB office, where your visa will be extended on the spot, is Chengde (see p.158); you can make it there and back in a day. If you have an emergency and require urgent assistance, dial ⓣ110 or ⓣ010/550100, and have a Chinese-speaker handy to help you.

Spectator sports Beijing's football team, Guo An, plays at the massive Workers' Stadium in the northeast of the city, off Gongren Tiyuchang Bei Lu (bus #110 along Dongdaqiao), every other Sunday afternoon at 3.30pm in season. There's a timetable outside the ticket office, which is just east of the north gate of the stadium. Tickets are cheap (¥30), and can be bought up to three days before from the office at the stadium's west gate, from the ticket line ⓣ010/4008101887, online at Ⓦwww.228.com.cn or on the day from a tout. Basketball is almost as popular and Beijing's Shougang play at the Workers' Stadium from Oct–March; exhibition matches are played at the superb Wukesong Arena (Ⓦwww.wukesongarena.com; ¥30; Wukesong subway stop), built for the Olympics.

Swimming If you just want a cheap swim, try the Ditan Swimming Pool at 8 Hepingli Zhong Jie (ⓣ010/64264483; ¥30); but serious swimmers should check out the Olympic-size pool in the Sino Japanese Centre (ⓣ010/64683311; ¥88), 40 Lianmaqiao Lu, by the Century Theatre. For family pool fun, visit the Splash Recreation Club at the *Sino Swiss Hotel* (9 Xiao Tianzhi Nan Lu,

Ⓣ010/64565588, Ⓦwww.sinoswisshotel.com; ¥130/day) which has hot springs and the capital's only indoor-outdoor pool. Some hotels open their lavish pools and gym facilities to non-guests; most impressive are the pools at the *Ritz-Carlton* (1 Jinchengfang Dong Jie, Ⓣ010/66016666; ¥220) and the *Doubletree by Hilton* (168 Guang'anmen Wai Dajie (Ⓣ010/63381888; ¥150). The famous Olympic Water Cube has re-opened as a water theme park, featuring spas, slides and a wave pool; (daily 10am–9.30pm; ¥200).

Travel agents CITS is at 103 Fuxingmennei Dajie (daily 8.30–11.30am & 1.30–4.30pm; Ⓣ010/66011122). They offer expensive tours, a tour guide and interpreter service, and advance ticket booking for trains, planes and ferries (from Tianjin), with a commission of around ¥20 added. Other CITS offices are in the *Beijing Hotel*, 33 Dongchang'an Jie (Ⓣ010/65120507) and the *New Century Hotel* (Ⓣ010/68491426), opposite the zoo. Good private alternatives to the state monolith, geared at corporate groups, include China Swan International Tours on the 4th floor of the Longhui Building, 1 Nanguang Nanli, Dongsanhuan Lu (Ⓣ010/67316393, Ⓦwww.china-swan.com) and BTG International at 206 Beijing Tourism Building (Ⓣ010/96906798, Ⓦwww.btgtravel.cn). For adventure travel within China, contact Wildchina, Room 801, Oriental Place, 9 Dongfang Dong Lu, Dongsanhuan Bei Lu (Ⓣ010/64656602, Ⓦwww.wildchina.com). Beijing's most unusual tour agency is Koryo Tours (27 Beisanlitun Nan [East Courtyard], Chaoyang District; Ⓣ010/64167544, Ⓦwww.koryogroup.com), who arrange visits (heavily controlled, of course) to the paranoid hermit kingdom of North Korea. Expect to pay at least US$2000 for the privilege.

Around Beijing

There are plenty of scenic spots and places of interest scattered in the plains and hills around the capital, and no visit would be complete without a trip to the **Great Wall**, accessible in three places within easy journey time of Beijing. The **Ming Tombs**, another remnant of imperial glory, are often combined with a trip to the nearby wall. In addition, the **Western Hills** shouldn't be overlooked, and if you're in the capital for any length of time, this large stretch of densely wooded parkland provides an invigorating breather from the pressures of the city. Further out, the **Jietai** and **Tanzhe temples** are pretty in themselves and, unlike the city's other temples, they're attractively situated.

The Great Wall

This is a Great Wall and only a great people with a great past could have a great wall and such a great people with such a great wall will surely have a great future.

Richard M. Nixon

Stretching from Shanhaiguan, by the Yellow Sea, to Jiayuguan Pass in the Gobi Desert, the **Great Wall** (长城, *chángchéng*) is an astonishing feat of engineering. The practice of building walls along China's northern frontier began in the fifth century BC and continued until the sixteenth century. Over time, this discontinuous array of fortifications and ramparts came to be known as **Wan Li Changcheng** (literally, "Long Wall of Ten Thousand Li", *li* being a Chinese measure of distance roughly equal to 500m), or "the Great Wall" to English-speakers. Even the most-visited section at **Badaling**, constantly overrun by Chinese and foreign tourists, is still easily one of China's most spectacular sights. The section at **Mutianyu** is somewhat less crowded; distant **Simatai** and **Jinshanling** are much less so, and far more beautiful. To see the wall in all its crumbly glory, head out to **Huanghua**. For other trips to unreconstructed sections, check out Ⓦwww.wildwall.com or contact Beijing Hikers at Ⓦwww.beijinghikers.com.

Some history

The Chinese have walled their cities since earliest times and during the Warring States period (around the fifth century BC) simply extended the practice to separate rival territories. The Great Wall's origins lie in these fractured lines of fortifications and in the vision of the first Emperor **Qin Shi Huang** who, having unified the empire in the third century BC, joined and extended the sections to form one continuous defence against barbarians.

Under subsequent dynasties, whenever insularity rather than engagement drove foreign policy, the wall continued to be maintained and, in response to shifting regional threats, grew and changed course. It lost importance under the Tang, when borders were extended north, well beyond it. The Tang was in any case an outward-looking dynasty that kept the barbarians in check far more cheaply by fostering trade and internal divisions. With the emergence of the insular Ming, however, the wall's upkeep again became a priority, and from the fourteenth to the sixteenth century military, technicians worked on its reconstruction. The Ming wall is the one that you see today.

The 7m-high, 7m-thick wall, with its 25,000 battlements, served to bolster Ming sovereignty for a couple of centuries. It restricted the movement of the nomadic peoples of the distant, non-Han minority regions, preventing plundering raids. Signals made by gunpowder blasts, flags and smoke swiftly sent news of enemy movements to the capital. In the late sixteenth century, a couple of huge Mongol invasions were repelled, at Jinshanling and Badaling. But a wall is only as strong as its guards, and by the seventeenth century the Ming royal house was corrupt and its armies weak; the wall was little hindrance to the invading Manchus. After they had established their own dynasty, the Qing, they let the wall fall into disrepair. Slowly it crumbled away, useful only as a source of building material – demolitions of old *hutongs* in Beijing have turned up bricks from the wall, marked with the imperial seal.

Now this great monument to state paranoia is great business – the restored sections are besieged daily by rampaging hordes of tourists – and is touted by the government as a source of national pride. Its image adorns all manner of products, from wine to cigarettes, and is even used – surely rather inappropriately – on visa stickers.

Badaling

The best-known section of the wall is at **Badaling**, 70km northwest of Beijing (八达岭, *bādálǐng*; daily 8am–4.30pm; ¥45). It was the first section to be restored (in 1957) and opened up to tourists. Here the wall is 6m wide, with regularly spaced watchtowers dating from the Ming dynasty. It follows the highest contours of a steep range of hills, forming a formidable defence, so much so that this section was never attacked directly but instead taken by sweeping around from the side after a breach was made in the weaker, low-lying sections.

Badaling may be the easiest part of the wall to get to from Beijing, but it's also the most packaged. At the entrance, a giant tourist circus – a plethora of restaurants and souvenir stalls – greets you. As you ascend to the wall, you pass a train museum (¥5), a cable car (¥30) and the **Great Wall Museum** (included in the main ticket). The wall museum, with plenty of aerial photos, models and construction tools, is worth a browse, though it's more interesting visited on the way down.

Once you're up on the wall, flanked by guardrails, it's hard to feel that there's anything genuine about the experience. Indeed, the wall itself is hardly original here, as the "restorers" basically rebuilt it wholesale on the ancient foundations. To get the best out of this part of the wall you need to walk – you'll quickly lose the crowds and, generally, things get better the further you go. You come to unreconstructed sections after heading 1km north (left) or 2km south (right). That's as far as you are allowed to go; guards posted here will turn you back.

Practicalities

As well as CITS, all the more expensive Beijing hotels (and a few of the cheaper ones) run **tours** to Badaling, usually with a trip to the Ming Tombs thrown in. If you come with a tour you'll arrive in the early afternoon, when the place is at its busiest, spend an hour or two at the wall, then return, which really gives you little time for anything except the most cursory of jaunts and the purchase of an "I climbed the Great Wall" T-shirt. It's just as easy, and cheaper, to travel under your own steam. The easiest way to get here is on bus #919 from Deshengmen (a 2min walk east from Jishuitan subway stop) – there's an ordinary service (2hr; ¥7) and a much quicker air-conditioned luxury bus (1hr; ¥12). Note that private minbuses also call themselves #919 and that you might get scalped on these; the real buses are larger and have "Deshengmen–Badaling" written in the window.

Or there are plenty of tourist buses (outward journeys daily 6–10am; every 20min; ¥110–130 for a return ticket): route #1 leaves from Qianmen, route #2 from the train station, and #4 from outside the zoo. The journey to Badaling on one of these takes about an hour and a half, and the buses visit the Ming Tombs (see p.137) on the way back.

Mutianyu

A two-kilometre section, the **Mutianyu Great Wall**, 90km northeast of the city (慕田峪, *mùtiányù*; daily 8am–5pm; ¥35), is more appealing to most foreign visitors than Badaling, as it has rather fewer tourist trappings. Passing along a ridge through some lush, undulating hills, this part of the wall is well endowed with guard towers, built in 1368 and renovated in 1983.

From the entrance, steep steps lead up to the wall; you can get a cable car up (¥35) though it's not far to walk. The stretch of wall you can traverse here is about 3km long (barriers in both directions stop you continuing any further). The atmospheric *Mutianyu Great Wall Guesthouse* (☎010/69626867; ❸), situated in a reconstructed watchtower 500m before the eastern barrier, is a good place for a quiet overnight stay, though be aware it has no plumbing; you have to call ahead.

To get here, take **bus #916** from Dongzhimen and get off at Mingzhu Square in Huairou, where you can catch a minibus to the wall (¥20 or so), or take bus #936 from Dongzhimen (note that there are a few different routes for this bus, so confirm with the driver that yours goes to Mutianyu Great Wall); it runs hourly from 7am–3pm and takes about two hours.

Alternatively, you can get tourist bus #6 (mid-April to mid-Oct, outward journeys daily 6.30am–8am; ¥45) from the #42 bus station, just south of Dongsi Shitiao subway stop; they'll wait around at the site for an hour or two before heading back to Beijing. Returning by other means shouldn't be a hassle, provided you do so before 6pm; plenty of minibuses wait in the car park to take people back to the city. If you can't find a minibus back to Beijing, get one to the town of **Huairou**, from where you can get regular bus #916 back to the capital – the last bus leaves at 6.30pm.

Simatai

Peaceful and semi-ruined, **Simatai** (司马台, *sīmǎtái*; daily 8am–4pm; ¥40), 110km northeast of the city, is the most unspoilt section of the Great Wall around Beijing. With the wall snaking across purple hills that resemble crumpled velvet from afar, and blue mountains in the distance, it fulfils the expectations of most visitors more than the other sections. At the time of writing though, the whole area was closed for a two-year renovation. It is due to re-open in 2012, and will no doubt have been spruced up considerably, so take the information below as provisional.

Most of this section dates back to the Ming dynasty, and sports a few late innovations such as spaces for cannon, with the inner walls at right angles to the outer wall to thwart invaders who breached the first defence.

From the car park, a winding path takes you up to the wall, where most visitors turn right. Regularly spaced watchtowers allow you to measure your progress uphill along the ridge. If you're not scared of heights you can take the cable car to the eighth tower (¥20). The walk over the ruins isn't an easy one, and gets increasingly precipitous after about the tenth watchtower. The views are sublime, though. After about the fourteenth tower (2hr on), the wall peters out and the climb becomes quite dangerous, and there's no point going any further.

Turning left when you first reach the wall, you can do the popular hike to Jinshanling in three hours (see p.136). Most people, though, do the walk in the other direction, as it's more convenient to finish up in Simatai.

Practicalities

The journey out from the capital to Simatai takes about three hours by private transport. **Tours** run from the backpacker hotels and hostels for around ¥150, generally once or twice a week in low season, daily in the summer, and sometimes offer overnight stays. Most other hotels can arrange transport, too (usually a minibus), though expect to pay a little more.

You can travel here independently, but considering the logistical hassles and expense, this is only worth doing if you want to stay for a night or two. To get here under your own steam, catch a direct Simatai bus from Dongzhimen bus station (buses leave 7–9am; ¥40) or take bus #980, #970 or #987 to **Miyun** (¥10) and negotiate for a minibus or taxi to take you the rest of the way (you shouldn't have to pay more than ¥100). Between mid-April and mid-October tourist bus #12 heads to Simatai (6am–8am; ¥95 including entrance ticket) from the #42 bus station south of Dongsi Shitiao subway stop, and from opposite Xuanwumen subway stop; buses return between 4pm and 6pm. A rented **taxi** will cost about ¥500 return, including a wait.

To get from Simatai back to Beijing, you can get a taxi from Simatai to Miyun (¥70 or so, after some negotiaton); from Miyun, the last public bus back to Beijing is at 4pm. Alternatively, wait at the Simatiai car park for a tourist bus; they start to head back to the city at 4pm.

The *Simatai Youth Hostel* (Ⓣ010/69035311), by the entrance, has **rooms** (¥160) and hard beds in an eight-bed dorm (¥70); there's hot water for two hours a day. You'll get rather better value if you head off with one of the locals who hang

> At all the less touristy places, each tourist or group of tourists will be followed along the wall by a villager selling drinks and postcards, for at least an hour; if you don't want to be pestered, make it very clear from the outset that you are not interested in anything they are selling – though after a few kilometres you might find that ¥5 can of Coke very welcome.

around the car park; they will charge ¥70 or so for a spare room in their house, though facilities will be simple, with only cold water on tap; ask, and your host will bring a bucket of hot water to the bathroom for you. As for **eating**, avoid the youth hostel's overpriced restaurant and head to one of the nameless places at the side of the car park, where the owners can whip up some very creditable dishes; if you're lucky, they'll have some locally caught wild game in stock.

Jinshanling

Jinshanling (金山岭长城, *jīnshānlǐng chángchéng*; ¥30), 10km west of Simatai, is one of the least-visited and best-preserved parts of the wall, with jutting obstacle walls and oval watchtowers, some with octagonal or sloping roofs. It's not easy to reach without your own transport, but there are plenty of tours out here from the hostels (¥180); they'll drop you off here in the morning, leave you to walk along the wall and pick you up at Simatai in the afternoon. Otherwise, a taxi from Miyun (see above for routes) will cost around ¥100.

Turn left when you hit the wall and it's a three-hour walk to Simatai along an unreconstructed section. You won't meet many other tourists, and will experience something of the wall's magnitude: a long and lonely road that unfailingly picks the toughest line between peaks. Take the hike seriously, as you are scrambling up and down steep, crumbly inclines, and you need to be sure of foot. Watch, too, for loose rocks dislodged by your companions. When you reach Simatai there's a ¥30 toll at the suspension bridge.

Finally, if you head right when you get onto the wall at Jinshanling, you quickly reach an utterly abandoned and overgrown section. After about four hours' walk along here you'll reach a road that cuts through the wall, and from here you can flag a bus back to Beijing. This is only recommended for the intrepid.

Hunghua

The section of the wall at **Huanghua** (黄花长城, *huánghuā chángchéng*; ¥25), 60km north of Beijing, is completely unreconstructed. It's a good example of Ming defences, with wide ramparts, intact parapets and beacon towers. You can hike along the wall for as long as you like, though some sections are a bit of a scramble. It's not too hard to get here: backpacker hotels have started taking tours, otherwise take bus #916 from Dongzhimen bus station to Huairou (¥8), and catch a minibus taxi from there (around ¥10; agree the fare before setting off, as the driver may try to overcharge foreigners). You'll be dropped off on a road that cuts through the wall. The section to the left is too hard to climb, but the section on the right, past a little reservoir, shouldn't present too many difficulties for the agile; indeed, the climb gets easier as you go, with the wall levelling off along a ridge.

The wall here is attractively ruined – so watch your step – and its course makes for a pleasant walk through some lovely countryside. Keep walking the wall for about 2km, to the seventh tower, and you'll come to steps that lead south down the wall and onto a stony path. Follow this path down past an ancient barracks to a pumping station, and you'll come to a track that takes you south back to the main road, through a graveyard and orchards. When you hit the road you're about 500m south of where you started. Head north and after 150m you'll come to a bridge where taxis (¥10) and buses to Huairou congregate. The last bus from Huairou to Beijing is at 6.30pm.

Jiankou

Every few years a new section of the Great Wall is discovered by travellers, somewhere that's not too tricky to get to but has yet to be commercialized, where you can hike along the wall alone, experiencing this winding mountain road in all its ruined glory. Once it was Simatai, then Huanghua, but now that these have been added to the tourist trail the new destination for the intrepid to head for is **Jiankou**, about 20km north of Huairou.

The wall here is white, as it's made of **dolomite**, and there is a hikeable and very picturesque section about 20km long that winds through thickly forested mountain. Note that much of the stone is loose, so you really need to watch your step. Some sections are pretty nervewracking, so steep that they have to be climbed on all fours. Don't take the trip without a local guide.

It's possible to **get here** and back in a day, if you leave very early, but you'd be better off planning to stay a night. First, take **bus #916** to Huairou then charter a minibus for about ¥50 to Xizhazi village (it'll take another hour and a half or so) where villagers will charge you a dubious entry fee of ¥20. The village should be considered **base camp** for the hike – plenty of local farmers rent out rooms, but it is recommended that you call in at the spartan but clean *Jiankou Zhao's Hostel* (dorms ¥15, rooms ❶). Mr. Zhao is full of information on the hike, and will either guide you himself or sort out someone else to do it. The home-cooked food, incidentally, is excellent.

From Xizhazi it takes an hour or so just to reach the wall, west of here – without a local to guide you it's easy to get lost on the way. Only the most determined choose to travel the full 20km hike from west to east; most people do the first 10km or so, or choose to do the most spectacular middle section, about 3km in length, easy to get to and with no tricky parts.

The far western end of the hike starts at **Nine Eye Tower**, one of the biggest watchtowers on the wall, and named after its nine peep holes. It's a tough 12km or so from here to the **Beijing Knot**, a watchtower where three walls come together. Around here the hiking gets easier and the views are spectacular, at least for the next 3 or 4km, till you reach a steep section called 'Eagle Flies Vertically'. Though theoretically you can scale this, then carry on for another 10km to Mutianyu, it is not recommended, as the hike gets increasingly dangerous, and includes some almost vertical climbs, such as the notorious "sky stairs". When you've had enough you'll need to head back to Xizhazi village, from where you'll have to negotiate a ride back to Huairou.

The Ming Tombs

After their deaths, all but three of the sixteen Ming-dynasty emperors were entombed in giant underground vaults, the **Shisan Ling** (十三陵, *shísān líng*; literally, "Thirteen Tombs", usually called the **Ming Tombs** in English). Two of the tombs, Chang Ling and Ding Ling, were restored in the 1950s; the latter was also excavated. The tombs are located in and around a valley 40km northwest of Beijing. The location, chosen by the third Ming emperor, Yongle, for its landscape of gentle hills and woods, is undeniably one of the loveliest around the capital, the site marked above ground by grand halls and platforms. That said, the fame of the tombs is overstated in relation to the actual interest of their site, and unless you've a strong archeological bent, a trip here isn't worth making for its own sake. The tombs are, however, very much on the tour circuit, being conveniently placed on the way to Badaling Great Wall (see p.133). The site also makes a nice place to picnic, especially if you just feel like taking a break from the city and its more tangible sights. To get the most out of the place, it's best not to stick to the tourist route between the car park and Ding Ling, but to spend a day here and hike around the smaller tombs farther into the hills. You'll need a map to do this – you'll find one on the back of some Beijing city maps, or you can buy one at the site (¥2).

The easiest way to get to the Ming Tombs is to take any of the **tourist buses** that go to Badaling (see p.133), which visit the tombs on the way to and from Beijing. You can get off here, then rejoin another tourist bus later, either to continue to Badaling or to return to the city. To get there on ordinary public transport, take bus #345 from Deshengmen Xi station to the terminus at Changping, then get bus #314 the rest of the way. All buses drop you at a car park in front of one of the tombs, Ding Ling.

The Spirit Way and Chang Ling

The approach to the Ming Tombs, the 7km-long **Spirit Way**, is Shisan Ling's most exciting feature, well worth backtracking along from the ticket office. The road commences with the **Dahongmen** (Great Red Gate), a triple-entranced triumphal arch, through the central opening of which only the emperor's dead body was allowed to be carried. Beyond, the road is lined with colossal stone statues of animals and men. Startlingly larger than life, they all date from the fifteenth century and are among the best surviving examples of Ming sculpture. Their precise significance is unclear, although it is assumed they were intended to serve the emperors in their next life. The animals depicted include the mythological *qilin* – a reptilian beast with deer's horns and a cow's tail – and the horned, feline *xiechi*; the human figures are stern, military mandarins. Animal statuary reappears at the entrances to several of the tombs, though the structures themselves are something of an anticlimax.

At the end of the Spirit Way stands **Chang Ling** (daily 8.30am–5pm; ¥35), which was the tomb of Yongle himself, the earliest at the site. There are plans to excavate the underground chamber, an exciting prospect since the tomb is contemporary with some of the finest buildings of the Forbidden City in the capital. At present, the enduring impression above ground is mainly one of scale – vast courtyards and halls, approached by terraced white marble. Its main feature is the Hall of Eminent Flowers, supported by huge columns consisting of individual tree trunks, which, it is said, were imported all the way from Yunnan in the south of the country.

Ding Ling

The main focus of the area is **Ding Ling** (daily 8.30am–5pm; ¥40), the underground tomb-palace of the Emperor Wanli, who ascended the throne in 1573 at the age of 10. Reigning for almost half a century, he began building his tomb when he was 22, in line with common Ming practice, and hosted a grand party within on its completion. The mausoleum, a short distance east of Chang Ling, was opened up in 1956 and found to be substantially intact, revealing the emperor's coffin, flanked by those of two of his empresses, and floors covered with scores of trunks containing imperial robes, gold and silver and even the imperial cookbooks. Some of the treasures are displayed in the tomb, a huge, musty stone vault, undecorated but impressive for its scale; others have been replaced by replicas. It's a cautionary picture of useless wealth accumulation, as pointed out by the tour guides.

The Western Hills

Like the Summer Palace (see p.114), the **Western Hills** (西山, *xīshān*) are somewhere to escape urban life for a while, though they're more of a rugged experience. Thanks to their coolness at the height of summer, the hills have long been favoured as a restful retreat by religious men and intellectuals, as well as politicians in the modern times – Mao lived here briefly, and the Politburo assembles here in times of crisis.

The hills are divided into three parks, the nearest to the centre being the **Botanical Gardens**, 3.5km northwest of the Summer Palace. Two kilometres farther west, **Xiangshan** is the largest and most impressive of the parks, but just as pretty is **Badachu**, its eight temples strung out along a hillside 2.5km to the south of Xiangshan.

The hills take roughly an hour to reach on public transport. You can explore two of the parks in one day, but each deserves a day to itself. For a weekend escape and some in-depth exploration of the area, the *Xiangshan Hotel*, close to the main entrance of Xiangshan Park, is a good base (Ⓣ010/62591166; Ⓦwww.xsfd.com ❻). A startling sight, the light, airy hotel is one of the city's more innovative buildings, something between a temple and an airport lounge. It was designed by I.M. Pei, who also designed the pyramid at the Louvre in Paris and the Bank of China building at Xidan.

The Botanical Gardens

The **Botanical Gardens** (植物园, *zhíwù yuán*; daily 6am–8pm; ¥5) are accessible by bus #331 from outside the Yuanmingyuan (see p.114) or #360 from the zoo, though the quickest way here would be to get a cab from Yiheyuan subway station. Two thousand varieties of trees and plants are arranged in formal gardens (labelled in English), at their prettiest in summer, though the terrain is flat and the landscaping is not as original as in the older parks. The impressive conservatory (¥50) has desert and tropical environments and a lot of fleshy foliage from Yunnan.

The main path leads after 1km to the **Wofo Si** (卧佛寺, *wòfó sì*; daily 8am–4.30pm; ¥5), whose main hall houses a huge reclining Buddha, more than 5m in length and cast in copper. With two giant feet protruding from the end of his painted robe, and a pudgy, baby-face, calm in repose, he looks rather cute, although he is not actually sleeping but dying – about to enter nirvana. Suitably huge shoes, presented as offerings, are on display around the hall. Behind the temple is a bamboo garden, from which paths wind off into the hills. One heads northwest to a pretty cherry valley, just under 1km away, where Cao Xueqiao is supposed to have written *The Dream of Red Mansions* (see p.992).

Xiangshan Park

Two kilometres west of the gardens lies **Xiangshan Park** (香山公园, *xiāngshān gōngyuán*; Fragrant Hills; daily 7am–6pm; ¥10; same buses as for the Botanical Gardens, stopping at the main entrance), a range of hills dominated by Incense Burner Peak in the western corner. It's at its best in the autumn (before the sharp November frosts), when the leaves turn red in a massive profusion of colour. Though busy at weekends, the park is too large to appear swamped, and is always a good place for a hike and a picnic.

Northeast from here, the **Zhao Miao** (Temple of Brilliance), one of the few temples in the area that escaped vandalism by Western troops in 1860 and 1900, was built by Qianlong in 1780 in Tibetan style, designed to make visiting Lamas feel at home. From here, follow the path west up to the peak (1hr) from where, on clear days, there are magnificent views down towards the Summer Palace and as far as distant Beijing. You can hire a horse to take you down again for ¥20, the same price as the cable car. Both drop you on the northern side of the hill, by the north entrance, a short walk from the superb **Biyun Si** (Azure Clouds Temple), just outside the park gate. A striking building, it's dominated by a north Indian-style dagoba and topped by extraordinary conical stupas. Inside, rather bizarrely, a tomb holds the hat and clothes of Sun Yatsen – his body was held here for a while before being moved in 1924. The giant main hall is now a maze of corridors lined with arhats, five hundred in all, and it's a magical place. The benignly smiling golden figures are all different – some have two heads or sit on animals, one is even pulling his face off – and you may see monks moving among them and bowing to each.

Badachu

Badachu, or the Eight Great Sights (八大处, *bādàchù*; daily 8am–5pm; ¥10), is a forested hill 10km south of Xiangshan Park and accessible on bus #347 from the zoo, or you can take the east–west subway line to its westernmost point, Pingguoyuan, and get a cab the rest of the way (¥15). Along the path that snakes around the hill are eight **temples**, fairly small affairs, but quite attractive on weekdays, when they're not busy. The new pagoda at the base of the path holds a Buddha tooth, which once sat in the fourth temple. The third, a nunnery, is the most pleasant, with a teahouse in the courtyard. There's a statue of the rarely depicted thunder deity inside, boggle-eyed and grimacing. As well as the inevitable cable car (¥50), it's also possible to slide down the hill on a metal track (¥40).

Tanzhe Si and Jietai Si

Due west of Beijing, two splendid temples sit in the wooded country outside the industrial zone that rings the city. Though **Tanzhe Si** and **Jietai Si** are relatively little-visited by tourists, foreign residents rate them as among the best places to escape the city smoke. Take a picnic and make a day of it, as getting there and back can be time-consuming.

Tourist bus #7 visits both temples (mid-April to mid-Oct outward journeys 7–8.30am; ¥38 return), giving you ninety minutes at each, before returning to Qianmen. Otherwise, you could ride the east–west subway line all the way to its western terminus at Pingguoyuan, then catch bus #931 (¥3; this bus has two routes, so make sure the driver knows where you're going) to Tanzhe Si (the last stop). From here you'll be able to find a taxi on to Jietai Si (¥20), from where you'll have to get a cab back to the city. Or you can save yourself some hassle by hiring a taxi to visit both temples, which should cost around ¥250 if you start from the city centre.

Tanzhe Si

Forty kilometres west of the city, **Tanzhe Si** (潭柘寺, *tánzhé sì*; daily 8am–6pm; ¥35) occupies the most beautiful and serene temple site anywhere near the city. It's Beijing's largest and one of the oldest, first recorded in the third century as housing a thriving community of monks. Wandering through the complex, past terraces of stupas, you reach an enormous central courtyard, with an ancient towering ginkgo that's more than a thousand years old (christened the "King of Trees" by Emperor Qianlong) at its heart. Across the courtyard, a second, smaller tree, known as "The Emperor's Wife", is supposed to produce a new branch every time a new emperor is born. From here you can take in the other temple buildings, on different levels up the hillside, or look around the lush bamboo gardens, whose plants are supposed to cure all manner of ailments. The spiky zhe (Cudrania) trees near the entrance apparently "reinforce the essence of the kidney and control spontaneous seminal emission".

Jietai Si

Twelve kilometres back along the road to Beijing, **Jietai Si** (戒台寺, *jiètái sì*; daily 8am–6pm; ¥35) is a complete contrast to the Tanzhe Si: sitting on a hillside surrounded by forbiddingly tall, red walls it looks more like a fortress than a temple. It's an extremely atmospheric, peaceful place, made slightly spooky by its dramatically shaped pines – eccentric-looking, venerable trees growing in odd directions. Indeed, one, leaning out at an angle of about thirty degrees, is pushing over a pagoda on the terrace beneath it. In the main hall is an enormous Liao-dynasty platform of white marble, 3m high and intricately carved with figures – monks, monsters (beaked and winged) and saints – at which novice monks were ordained. Another, smaller hall, holds a beautiful wooden altar that swarms with relief dragons.

Travel details

Trains

Beijing South (Yongdimen) to: Qingdao (8 daily; 6hr); Shanghai (7 express daily; 11hr); Tianjin (frequent; 30min).
Beijing Zhan to: Baotou (daily; 12hr); Beidaihe (3 daily; 3–5hr); Changchun (daily; 6–12hr); Chengde (4 daily; 4hr); Dalian (3 daily; 11hr); Dandong (daily; 13hr); Datong (8 daily; 7hr); Fuzhou (daily; 20hr); Hangzhou (daily; 13–21hr); Harbin (5 daily; 8–15hr); Hohhot (8 daily; 11hr); Ji'nan (8 daily; 3–7hr); Lhasa (daily; 44hr; requires travel permit); Nanjing (daily; 16hr); Shanhaiguan (5 daily; 2–6hr); Shenyang (8 daily; 5–12hr); Tai'an (2 daily; 3–6hr); Yantai (daily; 14hr).
Xi Zhan to: Changsha (frequent; 15hr); Chengdu (3 daily; 25–30hr); Chongqing (3 daily; 25hr); Guangzhou (4 daily; 21hr); Guilin (3 daily; 22hr); Guiyang (4 daily; 30hr); Hong Kong (daily; 24hr); Kunming (2 daily; 38hr);Lanzhou (5 daily; 20hr); Luoyang (6 daily; 9hr); Nanchang (8 daily; 11–20hr); Nanning (daily; 28hr); Shijiazhuang (frequent; 3hr); Taiyuan (10 daily; 4hr); Ürümqi (daily; 40hr); Xi'an (12 daily; 12hr); Yichang (daily; 21hr); Zhanjiang (daily; 27hr); Zhengzhou (frequent; 9hr). As well as the above, there are weekly services from Xi Zhan to Moscow and Ulaan Baatur; see p.81 for details.

Buses

There is little point travelling to destinations far from Beijing by bus; the journey takes longer than the train and is far less comfortable. The following destinations are within bearable travelling distance. Services are frequent, usually hourly during the day, with a few sleeper buses travellling at night. Note that there are also private bus services to Tianjin and Chengde from outside the main train station, Beijing Zhan.
Deshengmen bus station to: Chengde (4hr); Datong (10hr).
Haihutun bus station to: Shijiazhuang (10hr); Tianjin (2hr).
Majuan bus station to: Beidaihe (9hr); Shanhaiguan (9hr; express service 5hr).

Flights

Beijing to: Baotou (1hr 30min); Beihai (4hr); Changchun (1hr 45min); Changsha (2hr); Chengdu (2hr 30min); Chifeng (3hr); Chongqing (2hr 40min); Dalian (1hr 20min); Dandong (1hr 20min); Fuzhou (2hr 50min); Guangzhou (3hr); Guilin (3hr); Guiyang (4hr 45min); Haikou (3hr 45min); Hangzhou (1hr 50min); Harbin (2hr); Hefei (2hr); Hohhot (1hr 10min); Hong Kong (3hr); Huangshan (2hr); Huangyan (2hr 40min); Jiamusi (2hr); Jilin (1hr 50min); Ji'nan (1hr); Jingjinag (2hr 30min); Jinzhou (1hr 20min); Kunming (3hr 30min); Lanzhou (2hr 20min); Lhasa (4hr); Lianyungang (5hr 30min); Linyi (2hr 30min); Liuzhou (2hr 45min); Luoyang (1hr 40min); Mudanjiang (1hr 50min); Nanchang (2hr); Nanjing (1hr 45min); Nanning (3hr 30min); Nantong (2hr 30min); Nanyang (1hr 30min); Ningbo (2hr 20min); Qingdao (1hr 15min); Qiqihar (2hr); Sanya (5hr 20min); Shanghai (1hr 50min); Shantou (3hr); Shenyang (1hr); Shenzhen (3hr 10min); Taiyuan (1hr 10min); Tongliao (1hr 45min); Urümqi (3hr 50min); Weifang (1hr); Wenzhou (2hr 20min); Wuhan (2hr); Wuyishan (1hr 45min); Xiamen (2hr 50min); Xi'an (1hr 30min); Xining (2hr 30min); Xuzhou (1hr 15min); Yanan (1hr 20min); Yanji (2hr); Yantai (1hr); Yibin (3hr 45min); Yinchuan (2hr); Zhangjiajie (3hr); Zhengzhou (1hr 20min); Zhuhai (3hr 30min).

CHAPTER 2

Highlights

* **Tianjin** Glimpse dilapidated colonial architecture and browse the souvenir markets of this huge city. See p.144

* **Beidaihe beachfront** Once the pleasure preserve of colonists, then Communists, the summer sands are now chock-a-block with the bikini-clad masses. See p.151

* **Shanhaiguan** A dusty relic of a walled city on the Bohai Gulf, where you can follow the Great Wall until it disappears dramatically into the sea. See p.155

* **Chengde** The summer playground of emperors, whose many palaces and temples have been restored to the delight of Beijing day-trippers. See p.158

▲ Imperial Summer Palace, Chengde

Hebei and Tianjin

A somewhat anonymous region, Hebei has two great cities at its heart – Beijing and Tianjin – both of which long ago outgrew the province and struck out on their own as separate municipalities. In the south, a landscape of flatlands is spotted with heavy industry and mining towns – China at its least glamorous – which are home to the majority of the province's seventy million inhabitants. Though most travellers pass through here on their way to or from the capital, few stop. The sparsely populated tableland to the north, rising from the **Bohai Gulf**, holds more promise. For most of its history this marked China's northern frontier, and was the setting for numerous battles with invading forces; both the **Mongols** and the **Manchus** swept through, leaving their mark in the form of the **Great Wall**, winding across lonely ridges.

The first sections of the wall were built in the fourth century AD, along the Hebei–Shanxi border, in an effort to fortify its borders against aggressive neighbours. Two centuries later, Qin Shi Huang's Wall of Ten Thousand Li (see p.132) skirted the northern borders of the province. The parts of the wall visible today, however, are the remains of the much younger and more extensive Ming-dynasty wall, begun in the fourteenth century as a deterrent against the Mongols. You can see the wall where it meets the sea at **Shanhaiguan**, a fortress town only a few hours by train from Beijing. If you're in the area, don't miss the intriguing seaside resort of **Beidaihe**, along the coast to the south, whose beaches host summer vacationers and dwindling numbers of Communist Party elite. Well north of the wall, the town of **Chengde** is the province's most visited attraction, an imperial base set amid the wild terrain of the Hachin Mongols and conceived on a grand scale by the eighteenth-century emperor Kangxi, with temples and monuments to match. All three towns are popular spots with domestic tourists, particularly Beijingers snatching a weekend away from the capital's bustle and stress. The Chinese like their holiday spots the way they like their restaurants – *renao* (literally "hot and noisy") – but it's easy to beat the crowds and find some great scenery.

Tianjin, an industrial giant and former concession town with a distinctly Western stamp, is worth a day-trip on the super-fast express train from Beijing to see its hodgepodge of colonial architecture and modern skyscrapers.

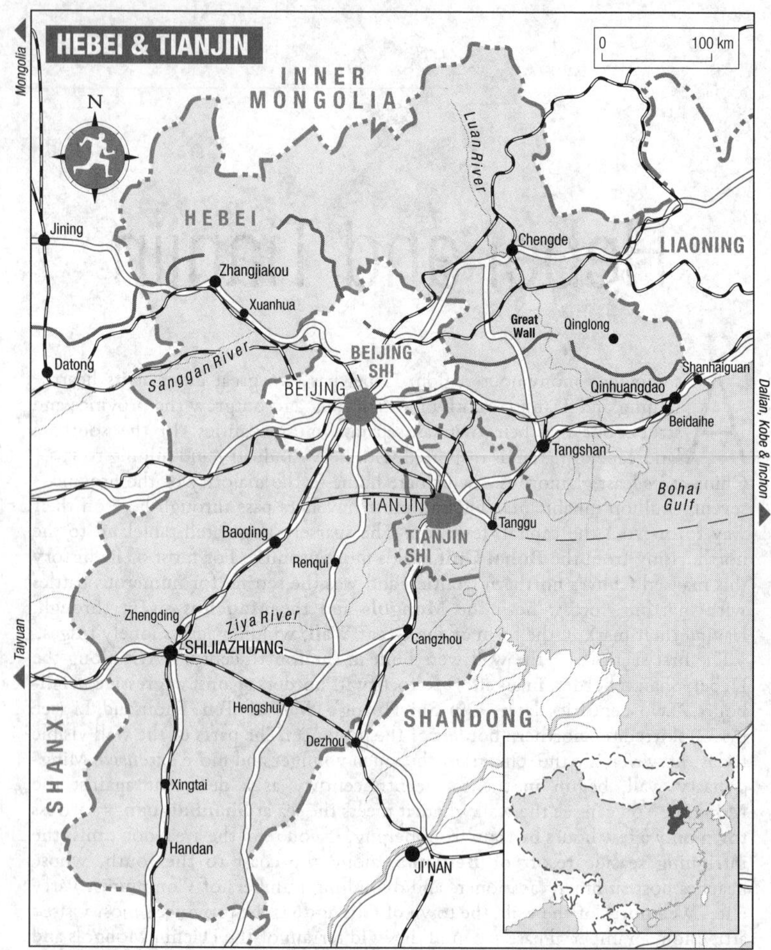

Tianjin

And there were sections of the city where different foreigners lived – Japanese, White Russians, Americans and Germans – but never together, and all with their own separate habits, some dirty, some clean. And they had houses of all shapes and colours, one painted in pink, another with rooms that jutted out at every angle like the backs and fronts of Victorian dresses, others with roofs like pointed hats and wood carvings painted white to look like ivory.

Amy Tan, *The Joy Luck Club*

Massive and dynamic, **TIANJIN** (天津, *tiānjīn*) is China's third-largest city, located near the coast some 80km east of Beijing. The city has few actual sights; its streetscapes – ageing nineteenth- and early twentieth-century foreign architecture, mostly European, juxtaposed with the concrete-and-glass monoliths of wealthy contemporary China – are its most engrossing attractions. Locals say, not altogether with pride, that the city has become a massive construction site, requiring a new map to be printed every three months. Though wide swaths of the city are being redeveloped, much of the colonial architecture has been placed under protection, though not from over-zealous renovation – look for the distinctive plaques on the relevant buildings. Feng Jicai, one of China's best-known writers and a Tianjin resident, led a campaign to preserve the old city, noting, "Once a nation has lost its own culture, it faces a spiritual crisis more dreadful than that brought on by material poverty. If you regard a city as having a spirit, you will respect it, safeguard it, and cherish it. If you regard it as only matter, you will use it excessively, transform it at will, and damage it without regret." Contemporary Tianjin is an illustration of the latter, an unwieldy fusion of Beijing's bustle and Shanghai's Bund, though delivered without the character of either.

Nevertheless, Tianjin has enough architectural attractions and shopping opportunities, particularly for antiques, to justify a day-trip from the capital, especially now the city is within easier reach of Beijing than many of the capital's own suburbs, thanks to the high-speed train link, a legacy of the 2008 Olympics, which means it takes just thirty minutes to shuttle between the two. On the journey you may well be joined by young Beijingers coming to shop for clubwear, older residents in search of curios and businesspeople on their way to the next deal.

Though today the city is given over to industry and commerce, it was as a **port** that Tianjin first gained importance. When the Ming emperor Yongle moved the capital from Nanjing to Beijing, Tianjin became the dock for vast quantities of rice paid in tribute to the emperor and transported here from all over the south via the Grand Canal. In the nineteenth century, the city caught the attention of the seafaring Western powers, who used the boarding of an English ship by Chinese troops as an excuse to declare war. With well-armed gunboats, they were assured of victory, and the Treaty of Tianjin, signed in 1856, gave the Europeans the right to establish nine concessionary bases on the mainland, from which they could conduct trade and sell opium.

These separate **concessions**, along the banks of the Hai River, were self-contained European fantasy worlds: the French built elegant chateaux and towers, while the Germans constructed red-tiled Bavarian villas. The Chinese were discouraged from intruding, except for servants, who were given pass cards. Tensions between the indigenous population and the foreigners exploded in the **Tianjin Incident** of 1870, when a Chinese mob attacked a French-run orphanage and killed the nuns and priests in the belief that the Chinese orphans had been kidnapped and were merely awaiting the pot. Twenty Chinese were beheaded as a result, and the prefect of the city was banished. A centre for secretive anti-foreign movements, the city had its genteel peace interrupted again by the **Boxer Rebellion** in 1900 (see p.950), after which the foreigners leveled the walls around the old Chinese city to enable them to see in and keep an eye on its residents.

Arrival

The city's huge **main train station** (天津站, *tiānjīn zhàn*) is conveniently located just north of the Hai River; with the town centre just to the south (take bus #24). There are two other stations in town: **North** (北站, *běi zhàn*), where you are likely to arrive if you have come from northeast China; and **West** (西站, *xīzhàn*), which is on the main line between Beijing and destinations farther south. Trains terminating in Tianjin may call at one of the other stations before reaching the main station. The most stylish way to arrive is on one of the high-speed bullet trains (¥58), which leave Beijing every 20 minutes, reach Tianjin's main station in 30 minutes and plough along at a top speed of 340 km/hr.

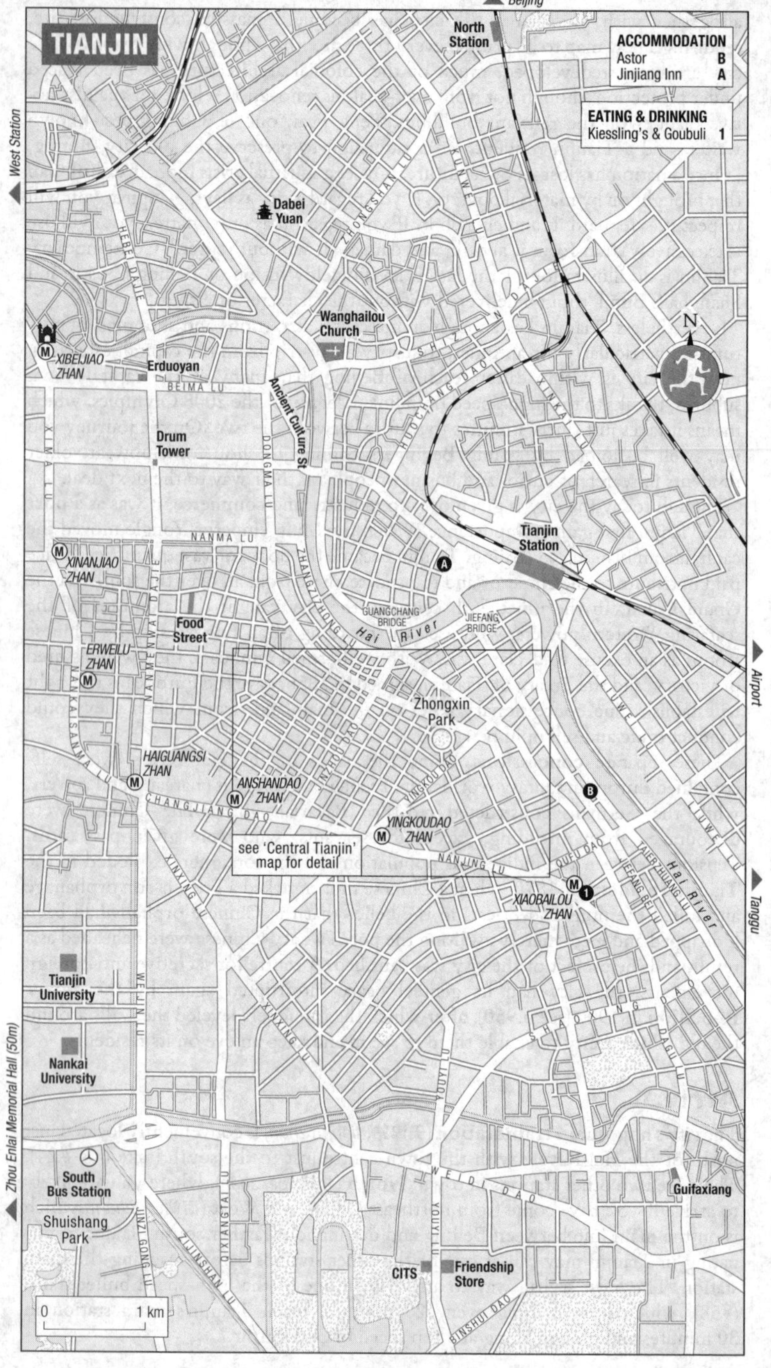
TIANJIN
ACCOMMODATION
Astor B
Jinjiang Inn A
EATING & DRINKING
Kiessling's & Goubuli 1
Beijing
North Station
West Station
Dabei Yuan
Wanghailou Church
XIBEIJIAO ZHAN
Erduoyan
Drum Tower
Ancient Culture St
XINANJIAO ZHAN
Food Street
ERWEILU ZHAN
Tianjin Station
GUANGCHANG BRIDGE
JIEFANG BRIDGE
Hai River
Airport
Zhongxin Park
HAIGUANGSI ZHAN
ANSHANDAO ZHAN
YINGKOUDAO ZHAN
see 'Central Tianjin' map for detail
XIAOBAILOU ZHAN
Tanggu
Tianjin University
Nankai University
Zhou Enlai Memorial Hall (50m)
South Bus Station
Shuishang Park
Guifaxiang
CITS
Friendship Store
0 1 km
ZHONGSHAN LU
KUNWEI LU
HEBEI DAJIE
SHIZILIN DAJIE
BEIMA LU
HUOCHANG DAO
XINKAI LU
XIMA LU
DONGMA LU
NANMA LU
ZHANGZIZHONG LU
NANMENWAI DAJIE
NANKAI SANMA LU
CHANGJIANG DAO
YINGKOU DAO
NANJING LU
QUFU DAO
LIUWEI LU
TAIERZHUANG LU
JIEFANG BEI LU
XINXING LU
WEIJIN LU
SHAOXING DAO
DAGU LU
YOUYI LU
WEIDI DAO
QIXIANGTAI LU
ZIJINSHAN LU
JINZI GONG LU
BINSHUI DAO

The only **buses** serving Tianjin's large international **airport**, 15km east of the city, are Air China shuttles coinciding with their flights; a taxi into the centre from the airport should cost around ¥50.

City transport

Downtown and the old concession areas are just small enough to explore on foot, which is fortunate, as the **bus** network is both complicated and overcrowded, though bus maps are available around the train stations. Some useful routes include **#24**, which runs from the West Station into town, then doubles back on itself and terminates at the main station; **#1**, which runs from the North Station into town, terminating at Zhongxin Park (中心公园, *zhōngxīn gōngyuán*), the northern tip of the downtown area; and **#50**, which meanders into town from the main train station and takes you close to the Xikai Catholic Church (西开教堂, *xī kāi jiàotáng*). Bus fares are a standard ¥1.5 throughout the city centre.

An alternative to the fiendish bus system is the **subway** (from ¥2/journey), which runs south from the West Station, stopping near the Drum Tower and along Nanjing Lu, which is close to the main downtown shopping area. **Taxis** are plentiful – ¥15 is sufficient for most journeys around town.

Accommodation

Thanks to the city's new-found proximity to Beijing via the high-speed train, there is little reason for the casual visitor to overnight in Tianjin, but if a hotel is required there are some decent options.

Astor (利顺德饭店, *lì shùndé fàndiàn*) 33 Tai'er Zhuang Lu ⓣ022/23311688, ⓦwww.luxurycollection.com/astor. Located in a stylish British mansion more than 100 years old, this hotel has recently undergone massive renovation and has to be the most luxurious in the city. ❾

Friend (富蓝特大酒店, *fù lán tè dà jiǔdiàn*) 231 Xinhua Lu ⓣ022/83326399. Very friendly, clean, and a bargain by Tianjin standards. Across the street from *Friendship*'s East Building, and much more welcoming. ❹

Friendship Hotel (友谊宾馆, *yǒuyì bīnguǎn*) 176 Xinhua Lu ⓣ022/58291888. Directly opposite *Friend* is the budget wing of this hotel whose main building, round the corner on Nanjing Lu, was another closed for renovation at the time of writing. Rooms here are comfortable, clean and reasonably priced. ❸

Jinjiang Inn (锦江宾馆, *jǐnjiāng bīnguǎn*) 17 Jinbu Dao ⓣ022/58215018. A cheap chain hotel close to the station (150m from south exit #4) with clean, standard rooms. ❸

The City

The part of the city of interest to visitors – the dense network of ex-concession streets south and west of the central train station, and south of the **Hai River** (海河, *hǎi hé*) – is fairly compact. Many pinyin street signs help in navigating the central grid of streets, as do plenty of distinctive landmarks, notably the T-shaped pedestrianized shopping district of **Binjiang Dao** and **Heping Lu** at Tianjin's heart.

The **old city** was strictly demarcated into national zones, and each section of the city centre has retained a hint of its old flavour. The area northwest of the main train station, on the west side of the Hai River, was the old Chinese city. Running from west to east along the north bank of the river were the Austrian, Italian, Russian and Belgian concessions, though most of the old buildings here have been destroyed. Unmistakeable are the chateaux of the French concession, which now make up the downtown district just south of the river, and the haughty mansions the British built east of here. Farther east, also south of the river, the architecture of an otherwise unremarkable district has a sprinkling of stern German constructions.

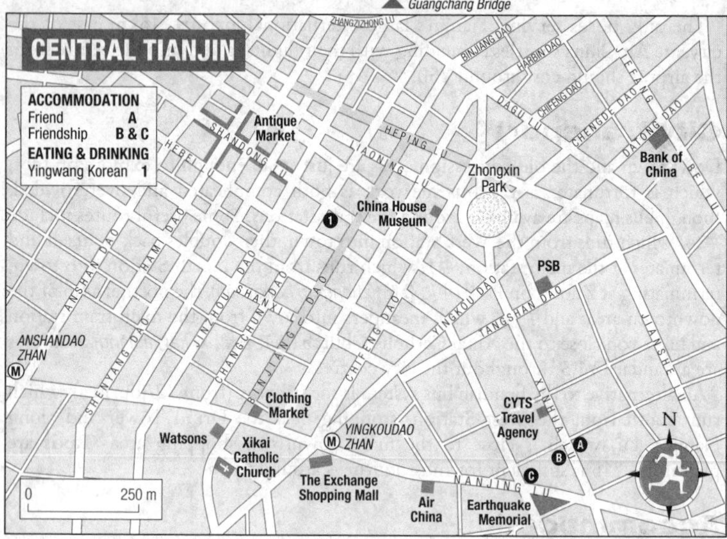

Downtown Tianjin

The majority of Tianjin's colonial buildings are clustered in the grid of streets on the southern side of the river. From the main train station, you can approach it via Jiefang Bridge, built by the French in 1903, which leads south along the heavily restored/developed **Jiefang Bei Lu**, an area given an oddly continental feel by the pastel colours and wrought-iron scrollwork balconies of the French concession. This is at its most appealing around the glorified roundabout known as **Zhongxin Park** which marks the southeastern end of the main shopping district, an area bounded by Dagu Lu, Jinzhou Dao and Chifeng Dao. Heping Lu and Binjiang Dao are the two busiest streets. Though stuffed with fashionably dressed shoppers, these narrow tree-lined streets have a pleasingly laidback feel, and the two busiest – Heping Lu and Binjiang Dao – are pedestrianized and lined with sculptures and benches. While most people won't feel the need to go inside, the **China House Museum** (房子博物馆, *fángzi bówù guăn*; ¥35) on Chifeng Dao, which traces the history of porcelain, is a must-see for its (frankly insane) premises – a colonial mansion clad entirely in broken pottery, replete with extensive additional curlicues.

The antique market

Just west of here is a shopping district of a very different character, the **antique market** (旧货市场, *jiù huò shìchăng*; daily 8am–5pm), centred on Shandong Lu but spilling over into side alleys. A great attraction even if you have no intention of buying, the alleys are lined with dark, poky shops, pavement vendors with their wares spread out in front of them on yellowed newspapers and stallholders waving jade and teapots in the faces of passers-by. The market expands and contracts according to the time of year (small in winter, big in summer) but it's always at its largest on Sundays, swelled by Beijingers here for the weekend. It's generally cheaper than any in the capital, though you still have to look hard for a bargain.

The variety of goods on display is astonishing: among the standard jade jewellery, ceramic teapots, fans and perfume bottles are Russian army watches, opium pipes, snuffboxes, ornate playing cards, old photographs, pornographic paintings and rimless sunglasses. Look out for the stalls selling picture postcards of revolutionary dramas depicting synchronized ballet dancers performing graceful, mid-air leaps with hand grenades. Bargaining is mandatory; be aware that much of the stuff is fake.

Around Nanjing Lu

At the southern end of Binjiang Dao, the **Xikai Catholic Church** (西开教堂, *xī kāi jiàotáng*; daily 5.30am–4.30pm) is a useful landmark and one of the most distinctive buildings in the city, with its odd facade of horizontal brown and orange brick stripes topped with three green domes. The diffuse zone of unremarkable buildings east of here, around Nanjing Lu, is notable only for the **Earthquake Memorial** (抗震纪念碑, *kàngzhèn jìniànbēi*) opposite the *Friendship Hotel*. More tasteful than most Chinese public statuary, this hollow pyramid commemorates the 250,000 people who died in the 1976 earthquake in Tangshan, a city to the northeast.

North of the centre

The main sight in the northern part of the city, best reached by taxi, is the **Dabei Yuan** (大悲院, *dà bēi yuàn*; daily 9am–4.30pm; ¥10), located on a narrow alleyway off Zhongshan Lu. Tianjin's major centre for Buddhist worship, it's easy to find as the alleys all around are crammed with stalls selling a colourful mix of religious knick-knacks: incense, tapes of devotional music, mirror-glass shrines and ceramic Buddhas with flashing lights in their eyes. Large bronze vessels full of water stand outside the buildings, a fire precaution that has been in use for centuries. Outside the first hall, which was built in the 1940s, the devout wrap their arms around a large bronze incense burner before lighting incense sticks and kowtowing. In the smaller, rear buildings – seventeenth-century structures extensively restored after the Tangshan earthquake – you'll see the temple's jovial resident monks, while small antique wood and bronze Buddhist figurines are displayed in a hall in the west of the complex.

The stern **Wanghailou Church** (望海楼教堂, *wàng hǎi lóu jiàotáng*) stands not far south of Dabei Yuan, over Shizilin Dajie on the north bank of the river. Built in 1904, it has an austere presence thanks to the use of dark stone and is the third church to stand on this site – the first was destroyed in the massacre of 1870 (see p.145), a year after it was built, and the second was burnt down in 1900 in the Boxer Rebellion. It's possible to visit during the week, but the Sunday morning Chinese-language services (7am) make a stop here much more interesting.

Ancient Culture Street

A short walk southwest of Wanghailou Church, the more prosaic **Ancient Culture Street** (古文化街, *gǔwénhuà jiē*) runs off Beima Lu just west of the river, its entrance marked by a colourful arch. Like Liulichang Jie in Beijing, this is a re-creation of a nineteenth-century Chinese street – minus the beggars and filth and plus the neon "OK Karaoke" signs – designed as a tourist shopping mall. It's fake but undeniably pretty, with carved balconies and columns decorating the facade of red and green wooden shops topped with curling, tiled roofs. The shops sell pricey "antiques" and souvenirs, and there's an especially large range of teapots. Look out for the stalls selling *chatang*, soup made with millet and sugar; the stallholders attract customers by demonstrating their skill at pouring boiling soup from a long, dragon-shaped spout into four bowls all held in one hand. About halfway down the street is the entrance to the heavily restored **Sea Goddess Temple** (天后宫, *tiānhòu gōng*; daily 9am–5pm; ¥3), originally built in 1326 and supposedly the oldest building in Tianjin. There's an exhibition of local crafts in the side halls.

The Drum Tower and around

Just west of Ancient Culture Street, the recently built, characterless **Drum Tower** (鼓楼, *gǔlóu*; daily 9am–4.30pm; free) stands in what was once a quiet network of *hutongs* demarcated by four "horse" (*ma*) streets – **Beima**, **Nanma**, **Dongma** and **Xima**. The original *hutongs* have been swept away, replaced by new pseudo-*hutongs* packed to the rooflines with shops selling souvenirs and antiques.

The **mosque** (清真寺, *qīngzhēnsì*), farther west off Dafeng Lu, is an active place of worship, and you're free to wander around the buildings, though only Muslims may enter the prayer halls. It's a fine example of Chinese Muslim architecture, with some striking wood carvings of floral designs in the eaves and around the windows.

Zhou Enlai Memorial Hall

Southwest of the centre is the massive **Zhou Enlai Memorial Hall** (周恩来纪念馆, *zhōu ēnlái jìniànguǎn*; daily 8am–5pm; ¥15), paying tribute to Tianjin's most famous resident. A bunker perched on the northern edge of Shuishang Park, the hall features a few wax figures, Zhou's aeroplane and limousine and scattered English explanations of his achievements – though it's not so much an analysis of the difficulties in being Chairman Mao's right-hand man as a paean to his marriage to fellow comrade Deng Yingchao. Try not to crack up when reading the description of the couple's bond: "Cherishing the same ideals, following the same path, and comrade-in-arms affection tied them in love relations." The events around the Cultural Revolution, from which Zhou's legacy derives most of its strength, are curtly summarized thus: "He frustrated the attempts of the Gang of Four." To get here, take bus #8 from Tianjin Station and get off at Shuishang Park near the statue of Nie Zhongjie, a general who is depicted on horseback.

Eating

Make sure you don't leave Tianjin without sampling some of its famous cakes and pastries. **Erduoyan** (耳朵眼, *ěrduo yǎn*), rice-powder cakes fried in sesame oil with a name which literally means "ear hole", and **mahua**, fried dough twists, are particular specialities available at shops on Ancient Culture Street and elsewhere.

Downtown, the side streets around Heping Lu (close to Zhongxin Park) are home to local restaurants that are often worth sampling. Heping Lu itself is rife with Western fast-food chains.

Food Street (食品街, *shípǐn jiē*) East of Nanmenwai Dajie, on Qingyi Dajie. A cheerful two-storey mall, this is the best place to eat in Tianjin, though standards have slipped a little over the years. With so many restaurants crammed in, there's something to suit all budgets and tastes.

Kiessling's (起士林西式餐厅, *qǐ shì lín xī shì cāntīng*) & **Goubuli** (狗不理包子铺, *gǒu bùlǐ bāozi pù*) 333 Zhejiang Lu, just off Nanjing Lu, hidden behind the be-domed and be-columned concert hall. Formerly Austrian-owned, this restaurant has been around for nearly 100 years, and still serves Western food: breaded fish fillets, mashed potatoes, pasta and so forth. The beer hall and dining room on the top level is worth a stop, if only for their home-brewed dark beer. Across the road is a branch of Tianjin's famous *Gobuli* dumpling chain.

Yingwang Korean (英王韩国饭, *yīng wáng háng guó fàn*) Junction of Shandong Lu and Changchun Dao. One of a cluster of simple fastish-food restaurants around this junction. Spicy Korean standards for ¥20–30, a good option if browsing the market has worked up an appetite.

Listings

Airlines Air China (daily 8am–4.30pm; ⓣ022/83311666) is at 113 Nanjing Lu.

Banks and exchange The Bank of China (daily 8am–5pm) is at 80 Jiefang Bei Lu, on the corner of Datong Dao.

Mail The post office (daily 9am–6.30pm) is just east of Tianjin Station.

PSB 30 Tangshan Dao.

Shopping As well as the clothing and antique markets in the city centre, Tianjin is renowned for its handmade rugs and carpets, featuring bright, complex, abstract patterns. They're not cheap, and are best bought directly from the factories in the suburbs. Tianjin is also noted for its kites and its bright woodblock prints of domestic subjects, pinned up for good luck at Chinese New Year; the latter are made and sold at the Yangliuqing Picture Studio, which has an outlet on Ancient Culture St. **Travel agents** CITS (☎022/28358866 ext 102) is at 22 Youyi Lu, opposite the Friendship Store. They don't impart much information, but they will book train and boat tickets for onward travel. Closer to the centre, CYTS (☎022/23035678), on the fourth floor at 166 Xinhua Lu, are helpful and speak some English.

Beidaihe to Shanhaiguan

On the **Bohai Gulf**, 300km east of Beijing, lies the rather bizarre seaside resort of **Beidaihe**. The coastline, reminiscent of the Mediterranean – rocky, sparsely vegetated, erratically punctuated by beaches – was originally patronized a hundred years ago by European diplomats, missionaries and businessmen, who can only have chosen it out of homesickness. They built villas and bungalows here, and reclined on verandas sipping cocktails after indulging in the new bathing fad. After the Communist takeover, the village became a pleasure resort for Party bigwigs, reaching its height of popularity in the 1970s when seaside trips were no longer seen as decadent and revisionist. Though you'll still see serious men in uniforms and sunglasses licking ice creams, and black Audis with tinted windows (the current cadre car of choice) cruising the waterfront, most of Beidaihe's visitors nowadays are ordinary, fun-loving tourists, usually relatively well-heeled Beijingers. In high season (May–Aug), when the temperature is steady around the mid-20s Celsius and the water warm, it's a fun place to spend the day.

Only 25km or so to the northeast, **Shanhaiguan** makes a good base if you're touring the area – cheaper than Beidaihe, and with year-round appeal. The central area is small enough to walk around, and though the town is rapidly being redeveloped, it can still be a peaceful stop, particularly if you nab a room inside the city walls. The surrounding countryside contains some fine sturdy fortifications and remnants of the **Great Wall**.

This part of the Bohai Gulf is quickly and conveniently reached from Beijing on the express train service which calls most regularly at the travel hub **Qinhuangdao**. Midway between Beidaihe and Shanhaiguan, it's an industrial city and charmless modern port, but once here getting around is straightforward; see the relevant accounts below for arrival and information details. In the unlikely event you do get stuck in Qinhuangdao, you could do worse than stay at the *Haiyue Hotel* (海岳大厦, *hǎiyuè dàshà*; ☎0335/3065760; ⑤), 159 Yingbin Lu; walk south from the train station concourse and the hotel is on the west side of the road.

Beidaihe and around

It wasn't so long ago that **BEIDAIHE** (北戴河, *běidàihé*) had strict rules restricting where foreigners could bathe. West Beach was reserved for *waiguoren* after they were granted access in 1979, with guards posted to chase off Chinese voyeurs interested in glimpsing their daringly bourgeois swimming costumes; for visiting Chinese, dark swimsuits were compulsory to avoid the illusion of nudity. These days things have changed: skimpy bikinis are now de rigueur and the town is a fascinating mix of the austerely communist and the gaudy kitsch of any busy seaside resort. Some of the barriers remain though, with choice bits of the coastline reserved for party officials and those from the PLA lucky enough to be granted a holiday here – it can be a bemusing sight to see the colourful holidaying hordes crammed onto the sand cheek-by-jowl while, just a few metres away, a lone soldier sits under a canopy guarding a pristine stretch of smooth, golden – and deserted – beach.

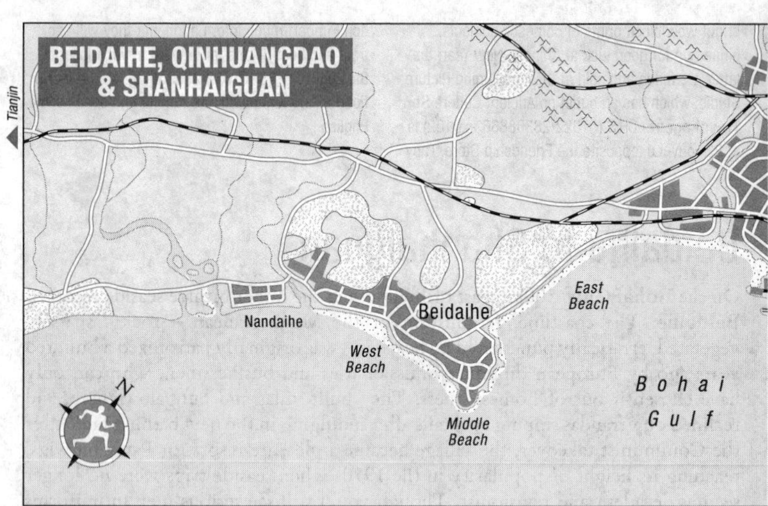

Arrival and information

Beidaihe's **train station** is inconveniently located 15km west of town; bus #5 (¥1) will take you from here into the centre – the bus leaves from a stop about 140m to the left out of the station. Any time you arrive, there'll be private minibuses and taxis waiting; bargain hard to get the fare down below ¥50. If you arrive in **Qinhuangdao** train station, you can either hop on one of the regular local trains to Beidaihe, or catch bus #34 (¥2) heading west from just outside the station square; at its terminus switch to a #33 which will take you into Beidaihe. The whole bus trip takes around forty minutes. A taxi is faster and will cost about ¥70. From Beidaihe's **bus station**, it's a fifteen-minute walk down to Middle Beach.

Taxis around town cost ¥10, but once at the beach Beidaihe is small enough to get around easily on foot. The Beidaihe **CITS** (Ⓣ0335/4041748) is at 4 Jinshanzui Lu, though those arriving by train will find it more convenient to use the tourist information booth at the station.

Accommodation

Beidaihe's **accommodation** is most in demand between May and August; although out of season room prices are often slashed by half, most of the budget hotels do not accept foreigners, making a summer stay in Beidaihe an expensive prospect. Popular with Russian tour groups, the *Diplomatic Missions Guesthouse* (外交人员宾馆, *wàijiāo rényuán bīnguǎn*; Ⓣ0335/4280600, Ⓦwww.bsbdm.com.cn; ⑧–⑨) at 1 Baosan Lu, is in a quiet street ten minutes' walk north of Middle Beach. It's a complex of villas set among gardens of cypress and pine, with a karaoke bar, a nightclub, a tennis court, a gym and a good outdoor restaurant featuring barbecues in the summer, and also has a new annexe on Haining Lu. Other foreigner-friendly options include *Tiger Rock* (老虎石宾馆, *lǎohǔ shí bīnguǎn*; Ⓣ0335/4682666; ⑥) and the *Jinhai* (金海宾馆, *jīnhǎi bīnguǎn*; Ⓣ0335/4030048, Ⓦwww.bdhmk.com; ⑤), both well located right next to the beach, if a little bland. Further away in a quiet cove on Zhonghaitan Lu is the *Jinshan* (金山宾馆, *jīnshān bīnguǎn*; Ⓣ0335/4041338; ⑥) a three-star complex with a pool.

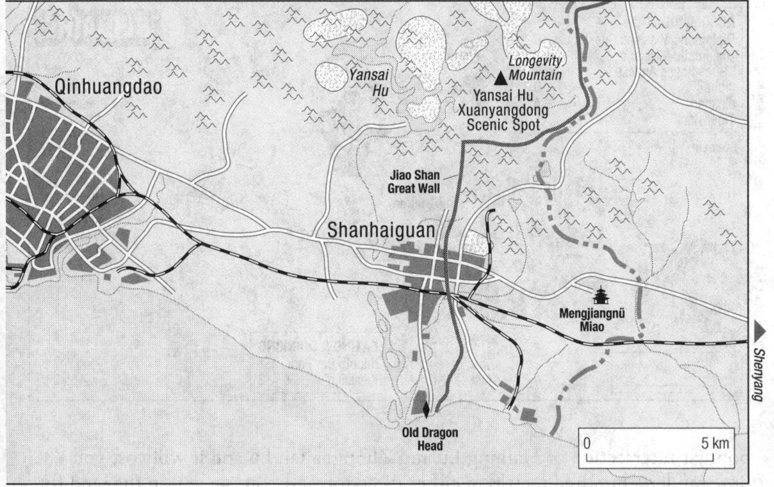

The Town

Much of Beidaihe shuts down during colder months; the streets along the seafront are at their liveliest from May to August – most buildings are either restaurants, with crabs and prawns bobbing about in buckets outside, or shops selling Day-Glo swimsuits, inflatables, snorkelling gear, souvenirs and a menagerie of animals tastefully sculpted from shells and raffia. The main streets of interest here are **Zhonghaitan Lu** running east–wast along the seafront, **Dongjing Lu** which runs parallel a few hundred metres back from the beach, and **Haining Lu** which runs north–south and intersects both. It's around these three that you'll find the busiest stretch of hotels, cafés and tourist shops. This central area has been given a colonial German facelift with older buildings restored and newer ones fitted out with timber-frame cladding – but the overall flavour is Sino-Russian, with signs in Cyrillic catering to the huge contingent of holiday-makers for whom Beidaihe represents a cheap break from Siberian climes.

Away from the sea, up the hill, the tree-lined streets are much quieter, and the majority of the town seems to consist of nondescript compounds hosting guest-houses, **villas** and sanatoriums, some open to paying guests and others set aside for the Party, PLA or state-run companies who reward favoured cadres/soldiers/workers with trips to the seaside. Rumour has it that every Politburo member once had a residence here, and many probably still do.

On the far western side of town, 500m back from the beach, **Lianfengshan Park** (联峰山公园, *liánfēngshān gōngyuán*) is a hill of dense pines with picturesque pavilions and odd little caves, a good place to wander and get away from the crowds for a while, and also a popular spot with birdwatchers. Atop the hill is the **Sea Admiring Pavilion**, which has good views of the coast. Also here is a quiet temple, **Guanyin Si**.

The beaches

On Beidaihe's three beaches, stirring revolutionary statues of lantern-jawed workers and their wives and children stand among the throngs of bathers. **Middle Beach** (中海滩, *zhōnghǎi tān*), really many small beaches with rocky outcrops in between, is the most convenient and popular. Enter the beach at the

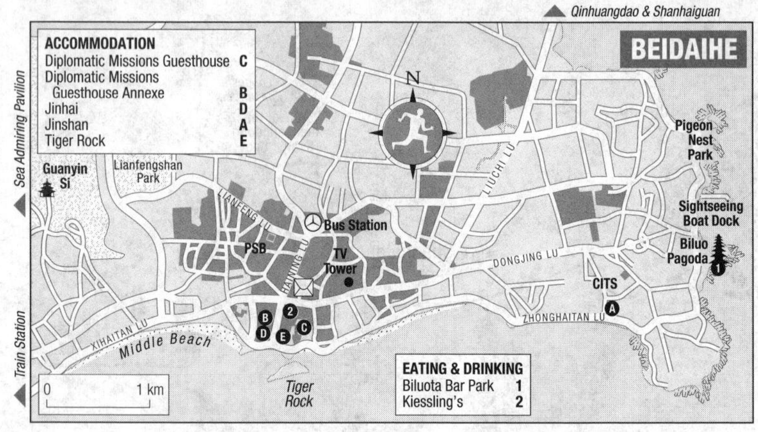

popular intersection of Haining Lu and Zhonghaitan Lu and it will cost you ¥8, but wander a hundred metres in either direction and you can get on the sand for free. The promenade at the back is much like any in the world, lined with seafood restaurants and soft-drink and ice-cream vendors. You can also hire bicycles here for up to three people on one machine (a thrandom?) at ¥20/30/40 per hour, depending on the number of saddles, plus ¥200 deposit. **West Beach** (西海滩, *xīhǎi tān*) is more of the same, but a little quieter. East of the resort, stretching 15km to Qinhuangdao, is **East Beach** (东海滩, *dōnghǎi tān*; take bus #1 or #34), popular with cadres and sanatorium patients for its more sedate atmosphere. The beach is long enough for you to be able to find a spot where you can be alone, though much of the muddy shoreline isn't very attractive. At low tide its wide expanse is dotted with seaweed collectors in rubber boots.

At the southern tip of East Beach is Pigeon Nest or **Geziwo Park** (鸽子窝公园, *gēzǐwō gōngyuán*; ¥12; bus #1, #34), a 20m-high rocky outcrop named for the seagulls fond of perching here, presumably by someone who wasn't skilled in bird identification. It's a popular spot for watching the sunrise. Mao sat here in 1954 and wrote a poem, "Ripples sifting sand/Beidaihe", which probably loses something in translation. Just before Pigeon Nest Park, the bus stops near the dock for Beidaihe's **sightseeing boats**, which in season leave regularly during the day to chug up and down the somewhat underwhelming coast (1hr; ¥32).

Eating and drinking

Foodwise, Beidaihe is noted for its crab, cuttlefish and scallops. Try one of the innumerable small **seafood** places on Haining Lu, where you order by pointing to the tastiest looking thing scuttling or slithering around the bucket, or *Kiessling's* (起士林西式餐厅, *qǐ shì lín xī shì cāntīng*), on Dongjing Lu near the *Diplomatic Missions Guesthouse*. Originally Austrian, this restaurant has been serving the foreign community for most of the last century and is now part of a larger hotel complex – look for the gateway with a large "K" at the top. The reasonably priced menu has a fair Western selection, though tends towards borscht rather than burgers, and you'll have more to choose from if you read Russian. The café out front is probably the best place in town for breakfast, offering good pastries and bread.

For nightlife, the *Biluota Bar Park* (碧螺塔酒吧公园, *bì luó tǎ jiǔbā gōngyuán*; ¥30 entry) based around a modern pagoda resembling the inside of a seashell, is trying hard to market itself as the place to go out, but a couple of beers in one of the restaurants along the beachfront in town would probably be more fun.

Around Beidaihe

Justifiably popular with birdwatchers, the countryside around Beidaihe – a stopping-off point for Siberian and red-crowned cranes migrating to Dongbei in May – has been designated a **nature reserve**; the Beidaihe CITS is a useful point of contact for the ornithologically minded.

Fifteen kilometres west along the coast, **NANDAIHE** (南戴河, *nándàihé*) is a tourist resort constructed to take advantage of Beidaihe's popularity. With 3km of beach and a few parks and viewpoints, it's the same sort of thing as Beidaihe but more regimented and artificial; frequent minibuses come here from the Beidaihe bus station. The main attraction in Nandaihe is **Golden Beach** (¥100) to the west, where you can go "sand sliding" down the steep dunes on a rented sledge – great fun, but remember to keep your feet and elbows up. Foreigners can stay here at the *Nandaihe Beach House* resort complex (Ⓣ0335/4050292, Ⓦwww.ndh.com.cn; ❺).

Shanhaiguan and beyond

A town at the northern tip of the Bohai Gulf, **SHANHAIGUAN** (山海关, *shānhǎiguān*) "the Pass Between the Mountains and the Sea", was originally built during the Ming dynasty as a fortress to defend the eastern end of the **Great Wall**. The wall crosses the Yanshan mountains to the north, forms the east wall of the town and meets the sea a few kilometres to the south. Far from being a solitary castle, Shanhaiguan originally formed the centre of a network of defences: smaller forts, now nothing but ruins, existed to the north, south and east, and beacon towers were dotted around the mountains. The town's obvious tourist potential is now being tapped, and extensive demolition and reconstruction continues within the city walls as the tide of tourist buses visiting the town grows ever larger. It's obvious not much money has made its way into the town outside the battlements, and aside from the reconstructed streets (now given over to tourist shops and restaurants) the *hutongs* of the old town are squalid and crumbling. That said, the odd courtyarded gem makes Shanhaiguan a good place to explore on foot and an excellent base for visiting the Great Wall sites of **Lao Long Tou** and **Jiao Shan.**

Local buses from Qinhuangdao run along Guancheng Nan Lu, with a stop just outside the southern city gate, while the **train station** is a few hundred metres south of the city wall.

Accommodation

Frustratingly for budget travellers, **accommodation** options for foreigners are limited to the more expensive end of the market; at time of writing only one hotel inside the city walls accepted non-Chinese-ID holders. The palatial *A Jingshan Hotel* (京山宾馆, *jīngshān bīnguǎn*; Ⓣ0335/5132188; ❹) was built to imitate a Qing mansion, with high ceilings, decorative friezes, curling roofs and red-brick walls and balconies, and, especially considering its monopoly, is remarkably good value. **Outside the city wall**, budget hotels line the street running up from the train station, all of which are unfortunately off limits, but it may be worth enquiring just in case rules change. The only other option is the *Boyi Business Hotel* (博逸酒店, *bóyì jiǔdiàn*; Ⓣ0335/5139888; ❺) at 107 Guancheng Nanlu, a smart if characterless place to stay.

The Town

Shanhaiguan is still arranged along its original plan of straight boulevards following the points of a compass, intersected with a web of alleys. Dominating the town is a fortified gatehouse in the east wall, the **First Pass Under Heaven** (天下第一关, *tiānxiàdìyī gūan*), which for centuries was the entrance to the Middle

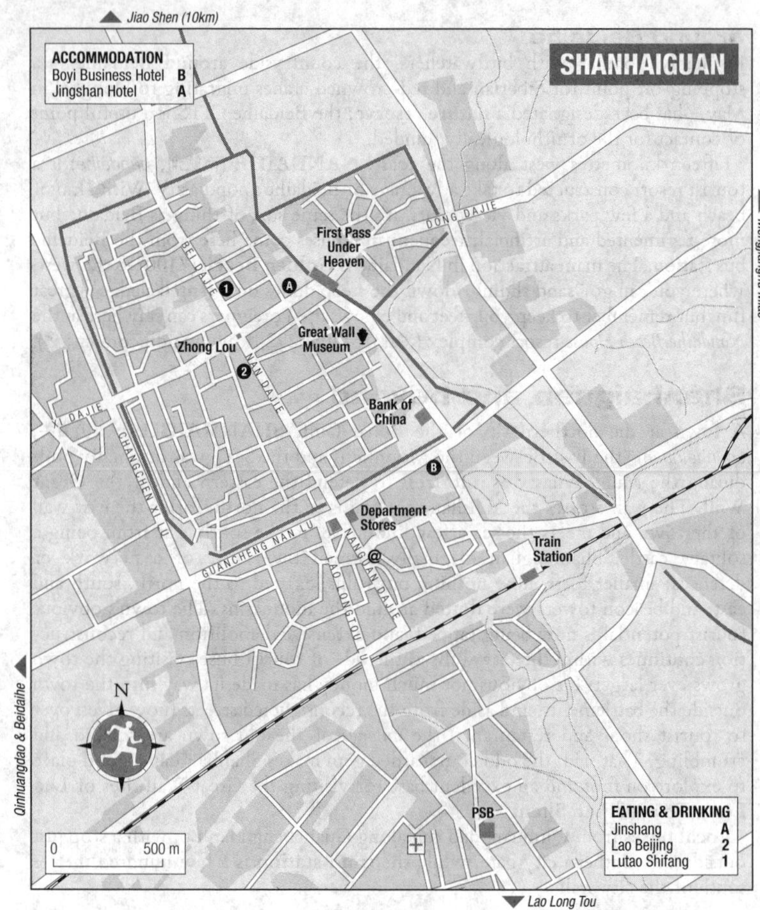

Kingdom from the barbarian lands beyond. An arch topped by a two-storey tower, the gate makes the surrounding buildings look puny and it must have looked even more formidable when it was built in 1381, with a wooden drawbridge over a moat 18m wide, and three outer walls for added defensive strength. The arch remained China's northernmost entrance until 1644, when it was breached by the Manchus.

These days, the gate is overrun by hordes of marauding tourists, and is at its best in the early morning before most of them arrive. The gate's name is emblazoned in red above the archway, calligraphy attributed to Xiao Xian, a Ming-dynasty scholar who lived in the town. A steep set of steps leads up from Dong Dajie to the impressively thick wall, nearly 30m wide. The tower on top, a two-storey, 10m-high building with arrow slits regularly spaced along its walls, is now a **museum** containing weapons, armour and costumes, as well as pictures of the nobility, who are so formally dressed they look like puppets. It's possible to stroll a little way along the wall in either direction; the wall is scattered with pay-per-view telescope and binocular stands, which afford a view of tourists on the Great Wall at Jiao Shan several kilometres to the north (see p.158), where the wall zigzags and dips along vertiginous peaks before disappearing over the horizon. A sliding scale of **multitickets** to visit the gate and Shanghaiguan's other attractions ranges from ¥40 for the First Pass Under Heaven alone to ¥100 for this and six other sights, including the museum and the Drum Tower. There's plenty of tat for sale at the wall's base, including decorated chopsticks, hologram medallions and jade curios, while in a courtyard to the northern side, a statue of Xu Da, the first general to rule the fort, frowns sternly down on the scene.

Follow the city wall south from the gate and you come to the **Great Wall Museum** (长城博物馆, *chángchéng bówùguǎn*; daily 8am–4pm). A modern, imitation Qing building, it has eight halls showcasing the history of the region in chronological order from Neolithic times; photographs of visiting presidents and secretary-generals show what a tourist draw the town has become. In addition to the tools used to build the wall, the vicious weaponry used to defend and attack it is also on display, including mock-ups of siege machines and broadswords that look too big to carry, let alone wield. The last three rooms contain dioramas, plans and photographs of local historic buildings. Inside the final room is a model of the area as it looked in Ming times, giving an idea of the extent of the defences, with many small outposts and fortifications in the district around. It's much better than any CITS map or glossy brochure and should inspire exploration into the surrounding countryside.

Eating

For **food**, the *Jingshan*'s fancy restaurant serves up huge dishes at reasonable prices, and has an English-language menu. For cheap eats and those arriving by train, the street running between the station and the city wall is packed with simple canteens; in the old town there are several restaurants along the main street including the standard *Lao Beijing* (老北京, *lǎo Běijīng*) and friendly *Lutao Shifang* (禄涛食坊, *lù tāo shí fāng*).

The Great Wall beyond Shanhaiguan

You'll see plenty of tourist **minibuses** grouped around the major crossroads in town and at the station, all serving the sights outside Shanhaiguan. Public **buses** also travel these routes, but if you have the time you're best off travelling by **bike**: the roads are quiet, the surrounding countryside is strikingly attractive and there are any number of pretty places off the beaten track where you can escape the crowds.

Intrepid hikers could try and make it to **Yansai Hu** (燕塞湖, *yànsài hú*), a lake in the mountains directly north of Shanhaiguan, or to **Longevity Mountain** (长寿山, *chángshòu shān*), a hill of rugged stones east of the lake, where many of the rocks have been carved with the character *shou* (longevity). There's also a mountain pool here, a good place for a quiet swim.

Lao Long Tou

Follow the remains of the Great Wall south and after 4km you'll reach **Lao Long Tou** (老龙头, *lǎolóng tóu*; Old Dragon Head, after a large stone dragon's head that used to look out to sea here; daily 7.30am–5pm; ¥50), the point at which the wall hits the coast – literally jutting out into the water. Bus #24 heads here from Lao Longtou Lu, near Shanhaiguan's train station. A miniature fortress with a two-storey temple in the centre stands right at the end of the wall. Unfortunately everything here has been so reconstructed it all looks brand new, and is surrounded by a rash of tourist development. The rather dirty beaches either side of the wall are popular bathing spots.

Walk for a few minutes past the restaurants west of Lao Long Tou and you'll come to the old British Army **barracks**, on the right; this was the beachhead for the Eight

Allied Forces in 1900, when they came ashore to put down the Boxers. A plaque here reminds visitors to "never forget the national humiliation and invigorate the Chinese nation". Do your part by taking care not to trample the lawn.

Mengjiangnü Miao

Some 6.5km northeast of town is **Mengjiangnü Miao** (孟姜女庙, *mèngjiāngnǚ miào*; daily 7.30am–5pm; ¥25), a temple dedicated to a legendary woman whose husband was press-ganged into one of the Great Wall construction squads. He died from exhaustion, and she set out to search for his body to give him a decent burial, weeping as she walked along the wall. So great was her grief, it is said, that the wall crumbled in sympathy, revealing the bones of her husband and many others who had died in its construction. The temple is small and elegant, with good views of the mountains and the sea. Statues of the lady herself and her attendants sit looking rather prim inside. To get here, take bus #23 from outside Shanhaiguan's south gate.

Jiao Shan

A couple of kilometres to the north of Shanhaiguan, it's possible to hike along the worn remains of the Great Wall all the way to the mountains. Head north along Bei Dajie and out of town, and after about 10km you'll come to a reconstructed section known as **Jiao Shan** (角山, *jiăo shān*; daily 8am–4pm; ¥30), passing the ruins of two forts – stone foundations and earthen humps – along the way. A steep path from the reconstructed section takes you through some dramatic scenery into the Yunshan mountains, or you can cheat and take the cable car (¥30 one-way, ¥50 return).

The further along the wall you go the better it gets – the crowds peter out, the views become more dramatic, and once the reconstructed section ends, you're left standing beside – or on top of – the real, crumbly thing. Head a few kilometres further east and you'll discover a trio of passes in the wall, and a beacon tower that's still in good condition. You can keep going into the mountains for as long as you like, so it's worth getting here early and making a day of it. A pedicab or taxi back into town from Jiao Shan's car park costs ¥5.

Chengde

CHENGDE (承德, *chéngdé*), a country town 250km northeast of Beijing, sits in a river basin on the west bank of the Wulie River, surrounded by the Yunshan mountain range. It's a quiet, unimportant place, rather bland in appearance, but on its outskirts are some of the most magnificent examples of imperial architecture in China, remnants from its glory days as the **summer retreat** of the Manchu emperors. Gorgeous temples punctuate the cabbage fields around town, and a palace-and-park hill complex, **Bishu Shanzhuang**, covers an area nearly as large as the town itself. In recent years Chengde has once more become a summer haven, justly popular with weekending Beijingers escaping the capital.

Some history

Originally called "Rehe", the town was discovered by the Qing-dynasty emperor **Kangxi** at the end of the seventeenth century, while marching his troops to the Mulan hunting range to the north. He was attracted to the cool summer climate and the rugged landscape, and built small lodges here from which he could indulge in a fantasy Manchu lifestyle, hunting and hiking like his northern ancestors. The building programme expanded when it became diplomatically useful to spend time north of Beijing, forging closer links with the troublesome Mongol tribes. Chengde was a thoroughly pragmatic creation, devised as an effective means of defending the empire by overawing Mongol princes with splendid audiences, hunting parties and impressive military manoeuvres.

Construction of the first palaces started in 1703. By 1711 there were 36 palaces, temples, monasteries and pagodas set in a great walled park, its ornamental pools and islands dotted with beautiful pavilions and linked by bridges. Craftsmen from all parts of China were invited to work on the project; Kangxi's grandson, **Qianlong** (1736–96), added another 36 imperial buildings during his reign, which was considered to be the heyday of Chengde.

In 1786, the **Panchen Lama** was summoned from Tibet by Qianlong for his birthday celebrations. This was an adroit political move to impress the followers of Lamaist Buddhism. The Buddhists included a number of minority groups who were prominent thorns in the emperor's side, such as Tibetans, Mongols, Torguts, Eleuths, Djungars and Kalmucks. Some accounts (notably not Chinese) tell how Qianlong invited the Panchen Lama to sit with him on the Dragon Throne, which was taken to Chengde for the summer season. He was certainly feted with honours and bestowed with costly gifts and titles, but the greatest impression on him and his followers must have been made by the replicas of the Potala and of his own palace, constructed at Chengde to make him feel at home – a munificent gesture, and one that would not have been lost on the Lamaists. However, the Panchen Lama's visit ended questionably when he succumbed to smallpox, or possibly poison, in Beijing and his coffin was returned to Tibet with a stupendous funeral cortege.

The first **British Embassy** to China, under Lord Macartney, visited Qianlong's court in 1793. Having sailed up the river to Beijing in a ship whose sails were painted with characters reading "Tribute bearers from the vassal king of England", they were somewhat disgruntled to discover that the emperor had decamped to Chengde for the summer. However, they made the 150km journey there, in impractical European carriages, where they were well received by the emperor, though the visit was hardly a success. Macartney caused an initial stir by refusing to kowtow, while Qianlong was disappointed with the gifts the British had brought and, with Manchu power at its height, rebuffed all British trade demands, remarking: "We possess all things. I set no value on objects strange or ingenious, and have no use for your country's manufactures." His letter to the British monarch concluded, magnificently, "O king, Tremblingly Obey and Show No Negligence!"

Chengde gradually lost imperial popularity when it came to be seen as unlucky after emperors Jiaqing and Xianfeng died here in 1820 and 1860 respectively. The buildings were left empty and neglected for most of the twentieth century, but largely escaped the ravages of the Cultural Revolution. Restoration, in the interests of tourism, began in the 1980s and is ongoing.

Arrival and information

From Beijing, reaching Chengde takes more than four hours on even the fastest trains, chugging through the rolling countryside around the Great Wall before arriving at the **train station** in the south of town. By bus the scenery is similarly spectacular and takes about the same amount of time, though you run greater risk of traffic and weather delays. Buses to and from Beijing (¥70 from Beijing Train Station) terminate just outside the *Yunshan Hotel*. Onward tickets and tours can be booked from **CITS** on Lizhengmen Dajie (Ⓣ0314/2027483), but similar services are available at most hotels.

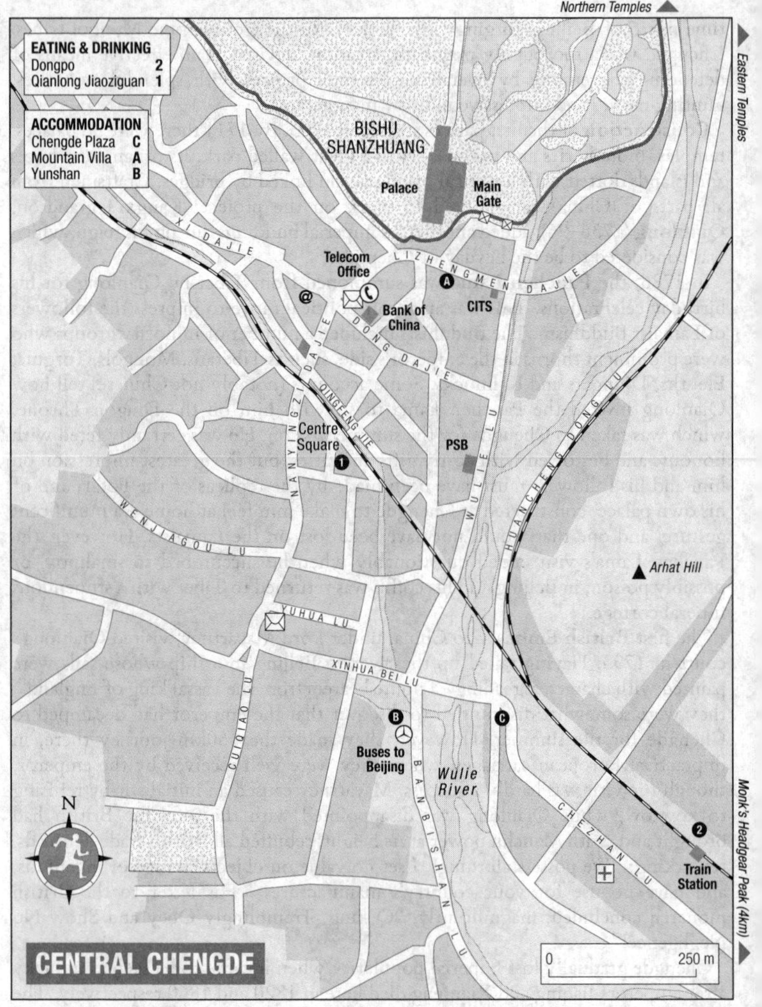

City transport

Getting around Chengde by public transport isn't easy, as **local buses** are infrequent and always crammed. Buses #5 and #11, which go from the train station to the mountain resort, Bishu Shanzhuang (避暑山庄, *bishŭ shānzhuāng*), and bus #6, from the resort to the Puning Si (普宁寺, *pŭníng si*; see p.164), are the most useful. **Taxis** are easy to find, but the drivers are often unwilling to use their meters – a ride around town shouldn't cost more than ¥10. At peak hours during the summer the main streets are so congested that it's quicker to walk, and the town is just about small enough to cover on foot.

Probably the best way to see everything in a short time is to take a minibus or a bike around the temples one day and explore the mountain resort the next - you can charter a taxi or a minibus for around ¥200 a day (bargain hard) and create your own itinerary. Bikes are available for rent from the *Mountain Villa Hotel*, hotels will be able to help with chartering a minibus and if you only need a taxi, flag one down and haggle.

Accommodation

There are plenty of **hotels** in Chengde town itself, plus a couple of expensive places inside Bishu Shanzhuang. Unfortunately, as with elsewhere in Hebei, strict enforcement of local government rules means foreigners are barred from cheaper accommodation. On the plus side, rates at approved hotels are highly negotiable and off-peak discounts of up to two-thirds are available.

Chengde Plaza (承德大厦, *chéngdé dàshà*) Chezhan Lu ⓣ0314/2088808. This hugely ugly fifteen-storey concrete block is convenient for the station, but in an uninteresting area of town. Rooms are smart and clean if a little over-fussy. The best thing about staying here is that, once inside, you no longer have to look at the outside of it. ❺

Mountain Villa (山庄宾馆, *shānzhuāng bīnguǎn*) 127 Xiaonanmen (entrance on Lizhengmen Dajie) ⓣ0314/2025588. This grand, well-located complex has huge rooms, high ceilings and a cavernous, gleaming lobby, and is extremely popular with tour groups. The large rooms in the main building are nicer but a little more expensive than those in the ugly building round the back, and there are some very cheap rooms in the basement. Buses #5 or #11 from the train station will get you here. ❹–❼

Qiwanglou (倚望楼宾馆, *yǐwànglóu bīnguǎn*) Around the corner and uphill from the Bishu Shanzhuang main entrance ⓣ0314/2024385. A well-run hotel in a pleasing imitation Qing-style building, and the grounds make for an interesting walk even if you're not staying here. ❺

Shang Ke Tang (上客堂宾馆, *shàng kè táng bīnguǎn*) Puning Si ⓣ0314/2058888. This interesting hotel's staff wear period clothing and braided wigs befitting the adjoining Puning temple, and glide along the dim bowels of the complex to lead you to appealingly rustic rooms. ❺

Yunshan (云山饭店, *yún shān fàndiàn*) 2 Banbishan Lu ⓣ0314/2055588. This modern block was once popular with tour groups, before being trumped by the *Mountain Villa*. The second-floor restaurant is good, the plushest in town, and not too expensive. A 10min walk from the train station. ❼

The Town

Bishu Shanzhuang lies in the north of the town, while farther north and to the east, on the other side of the river, stand Chengde's eight imposing **temples**. The majority of Chengde's one-million-strong population live in a semi-rural suburban sprawl to the south of the centre, leaving the city itself fairly small-scale – its new high-rises yet to obscure the view of distant mountains and fields. However, hundreds of thousands of visitors come here each year, and on summer weekends in particular, the town can be packed with tourists, its main artery, **Nanyingzi Dajie**, clogged with traffic. The street is much more pleasant in the evening, when a **night market** stretches all the way down it. In addition to snacks, many vendors sell antiques and curios that are generally cheaper than in Beijing or Tianjin, but you'll have to bargain hard and don't expect everything to be genuine.

Bishu Shanzhuang

Surrounded by a 10km-long wall and larger than the Summer Palace in Beijing, **Bishu Shanzhuang** (避暑山庄, *bìshǔ shānzhuāng*; also referred to as the Mountain Resort; daily 8am–5.30pm; April 16–Oct 15 ¥120, Oct 16–April 15 ¥90; combined ticket for the park and the palace) occupies the northern third of the town's area. This is where, in the summer months, the Qing emperors lived, feasted, hunted, and occasionally dealt with affairs of state. The palace buildings just inside the main entrance are unusual for imperial China as they are low, wooden and unpainted – simple but elegant, in contrast to the opulence and

grandeur of Beijing's palaces. It's said that Emperor Kangxi wanted the complex to mimic a Manchurian village, to show his disdain for fame and wealth, though with 120 rooms and several thousand servants he wasn't exactly roughing it. The same principle of idealized naturalness governed the design of the park. With its twisting paths and streams, rockeries and hills, it's a fantasy re-creation of the rough northern terrain and southern Chinese beauty spots that the emperors would have seen on their tours. The whole is an attempt to combine water, buildings and plants in graceful harmony. Lord Macartney noted its similarity to the "soft beauties" of an English manor park of the Romantic style.

Covering the whole park and its buildings takes at least a day, and an early start is recommended. It's at its nicest in the early morning anyway, when a vegetable market sets up just outside the front gate, and old people practise *tai ji* or play Go by the palace. The park is simply too big to get overcrowded, and if you head north beyond the lakes, you're likely to find yourself alone.

The palace

The **main gate**, Lizhengmen, is in the south wall, off Lizhengmen Dajie. The **palace quarter**, just inside the complex to the west of the main gate, is built on a slope, facing south, and consists of four groups of dark wooden buildings spread over an area of 100,000 square metres. The first, southernmost group, the Front Palace, where the emperors lived and worked, is the most interesting, as many of the rooms have been restored to their full Qing elegance, decked out with graceful furniture and ornaments. Even the everyday objects are impressive: brushes and ink stones on desks, ornate fly whisks on the arms of chairs, little jade trees on shelves. Other rooms house displays of ceramics, books and exotic martial-art weaponry. The Qing emperors were fine calligraphers, and examples of their work appear throughout the palace.

There are 26 buildings in this group, arranged south to north in nine successive compounds, which correspond to the nine levels of heaven. The main gate leads into the **Outer Wumen**, where high-ranking officials waited for a single peal of a large bell, indicating that the emperor was ready to receive them. Next is the **Inner Wumen**, where the emperor would watch his officers practise their archery. Directly behind, the **Hall of Frugality and Sincerity** is a dark, well-appointed room made of cedarwood, imported at great expense from south of the Yangzi River by Qianlong, who had none of his grandfather Kangxi's scruples about conspicuous consumption. Topped with a curved roof, the hall has nine bays, and patterns on the walls include symbols of longevity and good luck. The **Four Knowledge Study Room**, behind, was where the emperor worked, changed his clothes and rested. A vertical scroll on the wall outlines the knowledge required of a gentleman: he must be aware of what is small, obvious, soft and strong.

The main building in the **Rear Palace** is the **Hall of Refreshing Mists and Waves**, the living quarters of the imperial family, and beautifully turned out in period style. It was in the west room here that Emperor Xianfeng signed the humiliating Beijing Treaty in the 1850s, giving away more of China's sovereignty and territory after their defeat in the Second Opium War. The **Western Apartments** are where the notorious Cixi, better known as the Dowager Empress (see p.115), lived when she was one of Xianfeng's concubines. A door connects the apartments to the hall, and it was through here that she eavesdropped on the dying emperor's last words of advice to his ministers, intelligence she used to force herself into power.

The other two complexes are much smaller. The **Pine and Crane Residence**, a group of buildings parallel to the front gate, is a more subdued version of the Front Palace, home to the emperor's mother and his concubines. In the **Myriad Valleys of Rustling Pine Trees**, to the north of here, Emperor Kangxi read books and granted audiences, and Qianlong studied as a child. The group of structures southwest of the main palace is the **Ahgesuo**, where male descendants of the royal family studied during the Manchurian rule; lessons began at 5am and finished at noon. A boy was expected to speak Manchu at 6, Chinese at 12, be competent with a bow by the age of 14 and marry at 16.

The grounds

The best way to get around the **lake area** of the park – a network of pavilions, bridges, lakes and waterways – is to rent a **rowing boat** (¥10–50/hr). Much of the architecture here is a direct copy of southern Chinese buildings. In the east, the **Golden Hill**, a cluster of buildings grouped on a small island, is notable for a hall and tower modelled after the Golden Hill Monastery in Zhenjiang, Jiangsu Province. The **Island of Midnight and Murmuring Streams**, roughly in the centre of the lake, holds a three-courtyard compound which was used by Kangxi and Qianlong as a retreat, while the compound of halls, towers and pavilions on **Ruyi Island**, the largest, was where Kangxi dealt with affairs of state before the palace was completed.

Just beyond the lake area, on the western side of the park, is the grey-tiled **Wenjinge**, or Knowledge Imparting Library, surrounded by rockeries and pools for fire protection. From the outside, the structure appears to have two storeys. In fact there are three – a central section is windowless to protect the books from the sun. Sadly, the building is closed to the public.

A vast expanse of **grassland** extends from the north of the lake area to the foothills of the mountains, comprising Wanshun Wan (Garden of Ten Thousand Trees) and Shima Da (Horse Testing Ground).

The hilly area in the northwest of the park has a number of rocky valleys, gorges and gullies with a few tastefully placed lodges and pagodas. The deer, which graze on tourist handouts, were reintroduced after being wiped out by imperial hunting expeditions.

The temples and Sledgehammer Rock

The **temples** (daily 8am–5.30pm) in the foothills of the mountains around Chengde were built in the architectural styles of different ethnic nationalities, so that wandering among them is rather like being in a religious theme park. This isn't far from the original intention, as they were constructed less to express religious sentiment than as a way of showing off imperial magnificence, and also to make envoys from anywhere in the empire feel more at home. Though varying in design, all the temples share **Lamaist features** – Qianlong found it politically expedient to promote Tibetan and Mongolian Lamaism as a way of keeping these troublesome minorities in line. The temples are now in varying states of repair, having been left untended for decades. Originally there were twelve, but two have been destroyed and another two are dilapidated.

The best way to see the temples is to **rent a bicycle** (ask at your hotel; the *Qiwanglou* and *Mountain Villa* have bikes to rent): the roads outside the town are quiet, it's hard to get lost and you can dodge the tour groups. A good itinerary is to see the northern cluster in the morning, return to town for lunch (it's impossible to cross the river to the eastern temples from outside town) and in the afternoon, head for the Pule Si and **Sledgehammer Rock**, a bizarre protuberance that dominates the eastern horizon of the town. Before you head back to the centre, you can check out the small, peaceful Anyuan and Puren temples.

The northern temples

Just beyond the northern border of Bishu Shanzhuang are five temples that were once part of a string of nine. Three of these deserve special attention but the **Puning Si** (普宁寺, *pǔníng sì*; Temple of Universal Peace; April 1–Oct 31 ¥80; Nov 1–March 31 ¥60; joint ticket includes Puning Si and Puyou Si) is a must, if only for the awe-inspiring statue of Guanyin, the largest wooden statue in the world. This is the only working temple in Chengde, with shaven-headed Mongolian monks manning the altars and trinket stalls, though the atmosphere is not especially spiritual – it's usually clamorous with day-trippers, some of whom take outrageous liberties, judging by the sign that says "No shooting birds in the temple area". There are rumours the monks are really paid government employees working for the tourist industry, though the vehemence with which they defend their prayer mats and gongs from romping children suggests otherwise.

The Puning Si was built in 1755 to commemorate the Qing victory over Mongolian rebels at Junggar in northwest China, and is based on the oldest Tibetan temple, the Samye. Like traditional Tibetan buildings, it lies on the slope of a mountain facing south. In the **Hall of Heavenly Kings**, the statue of a fat, grinning monk holding a bag depicts Qi Ci, a tenth-century character with a jovial disposition, believed to be a reincarnation of the Buddha. In the **East Hall**, the central statue, flanked by *arhats*, depicts Ji Gong, a Song-dynasty monk who was nicknamed Crazy Ji for eating meat and being almost always drunk, but who was much respected for his kindness to the poor.

The rear section of the temple, separated from the front by a wall, comprises 27 Tibetan-style rooms laid out symmetrically, with the **Mahayana Hall** in the centre. Some of the buildings are actually solid (the doors are false), suggesting that the original architects were more concerned with appearances than function. The hall itself is dominated by the 23m-high wooden **statue of Guanyin**, the Goddess of Mercy. She has 42 arms with an eye in the centre of each palm, and three eyes on her face, which symbolize her ability to see into the past, present and future. The hall has two raised entrances, and it's worth looking at the statue from these upper viewpoints as they reveal new details, such as the eye sunk in her belly button, and the little Buddha sitting on top of her head.

On the thirteenth day of the first lunar month (Jan or Feb), the monks observe the ritual of **catching the ghost**, during which a ghost made of dough is placed on an iron rack while monks dressed in white dance around it, then divide it into pieces and burn it. The ritual is thought to be in honour of a ninth-century Tibetan Buddhist, Lhalung Oaldor, who assassinated a king who had ordered the destruction of Tibetan Buddhist temples, books and priests. The wily monk entered the palace on a white horse painted black, dressed in a white coat with a black lining. After killing the king, he washed the horse and turned the coat inside out, thus evading capture from the guards who did not recognize him.

The Xumifushouzhi Miao and Putuozongcheng Miao

Recently restored, the **Xumifushouzhi Miao** (须弥福寿之庙, *xūmífúshòu zhīmiào*; April 1–Oct 31 ¥80; Nov 1–March 31 ¥60; joint ticket includes Putuozongcheng Miao and Shuxiang Si), just southwest of Puning Si, was built in 1780 in Mongolian style for the ill-fated sixth Panchen Lama when he came to Beijing to pay his respects to the emperor (see p.159).

Next door to the Xumifushouzhi Miao, the magnificent **Putuozongcheng Miao** (普陀宗乘之庙, *pŭtuó zōngchéng zhīmiào*; Temple of Potaraka Doctrine) was built in 1771 and is based on the Potala Palace in Lhasa. Covering 220,000 square metres, it's the largest temple in Chengde, with sixty groups of halls, pagodas and terraces. The grand terrace forms a Tibetan-style facade screening a Chinese-style interior, although many of the windows on the terrace are fake, and some of the whitewashed buildings around the base are merely filled-in shapes. Inside, the West Hall is notable for holding a rather comical copper statue of the Propitious Heavenly Mother, a fearsome woman wearing a necklace of skulls and riding side-saddle on a mule. According to legend, she vowed to defeat the evil demon Raksaka, so she first lulled him into a false sense of security – by marrying him and bearing him two sons – then swallowed the moon and in the darkness crept up on him and turned him into a mule. The two dancing figures at her feet are her sons; their ugly features betray their paternity.

It's easy to walk or cycle between the two westernmost temples, and even on to Puning Si, though this last section is busy, tedious and best navigated by taxi. Between the first two, a west-to-east course is recommended – you'll see the temples on your left, the fortress on your right, and Sledgehammer Rock erect in the distance.

The eastern temples

The three **eastern temples** (8.30am–4.30pm; ¥50 joint ticket includes Pule Si, Anyuan Miao and Qingchuifeng Scenic Area) are easily accessible off a quiet road that passes through dusty, rambling settlements, 3km to 4km from the town centre. From Lizhengmen Dajie, cross over to the east bank of the river and head north.

The **Puren Si** (溥仁寺, *pŭrén sì*; Temple of Universal Benevolence) is the first you'll reach and the oldest in the complex, but is closed to tourists. It was built by Kangxi in 1713, as a sign of respect to the visiting Mongolian nobility, who came to congratulate the emperor on the occasion of his sixtieth birthday.

The **Pule Si** (普乐寺, *pŭlè sì*; Temple of Universal Happiness) farther north was built in 1766 by Qianlong as a place for Mongol envoys to worship, and its style is an odd mix of Han and Lamaist elements. The Lamaist back section, a triple-tiered terrace and hall, with a flamboyantly conical roof and lively, curved surfaces, steals the show from the more sober, squarer Han architecture at the front. The ceiling of the back hall is a wood-and-gold confection to rival the Temple of Heaven in Beijing. Glowing at its centre is a mandala of Samvara, a Tantric deity, in the form of a cross. The altar beneath holds a Buddha of Happiness, a life-size copper image of sexual congress; more cosmic sex is depicted in two beautiful mandalas hanging outside. Outside the temple, the view from the car park is spectacular, and just north is the path that leads to **Sledgehammer Rock** and the cable car.

The less interesting **Anyuan Miao** (安远庙, *ānyuǎn miào*; Temple of Appeasing the Borders) is the most northerly of the group. It was built in 1764 for a troop of Mongolian soldiers who were moved to Chengde by Qianlong, and has a delightful setting on the tree-lined east bank of the Wulie River.

Sledgehammer Rock and beyond

Of the scenic areas around Chengde, the one that inspires the most curiosity is **Sledgehammer Rock** (棒锤山, *bàngzhōng shān*; ¥50). Thinner at the base than at the top, the towering column of rock is more than 20m high, and skirted by stalls selling little models and Sledgehammer Rock T-shirts. According to legend, the rock is a huge dragon's needle put there to plug a hole in the peak, which was letting the sea through. The rock's obviously phallic nature is tactfully not mentioned in tourist literature, but is acknowledged in local folklore – should the rock fall, it is said, it will have a disastrous effect on the virility of local men.

The rock is a couple of kilometres on foot from the Pule Si, or there's a **cable car** option (¥45), offering impressive views. On the south side of the rock, at the base of a cliff, is **Frog Crag** (蛤蟆石, *hámá shí*), a stone that vaguely resembles a sitting frog – the 2km walk here is pleasant, if the frog itself disappoints. Other rocky highlights within walking distance are **Arhat Hill** (罗汉山, *luóhàn shān*), on the eastern side of the river, meant to look like a reclining Buddha, and **Monk's Headgear Peak**, 4km south of town, the highest point in the area and best reached by bike – head south down Chezhan Lu.

Eating and drinking

Chengde is located in Hebei's most fertile area, which mainly produces maize and sorghum but also yields excellent local chestnuts, mushrooms and apricots. This fresh produce, plus the culinary legacy of the imperial cooks, means you can eat very well. The town is also noted for its wild game, particularly deer (*lurou*), hare (*yetou*) and pheasant (*shanji*), and its **medicinal juice drinks**: almond juice is said to be good for asthma; date and jujube juice for the stomach; and *jinlianhua* (golden lotus) juice for a sore throat. Local **cakes**, such as the glutinous Feng family cakes, once an imperial delicacy but now a casual snack, can be found in the stalls on Yuhua Lu and Qingfeng Jie.

There are plenty of **restaurants** catering to tourists on Lizhengmen Dajie, around the main entrance to Bishu Shanzhuang. The small places west of the *Mountain Villa* hotel are fine, if a little pricey, and lively on summer evenings, when rickety tables are put on the pavement outside. A meal for two should cost about ¥80, and plenty of diners stay on drinking well into the evening. The best *jiaozi* in town are served at *Qianlong Jiaoziguan* (乾隆饺子馆, *qiánlóng jiǎoziguǎn*), just off Centre Square, a park at the heart of the shopping district. Nearby, **Qingfeng Jie** is an old, charmingly seedy street of restaurants and salons, and is a great place to have a satisfying *shaguo* – a veggie claypot costs ¥6, a meat-based one ¥10.

Opposite the train station, the *Dongpo* (东坡, *dōngpō*) serves outstanding meals while, inside Bishu Shanzhuang itself, *Fangyuan Restaurant* (芳园居, *fāngyuánjū*) offers imperial cuisine, including such exotica as "Pingquan Frozen Rabbit".

Travel details

Trains

Beidaihe to: Beijing (15 daily; 2–5hr); Qinhuangdao (19 daily; 20min); Shanhaiguan (17 daily; 40min); Shenyang (17 daily; 2–7hr); Tianjin (15 daily; 3–4hr).
Chengde to: Beijing (6 daily; 4–6hr); Dandong (1 daily; 16hr); Shenyang (2 daily; 12–13hr).
Qinhuangdao to: Beidaihe (18 daily; 20min); Beijing (25 daily; 2hr–5hr 30min); Shanhaiguan (43 daily; 20min); Shenyang (41 daily; 2–7hr); Tianjin (frequent; 3hr–4hr 15min).
Shanhaiguan to: Beidaihe (frequent; 1hr); Beijing (frequent; 2hr 40min–5hr 40min); Qinhuangdao (frequent; 15min); Shenyang (frequent; 4hr–6hr 30min); Tianjin (43 daily; 2hr–5hr 30min).
Tianjin to: Beidaihe (20 daily; 2hr 30min–5hr); Beijing (76 daily; 30–90min); Guangzhou (3 daily; 25hr); Jilin (3 daily; 16hr); Qinhuangdao (44 daily; 2–5hr); Shanghai (10 daily; 9–17hr); Shanhaiguan (45 daily; 3–5hr); Xi'an (4 daily; 17–19hr).

Buses

Beidaihe to: Beijing (4hr); Qinhuangdao (20min); Shanhaiguan (40min); Tianjin (3hr 30min).
Chengde to: Beijing (4–5hr); Tianjin (4hr).
Qinhuangdao to: Beidaihe (20min); Beijing (5hr); Shanhaiguan (20min); Tianjin (4hr).
Shanhaiguan to: Beidaihe (40min); Beijing (5hr 20min); Qinhuangdao (20min); Tianjin (4hr 30min).
Tianjin to: Beidaihe (3hr 30min); Beijing (2hr); Chengde (4hr); Qinhuangdao (4hr); Shanhaiguan (4hr 20min).

Ferries

Tianjin (Tanggu) to: Dalian (March–Oct daily; rest of year every other day; 13–15hr); Inchon (South Korea; 2 weekly; 26hr); Kobe (Japan; weekly; 51hr).

Flights

Qinhuangdao to: Dalian (3 weekly; 1hr).
Tianjin to: Changsha (4 weekly; 1hr 40min); Chengdu (daily; 2hr 20min); Dalian (daily; 50min); Fuzhou (3 weekly; 3hr 50min); Guangzhou (4 daily; 3hr); Guilin (2 weekly; 4hr 30min); Haikou (daily; 3hr 15min); Hangzhou (5 weekly; 1hr 30min); Harbin (daily; 3hr); Hong Kong (daily; 3hr 15min); Kunming (8 weekly; 3hr 20min); Nanjing (daily; 1hr 40min); Ningbo (daily; 3hr 10min); Qingdao (daily; 1hr); Shanghai (daily; 1hr 45min); Shenyang (8 weekly; 1hr 20min); Shenzhen (daily; 2hr 45min); Taiyuan (daily; 1hr); Wuhan (7 weekly; 2hr 30min); Xiamen (5 weekly; 2hr 30min); Xi'an (daily; 2hr); Zhengzhou (daily; 1hr 10min).

CHAPTER 3 **Highlights**

* **The Imperial Palace, Shenyang** Pre-empting Beijing's Forbidden City, this was the historical seat of the Manchus before they seized the capital. See p.175
* **Old Yalu Bridge, Dandong** Walk halfway to North Korea on this structure, bombed by the US during the Korean War. See p.183
* **Puppet Emperor's Palace, Changchun** The second act of the "last emperor" Puyi's life was played out here, where he was installed by the Japanese as leader of Manchuria. See p.187
* **Changbai Shan** The northeast's loveliest nature reserve – see the crater lake and root around for wild ginseng, though beware of North Korean border guards. See p.189
* **Winter ice festivals** Most Manchurian metropolises have one, but Harbin's is the biggest and best, with illuminated ice sculptures that tower higher by the year. See p.196
* **Zhalong Nature Reserve** Birdwatchers flock to the reedy lakes west of Harbin, where the red-crowned crane and thousands of its cousins breed. See p.200

▲ Dandong residents practicing *tai ji*, with Old Yalu Bridge in the background

Dongbei

Dongbei (东北, *dōngběi*) – or, more evocatively, Manchuria – may well be the closest thing to the "real" China that visitors vainly seek in the well-travelled central and southern parts of the country. Not many foreign tourists get up to China's northernmost arm, however, due to its reputation as an inhospitable wasteland: "Although it is uncertain where God created paradise", wrote a French priest when he was here in 1846, "we can be sure he chose some other place than this." Yet, with its immense swaths of fertile fields and huge **mineral resources**, Dongbei is metaphorically a treasure house. Comprising **Liaoning**, **Jilin** and **Heilongjiang** provinces, it is economically and politically among the most important regions of China, and, for much of its history, the areas has been fiercely contested by Manchus, Nationalists, Russians, Japanese and Communists.

With 4000km of sensitive border territory alongside North Korea and Russia, Dongbei is one of China's most vulnerable regions strategically; as well, economic pressures have made it prone to internal unrest, with worker protests common and a widening gap between haves and have-nots that is threatening to become a chasm. In the heady days of a planned economy, Dongbei's state-owned enterprises produced more than a third of the country's heavy machinery, half its coal and oil and most of its automobiles and military equipment. Since market reforms, however, lay-offs have been brutal, with unofficial statistics suggesting fifty percent unemployment in some areas.

Tourism – what there is of it (a good portion of it is domestic) – has become the leading growth industry. The region is cashing in on its colourful history, seen most vividly in the preservation of long-ignored Russian and Japanese colonial architecture, some of which you can actually stay in. In Liaoning, the thriving port of **Dalian** sports cleaned-up beaches, a cliffside drive, and restored Russian and Japanese neighbourhoods. Dandong, the country's window on North Korea, features a promenade on the Yalu River and a fascinating Korean War museum. China's other Forbidden City – the restored **Manchu Imperial Palace** – and the tombs of the men who established the Qing dynasty draw tourists to Liaoning's otherwise bland capital, **Shenyang**. To the north in Jilin province, **Jilin city** is famed for the ice-coated trees that line its riverfront in winter, and ski resorts dot the outskirts of town. In the provincial capital, **Changchun**, the Puppet Emperor's Palace memorializes Puyi's reign as "emperor" of the Japanese state Manchukuo. Evidence of Heilongjiang province's border with Russia can be seen throughout its capital, **Harbin**: a restored central shopping district preserves the city's old architecture, while a museum set in an Orthodox cathedral ensures China's northernmost metropolis is known for more reasons than its world-famous Ice Festival. Beyond Harbin, Dongbei's northeast is little visited by Western tourists, with the main draw being the Zhalong Nature Reserve, near Qiqihar. If you're journeying any further, it's likely you'll be on the **Trans-Manchurian train** and on your way to Russia, via Hailar and Manzhouli, both in **Inner Mongolia** (see p.200 for more on sights there).

Visitors to these parts tend to come for quite specific reasons. Dongbei's **geography**, a terrain of fertile plains, rugged mountains and forests, is itself an attraction, and hikers and birdwatchers will both find places to indulge their passions. Although long derided by Han Chinese as "the land beyond the pale", the region "outside" the Great Wall is home to several protected reserves, most famously the mountainous **Changbai Shan Nature Reserve** in Jilin province near the Korean border, where a huge lake, Tian Chi, nestles in jaw-dropping

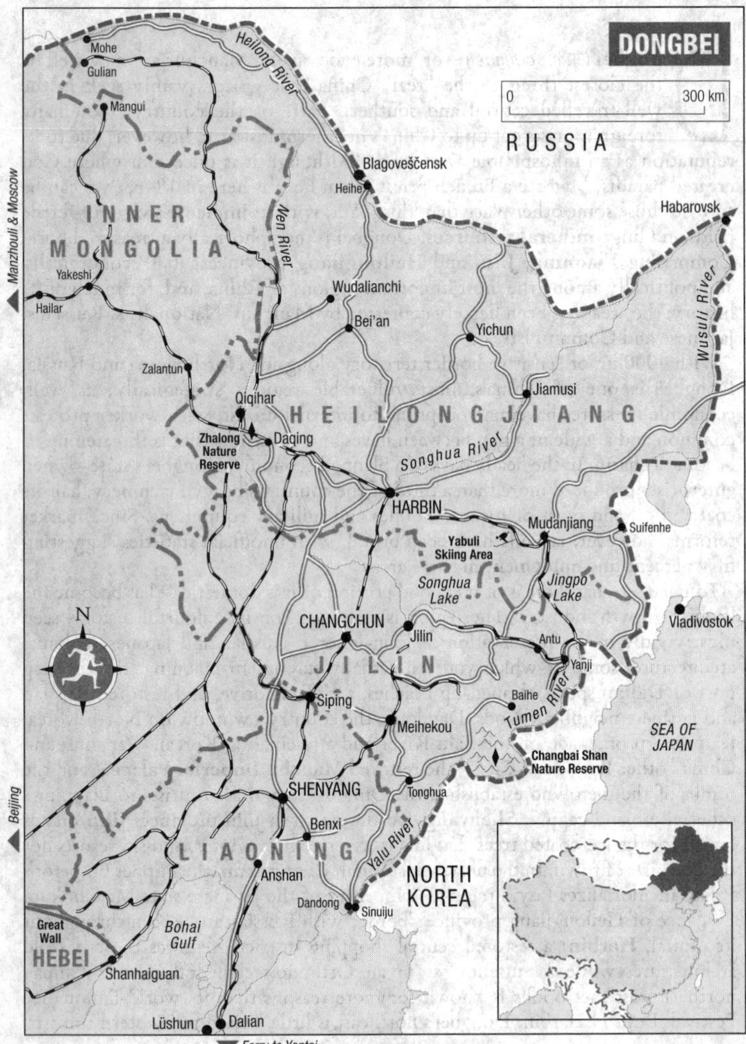

scenery. **Zhalong Nature Reserve**, in Heilongjiang, is a summer breeding ground for thousands of species of birds, including the rare red-crowned crane. Some visitors call in for **study** purposes, too. Foreign students find an environment free of thick accents – perfect for practising Chinese – and scholars of recent **Chinese history** couldn't choose a better place to explore: Dongbei's past one hundred years of domestic and international conflicts have heavily influenced the shape of the PRC today. Those interested in the **Russo-Japanese War** can follow the route of the Japanese advance from Port Arthur (now Lushun, near Dalian) to Mukden (today's Shenyang); check out *The Asian Writings of Jack London*, which contains the columns he wrote on assignment for the *San Francisco Examiner*, and *Thirty Years in Moukden* by Scottish missionary Dugald Christie. Puyi's autobiography, *From Emperor to Citizen*, lends insight to Manchukuo, and Ha Jin's *Ocean of Words* shows what life was like patrolling the Heilongjiang–Siberian border in the tense 1970s.

Dongbei's **climate** is one of extremes: in summer, it is hot, and in winter it is very, very cold, with temperatures as low as -30°C and howling Siberian gales. But there is skiing, sledding and skating all winter, plus January **ice festivals** in Jilin and Harbin.

Thanks to Dongbei's export-based economy, there's an efficient **rail system** between the cities and an extensive highway network. The region's **food** is heavily influenced by neighbouring countries, and every town has a cluster of Korean, Japanese and, up north, Russian restaurants. The specialities are also quite diverse, ranging from fresh crabs in Dalian and *luzi yu* river fish in Dandong to silkworms in the countryside (a mushy, pasty-tasting local delicacy).

Some history

The history of Manchuria proper begins with **Nurhaci**, a tribal leader who in the sixteenth century united the warring tribes of the northeast against the corrupt central rule of Ming-dynasty **Liaoning**. He introduced an **alphabet** based on the Mongol script, administered Manchu law and, by 1625, had created a firm and relatively autonomous government that was in constant confrontation with the Chinese. Subsequently, **Dorgun** was able to go a stage further, marching on Beijing with the help of the defeated Ming general Wu Sangui. In 1644, the **Qing dynasty** was proclaimed, and one of Nurhaci's grandsons, **Shunzhi**, became the first of a long line of Manchu emperors, with his uncle Dorgun as regent.

Keen to establish the Qing over the whole of China, the first **Manchu emperors** – Shunzhi, Kangxi and Qianlong – did their best to assimilate Chinese customs and ideas. They were, however, even more determined to protect their homeland, and so the whole of the northeast was closed to the rest of China. This way they could guard their monopoly on the valuable **ginseng trade** and keep the agricultural Han Chinese from ploughing up their land, a practice that often resulted in the desecration of the graves of the Manchus' ancestors. But isolationism was a policy that could not last forever, and the eighteenth century saw increasing migration into Manchuria. By 1878, these laws had been rescinded, and the Chinese were moving into the region by the million, escaping the flood-ravaged plains of the south for the fertile northeast.

All this time, Manchuria was much coveted by its neighbours. The **Sino-Japanese War** of 1894 left the Japanese occupying the Liaodong Peninsula in the south of Liaoning province, and the only way the Chinese could regain it was by turning to **Russia**, also hungry for influence in the area. The deal was that the Russians be allowed to build a **rail line** linking Vladivostok to the main body of Russia, an arrangement that in fact led to a gradual and, eventually, complete occupation of Manchuria by the imperial Russian armies. This was a bloody affair, marked by atrocities and brutal reprisals, and was followed in 1904 by a Japanese declaration of war in an attempt to usurp the Russians' privileges for themselves.

The **Russo-Japanese War** concluded in 1905 with a convincing Japanese victory, though Japan's designs on Manchuria didn't end there. The Japanese population doubled between 1872 and 1925, creating the perceived need to expand its territories; this, coupled with a disastrous economic situation at home and an extreme militaristic regime, led to their invasion of the region in 1932, establishing the puppet state of **Manchukuo**. This regime was characterized by horrific and violent oppression – not least the secret germ-warfare research centre in **Pingfang**, where experiments were conducted on live human subjects. Rice was reserved for the Japanese, and it was a crime for the locals to eat it. It was only with the establishment of a united front between the Communists and the Guomindang that Manchuria was finally rid of the Japanese, in 1945, although it was some time (and in spite of a vicious campaign backed by both Russia and the USA against the Communists) before Mao finally took control of the region.

Relations with **Russia** dominate recent history. In the brief romance between the two countries in the 1950s, Soviet experts helped the Chinese build efficient, well-designed factories and workshops in exchange for the region's agricultural products. These factories laid the foundation for China's automobile industry: the **First Automobile Works** (FAW) in Changchun, for example, began production then, and now has a joint venture with VW and Audi. In the 1960s, relations worsened, the Soviets withdrew their technical support and bitter **border disputes** erupted, notably around the Wusuli (Ussuri) River, where hundreds of Russian and Chinese troops died fighting over an insignificant island in the world's first military confrontation between communist states. An extensive network of nuclear shelters was constructed in northeastern cities. Following the collapse of the Soviet Union, military build-ups around the border areas and state paranoia have lessened, and the shelters have been turned into underground shopping malls. Russian faces can again be seen on the streets, often **traders**, legal and otherwise, buying up consumer goods to take over the border now that Russia's own manufacturing industry has almost collapsed.

Shenyang

SHENYANG (沈阳, *shěnyáng*), the capital of Liaoning province (辽宁, *liáoníng*) and unofficial capital of the northeast, is both a railway junction and banking centre that's served as host to the Manchus, Russians, Japanese, Nationalists and then Communists. An hour's flight from Beijing, the city likens itself to the capital; any cabbie here will delight in telling you that they have the only other Imperial Palace in China.

Shenyang does indeed resemble the capital, but only in its wide, characterless avenues walled by Soviet-style matchbox buildings and glassy towers. In fact, the most remarkable thing about Shenyang is that it isn't remarkable at all. All the ingredients for an interesting visit are here: China's other Forbidden City, constructed by Manchus before their takeover of the Ming dynasty; a stunning monument to Chairman Mao built during the frenzied height of the Cultural Revolution; the tombs of two former emperors; architecture left over from Japan's occupation, including one of China's loveliest hotels. The list goes on. And a list is what Shenyang feels like, a collection of curios out of context in their industrial surroundings, with little to detain you for more than a brief stop.

Though well known in China as an important power base for the more radical hardline factions in Chinese politics (Mao's nephew, Yuanxin, was deputy Party secretary here until he was thrown in jail in 1976), Shenyang had its real heyday in the early seventeenth century. Nurhaci declared the city (then known as Mukden) the first capital of the expanding Manchu empire. He died in 1626, as work on his palace was just beginning, and was succeeded by his eighth son, **Abahai**, who consolidated and extended Manchu influence across northern China. When the Manchus, having defeated the resident Ming, moved to Beijing in 1644 and established the Qing dynasty, Shenyang declined steadily in importance. The city began to take on its modern, industrial role with the arrival of the Russians in the nineteenth century, who made it the centre of their rail-building programme. Years later, the puppets of the Japanese state also set up shop here, exploiting the resources of the surrounding region and building an industrial infrastructure whose profits and products were sent home to Japan.

Arrival

Shenyang's international **airport**, the busiest in the northeast, lies 20km south of the city. It's linked to the CAAC office in the centre by an airport bus (¥15), while a taxi into town should cost around ¥90.

Five lines converge on Shenyang's two main **train stations**. If you've come from Beijing or farther south, you'll arrive first at the **South station** (南站, *nánzhàn*),

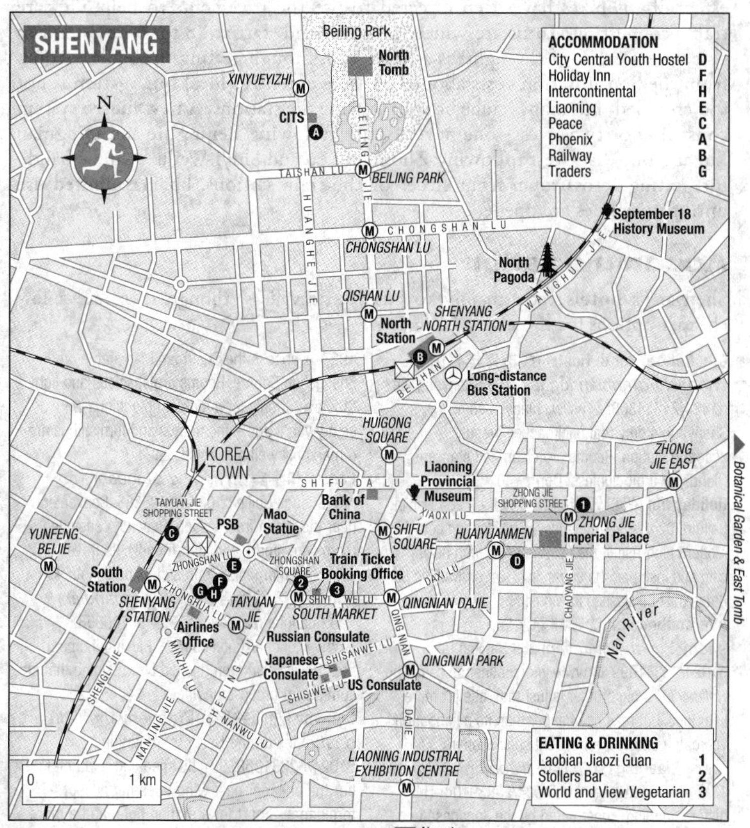

which is larger and more central. The newer **North station** (北站, *běizhàn*), serving destinations to the north (and the terminus for express Beijing trains), is a bit out of the centre; take trolleybus #5 from here to **Zhongshan Square** (中山广场, *zhōngshān guǎngchǎng*) and the South station (also served from here by bus #203). The North station ticket hall is to the right as you look at the station, while the booking office at the South station is in a large hall to the left. Tickets for services leaving from the North station can be bought from the South station, and vice versa; double-check which station the train you want actually leaves from. The gleaming, futuristic **long-distance bus station** (referred to locally as the express-bus station; 快速客运站, *kuàisù kèyùnzhàn*) is near the North station. To get to the centre from here, catch one of the many minibuses plying the route, or take a taxi (¥10).

If you're entering the city by train and planning on moving on immediately to a major city by bus, get off at the North station, where coaches depart from the east side of the concourse to Beijing (7–8hr) and Dalian (5hr). For Jilin (4hr), Changchun (3hr) and Harbin (6hr) services, walk one block south to the long-distance bus station.

City transport

Shenyang is very spread out, and trying to walk anywhere is frustrating, especially as bikes have been directed to use the pavements to help alleviate traffic congestion. **Taxis** are widely available and start at ¥8 for 3km; a taxi to or between most of the sights is around ¥25, though getting to the East Tomb from the South station costs about ¥60. The extensive local **bus system** is not too crowded; bus maps can be bought outside the stations. A new **metro** system consisting of two lines – one north–south following Beijing Jie and Qingnian Lu, and one east–west following Zhonghua Lu and Shiyi Weilu – can be handy for getting across town from either of the train stations, but has limited use until future lines are opened.

Accommodation

Shenyang's **hotels** cater mainly to business travellers, though there are a few cheaper options for those on a budget.

City Central Youth Hostel (成市青年旅馆, *chéngshì qīngnián lǚguǎn*) 103 Shenyang Jie ⓣ024/24844868, ⓦwww.chinayha.com. Shenyang's only real backpacker-friendly accommodation. Rooms are clean and staff are friendly, if a bit clueless. Dorm ¥40, ❷

Holiday Inn (假日饭店, *jiàrì fàndiàn*) 204 Nanjing Beilu ⓣ024/23341888, ⓦwww.holiday-inn.com. Modern high-rise in the heart of town, with health club and Irish bar; the entrance is just off Nanjing Lu. Rates may be slashed in winter. ❼

Intercontinental (沈阳洲际酒店, *shěnyáng zhōujì jǔdiàn*) 208 Nanjing Beilu ⓣ024/23341999, ⓦwww.intercontinental.com. The *Holiday Inn*'s big brother is just that little bit more luxurious, but may be cheaper than its neighbour if you catch one of the frequent special offers. ❼

Liaoning (辽宁宾馆, *liáoníng bīnguǎn*) 97 Zhongshan Lu ⓣ024/23839104. This historic lodging, constructed by the Japanese in 1927, overlooks the Chairman Mao statue on Zhongshan Square. Rooms are spacious and light. Stop over if only for a look at how things were eighty years ago – the fittings and furnishings are remarkably well preserved. ❹

Peace (和平宾馆, *hépíng bīnguǎn*) 104 Shengli Beijie ⓣ024/23498888. Conveniently near the South train station. Recently renovated rooms are smart, and staff friendly. Its travel service can organize train and plane tickets. ❸

Phoenix (凤凰饭店, *fènghuáng fàndiàn*) 109 Huanghe Nan Dajie ⓣ024/86105858, ⓦwww.phoenixhotel.com.cn. Plush behemoth near Beiling Park, refurbished but retaining that old communist group-tour vibe. ❹

Railway (沈阳铁路大厦, *shěnyáng tiělù dàshà*) Inside the North train station ⓣ024/62231888. Strictly speaking two hotels, but the cheaper east wing does not accept foreigners. Smart for a station hotel and a more than adequate place to crash if arriving late or departing early. ❹

Traders (商贸饭店, *shāngmào fàndiàn*) 68 Zhonghua Lu ⓣ024/23412288, ⓦwww.shangri-la.com. The most luxurious place to stay in Shenyang, as befitting its *Shangri-La* connections, and priced to match. The opulence of the lobby is matched by that of the rooms. ❼

The City

Shenyang has some great examples of uncompromising Soviet-style building, and you may well find yourself staying in one. The giant **Mao statue** in **Zhongshan Square** (中山广场, *zhōngshān guǎngchǎng*), erected in 1969, is by far the most distinctive landmark, its base lined with strident, blocky peasants, Daqing oilmen, PLA soldiers and students, though the Little Red Books they were waving have mostly been chipped off. Above them, the monolithic Mao stands wrapped in an overcoat, a bald superman whose raised hand makes him look as if he's directing traffic. Head in the direction he's facing, and you'll hit one of the the city's main shopping districts, centred around Zhongshan Lu, Zhonghua Lu and Taiyuan Jie, which abound with department stores.

The **Liaoning Provincial Museum** (辽宁省博物馆, *liáoníngshěng bówùguǎn*; Tues–Sun 9am–5pm; free, last entry 3.30pm), in the heart of the downtown, is one of the largest museums in the northeast; exhibits include paintings, copperware, pottery and porcelain. Perhaps most interesting are the fragments of oracle bones used for divination, featuring some of the earliest examples of written Chinese.

The Imperial Palace

More rewarding than the city centre are the Manchu structures on the outskirts of Shenyang, starting with the **Imperial Palace** (沈阳故宫, *shěnyáng gùgōng*; daily 8am–5pm; ¥50). Begun in 1626, it's a vastly scaled-down replica of Beijing's Forbidden City. Located in what was the centre of the old city but is now largely shopping malls (bus #237 comes here from the South station), the complex divides into three main sections. The first, the Cong Zhen Dian, is a low, wooden-fronted hall where the Qing dynasty was proclaimed and which was used by ministers to discuss state affairs. Beyond here, in the second courtyard, stands the Phoenix Tower, most formal of the ceremonial halls, and the Qing Ning Lou, which housed bedrooms for the emperor and his concubines. In the eastern section of the complex, the Da Zheng Dian is a squat, octagonal, wooden structure in vivid red and lacquered gold, with two pillars cut with writhing golden dragons in high relief. Here, the emperor Shunzhi was crowned before seizing Beijing – and the empire – in 1644. Just in front stand ten square pavilions, the Shi Wang, once used as offices by the chieftains of the Eight Banners (districts) of the Empire, and now housing a collection of bizarrely shaped swords and pikes. Take time to wander away from the groups amid the side palaces, and note the Manchu dragons in bas-relief, unique to this palace.

The tombs

From the Imperial Palace, bus #213 will get you to the **North Tomb** (北陵, *běi líng*; daily 8.30am–5pm; ¥30) in Beiling Park (park entry ¥6); bus #220 also heads there from the South station. The tomb is where Abahai is buried, and though it was his father Nurhaci who was the real pioneering imperialist, Abahai got the better crypt. The well-preserved complex, constructed in 1643, is entered through a gate to the south, either side of which are pavilions; the easternmost was for visiting emperors to wash and refresh themselves, the westernmost for sacrifices of pigs and sheep. A drive flanked with statues of camels, elephants, horses and lions leads to the Long En Hall, which contains an altar for offerings and the spirit tablets of the emperor and his wife. Their tree-covered burial mounds are at the rear, where you'll also find a fine dragon screen.

Outside the tomb area, **Beiling Park** comes alive in winter with snow sculptures, and ice skates and *pali* – wooden sleds with blades on the bottom, which you move using two metal ski poles while seated – available for rent.

The more restrained **East Tomb** (东陵, *dōng líng*; daily 7am–6pm; ¥30), built in 1629 as the last resting place of Nurhaci, is set among conifers next to **Dongling Park** (daily 9am–4.30pm; ¥2) in the east of the city. Buses #168 and #218 come here from the stop one block north and one block east of the Imperial Palace. The tomb is less monumental in layout than Abahai's and shows more signs of age, but it's still an impressive structure, with fortified walls and a three-storey tower. One hundred and eight steps (the number of beads on a Buddhist rosary) lead into the main gate, while all around the tomb are walking trails into the woods covering Mount Tianzhu – a hill, really.

The rest of the city

Aside from the major imperial relics, Shenyang's sights are something of a disappointment. Of the four pagodas and four temples that once stood at the limits of the city, one on each side, the only one in a reasonable state is the **North Pagoda** (北塔, *běi tă*; daily 9am–4.30pm; free), north of the long-distance bus station. The pagoda contains a sky and earth Buddha (Tiandifu), a carnal image of twin Buddhas rarely found in Chinese temples. Not far away, you'll find the huge concrete edifice of the **September 18 History Museum**, 46 Wanghua Nanjie (九一八历史博物馆, *jiŭyībā lìshĭ bówùguăn*; daily 9am–4.30pm; free), which focuses on Japan's invasion of Shenyang in 1931, telling the story through a predictable array of black-and-white photos, maps and rusty weapons. It's a "patriotic education base", so the tone of the Chinese-only captions is easy to guess. Bus #213 from the North Tomb stops here as well as near the North Pagoda.

A half-hour bus ride (#168) outside town, **Shenyang Botanical Garden** (沈阳世博园, *shěnyáng shì bó yuán*; daily 8am–5pm; ¥20–60) is a vast area featuring formal gardens from all over China and the world. Some of the attempts at foreign gardens may be a little wide of the mark, but it makes for a great escape from the dust of the city.

You'll have to time it right to enjoy another amusement: from December to February, the town hosts the increasingly popular **Shenyang International Ice and Snow Festival**, held at Qipanshan, 17km outside town to the northeast.

Eating and drinking

The lack of a defined cuisine in Sheyang can be a bit of a letdown, but at least there's plenty of choice. **Shiyi Weilu** (十一纬路, *shíyīwěilù*) is packed with restaurants of all kinds, and there are some tasty bargains in the Korea Town area at the western end of Shifu Da Lu. For **street food**, the alleys running south from Zhong Jie – a popular shopping street that dates back to 1636 – are lined with barbecues. Shenyang's most famous restaurant is *Laobian Jiaozi Guan* (老边饺子馆, *lăobiān jiăoziguăn*), a rough-and-ready dumpling house. Sadly the original premises – a huge dining room opposite the South Station at 55 Shengli Beijie – have disappeared behind scaffolding (and may or may not reopen), but another branch at 6 Zhong Jie is still doing a roaring trade. The top pub in town is *Stroller's Bar (*流浪者酒吧, *liúlàngzhě jiŭbā*), at 36 Bei Wujing Jie, near the junction with Shiyi Weilu. Beers start from ¥25; food, including T-bone steak and French onion soup, ranges from ¥40 to ¥80. The curiously titled *World and View Vegetarian (*素食馆, *sù shí guăn*), on the north side of Shiyi Weilu near the junction with Bei Yijing Jie, is the place to go if meat is off your menu.

Listings

Airlines CAAC (daily 8am–6pm; ⓣ024/89392520) is at 117 Zhonghua Lu. Plane tickets can also be bought from hotels or from CITS.

Banks and exchange Bank of China (Mon–Fri 8.30am–5pm, Sat & Sun 9am–4pm), 253 Shifu Da Lu.

Consulates The Japanese, Russian and US consulates are all in the same road, Shisiwei Lu, in the south of the city. Reports on whether Russian visas can be obtained easily here aren't encouraging; it's better to apply in Beijing.

Mail and telephones Shenyang's main post office (Mon–Fri 8am–6pm) is at 32 Zhongshan Lu.

PSB On Zhongshan Lu, by the Mao statue (Mon–Fri 8am–5pm).

Travel agents The CITS has offices at 113 Nan Huanghe Dajie (ⓣ024/86131251) and on Shifu Dalu (ⓣ024/85850808), at the junction with Xishuncheng Jie, next to Tesco (yes, Tesco).

Dalian and around

A modern, sprawling city on the Yellow Sea, **DALIAN** (大连, *dàlián*) is one of China's most cosmopolitan cities, partly because it has changed hands so often. As the only ice-free port in the region, it was eagerly sought by the foreign powers that held sway over China in the nineteenth century. The Japanese took the city in 1895, only to lose it a few years later to the Russians, who saw it as an alternative to ice-bound Vladivostok. In 1905, after decisively defeating the Russian navy, the Japanese wrested it back and remained in control for long enough to complete the construction of the port facilities and city grid – still visible in the many traffic circles and axial roads. After World War II, the Soviet Union occupied the city for ten years, finally withdrawing when Sino–Soviet relations improved.

The "foreign devils" are still here, though they're now invited: Dalian has been designated a Special Economic Zone, one of China's "open-door" cities, with regulations designed to attract overseas investment. As a result, it is busier than

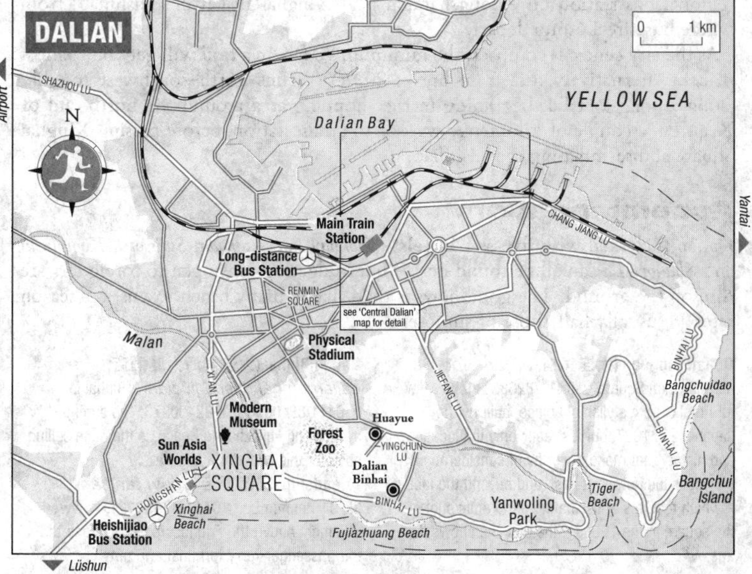

ever, the funnel for Dongbei's enormous natural and mineral wealth and an industrial producer in its own right, specializing in petrochemicals and shipbuilding. Unlike most Chinese metropolises, the city boasts green spaces and an excellent traffic control system, both the handiwork of the high-flying former mayor turned national commerce minister and Politburo member Bo Xilai. Despite his leaving the city in 2003, locals still seem to admire him as much as they do Dalian's football team, Shide, which won the Chinese league ten times in 22 years, contributed six players to the country's 2002 World Cup squad (the last time the national team qualified) and were the home team of one of the country's first footballing exports, Sun Jihai.

Still, Dalian manages to be a leisurely place, popular with tourists who come here for the scenic spots and beaches outside the city, to recover their health in sanatoriums and to gorge themselves on seafood.

Arrival and city transport

Dalian sits at the southern tip of the Liaodong Peninsula, filling a piece of land that's shaped like a tiger's head – the result, local legend has it, of a mermaid flattening the animal into land as punishment for eating the fiancé of a beautiful girl. The city has four main sections: Zhongshan Square (中山广场, *zhōngshān guǎngchǎng*), at the tiger's eye; Renmin Square (人民广场, *rénmín guǎngchǎng*), at his ear; the beaches, at his mouth and throat; and Heishijiao (黑石礁, *hēishí jiāo*; Black Coral Reef), across the Malan River to the west of town.

A taxi to or from the **airport**, 12km northwest of the city, should cost ¥35, or there's a regular airport bus (¥5) to and from Shengli Square. The main **train station** (there are three in total) and **passenger-ferry** terminal (for services to Yantai) are within 1km of Zhongshan Square. Long-distance buses pick up and drop off passengers around Shengli Square, outside the train station – if you're on an express bus from Beijing, you'll probably be dropped here – while the main bus station is located at the terminus of bus #201, around 1km to the west. You'll need to check where to board your bus when you buy your ticket. There's also a further regional bus station on Zhongshan Lu near Xinghai Beach in Heishijiao, from where buses to Lüshun depart.

As the city centre is compact, the minimum ¥8 fare in a **taxi** will get you to most places. Alternatively, the tram line, #202 (¥1), runs north–southwest roughly along Zhongshan Lu, beginning in the shopping area around the north end of Xi'an Lu, a couple of kilometres west of the train station, before passing Xinghai Square and terminating at Heishijiao.

Accommodation

Dalian is choked with five-star **hotels** – *Holiday Inn*, *Ramada*, *Swissotel*, *Kempinski* and *Shangri-La* can all be found here – but budget options open to foreigners are thin on the ground. The good news is that, like in many beach towns, off-season rates are usually half those of summer's.

Dalian Binguan (大连宾馆, *dàlián bīnguǎn*) 4 Zhongshan Square ⓣ0411/82633111, ⓦwww.dl-hotel.com. A stylish old place, built by the Japanese in 1927, but it's really only the location and history that make it worthy of consideration; service is indifferent at best, and beyond the lobby – which features a fascinating panoramic shot of the square in the 1920s – the building shows its age. ❺

Dalian Binhai (大连滨海大厦酒店, *dàlián bīnhǎi dàshà jiǔdiàn*) 2 Binhai Lu ⓣ0411/82406666, ⓕ82400873. The setting, overlooking Fujiazhuang Beach, is the main selling point for this two-star affair. ❹

Friendship (友谊饭店, *yǒuyí fàndiàn*) 3F, 91 Renmin Lu ⓣ0411/82634121, ⓦwww.dlfsh.cn. Above the Friendship Store, close to the passenger-ferry terminal and newly renovated, this state-owned enterprise is clean and comfortable. 5

Furama (富丽华大酒店, *fùlìhuá dàjiǔdiàn*) 60 Renmin Lu ⓣ0411/82630888, ⓦwww.furama.com.cn. A very upscale Japanese hotel, the *Furuma* has every imaginable facility, a lobby big enough for Shide to play in and palatial rooms. 7

Home Inn (如家酒店, *rújiā jiǔdiàn*) 92 Renmin Lu ⓣ0411/39858588, ⓦwww.homeinns.com. Budget Chinese hotel chain offering tidy, moderately priced rooms near the centre. 4

Huayue (海悦酒店, *hǎi yuè jiǔdiàn*) 1 Yingchun Lu ⓣ0411/82588666. A former youth hostel, the renamed and renovated building now bills itself a business hotel. This means the carpets are new, but even so, there are few useful services offered. The price (if you bargain a bit you can still bag yourself a bed here for under ¥100) is the sole justification for a trip out from the station (buses #404, #702 or minibus #525; taxi ¥15). 3

Ramada (九洲华美达酒店, *jiǔzhōu huáměidá jiǔdiàn*) 18 Shengli Square ⓣ0411/82808888, ⓦwww.ramada.com. Four-star luxury in the heart of town next to the train station, overlooking Shengli Square. 6

The City

The hub of Dalian is **Zhongshan Square** (中山广场, *zhōngshān guǎngchǎng*), really a circle, whose spokes are some of the most interesting streets in the city. Japanese and Russian buildings, *KFC* and *McDonald's*, girls in miniskirts and Western dance music blaring from the shops give the area an international

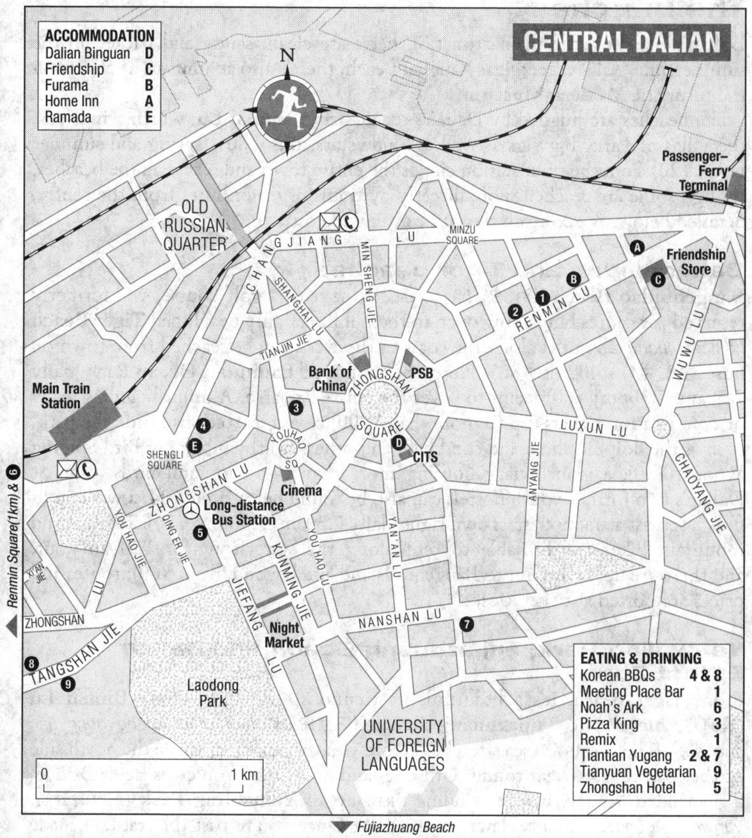

flavour. The main shopping strips are Shanghai Lu and Tianjin Jie, which now house massive malls. Continue northwest on Shanghai Lu and cross the railroad tracks to reach the old **Russian quarter** (老俄罗斯风景区, *lǎoéluósī fēngjǐngqū*). This neighbourhood used to house Russia's gentry, though today each peeling mansion is home to several families. The pedestrian street takes you past restored pistachio-coloured facades and street vendors selling Russian cigarettes, lighters, vodka and Soviet pins. It's hardly an authentic colonial avenue, but step west into one of the lanes and you've gone back a century. Ask nicely and you may even get to see inside the homes.

Follow Zhongshan Lu west past Shengli Square, the train station and the meandering shopping lanes of Qing Er Jie to reach **Renmin Square** (人民广场, *rénmín guǎngchǎng*), large, grassy and lit with footlights at night. It's a long walk from the train station, but several buses ply the route, among them #15, #702 and #801. The neighbourhoods to the south of the square retain their Russian colonial architecture, and their narrow, tree-lined streets make for excellent wandering.

South of the train station is the Japanese-designed **Laodong Park**. **Nanshan**, the hilly neighbourhood across the street east of the park, was once home to the Japanese community; now, the cream-coloured, red-roofed villas are being renovated by nouveau riche Chinese.

The beaches

Dalian's **beaches**, the main attraction here, are clean, sandy and packed in the summertime. All are free; near Xinghai Beach, there's also an unusual attraction in the futuristic **Modern Museum**.

The beaches are hugged by Dalian's scenic drive, **Binhai Lu**, which winds past the villas of Party bigwigs as well as Shide stars. Bus #801 (spring and summer only; ¥20) from the train station circles the entire town and serves all the beaches, though some are reached more directly by trams or other buses from the centre, detailed below. A taxi from the city centre will cost ¥40.

Bangchuidao and Tiger beaches

Bangchuidao Beach (棒棰岛, *bàngchúidǎo*), next to a golf course, was formerly reserved for cadres but is now open to the public. Highly developed **Tiger Beach** (老虎滩, *lǎohǔ tān*), next along the coast to the west, can be reached from town on buses #2, #4, #402 or #801. Here, the funfair of **Laohutan Ocean Park** (daily 7.30am–5.30pm; ¥60) seems to cover the entire bay area. A mind-boggling array of combination tickets (up to more than ¥200) covers attractions inside the park, such as the dolphin show and coral hall, and others nearby including Bird Singing Woods (¥30), a giant aviary housing more than two thousand birds. One of Dalian's two former youth hostels can also be found here: **Boat 104**, a warship, is now a tourist attraction in its own right (daily 7.30am–5.30pm; ¥20). Tandem and mountain bikes are available to rent along the waterfront for ¥20 an hour, and there are boat trips out to Bangchui Island and beyond (from ¥60); routes and prices are posted at ticket kiosks.

Yanwoling Park, Fujiazhuang Beach and Dalian Forest Zoo

From Tiger Beach, it's a beautiful, if strenuous, 7km hike along **Binhai Lu** (滨海路, *bīnhǎilù*) to **Fujiazhuang Beach** (傅家庄公园浴场, *fùjiāzhuāng gōngyuán yùchǎng*). The turquoise sea stretches before you to the south, while the north side of the road is green year round with trees and new grass. You cross Beida Bridge, a suspended beauty, before winding 3km up to **Yanwoling Park** (燕窝岭公园, *yànwōlǐng gōngyuán*; daily dawn–dusk; ¥10). Once you're past the statue – made from shells – of a little boy with seagulls, there's a profusion of maintained trails and stairs to take you down to the sea. One particularly nice hike, signed in English, ends up at Sunken Boat Rock, a cove where starfish cling to rocks and the only sounds are those of the waves. Don't attempt to swim here, due to the dangerously strong currents.

Continuing 4km west on Binhai Lu, you wind downhill to **Fujiazhuang Beach** (daily dawn–dusk), sheltered from the wind in a rocky bay and less developed than Tiger Beach. You can charter speedboats from here to outlying islands, while a trip west to Xinghai Beach and back costs around ¥60 depending on your bargaining skills. At the back of the beach are plenty of good, open-air seafood restaurants; expect to pay around ¥100 for a meal for two.

A couple of kilometres northwest along Binhai Lu, you'll come to **Dalian Forest Zoo** (森林动物园, *sēn lín dōngwùyuán*; daily 8am–5pm; adults ¥120, students/OAPs ¥60, children under 1.3m free). Naturally, the stars of the show here are the pandas, with both giant and smaller red varieties represented, though the big cats and performing parrots are also popular.

The Modern Museum and Xinghai Beach

On the northwest shoulder of the massive **Xinghai Square** (星海广场, *xīnghǎi guǎngchǎng*; tram #202 comes here from Xi'an Lu), beside the Malan River, the **Modern Museum** (现代博物馆, *xiàndàibówùgǔan*; daily 9am–5pm; ¥30) showcases Dalian's idealized future. Visitors can drive mock streets, steer an oil tanker into the port on a simulator or ride a flying carpet through pollution-free skies. The museum (the brainchild of former mayor Bo Xilai) isn't all pie in the sky – UN awards attest to the success of the city's ongoing urban revamp.

Xinghai Beach (星海公园浴场, *xīnghǎi gōngyuán yùchǎng*; daily 7am–9pm) is a long walk or short tram ride southwest along Zhongshan Lu from the Modern Museum (take bus #202 three stops to the Medical University). Besides the usual fairground rides, souvenir stands and restaurants, the beach features a trio of attractions in the form of **Sun Asia Ocean World** (圣亚海洋世界, *shèngyà hǎiyán shìjiè*; 9am–4pm; ¥100), **Sun Asia Polar World** (same hours; ¥80) and **Sun Asia Coral World** (same hours; ¥50). Combination tickets for two or more of the "worlds" offer a money-saving option of sorts.

Eating

Dalian is full of **restaurants**, especially around Shengli Square, and just south and west of here on the pedestrian streets bordered by Qing Er Jie and Jiefang Lu. For simple, affordable fare, head south from Zhongshan Square toward the University of Foreign Languages: Yan'an Lu is lined with restaurants. There's a stretch of Korean barbecue joints along Gao Er Ji Lu, a block south of Renmin Square; simply follow the smoke and bustle, and the touts out front will wave you in. More conveniently, there's a similar option close to the train station on Changjiang Lu.

For seafood away from the beaches, don't miss one of Dalian's many branches of *Tiantian Yugang Jiulou* (天天渔港酒楼, *tiāntiānyúgǎng jiǔlóu*). The one near the university, at 20 Jilin Jie, is usually packed with people enjoying draught beer and fresh steamed crab; dinner for two with drinks comes to around ¥150. You'll have to shell and eat the thing with chopsticks, so wear clothes you don't mind getting splattered. There's a more central branch at 10 Renmin Lu.

There are passable pizzas and other Western food at *Pizza King* (比萨王, *bǐsà wáng*) on Youhao Lu. If you're craving something a bit different, the enormous *Zhongshan Hotel* (中山大酒店, *zhōngshāndàjǐudian*) at 3 Jiefang Lu, just south of Shengli Square, has an Indian restaurant on the fifth floor and a Russian restaurant on the 38th. Both have live music and dance performances. Vegetarians can head for the hard-to-find *Tianyuan Vegetarian* (天缘素食店, *tiānyuán sùshídiàn*; ⓣ0411/83673110), just past the small but colourful Songshan Temple a short way along Tangshan Jie, for a fix of cheap meat-like tofu dishes.

Drinking and entertainment

Dalian has lots of **bars**; among the liveliest is the reliable *Meeting Place Bar* (互情酒吧, *hùqíng jiŭbā*), 12 Renmin Lu. It has tattooed, English-speaking bartenders, live rock music, imported beers and the requisite Russian prostitutes. Next door is *Remix*, which claims the mantle of choicest hip-hop club in town. *Noah's Ark* (诺亚方舟酒吧, *nuòyǎ fāngzhōu jiŭbā*), at 32 Wusi Lu, across the street from Renmin Square, is a long-standing favourite for live music; look for the wooden wagon out front.

Listings

Banks and exchange The Bank of China (Mon–Fri 8.30am–noon & 1–5pm) is at 9 Zhongshan Square.
Buses From the long-distance bus station, there are buses to Shenyang, Dandong and other provincial towns. Tickets can be bought the night before to avoid queues. More convenient are the luxury buses to Shenyang and Beijing, which depart throughout the day from the north and east sides of Shengli Square; tickets can be bought on the bus.
Ferries Services from Dalian have been greatly reduced, with Yantai, directly to the south across the Bo Hai bay, growing in importance. The ferry to Yantai itself is a full day faster than the train, and cheaper (6hr; ¥100–800). From Yantai, there are frequent connections to Qingdao (4hr). Tickets can be bought in advance from the passenger-ferry terminal on Yimin Jie in the northeast of the city or from one of the many windows both at and around the train station. A train ferry also runs from Dalian to Yantai (ⓦwww.sbtf.com.cn) with fares ¥180–680. A twice-weekly service also runs to Incheon in South Korea (18hr; ¥920–1848).
Football The Physical Stadium, just southwest of Renmin Square on Wusi Lu, is the venue for Dalian Shide matches (late March until Oct). Seats go for ¥40 – buy tickets at the stadium.
Internet Many internet cafés can be found in the area surrounding the University of Foreign Languages, south of Zhongshan Square.
Mail and telephones The post office (Mon–Sat 8am–6pm) is next to the main train station.
PSB Centrally located on the northeast side of Zhongshan Square (daily 8am–4.30pm).
Trains Tickets are easy to buy at the main train station. The ticket windows are on the ground floor, outside and to the left of the station's main entrance.
Travel agents CITS (daily 8.30am–4.30pm; ⓣ0411/83691159, ⓦwww.citsdl.com), 10F, Wanda Plaza, Zhongshan Square. Most hotels also have their own ticketing and tour offices.

Dandong

Once an obscure port tucked away in the corner of Liaoning province at the confluence of the Yalu River and the Yellow Sea, **DANDONG** (丹东, *dāndōng*) is now a popular weekend destination for Chinese, who come to gaze across the border into North Korea – the listless Korean city of Sinuiju (Xinyizhou in Chinese) lies on the other side of the Yalu River. South Koreans, too, come to look across at their northern neighbours, while foreigners from further afield visit for the massive memorial and museum dedicated to the defence of China's communist neighbour against imperialists during the Korean War. All in all, Dandong makes a worthwhile weekend trip out of Beijing or a stopover while touring the sooty northeast, as well as a convenient departure point for the Changbai Shan Nature Reserve (see p.189).

Arrival and city transport

Arriving at Dandong **train station**, or at the long-distance bus station just to the north, puts you right in the centre of town, a gleaming marble-paved square featuring a statue of Mao Zedong, about 1km north of the **Yalu River** (鸭绿江, *yālùjiāng*). Dandong has a small **airport** 14km southwest of town, and there's a ferry terminal 38km away, where vessels from South Korea dock. **Taxis** in Dandong charge a minimum of ¥5, which is sufficient for rides around town.

Accommodation

Dantie Dajiudian (丹铁大酒店, *dāntiě dàjiǔdiàn*) Train Station Square ⓣ0415/2307777. Situated within the station itself, this is convenient if arriving late or leaving early; rooms are not too shabby. ❷

Kaixuan (凯旋宾馆, *kǎixuán bīnguǎn*) 9 Shiwei Lu ⓣ0415/2125566. North of the Yalu Bridge, the *Kaixuan* has clean triples from less than ¥100 per bed, breakfast included. ❸

Yalu River Guesthouse (鸭绿江大厦, *yālùjiān dàshà*) 87 Jiuwei Lu ⓣ0415/2125901, ⓦwww.yaluriverhotel.cn. A Sino-Japanese effort – though the rooms have seen better days they are more than adequate, even coming equipped with satellite TV. Staff are helpful, and the ticket service is able to deal with onward travel requests. ❹

Yinghua Dajiudian (樱花大酒店, *yīnghuā dàjiǔdiàn*) 2 Liuwei Lu ⓣ0415/2100999. Boasting views across the river and large rooms equipped with broadband internet access, this is a decent and reasonably priced bet if you're on a business trip. ❸

Zhonglian (中联大酒店, *zhōnglián dàjiǔdiàn*) 62 Binjiang Zhonglu ⓣ0415/2333333, ⓦwww.zlhotel.com.cn. The poshest accommodation in town, this waterfront hotel looks out across the bombed-out bridge toward North Korea. As well as smart rooms with great views, they offer an exceedingly helpful lobby travel service. ❻

The City

Dandong remains small enough to feel human in scale, and the tree-lined main streets are uncrowded, clean and prosperous. A strong Korean influence can be felt: vendors along the riverfront promenade sell North Korean stamps, bearing slogans in Korean such as "Become human gun bombs!" and North Korean TV is on view in Dandong hotels.

On foot, the nearest you can get to the North Korean soil without a visa is halfway across the river, on the **Old Yalu Bridge** (鸭绿断桥, *yālù duànqiáo*; daily 8.30am–5pm; ¥15) in the south of town, next to the new bridge. The Koreans have dismantled their half but the Chinese have left theirs as a memorial, complete

Moving on from Dandong

Dandong is well connected to the rest of northeast China, with **trains** arriving and departing daily. Tickets are easy enough to get from the train station and can also be booked through CITS (ⓣ0415/2123688, ⓦwww.ddcits.com), just north of the Shiwei Lu/Jiang Chen Dajie intersection. There are **flights** to Sanya, Shanghai and Shenzhen; CITS can book these too, though most hotels will either be able to reserve tickets for you or point you in the right direction. If you're planning to head off to the **Changbai Shan Nature Reserve**, you'll need to get the 6.30am or 8.50am bus to Tonghua (8–10hr; ¥60); buy a ticket the night before from the efficient booking office at the bus station. **Taxis** heading to Shenyang ply for passengers on the west side of the station concourse (¥70/person), which works out faster than taking the train.

If you're desperate to visit **North Korea**, arrange a tour with the Beijing-based Koryo Tours (ⓦwww.koryogroup.com), run by Englishman Nick Bonner.

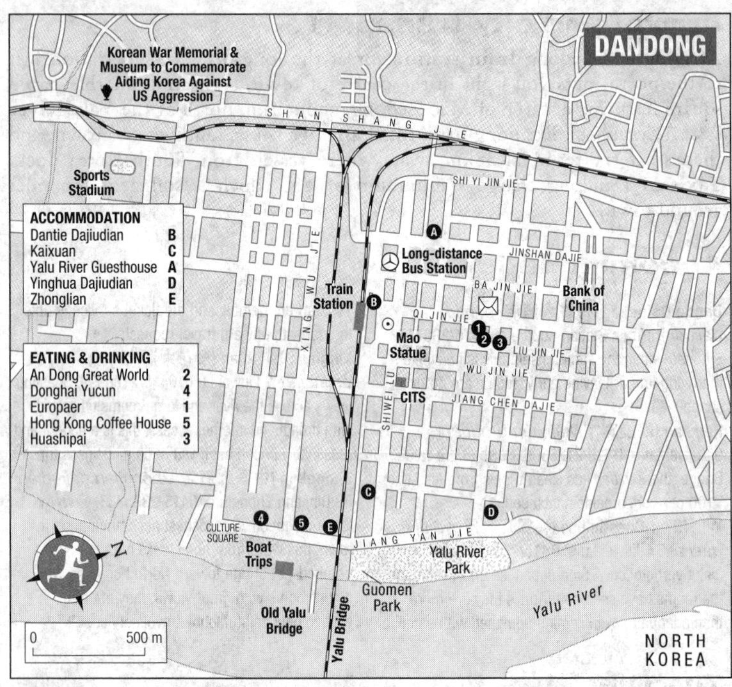

with thirty framed photos of its original construction by the Japanese in 1911, when the town was called Andong. The bridge ends at a tangled mass of metal that resulted from American bombing in 1950 in response to the Chinese entering the Korean War. Several viewing platforms are on site, along with pay-telescopes trained on Sinuiju on the far bank.

From 8am, boats set out from all along Dandong's promenade, by the bridge, on thirty-minute trips across the river (costing ¥20 in a large boat that leaves when full, or ¥35 per person for a zippy six-seater). The boats take you into North Korean waters to within a few metres of shore, where you can do your part for international relations by waving at the soldiers shouldering automatic rifles. Photography is allowed, but most foreign tourists keep their cameras packed away: there isn't much to see on Sinuiju's desultory shore, save for some rusting ships and languid civilians. If you've an interest in visiting, it's best to check the current situation with Dandong's CITS (see box, p.183), though foreigners will almost certainly be forbidden from joining their North Korean tour.

The **Dandong side** of the river is a boomtown in comparison. The riverside by the bridges is the most scenic area, full of strolling tourists, particularly in the early evening. Nearby is **Yalu River Park** (鸭绿江公园, *yālǜjiān gōngyuán*), where you can drive bumper cars and pay ¥1 to sit on a patch of downy green grass. At the western end of the riverside promenade, **Culture Square** (文化广场, *wénhuà guǎngchǎng*) is a well-lit local evening hangout.

The Museum to Commemorate Aiding Korea Against US Aggression

Built in 1993, the huge, macabre **Museum to Commemorate Aiding Korea Against US Aggression** (抗美援朝纪念馆, *kàngměi yuáncháo jìniànguǎn*; daily 8am–4.30pm; ¥40) feels like a relic of the Cold War. It has nine exhibition halls on the Korean War, full of maps, plans, dioramas, machine guns, hand grenades, photographs (almost all of which are captioned in English), and sculptures of lantern-jawed Chinese and Korean soldiers. A few large plaques in each hall spell out, in English and Chinese, the basic theme of each room – tending to be along the lines of "the Americans were terrible aggressors, China heroically won the war after stepping in to help its Korean brothers and sisters." The trifling details that the North kicked off the war by invading the South, and that at best the conflict (which has still never officially ended) was a draw, are conspicuous by their absence.

In a field behind the museum, a collection of Chinese and captured US aircraft and artillery are on display, while a paintball area, assault course and fighter plane simulator help crank up the fun factor. Purchase another ticket (¥15) and you can climb up inside the huge memorial next to the museum – surrounded by statues of burly Chinese soldiers trampling US army helmets underfoot – for a view over Dandong and into North Korea.

The museum is in the northwest of the city and can be reached on buses #1, #3, #4 or #5 from the station; get off by the sports stadium and walk north for five minutes. If you've developed a thirst by the time you arrive, note the ice-cold Coca-Colas for sale at the entrance to the compound, next to Jiang Zemin's large plaque swearing eternal North Korean–Sino friendship.

Eating

Restaurants in Dandong cater to masses of weekenders craving freshwater fish and Korean dishes. Try the local *luzi yu*, a river fish, at *Donghai Yucun* (东海渔村, *dōnghǎi yúcūn*), no. 42, Block E (promenade buildings are labelled with letters), west of the Yalu Bridge. All dishes here are served with glutinous rice, soup, bread and dumplings, and a feast for two is a bargain at around ¥80. Eateries stretch the length of the promenade, many following the popular northern style of having plates of food out ready for you to choose from. For an enlightening start to your morning, check out the latest North Korean TV news at *Hong Kong Coffee House* (香港咖啡厅, *xiānggǎng kāfēitīng*), no. 32, Block D, where strong Korean coffee is ¥20.

In the centre, a clutch of restaurants nestles around the junctions of Liuwei Lu, Qi Jin Jie and Liu Jin Jie. There are Western dishes available at *Europaer* (欧罗巴, *ōuluóbā*) and *Huashipai* (华士派, *huáshìpài*), both serving pizzas from ¥30 and steak for about ¥50, while *An Dong Great World* (安东大世界, *āndōng dàshìjiè*), opposite Huashipai, is a posh dim sum restaurant that stays open late, though check the price of each plate as you order or you could be in for a nasty surprise when the bill comes. For local and Korean dishes, a string of restaurants runs north along San Jin Jie from its junction with Shiwei Lu.

Listings

Banks and exchange There is a Bank of China on the waterfront at Culture Square. US, Hong Kong and Japanese money can also be changed at the *Yalu River Guesthouse*.

Mail and telephones The central post office (daily 8am–5.30pm) can be found on Qi Jing Jie, the main road running east from the station and site of a bustling night market. Another outpost can be found at Culture Square.

Changchun and Jilin

The cities of Jilin province bore the brunt of Japanese, Russian and Chinese communist planning more than anywhere in China. This was due to Jilin's vast mineral reserves, deposits of coal and iron ore that transformed the area into a network of sprawling industrial hubs, and, for thirteen years, the seat of the Japanese Manchukuo government. The closing of state-owned factories has resulted in massive lay-offs, but not all is glum, as tourism has crept in as one of the few growth industries. Roads have been improved, the rail network is thorough and easy to use, most hotels are delighted to see foreigners, and winter brings low-cost skiing and sledding. Popular with both domestic and South Korean tourists is the **Changbai Shan Nature Reserve** (see p.189), a swath of mountain and forest that boasts breathtaking scenery in the far eastern section of the province, along the North Korean border. The most convenient jumping-off point for Changbai Shan is **Jilin city**, which has little by way of sights, but great winter sports. Some 90km to the west, **Changchun** is the provincial capital and former capital of Manchukuo. The city retains much imperial architecture and design, with straight boulevards and squares throughout.

Jilin province is famous in its own country for **er ren zhuan**, a form of theatre closer to vaudeville than Beijing opera, incorporating dancing, singing, baton-twirling, costume changes and soliloquies. A typical performance sees a man and woman regaling the audience with a humorous tale of their courtship and love. CDs of the genre are available at stores, and you may be able to get into a performance with translation via CITS, or you could just ask a cabbie or local to point you to a theatre.

Changchun

CHANGCHUN (长春, *chángchūn*) has historical notoriety from its role as Hsinking, capital of Manchukuo, the Japanese-controlled state from 1932 to 1945 that had Xuantong (better known as Puyi) as its emperor. Now a huge, sprawling industrial city, it's also renowned for its many colleges, its movie studio and the Number One Automobile Factory, producer of the ubiquitous Liberation Truck and Red Flag sedans, though in these joint-venture days the majority of the city's auto production focuses on VWs.

Arrival and information

Numerous flights connect Changchun with every major city in China. A bus from the **airport** (40min; ¥20), 10km northwest of town, drops you outside the *CAAC Hotel* (ⓣ0431/82988888) at 480 Jiefang Dalu, about 3km south of the train station. Both **train** and **bus stations** are in the north of town, with frequent connections to the rest of the northeast. Chinese-only maps are available from the train station and newsstands (¥2). CITS (ⓣ0431/86909076) is at 1296 Xinmin Dajie, at the very southern end of the road.

Accommodation

Chunyi Hotel (春谊宾馆, *chūnyí bīnguǎn*) Directly across from the station's south exit ⓣ0431/82096888. Built in 1909 by the Japanese, the province's oldest inn is hardly beautiful, but good value for cleanliness, location and price. ❹

International Hotel (国际大厦酒店, *guójìdàshàjiǔdiàn*) 568 Xi'an Da Lu ⓣ0431/88485116. A more than adequate business hotel. ❺

Postal Hotel (邮政宾馆, *yóuzhèng bīnguǎn*) Train Station Square, just left out of the station. Once renovations are complete (sometime in 2011), smart rooms at a similar price to the *Rail Station* (see below) should be available here. ❸

Rail Station Hotel (铁路宾馆, *tiělù bīnguǎn*) In the station building ⓣ0431/86128027. The most convenient place in town to stay, but they can be picky about taking foreigners. ❷

Shangri-La (香格里拉饭店, *xiānggélǐlā fàndiàn*) 569 Xi'an Da Lu ⓣ0431/88981818, ⓦwww.shangri-la.com. In the centre of the new commercial district, this is the town's five-star option. ❾

Wenhua Square and the Geological Palace

A good, if long, introduction to the city is to stroll south from the train station down the main artery, **Renmin Dajie** (人民大街, *rénmíndàjīe*), past Japan's former Kwangtung Army Headquarters (identifiable by its spiky eaves) to Renmin Square and then west to **Wenhua Square**. The latter is the second-largest square in the world (after Tian'anmen), and was to be the site of Puyi's palace. Today, it's a large paved expanse with statues of a muscular naked man, standing with his arms raised in liberation, and a reclining naked woman marking its centre. All that remains of the planned palace are its foundations, topped by the so-called **Geological Palace** (地质宫博物馆, *dìzhígōng bówùguǎn*; daily 8.30am–4.30pm; ¥10). Inside, rows upon rows of minerals attest to Jilin's abundant resources. Bored school groups come to life when they see the pair of dinosaur skeletons, including a "Manchusaurus".

The Puppet Emperor's Palace

Changchun's only notable attraction is the **Puppet Emperor's Palace** (伪皇宫, *wěihuáng gōng*; daily: summer 8.30am–4.20pm; winter 8.30am–3.40pm; ¥80), in the east of the city on the route of buses #10, #125, #264 and #268 from the train station, though most entertainingly accessed through the bustling Guangfu Lu market just west of the palace. In 1912, at the age of 8, Puyi ascended to the imperial throne in Beijing, at the behest of the dying Dowager Cixi. Although forced to abdicate that same year by the Republican government, he retained his royal privileges, continuing to reside as a living anachronism in the Forbidden City. Outside, the new republic was coming to terms with democracy and the twentieth century, and Puyi's life, circumscribed by court ritual, seems a fantasy in comparison. In 1924, he was expelled by Nationalists uneasy at what he represented, but the Japanese protected him and eventually found a use for him here in Changchun as a figure who lent a symbolic legitimacy to their rule. After the war, he was re-educated by the Communists and lived the last years of his life as a gardener. His story was the subject of Bernardo Bertolucci's lavish film *The Last Emperor*.

Like its former occupant, the palace is really just a shadow of Chinese imperial splendour, a poor miniature of Beijing's Forbidden City, but in its defence, it does boast a swimming pool and horse racing track (¥10), both of which its ancient forebear lacks. This luxurious retreat, though, was only meant to be temporary, until his grand abode proper was completed at Culture Square.

The **Museum of North East China's Occupation by Japan** (¥20), on the same site, documents Japan's brutal invasion and rule. On a lighter note, be sure to see the restored Japanese garden, one of Changchun's most tranquil spots.

Eating and drinking

The city's main **bar** and **restaurant** area lies around 1km south down Tongzhi Jie, running into side alleys between Qinghua Lu and Xikang Lu. Closer in is *Xiang Yang Tun Fanguan* (向阳屯饭馆, *xiàngyángtún fàngǔan*), a traditional Dongbei restaurant – the log piles outside attest to the fact that everything here is still cooked on wood-fired stoves. To get here, walk south on Tongzhi Jie from the *Shangri-La* and turn left at Dong Chaoyang Lu; the restaurant is on the left-hand side, at no. 433. The rustic facade is impossible to miss.

Listings

Banks and exchange Bank of China (Mon–Fri 8.30am–4.30pm) is just north of the *Shangri-La*, at 699 Xi'an Dalu.

Mail and telephones The post office (daily 8.30am–4.30pm) is just to the left as you exit the train station.

PSB 99 Renmin Dajie.

Jilin and around

Known as Kirin during the Manchukuo time, **JILIN** (吉林, *jílín*) is split in two by the Songhua River, with the downtown area spread along its northern shore. The waterside promenade makes for a pretty walk, especially in winter, when the trees are coated in frost – a phenomenon, known as *shugua* in Chinese, that results from condensation from the city's hydroelectric dam at Songhua Hu. It's Jilin's claim to fame, along with an ice festival in January and three neighbouring parks for skiing and sledding. This makes winter the ideal time to visit, though the parks – Beishan, Jiangnan and Jiangbei – are nice enough in summer. **Beishan** (北山公园, *běishān gōngyuán*), in the west of town at the terminus of bus routes #7 and #107, is the best known of the three. It's filled with pathways and temples, the most interesting of which is Yuhuangge (Jade Emperor's Temple), where rows of fortune-tellers gather out front.

A reminder of the past, Jilin's **Catholic church** (天主堂, *tiānzhǔ táng*) is the town's prettiest building, constructed in 1917 at 3 Songjiang Lu, the road bordering the river promenade. Next door is a hospice for the elderly, which perhaps helps explain why the median age of a Jilin Catholic appears to be 80.

Arrival and information

Jilin's small **airport** is located 25km northwest of town; a taxi into the centre will cost ¥50. Taxi fares begin at ¥5, which should cover most rides within town. The central **train** and **bus stations** are around 2km north of the river, but note that departing from Changchun offers many more destination options. If you're going to Changbai Shan, it's worthwhile talking to the **CITS** office (Ⓣ0432/2435819) on Jiang Wan Lu. The main **Bank of China** (daily 8am–5pm) and **post office** (8am–5pm) are across from each other on opposite sides of Jilin Dajie (吉林大街, *jílíndàjīe*), just north of the bridge. For **internet** access, Chongqing Jie, a road that runs diagonally northeast from the post office to the train station, has several places to choose from near the intersection with Shanghai Lu.

Accommodation and eating

The *Jilin International* (吉林国际大酒店, *jílín guójì dàjiǔdiàn*; Ⓣ0432/66571888; ❷), at 20 Zhongxing Jie, offers comfortable **accommodation** right in front of the train station. A smarter in-town choice is the *Angel Hotel* (天使宾馆, *tiānshǐ bīnguǎn*; Ⓣ0432/2481848; ❸), 2 Nanjing Jie, near the Catholic church, off the main north–south road, Jilin Dajie. Where Tianjin Lu meets the river, at 1 Songjiang Donglu, the *Shenzhou Hotel* (神州大酒店, *shénzhōu dàjiǔdiàn*; Ⓣ0432/2161000; ❸) is about the smartest Jilin has to offer.

Chongqing Jie is lined with good **restaurants**, including a "Dumpling King", *Dongfang Jiaozi Wang* (东方饺子王, *dōngfāng jiǎoziwáng*), south of the *Jilin International*.

Songhua Hu

Twenty kilometres east of Jilin is **Songhua Hu** (松花湖, *sōnghuā hú*), a deep, very attractive lake, surrounded by hills in a large forested park. A taxi to this popular local beauty spot should cost about ¥50, and there are rowing boats for rent. Unlike most Chinese scenic attractions, Songhua Hu seems big enough to absorb the impact of all its visitors, and even on weekends it's possible to escape to some peaceful spot.

At the lake's southern end is the huge **Fengman Dam**, a source of great local pride. Although in recent years the Songhua River's level has dropped by half (a result of extensive tree felling in its catchment area), the river floods every year, and at least a couple of the dam's four sluice gates have to be opened. With ruthless Chinese pragmatism, cities in Dongbei have been graded in order of importance in the event that the annual floods ever become uncontrollable. Jilin is judged more important than Harbin, so if the river does ever flood disastrously, Jilin will be spared and Harbin submerged.

Local ski areas

In winter, the area around the lake is great for skiing and sledding, and ski packages are available through Jilin's tourist agencies. Closest to Jilin city, on bus routes #9 and #33, is **Zhuque Shan** (朱雀山, *zhūquè shān*), a park also known for its hiking and temples. It's 14km southeast of Jilin; a taxi is around ¥40 from the train station. After you're dropped off, you have to walk 1km to the park. There are two small slopes, one for skiing and one for sledding. The sleds are actually two downhill skis nailed together with a piece of raised plywood, and they really fly if you get a running start and bellyflop. A good restaurant seats guests on a *kang*, a heated raised platform that provides a nice vantage point over the hill. Foreigners are a rarity, and the staff and patrons a lot of fun.

Jilin also has two first-class ski areas, replete with chairlifts – transport and lift tickets plus equipment rental at **Songhua Hu Huaxue Chang** (松花湖滑雪场, *sōnghuā hú huáxuěchǎng*; ⓣ0432/4697666) and **Beida Hu Huaxue Chang** (北大湖滑雪场, *běidàhú huáxuěchǎng*; ⓣ0432/4202168) are considerably more expensive, not to mention vastly more professional, than at Zhuque Shan. To get to the Songhua Hu resort, take bus #9 or #33 to the small district of Fengman (30min) and continue by taxi, or get a taxi all the way from Jilin city (26km) for about ¥50. Transport to the bigger Beida Hu ski area, 56km southeast of Jilin, is easiest by taxi (¥120), though in winter months hourly buses also make the trip (1hr 30min; ¥20).

Changbai Shan Nature Reserve

The **Changbai mountains** run northeast to southwest along the Chinese–Korean border for more than 1000km. With long, harsh winters and humid summers, this is the only mountain range in east Asia to possess alpine tundra, and its highest peak, Baitou Shan (2744m), is the tallest mountain on the eastern side of the continent. The huge lake, **Tian Chi**, high in the Changbai mountains, is one of the highlights of Dongbei, as is the surrounding area, the beautiful **Changbai Shan Nature Reserve** (长白山自然保护区, *chángbáishān zìrán bǎohùqū*). With jagged peaks emerging from swaths of lush pine forest, this is remote, backwater China, difficult to access even after recent improvements in infrastructure. Heading a little off the tourist track into the wilderness is the way to get the most out of the area, though you need to come well prepared with all-weather gear, whatever the time of year.

Established in 1961, the nature reserve covers more than 800 square kilometres of luxuriant forest, most of which lies 500m to 1100m above sea level. At the base

Ginseng

Ginseng has been collected as a medicinal plant for millennia, and the first Chinese pharmacopoeia, written in the first century, records its ability to nourish the five internal organs, sharpen intelligence, strengthen *yin* (female energy) and invigorate *yang* (male energy).

It is the ginseng root that is prized. It's quite conceivable to search for weeks and not find a single specimen, and ginseng hunters have even disappeared, the combination of which has given rise to a host of **superstitions**. The roots are said to be guarded by snakes and tigers, and legend has it that if a hunter should dream of a laughing, white-bearded man or a group of dancing fairies, he must get up, remain silent, and walk off into the forest. His colleagues must follow without speaking to him, and he will lead them to a root.

Changbai ginseng is regarded as the finest in China. Ginseng hunters in Changbai work in summer, when the plant can be spotted by its red berries. One way to find it is to listen for the call of the Bangchui sparrow, which becomes hoarse after eating ginseng seeds. When a ginseng is found, a stick is planted in the ground and a red cloth tied to it: according to tradition, the cloth stops the ginseng child – the spirit of the root – from escaping.

Ginseng generally grows in the shade of the Korean pine, and it is said that a plant of real medicinal value takes fifty years to mature. The plants are low-growing, with their roots pointing upwards in the topsoil. Digging one out is a complex, nail-biting operation, because if any of the delicate roots are damaged, the value of the whole is severely diminished. Roots are valued not just by weight, but by how closely the root system resembles a human body, with a head and four limbs. If you find a wild root, you're rich, as Changbai ginseng sells for ¥1000 a gram. Artificially reared ginseng is worth a fraction of this.

of the range, the land is dense with huge Korean pines, which can grow up to 50m tall, and mixed broadleaf forest. The rare Manchurian fir is also found here. Higher altitudes are home to the Changbai Scotch pine, recognizable by its yellow bark, and the Japanese yew. As the climate becomes colder and damper higher up, the spruces and firs get hardier before giving way to a layer of sub-alpine grassland with colourful alpine plants. Animal species on the reserve include the leopard, lynx, black bear and Siberian tiger, all now protected, though decades of trapping have made them rarities. Notable bird species include the golden-rumped swallow, orioles and the ornamental red crossbill. The area is rich in medicinal plants, too, and has been a focus of research since the eleventh century. The Chinese regard the region as the best place in the country for **ginseng** and deer antlers, both prized in traditional remedies, and the reserve's rare lichens have been investigated as a treatment for cancer.

Visitors, mostly domestic tourists, South Koreans and Japanese, come here in great numbers, and a tourist village has grown up on the mountain, with the result that the scenery and atmosphere are somewhat marred by litter, souvenir stalls and hawkers. Not all visitors are here for the landscape – plenty come to search for herbs, and many of the Japanese are here to catch butterflies (to keep) and ants (to eat).

The **weather** in the region is not kind and can change very suddenly. In summer, torrential rain is common, and at any time of year cloud and mist can make it impossible to see ten metres ahead of you, let alone the grandeur of Tian Chi lake. Chinese-speakers can call the park's **tourist office** (Ⓣ0433/5710778) to check on conditions. Given the climate, the best time to visit is between June and September; at other times, heavy snows can close roads.

Reaching the reserve

Changbai Shan (长白山, *chángbái shān*) is a long way from anywhere, and the easiest way to get there is by booking one of the three-day, two-night tours arranged through CITS in Jilin (see p.188). These cost more than ¥1000, including park entrance fees and accommodation, but stop at all the must-sees, including Tian Chi. There are good train and bus links, however, and independent travel is perfectly feasible.

At the base of the mountain, **Baihe** village is the rail terminus for Changbai Shan. The most convenient approach is from the north via bus from Jilin to Baihe (4hr; ¥50). From Changchun, train #K7388/7389 departs daily at 2.30pm, arriving in Baihe at 5.45am the next day. You can also approach from Dandong to the south: two daily buses depart before 9am for Tonghua (通化, *tōnghuà*; 7hr; ¥60), a regional rail hub, arriving in plenty of time to catch the 10pm night train to Baihe, which gets in at 5.45am; if you miss that, there are three morning trains for Baihe, departing at 3am, 6.30am and 8am, the latest of which arrives in Baihe at 2.30pm. Approaching from Beijing, there is a daily overnight train to Tonghua, which departs at 2.45pm and arrives in Tonghua at 7am the next day.

The train is also the best overland route back out of the Changbai Shan region, with daily direct runs from Tonghua to Shenyang and Beijing. There are also four buses daily from Baihe to **Yanji**, in China's Korean Autonomous Prefecture, from where you can transfer west to Jilin and Changchun, or north towards Harbin.

Baihe

Once a logging village in its own right, **BAIHE** (白河, *báihé*) is now little more than a staging post for tourists visiting Changbai Shan Nature Reserve, 20km away. Arrival at the train station is bedlam; you can collect your thoughts over a steaming cup of tea in the *Yanleyuan Restaurant*, also in the car park square.

There are **hotels** around the train and bus stations and in the commercial area, called Erhao Baihe Zhan (二号白河站, *èrhào báihé zhàn*). Around the train station, the *Hongda Binguan* (宏达宾馆, *hóngdá bīnguǎn*; ❶–❷) runs a virtual cartel, with places to stay on both sides of the station car park: the *Hongda* itself is on the right as you get off the train and the cheaper *Ding Jia*, where you can get a bed for around ¥20, on the left.

If the spartan budget options around the station don't suit, it's only a ¥5 taxi ride to *Erdao Baihe Zhan*, where there is a string of smarter establishments along the main road to choose from. Not as tacky as it sounds, the *Landmark Resort* (Ⓣ0433/5712422; ❹) has smart, clean rooms; directly opposite, the renovated *Xinda Binguan* (信达宾馆, *xìndá bīnguǎn*; Ⓣ0433/5720111; ❺) is one of the best in this part of town. You can bargain at the *Yongxu Binguan* (永旭宾馆, *yǒngxù bīnguǎn*; Ⓣ0433/5713588; ❹), at the top of the street, when rooms outnumber tourists.

The reserve

It is surely only a matter of time before **Tian Chi** (天池, *tīanchí*), a dramatic volcanic crater lake 5km across, encircled by angular crags, gushing waterfalls and snow-capped peaks, takes its place alongside Beijing's Forbidden City and Xi'an's Terracotta Army as one of China's must-see wonders. The effort of climbing the thousand or so concrete steps to reach the lake, not to mention all the trouble of getting to the reserve in the first place, is forgotten as you cross the boulder-strewn snow field to what must be one of the most spectacular views anywhere in the world.

Tian Chi is the undisputed jewel of the reserve. Of the other specific sights, **Small Tian Chi** is almost laughable when compared to its larger sibling, though the **Underground Forest** (地下森林, *dìxià sēnlín*) – a tree-filled canyon – is an unexpected wonder.

Despite its remoteness, Changbai Shan averages around 10,000 visitors a day in summer – and as you're herded from one spot to the next, it's easy to feel the outdoors experience has been diluted a bit. Getting away from the crowds is the key to a rewarding visit. Head off on your own and you can quickly be swallowed up in the wilderness, but be careful around Tian Chi; the lake straddles the Chinese–North Korean border – if you stray across, you're subject to arrest and charges of espionage. At the height of the Cultural Revolution, Chairman Mao ordered that the line be demarcated, but it isn't clearly marked on the ground.

Reserve practicalities

The bus trip from **Baihe** to the main gate of the reserve takes 45min (¥35), from where park shuttles run up and down the mountain. The last buses return to Baihe around 4pm. Alternatively, you can charter a taxi from anywhere in Baihe, which should cost around ¥100 for a round-trip to the gates of the reserve and back – don't pay the full amount until you have been safely returned to where you came from.

Entry to the reserve (daily 7.30am–6pm) costs ¥100, half-price for students and other groups spelled out in minute detail at the ticket office. However, there's an additional ¥45 fee for using the parks "eco" buses (or ¥80 if you opt for a decidedly non-eco 4WD), which, considering it is 16km from the entrance to Tian Chi (a ticket for which costs a further ¥25), all uphill, is an unavoidable expense.

Among the cluster of **hotels** inside the park are *Athletes' Village* (运动员村宾馆, *yùndòngyuáncūn bīnguǎn*; ⓣ0433/5746066; ❻) and *Cuckoo Villas* (杜鹃山庄, *dùjuān shānzhuāng*; ⓣ0433/5746099; ❺), which represent the cheap to mid-range options. At the upper end of the spectrum, popular with the many Korean tour groups who visit, are the *International Tourist Hotel* (长白山国际旅游宾馆, *chángbáishān guójìlǚyóu bīnguǎn*; ⓣ0433/5746001; ❼), which has rooms with views of a waterfall, and the *Heaven Springs Hotel* (天上温泉宾馆, *tiānshàng wēnquán bīnguǎn*; ⓣ0433/5822157; ❼), which has a hot-spring swimming pool, filled by sulphurous waters bubbling up from beneath the mountains.

Harbin and beyond

The capital of Heilongjiang province, **HARBIN** (哈尔滨, *hāěrbīn*) is probably the northernmost city of interest to visitors, the last before you hit the sub-Siberian wilderness and its scattering of oil and mining towns. It's worth a visit for its winter **Ice Festival** alone, but it's also one of the few northern cities with a distinctive character, the result of colonialism and cooperation with nearby Russia.

Harbin was a small fishing village on the Songhua River until world history intervened. In 1896, the Russians obtained a contract to build a rail line from Vladivostok through Harbin to Dalian, and the town's population swelled to include 200,000 foreigners. More Russians arrived in 1917, this time White Russian refugees fleeing the Bolsheviks, and many stayed on. In 1932, the city was briefly captured by Japanese forces invading Manchuria, then in 1945 it fell again to the Russian army, who held it for a year before Stalin and Chiang Kai-shek finally came to an agreement. Harbin reverted to the Chinese, though when the

Russians withdrew, they took with them most of the city's industrial plant. Things haven't been totally peaceful since – Harbin was the scene of fierce factional fighting during the Cultural Revolution, and when relations with the Soviet Union deteriorated, the inhabitants looked anxiously north as fierce border skirmishes took place.

Not surprisingly, the city used to be nicknamed "Little Moscow", and though much of the old architecture has been replaced with sterile blocks and

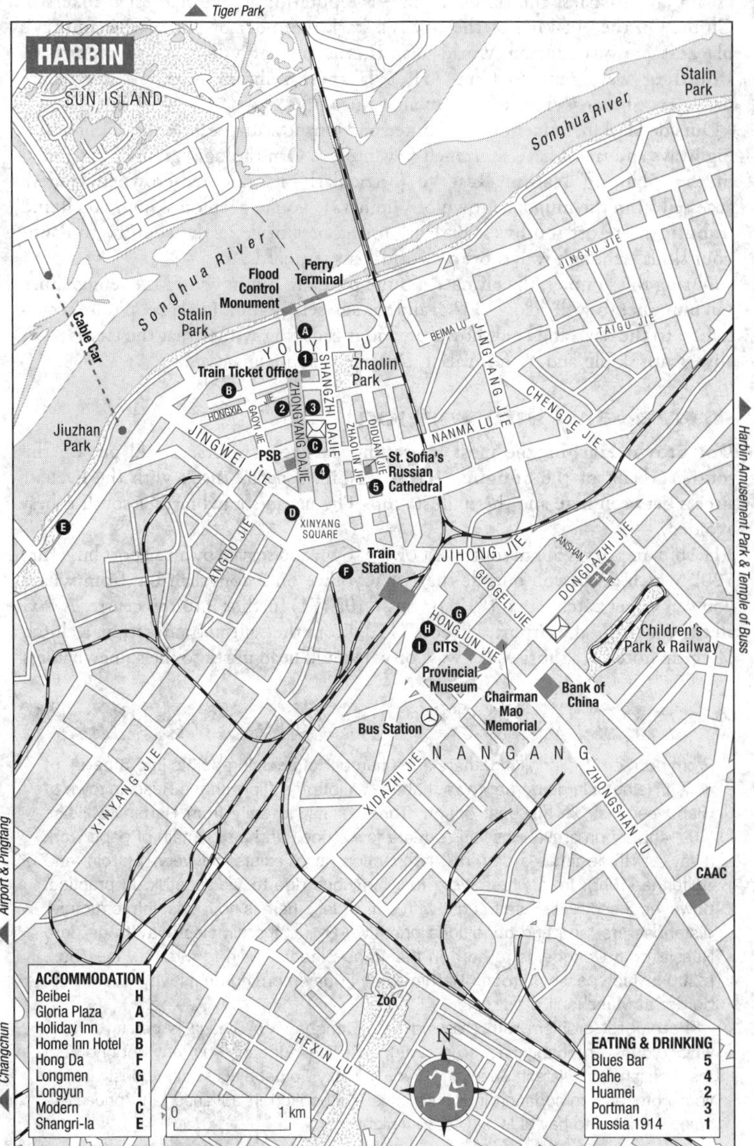

skyscrapers, corners of Harbin still look like the last threadbare outpost of imperial Russia. Leafy boulevards are lined with European-style buildings painted in pastel shades, and bulbous onion domes dot the skyline. The city's past is celebrated with a restored shopping street, **Zhongyang Dajie** (中央大街, *zhōngyāng dàjiē*), as well as in a Russian cathedral that now houses a photographic history of Harbin. There are several Russian restaurants, and the locals have picked up on some of their neighbour's customs: as well as a taste for ice cream and pastries, the residents have a reputation as the hardest drinkers in China. On the outskirts of the city is a stark reminder of one of the country's blackest periods: during World War II, the former village, now suburb, of **Pingfang** was home to Unit 731, a Japanese military research base where prisoners of war were used as human guinea pigs.

Outside Harbin, attractions are limited and journeys can be arduous, though new highways and trains have shortened travel times. Ornithologists will be interested in the **Zhalong Nature Reserve** (particularly its rare red-crowned cranes), accessed from the mundane town of Qiqihar. If you're keen on skiing, you'll find **Yabuli**, the resort southwest of Harbin, the best place in the country to flaunt your skills – though well short of world-class standards.

During the summer, the **climate** is quite pleasant, but in winter the temperature can plummet to well below -30°C, and the sun sets at 4pm. Local people are accustomed to the dark and cold, however, and it is during winter that the city is most alive, with skiing and ice festivals in December and January.

Arrival and information

Downtown Harbin, the most interesting part for visitors, is laid out on the southern bank of the **Songhua River** (松花江, *sōnghuā jiāng*), with the liveliest streets between here and the train station. The urban sprawl farther south is best avoided.

Harbin **airport** is 50km southwest of the town and served by an airport bus (1hr; ¥20), which drops you outside the CAAC office on Zhongshan Lu, from where you can either catch a taxi (¥12) or bus #103 (¥1) further into the centre. A taxi all the way from the airport will cost ¥150. From the central train station, a clutch of cheap hotels is a short walk away, or you could head north to the somewhat less

Crossing into Siberia

From northern Heilongjiang, there are a number of crossing points into **Siberia**, of which Heihe, a large border town that sees a lot of traffic with the Russian town of Blagoveščensk, is the best option. Three trains go daily from Harbin to Heihe (10–14hr); upon arrival Russia is a mere few strides and a mountain of paperwork away. A three-times-a-day rail connection also exists between Harbin and Suifenhe (10hr), from where it's a four-hour bus ride to Vladivostok. In practice, however, these routes are fraught with difficulties; there is no tourist infrastructure, distances are long and conditions primitive. By far the simplest way to get into Russia from Dongbei is to hop on the Trans-Siberian train to Moscow (see box, p.200), which passes through Harbin every Friday morning on its way west to the border at Manzhouli.

The biggest problem with crossing from Dongbei into Siberia is getting a visa, which you will probably have to sort out in Beijing, although you may get one from the Russian Consulate in Shenyang if you're lucky. To get a two-week tourist visa, all your hotel accommodation in Russia must be booked in advance, and prices are steep – expect to pay at least US$50 a night.

seedy and hectic central streets. The long-distance **bus station** is on Songhuajiang Jie, across from the train station.

To save doing battle at the station, consider buying train tickets from the **ticket office** on the first floor of the *Jingu Hotel*, opposite *Russia 1914*, at the north end of Zhongyang Dajie at its junction with Shangyou Jie. The same office also sells air tickets.

City transport

For getting around the city, the most useful **bus** is #103, which runs between Zhongshan Lu and **Zhaolin Park** (兆林公园, *zhàolín gōngyuán*) just east of Zhongyang Dajie. Taxi fares around the city start at ¥8 for the first 3km; Harbin has lots of one-way streets, so don't panic if it seems your driver is lapping the block. In summer, regular **boats** cross the Songhua (¥10 return). Good English **maps** of the city are sold in the gift shop at the *Holiday Inn*; Chinese-only versions are widely available (¥6).

Accommodation

The hotels around Zhongyang Dajie are the best option if you're staying for any length of time. There's a cluster around the train station – and the train station itself possesses the grim *Station Hotel* – but the area is noisy, dirty and crowded.

Beibei (北北大酒店, *běiběi dàjiǔdiàn*) Directly across from the train station ⓣ0451/82570960, ⓦwww.beibeihotel.com. Handy location and can be good value, but make sure you see any rooms before agreeing to stay. ❸

Gloria Plaza (饥菜花园大酒店, *jīcài huāyuán dàjiǔdiàn*) 259 Zhongyang Dajie ⓣ0451/8670000. Smart four-star affair perched at the top of Zhongyang Dajie, looking out across the river toward Sun Island. ❻

Holiday Inn (万达假日饭店, *wàndájiàrì fàndiàn*) 90 Jingwei Jie ⓣ0451/84887205, ⓦwww.holidayinn.com/harbinchn. Fading a bit, but has a good location at the head of Zhongyang Dajie and a very helpful English-speaking staff. ❻

Home Inn (如家酒店, *rújīajiǔdiàn*) 51 Shangyou Jie ⓣ0451/57645999, ⓦwww.homeinns.com. The same as any other *Home Inn* in the country – characterless, sterile, clean and good value. Excellent location helps. ❸

Hongda (宏达宾馆, *hóngdá bīnguǎn*) 2 Shangzhi Dajie ⓣ0451/84637582. Clean, friendly, cheap, and just a five-minute walk from Zhongyang Dajie. Breakfast included. ❷

Longmen (龙门大厦, *lóngmén dàshà*) 85 Hongqi Jie ⓣ0451/86791999. A grand old place built in 1901 as the *Chinese Eastern Railway Hotel*, this restored gem is a snapshot of Harbin's bicultural past and worth visiting even if you don't stay. ❺

Longyun (龙运宾馆, *lóngyùn bīnguǎn*) Train Station Square ⓣ0451/82830102. A clean, modern and surprisingly smart place a few doors to the right of the *Beibei* as you exit the train station. ❹

Modern (马达尔宾馆, *mădá'ěr bīnguǎn*) 89 Zhongyang Dajie ⓣ0451/84884199, ⓦhotel.hrbmodern.com. The name is a misnomer, as this place was built in 1906 and survives as Harbin's oldest hotel. An elegant building on one of the city's busiest streets, it's bursting with character. From Zhongyang Dajie, you enter via a ground-floor restaurant. ❻

Shangri-La (香格里拉大饭店, *xiānggélǐlā dàfàndiàn*) 555 Youyi Lu ⓣ0451/84858888, ⓦwww.shangri-la.com. Harbin's only five-star hotel overlooks Stalin Park, Zhongyang Dajie and Zhaolin Park, making rooms here during the Ice Festival like gold dust. Book early. ❾

The City and around

Harbin is more a place to shop and explore the streets than any sort of cultural centre. A good starting point is the **Daoli** district, in the triangle outlined by Diduan Jie and Jingwei Jie, where there are plenty of brand-name clothing boutiques, fur shops and department stores. The smaller streets and alleys around here are the best places to see the city's Russian architecture, with its stucco facades and elegant balconies. There's an extensive market selling women's clothes off

Harbin's Ice Festival

In compensation for the cruel winter weather, the annual **Ice Festival** (冰灯节, *bīngdēngjié*), centred on Zhaolin Park, is held from January 5 to February 5 – though with the influx of tourists, the dates extend each year. Sculptors, some of them teenagers, work twelve-hour days in -20°C December weather to help transform the park into a fairy-tale landscape: the magnificent ice sculptures they create are sometimes entire buildings, complete with slides, stairways, arches and bridges. Carved with chainsaws and picks, the creations often have coloured lights inside to heighten the psychedelic effect. Highlights of past festivals have included detailed replicas of St Paul's Cathedral and life-size Chinese temples, though these days cartoon characters outnumber more traditional Chinese subject matter. Over on Sun Island, a snow sculpture display is held, the highlights of which are the toboggan and snow-tube pistes. It's as much fun watching ecstatic Chinese bounce down the slopes as it is sledding. You can walk across the river yourself or even take a horse-drawn carriage. Festival's end is marked with fireworks and pickaxes; visitors are encouraged to destroy the icy artwork by hand.

Xinyang Square, while the best large department stores are on **Diduan Jie** and **Zhongyang Dajie** (中央大街, *zhōngyāng dàjiē*).

Shops along the latter road have all been restored, with plaques out front in English detailing their past lives as colonial homes and stores. Make sure you go in the department store at no. 107, if only to see its spectacular skylight and rendition of a section from Michelangelo's Sistine Chapel mural, which hangs on the back wall. There are good restaurants and bars along the numbered streets running off Zhongyang Dajie, which is paved with cobblestones and closed to cars and bicycles. At the north end, a modern shopping mall, including a Walmart, rather encroaches on the atmosphere, but can be useful for locating Western "essentials". In winter, ice sculptures line the street, while summer sees pavement cafés set up.

The cathedral and around

The most interesting formal sight in Harbin has to be the **Russian Orthodox cathedral** (St Sofia's, built in 1907) on Zhaolin Jie. Set in its own square and restored to all its onion-domed glory, the cathedral now houses the **Harbin Architecture and Art Centre** (哈尔滨建筑艺术馆, *hā'ěrbīn jiànzhú yìshùguǎn*; daily 8.30am–5pm; ¥20), with a photographic survey of Harbin's history as a Russian railway outpost. On summer evenings, the area around the cathedral comes alive with impromptu badminton games, ladies displaying their fan-dancing skills and – the highlight – a well-choreographed display from the square's fountains. They are roped off, but it is never long before someone charges into the maelstrom.

Due to frosty relations with the Soviet Union in the 1960s and 70s (subject of Ha Jin's excellent *Ocean of Words*, a book of short stories by a former PLA soldier who was based on the Siberian border), Harbin also boasts a network of underground bomb shelters turned shopping malls. You can enter at the train station and walk all the way to Dongdazhi Jie and beyond.

Along Dongdazhi Jie

Southeast from the train station, a Russian-era mansion, the mansard-roofed **Chairman Mao Memorial** (毛主席纪念馆, *máozhǔxí jìniànguǎn*; daily 9am–4pm;

¥6) is named for its most famous post-Revolution guest. The home is at the junction of Hongjun Jie and Dongdazhi Jie, next to the *Sinoway Hotel*. Diagonally across the street, at 48–50 Hongjun Jie, is the **Provincial Museum** (黑龙江博物馆, *hēilóngjiāng bówùguǎn*; daily 9am–4pm; ¥10). Entered through an anonymous set of doors between a sports shop and a shoe shop, the collection has certainly seen better days. With virtually no English explanations, there would be no reason to visit were it not for the dinosaur, mammoth and woolly rhino skeletons secreted away upstairs. Just beyond, the junction with Guogeli Jie is an up-and-coming area for drinking and shopping. One spin-off of improved Sino-Indian relations is the mall called India Street, where bemused Indian shopkeepers sell trinkets and curry to camera-wielding Chinese tourists.

Out from the centre, there are some nice old working churches in the Nangang District. At 25 Dongdazhi Jie is a German Lutheran chapel built in 1914, while just a little further on at no. 268 you can peek inside an onion-domed Russian Orthodox building.

Continuing northeast along Dongdazhi, you'll eventually come to a long street market, hawking the usual collection of clothes, shoes and DVDs. This in turn leads to the **Temple of Bliss** (吉乐寺, *jílè sì*; daily 8am–4pm; ¥10), surrounded by tourist shops and stalls. Built in the 1920s, the Buddhist complex includes an impressive seven-tiered pagoda, and the smattering of monks suggests there is at least some genuinely religious, as well as mercantile, activity. At the end of all this lies **Harbin Amusement Park** (哈尔宾游乐园, *hā'ěrbīn yóulèyuán*), its huge ferris wheel dwarfing the only in-town competition at Zhaolin Park (兆林公园, *zhàolín gōngyuán*).

Along the river

The riverbank area is another worthwhile district to explore, starting from the **Flood Control Monument** (防洪纪念碑, *fánghóng jìniànbēi*) at the bottom of Zhongyang Dajie. Built in 1958, the monument commemorates the many thousands who have died in the Songhua floods, and has been updated to mark floods from the summers of 1989 and 1998. The square here is a popular hangout for local people, who gather to feed pigeons and fly kites, as is **Stalin Park** (斯大林公园, *sīdàlín gōngyuán*), a strip of land along the east bank of the river that's particularly lively on weekends. People come to what must be China's last public memorial to Stalin in order to wash their clothes, meet and chat, even bathe in the river – the last is not a good idea, as levels of pollution are so high that fish can no longer survive. Others cluster around palm-readers and storytellers who relate old Chinese folk legends. Just southeast of the monument, **Zhaolin Park**, unremarkable in summer, is host to the spectacular winter Ice Festival (see box opposite).

In winter, the Songhua River freezes solid and you can take a horse carriage, rent a go-kart or walk across – the ice is so thick it will support a fully loaded bus or lorry and gets used as a road. In summer, **ferries** (¥10 return) leave from near the Flood Control Monument for the northern bank and the busy resort and sanatorium village of **Taiyang (Sun) Island** (太阳岛, *tàiyáng dǎo*; daily 8am–5pm; ¥30/¥150 during the ice festival). You can also access Sun Island by cable car (¥50 one way). The island is an enormous park and leisure complex, with lakes for boating, swimming pools and fairground rides, as well as an infamous **Tiger Park** (东北虎林园, *dōngběihǔ línyuán*; daily 9am–4pm; ¥65); supposedly a refuge and breeding centre for the critically endangered Siberian tiger, this place smells more of commerce than conservation as park staff encourage visitors (for a small fee) to release domestic livestock to be stalked, slain and eaten.

Pingfang: unit 731

Harbin's most notorious location lies out in the suburbs, a forty-minute bus journey southwest of the centre, in **PINGFANG**. This was the home of a secret Japanese research establishment during World War II, now open to the public as a **museum** (平方, *píngfāng*; daily 9–11.30am & 1–3.30pm; ¥20). Here, prisoners of war were subjected to horrendous torture – being injected with deadly viruses, dissected alive, and frozen or heated slowly until they died – under the pretense of scientific experimentation. More than three thousand people from China, Russia and Mongolia were murdered by troops from unit 731 of the Japanese army. After the war, the Japanese tried to hide all evidence of the base, and its existence only came to light through the efforts of Japanese investigative journalists. It was also discovered that, as with scientists in defeated Nazi Germany, the Americans gave the Japanese scientists immunity from prosecution in return for their research findings.

A couple of hundred metres from the terminus of bus #338, which you can catch one street west of Harbin's central train station square, the museum mostly comprises photographs labelled in Chinese. Looking at the displays, which include a painting of bound prisoners being used as bomb targets, you can begin to understand why Chinese antipathy towards Japan runs so deep.

Eating, drinking and nightlife

Aside from expensive regional delicacies such as bear paw and deer muzzle, available in upmarket hotels, **food** in Harbin is good value. Influenced by Russian cuisine, local cooking is characterized by the exceptionally heavy use of garlic – and a lot of potato. A favourite local dish is *xiaoji dunmogu* (chicken and stewed mushrooms). In summer and during the busy winter periods, tented areas resembling outdoor German beer halls spring up on the fringes of Zhongyang Dajie. They're great spots to enjoy piping-hot barbecued skewers and a stein or two of ice-cold Harbin beer.

For **bars**, try Guogeli Jie east of the train station, somewhat of an unsalubrious area, or along the river, where drinking establishments tend to have a Russian theme. The top **nightlife option** is *Blues Bar* (布蓝斯酒吧, *bùlánsī jiǔbā*) at 100 Diduan Jie, where Russian and Chinese students – plus a rogues' gallery of older folk – dance the night away on weekends.

Dahe (大和美食日本菜, *dàhé měishí rìběncài*) 60 Xi 14 Dao Jie. Reasonably priced Japanese restaurant serving all the favourites, from steaming bowls of udon noodles to well-sculpted plates of sashimi.

Huamei (华梅饭店, *huáméi fàndiàn*) 112 Zhongyang Jie. A Harbin institution, food here is basic but good – the stroganoff comes particularly recommended – and unless you go for caviar, it won't break the bank.

Portman (波特曼西餐厅, *bōtèmàn xīcāntīng*) 53 Xi Qidao Jie. A European-style pub and grill with a heavily Russian-influenced menu.

Russia 1914 (俄罗斯一九一四, *éluósī yījiǔyīsì*) 57 Xi Toudao Jie. The perfect place for afternoon tea, with atmosphere to match – you can almost imagine yourself back in the early 1900s. Main meals are also served, but if you're just after a little pick-me-up, it's hard to beat a cup of tea with Russian bread and jam.

Listings

Airlines The CAAC sales office is at 99 Zhongshan Lu (☎0451/82651188); airport buses run from outside every 20min (1hr; ¥20). If you're leaving the city by plane, allow an hour to get to the airport through the traffic.

Banks and exchange The Bank of China is on Zhongshan Lu (Mon–Fri 8am–noon & 1–5pm). The foreign-exchange counter is upstairs. You can also change money at its branch at 37 Zhaolin Jie (same hours).

Internet There are plenty of internet cafés throughout town, including one directly opposite the train station, next door to the *Longyun*; another across the street from the Hongda at 4 Shangzhu Dajie; and several on side streets running off Zhongyang Dajie.

Mail and telephones The main post office is at 51 Jianshe Jie (Mon–Sat 8am–6pm).

PSB 26 Duan Jie, off Zhongyang Dajie (Mon–Fri 8–11am & 2–5pm).

Travel agents CITS (Ⓣ0451/53661191, Ⓦwww.hljcits.com), at 68 Hongjun Jie, is friendly and dependable, and the similarly titled CTIS (Ⓣ0451/53665858), round the corner from the railway station at 14 Songhuajiang Jie, specializes in tours across the province. Both can organize ski packages to Yabuli, but with transport to the resort so plentiful, and accommodation at the slopes only available through *Sun Mountain Resort* (see p.200), it can be just as easy to arrange independently.

Yabuli

Regarded as the premier ski destination in China, **YABULI** (亚布力, *yàbùlì*) resort's 3800m piste spreads across the southern side of Guokui (literally Pot-lid) Mountain (1300m), 194km southeast of Harbin. Six lifts shuttle an average of 10,000 skiers per day during the winter months. Although popular, the pistes are nowhere near as good as those in Europe, North America or Japan, nor are they cheap to ski. If you're after a proper skiing holiday, this is not really the place, and the slopes cropping up outside most northern cities offer

Dongbei's minority communities

After forcing minority communities to embrace official communist culture during the 1950s and 60s, the Chinese government now takes a more enlightened – if somewhat patronizing – approach to the minority nations of the north. The **Manchu** people, spread across Inner Mongolia and Dongbei, are the most numerous and assimilated. Having lived so long among the Han, they are now almost identical, though Manchus tend to be slightly taller, and Manchu men have more facial hair. Manchus are noted for an elaborate system of etiquette and will never eat dog, unlike their Korean neighbours, who love it. The "three strange things" that the southern Chinese say are found in the northeast are all Manchu idiosyncrasies: paper windows pasted outside their wooden frame, babies carried by their mothers in handbags and women smoking in public (the latter, of course, can be a habit of Han and every other ethnicity in large cities).

In the inhospitable northern margins of Dongbei live small communities such as the **Hezhen**, one of the smallest minority nations in China with an estimated 1400 members. Inhabiting the region where the Songhua, Heilong and Wusuli (Ussuri) rivers converge, they're known to the Han Chinese as the "Fish Tribe", and their culture and livelihood centre around fishing. Indeed, they're the only people in the world to make clothes out of fish skin: the fish is gutted, descaled, then dried and tanned and the skins sewn together to make light, waterproof coats, shoes and gloves. More numerous are the **Daur**, 120,000 of whom live along the Nenjiang River. They are fairly seamlessly assimilated these days, but still retain distinctive marriage and funerary traditions, and have a reputation for being superb at hockey, a form of which they have played since the sixth century.

However, perhaps the most distinctive minority are the **Oroqen**, a tribe of nomadic hunters living in patrilineal clan communes called *wulileng* in the northern sub-Siberian wilderness. Although they have recently adopted a more settled existence, their main livelihood still comes from deer-hunting, while household items, tools and canoes are made from birch bark by Oroqen women. Clothes are fashioned from deer hide, and include a striking hat made of a roe deer head, complete with antlers and leather patches for eyes, which is used as a disguise in hunting.

To Russia on the Trans-Manchurian

For those with time and a little bit of patience to spare, the evocatively named **Trans-Manchurian railway** is one of the best ways to enter or exit China. The line barrels northeast out of Beijing, eventually crossing the Russian border to connect with its far more illustrious sibling, the Trans-Siberian. Indeed, once a week **direct trains** run the route all the way between Beijing and Moscow, avoiding Mongolia and thus the necessity of acquiring an extra visa. The trip takes around six days, starting in Moscow on Friday evening, and Beijing on Saturday evening; trains are extremely comfortable, with private rooms and restaurant cars (see p.31 for more). **Visas** must be arranged in advance both ways, and the difficulty of acquiring a Russian one (not to mention buying the ticket itself) means that many choose to organize the trip through a travel agency; see p.30 for recommended operators. Prices vary enormously depending upon whether you go through an agency or do things by yourself; CITS in Beijing (p.81) sell Moscow tickets from US$710.

With a little advance planning, it'll be possible to visit other Russian cities before hitting Moscow, with the Siberian city of Irkutsk a favourite thanks to its proximity to Lake Baikal, the world's largest body of fresh water. Easier to organize are stops at Chinese cities on the way: Shenyang (p.172), Changchun (p.186) and Harbin (p.192) all have their merits, and new high-speed services have cut travel times considerably. From Harbin, the train cuts through **Inner Mongolia** (see pp.217–219 for more on this province's history and attractions) before hitting the Russian border, passing through the pleasant towns of Hailar and Manzhouli.

Hailar

With rail connections as well as an airport, **HAILAR** (海拉尔, *hǎilā'ěr*) is the main transport hub of the region, and a centre for grassland visits. The town of Hailar itself is of minimal interest, its main attraction the **network of tunnels** used by the Japanese army during World War II; the site can only be reached by a bumpy taxi ride

much better value for money and are easier to get to. Nevertheless, a trip can still be good fun if expectations are kept in check.

Ski season runs from October to March, and the only place to stay at Yabuli is the *Sun Mountain Resort* (阳光度假村, *yánggūangdùjiàcūn*; ⓣ0451/53458888, ⓦwww.yabuliski.com; ❻–❾). Packages covering travel, accommodation and skiing can be booked at CITS and other travel agents in Harbin and throughout China, but are fairly simple to organize independently.

Qiqihar and the Zhalong Nature Reserve

A four-hour bus ride west of Harbin, **QIQIHAR** (齐齐哈尔, *qíqíhāěr*) is one of the northeast's oldest cities, and still a thriving industrial centre. Alas, it's more fun to say the city's name aloud than to stay here for more than a day. The only real reason to come is to visit the **Zhalong Nature Reserve** (扎龙自然保护区, *zhālóng zìrán beohùqū*; ¥20), 30km southeast from town. This marshy plain abounds in shallow reedy lakes and serves as the summer breeding ground of thousands of species of birds, including white storks, whooper swans, spoonbills, white ibis and – the star attractions – nine of the world's fifteen species of crane. Most spectacular of these is the endangered red-crowned crane, a lanky black-and-white bird over 1m tall, with a scarlet bald patch. It has long been treasured in the East as a paradigm of elegance – the Japanese call it the Marsh God – and is a popular symbol of longevity, living as long as sixty years. The birds mate for life, and the

(¥30 return) from the train station. The chief reason most visitors come to Hailar, however, is to see the North Mongolian **Hulunbuir grasslands** (呼伦贝尔草原, *hūlúnbèi'ěr cǎoyuán*), an apparently limitless rolling land of plains and low grassy mountains. As elsewhere in Inner Mongolia, there are the CITS-approved villages of Mongol herders; though you could try to strike off independently, it's worth noting that the grassland **tours** here don't attract hordes of people. A day-trip from Hailar to eat a traditional mutton banquet on the grasslands, for a group of four people, costs around ¥350 each, or double that to stay the night. For bookings and more information, contact CITS (Ⓣ0470/8224017) at their office on the third floor of *Beiyuan Hotel* (北苑宾馆, *běiyuàn bīnguǎn*; Ⓣ0470/8235888; ❹), itself one of the better **accommodation** options in town.

Manzhouli

A few hours to the west of Hailar is **MANZHOULI** (满洲里, *mǎnzhōulǐ*), a bustling centre for cross-border commerce whose wholesale demolition, renovation and development – much of which has involved the surreal addition of Versailles-inspired facades to communist tower blocks – has left it with little atmosphere, though it's worth a visit for trips to the surrounding countryside, as well as air fresher than you may have experienced elsewhere in China. There are plenty of **hotels** in town, and **eating** is a treat if you love Russian food. Those staying the night may care to visit the great lake **Dalai Hu** (达赉湖, *dálài hú*; Hulun Nur in Mongolian), a shallow expanse of water set in marshy grazing country where flocks of swans, geese, cranes and other migratory birds come to nest. In June and July, the grasslands in this region are said to be the greenest in all Mongolia, and coming here may be the most rewarding – and least expensive – way to see Inner Mongolia's grasslands. A taxi from town will cost ¥200 round-trip.

female only lays one or two eggs each season, over which the male stands guard. The best time to visit the reserve is from April to June, when the migrants have just arrived, though the viewing season extends through September. Walking around the reserve, although not forbidden, is not encouraged by the keepers – or by the murderous swarms of mosquitoes. Come prepared, and bring binoculars if you can, too. Dedicated ornithologists might like to spend a few days here, but for most people an afternoon crouched in the reedbeds will be enough.

Practicalities

Buses to the reserve (1hr; ¥5) leave from Qiqihar's bus station, 1km south down Longhua Lu, on the left, and also from in front of the train station. A **taxi** will cost ¥150 return, depending on how long you make the driver wait around. Splendid though the birds are, it can be difficult to fill the hours the bus timetable obliges you to spend in Qiqihar, so consider devoting part of your visit to the **flat-bottomed-boat tour** that leaves from the reserve entrance; book through CITS (Ⓣ0452/2474646).

Visitors to Zhalong have to stay in Qiqihar, where a number of new business **hotels** have sprung up. The reasonably priced *Civil Aviation* (民航宾馆, *mínhángbīngǔan*; Ⓣ0452/2388888; ❷) at 12 Pukui Lu, is close to the station and, while nothing special, offers value and cleanliness as well as convenience.

Travel details

Trains

Changchun to: Beijing (12 daily; 6–15hr); Dandong (2 daily; 9hr); Harbin (32 daily; 2–3hr); Jilin (11 daily; 1hr 30min–2hr); Shenyang (42 daily; 2–4hr); Tonghua (2 daily; 6–8hr).
Dalian to: Beijing (2 daily; 10–11hr); Dandong (daily; 10hr 30min); Harbin (6 daily; 9–13hr); Shenyang (30 daily; 3hr 30min–6hr).
Dandong to: Beijing (2 daily; 14–21 hr); Changchun (2 daily; 9hr); Dalian (daily; 11 hr); Shenyang (10 daily; 3–5hr).
Harbin to: Beijing (10 daily; 10–18hr); Changchun (32 daily; 2–3hr); Daqing (27 daily; 1hr 30min–3hr); Jilin (2 daily; 5–6hr); Moscow (weekly; 6 days); Qiqihar (21 daily; 3–4hr); Shanghai (daily; 31hr); Shenyang (33 daily; 5–7hr).
Jilin to: Beijing (2 daily; 11–17hr); Changchun (11 daily; 1hr 30min–2hr); Dalian (3 daily; 13–15hr); Harbin (4 daily; 5–6hr); Shenyang (12 daily; 5hr–9hr 30min).
Qiqihar to: Bei'an (3 daily; 4hr); Beijing (4 daily; 15–20hr); Hailar (6 daily; 7hr 30min–13hr); Harbin (21 daily; 3–4hr).
Shenyang to: Beijing (32 daily; 4–17hr); Changchun (46 daily; 2–4hr); Dalian (31 daily; 3hr 30min–6hr); Dandong (9 daily; 3hr 30min–6hr); Harbin (32 daily; 3–7hr); Jilin (11 daily; 5hr–11hr 30min); Tonghua (3 daily; 6–7hr).
Tonghua to: Baihe (3 daily; 6hr 30min–8hr); Beijing (daily; 15hr 30min); Changchun (2 daily; 7–8hr); Shenyang (4 daily; 6hr–7hr 30min).

Buses

Bus connections are comprehensive and can be picked up to all major towns from the bus station or in front of the train station. For some stretches, buses are **faster** and more **convenient** than trains, especially from Harbin to the west and south; Changchun to Jilin and Shenyang; and Shenyang to Dalian. Away from the major cities, however, roads turn rough and the journeys arduous.

Ferries

Dalian to: Tanggu (for Tianjin; daily or alternate days; 13–15hr); Weihai (2 daily; 8hr); Yantai (6 daily; 6hr).
Dandong to: Inchon (South Korea; 3 weekly; 20hr).
Harbin to: Jiamusi (daily in summer; 18hr).

Flights

Besides the domestic services listed, some useful international connections serve this part of China, including flights from Changchun to Seoul; from Dalian to Fukuoka, Hiroshima, Nagoya, Osaka, Seoul, Tokyo and Vladivostok; and from Shenyang to Bangkok, Osaka, Pyongyang, Seoul and Tokyo.
Changchun to: Beijing (11 daily; 1hr 30min); Chengdu (5 weekly; 5hr); Chongqing (3 weekly; 4hr 40min); Dalian (4 daily; 1hr 10min); Fuzhou (2 weekly; 4hr 20min); Guangzhou (daily; 5hr 40min); Hangzhou (daily; 2hr 50min); Hong Kong (2 weekly; 4hr 30min); Ji'nan (daily; 1hr 55min); Kunming (3 weekly; 6hr); Nanjing (daily; 2hr 15min); Qingdao (daily; 1hr 35min); Shanghai (3 daily; 2hr 30min); Shenzhen (3 daily; 5hr); Xiamen (8 weekly; 5hr); Xi'an (3 weekly; 4hr 10min); Yanji (2 daily; 1hr); Yantai (daily; 2hr 25min).
Dalian to: Beijing (12 daily; 1hr 10min); Changchun (3 daily; 1hr); Changsha (2 daily; 3hr 40min); Chengdu (2 daily; 3hr 40min); Chongqing (4 weekly; 3hr); Fuzhou (daily; 3hr 30min); Guangzhou (3 daily; 3hr 15min); Guilin (2 weekly; 4hr 25min); Haikou (daily; 3hr 35min); Hangzhou (2 daily; 2hr); Harbin (3 daily; 1hr 25min); Hefei (weekly; 1hr 50min); Hong Kong (daily; 3hr 25min); Jilin (3 weekly; 1hr 20min); Ji'nan (2 daily; 1hr); Kunming (daily; 5hr); Luoyang (3 weekly; 1hr 40min); Nanjing (3 daily; 1hr 30min); Ningbo (daily; 1hr 50min); Qingdao (5 daily; 40min); Qinhuangdao (3 weekly; 1hr); Sanya (3 weekly; 6hr 30min); Shanghai (7 daily; 1hr 30min); Shenyang (daily; 50min); Shenzhen (3 daily; 4hr 50min); Taiyuan (daily; 3hr 30min); Tianjin (2 daily; 1hr); Wenzhou (daily; 2hr); Wuhan (8 weekly; 3hr); Xiamen (2 daily; 3hr 35min); Xi'an (daily; 2hr 20min); Yanji (daily; 2hr 30min); Yantai (daily; 35min); Zhengzhou (9 weekly; 1hr 45min).
Dandong to: Sanya (3 weekly; 6hr 25min); Shanghai (3 weekly; 2hr 20min); Shenzhen (3 weekly; 5hr 35min).
Harbin to: Beijing (13 daily; 1hr 50min); Chengdu (daily; 5hr 50min); Chongqing (4 weekly; 3hr 50min); Dalian (4 daily; 1hr 20min); Fuzhou (daily; 4hr 25min); Guangzhou (2 daily; 5hr 35min); Guiyang (3 weekly; 5hr 35min); Haikou (4 weekly; 5hr 30min); Hangzhou (daily; 3hr 10min); Hong Kong (4 weekly; 4hr 40min); Ji'nan (daily; 2hr 10min); Kunming (daily; 7hr); Nanjing

(daily; 3hr 50min); Ningbo (4 weekly; 3hr); Qingdao (4 daily; 1hr 50min); Sanya (4 weekly; 7hr); Shanghai (7 daily; 2hr 40min); Shenyang (2 daily; 55min); Shenzhen (daily; 5hr); Tianjin (daily 3hr); Wenzhou (5 weekly; 4hr 30min); Wuhan (daily; 4hr); Xiamen (2 daily; 5hr); Xi'an (daily; 3hr); Zhengzhou (7 weekly; 3hr 40min).

Jilin to: Beijing (4 weekly; 1hr 40min); Dalian (3 weekly; 1hr 20min); Guangzhou (2 weekly; 6hr 35min); Shanghai (2 weekly; 2hr 30min).

Qiqihar to: Beijing (3 weekly; 1hr 50min); Guangzhou (2 weekly; 5hr 55min); Shanghai (2 weekly; 2hr 50min).

Shenyang to: Beijing (7 daily; 1hr 15min); Changsha (daily; 3hr); Chengdu (daily; 4hr 30min); Chongqing (daily; 3hr 15min); Dalian (daily; 50min); Fuzhou (daily; 2hr 50min); Guangzhou (3 daily; 3hr 45min); Guiyang (3 weekly; 4hr 40min); Haikou (daily; 5hr 30min); Hangzhou (daily; 2hr 20min); Harbin (2 daily; 1hr); Hefei (4 weekly; 1hr 45min); Hohhot (3 weekly; 1hr 30min); Hong Kong (4 weekly; 4hr 35min); Ji'nan (daily; 1hr 20min); Kunming (2 daily; 5hr 10min); Lanzhou (7 weekly; 3hr 10min); Nanjing (6 weekly; 1hr 50min); Ningbo (daily; 2hr 10min); Qingdao (2 daily; 1hr 10min); Sanya (daily; 5hr 30min); Shanghai (8 daily; 2hr); Shantou (2 weekly; 4hr); Shenzhen (4 daily; 4hr); Shijiazhuang (4 weekly; 1hr 40min); Taiyuan (2 daily; 1hr 40min); Tianjin (8 weekly; 1hr 20min); Ürümqi (3 weekly; 6hr 30min); Wenzhou (daily; 2hr 35min); Wuhan (daily; 3hr 25min); Xiamen (2 daily; 3hr 10min); Xi'an (daily; 2hr 30min); Yanji (2 daily; 1hr 10min); Yantai (daily; 1hr); Zhengzhou (daily; 2hr); Zhuhai (2 weekly; 6hr 30min).

CHAPTER 4 Highlights

* **The grasslands** Explore the rolling green horizons of Inner Mongolia's "grass sea" – such as those near Hohhot – and sleep in a Mongol yurt. See p.229

* **Yungang Caves** See glorious Buddhist statuary from the fifth century, nestling in grottoes near Datong. See p.234

* **Walking Wutai Shan** The least developed of China's four Buddhist mountains is actually five flat peaks, perfect for independent exploration. See p.238

* **Pingyao** An intact Ming-era walled city, home to winding back alleys and a number of atmospheric hotels and guesthouses. See p.244

* **The Terracotta Army** No visit to China is complete without a peek at these warrior figurines, guarding the tomb of Qin Shi Huang near Xi'an. See p.265

* **Longmen Caves, Luoyang** Walk along a riverside promenade past caves peppering limestone cliff faces, containing more than 100,000 Buddhist carvings. See p.277

▲ Pingyao

The Yellow River

From its lofty source on the Tibetan plateau, the famed **Yellow River** (黄河, *huánghé*) runs for almost 5500km before emptying into the Yellow Sea, making it China's second-longest waterway, and the sixth longest in the world. The river's etymology stems from the vast quantities of **loess** it carries, a yellow silt which has clogged and confused its course over the years. However, the river's popular nickname, "China's Sorrow", hints at the **floods** and changes of course that have repeatedly caused devastation – the waterway is often likened to a dragon, a reference not just to its sinuous course, but also to its uncontrollable nature, by turns benign and malevolent. On the flipside, it provides much-needed irrigation to areas otherwise arid and inhospitable, and has created some of China's most distinctive landscapes, barrelling past colossal sand dunes before sliding along pancake-flat plains scarred with deep, winding crevasses.

Such is the length of the Yellow River that the first and last major cities it hits – Lanzhou and Ji'nan – are actually covered in other chapters (see p.814 & p.298, respectively). In between, the river flows through **Ningxia**, **Inner Mongolia**, **Shanxi**, **Shaanxi** and **Henan**, and has played a vital role in the history, geography and fortunes of each province, but sadly the capricious nature of the river makes river travel impossible in the region.

In **Ningxia**, a tiny province with a substantial Hui minority, you can witness the river's mighty waters running between desert sand dunes at the resort of **Shapotou**. Rarely visited by foreign tourists, Ningxia also offers quiet, attractive cities, while the provincial capital of **Yinchuan** is a base for fascinating sights such as the mausoleums of the Western Xia, ancient reminders of a long-extinct culture. The river then slides into **Inner Mongolia**, passing through the super-industrial city of Baotou, jump-off point for the supposed **tomb of Genghis Khan**. The grasslands surrounding the provincial capital of **Hohhot** make it possible to catch a glimpse of the Mongols' ancient and unique way of life – you can sleep in a nomad's yurt, sample Mongol food and ride a horse across the grasslands, all within half a day's train journey from Beijing. Further downstream, **Shanxi** province boasts some great attractions, most notably the **Yungang cave temples**, and the beautiful holy mountain of **Wutai Shan**. Dotted around the small towns along the single rail line leading south to the Yellow River plain are quirky temples and villages that seem stuck in the nineteenth century. **Shaanxi** province is more of the same, yet its wealthy and historically significant capital city, **Xi'an**, is one of China's biggest tourist destinations, with as many temples, museums and tombs as the rest of the region put together, and the **Terracotta Army** deservedly ranking as one of China's premier sights. The city is also home to a substantial **Muslim** minority, whose cuisine is well worth sampling. Within easy travelling distance of here, following the Yellow River east, are two more

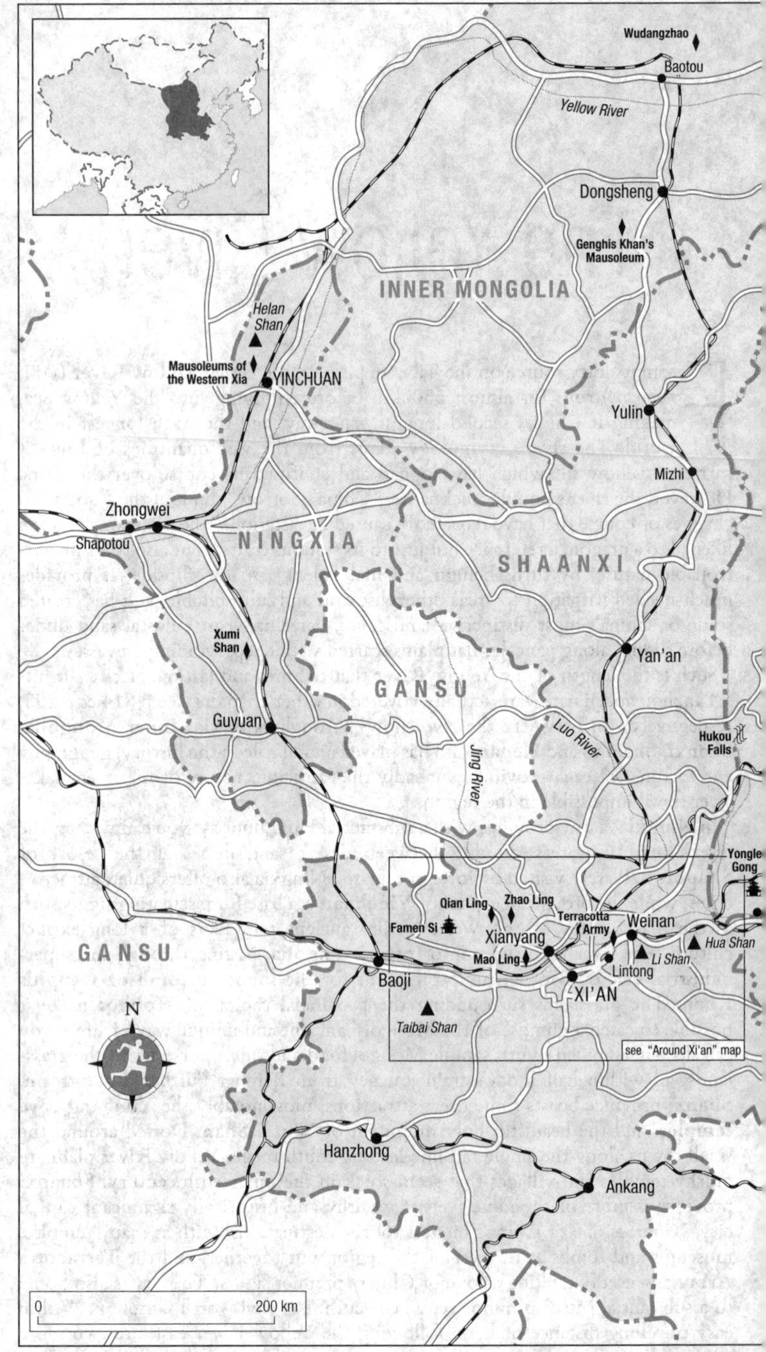
Wudangzhao
Baotou
Yellow River
Dongsheng
Genghis Khan's Mausoleum
INNER MONGOLIA
Helan Shan
Mausoleums of the Western Xia
YINCHUAN
Yulin
Mizhi
Zhongwei
Shapotou
NINGXIA
SHAANXI
Xumi Shan
Yan'an
GANSU
Guyuan
Luo River
Jing River
Hukou Falls
Yongle Gong
Qian Ling
Zhao Ling
Famen Si
Terracotta Army
Weinan
Xianyang
Hua Shan
GANSU
Mao Ling
Li Shan
Lintong
Baoji
XI'AN
N
Taibai Shan
see "Around Xi'an" map
Hanzhong
Ankang
0
200 km

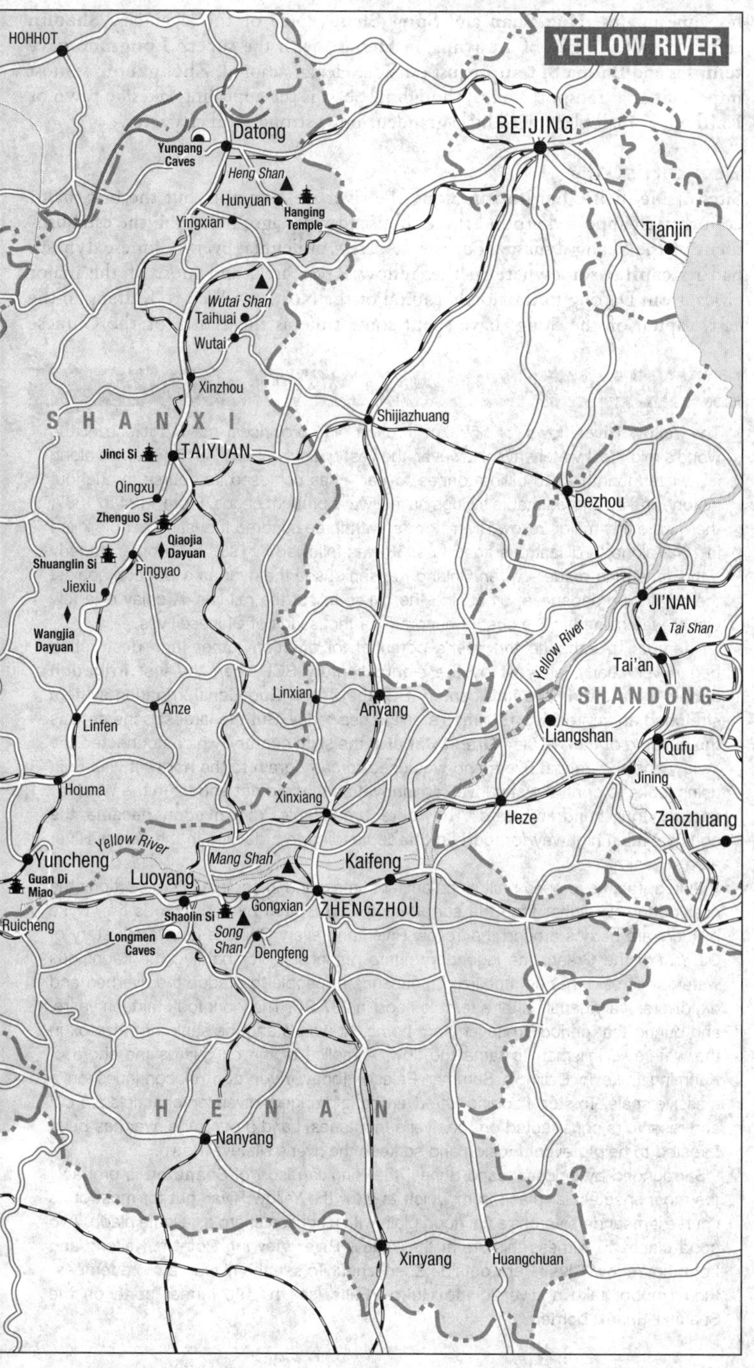
YELLOW RIVER
HOHHOT
Datong
Yungang Caves
Heng Shan
Hunyuan
Hanging Temple
Yingxian
BEIJING
Tianjin
Wutai Shan
Taihuai
Wutai
Xinzhou
SHANXI
Shijiazhuang
Jinci Si
TAIYUAN
Qingxu
Zhenguo Si
Qiaojia Dayuan
Shuanglin Si
Pingyao
Jiexiu
Wangjia Dayuan
Dezhou
JI'NAN
Tai Shan
Yellow River
Tai'an
SHANDONG
Linxian
Anyang
Anze
Linfen
Liangshan
Qufu
Jining
Houma
Xinxiang
Heze
Zaozhuang
Yellow River
Yuncheng
Guan Di Miao
Mang Shan
Kaifeng
Luoyang
Gongxian
ZHENGZHOU
Shaolin Si
Ruicheng
Longmen Caves
Song Shan
Dengfeng
HENAN
Nanyang
Xinyang
Huangchuan

holy mountains, **Hua Shan** and **Song Shan** (home of the legendary **Shaolin temple**), and the city of **Luoyang** in **Henan**, with the superb **Longmen cave temples** and **Baima Si temple** just outside. Henan's capital, **Zhengzhou**, is most important as a transport nexus, though just east is the appealing lakeside town of **Kaifeng**, a small place with little grandeur but a strong local character.

Some history

Sites of **Neolithic habitation** along the river are common, but the first major conurbation appeared around three thousand years ago, heralding the establishment of the Shang dynasty. For the next few millennia, every Chinese dynasty had its **capital** somewhere in the Yellow River area, and most of the major cities, from Datong in the north, capital of the Northern Wei, to Kaifeng in the east, capital of the Song, have spent some time as the centre of the Chinese

The Yellow River

The **Yellow River** flows for 5500km through nine provinces, making it one of the world's mightiest waterways. However, the vast quantity of **silt** the river carries along its twisted length – 1.6 billion tonnes a year – has confused its course throughout history, and its unpredictable swings have always brought chaos. From 1194 to 1887, there were fifty major Yellow River **floods**, with three hundred thousand people killed in 1642 alone. A disastrous flood in 1933 was followed in 1937 by another tragedy – this time man-made – when Chiang Kai-shek used the river as a weapon against the advancing Japanese, breaching the dykes to cut the rail line. A delay of a few weeks was gained at the cost of hundreds of thousands of Chinese lives.

Attempts to enhance the river's potential for creation rather than destruction began very early, at least by the eighth century BC, when the first **irrigation canals** were cut. In the fifth century BC, the Zheng Guo Canal irrigation system stretched an impressive 150km; it's still in use today. But the largest scheme was the building of the 1800km **Grand Canal** in the sixth century, which connected the Yellow and the Yangzi rivers and was used to carry grain to the north. It was built using locks to control water level, an innovation that did not appear in the West for another four hundred years. The more predictable Yangzi soon became the county's main highway for food and trade, leading to a decline in the Yellow River area's wealth.

Dykes, too, have been built since ancient times, and in some eastern sections the river bottom is higher than the surrounding fields, often by as much as 5m. Dyke builders are heroes around the Yellow River, and every Chinese knows the story of Da Yu (Yu the Great), the legendary figure responsible for battling the capricious waters. It is said that he mobilized thousands of people to dredge the riverbed and dig diversionary canals after a terrible flood in 297 BC. The work took thirteen years, and during that period Yu never went home. At work's end, he sank a bronze ox in the waters, a talisman to tame the flow. A replica of the ox guards the shore of Kunming Lake in Beijing's Summer Palace. Today, **river control** continues on a massive scale. To stop flooding, the riverbed is dredged, diversion channels are cut and reservoirs constructed on the river's tributaries. Land around the river has been forested to help prevent erosion and so keep the river's silt level down.

Surrounded by colossal sand dunes, the Ningxia resort of **Shapotou** is probably the most spectacular place from which to view the Yellow River, but for most of its course it meanders across a flat flood plain with a horizon sharp as a knife blade. Two good places to witness this are at the **Yellow River Viewing Point** in Kaifeng and from the **Yellow River Park** outside Zhengzhou. To see the river in a more tempestuous mood, take a diversion to **Hukou Falls** (see p.249), farther north on the Shaanxi–Shanxi border.

universe. With the collapse of imperial China, the area sank into provincialism, and it was not until late in the twentieth century that it again came to prominence. The old capitals have today found new leases of life as industrial and commercial centres, and thus present two sides to the visitor: a rapidly changing, and sometimes harsh, modernity; and a static history, preserved in the interests of tourism. This latter feature contrasts strongly with, for instance, southwestern China, where temples might double as tourist attractions but are also clearly functional places of worship; here, most feel much more like museums – even if they seldom lack grandeur.

Ningxia

Squeezed between Inner Mongolia, Gansu and Shanxi, **Ningxia** (宁夏, *níngxià*) is the smallest of China's provinces, and an autonomous region for the **Hui** minority (see below). Historically, the area has never been a secure one for the Chinese: almost every dynasty built its section of **Great Wall** through here and, in the nineteenth century, the Hui people played an active part in the Muslim rebellions, which were subsequently put down with great ferocity by the Qing authorities. Until recent times, Ningxia's very existence as a separate zone remained an open question; having first appeared on the map in 1928, the region was temporarily subsumed by Gansu in the 1950s before finally reappearing again in 1958. It appears that the authorities of the People's Republic could not make up their

The Hui

Hui (回, *húi*) is a vague term, applied to followers of the **Muslim faith** all over China who have no other obvious affiliation bar Islamic dress and the absence of pork in their diets. Most Hui are descended from Middle Eastern traders who arrived in China over a thousand years ago; men can usually be distinguished by their skullcaps, women often wear headscarves or veils, while the sprouting of minarets is the most obvious sign that you're in a Hui-populated area. While remaining Muslim, the Hui have otherwise long since integrated with Han culture; barring a few Persian or Islamic words, they speak Chinese as their mother tongue.

Ningxia is the officially designated homeland of the Hui, who today make up about thirty percent of the province's tiny population of four million. However, pockets of Hui can be found all over China; indeed, most do not live in Ningxia at all, but are scattered around neighbouring regions – particularly Gansu and Shaanxi – to the point where they often seem strangely absent within what is supposed to be "their" land. In Ningxia, as with all the autonomous regions of the Northwest, the central government has steadily encouraged **Han immigration** – or colonization – as a way of tying the area to the Chinese nation, but the situation of the Hui people is not comparable with that of the disaffected Uyghurs or Tibetans, since there is no talk whatsoever of secession.

The Hui population of Ningxia's major cities is rather low, but to immerse yourself more fully in the culture take a trip to Guyuan (see p.216), the Muslim districts in Xi'an (see p.256), or the Lanzhou–Linxia route in Gansu province (see p.820).

minds whether the Hui population was substantial enough to deserve its own autonomous region, in the same way as the Uyghurs and the Mongols.

Despite a certain degree of industrialization since the Communists came to power, Ningxia remains an underdeveloped area. For visitors, the rural scenes provide the charm of the place, but this province is one of the poorest in the country. Geographically, the area is dominated by coalfields and the **Yellow River**, without which the hilly south of the province, green and extremely beautiful, would be barren and uninhabitable desert. Unsurprisingly, the science of **irrigation** is at its most advanced here: two thousand years ago, the great founding emperor of China, Qin Shi Huang, sent a hundred thousand men here to dig irrigation channels. To those ancient systems of irrigation, which are still used to farm cereal crops, have now been added ambitious reforestation and desert reclamation projects. Some of these can be visited, particularly around the city of **Zhongwei**. Other sights include the capital **Yinchuan**, which makes a pleasant stopover, and one relic from an obscure northern branch of the Silk Road, the delightful **Xumi Shan Grottoes**, located well away from the Yellow River in the southern hills.

Zhongwei and Shapotou

The mini-city of **ZHONGWEI** (中卫, *zhōngwèi*) lies right alongside one of the Yellow River's most curious stretches – just west of town, the waterway can be seen roaring past an expanse of **sand dunes**, providing a rare opportunity to see a river of such size in **desert** terrain. The river essentially moulded the Zhongwei of today – historically, the old walled city was said to have had no north gate – simply because there was nothing more to the north of here. It remains in a potentially awkward location, between the fickle **Yellow River** to the south and the sandy Tenger Desert to the north, but today Zhongwei is surrounded by a rich belt of irrigated fields, and the desert is kept at bay through reforestation projects. The river outside the town, at **Shapotou**, is a splendid sight and should definitely be visited if you are in the area.

Zhongwei itself is based around a simple crossroads, with a traditional **Drum Tower** (鼓楼, *gŭlóu*) at the centre, just south of the train station. It's small enough to walk everywhere, although an absurd number of taxis – perhaps more numerous than non-taxis – are available to ferry you around. The town has one intriguing sight, the **Gao Miao** (高庙, *gāomiào*; daily 8am–6pm; ¥20), a quite extraordinary temple catering for a number of different religions, including Buddhism, Confucianism and Taoism. Originally constructed in the early fifteenth century, and rebuilt many times, the temple is now a magnificent jumble of buildings and styles. From the front entrance you can see dragon heads, columns, stairways and rooftops spiralling up in all directions; the left wing contains vivid sculptures of five hundred *arhats*, while the right wing is a mock hell. Altogether, there are more than 250 temple rooms, towers and pavilions. The Gao Miao lies between the train station and Drum Tower, a few minutes' walk from either.

Arrival

All trains on the main Lanzhou–Beijing (via Inner Mongolia) rail line call at Zhongwei, but services are not that regular. Branch lines also serve Wuwei in Gansu province and Baoji in Shaanxi. Zhongwei's **train station** is just off the north arm of the crossroads; the new long-distance **bus station** is a few kilometres east of the Drum Tower and has connections to Guyuan farther south and Wuwei in Gansu province. Buses to and from Yinchuan run frequently, and you'll be given the choice of regular buses or more expensive express services that utilise the new highway.

Accommodation

If you're arriving in Zhongwei by train, you'll find scores of **accommodation** options right outside the station, though the cheapest usually turn foreigners away, and such is the popularity of Shapotou that all establishments can be fully booked on weekends. The hotel in Shapotou (see below) is the best-value place to stay in any case.

Aijia Easy Hotel (爱家酒店, *àijīa jiǔdiàn*) Changcheng Donglu ☎0955/7037777. This well-run little hotel is superb value for money, its clean rooms a welcome change from the grotty neighbouring options available for similar prices. Usually fully booked on weekends. ❸

Railway Hotel (铁路宾馆, *tiělù bīnguǎn*) Renmin Square ☎0955/7031948. A nice, clean and friendly place offering double rooms with bath, though hot water is only available in the morning and evening. ❷

Shapo Shanzhuang (沙坡山庄, *shāpō shānzhuāng*) Shapotou ☎0955/7689073. Delightful hotel in a very cool and pleasant location near the Shapotou tourist complex, with gardens full of trees and vine trellises. It has well-designed doubles with bath and, despite the tourist draw just down the road, is rarely busy. Only open April–Oct. ❸

Zhongwei Dajiudian (中卫大酒店, *zhōngwèi dàjiǔdiàn*) Bei Dajie ☎0955/7025555. Plush place offering generous discounts out of season, more or less opposite the entrance to the Gao Miao. ❺

Eating

For **food**, the train station square is alive most evenings with stands peddling barbecued meat. For another form of local flavour check out the ¥2.5 beef noodles at *Mouwu Niurou Mianguan* (某五牛肉面馆, *mǒuwǔ niúròumiàn guǎn*), just south of the square on the left. You'll also find *Laomao Shouzhua Meishilou* (老毛手抓美食楼, *lǎomáo shǒuzhuā měishílóu*), a good-value Muslim restaurant, northwest of the Drum Tower (meals around ¥20 including beer).

Listings

Bank The main Bank of China is immediately to the southeast of the Drum Tower.
Internet Available from the net bar on the southeast corner of Renmin Square.
Mail and telephones There's a post office on Zhongshan Jie, a small lane several minutes' walk along Xi Dajie from the centre; you can also make long-distance phone calls from here.
Tours Tours of the Tenger Desert, as well as Yellow River tours and camping trips, can be booked from the Shapotou Travel Service (☎0955/7014880), just outside the Zhongwei Binguan, a few minutes' walk west of the Drum Tower.

Shapotou

SHAPOTOU (沙坡头; *shāpōtóu*), 16km west of Zhongwei, is a tourist resort of sorts by the banks of the Yellow River. Most people come on a day-trip, but you can easily spend an enjoyable night or two here at the nearby *Shapo Shanzhuang* (see above). The main pleasure of the place is in the contrast between the leafy, shady banks of the river itself, and the harsh desert that lies just beyond. The main focus is a **tourist resort** (¥90, ¥65 Nov–March), a charming yet slightly Disneyfied place, with cafés and outdoor restaurants. Among the activities on offer are ferry rides (from ¥100), ziplines over the river (¥80), sand-skiing (¥30 including cable-car ride) and camel rides (from ¥30). There's very little shade in the complex, so bring a hat and sunscreen if it's sunny. Additionally, the **Shapotou Desert Research Institute** (entry free with tourist resort ticket) has been based here for forty years, working on ways to conquer the sands. Travelling either by bus or train between Zhongwei and Shapotou, you'll see some of the fruits of their labour in the chequerboard grid of straw thatch implanted to hold the sands in place and provide irrigation.

There are two main entrances to the resort, one to the south, and another high up to the north; the latter is preferable, since from here you can slide down a huge sand dune to get to the main resort area. The southern entrance is accessible by **minibus** (every 30min; ¥5) from central Zhongwei, but the bus stops are scattered around town and hard to hunt down. Additionally, they crawl through myriad neighbourhoods on their way to the resort, meaning that the short journey takes almost an hour – it's far easier to grab a **taxi** (¥30).

Yinchuan and around

The capital of Ningxia, **YINCHUAN** (银川, *yínchuān*) is a bland modern city possessing little of tourist interest, and is frustratingly spread out, even by Chinese standards. However, it's worth dropping by to see some excellent historical sights on the city's periphery: from 1038 Yinchuan (then Xingqing) was capital of the **Western Xia kingdom**, an independent state which survived for less than two hundred years (see p.215). It was virtually forgotten about until the early twentieth century, when the archeological remains of the kingdom started being recognized for what they were; you should definitely make a visit to their weathered **mausoleums**, some 20km outside the city.

Arrival

Yinchuan is divided into three parts from east to west: Xixia, Jinfeng and Xingqing. All the main sights and the main bus station are located in **Xingqing**. The train station lies inconveniently in the west end of **Jinfeng**, some 12km away from Xingqing; given this location it may be wise to buy tickets at the downtown booking office (daily 9am–6pm) on Xinhua Xi Jie.

Yinchuan's new **airport** lies 15km southeast of Xingqing. Airport buses (¥15) depart from outside the *Civil Aviation Hotel* (see opposite) on the hour. Most **buses** arrive frustratingly far away at a new terminal 7km to the south of central Xingqing. A **taxi** into town will cost about ¥15, while it's more like ¥20 from the **train station**, way to the west.

Accommodation and eating

Accommodation in Yinchuan can be amazingly tight in midsummer: Chinese tourists flock here and you may end up doing a lot of traipsing around to find a place. There's a clutch of scruffy guesthouses directly to the left outside the train station, but since there's absolutely nothing to see in the area, it's best to stay in **Xingqing**.

The culinary scene is pretty poor, though one decent place to **eat** is ★ *Yingbin Lou* (迎宾楼, *yíngbīn lóu*), a smart Muslim restaurant serving lamb hotpots, kebabs, noodles and eight-treasure tea.

Jinfeng and Xixia

Jixiang Youth Hostel (吉祥青年旅馆, *jíxiáng qīngnián lǚguǎn*) 86 Huaiyuan Xilu ⓣ0951/2023021. Mixed reviews for Ningxia's only hostel: some find the staff friendly, others are disappointed by the service and location. Still, at ¥70 for a cosy room and ¥35 for a dorm bed, it's good value, and though there's nothing to see in this university district you're handily placed for the Western Xia tombs. ❶

Railway Hotel (铁道宾馆, *tiědào bīnguǎn*) ⓣ0951/3962118. Off Xingzhou Bei Jie, over to the left of the station exit. Rooms are spartan but adequate, yet overpriced. ❹

Xingqing

Civil Aviation Hotel (民航大厦, *mínháng dàshà*) ⓣ0951/4090888. Swanky place near the mosque, with super-comfy rooms and attentive staff. Very convenient for the airport, too, since the shuttle bus stops right outside. ❻

Gulou (鼓楼饭店, *gǔlóu fàndiàn*) 26 Jiefang Dong Jie ⓣ0951/6028784. Well located beside the Gulou (Drum Tower), this little hotel has comfortable and affordable doubles, though they could do with a lick of paint and new bathrooms. ❸

Ningfeng (宁丰宾馆, *níngfēng bīnguǎn*) Jiefang Dong Jie ⓣ0951/6027224. Smart-looking place, with good doubles and flustered staff. ❹

Rainbow Bridge (虹桥大酒店, *hóngqiáo dàjiǔdiàn*) Jiefang Xi Jie ⓣ0951/6918888, ⓕ6918788. Though not as colourful as its name suggests, this four-star block is one of the plushest hotels in town, with a good and expensive restaurant. Rooms range from moderately priced to downright expensive. ❻

The City

Yinchuan's sights, all in Xingqing, can be visited on foot in a single day. The best place to start exploring is the centre of the city, based around the eastern part of Jiefang Jie, which is dominated by a couple of well-restored, traditionally tiered Chinese towers guarding the main intersections. From the west, the first of these is the **Drum Tower** (鼓楼, *gŭlóu*) at Gulou Jie, while the second, one block farther east, is the four-hundred-year-old **Yuhuang Pavilion** (玉皇阁, *yùhuáng gé*; ¥5), at Yuhuangge Jie, which also contains a tiny exhibition room.

Further south the **Nanguan Grand Mosque** (南关清真寺, *nánguān qīngzhēn sì*; daily 8am–7pm; ¥10), the biggest mosque in Yinchuan, is one of the few places in town you'll find Hui in any appreciable numbers. First built in 1915, it was rebuilt in 1981 after years of damage and neglect during the Cultural Revolution, but now looks something like a leisure centre with minarets.

To the west are the **Regional Museum** (宁夏博物馆, *níngxià bówùguăn*) and **Chengtiansi Ta** pagoda (承天寺塔, *chéngtiānsì tă*; also known as West Pagoda; daily 8am–6pm; ¥20), on the same site. The museum contains some interesting English-labelled exhibitions, including relics from the Xixia mausoleum. Outside, the twelve-storey pagoda, in classic Chinese style, is a place of worship for Buddhists. It was built around 1050 during the time of the Western Xia with the top six storeys rebuilt during the Qing dynasty. You can climb the octagonal tower right to the top for excellent views.

Listings

Airlines The main CAAC office is at the Changcheng Dong Lu/Shengli Jie intersection (daily 8am–10.30pm; ⓣ0951/6913456). It also has a branch in the main post office of Xingqing, at window 8. Better domestic flight deals can be obtained at a private Airline Ticket office at the northeast corner of the Yuhuangge junction.

Banks The main Bank of China is in the western part of Xingqing, on Jiefang Xi Jie; the branch on Yuhuangge Bei Jie has an ATM.

Bookshop The Foreign Language Bookstore (daily 9am–6.30pm), at the corner of Jiefang Xi Jie and Jining Jie, is well stocked with English novels as well as local maps.

PSB At the corner of Beijing Dong Lu and Yuhuangge Bei Jie (Mon–Thurs 8am–noon & 2.30–6.30pm, Fri 2.30–6.30pm; ⓣ0951/6915080).

Travel agents Ningxia CITS (ⓣ0951/6732749, ⓦwww.nxcits.com) is on the first floor of 375 Beijing Dong Lu. Ningxia Merchants International Tour (ⓣ0951/5064333, ⓦwww.cmitnx.com) is at 365 Jiefang Xi Jie. Both can provide English-speaking tour guides and organize tours of areas outside the city.

Around Yinchuan

A few interesting spots outside Yinchuan can comfortably be visited as day-trips, especially if using the **tourist buses** which head to the main sights from various parts of town – ask at your accommodation for timetables and advice from your part of town.

Mausoleums of the Western Xia

The **Mausoleums of the Western Xia** (西夏王陵, *xīxià wánglíng*; daily 8am–6pm; ¥60), about 10km west of the new city, stand as monuments to the nine kings of Western Xia, whose kingdom was based at Yinchuan (see opposite). The site is spectacular and atmospheric, with towering, haystack-shaped piles of brown mud bricks, slowly disintegrating and punctuating the view around the Helan Shan range. The entrance fee includes transport within the complex to the museum, figure gallery and the biggest mausoleum of the nine. Interesting items in the museum include the original pieces of the Lishi pillar support and some terracotta bird ornaments with human faces.

The Xi Xia kingdom

The ancient feudal **Xi Xia kingdom** (Western Xia Kingdom; 1038–1227 AD) encompassed a vast expanse of land, overlapping regions of what is now Ningxia, Gansu and Shaanxi provinces. Established by the nomadic Dangxiang clan of Qiang ancestry, the kingdom had twelve kings and developed its own **written language**, which combines influences from Mongolian, Tibetan and Chinese. The Xi Xia territory survived prior to independence by playing off the Song or Liao dynasties against each other. In 1038, **Li Yuanhao**, leader of Xi Xia, was militarily powerful enough to oppose Song jurisdiction and thus this third kingdom was created. A prosperous period ensued as the kingdom benefited from controlling the trade routes into central Asia. The new era saw a time of great **cultural development**, a state academy was erected, and future officials took Confucian examinations. Less emphasis, however, was placed on military matters, and in 1227 the Xi Xia were obliterated by the Mongol empire of **Genghis Khan**.

The cheapest way to reach the site is to take **minibus** #2 (¥2) from the west of Gulou Jie/Xinhua Dong Jie junction to Xixia Square. From here you can take a taxi (¥15) for the last 10km.

Helan Shan and around

The **Helan Shan** (贺兰山, *hèlán shān*) mountain ranges themselves are also of interest. The **Rolling Bell Pass** (滚钟口, *gǔnzhōng kǒu*; ¥31), about 25km west of Xixia, where Li Yuanhao (see below) built his summer palace, is a pleasant resort with attractive, historic buildings and plenty of opportunities for hiking around the hills and admiring the views. Six or seven kilometres north of here are the **Baisikou Shuang Ta** (拜寺口双塔, *bàisìkǒu shuāng tǎ*), a couple of 12m-high pagodas guarding another pass. A few more kilometres to the east is the **China West Film Studio** (镇北堡中国西部影视城, *zhènběibǎo zhōngguó xībù yǐngshìchéng*; daily 8am–6pm; ¥60) where the film *Red Sorghum*, directed by Zhang Yimou, was shot. The stunning film depicts village life in northwest China during the period leading up to World War II – in part a rural idyll, in part a brute struggle to survive. The scenes of dry, dusty hillsides alternating with the lush fields of sorghum are a fair record of how Ningxia still looks today. Get the #16 bus from Nanmen station. Fairly extensive galleries of engraved **rock art** have been found spread out near here at **Suyu Kou National Park** (苏峪口国家公园, *sūyù kǒu guójiā gōngyuán*; ¥40); you can also hike to the peak of Helan Shan. Merchants International Tour (see opposite) offers a **tour** of these places from Yinchuan for ¥400 including a car and an English tour guide; otherwise you can hire a taxi on the street for no more than ¥300.

Sha Hu

About 45km north of Yinchuan is the beautiful **Sha Hu** (沙湖, *shā hú*; ¥120 including a return trip by boat across the lake), or "Sand Lake". This is a developing summer resort *par excellence*, with swimming, sand dunes, rafting and beautiful scenery. During winter the lake freezes over, making an ideal skating rink, though most tourists arrive in summer to view the expansive lily ponds. Camel rides and caravan trips are also offered in the desert nearby. **Accommodation** at the comfortable *Qingxin Fandian* (❹) is available in summer. You can get there from the Tour Bus Station (also known as North Bus Station) on Qinghe Jie; an hourly direct bus (¥10) leaves from 10.30am till early evening (1hr).

Southern Ningxia

Located in the remote, impoverished southern part of Ningxia, the town of **Guyuan** has seen very little tourist traffic. Only in 1995 did it finally join the rail network, with the opening of the Zhongwei–Baoji line. Aside from a ruinous stretch of the **Great Wall**, built in the Qin dynasty, 5km north of town (you'll see it in passing), the main interest here is in the Buddhist grottoes at **Xumi Shan**, a major relic of the Silk Road, curiously marooned far to the north of the main route from Lanzhou to Xi'an. The great Taoist temple **Kongtong Shan** (see p.814) at Pingliang in Gansu is only two hours from Guyuan, another possible day-trip. The hills along the road from Gansu have been terraced for centuries; every patch of land in the vast landscape is under cultivation, with terraces laddering up the slopes and flowing round every tiny hillock and gully in fantastic swirls of colour.

The high pass on the border with Gansu, **Liupan Shan** (which you cross on the way to or from Tianshui), is also famous for the fact that the Long Marchers managed to elude pursuing Guomindang forces here in the 1930s; a commemorative stone marks the spot.

Guyuan

A useful place to base yourself for a visit to the Xumi Shan grottoes, **GUYUAN** (固原, *gùyuán*) is itself of no special interest. Although trains now pass through on their way between Zhongwei and Baoji in Shaanxi province, the **train station** is inconveniently located several kilometres from town. It's easier to rely on long-distance **buses** connecting Guyuan with Xi'an to the east, Lanzhou and Ürümqi to the west. There are also frequent connections to Yinchuan (every 40min 8am–5.30pm; ¥50). Bus #1 (¥1) links the train station and the bus station in town; there is no signpost, so simply flag down the bus at the junction outside the train station. A taxi to anywhere in town costs ¥5, and there's plenty of **accommodation** outside both the bus and train stations.

There's one daily direct **bus to Xumi Shan** from Guyuan, but at the wretchedly inconvenient time of 2pm – you'd have to stay the night. To make a day-trip of it, head from Guyuan to the small town of **Sanying** (hourly; 1hr; ¥5), and tell the driver that you want to see the grottoes. From the drop-off point in Sanying, hire a minivan for the thirty-minute drive to the caves; a return trip (including 2hr wait while you look around) should cost about ¥50. There's a **drinks and snacks** kiosk at the grottoes' car park, plus a basic **hotel** if you need to stay the night.

The Xumi Shan grottoes

The dramatic **Xumi Shan grottoes** (须弥山, *xūmí shān*; daily; ¥30) lie about 55km northwest of Guyuan. One hundred and thirty-eight caves have been carved out from the rusty red sandstone cliff face on five adjoining hillsides, and a large number of statues – primarily from Northern Wei, Sui and Tang dynasties – survive, in a somewhat diminished state. With a beautifully secluded natural backdrop, the grottoes occupy a huge site, the red cliffs and shining tree-covered slopes commanding panoramic views. The last stage of the journey there takes you through one of the remotest corners of rural China where, at the height of summer, you can see the golden wheat being cut by hand, then spread out over the road to be ground by passing vehicles.

The site takes at least two hours to walk around. After entering the cliffs area, bear left first for Cave no. 5 and the **Dafo Lou**, a statue of a giant 20m-high Maitreya Buddha facing due east. Originally this Buddha was protected by a wall that has long since fallen away. Head back to the entrance and you'll see the five hillocks lined up along an approximate east–west axis, each with one key sight and a cluster of caves. After the Dafo Lou, the second major sight you come to is the **Yuanguang Si**, a temple housing caves 45, 46 and 48, where statues were built during the North Zhou and Tang dynasties. You'll need to ask the nun to open the caves. Looking at their smoky-coloured surface today, it is hard to imagine that all Buddha statues were once coated in gold. From here you have to cross a bridge and bear left to reach **Xiangguo Si**, centred around the magnificent Cave no. 51 with its 5m-high Buddha seated around a central pillar. Returning to the bridge, walk underneath it and up the dry river bed towards the cliff, to reach **Taohua Dong** (Peach Blossom Cave).

Inner Mongolia

Mongolia is an almost total mystery to the outside world, its very name being synonymous with remoteness. For hundreds of years, landlocked between the two Asian giants Russia and China, it seems to have been doomed to eternal obscurity, trapped in a hopeless physical environment of fleeting summers and interminable, bitter winters. And yet, seven hundred years ago the people of this benighted land suddenly burst out of their frontiers and for a century subjugated and terrorized almost all of the Eurasian landmass.

Visitors to the **autonomous region of Inner Mongolia** will not necessarily find many signs of this today. The modern-day heirs of the Mongol hordes are not only placid – quietly going about their business of shepherding, herding horses and entertaining tourists – but, even here, are vastly outnumbered by the Han Chinese

Staying in a yurt

In regions that still harbour semi-nomadic herders, such as Inner Mongolia's grasslands (see p.229) and around Tian Chi (see p.856) in Xinjiang, it's often possible to ask a local family to put you up in their **yurt** (*mengu bao* in Mandarin). The genuine article is a circular felt tent with floor rugs as the only furniture, horsehair blankets, a stove for warmth, and outside toilets. Though it's a well-established custom to offer lodging to travellers, remember that few people in these regions have had much contact with foreigners, and misunderstandings can easily arise. You'll need to haggle over the price with your hosts; around ¥55 should cover bed and simple meals of noodles and vegetables. In addition, it's a good idea to bring a **present** – a bottle of *baijiu*, a clear and nauseatingly powerful vodka-like spirit, rarely goes amiss. Liquor stores, ubiquitous in Chinese cities and towns, are the obvious place to buy the stuff, but you'll also find it on sale at train and bus stations, restaurants, hotels, shops and airports. You might also want to bring a torch and bug spray for your own comfort.

Local tour companies may be able to arrange yurt accommodation, though where Chinese tour groups are commonplace, you may be treated to a very artificial experience – often basically just a concrete cell "dolled" up in yurt fashion, with karaoke laid on in the evenings. If you want something better than this, it's worth at least asking to see photos of the interior when making a booking.

(by seventeen million to two million). In addition, this is, and always has been, a sensitive border area, and there are still restrictions on the movements of tourists in some places, despite the demise of the Soviet Union.

Nevertheless, there are still traces of the "real" Mongolia out there, in terms of both landscape and people. Dotting the region are enormous areas of **grassland**, gently undulating plains stretching to the horizon and still used by nomadic peoples as pastureland for their horses. Tourists are able to visit the grasslands and even stay with the Mongols in their yurts, though the only simple way to do this is on an **organized tour** out of the regional capital **Hohhot** – an experience rather short on authenticity. If you don't find what you are looking for in the Hohhot area, however, don't forget that there is a whole vast swath of Mongolia stretching up through northeastern China that remains virtually untouched by Western tourists; see the Dongbei chapter, p.200.

Some history

Genghis Khan (1162–1227) was born, ominously enough, with a clot of blood in his hand. Under his leadership, the Mongols erupted from their homeland to ravage the whole of Asia, butchering millions, razing cities and laying waste to all the land from China to eastern Europe. It was his proud boast that his destruction of cities was so complete that he could ride across their ruins by night without the least fear of his horse stumbling.

Before Genghis exploded onto the scene, the nomadic Mongols had long been a thorn in the side of the city-dwelling Chinese. Construction of the **Great Wall** had been undertaken to keep these two fundamentally opposed societies apart. But it was always fortunate for the Chinese that the early nomadic tribes of Mongolia fought as much among themselves as they did against outsiders. Genghis Khan's achievement was to weld together the warring nomads into a fighting force the equal of which the world had never seen: the secret of his success was skilful **cavalry tactics**, acquired from long practise in the saddle on the wide-open Mongolian plains. Frequently his armies would rout forces ten or twenty times their size.

Led by Genghis, the Mongols unleashed a massive onslaught on China in 1211. The Great Wall proved no obstacle, and with two hundred thousand men in tow Genghis cut a swath across northwest China towards Beijing. It was not all easy progress, however – so great was the destruction wrought in northern China that **famine and plague** broke out, afflicting the invader as much as the invaded. Genghis Khan himself died (of injuries sustained in falling from his horse) before the **capture of Beijing** had been completed. His body was carried back to Mongolia by a funeral cortege of ten thousand, who murdered every man and beast within ten miles of the road so that news of the Great Khan's death could not be reported before his sons and viceroys had been gathered from the farthest corners of his dominions. The whereabouts of his **tomb** is uncertain, though according to one of the best-known stories his ashes are in a mausoleum near Dongsheng (see p.222), south of Baotou.

In the years after Genghis Khan's death, the fate of both China and of distant Europe teetered together on the brink. Having conquered all of Russia, the Mongol forces were poised in 1241 to make the relatively short final push across Europe to the Atlantic, when a message came from deep inside Asia that the invasion was to be cancelled. The decision to spare Western Europe cleared the way for the **final conquest of China** instead, and by 1271 the Mongols had established their own dynasty – the **Yuan**. It was the first time the Chinese had come under foreign rule. The Yuan is still an era about which Chinese historians can find little good to say, though the boundaries of the empire were expanded considerably, to include

Kublai Khan

In Xanadu did Kubla Khan
A stately pleasure dome decree...

Immortalized not only in the poetry of Samuel Taylor Coleridge but also in the memoirs of Marco Polo, **Kublai Khan** (1215–94) – known to the Chinese as Yuan Shizu – is the only emperor popularly known by name to the outside world. And little wonder: as well as mastering the subtle statecraft required to govern China as a foreigner, this grandson of Genghis Khan commanded an **empire** that encompassed the whole of China, Central Asia, southern Russia and Persia – a larger area of land than perhaps anyone in history has ruled over, before or since. And yet this king of kings had been born into a nomadic tribe which had never shown the slightest interest in political life, and which, until shortly before his birth, was almost entirely illiterate.

From the beginning, Kublai Khan had shown an unusual talent for politics and government. He managed to get himself elected **Khan of the Mongols** in 1260, after the death of his brother, despite considerable opposition from the so-called "steppe aristocracy" who feared his disdain for traditional Mongolian skills. He never learned to read or write Chinese, yet after audaciously establishing himself as **Emperor of China**, proclaiming the Yuan dynasty in 1271, he soon saw the value of surrounding himself with advisers steeped in Confucianism. This was what enabled him to set up one hundred thousand Mongols in power over perhaps two hundred million Chinese. As well as **reunifying China** after centuries of division under the Song, Kublai Khan's contributions include establishing **paper money** as the standard medium of exchange, and fostering the **development of religion**, Lamaist Buddhism in particular. Above all, under his rule China experienced a brief – and uncharacteristic – period of **cosmopolitanism** which saw not only foreigners such as Marco Polo promoted to high positions of responsibility, but also a final flowering of the old Silk Road trade, as well as large numbers of Arab and Persian traders settling in seaports around Quanzhou in southeastern China.

Ironically, however, it was his admiration for the culture, arts, religion and sophisticated bureaucracy of China – as documented so enthusiastically by Marco Polo – that aroused bitter hostility from his own people, the Mongols, who despised what they saw as a betrayal of the ways of Genghis Khan. Kublai Khan was troubled by skirmishing nomads along the Great Wall just as much as his more authentically Chinese predecessors, forcing the abandonment of **Xanadu** – in Inner Mongolia, near the modern city of Duolun – his legendary summer residence immortalized in Coleridge's epic poem, *The Ballad of Kublai Khan*. Today virtually nothing of the site remains.

Yunnan and Tibet for the first time. The magnificent zenith of the dynasty was achieved under **Kublai Khan**, as documented in Marco Polo's *Travels* (see above). Ironically, however, the Mongols were able to sustain their power only by becoming thoroughly Chinese, and abandoning the traditional nomadic Mongol way of life. Kublai Khan and his court soon forgot the warrior skills of their forefathers, and in 1368, less than a hundred years later, the Yuan, a shadow of their former selves, were **driven out of China** by the Ming. The Mongols returned to Mongolia, and reverted to their former ways, hunting, fighting among themselves and occasionally skirmishing with the Chinese down by the Wall. Astonishingly, history had come full circle.

Thereafter, Mongolian history moves gradually downhill, though right into the eighteenth century they maintained at least nominal control over many of the lands to the south and west originally won by Genghis Khan. These included

Tibet, from where **Lamaist Buddhism** was imported to become the dominant religion in Mongolia. The few Tibetan-style monasteries in Mongolia that survive bear important testimony to this. Over the years, as well, came **settlers** from other parts of Asia: there is now a sizeable Muslim minority in the region, and under the Qing many Chinese settlers moved to Inner Mongolia, escaping overpopulation and famine at home, a trend that has continued under the Communists. The incoming settlers tried ploughing up the grassland with disastrous ecological results – wind and water swept the soil away – and the Mongols withdrew to the hills. Only recently has a serious programme of land stabilization and reclamation been established.

Sandwiched between two imperial powers, Mongolia found its independence constantly threatened. The Russians set up a protectorate over the north, while the rest came effectively under the control of China. In the 1930s, Japan occupied much of eastern Inner Mongolia as part of Manchuguo, and the Chinese Communists also maintained a strong presence. In 1945 Stalin persuaded Chiang Kai-shek to recognize the independence of **Outer Mongolia** under Soviet protection as part of the Sino-Soviet anti-Japanese treaty, effectively sealing the fate of what then became the Mongolian People's Republic. In 1947, **Inner Mongolia** was designated the first autonomous region of the People's Republic of China.

Baotou and around

Just three hours to the west of Hohhot by train or bus lies Inner Mongolia's biggest and bleakest city, **BAOTOU** (包头, *bāotóu*). Its primary significance is as the chief iron- and steel-producing centre in China: if you're arriving at night from the direction of Yinchuan, your first glimpse of the city is likely to be of satanic fires burning in the great blast furnaces. The sky over the western half of Baotou glows a more or less permanent yellow, orange and purple. For visitors, there can be something magnificent about Soviet ugliness on such a scale, but otherwise, apart from a few minor sights, including **Wudangzhao**, an attractive Tibetan-style monastery nearby, the city does not have much to offer. One further site of interest, **Genghis Khan's Mausoleum** – which is unlikely to be the real thing – lies well to the south of Baotou near the town of **Dongsheng**.

Arrival and information

A colossal city stretching for kilometres in all directions, Baotou comprises three main areas: **Donghe** (东河, *dōnghé*), the ramshackle, oldest part of town, to the east, and **Qingshan** (青山, *qīngshān*) and **Kundulun** (昆都仑, *kūndū lún*) to the west. Qingshan is a shopping and residential area, while Kundulun includes the iron- and steelworks on its western edge. The three parts of the city are well connected by frequent buses (#5 and #10; ¥2), which take thirty to forty minutes to travel between Donghe and Kundulun. Taxis begin at ¥6 for the first 3km, charging ¥1.2 per additional kilometre. Traversing Baotou, this can add up quickly.

There are two major **train stations**, one in West Baotou (Baotou Zhan), and one in Donghe (Baotou Dong Zhan). All through trains, including express trains from Beijing and Lanzhou, stop at both stations. Train tickets can be bought at the **booking office** on the east of A'Erding Square. The **bus station** is right opposite the Donghe train station; buy tickets for Hohhot here. For Dongsheng (every 30min), you also buy your ticket inside the bus station, though in warm months the touts will find you before you can say "Genghis Khan". The **airport** is just a couple of kilometres south of the Donghe train station.

Accommodation and eating

Of the two ends of town, **Donghe** is the more convenient place **to stay** for trips to Genghis Khan's mausoleum, though sadly there isn't much choice here. If you want to stay in **Kundulun**, be warned that the hotels in this part of town are a long way from the central station, though bus #1 from the station will take you to Gangtie Dajie. Baotou isn't famous for its cuisine, and restaurants here are average to say the least. However, it's a great place for **snack food**, which can be found in abundance in and around the Baobai shopping district on Gangtie Dajie, most notably across the street from *KFC*.

Donghe

West Lake Hotel (西湖宾馆, *xīhú bīnguǎn*) ⓣ0472/4187101. The best of the very limited options in this part of town. From the train station, walk straight up the main road, Nanmenwai Dajie; the hotel is at no. 10, on the right, before the intersection with Bayan Tala Dajie. ❹

Kundulun

Bao Yuan Binguan (包院宾馆, *bāoyuàn bīnguǎn*) ⓣ0472/6942628. For low prices *and* a good location, look no further than this hotel, opposite the entrance to Bayi Park – just don't expect much in the way of a cheery welcome or decor. Dorm beds from ¥18. ❷

Baotou Hotel (包头宾馆, *bāotóu bīnguǎn*) ⓣ0472/5362266, ⓦwww.baotouhotel.com.cn. A good bet, and on the main east–west Gangtie Dajie, a few hundred metres west of A'Erding Square. Following a makeover, the old building is now very comfortable, so push for a room here rather than in the "new" block. ❹

Haide (海德酒店, *hǎidé jiǔdiàn*) ⓣ0472/5365555, ⓦwww.hd-hotel.com.cn. The most upmarket hotel in town, opposite the *Baotou Hotel*, is a five-star establishment, with all the service and facilities you would expect. It's pricey but often gives 25 percent discounts. ❽

Shenhua International (神华国际大酒店, *shénhuá guójì dàjiǔdiàn*) ⓣ0472/536888. A tall edifice behind A'Erding Square at 17 Shaoxian, with its own pool, sauna and gym. ❼

Listings

Airlines The CAAC office (ⓣ0472/2118966) is on the south side of Gangtie Dajie, east of the post office, though the better hotels can also book for you.

Banks and exchange To change travellers' cheques, go to the main office of the Bank of China (daily 8am–6pm) in Kundulun, on the main road just east of A'Erding Square. There are ATMs further up the street at the Baibao branch. In Donghe there's a branch 50m north of the train station on the western side of Nanmenwai Dajie; it has an ATM and also changes cash.

Internet There's an internet café on the crossroads of Gangtie Dajie and Minzu Xi Lu, just west of the *Baotou Hotel*.

Mail and telephones The main post and telecommunications office is in Kundulun near the Bank of China, and there's also a post office in Donghe.

Travel agents There's a CTS office (ⓣ0472/2118966) just northwest of the *Baotou Hotel* on Wulan Dao.

Wudangzhao and the Yellow River

The one definite attraction in the Baotou area, **Wudangzhao** (五当召, *wǔdāng zhào*; daily 8am–6pm; ¥20) is the best-preserved Lamaist monastery still functioning in Inner Mongolia, one of the results of the Mongolian conquest of Tibet in the thirteenth century. For centuries afterwards, the roads between Tibet and Mongolia were worn by countless pilgrims and wandering monks bringing Lamaist Buddhism to Mongolia. This particular monastery, of the Yellow Sect, was established in 1749 and at its height housed twelve hundred lamas; seven generations of Living Buddhas were based here, the ashes of whom are kept in one of the halls. Today, however, the few remaining monks are greatly outnumbered by tourists from Baotou, and sadly their main duties now seem to involve hanging around at the hall entrances to check tourists' tickets.

Set in a pretty, narrow valley about 70km northeast of Baotou, the monastery can be reached by catching bus #7 (¥10) from outside the Donghe train station to the terminus at Shiguai. The monastery is another 25km on – if you arrive early enough there are one or two minibuses that go on to it from here, otherwise take a taxi from Shiguai (¥30). Once at the monastery, you can hike off into the surrounding hills and, if you're keen, you should be able to **stay** in the pilgrims' hostel in the monastery as well. Returning to Baotou is fairly easy as there are various minibuses and other tour vehicles plying the route, up to around 5pm. Hiring a taxi for the round-trip to the temple should cost ¥150.

The Yellow River

The other main sight in the Baotou area is the **Yellow River** (黄河, *huánghé*), worth having a look at, if only to ruminate on its historical significance. When the Chinese built the Great Wall far to the south, the area between the Inner Mongolian loop of the Yellow River and the Wall became known as the **Ordos** and remained the dominion of the nomad. However, to the Chinese the Yellow River seemed like the logical northern limit of China. The Qing eventually decided matters once and for all not only by seizing control of the Ordos, but also by moving north of the river into the heart of Mongolia. Today, the whole Yellow River region, from Yinchuan in Ningxia province up to Baotou and across to Hohhot, is thoroughly irrigated and productive land – without the river, it would be pure desert. You can take a stroll along the northern bank of the Yellow River by taking **bus** #18 (¥2) from in front of Donghe train station for about 6km to the new bridge. The river here is around a kilometre wide, shallow, sluggish and chocolate brown.

Genghis Khan's Mausoleum

The first thing to be said about **Genghis Khan's Mausoleum** (成吉思汗陵园, *chéngjísīhàn língyuán*; daily 24hr; ¥90) is that it's not all it's cracked up to be: it probably isn't the tomb of Genghis Khan, and it isn't a particularly attractive place anyway, but can nonetheless be fascinating as an insight into the modern cult of the famous warrior. There are no English captions for the exhibits.

Genghis Khan is known to have died in northern China, but while his funeral cortege may have passed through this region on its way back to Mongolia, the story that the wheels of his funeral cart got stuck in the mud here, resulting in his burial on the spot, is almost certainly apocryphal. At best, scholars believe, the site contains a few of the warrior's relics – perhaps weapons. The real tomb is thought to be on the slopes of Burkhan Khaldun, in the Hentei Mountains, not far to the east of Ulan Bator in Outer Mongolia. The reason it came to be so strongly believed that the Khan was buried here in China appears to be that the tribe who were charged with guarding the real sepulchre eventually drifted down across the Yellow River to the Ordos – but continued to claim the honour of being the official guardians of the tomb.

The tomb's alleged **relics** have a murky political history. Several times they have been removed, and later returned, the most recent occasion being during World War II, when the Japanese seized them. Apparently the Japanese had plans to set up a puppet Mongol state, centred around a Genghis Khan shrine. They even drew up plans for an elaborate mausoleum to house them – plans that were then commandeered by the Chinese Communists who, having safely returned the relics from a hiding place in Qinghai, built the mausoleum for themselves in 1955 as a means of currying favour with the Mongolian people.

The site

The main part of the cement mausoleum is formed by three connecting halls, shaped like Mongolian yurts. The corridors connecting the halls are adorned with bizarre murals supposedly depicting the life of Genghis Khan – though note the women in Western dress (1890s-style). In the middle of the main hall stands a 5m-high marble **statue** of Genghis before a map of his empire. Whatever the truth about the location of his burial place, the popular view among Mongolians, both in China and in the Republic of Mongolia, is that this is a holy site: the side halls, all very pretty, have ceremonial yurts, altars, burning incense, hanging paintings and Mongolian calligraphy, and offerings as though to a god. Some bring offerings – not the usual apples and bread, but bottles of rotgut *baijiu* on sale in the souvenir shop – and bow in penitence. Others, including several of the female staff, get drunk early and keep sipping until they're surly – or extremely affectionate; be prepared for anything as the site attracts its fair share of dodgy characters, including about fifteen "hairdressers" just outside. There's a small, free **museum** by the ticket office with a few relics.

Special **sacrificial ceremonies** take place here four times a year on certain days of the lunar calendar – the fifteenth day of the third lunar month, the fifteenth day of the fifth lunar month, the twelfth day of the ninth month and the third day of the tenth month. On these occasions, Mongolian monks lead solemn rituals that involve piling up cooked sheep before the statue of the khan. The ceremonies are attended not only by local people, but also by pilgrims from the Republic of Mongolia itself.

Practicalities

The most common approach to the site is from Baotou: take a bus (1hr; ¥32) from outside the Donghe train station to the coal-mining town of **DONGSHENG** (东胜, *dōngshèng*), 50km from the mausoleum, or one of the four daily train services between the cities. From Dongsheng to the mausoleum it takes a further hour on a new road by bus (¥7), and outside of summer there are only a few departures per day; if you don't want to spend the night, you should aim to catch a bus by 12.30pm. To return to Dongsheng from the mausoleum, simply stand in the road and flag down a passing minibus. It would be possible, if you left Baotou very early in the morning, to reach the mausoleum and make it back the same evening – the last bus from Dongsheng to Baotou leaves at about 6pm. It's a tiring trip, though, and spending a night in up-and-coming Dongsheng is the most pleasant way to do it.

If you need a bed, you can **stay** either in Dongsheng, or at the mausoleum itself; the latter option means sleeping in the (very) fake yurts on the grounds (¥40–50/person). There are no showers. One of the cheapest places to stay **in Dongsheng** is the fading *Jiaotong* (交通宾馆, *jiāotōng bīnguǎn*; ⓣ0477/8321575; ❷), which is part of the bus station itself – turn right as you exit, then right again. A better bet is a few minutes' walk south down the main street, away from the bus station, to the *Dongsheng* (东胜宾馆, *dōngshèng bīnguǎn*; ⓣ0477/8327333; ❸). Tour groups stay at the three-star *Tianjiao Hotel* (天骄宾馆, *tiānjiāo bīnguǎn*; ⓣ0477/8533888; ❼), at 102 Dalate Nan Lu.

For **food**, Hangjin Bei Lu and Yijinhuoluo Xi Jie both have Chinese fast-food and Lanzhou-style hand-pulled noodle (*lamian*) restaurants; *Maikeni* and *Xin Xin* are popular.

Hohhot and around

There has been a settlement at **HOHHOT** (呼和浩特, *hūhé hàotè*) since the time of the Ming dynasty four hundred years ago, though it did not become the capital of Inner Mongolia until 1952. Until relatively modern times, it was a small town centred on a number of **Buddhist temples**. The temples are still here, and although it's now a major city, Hohhot manages to be an interesting blend of the old and the new, and a relatively green and leafy place in summer – which is fitting, as the town's Mongolian name means "green city". As well as the shiny new banks and department stores downtown, there's an extensive area in the south of the town with old, narrow streets built of black bricks and heavy roof tiles. These days Hohhot is largely a Han city, though there is also a Hui and a Mongol presence; it's worthwhile tracking down the vanishing **Mongol** areas, not least to try some of their distinctive **food**. The other reason for visiting Hohhot is its proximity to some of the famous Mongolian **grasslands** within a 100km radius of the city.

Arrival

Hohhot is a fairly easy place to navigate. The heart of the modern commercial city, including most hotels, lies in the blocks to the south of the **train and bus stations**, while the old city and its flamboyant temples – in a seemingly permanent state of renovation – are southwest of the central Qingcheng Park. Hohhot's Baita **airport** lies 35km east of the city, and the airport bus (30min; ¥5) drops arriving passengers at the CAAC office on Xilin Guole Lu, the road running south from the bus station. A taxi will cost ¥20.

In summer, travellers arriving by train, in particular, are often subjected to furious and persistent harassment by travel agents' touts trying to sell them grassland tours. The only practical way to escape the melee is to get into a **taxi** – the minimum fare is ¥6, sufficient for most rides within the city.

Accommodation

Hohhot's **accommodation scene** is changing rapidly, and as the old favourites by the train station fall prey to the wrecking ball, demand is being met by more modern and central establishments.

Anda Guesthouse (安达宾馆, *āndá bīnguǎn*) Qiaokou Xi Jie ⓣ0471/6918039, ⓦwww.andaguesthouse.com. Friendly little youth hostel, with cheap dorm beds, and pleasant private rooms. The owner is a fountain of local knowledge, and will be able to rustle up a tailor-made grasslands trip in no time. The hostel is almost impossible to find independently – call ahead and you'll be picked up at the train station. ❷

Boyou Hotel (博友宾馆, *bóyǒu bīnguǎn*) 126 Xilin Guole Lu ⓣ0471/6293222. Just 300m south of the train station, this new venture is well looked

Moving on from Hohhot

There are daily trains to the Mongolian border town of **Erlianhot** (see p.228), posted "Erlian" on schedules. Train #4602/3 departs Hohhot at 10.30pm, arriving at 7.18am the next day. Alternatively, train #5712/13 leaves Hohhot at 8.10am, pulling in at 7.32pm after rolling through the grasslands. Note that this view of the pastures will be far more relaxing, quiet and comfortable than joining one of many group tours.

To **Baotou**, buses run every ten minutes from 7am (1hr 30min; ¥30) from the long-distance bus station next to the train station. There are also buses every thirty minutes from 6.30am to 6.30pm to **Dongsheng** (3hr; ¥55) where there are no shortage of buses and tours to Genghis Khan's Mausoleum (see p.222).

Hohhot is linked by **train** to **Lanzhou** to the west, **Beijing** to the east and **Hailar** (a 38hr journey via Beijing) to the northeast. There are also trains to **Ulan Bator** in the Republic of Mongolia (see p.228). Leaving Hohhot by train, you can seek the help of a travel agent to procure tickets for a small commission. You'll need to give them at least 36 hours' notice for a hard sleeper – or try your luck at the station ticket office, which is often hideously crowded with migrant workers.

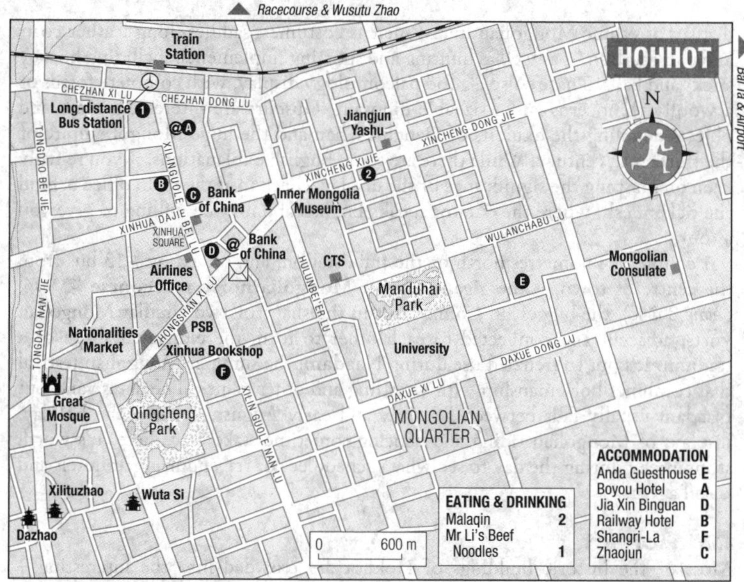

after by staff who are happy to help. The doubles with shared bathroom are excellent value at ¥68, while standard doubles are still keen at ¥120. 2

Jia Xin Binguan (家馨宾馆, *jiāxīn bīnguǎn*) Malan Qiate Xi Jie ⊕0471/6287766. Compact and bijou, this clean and nicely decorated family-run hotel has a good location and discounts to match. 3

Railway Hotel (铁路宾馆, *tiělù bīnguǎn*) 131 Xilin Guole Lu ⊕0471/6933377. Budget hotel with welcoming staff and clean facilities, far enough south of the train station to escape the attention of touts. They are also happy to book train tickets for guests. 3

Shangri-La (香格里拉酒店, *shānggélǐlā jiǔdiàn*) Xilin Guole Nan Lu ⊕0471/3366888, ⓦwww.shangri-la.com. You'll have to travel for hundreds of kilometres to find better rooms – this is Hohhot's newest and plushest hotel, with superb standards of service and great views from the higher floors. 8

Zhaojun (昭君大酒店, *zhāojūn dàjiǔdiàn*) 69 Xinhua Dajie ⊕0471/6668888, ⓦwww.zhaojunhotel.com.cn. A well-organized and comfortable place in the centre of town, diagonally across from Xinhua Square. The travel service in the lobby has information in English on their grassland and Genghis Khan Mausoleum tours. 6

The City

Hohhot focuses on **Xinhua Square**, at the junction of Xilin Guole Lu and the east–west axis Xinhua Dajie; early in the morning it becomes a giant exercise yard for hundreds of people. There is just one historic building marooned in this new part of town: this is the **Jiangjun Yashu** (将军衙署, *jiāngjūn yáshǔ*; daily 8am–4.30pm; ¥10), actually the office of a prominent Qing-dynasty general, even though it looks like a temple. Now it's a tiny museum with some bizarre modern Buddhist art mingling with Qing office furniture at the back. The best reason to come here is to see the scale model of ancient Hohhot, back before the city walls and temples were replaced with boulevards and banks. From the train station, bus #3 (¥1) will bring you here.

Also on the route of bus #3, the **Inner Mongolia Museum** (内蒙古博物馆, *nèiménggǔ bówùguǎn*; daily 9am–5pm; ¥10), on the corner of Xinhua Dajie and Hulunbei'er Lu, is well worth a visit. In the downstairs exhibition, there's a large display of ethnic Mongolian items, such as costumes, saddles, long leather coats and cummerbunds, as well as hunting and sporting implements, including hockey sticks and balls. There's also a good paleontology display, with complete fossils of a woolly rhinoceros and a sizeable dinosaur. Upstairs are interesting maps and objects detailing the exploits of Genghis Khan and the huge Mongol empire of the thirteenth century. While there are some English explanations, if you're truly keen on grasping the significance of the display, check in at the main office behind the ticket desk, where the curator speaks English and may be willing to give you a tour.

A couple of kilometres north of the train station, and served by #13 bus from the centre of town, is the gigantic **Inner Mongolia horse racecourse** (赛马场, *sàimă chăng*), the biggest in China, built in the shape of two circular Mongolian yurts, adjacent and connected to each other to form the elongated shape of a stadium. It's put to frenzied use during **Naadam**, the summer Mongolian festival that combines horsemanship with wrestling and other games. The dates vary, but Naadam usually falls between late July and early August. Outside the holiday, displays of Mongolian riding and dancing sometimes take place here. It's worth stopping by during the day to see what's scheduled, or try enquiring at hotels and travel agents.

Old Hohhot

Most of the historic buildings of Hohhot are crowded into the interesting – though fast-disappearing – old southwestern part of the city, where you can enjoyably spend half a day simply ambling around. From the train station, buses #6, #7 and #8 run here – get off at the Hui Middle School stop. You'll immediately see the Chinese-style minaret (topped with a pagoda roof) of the **Great Mosque** (清真大寺, *qīngzhēn dàsì*). This attractive black-brick building, situated at the southern end of Zhongshan Lu, blends traces of Chinese and Arabic style. The Hui people who worship here are extremely friendly, and will probably be delighted if you ask to look round the mosque. The surrounding streets comprise the Muslim area of town, and besides a lot of old men with wispy beards and skull-caps, you'll find a good, if dwindling, array of noodle and kebab shops in the immediate area.

Walking south from the mosque for about fifteen minutes along the main road leads you to a couple of Buddhist temples. The biggest of these is the **Dazhao** (大召, *dàzhāo*; daily 8am–5.30pm; ¥30), down a side street west of the main road. Constructed in 1579, and recently the subject of a typically gaudy renovation, the structure was dedicated in the late seventeenth century to the famous Qing emperor Kangxi – a gold tablet with the words "Long Live the Emperor" was set before the silver statue of Sakyamuni, and in the main hall murals depicting the visit of Kangxi can still be seen.

Just a few minutes from the Dazhao, over on the other side of the main road, is **Xilituzhao** (席力图召, *xílìtú zhào*; daily 8am–5.30pm; ¥10), another temple of similar scale and layout to the Dazhao, and dating from the same era, though it too has been restored since the destruction of the Cultural Revolution. The dagoba is interesting for featuring Sanskrit writing above Chinese dragons above Tibetan-style murals. Since 1735 this has been the official residence of the reincarnation of the Living Buddha, who is in charge of Buddhist affairs in the city.

Farther east, across what used to be the alleyways of the old city you'll come to Hohhot's most attractive piece of architecture, known as the **Wuta Si** (五塔寺, *wŭtă sì*; Five Towers Temple; daily 8am–5.30pm; ¥35). Built in 1727, in Indian style, this composite of five pagodas originally belonged to the Ci Deng Temple, which no longer exists. It's relatively small, but its walls are engraved with no fewer than

1563 Buddhas, all in slightly different postures. Currently stored inside the pagoda building is a rare, antique Mongolian cosmological map that marks the position of hundreds of stars.

Eating and drinking

The highlight of eating in Hohhot is dining on **Mongolian food**. Mongolian **hotpot**, or *shuan yangrou*, is best shared with friends and beer. It's a do-it-yourself meal: piles of thinly sliced mutton, ordered by the *jin*, are cooked by being dropped into a cauldron of boiling water at the table, then quickly removed and dipped into a spicy sesame sauce. Tofu, glass noodles, cabbage and mushrooms will often go into the pot too. Many restaurants in Hohhot serve *shuan yangrou* – the most famous being *Malaqin Restaurant* (马拉沁饭店, *mălāqìn fàndiàn*) on Xincheng Xi Jie, a few blocks east of Hulunbei'er Lu. Dinner with plenty of beer shouldn't cost more than ¥40 per head.

For an even more exotic meal, however, with the focus on Mongolian dairy products, head for the **Mongolian quarter** in the southeast of town. Bus #4 comes down here – get off at Daxue Xi Jie just south of the university. During term time, this area is packed with students eating and shopping; their increased spending power has seen many of the old eating places morph into clothing boutiques, but any restaurant with Mongolian letters above the door is worth trying. For an excellent breakfast or lunch, order a large bowl of sugary milk tea, and *chaomi* (buckwheat), *huangyou* (butter), *nailao* (hard white cheese) and *naipi* (a sweetish, biscuit-like substance formed from the skin of boiled milk). Toss everything into the tea, and eat it with chopsticks – it's surprisingly delicious. To make this into a substantial meal, eat it with *mengu baozi* or *jianbing* – dough stuffed with ground mutton, respectively steamed or fried. If you're pressed for a meal near the train station, there's a *Mr Li's Beef Noodle* branch (美国加洲牛肉面大王, *měiguó jiāzhōu niúròumiàn dàwáng*) on Chezhan Lu that serves up reasonable noodle staples.

Listings

Airlines CAAC (Mon–Sat 8am–9pm; ⓣ0471/6963160), Xilin Guole Lu, just south of Xinhua Square.

Banks and exchange The easiest place to change money and travellers' cheques is at the *Zhaojun* hotel, which offers the same rates as the bank without the queuing and form-filling. The head office of the Bank of China (daily 8am–5.30pm), across the road from the hotel, is equipped with ATMs, as is the branch opposite the post office at 19 Zhongshan Xi Lu.

Bookshop The Foreign Language Bookstore on Xilin Guole Lu, across the road from Xinhua Square has a poor selection of works in English.

Consulate The Republic of Mongolia consulate (Mon, Tues & Thurs 8.30am–noon; ⓣ0471/4303254) is in the east of the city, at 5 Wulanzaigu. Visas are fairly easy to obtain, though they cost ¥500 for a month and may take some time to be issued. US citizens do not need visas for stays up to thirty days.

Internet The Green Net Café (9am–7pm) on the fourth floor of the tech goods centre on the corner of Zhongshan Xi Lu and Yingbin Xi Lu (opposite the post office) charges ¥3/hour. The *Zhaojun* hotel offers access in its business centre for ¥33/hour.

Mail and telephones The main post office (daily 8am–6pm) is on the northeastern corner of the train station square, and offers Western Union money transfer services should you find yourself in dire straits. There's another on the south side of Zhongshan Lu, just east of Xilin Guole Lu (Mon–Sat 8am–7pm). The Telecom Centre is adjacent (daily 8am–6pm), with a small 24hr office.

PSB In the government building to the south of the junction between Zhongshan Lu and Xilin Guole Lu.

Travel agents There are numerous travel agents in town, many of whom will find you before you find them. They nearly all have English-speaking employees, and deal in grassland tours as well as booking train tickets. These are the best form of access to the grasslands: your accommodation will also be able to organize trips, but for a much higher price.

Around Hohhot

There are a few more sights scattered around the outer suburbs of Hohhot, some of which can be reached on city buses. The **Tomb of Wang Zhaojun** (昭君墓, *zhāojūn mù*; daily 9am–5pm; ¥18) about 8km to the south of Hohhot, is the burial site of a Tang-dynasty princess sent from what is today Hubei to cement Han-Mongol relations by marrying the king of Mongolia. It isn't spectacular – a huge mound raised from the plain and planted with gardens, in the centre of which is a modern pavilion – but the romantic story it recalls has important implications for modern Chinese politics, signifying the harmonious marrying of the Han with the minority peoples. In the rose garden, among pergolas festooned with gourds, is a tiny museum devoted to Zhaojun, containing some of her clothes, including a tiny pair of shoes, plus jewels, books and a number of steles. You can reach the tomb on the #44 minibus (¥1.5), or by walking due south along the main road from the Great Mosque in the west of town.

Not accessible by bus, but well worth the effort to reach, is the **Wusutu Zhao** complex (乌素图召, *wūsùtú zhào*), the only temple in Mongolia to have been designed and built solely by Mongolians. Boasting buildings in Mongolian, Tibetan and Han styles, it lies 12km northwest of Hohhot, south of the Daqing Mountain and in attractive countryside separated from the city by the new expressway. Admission to each of the four neighbouring temples is ¥3, collected by an elderly monk who will probably be surprised to see you. There are still no souvenir stands, no gaudy refurbishments, so take the time to scour the Ming-era murals within and the ornate woodcuts attached to sticks at the base of the Buddhas. The surrounding grasslands and trails into the mountains make for a relaxing day out. To get here from the train station, take bus #5 to its terminus and hire a taxi from there, a ride which shouldn't come to more than ¥20, though

On to Outer Mongolia

Should you require them, visas for the Republic of Mongolia, otherwise known as **Outer Mongolia**, are available in Hohhot and Beijing.

Currently, only MIAT (Meng Hang, the national airline of the Mongolian Republic) has flights **from Hohhot** to Ulan Bator; tickets can be bought at the office in the Mongolian consulate for around ¥3500. Air China and MIAT both fly three times weekly **from Beijing** to Ulaan Baatar; tickets for the two-hour flight cost around ¥2000 one way, while the **direct train**, which takes about 36 hours, is cheaper at ¥550.

Alternatively, you can do the journey in stages from Hohhot. The first leg is to get to the border at Erlianhot (*èrlián hàotè*), shortened to Erlian on timetables. Two **direct trains** run daily (9–11hr; ¥73). Or you can break the trip and soak up more of the grasslands by stopping in Jining (2hr; ¥22), then change to the Erlianhot train (4 daily; 4–7hr; ¥46).

Crossing the border at Erlianhot is still something of a hassle if you are not on a through train. Assuming you arrive in the evening you'll certainly have to spend one night here. In the morning there's one local bus that does the 7km trip across to the Mongolian town of **Zamen Uud**, though you may wait hours for it to leave. From there to Ulan Bator it's an eighteen-hour train journey.

Erlianhot itself is a curious border town in the middle of nowhere, catering mostly to Mongolian nomads and shepherds coming to do their shopping. It's also a famous centre for wool production. Twice a week its train station briefly fills with foreigners as the Trans-Mongolian Express comes through on its way to or from Moscow – there's even a disco and a bar here for their entertainment. Eat all you can in town, because the food in Outer Mongolia is notoriously poor.

unless you're prepared to hire the taxi for a half day, you'll probably have to walk back to the bus stop later, about an hour's hike along a busy road.

Slightly farther out is one more site that you can reach only by taxi: the **Bai Ta**, or White Pagoda (白塔, *bái tǎ*; daily dawn–dusk; ¥5), about 17km east of the city, is an attractive, 55m-high wood-and-brick construction, erected in the tenth century and covered in ornate carvings of coiling dragons, birds and flowers on the lower parts of the tower. You can reach it by following Xincheng Xi Jie east out of the city – it's a possible stop on the way to the airport.

The grasslands

Mongolia isn't all one giant steppe, but three areas in the vicinity of Hohhot are certainly large enough to give the illusion of endlessness. These are **Xilamuren** (希拉穆仁草原, *xīlāmùrén cǎoyuán*), which begins 80km north of Hohhot; **Gegentala** (格根塔拉草原, *gégēntǎlā cǎoyuán*), 70km further north; and **Huitengxile** (辉腾锡勒草原, *huīténgxīlè cǎoyuán*), 120km northeast of Hohhot. It's hard to differentiate between them, save to say that Xilamuren – the only one of the three that can feasibly be reached independently – is probably the most visited and Gegentala the least. Bear in mind that your grassland experience in the immediate area of the regional capital is likely to be a rather packaged affair, and a visit to a grassland in another, remoter part of the region (such as Hailar – see p.200) may well give you a more authentic flavour of Mongolia.

The most convenient way to visit the grasslands is to take one of the **grassland tours**, which Westerners rarely enjoy but east Asian tourists seem to love – or at least put up with in good humour. The tours always follow a similar pattern, with visitors based at a site comprising a number of **yurts**, plus a dining hall, kitchen and very primitive toilets. The larger sites, at Xilamuren, are the size of small villages. Transport, meals and accommodation are all included in the price, as are various unconvincing "Mongolian entertainments" – wrestling and horseriding in particular – and visits to typical Mongol families in traditional dress. Only the food is consistently good, though watch out for the local firewater, *baijiu*, which you're more or less forced to drink when your Mongolian hosts bring silver bowls of the stuff round to every table during the evening banquet. The banquet is followed by a fairly degenerate evening of drinking, dancing and singing.

If you accept the idea that you are going on a tour of the grasslands primarily to participate in a bizarre social experience, then you'll get much more out of it. Besides, it is perfectly possible to escape from your group if you wish to do so. You can hire your own horse, or head off for a hike. If your stay happens to coincide with a bright moon, you could be in for the most hauntingly beautiful experience of your life.

Practicalities

A two-day **tour** (with one night in a yurt) is definitely enough – in a group of four or five people, this should come to around ¥450 each. Some travel services can tack smaller parties onto existing groups. Bear in mind that if you choose this option, you may find yourself sleeping crushed into a small yurt with six others who don't speak your language, and consequently the tour may not be in English, even if you've specifically requested that it should be.

Travelling independently to the Xilamuren grassland can work out a good deal cheaper than taking a tour. Store your luggage at your hotel in Hohhot, and catch a bus from the long-distance bus station (90min; ¥20) to the small settlement of **Zhaohe**, adjacent to the grassland. When you get off you will be accosted by people offering to take you to their yurts – try to negotiate an all-inclusive daily rate of about ¥50 per person, for food and accommodation, before you accept any offer. You aren't exactly in the wilderness here, but you can wander off into the grass and soon find it. Return buses to Hohhot run regularly throughout the day.

Shanxi

Shanxi province (陕西, *shǎnxī*), with an average height of 1000m above sea level, is one huge mountain plateau. Strategically important, bounded to the north by the Great Wall and to the south by the Yellow River, it was for centuries a bastion territory against the northern tribes. Today, its significance is economic: this is China's most **coal-rich** province, with 500 million tons mined here annually, a quarter of the national supply. Around the two key towns, **Datong** and the capital **Taiyuan**, open-cast mining has obliterated large parts of the countryside, and over a million people had to be recently rehoused due to land subsidence in the region.

Physically, Shanxi is dominated by the proximity of the Gobi Desert, and wind and water have shifted sand, dust and silt right across the province. The land is farmed, as it has been for millennia, by slicing the hills into steps, creating a plain of ribbed hillocks that look like the realization of a cubist painting. The dwellings in this terrain often have mud walls, or are simply caves cut into vertical embankments, seemingly a part of the strange landscape. Great tracts of this land, though, are untillable, due to **soil erosion** caused by tree felling, and the paucity of rainfall, which has left much of the province fearsomely barren, an endless range of dusty hills cracked by fissures. Efforts are now being made to arrest **erosion** and the advance of the desert, including a huge tree-planting campaign. Sometimes, you'll even see wandering dunes held in place by immense nets of woven straw.

While Shanxi's cities are generally functional and laminated in coal dust, once you get beyond them – sometimes not even very far – things improve dramatically. Tourism staff in the province call it a "museum above the ground", a reference to the many unrestored but still intact **ancient buildings** that dot the region, some from dynasties almost unrepresented elsewhere in China. Just outside Datong, the

Cave houses

A common sight among the folds and fissures of the dry loess plain of northern Shanxi (and neighbouring Shaanxi) are **cave dwellings**, a traditional form of housing that's been in use for nearly two thousand years. Hollowed into the sides of hills terraced for agriculture, they house more than eighty million people, and are eminently practical – cheap, easy to make, naturally insulated and long-lasting. In fact, a number of intact caves in Hejin, on the banks of the Yellow River in the west of the province, are said to date back to the Tang dynasty. Furthermore, in a region where flat land has to be laboriously hacked out of the hillside, caves don't take up land that could be cultivated.

The **facade** of the cave is usually a wooden frame on a brick base. Most of the upper part consists of a wooden lattice – designs of which are sometimes very intricate – faced with white paper, which lets in plenty of light, but preserves the occupants' privacy. Tiled eaves above protect the facade from rain damage. Inside, the **single-arched chamber** is usually split into a bedroom at the back and a living area in front, furnished with a *kang*, whose flue leads under the bed and then outside to the terraced field that is the roof – sometimes, the first visible indication of a distant village is a set of smoke columns rising from the crops.

Such is the popularity of cave homes that prosperous cave dwellers often prefer to build themselves a new courtyard and another cave rather than move into a house. Indeed, in the suburbs of towns and cities of northern Shaanxi, **new concrete apartment buildings** are built in imitation of caves, with three windowless sides and an arched central door. It is not uncommon even to see soil spread over the roofs of these apartments with vegetables grown on top.

Yungang cave temples are among China's major Buddhist art sites, easily taken in en route between Beijing and Hohhot in Inner Mongolia. Not quite as accessible, **Wutai Shan** is a holy mountain on the northeastern border with Hebei, with an unusually devout atmosphere and beautiful alpine scenery. Farther south, all within a bus ride of the towns spread along the rail line between Taiyuan and Xi'an, are a host of little places worth a detour, the highest profile of which is **Pingyao**, an old walled town preserved entirely from its Qing-dynasty heyday as a banking centre. Southwest of here and surprisingly time-consuming to reach, the Yellow River presents its fiercest aspect at **Hukou Falls**, as its chocolate-coloured waters explode out of a short, tight gorge.

Datong and around

Don't let first appearances deceive you – gritty, polluted and unattractive it may be, but **DATONG** (大同, *dàtóng*) is the main jumping-off point for two of northern China's most spectacular sights. The phenomenal **Yungang Caves** and the gravity-defying **Hanging Temple** can both be chalked off in a single day, while the latter can be combined with a visit to **Heng Shan**, one of the five holy mountains of Taoism, or on the way to the Buddhist centre of **Wutai Shan** (see p.239).

Datong throws a few sights of its own into the ring, relaying a tale of two non-Han dynasties. The Turkic **Toba** people took advantage of the internal strife afflicting central and southern China to establish their own dynasty, the **Northern Wei** (386–534 AD), taking Datong as their capital in 398 AD. Though the period was one of discord and warfare, the Northern Wei became fervent Buddhists and commissioned a magnificent series of **cave temples** at Yungang, just west of the city. Over the course of almost a century, more than a thousand grottoes were completed, containing over fifty thousand statues, before the capital was moved south to Luoyang, where construction began on the similar Longmen Caves (see p.277).

A second period of greatness came with the arrival of the Mongol **Liao dynasty**, also Buddhists, who made Datong their capital in 907. Their rule lasted two hundred years, leaving behind a small legacy of statuary and some fine temple architecture, notably in the **Huayan** and **Shanhua temples** in town, and a **wooden pagoda**, the oldest in China, in the nearby town of **Yingxian**. Datong

remained important to later Chinese dynasties for its strategic position just inside the Great Wall, south of Inner Mongolia, and the tall **city walls** date from the early Ming dynasty.

Arrival, information and city transport

Free shuttle buses plough the 15km from Datong's **airport** to the city centre; failing this, you'll have to take a taxi (¥65). The **train station** is on the city's northern edge, and on arrival you may be grabbed by a representative of the helpful **CITS office** (6.30am–6.30pm; ⓣ13008088454), at first indistinguishable from other pushy touts and taxi drivers, but far more useful. If you don't meet them at the station, make for their office inside the *Taijia* hotel, or call them – they can arrange discount accommodation and organize tours and train tickets. The long-distance **Xinnan bus station** (新南站, *xīnnán zhàn*) is around 5km south of the centre on the #30 bus route to the train station via Xinjian Nan Lu and Xinjian Bei Lu; other possible arrival points include the more central **Regional bus station** (长途汽车站, *chángtú qìchēzhàn*) and the tiny **North bus station** (汽车北站, *qìchē běizhàn*) just south of the train station area.

Datong has numerous **bus routes** (¥1), while **taxis** cruise the streets; flag fare is ¥5, and a ride within town should be under ¥10. **Walking** around the city is tiring, as it's quite spread out, roads are tediously straight and Datong's dry air can leave you feeling parched.

Accommodation

The city's budget **accommodation** options are clustered around the train station, with some good-value mid-range options in the city centre. Very little stands out at the cheapest end of the scale, so budget travellers – or anyone, really – may care to arrive in the morning, see the sights and grab a night train out.

Garden Hotel (花园大饭店, *huāyuán dàfàndiàn*) 59 Da Nan Jie ⓣ0352/5865825, ⓕ5865824. The city's top-end option, with good service, crisp linen on the beds and an excellent location. There's also a Brazilian buffet – incongruous in dusty Datong, but quite a pleasant surprise. Free wi-fi. ❽

Hongqi (红旗大饭店, *hóngqí dàjiǔdiàn*) Train station square ⓣ0352/5366888, ⓕ5366222. Highly convenient for the train station, this hotel is perfectly acceptable for the price, with the free breakfasts going down particularly well. ❺

Taijia (泰佳宾馆, *tàijiā bīnguǎn*) Jianbei Jie ⓣ0352/5101816. This grubby hotel is pretty much the cheapest acceptable lodging near the station, and the base of the city's CITS office, who will probably try to push you here. Have a good look at the room before agreeing to stay, though. ❸

Yungang International (云冈国际酒店, *yúngāng guójì jiǔdiàn*) 38 Da Xi Jie ⓣ0352/5869999, ⓕ5869666. Surprisingly cheap, given its appearance – all marble and chandeliers, providing an oasis of calm in this hectic city. Rooms are excellent, and even the café and bar are appealing. ❼

Moving on from Datong

The **CAAC office** (daily 8.30am–5pm; ⓣ0352/2052777 or 2043388) is at 1 Nanguan Nan Jie, with several flights weekly to Beijing, Shanghai and Guangzhou. Free shuttle buses to the **airport** start from outside the *Datong Hotel* (大同宾馆), just a block to the south. **Train tickets** are straightforward enough to buy at the station, or at the advance-ticket office (8am–12.30pm & 2.30–6pm) at the corner of Nanguan Nan Jie and Nanguan Xi Jie.

The main **long-distance bus station** is the Xinnan station south of town on the #30 bus route, for services to Taiyuan and Yingxian. Try the Yantong Xi Lu depot for departures to **Hunyuan**, **Baotou** and **Beijing**; the North bus station for Wutai Shan; and the train station forecourt for shared taxis and minibuses to Beijing or Taiyuan.

The City

The yellow earthen **ramparts** that once bounded the old city are still quite impressive, though now demolished in places – the best stretches are in the east of the city. Inside the walls, aside from the main sights there are a good number of small temples and old monuments hidden away in the backstreets, which themselves are full of a gritty atmosphere that those who don't have to live here might just find appealing.

The Drum Tower and Nine Dragon Screen

Just south of the crossroads of Da Xi Jie and Da Bei Jie, at the heart of the city, Datong's three-storey **Drum Tower** (鼓楼, *gŭlóu*) dates back to the Ming dynasty. You can't go inside, but it makes a useful landmark. A little way east on the south side of Da Dong Jie, the **Nine Dragon Screen** (九龙壁, *jiŭlóng bì*; 7.30am–7.30pm; ¥10) is the largest of several similar Ming-dynasty screens around the city; a lively 45m-long relief of nine sinuous dragons depicted in 426 multicoloured glazed tiles, rising from the waves and cavorting among suns. The only other dragon screens of this age are in Beijing, the main difference here being that these dragons have only four claws, indicating the dwelling of a prince, not an emperor (whose dragons had five claws). Originally, the screen stood directly in front of a palace, destroyed in the fifteenth century, as an unpassable obstacle to evil spirits, which, it was thought, could only travel in straight lines. A long, narrow pool in front of the screen is meant to reflect the dragons and give the illusion of movement when you look into its rippling surface.

Huayan Si

The area to the southwest of the main crossroads was being redeveloped – again – at the time of writing, and despite using the usual bringing-tradition-to-the-modern-day template, the results were looking rather encouraging. West of this area are the remaining buildings of **Huayan Si** (华严寺, *huáyán sì*), originally a large temple dating to 1062 AD during the Liao dynasty and now forming two complexes. The **Upper Temple** (daily 8am–6.30pm; ¥20), the first one you come to, is a little shabby, but its twelfth-century **Main Hall** is one of the largest in China, and is unusual for facing east – it was originally built by a sect that worshipped the sun. The roof is superb, a Tang-style design with two vertical "horns" fashioned to look like lions doing handstands. The cavernous interior has some wonderful Ming statuary including twenty life-size guardians, gently inclined as if listening attentively, but the main draw is the Qing-dynasty **frescoes** completely covering the walls, depicting Buddha's attainment of nirvana.

Turn right out of the entrance to this complex and you come to the **Lower Temple** (daily 8am–6.30pm; ¥20), notable for its rugged-looking hall, a rare Liao-dynasty construction from 1038, complete with contemporary statues. Halls surrounding the front courtyard form a **museum** of regional discoveries spanning the Liao, Jin, Khitan and Yuan eras.

Shanhua Si

South of the Drum Tower on Da Nan Jie and tucked away behind the *Yonghe* restaurant is the **Shanhua Si** (善化寺, *shànhuà sì*; daily 8am–6pm; ¥20). A temple has stood here since the Tang dynasty, though what you see is a Ming restoration of a Jin structure. The buildings have a solid presence very different from the delicate look of later Chinese temples, and are impressive for their obvious age alone – one dates from 1154. The Jin-dynasty statues in the main hall, five Buddhas in the centre with 24 *lokapalas* (divine generals) lined up on either side, are exceptionally finely detailed. One of the outlying courtyards sports a **five-dragon screen**, relocated from a monastery that once stood to the south of the city.

Eating and drinking

Datong is far enough north for **mutton hotpot** to figure heavily in the local cuisine, along with potatoes, which you can buy, processed into a starchy jelly and seasoned with sauces, from street stalls. Other typically northern dishes available are *zongyi* (glutinous rice dumplings) and *yuanxiao* (sweet dumplings). There are plenty of inexpensive dumpling places up around the train station area, and also snack-stands serving cheap *xiao mian*, the local form of noodles.

Deyue Lou (得月楼, *déyuè lóu*) Yantong Xi Lu. Muslim-run venue serving the local variety of hotpot in distinctive conical pots. ¥30 should buy enough meat and veggies for two.

Habitat Xinjian Nan Lu. Expat-oriented bar across from Hongqi Square, with beer from ¥10. Frequent live music, and it can get lively on Friday and Saturday evenings.

Yonghe Restaurant (永和中餐厅, *yǒnghé zhōngcāntīng*) Da Nan Jie. Colossal venue with a hotpot section, a snack section and a restaurant specializing in Sichuanese and Cantonese cooking. Prices for regular dishes are very reasonable, with many under ¥20.

Listings

Banks and exchange The main Bank of China (Mon–Fri 8am–6pm) on Yingbin Xi Lu can cash travellers' cheques, and there's a small branch with an ATM at the southern end of Da Nan Jie.

Hospital People's Hospital No. 3 is in the south of the city on Yingbin Xi Lu, just west of the crossroads with Xinjian Nan Lu.

Left luggage There's an office outside the train station on the western side of the concourse (¥5).

Mail and telephones The large Russian-looking stately building fronting Hongqi Square, south of Da Xi Jie, houses both the post office (daily 8am–6pm) and a 24hr telecom office. Droves of women stand about selling cut-rate IC and IP phone cards.

PSB The police station (Mon–Sat 8.30am–noon & 2.30–6pm) is on Xinjian Bei Lu, 200m north of the post office; take along a Mandarin-speaker, since they're not particularly heedful of travellers' needs.

Travel agents The CITS office at the *Taijia* (see p.232) is able to book train and plane tickets for a ¥30–50 mark-up. They also offer day-trips for ¥100/person (transportation only) to Yungang Caves and the Hanging Temple; the Hanging Temple and Wooden Pagoda; and the caves and city temples.

Around Datong

The sights outside the city are far more diverting than those within. In addition to the **Yungang Caves**, several ancient buildings dotted around in nearby country towns are also worth checking out. Roads are sometimes bumpy and often blocked in winter, when transport times can double, but at least journeys are enlivened by great views: the lunar emptiness of the fissured landscape is broken only occasionally by villages whose mud walls seem to grow out of the raw brown earth. Some of the villages in the area still have their **beacon towers**, left over from when this really was a wild frontier.

Some **maps** of Datong include plans of Hunyuan and Yingxian, together with area maps showing the roads, so are worth picking up before you go. Getting around to all the sites on teeth-rattling public buses can be time-consuming, so consider taking a **CITS tour** – see Datong "Listings" above for details. A **taxi** to the caves and the Hanging Temple will cost around ¥300.

The Yungang Caves

Just 16km west of Datong, the monumental **Yungang Caves** (云冈石窟, *yúngāng shíkū*; daily 8am–6.30pm; ¥130), a set of Buddhist grottoes carved into the side of

Building the Yungang Caves

Construction of the Yungang Caves began in 453 AD, when Datong was the capital of the Northern Wei dynasty, and petered out around 525, after the centre of power moved to Luoyang. The caves were made by first hollowing out a section at the top of the cliff, then digging into the rock, down to the ground and out, leaving two holes, one above the other. As many as forty thousand craftsmen worked on the project, coming from as far as India and Central Asia, and there is much foreign influence in the **carvings**: Greek motifs (tridents and acanthus leaves), Persian symbols (lions and weapons), and bearded figures, even images of the Hindu deities Shiva and Vishnu, are incorporated among the more common dragons and phoenixes of Chinese origin. The soft, rounded modelling of the **sandstone figures** – China's first stone statues – lining the cave interiors has more in common with the terracotta carvings of the Mogao Caves near Dunhuang in Gansu, begun a few years earlier, than with the sharp, more linear features of Luoyang's later limestone work. In addition, a number of the seated Buddhas have sharp, almost Caucasian noses.

The caves' present condition is misleading, as originally the cave entrances would have been covered with wooden facades, and the sculptures would have been faced with plaster and brightly painted; the larger sculptures are pitted with regular holes, which would once have held wooden supports on which the plaster face was built. Over the centuries, some of the caves have inevitably suffered from weathering, though there seems to have been little vandalism, certainly less than at Luoyang.

a sandstone cliff, are a must. Built around 400 AD at a time of Buddhist revival, the caves were the first and grandest of the three major Buddhist grottoes, the other two being the Longmen Caves in Luoyang (p.277) and the Mogao Caves in Gansu (p.842). These are the best preserved, but prepare to be disappointed by their surroundings – the atmosphere has for years been blighted by nearby coal mines, and the benefits afforded by the recent addition of parkland have been eroded by a huge and even more recently built shopping mall. However, it's still well worth the trip. There are two ways to get to the caves – **bus #3-2** (every 10–15min; ¥2) heads from the train station via Xinjian Bei Lu and Xinjian Nan Lu, though since it can take over half an hour just to escape the city, many prefer to take a **taxi** (¥50).

Arranged in three **clusters** (east, central and west) and numbered east to west from 1 to 51, the caves originally spread across an area more than 15km long, though today just a kilometre-long fragment survives. If it's spectacle you're after, just wander at will, but to get an idea of the changes of style and the accumulation of influences, you need to move sequentially between the three clusters. The earliest group is caves 16–20, followed by 7, 8, 9 and 10, then 5, 6 and 11 – the last to be completed before the court moved to Luoyang. Then followed 4, 13, 14 and 15, with the caves at the eastern end – 1, 2 and 3 – and cave 21 in the west, carved last. Caves 22–50 are smaller and less interesting.

The eastern and central caves

The easternmost caves are slightly set apart from, and less spectacular than, the others. **Caves 1 and 2** are constructed around a single square central pillar, elaborately carved in imitation of a wooden stupa but now heavily eroded, around which devotees perambulated. **Cave 3**, 25m deep, is the largest in Yungang – an almost undecorated cavern, it may once have been used as a lecture hall – while **cave 4** has a central pillar carved with images of Buddha.

The most spectacular caves are numbers 5–13, dense with **monumental sculpture**. Being suddenly confronted and dwarfed by a huge, 17m-high Buddha as you walk into **cave 5**, his gold face shining softly in the half-light, is an awesome, humbling experience. Other Buddhas of all sizes, a heavenly gallery, are massed in niches that honeycomb the grotto's gently curving walls, and two Bodhisattvas stand attentive at his side.

Cave 6, though very different, is just as arresting. A wooden facade built in 1652 leads into a high, square chamber dominated by a thick central pillar carved with Buddhas and Bodhisattvas in deep relief, surrounded by flying Buddhist angels and musicians. The vertical grotto walls are alive with images, including reliefs depicting incidents from the **life of the Buddha** at just above head height, which were designed to form a narrative when read walking clockwise around the chamber. Easy-to-identify scenes at the beginning include the birth of the Buddha from his mother's armpit, and Buddha's father carrying the young infant on an elephant. Buddha's first trip out of the palace, which is depicted as a schematic, square Chinese building, is shown on the east wall of the cave, as is his meeting with the grim realities of life, in this case a cripple with two crutches.

Caves 7 and 8 are a pair, both square, with two chambers, and connected by an arch lined with angels and topped with what looks like a sunflower. The figures here, such as the six celestial worshippers above the central arch, are more Chinese in style than their predecessors in caves 16–20, perhaps indicating the presence of craftsmen from Gansu, which the Wei conquered in 439 AD.

The columns and lintels at the entrances of **caves 9, 10 and 12** are awash with sculptural detail in faded pastel colours: Buddhas, dancers, musicians, animals, flowers, angels and abstract, decorative flourishes (which bear a resemblance to Persian art). Parts of cave 9 are carved with imitation brackets to make the interior resemble a wooden building.

The outstretched right arm of the 15m-high Buddha inside **cave 13** had to be propped up for stability, so his sculptors ingeniously carved the supporting pillar on his knee into a four-armed mini-Buddha. The badly eroded sculptures of **caves 14 and 15** are stylistically some way between the massive figures of the early western caves and the smaller reliefs of the central caves.

The western caves

Compared to the images in the central caves, the figures in these, the **earliest caves** (16–20) are simpler and bolder, and though they are perhaps more crudely carved, they are at least as striking. The **giant Buddhas**, with round faces, sharp noses, deep eyes and thin lips, are said to be the representations of five emperors. Constructed between 453 and 462 AD, under the supervision of the monk Tan Hao, all are in the same pattern of an enlarged niche containing a massive Buddha flanked by Bodhisattvas. The Buddha in **cave 16**, whose bottom half has disintegrated, has a knotted belt high on his chest, Korean-style. The Buddhas were carved from the top down, and when the sculptors of the Buddha in **cave 17** reached ground level they needed to dig down to fit his feet in. The same problem was solved in **cave 18** by giving the Buddha shortened legs. The 14m-high Buddha in **cave 20**, sitting open to the elements in a niche that once would have been protected by a wooden canopy, is probably the most famous, and certainly the most photographed.

The small caves 21–51, the least spectacular of the set, are not much visited, but the ceiling of **cave 50** is worth a look for its flying elephants, which also appear in **cave 48**, and in **caves 50 and 51** there are sculptures of acrobats.

The Hanging Temple and Heng Shan

Clinging to the side of a sheer cliff face, the **Hanging Temple** (悬空寺, *xuánkōng sì*; daily 7am–6pm; ¥130) is one of the most visually arresting sights in all China, and a must-see for those visiting Datong. Exceptions could be made for those who suffer from vertigo – literally translating as "Temple Suspended in the Void", its buildings are anchored by wooden beams set into the rock. There's been a temple on this site since the Northern Wei, though the buildings were periodically destroyed by the flooding of the Heng River (now no longer there, thanks to a dam upstream), occasioning the temple to be rebuilt higher and higher each time. Your first glimpse of it will be spectacular enough, but things get a great deal more atmospheric once you're inside the rickety, claustrophobic structure. Tall, narrow stairs and plank walkways connect the six halls – natural caves and ledges with wooden facades – in which shrines exist to Confucianism, Buddhism and Taoism, all of whose major figures are represented in nearly eighty statues in the complex, made from bronze, iron and stone.

The Hanging Temple sits on the valley road that runs up to **Heng Shan** (恒山, *héngshān*; 8am–6pm; ¥60), a range of peaks around 80km southeast of Datong near the town of Hunyuan. This is one of China's five main Taoist mountains – its history as a religious centre stretches back more than two thousand years, and plenty of emperors have put in an appearance here to climb the highest peak, Xuanwu (2000m), a trend begun by the very first emperor, Qin Shi Huang. From the base of the mountain, an easy climb takes you to Heng Shan's main temple, **Hengzong Si**, via switchbacking paths through other smaller temples, about a thirty-minute walk up and twenty minutes down (a cable-car round trip costs ¥42). Heng shan's peak lies another forty minutes uphill from Hengzong Si, and might be the quietest place left on the mountain.

Practicalities

Getting to the Hanging Temple is usually straightforward enough, with regular **buses** from Datong's regional bus station (1hr 30min; ¥31), including a few that start their journey outside the train station. Don't be surprised if you're bundled into a free taxi for the last leg of the journey. Finding a bus back can be a chore, in which case hop in a taxi (¥15–20) to the nearby town of **Hunyuan** (浑圆, *húnyuán*), which has regular buses back to Datong, the last leaving at around 6pm. To get to Heng Shan, it's best to head first to Hunyuan, then take a cab the rest of the way (¥30).

Restaurants at Heng Shan are a ridiculous rip-off, and at the time of writing there were none at all at the Hanging Temple – bring your own food.

The Wood Pagoda

At the centre of the small town of **Yingxian** (应县, *yìngxiàn*), 75km south of Datong, the stately **Wood Pagoda** (应县木塔, *yìngxiàn mùtǎ*; daily 8am–6pm; ¥61), built in 1056 in the Liao dynasty, is one of the oldest wooden buildings in China, a masterful piece of structural engineering that looks solid enough to stand here for another millennium. The "Woody Tower", as the English sign explains, reaches nearly 70m high and is octagonal in plan, with nine internal storeys, though there are only six layers of eaves on the outside.

The first storey is taller than the rest with extended eaves held up by columns forming a cloister around a mud-and-straw wall. The original pagoda was constructed without nails, though there are plenty in the floors nowadays. The ceilings and walls of the spacious internal halls are networks of beams held together with huge, intricate **wooden brackets**, called *dougongs*, of which there are nearly sixty different kinds. Interlocking, with their ends carved into curves and layered one on top of another, these give the pagoda a burly, muscular appearance, and as structural supports they perform their function brilliantly – the building has survived seven earthquakes.

Originally, each storey had a statue inside, but now only one remains, an 11m-tall Buddha with facial hair and stretched-out earlobes – characteristic of northern ethnic groups, such as the Khitan, who came to power in Shanxi during the Liao dynasty (916–1125 AD). During a recent renovation, a cache of **treasures** was found buried underneath the pagoda, including Buddhist sutras printed using woodblocks dating back to the Liao.

Buses to Yingxian from Datong take two hours and leave from the Xinnan station (p.232). **Yingxian's bus station** is on the western section of the town's main east–west road, about 1km southwest of the pagoda. From Yingxian, there are buses to Hunyuan, about 50km away, for Heng Shan and the Hanging Temple; these leave every hour until 5pm – also the time of the last bus back to Datong. Alternatively, if you start early you can just about manage to see both the Hanging Temple and the Wood Pagoda by public transport in one (long) day. Note that it's also possible to stay in Yingxian.

Wutai Shan

One of China's four Buddhist mountains, the five flat peaks of **WUTAI SHAN** (五台山, *wǔtái shān*) – the name means "Five-terrace Mountain" – rise around 3000m above sea level in the northeastern corner of Shanxi province, near the border with Hebei. The long bus ride here is rewarded with fresh air, superb scenery, some fascinating temple architecture and a spiritual (if not always peaceful) tone.

Though increasingly accessible today, the mountain's formerly remote location has always given it a degree of protection, and many of Wutai Shan's forty temples have survived the centuries intact – one reason why the mountains gained World Heritage status in 2009. The monastic village of **Taihuai** is the focus, sitting in a depression surrounded by the five holy peaks; highlights are its ninth-century **revolving bookcase** of the Tayuan Si and **two ancient temples**, the Song-dynasty Foguang and the Tang-dynasty Nanchan. All the temples today are working and full of resident clergy, despite an escalating number of tour groups trudging around them in peak season – though you'll also see a surprising number of ordinary Chinese people here as **pilgrims**, thumbing rosaries and prostrating themselves on their knees as they clamber up the temples' steep staircases.

The hordes of tourists that descend upon Wutai Shan in warmer months sometimes put paid to genuine feelings of remoteness. Crowds die down between October and April, though you will have to come prepared for some low temperatures and possible blizzards. Whatever the time of year, don't **hike** off into the hills around Taihuai without some warm, weatherproof gear, food and water, and a torch, even though in good weather the trails here present no special difficulties. Allow plenty of time for hikes, as the paths are hard to find in the dark and even in summer the temperature drops sharply at sundown.

Some history

Wutai Shan was an early bastion of Buddhism in China, a religious centre at least since the reign of Emperor Ming Di (58–75 AD). At that time, a visiting Indian monk had a vision in which he met **Manjusri** (**Wenshu**), the Buddhist incarnation of Wisdom, who is usually depicted riding a blue lion and carrying a manuscript (to represent a sutra) and a sword to cleave ignorance. By the time of the Northern Wei, Wutai Shan was a prosperous Buddhist centre, important enough to be depicted on a mural at the Dunhuang Caves in Gansu. The mountain reached its height of popularity in the Tang dynasty, when there were more than two hundred temples scattered around its peaks. In the fifteenth century, the founder

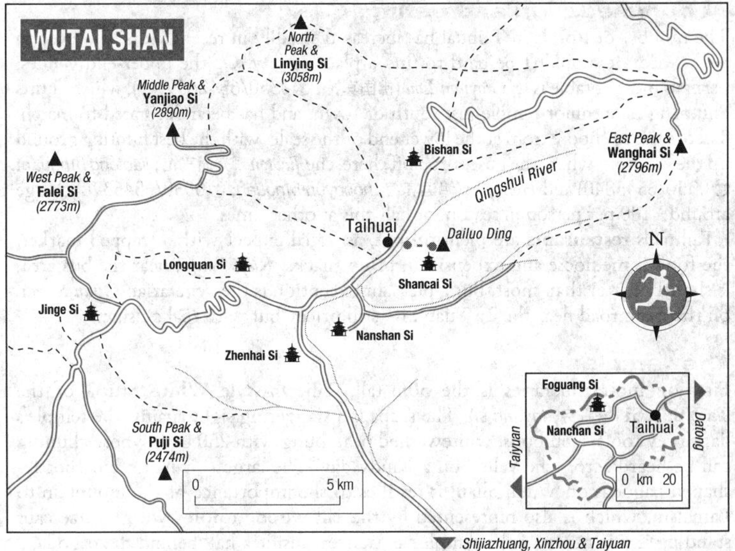

of the **Yellow Hat order**, now the dominant Buddhist sect in Tibet, came to the area to preach; Manjusri is particularly important in Tibetan and Mongolian Buddhism, and Wutai Shan remains an important pilgrimage place for Lamaists.

Taihuai

Also known as "Wutai Shan" (but not "Wutai", another township), **Taihuai** (台怀, *táihuái*) is a strip of tourist facilities and temples spread along about a kilometre of road, overlooked by high, dark brown hills. This is base camp for Wutai Shan trekkers, and its relaxed atmosphere – together with the physical exertion of climbing the hills – encourages an overnight stay, rather than a day-trip from Datong or Taiyuan.

Orientation is easy: uphill along the road is north, with the main batch of temples, which have all expanded into one another, immediately to the west, and a smaller group of pavilions studding the steep hillside to the east across a river; entrance fees to the most popular spots hover around the ¥5 mark.

Arrival and information

Getting to Taihuai is straightforward, though access can be restricted outside the warmer months. The nearest **train station**, also known as Wutaishan, is ninety minutes away on the Beijing–Taiyuan line, and connected through the day to Taihuai by taxis and shuttle buses. By **bus**, you can get here in summer from Datong's North long-distance bus station (4hr 30min), though the road crosses a high pass, which can see it closed at short notice by snow; and more reliably from Taiyuan's East bus station (5hr). Note that some travellers who have arrived after dark have reported being turfed out of their bus outside Taihuai, and encouraged to stay at a particular hotel. You will, however, be asked to leave the bus at some point to pay the mountain's **entry** fee (¥168).

The Bank of China in the central temple district has an **ATM** and can usually change money, but it's wise to arrive with enough yuan to last the duration of the visit.

Accommodation and eating

The number of **hotels** in Taihuai has increased steadily in recent years, and even in peak season it shouldn't be hard to find a place to stay. Of the upper-end venues, perhaps most notable is the *Foyuan Lou* (佛国宾馆; ⓣ0350/6542659; ❺), which abutts Shuxiang Si, a minor temple just south of town, and has been decorated to match. There's less to choose from at the lower end of the scale, with the best hunting ground up the hill from where the buses drop off; here, the *Jiaotong* (交通宾馆; *jiāotōng bīnguǎn*; ⓣ0350/6545840) and *Hongyun* (鸿运宾馆, *hóngyùn bīnguǎn*; ⓣ0350/6545378) charge around ¥100 per person in season, or half this at other times.

Taihuai's **restaurants** are plentiful but, as you'd expect with a trapped market, the food is mediocre and expensive – bring snacks. *Ruyi Fanfu*, near the bus area, is slightly better than most, but a pleasant exception is the vegetarian *Quan Suzai*, on the main road near the Ta Yuan Si – still pricey but with real cuisine.

The temples

First on most itineraries is the 50m-tall, Tibetan-style **White Stupa** of the **Ta Yuan Si** (塔院寺, *tǎyuàn sì*). The stupa is a staggering sight against the temple's dark grey roofs, a bulbous, whitewashed peak hung with 250 bells whose chiming can be heard across the valley on a windy day. The largest of many such bottle-shaped pagodas on Wutai Shan, it testifies to the importance of the mountain to Lamaism, which is also represented by the tall **wooden poles** with bronze caps standing inside many of the temple's entrances. Inside a hall behind the pagoda, a Ming-dynasty, two-storey library was built to house a bizarre and beautiful revolving **wooden bookcase**, much older than the rest of the complex. Its 33 layers of shelves, split into cubbyholes and painted with decorative designs, hold volumes of sutras in Tibetan, Mongolian and Chinese. Not far from **Shanhai Lou**, the chunky main gate of the temple – which you can climb for views – is the **Chairman Mao Memorial Hall**, whose placement at the heart of one of Buddhism's most sacred sights is in decidedly poor taste.

Just north of Ta Yuan Si's entrance, **Luohou Si** (罗喉寺, *luóhóu sì*) is a Ming-dynasty reconstruction of a Tang temple. Crowds gather to gawk at the spinning round wooden altar in the main hall with a wave design at its base supporting a large wooden lotus with moveable petals. A mechanism underneath opens the petals to reveal four Buddhas sitting inside the flower.

The **Xiantong Si** (显通寺, *xiǎntōng sì*), just uphill from the Ta Yuan Si, reputedly dates back to 68 AD, and so is one of the oldest Buddhist sites in China. The main sights here are the whitewashed **Beamless Hall**, built in brick to resemble a wooden structure; and the dazzling 5m-high **Bronze Palace**, constructed entirely of the metal and recently gilded. Its walls and doors are covered with animal and flower designs on the outside and rank upon rank of tiny Buddhas on the inside, along with an elegant bronze Manjusri Buddha sitting on a human-faced lion. The grounds also house an interesting sundial, which uses zodiac animals to depict the hours.

Sitting on the hill behind Luohou Si, via a splendid statue of Manjusri surrounded by *arhats* and clouds at the **Yuanzhao Si** (圆照寺, *yuánzhào sì*), and atop a stone staircase of 108 steps, is the **Pusa Ding**. This Ming and Qing complex once accommodated emperors Kangxi and Qianlong, hence the yellow roof tiles and dragon tablet on the stairway, both indicating imperial patronage. This is a great destination for a first day in town, as it affords an aerial view of the valley and is a good way to warm up for longer hikes to higher temples.

Around Taihuai

Few tourists get very far out of Taihuai; it's certainly worth the effort, however, as not just the temples, but also the views and the scenery, are gorgeous. The following are all within an easy day's hike from Taihuai, though you can also hire a **tour taxi** at the central car park for any combination of sights, ranging from ¥50 for a simple tour of nearby temples, to over ¥200 for a trip including the farthest sights. Ticket prices for the temples themselves are all ¥4 or so, unless otherwise stated.

Outlying temples

For an excellent view of Taihuai, **Dailuo Ding** (黛螺顶, *dàiluó dǐng*), the hillside overlooking the town to the east, is well worth a trip; you can walk up the steep stone staircase in about twenty minutes or take a cable car most of the way (¥25 one-way). At the top is **Shancai Si** (山财寺, *shāncái sì*), a tiny but beautiful temple with unpretentious halls dedicated to Manjusri.

The **Nanshan Si** (南山寺, *nánshān sì*) sits in a leafy spot halfway up Yangbai Shan, a hilltop 5km south of Taihuai. It's again approached by a steep flight of stairs, its entrance marked by a huge screen wall of cream-coloured brick. More decorated brickwork inside, including fake brackets and images of deities in flowing robes, is the temple's most distinctive feature. Eighteen Ming images of *lohans* in the main hall are unusually lifelike and expressive; one gaunt figure is sleeping with his head propped up on one knee, his skin sagging over his fleshless bones. Two kilometres southwest of here, the **Zhenhai Si** (镇海寺, *zhènhǎi sì*), sitting at an altitude of 1600m just off the road, seems an odd place to build a temple celebrating the prevention of floods, although legend has it that Manjusri tamed the water of the spring that now trickles past the place. During the Qing dynasty, a monk called Zhang Jia, reputed to be the living Buddha, stayed here; he is commemorated with a small pagoda south of the temple.

The **Longquan Si** (龙泉寺, *lóngquán sì*) is on the west side of the Qingshui River, 5km southwest of Taihuai, just off the main road, and easily accessible by bus from town. Its highlight is the decorated **marble entranceway** at the top of 108 steps, whose surface is densely packed with images of dragons, phoenixes and foliage. The rest of the temple seems sedate in comparison, though the Puji Pagoda inside is a similar confection – a fat stupa carved with guardians, surmounted by a fake wooden top and guarded by an elaborate railing. Both structures are fairly late, dating from the beginning of the twentieth century.

The **Bishan Si** (碧山寺, *bìshān sì*), 2km north of the town, was originally used as a reception house for monks and *upasaka* (lay Buddhists). The Ming building holds many Qing sculptures, including a white jade Buddha donated by Burmese devotees.

The far temples

Too far to reach on foot, the following temples and peaks are all served by minibuses or taxis from Taihuai, organized yourself or through the hotels. Preserved from vandalism by their inaccessibility, the temple complexes include some of the oldest buildings in the country.

The **Jinge Si** (金阁寺, *jīngé sì*; ¥4) is 10km southwest of Taihuai, and worth the trip for an impressive 17m-tall Guanyin inside – the largest statue at Wutai Shan. Some of the original Tang structure remains in the inscribed base of the pillars. Ask if you can stay in their **pilgrims' accommodation**, a useful base from which to walk the trails behind the complex.

The superb Nanchan Si and Foguang Si require a considerable diversion to reach. The **Nanchan Si** (南禅寺, *nánchán sì*; ¥10) is about 60km southwest of Taihuai, a little way off the road from Taiyuan, near the county town of **Wutai**. Tour buses from Taiyuan sometimes stop here on their way into Taihuai; otherwise, you can catch a bus to Wutai, then get a motor-rickshaw to the village of **Dong Ye** (东冶, *dōng yě*). A large sign here points the way, but it's another 7km along a rough road to the complex. The temple's small **main hall**, built in 782, is the oldest wooden hall in China. Two inward-curving peaks sit at the ends of the roof ridge – all features characteristic of very early Chinese architecture. The hall of the Jin-dynasty **Yanqing Si** (延庆寺, *yánqìng sì*), accessible by a short path behind the Nanchan Si and included in the ticket price, is somewhat dilapidated but notable for quirky architectural detail, particularly the carved demons' heads, which sit atop the two columns on either side of its main entrance.

The **Foguang Si** (佛光寺, *fóguāng sì*; ¥10), 40km west of Taihuai, is a museum complex of more than a hundred buildings, mostly late, but including Wutai Shan's second Tang-dynasty hall, built in 857, whose eaves are impressive for the size and complexity of their interlocking *dougongs*. The walls inside the hall are decorated with lively Tang and Song paintings of Buddhist scenes. To get here, catch a **morning bus** (¥10) from Taihuai to **Doucun**, where you'll be dropped at the junction near a large sign pointing the way to Foguang. It's a 5km walk from here along a dusty road to the temple, or you can negotiate an onward round trip with a vehicle for around ¥150.

The peaks

The five flat **peaks** around Taihuai – north, south, east, west and middle – are all approximately 15km away and considerably higher than Taihuai, with the tallest at over 3000m above sea level. On each summit sits a small temple, and pilgrims endeavour to visit each one, a time-consuming process even with the help of minibuses that go some way up each mountain. In the past, the truly devout took up to two years to reach all the temples on foot, but today most visitors make do with looking at the silhouette of the summit temples through the telescopes of entrepreneurs in town. The **South Peak** is regarded as the most beautiful, its slopes described in a Ming poem as "bedecked with flowers like a coloured silk blanket", but you can't beat a crowd-free sunrise on the **East Peak**.

Taiyuan

Industrial powerhouse and the capital of Shanxi province, **TAIYUAN** (太原, *tàiyuán*) is a victim of its own excellent transport connections – with Pingyao so close, and Beijing just a few hours away by D-class train, there's no real need to stay the night here, but those who do so will find it an agreeable place.

Arrival and information

Taiyuan is a huge, sprawling place, though fortunately most of the transit points and attractions, along with plenty of accommodation, are within striking distance of the city centre along **Yingze Dajie**, which cuts east–west across town. The **airport** is 15km southeast of the city, a ¥60 ride away by taxi, or ¥2 on bus #201; there's a China Eastern office on Yingze Dajie. The **train station** is conveniently located at the eastern end of the same road, and has express services to Beijing (Xi'an will soon follow) and clunkers to Pingyao. Most will head to and from Pingyao by **bus** from the Jiannan station, 3km south of the centre, some stopping off en route to see the Qiao Family Mansion (see p.249). The East bus station, 1.5km east of the train station on Wulongkou Jie, is where you'll wind up coming from Wutai Shan; the **regional bus station** at the eastern end of Yingze Dajie handles express services from Datong.

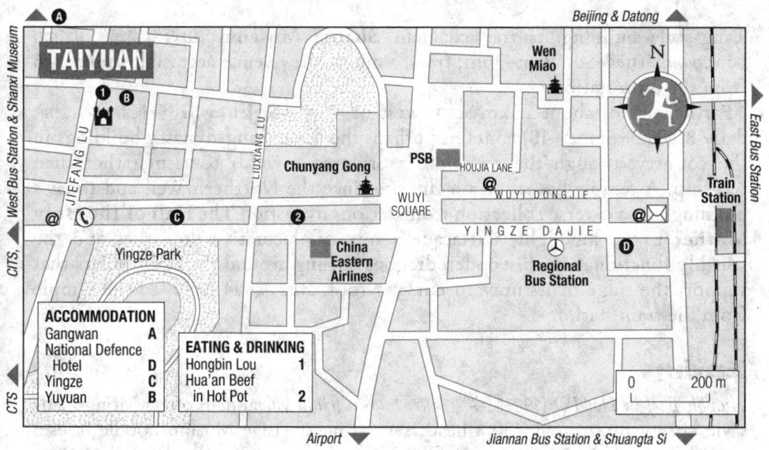

The CITS office (ⓣ0351/4063562) is on Yingze Dajie, though the nearby CTS office on Xinjian Nan Lu (ⓣ0351/4946300) is perhaps a better choice, as staff can arrange discounts on accommodation and a variety of excursions.

Accommodation

Taiyuan's **accommodation** places are spread right across town, with the cheaper options up near the train station.

Gangwan (港湾大酒店, *gǎngwān dàjiǔdiàn*) 87 Xinjian Lu ⓣ0351/8225655 or 82225699. Ordinary but clean and quiet mid-range Chinese urban hotel, a bit far from transit points but probably better for it. The attached restaurant is good. ⑤

National Defence Hotel (国防宾馆, *guófáng bīnguǎn*) 12 Yingze Dajie ⓣ0351/8822209, ⓕ4124029. Rooms here are a little disappointing, given the presentable lobby, but good value nonetheless. Those travelling in small groups may be able to wangle one of the dorm rooms. ④

Yingze (迎泽宾馆, *yíngzé bīnguǎn*) 189 Yingze Dajie ⓣ0351/8828888, ⓦwww.sxyzhotel.com. This stylish four-star hotel has its own café, bookshop and tour company, and is thick with visiting dignitaries and upmarket domestic tourists. There's another, much less presentable *Yingze* just to the east. ⑧

Yuyuan (豫园宾馆, *yùyuán bīnguǎn*) Kaihuasi Jie, just east off Jiefang Lu ⓣ0351/8823333, ⓕ2024433. A good, if slightly expensive mid-range option, set in a quiet street in an interesting part of town. ⑧

The city and around

If you have time to kill between trains, there are a few sights to keep you occupied. Just off Yingze Dajie, **Chunyang Gong** (纯阳宫, *chúnyáng gōng*; daily 9am–5pm; ¥10) is a Ming temple complex of small, multistorey buildings and interconnected courtyards dedicated to the Taoist deity Lü Dongbin; there's a small and vaguely diverting museum on site. Similarly, there are attractive Ming buildings at **Wen Miao** (文庙, *wén miào*; daily 9am–noon & 2.30–5pm; free), a Confucius Temple east of here off Jianshe Bei Lu. A tour of the city's ancient buildings is completed with a look at the two 50m-tall pagodas of the **Shuangta Si** (双塔寺, *shuāngtǎ sì*; daily 8am–8pm; ¥20), south of the train station off Shuangta Bei Lu. These were built by a monk called Fu Deng in the Ming dynasty, under the orders of the emperor, and today have become a symbol of the city. You can climb the thirteen storeys for a panoramic view of Taiyuan. Way out west across the Fenhe River, and housed in a distinctive

Tang-style building, is the excellent **Shanxi Museum** (山西博物馆, *shānxī bówùguǎn*; Tues–Sun 9am–5pm; free), a multistorey venue accessible on bus #6 from the train station.

Farther afield, about 25km southwest of Taiyuan, **Jinci Si** (晋祠寺, *jìncí sì*; daily 8.30am–6pm; ¥40) contains perhaps the finest Song-dynasty buildings in the country, though the complex is oriented towards tourism rather than worship. A temple has stood on the site since the Northern Wei, and today's buildings are a diverse collection from various dynasties. The **Hall of the Holy Mother** is the highlight, its facade a mix of decorative flourishes and the sturdily functional, with wooden dragons curling around the eight pillars that support the ridge of its upward-curving roof. **Bus** #804 heads to the temple from the train station.

Eating

Hua'an Beef in Hot Pot (华安肥牛迎择店, *húa'ān féiniú yíngzédiàn*) offers Mongolian-style hotpot for around ¥30 a head; several inexpensive Muslim noodle houses surround the **old Mosque** on Jiefang Lu; and the nearby *Hongbin Lou* (鸿宾楼, *hóngbīn lóu*) restaurant serves cheap roast duck.

Pingyao and around

The tiny town of **PINGYAO** (平遥, *píngyáo*) has steadily become an understated travel favourite in recent times, and for good reason – not only does it form a logical stopover point between Beijing and Xi'an, but its wall-bound core – almost entirely filled with traditional eighteenth- and nineteenth-century buildings – provides something of a step back in time. This is one of the most authentic old

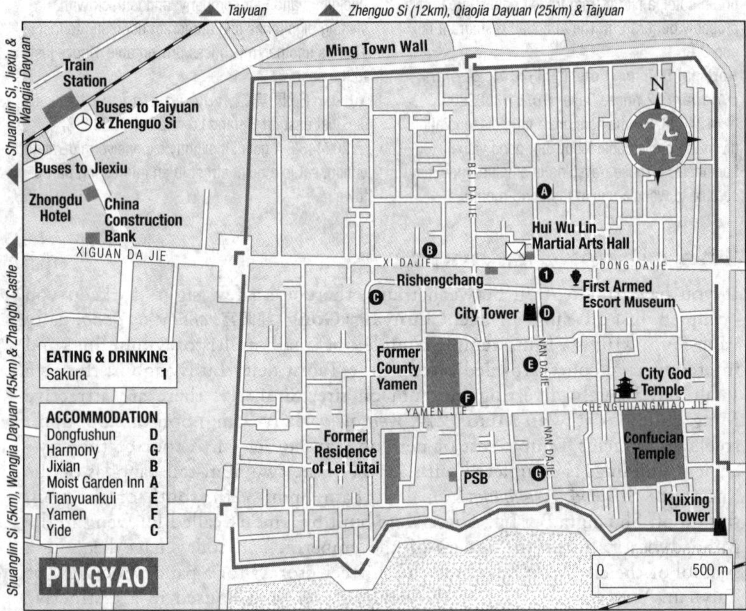

towns in China, and provides travellers with the chance to sleep on traditional Shanxi beds (*kang*) raised up on platforms – in charismatic old courtyard mansions. Things have changed recently thanks to the soft wrecking ball of domestic tourism, but take a few steps away from the restaurants and souvenir stands of the (pedestrianized) main streets, and you're in another world. Throw in a couple of fine rural **temples** and some impressive **fortified clan villages**, all within day-trip distance, and staying overnight becomes a pleasurable necessity, rather than a possibility.

Pingyao reached its zenith in the Ming dynasty, when it was a prosperous **banking centre**, one of the first in China, and its wealthy residents constructed luxurious **mansions**, adding **city walls** to defend them. In the course of the twentieth century, however, the town slid rapidly into provincial obscurity, which kept it largely unmodernized. Inside the town walls, Pingyao's narrow streets, lined with elegant Qing architecture – no neon, no white tile, no cars – are a revelation, harking back to the town's nineteenth-century heyday. Few buildings are higher than two storeys; most are small shops much more interesting for their appearance than their wares, with ornate wood-and-painted-glass lanterns hanging outside, and intricate wooden latticework holding paper rather than glass across the windows.

Arrival and information

Pingyao may soon receive high-speed **trains** on the new Taiyuan–Xi'an line, but for now you'll have to head to the tiny station just northwest of the walls in a grubby, shambolic bit of town. This is also where **buses** set down and congregate – there are plentiful buses from Taiyuan, and one fast bus daily direct from Xi'an. It's only a ten-minute walk to accommodation, but if your bags are heavy a swarm of **bicycle rickshaws** and **electric buggies** will offer to carry you – ¥5 is a decent fare.

There's a bank in town (see p.247) that can handle foreign currency transactions, but it's still wise to **load up on cash** before you get here.

Accommodation

Staying overnight in Pingyao is a must: all of the following places are housed in atmospheric **mansions** with stone courtyards, wooden window screens, traditional furniture and *kang* to sleep on. Although offering much the same in the way of decor, prices vary quite a lot – you'll pay most along Xi Dajie, since that's where Chinese groups tend to head. Lodgings can fill up quickly – especially at weekends or during holidays – so it's best to book in advance.

Moving on from Pingyao

Unless you're heading to Taiyuan, to which there are regular **buses** from outside the train station, you'll probably need to leave Pingyao by train, though there's also an **express bus** to Xi'an, which you can book through some of the accommodation listed on p.246 or the *Zhongdu Binguan* just across from the train station. **Trains** head to Taiyuan (1hr 30min), Beijing (12hr), Xi'an (11hr) and Linfen (2hr 30min), and seats, at least, are easy enough to buy yourself at the station, where some staff speak a little English. Sleepers are harder to get, though hotels in Pingyao have sorted out a system where they book your ticket through Beijing or Xi'an and then get a photocopy of it, which you use in place of the real thing – it sounds like a scam, but reports say that it works. Expect a ¥40 fee per ticket for this.

Dongfushun (东副顺民俗栈, *dōngfùshùn mínsúzhàn*) 38 Nan Dajie ⓣ0354/5686003, ⓕ5685005. Occupies a superb location in a restored 200-year-old home near the Bell Tower, with inexpensive rooms. ❸

Harmony (和议昌客栈, *héyìchāng kèzhàn*) 165 Nan Dajie ⓣ0354/5684952 or 13593085633. Presided over by a cheery, English-speaking local couple, this was already the most popular budget choice in town even before their relocation to a superbly designed courtyard mansion. Facilities include bike rental, free internet, free train station pick-up and a good bar, and they also run tours to Zhangbi castle (see p.250). Dorms from ¥30. ❷

Jixian (集贤客栈, *jíxián kèzhàn*) 87 Xi Dajie ⓣ0354/5683458 or 13753421144. Former silk merchant's house and a bit more dolled up with silk draperies than most, especially in the bedrooms. Good deal for this location. ❺

Moist Garden Inn (润泽苑民俗客栈, *rùnzéyuàn mínsú kèzhàn*) Hongshengmiao Jie, about 100m north of the post office and to the east ⓣ0354/5681777, ⓦpykz518.com. A family-run place in a rustic part of town, not as smartened up as other options in town, and no English spoken, but their most expensive rooms are still cheaper than a double anywhere else, and are beautifully decorated. ❷–❸

Tianyuankui (天元奎客栈, *tiānyuánkuí kèzhàn*) 73 Nan Dajie ⓣ0354/5680069, ⓦwww.pytyk.com. This is the liveliest of the central guesthouses, though it can get a bit noisy when the town is busy. ❺

Yamen (衙门官舍, *yámén guānshè*) 68 Yamen Jie ⓣ0354/5683539, ⓕ5683975. IYHA hostel with spacious – if slightly musty – rooms set in a lovely building. Service standards have declined slightly over the years, meaning that it's better to go elsewhere if you want tour advice. Dorms from ¥20. ❷

Yide (一得客栈, *yīdé kèzhàn*) 16 Sha Xiang, just south off Xi Dajie ⓣ0354/5685988, ⓦwww.yide-hotel.com. Eighteenth-century building hidden at the end of a quiet lane and surrounded by several other courtyard homes. Rooms are cosy, and the restaurant is a good place to dine even if you're not staying. ❺

The Town

Massive **walls**, pierced by regular gates, enclose Pingyao on four sides, making navigation a doddle. The central streets are closed to cars, though are usually so congested with bicycles and pedestrians that the lattice of narrow backstreet alleys make an attractive diversion. This is especially true at night, when the glow from nearby houses shows the way – though small kids stay off the street after dark, haunted by their parents' tales of returning Ming-era **ghosts** who, it's said, navigate the unchanged alleys with ease.

Entry to the town itself is free, but to visit the attractions you have to buy an **all-inclusive ticket** (¥120), which covers nineteen of the city buildings, plus the walls. Sold at most places it's used to gain entry to, it's valid for two days. Visitors may get just as much of a kick nosing around the various guesthouses as they would ticking off the sights, while cycling around the interior perimeter road is almost as much fun as walking around the wall itself, providing views of Pingyao at its most Pingyaoesque.

The town walls

From various access points around their 6km length, steps lead up to the Ming **town walls** (daily 8am–6.30pm), 12m high and crenellated, and punctuated with a watchtower every 50m or so. You can walk all the way around them in two hours, and get a good view into some of the many courtyards inside the walls. A belt of sculpted **parkland** is sprouting up outside, scheduled for completion in 2012, when the final pockets of housing will have been removed and their former inhabitants placed in new blocks just outside the town centre. The structures where the wall widens out are *mamian* (literally, horse faces), where soldiers could stand and fight. At the southeast corner of the wall, the **Kuixing Tower** (奎星楼, *kuíxīnglóu*), a tall, fortified pagoda with a tiled, upturned roof, is a rather flippant-looking building in comparison to the martial solidity of the battlements.

Other sights

It's also possible to climb the **City Tower** (市楼, *shìlóu*; ¥5) on central Ming Qing Jie, a charming little building that provides a fantastic rooftop view of the old city. The eave decoration includes colourful reliefs of fish and portly merchants, and guardian statues of Guanyin and Guandi face north and south respectively.

At the western end of Dong Dajie, you can look around the **Rishengchang** (日升昌, *rìshēngchāng*; daily 9am–5pm), a bank established in 1824, the first in the country and one of the first places in the world where cheques were used. During the Qing, more than four hundred financial houses operated in Pingyao, handling over eighty million ounces of silver annually. After the Boxer Rebellion, Dowager Empress Cixi came here to ask for loans to pay the high indemnities demanded by the Eight Allied Forces. Soon after, the court defaulted, then abdicated, and the banks dried up. Hong Kong and Shanghai took over Pingyao's mantle, rendering the city an isolated backwater.

There are many, many other **museums** in town (all included in the entry price and open around 8am–6pm), but after visiting a few you'll find the exhibits are repetitive and nowhere near as interesting as the buildings themselves, which are probably much like your accommodation. Still, they give a good excuse to wander, and some – like the two **armed escort museums** and former **Hui Wu Lin martial arts training hall** (汇武林博物馆, *huìwǔlín bówùguǎn*) – are, given the need to protect the city's financial reserves from banditry, also relevant to Pingyao's history. Worthwhile options include the **Former County Yamen** (平遥县衙门, *píngyáoxiàn yámén*; daily 8am–6.30pm), a massive complex on Yamen Jie, which housed the town's administrative bureaucracy (the prisons were in use until the 1960s); the **Former Residence of Lei Lütai** (雷撸汰故居, *léilǔtài gùjū*; daily 8am–7pm), Rishengchang's founder; the ramshackle **City God Temple** (城隍庙, *chénghuáng miào*) on Chenghuang Miao Jie; and the large **Confucian Temple** (文庙, *wénmiào*), also on Chenghuang Miao Jie.

Eating

Eating in Pingyao is quite fun, with a score of restaurants – none particularly noteworthy – along Ming Qing Jie offering a similar run of tasty, well-presented **local dishes**, though prices are tourist-inflated, and portions not always that large. Things to look for include salted, five-spiced beef; wild greens; yams; flat "mountain noodles" (served on their edges in a steamer); and "cat's ear noodles" (triangular flecks of dough flicked into boiling water). For **Western food**, try *Sakura* (part of a national chain beloved of backpackers) or the *Harmony Guesthouse*, both of which have pretty decent kitchens and inexpensive coffee. For cheap **Chinese staples**, head to the western end of Xi Dajie, or the streets between the West Gate and the train station.

Listings

Banks and exchange The Construction Bank is just outside the west gate. If you need money, some hotels cash foreign notes.

Bike rental Bikes are available from some of the guesthouses, and agencies with English signs along Xi Dajie (¥10/day, ¥100 deposit).

Clinics There's a helpful clinic at 43 Dong Dajie (☎0354/5683732).

Mail The post office is at 1 Xi Dajie (daily 8am–6pm).

PSB At 110 Zhoubi Nan Jie, near the Former County Yamen. They might be willing to extend a visa, but it would be better to do this in Taiyuan.

Shopping Anywhere along Ming Qing Jie and the first section of Xi Dajie that isn't a restaurant or hotel will be selling souvenirs – lacquerware, papercuts, embroideries and the usual run of "new antiques", along with martial-arts weaponry. Prices are good after haggling.

Around Pingyao

Two **temples** near Pingyao – one full of superb statues, the other interesting for its age – are easy to visit from town. Further afield, a couple of Ming-dynasty **fortified mansions** standing starkly amongst the surrounding hills would be even more impressive if you hadn't seen Pingyao first, but are anyway worth the minimal effort it takes to reach them – one is even on the bus route to Taiyuan.

Shuanglin Si

The **Shuanglin Si** (双林寺, *shuānglín si*; daily 8am–6pm; ¥25) stands 5km southwest of Pingyao, just off the main road to Jiexiu – cycle, catch a Jiexiu-bound bus from near the train station, or haggle with a taxi (try ¥25 for the round trip with wait). Originally built in the Northern Wei, the present buildings, ten halls arranged around three courtyards, are Ming and Qing.

The complex looks more like a fortress from the outside, being protected by high walls and a gate. Once you're inside, the fine architecture pales beside the contents of the halls, a treasury of 1600 coloured terracotta and wood **sculptures** dating from the Song to the Qing dynasties. They're arranged in tableaux, with backgrounds of swirling water or clouds, turning the dusty wooden halls into rich grottoes. Some of the figures are in bad shape but most still have a good deal of their original paint, although it has lost its gaudy edge. It's worth hiring a **guide** (ask at your accommodation), as each hall and each row of statues has intriguing elements, such as the statue of the husband and wife who lived here and protected the temple during the Cultural Revolution.

The horsemen dotted in vertical relief around the **Wushung Hall**, the first on the right, illustrate scenes from the life of Guandi, the god of war, but the figures in most of the halls are depictions of Buddha or saints and guardians. The **eighteen arhats** in the **second hall**, though unpainted, are eerily lifelike, and somewhat sinister in the gloom with their bulging foreheads, long tapering fingernails and eyes of black glass that follow you round the room. In the **third hall**, the walls are lined with elegant 20cm-high Bodhisattvas inclined towards a set of larger Buddha figures at the centre like so many roosting birds. The statue of **Guanyin** – sitting in a loose, even provocative, pose – is probably a reflection of the confidence and pride Pingyao enjoyed during its economic heyday.

Zhenguo Si

Out in the fields 12km northeast of Pingyao – catch bus #9 from outside the train station – **Zhenguo Si** (镇国寺, *zhènguó sì*; daily 8am–6pm; ¥20) is a quiet, forgotten place, fronted by gnarled old trees. It's surprising then to find one of China's **oldest wooden buildings** here: the Wanfo Hall was built in 963 AD and looks like it hasn't been touched since, with an amazingly complex system of brackets holding the roof up and full of contemporary, Indian-influenced statuary. At the rear, the upper hall has some Qing frescoes of the life of Buddha, all set in a Chinese context, while the Ming-dynasty **Dizang Hall** is a riot of paintings of the King of Hell and his demons handing out punishments to sinners.

Family mansions

The **Wang Family Mansion** (王家大院, *wángjiā dàyuàn*; daily 8am–5pm; ¥66) is more like a huge, fortified castle than a private residence. Some 45km southwest of Pingyao, it's reached via the town of **Jiexiu** (介休, *jièxiū*): catch a Jiexiu bus from outside Pingyao's train station (1hr; ¥5), then minibus #11 from Jiexiu's train station to the mansion (30min; ¥4). Set among stark brown hills, the location, the enormous scale and – especially – the details of the mansion buildings are all astounding, with high brick walls surrounding an intricate and vast collection of interconnected Qing-dynasty courtyards, halls (around a thousand), gardens, galleries, triumphal archways and screens, all built in carved grey stone along a rigidly symmetrical plan. The Wangs settled here at the end of the Mongol dynasty and built this complex in the early nineteenth century, after the family struck it rich not only in commerce but also political appointments; the infamous **Empress Dowager Cixi** stayed a night here while fleeing to Xi'an after the Boxer Rebellion in 1901. The complex is in two sections, joined by a stone bridge over a gully, and you could easily spend half a day here getting lost amongst the architecture.

The similar but much more comfortably scaled **Qiao Family Mansion** (乔家大院, *qiáojiā dàyuàn*; daily 8am–5pm; ¥66) lies 25km northeast of Pingyao near the hamlet of **Leguan Zhen**. Check with accommodation about transport, or cast around for buses outside the train station to Leguan Zhen (1hr; ¥4) and then get a motor-rickshaw (¥10). The mansion was used as a setting by Zhang Yimou for his

Breaking the journey between Pingyao and Xi'an

Pingyao and Xi'an are firm favourites on the China travel map, and good transport connections mean most travellers race directly between the two. However, some interesting sights lie just off this route, and are not particularly hard to reach through the transit towns of Linfen, Yuncheng and Ruicheng, all of which have plentiful accommodation around their main transport terminals.

About 140km south of Pingyao, **Linfen** (临纷, *línfēn*) is a transit point for **Hukou Falls** (壶口瀑布, *húkǒu pùbù*; ¥60), the Yellow River at its most impressively turbulent. The mighty river's span approaches 400m at this point, yet it suddenly finds itself forced through a gap only 20m wide – the resultant torrent is predictably fierce, and predictably loud. The falls are regarded by the Chinese as one of their premier beauty spots, but you may question whether reaching them was worth the effort – they're a 150km-long, four-hour-plus bus-ride from Linfen (and also accessible from Yan'an; see p.273), yet the remoteness of their location is shattered by ranks of souvenir stands. The CITS (☎0357/3330281) often runs tours from the south side of Linfen train station plaza, or can recommend where to pick up a **tourist minibus**.

Farther south, the city of **Yuncheng** (运城, *yùnchéng*) is a springboard to the **Guan Di Miao** (关帝庙, *guāndì miào*; daily 8am–6.30pm; ¥48, ¥20 to ascend main hall), a fine Qing-dynasty temple popular with the Taiwanese. This was the birthplace of **Guan Di** (aka Guan Yu), a general of the Three Kingdoms period (220–280 AD; see p.945) who epitomized all the classical martial virtues, which included finally choosing execution over betraying his oath brother, Liu Bei. Later deified as god of war, his temple (founded in 589 AD, though the present structure is eighteenth-century) is appropriately robust, looking more like a castle, with high battlements and thick wooden doors. It lies around 20km southwest of Yuncheng in the small country town of **Jiezhou** (解州, *jièzhōu*), accessible by bus #11 from opposite Yuncheng's train station concourse.

A 75km bus ride from Yuncheng will bring you to **Ruicheng** (芮城, *ruìchéng*), jump-off point for the nearby Taoist temple of **Yongle Gong** (永乐宫, *yǒnglè gōng*; daily 8.30am–6pm; ¥50), most notable for its excellent murals, and located at the terminus of bus #2. Its name derives from the position it once held in the village of Yongle, farther south on the banks of the Yellow River. It was moved brick by brick in 1959, when the dam at Sanmenxia was built and Yongle disappeared beneath the water.

film *Raise the Red Lantern*, in which the labyrinthine layout of the place symbolizes just how restricted life was for women in classical China.

Zhangbi Castle

About 40km southwest of Pingyao, **Zhangbi Castle** (张壁古堡, *zhāngbì gŭbăo*; daily 8am–6pm; ¥60 including guide) was built at the beginning of the seventh century, yet was only recently added to Shanxi's litany of subterranean tourist sights. Though pleasant enough on the surface, the castle is more famed for its network of **underground tunnels**, most of which were added by the Sui dynasty for protection against Tang invasion. Once in control, the Tang added a few tunnels of their own, and explorations of the resultant warren – a multilayered beast which dives over 20m beneath the surface – are thoroughly enjoyable. The labyrinthine nature of the tunnels makes **hiring a guide** all but essential, even more so since doing so will also get you a tour of **Zhangbi Village**, a pleasing, ramshackle hotchpotch of Yuan, Ming and Qing buildings. There's no public transport to Zhangbi; it's best to join one of the **tours** organized by *Harmony* in Pingyao (see p.246).

Shaanxi and Henan

The provinces of **Shaanxi** and **Henan** are both remarkable for the depth and breadth of their history. The region itself is dusty, harsh and unwelcoming, with a climate of extremes: in winter, strong winds bring yellow dust storms, while summer is hot and officially the rainy season. But, thanks to the Yellow River, this was the cradle of Chinese history, and for millennia the centre of power for a string of dynasties, the remains of whose capital cities are strung out along the southern stretch of the plain.

Of these ancient cities, none is more impressive than thriving **Xi'an**, now the capital of Shaanxi province and perhaps the most cosmopolitan city in China outside the eastern seaboard. It also retains copious evidence of its former glories – most spectacularly in the tomb guards of the great emperor Qin Shi Huang, the renowned **Terracotta Army**, but also in a host of temples and museums. The whole region is crowded with buildings that reflect the development of **Chinese Buddhism** from its earliest days; one of the finest is the **Baima Si** in **Luoyang**, a city farther east, thought by the ancient Chinese to be the centre of the universe. The **Longmen Caves**, just outside the city, are among the most impressive works of art in China, but also rewarding are excursions in the area around, where two holy mountains, **Hua Shan** and **Song Shan**, one Buddhist, one Taoist, offer a welcome diversion from the monumentality of the cities. **Zhengzhou**, farther east, the capital of Henan, has less of interest beyond a good museum but the nearby former Song-dynasty capital of **Kaifeng** is a pretty and quiet little place, though little remains of its past thanks to its proximity to the treacherous Yellow River. If you've had enough of the relics of ancient cultures, get a glimpse of recent history at **Yan'an** in northern Shaanxi, the isolated base high in the loess plateau to which the Long March led Mao in 1937.

Xi'an

There's no doubting the historical pedigree of **XI'AN** (西安, *xī'ān*). Between 1000 BC and 1000 AD, it served as the **imperial capital** for no fewer than eleven dynasties, and as such it comes as no surprise that the place is filled with, and surrounded by, a wealth of important sites and relics. The list, which is growing with each passing decade, includes **Neolithic Banpo**, the **Terracotta Army** of the Qin emperor, the Han and Tang **imperial tombs**, and, in the city itself, two Tang-dynasty **pagodas**, the **Bell and Drum towers** and the **Ming city walls**, as well as two excellent **museums** holding a treasury of relics from the most glamorous parts of Chinese history.

However, visitors are also advised to prepare for a modicum of disappointment. Historically significant though it may be, today's Xi'an is a manufacturing city of five million inhabitants, filled with traffic and prone to heavy **pollution** – issues that can make visits to the outlying sights a bit of a chore. Yet most visitors are able to see past these failings, perhaps best evidenced by a large foreign community, many of whom come to study, as the colleges are regarded as some of the best places to learn Chinese outside of Beijing.

Some history

Three thousand years ago, the western Zhou dynasty, known for their skilled bronzework, built their capital at **Fenghao**, a few kilometres west of Xi'an – one of their chariot burials has been excavated nearby. When Fenghao was sacked by northwestern tribes, the Zhou moved downriver to **Luoyang** and, as their empire continued to disintegrate into warring chiefdoms, the nearby Qin kingdom expanded. In 221 BC, the larger-than-life **Qin Shi Huang** united the Chinese in a single empire, the Qin, with its capital at **Xianyang**, just north of Xi'an. The underground **Terracotta Army**, intended to guard his tomb, are this tyrant's inadvertent gift to today's tourist prosperity.

His successors, the **Han**, also based here, ruled from 206 BC to 220 AD. Near-contemporaries of Imperial Rome, they ruled an empire of comparable size and power. Here in Xi'an was the start of the **Silk Road**, along which, among many other things, Chinese silk was carried to dress Roman senators and their wives at the court of Augustus. There was also a brisk trade with south and west Asia; Han China was an outward-looking empire. The emperors built themselves a new, splendid and cosmopolitan capital a few kilometres northwest of Xi'an, which they called **Chang'an** – Eternal Peace. Its size reflected the power of their empire, and records say that its walls were 17km round with twelve great gates. When the dynasty fell, Chang'an was destroyed. Their **tombs** remain, though, including Emperor Wu's mound at **Mao Ling**.

It was not until 589 that the **Sui** dynasty reunited the warring kingdoms into a new empire, but their dynasty hardly lasted longer than the time it took to build a new capital near Xi'an, called **Da Xingcheng** – Great Prosperity. The **Tang**, who replaced them in 618, took over the capital, overlaying it with their own buildings in a rational grid plan that became the model not only for many other Chinese cities, but also the contemporary Japanese capital Hei'an (now Kyoto). During this time, the city became one of the biggest in the world, with over a million inhabitants.

The Tang period was a **golden age** for China's arts, and ceramics, calligraphy, painting and poetry all reached new heights. Its sophistication was reflected in its religious tolerance – not only was this a great period for **Buddhism**, with monks busy translating the sutras that the adventurous monk **Xuan Zong** had brought back from India, but the city's **Great Mosque** dates from the Tang, and one of the steles in the Provincial Museum bears witness to the founding of a chapel by Nestorian Christians.

After the fall of the Tang, Xi'an went into a long **decline**. It was never again the imperial capital, though the Ming emperor Hong Wu rebuilt the city as a gift for his son; today's great walls and gates date from this time. Occasionally, though, the city did continue to provide a footnote to history. When the Empress Dowager Cixi had to flee Beijing after the Boxer Rebellion, she set up her court here for two years. In 1911, during the uprising against the Manchu Qing dynasty, the Manchu quarter in Xi'an was destroyed and the Manchus massacred. And in 1936, Chiang Kai-shek was arrested at Huaqing Hot Springs nearby in what became known as the Xi'an Incident (see p.265).

Arrival and information

Xi'an's **airport**, 40km northwest of the city, is connected to town by regular **airport buses** (6am–8pm; ¥25), which drop passengers off at the *Melody Hotel*, just west of the Bell Tower. A taxi costs ¥120, and it's best to negotiate the fare in advance rather than risk being taken a long way round on the meter. At the airport, there are several ATMs upstairs in the departures area.

The busy **train station**, in the northeast corner of town, just outside the city walls, is a major stop on routes from Zhengzhou, Beijing, Chengdu and Lanzhou. City buses leave from the tangled north end of Jiefang Lu, just south of the station – buses #206, #205, #201 and #610 (aka tourist bus #8) will get you to the Bell and Drum tower area – while taxis congregate on the western side of the station

Moving on from Xi'an

Air tickets can be arranged through all accommodation; if hostels try to charge mark-ups, go elsewhere. The **airport bus** (¥25) leaves from outside the *Melody Hotel* on Xi Dajie on the hour from 6am to 7pm, and takes around an hour; buy tickets on board. Taxis hang around the same place; they'll take four people for ¥120 and will stick solo passengers in with others to make up numbers. There's a **hotel** in the basement of the airport charging ¥100 for two hours if you need a rest and brush-up.

Train tickets are a nightmare to get at the station; either use your accommodation (hostels charge around ¥40 a ticket) or one of several **advance-ticket offices** scattered around, where the fee is only ¥5. There's a massive one at the corner of Jiefang Lu and Xiwu Lu (8am–midnight), and a smaller branch on Jianguo Lu between Dong Qi Lu and Dong Liu Lu.

There are masses of **buses** heading towards Luoyang, Zhengzhou, Yan'an and Taiyuan from the main station at the top of Jiefang Lu.

concourse. At the time of writing, a new train station – **Xi'an North** – was under construction, and on completion will receive high-speed services from Beijing.

The main **bus station** (省汽车站, *shěng qìchēzhàn*) faces the train station at the top of Jiefang Lu; take the same buses from train station into town. Other major depots include the **East bus station** (客运东站, *kèyùn dōngzhàn*), 2km outside the walls on Changle Lu; the **Shichang bus depot** (市长途汽车站, *shìchángtú qìchēzhàn*), just outside the southwestern corner of the walls (take bus #15 to the Drum Tower); and the **Chengnan depot** (城南汽车站, *chéngnán qìchēzhàn*), about 3km south of the walls on Zhuque Dajie – take a taxi.

City **maps** (¥5), some in English, are available everywhere and are worth picking up immediately, as bus routes are continually amended.

City transport

The largest concentration of **city buses** is found outside the train station at the northern end of Jiefang Lu. There are other clusters just outside the South Gate, and at the southern end of Yanta Lu, just north of the Big Goose Pagoda. Normal buses cost ¥1, fancier ones with air conditioning ¥2. **Bus #610** (aka **tourist bus #8**) is particularly useful, as it links most of the sights. Otherwise, there are plenty of green **taxis** cruising the streets, and they can be hailed anywhere. Most destinations within the city walls are within the ¥6 flag fare.

As the streets are wide and flat, **cycling** is a good way to get around. All the main streets have cycle lanes, controlled at major intersections by officials with flags. There are, however, few bike parks, and most people risk a (rarely enforced) ¥10 fine by leaving their bikes padlocked to railings. Make sure you have a good security chain, especially if your bike is anything other than a downbeat Flying Pigeon. For **rental places**, see p.261.

A new **metro** system was nearing completion at the time of writing – a controversial project considering the city's complex archeology, but one that may reduce its snarling road traffic. Line 2, running north–south, should be ready in late 2011, with east–west Line 1 following in late 2012.

Accommodation

Xi'an is firmly on the tourist itinerary, and **accommodation** abounds, ranging from a slew of inexpensive hostels through a couple of good-value motel options and on to upmarket international hotel chains. As plenty of these are located within the city walls, close to the most interesting bits of Xi'an and with easy access to the tourist sights, there seems little point in staying outside, in the drabber, more modern parts of town. It's a good idea to **book ahead**, especially for the hostels, all of which offer internet, laundry, food and beer, and usually free pick-up from the train station.

Bell Tower (钟楼饭店, *zhōnglóu fàndiàn*) 110 Nan Dajie ⓣ029/87600000, ⓦwww.belltowerhtl.com. Massively popular with tour groups, this smart hotel has a great location opposite the southwest corner of the Bell Tower, right in the centre of town. ⑧

Hang Tan Inn (磺唐旅舍, *huángtáng lǚshè*) 7 Nanchang Xiang ⓣ029/87231126, ⓦwww.itisxian.com. Newly moved to a pleasant location just northeast of the Bell Tower, this hostel, a long-time favourite, has lost none of its charm – think friendly staff, comfy beds, good Western breakfasts and fun theme evenings. Dorms from ¥30, rooms ③

Hyatt Regency (凯悦饭店, *kǎiyuè fàndiàn*) 158 Dong Dajie, just east of Heping Lu ⓣ029/87691234, ⓦxian.regency.hyatt.com. Swanky rooms cascade up along the inside-of-a-pyramid style beloved of the chain – well located, and suitably popular with tour groups and business folk. ⑨

Ibis 59 Heping Lu ⓣ029/87275555, ⓦwww.accorhotels.com. Blocky and unadventurous it may appear from the outside, but rooms here are a real bargain, even if the beds are a little firm for some tastes. Staff speak English and score good service marks. ④

Jinjiang Inn (锦江之星旅馆, *jǐnjiāng zhīxīng lǚguǎn*) 110 Jiefang Lu ⓣ029/87452288, ⓦwww.jinjianginns.com. The town's outstanding bargain for a double or twin, with the lowest rates cheaper than some of the backpacker hotel doubles; rooms are simple, smart and modern, with an internet socket. ④

Seven Sages 1 Beixin Jie ⓣ029/87444087 or 81709181. A hostel housed in a grey-brick courtyard building formerly used as headquarters of the 8th Route Army in the 1930s. Rooms are clean and simple with modern bathrooms, and though a little distant from the centre it's close to the bus and train stations. Dorms from ¥20, rooms ②

Shuyuan (书院旅舍, *shūyuàn lǚshè*) West of the South Gate ⓣ029/87287721, ⓦwww.hostelxian.com. Appealingly ramshackle hostel facing the city walls. The building is based on a traditional courtyard plan, and rooms are generally fine, if occasionally a little musty. Dorms from ¥30, rooms ④

Sofitel (索菲特, *suǒfēitè guójì fàndiàn*) 319 Dongxin Jie ⓣ029/87928888, ⓦwww.sofitel.com. Part of a large complex of high-class hotels, the twin *Sofitel* buildings boast scented lobbies, intricately designed interiors, and plush rooms, presided over by a young and energetic staff, all of whom are bilingual. ⑨

Wuyi (五一饭店, *wǔyī fàndiàn*) 351 Dong Dajie ⓣ029/87681098, ⓕ87213824. Take bus #611 from the station. In a superb location tucked behind a dumpling shop in the centre of town, this little hotel has character, is good value and houses an excellent restaurant. Deservedly popular and often full. ⑤

Xiangzimen (湘子门国际青年旅舍, *xiāngzǐmén guójì qīngnián lǚshè*) 16 Xiangzi Miao Jie ⓣ029/62867888, ⓦwww.yhaxian.com. Beautiful old courtyard mansion hostel with wooden fittings – there's nothing else like this closer than Pingyao. The downstairs doubles are decent but windowless and claustrophobic; better to try rooms in the new wing. Dorms ¥30, rooms ④

The City

Central Xi'an is bounded by city walls, with a bell tower marking the crossroads of the four main streets. Getting around this area is a doddle, since the street layout closely follows the ordered **grid plan** of the ancient city, with straight, wide streets running along the compass directions; the only exception is the **Muslim Quarter**, northwest of the Bell Tower, around whose unmarked winding alleys it's easy (and not necessarily unpleasurable) to get lost.

Downtown Xi'an, inside the walls, is just about compact enough to get around on foot, with enough sights to fill a busy day. To the southeast you'll find the **Beilin Museum**, which holds a massive collection of steles, next to the **city walls**, imposing remnants of Imperial China. Contrast is provided by the **Muslim Quarter** northwest of the Drum Tower, which preserves a different side of old China in a labyrinth of alleys centring on the **Great Mosque**.

The area south of the Ming-dynasty city walls is scattered with architecture from the Han and Tang dynasties. The excellent **Shaanxi History Museum** and the small **Daxingshan Si** sit between the two **Goose pagodas** and their temples, which are some of Xi'an's oldest buildings, and certainly the most distinctive.

The most useful **bus** for sightseeing is #610, also labelled as tourist bus #8 in Chinese, which runs from the train station via Bei Xin Jie, Bei Dajie, the Bell and Drum towers, then south off Xi Dajie down Guangji Jie to Small Goose Pagoda, Daxingshan Si, the History Museum and on to the Big Goose Pagoda.

Downtown Xi'an

In the heart of town, the **Bell Tower** (钟楼, *zhōng lóu*; daily 8am–9pm; ¥27, or ¥40 including the Drum Tower) stands at the centre of the crossroads where the four main streets meet. The original tower was raised two blocks west of here in 1384, at the centre of the Tang-dynasty city; the present triple-eaved wooden structure standing on a brick platform was built in 1582 and restored in 1739. You can enter only via the subway on Bei Dajie, where you buy your ticket and where you must leave any large bags. Inside is an exhibition of chimes and a bronze bell (not the original). A balcony all the way around the outside provides a view of the city's traffic.

Just west of the Bell Tower is the **Drum Tower** (鼓楼, *gŭlóu*; daily 8am–6pm, in summer till 10pm; ¥27, or ¥40 including the Bell Tower). It's a triple-eaved wooden building atop a 50m-long arch straddling the road. You enter up steps on the eastern side, to find a row of drums that used to be banged at dusk, a complement to the bell in the Bell Tower, which heralded the dawn.

The Muslim Quarter

North of the Drum Tower, the scale of Xi'an's streets constricts, and the narrow alleys lined with cramped half-timbered, two-storey buildings feel more like a village than a sprawling provincial capital. This is the **Muslim Quarter**, for centuries the centre for Xi'ans Hui population; numbering thirty thousand today, they're said to be descended from eighth-century Arab soldiers. **Beiyuanmen**, the street that runs north from the Drum Tower gate, is flagstoned and lined with Muslim restaurants, all packed out and lively in the evening. Just north of the tower, the narrow, covered alley of **Huajue Xiang** – essentially one long line of tourist tat – heads to the **Great Mosque** (清真大寺, *qīngzhēn dàsì*; daily 8am–6pm; April–Oct ¥25, Nov–March ¥15); a more interesting approach can be made on the small roads running up the western and northern sides of the complex. The largest mosque in China, it was originally established in 742, then rebuilt in the Qing dynasty and heavily restored. An east–west facing complex that integrates Arabic features into a familiar Chinese design, it's a calm place, untouched by the hectic atmosphere of the streets outside.

The Muslim Quarter extends west from here towards the city wall. There are a couple of targets: the **produce market**, including antiques and pet stalls, in the streets north off Miaohou Jie (the western extension of Xiyang Shi Jie); and the small **West Mosque** (西清真寺, *xīqīngzhēn sì*), at the end of Miaohou Jie. Streets along the way are full of poky stalls selling Muslim food (see p.260).

The Beilin Museum

Heading south from the Bell Tower along Nan Dajie, a street of department stores and offices, you come to Yongning, the huge **south gate**. A turn east takes you along **Shuyuanmen**, a pleasant, cobbled street of souvenir shops, art stores and

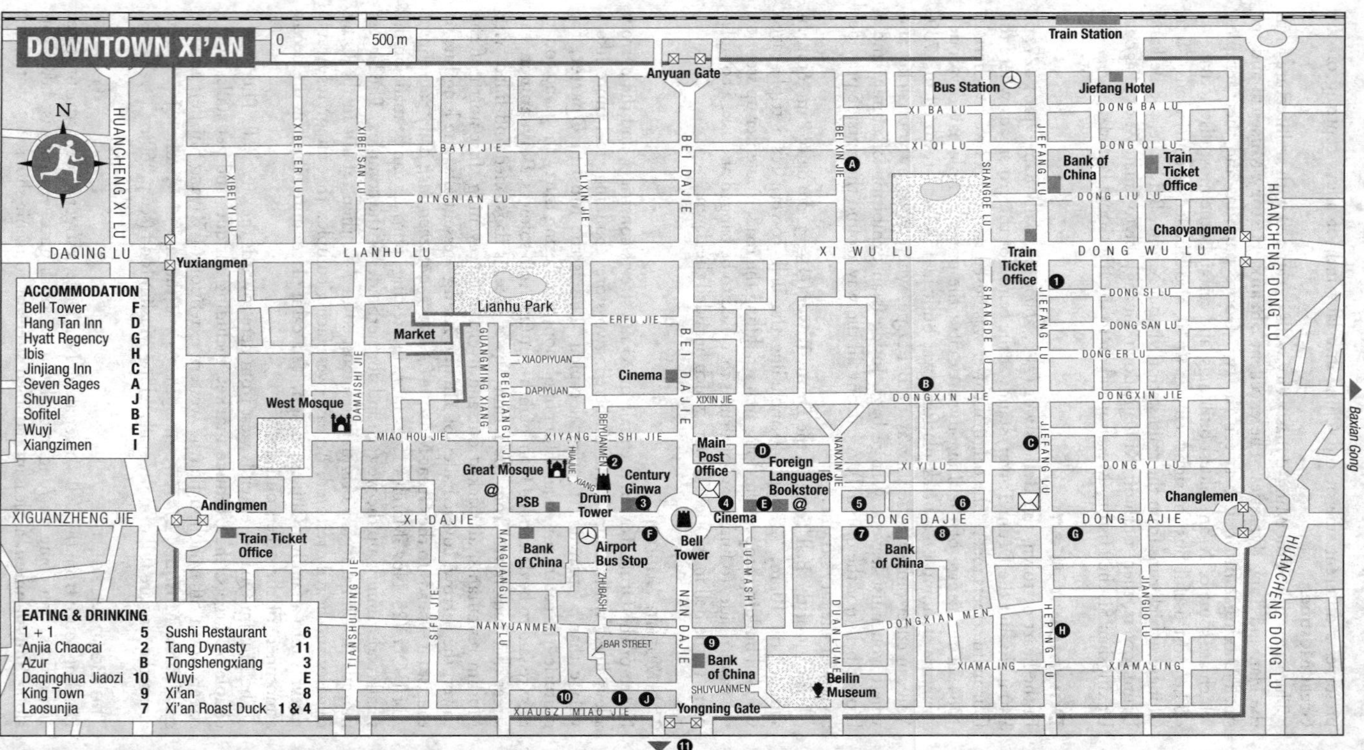

ACCOMMODATION

Bell Tower	F
Hang Tan Inn	D
Hyatt Regency	G
Ibis	H
Jinjiang Inn	C
Seven Sages	A
Shuyuan	J
Sofitel	B
Wuyi	E
Xiangzimen	I

EATING & DRINKING

1 + 1	5
Anjia Chaocai	2
Azur	B
Daqinghua Jiaozi	10
King Town	9
Laosunjia	7
Sushi Restaurant	6
Tang Dynasty	11
Tongshengxiang	3
Wuyi	E
Xi'an	8
Xi'an Roast Duck	1 & 4

antique shops traversing the heart of Beilin, a touristy artists' quarter (see p.258 for more about shopping here).

About 500m east along here is an access point for the city walls and the **Beilin Museum** (碑林博物馆; *bēilín bówùguǎn*; daily 8.30am–6.30pm; March–Sept ¥45, otherwise ¥30), a converted Confucian temple. Aside from an annexe on the west side, which holds an exhibition of chronologically arranged **Buddhist images** where you can follow the evolution of styles over the centuries, the museum's main focus is six halls containing more than a thousand **steles**. The **first hall** contains the twelve Confucian classics – texts outlining the Confucian philosophy – carved onto 114 stone tablets, a massive project ordered by the Tang emperor Wenzong in 837 as a way of ensuring the texts were never lost or corrupted by copyists' errors. The **second hall** includes the **Daqing Nestorian tablet**, on the left as you go in, recognizable by a cross on the top, which records the arrival of a Nestorian priest in Chang'an in 781 and gives a rudimentary description of Christian doctrine. In the **third hall**, one stele is inscribed with a **map of Chang'an** at the height of its splendour, when the walls were extensive enough to include the Big Goose Pagoda within their perimeter. Rubbings are often being made in the **fourth hall**, where the most carved drawings are housed; thin paper is pasted over a stele and a powdered ink applied with a flat stone wrapped in cloth. Among the steles is an image called the "God of Literature Pointing the Dipper", with the eight characters that outline the Confucian virtues – regulate the heart, cultivate the self, overcome selfishness and return propriety – cleverly made into the image of a jaunty figure. "To point the dipper" meant to come first in the exams on Confucian texts, which controlled entry to the civil service.

The city walls

Imposing enough to act as a physical barrier between the city centre and the suburbs, Xi'an's **city walls** (daily: summer 7am–9.30pm; rest of year 8am–6pm; ¥40) were originally built of rammed earth in 1370 on the foundation of the walls of the Tang-dynasty imperial city, though they took their modern form in 1568, when they were faced with brick. Recently restored, the walls are the most distinctive feature of the modern city, forming a 12m-high rectangle whose perimeter is nearly 14km in length. Some 18m wide at the base, they're capped with crenellations, a watchtower at each corner and a fortress-like gate in the centre of each side. Originally, the city would have been further defended with a moat and drawbridges, but today the area around the walls is a thin strip of parkland, created after a major restoration in 1983.

You can **ascend** the wall from the **four main gates**. An **electric shuttle** runs around (¥50 for the circuit, or ¥5 to the next of fifteen stations), but more fun are the **rentable bikes** (¥20/100min, just enough time to get around; you can't bring your own bike up here) – if prepared with food and drinks, you can spend the better part of a day exploring Xi'an from the wall.

The Small Goose Pagoda and the Daxingshan Si

The **Xiaoyan Ta** or **Small Goose Pagoda** (小雁塔; *xiǎoyàn tǎ*; daily 8am–6pm; March–Sept ¥25, otherwise ¥18) is southwest of the Yongning gate on Youyi Xi Lu. A 45m-tall, delicate construction, founded in the Tang dynasty in 707 to store sutras brought back from India, the pagoda sits in what remains of the Jianfu Si. Two of the pagoda's original fifteen storeys were damaged in an earthquake, leaving a rather abrupt jagged top to the roof, to which you can ascend for a view of the city. A shop at the back of the complex sells Shaanxi folk arts.

Just south of here on Xingshan Xijie, in Xinfeng Park, accessible down a narrow market street, the small **Daxingshan Si** (大兴善寺; *dàxīngshàn sì*; daily

8am–5pm; ¥20) is usually overlooked by visitors, but is worth a visit. This is the only working Buddhist temple in Xi'an; it was destroyed in the Tang persecution of Buddhism, and thus today's buildings are mainly Qing. Monks in baggy orange trousers will write your name on a prayer sheet in the main hall for a donation.

Shaanxi History Museum

One of the city's major highlights, the **Shaanxi History Museum** (陕西历史博物馆; *shǎnxīlìshǐ bówùguǎn*; Wed–Mon; free) is an impressive modern building within walking distance of the Daxingshan Si and the Big Goose Pagoda. The exhibition halls are spacious, well laid out, and have English captions, displaying to full advantage a magnificent collection of more than three thousand relics.

The **lower floor**, which contains a general survey of the development of civilization until the Zhou dynasty, holds mostly weapons, ceramics and simple ornaments – most impressive is a superb set of Western Zhou and Shang **bronze vessels** covered in geometric designs suggestive of animal shapes, used for storing and cooking ritual food. Two **side halls** host themed exhibitions. The **western hall** holds bronzes and ceramics, in which the best-looking artefacts are Tang. Large numbers of ceramic **funerary objects** include superbly expressive and rather vicious-looking camels, guardians and dancers. The **eastern hall** holds a display of Tang **gold and silver**, mainly finely wrought images of dragons and tiny, delicate flowers and birds, and an exhibition of Tang costume and ornament.

The two **upstairs galleries** display relics from the Han through the Qing dynasties; notable are the Han ceramic funerary objects, particularly the model houses.

Shopping in Xi'an

Xi'an is an excellent place to pick up souvenirs and antiques, which are generally cheaper and more varied than in Beijing, though prices have to be bartered down and the standard of goods, especially from tourist shops, is sometimes shoddy. Shopping is also an enjoyable evening activity, since the markets and department stores are open until 10pm – the Muslim Quarter and Beilin make for an entertaining stroll under the stars, where the nocturnal hawkers sell everything from dinner to souvenir silk paintings.

Artwork

Xi'an has a strong artistic pedigree, and the **paintings** available here are much more varied in style than those you see elsewhere in China. As well as the widespread line-and-wash paintings of legendary figures, flowers and animals, look for bright, simple **folk paintings**, usually of country scenes. A traditional Shaanxi art form, appealing for their decorative, flat design and lush colours, these images were popular in China in the 1970s for their idealistic, upbeat portrayal of peasant life. A good selection is sold in a shop just behind the Small Goose Pagoda and in the temple compound, as well as outside the Banpo Museum (see p.262). For **rubbings** from steles, much cheaper than paintings and quite striking, try the Big Goose Pagoda and Shuyuanmen, especially around the Beilin Museum, which is also a great area to find **calligraphy and paintings**. The underground pedestrian route at the South Gate includes an interesting diversion down an old bomb shelter tunnel to Nan Shang Jie, where **papercuts** are for sale.

Strong competition means you can pick up a painting quite cheaply if you're prepared to **bargain** – a good, sizeable work can be had for less than ¥150. Beware the bright young things who introduce themselves as art students whose class

The Dacien Si and Big Goose Pagoda

The **Dacien Si** (大慈恩寺; *dàcíēn sì*; daily 8am–6.30pm; ¥25), in the far south of town, 4km from the city walls at the end of Yanta Lu, is the largest temple in Xi'an. The original, destroyed in 907, was even bigger: founded in 647, it had nearly two thousand rooms, and a resident population of more than three hundred monks. The surrounding area is a bit of a circus nowadays, with the armies of souvenir sellers dwarfed by a crowd-pulling **musical fountain**, arranged in steps, which fills the northern approach to the temple. The main entrance, however, is to the south, and inside the walls the atmosphere is much calmer, though still oriented towards tourism rather than worship, even though there are resident monks here.

The most famous person associated with the temple is **Xuanzang**, the Tang monk who made a pilgrimage to India and returned with a trove of sacred Buddhist texts (see p.864). At his request, the Dayan Ta, or **Big Goose Pagoda** (大雁塔; *dàyàn tă*; daily 8am–6pm; ¥50, plus ¥25 to climb) was built of brick at the centre of the temple as a fireproof store for his precious sutras. More impressive than its little brother, the Big Goose Pagoda is sturdy and angular, square in plan, and more than 60m tall. As you go in, look for a famous **tablet** on the right showing Xuanzang dwarfed by his massive bamboo backpack, rubbings of which are sold all over the city. The pagoda has **seven storeys**, each with large windows (out of which visitors throw money for luck). The area surrounding the complex has been heavily redeveloped in recent years, to the delight of some locals, and the chagrin of others.

The Baxian Gong

The **Baxian Gong** (八仙宫; *bāxiān gōng*; ¥3), Xia'an's largest Taoist temple, lies in a shabby area east of the city walls – probably the easiest way to get here is to catch bus

happens to be having an exhibition. They're essentially touts who will lead you to a room full of mediocre work at inflated prices.

Souvenirs

Beiyuanmen and Huajue Xiang, the alley that runs off to the Great Mosque, are the places to go for **small souvenirs**, engraved chopsticks, teapots, chiming balls and the like. Clusters of stalls and vendors swarm around all the tourist sights, and are often a nuisance, though the stalls around the Great Mosque are worth checking out – you'll see curved Islamic **shabaria** knives among the Mao watches and other tourist knick-knacks.

For a personalized souvenir, try the **seal engravers** along Shuyuanmen, where you'll also find a variety of **artists' materials** – calligraphy sets and the like.

Antiques

Antiques abound in Xi'an, but be aware that many – however dusty and worn – are reproductions. The best place to go for **antiques** is the **City Antiques Market**, about a block south of the Small Goose Pagoda, on Zhuque Dajie. This is pretty good, with some genuine antiques and oddities (such as old military gear) at reasonable prices, and Mao-era artwork with price tags that show the dealers here know how much these things sell for overseas. Another good place is the market outside **Baxian Gong**, which is biggest on Wednesdays and Sundays; many vendors are villagers from the outlying regions who look as if they are clearing out their attics. You can find some unusual items here, such as books and magazines dating from the Cultural Revolution containing rabid anti-Western propaganda, Qing vases, opium pipes, and even rusty guns.

Paomo

It would be a shame to leave Xi'an without sampling **paomo** (泡馍), its signature dish. This is basically a meat soup – there are both lamb (*yangrou paomo*) and beef (*niurou paomo*) versions – poured over a bowlful of tiny bread cubes. At many restaurants, diners are given discs of bread and encouraged to do the cubing themselves. Most foreigners seem to prefer the taste and texture of larger chunks – this will likely be met with a scornful look from your waitress, since locals take their time with this process, producing something almost akin to breadcrumbs. The bowl is then taken to the kitchen and piled with shredded meat and noodles, and it's all served with cloves of pickled garlic and chilli paste for you to tip in as required.

#203 east along Dong Dajie, get off at the first stop outside the walls, and head north with a map. It's said to be sited over the wine shop where **Lü Dongbin**, later one of the Eight Immortals (see p.243), was enlightened by Taoist master Han Zhongli. Containing an interesting collection of steles, including pictures of local scenic areas and copies of complex ancient medical diagrams of the human body, the temple is the setting for a popular **religious festival** on the first and fifteenth day of every lunar month. However, it is probably of most interest to visitors for the **antiques market** that takes place outside every Wednesday and Sunday (see p.259).

Eating

Xi'an is a great place to eat, though the best of the **local food** is fairly rough and ready, most enjoyably consumed in the Muslim Quarter's hectic, open-fronted restaurants – an excellent primer for those pushing on west to Xinjiang. Here you'll find *liang fen* (cold, translucent noodles shaved off a block of beanstarch jelly and served with a spicy sauce), *hele* (buckwheat noodles) and *mianpi* (flat noodles made of refined wheat dough); huge rounds of flat bread, which make an excellent accompaniment to a handful of grilled mutton skewers; **sweets** such as steamed "eight treasure pudding" (glutinous rice cooked in a tiny wooden pot and dusted with sugar and sesame); and preserved fruits heaped on plates. The most widely touted Xi'an dish, however, is *paomo* (see above).

Anjia Chaocai (安家炒菜, *ānjiā chǎocài*) Beiyuanmen. One of the busiest, nosiest and cleanest of many similar Muslim restaurants on this street, with excellent kebabs, cold noodles and vegetable dishes. They also serve beer, unlike some of the stricter establishments. Getting all your food served at the same time takes some doing though, as kebabs are grilled in huge batches.

Azur 319 Dongxin Jie. Located in the east wing of the *Sofitel* (see p.254) and entered through a panoply of hanging cuboid lanterns, this is perhaps the most stylish venue in town, blending the cuisines of North Africa, southern Europe and the eastern Mediterranean. The lunch buffets are immaculate, if pricey, while it's also a good place to drop in for an evening tipple.

Daqinghua Jiaozi (大青花饺子, *dàqīnghuā jiǎozi*) Wuyuemiaomen, facing up Dachejia Gang. Decent Dongbei restaurant decked in hefty yellow pine furniture with cannons and sabres as decor. *Jiaozi* are not what they do best; go for the whole stewed pork leg, cold spiced *mu'er* fungus, steamed bitter gourd and sweetcorn with peas, all visible on a large picture menu. They often give you complimentary soup and honeyed potatoes. Even with beer, four people can fill up here for under ¥100.

King Town (秦唐一号中国餐馆, *qíntáng yīhào zhōngguó cānguǎn*) 176 Dongmu Tuoshi. Smart, excellent Sichuanese restaurant, with a casual snack area at street level and a more formal restaurant upstairs where you can pay over ¥50 a head.

Laosunjia (老孙家, *lǎosūnjiā*) Xiyang Shi Jie in the Muslim Quarter, and also at 364 Dong Dajie. *Yangrou paomo* (see above) is the house speciality here, and they've been serving it up for over a century – perhaps one reason for the occasionally surly service. The Xiyang Shi Jie branch is down to earth, the Dong Dajie one more refined but three times the price.

Sushi Restaurant (回转寿司店, *huízhuăn shòusīdiàn*) 223 Dong Dajie. Authentic and reasonably priced sushi bar. You can either sit and select from the conveyor belt, or order pricier options from one of the booths.
Tang Dynasty (唐乐宫, *tánglè gōng*) 75 Chang'an Beidajie ⓣ029/87822222, ⓦwww.xiantangdynasty.com. Speciality dumplings and a daily Cantonese lunch buffet. Dinner is an imperial-style banquet followed by a cultural show (see below).
Tongshengxiang (同盛祥, *tóngshèngxiáng*) In the block of restaurants behind and just west of the Bell Tower, Xi Dajie. This multistoreyed Muslim place is famous for its *paomo* and *tangbao* (soup buns).
Wuyi (五一饭店, *wŭyī fàndiàn*) 351 Dong Dajie. Outside, there's a row of windows from which steamed buns are sold, with a similar counter inside offering a huge range of local snacks, from noodles to soups, meats and vegetable dishes – pick up a tray, point to what you want, pay at the till and then sit down and eat. Great for a Chinese breakfast or a light meal, with most dishes under ¥10.
Xi'an (西安宾馆, *xīān bīnguăn*) 298 Dong Dajie. A restaurant famed as the place where the plotters of the Xi'an Incident (see p.265) met to form their plan to kidnap Chiang Kai-shek. The downstairs canteen is all right, with set breakfasts and lunch buffets for ¥10–22 (the *Wuyi* is better), but the upstairs restaurant is excellent, with banquet dishes such as gourd-shaped chicken. Expect to pay ¥60 a head.
Xi'an Roast Duck (西安烤鸭店, *xīān kăoyādiàn*) 368 Dong Dajie, and also on the corner of Jiefang Lu and Dong Si Lu. This otherwise unassuming, two-floor restaurant is usually crowded at lunch. Cafeteria-style downstairs, dining room upstairs. A whole duck (enough for 2/3 people) costs around ¥65.

Drinking and entertainment

Though not as lively as Beijing or Shanghai, Xi'an has a large student population and general prosperity that make it more exciting at night than most other Chinese cities. The easiest place to start is the **bar street** area on **Defu Lu**, just north of the *Xiangzimen* hostel, which is lined with Western-style pubs – none are particularly remarkable, but since all can be peeked inside from the street it's easy to find the best venue on any given night. Tuesday is the most popular night to go to the **clubs**. A favourite spot with foreign students is *1+1* on Dong Dajie – the music is a typical mix of hip-hop and techno.

For a meal with a difference, pop along to *Tang Dynasty* (see above), where dinner (¥500) is followed by a 90min **cultural show**. There are also dinnerless shows, which cost ¥220. Tickets can be bought in advance from the theatre lobby on the ground floor, though some accommodation can get you in at a discounted rate. Alternatively, free musical **fountain shows** take place each evening at 9pm just north of the Big Goose Pagoda.

Listings

Banks and exchange Convenient branches of the Bank of China with ATMs are marked on our "Downtown Xi'an" map. Cash can be exchanged at the business centres of the larger hotels and many other banks.
Bike rental Hostels rent bikes for around ¥20/day, with a deposit of up to ¥200.
Bookshop The Foreign Languages Bookstore on Dong Dajie has a wide selection of books about China – and Xi'an in particular – together with the standard English-language novels.
Cinema The big complex at 379 Dong Dajie shows the occasional dubbed foreign action-movie.
Guides English-speaking Frank Che (ⓣ029/81909165, ⓔchexing_2000@yahoo.com) is especially good at organizing trips to try and see wild pandas around the reserve at Foping.
Hospital The Provincial Hospital is on Youyi Xi Lu, just west of the intersection with Lingyuan Lu.
Internet Hostels all offer free access. The best netbar (¥2/hr) in town is on the 5th floor of the Parkson Building on Xi Dajie – enter via the external glass lift underneath the huge gateway at the mouth of Beiguang Jie. There's another one next to the main bus station.
Mail and telephones The central post office (8am–8pm) faces the Bell Tower at the intersection of Bei Dajie and Dong Dajie. The "Telecom district", with phone emporiums and card sellers, is around the intersection of Bei Dajie and Xixin Jie.

Massage There's a centre staffed by blind masseuses at 118 Beiyuanmen, in the Muslim Quarter – look for the English sign on the west side of the street. ¥50 will get you an hour of excellent pressure-point manipulation.
PSB 138 Xi Dajie (Mon–Sat 8am–noon & 3–5pm).
Travel agents All hostels can book you on local tours, and some act as agents for Yangzi ferries, too; you don't have to be staying with them either. Hotels and motels also have tour desks, though you're likely to be bundled in with Chinese-speaking groups if you use them. The main office of CITS is at 48 Chang'an Lu (daily 8am–6pm; ⓣ 029/85399999); they can arrange tours and hire minibuses seating 5–6 for ¥400/day.

Around Xi'an

You could spend days on excursions **around Xi'an**: look at any tourist map and you'll see how dense with attractions the area is. Excavations and renovations are ongoing, meaning that new attractions are being added to the list each year. For now, people swarm to see the **Terracotta Army** and **Banpo Museum** at least, though two recommended attractions off the tour-group itinerary are the **Famen Si**, with a superb museum attached – which is a little too remote for most visitors – and the exhausting but highly scenic holy mountain of **Hua Shan**.

The cheapest option – though not the quickest – is to take **local buses** to the sights. This works best along the eastern route, with the Huaqing Pool, Lintong Museum and the Terracotta Army covered by **bus #306** (aka **tourist bus #5**) from the east side of the train station square, and the Banpo Museum accessible by city buses. See accounts below for specific details.

Banpo Museum

The **Banpo Museum** (半坡博物馆, *bànpō bówùguǎn*; daily 8am–5pm; ¥35), 8km east of the centre, is the first stop on most eastern tours. To get here yourself catch city **bus #240** from the top of Jiefang Lu near the train station; it's about an hour's ride. The ticket affords access to both the museum and the model village (same hours), though the latter is a waste of time. The site as a whole is not visually spectacular, so some imagination is required to bring it alive.

Xi'an tours

The easiest way to see the sights around Xi'an is to get up early and take one of the many **tours** on offer. There are two routes: the popular **eastern route** covers the Huaqing Pool and the Lintong Museum, the Terracotta Army, the Tomb of Qin Shi Huang and the Banpo Museum; the **western route**, going to the Imperial Tombs and the Famen Si, is less popular as more travel time is involved, and it's more expensive (it's also harder to find anyone running it off season). The best tours leave by 8am.

Most hotels, and all hostels, can arrange such tours, sometimes even with no advance notice. Prices for the eastern route can vary from ¥140 for the Terracotta Army only, to over ¥300 including all aforementioned sights. A comprehensive tour of the western route will also cost around ¥300 – some operators tempt customers by knocking the price down, then also knock Famen Si off the itinerary, so clarify its inclusion beforehand. It's possible to take cheaper tours, aimed at domestic tourists, from the agencies based in front of the **Jiefang** hotel – these are the civilized faces of the seething mass of **private tour buses** fighting to exit the car park east of the train station square.

One unusual option offered by the hostels is a full day-trip southwest to a **panda reserve** at Foping in the Qingling mountains (¥220), where you can see captive animals and tour the research centre.

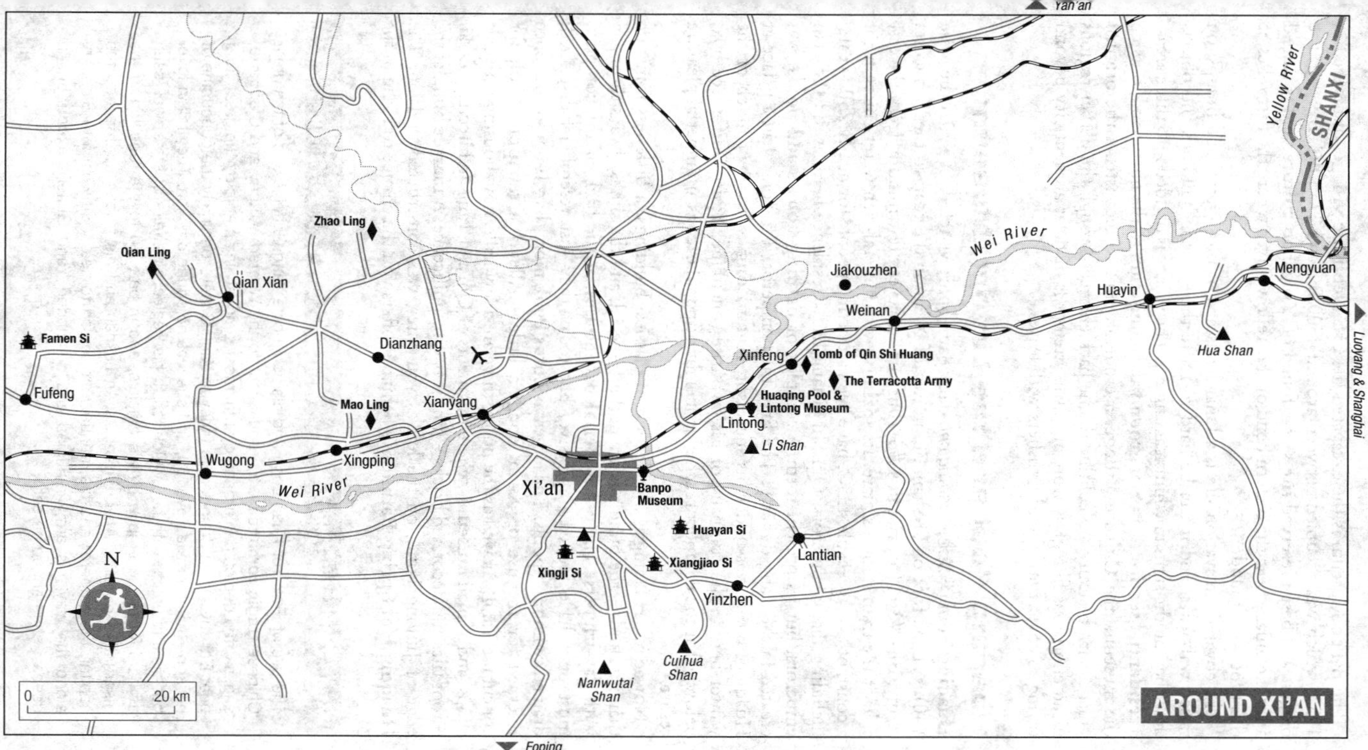

AROUND XI'AN
Luoyang & Shanghai
Yan'an
Foping
SHANXI
Yellow River
Wei River
Wei River
Mengyuan
Hua Shan
Huayin
Jiakouzhen
Weinan
Tomb of Qin Shi Huang
The Terracotta Army
Xinfeng
Huaqing Pool & Lintong Museum
Lintong
Li Shan
Lantian
Yinzhen
Huayan Si
Xiangjiao Si
Cuihua Shan
Banpo Museum
Nanwutai Shan
Xi'an
Xingji Si
Xianyang
Dianzhang
Zhao Ling
Mao Ling
Xingping
Qian Xian
Wugong
Qian Ling
Famen Si
Fufeng
N
0
20 km

The Banpo Museum is the excavated site of a **Neolithic village**, discovered in 1953, which was occupied between around 4500 BC and 3750 BC. Banpo is the biggest and best-preserved site so far found of **Yangshao culture**, and is named after the village near the eastern bend of the Yellow River where the first relics of this type were found.

The covered excavation site is a lunar landscape of pits, craters and humps, on raised walkways, and it can be hard to relate these to the buildings and objects described on the signs in whimsical English. The village is divided into three areas: a **residential section**; a **burial ground** and a **museum**, to the north; and, outside the museum, the **Culture Village**, a crude attempt to reconstruct the original village – it's basically a Neolithic theme park entered through the nether regions of an enormous fibreglass woman. Little attempt is made at authenticity beyond trying to cover the fire extinguishers with leaves.

Huaqing Pool and the Lintong Museum

Huaqing Pool (华清池, *huáqīng chí*; daily 8am–5pm; March–Oct ¥70, otherwise ¥40) is at the foot of Li Shan, 30km east of Xi'an on the road to the Terracotta Army. **Bus #306** (**tourist bus #5**) runs out here every few minutes from the east side of the train station square. Its **springs**, with mineral-rich water emerging at a constant and agreeable 43°C, have been attracting people for nearly 2500 years, including many emperors. Qin Shi Huang had a residence here, as did the Han emperors, but its present form, a complex of **bathing houses and pools**, was created in the Tang dynasty. The first Tang emperor, Tai Zong, had a palace at Huaqing, but it was under his successor, **Xuan Zong**, who spent much of the winter here in the company of his favourite concubine, **Yang Guifei** (see box, below), that the complex reached its height of popularity as an imperial pleasure resort.

Nowadays, Huaqing is a collection of classical buildings, a little less romantic than it sounds – the buildings are nothing special, and the site is always thronged with day-trippers. The old **imperial bathhouses**, at the back of the complex, must once have looked impressive, but today they just resemble half-ruined, drained swimming pools. The largest is **Lotus Pool**, more than 100m square, once reserved for the use of Xuan Zong; a little smaller is **Crabapple Pool**, for concubine Yang. As well as the pools, there are a few halls, now housing souvenir shops, and a small **museum**, where fragments of Qin and Tang architectural detail – roof tiles and decorated bricks – hint at past magnificence. A **marble boat**, at the edge of Jiulong Pond, on the left as you enter, was constructed in 1956. The **Huaqing Hot Spring Bathhouse** behind it offers you the chance to bathe in the

Xuan Zong and Yang Guifei

The tale of Emperor Xuan Zong and his concubine Yang Guifei is one of the great Chinese **tragic romances**, the equivalent to the Western Antony and Cleopatra, and is often depicted in art and drama, most famously in an epic by the great Tang poet Bai Juyi. Xuan Zong took a fancy to Yang Guifei – originally the concubine of his son – when he was over 60, and she was no spring chicken. They fell in love, but his infatuation with her, which led to his neglect of affairs of state, was seen as harmful to the empire by his officials, and in part led to the rebellion of the disgruntled general, **An Lushan**. As An Lushan and his troops approached the capital, the emperor and his retinue were forced to flee southwest into Sichuan; along the way, his army mutinied and demanded Yang Guifei's **execution**. In despair, she hanged herself.

The Xi'an Incident

Huaqing Pool's modern claim to fame is as the setting for the **Xi'an Incident** in 1936, when **Chiang Kai-shek** was arrested by his own troops and forced to sign an alliance with the Communists. The story is a little more complicated than this. As Japanese troops continued to advance into China, Chiang insisted on pursuing his policy of national unification – meaning the destruction of the Communists before all else. In December 1936, he flew to Xi'an to overlook another extermination campaign. The area was under the control of **Marshal Zhang Xueliang** and his Manchurian troops. Although GMD supporters, they, like many others, had grown weary of Chiang's policies, fuelled by the fact that their Manchurian homeland was now occupied by the Japanese. In secret meetings with Communist leaders, Zhang had been convinced of their genuine anti-Japanese sentiments, and so, on the morning of December 12, Nationalist troops stormed Chiang's headquarters at the foot of Li Shan, capturing most of the headquarters staff. The great leader himself was eventually caught halfway up the slope in a house at the back of the complex, behind the pools – a neo-Grecian pavilion on the lower slopes of the mountain marks the spot. Still in his pyjamas and without his false teeth, he had bolted from his bed at the sound of gunfire. Chiang was forced to pay a heavy ransom but was otherwise unharmed, his captors allowing him to remain in control of China – provided that he allied with the Communists against the Japanese. Today, tourists line up here to don GMD uniforms and have their pictures taken.

waters; for a steep ¥70 you are shut in a room that looks like a mid-range hotel room (complete with a photo of a glossy tropical paradise on the wall and little plastic bottles of shampoo) with a bath and a shower. Better is the **public bathhouse** at the front of the complex, on the left of the gate as you go in, where you can bathe in a communal pool for ¥20; you'll need to take your own towel and soap.

The Lintong Museum

The **Lintong Museum** (临潼博物馆, *líntóng bówùguǎn*; daily 8am–6pm; ¥25) nearby provides a rewarding diversion while visiting Huaqing Pool; turn right out of the pool complex, then run a gauntlet of souvenir sellers for 150m and you'll see the museum on your right. Though small and relatively expensive, it's worth it for a varied collection that includes silver chopsticks and scissors, a bronze jar decorated with human faces, a crossbow and numerous Han funerary objects. The best exhibit, a **Tang reliquary** unearthed nearby, is in the second of the three rooms. Inside a stone stupa about a metre high, decorated with images of everyday life, was found a silver coffin with a steep sloping roof, fussily ornamented with silver spirals, strings of pearls and gold images of monks on the side. Inside this, a gold coffin about 7cm long held a tiny glass jar with a handful of dust at the bottom. These delicate relics, and the dust, optimistically labelled "ashes of the Buddha", though crudely exhibited in what look like Perspex lunchboxes, are more interesting than anything at Huaqing Pool.

The Terracotta Army and Tomb of Qin Shi Huang

The **Terracotta Army** – probably the highlight of a trip to Xi'an – and the **Tomb of Qin Shi Huang**, which it guards, are 28km east of Xi'an, just beyond Huaqing Pool. Plenty of tours come here, giving you two hours at the army and twenty minutes at the tomb. Alternatively, it's easy enough to get here by yourself on **bus**

#306 (¥7) from the east side of the Xi'an train station; the journey takes an hour. More expensive, but a little quicker, are the **minibuses** (¥26) that leave from the same place. You get dropped off in a vast car park at the start of a newly built tourist complex of industrial proportions whose main purpose seems to be to channel visitors through a kilometre-long gauntlet of overpriced restaurants and souvenir stalls. The food is diabolical, and it's best to eat before you go. Both the army and the tomb are now accessed with one single ticket, costing ¥150 during high season, and ¥120 at other times.

The Terracotta Army

No records exist of the **Terracotta Army** (兵马俑; *bīngmǎ yǒng*), which was set to guard Qin Shi Huang's tomb over two thousand years ago, and was only discovered by peasants sinking a well in 1974. Three rectangular vaults were found, constructed of earth with brick floors and timber supports. Today, **hangars** have been built over the excavated site so that the ranks of soldiers – designed never to be seen, but now one of the most popular tourist attractions in China – can be viewed in situ. You can take photos, but are not meant to use tripods or flash.

Qin Shi Huang

Though only 13 when he ascended the throne of the western state of Qin in 246 BC, within 25 years **Qin Shi Huang** had managed to subjugate all the quarrelsome eastern states, thus becoming the first emperor of a **unified China**. "As a silkworm devours a mulberry leaf, so Qin swallowed up the kingdoms of the Empire", or so the first-century BC historian Sima Qian put it. During his eleven years as the sole monarch of the Chinese world, Qin Shi Huang set out to transform it, hoping to create an empire that his descendants would continue to rule for "ten thousand years". His reign was marked by centralized rule, and often **ruthless tyranny**. As well as standardizing weights and measures (even the width of cartwheels) and ordering a unified script to be used, the First Emperor decreed that all books, except those on the history of the Qin and on such practical matters as agriculture, be destroyed, along with the scholars who produced them. It was only thanks to a few Confucian scholars, who hid their books away, that any literature from before this period has survived.

As well as overseeing the construction of roads linking all parts of the empire, mainly to aid military operations, Qin Shi Huang began the construction of the **Great Wall**, a project that perhaps – more than any of his harsh laws and high taxes – turned the populace, drummed into constructing it, against him. Ambitious to the end, Qin Shi Huang died on a journey to the east coast seeking the legendary island of the immortals and the secret drug of longevity they held. His entourage concealed his death – easy to do as he lived in total seclusion from his subjects – and on their return installed an easily manipulated prince on the throne. The empire soon disintegrated into civil war, and within a few years Qin Shi Huang's capital at Xianyang had been destroyed, his palace burnt and his tomb ransacked.

It is possible that Qin Shi Huang, seen as an archetypal tyrant, has been harshly judged by history, as the story of his reign was written in the Han dynasty, when an eastern people whom he subjugated became ascendant. They are unlikely to have been enamoured of him, and the fact that the Terracotta Army faces east, the direction from where Qin Shi Huang thought threats to his empire would come, indicates the animosity that existed. The outstanding artistry of the terracotta figures has revised the accepted view of the Qin dynasty as a time of unremitting philistinism, and his reign has been reassessed since their discovery. Mao Zedong, it is said, was an admirer of his predecessor in revolution.

Vault 1

Vault 1 is the largest, and about a fifth of the area has been excavated, revealing more than a **thousand figures** (out of an estimated eight thousand) ranked in battle formation and assembled in a grid of 6m-deep corridors. Facing you as you enter the hangar, this is one of the most memorable sights in China; you can inspect the static soldiers at closer range via raised walkways running around their perimeter. Averaging 1.8m in height, the figures are hollow from the thighs up; head and hands were modelled separately and attached to the mass-produced bodies. Each soldier has **different features** and expressions and wears marks of rank; some believe that each is a portrait of a real member of the ancient Imperial Guard. Their hair is tied in buns and they are wearing knee-length battle tunics; the figures on the outside originally wore leather armour, now decayed. Traces of **pigment** show that their dress was once bright yellow, purple and green, though it's grey now. Originally, the troops carried real bows, swords, spears and crossbows, more than ten thousand of which have been found. The metal weapons, made of sophisticated alloys, were still sharp when discovered, and the arrowheads contained lead to make them poisonous.

A central group of **terracotta horses** is all that remains of a set of chariots. These wore harnesses with brass fittings and have been identified as depicting a breed from Gansu and Xinjiang. Each has six teeth, an indication that they are in their prime.

Vaults 2 and 3

Vault 2 is a smaller, L-shaped area, still under excavation; it's thought to hold more warriors than vault 1. The four groups here – crossbowmen, charioteers, cavalry and infantry – display more variety of posture and uniform than the figures in the main vault, though a large number of smashed and broken figures make the scene look more like the aftermath of a battle than the preparation for one. Four exceptional figures found here are exhibited at the side: a kneeling **archer**, a **cavalryman** leading a horse, an **officer** with a stylish goatee and the magnificent figure of a **general**, 2m tall, wearing engraved armour and a cap with two tails. Also on show are some of the weapons discovered at the site, including a huge bronze battle-axe.

The much smaller **vault 3**, where 68 figures and a chariot have been found, seems to have been battle headquarters. Armed with ceremonial *shu*, a short bronze mace with a triangular head, the figures are not in battle formation but form a guard of honour. Animal bones found here provide evidence of ritual sacrifices, which a real army would have performed before going into battle. A photo exhibition of plaster replicas gives some idea of how the figures would have been painted. At times, you'll find a half-blind peasant signing postcards in the shop at vault 2; this is **Yang Zhifa**, the man who discovered it all in 1974.

The rest of the site

At the side of vault 2 is a small **museum** where two magnificent **bronze chariots**, found in 1982 near Qin Shi Huang's tomb, are displayed in glass cases. They're about half actual size. The front one, depicting the Imperial Fleet leader's chariot, has four horses and a driver, and is decorated with dragon, phoenix and cloud designs, with a curved canopy and a gold-and-silver harness. Behind the driver is a large compartment featuring a silver door-latch and windows that open and close. The chariot at the back was the emperor's and has seats and beds in the rear. Both chariots were made with astonishing attention to detail; even the driver's knuckles, nails and fingerprints are shown. Another museum holds small artefacts found around the area, including a skull with an arrowhead still embedded in it, and a few kneeling pottery attendants, the only **female figures** depicted.

The Tomb of Qin Shi Huang

The **Tomb of Qin Shi Huang** (秦始皇陵, *qínshĭhuáng líng*; same ticket as Terracotta Army) is now no more than an artificial hill, nearly 2km west of the Terracotta Army; there's no transport so you'll have to walk. The burial mound was originally at the southern end of an inner sanctuary with walls 2.5km long, itself the centre of an outer city stretching for 6km, none of which remains. There's not much to see here; hassled at every step by souvenir sellers, you can walk up stone steps to the top of the hill, where you have a view of fields scraped bare for agriculture. According to accounts by **Sima Qian** in his *Historical Records*, written a century after the entombment, 700,000 labourers took 36 years to create an imperial city below ground, a complex full of wonders: the heavens were depicted on the ceiling of the central chamber with pearls, and the geographical divisions of the earth were delineated on a floor of bronze, with the seas and rivers represented by pools of mercury and made to flow with machinery. Automatic crossbows were set to protect the many gold and silver relics. Abnormally high quantities of **mercury** have recently been found in the surrounding soil, suggesting that at least parts of the account can be trusted. Secrecy was maintained, as usual, by killing most of the workmen. The tomb has yet to be excavated; digs in the surrounding area have revealed the inner and outer walls, ten gates and four watchtowers.

West of the city

Except for the museum at **Xianyang**, the tombs, temples and museums west of Xi'an are a little far out to be visited conveniently. Trying to get around yourself is tricky, as the only place served by regular **country buses** is Xianyang, though it's also possible to get to Qian Ling and Famen Si independently. **Tours** start early and get back late, with the sights thinly spread out in a long day of travelling across stark loess plains, but the museums are stimulating and it's good to get the feel of the tombs from which so many museum treasures come, even though most are little more than great earth mounds. The farthest sight, the **Famen Si**, is also the most rewarding.

Xianyang

XIANYANG (咸阳, *xiányáng*), now a nondescript city 60km northwest of Xi'an (buses from the main long-distance bus station take 1hr 30min), was the centre of China a couple of millennia ago, the site of the capital of **China's first dynasty**, the Qin. Little evidence remains of the era, however, except a flat plain in the east of the city that was once the site of Qin Shi Huang's palace. Relics found here, mostly unspectacular architectural details of more interest to archeologists – roof tiles, water pipes, bricks and so on – are in the **city museum** (daily 8am–5.30pm; ¥20) on Zhongshan Lu, a converted Confucian temple. From the Xianyang bus station, the museum is about 2km away: turn left on to Xilan Lu, then immediately left on to Shengli Anding Lu, which turns into Zhongshan Lu when it crosses Leyu Lu – the museum is on Zhongshan Lu, on the left. Star of the collection is a **miniature terracotta army** unearthed from a tomb, probably of a high official, 20km away, a lot less sinister than the real thing as each of the nearly three thousand terracotta figures is about 50cm high; some still have traces of their original bright paint scheme, which show that the designs on their shields varied widely. The warriors are fairly crude, but the horses are well done.

The Imperial Tombs

The area around Xi'an was the location of multiple ancient capitals spanning multiple dynasties over more than a thousand years; the result is one of the richest archeological areas in China. The many **Imperial Tombs** scattered along the Wei

River valley to the west of Xi'an are largely Han- and Tang-dynasty structures, less touristy than other sites in Xi'an, and a good way to escape the eastbound crowds and see a bit of the countryside.

Mao Ling

The resting place of the fifth Han emperor, Wu Di (157–87 BC), **Mao Ling** (茂陵, *màolíng*; daily 8am–5pm; ¥28), 40km west of Xi'an, is the largest of the twenty Han tombs in the area. It's a great green mound against the hills, which took more than fifty years to construct and contains, among many treasures, a full **jade burial suit** – jade was believed to protect the corpse from decay and therefore enhanced the possibilities of longevity of the soul. A dozen **smaller tombs** nearby belong to the emperor's court and include those of his favourite concubine and his generals, including the brilliant strategist **Huo Qubing** who fought several campaigns against the northern tribes (the Huns) and died at the age of 24. A small **museum** displays some impressive relics, including many massive stone sculptures of animals that once lined the tombs' spirit ways, simplified figures that look appealingly quirky; look for the frogs and a cow, and the horse trampling a demonic-looking Hun with its hooves, a macabre subject made to look almost comical.

Qian Ling

Qian Ling (乾陵, *qián líng*; daily 8am–5pm; March–Oct ¥45, otherwise ¥25) is 80km northwest of Xi'an, and usually the second tomb tour after Mao Ling. To get here under your own steam, take tour bus line #2 (3hr; ¥28) from the east side of the Xi'an train station. This hill tomb, on the slopes of Liang Shan, is where **Emperor Gao Zong** and his empress **Wu Zetian** were buried in the seventh century.

The **Imperial Way** leading to the tombs is formed from two facing rows of carved stone figures of men and flying horses, and with two groups of (now headless) mourners – guest princes and envoys from tribute states, some with their names on their backs. The tall stele on the left praises Gao Zong; opposite is the uninscribed **Wordless Stele**, erected by the empress to mark the supreme power that no words could express.

Seventeen **lesser tombs** are contained in the southeast section of the area. Among the five excavated since 1960 here is the **tomb of Prince Zhang Huai**, second son of Gao Zong, forced to commit suicide by his mother Wu Zetian (see p.270) during one of her periodic purges of those opposing her rise to power. At this tomb you walk down into a vault frescoed with army and processional scenes, a lovely tiger with a perm in the dip on either side. One fresco shows the court's welcome to visiting foreigners, with a hook-nosed Westerner depicted. There are also vivid frescoes of polo playing and, in the **museum** outside, some Tang pottery horses.

Princess Yong Tai's tomb (¥20) is the finest here – she was the emperor's granddaughter. Niches in the wall hold funeral offerings, and the vaulted roof still has traces of painted patterns. The passage walls leading down the ramp into the tomb are covered with murals of animals and guards of honour. The court ladies are still clear, elegant and charming after 1300 years, displaying Tang hairstyles and dress. At the bottom is the great tomb in black stone, lightly carved with human and animal shapes. Some 1300 gold, silver and pottery objects were found here and are now in Xi'an's Shaanxi History Museum (see p.258). At the mouth of the tomb is the traditional **stone tablet** into which the life story of the princess is carved – according to this, she died in childbirth at the age of 17, but some records claim that she was murdered by her grandmother, the empress Wu Zetian. The **Shun mausoleum** of Wu's own mother is small, but it's worth a look

Empress Wu Zetian

The rise to power of **Empress Wu Zetian** is extraordinary. Originally the **concubine** of Emperor Gao Zong's father, she emerged from her mourning to win the affections of his son, bear him sons in turn, and eventually marry him. As her husband ailed, her power over the administration grew until she was strong enough, at his death, to usurp the throne. Seven years later she was declared empress in her own right, and ruled until being forced to abdicate in favour of her son shortly before her death in 705 AD. Her reign was notorious for intrigue and bloodshed, but even her critics admit that she chose the right ministers for the job, often solely through merit. The heavy negative historical criticism against her may be solely because she was a woman, as the idea of a female in a position of authority is entirely contrary to Confucian ethics (her title was "Emperor", there being no female equivalent for so exalted a position). For more about Wu Zetian, see also Chapter 12 "Sichuan and Chongqing", p.763.

for the two unusually splendid granite figures that guard it: a 3m-high lion and an even bigger unicorn.

Zhao Ling

At **Zhao Ling** (昭陵, *zhāo líng*; daily 8am–6pm; ¥15), east of Qian Ling and 70km northwest of Xi'an, nineteen **Tang tombs** include that of Emperor Tai Zong. Begun in 636 AD, this took thirteen years to complete. Tai Zong introduced the practice of building his tomb into the hillside instead of as a tumulus on an open plain. From the main tomb, built into the slope of Jiuzou, a great cemetery fans out southeast and southwest, which includes 167 lesser tombs of the imperial family, generals and officials. A small **museum** displays stone carvings, murals and pottery figures from the smaller tombs.

Famen Si

The extraordinary **Famen Si** (法门寺, *fămén sì*; daily 8am–6pm; March–Oct ¥120, otherwise ¥90), 120km west of Xi'an, home of the finger bone of the Buddha, and the nearby **museum** containing an unsurpassed collection of Tang-dynasty relics, are worth the long trip it takes to get out here. The easiest way is to join a tour (see p.262), but failing that, catch **tour bus #2** (3hr) at the Xi'an train station, across the concourse on the east side in front of the *Jiefang* hotel; it also stops at Qian Ling. Hostels charge ¥800 for an eight-person **minibus** to the temple, which isn't such a bad deal. Otherwise, take the hourly **bus to Fufeng** from Xi'an's long-distance bus station (4hr), from where you can catch a minibus to the temple (20min).

In 147 AD, King Ashoka of India, to atone, it is said, for his warlike life, distributed precious **Buddhist relics** (*sarira*) to Buddhist colonies throughout Asia. One of the earliest places of Buddhist worship in China, the Famen Si was built to house his gift of a **finger**, in the form of three separate bones. The temple enjoyed great fame in the Tang dynasty, when Emperor Tuo Bayu began the practice of having the bones temporarily removed and taken to the court at Chang'an at the head of a procession repeated every thirty years; when the emperor had paid his respects, the finger bones were closed back up in the **crypt** underneath the temple stupa, together with a lavish collection of offerings. After the fall of the Tang, the vault was forgotten about until the protective stupa above collapsed in 1981, revealing the most astonishing array of Tang precious objects, and at the back, concealed inside box after box, the legendary finger of the Buddha.

Today, the temple is a popular place of pilgrimage. The stupa and crypt have been rebuilt, with a **shrine** holding the finger at the crypt's centre. A praying monk is always in attendance, sitting in front of the finger, next to the safe in which it is kept at night (if it's not being exhibited elsewhere, as happens periodically). Indeed, the temple's monks are taking no chances, and the only entrance to the crypt is protected by a huge metal door of the kind usually seen in a bank. You can look into the original crypt – at 21m long, the largest of its kind ever discovered in China – though there's not much to see now.

The museum

The **museum** west of the temple houses the well-preserved Tang relics found in the crypt, and is certainly one of the best small museums in China. Exhibits are divided into sections according to their material, with copious explanations in English. On the lower floor, the **gold and silver** is breathtaking for the quality of its workmanship: especially notable are a silver incense burner with an internal gyroscope to keep it upright; a silver tea basket, the earliest physical evidence of tea-drinking in China; and a gold figure of an elephant-headed man. Some unusual items on display are twenty **glass plates and bottles**, some Persian, with Arabic designs, some from the Roman Empire, including a bottle made in the fifth century. Glassware, imported along the Silk Road, was more highly valued than gold at the time, as none was made in China.

At the centre of the main room is a gilded **silver coffin**, which held one of the finger bones, itself inside a copper model of a stupa, inside a marble pagoda. Prominent upstairs is a gold-and-silver **monk's staff**, which, ironically, would have been used for begging alms, but the main display here is of the **caskets** that the other two finger bones were found in – finely made boxes of diminishing size, of silver, sandalwood, gold and crystal, which sat inside each other, while the finger bones themselves were in tiny jade coffins.

South of the city

In the wooded hilly country south of Xi'an, a number of important **temples** serve as worthy focal points for a day's excursion. The **Xingjiao Si**, 24km southeast of the city on a hillside by the Fan River, was founded in 669 AD to house the ashes of the travelling monk Xuanzang (see p.864), whose remains are underneath a square stupa at the centre of the temple. The two smaller stupas either side mark the tombs of two of his disciples. Beside the stupa, a pavilion holds a charming and commonly reproduced stone carving of Xuanzang looking cheery, despite being laden down under a pack. Little remains of the **Huayan Si**, on the way to the Xingjiao Si, except two small brick pagodas, one of which holds the remains of the monk Dushun, one of the founders of Zen Buddhism. The **Xingji Si**, 5km west of here, has a ten-storey pagoda, which covers the ashes of Shandao, founder of the Jingtu sect.

No tours visit the temples, but the sites are accessible by **bus #215**, which leaves from just outside Xian's south gate. Ride right to the last stop, then take a rickshaw to the temples; you'll have to negotiate a return trip.

Hua Shan

The five peaks of **Hua Shan** (华山, *huáshān*; ¥70 entrance fee), 120km east of Xi'an, were originally known as Xiyue (Western Mountain), because this is the westernmost of the five sacred Taoist mountains. It's always been a popular place for pilgrimage, though these days people puffing up the steep, narrow paths or enjoying the dramatic views from the peaks are more likely to be tourists.

Arrival

As Hua Shan lies between Xi'an and Luoyang, you can take in the mountain en route between the two cities, as an excursion from Xi'an, or on the way to Xi'an from Ruicheng in Shanxi. **Tour bus #1** from Xi'an's train station concourse takes two hours to get to the east gate and cable car. The last buses back to Xi'an leave from each gate at around 5.30pm, but walk to the main road and you'll find private minibuses leaving as late as 8pm. A **day-tour** organized by hostels in Xi'an, including transport, cable car, entry and occasionally a light breakfast, costs around ¥390 per person, or you can rent an eight-person minibus through them for around ¥800.

You can also get here by **train** to Hua Shan station, about 20km to the east of either of the mountain gates, and on the new high speed Xi'an–Zhengzhou line. From the station, **public buses** (¥3) will drop you at Yuquan Jie, the street that runs uphill to the Yuquan Si temple and the hiking trail. **Private minibuses** follow the same route, but go straight to Yuquan Si (¥5). A taxi should cost ¥20 to either gate from the train station.

Climbing Hua Shan

There's a Chinese saying, "There is one path and one path only to the summit of Hua Shan", meaning that sometimes the hard way is the only way. This isn't so true today, perhaps, what with a **cable car** (¥150 return) running from the east gate – the ride doesn't go to the peak, but does put you above the toughest climbs. The original, arduous **old route** begins at the **west gate** and **Yuquan Si** (Jade Spring Temple), dedicated to the tenth-century monk Xiyi who lived here as a recluse. From here, every few hundred metres you'll come across a wayside refreshment place offering stone seats, a burner, tea, soft drinks, maps and souvenirs – the higher you go, the more attractive the knobbly walking sticks on sale seem. In summer, you'll be swept along in a stream of Chinese, mostly young couples, dressed in their fashionable, but often highly impractical, holiday finest, including high-heeled shoes.

Known as the **Eighteen Bends**, the deceptively easy-looking climb up the gullies in fact winds for about two hours before reaching the flight of narrow stone steps that ascend to the first summit, **North Peak** (1500m). The mountain was formerly dotted with temples, and there are still half a dozen. Many people turn back at this point, although you can continue to **Middle Peak** next, then East, West and South peaks (each at around 2000m), which make up an **eight-hour circuit trail**.

Though the summits aren't that high, the gaunt rocky cliffs, twisted pines and rugged slopes certainly look like genuine mountains as they swim in and out of the mist trails. It's quite possible to ascend and descend the mountain in a single day, especially if you use the cable car. The going is rough in places and a few of the upper paths require a head for heights, with chain handrails, wooden galleries and rickety ladders attached at difficult points. Some people arrive in the evening and climb by moonlight in order to see the **sunrise** over the Sea of Clouds from Middle or East Peak. If you plan to climb at night, be sure to take some warm clothes and a flashlight with spare batteries.

Accommodation and eating

There are several **places to stay** on Yuquan Jie: the *Huaiying Dajiudian* (❸, dorms ¥30) is a popular staging point for night ascents, while the nearby *Huashan Kezhan* (❻) is a tremendous step up in class. There are also hotels about every 5km along the **circuit route**, including ones abutting the North, East and West peaks. The *East Peak Guesthouse* (❽) is a particular favourite with sun watchers – but don't expect light, heat or a private bathroom at these places, and if you plan to stay the night on the mountain it's a good idea to take your own sleeping bag. These places are at least easy to find, though, and hotel touts waylay travellers along the route.

The nicest thing to be said about the **food** near the east gate and on the mountain is that it's palatable. It's also more expensive the higher you go. If you're on a tight budget, stock up beforehand. There is a small **convenience store** just uphill from the *Huaiying*, and plenty of noodle restaurants nearby as well.

The Communists in Yan'an

Some way to the north of Xi'an lies the town of **Yan'an**, an unprepossessing place which nevertheless played a major role in China's recent history. The arrival of the Communists in Yan'an in October 1935 marked the end of the **Long March**, an astonishing and now semi-mythical journey in which eighty thousand men, women and children of the Red Army fled their mountain bases in Jiangxi province to escape encirclement and annihilation at the hands of the Nationalists (see p.951).

When Mao finally arrived in Yan'an there were only about five thousand still with him, but here they met up with northern Communists who had already established a soviet. Gradually, stragglers and those who had been sent on missions to other parts arrived to swell their numbers. The **Yan'an soviet** came to control a vast tract of the surrounding country, with its own economy and banknotes to back the new political system. Soldiers in China usually lived parasitically off the peasants unfortunate enough to be in their way, but Mao's troops, trained to see themselves as defenders of the people, were under orders to be polite and courteous and pay for their supplies. **Mao** wrote some of his most important essays here, including much that was later included in the Little Red Book.

Arranged in a Y-shape around a fork of the Yan River, today's Yan'an (延安, *yán'ān*) is a dour and rather unappealing place rarely visited by foreigners, but there are a few sights on hand to detain the curious. Foremost are the **Yangjialing Revolutionary Headquarters** (杨家岭革命旧址, *yángjiālǐng gémìng jiùzhǐ*; daily 8am–5.30pm; ¥10), northwest of town on the #3 bus route. These were home to the Communist leaders in the early 1940s, a time when Mao began to look beyond fighting off the Japanese and Guomindang, and conceptualized what a Communist Chinese state would be like. Cut into the hillside above are the residences of Mao, Zhou Enlai, Liu Shaoqi, Zhu De and the like. The **Wangjiaping Revolutionary Headquarters** (王家坪革命旧址, *wángjiāpíng gémìng jiùzhǐ*; daily 7am–7pm; ¥10), a clutch of simple, low buildings of white plaster over straw, mud and brick where Mao and company lived and worked in the late 1940s, are just around the corner from the Revolutionary Museum. The unassuming **Fenghuangshan Revolutionary Headquarters** (凤凰山革命旧址, *fènghuángshān gémìng jiùzhǐ*; daily 8am–5.30pm; ¥7) served as the initial residence of the Communists; in 1937 and 1938, the two main rooms in the western courtyard functioned as Mao's bedroom and study, and still house his wooden bed, desk with chairs and a latrine. Lastly, the **Revolutionary Museum** (延安革命纪念馆, *yán'ān gémìng jìniàngǎun*; daily 8am–6pm; ¥15) in the northwest corner of town holds a massive collection of artefacts and propaganda pictures.

Yan'an's **train station** is in the far south of town, a long way from anything interesting. **Bus #2**, which heads up through the centre of town near the **accommodation**, is the most useful service to catch from here. **Long-distance buses**, which are faster than the train, arrive either at the train station concourse or the **bus station**, about 1km east of the town centre.

Luoyang and around

The sprawling city of **LUOYANG** (洛阳, *luòyáng*) lies in the middle reaches of the Yellow River valley in Henan province. It's most commonly used as a hub for the famed **Longmen Caves**, one of China's three major rock art galleries, which lie just to the south. In addition, it's within striking distance of **Song Shan** and **Shaolin Si**. These ancient sights hint at a rich history – Luoyang has, indeed, been occupied since Neolithic times, and served as China's capital at various points from the Zhou through to 937 AD. Confucius once studied here, and this is where Buddhism first took root in China in 68AD. While the industrial and drab modern city itself retains no atmosphere of past glories, the outlying fields are dotted with earthern **tomb mounds** of former officials and wealthy citizens, and there are two outstanding Buddhist sites nearby: the aforementioned Longmen Caves, and the venerable **Baima Si**.

Arrival and city transport

Luoyang's tiny **airport**, 20km north of town, is served by bus #83 to the massive **train station**, a major intersection on China's north–south and east–west lines; the station is in the town's busy and unattractive northern extremity. The **bus stations** are here, too: most services use the big one east of the train station square, but there's also the Jinyuan depot, west of the train station, which handles inter-provincial destinations.

The train station area is also the place to pick up **city buses**, including those to Baima Si and the Longmen Caves (see accounts for details), while touts for buses

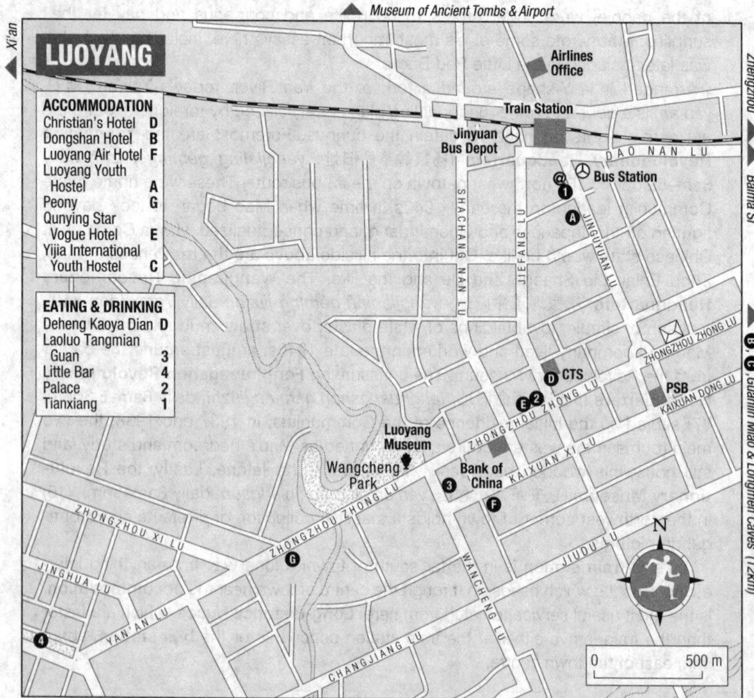

to Shaolin Si (p.281) hang around outside the main bus station, and are not shy of grabbing customers. **Taxis** are plentiful, and have a ¥6 flag fare.

Accommodation

Basing yourself in one of the **budget options** near Luoyang's train station isn't such a bad idea, as there are good connections to the sights and transport out once you've finished. Yet the centre of town is cleaner, and the accommodation more upmarket. There's even an option out near the Longmen Caves.

Christian's Hotel 56 Jiefang Lu ⓣ0379/63266666. Chic new hotel with themed floors – stay in European, Chinese or even Balinese style. Service is excellent, and rooms are very good value for the price. ❻

Dongshan Hotel (东山宾馆, *dōngshān bīnguǎn*) Longmen Caves ⓣ0379/64686000, ⓦwww.lydongshanhotel.cn. On a hilltop overlooking the Longmen Caves, this resort-style hotel boasts almost 100 elegant rooms, a free gym and a few interesting quirks, such as piped spring water and a superb night-time view of the caves from a fourth-floor bar. The downside of its remote location is that you're almost obliged to dine on site. ❽

Luoyang Air Hotel (洛阳航空大厦, *luòyáng hángkōng dàshà*) Junction of Fanglin Lu and Kaixuan Xi Lu ⓣ0379/3944668, ⓕ3915552. Take a taxi from the station. Staff at this nine-storey place wear the most stylish uniforms of any Luoyang hotel, and the guests – plenty of pilots and flight attendants – are pretty chic, too. The lobby, appropriately, looks like an airport lounge. ❺

Luoyang Youth Hostel (洛阳国际青年旅舍, *luòyáng guójì qīngnián lǚshè*) 72 Jinguyuan Lu ⓣ0379/65260666, ⓕ63305858. A short walk from the train and bus stations; go into the empty lobby and take the lift to the third floor. Rooms are kept spick-and-span, and there's a kitchen and washing machine, though the service isn't always that hot. Dorms from ¥30, rooms ❸

Peony (牡丹大酒店, *mǔdān dàjiǔdiàn*) 15 Zhongzhou Zhong Lu ⓣ & ⓕ0379/6468000. The most upmarket place in town, charging up to ¥2400 for the most luxurious rooms. All mod cons provided, and there's a good, though expensive, restaurant. ❽

Qunying Star Vogue Hotel (群英之皇的酒店, *qúnyīng zhīhuāngde jiǔdiàn*) 266 Zhongzhou Zhong Lu ⓣ0379/62983198, ⓕ62683001. Cute boutique motel with colourful, frivolous decor usually alien to Chinese accommodation. Relatively pricey, though you can haggle them down a fair bit. ❻

Yijia International Youth Hostel (一家国际青年旅舍, *yī jiā guójì qīngnián lǚshè*) 329 Zhongzhou Dong Lu ⓣ0379/63512311. Despite its slightly awkward location east of the centre (¥10 by taxi, ¥1 on bus #5), this is a prime target for savvy backpackers, presided over by winningly helpful staff who are particularly good at organizing trips out of town. Dorms from ¥40, rooms ❷

The City

Luoyang's two sole sights are located along Zhongzhou Zhong Lu, around 2km southwest of the station – catch bus #40 down Jiefang Lu, or #50 down Jinguyuan Lu. **Wangcheng Park** (王成公园, *wángchéng gōngyuán*; daily 5am–9.30pm; ¥5), at its best in April when the peonies are blooming, is a popular recreation spot at dawn, and overlies the site of the **Zhou capital**, though very few authentic remains are on show.

Instead, most of what has been left of the city's dynastic importance is gathered into the **Luoyang Museum** (洛阳博物馆, *luòyáng bówùguǎn*; daily 9am–5.30pm; ¥20), just east of the park, a surprisingly bright and well-captioned exhibition inside a grubby building. The area around Luoyang entered the Bronze Age before the rest of China, so the **Shang bronzes** are especially extensive; look, too, for an endearing **jade tiger** from the Zhou, as well as some Indian-influenced **Wei statuary**, and a model farm from a Han tomb, with a sow and her row of piglets. As usual, the Tang wins hands down for pottery, with their multicoloured, expressive camels and several hook-nosed, pointy-chinned foreigners, and for

Luoyang's peonies

It's said that in 800 AD the Tang Empress Wu Zetian, enraged that the **peonies**, alone among flowers, disobeyed her command to bloom in the snow, banished them from her capital at Chang'an. Many were transplanted to Luoyang (the secondary capital) where they flourished, and have since become one of the city's most celebrated attractions, the subject of countless poems and cultivation notes. Luoyang now boasts over 150 varieties of peony, which have found their way onto every available patch or scrap of ground – a splendid sight when they flower in spring. The peony motif is also everywhere in the city, from trellises to rubbish bins.

gold and silver, where their ornate decorative objects show the influence of Persian and Roman styles.

Eating and drinking

As far as **restaurants** go, the Sichuanese have landed and taken over Luoyang, though there are a couple of places where dishes don't arrive smothered in chillies. For cheap noodles and dumplings, try the snack stalls near the station. There's also a knot of **cafés** at the south end of Shachang Nan Lu, near the junction with Kaixuan Xi Lu. As for **bars**, one favourite with local expats is the *Little Bar*, west of the centre on Mudan Square.

Deheng Kaoya Dian (德恒烤鸭店, *déhéng kaōyā diàn*) Tanggong Xi Lu. Famous roast-duck restaurant with smart antique-style furnishings but not especially expensive – a whole duck is around ¥60.

Laoluo Tangmian Guan (老雒汤面馆, *lǎoluò tāngmián guǎn*) Wangcheng Lu, just south of the park and museum. Good, old-style place for snacks and light meals; downstairs canteen and more formal rooms above. Not expensive in any case.

Palace (宫邸, *gōng dǐ*) Corner of Jiefang Lu and Zhongzhou Zhong Lu. New restaurant-bar offering eclectic mix of Sichuanese, pizza and Japanese dishes, plus lots of beer. A bit pricey for what you get, but good atmosphere.

Tianxiang (天香饭店, *tiānxiāng fàndiàn*) 56 Jingyuyuan Lu. Crowded, smoky and inexpensive Sichuanese restaurant, very popular and with decent food. They have an English menu of sorts, too. Part of a hotel of the same name.

Listings

Airlines CAAC are at 196 Dao Bei Lu (☎0379/3935301), 200m north of the station. There's a China Southern office on Zhongzhou Zhong Lu, just east of Jiefang Lu.

Banks and exchange The Bank of China (daily 8am–5pm) is on the corner of Zhongzhou Zhong Lu and Shangchang Nan Lu.

Mail The post office (Mon–Sat 8am–6pm) is on the north side of Zhongzhou Zhong Lu, near the junction with Jinguyuan Lu.

PSB The PSB is at 1 Kaixuan Xi Lu (Mon–Sat 8am–noon & 2–6pm).

Travel agents and tours If your accommodation can't help out, the CTS (☎0379/65372020 or 13592058448) are in the *Yinyan* hotel on Tanggong Xi Lu. A standard day-tour of the sights in the vicinity of town, including Baima Si and Shaolin Si, costs around ¥55.

Around Luoyang

The main destination around Luoyang lies south at the **Longmen Caves**. However little you know about Buddhism or about sculpture, you cannot help but be impressed by the scale and complexity of the work here and by the extraordinary contrast between the power of the giant figures and the intricate delicacy of the miniatures. Nearby, you can also visit **Guanlin Miao**, a memorial temple to

Three Kingdom hero Guan Di. The other major sight is the Buddhist temple of **Baima Si**, which lies east of the city; and there's also an interesting, if not very well-presented, **Museum of Ancient Tombs** northwest of Luoyang, where you can see the interiors of the mounds that dot the local fields. All these can be visited on **public buses** from Luoyang, and you could pack the lot into one very busy day. Alternatively, all but the museum are served by private **tourist minibuses**, which run from outside the station. If you're heading east to Song Shan or Zhengzhou after Luoyang, Baima Si is on the way and makes a good spot to break the journey; day-tours to Shaolin Si tend to stop off here, too.

The Longmen Caves

A UNESCO World Heritage Site, the **Longmen Caves** (龙门石窟, *lóngmén shíkū*; daily 7.30am–5.30pm; ¥120) are a spectacular parade of Buddhist figurines and reliefs. **Bus #81** (¥1.50) runs here from the east side of the train station via Jingguyuan Lu, turning east onto Zhongzhou Zhong Lu and then south down Dingding Lu and Longmen Lu to its terminus at the caves; the journey can take up to an hour, though it's only 12km south of town. A metered **taxi** ride will set you back between ¥30 and ¥50. The roadhead is a kilometre short of the caves, and if you don't fancy a walk through the souvenir stalls, head down to the river and follow it to the entrance. The site is very busy in the summer, overrun with tourists posing in the empty niches for photos, and also very hot and exposed – try to visit early on.

The caves have been beautifully renovated and feature English labelling. Starting from the entrance at the northern end and moving south down the group, the following are the largest and most important carvings, which stand out due to their size. The three **Bingyang caves** are early; the central one, commissioned by Emperor Xuan Wu to honour his parents, supposedly took 800,000 men working from 500 to 523 AD to complete. The eleven statues of Buddha inside show northern characteristics – long features, thin faces, splayed fishtail robes – and traces of Greek influence. The side caves, completed under the Tang, are more natural and voluptuous, carved in high relief. **Wanfo** (Cave of Ten Thousand Buddhas), just south of here, was built in 680 by Gao Zong and his empress Wu Zetian, and has fifteen thousand Buddhas carved in tiny niches, each one different and the smallest just 2cm high. **Lianhua** (Lotus Flower Cave) is another early one,

Creating the caves

Over the years, 1350 caves, 750 niches and 40 pagodas containing 110,000 statues were carved out of the limestone cliffs bordering the Yi River to create the Longmen Caves. Stretching more than one kilometre in length, the carvings were **commissioned** by emperors, the imperial family, other wealthy families wanting to buy good fortune, generals hoping for victory, and religious groups. The Toba Wei began the work in 492 AD, when they moved their capital to Luoyang from Datong, where they had carved the Yungang Caves (see p.234). At Longmen, they adapted their art to the different requirements of a harder, limestone surface. Three sets of caves, Guyang, Bingyang and Lianhua, date from this early period. Work continued for five hundred years and reached a second peak under the Tang, particularly under Empress Wu Zetian, a devoted adherent of Buddhism.

There's a clearly visible progression from the early style brought from Datong, of simple, rounded, formally modelled holy figures, to the complex and elaborate, but more linear, Tang carvings, which include women and court characters. In general, the Buddhas are simple, but the sculptors were able to show off with the attendant figures and the decorative flourishes around the edges of the caves.

dating from 527, and named after the beautifully carved lotus in its roof; while at **Moya Sanfo** you can see an incomplete trinity, abandoned when the Tang dynasty began to wobble. But by far the most splendid is **Fengxian** (Ancestor Worshipping Cave), where an overwhelming seated figure of Vairocana Buddha, 17m high with 2m-long ears, sits placidly overlooking the river, guarded by four warrior attendants (though the westerly two are almost completely gone) who are grinding malevolent spirits underfoot. **Medical Prescription Cave**, built in 575, details several hundred cures for everything from madness to the common cold. **Guyang** is the earliest of all, begun in 495, where you can still see traces of the vivid paintwork that originally gave life to these carvings. There's a central Buddha and nineteen of the "Twenty Pieces", important examples of ancient calligraphy. From the end of the west bank you can cross the bridge to the east side, for a good view of the caves peppering the opposite bank like rabbit warrens.

Guanlin Miao

On its way back to Luoyang from the Longmen Caves, bus #81 stops 7km south of town outside the red-walled **Guanlin Miao** (关林苗, *guānlín miào*; daily 8am–5pm; ¥30) a complex dedicated to **Guan Di** – also known as Guang Gong and Guan Yu – loyal general of Liu Bei of the Three Kingdoms period (see p.945). He was captured and executed by the King of Wu who sent his head to Cao Cao, King of Wei, hoping in this way to divert on to the Wei any revenge that might be coming. Cao Cao neatly sidestepped this grisly game of pass-the-parcel by burying the head with honour in a tomb behind the temple, now a wooded, walled mound.

Despite its military theme, the temple is beautiful and rather peaceful, the elegant Ming buildings highly carved and richly decorated. Especially fine are the carved stone lionesses lining the path to the Main Hall. Each has a different expression and a different cub, some riding on their mother's back, some hiding coyly behind her paws. In the first hall, look carefully at the eaves for rather comical images of Guan Di fighting – he's the one on the red horse, a faithful animal called **Red Hare** – and leading an army engaged in sacking a city engulfed by carved wooden flames. Inside, stands a 7m-tall statue of the general, resplendent in technicolour ceremonial robes with a curtain of beads hanging from his hat.

The Baima Si

Historic, leafy **Baima Si** (白马寺, *báimǎ sì*; White Horse Temple; daily 7.30am–5.30pm; ¥40), 12km east of Luoyang at the end of the #56 bus route from the train station (¥1.50), is attractive for its ancient buildings and devotional atmosphere. You'll be dropped either on the side of the road or at the car park, from where it's a dash through a stretch of souvenir shops to the ticket window.

Founded in 68 AD, the Baima Si has some claim to being the first Buddhist temple in China. Legend says that the Emperor Mingdi of the Eastern Han dreamed of a golden figure with the sun and moon behind its head. Two monks sent to search for the origin of the dream reached India and returned riding white horses with two Indian monks in tow, and a bundle of sutras. This temple was built to honour them, and its layout is in keeping with the legend: there are two stone horses, one on either side of the entrance, and the tombs of the two monks, earthen mounds ringed by round stone walls, lie in the first courtyard.

Home to a thriving community of monks, the Baima Si is primarily a place of worship, and over-inquisitive visitors are tactfully but firmly pointed in the right direction. Inside the temple, you'll find this a placid place, its silence only pricked by the sound of gongs or the tapping of stonemasons carving out a stele. Beyond the Hall of Celestial Guardians, the **Main Hall** holds a statue of Sakyamuni flanked by the figures of Manjusri and Samantabhadra. Near the Great Altar is an ancient bell weighing more than a tonne; as in the days when there were over ten thousand Tang monks here, it is still struck in time with the chanting. The inscription reads: "The sound of the Bell resounds in Buddha's temple causing the ghosts in Hell to tremble with fear". Behind the Main Hall is the **Cool Terrace** where, it is said, the original sutras were translated. Offerings of fruit on the altars, multicoloured cloths hanging from the ceilings and lighted candles in bowls floating in basins of water, as well as the heady gusts of incense issuing from the burners in the courtyards, indicate that, unlike other temples in the area, this is the genuine article.

The Museum of Ancient Tombs

In a patch of open land around 6km northwest of the city (catch bus #83 from the east side of the train station), the **Museum of Ancient Tombs** (洛阳古墓博物馆, *luòyáng gǔmù bówùguǎn*; daily 8am–5pm; ¥20) contains the relocated brick interiors of two dozen tomb mounds from the Luoyang area dating from the Western Han to Northern Song. Most had been robbed, and the museum is very neglected, but it does give a more human view of the times when compared with Longmen's overwhelming scale.

The tombs are arranged underground around a central atrium, into which you descend from beside souvenir stalls (there are no signs, but the helpful stallholders will point the way). Each is entered through a short tunnel, and is very small – you can barely stand in a couple – but decorated brickwork and frescoes liven the whole thing up. Best, however, is **Jing Ling**, the tomb of Xuan Wu of the Northern Wei, which stands just outside the museum grounds – again, there's no sign but you can't miss the huge earth hillock. This hasn't been relocated, and you descend a 50m-long ramp into Xuan Wu's tomb chamber – guarded by two sneering demons – where his sarcophagus remains.

Song Shan

The seventy peaks of the **Song Shan** (嵩山, *sōngshān*) range stretch over 64km across Dengfeng county, midway between Luoyang and Zhengzhou. When the Zhou ruler Ping moved his capital to Luoyang in 771 BC, it was known as Zhong Yue, Central Peak – being at the axis of the **five sacred Taoist mountains**, with Hua Shan to the west, Tai Shan to the east, Heng Shan to the south and another Heng Shan to the north. The mountains, thickly clad with trees, rise from narrow, steep-sided rocky valleys and appear impressively precipitous, though with the highest peak, Junji, at just 1500m, they're not actually very lofty. When the summits emerge from a swirling sea of cloud, though, and the slopes are dressed in their brilliant autumn colours, they can certainly look the part.

Given its importance to Taoism, it's ironic that the busiest sight at Song Shan today is in fact the **Shaolin Si**, a Buddhist temple famed not just as one of the earliest dedicated to the Chan (Zen) sect, but also where **Chinese kung fu** is said to have originated. A major Taoist temple survives, too, in the **Zhongyue Miao**, though it's by no means as busy. The mountain ranges themselves are another draw, with numerous paths meandering around the valleys, passing temples, pagodas and guard towers, and some wonderful views. Unlike at other holy mountains, there is no single set path, and, as the slopes are not steep and the undergrowth is sparse, you can set out in any direction you like. Song Shan's sights aren't close to one another, so you won't be able to do more than one or two a day and count on getting back to Dengfeng before nightfall.

You can visit Song Shan on a **day-trip** from either **Luoyang** or **Zhengzhou**, though it's more satisfying – and certainly less rushed – to base yourself in the town of **Dengfeng**, from where you can explore Shaolin Si, Zhongyue Miao and a couple of other nearby sites at your own pace. Buses from Luoyang pass Shaolin on the way to Dengfeng, so you can always get off here first. **Maps** of the area are included on the back of local maps of Zhengzhou (available in Zhengzhou, and possibly Luoyang), or can be bought at Dengfeng and Shaolin.

Arrival

Tours to Song Shan and Shaolin Si are easy to organize through accommodation in both Luoyang and Zhengzhou, but it's also quite simple to make the trip on public transport. The small market town of **Dengfeng** (登封, *dēngfēng*) functions as the main base for Song Shan. Its **bus station** is about 3km southeast of the centre; bus #1 or #3 (¥1) will get you to the main drag, Zhongyue Dajie; a taxi will cost about ¥5. To head **to Shaolin Si** from town, walk west (uphill) along Zhongyue Dajie and look for buses marked "Shaolin" in Chinese (少林, *shàolín*) hanging around outside the little bus station compound. Buses run from dawn until dusk and the ¥2 ride takes about twenty minutes; a taxi will cost ¥25 each way.

Accommodation

Visitors to Song Shan can choose to stay in Dengfeng, or around the Shaolin temple itself. The two best **places to stay** in **Dengfeng** are the motel-like *Shaolin Binguan* (少林宾馆, *shàolín bīnguǎn*; ⓣ0371/62856188, ⓦwww.shaolinhotel.com; ❽), at 66 Zhongyue Dajie, a great place amenable to bargaining, as rates can be halved quite easily at most times; and the *Gaotian Jiudian* (高天酒店, *gāotiān jiǔdiàn*; ⓣ0371/2885200, ⓕ2885201; ❹), further east at 166 Zhongyue Dajie. If you're on a tight budget, it's cheaper to stay around **Shaolin Si** – there are a host of identical, simple hotels near the bus park on the road towards Dengfeng (beds ¥50–75, rooms ❸). A large step up in class is the modern and comfortable *Zen International Hotel* (禅居国际饭店, *chán jū guójì fàndiàn*; ⓣ0371/6275666, ⓕ62745555; ❺), behind the kung fu show hall.

Zhongyue Miao

The **Zhongyue Miao** (中岳庙, *zhōngyuè miào*; daily 8am–6pm; ¥30), on the eastern edge of Dengfeng on the #2 bus route from Shaolin Dadao, is a huge Taoist temple founded as long ago as 220 BC, though the buildings here today date from the Ming. Inside, it's an attractive place, with spacious, wooded courtyards and brilliantly coloured buildings standing out against the grey and green of the mountain behind. If you've just come from crowded Shaolin, the quiet, calm atmosphere of this working Taoist monastery is particularly striking.

A series of gateways, courtyards and pavilions leads to the **Main Hall** where the emperor made sacrifices to the mountain. The Junji Gate, just before the hall, has two great sentries, nearly 4m high, brightly painted and flourishing their weapons. The courtyard houses gnarled old cypresses, some of them approaching the age of the temple itself, and there are four Song-dynasty **iron statues** of guardian warriors in martial poses on the eastern side. The **Bedroom Palace** behind the Main Hall is unusual for having a shrine that shows a deity lying in bed. Contemporary worshippers tend to gravitate to the back of the complex, where you may see people burning what look like little origami hats in the iron burners here, or practising *qi gong*, exercises centring around control of the breath.

If you go to the back of the complex, past the monks' quarters on the right, you come to the temple's back exit, where you are charged ¥2 for the privilege of walking 200m up stone steps to a little **pagoda** on a hill behind the temple. From here, paths take you through pinewoods to the craggy peaks of the mountain, a worthwhile afternoon's excursion and a rare chance for solitude; the only other person you are likely to see is the odd shepherd.

Other sights around Dengfeng

Three kilometres north of Dengfeng at the top end of Songshan Lu, the **Songyang Academy** (嵩阳书院, *sōngyáng shūyuàn*) consists of a couple of lecture halls, a **library** and a memorial hall, founded in 484 AD, which was one of the great centres of learning under the Song. Many famous scholars from history lectured here, including Sima Guang and Cheng Hao. In the courtyard are two enormous cypresses said to be three thousand years old, as well as a stele from the Tang dynasty. The path beyond climbs to Junji Peak and branches off to the **Songyue Temple Pagoda** (嵩岳寺塔, *sōngyuèsì tǎ*), 5km north of Dengfeng. Built at the beginning of the sixth century by the Northern Wei, this 45m-high structure is both the oldest pagoda and the oldest complete brick building in China, rare for having twelve sides.

Around 12km southeast of Dengfeng, in the town of Gaocheng, the **Guanxing Observatory** (观星台, *guānxīng tái*) was built in 1279 and designed by Gui Shou Jing to calculate the solstices. It's a fascinating, sculptural-looking building, an almost pyramidal tower with a long straight wall marked with measurements running along the ground behind it. A round trip by taxi should cost about ¥40, including waiting time.

Shaolin Si

Around 13km west of Dengfeng, through rugged, mountainous countryside and a main road lined with martial-arts schools, **Shaolin Si** (少林寺, *shàolín sì*; daily 8am–6pm; ¥100) is a place of legends. This is the temple where the sixth-century founder of Buddhism's Chan (Zen) sect, **Bodhidarma**, consolidated his teachings in China, and also where – surprisingly, given Buddhism's peaceful doctrines – **Chinese kung fu** is said to have originated. Today, it's a tourist black spot, packed with noisy groups and commercial enterprises, and a complete non-starter if you're seeking any form of spiritual enlightenment – though as an entertaining look into modern China's kung fu cult, it's a lot of fun. In September, the place is particularly busy, filling up with martial-arts enthusiasts from all over the world who come to attend the international **Wushu Festival**.

The original Shaolin Si was built in 495 AD. Shortly afterwards, the Indian monk **Bodhidarma** (known as **Da Mo** in China) came to live here after visiting the emperor in Nanjing, then crossing the Yangzi on a reed (depicted in a tablet at the temple). As the temple has been burned down on several occasions – most recently in 1928, by the warlord Shi Yousan – the buildings you see here today are mostly reconstructions in the Ming style, built over the last twenty years. Despite this, and the incredible density of tourists, the temple and surroundings are beautiful, and the chance to see some impressive martial-art displays here make it well worth the trip.

The temple and around

All transport drops you at the mouth of a long plaza lined with souvenir shops selling a startling array of weapons, from swords to throwing stars and

Shaolin kung fu

Kung fu was first developed at the Shaolin Si as a form of gymnastics to counterbalance the immobility of meditation. The monks studied the movement of animals and copied them – the way snakes crawled, tigers leapt and mantises danced – and coordinated these movements with meditational breathing routines. As the temple was isolated it was often prey to bandits, and gradually the monks turned their exercises into a form of self-defence.

The monks owed their strength to rigorous **discipline**. From childhood, monks trained from dawn to dusk, every day. To strengthen their hands, they thrust them into sacks of beans, over and over; when they were older, into bags of sand. To strengthen their fists, they punched a thousand sheets of paper glued to a wall; over the years, the paper wore out and the young monks punched brick. To strengthen their legs, they ran around the courtyard with bags of sand tied to their knees, and to strengthen their heads, they hit them with bricks.

Only after twenty years of such exercises could someone consider themselves proficient in kung fu, by which time they were able to perform incredible **feats**, examples of which you can see illustrated in the murals at the temple and in photographs of contemporary martial-arts masters in the picture books on sale in the souvenir shops. Apart from breaking concrete slabs with their fists and iron bars with their heads, the monks can balance on one finger, take a sledgehammer blow to the chest, and hang from a tree by their neck. Their **boxing routines** are equally extraordinary, their animal qualities clearly visible in the vicious clawing, poking, leaping and tearing that they employ. One comic-looking variation that requires a huge amount of flexibility is **drunken boxing**, where the performer twists, staggers and weaves as if inebriated – useful training given that Shaolin monks are allowed alcohol.

Yet the monks were not just fighters – their art was also intended as a technique to reach the goal of inner peace; as many hours were spent **meditating and praying** as in martial training. They obeyed a moral code, which included the stricture that only

poleaxes. The **ticket office** is hidden away on the left just before the huge stone archway; included in the price is entry to a **kung fu show**, which you shouldn't miss. Once through the gates, walk downhill where the road passes two huge open areas packed in the morning and afternoons with hundreds of **martial-arts students** in tracksuits, arranged in small groups and practising jumps, throws, kicks and weapons routines. Just on from here and to the right is the **kung fu show hall**, with performance times (around 5 daily) posted outside. The half-hour performance is a cut-down version of the stage show that regularly tours the world, with demonstrations of Shaolin's famous stick fighting and animal-style kung fu, all pretty electrifying if you haven't seen it before.

From here, it's about 500m to the **temple entrance** and a walkway past rows of steles commemorating visits by foreign kung fu schools (look, too, for trees here with holes drilled in the bark by kung fu practioners' fingers). At the end is a boxy pavilion housing two fearsome demon statues that tower overhead, fists raised, past which is the first courtyard. On the right here are two large glassed-in tablets from 728 AD, raised by the emperor **Taizong** after thirteen of Shaolin's monks had aided him against the rebel Wang Shichang; in gratitude, he passed an edict allowing monks at the temple to eat meat and drink wine. Another stele over towards the left has a wonderful, single brush-stroke image of Da Mo. The temple's succession of halls are quite small and simple, but two at the rear of the complex are worth attention: **Qianfo Hall**, whose brick floor is dented from where the monks used to stamp during their kung fu training; and the **White** fighting in self-defence was acceptable, and killing your opponent was to be avoided if possible. These rules became a little more flexible over the centuries as emperors and peasants alike sought their help in battles, and the Shaolin monks became legendary figures for their interventions on the side of righteousness.

The monks were at the height of their power in the Tang dynasty, though they were still a force to be reckoned with in the Ming, when **weapons** were added to their discipline – most famously their athletic stick routine. However, the temple was sacked during the 1920s and again in the 1960s during the Cultural Revolution, when the teaching of kung fu in China was **banned** and Shaolin's monks persecuted and dispersed. Things picked up again in the 1980s, when, as a result of Jet Li's enormously popular first film *Shaolin Temple*, there was a **resurgence** of interest in the art. The old masters were allowed to teach again, and the government realized that the temple was better exploited as a tourist resource than left to rot.

Evidence of the popularity of kung fu in China today can be seen not just at the tourist circus of the Shaolin Si, but in any cinema, where **kung fu films**, often concerning the exploits of Shaolin monks, make up a large proportion of the entertainment on offer. Many young Chinese today want to study kung fu, and to meet demand numerous **schools** have opened around the temple. Few of them want to be monks, though – the dream of many is to be a movie star.

Inevitably, such attention and exploitation has taken its toll on Shaolin Si's original purpose as a Buddhist monastery. While the monks here are undoubted skilled fighters, the temple's primary drive today is less towards the spiritual and more about the travelling shows and protecting commercial interests – they are currently pursuing efforts to trademark the name "Shaolin", in order to capitalize on its use by everything from martial-arts outfits to beer companies. For a good account of what it's like to live and train here, and the challenges that the modern temple faces, read *American Shaolin* by Matthew Polly (see p.988).

Robe Hall, where Ming-dynasty **murals** covering two walls depict Taizong being saved by the monks.

The **Ta Lin** (塔林, *tǎlín*), 200m farther up the hill past the temple entrance, is where hundreds of stone pagodas, memorials to past monks, are tightly grouped together in a "forest". Up to 10m tall, and with stepped, recessed tops, these golden stone structures look particularly impressive against the purple mountain when snow is on the ground. The earliest dates to 791 AD and commemorates a monk named Fawan, while the forest is still being added to as monks die.

Beyond here the mountain can be ascended by cable car or stone steps, but there is not much to see except the **cave** where Bodhidarma supposedly passed a nine-year vigil, sitting motionless facing a wall in a state of illumination (the mystic knowledge of the Nothingness of Everything). You can save yourself some effort by paying a few yuan to look at it from the road through a high-powered telescope.

Eating

The accommodation options on p.280 all have **restaurants**, but the best is the one at the *Zen International Hotel*, which offers huge vegetarian lunch buffets at ¥25 a head. Otherwise, there's not much to eat in the area beyond a few snacks sold at stalls along the main path. In Dengfeng, there are numerous dumpling places scattered around, or head to the frenetic **night market** in the lane directly facing the *Shaolin* hotel for street food.

Zhengzhou and around

Close to the south bank of the Yellow River, **ZHENGZHOU** (郑州, *zhèngzhōu*) lies almost midway between Luoyang to the west and Kaifeng to the east. The walled town that existed here 3500 years ago was probably an early capital of the Shang dynasty, and excavations have revealed bronze foundries, bone-carving workshops and sacrificial altars. Today's Zhengzhou, however, is an entirely modern city, rebuilt virtually from scratch after heavy bombing in the war against Japan. Despite the resultant dearth of historical sights, and the industrial trappings inevitably springing from a position atop China's two main rail routes, Zhengzhou is one of the most pleasant large cities in the Chinese interior, its broad, leafy avenues lined with shopping malls and boutiques. Kaifeng and Luoyang are easily accessible, and you can take a bus trip to Song Shan, but decent hotels and restaurants – and one excellent **museum** – mean Zhengzhou is worth a night's stay.

Arrival

Zhengzhou **airport** lies well to the east of the city; a taxi into the centre should cost ¥80, while hourly **CAAC buses** cost ¥15 and terminate at the Aviation Building on

Moving on from Zhengzhou

The main **CAAC ticket office** is at the Aviation Building, 3 Jinshui Lu (open 24hr; Ⓣ0371/5991111), where the airport bus departs from (see opposite). **Train tickets** can be hard to buy at the station due to the overwhelming crowds – there are advance-booking booths open from 8am–noon and 2.30–5pm up near the Henan Provincial Museum on Huayuan Lu, again on Huayuan Lu north of the Jinshui Lu intersection, and inside the regional bus station on Erma Lu, 500m north of the train station; see the map for locations. You can also book plane and train tickets through some accommodation, or from **Henan Tourism** (Ⓣ0371/65959892 or 68262900), north of the *Sofitel* on Jinshui Lu. **Bus tickets** to all major regional destinations are easy to get at the horde of windows surrounding the main bus station; **day-trips to Shaolin** leave from in front of the train station around 8am, when you'll find minibuses lined up.

Jinshui Lu, from where bus #26 will get you to the train station. The **train station** is fronted by a bustling square and faces the main **long-distance bus station**, though there are also the usual run of other depots scattered around the city's edges.

City transport

Work is now underway on a new **subway** system, with the first line scheduled for completion in 2013. Until then, visitors will have to stick to the city **bus** network – there are two clusters of **terminals** on either side of the square outside the train station – and **taxis**, which have a ¥7 minimum charge. **Maps** in Chinese with details of bus routes are available outside the train station.

Accommodation

If you've only come to Zhengzhou in transit, it makes sense to stay around the train station area, where there's plenty of inexpensive, decent accommodation, though it can get noisy. There are also a couple of motel and upmarket hotel options further out, in less crowded settings.

Home Inn (如家酒店, *rújiā jiǔdiàn*) 68 Chengdong Lu Ⓣ0371/66380188, Ⓦwww.homeinns.com. You can't miss this bright yellow, friendly motel, whose smart modern doubles have free wi-fi access and passably comfy beds. Bus #33 from the station stops nearby. ❹

Sofitel (索菲特国际饭店, *suǒfēitè guójì fàndiàn*) 289 Chengdong Lu Ⓣ0371/65950088, Ⓦwww.sofitel.com. Don't let the ugly exterior throw you – this is the most comfortable of Zhengzhou's five-stars, and the most popular with business travellers, thanks to appealing rooms and a clutch of excellent bars and restaurants. ❾

Tian'e (天鹅宾馆, *tiān'é bīnguǎn*) Ⓣ0371/66768599. There's one of these outside most large train stations in China – a blocky, bare-bones hotel with an enormous stack of budget rooms, including dormitories that staff are rarely willing to let foreigners anywhere near. ❹

Zhengzhou (郑州饭店, *zhèngzhōu fàndiàn*) 8 Xinglong Jie Ⓣ0371/66760038, Ⓕ66760469. Ahead and on the left as you leave the train station. A huge, fairly modern hotel with hundreds of rooms, which are well furnished and spacious, if a little under-maintained. Bargain and they drop the rate considerably. ❻

The City

The hub of downtown Zhengzhou is the **Erqi Pagoda** (二七塔, *èrqī tǎ*; daily 8.30am–6pm; ¥5), a twin-towered, seven-storey structure built to commemorate those killed in a 1923 Communist-led rail strike that was put down with great savagery by the warlord Wu Pei Fu. To the north, **Renmin Park** (人民公园, *rénmín gōngyuán*) is where to head if you need some space; there's paving everywhere but also plenty of trees.

East of the Erqi Pagoda, there's a remnant of **old Zhengzhou** in its ancient **city walls**, rough earthen ramparts 10m high, originally built more than two thousand years ago. There's a path along the top, and you can walk for about 3km along the south and east sections (the west section has been destroyed by development), descending to cross the main roads along the way. Planted with trees, the walls are now used by the locals as a short cut and a park, full of courting couples, kids who slide down the steep sides on metal trays, and old men who hang their cagebirds from the trees and sit around fires cooking sweet potatoes. Indeed, the charm of the wall comes from the way it has been incorporated by the inhabitants – it doesn't seem to occur to anyone to treat it as a historical monument. While you're in the area, **Chenghuang Miao** (城隍庙, *chénghuáng miaò*; daily 8am–6pm), on the north side of Shangcheng Lu, is worth a look as the most interesting of Zhengzhou's temples, with well-observed images of birds decorating the eaves of the first hall, underneath roof sculptures of dragons and phoenixes. Murals in the modern Main Hall owe much to 1950s socialist realism, and surround a sculpture of a stern-looking Chenghuang, magisterial defender of city folk, who sits flanked by two attendants.

Zhenghou's modern face is perhaps best appreciated a way to the east, at **Ruyi Lake** (如意湖; *rú yì hú*), whose western shore is fringed with parkland, as well as the five huge, golden egg-buildings that make up the new **Henan Art Center**.

Henan Provincial Museum

A giant stone pyramid at the northern end of Jingqi Lu, the modern **Henan Provincial Museum** (河南省博物院, *hénánshěng bówùyuàn*; daily 8.30am–6.15pm; ¥20; English audio-guide ¥30) boasts an outstanding collection of relics unearthed in the region, dating back to when Henan was the cradle of Chinese civilization. As you move clockwise, each hall covers a particular stage of regional history, beginning with the stone age: look for **oracle bones** inscribed with the ancestors of modern Chinese script unearthed from **Anyang**, 200km north of Zhengzhou, site of China's Shang-dynasty capital; and some outstanding **bronzes**, from the Shang to Tang periods, including large tripods and tiny animal figures used as weights. By far the most interesting pieces, however, are the **Han pottery**, with scale models of houses showing defensive walls and towers, models of domestic animals, and huge numbers of human figurines – dancers, musicians, soldiers, court ladies – all leaving the impression that the Han were an articulate, fun-loving people who liked to show off. To get here, take bus #32 from the south side of the train-station area.

Eating, drinking and entertainment

Zhengzhou has abundant **eating options**. Around the train station there are plenty of small **noodle and snack restaurants**, all much the same, and enormous numbers of shops selling travellers' nibbles – walnuts, oranges and dates – which testify to the great number of people passing through here every day. For something a bit smarter, there's the popular *Huayuchuan* restaurant (华豫川酒家, *huáyùchuān jiǔjiā*) at 59 Erqi Lu, a Sichuanese chain with a photo menu and well-presented dishes such as tea-smoked duck and garlic pork costing around ¥20; and the *Kaoya Dian* (烤鸭店, *kǎoyādiàn*) just up the road, which is where to get Beijing-style roast duck. Another good option is the *Wenxin Canyin* (温馨餐饮, *wēnxīn cānyǐn*), a regional restaurant up near the museum on Jinqi Lu, packed out at lunchtime. Pricey Shandong cuisine can be had at the *Jingya* (净雅, *jìng yǎ*), more or less opposite the *Sofitel* on Chengdong Lu.

For an evening **drink**, there are numerous bars off Jingliu Lu, the two best being *Garden Lounge* (known locally as *Amy's*), and the *Target Pub*. These are also the best places to head for up-to-date information about the clubbing scene.

Listings

Banks and exchange The main Bank of China is on Jinshui Lu; the closest branch to southern accommodation is on Dong Dajie – both have ATMs.
Mail and telephones The principal post office (Mon–Fri 8am–8pm) is next to the train station on the south side, with a 24hr telecom office next door.
PSB The visa section is at 70 Erqi Lu (Mon–Fri 8.30am–noon & 3–6pm; ⓣ0371/69620359).

The Yellow River Scenic Area

Zhengzhou is one of the most convenient bases from which to view the famed Yellow River , which slides by just 28km to the north. Bus #16, which leaves from Minggong Lu just outside Zhengzhou's train station, terminates at the **Yellow River Scenic Area** (黄河公园, *huánghé gōngyuán*; daily 8am–6pm; ¥40), really a stretch of typical Chinese countryside, incorporating villages and allotments, that you have to pay to get into because it has a view of the river. Despite the waterway's dusty environs, and the pancake-flat terrain stretching into the distance from its north bank, parts of this large scenic area are surprisingly verdant, incorporating forested hills, crumbly temple buildings, lakeside pavilions and large statues of dynastic emperors (including one Mount Rushmore-like design). You can spend an afternoon here walking, horse-trekking – an escorted, hour-long trot should cost about ¥20 – or taking a speedboat ride along the river. From the hilltops you have a good view over the river and the plain of mud either side of it. It's hard to imagine that in 1937, when Chiang Kai-shek breached the dykes 8km from the city to prevent the Japanese capturing the rail line, the Yellow River flooded this great plain, leaving more than a million dead and countless more homeless.

Kaifeng

Located on the alluvial plains in the middle reaches of the Yellow River 70km east of Zhengzhou, **KAIFENG** (开封, *kāifēng*) is an ancient capital with a history stretching back over three thousand years. However, unlike other ancient capitals in the area, the city hasn't grown into an industrial monster, and remains pleasingly compact, with most of its sights in a fairly small area within the walls. While not an especially attractive town, its low-key ambience and sprinkling of older temples and pagodas encourage a wander, and the longer you stay, the more you register the town's distinctive local character. In all, this a worthwhile place to spend a couple of days, especially if you've grown weary of the scale and pace of most Chinese cities.

Some history

First heard of as a Shang town around 1000 BC, Kaifeng had its heyday during the Song dynasty between 960 and 1127 AD, when the city became the political, economic and cultural centre of the empire. A famous 5m-long horizontal **scroll** by Zhang Azheduan, *Qingming Shang He* (*Along the River at the Qingming Festival*), now in the Forbidden City in Beijing, unrolls to show views of the city at this time, teeming with life, crammed with people, boats, carts and animals. It was a great age for painting, calligraphy, philosophy and poetry, and Kaifeng was famed for the quality of its textiles and embroidery, and for its production of ceramics and printed books. It was also the home of the first mechanical timepiece in history, Su Song's **astronomical clock tower** of 1092, which worked by the transmission of energy from a huge water wheel.

Some of this artistic heritage survives – the nearby town of Zhuxian Zhen is still known for its **New Year woodblock prints** – but Kaifeng's Golden Age ended

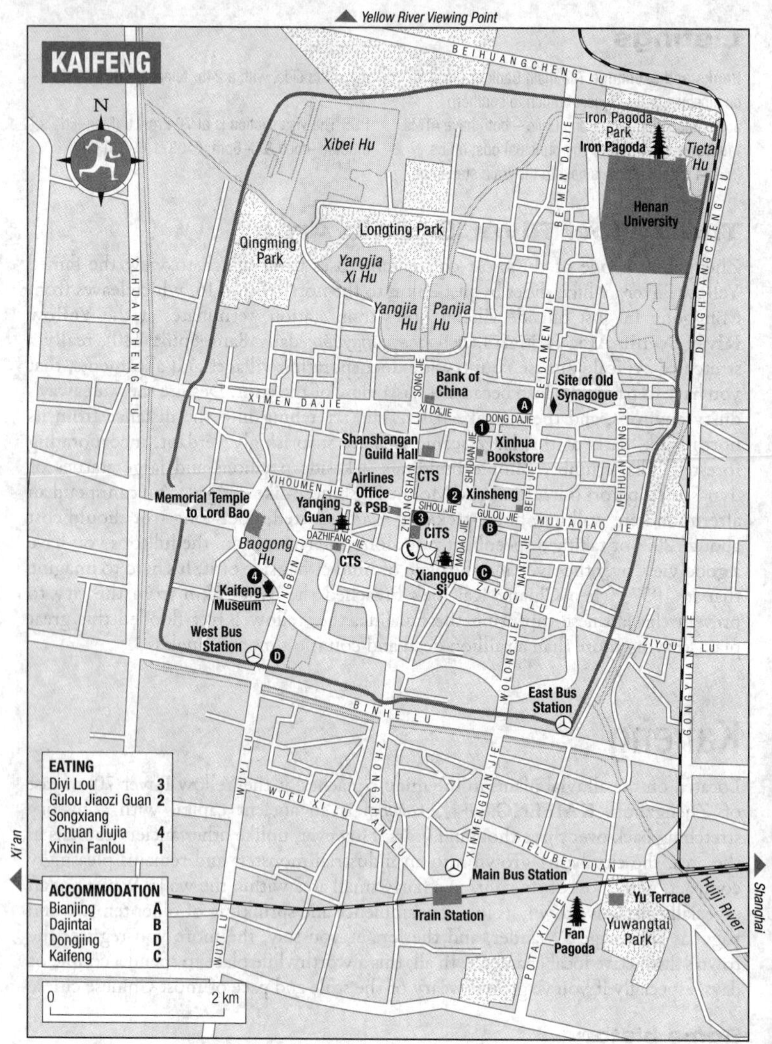

suddenly in 1127 when Jurchen invaders overran the city. Just one royal prince escaped to the south, to set up a new capital out of harm's reach at Hangzhou beyond the Yangzi, though Kaifeng itself never recovered. What survived has been damaged or destroyed by repeated **flooding** since – between 1194 and 1887 there were more than fifty severe incidents, including one fearful occasion when the dykes were breached during a siege and at least 300,000 people are said to have died, among which were many of Kaifeng's **Jewish community**.

Arrival and city transport

The **train station**, on the Xi'an–Shanghai line, is in a dull, utilitarian area outside the walls, about 2km south of the centre. The main long-distance **bus station** is

Moving on from Kaifeng

The nearest **airport** to Kaifeng is Zhengzhou; buy air tickets at the CAAC office (8am–7pm; ⓣ0378/5955555) at the southwest corner of Zhongshan Lu and Sihou Jie. The **train station** is small and not too hard to figure out; buy tickets here or through CITS or CTS if your accommodation can't help. Most **buses** departing for major destinations leave from the main station, though if you're heading to Zhengzhou or Heze (for connections to Qufu in Shandong) try the west station first.

here, too, though you might also wind up at the smaller west or east bus stations, near the southern walls – all are on **city bus routes**. You can bargain with a rickshaw or taxi (¥5–10) for a ride to accommodation from any of the stations. **Maps** of Kaifeng cost around ¥3 at arrival points.

Accommodation

Despite Kaifeng's small size, it has several good-value **hotels**, though bargain motels have yet to put in an appearance. The *Dajintai* is the budget hotel of choice.

Bianjing (汴京饭店, *biànjīng fàndiàn*) Corner of Dong Dajie and Beidamen Jie ⓣ0378/2886699, ⓕ2882449. Bus #3 from the train station. A large, pink-and-white wedding cake of a place, which recent renovations have given pretensions to luxury. ❺

Dajintai (大金台旅馆, *dàjīntái lǚguǎn*) Gulou Dajie ⓣ0378/2552888. On the route of bus #4. In the heart of the night market and most interesting section of town, this hotel dates from the end of the Qing dynasty, and is the best budget place to stay. Try to score one of the comfy renovated doubles. Dorm beds ¥60, rooms ❸

Dongjing (东京大饭店, *dōngjīng dàfàndiàn*)14 Yingbin Lu ⓣ0378/3989388, ⓕ3938861. A short walk from the west bus station, and buses #1 and #9 come here from the train station. This compound of buildings, set in a park just inside the walls in the south of the city, looks like a health sanatorium, and is suitably quiet, low-key and comfortable, with a good range of services, including a post office. ❹

Kaifeng (开封宾馆, *kāifēng bīnguǎn*) 66 Ziyou Lu ⓣ0378/5955589, ⓦwww.kaifengbinguan.com. Bus #9 from the train station. This central, three-star hotel in a large, attractive compound off the street is where most tour groups end up. It has four buildings and a range of rooms, including triples and quads. Comfortable without being ostentatious, and surprisingly inexpensive. ❺

The Town

Central Kaifeng, bounded by walls roughly 3km long at each side, is fairly small, and most places of interest lie within walking distance of one another. The town is crisscrossed by canals, once part of a network that connected it to Hangzhou and Yangzhou in ancient times.

The **town walls**, tamped earth ramparts, have been heavily damaged and there's no path along them, but they do present a useful landmark. **Shudian Jie** – Bookshop Street – is at the centre of town, a scruffy run of two-storey imitation Qing buildings with fancy balconies. Many shops here do indeed sell books, from art monographs to pulp fiction with lurid covers. In the evening, the street transforms into a busy **night market**, when brightly lit stalls selling mostly underwear, cosmetics and plastic kitchenware line its length; it's somewhere to join the locals for a wander and to feast from the numerous **food stalls** that set up around the crossroads with Sihou Jie (see p.292).

Some of Kaifeng's most interesting old buildings are in this area, too. In a lane running west off Shudian Jie to parallel Zhongshan Lu, the **Shanshangan Guild Hall** (陕山甘会馆, *shǎnshāngān huìguǎn*; daily 8am–6.30pm; ¥20) is a superb example of Qing-dynasty architecture at its most lavish. It was established by

Kaifeng's Jews

A number of families in Kaifeng trace their lineage back to the **Jews**, though these origins remain a mystery. It's likely that their ancestors came here from central Asia around 1000 AD, when trade links between the two areas were strong. The community was never large, but it seems to have flourished until the nineteenth century, when – perhaps as a result of disastrous floods, including one in 1850 that destroyed the synagogue – the Kaifeng Jews almost completely died out. However, following the atmosphere of greater religious tolerance in contemporary China, many Jews have begun practising their faith again. You can see a few relics from the synagogue in the museum, including three steles that once stood outside it, but most, such as a *Torah* in Chinese now in the British Museum, are in collections abroad.

merchants of Shanxi, Shaanxi and Gansu provinces as a social centre and has the structure of a flashy, ostentatious temple. The woodcarvings on the eaves are excellent, including lively and rather wry scenes from the life of a travelling merchant – look for the man being dragged along the ground by his horse in the Eastern Hall – and groups of gold bats (a symbol of luck) beneath images of animals and birds frolicking among bunches of grapes.

Head back on to Shudian Jie and walk two blocks south and you reach Ziyou Lu, just east along which you'll find the **Xiangguo Si** (相国寺, *xiàngguó sì*; daily 7am–7pm; ¥30), which was founded in 555 AD. The simple buildings here today are Qing style, with a colourful, modern frieze of *arhats* at the back of the Main Hall, and an early Song-dynasty bronze Buddha in the Daxiong Baodian (Great Treasure House). In an unusual octagonal hall at the back you'll see a magnificent four-sided Guanyin carved in ginkgo wood and covered in gold leaf, about 3m high.

A kilometre west, along Ziyou Lu, is the **Yanqing Guan** (延庆观, *yánqìng guān*; daily 8am–7pm; ¥15), whose rather odd, knobbly central building, the **Pavilion of the Jade Emperor**, is all that remains of a larger complex built at the end of the thirteenth century. The outside of this octagonal structure of turquoise tiles and carved brick is overlaid with ornate decorative touches; inside, a bronze image of the Jade Emperor sits in a room that is by contrast strikingly austere. The rest of the complex looks just as old, though the images of kangaroos among the animals decorating the eaves suggest otherwise.

Baogong Hu

Within walking distance of Yanqing Guan is **Baogong Hu** (包公湖, *bāogōng hú*), one of the large lakes inside Kaifeng, whose undisturbed space helps give the town its laidback feel. On a promontory on the western side, and looking very attractive from a distance, the **Memorial Temple to Lord Bao** (包公祠, *bāogōng cí*; daily 8am–6pm; ¥20) is a modern imitation of a Song building holding an exhibition of the life of this legendary figure who was Governor of Kaifeng during the Northern Song. Judging from the articles exhibited, including modern copies of ancient guillotines, and the scenes from his life depicted in paintings and waxworks, Lord Bao was a harsh but fair judge, who must have had some difficulty getting through doors if he really wore a hat and shoes like the ones on display. A substantial mansion on the south side of the lake, the **Kaifeng Museum** (开封博物馆, *kāifēng bówùguăn*; daily 8.30–11.30am & 2.30–5.30pm; ¥10), holds steles recording the history of Kaifeng's Jewish community that used to stand outside the synagogue, and a good exhibition of local folk art.

Song Jie, Yangjia Hu, Qingming and Longting parks

At the north end of Zhongshan Lu and under a stone archway, **Song Jie** (宋都御街, *sòngdū yùjiē*) is a street of antique-style tourist shops built over the site of the Song-dynasty Imperial Palace. The shops sell handmade paper, paintings, reproduction classical scrolls and, around Chinese New Year, brightly coloured woodblock prints of animals and legendary figures, which people paste on their doors for good luck. In the winter, when the tourists have gone, many of the shops switch to selling household goods.

Song Jie runs up to a large **plaza**, often full of people strolling and flying kites, beyond which is **Yangjia Hu** (杨家户, *yángjiā hú*), originally part of the imperial gardens but now at the centre of a large warren of carnival-like tourist traps arranged around the lakeshore. At **Qingming Park** (清明上河园, *qīngmíng shànghéyuán*; daily 9am–10pm; ¥80), west of the lake, you can walk through a realized version of *Qingming Shang He*, wandering to your heart's content past costumed courtesans and ingratiating shopkeepers. **Longting Park** (龙亭公园, *lóngtíng gōngyuán*; daily 6am–6.30pm; ¥35), across the causeway and on the northern shore of Yangjia Hu, has a somewhat desolate feel, though it makes for good people-watching when the crowds are out.

Iron Pagoda Park

From the centre of town, buses #1 and #3 go to the far northeast corner of the city walls, to **Iron Pagoda Park** (铁塔公园, *tiětǎ gōngyuán*; daily 8am–6pm; ¥20), which is only accessible off Beimen Dajie. At its centre you'll find the 13-storey, 56m-high **Iron Pagoda** that gives it its name, a striking Northern Song (1049 AD) construction so named because its surface of glazed tiles gives the building the russet tones of rusted iron. Its base, like all early buildings in Kaifeng, is buried beneath a couple of metres of silt deposited during floods. Most of the tiles hold relief images, usually of the Buddha, but also of Buddhist angels, animals and abstract patterns. You can climb up the inside for an extra ¥10.

Outside the walls

Three kilometres southeast of the city centre – a cab is the best way to get here, as it's a dusty, drab walk – **Yuwangtai Park** (禹王台公园, *yǔwángtái gōngyuán*; daily 7am–7pm; ¥10) surrounds the **Yu Terrace**, an earthen mound now thought to have been a music terrace that was once the haunt of Tang poets. The park, dotted with pavilions and commemorative steles, is pleasant in summer when the many flower gardens are in bloom.

Not far from here, its top visible from the park, the **Fan Pagoda** (繁塔, *fán tǎ*; 7am–7pm; ¥5) is not in a park as maps say, but sits between a car repair yard and a set of courtyards in a suburbia of labyrinthine alleyways; the only approach is from the western side. The fact that the local inhabitants tie their washing lines to the wall around the base and peel sweetcorn in the courtyard adds to the charm of the place. Built in 997 AD, and the oldest standing building in Kaifeng, this dumpy hexagonal brick pagoda was once 80m tall and had nine storeys; three remain today, and you can ascend for a view of rooftops and factories.

From a bus station on the west side of Beimen Dajie, opposite the entrance to the Iron Pagoda Park, it's worth catching bus #6 to the **Yellow River Viewing Point** (黄河公园, *huánghé gōngyuán*), 11km north of town, especially if you haven't seen the river before. From the pavilion here you can look out onto a plain of silt that stretches to the horizon, across whose dramatic emptiness the syrupy river meanders. Beside the pavilion is an **iron ox**, which once stood in a now submerged temple. It's a cuddly looking beast with a horn on its head that makes it look like a rhino sitting on its hind legs. An inscription on the back reveals its original function – as a charm to ward off floods, a tradition begun by the legendary flood-tamer Da Yu (see p.208).

Eating

The best **place to eat** is the **night market** on Shudian Jie, where the food, as well as the ambience, is good. Here you'll find not just the usual staples such as *jiaozi*, made in front of you, and skewers of mutton cooked by Uyghur peddlers, but also a local **delicacy** consisting of hot liquid **jelly**, into which nuts, berries, flowers and fruit are poured. You can spot jelly stalls by the huge bronze kettle they all have, with a spout in the form of a dragon's head. There's also a good veggie restaurant in the grounds of the Xiangguo Si (p.290), while those visiting during the Mid-Autumn Festival should look out for Kaifeng's unique **mooncakes** – the usual thickness, but nearly half a metre wide.

Diyi Lou (第一楼, *dìyīlóu*) 43 Sihou Jie. This smart spot is famous for its *baozi*, but in autumn also serves delicious little river crabs stir-fried with chillies, which you eat whole, shells and all. Dinner for two with drinks should come to around ¥60.

Gulou Jiaozi Guan (鼓楼饺子馆, *gŭlóu jiăoziguăn*) Corner of Shudian Jie and Sihou Jie. Housed in a mock Qing structure at the corner of Gulou Jie and Shudian Jie, this three-storey venue whips up round after round of succulent dumplings, and boasts tremendous views of the night market from its upper levels.

Songxiang Chuan Jiujia (宋像川酒家, *sòngxiàngchuān jiŭjiā*) A good, straightforward Sichuanese restaurant just on the corner of Yingbin Lu, and the best bet should you need lunch near the museum.

Xinxin Fanlou (新新饭楼, *xīnxīn fànlóu*) At the north end of Shudian Jie near the intersection with Dong Dajie, this is a busy Muslim place selling *baozi* at ¥5 a steamer and roast duck for just ¥40.

Listings

Banks and exchange The main Bank of China is on the corner of Xi Dajie and Song Jie, and there are several major banks with ATMs on Zhongshan Lu.
Bookshops Shudian Jie is lined with shops catering to most tastes. The Xinhua Bookstore, on the east side of the street just north of Xi Dajie, has a limited selection of English books, but they do sell good maps.
Internet A large, clean internet bar (24hr; ¥1.5/hr) is just down the alley behind the PSB office.
Mail and telephones There's a large post office (Mon–Fri 8am–noon & 2.30–6pm) on Ziyou Lu, with a 24hr telecom office next door.
PSB The main police station is on Zhongshan Lu. Windows #3 and #4 deal with visas; a visa extension (¥120) can take 10min.
Shopping Kaifeng is a good place to find paintings and calligraphy, among the best buys in China. The obvious thing to pick up is a full-size reproduction of the *Qingming Shang He* scroll, which shouldn't set you back more than ¥50. Try the shops on Song Jie and stalls at the night market on Shudian Jie.
Travel agents CTS have an office directly opposite Yanqing Guan on Dazhifang Jie (ⓣ0378/3931861 or 3268689). The CITS (ⓣ0378/5650712, ⓕ5650711) are across from the PSB on Zhongshan Lu; the only thing you'll possibly need them for is buying train tickets.

Travel details

Trains

Times given are for the fastest possible connections; there are usually slower services available at a slightly cheaper price.

Baotou to: Beijing (many daily; 12hr); Dongsheng (4 daily; 2hr); Hohhot (many daily; 2hr); Lanzhou (3 daily; 15hr); Yinchuan (5 daily; 7hr).

Datong to: Baotou (many daily; 6hr); Beijing (many daily; 6hr); Hohhot (many daily; 4hr); Lanzhou (1 daily; 21hr); Linfen (5 daily; 10hr); Taiyuan (12 daily; 5hr 30min); Xi'an (2 daily; 17hr).

Hohhot to: Baotou (many daily; 2hr); Beijing (many daily; 10hr); Taiyuan (2 daily; 12hr);

Ulan Bator (daily; 25hr); Xi'an (daily; 21hr).
Hua Shan to: Xi'an (many daily; 50min); Yuncheng (7 daily; 1hr 50min).
Kaifeng to: Shanghai (11 daily; 6hr 30min); Xi'an (many daily; 7hr); Yanzhou (7 daily; 3hr 15min); Zhengzhou (many daily; 30min).
Luoyang to: Beijing (7 daily; 7hr 15min); Shanghai (7 daily; 14hr); Xi'an (many daily; 4hr 30min); Zhengzhou (many daily; 1hr 30min).
Pingyao Beijing (3 daily; 12hr); Taiyuan (hourly; 1hr 20min).
Taiyuan to: Beijing (16 daily; 3hr 10min); Datong (12 daily; 5hr 30min); Luoyang (2 daily; 11hr 40min); Pingyao (hourly; 1hr 20min); Xi'an (5 daily; 10hr); Zhengzhou (4 daily; 4hr 30min).
Xi'an to: Baoji (many daily; 1hr 20min); Beijing (11 daily; 11hr); Datong (2 daily; 16hr); Guangzhou (5 daily; 22hr); Hua Shan (many daily; 50min); Lanzhou (many daily; 6hr 20min); Luoyang (many daily; 4hr 30min); Shanghai (10 daily; 14hr); Taiyuan (5 daily; 10hr); Ürümqi (10 daily; 28hr); Xining (10 daily; 9hr); Zhengzhou (many daily; 2hr).
Yinchuan to: Baotou (5 daily; 7hr); Beijing (4 daily; 19hr); Guyuan (5 daily; 6hr 30min); Lanzhou (4 daily; 8hr); Xi'an (4 daily; 14hr); Zhongwei (10 daily; 2hr 30min).
Zhengzhou to: Beijing (many daily; 5hr); Guangzhou (16 daily; 15hr); Luoyang (many daily; 1hr 30min); Shanghai (17 daily; 7hr); Taiyuan (4 daily; 4hr); Xi'an (many daily; 2hr).
Zhongwei to: Guyuan (7 daily; 4hr); Hohhot (3 daily; 11hr); Lanzhou (5 daily; 6hr); Yinchuan (10 daily; 2hr 30min); Wuwei (3 daily; 4hr).

Buses

Baotou to: Dongsheng (hourly; 2hr 30min); Hohhot (every 30min; 2hr 30min).
Datong to: Taiyuan (3hr 30min); Wutai Shan (5hr).
Dengfeng to: Luoyang (1hr 20min); Zhengzhou (1hr 30min).
Hohhot to: Baotou (every 30min; 2hr 30min).
Kaifeng to: Heze (for Qufu or Ji'nan; 3hr); Zhengzhou (1hr 30min).
Linfen to: Pingyao (3hr); Taiyuan (3hr); Yuncheng (3hr).
Luoyang to: Dengfeng (1hr 20min); Ruicheng (4hr); Yuncheng (4hr).
Pingyao to: Taiyuan (2 hr); Xi'an (7hr).
Taiyuan to: Datong (3hr 30min); Pingyao (2hr); Wutai Shan (4hr); Yuncheng (7hr).
Xi'an to: Hua Shan (2hr 30min); Pingyao (7hr); Ruicheng (3hr).
Yinchuan to: Guyuan (7hr); Lanzhou (14hr); Xi'an (12hr); Zhongwei (4hr).
Yuncheng to: Linfen (3hr); Ruicheng (2hr); Taiyuan (4hr 30min); Xi'an (3hr).
Zhengzhou to: Dengfeng (1hr 30min); Kaifeng (1hr 30min); Luoyang (2hr 30min).
Zhongwei to: Guyuan (5hr); Shapotou (1hr); Yinchuan (3hr).

Flights

Among international connections from this part of China, there are flights from Hohhot (Ulan Batur), Ji'nan (Seoul, Singapore), Qingdao (Busan, Fukuoka, Nagoya, Osaka, Seoul, Taipei, Tokyo), Xi'an (Bangkok, Busan, Fukuoka, Nagoya, Seoul, Taipei, Tokyo) and Zhengzhou (Bangkok, Kuala Lumpur, Seoul, Taipei).
Baotou to: Beijing (3 daily; 55min); Shanghai (2 daily; 2hr 25min).
Datong to: Beijing (daily; 1hr); Shanghai (2 weekly; 2hr 10min).
Hohhot to: Beijing (9 daily; 1hr 10min); Guangzhou (1–3 daily; 3hr); Shanghai (5 daily; 2hr 30min); Shenyang (1–3 daily; 1hr 30min); Shenzhen (2–3 daily; 3hr); Tianjin (2–4 daily; 1hr); Xi'an (2 daily; 1hr 30min).
Luoyang to: Beijing (2 daily; 1hr 30min); Chengdu (3 weekly; 1hr 50min); Guangzhou (4 weekly; 2hr); Hangzhou (3 weekly; 1hr 40min); Shanghai (daily; 1hr 30min); Shenzhen (2 weekly; 2hr).
Taiyuan to: Beijing (7 daily; 1hr); Chengdu (2–3 daily; 2hr); Chongqing (3 daily; 1hr 50min); Guangzhou (6–7 daily; 2hr 40min); Nanjing (6–7 daily; 1hr 35min); Shanghai (10 daily; 1hr 55min); Tianjin (3 daily; 1hr); Xi'an (2–4 daily; 1hr).
Xi'an to: Beijing (hourly; 2hr); Chengdu (8 daily; 50min); Chongqing (8–9 daily; 1hr 15min); Dalian (3–4 daily; 2hr); Dunhuang (2–3 daily; 2hr 50min); Guangzhou (11–13 daily; 2hr 25min); Guilin (6 daily; 1hr 40min); Hong Kong (3 daily; 2hr 30min); Ji'nan (3–4 daily; 1hr 30min); Kunming (2–3 daily; 2hr); Lanzhou (6–8 daily; 1hr 10min); Nanjing (7 daily; 1hr 50min); Qingdao (5–6 daily; 1hr 50min); Shanghai (hourly; 1hr 50min); Taiyuan (2–4 daily; 1hr).
Yinchuan to: Beijing (9 daily; 2hr); Chengdu (2 daily; 2hr); Guangzhou (4 weekly; 4hr); Lanzhou (daily; 50min); Nanjing (2 daily; 3hr 30min); Shanghai (daily; 3hr 30min); Ürümqi (3 daily; 3hr); Xi'an (12 daily; 50min).
Zhengzhou to: Beijing (7 daily; 1hr 10min); Chengdu (3–4 daily; 1hr 40min); Chongqing (5 daily; 1hr 40min); Guangzhou (9 daily; 2hr); Hong Kong (daily; 2hr 35min); Kunming (6 daily; 2hr 20min); Lanzhou (3 daily; 1hr 40min); Nanjing (2 daily; 1hr); Qingdao (3 daily; 1hr 10min); Shanghai (11 daily; 1hr 40min).

CHAPTER 5

Highlights

✱ **Wangfu Chizi, Ji'nan** Swim with China's fittest pensioners at this open-air pool, fed by hot springs. **See p.300**

✱ **The Grand Canal** The original source of the region's wealth, and a construction feat to rival the Great Wall. **See p.324**

✱ **Suzhou** A striking medley of tree-lined canals, ramshackle homes, old stone bridges and hi-tech factories. **See p.335**

✱ **Xi Hu, Hangzhou** You will get great vistas from this beautiful lake, best appreciated by cycling the area. **See p.347**

✱ **Moganshan** An old colonial hill resort that has become fashionable as a summer retreat – it's a great spot for a brisk hike. **See p.352**

✱ **Shaoxing** Charismatic backwater once home to writer Lu Xun, whose elegant mansion – now a museum – offers a glimpse into a vanished world. **See p.353**

✱ **Putuo Shan** A tranquil island of Buddhist temples and beaches. **See p.356**

▲ Traditional riverside houses in Suzhou

5

The eastern seaboard

China's eastern seaboard stretches for almost 2000km between the mouths of the Yellow and Yangzi rivers, both of which have played a vital role in the country's history. The murky Yellow River finally pours into the sea from **Shandong** province, and its dusty basin provided China with its original heartland. However, it was the greenness and fertility of the **Yangzi River estuary** that drew its people south, and provided them with the wealth and power needed to sustain a huge empire. The provinces of **Jiangsu** and **Zhejiang**, which today flank the metropolitan area of Shanghai (see p.363), have played a vital part in the cultural and economic development of China for the last two thousand years. No tour of eastern China would be complete without stopovers in some of their classic destinations.

Shandong province is home to some small and intriguing places: **Qufu**, the birthplace of Confucius, with its giant temple and mansion; **Tai Shan**, the most popular holy mountain in the area; and the coastal city of **Qingdao**, which offers a couple of beaches and a ferry service to South Korea. Over in **Jiangsu** province there's **Nanjing**, China's large but likeable "southern capital", and wonderful **Suzhou**, whose centre is crisscrossed by gorgeous **canals**, and dotted with classically designed **gardens**. Heading further south to Zhejiang province one will undoubtedly stumble across **Hangzhou**, which Marco Polo termed "the most beautiful and magnificent city in the world"; its Xi Hu (West Lake), still recognizable from classic scroll paintings, is deservedly rated as one of the most scenic spots in China. The same can be said of the enchanting island of **Putuo Shan**, which juts out of the sea just east of the mainland.

The prosperity of the region means that its **accommodation** is on the expensive side, with the cheapest hotels dipping only slightly below ¥200 for a double room – though there are excellent youth hostels in almost all tourist centres. The downside of this relative affluence means that the area suffers from chronic **overpopulation** – including Shanghai, the eastern seaboard is home to going on for 250 million people, meaning that if somehow cleaved from China it would be the **world's fourth most populous country**; Shandong alone would rank twelfth. However, this makes for excellent **transport** connections: comfortable modern buses run along the many intercity expressways, and are often the best way to make relatively short trips, while train connections are also good, with a growing number of high-speed lines.

Shandong's **climate** is more or less proximate to that of Beijing, but the area around the Yangzi River, despite being low-lying and far from the northern plains, is unpleasantly cold and damp in winter, and unbearably hot and sticky during the summer months when most people choose to visit – Nanjing's age-old reputation as one of the "three furnaces" of China is well justified. If possible, try to visit in **spring** (mid-April to late May), during which a combination of rain

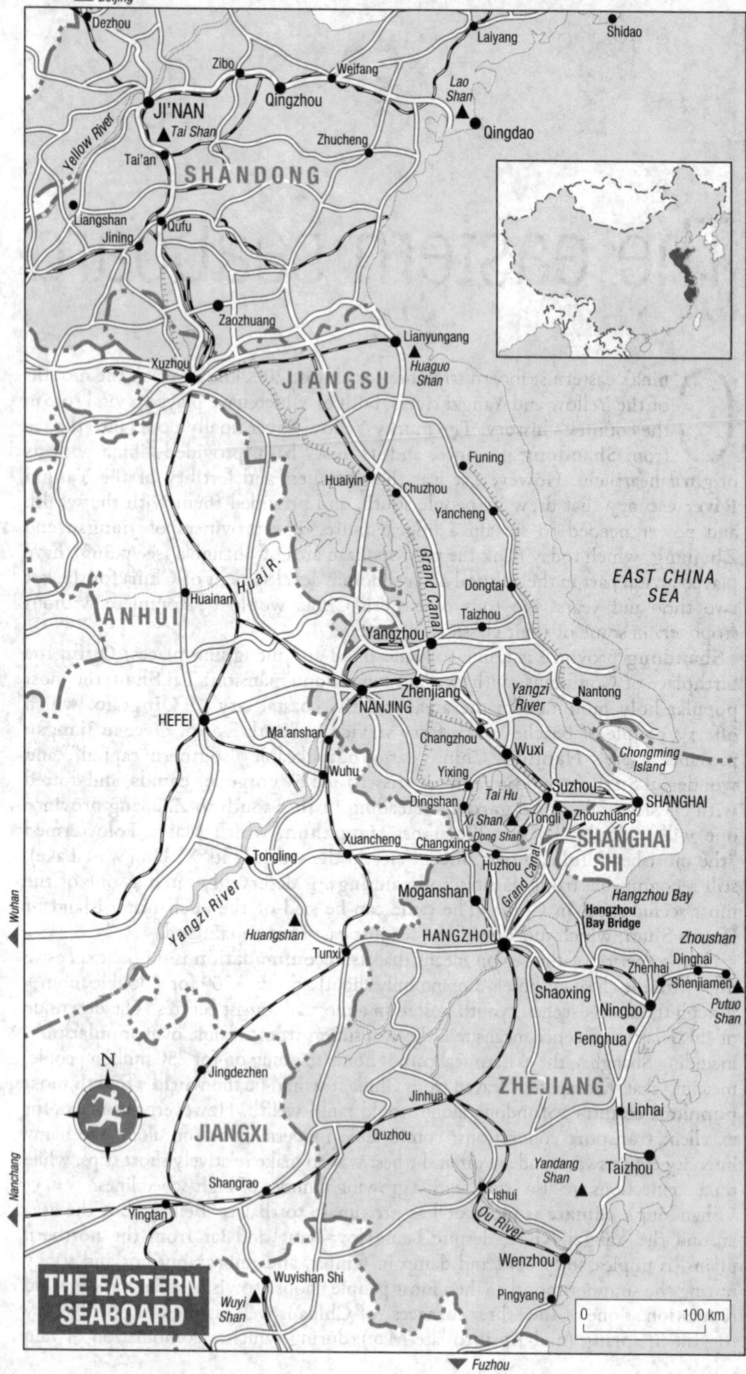
THE EASTERN SEABOARD
Beijing
Dezhou
Laiyang
Shidao
Zibo
Weifang
JI'NAN
Qingzhou
Lao Shan
Qingdao
Yellow River
Tai Shan
Zhucheng
Tai'an
SHANDONG
Liangshan
Qufu
Jining
Zaozhuang
Lianyungang
Huaguo Shan
Xuzhou
JIANGSU
Funing
Huaiyin
Chuzhou
Yancheng
Grand Canal
EAST CHINA SEA
Huai R.
Dongtai
Huainan
ANHUI
Taizhou
Yangzhou
Zhenjiang
Yangzi River
Nantong
NANJING
HEFEI
Ma'anshan
Changzhou
Wuxi
Chongming Island
Wuhu
Yixing
Tai Hu
Suzhou
SHANGHAI
Dingshan
Xi Shan
Tongli
Zhouzhuang
Xuancheng
Changxing
Dong Shan
SHANGHAI SHI
Tongling
Huzhou
Moganshan
Hangzhou Bay
Hangzhou Bay Bridge
Wuhan
Yangzi River
Huangshan
HANGZHOU
Zhoushan
Tunxi
Dinghai
Zhenhai
Shenjiamen
Shaoxing
Putuo Shan
Ningbo
Fenghua
N
Jingdezhen
ZHEJIANG
Jinhua
Linhai
JIANGXI
Quzhou
Nanchang
Yandang Shan
Taizhou
Shangrao
Lishui
Yingtan
Ou River
Wenzhou
Wuyishan Shi
Wuyi Shan
Pingyang
0
100 km
Fuzhou

showers, sunshine and low humidity gives the terrain a splash of green as well as putting smiles on the faces of residents emerging from the harsh winter.

Some history

The fertility of the Yellow River flood plain means that human settlements have existed in Shandong for more than six thousand years, with **Neolithic remains** indicating a sophisticated agricultural society. In the Warring States Period (720–221 BC), Shandong included the states of Qi and Lu, and the province is well endowed with **ancient tombs and temples**, not least thanks to the efforts of its most illustrious son, **Confucius**.

The story of the Yangzi basin begins in the sixth century BC when the area was part of the state of Wu and had already developed its own distinct culture. The flat terrain, the large crop yield and the superb communications offered by coastal ports and navigable waterways enabled the principal towns of the area to develop quickly into important **trading centres**. These presented an irresistible target for the expanding Chinese empire under the Qin dynasty, and in 223 BC the region was annexed, immediately developing into one of the economic centres of the empire. After the end of the Han dynasty in the third century AD, several regimes established short-lived capitals in southern cities; however, the real boost for southern China came when the Sui (589–618 AD) extended the **Grand Canal** to link the Yangzi with the Yellow River and, ultimately, to allow trade to flow freely between here and the northern capitals. With this, China's centre of gravity took a decisive shift south. Under later dynasties, Hangzhou and then Nanjing became the greatest cities in China, each serving as capital of the country at some point, and acting as counter-weights to the bureaucratic tendencies of Beijing since its own accession to power.

The area's recent history, though, has been dominated by **foreign influence** and its ramifications. The **Treaty of Nanking**, which ceded Hong Kong to Britain, was signed in Nanjing in 1841, after which the city itself became a treaty port. In 1897, the Germans arrived in Shandong, occupying first the port of **Qingdao** and then the capital, **Ji'nan**, their influence spreading further as they built a rail system across the province. Resentment at this interference, exacerbated by floods and an influx of refugees from the south, combined at the turn of the twentieth century to make Shandong the setting for the **Boxer Rebellion** (see p.950). Moving on a few decades, Nanjing was to suffer one of the world's worst ever massacres, with an estimated 300,000 civilians killed by Japanese soldiers in what is now known as the **Rape of Nanking** (see p.325).

Shandong

Shandong province (山东, *shāndōng*), a fertile plain through which the Yellow River completes its journey, was once one of the poorest regions of China, overpopulated and at the mercy of the river, whose course has continually shifted, bringing chaos with every move. Times have changed, and it is now one of the most **prosperous** provinces in the land. Visitors may also remark upon the friendliness of the people, who are proud of their reputation for hospitality, a tradition that goes right back to **Confucius**, a Shandong native who declared in *The Analects*, "Is it not a great pleasure to have guests coming from afar?"

Despite Shandong's new-found wealth, some of its most appealing attractions are as old as the hills. One actually *is* a hill, albeit a rather large one – **Tai Shan**, China's holiest Taoist mountain, and a favourite with hikers and temple-hunters alike. Also popular is little **Qufu**, formerly home to Confucius, and presently home to a magnificent temple complex. The coast is lined with colossal cities, of which **Qingdao** proves the most popular with visitors, as much for its beer as its ferry connections to Korea.

As far as tourists are concerned, there's little reason to stray from these areas, though other port cities offer **ferries** to South Korea and elsewhere in China, while highways are good and bus services frequent. The province is also home to new **high-speed rail** lines, which zip from Beijing to Qingdao (via Ji'nan) and Taishan.

Ji'nan

The Shandong capital of **JI'NAN** (济南, *jǐ'nán*) stands on the site of one of China's **oldest settlements** – pottery unearthed nearby has been dated to over four thousand years ago – but is today a bright, modern and youthful place with wide boulevards and gleaming towers. It is famous throughout China for its **natural springs**, clear blue upwellings that are set among several urban parks and must rank as some of the cleanest water available in any Chinese city. **Baotu Spring** is

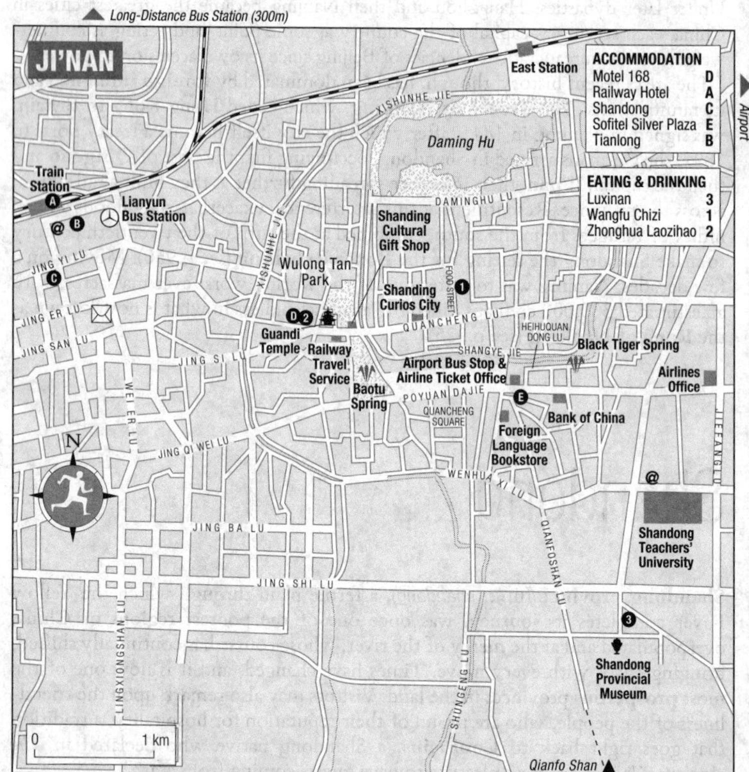

the most famous, though similar delights are on offer at **Wulong Tan Park**; most notable, however, is secluded **Wangfu Chizi**, an open-air pool which gives visitors a rare chance to bathe amid grey *hutong* architecture. There are also non-watery sights available, particularly the **provincial museum** and the steep hillside at **Qianfo Shan**, both at the city's southern limits and a good way to fill in time in transit.

Arrival and city transport

Ji'nan's **airport**, with international connections to Japan, South Korea and Hong Kong, is 40km northeast of the city. A private company operates airport shuttles (6am–6pm; ¥20; 30min), which drop you outside the airline ticket office opposite the *Sofitel Silver Plaza* hotel. Taxis from the airport into the city cost just over ¥100. The large and noisy main **train station**, at the junction of the Beijing–Shanghai line, and the line that goes east to Yantai and Qingdao, is in the northwest of town. The **long-distance bus station** is nearly 2km due north of the train station in a wretched part of town, with bus #84 running between the two, though you could also wind up at the **Lianyun bus station** on the train station square, which has connections to cities within Shandong.

Many of the **city's bus routes** begin from the train station, and **taxis** are cheap, the ¥6 basic fare just about covering trips around the city centre – these are your best option in most cases for reaching accommodation on arrival.

Accommodation

Ji'nan's **hotel** situation is a little limited, with foreigners excluded from the cheapest places. The train station touts are OK, but make it very clear how much you're willing to pay if you don't want an endless run-around, and avoid the *Hongya*, whose staff are masters at finding reasons not to refund your room deposit.

Motel 168 (莫泰连锁旅店, *mòtài liánsuǒ lǚdiàn*) Puli Jie ⓣ0531/86168168 or 81679999, ⓦwww.motel168.com. An excellent choice, with clean rooms, friendly staff and a superb location alongside Wulong Tan Park. All rooms cost under ¥200, which makes it all the more surprising that the place boasts a few stylish touches. It's often full, so book ahead. ③

Railway Hotel (铁道大酒店, *tiědào dàjiǔdiàn*) On the train station square ⓣ0531/86328888. Three-star, comfy place attached to the station front, convenient for transport. Ask about discounts – rack rates can often be halved. ⑤

Shandong (山东宾馆, *shāndōng bīnguǎn*) Jingyi Lu, about 500m south of the train-station area ⓣ86057881, ⓦwww.jnsdhotel.com. Elderly building with reasonably maintained rooms and grumpy staff but the cheapest deal in town for foreigners after you haggle over the rates. Beds ¥50, rooms ③

Sofitel Silver Plaza (索菲特银座大酒店, *suǒfēitè yínzuò dàjiǔdián*) 66 Luoyuan Dajie ⓣ0531/86068888, ⓦwww.sofitel.com. The pinnacle of luxury in Ji'nan, right in the heart of the city with views of Quancheng Square. Rates often discounted by half or more. ⑨

Moving on from Ji'nan

The main **CAAC office** (8am–5.30pm; ⓣ0531/86988777) is at 95 Jiefang Lu, though it's far easier to get your tickets and airport shuttles from the airline ticket office across from the *Sofitel*. **Train tickets** are not hard to get at the station, though there's also the large Railway Travel Service (8.30am–5pm; ⓣ0531/81817171), opposite Wulong Tan Park, which can also reserve flights. For **buses** to Qingdao, Tai'an and Qufu, try the Lianyun bus station before heading out to the main long-distance station, though you'll probably need this for travel outside the province.

Tianlong (天龙大酒店, *tiānlóng dàjiǔdiàn*) On the train-station square ⓣ0531/86328888. Grubby little place adjacent to the *Railway Hotel*, and usually far cheaper, with singles sometimes clocking in at under ¥70 – one for budget travellers with an early morning train to catch. ❷

The City

Ji'nan is pretty spread out, though there's something of a downtown focus around the oblong vastness of **Quancheng Square**, surrounded by shopping precincts and close to several of the city's parks. Immediately west, **Baotu Spring** (趵突泉, *bàotū quán*; 7am–5.30pm; ¥40) is enclosed in a pleasant park, but the entrance fee is absurd; better head just north to **Wulong Tan Park** (五龙潭公园, *wǔlóngtán gōngyuán*; 7am–5.30pm; ¥5), whose springs – some of which have been enclosed in goldfish-filled ponds – were mentioned in the *Spring and Autumn Annals*, government texts of 694 BC. In the summer, it'll be tempting to take off your shoes and wade through the shallower ponds. Just outside the south gate is a tiny **Guandi Temple** (关帝庙, *guāndìmiào*), noted as the site where eunuch An Dehai, manipulative confidant of the Qing Empress Dowager Cixi, was executed by governor Ding Baozhen (after whom the Sichuanese dish "Gongbao Jiding" is named). In the east of the park is a modern hall to one of China's most famous female poets, **Li Qingzhao**, who was born in 1084 in Ji'nan – it contains extracts from her work and paintings by well-known contemporary artists.

Just over a kilometre north of Quancheng Square on the route of bus #11 from the train station, **Daming Hu** (大明湖, *dàmíng hú*; daily 6am–6pm; ¥30, or ¥40 including boat trip) is surrounded by some quaint gardens, pavilions and bridges, and the lake is edged with willow trees and sprinkled with water lilies. About the same distance east, behind a wall on Heihuquan Dong Lu, the famous **Black Tiger Spring** (黑虎泉, *hēihǔ quán*; open all day; free) rises from a subterranean cave and emerges through tiger-headed spouts into a canal that once formed the old city's moat. People come here to fill up jerrycans from the spring and play in the water.

Ji'nan's secret spring

Ji'nan is justly famed for its springs, but very few outsiders are aware of the quirkiest one in town – possibly the best-kept travel secret in the whole of Shandong. You won't find **Wangfu Chizi** (王府池子, *wángfǔ chízi*) on any tourist maps, and the pool's location at the centre of a labyrinthine tangle of alleyways makes it doubly difficult to track down, but your efforts will not go unrewarded. Edged with grey *hutong* buildings, this is essentially an **open-air swimming pool**, and the fact that it remains such an integral part of local life makes for quite a spectacle – lines of elderly men bob up and down on their daily laps, housewives engage in casual conversation while semi-naked and local youths whoop and holler as they scrub themselves clean on the western bank. The water quality isn't superb – spit, cigarette butts and ice-cream wrappers are inevitable – but it's hard to resist the temptation to join in the fun, even more so when being persuaded by a gaggle of bronzed and finely chiselled pensioners. There's also a bit of **history** in the air – as may be inferred from its name, which roughly translates as "King's Abode Pool", Wangfu Chizi was once the property of a local prince, and the family still living on the north bank are descendants of former royal bodyguards. The pool maintains a temperature of around 18°C throughout the year, making for an ethereal effect in the winter, when mist rises from the waters and makes silhouettes of the swimmers. It's also worth dropping by in the late evening, when locals drain draught beer on the south bank while listening to the gentle lapping of waves.

Qianfo Shan and the Shandong Provincial Museum

A scenic spot worth a trip is **Qianfo Shan** (千佛山, *qiānfóshān*; daily 8am–6pm; ¥30), to the south of the city, on the route of bus #K54, which leaves from a terminus in the southwest corner of Daming Hu; the journey is about 5km. The mountainside is leafy and tracked with winding paths, the main one lined with painted opera masks. Most of the original statues that once dotted the slopes, freestanding images of Buddhas and Bodhisattvas, were destroyed by Red Guards, but new ones are being added, largely paid for by donations from Overseas Chinese. It's quite a climb to the summit (2hr), but the sculptures, and the view, get better the higher you go. Behind the **Xingguo Si** near the top are some superb sixth-century Buddhist carvings.

Near the mountain, and accessible on the same bus, the **Shandong Provincial Museum** (山东省博物馆, *shāndōngshěng bówùguǎn*; Mon–Fri 8.30–noon & 2–6pm, Sat & Sun 9am–4.30pm; ¥10) contains a number of fine Buddhist carvings as well as exhibits from the excavations at Longshan and Dawenkou, two nearby Neolithic sites noted for the delicate black pottery unearthed there. The remains date back to 5000 to 2000 BC. There's also a 22m-long Ming-dynasty **wooden boat**, excavated from the marshes southwest near Liangshan (setting for China's Robin Hood epic, *Outlaws of the Marsh*) and, in the basement, a huge and well-presented collection of Han **pictorial tomb reliefs** and Tang-dynasty tombstones.

Eating

To fill up inexpensively, there are plenty of noodle places around the train station, while south of Black Tiger Spring on Poyuan Dajie you'll find a string of **Mongolian hotpot restaurants**, easily identifiable by the copper funnel hotpots outside.

Luxinan (鲁西南风味楼, *lǔxīnán fēngwèilóu*) 150 Lishan Lu. A good choice for those visiting the museum, serving Shandong fare and regular Chinese staples at reasonable prices.

Wangfu Chizi (王府池子, *wángfǔ chízi*) The no-name snack shack at the Wangfu Chizi (see opposite) is the most atmospheric place to eat in town, with old men in bathing suits dropping by for snails, peanuts, barbecued shrimp and the like between swims, and occasionally somersaulting into the pool from above your head. Also a grand place for beer in the evenings – the local draught uses water from the Baotu Springs.

Zhonghua Laozihao (中华老字号, *zhōnghuá lǎozihào*) Puli Jie. This decades-old dumpling restaurant is something of a local institution, and is handily located just west of Wulong Tan Park.

Listings

Bank and exchange The Bank of China (Mon–Fri 8.30am–5pm) is on Poyuan Dajie, just east of the *Sofitel*.

Bookshop The Foreign Language Bookstore is on Chaoshan Jie southwest of the *Sofitel*.

Internet There's access on the third floor of the Tianlong department store on the train station square.

Mail and telephones Ji'nan's main post office (8am–4.30pm) is a red-brick building on Jing Er Lu, just west of Wei Er Lu. There's a 24hr telecom office inside.

Shopping There are two good spots for antiques and souvenirs on Quancheng Lu: Shandong Curios City in a mock-Ming shopping complex; and the higher-end Shandong Cultural Gift Shop at the southeastern corner of Wulong Tan Park.

Tai'an and Tai Shan

Tai Shan is not just a mountain, it's a god. Lying 100km south of Ji'nan, it's the easternmost and holiest of China's five holy Taoist mountains (the other four being Hua Shan, the two Heng Shans and Song Shan), and has been worshipped by the Chinese for longer than recorded history. It is justifiably famed for its scenery and the ancient buildings strung out along its slopes. Once host to emperors and the devout, it's now Shandong's biggest tourist attraction: the ascent is engrossing and beautiful – and very hard work.

The small town of **Tai'an** lies at the base of the mountain, and for centuries has prospered from the busy traffic of pilgrims coming to pay their respects. You'll quickly become aware just how popular the pilgrimage is – on certain holy days ten thousand people might be making their way to the peak, and year-round the town sees over half a million visitors.

Tai'an

TAI'AN (泰安, *tài'ān*) is unremarkable but not unpleasant. It's just small enough to cover on foot, though few people pay it much attention; the town is overshadowed, literally, by the great mountain just to the north. Dongyue Dajie is the largest street, a corridor of high-rises running east–west across town. Qingnian Lu, the main **shopping street**, runs off its eastern end. The trailhead is reached on Hongmen Lu, which is flanked by a string of souvenir shops selling shoes and gnarled walking sticks made from tree roots. Just south of Daizhong Dajie, in the north, are some busy **market streets** selling medicinal herbs that grow on the mountain, such as ginseng, the tuber of the multiflower knotweed, and Asian puccoon, along with strange vegetables, bonsai trees and potted plants.

Arrival and town transport

Tai'an's **train station** is on the Ji'nan–Shanghai line, and exiting into the square outside you'll be greeted by a mob of eager taxi drivers. The minimum fare of ¥5 is sufficient for rides around town, with no more than ¥10 required to reach the mountain. There is a helpful **tourist office** (24hr) in front of the train-station exit (bypass the uninformative tourist office *inside* the station) that sells a useful English map of the area (¥5). **Long-distance buses** from Ji'nan and Qufu terminate at the **Tai'an bus station** on Sanlizhuang Lu, south of the train station, though it's

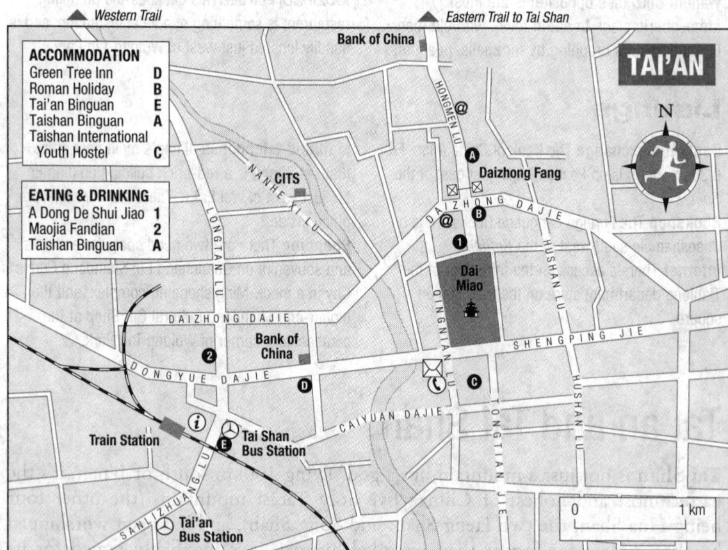

possible you'll end up at the Tai Shan depot just east of the train station. Both the train station and the Tai'an bus station have **left-luggage** facilities charging about ¥2 per day. Most of Tai'an's **city buses** run along Dongyue Dajie, just north of the station: bus #3 links both the western and eastern trailheads; #14 also goes to the eastern trailhead via Daizhong Dajie.

Accommodation

There's a mess of **places to stay** around the arrival points, and you might get in to the cheapest places – they're signed in Chinese only – if you speak some Chinese. A slightly more upmarket group of hotels is clustered up between Dai Miao and the eastern trail on Hongmen Lu, while there's also **accommodation on Tai Shan** itself, but it's expensive for what you get – see p.306 for details.

Green Tree Inn (格林豪泰, *gélín háotài*) 53 Dongyue Dajie ⓣ0538/8169999. Surprisingly plush for the price, the corridors of this new hotel are lined with carpets of brown and gold, which lead to well-appointed rooms with flatscreen televisions. ❹

Roman Holiday (罗马假日商务酒店, *luômǎ jiàrì shāngwù jiǔdiàn*) 18 Hongmen Lu ⓣ0538/6279999, ⓕ6278889. Motel-like venue that's excellent value for the price, and usefully located between Dai Miao and the eastern trailhead. Frosted glass walls mean that some bathrooms are a little visible from the beds, but some strategic curtain placement may come to the aid of those who want a little privacy. Do ensure first that your room has a window – some don't. ❸

Tai'an Binguan (泰安宾馆, *tài'ān bīnguǎn*) Sanlizhuang Lu ⓣ0538/6911111. Just across from the train station, which is at least one reason to recommend it. Rooms are clean, if a little worn, and the service rather surly. ❷

Taishan Binguan (泰山宾馆, *tàishān bīnguǎn*) ⓣ0538/8224678, ⓕ8221432. Five-storey venue that's one of the best-run places in town – smart but casual, and boasting terrific views from north-facing rooms. The on-site restaurant is a good place to try Tai Shan carp (see p.304). ❺

Taishan International Youth Hostel (泰山国际青年旅舍, *tàishān guójì qīngnián lǚshè*) 8 Fuqian Lu ⓣ0538/6285196. Handily located a short walk from Dai Miao, this is a bit of a treat, with friendly staff, pine-clad dormitories and a reception desk that doubles as a café and bar of sorts. It's tucked away in a small alley behind a covered shopping arcade. Dorm beds ¥40, doubles ❸

Dai Miao

Dai Miao (岱庙, *dài miào*; daily 8am–5pm; ¥20), the temple where emperors once made sacrifices to the mountain, is the traditional starting point for the procession up Tai Shan. It's a magnificent structure, with yellow-tiled roofs, red walls and towering old trees, one of the largest temples in the country and one of the most celebrated. Though it appears an ordered whole, the complex is really a blend of buildings from different belief systems, with veneration of the mountain as the only constant factor – the peak is, suitably, visible from many of the most important parts of the complex.

The Main Hall, **Tiankuangdian** (Hall of the Celestial Gift), is matched in size only by halls in the Forbidden City and at Qufu. The hall's construction started as early as the Qin dynasty (221–206 BC), though expansion and renovation have gone on ever since, particularly during the Tang and Song dynasties. Inside is a huge **mural** covering three of the walls, a Song-dynasty masterpiece depicting the Emperor Zhen Zong as the God of Tai Shan on an inspection tour and hunting expedition. The mural is fairly worn overall but you can still see most of the figures of its cast of thousands, each rendered in painstaking detail. There is also a **statue** of the God of Tai Shan, enthroned in a niche and dressed in flowing robes, holding the oblong tablet that is the insignia of his authority. The five sacrificial vessels laid before him bear the symbols of the five peaks.

The surrounding courtyards, halls and gardens are used a museum for **steles**; the oldest, inside the **Dongyuzuo Hall**, celebrates the visit of Emperor Qin and his son in the third century BC. Many of the great calligraphers are represented here and even the untrained Western eye can find something to appreciate. Charcoal rubbings of the steles can be bought from the mercifully discreet souvenir shops inside the temple complex. The courtyards are also well wooded with cypresses – including five supposedly planted by the Han emperor Wu Di – ginkgos and acacias.

In a side courtyard at the back of the complex is the **Temple of Yanxi**. A Taoist resident on the mountain, Yanxi was linked with the mountain cult of the Tang dynasty. A separate Taoist hall at the rear is devoted to the Wife of the Mountain, a deity who seems somewhat of an afterthought, appearing much later than her spouse. To head back to the main entrance, it's possible to take a walk along the **western wall**, which offers superb views of the complex innards.

Eating and drinking

A speciality of **Tai'an cuisine** is red-scaled carp, fresh from pools on the mountain and fried while it's still alive. Other dishes from the mountain include chicken stewed with *siliquose pelvetia* (a fungus only found within 2m of the ancient pine trees around the Nine Dragon Hill), coral herb and hill lilac. The best place to try these things is in the *Taishan Binguan*, where a meal, with vegetable and meat dishes as well as drinks, should come to around ¥80 per head. If this is too much, try *A Dong De Shui Jiao* (阿东的水饺, *ādōng de shuǐjiǎo*), further south on Hongmen Lu, a popular, busy place serving Chinese staples. Down near the train station, *Maojia Fandian* (毛家饭店, *máojiā fàndiàn*) is an upmarket place offering excellent Hunanese food, such as chilli-smoked meat and dry-fried beans (complete with photo menu), at around ¥20 per main.

Listings

Banks and exchange The main Bank of China is located at 48 Dongyue Dajie, though a small branch with an ATM is uphill from the *Taishan Binguan*.

Internet There's an internet café just uphill from the *Taishan Binguan*, another not far to the south on Dai Zhong Dajie, and a third opposite the *Yulong Binguan* on Longtan Lu.

Mail The post office (Mon–Fri 8am–6pm) is on Dongyue Dajie, near the junction with Qingnian Lu.

Tai Shan

More so than any other holy mountain, **Tai Shan** (泰山, *tàishān*) was the haunt of emperors, and owes its obvious glories – the temples and pavilions along its route – to the patronage of the imperial court. From its summit, a succession of emperors surveyed their empires, made sacrifices and paid tribute. Sometimes, their retinues stretched right from the top to the bottom of the mountain, 8km of pomp and ostentatious wealth. In 219 BC, Emperor Qin Shi Huang had **roads** built all over the mountain so that he could ride here in his carriage under escort of the royal guards when he was performing the grand ceremonies of *feng* (sacrifices to heaven) and *chan* (offerings to earth). Various titles were offered to the mountain by emperors keen to bask in reflected glory. As well as funding the temples, emperors had their visits and thoughts recorded for posterity on steles here, and men of letters carved poems and tributes to the mountain on any available rockface. Shandong-native Confucius is also said to have made a trip here, and there is a temple in his honour in the shadow of the highest peak.

In recent years, this huge open-air museum has mutated into a religious theme park, and the path is now thronged with a constant procession of **tourists**. There are photo booths, souvenir stalls, soft-drinks vendors and teahouses. You can get your name inscribed on a medal, get your photograph taken and buy

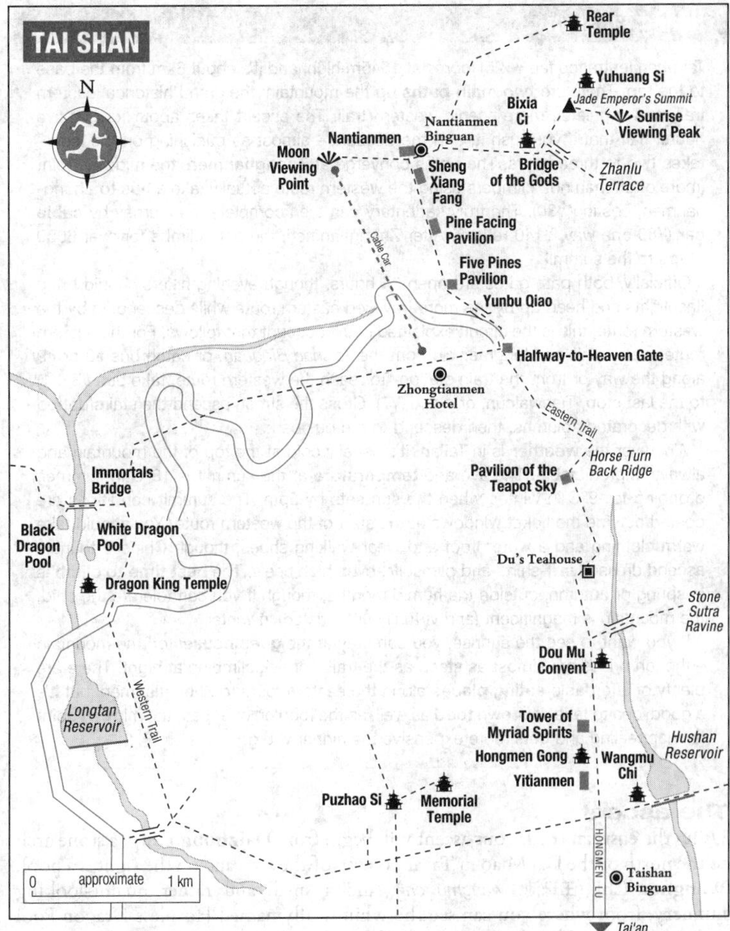

medicinal herbs from vendors squatting on walls. Halfway up, there's a **bus station** and **cable car**. Yet Tai Shan retains an atmosphere of grandeur; the buildings and the mountain itself are magnificent enough to survive their trivialization.

It is surprising, though, to see that numbering among the hordes of tourists are a great many genuine **pilgrims**. Taoism, after a long period of communist proscription, is again alive and flourishing, and you're more than likely to see a bearded Taoist monk on the way up. Women come specifically to pray to **Bixia Yuan Jun**, the Princess of the Rosy Clouds, a Taoist deity believed to be able to help childless women conceive. Tai Shan also plays an important role in the **folk beliefs** of the Shandong peasantry (tradition has it that anyone who has climbed Tai Shan will live to be 100). The other figures you will see are the streams of **porters**, balancing enormous weights on their shoulder poles, moving swiftly up the mountain and then galloping down again for a fresh load; they may make three trips a day, six days a week.

Hiking Tai Shan

Tai Shan (entrance fee ¥125) looms at 1545m high, and it's about 8km from the base to the top. There are **two main paths** up the mountain: the grand historical eastern trail, and a quieter, more scenic western trail. The ascent takes about four or five hours, half that if you rush it, and the descent – almost as punishing on the legs – takes two to three hours. The paths converge at **Zhongtianmen**, the midway point (more often than not, climbers using the western route actually take a **bus** to Zhongtianmen, costing ¥30). The truly sedentary can then complete the journey by **cable car** (¥80 one way, ¥140 return). After Zhongtianmen, the path climbs for over 6000 **steps** to the summit.

Officially, both path gates are open 24 hours, though evening hikers should bring flashlights and head up by the more travelled eastern route while descending by the western route; this is the circuit explained in the account that follows. For the eastern route, walk uphill on Hongmen Lu from the *Taishan Binguan*, or catch bus #3 or #9 along the way or from the train station. To reach the western route, take bus #3 (¥1) to the last stop, Tianwaicun, or a taxi (¥7). Cross the street, ascend the stairs dotted with decorated columns, then descend to the bus park.

Whatever the **weather** is in Tai'an, it's usually cold at the top of the mountain and always unpredictable. The average **temperature** at the summit is 18°C in summer, dropping to -9°C in winter, when the sun sets by 5pm. The summit conditions are posted outside the ticket windows at the start of the western route. You should take warm clothing and a waterproof and wear walking shoes, though Chinese tourists ascend dressed in T-shirts and plimsolls, even high heels. The **best time to climb** is in spring or autumn, outside the humid months, though if you can tolerate the cold, the mountain is magnificent (and virtually untouristed) in winter.

If you want to see the sunrise, you can stay at the **guesthouses** on the mountain – though prices are almost as steep as the trail – or risk climbing at night. There are plenty of affordable **eating places** along the eastern route to Zhongtianmen, but it's a good idea to take your own **food** as well, as the food on offer past the midway point is unappealing and gets more expensive the higher you go.

The ascent

Using the **eastern trail**, your ascent will begin from **Daizhong Fang**, a stone arch to the north of the Dai Miao in Tai'an. North of the arch and on the right is a pool, **Wangmu Chi** (王母池, *wángmǔ chí*), and a small and rather quaint-looking nunnery, from where you can see the whimsically named Hornless Dragon Pool and Combing and Washing River. In the main hall of the nunnery is a statue of Xiwang Mu, Queen Mother of the West, the major female deity in Taoism.

Yitianmen to Zhongtianmen

About 500m up is the official start of the path at the **First Heavenly Gate** (一天门, *yītiānmén*). This is followed by a Ming arch, said to mark the spot where Confucius began his climb, and the **Red Gate Palace** (红门宫, *hóngmén gōng*), where emperors used to change into sensible clothes for the ascent, and where you buy your ticket, which includes insurance. Built in 1626, Hongmen Gong is the first of a series of temples dedicated to the Princess of the Rosy Clouds. It got its name from the two red rocks to the northwest, which together resemble an arch.

There are plenty of buildings to distract you around here. Just to the north is the Tower of Myriad Spirits, and just below that the Tomb of the White Mule is said to be where the mule that carried the Tang emperor Xuan up and down the mountain finally dropped dead, exhausted. Xuan made the mule a posthumous general and at least it got a decent burial. The next group of buildings is the former **Dou Mu Convent** (斗母宫, *dǒumǔ gōng*), a hall for Taoist nuns. Its date of founding is uncertain, but it was reconstructed in 1542. Today, there are three halls, a drum tower, a bell tower and an ancient, **gnarled tree** outside, which is supposed to look like a reclining dragon. Like all the temple buildings on the mountain, the walls are painted with a blood-red wash, here interspersed with small grey bricks.

North of here, a path veers east off the main route for about a kilometre to the **Stone Sutra Ravine** (经石谷, *jīngshí gǔ*) where the text of the Buddhist Diamond Sutra has been carved on the rockface. This is one of the most prized of Tai Shan's many calligraphic works, and makes a worthwhile diversion as it's set in a charming, quiet spot. Back on the main path, don't miss **Du's Teahouse**, built on the spot where, more than a thousand years ago, General Cheng Yao Jing Tang planted four pines, three of which are still alive. The teahouse and everything in it is quaintly built out of polished tree roots, and the "maiden tea" is excellent, and a speciality of this mountain area.

After a tunnel of cypress trees, and the **Pavilion of the Teapot Sky** (壶天阁, *hútiān gé*), so called because the peaks all around supposedly give the illusion of standing in a teapot, you see a sheer cliff rising in front of you, called **Horse Turn Back Ridge** (回马岭, *huímǎlǐng*). This is where Emperor Zhen Zong had to dismount because his horse refused to go any farther. Not far above is **Halfway-to-Heaven Gate** (中天门, *zhōngtiānmén*), the midpoint of the climb. There are some good views here, though the **cable car** will be the most welcome sight if you're flagging. The pleasant *Zhongtianmen Hotel* is situated here (中天门宾馆, *zhōngtiānmén bīnguǎn*; ⓣ0538/8226740; ④), plus a collection of dull restaurants. Confusingly, you have to descend two staircases and then follow the road round to continue the climb.

Zhongtianmen to the top

The next sight is **Cloud Stepping Bridge** (云步桥, *yúnbù qiáo*), after which you arrive at **Five Pines Pavilion**, where the first Qin emperor took shelter from a storm under a group of pines. The grateful emperor then promoted the lucky pine trees to ministers of the fifth grade. From here you can see the lesser peaks of Tai Shan: the Mountain of Symmetrical Pines, the Flying Dragon Crag and Hovering Phoenix Ridge.

Farther up you pass under the **Archway to Immortality** (升仙房, *shēngxiān fáng*), which, according to mountain myth, assures your longevity and provides the viewpoint that inspired Tang poet Li Bai to write: "In a long breath by the heavenly gate, the fresh wind comes from a thousand miles away", though by this point most climbers are long past being able to appreciate poetry.

The **final section** of the climb is the hardest, as the stone stairs are steep and narrow, and ascend almost vertically between two walls of rocks (often through thick white mist) – almost everyone by this point is unashamedly grasping the handrails as they haul themselves upwards. And then suddenly you're at the top on **Tian Jie** (Heaven Street), a tourist strip where you can buy "I climbed Tai Shan" T-shirts, slurp a pot noodle and get your picture taken dressed as an emperor. There are a couple of **restaurants** here, **hotels** and a few **shops**. This thriving little tourist village represents a triumph of the profit motive over the elements; it's often so misty you can hardly see from one souvenir stall to the next. If you want to **stay the night**, try and negotiate a discount at the wildly overpriced *Nantianmen Binguan* (南天门宾馆, *nántiānmén bīnguǎn*; ⓣ0538/8330988; dorm beds ¥70, rooms ⑧), which also has a restaurant.

The **Bixia Ci** (碧霞寺, *bìxiá cí*), on the southern slopes of the summit, is the final destination for most of the bona fide pilgrims, and offerings are made to a bronze statue of the princess in the main hall. It's a working temple and its guardians enforce strict rules about where the merely curious are allowed to wander. It's also a splendid building, the whole place tiled with iron to resist wind damage, and all the decorations are metal, too. The bells hanging from the eaves, the mythological animals on the roof, and even the two steles outside are bronze. From 1759 until the fall of the Qing, the emperor would send an official here on the eighteenth day of the fourth lunar month each year to make an offering. Just below is a small **shrine to Confucius**, at the place where he was supposed to have commented, "the world is small".

At the **Jade Emperor Temple** (玉皇寺, *yùhuáng sì*), you have truly arrived at the **highest point** of the mountain, and a rock with the characters for "supreme summit" and "1545m" carved on it stands within the courtyard. In Chinese popular religion, which mixes Taoism and Confucianism with much earlier beliefs, the Jade Emperor is the supreme ruler of heaven, depicted in an imperial hat with bead curtains hanging down his face. Outside the temple is the **Wordless Monument**, thought to have been erected by Emperor Wu more than two thousand years ago. The story goes that Wu wanted to have an inscription engraved that would do justice to his merits. None of the drafts he commissioned came up to scratch, however, so he left the stele blank, leaving everything to the imagination.

Southeast of here is the peak for **watching the sunrise** (4.45am in June, 7am in December). It was here that the Song emperor performed the *feng* ceremony, building an altar and making sacrifices to heaven. On a clear day, you can see 200km to the coast, and at night you can see the lights of Ji'nan. There are numerous **trails** from here to fancifully named scenic spots – Fairy Bridge, Celestial Candle Peak and the like. If the weather is good, it's a great place for aimless wandering.

The descent

The best way down is along the **western trail**, which is longer, quieter and has some impressive views. It starts at Zhongtianmen, loops round and joins the main trail back at the base of the mountain. Midway is the **Black Dragon Pool**, a dark, brooding pond, home of the Tai Shan speciality dish, red-scaled carp, once so precious that the fish was used as tribute to the court. Near the bottom, the **Puzhao Si** (普照寺, *pǔzhào sì*) is a pretty, mostly Qing, temple complex. It's east of the western trail, though access is via the road that runs around the base of the mountain.

Qufu and around

Though it may, at first glance, appear to be little more than a small town in the south of Shandong, **QUFU** (曲阜, *qǔfù*) is actually of immense historical and cultural importance. **Confucius** (孔子, *kǒngzǐ*) was born here around 551 BC, and, having spent his life teaching his moral code – largely unappreciated by his contemporaries – was buried just outside the town, in what became a sacred burial ground for his clan, the Kong. His teachings caught on after his death, however, and despite periodic purges (most recently during the Cultural Revolution), they have become firmly embedded in the Chinese psyche. All around the town is architectural evidence of the esteem in which he was held by successive dynasties – most monumentally by the Ming, who were responsible for the two dominant sights, the **Confucius Temple** and the **Confucius Mansion**, whose scale seems more suited to Beijing. For more on Confucius and Confucianism, see p.311.

Qufu is an interesting place to stop over for a few days, with plenty to see concentrated in an area small enough to walk around. As it's a major tourist destination, however, you'll have to expect the usual crowds and hustles – especially around the end of September, **on Confucius's birthdate** in the lunar calendar, when a **festival** is held here and reconstructions of many of the original rituals are performed. If it all gets too much, there are places to escape amid old buildings, trees and singing birds, such as the **Confucian Forest** to the north.

Arrival and information

The **train station** is 5km east of central Qufu, at the end of the #5 bus route. This runs into town past the **bus station**, from where you can get transport to Heze (for Kaifeng), Ji'nan, Tai'an, Qingdao, Yantai and Zhengzhou. A booking office for train and airline tickets (the nearest airport is Ji'nan's) is southeast across the street from the bus station.

City transport

Once in town, the only **city bus** you'll need is the #1, which runs up Gulou Beijie to the Confucian Forest. Otherwise, grab a **cycle-rickshaw**, whereby the passenger is slung low in the front, giving an uninterrupted dog's-eye view of the street. A ride anywhere in town should cost ¥3–5. There are also horse-drawn gypsy-style **carts**, strictly for tourists, so not cheap. A **taxi** in town will start at ¥6.

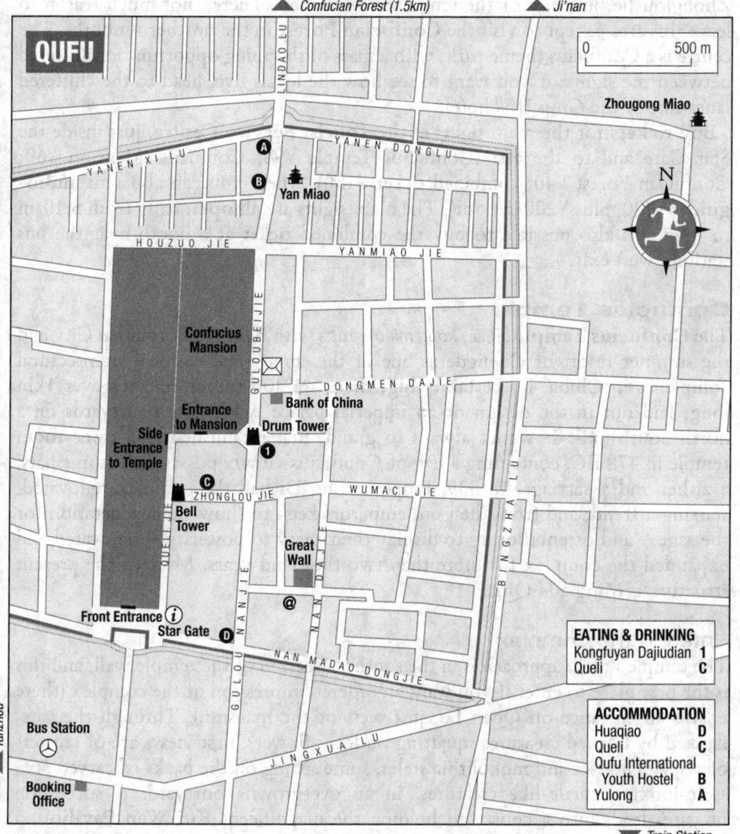

Accommodation

Accommodation in Qufu is surprisingly patchy, given the city's popularity with domestic tourists, and higher-end places are almost non-existent.

Huaqiao (华侨宾馆, *huáqiáo bīnguǎn*) In through the walls and left on Nan Madao Dong Jie ⓣ1395/3711550. A comfy but basic hotel, whose lobby is accessed through a bubble tea café. Avoid the bubble tea at all costs. Doubles with/without a/c ❷

Queli (阙里宾舍, *quèlǐ bīnshè*) 1 Queli Jie ⓣ0537/4866523, ⓦwww.quelihotel.com. Located right next to the Confucius Temple and Mansion, this is the only real higher-end accommodation in town. Because of their trapped market, rooms are relatively poor value for money, but have satellite TV, 24hr hot water and English-speaking staff. ❻

Qufu International Youth Hostel (曲阜国际青年旅舍, *qǔfù guójì qīngnián lǚshè*) Gulou Beijie ⓣ0537/4418989, ⓦwww.yhachina.com. A pleasant, wel-run hostel, with decent bedrooms, amiable staff and a terrific bar that serves the best – actually, the only – espresso in town. Dorm ¥35, rooms ❸

Yulong (裕隆大饭店, *yùlóng dàfàndiàn*) 1 Gulou Beijie ⓣ0537/4413469, ⓕ4413209. New, ordinary Chinese tourist hotel, a bit out of the way and hence underpatronized – which means it's easier to bargain rates down. ❹

The Town

Orientation is easy, as the centre of town lies at the crossroads of Gulou Dajie and Zhonglou Jie, just east of the temple and mansion. There's not much reason to leave this area except to visit the **Confucian Forest** in the northern suburbs. The centre is a Confucius theme park, with a mass of shopping opportunities clustered between the sights; if you want to see how the locals live, head to the cluttered lanes east of the *Great Wall* hotel.

Buy **tickets** for the main sights at the **Tourist Service Centre**, just inside the Star Gate and to the east (Confucius Temple ¥90; Confucius Mansion ¥60; Confucian Forest ¥40; combined ticket ¥150), where you can also rent **audio-guides** (¥20, plus ¥200 deposit). The main sights are all **open** daily from 8.10am to 5pm. It's also possible to buy the combined ticket at a booth near the bus station's west exit.

Confucius Temple

The **Confucius Temple** (孔庙, *kǒng miào*) ranks with Beijing's Forbidden City and the summer resort of Chengde as one of the three great classical architectural complexes in China. It's certainly big: there are 466 rooms, and it's over 1km long, laid out in the design of an imperial palace, with nine courtyards on a north–south axis. It wasn't always so grand, first established as a three-room temple in 478 BC, containing a few of Confucius's lowly possessions: some hats, a zither and a carriage. In 539, Emperor Jing Di had the complex renovated, starting a trend, and from then on, emperors keen to show their veneration for the sage – and ostentatiously to display their piety to posterity – renovated and expanded the complex for more than two thousand years. Most of the present structure is Ming and Qing.

Entering the complex

The temple's main approach is in the southern section of the temple wall, and this is the best place to enter if you want an ordered impression of the complex (there is also an entrance on Queli Lu, just west of the mansion). Through the gate, flanked by horned creatures squatting on lotus flowers, first views are of clusters of wiry cypresses and monolithic steles, some sitting on the backs of carved *bixi*, stoic-looking turtle-like creatures, in an overgrown courtyard. A succession of gates leads into a courtyard holding the magnificent **Kui Wen Pavilion**, a

Confucianism in modern China

When the **Communists** came to power they saw **Confucianism** as an archaic, feudal system and an **anti-Confucius campaign** was instigated, which came to a climax during the Cultural Revolution. Now, however, Conservatives frightened by the pace of change, the growing generation gap and the new materialism of China are calling for a **return to Confucian values** of respect and selflessness, just as their nervous counterparts in the West preach a return to family values. Confucian social morality – obeying authority, regarding family as the seat of morality and emphasizing the mutual benefits of friendship – is sometimes hailed as one of the main reasons for the success of East Asian economies, just as Protestantism provided the ideological complement to the growth of the industrialized West.

Most of the Confucian buildings in Qufu have been recently renovated, but this is strictly in the interests of **tourism**, not worship. Confucianism as a moral force was thought to have died, yet the ability of Chinese traditions to survive modernization and suppression always surprises observers. As one Chinese visitor commented, "Confucius is the one Chinese leader who never let the people down".

three-storey wooden building constructed in 1018 with a design unique in Chinese classical architecture – a triple-layered roof with curving eaves and four layers of crossbeams. It was renovated in 1504 and has since withstood an earthquake undamaged, an event recorded on a tablet on the terrace. To the east and west, the two pavilions are abstention lodges where visiting emperors would fast and bathe before taking part in sacrificial ceremonies.

The **thirteen stele pavilions** in the courtyard beyond are worth checking out, containing 53 tablets presented by emperors to commemorate their visits, and gifts of land and funds for renovations made to the Kong family. The earliest are Tang and the latest are from the Republican period. Continuing north, you come to **five gates** leading off in different directions. The eastern ones lead to the hall where sacrifices were offered to Confucius's ancestors, the western to the halls where his parents were worshipped, while the central Gate of Great Achievements leads to a large pavilion, the **Apricot Altar**. Tradition has it that Confucius taught here after travelling the country in search of a ruler willing to implement his ideas. The cypress just inside the gate was supposed to have been planted by Confucius himself, and its state of health is supposed to reflect the fortunes of the Kongs.

The Hall of Great Achievements

The **Hall of Great Achievements** (大成殿, *dàchéng diàn*), behind the Apricot Altar, is the temple's grandest building, its most striking feature being 28 **stone pillars** carved with bas-relief dragons, dating from around 1500. Each pillar has nine gorgeous dragons, coiling around clouds and pearls towards the roof. There is nothing comparable in the Forbidden City in Beijing, and when emperors came to visit, the columns were covered with yellow silk to prevent imperial jealousy. Originally, the temple was solely dedicated to the worship of Confucius, but in 72 AD, Emperor Liu Zhuang offered sacrifices to his 72 disciples, too. Five hundred years later, Zhen Guan of the Tang dynasty issued an edict decreeing that 22 eminent Confucians should also be worshipped. Emperors of later dynasties (not wishing to be outdone) added more, and there are presently 172 "eminent worthies".

Behind the main hall is the inner hall for the worship of **Confucius's wife**, **Qi Guan**, who also, it seems, merited deification through association (though Confucian values placed women way down the social hierarchy, with wives less important than their sons, and daughters-in-law less important than anybody).

The phoenixes painted on its columns and ceiling are symbols of female power, in the same way as the dragon symbolizes masculinity.

Beyond is the **Hall of the Relics of the Sage**, where 120 carved stone plates made in the sixteenth century from Song paintings depict scenes from Confucius's life. They begin with Confucius's mother praying for a son, and end with his disciples mourning at his grave.

The Hall of Poetry and Rites and the Lu Wall

The **eastern axis** of the temple is entered here, through the **Gate of the Succession of the Sage** next to the Hall of Great Achievements. Here is the **Hall of Poetry and Rites** (诗社堂, *shīshè táng*) where Confucius was supposed to have taught his son, Kong Li, to learn poetry from the *Book of Odes* in order to express himself, and ritual from the *Book of Rites* in order to strengthen his character.

A solitary wall in the courtyard is the famous **Lu Wall**, where Kong Fu, a ninth-generation descendant of Confucius, hid the sage's **books** when Qin Shi Huang, the first emperor (see p.266), persecuted the followers of Confucius and burned all his books. Several decades later, Liu Yu, prince of Lu and son of the Emperor Jing Di, ordered Confucius's dwelling to be demolished in order to build an extension to his palace, whereupon the books were found, which led to a schism between those who followed the reconstructed version of his last books, and those who followed the teachings in the rediscovered originals. In the east wall of the temple, near the Lu Wall, an unobtrusive gate leads to the legendary **site of Confucius's home**, sandwiched between the spectacular temple and the magnificent mansion, a tiny square of land just big enough to have held a couple of poky little rooms.

The western section

The **western section** is entered through the Gate of He Who Heralds the Sage, by the Hall of Great Achievements. A paved path leads to a high brick terrace on which stands the five-bay, green-tiled **Hall of Silks and Metals** and the **Hall of He Who Heralds the Sage**, built to venerate Confucius's father, **Shu Lianghe**. He was originally a minor military official who attained posthumous nobility through his son. Behind is, predictably, the Hall of the Wife of He Who Heralds the Sage, dedicated to Confucius's mother.

Confucius Mansion

The First Family Under Heaven – the descendants of Confucius – lived continuously at the **Confucius Mansion** (孔府, *kǒng fǔ*), accessible off Queli Jie in the centre of town, for more than 2500 years, spanning 74 generations. The opulence and size of the mansion testifies to the power and wealth of the **Kong clan** and their head, the **Yansheng Duke**. Built on a north–south axis, the mansion is loosely divided into living quarters, an administrative area and a garden. In the east is a temple and ancestral hall, while the western wing includes the reception rooms for important guests and the rooms where the rites were learned.

Intricate and convoluted, this complex of twisting alleyways and over 450 rooms (most of them sixteenth-century) has something decidedly eccentric about it. Inside lies a central courtyard lined with long, narrow buildings, which were once administrative offices; now they hold a few trinket shops. The **Gate of Double Glory** to the north was opened only on ceremonial occasions or when the emperor dropped in. To its east and west are **old administrative departments**, modelled after the six ministries of the imperial government: the Department of Rites was in charge of ancestor worship; the Department of Seals concerned with jurisdiction and edicts; then followed Music, Letters and Archives, Rent Collection and Sacrificial Fields. Beyond the Gate of Double Glory, the **Great Hall** was

Grand designs: Chinese architecture

Though much of urban China has been ripped up and rebuilt in the last fifty years, there are enough beautiful ancient buildings left – mostly temples and palaces – to illustrate three thousand years of illustrious architectural history. There is a remarkable consistency across centuries – marked by a historical adherence to the rules of feng shui – with only minor variations by dynasty, and it doesn't take a visitor long to grasp the fundamentals of Chinese design.

Wudang Shan, Hubei province ▲

Foshan Ancestral Temple, Guangdong ▼

Temples and palaces

Traditional temples and palaces follow a basic building structure. The foundations form a raised platform of earth, brick or stone, while columns rest on separate bases with their heads linked by beams running lengthways and across. Above this, beams are raised on posts set on the beam below to create an interlocking structure that rises to the point of the roof – here, posts at the centre support the roof ridge. This produced a characteristic **curved roofline**, felt to confer good luck. Scale and space were ultimately limited by a lack of arches, but this design was solid enough to allow the use of heavy **ceramic roof tiles**.

These features reached a peak of sophistication during the Tang and Song eras. Later restorations, such as the temples at **Wudang Shan**, convey something of the period's spirit. Two regional styles also developed: **northern** architecture was comparatively restrained and sober, while the **southern style** featured exaggerated curves and ornamentation; Guangdong's **Foshan Ancestral Temple** is a classic example of the latter.

Imperial buildings were distinguished by four-sided roofs, high platforms, wide staircases and by special yellow glazed tiles for the roofs.

Homes

Domestic architecture shares many guiding principles of temple and palace design, with curved rooflines and the use of *feng shui*-influenced spirit walls or mirrors, the latter placed over external doorways to repulse demons. Older homes with these basic features can be found across China, but in many cases, practical considerations – namely the climate – created distinctive **local styles**. Northern China's cold

Feng shui

Whatever the scale of a building project, the Chinese consider divination using **feng shui** an essential part of the initial preparations. Literally meaning "wind and water", feng shui is a form of **geomancy**, which assesses how buildings must be positioned so as not to disturb the spiritual attributes of the surrounding landscape. This reflects **Taoist cosmology**, which believes that the disruption of a single element can cause potentially dangerous alterations to the whole. It's vital, therefore, that sites – whether for peasant homes or entire cities such as Beijing – be favourably orientated according to points on the compass and protected from local "unlucky directions" by other buildings, walls, hills, mountain ranges, water or even a Terracotta Army.

winters and hot summers spawned solidly insulated brick walls, while more stable, subtropical southern temperatures encouraged the use of open eaves, internal courtyards and wooden lattice screens to allow air to circulate freely.

Rural areas are good places to find more traditional or unusual types of residential architecture. In the mountainous border areas between Guizhou and Guangxi provinces, ethnic Dong and Miao build huge, two- or three-storey wooden houses from local cedar. The Dong are also known for their wooden drum towers and wind-and-rain bridges. Another ethnic group, the Hakka, build immense, circular stone clan or family mansions – some of which can accommodate hundreds of people; these were originally built for defensive purposes in their Guangdong-Fujian homelands. Extreme adaptation to local conditions can be seen in Shaanxi province, where underground homes, cool in summer and warm in winter, have been excavated.

▲ Geomancy compass

▼ Wind-and-rain bridge, Chengyang

▼ Hakka circular homes, Fujian province

Expo 2010 China Pavilion, Shanghai ▲

CCTV Building, Beijing ▼

Modern architecture

Under the Communists, a brutally functional **Soviet style** became the norm – everything from factories to hotels was built as identical drab, grey boxes. Since China opened up to the West and capitalism, however, a more "international" look has taken hold, as seen in the gleaming high-rises going up across the country. Here you'll often see attempts to marry the traditional Chinese idiom with current needs.

In recent years, the urban landscape has been ripped up and reconstructed yet again. Old towns such as **Lijiang**, featuring cobbled lanes and "ethnic" building styles in wood and stone are being resurrected; at the other end of the scale, prestige projects by world-renowned architects have been springing up in Shanghai and Beijing - motivated by the desire to present China's urban hubs as dynamic, hip cities.

Four modern masters

CCTV Building, Beijing Dutch firm OMA designed this truly bizarre structure, a double "Z" with a hole in the middle and no right angles, nicknamed "the Twisted Doughnut".

National Centre for the Performing Arts, Beijing Known as "the Egg", this Paul Andreu-designed structure features three halls under a dome at the centre of an artificial lake.

National Olympic Stadium, Beijing Herzog and de Meuron designed the stadium to resemble a bird's nest, and though now rather underused, it's still an iconic image to the Chinese.

Xintiandi, Shanghai Complex of accommodation and restaurants that is a rare example of an extravagant architectural gesture that's still recognizably Chinese, a collection of *shikumen* – houses with stone gateways, painstakingly reconstructed with original materials. see p.389.

The Yansheng Duke and the Kong family

The status of the **Yansheng Duke** – the title given to Confucius's direct male descendant – rose throughout imperial history as emperors granted him increasing **privileges and hereditary titles**; under the Qing dynasty, he enjoyed the unique privilege of being permitted to ride a horse inside the Forbidden City and walk along the Imperial Way inside the palace. Emperors presented the duke with large areas of sacrificial fields (so called because the income from the fields was used to pay for sacrificial ceremonies), as well as exempting him from taxes.

As a family, the Kongs remained close-knit, practising a severe interpretation of **Confucian ethics**. For example, any young family member who offended an elder was fined two taels (about 70g) of silver and battered twenty times with a bamboo club. Strict rules governed who could go where within the house, and when a fire broke out in the living quarters in the last century it raged for three days as only twelve of the five hundred hereditary servants were allowed to go into the area to put it out. A female family member was expected to obey her father, her husband and her son. One elderly Kong general, after defeat on the battlefield, cut his throat for the sake of his dignity. When the news reached the mansion, his son hanged himself as an expression of filial piety; after discovering the body, his wife hanged herself out of female virtue. On hearing this, the emperor bestowed the family with a board, inscribed "A family of faithfulness and filiality".

The Kong family enjoyed the good life right up until the beginning of the twentieth century. **Decline** set in rapidly with the downfall of imperial rule, and in the 1920s the family was so poor that when wine was required for entertaining a guest, the servants bought it out of their own pocket, as a favour to their masters. In 1940, the last of the line, **Kong Decheng**, fled to Taiwan during the Japanese invasion, breaking the tradition of millennia. His sister, **Kong Demao**, penned *In the House of Confucius*, a fascinating account of life lived inside this strange family chained to the past; it's available in foreign-language bookstores. Half of Qufu now claims descent from the Kongs, who are so numerous there is an entire local telephone directory dedicated to the letter K.

where the Yansheng Duke sat on a wooden chair covered with a tiger skin and proclaimed edicts. The flags and arrow tokens hanging on the walls are symbols of authority. Signs next to them reading "Make way!" were used to clear the roads of ordinary people when the duke left the mansion.

The next hall was where the duke held examinations in music and rites, and beyond it lies the **Hall of Withdrawal**, where he took tea. The hall contains two sedan chairs; the green one was for trips outside the mansion, the red one for domestic use.

The residential apartments

The **residential apartments** of the mansion are to the north, accessible through gates that would once have been heavily guarded; no one could enter of their own accord under pain of death. Tiger-tail cudgels, goose-winged pitchforks and golden-headed jade clubs used to hang here to drive the message home. Even the water-carrier was not permitted, and emptied the water into a stone trough outside that runs through the apartment walls. On a screen inside the gates is a painting of a *tan*, an imaginary animal shown eating treasures and greedily eyeing the sun. Feudal officials often had this picture painted in their homes as a warning against avarice.

The first hall is the seven-bay **Reception Hall**, where relatives were received, banquets held and marriage and funeral ceremonies conducted. Today, the only remnants of its once-salubrious past are several golden throne chairs and ornate staffs. Directly opposite the Reception Hall, the **central eastern room** contains a set of furniture made from tree roots, presented to the mansion by Emperor Qianlong – an original imperial decree lies on the table. Elsewhere in the central eastern room, check out the dinner service; it contains 404 pieces, including plates shaped like fish and deer, for consumption of the appropriate animals. Banquets for honoured guests could stretch to 196 courses.

Past the outbuildings and through a small gate, you reach the **Front Main Building**, an impressive two-storey structure in which are displayed paintings and clothes. The eastern central room was the home of **Madame Tao**, wife of Kong Lingyi, the 76th duke. Their daughter, Kong Demao, lived in the far eastern room, while Kong Lingyi's concubine, Wang, originally one of Tao's handmaids, lived in the inner western room. It doesn't sound like an arrangement designed for domestic bliss; indeed, whenever the duke was away, Madame Tao used to beat Wang with a whip she kept for the purpose. When Wang produced a male heir, Tao poisoned her. A second concubine, Feng, was kept prisoner in her rooms by Tao until she died.

The duke himself lived in the **rear building**, which has been left as it was when the last duke fled to Taiwan. Behind that is the garden where, every evening, flocks of **crows** come to roost noisily. Crows are usually thought to be inauspicious in China, but here they are welcome, and said to be the crow soldiers of Confucius, who protected him from danger on his travels. To the southeast of the inner east wing is a four-storey building called the **Tower of Refuge**, a planned retreat in the event of an uprising or invasion. The first floor was equipped with a moveable hanging ladder, and a trap could be set in the floor. Once inside, the refugees could live for weeks on dried food stores.

The temple

In the east of the complex you'll find the family temple, the Ancestral Hall and residential quarters for less important family members. The **temple** is dedicated to the memory of Yu, wife of the 72nd duke, and daughter of Emperor Qianlong. The princess had a mole on her face, which, it was predicted, would bring disaster unless she married into a family more illustrious than either the nobility or the highest of officials. The Kongs were the only clan to fulfil the criteria, but technically the daughter of the Manchu emperor was not allowed to marry a Han Chinese. This inconvenience was got around by first having the daughter adopted by the family of the Grand Secretary Yu, and then marrying her to the duke as Yu's daughter. Her dowry included twenty villages and several thousand trunks of clothing.

The rest of town

Not far to the east of the gate of the Confucius Mansion is the Ming **Drum Tower** (鼓楼, *gǔlóu*), which forms a pair with the **Bell Tower** (钟楼, *zhōng lóu*) on Queli Jie. The drum was struck to mark sunset, the bell to mark sunrise, and at major sacrificial ceremonies they would be sounded simultaneously. You can't go inside either.

A little way northeast of the Confucius Mansion is the **Yan Miao** (颜庙, *yán miào*; 8am–5pm; ¥10), a smaller temple dedicated to Yan Hui, who was regarded as Confucius's greatest disciple and sometimes called "The Sage Returned". A temple has been situated here since the Han dynasty, though the present structure is Ming. It's attractive, quieter than the Confucius Temple, and contains some impressive architectural details, such as the dragon pillars on the main hall, and a dragon head embedded in the roof. The eastern building now contains a display of locally excavated Neolithic and Zhou pottery.

The **Zhougong Miao** (周公庙, *zhōugōng miào*; 7.30am–4.30pm; ¥5) in the northeast of town is dedicated to a Zhou-dynasty duke, a statue of whom stands in the main hall, together with his son Bo Qin and Bo Qin's servant. Legend has it that Bo Qin was a rasher man than his father, and the duke, worried that his son would not act sensibly in state matters, inscribed a pithy maxim from his own political experience on a slate and directed the servant to carry it on his back. Whenever Bo Qin was about to do something foolish, the ever-present servant would turn his back so Bo Qin would think again. The open terrace before the hall, where sacrifices were made to the duke, contains a striking stone incense burner carved with coiling dragons.

The Confucian Forest

The **Confucian Forest** (孔林, *kǒng lín*) is in the suburbs 3km north of the town centre, reachable by cycle-rickshaw or bus #1 up Gulou Nanjie. You can rent **bikes** (¥5) at the gates, which is good because the area is really too large to explore thoroughly on foot. The forest is the **burial ground** of the Kongs and, like the temple, it expanded over the centuries from something simple and austere to a grand complex, in this case centring around a single grave – **the tomb of Confucius**. Confucian disciples collected exotic trees to plant here, and there are now more than a hundred thousand different varieties. Today, it's an atmospheric place, sculptures half concealed in thick undergrowth, tombstones standing aslant in groves of ancient trees and wandering paths dappled with sunlight. A great place to spend an afternoon, it's one of the few famous scenic spots in China that it's possible to appreciate unaccompanied by crowds.

Running east from the chunky main gate, the imperial carriageway leads to a gateway and an arched stone bridge, beyond which is the spot where Confucius and his son are buried. The **Hall of Deliberation**, just north of the bridge, was where visitors put on ritual dress before performing sacrifices. An avenue of name-chop carvers and souvenir stalls, then of carved stone animals, leads to the **Hall of Sacrifices**, and behind that to a small grassy mound – the **grave**. Just to the west of the tomb, a hut, looking like a potting shed, was where Confucius's disciples each spent three years watching over the grave. Confucius's son is buried just north of here. His unflattering epitaph reads: "He died before his father without making any noteworthy achievements".

According to legend, before his death Confucius told his disciples to bury him at this spot because the *feng shui* was good. His disciples objected, as there was no river nearby. Confucius told them that a river would be dug in the future. After the first Qin emperor, Qin Shi Huang, unified China, he launched an anti-Confucian campaign, burning books and scholars, and tried to sabotage the grave by ordering a river to be dug through the cemetery, thus inadvertently perfecting it.

Eating, drinking and nightlife

Local specialities include fragrant rice and boiled **scorpions** soaked in oil. The Kong family also developed its own **cuisine**, featuring dishes such as "Going to the Court with the Son" (pigeon served with duck) and "Gold and Silver Fish" (a white and a yellow fish together). It's possible to sample this refined cuisine at the *Queli* hotel and the *Kongfuyan Dajiudian* (孔府宴大酒店, *kǒngfǔyàn dàjiǔdiàn*) near the Drum Tower, though count on up to ¥200 per head. There are also many smaller places around town offering much cheaper **set menus** of these things: six dishes and a soup at ¥30 per person, eight dishes and soup ¥60 and so on. They all have boards outside listing their prices.

At night, Wumaci Dajie fills up with open-air **food stalls**, offering tasty-looking hotpots and stews. The food's not bad and the atmosphere is lively, though make sure you know the price before you order anything. Otherwise, backstreets such as Nan Dajie, east of the *Great Wall* hotel, are thick with hole-in-the-wall noodle and stir-fry places, where you can fill up for under ¥10. Lastly, **Western food** and **coffee** are available at the youth hostel (p.310).

Listings

Banks and exchange There's a Bank of China near the corner of Dongmen Dajie and Gulou Nanjie.

Mail The post office is near the corner of Dongmen Dajie and Gulou Beijie.

Shopping There are plenty of stalls and shops selling tourist gimmicks all through town. The Confucian connection has been exploited to the hilt, with Confucius fans, beer, sweets and something called the "Confucius Treasure Box", which claims to include an acorn from the Confucian Forest and sand from the great sage's grave. Pick up a book of translated Confucian sayings at the *Queli* hotel, but beware price tags covering the actual printed price on these. While steering clear of Confucian paraphernalia, it's worth checking out the chops (which can be carved with your name in a few minutes), rubbings taken from the steles in the temple and locally crafted pistachio carvings. Get your scorpion essence – a local product, advertised as a general tonic – in the department stores on Wumaci Jie.

Qingdao and around

The eastern Shandong port city of **QINGDAO** (青岛, *qīngdǎo*) sprang to prominence in 1897, when Germany's **Kaiser Wilhelm**, wanting to extend his country's sphere of influence in the East, **annexed** the city after two German missionaries were murdered here during the **Boxer Rebellion** (see p.950). Following the

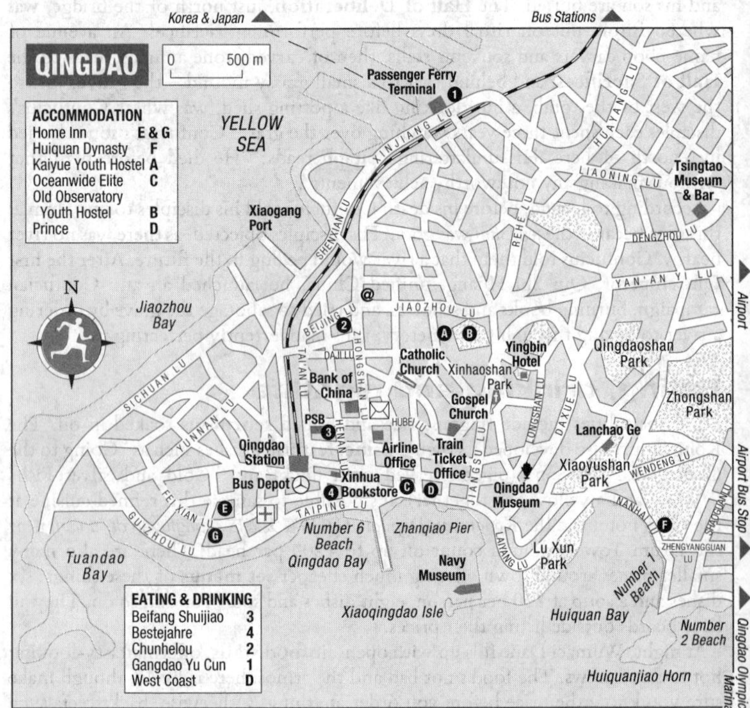

Kaiser's hysterical speech (which coined the phrase "Yellow Peril"), the feeble Manchu court ceded the territory for 99 years, along with the right to build the Shandong rail lines. Qingdao made an ideal deep-water base for the German navy, and while they were here they established a **brewery** producing the now world-famous Tsingtao Beer (Tsingtao is the old transliteration of Qingdao). However, the city was forcibly taken from Germany in 1914 by the **Japanese** and later gifted to Japan at the Treaty of Versailles, an event that led to nationwide demonstrations – the beginning of the May Fourth Movement (see p.951). Qingdao was returned to China in 1922.

Modern Qingdao is still a very important **port**, China's fourth-largest, but the **old town**, which once was a museum piece of red-roofed Bavarian architecture, is today being run down and neglected as a huge, modern industrial city cut by multilane highways sprouts 5km to the east; pretty much the only reason to head this way is for the year-round **ferry connections** to South Korea and Japan. While you're here, though, you can check out some decent white-sand **beaches** dotted along the shoreline – indeed, the city was chosen to host the sailing events of the 2008 Olympics – and a worthwhile day-trip east to **Lao Shan**, one of China's most famous peaks.

Arrival and information

The **old town**, in the southwest side of the city, is fairly close to the beaches and most transit points. North–south **Zhongshan Lu** is the main shopping district here, with a mesh of roads and lanes spread either side.

The **airport**, 30km to the northeast, is served by an **airport bus** (¥15) to **Qingdao station**, newly restored and conveniently located in the area of greatest tourist interest. There's a small **bus** depot in this area, but most long-distance services will arrive about 5km to the north – bus #5 runs from here down to the seafront at Taiping Lu. The **passenger-ferry terminal** (大港客运站, *dàgǎng kèyùnzhàn*) is again north of the old town – turn right out of the terminal and catch bus #303 to the old train-station area, or #8 to Zhongshan Lu. **Taxis** start at ¥7, though expect to pay more than double this to get to the eastern part of town.

There's plenty of expat-oriented **information** at Ⓦmyredstar.com. The *Red Star* team put out an excellent monthly magazine, as well as a quirky pack of cards highlighting 52 top Qingdao venues.

Moving on from Qingdao

There's an **airlines office** (Ⓣ0532/2895577) at 29 Zhongshan Lu; the airport bus leaves from outside the *Haitian Dajiudian* in the modern, eastern part of town, between 6am and 9pm. **Trains** run north to Yantai, and west to Ji'nan and beyond. There's a **train ticket office** inside a compound shared with a carwash on Yishui Lu (an eastern continuation of Hubei Lu); otherwise, ask at accommodation or head to the station. For **buses**, try the depot south of the train station first, which has departures to Yantai, Beijing, Shanghai, Ji'nan and Xi'an.

There are also **international ferries** from the passenger-ferry terminal on Xinjiang Lu to Incheon in South Korea, and Shimonoseki in Japan. Ferries to **Incheon** – a major city just one hour from Seoul by subway train – leave on Monday, Wednesday and Friday; the journey takes 16 hours, and tickets cost from ¥750–1090. Ferries to **Shimonoseki** leave on Mondays and Thursdays, take 36 hours and cost ¥1100–4400. You will also have to pay **departure tax** of around ¥60.

Accommodation

Qingdao's old town has abundant **accommodation**, and though the city's newest, flashest places are much further east, there's a good range here.

Home Inn (如家酒店, *rújiā jiǔdiàn*) 52 Danxian Lu, just off Guizhou Lu ⓣ0532/82669000, ⓦwww.homeinns.com. Usual good value offered by this new, clean motel chain – book ahead if possible. There's another branch nearby at 62 Fuzhou Lu, if they're full here. ❸

Huiquan Dynasty (汇泉王朝大酒店, *huìquán wángcháo dàjiǔdiàn*) 9 Nanhai Lu ⓣ0532/82999888, ⓕ82871122. A well-located four-star hotel – the beach is directly opposite. ❽

Kaiyue Youth Hostel (凯越国际青年旅馆, *kǎiyuè guójì qīngnián lǚguǎn*) 31 Jining Lu ⓣ0532/82845450, ⓦwww.yhaqd.com. Situated near some of the town's older colonial quarters, and inside what was once a church, this is a lovely place to stay, and the staff can organize all watersports plus kite-flying activities. Dorms from ¥45, standard doubles ❷, family rooms ❸

Oceanwide Elite (泛海名人酒店, *fànhǎi míngrén jiǔdiàn*) 29 Taiping Lu ⓣ0532/82996699, ⓦwww.oweh.com. In an excellent location opposite Zhanqiao Pier, this immaculate four-star hotel has an impressive interior and all the facilities you'd expect. Keep an eye out for whopping discounts in the off-season. ❽

Old Observatory Youth Hostel (奥博维特国际青年旅馆, *àobówéitè guójì qīngnián lǚguǎn*) 21 Guanxiang Er Lu ⓣ0532/82822626, ⓦhostelqingdao.com. Housed in a former observatory, this offers (predictably) good views, best taken in over coffee or beer from its rooftop café. Pick-up is available from the train station or ferry terminal. Dorms from ¥60, doubles ❸

Prince (栈桥宾馆, *zhànqiáo bīnguǎn*) 31 Taiping Lu ⓣ0532/82888666, ⓕ82870936. Elderly hotel, but with heaps of character from the wood-panelled lobby upwards, and featuring an excellent restaurant on the lobby floor (see p.320). Sun Yatsen stayed here once, too. ❼

The City

The main thing to do in Qingdao is to wander through the **old German town**, where some quiet back lanes retain a century-old ambience, or to head down to the **waterfront**, where besides the beaches there's an offbeat museum.

Anchoring the old German town is the fine **Catholic Church** (天主教堂, *tiānzhǔ jiàotáng*; Mon–Sat 8am–5pm, Sun noon–5pm; ¥5), whose distinctive double spires can be seen from all over the western parts of the city. The streets east of here are interesting, some cobbled, many lined with pink buildings with black iron balconies overlooking the street; there's also the 1908 **Gospel church** (基督教堂, *jīdū jiàotáng*), built of solid stone and with a dark blue tin clocktower, on Jiangsu Lu. East again, the **Yingbin Hotel** on Longshan Lu (迎宾馆, *yíngbīnguǎn*; daily 8.30am–4.30pm; ¥15) is an incredible, Disney-style fortress built in 1905. It's worth a tour, as the German Governor-General, the warlord Yuan Shikai and Chairman Mao have lodged here in their time. South of here, the **Qingdao Museum** on Daxue Lu (青岛市博物馆, *qīngdǎoshì bówùguǎn*; Tues–Sun 8.30am–5pm; ¥15) is housed in a beautiful, temple-like building, which in the 1930s was the headquarters of the sinister-sounding Red Swastika Association, a welfare institute. There's a collection of paintings here from the Yuan through to Qing dynasties, and four large **Buddhas** dating back to 500–527 AD – slim striking figures with bulbous, smiling heads, one hand pointing upward to heaven, the other down to the earth.

One last essential sight is the **Tsingtao Museum and Bar** (青岛啤酒博物馆, *qīngdǎo píjiǔ bówùguǎn*; daily 8.30am–4.30pm; ¥50; ⓣ0532/8383 3437), around 1.5km northeast of the Gospel Church, at 56 Dengzhou Lu. Though the museum itself is pretty tame, the ticket includes three glasses of beer, and the **bar** here will let you buy more.

The waterfront

Qingdao's **beaches**, with fine white sand, are busy places in the summer, when holidaymakers come to promenade or just slump and look out to sea against a backdrop of pine trees. **Kite flying** is popular, too – some of the country's best kites are made at the nearby city of Weifang.

Closest to the old town, **Number 6 beach** is at the bottom of Zhongshan Lu; it's small but has the liveliest social scene, with crowds promenading along **Zhanqiao Pier** and numerous little stalls lining Taiping Lu selling gaudy swimsuits and cheap souvenirs. Follow the bay around east of the pier and you reach the **Navy Museum** (海军博物馆, *hǎijūn bówùguǎn*; daily 8am–5pm; ¥30), where a decommissioned **submarine** and a **destroyer** sit in the water. You're required to leave cameras at the ticket booth, which seems a little oversensitive as both exhibits are virtually antiques. The submarine is the most interesting, its narrow, dark rooms arrayed with masses of chunky old valves, dials, levers and knobs, many of them bearing Russian markings.

East along Laiyang Lu is pleasant **Lu Xun Park** (鲁迅公园, *lǔxùn gōngyuán*; free), a strip of pine trees and benches above the rocky coast, and then the old town ends abruptly with a flurry of high-rises and paved plazas at **Number 1 beach**, the biggest (580m long) and best. In season, it's packed with ice-cream vendors, trinket stalls and a rash of photographers. There are beachball-shaped changing huts, showers, multicoloured beach umbrellas, and designated swimming areas marked out with buoys and protected by shark nets. The water, however, is like Chinese soup – murky and warm, with unidentifiable things floating in it – so swimming is not recommended. If it feels too crowded here, head east to the more sheltered **number 2 and 3 beaches**, popular with the older, sanatorium-dwelling crowd. At the eastern end of Number 2 beach stands the **former German Governor's Residence**, a grand castle looking out to sea.

Eating, drinking and nightlife

Qingdao has ample **restaurants** to choose from. The speciality is seafood; mussels and crabs here are particularly good. There are plenty of small, noisy and busy **seafood places** in the streets leading down to the coast, where competition means standards are high, and, with some exceptions, costs are reasonably low. **Nightlife**

Tsingtao Beer

Many a Western traveller arrives in Qingdao with a nagging sense of familiarity regarding the city's name. It usually doesn't take too long to be put straight – this is the home of **Tsingtao**, China's undisputed number-one beer. The confusion stems from its non-pinyin romanization, which can be directly attributed to the brewery's age; it was started way back in 1903 (when Chinese used the Wade-Giles transliteratory system) as a German-British joint venture, before coming under **Japanese** control during their occupation of Qingdao. The Japanese ramped up production and essentially transformed Tsingtao from a pumped-up microbrewery to a national success story. During the first decades of **Communist control**, Tsingtao beer was pretty much the only product exported from China.

As in the rest of China, bottles of Tsingtao can be bought all over the city. However, it would be a shame to leave Qingdao without buying the unpasteurized **draught** version, sold in plastic bags on the streetsides – getting the nectar into the bag without spillage is something of an art form. Tsingtao also takes pride of place during the **International Beer Festival**, which occurs each August at International Beer City, way out to the east of town.

isn't as exciting in the Old Town as you'll find out east in the city centre – see Ⓦmyredstar.com for up-to-date listings information.

Beifang Shuijiao (北方水饺, *běifāng shŭijiăo*) 26 Hubei Lu. At the corner of Henan and Hubei streets, this specializes in *jiaozi* and other northern fare. They have an English menu, and two can eat well for ¥40.

Bestejahre (百事特雅大厦, *băishìtèyă dàshà*) Taiping Lu. The Bestejahre building, just across from the Number 6 beach, houses a café, pizzeria, dumpling restaurant and a Japanese place.

Chunhelou (春和楼饭店, *chūnhélóu fàndiàn*) 146 Zhongshan Lu. This famous spot – heaving in the evenings – offers generous portions and highly recommended spicy chicken.

 **Gangdao Yu Cun** (港岛渔村, *găngdăo yúcūn*) 10 Xinjiang Lu. Right around the corner from the ferry terminal, and perfect for a first or last meal in China. Portions are huge, and chosen from a hanging picture menu – highly recommended is *jinsha yipin jialai*, a Shandong speciality made from aubergine segments stuffed with mince then fried. Service is also friendly to a fault, right from the inevitable "Hello!" as you enter.

West Coast 31 Taiping Lu. There are surprisingly reasonable prices on the menu at this restaurant, which sits pretty in the bowels of the *Prince* hotel, and offers shimmery ocean views with echoes of the French Riviera. Fish is the speciality, including sea bass and Japanese-style sashimi, but simple mains (¥20 or so) are on offer for those who want a promenade view without breaking the bank.

Listings

Banks and exchange The Bank of China (Mon–Fri 8.30am–5pm, Sat & Sun 9.30am–4pm), which has an ATM, is at 62 Zhongshan Lu.

Bookshop The Xinhua Bookstore is at 10 Henan Lu, just south of Hubei Lu.

Internet A large, comfortable internet café (¥2/hr) is at the corner of Zhongshan Lu and Jiaozhou Lu.

Mail and telephones The main post office and telecom building (Mon–Sat 8am–6pm) is about halfway along Zhongshan Lu.

PSB The PSB (Mon–Sat 8am–noon & 2–7pm) is at 29 Hubei Lu, not far from the train station.

Lao Shan

The **Lao Shan** (崂山, *láoshān*) area, 400 square kilometres of rugged, mountainous coast 40km east of Qingdao, is an easy day-trip from the city. **Minibus tours** (¥65) depart in the early morning from Taiping Lu, west of the pier; **public bus** #304 (¥8) leaves frequently from the east side of the train station, dropping you at **Wu Kou**, the easternmost part of the area. Plenty of other buses come here from other parts of Qingdao, plus there are paths, cable cars and shuttle buses between the sights, so getting around and back to town afterwards is not a problem. It's definitely worth getting a **map**, however – detailed spreads of Lao Shan are printed on the back of most city maps.

Lao Shan is a good place to **hike** around, as the whole area is dotted with caves, springs and waterfalls amid striking scenery, and with a bit of effort it's possible to lose the crowds and trinket stalls. Writers have been inspired by the landscape for centuries – *Strange Stories from a Chinese Studio* by the Qing-dynasty author **Pu Songling** (see p.993) was written here – and have left noble graffiti in the form of poems and sage reflections cut into rocks all round the area. Jiushui Valley here is also the source of **Lao Shan mineral water**, which gives Tsingtao beer its taste; it's one of the few Chinese mineral waters that doesn't taste of swimming pools.

Around the mountain

On a clear day, the **coastal road route** from Qingdao is spectacular, winding precariously along clifftops. On the way you'll pass the **Stone Old Man**, a 10m-high rock standing in the sea, said to be the petrified body of a man who turned to stone after his daughter was kidnapped by Longwang, the King of the East Sea.

You'll be charged ¥50 entrance (¥30 off season) near **Lao Shan village**, after which there are various routes out to the sights. One of these, heading southeast, takes you to a village at the foot of Lao Shan, from where a pathway of stone steps, constructed a century ago by the enterprising German Lao Shan Company to cater for their compatriots' weakness for alpine clambering, runs all the way to the summit and then back down a different route on the other side. The **path** climbs past gullies and woods, streams and pools, and the ascent takes about two hours. There's a temple halfway up, where you can fortify yourself with fruit and tea for the final haul. At the **summit**, 1133m above sea level, a ruined temple now houses a meteorological station. The view is great, and gets even better as you descend by the alternative route back to the village.

Other scenic spots have a religious connection. On **Naloyan Shan**, 2km northeast of Lao Shan, is a cave in which the Naloyan Buddha was said to have meditated, and on the coast just north of here the **Baiyun Cave** was once the home of a famous monk, Tian Baiyun. Ever since, it has been seen as an auspicious place to meditate. **Mingxia Cave**, 3km farther south down the coast, on the slopes of Kunyu Shan, was written about by a famous Taoist, Qiu Changchun. Inside the cave are stones that reflect the rays of the morning sun, and the flat area outside is a good vantage point from which to watch the sunset.

Well worth a visit is the **Taiqing Gong** (¥15), a temple to the south of Lao Shan, by the coast, and close to the boat dock. It's the oldest and grandest of Lao Shan's temples, consisting of three halls set amid old trees – some dating back to the Han and Tang dynasties – and flower gardens. Outside the first hall are two camellias about which Pu Songling wrote a story. There are nine other temples nearby, which, though smaller, are quiet, peaceful places.

Yantai

On the Yellow Sea in northern Shandong, **YANTAI** (烟台, *yāntái*) is a modern and bustling place with a burgeoning port, and one of the fastest-growing cities in a land full of them. Despite its financial success, tourist sights are thin on the ground and things are rather pricey relative to most other places in northern China – the main reason to visit the area is to pick up **ferries** to Dalian, or even Korea (see p.322).

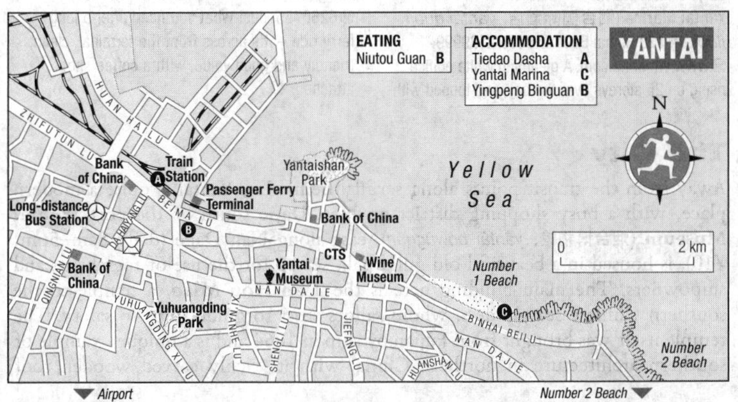

Ferries to Korea

In addition to services from Qingdao (see p.316), two other Shandong ports – Yantai and Weihai – offer ferry connections to **Incheon**, a major city in South Korea, only one hour from Seoul by subway train. **Tickets** can be bought in advance, or at the terminals themselves. There are several classes on each vessel, with gradations in price as you move down the scale. You will also have to pay a **departure tax** of around ¥60.

Ferries leave **Yantai** on Monday, Wednesday and Friday; the journey takes 12 hours and tickets start at ¥960. Tickets can be bought at the terminal, or from CTS (Ⓣ0535/6231539, 6216533 or 6611582), on Beima Lu. From **Weihai** (威海, *wēihǎi*), 80km east of Yantai, ferries leave on Sunday, Tuesday and Thursday; the journey takes 14 hours and tickets start at ¥750. Tickets can be booked at the port, and most accommodation in town.

Arrival

Yantai's **airport** is 15km south of the city; bus #9 runs from here to the train station, or a taxi will cost around ¥60. The other arrival points are fairly closely grouped in the northwest of town: on Beima Lu, the **train station**, on lines to Qingdao and Ji'nan, is just west of the **port**, which handles ferries from Dalian (several times a day; 4hr; ¥170) and Incheon. **Buses** usually use the main long-distance station about 1km west of the train station on Qingnian Lu, though sometimes you get dropped in the train station forecourt.

Accommodation and eating

The rail and port areas are flooded with **hotels** charging just ¥100 for a double, though not all will take foreigners.

For **eating**, the 24hr noodle and dumpling place next to the *Tiedao Dasha*, and a Korean barbecue place called the *Niutou Guan* next to the *Yingpeng Binguan*, make the best alternatives to dining at your accommodation, or you can try the street stalls in the back lanes between Beima Lu and Nan Dajie.

Tiedao Dasha (铁道大厦, *tiědào dàshà*) Ⓣ0535/2961188, Ⓕ6261391. Immediately west of the train station, this has small rooms but is otherwise a good budget choice, and not too noisy despite the location. ❷

Yantai Marina (烟台国际酒店, *yāntái guójì jiǔdiàn*) 128 Binhai Beilu Ⓣ0535/2129999, Ⓦwww.ytmarina.com. A gleaming white edifice rising up 25 storeys over the bay, and topped with a revolving restaurant. Views from the upper floors are predictably superb, though you'll have to pay extra for a sea-facing room. ❼

Yingpeng Binguan (鹰鹏宾馆, *yíngpéng bīnguǎn*) 59 Beima Lu Ⓣ0535/620655, Ⓕ6260755. Just what you need after a long ferry ride – it's across from the terminal, clean, friendly and good value, with a coffee shop attached. ❸

The City

Away from the transit points along scruffy Beima Lu, Yantai is quite a modern place, with a busy shopping district on **Nan Dajie** south of the port. **Yantai Museum** (烟台博物馆, *yāntái bówùguǎn*), east along Nan Dajie (daily 8am–5pm; ¥10), is housed in a beautiful old guild hall, set up for the use of merchants and shipowners. The main building here is the **Tian Hou Miao**, a temple to the southern Chinese sea goddess, whom sailors trust to guide ships to safety. The temple itself was brought from Fujian by ship in 1864 and is a unique example of southern architecture in northern China, with its richly carved wooden roof beams, eaves and panels illustrating historical scenes, and sweeping, pronged roofline fancifully ornamented with mythical figures in wood, stone and glazed ceramics. The whole temple complex is set in a little garden with pools and a stage (the goddess is said to have been fond of plays).

A twenty-minute walk northeast, the **Wine Museum** (张继酒文博物馆, *zhāngjí jiǔwén bówùguǎn*; daily 9am–5pm; ¥30, or ¥50 including wine tasting) on Beima Lu is worth a look, not so much for the humdrum historical exhibits but because – almost uniquely in China – they produce a grape wine that is better than just drinkable. Make sure you descend in to the vast **cellar** where, sitting proud and beribboned among lesser casks, are the three-century-old "Barrel Kings", each holding fifteen tons. You can have a go at bottling in cellar 4, or make your way straight to the **bar** in cellar 5 for your samples – the twelve-year-old red is excellent, as is their brandy, both of which are on sale in the museum shop.

After this you've pretty well exhausted Yantai's attractions, though the **seafront** is pleasant on a good day. **Yantaishan Park** (烟台山公园, *yāntáishān gōngyuán*; ¥8), marking the eastern edge of the port area, features a steep hill where the locals used to keep an eye out for pirates, latticed with twisting paths, pavilions, a couple of former European consulates and an old Japanese military camp. The city's two **beaches** are both east of here, but they're not great – littered, windy and hemmed in by unattractive buildings. Number 2 beach, the farther of the two, is the better, though the water is very polluted.

Listings

Banks and exchange The main Bank of China (Mon–Fri 8am–noon & 2–5pm), which has an ATM, is on the corner of Qingian Lu and Nan Dajie.

CAAC The office (☎0535/6669777) is on Da Haiyang Lu, near the train station.

Mail The post office (Mon–Fri 8am–6pm) is on Nan Dajie, near the corner of Da Haiyang Lu.

Jiangsu

Jiangsu (江苏, *jiāngsū*) is a long, narrow province hugging the coast south of Shandong. Low-lying, flat and wet, it is one of China's most fertile and long-inhabited areas. Today, much of it is industrial sprawl, which is why it's one of China's richest areas, but there are a few gems among all the new factory towns; provincial capital **Nanjing** is one of the country's great historical cities, while **Suzhou** is an ancient city famous throughout China for its gardens and silk production.

Visiting the region, you find yourself in a world of **water**. The whole area is intensively drained, canalized, irrigated and farmed, and the rivers, canals and lakes which web the plain give it much of its character. The traditional way to travel here was by **boat**, though passenger traffic has dwindled away to near-extinction. The traditional route across Jiangsu was the **Grand Canal** (see p.324), once navigable all the way from Hangzhou in Zhejiang province to Beijing. The province's other great water highway – the **Yangzi River** – connects Nanjing with Shanghai, ensuring that trade from both east and west continues to bring wealth to the region.

Jiangsu **cuisine** tends to be on the sweet side and is characterized by an emphasis on flavour rather than texture, and by the use of wine in cooking. That said, one of the best-known dishes, *yanshui ya* (brine duck), has none of these qualities. The

The Grand Canal

The **Grand Canal** (大运河, *dàyùnhé*), at 1800km the longest canal on earth, ranks alongside the Great Wall of China as the country's greatest engineering achievement. The first sections were dug about 400 BC, probably for military purposes, but the historic task of linking the Yellow and the Yangzi rivers was not achieved until the early seventh century AD under the Sui emperor Yang Di, when as many as six million men may have been pressed into service for its construction.

Locals like to point out that whereas the Great Wall was designed to stop contact and communication, the canal was made to further it. The original function of the canal was specifically to join the fertile rice-producing areas of the Yangzi with the more heavily populated but barren lands of the north, and to alleviate the effects of regular crop failures and famine. Following its completion, however, the canal became a vital element in the expansion of **trade** under the Tang and Song, benefiting the south as much as the north. Slowly the centre of political power drifted south – by 800 AD the Yangzi basin was taking over from the Yellow River as the chief source of the empire's finances, a transformation that would bring an end to the long domination of the old northern capitals, and lead to Hangzhou and Nanjing becoming China's most populous and powerful cities.

By the twelfth century, the provinces of Jiangsu and Zhejiang had become the economic and political heart of China. The Song dynasty moved south and established a capital at **Hangzhou** and the Ming emperors subsequently based themselves in **Nanjing**. During this period, and for centuries afterwards, the canal was constantly maintained and the banks regularly built up. A Western traveller, Robert Morrison, journeying as late as 1816 from Tianjin all the way down to the Yangzi, described the sophisticated and frequent locks and noted that in places the banks were so high and the country around so low that from the boat it was possible to look down on roofs and treetops.

Not until early in the twentieth century did the canal seriously start falling into **disuse**. Contributing factors included the frequent flooding of the Yellow River, the growth of coastal shipping and the coming of the rail lines. Unused, much of the canal rapidly silted up. But since the 1950s its value has once more been recognized, and renovation undertaken. The stretch **south of the Yangzi**, running from Zhenjiang through Changzhou, Wuxi and Suzhou, is now navigable year-round, at least by flat-bottomed barges, since passenger services have been killed off by new highways and high-speed trains. **North of the Yangzi**, the canal is seasonably navigable virtually up to Jiangsu's northern border with Shandong, and major works are going on to allow bulk carriers access to the coal-producing city of Xuzhou. Beyond here, towards the Yellow River, sadly the canal remains impassable.

duck is first pressed and salted, then steeped in brine and baked; the skin should be creamy-coloured and the flesh red and tender. Other Jiangsu dishes worth trying include *majiang yaopian* (pig's intestines), jiwei xia (a lake crustacean vaguely resembling a lobster, but much better tasting, locals affirm) and *paxiang jiao* (a type of vegetable that resembles banana leaves).

Nanjing

Formerly known in the West as Nanking, the colossal city of **NANJING** (南京, *nánjīng*) handles its size well. With leafy, shaded avenues and a generally laidback air, it's one of those cities that's perhaps better to live in than visit – accordingly, many simply pass through on their way to Shanghai, Suzhou or Hangzhou, but a wealth of historic sites means that it's well worth a few days of anyone's time. Its very name, "Southern Capital", stands as a direct foil to the "Northern Capital" of Beijing, and the city is still considered the rightful capital of China by many Overseas Chinese, particularly those from Taiwan. Today, it's a prosperous city, benefiting both from its proximity to Shanghai and from its gateway position on the **Yangzi River**, which stretches away west deep into China's interior. With broad, tree-lined boulevards and balconied houses within Ming walls and gates, Nanjing is also one of the most attractive of the major Chinese cities, and although it has become rather an expensive place to visit, it offers a fairly cosmopolitan range of tourist facilities.

Some history

Occupying a strategic site on the south bank of the Yangzi River, Nanjing has had an important role from the earliest times, though not until 600 BC were there the beginnings of a walled city. By the time the Han empire broke up in 220 AD, Nanjing was the capital of half a dozen local dynasties, and when the Sui reunited China in 589, the building of the **Grand Canal** (see opposite) began to considerably increase the city's economic importance. During the Tang and Song periods, the city rivalled nearby Hangzhou as the wealthiest in the country, and in 1368 the first emperor of the Ming dynasty decided to establish Nanjing as the **capital** of all China.

Although Nanjing's claims to be the capital would be usurped by the heavily northern-based Qing dynasty, for centuries thereafter anti-authoritarian movements associated themselves with efforts to restore the old capital. For eleven years in the mid-nineteenth century, the **Taiping rebels** (see p.330) set up the capital of their Kingdom of Heavenly Peace at Nanjing. The siege and final recapture of the city by the foreign-backed Qing armies in 1864 was one of the saddest and most dramatic events in China's history. After the Opium War, the **Treaty of Nanking** which ceded Hong Kong to Britain was signed here in 1841, and Nanjing itself also suffered the indignity of being a treaty port. Following the overthrow of the Qing dynasty in 1911, however, the city flowered again and became the provisional capital of the new Republic of China, with Sun Yatsen as its first president.

In 1937, the name Nanjing became synonymous with one of the worst atrocities of World War II, after the so-called **Rape of Nanking**, in which invading Japanese soldiers butchered an estimated 300,000 civilians. Subsequently, Chiang Kai-shek's government escaped the Japanese advance by moving west to Chongqing, though after Japan's surrender and Chiang's return, Nanjing briefly resumed its status as the official capital of China. Just four years later, however, in 1949, the victorious Communists decided to abandon Nanjing as capital altogether, choosing instead the ancient – and highly conservative – city of Beijing in which to base the country's first "modern" government.

Arrival and city transport

Nanjing Lukou Airport lies literally in the middle of rice paddies 42km to the southeast of the city. Frequent CAAC buses (¥25) run two routes into town, one terminating at Tianjin Lu Xinghan Building on Hanzhong Lu near Xinjiekou, and the other at the main CAAC office on Ruijin Lu, in the southeast of town. The first of these can be tricky to find for those on their way back to the airport – the bus leaves from a stop well off the road, behind an ugly blue building.

The city's broken Ming **walls** are still a useful means of orientation, and the main streets run across town between gates in the city wall. To the northeast of the wall is the **main train station**, connected by subway to the city centre. There's a faint

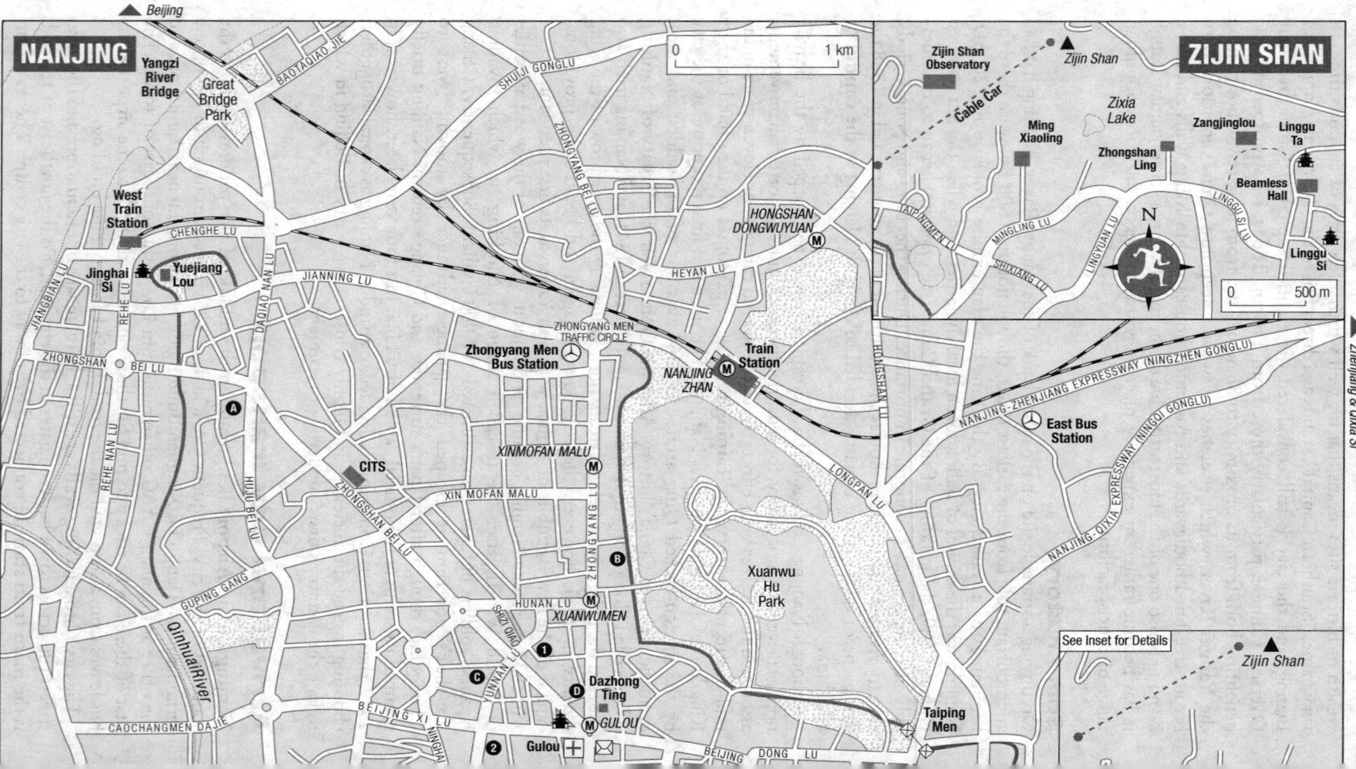
NANJING
Beijing
Yangzi River Bridge
Great Bridge Park
BAOTAQIAO JIE
SHUIJI GONGLU
0 1 km
West Train Station
CHENGHE LU
Jinghai Si
Yuejiang Lou
JIANGBIAN LU
REHE LU
DAQIAO NAN LU
JIANNING LU
ZHONGYANG BEI LU
HONGSHAN DONGWUYUAN
HEYAN LU
ZHONGYANG MEN TRAFFIC CIRCLE
Zhongyang Men Bus Station
Train Station
NANJING ZHAN
ZHONGSHAN BEI LU
REHE NAN LU
HUJU BEI LU
CITS
XINMOFAN MALU
XIN MOFAN MALU
ZHONGYANG LU
HUNAN LU
XUANWUMEN
SHIZI QIAO
YUNNAN LU
GUPING GANG
QinhuaiRiver
CAOCHANGMEN DAJIE
BEIJING XI LU
NINGHAI
Dazhong Ting
GULOU
Gulou
BEIJING DONG LU
Xuanwu Hu Park
LONGPAN LU
HONGSHAN LU
Taiping Men
East Bus Station
NANJING-ZHENJIANG EXPRESSWAY (NINGZHEN GONGLU)
NANJING-QIXIA EXPRESSWAY (NINGQI GONGLU)
Zhenjiang & Qixia Si
See Inset for Details
Zijin Shan
ZIJIN SHAN
Zijin Shan Observatory
Cable Car
Zixia Lake
Ming Xiaoling
Zhongshan Ling
Zangjinglou
Linggu Ta
Beamless Hall
Linggu Si
LINGGU SI LU
TAIPINGMEN LU
MINGLING LU
SHIXIANG LU
LINGYUAN LU
N
0 500 m

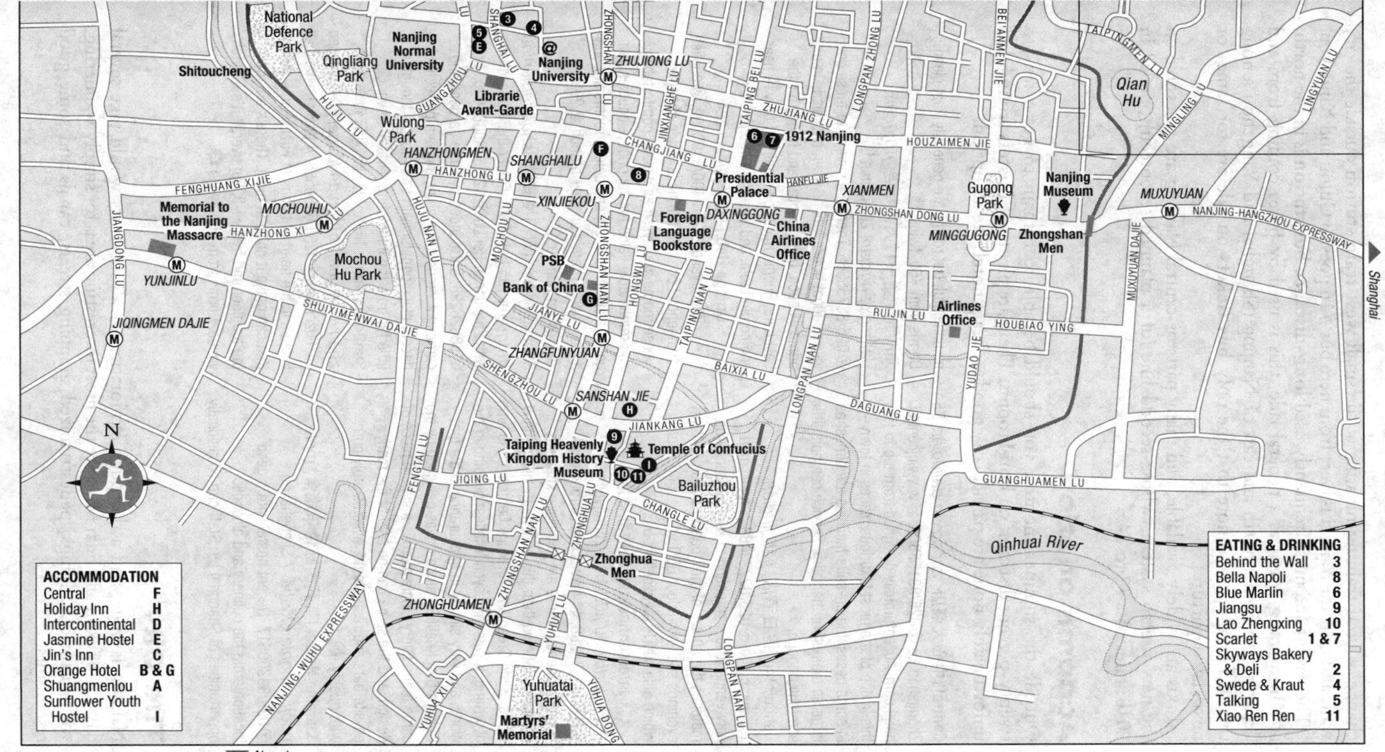
National Defence Park
Shitoucheng
Qingliang Park
Nanjing Normal University
Nanjing University
Librarie Avant-Garde
Wulong Park
HANZHONGMEN
SHANGHAILU
XINJIEKOU
1912 Nanjing
Presidential Palace
DAXINGGONG
Foreign Language Bookstore
China Airlines Office
XIANMEN
Gugong Park
MINGGUGONG
Nanjing Museum
Zhongshan Men
MUXUYUAN
Qian Hu
Shanghai
Memorial to the Nanjing Massacre
MOCHOUHU
Mochou Hu Park
YUNJINLU
JIQINGMEN DAJIE
PSB
Bank of China
ZHANGFUYUAN
SANSHAN JIE
Airlines Office
Taiping Heavenly Kingdom History Museum
Temple of Confucius
Bailuzhou Park
Zhonghua Men
ZHONGHUAMEN
Qinhuai River
Yuhuatai Park
Martyrs' Memorial
Airport
N
ACCOMMODATION
Central F
Holiday Inn H
Intercontinental D
Jasmine Hostel E
Jin's Inn C
Orange Hotel B & G
Shuangmenlou A
Sunflower Youth Hostel I
EATING & DRINKING
Behind the Wall 3
Bella Napoli 8
Blue Marlin 6
Jiangsu 9
Lao Zhengxing 10
Scarlet 1 & 7
Skyways Bakery & Deli 2
Swede & Kraut 4
Talking 5
Xiao Ren Ren 11
SHANGHAI LU
GUANGZHOU LU
HUJU LU
ZHONGSHAN LU
ZHUJIONG LU
JINXIANGHE LU
TAIPING BEI LU
ZHUJIANG LU
LONGPAN ZHONG LU
BEI'ANMEN JIE
TAIPINGMEN LU
LINGYUAN LU
MINGLING LU
HOUZAIMEN JIE
CHANGJIANG LU
HANZHONG LU
HANFU JIE
FENGHUANG XIJIE
ZHONGSHAN DONG LU
NANJING-HANGZHOU EXPRESSWAY
JIANGDONG LU
HANZHONG XI
HUJU NAN LU
MOCHOU LU
ZHONGSHAN NAN LU
HONGWU LU
TAIPING NAN LU
MUXUYUAN DAJIE
SHUIXIMENWAI DAJIE
JIANYE LU
RUIJIN LU
HOUBIAO YING
LONGPAN NAN LU
BAIXIA LU
YUDAO JIE
SHENGZHOU LU
DAGUANG LU
JIANKANG LU
FENGTAI LU
JIQING LU
GUANGHUAMEN LU
CHANGLE LU
ZHONGHUA LU
NANJING-WUHU EXPRESSWAY
YUHUA LU
YUHUA XI LU
YUHUA DONG

chance of your train terminating at the small **west train station** outside the city walls and near the Yangzi River; from here bus #16 goes to Gulou and Xinjiekou.

The largest and most frequently used **long-distance bus station** is in the north, at **Zhongyang Men**; as a general rule, this is used by buses coming from and departing to points north and east of Nanjing (Shanghai and Yangzhou among them). Leaving town, note that the only **bus tickets** on sale are for same- or next-day departures.

Taxis are widely available, and many parts of central Nanjing are accessible on the new **metro** system, whose second line (of a planned seventeen) opened in 2010; fares cost ¥2 to ¥4.

Accommodation

Outside the summer months, you should be able to bargain to get a ten- to twenty-percent discount on **hotel** rooms. There are plenty of **hostels** around, but unfortunately none are particularly good – cheap motels are an option.

Central (中心大酒店, *zhōngxīn dàjiǔdiàn*) 75 Zhongshan Lu ⓣ025/83155888, ⓦwww.njcentralhotel.com. Adventurously designed from top to toe, this is one of the most luxurious places in town – in some cases, the en-suite facilities are almost as large as the rest of the room. Service can be a little scratchy, though. ❼

Holiday Inn (假日酒店, *jiàrì jiǔdiàn*) 1 Jiankang Lu ⓣ025/82233888. Super-smart new venue whose attention to service standards matches the quality of their peaceful rooms. Warm evenings see an outdoor BBQ on the third floor, which also sports an excellent bar. ❾

Intercontinental (绿地洲酒店, *lǜdìzhōu jiǔdiàn*) 1 Zhongyang Lu ⓣ025/83538888, ⓦwww.ichotelsgroup.com/intercontinental. There are few more stunning hotels in all China than this behemoth, filling many floors of the Greenland Financial Center. At the time of writing, it was the seventh-tallest building in the world, and very similar in appearance to the first – Dubai's Burj Khalifa – since it was designed by the same team. Every single room is a superb piece of design, and the same can be said of the many on-site bars and restaurants, which simply purr with quality. ❾

Jasmine Hostel (茉莉国际青年旅舍, *mòlì guójì qīngnián lǚshè*) 7 Shanghai Lu ⓣ025/83300517. Decent hostel with a good location amid the culinary and alcoholic opportunities of Shanghai Lu. Staff can occasionally be unhelpful, but rooms are generally kept clean. Dorms from ¥50, twins ❹

Jin's Inn (金一村大方巷店, *jīnyīcūn dàfāngxiàngdiàn*) 26 Yunnan Lu ⓣ025/83755666. There are several of these good-value budget hotels around town but this is in a prime location, being central and handy for the best bars. Rooms might be small but they're neat and comfortable, and have free internet. ❸

Orange Hotel (桔子, *jiézi*) 224 Zhongyang Lu ⓣ0400/8190099, ⓦenglish.orangehotel.com.cn. Terrific lakeside cheapie whose rooms are stylish as well as comfortable, and remarkable value for the price – doubles can go for as little as ¥220, and deluxe rooms are only a little more. There's another branch at 288 Zhongshan Nan Lu. ❺

Shuangmenlou (双门楼宾馆, *shuāngménlóu bīnguǎn*) 185 Huju Bei Lu, near the intersection with Zhongshan Bei Lu ⓣ025/58800888 ext 80, ⓕ58826298. Surrounded by large gardens and carrying a vague colonial air, this is a perfectly decent place popular with tour groups, though a little far from the interesting parts of town. ❻

Sunflower Youth Hostel (蘸园国际青年旅舍, *zhānyuán guójì qīngnián lǚshè*) 80 Zhanyuan Lu, Fuzi Miao ⓣ025/66850566. A basic hostel well located in the heart of things at Fuzi Miao – though that can make it noisy at night. There's a bar on the top floor and free wi-fi, but overall it's a patchy venue. Dorms from ¥50, twins ❹

The City

Nanjing is huge, and a thorough exploration of all its sights would take several days. Xinjiekou and Fuzi Miao are the most interesting areas for simply wandering, with historic buildings, pedestrianized shopping streets, canals and some good restaurants.

Many of the main sights can be taken in on the convenient **metro line 1 route** from the train station in the north to Yuhuatai Park in the south. This will get you to **Xuanwu Hu Park** and its glorious lake, the opulent **Presidential Palace** and **Fuzi Miao** temple. To the west there are a number of sights around the **Yangzi River**, while rising to the east are the slopes of **Zijin Shan**, a mountain spotted with historical sights.

Xuanwu Hu Park

North of the centre, to the east of Zhongyang Lu and south of the train station, the enormous **Xuanwu Hu Park** (玄武湖公园, *xuánwǔhú gōngyuán*; daily 5am–9pm; ¥20) comprises mostly water, with hills on three sides and the city wall skirting the western shore. Formerly a resort for the imperial family and once the site of a naval inspection by Song emperor Xiaowu, it became a park in 1911 and is a pleasant place to mingle with the locals who come here en masse at weekends. The lake contains five small **islets** linked by causeways and bridges, with restaurants, teahouses, pavilions, rowing boats, paddle boats, places to swim, an open-air theatre and a zoo. The southern end of the park contains one of the better-preserved reaches of the city wall. Xuanwu Gate, just outside Xuanwumen metro station, is the most convenient way to enter the park.

The Presidential Palace

Close to Daxinggong station on metro line 2 is the **Presidential Palace** (总统府, *zǒngtǒng fǔ*; daily 8am–5pm; ¥40) located in the Suzhou-esque garden, Xu Yuan. Both palace and garden were built more than six hundred years ago for a Ming prince, and were subsequently turned into the seat of the provincial governor under the Qing. In 1853 the building was seized by the armies of the Taiping Heavenly Kingdom and converted into the headquarters of Taiping leader Hong Xiuquan. After the overthrow of the Qing, it became the Guomindang government's Presidential Palace. It was from here, in the early decades of the twentieth century, that first Sun Yatsen and later Chiang Kai-shek governed China. Visiting the palace today, you'll see exhibitions on the Taiping Uprising and the life and times of Sun and Chiang.

Fuzi Miao

Near Sanshan Jie station on metro line 1 is the **Temple of Confucius** (夫子庙, *fūzǐ miào*) area, which begins south of Jiankang Lu and harbours a noisy welter of street vendors, boutiques, arcades and restaurants. The central **temple** (daily 8am–9.30pm; ¥15) resembles a theme park inside, complete with mannequins in period costume. The temple is hardly worth bothering about, but there is an attractive waterfront area along the canal here (where the Tang poet Liu Yuxi composed his most famous poem, *Wuyi Lane*), along which you can pick up **leisure boats** (electric ¥20, paddle ¥10; 30min) that trundle south to Zhonghua Men. Cross the canal in front of the temple, and a short walk southeast will bring you to a small park, **Bailuzhou** (白鹭洲, *báilù zhōu*). This ancient corner of the city remained the Chinese quarter after the arrival of the Manchu Qing dynasty in the seventeenth century, and there are still a few traditional houses.

Ten minutes' walk west of the Temple of Confucius and right on the small Zhanyuan Lu, just east of Zhonghua Lu, is the **Taiping Heavenly Kingdom History Museum** (太平天国历史博物馆, *tàipíngtiānguólìshǐ bówùguǎn*; daily 8am–4.30pm; ¥10), well worth a visit. The sad but fascinating story of the Taiping Uprising (see box, p.330) is told here in pictures and relics, with English captions. The building itself was the residence of Xu Da, a Ming prince, and became the home of one of the rebel generals during the uprising.

The Taiping Uprising

One of the consequences of the weakness of the Qing dynasty in the nineteenth century was the extraordinary **Taiping Uprising**, an event that would lead to the slaughter of millions, and which has been described as the most colossal civil war in the history of the world. The Taipings were led by **Hong Xiuquan**, failed civil-service candidate and Christian evangelist, who, following a fever, declared himself to be the younger brother of Jesus Christ. In 1851, he assembled 20,000 armed followers at **Jintian village**, near Guiping in Guangxi province, and established the **Taiping Tianguo**, or Kingdom of Heavenly Peace. This militia routed the local Manchu forces, and by the following year was sweeping up through Hunan into central China. They **captured Nanjing** in 1853, but though the kingdom survived another eleven years, this was its last achievement. Poorly planned expeditions failed to take Beijing or win over western China, and Hong's leadership – originally based on the enfranchisement of the peasantry and the outlawing of opium, alcohol and sexual discrimination – devolved into paranoia and fanaticism. After a gigantic struggle, **Qing forces** finally managed to unseat the Taipings when Western governments sent in assistance, most notably in the person of Queen Victoria's personal favourite, Charles "Chinese" Gordon.

Despite the rebellion's ultimately disastrous failure and its overtly Christian message, the whole episode is seen as a precursor to the arrival of Communism in China. Indeed, in its fanatical rejection of Confucianism and the incredible damage it wrought on buildings and sites of historic value, it finds curious echoes in Mao Zedong's Cultural Revolution.

Zhonghua Men and Yuhuatai Park

Zhonghua Men (中华门, *zhōnghuá mén*) in the far south is now largely bereft of its wall and isolated in the middle of a traffic island, just inside the river moat near a metro station of the same name. This colossal gate actually comprises four gates, one inside another, and its seven enclosures were designed to hold three thousand men in case of enemy attack, making it one of the biggest of its kind in China. Today you can walk through the central archway and climb up two levels, and up above, there's a tremendous view of the city spread out beyond.

The road south, across the Qinhuai River, between Zhonghua Men and Yuhuatai Park, is an interesting stretch lined with two-storey wooden-fronted houses, many with balconies above, while below are small shops and workshops. The trees lining the pavement provide shade as well as room to hang birdcages, pot plants and laundry. Just beyond, the road reaches a small hill, now a park known as **Yuhuatai** (雨花台公园, *yǔhuātái gōngyuán*; daily 6am–6.45pm; ¥25). After 1927 the hill was used as an execution ground, and the Guomindang is said to have murdered vast numbers of people here. The spot is now marked by a **Martyrs' Memorial**, a colossal composite of nine 30m-high figures, worth seeing as a prime example of gigantic Chinese Socialist Realism.

Around the Yangzi River

The far northwest of town in the area of the **Yangzi River** offers a modicum of interest. The **Nanjing Treaty Museum**, located in **Jinghai Si** (静海寺, *jìnghǎi sì*; daily 8am–4.30pm; ¥6), lies very near the west train station off Rehe Lu. It was in this temple that the British and Chinese negotiated the first of the many unequal treaties in the wake of the Opium War in 1843 (the treaty was later signed on a British naval ship in Nanjing harbour). Unfortunately, the museum's detailed exposition of fractious Sino-British relations throughout the nineteenth and twentieth centuries is in Chinese only, but the temple is pleasant to stroll around nonetheless. It was originally built in the Ming dynasty by Emperor Chengzu to honour the Chinese Muslim naval hero **Zhenghe**, who led the Chinese fleet on exploratory voyages to East Africa and the Persian Gulf; you'll see his name commemorated throughout the city.

Rising up behind the temple is **Shizi Shan** (狮子山, *shīzishān*; ¥40; elevator ¥3), a small mountain topped with an ornate, multistorey building, the **Yuejiang Lou** (阅江楼, *yuèjiāng lóu*). While the structure is of little historical importance, its size alone makes it worth a look, and from the top level there's a tremendous view of the city on one side and the Yangzi on the other.

If you're in this area you should definitely take a look at the 1500m-long **double-decker bridge** over the river, still a source of great pride to the Chinese who built it under their own steam after the Russians pulled out in 1960. Before the bridge was built, it took ninety minutes to ferry trains and road vehicles across the river. For a great view of the structure and the banks of the Yangzi, head for **Great Bridge Park** (大桥公园, *dàqiáo gōngyuán*; daily 7am–4.30pm) on the eastern bank; you can take a lift up to a raised platform above the upper (road) deck of the bridge, for ¥4. Bus #15 heads to the park from Zhongyang Men and Gulou.

Some way west of the river is the must-see **Memorial to the Nanjing Massacre** (南京大屠杀纪念馆, *nánjīngdàtúshā jìniànguǎn*; Tues–Sun 8.30am–4.30pm; free). This grim, gravelly garden includes a gruesome display of victims' skulls and bones, half-buried in the dirt, as well as a clearly labelled (in English) photographic account of the sufferings endured by the Chinese at the hands of the Japanese army during World War II. It's right next to Yunjinlu station on metro line 2.

The Nanjing Museum and Zhongshan Men

East of the centre, and a short walk from Minggugong station on metro line 2, the huge **Nanjing Museum** (南京博物馆, *nánjīng bówùguǎn*; daily 9am–4pm; ¥20) is one of the best provincial museums in China, especially in terms of clarity of explanations – nearly everything is labelled in English. Highlights include some superb silk-embroidered sedan chairs and several heavy cast bronzes, dating from as early as the Western Zhou (1100–771 BC). The jade and lacquerwork sections, as well as the model Fujian trading ships, are also well worth seeing.

A short walk east of the museum is **Zhongshan Men** (中山门, *zhōngshān mén*), the easternmost gate of the ancient city walls. You can climb to the top of the wall

Nanjing's city walls

Though Nanjing was walled as many as 2500 years ago, the present **city wall** is basically the work of the first Ming emperor, who extended and strengthened the earlier walls in 1369–73. His wall, built of brick and more than 32km long, followed the contours of the country, skirting Xuanwu Hu in the north, fringing Xijin Shan in the east, and tracing the Qinhuai River (which doubled as a moat) to the west and south. The wall was mainly paid for by rich families resettled here by the emperor: one third of it was "donated" by a single native of Wuxiang in Zhejiang province. Its construction employed 200,000 conscripts, who ensured that the bricks were all the same size and specification, each one bearing the names of the workman and overseer. They were held together, to an average height of 12m and a thickness of 7m, by a mixture of lime and glutinous rice paste.

The original structure, of red rock in places, is still plainly visible along a 300m section of the wall at the so-called **Shitoucheng**, in the west of the city between Caochangmen Dajie and Fenghuang Jie. You can see it from bus #18, which runs outside the walls between Xinjiekou and the west train station.

here, and walk along a little way to the north before the structure crumbles into a small lake, Qian Hu. It's surprisingly spacious and peaceful on the top and affords excellent views.

Zijin Shan

Not far outside Zhongshan Men is **Zijin Shan** (紫金山, *zǐjīn shān*; Purple Gold Mountain), named after the colour of its rocks. Traditionally, the area has been a cool and shady spot to escape the furnace heat of Nanjing's summer, with fragrant woods and stretches of long grass, but also here are the three most visited sites in Nanjing. Of these, the centrepiece, right in the middle of the hill, is **Zhongshan Ling**, the magnificent mausoleum of China's first president, Sun Yatsen. To the east of Zhongshan Ling is the **Linggu Si** complex, and to the west are the ancient **Ming Xiaoling**, tombs of the Ming emperors who ruled China from Nanjing.

Visiting the three main sites on Zijin Shan can easily take a full day. Bus #9 goes to Zhongshan Ling via Linggu Si from Xinjiekou, while bus #20 heads to Ming Xiaoling from Gulou. Private minibuses and a host of private operators also make the trek from the train station square. Perhaps the best way to visit all three without backtracking is to catch a bus from town to either Ming Xiaoling or Linggu Si, and then walk to the other two sites. Various half-day **bus tours** are also available from town; ask at any travel service or upmarket hotel. If you're interested in an overview of the whole mountain, you can ride the **cable car** (one way ¥25, return ¥45) to the peak from a station about 1km east of Taiping Men, the gate by the southern end of Xuanwu Hu Park.

Linggu Si and Linggu Ta

Starting from the eastern side of the hill, farthest from the city, the first sight on Zijin Shan is the collection of buildings around **Linggu Si** (灵谷寺, *línggǔ sì*; daily 8am–5pm; ¥15 entry to the site). If you arrive here by bus, the main building in front of you is the so-called **Beamless Hall**. Completed in 1381, and much restored since, it's unusual for its large size and particularly for its self-supporting brick arch construction, with five columns instead of a central beam. The hall was used to store Buddhist sutras before the Taiping rebels made it a fortress; now it's an exhibition hall. A couple of minutes' walk southeast from the Beamless Hall is the Linggu Si itself, a very much smaller and much restored version of its original self – and still attended by yellow-robed monks.

Leading northwest from the Linggu buildings, a delightful footpath through beautiful cypresses and pines leads to **Linggu Ta** (灵谷塔, *línggǔ tǎ*), an octagonal, nine-storey, 60m-high pagoda, dating back to the 1930s and built as a monument to Guomindang members killed in the fighting against insurgent Communists in 1926–27. It's well worth climbing up for the views over the surrounding countryside.

Sun Yatsen Mausoleum

Dr Sun Yatsen, the first president of post-imperial China, is the only hero revered by Chinese jointly on both sides of the Taiwan Straits. The former leader's **mausoleum** (中山陵, *zhōngshān líng*; daily 6.30am–6.30pm; ¥80), with its famous marble stairway soaring up the hillside, is one of the most popular sites in the country for Chinese tourists. Walking up the steps is worth it for the great views back down the stairs and across the misty hills to the south.

An imposing structure of white granite and blue tiles (the Nationalist colours) set off by the green pine trees, the mausoleum was completed in 1929, four years after Sun Yatsen's death. From the large bronze statue at the bottom, 392 marble steps lead up to the Memorial Hall, dominated by a 5m-tall seated white marble figure of the great man himself. Beyond the figure is the burial chamber, with another marble effigy lying on the stone coffin; according to unsubstantiated rumours, the bones were removed from the coffin to Taiwan by fleeing Guomindang leaders in 1949. The Guomindang ideals – Nationalism, Democracy and People's Livelihood – are carved above the entrance to the burial chamber in gold on black marble.

Ming Xiaoling Mausoleum

A walk of half an hour or so along the road west from Zhongshan Ling brings you to the **Ming Xiaoling** (明孝陵, *míngxiào líng*; daily 8am–5.30pm; ¥70), the burial place of Zhu Yuanzhang, founder of the Ming dynasty and the only one of its fourteen emperors to be buried at Nanjing (his thirteen successors are all buried in Beijing; see p.137). So colossal was the task of moving earth and erecting the stone walls that it took two years and a hundred thousand soldiers and conscripts to complete the tomb in 1383. Although the site was originally far larger than the Ming tombs near Beijing, its halls and pavilions, and 22km-long enclosing vermilion wall, were mostly destroyed by the Taipings. Today what remains is a walled collection of trees, stone bridges and dilapidated gates leading to the lonely mound at the back containing the (as yet unexcavated) burial site of the emperor and his wife, as well as the fifty courtiers and maids of honour who were buried alive to keep them company.

The Ming Xiaoling actually comprises two parts, the tomb itself and the approach to the tomb, known as Shandao (Sacred Way) or, more commonly, **Shixiang Lu** (石像路, *shíxiàng lù*; daily 8am–6.30pm; ¥10) – which leads to the tomb at an oblique angle as a means of deterring evil spirits, who can only travel in straight lines. It's a strange and magical place to walk through, the road lined with twelve charming pairs of stone animals – including lions, elephants and camels – and four pairs of officials. Most people visit the tomb first and the approach afterwards, simply because the road from Zhongshan Ling arrives immediately outside the tomb entrance. To reach the Sacred Way from the tomb entrance, follow the road right (with the tomb behind you) and then round to the left for about fifteen minutes.

Next to Ming Xiaoling is the entrance to **Zixia Hu** (紫霞湖, *zǐxiá hú*; daily 7am–6pm; ¥10), a small lake whose wooded surroundings are perfect for a stroll at any time of year. In summer, the lake is open for swimming, although you should avoid the weekends when the place is full of locals escaping the heat of the city.

One more sight here is the **Zijin Shan Observatory** (¥15), built in 1929 high on one of the three peaks where the Taipings formerly had a stronghold. For fresh air and good views of Nanjing, try to find a minibus heading this way.

Eating

Nanjing has a wide selection of local, regional Chinese and foreign foods, often at much more reasonable prices than their counterparts in nearby Shanghai. It's an especially great place to sample **Jiangsu cuisine**, the best areas for which are north of Gulou along Zhongyang Lu and northwest along Zhongshan Bei Lu.

The presence of a heavy contingent of foreign students in the city, as well as a growing population of expatriate and home-grown business people, ensures a scattering of highly **Westernized restaurants and bars**, which are not necessarily expensive. Xinjiekou and Fuzi Miao are generally good districts to browse for restaurants, but for a staggering variety of Asian food – including just about every kind of Chinese cuisine, plus Indian, Japanese and Thai – head for pedestrianized **Shizi Qiao**, off Hunan Lu to the west of Xuanwu Hu Park.

Behind the Wall 150 Shanghai Lu. Head a few metres uphill along the alley here, called Nan Xiu Cun, and go up the nondescript staircase on the left, which leads to the patio entrance. Great Mexican-style food, especially the quesadillas and enchiladas. In decent weather, the patio is perfect for quiet lunches and livelier evening barbecues.

Bella Napoli 75 Zhongshan Dong Lu, just east from Xinjiekou. Good, if slightly overpriced, Italian food; the pizzas are a better bet than the pasta.

Jiangsu (江苏, *jiāngsū*) 26 Jiankang Lu, just east of Zhonghua Lu. One of the most upmarket places to try Jiangsu food – brine duck is a speciality.

Lao Zhengxing (老正兴菜馆, *lǎozhèngxīng càiguǎn*) 119 Gongyuan Jie, near Fuzi Miao. A favourite of GMD officials in the 1930s, this is a lively place with interesting local dishes, backing onto the river.

Skyways Bakery & Deli 160 Shanghai Lu. Fantastic deli sandwiches on offer at this expat magnet: they bake their own baguettes, ciabatta and cookies, and have a caseful of handmade confections and cakes, as well as passable coffee. Daily 9am–9.30pm.

Swede & Kraut 14 Nan Xiu Cun, off Shanghai Lu ⓣ025/86638798. Sharing management with *Skyways*, this does by far the best Western food in the city, and isn't too pricey either. The pasta and bread are all home-made. The lasagne and fettuccine especially are scrumptious, and the steaks are great, too.

Xiao Ren Ren (小人人食品店, *xiǎorénrén shípǐngdiàn*) 97 Gongyuan Jie, Fuzi Miao. Friendly place designed in the style of a traditional teahouse, with musicians serenading patrons. You can try a selection of local delicacies for just ¥40.

Drinking and entertainment

Nanjing **nightlife** is nowhere near as varied as Shanghai's, though there are a few bars and clubs that see a regular mix of foreigners and Chinese. For a civilized night out, the 1912 Nanjing complex, on Taiping Bei Lu, is the local answer to Shanghai's Xintiandi, a pedestrianized zone of restored buildings now housing upscale bars and restaurants.

Nanjing's **cultural life** is sadly lagging far behind Shanghai's, though your visit might coincide with infrequent acrobatics or Chinese opera performances somewhere in town. The expat-oriented **listings** magazine *Map* (ⓦwww.maiqiu.cn) can be found at most bars and restaurants geared up for foreign custom.

Behind the Wall 150 Shanghai Lu. This restaurant (see p.333) really comes alive in the evenings, with good beer on tap and occasional Latin-tinted live music.

Blue Marlin At the north end of the 1912 Nanjing complex, Taiping Bei Lu. Above the restaurant is a dance floor and terrace with occasional Latin dance nights. Staff are often willing to plug your iPod into their sound system.

Scarlet 34-1 Hubei Lu, an alley south of Yunnan Lu; a second branch is at the northern end of the 1912 Nanjing complex. Two-storey bar that's the late-night venue of choice with most expat residents, with the occasional Western DJ playing dance sounds and rock. Daily until 2am.

Talking Off Shanghai Lu and 9 Ninghai Lu. Cheap beer and a lively atmosphere mean that the two *Talking* bars are hugely popular with local expats, as well as locals that fancy practising their English.

Listings

Airlines The main CAAC reservations and ticketing office (daily 7.30am–10pm; ⓣ025/84499378) is at 52 Ruijin Lu in the southeast of town. China Eastern Airlines' head office (daily 8.30am–5.30pm; ⓣ025/84454325) is at the corner of Changbai Jie and Zhongshan Dong Lu.

Banks and exchange The Bank of China head office (daily 8.30am–5pm), with a 24hr ATM, is due south of Xinjiekou on Zhongshan Nan Lu.

Bookshops The Foreign Language Bookstore on Zhongshan Dong Lu has a few English-language books, though it's usually just business biographies and Harry Potter. The superbly atmospheric Librarie Avant-Garde on Guangzhou Lu – it's a converted underground car-park – has a few foreign-language books.

Hospital The most central hospital is the Gulou Hospital, on Zhongshan Lu just south of the Gulou intersection.

Mail and telephones Nanjing's main post office (daily 8am–6.30pm), offering international phone and fax calls as well as postal services, faces the Gulou traffic circle. There's also a post office at 19 Zhongshan Lu, just north of Xinjiekou.

Travel agents Nearly all hotels have their own travel agencies. CITS (Mon–Fri 8.30am–noon & 2–5pm, Sat & Sun 9am–4pm; ⓣ025/83538564, ⓕ83538561) is at 202 Zhongshan Bei Lu.

Suzhou and around

With its centre riddled with **classic gardens** and picturesque **canals**, the ancient city of **SUZHOU** (苏州, *sūzhōu*) is justly one of eastern China's biggest tourist draws. Whereas most Chinese cities are busy building themselves up from the inside out, parts of central Suzhou remain remarkably quaint and calm – no mean feat in a city of over six million. As if greenery and waterways were not enough, Suzhou has also long been famed for its **silk** production, making it one of China's best places in which to shop for said commodity.

Just forty minutes from Shanghai by high-speed train, many choose to visit Suzhou on a day-trip, though to do so would be something of a mistake unless you're pressed for time, for it's only in the evening that the true soul of the city can be appreciated. Those who stay the night will see the soft light of innumerable **paper lanterns** dappling the canalsides, whose paved lanes make Suzhou one of those rare places that looks fantastic in the rain. Additionally, those who fight their way through the industrial areas surrounding the city can make their way to one of several smaller **canaltowns**, or the majestic lake of **Tai Hu**.

Some history

He Lu, semi-mythical ruler of the Kingdom of Wu, is said to have founded Suzhou in 600 BC as his capital, but it was the arrival of the **Grand Canal** more than a thousand years later that marked the beginning of the city's prosperity. The **silk trade** too was established early here, flourishing under the Tang and thoroughly booming when the whole imperial court moved south under the Song. To this day, silk remains an important source of Suzhou's income.

With the imperial capital close by at Hangzhou, Suzhou attracted an overspill of scholars, officials and merchants, bringing wealth and patronage with them. In the late thirteenth century, Marco Polo reported "six thousand bridges, clever merchants, cunning men of all crafts, very wise men called Sages and great natural physicians". These were the people responsible for carving out the intricate gardens that now represent Suzhou's primary attractions. When the first Ming emperor founded his capital at Nanjing, the city continued to enjoy a privileged position within the orbit of the court and to flourish as a centre for the production of woodblock and the weaving of silk. The business was transformed by the gathering of the workforce into great sheds in a manner not seen in the West until the coming of the Industrial Revolution three centuries later.

Until recently, Suzhou's good fortune had been to avoid the ravages of history, despite suffering brief periods of occupation by the Taipings (see p.330) in the 1860s and by the Japanese during World War II. The 2500-year-old city walls, however, which even in 1925 were still an effective defence against rampaging warlords, were almost entirely demolished after 1949, and the parts of the **old city** that still survive – moats, gates, tree-lined canals, stone bridges, cobblestoned streets and whitewashed old houses – are disappearing fast.

Arrival and information

Nearly all travellers arrive by **train**, with Suzhou's newly refurbished station lying on the main Shanghai–Nanjing rail line. A number of **tourist bus** routes head into the centre (Y2 and Y5 are most convenient), or it's a short taxi ride.

Suzhou has two main bus stations: the **North bus station**, which has regular connections with Shanghai and Wuxi; and the **South bus station**, which sees arrivals from points south including Hangzhou. There's no airport at Suzhou,

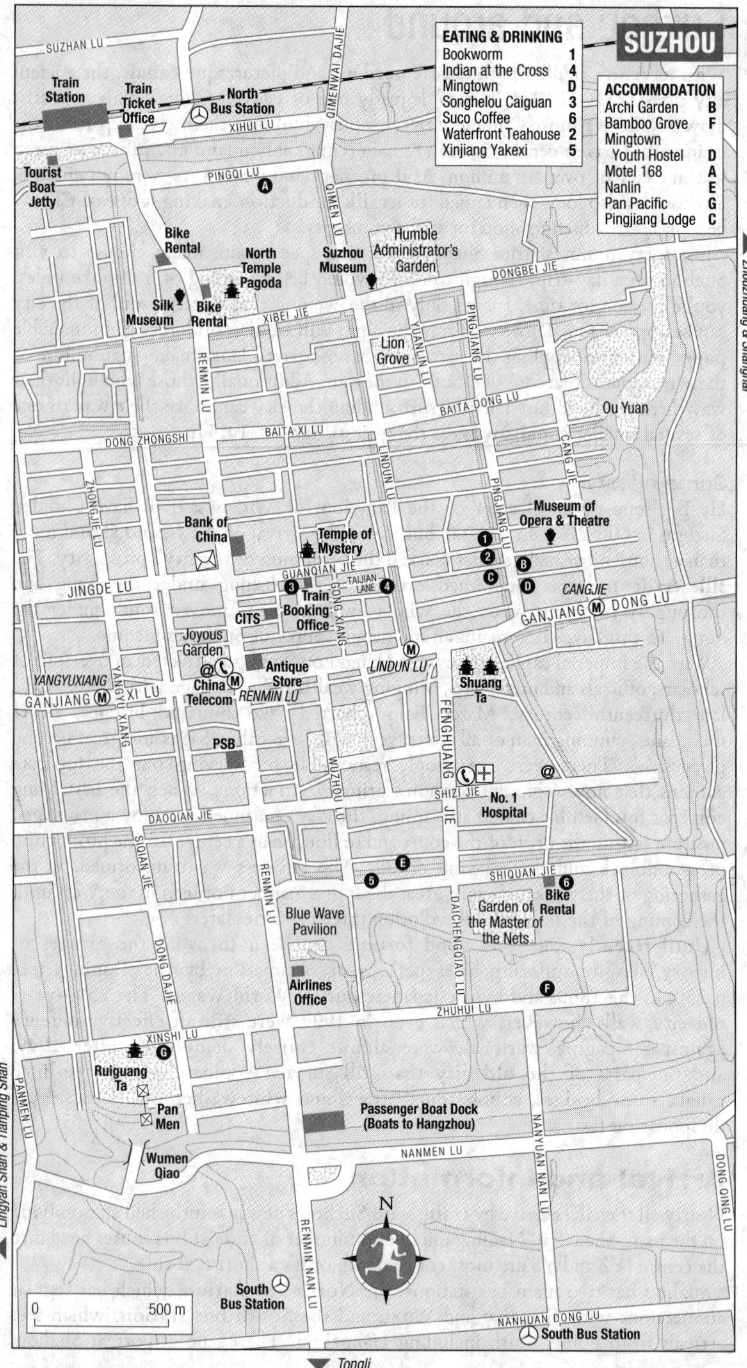
SUZHOU
EATING & DRINKING
Bookworm 1
Indian at the Cross 4
Mingtown D
Songhelou Caiguan 3
Suco Coffee 6
Waterfront Teahouse 2
Xinjiang Yakexi 5
ACCOMMODATION
Archi Garden B
Bamboo Grove F
Mingtown Youth Hostel D
Motel 168 A
Nanlin E
Pan Pacific G
Pingjiang Lodge C
SUZHAN LU
Train Station
Train Ticket Office
North Bus Station
XIHUI LU
QIMENWAI DAJIE
PINGQI LU
Tourist Boat Jetty
QIMEN LU
Humble Administrator's Garden
Bike Rental
North Temple Pagoda
Suzhou Museum
DONGBEI JIE
Zhouzhuang & Shanghai
Silk Museum
XIBEI JIE
YUANLIN LU
PINGJIANG LU
Lion Grove
RENMIN LU
BAITA DONG LU
Ou Yuan
BAITA XI LU
DONG ZHONGSHI
LINDUN LU
CANG JIE
ZHONGJIE LU
Museum of Opera & Theatre
Bank of China
Temple of Mystery
JINGDE LU
GUANQIAN JIE
TAIJIAN LANE
CANGJIE
Train Booking Office
GONG XIANG
GANJIANG DONG LU
CITS
Joyous Garden
Antique Store
LINDUN LU
YANGYUXIANG
YANGYU XIANG
China Telecom
RENMIN LU
Shuang Ta
GANJIANG XI LU
PSB
FENGHUANG JIE
WUZHOU LU
SHIZI JIE
No. 1 Hospital
DAOQIAN JIE
SIQIAN JIE
SHIQUAN JIE
Bike Rental
Blue Wave Pavilion
Garden of the Master of the Nets
DONG DAJIE
DAICHENGQIAO LU
Airlines Office
ZHUHUI LU
XINSHI LU
Ruiguang Ta
Pan Men
PANMEN LU
Lingyan Shan & Tianping Shan
Passenger Boat Dock (Boats to Hangzhou)
NANMEN LU
Wumen Qiao
NANYUAN LU
DONG QING LU
RENMIN NAN LU
N
South Bus Station
0
500 m
NANHUAN DONG LU
South Bus Station
Tongli

though there are regular buses to both of Shanghai's airports, and the city has a CAAC office for bookings (see p.341). For other information, it's best to ask at your accommodation.

City transport

Taxis are your best bet for getting around Suzhou's small centre, though the city is embarking on construction of a **metro** network – the first line should be ready by 2012, with more to follow. More unique are **canal boat tours** of the city, which cost from ¥70 and can be arranged at the Boat Dock to the south of town, and booths just south of the Humble Administrator's Garden. Enterprising local boatsmen may offer you a ride – it's around ¥100 per boat for a 40-minute trip.

Accommodation

Suzhou has some excellent accommodation options for all budgets. The main **hotel** area is in the south of the city, around **Shiquan Jie**, though travellers are increasingly falling for the more rustic appeal of **Pingjiang Lu**, to the east. Prices tend to fall heavily out of season.

Archi Garden (築園, *zhúyuán*) 31 Pingjiang Lu ⓣ0512/65810618. A place for Suzhou's artier visitors, featuring just four spartan but immaculate rooms – think sliding doors, white linen and an atmosphere so quiet you could hear a pin drop. The lobby also functions as a café, gallery and style-book library. Highly recommended. 5

Bamboo Grove (竹辉饭店, *zhúhuī fàndiàn*) 168 Zhuhui Lu ⓣ0512/65205601, ⓦwww.bg-hotel.com. A tour-group favourite, this efficient Japanese-run four-star hotel imitates local style with black-and-white walls and abundant bamboo in the garden. It has a couple of good restaurants, too. 6

Mingtown Youth Hostel (明堂青年旅舍, *míngtáng qīngnián lǚshè*) 28 Pingjiang Lu ⓣ0512/65816869. Filled with character, this friendly canalside venue is hugely popular with budget travellers – singles and doubles are remarkably stylish for the price, with wooden furniture and excellent en-suite facilities. Dormitories can get a little stuffy, though. Dorm beds from ¥50, doubles 3

Motel 168 (莫泰连锁旅店, *mòtài liánsuǒ lǚdiàn*) 16 Pingqi Lu ⓣ0512/82106666. Though it's a little out of the way, this chirpily decorated, no-frills chain hotel is very competitively priced. 2

Nanlin (南林饭店, *nánlín fàndiàn*) 20 Gun Xiu Fang, Shiquan Jie ⓣ0512/68017888, ⓦwww.nanlin.com. A big three-star garden-style affair with an immaculate lobby. The new wing has luxury rooms, while the old wing still offers reasonably priced doubles and triples. 8

Pan Pacific (吴宫泛太平洋酒店, *wúgōng fàntài píngyáng jiǔdiàn*) 259 Xinshi Lu ⓣ0512/65103388, ⓦwww.panpacific.com. Formerly the *Sheraton*, this top-end hotel was modelled on the eponymous old city gate (see p.340) – cheesy, perhaps, but somehow it works. Rooms are nothing short of superb, the staff are sprightly and informative, while the outside gardens could function as a tourist draw in themselves. Occasional big discounts for those booking online. 8

Pingjiang Lodge (平江客栈, *píngjiāng kèzhàn*) 33 Pingjiang Lu ⓣ0512/65233888, ⓦwww.the-silk-road.com. Part of a small yet nationwide chain of "culture hotels", this appealingly rustic venue seeks to recreate the charm of old Suzhou. Its rooms have been traditionally styled, and prove particularly popular with Chinese families. 5

The City

Lying within a rectangular moat formed by canals, the historic town's clear grid of streets and waterways makes Suzhou a relatively easy place in which to get your bearings. The traditional commercial centre of the city lies around **Guanqian Jie**, halfway down Renmin Lu, an area of cramped, animated streets thronged with small shops, teahouses and restaurants, though savvy travellers are now heading to **Pingjiang Lu**, a canalside street which is fast becoming a local version of Beijing's Nanluogu Xiang (see p.110), blending a traditional vibe with modern cafés and galleries.

Suzhou's gardens

Gardens, above all, are what Suzhou is all about. They have been laid out here since the Song dynasty, a thousand years ago, and in their Ming and Qing heyday it is said that the city had two hundred of them. Some half-dozen major gardens have now been restored, as well as a number of smaller ones. Elsewhere in China you'll find grounds – as at Chengde or the Summer Palace outside Beijing – laid out on a grand scale, but the gardens of Suzhou are tiny in comparison, often in small areas behind high compound walls, and thus are far closer to the true essence of a Chinese garden.

Chinese gardens do not set out to improve upon a slice of nature or to look natural, which is why many Western eyes find them hard to accept or enjoy. They are a serious art form, the garden designer working with rock, water, buildings, trees and vegetation in subtly different combinations; as with painting, sculpture and poetry, the aim is to produce for contemplation the **balance**, **harmony**, **proportion** and **variety** which the Chinese seek in life. The wealthy scholars and merchants who built Suzhou's gardens intended them to be enjoyed either in solitude or in the company of friends over a glass of wine and a poetry recital or literary discussion. Their designers used little pavilions and terraces to suggest a larger scale, undulating covered walkways and galleries to give a downward view, and intricate interlocking groups of rock and bamboo to hint at, and half conceal, what lies beyond. Glimpses through delicate lattices, tile-patterned openings or moon gates, and reflections in water created cunning perspectives which either suggested a whole landscape or borrowed outside features (such as external walls of neighbouring buildings) as part of the design, in order to create an illusion of distance.

Among the essential features of the Suzhou gardens are the white pine trees, the odd-shaped rocks from Tai Hu and the stone tablets over the entrances. The whole was completed by animals – there are still fish and turtles in some ponds today. **Differences in style** among the various gardens arise basically from the mix and balance of the ingredients; some are dominated by water, others are mazes of contorted rock, yet others are mainly inward-looking, featuring pavilions full of strange furniture. Almost everything you see has some symbolic significance – the pine tree and the crane for long life, mandarin ducks for married bliss, for example.

Among the Chinese, Suzhou is one of the most highly favoured tourist destinations in the country, and the city is packed with visitors from far and wide. This can make for a festive atmosphere, but it also means that you are rarely able to appreciate the **gardens** in the peace for which they were designed. The most famous ones attract a stream of visitors year-round, but many of the equally beautiful yet lesser-known gardens, notably Canglang Ting and Ou Yuan, are comparatively serene and crowd-free; the best strategy is to visit one or two of the popular gardens before 10am and spend the rest of the day in the smaller gardens. **Prices** for many of these sights are slightly lower in the off-season.

North Temple Pagoda and the Silk Museum

A few minutes' walk south down Renmin Lu from the train station, the **North Temple Pagoda** (北寺塔, *běisì tǎ*; daily 7.45am–5pm; ¥35) looms up unmistakeably. On the site of the residence of the mother of Wu Kingdom king Sun Quan, the structure was first built in the third century AD, and rebuilt in 1582. The pagoda is, at 76m, the tallest Chinese pagoda south of the Yangzi, though it retains only nine of its original eleven storeys. Climbing it gives an excellent view over some of Suzhou's more conspicuous features, and there's also a very pleasant teahouse on site. Virtually opposite is the **Silk Museum** (丝绸博物馆, *sīchóu bówùguǎn*; daily 9am–5.30pm; ¥10), one of China's better-presented museums.

There are looms, weaving machines and reproductions of early silk patterns, but the most riveting display is the room full of silkworms munching mulberry leaves and spinning cocoons.

Suzhou Museum, the Humble Administrator's Garden and Lion Grove

Designed by China's premier architect, IM Pei, the **Suzhou Museum** (苏州博物馆, *sūzhōu bówùguǎn*; daily 8.15am–4.15pm; free) is by far the most successful of the many attempts to update Suzhou's characteristic white wall and black beam style. The collection, though small, is pretty good too, and there are plenty of English captions. Some exquisitely delicate china and jade pieces are on show in the first two galleries – look out for the ugly toad carved out of jasper – but the museum's highlight is the craft gallery, which holds some fantastically elaborate carvings of Buddhist scenes in bamboo roots. Only a certain number of visitors are allowed in at any time, meaning that you may be **queueing** for some time in peak season unless you get here early.

Just next door lies the largest of the Suzhou gardens, covering forty thousand square metres, the **Humble Administrator's Garden** (拙政园, *zhuózhèng yuán*; ¥70). It's based on water and set out in three linked sections: the eastern part (just inside the entrance) consists of a small lotus pond and pavilions; the centre is largely water, with two small islands connected by zigzag bridges, while the western part has unusually open green spaces. Built at the time of the Ming by an imperial censor, Wang Xianchen, who had just resigned his post, the garden was named by its creator as an ironic lament on the fact that he could now administer nothing but gardening.

A couple of minutes south is another must-see garden, the **Lion Grove** (狮子林, *shīzi lín*; daily 7.30am–4.30pm; ¥30). Tian Ru, the monk who laid this out in 1342, named it in honour of his teacher, Zhi Zheng, who lived on Lion Rock Mountain, and the rocks of which it largely consists are supposed to resemble the big cats. Once chosen, these strange water-worn rocks were submerged for decades in Tai Hu (p.342) to be further eroded. Part of the rockery takes the form of a convoluted labyrinth, from the top of which you emerge occasionally to gaze down at the water reflecting the green trees and grey stone. Qing emperors Qianlong and Kangxi were said to be so enamoured of these rockeries that they had the garden at the Yuanmingyuan Palace in Beijing (p.114) modelled on them.

The Temple of Mystery and the Joyous Garden

Moving south from here, you arrive at the intriguingly named **Temple of Mystery** (玄妙观, *xuánmiào guān* ; daily 7.30am–4.30pm; ¥10), rather incongruously located at the heart of the modern city's consumer zone. Founded originally during the Jin dynasty in the third century AD, the temple has been destroyed, rebuilt, burned down and put back together many times during its history. For centuries it was the scene of a great bazaar where travelling showmen, acrobats and actors entertained the crowds. Nowadays the complex, still an attractive, lively place, basically consists of a vast entrance court full of resting locals with, at its far end, a hall of Taoist deities and symbols; it's all encircled by a newly constructed park.

A few minutes southwest is **Joyous Garden** (怡园, *yíyuán*; daily 7.30am–11pm; ¥15), laid out by official Gu Wenbin. Late Qing-dynasty, and hence considerably newer (and less popular) than the others, it is nevertheless supposed to encompass all the key features of a Chinese garden; unusually, it also has formal flowerbeds and arrangements of coloured pebbles.

The Museum of Opera and Theatre and Ou Yuan

A ten-minute walk along narrow lanes due east from Guanqian Jie, the rooms of the unusual and memorable **Museum of Opera and Theatre** (戏曲博物馆, *xìqǔ bówùguǎn*; daily 8.30am–4.30pm; ¥8) are filled with costumes, masks, musical instruments, and even a full-sized model orchestra, complete with cups of tea, though the building itself is the star, a Ming-dynasty theatre made of latticed wood. The Suzhou area is the historical home of the 5000-year-old **Kun Opera** style, China's oldest operatic form – Beijing Opera has existed for a mere 3000 years. Kun is distinguished by storytelling and ballad singing, performed in the Suzhou dialect.

A five-minute walk northeast of the museum, abutting the outer moat and along a canal, is the **Ou Yuan** (耦园, *ǒuyuán*; daily 8am–5pm; ¥15), whose greatest asset is its comparative freedom from the loudhailer-toting tour groups that crowd the other gardens. Here a series of hallways and corridors opens onto an intimate courtyard, with a pond in the middle surrounded by abstract rock formations and several relaxing teahouses. The surrounding area houses some of the loveliest architecture, bridges and canals in Suzhou.

Shuang Ta and the Dark Blue Wave Pavilion

Several blocks east of Renmin Lu and immediately south of Ganjiang Lu, the twin towers known as **Shuang Ta** (双塔, *shuāng tǎ*; daily 7am–4.30pm; ¥4) are matching slender pagodas built during the Song dynasty by a group of students wishing to honour their teacher. Too flimsy to climb, the pagodas sprout from a delightful patch of garden. At the other end is a teahouse crowded in summer with old men fanning themselves against the heat.

A kilometre or so farther southwest of here, just beyond Shiquan Jie, the under-visited but intriguing **Blue Wave Pavilion** (沧浪亭, *cānglàng tíng*; daily 8am–5pm; ¥15) is the oldest of the major surviving gardens, near the corner of Renmin Lu and Zhuhui Lu. Originally built in the Song dynasty by scholar Su Zimei around 1044 AD, it's approached through a grand stone bridge and ceremonial marble archway. The central mound inside is designed to look like a forested hill.

Garden of the Master of the Nets

The **Garden of the Master of the Nets** (网师园, *wǎngshī yuán*; daily 7.30am–5pm; ¥30) is a tiny, intimate place considered the finest of Suzhou's gardens by many a connoisseur. Started in 1140, it received its curious name because the owner, a retired official, decided he wanted to become a fisherman. Nowadays, it boasts an attractive central lake, minuscule connecting halls, pavilions with pocket-handkerchief courtyards and carved wooden doors – and rather more visitors than it can cope with. The garden is said to be best seen on moonlit nights, when the moon can be seen three times over from the Moon-watching Pavilion – in the sky, in the water and in a mirror. The garden's other main features are its delicate latticework and fretted windows, through which you can catch a series of glimpses – a glimmer of bamboo, dark interiors, water and a miniature rockery framed in the three windows of a study. Outside the dead winter months Wangshi Yuan plays host to nightly arts performances.

Pan Men and around

In the far southwestern corner of the moated area is one of the city's most pleasant districts, centred around **Pan Men** (盘门, *pánmén*) and a stretch of the original city wall, built in 514 BC by King Helu of the Wu Kingdom; the gate is the only surviving one of eight that once surrounded Suzhou. The best approach to this area is from the south, via **Wumen Qiao** (吴门桥, *wúmén qiáo*), a delightful high-arched bridge (the tallest in Suzhou) with steps built into it; it's a great vantage point for watching the canal traffic. Just inside Pan Men sits the dramatic **Ruiguang Ta** (瑞光塔, *ruìguāng tǎ*; ¥6), a thousand-year-old pagoda now rebuilt from ruins, once housing a rare Buddhist pearl stupa (since moved to the Suzhou Museum).

Eating, drinking and entertainment

Suzhou cooking, with its emphasis on fish from the nearby lakes and rivers, is justly renowned; specialities include *yinyu* ("silver fish") and *kaobing* (grilled pancakes with sweet filling). The town is well stocked with **restaurants** for all budgets – in addition to those reviewed below, flanking *Songhelou* on Taijian Lane are four other restaurants of repute: the *Dasanyuan*, *Deyuelou*, *Wangsi* and *Laozhengxing*, all of which claim more than one hundred years of history, are big, busy and good for a splurge on local dishes, with foreigner-friendly staff and menus.

The town holds little in the way of **nightlife**, but there are a few bars along Shiquan Jie. There's also a nightly **opera extravaganza** at the Master of the Nets garden (spring–autumn 7.30–10pm; ¥80 including admission to garden), featuring eight displays of the most prominent forms of Chinese performing arts, from Beijing Opera to folk dancing and storytelling.

Restaurants

Indian at the Cross Off Lindun Lu. New location, same cheap curries, and quite a treat if you've been racing around the provincial backwaters. Daily 11am–2pm & 5–11pm.

Mingtown (明堂, *míngtáng*) 28 Pingjiang Lu. Just down the road from the hostel (see p.337), and popular with backpackers on account of some tasty food, decent coffee and an only-slightly-wonky pool table. Good for a Western breakfast, and turns into a bar of sorts in the evening.

Songhelou Caiguan (松鹤楼, *sōnghèlóu*) Taijian Lane, 200m east of Renmin Lu. The most famous restaurant in town – it claims to be old enough to have served Emperor Qianlong. The menu is elaborate and long on fish and seafood (crab, eel, squirrel fish and the like), though not cheap at around ¥150 a head. There are four good places nearby on Taijian Lane; see above.

Xinjiang Yakexi (新疆亚克西, *xīnjiāng yǎkèxī jiǔlóu*) 768 Shiquan Jie. Xinjiang comfort food – pulled noodles with vegetables (*latiaozi*) and naan bread, among others – in a bright dining room bustling with local Uyghurs and tourists. Open late.

Cafés and teahouses

Bookworm 77 Shiquan Jie ⓦ www.chinabookworm.com. Like the chain's mothership in Beijing (p.117), this place is ground zero for local expats, though visitors will also be able to take part in the many events that they organize, or just pop by for coffee or a drink. There's a smaller, more secluded version of the same resting above a canal on Pingjiang Lu.

Suco Coffee (苏卡咖啡, *sūkǎ kāfēi*) 357 Shiquan Jie. A café with excellent smoothies, and they'll recommend a brand of Chinese tea according to your star sign. Wi-fi and comfy seating make it a good place to linger.

Waterfront Teahouse (运河茶馆, *yùnhé cháguǎn*) 36 Pingjiang Lu. Traditional canalside venue with tiny seats on the outside veranda, and slightly fancier places to park your posterior inside. The former are recommended, for this place offers a simply splendid view of local canal life over a latte or herbal tea. Walk past at night if you can – the sight of soft light pouring through its latticed windows is rather magical.

Listings

Airlines The main CAAC reservations and ticketing office (daily 8am–7pm; ⓣ0512/65104881) is at 943 Renmin Lu, a few minutes' walk south of Ganjiang Lu.

Banks and exchange The Bank of China head office (daily 8.15am–5.15pm) is on Renmin Lu, in the centre of town, just north of Guanqian Jie.

Bike rental Many gift shops along Shiquan Jie rent bikes, as do a couple of storefronts just north of the Silk Museum. They charge ¥15–25/day with a deposit of a few hundred yuan (or a passport).

Hospital The No. 1 Hospital is at the junction of Fenghuang Jie and Shizi Jie.

Mail Suzhou's main post office (daily 8am–8pm) is at the corner of Renmin Lu and Jingde Lu.
PSB On Renmin Lu, at the junction with the small lane Dashitou Xiang.
Shopping There are numerous opportunities to shop for silk in Suzhou, although be aware of outrageous prices, especially in the boutiques along Shiquan Jie and Guanyin Jie, and the night market on Shi Lu. Bargain hard, as these sellers can quote prices up to ten times the going rate. The King Silk Store next to the Silk Museum has a good selection, including great duvets starting at just over ¥300. The Antique Store along Renmin Lu at Ganjiang Dong Lu is the place for old furniture, while paintings and embroidery are on hand in a pavilion near the corner of Renmin Lu and Baita Xi Lu, and in the shops along Shiquan Jie.
Trains There's a booking office (daily 8am–8pm) 50m south of Xuanmiao Guan on the west side of Gong Xiang. CITS and most hotels will book tickets for a commission.
Travel agents CITS (☎0512/65155207) is next to the *Lexiang Hotel* on Dajing Xiang. Nearly all hotels have their own travel agencies.

Tongli

Suzhou is surrounded by a clutch of **canal towns**, each of them boasting scores of traditional buildings and bridges. Unfortunately, while the structures themselves have been protected (and, in many cases, reconstructed) by local authorities, the once-bucolic atmosphere of these towns has been sullied by their popularity with domestic tourists – it's hard to appreciate their beauty when every third house rents garish faux Qing-dynasty clothing to camera-toting groups. Indeed, some canals in Suzhou itself could be said to exude a more laidback atmosphere.

However, it's worth visiting one of the canal towns, and **TONGLI** (同里, *tónglǐ*; ¥80), 23km from Suzhou, remains the best example – every house backs on to canals, there are 49 stone bridges, and nearly all movement takes place by boat. The main street has become very touristy, but a little exploration along the back alleys will reveal canals shaded by stately bridges, overhanging willows, lazing elderly folk, putt-putting barges and rural splendour. The top sight here is the UNESCO World Heritage Site, **Tuisi Yuan** (退思远, *tuìsī yuǎn*; daily 7.45am–5.30pm; ¥25), a late-Qing garden that rather resembles Suzhou's Ou Yuan (see p.340). It was built by disillusioned retired official Ren Lansheng in 1886 as a place to retreat and meditate – though you'll have to come in the early morning, before the tour groups arrive, if that is your intention. Few visitors can resist popping into the **Sex Museum** (性文化博物馆, *xìngwénhuà bówùguǎn*; daily 8am–5.30pm; ¥20) just around the corner; set up by single-minded sexologist Liu Dalin, the collection of ancient dildoes, foot-binding tools, graphic bronzes, erotic scroll paintings and the like are all presented with explanations of their historical context. It's all rather less titillating and more informative than you might expect.

You can reach Tongli from either of Suzhou's **bus** stations (45min; ¥7), and it also has a daily connection with Shanghai.

Tai Hu

Thirty-five kilometres west of Suzhou lies the enormous **Tai Hu** (太湖, *tàihú*), one of the largest freshwater lakes in China. It's a popular focus for a day out, though there's not much to do but wander the wooded hills around the shore. From Suzhou train station, take a minibus to rural Dongshan (1hr), which sits at the end of a long promontory. Here, you can pop into the lovely **Zijin An** (紫金庵, *zǐjīn'ān*; daily 7.30am–5pm; ¥20), a nunnery notable for its ancient statuary and location in a secluded wood surrounded by sweet-smelling orange groves. Then it's an easy hike up to Longtou Shan, or Dragon's Head Mountain. If the peak's not shrouded, there are stunning views of the surrounding tea plantations and the lake. Head back to Dongshan and walk northwest and you'll come to the pier for ferries to the nearby island of **Xishan** (¥5). There are plenty of woods to wander through before returning to Dongshan for a minibus back to Suzhou.

Zhejiang

ZHEJIANG (浙江, *zhèjiāng*), one of China's smallest provinces but also one of the wealthiest, is made up of two quite different areas. The northern part shares its climate, geography, history and the Grand Canal with Jiangsu – the land here is highly cultivated, fertile and netted with waterways, hot in summer and cold in winter. The south, however, has much more in common with Fujian province, being mountainous and sparsely populated in the interior, thriving and semitropical on the coast.

Cities througout the province tend to have an attractive, prosperous air. **Hangzhou**, the terminus of the Grand Canal, is one of the greenest and most visually appealing cities in China, with its famous lake a former resort of emperors; it's still a centre for silk, tea and paper-making. Nearby **Shaoxing**, a charming small town threaded by canals, offers the chance to tour its beautiful surroundings by boat. Off the coast, and accessible from Shanghai, **Putuo Shan** is a Buddhist island with more temples than cars; as fresh, green and tranquil as eastern China gets.

Hangzhou and around

Few cities are as associated with a tourist draw as the Zhejiang capital of **HANGZHOU** (杭州, *hángzhōu*), which has found fame for one simple reason – **Xi Hu**, a large lake right in the centre of the action. Encircled by gardens and a wreath of willow trees, crisscrossed with ancient walkways and bridges and punctuated by the odd temple or pagoda, the lake exudes an old-style Oriental air increasingly hard to find in modern China, and is a must-see if you're in this part of the land.

However, this beauty has come at a price. The city is particularly busy at weekends, when it's packed with trippers escaping from the concrete jungle of Shanghai, and in summer, when the whole country seems to be jostling for space around the lakeshore. This popularity has pushed up hotel prices, but it also brings advantages: there are plenty of restaurants, the natural environment is being protected and the bulk of the Taiping destruction to the temples and gardens on the lakeside has been repaired. Most of the places to see can be visited on foot or by bicycle, though those following the latter course of action should avoid evening rush hour like the plague – this is a city of around four million people, and the lake makes for something of a traffic obstacle.

Finally, much further afield, the old colonial hill resort of **Moganshan** is today making a comeback as a place for city slickers to escape the **heat**, which reaches oppressive levels in summer months.

Some history

Hangzhou has little in the way of a legendary past or ancient history, for the simple reason that the present site, on the east shore of Xi Hu, was originally under water. Xi Hu itself started life as a wide shallow **inlet** off the bay, and it is said that Emperor Qin Shihuang sailed in from the sea and moored his boats on what is now the northwestern shore of the lake. Only around the fourth century AD did river currents and tides begin to throw up a barrier of silt, which eventually resulted in the formation of the lake.

However, Hangzhou rapidly made up for its slow start. The first great impetus came from the building of the **Grand Canal** at the end of the sixth century (see p.324), and Hangzhou developed with spectacular speed as the centre for trade between north and south, the Yellow and Yangzi river basins. Under the **Tang dynasty** it was a rich and thriving city, but its location between lake and river made it vulnerable to the fierce equinox tides in Hangzhou Bay; the problem of **floods** – and the search for remedies – was to recur down the centuries.

During the **Song dynasty**, Hangzhou received its second great impetus when the encroachment of the Tartars from the north destroyed the northern capital of Kaifeng and sent remnants of the imperial family fleeing south in search of a new base. The result of this upheaval was that from 1138 until 1279 Hangzhou became the **imperial capital**. There was an explosion in the silk and brocade industry, and indeed in all the trades that waited upon the court and their wealthy friends. Marco Polo, writing of Hangzhou towards the end of the thirteenth century, spoke of "the City of Heaven, the most beautiful and magnificent in the world". So glorious was the reputation of the city that it rapidly grew overcrowded. On to its sandbank Hangzhou was soon cramming more than a million people, a population as large as that of Chang'an (Xi'an) under the Tang, but in a quarter of the space – tall wooden buildings up to five storeys high were crowded into narrow streets, creating a ghastly fire hazard.

Hangzhou ceased to be a capital city after the Southern Song dynasty was finally overthrown by the Mongols in 1279, but it remained an important centre of commerce and a place of luxury, with **parks and gardens** outside the ramparts and hundreds of boats on the lake. Although the city was largely destroyed by the **Taiping Uprising** (see p.330), it recovered surprisingly quickly, and the **foreign concessions** established towards the end of the century stimulated the growth of new industries alongside traditional silk.

Arrival and information

Hangzhou's **airport** is 15km north of town, and connected by CAAC bus (¥5) to the main CAAC office on Tiyuchang Lu. The **train station** is 2km east of the city centre. Reaching the lake from here on foot takes about forty minutes; otherwise, take bus #7 direct to the lake or #151 as far as Yan'an Lu. A few trains, including some from Shanghai, stop only at the remote **East** or **South train stations**; from these, buses #48 and #301 go to the northeastern lakefront. A 450km/hr **maglev line** from Shanghai – an extension of the line from Pudong Aiport (see p.369) – was scheduled to open in time for the Shanghai Expo in 2010, but a bout of rare umming and aahing meant that it only received "final approval" in March of that year. No timetable had been agreed at the time of writing, and a huge question mark still hovered over the entire project.

Buses use a number of stations ringing Hangzhou. Eastern arrivals and departures to Shaoxing and Fuzhou use the **east bus station** in the northeast of town, which is connected by bus #K35 to the centre of town. The **north bus station** (bus #155 runs the 9km to the centre) serves Shanghai and Jiangsu, though frequent private buses on these routes use the train station square. Huangshan services use the **west bus station** on Tianmushan Lu (bus #49 travels the 8km to the centre). Wenzhou and Fujian province buses leave from the **southeast bus station**, a five-minute walk south of the main train station on the corner of Dongbao Lu and Qiutao Lu.

Hangzhou is one of the very few Chinese cities with **visitor information booths** around town. The larger **Hangzhou Tourist Centre** (ⓣ0571/96123) is in front of the train station, between the public bus stops; they run one-day tours of Hangzhou and surrounding canal towns and cities, as well as shuttles to Shanghai's Pudong airport. There's another decent office on Yan'an Lu.

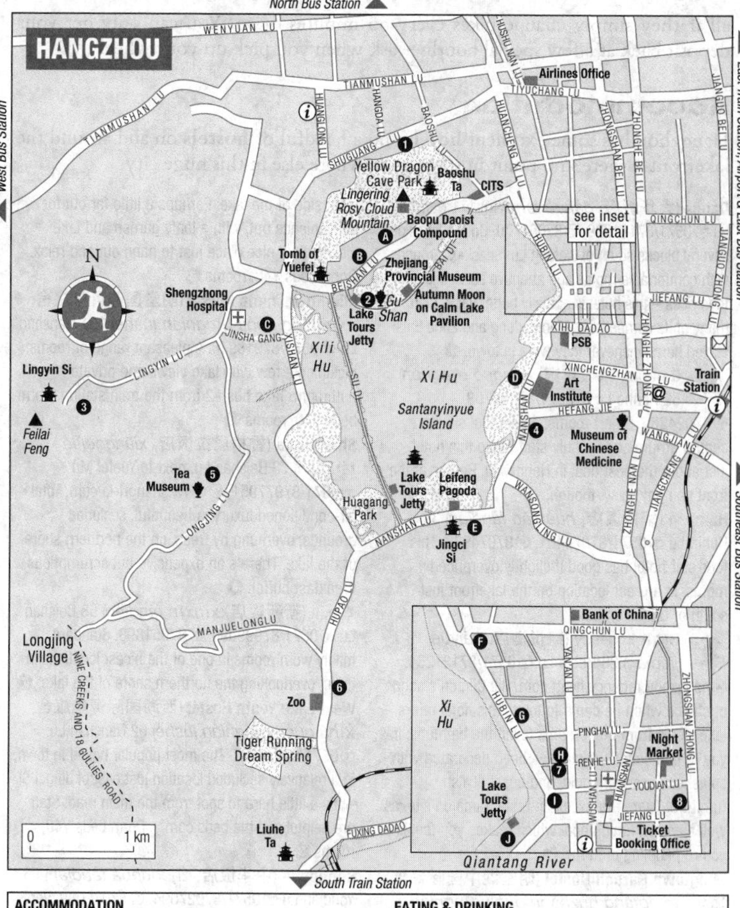

ACCOMMODATION			
Dahua	J	Mingtown Youth Hostel	D
Dongpo	H	Shangri-La	B
Huaqiao	F	West Lake Youth Hostel	E
Hyatt Regency	G	Xinxin	A
Mingtown Garden Hostel	C	Zhonghua	I

EATING & DRINKING			
Green Tea	5	Tianwaitian	3
Kuiyuan Guan	8	Vienna Coffee House	1
Ladinna	4	Zhiweiguan	7
Louwailou	2		
The Norway Woods	6		

City transport

Taxis are currently the best way to get around town; a ¥10 ride should cover any destination in central Hangzhou. However, there are some useful **tourist bus** routes around the lake shore; ask for information at any of the many tourist booths. Additionally, a new **metro** system is scheduled to open its first line by 2012.

It would be a shame to leave Hangzhou without taking a **boat ride** on Xi Hu (see p.346 for more), while renting a **bike** to race around the lake is also an option. These are available for rent at all hostels for around ¥10 per hour, but the city authorities have laid on an astonishing 50,000 bikes at the same rate, available outside all tourist booths for a deposit of ¥400. They're free for the first hour, and young Chinese travellers have cottoned onto the fact that they don't have to pay at all if they simply change bikes every 55 minutes or so. You can only get your deposit back at a few special booths – ask when you pick up your wheels.

Accommodation

Hangzhou has some excellent **hotels** and a handful of **hostels** on and around the lakefront – there's no point in staying anywhere else in this huge city.

Dahua (大华饭店, *dàhuá fàndiàn*) 171 Nanshan Lu ⓣ0571/87181888, ⓕ87061770. On the lakeside, several blocks south of Jiefang Lu. Spacious grounds with comfortable rooms and attentive service justify the prices – this hotel is actually better value than many of its competitors. Mao Zedong and Zhou Enlai stayed here whenever they were in town. ❼

Dongpo (东坡宾馆, *dōngpō bīnguǎn*) 52 Renhe Lu ⓣ0571/87069769, ⓕ87024266. Smart rooms, a beautiful six-storey central atrium and friendly staff make this hotel just about the best deal in Hangzhou. Rooms at the front can get noisy, though. ❹

Huaqiao (华侨饭店, *huáqiáo fàndiàn*) 39 Hubin Lu ⓣ0571/87074401, ⓕ87074978. This four-star hotel has good if slightly overpriced rooms, in a great location on the lakefront just south of Qingchun Lu. ❻

Hyatt Regency (凯悦酒店, *kǎiyuè jiǔdiàn*) 28 Hubin Lu ⓣ0571/87121234, ⓦhangzhou.regency.hyatt.com. Bill Clinton's abode of choice when he came to town, this hotel offers lake views from most rooms (even the bathtubs, if you're in a suite), which have been decorated with splashes of red and gold, and boast stylish furniture. There are excellent restaurants on site, as well as a swimming pool which makes you feel like you're paddling in Xi Hu. ❾

Mingtown Garden Hostel (明堂湖中国际青年旅舍, *míngtáng húzhōng guójì qīngnián lǚshè*) 4 Zhaogong Causeway ⓣ0571/87875883. This mellow hostel is in a refurbished villa at the west side of the lake. Perhaps a little far out for convenience but, with a leafy garden and lake views, it's a nice place just to hang out and relax. Dorm beds ¥40, rooms ❸

Mingtown Youth Hostel (明堂国际青年旅舍, *míngtáng guójì qīngnián lǚshè*) 101 Nanshan Lu ⓣ0571/87918948. A pleasant range of rooms, including a few with lake views and private bathroom. Take bus #2 from the train station. Dorm beds ¥40, rooms ❸

Shangri-La (香格里拉饭店, *xiānggélǐlā fàndiàn*) 78 Beishan Lu, next to Yuefei Mu ⓣ0571/87977951, ⓦwww.shangri-la.com. Total air-conditioned luxury in beautiful, secluded grounds, overhung by trees, on the northern shore of the lake. There's an expensive but scrumptious breakfast buffet. ❾

Xinxin (新新饭店, *xīnxīn fàndiàn*) 58 Beishan Lu ⓣ0571/87999090, ⓕ87051898. Standard, mildly worn rooms in one of the nicest locations in town, overlooking the northern shore of the lake. ❼

West Lake Youth Hostel (西湖国际青年旅舍, *xīhú guójì qīngnián lǚshè*) 62 Nanshan Lu, ⓣ0571/87027027. The most popular hostel in town, in a relatively secluded location just east of Jingci Si – it's a little hard to spot from the main road. Staff are helpful and the beds comfy. Dorm beds ¥40, rooms ❸

Zhonghua (中华饭店, *zhōnghuá fàndiàn*) 55 Youdian Lu ⓣ0571/87027094, ⓕ87077089. Very central, between the lakefront and Yan'an Lu, this place offers good single and double rooms. ❺

The City

Xi Hu is, of course, Hangzhou's focal point. Within the lake area itself are various **islands** and causeways, while the shores are home to endless **parks** holding

Boat trips on Xi Hu

One of the loveliest things to do in Hangzhou is take a boat trip on the lake. Tourist boats (¥45, including entrance fees for Santanyinyue) launch from the two lake tour jetties and head directly for the **islands**. Then there are the freelance boatmen in small canopied boats, who fish for tourists along major lakeside gathering points, especially the causeways, and charge ¥160 for 40 minutes for up to six people. You can also take out a boat of your own – either electric putt-putters for four people (¥80/40min; ¥200 deposit), or paddle boats (¥40/30min).

Hangzhou's most famous individual sights, ranging from the extravagant and historic **Yuefei Mu** (Tomb of Yuefei) to the ancient hillside Buddhist carvings of **Feilai Feng** and its associated temple, the **Temple of the Soul's Retreat**, one of China's largest and most renowned. Farther afield the terrain becomes semi-countryside, where beautiful tea plantations nestle around the village of **Longjing**, while there are excellent walking opportunities south down to the **Qiantang River**.

With most of Hangzhou's sights located on or near the lakeshore, you'll find that the ideal way to get between them is by **bike**; otherwise you can use local buses or simply walk. Outside the sweltering summer, it's possible to walk round the lake's entire circumference in one day, but you wouldn't have time to do justice to all the sights en route.

Xi Hu

A voyage on this lake offers more refreshment and pleasure than any other experience on earth...

Marco Polo

Xi Hu (西湖, *xīhú*) forms a series of landscapes with rock, trees, grass and lakeside buildings all reflected in the water and backed by luxuriant wooded hills. The "West Lake" itself stretches just over 3km from north to south and just under 3km from east to west, though the surrounding parks and associated sights spread far beyond this. On a sunny day the colours are brilliant, but even with grey skies and choppy waters, the lake views are soothing and tranquil; for the Chinese they are also laden with literary and historic associations. Although the crowds and hawkers are sometimes distracting, the area is so large that you can find places to escape the hubbub. A good time to enjoy the lake is sunrise, when mellow *tai ji* practitioners hone their craft against a backdrop of early-morning mists.

As early as the Tang dynasty, work was taking place to control the waters of the lake with dykes and locks, and the two **causeways** that now cross sections of the lake, Bai Di across the north and Su Di across the west, originated in these ancient embankments. Mainly used by pedestrians and cyclists, the causeways offer instant escape from the noise and smog of the built-up area to the east. Strolling the causeways at any time, surrounded by clean, fresh water and flowering lilies, is a pleasure and a favourite pursuit of Chinese couples. The western end of Bai Di supposedly offers the best vantage point over the lake.

Bai Di and Gu Shan

Bai Di (白堤, *báidī*) is the shorter and more popular of the two causeways, about 1500m in length. Starting in the northwest of the lake near the *Shangri-La* hotel, it runs along the outer edge of Gu Shan before crossing back to the northeastern shore, enclosing a small strip known as Beili Hu (North Inner Lake). The little island of **Gu Shan** (孤山, *gūshān*) in the middle of the causeway is one of Hangzhou's highlights, a great place to relax under a shady tree. Bursting with chrysanthemum blossoms in the spring and sprinkled with pavilions and pagodas, this tiny area was originally landscaped under the Tang, but the present style dates from the Qing, when Emperor Qianlong built himself a palace here, surrounded by the immaculate **Zhongshan Park** (中山公园, *zhōngshān gōngyuán*). Part of the palace itself, facing south to the centre of the lake, is now the **Zhejiang Provincial Museum** (浙江博物馆, *zhèjiāng bówùguăn*; Mon noon–4pm, Tues–Sun 9am–4pm; free), a huge place with clear English captions throughout and a number of different wings. The main building in front of the entrance houses historical relics, including some superb bronzes from the eleventh to the eighth century BC. Another hall centres on coin collections and has specimens of the world's first banknotes, dating to the Northern Song. New galleries outside hold displays of painting and Tibetan Buddha statues.

The curious **Xiling Seal Engravers' Society** (西泠印社, *xīlíng yìnshè*; daily 9am–5pm; ¥5), founded in 1904, occupies the western side of the hill, next to the *Louwailou* restaurant. Its tiny park encloses a pavilion with a pleasant blend of steps, carved stone tablets, shrubbery and, nearby, a small early Buddhist stupa; drop by here in summer and you can often see the engravers at work. On the southeastern side of the hill by the water is another of Qianlong's buildings, the **Autumn Moon on a Calm Lake Pavilion**, which is the perfect place to watch the full moon. It's a teahouse now, very popular after sunset and full of honeymooners. The low stone **Broken Bridge**, at the far eastern end of the causeway, gets its name because winter snow melts first on the hump of the bridge, creating the illusion of a gap.

Su Di and Santanyinyue Island

The longer causeway, **Su Di** (苏堤, *sūdī*), named after the Song-dynasty poet-official Su Dong Po, who was governor of Hangzhou, starts from the southwest corner of the lake and runs its full length to the northern shore close to Yuefei Mu. Consisting of embankments planted with banana trees, weeping willows and plum trees, linked by six stone-arch bridges, the causeway encloses a narrow stretch of water, **Xili Hu**. East of the causeway and in the southern part of the lake is the largest of the islands here, **Xiaoying**, built up in 1607. It's better known as **Santanyinyue** (三潭印月, *sāntán yìnyuè*), meaning "Three Flags Reflecting the Moon", after the three "flags" in the water – actually stone pagodas, said to control the evil spirits lurking in the deepest spots of the lake. Bridges link across from north to south and east to west so that the whole thing seems like a wheel with four spokes, plus a central hub just large enough for a pavilion, doubling as a shop and a restaurant. The ¥20 admission fee to get onto the island is usually included if you take one of the tourist boat rides here.

The lakeshore

The account here assumes you start from the northeast of the lake on Beishan Lu and head anticlockwise, in which case the seven-storey **Baoshu Ta** (报数塔, *bǎoshū tǎ*) on Baoshi Shan is the first sight you'll encounter. Looming up on the hillside to your right, the pagoda is a 1933 reconstruction of a Song-dynasty tower, and a nice place to walk to along hillside tracks. From Beishan Lu a small lane leads up behind some buildings to the pagoda. Tracks continue beyond, and you can climb right up to **Lingering Rosy Cloud Mountain** (栖霞山, *qīxiá shān*) above the lake. About halfway along this path you'll see a yellow-walled monastery with black roofs lurking below to your left, the **Baopu Daoist Compound** (包朴道远, *bāopǔ dàoyuàn*). It's well worth a stop, especially in the late afternoon, if only because you might be able to discreetly watch one of the frequent ancestral worship ceremonies that are held here, with priests clad in colourful garb and widows clutching long black necklaces to pay tribute to their husbands. If you climb the stairs, you will find several smaller halls where old men practise their calligraphy and young women play the *pipa*.

Back on the path along the ridge above the monastery, you can stroll past **Sunrise Terrace**, traditionally the spot for watching the spring sun rise over the lake and Gu Shan. If you continue west, you'll eventually reach some steep stone stairs which will bring you back down to the road, close to the Yuefei Mu at the northwest end of the lake, next to the *Shangri-La* hotel.

Tomb of Yuefei and Yellow Dragon Cave Park

The **Tomb of Yuefei** (岳飞墓, *yuèfēi mù*; daily 7.30am–5.30pm; ¥25) is one of Hangzhou's big draws, the twelfth-century Song general Yuefei being considered a hero in modern China thanks to his unquestioning patriotism. Having emerged victorious from a war against barbarian invaders from the north, Yuefei was falsely charged with treachery by a jealous prime minister, and executed at the age of 39. Twenty years later, the subsequent emperor annulled all charges against him and had him reburied here with full honours. Walk through the temple to reach the tomb itself – a tiny bridge over water, a small double row of stone men and animals, steles, a mound with old pine trees and four cast-iron statues of the villains, kneeling in shame with their hands behind their backs. The calligraphy on the front wall of the tomb reads, "Be loyal to your country".

Immediately west of Yuefei's tomb is a lane leading away from the lake and north into the hills behind. Thirty minutes' walk along here eventually leads to the **Yellow Dragon Cave Park** (黄龙洞公园, *huánglóngdòng gōngyuán*; daily 6.30am–4pm; ¥15), to the north of Qixia Shan. The park can also be approached from the roads to the north of here, south of Hangzhou University. The main area of the park is charmingly secretive, sunk down between sharply rising hills with a pond, teahouses, a shrine to Yue Lao (the Chinese god of arranging marriages), cherry blossoms in the early spring and a pavilion where musicians perform traditional music.

Huagang Park, Jingci Si and the Museum of Chinese Medicine

On a promontory in the southwestern corner of the lake, the small Song-era **Huagang Park** (花港公园, *huāgǎng gōngyuán*) contains a pond full of enormous fish, and there are also wonderful stretches of grass and exotic trees under which to relax. East of here, by the southern shore of Xi Hu, is another temple, **Jingci Si** (净慈寺, *jìngcí sì*; daily 7.30am–5pm; ¥10), which has been fully restored; tourist buses #1 and #2 run past.

Finally, a kilometre east of the lake is the **Huqingyu Tang Museum of Chinese Medicine** (胡清余堂中药博物馆, *húqìngyútáng zhōngyào bówùguǎn*; daily 8am–5pm; ¥10), which traces the complicated history of Chinese medicine from its roots several thousand years ago. The museum is housed in a traditional medicine shop, an architectural gem hidden down a small alley off Hefang Jie. On Hefang Jie itself, look for the white wall with seven large characters and turn down the first alley along its west side; the museum is on the right after about 30m.

West of the lake: Feilai Feng and the Temple of the Soul's Retreat

Three kilometres west, away from the lake (take bus #7 from Yuefei Mu to its terminus), Hangzhou's most famous sights are scattered around **Feilai Feng** (飞来峰, *fēilái fēng*; daily 5.30am–5.30pm; ¥25). The hill's bizarre name – "The Hill that Flew Here" – derives from the tale of an Indian Buddhist devotee named Hui Li who, upon arrival in Hangzhou, thought he recognized the hill from one back home in India, and asked when it had flown here. Near the entrance is the **Ligong Pagoda**, constructed for him. If you turn left shortly after entering the site, you'll come to a surprisingly impressive group of fake rock carvings, replicas of giant Buddhas from all over China. To the right of the entrance you'll find a snack bar and beautiful views over the neighbouring tea plantations up the hill.

The main feature of Feilai Feng is the hundreds of **Buddhist sculptures** carved into its limestone rocks. These date from between the tenth and fourteenth centuries and are the most important examples of their type to be found south of the Yangzi. Today the little Buddhas and other figurines are dotted about everywhere, moss-covered and laughing among the foliage. It's possible to follow trails right up to the top of the hill to escape the tourist hubbub.

Deep inside the Feilai Feng tourist area you'll eventually arrive at the **Temple of the Soul's Retreat** (灵隐寺, *língyǐn sì*; daily 7.30am–4.30pm; ¥20), one of the biggest temple complexes in China. Founded in 326 AD by Hui Li, who is buried nearby, it was the largest and most important monastery in Hangzhou and once had three thousand monks, nine towers, eighteen pavilions and 75 halls and rooms. Today it is an attractive working temple with daily services, usually in the early morning or after 3pm.

In the 1940s the temple was so badly riddled with woodworm that the main crossbeams collapsed onto the statues; the 18m-high Tang statue of Sakyamuni is a replica, carved in 1956 from 24 pieces of camphorwood. Elsewhere in the temple, the old frequently brushes against the new – the **Hall of the Heavenly King** contains four large and highly painted Guardians of the Four Directions made in the 1930s, while the Guardian of the Buddhist Law and Order, who shields the Maitreya, was carved from a single piece of wood eight hundred years ago.

Southwest of the lake

Down in the southwestern quarter of the lake, in the direction of the village of Longjing, the dominant theme is **tea production**: gleaming green tea bushes sweep up and down the land, and old ladies pester tourists into buying fresh tea leaves. Fittingly, this is where you'll find the **Tea Museum** (茶博物馆, *chá bówùguǎn*; daily 8am–5pm; free), a smart place with lots of captions in English, covering themes such as the history of tea and the etiquette of tea drinking. Bus #27 from Pinghai Lu in the town centre comes here; get off more or less opposite the former *Zhejiang Hotel*, then head southwest to the museum along a small lane just to the north of, and parallel to, the main road.

A couple of kilometres further southwest, the village of **LONGJING** (龙井, *lóngjǐng*), with tea terraces rising on all sides behind the houses, is famous as the origin of **Longjing tea**, perhaps the finest variety of green tea produced in China. Depending on the season, a stroll around here affords glimpses of leaves in different stages of processing – being cut, sorted or dried. You'll be pestered to sit at an overpriced teahouse or to buy leaves when you get off the bus – have a good look around first, as there is a very complex grading system and a huge range in quality and price. The **Dragon Well** itself – that's what Longjing means – is at the end of the village, a group of buildings around a spring, done up in a rather touristy fashion. Bus #27 runs to Longjing from the northwestern lakeshore, near the Tomb of Yuefei; alternatively, you can actually hike up here from the Qiantang River (see below).

South of the lake

The area to the south and southwest of Xi Hu, down to the Qiantang River, is full of trees and gentle slopes. Of all the parks in this area, perhaps the nicest is the **Tiger Running Dream Spring** (虎跑梦泉, *hǔpǎomèng quán*; daily 8am–5pm; ¥15). Bus #504 and tourist bus #5 both run here from the city centre, down the eastern shore of the lake, while tourist bus #3 passes close by on the way down from Longjing. The spring (originally found by a ninth-century Zen Buddhist monk with the help of two tigers, according to legend) is said to produce the purest water around, the only water that serious connoisseurs use for brewing the best Longjing teas. For centuries, this has been a popular site for hermits to settle and is now a large forested area dotted with teahouses, shrines, waterfalls and pagodas.

A few more stops south on bus #308 takes you to the 1000-year-old **Liuhe Ta** (六和塔, *liùhé tǎ*; daily 7am–5.30pm; ¥20, tower ¥10), a pagoda occupying a spectacular site overlooking the Qiantang River, a short way west of the rail bridge. The story goes that a Dragon King used to control the tides of the river, wreaking havoc on farmers' harvests. Once a particularly massive tide swept away the mother of a boy named Liuhe to the Dragon King's lair. Liuhe threw pebbles into the river, shaking the Dragon Palace violently, which forced the Dragon King to return his mother to him and to promise never again to manipulate the tides. In appreciation villagers built the pagoda, a huge structure of wood and brick, hung with 104 large iron bells on its upturned eaves. Today, ironically, the pagoda is a popular vantage point from which to view the dramatic **tidal bores** during the autumn equinox.

Twenty minutes' walk upriver west from the pagoda, at the #4 bus terminus, a lane known as **Nine Creeks and Eighteen Gullies** runs off at right angles to the river and up to Longjing. This is a delightful narrow way, great for a bike ride or a half-day stroll, following the banks of a stream and meandering through paddy fields and tea terraces with hills rising in swelling ranks on either side. Halfway along the road, a restaurant serving excellent tea and food straddles the stream where it widens into a serene lagoon.

Eating, drinking and nightlife

As a busy resort for local tourists, Hangzhou has plenty of good **places to eat**. The wedge-shaped neighbourhood between Hubin Lu and Yan'an Lu is home to a number of Chinese restaurants and fast-food joints, while touristy Hefang Jie is also a good spot for Chinese restaurants and snacks. Lastly, the area between Shuguang Lu and the park has its own little cultural microclimate – downmarket and sometimes downright seedy, but fascinating nonetheless.

Many Chinese tourists make it a point to visit one of the famous historical restaurants in town: both *Louwailou* (Tower Beyond Tower) and *Tianwaitian* (Sky Beyond Sky) serve local specialities at reasonable prices, while a third, *Shanwaishan* (Mountain Beyond Mountain), has garnered a bad reputation over the years. All three were named after a line in Southern Song poet Lin Hejin's most famous poem: "Sky beyond sky, Mountain beyond mountain and tower beyond tower/ Could song and dance by West Lake be ended anyhow?"

For **nightlife**, Nanshan Lu and Shuguang Lu are the best bar strips in the Xi Hu area; for good information about bars and restaurants, check Ⓦwww.morehangzhou.com and www.viewhangzhou.com.

Restaurants

Green Tea (绿茶, *lǜ chá*) 83 Longjing Lu, ⓣ0571/87888022. Sitting amid tea plantations, and next door to the Tea Museum itself (opposite), this out-of-the-way restaurant is quite a treat, a rickety pine structure sitting lakeside. Its collection of dishes is extensive but the barbecued beef deserves a special mention. Packed most evenings, so book ahead.

Kuiyuan Guan (奎元馆, *kuíyuán guǎn*) Jiefang Lu, just west of Zhongshan Zhong Lu (go through the entrance with Chinese lanterns hanging outside, and it's on the left, upstairs). Specializes in more than forty noodle dishes for all tastes, from the mundane (beef noodle soup) to the acquired (pig intestines and kidneys). Also offers a range of local seafood delicacies.

Ladinna (拉丁娜, *lādīngnà*) 176-1 Nanshan Lu. This Brazilian *churrasqueria* is quite the treat for those who've been in China for a while: ¥58 will find round after round of skewered, barbecued meat arriving at your table until you reluctantly wave the waiter away.

Louwailou (楼外楼, *lóuwài lóu*) Gu Shan Island. The best-known restaurant in Hangzhou, whose specialities include *dongpo* pork, fish-shred soup and beggar's chicken (a whole chicken cooked inside a ball of mud, which is broken and removed at your table). Lu Xun and Zhou Enlai, among others, have dined here. Standard dishes cost around ¥45.

Tianwaitian (天外天, *tiānwài tiān*) At the gate to Feiliai Feng and Lingyin Si. Chinese tourists flock here to sample the fresh seafood, supposedly caught from Xi Hu. Not as good as *Louwailou*, though. Dishes around ¥50.

Zhiweiguan (知味观, *zhīwèi guān*) Renhe Lu, half a block east of the lake. In a very urbane atmosphere, with piped Western classical music, you can enjoy assorted *dianxin* by the plate for around ¥20, including *xiao long bao* (small, fine stuffed dumplings) and *mao erduo* (fried, crunchy stuffed dumplings). The *huntun tang* (wuntun soup) and *jiu miao* (fried chives) are also good.

Bars and cafés

The Norway Woods (挪威森林, *nuówēi sēnlín*) Hupao Lu. A little out of the way, en route to the Tiger Running Dream Spring (opposite), this bar is certainly worth a beer or three of your time. As its name suggests, there's a focus on nature, with a stream running past a large outdoor area, whose surrounding trees make an admirable effort to drown the din from the road.

Vienna Coffee House (维也纳咖啡厅, *wéiyěnà kāfeītīng*) 91 Shuguang Lu. A branch of the famous Shanghai café, and a little slice of *fin-de-siècle* Austria – good coffee, great cakes, and superb tiramisu. Also has free wi-fi, for those desperate to upload shots of Xi Hu to social networking sites.

Listings

Airlines The main CAAC reservations and ticketing office (daily 7.30am–8pm; reservations ⓣ0571/86662391; domestic flight schedules ⓣ0571/85151397) is at 390 Tiyuchang Lu in the north of town. CAAC buses to the airport (5.45am–8pm; ¥15) leave from here every 30min.

Banks and exchange The Bank of China head office is at 140 Yan'an Bei Lu (daily 8am–5pm), immediately north of Qingchun Lu.

Bike rental Hangzhou's Freedom Network Bike Rental (see p.345) is one of the best operations of its kind in China.

Hospital The most central is the Shengzhong, on Lingyun Lu, west of the lake.

Mail The main post office is just north of the train station on Huancheng Dong Lu.

PSB For visa extensions, enquire at the PSB in the centre of town, on the southwest corner of the junction between Jiefang Lu and Yan'an Lu.

Shopping The most touristed concentration of souvenir outlets – selling silk, tea and crafts – is along Hefang Jie. An L-shaped night market bends around the western end of Renhe Lu, with street sellers peddling a proletarian jumble of wares, ranging from watches to DVDs to Little Red Books. The ritziest brand names are all on Hubin Lu, right on the waterfront.

Trains The main train station contains a very convenient soft-seat ticket office (daily 8am–7pm) for foreigners on the north side of the station building at street level, left as you enter the station. An equally convenient soft-seat waiting room (daily 6am–midnight) is just around the corner on the station's front facade. Tickets can be bought at an outlet just north of the junction between Jiefang Lu and Huanshan Lu.

Travel agents CITS (daily 8.30am–5pm; ⓣ0571/85059033, ⓕ85059052) is on the north shore of the lake, on a hillock above the junction of Beishan Lu and Baoshu Lu. Nearly all Hangzhou hotels have their own travel agencies, usually more helpful than CITS.

Moganshan

The hill station of **MOGANSHAN** (莫干山, *mògān shān*), 60km north of Hangzhou, was popular before World War II with the fast foreign set and has recently reprised its former role as a resort to escape the stifling summer heat. The old European-style villas and po-faced communist-style sanatoriums are being restored and turned into guesthouses, bars and cafés. There's little to do here but wander the incongruously European-looking village, hike in the bamboo woods and enjoy the views. It's lovely, but get here sooner rather than later, before it all gets overdeveloped.

You can get here by **bus** from Hangzhou's north bus station, which will drop you off at the base of the mountain in Wukang; a taxi the rest of the way costs around ¥55, and there's a fee of ¥80 for entering the resort.

Moganshan has a surfeit of faded, Chinese-style two-star **accommodation**, fine if you just want a bed, from ¥150. The *Du Yuesheng Villa* (杜月笙别墅, *dùyuèshēng biéshù*; ⓣ0572/8033601; ❾), once owned by the gangster himself (see p.381) and now operated by the *Radisson* chain, is upmarket but a little overpriced. For **food**, Yinshan Jie is lined with restaurants offering local specialities such as wild game; recommended is the bar-cum-restaurant at the *Moganshan Lodge* (ⓣ0572/8033011; ⓦwww.moganshanlodge.com) in a wing of the *Songliang Shanzhuang* (松梁山庄, *sōngliáng shānzhuāng*). The helpful owners will point you in the right direction for good local walks. There are no **ATMs** in town, so arrive with enough money to last your stay.

Shaoxing and around

Located south of Hangzhou Bay in the midst of a flat plain crisscrossed by waterways and surrounded by low hills, **SHAOXING** (绍兴, *shàoxīng*) is one of the oldest cities in Zhejiang, having established itself as a regional centre in the fifth century BC. During the intervening centuries – especially under the Song, when the imperial court was based in neighbouring Hangzhou – Shaoxing remained a flourishing city, though the lack of direct access to the sea has always kept it out of the front line of events.

For the visitor, Shaoxing is a quieter and more intimate version of Suzhou, combining attractive little sights with great opportunities for boating around classic Chinese countryside. It's a small city that seems to have played a disproportionate role in Chinese culture – some of the nation's more colourful characters came from here, including the mythical tamer of floods Yu the Great, the wife-murdering Ming painter Xu Wei, the female revolutionary hero Qiu Jin and the great twentieth-century writer Lu Xun, all of whom have left their mark on the city.

Near Shaoxing is **Jian Hu**, a lake whose unusual clarity has made the city known throughout China for its alcohol. Most famous are the city's sweet **yellow rice wine**, made from locally grown glutinous rice, and its ruby-coloured **nu'er hong wine**, traditionally the tipple brides sipped to toast their new husbands – it was bought when the bride was born, and buried in the backyard to age.

Arrival and information

Shaoxing's **train station** is in the far north of town, and the rail line that comes through here is a spur running between Hangzhou and the city of Ningbo. Bus #2 runs from here along Jiefang Lu to the southern end of the city. If you're coming from Hangzhou or Ningbo by bus, you'll probably arrive at the Keyun

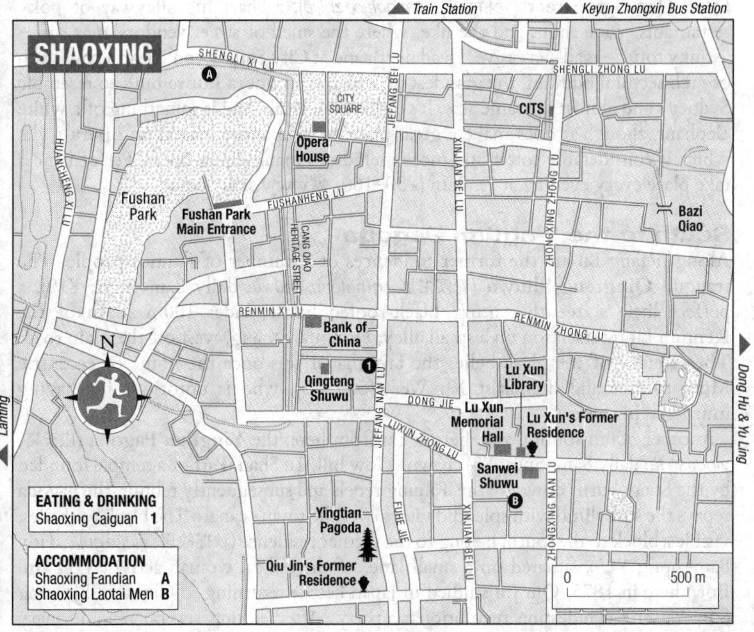

Zhongxin, a **bus station** in the far northeast of town, in which case take bus #3 to the city centre.

The main **Bank of China** (daily 7.30am–5.30pm) is on Renmin Xi Lu. **CITS** (Ⓣ0575/5200079), at 288 Zhongxing Zhong Lu, can arrange tours of the surrounding area as well as book onward travel.

Accommodation

The most upmarket **hotel** in town is the Ming-style *Shaoxing Fandian* on Shengli Lu (绍兴饭店, *shàoxīng fàndiàn*; Ⓣ0575/5155888; ⑥), a huge and charming place in grounds so large that you can travel around them by boat. It's a couple of hundred metres west of Jiefang Lu; bus #30 heads there from the train station. Otherwise, consider the *Shaoxing Laotai Men* (绍兴老台门旅店, *shàoxīng lǎotáimén lǚdiàn*; ②), housed in an old courtyard building on Luxun Zhong Lu; it's all rather rickety, but with its period fittings has something of the feel of a country inn.

The city and around

Although Shaoxing's immediate centre comprises a standard shopping street, elsewhere there are running streams, black-tiled whitewashed houses, narrow lanes divided by water, alleys paved with stone slabs and back porches housing tiny kitchens that hang precariously over canals.

Fushan Park and around

Fushan Park (府山公园, *fǔshān gōngyuán*; daily 8am–4.30pm), in the west of town, is as good a place as any to get your bearings, with a view over the town's canals and bridges from the top; the main entrance to the park is on Fushanheng Lu. Just north of the entrance, the **Yue Terrace** (¥8) is a grand memorial hall with a lovely garden. Coming out of the park, turn east along Fushanheng Lu and you'll arrive at **Cang Qiao Heritage Street** (仓桥直街, *cāngqiáo zhíjiē*), a charming alleyway of poky restaurants, wine shops and the like, where the smell of street vendors' *chou dofu* – "stinky tofu" – is all-pervasive. Head north and at City Square you'll find a collection of architectural oddities, the grandest of which is an **opera house** built to resemble Sydney's and almost the same size. It's disliked by locals, and is something of a white elephant, though it does make a great place to sample the local **Yue opera** style, which is considerably softer and more melodious than Beijing opera. Performances take place every evening at 7.30pm (¥50–160; Ⓦwww.sxdjy.com).

South to the Yingtian Pagoda

Along Jiefang Lu are the former residences of a number of famous people. The tranquil **Qingteng Shuwu** (青藤书屋, *qīngténg shūwū*; daily 8am–5pm; ¥10), a perfect little sixteenth-century black-roofed house, hides 100m south of the Renmin Lu intersection on a small alley, Houguan Xiang, west off the main road. The serenity of the place belies the fact that it was once the home of eccentric Ming painter and dramatist Xu Wei (1521–93), who is notorious for having murdered his wife.

Another 500m south down Jiefang Lu from here, the **Yingtian Pagoda** (应天塔, *yìngtiān tǎ*; daily 8am–5pm; ¥5) crowns a low hill, Tu Shan. Part of a temple founded by the Song, burnt down by the Taiping rebels and subsequently rebuilt, the pagoda repays the stiff climb with splendid views over the town's canals. The black roof tiles, visible a block to the south, belong to the former residence (秋瑾故居, *qiūjǐn gùjū*; daily 8am–5pm; ¥15), situated on a small lane, of the radical woman activist **Qiu Jin**. Born here in 1875, Qiu Jin studied in Japan before returning to China and joining Sun Yatsen's clandestine revolutionary party. After editing several revolutionary papers in Shanghai and taking part in a series of abortive coups, she was captured and executed in Hangzhou in 1907 by Qing forces.

Lu Xun sights

East, of Jiefang Lu, down Luxun Lu, are several sights associated with the writer **Lu Xun** (see p.991), all open daily from 8am to 5pm; a combined ticket to see them all costs ¥120. Lu Xun's childhood and early youth were spent in Shaoxing, and local characters populate his books. Supposedly, he based his short story *Kong Yi Ji*, about a village idiot who failed the imperial exams and was thus ostracized from mainstream society, in part on observations in a bar that used to stand on this street. A few minutes farther east from the **Lu Xun Memorial Hall** (鲁迅纪念馆, *lŭxùn jìniànguăn*), beyond the plain **Lu Xun Library**, you'll find **Lu Xun's Former Residence** (鲁迅故居, *lŭxùn gùjū*), now converted into a **Folk Museum**. If you've seen the high, secretive outer walls so many compounds have, you'll find it a refreshing change to get to look at the spacious interior and numerous rooms inside a traditional house; drop in here for a wander through the writer's old rooms and for a stroll in his garden. Immediately across the road from the museum is the **Sanwei Shuwu** (三味书屋, *sānwèi shūwū*), the small school where Lu Xun was taught as a young boy. In the one room to see, there's a small desk on which you'll find a smooth stone and a bowl of water, in former times the only available tools for calligraphy students too poor to buy ink and paper. Visitors are supposed to write their names in water on the stone for luck.

One nearby sight definitely worth seeking out predates Lu Xun by several hundred years. About 1km to the northeast of the Lu Xun buildings, in the east of the town and in the heart of one of Shaoxing's most picturesque and traditional neighbourhoods, is the most famous of all the town's old bridges, **Bazi Qiao** (八子桥, *bāzĭ qiáo*). This thirteenth-century piece of engineering, which acquired its name because it looks like the Chinese character for the number eight, is still very much in use. A small alley called Baziqiao Zhi Jie runs east off Zhongxing Zhong Lu to the bridge.

Dong Hu

Easily accessible from town, the photogenic **Dong Hu** (东湖, *dōnghú*; daily 7am–5.30pm; ¥40) is a twenty-minute ride away on the #1 bus route. Despite appearances, the lake is not a natural one. In the seventh century the Sui rulers quarried the hard green rock east of Shaoxing for building, and when the hill streams were dammed, the quarry became a lake to which, for picturesque effect, a causeway was added during the Qing. The cliff face and lake are now surrounded by a maze of streams, winding paths, pagodas and stepping-stone bridges. Once inside the site, you can rent a little three-person boat (¥40) to take you around the various caves, nooks and crannies in the cliff face. You can choose to be dropped on the opposite shore, from where a flight of steps leads up to a path running to the clifftop, offering superb views over the surrounding paddy fields.

The last bus back to Shaoxing leaves around 5.30pm, though you can take a **boat** back instead (45min; ¥65/boat), or continue through the network of waterways on to Yu Ling (see below); this is a great trip (1hr 20min; ¥100/boat) in a long, slim, flat-bottomed vessel, the boatman steering with a paddle and propelling the boat with his bare feet on the loom of the long oar.

Yu Ling

Yu Ling (禹陵, *yŭlíng*; daily 8am–4pm; ¥50), 6km southeast of Shaoxing and linked to town by bus #2, is a heaped-up chaos of temple buildings in a beautiful setting of trees, mossy rocks and mountains. Yu, the legendary founder of the Xia dynasty, around 2000 BC, earned his title "Tamer of Floods" by tossing great rocks around and dealing with the underwater dragons who caused so many disasters. It took him eight years to control a great flood in the Lower Yangzi. The first temple was probably built around the sixth century AD, while Yu's tomb may be Han-dynasty. The temple today, most recently restored in the 1930s, contains a large painted figure of Yu and scores of inscribed tablets. Outside, the tall, roughly shaped tombstone is sheltered by an elegant open pavilion. The vigorous worshipping you'll see inside the temple shows what a revered figure Yu still is in modern China.

Eating

You'll find a few **restaurants** in Shaoxing, around the northern half of Jiefang Bei Lu. The restaurant in the *Shaoxing Fandian* (see p.354) is good, serving several dishes in the local *mei* (charcoal-grilled) style. Dried freshwater fish is a great speciality in Shaoxing, as is the yellow rice wine that's these days more commonly used for cooking than drinking – *shaoxing ji* (Shaoxing chicken) is a classic dish prepared with it. To sample local cuisine in upscale surroundings, visit the *Shaoxing Caiguan* (绍兴菜馆, *shàoxīng càiguǎn*) on Jiefang Lu. While walking around town you might be struck by the huge number of stalls selling that malodorous staple of Chinese street life, *chou doufu* (smelly tofu). The recipe was allegedly created by a Shaoxing woman who, tired of her limited cooking prowess, decided to experiment by throwing a variety of spices into a wok with some tofu.

Putuo Shan

The Buddhist island of **Putuo Shan** (普陀山, *pǔtuó shān*) is undoubtedly one of the most charming places in eastern China. A combination of religious reverence and relative inaccessibility means that it has no honking cars or department stores, only endless vistas of blue sea, sandy beaches and lush green hills dotted with ancient monasteries. As such, it's an ideal place to escape the noise, traffic and dirt of the big cities, but such appeal means that it's far better to visit midweek if possible – Putuo Shan is just twelve square kilometres in area, and can get swamped with tourists on weekends. Indeed, the best times to come are April, May, September and October, when the weather is warm and the island not especially busy. Bring walking shoes, too; you'll get much more out of the place if you walk between the attractions rather than taking the tour buses.

Over the years more than a hundred monasteries and shrines were built at Putuo Shan, with magnificent halls and gardens to match. At one time there were four thousand monks squeezed onto the island, and even as late as 1949 the Buddhist

The cult of Guanyin

Putuo Shan has been attracting Buddhist pilgrims from all over northeast Asia for at least a thousand years, and there are many tales accounting for the island's status as the centre of the **cult of Guanyin** (观音; *guānyīn*), Goddess of Mercy. According to one, the goddess attained enlightenment here; another tells how a Japanese monk named Hui'e, travelling home with an image of the goddess, took shelter here from a storm and was so enchanted by the island's beauty that he stayed, building a shrine on the spot. With the old beliefs on the rise again, many people come specifically to ask Guanyin for favours, often to do with producing children or grandchildren. The crowds of Chinese tourists carry identical yellow cotton bags which are stamped with symbols of the goddess at each temple, sometimes in exchange for donations.

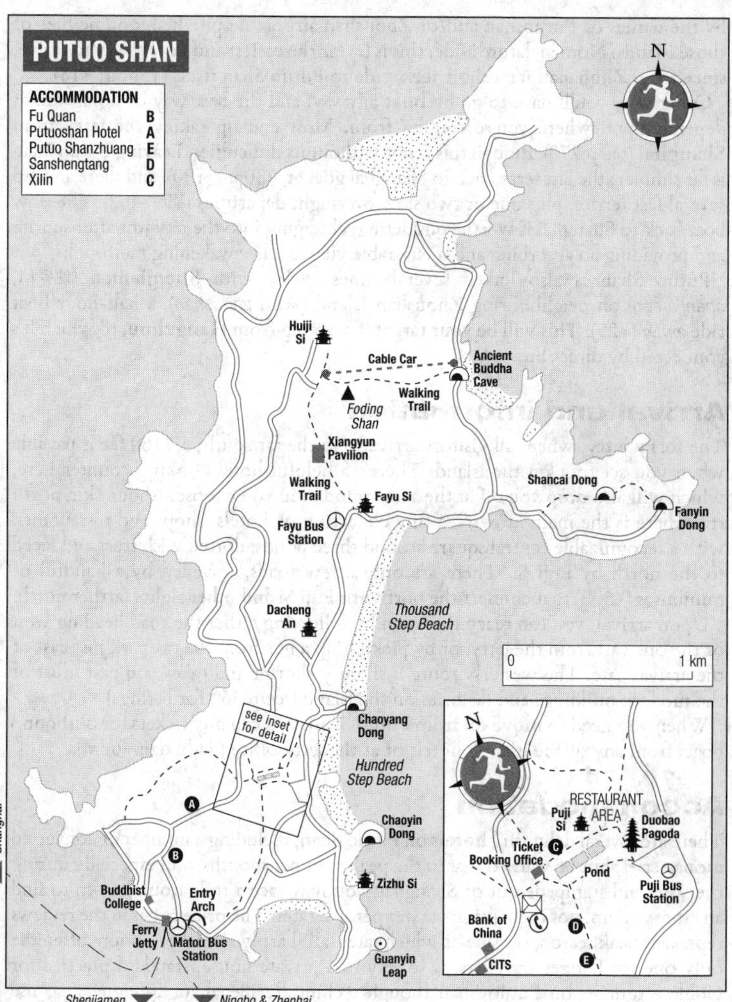

community numbered around two thousand. Indeed, until that date secular structures were not permitted on the island, and nobody lived here who was not a monk. Although there was a great deal of destruction on Putuo Shan during the Cultural Revolution, many treasures survived, some of which are in the Zhejiang Provincial Museum in Hangzhou (see p.347). Restoration continues steadily, and the number of monks has grown from only 29 in the late 1960s to several hundred. Three principal monasteries survive – **Puji**, the oldest and most central; **Fayu**, on the southern slopes; and **Huiji**, at the summit.

Access to the island

Putuo Shan has no **airport**, though there is one named after it on the neighbouring island of **Zhujiajian** (朱家尖, *zhūjiājiān*), which somewhat confusingly goes by the names of Putuoshan and/or Zhoushan airport despite being on neither of those islands. Nomenclature aside, this is by far the easiest and fastest way to arrive, since from Zhujiajian it's a short ferry ride to Putuo Shan itself (15min; ¥18).

Otherwise, you'll have to go by **boat** anyway, and the best way of doing things depends upon where you're coming from. Most end up taking the ferry from **Shanghai** (see p.270), though this is not without its difficulties. Leaving Putuo Shan is far simpler; the last ferry back to Shanghai goes at 4.30pm (¥90), and there are also several fast ferries, plus one or two slow overnight departures (¥99–462). The slow boat back to Shanghai is worth considering, chugging into the city just after sunrise and providing an absorbing and memorable view of the awakening metropolis.

Putuo Shan is also linked several times a day with **Shenjiamen** (沈家门, *shěnjiāmén*) on neighbouring Zhoushan Island (舟山, *zhōushān*), a half-hour boat ride away (¥25). This will be your target if arriving from **Hangzhou**, to which it's connected by direct bus.

Arrival and information

The **ferry jetty**, where all visitors arrive, is in the far south; a ¥160 fee is payable when you set foot on the island. There's a helpful hotel booking counter here, which will also drop you off at the accommodation you choose. About 1km north from here is the main "town", a tiny collection of hotels, shops and restaurants, with a recognizable central square around three ponds, dotted with trees and faced to the north by Puji Si. There are only a few roads, travelled by a handful of minibuses (¥5–8) that connect the port with Puji Si and other sights farther north.

Upon arrival, you can reach the town by following either the road heading west or the one east from the jetty, or by picking up a bus from the car park just east of the arrival gate. The westerly route is slightly shorter and takes you past most of the modern buildings and facilities on the island (see p.360 for listings).

When you need to **move on** from Putuo Shan, you can buy tickets for outbound boats from any of the island's hotels or at the jetty office (daily 6am–6pm).

Accommodation

There are several delightful **hotels** on Putuo Shan, including a number of converted monasteries, but be warned that in the peak summer months, and especially during the weekend stampede out of Shanghai, you may face a trek around town to find an empty room, not to mention very expensive rates. The price codes in the reviews represent peak season, outside of which rates fall sharply. Another option, often the only one for budget travellers, is to stay in a private house, standard practice for Chinese tourists on Putuo Shan though technically illegal for foreigners, so use your discretion. It's not hard to find people with houses to let – they congregate at the jetty pier, and you should be able to bargain them down to around ¥150 per person, depending on the season. A third option, pursued especially by younger foreign travellers, is to crash on one of the island's two beaches for the night.

Fu Quan (副泉山庄, *fúquán shānzhuāng*) ⓣ0580/6092069. The sign is only in Chinese and easy to miss, though not far from the jetty. Basic but agreeable rooms. ❹

Putuoshan Hotel (普陀山大酒店, *pǔtuóshān dàjiǔdiàn*) On the main west road from the jetty to the town ⓣ0580/6092828, ⓦwww.putuoshanhotel.com. Very easy to spot, thanks to its spacious grounds and opulent design, this is the best hotel on the island, with cheaper prices than some less salubrious competitors. Traditional Chinese furniture in the classier rooms, and an on-site vegetarian restaurant. ❻

Putuo Shanzhuang (普陀山庄宾馆, *pǔtuóshānzhuāng bīnguǎn*) Just south of the *Sanshengtang* ⓣ0580/6091530, ⓕ6091228. A beautiful, relatively isolated and extremely comfortable option set on the wooded hillside opposite Puji Si. ❻

Sanshengtang (三圣堂饭店, *sānshèngtáng fàndiàn*) ⓣ0580/6091277, ⓕ6091140. On the eastern route from the jetty to town, this is just a couple of minutes due south of the centre on a small path. It's quite an attractive place, styled like a temple, but they tend to surcharge foreigners by fifty percent. ❼

Xilin (锡麟饭店, *xīlín fàndiàn*) Right on the central square, to the west of Puji Si ⓣ0580/6091303, ⓕ6091199. Features an entrance that makes it look like a temple, plus a good restaurant; you may be able to persuade them to waive their foreigners' surcharge. ❻

The island

The three main temples on the island are in extremely good condition, recently renovated, with yellow-ochre walls offsetting the deep green of the mature trees in their forecourts. This is particularly true of **Puji Si** (普济寺, *pŭji sì*; daily 6am–9pm; ¥5), right in the centre of the island, built in 1080 and enlarged by successive dynasties. Standing among magnificent camphor trees, it boasts a bridge lined with statues and an elegantly tall pagoda with an enormous iron bell.

South of here and just to the east of the square ponds is the five-storey **Duobao Pagoda** (多宝塔, *duōbăo tă*). Built in 1334 using stones brought over from Tai Hu in Jiangsu province, it has Buddhist inscriptions on all four sides. Twenty minutes' walk farther south down on the southeastern corner of the island is a cave, **Chaoyin Dong** (潮音洞, *cháoyīn dòng*). The din of crashing waves here is remarkable, thought to resemble the call of Buddha (and hence this was a popular spot for monks to commit suicide in earlier days). The neighbouring **Zizhu Si** (紫竹寺, *zĭzhú sì*; daily 6am–6pm; ¥5 including admission to Chaoyin Dong), meaning "Temple of Violet Bamboo", is one of the less touristed temples on the island and, for that reason alone, a good spot to observe the monks' daily rituals.

On the island's southern tip is Putuo's most prominent sight, the **Guanyin Leap** (观音跳, *guānyīn tiào*; daily 7am–5pm; ¥6), a headland from which rises a spectacular 33m-high bronze-plated statue of the Goddess of Mercy, visible from much of the island. In her left hand, Guanyin holds a steering wheel, symbolically protecting fishermen from violent seastorms. The pavilion at the base of the statue holds a small exhibit of wooden murals recounting how Guanyin aided Putuo villagers and fishermen over the years, while in a small room directly underneath the statue sit four hundred statues representing the various spiritual incarnations of Guanyin. The view from the statue's base over the surrounding islands and fishing boats is sublime, especially on a clear day.

North of the town

The two temples in the northern half of the island, Huiji Si and Fayu Si, make for a pleasant day-trip from town. They're conveniently connected to the southern half by minibuses departing from the Puji bus station just southeast of the central square, and there are minibuses between the temples as well.

Huiji Si (慧济寺, *huìjì sì*; daily 6.30am–5pm; ¥5) stands near the top of **Foding Shan** (佛顶山, *fódĭng shān*), whose summit provides spectacular views of the sea and the surrounding islands. You can hike up or use the **cable car** (daily 7am–5pm; ¥40/return, ¥25 one-way) from the minibus stand. The temple itself, built mainly between 1793 and 1851, occupies a beautiful site just to the northwest of the summit, surrounded by green tea plantations. The halls stand in a flattened area between hoary trees and bamboo groves, the greens, reds, blues and gold of their enamelled tiles gleaming magnificently in the sunshine. There's also a vegetarian restaurant here.

You can head down along a marked path towards the third major temple, Fayu Si, the whole walk taking about an hour. Shortly after setting off, you'll see a secondary track branching away to the left towards the **Ancient Buddha Cave**, a delightfully secluded spot by a sandy beach on the northeastern coast of the island; give yourself a couple of hours to get there and back. Back on the main path, the steep steps bring you to the **Xiangyun Pavilion**, where you can rest and drink tea with the friendly monks.

Thirty minutes farther on you'll reach the **Fayu Si** (法雨寺, *fǎyǔ sì*; daily 6.30am–5.30pm; ¥5), another superb collection of more than two hundred halls amid huge green trees, built up in levels against the slope during the Ming. With the mountain behind and the sea just in front, it's a delightful place to sit in peaceful contemplation. The Daxiong Hall has been brilliantly restored, and the Dayuan Hall has a unique beamless arched roof and a dome, around the inside of which squirm nine carved wooden dragons. This hall is said to have been moved here from Nanjing by Emperor Kangxi in 1689. Its great statue of **Guanyin**, flanked by monks and nuns, is the focal point of the goddess's birthday celebrations in early April, when thousands of pilgrims and sightseers crowd onto the island for chanting and ceremonies that last all evening.

Occasional minibuses head out along the promontory immediately east of Fayu Si to **Fanyin Dong** (梵音洞, *fányīn dòng*; daily 8am–4.30pm; ¥5), a cave whose name derives from the resemblance of the sound of crashing waves to Buddhist chants. The cave is set in the rocky cliff, with a small shrine actually straddling a ravine. Walking around on the promontory is a pleasure given the absence of crowds and the difficulty of getting lost.

You'll appreciate Putuo's beauty much more by making the trip to Huiji Si and Fayu Si **on foot** via the two excellent **beaches** that line the eastern shore: Qianbu Sha (Thousand Step Beach; ¥12 until 5pm, free afterwards) and Baibu Sha (Hundred Step Beach; ¥10 until 5pm, free afterwards). In summer, it's possible to bring a sleeping bag and camp out on either beach – be sure to bring all your supplies from town as there are no stores or restaurants nearby. The beaches are separated by a small headland hiding the **Chaoyang Dong** (潮阳洞, *cháoyáng dòng*). Just inside this little cave there's a teahouse and a seating area overlooking the sea, while from the top of the headland itself you'll get great views. One kilometre south of Fayu Si, the **Dacheng An** (大乘庵, *dàchèng' ān*; daily 8am–5.30pm; ¥1) is a nunnery notable for the reclining Buddha downstairs in the main hall, and the thousands of tiny seated Buddhas upstairs.

Eating

Most **food** must be brought in from the mainland and is, therefore, expensive. The lane running northeast away from Puji Si, as well as the road between the jetty departure and arrival points, both have some dingy-looking places specializing in seafood (fish, molluscs, eel) though they also do standard dishes and noodles. All the main temples have simple vegetarian restaurants, and there's an upscale vegetarian place attached to the *Putuoshan Hotel*.

Listings

Airlines The main CAAC reservations and ticketing office (daily 7.30am–8pm; reservations ⓣ0571/86662391; domestic flight schedules ⓣ0571/85151397) is at 390 Tiyuchang Lu in the north of town. CAAC buses to the airport (5.45am–8pm; ¥15) leave from here every 30min. There's a ticket office where you can book domestic flights at the northwestern corner of the central square.

Banks and exchange The Bank of China (daily 8–11am & 1–4.30pm; ATM 24hr) is on the westerly route into town from the ferry jetty.

Mail and telephones The post office and China Telecom office are just past the Bank of China, up a small lane to to the right, just before the *Xilin* hotel.

Travel agents The CITS office is on the westerly route into town from the ferry jetty, just before the Bank of China.

Travel details

Trains

Times given are for the fastest possible connections; there are usually slower services available at a slightly cheaper price.

Hangzhou to: Beijing (4 daily; 11hr 30min); Guangzhou (5 daily; 16hr); Nanjing (frequent; 4hr 20min); Shanghai (frequent; 1hr 20min); Shaoxing (frequent; 20min); Suzhou (frequent; 3hr).

Ji'nan to: Beijing (many daily; 3hr); Qingdao (many daily; 2hr 15min); Qufu (3 daily; 2hr 20min); Shanghai (16 daily; 7hr 40min); Taishan (many daily; 50min); Yantai (8 daily; 6hr 30min).

Nanjing to: Beijing (12 daily; 8hr); Chengdu (5 daily; 27hr); Hangzhou (frequent; 4hr 20min); Shanghai (frequent; 2hr); Suzhou (frequent; 1hr 30min); Xi'an (12 daily; 12hr).

Qingdao to: Beijing (8 daily; 5hr 40min); Ji'nan (many daily; 2hr 15min); Yantai (1 daily; 4hr 15min).

Qufu Ji'nan (3 daily; 2hr 20min); Taishan (2 daily; 1hr 40min).

Shaoxing to: Hangzhou (frequent; 20min).

Suzhou to: Hangzhou (frequent; 3hr); Nanjing (frequent; 1hr 30min); Shanghai (frequent; 36min).

Taishan (Tai'an) to: Beijing (13 daily; 3hr 40min); Ji'nan (many daily; 50min); Qufu (2 daily; 1hr 40min).

Yantai to: Beijing (1 daily; 14hr 20min); Ji'nan (8 daily; 6hr 45min); Qingdao (1 daily; 4hr 30min).

Buses

There are frequent departures on many of the routes listed below, though if your journey is a lengthy one, it's advisable to try to set off before noon.

Hangzhou to: Huang Shan (4hr); Nanjing (4hr); Shanghai (2hr 30min); Shaoxing (1hr 30min); Suzhou (2hr); Wenzhou (4hr 30min).

Ji'nan to: Qingdao (4hr 30min); Qufu (2hr 30min); Tai'an (1hr 30min).

Nanjing to: Hangzhou (5hr); Hefei (7hr); Huang Shan (5hr); Qingdao (12hr); Shanghai (4–5hr); Suzhou (3–4hr).

Qufu to: Heze (for Kaifeng; 3hr); Ji'nan (2hr 30min); Qingdao (6hr); Tai'an (1hr).

Shaoxing to: Hangzhou (1hr 30min).

Suzhou North station to: Nanjing (3hr); Shanghai (1–2hr).

Suzhou South station to: Hangzhou (4hr); Tongli (1hr); Zhouzhuang (2hr).

Tai'an to: Ji'nan (1hr 30min); Qufu (1hr); Zhengzhou (7hr).

Ferries

Putuo Shan to: Shanghai (several daily; 4hr express, 10hr overnight); Shenjiamen (at least 7 daily; 30min); Zhujiajian (every 15min; 15min).

Qingdao to: Incheon (South Korea; 3 weekly; 16hr); Shimonoseki (Japan; 2 weekly; 36hr).

Weihai to: Incheon (South Korea; 3 weekly; 14hr).

Yantai to: Dalian (daily; 4hr); Incheon (South Korea; 3 weekly; 14hr).

Flights

Among international connections from this part of China, there are flights from Hangzhou (Amsterdam, Busan, Kuala Lumpur, Osaka, Seoul, Singapore, Tokyo), Ji'nan (Seoul, Singapore), Nanjing (Frankfurt, Osaka, Seoul, Singapore, Tokyo) and Qingdao (Osaka, Seoul, Tokyo).

Hangzhou to: Beijing (frequent; 2hr); Chengdu (10 daily; 2hr 30min); Guangzhou (frequent; 2hr); Guilin (5 daily; 2hr); Hong Kong (7 daily; 2hr); Kunming (6 daily; 2hr); Qingdao (8 daily; 1hr 30min); Shanghai (3 daily; 20min); Shenzhen (10 daily; 2hr); Xiamen (4–5 daily; 1hr 10min); Xi'an (7 daily; 2hr).

Ji'nan to: Beijing (3–4 daily; 1hr); Chengdu (5–6 daily; 2hr 15min); Chongqing (6 daily; 2hr); Guangzhou (6 daily; 2hr 30min); Hong Kong (daily; 2hr 55min); Kunming (5–6 daily; 3hr); Nanjing (2 daily; 1hr); Shanghai (hourly; 1hr 20min); Xi'an (3–4 daily; 1hr 30min); Yantai (1–2 daily; 50min).

Nanjing to: Beijing (frequent; 1hr 30min); Chengdu (7 daily; 2hr 20min); Chongqing (5 daily; 2hr 20min); Dalian (4 daily; 1hr 30min); Guangzhou (11 daily; 2hr); Guilin (4 daily; 2hr); Haikou (5 daily; 2hr 25min); Hong Kong (7 daily; 2hr 20min); Kunming (5 daily; 2hr 40min); Qingdao (5 daily; 1hr); Shenzhen (8 daily; 2hr); Xiamen (4–5 daily; 1hr 40min); Xi'an (4 daily; 2hr).

Qingdao to: Beijing (hourly; 1hr 15min); Chengdu (4 daily; 2hr 30min); Chongqing (3 daily; 1hr 30min); Guangzhou (8 daily; 3hr); Hangzhou (10 daily; 1hr 30min); Hong Kong (1–2 daily; 3hr); Kunming (1–2 daily; 3hr); Nanjing (3–5 daily; 1hr); Shanghai (hourly; 1hr 15min); Xi'an (5–6 daily; 1hr 50min); Zhengzhou (3 daily; 1hr 10min).

Yantai to: Beijing (7–8 daily; 1hr 15min); Hong Kong (2 weekly; 3hr 30min); Ji'nan (1–2 daily; 50min); Nanjing (1–2 daily; 1hr 20min); Shanghai (9 daily; 1hr 30min).

CHAPTER 6 Highlights

* **The Bund** Fusty colonial architecture and brash modernity stare each other down over the Huangpu River. See p.376

* **Huangpu boat trips** Get out on the river for a sense of the maritime industry that's at the heart of the city's success. See p.377

* **Shanghai World Financial Centre observation platform** The view from the top floor of Shanghai's finest building is simply awesome. See p.382

* **Shanghai Museum** A candidate for the best museum in the country, with a wide range of exhibits housed in a building that's shaped like an ancient Chinese pottery vessel. See p.384

* **Moganshan Art District** Fascinating arts venue full of trendy galleries and studios. See p.387

* **Yu Yuan** An elegant Chinese garden with opportunities to snack and sip tea in the vicinity. See p.388

* **Tianzifang** Intriguing, fun shopping district of traditional housing turned into boutiques See p.390

▲ Moganshan Art District

6

Shanghai and around

After years of stagnation, the great metropolis of **SHANGHAI** (上海, *shànghǎi*) is undergoing one of the fastest economic expansions the world has ever seen. Nearly a third of China's exports come from the area and it attracts almost a quarter of all the country's foreign investment, more than any single developing country. As Shanghai begins to recapture its position as East Asia's leading business city, a status it last held before World War II, the skyline is filling with skyscrapers, and there are over four thousand now, more than twice as many as in New York. Gleaming shopping malls, luxurious hotels and prestigious arts centres are rising alongside. Shanghai's 21 million residents enjoy the highest incomes on the mainland, and there's plenty for them to splash out on; witness the rash of celebrity restaurants and designer flagship stores. In short, it's a city with a swagger, bursting with nouveau-riche exuberance and elan.

And yet, for all the modernization, Shanghai is still known in the West for its infamous role as the base of **European imperialism** in mainland China. Whichever side you were on, life in Shanghai then was rarely one of moderation. China's most prosperous city, in large part European- and American-financed, Shanghai introduced Asia to electric light, boasted more cars than the rest of the country put together, and created for its rich citizens a world of European-style mansions, tree-lined boulevards, chic café society, horse-racing and exclusive gentlemen's clubs. Alongside, and as much part of the legend, lay a city of singsong girls, warring gangsters and millions living in absolute poverty.

When the Communists marched into Shanghai in May 1949, they took control of the most important business and trading centre in Asia, an international port where vast fortunes were made. Their movement may have been born here, yet they never trusted the place; for most of the communist period, the central government in Beijing deliberately ran Shanghai down, siphoning off its surplus to other parts of the country, to the point where the city came to resemble a living museum, housing the largest array of **Art Deco architecture** in the world and frozen in time since the 1940s. Parts of the city still resemble a 1920s vision of the future, a grimy metropolis of monolithic Neoclassical facades, threaded with overhead cables and walkways, and choked by vast crowds and rattling trolleybuses.

Yet the Shanghainese never lost their ability to make waves for themselves. The present boom dates back to 1990, with the opening of the "New Bund" – the Special Economic Zone across the river in Pudong. Ever since, the city has enjoyed double digit growth, and what was once a sleepy suburb of rice fields now looks like a city of the future, quite literally – when sci-fi film *Code 46* was shot here, no CGI was used.

Not that the old Shanghai is set to disappear overnight. Most of the urban area was partitioned between foreign powers until 1949, and their former embassies, banks and official residences still give large sections of Shanghai an early twentieth-century European flavour. It's still possible to make out the boundaries of what used to be the foreign concessions, with the bewildering tangle of alleyways of the old Chinese city at its heart. Only along the Huangpu waterfront, amid the stolid grandeur of the **Bund**, is there some sense of space – and here you feel the past more strongly than ever. It's ironic that the relics of hated foreign imperialism are now protected as city monuments.

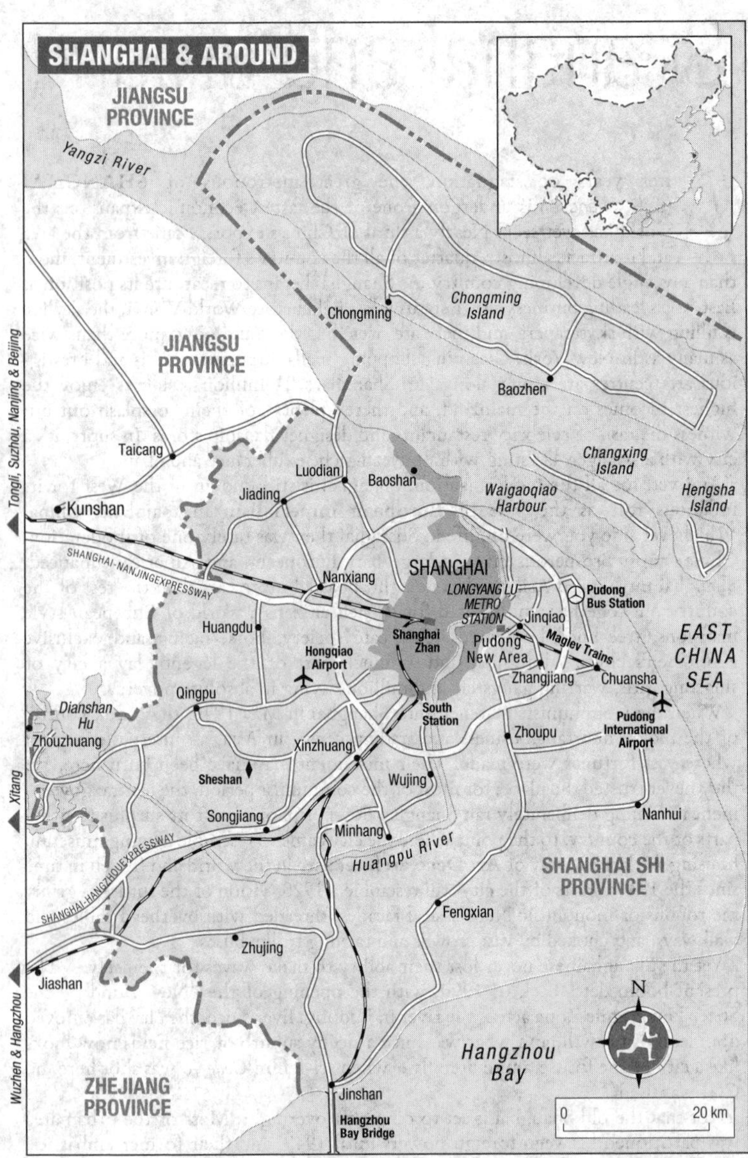

Like Hong Kong, its model for economic development, Shanghai does not brim with obvious attractions. Besides the Shanghai Museum, the Suzhou-reminiscent gardens of Yu Yuan, and the Huangpu River cruise, there are few tourist sights with broad appeal. But the beauty of visiting Shanghai lies in its less apparent pleasures: Shanghai is one of the few Chinese cities that rewards aimless wandering, and it's fascinating to stroll the Bund, explore the pockets of colonial architecture in the former French Concession, or get lost in the old city's alleys. The place absolutely excels in all materialistic pleasures, so make sure you sample the exploding restaurant and nightlife scenes, and budget some time for serious shopping. Perhaps the greatest fascination is in simply absorbing the splendour of a city so extravagantly on the up.

Some history

Contrary to Western interpretations, Shanghai's history did not begin with the founding of the British Concession in the wake of the First Opium War. Located at the confluence of the Yangzi River, the Grand Canal and the Pacific Ocean, Shanghai served as a major commercial port from the Song dynasty, channelling the region's extensive cotton crop to Beijing, the hinterland and Japan. By the Qing dynasty, vast **mercantile guilds**, often organized by trade and bearing superficial resemblance to their Dutch counterparts, had established economic and, to some extent, political control of the city. Indeed, the British only chose to set up a treaty port in Shanghai because, in the words of East India Company representative Hugh Lindsay, "the city had become the principal emporium of Eastern Asia" by the 1840s.

After the **Opium Wars**, the British moved in under the Treaty of Nanking in 1842, to be rapidly followed by the French in 1847. These two powers set up the first **foreign concessions** in the city – the British along the Bund and the area to the north of the Chinese city, the French in an area to the southwest, on the site of a cathedral a French missionary had founded two centuries earlier. Later the Americans (in 1863) and the Japanese (in 1895) came to tack their own areas onto the British Concession, which expanded into the so-called International Settlement. Traders were allowed to live under their own national laws, policed by their own armed forces, in a series of privileged enclaves that were leased indefinitely. By 1900, the city's favourable position, close to the main trade route to the major silk- and tea-producing regions, had allowed it to develop into a sizeable port and manufacturing centre. At this time, it was largely controlled by the "Green Gang", the infamous Chinese crime syndicate founded in the 1700s by unemployed boatmen, which by the 1920s ran the city's vast underworld. Businessmen and criminals who flouted the Green Gang's strict code of behaviour were subject to "knee-capping" punishment – having every visible tendon severed with a fruit knife before being left to die on a busy sidewalk.

Shanghai's cheap workforce was swollen during the Taiping Uprising (see p.330) by those who took shelter from the slaughter in the foreign settlements, and by peasants attracted to the city's apparent prosperity. Here China's first urban proletariat emerged, and the squalid living conditions, outbreaks of unemployment and glaring abuses of Chinese labour by foreign investors made Shanghai a natural breeding ground for **revolutionary politics**. The Chinese Communist Party was founded in the city in 1921, only to be driven underground by the notorious massacre of hundreds of strikers in 1927.

Inevitably, after the Communist takeover, the bright lights dimmed. The foreign community may have expected "business as usual", but the new regime was determined that Shanghai should play its role in the radical reconstruction of China. The worst slums were knocked down to be replaced by apartments, the gangsters

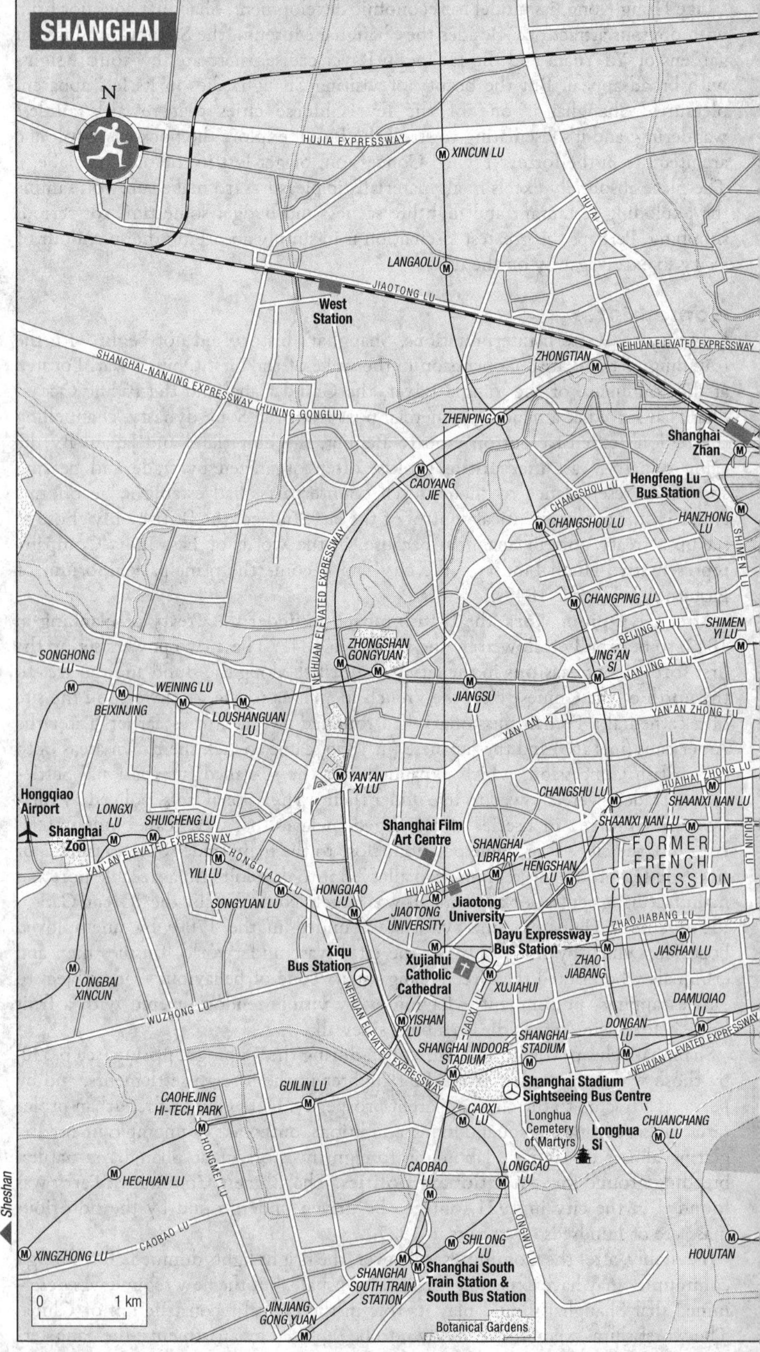
SHANGHAI
HUJIA EXPRESSWAY
XINCUN LU
HUTAI LU
LANGAOLU
JIAOTONG LU
West Station
SHANGHAI-NANJING EXPRESSWAY (HUNING GONGLU)
NEIHUAN ELEVATED EXPRESSWAY
ZHONGTIAN
ZHENPING
Shanghai Zhan
CAOYANG JIE
Hengfeng Lu Bus Station
CHANGSHOU LU
HANZHONG LU
SHIMEN LU
CHANGPING LU
SHIMEN YI LU
BEIJING XI LU
ZHONGSHAN GONGYUAN
SONGHONG LU
JING'AN SI
NANJING XI LU
WEINING LU
JIANGSU LU
BEIXINJING
LOUSHANGUAN LU
YAN'AN ZHONG LU
YAN' AN XI LU
YAN'AN XI LU
HUAIHAI ZHONG LU
Hongqiao Airport
LONGXI LU
SHUICHENG LU
CHANGSHU LU
SHAANXI NAN LU
Shanghai Zoo
YAN'AN ELEVATED EXPRESSWAY
Shanghai Film Art Centre
RUIJIN LU
HONGQIAO LU
SHANGHAI LIBRARY
FORMER FRENCH CONCESSION
YILI LU
HENGSHAN LU
HUAIHAI XI LU
Jiaotong University
SONGYUAN LU
HONGQIAO LU
JIAOTONG UNIVERSITY
ZHAOJIABANG LU
Dayu Expressway Bus Station
JIASHAN LU
Xiqu Bus Station
Xujiahui Catholic Cathedral
ZHAO-JIABANG
XUJIAHUI
LONGBAI XINCUN
DAMUQIAO LU
WUZHONG LU
CAOXI LU
YISHAN LU
DONGAN LU
SHANGHAI STADIUM
SHANGHAI INDOOR STADIUM
NEIHUAN ELEVATED EXPRESSWAY
Shanghai Stadium Sightseeing Bus Centre
GUILIN LU
CAOHEJING HI-TECH PARK
CAOXI LU
Longhua Cemetery of Martyrs
Longhua Si
CHUANCHANG LU
HONGMEI LU
HECHUAN LU
CAOBAO LU
LONGCAO LU
LONGWU LU
Sheshan
CAOBAO LU
XINGZHONG LU
SHILONG LU
HOUTAN
SHANGHAI SOUTH TRAIN STATION
Shanghai South Train Station & South Bus Station
0 1 km
JINJIANG GONG YUAN
Botanical Gardens

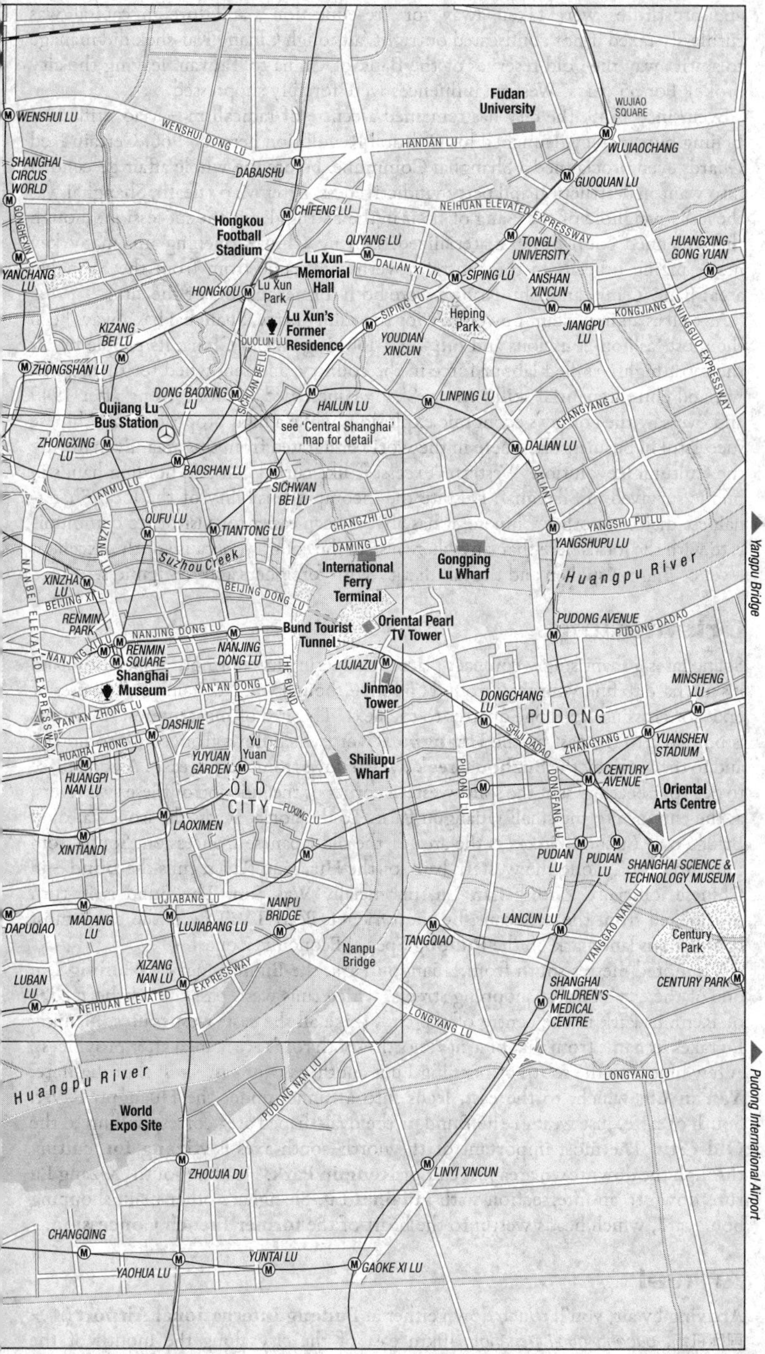

Fudan University
WUJIAO SQUARE
WENSHUI LU
WENSHUI DONG LU
HANDAN LU
WUJIAOCHANG
SHANGHAI CIRCUS WORLD
DABAISHU
GUOQUAN LU
NEIHUAN ELEVATED EXPRESSWAY
CHIFENG LU
Hongkou Football Stadium
GONGHEXIN LU
QUYANG LU
TONGJI UNIVERSITY
HUANGXING GONG YUAN
YANCHANG LU
Lu Xun Memorial Hall
DALIAN XI LU
SIPING LU
ANSHAN XINCUN
HONGKOU
Lu Xun Park
Lu Xun's Former Residence
SIPING LU
Heping Park
KONGJIANG LU
JIANGPU LU
KIZANG BEI LU
DUOLUN LU
YOUDIAN XINCUN
NINGGUO EXPRESSWAY
ZHONGSHAN LU
SICHUAN BEI LU
DONG BAOXING LU
LINPING LU
HAILUN LU
Qujiang Lu Bus Station
see 'Central Shanghai' map for detail
CHANGYANG LU
ZHONGXING LU
DALIAN LU
BAOSHAN LU
SICHWAN BEI LU
TIANMU LU
DALIAN LU
QUFU LU
TIANTONG LU
CHANGZHI LU
YANGSHU PU LU
XIZANG LU
DAMING LU
YANGSHUPU LU
Suzhou Creek
International Ferry Terminal
Gongping Lu Wharf
Huangpu River
Yangpu Bridge
XINZHA LU
BEIJING XI LU
BEIJING DONG LU
NANBEI ELEVATED EXPRESSWAY
RENMIN PARK
NANJING DONG LU
Bund Tourist Tunnel
Oriental Pearl TV Tower
PUDONG AVENUE
PUDONG DADAO
NANJING XI LU
RENMIN SQUARE
NANJING DONG LU
LUJIAZUI
Shanghai Museum
YAN'AN DONG LU
THE BUND
Jinmao Tower
MINSHENG LU
DONGCHANG LU
YAN'AN ZHONG LU
PUDONG
DASHIJIE
SHIJI DADAO
ZHANGYANG LU
YUANSHEN STADIUM
HUAIHAI ZHONG LU
YUYUAN GARDEN
Yu Yuan
Shiliupu Wharf
HUANGPI NAN LU
OLD CITY
PUDONG LU
DONGFANG LU
CENTURY AVENUE
Oriental Arts Centre
FUXING LU
LAOXIMEN
XINTIANDI
PUDIAN LU
PUDIAN LU
SHANGHAI SCIENCE & TECHNOLOGY MUSEUM
LUJIABANG LU
NANPU BRIDGE
DAPUQIAO
MADANG LU
LUJIABANG LU
TANGQIAO
LANCUN LU
Nanpu Bridge
YANGGAO NAN LU
Century Park
XIZANG NAN LU
LUBAN LU
NEIHUAN ELEVATED EXPRESSWAY
SHANGHAI CHILDREN'S MEDICAL CENTRE
CENTURY PARK
LONGYANG LU
LONGYANG LU
Huangpu River
PUDONG NAN LU
World Expo Site
Pudong International Airport
ZHOUJIA DU
LINYI XINCUN
CHANGQING
YUNTAI LU
YAOHUA LU
GAOKE XI LU

and prostitutes were taken away for "re-education", and foreign capital was ruthlessly taxed if not confiscated outright (although Chiang Kai-shek did manage to spirit away the gold reserves of the Bank of China to Taiwan, leaving the city broke). For 35 years, Western influences were forcibly suppressed.

Even since 1949, the city has remained a centre of radicalism – Mao, stifled by Beijing bureaucracy, launched his Cultural Revolution here in 1966. Certain Red Guards even proclaimed a Shanghai Commune, before the whole affair descended into wanton destruction and petty vindictiveness. After Mao's death, Shanghai was the last stronghold of the Gang of Four in their struggle for the succession, though their planned coup never materialized. During China's opening up, many key modernizing officials in the central government came from from the Shanghai area; Jiang Zemin and Zhu Rongji were both former mayors of the city.

As well as an important power base for the ruling party, Shanghai has always been the most fashion-conscious and **outward-looking** city in China, its people by far the most highly skilled labour force in the country, and renowned for their quick wit and entrepreneurial skills. Many Shanghainese fled to Hong Kong after 1949 and oversaw the colony's economic explosion, while a high proportion of Chinese successful in business elsewhere in the world emigrated from this area. Even during the Cultural Revolution, Western "excesses" like curled hair and holding hands in public survived in Shanghai. Despite the incomprehensibility of the local Shanghainese dialect to other Chinese, it has always been easier for visitors to communicate with the locals here than anywhere else in the country, because of the excellent level of English spoken and the familiarity with foreigners and foreignness.

Orientation

Shanghai is a surprisingly compact place, considering its enormous population, and it's not hard to find your way around on foot – though you'll certainly need buses or taxis for crossing from one quarter to the next. The area of most interest to visitors is bordered to the east by the **Huangpu River** (which flows from south to north), and to the north by the **Suzhou Creek** (which flows from west to east). A good place to get your bearings is at the southwestern corner of the junction of these two rivers, at the entrance to the small Huangpu Park. To the north, across the iron Waibaidu Bridge over Suzhou Creek, is the area of the old Japanese Concession. South from Huangpu Park, along the western bank of the Huangpu River, runs the **Bund** – in Chinese, officially **Zhongshan Lu**, unofficially **Wai Tan**. The Bund is in turn overlooked from the east bank by the Oriental Pearl TV Tower, the city's most conspicuous landmark, in the **Pudong** Special Economic Zone.

A hundred metres south from Huangpu Park, the Bund is met by **Nanjing Lu**, one of the city's busiest shopping streets, which runs west, past the northern edge of Renmin Park in the centre of the city. (Like all the east–west routes, Nanjing Lu takes its name from that of a city; north–south roads are named after provinces.) A few blocks to the south of Nanjing Lu is another major east–west thoroughfare, **Yan'an Lu**, which, to the east, leads into a tunnel under the Huangpu River. South of here, just west of the Bund, is the oval-shaped area corresponding to the **Old City**. The most important of the north–south axes is **Xizang Lu**, cutting through the downtown area just east of **Renmin Park**. Heading south, Xizang Lu runs down to an intersection with **Huaihai Lu**, Shanghai's other main shopping boulevard, which heads west into the heart of the **former French Concession**.

Arrival

Arriving by air, you'll touch down either at **Pudong International Airport** (浦东国际机场, *pǔdōng guójì jīchǎng*), 40km east of the city along the mouth of the

Yangzi River, or at the recently spruced up **Hongqiao Airport** (虹桥机场, *hóngqiáo jīchǎng*), 15km west of the city. Pudong handles most international flights, with the smaller Hongqiao servicing domestic flights.

The most romantic way to get into town from Pudong is on the world's only commercial **Maglev train** (磁悬浮列车, *cíxuánfú lièchē*; daily 7am–9pm; every 20min), suspended above the track and propelled by the forces of magnetism. It whizzes from Pudong to Longyang Lu subway station in the eastern suburbs in eight minutes, accelerating to 430km/hr in the first four minutes, then immediately starting to decelerate. As you near top speed – there's a digital speedometer in each cabin – the view from the windows becomes an impressionistic blur. Tickets cost ¥50 one-way, ¥40 if you show a plane ticket. Never mind that the Maglev terminal is a few minutes' walk from the airport, and that Longyang Lu subway is still a long way from the centre of town –you may never get another chance to go this fast on land.

A **taxi** from Pudong to the Bund should cost around ¥150, to Nanjing Xi Lu around ¥130, or you can board an **airport bus** (飞机场特快汽车, *fēijīchǎng tèkuài qìchē*). There are stops opposite the exit gates, and eight routes to choose from, with departures every fifteen minutes until the last plane lands; tickets cost around ¥20. The journey into town takes around ninety minutes. Bus #2 is generally the most useful as it goes to the Jing'an subway stop in the city centre. Bus #1 goes to Hongqiao Airport; bus #3 goes to the *Galaxy Hotel*, in the Hongqiao business district in the west of the city, and then to Xujiahui; bus #4 goes to Hongkou Stadium, in the north; bus #5 goes to Shanghai Zhan train station; bus #6 goes to Zhonghsan Park, bus #7 to the south railway station, in the southern suburbs. The only one with a drop off in Pudong is bus #5 (Dongfang Hospital).

These days you can also take the **subway** straight into town (上海地铁, *shànghǎi dìtiě*; ¥7); this isn't as convenient as it should be, as the trip takes ninety minutes (so isn't any faster than the bus), you'll have to wait for up to twenty minutes to change trains onto Line 2 at Guanglan Lu station, and the line closes at 4pm.

On the second floor, opposite exit 18, there are long-distance coaches, leaving hourly, which will take you to Suzhou, Nanjing and Hangzhou; tickets cost around ¥50–80. Your best route **out of Hongqiao Airport** is to take the subway (line 2), though a taxi to Nanjing Xi Lu only costs about ¥45, and to the Bund about ¥60; on busy times such as Friday nights, you can wait more than an hour for a cab at the rank – walk to departures and pick up one that's just dropped someone off, or get on any bus for a couple of stops and hail one there. Buses leave from the parking lot: bus #1 goes to Pudong International Airport, the airport shuttle goes to Jing'an Temple subway stop in the city centre, bus #925 goes to Renmin Square and bus #941 goes to the Shanghai Zhan. Each of these bus rides from Hongqiao can take up to an hour depending on traffic.

By train

The main **train station** (上海火车站, *shànghǎi huǒchēzhàn*) is to the north of Suzhou Creek. City buses are not an easy way to get out of the station area; you're better off taking subway line #1 or a taxi, the latter not likely to cost more than ¥15–20. There's an official rank outside the station and no trouble with drivers hustling foreigners. You may well arrive at the big new **Shanghai South station** (上海南站, *shànghǎi nān zhàn*) if you have come from cities south of here, such as Ningbo or Hangzhou; it's on the subway (lines 1 and 3).

By bus and boat

Hardly any tourists arrive in Shanghai by **bus**; if you do you'll probably be dropped at either the new South bus station, or, more likely, at the main train station, both of which are attached to the subway. Some buses arrive at **Hengfeng Lu bus station** (横峰公共汽車站, *héngfēng gōnggòngqìchē zhàn*), a short walk from the main station. If you're unlucky, you might be dropped at **Pudong bus station**, in the far east of the city (浦东公共汽車站, *pŭ dōng gōnggòngqìchē zhàn*); a cab from here to the centre of town will cost ¥100 or so, so instead get a cab to the nearest subway station, Chuansha Lu, a couple of kilometres southwest. A few services use the bus station on Qiujiang Lu, next to the Baoshan Lu subway station.

An enjoyable way to arrive in Shanghai is by **boat**, whether from Japan, Korea, the towns along the coast or inland up the Yangzi. The Yangzi ferries and coastal boats to and from Ningbo and Putuo Shan sail south right past the Bund to the **Shiliupu wharf**, linked by bus #55 to the northern end of the Bund. Coastal boats to and from Qingdao and Fuzhou use the **Gongping Lu wharf** (公平路码头, *gōngpínglù mătóu*), which is only about twenty minutes' walk to the northeast of the Bund or a short ride on bus #135, while boats from Japan and South Korea dock at the **International Ferry Terminal** (国际客运码头, *guójì kèyùn mătóu*), about ten minutes' walk east of the Waibaidu Bridge.

Information

You can pick up free leaflets, containing basic tourist information, at the upmarket hotels and at the airport. Much more useful, though, are the **free magazines** aimed at the expat community, such as *City Weekend* (Ⓦwww.cityweekend.com.cn/shanghai) and *Time Out Shanghai*, which you can pick up at most expat hangouts. All have listings sections including restaurants, club nights and art events, with

Moving on from Shanghai

The limited hours of the Maglev trains means you won't be able to make use of them if flying out of Pudong International Airport early in the morning or late in the evening. For details of airline offices in town, see p.407.

By train

The soft-seat waiting room in **Shanghai Station** (上海火车站, *shànghăi huŏchēzhàn*; enter from the forecourt, near the eastern end; there's an English sign) has an office that sells train tickets (daily 7am–9pm; same-day and next-day travel only) – hard seat and sleeper as well as soft. Alternatively, the *Longmen Hotel*, a couple of minutes west of the station square, has a foreigners' ticket office (daily 7am–5.30pm & 6–9pm) in the lobby, which sells tickets for up to ten days in advance – mainly to Nanjing and Hangzhou, and for sleepers to a few important destinations such as Beijing or Guangzhou. To book up to a week in advance of your journey, buy tickets from a hotel (sometimes for a small commission), from CITS (daily 8.30–11.30am & 1–4.45pm), in the Shanghai Centre, or from a train-ticket booking office, where you'll rarely have to queue; there are handy ones at 77 Wanhangdu Lu (near Jing'an Temple), 108 Nanjing Xi Lu, 2 Jinling Dong Lu, and 257 Dongfang Lu, all of which are open daily (8am–5pm); these offices will only sell the "soft class" tickets, where you pay a little more for a well-padded seat.

By bus

For a few destinations, for example Suzhou and Hangzhou, buses might offer a convenient way to leave the city: they're slightly cheaper than trains, and it's easy to get a seat. The widest range of services is from the new **Shanghai South bus station** (上海南站, *shànghăi nān zhàn*), underneath Shanghai South train station. Private buses for destinations in Jiangsu and Zhejiang provinces leave from the western part of the train station addresses written in pinyin and Chinese, but no maps. Smart Shanghai (Ⓦwww.smartshanghai.com) is a good listings website that includes maps and user-submitted reviews.

Various glossy English-language **maps** are available, including the *Shanghai Official Tourist Map*, which is paid for by advertising and is issued free in hotels and from the tourist kiosk in the Renmin Square subway station. Additionally, bus routes can be found on the *Shanghai Communications Map*, which is widely available from street vendors, though this has street names in Chinese only.

City transport

The clean, efficient **Shanghai subway** (上海地铁, *shànghǎi dìtiě*; daily 5.30am–11pm) comprises eleven lines, but only three or four are particularly useful for visitors. Line #1 runs north–south, with useful stops at the railway station, People's Square, Changshu Lu (for the Old French Concession), Xujiahui and Shanghai Stadium. Line #2 runs east–west with stops at Jing'an Temple, Henan Lu and, in Pudong, Lujiazui and the Science and Technology Museum. The lines intersect at the enormous People's Square station (take careful note of the wall maps here for which exit to use). Lines #4 to #7 are much less used by visitors, and mainly serve commuters. Line#8 is north–south, with handy stops at Hongkou Stadium, Qufu Lu, and Laoximen (for the Old City), and east–west line #10 has useful stops at Yu Yuan and Xintiandi.

Tickets cost from ¥3 to ¥7, according to the distance travelled. They can be bought either from touch-screen machines (there's an option for English) or from vendors. Alternately, you can purchase a stored-value card for a refundable ¥20,

square, and from nearby **Hengfeng bus station** (横峰公共汽車站, *héngfēng gōnggòngqìchē zhàn*), but their fares are nearly as expensive as the train. You can buy tickets there or from a kiosk just south of the Shanghai Museum. The **Qiujiang Lu bus station** (虬江路公共汽車站, *qiújiāng lù gōnggòngqìchē zhàn*) has more reasonable fares, yet less comfortable buses, mainly leaving for Hangzhou and towns in Jiangsu. Services for a few destinations within Shanghai Shi leave from the Xiqu bus station (bus #113 from the train station) or a nameless bus stop on Shanxi Nan Lu, outside the Wenhua Guangchang, just south of Fuxing Lu. For these buses, you pay on board.

By boat

For ferries to **Putuo Shan**, see p.357. Two shipping companies sail weekly from the **international ferry terminal** (国际客运码头, *guójì kèyùn mǎtóu*), to **Kōbe** and **Ōsaka** in Japan. The ferry to Ōsaka leaves on Tuesdays at 11am and takes two nights, arriving on Thursday morning; fares start at ¥1300 for a roll-up bed on the floor of a common room, though a bunk in a four-bed cabin is not much more expensive. Return tickets cost an extra fifty percent or so – for more details see Ⓦwww.shanghai-ferry.co.jp. You can book a ticket at CITS (see p.408) or by emailing Ⓔzhangyz@suzhaohao.com; you'll be given a reference number and can pick up and pay for your ticket at the ferry port on the day.

The ship to Kōbe leaves every Saturday at 1pm and arrives on Monday at 10.30am; fares for this trip start at ¥1300 – check Ⓦwww.chinajapanferry.com for more details and to book your ticket.

Both ferries are run by a Japanese company, and are perfectly comfortable, but take some food as the restaurant is expensive. When you arrive in Japan you'll find yourself dumped in an industrial port with no banks or foreign exchanges nearby, so take some Japanese yen with you.

Useful Shanghai bus routes

North–south

#18 (trolleybus) From Lu Xun Park, across Suzhou Creek and along Xizang Lu.

#41 Passes Tianmu Xi Lu, in front of Shanghai Zhan and goes down through the former French Concession to Longhua Cemetery.

#64 From Shanghai Zhan, along Beijing Lu, then close to Shiliupu wharf on the south of the Bund.

#65 From the top to the bottom of Zhongshan Lu (the Bund), terminating in the south at the Nanpu Bridge.

East–west

#19 (trolleybus) From near Gongping Lu wharf in the east, passing near the *Pujiang Hotel* and roughly following the course of Suzhou Creek to Yufo Si.

#20 From Jiujiang Lu (just off the Bund) along Nanjing Dong Lu, past Jing'an Si, then on to Zhongshan Gongyuan in the west of the city.

#42 From Guangxi Lu (just off the Bund), then along Huaihai Lu in the former French Concession.

#135 From Yangpu Bridge in the east of the city to the eastern end of Huaihai Lu, via the Bund.

which you can top up with as much as you like. You'd need to be in the city for at least a couple of weeks to make it worthwhile.

Local buses run everywhere from around 4am to 10.30pm, but they are crowded (especially during rush hour) and slow, stops are far apart, and few lines travel from one side of the city to the other. Fares are ¥2; buy your ticket from the conductor on board. Services with numbers in the 300s are night buses; those in the 400s cross the Huangpu River. Most large fold-out city maps show bus routes, usually as a red or blue line with a dot indicating a stop. Sightseeing buses for tourist sights in the outskirts leave from the Shanghai Stadium (see p.395).

Taxis are very easy to get hold of and, if you're not on a very tight budget, they are often the most comfortable way to get around – fares usually come to ¥20–40 for rides within the city, with a flagfall of ¥11 (¥14 at night). Few drivers speak English, so it helps to have your destination written in Chinese. The only hassle you're likely to suffer is from drivers who take you on unnecessarily long detours, but if you sit in the front seat and hold a map on your lap they usually behave themselves. Drivers also ask if you want to use the elevated expressway – *zou gao jia* – at busy times; it'll be quicker but tends to involve slightly greater distances and is thus more expensive.

Accommodation

Accommodation in Shanghai is plentiful, and in places highly stylish, but prices are higher than elsewhere in China. The **grand old-world hotels** that form so integral a part of Shanghai's history cost at least US$150 per night these days, and for comfort and elegance have been overtaken by new arrivals, such as the clutch of boutique hotels.

If you want to be near the centre of the action, go for somewhere around Renmin Park or the Bund; there are options here for all budgets. For style and panache, head to the genteel former French Concession, where attractive mid-range hotels are close to upmarket dining and nightlife. For the latest in corporate chic, Pudong has the fanciest options, but the area is rather dull.

If you're simply looking for somewhere that's good value and convenient, stay in the outskirts near a subway station.

At all but the cheapest hotels, rack rates should not be taken seriously; it's almost always possible to bargain the rate down, by as much as two thirds off-season.

The Bund and around

Captain Hostel (船长酒店, *chuánzhǎng fàndiàn*) 37 Fuzhou Lu ⓣ021/63235053, ⓦwww.captainhostel.com.cn. Doubles at this place off the Bund are pricey, but it's of most interest for its clean, cheap dorms, all made to look like cabins. Staff are dressed in sailor suits – though it hasn't made them any jollier. The *Captain Bar* on the sixth floor has great views of Pudong (see p.403). Internet access is a steep ¥20/hr, bike rental ¥2/hr (guests only), and there's free use of the washing machine. There's a second branch just around the corner, at 7 Yan'an Dong Lu. Beds in an eight-bed dorm ¥80, rooms ❻

CHAI Shanghai Living (上海灿客栈, *Shànghǎi cànkèzhàn*) 400 Suzhou Bei Lu ⓣ021/63561812, ⓦwww.chailiving.com. Luxury serviced apartments in a shabby, genteel Art Deco apartment block. There's no lobby to speak of – you'll be met on arrival by the service manager, Mr. Li – and your neighbours will be locals who hang their washing and practice *tai ji* in the corridors. Each well-designed apartment has underfloor heating and fully equipped kitchens; go for one with a view of Pudong. ❼

Fairmont Peace (和平饭店, *hépíng fàndiàn*) Junction of the Bund and Nanjing Dong Lu ⓣ021/63216888, ⓦwww.shanghaipeacehotel.com. Occupying both sides of the road, this was formerly the *Cathay Hotel*, the most famous hotel in Shanghai, home to the *Jazz Bar* and still well worth a visit to admire the lobby's Art Deco interiors. The long list of illustrious previous guests includes Charlie Chaplin and Noel Coward. In the modern era its star faded thanks to bad management, but its fotunes have, hopefully, been turned around, as the hotel is now run by the *Fairmont* group. ❾

Metropole (新城饭店, *xīnchéng fàndiàn*) 180 Jiangxi Nan Lu ⓣ021/63213030. Just off the Bund and dating from 1931, this is one of the more affordable of the older hotels, but like the others it suffers from uninspired renovation and old-fashioned service. There's a great Art Deco lobby and exterior, but the rooms are plain. ❽

Mingtown Hikers Hostel (明堂上海旅行者国际青年旅馆, *míngtáng shànghǎi lǚxíngzhě guójì qīngnián lǚguǎn*) 450 Jiangxi Zhong Lu ⓣ021/63297889. Very well located just northwest of the Bund, this cheap-and-cheerful hostel has wi-fi and a lively bar. Four- and six-bed dorms ¥45; rooms with shared bathrooms ❸, en-suite rooms ❹

Peninsula (上海半岛酒店, *shànghǎi bàndǎo jiǔdiàn*) 32 Zhongshan Dong Lu ⓣ021/23272888, ⓦwww.pensinsula.com/shanghai. The latest incarnation of the exclusive Hong Kong brand is the first new hotel to open on the Bund in 20 years. In keeping with the area, it's gone for a traditional, Art Deco look; rather sinister black marble corridors lead to the white columned lobby, where a quartet plays and the local elite drink afternoon tea. ❾

Pujiang (浦江饭店, *pǔjiāng fàndiàn*) 15 Huangpu Lu ⓣ021/63246388, ⓦwww.pujianghotel.com. Located across the Waibaidu Bridge north of the Bund and slightly to the east, opposite the blue Russian Consulate building. Formerly the *Astor Hotel*, and dating back to 1846, this is a pleasingly old-fashioned place with creaky wooden floors and high ceilings, and the antiquated look of a Victorian school. ❻

Shanghai Mansions (Broadway Mansions) (上海大厦, *shànghǎi dàshà*) 20 Suzhou Bei Lu ⓣ021/63246260. This is the huge, ugly lump of a building on the north bank of Suzhou Creek, visible from the north end of the Bund. Rooms get pricier the higher up you go. ❽

Pudong

Grand Hyatt (浦东金茂凯悦大酒店, *pǔdōng jīnmàokǎiyuè dàjiǔdiàn*) Jinmao Tower, 88 Shijia Dadao ⓣ021/50491234, ⓦwww.shanghai.hyatt.com. Taking up the top floors of the magnificent Jinmao Tower, there's no doubt the place is fantastic – awesome views, great design, lots of lucky numbers (555 rooms, 88 storeys) – but, it has to be said, the area is hardly interesting. *Cloud Nine Bar* (see p.403) is on the top floor. ❾

Park Hyatt 100 Century Ave ⓣ021/68881234, ⓦwww.shanghai.park.hyatt.com. This stylish, ultra-modern business hotel, located on floor 79 in the World Financial Centre, has stolen the "highest hotel in the world" crown from its sister in the Jinmao Tower. Surprisingly large rooms have great views, and on-site attractions include an infinity pool and a spa. On the downside, the area is rather soulless. ❾

Pudong Shangri-La (柏悦酒店, *bóyuè jiǔdiàn*) 33 Fucheng Lu ⓣ021/68828888, ⓦwww.shangri-la.com/shanghai. The other monster hotel in Pudong, with almost a thousand rooms. Popular with upscale business travellers for comfort, convenience and, of course, the views through the huge windows. ❾

The former French Concession

88 Xintiandi (88 新天地, *bā shí bā xīn tiān dì*) 380 Huangpi Bei Lu ⓣ021/53838833, ⓦwww.88xintiandi.com. Fifty-room boutique hotel at the edge of the yuppie theme park that is the Xintiandi complex. The best rooms have a view of the lake. There's a pool, and guests can use the adjacent spa and fitness centre. The no-smoking floors are a nice touch. Convenient for Huangpi Nan Lu subway stop. ❾

B'LaVii House (宝丽会馆, *bǎolì huìguǎn*) 285 Hunan Lu ⓣ021/64677171, ⓦwww.blavii.com. This elegant, well-appointed French concession mansion has rooms arranged around a courtyard, all individually decorated, though a common theme is dark wood furniture and red lacquer. The area is quiet and civilized, and there are plenty of dining options nearby. Booking essential. ❼

Dong Hu (东湖宾馆, *dōnghú bīnguǎn*) 70 Donghu Lu, one block north of Huaihai Zhong Lu ⓣ021/64158158, ⓦwww.donghuhotel.com. Of the seven buildings that make up the *Dong hu,* the villas on the south side are the most interesting, with a chequered past; they served as an opium warehouse and the centre of gangland operations in the 1920s and 1930s. Make sure you get a room in here (Building One), and not the dull new block over the road. The good location and the pleasant gardens make this one of the best hotels in its price range. ❻–❽

Hengshan Moller Villa (衡山马勒墅饭店, *héng shān mǎ lè shù fàn diàn*) 30 Shaanxi Nan Lu ⓣ021/62478881, ⓦwww.mollervilla.com. Describing itself as a boutique heritage hotel, the main building here is a gorgeous Scandinavian gothic fantasy built in the 1930s. You can stay in the villa's well-appointed rooms, with their balconies and fireplaces, but they're expensive; most rooms are in a three-storey block just behind. ❼

The Nine 9 Jianguo Xi Lu, by Taiyuan Lu ⓣ021/64719950. A select boutique hotel in an old villa, with the feel of a private club; there are only five rooms, all tricked out with antiques. It's very discreet and there's not even a sign – look for the sturdy gates. Good dinners at the long table. Reservations essential. ❾

Okura Garden (花园饭店, *huā yuán fàn diàn*) 58 Maoming Nan Lu ⓣ021/64151111, ⓦwww.gardenhotelshanghai.com. Japanese-managed luxury mansion; the grounds are lovely, and the lobby, which used to be the Cercle Sportif French Club, has some great Art Deco detailing; but the rooms, in a giant new monolith looming at the back, are a little nondescript. ❽

Old House Inn (老时光餐厅酒吧, *lǎo shíguāng cāntīng jiǔbā*) 16 Lane 351, Huashan Lu, by Changshu Lu ⓣ021/62486118, ⓦwww.oldhouse.cn. A small guesthouse in a sympathetically restored *shikumen* house. The dozen rooms are comfortable, though the corridors are authentically poky. Free wi-fi. You'll need to book in advance. ❼

Quintet Bed & Breakfast (五重奏旅店, *wǔ chóngzòu lǚdiàn*) 808 Changle Lu, near Changshu Lu ⓣ021/62499088, ⓦwww.quintet-shanghai.com. This courtyard house has been smartly converted into an exclusive guesthouse, with each room designed around a theme. Staff are knowledgable, and the whole place is non-smoking. Not many business facilities, but this would be ideal for tourists looking for something a little different. Reservations essential. ❻

Ruijin Guesthouse (瑞金宾馆, *ruìjīn bīnguǎn*) 118 Ruijin Er Lu (main entrance on Fuxing Lu) ⓣ021/64725222, ⓦwww.ruijinhotelsh.com. Cosy and exclusive Tudor-style villas in manicured gardens. It's not quite the fabulous destination it could be thanks to occasionally lacklustre service, but is still recommended. Ask for Building One, where Mao used to stay. ❾

Taiyuan Villa (太原别墅, *tài yuán bié shù*) 106 Taiyuan Lu, by Yongjia Lu ⓣ021/64716688. If you don't mind a 10-minute walk to the nearest subway, this historic villa set in lovely grounds in a quiet former French Concession street is one of the best places to stay in this price range. Dark wood panelling in the rooms adds to the period charm. ❽

Jing'an

LeTour Travelers's Rest Youth Hostel (乐途国际青年旅舍, *lètú guójì qīngnián lǚshè*) Lane 36, 319 Jiaozhou Lu ⓣ021/62671912, ⓦwww.letourshanghai.com. This huge hostel was once a factory and though it's been livened up, concrete floors give it an industrial feel. The newly refurbished rooms are small, but this place boasts the most facilities of any hostel; as well as kitchen, rooftop bar, bike hire, and free wi-fi, there's a DVD room, a mini gym and a ping pong table. It's ten minutes' walk north from Jing'an Lu subway stop, and can be hard to find first time, as it's located down a narrow alley just off busy Bai Lan Lu. Look out for the big green building and if you reach Wuding Lu you've gone too far. Dorms ¥90, rooms ❹

Puli (璞丽酒店, *púlì jiǔdiàn*) 1 Changde Lu ⓣ021/32039999, ⓦwww.thepuli.com. This attractive new hotel is coolly minimal, with a handsome library and spa attached. Rooms have wooden floors, grey slate walls and stylish if rather impractical sinks. Ask for a view of Jing'an Park. ⑨

URBN Hotel (雅悦酒店, *yǎyuè jiǔdiàn*) 183 Jiaozhou Lu ⓣ021/51534600, ⓦwww.urbnhotels.com. Though it doesn't quite live up to its considerable hype, this hip little hotel is still pretty good value for this price range. The typical Shanghai idea of stylishness – low lighting and rough grey brick – is leavened with quirky touches, such as porthole-like doors and a wall made of leather suitcases behind reception. Breakfast is not included, and is rather pricey, so pop to the *Aura* café next door. ⑨

Around Renmin Square

24K Hotel (24K国际连锁酒店, *24K guójì liánsuǒ jiǔdiàn*) 155 Weihai Lu ⓣ021/51181222 555 Fuzhou Lu ⓣ021/51503588, ⓦ24khotels.com. This frills business hotel chain scores for chirpy design and good value. Not much English is spoken. Both branches are on busy roads not far from People's Square, and walkable from the subway. Free wi-fi, and there's even a machine that dispenses medicines in the lobby. ④

JW Marriot (明天广场JW万怡酒店, *míng tiān guǎng chǎng JW wàn yí jiǔ diàn*) Tomorrow Square, 399 Nanjing Xi Lu ⓣ021/53594969, ⓦwww.marriott.com. Housed in the top floors of one of Shanghai's most uncompromising landmarks (something like an upraised claw), this swanky venue is both well located and has magnificent views, making it one of the finest top-end destinations. ⑨

Mingtown Etour Hostel (上海明堂新易途国际青年旅馆, *shàng hǎi míngtáng xīnyìtú guójì qīngnián lǚguǎn*) 57 Jiangxi Zhong Lu ⓣ021/63277766. This is the best of the cheapies, being very well located – tucked in the alleyway behind Tomorrow Square, right beside Renmin Park – yet quiet and surprisingly affordable. Everything centres on a relaxing courtyard. Rooms vary, so ask to see a few – one or two have balconies. Bathrooms are shared between two or three rooms. Internet is free, but there are only two computers. Dorms ¥80, rooms ③

Radisson New World (新世界丽笙大酒店, *xīn shì jiè lì shēng dàjiǔdiàn*) 88 Nanjing Dong Lu ⓣ021/63599999, ⓦwww.radisson.com. A new and swish venue that has quickly become popular, offering a convenient location right at the corner of bustling Nanjing Lu, and, in general, a slick upscale experience. ⑨

Westin (威斯汀大酒店, *weī sī tīng dà fàn diàn*) 88 Henan Zhong Lu ⓣ021/63351888, ⓦwww.westin.com/shanghai. Chinese luxury hotels usually try to impress with either a water feature or palm trees in the lobby; the over-the-top Westin goes for both, and then, as if that weren't enough to declare its intentions, the building has a crown on top. Rooms aren't so flashy, which is a good thing; ask for one with a view. Good on-site restaurants and spa. ⑧–⑨

The City

Although most parts of Shanghai that you are likely to visit lie to the west of the **Huangpu River** and its colonial riverfront, the **Bund**, the most easily recognizable landmark in the city is on the east side – the daft, rocket-like Oriental Pearl TV Tower. The best way to check out both banks of the Huangpu River and their sights is to take a splendid **Huangpu River tour**.

Nanjing Lu, reputedly the busiest shopping street in China, runs through the heart of downtown Shanghai. Headed at its eastern end by the famous **Peace Hotel**, the road leads west to **Renmin Park**, which today houses the excellent **Shanghai Museum** as well as a couple of decent art galleries. The other main sights lie about 1500m south of Nanjing Lu in the **Old City**, the longest continuously inhabited part of Shanghai, with the **Yu Yuan** – a fully restored classical Chinese garden – and bazaars at its heart. To the southwest of here lies the marvellous **former French Concession**, with its cosmopolitan cooking traditions, European-style housing and revolutionary relics. The energetic eating and nightlife centre of Shanghai, **Huaihai Lu**, serves as the area's main artery.

Farther out from the centre remains a scattering of sights. Just west of Shanghai Zhan is the fascinating **Moganshan Art District**, an old factory full of art galleries and studios. North of Suzhou Creek is the interesting **Lu Xun Park**, with its monuments to the great twentieth-century writer, Lu Xun, while Duolun Culture Street, with its quirky museums and shops, is a lovely place to while away an afternoon. Finally, in the far west are two of Shanghai's most important surviving religious sites: the **Longhua Si** and the **Yufo Si**.

The Bund and the Huangpu River

Shanghai's original signature skyline, and the first stop for any visitor, is the **Bund** (外滩, *wàitān*), a strip of grand colonial edifices on the west bank of the Huangpu River, facing the flashy skyscrapers of Pudong on the opposite shore. Since 1949, it's been known officially as Zhongshan Lu, but it's better known among locals as Wai Tan (literally "Outside Beach"). Named after an old Anglo-Indian term, "bunding" (the embanking of a muddy foreshore), the Bund was old Shanghai's commercial heart, with the river on one side, the offices of the leading banks and trading houses on the other. During Shanghai's riotous heyday it was also a hectic working harbour, where anything from tiny sailing junks to ocean-going freighters unloaded under the watch of British – and later American and Japanese – warships. Everything arrived here, from silk and tea to heavy industrial machinery. Amid it all, wealthy foreigners disembarked to pick their way to one of the grand hotels through crowds of beggars, hawkers, black marketeers, shoeshine boys, overladen coolies and even funeral parties – Chinese too poor to pay for the burial of relatives would launch the bodies into the river in boxes decked in paper flowers.

Today, it's the most exclusive chunk of real estate in China, with pretensions to becoming the nation's Champs-Elysées; the world's most luxurious brands have set up shop here and there are a clutch of ritzy hotels and celebrity restaurants (though if you just want to eat, rather than have a gourmet experience, choice is rather limited).

Around Waibaidu Bridge

Before tackling the Bund, have a look at the Main Post Office, just north of it, built in 1931, and easily recognizable by its clocktower. It's the only Bund building that has never been used for anything but its original function. It houses the **Shanghai Post Museum** (上海邮政博物馆, *shànghǎi yóuzhèng bówùguǎn*; Wed, Thurs, Sat & Sun 9am–4pm; ¥5) on the third floor, which is more interesting than it sounds. The collection of letters and stamps is only mildly diverting, but the new atrium is very impressive, and the view of the Bund from the grassed-over roof is superb.

The northern end of the Bund starts from the confluence of the Huangpu and Suzhou Creek, by **Waibaidu Bridge** (外白渡桥, *wàibáidù qiáo*), and runs south for 1500m to Jinling Dong Lu, formerly Rue du Consulat. At the outbreak of the Sino-Japanese War in 1937, Waibaidu bridge formed a no-man's-land between the Japanese-occupied areas north of Suzhou Creek and the **International Settlement** – it was guarded at one end by Japanese sentries, the other by British. Today, though most ships dock farther downstream, the waterways are still well-used thoroughfares, and the Bund itself is a popular place for an after-dinner stroll or

Huangpu River tours

One highlight of a visit to Shanghai, and the easiest way to view the edifices of the Bund, is to take one of the **Huangpu River tours** (黄浦江旅游, *huángpǔjiāng lǚyóu*). These leave a wharf near the end of Nanjing Dong Lu. You can book tickets at the jetty (daily 8am–4.30pm).

The hour-long round trip south to the Yanpu Bridge and back costs ¥100, but the classic cruise here is the three-hour-long, 60km journey to the mouth of the Yangzi and back. There are departures daily at 9am and 2pm, and tickets start at ¥200, with higher prices offering armchairs, a higher deck, tea and snacks. On the tour, you're introduced to the vast amount of shipping that uses the port, and you'll also be able to inspect all the paraphernalia of the shipping industry, from sampans and rusty old Panamanian-registered freighters to sparkling Chinese navy vessels. You'll also get an idea of the colossal construction that is taking place on the eastern shore, before you reach the mouth of the Yangzi River itself, where the wind kicks in and it feels like you're almost in open sea. There are also several hour-long night cruises, with boats departing between 7pm and 8.30pm (¥100). Tours do not run in foggy or windy weather (for current information, call ⓣ021/63744461; Chinese only).

morning exercises, while tourists from all over China patrol the waterfront taking photos of each other against the backdrop of the Oriental Pearl TV Tower.

The first building south of the bridge was one of the cornerstones of British interests in old Shanghai, the **former British Consulate**, once ostentatiously guarded by magnificently dressed Sikh soldiers. The blue building just to the northeast of here across the Suzhou Creek still retains its original function as the **Russian Consulate**. Right on the corner of the two waterways, **Huangpu Park** (黄浦公园, *huángpǔ gōngyuán*) was another British creation, the British Public Gardens, established on a patch of land formed when mud and silt gathered around a wrecked ship. Here, too, there were Sikh troops, ready to enforce the rules that forbade Chinese from entering, unless they were servants accompanying their employer. After protests, the regulations were relaxed to admit "well-dressed" Chinese, who had to apply for a special entry permit. Though it's firmly established in the Chinese popular imagination as a symbol of Western racism, there's no evidence that there ever was a sign here reading "no dogs or Chinese allowed". These days, the park contains a stone monument to the "Heroes of the People", and is also a popular spot for citizens practicing *tai ji* early in the morning, but it's best simply for the promenade that commands the junction of the two rivers.

Walking down the Bund, you'll pass a succession of grandiose Neoclassical edifices, built to house the great foreign enterprises.

The Peace Hotel and the Bank of China

Straddling the eastern end of Nanjing Lu is one of the most famous hotels in China, the **Fairmont Peace Hotel** (和平饭店, *hépíng fàndiàn*), formerly the *Cathay Hotel*. The place to be seen in prewar Shanghai, it offered guests a private plumbing system fed by a spring on the outskirts of town, marble baths with silver taps, and vitreous china lavatories imported from Britain. Noel Coward is supposed to have stayed here while writing *Private Lives*. The *Peace* today is worth a visit for a walk around the lobby and upper floors to take in the Art Deco elegance.

Next door to the *Peace*, at no. 19 on the Bund, the **Bank of China** was designed in the 1920s by Shanghai architectural firm Palmer & Turner, who brought in a Chinese architect to make the building "more Chinese" after construction was

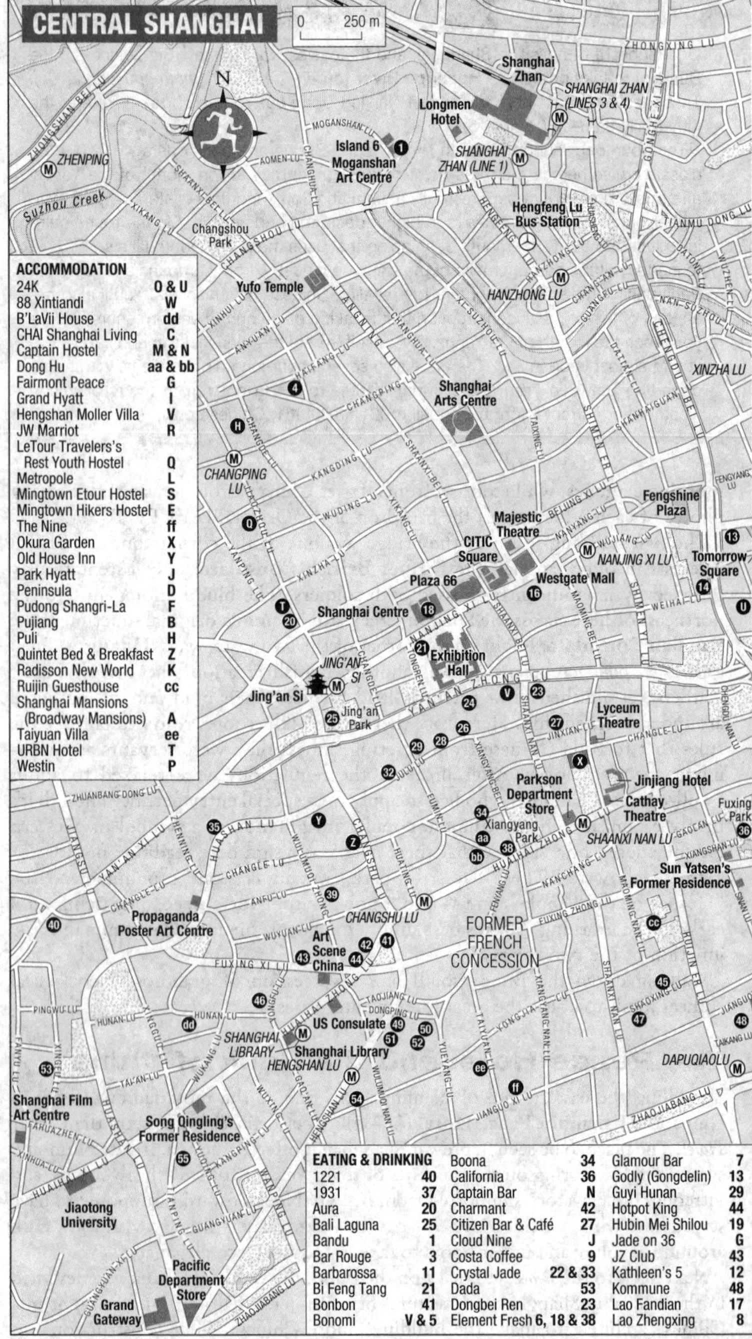
CENTRAL SHANGHAI
0 250 m
N
ACCOMMODATION
24K O & U
88 Xintiandi W
B'LaVii House dd
CHAI Shanghai Living C
Captain Hostel M & N
Dong Hu aa & bb
Fairmont Peace G
Grand Hyatt I
Hengshan Moller Villa V
JW Marriot R
LeTour Travelers's Rest Youth Hostel Q
Metropole L
Mingtown Etour Hostel S
Mingtown Hikers Hostel E
The Nine ff
Okura Garden X
Old House Inn Y
Park Hyatt J
Peninsula D
Pudong Shangri-La F
Pujiang B
Puli H
Quintet Bed & Breakfast Z
Radisson New World K
Ruijin Guesthouse cc
Shanghai Mansions (Broadway Mansions) A
Taiyuan Villa ee
URBN Hotel T
Westin P
EATING & DRINKING
1221 40
1931 37
Aura 20
Bali Laguna 25
Bandu 1
Bar Rouge 3
Barbarossa 11
Bi Feng Tang 21
Bonbon 41
Bonomi V & 5
Boona 34
California 36
Captain Bar N
Charmant 42
Citizen Bar & Café 27
Cloud Nine J
Costa Coffee 9
Crystal Jade 22 & 33
Dada 53
Dongbei Ren 23
Element Fresh 6, 18 & 38
Glamour Bar 7
Godly (Gongdelin) 13
Guyi Hunan 29
Hotpot King 44
Hubin Mei Shilou 19
Jade on 36 G
JZ Club 43
Kathleen's 5 12
Kommune 48
Lao Fandian 17
Lao Zhengxing 8
Shanghai Zhan
SHANGHAI ZHAN (LINES 3 & 4)
Longmen Hotel
Island 6 Moganshan Art Centre
SHANGHAI ZHAN (LINE 1)
ZHENPING
Suzhou Creek
Changshou Park
Hengfeng Lu Bus Station
Yufo Temple
HANZHONG LU
XINZHA LU
Shanghai Arts Centre
CHANGPING LU
Fengshine Plaza
Majestic Theatre
CITIC Square
NANJING XI LU
Tomorrow Square
Plaza 66
Westgate Mall
Shanghai Centre
Exhibition Hall
JING'AN SI
Jing'an Si
Jing'an Park
Lyceum Theatre
Jinjiang Hotel
Parkson Department Store
Cathay Theatre
Fuxing Park
Xiangyang Park
SHAANXI NAN LU
Sun Yatsen's Former Residence
Propaganda Poster Art Centre
CHANGSHU LU
FORMER FRENCH CONCESSION
Art Scene China
US Consulate
SHANGHAI LIBRARY
Shanghai Library
HENGSHAN LU
DAPUQIAOLU
Shanghai Film Art Centre
Song Qingling's Former Residence
Jiaotong University
Pacific Department Store
Grand Gateway
ZHONGXING LU
MOGANSHAN LU
AOMEN LU
TIANMU XI LU
TIANMU DONG LU
GONGHE XIN LU
CHANGSHOU LU
XIKANG LU
SHAANXI BEI LU
ZHONGSHAN BEI LU
CHENGDU BEI LU
XI SUZHOU LU
CHANG'AN LU
NAN SUZHOU LU
CHANGPING LU
KANGDING LU
WUDING LU
XINZHA LU
BEIJING XI LU
NANYANG LU
WEIHAI LU
YAN'AN ZHONG LU
YAN'AN XI LU
JULU LU
CHANGLE LU
HUAIHAI ZHONG LU
NANCHANG LU
FUXING ZHONG LU
FUXING XI LU
ANFU LU
WUYUAN LU
HUASHAN LU
HUNAN LU
JIANGSU LU
ZHAOJIABANG LU
JIANGUO XI LU
HENGSHAN LU
GUANGYUAN LU
XINHUA LU
HUAIHAI XI LU
RUIJIN ER LU
SHAOXING LU
MAOMING NAN LU
SHIMEN ER LU

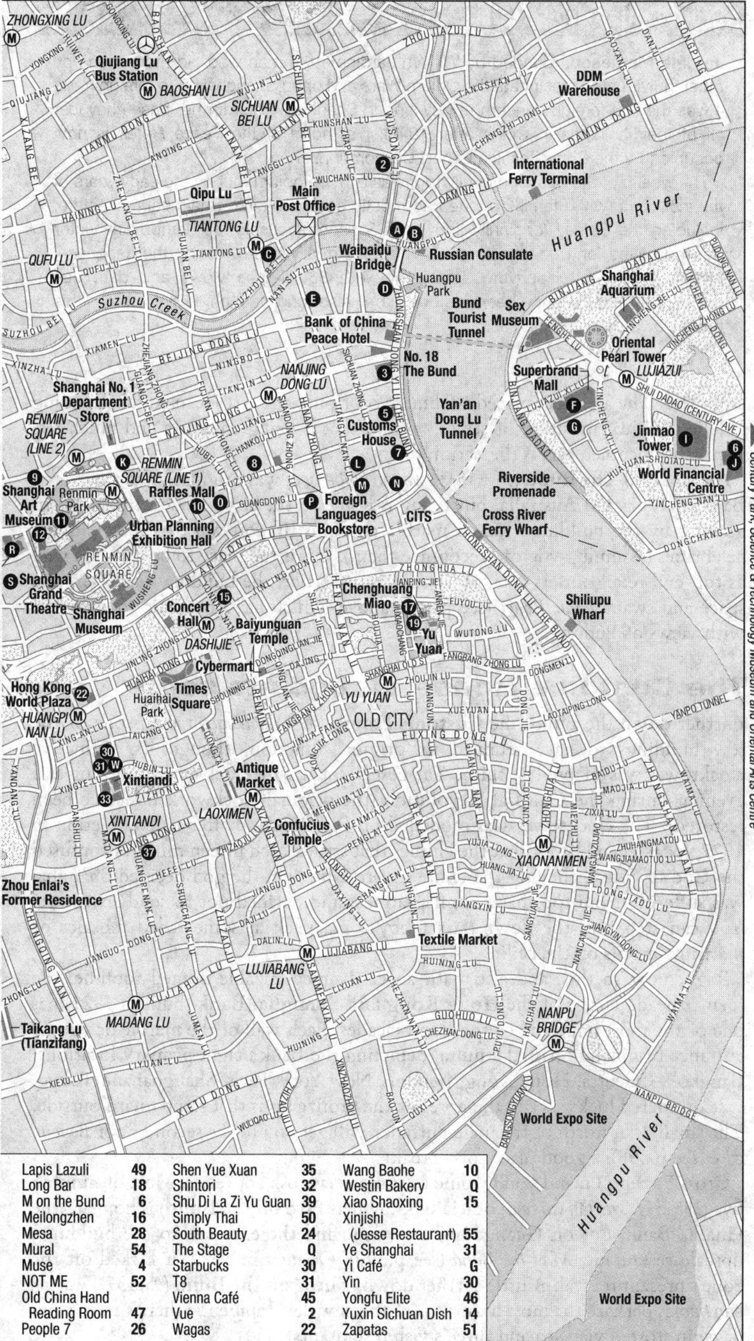

Lapis Lazuli	49	Shen Yue Xuan	35	Wang Baohe	10
Long Bar	18	Shintori	32	Westin Bakery	Q
M on the Bund	6	Shu Di La Zi Yu Guan	39	Xiao Shaoxing	15
Meilongzhen	16	Simply Thai	50	Xinjishi	
Mesa	28	South Beauty	24	(Jesse Restaurant)	55
Mural	54	The Stage	Q	Ye Shanghai	31
Muse	4	Starbucks	30	Yi Café	G
NOT ME	52	T8	31	Yin	30
Old China Hand		Vienna Café	45	Yongfu Elite	46
Reading Room	47	Vue	2	Yuxin Sichuan Dish	14
People 7	26	Wagas	22	Zapatas	51

Great British drug dealers

Jardine Matheson, founded by William Jardine – the man who did more than any other individual to precipitate the Opium Wars and open Shanghai up to foreign trade – was the first foreign concern to buy land in Shanghai. Their former base (they lost all of their holdings in China after 1949), just north of the *Peace Hotel*, is now occupied by the China Textiles Export Corporation.

The wealth of the Sassoon family too, was built on opium, but by the early years of the last century, the family fortune had mostly been sunk into Shanghai real estate, including the *Cathay* (originally known as *Sassoon House*). The flamboyant Victor Sassoon lived long enough to see his hotel virtually destroyed by the Japanese, including his rooftop private apartment, with 360-degree views and dark oak panelling (it has recently been restored), but also long enough to get most of his money away to the Bahamas.

complete. The architect placed a Chinese roof onto the Art Deco edifice, creating a delightful juxtaposition of styles, an idea that is being endlessly and much less successfully copied across the nation today.

Number 18 The Bund (外滩18号, *wàitān shíbā hào*) was originally the Chartered Bank of India and Australia, but today is home to the city's ritziest shops, given gravitas by the building's Italian marble columns. If you want to spot Chinese celebrities (assuming you can recognize them), this is the place to be seen. As well as top-end retail outlets such as Younik and Cartier, the building houses an arts space and swanky *Bar Rouge* (see p.403) above, which has a fantastic roof terrace with views of Pudong.

The Customs House and points south

Further down the Bund, the **Customs House** (海关楼, *hǎiguān lóu*) is one of the few buildings to have retained its original function, though its distinctive clocktower was adapted to chime *The East is Red* at six o'clock every morning and evening during the Cultural Revolution (the original clockwork has since been restored). The clocktower was modelled on Big Ben, and after its completion in 1927, local legend had it that the chimes that struck each fifteen minutes confused the God of Fire: believing the chimes were a firebell, the god decided Shanghai was suffering from too many conflagrations, and decided not to send any more. You can step into the downstairs lobby for a peek at some faded mosaics of maritime motifs on the ceiling.

Right next to this, and also with an easily recognizable domed roofline, the former headquarters of the **Hong Kong and Shanghai Bank** (built in 1921) has one of the most imposing of the Bund facades. Each wall of the marble octagonal entrance originally boasted a mural depicting the Bank's eight primary locations: Bangkok, Calcutta, Hong Kong, London, New York, Paris, Shanghai and Tokyo. It's considered lucky to rub the noses of the bronze lions that stand guard outside. The small door north of the main entrance will get you to the second floor *Bonomi* café (see p.398), a good place for a break.

Cross Fuzhou Lu and you'll come to some very posh addresses. Most of number five (外滩5号, *wài tān wǔ hào*; officially known as **Five on the Bund**) is home to the Huaxia Bank, but on Guangdong Lu you'll find the entrance to the building's upscale restaurant, *M of the Bund* (see p.399). Opened in 1999, it kicked off the zone's present revival. A little further down, **Three on the Bund** (外滩3号, *wài tān sān hào*) is perhaps the most luxurious of the new developments: there's an Armani flagship store, Evian spa and three swish restaurants.

The east bank of the Huangpu: Pudong district

Historically, **Pudong** (浦东, *pŭdōng*) has been known as the "wrong side of the Huangpu" – before 1949, the area was characterized by unemployed migrants, prostitution, murders and the most appalling living conditions in the city. It was here that bankrupt gamblers would "*tiao huangpu*", commit suicide by drowning themselves in the river. Shanghai's top gangster, Du Yuesheng, more commonly known as "Big-eared Du", learned his trade growing up in this rough section of town. In 1990, however, fifteen years after China's economic reforms started, it was finally decided to grant the status of Special Economic Zone (SEZ) to this large tract of mainly agricultural land, a decision which, more than any other, is now fuelling Shanghai's rocket-like economic advance. The skyline has since been completely transformed from a stream of rice paddies into a sea of cranes, and ultimately a maze of skyscrapers that seemingly stretches east as far as the eye can see.

The bustling street life that so animates the rest of Shanghai is striking by its absence, but Pudong can be very rewarding. There are two areas that are really interesting; the first is the battery of skyscrapers in **Lujiazui**, just across the water from the Bund, where you'll find the bulbous **Oriental Pearl TV Tower**, the **World Financial Centre** and the elegant **Jinmao Tower**, all of which offer sublime views across the city. Several museums have been plonked here, to take advantage of the huge crowds of Chinese tourists who flock to the Pearl TV Tower. Of these, the **Museum of History** is fun, and the **China Sex Culture Exhibition** is intriguing.

From Liujiazui, the eight-lane Century Avenue zooms for 4km to one of the city's few spacious green spaces, **Century Park**, where you'll find the **Science and Technology Museum**, the city's busiest fake **market**, and the **Oriental Arts Centre**.

Lujiazui

Lujiazui (陆家嘴, *lùjiāzuĭ*) is, above all, an area of **commerce**, with few activities of interest to the visitor besides giving your neck a good workout as you gaze upwards at the skyline. Ascending the 457m-high **Oriental Pearl TV Tower** (东方明珠广播电视塔, *dōngfāng míngzhū guăngbō diànshìtă*; daily 8am–9.30pm; ¥70 to go to the top bauble) to admire the giddying views has become a mandatory pilgrimage for most Chinese visitors to Shanghai, despite the ridiculously high entrance fee, long queue for the lift, and rather tatty interior.

You can get a better view from a much nicer building by ascending to the observation platform at the top of the **Jinmao Tower** (金茂大厦, *jīnmào dàshà*; daily 7am–9.30pm; ¥88; enter from the building's north side), although there are also great (free) views to be had by going in the front door (in the east) and up to the hotel lobby on the 54th floor, where you can take advantage of the *Hyatt*'s comfy, windowside chairs. But to observe the panorama in style, put on your best clothes

Getting to Pudong

The simplest way to reach the area is to catch the **subway**, which whooshes passengers from Renmin Square to downtown Pudong in less than three minutes; otherwise, several **minibuses** cross under the river using the Yan'an Dong Lu tunnel. For a more picturesque trip, catch the double-decker **ferry** (¥1) from the Bund opposite the eastern end of Jinling Lu. There's also a **Tourist Tunnel** (外滩观光隧道, *wài tān guān guāng suì dào*) under the river (entrance in the subway opposite Beijing Dong Lu; ¥45 one-way, ¥55 return), in which you're driven past a silly light show.

and pay a nighttime trip to the hotel bar *Cloud Nine*, on the 87th floor of the same building (see p.403).

World Financial Centre

The best views of the city are from the observation deck at the top of the 492m Shanghai **World Financial Centre** (环球金融中心, *huánqiú jīnróng zhōngxīn*; daily 8am–11pm, last admission 10pm; Ⓦwww.swfc-observatory.com), China's tallest building. In contrast to its elegant neighbour, the Jinmao Tower, its lines are simple: it's just a tapering slab whose most distinctive feature is the hole in the top. Locals call it "the bottle opener". That hole was originally meant to be circular, but was redesigned as an oblong when the mayor complained that it would look like a Japanese flag hovering over the city.

The entrance and ticket office is in the southwest side. There are three ticket prices, depending on how high up you want to go; for the little deck on 94 (423m), it's ¥100; for that and the larger lounge on 97 (439m), which also has the souvenir- and coffee shop, it's ¥110; and for access to those two and the top deck (474m), the strip above the hole, it's ¥150. The top level is by far the most impressive and now you're here you may as well bite the pricey bullet and go all the way to the top, where you'll be greeted by a magnificent 360-degree view across the city. Hardened glass tiles in the floor even allow you to look right down between your feet. Landmarks are pointed out in the booklet that comes with your ticket, and you can get a photo printed for ¥50. The view is at least as impressive at night. Heading back down, you'll pass an *Element Fresh* and a *Costa Coffee* (see p.398) on the second floor.

Binjiang Dadao and around

The riverside promenade, **Binjiang Dadao** (滨江大道, *bīnjiāng dàdào*), is close enough to the Huangpu to hear the slap of the water, and it's the only place in Liujiazui where a walk can feel rewarding. The north end of the promenade is close to the exit of the Bund Tourist Tunnel, and it's here you will find the absorbing **China Sex Culture Exhibition** (中华性文化博物馆, *zhōnghuá xìngwénhuà bówùguǎn*; daily 8am–10pm; ¥20), the private collection of a single-minded academic, Liu Dalin. As well as plenty of rather twee pornographic images and jade phalluses, there is a "widow's pillow" – a headrest with a secret dildo compartment – a tool for expanding anuses, a knife used to turn men into eunuchs, and a saddle with a wooden stump for punishing adulterous women. It's the only museum of its kind in China and corporate Pudong seems an incongruous place to put it.

Century Park and around

Century Boulevard (世纪大道, *shìjì dàdào*) runs arrow-straight for 4km to Century Park, one of Shanghai's largest green spaces. The simplest way to get here is on the subway; the Shanghai Science and Technology Museum stop (labelled in English) is three stops east of Lujiazui, and just north of the park, and plays host, incongruously, to a huge fake market (see p.406). There are some striking new buildings here, not high-rises for once, foremost among which is the **Science and Technology Museum** itself (上海科技馆, *shànghǎi kējìguǎn*; daily 9am–5pm; ¥60, students ¥45; Ⓦwww.sstm.org.cn), though it's rather too big perhaps, as the cavernous halls make some of the twelve exhibitions look threadbare – there isn't much English explanation or quite enough interactivity. The section on space exploration is good – a big topic in China right now, with the nation fully intending to get to the moon as soon as possible – with real spacesuits, models of spacecraft and the like, and in the section on robots you can take on a robotic arm at archery and play a computer at Go. The most interesting sections, however, are the **cinemas**: the space theatre (every 40min; ¥40) shows astronomical films; the two IMAX domes in the basement (hourly 10.30am–4.30pm; ¥40) show cartoons; while the IWERKS dome on the first floor (every 40min; ¥30) is an attempt to take the concept of immersive realism even further – as well as surround sound and images there are moving seats, and water and wind effects.

Just north of the museum, the **Oriental Arts Centre** (上海东方艺术中心, *shànghǎi dōngfāng yìshùzhōngxīn*; see p.406) is a magnificent, glass-faced, flower-shaped building that houses a concert hall, opera theatre, exhibition space and performance hall – they're the petals. It was designed by French architect Paul Andreu, who also created the new opera house in Beijing.

From here it's a pleasant ten-minute stroll along a pedestrian walkway to **Century Park** (though the park also has its own subway stop; 世纪公园, *shìjì gōngyuán*; daily 7am–6pm; ¥10). The park is spacious, the air is clean and it's possible to feel that you have escaped the city. You can hire a tandem bike (¥20/hr) – sadly you're not allowed to ride your own bicycle – and pedalos are available to rent on the central lake (¥25/hr).

Nanjing Lu and around

Stretching west from the Bund through the heart of Shanghai lie the main commercial streets of the city, among them one of the two premier shopping streets, **Nanjing Lu** (南京路, *nánjīng lù*), with its two major parallel arteries, **Fuzhou Lu** (福州路, *fúzhōu lù*) and **Yan'an Lu** (延安路, *yán'ān lù*). In the days of the foreign concessions, expatriates described Nanjing Lu as a cross between Broadway and Oxford Street. It was also at this time that Nanjing Lu and Fuzhou Lu housed numerous teahouses that functioned as the city's most exclusive brothels. Geisha-like *shuyu* (singer/storyteller girls) would saunter from teahouse to teahouse, performing classical plays and scenes from operas, and host banquets for guests. In a juxtaposition symbolic of prewar Shanghai's extremes, strings of the lowest form of brothel, nicknamed *dingpeng* ("nail sheds" because the sex, at ¥0.3, was "as quick as driving nails"), lay just two blocks north of Nanjing Dong Lu, along Suzhou Creek. The street was dubbed "Blood Alley" for the nightly fights between sailors on leave who congregated here.

Nanjing Dong Lu

On its eastern stretch, the garish neon lights and window displays of **Nanjing Dong Lu** (南京东路, *nángjīng dōng lù*) are iconic; come here in the evening to appreciate the lightshow in its full tacky splendour. But the shopping is not what it once was, with the emphasis now firmly on cheap rather than chic.

Warning: the tea scam

Foreigners in tourist areas of Shanghai will inevitably be approached by young girls and sweet-looking couples claiming to be art students or asking to practice their English. They are very skilled scam artists, and their aim is to befriend you, then coax you into visiting a bogus art gallery or teahouse. After a few cups of tea, you'll be presented with a bill for hundreds or even thousands of yuan, your new friends will disappear and some large gentlemen will appear. Never drink with a stranger unless you've seen a price list.

Number 635 was once the glorious **Wing On** emporium, and diagonally opposite was the **Sincere**. These were not just stores: inside, there were restaurants, rooftop gardens, cabarets and even hotels. The **Shanghai Department Store** near Guizhou Lu at no. 800, once the largest in China, is still going, and is still a place of pilgrimage for out-of-towners, but it's not as spectacular as it once was. Off the circular overhead walkway at the junction between Nanjing Dong Lu and Xizang Zhong Lu, just northeast of Renmin Park, is the grandest of the district's department stores, the venerable **Shanghai No. 1 Store**.

If you're looking for cheap clothes, you'll be spoilt for choice, but for something distinctly Chinese you'll have to look a bit harder. Your best bet for curiosities is to head to the **Shanghai First Food Store** at the west end of the street, at no. 720. The Chinese often buy food as a souvenir, and this busy store sells all kinds of locally made gift-wrapped sweets, cakes and preserves, as well as tea and tasty pastries.

Renmin Square

Its perimeters defined by the city's main arteries – Xizang, Nanjing and Yan'an roads – **Renmin Square**, or People's Square (人民广场, *rénmín guǎngchǎng*), is the modern heart of Shanghai. The area of Renmin Square was originally the site of the Shanghai racecourse, built by the British in 1862. The races became so popular among the foreign population that most businesses closed for the ten-day periods of the twice-yearly meets. They soon caught on with the Chinese, too, so that by the 1920s the Shanghai Race Club was the third-wealthiest foreign corporation in China. It was converted into a sports arena in 1941 by Chiang Kai-shek, who thought gambling immoral. During World War II the stadium served as a holding camp for prisoners and as a temporary mortuary; afterwards, most of it was levelled, and while the north part was landscaped to create Renmin Park, the rest was paved to form a dusty concrete parade ground for political rallies. Only the racecourse's clubhouse survives, as the venue for the Shanghai Art Museum.

There's an impressive clutch of sights, with the **Shanghai Museum**, **Urban Planning Exhibition Hall**, **Shanghai Art Museum** and little **Museum of Contemporary Art** all within walking distance of each other. Add to that an unexpectedly peaceful park, and you have one of Shanghai's most rewarding destinations.

The easiest way to get here is on the subway, as Renmin Square is at the interchange of lines #1 and #2.

The Shanghai Museum

The unmistakeable pot-shaped **Shanghai Museum** (上海博物馆, *shànghǎi bówùguǎn*; daily 9am–5pm; free; audio-guide ¥40, with ¥400 deposit) is one of the city's highlights, with a fantastic, well-presented collection. On the ground floor, the gallery of ancient **bronzes** holds cooking vessels, containers and weapons, many covered with intricate geometrical designs that reference animal shapes – check out the cowrie container from the Western Han dynasty, with handles shaped like stalking tigers. Most of the exhibits in the sculpture gallery next door are of religious figures – boggle-eyed temple guardians, serene Buddhas and the like, including a row of huge, fearsome Tang-dynasty heads. Tang-dynasty figurines again steal the show in the first-floor ceramics gallery, in the form of multicoloured ferocious-looking beasties placed to guard tombs.

On the second floor, skip the calligraphy and carved seals unless you have a special interest and investigate the **painting** gallery, which shows some amazingly naturalistic Ming-dynasty images of animals. The colourful top-floor exhibition dedicated to Chinese **minority peoples** is the museum highlight. One wall is lined with spooky lacquered masks from Tibet and Guizhou, while nearby are colourfully decorated boats from the Taiwanese minority, the Gaoshan. The silver ceremonial headdresses of southwest China's Miao people are breathtaking for their intricacy, if rather impractical to wear. Elaborate abstract designs turn the Dai lacquered tableware into art. In the section on traditional costumes, look out for the fish-skin suit made by the Hezhen people of Dongbei, in the far north.

Shanghai Urban Planning Exhibition Hall and Shanghai Grand Theatre

It's revealing of the Shanghai mindset that one of the city's grandest museums is dedicated not to the past but the future: the **Shanghai Urban Planning Exhibition Hall** (城市规划展示馆, *chéngshì guīhuà zhǎnshìguǎn*; daily 9am–5pm; ¥30) is interesting for its insight into the grand ambitions and the vision of the city planners, though if you're not keen on slick propaganda presentations it can be safely skipped. Most worthy of note is the tennis-court sized model of the city on the second floor, showing what it will (hopefully) look like in 2020. There's no room in this brave new world for shabby little alleyways; it's a parade ground of skyscrapers and apartment blocks in which, according to this model, the whole of the Old City (see p.387) is doomed.

Continuing west from here, past frumpy City Hall, brings you to the impressive **Shanghai Grand Theatre** (上海大剧院, *shànghǎi dàjùyuàn*), distinguished by its convex roof and transparent walls and pillars (see p.406). There's a café on site, and a good shop sells reasonably priced DVDs and CDs.

Shanghai Art Museum

Beyond the Grand Theatre, turning right along Huangpi Bei Lu will bring you to the **Shanghai Art Museum** (上海美术馆, *shànghǎi měishùguǎn*; Tues–Sun 9am–5pm, no entry after 4pm; ¥20; Ⓦwww.cnarts.net/shanghaiart), whose distinctive clocktower was once nicknamed "Little Ben". You can see hints of its former function as the racecourse clubhouse in the equestrian detailing on the balustrades. There's no permanent exhibition, but its shows of contemporary art are always worth a wander round, and it's a must during the Biennale every other autumn (see p.404), when it's full of work by the hottest international artists and you'll have to queue to get in. The third-floor café is okay but you'd be better off heading up to *Kathleen's 5* restaurant (see p.399) on the top floor for afternoon tea and fantastic views over the square.

Renmin Park

Just east of the Art Museum is the north gate to lovely **Renmin Park** (人民公园, *rénmín gōngyuán*). It's surprisingly quiet, with rocky paths winding between shady groves and alongside ponds – the only sign that you are in the heart of a modern city is the view of skyscrapers looming above the treetops. Crossing the lotus pond brings you to the glass-walled **Museum of Contemporary Art** (上海当代, 艺术馆 *shànghǎi dāngdài yìshùguǎn*; MoCA; daily 10am–6pm; ¥20, students free; Ⓦwww.mocashanghai.org). This attractive, privately funded museum has no permanent collection but its themed shows are imaginatively curated, and the museum holds regular talks and tours; check the website for details.

Nanjing Xi Lu

The historic **Pacific** and **Park hotels** stand on Nanjing Xi Lu opposite Renmin Park. The *Park Hotel* (国际饭店, *guójì fàndìan*), for many years the tallest building in Shanghai, once had a reputation for superb food as well as for its dances, when the roof would be rolled back to allow guests to cavort under the stars. Latterly, Mao Zedong always stayed here when he was in Shanghai. Today, however, it has been stripped of most of its old-world charm. The *Pacific Hotel* (金门大酒店, *jīnmén dàjiǔdiàn*), by contrast, a few metres to the east of the *Park*, is still worth having a look at, both for its ostentatious facade and for the fabulous plaster reliefs in the lobby.

The western end of Nanjing Xi Lu was known to "Shanghailanders" (the Europeans who made their homes here) as Bubbling Well Road, after a spring that used to gush at the far end of the street. Then, as today, it was one of the smartest addresses in the city, leading into tree-lined streets where Westerners' mock-Tudor mansions sheltered behind high walls. Now it's also the location of a number of luxury hotels, including the **Shanghai Centre** (上海商城, *shànghǎi shāngchéng*), a complex of luxury shops, restaurants and residential flats centred around the five-star *Portman Hotel*.

Opposite the Shanghai Centre, the gigantic Stalinist wedding cake that is the **Exhibition Hall** (展览馆, *zhǎnlǎnguǎn*) is worth seeing for its colossal ornate entrance, decorated with columns patterned with red stars and capped by a gilded spire. Constructed by the Russians in 1954, it was originally known as the Palace of Sino-Soviet Friendship and housed a permanent exhibition of industrial products from the Shanghai area – in recent years, it has become a venue for trade fairs.

Jing'an Si

Also at this end of Nanjing Xi Lu, a few hundred metres west of the Shanghai Centre, **Jing'an Si** (静安寺, *jìng'ān sì*; daily 7.30am–5pm; ¥10) is a small active temple nestling beside the tiny **Jing'an Park** (静安公园, *jìngān gōngyuán*) and under looming high-rises. Building work first began on the temple during the Three Kingdoms period, and its apparent obscurity belies its past as the richest Buddhist foundation in the city, headed by legendary abbot Khi Vehdu, who combined his abbotly duties with a gangster lifestyle. The abbot and his seven concubines were shadowed by White Russian bodyguards, each carrying a leather briefcase lined with bulletproof steel, to be used as a shield in case of attack. Today, the temple is the primary place of ancestral worship in the city, although an equal number of people come to pray for more material reasons – worshippers eagerly throw coins into incense burners in the hope that the gods will bestow financial success. Bus #20 runs here from Renmin Square, while a stop on subway line #2 lies underneath.

Yufo Si

Three kilometres north of the Jing'an Si is the **Yufo Si**, the **Jade Buddha Temple** (玉佛寺, *yùfó sì*; daily 8am–5pm; ¥15), a much more interesting and attractive complex. The pretty temple buildings have flying eaves, complicated brackets and intricate roof and ceiling decorations. It's a lively place of worship, with gusts of incense billowing from the central burner, and worshippers kowtowing before effigies and tying red ribbons to the branches of trees, decorative bells and the stone lions on the railings.

The star attractions here, though, are the relics. Two jade Buddhas were brought here from Burma in the 1882, and the temple was built to house them. The larger, at nearly 2m tall, sits in its own separate building in the north of the temple, and costs an extra ¥10 to see. It was carved from a single block of milky-white jade and is encrusted with agate and emerald. The second statue, in the Western Hall, is a little smaller, around 1m long, but easier to respond to. It shows a recumbent Buddha, at the point of dying (or rather entering nirvana), with a languid expression on his face, like a man dropping off after a good meal.

The central Great Treasure Hall holds three huge figures of the past, present and future Buddhas, as well as the temple drum and bell. The gods of the twenty heavens, decorated with gold leaf, line the hall like guests at a celestial cocktail party, and a curvaceous copper Guanyin stands at the back. It's all something of a retreat from the material obsessions outside, but it's still Shanghai; religious trinkets, such as fake money for burning and Buddhas festooned with flashing lights, are for sale everywhere and the monks are doing a roaring trade flogging blessings.

Moganshan Art District

An old factory beside Suzhou Creek in the north of the city, 3km northeast of the Yufo Temple, **Moganshan Arts District** (莫干山路50号, *mògānshānlù wŭshíhào*) is a complex of studios and galleries that makes up the city's biggest arts scene. The nearest subway stop to Moganshan is at Shanghai Zhan, a ten-minute walk away; otherwise, you'll have to take a cab.

Attracted by cheap rents, artists took over the abandoned buildings at 50 Moganshan Lu and used them as studios. Then the art galleries moved in, and now the design studios and cafés and more commercial galleries are arriving. What makes it fascinating – at the moment – is the way the area is both shabby and sophisticated, jumbling together paint-spattered artists, slick dealers, pretentious fashionistas and baffled locals. Most of the smaller galleries double as studios and there's something for all tastes, so expect to spend at least a morning poking around. Many of the galleries are closed on Mondays, and there's a map on the wall to the right of the entrance.

Of the 35 or so **galleries**, one of the biggest is Eastlink (daily 10am–5.30pm; ⓣ021/62769932, ⓦwww.eastlinkgallery.cn) on the fifth floor of Building 6; it's the oldest gallery here, resolutely resisting commercial pressures to water down its content. Another heavy hitter is ShangART (daily 10am–6pm; ⓣ021/63593923, ⓦwww.shangartgallery.com), housed in buildings 16 and 18. The most credible gallery is the Bizart Centre on the fourth floor of Building 7 (Mon–Sat 11am–6pm; ⓣ021/62775358, ⓦwww.biz-art.com); it's a not-for-profit space that promotes Chinese and foreign contemporary art, with an artist-in-residence programme. The ArtSea Studio and Gallery, on the second floor of Building 9 (Wed–Sun 10am–6pm; ⓣ021/62278380) is the best photography gallery. You're probably all arted out now, so have a coffee at the nearby *Bandu* café (see p.398).

The Old City

The **Old City** (老城, *lăochéng*) is that strange oval on the map, circumscribed by two roads, Renmin Lu and Zhonghua Lu, which follow the old path of the city walls. The Old City never formed part of the International Settlement and was known by the foreigners who lived in Shanghai, somewhat contemptuously, as the **Chinese City**. Based on the original **walled city** of Shanghai, which dated back to the eleventh century, the area was reserved in the nineteenth and early twentieth centuries as a ghetto for vast numbers of Chinese who lived in conditions of appalling squalor, while the foreigners carved out their living space around them. The easiest approach from Nanjing Dong Lu is to walk due south along Henan Lu or Sichuan Lu; or just take the subway to the Yu Yuan stop.

Tree-lined ring roads had already replaced the original walls and moats as early as 1912, and sanitation has obviously improved vastly since the last century, but to cross the boundaries into the Old City is still to enter a different world. The twisting alleyways are a haven of free enterprise, bursting with makeshift markets selling fish, vegetables, cheap trinkets, clothing and food. Ironically, for a tourist entering the area, the feeling is like entering a Chinatown in a Western city. The centre of activity today is an area known locally as **Chenghuang Miao** (after a local temple), surrounding the two most famous and crowded tourist sights in the whole city, the **Yu Yuan** and the **Huxin Ting** teahouse, both located right in the middle of a new, touristy bazaar that caters to the Chinese visitors who pour into the area. "Antiques", scrolls and kitsch souvenirs feature prominently, and there are also lots of good places to eat Shanghainese *dianxin*, some more reasonable than others (see "Restaurants", p.399).

Yu Yuan

A classical Chinese garden featuring pools, walkways, bridges and rockeries, the **Yu Yuan** (豫园, *yùyuán*; daily 8.30am–5.30pm; ¥40) was created in the sixteenth century by a high official in the imperial court in honour of his father. The Yu Yuan is less impressive than the gardens of nearby Suzhou, but given that it predates the relics of the International Settlement by some three hundred years, the Shanghainese are understandably proud of it. Despite fluctuating fortunes, the garden has surprisingly survived the passage of the centuries. It was spared from its greatest crisis – the Cultural Revolution – apparently because the anti-imperialist "Little Sword Society" had used it as their headquarters in 1853 during the Taiping Uprising. Garden connoisseurs today will appreciate the whitewashed walls topped by undulating dragons made of tiles, and the huge, craggy and indented rock in front of the Yuhua Tang (Hall of Jade Magnificence). During the Lantern Festival on the fifteenth day of the traditional New Year, ten thousand lanterns (and an even larger number of spectators) brighten up the garden.

After visiting the garden, you can check out the delightful **Huxin Ting** (湖心亭茶馆, *húxīntíng cháguǎn*; daily 8am–9pm), a two-storey teahouse on an island at the centre of an ornamental lake, reached by a zigzagging bridge. The Queen of England and Bill Clinton, among other illustrious guests, have dropped in for tea. These days it's a bit pricey at ¥50 for a limitless cup of tea, but you're welcome to poke about.

The antique markets

If you're in Chenghuang Miao early on Sunday morning (8–11am is the best time, though trade continues into mid-afternoon), you can visit a great **market** on Fuyou Lu (福佑路, *fúyòu lù*), the small street running east–west along the northern edge of Yu Yuan. The market has a raw, entrepreneurial feel about it; all sorts of curios and antiques – mostly fakes – ranging from jade trinkets to Little Red Books can be found here, though you'll have to bargain fiercely if you want to buy.

Just outside the Old City, in a small alley called Dongtai Lu leading west off Xizang Nan Lu, is the largest permanent **antique market** in Shanghai (东台路, *dōngtái lù*; daily 10am–4pm). Even if you're not interested in buying, this is a fascinating area to walk around. The range is vast, from old Buddhas, coins, vases and teapots to mahjong sets, renovated furniture and Cultural Revolution badges. As with all antique markets in China, the vast majority of goods are fake.

The former French Concession

Established in the mid-nineteenth century, the **former French Concession** (法租界, *fǎzūjiè*) lay to the south and west of the International Settlement, abutting the Chinese City. Despite its name, it was never particularly French: before 1949, in fact, it was a low-rent district mainly inhabited by Chinese and White Russians. Other Westerners looked down on the latter as they were obliged to take jobs that, it was felt, should have been left to the Chinese.

The French Concession was notorious for its lawlessness and the ease with which police and French officials could be bribed, in contrast to the well-governed areas dominated by the British. This made it ideal territory for gangsters, including the king of all Shanghai mobsters, Du Yuesheng, the right-hand man of Huang Jinrong. For similar reasons, **political activists** also operated in this sector – the first meeting of the Chinese Communist Party took place here in 1921, and both Zhou Enlai and Sun Yatsen, the first provisional President of the Republic of China after the overthrow of the Qing dynasty, lived here. The preserved former homes of these two in particular (see below) are worth visiting simply because, better than anywhere else in modern Shanghai, they give a sense of how the Westerners, and the Westernized, used to live.

Certain French characteristics have lingered here, in the local chic and in a taste for bread and sweet cakes – exemplified in **Huaihai Lu**, the main street running through the heart of the area. Not as crowded as Nanjing Lu, Huaihai Lu is considerably more upmarket, particularly in the area around **Maoming Lu** and **Shanxi Lu**, where fashion boutiques, extremely expensive department stores and excellent cake shops abound.

Xintiandi

Although it might seem like an obvious idea, the **Xintiandi** development (新天地, *xīntiāndì*), which comprises two blocks of renovated and rebuilt *shikumen* converted into a genteel open-air mall, was the first of its kind in China. It has met with such success that now town planners all over the country are studying its winning formula. Paved and pedestrianized, with narrow lanes (*longtang*) opening out onto a central plaza, Xintiandi is a great place to wind down or linger over a coffee, with upscale restaurants (see p.400) and shops (see p.405) and plenty of outside seating for people-watching. The easiest way to get here is to take the subway to Huangpi Nan Lu and walk south for five minutes, or get out at Xintiandi and walk north.

Shikumen Open House Museum

The **Shikumen Open House Museum** (石库门民居陈列馆, *shíkùmén chénglièguǎn mínjū*; daily 10am–10pm; ¥20), at the bottom end of Xintiandi north block, does an excellent job of evoking early twentieth-century Chinese gentility. This reconstruction of a typical *shikumen* is filled with everyday objects – typewriters, toys, a four-poster bed and the like – so it doesn't look as bare as the "former residences" elsewhere in the city. A top-floor display details how Xintiandi came about, admitting that most of it was built from scratch. A quote on the wall is perhaps more revealing than was intended: "Foreigners find it Chinese and Chinese find it foreign."

The First National Congress of the Chinese Communist Party

On the east side of the complex, at the junction of Xingye Lu and Huangpi Nan Lu, you'll find, rather incongruously, one of the shrines of Maoist China, the **First**

National Congress of the Chinese Communist Party (中国一大会址纪念 馆, *zhōngguó yīdàhuìzhǐ jìniànguǎn*; daily 9am–5pm, last admission 4pm; free). The official story of this house is that on July 23, 1921, thirteen representatives of the Communist cells that had developed all over China, including its most famous junior participant, Mao Zedong, met here to discuss the formation of a national party. The meeting was discovered by a French police agent (it was illegal to hold political meetings in the French Concession), and on July 30 the delegates fled north to nearby Zhejiang province, where they resumed their talks in a boat on Nan Hu. Quite how much of this really happened is unclear, but it seems probable that there were in fact more delegates than the record remembers – the missing names would have been expunged according to subsequent political circumstances. There's a little exhibition hall downstairs, where relics from the period such as maps, money and a British policeman's uniform and truncheon are more interesting than the comically outdated propaganda rants. The last room has a waxwork diorama of Mao and his fellow delegates.

The former residences

From Xintiandi it's a short walk to Sinan Lu, where you'll find the **Former Residence of Sun Yatsen**'s, the first president of the Chinese Republic, and his wife, Song Qingling (孙中山故居, *sūnzhōngshān gùjū*; daily 9am–4.30pm; ¥8). The dry exhibition of the man's books and artefacts is nothing special, but just as an example of an elegantly furnished period house it is worth a look.

Head south down Sinan Lu and you enter a smart neighbourhood of old houses. Five minutes' walk brings you to one you can get into, the **Former Residence of Zhou Enlai** at no. 73 (周恩来故居, *Zhōuēnlái gùjū*; daily 9am–4pm; ¥2). Zhou was Mao's right hand man, but he has always been looked upon with rather more affection than the Chairman. When he lived here he was head of the Shanghai Communist Party, and as such was kept under surveillance from a secret outpost over the road. There's not, in truth, a great deal to see, beyond a lot of hard beds on a nice wooden floor. The house has a terrace at the back with rattan chairs and polished wooden floors, and its garden, with hedges and ivy-covered walls, could easily be a part of 1930s suburban London.

Taikang Lu (Tianzifang)

As you continue further south along Sinan Lu from the former residences, the area begins to feel earthier; but head right to the end of the road and a right turn onto **Taikang Lu** (泰康路, *tàikāng lù*) will bring you to the latest fashionably artsy shopping and lunching quarter, **Tianzifang** (田子坊, *tiánzifāng*). You'll have to look hard to find the unassuming entrance, an arch over alley 210, which stretches north off Taikang Lu. It leads onto Taikang Art Street, a narrow north–south alleyway that is the central artery for an expanding web of alleys filling up with trendy boutiques, coffee shops, handmade jewellery stores, art galleries, interior design consultancies and the like, all housed in converted *shikumen* houses. At its northern end, it comes out at Sinan Lu, but don't even try to come in from there – the entrance is really tough to find.

Inevitably, the place gets compared with Xintiandi; but whereas the architecture there is modern pastiche, this is a set of real, warts-and-all *longtangs*, with the result that it's quainter, shabbier and more charming. There are still plenty of local families around, who continue, boutiques or no boutiques, to hang their woolly underwear out to dry, and old folk shuffle round in their pyjamas, studiously ignored by the chic ladies who lunch. If you're looking for an artsy knick-knack or accessory, quirky souvenir, tasteful homeware or a designer original, this is the place to come; an emphasis on local design and creativity rather than brands makes this the **best shopping experience** in the city. There's a tourist information booth just inside the entrance and next to that, a map shop; you might balk at paying ¥5 for a glossy sheet of paper, but really the map is invaluable as the alleys are something of a warren.

For gorgeous clothes by local designers, head to Insh and La Vie (see p.406) or Nuomi (12, Lane 274; ⓣ021/64663952), and for lovely cashmere scarves check out Scarf City (46, Lane 248; ⓣ021/54650296). More affordable are the witty T-shirt designs offered by Plastered (49, Lane 248; ⓣ021/21539477) and Shirtflag (see p.406) and the tasteful, eco-friendly soft furnishings from Nest (2F, building 3, Lane 210). For a coffee stop, central *Kommune* (see p.398) is a local institution.

Ruijin Lu and Maoming Lu

As you head west, the south section of **Ruijin Er Lu** (瑞金二路, *ruìjīn èr lù*) is busy and cramped but there's a wonderful escape in the form of the stately **Ruijin Guesthouse** (瑞金宾馆, *ruìjīn bīnguǎn*), just south of Fuxing Zhong Lu. This Tudor-style country manor was home in the early twentieth century to the Morris family, owners of the *North China Daily News*; Mr Morris raised greyhounds for the Shanghai Race Club and the former Canidrome dog track across the street. The house, having miraculously escaped severe damage during the Cultural Revolution because certain high-ranking officials used it as their private residence, has now been turned into a pleasant inn. Even if you're not a guest, you're free to walk around the spacious, quiet grounds, where it's hard to believe you're in the middle of one of the world's most hectic cities.

The two plush **hotels** north of here, the *Okura Garden* (上海花园饭店, *shànghǎi huāyuán fàndiàn*; see p.374) and the *Jinjiang* (锦江之星, *jǐnjiāngzhīxīng*), are worth a visit for glimpses of past luxuries. The *Okura*, originally the French Club, or Cercle Sportif Français, was taken over by the Americans during World War II and converted by the egalitarian communists into the People's Cultural Palace. Anyone can wander round the lovely gardens and go in to look at the sumptuous ceiling design of stained glass on the ballroom.

The *Jinjiang* compound opposite includes the former **Grosvenor Residence** complex, the most fashionable and pricey address in pre-World War II Shanghai. The Grosvenor has recently been modernized, but the *VIP Club* still retains much of its 1920s architecture and Great Gatsby ambience. Non-guests might be able to sneak a peek by taking the elevator to the top floor of the Old Wing of the *Jinjiang*, where the club is located, although gaining entrance to one of the twenty astonishingly beautiful refurbished Art Deco VIP mansion rooms on the floors directly below (a snip at US$800/night), might prove slightly more difficult.

If you keep walking up Maoming Nan Lu you come to the Art Deco **Lyceum Theatre** (兰心大戏院, *lánxīn dàxìyuàn*), built in 1931 and once home to the British Amateur Dramatic Club. It now holds nightly acrobatic shows (see p.404).

Around Changshu Lu

West of Changshu Lu subway station you really get a good idea of what the French Concession is all about. Many of the villas here have been converted to embassy properties (the more sensitive are guarded by soldiers with fixed bayonets) and there are also plenty of upmarket, expat-oriented restaurants, a fair few beauty salons and, oddly, not that many shops. It's more a place to soak up atmosphere on a sunny day than to take in specific sights.

Fuxing Xi Lu (复兴西路, *fùxīng xī lù*) is a discreetly charming street, typical of the area, with a winning combination of artsiness, idiosyncratic low-rise buildings and coffee stops. **Art Scene China** (艺术景画廊, *yìshùjǐng huàláng*), an art gallery inside a restored villa, in an alley just off the southern side of the street, is always worth popping into. Their stable of artists produces painterly, tasteful work that's neither trendy nor gaudy. Have a look at the workshop of Shanghai Trio, next door (see p.406), for cute bags. A little further up are cafés *Urban Tribe* and *Boona* (see p.398); the prestigious *Yongfu Elite* (see p.403), a great place for a pre-dinner cocktail, is just around the corner, too.

A pleasant ten-minute stroll away on Huashan Lu, the **Propaganda Poster Centre** (宣传画年画艺术中心, *xuānchuánhuàniánhuà yìshùzhōngxīn*; daily 9.30am–4.30pm; ¥25; ⓣ021/62111845) is an abrupt change of tone, providing a fascinating glimpse into communist China – you will not come across a more vivid evocation of the bad old days of Marx and Mao. To find the place, present yourself to the security guard at the entrance to 868 Huashan Lu. He'll give you a name card with a map on the back showing you which Building in the complex beyond to head for – the centre is a basement flat in building 4. The walls are covered with Chinese Socialist Realist posters, over three thousand examples arranged chronologically from the 1950s to the 1970s, which the curator will talk you round, whether or not you understand his Chinese. There are, fortunately, English captions. With slogans like "the Soviet Union is the stronghold of world peace" and "hail the over-fulfillment of steel production by ten million tons" and images of sturdy, lantern-jawed peasants and soldiers defeating big-nosed, green-skinned imperialists or riding tractors into a glorious future, the black-and-white world view of communism is dramatically realized.

Former Residence of Song Qingling

Some twenty minutes' walk southwest from Hengshan Lu subway station, at 1843 Huaihai Xi Lu, is the **Former Residence of Song Qingling** (宋庆龄故居, *sòngqìnglíng gùju*; daily 9–11am & 1–4.30pm; ¥8). As the wife of Sun Yatsen, Song Qingling was part of a bizarre family coterie – her sister Song Meiling was married to Chiang Kai-shek and her brother, known as T.V. Soong, was finance minister to Chiang. Once again, the house offers a charming step back into a residential Shanghai of the past, and although this time the trappings on display – including her official limousines parked in the garage – are largely post-1949, there is some lovely wood panelling and lacquerwork inside the house. Song Qingling lived here on and off from 1948 until her death in 1981.

Western Shanghai

Due west from the city there is less to see, with a sprinkling of sights too far apart to walk between. If you follow Nanjing Lu beyond Jing'an Si, it merges into Yan'an Lu, which (beyond the city ring road) eventually turns into Hongqiao Lu, the road that leads to the airport. Shortly before the airport it passes **Shanghai Zoo** (上海动物园, *shànghǎi dòngwùyuán*; daily 6.30am–4.30pm; ¥20), a massive affair with more than two thousand animals and birds caged in conditions that, while not entirely wholesome, are better than in most Chinese zoos. The stars, inevitably, are the giant pandas. The zoo grounds used to serve as one of pre-1949 Shanghai's most exclusive golf courses. Next door, at 2409 Hongqiao Lu, stands the mansion that once functioned as the **Sassoons' home**, and which originally boasted a fireplace large enough to roast an ox; the central room, since renovated, resembled a medieval castle's Great Hall. Victor Sassoon, who used this mansion as a weekend residence (his other pad was the top-floor apartment of the *Peace Hotel*), only allowed for the design of two small bedrooms because he wanted to avoid potential overnight guests. It has served since as a Japanese naval HQ, a casino and as the private villa of the Gang of Four, but now suffers the relative ignominy of being rented out as office space. Bus #57 from the western end of Nanjing Lu will bring you out here. The side gate is sometimes open if you wish to take a peek.

The Xujiahui Catholic Cathedral

The **Xujiahui Catholic Cathedral** (圣依纳爵主教座堂, *shèngyīnàjué zhǔjiào zuòtáng*) in the southwest of the city is one of many places of public worship that have received a new lease of life in recent years. Built in 1846 on the grave of Paul Xu Guangqi, the first Jesuit convert, it was closed for more than ten years during the Cultural Revolution, reopening in 1979. Most of the cathedral library's 200,000 volumes, as well as the cathedral's meteorological centre (built at the same time as the cathedral and now housing the Shanghai Municipal Meteorology Department), survive on the grounds.

Longhua Cemetery of Martyrs and Longhua Si

Southeast of the Xujiahui Cathedral, **Longhua Cemetery of Martyrs** (龙华烈士陵园, *lónghuá lièshì língyuán*; daily 6.30am–4pm; cemetery ¥1, exhibition hall ¥5) is a park commemorating those who died fighting for the cause of Chinese communism in the decades leading up to the final victory of 1949. In particular, it remembers those workers, activists and students massacred in Shanghai by Chiang Kai-shek in the 1920s – the site of the cemetery is said to have been the main execution ground. In the centre is a glass-windowed, pyramid-shaped **exhibition hall** with a bombastic memorial to 250 communist martyrs who fought Chiang's forces. The cemetery is a short walk south from the terminus of bus #41, which you can catch from Huaihai Zhong Lu near Shanxi Nan Lu, or from Nanjing Xi Lu near the Shanghai Centre.

Right next to the Cemetery of Martyrs is one of Shanghai's main religious sites, the **Longhua Si** (龙华寺, *lónghuá sì*; daily 5.30am–4pm; ¥10), and its associated tenth-century pagoda. The **pagoda** itself is an octagonal structure about 40m high (until the feverish construction of bank buildings along the Bund in the 1910s, the pagoda was the tallest edifice in Shanghai), its seven brick storeys embellished with wooden balconies and red-lacquer pillars. After a long period of neglect (Red Guards saw it as a convenient structure to plaster with banners), an ambitious re-zoning project has spruced up the pagoda and created the tea gardens, greenery and shop stalls that now huddle around it.

Though there has been a temple on the site since the third century, the halls are only around a century old. It's the most active Buddhist site in the city, and a centre for training monks. On the right as you enter is a bell tower, where you can strike the bell for ¥10 to bring you good luck. On Chinese New Year, a monk bangs the bell 108 times, supposedly to ease the 108 "mundane worries" of Buddhist thought. You can whack it yourself, any time, for ¥10; three hits is considered auspicious.

Botanical Gardens

Taking bus #56 south down the main road, Longwu Lu, just to the west of the Longhua Si site, will bring you to the **Botanical Gardens** (上海植物园, *shànghǎi zhíwùyuán*; daily 7am–4pm; ¥15). More than nine thousand plants are on view in the gardens, including two pomegranate trees that are said to date from the reign of Emperor Qianlong in the eighteenth century; despite their antiquity, they still bear fruit. Look out, too, for the orchid chamber, where more than a hundred different varieties are on show.

North of Suzhou Creek

North across the Waibaidu Bridge from the Bund, you enter an area that, before the war, was the Japanese quarter of the International Settlement, and which since 1949 has been largely taken over by housing developments. The obvious interest lies in the Lu Xun Park area (also known Hongkou Park), and its monuments to the political novelist Lu Xun, although the whole district is lively and architecturally interesting.

From East Baoxing road subway station, on line #3, it's a short walk to **Duolun Lu** (多伦文化名人街, *duōlún wénhuà míngrénjiē*), a heritage street of antique and bric-a-brac shops housed in elegant imitation Qing buildings. The best thing about it is the *Old Film Café* (see p.399), charmingly decorated with film posters, and the seven-storey **Duolun Museum of Modern Art** (多伦现代美术馆, *duōlún xiàndài měishùguǎn*; Tues–Sun 10am–6pm; ¥10; ⓦwww.duolunart.com). There's no permanent show, but check the website to see what's on.

Lu Xun Park (鲁迅公园, *lǔxùn gōngyuán*; daily 6am–7pm), five minutes' stroll north of here, is one of the best places for observing Shanghainese at their most leisured. Between 6am and 8am, the masses undergo their daily *tai ji* workout; later in the day, amorous couples frolic on paddle boats in the park lagoon and old men teach their grandkids how to fly kites. The park is also home to the pompous **Tomb of Lu Xun**, complete with a seated statue and an inscription in Mao's calligraphy, which was erected here in 1956 to commemorate the fact that Lu Xun had spent the last ten years of his life in this part of Shanghai. The tomb went against Lu Xun's own wishes to be buried simply in a small grave in a western Shanghai cemetery. The novelist is further commemorated in the **Lu Xun Memorial Hall** (鲁迅纪念馆, *lǔxùn jìniànguǎn*; daily 9–11am & 1.30–4pm; free), also in the park, to the right of the main entrance. Exhibits include original correspondence, among them letters and photographs from George Bernard Shaw.

A block southeast of the park on Shanyin Lu (Lane 132, House 9), the **Former Residence of Lu Xun** (鲁迅故居, *lǔxùn gùjū*; daily 9am–4pm; ¥8) is worth going out of your way to see, especially if you have already visited the former residences of Zhou Enlai and Sun Yatsen in the French Concession (see p.390). The sparsely furnished house where Lu Xun and his wife and son lived from 1933 until his death in 1936 offers a fascinating glimpse into typical Japanese housing of the period – a good deal smaller than their European counterparts, but still surprisingly comfortable.

Outside the city

Shanghai Shi (Shanghai Municipality) covers approximately two thousand square kilometres, comprising ten counties and extending far beyond the limits of the city itself. Surprisingly, very little of this huge area is ever visited by foreign tourists, though there are a couple of interesting sights. Most can be visited by tour bus – services leave from 1111 Caoxi Bei Lu, near Shanghai Stadium.

The most obvious of these is **She Shan** (佘山, *shéshān*; daily 7.30am–4pm; ¥30), about 30km southwest of the city. Such is the flatness of the surrounding land that

She Shan, which only rises about 100m, is visible for miles around. The hill is crowned by an impressive **basilica**, a legacy of nineteenth-century European missionary work – She Shan has been under the ownership of a **Catholic** community since the 1850s – though the present church was not built until 1925.

It's a pleasant walk up the hill at any time of year, or a cable-car ride if you prefer (¥10), past bamboo groves and the occasional ancient pagoda. Also on the hill are a **meteorological station** and an old **observatory**, the latter containing a small exhibition room displaying an ancient earthquake-detecting device – a dragon with steel balls in its mouth that is so firmly set in the ground that only movement of the earth itself, from the vibrations of distant earthquakes, can cause the balls to drop out. The more balls fall, the more serious the earthquake.

The eastern side of the hill has been redeveloped as a ninety-acre **sculpture park** (daily 8am–6pm; ¥80), including the artificial Moon Lake. There's nothing particularly distinguished about the thirty or so works of art, but they serve as handy way stations on a pleasant walk. With a long artificial beach around a lake, manicured lawns and plenty of playgrounds, this makes a good retreat to take the kids and is busy with families at the weekend. Rowing boats can be rented for ¥60 an hour.

You can reach She Shan on subway Line #9; it's about forty minutes from Xujiahui to the She Shan stop. A ten-minute walk west brings you first to the sculpture park; the road curves south to get around the hill itself.

The canal towns

An extensive canal system once transported goods all around imperial China, and the attractive water towns that grew up around them – notably **Zhouzhuang**, **Xitang** and **Tongli** – present some of eastern China's most distinctive urban environments. Whitewashed Ming and Qing timber buildings back onto the narrow waterways, which are crossed by charming humpback stone bridges; travel is by foot or punt as the alleys are too narrow for cars.

Today, these sleepy towns are a popular escape from the city, and each has become a nostalgia theme park for the urban sophisticate. They're fine as day-trips but don't expect much authenticity – there are far more comb shops than dwellings – and don't come on weekends, when they're overrun. All charge an **entrance fee**, which also gets you into the historical buildings, mostly the grand old houses of wealthy merchants.

By far the easiest way to get to these places is from the **Shanghai Stadium Sightseeing Bus Centre** (上海体育馆旅游集散中心, *shànghǎi tǐyùguǎn lǚyóu jísànzhōngxīn*; information ⓣ021/64265555) at 666 Tianyaoqiao Lu, on the south side of the Shanghai Stadium, a ten-minute walk from the subway stop of the same name. Tour buses leave between 7.30am and 10.30am, returning in the afternoon. Tickets, priced around ¥150, are available up to a week in advance from the main booking office, where staff speak English, or you can order tickets up to three days in advance from a freephone number (ⓣ4008872626) and they'll deliver them to your hotel for a fee of between ¥10 and ¥30. A guide is provided (non-English speaking), though you are free to wander off on your own. Otherwise, a taxi will cost in the region of ¥500.

Zhouzhuang

Twenty kilometres west of the city, just across the border into Jiangsu province, **ZHOUZHUANG** (周庄, *zhōuzhuāng*; ¥100) is the most accessible of the canal towns. Buses make the run regularly from the Sightseeing Bus Centre stop by

Shanghai Stadium (1hr 30min; buses depart at 7am, 8.30am, 9am, 9.30am & 10am, and return between 4.30pm & 5.30pm).

Lying astride the large Jinghang Canal connecting Suzhou and Shanghai, Zhouzhuang grew prosperous from the area's brisk grain, silk and pottery trade during the Ming dynasty. Many rich government officials, scholars and artisans moved here and constructed beautiful villas, while investing money into developing the stately stone bridges and tree-lined canals that now provide the city's main attractions.

The biggest mansion is the **Shen House** in the east of town, built in 1742. Over a hundred rooms (not all of them open) are connected by covered colonnades, with grand public halls at the front and the more intimate family chambers at the back. Period furnishings help evoke a lost age of opulence, though it is all rather dark; the neat gardens offer a pleasant contrast.

Zhouzhuang's most highly rated views are of the pretty sixteenth-century twin **stone bridges** in the northeast of town. Also firmly on the itinerary are a **boat ride** round the canals (¥80) and lunch – there are no shortage of restaurants, all offering the local specialities of pig's thigh, meatballs and clams as a set meal (around ¥60/head).

Xitang

XITANG (西塘, *xītáng*; ¥50, ¥100 including all entrance fees; free on Sun afternoon and Fri morning) is short on specific sights, although the lanes, canals and bridges are undeniably picturesque. And if it rains, at least you'll be dry: the locals, tired of the wet climate, built roofs over the main alleyways, the biggest of which is over 1km long. It runs alongside the central canal, and is lined with restaurants and stalls housed in half-timbered buildings. There are plenty of riverside restaurants serving up local specialities such as pork with sweet potatoes.

To get to Xitang, take a sightseeing bus from Shanghai Stadium, which leaves at 8.45am and returns at 4pm; the journey takes two hours. To get here under your own steam, take a bus from the South bus station to Jiashan (hourly; ¥28), then take one of the many minibuses for the short hop to Xitang. If you want to stay the night, head for the *Xitang Youth Hostel* at 6 Tangjia Lane, off Xi Xia Jie on the west side of town, which offers simple rooms and dorms (西塘国际青年旅舍, *xītáng guójì qīngnián lǚshè*; ⓣ0512/65218885; ❶–❸) or for something a little more upmarket try the *Jinshui Lou Ge* (近水楼阁客栈, *jìnshǔi lóugé kèzhàn* ; ⓣ133/75731700; ❺) at 10 Chaonan Dai, whose rooms are full of reproduction Ming-dynasty furniture.

Tongli

Of all the canal towns, **TONGLI** (同里, *tónglǐ*; ¥80), around 80km from Shanghai, has the best sights, and with more than forty humpback bridges (some more than a thouand years old) and fifteen canals it offers plenty of photo ops. The town's highlight is the UNESCO World Heritage Site **Tuisi Garden** (退思园, *tuìsī yuán*; daily 8am–6pm; ¥40), built by disillusioned retired official Ren Lansheng in 1886 as a place to retreat and meditate – though you'll have to come in the early morning, before the tour groups arrive, to appreciate the peacefulness of the place. With its harmonious arrangements of rockeries, pavilions and bridges, zigzagging over carp-filled ponds, it is comparable to anything in Suzhou. The nearby **Sex Museum** (中华性文化博物馆, *zhōnghuá xìngwénhuà bówùguǎn*; daily 8am–5.30pm; ¥20), housed in a former girls' school, is a branch of the museum in Pudong (see p.382), with similar exhibits – figurines of Tang-dynasty prostitutes, special coins for use in brothels and a wide range of occasionally eye-watering dildos.

Buses from the Sightseeing Bus Centre by the Shanghai Stadium (see above) depart at 8.30am, take around 1hr 30min to get here, and return around 5pm.

Wuzhen

As it's a little further out than other canal towns (two hours by bus), sedate **WUZHEN** (乌镇, *wūzhèn*) is much less busy; if you're headed out on the weekend, this is the one to go to as the others will be choked. Entrance is ¥100, and your ticket gets you into all the local sights; make sure you pick up a map at the nearby visitor's centre. The prime draw here is the cute little **Xiuzhen Taoist Temple** and its collection of folk art, including intricate wood carving and leather shadow puppets; you can watch the latter in action at the nearby playhouse, which has shows every hour until 5pm.

Several of the houses are used to demonstrate local crafts such as silk painting or printing using dyes made from tea leaves, or as museums; check out the intricately carved pieces of the Hundred Bed Museum. The Fanglu Paviliion, near the centre of town, is today a teahouse with picturesque views over the canal, and makes a good place for a rest, though as ever in these places, you won't find it cheap (¥28 a pot).

Wuzhen is especially nice at night, when most of the visitors have left and the town is bathed in a romantic glow by lanterns; if you want to **stay** over, try the *Wuzhen Guesthouse* (ⓣ573/88731230, ⓦwww.wuzhen.com.cn), which has properties all over town (❸–❻), all run by local families. To do this you'll have to make your own arrangements to get here: take a bus to Jiaxing from the South bus station and then get a minibus for the last leg of the trip. For a **day trip**, buses from the Sightseeing Bus Centre by the Shanghai Stadium (see above) depart at 8.30am and return around 5pm.

Eating, drinking, nightlife, entertainment and shopping

Food in Shanghai is fantastic; though there are fairly few options to eat cheap street food, most forms of international cuisine are widely available and there are plenty of classy **restaurants**. You're similarly spoilt for choice when it comes to entertainment; the arts scene has got considerably livelier of late, with a number of new arts centres and plenty of new galleries offering something for all tastes. The **bar and club scene** is excellent; though Beijing is the place to go for live music, Shanghai has the edge when it comes to clubbing. **Shopping** is another diverting pastime, with the best choice of souvenirs and consumables in the country; in particular, Shanghai has the best fashion stores in China.

Eating

If you are arriving from other areas of China, be prepared to be astounded by the excellent **diversity** of food in Shanghai, with most Chinese regional cuisines represented, as well as an equally impressive range of foreign cuisine, including Brazilian, Indian, Japanese and European. It's hard to believe that up until the early 1990s, simply getting a table in Shanghai was a cut-throat business.

Compared to, for example, Sichuan or Cantonese, **Shanghai cuisine** is not particularly well known or popular among foreigners. Most of the cooking is done with added ginger, sugar and Shaoxing wine, but without heavy spicing. There are some interesting dishes, especially if you enjoy exotic seafood. Fish and shrimp are considered basic to any respectable meal, and eels and crab may appear as well. In season (Oct–Dec), you may get the chance to try *dazha* crab, the most expensive and, supposedly, the most delicious. Inexpensive **snack food** is easily available in almost any part of the city at any time of night or day – try *xiao long bao*, a local dumpling speciality.

Breakfast, cafés and fast food

Global fast-food chains are everywhere; but rather better (and certainly healthier) are Asian chains such as *Yoshinoya*, *Kung Fu Catering* and *Ajisen* (for noodles and rice dishes). Every mall and shopping centre has a cluster of **fast-food restaurants**, either in the basement or on the top floor. A good one is in the basement of Raffles Mall on Fuzhou Lu; Megabite on the sixth floor is a huge food court.

Shanghai does **cafés** very well. As any tourist itinerary here involves lots of fairly unstructured wandering around, visitors might find themselves spending more time than they thought people-watching over a cappuccino. All the cafés listed below have free wi-fi.

Visitors craving a good Western breakfast should head to a *Wagas* or *Element Fresh* (see below).

Aura (埃哇餐厅, *āiwā cāntīng*) 171 Jiaozhou Lu. This crisply decorated and cosy little hideaway is aimed at the trendsetters staying at the *URBN* hotel next door. Coffee or a milkshake is ¥25, but their pizzas, starting at ¥40, are good value. Daily 9am–11pm.

Bandu (半度音乐, *bàn dù yīn yuè*) 50 Moganshan Lu, near Changhua Lu. The best of the Moganshan Art District (see p.387) cafés, this intimate hideaway hosts performances of Chinese folk music every Sat at 8pm. Daily 11am–11pm.

Barbarossa (芭芭露莎, *bā bā lù shā*) 231 Nanjing Xi Lu, inside Renmin Park. This mellow, onion-domed Arabian fantasy is beautifully situated by the lotus pond in Renmin Park. It's also a bar and a restaurant, but don't eat here as the food is overpriced. Makes a great pitstop for anyone doing the sights in nearby Renmin Square. Daily 10.30am–2am.

Bonomi (波诺米饭店, *bōnuò mǐ fàndiàn*) Room 226, 12 Zhongshan Dong Yi Lu; *Hengshan Moller Villa*, 30 Shaanxi Nan Lu. This stylish Italian chain is a winner thanks to the fantastic locations of its restaurants. The one on the Bund, secreted on the second floor of the former HSBC, feels like a secret club (see p.380), and there's a nice terrace, too. The branch inside the *Hengshan Moller Villa* (see p.398) also has a lovely terrace, overlooking the garden. You won't mind paying ¥25 for a coffee with views like this. Daily 8am–10pm.

Boona 88 Xinle Lu. Writing a business plan on a Mac laptop is not mandatory at this artsy little café but would certainly help you fit in. The paintings and photos are all for sale. Afternoon tea is ¥28.

Citizen Bar and Café (天台餐厅, *tiān tái cān tīng*) 222 Jinxian Lu ⓣ021/62581620. A great continental-style café tucked away in a gentrified neighbourhood. A good brunch place, with a wide choice of bar snacks, and a very civilized venue for a pre-dinner cocktail or a slice of apple pie. Daily 11am–1am.

Costa Coffee 388 Nanjing Xi Lu; east side of the Bund, opposite Beijing Dong Lu. The latest coffee colonizers are from the UK, and they're spreading fast, with twenty branches in Shanghai already. Hard to get excited about, but at least it's better than *Starbucks*. Both the above branches are handy, as there aren't too many cafés in the area. Daily 9am–10pm.

Element Fresh (新元素, *xīn yuán sù*) Shanghai Centre (east side), 1376 Nanjing Xi Lu (daily 7am–11pm); 4F, KWah Centre, 1028 Huaihai Zhong Lu (daily 7am–11pm); Level 2, World Financial Centre, Century Ave; ⓦwww.elementfresh.com. This airy, informal bistro is the best place in town for a Western breakfast (they're open early), with plenty of options both hearty and healthy; it won't cost you more than ¥60 and includes limitless coffee. Free delivery.

Kommune (公社酒吧, *gōng shè jiǔ bā*) 210 Taikang Lu, Building 7, near Sinan Lu. Hip, if pricey, café hidden at the heart of Taikang Lu (see p.390) – head north up the alley, take the first left and it's just there. Very popular with the designer set, especially for weekend brunch, when the courtyard outside fills up. There's an Australian-style barbecue (all you can eat ¥148) every Wednesday night. Deli sandwiches for ¥38. Daily 9am–10pm.

Old China Hand Reading Room (汉源书屋, *hàn yuán shū wū*) 27 Shaoxing Lu, by Shaanxi Nan Lu ⓣ021/64732526. Bookish but not fusty, this is the place to come for leisured reflection. There's a huge collection of tomes to peruse or buy, many printed by the café press, which specializes in coffee-table books about French Concession architecture. Afternoon coffee with a scoop of ice cream and biscuits is ¥45. No meals. Daily 10am–midnight.

Old Film Café (老电影咖啡吧, *lǎo diàn yǐng kā fēi bā*) 123 Duolun Lu, by Sichuan Bei Lu ⓣ021/56964763. If you're in the area, this charming old house full of period detail and wallpapered with old film ads is great for refreshments. Film buffs will be excited by the possibility of the owners screening their fine collection of old Chinese and Russian films – just ask.

Starbucks House 18, North Block Xintiandi; Binjiang Dadao. The coffee colonizers have spread all over the city, so you're never far from an overpriced shot of caffeinated mud. The two stores above are the best, notable for having pleasant outdoor seating.

Vienna Café (维也纳咖啡馆, *wéi yě nà kā fēi guǎn*) 25 Shaoxing Lu, near Ruijin Lu ⓦwww.viennashanghai.com. Popular and charming Austrian-style French Concession café, almost managing that fin-de-siecle vibe. You can't fault their strudel or Kaiserchmarn – pancake served with apple sauce. Daily 8am–8pm.

Wagas (沃歌斯, *wò gē sī*) Shop G107, Hong Kong World Plaza, 300 Huaihai Zhong Lu; CITIC Square basement, 1168 Nanjing Xi Lu, near Jiangning Lu. Good-looking yet wholesome food, decor and staff at this New York-style deli. Order their Western breakfast before 10am and it's half price (only ¥27) – and add coffee for ¥10. Smoothies and frappes for just over ¥30; wraps and sandwiches are a little more. Daily 7.30am–11pm.

Westin Bakery The *Westin Bund Center*, 88 Henan Zhong Lu. This bakery, tucked at the back of the over-the-top *Westin* hotel lobby (see p.375), deserves a mention for being understated and good value (unlike the hotel). Tasty cakes, tarts and coffees. Treat yourself to a lychee vodka truffle (¥7).

Restaurants

Restaurants are more expensive in Shanghai than elsewhere in China, although prices remain reasonable by international standards; most dishes at Chinese restaurants are priced around ¥35, and even many upmarket Western restaurants have meal specials that come to less than ¥90. The reviews give phone numbers for those places where reservations are advisable. Restaurant opening hours are the same as the rest of the country, though generally speaking expat places are open a little later; places with unusually long hours are marked.

The Bund, Nanjing Dong Lu, Renmin Park and around

The **Bund** itself has a number of upmarket restaurants in some of the old Art Deco buildings, most notably *M on the Bund*.

Godly (Gongdelin) (功德林素食馆, *gōngdélín sùshíguǎn*) 445 Nanjing Xi Lu. A vegetarian restaurant with templey decor, specializing in fake meat dishes. It's all rather hit-and-miss; try the meatballs, roast duck, crab and ham, but avoid anything meant to taste like fish or pork, and be wary of ordering just vegetables, as they'll turn up too oily. Staff could be livelier. Around ¥60/head.

Kathleen's 5 (赛马餐饮, *saì mǎ cān yǐn*) 5F, Shanghai Art Museum, 325 Nanjing Xi Lu ⓣ021/63272221. Great location – an elegant glass box on top of the old Shanghai Art Museum building, with views over Renmin Square. The Western food is not quite as inspiring, but the three-course lunch sets (¥140) are decent value, as is the afternoon tea set (¥88). Try the crab-meat tower – which includes avocado and mango – as a starter and follow with the cod or lamb. Good for a date.

Lao Zhengxing (老振兴餐馆, *lǎo zhèn xīng cān guǎn*) 556 Fuzhou Lu. This unassuming restaurant is perennially popular for its light, non-greasy Shanghai cuisine. Good for seafood and famous for herring; try "squirrel fish" and a selection of dumplings. A good introduction to genuine local cuisine. Around ¥70/person.

M on the Bund (米氏西餐厅, *mǐshì xīcāntīng*) 7F, 5 Wai Tan, entrance at Guang Dong Lu ⓣ021/63509988. Worth eating at for the extraordinary view overlooking the Bund. Some complain that as a fine-dining experience it isn't all that great, but the Mediterranean-style cuisine is some of the classiest (and most expensive) food in town, and the set lunch (¥98) is good value. If you're going to splash out, try the grilled salmon and finish with pavlova.

The Stage Level 1, The *Westin Bund Center*, 88 Henan Zhong Lu, near Guangdong Lu ⓣ021/3350577. The "it" place for a buffet brunch – ¥520 for as much as you can eat and drink, including champagne and caviar. Come hungry and not too hungover, and pig out. Daily 6am–12am.

Wang Baohe (王宝和酒家, *wáng bǎo hé jiǔ jiā*) 603 Fuzhou Lu ⓣ021/63223673. Wang Baohe bills itself as the "king of crabs and ancestor of wine". It's been around for more than 200 years, so it must be doing something right, and is famous for its hairy crab set meals, which start at ¥200/person.

Yuxin Sichuan Dish (渝信川菜, *yú xìn chuān cài*) 3F, 333 Chengdu Bei Lu ⓣ021/52980438. Super-spicy Sichuan food in a no-nonsense dining hall. Very popular with families and the white-collar crowd, so a reservation is recommended. Go for the *kou shui* ji (saliva chicken) and *sha guo yu* (fish pot) and work on developing a face as red as the peppers. Little English is spoken, but there's a picture menu.

The Old City

The Yu Yuan area has traditionally been an excellent place for **snacks** – *xiao long bao* and the like – eaten in unpretentious surroundings. Although the quality is generally superb and prices very low, there is a drawback in the long lines that form at peak hours. Try to come outside the main eating times of 11.30am to 1.30pm, or after 5.30pm. Among the snack bars in the alleys around Yu Yuan, perhaps the best is *Lubolang* with a large variety of dumplings and noodles. Very close to the Yu Yuan entrance is the *Hubin Mei Shilou* (湖滨美食楼, *húbīn měi shí lóu*), which serves a delicious sweet bean *changsheng zhou* (long-life soup). The *Lao Fandian* (老饭店, *lǎo fàndiàn*), just north of Yu Yuan at 242 Fuyou Lu, is one of the most famous restaurants in town for local Shanghai food, though prices are slightly inflated. For quick bites, check out the satay, noodle and corn-on-the-cob stands lining the street bordering the western side of Yu Yuan bazaar.

The former French Concession and western Shanghai

This is the area where most expats eat and correspondingly where prices begin to approach international levels. The compensation is that you'll find menus in English, and English will often be spoken, too. For travellers tired of Chinese food, Huaihai Lu and Maoming Lu brim with **international cuisine**. Many excellent **Shanghainese** and **Sichuanese** restaurants also cluster in the alleys around Huaihai Lu, at prices much lower than for international food. Huaihai Lu itself is lined with fast-food joints, bakeries and snack stalls.

Xintiandi (新天地, *xīntiāndì*) on Taicang Lu is an "olde worlde" renovated courtyard complex of fancy cafés, bars and more than 25 restaurants (pick up the handy map at the entrance), all rather pricey – you won't get away with paying much less than ¥100 a head.

1221 (一二二一酒家, *yī èr èr yī jiǔjiā*) 1221 Yan'an Xi Lu. A little out of the way, a ten-minute walk east of Yan'an Lu subway stop (though bus #71 stops right outside), this is one of the city's best and most creative Shanghainese restaurants, attracting a mix of locals and expatriates. The drunken chicken and *xiang su ya* (fragrant crispy duck) are excellent, as are the onion cakes. Good choice for vegetarians, too.

1931 (一九三一饭店, *yījiǔsānyī fàndiàn*) 112 Maoming Nan Lu, just south of Huaihai Zhong Lu ⓣ021/64725264. The right mix of Shanghainese, Japanese and Southeast Asian cuisines and reasonably priced, good-sized portions characterize this civilized little place. ¥150/person.

Bali Laguna (巴厘岛, *bā lí dǎo*) 189 Huashan Lu, inside Jing'an Park, near Yan'an Lu ⓣ021/6248 6970. A popular, classy Indonesian restaurant beautifully situated in quiet Jing'an Park. Good place for a date. The seafood curry (¥88) is served inside a pineapple. ¥140/person.

Bi Feng Tang (避风塘, *bì fēng táng*) 1333 Nanjing Xi Lu, by Tongren Lu; 175 Changle Lu. This cheap and tasty Cantonese fast-food diner makes a great last spot on a night out (though beware the merciless lighting). There's a picture menu, and you can't go far wrong with their many dim sum and dumpling options. Finish off with custard tarts. Open 24hr.

Charmant (小城故事, *xiǎo chéng gù shì*) 1414 Huaihai Zhong Lu ☎021/64318027. Great Taiwanese place – convenient, cheap, functioning as much as a café as a restaurant – that's open till the early hours, handy after a night of drinking in the former French Concession. Daily 11.30am–4am.

Crystal Jade (翡翠酒家, *fěi cuì jiǔ jiā*) Unit 12A-B, 2F, Building 7, South Block, Xintiandi ☎021/63858752; B110 Hong Kong World Plaza, 300 Huaihai Zhong Lu. Great Hong Kong food, sophisticated looks and down-to-earth prices make this the place to eat in Xintiandi, and the best place in town for dim sum. Try the barbecued pork – and leave room for mango pudding. The second branch in the Hong Kong World Plaza is not as swanky, but is less busy. Cheaper than it looks, at around ¥80/head.

Dongbei Ren (东北人, *dōng běi rén*) 1 Shaanxi Nan Lu, by Yan'an Zhong Lu ☎021/52289898. Hale and hearty, the way those sturdy *dongbei ren* – northeasterners – like it. It's all meat and potatoes, much like Scottish fare (must be something to do with the cold). Try the dumplings, lamb skewers and braised pork shank. ¥60/head.

Guyi Hunan (古意湘味浓, *gǔ yì xiāng wèi nóng*) 89 Fumin Lu, near Julu Lu ☎021/62495628. This stylish, popular place is the best in the city to sample Hunan cuisine – known for being hot and spicy and for its liberal use of garlic, shallots and smoked meat. Go for the chilli-spinkled spareribs, fish with beans and scallions or tangerine-peel beef, which tastes better than you might expect, or try the chef's speciality, open face fish. About ¥100/head.

Hotpot King (来福楼, *lái fú lóu*) 2F, 146 Huaihai Zhong Lu, by Fuxing Xi Lu ☎021/64736380. English menus, understanding staff and tasteful decor make this an accessible way to sample a local favourite. Order lamb, glass noodles, mushrooms and tofu (at the least) and chuck them into the pot in the middle of the table. Perfect for winter evenings. ¥70/person. Daily 11am–4am.

Lapis Lazuli (藏龙坊, *cáng lóng fāng*) 9 Dongping Lu, near Hengshan Lu ☎021/64731021. Pleasant, clubby hideaway, very stylish if a bit dark, serving reasonably priced continental food. The intimate outdoor terrace makes this a great place for a date on a summer evening. Try the seafood risotto. About ¥100/head.

Meilongzhen (梅龙镇酒家, *méi lóng zhèn jiǔjiā*) 22 Lane 1081, Nanjing Xi Lu ☎021/62535353. A Shanghai restaurant with a dash of Sichuan spiciness; it's very popular, so best reserve. It's tucked behind Nanjing Lu, but you can't miss the colourful arched doorway. Go for twice-cooked pork, drink eight-treasure tea – check out the long-spouted kettles – and finish off with a sugar-roasted banana. ¥90/person.

Mesa (梅萨, *méi sà*) 748 Julu Lu, near Fumin Lu ☎021/62899108. Fine dining, Western-style, in a stylish converted factory. Try the carpaccio of beef or seared duck breast but leave room for the dessert tasting platter. Service could be a tad better but they're trying. The bar upstairs, *Manifesto*, is handy. Daily 10am–late.

Shen Yue Xuan (申粤轩饭店, *shēnyuè xuān fàndiàn*) 849 Huashan Lu ☎021/62511166. The best Cantonese place in Shanghai, with scrumptious dim sum at lunchtime and pleasant, if cavernous, decor. In warmer weather, you can dine alfresco in the garden, a rarity for a Cantonese restaurant. Dinner for two comes to around ¥120/head, drinks included.

Shintori (新都里餐厅, *xīndūlǐ cāntīng*) 803 Lulu Lu, three blocks south of Hengshan Lu ☎021/64672459. Take someone you want to impress to this nouvelle Japanese trendsetter: the buffet will set you back around ¥300. Entertaining presentation (such as plates made of ice) will give you something to talk about, though you'd better order a lot or you'll be bitching about the small portions. Finish with green tea tiramisu (¥60).

Shu Di La Zi Yu Guan (蜀地辣子鱼馆, *shǔdìlàzǐ yúguǎn*) 187 Anfu Lu, on the corner with Wulumuqi Zhong Lu. Never mind the tacky decor – concentrate on the excellent, inexpensive Sichuan and Hunanese cuisine. A big pot of Sichuan spicy fish is a must, but also recommended is *zhu xiang ji* (bamboo fragrant chicken) and old fave, *mala doufu* (spicy tofu).

Simply Thai (天泰餐厅, *tiāntài cāntīng*) 5-C Dongping Lu ☎021/64459551. The best of the city's Thai joints, with good, eclectic dishes and a smart but informal setting, including a leafy courtyard. Try the stir-fried asparagus and fish cakes. The Xintiandi branch is not nearly as good.

South Beauty (俏江南, *qiào jiāng nán*) 881 Yan'an Lu, opposite the Exhibition Hall ☎021/62475878. Upmarket Sichuan food in what looks like an English country house. The house speciality is beef in boiling oil – cooked at your table. ¥200/person.

T8 House 8, North Block, Xintiandi, Taicang Rd ☎021/63558999. Fine continental-style dining, courtesy of a Swedish chef, in an elegant reconstruction of a courtyard house. Reserve, and ask for one of the booths at the back. Start with a lobster congee and follow with a goat cheese roulade, or splash out on the seven-course tasting menu (¥788). Fabulous desserts include a chocolate addiction platter. ¥400/head.

Xiao Shaoxing (小绍兴饭店, *xiǎo shàoxīng fàndiàn*) Yunnan Lu (east side), immediately north of Jinling Dong Lu. Famous in Shanghai for its *bai qie ji* (chicken simmered in wine), although adventurous diners might also wish to sample the blood soup or chicken feet.

Xinjishi (Jesse Restaurant) (新吉士餐厅, *xīn jí shì cān tīng*) 41 Tianping Lu; Shop 9, North Block, Xintiandi, 181 Taicang Lu ⓣ021/63364746 ⓦwww.xinjishi.com. The decor is a bit tatty at the tiny, original branch on Tianping Lu, but there's nothing wrong with the tasty homestyle cooking, with dishes from all over the country. Go for the red cooked pork and other local faves. The second branch at Xintiandi, with its traditional styling, looks better, but the food is not as good. You'll certainly have to reserve. Daily 11am–2pm & 5–9.30pm.

Ye Shanghai (夜上海, *yè shàng hǎi*) House 6, North Block, Xintiandi, 338 Huangpi Nan Lu ⓣ021/63112323. Shanghai cuisine in an upmarket pastiche of colonial grandeur – so lots of red lanterns and dark wood. A good introduction to local tastes – particularly recommended are the drunken chicken, prawns with chilli sauce and the many crab dishes. Around ¥200/person.

Yin (音, *yīn*) 2F, 4 Hengshan Lu, Near Wulumuqi Lu ⓣ021/54665070. Hardwood floors and screens create an intimate atmosphere, and the food is similarly tasteful, well thought through and understated. No MSG is used, and all dishes – Shanghai staples – are light and not oily. A great place to sample local cuisine such as eggplant pancakes. Set menu is ¥100/person.

Pudong

There's nothing particularly mid-range around **Lujiazui**; either head to a mall for the cheap and cheery food court, or a hotel for a fabulous, if pricey, culinary experience.

Jade on 36 36F, Tower 2, Pudong *Shangri-La*, 33 Fucheng Lu ⓣ021/68823636, ⓦwww.shangri-la.com. Celebrity chef Fabrice Giraud's classic French food in a grand venue, which has an amazing view of the Bund. Foie gras, prawn and beef rib recommended but be warned, it's very pricey; at least ¥450/head.

Yi Café Level 2, Tower 2, Pudong *Shangri-La*, 33 Fucheng Lu ⓣ021/58775372, ⓦwww.shangri-la.com. This slickly designed place is the best of the hotel buffets. All you can eat – and there's an enormous choice, with ten show kitchens – for ¥268, plus fifteen-percent service charge. Go hungry. Very popular for Sun brunch (11am–2pm). Daily 6am–1am.

Drinking and nightlife

Western-style **bars** are found mostly in the Huaihai Lu area, nearly all of which serve food, and some of which have room for dancing. Bars tend to cluster in districts; Julu Lu, Tongren Lu and Maoming Nan Lu each have a dense concentration of venues, though some have a sleazy edge. There are also plenty of rather more upmarket places for a drink in Xintiandi.

You'll find the full range of drinks available, though beer is usually bottled rather than draught and prices are on the high side; reckon on ¥30–60 per drink in most places. This hasn't stopped the development of a jumping, occasionally sleazy, nightlife, though the scene is patently focused on expats and the moneyed Chinese elite.

The **club** scene will be eerily familiar to anyone who's been clubbing in any Western capital – you won't hear much in the way of local sounds – but at least door prices are much cheaper, never more than ¥100. One Chinese innovation is the addition of karaoke booths at the back; another, much less welcome, is the annoying practice of having to pay to sit at a table. Most places have international DJs, and plenty of famous faces have popped in for a spin of the decks. Wednesday is (usually) ladies night, Thursday is hip-hop night, and, of course, the weekends are massive. There are also dance floors in bar *Rouge*, *Dada*, *NOT ME* and *Zapatas*, reviewed below.

Bars

Bar Rouge 7F, Bund 18, 18 Zhongshan Dong Yi Lu, near Dianchi Lu. Staff are snobbish, clientele are pretentious, but the terrace has unrivalled views over the Bund. ¥50 cover on weekends and you won't get much change from a red bill for a drink.

Captain Bar (船长酒吧, *Chuánzhăng jiŭbā*) 6F, *Captain Hostel*, 37 Fuzhou Lu, by Sichuan Zhong Lu. This relaxed venue scores for its terrace with a great view of Pudong. It sits atop a backpacker hotel (see p.373), though most guests are put off by the prices – draught beer ¥40.

Cloud Nine 87th floor, *Grand Hyatt*, Jinmao Tower, 88 Shiji Dadao, Pudong ⓣ021/50491234. Inside, it's all rather dark and metallic, but the view is great. Pick a cloudless day, and arrive soon after opening time (6pm) to bag one of the coveted windowside tables facing Puxi. ¥120 minimum spend/person, which will only get you one cocktail.

Dada 115 Xingfu Lu, between Fahuazhen Lu and Pingwu Lu, behind *Logo Bar*. It might be a bit of a way out, but this clubby lounge bar is worth searching out for its laidback ambience and hip young crowd. Music, mostly house and electro, is by talented independent promoters Antidote. Look out for their special events – check flyers around town.

Glamour Bar 6F, *M on the Bund*, 20 Guangdong Lu, by Zhonghsan Dong Yi Lu ⓦwww.m-theglamourbar.com. Pink, frivolous and fabulous, this is Shanghai's destination du jour for poseurs. Good view of the Bund though, and there's a schedule of cultural events. Cocktails from ¥65 (great mojitos).

JZ Club 46 Fuxing Xi Lu, near Yongfu Lu ⓦwww.jzclub.cn. A popular venue, dark but not smoky, with live jazz every night from 10pm. Pricey drinks (starting at ¥45) but there's no cover.

Long Bar 2F, Shanghai Centre, 1376 Nanjing Xi Lu. Comfy expat bar, for networking and post-work drinks. Beers from ¥35.

Mural 697 Yongjia Lu, near Hengshan Lu ⓦwww.muralbar.com. Cheap and cheery basement venue, incongruously decorated like a Buddhist cave, popular for its ¥100 open bar on Fri nights.

NOT ME 21 Dongping Lu, near Hengshan Lu ⓣ021/64330760, ⓦwww.not-me.com. Though it's surrounded by dodgy venues, and doesn't look too different from them with its purple walls and white leather decor, this is actually one of Shanghai's hippest hangouts, one of the few to host independent promoters. All-you-can-drink deals are every Mon and Tues, Thurs is indie night, and it's invited DJs on the weekend. No cover, and reasonably priced drinks.

People 7 805 Julu Lu, close to Fumin Lu. This very hip bar trades on its exclusivity. Not only is there no sign, there's even a special code to get in: put your hands into the third and seventh of the nine lighted holes outside. A door slides back revealing a two-storey lounge bar with walls of exposed concrete, spotlights, comfy white sofas and a long eerily lit bar. The quirky elements – glasses with curved bottoms so they keep rolling round, baffling toilet doors with fake handles – will either delight or annoy.

Vue 32–33F, *Hyatt on the Bund* hotel, 199 Huangpu Lu, north of Suzhou Creek. Another *Hyatt*-run Shanghai "must do", this sleek designer bar has fantastic views of the Bund, and there's a jacuzzi on the outdoor terrace so take your swimwear (or rent it from the bar). Cocktails for around ¥80.

Yongfu Elite (雍福会, *yōngfú huì*) 200 Yongfu Lu, by Hunan Lu. A former private members' club now open to the public, this fabulously opulent villa has vintage everything; heaven forbid that you spill a drink. Sip cocktails (which start at ¥60) on the veranda under the gaze of the garden's huge Buddha statue, and feel like a film star.

Zapatas (长廊酒吧, *chángláng jiŭbā*) 5 Hengshan Lu, near Dongping Lu ⓦwww.zapatas-shanghai.com. No self-respecting Mexican anarchist would be seen dead in the company of this lascivious frat-house crowd. Never mind, it's a heaving party on their Mon and Wed "free margaritas for the ladies before midnight" special. You enter through the garden of *Sasha's*, the nearby restaurant.

Clubs

Bonbon 2F Yunhai Tower, 1329 Huaihai Zhong Lu ⓦwww.clubbonbon.com. *Bonbon* is packed with a raucous young crowd, even on weekdays; Tues is popular. Hip-hop on Thurs. Cover charge ¥40–100.

California 2A Gaolan Lu, entertainment complex Park 97, inside Fuxing Park ⓦwww.lankwaifong.com. So red inside it's like being inside a liver; not inappropriately then, it's a meat market. This house club is more upscale than most and popular with both locals and expats. Mon–Thurs & Sun 8pm–2am, Fri & Sat 9pm–late.

Muse (同乐坊, *tónglè fāng*) 68 Yuyao Lu, New Factories, near Xikang Lu ⓦwww.museshanghai.com. Big and glitzy club, with house music downstairs, and hip-hop up. Open till 2am on weekdays, 4am on weekends. ¥70.

Entertainment

Most visitors take in an **acrobatics show** and perhaps the **opera**, but equally worthy of note are the flourishing contemporary art and music scenes. The **Shanghai Arts Festival** (Ⓦwww.artsbird.com) is held from mid-October to mid-November – though you'd be forgiven for not noticing it, arts programming does much better during the period, with lot of visiting shows. For listings of big cultural spectaculars such as visiting ballet troupes, check the *China Daily*, but for the lowdown on punk gigs, underground art shows and the like, get an up-to-date expat magazine such as *cityweekend* or check Ⓦwww.smartshanghai.com.

The simplest way to get **tickets** is at the box office before the show starts, or a few days earlier if there's any danger that it will sell out. You can also buy tickets from the booking centre behind the Westgate Mall on Nanjing Xi Lu.

The contemporary art scene can be conveniently checked out at the Moganshan Art District (see p.387). The next **Shanghai Biennale**, held in venues all over town, is in 2012 (Ⓦwww.shanghaibiennale.com).

Acrobatics

There are three main venues for the perennially popular **acrobatics**; the **Shanghai Circus World** in the far north of the city (上海马戏城, *shànghǎi mǎxìchéng*; 2266 Gonghe Xin Lu; performances daily 7.30pm; tickets ¥80–580; Ⓣ021/66527750, Ⓦwww.era-shanghai.com) puts on a nightly show "ERA: the Intersection of Time", but never mind the daft name, this is a good old-fashioned spectacular, in a specially built dome. The shows at the **Shanghai Centre's theatre** (上海商城剧院, *shànghǎi shāngchéng jùyuàn*; 1376 Nanjing Xi Lu, by Xikang Lu; performances daily at 7.30pm; tickets ¥100–280; Ⓣ021/62798948, Ⓦwww.shanghaicentre.com) and the **Lyceum** (兰心大戏院, *lánxīn dàxìyuàn*; 57 Maoming Nan Lu; performances daily 7.30pm; tickets ¥150–250; Ⓣ021/62565544) are lighter on the glitz but full of breathtaking feats.

Cinema

China's first **movie studios** were in Shanghai, in the 1930s (see p.979), and you can see old classics such as *Sister Flower* and *The Goddess* – both surprisingly hard-hitting naturalistic tragedies – at the *Old Film Café* (see p.399). The studios might have gone but, increasingly, you can find Shanghai depicted on film, most succesfully in Lou Ye's tragic love story *Suzhou Creek* (2002). The best of many concession era "lipstick and *qipao*" films is *Shanghai Triad* (1995). The brutal end to those days is shown in Steven Spielberg's decent adaptation of J.G. Ballard's classic novel, *Empire of the Sun* (1987).

Two cinemas that show foreign blockbusters in their original languages are the **UME International Cineplex** (新天地国际影城, *xīntiāndì guójì yǐngchéng*; Fifth Floor, South Block, Xintiandi; tickets from ¥50; Ⓣ021/6373333 – an English schedule follows the Chinese when you call, Ⓦwww.ume.com) and the **Paradise Warner International City** (永华电影城, *yǒng huá diàn yǐng chéng*; Sixth Floor, Grand Gateway, 1 Hongqiao Lu, Xujiahui; tickets from ¥50; Ⓣ021/64076622, Ⓦwww.paradisewarner.com). They also show all the latest Chinese releases, though in Mandarin Chinese only, as does Shanghai's other giant multiplex, the **Broadband International Cineplex** (万裕国际影城, *wànyù guójì yǐngchéng*; Sixth Floor, Times Square, 99 Huaihai Lu, near Huangpi Nan Lu subway station; tickets from ¥50; Ⓣ021/63910363, Ⓦwww.swy99.com).

For **art-house** flicks, in addition to the possibilities above there's a popular screening club at *Dada* (see p.403) every Tuesday night at 9pm, and one at the *Vienna Café* (see p.399) every Thursday at 7.30pm. In mid-June the city hosts the **Shanghai International Film Festival** (Ⓦwww.siff.com), when there is much more varied fare on offer.

Music

A number of new world-class venues are sating local demand for **classical music** and imported **musicals**. The Shanghai Cultural Information and Booking Centre has a comprehensive website with the schedules of all the most popular venues (Ⓦwww.culture.sh.cn/English, reservations on Ⓣ021/62172426), as has the China Ticket Online (Ⓦshdx.piao.com.cn/en_piao, reservations Ⓣ021/63744968). At both, tickets can be booked over the phone then delivered to your hotel or home at no extra charge, provided you book more than three days before the performance. Ticket prices vary, but you can expect to pay around ¥100, three times that for the best seats.

Jazz is perennially popular; check out *JZ Club* (see p.403). The **indie music** scene is not as good as Beijing's, but it's there, and it is worth dipping a toe into.

Majestic Theatre (美琪大剧院, *měi qí dà jù yuàn*) 66 Jiangning Lu, near Nanjing Xi Lu Ⓣ021/62174409. When built in 1941 this was one of Asia's best theatres. It usually shows musicals, but has some English-language drama.

Oriental Arts Centre (上海东方艺术中心, *shàng hǎi dōng fāng yì shù zhōng xīn*) 425 Dingxiang Lu, near Century Ave Ⓣ021/68541234. There's no doubt that this is one of Asia's most important concert venues but at present this fantastic, forty thousand-square-metre behemoth (see p.405) struggles to fill its schedule. Hosts a little bit of everything, but comes into its own as a concert venue, as the acoustics are superb.

Shanghai Concert Hall (上海音乐厅, *shànghǎi yīnyuètīng*) 523 Yan'an Dong Lu, near Xizang Zhong Lu Ⓣ021/63862836. This beautiful old building was moved 60m east in 2003, at tremendous cost, to get it away from the din of Yan'an Lu. Today, it's the premier venue for classical music. Tickets from ¥80.

Shanghai Grand Theatre (上海大剧院, *shànghǎi dàjùyuàn*) 300 Renmin Dadao Ⓣ021/63273094. Lovely building that puts on popular contemporary dramas, operas and classical ballets, and plays host to most of the visiting musicals. Regular performances by the in-house Shanghai Symphony Orchestra.

Yuyingtang (育音堂, *yùyīntáng*) 851 Kaixuan Lu, by Yan'an Xi Lu subway stop Ⓣ021/52378662, Ⓦwww.yuyintang.org. This is ground zero for the Converse-and-black-nail-varnish set. Rock/punk and electro gigs every weekend with a varying cover of around ¥30. With concrete floors and graffittied walls, it's all pretty rough and ready, but the sound system is surprisingly good, and bottles of beer are only ¥15. The promoters are always getting in trouble with the authorities, and move often, so check the place is still here before you turn up.

Shopping

The **shopping** is great in Shanghai, and it's a rare visitor who doesn't end up having to buy another bag to keep all their new goodies in. The Shanghainese love luxury goods, and it's not uncommon to find young women spending several months' salary on a handbag, but all those glitzy brand names that give the streets such a lot of their shine are not good value; high-end goods and international brands are generally twenty percent more expensive than they would be in the West. Ignore them, and instead plunge into the fascinating world of the backstreet boutiques and markets.

Fake markets

There are several **fake markets** catering largely to foreigners (all open daily 9am–8pm). As well as clothes, there are trainers, sunglasses, bags and watches on sale. The biggest and most convenient is the **Yatai Xinyang Fashion & Gift market** (亚太新阳服饰礼品市场, *yàtàixīnyáng fúshì lǐpǐn shìchǎng*) in the Science and Technology Museum subway station, its entrance close to the ticketing machines. As well as the usual fake shoes, bags and clothes there are plenty of tailors, and there's a whole zone for jewellery. **Qipu Road Market** (七浦路和河南北路, *qīpǔlù hé hénánběilù*) at 183 Qipu Lu is just northeast of the Bund. Not everything is a copy; some of this stuff, mainly the jeans and trainers, is made in the same factories as the real thing. You'll have to bargain harder here than anywhere else in the city; the pushy vendors commonly start at ten or twenty times the real price, and it pays to shop around as plenty of people are selling the same thing.

Clothes

Sartorial elegance is something of a local obsession, so you're spoilt for choice if you're looking for **clothes**. If you want to see international designer clothes in showpiece stores head to Plaza 66 or the Bund. The chicest shopping is to be had in the former French Concession; central Huaihai Zhong Lu itself is full of familiar brands, but the streets off it – such as Nanchang, Shanxi Nan Lu and Maoming Lu – are full of fascinating little boutiques, which make this the place to forage for fashionable gear.

Getting **tailored** clothes is a recommended Shanghai experience, as it will cost so much less than at home and the artisans are skilled (provided you're clear about exactly what you're after) and quick. At the **textile market** at 399 Lujiabang Lu (南外滩轻纺面料市场, *nánwàitān qīngfǎng miànliào shìchǎng*; Old City, near Liushui Lu; daily 10am–7pm) on-site tailors will make you a suit for around ¥500, including material (you'll have to barter a bit), which will take a couple of days. If you're looking for a tailored *qipao*, your best bet is to head to one of the dozen or so specialist stores on Maoming Nan Lu, just south of Huaihai Lu, or head for Hanyi Cheongsam at 221 Changle Lu (Ⓣ021/54044727). For reasonably priced (¥500 or so) handmade shoes try the Yanye Shoe Studio at 893 Huashan Lu (Ⓣ13162705506), though they'll take a couple of weeks.

For designer clothes at bargain basement prices, head to a **factory overstock** shop. These will be unpromising from the outside, possibly won't have a name, and will usually carry their own lines in the window, with the good stuff hung rather negligently on a rail at the back. The place to start looking is Ruijin Er Lu, at the intersection with Huaihai Zhong Lu. Head south down the street then turn onto Nanchang Lu – look in any clothes shop that's busy on the way. A second concentration of these stores is on Fuxing Zhong Lu, east of Baoqing Lu. Or find your way to a branch of overstock chain Hot Wind (Ⓦwww.hotwind.net): there are convenient ones at 358 Huaihai Zhong Lu (by Huangpi Nan Lu subway station exit three); 127 Ruijin Yi Lu; and 106 Ruijin Yi Lu. They put their own label over the original – you have to scrape it off with a fingernail.

The place to start looking for interesting local designers is Tianzifang (see p.390); check out Insh (Ⓣ021/64665249; Ⓦwww.insh.com.cn) at 200 Taikang Lu, La Vie (Ⓣ021/64453585; Ⓦwww.lavie.com.cn) at Courtyard 7, Lane 210 and Nuomi at 274, Lane 12. Here too, you'll find plenty of artsy knick-knacks, handmade jewellery and the like; check out the Tian Zi Fang Leather workshop at no. 15, lane 210, which sells bags and belts; Cholon at no.3, lane 108, which sells Vietnamese homeware; Hari Rabu at House 6, Lane 210, which has a Shanghai take on Indonesian curios; and Jooi Design (Ⓦ www.jooi.com) on the second floor at Studio 201 of the International Artist Factory, which has some great cushion covers and embroidered evening bags.

Souvenirs, electronics and books

If you're looking to do some souvenir shopping in a hurry, head to the bazaar around the Yu Yuan. The best places to shop for **electronic goods** are the giant tech-souks **Cybermart** (赛博数码广场, *saìbó shùmǎ guǎngchǎng*), on Huahai Zhong Lu, near the intersection with Xizang Nan Lu; **Subway City**, at 111 Zhaojiabang Lu, by Caoxi Bei Lu, in the basement of the mall shaped like a giant bubble (Xujiahui subway); and **Pacific Digital Plaza** (太平洋数码广场, *tàipíngyáng shùmǎ guǎngchǎng*), at 117 Zhaojiabang Lu (Xujiahui subway). Obscure brand laptops, MP3 players, memory sticks, RAM, and low-end accessories such as headphones can be very cheap. Shop around, as many of the stalls sell the same things, and barter (though this isn't the fake market; you'll get at most fifteen percent off the asking price). Test everything thoroughly, and remember that for the majority of this stuff the warranty is not valid internationally.

For **books**, head to Chaterhouse, in the basement of Times Square at 93 Hauihai Zhong Lu (时代豪庭, *shídài háotíng*), whose good selections of imported English-language books cost a little more than they would at home. The Foreign Languages Bookstore at 390 Fuzhou Lu is a useful resource, with plenty of English-language guides and the like; the novels, published by Chinese publishers, are cheap.

Listings

Airlines Aeroflot, *Donghu Hotel*, Donghu Lu ⓣ64158158; Air China, 24H Room 101B, Changfeng Centre, 1088 Yan'an Xi Lu, near Fanyu Lu ⓣ52397227; Air France Room 3901, Ciro's Plaza, 388 Nanjing Xi Lu ⓣ4008808808; All Nippon Airways (ANA), Shanghai Centre, 1376 Nanjing Xi Lu ⓣ62797000; Asiana Airlines, 2000 Yan'an Xi Lu ⓣ62709900; Cathay Pacific, Room 2104, 138 Shanghai Plaza, Huaihai Zhong Lu ⓣ63756000; China Eastern Airlines, 200 Yan'an Xi Lu ⓣ62472255; China Southern Airlines, 227 Jiangsu Lu ⓣ62262299; JAL (Japan Airlines), 7F, Huaihai International Plaza, 1045 Huaihai Zhong Lu ⓣ62883000; KLM/Northwest Airlines, Room 207, Shanghai Centre, 1376 Nanjing Xi Lu t68846884; Korean Air, 2099 Yan'an Lu ⓣ62758649; Lufthansa, 3F, 1 Building, Corporate Av, 222 Hubin Lu ⓣ53524999; Malaysia Airlines, Suite 560, Shanghai Centre, 1376 Nanjing Xi Lu ⓣ62798607; Qantas Airways, 32F, K. Wah Centre, 1010 Huaihai Zhong Lu, near Xiangyang Nan Lu ⓣ8008190089; Singapore Airlines, Plaza 66, Tower 1, 1266 Nanjing Xi Lu ⓣ62887999; Thai Airways, Unit 105, Kerry Centre, 1515 Nanjing Xi Lu ⓣ52985555; United Airlines, Room 3301, Central Plaza, 381 Huaihai Zhong Lu ⓣ33114567; Virgin Atlantic Suite 221, 2F, 12 The Bund ⓣ53534600.

American Express Room 206, Shanghai Centre, 1376 Nanjing Xi Lu (Mon–Fri 9am–5.30pm; ⓣ021/62798082).

Banks and exchange The head office of the Bank of China is at 23 Zhongshan Lu (The Bund), next to the *Peace Hotel* (Mon–Fri 9am–noon & 1.30–4.30pm, Sat 9am–noon). Next door is a Citibank ATM machine with 24hr access.

Consulates Australia, 22F, 1168 Nanjing Xi Lu ⓣ22155200, Ⓦ www.shanghai.china.embassy.gov.au; Canada, Room 604, West Tower, Shanghai Centre, 1376 Nanjing Xi Lu ⓣ32792800, www.china.gc.ca; New Zealand, 15F, Qihua Building, 1375 Huaihai Zhong Lu ⓣ64711127; Republic of Ireland, 700A Shanghai Centre, 1376 Nanjing Xi Lu ⓣ62798729, Ⓦ www.embassyofireland.cn/Ireland/consulate.htm; South Africa, Room 2706, 220 Yanan Zhong Lu ⓣ53594977; UK, Room 301, West Tower, Shanghai Centre, 1376 Nanjing Xi Lu ⓣ62797650; US, 1469 Huaihai Zhong Lu ⓣ62797662, Ⓦ shanghai.usembassy-china.org.cn.

Football During the football season (winter) you can watch Shanghai's main team, Shenhua (Ⓦ www.shenhua.com.cn) play every other Sun at 3.30pm at the 35,000-seat Hongkou Football Stadium, 444 Dongjianwan Lu, in the north of town. Tickets are ¥30 and can be bought at the ground on the day.

Hospitals A number of the city's hospitals have special clinics for foreigners, including the Huadong Hospital (Ⓣ 021/62483180) at 221 Yan'an Xi Lu and the Hua Shan Hospital (go to the eighth floor; Ⓣ 021/62489999 ext 2531) at 12 Wulumuqi Lu. You'll find top-notch medical care at World Link Medical and Dental Centres (Ⓣ 021/62797688, Ⓦ www.worldlink-shanghai.com) in Suite 203 of the Shanghai Centre West Tower at 1376 Nanjing Xi Lu, but they are pricey at ¥700/consultation.

Internet Netbars are dotted around the back streets (¥3/hr; 24hr); you'll need to show your passport before you're let near a computer. There's a handy internet office in the basement of the Shanghai Library at 1555 Huaihai Zhong Lu (daily 8.30am–8pm; ¥4/hr).

Mail The main post office (see p.376) is at 1 Sichuan Bei Lu, just north of and overlooking Suzhou Creek. It offers a very efficient parcel service; the express option can get packages to Britain or the US within two days. Poste restante arrives at the Bei Suzhou Lu office across the street – each separate item is recorded on a little slip of cardboard in a display case near the entrance. Both the main post office and the poste restante service are open daily (9am–7pm). Branch post offices dot the city, with convenient locations along Nanjing Dong Lu, Huaihai Zhong Lu, in the Portman Centre, and near the Huangpu River ferry jetties at the corner of Jinling Dong Lu and Sichuan Bei Lu.

PSB 210 Hankou Lu, near the corner of Henan Zhong Lu. For visa extensions, go to 1500 Minsheng Lu, in Pudong, near Yinchun Lu (Science and Technology Museum subway stop; Mon–Fri 9am–11.30pm & 1.30–4.30pm). The visa office is on the third floor.

Travel agents CITS has an office (Ⓣ 021/63233384, Ⓕ 63290295) at 66 Nanjing Dong Lu, providing travel and entertainment tickets, with a small commission added on. There's another CITS office (Ⓣ 021/62898899) at 1277 Beijing Xi Lu, as well as a transport ticket office just off the Bund at 2 Jinling Dong Lu; all branches are open daily (8.30am–5pm). Most hotels have travel agencies offering the same services.

Travel details

Trains

Shanghai Station to: Beijing (3 daily, 11hr; express trains leave from the south station); Changzhou (frequent; 1–3hr); Chengdu (3 daily; 35–42hr);Guangzhou (4 daily; 15–20hr); Harbin (daily; 33hr); Hefei (13 daily; 4hr); Hong Kong (daily; 32hr); Huangshan (2 daily; 12hr); Lanzhou (4 daily; 25hr); Nanjing (frequent; 2–3hr); Qingdao (2 daily; 10–18hr); Shaoxing (6 daily; 3–5hr); Shenyang (4 daily; 15–26hr); Suzhou (frequent; 1hr; express trains leave from Hongqiao station); Tai'an (for Qufu; daily; 25hr); Ürümqi (daily; 45hr); Wuxi (frequent; 1hr); Xi'an (8 daily; 14–21hr); Xuzhou (frequent; 5hr); Zhengzhou (frequent; 7–14hr); Zhenjiang (frequent; 1–3hr).

Shanghai South Station to: Beijing (7 express daily, 10hr); Changsha (4 daily; 8–14hr); Chongqing (2 daily; 30–44hr); Fuzhou (10 daily; 7hr); Guilin (3 daily; 24hr); Hangzhou (frequent; 2hr); Kunming (3 daily; 42hr); Nanchang (8 daily; 10hr); Nanning (2 daily; 28hr); Ningbo (frequent; 3hr); Xiamen (2 daily; 30hr).

Shanghai Hongqiao station to: Suzhou (frequent expresses daily; 30min).

Buses

Shanghai to: Hangzhou (frequent; 3hr); Lianyungang (5 daily; 8hr); Nanjing (frequent; 4hr); Shaoxing (6 daily; 4hr); Suzhou (frequent; 1hr); Wenzhou (3 daily; 12hr); Wuxi (35 daily; 3hr); Yangzhou (13 daily; 5hr); Zhouzhuang (4 daily; 1hr 30min).

Ferries

Shanghai to: Inchon (South Korea; weekly; 22hr); Kobe (Japan; 1 weekly; 38hr); Osaka (Japan; 1 weekly; 36hr); Putuo Shan (4 daily; 4–12hr).

Flights

Shanghai to: Baotou (2 weekly; 2hr 50min); Beijing (16 daily; 1hr 50min); Changsha (5 daily; 4hr); Changchun (4 daily; 2hr 45min); Chengdu (12 daily; 2hr 45min); Chongqing (8 daily; 2hr 30min); Dalian (5 daily; 1hr 30min); Fuzhou (11 daily;

1hr 30 min); Guangzhou (10 daily; 2hr); Guilin (4 daily; 2hr 20min); Haikou (4 daily; 3hr); Harbin (2–4 daily; 2hr 40min); Hefei (4 daily; 1hr); Hohhot (3 weekly; 2hr 20min); Hong Kong (19 daily; 2hr 10min); Huangshan (3 daily; 1hr); Kunming (9 daily; 3hr); Lanzhou (1–2 daily; 3hr); Lhasa (2 weekly; 6hr); Lijiang (daily; 4hr 30min); Macau (2 daily; 2hr 20 min); Nanning (2 daily; 3hr); Ningbo (daily; 40min); Qingdao (daily; 1hr 20min); Shenzhen (daily; 2hr); Taiyuan (daily; 2hr); Tianjin (8 daily; 1hr 30min); Ürümqi (4 daily; 5hr); Wenzhou (1–3 daily; 1hr); Wuhan (3 daily; 1hr); Xiamen (3 daily; 1hr 30min); Xi'an (7 daily; 2hr 15min); Xining (daily; 4hr); Yichang (2 daily; 1hr 30min).

CHAPTER 7 Highlights

* **Yixian** An amazing collection of antique Ming villages, used atmospherically in Zhang Yimou's film *Raise the Red Lantern*. See p.425

* **Huang Shan** Arguably China's most scenic mountain, wreathed in narrow stone staircases, contorted trees and cloud-swept peaks. See p.425

* **Hubei Provincial Museum, Wuhan** On show here are 2000-year-old relics from the tombs of aristocrats, including a lacquered coffin and an orchestra of 64 giant bronze bells. See p.434

* **Shennongjia Forest Reserve** Wild and remote mountain refuge of the endangered golden monkey and (allegedly) the enigmatic *ye ren*, China's Bigfoot. See p.440

* **Wudang Shan** Temple-covered mountains at the heart of Taoist martial-art mythology; it's said this is where *tai ji* originated. See p.441

* **Jingdezhen** China's porcelain capital for the last six centuries, with a fine ceramic history museum and busy street markets. See p.468

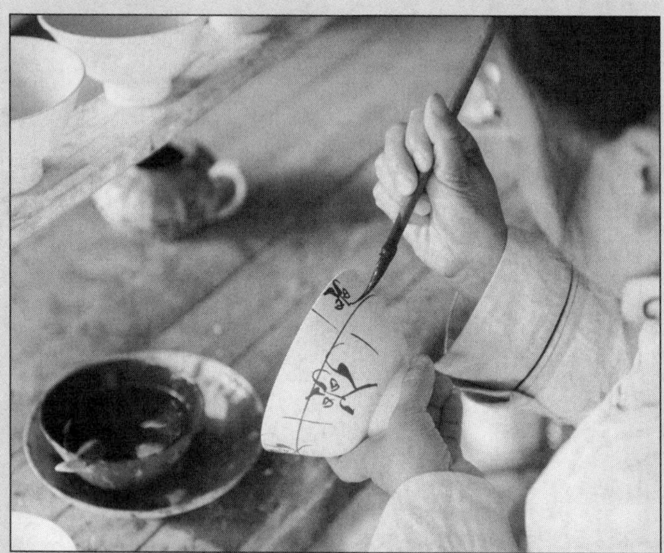

▲ Ancient Porcelain Workshop in Jingdezhen, Jiangxi

The Yangzi basin

Having raced out of Sichuan through the narrow Three Gorges, the **Yangzi** (here known as the **Chang Jiang**) widens, slows down and loops through its flat, low-lying middle reaches, swelled by lesser streams and rivers that drain off the highlands surrounding the four provinces of the Yangzi basin: **Anhui**, **Hubei**, **Hunan** and **Jiangxi**. As well as watering one of China's key rice- and tea-growing areas, this stretch of the Yangzi has long supported trade and transport; back in the thirteenth century, Marco Polo was awed by the "innumerable cities and towns along its banks, and the amount of shipping it carries, and the bulk of merchandise that merchants transport by it". Rural fringes away from the river – including much of Anhui and Jiangxi provinces – remain some of the least developed regions in central China, a situation the mighty **Three Gorges Dam** on the border between Hubei and Chongqing, whose hydroelectric output powers a local industrial economy to rival that of the east coast, is going some way to address.

The river basin itself is best characterized by the flat expanses of China's two largest freshwater lakes: **Dongting**, which pretty well marks the border between Hunan and Hubei, and **Poyang**, in northern Jiangxi, famed for porcelain produced at nearby **Jingdezhen**. Riverside towns such as **Wuhu** in Anhui also hold interest as working ports, where it's possible to see traditional river industries – fish farming, grain, rice and bamboo transportation – exist alongside newer ventures in manufacturing. Strangely enough, while all four regional capitals are located near water, only **Wuhan**, in Hubei, is actually on the Yangzi, a privileged position that has turned the city into central China's liveliest urban conglomeration. By contrast, Anhui's **Hefei** and Jiangxi's Nanchang seem somewhat dishevelled. Long settlement of the capitals has, however, left a good deal of history in its wake, from well-preserved Han-dynasty tombs to whole villages of Ming-dynasty houses, and almost everywhere you'll stumble over sites from the epic of *The Three Kingdoms*, making the tale essential background reading (see box, p.993). Many cities also remain studded with hefty European buildings, a hangover from their being forcibly opened up to foreign traders as **Treaty Ports** in the 1860s, following the Second Opium War. Perhaps partly due to these unwanted intrusions, the Yangzi basin can further claim to be the **cradle of modern China**: Mao Zedong was born in Hunan; Changsha, Wuhan and Nanchang are all closely associated with Communist Party history; and the mountainous border between Hunan and Jiangxi was both a Red refuge during right-wing purges in the late 1920s and the starting point for the subsequent Long March to Shaanxi.

Away from the river, wild mountain landscapes make for excellent hiking, the prime spot being **Huang Shan** in southern Anhui, followed by Hubei's remote

Shennongjia Forest Reserve, and **Wulingyan Scenic Reserve** (known locally as Zhangjiajie) in Hunan's far west. Pilgrims also have a selection of Buddhist and Taoist holy mountains to scale – Hubei's **Wudang Shan** is outstanding – and less dedicated souls can find pleasant views at the mountain resort town of **Lu Shan** in Jiangxi. As an alternative to the better-known Huang Shan, Anhui's **Jiuhua Shan** has many advantages: it's lower (the highest peak is a little over 1300m), the walking is considerably easier and there's plenty of interest beyond the scenery.

In theory, **getting around** isn't a problem. **Rail** lines from all over China cross the region, and **buses** and swifter, pricier minibuses link cities to the remotest of corners. **Ferries**, once the principal mode of transport, have been superseded, with passenger services now limited to the stretch between Wuhan and Chongqing. Autumn is probably the most pleasant time of year, though even winters are generally mild, but near-constant rains and consequential lowland flooding plague the summer months. In 1998, **floods** claimed four thousand lives, wiped out entire villages, isolated cities and destroyed millions of hectares of crops, and a similar disaster was only narrowly averted in 2002. In 2010, torrential rains upstream saw the **Three Gorges Dam** – trumpeted as the solution to the region's water management problems – put to its stiffest test since completion, amid swift backpedalling from its supporters: while the dam held, both land and people felt the destructive effects of the flooding. During building it was claimed the dam could deal with everything but a "once in 10,000 year flood", by 2007 that had been reduced to "once every 1000 years" and in 2008 to "once in every 100 years". By 2010, Chinese lawmakers were saying the dam's flood prevention abilities were "limited" and "should not be overestimated".

Sanguo: The Three Kingdoms

The empire, long divided, must unite; long united, must divide. Thus it has ever been.

So, rather cynically, begins one of China's best-known stories, the fourteenth-century historical novel **Romance of the Three Kingdoms** (三国, *sān guó*). Covering 120 chapters and a cast of thousands, the story touches heavily on the Yangzi basin, which, as a buffer zone between the Three Kingdoms, formed the backdrop for many major battles and key events. Some surviving sites are covered in this chapter and elsewhere in the guide.

The *Romance of the Three Kingdoms* is essentially fictionalized, though well founded in historical fact. Opening in 168 AD, the tale recounts the decline of the Han empire, how China was split into three states by competing warlords, and the subsequent (short-lived) reunification of the country in 280 AD under a new dynasty. The main action begins in 189 AD. At this point, the two protagonists were the villainous **Cao Cao** and the virtuous **Liu Bei**, whose watery character was compensated for by the strength of his spirited sworn brothers **Zhang Fei** and **Guan Yu** – the latter eventually becoming enshrined in the Chinese pantheon as the red-faced god of war and healing. Having put down the Yellow Turban taoist secret society uprising in 184 AD in the name of the emperor, both Cao and Liu felt their position threatened by the other; Cao was regent to the emperor **Xian**, but Liu had a remote blood tie to the throne. Though both claimed to support the emperor's wishes, Cao and Liu began fighting against each other, with Cao being defeated in Hubei at the **Battle of the Red Cliffs** (208 AD) after Liu engaged the aid of the wily adviser **Zhuge Liang**, who boosted Liu's heavily outnumbered forces by enlisting the help of a third warlord, **Sun Quan**.

Consolidating their positions, each of the three formed a private kingdom: Cao Cao retreated north to the Yellow River basin where he established the state of **Wei** around the ailing imperial court; Sun Quan set up **Wu** farther south along the lower Yangzi; while Liu Bei built a power base in the riverlands of Sichuan, the state of Shu. The alliance between Shu and Wu fell apart when Sun Quan asked Guan Yu to betray Liu. Guan refused and was assassinated by Sun in 220 AD. At this point Cao Cao died, and his ambitious son, **Cao Pi**, forced the emperor to abdicate and announced himself head of a new dynasty. Fearing retaliation from the state of Shu after Guan Yu's murder, Sun Quan decided to support Cao Pi's claims, while over in Shu, Liu Bei also declared his right to rule.

Against Zhuge Liang's advice, Liu marched against Wu to avenge Guan Yu's death, but his troops mutinied, killing Zhang Fei. Humiliated, Liu withdrew to Baidicheng in the Yangzi Gorges and died. With him out of the way, Cao Pi attacked Sun Quan, who was forced to renew his uncomfortable alliance with Shu – now governed by Zhuge Liang – to keep the invaders out of his kingdom. By 229 AD, however, things were stable enough for Sun Quan to declare himself as a rival emperor, leaving Zhuge to die five years later fighting the armies of Wei. Wei was unable to pursue the advantage, as a coup against Cao Pi started a period of civil war in the north, ending around 249 AD when the **Sima clan** emerged victorious. Sun Quan died soon afterwards, while Shu abandoned all claim to the empire. Wei's Sima clan founded a new dynasty, the **Jin**, in 265 AD, finally overpowering Wu and uniting China in 280 AD.

Anhui

Despite a government vision of **Anhui** (安徽, *ānhuī*) as a wealthy corridor between coast and interior, the region continues to live up to its reputation as eastern China's poorest province. It has a long history, however, and not all of it bad. Million-year-old remains of the proto-human *Homo erectus* have been found here, while Shang-era copper mines in southern Anhui fuelled China's Bronze Age. The province later became known for its artistic refinements, from decorative Han tombs through to Song-dynasty porcelain and Ming architecture.

Any success, however, has been in the face of Anhui's unfriendly geography. Arid and eroded, the north China plains extend into its upper third as far as the **Huai River**, and while the south is warmer and wetter, the fertile wooded hills soon climb to rugged mountains, where little can grow. Historically, though, the flood-prone **Yangzi** itself has ensured Anhui's poverty by regularly inundating the province's low-lying centre, which would otherwise produce a significant amount of crops. Until recently, a lack of bridges across the river also created a very physical division, separating the province's mountainous south from its more settled regions. Despite improvements in infrastructure since the 1990s, including the expansion of highways and railways, Anhui seems to remain, rather unfairly, as economically retarded as ever.

For the visitor, this isn't all bad news. Neither **Hefei** – the provincial capital – nor the north has much beyond history; yet there are compensations for Anhui's lack of development south of the Yangzi. Here, superlative mountain landscapes at **Huang Shan** and the collection of Buddhist temples at **Jiuhua Shan** have been pulling in sightseers for centuries, and there's a strong cultural tradition stamped on the area, with a substantial amount of antique rural architecture surviving intact around **Tunxi**. A riverside reserve near Xuancheng protects the **Chinese alligator**, one of the world's most endangered animals, though another local species, the **Yangzi river dolphin**, is now classified extinct.

Flooding aside (and there's a near guarantee of this affecting bus travel during the summer months), the main problem with finding your way around Anhui is that many towns have a range of aliases, and can be differently labelled on maps and timetables. **Rail lines** connect Hefei to Nanjing through **Wuhu** – Anhui's major port – with other lines running west towards Changsha, north to Xi'an and Beijing, and south from Tunxi to Jiangxi.

Hefei

Nestled in the heart of the province but generally overlooked in the rush to cross the Yangzi and reach Huang Shan, Anhui's capital, **HEFEI** (合肥, *héféi*) gets few chance visitors. Only developed as a modest industrial base after 1949, Hefei's sole points of interest are a couple of **historical sites** and an unusually thorough **museum**. The street layout retains its concentric ring-roads of yore, which can make navigation confusing, but aside from that, with its concrete highrises and *KFC*s, there's little to differentiate Hefei from countless other modern Chinese cities. Nevertheless, it's a comfortable enough place to stay, can be a handy transport hub and the locals will be happy, if perhaps surprised, to see you.

Arrival and information

Luogang airport is about 11km from the city, and reachable by taxi (¥40). The **airlines office** (daily 8am–10pm; ⓣ0551/2886626), whose entrance doubles as a florist's, is on Huizhou Dadao. The **train station** is 3km northeast of the centre at the end of Shengli Lu – bus #119 runs down Shengli Lu and into town along Changjiang Lu – with lines servicing Bozhou, Shanghai, Guangzhou, Chengdu, Xiamen and Beijing. There's a train ticket booth, attached to a travel agency selling air tickets, a little north from **Changjiang Lu** (长江路, *chángjiānglù*) – the main street – along the west side of Fuyang Lu.

Hefei's main **bus station**, on Mingguang Lu, handles traffic from all over Anhui and adjacent provincial capitals, though there are just as many services from the chaotic clutch of **minibus depots** nearby on Shengli Lu – leaving, you'll have to hunt around stations for the right vehicle.

Accommodation

Hefei has a range of unremarkable **places to stay**. Some of the budget hotels near the bus stations have cheap dorm beds.

7 Days Inn (7天连锁酒店, *qī tiānliánsuǒjiǔdiàn*) 299 Changjiang Zhong Lu ⓣ0551/2248177. Right in the centre of town, this characterless but scrupulously clean chain hotel is undeniably great value. ❸

Anhui Hotel (安徽饭店, *ānhūifàndiàn*) 88 Meishan Lu ⓣ0551/221888888, ⓔanhuihtl@mail.hf.ah.cn. Smart business hotel marred by its faded exterior. Staff speak English and rooms are of a decent standard. ❺

Donghai Fandian (东海饭店, *dōnghǎi fàndiàn*) 139 Mingguang Lu ⓣ0551/4693004. The best-value budget accommodation in town, with small, comfortable doubles and larger twin rooms. ❷

Hilton (希尔顿酒店, *xīěrdùnjiǔdiàn*) 198 Shengli Lu ⓣ0551/2808888, ⓔhefei@hilton.com.

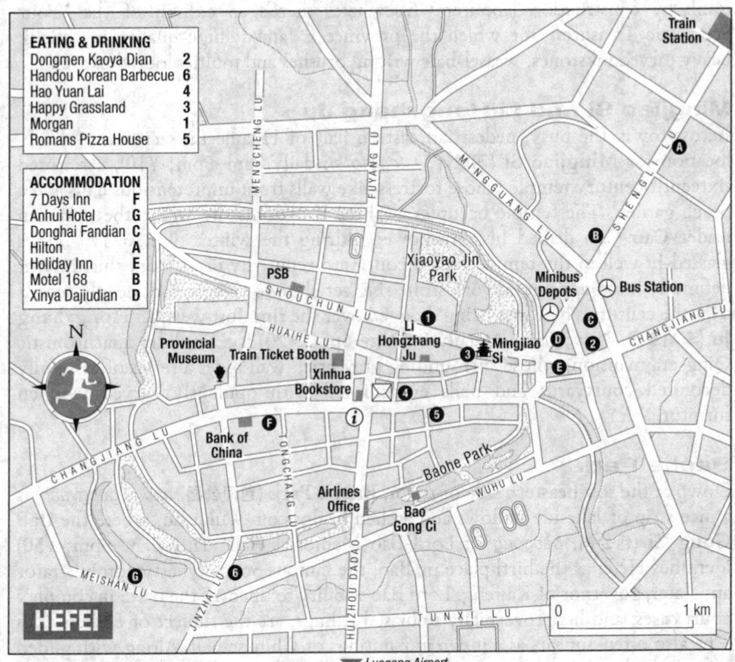

A huge, opulent lobby, quality rooms and all the other services you would expect at a Hilton. ❼

Holiday Inn (古井假日酒店, *gǔjǐng jiàrì jiǔdiàn*) 1104 Changjiang Lu ⓣ0551/2206666, ⓦwww.holiday-inn.com/hefeichina, ⓔhihfe@mail.hf.ah.cn. The usual range of facilities, along with a surprisingly good and inexpensive 24hr noodle bar. There's also a coffeeshop alongside the fifth-floor reception. ❼

Motel 168 (莫泰连锁旅店, *mòtàiliánsuǒ lǚdiàn*) Shengli Lu ⓣ0551/5186777. Another of China's growing phalanx of budget chain hotels is just a quick hop from either station. Smart, good-value, clean rooms. ❹

Xinya Dajiudian (新亚大酒店, *xīnyà dàjiǔdiàn*) Near the bus stations on Shengli Lu ⓣ0551/2203088, ⓦwww.xinyahotel.cn. The once-upmarket lobby is reflected in the worn furnishings upstairs, but rooms are large, everything works and the staff are happy to have you. ❹

The City

Ringed by parkland and canals – the remains of Ming-dynasty moats – downtown Hefei resembles a suburban high street more than a provincial capital. The few sights worth mentioning aren't too far off that main strip.

The Provincial Museum

The **Provincial Museum** on Mengcheng Lu (省博物馆, *shěng bówùguǎn*; Tues–Sun 9am–5pm; free) provides sound evidence of Anhui's contributions to Chinese culture. A walk-through plaster cave of plastic dinosaurs follows on from a cast of the *Homo erectus* cranium from Taodian in the south of the province, proudly displayed in an oversized glass case. Comparatively recent history emerges in a few Stone Age items and an exceptional Shang bronze urn decorated with tiger and dragon motifs. Also interesting are the carved blocks taken from Han-dynasty mausoleums – Chinese-speakers might be able to decipher the comments about the Cao family (of *The Three Kingdoms* fame) incised into the bricks of their Bozhou tomb by construction labourers. Elsewhere, there's an exhibit of the "Four Scholastic Treasures" for which the province is famed: high-quality ink sticks, heavy carved inkstones, weasel-hair writing brushes and multicoloured papers.

Mingjiao Si and Li Hongzhang Ju

Across town, the busy, pedestrian eastern half of Huaihe Lu seems an unlikely location for **Mingjiao Si** (明教寺, *míngjiào sì*; daily 7am–6pm; ¥10), a restored sixteenth-century temple whose fortress-like walls front unpretentious halls and a peach garden. The temple occupies a Three Kingdoms site where the northern leader **Cao Cao** drilled his crossbowers during the winter of 216–17 AD. A glassed-in well in the temple's main courtyard reputedly dates from this time; it definitely looks ancient, a worn stone ring set close to the ground, deeply scored over the centuries by ropes being dragged over the rim. Just west, **Li Hongzhang Ju** (李鸿章居, *lǐhóngzhāng jū*; daily 8.30am–6pm; ¥20) is a similarly anachronistic Qing-era mansion, whose surrounding grey brick wall hides a series of tastefully decorated courtyards and halls embellished with opulently carved wooden furniture.

Baohe Park

Down at the southeastern side of town, **Baohe Park** (包河公园, *bāohé gōngyuán*) is a nice strip of lakeside willows and arched bridges off Wuhu Lu, where the **Bao Gong Ci** (包公祠, *bāogōng cí*; Lord Bao Memorial Hall; daily 8am–6pm; ¥50) identifies Hefei as the birthplace of Bao, the famous Song-dynasty administrator and, later, governor of Kaifeng. Lord Bao's ability to uncover the truth in complex court cases, and his proverbially unbiased rulings, are the subject of endless tales – he also often appears as a judge in paintings of Chinese hell. Along with gilded statues, some waxworks bring a couple of well-known stories to life: look for Lord Bao's dark face, improbably "winged" hat and the three axes – shaped as a dragon, tiger and dog – he had made for summary executions; the implement used was chosen according to the status of the condemned.

Eating, drinking and entertainment

Off the Huaihe Lu pedestrian street, a warren of alleys holds **stalls** and **canteens** where you can fill up on stir-fries, noodle soups and river food. There's an excellent hotpot to be had at *Happy Grassland* (欢乐牧场火锅, *huānlèmùchǎnghuǒguō*), in a cavernous basement next door to Mingjiao Si, where friendly staff will help you pick your way through the menu, and more DIY fare on the southwest side of town at *Handou Korean Barbecue* (韩都烤肉餐厅, *hándoū kǎoyā cāntīng*), if you fancy cooking your own steak at the table. Round the corner from the *Donghai Fandian*, the *Dongmen Kaoya Dian* (东门烤鸭店, *dōngmén kǎoyā diàn*) is a fantastic, hugely popular example of a dying breed of basic Chinese canteen – no frills, but the open kitchen turns out lots of tasty dishes for just a few yuan each. *Romans Pizza Housh* (罗麦斯意大利比萨屋, *luómàisīyìdàlìbǐsàwū*), on Changjiang Lu, is better at cooking than spelling; nearby are the usual plethora of Western fast-food outlets and, for a steak meal, *Hao Yuan Lai* (好缘来, *haǒyuán laí*; ¥35 and up).

Morgan, on Shouchun Lu, is a fair approximation of a Western **bar**, while there are a couple of more upmarket watering holes toward the train station in the *Hilton*. Further evening entertainment can be had browsing the **night markets** that spring up in the streets north of Huaihe Lu, as well as around the junction of Shengli Lu and Mingguang Lu, and opposite the train station.

Listings

Banks and exchange The Bank of China (Mon–Fri 8.30am–5.30pm) is on Changjiang Lu.
Bookstores The Xinhua Bookstore on Changjiang Lu has some books in English – including translated Chinese novels – on the second floor.
Hospital There's one with English-speaking doctors at the junction of Tongchang Lu and Changjiang Lu.
Internet Upstairs at the post office (below).
Mail The post office (daily 8am–6pm) is on Changjiang Lu.
PSB On Shouchun Lu, a few blocks north of Changjiang Lu.
Travel agents A tourist information office/travel agency sits on the corner of Changjiang Lu and Huizhou Dadao.

Northern Anhui

Cynics say that northern Anhui's high points are its roads, which run on flood-proof embankments a few metres above pancake-flat paddy fields. Certainly, about the only geographic features are **rivers** such as the **Huai He**, setting for the rather drab industrial centre of **Bangbu** (蚌埠, *bàngbù*). The **battle of Huai Hai** took place nearby in 1948, when a million Guomindang and PLA combatants fought a decisive encounter in which the guerrilla-trained Communists overran Chiang Kai-shek's less flexible forces. A demoralized GMD surrendered in Beijing in January the next year, and though war resumed when the two sides couldn't agree on terms, it was largely a mopping-up operation by the Communists against pockets of GMD control.

All this is mainly background for what you'll see along the way, but anyone interested in traditional Chinese medicine will find attractions at **Bozhou**, which is worth a day's scrutiny on the long haul into or out of the province. There are **minibuses** throughout the day from Hefei's Shengli Lu depots.

Bozhou

BOZHOU (亳州, *bózhōu*) lies in Anhui's northwestern corner, around five hours from Hefei, the journey taking in scenes of river barges loading up with coal, red-brick villages, and a level horizon pierced by kiln chimneys. The city's fame rests on it being the largest marketplace in the world for traditional **Chinese medicine**; as the birthplace of **Hua Mulan**, heroine of Chinese legend and Disney animation; and as the ancestral home of *The Three Kingdoms'* **Cao Cao**, traditionally portrayed as a self-serving villain whose maxim was "Better to wrong the world than have it wrong me".

Orientation and arrival

Bozhou's centre is a 2km-wide grid just south of the slow-flowing **Wo He River**, the main roads being the east–west Renmin Lu and the north–south Qiaoling Lu that intersect on the eastern side of town. The **train station** is about 3km southeast – best reached by taxi – and has a few services down to Hefei each day. An alternative rail option is to catch a bus south to Fuyang (around 90min), which is on the Beijing–Jiujiang and Hefei–Zhengzhou lines. The two adjacent **bus stations** on Qiaoling Lu mostly serve Hefei, Fuyang or local destinations, with a few long-distance buses to adjoining provinces.

The **Bank of China** is also on the crossroads, with the main **post office** 500m west on Renmin Zhong Lu.

The City

About 3km southeast of the centre, the eastern end of Zhan Qian Lu (the train station approach road) sets up on weekdays as a **medicinal market**, attracting around 60,000 traders daily from all over China and Southeast Asia. The main **Chinese Medicinal Products Marketplace** (中药材交易中心, *zhōngyàocái jiāoyìzhōngxīn*) is a huge building on the south side of the road, packed to the rafters with bales of dried plants, fungi – including the bizarre caterpillar fungus, or *cordyceps* – and animals (or bits of them). The market and its strangely reassuring smell alone justify the trip, but you need to arrive early – perhaps coming to town the night before – as the indoor market closes at 10am.

The rest of Bozhou is for history buffs. On the south side of Renmin Zhong Lu, **Dixia Yunbing Dao** (地下运兵道, *dìxià yùnbīngdào*; ¥20) is a 100m-long tunnel Cao Cao had installed so his troops could take an invading army by surprise. North from here, Renmin Bei Jie is the heart of Bozhou's **Muslim quarter**, full of noodle-, bread- and mutton kebab-vendors, and containing a couple of small mosques.

Bozhou's architectural masterpiece is **Huaxi Lou** (花戏楼, *huāxì lóu*; ¥20), a seventeenth-century guild-temple theatre at the river end of Nanjing Gang. Sporting skilfully carved brick and wood embellishments, the theatre is named after the Han-dynasty doctor **Hua Tuo**, the first person credited with using anaesthetics during surgery, and who was bumped off by Cao Cao after refusing to become the warlord's personal physician. The friezes surrounding the stage show several well-known *The Three Kingdoms* set pieces, while the theatre's rear hall contains a collection of Neolithic stone axes and Eastern Han artefacts unearthed nearby.

Accommodation and eating

The intersection of Renmin Lu and Qiaoling Lu, about 500m south of the bus stations, marks a heap of **accommodation** options. The three-star *Gujing Dajiudian* (古井大酒店, *gǔjǐng dàjiǔdiàn*; ⓣ0558/5521298; ❸) has some pretensions to comfort with the usual cloned Chinese-hotel rooms replete with bad carpets and loose fittings.

Hotpot and noodle stalls abound in the alleys off the crossroads, and the *Gujing Dajiudian*'s **restaurant** offers tasty, if pricey, standard Chinese fare.

The Yangzi: Ma'anshan and Xuancheng

The **Yangzi** (长江, *chángjiāng*) flows silt-grey and broad for 350km across Anhui's lower third, forming a very visible geographic boundary – the fact that as recently as 1995 the only way to cross the river was by ferry is an indication of the province's chronic underdevelopment. It's now bridged in the east at Wuhu (芜湖, *wúhú*) and roughly halfway along at Tongling (铜岭, *tónglǐng*) where a reserve was at the forefront of unsuccessful efforts to save the *baiji*, or **Yangzi river dolphin** (白鳍河, *báijì hé*). Though the animals – 2.5m-long white river dolphins with a long thin snout and a stubby dorsal fin – were common as recently as the 1970s, a 2007 survey of the river failed to find a single one, the species' demise linked to industrial pollution, river traffic and net fishing. The dolphins may linger on only in Tongling's **Baiji beer**, which has their Latin name, *Lipotes vexillifer*, stamped on the bottle cap.

Most of the riverside towns don't really justify special trips, but **Ma'anshan** and **Xuancheng** offer a modicum of interest for their poetic and herpetological associations, respectively.

Ma'anshan

MA'ANSHAN (马鞍山, *mǎ'ān shān*) is notable for cliffside scenery at **Cuiluo Shan** (翠螺山, *cuìlúo shān*; ¥40), twenty minutes on bus #4 from the bus or train station, and its vast expanse of parkland dotted with halls and pavilions commemorating Tang-dynasty poet **Li Bai** (aka Tai Bai, see p.993). Inspired by the scenery, Li Bai wrote many of his works here; he drowned nearby in 762 AD after drunkenly falling out of a boat while trying to touch the moon's reflection.

Ma'anshan's **bus** and **train stations** are on Hongqi Lu, which leads down to the town centre (head left out of the bus station or right out of the train station). There's a *Motel 168* (莫泰连锁旅店, *mòtàiliánsuǒ lǚdiàn*; Ⓣ0555/2753333; ❸) at 14 Hubei Lu, a fifteen-minute walk from the stations down Hongqi Lu and then left along the edge of Yushan Lake. The **Bank of China** and **post office** are both on Hubei Lu.

Xuancheng

Two hours by bus to the southeast of Wuhu, **XUANCHENG** (宣城, *xuānchéng*) is an untidy but friendly place worth visiting for its **Chinese alligator-breeding centre** (扬子鳄养殖场, *yángzǐè yǎngzhíchǎng*; daily 8am–5pm; ¥30). Wild populations of these timid alligators are few and confined to Anhui, with their habitat ever more encroached upon, but a breeding programme has boosted their captive numbers here to ten thousand; it's a rare opportunity to see these animals up close. Tourist bus #5 from the bus station runs to the centre.

Xuancheng is about 2km across, with the **train station** on the eastern side and the main **bus station** to the southwest. For **accommodation**, the *Xuanzhou Binguan* is on Zhuangyuan Lu (宣州宾馆, *xuānzhōu bīnguǎn*; Ⓣ0563/3022957; ❸), near the bus station.

Jiuhua Shan

A place of worship for fifteen hundred years, **JIUHUA SHAN** (九华山, *jiǔhuá shān*; also known as Nine Glorious Mountains, a name bestowed by the Tang man of letters Li Bai on seeing the major pinnacles rising up out of clouds) has been one of China's sacred Buddhist mountains ever since the Korean monk **Jin Qiaojue** (believed to be the reincarnation of the Bodhisattva Dizang, whose doctrines he preached) died here in a secluded cave in 794 AD. Today, there are more than seventy temples – some founded back in the ninth century – containing a broad collection of sculptures, religious texts and early calligraphy, though there are also plenty of visitors (many of them overseas Chinese and Koreans) and some outsized building projects threatening to overwhelm Jiuhua Shan's otherwise human scale. Even so, an atmosphere of genuine devotion is clearly evident in the often austere halls, with their wisps of incense smoke and distant chanting.

Arrival and mountain access

Though it's 60km south of the Yangzi and remote from major transport centres, Jiuhua Shan is straightforward enough to reach, with direct **buses** at least from Hefei, Tangkou, Taiping (Huang Shan), Tongling and Guichi. Other traffic might drop you 25km to the northeast at **Qingyang** (青阳, *qīngyáng*), from where

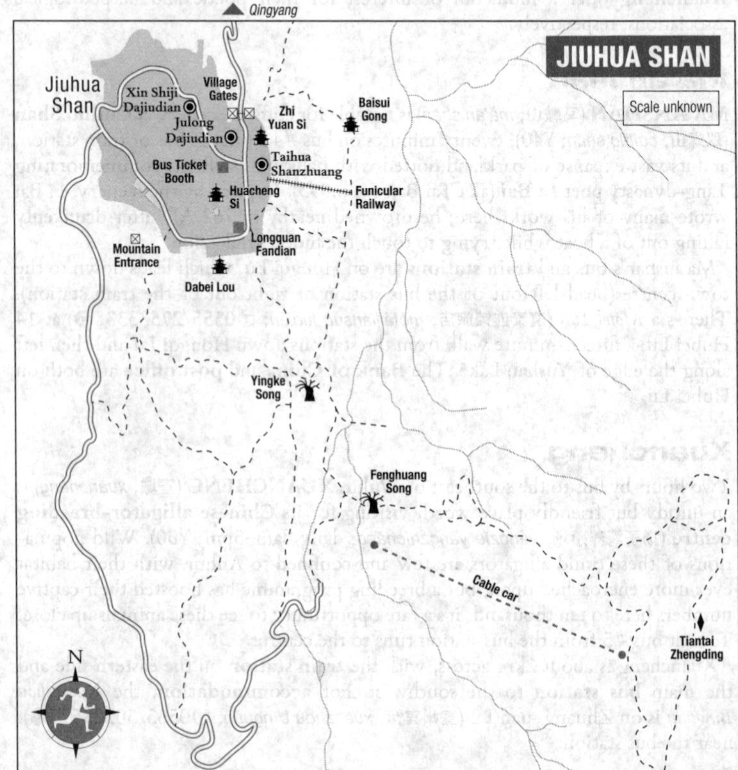

mountain **minibuses** (¥10) leave when full throughout the day; in case you arrive late, there's a cheap hotel attached to the bus station here.

The twisting Jiuhua Shan road passes villages scattered amidst the moist green of rice fields and bamboo stands, white-walled houses built of bricks interlocked in a "herringbone" pattern, with some inspiring views of bald, spiky peaks above and valleys below. The road ends at picturesque **Jiuhua Shan village**, where the mountain's accommodation and the most famous temples huddle around a couple of cobbled streets and squares, all hemmed in by encircling hills. Upon arrival at the village gates you'll have to pay an **entry fee** (March–Nov ¥190; Dec–Feb ¥140). From here the road runs up past a host of market stalls selling postcards, trinkets, and waterproof maps and umbrellas for the frequently sodden weather.

About 100m along, the road divides around the village in a 2km circuit; a booth selling onward bus tickets is just down on the right here, while the core of the village lies straight ahead. Long-distance transport to Hefei, Nanjing, Tangkou, Taiping, Tunxi and Shanghai congregates first thing in the morning near the booth, or you can pick up minibuses to Qingyang and look for connections there.

Accommodation and eating

You'll be grabbed on arrival and offered all manner of **accommodation**, most of it decent value. For more upmarket facilities try *Julong Dajiudian*, to the right of the village gates behind an illuminated fountain (聚笼大酒店, *jùlóng dàjiŭdiàn*; ⓣ0566/2831368; ❼), though check rooms for dampness first. On the other side of the street, *Zhiyuan Si* (执园寺, *zhíyuán sì*; ¥30) has extremely bare beds that may be available to tourists – though they're designed for itinerant monks. Up the main street on the left, look for steps and an English sign above a car park for *Taihua Shanzhuang* (太华山庄, *tàihuá shānzhuāng*; ⓣ0566/2831340, Ⓔjhswwx@163.com; ❹), a hospitable guesthouse with constant hot water and a very helpful travel service, although they don't speak English. For cheaper lodgings head up the hill past the bus ticket booth, where there are several smaller hotels with simple, shabby rooms (❷–❸). Numerous places to **eat** offer everything from cheap buns to expensive game dishes.

On Jiuhua Shan

Just inside the village gates, **Zhiyuan Si** (执园寺, *zhíyuán sì*; free) is an imposing Qing monastery built with smooth, vertical walls, upcurving eaves and a yellow-tiled roof nestled up against a cliff. Despite a sizeable exterior, the numerous little halls are cramped and stuffed with sculptures, including a fanged, bearded and hooknosed thunder god bursting out of its protective glass cabinet just inside the gate. Head for the main hall, in which a magnificently gilded Buddhist trinity sits solemnly on separate lotus flowers, blue hair dulled by incense smoke, and ringed by *arhats*. This makes quite a setting for the annual **temple fair**, held in Dizang's honour on the last day of the seventh lunar month, when the hall is packed with worshippers, monks and tourists. Make sure you look behind the altar, where Guanyin statuettes ascend right to the lofty wooden roof beams.

If you follow the main road around through the village, the next temple of note is the new and garish **Dabei Lou** (大悲楼, *dàbēi lóu*; ¥6), which sports some hefty carved stonework; more or less opposite, **Huacheng Si** (化城寺, *huàchéng sì*; ¥8) is the mountain's oldest surviving temple, which may date as far back as to the Tang, though it has been comprehensively restored. The stone entrance is set at the back of a large cobbled square whose centrepiece is a deep pond inhabited by some giant goldfish. Inside, Huacheng's low-ceilinged, broad main hall doubles as a museum, with paintings depicting the life of Jin Qiaojue from his sea crossing to China (accompanied only by a faithful hound) to his death at the age of 90, and the discovery of his miraculously preserved corpse three years later.

To the peaks

The mountain's official "entrance" is marked by a huge ornamental gateway and temple about 500m past Dabei Lou on the main road, though well-concealed, smaller flagstoned paths ascend from behind Zhiyuan Si and at the corners of the main road in the village. There's also a **funicular railway** (缆车站, *lǎnchē zhàn*; one-way; March–Nov ¥55, Dec–Feb ¥40) from the main street near Longquan Fandian to the ridge above. Using these access points, you can do a good, easy circuit walk on the ridges just above the village in about an hour, or extend this to a full day's hike up around Jiuhua's higher peaks – though again, you can save time by using park buses and the cable car. To get on the circuit, walk past Dabei Lou to where the road bends sharply right. Steps ascend from here to a temple complex whose entrance-hall atrium contains some gruesomely entertaining, life-size sculptures of Buddhist hell. These are so graphic that it's hard not to feel that the artists enjoyed their task of depicting sinners being skewered, pummelled, strangled, boiled and bisected by demons, the virtuous looking down, doubtless exceedingly thankful for their salvation. Beyond the temple, a few minutes' walk brings you to a meeting of several paths at **Yingke Song** (迎客松, *yíngkè sōng*; Welcoming Guest Pine). Bear left and it's a couple of kilometres past several pavilions and minor temples to **Baisui Gong** (百岁宫, *bǎisuì gōng*; ¥8), a plain, atmospheric monastery whose interior is far from weatherproof, with clouds drifting in and out of the main hall. A rear room contains the mummy of the Ming priest Wu Xia, best known for compiling the Huayan *sutras* in gold dust mixed with his own blood; his tiny body is displayed seated in prayer, grotesquely covered in a thick, smooth skin of gold leaf. Steps descend to Zhiyuan Si, or you can take the funicular railway down to the main street.

To reach the upper peaks, turn right at Yingke Song, and you've a two-hour climb ahead of you via **Fenghuang Song** (凤凰松, *fènghuáng sōng*; Phoenix Pine), more temples, wind-scoured rocks, and superb scenery surrounding the summit area at **Tiantai Zhengding** (天台正顶, *tiāntái zhèngdǐng*; Heavenly Terrace). There's also a **cable car** (索道站, *suǒdào zhàn*; one-way; March–Nov ¥75; Dec–Feb ¥55) from Fenghuang Song to just below the peaks. The truly indolent can catch a **minibus** from the entrance gate all the way to the Fenghuang Song terminus; these buses are included in the Jiuhua Shan entry fee.

Tunxi, Shexian and Yixian

The most obvious reason to stop in **Tunxi**, down near Anhui's southernmost borders, is for its transport connections to Huang Shan, 50km off to the northwest (see p.425): Tunxi has the closest airport and train station to the mountain, and many long-distance buses pass through as well. However, if you've even the slightest interest in classical **Chinese architecture**, then Tunxi and its environs are worth checking out in their own right. Anhui's isolation has played a large part in preserving a liberal sprinkling of seventeenth-century monuments and homes in the area, especially around **Shexian** (歙县, *shèxiàn*) and **Yixian** (黟县, *yīxiàn*).

Any exploration of Shexian will reveal traditional Ming and Qing architectural features, most notably the *paifang* or ornamental archways – there are over eighty of these in **She County** alone. Wood or stone, *paifang* can be over 10m in height, and are finely carved, painted or tiled, the central beam often bearing a moral inscription. They were constructed for a variety of reasons, foremost among which, cynics would argue, was the ostentatious display of wealth. This aside, the gateways were built to celebrate or reward virtuous behaviour, family success, important historical events or figures, and to reflect prevailing values such as filial piety; as such, they provide a valuable insight into the mores of the time.

Tunxi

An old trading centre, **TUNXI** (屯溪, *túnxī*; aka Huang Shan Shi) is set around the junction of two rivers, with the original part of town along the north bank of the Xin'an Jiang at the intersection of Huang Shan Lu and Xin'an Lu, and a newer quarter focused around the train and bus stations 1km or so to the northeast. If you've time to spare, try tracking down two Ming-dynasty houses in Tunxi's eastern backstreets (neither is well marked). The more easterly house is that of the mathematician **Cheng Dawei** (程大位居, *chéngdàwèi jū*); the other, closer to the old town, is known as the **Cheng Family House** (程氏三宅, *chéngshì sānzhái*). Both are classic examples of the indigenous **Huizhou style**, of which you'll find plenty more at Shexian or Yixian. Their plan, of two floors of galleried rooms based around a courtyard, became the template for urban domestic architecture in central and eastern China.

For more, head down to Tunxi's historic, flagstoned **Lao Jie** (老街, *lǎojiē*; Old Street), a westerly continuation of Huang Shan Xi Lu. Here, a long stretch of Ming **shops** running parallel to the river have been restored, selling local teas, medicinal herbs and all manner of artistic materials and "antiques" – inkstones, brushes, Mao badges, decadent advertising posters from the 1930s and carved wooden panels prised off old buildings. Look out for the characteristic horse-head gables rising out below the rooflines in steps. These originated as fire baffles

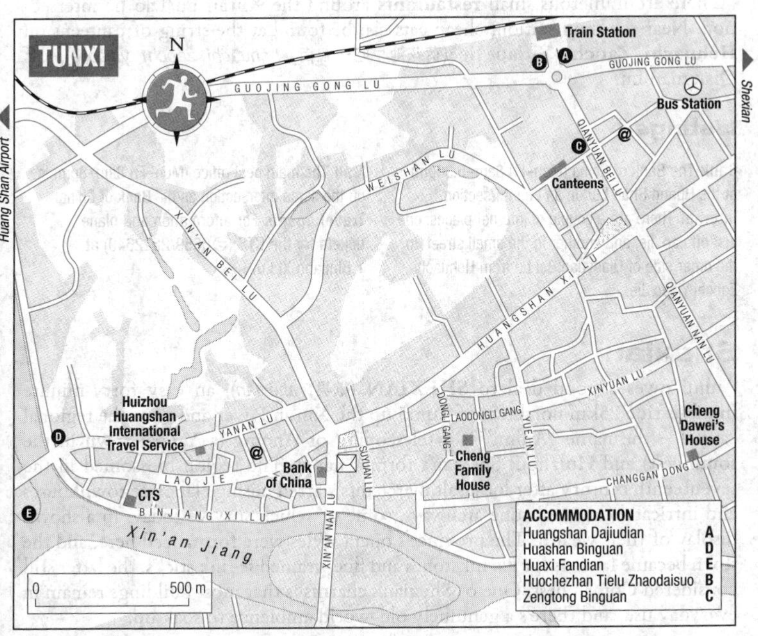

between adjoining houses, stopping the spread of flames from building to building, but became increasingly decorative.

Arrival and city transport

A taxi into the centre from busy **Huang Shan airport**, around 10km west of town, should cost around ¥20 on the meter. The **train station** is at the northern city limits on the end of Qianyuan Bei Lu; there are connections to Hefei (via Xuancheng and Wuhu), Nanchang, Shanghai, Xiamen and Beijing, along with useful, though ploddingly slow, "K" trains southwest to Jingdezhen. Tangkou **minibuses** prowl the station forecourt, while Tunxi's **bus station** occupies an entire block 250m east, off Guojing Gong Lu, with frequent services for Shexian, Yixian, Tangkou and Taiping, and long-distance departures to Jiuhua Shan, Wuhu, Hefei, Shanghai, Jiujiang, Nanchang and even Guangzhou.

A couple of **city buses** run around Tunxi: from the train station, #6 takes a back road into town, while #12 follows Huang Shan Xi Lu southwest from the bus station – either route is a twenty-minute walk.

Accommodation and eating

Convenient, if underwhelming, **places to stay** surround the train station, the best of which are the smart *Huangshan Dajiudian* (黄山大酒店, *huángshān dàjiǔdiàn*; ⓣ0559/2345188; ❸) directly opposite, and the nearby *Zengtong Binguan* (政通宾馆, *zhèngtōng bīnguǎn*; ⓣ0559/2112968; ❹), with comfortable, modern rooms. The *Huochezhan Tielu Zhaodaisuo* (火车站铁路招待所, *huǒchēzhàn tiělù zhāodàisuǒ*; ⓣ0559/2113699; ❷) is immediately to the right out of the train station and, for the price, has acceptable, tidy rooms. Near the old town and next to the bridge on Yanan Lu is the smart *Huashan Binguan* (华山宾馆, *huáshān bīnguǎn*; ⓣ0559/2328888; ❼), while on the opposite side of the river, the *Huaxi Fandian* is quiet and pleasant (花溪饭店, *huāxī fàndiàn*; ⓣ0559/2328000; ❼).

There are numerous small **restaurants** around the Xin'an Lu/Lao Jie intersection. Near the train station, cheap eats can be found at the string of canteens on **Hehuachi Zaochi Yitiao Jie** (荷花池早吃一条街, *héhuāchí zǎochī yìtiáojiē*), off Qianyuan Lu.

Listings

Bank The Bank of China (Mon–Fri 8am–5.30pm) is at the Huang Shan Lu/Xin'an Lu intersection.

Internet There are a couple of internet places: one just off Lao Jie, and another in the small street on the other side of Qianyuan Bei Lu from Hehuachi Zaochi Yitiao Jie.

Mail The main post office (Mon–Fri 8am–8pm) is on the same intersection as the Bank of China.

Travel agents For information and plane tickets try the CTS (ⓣ0559/2522649) at 1 Binjiang Xi Lu.

Shexian

Anhui owes a good deal to **SHEXIAN** (歙县, *shèxiàn*), an easy forty-minute minibus ride 25km northeast of Tunxi up the Xin'an River and once the regional capital – the name "Anhui" is a telescoping of Anqing (a Yangzi town in the southwest) and Huizhou, Shexian's former name. The region blossomed in the seventeenth century after local salt merchants started raising elaborate townhouses and intricately carved stone archways, some of which survive today, in a showy display of their wealth. The province's opera styles were formalized here, and the town became famous for *hui* inkstones and fine-grained *she* ink sticks, the latter still considered China's best. One of Shexian's charms is that most buildings remain in everyday use, and there's a genuinely old-world ambience to soak up.

Shexian's **bus station** is out on the highway. Don't stop for the "guides" and motor-rickshaw drivers who await – just take the bridge over the river and carry straight on past 100m of uninspiring, concrete-and-tile buildings; at the end of the road turn right, then take the first left, and you're walking up **Jiefang Jie**, off which run the narrow lanes that comprise the older part of town. To the sides you'll see the restored **Nan Lou** (南楼, *nánlóu*) and **Yanghe Men** (阳和门, *yánghé mén*) gate towers; straight ahead, however, Jiefang Jie runs under the smaller but highly decorative **Xuguo archway** (许国石坊, *xǔguó shífāng*) one of the finest in the region. Nearby are souvenir stalls and a bookshop, where you should pick up a **map** of Shexian (¥5) with all the streets and points of interest marked. You could just walk at random, snacking on traditional "pressed buns", but for a detailed look, seek out **Doushan Jie** (斗山街, *dǒushān jiē*), a street full of well-preserved Huizhou-style homes – choose one or more that looks appealing and pay (¥20) at the door for a poke around. When you've had enough, return to the station and get a Tunxi-bound minibus to drop you off around 5km down the highway, then walk or catch a motorbike-rickshaw for the last 3km to where the **Tangyue arches** (堂越牌坊, *tángyuè páifāng*; ¥50) form a strange spectacle of seven ornamental gates – a sentimental story behind the erection of each – standing isolated in a row in a field.

Yixian and around

YIXIAN (黟县, *yīxiàn*), 60km due west of Tunxi, should really only be seen as a stepping stone to the surrounding picturesque villages, two of which have been recognized as UNESCO World Heritage sites. One of those, **Xidi** (西递, *xīdì*; entry ¥104), is the pick of the bunch and hence the most visited; a particularly attractive place comprising some 120 eighteenth-century houses set along a riverbank. There are endless examples of carved gilded wooden screens and panels inside the houses, as well as thin line paintings on front walls showing pairs of animals or "double happiness" characters. Mirrors placed above the three-tiered door lintels reflect bad luck or reveal a person's true character – a useful tool for judging the nature of strangers. The other, **Hongcun** (宏村, *hóngcūn*), is also a fine spot, whose street plan resembles (with some imagination) the body of a buffalo, complete with horns, body and legs, while nearby **Nanping** (南屏村, *nánpíng cūn*), another preserved village of similar vintage, was used as a set in Zhang Yimou's disturbing film *Judou*. Combined admission for both Hongcun and Nanping is ¥104. Tourist buses from Tunxi bus station run direct to Xidi and Hongcun, while more regular minibus services shuttle to the villages from Yixian bus station. A more straightforward way to get around is to charter a cab from Yixian, which should cost around ¥150 for the day, but you'll need to haggle.

Huang Shan

Rearing over southern Anhui, **Huang Shan** (黄山, *húangshān*) – the Yellow Mountains – is among eastern China's greatest sights. It's said that once you've ascended these peaks you will never want to climb another mountain, and certainly the experience is staggeringly scenic, with pinnacles emerging from thick bamboo forests, above which rock faces dotted with ancient, contorted pine trees disappear into the swirling mists. Huang Shan's landscape has left an indelible impression on Chinese art, with painters a common sight on the paths, huddled in padded jackets and sheltering their work from the drizzle beneath umbrellas – the more serious of them spend months at a time up here.

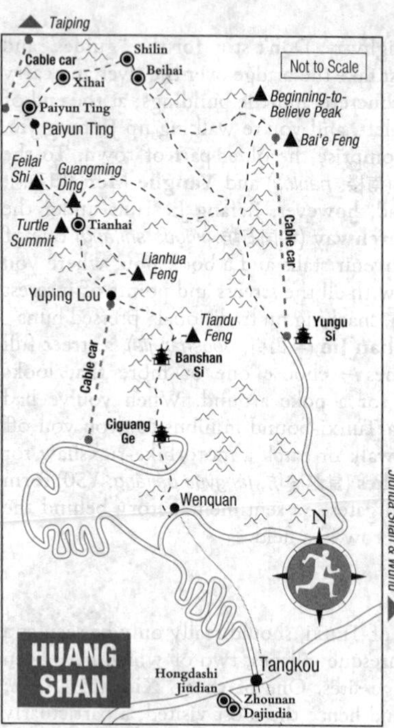

As a pilgrimage site trodden by emperors and Communist leaders alike, Huang Shan is regarded as sacred in China, and it's the ambition of every Chinese to conquer it at least once in their lifetime. Consequently, don't expect to climb alone: noisy multitudes swarm along the neatly paved paths, or crowd out the three cable-car connections to the top. All this can make the experience depressingly like visiting an amusement park, but then you'll turn a corner and come face to face with a huge, smooth monolith topped by a single tree, or be confronted with views of a remote square of forest growing isolated on a rocky platform. Nature is never far away from reasserting itself here.

Accessing Huang Shan

Transport pours into the Huang Shan region from all over eastern China. There are direct **buses** from Shanghai, Hangzhou and Nanjing, as well as Jiuhua Shan, Wuhu, Hefei and other places within Anhui. Much of this, and all **rail** and **air** traffic, passes through Tunxi (aka Huang Shan Shi; see p.423), with regular shuttle buses (¥13) connecting the train and bus stations here with Huang Shan's main gateway at **Tangkou**, 50km northwest of Tunxi on the mountain's southern foothills. Alternatively, **Taiping** is a lesser-used access point to the north of the mountain on the Jiuhua Shan–Tangkou road. Be aware that some long-distance buses go directly to Tangkou or Taiping, and might refer to these towns as "Huang Shan" on their timetables.

Tangkou (汤口, *tāngkǒu*) is the starting point for Huang Shan's two **hiking trails** and parallel **cable cars** (索道站, *suǒdào zhàn*; daily 8am–4.30pm; March–Nov ¥80, Dec–Feb ¥65). An additional cable car (same prices) is accessed from Taiping (太平, *tàipíng*) by catching a minibus from the main-street bus station for the 22-km ride to the terminus at Songgu. Note that queues for peak-bound cable cars can be quite long (there's usually less of a wait to go down) and that services are suspended during windy weather. The Huang Shan **entry fee** (March–Nov ¥230, Dec–Feb ¥150) is payable at the start of the trails or at the cable-car ticket offices. The cable cars take upwards of twenty minutes; you'll need between two and eight hours to walk up, depending on whether you follow the easier eastern route or the lengthy and demanding western route. Once at the top, there's a half-day of relatively easy hiking around the peaks. Ideally, plan to spend two or three days on the mountain to allow for a steady ascent and circuit, though it's quite feasible to see a substantial part of Huang Shan in a full day.

Practicalities

There's **accommodation** (mostly fairly expensive) and **food** available in Tangkou, Taiping and on the mountain itself, but you'll need to come prepared for steep paths, rain and winter snow – all an essential part of the experience. Note that in winter, hotels either dramatically drop their prices or close shop until spring. Accommodation in Tangkou and Taiping will store surplus gear; just bring a daypack, suitable footwear and something warm for the peak.

There are branches of the **Bank of China** in Tangkou, Wenquan and on the mountaintop, and Tangkou has an **internet café**, too.

Tangkou and Wenquan

Two hours from Tunxi, **TANGKOU** (汤口, *tāngkǒu*) is an unattractive jumble of narrow lanes, hotels and restaurants on the Taohua Gully, where roads from Wuhu, Tunxi and Jiuhua Shan meet. From here another road runs up the mountain to further accommodation 3km along at Wenquan, where the road divides and continues to the two trailheads.

Minibuses from Tunxi and Jiuhua Shan collect and drop off at Tangkou's central bridge, while the **long-distance bus stop** is 1km up the Wenquan road, near Huang Shan's official entrance. Tangkou's **places to stay** are of most interest to late arrivals: just off the main road, the *Hongdashi Jiudian* (洪大师酒店, *hóngdàshī jiǔdiàn*; ⓣ0559/5562577; ❷) has clean, comfortable rooms, as does the *Mingfang Dajiudian* (名方大酒店, *míngfāng dàjiǔdiàn*; ⓣ0559/5562387; ❷) next door. Alternatively, try the cheaper Chinese-oriented *Dazhong* (大众饭店, *dàzhòng fàndiàn*; ⓣ0559/5562453; ❷).

The cheapest spots to **eat** are at tables under the bridge, but there are a host of canteens all around the town, whose owners will drag you in as you walk past. Some have bilingual menus offering arresting delights such as squirrel hotpot and scrambled mountain frog, as well as more conventional dishes – if there's no price on the menu, agree the cost in advance to avoid being ripped off. You can also pick up umbrellas, walking sticks, warm clothes and mountain maps from hawkers and stalls around Tangkou. Heading up the mountain, minibuses wait on the Wenquan road, where you'll have to bargain hard for reasonable fares – around ¥5 to Wenquan and ¥10 to the eastern route at Yungu Si.

Wenquan

About 3km uphill from Tangkou where the mountain's two main ascent routes diverge, **WENQUAN** (温泉, *wēnquán*) is an altogether more pleasant prospect, surrounded by pine and bamboo forest and perched above the clear blue Taoyuan Stream and a noisy waterfall. The first thing you'll see here is the arched bridge over the gully, where the road heads on 8km to the eastern route's trailhead; follow the footpath upstream and it's about half an hour to **Ciguang Ge** (慈光阁, *cíguāng gé*; Merciful Light Pavilion), at the start of the western route. A minibus to either trailhead from Wenquan costs ¥5.

Places to stay are on either side of the stream. On the near side, the *Taoyuan Binguan* (桃源宾馆, *táoyuán bīnguǎn*; ⓣ0559/5562666; ❻) is one of the smarter options, while the new *Best Western Wenquan Dajiudian* (温泉大酒店, *wēnquán dàjiǔdiàn*; ⓣ0559/5582222; ⓦwww.bwhuangshan.com; ❻) is a hot springs resort hotel that dominates the area.

Huang Shan hikes

Huang Shan barely rises above 1870m, but as you struggle up either of the staircases on the trails it can begin to feel very high indeed. The **eastern route** is by far the easier; the road from Wenquan ends at **Yungu Si** (云谷寺, *yúngǔ sì*; Cloud Valley Temple), where a cable car can whisk you to the summit area at **Bai'e Feng** (白鹅峰, *bái'é fēng*) in twenty minutes – once you've queued two hours or so for your turn.

Alternatively, you can climb the steps to Bai'e Feng in under three hours, though the forest canopy tends to block views and the path is thick with **porters** ferrying laundry, rubbish and building materials up and down the slopes.

In contrast, the exceptional landscapes on the 15-km **western route** are accompanied by up to eight hours of exhausting legwork – though you can shorten things by catching another gondola between the trailhead at Ciguang Ge and **Yuping Lou** (玉屏楼, *yùpíng lóu*). There are around two thousand steps from the Ciguang Ge to **Banshan Si** (半山寺, *bànshān sì*), the misleadingly named Midway Monastery, after which things start to get interesting as you continue up an increasingly steep and narrow gorge. The rocks are huge, their weirdly contorted figures lending some credence to the usual gamut of names hailing from ancient times, and the broken hillside is riddled with caves. A steep, hour-long detour from Banshan – not a climb for those nervous of heights – follows steps cut into the cliffs up to **Tiandu Feng** (天都峰, *tiāndū fēng*; Heavenly City Peak), where **Jiyu Bei** (鲫鱼背, *jìyú bèi*; Kingfish Ridge), a narrow path extending over a precipice, provides Huang Shan's most spectacular views.

Back on the main track, the beautifully positioned **Yuping Lou** (玉屏楼, *yùpíng lóu*; Jade Screen Pavilion) is the true halfway house at around three hours into the journey. The vegetation thins out here, exchanged for bare rocks with only the occasional wind-contorted tree, one of which, **Yingke Song** (迎客松, *yíngkèsōng*; Welcoming Guest Pine), has been immortalized in countless scroll paintings, photographs, cigarette packets and beer labels. The steps wind on up to a pass where more strange rocks jut out of the mist; bear right for the climb to Huang Shan's apex at **Lianhua Feng** (莲花峰, *liánhuāfēng*; Lotus Flower Peak; 1864m) or press on to accommodation at *Tianhai Binguan* (天海宾馆, *tiānhǎi bīnguǎn*; ⓣ0559/5582708; ⑨). From here, it's just a short climb to where you finally reach the peak circuit at **Guangming Ding** (光明顶, *guāngmíng dǐng*; Brightness Summit), with a TV tower and weather station off to the right, and **Feilai Shi** (飞来石, *fēilái shí*; "Rock Flown From Afar") ahead.

The peak circuit

It takes around three hours to **circuit the peaks**. North (anticlockwise) from the eastern steps and **Bai'e Feng** (白鹅峰, *bái'é fēng*) cable-car terminus, the first stop is where a track leads out to **Shixin Feng** (Beginning-to-Believe Peak). This cluster of rocky spires makes a wonderful perch to gaze down to lowland woods and rivers, with white-rumped swifts and pine and rock silhouettes moving in and out of shifting silver clouds. Tour groups concentrate on the higher levels, so the lower stairs are more peaceful.

From here, the path continues round to the first of a few **accommodation** options. Staying here is far from cheap, but most hotels offer significant reductions early in the week. Despite its mountain-top location, the comfortable *Beihai Binguan* (北海宾馆, *běihei bīnguǎn*; ⓣ0559/5582555; ⑧) boasts a Bank of China and ATM. Crowds congregate each morning on the terrace nearby to watch the sunrise over the "northern sea" of clouds, one of the most stirring sights on the mountain. The views are good even without the dawn, and the area tends to be busy all day. Straight ahead, a side track leads to the cosy *Shilin Dajiudian* (石林大酒店, *shílín dàjiǔdiàn*; ⓣ0559/5584040, ⓦwww.shilin.com; ⑧); another twenty minutes on the main path brings you to the well-placed *Xihai Fandian* (西海饭店, *xīhǎi fàndiàn*; ⓣ0559/5588888, ⓦwww.hsxihaihotel.cn; ⑦), the perfect spot to sip drinks on the terrace and watch the sunset over the "western cloud sea".

It's another ten minutes or so from Xihai to where the track splits at the mountain's least expensive accommodation, the *Paiyun Ting Binguan* (排云亭宾馆, *páiyúntíng bīnguǎn*; ⓣ0559/5581558, ⓔhspyl@sohu.com; ⑦). Ahead is the

Taiping **cable-car station** (索道站, *suǒdào zhàn*) down to Songgu (see p.426). Stay on the main track for **Paiyun Ting** (排云亭, *páiyún tíng*; Cloud-dispelling Pavilion); on a clear day you'll see a steep gorge squeezed between jagged crags below, all covered in pine trees and magnolias. Farther round, the lonely tower of **Feilai Shi** (飞来石, *fēilái shí*) looks across at cascades that are especially evident after rain. Beyond here, the path undulates along the cliff edge to where the western steps descend on the right (below the TV tower and weather station), and then winds back to the Bai'e Feng cable car.

Hubei

HUBEI (湖北, *húběi*) is Han China's agricultural and geographic centre, mild in climate and well watered. Until 280 BC this was the independent state of **Chu**, whose sophisticated bronzeworking skills continue to astound archeologists, but for the last half-millennium the province's eastern bulk, defined by the low-lying Jianghan plain and spliced by waterways draining into the Yangzi and Han rivers, has become an intensely cultivated maze of rice fields so rich that, according to tradition, they alone are enough to supply the national need. More recently, Hubei's central location and mass of transport links into neighbouring regions saw the province become the first in the interior to be heavily industrialized. The colossal **Three Gorges hydroelectric dam** upstream from Yichang (see p.437), car manufacturing – up and running with the help of foreign investment – and long-established iron and steel plants provide a huge source of income for central China.

As the "Gateway to Nine Provinces", skirted by mountains and midway along the Yangzi between Shanghai and Chongqing, Hubei has always been of great strategic importance, and somewhere that seditious ideas could easily spread to the rest of the country. The central regions upriver from the capital, **Wuhan**, feature prominently in the *Romance of the Three Kingdoms* – the port of **Jingzhou** for one retaining its period associations, while **Wuhan** thrives on industry and river trade, and played a key role in China's early twentieth-century revolutions. In the west, the ranges that border Sichuan contain the holy peak of **Wudang Shan**, alive with Taoist temples and martial-arts lore, and the remote **Shennongjia Forest Reserve**, said to be inhabited by China's yeti.

Wuhan

One way or another, almost anyone travelling through central China has to pass through **WUHAN** (武汉, *wǔhàn*), Hubei's vast capital. The name is a portmanteau label for three original settlements: **Wuchang** (武昌, *wǔchāng*), **Hankou** (汉口, *hànkǒu*) and **Hanyang** (汉阳, *hànyáng*), separated by the Han and Yangzi rivers, but now connected by bridges, tunnels and ferries. Wuhan's sheer size – the population approaches ten million people – lends atmosphere and significance, even if the city is not a traditional tourist centre. Nonetheless it's an upbeat, characterful metropolis, and Hankou's former role as a foreign concession has left plenty of colonial European heritage in its wake, while the **Provincial Museum** in Wuchang is one of China's best. There are also a couple of temples and historical monuments to explore, some connected to the **1911 revolution** that ended two thousand years of imperial rule. On the downside, Wuhan has a well-deserved reputation – along with Chongqing and Nanjing – as one of China's three summer "furnaces": between May and September you'll find the streets melting and the gasping population surviving on a diet of watermelon and iced treats.

Arrival

More than 10km across, Wuhan has an extensive choice of transit points – there are three **train stations** and at least three long-distance **bus stations**. Train and bus timetables usually spell out the district where services arrive, though the new high-speed rail terminal is simply known as "Wuhan Station". Most people understandably stay on the northern bank of the Yangzi in Hankou, the city's trade and business centre, which boasts the best services and accommodation. South across the Han River is lightly industrial Hanyang, while Wuchang recedes southeast of the Yangzi into semi-rural parkland.

Tianhe airport (天河飞机场, *tiānhé fēijīchǎng*) sits 30km to the north of Wuhan, with good bus links (¥15–30) running to the China Southern airline office on Hangkong Lu in Hankou and the long-distance bus stations. A taxi will cost around ¥90. Rail services from the north tend to terminate at Hankou's train station, along Fazhan Dadao, while those from the south favour Wuchang's station, on the other side of town on Zhongshan Lu. The **high-speed rail station** (武汉火车站, *wǔhànhuǒchēzhàn*), in northeast Wuchang, will eventually be connected to the city via metro line #4, but coaches also ply the route to bus stations around town (¥12; 45min–1hr).

Arriving **by bus** could put you at any one of the major long-distance bus stations – on Jiefang Dadao in downtown Hankou, on Hanyang Dadao in Hanyang, or near Wuchang's train station on Zhongshan Lu – irrespective of where you're coming from; there are also several private bus depots outside the **Yangzi ferry terminal** (武汉港客运站, *wǔhàngǎng kèyùnzhàn*) and along Yanhe Dadao in Hankou. At least there's no confusion with ferries – passengers arrive at the ferry terminal on Yanjiang Dadao in Hankou.

City transport

Wuhan is too large to walk, though the overloaded bus and trolleybus systems seldom seem to be much quicker. The main city-bus termini are at Hankou and

Useful bus routes

The most convenient bus for **sightseeing** is the "Electric Special #1" (电一专路, *diànyī zhuānlù*), not to be confused with any other #1 bus or trolleybus – the characters for **dian zhuan** are displayed either side of the number. It runs from Yanhe Dadao in Hankou, via Hanyang and the Great Changjiang Bridge (长江大桥, *chángjiāng dàqiáo*), and then links the Yellow Crane Tower with Changchun Guan and the Provincial Museum. Other noteworthy services are:

#38 From Hankou train station through the downtown concession area, terminating along the river on Yanjiang Dadao near the Flood Control Monument (防洪纪念碑, *fánghóng jìniànbēi*).

#503 From Wuchang train station to the Yangzi ferry terminal.

#507 Between Hankou and Wuchang train stations, via the Yangzi ferry terminal, taking 45–90min, depending on traffic.

#595 Connects Hankou train station with the Yangzi ferry terminal.

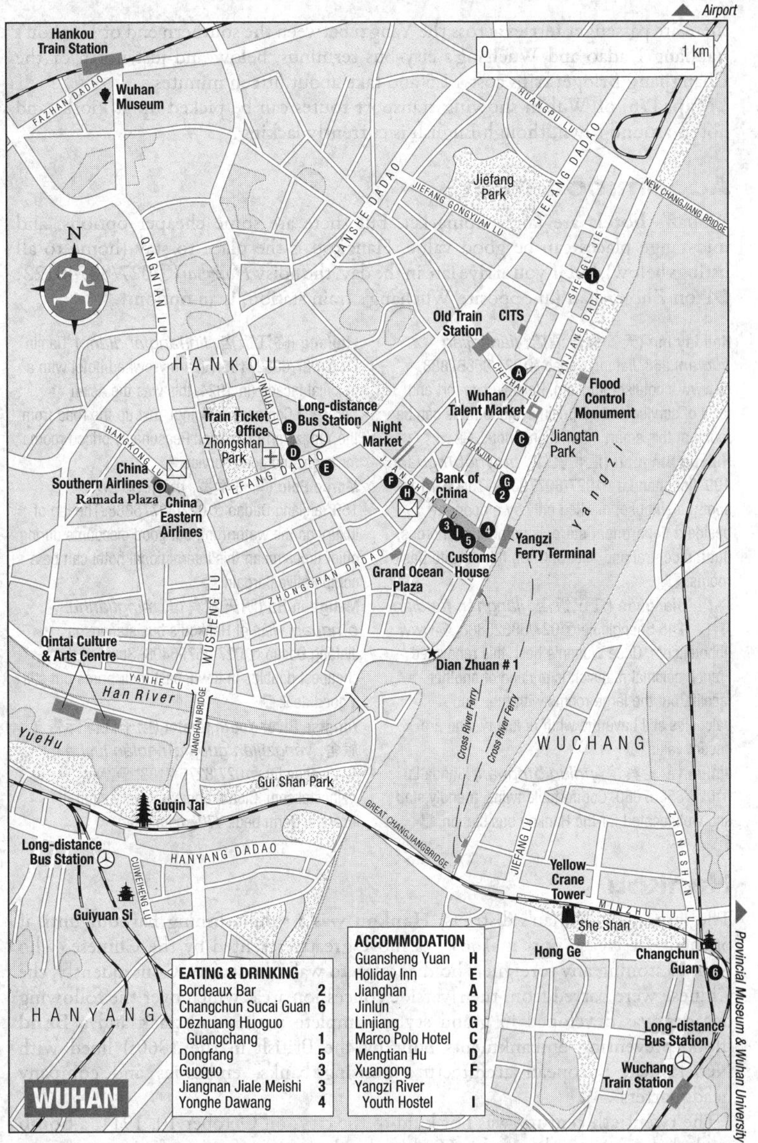

Wuchang train stations, and beside the Yangzi ferry terminal on Yanjiang Dadao. Services are regular and cheap – it only costs ¥2 between Wuchang and Hankou stations – and crawl out to almost every corner of the city between around 6am and 10pm.

Taxis are ubiquitous and, at ¥8 for the first 2km, not too expensive. The city's **metro** is expanding, and lines #2 and #4, crossing the river, are due to open in 2012 to join Hankou's extended line #1, an elevated rail roughly following the curve of the river between Jiefang and Zhongshan Dadaos. During daylight hours, there are passenger ferries across the Yangzi between the southern end of Hankou's Yanjiang Dadao and Wuchang's city-bus terminus, below and just north of the Changjiang Bridge; trips cost ¥1.5 and take about fifteen minutes.

Maps (¥6) of Wuhan showing transport routes can be picked up at kiosks and hotels around town, though English is currently lacking.

Accommodation

Wuhan's **hotels** are fairly upmarket, but there are some cheaper options, and mid-range places can be good value. Hangkou is the place to stay (home to all listings below), but if you arrive late in the day, the noisy *Hanghai* (Ⓣ027/88740122; ❹), on Zhongshan Lu opposite Wuchang's train station, is an option.

Holiday Inn (天安假日酒店, *tiānānjiàrì jiǔdiàn*) 868 Jiefang Dadao Ⓣ027/85867888, Ⓦwww.ichotelsgroup.com. Reliable comfort and level of service and surprisingly good rates can be found at this smart international hotel. ❻

Huiyue Binguan (汇悦宾馆, *huìyuèbīnguǎn*) 109 Jianghan Lu Ⓣ027/82779069. This hard-to-spot guesthouse, marked only by a doorway beside a department store, is nothing glamorous, but it's central and cheap. Often full despite basic rooms. ❸

Jianghan (江汉饭店, *jiānghàn fàndiàn*) 245 Shengli Jie Ⓣ027/68825888, Ⓦwww.jhhotel.com. Once Wuhan's best, this renovated French colonial mansion is in need of another facelift, but the large rooms with tubs and balconies still have the whiff of luxury, and are decent value. ❺

Jinlun (金轮宾馆, *jīnlún bīnguǎn*) Xinhua Lu Ⓣ027/85807060. Comfortable twins, friendly staff and well located for the Hankou bus station. ❹

Linjiang (临江饭店, *línjīangfàndìan*) 1 Tianjin Lu Ⓣ027/68826185. An army-owned hotel with a colonial facade (in 1924, this was the Asian Kerosene Company building), just up the road from the Yangzi ferry terminal. Reasonably priced rooms for town, and good service. ❸

Marco Polo (马哥孛罗, *mǎgēbóluō*) 159 Yanjiang Dadao Ⓣ027/82775888. The lap of luxury on the waterfront, but good discounts during quiet times mean this international hotel can be a comparative bargain. ❼

Mengtian Hu (明天湖宾馆, *míngtiānhú bīnguǎn*) West of Hankou's bus station, on Jiefang Dadao Ⓣ027/85796408. Some of the cheapest doubles in town, past their prime but still a good deal. ❷

Yangtse River Youth Hostel (扬子江国际青年旅舍, *yángzǐjiān guójì qīngnián lǚshè*) 47 Jianhan Lu Ⓣ027/8275 7188, Ⓦwww.yzjhostel.com. Clean rooms in a very central location. Dorm beds ¥70, rooms ❸

Hankou

The largest of Wuhan's districts, **Hankou** was a simple fishing harbour until it opened as a treaty port in 1861 – a move greatly resented by the Chinese, who took to stoning any foreigners bold enough to walk the streets. Consequently, the Chinese were barred from the riverside concession area, which over the following decades was developed in grand style, complete with a racetrack and a **Bund** (flood-preventing embankments built by the British in the 1860s) lined with Neoclassical European architecture housing banks, embassies and company headquarters.

The twentieth century was not kind to the city: on October 10, 1911, a **bomb** exploded prematurely at the Hankou headquarters of a revolutionary group linked to Sun Yatsen, keen on replacing imperial rule with a democratic government. Imperial troops executed the ringleaders, sparking a citywide uprising against the Manchus, which virtually levelled Hankou and soon spread across China, forcing the last emperor, Pu Yi, to abdicate. A Republican government under Sun Yatsen was duly elected in Nanjing the following year. The foreign concession was rebuilt, but anti-Western riots broke out in 1925 and again in 1927, prompting their return to Chinese administration. A few months later, the Guomindang stormed through on their Northern Expedition, returning briefly in

1937 to establish a national government in town before being forced farther west by the Japanese. Thirty years later, Hankou saw more fighting, this time between the PLA and various Red Guard factions, who had been slugging it out over differing interpretations of Mao's Cultural Revolution.

Exploring the district

Bursting with traffic and crowds, Hankou is a place to walk, shop, eat, spend money and watch others doing the same. The main thoroughfare is **Zhongshan Dadao** (中山大道, *zhōngshān dàdào*) a packed, 3km-long stretch of restaurants, stores and shopping plazas. Surprisingly, given the city's history, Hankou's **colonial quarter** survives largely intact, restored during a big clean-up project in 2001. Aside from the racetrack, now the watery **Zhongshan Park** (中山公园, *zhōngshān gōngyuán*) near the corner of Jiefang Dadao and Qingnian Lu, the colonial core lies mostly between the eastern half of Zhongshan Dadao and the river. The best sections are along the former Bund, renamed **Yanjiang Dadao,** and the pedestrianized **Jianghan Lu**. The two roads converge at the mighty **Customs House** (武汉海关, *wǔhàn hǎiguān*), a solid Renaissance edifice with imposing grey-stone portico and Corinthian capitals. The Bund itself is still visible and has been turned into **Binjiang** (滨江公园, *bīnjiānggōngyuán*) and **Jiang Tan** (江滩公园, *jiāngtāngōngyuán*) **parks**, popular places to stroll of a stifling summer evening. Many buildings in the area have plaques in English outlining their history; some to look for include the unusual seven-storey Art Deco/Modernist exterior of the former **Siming Bank** at 45 Jianghan Lu, and the brick "**Wuhan Talent Market**" on Yanjiang Dadao – once the US Consulate. **The Bank of China**, at the intersection of Jianghan Lu and Zhongshan Dadao, retains its period interior of wooden panelling and chandeliers, while Hankou's **old train station** on Chezhan Lu sports a French Gothic shell.

If you're up near Hankou's current train station, drop in to **Wuhan Museum** (武汉博物馆, *wǔhàn bówùguǎn*; daily 9am–5pm), which houses an outstanding collection of local cultural relics. In particular, there's a wonderful Ming-dynasty painting of the Yueyang Tower in Hunan (see p.453) and a 1700-year-old bronze mirror decorated with scenes from Han-dynasty mythology, the Book of Songs.

Hanyang

From Hankou, you can cross the Han River into **Hanyang** by bus over the short Jianghan Bridge between Yanhe Dadao and eastern Hanyang's **Gui Shan Park** (龟山公园, *guīshān gōngyuán*). Settled as far back as 600 AD, Hanyang remained insignificant until the late nineteenth century when the viceroy Zhang Zhidong built China's first large-scale steel foundry here as part of the "Self-Strengthening Movement" – a last-ditch effort to modernize China during the twilight years of the Qing dynasty.

Hanyang remains Wuhan's principal manufacturing sector; the two huge modern auditoriums that make up **Qintai Culture and Arts Centre** (琴台剧场, *qíntáijùchǎng*) on the South Bank suggest an attempt to spruce up the district, but it remains distinctly shabby compared to its neighbours. The Jianghan Bridge runs south to the western end of Gui Shan Park, from whose hills the Xia king **Yu** is said to have quelled floods four thousand years ago. Through the park and past the impressive lotus blooms, **Guqin Tai** (古琴塔, *gǔqíntǎ*; Ancient Lute Platform; ¥15) was the haunt of legendary strummer **Yu Boya**, who played over the grave of his friend Zhong Ziqi and then smashed his instrument because the one person able to appreciate his music was dead.

Guiyuan Si

Around 1km further south, **Guiyuan Si** (归元寺, *guīyuán sì*; daily 8.30am–5pm; ¥10) is a busy Buddhist monastery on Guiyuan Lu, off the main Hangyang Dadao, behind the long-distance bus station. The temple's scripture collection – which includes a complete seven-thousand-volume set of the rare **Longcan Sutra** – has made it famous among Buddhist circles. Of more general interest are several hundred individually styled saintly statues in the Arhat Hall as well as the statue of Sakyamuni in the main hall, a gift from Burma in 1935, carved from a single block of white jade.

Wuchang

Wuchang, on the right bank of the Yangzi, was founded as Sun Quan's walled capital of Wu during the Three Kingdoms period. Tang rulers made the city a major port, which, under the Mongols, became the administrative centre of a vast region covering present-day Hunan, Hubei, Guangdong and Guangxi provinces.

During the 1910 insurrection, Wuchang hosted appalling scenes when ethnic Han troops mutinied under a banner proclaiming "Long live the Han, Exterminate the Manchu" and accordingly slaughtered a Manchu regiment and over eight hundred civilians. The city and its bureaucracy survived, and nowadays Wuchang comprises government offices and the huge Wuhan University campus. Highlights include the **Taoist Changchun Guan**, the **Yellow Crane Tower** – the greatest of the Yangzi's many riverside pavilions – the **Provincial Museum** and the increasingly developed lakeside areas around **Dong Hu** (东湖, *dōng hú*).

Yellow Crane Tower and around

The road from Hanyang to Wuchang crosses the Great Changjiang Bridge, before the 1957 construction of which all traffic – rail included – had to be ferried 1500m across the river. On the far side, Wuluo Lu curves around **She Shan** (蛇山, *shéshān*; Snake Hill), which is overlooked by the bright tiles and red columns of the 50m-high **Yellow Crane Tower** (黄鹤楼, *huánghèlóu*; ¥80; daily 7.30am–5pm). It's no less magnificent for being an entirely modern Qing-style reproduction, 1km from where the original third-century structure burned down in 1884. Legend has it that She Shan was once home to a Taoist Immortal who settled his tab at a nearby inn by drawing a picture of a crane on the wall, which would fly down at intervals and entertain the guests. A few years later the Immortal flew off on his creation, and the landlord, who doubtless could afford it by then, built the tower in his honour. Climb (or take the lift) to the top to see Wuhan and the Yangzi at their best.

At the southern foot of She Shan, **Hong Ge** (红阁, *hónggé*; Tues–Sun 9am–5pm; free) is a colonial-style red-brick mansion that housed the Hubei Military Government during the 1910 uprising. A bronze Sun Yatsen stands in front, though at the time he was abroad raising funds. Follow Wuluo Lu east for 1km and you'll be standing outside the russet walls of **Changchun Guan** (长春观, *chángchūn guān*; ¥10), a Taoist complex that made its name through the Yuan-dynasty luminary **Qiu Chuzi**, who preached here and later founded his own sect. The halls are simply furnished with statues of the Three Purities, the Jade Emperor and other Taoist deities, while a side wing has been co-opted as a pharmacy, where Chinese-speakers can have their vital signs checked by a traditional doctor and buy medicines. Next door, Changchun's **vegetarian restaurant** is well worth a visit.

Hubei Provincial Museum

From the Yellow Crane Tower, it's around twenty minutes by bus to the **Hubei Provincial Museum** (湖北省博物馆, *húběishěng bówùguǎn*; Tues–Sun 9am–5pm, no admission after 3.30pm; ¥50) on Donghu Lu. The museum's display of items unearthed from the Warring States Period's tomb of the Marquis Yi deserves a good hour of your time – especially if you're planning on visiting similar collections at Jingzhou (see p.437) or Changsha (see p.446).

The marquis died in 433 BC and was buried in a huge, multilayered, wooden lacquered coffin at nearby Suizhou, then a major city of the state of Zeng. His corpse was accompanied by fifteen thousand bronze and wooden artefacts, 21 women and a dog. The museum's comprehensive English explanations of contemporary history and photos of the 1978 excavation put everything in perspective. Don't miss the impressive orchestra of 64 bronze bells, ranging in weight from a couple of kilos to a quarter of a tonne, found in the waterlogged tomb – the largest such set ever discovered – along with the wooden frame from which they once hung in rows. Played with hand-held rods, each bell can produce two notes depending on where it is struck – the knowledge of metals and casting required to achieve this initially boggled modern researchers, who took five years to make duplicates – and there are brief performances every hour or so in the museum's auditorium. More than a hundred other musical instruments are on display, including stone chimes, drums, flutes and zithers, along with spearheads and a very weird brazen crane totem sprouting antlers – an inscription suggests that this was the marquis's steed in the afterlife.

Dong Hu

The shores of vast **Dong Hu** (东湖, *dōng hú*; East Lake) not only host the high-speed rail station, the provincial museum and the university, but also have designated **scenic areas** in their own right. It is a lovely spot, and locals will proudly tell you that their East Lake is five times the size of Hangzhou's considerably more famous West Lake. **Moshan** (磨山风景区, *móshānfēngjǐngqū*), the pick of the scenic locations, is known for its springtime plum and cherry blossoms, on view at Wuhan's **Botanical Gardens** (磨山植物园, *móshānzhíwùyuán*; daily 8am–5.30pm; ¥40); it can be reached on buses #401 or #413 from the Yellow Crane Tower. Also on the shores of the lake, a ten-minute walk from the Provincial Museum at 56 Donghu Lu, lies one of Mao's holiday homes, **Meiling Villa** (毛泽东美龄别墅, *máozédōngmeǐlíngbiéshù*; daily 8am–5pm; ¥20). This was a private retreat for the Chairman and other leading Politburo members, and is hosted meetings with the likes of President Nixon and Henry Kissinger. While the nearby lake is still home to several popular swimming areas for use by the proletariat, Mao ensured his villa included a near-Olympic-sized indoor pool for personal use.

Eating and drinking

Wuhan's food reflects its position midway between Shanghai and Chongqing, and **restaurants** offer a good balance of eastern-style steamed and braised dishes – particularly fish and shellfish – along with some seriously spicy Sichuanese food. There's also a strong snacking tradition in town, with many places specializing in **dumplings**: various types of *shaomai*; *tangbao*, soup buns stuffed with jellied stock which burst messily as you bite them, much to the amusement of other diners; and *doupi*, sticky rice packets stuffed with meat and rolled up in a beanpaste skin.

Hankou has the best of the restaurants, mostly concentrated along Zhongshan Dadao and its offshoots. There is also a healthy stock of busy canteens and holes in the wall, particularly on the north side of Jiefang Dadao near the junction with Xinhua Lu. Western-style cafés and bars have sprung up along Yanjiang Dadao and Jianghan Lu, with **nightclubs** populating the basement of the ferry terminal.

Hankou

Bordeaux Bar (波尔图酒吧, *bōěrtú jiǔbā*) Just west of the *Linjiang* hotel on Yanjiang Dadao. One of many such café-bars in the area, replete with pavement tables and dimmed lighting. The Western-style pasta and steak dishes, along with Chinese fare, are expensive; expect at least ¥100/head.

Dezhuang Huoguo Guangchang (德庄火锅广场, *dézhuāng huǒguō guǎngcheng*) Corner of Yanjiang Dadao and Eryao Lu. If you're craving northern-style hotpot, this is the place to come – big, bright, noisy and inexpensive.

Dongfang (东方, *dōngfāng*) Near the Customs House on Jianghan Lu. A comfortable and popular place to take a breather from all that strenuous shopping and tuck into some tasty hotpots (¥35).

Guoguo (锅锅, *guōguō*) Jiaotong Lu. Ridiculously popular canteen serving excellent, inexpensive dumplings. Order at the counter, then wait in line.

Jiangnan Jiale Meishi (江南家乐美食, *jiāngnánjiālèmeǐshí*) Two doors up from *Guoguo*, this busy canteen serves up the whole range of local delicacies at just a fraction of the cost of the more proper restaurants.

Yonghe Dawang (永和大王, *yǒnghé dàwáng*) Across from the ferry terminal on Yanjiang Dadao, and elsewhere. Open around the clock, this restaurant chain's logo looks suspiciously like KFC's but the food is very different: big bowls of beef noodle soup or *doujiang*, steamed buns and fried rice.

Wuchang

Changchun Sucai Guan (长春素菜馆, *chángchūn sùcàiguǎn*) Wulou Lu. Vegetarian restaurant with Ming decor and a resolutely Chinese menu. The "beef" and "chicken" are made from bean-curd sheets, "prawns" from bean starch, and so on. Portions are good, liberally laced with chillies and aniseed, and very tasty. Mains from ¥30 or so.

Listings

Banks and exchange The Bank of China (Mon–Sat 8.30am–5pm) is on Zhongshan Dadao, in Hankou.

Bookshops The Xinhua bookstore, just west of the Jianghan Lu/Zhongshan Dadao intersection in Hankou, has plenty of maps and some English titles, including abridged texts of Chinese classics.

Cinema There are at least two screens in Hankou; one at Warner Village in Walmart near the Mingcheng Plaza on Zhongshan Dadao, and the other near the former US Consulate on Yanjiang Dadao.

Hospitals The Tongji, east of the Jiefang Dadao/Qingnian Lu crossroads in Hankou, is considered Wuhan's best. Another good place to go for acupuncture and massage is the hospital attached to the Hubei Traditional Medicine College, just north of She Shan, Wuchang.

Internet In Hankou, there are internet bars on the second floor of the cinema complex on Yanjiang Dadao and east of the *Holiday Inn* on Jiefang Dadao. In Wuchang there's one on Wulou Lu, west of Zhongshan Lu.

Left luggage There are booths charging ¥2 a bag at the bus (daily 8am–8pm) and train stations (24hr).

Mail and telephones The main post offices, with IDD phones, are on Zhongshan Dadao and at the junction of Hangkong Lu and Qingnian Lu, Hankou (daily 8am–6pm). There is no GPO as such, so ensure that poste-restante mail addresses use the street name and "Hankou", or it could end up anywhere in the city.

Markets and shopping For "antique" souvenirs, try the shops at the Hubei Provincial Museum, Wuchang. Hankou's old concession area, north of Zhongshan Dadao, has the liveliest market activity, mostly revolving around fruit and vegetables. Like most Chinese cities, Hankou is a very good place to buy clothes – hit the new Grand Ocean Plaza or the Walmart Super Centre, both on Zhongshan Dadao, or numerous smaller shops nearby, many with unfortunate names such as the "Ebola" clothes shop on Zhongshan Dadao.

Pharmacies In addition to smaller places elsewhere, Hankou's Hangkong Lu has a string of pharmacies stocking traditional and modern medicines, the biggest of which is the Grand Pharmacy, or, according to the English sign, the "Ark of Health".

Travel agents These abound around the Yangzi ferry terminal and the Hankou long-distance bus station. Alternatively, CITS here are a well-informed, English-, German- and French-speaking agency which can organize Three Gorges cruises and trips to Shennongjia and Wudang Shan; they're located just north of the *Jianghan* hotel at 909 Zhongshan Dadao, Hankou (Ⓣ027/82787386).

Up the Yangzi: Wuhan to Yichang

The flat, broad river plains west of Wuhan don't seem too exciting at first, but historic remains lend solid character along the way. It takes around 36 hours to navigate upstream from Wuhan via Jingzhou to **Yichang**, from where the exciting journey through the Yangzi Gorges and on to Chongqing begins. Most boats, however, don't stop along the way, so if you want to see anything it's more convenient – and far quicker – to use the **Wuhan–Jingzhou–Yichang expressway**, which cuts the journey time to Yichang down to less than four hours.

Jingzhou Shi and around

Around 240km west of Wuhan on the highway to Yichang, **JINGZHOU SHI** (荆州市, *jīngzhōushì*) lies on the north bank of the Yangzi, where the Wuhan–Yichang expressway joins the highway up to Xiangfan in northern Hubei. The city divides into two districts: easterly **Shashi** is an indifferent modern port, while **Jingzhou**, 10km west, is ringed by around 8km of moats and well-maintained, 7m-high battlements built by *The Three Kingdoms* hero Guan Yu.

From Shashi's long-distance bus station on Taqiao Lu, city bus #1 runs west into Jingzhou through the **east gate**, trundles down past Jingzhou's own long-distance bus station on Jing Nan Lu, turns into **Jingzhong Lu** and finally terminates by the **west gate**. Walls aside, there's not much to be impressed with in this forty-minute trawl, but walk 100m back along Jingzhong Lu from the bus stop and you'll be outside **Jingzhou Museum** (荆州博物馆, *jīngzhōubówùgǔan*; daily 8.30am–5.30pm; free), which includes a fantastic collection of Western Han tomb remains that were found a few kilometres north at Fenghuang Shan. More than 180 tombs dating from the Qin era to the end of the Western Han (221 BC–24 AD) have been found, an impressive range for a single site; the exhibition here focuses on the tomb of a court official named Sui. In many regards the items on display are similar to those in Wuhan's provincial museum (see p.434) – the house-like sarcophagi and copious lacquerwork, for example – but the bonus here is Sui's astoundingly well-preserved **corpse**, along with some comfortingly practical household items and wooden miniatures of his servants. The site where many of these items were discovered is still undergoing excavation and can be visited an hour to the north at **Xiongjia Zhong** (¥30); buses run here from the bus station or charter a taxi for ¥100–150. *Romance of the Three Kingdoms* aficionados should visit **Kaiyuan Guan**, next door to the museum, a tiny, elderly temple dedicated to Guan Yu and set among overgrown gardens.

There are **buses** both ways along the expressway until early evening from either Jingzhou's or Shashi's long-distance bus stations, with at least eight additional services north to Xiangfan throughout the day. There's basic accommodation (❸–❹) around both bus stations.

Yichang and the Three Gorges Dam

You may well end up spending a night at **YICHANG** (宜昌, *yíchāng*) a transport terminus on the Yangzi 120km upstream from Jingzhou and virtually in the shadow of the **Three Gorges Dam**. Ringed by car showrooms (western Hubei has long been a car manufacturing centre), the town is where visitors land after riding ferries and hydrofoils down from neighbouring Chongqing through the Three Gorges – or it can be used as a staging post for visiting the dam itself. Wild **Shennongjia Forest Reserve** is a bus ride away to the north.

Remnants of Yichang's treaty port days provide a dash of character, such as the **St Francis Cathedral** (圣方济各堂, *kūfāngjǐ gětáng*) on Zili Lu. Early evening is a good time to head down to the river and watch crowds flying kites, gorging themselves on shellfish at nearby street restaurants or cooling off with an ice cream.

Arrival

Yichang stretches along the Yangzi's northern bank for around 5km, directly below the relatively small Gezhou dam. **Sanxia airport** (三峡机场, *sānxiá jīchǎng*) is 10km east of town, a ¥60 taxi-ride away. The **train station** is at the north side of town atop a broad flight of steps, while the main **long-distance bus station** (长汽车客运站, *chángqìchēkèyúnzhàn*) is 500m to the east. Buses might also terminate south across town next to the **Yangzi ferry terminal** (水路客运站, *shuǐlù kèyùnzhàn*). Hydrofoils from Wanzhou dock at the **Taiping Xi hydrofoil port** (太平溪码头, *tàipíngxī mǎtóu*) above the Three Gorges Dam; the hydrofoil company lays on free transport to town. A **taxi** costs a fixed ¥6 within the city centre.

Accommodation

Yichang's **cheapest accommodation** option is the *Dili Binguan* at 135 Dongshan Dadao (帝丽宾馆, *dìlì bīnguǎn*; ⓣ0717/6054300; ❷), tucked down an alley beside the SPAR supermarket. For budget hotels with smarter rooms and amenities like internet connection and on-site cafés, head to the *Manor Hotel*, off the street at 105 Dongshan Dadao (山庄商务酒店, *shānzhuāng shāngwù jiǔdiàn*; ⓣ0717/6084500; ❸); the *Rest Motel*, 31 Yunji Lu (锐思特汽锁酒店, *dùisītè qìsǔo jiǔdiàn*; ⓣ0717/6236888, ⓦwww.restmotel.com.cn; ❸); or the *Wanhao Motel*, 115 Dongshan Dadao (万豪快酒店, *wànháo kuài jiǔdiàn*; ⓣ0717/8867888; ❸). The best-value upmarket option is the *Yichang International* at 121 Yanjiang Dadao (国际大酒店, *guójìdàjiǔdiàn*; ⓣ0717/8866999; ❺), which features its own brewery, a revolving restaurant and 24-hour café.

Moving on from Yichang

Plane, ferry, hydrofoil and train **tickets** are most easily booked through accommodation tour desks – you don't have to be staying to use these – though train tickets come with a fee, so you might want to buy them yourself at the station. The main **CITS office** at 100 Yiling Lu (ⓣ0717/6911998 or 6908582) is staffed by helpful English-speakers and can also arrange all Three Gorge cruise tickets, plus tours to Zhangjiajie (p.456) and Shennongjia (p.440).

Public ferry tickets upstream to Wushan, Fengjie, Wanxian, Shibaozhai, Fengdu and Chongqing can be bought at the Yangzi Ferry Terminal booking office – see p.438 for more about classes and conditions. **Fares** to Chongqing range from ¥152 for a berth in an open dorm to ¥884 (per person) for a private cabin. Departure times are posted on a board outside.

There are five **hydrofoils** daily through the Three Gorges to Wanzhou (5hr; ¥300); the only stop along the way is at Fengjie. They leave from the Taiping Xi dock above the Three Gorges Dam, and the hydrofoil company lays on a shuttle bus from their office in the west of town; when you buy your ticket, get the agent to write down the address to show a cab driver. Hydrofoil staff sell tickets on board for express buses from Wanzhou's hydrofoil terminal to **Chongqing**'s north train station (3hr; ¥100).

Yichang's **long-distance bus station** has an English-speaking information desk, a left-luggage office that stays open until 8pm and departures to almost everywhere between Chongqing and Shanghai. Xingshan, Xiangfan, Jingzhou and Wuhan are also reachable by minibuses from the bus-station forecourt.

If you're travelling by **train**, it's a smooth ride up to Zhengzhou in Henan, or south to Zhangjiajie in Hunan. There are direct **flights** from Yichang to Shenzhen, Beijing, Shanghai, Chengdu, Chongqing, Guangzhou, Lanzhou and Xi'an, but seats are very expensive. The airport is a ¥60 taxi ride east of town.

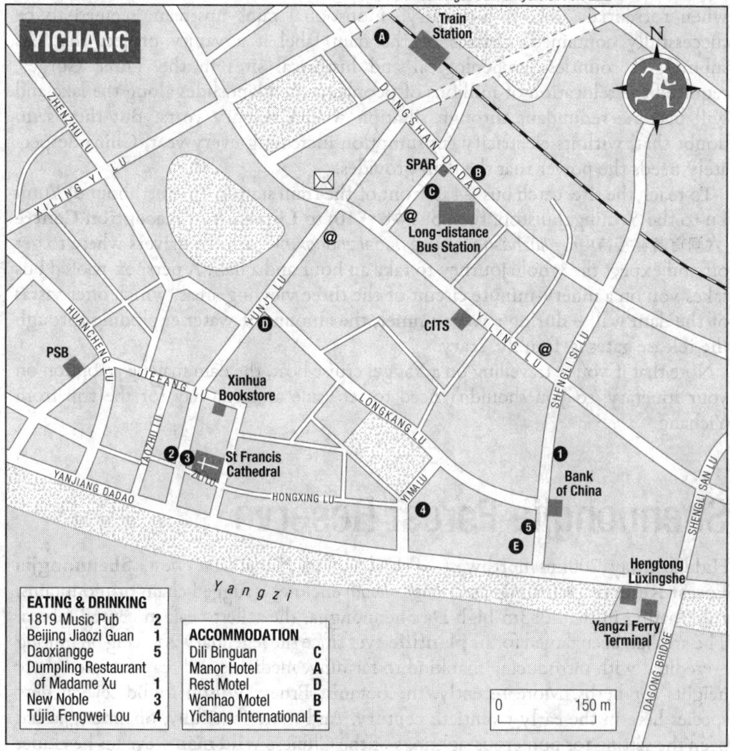

Eating, drinking and nightlife

Basic **Chinese food** can be found at the handful of stir-fry places near the port along Yanjiang Dadao. A block west at 33 Yi Ma Lu, *Tujia Fengwei Lou* (土家风味楼, *tǔjiā fēngweì lóu*; ⓣ0717/6230577) specializes in local homestyle dishes, including very spicy hotpots. There are several good options on nearby Shengli Si Lu, including the moderately flash *Daoxiangge*, no. 31 (稻香阁, *dàoxiānggé*; ⓣ0717/6222107), whose menu runs from Chinese staples to game meats; and inexpensive dumpling restaurants such as *Beijing Jiaozi Guan* (北京饺子馆, *běijīng jiǎoziguǎn*) and the English-signed *Dumpling Restaurant of Madame Xu*. For pizza, steak and other Western meals, head to the *New Noble* (新贵族, *xīnguìzú*), one of several cafés at the river end of Yunji Lu. The *1819 Music Pub* opposite is packed out most nights for **live bands** or DJs.

The Three Gorges Dam

The **Three Gorges Dam** (长江三峡大坝, *chángjiāng sānxiá dàbà*; ¥105), the world's most ambitious **hydroelectric project**, is 35km west of Yichang at Sandouping. The statistics are impressive: completed in 2006, the dam wall has raised water levels upstream by up to 175m and holds back a 660km-long lake; and when it becomes fully operational around 2012, the turbines will generate 22.5 GW (gigawatts) of power – about ten percent of the entire country's needs. It's hoped that the dam will help control the disastrous summer **flooding** which has long afflicted the lower Yangzi – something that received its first serious test in 2010, when torrential "once-in-a-century" monsoonal rains upstream seemed to be successfully contained. **Critics** of the dam label it a vanity project that has submerged countless archeological and historical sites in the Three Gorges, required the relocation of millions of people, caused landslides along the lake and will become redundant through siltation within seventy years. But there's no doubt that, with its electricity consumption increasing every year, China desperately needs the power that the dam provides.

To reach the site, catch bus #4 in front of the train station on (northbound) Yunji Lu to the Yemingzhu stop, then bus #8 (¥10) to **Liuzhashou Reception Centre** (六闸首游客接待中心, *liùzháshoǔ youkè jīedaì zhōngxīn*) – ask the drivers where to get off and expect the whole journey to take an hour and a half. A perspex-roofed bus takes you on a ninety-minute circuit of the three viewing areas, which offer vistas of the dam wall – during a wet summer, the amount of water exploding through the release gates is, frankly, scary.

Note that if you're travelling on a Yangzi cruise boat, the dam may be an option on your itinerary, so you shouldn't need to set aside an extra day for the trip from Yichang.

Shennongjia Forest Reserve

Hidden away 200km northwest of Yichang in Hubei's far west, **Shennongjia Forest Reserve** (神农架林区, *shénóngjià línqū*) encloses a rugged chain of mountains, culminating in the 3053m-high Da Shennongjia, the tallest peak in central China. The area has been famed for its **plantlife** ever since the legendary Xia king Shennong – credited with introducing mankind to farming, medicine and tea – scoured these heights for herbs. More recently, the botanist Ernest Wilson found several new species here in the early twentieth century. And more fancifully, Shennongjia has been the setting for numerous sightings of the Chinese **wild man** – even if he eludes you, there's a chance of seeing endangered **golden monkeys** here.

As parts of the reserve are **militarily sensitive**, it's best to visit Shennongjia on a **CITS tour** from Yichang. Chinese-language versions cost ¥400 per person, including transport, basic accommodation and a whip around the highlights; for more comfort, longer on site and an English-speaking guide you're looking at twice this. If you want to travel **independently**, the only area open to foreigners is at **Muyu Zhen**, which you can reach on public transport (see below). CITS might be able to arrange PSB **permits** for other areas, but whatever you do, avoid Shennongjia town (known locally as Songbai or Songbo): arrive here and you will be arrested, fined and booted out.

To Muyu Zhen and the reserve

There's one direct early-morning **bus** from Yichang's long-distance bus station to Muyu Zhen; alternatively, catch one of the frequent **minibuses** to **Xingshan** (兴山, *xīngshān*; 4hr; ¥65). Either way, the road climbs through well-farmed, increasingly mountainous country overloaded with hydroelectric stations. Tell the driver where you're headed and he'll make sure you get out at the right place to catch onward transport to Muyu Zhen (¥20; 2hr).

MUYU ZHEN (木鱼镇, *mùyúzhèn*) – also known as Muyu or Yuzhen – is a service centre spread along the main road 17km south of the reserve. **Hotels** are surprisingly upmarket, including the comfortable *Shennong Shanzhuang* (神农山庄, *shénnóng shānzhuāng*; Ⓣ0719/3452513, Ⓕ0719/3452520; ⑤), *Jiari Jiudian* (假日酒店, *jiărì jĭudiàn*; ⑤) and *Tianlü Binguan* (天绿宾馆, *tiānlǜ bīnguǎn*; Ⓣ0719/3385916; ④).

Cheaper rooms are available at the *Jiaxin Binguan* (佳信宾馆, *jiāxìn bīnguǎn*; ⓣ0719/3384845; ❸).

To **reach the reserve** from Muyu, either flag down Songbai-bound **buses** on the main road (note that the reserve gates are as far up this road as foreigners are allowed to travel) or bargain with the Xingshan **minibus** drivers for a charter (about ¥50 to the reserve gates, or ¥400 for the day), who otherwise run back to Xingshan until the afternoon.

Exploring the reserve

Once at the reserve entrance, known as **Yazikou** (鸭子口, *yāzikǒu*), you hand over the **entry fee** (¥140, bus through reserve ¥90) and add your name and passport number to the list of the few foreigners who make it here each year. Perhaps because of the military area to the north – but also because Shennongjia is fairly remote – staff here are very paranoid about visitors getting lost: wander off alone and you're likely to return to a police search. If you want to explore, ask someone to accompany you.

From the gates, 6km of gravel track runs southwest up a once-logged valley to the couple of Forestry Department buildings that comprise **Xiaolong Tan** (小龙潭, *xiǎolóng tán*), where close-up views of **golden monkeys** (金丝猴, *jīnsīhóu*) are available at the "animal hospital" here. There's also a **Wild Man museum**, where paintings, newspaper clippings, maps and casts of footprints document all known encounters with the gigantic, shaggy, red-haired **ye ren**, first seen in 1924. The creature was most recently spotted in June 2003 by a party of six, including a local reporter, who described the beast as being 1.65m tall, of greyish hue, with shoulder-length hair and a footprint measuring some 30cm.

Assuming you can arrange it with staff, there are some good walking tracks around Xiaolong Tan. One route (much of it along a vehicle track) climbs south, for around 2.5km, to a forest of China firs on the slopes of **Jinhou Ling** (金猴岭, *jīnhóu lǐng*), a prime spot to catch family groups of golden monkeys foraging first thing in the morning. Favouring green leaves, stems, flowers and fruit, the monkeys live through the winter on lichen and moss, which cover the trees here. The males especially are a tremendous sight, with reddish-gold fur, light blue faces, huge lips and no visible nose. A far rougher trail continues to the top of the mountain in four hours. Alternatively, a more relaxed, 3km stroll north of Xiaolong Tan is **Dalong Tan** (大龙潭, *dàlóng tán*), a cluster of run-down huts by a stream, from where there's an undemanding 8km walk up the valley to **Guanyin Cave** (观音洞, *guānyīn dòng*). Most of this is through open country, which gets plenty of wildflowers in the spring; birders can spot **golden pheasants** (红胸山鸡, *hóngxiōng shānjī*) and grouse-like **tragopans** (红胸角稚, *hóngxiōng jiǎozhì*).

The gravel road from Xiaolong Tan curves westwards up the valley, climbing almost continually along the ridges and, in clear weather, affording spectacular views. On the way, you'll cross **Da Shennongjia** (大神农架, *dà shénnóngjià*), though the rounded peak is barely noticeable above the already high road. Better are the cliffscapes about 10km along at **Fengjing Ya** (风景垭, *fēngjīng yà*) and the "forest" of limestone spires where the road finally gives up the ghost 17km due west of Xiaolong Tan at **Banbi Yan** (板壁岩, *bǎnbì yán*).

Wudang Shan

Hubei's river plains extend well into the province's northwest, where they reluctantly cede to mountain ranges butting up against Henan, Shaanxi and Sichuan. The region's peaks are steeped in legends surrounding **Wudang Shan** (武当山, *wǔdāngshān*), the Military Mountain, known for its Taoist temples and fighting style. A relatively easy ascent, coupled with the mountain's splendid scenery and the availability of transport from Wuhan, Xi'an and Yichang, make this an appealing trip.

Wudang Shan's 72 pinnacles have, since Tang times, been liberally covered in **Taoist temples**. Those that survived a wave of thirteenth-century revolts were restored following proclamations for the development of religion under the Ming emperor **Cheng Zi** in 1413 – the work took three hundred thousand labourers ten years to complete – and the mountain is currently enjoying another bloom of tourist-funded religious fervour, with many of the temples emerging fabulously decorated after decades of neglect.

To foreigners, Wudang Shan is most famous for its **martial arts**, which command as much respect as those of Henan's Shaolin Monastery (see p.281). It's said that the Song-dynasty monk **Zhang Sanfeng** developed Wudang boxing – from which *tai ji* is derived – after watching a fight between a snake and a magpie, which revealed to him the essence of *neijia*, an internal force used (in typical Taoist manner) to control "action" with "non-action". Fighting skills would also have come in handy considering the vast number of outlaws who've inhabited these mountains over the centuries. The rebel peasant Li Zicheng amassed his forces and

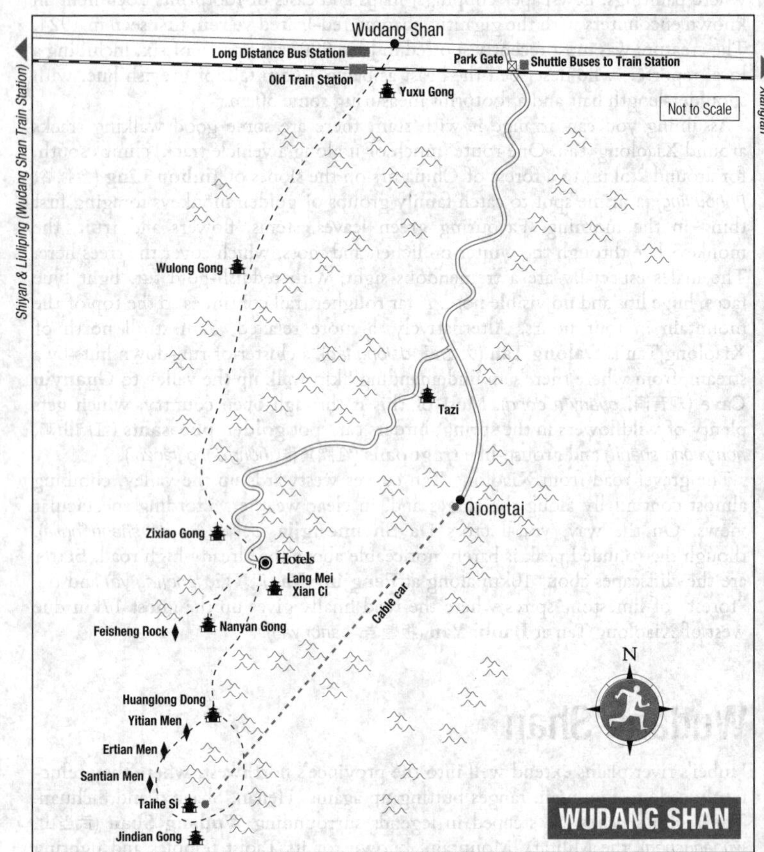

eventually deposed the last Ming emperor from here – there's a tablet recording the suppression of the Red Turbans on the mountain by Qing troops in 1856. More recently, the Communist Third Front Army found sanctuary here in 1931, after their march from Hong Lake in southern Hubei.

On a more peaceful note, Wudang Shan was also the retreat of **Emperor Zhen Wu**, who cultivated his longevity in these mountains during the fifteenth century, and whose portly statue graces many local temples. His birthday is celebrated locally on the third day of the third lunar month, a good time to visit the mountain. Wudang's valuable plants later attracted the attention of the sixteenth-century pharmacologist **Li Shizhen**, who included four hundred local species among the 1800 listed in his *Materia Medica*, still an important reference work on the medicinal use of Chinese herbs.

Wudang Shan Shi

About 120km west of **Xiangfan** (襄樊, *xiāngfán*), the small market town of **Wudang Shan Shi** (武当山市镇, *wǔdāngshān shìzhèn*) sits with the famed mountain range rising immediately to its south. Confusingly, **Wudang Shan train station** is no longer actually in the town, but has been relocated to **Liuliping** (六里坪, *liùlǐpíng*), 15km to the west. While hardly as convenient, it's still straightforward to catch a bus (¥5) or taxi to Wudang Shan from there. Regular buses also run to Wudang Shan Shi from the train station in **Shiyan** (十堰, *shíyàn*), a further 10km to the west (¥10).

Arrival and information

Wudang Shan town is not a big place, stretching for a couple of kilometres along the main road, **Taihe Lu** (太和路, *tàihélù*), with a few side streets branching off, bounded in by the mountains to the south and the Tai River to the north and west. The **bus station** is north of Taihe Lu on Chezhan Lu – the approach to the old train station – while the main entrance to the mountain lies uphill at the east end of town, opposite the toll gate for the nearby motorway. In town, you'll also find a **Bank of China**, a couple of **supermarkets** and lots of shops selling swords.

Accommodation

Accommodation is plentiful along Taihe Lu and tends toward the cheap, no-frills end of the market, though en suite rooms with air-conditioning and hot water are the norm. Prices can climb unreasonably at peak times, and there's little reason to stay in town unless you have transport to catch. The *Xuanwu Jiudian* (玄武酒店, *xuánwǔ jiǔdiàn*; Ⓣ0719/5666013; ❸) on Taihe Lu opposite the bus station is one of many similar places with clean rooms; it's worth haggling a bit.

The Town

South down Huangbang Lu is the new **Wudang Shan Museum** (武当山博物馆, *wūdāngshān bówùgǔan*; free), which traces the history of martial arts here and includes plenty of English. To the north, up the semi-pedestrianized Puxing Jie and under the railway arch, is **Yuxu Gong** (玉虚宫, *yùxū gōng*), the largest temple complex in Wudang Shan before it burned down in 1745. It's currently just a few vegetated pavilions around a flagstoned square, but unlikely to stay an undeveloped tourist attraction for long.

For those interested in learning some Wudang *wushu*, there are several academies: try the Jing Wu Martial Arts School (Ⓣ0719/5666666, Ⓦwww.wdsws.com) or Chuanzhen Martial Arts Institute (Ⓣ13972471458, Ⓦwww.gongfuchina.com.cn), where you should be able to negotiate a short course from around ¥200 per day.

The mountain

It's possible to **hike** from town to summit in about eight hours – the footpath starts near the old train station – though most people catch one of the park buses to **Nanyan** (南岩, *nányán*), around three-quarters of the way up and where in-park accommodation is most abundant.

At the main park gate keep straight ahead, past the souvenir shops and restaurants, to the **ticket office**. Here you can purchase your **park ticket** (¥140; unlimited time but only valid for a single entry), your all-but-compulsory **bus ticket** (¥70; unlimited use of buses within the park – all other transport is prohibited) and your park map (¥3 Chinese; ¥8 English), and drop off any luggage you don't want to haul up the mountain (¥10/item/day). You'll be funnelled through some turnstiles to the bus stop, ready to be whisked up the mountain.

An alternative to Nanyan, and a popular option for those not planning to spend the night, is to catch the bus to **Qiongtai** (琼台, *qióngtaí*), from where a **cable car** (索道站, *suǒdào zhàn*; ¥80 return) saves the effort of sweating up the steps to the top (and back down again), making a one-day visit a far more realistic proposition.

Accommodation

Places to stay line the road at Nanyan for the few hundred metres between the bus drop-off and the start of the trails to **Tianzhu Peak** (天主蜂, *tiānzhǔfēng*) and **Nanyan Gong** (南岩宫, *nányán gōng*). Advertised rates are outrageous, but only apply when demand outstrips supply – come on a Sunday or at the beginning of the week when it's quieter and you can pretty much name your price. Quality of rooms is similar across the board – modern, prematurely aged and basically clean – but check when hot water is available. The first hotel after the bus stop is the *Xianghe Shanzhuang* (祥和山庄, *xiánghéshānzhuāng*; ⓣ0719/5689018; ❸), where you can bargain for room rates, while at the far end of the road is the smarter **Nanyan Binguan** (南岩宾馆, *nányán bīnguǎn*; ⓣ0719/5689182; ❹). There's also a **hostel** at the summit (dorm beds ¥30, rooms ❹), part of the temple complex on **Tianzhu Feng** (天主蜂, *tiānzhǔfēng*; Pillar of Heaven Peak); Chinese-speakers will find the monks' company well worth enduring the spartan facilities.

Nanyan Gong and Zixiao Gong

A path from the top end of the hotel area leads to **Nanyan Gong** (南岩宫, *nányán gōng*), perched fortress-like on a precipice. The halls are tiny and austere, carved as they are out of the cliff face, but the main sight is **Dragon Head Rock**, a 2m-long slab sculpted with swirls and scales, which projects straight out over the void. Before it was walled off, countless people lost their lives trying to walk to the end with a stick of incense.

About 3km (and one bus stop) downhill from Nanyan is **Zixiao Gong** (紫霄宫, *zǐxiāo gōng*; the Purple Cloud Palace), a huge early-Ming temple complex whose pattern of successively higher platforms appears to mimic the structure of the hills above. Pleasantly active with monks, tourists and the occasional mendicant traveller, the place is becoming the mountain's most important monastery. Through the gates, a broad stone staircase climbs between boxy Tang pavilions housing massive stone tortoises to the main hall, whose exterior is lightened by the graceful sweep of its tiled roof. Inside is a rare wooden spiral cupola and a benevolent statue of the Yellow Emperor; surrounding courtyards are sometimes used for martial-arts displays.

Tianzhu

It's only a 4km walk, but, with much of it being up and down stone steps, it takes two to three hours to get from Nanyan to the top of **Tianzhu Peak** (天主蜂, *tiānzhǔfēng*), the highest here, at 1600m – a waterproof or umbrella may come in handy as protection against Wudang Shan's famously unpredictable weather. One way to keep your mind off the endless steps is to watch out for the colourful variety of **birds** in the forest, including boisterous red-billed magpies with graceful blue tails, and magnificent golden pheasants. You'll soon arrive at **Lang Mei Xian Ci** (榔梅仙祠, *lángméi xiāncí*), a small shrine dedicated to Zhang Sanfeng and his contribution to Chinese martial arts – there's a statue of him along with a cast-iron halberd in one hall, and Chinese-only accounts of his development of Wudang boxing in adjoining rooms.

Halfway up to Tianzhu the path divides at **Huanglong Dong** (黄龙洞, *huánglóng dòng*; Yellow Dragon Cave) to form an eventual circuit via the peak; turn left for the longer but less-steep "hundred-step-ladder" (a lie, it's considerably more) route to the peak, with superb views through the canopy of cloud-swept, apparently unscalable cliffs. A surprisingly short time later you'll find yourself on top of them, outside the encircling wall that has turned Tianzhu and its temples into a well-defended citadel. Inside, the Ming-dynasty **Taihe Gong** (太和宫, *tàihé gōng*) is impressive for the atmosphere of grand decay enclosed by the thick green tiles and red walls of **Huangjing Hall** (皇经堂, *huángjīng táng*), where monks stand around the cramped stone courtyards or pray in the richly decorated, peeling rooms squeezed inside. From here you can ascend to where the mountain is literally crowned by **Jindian Gong** (金殿宫, *jīndiàn gōng*; Golden Palace Temple), a tiny shrine with a gilded bronze roof embellished with cranes and deer, whose interior is filled by a statue of armour-clad Zhen Wu sitting behind a desk in judgement; it's an extra ¥20 to climb the stairs to the shrine. Views from the front terrace (clearest in the morning) look down from the top of the world, with sharp crags dropping away through wispy clouds into the forest below. For an alternative descent, follow the stairs off Jindian Gong's rear terrace, which return to Huanglong Dong down some very rickety steps via **Santian Men** (三天门, *sāntiān mén*), the Three Sky Gates.

Hunan

For many travellers, their experience of **Hunan** (湖南, *húnán*) is a pastiche of the tourist image of rural China – a view of endless muddy tracts or paddy fields rolling past the train window, coloured green or gold depending on the season. But the bland countryside, or rather the peasants farming it, has greatly affected the country's recent history. Hunan's most famous peasant son, **Mao Zedong**, saw the crushing poverty inflicted on local farmers by landlords and a corrupt government, and the brutality with which any protests were suppressed. Though Mao is no longer accorded his former god-like status, monuments to him litter the landscape around the provincial capital **Changsha**, which is a convenient base for exploring the areas where he spent his youth. By contrast, the historical town of **Yueyang** in northern Hunan, where the Yangzi meanders past **Dongting Hu**, China's second largest lake, offers more genteel attractions. Both Hunan and Hubei – literally "south of the lake" and "north of the lake" respectively – take their names from this vast expanse of water, which also provided the origins of dragon-boat racing. South of Changsha, **Heng Shan** houses a pleasant assortment of mountain temples, while **Wulingyuan Scenic Reserve** in the far west boasts inspiringly rugged landscapes. A few hours south of here lies the picturesque town of **Fenghuang**, where you'll find remnants of the Southern Great Wall.

Changsha and around

There's little evidence at street level to suggest that **CHANGSHA** (长沙, *chángshā*), Hunan's rather modern, high-rise filled capital, has been inhabited for three thousand years, though archeological evidence suggests this is the case. Its importance as a river town has been appreciated for millennia, as demonstrated by both a **Qin** invasion in 280 BC and Changhsa's demarcation as a treaty port more than two thousand years later in 1903. Europeans found, however, that the Hunanese had a very short fuse (something other Chinese already knew): after the British raised the market price of rice during a famine in 1910, the foreign quarter was totally destroyed by rioting. Guomindang forces torched much of the city in 1938 as they fled the Japanese advance, and modern developments have claimed the rest. Ancient sites and objects occasionally surface – such as Shang-era bronze wine jars and the magnificently preserved contents of three Han burial mounds – but usually only during the digging of foundations for another flyover.

Primarily, Changsha is known for its links with **Mao**, who arrived here in 1911 at the age of eighteen as nationwide power struggles erupted following the collapse of the Manchu dynasty. By 1918 there was a real movement for Hunan to become an independent state and, for a time, this found favour with local warlord **Zhao Hendi**, who soon turned violently on his own supporters. Mao, back in Shaoshan heading a Communist Party branch, was singled out for persecution and in 1925 fled to Guangzhou, taking up a teaching post at the Peasant Movement Training Institute. Within three years he returned to Hunan, organizing the abortive **Autumn Harvest Uprising** and establishing guerrilla bases in rural Jiangxi.

Mao was by no means the only young Hunanese caught up in these events, and a number of his contemporaries surfaced in the Communist government, including **Liu Shaoqi**, Mao's deputy until he became a victim of the Cultural Revolution; former CCP chief, **Hu Yaobang**; and **Hua Guofeng**, Mao's lookalike and briefly empowered successor. Today, away from the bustling shopping district and vibrant nightlife, sights linked to the Chairman still account for the majority of Changsha's formal attractions, though there are also some parks to wander around and a fascinating **Provincial Museum**. Day-trips include **Mao's birthplace** at Shaoshan, 90km to the southwest, and the famous tower at Yueyang (see p.453), 120km to the north, both of which are easily reached by local rail.

Arrival and city transport

The bulk of Changsha is spread east of the **Xiang River** (湘江, *xiāngjiāng*), and the city's name – literally "Long Sand" – derives from a narrow midstream bar now called **Juzi Dao** (桔子岛, *júzi dǎo*; Tangerine Island). The lengthy Xiangjiang Bridge, which links the city to the west-bank suburbs, Hunan University and Yuelu Park, spans the river. **Wuyi Dadao** (五一大道, *wǔyīdàdaò*) is Changsha's main drag and forms an unfocused downtown district as it runs broad and straight for 4km across the city.

The city's Huanghua **airport** (黄花飞机场, *húanghūafēijīchǎng*), 15km east of town, is connected to the airline offices on Wuyi Dadao by a shuttle bus (¥16) or taxi (¥100). Changsha's train **station**, at the eastern end of Wuyi Dadao, is conveniently central, but the three main long-distance **bus stations** are all several kilometres out of town in the suburbs, and you could easily wind up at any of them; to reach the train station, catch city bus #126 from the east bus station (4km), bus #302 from

Moving on from Changsha

There are **flights** from Changsha to Hefei, Yichang, Zhangjiajie, Shanghai, Beijing and everywhere else between Hong Kong and Ürümqi. Between 7am and 9pm, half-hourly buses head to the airport from the airline office, which is in the same buiding as the *Civil Aviation* hotel on Wuyi Dadao (daily 6.30am–8pm; ⓣ0731/84112222).

Leaving by **bus**, use the east bus station for eastern destinations, the west for western ones, and the south for southern – though the **train** is a better option for almost all travel. Trains head north from Changsha to Yueyang and Hubei province; west to Guizhou, Jishou and Zhangjiajie; east to Nanchang in Jiangxi; and south via Hengyang to Guangdong and Guangxi. There's also a special tourist train daily to Shaoshan. Currently, the fastest train to Zhangjiajie takes a mere five hours, but departs at 2.39am – other services that are not much slower depart later in the morning and at night, but there's little during the day. At the station, ticket offices on the south side of the square (daily 6am–11pm) are constantly crowded; better to use one of the in-town kiosks, which also sell bus tickets. Changsha is also one of the first cities connected to China's new **High-Speed Rail Network**. Sitting on what will eventually be the Beijing to Hong Kong line, the huge, airport-like **South Station**, or *Gaotie Zhan*, is several kilometres south of the city centre – around ¥30 in a taxi – with 200kmph services currently running north to Wuhan (1hr 40min) and south to Guangzhou South (2hr 30min).

the west bus station (8km) or bus #7 from the south bus station (10km). A **metro** line, currently under construction, is due to open in 2013. The city also sits on the new **high-speed rail** line running between Wuhan and Guangzhou, and the higher ticket prices can prove money well spent as the 200km locomotives knock hours off journey times. The station (南站, *nánzhàn*), south of the centre, can be reached for around ¥30 in a taxi.

Changsha's **city buses** run between about 6am and 9pm and almost all originate, or at least stop, at the train-station square. Chinese maps of the city, with the bus routes clearly marked, are easily picked up from street vendors at arrival points.

Accommodation

There's a fair choice of **hotels** in Changsha, though almost entirely aimed at business rather than budget travellers.

Changsha International Youth Hostel (长沙国际青年旅舍, *chángshāgúojìqīngníanlǚshè*) 61 Gongshang Lane, off Dongfeng Lu, north of the Provincial Museum ⓣ0731/2990202, ⓦwww.yhachangsha.com. A newly established, friendly hostel with English-speaking staff. A little out of the way, but the only place in town you're likely to bump into backpackers – give reception a call and they will guide you in. Dorm beds ¥30, room ❶

Civil Aviation (民航大酒店, *mínháng dàjiǔdiàn*) 47 Wuyi Dadao ⓣ0731/29125888, ⓕ2915800. A well-run and tidy airlines-owned operation, though it can get busy with tour groups. ❹

Dolton (通程国际大酒店, *tōngchéng guójì dàjiǔdiàn*) 159 Shaoshan Lu ⓣ0731/4168888, ⓦwww.dolton-hotel.com. The height of luxury in Changsha, an opulent sprawl of marble and chandeliers, with five-star service. Worth dropping in, if only to meet the over-enthusiastic doorman. ❻

Green Tree Inn (格林豪泰酒店, *gélínhaótaìjiǔdiàn*) 98 Shaoshan Lu ⓣ0731/8186998, ⓦwww.998.com, ⓔliuky@998.com. Chain hotel offering decent, good-value rooms, though some are better kept than others – don't be shy about asking to see several options. There's also a *7 Days Inn* a few doors up. ❸

Home Inn (如家酒店, *rújiājiǔdiàn*) 34 Wuyi Dadao ⓣ0731/82918666. Very close to the train station, for genuinely comfortable ensuite rooms with internet access. ❸

Lianjing Jiudian (联京酒店, *liánjīng jiǔdiàn*) 290 Chezhan Lu ⓣ0731/82169218. Friendly, but slightly run-down affair, just around the corner from the train station. ❷

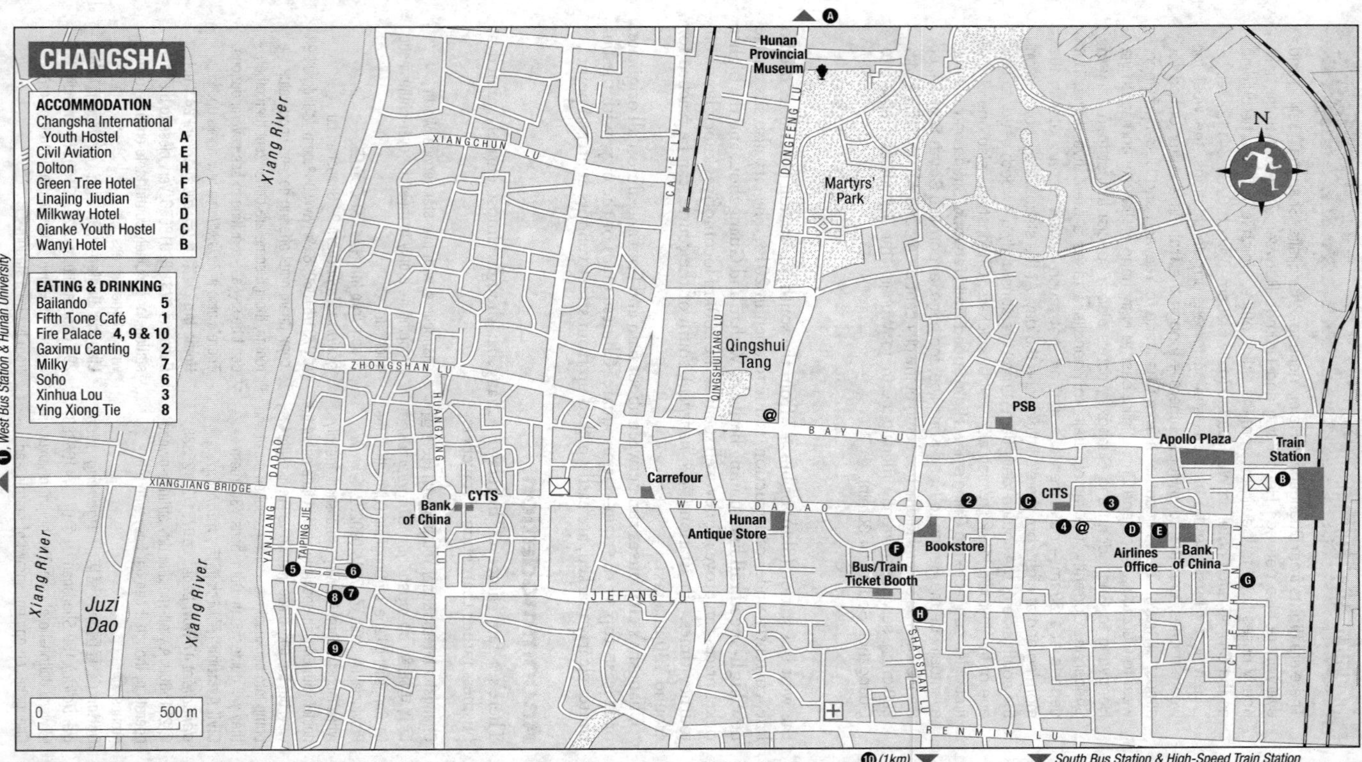
CHANGSHA
ACCOMMODATION
Changsha International Youth Hostel A
Civil Aviation E
Dolton H
Green Tree Hotel F
Linajing Jiudian G
Milkway Hotel D
Qianke Youth Hostel C
Wanyi Hotel B
EATING & DRINKING
Bailando 5
Fifth Tone Café 1
Fire Palace 4, 9 & 10
Gaximu Canting 2
Milky 7
Soho 6
Xinhua Lou 3
Ying Xiong Tie 8
0 500 m
1, West Bus Station & Hunan University
Airport & East Bus Station
South Bus Station & High-Speed Train Station
10 (1km)
A
Hunan Provincial Museum
Martyrs' Park
Qingshui Tang
PSB
Apollo Plaza
Train Station
CITS
Bookstore
Airlines Office
Bank of China
Bus/Train Ticket Booth
Hunan Antique Store
Carrefour
CYTS
Bank of China
Xiang River
Juzi Dao
XIANGCHUN LU
CAI'E LU
DONGFENG LU
QINGSHUITANG LU
ZHONGSHAN LU
HUANGXING LU
BAYI LU
WUYI DADAO
JIEFANG LU
SHAOSHAN LU
CHEZHAN LU
RENMIN LU
XIANGJIANG BRIDGE
YANJIANG DADAO
TAIPING JIE
N

Milkyway Hotel (银河大酒店, *yínhé dàjiǔdiàn*) 59 Wuyi Dadao ☎0731/84111818. Don't be fooled by the tacky glass-and-chrome exterior, as the inside has had a complete overhaul. State of the art, neo-Qing decor and attentive staff make for a very pleasant stay. ❹

Qianke Youth Hostel (迁客青年旅馆, *qiānkèqīngniánlǚguǎn*) 186 Wuyi Dadao ☎0731/84465485. Not genuinely IYHA affiliated, but this recently redecorated, if spartan, hostel has clean, cheap doubles. ❷

Wanyi Hotel (万怡商里务酒店, *wànyíshānglǐwùjiǔdiàn*) Train Station Square ☎0731/82279988, ⓦwww.wanyihotel.com. The smarter of two hotels in the station square – as usual you're paying for location rather than comfort, but it's a fair-ish deal. ❷

The City

Changsha's a clean, well-ordered city, and its denizens are noticeably friendly – don't be surprised if you acquire a guide while walking around. The main **shopping district** springs from the junction of Wuyi Dadao and the pedestrianized Furong Lu (芙蓉路, *fúrónglù*), a noisy, intensely crowded area loaded with shopping plazas, Western fast-food chains and teenagers. A little further west, running between Wuyi Lu and Jiefang Lu, **Taiping Jie** (太平街, *taìpíngjiē*) – a sympathetically reconstructed old street – hosts cafés, bars, boutiques and some tourist shops, and is likely to be of more interest.

Qingshui Tang

Qingshui Tang (清水潭, *qīngshuǐ tán*; Clearwater Pool; daily 8am–4.30pm; free; bus #113 stops outside), on Bayi Lu, is Mao's former Changsha home and the site of the first local Communist Party offices. A white marble statue of Mao greets you at the gate, and the garden walls are covered with stone tablets carved with his epigrams. Near the **pool** is a scruffy vegetable patch and the reconstructed room in which Mao and his second wife, Yang Kaihui (daughter of Mao's stoical and influential teacher, Yang Changji), lived after moving here from Beijing following their marriage in 1921. There's also a display of peasant tools – a grindstone, thresher, carrypole and baskets – and a short history of Chinese agriculture. On the same grounds, a brightly tiled **museum** contains a low-key but interesting collection of historical artefacts, including a clay tomb figurine of a bearded horseman and a cannon that was used to defend the city against Taiping incursions in 1852. These pieces lead to a depressing photographic record of Guomindang atrocities and eulogies to Mao, Zhou Enlai and others. Outside, on Qingshuitang Lu, are a number of antique stores – at weekends an informal and jolly antique market lines the pavement.

Martyrs' Park and Hunan Provincial Museum

From Qingshui Tang, follow Qingshuitang Lu north and then head east for 500m to the gates of **Martyrs' Park** (烈士公园, *lièshì gōngyuán*; free). Though it's often crowded, plenty of shade, as well as lakes, bridges and pagodas make the park a perfect place to stroll. The main reason to head up this way, though, is to visit **Hunan Provincial Museum** (湖南省博物馆, *húnánshěng bówùguǎn*; daily 8.45am–4pm; free; bus #126, from the station via Wuyi Dadao, stops outside), entered from Dongfeng Lu at the park's northwestern corner. One of Changsha's highlights, the museum is dominated by the Han-era tomb of **Xin Zui**, the Marquess of Dai. Xin Zui died around 160 BC, and her subterranean tomb – roughly contemporary with similar finds at Jingzhou (see p.437) and Wuhan (see p.429) – was one of three discovered in 1972 during construction work at Mawangdui, about 4km northeast (the others contained her husband and son). Thanks to damp-proof rammed walls of clay and charcoal, a triple wooden sarcophagus, and wrappings of linen and silk, the marquess' body was so well preserved that modern pathologists were able to determine that she suffered from tuberculosis, gallstones, arteriosclerosis and bilharzia when she died at age 50. The sarcophagi are in a side hall, while access to the mummy is through a basement display of embroideries, lacquered bowls and coffins, musical instruments, wooden tomb figures and other funerary offerings. Taoist texts written on silk were also found in the tomb, and one piece illustrating *qi gong* postures is on display. Xin Zui herself lies in a fluid-filled tank below several centimetres of perspex, a gruesome white doll, with her internal organs displayed in jars.

Around the river

Crossing the river affords a good opportunity to look across at Changsha's evolving skyline, and also to gaze down upon **Juzi Dao** (桔子岛, *júzi dǎo*; Tangerine Island), which was settled by Europeans following the riots of 1910. Several of their former homes are still standing, though they've suffered overenthusiastic renovation. The southern tip of the island is a neatly laid out park, while the northern two-thirds is given over to a new pavilion and hotel complex. Legend has it that Mao used to swim to shore from the southern tip of the island, a feat he repeated on his 65th birthday as one of his famous river crossings.

On the other side of the river, **Hunan University's campus** (湖南大学, *húnán dàxué*) sits south of **Yuelu Shan park** (岳麓山, *yuèlù shān*), where paths meander uphill, making for a pleasant stroll through some woodland to **Wangxiang Ting** (望乡亭, *wàngxiāng tíng*), a pavilion with views over the city. On the way, the small **Aiwan Ting** (爱晚亭, *àiwǎn tíng*; Loving the Dusk Pavilion), built in 1792, was one of Mao's youthful haunts, and a tablet bears his calligraphy.

A little west of here, **Lushan Si** (麓山寺, *lùshānsì*) dates from the Western Jin dynasty (263–316 AD), making it one of the oldest monasteries in Hunan; the enormous yew tree immediately in front of the temple is said to be of a similar age.

Eating, drinking and entertainment

Strong flavours and copious chillies are the signatures of **Hunanese food** – Mao himself claimed that it was the fiery food that made locals so (politically) red. Pungent regional specialities include air-cured and chilli-smoked meat; dong'an (chicken), seasoned with a vinegar-soy dressing; *gualiang fen*, a gelatinous mass of cold rice noodles covered in spicy sauce; and *chou doufu* (literally "stinky tofu"), deep-fried fermented bean-curd. There are numerous places at which to experience these firsthand, as well as a plethora of Western-style **cafés** and **bars**, particularly plentiful around Taiping Lu and the western end of Jiefang Lu). For **nightclubs**, the two most popular are currently *Soho* and *Milky* (乐巢酒吧, *lèchaójiǔbā*; Ⓦ www.milkybar.cn) on Jiefang Xi Lu, and there are also several **live music** venues, including *Freedom House* on Taiping Jie.

Bailando South end of Taiping Jie. More a bar than a restaurant, but this place does okay Mexican food – you could do worse if looking for a Western option that's not pizza, fried chicken or burgers.

Fifth Tone Cafe (第五调咖啡店, *dìwǔdiaòkāfeīdiàn*) Just off Xinmin Lu, close to Hunan University and Yuelu Shan park ⓣ0731/8805303. Relaxed and über-friendly American-run coffee shop with decent espresso, a selection of freshly baked cakes and free wi-fi. Call if you need directions. Mon–Sat 2–10pm.

Fire Palace (火宫饭店, *huǒgōng fàndiàn*) There are three branches of this riotously good restaurant: at 507 Shaoshan Bei Lu, on Wuyi Dadao and at the western end of Jiefang Lu. The original on Shaoshan Lu is the best – a busier, noisier and more enjoyable place to wolf down Hunanese food would be hard to imagine. Get an order card from the waitress, request some dark Baisha beer, and stop trolleys loaded with small plates of goodies as they pass.

Gaximu Canting (咖稀穆餐厅, *jiāxīmù cāntīng*) Wuyi Dadao. A great Muslim eatery, this one is fairly upmarket but affordable nevertheless. There's a choice of *lamian* (stretched noodles), hefty meat skewers or dumplings. Dishes from ¥5.

Xinhua Lou (新华楼, *xīnhuá lóu*) Eastern end of Wuyi Dadao. Another excellent place for local dishes, with trolleys of smoked tofu and meats, crisp cold vegetables dressed in sesame oil, black-skinned-chicken soup, preserved eggs and a huge range of dumplings being wheeled around between 6.30am and 1.30am. ¥2–10 a dish.

Ying Xiong Tie (英雄帖, *yīnxióngtiě*) Hidden away in a courtyard just off Jiefang Lu. Lively and traditional, this Hunanese restaurant dispenses with the hassle of a menu. Instead just tell the staff what you want – chicken, beef, pork, fish, tofu, vegetables, etc – and a few minutes later they'll bring you a steaming plate of spicy deliciousness.

Listings

Banks and exchange The principal Bank of China (Mon–Sat 8am–noon & 2.30–5pm) is near the train station on Wuyi Dadao. Upmarket hotels such as the *Dolton* also change travellers' cheques, and might not mind whether you're staying or not.

Hospital Global Doctor Clinic, Hunan brain hospital, 427 Furong Zhong Lu, Section 3, ⓣ0731/85230250.

Internet There are internet cafés throughout the city, generally charging ¥3/hr; a convenient option is the one on the second floor of the *Sanjiu Chunyun* hotel, while there are others near the airlines office on Wuyi Dadao and near the entrance to Qingshui Tang on Bayi Lu.

Left luggage Both the train and bus stations have left-luggage offices.

Mail and telephones The most convenient post office – with parcel post and international phones – is in the train-station square.

PSB The Foreign Affairs Department of the PSB (Mon–Fri 8am–noon & 2.30–5.30pm; ⓣ0731/84590788) is on Bayi Lu at its junction with Chengdao Lu.

Shopping Changsha has long had a reputation for silk embroidery, which you can buy at various stores along Wuyi Dadao. Taiping Jie has a smattering of shops selling pottery and other souvenirs, and there are antique stores along Qingshuitang Lu.

Travel agents CITS are at 160 Wuyi Dadao (ⓣ0731/84468929), and can organize tours. Hunan Shida Travel Service (ⓣ0731/4131177) is on Bayi Lu.

Shaoshan

Mao Zedong's birthplace, the hamlet of **SHAOSHAN** (韶山, *sháoshān*), lies 90km to the southwest of Changsha, a fine day-trip from the provincial capital through the Hunanese countryside. Established as a pilgrimage site for idolatrous Red Guards during the Cultural Revolution, Shaoshan seethes with Chinese tourists, who – following a low point in Mao's reputation through the 1980s – have started to flock back to visit the Great Helmsman's hometown. The best way to get here is on the special train from Changsha, which departs daily at 6.30am for the two-and-a-half-hour journey (¥101 return; returns from Shaoshan at 4.30pm). Alternatively, tour buses leave from the square outside the train station ticket office at 7am (guided day-tour ¥150).

Shaoshan contains two settlements: a knot of hotels and services that have sprung up around the railhead and long-distance bus depot, and **Shaoshan Dong**, the village itself, some 6km distant. Patriotic jingles and a large portrait of Mao greet arrivals at the train station, as do minibuses heading up to the village. Unless you're planning to stay overnight or are hungry – in which case there's a cheap hotel (❸) and several restaurants ahead and round to the right near the bus depot – you should hop directly onto a minibus.

Shaoshan Dong: Mao Zedong sights

The first place to disembark is just before the village proper outside **Mao's Family Home** (毛泽东故居, *máozédōng gùjū*; daily 8am–5pm; free), a compound of bare adobe buildings next to a lotus-filled pond, where Mao was born on December 26, 1893. The home is neatly preserved, with a few pieces of period furniture, the odd photograph, and wonderfully turgid English explanations completing the spartan furnishings. Here he led a thoroughly normal childhood, one of four children in a relatively wealthy peasant household that comfortably survived the terrible famines in Hunan during the first decade of the twentieth century. Though a rebellious youth, he did not become politicized until he moved to Changsha in his late teens.

Just up the road is the huge village square where, next to a bronze statue of an elderly Mao and a swarm of souvenir stalls, stands the **Mao Zedong Exhibition Hall** (毛泽东纪念馆, *máozédōng jìniànguǎn*; daily 8am–5pm; ¥15). Photos and knick-knacks chart Mao's career, though today there's a great distinction between Mao the heroic revolutionary and the character who inflicted the **Great Leap Forward** – the disastrous movement which was meant to bring Chinese industrial output up to Western levels – and Cultural Revolution on his country. The exhibition reflects this: noticeable omissions include the Little Red Book and just about any mention of the years between 1957 and his funeral in 1976. Next door to the museum is the former **Mao Ancestral Temple** (毛氏宗祠, *máoshì zōngcí*; free), now a memorial to the leader's early work among the peasants here.

After his Great Leap Forward had begun to falter, Mao returned to Shaoshan in 1959 to interview peasants on the movement's shortcomings. He can't have liked what he heard; on his final visit in 1966 at the start of the Cultural Revolution, he kept himself aloof near the reservoir in a secret retreat, poetically named **Dishui Dong** (滴水洞, *dīshuǐ dòng*; Dripping Water Cave; ¥30), to which you can catch a minibus. Alternatively, the elegant pavilion atop Shaoshan peak overlooks the local landscape – not really typical, given the amount of tourist revenue, but a nice scene of healthy fields and bamboo thickets.

Accommodation and eating

There are a few **restaurants** and **places to stay** in Shaoshan village around the square, including the *Shaoshan Binguan* (韶山宾馆, *sháoshān bīnguǎn*; ⓣ0731/55685262; ⑤) in the square itself, with a jumble of very ordinary rooms around an ornamental pool.

Yueyang

YUEYANG (岳阳, *yuèyáng*), a major riverside city on the Beijing–Guangzhou rail line and stop for Yangzi ferries, lies 160km southwest of Wuhan and 120km north of Changsha. The city also perches on the eastern shores of **Dongting Hu** (洞庭湖, *dòngtínghú*), China's second largest freshwater lake, covering 2500 square kilometres. Fringed with reeds and lotus ponds, villages farming rich cane and paddy fields surround the lake; many locals also earn a livelihood from fishing. Despite accelerating tourism and an unpleasantly down-at-heel new city springing up in the background, it remains a reasonable place to spend the day while in transit, thanks to the impressive **Yueyang Tower** (岳阳楼, *yuèyáng lóu*) – frequently packed with Chinese tourists – and some historical links to the nationwide sport of dragon-boat racing.

Arrival and information

Yueyang's **bus** and **train** stations are on opposite sides of a huge, multilevel roundabout 3km east of the city centre down Baling Lu. From here it's a simple bus trip to the lake and then north along Dongting Bei Lu to the Yueyang Tower – city buses #1 to #9 all run to the tower, but for easier navigation, pick up a map on arrival. Yangzi ferries stop 17km north of the city at **Chenglingji** (城陵矶, *chénglíng jī*), where bus #1 connects with the train station.

The English-speaking **CITS** (daily 9–11.30am & 2–5pm; ⓣ0730/8282222), located inside the *Yunmeng Hotel* on Yunmeng Lu, can arrange tours to lakeside sights. There's a **post office** on Baling Lu towards the bus and train stations (daily 8am–6pm), and a Bank of China to the right from the train station on Zhanqian Lu.

There's a range of **places to stay** around the bus and train stations and the Yueyang Tower, though it isn't worth overnighting here except during the Dragon Boat Festival.

The City

Yueyang's main street, **Baling Lu**, runs west for 5km, bare, broad and numbingly straight right up to **Nanyuepo docks** (南越码头, *nányuè mǎtóu*) on the lakeshore. Here it's crossed by Dongting Lu, with the Yueyang Tower and most of the services close to this junction. On Dongting Bei Lu, the **Yueyang Tower** (岳阳楼, *yuèyáng lóu*; daily: summer 7am–6.25pm; winter 7.30am–5.55pm; ¥46) rises from walled ramparts overlooking Dongting Hu, but the site was originally a mere platform where the **Three Kingdoms** general **Lu Su** reviewed his troops. It was through Lu's diplomacy that the armies of his native Wu and those of Shu were united against the overwhelming forces of Wei, who were subsequently defeated in 208 AD at the Battle of the Red Cliffs. A tower was first built here in 716, but today's 20m-tall timber edifice is of Qing design. Three upward-curving, yellow-glazed roofs are supported by huge, blood-red pillars of *nanmu* (southernwood); with its screens, eaves and crossbeams decorated with animal carvings, the tower makes a striking spectacle. Climb up to take in grand views of the lake, which quickly whips up into a stormy sea at the first breath of wind.

Flanking the tower are two lesser pavilions: **Xianmei Ting** (Immortal's Plum) – named after the delicately etched blossom design on a Ming stone tablet within – and **Sanzui Ting** (Thrice Drunk). This recalls the antics of **Lu Dongbin**, one of

Qu Yuan and the Dragon Boat Festival

The former state of **Chu**, which encompassed northern Hunan, was under siege in 278 BC from the first stirrings of the ambitious Qin armies, who later brought all of China under their control. At the time, Dongting was the haunt of the exiled poet-governor **Qu Yuan**, a victim of palace politics but nonetheless a great patriot of Chu. Hearing of the imminent invasion, Qu picked up a heavy stone and drowned himself in the nearby Miluo River rather than see his beloved state conquered. Distraught locals raced to save him in their boats, but were too late. They returned later to scatter *zongzi* (packets of meat and sticky rice wrapped up in reeds and lotus leaves) into the river as an offering to Qu Yuan's spirit.

The **Dragon Boat Festival**, held throughout China on the fifth day of the fifth lunar month (June or July), commemorates the rowers' hopeless rush – though many historians trace the tradition of food offerings and annual boat races to long before Qu's time. At any rate, it's a festive rather than mournful occasion, with the consumption of huge quantities of steamed *zongzi* and keen competition between local dragon-boat teams, who can be seen practising in their narrow, powerful crafts months before the event to the steady boom of a pacing drum. It's a lively spectator sport, with crowds cheering the rowers along, but you need to be up early to get the most from the ceremonies (for example, the dedication of the dragon-headed prows) as the race itself lasts only a few minutes. In Yueyang, the race is staged on the Miluo River (汨罗江, *mìluó jiāng*) south of town; contact CITS for details.

the Taoist Eight Immortals, who regularly visited the pavilion to down a wine gourd or two; there's a comic painting of this inside. Lu is also credited with populating Dongting Hu with shoals of silvery fish by tossing woodshavings into the water. Xiao Qiao, the wife of another historic general, lies buried at the northern end of the surrounding gardens, the grassy mound honoured by a tablet bearing the calligraphy of the renowned Song-dynasty poet, **Su Dongpo**.

Stores in Yueyang sell the very expensive **silver needle tea**, the main produce of **Junshan Dao** (君山岛, *jūnshān dǎo*), an island half an hour away by boat across the lake. Said to impart longevity, the tea was once paid in tribute to the emperor, and has tips that look like pale green twists; pour boiling water over them, inhale the musty vapour and watch them bob up and down in the glass. A spoonful sells for around ¥5.

Heng Shan

Some 120km south of Changsha, the **Heng Shan** (衡山, *héngshān*) region is one of China's holiest sites. Spread over 80km or so, the ranges form scores of low peaks dressed in woodland with a smattering of **Buddhist and Taoist temples**, some of which were established more than 1300 years ago. It's somewhere to relax and admire the scenery (frosted in winter, golden in autumn and misty year-round), either tackling the easy walks between shrines on foot, or resorting to local transport to ascend the heights.

Confusingly, it's **Nanyue**, a district of Hengyang city, not the nearby Hengshan town, that marks the starting point up into the hills. Early-morning **buses** from Changsha or Shaoshan take around three hours to reach Nanyue via Xiangtan. If you're coming from the south by road or rail from Shaoguan in Guangdong province or Guilin in Guangxi, you'll arrive in **Hengyang** (衡阳, *héngyáng*), where minibuses to Nanyue leave for the hour-long trip from the depot on Jiefang Lu – bus #1 connects Hengyang's nightmarishly busy **train station** with this depot, across the river. Alternatively, leave the train farther on at Hengshan town, where regular minibuses cover the 20km trip west to Nanyue.

Nanyue

Banners strung across the highway welcome visitors to **NANYUE** (南岳, *nányuè*; South Mountain), a small but expanding village of old flagstoned streets and new hotels set around **Nanyue Damiao** (南岳大庙, *nányuè dàmiào*) and **Zhusheng Si** (祝圣寺, *zhùshèng sì*), the two largest and most architecturally impressive temple complexes in the area. The Changsha–Hengyang highway runs along the eastern side of the village, with the **bus station** at its southern end, where map sellers, rickshaw drivers and hotel touts descend on new arrivals. Midway along the highway an ornamental stone archway forms the "entrance" to the village proper and leads through to the main street, Dongshan Lu. Here you'll find a mass of **restaurants**, whose staff will call you over as you pass – as always, establish prices before you order. Many of these places also offer basic **accommodation** for about ¥35 a bed, but there are plenty of easy-to-find hotels in the vicinity (❸–❹).

Nanyue Damaio

Off Dongshan Lu, streets lead through the old village centre to **Nanyue Damiao** (南岳大庙, *nányuè dàmiào*; ¥15). The site has served as a place of worship since at least 725 AD – some say that it was sanctified in Qin times – but the older buildings succumbed to fire long ago and were replaced in the nineteenth century by a smaller version of Beijing's Forbidden City. It's a lively place, echoing with bells and thick with smoke from incense and detonating firecrackers – there are furnaces in the courtyards to accommodate the huge quantities offered up by the crowds. Seventy-two pillars, representing Heng Shan's peaks, support the massive wooden crossbeams of the main hall's double-staged roof, and gilt phoenixes loom above the scores of kneeling worshippers paying homage to Taoist and Buddhist deities. Other halls in the surrounding gardens are far more humble but boast detailed carvings along their eaves and exterior alcoves.

Zhusheng Si

Far quieter, with fewer tourists and more monks in evidence, is **Zhusheng Si** (祝圣寺, *zhùshèng sì*), a short walk left out of the temple gates. A purely Buddhist site originating around the same time as Nanyue, the entire monastery – whose name translates as "Imperial Blessings" – was reconstructed for the anticipated visit of **Emperor Kangxi** in 1705, but he never showed up. The smaller scale and lack of pretence here contrast with Nanyue's extravagances, though there's a series of five hundred engravings of Buddhist *arhats* set into the wall of the rear hall, and a fine multifaced and many-handed likeness of Guanyin to seek out among the charming courtyards.

In the hills

There's a good day's walking to be had between Nanyue and **Zhurong Gong** (祝融殿, *zhùróng diàn*), a hall perched on Heng Shan's 1290m apex, 15km from town. Even major temples along the way are small and unassuming, requiring little time to explore, and tracks are easy, so around eight hours should be sufficient for a return hike along the most direct route – though you'd need at least ten hours to see everything on the mountain. **Minibuses** run between Nanyue and **Shangfeng Si** (上封寺, *shàngfēng sì*; ¥10), below the summit, in under an hour. **Food stalls** lurk at strategic points, so there's no need to carry much beyond something to keep out any seasonally inclement weather at the top.

Take the main road through Nanyue to the park gates behind Nanyue Damiao, where the admission **fee** (¥80) covers entry to all temples and includes a bilingual map of the mountain. The first two hours are spent passing occasional groups of descending tourists and black-clad Taoists, as the road weaves past rivers and patches of farmland before reaching the temple-like Martyrs' Memorial Hall, built to commemorate those killed during the 1911 revolution. Entering pine forests shortly thereafter, you'll find **Xuandu Si** (玄都寺, *xuándū sì*), which marks the halfway point (it's also known as the Midway Monastery) and is Hunan's Taoist centre, founded around 700 AD. Even so, an occasional Buddhist saint graces side shrines, but the best feature is the unusually domed ceiling in the second hall, watched over by a statue of Lao Zi holding a pill of immortality.

The rest of the ascent passes a handful of functioning, day-to-day temples with monks and nuns wandering around the gardens – **Danxia Si** (丹霞寺, *dānxiá sì*) and **Zushi Gong** (祖师宫, *zǔshī gōng*) are larger than most – before arriving outside **Shangfeng Si**'s red timber halls, which mark the minibus terminus. Overpriced **hotels** cater to those hoping to catch the dawn from the sunrise-watching terrace, a short walk away below a radio tower. On a cloudy day, it's better to push on for a further twenty minutes to the summit, where **Zhurong Gong** (祝融殿, *zhùróng diàn*), a tiny temple built almost entirely of heavy stone blocks and blackened inside from incense smoke, looks very atmospheric as it emerges from the mist. For the descent, there's always the bus, or an alternative track (shown on local maps) from Xuandu Si which takes in Lingzhi spring, the Mirror Grinding Terrace and the bulky Nantai Monastery, before winding back to town past the quiet halls of **Huangting Si** (黄庭寺, *huángtíng sì*), another sizeable Taoist shrine.

Wulingyuan (Zhangjiajie)

Hidden away in the northwestern extremities of Hunan, **Wulingyuan Scenic Reserve** (武陵源风景区, *wǔlíngyuán fēngjǐngqū*), widely known as **Zhangjiajie** (张家界, *zhāngjiājiè*), protects a mystical landscape of sandstone shelves and fragmented limestone towers, often misted in low clouds and scored by countless streams, with practically every horizontal surface hidden under a primeval, subtropical green mantle. It's so otherworldly that it is claimed (spuriously) these pinnacles provided inspiration for the landscapes in James Cameron's movie *Avatar*. The park however, is stunning enough without the injection of science fiction: among the 550-odd tree species (twice Europe's total) within its 370 square kilometres are rare **dove trees**, **ginkgos** and dawn **redwoods** – the last identified by their stringy bark and feathery leaves; now popular as an ornamental tree, until 1948 they were believed extinct. The **wildlife** list is impressive, too, including civets, giant salamanders, monkeys and gamebirds. The region is also home to several million ethnic **Tujia**, said by some to be the last descendants of western China's mysterious prehistoric Ba kingdom. On the downside, despite the UNESCO World Heritage listing, a total fire ban (smoking included) and a generous number of erosion-resistant paths, Wulingyuan is beginning to suffer from its popularity. Depending on your point of view, the giant **Heavenly Elevator** constructed up the side of one of the peaks (at 326m, by some reckoning the tallest in the world) is either a wonder of modern engineering or an outrageous blot on an otherwise unspoilt landscape; as well, more accessible parts of the reserve are often almost invisible under hordes of litter-hurling tour groups, despite the admission fee reaching an exorbitant ¥248.

Practicalities

Most visitors base themselves on the southern boundaries of the reserve at **Zhangjiajie village** (张家界国家森林公园管理处, *zhāngjiājiè guójiā sēnlín gōngyuán guǎnlǐchù*), where there's certainly enough to keep you occupied for a few days. It's also possible to organize extended walks north to **Tianzi Mountain** (天子山, *tiānzǐ shān*), or east to the **Suoxi Valley** (索溪, *suǒxī*). There are villages and stalls along the way supplying **accommodation** and **food**, but take water and snacks on long journeys. You'll need comfortable walking shoes and the right seasonal dress – it's humid in summer, cold from late autumn, and the area is often covered in light snow early in the year.

Note that **accommodation** prices double at weekends and holidays, when crowds are at their worst and train tickets are in short supply. If you're on a Chinese package tour to Wulingyuan, they may try to sting you for ¥50–100 based on a supposedly higher foreigners' entrance fee to the reserve, but there is no discriminatory pricing here. If the tour staff won't back down, tell them you'll pay the surcharge yourself at the gates.

Zhangjiajie Shi

ZHANGJIAJIE SHI (张家界市, *zhāngjiājiè shì*) is the regional hub, 33km south of the reserve. The **bus station** is fairly central, but the **train station** and ticket office are a further 9km south, and the **airport** is a similar distance to the west. Minibuses prowl arrival points for the hour-long journey to the reserve at either Zhangjiajie village (¥6) or Suoxi (¥10).

It's only worth **staying here** if you arrive too late to get the last bus to the park (around 7pm). There are a host of mediocre **hotels** in town – the *Wuling Hotel* is the best of these (武陵宾馆, *wǔlíng bīnguǎn*; ⓣ0744/8225088; ❹).

Leaving, there are regular **buses** covering the journey to Changsha and down to Jishou for Fenghuang. **Trains** are faster; direct services head east to Changsha, north to Yichang in Hubei, and south to Jishou and Liuzhou in Guangxi. For Guizhou and points west you'll have to change trains at the junction town of Huaihua, four hours to the southwest – sleeper tickets out of Huaihua are hard to come by at the station, but you may be able to upgrade on board. You can also **fly** from Zhangjiajie Shi to Changsha and a half-dozen other provincial capitals.

Zhangjiajie village and around

ZHANGJIAJIE VILLAGE (张家界国家森林公园管理处, *zhāngjiājiè guójiā sēnlín gōngyuán guǎnlǐchù*) is simply a couple of streets in the valley at the reserve entrance, overflowing with map- and souvenir-sellers, pricey **restaurants**, a **post office** and **places to stay**. You should ask around about basic hotels within the reserve, which are recommended for getting away from it all.

The best-value option in the village is the Tujia-run *Minsu Shanzhuang* (民俗山庄, *mínsú shānzhuāng*; ⓣ0744/5719188; ❷), a wooden building at the bottom of town. Farther up is one of the village's better hotels, the *Xiangdian Shanzhuang* (香殿山庄, *xiāngdiàn shānzhuāng*; ⓣ0744/5712999; ❺). Its travel service is fairly helpful with general hiking advice, and can arrange whitewater rafting day-tours in the Suoxi Valley (¥250/person).

The reserve

With a dense forest of tall, eroded karst pinnacles splintering away from a high plateau, Zhangjiajie's scenery is awesomely poetic – even Chinese tour groups can be hushed by the spectacle. The road through the village leads downhill past a throng of Tujia selling medicinal flora and cheap plastic ponchos at the **reserve entrance**, where you buy your ticket (¥248, valid for two days).

The left path here follows a four-hour circuit along a short valley up to **Huangshi village** (黄石寨, *huángshí zhài*), on the edge of a minor, island-like plateau surrounded by views of the area. There's also a **cable car** to the top (索道站, *suǒdào zhàn*; ¥48 each way). The right path offers several options, the shortest of which (again, around 4hr) runs along **Golden Whip Stream**, branching off to the right and returning to base through a particularly dense stand of crags below two facing outcrops known as the **Yearning Couple** (engraved tablets along the path identify many other formations). Alternatively, bearing left after a couple of kilometres – consult a map – takes you up past **Bewitching Terrace** (迷魂台, *míhún tái*) into the **Shadao Valley**. From here, basic trails continue through magnificent scenery around the western edge of the plateau to **Black Dragon village** (黑龙寨, *hēilóng zhài*), then circuit back to the park gates. This is a lengthy day's walk, and you won't see many other tourists along the way.

Suoxi Valley and Tianzi Shan

With many of the same facilities as Zhangjiajie, **SUOXI VILLAGE** (索溪峪镇, *suǒxīyù zhèn*) makes a good base for exploring the east and north of the reserve. Set in the **Suoxi Valley**, it's 10km as the crow flies from Zhangjiajie but the better part of a day away on foot (you can also get between the two by local bus). Attractions here include groups of rhesus monkeys and relatively open river gorges where it's possible to **cruise** – or even go whitewater rafting – between the peaks. Around the 2km-long **Baofeng Hu** (宝峰湖, *bǎofēng hú*), a lake accessed by a ladder-like staircase from the valley floor, there's a chance of encountering golden pheasants, the grouse-like tragopans and **giant salamanders** – secretive, red-blotched monsters which reach 2m in length; considered a great delicacy, they're sometimes seen in the early mornings around Baofeng's shore. There's also **Huanglong Dong** (黄龙洞, *huánglóng dòng*; Yellow Dragon Cave), a few kilometres east of Suoxi, a mass of garishly lit limestone caverns linked by a subterranean river, and **Hundred Battle Valley**, where the Song-dynasty Tujia king, Xiang, fought imperial forces.

The **Tianzi Shan** region, which basically covers the north of the park, is named after an isolated 1250m-high peak and contains most of Wulingyuan's caves. It's probably best visited from Suoxi village, where there's a possible circuit of 30km setting off along the **Ten-li Corridor** (十里画廊, *shílǐ huàláng*). High points include the mass of lookouts surrounding **Shentangwan** (神堂湾, *shéntáng wān*), a valley thick with needle-like rocks where Xiang is said to have committed suicide after his eventual defeat; **Immortals' Bridge** (仙人桥, *xiānrén qiáo*), a narrow strip of rock bridging a deep valley; and the astounding, 330m-high **Bailong Elevator** at Yuanjiajie (袁家界百龙电梯, *yuánjiājièbaǐlóngdiàntī*; ¥56 each way). Instead of returning to Suoxi, you can continue past the mountain to **TIANZI SHAN VILLAGE** (天子山镇, *tiānzǐ shānzhèn*), spend the night in the guesthouse there (❸), and then either hike south to Zhangjiajie or leave Wulingyuan by catching a bus first to Songzhi (45km) and then on to Dayong (another 60km).

Fenghuang and around

Two hours south of Zhangjiajie by road or rail is **Jishou**, the jumping-off point for the charming town of **FENGHUANG** (凤凰, *fènghuáng*), with its stilted houses, flagstoned streets and communities of Miao and Tujia peoples. Fenghuang is a great place to unwind for a couple of days: it's relatively unspoilt by modern development (but does get packed with visitors in summer), the town's twelve-hundred-year **history** is evident in its narrow winding streets and the renovated **Southern Great Wall** can be explored nearby.

Arrival

Heading to Fenghuang by train, you'll need to get off at nearby **Jishou** (吉首, *jíshoŭ*), where a bus or a taxi (¥5) over the bridge takes you to the bus station on Wuling Lu, just off the main Tuan Jie Lu. Hop one of the regular shuttle **buses** (¥12), which run until 6pm or so, to take you the remaining seventy minutes. If you are coming from Yichang you will probably arrive too late and have to stay overnight. Alternatively, there are direct buses to Fenghuang from Sichuan and Hunan, or you can **fly** into **Tongren** (铜仁市, *tóngrénshì*) in Guizhou and get a bus (3–4hr) to Fenghuang, although flying in does take some of the romance out of the venture.

On reaching Fenghuang, buses will either drop you at Nanhua Lu bridge or halfway down Fenghuang Lu. From either destination the old town is walking distance, but anywhere in town is reachable for ¥5 in a taxi.

When **leaving**, buses depart from the **New North Station** (新北站, *xīnbeǐzhàn*), a kilometre or so out of town up Fenghuang Lu.

Accommodation

Fenghuang International Youth Hostel (青年旅馆, *qīngnián lǚguǎn*) ⓣ0743/3260546, ⓦwww.yhachina.com. Usually staffed by students, whose lack of experience is tempered by their eagerness to help; low prices and an excellent location also aid the cause. Dorm beds ¥20, rooms ❷

Fengtian Hotel (凤天宾馆, *fèngtiān bīnguǎn*) 8 Nanhua Lu ⓣ0743/3501000. Recently built four-star affair, tastefully furnished, with 24hr hot water and heating to boot. A nice way to treat yourself if you have been enduring unheated guest-houses. ❹

Government Hotel (政府宾馆, *zhèngfǔ bīnguǎn*) Xi Men Po, off Nanhua Lu ⓣ0743/3221690. The hotel moved not long ago to a new building; until the fixtures and fittings get too worn, it's a fair deal in a good location. ❹

Guyun Binguan (古韵宾馆, *gǔyún bīnguǎn*) 52 Lao Cai Jie, near the old city wall by the river ⓣ0743/3500077. Rising from the ashes of an old

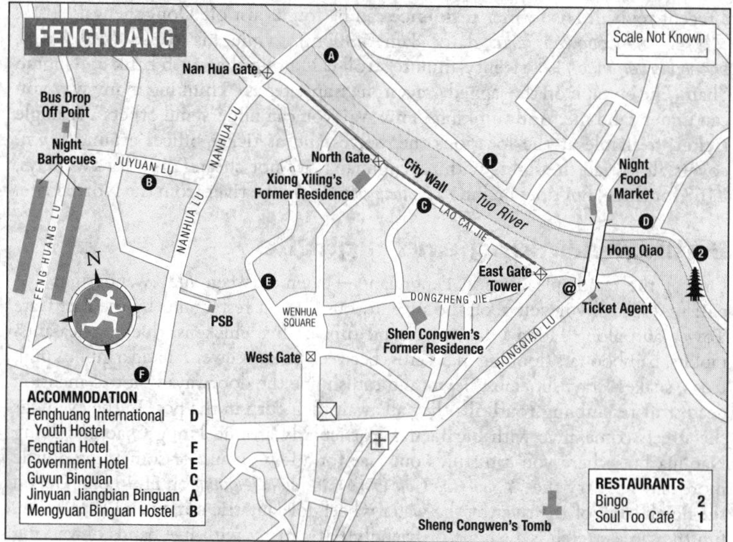

courtyard dwelling, this spot has clean rooms but unfortunately little in the way of atmosphere. ❷

Jin Lai Hotel (金来宾馆, *jīnlái bīnguǎn*) 4 Guangming Dong Lu ☎0743/8721188. The best of a smattering of accommodation near the train station, with the best mix of values and facilities. ❸

Jinyuan Jiangbian Binguan (金源江边宾馆, *jīnyuán jiāngbiān bīnguǎn*) 94 Lao Gong Shao ☎13974346711. Ideally situated by the river, just below the Nanhua bridge, this traditional-style, family-run hotel boasts good views, but icy rooms outside summer. ❷

Mengyuan Binguan Hostel (梦源宾馆, *mèngyuán bīnguǎn*) Ku Yuan Lu, just off Nanhua Lu ☎0743/2150721. A good budget option outside the old town and close to bus drop-off points. Spotless rooms, hot water and a good on-site restaurant make it a viable option. ❷

The Town

Fenghuang is a small, easily navigable place largely south of the Tuo River, which runs roughly west to east. The old town is bounded on its north side by the river, with a restored section of the city's Ming walls running along the riverbank, punctuated from west to east by the splendid Nanhua, North and East gates. The principal thoroughfare, **Dongzheng Jie**, is a pedestrianized alley squeezing its way through from Wenhua Square, in the centre, to the East gate and **Hong Qiao**, a 300-year-old covered bridge. To the west and south, Nanhua Lu and Hong Qiao Lu define the old town, the latter curling north from the southeast corner of town to end up at Hong Qiao.

Fenghuang is the hometown of several important Chinese, including **Xiong Xiling**, an ethnic Miao who became premier of China's first republican government. Near the North Gate, you can visit his **former home** (熊希龄故居, *xióngxīlíng gùjū*; daily 8am–5.30pm), a simple affair preserved as it was and holding a few photos, including those of his three wives, with some English captions.

Shen Congwen (1902–88), one of China's greatest writers and also Miao, was from Fenghuang, and many of his stories centre on the Miao people and the landscapes of Western Hunan (*Recollections of West Hunan* is available in English). In 1949, Shen's writing was banned in both mainland China and Taiwan after he failed to align with either, effectively ending his career, but his works have enjoyed a recent revival. His former **residence** can be found just off Dongzheng Jie (沈从文故居, *shěncóngwén gùjū*; daily 8am–5.30pm), while his **tomb** (沈从文墓地, *shěncóngwén mùdì*) is a twenty-minute stroll east along the south bank at Tingtao Shan. The epitaph on the jagged gravestone translates as "Thinking in my way you can understand me. And thinking in my way you can understand others". A single **ticket**, available at the locations themselves and at ticket offices around town, covers almost all the sights within Fenghuang; it's not cheap (¥148 for two days, ¥168 for three) but does include a *sampan* trip down the river from the North Gate.

Eating, drinking and nightlife

One of the major pleasures in Fenghuang – taken between alley wanderings – is **eating**, especially if you're on the adventurous side. At restaurants by the East Gate Tower and along Hong Qiao, cages and tubs of live chickens, ducks, pheasants, rabbits, bamboo rats (looking like a cross between a giant sewer rat and a guinea pig), frogs, snakes, crayfish, crabs, newts and catfish line the doorways – not to mention dead stuff resembling **roadkill**; they all await their turn in the pot. In the evenings the streets come alive with **barbecues**, particularly around Hong Qiao and along Nanhua Lu, where you can stuff your face for a few yuan. For something a little more laid-back try the *Soul Too Café* (素咖啡馆, *sù kāfēiguǎn*) on Hui Long Ge, on the north bank of the river by the water wheel, for fantastic **coffee** and cheesecake. On the same stretch is a gaggle of friendly **bars**, many with live bands of varying quality, though invariably loud. If you fancy a quieter night, walk over by the pagoda to a place called *Bingo* (边各, *biāngè*) that is full of quiet hideyholes, has a good selection of pizzas and pastas, and can turn out vegetarian dishes on request.

Listings

Hospital On Hong Qiao Lu, between the West and South gates to the old town.

Internet Two cafés are on the south side of the Hong Qiao bridge.

Mail and telephones The post office is in the new town on Hong Qiao Lu, between the West and South gates to the old town. Near the *Government Hotel*, a couple of shops offer international phone services.

PSB Just off Nanhua Lu near the *Government Hotel*.

Travel agent Cross over to the south side of the Hong Qiao bridge.

Around Fenghuang

The pretty countryside near Fenghuang has some worthwhile and easily accessible sights, the nearest being the **Southern Great Wall** (南方长城, *nánfāng chángchéng*), which, astonishingly, wasn't recognized for what it was until 2000. Originally constructed in 1554 as a defence against the Miao, the wall ran for around 190km from Xiqueying in western Hunan to Tongren in Guizhou. There are several hundred metres of intact wall at a site 13km west from Fenghuang, the journey to which takes around half an hour by bus from a roundabout at the western end of Jianshe Lu. A ticket to the site (¥45) grants you access to the newly renovated wall, which, while not as rugged as its northern counterpart, is nevertheless impressive and significantly less visited; if you come in winter you'll probably have the place to yourself.

Ten kilometres from the wall, **Huangsi Qiao** (黄丝桥, *huángsīqiáo*; Huang's Silk Bridge) is another ancient settlement, which prospered after Huang, a silk merchant, decided to build a bridge to attract people to the town. A smaller version of Fenghuang, with attractive stilted houses, the town is only half a kilometre across and has gate towers to the north, east and west. You can get here by bus from the wall or Fenghuang (¥3; 30min).

If you want to see more of the Miao or acquire some of their **handicrafts**, you could head to **Alaying** (阿拉营, *ālāyíng*), 7km west of the Great Wall, where market days (on dates ending with a 2 or 7, as is the local practice) attract the surrounding villagers. Buses leave for Alaying from the western end of Jianshe Lu in Fenghuang (¥5; 1hr).

Jiangxi

Caught between the Yangzi in the north and a mountainous border with Guangdong in the south, **Jiangxi province** (江西, *jiāngxī*) is generally considered a bit of a backwater, but to dismiss it out of hand is to ignore some significant attractions. Here you will find at least a couple of mountain ranges worth hiking, some major revolutionary history and a town that has been producing the highest quality ceramics for almost six and a half centuries.

Inhabited for some four thousand years, the province's first major influx of settlers didn't arrive until about two thousand years ago, with the northern half benefiting most as migrants began farming the plain around **Poyang Hu**, China's largest freshwater lake. A network of rivers covering the province drains into Poyang, and when the construction of the Grand Canal created a route through Yangzhou and the lower Yangzi in the seventh century, Jiangxi's capital, **Nanchang**, became a key point on the great north–south link of inland waterways. The region enjoyed a long period of quiet prosperity until coastal shipping and the opening up of treaty ports took business away in the 1840s. The twentieth century saw the province's fortunes nosedive: the population halved as millions fled competing warlords and, during the 1920s and 30s, fighting between the Guomindang and Communist forces raged in the southern Jinggang Shan ranges. This conflict eventually led to an evicted Red Army starting on their Long March across China.

Things picked up after the Communist takeover, and a badly battered Nanchang licked its wounds and reinvented itself as a centre of heavy industry. Transport links provided by the Poyang and Yangzi tributaries have also benefited the east of the province, where **Jingdezhen** retains its title as China's porcelain capital. North of the lake, **Jiujiang** is a key Yangzi port on the doorsteps of Anhui and Hubei, while the nearby mountain area of **Lu Shan**, also easily visited from Nanchang, offers a pleasant reminder of Jiangxi's past, when it served as a summer retreat for Chinese literati and colonial servants.

Nanchang

Hemmed in by hills, **NANCHANG** (南昌, *nánchāng*) sits on Jiangxi's major river, the Gan Jiang (赣江, *gànjiāng*), some 70km south of where it flows into Poyang Hu (鄱阳湖, *póyánghú*). Built on trade, Nanchang has served as a **transport hub** for central-southern China and established itself a handy base for car and plane manufacturers – Ford now has a plant here assembling vans. More recently, the city has traded in its reliance on heavy industry – which gave the city a sullen, Soviet atmosphere – for consumerism, tossing up office blocks and shopping malls with abandon.

The Guomindang army occupied the city in December 1926, but when Chiang Kai-shek broke with the Communists the following year, Zhou Enlai and Zhu De, two Communist officers, mutinied and took control of the city with thirty thousand troops. They were soon forced to flee into Jiangxi's mountainous south, but the anniversary of the uprising – August 1, 1927 – is still celebrated as the birth of the People's Liberation Army and the PLA flag remains emblazoned with the Chinese characters "8" and "1" (八一, *bāyī*) for the month and day.

Arrival and city transport

Nanchang sprawls eastward from the Gan Jiang, but the centre is a compact couple of square kilometres between the river and Bayi Dadao.

From **Changbei International Airport** (昌北国际机场, *chāngběi guójì jīchǎng*), 23km north of the centre, there's an airport bus (¥15) that will drop you at the *Civil Aviation Hotel* (民航大酒店, *mínháng dàjiǔdiàn*) on Hongcheng Lu. Alternatively, taxis can whisk you into town (¥70). Other transit points are more central. Nanchang's **train station** is 700m east of the Fushan roundabout at the end of Zhanqian Lu. The **long-distance bus station** is 1km away on Bayi Dadao. Taxis (¥6 standing charge) cruise downtown arrival points, while city bus #2 runs from the train station along Bayi Dadao and then makes a circuit of the central area, passing or coming close to all the hotels.

Accommodation

There's a good range of accommodation in town, much of it relatively close to the train and bus stations.

7 Days Inn (7天连锁酒店, *qītiānliánsuǒjiǔdiàn*) 142 Bayi Dadao ⓣ0791/8857688. Excellent location across from the bus station, clean modern rooms and attentive, friendly staff. ❸

Gloria Plaza (凯莱大酒店, *keilái dàjijdiàn*) 88 Yanjiang Bei Lu ⓣ0791/6738855, ⓦwww.gphnanchang.com, ⓔgloria@gphnanchang.com. Modern, international-style joint-venture hotel, the most foreigner-friendly in Nanchang and worth visiting for its Western food. ❻

Hua Guang Binguan (华光宾馆, *huáguāng bīnguǎn*) 58 Xiangshan Bei Lu ⓣ0791/6777222. New, friendly place in the heart of town. Clean, stylish rooms and corridors oddly lit with electric blue light. ❷

Lijing Hotel (丽景酒店, *lìjǐngjiǔdiàn*) 122 Bayi Dadao ⓣ0791/8801199, ⓦwww.brly.cn. Smart three-star venture, good value, with attentive staff. ❹

Ruidu (瑞都大酒店, *ruìdū dàjiǔdiàn*) 399 Guangchang Lu ⓣ0791/6201888. An

Moving on from Nanchang

You can **fly** from Nanchang to Beijing, Shanghai, Guangzhou and a handful of other cities. Zhanqian Lu is teeming with airline agents, and most hotels can book flights. China Eastern (ⓣ0791/8514195) is on Beijing Lu.

Nanchang lies on the Kowloon–Beijing **train line** and just off the Shanghai–Kunming line, with connections through easterly Yingtan down into Fujian province. Sleeper tickets are pretty easy to obtain, but prepare for mighty queues at the station; alternatively, there are travel agencies and a train ticket office on Supu Lu near the Mayflower.

The **bus station** looks huge and crowded, but the ticket office is user-friendly and there's no problem getting seats. Minibuses and smart coaches operate throughout the day along fast expressways to Jiujiang, Lu Shan and Jingdezhen, with daily services within Jiangxi to Jinggang Shan and Ganzhou, and further afield to Wuyi Shan in Fujian and destinations across central China.

upmarket place, nicely located on the southeast corner of Renmin Square. ❺

Welcome Inn (唯客酒店, *wéikèjiǔdiàn*) 70 Louyang Lu ☎0791/8168168, Ⓦwww.chnwelcomeinn.com. Another mid-range chain hotel in a great location, this time next to the train station. Not the cheapest here but by far the cleanest, most comfortable and best value. ❹

Xingqiu Hotel (星球宾馆, *xīngqiúbīnguǎn*) Erqi Beilu ☎0791/6126668. One in a string of tired flophouses, only worth considering if you want to stay close to the train station. ❸

The City

Nanchang's older relics, the Cold-War-era **Exhibition Hall** and revolutionary **Bayi Monument** (八一纪念塔, *bāyī jìniàntǎ*), both on the central **Renmin Square** (人民广场, *rénmín guǎngchǎng*), are overshadowed by their modern neighbours: skyscrapers and shopping malls. Running west of the square, Zhongshan Lu takes you to the heart of Nanchang's bustling shopping district, past the water and greenery of **Bayi Park** (八一公园, *bāyī gōngyuán*) to the north and, further along, the **August 1 Uprising Museum** (八一纪念馆, *bāyī jìniànguǎn*; daily 8am–5pm, last entry 3.30pm; free). Formerly a hotel, this was occupied by the embryonic PLA as their 1927 Headquarters and is mostly of interest as an example of Nanchang's colonial architecture; as a museum it is disappointingly dull.

Opposite the top end of Bayi Park and set back off Minde Lu, **Youmin Si** (佑民寺, *yòumín sì*; ¥2) is a Buddhist temple dating back to 503 AD, which Nanchang's Red Guards were especially diligent in wrecking at the start of the Cultural Revolution. Three restored halls include a striking, 10m-high standing Buddha, rising out of a lotus flower. East of here, an austere grey brick house on the corner of Huayuanjiao Jie is **Zhu De's former residence** (朱德旧居, *zhūdé jiùjū*; daily

8am–5.30pm; free). Like at the Uprising Museum, the exhibits are hardly captivating – Chinese-captioned photographs of Zhu De and Zhou Enlai, Zhu's bedroom and a few personal effects, including his gun.

Tengwang Pavilion and the Provincial Museum

The mighty **Tengwang Pavilion** (滕王阁, *téngwáng gé*; daily: summer 7.30am–5.30pm; winter 8am–4.30pm; ¥50) overlooks the river on Yanjiang Lu, 1km or so west of Youmin Si. There have been 26 consecutive towers built here since the first was raised more than a thousand years ago in memory of a Tang prince. The present "Song-style" building was completed in 1989 but has an impressive pseudo-old exterior nonetheless. There's not much reason to enter: the upper-level balconies offering less-than aerial views of a drab cityscape.

South of the pavilion, bridges off Yanjiang Lu cross to the surreal **Provincial Museum** (省博物馆, *shěng bówùguǎn*; Tues–Sun 9am–5pm; free), a huge, futuristic complex of marble and green glass towers that is perennially deserted. The collection features several floors of local porcelain and a dinosaur exhibition.

Southern Nanchang

West of the Fushan roundabout off Zhanqian Lu (bus #5 passes by on its route between the roundabout and Xiangshan Lu), you'll find **Shengjin Ta** (绳金塔, *shéngjīn tǎ*; daily 7am–6pm; ¥15). Legend has it that the city will fall if the seven-storey pagoda is ever destroyed, a warning still taken fairly seriously despite the fact that Shengjin has already been demolished several times, most recently in the early eighteenth century. The area's restored streets and teahouses make this market quarter worth a wander.

For a reprieve from the city, catch bus #20 from Yanjiang Lu 5km south to the **Bada Shanren Museum** (八大山人纪念馆, *bādàshānrén jìniànguǎn*; Tues–Sun 9am–4.30pm; ¥20). This whitewashed Ming-era compound set in parkland was the studio of the painter Zhu Da, also known as Bada Shanren, a wandering Buddhist monk of royal descent who came to live in this former temple in 1661 and was later buried here. He is said to have painted in a drunken frenzy – his pictures certainly show great spontaneity. There are a number of originals displayed inside and some good reproductions on sale.

Eating, drinking and nightlife

Nanchang's **gastronomy** covers everything from dumpling houses and spicy Hunanese restaurants to the regional Gan cooking – lightly sauced fresh fish, crayfish, snails and frogs. Soups are a Jiangxi favourite – egg and pork soup is a typical breakfast – often served in huge pots as communal affairs. Restaurants are spread all over the city, though the streets around Bayi Park have the highest concentration and **Yongshu Lu** (永叔路, *yǒngshūlù*) is lined with eateries, from holes in the wall to fancy hotel restaurants. Cafés and coffee shops are on the rise, including *My Café*, on Minde Lu near Supu Lu, a relaxing place to spend a couple of hours sipping Earl Grey. The locals are also renowned for enjoying a night on the tiles, and Minde Lu hosts several **bars** and **nightclubs** – try *Bar 97* or one of the other pubs along the same street, Rongmen Lu (榕门路, *róngménlù*), for a relaxed drink, and the *Mayflower* (五月花, *wǔyuèhuā*) further east if you fancy a dance as well.

Haokoufu Xiaochi (好口福小吃, *haǒkoǔfúxiaǒchī*) 46 Zhongshan Lu. Crowded canteen-style dining: ordering is easy (the food's on display), though payment via a swipe card system is more complicated than necessary.

Hao Yuan Lai (好缘来, *haǒyuánlai*) 175 Minde Lu, next to Youmin Si. Sizzling steaks

from ¥30, plus delicious Chinese snacks, biscuits and dumplings from ¥8 a plate.
Hunan Wang Caiguan (湖南王菜馆, *húnánwáng càiguăn*) Supu Lu. Popular, mid-range Hunanese restaurant, where you can sweat over your red-braised pork while enjoying the views overlooking Bayi Park.
Ming Dynasty (明朝铜鼎煨汤府, *míngcháo tóngdĭng wèitāngfŭ*) Bayi Dadao, next to the Jiangnan Fandian. The big bronze cauldron outside marks this as a Jiangxi-style soup restaurant. Individual pots from ¥18 or three- to four-person pots from ¥30.

Listings

Bank and exchange The main Bank of China is on Zhanqian Xi Lu just off the Fushan roundabout, and there's another large branch in the south-eastern corner of Renmin Square (both Mon–Fri 8am–5.30pm).
Hospital First City Hospital, Xiangshan Lu ☎0791/8862261.
Internet There are internet bars scattered across the city, including one on Xiangshan Lu near the intersection with Dieshan Lu and another just west of Bayi Park on Minde Lu.
Left luggage Offices at train and bus stations open roughly daily 6am–7pm.
Mail and telephones The main post office and the telecommunications building (both daily 8am–6pm) are near each other at the corner of Bayi Dadao and Ruzi Lu.
PSB On Shengli Lu, just north of Minde Lu (daily 8am–noon & 2.30–5.30pm; ☎0791/8892000).
Shopping Nanchang Department Store, the city's largest and best-stocked department store, hides behind a 1950s frontage west of Renmin Square along Zhongshan Lu. Zhongshan Lu itself and the pedestrianized southern stretch of Shengli Lu are rife with clothing stores and boutiques. A good supermarket is Walmart, on the second floor of the shopping centre at the northern end of Renmin Square. For a big range of porcelain, name chops and paintings, try the Jiangxi Antique Store on Minde Lu.

Jiujiang and Lu Shan

Set on the Yangzi 150km north of Nanchang, **Jiujiang** had its heyday in the nineteenth century as a treaty port, and now serves as a jumping-off point for tourists exchanging the torrid lowland summers for Lu Shan's cooler climes. Trains on the Kowloon–Beijing line stop at Jiujiang, while fast buses from Nanchang run throughout the day to both Jiujiang and **Lu Shan**.

Jiujiang

A small but important staging post for river traffic, **JIUJIANG** (九江, *jiŭjiāng*) grew wealthy during the Ming dynasty through trade in Jingdezhen porcelain. Largely destroyed during the Taiping Uprising, the town was rebuilt as a treaty port in the 1860s, and today enjoys a low-scale renaissance, its docks busy once again from dawn till dusk.

Arrival and information

Jiujiang's centre is laid out in a narrow strip between the north shore of **Gantang Hu** (甘棠湖, *gāntáng hú*) and the Yangzi: Xunyang Lu runs west from the top of the lake out to the highway, while parallel Binjiang Lu is 100m farther north and follows the riverbank.

The **train station** is 3km southeast of the centre at the bottom end of Gantang Hu – catch #1 to the bus station – and has regular links to Nanchang (90min) and Hefei (4–5hr). The **long-distance bus station** is 1500m east down Xunyang Lu, with buses back to Nanchang until 7pm, earlier for Lu Shan, and others to Wuhan and Nanjing. On Xunyang Lu between here and the lake you'll find a **Bank of China** (Mon–Fri 8am–5pm).

The Town

The picturesque **Yanshui Pavilion** (烟水亭, *yānshuǐ tíng*; daily 8am–8pm; ¥10), a Ming construction commemorating the Tang poet-official **Li Bai** – responsible for the causeway and the restored moon-shaped sluice gate – completely occupies a tiny islet in the lake. On Binjiang Lu northeast of Gantang Hu, **Xunyang Lou** (寻阳楼, *xúnyáng lóu*; daily 8am–6.30pm; ¥6) is an "antique" wooden wine house (built in 1986 to replace a Tang-dyasty structure) facing out across the Yangzi. The original building was the setting for a scene in *Outlaws of the Marsh* (aka *The Water Margin*), China's Robin Hood legend, which provides the theme for much of the decor. Upstairs, the restaurant is worth visiting at lunchtime for dongpo rouding (steamed and braised pork belly), river fish, "Eight Treasure" duck, scrambled eggs and green pepper, or *sunyang dabing* (a pancake invented by one of the legendary outlaws).

Accommodation and eating

Jiujiang's most convenient **accommodation** is on Xunyang Lu between the bus station and the lake. The *Xinhua Binguan* (新华宾馆, *xīnhuá bīnguǎn*; ⓣ0792/8989222; ❷) is the best value, past its prime but comfortable nevertheless. Nearby, the modern *Huifeng Binguan* (荟丰宾馆, *huìfēng bīnguǎn*; ⓣ0792/8985188; ❸) has chrome fittings and enormous glass-screened bathrooms, while more traditional rooms are available at *Bailu Binguan* (白鹿宾馆, *báilù bīnguǎn*; ⓣ0792/8980866; ❸), a smart place popular with tour groups.

On summer evenings everyone heads down Xunyang Lu to window-shop and **eat** at one of the pavement cafés on Gantang's north shore – a great spot from which to admire Lu Shan across the water while gorging on crayfish, sautéed frogs and freshwater snails.

Lu Shan

Lu Shan's (庐山, *lúshān*) range of forested peaks rises abruptly from the level shores of Poyang Hu to a dizzying 1474m, its cool heights bringing welcome relief from the summer cauldron of the Yangzi basin. Developed in the mid-nineteenth century by Methodist minister-turned-property-speculator **Edward Little** as a hill-station-style resort for European expats, it saw the Chinese elite move in soon after foreigners lost their grip on the region. Chiang Kai-shek built a summer residence and training school for officials here in the 1930s, and, twenty years later, Lu Shan hosted one of the key meetings of the Maoist era. Today, proletarian holidaymakers pack out its restaurants and tramp its paths, and the mansions have been converted into hotels to accommodate them. Crowds reach plague proportions between spring and autumn, so winter – though very cold – can be the best season to visit, and a weekend's walking is enough for a good sample of the scenery.

Guling

The 30km trip from Jiujiang takes around an hour and a half on the sharply twisting road, with sparkling views back over the great lake and its junction with the Yangzi. There's a pause at the top gates for passengers to pay the steep entry fee (¥180), then it's a short way to **GULING** (牯岭, *gǔlǐng*) township in Lu Shan's northeastern corner, whose handful of quaintly cobbled streets, European stone villas and bungalows are the base for further exploration. There are some sights around town, though these are generally only of interest to those making revolutionary pilgrimages: the **Meilu Villa** on He Xi Lu (美庐别墅, *měilú biéshù*; daily 8am–6pm; ¥15), is a former residence of both Chiang Kai-shek (it's named after his wife, Song Meiling) and Mao Zedong. Not far away are **Zhou Enlai's**

Residence (周恩来故居, *zhōuēnlaígùjū*; daily 8am–6pm; ¥10), the **People's Hall** (人民剧院, *rénmín jùyuàn*; daily 8am–5pm; ¥20), venue of many a historic meeting – including one in 1959 when Marshal Peng Dehui openly criticized the Great Leap Forward, and was subsequently denounced as a "Rightist" by Mao, triggering the Cultural Revolution – and the **Lu Shan Museum** (庐山博物馆, *lúshānbówùguǎn*; daily 8am–5.30pm; free), where Mao apparently also once laid his head. A bigger attraction for most foreign visitors is the combination of stunning scenery and cool mountain air.

Buses arrive on He Dong Lu immediately after emerging from a tunnel into town (though minibuses from Jiujiang might terminate anywhere). Fifty metres downhill on the right is a pedestrian mall leading through to Guling Jie. Most essential services are either in the mall or on Guling Jie, where you'll find shops selling **maps**, a **post office**, **Bank of China** and a **market** selling fruit and veg.

Leaving Lu Shan is simple, with hourly buses to Jiujiang and Nanchang, and less regular services for farther afield. If you can't find a direct service for where you're headed, go first to Jiujiang for Wuhan and points east, and Nanchang for southern or westerly destinations.

Accommodation and eating

Summers are very busy – arrive early on in the day to ensure a room – and expensive, with **hotel**-owners raising their rates (price codes below apply to summer) and refusing to bargain. Rates tumble during winter months, when it gets cold enough to snow, so check the availability of heating and hot water.

There are plenty of **restaurants** in Guling, mostly good value, and some post their menus and prices outside. For local flavours – mountain fungus and fish – try the stalls and open restaurants around the market, or the *Wurong Canting*, above a teashop in the mall.

Guling Fandian (牯岭饭店, *gŭlĭng fàndiàn*) 7 He Xi Lu ⓣ0792/8282435. About 100m downhill from the bus stop. One of the cheaper places in town, reflected in a lack of luxury, but rooms are serviceable and staff helpful. ③

Lushan Binguan (庐山宾馆, *lúshān bīnguǎn*) 446 He Xi Lu ⓣ0792/8295203, ⓕ8282843. Ten minutes farther on past the *Guling*, this is a heavy stone mansion with pleasant, comfortable rooms, good-value suites and a fine restaurant. ⑤

Lushan Dasha (庐山大厦, *lúshān dàshà*) 506 He Xi Lu ⓣ0792/8282178. Another five minutes from the *Lushan Binguan*, a regimental exterior betrays this hotel as the former Guomindang Officers' Training Centre; rooms are well furnished and comfortable. ③

Lushan Villas (庐山别墅, *lúshān biéshù*) ⓣ0792/8282927, ⓕ8282387. Nice quiet location off He Xi Lu and next to Meilu Villa. The rooms are in a group of renovated cottage villas named after different historic figures, and there are two excellent restaurants on site. ⑨

Into the hills

Covering some 500 square kilometres, Lu Shan's highlands form an elliptical platform tilted over to the southwest, comprising a central region of lakes surrounded by pine-clad hills, with superb rocks, waterfalls and views along the vertical edges of the plateau. **Hiking** is undoubtedly one of the area's greatest pleasures, and there are a number of trails laid out within the park – maps of varying detail are widely available. Although it can be tempting to try to walk everywhere, some of the paths lie quite a distance from Guling and it's well worth taking advantage of park transport to save your energy for the trails proper.

For an easy walk out from town (3hr round-trip), follow the road downhill to the southwest from Guling Lu and the Jiexin Garden to the far end of **Ruqin Hu** (如琴湖, *rúqín hú*), where you pick up the Floral Path. This affords impressive views of the Jinxui Valley as it winds along Lu Shan's western cliff edge past **Xianren**

Dong (仙人洞, *xiānrén dòng*; the Immortal's Cave), once inhabited by an ephemeral Taoist monk and still an active shrine, complete with a slowly dripping spring.

The most spectacular scenery can be found on Lu Shan's **southern fringes**. Proper exploration requires a full day's hike, and this is one even hardened walkers should hop on a bus for. **Lulin Hu** (芦林湖, *lúlín hú*) is a nice lakeside area with the attractive Dragon Pools and elderly Three Treasure trees over to the west. Due east of here – about 5km by road but less along walking tracks – is China's only subalpine **botanical garden** (植物园, *zhíwù yuán*), the finest spot in Lu Shan to watch the sunrise, though the peaks are famously often obscured by mist and clear days are a rarity; even the local brew is suitably known as "Cloud Fog Tea".

Jingdezhen

Across Poyang Hu from Nanchang and not far from the border with Anhui province, **JINGDEZHEN** (景德镇, *jǐngdézhèn*) has been producing **ceramics** for at least two thousand years. Lying in a river valley not only rich in clay but also the vital feldspar needed to make porcelain, the city's defining moment came in the fourteenth century: China's capital was at Nanjing, and Jingdezhen was considered conveniently close to produce porcelain for the Ming court. An imperial kiln was built in 1369 and its wares became so highly regarded – "as white as jade, as thin as paper, as bright as a mirror, as tuneful as a bell" – that Jingdezhen retained official favour even after the Ming court moved to Beijing fifty years later.

As demand grew, workshops experimented with new glazes and a classic range of decorative styles emerged: *qinghua*, blue and white; *jihong*, rainbow; *doucai*, a blue-and-white overglaze; and *fencai*, multicoloured famille rose. The first examples reached Europe in the seventeenth century and became so popular that the English word for China clay – *kaolin* – derives from its source nearby at Gaoling. Factories began to specialize in export ware shaped and decorated in European-approved forms, which reached the outside world via the booming Canton markets: the famous Nanking Cargo, comprising 150,000 pieces salvaged from the 1752 wreck of the Dutch vessel *Geldermalsen* and auctioned for US$15 million in 1986, was one such shipment. Foreign sales petered out after European ceramic technologies improved at the end of the eighteenth century, but Jingdezhen survived by sacrificing innovation for cheaper production-line manufacturing. Today, it's a scruffy, heavily polluted city, mostly as a result of the scores of smoky kilns that still employ some fifty thousand people and turn out the goods.

Arrival and information

It's three and a half hours by bus to Jingdezhen from Nanchang, or four and a half by train. Coming from Fujian, there are a couple of direct trains every day from **Fuzhou** (13hr); you can also catch one of the more regular services to **Yingtan** (8hr) and change there. It's easy to get here by bus or train from Anhui, and there are trains from Nanjing and Shanghai as well.

The town is concentrated on the east bank of the Chang Jiang – not the Yangzi, but a lesser river of the same name. Zhushan Lu runs east from the river for a kilometre to the central Guangchang, a broad, paved square where children fly kites. The **train station** is 1500m southeast of Guangchang on Tongzhan Lu, while the long-distance **bus station** is 3km west across the river – bus #28 connects the two via Zhushan Lu and Guangchang.

For factory tours or ticket booking there's a **CITS** (Mon–Sat 9am–5.30pm; ⓣ0798/8629999) in the *Binjiang Hotel* by the river on Zhushan Xi Lu. You'll find the **Bank of China** on the way into town on Ma'anshan Lu; the main **post office** is west of the river on Zhushan Lu, and there's a small **internet bar** (¥2/hr) on Ma'anshan Lu near the junction with Tongzhan Lu.

Food stalls offering hotpots and stir-fries can be found east of Guangchang along Tongzhan Lu.

Accommodation

It's just as well that many visitors treat Jingdezhen as a day-trip, as **accommodation** prospects are mediocre. The best option near the train station is *Bandao International Hotel* at 121 Tongzhan Lu (半岛国际酒店, *bàndaǒguójìjiǔdiàn*; ⓣ0798/8533333; ❹); around the Guangchang, try the welcoming *Jinsheng Dajiudian* on the north side of Zhushan Zhong Lu (金盛大酒店, *jīnshèng dàjiǔdiàn*; ⓣ0798/8207818; ❷), west of the square.

The Town

The only available vistas of Jingdezhen are from the four-storey **Longzhu Ge** on Zhonghua Bei Lu (龙珠阁, *lóngzhū gé*; daily 8.30am–5.30pm; ¥15), a pleasant construction in wood and orange tiles along the lines of Hunan's Yueyang Tower (see p.453); it also contains a small porcelain museum of nominal interest. From the top, the town's smoggy horizon, a patchwork of paddy fields and tea terraces, is liberally pierced by tall, thin smokestacks, which fire up by late afternoon.

But it's porcelain, not views, that drives Jingdezhen. There are plenty of shops aimed at tourists, but it's more fun to head to the **markets**. On Jiefang Lu, south of the central square, the pavements are clogged by stacks of everything that has ever been made in porcelain: metre-high vases, life-sized dogs, Western- and Chinese-style crockery, antique reproductions including yellow- and green-glazed Tang camels, ugly statuettes and simple porcelain pandas. Haggling can be fun, but it's just as entertaining to watch other people and wonder how they are going to get their new acquisitions home – and where on earth they'll put them once they do.

The Museum of Ceramic History

To experience the manufacturing side of things, either join a CITS factory tour or visit the **Museum of Ceramic History** (陶瓷历史博物馆, *táocí lìshǐ bówùguǎn*; daily 8am–5pm; ¥50). Normally the museum is a bit quiet, but if a big tour party is expected, the workshops get fired up and it's much more entertaining.

The museum is out of town on the west side of the river – take bus #15 or #19 to Cidu Dadao, then cross the road and head under the ornamental arch opposite. A fifteen-minute walk through fields leads to a surprising collection of antique buildings divided into two sections. A Ming mansion houses the museum itself, and its ornate crossbeams, walled gardens and gilt eave screens are far more interesting than the second-rate ceramics display, though this covers everything from 1000-year-old kiln fragments through to the Ming's classic simplicity and overwrought, multicoloured extravagances of the late nineteenth century. Next door, another walled garden conceals the **Ancient Porcelain Workshop**, complete with a Confucian temple and working pottery, where the entire process of throwing, moulding and glazing takes place. Out back is a rickety two-storey kiln, packed with all sizes of the unglazed yellow pottery sleeves commonly seen outside local field kilns – these shield each piece of porcelain from damage in case one explodes during the firing process.

Southern Jiangxi

When Zhou Enlai and Zhu De were driven out of Nanchang after their abortive uprising, they fled to the **Jinggang Shan** (井岗山, *jǐnggāng shān*) ranges, 300km southwest along the mountainous border with Hunan. Here they met up with Mao, whose Autumn Harvest Uprising in Hunan had also failed, and the remnants of the two armies joined to form the first real PLA divisions. Their initial base was near the country town of **Ciping** (茨坪, *cípíng*), and, though they declared a Chinese Soviet Republic in 1931 at the Fujian border town of Ruijin, Ciping was where the Communists stayed until forced out by the Guomindang in 1934.

Today, Jinggang Shan is reasonably accessible thanks to new roads, though it doesn't attract huge numbers of tourists, making the picture-perfect forest scenery and meandering hiking trails an attractive proposition. Ciping, Jingangshan's main town, is eight hours by bus from Nanchang, but the park also has its own train station – albeit a good forty minutes by bus or taxi from Ciping at the top of the mountain – with three daily trains from Nanchang (3–4hr) to the north and one from Shenzhen in the south (6hr 30min).

Ciping and Jinggang Shan

CIPING (茨坪, *cípíng*) is little more than a village. Completely destroyed by artillery bombardments during the 1930s, it was rebuilt after the Communist takeover and has recently been remodelled to take better advantage of tourism. It is unintentionally ironic that that the heart of Ciping, once the frontline of the Communist cause, is now a soulless market selling tourist tat commemorating the bloody struggle. The main streets form a 2km elliptical circuit, the lower half of which is taken up with a lake surrounded by well-tended gardens.

Arrival and information

Ciping's **bus station** is on the northeastern side of the circuit, served by buses from Nanchang and Ganzhou, and also Hengyang in Hunan province, from where there are transport links into southern and central China. **Maps** of the town and surrounding area can be bought virtually everywhere (¥5).

Ciping is singularly lacking in travel agencies; the only place to get **train tickets** – aside from the train station an hour down the mountain at Jinggangshan Shi (井岗山市, *jǐnggānshān shì*) – is out beyond the *Nanhu Binguan* (see below) at the *Shengdi Shanzhuang* hotel (圣地山庄, *shèndìshānzhuāng*; ⓣ0796/7027248; ❹), which has a ticket office hidden away behind reception.

Regular buses (running around every 90min; ¥10) serve the train station, and taxis also ply the route (¥60–70). Nearer the centre, the **Bank of China** (Mon–Fri 9–11.30am & 2–5pm) is just downhill from the Former Revolutionary Headquarters (see below).

Accommodation

There is a host of budget and mid-range **places to stay** (❸) near the bus station. Alternatively, walking down hill from the bus station, take the first street on the right and cut through Ciping's tourist market to the fading *Jinggang Shan Binguan* (井岗山宾馆, *jǐnggāngshān bīnguǎn*; ⓣ0796/6552272, ⓦwww.jgshotel.cn; ❹), a former favourite with party cadres. South from here are plenty more decent hotels, culminating in the huge, marble-clad *Nanhu Binguan* (南湖宾馆, *nánhúbīnguǎn*; ⓣ0796/6556666; ❼).

The village

Ciping's austere historical monuments can be breezed through fairly quickly, as it's the surrounding hills that best recreate a feeling of how Communist guerrillas might have lived. Five minutes west of the bus station at the top end of town is the **Martyrs' Tomb** (烈士纪念堂, *lièshì jìniàntáng*), positioned at the top of a broad flight of stairs and facing the mountains that the fighters it commemorates died fighting for. It also overlooks the tourist market. Farther round the circuit is the almost comically overbearing **Revolutionary Museum** (井岗山博物馆, *jǐnggāngshān bówùguǎn*; daily 8am–4pm: free), built in the monumental style so beloved of totalitarian regimes. Steps lead up behind to a vast statue commemorating the Communist struggle, from where there would be a great view across the valley – if the museum were not blotting it out. Exhibitions mainly consist of maps and dioramas showing battlefields and troop movements up until 1930, after which the Communists suffered some heavy defeats. There are also busts of prominent revolutionaries, paintings of a smiling Mao preaching to his peasant armies and cases of the spears, flintlocks and mortars that initially comprised the Communist arsenal. Across the park, a group of mud-brick rooms form a reconstruction of the **Former Revolutionary Headquarters** (革命旧居群, *gémìng jiùjūqún*; daily 8am–4pm). As the site marking where Mao and Zhu De coordinated their guerrilla activities and the start of the Long March, it is the town's biggest attraction as far as visiting cadres are concerned. While the museum is free, the Former Revolutionary Headquarters and Martyrs' Tomb can only be visited using the **Jingganshan Park entry ticket** (¥156).

Jinggang Shan

Having waded through the terribly serious displays in town, it's nice to escape into **Jinggang Shan**'s (井岗山, *jinggāng shān*) surprisingly wild countryside. Some of the peaks provide glorious views of the sunrise – or frequent mists – and there are colourful plants, natural groves of pine and bamboo, deep green temperate cloud forests, and hosts of butterflies and birds.

Though still stunning, the park is not the wild frontier it once was, and tourist transport now runs to and from Ciping and around the park. There is also a fairly hefty **entry fee** of ¥156, plus ¥70 for use of the buses. Tickets are valid for 48 hours and can be bought from a dedicated agency next to the Bank of China in Ciping.

One of the nicest areas to explore is **Wulong Tan** (五龙潭, *wǔlóng tán*; Five Dragon Pools), about 8km north along the road from the Martyrs' Tomb. A footpath from the roadhead leads past some poetically pretty waterfalls dropping into the pools (of which there are actually eight) between a score of pine-covered peaks. The same distance south is Jinggang Shan itself, also known as **Wuzhi Feng** (五指峰, *wǔzhǐ fēng*; Five Finger Peak), apex of the mountains at 1586m. The more well-trodden trails are obvious and well signposted in English, though they can become slippery in the wet. As the trees and waterfalls below slide in and out of the clouds, the peace and beauty make it hard to imagine it as the cradle of guerrilla warfare for the Communists back in the 1920s and 30s.

Ganzhou

Four hours south of Jinggang Shan, **GANZHOU** (赣州, *gànzhōu*) is not a choice destination in itself, but anyone busing to Jinggangshan from Guangdong will most likely stop over here.

Formerly a strategic port between central and southern China, the town sits on a triangular peninsula where two rivers, the **Gong Shui** (贡水, *gòngshuǐ*) and **Zhang Shui** (章水, *zhāngshuǐ*), combine to form the **Gan Jiang** (赣江, *gànjiāng*),

The Long March

In 1927, **Chiang Kai-shek**, the new leader of the Nationalist Guomindang (GMD) government, began an obsessive war against the six-year-old Chinese Communist Party, using a union dispute in Shanghai as an excuse to massacre their leadership. Driven underground, the Communists set up half a dozen remote rural bases, or soviets, across central China. The most important of these were the **Fourth Front army** in northern Sichuan, under the leadership of Zhang Guotao; the **Hunan soviet**, controlled by the irrepressible peasant general **He Long**; and the main **Jiangxi soviet** in the Jinggang Mountains, led by **Mao Zedong** and **Zhu De**, the Communist Commander-in-Chief.

Initially poorly armed, the Jiangxi soviet successfully fought off GMD attempts to oust them, acquiring better weapons in the process and swelling their ranks with disaffected peasantry and defectors from the Nationalist cause. But they over-estimated their position and in 1933, abandoning Mao's previously successful guerrilla tactics, they were drawn into several disastrous pitched battles. Chiang, ignoring Japanese incursions into Manchuria in his eagerness to defeat the Communists, blockaded the mountains with a steadily tightening ring of bunkers and barbed wire, systematically clearing areas of guerrillas with artillery bombardments. Hemmed in and facing eventual defeat, the First Front army, comprising some eighty thousand Red soldiers, decided to break through the blockade in October 1934 and retreat west to team up with the Hunan soviet – marking the beginning of the **Long March**.

Covering a punishing 30km a day on average, the Communists moved after dark whenever possible so that the enemy would find it difficult to know their exact position; even so, they faced daily skirmishes. One thing in their favour was that many putative GMD divisions were, in fact, armies belonging to local warlords who owed a token allegiance to Chiang Kai-shek, and had no particular reason to fight once it became clear that the Red Army was only crossing their territory. But after incurring severe losses during a battle at the Xiang River near Guilin in Guangxi, the marchers found their progress north impeded by massive GMD forces, and were obliged to continue west to Guizhou, where they took the town of Zunyi in January 1935. With their power structure in disarray and with no obvious options left, an emergency meeting of the Communist Party hierarchy was called – the **Zunyi Conference**. Mao emerged as the undisputed leader of the Party, with a mandate to "go north to fight the Japanese" by linking up with Zhang Guotao in Sichuan. In subsequent months they circled through Yunnan and Guizhou, trying to shake off the GMD, routing twenty regiments of the Guangxi provincial army at the Loushan

which flows north from here all the way to Nanchang and Poyang Hu. During the 1930s, Chiang Kai-shek's son was governor here, doubtless keeping a close watch on the events at Jinggang Shan. The peninsula's northern end is enclosed by several kilometres of stone battlements; at the very tip, **Bajing Park** (八境公园, *bājìng gōngyuán*) is enlivened by Bajing Tai, a fort whose rusting cannon overlook barges negotiating the river junction below. Exiting the park, you can follow the walls southeast down Zhongshan Lu through to the old **east gate** (建看门, *jiànkānmén*). At weekends there's a small street market here, with fishermen selling their catches, food stalls, fortune-tellers and hawkers of all kinds. A low **pontoon bridge** (东河浮桥, *dōnghéfúqiaó*), runs across the river here to the far bank, and a stroll across to experience the village atmosphere oppositte is highly recommended. In the early evening you'll see hardy swimmers taking to the none-too-inviting waters, an activity they proudly claim to carry out every day of the year.

Back inside the city, the narrow side streets at the north end of Zhongshan Lu comprise the last vestiges of the **old town**. By turns squalid and picturesque, it's

Pass in the process; they then suddenly moved up into Sichuan to cross the Jinsha River and, in one of the most celebrated and heroic episodes of the march, took the Luding Bridge across the Dadu River (see p.795). Now they had to negotiate Daxue Shan (Great Snowy Mountains), where hundreds died from exhaustion, exposure and altitude sickness before the survivors met up on the far side with the Fourth Front army.

The meeting between these two major branches of the Red Army was tense. Mao, with Party backing, wanted to start resistance against the Japanese, but Zhang, who felt that his better-equipped forces and better education gave him superiority, wanted to found a Communist state in Sichuan's far west. Zhang eventually capitulated, and he and Mao took control of separate columns to cross the last natural barrier they faced, the Aba grasslands in northern Sichuan. But here, while Mao was bogged down by swamps, hostile nomads and dwindling food reserves, Zhang's column suddenly retreated to Garzê, where Zhang set up an independent government. Mao and what remained of the First Front struggled through southern Gansu, where they suffered further losses at the hands of Muslim supporters of the GMD, finally arriving in Communist-held Yan'an, Shaanxi province, in October 1935. While the mountains here were to become a Communist stronghold, only a quarter of those who started from Jiangxi twelve months before had completed the 9500km journey. For his part, Zhang was soon harried out of western Sichuan by Chiang's forces, and after meeting up with He Long, he battled through to Shaanxi, adding another twenty thousand to the Communist ranks. Here he made peace with Mao in October 1936, but later defected to the GMD.

Immediately after the Long March, Mao admitted that in terms of losses and the Red Army's failure to hold their original positions against the Nationalists, the Guomindang had won. Yet in a more lasting sense, the march was an incredible success, uniting the Party under Mao and defining the Communists' aims, while changing the Communists' popular image from simply another rebel group opposing central authority into one of a determined and patriotic movement. After Zunyi, Mao turned the march into a deliberate propaganda mission to spread the Communist faith among the peasantry, opening up prisons in captured GMD towns and promoting tolerance and cooperation with minority groups (though not always successfully). As Mao said, "Without the Long March, how could the broad masses have learned so quickly about the existence of the great truth which the Red Army embodies?"

incredibly atmospheric, the buildings slowly decaying as they await the inevitable wrecking ball. **Bajing Lu**, running south from the park, is full of antique shops, and there are a couple of minor temples: the tallest, the 42m-high **Ciyun Pagoda** (慈云塔, *cīyúntǎ*), is a short walk southwest of the old east gate. If you are around for longer you may want to make the journey 12km northwest to see the **Tongtian rock formations** (通天岩景区, *tōngtiānyánjǐngqū*) and Buddhist carvings.

Arrival and information

The centre is only a couple of kilometres across, with Nanmen **Guangchang** (南门广场, *nánméngŭangchǎng*; South Gate Square) as its hub. From here, Wenqing Lu runs north through the centre to Bajing Park and the river, lined with clothes shops and restaurants, while Hongqi Lu runs east–west.

The **long-distance bus station** is on Bayi Si Dadao, 2km from the centre at the southeastern corner of town, a relentlessly unappealing area. The **train station** is farther out in the same direction; from either station, bus #2 will get you to

Nanmen Guangchan. You can get a **map** of the city centre (¥5) from newsstands at either station to help you find your bearings.

Leaving, trains head to Jinggang Shan, Nanchang, Jiujiang, Wuhan, Hefei and well beyond, with useful buses south to Shaoguan and Guangzhou in Guangdong.

The main **Bank of China** is halfway up Wenqing Lu and a post office can be found on Nanmen Guangchang.

Accommodation and eating

There are a few cheap **hotels** around the bus station on Bayi Si Dadao (❷), practical if you've an early morning departure but with little else to recommend them. You're probably better off splashing out at the *Gandian Dasha*, near Nanmen Guangchang at 29 Hongqi Dadao (赣电大厦, *gandiàndàshà*; Ⓣ0797/8202388, Ⓦwww.gandianhotel.com.cn; ❺) – or any one of a number of decent hotels on the way into town.

As for **eating**, on Zhongshan Lu opposite the East Gate, the historic *Tai Zi Loum: 1939* (太子楼1939, *taìzĭloúyījiǔsanjiǔ*) restaurant is in the building of a former bank owned by Chiang Kai-shek's son and serves up excellent examples of all the Chinese standards. If you're after something Western, head to Wenqing Lu, north of Nanmen Guangchang, which numerous fast-food joints and a *Starbucks* look-alike at the junction with Qingnian Lu.

Travel details

Trains

Bozhou to: Beijing (7 daily; 8–10hr); Hefei (10 daily; 4–5hr); Nanchang (13 daily; 7–10hr); Shanghai (1 daily; 14hr).

Changsha to: Beijing (18 daily; 13–21hr); Guangzhou (68 daily; 2hr 30min–10hr); Guilin (9 daily; 7–10hr); Guiyang (5 daily; 12–13hr); Hengyang (60 daily; 30min–2hr); Nanchang (2 daily; 3hr–5hr 30min); Shaoshan (daily; 2hr 30min); Shenzhen (8 daily; 9–12hr); Wuhan (76 daily; 1hr 30min–5hr); Yueyang (49 daily; 30min–2hr); Zhangjiajie (7 daily; 5–11hr).

Ganzhou to: Beijing (4 daily; 18–24hr); Guangzhou (6 daily; 6hr–8hr 30min); Hefei (4 daily; 10hr–12hr 30min); Jinggang Shan (daily; 5hr); Jiujiang (20 daily; 6–8hr); Nanchang (27 daily; 4–6hr); Shenzhen (16 daily; 6hr–8hr 30min); Wuhan (4 daily; 8–11hr).

Hefei to: Beijing (5 daily; 9hr 30min–17hr 30min); Bozhou (10 daily; 4hr–5hr 30min); Ganzhou (4 daily; 11–13hr); Jingdezhen (2 daily; 8hr 30min–9hr); Jiujiang (6 daily; 4–6hr); Nanchang (6 daily; 6–8hr); Nanjing (19 daily; 1–5hr); Shanghai (15 daily; 3–10hr); Tunxi (3 daily; 6hr); Wuhu (24 daily; 2hr); Xian (5 daily; 14–17hr).

Jingdezhen to: Hefei (2 daily; 11hr); Nanchang (3 daily; 4hr 30min–6hr 30min); Shanghai (daily; 16hr 30min); Tunxi (11 daily; 2hr 30min–5hr).

Jiujiang to: Ganzhou (19 daily; 6–9hr 30min); Hefei (6 daily; 4–5hr); Nanchang (42 daily; 1hr 30min–2hr 30min); Shanghai (daily; 12hr).

Nanchang to: Beijing (12 daily; 11hr 30min–22hr); Changsha (2 daily; 4–5hr); Fuzhou (9 daily; 2–13hr 30min); Ganzhou (27 daily; 4hr–5hr 30min); Guangzhou (7 daily; 10hr 30min–14hr); Hefei (6 daily; 5hr 30min–7hr); Jingdezhen (3 daily; 4hr 30min); Jinggang Shan (3 daily; 3–4hr); Jiujiang (43 daily; 1–3hr); Shanghai (7 daily; 5hr 30min–11hr); Shenzhen (13 daily; 10–14hr 30min); Tunxi (1 daily; 8hr 30min); Wuhan (22 daily; 3hr 30min–8hr 30min); Xiamen (5 daily; 15–17hr); Yingtan (31 daily; 1hr 30min–2hr).

Tunxi to: Beijing (daily; 20hr); Hefei (3 daily; 7–8hr); Jingdezhen (11 daily; 2hr 30min–5hr); Nanchang (daily; 9hr); Nanjing (9 daily; 6hr–7hr 30min); Shanghai (2 daily; 12hr 30min–14hr 30min).

Wudang Shan to: Beijing (2 daily; 18hr–19hr 30min); Hefei (2 daily; 18hr 30min–19hr 30min); Shanghai (3 daily; 22–25hr); Wuhan (9 daily; 6–8hr).

Wuhan to: Beijing (26 daily; 8hr 30min–18hr); Changsha (76 daily; 1hr 30min–6hr); Ganzhou (4 daily; 8–12hr); Guangzhou (59 daily; 3hr 30min–15hr); Nanchang (22 daily; 3hr 30min–9hr); Shiyan (17 daily; 4hr–8hr 30min); Wudang Shan (9 daily; 5–8hr); Yueyang (53 daily; 1–4hr); Xi'an (11 daily;

10–18hr); Xiangfan (25 daily; 2–5hr).
Wuhu to: Hefei (25 daily; 2hr); Ma'anshan (20 daily; 1hr); Nanjing (20 daily; 2–4hr); Shanghai (2 daily; 7hr 30min–9hr).
Xiangfan to: Shiyan (33 daily; 2–3hr); Wudang Shan (18 daily; 2hr); Wuhan (25 daily; 2–5hr); Yichang (9 daily; 3hr); Zhangjiajie (6 daily; 6–9hr).
Yichang to: Beijing (daily; 21hr); Xi'an (daily; 18hr); Xiangfan (3hr); Zhangjiajie (3 daily; 5hr).
Yueyang to: Changsha (36 daily; 30min–2hr); Wuhan (47 daily; 1hr–4hr 30min).
Zhangjiajie to: Changsha (6 daily; 5–7hr); Huaihua (for connections to Guiyang or Changsha; 11 daily; 3hr 30min–8hr); Jishou (for Fenghuang; 12 daily; 2–5hr); Xiangfan (6 daily; 7–10hr); Yichang (3 daily; 4hr 30min–6hr).

Buses

Changsha to: Fenghuang (6hr); Heng Shan (3hr); Jiujiang (13hr); Nanchang (6hr); Wuhan (4hr); Yichang (6hr); Yueyang (3hr); Zhangjiajie (7hr).
Ciping (Jinggang Shan Shi) to: Ganzhou (5hr); Hengyang (8hr); Nanchang (8hr); Taihe (for Jinggang Shan; 2hr).
Hefei to: Bozhou (5hr); Huainan (2hr); Jiuhua Shan (5hr); Jiujiang (5hr); Ma'anshan (3hr); Nanchang (6hr); Nanjing (3hr); Shouxian (2hr); Tongling (3hr); Tunxi (5hr); Wuhan (6hr); Wuhu (2hr).
Jingdezhen to: Jiujiang (1–2hr); Nanchang (3hr); Tunxi (3hr 30min); Yingtan (3hr).
Jiuhua Shan to: Hefei (5hr); Qingyang (30min); Taiping (3hr); Tangkou (4hr); Tongling (2hr); Wuhu (3hr).
Jiujiang to: Changsha (13hr); Hefei (5hr); Jingdezhen (1–2hr); Lu Shan (1hr 30min); Nanchang (2hr); Wuhan (4hr).
Jishou to: Fenghuang (1hr 30min).
Nanchang to: Changsha (6hr); Ciping (8hr); Hefei (6hr); Jingdezhen (3hr); Jinggang Shan (6hr); Jiujiang (2hr); Lu Shan (4hr); Wuhan (6hr); Yingtan (2hr 30min).
Tunxi to: Hefei (5hr); Jingdezhen (3hr 30min); Jiuhua Shan (5hr); Nanjing (6hr); Shanghai (12hr); Shexian (1hr); Tangkou (1hr); Tongling (4hr); Wuhu (3hr); Yixian (2hr).
Wuhan to: Changsha (4hr); Hefei (6hr); Jingzhou (3hr 30min); Jiujiang (4hr); Nanchang (6hr); Xiangfan (5hr); Yichang (4hr); Yueyang (4hr).
Wuhu to: Hefei (2hr); Jiuhua Shan (3hr); Ma'anshan (1hr); Nanjing (3hr); Tongling (2hr); Tunxi (3hr); Xuancheng (2hr).
Xiangfan to: Jingzhou (4hr 30min); Wudang Shan (2hr); Wuhan (5hr); Yichang (5hr).
Yichang to: Changsha (6hr); Jingzhou (1hr 30min); Jiujiang (12hr); Wuhan (4hr); Xiangfan (5hr); Xing Shan (4hr).
Zhangjiajie to: Changsha (7hr); Jishou (for Fenghuang; 2hr).

Ferries

Wuhan to: Chongqing (daily; 5 days).
Yichang to: Chongqing (daily; 11hr by hydrofoil, otherwise 2–4 days).

Flights

Changsha to: Beijing (6 daily; 2hr); Chongqing (2 daily; 1hr 15min); Guangzhou (3 daily; 1hr); Hefei (daily; 1hr 35min); Hong Kong (7 weekly; 1hr 30min); Shanghai (6 daily; 1hr 30min); Shenzhen (6 daily; 1hr 10min); Tianjin (5 weekly; 1hr 40min); Zhangjiajie (daily; 40min).
Hefei to: Beijing (3 daily; 1hr 40min); Changsha (daily; 1hr 35min); Guangzhou (3 daily; 1hr 50min); Nanchang (2 weekly; 1hr); Shenzhen (2 daily; 2hr); Tunxi (daily; 40min); Xiamen (daily; 1hr 35min); Xi'an (daily; 1hr 30min).
Nanchang to: Beijing (5 daily; 2hr); Chengdu (daily; 2hr); Guangzhou (3 daily; 1hr 10min); Hefei (2 weekly; 1hr); Kunming (daily; 2hr); Shanghai (5 daily; 1hr); Tunxi (2 weekly; 50min).
Tunxi (Huang Shan) to: Beijing (2 weekly; 2hr); Guangzhou (2 daily; 1hr 30min–3hr 10min); Hefei (daily; 40min); Nanchang (2 weekly; 50min); Shanghai (daily; 1hr).
Wuhan to: Beijing (7 daily; 1hr 50min); Guangzhou (5 daily; 1hr 30min); Hong Kong (daily; 1hr 50min); Shanghai (10 daily; 1hr 15min).
Yichang to: Beijing (daily; 2hr); Chongqing (daily; 1hr 20min); Guangzhou (daily; 1hr 45min); Shanghai (2 weekly; 1hr 30min).
Zhangjiajie to: Changsha (daily; 40min).

CHAPTER 8 Highlights

* **Wuyi Shan** Dramatic gorges and great hiking trails amongst some of the finest scenery in southern China. See p.484

* **Gulangyu Islet** Uniquely relaxing island sporting vehicle-free streets, European-style colonial mansions and sea views. See p.497

* **Hakka mansions** These circular mud-brick homes, sometimes housing upwards of four hundred people, are China's most distinctive traditional architecture. See p.499

* **Cantonese food** Sample China's finest cuisine, from dim sum to roast goose, in one of Guangzhou's restaurants. See p.520

* **Chaozhou** Old town with Ming-dynasty walls, some great street life, the famous Kaiyuan Si – and more good food. See p.541

* **Hainan Island** Soak up the sun while swimming and surfing at the country's best beaches. See p.551

▲ Hakka mansion, Nanjing

Fujian, Guangdong and Hainan Island

There's something very self-contained about the provinces of **Fujian**, **Guangdong** and **Hainan Island**, which occupy 1200km or so of China's convoluted southern seaboard. Though occasionally taking centre stage in the country's history, the provinces share a sense of being generally isolated from mainstream events by the mountain ranges surrounding Fujian and Guangdong, physically cutting them off from the rest of the empire. Forced to look seawards, the coastal regions have a long history of contact with the outside world, continually importing – or being forced to endure – foreign influences and styles. This is where Islam entered China, and porcelain and tea left it along the **Maritime Silk Road**; where the mid-nineteenth-century theatricals of the Opium Wars, colonialism, the Taiping Uprising and the mass overseas exodus of southern Chinese were played out; and where today you'll find some of China's most Westernized cities. **Conversely**, the interior mountains enclose some of the country's wildest, most remote corners, parts of which were virtually in the Stone Age within living memory.

Possibly because its specific attractions are thinly spread, the region receives scant attention from visitors. Huge numbers do pass through Guangdong, in transit between the mainland and Hong Kong and Macau, but only because they have to, and few look beyond the overpowering capital, **Guangzhou**. Yet while the other two regional capitals – **Fuzhou** in Fujian, and Hainan's **Haikou** – share Guangzhou's modern veneer, all three also hide temples and antique architecture that have somehow escaped developers, and other towns and cities in the region have managed to preserve their old, character-laden ambience intact. The pick of these are the Fujian port of **Xiamen**, where parts of the city seem almost frozen in time, and **Chaozhou** in eastern Guangdong, staunchly preserving its traditions in the face of the modern world.

Indeed, a sense of local tradition and of being different from the rest of the country pervades the whole region, though this feeling is rarely expressed in any tangible way. **Language** is one difference you will notice, however, as the main dialects here are Cantonese and Minnan, whose rhythms and tones are recognizably removed from Mandarin, even if you can't speak a word of Chinese. Less obvious are specific **ethnic groups**, including the **Hakka**, a widely spread Han subgroup whose mountainous Guangdong-Fujian heartland is dotted with

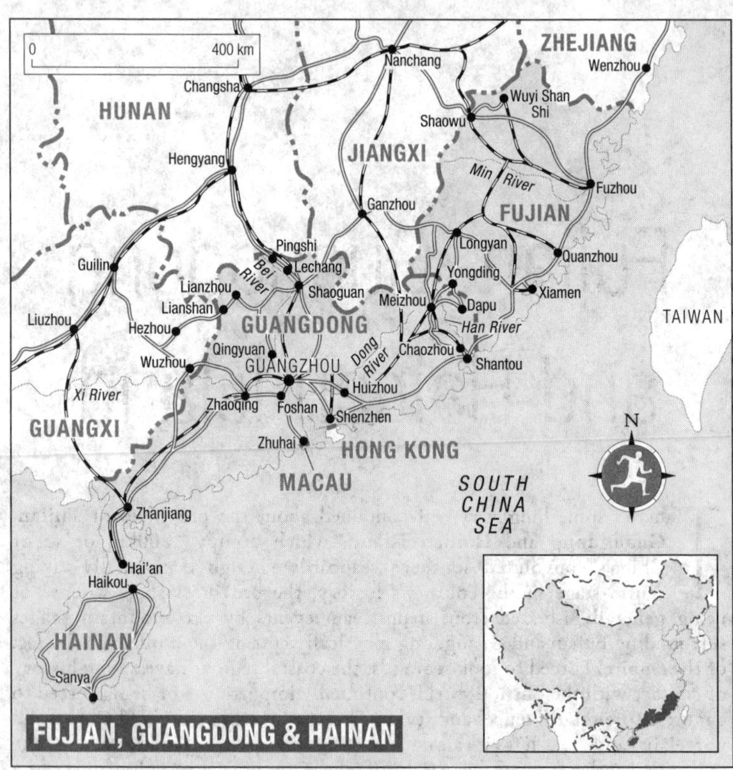

fortress-like mansions; the Muslim **Hui**, who form large communities in Guangzhou, coastal Hainan and in **Quanzhou** in Fujian; and the **Li**, Hainan's animistic, original inhabitants.

While a quick look around much of the coastal areas here leaves a gloomy impression of uncontrolled development and its attendant ills, most of this is actually contained within various **Special Economic Zones** (SEZs), specifically created in the mid-1980s as a focus for heavy investment and industrialization. Beyond their boundaries lurk some respectably wild – and some nicely tamed – corners where you can settle back and enjoy the scenery. Over in western Guangdong, the city of **Zhaoqing** sits beside some pleasant lakes and hills, while the **Wuyi Shan** range in northeastern Fujian contains the region's lushest, most picturesque mountain forests. Way down south lie the country's best **beaches** – encouraging the tourist industry to hype Hainan as "China's Hawaii" – and there's also a limited amount of hiking to try, through the island's interior highlands.

Anyone wanting to stop off and explore will find plentiful local and long-distance **transport**, though **accommodation** can be expensive and suffers huge seasonal fluctuations in price. The **weather** is nicest in spring and autumn, as summer storms from June to August bring sweltering heat, extreme humidity, thunder, afternoon downpours and floods. In contrast, the higher reaches of the Guangdong-Fujian border can get very cold in winter.

Fujian

FUJIAN (福建, *fújiàn*), on China's southeastern coast, is well off the beaten track for most Western travellers, which is a pity because the province possesses not only a wild mountainous interior, but also a string of old ports, including **Xiamen** (厦门, *xiàmén*), probably China's most relaxed coastal city. From Hong Kong, the well-trodden routes head directly west towards Guilin, or north to Shanghai, but a detour to Xiamen makes an excellent introduction to mainland China.

Culturally and geographically, the province splits into distinct halves. One is made up of large, historical seaports and lush, semitropical coastal stretches, whose sophisticated population enjoys warm sun and blossoming trees even in January. The other is the rugged, mountainous and inaccessible interior, freezing cold in winter, home to around 140 different local dialects and with a history of poverty and backwardness: when the Red Army arrived in the 1960s they found communities unaware that the Qing dynasty had been overthrown, and even today, the area is wild enough to harbour the last remaining **South China tigers**. However, while inland Fujian until recently knew very little even of China, contacts between the coastal area and the outside world had been flourishing for centuries. In the Tang dynasty, the port of **Quanzhou** (泉州, *quánzhōu*) was considered on a par with Alexandria, and teemed with Middle Eastern traders, some of whose descendants still live in the area today. So much wealth was brought into the ports here that a population explosion led to mass emigration, and large parts of the Malay Peninsula, the Philippines and Taiwan were colonized by Fujianese. In the early eighteenth century this exodus of able-bodied subjects became so drastic that the imperial court in distant Beijing tried, ineffectually, to ban it.

Today the interior of Fujian remains largely unvisited and unknown, with the exception of the scenic **Wuyi Shan** (武夷山风景区, *wǔyíshān fēngjǐng qū*) area in the northwest of the province, and the **Hakka regions** around southwesterly **Yongding** (永定, *yǒngdìng*). The coast, however, is booming, with colossal investment pouring in from both Hong Kong and neighbouring Taiwan, many of whose citizens originate from the province and speak the same dialect. The cities of **Fuzhou** (福州, *fúzhōu*) and Xiamen are among the wealthiest in the country, particularly Xiamen, with its clean beaches, charming streets and shopping arcades. The proximity of Taiwan accounts not only for the city's rapid economic development and the proliferation of first-class tourist facilities, but also for the occasional outbreak of tension. During Taiwanese elections, mainland authorities often hold military exercises just off the coast as a gentle reminder to the Taiwanese not to vote for separatist candidates – a tactic which usually backfires, as demonstrated by the back-to-back election victories of pro-independence Chen Shui-Bian in 2000 and 2004, while military exercise-free elections in 2008 saw Beijing-friendly candidate Ma Yingjiu sweep to power. Cross-straits business manages to smooth over the cracks somewhat, but the hundreds of missiles pointing from the mainland to Taiwan remain.

Getting around Fujian has become easier in recent years, with a fast coastal expressway linking the main cities with neighbouring Zhejiang and Guangdong provinces. To reach the interior wilds of Wuyi Shan, you're better off catching a train, with separate lines from Fuzhou, Quanzhou and Xiamen; Fuzhou also has a decent link through to Jiangxi province, and there's another track west to Meizhou in Guangdong from Xiamen and Quanzhou. Otherwise, train travel within or beyond the province is circuitous and very slow.

Fuzhou

Capital of Fujian Province, **FUZHOU** (福州, *fúzhōu*) is a comfortably modern city, with shiny skyscrapers looming over the main roads. An important trading centre for more than a thousand years, it was visited by Marco Polo during the Yuan dynasty. In the fifteenth century, Fuzhou shipbuilders earned themselves the distinction of building the world's largest ocean-going ship, the *Baochuan*, sailed by the famous Chinese navigator **Zheng He**, who used it to travel all around Asia and Africa. One thing Polo noted when he was here was the high-profile presence of Mongol armies to suppress any potential uprisings; the city is no less well defended today, forming the heart of Fujian's military opposition to Taiwan. There's precious little to detain casual visitors, and the city is probably best used as a springboard for reaching the tourist-friendly wilds of Wuyi Shan.

Arrival and information

Flowing east–west through the city, the **Min River** (闽江, *mǐnjiāng*) roughly delineates the southern border of Fuzhou. The 5km-long main north–south axis, called **Wusi Lu** (五四路, *wǔsìlù*) in the north, and **Wuyi Lu** (五一路, *wǔyīlù*) farther south, cuts right through the city, intersecting with Dong Jie (东街, *dōngjīe*), and farther south with Gutian Lu (古田路, *gǔtíanlù*), marking the centre of the city at **Wuyi**

Moving on from Fuzhou

For booking **tours** to Wuyi Shan, or plane tickets, approach CTS (☎0591/88371588) a little way west down Hu Dong Lu from the *Minjiang* hotel.

By air

You can **fly** from Fuzhou to Wuyi Shan and a host of major cities, including Hong Kong and Macau; the CAAC **ticket office** is on Wuyi Lu (daily 8am–8pm; ☎0591/968899 or 83345988). Travelling to the **airport**, pick up the bus from the courtyard of the *Minhang* hotel, next door – the journey takes an hour and you'll need to get to the airport at least an hour before your departure.

By train

Fuzhou is the terminus for a couple of fairly remote **rail lines**. Heading northwest, trains run to Wuyi Shan, and through into Jiangxi and the rest of China; be aware that most trains to Guangdong province also travel this way and so take much longer than you'd expect. The new line west from Fuzhou, via Longyan to Meizhou in eastern Guangdong, has sparse services at present, and it may well be faster to take a bus for these destinations. The **ticket office** is in the western part of the station (to the left as you face it), or there are at least three ticket offices in town where you can buy train and bus tickets – on Hualin Lu opposite the *Best Western*, on Wuyi Lu on the ground floor of a *Super 8*, and just off Hu Dong Lu, first left past CTS – you'll almost certainly need to reserve sleeper berths at least a day in advance.

By bus

Long-distance buses to everywhere in Fujian and neighbouring provinces leave from both bus stations. There are several sleepers daily to Wuyi Shan, and constant departures along the coastal expressway to Quanzhou, Xiamen and Guangdong province; remember that there's a huge price discrepancy between standard and luxury buses, but also often an equally huge discrepancy in the time taken to reach your destination. The express bus station next to the *Minjiang* serves Guangzhou, Shanghai and other distant destinations.

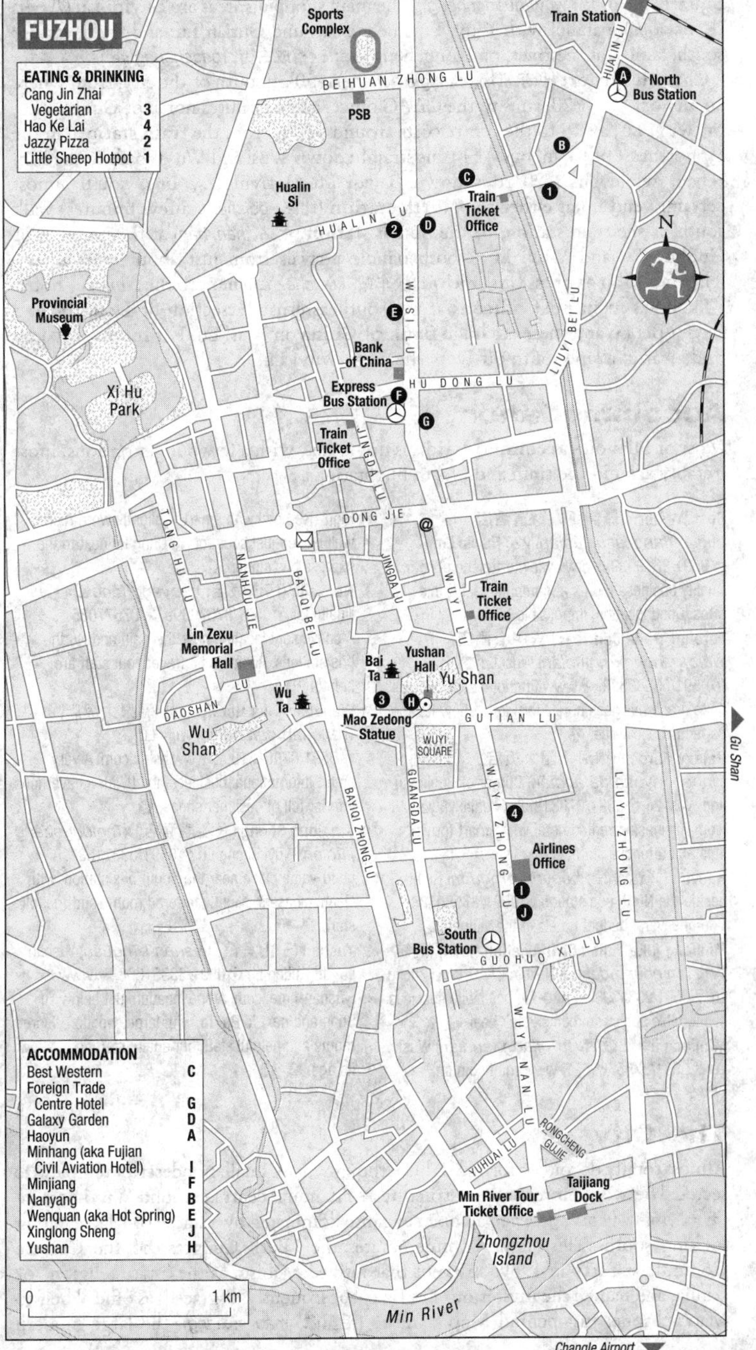

FUZHOU
EATING & DRINKING
Cang Jin Zhai Vegetarian 3
Hao Ke Lai 4
Jazzy Pizza 2
Little Sheep Hotpot 1
Sports Complex
Train Station
HUALIN LU
North Bus Station
BEIHUAN ZHONG LU
PSB
Hualin Si
HUALIN LU
Train Ticket Office
Provincial Museum
WUSI LU
LIUYI BEI LU
Bank of China
Xi Hu Park
HU DONG LU
Express Bus Station
Train Ticket Office
JINGDA LU
DONG JIE
TONG HU LU
NANHOU JIE
BAYIQI BEI LU
JINGDA LU
WUYI LU
Train Ticket Office
Lin Zexu Memorial Hall
LU
Bai Ta
Yushan Hall
Yu Shan
Wu Ta
DAOSHAN
Mao Zedong Statue
GUTIAN LU
Gu Shan
Wu Shan
WUYI SQUARE
GUANGDA LU
BAYIQI ZHONG LU
WUYI ZHONG LU
LIUYI ZHONG LU
Airlines Office
South Bus Station
GUOHUO XI LU
WUYI NAN LU
ACCOMMODATION
Best Western C
Foreign Trade Centre Hotel G
Galaxy Garden D
Haoyun A
Minhang (aka Fujian Civil Aviation Hotel) I
Minjiang F
Nanyang B
Wenquan (aka Hot Spring) E
Xinglong Sheng J
Yushan H
RONGCHENG GUJIE
YUHUAI LU
Taijiang Dock
Min River Tour Ticket Office
Zhongzhou Island
0
1 km
Min River
Changle Airport

Square (五一广场, *wǔyī guǎngchǎng*). The main shopping areas are **Bayiqi Lu** (八一七路, *bāyīqīlù*), parallel with Wuyi Lu; the area around Gutian Lu; and much farther south, almost at the river, on Rongcheng Gujie (榕成古街, *róngchénggǔjīe*).

Changle airport (长乐机场, *chánglè jīchǎng*) is 50km south of the city, from where an **airport bus** (¥20) runs to the CAAC office, a few minutes north of Guohuo Lu, on Wuyi Lu; a taxi to the centre costs around ¥200. From the **train station**, in the far northeast of town, bus #51 runs straight down Wusi and Wuyi roads to the Min River, while bus #20 runs down Bayiqi Lu. Arriving **by bus**, you'll almost certainly end up at either the **North station** (北站, *běizhàn*), a few minutes' walk south of the train station, or the **South station** (南站, *nánzhàn*) at the junction of Guohuo Lu and Wuyi Lu – both handle arrivals from just about everywhere. There's also an **express bus station** (快车站, *kùaichēzhàn*) next to the *Minjiang* hotel.

Fuzhou's main **post office** is at the southeastern intersection of Dong Jie and Bayiqi Bei Lu and there is a huge **Bank of China** on Wusi Lu. For **internet**, you'll find a bar in a lane south off Dong Jie, near Wuyi Lu.

Accommodation

Most of Fuzhou's **accommodation** is upmarket, with a few budget options, most notably around the train and North bus stations.

Best Western (最佳西方财富酒店, *zuìjiāxīfāngcáifù jiǔdiàn*) 220 Hualin Lu ⓣ0591/88199999, ⓦwww.bwfortunehotel.com. Quality business rooms at competitive, flexible rates. Good location, impossible to miss. ❼

Foreign Trade Centre (外宾中心酒店, *wàibīnzhōngxīn jiǔdiàn*) Wusi Lu ⓣ0591/63388888, ⓦwww.fjftchotel.com. Still quite grand business hotel starting to show its age. Perfectly good value. ❼

Galaxy Garden (银河花园大饭店, *yínhéhuāyuán dàfàndiàn*) Corner of Hualin Lu and Wusi Lu ⓣ0591/87831888, ⓔgalaxy88@126.com Business-oriented hotel with smart furnishings and attentive staff. ❻

Haoyun (好运宾馆, *hǎoyùn bīnguǎn*) Right beside the North bus station ⓣ0591/87580888. One of several budget hotels in the vicinity. ❸

Minhang (aka Fujian Civil Aviation Hotel) (民航大厦, *mínháng dàsha*) Next to CAAC, Wuyi Zhong Lu ⓣ0591/83343988. CAAC-run hotel with spacious, comfortable and clean rooms. A fair deal. ❻

Minjiang (闽江饭店, *mǐnjiāng fàndiàn*) Wusi Lu ⓣ0591/87557895, ⓦwww.mjht.com.cn. High-rise hotel with smart, if slightly worn rooms, well placed just south of Hu Dong Lu next to the express bus station. ❻

Nanyang (南洋饭店, *nányáng fàndiàn*) Hualin Lu ⓣ0591/87579699, ⓕ87577085. A convenient location near the train and North bus stations. Rooms a bit frayed, but staff are helpful. ❸

Wenquan (aka Hot Spring) (温泉大饭店, *wēnquán dàfàndiàn*) Wusi Lu ⓣ0591/87851818, ⓦwww.hshfz.com. A very smart international business hotel with a cavernous interior full of designer shops. ❽

Xinglong Sheng (兴隆盛酒店, *xīnglóngshèng jiǔdiàn*) Wuyi Zhong Lu ⓣ0591/83371037. A good-value place near the South bus station, with clean, pleasant, slightly tattered rooms and friendly staff. ❷–❸

Yushan (于山宾馆, *yúshān bīnguǎn*) Yushan Lu, off Gutian Lu ⓣ0591/83351668, ⓦwww.yushan-hotel.com. A fine location just below Yu Shan and next to Bai Ta, with large, wooden-floored rooms and helpful staff, but again, starting to show its age. ❺–❻

The City

Almost totally devoid of formal sights – though many small, nondescript temples are secreted between more modern structures – Fuzhou is centred around **Wuyi Square** (五一广场, *wǔyī guǎngchǎng*), an open expanse dominated by a statue of Mao Zedong looking south. This statue commemorates the Ninth Congress of the Chinese Communist Party in 1969, an event that ratified Maoism as the "state religion" of China, and named the mysterious Lin Biao (subsequently disgraced) as official heir to Mao's throne. Just behind **Mao's statue** (毛塑像, *máo sùxiàng*), the large modern building, **Yushan Hall**, is sometimes used for exhibitions – climbing up a path to the west of it lands you at the gates of **Yu Shan** (玉山, *yùshān*; Jade Hill). The main sights here are the 1000-year-old **Bai Ta** (白塔, *báitǎ*), a whitewashed pagoda located beside a temple, and a small exhibition of the contents of a local Song-dynasty tomb, which includes the preserved bodies of a man and a woman and some silk garments.

West of the city centre

West from Yu Shan is **Bayiqi Lu** (八一七路, *bāyīqīlù*), a busy, crowded avenue at the heart of Fuzhou's shopping district. On the far side is another small hill, Wu Shan. The flat summit, fringed with banyan trees, is capped by a small temple and **Wu Ta** (乌塔, *wūtǎ*), a black granite pagoda dating back to the same era as the white Bai Ta, and containing some attractive statuary. North from here on the corner of Daoshan Lu and Nanhou Jie, you'll find the **Lin Zexu Memorial Hall** (林则徐纪念馆, *línzéxú jìniànguǎn*; daily 8.30am–5pm; free), a quiet, attractive couple of halls and courtyards with funereal statues of animals. Lin Zexu (1785–1850) is fondly remembered as the patriotic Qing-dynasty official who fought against the importation of opium by foreigners – even writing persuasive letters to Queen Victoria on the subject. His destruction of thousands of chests of the drug in 1840 sparked the first Opium War and, rather unfairly, he was exiled to Xinjiang.

North of the city centre

Running north from behind Yushan Hall is **Jingda Lu** (井大路, *jǐngdà lù*), Fuzhou's second shopping street. A far more intimate affair than Wuyi Lu, Jingda is home to hundreds of clothing boutiques selling a variety of designer- (some genuine) and Chinese-brand garments. While not quite up to Shanghai shoppers' standards, prices are lower and there is the odd hidden gem waiting to be found.

The northwest of the city is dominated by **Xi Hu Park** (西湖公园, *xīhú gōngyuán*; daily 7am–9pm; free), whose main entrance faces southerly Tong Hu Lu – you can get here on bus #1 or #2 from the southern end of Bayiqi Lu, or #810 from the train station. The park, mostly comprising an artificial lake formed by excavations some seventeen hundred years ago, is a good spot to go boating or stroll with the masses on a hot day. Within the grounds, staff at the modern but unfrequented **Fuzhou Provincial Museum** (福建省博物馆, *fújiànshěng bówùguǎn*; Tues–Sun 9am–5pm; free) will be delighted to see you. Among thousands of pieces of porcelain and examples of primitive iron tools is a 3500-year-old coffin-boat removed from a Wuyi Shan cave, but the real highlight for children young and old has to be the dinosaur collection in the Natural History building. Regular art exhibitions are also hosted in the museum's ground-floor gallery.

Gu Shan

Fuzhou's most-touted tourist attraction is **Gu Shan** (鼓山, *gǔshān*; Drum Mountain), about 9km east of the city. To get here, catch one of the regular **minibuses** from the Nanmen terminus on Guangda Lu, just west of Wuyi Square (¥10); it's an attractive 45-minute journey through forested hills, with sweeping views as the road starts climbing. The Gu Shan area offers woodland walks as well as scattered sights, including the thousand-year-old, heavily restored **Yongquan Si** (永泉寺, *yǒngqúansì*), which gets phenomenally crowded at weekends. One way to escape the crowds is to climb the 2500 stone steps (allow around an hour; your knees will want plenty of rests) behind the temple to the wooded summit of Gu Shan.

Eating and drinking

For such a major city, parts of central Fuzhou suffer a serious lack of **restaurants**, though Western and Chinese fast-food chains are everywhere. For **snacks**, hole-in-the-wall operations surround transit points, while street vendors peddle small, bagel-like *gua bao* (刮包, *gūabāo*; "cut buns"), stuffed with vegetables or a slice of spiced, steamed pork. Otherwise, the highest concentration of places to eat is along downtown Dong Jie. Branches of *Hao Ke Lai* (豪客来, *háokèlái*), serving Sichuan-style cold spiced meats and vegetables, along with soups, noodles, spring rolls and local buns, all at a few yuan a serve, are scattered around the centre – look for the yellow-and-green sign spelling out "Houcaller".

For a city that is sweltering for most of the year, **hotpot** (火锅, *hŭogūo*) is inordinately popular – there's a busy branch of the *Little Sheep* (小肥羊, *xĭaoféiyáng*) chain not far from the North bus station with another, smarter hotpot place upstairs in the building next door. Vegetarians can satisfy their cravings at *Cang Jin Zhai* (仓锦斋, *cāngjĭn zhāi*) at the western end of Yu Shan Lu, a rare Buddhist-themed restaurant that also indulges customers wishing to smoke and drink, or in the temple restaurant a hundred metres up the road. Steak houses abound, while *Jazzy Pizza*, at the junction of Haulin Lu and Wusi Lu, also does pasta. For **nightlife**, the main bar and club area is along Dong Jie at "Dongjie Kou" (东街口, *dōngjīekŏu*), its junction with Bayiqi Bei Lu, but a couple of more relaxed pubs opposite the south gate of Xi Hu park (西湖公园南门, *xīhú gōngyuánnánmén*) are probably more to Western tastes.

Wuyi Shan

Away in the northeast of the province, 370km from Fuzhou and close to the Fujian-Jiangxi border, the **WUYI SHAN** (武夷山风景区, *wŭyíshān fēngjĭng qū*) area contains some of the most impressive scenery in southern China. It's about the only inland part of Fujian regularly visited by tourists, and consists of two principal parts: the **Jiuqu River** (九曲溪, *jiŭqŭ xī*), which meanders at the feet of the mountains, and the **Thirty-Six Peaks** (三十六峰, *sānshíliufēng*), which rise up from the river, mostly to its north. With peaks protruding from low-lying mists, the scenery is classic Chinese scroll-painting material, and the park, dotted with small, attractive villages, can be a tremendous place to relax for a few days, offering clean mountain air and leisurely walks through a landscape of lush green vegetation, deep red sandstone mountains, soaring cliff faces, rock pools, waterfalls and caves. Despite the remoteness, Wuyi is surprisingly full of tourists – especially Taiwanese

Bamboo-raft trips

The traditional way to appreciate Wuyi Shan is to take a two-hour **bamboo-raft trip** along the Jiuqu River. Rafts leave daily between 7.30am and around 4pm all year round, from the small village of **Xingcun**, which you can reach on public buses from Wuyi Shan Shi and Wuyigong (both ¥2.5). On arrival, locals will happily point you towards the river where boatmen wait to pick up tourists. Tickets cost ¥100 and rafts only set off when they have the necessary six people. Be prepared to be pushed, tugged, shouted at and generally cajoled into taking the final seat on a raft that is waiting to leave – even if you are travelling in a pair. At busy times the river becomes a noisy bamboo conveyor-belt, but, although it is hardly the tranquil experience it may once have been, from the first crook in the meandering river right up to the ninth, you'll still have stupendous gorge scenery all the way. Watch out for the odd, boat-shaped **coffins** in caves above the fourth crook; they are said to be four thousand years old, and appear similar to those in Gongxian and along the Little Three Gorges in Sichuan (see p.786).

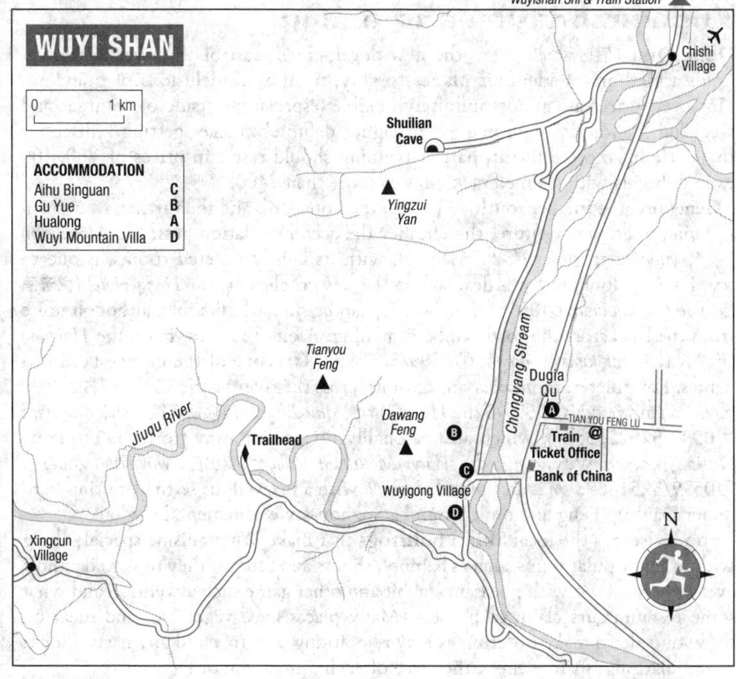

– in high summer, so a visit off-season might be preferable, when you'll also see the mountaintops cloaked with snow. Sadly, as Wuyi Shan has developed into a major attraction, tourists have become regarded as fair game for some serious overcharging – in restaurants check the price of everything before you tuck in.

Wuyigong and Wuyishan Shi

The sixty-square-kilometre site is bordered by the **Jiuqu (Nine-Twisting) River** (九曲溪, *jiǔqǔ xī*) to the south, which runs its crooked course for some 8km between **Xingcun village** (腥村, *xīng cūn*) to the west, and the main village in the area, **WUYIGONG** (武夷宫, *wǔyí gōng*) to the east – where it joins the **Chongyang Stream** (崇阳溪, *chóngyáng xī*) which runs from north to south, demarcating the park's eastern border. There is a strip of tourist hotels, restaurants, shops, and bus- and plane-ticket booking offices, along with a **Bank of China** (daily 8am–5.30pm), immediately east of the stream, just before the bridge. Over the bridge 1km or so, Wuyigong lies in the cleft between the junction of the two waterways and contains a bus stop and some hotels.

Most transport arrives 15km north of the park at **WUYISHAN SHI** (武夷山市, *wǔyíshān shì*), the regional town. You can get here by **train** from Fuzhou, Quanzhou or Xiamen, or by **sleeper bus** (¥80–100) from Fuzhou. The alternative is to **fly** from Fuzhou (¥380 each way), Xiamen and other cities across China; **Wuyi airport** is at the village of **Chishi** (赤石, *chìshí*), a few kilometres to the northeast of the scenic area and to the south of Wuyishan Shi. Frequent minibuses connect Wuyishan Shi and the airport with Wuyigong. Fuzhou's CTS (see p.480) also runs **tour buses** direct to Wuyigong. A **taxi** from the train station to Wuyigong will cost around ¥40.

Accommodation and eating

Dujia Qu (度假区, *dùjiàqū*), as the new development east of the river is known, holds a plethora of identikit **places to stay**, many with delusions of grandeur. However, prices are almost infinitely flexible (especially outside of summer and weekends), and, although being a foreigner definitely makes getting a discount that little bit more difficult, hard bargaining should result in prices of ¥80–100 even in hotels with claimed rack rates of more than ¥400.

Generally, the further south you go on the hotel strip and the further away from the main road you venture, the cheaper the accommodation gets; the *Moonbeam* (月光, *yùeguāng*; ⓣ0599/5253618; ③), with its lightly tattered rooms, is one to try if you're looking for a deal, while the newer, cleaner *Yue Hong Hotel* (悦宏酒店, *yue hong jiudian*; ⓣ0599/5252942; ④) can be similarly flexible, although noise from the bar across the road can be deafening. Along the main road, the *Hualong* (花龙大酒店, *huālóng dàjiǔdiàn*; ⓣ0599/5252999; ⑤) is one of the more established names. For quieter, more pleasant options, cross the river to the *Gu Yue* (古越山庄, *gǔyuè shānzhuāng*; ⓣ0599/5252916; ③) or *Aihu Binguan* (矮胡宾馆, *ǎihú bīnguǎn*; ⓣ0599/5252263; ③), which are reasonably priced and away from the bustle of Dujia. Toward Wuyigong, the *Wuyi Mountain Villa* (武夷山庄, *wǔyíshān zhuāng*; ⓣ0599/5251888; ⑦) is an upmarket place with a marvellous setting, resting hard under Dawang Feng and built around a Suzhou-style ornamental garden.

Foodwise, it's the local **Shilin bullfrogs** that make Wuyi cuisine special; along with other popular items such as bamboo shoots and fungus, they're served almost everywhere, along with pheasant, rabbit and other game such as venison and what some restaurateurs claim to be bear. Many places have vegetables and meat on show outside to make ordering as easy as pointing, but to avoid any nasty shocks – overcharging is rife – check the price of each dish as you order.

The Thirty-Six Peaks

A series of trails head north into the mountains from the main trailhead area at the base of **Tianyou Feng** (天游峰, *tiānyóu fēng*; Heavenly Tour Peak), about halfway between Xingcun and Wuyigong. Minibuses, motorcycle taxis and taxis all run here. A ticket covering entry to the trails costs ¥140 for one day, ¥150 for two days or ¥160 for three. The **mountains** look quite large and imposing, but in fact are relatively easy to climb. The summit of Tianyou Feng is no more than a thirty-minute clamber away from the ticket office. The best time to get up here is early morning, when you can catch the sunrise and watch the mists clear to reveal the nine crooks in the Jiuqu River. A number of tiny pavilions and **tea gardens** on the lower slopes can provide sustenance on the way up. **Tea** is a big deal in Fujian, and Wuyi Shan is famous as the original home of **Oolong**, one of the few types known by name in the West. Leaves for Oolong are picked when mature, then processed by alternate bruising, fermenting and airing before being fire-dried to create the distinctive taste; one of the best varieties is the widely available *tie guanyin cha* (铁观音茶, *tiěguānyīncha*; Iron Buddha Tea).

Another peak well worth the ascent is **Dawang Feng** (大王峰, *dàwáng fēng*; King of Peaks) at the easternmost end of the river, north of Wuyigong, and more of a gentle walk than a climb (2hr). If you have time, try to get to the **Shuilian Cave** (水帘洞, *shuǐlián dòng*), about 6km north of the river; you can walk along easy trails or take a minibus from the Tianyou Feng area or from Wuyigong. The cave is about halfway up a cliff of red sandstone, down which a large waterfall cascades in the summer months. You can sit in the adjacent teahouse, cut out of the rock, while the waterfall literally crashes down beside you. The walk between the cave and river passes tea plantations, more teahouses and all kinds of little sights, including **Yingzui Yan** (鹰嘴岩, *yīngzuǐ yán*; Eagle Beak Crag), whose main point of interest is the walkways leading to a set of caves where, during the Taiping Uprising, local bigwigs fled to escape persecution.

Quanzhou and around

I tell you that for one shipload of pepper which may go to Alexandria or to other places, to be carried into Christian lands, there come more than one hundred of them to this port.

Thus wrote Marco Polo when he visited **QUANZHOU** (泉州, *quánzhōu*), then called Zaytoun (from the Arabic word for olive, symbol of peace and prosperity), in the late thirteenth century. At this time, Quanzhou was a great port, one of the two largest in the world, exploiting its deep natural harbour and sitting astride trade routes that reached southeast to Indonesian Maluku, and west to Africa and Europe. It became uniquely cosmopolitan, with tens of thousands of Arabs and Persians settling here, some of them to make colossal fortunes – the Arabs of Quanzhou are also believed responsible for introducing to the West the Chinese inventions of the compass, gunpowder and printing.

The Song and Yuan dynasties saw the peak of Quanzhou's fortunes, when the old Silk Road through northwestern China into Central Asia was falling prey to banditry and war, deflecting trade seawards along the **Maritime Silk Road**. Polo was by no means the only European to visit Quanzhou around this time: the Italian **Andrew Perugia**, Quanzhou's third Catholic bishop, died here in 1332, having supervised the building of a cathedral; and fourteen years later the great Moroccan traveller **Ibn Battuta** saw the port bustling with large junks. But by the Qing era, the city was suffering from overcrowding and a decaying harbour, and an enormous **exodus** began, with people seeking new homes in Southeast Asia. According to Chinese government statistics, there are more than two million Quanzhounese living abroad today – which compares to just half a million remaining in the entire municipal area. Despite these depredations of history, Quanzhou today retains several reminders of its glorious past, and it's certainly worth a stopover between Fuzhou and Xiamen.

Arrival and information

You'll most likely arrive in Quanzhou by **bus** along the coastal expressway between Xiamen and Fuzhou. The imposing new **long-distance bus station** is in the southeast of town, 3km east down Quanxiu Jie (泉秀街, *qúanxìujīe*) from

Moving on from Quanzhou

There are frequent daytime **buses** from both new and old long-distance bus stations to Xiamen (¥20–40; 90min) and Fuzhou (¥35–70; 3hr), and to practically anywhere in southern China, from Ningbo and Hangzhou in the north, to Guangzhou and Shenzhen in the south. If you're catching a **night bus**, note that the left luggage office at the new station closes at 8pm sharp – anything still inside at the end of the day will stay locked there until morning. By **train**, there's a morning departure to Wuyi Shan, and slow services to Longyan, Yongding and Meizhou; a **ticket office** in town, on the ground floor of the *Bayi Hotel* (八一酒店, *bāyījiǔdiàn*) on Wenling Lu, saves trekking out to the station. In addition, the **CTS office** near the *Overseas Chinese Hotel* on Daxi Jie can make travel bookings for a fee.

Wenling Lu (温陵路, *wēnlínglù*). Orange bus #15 from outside will take you back northwest up to Wenling Lu; get off when you see the giant stone column on the roundabout, the Great Ocean department store or *McDonald's*, and you'll be close to the old long-distance bus station (see map below). Quanzhou's **train station** is about 5km east down Dong Hu Jie; bus #23 from outside will get you to the old long-distance bus station. There's also an **airport** about 20km southeast of town, from which you'll need to take a taxi (¥30–50).

The **Bank of China** (Mon–Fri 8am–5.30pm) is on Nanjun Lu (南俊路, *nánjùnlù*), while the enormous **post office** (Mon–Sat 8am–8pm) is on Wenling Lu. There are several **internet cafés** in the lane north of the Qingjing Mosque and more near the *Quanzhou* hotel.

Accommodation

Quanzhou has a selection of **budget accommodation**, and the following hotels are all fair value.

Great Wall (长城宾馆, *chángchéng bīnguǎn*) Wenling Lu ⓣ0595/22171688. Excellent value, good location and friendly staff. ❸

Huaqiao Zhijia (华侨之家, *huáqiáo zhījiā*) Southern end of Wenling Lu ⓣ0595/22175395. Spacious and comfortable rooms, if slightly threadbare. Also triples and quads from ¥25. ❸

Jinzhou (金州大酒店, *jīnzhōu dàjiǔdiàn*) Next to the old long-distance bus station on Quanxiu Lu ⓣ0595/22586788. Reasonably smart and comfortable, and quite convenient for the new bus station. ❺

Quanzhou (泉州酒店, *quánzhōu jiǔdiàn*) Zhuangfu Xiang ⓣ0595/22289958, ⓦwww.quanzhouhotel.com. A ludicrous Neoclassical white-and-gold monstrosity, right in the centre of town, just west of Zhongshan Zhong Lu. Rooms are of an international standard but, disappointingly, do

not quite live up to the kitschy grandeur of the hotel's exterior. Old wing ❻, new wing ❼

Quanhzhou Overseas Chinese Hotel (泉州华侨大厦, *quánzhōu huáqiáo dàshà*) Baiyuan Lu ⓣ0595/22282192, ⓦwww.overseaschinesehotel.com. Smart four-star business hotel right in the centre of town. ❹

The town and around

Quanzhou is a small, prosperous and, so far, sympathetically preserved town. Located entirely on the northeast bank of the Jin River, the majority of its sights can be reached on foot. The two major north–south streets are **Zhongshan Lu** (中山路, *zhōngshānlù*) and **Wenling Lu**, with the town centre falling mainly between these two. The oldest part of town lies to the west and up along the northern section of Zhongshan Lu, where you'll find attractively restored, colonial-era arcaded streets, lined with trees and packed with pedestrians and cyclists. As in Fuzhou, there are plenty of minor temples scattered around, perhaps the best of which is **Tianhou Gong** (天后宫, *tiānhòu gōng*), a large airy hall at the southern end of Zhongshan Lu, dedicated to southeastern China's most popular deity, the Heavenly Empress.

Along Tumen Jie

One of the town centre's most interesting areas lies north off **Tumen Jie** (涂门街, *túménjīe*), Quanzhou's main east–west street, which sports a surprisingly well-integrated collection of genuine antique buildings and modern shops with traditional flourishes. Heading northwest up Tumen Jie from its junction with Wenling Lu, you'll first encounter **Guandi Miao** (关帝庙, *guāndì miào*), a splendid and busy temple on the junction with Mingquan Lu, dedicated to the Three Kingdoms' hero turned god of war and healing, Guan Yu (see p.413). The temple's roofline is typically florid and curly, and the atmospheric interior – guarded by life-sized statues of soldiers on horseback – features low-ceilinged halls, smoke-grimed statues and wall engravings showing scenes from Guan Yu's life.

Almost the next building along, the granite **Qingjing Mosque** (清净寺, *qīngjìng sì*; daily 8am–5.30pm; ¥3) provides firm evidence of just how established the Arabs became in medieval Quanzhou. Founded by Arab settlers in 1009 and rebuilt by Persian Muslims three centuries later, Qingjing ranks as one of the oldest mosques in China and is highly unusual in being Middle Eastern in design, though only parts of the original buildings survive. The tall gate tower is said to be an exact copy of a Damascus original, its leaf-shaped archway embellished with fourteenth-century Arabic calligraphy and designs, while parts of the walls and supporting pillars of the original prayer hall stand alongside. A side room has a detailed account of the Arab presence in Quanzhou, with an English translation; the small, tiled building next door is the modern prayer hall. The "**Houcheng Tourism and Culture Street**" (后成街, *hòuchéngjīe*) behind the mosque is not as hokey as it sounds, containing some original buildings, most of which now hold antique- and souvenir shops and teahouses.

West between Qingjing Mosque and Zhongshan Lu, an ornamental gateway leads north to a broad paved square, at the back of which is a Confucian temple, **Fuwen Miao** (府文庙, *fǔwén miào*). This isn't of great importance, but the square is dotted with freshly restored examples of Quanzhou's **traditional domestic architecture**, all built of granite blocks and characteristic red bricks marked with dark chevrons, the roof ridges pulled up into projecting forks.

Other attractions include the renovated **Yuan Miao Guan** (元妙观, *yuánmiào guān*), a Taoist temple shoehorned between buildings on Zhuangyuan Jie; it has nothing to particularly recommend it over Guandi Miao but offers a fascinating insight into the painstaking workmanship and effort still expended in restoring these temples. **Cheng Tian Si** (承天寺, *chéngtiān sì*), a Buddhist monastery a little further southeast along Nanjun Lu, provides a wonderful oasis of calm in the heart of the city.

Kaiyuan Si

Quanzhou's most impressive historical remains are at **Kaiyuan Si** (开元寺, *kāiyuán sì*; daily 7.30am–5.30pm; ¥8), a huge, restful temple dotted with magnificent trees in the northwest of town on Xi Jie. Bus #2 runs up here from the old long-distance bus station, but it's much more interesting to follow the backstreets from the Tumen Jie/Zhongshan Lu intersection, through narrow lanes lined with old homes. Running past the temple, Xi Jie still looks very much as it must have done a hundred years ago or more. Founded in 686 AD, Kaiyuan was built, legend has it, after the owner of a mulberry grove dreamed a Buddhist monk asked him to erect a place of worship on his land. "Only if my mulberry trees bear lotus flowers", replied the owner dismissively – whereupon the lotus flowers duly appeared. In memory of this, an ancient mulberry in the temple courtyard bears the sign "Mulberry Lotus Tree". The two five-storey **stone pagodas** were added in the thirteenth century; apart from these, the whole complex was rebuilt during the Ming dynasty after being destroyed by fire.

The temple is highly regarded architecturally, not least for its details, which include one hundred stone columns supporting the roof of the main hall, most of which are carved with delicate musicians holding instruments or sacrificial objects. Having survived everything from earthquakes to the Red Guards, the unimaginably solid pagodas are also carved on each of their eight sides with two images of the Buddha; inside, one of them has forty Buddhist stories inscribed on its walls. The temple grounds also hold a special exhibition hall (¥2) housing the hull of a twelfth- or thirteenth-century wooden sailing vessel found in 1974 (a series of photos detail the stages of the excavation), still with the herbs and spices it had been carrying preserved in its hold.

The Maritime Museum

Across on the northeast side of town, a kilometre or so down Dong Hu Lu, just past its junction with Tian'an Bei Lu, the **Maritime Museum** (海外交通史博物馆, *hǎiwàijiāotōngshǐ bówùguǎn*; Tues–Sun 8.30am–5.30pm; free; bus #19 from the long-distance bus station) recalls Quanzhou's trading history and illustrates how advanced Chinese shipbuilders were, compared to their European contemporaries. Two floors of exhibits track the development of Chinese boatbuilding, reaching as far back as the Warring States period (around 500 BC). A corner devoted to the "Recovery of Taiwan from the Greedy Grasp of the Dutch Invaders and the Development of Foreign Trade" reinterprets **Koxinga**'s exploits (see p.494) in a modern light, but the museum's heart is its collection of lovingly made **wooden models**. There are hundreds of them, illustrating everything from small, coastal junks to Zheng He's mighty *Baochuan* – possibly the largest wooden vessel ever made – and ornate pleasure boats used by the wealthy for touring China's famous lakes and rivers.

While you're here, don't miss the first-floor collection of tombstones dating back to Quanzhou's heyday. Most of these are Muslim, but you'll also find those of Italians and Spaniards, Nestorian Christians from Syria, and the fourteenth-century Bishop, Andrew Perugia. In the back, stone pillars, lintels and statues show that there were also Hindus and Manichaeans (followers of a Persian religion that drew on Christianity, Jainism and Buddhism) in Quanzhou, each with their own places of worship – further proof of the city's cosmopolitan heritage.

Qingyuan Shan and Sheng Mu

A few sights just outside town warrant the effort of reaching them on local buses. The **Qingyuan Shan** (清源山, *qīngyuán shān*) scenic area is 3km to the north, with good views over Quanzhou from small crags and pavilions, though most people come out here for the huge stone **Laojun Yan** (老君岩, *lǎojūnyán*), a Song-dynasty sculpture of Laozi which is said to aid longevity if you climb onto its back and rub noses. Bus #3 comes up here from Tumen Jie and Zhongshan Zhong Lu.

East of the town centre on Donghu Jie, **Sheng Mu** (伊斯兰教圣墓, *yīsīlánjiào shèngmù*) is a Muslim cemetery housing the graves of two of Mohammed's disciples sent to China in the seventh century to do missionary work – and so presumably the first Muslims in China. There's little to see, but it's a peaceful, semi-forested place; catch bus #7 from Wenling Lu to the Sheng Mu stop. The entrance can be seen to the south of the road – when you glimpse a stone archway, take the alley leading towards it.

Around Quanzhou

About 60km east of Quanzhou, **CHONGWU** (崇武古城, *chóngwǔ gǔchéng*) is an old walled city built entirely of stone, now nicely restored as a huge museum piece. The adjacent new town has one of southern China's largest fishing fleets, with just about every man employed in this industry – the women work in local stone quarries, carting huge rocks around on carrypoles and wearing characteristic blue jackets and wide-brimmed straw hats. Slightly closer to the southeast is the town of **SHISHI** (石狮, *shíshī*; Stone Lion), from where you can pick up a ride for the 5km to the beautiful **Sisters-in-law Tower** (姑嫂塔, *gūsǎo tǎ*), another Song-dynasty monument, overlooking the sea. Finally, 30km south, just off the expressway to Xiamen and outside the town of Anhai, the spectacular 2km-long, 800-year-old **Anping Bridge** (安平桥, *ānpíng qiáo*) actually crosses a section of sea.

Eating and drinking

Food options around the new **long-distance bus station** include the all-you-can-eat pizza paradise that is *Happy-Tom* (快乐汤姆, *kuàilè tāngmǔ*) and the more urbane *Dawin Café Coffee Shop* (达文咖啡店, *dáwén kāfēidiàn*). In town, northern Zhongshan Lu, the area around Kaiyuan Si and the backstreets off Tumen Jie are thick with cheap noodle stalls and canteens. On Wenling Jie, try a barbecue at the *Korean Restaurant* (度彼岸韩国料理, *dùbǐàn hánguó liàolǐ*; best enjoyed if there is a group of you), near the *Great Wall*, or head north of the Bank of China on Nanjun Lu to *Qiwei Yazai* (奇味鸭仔, *qíwèi yāzǎi*), which specializes in roast duck.

For Western food, there are the ubiquitous fast-food chains, along with several cafés along Tumen Jie that serve sandwiches and grills, and several outlets of *Noble Family Steakhouse* (贵族世家牛排, *guìzúshìjiā niúpái*) around town. The *Quanzhou* hotel also has its own Western-style restaurant. For something more traditional, *Qing Qi Sheng Chadian* teahouse (请其神茶店, *qǐngqíshén chádiàn*) is in an old brick home, in the lane directly behind Qingjing Mosque, which also hosts a couple of Vietnamese restaurants.

Vegetarians should head to the swish but reasonably priced *Three Virtues Vegetarian Restaurant* (三德素食馆, *sāndé sùshíguǎn*) near Cheng Tian Si monastery upstairs at 124 Nanjun Lu. There's a vast English menu with mains for around ¥30.

Xiamen

Joined to the mainland by a 5km-long causeway **XIAMEN** (厦门, *xiàmén*), an island city traditionally known in the West as **Amoy**, is more focussed, prettier and more prosperous than the provincial capital Fuzhou. It also offers more to see, its preserved streets and buildings, shopping arcades and bustling seafront giving a

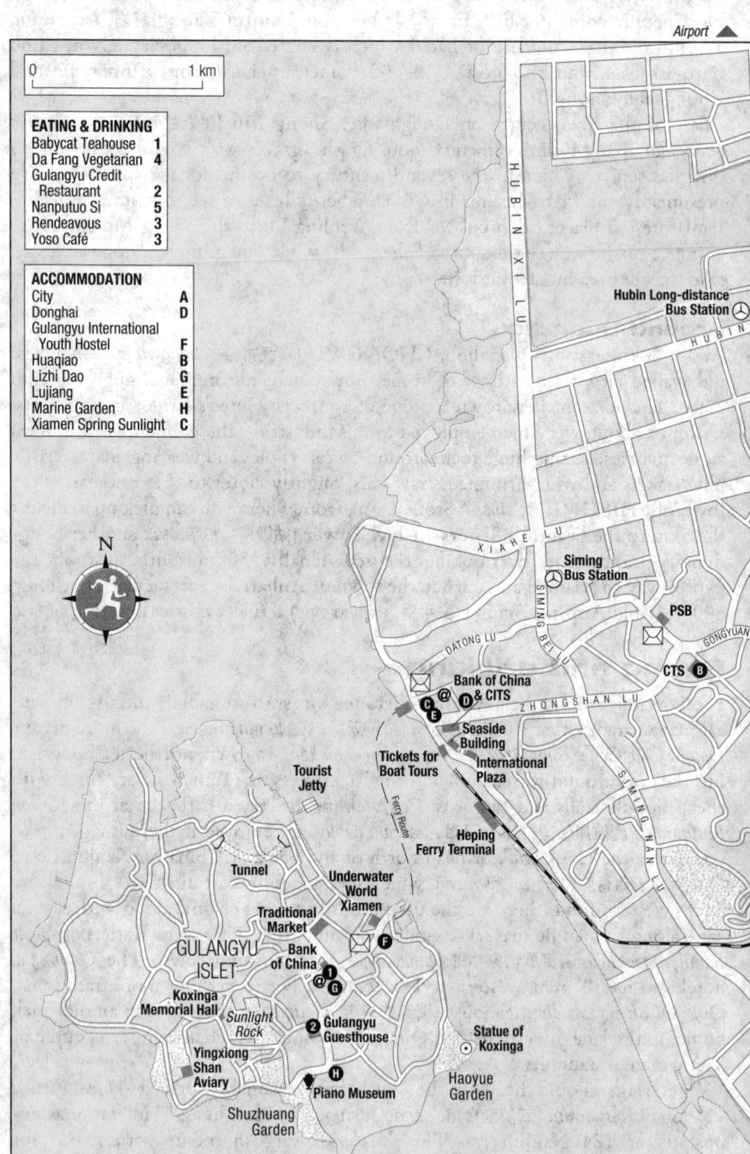

nineteenth-century flavour alongside its twenty-first century skyscrapers. One of China's most tourist-friendly cities, Xiamen is, in addition, the cleanest and, perhaps, most tastefully renovated city you'll see anywhere in the country, giving it the feel of a holiday resort. Compounding the resort atmosphere is the little island of **Gulangyu** (鼓浪屿, *gŭlàng yŭ*), a ten-minute ferry ride to the southwest, the old colonial home of Europeans and Japanese, whose mansions still line the island's traffic-free streets – staying here is highly recommended.

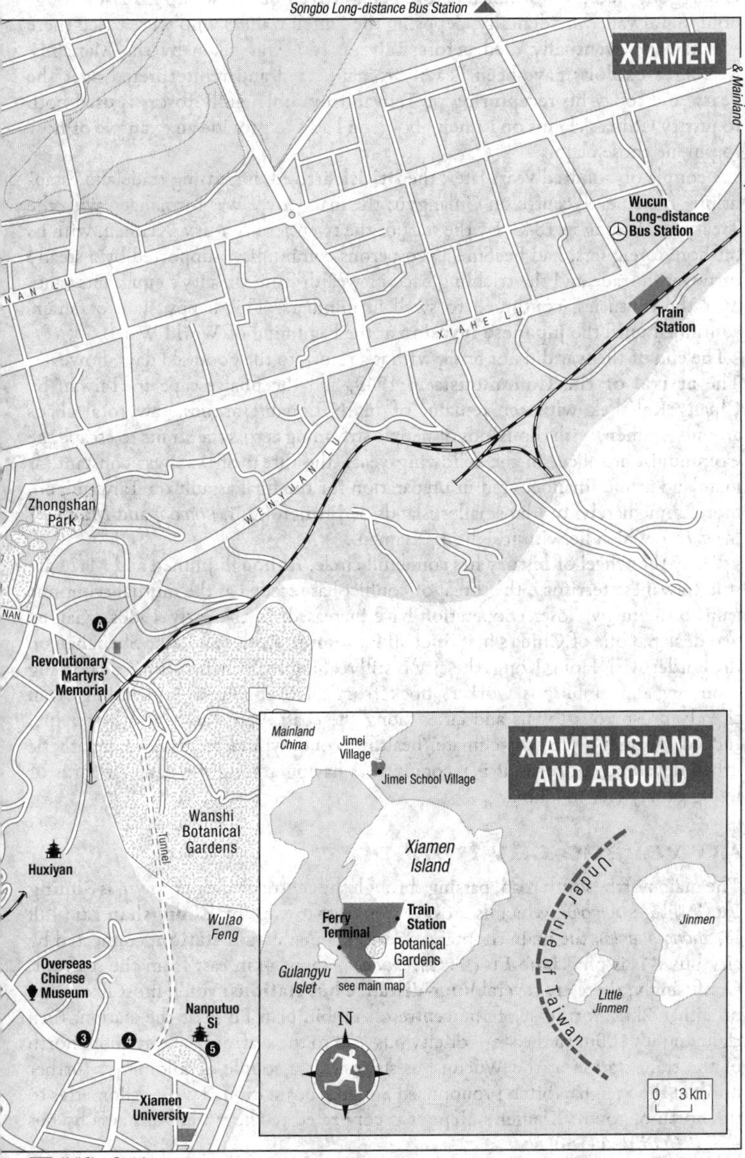

Some history

Founded in the mid-fourteenth century, Xiamen grew in stature under the Ming dynasty, becoming a **thriving port** by the seventeenth century, influenced by a steady succession of Portuguese, Spanish and Dutch fortune-hunters. When invading Manchu armies poured down from the north in the seventeenth century, driving out the Ming, Xiamen became a centre of resistance for the old regime. The pirate and self-styled **Prince Koxinga** (also known as Zheng Chenggong) led the resistance before being driven out to set up his last stronghold in Taiwan – incidentally, deposing the Dutch traders who were based there – where he eventually died before Taiwan, too, was taken by the Manchus. Koxinga's exploits have been heavily romanticized and reinterpreted over the years, and today his recapturing of Taiwan from unfriendly forces is used both to justify China's claims on its neighbour, and also to provide an example of how to pursue those claims.

A couple of hundred years later, the **British** arrived, increasing trade and establishing their nerve centre on Gulangyu; the manoeuvre was formalized with the Treaty of Nanjing in 1842. By the start of the twentieth century, Xiamen, with its offshore foreigners, had become a prosperous community, supported by a steady turnover in trade and the trickling back of wealth from the city's emigrants who, over the centuries, continued to swell in numbers. This happy state of affairs continued until the **Japanese invasion** at the beginning of World War II.

The end of the war did not bring with it a return to the good old days, however. The **arrival of the Communists** in 1949, and the final escape to Taiwan by Chiang Kai-shek with the remains of his Nationalist armies, saw total chaos around Xiamen, with thousands of people streaming across the straits to escape the Communist advance. In the following years, the threat of war was constant, as mainland armies manoeuvred in preparation for the final assault on Taiwan, and, more immediately, on the smaller islands of **Jinmen** (金门, *jīnmén*) and **Mazu** (马祖, *mǎzǔ*), which lie within sight of Xiamen.

Today the wheel of history has come full circle. Although Jinmen and Mazu are still Taiwanese territory, the threat of conflict has receded as the mutual economic gains brought by closer cooperation have increased. In the early 1980s, Xiamen was declared one of China's first **Special Economic Zones** and, like Shenzhen on the border with Hong Kong, the city is still reaping the benefits. It has a booming economy and ambitious workers flock from all over China – including from already prosperous towns and cities along the coast – in search of a better life. Indeed, Xiamen's pleasant climate, healthy economy and relatively sympathetic urban development mean it is recognized as having among the best standards of living of any city in China.

Arrival and city transport

The main north–south road, passing through the centre of the old town, is **Siming Lu** (思明路, *sīmínglù*), which is crossed from east to west by **Zhongshan Lu** (中山路, *zhōng shānlù*), the main shopping street. Xiamen's **train station**, connected by city bus #1, is on **Xiahe Lu** (夏禾路, *xiàhélù*), about 4km east from the seafront. Confusingly, there are several **long-distance bus stations**; you'll most likely end up either 2km northeast of the centre on Hubin Nan Lu (exit the station, turn right and it's 100m to the stop for city bus #23 to the seafront), about 200m north of the train station at the Wucun bus station, or a couple of kilometres further north at the Songbai (often pronounced Songbo) bus station. Twelve kilometres to the north of town, Xiamen's **airport** is connected to the waterfront area by bus #27 (¥6) or taxi (¥50).

Moving on from Xiamen

Xiamen is well placed for bus and plane connections, though rail lines – as usual in Fujian – are a bit unsatisfactory.

By bus

With three long-distance bus stations – **Hubin** (湖宾汽车站, *húbīn qìchēzhàn*), **Songbai** (松柏汽车站, *songbai qìchēzhàn*) and **Wucun** (捂村汽车站, *wǔcūn qìchēzhàn*) – Xiamen has frequent departures to **Fuzhou** and **Quanzhou** between about 6am and 10pm; several daily to **Longyan** and **Yongding**; and services at least daily to **Guangzhou** and **Shantou**. The problem is knowing which bus leaves from where. Fortunately, bus-station staff are sympathetic, giving times and instructions on how to get to the right departure point, whether you're at the right station or not. With this in mind, the **Siming Bus Station** (思明汽车站, *sīmíngqìchēzhàn*) in town is the easiest place to start, even though, if you're after a long-distance service, the bus you want is unlikely to actually leave from here.

CTS operates a rival private service, with buses leaving directly form their office on Xinhua Lu next to the *Huaqiao* hotel.

By air

Flights link Xiamen with Wuyi Shan, Fuzhou, Guangzhou and several other cities in eastern **China** as well as major destinations across the country; see Listings, p.498, for airline offices and travel agents.

By train

Rail lines run north from Xiamen to **Wuyi Shan** and **Jiangxi province**, and west into **Guangdong province** via **Longyan**. Services to Fuzhou are very circuitous; it's much faster to take the bus. Buying tickets is not too problematic, though queues at the station are often lengthy – there is an in-town booking office at Heping Ferry Terminal.

Buses cover the city and are fast, regular and cheap – rides cost ¥1–2. **Taxis** are also plentiful, costing upwards of ¥8 to hire. Vendors sell city **maps** (¥6) near the Gulangyu ferry terminal and outside the stations.

Accommodation

There's a good choice of **accommodation** in Xiamen, from mid-range to luxurious. Some of the best places to stay are on **Gulangyu Islet**; you'll have to carry your own luggage as there are no buses or taxis, but the picturesque surroundings more than compensate. Wherever you stay, make a point of bargaining – off-season discounts can slash rates in half.

Downtown Xiamen

City (厦门宾馆, *xiàmén bīnguǎn*) 16 Huyuan Lu ⓣ0592/2053333, ⓦwww.cityhotelxm.com. A modern, ultra-smart place to stay, built up a hillside and overhung by trees, yet not too remote. ⑦

Donghai (aka East Ocean) (东海大厦酒店, *dōnghǎi dàshà jiǔdiàn*) 1 Zhongshan Lu ⓣ0592/2021111, ⓦwww.easy-inn.cn. In a good location, behind the *Lujiang*, with nice rooms. ⑤

Huaqiao (华侨宾馆, *huáqiáo bīnguǎn*) Xinhua Lu ⓣ0592/2660888, ⓦwww.xmhqhotel.com.cn. Very smart, modern and well-serviced hotel, with airline agents and CTS conveniently located outside. ⑦

Lujiang (鹭江宾馆, *lùjiāng bīnguǎn*) 54 Lujiang Lu ⓣ0592/2022922, ⓦwww.lujiang-hotel.com. Occupying a prime site on the seafront in a well-maintained colonial building, this is an excellent hotel, and the ideal place to stay for views over Gulangyu Islet. The cheaper twins are rather small. ⑧

Xiamen Spring Sunlight (厦门春光酒店, *xiàmén chūnguāng jiǔdiàn*) Haihou Lu ⓣ0592/2665558. Good value, given the central location directly opposite the Gulangyu ferry terminal. Behind its colonial-style facade the interior is modern and spotless, if a little bland. ⑤

Gulangyu Islet

Gulangyu International Youth Hostel (国际青年旅舍, *gúojìqīngníanlǚshè*) 18 Lujiao Lu ⓣ0592/2066066, ⓦwww.yhagly.com. A quick left-right after the ferry and just up the hill on the left – offers small, very basic but clean rooms and all the normal YHA services: laundry, internet etc. Dorms ¥55–75, rooms ③

Lizhi Dao (aka Beautiful Island) (丽之岛酒店, *lìzhīdǎo jiǔdiàn*) 133 Longtou Lu ⓣ0592/2063309, ⓦwww.lzd-hotel.com. Very convenient, if suffering minor damp problems. The cheapest rooms are small and airless, but get one with a window and it's fair value. ③

Marine Garden (海上花园酒店, *hǎishàng huāyuán jiǔdiàn*) 27 Tianwei Lu ⓣ0592/2062688, ⓦwww.marinegardenhotel.com.cn. Just above Shuzhuang Garden, this plush, mildly garish faux-colonial place has quality rooms, a pool, tennis court and good views over the beach. ⑨

The City

The main pleasure in Xiamen, apart from visiting Gulangyu Islet, is simply walking the streets of the **old city** between Siming Lu and the seafront, its bustling narrow streets in total contrast to the skyscapers springing up over the rest of the city. Stroll down to the western end of Zhongshan Lu and you'll see the island of Gulangyu across the water. Several kiosks along the waterfront and on Gulangyu itself sell tickets for boat trips around island, and for a peek at the Taiwanese on neighbouring Jinmen. Prices start at ¥106 for an hour and forty minutes – for good views of Taiwan's front line bring binoculars. For a cheaper trip, go to the Gulangyu ferry terminal, from where there are tours that simply circle Gulangyu (30min; ¥15).

Southeast and east from the town centre there's a thin scattering of tourist sights. On Siming Nan Lu, about 2km south of Zhongshan Lu, you'll find the **Overseas Chinese Museum** (华侨博物馆, *huáqiáo bówùguǎn*; Tues–Sun 9.30am–4pm; free), which traces the history of the huge Fujianese diaspora around the world. The museum features pottery, bronzes, lots of photos and some amazing model boats, though little English. Another kilometre farther southeast (bus #1 to Xiada, Xiamen University) is the **Nanputuo Si** (南普陀寺, *nánpǔtuó sì*; daily 4am–6pm; ¥3), a temple complex established more than a thousand years ago. This is one of China's most organized, modern-looking Buddhist temples, its roofs a gaudy jumble of flying dragons, human figures and multicoloured flowers. Among its collection of treasures is a set of tablets carved by resistance fighters at the time of the early Qing, recording Manchu atrocities. Inside the main hall, behind the Maitreya Buddha, is a statue of **Wei Tuo**, the deity responsible for Buddhist doctrine, who holds a stick pointing to the ground – signifying that the monastery is wealthy and can provide board and lodging for itinerants. Today the temple is a huge draw for tour groups and has a well-known **vegetarian restaurant** (see p.498).

Immediately south of Nanputuo stands **Xiamen University** (厦门大学, *xiàmén dàxué*), from where you can cut through to Daxue Lu, the coastal road, which runs past attractive sandy beaches. A kilometre or so southwest is **Huli Shan Paotai** (胡里山炮台, *húlǐ shān pàotái*; Huli Mountain Gun Emplacement), at the terminus of bus #2. This nineteenth-century hunk of German heavy artillery had a range of 10km and was used during the Qing dynasty to fend off foreign imperialists. You can rent binoculars to look across to **Jinmen**, which lies less than 20km to the west.

A lengthy hike (at least 2hr) from the grounds of Nanputuo takes you up and over the forested **Wulao Shan** (五老山, *wǔlǎoshān*) behind the temple – you can also take bus #17 from outside Nanputuo's entrance to the same destination. Either way, you'll arrive at **Wanshi Botanical Gardens** (万石植物馆, *wànshí* *zhíwùguǎn*; daily 6am–6pm; ¥40), with their 4000 varieties of plant life including a redwood tree brought here by President Nixon in the 1970s. Southwest of the gardens' north (main) gate is the **Huxiyan** (虎溪岩, *hǔxī yán*; Tiger Stream Rock), built high on a rocky hillside. If you climb up you'll find a great little temple nestling amid a pile of huge boulders; slip through the cave to one side and climb the rock-hewn steps to the top. A second small temple right at the summit, **Bailu Dong** (白鹿洞, *báilù dòng*), commands spectacular views over the town and the sea.

Gulangyu Islet

Gulangyu Islet was Xiamen's foreign concession until World War II, and remains more-or-less architecturally intact. In summer and at weekends, the island is packed with tour groups, but the atmosphere remains generally restful – battery-powered golf-buggies (¥10 for a short journey, ¥50 for a round-island trip), for example, are the only vehicles allowed here. The narrow tangle of streets can be confusing, but the island's size (it's less than two square kilometres) means you can't go very far wrong. Though it's not worth walking a complete circuit – the northwest is exposed and empty – a stroll through the streets will uncover plenty of attractions, especially along **Fuzhou Lu** (福州路, *fúzhōulù*) and **Guxin Lu** (鼓新路, *gǔxīnlù*), overhung with flowers and blossom throughout the year.

From the disembarkation point, a splendid bronze sculpture of a giant octopus diagonally to your right marks the entrance to **Underwater World Xiamen** (海底世界, *hǎidǐ shìjiè*; daily 9.30am–4.30pm; ¥90, children and students ¥50), with walk-through aquariums, seal displays, penguins, turtles and a massive whale skeleton. Past here, follow Sanming Lu northwest and you'll come to the mouth of a **tunnel**, built in the 1950s when the threat of military confrontation with Taiwan seemed imminent, which burrows right underneath the hill. Don't go down the tunnel, but instead try finding your way back to the jetty through the back lanes – it makes for an excellent half-hour walk.

If you head southeast from the jetty, you'll pass a number of grand old buildings, including the former British and German consulates. The road continues on to the island's rocky eastern headland, now enclosed by **Haoyue Garden** (皓月园, *hàoyuè yuán*; ¥15), containing a gigantic granite **statue of Koxinga** (郑成功塑像, *zhèngchénggōng sùxiàng*) dressed in grand military attire and staring meaningfully out towards Taiwan. Shortly beyond the garden, the road heads west towards the middle of the island, bringing you to a sports ground and the old colonial **Gulangyu Guesthouse** (鼓浪屿宾馆, *gǔlàngyǔ bīnguǎn*). President Nixon stayed here on his 1972 trip, and it was, until recently, the haunt of Chinese VIPs – rumour has it the off-limits interior is preserved in all its 1920s opulence. For a closer glimpse of colonial life, the **Huaijiu Gulangyu Museum** (怀旧鼓浪屿馆, *húaijìugǔlàngyǔgǔan*; daily 8am–6pm; ¥60), up the alley on the north end of the sports ground, is not quite as grand as the guesthouse, but gives an idea of what life might once have been like.

Gulangyu practicalities

The **boat** to the island runs from 5.30am until just after midnight from the pier across from the *Lujiang* – the outbound journey on the lower deck is free and the upper deck is ¥1, while on the way back the lower and upper decks cost ¥8 and ¥9 respectively. The **island centre** – a knot of small streets with a **Bank of China**, a **post office**, and where **restaurants** and **cafés** are only outnumbered by souvenir shops – is directly ahead as you disembark from the ferry.

Due south, on the southern shore, the flower-filled **Shuzhuang Garden** (菽庄花园, *shūzhuāng huāyuán*; daily 6.30am–8pm; ¥30) boasts some nicely shaded areas for taking tea right by the sea. The **Piano Museum** (鼓浪屿钢琴博物馆, *gŭlàngyŭ gāngqín bówùguăn*) within is a reflection of the island's history with the instrument; foreigners began teaching locals here at the start of the twentieth century and the island has produced some of China's finest pianists.

The clean, sandy **beach** running west from the park is tempting for swimming when it's not too packed and is overlooked to the north by **Sunlight Rock** (日光岩, *rìguāng yán*; daily 6am–8pm; ¥60 includes cable-car ride), the highest point on Gulangyu (93m) and a magnet for tourists who ride up to the viewing platform to survey the entire island. At the foot of the rock (and covered by the same entrance ticket) is the **Koxinga Memorial Hall** (郑成功纪念馆, *zhèngchénggōng jìniànguăn*), which contains various relics, including Koxinga's jade belt and bits of his "imperial" robe. Follow the path along the coast from here – a beautiful walk on a bright day – and you pass below **Yingxiong Shan** (英雄山, *yīngxióng shān*), the top of which is enclosed in netting as an open-air **aviary** (included in Sunlight Rock ticket price), thick with tropical pigeons, egrets and parrots. A **multiticket** for entry to Haoyue and Shuzhuang Gardens, Sunlight Rock and Yingxiong Shan, available from any of the ticket kiosks dotted around, costs ¥80.

Eating and drinking

Xiamen has plenty of places to eat fresh **fish** and **seafood**, particularly oysters, crabs and prawns. Head for the restaurants around Gulangyu's market area – the curiously titled *Gulangyu Credit Restaurant* on Zhonghua Lu is particularly popular with Chinese tourists – or the backstreets behind the *Donghai*, but make sure you establish a price in advance: the seafood is usually sold by weight, not per portion. Nanputuo Si's **vegetarian restaurant** is expensive for what you get, with set meals at ¥30–80, depending on the number of dishes; two minutes up the road, *Da Fang* (大方素食馆, *dàfāng sùshíguăn*) is a cheaper vegetarian option. Nearby, a clutch of student-oriented **cafés** on Nanhua Lu offer Chinese and Western food, beers and cocktails, in a relaxed atmosphere with outdoor seating – try *Yoso* or *Rendeavous*. On **Gulangyu**, around the corner from the *Lizhi Dao*, the contemporary Taiwan-style *Babycat* teahouse (小猫茶馆, *xiăomāo cháguăn*) – a laidback coffee shop and café that does brisk trade in its famous traditional **Amoy pies** – has simple Western food, internet access and a resident celebrity feline.

Listings

Airlines Air China, *Huguang Dasha*, Hubin Dong Lu ⓣ0592/5084382; China Eastern, 311 Siming Nan Lu ⓣ0592/2028936; Malaysia Airlines, *Crowne Plaza* ⓣ0592/2023333; Philippine Airlines, *Marco Polo Hotel*, Jianye Lu ⓣ0592/2394729; Silk Air, International Plaza ⓣ0592/2053257; Thai Airways, International Plaza ⓣ0592/2261688.

Banks and exchange There are branches of the Bank of China (Mon–Fri 8.30am–noon & 2.30–5pm, Sat 8am–12.30pm) on Gulangyu Islet and on Zhongshan Lu, back from the seafront.

Consulates Philippines, near the geographic centre of Xiamen on Lianhua Bei Lu ⓣ0592/5130355.

Internet There are several internet bars in the lane directly north of the *Donghai*, parallel with Datong Lu; *Babycat* teahouse has wi-fi.

Mail and telephones Xiamen's main post office, where IDD telephone calls can also be made, is on the seafront, just north of the *Xiamen Spring Sunlight*, and there's another large branch on Xinhua Lu, south of the junction with Siming Dong Lu.

PSB Across from the Post Office on Gongyuan Nan Lu ⓣ0592/2262203.

Travel agents CTS, *Huaqiao* hotel, Xinhua Lu ⓣ0592/2025602; Xiamen Tourism Group, *Lujiang* ⓣ0592/2029933.

Southwestern Fujian: the Hakka homelands

Fujian's hilly southwestern border with Guangdong is an area central to the **Hakka**, a Han subgroup known to locals as *kejia* (客家, *kèjīa*; guest families) and to nineteenth-century Europeans as "China's gypsies". Originating in the Yangzi basin during the third century and dislodged ever southward by war and revolution, the Hakka today form large communities here, in Hong Kong and on Hainan island. They managed to retain their original languages and customs by remaining aloof from their neighbours in the lands in which they settled, a habit that caused resentment and led to their homes being well defended. While towns up this way are mostly unattractive low-level industrial settlements, the countryside is pretty in spring, and villages and hamlets around the focal city of **Yongding** (永定, *yongding*) sport fortress-like **Hakka mansions** built of stone and adobe. The largest are four or five storeys high, circular, and house entire clans.

If you can't find direct transport from coastal Fujian, aim first for **LONGYAN** (龙岩, *lóngyán*), a small city 170km northwest of Xiamen, where roads and separate rail lines from Fuzhou, Quanzhou and Xiamen converge to head west to Meizhou in Guangdong (see p.500). From the **train station** on the eastern edge of town, catch bus #14 over three bridges to Longzhou Xi Lu (龙州西路, *lóngzhōuxīlù*) and the **long-distance bus station**, 2km away and just south of Longyan's centre. Here you'll be mobbed by minibus drivers for the final 60km, hour-long run southwest to Yongding (¥10), through several Hakka towns marked by large, mud-brick mansions and, inevitably, surrounded by cement factories.

Yongding and around

Set on the edge of a flat river basin, ancient **YONGDING** (永定, *yǒngdìng*) has been recast as a heavily built-up, typically ugly place, whose residents are nevertheless very friendly toward the few foreigners who make it up here. The road from Longyan ends up at a **roundabout**, where you'll find the **bus station** and decent, if forgettable and slightly noisy, **accommodation** options. The best of these is the *Dongfu Jiudian* (东府酒店, *dōngfǔ jiǔdiàn*; Ⓣ0597/5830668; ❸), which has clean, pleasant rooms and helpful staff; the nearby *Jiari Lüguan* (假日旅馆, *jiàrì lǚguǎn*; ❷) and *Tianhe Lüguan* (天河旅馆, *tiānhé lǚguǎn*; Ⓣ0597/5835769; ❷) aren't quite as comfortable. From the roundabout, the main street runs west over the river and into town; on the far bank, Huancheng Dong Lu (环成东路, *húanchéngdōnglù*) forks left after 100m into a market area, while steps on the right climb a ridge to **Feng Shan park** (风山公园, *fēngshāngōngyúan*), with views across town and the countryside. If you carry straight on you'll reach the Bank of China. **Places to eat** surround the bus station and main streets; you'll find all sorts of rice noodles, snacks and **kourou** (口肉, *kǒuròu*), a Hakka dish made from slices of soya-braised pork belly on a bed of bitter kale. Daily buses **depart** to Meizhou in Guangdong, and Xiamen, and minibuses head through the day back to Longyan.

Hongkeng Cun and Zhencheng Lou

An hour's bus ride east of Yongding, **Zhencheng Lou** (振城楼, *zhènchéng lóu*) is considered to be the most perfect Hakka roundhouse or *tulou*. This century-old home forms the well-maintained, if slightly sterile, centrepiece of the **Hongkeng Cun tourist village** (洪坑村, *hóngkēngcūn*; ¥50): plain and forbidding on the outside, the huge outer wall encloses three storeys of galleried rooms looking inwards to a central courtyard where guests were entertained, and which contained

the clan shrine. The galleries are vertically divided into eight segments by thick fire walls, a plan that intentionally turns the building into a giant *bagua*, Taoism's octagonal symbol. This powerful design occurs everywhere in the region, along with demon-repelling mirrors and other Taoist motifs. An almost disastrous consequence of roundhouse design – which from above looks like a ring – was that (so locals say) the first US satellite photos of the region identified the houses as missile silos.

The tourist village is nice enough in itself, with other, more "authentic", houses (still lived in) laid out along a small stream. Those worth investigating include a 1920s schoolhouse; **Fuyu Lou**, the old *yamen* building; **Rushen**, one of the smallest multistorey roundhouses; and **Kuijiu**, a splendid, 165-year-old square-sided Hakka mansion, its interior like a temple squeezed into a box.

To get here from Yongding, jump on one of the regular direct **buses** (1hr; ¥16), which will drop you outside a row of **guesthouses** a few hundred metres from Zhencheng Lou itself. Guesthouse owners will meet you from the bus, offering modern rooms (❶–❷) or the chance to stay in the imposing but very ramshackle *Huangxin Lou* opposite (❶). Mr Li at the *Backpacker's Station* is particularly hospitable. From Zhencheng it's easy to organize trips (reckon on around ¥100 for a full day, but be prepared to haggle) to surrounding *tulou*, including **Chengqi Lou** (承启楼, *chéngqǐlóu*), the largest roundhouse of them all, built in 1709, with more than 300 rooms housing more than 400 people; **Tianluo Keng** (田螺坑, *tíanlúokēng*), a remote grouping of five large houses – including three roundhouses, one square walled house and one oval – that date back between two and three hundred years and still house around six hundred people; and **Yuchang Lou** (裕唱楼, *yùchānglóu*), the oldest and, at more than 21m, tallest of the roundhouses. Yuchang's five storeys have stood since 1309, despite a drunken 15° lean in its uprights.

Moving on from Zhencheng, you could take one of several daily buses to Yongding and Longyan from where it's a short skip into **Guangdong**. Alternatively, three daily direct buses head to **Xiamen**, 160km south on the Fujian coast (4hr 30min; ¥63). All leave from the unofficial-looking **bus station** opposite the **Hongkeng Tourist Village** bus park.

Guangdong

Halfway along **Guangdong**'s (广东, *gŭangdōng*) 800km coastline, rivers from all over the province and beyond disgorge themselves into the South China Sea, through the tropically fertile **Pearl River Delta**, one of China's most densely cultivated and developed areas. Perched right at the delta's northern apex and adjacent to both Hong Kong and Macau, the provincial capital **Guangzhou** (广州, *guăngzhōu*) provides many travellers with their first taste of mainland China. It's not everyone's favourite city, but once you've found your bearings among the busy roads and packed shopping districts, Guangzhou's world-famous **food** merits a stop, as does an assortment of museums, parks and monuments. The Pearl River Delta has a few patches of green and some history to pick up in passing, but it would be futile to pretend the area's focus is anything other than industry and commerce – as demonstrated by the city of **Shenzhen** (深圳, *shēnzhèn*) where China's "economic miracle" took its first baby steps.

Farther afield, the rest of the province is more picturesque. There are Buddhist temples and Stone Age relics around **Shaoguan** (韶关, *sháoguān*), up north by the Hunan and Jiangxi borders. Over in the east near Fujian, the ancient town of **Chaozhou** (潮州, *cháozhōu*) has well-preserved Ming architecture peppered amongst a warren of narrow streets, while nearby **Meizhou** (梅州, *méizhōu*) is a useful stepping stone to the ethnic Hakka heartland, set in the surrounding hills. The highlight of the region, though, lies to the east in the form of the fantastical towers around the town of **Kaiping** (开平, *kāipíng*), recognized as a UNESCO World Heritage Site in 2007. Not far away, **Zhaoqing** (肇庆, *zhàoqìng*) sports pleasant, formalized lakes and hilly landscapes, while those heading towards Hainan need to aim for the ferry port of **Hai'an** (海安, *hăi'ān*), down in Guangdong's southwestern extremities.

Guangdong has a generous quantity of rail and road traffic, and getting around is none too difficult, though often requires some advance preparation. Rail lines run north through Shaoguan and up into Hunan and central China, east to Meizhou, Shantou and Fujian, and west through Zhaoqing to Zhanjiang and Guangxi. River travel was, until recently, a highlight of the province, though the only easy excursions left are the fast hydrofoils between the Pearl River Delta towns and Hong Kong, and a day-cruise from the northern town of Qingyuan to some riverside temples. As for the **climate**, summers can be sweltering across the province, with typhoons along the coast, while winter temperatures get decidedly nippy up in the northern ranges – though it's more likely to be miserably wet than to snow, except around the highest mountain peaks.

Guangzhou

GUANGZHOU (广州, *guăngzhōu*), once known to the Western world as **Canton**, has for centuries been the point where China meets the rest of the world – commercially, militarily and otherwise. Increased competition from its noisy upstart neighbour, Shenzhen, and the flowering of Beijing and Shanghai may have diminished Guangzhou's role as a centre of international commerce, but the locals are secure in their history, and with the money continuing to roll in from the surrounding factories, you will hear no suggestions here that the city is a fading power. An expanding **metro** and **high-speed rail network** have made getting to and around the city a breeze, and triggered growth in previously unreachable districts.

True, Guangzhou's **sights** remain relatively minor, though a fascinating 2000-year-old tomb and palace site complement the obligatory round of temples. Yet the city is an enjoyable place, especially if you love to dine out. The Cantonese are compulsively garrulous, turning Guangzhou's two famous obsessions – **eating** and **business** – into social occasions, and filling streets, restaurants and buildings with the sounds of Yueyu, the Cantonese language.

Newer districts can pass as a blur of chrome and concrete, but make your way around on foot through the back lanes and you'll discover a very different city, one of flagstoned residential quarters, tiny collectors' markets and laundry strung on lines between buildings.

The emphasis, however, is undoubtedly on business over tourism; the **biannual Trade Fair** is the highlight for many in the city and commerce is Guangzhou's lifeblood, an ethos inspiring train-station pickpockets and company CEOs alike. In purely practical terms, however, while the city is expensive compared with some parts of China, it's far **cheaper** than Hong Kong, the place citizens here would most like you to consider their city alongside.

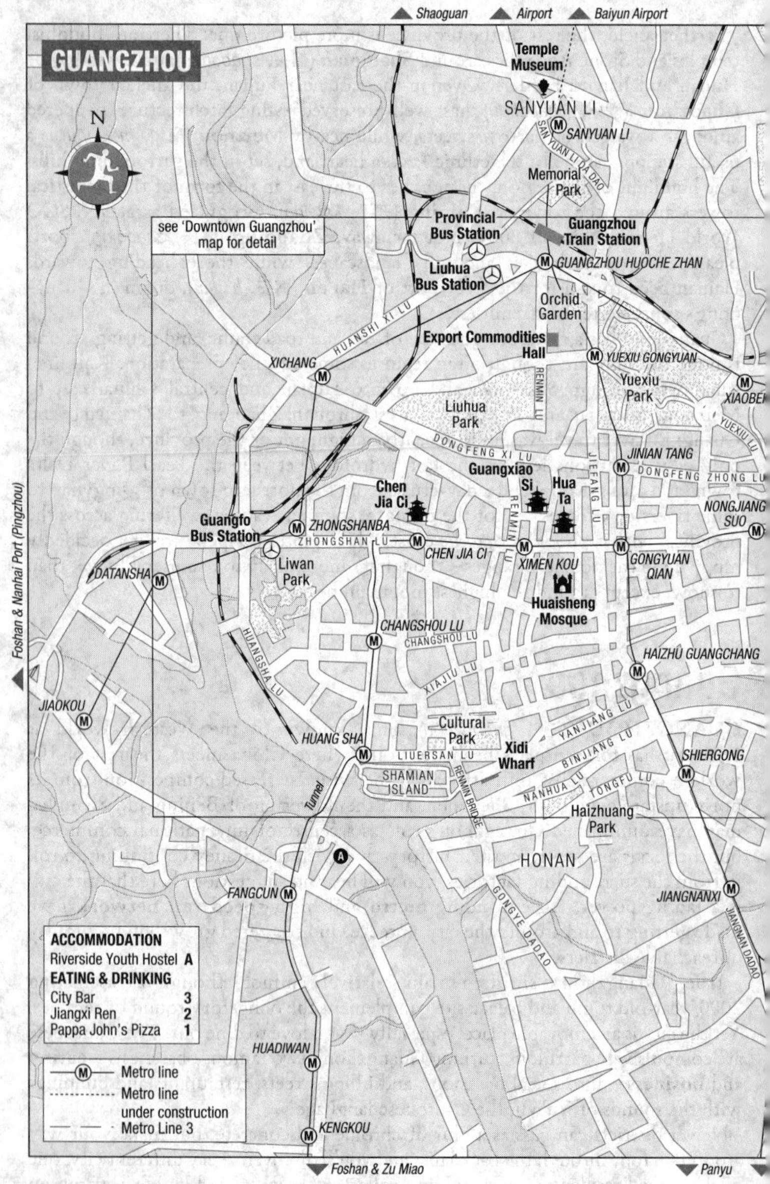

Some history

Legend tells how Guangzhou was founded by **Five Immortals** riding five rams, each of whom planted a sheaf of rice symbolizing endless prosperity – hence Guangzhou's nickname, **Yang Cheng** (Goat City). Myths aside, a settlement called **Panyu** had sprung up here by the third century BC, when a rogue Qin commander founded the **Nanyue Kingdom** and made it his capital. Remains of a contemporary **shipyard** uncovered in central Guangzhou during the 1970s suggest that the city had contact

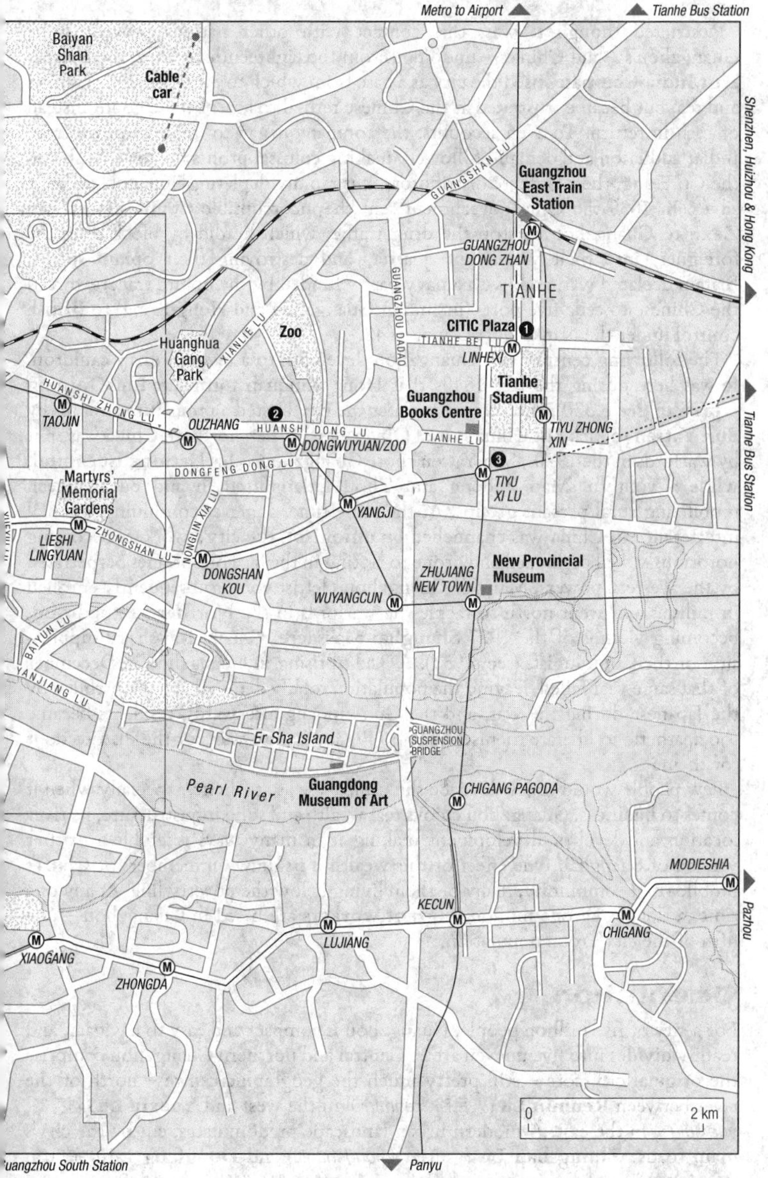

with foreign lands even then: there were merchants who considered themselves Roman subjects here in 165 AD, and from Tang times, vessels travelled to Middle Eastern ports, introducing **Islam** into China and exporting porcelain to Arab colonies in distant Kenya and Zanzibar. By 1405, Guangzhou's population of foreign traders and Overseas Chinese was so large that the Ming emperor Yongle founded a special quarter for them. When xenophobia later closed the rest of China to outsiders, Guangzhou became the country's main link with the rest of the world.

Restricted though it was, this contact with other nations proved to be Guangzhou's – and China's – undoing. From the eighteenth century, the **British East India Company** used the city as a base from which to purchase silk, ceramics and tea, but became frustrated at the Chinese refusal to accept trade goods instead of cash in return. To even accounts, the company began to import **opium** from India; addiction and demand followed, making colossal profits for the British and the Co Hong, their Chinese distributors, but rapidly depleting imperial stocks of silver. In 1839 the Qing government sent the incorruptible Commissioner **Lin Zexu** to Guangzhou to stop the drug traffic, which he did by blockading the foreigners into their waterfront quarters and destroying their opium stocks. Britain declared war, and, with a navy partly funded by the opium traders, forced the Chinese to cede five ports (including Guangzhou and Hong Kong) to British control under the Nanking Treaty of 1842.

The following century saw Guangzhou develop into a revolutionary cauldron. It was here during the late 1840s that Hong Xiuquan formulated his **Taiping Uprising** (see p.330), and sixty years later the city hosted a premature attempt by **Sun Yatsen** to kick out China's royal Qing rulers. When northern China was split by warlords in the 1920s, Sun Yatsen chose Guangzhou as his **Nationalist capital**, while a youthful Mao Zedong and Zhou Enlai flitted in and out between mobilizing rural peasant groups. At the same time, anger at continuing colonial interference in China was channelled by **unionism**, the city's workers becoming notoriously well organized and prone to rioting in the face of outrages perpetrated by the Western powers. Many of Guangzhou's leftist youth subsequently enrolled in militias and went north to tackle the warlords in the **Northern Expedition**, becoming victims of the 1927 **Shanghai Massacre**, Chiang Kai-shek's suppression of the Communists (see p.951). A Red uprising in Guangzhou in December of that same year failed, leaving the population totally demoralized. Controlled by the Japanese during the war, and the Guomindang afterwards, residents became too apathetic to liberate themselves in 1949, and had to wait for the PLA to do it for them.

Few people would today describe the Cantonese as apathetic, especially when it comes to **business**. Guangzhou enjoys real wealth and solid infrastructure, its river location and level of development making it in many ways resemble a grittier version of Shanghai. One effect of this wealth is its draw on members of China's mobile rural community, many of them living below the poverty line. At any one time, a staggering one million **migrant workers** are based in Guangzhou – one fifth of the city's total population.

Orientation

For a city of five million people, Guangzhou is compact and easy to navigate, and readily divides into five uneven areas. Central and northern Guangzhou comprise the original city core – still pretty much the geographic centre – north of the river between **Renmin Lu** (人民路, *rénmínlù*) in the west and **Yuexiu Lu** (越秀路, *yuèxiùlù*) in the east. A modern urban landscape predominates, cut by the city's main roads: **Zhongshan Lu** (中山路, *zhōngshānlù*) and **Dongfeng Lu** (东风路, *dōngfēng lù*) run east–west, and **Jiefang Lu** (解放路, *jiěfànglù*) and Renmin Lu (人民路, *rénmínlù*) run north–south. These streets are divided into north, south, east, west and central sections, with the exception of Zhongshan Lu, whose segments are numbered. It's not all relentless modernity and traffic, however: most of Guangzhou's historical sites are located here, along with two sizeable parks, **Yuexiu** (越秀公园, *yuèxiù gōngyuán*) and **Liuhua** (流花公园, *liúhuā gōngyuán*).

Western Guangzhou, the area west of Renmin Lu, is a thriving shopping and eating district centred on **Changshou Lu** (长寿路, *chángshòulù*). This formed a

Ming-dynasty overflow from the original city, and it retains its former street plan, though the narrow back lanes, old houses and markets are also ringed by main roads, such as waterfront **Liuersan Lu** (六二三路, *liùèrsānlù*). Right on the river here is the former foreigners' quarter of **Shamian Island** (沙面岛, *shāmiàn dǎo*). Over on the south bank, **Honan** (河南, *hénán*) was a seedy hotspot during the 1930s, though nowadays it's simply a smaller version of the Changshou Lu districts.

East of Yuexiu Lu the city opens up, as the main roads – Zhongshan Lu, Dongfeng Lu and Huanshi Lu, all lined with glassy corporate offices – run broad and straight through **Eastern Guangzhou** to culminate in the vast, open square and sports stadium at the centre of **Tianhe** (天河, *tianhé*). Nightlife is the east's biggest draw – many of Guangzhou's bars are out this way – while a few kilometres to the north is **Baiyun Shan** (白云山, *báiyún shān*), a formalized string of hills and parkland just beyond the city proper.

Arrival and information

Baiyun international airport (白云国际飞机场, *báiyúngúojìfēijīchǎng*) lies 20km north of the city centre – a plethora of **airport express buses head** to the centre and beyond (¥13–33). Taxis into the centre are also freely available (¥70–130), but it's more convenient to jump on the recently extended metro line #3. Ferries **from Hong Kong** dock at least an hour's taxi ride away at Nansha.

The city proper has two major **train** stations – **Guangzhou Station** (广州火车站, *guǎngzhōu huǒchēzhàn*) and **Guangzhou East** (东方火车站, *dōngfāng guǎngzhōu chēzhàn*) – and a third, **Guangzhou South Station** (广州南站, *gǔangzhōunánzhàn*), is in the city's Panyu district, around 17km south of the centre. This already runs high-speed services to Wuhan on a line that will eventually continue all the way to Beijing; it will also serve as the terminus for the high-speed Guangzhou–Shenzhen–Hong Kong rail line, will be linked to Zhuhai by light rail and will take on more services in time – check when you book your tickets.

Guangzhou Station, in the north of the city, is the most confrontational place to arrive, the vast square outside perpetually seething with passengers, hawkers and hustlers. Mainline services from most central, northern and western destinations terminate here. New arrivals exit on the west side of the square, convenient for the metro; for Shamian, take it south three stops to Gongyuan Qian interchange, then catch line #1 south to Huang Sha. Taxis and most city buses wait over on the east side; buses #5 and #31 run down to the Cultural Park near Shamian Island.

Guangzhou East Station is situated 5km east of the centre at Tianhe. Trains from Shenzhen stop here, along with the Kowloon Express, services from Shantou, Meizhou and western Fujian. From the basement, catch metro line #1 direct to the Huang Sha (黄沙, *huángshā*) stop for Shamian Island; for Guangzhou Station, take bus #271 or the metro, changing at Gongyuan Qian (公园前, *gōngyuán qián*). A taxi to the centre costs ¥30–40.

There are several major long-distance bus stations. West of Guangzhou train station on Huanshi Xi Lu, the **provincial bus station** (省汽车客运站, *shěngqìchē kèyùnzhàn*) handles arrivals from almost everywhere in the country, with more local traffic often winding up across the road at one of the number of depots that comprise **Liuhua station** (流花车客运站, *liúhuāchē kèyùnzhàn*). Buses from eastern Guangdong and central China might terminate out in the northeastern suburbs at **Tianhe bus station** (天河客运站, *tiānhé kèyùnzhàn*), from where it is simple to catch the metro into town.

Maps of varying detail and quality are sold for around ¥5 by hawkers at the train and bus stations, and at numerous bookshops, hotels and newsstands around the city. The current favourite is *The Tour Map of Guangzhou*, which has many of the sights marked in English, and should have a date on it – though it

Moving on from Guangzhou

Leaving Guangzhou requires advance planning, and you'll generally need a few days to arrange tickets or at least check out the options, especially for the train.

By air

With an **airport** designed to rival Hong Kong's – and considerably cheaper fares – Guangzhou is well connected by air to all major cities in China, many in Southeast Asia and increasingly more worldwide. The regional airline, China Southern (Ⓣ020/95539), has its headquarters just east of the central train station, with its well-organized ticket office upstairs (daily 9am–6pm). See "Listings", p.524, for international airline offices and travel agents. Airport buses (¥10–30) leave from outside China Southern (every 20min 5am–11pm), or there are taxis (¥100). The metro is expected to reach the airport sometime in 2011 and will whisk passengers into the centre of town in around 30min.

By train

Demand for train tickets out of Guangzhou is very high. Tickets become available three days before departure, but sleepers sell out swiftly, as do even hard seats on popular lines. There are several **advance-ticket offices** around town, where there's no commission and the queues are usually shorter than at the stations: the most convenient are down near the river at the northeastern corner of the Guangzhou Qiyi Lu/Yide Lu intersection; and west of the *Garden* hotel on Huanshi Zhong Lu. CITS Travel, 618 Jie Fang Bei Lu, just north of Gongyuan Qian metro station or CTS, next to the *Landmark*, can also be helpful with booking rail and flight tickets.

Paying an **agent** can cut out so much bother that it's money well spent, despite the service fees involved – upwards of ¥50 a ticket. Most agents, however, deal only with major destinations like Shanghai, Beijing, Hong Kong, Guilin and Xi'an.

Guangzhou Station handles virtually all destinations, though for Shenzhen or Hong Kong, Guangzhou East station may be a calmer alternative. The **ticket hall** is at the eastern end of the station; crowds are horrendous here at peak times, when entry is through guarded gateways that are closed off when the interior becomes too chaotic. Otherwise, you'll generally get what you want if you've a flexible schedule and are prepared to queue for an hour, though staff can be positively hostile.

Guangzhou East Station handles the Kowloon Express (12 daily 8.35am–9.20pm; ¥198–293), Shenzhen traffic (50 daily 6.30am–10.20pm; ¥75), eastern lines to

does not illustrate all of Guangzhou's two-hundred-plus bus routes, nor does it have a separate metro map. For Guangzhou's eating, drinking and bar scene, as well as other expat-related and **tourist information**, try Ⓦwww.cityweekend.com.cn/guangzhou.

City transport

Though the city is too big to walk everywhere, and bicycles are not recommended because of heavy traffic, expansion of the **metro** system to five lines means getting around Guangzhou is incredibly simple, and almost everywhere is within easy reach. Of the two most central lines, **line #1** runs diagonally across the city from Guangzhou East train station at Tianhe, through the centre along Zhongshan Lu, then turns south at Chen Jia Ci (陈家祠, *chénjiā cí*), past Shamian Island and across the river. **Line #2** runs south from Sanyuan Li (三元里, *sānyuán lǐ*) via Guangzhou train station, interchanging with line #1 at Gongyuan Qian, then crossing the river and heading east to Xilang (西朗, *xīlǎng*). Line #2 should connect to the airport in the future, and, when totally finished, line #1 will run as far as Foshan

Shantou and Fujian, and an increasing number of services north through central China.

Guangzhou South Station, best reached by metro, already carries high-speed services north as far as Wuhan and will be the hub for express services to Shenzhen and Hong Kong as well as light rail to Zhuhai. Given its vast size, more services are likely to be moved to arrive and depart from here.

By bus

Leaving Guangzhou by bus can be the cheapest of all exit options, and more comfortable than the average hard-seat experience if you have any distance to travel. Fast but relatively expensive **express buses** are very much the rage at present – especially around the Pearl River Delta and along the expressway to eastern Guangdong – so if money is your prime consideration, check to see whether there are any ordinary buses (*putong che*) to your destination, but don't forget to also ask how long these services will take.

The **provincial bus station** on Huanshi Xi Lu, diagonally opposite the main station, is always full of people, but tickets are easy to get – and there are at least daily departures to everywhere in Guangdong, and as far afield as Guizhou, Anhui, Hainan and Fujian provinces. Destinations within 100km or so of Guangzhou – including all Delta towns, Qingyuan and Huizhou – are covered from the **Liuhua bus station**, also on Huanshi Xi Lu. Buses for Shantou, Meizhou and points east mostly depart from the new **Tianhe bus station**, about 7km east of town. You can buy tickets for these at the provincial bus station – they'll stamp your ticket on the back for a free shuttle bus to the Tianhe station, which takes around thirty minutes.

Express buses to **Hong Kong** and **Macau** run by CTS and others depart from various hotels between 5.30am and 8pm; buy tickets at the departure points. For **Kowloon** – either Hong Kong Airport (3hr; around ¥255) or Kowloon Tong MTR (3hr; around ¥115) – try the *China Marriott* (26 daily), *Landmark* (16 daily), or *White Swan* (5 daily). For **Macau** (3hr 30min; ¥75), the *Landmark* has nine departures daily.

By boat

Guangzhou's **ferry port** is to the southeast at Nansha, and has six daily speedboats to and from Hong Kong (1hr; ¥116) but it currently takes at least an hour to get to Nansha from central Guangzhou.

(佛山, *fóshān*; see p.531). **Metro stations** can be hard to locate at street level, but are signposted from nearby roads; keep an eye out for the logo, rather like a "Y" made up of two red (or yellow) lines on a white (or yellow) background. **Fares** are ¥2–13, according to the number of stops from your starting point. Carriages have bilingual route maps, and each stop is announced in Mandarin and English.

If you can't get somewhere by metro, you'll find yourself using Guangzhou's cheap and slow **bus** and **trolleybus** network, which covers most of the city from ¥1 a ride. **Taxis** are plentiful and can be hailed in the street. Fares start at ¥7, but larger vehicles charge more – all have meters. Drivers rarely try any scams, though the city's complex traffic flows can sometimes make it seem that you're heading in the wrong direction.

Accommodation

Guangzhou's business emphasis means that true budget accommodation is limited, resign yourself to this and plan your finances accordingly. Prices can more than **double** during the fortnight-long trade fairs each April and October, when beds will be in short supply, but can be discounted by as much as fifty percent when fewer visitors are about. Every hotel has some sort of travel-booking service, while smarter places have their own banks, post offices, restaurants and shops.

Shamian Island is the best place to stay: a pleasant spot with well-tended parks, a bit of peace and plenty of places to eat. Otherwise, there are several relatively inexpensive hotels in central Guangzhou, mostly near the riverfront, and upmarket accommodation in the city's north and eastern quarters, where you will also find a few budget options near Guangzhou train station.

Shamian Island

The places reviewed below are marked on the map on p.518, unless otherwise noted.

7 Days Inn (7天连锁酒店, *qī tiānliánsuǒjiǔdiàn*) Huangsha Dadao ⓣ020/81259588, ⓦwww.7daysinnl.com. One of a growing chain of hotels offering cheap, clean accommodation across the country. Literally a thirty-second walk from Shamian Island. Characterless rooms but staff are helpful. Great value. ❸–❹

Customs Hotel (海关会议接待中心, *hǎiguān huìyì jiēdài zhōngxīn*) Shamian Dajie ⓣ020/81102388, ⓦwww.gzchotel.com. Well-located hotel aimed at Chinese businessmen, inside a former Customs House – though the interior is strictly modern. ❻

Guangzhou Youth Hostel (广州青年招待所, *guǎngzhōu qīngnián zhāodàisuǒ*) Shamian Si Jie ⓣ020/81218298, ⓦwww.gzyhostel.com. Across from the lavish *White Swan*, this is one of Shamian's cheaper options. Dorms can be damp, but other rooms are fairly presentable. Despite the name, not an actual IYHF hostel. Dorm beds ¥60, rooms ❺

Riverside Youth Hostel (广州江畔国际青年旅舍, *guǎngzhōujīangpàngúojìqīngníanlǚguǎn*) 15 Changdi St, Luju Rd, Liwan ⓣ020/22392500, ⓔrsjiangpan@yahoo.com.cn; see map, pp.510–511. Just across the water in Liwan district, this is Guangzhou's only genuine IYHA hostel. It provides all the services you would expect, plus there's an up-and-coming bar district in the surrounding area. Dorm beds ¥60, rooms ❸

Shamian (沙面宾馆, *shāmiàn bīnguǎn*) Shamian Nan Jie ⓣ020/81218359, ⓦwww.gdshamianhotel.com. Cheaper rooms are small and mostly windowless, but otherwise this is a very snug and comfortable option, with internet in every room. It's just around the corner from the youth hostel. ❺

Victory (aka Shengli) (胜利宾馆, *shènglì bīnguǎn*) Shamian Bei Jie and Shamian Si Jie ⓣ020/81216688, ⓦwww.vhotel.com. Formerly the *Victoria* in colonial days, this upmarket choice covers two separate buildings; the newly renovated annexe (on Si Jie) is both more luxurious and more expensive. Fifty-percent discounts are available outside of peak season. ❼

White Swan (白天鹅宾馆, *báitiān'é bīnguǎn*) Shamian Nan Jie ⓣ020/81886968, ⓦwww.whiteswanhotel.com. Once Guangzhou's most upmarket place to stay, this hotel is probably still the city's most famous, and a favourite with US citizens in town to adopt Chinese orphans. You'll find a waterfall in the lobby, river views, an on-site bakery and huge array of upmarket objets d'art. ❽

Central Guangzhou

The places reviewed below are marked on the map on pp.510–511.

Baigong (白宫酒店, *báigōng jiǔdiàn*) 13–17 Renmin Nan Lu ⓣ020/81925999, ⓦwww.baigong-hotel.com. Run-of-the-mill business hotel, where the rooms are past their prime and can get noisy. It is, however, also tidy, friendly and excellent value for the location. ❹

Beijing (北京大酒店, *běijīng dàjiǔdiàn*) 105 Xihao Er Lu ⓣ020/62793388, ⓕ81883799. Another typical inner-city Chinese hotel – smart lobby, slightly tarnished rooms, huge restaurant and, of course, a karaoke hall. Also has a travel booking centre. Easily confused with the similarly priced *New Beijing* across the street. ❸

Guangdong Guesthouse (广东宾馆, *guǎngdōng bīnguǎn*) 603 Jiefang Bei Lu ⓣ020/83332950, ⓦwww.ggh.com.cn. A huge complex of square concrete wings, Sinicized with green tiling and flared eaves. Quite comfortable, but fading around the edges. ❻

King Long Hotel (金隆酒店, *jīnlōngjǐudìan*) 505 Huifu Dong Lu ⓣ020/83190988, ⓔbook@gzkinglong.com. This modern neon-signed hotel sits above the *Lemon House* Vietnamese restaurant; its very central location also means it can be a bit noisy. Also rents rooms by the hour. ❺

Landmark (华厦大酒店, *huáxià dàjiǔdiàn*) 8 Qiaoguang Lu ⓣ020/83355988, ⓦwww.hotel-landmark.com.cn. Four-star business centre between a busy roundabout and the river. ❼

Northern and eastern Guangzhou

The places reviewed below are marked on the map on pp.502–503.

Baiyun City Hotel (白云城市酒店, *báiyúnchéngshìjiǔdiàn*) 179 Huanshi Xi Lu ⓣ020/86666889, ⓦwww.baiyuncityhotel.com. Right next to the China Southern office and Guangzhou train station, this used to be, but is no longer, IYHA affiliated. Very handy for the station but little else to recommend it. ❸

China Marriott (中国大酒店, *zhōngguó dàjiǔdiàn*) Liuhua Lu ⓣ020/86666888, ⓦwww.marriotthotels.com. Five-star labyrinth of red marble corridors opposite the Export Commodities Hall, with upmarket shopping malls and places to eat. You almost need a map to get around, but rooms are of a predictably high-quality standard. ❾

Dongfang (东方宾馆, *dōngfāng bīnguǎn*) 120 Liuhua Lu ⓣ020/86669900, ⓦwww.dongfanghotel-gz.com. Literally in the *Marriott*'s shadow, here's another five-star maze with a dazzling number of restaurants housed in smartly remodelled 1950s buildings. ❾

Garden (花园酒店, *huāyuán jiǔdiàn*) 368 Huanshi Dong Lu ⓣ020/83338989, ⓦwww.thegardenhotel.com.cn. The city's most opulent accommodation, this classier version of the *White Swan* – there's even a waterfall – is its superior in every respect but the setting. Pool and gym free for guests. ❾

Holiday Inn (文化假日酒店, *wénhuà jiàrì jiǔdiàn*) 28 Guangming Lu ⓣ020/61286868, ⓦwww.guangzhou.holiday-inn.com. The usual international-standard facilities and a cinema. ❽

Liuhua (流花宾馆, *liúhuā bīnguǎn*) 194 Huanshi Xi Lu ⓣ020/86668800, ⓦwww.lh.com.cn. Business hotel directly opposite the train station, with a broad range of rooms. ❼

Yishu (aka Art Hotel) (艺术宾馆, *yìshù bīnguǎn*) 698 Renmin Bei Lu ⓣ020/86670266. Tucked back from the street; look for the English name on a gateway out front and follow the driveway to the hotel. Nothing exceptional, but at least it's inexpensive, given its busy location near the Export Commodities Hall. ❹

The city centre

Central Guangzhou is basically a 2km-wide band running north from the river between Renmin Lu and Yuexiu Lu. As remnants of the **Nanyue Kingdom** illustrate, this was the core of the city from its very foundation around 220 BC, and sports a host of historical monuments from this time right up to the 1930s. Most of these are located south of **Dongfeng Lu** (东风路, *dōngfēnglù*) a mixed, rather scruffy mesh of old and new roads, alleys and businesses.

Around the Pearl River to Wuxian Guan

Lined with trees and a smattering of colonial-era buildings – such as the **Customs House** (广州海关, *guǎngzhōu hǎiguān*) – **Yanjiang Lu** (沿江路, *yánjīanglù*), the northern promenade along the **Pearl River** (珠江, *zhūjiāng*), is a good place to mill about on hot summer evenings.

Follow Yanjiang Lu to its eastern end and you'll find yourself crossing to **Er Sha Island** (二沙岛, *èrshādǎo*), the focus of much upmarket housing development and home to the **Guangdong Museum of Art** (广东美术馆, *guǎngdōng měishùguǎn*; Tues–Sun 9am–5pm; ¥15; ⓦwww.gdmoa.org). The museum holds one of China's largest collections of contemporary art and hosts special exhibitions.

Back in the centre, north from the river, **Yide Lu** (一德路, *yīdélù*) is stuffed with small shops selling toys and dried marine produce – jellyfish, shark's fin, fish maw and whole salted mackerel – along with sacks of nuts and candied fruit. Set north off the road, the **Sacred Heart Church** (圣心大教堂, *shèngxīn dàjiàotáng*) – also known as the Stone House – is a Gothic-style cathedral completed in 1888, impressive for its size and unexpected presence, though it's not generally open to the public. Three streets up from here on Huifu Xi Lu is **Wuxian Guan** (五仙观, *wǔxiān guān*; Five Immortals' Temple). Dating from 1377, the original wooden building isn't much to write home about, but there are some obviously ancient statues around the place: weathered guardian lions flank the way in, and some

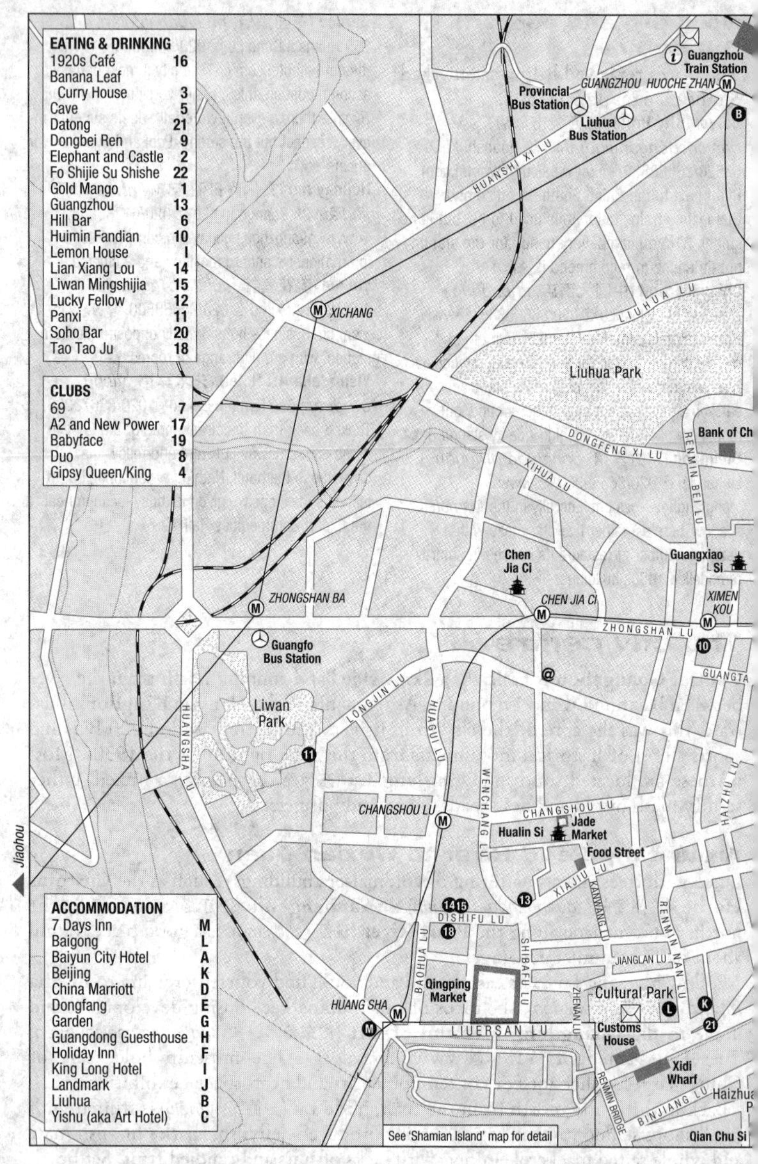

stylized Ming sculptures at the back look like giant chess pieces. The Five Immortals – three men and two women – are depicted too, riding their goatly steeds as they descend through the clouds to found Guangzhou. Also impressive is a fourteenth-century **bell tower** behind the temple, in which hangs a 3m-high, five-tonne bronze bell, silent since receiving the blame for a plague which broke out shortly after its installation in 1378 – it has been called the "Forbidden Bell" ever since.

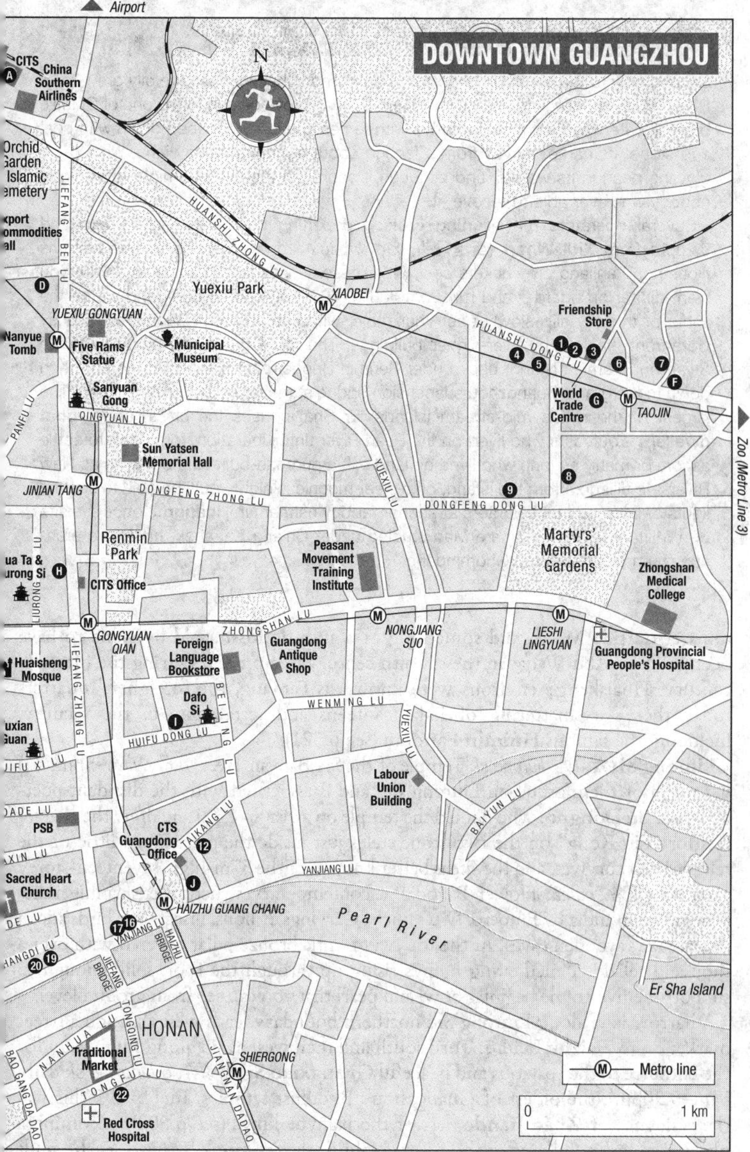

Huaisheng Mosque, Liurong Si and Guangxiao Si

A few blocks north of Wuxian Guan, the modern thoroughfare of Zhongshan Lu runs within striking distance of three of Guangzhou's most important temples – Ximen Kou or Gongyuan Qian are the closest metro stops. South of Zhongshan Liu Lu on Guangta Lu, **Huaisheng Mosque** (怀圣清真寺, *huáishèng qīngzhēn sì*) and its grey, conical tower, **Guangta**, loom over a surrounding wall that bars entry to non-Muslims. Looking like a lighthouse, Guangta is possibly the world's oldest

Pearl River cruises

Second only to the Yangzi in importance as an industrial channel, the oily grey **Pearl River** (珠江, *zhūjiāng*) originates in eastern Yunnan province and forms one of China's busiest waterways, continually active with ferries and barges loaded down with coal and stone. Its name derives from a legend about a monk named Jiahu, who lost a glowing pearl in its waters, and although it shone on the riverbed night after night, nobody was ever able to recover it.

Several operators run **evening cruises** departing daily between 7.20pm and 9.20pm from **Xidi Wharf** (西堤码头, *xīdī mǎtóu*), roughly opposite the Customs House on Yanjiang Lu – tickets cost ¥48. These cruises last 75 minutes – 90 if you want dinner on board – and run from ¥88 to ¥98. You can sit back and watch the lights of the city slip slowly past your table, with fine views of Guangzhou's busy waterfront, flanked by ever-higher buildings. The route takes you past the *White Swan* on Shamian Island, back under Renmin Bridge, past Haizhu Bridge and then down to the grand Guangzhou suspension bridge at the far end of Er Sha Island. The largest of the river's mid-stream islands, Er Sha, houses the city's former **boat dwellers** – outcasts who lived on the Pearl River until Liberation, forbidden to settle ashore or marry anyone who lived on land – in a purpose-built estate known as New Riverside Village. From the island, on a clear moonless night you'll be able to see the lights of international freighters at anchor far downstream in **Huangpu**, once the site of a Military Academy where Mao studied under Chiang Kai-shek, his future arch-enemy and leader of the Guomindang.

minaret outside Mecca and something of a stylistic fossil, said by some to have been built by Abu Waqas in the seventh century (see p.515). During the fifteenth century, Huaisheng's environs were known as Fanfang, the foreigners' quarter; today there's a smattering of halal canteens and restaurants in the vicinity, including the famous **Huimin Fandian** (see p.521).

Liurong Si (六榕寺, *liùróng sì*; Temple of the Six Banyan Trees; daily 9am–5pm; ¥5) lies north of the mosque on Liurong Lu, and is associated with the dissident poet-governor **Su Dongpo**, who named the temple on a visit in 1100 and drew the characters for "Liu Rong" on the two stone steles just inside the gates. Very little of the temple itself survives, and the site is better known for the 57m-high, seventeen-storey **Hua Ta** (花塔, *huātǎ*; Flower Pagoda), a contemporary structure enshrining relics brought from India by Emperor Wu's uncle. Carvings of lions, insects and birds adorn the pagoda's wooden eaves. At the top is a gigantic bronze pillar covered with over a thousand reliefs of meditating figures rising up through the roof, solid enough to support the five-tonne begging bowl and pearl that you can see from ground level.

A narrow lane along Liurong Si's northern boundary leads west through a street market on to Haizhu Bei Lu. Turn south and then west again along Jinghui Lu for the entrance to the spacious and peaceful **Guangxiao Si** (光孝寺, *guāngxiào sì*; daily 5am–5.30pm), the oldest of Guangzhou's Buddhist temples. In 113 BC this was the residence of **Zhao Jiande**, last of the Nanyue kings (see p.502), becoming a place of worship only after the 85-year-old Kashmiri monk **Tanmo Yeshe** built the first hall in 401 AD. The temple was later visited by Buddhist luminaries such as the sixth-century monk **Zhiyao Sanzang**, who planted the fig trees still here today; the Indian founder of Chan (Zen) Buddhism, **Bodhidharma**; and Chan's Sixth Patriarch, **Huineng** (for more on whom, see box, p.514). Again, none of the original buildings survive, but the grounds are well-ordered and enclose pavilions concealing wells and engraved tablets from various periods, while three halls at the back contain some imposing Buddha images; the westerly one is unusually reclining, while a more ordinary trinity fills the central hall.

Huifu Lu, Dafo Si and the Labour Union Building

Walking east from Wuxian Guan on Huifi Lu, where Vietnamese restaurants proliferate, you'll pass the small and unassuming **Dafo Si** (大佛寺, *dàfó sì*), the Big Buddha Temple, and reach the frenetically crowded shopping district along **Beijing Lu** (北京路, *běijīnglù*). Coming straight up from the river, look for the yellow 1920s **Labour Union Building** on Yuexiu Lu, later appropriated, somewhat cynically, as the Guomindang headquarters.

Peasant Movement Training Centre and Martyr's Memorial Gardens

Thanks to the subsequent career of its dean, Mao Zedong, Guangzhou's **Peasant Movement Training Institute**, on Zhongshan Lu (农民运动讲习所, *nóngmín yùndòng jiǎngxísuǒ*; Tues–Sun 9am–4.30pm; free), is the city's most frequented revolutionary site. It still looks like the Confucian Academy it was for six hundred years, before **Peng Pai**, a "rich peasant" from Guangdong, established the Institute in 1924 with Guomindang permission and 38 students. The school lasted just over two years, with Mao, Zhou Enlai and Peng Pai taking the final classes in August 1926, eight months before the Communist and Guomindang alliance ended violently in Shanghai. There's little to see; most poignant are the photographs of alumni who failed to survive the Shanghai Massacre and the subsequent **1927 Communist Uprising** in Guangzhou.

The scene of the latter event lies farther east along Zhongshan Lu at the **Martyrs' Memorial Gardens** (烈士陵园, *lièshì língyuán*; daily 6am–9pm). It was near here, on December 11, 1927, that a small Communist force under **Zhang Teilai** managed to take the Guangzhou Police Headquarters, announcing the foundation of the Canton Commune. Expected support never materialized, and on the afternoon of the second day Guomindang forces moved in; five thousand people were killed outright or later executed for complicity. Despite their history, the gardens are a jolly place and, as well as the evocatively titled Blood Spilled Pavilion, are also home to a boating lake, children's playground and roller-rink.

Northern Guangzhou

The area north between Dongfeng Lu and Guangzhou train station is primarily occupied by two huge **parks**, Liuhua and Yuexiu, the impressive **Nanyue Tomb**, an enormous leather goods market and the sole memento of a colonial-era confrontation further out beyond the station at **Sanyuan Li**.

Yuexiu Park

Yuexiu Park (越秀公园, *yuèxiù gōngyuán*; daily 6am–10pm; free) is China's biggest urban park, encompassing about 1.3 square kilometres almost half a square mile of sports courts, historic monuments, teahouses and shady groves. On the way here you'll pass a couple of notable buildings, most visibly the large rotunda and blue-tiled roof of the **Sun Yatsen Memorial Hall** on Dongfeng Zhong Lu (中山纪念堂, *zhōngshān jìniàn táng*; daily 8am–6pm), built on the spot where the man regarded by Guomindang and Communists alike as the father of modern China took the presidential oath in 1912. Inside it's a plain auditorium with seating for two thousand people, and is occasionally used as a concert hall. Far less obvious is **Sanyuan Gong** (三元宫, *sānyuán gōng*; Three Purities Temple; daily 8am–5pm) in the street immediately behind. Its entrance can be found by simply heading for the gaggle of hawkers touting brightly wrapped packs of ghost money and incense. This is actually the largest Taoist temple in Guangzhou, and the oldest, too – it was first consecrated in 319 – though the current arrangement of dark, spartan halls occupied by statues of Taoist deities is Qing. Gloomy furnishings aside, it's a

Chan Buddhism

Chan – known in Japan as **Zen** – believes that an understanding of the true nature of being can be achieved by sudden **enlightenment**, sparked by everyday, banal conversations or events. In this it differs from other forms of Buddhism, with their emphasis on the need for years of study of ritual and religious texts; though also using meditation and parables to achieve its ends, Chan therefore puts enlightenment within the grasp of even the most secular individual.

The founder of Chan was **Bodhidharma** (known as **Damo** in China), who arrived in Guangzhou from India around 520 AD intending to enrich China's rather formal, stodgy approach to Buddhism with his more lateral slant. After baffling the emperor with his teachings, Bodhidharma ended up at **Shaolin Si** in Henan; while there, exercises he taught the monks, to balance their long hours of meditation, are believed to have formed the basis of Chinese **kung fu** (see p.282). Shaolin subsequently became the centre for Chan Buddhism, spreading from there across China and into Japan and Korea.

Chan's most famous exponent was its Sixth Patriarch, **Huineng** (638–713). Huineng was from Guangzhou, but as a youth heard a wandering monk reciting sutras and was so impressed that he went to **Huangmei** in central China specifically to study Chan under the Fifth Patriarch, Hong Ren. Scorned by his fellow students for his rough southern manners, Huineng nonetheless demonstrated such a deep understanding of Chan that within a mere eight months he had achieved enlightenment on hearing the **Diamond Sutra** (which teaches how to recognize and dispense with illusions), and had been elected by Hong Ren to succeed him as patriarch, though the matter was kept secret at the time. Returning south to Guangzhou in 676, Huineng settled incognito at **Guangxiao Si**, where one day he heard two monks watching a flag and debating whether it was the wind or the flag that was moving. As they couldn't reach a decision, Huineng volunteered that neither was right – it was the mind that moved. His statement so stunned everyone present that he was invited to lecture, thereby revealing himself as the Sixth Patriarch (Hong Ren having died in the meantime). Huineng apparently spent his later years at **Nanhua Si** near Shaoguan in northern Guangdong.

busy place of worship, and there are a few splashes of red and gold in the painted bats, cranes and other Taoist motifs scattered around.

The park

While there are entrances at all points of the compass, Yuexiu's **front gate** is on Jiefang Bei Lu, a ten-minute walk north of San Yuan Gong. To the north of the porcelain dragons here are **Beixiu Hu** and the **Garden of Chinese Idiom**, where many strange stone and bronze sculptures lurk in the undergrowth, illustrating popular sayings. Head south, and you'll wind up at the much-photographed **Five Rams Statue** (五羊石像, *wǔyáng shíxiàng*), which commemorates the myth of Guangzhou's foundation – at least one of these is definitely not a ram, however.

Roughly in the middle of the park atop a hill, paths converge at **Zhenhai Lou** (镇海楼, *zhènhǎi lóu*), the "Gate Tower Facing the Sea", a wood-and-rendered-brick building that once formed part of the Ming city walls. Today it houses the **Municipal Museum** (广州博物馆, *guǎnzhōubówùgǔan*; daily 9am–5pm; ¥10), three floors of locally found exhibits ranging from Stone Age pottery fragments and ivory from Africa found in a Han-dynasty tomb, to fifth-century coins from Persia, a copy of *Good Words for Exhorting the World* (the Christian tract which inspired the Taiping leader, Hong Xiuquan), and nineteenth-century cannons tumbled about in the courtyard (two made by the German company, Krupp). A statue of Lin Zexu and letters from him to the Qing emperor documenting his disposal of the British opium stocks always draws big crowds of tongue-clicking Chinese.

The Nanyue Tomb and Liuhua Park

Five hundred metres north of Yuexiu Park's Jiefang Bei Lu entrance (and accessible on bus #5 or via the Yuexiu Gongyuan metro stop) looms the red sandstone facade of the **Nanyue Tomb** (西汉南越王墓, *xīhàn nányuèwángmù*; daily 9am–5.30pm, last admission 4.45pm; ¥12). Discovered in 1983 during foundation-digging for a residential estate, it houses the 2000-year-old site of the tomb of **Zhao Mo**, grandson of the Nanyue Kingdom's founder Zhao Tuo, and really deserves an hour of your time – there's an English-language **video** and a mass of exhibits.

Zhao Mo made a better job of his tomb than running his kingdom, which disintegrated shortly after his death: excavators found the tomb stacked with gold and priceless trinkets. They're on view in the museum, including a **burial suit** made from more than a thousand tiny jade tiles (jade was considered to prevent decay), and the ash-like remains of slaves and concubines immured with him. Several artefacts show Central Asian influence in their designs, illustrating how even at this early stage in Guangzhou's history there was contact with non-Chinese peoples. It's all fascinating and expertly presented, particularly worthwhile if you plan to visit contemporary gravesites in the Yangzi Basin or at Xi'an. Incidentally, Zhao Tuo's tomb still awaits discovery, though rumours of its fabulous treasures had eager excavators turning Guangzhou inside out as long ago as the Three Kingdoms period (220–280 AD).

West of the Nanyue Tomb between Liuhua Lu and Renmin Bei Lu, **Liuhua Park** (流花公园, *liúhuā gōngyuán*; daily 6am–10pm; free) is a large expanse of lakes, purpose-built in 1958 and pleasant enough during the week, though hellishly crowded at weekends. Liuhua means "Flowing Flowers", a name said to date back to the Han period when palace maids tossed petals into a nearby stream while dressing their hair.

The Orchid Garden and Islamic Cemetery

About 1km south of Guangzhou train station and surrounded by business hotels on Liuhua Lu and Renmin Lu, the **Export Commodities Hall** (中国出口商品交易会, *zhōngguó chūkǒushāngpǐn jiāoyìsuǒ*) hosts the city's **Trade Fair** each April and October, first held back in 1957 to encourage Western investments. This isn't the most pleasant area of town, but there is one oasis of peace and quiet: Guangzhou's delightful, though fairly small, **Orchid Garden**, off Jiefang Bei Lu (兰圃, *lánpǔ*; Mon–Fri 8am–6pm, Sat & Sun 8am–7pm; ¥8, ¥20 including tea in the central pavilion). Besides orchids, there are ponds surrounded by tropical ferns and lilies, winding stone paths, palms and giant figs with drooping aerial roots, and pink-flowering azaleas. Apart from the filtered traffic noise, it's hard to believe that the city lies just outside. Along the western edge of the garden, Guangzhou's **Islamic Cemetery** (清真古墓, *qīngzhēn gǔmù*) contains the tomb of **Abu Waqas**, a seventh-century missionary who brought Islam to China. The details are a little sketchy, however, as Abu Waqas supposedly died around 629, three years before Mohammed, and the Quran wasn't collated for another generation afterwards.

Sanyuan Li

For a return to earth after the Orchid Garden, continue up Jiefang Bei Lu for 1km after it crosses Huanshi Lu, past several giant buildings housing leather markets, to **Sanyuan Li** (三元里, *sānyuán lǐ*). A recently redeveloped part of the city, this was a separate village outside Guangzhou as of 150 years ago, and it was here that the **Sanyuan Li Anti-British Movement** formed in 1841 after the British stormed into the area during the First Opium War. Following months of abuse from the invaders, local workers and peasants rose under the farmer **Wei Shaoguang** and attacked the British camp, killing around twenty soldiers in an indecisive engagement before being dispersed by heavy rain. A **temple**, a 500m walk straight ahead from Sanyuan Li metro exit B, was built in 1860 on the sight of the battle and houses a small **museum** (三元里纪念博物馆, *sānyuánlĭ jìniàn bówùgǔan*; daily 9am–5pm; ¥2) exhibiting the peasants' armoury of farm tools and ceremonial weapons – don't take the turgid captions, the product of later propaganda, too seriously. A park featuring a **memorial** to the resistance (daily 5.45am–6pm; free) is also nearby, a few minutes' walk south from metro exit A1.

Western Guangzhou

Western Guangzhou, west of Renmin Lu and south of Dongfeng Xi Lu, features a charming warren of backroads and lanes around Changshou Lu, all stuffed to overflowing with market activity, restaurants and shops, which empty down near the waterfront opposite **Shamian Island**, a quiet haven of colonial mood and huge trees. North of the river, Zhongshan Lu continues westward through the area, cut by a score of roads running south to Liuersan Lu, along the river; south, the main roads are Nanhua Lu and Tongfu Lu.

Chen Jia Ci

Zhongshan Lu's western arm cuts through the tidy district of Liwan before heading over a tributary of the Pearl River and out of the city toward Foshan. About 2.5km from the Jiefang Lu intersection, a pedestrian walkway leads to **Chen Jia Ci** (陈家祠, *chénjiā cí*; Chen Clan Academy; daily 8.30am–5.30pm, last admission 5pm; ¥10). The story of its founding is unusual; subscriptions were invited from anyone named **Chen** – one of the most common Cantonese surnames – and the money raised went to build this complex, part ancestor temple where Chens could worship, part school where they could receive an education. The buildings form a series of rooms arranged around open courtyards, all decorated with the most garish tiles and gorgeously carved screens and stonework that money could buy in the 1890s. Have a good look at the extraordinary brick reliefs under the eaves, both inside and out. One of the first, on the right as you enter, features an opera being performed for what looks like a drunken horse, which lies squirming on the floor with mirth. Other cameos feature stories from China's "noble bandit" saga, *Outlaws of the Marsh*, and some of the sights around Guangzhou.

Changshou Lu and around

Below Zhongshan Lu, the ring of part of the old city walls can be traced along **Longjin Lu** in the north, and **Dishifu Lu** and others to the south. Though a couple of wide, modern main roads barge through, most of this district, with east–west **Changshou Lu** at its core, retains its Ming-dynasty street plan and a splash of early twentieth-century architecture, making for excellent random walks. In addition to some of Guangzhou's biggest shopping plazas and a crowd of markets spreading into each other south from Changshou Lu right down to the river, several **famous restaurants** are here, and the area is particularly busy at night.

Shops and markets selling jade run all the way from the pedestrian square on Xiajiu Lu right up to Changshou Lu, culminating in two multistorey jade shopping malls built on either side of the **Hualin Si** Buddhist temple (华林寺, *huálín sì*; daily 9am–5.30pm; ¥3), which was founded as a modest nunnery by the Brahman prince **Bodhidharma** in 527 (see box, p.514). After his Chan teachings caught on in the seventeenth century, the main hall was enlarged to house five hundred *arhat* sculptures ranged along the cross-shaped aisles, and Hualin remains the most lively temple in the city – during festivals you'll be crushed, deafened and blinded by the crowds, firecrackers and incense smoke.

From here, the best thing you can do is throw away your map and roam southward through the maze of alleys and Qing-era homes (some of which are protected historic relics), most likely emerging in the vicinity of the *Guangzhou* restaurant. Two streets lined with restored 1920s facades and pedestrianized at the weekends lie here – **Dishifu Lu** to the west and **Xiajiu Lu** to the east – and places to eat and shop are legion, the pavements always crammed to capacity. South again off Xiajiu Lu, you enter the upper reaches of the infamous **Qingping Market** (清平市场, *qīngpíng shìchǎng*), with each intersecting east–west lane forming dividing lines for the sale of different goods: dried medicines, spices and herbs, fresh vegetables, livestock, birds and fish. Once one of China's most challenging (tastewise, at least) – not to say gory – markets, this has been scaled down considerably in recent years with the removal of rare animals and large-scale streetside butchering, though it remains a lively and busy affair, amply illustrating the Cantonese demand for fresh and unusual food.

You exit Qingping onto Liuersan Lu, a recently widened road given a stack of flyovers to relieve chronic traffic congestion, and lined with palms, flowerbeds and fake colonial frontages mirroring the real thing opposite on Shamian Island. "Liuersan" means "6, 23", referring to June 23, 1925, when fifty people were shot by colonial troops during a demonstration demanding, among other things, the return of Shamian Island to Chinese control. East along Liuersan, the **Cultural Park** (文化公园, *wénhuà gōngyuán*; daily 6am–9.30pm; free), in the heart of the city's electronics market district, is a rather bland area of paving and benches, where gangs of children queue for their turn on arcade games and fairground rides, and theatre and sound stages host weekend performances of anything from local rock to opera.

Shamian Island

It's just a short hop across Liuersan Lu and a muddy canal – or head to Huang Sha (黄沙, *huángshā* – metro stop, then cross the bridge) – on to **Shamian Island** (沙面岛, *shāmiàn dǎo*), but the pace changes instantly, Guangzhou's busiest quarter exchanged for its most genteel. A tear-shaped sandbank about 1km long and 500m wide, Shamian was leased to European powers as an Opium War trophy, the French getting the eastern end and the British the rest. Here the colonials recreated their own backyards, planting the now massive **trees** and throwing up solid, Victorian-style **villas**, banks, embassies, churches and tennis courts – practically all of which are still standing. Iron gates on the bridges once excluded the Chinese from Shamian (as the Chinese had once forbidden foreigners to enter within Guangzhou's city walls), leaving the Europeans in self-imposed isolation from the bustle across the water. Shamian retains that atmosphere today, a quiet bolthole for many long-term travellers in the city. There's restricted traffic flow, and the well-tended architecture, greenery and relative peace make it a refreshing place to visit, even if you're not staying or sampling the restaurants and bars. As well as attracting tourists, Shamian's picturesqueness has also been well noted by local wedding photographers. Any visitor on a fair day will undoubtedly come across couples in full regalia standing in bushes or self-consciously tottering on the steps outside one colonial building or another having their pictures taken. The island, too, is home to the US Consulate dealing with the adoption of Chinese children by American parents, many of whom stay at the *White Swan* – accounting for both the large number of Westerners wheeling Asian babies around and also the inordinate number of shops selling baby clothes.

The main thoroughfare is east–west **Shamian Dajie**, with five numbered streets running south across the island. Wandering around, you'll find buildings have largely been restored to their original appearance – most were built between the

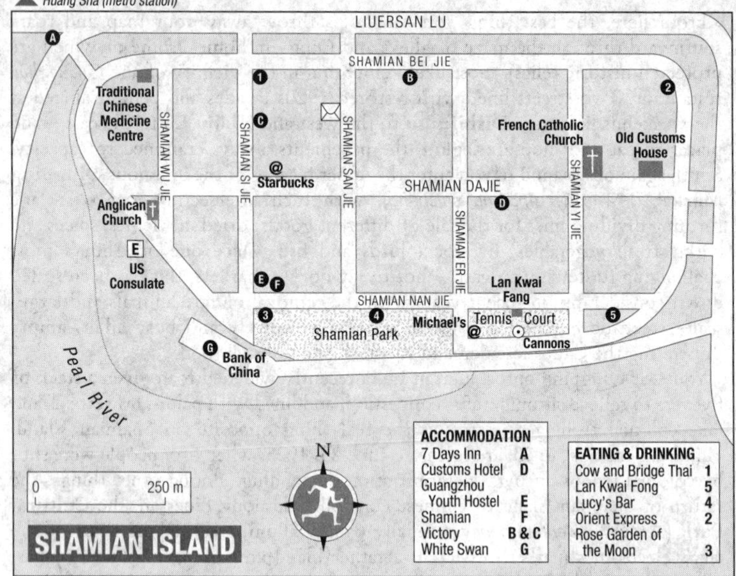

1860s and early twentieth century – with plaques sketching their history. Though sharing such a tiny area, the British and French seemingly kept themselves to themselves, building separate bridges, churches and customs houses; nothing is particularly worth searching out, but it's all great browsing. Next to the atypically modern *White Swan* hotel on the **Shamian Nan Jie** esplanade, a focus of sorts is provided by **Shamian Park** (沙面公园, *shāmiàn gōngyuán*), where two **cannons**, cast in nearby Foshan during the Opium Wars, face out across the river, and you might catch Cantonese opera rehearsals here on Saturday afternoons. The island's waterfront area is also the venue for Guangzhou's major Spring Festival **fireworks display**, held on the first night at around 9pm.

Honan

Honan (河南, *hénán*), the area immediately south of the river between westerly **Gongye Dadao** and **Jiangnan Dadao**, 1500m further east, can be reached on any of **three bridges**: Renmin Bridge, which connects Liuersan Lu with Gongye Dadao; and the closely spaced Jiefang and Haizhu bridges off Yanjiang Lu, which become Tongqing Lu and Jiangnan Dadao respectively. Metro line #2 runs along Jiangnan Dadao, with stations at Shiergong (市二宫, *shìèrgōng*) and Jiangnanxi (江南西, *jīangnánxī*).

Prior to 1949, Honan was Guangzhou's red-light district, crawling with opium dens, brothels and gambling houses, none of which survived the Communist takeover. Indeed, in 1984 Honan was chosen as a model of **Hu Yaobang**'s "Civic Spirit" campaign, which called on residents to organize kindergartens and old folks' clubs, and to keep their communities clean and safe. It's still a surprisingly calm and quiet corner of the city, the small flagstoned alleys off Nanhua Lu and Tongfu Lu kept litter-free and lined with austere, wooden-gated homes. During the **spring flower festival** (a southern Chinese tradition originating in Guangzhou) florist stalls along riverfront Binjiang Lu attract crowds from all over the city to buy blooms of every colour and shape for good luck in the coming year. There's also a big Cantonese-style **market** here – a rather more spirited affair than Qingping – in the backstreets southwest off the Nanhua Lu/Tongqing Lu junction.

Honan's sole formal sight is in **Haizhuang Park** (海幢公园, *hǎizhuàng gōngyuán*; daily 6.30am–5.30pm; free), sandwiched between Nanhua Lu and Tongfu Lu, about ten minutes' walk from Renmin Bridge. The buildings here have been returned to their original purpose as **Qian Chu Si** (千处寺, *qiānchù sì*; daily 8am–5pm), a sizeable Buddhist monastery. Renovations have spruced up the broad south hall, with its fine statuary and interlocked wooden-beam roof, so typical of south China's early Qing temple buildings – the flashing, coloured "haloes" surrounding several of the statues are less traditional touches.

Eastern Guangzhou and Baiyun Shan Park

Hemmed in on all other flanks by rivers and hills, Guangzhou inevitably expands east to accommodate its ever-growing population, and it's here you'll find the most "modern" parts of the city, shadowed by skyscrapers housing corporate headquarters and cut by several expressways. **Huanshi Lu** and **Dongfeng Lu** are the biggest of these, converging out in the northeastern suburbs at the vast open-plan district of **Tianhe** (天河, *tīanhé*). Much of the city's **expat community** is based out this way, and there are numerous Western-oriented **restaurants** and **bars** – if few actual sights – to recommend a visit. One exception is **Baiyun Shan Park** (白云山公园, *báiyún shān gōngyúan*), which lies immediately north of the city and offers an unexpectedly thorough escape.

Northeast off Huanshi Dong Lu along Xianlie Lu, **Huanghua Gang Park** (黄花岗公园, *huánghuā gāng gōngyuán*; daily 8am–5pm) recalls Sun Yatsen's abortive 1911 Canton Uprising in the **Mausoleum to the 72 Martyrs**, a very peculiar monument reflecting the nationalities of numerous donors who contributed to its construction – Buddhist iconography rubbing shoulders with a Statue of Liberty and an Egyptian obelisk. **Guangzhou Zoo**, about 1km farther out along Xianlie Lu (广州动物园, *guǎngzhōu dòngwùyuán*; daily 9am–4pm; ¥20; bus #6 from Dongfeng Lu, one block east of the Sun Yatsen Memorial Hall), is the third largest in the country. Conditions, however, are somewhat depressing – hardly mitigated by the draw of seeing a panda. Among other rarities are clouded leopards and several species of wildfowl.

You'll most likely find yourself out at **Tianhe**, the area surrounding the train station 2km due east of the zoo, en route to Guangzhou East train station. A vast planned area of concrete paving, broad roads and glassy towers, where pedestrians are reduced to insignificant specks, Tianhe has as its showpiece a huge **sports stadium** built for the 1987 National Games (Tiyu Zhong Xin metro).

Just south of here at Zhujiang New Town you can find the new, multimillion dollar **Provincial Museum** (省博物馆, *shěng bówùguǎn*; daily 9am–5pm). Shaped "like a moonlight treasure box", it boasts some awesome natural history exhibitions, including dinosaurs, as well as porcelain, calligraphy, paintings and carvings.

Baiyun Shan Park

Just 7km north of downtown, **Baiyun Shan** (白云山, *báiyún shān*; White Cloud Mountain) is close enough to central Guangzhou to reach by city bus, but open enough to leave all the city's noise and bustle behind. Once covered with monasteries, Baiyun's heavily reforested slopes now offer lush panoramas out over Guangzhou and the delta region. A **park** here encloses almost thirty square kilometres (¥10), its entrance a thirty-minute ride on bus #24 from the south side of Renmin Park, immediately northeast of the Jiefang Lu/Zhongshan Lu crossroads.

It's a good three-hour walk from the entrance off Luhu Lu to **Moxing Ling** (Star-touching Summit), past strategically placed teahouses and pavilions offering views and refreshments. There's also a **cable car** (¥30) from the entrance as far as the **Cheng Precipice**, a ledge roughly halfway to the top, which earned its name when the Qin-dynasty minister **Cheng Ki** was ordered here by his emperor to find a herb of immortality. Having found the plant, Cheng nibbled a leaf only to see the remainder vanish; full of remorse, he flung himself off the mountain but was caught by a stork and taken to heaven. Sunset views from the precipice are spectacular.

Eating

Eating out is the main recreation in Guangzhou, something the city is famous for and caters to admirably. Its restaurants, the best to be found in a province famed for its food, are justification enough to spend a few days in the city, and it would be a real shame to leave without having eaten in one of the more elaborate or famous **Cantonese places** – there's nothing to match the experience of tucking into a Cantonese spread while being surrounded by an enthusiastic horde of local diners. Locals are so proud of their cuisine that a few years ago it was hard to find anywhere serving anything else, though now you can also track down a good variety of Asian, European and even Indian food – not to mention regional Chinese. Some canteens open as early as 5am, and breakfast – including traditional dim sum – is usually served from 7am to 10am, later on Sundays or if the restaurant has a particularly good reputation. Lunch is on offer between 11am and 2pm, and dinner from 5pm to 10pm, though most people eat early rather than late.

Guangdong cooking

Guangdong cooking is one of China's four major regional styles and, despite northern critics decrying it as too uncomplicated to warrant the term "cuisine", it's unmatched in the clarity of its flavours and its appealing presentation. The style subdivides into **Cantonese**, emanating from the Pearl River Delta region; **Chaozhou**, from the city of the same name in the far east of Guangdong; and **Hakka**, from the northeastern border with Fujian, named after the Han subgroup with whom it originated. Though certain Chaozhou and Hakka recipes have been incorporated into the main body of Guangdong cooking – sweet-and-sour pork with fruit, and salt-baked chicken, for instance – it's Cantonese food that has come to epitomize its principles. With many Chinese emigrants leaving through Guangzhou, it's also the most familiar to overseas visitors, though peruse a menu here and you'll soon realize that most dishes served abroad as "Cantonese" would be unrecognizable to a local.

Spoiled by good soil and a year-round growing season, the Cantonese demand absolutely fresh ingredients, kept alive and kicking in cages, tanks or buckets at the front of the restaurant for diners to select themselves. Westerners can be repulsed by this collection of wildlife, and even other Chinese comment that the Cantonese will eat anything with legs that isn't a piece of furniture, and anything with wings that isn't an aeroplane. The cooking itself is designed to keep textures distinct and flavours as close to the original as possible, using a minimum amount of mild and complementary seasoning to prevent dishes from being bland. Fast stir-frying in a wok is the best known of these procedures, but slow-simmering in soy sauce and wine and roasting are other methods of teasing out the essential characteristics of the food.

No full meal is really complete without a simple plate of rich green and bitter **choi sam** (*cai xin* in Mandarin), Chinese broccoli, blanched and dressed with oyster sauce. Also famous is **fish and seafood**, often simply steamed with ginger and spring

Restaurants are pretty evenly spread across the city, though Dishifu Lu in the west, and Shamian Island, have a ridiculous quantity and variety between them. Ordering is a bit easier here than in the average Chinese city, as many restaurants have an **English menu** tucked away somewhere, even if these omit dishes that they believe won't appeal to foreigners. **Prices** vary greatly but expect upwards of ¥40 a head for a good Chinese meal, and ¥60 if you're after more exotic Asian or Western food.

You can eat for a fraction of this cost day or night at the city's numerous **food stalls** which, like the restaurants, are never far away (streets off Beijing Lu have the best selection). Here you can pick up a few slices of roast duck or pork on rice, meat and chicken dumplings, or noodle soups, usually for less than ¥10 a plate. Be sure to try a selection of **cakes** and the fresh tropical **fruits** too; local lychees are so good that the emperors once had them shipped direct to Beijing.

If Chinese dining just isn't for you, the **bars** and **cafés** listed below serve grills, sandwiches and counter meals as good as anything you'll get at home.

Central Guangzhou

1920s Café (一九二零餐厅, *yījiǔèrlíng cāntīng*) Yanjiang Lu. This refined German restaurant, with mains (¥50–130) including bratwürst, schnitzel, German noodles and sauerkraut, also has a pleasant, almost-riverside outdoor patio – perfect if you fancy knocking back a beer or two.

Datong (大同大酒家, *dàtóng dàjiǔjiā*) 63 Yanjiang Xi Lu. If you're after an authentically noisy, crowded dim sum session with river views, head here to floors 2, 5 or 6 between 7am and noon. They pride themselves on their roast suckling pig. Window seats are in high demand, so arrive early.

Huimin Fandian (aka Five Rams) (回民饭店, *huímín fàndiàn*) Southeast corner of the Renmin

onions – hairy crabs are a winter treat, sold everywhere – and nobody cooks **fowl** better than the Cantonese, always juicy and flavoursome, whether served crisp-skinned and roasted or fragrantly casseroled. Guangzhou's citizens are also compulsive snackers, and outside canteens you'll see **roast meats**, such as whole goose or strips of *cha siu* pork, waiting to be cut up and served with rice for a light lunch, or burners stacked with **sandpots** (*sai bo*), a one-person dish of steamed rice served in the cooking vessel with vegetables and slices of sweet *lap cheung* sausage. **Cake shops** selling heavy Chinese pastries and filled buns are found everywhere across the region. Some items like **custard tartlets** are derived from foreign sources, while roast-pork buns and flaky-skinned **mooncakes** stuffed with sweet lotus seed paste are of domestic origin.

Perhaps it's this delight in little delicacies that led the tradition of **dim sum** (*dian xin* in Mandarin) to blossom in Guangdong, where it's become an elaborate form of breakfast most popular on Sundays, when entire households pack out restaurants. Also known in Cantonese as **yum cha** – literally, "drink tea" – dim sum involves little dishes of fried, boiled and steamed snacks being stuffed inside bamboo steamers or displayed on plates, then wheeled around the restaurant on trolleys, which you stop for inspection as they pass your table. On being seated, you're given a pot of tea, which is constantly topped up, and a card, which is marked for each dish you select and which is later surrendered to the cashier. Try *juk* (rice porridge), spring rolls, buns, cakes and plates of thinly sliced roast meats, and small servings of restaurant dishes like spareribs, stuffed capsicum, or squid with black beans. Save most room, however, for the myriad types of little fried and steamed **dumplings** which are the hallmark of a dim sum meal, such as *har gau*, juicy minced prawns wrapped in transparent rice-flour skins, and *siu mai*, a generic name for a host of delicately flavoured, open-topped packets.

Lu/Zhongshan Lu crossroads. The city's biggest and most popular Muslim restaurant, serving lamb hotpots, roast duck, lemon chicken and spicy beef at reasonable prices.

Lemon House (越茗苑, *yuèmíng yuàn*) 507 Huifu Dong Lu. Serving up succulent, spicy Southeast Asian fare, *Lemon House* is locked in a constant battle with *Tiger Prawn* across the street for the mantle of best Vietnamese in town. Mains ¥30–50.

Lucky Fellow (幸运楼酒家, *xìngyùnlóu jiǔjiā*) Sixth floor of a shopping centre on the corner of Taikang Lu and Huilong Lu. This large, smart establishment serves up a range of Chinese cuisines, focusing on Cantonese – both the roast goose and fragrant chicken are excellent – and has an extensive English-language menu. It's all reasonably priced, with main dishes starting at ¥18.

Northern and eastern Guangzhou

Banana Leaf Curry House (蕉叶饮食, *jiāoyè yǐnshí*) Fifth floor, World Trade Centre, Huanshi Dong Lu. Good, eclectic mix of Thai, Malaysian and Indonesian fare, all authentically spiced. Not cheap, though; expect upwards of ¥70 a head.

Dongbei Ren (东北人, *dōngběi rén*) Opposite Liuhua Park on Renmin Bei Lu and on Dongfeng Dong Lu. Hugely popular nationwide chain serving Manchurian food. The sautéed corn kernels with pine nuts, steamed chicken with mushrooms, or eggs and black fungus are all good. Portions from ¥20.

Jiangxi Ren (江西人, *jiāngxī rén*) 475 Huanshi Dong Lu. It's easy to spot the huge earthenware jars outside this one, and the second-floor restaurant is decked out in Chinese "folksy" furnishings. The main thing to try here is the Jiangxi-style giant soups, enough for three or four people, at around ¥35–60; the duck and pear variety is excellent.

Papa John's Pizza (棒约翰中信餐厅, *bàngyuēhàn zhōngxìn cāntīng*) CITIC Plaza. Total American pizza experience housed on the second floor of a swish mall one metro stop from the eastern rail station. Everything much the same as you would expect at home, including the prices.

Western Guangzhou

Guangzhou (广州酒家, *guǎngzhōu jiǔjiā*) Corner of Wenchang Nan Lu and Xiajiu Lu; other branches citywide. The oldest, busiest and most famous restaurant in the city, with entrance calligraphy by the Qing emperor Kangxi and a rooftop neon sign flashing "Eating in Guangzhou". The menu is massive, and you won't find better crisp-skinned chicken or pork anywhere – bank on ¥80 a person for a decent feed. Service is brusque.

Lian Xiang Lou (莲香楼, *liánxiāng lóu*) 67 Dishifu Lu. Established in 1889 and famous for its mooncakes, baked dough confections stuffed with sweet lotus paste and shaped as rabbits and peaches, which you can buy from the downstairs shop. The upstairs restaurant does commendable roast suckling pig, brown-sauced pigeon, and duck fried with lotus flowers for about ¥30 a portion.

Liwan Mingshijia (荔湾名食家, *lìwān míngshíjiā*) 99 Dishifu Lu. Ming-style canteen and teahouse decked in heavy marble-and-wood furniture, crammed with diners wolfing down *dim-sum*-style snacks. Some of the finest *sheung fan* (stuffed rice rolls), *zongzi* (steamed packets of rice and meat) and *tangyuan* (glutinous riceballs filled with chopped nuts in a sweet soup) you'll find. No English and not much Mandarin spoken, but you can order by pointing to other people's dishes.

Panxi (泮溪酒家, *pànxī jiǔjiā*) Longjin Xi Lu, Liwan Park. The best thing about this Cantonese restaurant – a teahouse of ill repute in the 1940s – is the lakeside location and interesting dim sum selection. Main meals are undistinguished, however, and the English-language menu is disappointingly perfunctory. Inexplicably popular with tour groups, who apparently haven't discovered the far superior *Tao Tao Ju* (below).

Tao Tao Ju (陶陶居, *táotáo jū*) Dishifu Lu. Looks upmarket, with huge chandeliers, wooden shutters and coloured leadlight windows, but prices are mid-range and very good value. Roast goose is the house speciality, and they also do cracking seafood – plain boiled prawns or fried crab are both excellent – along with crisp-skinned chicken, lily-bud and beef sandpots, and a host of Cantonese favourites. Comprehensive English menu; mains ¥18–80.

Shamian Island

Cow and Bridge Thai (泰国牛桥, *tàiguó niúqiáo*) Shamian Bei Jie. Very formal place to dine on what is unquestionably the finest Thai food in Guangzhou, if not all China. The food is beautifully presented and the service impeccable. Main dishes are pricey, but turn to the back of the menu for cheaper options at ¥30 plus which are more than enough for one.

Lan Kwai Fong (兰桂坊, *lán guì feng*) Shamian Nan Jie. Taking its name from Hong Kong's central bar and restaurant district, this slightly pricey Guangdong restaurant's two outlets – one overlooking the tennis courts and one at the eastern end of the park – are extremely popular with locals, especially at the weekend. Mains ¥35+.

Lucy's Bar (露丝吧, *lùsī bā*) Shamian Nan Jie. Sit outside in the evening at this Westerner-oriented place and eat decent Mexican-, Thai- and Indian-style dishes, along with burgers, pizza and grills. Mains ¥30–100; beer ¥28 a pint.
Rose Garden of the Moon (玫瑰园西餐厅, *méiguìyuán xīcāntīng*) Shamian Nan Jie. Romantic, open-air restaurant set in the park and popular with couples. Nothing to cross town for but nice enough, with good river views and set meals from around the (Western) world from ¥78.
Station Western (车站西餐酒廊, *chēzhàn xīcān jiǔláng*) Shamian Bei Jie. If you fancy a break from the usual, this fancy French restaurant will serve you dinner either in the garden or aboard one of two luxury train carriages. The food doesn't quite justify the high prices (¥120 plus), but at least it's cheaper than riding the real Orient Express.

South of the river

Fo Shijie Su Shishe (佛世界素食社, *fóshìjiè sùshíshè*) Niu Nai chang Jie, south of Tongfu Lu, just west of the Red Cross Hospital. Down a small alley, this is hard to find but worth the effort. Look for the sign in Chinese and English reading *Fut Sai Kai*. Huge portions of vegetarian food; crispy chicken drumsticks in sweet-and-sour sauce, salt-fried prawns, chicken-ball casserole and the rest are all made from bean curd, with heaps of straightforward vegetable dishes too. Full English menu; in the restaurant upstairs most mains are under ¥30, while the canteen set menu downstairs is just ¥7.

Drinking, nightlife and entertainment

By Chinese standards, Guangzhou has good **nightlife**. A growing army of **clubs** in the central and eastern parts of the city range from warehouse-sized discos to obscure, almost garage-like affairs. Some have a **cover charge** though most make their money from pricey drinks. Expats favour the bars located in Guangzhou's eastern reaches along **Jianshe Lu** (建设六马路, *jiànshèliùmǎlù*) and **Huanshi East Road** (环市东路, *húanshìdōnglù*), where the booze is cheaper (¥25 a pint), pub-style meals can be had for ¥40, and the music is directed to Western tastes, while **Chang Di Dama Lu** (长堤大马路, *chángdīdàmǎlù*), just behind the waterfront, is an up-and-coming clubbing area. Club hours are from 8pm to 2am, bars are open anytime from lunch to 2am, but don't expect much to be happening before 9pm. Places come and go with frequency; while the ones reviewed below are good starting points, check out Ⓦwww.cityweekend.com.cn/guangzhou or www.gznightlife.com for the latest.

Bars

City Bar (城市酒吧, *chéngshì jiǔbā*) City Plaza, Tianhe Lu, Tianhe. Relaxed place to spend an hour or two over a Heineken before your train goes from Guangzhou East. Hard to find, the building is east of the better-signed Teem Plaza.
Elephant and Castle (大象堡酒吧, *dàxiàngbeo jiǔbā*) 363 Huanshi Dong Lu. Dim corners and a cramped bar make this a favourite with barfly foreigners, though it has a good beer garden and typically gets loud and busy as the evening progresses. Variable happy hours. Opens late afternoon.
Gold Mango (金芒果酒吧, *jīnmángguǒ jiǔbā*) 361 Huanshi Dong Lu. A bit of a pick-up joint on weekends, but cosy and laidback otherwise, with a welcoming staff and fine beer garden.
Hill Bar (小山吧, *xiǎoshān bā*) 367 Huanshi Dong Lu, across from the *Garden* hotel. Third choice in the trinity of adjacent expat bars, serving cheapish beer (¥25 a pint) and bar meals, with occasional live music.
Soho Bar (苏荷酒吧, *sūhéjiǔbā*) Yanjiang Lu, next to *Babyface*. Typical Chinese Western-style bar with Happy Hour deals. It's a good place to watch the crowds heading on their way into *Babyface* (see below).

Clubs

69 (六十九酒吧, *liùshíjiǔjiǔbā*) Heping Lu. One of a string of bars along this street in the Overseas Chinese Village. Nightly live music on two floors – everything from Canto-pop to Chinese rock and more offbeat local bands.
Á and New Power 183 Yanjiang Lu. Vast clubs next door to each other and aimed at Chinese punters, offering a range of music, floor shows and expensive drinks.
Babyface (娃娃脸, *wá wá liǎn*) 83 Chang Di Da Ma Lu (Yanjiang Lu). Offspring of the Beijing and Shanghai superclub, this far smaller version is expensive but a generally reliable facsimile of a Western disco.

Cave (墨西哥餐厅酒吧, *mòxīgē cāntīng jiǔbā*) Huanshi Dong Lu, west from the *Garden* hotel. Italian cantina and dance club, hidden down in a basement, with DJs or drummers playing to an ultraviolet-lit crowd.

Duo 16 Jianshe 6 ma Rd. Smart club and lounge bar with an array of different nights throughout the week.

Gipsy Queen/King (万紫千红酒吧, *wànzǐ qiānhóng jiǔbā*) 360 Huanshi Dong Lu, just west of *Cave*, this place is of a similar ilk, but has nightly shows around 10pm.

Shopping

Guangzhou's **shopping** ethos is very much towards the practical side of things. The **Changshou Lu** area in western Guangzhou is a mass of shopping plazas, designer clothes shops and boutiques, with **Beijing Lu** a similar, more central version; both have sections that are pedestrianized at weekends. To see where Guangzhou – and China – is heading, however, head to the shockingly modern and upmarket **Friendship Store** (友谊商店, *yǒuyìshāngdiàn*), five floors of expensive imported designer gear and some good-value, domestic formal wear; it's on easterly Taojin Lu, just off Huanshi Dong Lu.

For **souvenirs**, the streets running east off the southern end of Renmin Lu might give you some ideas. Yide Lu has several huge wholesale warehouses stocking **dried foods** and **toys** – action figures from Chinese legends, rockets and all things that rattle and buzz. Other shops in the area deal in **home decorations**, such as colourful tiling or jigsawed decorative wooden dragons and phoenixes, and at New Year you can buy those red-and-gold good-luck posters put up outside businesses and homes. For out-and-out tourist souvenirs, head first to the *White Swan* hotel on Shamian Island. Their batiks and clothing, carved wooden screens and jade monstrosities are well worth a look, if only to make you realize what a good deal you're getting when you buy elsewhere – such as in the shops just outside on Shamian Si Jie. Wende Lu, running south from Zhongshan Lu, and various small shops in the streets between Dishifu Lu and Liuersan Lu, have varying selections of authenticated antiques, jade, lacquerwork, scrolls, chops and cloisonné artefacts, identical to what you'll find in the Yue Hua stores in Hong Kong, but at half the price. The enormous **jade market** near Hualin Si (see p.516) is also worth a snoop.

Listings

Acupuncture The tourist-oriented Traditional Chinese Medicine Centre on Shamian offers foot massages, herbal baths, acupuncture and hot cupping from around ¥40.

Airlines China Southern Airlines, 181 Huanshi Dong Lu (☎020/95539), two doors east of the main train station; Malaysia Airlines (☎020/83358868) at the *Garden*, Huanshi Dong Lu.

Banks and exchange Bank of China branches in the enormous office in the centre of the city on Dongfeng Zhong Lu and outside the *White Swan*, Shamian Island (both open for currency exchange Mon–Fri 9am–noon & 2–5pm). Counters at the *Liuhua*, *China Marriott*, *Landmark* and *Garden* hotels change currency for non-guests.

Bookshops The Xinhua bookstore on Beijing Lu has an unexciting range of English literature and translated Chinese classics. The city's biggest bookstore, Guangzhou Books Centre, is at the southwest corner of Tianhe Square, Tianhe Lu, but there's little in English. Otherwise, the main source of reading material is the comprehensive and expensive range available at the *White Swan*.

Consulates Australia, 12th Floor, Development Centre, No. 3 Linjiang Rd, Zhujiang New City ☎020/38140111, visa office ☎020/38140250; Canada, Suite 801, China Hotel Office Tower, Liu Hua Lu ☎020/86116100; France, Room 803, *Guangdong International*, 339 Huanshi Dong Lu ☎020/83303405; Germany, Floor 14, Teem Tower, 208 Tianhe Lu ☎020/83130000; Italy, Room 1403, Heijing International Financial Plaza, 8 Huaxia Lu, Zhujiang New Town, Tianhe District ☎020/38396225; Japan, *Garden* hotel, 368 Huanshi Dong Lu ☎020/83343009; Malaysia, Floor 19, CITIC Plaza, 233 Tianhe Bei Lu ☎020/87395660; Netherlands, Floor 34, Teem

Mall, 208 Tianhe Lu ⓣ020/38132200; Philippines, Room 709, *Guangdong International*, 339 Huanshi Dong Lu ⓣ020/83311461; Thailand, Floor 2, *Garden* hotel, 368 Huanshi Dong Lu ⓣ020/83804277; UK, Floor 2, *Guangdong International*, 339 Huanshi Dong Lu ⓣ020/83143000; US, Shamian Nan Jie, Shamian Island ⓣ020/81218000; Vietnam, Floor 2, Building B, *Hotel Landmark Canton,* 8 Qiaoguang Lu, Haizhu Square ⓣ020/83305911; further information on consulates can be found on the Guangzhou local government's website (ⓦwww.gz.gov.cn). Consulates' visa sections are usually only open around 9–11.30am, and getting served isn't always easy.
Hospitals Call ⓣ120 for emergency services. There's an English-speaking SOS clinic based at the Ocean Pearl Tower in Zhujiang (ⓣ020/87351051). Other options include the Global Doctor Clinic at the Nō People's Hospital (ⓣ020/81045173) and the Red Cross Hospital, 396 Tongfu Zhong Lu (ⓣ020/84412233). There are English-speaking dentists at Sunshine Dental Clinic, 2 Tianhe Bei Lu (24hr English hotline; ⓣ020/38862888). For anything serious, though, you're better off heading to Hong Kong.
Internet Places can be found for as little as ¥2/hr. Most hotels offer wi-fi and some have their own terminals. *Starbucks* and other coffeehouses usually have free wi-fi. On Shamian Island, Michael's (daily 9am–9pm), at the south end of Shamian Er Jie, is principally a shop, but has a few internet-ready computers for ¥10/hr.
Interpreters The major hotels can organize interpreters for upwards of ¥600/day – you're also expected to cover all additional incidental costs such as meals and transport.
Left luggage Offices at the train (24hr) station, bus station (daily 8am–6pm) and most hotels.
Mail and telephones There are major post offices with IDD telephones, parcel post and poste restante on the western side of the square outside Guangzhou train station (daily 8am–8pm), and across from the Cultural Park entrance on Liuersan Lu (daily 8am–6pm). Shamian Island's post counter is open Mon–Sat 9am–5pm for stamps, envelopes and deliveries. All hotels have postal services and international call facilities.
PSB On the corner of Jiefang Lu and Dade Lu (Mon–Fri 8–11.30am & 2.20–5pm; ⓣ020/83115721).
Travel agents Try the following if hotels can't help with tours and transport reservations: CITS Travel, 618 Jie Fang Bei Lu, just north of Gongyuan Qian metro station (ⓣ020/22013539 or 22013546, ⓦwww.citsgd.com.cn), which can book tours, hotels and tickets within China, or CTS, next to the *Landmark* (ⓣ020/83336888, ⓦwww.chinatravelone.com). There is also a huge selection of travel agencies at Guangzhou East station.

The Pearl River Delta

At a glance, the **Pearl River Delta** (珠江三角洲, *zhūjīangsānjīaozhōu*) seems entirely a product of the modern age, dominated by industrial complexes and the glossy, high-profile cities of **Shenzhen** (深圳, *shēnzhèn*), east on the crossing to Hong Kong, and westerly **Zhuhai** (珠海, *zhūhǎi*), on the Macau border. Back in the 1980s these were marvels of Deng Xiaoping's reforms, rigidly contained **Special Economic Zones** of officially sanctioned free-market activities, previously anathema to Communist ideologies. Their success kickstarted a commercial invasion of the delta, obscuring an economic history dating back to the time of Song engineers who constructed irrigation canals through the delta's **five counties** – Nanhai, Panyu, Shunde, Dongguan and Zhongshan. From the Ming dynasty, local crafts and surplus food were exported across Guangdong, artisans flourished and funded elaborate guild temples, while gentlemen of leisure built gardens in which to wander and write poetry.

A planned high-speed rail link from Hong Kong to Guangzhou will cut through the delta in under an hour, and could easily cause you to overlook everything but the large urban agglomeration. But spend a little longer on your journey, or dip into the region on short trips from Guangzhou, and you'll find a good deal to discover beyond the factories, power stations and freeways. Don't miss **Foshan**'s (佛山, *fóshān*) splendid **Ancestral Temple**, or **Lianhua Shan**, a landscaped ancient quarry; historians might also wish to visit **Humen** (虎门, *hǔmén*), where the

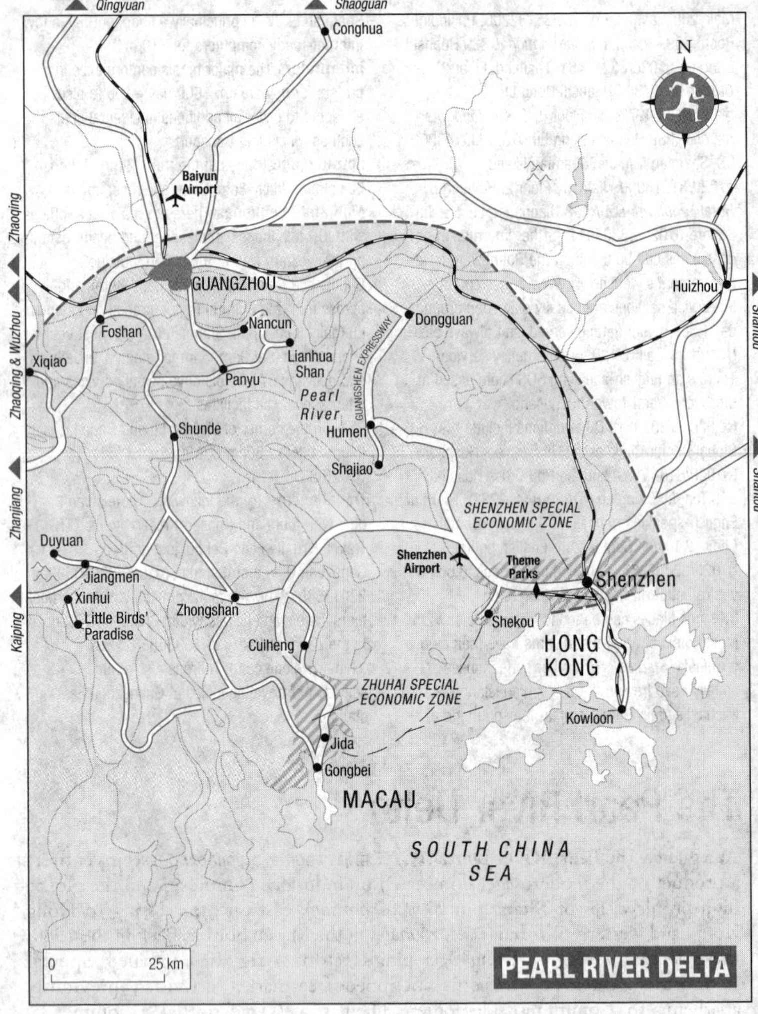

destruction of British opium in 1839 ignited the first Opium War, and **Cuiheng** (翠亨村, *cùihēng cūn*), home village of China's revered revolutionary elder statesman, **Sun Yatsen**.

The delta's western side is covered by a mesh of roads, and light-rail lines, either of which you'll be able to follow more or less directly south between sights to Zhuhai, 155km from Guangzhou. To the southeast, **Dongguan** (东莞, *dōng guăn*) is easily reachable by bus while trains shuttle between Guangzhou and Shenzhen in just minutes.

Southeast to Shenzhen

An hour southeast of Guangzhou down the expressway, **DONGGUAN** (东莞, *dōng guăn*) is the administrative seat of the delta's most productive county, its factories churning out textiles, electronic components and all manner of branded goods, some of them genuine.

If you stop in Dongguan to change buses on the way to **Humen** (see below), consider taking time to have a look at **Keyuan** (可园, *kěyuán*; daily 8am–5.30pm; ¥8) – whose name literally means "a garden worth visiting". To get here walk north from the **bus station** up Wantai Dadao for 250m, turn west along Keyuan Nan Lu, and it's about 1km away across the river. Laid out for the Qing minister Zhang Jingxiu, Keyuan puts its very limited space to good use, cramming passages, rooms, pavilions and devious staircases inside its walls. The most striking aspect, however, is the way it shuts out the rest of the city at ground level – though Dongguan's omnipresent motorways are only too obvious from the upper storey of the main **Yaoshi Pavilion**.

Humen and Shajiao

The routine industrial face of **HUMEN** (虎门, *hǔmén*; pronounced "Fumen" locally) ensures most visitors pass without a second look, but it also belies a colourful history. In 1839, after a six-week siege of the "Foreign Factories" in Guangzhou, the British were finally forced to hand over 1200 tons of **opium** to **Lin Zexu**, the Qing official charged with stopping the opium trade. The cargo was brought to Humen, mixed with quicklime, and dumped in two 45m pits on the beach 4km away at **Shajiao** (沙角, *shājiǎo*). Three weeks later the remains were flushed out to sea. Incensed, the British massacred the Chinese garrisons at Humen and on nearby **Weiyun Island**, and attacked Guangzhou. Lin got the blame, was exiled to the frontier province of Xinjiang, and replaced by an ineffectual nephew of the emperor, Yi Shan, later a signatory of the humiliating Guangzhou Treaty.

These bloodthirsty events are recounted at the **Lin Zexu Park Opium War Museum** on Jiefang Lu (林则徐公园 鸦片战争博物馆, *lín zéxú gōngyúan yāpìan zhànzhēng bówùgǔan*; daily 9am–5pm; ¥20), a twenty-minute walk between the skyscrapers northwest of Humen's bus station, and at the diorama-rich **Sea Battle Museum** (海战博物馆, *hǎizhànbówùgǔan*; daily 8.30am–5.30pm; ¥20) on Weiyuan Island – reached at the end of the #9 bus route. Nearby, **Weiyuan Fort** (威远炮台, *wēiyǔanpàotái*; daily 8.30am–6pm, ¥8), underneath Humen Bridge, provides a pleasant break from the city and a chance to see an actual historical site in the flesh – though most is covered by trees, the thick outer walls still look impregnable.

Shenzhen

Some Westerners may be familiar with **SHENZHEN** (深圳, *shēnzhèn*) as the global centre of iPod production, but the city's role in determining China's technology boom ensures that it's well known to all its countrymen. It was in this undeveloped fishing village – a tiny hamlet on the border with Hong Kong called Bao'an – that China's "economic miracle" was born back around 1979.

Thanks to its proximity to then-British-colony Hong Kong, the site was identified by Deng Xiaoping for the country's first "Special Economic Zone", an experiment in the freeing-up of markets that provided both the model for the subsequent move away from a controlled economy and the spark for meteoric growth. By 1990 the city had four harbours, its manufacturing industries were turning over $2 billion a year and a new nuclear power station was needed to cope with the energy demand. Delegations from all over China poured in to learn how to remodel their own businesses, cities and provinces.

Shenzhen may not have been the cause of capitalism in the People's Republic, but it has provided invaluable propaganda to those who promoted its virtues.

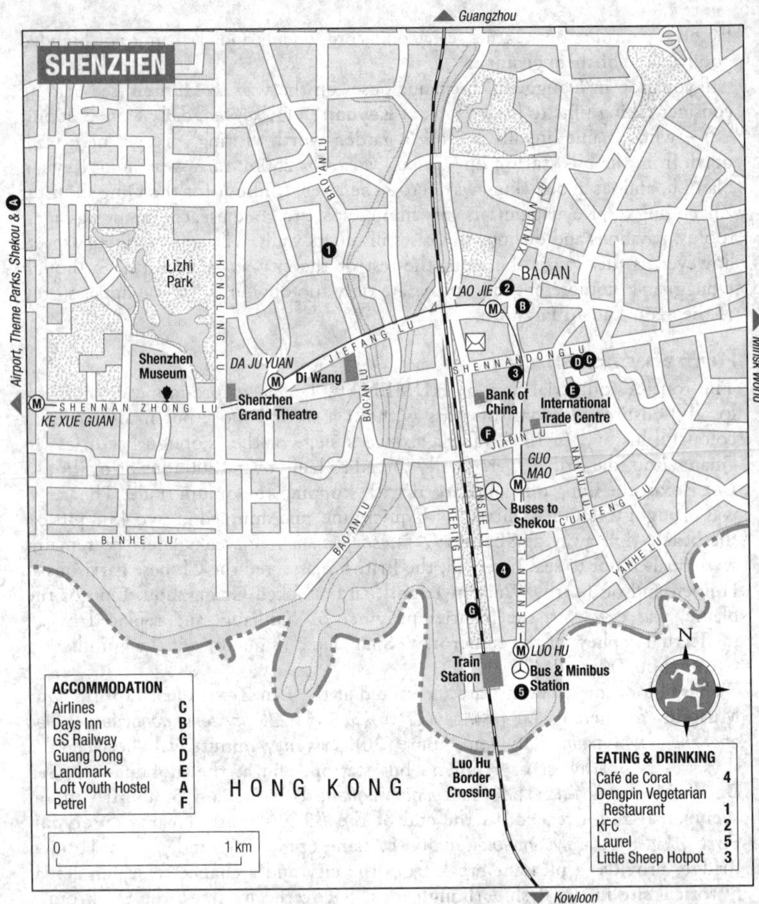

In 1992, Deng Xiaoping chose Shenzhen as the place to make his memorable "Poverty is not Socialism: to get rich is glorious" statement, voicing the Party's shift away from Communist dogma – and opening the gate for China's financial explosion.

Today, the city's gleaming skyscrapers – and ongoing construction – are testament to a continued success, as is the daily flow of thousands of commuters across the border, not just from Shenzhen to Hong Kong, but increasingly in the opposite direction. This doesn't necessarily mean there's much of interest to the casual visitor, who will find something of a shopper's paradise, a decent eating scene and a place so quickly changed that it can't shake a border-town seediness in areas, aided by pushy touts, beggars and pickpockets.

Arrival and information

A 5km-wide semicircle immediately north of the Hong Kong border, central Shenzhen is cut in half by the **rail line** that descends straight down Jianshe Lu to the Luo Hu border crossing. The border area itself is defined by the massive Luo Hu **bus station** to the east and **train station** to the west.

Moving on from Shenzhen

The **Hong Kong border** is open daily, from 6.30am to midnight. There's a lack of directional signs in the vicinity; you need to get on to the overpass from upstairs at the train station and then head south past souvenir stalls, roasted-meat vendors and pet shops. Border formalities on both sides are streamlined, and it shouldn't take more than an hour to find yourself on the other side, purchasing a ticket for the **KCR** (Kowloon–Canton Railway) train into Hong Kong.

Conventional **trains** to Guangzhou take around an hour (6.25am–10.30pm; ¥70), but a new high-speed line set to open in 2011 will slash that to just twenty minutes. Services will operate out of a new station in the city's Bao'an district. At the Lo Hu train station there is a designated Guangzhou **ticket office** at street level. Next door, another sells tickets on direct services to dozens of destinations across the country.

Buses leave regularly from the Luo Hu bus station for the delta, Guangzhou, the rest of Guangdong and many places in central China. For the **ferry**, bus #204 from Jianshe Lu will get you to the port at Shekou, alternatively a taxi will set you back around ¥80. From Shekou there are departures for Macau (6 daily; 1.30pm–7.30pm; 90min; ¥170), Zhuhai (every 30min; 7.30am–8.30pm; 1hr; ¥95), Hong Kong (5 daily; 7.45am–9.30pm; 1hr; ¥110) and Hong Kong Airport (hourly; 7.45am–9pm; 30min; ¥220). To confirm times call the ferry hotline (Ⓣ0755/26695600).

For **flights** into the rest of China, contact CAAC on Shennan Zhong Lu or go through one of the many online booking agencies such as Ⓦwww.elong.net (Ⓣ4006171717) or Ⓦwww.ctrip.com (Ⓣ4006199999) who will courier tickets direct to you. To get to the airport catch direct bus #330, take the metro to Shijiezhichuang and then take public bus #327, or get off the metro at Kexue Guan and catch the dedicated airport shuttle from outside the *Hualian* hotel (30–40min; ¥20). A taxi from the centre to the airport will cost ¥120–150.

Shuttle buses (30–40min; ¥20) operate between the **international airport**, 20km west of town, and the city centre; a taxi costs ¥120–150. The **port** lies 15km west of the centre, at **Shekou** (蛇口, *shékǒu*), from where you can catch bus #204 into town, or take a taxi for around ¥75.

Taxis and minibuses roam everywhere, and the city has an enviably efficient bus service, as well as a **metro system**; line #1 runs from Luo Hu (罗湖, *luóhú*; you will also see it spelled Lo Wu) in the southeast to Window on the World (世界之窗, *shìjiè zhīchuāng*) in the west of the city. The considerably shorter line #4 runs south from Shaoniangong to Huangang on the border with Lok Mau in Hong Kong. Fares are ¥2–5 and trains operate from 6.30am to 11pm.

As with most cities in China Shenzhen has its own expat blog/website (Ⓦwww.shenzenparty.com), which can be handy for the latest entertainment and other more practical info. There are **banks** at the border crossing, the airport, ferry terminal and some hotels, and an oversized **Bank of China** on Jianshe Lu (Mon–Fri 9am–5pm).

Accommodation

Shenzhen has a glut of central two- and three-star **hotels**, aimed at business travellers, almost all of which will usually offer a hefty discount on their advertised rack-rate. Many have good restaurants too, along with karaoke bars, interpreters, conference facilities, postal services and the like. A host of cheap (¥100–180), uninspiring options are to be found running north from the train station along Heping Lu, while more familiar names such as *Shangri-La*, *Novotel*, *Sheraton*, *Holiday Inn* and *Best Western* also have a presence.

Airlines (航空大酒店, *hángkōng dàjiǔdiàn*) Shennan Zhong Lu ⓣ0755/82237999 or 82310065. Good, comfortable rooms, a seafood restaurant and an expensive coffee shop. ❺–❻

Crowne Plaza Landmark (深圳富苑酒店, *shēnzhèn fùyuàn jiǔdiàn*) Nanhu Lu, corner of Shennan Zhong Lu ⓣ0755/82172288, ⓦwww.ichotelsgroup.com. One of Shenzhen's most upmarket venues, boasting a beautifully furnished neo-colonial interior and three restaurants. ❾

Days Inn (戴斯酒店, *dàisī jiǔdiàn*) 57 Yongxin Jie, Jiefang Lu ⓣ0755/82203333, ⓦwww.daysinn.cn. Close to the old town area, this chain hotel is a little shabby on the outside but more than presentable in. Handy for town-centre shopping and far enough from the train station to escape the worst of the city's less-desirable street life. ❻

GS Railway (广深铁路大酒店, *guǎngshēn tiělù dàjiǔdià*) Heping Lu ⓣ0755/2557318, ⓦwww.25591911.com. A little way north of the railway underpass, this is the nearest to the train station of a string of budget hotels along this street. Handy for the station, what it makes up for in practicality it loses in cleanliness and comfort, but the staff are friendly. ❹

Guang Dong (粤海酒店, *yuèhǎi jiǔdiàn*) Shennan Zhong Lu ⓣ0755/82228339, ⓦwww.gdhhotels.com. A smart business hotel with three restaurants, including a Japanese option. ❼

Loft Youth Hostel (侨城旅友国际青年旅舍, *qiáochéng lǚyǒu guójì qīnnián lǚshè*) 3 Enping Lu ⓣ0755/86095773, ⓔloftyha@yahoo.com.cn. A superior hostel backing onto the achingly cool "Loft," a former factory now housing art galleries, cafés, bars and trendy offices. Clean and modern with dorms, doubles, twins and triples, some en suite. Take metro line #1 to Qiaochengdong and leave by exit A. Walk straight ahead for a couple of minutes, turn right at the petrol station and you'll find the hostel behind the Konka building, just beyond the Loft complex. A bit out of the centre, but far more comfortable than options around the train station. Dorm beds ¥60, rooms ❹

Petrel (海燕大酒店, *hǎiyàn dàjiǔdiàn*) Jiabin Lu ⓣ0755/82232828. Smart, friendly option with views of Shenzen's skyline. Rooms are beginning to look frayed. ❺

The City

A bird's-eye view of this one-time fishing village can be taken from the observation platform on the 68th floor of the **Di Wang building** at the junction of Shennan Lu and Bao'an Nan Lu (地王大厦, *dìwáng dàshà*; 8.30am–10pm; ¥60), but for an up close glimpse of the city and its myriad shopping and eating options, a stroll along Renmin Lu, running northeast from the train station and **Luo Hu border crossing** (罗湖, *luóhú*; in Hong Kong you'll see the Cantonese rendering, Lo Wu) is a good introduction. The **Lou Hu Commercial City** (罗湖商业成, *lúohúshāngyèchéng*), immediately to your right as you clear customs on the border, is a chaotic trove of big-brand knock-offs hawking bags, watches, clothes, DVDs and all manner of electronics of questionable lineage. By contrast the **International Trade Centre** (国际贸易中心, *guójìmàoyì zhōngxīn*), a superior three-storey mall on the corner of Jiabin Lu, is a civilized affair populated with shoppers browsing upmarket jewellery and perfume. Push on over Jiefang Lu and you're in the tangle of narrow lanes that formed the **old town** of Bao'an; now a pedestrianized warren of shops selling cheap clothes, shoes, bags and the ubiquitous DVDs. Here, on Qingyuan Lu, was the historic site of China's first ever *McDonald's* restaurant, since replaced with larger premises and joined by *KFC*, *Starbucks* and *Pizza Hut*, amongst others.

For a shot of greenery, **Lianhuashan Park** (莲花山公园, *liánhuāshān gōngyuán*) sits north of the Shaoniangong northern terminus of metro line #4. After enjoying the day-glo marvels flying at Kite Square, head up the hill for a great view of the city where a giant bronze Deng Xiaoping gazes happily across the skyline – a sight for which he is largely responsible – toward Hong Kong.

If that sounds like too much effort, **Lizhi Park** (荔枝公园, *lìzhī gōngyuán*) by Da Ju Yuan metro station on Shennan Zhong Lu, is more central and a surprisingly refreshing open space with a fun boating lake. Across Hongling Lu on Shennan Zhong Lu, the **Shenzhen Museum** (深圳博物馆, *shēnzhèn bówùguǎn*; Tues–Sun 9am–5pm; free) holds thousands of paintings and works of calligraphy.

For Shenzhen's biggest guilty pleasure, hop on metro line #1 to its terminus at Shijiezhichuang, or catch bus #204 from Jianshe Lu for the thirty-minute ride west to the city's three biggest **theme parks**, situated next to each other on the Guangshen Expressway – look for a miniaturized Golden Gate Bridge spanning the road. **Window on the World** (世界之窗, *shìjiè zhīchuāng*; daily 9am–10pm; ¥120) is a collection of scale models of famous monuments such as the Eiffel Tower and Mount Rushmore, while **Splendid China** (锦绣中华, *jǐnxiù zhōnghuá*; daily 8am–5pm; ¥120) offers the same for China's sights. The latter's ticket also includes admission to the **Folk Culture Village** (民俗文化村, *mínsú wénhuàcūn*), an enjoyably touristy introduction to the nation's ethnic groups – there are yurts, pavilions, huts, archways, rock paintings and mechanical goats, with colourful troupes performing different national dances every thirty minutes. A short walk north gets you to **Happy Valley** (欢乐谷, *hūanlègǔ*; daily 9am–10pm; ¥150), Shenzhen's answer to Disneyland. It's best avoided at weekends and national holidays when waits can be interminable, but there are some genuinely exciting rides if you're into that kind of thing.

If you're after something completely different, jump aboard bus #202 or #205 from the bus depot by the border to **Minsk World** (明思克航空世界, *míngsīkè hángkōng shìjiè*; daily; ¥110), a decommissioned Russian aircraft carrier – complete with aircraft – moored at the docks for your entertainment.

Eating, drinking and nightlife

The cheapest places to **eat** are in the streets just north of Jiefang Lu, where Chinese canteens can fill you up with good dumplings, soups and stir-fries. There are also dozens of smarter options all through the centre.

For up-to-date info on Shenzhen's (predominantly expat and overseas Chinese) **nightlife**, check out Ⓦwww.shenzhenparty.com. The ultramodern **Grand Theatre** (深圳大剧院, *shēnzhèn dàjùyuàn*; Ⓦwww.szdjy.com.cn) on Shennan Zhong Lu stages everything from traditional Chinese opera to Disney musicals, while the Shekou port area, popular with expats, is the current centre of Shenzhen's **bar** and **club** scene. You can get to the port on the #204 bus from Jianshe Lu – it's a little further out than the theme parks.

Café de Coral (香港大家乐, *xiānggǎng dàjiālè*) Jianshe Lu. This Macanese chain provides quality Chinese food with a Western influence in a handy order-by-pictures format. A main meal with drink should set you back around ¥40. It can be standing room only at lunchtime.

Dengpin Vegetarian (登品素食府, *dēngpǐn sùshífǔ*) All but hidden on the third floor of the Jun Ting Ming Yuan, north of Bao'an Nan Lu's junction with Hongbao Lu. Choose the all-you-can-eat vegetarian buffet for ¥28 – a great way to try a bit of everything, along with dim sum – or order from the menu for a little more.

Laurel (丹桂轩酒楼, *dānguìxuān jiǔlóu*) Fifth floor of Louhu Commercial City in Railway Station Square. Some of the best Cantonese food in town, though not all of the specialities (eg snake) make it on to the English menu; best to break out the dictionary if you want something exotic. Expect ¥100/person.

Little Sheep Hotpot (小肥羊火锅, *xiǎoféiyáng huǒguō*) Renmin Lu at the junction with Shennan Zhong Lu. Seat yourself at a bubbling cauldron of the nationwide chain's signature spicy broth and order meat and vegetables to stew in it – best enjoyed by groups of three or more. Around ¥60/person.

The western delta: Foshan

Twenty-five kilometres southwest of Guangzhou, the satellite suburb of **FOSHAN** (佛山, *fóshān*) was once very much a town in its own right, with a history dating back to the seventh century. Along with the nearby village of **Shiwan**, Foshan became famous for its ceramics, silk, metalwork and woodcarving – a reputation it still enjoys – and the splendour of its **temples**, two of which survive on **Zumiao Lu**, a kilometre-long street shaded by office buildings and set in the heart of what was once the old town centre. At the southern end, **Zu Miao** (祖庙, *zǔmiào*; Ancestral Temple; daily 8.30am–6.30pm; ¥20) is a masterpiece of southern architecture, founded in 1080 as a metallurgists' guild temple. Ahead and to the left of the entrance is an elevated garden fronted by some locally made Opium War **cannons** – sadly for the Chinese, poor casting techniques and a lack of rifling made these inaccurate and liable to explode. Nearby, magnificent glazed **roof tiles** of frolicking lions and characters from local tales were made in Shiwan for temple restorations in the 1830s. The temple's **main hall** is on the left past here, its interior crowded with minutely carved wooden screens, oversized guardian gods leaning threateningly out from the walls, and a three-tonne **statue of Beidi**, God of the North, who in local lore controlled low-lying Guangdong's flood-prone waters – hence this shrine to snare his goodwill.

Opposite the hall is the elaborate masonry of the Lingying archway, similar to those at Shexian in Anhui province (see p.424). Foshan is considered the birthplace of Cantonese **opera**, and beyond the archway you'll find the highly decorative Wanfu stage, built in 1685 for autumnal performances given to thank the Divine Emperor for his bountiful harvests. Foshan is also renowned as a martial-arts centre, and there are exhibitions dedicated to past masters Yip Man, Bruce Lee's instructor, and, in the north of the complex, another to Huang Fei Hong, a doctor and fighter who has been the subject of many a movie.

A few blocks north, **Renshou Si** (仁受寺, *rénshòu sì*; Benevolent Longevity Temple; daily 8am–5pm; free) is a former Ming monastery whose southern wing, graced by a short seven-storey pagoda, is still consecrated. The rest has been cleaned out and turned into the **Foshan Folk Arts Research Institute** (daily 9am–5pm; free), a good place to look for souvenirs like excellent **papercuts** with definite Cultural Revolution leanings, showing the modernizing of rural economies. At the time of the Spring Festival, side halls are also full of celebratory lions, fish and phoenixes constructed from wire and coloured crepe paper.

About 1km due north of here on Songfeng Lu – continue up Zumiao Lu to its end, turn right and then first left – **Liang Yuan** (梁园, *liángyuán*; daily 8am–5.30pm; ¥10) is another of the delta's historic **gardens**, built between 1796 and 1850 by a family of famous poets and artists of the period. There are artfully arranged ponds, trees and rocks, and the tastefully furnished residential buildings are worth a look, but the real gem here is the **Risheng Study**, a perfectly proportioned retreat looking out over a tiny, exquisitely designed pond, fringed with willows.

Practicalities

Fenjiang Bei Lu forms the western boundary of the old town, running south for about 2km from the **train station**, over a canal, past the **long-distance bus station** and through to where the skyscrapers, which constitute Foshan's business centre, cluster around a broad roundabout. **Buses** from Guangzhou's Liuhua and Guangfo bus stations (¥15; 1hr) deposit you at **Zumiao station** (祖庙站, *zǔmiàozhàn*), just east of the roundabout on Chengmentou Lu; walk 50m east and you're at the bottom end of Zumiao Lu. Foshan's Guangzhou metro link began operation at the end of 2010, running from Zilang at the southern terminus of metro line #1; Zumiao has its own stop. To reach Zumiao Lu from the other stations, catch bus #1, #6 or #11, or walk down Fenjiang Bei Lu for about 700m, then east for a few minutes along tree-lined Qinren Lu to the intersection with Zumiao Lu. Foshan's main **Bank of China** (Mon–Fri 8.30am–5pm, Sat 9am–4pm) is between the two temples, as is a post office.

Around Panyu: Lian Hua Shan

A couple of attractive sights surround the town of **PANYU** (番禺, *pānyú*), now a district of Guangzhou, about 20km south of the city proper. The easiest way to get here is by jumping on the metro and getting off at Panyu Square on line #3.

Overlooking the Pearl River 15km east of Panyu, **Lian Hua Shan** (莲花山, *liánhuā shān*; daily 8am–4pm; ¥30) is an odd phenomenon, a mountain quarried as long ago as the Han dynasty for its red stone, used in the tomb of the Nanyue king, Zhao Mo. After mining it in such a way as to leave a suspiciously deliberate arrangement of crags, pillars and caves, Ming officials planted the whole thing with trees and turned it into a pleasure garden laid with lotus pools, stone paths and pavilions. A 50m-high pagoda was built in 1612, and the Qing emperor Kangxi added a fortress to defend the river. Still a popular excursion from Guangzhou, it's an interesting spot to while away a few hours, though frequently crowded.

For a livelier day-trip, you could visit the **Chime Long Theme Park Complex** (Ⓦwww.chimelong.com) close to Panyu's Hanxi-Changlong metro stop. The flagship **Chime Long Paradise** park (长隆欢乐世界, *chánglōnghūanlèshìjìe*; daily 9.30am–6pm; ¥180) boasts international-standard rides, while the **Xiangjiang Safari Park** (香江野生动物世界, *xīangjīang yěshēng dòngwù shìjiè*; same hours & price as above), a definite step up from Guangzhou's impoverished zoo, has pandas. The neighbourhood is also home to one of the world's largest water parks (same hours; ¥128), a crocodile park (same hours; ¥60) and a circus (shows daily 5.30 & 7.30pm; ¥180). Most are walkable from the metro but a shuttle bus exists, too. Tickets start at ¥150 for a single attraction but multitickets are also available.

Kaiping

Though more than 100km west of Guangzhou, the delta's excellent road network makes **KAIPING** (开平, *kāipíng*; Ⓦwww.kptour.com), recognized in 2007 as a UNESCO World Heritage Site, an excellent day-trip – just a couple of hours by bus from Guangzhou's long distance bus stations (every 30min 6am–8pm; ¥60). The town itself has no particular charm – its secret attractions lie dotted around the countryside beyond in the form of more than a thousand fantastical towers called **diaolou** (碉楼, *dīaolóu*). Looking like something Marco Polo might have dreamed up, the towers were built as protection against bandits and paid for with the proceeds of villagers who found success overseas in the late nineteenth and early twentieth centuries. Money was not all that flowed back, and the foreign influence is reflected in the myriad architectural styles adopted alongside more traditional Chinese features. Many of the remaining *diaolou* are in clusters, the main sites being the villages of **Zili** (自力村, *zìlìcūn*), **Majianglong** (马降龙村, *mǎjìanglóngcūn*), **Sanmenli** (三门里村, *sānménlǐcūn*) and **Jingjiangli** (锦江里村, *jǐnjīanglǐcūn*), where you will find **Ruishi Lou** (瑞石楼, *rùishílúo*), arguably the most majestic of the lot. Also falling under the umbrella of Kaiping are the **Li Garden and Mansion** (立园, *lìyúan*), a complex constructed by a wealthy businessman in the 1920s, and the town of **Chikan** (赤坎, *chìkǎn*), which has an impressively well-preserved waterfront dating from early last century.

Each village charges around ¥50 entry to their *diaolou*, and multilocation tickets are also available (at a discount); privately owned Ruishi Lou is, unfortunately, an exception, and costs an additional ¥20 to climb. It is only open at weekends.

Buses crisscross between the sites and Kaiping bus station, and it is perfectly possible to make it round hopping on and off these, but it can be more straightforward just to hire one of the many waiting taxis or minibuses for the day (this should be around ¥300, but be prepared to negotiate).

Shunde

Yet another antique garden, **Qinghui Gardens** (清晖园, *qīnghuī yuán*; daily 8am–6pm; ¥15), is one reason to pause in the county town of **SHUNDE** (顺德, *shùndé*), also known as Daliang Zhen, 50km south of Guangzhou. In the middle of town on Qinghui Lu, the well-kept gardens contain a series of square fish ponds surrounded by osmanthus, mulberry bushes and bamboo. The other highlight here is the *Qinghui Yuan* **restaurant** (daily 7–9am, 11am–2pm & 5–7pm), in the grounds of the gardens, which is revered for serving the very best in classic Cantonese cuisine. It is expensive – count on at least ¥75 a person – but the dishes are superb, with mild, fresh flavours that have to be taken slowly to be properly appreciated; their braised sea carp with garlic and ginger melts in the mouth. After eating, you can walk off your meal in the restored colonial-style streets behind the gardens off Hua Lu, where the old town centre mirrors Guangzhou's back lanes, with flagstones, markets and a fully restored street of colonial-era architecture. Alternatively, it's about 1km north across a huge open square and Wenxiu Lu to wooded and hilly **Feng Ling Park** (风岭公园, *fēnglǐng gōngyuán*), with the old Xishan Gumiao temple (西山古庙, *xīshān gǔmiào*) on the east side. Shunde is also home to not one but two **Bruce Lee museums** (李小龙博物馆, *lǐxiǎolóngbówùguǎn*). The first is based around a teahouse that Bruce supposedly visited during his one and only visit to the town when he was five years old; another, larger, effort in Bruce's ancestral home in nearby Shang village, **Jun'an district** (均安镇, *jūnānzhèn*; 30min taxi journey from the Qinghui Gardens), features costumes, photographs and poems and letters written by the martial-arts star. For the future, a giant statue and multimillion-dollar theme park are also rumoured.

Practicalities

The fastest way to get to Shunde from Guangzhou is on the new Guangzhou–Zhuhai MRT line, just three stops from Guangzhou South station. If you catch the bus (¥30), the **long-distance bus station** is on the highway about 3km south of Shunde centre; catch bus #9 from here to Qinghui Lu and the gardens. For a **place to stay**, there's the plush *New World Hotel* opposite the gardens at 150 Qinghui Lu (新世界大酒店, *xīnshìjièdàjiǔdiàn*; ⓣ0757/22218333, ⓦwww.shunde.newworldhotels.com; ❻); cheaper options exist throughout town.

Moving on, MRT is the best option for direct north–south travel, and if you can't find long-distance transport at the bus station, head to Guangzhou or Zhongshan and pick up services there.

Zhongshan and Cuiheng

Almost every town in China has a park or road named **Zhongshan**, a tribute to China's first Republican president, the remarkable **Dr Sun Yatsen**. Christened with the Cantonese name "Yatsen" (Yixian in Mandarin), while in exile in Japan he acquired the name Nakayama ("middle mountain"), the Chinese characters for which are pronounced "Zhongshan". Unless you need to change buses, there's no need to visit Zhongshan itself, a characterless county town 100km from Guangzhou, but 30km east on the coastal road to Zhuhai is the good doctor's home village of **CUIHENG** (翠亨村, *cùihēng cūn*), now the site of a **memorial garden** (孙中山故居, *sūnzhōngshān gùjù*; daily 8am–5pm; ¥20) celebrating his life and achievements. Buses from Zhongshan town and from Zhuhai (35km south) will set you down right outside the garden, where there are also a few cheap **places to eat** and to buy ice creams; it should be reachable as well on the new Guangzhou–Zhuhai MRT line.

Along with a banyan tree supposedly brought back from Hawaii and planted by Sun, the grounds incorporate a comprehensive museum of photographs, relics

Sun Yatsen

Born in 1866, **Sun Yatsen** grew up during a period when China laboured under the humiliation of colonial occupation, a situation justly blamed on the increasingly feeble Qing court. Having spent three years in Hawaii during the 1880s, Sun studied medicine in Guangzhou and Hong Kong, where he became inspired by that other famous Guangdong revolutionary, Hong Xiuquan (see p.504), and began to involve himself in covert anti-Qing activities. Back in Hawaii in 1894, he abandoned his previous notions of reforming the imperial system and founded the **Revive China Society** to "Expel the Manchus, restore China to the people and create a federal government". The following year he incited an uprising in Guangzhou under **Lu Haodong**, notable for being the first time that the green Nationalist flag, painted with a white, twelve-pointed sun (which still appears on the Taiwanese flag), was flown. But the uprising was quashed, Lu Haodong was captured and executed, and Sun fled overseas.

Orbiting between Hong Kong, Japan, Europe and the US, Sun spent the next fifteen years raising money to fund revolts in southern China, and in 1907 his new Alliance Society announced its famous **Three Principles of the People** – Nationalism, Democracy and Livelihood. He was in Colorado when the Manchus finally fell in October 1911; on returning to China he was made provisional president of the Republic of China on January 1, 1912, but was forced to resign in February in favour of the powerful warlord **Yuan Shikai**. Yuan established a Republican Party, while Sun's supporters rallied to the Nationalist People's Party – **Guomindang** – led by **Song Jiaoren**. Song was assassinated by Yuan's henchmen following Guomindang successes in the 1913 parliamentary elections, and Sun again fled to Japan. Annulling parliament, Yuan tried to set himself up as emperor, but couldn't even control military factions within his own party, which plunged the north into civil war on his death in 1916. Sun, meanwhile, returned to his native Guangdong and established an independent Guomindang government, determined to unite the country eventually. Though unsuccessful, by the time of his death in 1925 he was greatly respected by both the Guomindang and the four-year-old Communist Party for his lifelong efforts to enfranchise the masses.

(including the original Nationalist flag) and biographical accounts in English emphasizing the successful aspects of Sun Yatsen's career. There's also the solid, Portuguese-style family home where he lived between 1892 and 1895, "studying, treating patients and discussing national affairs with his friends". Behind Sun's home are some rather more typical period buildings belonging to the peasant and landlord classes, restored and furnished with wooden tables and authentic silk tapestries.

Zhuhai

ZHUHAI (珠海, *zhūhǎi*) is an umbrella name for the Special Economic Zone encompassing three separate townships immediately north of Macau: **Gongbei** (拱北, *gǒngběi*), on the border itself, and **Jida** (吉大, *jídà*) and **Xiangzhou** (香州珠海度假村, *xiāngzhōu zhūhǎi dùjiàcūn*), which make up the port and residential districts 5km to 10km farther up along the coast. Full of new offices, immensely wide roads and tasty economic incentives, Zhuhai has yet to blossom in the way that Shenzhen has – probably because Zhuhai's neighbour is Macau, not Hong Kong. Sights are few; the coastline hereabouts is pretty enough on a warm day, but there are few true beaches (though Lingjiaozui [菱角嘴, *língjiǎozuǐ*], in Jida [吉大, *jídà*], is best if you fancy a swim), and most people come for the border crossing or to take advantage of what amounts to a **duty-free enclave** aimed at Macanese day-trippers in Gongbei's backstreets. **Lianhua Lu** (莲花路, *liánhūalù*) is Gongbei's liveliest street, a kilometre's worth of hotels, restaurants and shops selling cheap clothes, household goods and trinkets you never realized you needed. South across a paved square, the **crossing into Macau** is concealed inside a huge shopping plaza – labelled "Gongbei Port" in gold on the red roof – where you can buy more of the same.

Practicalities

If you've just **walked across the border** – which is open 7am to midnight – into Zhuhai from Macau, you exit the customs building at Gongbei with Lianhua Lu and the two adjacent **bus stations** 250m diagonally across to the right. Buses go from both stations to the delta, Guangzhou and beyond, with the last bus to Guangzhou leaving at 10pm (3hr; ¥70). Once the **MRT** to Guangzhou is up and running, it will take just 45 minutes to go from here to Guangzhou South station. **Jiuzhou ferry port** is 5km up the road at Jida, with twice-hourly services to Shenzhen between 7.30am and 6pm (1hr; ¥70), and hourly departures to Hong Kong from 8am to 9.30pm (70min; ¥165). Buses #2, #4 and #13 (daily 6.30am–9.30pm) run up to the port from Gongbei, or you can hail a taxi (around ¥20).

For **accommodation**, there are dozens of mid-range places in Gongbei with almost identical facilities and prices (which can plummet considerably during the week): on Lianhua Lu, *Min'an* (民安酒店, *mín'ān jiǔdiàn*; ⓣ0756/8131168; ❺) is the pick of the bunch, with large, comfortable rooms and attentive staff, whilst the nearby *Changan* (昌安酒店, *chāngān jiǔdiàn*; ⓣ0756/8118828; ❺) is of a similar standard.

Northern Guangdong

Guangdong's hilly northern reaches form a watershed between the Pearl River Valley and the Yangzi Basin, guarding the main route through which peoples, armies and culture flowed between central China and the south – there are even remains of the physical road, broad and paved, up near **Meiling** on the Jiangxi border. Its strategic position saw the region occupied as long ago as the Stone Age, and it was later used by the Taiping rebels and the nineteenth-century Wesleyan Church, which founded numerous missions in northern Guangdong. Today, **Qingyuan** (清远, *qīngyuǎn*) and its pretty riverside temples lie only an hour northwest of Guangzhou by bus, while a host of offbeat attractions farther north around the rail town of **Shaoguan** (韶关, *sháoguān*) include **Danxia Shan** (丹霞山, *dānxiá shān*), a formalized mountain park. For those not continuing up into central China, Shaoguan is also a jumping-off point for a backwoods trip west **into Guangxi province** through ethnic Yao and Zhuang territories.

Qingyuan and around

Once a busy back-road market town surrounded by countryside thick with rice fields and mud-brick villages, **QINGYUAN** (清远, *qīngyuǎn*) is now, like much of the Pearl River Delta, an industrial jumble, with little of interest. Sitting on the banks of the **Bei River** (北江, *běijiāng*), about 80km northwest of Guangzhou by bus from the Liuhua station (1hr; ¥36), Qingyuan's allure is as a departure point for day-trips to the poetically isolated, elderly temple complexes of **Feilai** (飞来古寺, *fēilái gǔsì*) and **Feixia** (飞霞古寺, *fēilxiá gǔsì*), 20km upstream.

Buses from Guangzhou arrive at Qingyuan's **new bus station** (汽车总站, *qìchēzǒngzhàn*) about 3km south of the river; from here there are several daily buses to Shaoguan, and masses south to Guangzhou, Foshan and Shenzhen, but it should be noted there are few services after 8pm. From the new bus station take a taxi (¥30) out to the town docks at **Wuyi Matou** (五一马头, *wǔyīmǎtóu*), 14km to the east, where you will be able to charter a boat to Feilai and Feixia (up to ¥300 for a return trip, depending on your bargaining skills).

Bus #6 heads from the new station over the Beijiang Bridge and into town, whose kilometre-wide core – where you'll likely stay and eat if the need arises – is centred on the intersection of north–south **Shuguang Lu** and east–west **Xianfeng Lu**. A taxi will cost around ¥15.

There's a collection of noisy, inexpensive **hotels** on the roundabout at the northern end of Beimen Jie: *Sun Hua Yuan* (新花园酒店, *xīnhuāyuán jiǔdiàn*; ⓣ0763/3311138; ❸) is your best bet, with friendly staff and clean, functional rooms – those on the third floor have pleasant, communal balconies, albeit overlooking the road. There's also the plush and popular *Tianhu Dajiudian* (天湖大酒店, *tiānhú dàjiǔdiàn*; ⓣ0763/3820126; ❹), on the Shuguang Lu/Xianfeng Lu intersection. Most comfortable, convenient and expensive is the *Royal Crown Hotel* (华冠大酒店, *húaguāndàjīudìan*; ⓣ0763/387888; ❻), right next to the new bus station on Yanjiang Lu's junction with Fengming Lu.

In town, Nanmen Jie and Beimen Jie have the best **places to eat**; with options including river food at *Nandamen Jiudian* (南大门酒店, *nándàmén jiǔdiàn*), a café and restaurant alongside countless others running west along Yanjiang Lu, and *Zhiwei Guan* (之味馆, *zhīwèi guǎn*), a Cantonese diner on Beimen Jie.

About the only attraction within Qingyuan's town limits, **Tai He Temple** (太和古侗, *tài hé gǔdòng*; ¥15) is a series of Taoist pavilions dotting a path into the mountains north of town, plus a crystal-clear swimming pool filled from the mountain stream, children's roller coaster and bumper cars. The temple entrance is around ten minutes by motorbike taxi (¥10) from the #6 bus terminus. Further afield, the **Qing Xin Hot Springs Resort** (清心温场, *qingxin wenchang*; ¥50) is a favourite with locals and with some of China's best professional football teams. The resort can be reached in an hour from the old bus station opposite where bus #6 terminates (¥10).

Feilai and Feixia

Taking the boat from Wuyi Matou, it's a placid, hour-long journey upstream past a few brick pagodas, bamboo-screened villages and wallowing water buffalo being herded by children. Hills rise up on the right, then the river bends sharply east into a gorge and past the steps outside the ancient gates of **Feilai Gusi** (飞来古寺, *fēilái gǔsì*; ¥15), a romantically sited Buddhist temple whose ancestry can be traced back 1400 years. You'll only need about forty minutes to have a look at the ornate ridge tiles and climb up through the thin pine forest to where a modern pavilion offers pretty views of the gorge scenery. If you have time to spare before your boat heads on, the temple gates are a good place to sit and watch the tame cormorants sunbathing on the prows of their owners' tiny sampans.

Feixia

Some 3km farther upstream at the far end of the gorge, **Feixia Gusi** (飞霞古寺, *fēxiá gǔsì*; ¥35) is far more recent and much more extensive than Feilai Gusi in the scale and scope of its buildings. The name covers two entirely self-sufficient Taoist monasteries, founded in 1863 and expanded fifty years later, which were built up in the hills in the Feixia and Cangxia grottoes, with hermitages, pavilions and academies adorning the 8km of interlinking, flagstoned paths in between.

A couple of hours is plenty of time to have a look around. A broad and not very demanding set of steps runs up from the riverfront through a pleasant woodland where, after twenty minutes or so, you pass the minute Jinxia and Ligong temples, cross an ornamental bridge, and encounter **Feixia** itself. Hefty surrounding walls and passages connecting halls and courtyards, all built of stone, lend Feixia the atmosphere of a medieval European castle. There's nothing monumental to see – one of the rooms has been turned into a **museum** of holy relics, and you might catch a weekend performance of **traditional temple music** played on bells, gongs and zithers – but the gloom, low ceilings and staircases running off in all directions make it an interesting place to explore. If you walk up through the monastery and take any of the tracks heading uphill, in another ten minutes or so you'll come to the short **Changtian Pagoda** perched right on the top of the ridges, decorated with mouldings picked out in pastel colours, with views down over Feixia and the treetops. Another small temple next door offers food, drink and basic **accommodation** (❻).

Five minutes' walk east along the main track from Feixia brings you to the similar but smaller complex of **Cangxia**. Look for the garden with its fragrant white magnolia tree, an unusual, life-sized statue of the Monkey God, Sun Wu Kong, and some wonderful **frescoes** – one featuring an immortal crossing the sea on a fish, storm dragons and two golden pheasants.

Shaoguan

Many trains heading inland from Guangzhou call in at **SHAOGUAN** (韶关, *sháoguān*), 200km north; expresses cover the distance in just 45 minutes, while the majority of services do it in a more sedate couple of hours. An ancient city, Shaoguan was unfortunately the target of Japanese saturation bombing during the 1930s, which robbed the town of much of its heritage. Since the 1950s, textile mills and steelworks have ensured a moderate prosperity, if not a pretty skyline.

Arrival and information

Two major arrival points lie immediately east of the centre over the Zhen River, linked to Jiefang Lu by the Qujiang Bridge: the train station sits at the back of a big square, while the long-distance bus station is on its northeast edge. The **west bus station** (西站, *xīzhàn*), a kilometre away across the Wujiang Bridge, deals with arrivals and departures within the province, so if you're coming from Guangzhou (3hr; ¥70), this is where you will be dropped.

Onward train tickets are in short supply, as this is the main line north out of Guangdong and, despite a continuous stream of trains passing through, it's perpetually overcrowded, as is the train station itself. Long-distance buses – heading north to Jiangxi and Hunan, east to Huizhou and Chaozhou, south to Guangzhou and west to Lianshan – leave throughout the day. There are a couple of morning buses to Qingyuan, but for more services you should head to the west station. Taxis cruise the streets (¥5 within town), though the centre is so compact they are barely necessary, and minibuses out to nearby attractions leave from a depot in the southern corner of the train-station square. There's a **Bank of China** on Jiefang Lu (Mon–Fri 9am–5pm, Sat 10am–3pm), a **post office** on the south side of the train-station square, and several **internet bars** just north of Fengcai Ta on Dongti Lu.

Accommodation

For **accommodation**, there are several options around the station square itself, including the convenient but basic *Gangdu Jiu Dian* (港都酒店, *gǎngdūjiǔdiàn*; ⓣ0751/8252288; ❸), and the mid-range *Yuetong* (粤通世纪酒店, *yuètōng shìjì jiǔdiàn*; ⓣ0751/8229888; ❹), all but next door to each other on the north side of the square, and the superior *Royal Regent* (丽晶酒店, *lìjīng jiǔdiàn*; ⓣ0751/8210218, ⓔsgregent@pub.shaoguang.gd.cn; ❻) at the southwest corner. In town, Jiefang

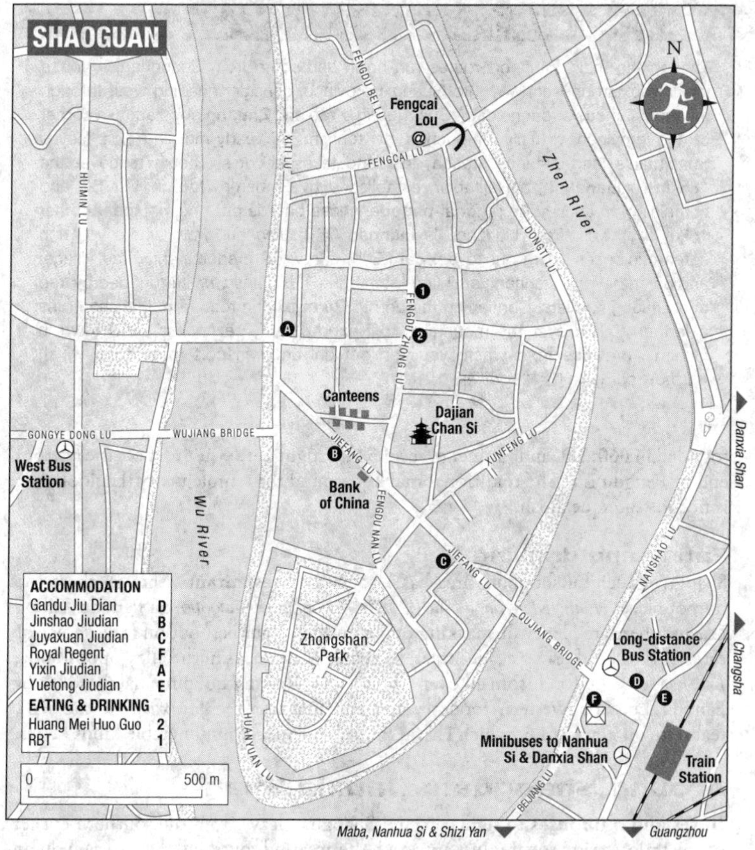

Lu offers the most options, including the smart *JinShao* (金韶酒店, *jīnsháojiǔdiàn*; ⓣ0751/8821888, ⓦwww.shaohuahotel.cn; ④) and the slightly pretentious *Juyaxuan* (聚雅轩酒店, *jùyǎxūanjǐudiàn*; ⓣ0751/8189333; ④), which also has a vaguely Western restaurant on the first floor. Elsewhere, the *Yixin* (壹心宾馆, *yìxīn bīnguǎn*; ⓣ0751/8889898; ③), at the junction of Fuxing Lu and Xidi Lu, has smart rooms, is bargainable and probably the best deal in town.

The Town

Shaoguan's downtown area fills a south-pointing **peninsula** shaped by the **Zhen River** (浈江, *zhēnjiāng*) on the east side and the **Wu River** (武江, *wǔjiāng*) on the west, which merge at the peninsula's southern tip to form the Bei River. The pedestrianized main street, Fengdu Lu, crossed by Fengcai Lu at the north end of town and Jiefang Lu in the south, runs vertically through the centre to the tree-lined **Zhongshan Park**. While there's plenty of activity in the clothing and trinket **markets** that fill the side streets off Fengdu Lu, and some crumbling colonial architecture, most of the town is functional and modern. The city sights, such as they are, comprise **Fengcai Lou** (风采楼, *fēngcǎi lóu*), a 1930s reconstruction of the old eastern city gate tower, up along Fengcai Lu; and **Dajian Chan Si** (大鉴禅寺, *dàjiànchán sì*), an insubstantial monastery with ancient heritage – it was

West into Guangxi

Though the main transport routes run north and south from Shaoguan, if you're looking for an unusual way into Guangxi province, consider heading west through the mountainous strongholds of Guangdong's **Yao** and **Zhuang** population, a corner of the province virtually untouched by tourism. An early-morning bus leaves Shaoguan's long-distance station daily and takes about six hours to cover the 185km to **Lianzhou**, a Han town established by Emperor Wudi in 111 BC and containing an ancient **hexagonal pagoda** whose base is of Song vintage. Another 15km southwest from Lianzhou is **Liannan** (连南, *líannán*), from where you can catch minibuses 10km out to **Sanpai** (三排, *sānpái*), a predominantly Yao village, and 35km beyond Liannan you'll find **Lianshan** (连山, *líanshān*), surrounded by Yao and Zhuang hamlets. Continuing through to **Guangxi**, the road from Lianshan runs a farther 100km over the mountains to **Hezhou** (贺州, *hèzhōu*), a small town in Guangxi province from where you can get onward transport to Wuzhou (悟州, *wùzhōu*) or Guilin (桂林, *gùilín*).

founded in 660 AD, and Huineng (see p.514) taught here – just east off the bottom end of Fengdu Lu. The traditional **market** around the temple is worth a look, but is not for the squeamish.

Eating and drinking

Shaoguan's central shopping area has a paucity of **restaurants**, though there is a hotpot place, *Huang Mei Xiang Guo* (煌妹香锅, *húangmèixīanggūo*) on Fengdu Zhong Lu, and there are plenty of snacking opportunities. Your best option for a choice of eateries is to head down a side street – a string of canteens in the alley opposite the *Jin Shao* serve up food from all over China – or to Jiefang Lu immediately south of Fengdu Lu. For Western food try the restaurant at the *Juyaxuan* or the *RBT* teahouse on Fengdu Lu, which has an English menu and innumerable kinds of tea.

Around Shaoguan: Danxia Shan

Buses and minibuses to sights around Shaoguan leave from the southern corner of the train-station square; just approach the area and touts will try to drag you on board. You will almost certainly be asked for at least double the correct fare and would be ill-advised to hand over any money without bargaining; nor should you get onto a partially empty vehicle unless you want a long wait. Alternatively, ask at the bus station to see if anything is heading your way.

The most interesting side trip is to UNESCO World Heritage Site **Danxia Shan** (丹霞山, *dānxiá shān*), a formation of vivid red sandstone cliffs lining the **Jin River** (锦江, *jǐnjīang*), 50km northeast of Shaoguan near the town of **Renhua** (仁化, *rénhùa*). Buses (¥10–15) drop you at the main gates, where you pay the **entry fee** (¥100 weekdays or ¥120 at weekends and holidays), which includes all minibus rides into and around the park, but not the cable car (¥55 round-trip) – note that the park buses stop around 5pm, and that the **last bus** back to Shaoguan passes the gates in the late afternoon.

The first place to aim for is **Yuan Shan Jing**, 2km inside the gates across the Jin, famous for **Yangyuan Shi** (阳元石, *yángyúanshí*), a rock that – though the description is less suitably applied to outcrops all over China – really does look like the male member. It's a tough climb to the summit of neighbouring (and less phallic) Yuan Shan, after which you can charter a **boat** (¥10 a person) or catch the bus for another couple of kilometres to Danxia Shan itself. The surrounding area is covered in 12km of paths, which rise steeply through woodland, past cliffside nunneries and rock formations, and up the various summits. You can stay overnight in the handful of **hotels** here (upward of ¥100) and rise early to catch the sunrise from the pavilion at the mountain's apex, **Changlao** – only an hour's climb – though the views are great all day long.

Nanling Forest Park

Another option for keen hikers is to use Shaoguan as a jumping-off point for **Nanling National Forest Park** (南岭国家森林公园, *nánlǐng gúojīasēnlín gǒngyúan*; ¥35; ⓣ0751/5232038, ⓦwww.english.eco-nanling.com), 80km to the northwest on the border with Henan province. The park takes in both the Guandong's largest remaining tract of virgin forest and its highest peak – Guangdong Shan at 1902m. Its 273 square kilometres contain countless walking trails allowing access to stunning peaks, valleys, gorges and waterfalls. To reach Nanling from Shaoguan's west station, take a direct bus (2hr; ¥20) to **Wuzhishan** (五指山, *wǔzhǐshān*), where the park entrance is located, or more frequent buses to the town of **Ruyuan** (乳源, *rǔyúan*), from where a second bus (¥10) or taxi (¥50) can take you the rest of the way. Accommodation in Wuzhishan is limited but the *Orange House* hotel (橙屋酒店, *chéngwūjǐudìan*; ⓣ0751/5232929; ❻), which also offers a campsite during summer (¥120 for a four-person tent), is more than comfortable.

Eastern Guangdong

Taken in one go, it's an arduous 600km journey east from Guangzhou to Xiamen in Fujian province, but there's a wealth of interesting territory to explore on the way. Only three hours away, **Huizhou**'s (惠州, *huìzhōu*) watery parkland makes it an excellent weekend bolthole from Guangzhou, while over near the Fujian border, **Chaozhou** (潮州, *cháozhōu*) is famed for its own cooking style and Ming-era architecture. With enough time, you could spend a few days farther north in the hilly country around **Meizhou** (梅州, *méizhōu*), investigating ethnic **Hakka culture** in its heartland. Getting around is easy: **expressways** from Guangzhou or Shenzhen run via Huizhou along the coast to **Shantou** (汕头, *shàntóu*) and on into Fujian, while the **rail line** from Guangzhou's East train station bends northeast from Huizhou to Meizhou – where an extension runs up to Yongding in Fujian – then down to Chaozhou and Shantou.

Chaozhou

On the banks of the Han River, **CHAOZHOU** (潮州, *cháozhōu*) is one of Guangdong's most culturally significant towns, yet manages to be overlooked by tourist itineraries and government projects alike – principally through having had its limelight stolen during the nineteenth century by its noisy southern sister, **Shantou** (汕头, *shàntóu*), just 40km away. In response, Chaozhou has become staunchly traditional, proudly preserving the architecture, superstitions and local character which Shantou, a recent, foreign creation, never had, making it a far nicer place to spend some time.

The city was founded back in antiquity, and by the time of the Ming dynasty had reached its zenith as a place of culture and refinement; the origins of many of the town's monuments date back to this time. A spate of tragedies followed, however. After an anti-Manchu uprising in 1656, only Chaozhou's monks and their temples were spared the imperial wrath – it's said that the ashes of the

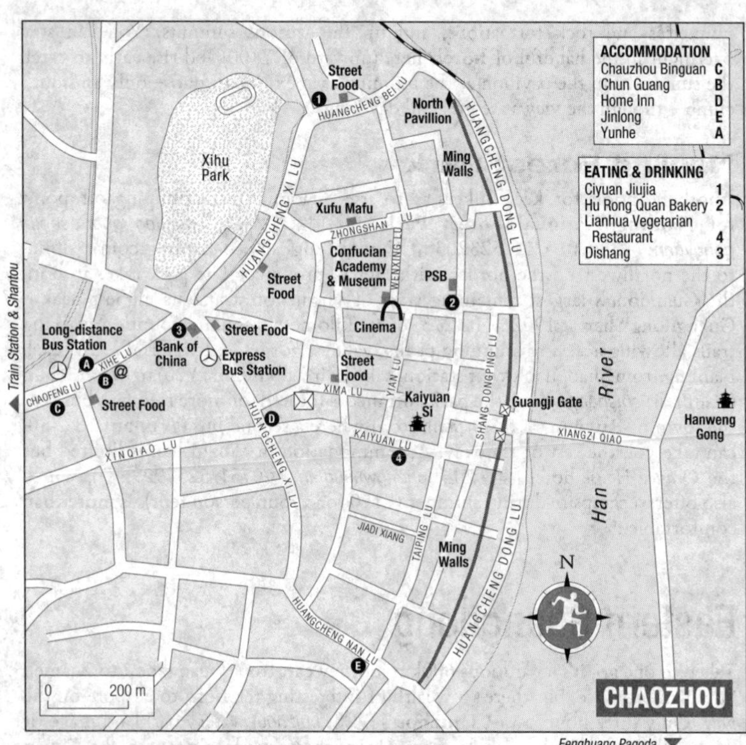

100,000 slaughtered citizens formed several fair-sized hills. The town managed to recover somehow, but was brought down again in the nineteenth century by famine and the Opium Wars, which culminated in Shantou's foundation. Half a million desperately impoverished locals fled Chaozhou and eastern Guangdong through the new port, many of them **emigrating** to European colonies all over Southeast Asia, where their descendants comprise a large proportion of Chinese communities in Thailand, Malaysia, Singapore and Indonesia. Humiliatingly, Shantou's rising importance saw Chaozhou placed under its administration until becoming an independent municipality in 1983, and real rivalry remains between the two.

For the visitor, Chaozhou is a splendid place. In addition to some of the most active and manageable street life in southern China, there are some fine historic **monuments** to tour, excellent shopping for local **handicrafts**, and a nostalgically dated small-town ambience to soak up. Chinese-speakers will find that Chaozhou's **language** is related to Fujian's *minnan* dialect, different from either Mandarin or Cantonese, though both of these are widely understood.

Arrival and information

On the western bank of the Han River, Chaozhou's **old town** comprises a 1500m-long oval enclosed by Huangcheng Lu, which, divided into north, south, east and west sections, follows the line of the **Ming-dynasty stone walls**. A stretch of these still faces the river on the centre's eastern side, while the city's modern fringe spreads west of Huangcheng Lu. The old town's main thoroughfares are Taiping Lu, orientated north–south, crossed by shorter Zhongshan Lu, Xima Lu and

Kaiyuan Lu, which all run east from Huangcheng Lu, through arched gates in the walls, and out to the river.

Chaozhou's **long-distance bus station** is just west of the centre on Chaofeng Lu; shuttles from Shantou wind up here too. The **train station** is about 5km northwest; on exiting, walk straight ahead out of the station and, taking your life in your hands, cross the main road to catch city buses #1 or #13 (daily 6.30am–8.30pm; ¥2), which run down to Huangcheng Lu. A taxi should cost around ¥14. **Motor- and cycle-rickshaws** – the only vehicles able to negotiate the old town's backstreets – are abundant, though once you are in town everything is within walking distance. There are branches of **Bank of China** (Mon–Fri 8.30–11.30am & 2–5pm) next to the Chaozhou Binguan and on the southern side of Xihe Lu at the junction with Huangcheng Xi Lu. There are also a few cheap **internet** places near here.

Moving on from Chaozhou, there are **buses** to Meizhou, Shantou, Guangzhou, Shenzhen and Fujian from the long-distance bus station, and **express coaches** east and west along the coastal road from a private station on Huangcheng Xi Lu. **Trains** (station ticket office open daily 6–11.30am & 1.30–5.30pm, or try the travel agency in the lobby of the *Yunhe Dajiudian*) run down to Shantou or back to Guangzhou via Meizhou and Huizhou. Shantou is quickest reached by bus, Meizhou by the train.

Accommodation

There are plenty of **places to stay** clustered around the bus station, with a number of good budget options.

Chaozhou Binguan (潮州宾馆, *cháozhōu bīnguǎn*) Opposite the long-distance bus station ⓣ0768/2333333, ⓦwww.chaozhouhotel.com. The smartest hotel in town, with large, clean rooms and many English-speaking staff. ❻

Chun Guang Dajiudian (春光大酒店, *chūnguāng dàjiǔdiàn*) Xihe Lu ⓣ0768/2681288. A clear rung or three down from the nearby *Chaozhou*, but if you're not after huge lobbies and room service, the rooms are perfectly adequate. ❸

Home Inn (如家酒店, *rújīajiǔdiàn*) Huangcheng Lu at junction with Kaiyuan Lu. ⓣ0768/2325666, ⓦwww.homeinns.com. Modern, good-value chain hotel; clean, comfortable, excellent service...but a little bit soulless. ❸–❹

Jinlong Binguan (金龙宾馆, *jīnlóng bīnguǎn*) Huangcheng Nan Lu ⓣ0768/2383888, ⓦwww.jinlong-hotel.com. Smart business hotel at the bottom of the old town: clean, comfortable and handily placed for reaching the town centre. ❺

Yunhe Dajiudian (云和大酒店, *yúnhé dàjiǔdiàn*) Across the road from the *Chun Guang* on Xihe Lu ⓣ0768/2136128. Don't be fooled by the Las Vegas light show on the outside: rooms here are far from five-star, but it is comfortable enough and has a certain kitsch charm. ❸

The Town

Chaozhou's **old quarter** may be past its heyday, but it remains a functioning part of town and the threat of the bulldozer is far less here than in almost any other city. In fact the biggest menace to the old city is over-enthusiastic renovation – pedestrianization and reconstruction on the main **Shang Dongping** shopping street to attract tourists is almost a bit too perfect, looking practically brand new despite the original buildings. A boom in souvenir stalls has started to rapidly displace the original traders, but turn down one of the anonymous alleys running towards Huangcheng Lu and you'll find an engaging warren of narrow streets packed with ageing but well-maintained colonial and traditional buildings. In the quieter residential back lanes, look for old wells, Ming-dynasty stone archways and antique family mansions, protected from the outside world by thick walls and heavy wooden doors, and guarded by mouldings of gods and good luck symbols. If you need a target, **Xufu Mafu** (许驸马府, *xǔfùmǎ fǔ*; daily 8.30am–5.30pm; ¥20) is a well-preserved mansion on an alley running parallel just behind Zhongshan Lu, 100m west of the junction with Wenxing Lu. Wander south down Wenxing

Lu and you'll come to both a Ming-style memorial archway and a former **Confucian academy** (海阳县儒学宫, *hǎiyángxiàn rúxuégōng*; daily 8am–5pm; ¥20) – now a newly renovated **museum**, full of prewar photos of town. Down in the south of town, **Jiadi Xiang**, a lane west off Taiping Lu, is an immaculate Qing period piece, its flagstones, ornamental porticos and murals (including a life-sized rendition of a lion-like *qilin* opposite no. 16) restored for the benefit of residents, not tourists. For a bit of space, head up to **Xihu Park** (西湖公园, *xīhú gōngyuán*; daily 8am–midnight; ¥8), just north of the old town across a "moat" on Huangcheng Xi Lu, where there's a dwarf pagoda, hillocks and some vegetated sections of the town walls.

Kaiyuan Si

If you bother with only one sight, however, make it **Kaiyuan Si** (开元寺, *kāiyuán sì*; daily 6am–6pm; ¥5) at the eastern end of Kaiyuan Lu. A lively Buddhist temple founded in 738 AD, it's still a magnet for pilgrims, though these days they are outnumbered by tourists and the inevitable beggars they attract. Three sets of solid wooden doors open onto courtyards planted with figs and red-flowered phoenix trees, where a pair of Tang-era **stone pillars**, topped with lotus buds, symbolically support the sky. The various halls are pleasantly proportioned, with brightly coloured lions, fish and dragons along the sweeping, low-tiled roof ridges. Off to the west side is a **Guanyin pavilion** with a dozen or more statues of this popular Bodhisattva in all her forms. Another room on the east side is full of bearded Taoist saints holding a *yin-yang* wheel, while the interior of the **main hall** boasts a very intricate vaulted wooden ceiling and huge brocade banners almost obscuring a golden Buddhist trinity.

The town walls and the east bank

About 250m east past the temple down Kaiyuan Lu you'll pass the 300-year-old **Matsu Miao** (妈祖庙, *māzǔmiào*) set below the **old town walls**. Seven metres high and almost as thick, these were only ever breached twice in Chaozhou's history, and more than 1500m still stand in good condition. The walls run from the **North Pavilion** (北亭, *běitíng*; daily 8.30am–5.30pm; ¥10), first constructed by the Song, past Guangji Gate and down as far as Huangcheng Nan Lu. There are access steps at several points along the wall, including above the main **Guangji Gate** (广济门, *guǎngjì mén*), where there's also a guard tower which houses an exhibition (daily 8.30am–5.30pm; ¥10) on the history of the adjacent **Xiangzi Qiao** (湘子桥, *xiāngzǐ qiáo*), a 500m-long bridge whose piles were sunk in the twelfth century. Newly rebuilt, the bridge reopened in 2009 after years of work and is an undeniably impressive sight (daily 10am–5pm; ¥50).

Shopping

Chaozhou is a great place to buy traditional arts and crafts. For something a bit unusual, the **hardware market**, just inside the Guangji Gate along Shangdong Ping Lu, has razor-sharp cleavers, kitchenware and old-style brass door rings. Temple trinkets, from banners to brass bells, ceramic statues – made at the nearby hamlet of Fengxi – and massive iron incense burners, are sold at numerous stores in the vicinity of Kaiyuan Si, also a good area to find ceramic tea sets and silk embroideries.

For those who enjoy haggling, an impromptu antiques market springs up most mornings along the pavement of Huangcheng Lu outside Xihu Park, and in the evenings a night market competes with motorcyclists and cars for road space along Kaiyuan Lu.

Eating, drinking and entertainment

Chaozhou's cooking style – light and sweet, with an emphasis on the freshness of ingredients – is becoming evermore popular in China, and thanks to emigrants from the region, it has long been unconsciously appreciated overseas. Seafood is a major feature, while local roast goose, flavoured here with sour plum – the use of fruit is a characteristic feature of the style, as is a garnish of fried garlic chips, a Southeast Asian influence – rivals a good Beijing duck. A good place to start looking is on Huangcheng Xi Lu, where a string of **restaurants** overlook Xihu Park, but wherever you are, and at pretty much any time of the day or night, you will never be far from **street stalls** doling out hotpots, noodles and other, less immediately recognizable dishes for just a few yuan.

Ciyuan Jiujia (瓷苑酒家, *cíyuàn jiǔjiā*) Huangcheng Xi Lu. Superb goose (around ¥100 for a whole bird), crispy-fried squid, steamed crab, fishball soup, fried spinach and a selection of dim sum.

Dishang Leisure Restaurant (迪尚餐厅, *díshàngcāntīng*) Xihe Lu, at junction with Huangcheng Lu. Westernish restaurant with an English menu featuring pizzas and steaks for ¥30 and up. Hardly an inspired option, but not bad for comfort food. For other, more familiar, Western food there is a trinity of well-known burger, chicken and pizza outlets at the junction of Huangcheng Lu and Kaiyuan Lu near the *Home Inn*.

Hu Rong Quan (胡荣泉, *húróng quán*) Taiping Lu. This bakery, specializing in mooncakes, makes the best spring rolls you'll ever eat, stuffed with spring onions, yellow beans, mushrooms and a little meat.

Lianhua Vegetarian Restaurant (莲华素食府, *liánhuāsùshífǔ*) Opposite Kaiyuan Si. Good meat-free restaurant, where a lunchtime six-dish set meal, including sweet-and-sour ribs and kebabs, will set you back about ¥20.

Meizhou and around

In the foothills of the Fujian border, 200km north of Chaozhou where rail lines from Guangzhou, Shantou and Fujian converge, **MEIZHOU** (梅州, *méizhōu*) is the ancestral home of a huge number of Overseas Chinese, whose descendants have begun to pump an enormous quantity of money back into the region. While not a pretty city, Meizhou is ethnically **Hakka** (see p.477) and is thus a fine place to pick up local background before heading off into their Fujian heartlands, just up the train line around Yongding.

Arrival and information

Meizhou lies on either side of the **Mei River** (梅江, *méijiāng*), with the older **town centre** on the north bank, connected to the newer south-bank districts by the **Meijiang** (梅江桥, *méijiāng qiáo*) and **Dongshan** (东山桥, *dōngshān qiáo*) bridges. The **long-distance bus station** is 1500m west of the centre on Meizhou Dadao, served by the #3 bus, while the **Yuemei bus station** (月梅汽车站, *yuèméi qìchēzhàn*) is a similar distance north at the terminus of the #4 bus route near the university; the **train station** lies 5km south of the river at the end of Binfang Dadao – catch a taxi (around ¥14) or city bus #4 (15min; ¥1.5) to the centre via the Dongshan Bridge.

The main **Bank of China** is south of the river on Meijiang Lu and there's another branch at the junction of Gongyuan Lu and Zhongyuan Lu (both Mon–Fri 8am–5pm). The **post office** is on Gingyuan Lu near the road off to the football stadium and there are a couple of **internet** places next door and over the road.

Moving on, there are regular buses to Dapu, Longyan and Xiamen in the east, and everywhere west back to Guangzhou and Shenzhen. Where you've a choice, trains are generally faster, though Fujian-bound services (to Yongding, Longyan, Xiamen and Fuzhou) are surprisingly infrequent. To save trekking out to the station, there is an in-town **ticket office** north of the river on Jinlilai Dajie.

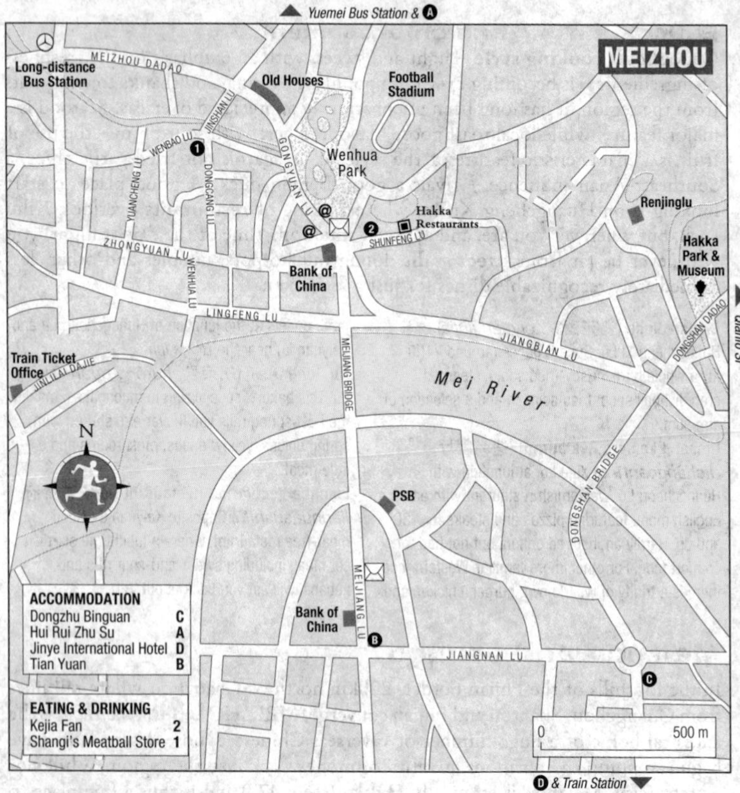

Accommodation

Places to stay are distributed on both sides of the river and are of varying quality. The majority of the newer, more modern hotels lie to the south.

Dongzhu Binguan 4 Binfang Dadao ⓣ0753/2181288. Smart new en-suite rooms just south of the river. ❸

Hui Rui Zhu Su (辉瑞住宿, *huīruì zhùsù*) Across the street from the Yuemei bus station, on Huanshi Bei Lu ⓣ0753/2356010. Cheap and basic, but clean. Intermittent hot water. ❷

Jinye International Hotel (金叶国际大酒店, *jīnyègúojìdàjĭudiàn*) 30 Binfang Dadao ⓣ0753/2355700, ⓦwww.mzjyhotel.com. With top-notch rooms, a pool, gym, spa and even a tennis court on the roof, this international business-standard hotel is excellent value if you fancy a night of luxury. ❻

Tian Yuan Dajiudian (田园大酒店, *tiányuán dàjiŭdiàn*) Meijiang Lu ⓣ0753/2163888, ⓦwww.2163888.com. Plush and modern affair, reliably comfortable and reasonably priced. ❹

The Town and around

Meizhou is a lightly industrial town, producing handbags and clothing, surrounded by hills and set in the fertile bowl of a prehistoric lake bed through which flows the convoluted **Mei River**. The scruffy centre is a two-square-kilometre spread on the north bank, connected to the neat, newer southern suburbs by the Meijiang and Dongshan bridges. As in Chaozhou, almost everything is within walking distance or the range of cycle-rickshaws.

Meizhou's social focus is **Wenhua Park** (文化公园, *wénhuà gōngyuán*) and the open square at the junction of various main roads immediately north of the Meijiang Bridge. The colonial-style shopfronts on Lingfeng Lu, which runs west along the riverfront, and the ageing alleys between here and Jinshan Lu are worth a wander, but with a succession of poorly built edifices dating from earlier this millennium standing derelict, and the buildings with real heritage crumbling even faster, it's clear the commercial balance within the town is shifting south of the river. But the park is pleasant enough, the university up on the hill ensures plenty of youthful vigour remains up north and, at night, older houses in nearby streets look very atmospheric, lit by tapers and red paper lanterns.

For local culture, head northeast off the square up Shunfeng Lu, and then follow the lanes and Chinese signs five minutes east to some algae-covered ponds outside **Renjinglu** (人境庐, *rénjìng lú*; daily 8am–5.30pm; ¥5), former home of Meizhou's nineteenth-century poet and diplomat, **Huang Zunxian**. You may have to knock on the door to get them to open up. It is the most ornate of several buildings around the ponds, the others being classically austere **Hakka town houses**, with high central gateways and square-sided walls and windows.

The Hakka theme continues just east of here at the impressive **Hakka Museum** (客家博物馆, *kèjīabówùgǔan*). An imposing modern building houses the museum, rubbing up against a couple of large, square-walled Hakka town houses, all in the pleasant environs of a well-manicured park. Despite a propensity to characterize the Hakka people as happy-go-lucky ethnics filling the air with their traditional jolly songs while they toil peacefully in the fields, the museum has some fascinating exhibits and insights (head upstairs for the more interesting displays), almost all with English captions. It's an excellent grounding if you plan to venture further into Hakka territory in the hills to the east.

Qianfo Si

A twenty-minute walk from here, **Qianfo Si** (千佛寺, *qiānfó sì*; Thousand Buddha Temple; ¥5) overlooks Meizhou 1km east of the Meijiang Bridge. Follow Dongshan Dadao north past the museum for about 200m, take the first right onto a new main road and then left up the hill as the road bends right – use the pagoda on the hill as a beacon to guide you in. There's a vegetarian restaurant among the group of buildings at the temple gates (see below) and another veggie teahouse serving snacks a bit further along. Above on the hill, the original temple and pagoda were demolished in 1995 in order to be totally rebuilt with expatriate funding and an attention to detail that has to be seen to be believed. The stonework is particularly accomplished, the temple pillars carved in deep relief with heroes and coiling dragons, while the base of the pagoda has finely executed scenes from Buddha's life.

Lingguang Si

One good day-trip from Meizhou is to head 50km east to **Yinna Shan** (阴那山, *yīnnà shān*), sanctified by the elderly temple of **Lingguang Si** (灵光寺, *língguāng sì*), founded in 861, though the present buildings are restored Qing. There are two 1000-year-old trees either side of the gate (a third died 300 years ago) and an extremely unusual wooden spiral ceiling in the main hall, the only other example being in a temple on Wudang Shan in Hubei province.

The temple is easily reached by direct bus (1hr; ¥12) from the Yuemei bus station. It's most pleasant in the morning, so try to get an early start and be sure to check when the last bus is returning.

Eating and drinking

The vegetarian restaurant at **Qianfo Si** serves outstanding meals daily at noon, but is strict on its timekeeping. The teahouse, also vegetarian, will serve at any time but is limited to meatless hot dogs and noodles. In town, carnivores can try the **Hakka specialities** sold at the smart *Kejia Fan* (客家饭, *kèjiā fàn*) and numerous family-run restaurants east of the square on Shunfeng Lu – juicy salt-baked chicken, wrapped in greaseproof paper (around ¥40 for a whole bird); little doughy rissoles made with shredded cabbage; and quick-fried cubes of bean curd, stuffed with pork and served in a gluey, rich sauce. For a take-away, hunt down Shangji's Meatball Store (尚记肉丸店, *shàngjì ròuwándiàn*) on Wenbao Lu in the western backstreets. **Hakka wine** is pretty nice by Chinese standards, similar to a sweet sherry and often served warm with ginger – most places to eat can provide a bottle. Meizhou's major speciality is **tea**, which grows in the surrounding hills, and alongside the standard Pu'ers and Tie Guanyins, the town has its very own **Meizhou Lu Cha** (梅州绿茶, *méizhōu lǜ chá*), of which the denizens are particularly proud.

Dapu and beyond

The best place to learn more about the Hakka and their extraordinary ancestral buildings is in the hills north and east of Meizhou. The small, dishevelled town of **Dapu** (大埔, *dàpǔ*), two hours and 100km east, **Longnan** to the north in Jianxi and, notably, **Zhencheng Lou** near **Yongding** in Fujian (p.499) to the east, are all worth a visit, with enormous mud-brick fortresses which have to be seen to be believed.

Yongding and Dapu can both be reached in a couple of hours or so on buses from Meizhou's Yuemai bus station, while for Longnan your best bet is to catch a train to Longchuan, just east of Meizhou, from where you'll be able to get a direct connection north.

Western Guangdong

While it's not an unpleasant area, there's very little to delay your passage across **western Guangdong** on the way to Guangxi or Hainan Island. Buses cover both routes quickly, but the rail line is the most convenient way to get to **Haikou**, although with only three services daily you may find yourself taking a bus to **Hai'an** (海安, *hǎi'ān*), from where there are regular ferries to Hainan. Either way, consider stopping off for a day or two at scenic **Zhaoqing** (肇庆, *zhàoqìng*), a local tourist attraction for more than a thousand years.

Zhaoqing and Dinghu Shan

Road, rail and river converge 110km west of Guangzhou at **ZHAOQING** (肇庆, *zhàoqìng*), a smart, modern city founded as a Qin garrison town to plug a gap in the line of a low mountain range. The first Europeans settled here as early as the sixteenth century, when the Jesuit priest **Matteo Ricci** spent six years in Zhaoqing using Taoist and Buddhist parallels to make his Christian teachings palatable. Emperor Wanli eventually invited Ricci to Beijing, where he died in 1610, having published numerous religious tracts. Since the tenth century, however, the Chinese have known Zhaoqing for the limestone hills comprising the adjacent **Qixing Yan Park** (七星岩公园, *qīxīngyán gōngyuán*), the Seven Star Crags. Swathed in mists and surrounded by lakes, they lack the scale of Guilin's peaks, but make for an enjoyable wander, as do the surprisingly thick forests at **Dinghu Shan** (鼎湖山, *dǐnghú shān*), just a short local bus ride away from town.

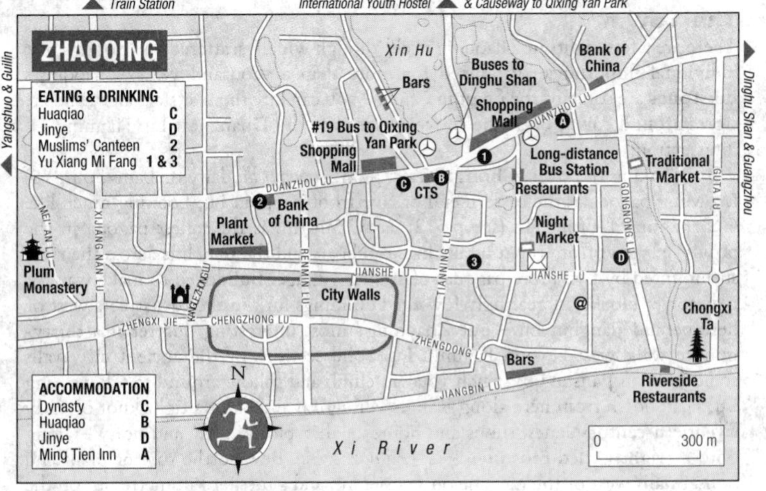

Arrival and information

Set on the north bank of the Xi, Zhaoqing is squashed between the river and the northerly lakes bordering Qixing Yan Park. Jianshe Lu and Duanzhou Lu run right across town east to west in numbered sections, crossed by **Tianning Lu**, which is oriented north–south between Qixing Yan Park's boundaries and the river. Zhaoqing's **train station** lies 5km away to the northwest – the #1 bus from outside the station will take you into town or a taxi will set you back about ¥12; the **long-distance bus station** is on Duanzhou Lu, 200m east of the northern end of Tianning Lu. **Taxis** can be hailed everywhere and buses ply the main routes but are unnecessary in the centre; Zhaoqing is somewhere to get about on foot. The main **Bank of China** is across the road 500m east (Mon–Fri 9am–noon & 2.30–5pm), and there's a **post office** (daily 8am–9pm) on Jianshe Lu.

Moving on, there are onward buses to Qingyuan, Shaoguan, Zhanjiang and just about everywhere between Guilin and Guangzhou – check which of Guangzhou's bus stations you're headed for before you board. Trains go to Nanning, Haikou (8hr), Guangzhou (2hr) and through to Shenzhen (3hr 30min) and Hong Kong (4hr). Staff at the **CTS** (daily 8am–9pm; ⓣ0758/2229908, ⓦwww.zqcts.com), just west of the *Huaqiao Dasha*, are helpful and some members speak English. You can buy train tickets upstairs and save yourself a journey out to the station.

Accommodation

The town has abundant **accommodation**, as does Dinghu Shan. Reasonable options in town include the *Huaqiao Dasha* (华侨大厦, *huáqiáo dàshà*; ⓣ0758/2232650, ⓦwww.zhaoqingtour.net.cn; ❹) on Duanzhou Lu; the excellent-value *Jinye Dasha* (金叶大厦, *jīnyè dàshà*; ⓣ0758/2221338; ❸), which also has a good restaurant, and the modern *Ming Tien Inn* (名典酒店, *míngdiǎn jiǔdiàn*; ⓣ0758/2293333, ⓦwww.mt-inn.com; ❹) on Duanzhou Lu east of the long-distance bus station, which has a passable café on the top floor serving Chinese and Western food. Probably Zhaoqing's most upmarket option, the central *Dynasty* (星湖大酒店, *xīnghú dà jiǔ diàn*; ⓣ0758/2238238, ⓦwww.dynastyhotel.cn; ❺) on Duanzhou Lu, has some rooms with a lake view out to the Seven Star Crags.

The Town

There are a few sights in Zhaoqing itself, though widely scattered and not of great individual importance. Produced for more than a thousand years, Zhaoqing's **inkstones** are some of the finest in China – you can buy them at stationery and art stores around town, or at the souvenir shops at the Duanzhou Lu/Tianning Lu intersection.

Overlooking the river, **Chongxi Ta** (崇禧塔, *chóngxī tǎ*; daily 8.30am–5pm; ¥5) is a Ming pagoda at the eastern end of riverfront Jiangbin Lu. Looking much like Guangzhou's Liurong Ta (see p.512), at 57.5m this is the tallest pagoda in the province; views from the top take in cargo boats and the red cliffs across the river surmounted by two more pagodas of similar vintage. Bulldozed to make way for new tower blocks, increasingly few aged buildings lurk in the backstreets west of here behind Jiangbin Lu – but Zhaoqing's most interesting quarter is a thirty-minute walk west beyond Renmin Lu. Solid sections of the ancient city walls stand here on Jianshe Lu, which you can climb and follow around to Chengzong Lu; head north from here along Kangle Zhong Lu and enter a tight knot of early twentieth-century lanes, shops and homes – all typically busy and noisy – along with a brightly tiled **mosque** (清真寺, *qīngzhēn sì*). Beyond the row of plant and bonsai stalls west of the mosque on Jianshe Lu, and a further kilometre out on the edge of town, the **Plum Monastery** (梅庵, *méiān*; daily 8.30am–5pm; ¥10), on Mei'an Lu, was established in 996 AD and has close associations with Huineng, founder of Chan Buddhism (see p.914). He is remembered in various paintings and sculptures here.

Arranged in the shape of the Big Dipper and said to be fallen stars, the seven peaks that make up **Qixing Yan Park** (七星岩公园, *qīxīngyán gōngyuán*; daily 7.30am–5.30pm; ¥60) rise 2km north of town on the far side of **Xing Hu** (星湖, *xīnghú*). To get here, go to the top end of Tianning Lu and cross over busy Duanzhou Lu to the paved area on the lakeshore, from where you can catch the #19 bus (15min; ¥1) along the **causeway** that continues north across Xin Hu. The crags are quite modest, named after objects they resemble – **Chanchu** (Toad), **Tianzhu** (Heavenly Pillar), **Shizhang** (Stone Hand). An interlocking network of arched bridges, pathways, graffiti-embellished caves and willows makes for a pleasantly romantic two-hour stroll.

Eating and drinking

There's a shortfall of **restaurants** along the main shopping street of Jianshe Lu, but explore off here and you'll find numerous places selling local *zongzi* (conical rice packets wrapped in a bamboo leaf), sandpots (stews served in earthenware pots) and light Cantonese meals. For something different try *Muslims' Canteen* (清真饭店, *qīngzhēn fàndiàn*) on Duanzhou Lu, which serves typical Hui food – lamb skewers, beef noodles, flat bread et al – at reasonable prices. There are a couple of branches of the Guangdong *Yu Xiang Mi Fang* (渔湘米坊, *yúxiāng mǐfāng*) chain, on Duanzhou Lu and Jianshe Lu, which have a good selection of cheap staples, dim sum and an English menu. A string of canteens near the night market at the north end of **Wenming Lu** (文明路, *wénmíng lù*) bustle every evening, but for something more refined check out the cluster of Cantonese restaurants with river views at the end of Gongnong Lu. A barrage of new shopping malls along the Southern shore of the lake are populated by Western favourites – *KFC*, *McDonald's* and *Pizza Hut* among them.

Besides the night market, there's little in the way of nightlife, but there are a couple of **bars** on the western edge of the lake and along the riverfront on Jiangbin Lu.

Dinghu Shan

Twenty kilometres east of Zhaoqing, the thickly forested mountains at **Dinghu Shan** (鼎湖山, *dǐnghú shān*) were declared China's first national park way back in 1956, have been incorporated into the UNESCO biosphere programme, and, it can seem, been made an obligatory school trip for every child in Guangdong. With well-formed paths giving access to a waterfall, temple and plenty of trees, the small area open to the public gets particularly crowded at the weekends, but at other times Dinghu Shan makes an excellent half-day out – particularly in summer, when the mountain is cooler than Zhaoqing. The **entry fee** (¥50) is a bit steep for what you get, but you could stay overnight to make the most of it – though rooms can be expensive: even the youth hostel charges ¥400 per room.

To reach Dinghu Shan, catch public bus #21 from the bottom end of Xin Hu (¥4); it takes thirty minutes and drops you off about 1km south of the reserve at Dinghu township, from where you can continue on foot or hire a motor-rickshaw uphill to the gates. A further kilometre brings you to a knot of restaurants and souvenir shops, where there's an *International Youth Hostel* (鼎湖山国际青年旅馆, *dǐnghúshān guójì qīngnián lǚguǎn*; Ⓣ0758/2621668; dorm beds ¥150, rooms ❻). Beyond here, the forest proper and walking track start, dividing either to follow a stream or to climb a flight of stairs to **Qingyun Si** (清云寺, *qīngyún sì*), a large temple with an expensive **vegetarian restaurant** open at lunchtime, and with restorations that have decked the exterior in awful green bathroom tiles while providing some accomplished statuary. The track along the stream takes you in ten minutes to a 30m-high **waterfall**, whose plunge pool has been excavated and turned into a swimming hole. A lesser-used track continues up the side of the falls and eventually up to a vehicle road, which you can follow across to the temple. It's a couple of hours' walk, but if you're not planning to stay the night be careful not to linger too long – the last bus back to Zhaoqing leaves at 5pm.

Zhanjiang and Hai'an

The only reason to make the long haul to **HAI'AN** (海安, *hǎi'ān*), 550km from Guangzhou at the province's southwestern tip, is to catch one of the regular ferries to **Hainan Island**. There are three direct trains from Guangzhou to Haikou each day via Zhaoqing; however, if you haven't managed to get one of these, or are travelling by bus, you may have to change at **ZHANJIANG** (湛江, *zhànjiāng*) en route to Hai'an; Zhanjiang's southern train station and bus station are next to each other on Jianshe Lu, and buses down to Hai'an take a little under three hours. From Hai'an's ramshackle bus station you can either walk (left out of the station and downhill) or take one of the free buses down to the ferry port. Ferries leave hourly, and it costs ¥30 for the ninety-minute journey.

Hainan Island

Rising out of the South China Sea between Guangdong and Vietnam, **HAINAN ISLAND** (海南岛, *hǎinándǎo*) marks the southernmost undisputed limit of Chinese authority, a 300km-broad spread of beaches, mountain scenery, history, myth and – most of all – the effects of exploitation. Today a province in its own right, Hainan was historically the "Tail of the Dragon", an enigmatic full stop to the Han empire and – in the Han Chinese mind – an area inhabited by unspeakably backward races, only surfacing into popular consciousness when it could be of use. Han settlements were established around the coast in 200 AD, but for millennia the island was only seen fit to be a place of exile. So complete was Hainan's isolation that, as recently as the 1930s, ethnic Li, who first settled here more than two thousand years ago, still lived a hunter-gatherer existence in the interior highlands.

Modern Hainan is no primitive paradise, however. After two years of naval bombardments, the island was occupied by the Japanese in 1939, and by the end of the war they had executed a full third of Hainan's male population in retaliation for raids on their forces by Chinese guerrillas. **Ecological decline** began in the 1950s during the Great Leap Forward, and escalated through the 1960s when large numbers of Red Guards were sent over from the mainland to "learn from the peasants" and became involved in the first large-scale **clearing of Hainan's forests** to plant cash crops. Successive governments have continued the process of stripping the island's natural resources and abandoning the inhabitants to fend for themselves, in an appalling example of **economic mismanagement**: while there are skyscrapers and modern factories around the cities, you'll also see country people so poor that they live in lean-tos made of mud and straw, which have to be rebuilt after each wet season. With the exception of ragged remnants clinging to the very tips of Hainan's mountains, rainforest has ceded to eroded plantations given over to experimentation with different crops – rubber, mango, coconuts and

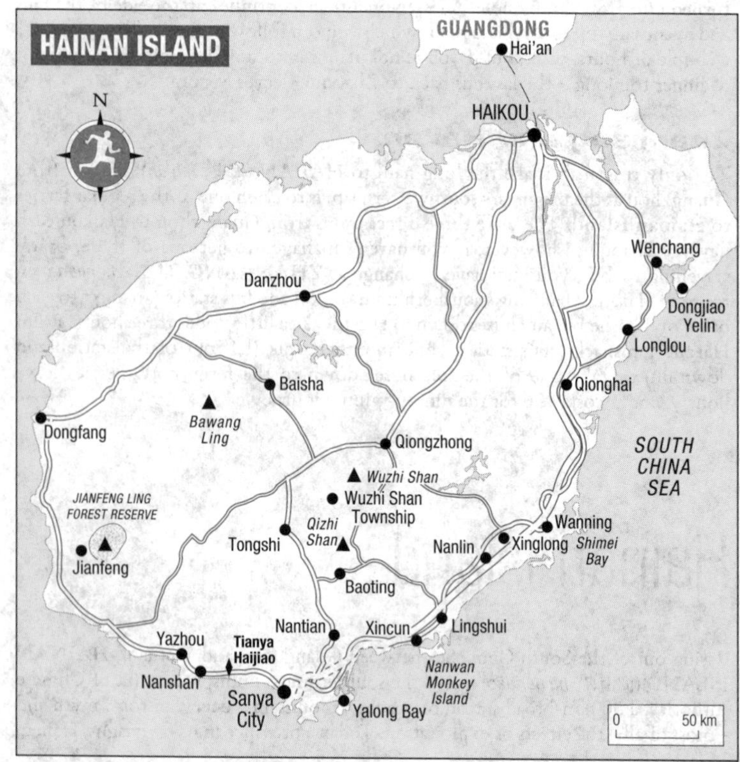

coffee – in the hope that a market will emerge. **Tourism** seems to be the sole reliable source of income, and everyone is desperate to be involved. Persistent marketing has made Hainan the place that all Chinese want to come for a holiday.

The most obvious reason to come is to flop down on the warm, sandy **beaches** near the southern city of **Sanya** (三亚, *sānyà*) – as a rest cure after months on the mainland, it's a very good one. Initially, there doesn't seem much more to get excited about. **Haikou** (海口, *hǎikǒu*), Hainan's capital, bears evidence of brief colonial occupation, but its primary importance is as a transit point, while Han towns along the **east coast** have only slightly more character and scenic appeal. Spend a little time and effort elsewhere, however, and things start to get more interesting: the highlands around the town of **Tongshi**, or **Wuzhi Shan Shi** (通什, *tōngshì* or 五指山市, *wǔzhǐ shān shì*), are the place to start looking for **Li culture**, and the mountainous southwest hides some forgotten **nature reserves**, where what's left of Hainan's indigenous flora and fauna hangs by a thread. There are even a handful of underwater sites off the southern coast, the only place in provincial China where those with the necessary qualifications can go **scuba diving**.

Hainan's extremely hot and humid **wet season** lasts from June to October. It's better to visit between December and April, when the climate is generally dry and tropically moderate, sunny days peaking around 25°C on the southern coast. **Getting to Hainan** is straightforward, with flights from all over the country to Haikou and Sanya, trains from Guangzhou and regular ferries from Guangzhou and Hai'an in Guangdong province and Beihai in Guangxi.

Once there, **getting around** is easy: Hainan's highways and roads are covered by a prolific quantity of local transport; high-speed buses link Haikou and Sanya in just three hours, while you can easily hop around the rest of the island by bus and minibus. Also note that, as a recognized tourist destination, Hainan, and Sanya in particular, is more expensive than the adjacent mainland – even Chinese tourists grumble about being constantly overcharged.

Haikou and the east coast

Haikou is Hainan's steamy capital, set at the north of the island and separated from Guangdong province by the 30km-wide Qiongzhou Channel. For most visitors, Haikou is little more than a transit stop en route to Sanya, but the city and nearby coastal towns are looking more and more to get their own piece of the tourist pie. If you can resist heading straight to Sanya, it's worthwhile spending a couple of days around here and hopping between towns along Hainan's **east coast** – home to some of the few surfable beaches in China. This is the part of Hainan longest under Han dominion, and it's a good way to get the feel of the island.

Haikou

Business centre, main port and first stop for newly arrived holidaymakers and hopeful migrants alike, **HAIKOU** (海口, *hǎikǒu*) has all the atmosphere of a typical Southeast Asian city. There's a smattering of French colonial architecture, a few parks and monuments, modern skyscrapers, broad streets choked with traffic and pedestrians, and the all-pervading spirit of commerce. An indication of the ethos driving Haikou is that nobody seems to be a local: officials, businessmen and tourists are all from the mainland, while Li, Miao and Hakka flock from southern Hainan to hawk trinkets, as do the Muslim Hui women selling betel nuts – all drawn by the opportunities that the city represents. More than anything, Haikou is a truly tropical city: humid, laidback, pleasantly shabby and complete with palm-lined streets, something particularly striking if you've just emerged from a miserable northern Chinese winter.

Arrival and information

Haikou's downtown area forms a compact block south of the waterfront Changti Dadao. The centre is marked by a busy circuit of wide one-way traffic flows and pedestrian overpasses surrounding Haikou Park, where much of the accommodation is located, with the most interesting shopping districts in the northerly old colonial quarter around Jiefang Lu and Bo'ai Bei Lu.

The **airport** is 25km southeast of town; shuttle buses run every thirty minutes (¥15) to (and from) the CAAC/China Southern office on Haixiu Dong Lu. A taxi will take around thirty minutes to the town centre and costs around ¥50; it's best to agree a price before you set off. The **New Port** is north of Changti Dadao on Xingang Lu, where most ferries pull in; those from Beihai in Guangxi sometimes use the **Xiuying Wharf** (秀英港, *xiùyīng gǎng*), 5km farther west along Binhai Dadao – you can take bus #6 to the centre from either. Buses from the mainland and Sanya wind up at the new **South Bus Station** on Longkun Lu, ¥20 in a taxi from the centre. The **train station** currently has three services a day to Guangzhou – buses #28 and #40 head to the centre from here, with the trip taking about an hour. Taxis are a little faster and cost around ¥60.

There's a general lack of tourist **information** in Haikou, with most agencies only geared to getting you to Sanya as fast as possible. If you plan to explore

Moving on from Haikou

Flying is the easiest way out of Haikou, with the city connected to Sanya and mainland locations between Harbin, Kunming and Hong Kong. Tickets for all airlines can be reserved at agents (see "Listings", p.558) or one of the numerous China Southern branches – the main office is in the CAAC (daily 8am–9.30pm; ⓣ0898/66525581), next to the *Civil Aviation* hotel on Haixiu Dong Lu.

Ferries shuttle between Haikou's New Port (新港, xīngǎng) and Hai'an (¥30; 90min) at Guangdong's southernmost tip, where buses meet ferries for the 150km run to Zhanjiang. There are also daily ferries from the New Port for Beihai (6pm; 12hr; cabins ¥120–360/person, depending on the number of berths) and a service to Guangzhou leaves three times a week (Tues, Thurs & Sat; 3.30pm; 19hr; ¥180–450) The ticket office (ⓣ0898/66243762) is open daily from 9am to 4pm, though most hotels and travel agencies in town will be able to make bookings a day ahead. There's usually no trouble getting a seat, though rough seas can suspend services.

The practicalities of getting out by **bus** are simple. The new **South Bus Station** handles **mainland traffic** – you'll find standard and luxury buses to destinations as far afield as Chongqing, Nanning, Jiujiang, Shenzhen and Guangzhou, and tickets include ferry costs – as well as coaches to **Sanya** (¥78; 3hr 30min), Tongshi (¥68; 4hr) and buses to Wenchang (¥18; 1hr). Smaller destinations on the east and west coasts are served by the East and West bus stations respectively – the East Station is 2km down Haifu Dadao, while the West Station lies way out on Haixiu Xi Lu.

The **railway link** from Sanya to Guangzhou – which sees the entire train go onto a boat – also calls in at Haikou, leaving eastward three times a day at 4am, 8.40pm and 10.50pm and taking eleven hours; you can book tickets for this, and mainland trains departing from Zhanjiang, at the CTS office on Haixiu Lu (Mon–Sat 9am–5.30pm) or at another branch in the *Hainan Overseas Chinese Hotel* (same hours; ⓣ0898/66778455). For those heading south to Sanya, trains from Haikou take 3hr 30min and leave at 2am, 9am and 6.40pm – a new **high-speed rail link** is due to open in 2011, cutting the journey time to just ninety minutes.

Hainan's backwaters, pick up a **map** of the island from hawkers or kiosks (¥7); some include spreads of Haikou, Sanya and Tongshi, along with detailed road maps of the island including even minor sights marked in English.

City transport

Haikou's **city bus service** is comprehensive and cheap, while **taxis** are so absurdly plentiful that you have only to pause on the street for one to pull up instantly – you will be expected to negotiate prices beforehand and, if done well, you may pay only two-thirds of the meter rate (check first with your hotel how much trips should cost).

Accommodation

There's plenty of central **accommodation** in Haikou, much of it conveniently located around Haikou Park. Room rates are always flexible; in summer, ensure that air conditioning is part of the bargain. Most hotels handle transport bookings and have their own restaurants.

7 Days Inn (7天连锁酒店, *qītiān liánsuǒjiǔdiàn*) 31 Wuzhishan Lu ⓣ0898/36355288, ⓦwww.7daysinn.cn. Clean, modern chain hotel, though there are plenty of other more interesting options in the same price range. ④

Banana Hostel (巴那那青年旅舍, *bānànà qīngnián lǚshè*) On east side of Renmin Ave, just north of the junction with Sandong Lu, in the north of town ⓣ0898/66286780, ⓦwww.haikouhostel.com. This IYHA establishment is the only accommodation in town geared towards budget travellers. Spacious, clean rooms are supplemented with a lively bar serving cold beer and basic food, as well as internet access, regular barbecues and staff who are an absolute mine of information on excursions and travel services. Hidden down an alley, it's slightly hard to find – the best bet is to call beforehand and someone will come out to meet you. Dorm beds ¥45, rooms ❸

Civil Aviation (海南民航宾馆, *hǎinán mínháng bīnguǎn*) Haixiu Dong Lu ⓣ0898/66506888. Smart hotel with light and airy rooms, very central and not bad value. ❹

Haikou Binguan (海口宾馆, *hǎikǒu bīnguǎn*) 4 Haifu Ave ⓣ0898/65351234, ⓦwww.haikouhotel.com.cn. Formerly Haikou's most prestigious accommodation, now revamped with a more contemporary feel. Comfortable rooms and friendly staff. ❺

Haikou Downtown (海口东堂, *hǎikǒu dōngtáng*) 38 Datong Lu ⓣ0898/66796999, ⓦwww.hnahotel.com. Luxury, international-standard business affair with all the trimmings. ❼

Hainan Overseas Chinese Hotel (海南华侨大厦, *hǎinánhúaqíaodàshà*) 17 Datong Lu ⓣ0898/66773288. A three-star business centre built in the early 1990s and beginning to look a bit threadbare, but comfortable enough and offering good discounts. ❹

Overseas (海外酒店, *hǎiwài jiǔdiàn*) 11 Wuzhishan Lu ⓣ0898/65235999, ⓦwww.jzoverseashotel.com. Fairly decent three-star venture, with tubs in each room taking advantage of a hot spring located 800m below the hotel. ❹

Songtao (松涛大厦, *sōngtāo dàshà*) 5 Wuzhishan Lu ⓣ0898/66729116, ⓕ66729006. One of Haikou's best deals, with cheap, spacious tiled rooms and slightly more expensive newly renovated options. ❸

The City

The **old quarter**, boxed in by Bo'ai Bei Lu, Datong Lu and pedestrianized Deshengsha Lu, is the best area to stroll through, with its grid of restored colonial architecture housing stores and businesses. **Jiefang Lu** and **Xinhua Lu** are the main streets here, especially lively in the evening when they're well lit and bursting with people out shopping, eating and socializing; there's also a busy **market** west of Xinhua. Otherwise, **Haikou Park** (海口公园, *hǎikǒu gōngyuán*) and its lake are small but quite pleasant, particularly in the early morning when the park comes to life with martial-art sessions, dancing and games of badminton.

Haikou has three formal sights, any of which will fill you in on Hainan's position in Han Chinese history, along with a beach to laze on.

Wugong Ci

Southeast of the centre along Haifu Lu, **Wugong Ci** (五公祠, *wǔgōng cí*; Five Officials' Memorial Temple; daily 8am–6pm; ¥20; bus #1 or minibus #217 down Haifu Lu) is a brightly decorated complex built in 1889 to honour Li Deyu, Li Gang, Li Guang, Hu Chuan and Zhao Ding, Tang men of letters who were banished here after criticizing their government. Another hall in the grounds commemorates Hainan's most famous exile, the poet **Su Dongpo**, who lived in the island's northwest between 1097 and 1100 and died on his way back to the imperial court the following year.

Xiuying Battery

About 5km west of the centre, **Xiuying Battery** (秀英古炮台, *xiùyīng gǔpàotái*) was built after the Chinese had apparently beaten off an attempted invasion by the French in the latter part of the nineteenth century, part of a string of coastal defences designed to deter foreign incursions along south China's coastline. Its basalt block walls conceal six 20cm naval cannons set in concrete bunkers, all connected by subterranean passageways. However, at the time of writing, despite featuring prominently on road signs, the battery was shut with no word on when, or if, the site would be re-opening to the public. To get there, catch minibus #32 from the south gate of Haikou Park.

Hai Rui Mu

A kilometre or so southwest of Xiuying on Qiuhai Avenue, a park and stone sculptures of lions surround **Hai Rui Mu**, tomb of the virtuous Ming-dynasty official Hai Rui (海瑞墓, *hǎiruì mù*; daily 8am–6pm; ¥10) – buses #28 and #40 from Haixiu Dong Lu stop near the junction of West Haixiu Lu and Qiuhai Avenue. Hai Rui's honesty, which earned him exile during his lifetime, caused a furore in the 1960s when historian **Wu Han** wrote a play called *The Dismissal of Hai Rui*, a parody of events surrounding the treatment of Marshal Peng Dehui, who had criticized Mao's Great Leap Forward. The play's suppression and the subsequent arrest of Wu Han, who happened to be a friend of Deng Xiaoping, are generally considered to be the opening events of the Cultural Revolution.

Holiday Beach

If all that is a bit too serious for you, Haikou boasts its own stretch of golden sand in the form of 6km-long **Holiday Beach** (假日海滩, *jiàrìhǎitān*) to the west of the city. While a good place to laze, it also has plenty of activities with windsurfers, kayaks and jet skis all for hire. It can get a bit crowded close to town, but keep heading west and the crowds thin out. To get here, catch bus #37 heading west from the clock tower on Changti Dadao near Renmin Dadao bridge, north of the town centre. A taxi will cost around ¥35.

Eating

Perhaps because Haikou is essentially a mainland Chinese colony, **food** here is not as exotic as you'd hope. The ingredients on display at market stalls are promising: green, unhusked coconuts (sold as a drink, but seldom used in cooking); thick fish steaks, mussels, eels, crab and prawns; exotic fruits; and, everywhere, piles of seasonal green vegetables. But Hainan's most famous dishes – Wenchang "white-cut" chicken, steamed duck and glutinous rice, and Dongshan mutton – are nothing extraordinary, though tasty.

The highest concentration of **restaurants** is in the old quarter along Jiefang Lu, where grilled chicken wings, kebabs and other snacks proliferate. A couple of palm-shaded cafés on the northern side of Haikou Park serve light snacks, fruit platters and endless teapots and make a good place to watch the world go by.

Coffee Time Jiefang Lu. Chinese interpretation of a Western restaurant. Prices are reasonable, with mains including pizza and steak going for ¥20–50, and the menu also boasts a vast array of teas, fresh juices and cocktails. Open until 1am.

Da Hong Bin Long Cha Dian (大红宾笼茶店, *dàhóngbīnlóngchádiàn*) Just up the road and round the corner from *Hunan Rent*. Come 3.30pm this dim sum place is heaving. Don't worry about the menu, just point at a selection of the deep-fried pastries, get yourself a pot of tea and soak up the atmosphere.

Ganghai Canting (港海餐厅, *gǎnghǎi cāntīng*) Jiefang Lu. Locals-oriented teahouse with tiled floor, dated wooden furniture and great dim sum.

Haikou Binguan (海口宾馆, *hǎikǒubīngǔan*) 4 Daying Houlu. With both Western and Chinese restaurants, this hotel is a good bet for local favourites, including steamed chicken in coconut milk and seafood rolls in coconut sauce. Not too expensive either – a whole chicken or duck costs around ¥60, with other dishes starting at ¥20.

Hainan Restaurant (琼菜坊, *qióngcàifāng*) Datong Lu, close to the *Hainan Overseas Chinese Hotel*. Does exactly what it says on the tin – lots of Hainan speciality foods and heavy on the seafood. No English menu but plenty of pictures to point at. Mains ¥30–50.

Hunan Ren (湖南人, *hù'nán ren*) Nanbao Lu. Smart, ethnic-looking place serving up traditional Hunan dishes at reasonable prices. One of the better options in the town centre.

Lao Xinjiang Fandian (老新疆饭店, *lǎoxīnjīangfàndiàn*) Wuzhishan Lu. Muslim restaurant selling hearty Uyghur fare – beef noodles, mutton and heavily seasoned lamb and chicken kebabs.

Tong Shan Tang Vegetarian (同善堂全素餐厅, *tóngshàntāng quánsùcāntīng*) 33 Haidian Sandong Lu, on north side of the road, 200m east of the junction with Heping Lu. This Buddhist gem has fake-meat versions of almost any Chinese dish you care to think of. A little hard to find, but worth the effort – look for the Buddhas in the window.

Listings

Banks and exchange There are numerous branches of the Bank of China, including opposite the *Huaqiao* and next to the *Haikou Downtown* on Datong Lu (Mon–Sat 8.30am–5.30pm).
Books The big Xinhua bookstore on Jiefang Lu, east of the post office, has a limited range of English classics on the third floor.
Hospital Hainan Provincial People's Hospital, Longhua Lu ⓣ0898/6225933.
Internet There's a net bar on the second floor of the shopping centre at the junction of Jichang Dong Lu and Daying Lu, near the *Overseas*.
Mail and telephones The main post office, with parcel post service, is on Jiefang Lu (24hr), and there are IDD phone places throughout the city.
PSB The Foreign Affairs Department is on Changti Dadao, just west of the junction with Longhua Lu.
Shopping Department stores along Haixiu Dong Lu sell indigenous products such as coconut coffee, coconut powder, coconut wafers, coconut tea, palm sugar and betel nut; clothing sections also stock Hainan shirts, which differ from their Hawaiian counterparts in their use of dragons instead of palm trees on bright backgrounds. Whole shark skins – like sandpaper – dried jellyfish and other maritime curiosities in the shops along Jiefang Lu are also worth a look.
Travel agents China Travel Air Service, next to the *Hainan Overseas Chinese Hotel* (ⓣ0898/66781735), are agents for a vast array of domestic and international carriers, including China Southern, Dragonair, Hainan Air, Cathay Pacific, Japan Airlines, Malaysia Airlines and Singapore Airlines.

The east coast

Most east-coast communities comprise small settlements of ethnic subgroups such as the Hakka, who were shuffled off the mainland by various turmoils, or returning Overseas Chinese deliberately settled here by the government, and many live by fishing, farming cash crops or pearl cultivation. Unless you plan to bask on the beaches at **Dongjiao Yelin** (东郊椰林, *dōngjiāo yélín*) and **Longlou** (龙楼, *lónglóu*), nowhere here takes more than half a day to look round, with the pick of the bunch being **Lingshui** (陵水, *língshuǐ*), a hamlet with a long history, unexpected Communist connections and a nearby wildlife reserve. Everywhere has **accommodation** (often near the bus stations) and places to eat, and **minibuses** are the best way to get around, with shuttle services running between towns from sunrise until after dark. Bear in mind that there are **no banks** capable of foreign currency transactions along the way, so carry enough cash to last until Sanya.

Wenchang, Dongjiao Yelin and Longlou

WENCHANG (文昌, *wénchāng*), a decent-sized county town 70km southeast of Haikou, is known to the Chinese as the ancestral home of the sisters **Song Qingling** and **Song Meiling**, wives to Sun Yatsen and Chiang Kai-shek respectively. Built up as a commercial centre in the nineteenth century by the French, it has now rather gone to seed, but you'll need to pass through to reach the beaches at **DONGJIAO YELIN** (东郊椰林, *dōngjiāo yēlín*), Hainan's first **coconut plantation**, and the marginally less developed **LONGLOU** (龙楼, *lónglóu*). Growing haphazardly, both are relaxing places to laze for a while, the palms forming a perfect backdrop to acres of white sands, and can be reached by direct bus from Wenchang. The #13 bus to Dongjiao (1hr; ¥7.5) terminates directly outside the *Prima Resort* (百莱玛度假村, *bǎiláimǎ dùjiàcūn*; ⓣ0898/6358222, ⓦwww.hainanprimaresort.com; ❹–❾), which has a range of comfortable wooden beachside bungalows and a few shabbier, cheaper rooms.

On arrival in Longlou (bus #9; 45min; ¥7), the best bet is to jump on a motor-taxi direct to the nearby **Qishuiwan beach** – the ten-minute journey should set you back about ¥5. Longlou's sole **hotel**, the *Longlou Jiudian* (龙楼酒店, *lónglóu jiǔdiàn*; ❷), has a rack rate of ¥150 that can be knocked down to less than half that. Next door is a basic but delicious and reasonably priced **seafood restaurant**.

Bo'ao, Wanning and Shimei Bay

BO'AO (博鳌, *bóaó*), about 50km south of Wenchang, is famous for an Asian business forum which is held here every year, but don't be fooled into thinking of this as any kind of commercial centre; beyond the developed centre things get rural very quickly. The beach can be reached on foot and is safe for swimming – just avoid the currents around the mouths of three rivers that arrive into the sea, which can be dangerous. To get here from Wenchang, catch a bus to Qionghai (琼海, *qiónghǎi*) and then change to city bus #2 to Bo'ao. For **accommodation** try the *Bo'ao Inn B&B* (博鳌老外家, *bóaólǎowàijīa*; Ⓣ13876271007, Ⓦwww.hainan-letsgo.com; ❻) on Wanghai Lu, owned and run by a hospitable American/Chinese couple.

Wanning (万宁, *wànníng*) is the next major town along the coast; rather than waste time here, continue south a few extra kilometres to **Shimei Bay** (石梅湾, *shíměi wān*). Exposed to waves from the Pacific, the beach here is popular with Hainan's embryonic surfing community and several outifts run trips from Sanya (for one of the better ones, try Ⓦwww.surfinghainan.com or call the owner, Brendon, on Ⓣ13519800103). Even if you're not catching waves, this is an idyllic spot where new hotels are only just getting a foothold.

Lingshui

An hour south of Shimei Bay, **LINGSHUI** (陵水, *língshuǐ*) has been around for a long time. They were forging iron tools and making pottery here as far back as the Han dynasty, while uncovered silver tomb ornaments point to the town being an important commercial centre by the time of the Ming dynasty. The town also played its part in modern history when, having shifted south from Qionghai, China's **first Communist government** convened here in 1928; it was still functioning when the Japanese stormed Hainan in February 1939, whereupon its members retreated into the hills to wage guerrilla war on the invaders with the help of the local Li population (for more on the Li, see the box on p.561). The Communists never forgot this, and once in power granted the district nominal self-rule as **Lingshui Li Autonomous County**.

Today, Lingshui's dozen or so narrow streets are set back off the highway where it bends sharply past town near the bus station. Around town you'll see remains of a Qing-dynasty monastery, the interior still decorated with original frescoes; a Communist Museum in another building of similar vintage (there's a cannon outside); and several fifty-year-old shops with what look like their original fittings. Wander off to Lingshui's fringes and you could be stepping back a hundred years, with lanes twisting into the countryside between walls surrounding family compounds, houses sporting decorative columns topped with lotus-bud motifs and courtyards thickly planted with slender areca palms, often with conical buckets strapped around the trunks. These catch falling betel nuts (*binlang*), a crop cultivated as a stimulant by the Li since at least Ming times. Women are the biggest users, but just about everyone in Lingshui seems to have stained their lips and teeth from chewing slices of the palm seed wrapped inside a heart-shaped pepper vine leaf.

Practicalities

Lingshui's main **bus station**, on a bend in the highway, is where most minibuses from Wanning drop off and where Sanya- and Haikou-bound vehicles depart. Coming from the south, you might end up at the minibus depot about 1km down the road on the Sanya side of town. For **accommodation**, try the rooms at the *Puli Binguan* (普利宾馆, *pǔlì bīnguǎn*; ⓣ0898/83325888; ❸) on the highway, five minutes north of the bus station, or smarter doubles at the nearby *Yiyuan Binguan* (怡园宾馆, *yíyuán bīnguǎn*; ⓣ0898/83311000; ❸), just off the main road. The best places to **eat** are around here too, with numerous bustling teahouses along the highway and backstreets.

Sanya and the southern coast

Across the island from Haikou on Hainan's central southern coast – some 320km direct down the expressway – **SANYA** (三亚, *sānyà*) is, sooner or later, the destination of every visitor to the island. Though relics at the westerly town of **Yazhou** prove that the area has been settled for close on a thousand years, Sanya City itself is entirely modern, and the old scruffy fishing port is transforming into a concrete high-rise holiday resort. Sanya is also the site of a major **naval base** and, according to US reports, a new James Bond-sounding underground nuclear submarine base, both maintained for monitoring events (and staking China's claims) in the South China Sea and beyond. Sanya came to international attention in 2001, when a **US spyplane** made a forced landing here after colliding with a Chinese fighter jet and, less weightily, has also twice hosted the Miss World contest. Generally, though, what pulls in the people – a huge number of whom are Russian – are Sanya's surrounding sights, especially **Dadonghai beach** (大东海, *dàdōng hǎi*). The Chinese also flock to legendary landmarks atop the **Luhuitou Peninsula** (鹿回头, *lùhuítóu*), a huge granite headland rising immediately south of the city, and west at the scenic spot of **Tianya Haijiao** (天涯海角, *tiānyá hǎijiǎo*), while foreigners generally find beach life suffices.

Farther afield, the coastal arc between Sanya and the western industrial port of **Dongfang** (东方, *dōngfāng*) sees few visitors. While Dongfang itself doesn't justify a trip, it's emphatically worth getting as far as **Jianfeng Ling** (尖峰岭, *jiānfēnglǐng*), the most accessible surviving fragment of Hainan's indigenous mountain **rainforest**. If this doesn't appeal, you can take advantage of plentiful transport north from Sanya to the Li stronghold of Tongshi, and on into the central highlands.

It must be said that though the beaches here are very pleasant, a trip to Sanya can also involve a few irritations, especially for those on a budget: at peak times – late June, July, August and Chinese New Year – rooms can be poor value; you'll have to watch for scams at cheaper restaurants; and foreign pedestrians are continually mobbed by taxi drivers and touts.

Arrival and city transport

The **Sanya area** comprises four sections: Sanya City, Dadonghai, the Luhuitou Peninsula – all fairly closely grouped – and Yalong Bay, a distant satellite tourist development. **Sanya City** occupies a 3km-long peninsula bounded west by the Beibu Gulf and east by the Sanya River. Aligned north–south, Jiefang Lu is the main road, forking at its southern end to run briefly southwest to the cargo wharves as Jiangang Lu, and east to form busy Gangmen Lu. Changing its name several more times, this extends 4km out to **Dadonghai** (大东海, *dàdōng hǎi*), a kilometre-long spread of hotels, restaurants and shops backing on to Dadonghai beach, beyond which are the start of routes to Haikou and Tongshi. Accessible by road from Dadonghai, the **Luhuitou Peninsula** (鹿回头, *lùhuítóu*) is separated from the cargo wharves by the harbour, while **Yalong Bay**

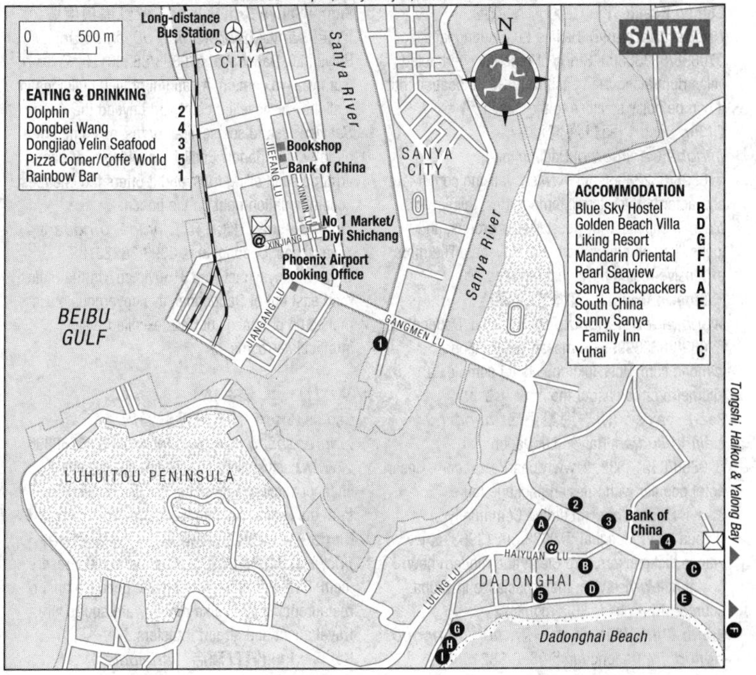

(亚龙湾, *yàlóng wān*) is a cluster of insular resorts along a single sandy beach 20km east of town.

Phoenix **airport** is about 15km to the west, from where you'll need to catch a taxi into the city (¥50–60). Sanya's main **long-distance bus station** is at the northern end of Jiefang Lu and handles normal and luxury buses to Haikou, and services to just about everywhere else on the island, including Dongfang, Tongshi and Wenchang. The **train station** lies just north of the bus station.

To **get around**, there's the usual overload of taxi cabs (who may be reluctant to take you anywhere for less than ¥10) and some motorcycle-and-sidecar assemblies as well as **public buses** – #2 and #8 run regularly between the long-distance bus station and Dadonghai, while bus #15 runs every fifteen minutes to Yalong Bay, via Jiefang Lu and the Summer Mall at Dadonghai. At Yalong Bay, get off at the giant stone totem pole from where you can walk through to the beach.

Accommodation

Sanya's accommodation is constantly developing, with increasing options across the board. The city itself is a pretty grotty place to stay, so most visitors head towards either the mostly cheap and cheerful **Dadonghai** or the more exclusive, and considerably pricier, **Yalong Bay**.

Dadonghai

Blue Sky Hostel (蓝天国际青年旅舍, *lántiān guójì qīngnián lǚshè*) Lanhai Xiang, Haiyun Lu, Dadonghai ⓣ13876791920, ⓔsy.youthhostel@gmail.com. This newly refurbished spot is backpacker central: free wifi internet, laundry facilities and English-speaking staff who can arrange anything from dive trips to hiking in the rainforest. Dorm beds ¥50, rooms ❹

Golden Beach Villa (金沙滩度假屋, *jīnshātāndùjiàwū*) Haihua Lu, Dadonghai ⓣ0898/88338800. String of recently overhauled villas right along the beachfront. Great location, but it can be noisy so close to the beach. ❻

Liking Resort (丽景海湾酒店, *lìjǐnghǎiwānjiǔdiàn*) Dadonghai ⓣ0898/88228666, ⓦwww.sanyaliking.com. More characterful than its contemporaries, this low-rise place is popular with Russian tour groups, and looks like something from 1950s Vegas. The more expensive rooms have vast terraces. ❼

Mandarin Oriental (文华东方酒店, *wénhúadōngfāngjiǔdiàn*) Yuhai Lu, Dadonghai ⓣ0898/88209999, ⓔmosan-reservations@mohg.com. Über-luxurious hotel complex a kilometre or so east of the main beach. ❾

Pearl Seaview (明珠海景酒店, *míngzhū hǎijǐng jiǔdiàn*) Haiyun Lu, Dadonghai ⓣ0898/88213838, ⓦwww.pearlresort.com. Resort hotel popular with Russian package tours. ❼

Sanya Backpackers Luming Community, Haihua Lu, Dadonghai ⓣ0898/88213963, ⓦwww.sanyabackpackers.com Clean and modern new hostel in low-rise villa; they specialize in scuba courses. Dorm beds ¥65, rooms ❹

South China (南中国大酒店, *nánzhōngguó dàjiǔdiàn*) Dadonghai ⓣ0898/88219888, ⓦwww.southchinahotel.com. Comfortable beachfront resort with all imaginable facilities, including a pool, gym and Western and Chinese restaurants. ❽

Sunny Sanya Family Inn (三亚红屋顶度假酒店, *sānyà hóngwūdǐng dùjià jiǔdiàn*) Haiyun Lu, Dadonghai ⓣ0898/88200128, ⓦwww.sunnysanya.com.cn. A handful of tiled buildings in a slightly dishevelled courtyard beyond the *Pearl Seaview*; ask to see several rooms, as some are a bit tatty, but friendly English-speaking staff can arrange snorkelling trips, and it offers the cheapest accommodation right on the beach. ❹

Yuhai Binguan (榆海宾馆, *yúhǎi bīnguǎn*) Yuya Dadao, Dadonghai ⓣ0898/38223188, ⓦwww.sanyayuhai.web.3150vip.cn. On the main road east out of Dadonghai, this cavernous place makes no pretences but has excellent-value, immaculate rooms. ❹

Yalong Bay

Cactus Resort (仙人掌度假酒店, *xiānrénzhǎng dùjiàjiǔdiàn*) ⓣ0898/88568866, ⓦwww.cactusresort.com. Alternative, slightly cheaper version of its sister, the *Gloria*. Set back from the beach, but with a better swimming pool. ❽

Gloria Resort (凯莱度假酒店, *kǎilái dùjià jiǔdiàn*) ⓣ0898/88568855, ⓦwww.gloriaresort.com. Five-star affair with private beach, a host of restaurants, a pool, bike rental, watersports hire, travel agent and airport transfers. ❾

Holiday Inn (假日酒店, *jiàrì jiǔdiàn*) ⓣ0898/88565666, ⓔhotel@holiday-inn-sanya.com. Another international effort, with all the facilities of its competitors. ❾

The City

Despite the area's resort image, **Sanya City** is not a tourist attraction, its proximity to the beaches only made apparent by the presence of matching-short-and-shirt-wearing holidaying mainlanders. Recent investment has given the downtown area the appearance of any other mildly prosperous Chinese city. Sanya's **No. 1 Market** (第一市场, *dìyī shìchǎng*), centred around Xinjian Jie running east off Jiefang Lu, is an interesting place to snack on local seafood and shop around the overstuffed open-fronted stores. Night or day, you can buy all manner of tropical fruits, along with clothes, boiled sweets by the kilo, kitchen hardware from coconut graters to giant cleavers and woks, and expensive imported toiletries, cigarettes and spirits smuggled in through Vietnam. The **wharf area**, where fishing boats cram together and blacksmiths hammer glowing metal in the shadow of ultramodern hotel blocks, is worth a look too.

Dadonghai and the Luhuitou Peninsula

Just 150m from the main road, often crowded and seasonally blistering hot, 3km-long **Dadonghai** (大东海, *dàdōng hǎi*) has pretty well everything you could ask for in a tropical beach: palm trees, white sands and warm, blue water. Beachside bars and kiosks renting out beach umbrellas, jet skis, catamarans and rubber rings complete the scene. Hugely popular with holidaying Russians, almost every shop along the strip has both Chinese and Cyrillic script, and this is one of the few places in China where, as a foreigner, you are likely to be addressed in Russian rather than English.

While it's all very relaxed for China, don't mellow too much, as unattended valuables will vanish, and women going topless, or any nudity – other than at the far eastern end of the beach where there's a nudist colony, mainly consisting of Chinese men well past the first bloom of youth – could lead to arrests.

The **Luhuitou Peninsula** (鹿回头, *lùhuítóu*) shouldn't take up much of your time. You can catch buses #2 or #8 heading west from Dadonghai to the summit entrance, where ¥68 gains access to the park around a ponderous granite statue depicting a Li legend about a deer transforming into a beautiful girl as it turned to face a young hunter – Luhuitou means "deer turns its head".

Eating and drinking

Given Sanya's tropical climate and location at China's southernmost point, there's something perverse about the bias towards northern and western Chinese **food** – probably explained by the fact that most of the restaurateurs are migrants from Sichuan and Dongbei. Like accommodation, eating here can be an expensive business, though the excellent seafood (almost all from Indonesia and the Philippines – Sanya's marine fauna is long fished out) is reasonably priced. The stretch of Haiyua Lu between the turn off to *Blue Sky* hostel and the junction with Haiyun Lu is home to Dadonghai's best-value and most varied selection of food – including Japanese, Italian and generic Western restaurants, along with a string of small Chinese seafood canteens which spill out onto the street at night. Don't eat anywhere – especially cheaper spots – without getting solid confirmation of prices, or you could end up being asked to pay vastly over the odds.

As far as **nightlife** is concerned, Chinese interpretations of Western nightclubs abound, although smaller, more authentic Western bars, such as *Rainbow*, are slowly appearing.

Restaurants

Beachfront Seafood Just above the beach near the *South China* hotel, Dadonghai. A surprisingly romantic place to eat in the evening: select fish, crabs, lobster, prawns and other seafood from the live tanks and say how you want it cooked, order a couple of beers, then kick back at outdoor tables under the coconut trees. A *jin* of prawns is about ¥40.

Dongbei Wang (东北王, *dōngběi wáng*) On the highway, Dadonghai. Lively, enjoyable Manchurian restaurant, with an illustrated menu. Portions are huge and the service good. The fried whole fish with pine nuts is a treat, as are cold shredded beef with aniseed, and a stir-fried mix of peas, pine nuts and corn kernels. ¥60 will feed two.

Dongjiao Yelin Seafood (东郊椰林海鲜城, *dōngjiāoyēlín hǎixiānchéng*) Yayu Lu, Dadonghai. A warehouse of a restaurant, offering a glut of seafood and Hainanese dishes in an opulent setting. Expensive.

Pizza Corner/Coffee World (品可诺, *pǐnkěnùo*) On the ground floor of the *Herton Hotel*, where Haihua Lu meets the beach. Provides coffee, pizzas, a selection of Western food and a vast array of cold drinks from around ¥40. Also has free wi-fi.

Bars

Dolphin (海豚酒吧, *hǎitúnjiǔbā*) Opposite the *City Hotel* on Yayu Lu, Dadonghai. Like *Rainbow*, this place offers the standard Western sports bar experience, but closer to Dadonghai. A blessedly conservative option.

Rainbow (云博西餐酒吧, *yúnbó xīcān jiǔbā*) On the waterfront of the wharf just off Gangmen Lu. *Rainbow* would not be out of place in the bar districts of Shanghai or Beijing. Big-screen sports, darts and shuffleboard are all on offer, alongside decent quality, if marginally too expensive, drinks and food.

Sky Bar (天空酒吧, *tīankōngjiǔbā*) Haiyun Lu, Dadonghai. Inexplicably popular bar/nightclub home to banging Euro-techno and provocatively dressed, shape-throwing Russians.

Listings

Airlines Most hotels have airline agents on hand. The Phoenix airport booking office is at the junction of Gangmen Lu and Jiefang Lu, Sanya (Mon–Sat 9am–noon & 1.30–5pm; ☎0898/ 88277409). There's also a major Hainan Air booking office beside the bus station (☎0898/88267988).

Banks and exchange The main Bank of China, on Jiefang Lu in Sanya (Mon–Fri 9am–5pm), is excruciatingly understaffed and slow. There's another branch opposite the bus station (same hours) as well as a Dadonghai branch (same hours), but the latter has been known to refuse to cash travellers' cheques.

Internet There's an internet café on the third floor of the Haitian bookstore, near the Bank of China on Jiefang Lu, Sanya, and a few more west of the post office on Xinjiang Lu. In Dadonghai, the hostels have internet access, as does *Ultra Speed* café, near the *Chuanya*.

Mail There are post offices on Xinjiang Lu, Sanya, and on the highway at Dadonghai (daily 7.30am–6pm).

Scuba diving Low visibility and maximum depths between 10m and 30m don't make Hainan the most exciting location for this, but it can be good fun and there's always the novelty of having dived in China. The three areas are at Yalong Bay, east of Sanya (best for its moderate coral growth, and a variety of fish and lobster); Tianya Haijiao, over to the west (good for molluscs, but extremely shallow); and the coral islands, also west (these are the deepest sites). Staff are NAUI/PADI qualified, hire gear is of reasonable quality, and you'll be expected to flash a C-card or make do with an introductory "resort" dive (¥260). Two shore dives cost ¥410, two boat dives ¥610, and a single dive at Yalong Bay will set you back ¥660. Bookings can be made through virtually any hotel, but touts who are more amenable to bargaining often patrol the beachfront at Dadonghai. Prices at Yalong will typically be 50–100 percent more than at Dadonghai for what will very likely be a similar, if not identical, service.

Shopping Sanya is a good place to pick up pearls, white, pink, yellow or black. The best buys are from local hawkers on Dadonghai beach, who sell strings of "rejects" for ¥40 or less with hard bargaining. Most of these pearls are perfectly genuine, just not of good enough colour, shape or size for commercial jewellery. If in doubt, scratch the surface – flaking indicates a thinly coated plastic bead.

Travel agents Any of the hotels or hostels, even those without their own travel desks, will arrange scuba diving, climbing, coral island or fishing trips and, if not able to actually book air tickets themselves, will be more than happy to point you in the direction of one of the many travel agencies in the town that can.

Around Sanya

For a very Chinese tourist experience, bus #15 from Dadonghai can cart you out 20km east of the city to **Tianya Haijiao** (天涯海角, *tiānyá hǎijiǎo*; ¥65), a long beach strewn with curiously shaped boulders, whose name roughly translates as the "ends of the earth". This isn't as fanciful as it sounds, as for Hainan's scholarly political exiles this was just about as far as you could possibly be from life's pinnacle at the imperial court. The modern world has unfortunately descended very heavily on the area, however, and a new township with expensive accommodation and restaurants, ever-escalating entry fees to the beach itself and overly persistent hawkers makes for an irritating time. Chinese come in their thousands to have their photographs taken next to rocks inscribed with big red characters marking them as the "Sweetheart Stones", or "Limit of the Sky, Edge of the Sea". An overpriced and overexploited attraction, if nothing else Tianya Haijiao provides a wonderful opportunity for people-watching.

Yazhou

Another 15km west, beyond a luxurious golf course, **YAZHOU** (崖州, *yázhōu*), has transformed from one of Hainan's biggest towns into a mere bottleneck for through traffic. It's chiefly known as the place where the thirteenth-century weaver **Huang Daopo** fled from her native Shanghai to escape an arranged marriage. After forty years living with the coastal Li, she returned to northern

The South China Sea islands

Chinese maps of China always show a looped extension of the southern borders reaching 1500km down through the South China Sea to within spitting distance of Borneo, enclosing a host of reefs and minute islands. These sit over what might be major **oil and gas reserves**, and are consequently claimed by every nation in the region – China, Malaysia, the Philippines, Taiwan and Vietnam have all put in their bids, based on historical or geographic associations. Occupied by Japan during the 1940s but unclaimed after World War II, the **Spratly and Paracel islands** are perhaps the most contentious groups. Vietnam and China both declared ownership of the Paracels in the 1970s, coming to blows in 1988 when the Chinese navy sank two Vietnamese gunboats. Then the Philippines stepped in in 1995, destroying Chinese territorial markers erected over the most westerly reefs in the Spratly group and capturing a nearby Chinese trawler. Ongoing minor brawls encouraged the nations of the region – including China – to hammer out a landmark agreement in November 2002, which basically allows access for all, while territorial disputes are settled one by one. This is likely to be a relief to companies such as the US conglomerate Exxon, who – despite the fact that guaranteed oil reserves have yet to be found – are already investing in the region.

China in 1295 and introduced their superior textile techniques to the mainland. Get off the bus when you see the reconstructed Ming city gate and walk through it to a tiny **temple museum**, which includes traditional Li clothing and a Hui headstone and mosque oil lamp. The Hui have been on Hainan for centuries – some say they were originally Song-dynasty refugees from Vietnam, others that they're a relic of the old Maritime Silk Road – and the countryside hereabouts is peppered with their distinctive cylindrical graves. Walk back onto the main road and continue 1km or so west out of town, and you'll find a 400-year-old, seven-storey brick pagoda leaning at a rakish angle next to a school – one of the few genuinely old structures on the island. The last direct transport back to Sanya leaves in the late afternoon.

Nantian and Nanshan

Two popular day-trips from Sanya are to the hot spring resorts of Nantian, an hour northeast of the city, and Nanshan, a spectacularly upmarket Buddhist retreat 20km further along the coast beyond Tianya Haijiao. **NANTIAN** (南田, *nántián*), a wholly secular affair, consists of a complex of pools sourced from natural hot springs and includes play pools with slides as well as more secluded hot tubs and a pool filled with kissing fish that provide a natural exfoliation service, happily, and ticklishly, nibbling away at any dead skin they can find. Most hotels in Dadonghai sell tickets for Nantian (¥198) and will also arrange transport for a fee; you can hail yourself a taxi for around ¥100 one-way. Male bathers should be warned that on the somewhat dubious grounds of hygiene they will be required to don figure-hugging Chinese-style trunks before being allowed into the pools. Buying a pair of the lycra wonders will set you back around ¥20 at Dadonghai, or ¥60 at Nantian itself. For women a standard bikini is acceptably clean.

A similar distance in the opposite direction, **NANSHAN** (南山, *nánshān*; ¥150; ⓣ0898/88837985) is a Buddhist retreat-cum-luxury spa that centres on a 108m-high statue of Buddha rising up out of the sea. It also has a temple complex, hot springs, immaculate gardens, a highly regarded vegetarian restaurant and luxury accommodation (⑨). The pervading atmosphere of commerce detracts slightly from the experience of what is, undoubtedly, a stunning location. To get there catch bus #15 west to Tianya Haijiao, from where a taxi (¥30) is the only way to cover the remaining 20km to Nanshan itself.

West to Jianfeng and Dongfang

There are departures from Sanya's long-distance bus station for the 165km run to the western port of Dongfang, up the coast beyond Yazhou; you could also travel there in stages by minibus. This side of the island is incredibly poor and undeveloped compared with the east, partly because it's too remote to benefit from tourism, but also because the main sources of income here are various forms of mining, an industry that sees little financial returns for local communities.

The real reason to head out this way is to spend a day at **Jianfeng Ling Forest Reserve** (尖峰岭热带原始森林 自然保护区, *jiānfēnglǐng rèdài yuánshǐ sēnlín zìránbǎohùqū*), a small indication of what the whole of southwestern Hainan looked like before the 1960s. Head first for **JIANFENG** (尖峰, *jiān fēng*) township, which lies at the base of the distinctively peaked Jianfeng range some 10km east of the coastal road, about 115km from Sanya. Dongfang-bound transport can drop you at the turning, from where you can walk or wait for the next passing vehicle to pick you up. A dusty little hollow where pigs and dogs roam the streets, Jianfeng has two teahouses and around a hundred homes. The sole **guesthouse** (❸) is a friendly place with a fine **restaurant** (try the chicken with locally grown cashew nuts), functioning plumbing and electric power.

The reserve is in the mountains at Tianchi, 18km beyond Jianfeng. To reach it, jump on a motorbike taxi (¥50). **Jianfeng Ling** – the mountain range – was aggressively logged until 1992, when a UNESCO survey found 400 types of butterfly and 1700 plant species up here and persuaded the Chinese government to establish the reserve, leaving a sharp-edged forested crown above bare lowland slopes. Though commercial timber stands have since been planted, locals have been left without a livelihood for the time being, a problem slightly eased by aid packages from the Asian Development Bank. The dirt road to the summit ends on the forest's edge at a group of stores, a small restaurant, a botanical research station and a little-frequented **hotel** (❹), whose staff will be most surprised to see you. A tiled gateway marks the reserve entrance about 100m back up the road, from where partially paved paths lead off uphill for an hour-long circuit walk taking in some massive trees, vines, orchids, ferns, birds, butterflies and beautiful views from the 1056m ridge. After dark, if you're armed with a torch and some caution, it's a good place to look for small mammals and reptiles.

Wuzhishan and the highlands

Just 100km north of Sanya and lying on the main inland route between Hakou and Sanya, **Wuzhishan's** quiet pace and large concentration of Li make it the favoured place to start delving into **Hainan's highlands**. Not that many do – despite evidence of long association with Li and Miao peoples, the island's central core gets scant attention from visitors.

Wuzhishan and around

Lacking heavy traffic or industry, pocket-sized **Wuzhishan** (通什, *tōngshí* or 五指山市, *wǔzhǐ shān shì*; previously known as Tongza), two hours north of Sanya, is a pleasantly unpolluted spot to hang out for a day or two, surrounded by pretty countryside. Energetic hikers might want to go scrambling up nearby **Qizhi Shan** (七指山, *qīzhǐ shān*) and **Wuzhi Shan**, whose summits are both steeped in local lore. Before 1987, Tongshi was also capital of Hainan's autonomous Li government, until it blew a billion-yuan road grant by importing luxury goods from Hong Kong and Vietnam, and building the palatial offices, now **Qiongzhou University** (琼州大学, *qióngzhōu dàxué*), on the hill above town. When Beijing caught on to what was happening, they sacked the local government and put the region under their direct control, a move that, while justified, was greatly resented by the Li.

The Town

Reached via a street running uphill just beyond the bus station, and then past the ostentatious green-tiled **university**, the **Nationality Museum** (民族博物馆, *mínzú bówùguăn*; daily 8am–5.30pm; ¥10) affords views across town to the aptly named **Nipple Mountain**, 5km away to the west, while the collection itself is excellent. Historical exhibits include prehistoric stone tools and a bronze drum decorated with sun and frog motifs, similar to those associated with Guangxi's Zhuang; Ming manuscripts about island life; Qing wine vessels with octopus and frog mouldings; and details of the various modern conflicts culminating in the last

Li and Miao

Hainan's million-strong **Li** population take their name from the big topknot (*li*) which men once wore. Archeological finds and traditions shared with other southwestern Chinese peoples point to their arriving on Hainan from Guangxi about 200 BC, when they occupied the coast and displaced the aboriginal inhabitants. Driven inland themselves by later Han arrivals, the Li finally settled Hainan's central highlands (though a few remained on the coast) and spent the next two thousand years as rice farmers and hunters, living in villages with distinctive tunnel-shaped houses, evolving their own shamanistic religion, and using poisoned arrows to bring down game. **Li women** have long been known for their **weaving** skills, and the fact that, until very recently, many got their faces heavily **tattooed** with geometric patterns – apparently to make them undesirable to raiding parties of slavers from the coast, or rival **clans**. The latter form five major groups – Ha, Qi, Yun, Meifu and Cai – and they have never coexisted very well, quarrelling to this day over territorial boundaries and only really united in their dislike of external rulers.

Though actively supporting Communist guerrillas against the Japanese, the Li have no great affection for the Han as a whole, and there were fourteen major rebellions against their presence on the island during the Qing era alone. Superficially assimilated into modern China, the Li would probably revolt again if they felt they could get away with it. They are, however, pretty friendly towards outside visitors, and though traditional life has all but vanished over the last half-century, there are still a few special events to watch out for. Best is the **San Yue San festival** (held on the third day of the third lunar month), the most auspicious time of the year in which to choose a partner, while in more remote corners of the highlands, **funerals** are traditionally celebrated with gunfire and three days of hard drinking by male participants.

Touted as Hainan's second "native minority" by the tourist literature, the **Miao** are in fact comparatively recent arrivals, forcibly recruited from Guizhou province as **mercenaries** to put down a Li uprising during the Ming dynasty. When the money ran out, the Miao stopped fighting and settled in the western highlands, where today they form a fifty-thousand-strong community. The US adventurer Leonard Clark, who traversed the highlands in 1937, reported them as living apart in the remotest of valleys, though they now apparently intermarry with the Li (for more on the Miao, see p.672).

pocket of Guomindang resistance being overcome in 1950. Artefacts and photos illustrate Hainan's cultural heritage, too – Li looms and textiles, traditional weapons and housing, speckled pottery from Dongfang and pictures of major festivals. Back across the river, you can tour the town centre's handful of streets and modern concrete-and-tile buildings in around thirty minutes. **Henan Lu** runs west along the waterfront from the bridge; two blocks back, Tongshi's **public square** is a sociable place to hang out after dark and meet people, full of tables serviced by drink and snack vendors, its crowds watching open-air table-tennis tournaments and queuing for the cinema. Nearby, on **Jiefang Lu**, there's a chance to see dark-dressed Miao and the occasional older Li women with tattoos at the daily **market**, whose wares include sweet, milky-white spirit sold in plastic jerry cans, deer and dog meat, and barbecued **rat**.

You can see more of the Li by catching a minibus 2km south to the tacky displays at **Fanmao Li Village**, but there's more to be said for just heading off into the countryside on foot. From the north side of the bridge, follow Hebei Xi Lu west along the river for 150m to a grossly patronizing **statue** of grinning Li, Miao and Han characters standing arm in arm. Take the road uphill from here past the *Tongzha Resort Hotel* (see below) and keep going along the dusty road as long as you like, through vivid green fields and increasingly poor villages, ultimately built of mud and straw and surrounded by split bamboo pickets to keep livestock in. Among these you'll see more substantial barns with traditional tunnel shapes and carved wooden doors.

Practicalities

Set at the base of low hills, Wuzhishan's tiny centre sits on the southern bank of a horseshoe bend in the generally unimpressive **Nansheng River**. The main road comes up from the coast as **Haiyu Lu**, skirts the centre, crosses over the river and passes the **post office**, turns sharply left past the **bus station**, and bends off north through the island toward Qiongzhong and Haikou. Buses head from the station to Baoting, Baisha, Qiongzhong, Haikou, Sanya and Wuzhi Shan. There are a couple of **internet cafés** around the bus station, but there's no **Bank of China** in town.

Wuzhishan's very reasonable **accommodation** prices are a relief after Sanya. Directly opposite the bus station's main door, *Jinyuan Dajiudian* has clean, tiled rooms (金源大酒店, *jīnyuán dàjiǔdiàn*; ⓣ86622942; ❷), as does the slightly nicer *Guolü Binguan* (国旅宾馆, *guólǚ bīnguǎn*; ⓣ86633158; ❸), which can be reached by turning left out of the bus station and following the road round to the right as it turns toward the river. Easily the town's best accommodation is the *Wuzhishan Tongza Resort Hotel* (通什旅游山庄, *tōngshí lǚyóu shānzhuāng*; ⓣ86623188; ❻) on the northeastern edge of town, whose characterful rooms have balconies looking out to the hills; there's a swimming pool to cool down in after a hike.

Teahouses near the market fill with sociable crowds on most mornings, which is also a good time to **eat** dim sum in *Shan Cheng Chazhuang* (山城茶庄, *shānchéng cházhuāng*) on Jiefang Lu – an extraordinary institution whose men's-club atmosphere is compounded by a card-gaming hall out the back; *hainan gau* here are sticky rice packets with coconut and banana. The *Tongza Resort Hotel* has a reasonable restaurant with an English menu of sorts, and there are plenty of canteens around the bus station.

Wuzhi Shan and Qizhi Shan

Several Li myths explain the formation of **Wuzhi Shan** (Five-Finger Mountain), whose 1867m-high summit rises 30km northeast of Tongshi at Hainan's apex.

In one tale, the mountain's five peaks are the fossilized fingers of a dying clan chieftain, while another holds that they represent the Li's five most powerful gods. Either way, Wuzhi Shan was once a holy site drawing thousands of people to animist festivals. Though the mountain is rarely a place of pilgrimage today, more remote villages in this part of Hainan maintain the old religion, raising archways over their gates, which are occasionally embellished with bull or chicken heads. It's still possible to climb the mountain – take a bus from Wuzhishan to **Shuiman**, then use local transport (motorcycle taxi) or walk the final 3km or so to the trailhead. From here it's a steep and slippery three-hour scramble to the peak, initially through jungly scrub, then pine forests. Although it's often clouded over, the summit offers further contorted pines, begonias and views.

Qizhi Shan (Seven-Finger Mountain), representing seven lesser Li immortals being vanquished by Wuzhi's five, lies about 40km by road southeast of Tongshi via sleepy **Baoting** (保亭, *bǎotíng*). This makes another good place from which to wander aimlessly off into the countryside, and you can get to the base of the mountain by catching available transport 10km east to **Shiling**, and thence 11km north to **Ba Cun**. The climb is shorter than that at Wuzhi Shan, but much harder.

Travel details

Trains

Chaozhou to: Guangzhou (2 daily; 6hr 30min–8hr); Huizhou (3 daily; 4hr 30min–6hr); Meizhou (3 daily; 2hr); Shantou (4 daily; 30min).
Fuzhou to: Beijing (2 daily; 20–35hr); Longyan (2 daily; 10hr); Meizhou (1 daily; 13hr); Nanchang (9 daily; 2–12hr); Shanghai (11 daily; 6–16hr); Shenzhen (1 daily; 18hr); Wuyi Shan (8 daily; 4hr 30min–6hr 30min); Yongding (1 daily; 11hr).
Guangzhou to: Beijing (6 daily; 21–27hr); Changsha (67 daily; 2hr 30min–10hr); Chaozhou (2 daily; 6hr 30min–7hr); Chengdu (4 daily; 27–39hr); Foshan (17 daily; 45min); Ganzhou (6 daily; 7hr); Guilin (2 daily; 11hr); Guiyang (5 daily; 21hr); Haikou (3 daily; 11hr); Huizhou (13 daily; 2hr); Kowloon (1 daily; 2hr); Kunming (3 daily; 26hr); Meizhou (4 daily; 6hr); Nanchang (7 daily; 12hr); Nanning (5 daily; 13hr); Shanghai (5 daily; 16–20hr); Shantou (2 daily; 8hr); Shaoguan (75 daily; 45min–4hr); Shenzhen (every 30min; 1–2hr); Wuhan (57 daily; 4–13hr); Xiamen (3 daily; 14hr); Xian (5 daily; 21–30hr); Zhanjiang (1 daily; 23hr); Zhaoqing (17 daily; 2hr).
Haikou to: Beijing (1 daily; 32hr); Guangzhou (3 daily; 10hr 30min–12hr); Shanghai (1 daily; 33hr).
Huizhou to: Chaozhou (3 daily; 4hr 30min–6hr); Guangzhou (13 daily; 1hr 30min–2hr 30min); Meizhou (6 daily; 4hr); Nanchang (21 daily; 8hr 30min–10hr 30min); Shantou (3 daily; 5–6hr 30min); Wuhan (3 daily; 12hr 30min–16hr).
Meizhou to: Chaozhou (3 daily; 2hr); Fuzhou (1 daily; 12hr); Guangzhou (4 daily; 5hr 30min); Huizhou (6 daily; 3hr 30min); Longyan (4 daily; 3hr); Shantou (3 daily; 2hr 30min); Yongding (3 daily; 1hr 45min).
Shantou to: Chaozhou (4 daily; 30min); Guangzhou (2 daily; 7–8hr); Huizhou (3 daily; 5–6hr 30min); Meizhou (3 daily; 2hr 30min).
Shaoguan to: Changsha (48 daily; 1hr 30min–6hr 30min); Guangzhou (74 daily; 30min–2hr 30min); Hengyang (62 daily; 1hr–4hr 30min).
Shenzhen to: Changsha (8 daily; 9–11hr); Fuzhou (1 daily; 18hr); Ganzhou (16 daily; 5hr 30min–8hr 30min); Guangzhou (99 daily; 50min–2hr); Shantou (1 daily; 8hr 30min); Shaoguan (10 daily; 4–5hr); Wuhan (5 daily; 11hr 30min–18hr).
Wuyi Shan to: Beijing (1 daily; 15hr); Fuzhou (8 daily; 4hr 30min; 7hr); Shanghai (3 daily; 10hr); Xiamen (1 daily; 12hr).
Xiamen to: Guangzhou (3 daily; 14hr 30min); Nanchang (5 daily; 15–17hr); Nanjing (1 daily; 30hr); Shanghai (2 daily; 8hr); Wuyi Shan (1 daily; 13hr 30min); Xi'an (1 daily; 37hr).
Zhaoqing to: Guangzhou (18 daily; 2hr); Sanya (3 daily; 12hr–13hr 30min); Shenzhen (1 daily; 4hr)

Buses

Generally, there are countless services between the places listed below (see text for exceptions),

though smaller towns may cease to see any traffic after 8pm.
Chaozhou to: Guangzhou (6hr); Huizhou (4hr); Meizhou (3hr); Shantou (1hr); Shenzhen (5hr); Xiamen (5hr 30min).
Fuzhou to: Guangzhou (12hr); Longyan (7hr); Nanchang (9hr); Ningbo (9hr); Quanzhou (2hr 30min); Shantou (7hr); Shenzhen (12hr); Wenzhou (7hr); Wuyi Shan (7hr); Xiamen (4hr).
Guangzhou to: Beihai (24hr); Changsha (20hr); Chaozhou (7–8hr); Dongguan (1hr); Foshan (1hr); Fuzhou (12hr); Ganzhou (11hr); Guilin (13hr); Haikou (12hr); Huizhou (2hr); Jiangmen (2hr); Kowloon (3hr); Meizhou (12hr); Nancun (1hr); Nanning (30hr); Panyu (1hr); Qingyuan (1hr); Shantou (6hr); Shaoguan (4hr); Shenzhen (3hr); Shunde (1hr 30min); Xiamen (9hr); Zhangjiang (5hr); Zhaoqing (2hr); Zhuhai (3hr).
Haikou to: Chongqing (28hr); Guangzhou (12hr); Guilin (12hr); Lingshui (3hr); Qionghai (2hr 30min); Sanya (3–5hr); Shenzhen (15hr); Tongshi (4hr); Wanning (3hr); Wenchang (1hr); Zhanjiang (5hr).
Huizhou to: Chaozhou (4hr); Guangzhou (2hr); Meizhou (5hr 30min); Shantou (4hr); Shenzhen (2hr).
Meizhou to: Chaozhou (3hr); Dapu (2hr); Guangzhou (12hr); Huizhou (5hr 30min); Longyan (4hr); Shantou (4hr); Shaoguan (12hr); Shenzhen (10hr); Xiamen (9hr); Yongding (4hr).
Qingyuan to: Foshan (2hr); Guangzhou (1hr); Shaoguan (3hr); Shenzen (2hr 30min); Zhaoqing (5hr).
Quanzhou to: Fuzhou (2hr 30min); Guangzhou (10hr); Hangzhou (11hr); Longyan (5hr); Ningbo (11hr); Shenzen (10hr); Xiamen (1hr 30min).
Sanya to: Dongfang (3hr); Haikou (3–5hr); Lingshui (2hr); Qionghai (4hr 30min); Tongshi (2hr); Wanning (3hr); Wenchang (4hr); Yazhou (1hr).
Shantou to: Chaozhou (1hr); Fuzhou (7hr); Guangzhou (6hr); Huizhou (4hr); Meizhou (4hr); Shenzhen (6hr); Xiamen (5hr).
Shaoguan to: Chaozhou (12hr); Ganzhou (4hr); Guangzhou (4hr); Huizhou (4hr); Lianshan (5hr); Meizhou (12hr); Pingshi (4hr); Qingyuan (3hr).
Shenzhen to: Chaozhou (7hr); Dongguan (2hr); Fuzhou (12hr); Guangzhou (3hr); Haikou (15hr); Hong Kong (2hr); Huizhou (2hr); Meizhou (10hr); Shantou (6hr); Yangshuo (10hr); Zhanjiang (7hr).
Xiamen to: Chaozhou (5hr 30min); Fuzhou (4hr); Guangzhou (9hr); Longyan (5hr); Meizhou (9hr); Quanzhou (1hr 30min); Shantou (5hr 30min); Shenzhen (9hr); Wenzhou (18hr); Yongding (5hr).
Yongding to: Longyan (1hr); Meizhou (4hr); Xiamen (5hr); Zhiling (1hr).
Zhanjiang to: Guangzhou (5hr); Hai'an (3hr); Haikou (5hr); Shenzhen (7hr); Zhaoqing (7hr).
Zhaoqing to: Guangzhou (2hr); Guilin (10hr); Qingyuan (5hr); Yangshuo (8hr 30min); Zhanjiang (7hr).
Zhuhai to: Cuiheng (1hr); Foshan (3hr); Fuzhou (15hr); Guangzhou (3hr); Guilin (13hr); Haikou (15hr); Jiangmen (2hr); Shunde (2hr 30min); Zhongshan (1hr).

Ferries

Guangzhou to: Hong Kong (2 daily; 2hr 30min).
Hai'an to: Haikou (10 daily; 1hr 30min).
Haikou to: Beihai (3 daily; 11hr); Hai'an (10 daily; 1hr 30min); Hong Kong (2 weekly; 25hr).
Shenzhen to: Hong Kong (20 daily; 1hr); Macau (daily; 2hr); Zhuhai (20 daily; 1hr).
Xiamen to: Hong Kong (1 weekly; 18hr).
Zhaoqing to: Hong Kong (1 daily; 4hr).
Zhuhai to: Hong Kong (10 daily; 1hr); Macau (5 daily; 20min); Shenzhen (20 daily; 1hr).

Flights

Besides the domestic flights listed here, Guangzhou is linked by regular services to major Southeast Asian cities and increasingly more destinations worldwide.
Fuzhou to: Beijing (6 daily; 2hr 30min); Guangzhou (1 daily; 1hr 30min); Haikou (6 weekly; 2hr); Hong Kong (3 daily; 1hr 30min); Shanghai (7 daily; 1hr 10min); Shenzhen (2 daily; 1hr 20min); Wuyi Shan (5 weekly; 30min); Xiamen (1 daily; 30min).
Guangzhou to: Beihai (2 daily; 1hr 20min); Beijing (20 daily; 2hr 45min); Changsha (3 daily; 1hr); Chengdu (10 daily; 2hr); Chongqing (10 daily; 1hr 35min); Dalian (2 daily; 3hr); Fuzhou (1 daily; 1hr 30min); Guilin (4 daily; 1hr); Guiyang (5–6 daily; 1hr 15min); Haikou (7–10 daily; 1hr); Hangzhou (14 daily; 1hr 45min); Harbin (2 daily; 4hr 15min); Hefei (3 daily; 1hr 45min–3hr); Hohhot (3 weekly; 3hr 10min); Hong Kong (7 daily; 40min–1hr); Kunming (6 daily; 2hr); Lanzhou (2 daily; 3hr); Meizhou (1 daily; 50min); Nanchang (3 daily; 1hr); Nanjing (6 daily; 2hr); Nanning (4–5 daily; 1hr 20min); Qingdao (4 daily; 2hr 40min–3hr 20min); Sanya (10 daily; 1hr 20min); Shanghai (25 daily; 2hr); Shantou (2–4 daily; 40min); Tianjin (2 daily; 2hr 30min); Ürümqi (3 weekly; 5hr); Wuhan (5 daily; 1hr 30min); Xiamen (4 daily; 1hr); Xi'an (6 daily; 2hr 30min); Yichang (daily; 1hr 45min); Zhengzhou (4 daily; 2hr).
Haikou to: Beihai (1 daily; 40min); Beijing (6 daily; 3hr 30min); Changsha (1–2 daily; 1hr 40min); Chengdu (1 daily; 2hr); Guangzhou (9 daily; 1hr); Guilin (1 daily; 1hr 20min); Hong Kong (1 daily; 1hr); Kunming (2 daily; 1hr 40min); Nanjing (1 daily; 2hr); Shanghai (5 daily;

2hr 20min); Shenzhen (11 daily; 1hr); Wuhan (2–3 daily; 3hr 20min); Xiamen (1–2 daily; 1hr 30min); Xi'an (3 daily; 3hr–3hr 30min); Zhanjiang (2 daily; 30min); Zhuhai (1–2 daily; 1hr).
Sanya to: Beijing (5 daily; 3hr 30min); Guangzhou (10 daily; 1hr 10min); Hong Kong (6 weekly; 1hr 30min); Shanghai (4–5 daily; 2hr 30min–4hr); Shenzhen (3–4 daily; 1hr 15min).
Shenzhen to: Beihai (1daily; 1hr); Beijing (17–19 daily; 3hr); Changsha (5 daily; 1hr); Chengdu (9 daily; 2hr 15min); Chongqing (10 daily; 2hr 35min); Fuzhou (1–2 daily; 1hr); Guilin (3 daily; 1hr); Guiyang (4 daily; 1hr 30min); Haikou (13 daily; 1hr); Hangzhou (8 daily; 1hr 50min); Harbin (1 daily; 4hr); Hefei (2 daily; 2hr); Kunming (3–4 daily; 2hr); Nanchang (1–2 daily; 1hr); Nanjing (5 daily; 2hr); Sanya (3–4 daily; 1hr 15min); Shanghai (many daily; 2hr); Wuhan (5 daily; 1hr 30min); Xiamen (2 daily; 1hr); Xi'an (5 daily; 2hr 20min).
Wuyi Shan to: Fuzhou (5 weekly; 30min); Shanghai (5 weekly; 1hr); Xiamen (5 weekly; 40min).
Xiamen to: Beijing (4–5 daily; 2hr 30min); Fuzhou (1 daily; 30 min); Guangzhou (4 daily; 1hr); Hefei (1 daily; 1hr 35min); Hong Kong (2–3 daily; 1hr); Macau (1–2 daily; 1hr 20min); Shanghai (12–13 daily; 1hr 30min); Shenzhen (3–4 daily; 1hr 10min); Wuyi Shan (4 weekly; 40min).

CHAPTER 9

Highlights

* **Star Ferry** The crossing from Tsim Sha Tsui to Hong Kong Island is the cheapest harbour tour on earth – and one of the most spectacular. See p.584

* **Harbour view from The Peak** At dusk, watch the city's dazzling lights brighten across Hong Kong, the harbour and Kowloon. See p.592

* **Sai Kung Peninsula** Get away from the crowds and concrete, amid beautiful seascapes, beaches and wild countryside in this often overlooked corner of Hong Kong. See p.605

* **Ngong Ping 360** Amazing vistas of Lantau's coast, mountains and Big Buddha on this cable-car ride from Tung Chung to Po Lin Monastery. See p.609

* **Dim sum** Tuck in to an authentic dim sum lunch alongside enthusiastic families – try the *har gau* (prawn dumplings) and barbecue pork buns. See p.610

* **Old Macau** Hunt for bargain rosewood furniture and traditional clothing in central Macau's cobbled streets. See p.624

* **Coffee, tarts and port** Thanks to Macau's Portuguese heritage, most cafés and restaurants serve ink-black coffee, delicious custard tarts and port wine – almost unknown elsewhere in China. See p.632

▲ View of Hong Kong from the Kowloon waterfront

9

Hong Kong and Macau

The handover of **Asia's last two European colonies**, Hong Kong in 1997 and Macau in 1999, opened new eras for both places. While their colonial heritage remains obvious, the essentially Chinese character underlying these two **SARs**, or "Special Administrative Regions of China" is increasingly apparent: after all, Hong Kong and Macau's population is 97 percent **Chinese**, the dominant language is Cantonese, and there have always been close ties – if often tinged with suspicion – with the mainlanders just over the border.

It is hard to overstate the symbolic importance that the handovers had for the Chinese as a whole, in sealing the end of centuries of foreign domination with the return of the last pieces of foreign-occupied soil to the motherland. The people of Hong Kong and Macau also widely supported the transfer of power – if only to see how much leeway they could garner under the new administration. Both entities now find themselves in the unique position of being capitalist enclaves subject to a communist state, under the relatively liberal "**One Country, Two Systems**" policy coined by the late Chinese leader Deng Xiaoping.

First under colonial and now mainland Chinese rule, Hong Kong and Macau's citizens have never had a say in their futures, so they have concentrated their efforts on other things – notably, **making money**. With its emphasis on economics and consumerism, **Hong Kong** offers the greatest variety and concentration of **shops and shopping** on earth, along with a colossal range of **cuisines**, and vistas of sea and island, green mountains and futuristic cityscapes. The excellent **infrastructure**, including the efficient public transit system, the helpful tourist offices and all the other facilities of a genuinely international city make this an extremely soft entry into the Chinese world.

While Hong Kong is a place to do business, **Macau** has leapt ahead in recent years as a haven for **gambling**, a veritable Las Vegas of the East, with thirty-odd casinos. Their wealth has funded a modern cityscape, but evidence of its colonial past persist in extensive quarters of Mediterranean-style architecture, along with Portuguese wine and Macanese cooking, a fusion of colonial and Chinese styles.

Visitors will spend more **money** here than elsewhere in China, though public transport and food are good value – even if accommodation is always pricey for what you get. Travellers on a tight **budget** who stay in dormitories can just about get by on HK$350 a day, though at the other end of the market in hotels, restaurants and shops, prices quickly rise to international levels.

Hong Kong

HONG KONG – more fully known as the Hong Kong SAR – wears a lot of hats: despite emerging competition from Shanghai, it remains one of the world's largest financial hubs; its modern face hides a surprisingly traditional culture; and it's also an experiment in governance with which the mainland authorities hope to win over a recalcitrant Taiwan. There's an unrelenting striving for wealth and all its rewards here too, though Hong Kong's famous addiction to money and brand names tends to mask the fact that most people work long hours and live in crowded, tiny apartments. On the other hand, the city is bursting with energy and the population of seven million is sophisticated and well informed compared to their mainland cousins, the result of a relatively free press. The urban panorama of sky-scrapered Hong Kong Island, seen across the harbour from Kowloon, is stunning, and you'll find a wealth of undeveloped rural areas within easy commuter range of the hectic centre and its perennial, massive engineering projects.

Hong Kong comprises 1100 square kilometres of the south China coastline and a number of islands east of the Pearl River Delta. The principal urban area is spread along the north shore of **Hong Kong Island**, which offers not only traces of the **old colony** – from English place names to ancient, double-decker trams trundling along the shore – but also superb **modern cityscapes** of towering buildings teetering up impossible slopes, along with whole districts dedicated to selling traditional Chinese medicine and herbs. The south of the island offers several decent **beaches**, a huge **amusement park**, and even **hiking** opportunities.

Immediately north across Victoria Harbour from Hong Kong Island, the **Kowloon Peninsula** – and especially its tip, **Tsim Sha Tsui** – is the SAR's principal tourist trap, boasting a glut of accommodation, and shops offering an incredible variety of goods (not necessarily at reasonable prices, though). North of Tsim Sha Tsui, Kowloon stretches away into the **New Territories**, a varied area of **New Towns** and older villages, secluded beaches and undeveloped country

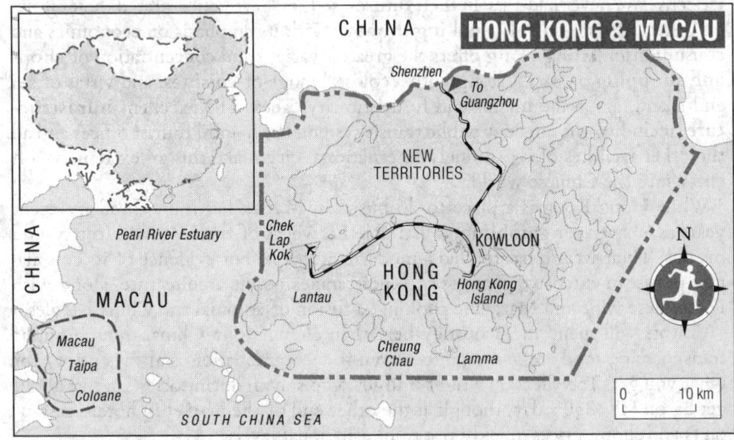

parks. In addition, the **Outlying Islands** – particularly **Lamma** and **Lantau** – are well worth a visit for their seafood restaurants and further rural contrasts to the hubbub of downtown Hong Kong.

Hong Kong has its own separate currency, the **Hong Kong dollar**, which is pegged at around $8 to the US dollar and so is currently worth a little less than the Chinese yuan. Yuan cannot officially be used in Hong Kong, though a few stores will take them. In this chapter, the symbol "$" refers to Hong Kong dollars throughout, unless stated.

Some history

While the Chinese justifiably argue that Hong Kong was always Chinese territory, the development of the city only began with the **arrival of the British** in Guangzhou in the eighteenth century. Having initially been rebuffed in their attempts to engage in profitable trade with China, the British found a valuable market for Indian opium; Chinese attempts to stop the trade precipitated the **Opium Wars** (see p.949); and the ensuing **Treaty of Nanking** (1842) ceded a small, thinly populated offshore island – Hong Kong – to Britain. Following more gunboat diplomacy eighteen years later, the **Treaty of Peking** granted Britain the Kowloon Peninsula, too, and in 1898 Britain secured a 99-year lease on an additional one thousand square kilometres of land north of Kowloon, later known as the New Territories.

Originally a seedy merchants' colony, by 1907 Hong Kong had a large enough manufacturing base to voluntarily drop the drug trade. Up until World War II, the city prospered as turmoils in mainland China drove money and **refugees** south into the apparently safe confines of the British colony. This confidence proved misplaced in 1941 when **Japanese forces** seized Hong Kong along with the rest of eastern China, though after Japan's defeat in 1945, Britain swiftly reclaimed the colony, stifling putative attempts by the residents to garner some independence. As the mainland fell to the Communists in 1949, a new wave of refugees – many of the wealthier ones from Shanghai – swelled Hong Kong's population threefold to 2.5 million, causing a housing crisis that set in motion themes still current in the SAR: **land reclamation**, the need for efficient infrastructure, and a tendency to save space by building upwards.

The early **Communist era** saw Hong Kong leading a precarious existence. Had China wished, it could have rendered the existence of Hong Kong unviable by a naval blockade, by cutting off water supplies, by a military invasion – or by simply opening its border and inviting the Chinese masses to stream across in search of wealth. That it never wholeheartedly pursued any of these options, even at the height of the Cultural Revolution, was an indication of the huge **financial benefits** that Hong Kong's international trade links, direct investment and technology transfers brought – and still brings – to mainland China.

In the last twenty years of British rule, the spectre of **1997** loomed large. Negotiations on the future of the colony led in 1984 to the **Sino-British Joint Declaration**, paving the way for Britain to hand back sovereignty of the territory in return for Hong Kong maintaining its capitalist system for fifty years. However, it appeared to locals that Hong Kong's lack of democratic institutions – which had suited the British – would in future mean the Chinese could do what they liked. Fears grew that repression and the erosion of freedoms such as travel and speech would follow the handover. The constitutional framework provided by the **Basic Law** of 1988, in theory, answered some of those fears, illustrating how the "One Country, Two Systems" policy would work. But the next year's **crackdown in Tian'anmen Square** only seemed to confirm the most pessimistic views of what might happen following the handover, especially to members of Hong Kong's

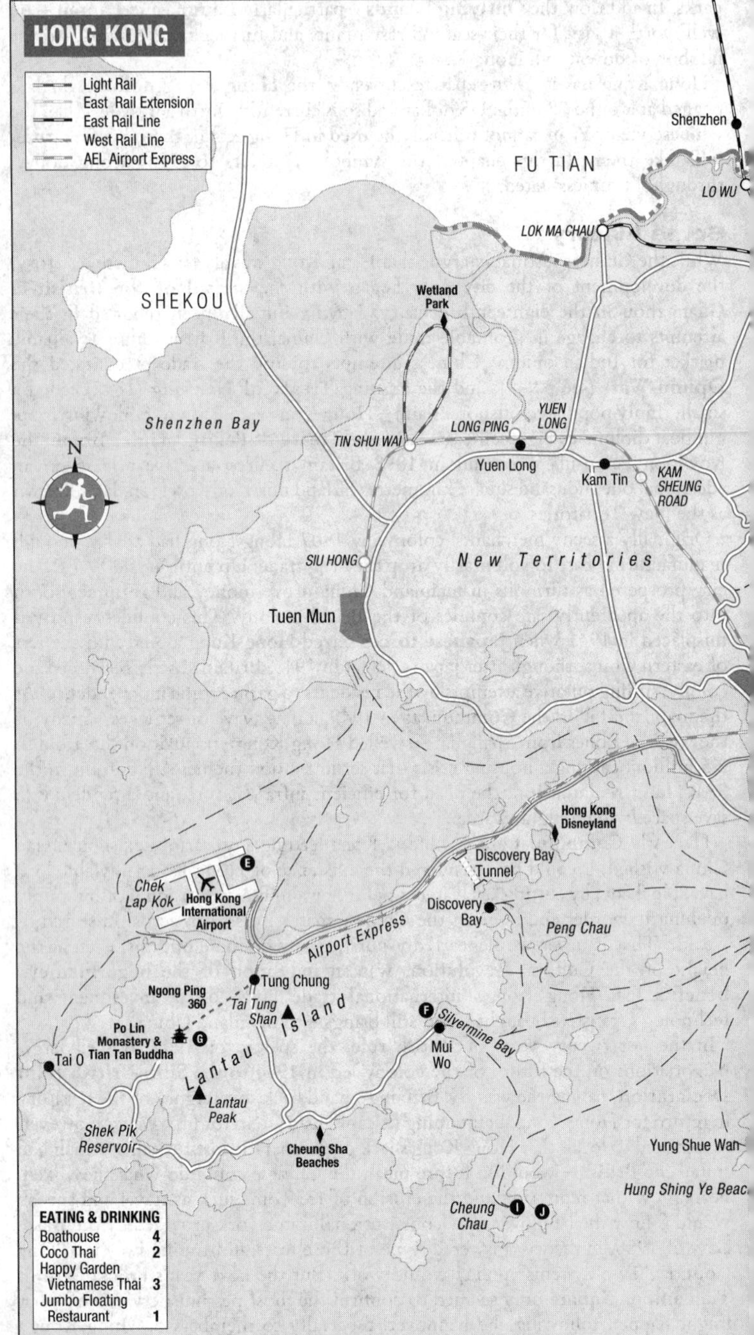
HONG KONG
Light Rail
East Rail Extension
East Rail Line
West Rail Line
AEL Airport Express
Shenzhen
FU TIAN
LO WU
LOK MA CHAU
SHEKOU
Wetland Park
Shenzhen Bay
N
YUEN LONG
LONG PING
TIN SHUI WAI
Yuen Long
Kam Tin
KAM SHEUNG ROAD
SIU HONG
New Territories
Tuen Mun
Hong Kong Disneyland
Discovery Bay Tunnel
Chek Lap Kok
Hong Kong International Airport
Discovery Bay
Peng Chau
Airport Express
Tung Chung
Ngong Ping 360
Tai Tung Shan
Lantau Island
Po Lin Monastery & Tian Tan Buddha
Silvermine Bay
Mui Wo
Tai O
Lantau Peak
Shek Pik Reservoir
Cheung Sha Beaches
Yung Shue Wan
Hung Shing Ye Beac
Cheung Chau
EATING & DRINKING
Boathouse 4
Coco Thai 2
Happy Garden Vietnamese Thai 3
Jumbo Floating Restaurant 1

9 HONG KONG AND MACAU

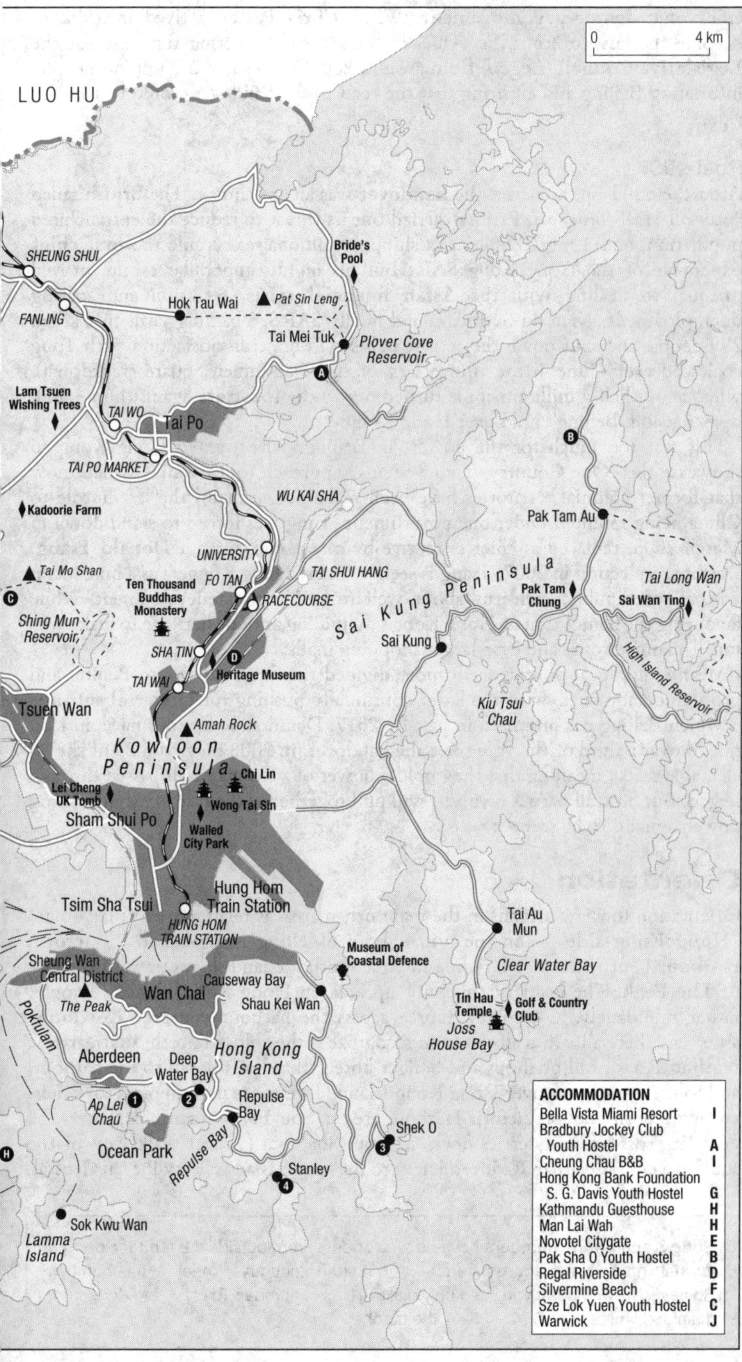

0 4 km
LUO HU
SHEUNG SHUI
FANLING
Hok Tau Wai
Pat Sin Leng
Bride's Pool
Tai Mei Tuk
Plover Cove Reservoir
A
Lam Tsuen Wishing Trees
TAI WO
Tai Po
TAI PO MARKET
B
Kadoorie Farm
WU KAI SHA
Pak Tam Au
UNIVERSITY
Tai Mo Shan
TAI SHUI HANG
Sai Kung Peninsula
Tai Long Wan
C
Ten Thousand Buddhas Monastery
FO TAN
RACECOURSE
Pak Tam Chung
Sai Wan Ting
Shing Mun Reservoir
SHA TIN
D
Sai Kung
TAI WAI
Heritage Museum
High Island Reservoir
Tsuen Wan
Amah Rock
Kiu Tsui Chau
Kowloon Peninsula
Chi Lin
Lei Cheng UK Tomb
Wong Tai Sin
Sham Shui Po
Walled City Park
Hung Hom Train Station
Tsim Sha Tsui
HUNG HOM TRAIN STATION
Tai Au Mun
Museum of Coastal Defence
Clear Water Bay
Sheung Wan
Central District
Causeway Bay
Wan Chai
The Peak
Shau Kei Wan
Tin Hau Temple
Golf & Country Club
Pokfulam
Joss House Bay
Hong Kong Island
Aberdeen
Deep Water Bay
Ap Lei Chau
Repulse Bay
Shek O
Ocean Park
Repulse Bay
Stanley
H
Sok Kwu Wan
Lamma Island
ACCOMMODATION
Bella Vista Miami Resort I
Bradbury Jockey Club Youth Hostel A
Cheung Chau B&B I
Hong Kong Bank Foundation S. G. Davis Youth Hostel G
Kathmandu Guesthouse H
Man Lai Wah H
Novotel Citygate E
Pak Sha O Youth Hostel B
Regal Riverside D
Silvermine Beach F
Sze Lok Yuen Youth Hostel C
Warwick J

embryonic **democracy movement**. When **Chris Patten** arrived in 1992 to become the last governor, he cynically broadened the voting franchise for the **Legislative Council** (**Legco**) from around 200,000 to some 2.7 million people, infuriating Beijing and ensuring that the road to the handover would be a rough ride.

Post-1997

After the build-up, however, the **handover** was an anticlimax. The British sailed away on HMS *Britannia*, Beijing carried out its threat to reduce the enfranchised population, and Tung Chee-hwa, a shipping billionaire, became the **first chief executive** of the Hong Kong SAR. But his highly unpopular tenure proved unequal to dealing with the **Asian financial crisis**, recession and soaring unemployment, avian flu outbreaks and finally SARS, a baffling virus that killed 299 people and shut down the tourist industry. Public dissatisfaction with Tung coalesced every June 4 (the anniversary of the Tian'anmen Square crackdown), when about half a million people turned out to **demonstrate** against him – and, by extension, Beijing's hold over Hong Kong.

This was too much for the powers in Beijing, who wanted Hong Kong to showcase the "One Country, Two Systems" approach to **Taiwan** – which, now that former colonial territories have been reclaimed, remains the last hurdle to China being reunited under one government. Tung was forced to stand down in March 2005, replaced as chief executive by career civil servant **Donald Tsang**. Despite re-election in 2007, Tsang is seen by many Hong Kongers as a bureaucrat who ignores public concerns about welfare and urban redevelopment, while favouring the demolition of Hong Kong's dwindling antique heritage to make way for ill-planned roads and ever-larger shopping malls.

Meanwhile, local politics seem more divided than ever along pro-Beijing and pro-democracy lines, with the latter continually pushing for **universal suffrage** – which Beijing has promised in part by 2017. Democratic factions have, in fact, polled over a third of the vote since the handover (in 2008 they won 23 of the 30 electable seats), meaning that they hold a power of veto over bills passed through Legco. But how all parties involved will pull together in the face of China's rising power remains to be seen.

Orientation

Orientation for new arrivals in the main urban areas is relatively easy: if you are "**Hong Kong-side**" – on the north shore of Hong Kong Island – **Victoria Harbour** lies to your north, while to your south the land slopes upwards steeply to **The Peak**. The heart of this built-up area on Hong Kong Island is known, rather mundanely, as **Central**. North across the harbour you are "**Kowloon-side**", and here all you really need to recognize is the colossal north–south artery, **Nathan Road**, full of shops and budget hotels, that leads down to the harbour, and to the view south over Hong Kong Island. Two more useful points for orientation on both sides of Victoria Harbour are the **Star Ferry terminals**, where the popular cross-harbour ferries dock, in Tsim Sha Tsui (a short walk west of the southern end of Nathan Road) and next to the Outer Islands Ferry Pier in Central.

Hong Kong phone numbers have no area codes. From outside the territory, dial the normal international access code + ⓣ852 (the "country" code) + the number. However, **from Macau** you need only dial ⓣ01 + the number. To call Hong Kong from mainland China, dial ⓣ00 + 852 + the number.

Arrival

Currently, nationals of the US, Canada, South Africa, Australia and New Zealand receive a three-month tourist **visa** on arrival in Hong Kong; British nationals can stay for six months. For present information, contact your local HKTB office or check Ⓦwww.immd.gov.hk/ehtml/hkvisas_4.htm.

Public transport is very organized and even first-time arrivals are unlikely to face any particular problems in reaching their destination within the city – apart from communicating with taxi drivers or reading the destinations on minibuses. All signs are supposed to be written in English and Chinese (although the English signs are sometimes so discreet as to be invisible), and travel times from the main international arrival points are reasonable, though road traffic is often heavy.

By plane

Hong Kong International Airport is located at **Chek Lap Kok**, off the north coast of Lantau Island. The fastest way into town is from inside the terminal aboard the **Airport Express (AEL)** rail service; rains depart every eight minutes between 5.50am and 1am to Kowloon (19min; $90) and Central on Hong Kong Island (23min; $100). Once in town at either the Kowloon or Hong Kong AEL stations, you'll find taxi ranks and **free hotel shuttle buses** (coloured blue and marked with a "K"), which, even if you're not staying at one of the hotels they serve, can deliver to within a short walk of most accommodation.

A more complicated but cheaper rail option is to catch an #S1, #S56 or #S64 bus to **Tung Chung MTR Station** ($4), and then take the Tung Chung Line into town along a parallel route to the AEL (around $25). It's slower, with more stops, but the advantage here is that you can change trains at Lai King Station, and get on the Tsuen Wan Line via Mong Kok, Jordan and Tsim Sha Tsui – useful for reaching Kowloon's accommodation.

Cheaper again, but far slower, is to take one of the dozen **Airbus routes** into town – their departure points are clearly signposted in the terminal. The airport customer-service counters sell tickets and give change, while on the buses themselves you need to have the exact money. All routes have regular departures between 6am and midnight, and there's plenty of room for luggage. The most useful include the #A11 and #A12 to Causeway Bay on Hong Kong Island via Sheung Wan, Central, Admiralty and Wan Chai; and the #A21 to Hung Hom Station via Tsim Sha Tsui, Jordan and Yau Ma Tei.

Taxis into the city are metered and reliable (see p.582 for more). You might want to get the tourist office in the Buffer Hall to write down the name of your destination in Chinese characters for the driver, though they should know the names of the big hotels in English. It costs roughly $300 to get to Tsim Sha Tsui, about $350 for Hong Kong Island (and so is cheaper than the AEL for a group). There may be extra charges for luggage and for tunnel tolls – on some tunnel trips the passenger pays the return charge, too. **Rush-hour traffic** can slow down journey times considerably, particularly if you're using one of the cross-harbour tunnels to Hong Kong Island.

In-town check-in

Leaving by air, many international airlines allow you to **check-in** for your flight, including checking through your in-hold luggage, up to 24hr in advance at the Hong Kong and Kowloon AEL stations. This is useful if you have a late flight and don't want to drag your luggage around with you after checking out of your hotel, but also means you don't have to join the often lengthy check-in queues at the airport.

The airport is open 24hr, and if you find yourself involved in a very late or early arrival, **night buses** include the #N11 to Central and the #N21 to Tsim Sha Tsui - otherwise you'll have to take a taxi.

By train and bus

Express trains **from China** arrive at **Hung Hom Railway Station** in Tsim Sha Tsui East (Ⓦwww.mtr.com.hk/eng/intercity/index.html). You'll also end up here if you crossed the border on foot **from Shenzhen** to Lo Wu, then caught the East Rail Line down through the New Territories. At Hung Hom, signposted walkways lead to a city bus terminal, taxi rank and – ten minutes around the harbour – the Hung Hom Ferry Pier to Wan Chai or Central (daily 7am–7pm, though there has been talk of closing this route for some time). For Tsim Sha Tsui, stay in the station and catch the MTR for one stop south to its terminus at Tsim Sha Tsui East Station, which exits into Middle Road (see map, p.583).

There are also regular daily **buses** from Guangzhou, Shenzhen and Shenzhen Airport operated by CTS and others; these arrive in either Kowloon or Wan Chai.

By ferry

Two ferry terminals handle regular ferries from Macau and from Shekou (Shenzhen): the **Hong Kong–Macau Ferry Terminal** is in the Shun Tak Centre, on Hong Kong Island, from where the Sheung Wan MTR Station and numerous bus lines are directly accessible; while the **Hong Kong China Ferry Terminal**, which also handles ferries from the Pearl River Delta, is in downtown Tsim Sha Tsui, on Canton Road. For more on Macau and Shekou ferries, see p.622 and below. There is also a berth for international cruise liners at Ocean Terminal in Tsim Sha Tsui.

Information, maps and the media

The **Hong Kong Tourism Board** or **HKTB** (daily 9am–6pm; Ⓣ2508 1234, Ⓦwww.discoverhongkong.com) issues more leaflets, pamphlets, brochures and maps than the rest of China put together. Their three downtown **offices**

Moving on: routes into mainland China

To enter China you need a **visa**. If you haven't picked one up from a Chinese consulate or embassy at home, it's quickest to obtain one through a **travel agency** (see p.619) or through your accommodation, many of which offer the service; agents can also arrange hotel accommodation and onward journeys into China. **Visa fees** vary between $200 and $600 or above, according to your nationality, whether you want a single-entry or double-entry, one-month, three-month or six-month visa, and whether you want fast (same-day) processing, or can wait two to three days. **Beware**: visas issued in Hong Kong are only **extendable once** on the mainland; and can wait some multi-entry visas require you to **leave China** every thirty days even if valid, for instance, for a six-month period.

By bus, CTS (see p.619 for address; Ⓦctsbus.hkcts.com) and many other companies run frequent services from downtown Hong Kong to Shenzhen or Shenzhen airport (1hr 40min; $50–100) and Guangzhou (3hr 30min; $90).

Trains from Hung Hom station in East Kowloon run to Guangzhou East (12 daily; 2hr; $190); Shanghai (1 on alternate days; 19hr; soft/hard sleeper $840/550); and Beijing West (1 on alternate days; 23hr; soft/hard sleeper $935/600). Tickets are available **online** (Ⓦwww.it3.mtr.com.hk/b2c) – though you have to collect them in Hong Kong – or from Hung Hom Station. You can also reach Guangzhou via (daily 8am–8pm) are in the Star Ferry Terminal in Tsim Sha Tsui; near Exit F, Causeway Bay MTR Station; and in an old railway carriage outside the Peak Mall, on The Peak. English-speaking staff at all three provide sound, useful advice on accommodation, shopping, restaurants, bus routes and hiking trails – or can tell you how to find out yourself. In addition, they run tours and organize short **free courses** on *tai ji*, Cantonese Opera, tea appreciation and more, for which you need to sign up a day in advance.

Free HKTB **maps**, and the maps in this book, should be enough for most purposes, though street atlases such as the paperback *Hong Kong Guidebook*, which includes all bus routes, can be bought from bookstores (see p.618). Free **listings magazines**, providing up-to-date information on restaurants, bars, clubs, concerts and exhibitions, include the trendy *HK Magazine* (Ⓦwww.hk-magazine.com) and acerbic *BC Magazine* (Ⓦwww.bcmagazine.net), both available in hotels, cafés and restaurants. *Time Out Hong Kong* (Ⓦwww.timeout.com.hk; $18) offers much the same, with perhaps more weighty reviews.

Hong Kong's two English-language **daily papers** are the *South China Morning Post*, whose bland coverage of regional news does its best to toe the party line, and the *Standard*, a business-oriented freebie which can be outspoken about politicians' failings. Other international papers, such as the local edition of the *Herald Tribune*, and journals such as *Time* and *Newsweek*, are widely available.

City transport

Hong Kong's public transport system is efficient, extensive and inexpensive – though best avoided during the weekday **rush hours**, which last between about 7–9am and 5–7pm. If you plan to travel a good deal, get hold of an **Octopus Card** (Ⓦwww.octopus.com.hk), a rechargeable stored-value ticket that can be used for travel on all MTR services (including lines through the New Territories and the AEL), most buses and most ferries (including the Star Ferry and main inter-island services). The card itself costs $50 and you add value to it by feeding it and your money into machines in the MTR. The fare is then electronically deducted each time you use the card by swiping it over yellow sensor pads at station turnstiles or,

Shenzhen by riding the East Rail Line up to the border at Lo Wu, crossing into Shenzhen on foot, and then picking up one of the hourly trains to Guangzhou from there (about $120 in total).

By ferry, your first option – assuming you already have a valid visa for China – is direct **from Hong Kong International Airport** to either Shekou (for Shenzhen) or Nansha (for Guangzhou), with either Chu Kong Ferries (Ⓦwww.cksp.com.hk) or TurboJet (Ⓦwww.turbojet.com.hk); follow signs from inside the transit terminal to the "Sky Pier". Crossings take around an hour, cost in the region of $220, and run from about 9am–7pm. Otherwise, the **China Ferry Terminal** on Canton Road, Tsim Sha Tsui, is the main departure point for destinations all over the Pearl River Delta, including Shekou and Nansha, mostly operated by Chu Kong Ferries (Ⓦwww.cksp.com.hk).

Finally, you can **fly** from Hong Kong to all major Chinese cities on regional Chinese carriers. However, airfares from Hong Kong are vastly more expensive than on the mainland, and you'll save a lot of money **flying from Shenzhen airport**, easily reached by bus in just two hours from downtown Hong Kong – any travel agent can book you a ticket ($100). The bus drops you at the border, you walk 500m to the other side via HK and Chinese customs, and then pick up another bus to the airport. Buses run every fifteen minutes, so don't worry if you get stuck in a passport queue along the way.

Free things

Hong Kong might be an expensive place compared with the Chinese mainland, but there are a number of **free things** to take advantage of while you're here. These include entry to all downtown parks, plus the Zoological and Botanical Gardens (p.592); the Edward Youde Aviary and the Museum of Teaware in Hong Kong Park (p.592); all government-run museums on Wednesdays; martial-arts performances in Kowloon Park on Sunday afternoons (p.600); the ferry ride through Aberdeen Harbour to the *Jumbo* floating restaurant (p.613); Mong Kok's bird and goldfish markets (p.600); harbour views from Tsim Sha Tsui waterfront (p.599) and the Bank of China tower (p.589); and introductory cultural courses, plus a harbour cruise, offered by the HKTB (p.580).

on a bus, beside the driver. Octopus cards can also be used in many retail outlets, including Park'n'shop supermarkets, *Maxim's* restaurants and 7–11 stores.

Trains

Hong Kong's trains are all operated by **MTR** (Mass Transit Railway; Ⓦwww.mtr.com.hk), and you buy single-journey **tickets** ($4–11) from easy-to-use dispensing machines at the stations, or use an Octopus Card. Clear, colour-coded **maps** can be found at all stations and on tourist maps handed out by the HKTB. Services run between about 6am and 1am.

People usually use the term **MTR** to refer to the four, mostly underground, lines connecting Hong Kong Island's north shore with Kowloon (though there are plans to extend these to the south of Hong Kong Island). Other important routes include the **West Rail Line** and **East Rail Line** from Kowloon into the New Territories; lines out to Disney and Tung Chung on **Lantau Island**; and the **AEL** (see p.579), which connects the downtown to the Airport. There's also the **LRT** (Light Rail Transit), which connects the New Territories towns of Tuen Mun and Yuen Long, though tourists rarely use it except to reach the Hong Kong Wetland Park (see p.603).

Trams

Trams have been rattling along Hong Kong Island's north shore since 1904 and, despite being an anachronism in such a hi-tech city, they are as popular as ever with locals and tourists alike, especially for the night-time view from the upstairs deck. The trams run between Kennedy Town in the west and Shau Kei Wan in the east, via Central, Wan Chai and Causeway Bay (some going via Happy Valley; check the front of the tram). You board the tram at the back, and swipe your Octopus Card or drop the money in the driver's box ($2; $1 for senior citizens and children; no change given) when you get off.

Buses, taxis and cars

Hong Kong's double-decker **buses** are comfortable and air-conditioned, and are essential for reaching the south of Hong Kong Island and parts of the New Territories. You swipe your card or pay as you board (exact change is required); the amount is often posted up on the timetables at bus stops, and fares range from $1.20 to $45. The HKTB issues up-to-date information on bus routes, including the approximate length of journeys and cost. The **main bus terminal** in Central is at Exchange Square, though some services start from outside the Star Ferry Terminal/Outlying Islands Ferry Pier. In Tsim Sha Tsui, Kowloon, the main bus terminal is currently in front of the Star Ferry Terminal – though there is talk of shifting it elsewhere.

As well as the big buses, there are also red- or green-striped **minibuses** and **maxicabs**, which have set stops but can also be hailed (not on double yellow

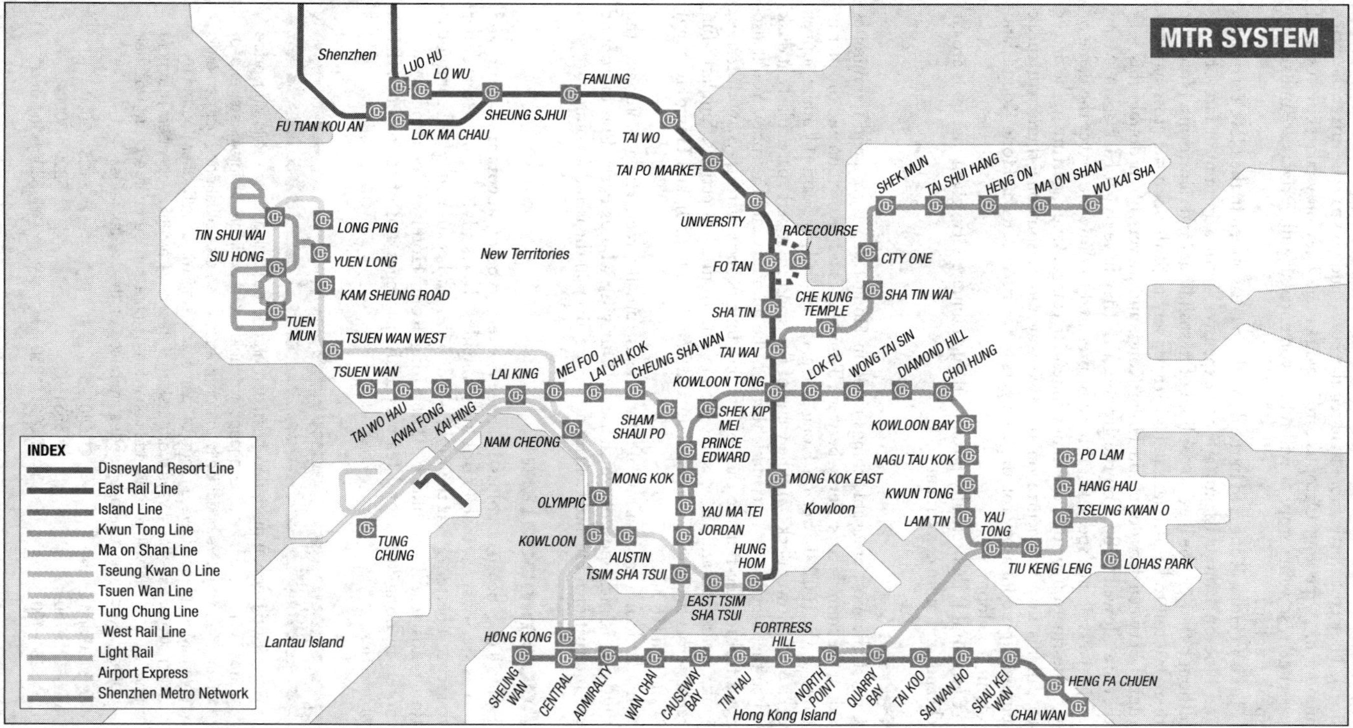

MTR SYSTEM

Shenzhen
LUO HU
LO WU
FANLING
FU TIAN KOU AN
LOK MA CHAU
SHEUNG SJHUI
TAI WO
TAI PO MARKET
UNIVERSITY
RACECOURSE
FO TAN
SHA TIN
TAI WAI
KOWLOON TONG
MONG KOK EAST
HUNG HOM
EAST TSIM SHA TSUI

SHEK MUN
TAI SHUI HANG
HENG ON
MA ON SHAN
WU KAI SHA
CITY ONE
SHA TIN WAI
CHE KUNG TEMPLE

TIN SHUI WAI
SIU HONG
LONG PING
YUEN LONG
KAM SHEUNG ROAD
TUEN MUN
TSUEN WAN WEST
New Territories

TSUEN WAN
TAI WO HAU
KWAI FONG
KAI HING
LAI KING
MEI FOO
LAI CHI KOK
CHEUNG SHA WAN
SHAM SHAUI PO
SHEK KIP MEI
PRINCE EDWARD
MONG KOK
YAU MA TEI
JORDAN
AUSTIN
TSIM SHA TSUI
NAM CHEONG
OLYMPIC
KOWLOON
TUNG CHUNG
Lantau Island

LOK FU
WONG TAI SIN
DIAMOND HILL
CHOI HUNG
KOWLOON BAY
NAGU TAU KOK
KWUN TONG
LAM TIN
YAU TONG
Kowloon
TIU KENG LENG
PO LAM
HANG HAU
TSEUNG KWAN O
LOHAS PARK

HONG KONG
SHEUNG WAN
CENTRAL
ADMIRALTY
WAN CHAI
CAUSEWAY BAY
TIN HAU
FORTRESS HILL
NORTH POINT
QUARRY BAY
TAI KOO
SAI WAN HO
SHAU KEI WAN
HENG FA CHUEN
CHAI WAN
Hong Kong Island

INDEX

- Disneyland Resort Line
- East Rail Line
- Island Line
- Kwun Tong Line
- Ma on Shan Line
- Tseung Kwan O Line
- Tsuen Wan Line
- Tung Chung Line
- West Rail Line
- Light Rail
- Airport Express
- Shenzhen Metro Network

lines). They cost a little more than regular buses, and you pay the driver the exact amount or swipe your Octopus card as you enter. They only take sixteen seated passengers, so won't stop, or will refuse you entry, if full. Drivers are unlikely to speak English.

Taxis in Hong Kong (red in the downtown areas, green in the New Territories and blue on Lantau Island) are not expensive, with a minimum fare of $18, although they can be hard to get hold of in rush hours and rainstorms. Note that there is a toll to be paid (around $5–15) on any trips through the cross-harbour tunnel between Kowloon and Hong Kong, and drivers often double this – as they are allowed to do – on the grounds that they have to get back again. Many taxi drivers do not speak English, so be prepared to show the driver the name of your destination written down in Chinese. If you get stuck, gesture to the driver to call his dispatch centre on the two-way radio; someone there will speak English. It is obligatory for all passengers to wear seat belts on Hong Kong Island and in Kowloon.

Car rental is theoretically possible, though unnecessary, given that taxis are far cheaper and more convenient.

Ferries

One of the most enjoyable things to do in Hong Kong is to spend ten minutes riding the humble **Star Ferry** between Tsim Sha Tsui in Kowloon and the pier in front of the IFC2 Tower on Hong Kong Island (daily 6.30am–11.30pm; upper deck $2.50, lower deck $2). The views of the island are superb, particularly at dusk when the lights begin to twinkle through the humidity and the spray. You'll also get a feel for the frenetic pace of life on Hong Kong's waterways, with ferries, junks, hydrofoils and larger ships looming up from all directions. Similarly fun ferries cross between Tsim Sha Tsui and Wan Chai ($2.50), and Hung Hom and Wan Chai ($6.30).

In addition, a large array of other boats runs between Hong Kong and the Outlying Islands, most of which use the **Outlying Islands Ferry Pier** in front of the International Finance Centre; details are given in the island accounts.

Accommodation

Hong Kong boasts a colossal range of every type of **accommodation**, and rooms are always available. **Booking ahead** is always advisable however, either to secure a better rate at the higher-end places, or because budget accommodation tends to fill up quickly. The Hong Kong Hotels Association (Ⓦwww.hotels-in-hong-kong.com) features deals, packages and offers for all HKHA properties.

Accommodation price codes

Hong Kong accommodation has been graded according to the following **price codes**, which represent the cheapest double room available to foreigners, except where the text refers specifically to dorm beds, when the actual price per person is given. Most places have a range of rooms, and staff will usually offer you the more expensive ones – it's always worth asking if they have anything cheaper. The more upmarket hotels will levy an additional ten-percent service charge on top of their quoted room rates. Our price codes are based on the pre-tax rates.

❶ $120 and under	❹ $401–550	❼ $1251–2000
❷ $121–250	❺ $551–900	❽ $2001–3000
❸ $251–400	❻ $901–1250	❾ $3001 and over

At the upper end of the market are some of the best **hotels** in the world, costing several thousand dollars a night, though less renowned places offering motel-like facilities start around $600. The lower end of the market is served by **guesthouses and hostels**, the bulk of which are squeezed into blocks at the lower end of Nathan Road – though there are even a few on the Outlying Islands. Always check these rooms for size (many are minuscule), whether they have a window, and whether you have to pay extra for the use of air conditioning. Even these are not that cheap, however – you'll be lucky to find a double for less than $300, though shared **dormitory accommodation** can come in as low as $100–150 a night for a bed.

The **Hong Kong Youth Hostels Association** (Ⓦwww.yha.org.hk) also operates seven self-catering hostels – mostly a long way from the centre – offering dormitory accommodation for IYHF members from $90. Finally, you can also **camp for free** at the 38 campsites run by the Agriculture, Fisheries and Conservation Department (Ⓦwww.afcd.gov.hk), mostly in relatively remote sites inside Hong Kong's Country Parks. Facilities are basic – pit latrines and tank water which must be boiled – and you'll need to be self-sufficient. Pitches are available on a first-come, first-served basis, so get in early at weekends and holidays.

Hong Kong Island

Accommodation on the island is mostly upmarket, though there's a small budget enclave in **Causeway Bay** (with prices a tad higher than Kowloon's), and the secluded, basic but excellent *Mount Davis Youth Hostel*. The places below are marked on the map on pp.590–591.

Bin Man Hostel 1F, Central Building, 531 Jaffe Rd, Causeway Bay Ⓣ2833 2063, Ⓕ2838 5651. Tiny, clean but elderly rooms in this budget hotel, well located for Causeway Bay's attractions. ❸

Garden View International House 1 MacDonnell Rd, Mid-Levels Ⓣ2877 3737, Ⓦwww.ywca.org.hk. This comfortable YWCA-run hotel is off Garden Rd, south of the Zoological and Botanical Gardens. Maxicab #1A from outside the Star Ferry Terminal and Central MTR runs past. Prices change considerably depending on demand, but their cheaper rates are a very good deal. ❼

Hotel LKF 33 Wyndham St, Lan Kwai Fong, Central Ⓣ3518 9688, Ⓦwww.hotel-lkf.com.hk. Boutique design, but generously-sized rooms, make this pricey, slick operation a stylish place to stay in the heart of Hong Kong's business and shopping district. ❽

Hostel HK 3F, Paterson Building, 47 Paterson St Ⓣ2392 6868, Ⓦwww.hostel.hk. No sign makes this tricky to find, but the friendly atmosphere and above-average rooms – plus free laundry – make it worth the effort. ❸

King's Hotel 303 Jaffe Rd, Wan Chai Ⓣ3188 2277, Ⓦwww.kingshotelhk.com. Quirky boutique hotel with a "cyber" theme resulting in a sort of minimalist sci-fi decor. Rooms come with broadband-enabled computers and plasma-screen TVs, and regular deals can halve rates. ❺

Mandarin Oriental 5 Connaught Rd, Central Ⓣ2522 0111, Ⓦwww.mandarinoriental.com/hongkong. Unassumingly set in a plain concrete box, this is one of the best hotels in the world, with unmatched service. The hotel lobby is also a great place to people-watch – anyone who's anyone in Hong Kong eats or drinks here. Internet rates begin at $2900. ❾

Mount Davis Youth Hostel Mount Davis Ⓣ2817 5715, Ⓦwww.yha.org.hk. Perched on the top of a mountain above Kennedy Town, this self-catering retreat has superb, peaceful views over the harbour. Getting here, however, is a major expedition, unless you catch the infrequent shuttle bus from the ground floor of the Shun Tak Centre (Hong Kong–Macau Ferry Terminal) – phone the hostel for times. Otherwise, catch bus #5 from Admiralty or minibus #3A from the Outlying Islands Ferry Pier in Central and get off near the junction of Victoria Rd and Mount Davis Path; walk back 100m from the bus stop and you'll see Mount Davis Path branching off up the hill – the hostel is a 35min walk. If you have much luggage, get off the bus in Kennedy Town and catch a taxi from there (around $50 plus $5 per item of luggage). Dorms $90, doubles/family rooms ❷–❺

Park Lane 310 Gloucester Rd, Causeway Bay Ⓣ2293 8888, Ⓦwww.parklane.com.hk. Located right on Victoria Park, this plush hotel is conveniently sited for the shopping and eating delights of Causeway Bay. ❾

Kowloon

Most of the accommodation listed below is conveniently central, within fifteen minutes' walk of the Tsim Sha Tsui Star Ferry Terminal. For a less claustrophobic atmosphere, however, try locations in Jordan and Yau Ma Tei, which are all located near MTR stations. Places listed represent a fraction of the total on offer, and it is always worth having a look at several options. The places below, including **Chungking and Mirador mansions**, are marked on the map on p.598.

Anne Black Guesthouse (YWCA) 5 Man Fuk Rd, Yau Ma Tei ⓣ2713 9211, ⓦwww.ywca.org.hk. Not far from the Yau Ma Tei MTR, this YWCA pension is surprisingly smart, light and airy, with a choice of either shared or en-suite bathrooms. Check the website for discounts. ❺

Benito 7–7B Cameron Rd, Tsim Sha Tsui ⓣ3653 0388, ⓦwww.hotelbenito.com. Bright, clean and modern boutique hotel close to everything that matters in Tsim Sha Tsui. Cheaper rooms are only fractionally larger than in a guesthouse, however. ❼

Luxe Manor 39 Kimberley Rd, Tsim Sha Tsui ⓣ3763 8888, ⓦwww.theluxemanor.com. Another boutique option, with stylish, strikingly themed rooms which will either appeal or appall. Their *Aspasia* restaurant draws the chic and almost-famous to dine. ❼

King's de Nathan 473–473A Nathan Rd, Yau Ma Tei, immediately south of the Yau Ma Tei MTR ⓣ2780 1281, ⓦwww.kingsdenathan.com. Probably the cheapest "real" hotel in town, with modern furnishings and reasonably sized rooms for the price. ❺

Nathan 378 Nathan Rd, Jordan ⓣ2388 5141, ⓦwww.nathanhotel.com. Smart, good-value hotel. Located in a slightly characterless area, though close to the night market and within easy reach of the MTR. ❼

Peninsula Hotel Salisbury Rd, Tsim Sha Tsui ⓣ2920 2888, ⓦwww.peninsula.com. One of the classiest hotels in the world, which has been overlooking the harbour and Hong Kong Island for eighty years. Check the website for package rates. ❾

The Salisbury (YMCA) 41 Salisbury Rd, Tsim Sha Tsui ⓣ2268 7888, ⓦwww.ymcahk.org.hk. Superb location next door to the *Peninsula Hotel* and with views over the harbour and Hong Kong Island; facilities include indoor pools, a fitness centre and squash court. For the price, the doubles are unbeatable value; relatively expensive four-bed dorms with attached shower are also available. Dorms $240, rooms ❺–❻.

Sealand House Block D, 8F, Majestic House, 80 Nathan Rd, Tsim Sha Tsui ⓣ2368 9522, ⓦwww.sealandhouse.com.hk. Located inside a residential block across from Kowloon Mosque, this is the cleanest, roomiest and friendliest of the upper-price-range guesthouses, with a choice of shared or en-suite facilities. ❸

Chungking Mansions

Set at the southern end of Nathan Road, **Chungking Mansions** is an ugly monster of a building, its lower three floors forming a warren of tiny shops and Central Asian restaurants, the upper sixteen storeys crammed with budget guesthouses. While the Mansions has a reputation for sleaze and poor maintenance, recent attention from the health and safety departments have wrought great changes: downstairs remains pretty lively, but the guesthouses are generally well-run, if cramped and sometimes windowless. The building is divided into five blocks, lettered A to E, each served by two tiny lifts that are subject to long queues.

Chungking House Block A, 4F and 5F ⓣ2739 1600, ⓦwww.chungkinghouse.com. Long-running place with decent-sized rooms; cheaper ones are not such a good deal though. Single ❷, double ❸

Dragon Inn Block B, 3F ⓣ2367 7071, ⓦwww.dragoninn.info. No-nonsense but friendly manager and bright rooms (within the Mansions' limits, at any rate) make this a good choice – though it's worth paying the extra for a/c. ❸

Germany Hostel Block D, 6F ⓣ3105 1830, ⓦwww.germanyhostelhk.com. A real gem of a place: clean, exceptionally friendly and they've taken trouble to make the admittedly small rooms as welcoming and bright as possible. ❶–❸

Hawaii Block A, 1F ⓣ2366 6127. Older place in good condition that offers minimum space at minimum cost. Dorms $70, doubles ❷

Welcome Guesthouse Block A, 7F ⓣ2721 7793, ⓕ2311 5558. A good choice, offering a/c doubles with and without shower. Nice clean rooms, luggage storage, laundry service and China visas available. ❷

Yan Yan Guesthouse Block E, 8F ⓣ2366 8930, ⓕ2723 5671. Helpful staff renting out doubles with all facilities; you could sleep three in some – at a squeeze – making them good value. ❷

Mirador Mansions

This is another block at 54–64 Nathan Rd, on the east side, in between Carnarvon Road and Mody Road, right next to the Tsim Sha Tsui MTR Station. Dotted about, in among the residential apartments, are large numbers of guesthouses. **Mirador Mansions** is cleaner and brighter than Chungking Mansions, and queues for the lifts are smaller.

Cosmic 12F ⓣ2369 6669, ⓦwww.cosmicguesthouse.com. No frills or excess space, even for this sort of guesthouse, but it's a friendly place with helpful management. ❸

Garden Hostel Flat F4, 3F ⓣ2311 1183. A friendly travellers' hangout, with washing machines, lockers and a patio garden. A *wing chun* martial-arts school is also based here, and you can arrange lessons with them. Mixed and women-only dorms; beds get cheaper if you pay by the week. Beware touts for other hostels using the same name – this is the real one. Dorms $60, rooms ❷

Mei Lam Guesthouse Flat D1, 5F ⓣ2721 5278. Helpful, English-speaking owner and very presentable singles and doubles, all spick-and-span, with full facilities. Worth the higher-than-usual prices. ❸

The New Territories and Outlying Islands

The **New Territories** and **Outlying Islands** offer an attractive escape from the city's congestion. You won't be the only one who is tempted by the idea, though – always book in advance, especially at weekends and during holidays. Most of Hong Kong's **youth hostels** are here; all are self-catering, require you to be a YHA member, and are too remote to be used as a base for exploring the rest of Hong Kong. Commuting from Lamma or Cheung Chau, however, is feasible – guesthouses here raise their rates at weekends but also offer package deals for a week or more. The HKTB can further advise about holiday flats on the islands. The places below are marked on the map on pp.576–577.

New Territories

Bradbury Jockey Club Youth Hostel 66 Tai Mei Tuk Rd, Tai Mei Tuk, Tai Po ⓣ2662 5123, ⓦwww.yha.org.hk. Not too hard to reach: ride the East Rail Line train to Tai Po, then bus #75K to Tai Mei Tuk. From the bus stop, walk towards the Plover Cove Reservoir and the hostel is a few minutes ahead on the left. Lots of boating, walking and cycling opportunities. Two- to eight-bed rooms ❶–❸

Pak Sha O Youth Hostel Pak Sha O, Hoi Ha Rd, Sai Kung ⓣ2328 2327. From Sai Kung town, catch green minibus #7 going to Hoi Ha and tell the driver where you're heading; it's a short walk from the road. Great for access to Hong Kong's cleanest, most secluded snorkelling beaches. Dorms $90, camping $35.

Regal Riverside Hotel 34–36 Tai Chung Kiu Rd, Sha Tin ⓣ2649 7878, ⓦwww.regalhotel.com. The New Territories' best hotel – though there's not a lot of competition – right in the centre of Sha Tin. This comfortable place often appears in holiday packages; there's a fine Asian lunch buffet served here and a free shuttle bus to Tsim Sha Tsui, too. Check their website for discounted rates. ❺

Outlying Islands

Bella Vista Miami Resort East Bay, Cheung Chau ⓣ2981 7299, ⓦwww.miamicheungchau.com.hk. A huge number of rooms located in a residential block near the east beach; check the website for pictures. The cheaper options are best avoided while the better rooms are worth the price. Sun–Fri ❸, Sat ❹

Cheung Chau B&B Tung Wah Beach, Cheung Chau ⓣ2986 9990, ⓦwww.bbcheungchau.com.hk. Just back from the beach along the access road from the village, this is a genuine, modern B&B with a welcoming atmosphere and excellent furnishings. Sun–Fri ❹, Sat ❺

Hong Kong Bank Foundation S. G. Davis Youth Hostel Ngong Ping, Lantau Island ⓣ2985 5610. From the Ngong Ping bus terminal (p.609) follow the paved footpath south, away from the Tian Tan Buddha and past the public toilets. It's a 10min walk and well signposted. Basic dorms and tent pitches at the base of Lantau Peak, and you can eat at the nearby Po Lin Monastery. It's cold on winter nights, though – bring a sleeping bag. Dorms $90, camping $35.

Kathmandu Guesthouse Yung Shue Wan, Lamma ⓣ2982 0028. Above Bubbles Laundry in Yung Shue Wan town, this hostel-like place has been going forever and offers dorm beds as well as doubles at some of the lowest rates on the island. Don't expect any luxuries. Beds $110 weekdays, $150 at weekends; doubles ❸

Man Lai Wah Hotel Yung Shue Wan, Lamma ⓣ2982 0220. Right ahead from the ferry pier, this great low-key place has small, double-bed flats with balconies and harbour views. ④

Novotel Citygate 51 Man Tung Rd, Tung Chung, Lantau ⓣ3602 8888, ⓦwww.novotel.com. Right next to the Tung Chung MTR and Ngong Ping 360, just five minutes from the airport. Rates are a bargain compared to the downtown areas and the website often advertises inexpensive last-minute deals. ⑦

Silvermine Beach Hotel 648 Silvermine Bay, Mui Wo, Lantau ⓣ2984 8295, ⓦwww.resort.com.hk. Superbly located right on the beachfront, a few minutes' walk from the Mui Wo Ferry Pier. The rooms are comfortable and quiet, with excellent-value long-term packages available. The restaurant spilling out onto the terraces offers popular barbecues and Thai grub. ⑥, sea view ⑦

Warwick Hotel East Bay, Cheung Chau ⓣ2981 0081, ⓦwww.warwickhotel.com.hk. Overlooking Tung Wan Beach, this is the most upmarket and expensive of Cheung Chau's accommodation, with a swimming pool and restaurant. Rooms have balconies, private baths, cable TV, and good-value weekly rates. Sun–Fri ⑥, Sat ⑦

Hong Kong Island

As the oldest colonized part of Hong Kong, its administrative and business centre, and site of some of the most expensive real estate in the world, **Hong Kong Island** is naturally the heart of the whole territory. Despite this, it measures just 15km across, with development concentrated along its **north shore** – a frenetically crowded and entertaining area of shops, restaurants, bars and financial institutions – and the far greener, mellower **south coast**, which actually sports a few beaches. Hills between the two rise to **The Peak**, which offers some of the island's best scenery and its freshest air. **Transport** around the island is easy, with the MTR and trams covering the north shore, and plentiful buses throughout.

The north shore

The island's **north shore**, overlooking **Victoria Harbour** to Kowloon, focuses on a narrow 6km-long financial, commercial and entertainment district. At its core, **Central** sprouts an astounding array of hi-tech towers, edged to the west by **Sheung Wan**'s smaller-scale and traditional Chinese businesses. Behind this the land climbs steeply, past parks and knots of restaurants and bars, to **The Peak**, a superb escape from street-level claustrophobia with unequalled views over the city. Back along the harbour and moving east through **Wan Chai** towards **Causeway Bay**, the emphasis shifts from finance to wining, dining and shopping – not to mention gambling, with Hong Kong's main horse racetrack located nearby at **Happy Valley**. Further east again, it's worth heading out to **Shau Kei Wan** to visit the **Museum of Coastal Defence**, built inside an old fortification.

The most obvious **arrival points** on the island are Central MTR Station, or adjacent bus stations, but it's far more romantic to catch the **Star Ferry** from Tsim Sha Tsui, which docks immediately east of the Outlying Islands Ferry Pier. Aside from the MTR Island Line, buses and trams, you should make use, too, of the outdoor **Mid-Levels Escalator**, which runs uphill from Central, and the extensive system of **elevated walkways** that link many buildings between Sheung Wan and the Bank of China tower.

Note that the whole harbourside area between Central and Wan Chai is undergoing extensive **land reclamation** at present to provide space for a congestion-relieving expressway, plazas and parkland.

Central

Central takes in the densely crowded heart of Hong Kong's financial district, and extends for a few hundred metres in all directions from Central MTR Station. The main west–east roads here are Connaught Road, Des Voeux Road and Queen's Road, with a mesh of smaller streets heading south and uphill.

For those arriving on the Star Ferry, an elevated walkway leads from the terminal between the post office and the **International Finance Centre (IFC)**. The centre itself houses a **mall** and the AEL terminus, while above it rears the 88-storey, 420m-high **IFC2**. This is so beautifully proportioned that it's not until you see the top brushing the clouds that you realize the tower stands half as high again as anything else in the area. Sadly, you can't ride the lift up for views, though there's a virtual 360-degree version on the IFC website (Ⓦwww.ifc.com.hk/english). IFC2 was Hong Kong's tallest building until 2010, when the **ICC Tower** sprouted across the harbour in West Kowloon (see p.597).

Continue straight ahead on the walkway, and you pass between **Jardine House** (the tower full of portholes) and **Exchange Square**, before descending into the heart of an extremely upmarket shopping area along **Des Voeux Road** – easily recognizable from its tramlines. The smartest mall here is the **Landmark**, on the corner with Pedder Street, though the best-known shop is undoubtedly **Shanghai Tang** on tiny Theatre Lane between Des Voeux and Queen's Roads (next to Exit D2 from Central MTR), specializing in pricey designer garments in bright colours, recalling traditional Chinese wear.

South of Queen's Road, the land begins to slope seriously upwards, making walking laborious in hot weather. Head up D'Aguilar Street, and you'll enter the **Lan Kwai Fong** area, Central's barfly district, stuffed with theme bars and restaurants that now overflow into several neighbouring streets, including Wing Wah Lane (locally known as "Rat Alley"). Also of interest here is the **Luk Yu Tea House** (see p.610) a 1930s-style establishment on Stanley Street.

East of the Landmark along Queen's Road lie two extraordinary buildings whose hi-tech appearances mask deeply traditional Chinese beliefs. The **Hong Kong and Shanghai Bank (HSBC)** dates from 1985; designed by Sir Norman Foster, it reputedly cost over US$1 billion. The whole building is supported off the ground so that it's possible to walk right underneath – a necessity stipulated by the *feng shui* belief that the centre of power on the island, Government House, which lies directly to the north of the bank, should be accessible in a straight line from the main point of arrival on the island, the Star Ferry. From underneath, the building's insides are transparent, and you can look up into its heart through the colossal glass atrium.

Past the HSBC, the 300m-high, blue-glass and steel **Bank of China** was designed by a team led by the renowned I.M. Pei. In *feng shui* terms, the bank's threatening, knife-like tower can be seen like a lightning conductor, drawing good luck down from the sky before any can reach its shorter rival next door. There are exceptional **views** from long windows on the 43rd floor – you're allowed up during office hours. Below, **Statue Square** is an oddly empty space, sided to the east by the anachronistic, domed, granite **Legco Building**, century-old home of the Legislative Council, Hong Kong's equivalent of a parliament.

The Mid-Levels Escalator

Head east along Queen's Road from the Central MTR – or follow walkways from the International Finance Centre – and you'll reach the covered **Mid-Levels Escalator**, which rises in sections 800m up the hill as far as Conduit Road and the trendy **Mid-Levels** residential area. During the morning (6–10am), when people are setting out to work, the escalators run downwards only; from 10.20am to midnight they run up. Places to get off and explore include the restaurant district between Wellington Street and Lyndhurst Terrace; the narrow lanes west of the escalator between Queen's Road and Hollywood Road, full of crowded produce markets and small shops specializing in domestic goods; **Hollywood Road** itself,

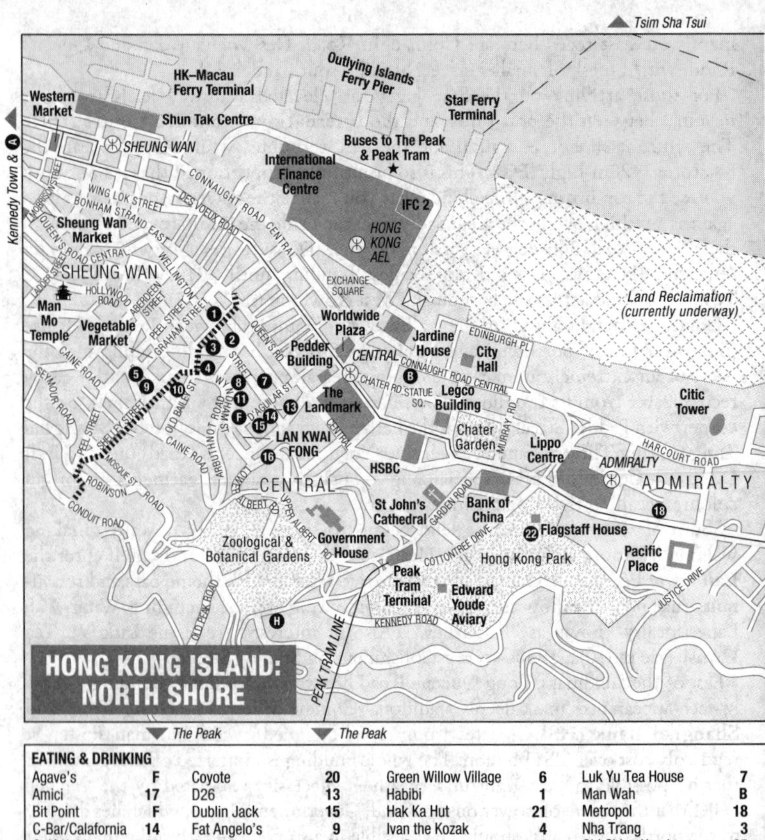

EATING & DRINKING

Agave's	F	Coyote	20	Green Willow Village	6	Luk Yu Tea House	7
Amici	17	D26	13	Habibi	1	Man Wah	B
Bit Point	F	Dublin Jack	15	Hak Ka Hut	21	Metropol	18
C-Bar/Calafornia	14	Fat Angelo's	9	Ivan the Kozak	4	Nha Trang	3
Café Habitu	26	Flying Pan	10	La Pampa	5	Old China Hand	25
Carnegie's	23	Fook Lam Moon	27	Le Jardin	11	Padang	12
Chippy	2	Fringe Club	16	Lok Cha Teahouse	22	The Pawn	28

lined with antique shops and fine art galleries (see p.615); and the restaurant, bar and café district of **Soho**, laid out along Elgin and Staunton streets.

Sheung Wan

West of Central, **Sheung Wan**'s major landmark is the waterfront **Shun Tak Centre**, edged in red and housing both the Hong Kong–Macau Ferry Terminal and Sheung Wang MTR station. The main road here, Connaught, is crammed with traffic and the area looks no different from Central, but venture inland and things begin to change rapidly.

First stop is **Western Market** (daily 10am–7pm), a brick Edwardian-era building featuring ground-floor tourist tack and good-value fabric shops upstairs. Follow **Morrison Street** uphill from here and you'll soon cross **Bonham Strand**; head west and you enter a web of lanes centred around **Bonham Strand West**, **Queen's Road West** and **Wing Lok Street** whose shops specialize in dried foods and traditional Chinese medicine products such as birds' nests, ginseng, assorted marine creatures, deer antlers, edible fungus and aromatic fruits. There's a fine line between food and medicine in China, but the best way of telling the difference

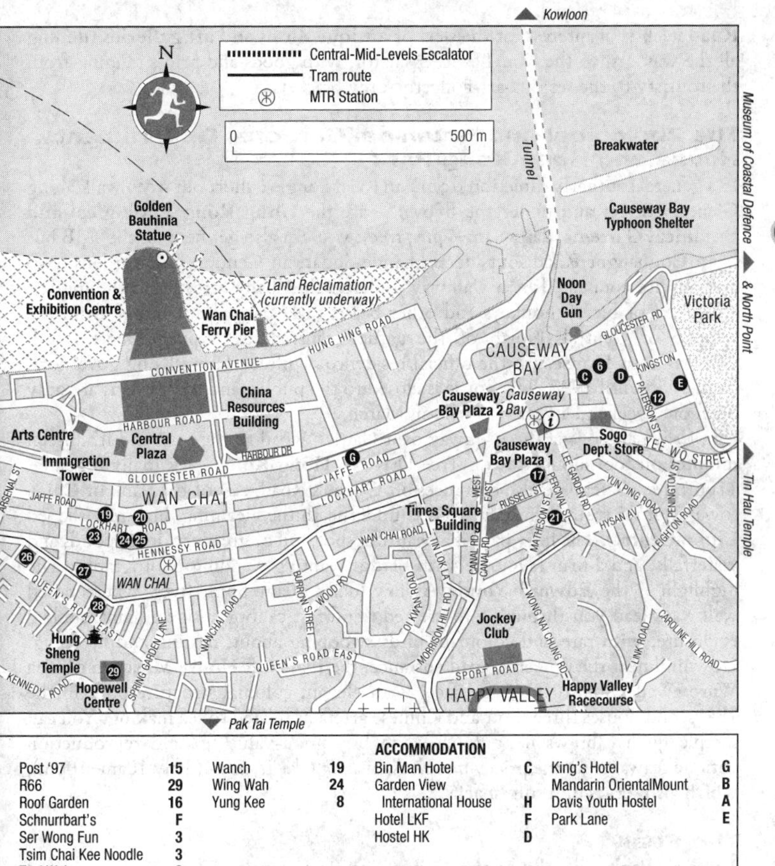

here is seeing what is displayed in tiny red- and -gold gift packages (rare medicines), and what is shifted by the sackful (usually food). Further up Morrison Street, **Sheung Wan Market** is a multistorey maze of Chinese shoppers after fresh vegetables, fish and meat, with an inexpensive **cooked food** area up top.

Morrison Road dead-ends at Queen's Road; turn east, and you'll soon see **Ladder Street**, a set of steep, broad stone steps heading uphill. This is one of many such stairways scattered between here and Central, a relic of the nineteenth-century sedan-chair carriers, who used them to get their loads up the hillsides. Halfway up Ladder Street, **Upper Lascar Row**, commonly known as **Cat Street**, is wall-to-wall with curio stalls loaded with coins, ornaments, jewellery, Chairman Mao badges and chops.

At the top of Ladder Street, the 150-year-old **Man Mo Temple** (daily 10am–6pm) on Hollywood Road is notable for its great hanging coils of incense suspended from the ceiling, filling the interior with eye-watering, aromatic smoke. The two figures on the main altar are the Taoist gods of Literature (*man* in Cantonese) and the Martial Arts (*mo*). Located as it is in a deeply traditional area, this is one of the most atmospheric temples to visit in Hong Kong. **Hollywood**

Road itself is of interest for the slew of **antique shops and art galleries** running all the way east to the Mid-Levels Escalator, with goods and prices ranging from the touristy to the serious-art-collector-only brackets.

The Zoological and Botanical Gardens, Government House and Hong Kong Park

In a general southerly direction from Lan Kwai Fong – a short but steep walk along Glenealy Street and under the flyover – are the **Hong Kong Zoological and Botanical Gardens** (daily 6am–7pm; free); you can also get here on the #3B bus from Connaught Road, outside Exchange Square in Central. The gardens' two sections are connected by a walkway underneath Albany Street, and the modest collection of birds, monkeys and other beasts makes a pleasant refuge from the hubbub of Central. North of the gardens, just across Upper Albert Road, **Government House** was the official residence of fifteen Hong Kong governors, from 1855 until 1997. The house is closed to the public, and the gardens are only open one weekend a year – usually in March.

Exit the gardens via the walkway over Garden Road to the east, and it's fifteen minutes on foot along Cotton Tree Drive to **Hong Kong Park** (daily 6.30am–11pm; free). There are also entrances off Queen's Road, east of the Bank of China tower, not far from Admiralty MTR (underneath the gleaming, bizarrely shaped **Lippo Centre**). The hilly park is a beautiful spot, full of greenery, lotus ponds and waterfalls, and a firm favourite with **brides** wanting wedding photographs. The highlight is the **Edward Youde Aviary** (daily 10am–5pm; free), where raised walkways lead you through a re-created rainforest canopy inside a giant meshed enclosure, with rare and colourful birds swooping about, nesting and breeding. Downhill near the Queen's Road entrance, the **Flagstaff House Museum of Tea Ware** (Wed–Mon 10am–5pm; free) is an elegant colonial structure built in the 1840s, and houses three thousand Chinese artefacts related to tea making. You can sample quality brews next door – and buy good-value tea and reproduction antique teaware – at the pricey but pleasant *Lock Cha Teahouse* (daily 10am–10pm), which also serves dim sum snacks.

The Peak

Victoria Peak – usually known as just **The Peak** – rises 552m over Central and Victoria Harbour. Since the 1870s, The Peak has been the premier address for Hong Kong's elite – which these days usually means Chinese tycoons – and reasons to come up here include not just the superb vistas and forest walks, but also the ascent in the **Peak Tram** (daily 7am–midnight; $25 one-way, $36 return; Octopus cards valid; Ⓦwww.thepeak.com.hk). This is, in fact, a funicular railway, which runs from the **Peak Tram terminal** in Garden Road in Central, most easily reached aboard bus #15C from outside the Outlying Islands Ferry Pier (daily 10am–11.40pm; approximately every 30min; $3.50). The track is incredibly steep, climbing the 386 vertical metres to its upper terminus in about eight minutes.

For an equally fun ride, sit upstairs at the front of **bus #15** (daily 6.15am–midnight; $9.80) as it tackles low branches and hairpin bends on the half-hour ascent from Exchange Square bus station. Fitness fanatics can **walk** up, too, though for most people walking down is a more realistic option.

All ways up terminate around the ugly, wok-shaped **Peak Tower**, featuring lookout platforms ($20) and a branch of Madame Tussauds, with wax models ranging from Zhang Zemin to Jackie Chan. Opposite is the **Peak Galleria** mall, full of souvenir shops and cafés – the best value of which is the *Pacific Coffee Company*, which has a huge viewing window. Wherever you get them from, **views** from up here are stupendous, down over the island's intensely crowded north shore (incredibly, you're not much higher here than the top of IFC2), across the busy harbour to a lower-rise, unspectacular Kowloon and the green peaks of the New Territories.

To reach the actual peak from this area, follow **Mount Austin Road** for twenty minutes to its end at the Victoria Peak Garden, formerly the site of the governor's residence – the actual summit, now crowned with transmitter masts, is walled off, but the views are still good. There's also an attractive, signposted hour-long **Peak Circuit walk** via Lugard and Harlech roads, an easy stroll through shady forest with surprisingly large, old trees in places, plus more sweeping views down over the SAR.

An excellent way to **descend** The Peak is to walk down one of several tracks, the quickest being the **Old Peak Road**, a little hard to find around the side of the Peak Tower. A steep, twenty-minute hike lands you among high-rise residences southwest of the Zoological and Botanical Gardens, which you can reach by continuing down the road for a further fifteen minutes.

Wan Chai

East from Central, **Wan Chai** is a nondescript district of broad, busy main roads and more towers, though these mainly house commercial, rather than financial, institutions. Back in the 1950s, **Wan Chai** was a thriving red-light district, famed as the setting for Richard Mason's novel *The World of Suzy Wong*, and there's still a vaguely sleazy feel to its core of **bars** and clubs. The main arteries here are parallel **Hennessy Road**, **Lockhart Road** – both lined with shops, restaurants and businesses – and the waterfront expressway, **Gloucester Road**. Wan Chai MTR Station is on Hennessy Road, while trams use Johnston Road, one block south; either are within walking distance of the sights.

Sights, however, are few. The most striking building is the **Hong Kong Convention and Exhibition Centre**, which juts out into the harbour and plausibly resembles a manta ray. This is where the British formally handed Hong Kong back to the Chinese in June 1997, and as such is a huge draw for mainland tourists, who pose beside the **Golden Bauhinia statue** behind, flanked by both the Chinese and Hong Kong SAR flags.

Immediately south across Gloucester Road soars the 78-storey **Central Plaza**, whose glowing cladding changes colour every fifteen minutes from 6pm to 6am. For splendid **360-degree views** over the city, catch the lift to the (free) public viewing area on the 46th floor. If you like your views with afternoon tea, however, try *R66* (see p.612) on the 66th floor of the **Hopewell Centre**, further inland on Queen's Road East.

Elsewhere, Wan Chai's emphasis is more functional, though there are many backstreet **markets**, such as the flower and bird market down Tai Wong Street West, opposite the tiny **Hung Sheng Temple** on Queen's Road East. More imposing is the **Pak Tai Temple** (daily 8am–6pm), at the head of Stone Nullah Lane, dedicated to the flood-quelling God of the North – look for the lively pottery figures from Chinese legend adorning the roof ridges.

Causeway Bay

East from Wan Chai, you can reach **Causeway Bay** by MTR or trams along **Yee Wo Street**, a continuation of Hennessy Road. The atmosphere here is lively, the streets loaded with restaurants and accommodation, and with scores of seething shopping and entertainment plazas dotted around. The biggest of these is **Times Square** (take Exit A from Causeway Bay MTR), two towers constructed in 1993 and packed with themed shopping over sixteen floors.

These range from computers to haute couture, a cinema multiplex and four floors of restaurants.

Causeway Bay's sole tourist sight is the waterfront **Noon Day Gun** – immortalized in Noel Coward's song *Mad Dogs and Englishmen*. This small naval cannon is still fired off with a loud report every day at noon, a habit dating back to the early days of the colony; at other times, there's nothing to see, however. The gun is most easily reached via a tunnel underneath Victoria Park Road from the car park next to the *Excelsior Hotel*.

The eastern part of Causeway Bay is dominated by **Victoria Park**, an extensive, open space containing swimming pools and other sports facilities. This has become the location for the annual candlelit vigil held on June 4 to commemorate the victims of Tian'anmen Square, in addition to hosting Hong Kong's largest Chinese New Year fairs. Come early in the morning and you'll see dozens of people practising *tai ji*. Down at the southeastern corner of the park, right by Tin Hau MTR (Exit A), is the 200-year-old **Tin Hau Temple** (daily 7am–7pm), a rather dark, gloomy place surrounded unhappily by skyscrapers. Tin Hau is the name given locally to the Goddess of the Sea, and her temples can be found throughout Hong Kong, originally in prominent positions by the shore but often marooned by land reclamation far inland. You can also reach this Tin Hau Temple on any tram heading for North Point; get off immediately after passing Victoria Park on your left.

Happy Valley

Happy Valley is a mostly low-lying area south of Wan Chai and Causeway Bay, notable for its huge multi-ethnic **cemeteries**, which cover a hillside to the west. But – as its Cantonese name, *Pau Ma Dei* or "Horse Racetrack" makes clear – Happy Valley really means only one thing for the people of Hong Kong: horse racing, or, more precisely, gambling. The **Happy Valley Racecourse**, which dates back to 1846, is where you can witness Hong Kong at its rawest and most grasping: entrance to the public enclosure is just $10, with races almost every Wednesday during the racing season (Sept–July). Otherwise, enquire at HKTB about their "Come Horse-racing Tour" ($690–1260 depending on the event; age and dress regulations apply), which includes transportation to and from the track, entry to the Members' Enclosure and a buffet meal at the official Jockey Club – and tips on how to pick a winner. Happy Valley can be reached from Central or Causeway Bay on a spur of the tramline, or on bus #1 from Central.

The Museum of Coastal Defence

Around 6km east of Causeway Bay, the splendid **Museum of Coastal Defence** (Fri–Wed 10am–5pm; $10) is located inside the 1887 Lei Yue Mui Fort, which itself is built into a hill overlooking the eastern end of the harbour. Aside from views on a sunny day from gun emplacements pointing seawards, the former barracks and ammunition rooms are now filled with artefacts, manneqins and photographs covering the period from the Ming dynasty to the handover. You can get here on the Island Line MTR to Shau Kei Wan; take Exit B1 and follow the signs for ten minutes via Shau Kei Wan Street East and busy Tun Hei Road.

Moving on from Shau Kei Wan, bus #9 runs from outside the MTR station to beaches at Shek O (see p.597).

The south coast

On its south side, Hong Kong Island straggles into the sea in a series of dangling peninsulas and inlets. The atmosphere is far quieter here than on the north shore, and the climate warmer and sunnier. You'll find not only separate towns such as **Aberdeen** and **Stanley**, with a flavour of their own, but also beaches, including those at popular **Repulse Bay** and, farther east, at the remoter outpost of **Shek O**. Especially if you're travelling with children, you should consider a visit to **Ocean Park**, a huge adventure theme park with a wonderful aquarium, just beyond Aberdeen.

There is no MTR line to the south coast as yet, but **buses** are plentiful to all destinations, and nowhere is more than an hour from Central.

Aberdeen

Aberdeen is the largest separate town on Hong Kong Island, with a population of more than sixty thousand living in garishly coloured tower blocks around the sheltered **harbour**. This is a **fishing port**, its fleet of family-run trawlers providing around a third of Hong Kong's fish and prawn catch. You can appreciate the fleet's size during the fishing **moratorium** (June–July), when the harbour is packed to capacity with freshly scrubbed vessels. The harbour is also the venue for the annual **Dragon-Boat Festival** held on the fifth day of the fifth lunar month (usually in June), one of the biggest in Hong Kong.

To reach Aberdeen, catch **bus #70** from Exchange Square in Central (15min). From the bus stop, cross over or under Aberdeen Praya Road to reach the harbour, where there's a busy early-morning co-operative **fish market** and, through the day, women waiting to solicit your custom for a **sampan tour** (around $50/person for a 30min ride, irrespective of the number of travellers). The trip offers photogenic views of houseboats complete with dogs, drying laundry and outdoor kitchens, as well as luxury yachts, boat yards and **floating restaurants**, which are especially spectacular when lit up at night.

Cheapskates can, in fact, enjoy a ten-minute **free harbour trip** by catching a ferry to the garishly decorated three-floor *Jumbo Restaurant* (Mon–Sat 11am–11.30pm, Sun 7am–11.30pm; see p.613) from a signed dock with a red gateway near the fish market; there's no pressure to actually have a meal here if you just want to look around. You'll also pass through the harbour if you use the **Aberdeen–Lamma ferry** (see p.606), so again won't need to pay for a separate tour.

Moving on, bus #73 links Aberdeen to Repulse Bay, Deep Water Bay and Stanley; Ocean Park is better reached on the #48.

Ocean Park

Ocean Park (daily 9.30am–7pm; $250, children aged 3–11 $125, children under 3 free; Ⓦ www.oceanpark.cn), a gigantic theme and adventure park, covers an entire peninsula to the east of Aberdeen. The price of the ticket is all-inclusive, and once you're inside, all rides and shows are free. You could easily spend the best part of a day here, and at weekends in summer you may find yourself frustrated by queues at the popular attractions, so make sure you arrive early in order to enjoy yourself at a relaxed pace. **Bus #260** runs to the main eastern entrance from the Exchange Square station via Admiralty MTR (daily; approximately every 15min; 9am–6.30pm).

In the face of fierce **competition** from Disney over on Lantau, the park is busy repositioning itself, balancing its fairground rides with displays about wildlife and the natural world. Star attractions are four **giant pandas** (two of them presents from the mainland government to celebrate the tenth anniversary of the handover), for whom a special $80-million, 2000-square-metre complex was created, complete with kitchen, clinic, fake slopes and misting machines to mimic a mountain atmosphere.

The first area you'll see is the Lowland section, which includes some life-size moving dinosaur models and a butterfly house – from here, there's a peaceful 1.5km **cable-car ride** to the Headland section at the tip of the peninsula. This is where you'll find scary rides such as the Dragon roller coaster and Abyss Turbo

Drop; a walk-through **aquarium**, where you can view sharks nose-to-nose through glass; the **Ocean Theatre**, where trained dolphins and sea lions perform; plus the **Atoll Reef**, a huge coral-reef aquarium that contains more than five thousand fish. Outdoor covered **escalators** take you back to ground level at the western gate, via the **Raging River** ride – expect to get soaked.

Moving on, bus #629 runs from Ocean Park's western entrance back to Admiralty MTR; from the eastern gate, bus #48 takes you to Aberdeen while #73 continues eastwards along the coastal beaches to Stanley.

Deep Water Bay, Repulse Bay and beyond

The 7km-long coastal strip east of Ocean Park forms several pleasant sandy **bays** linked to everywhere between Aberdeen and Stanley by **bus** #73, and to Ocean Park, Stanley and Central by bus #260. While the beaches offer a nice break from urban Hong Kong and there are plenty of good seafront **restaurants** out this way, note that the water is generally too polluted for swimming, the shoreline is increasingly built up, and the sand often packed to capacity through the summer and at weekends.

Deep Water Bay is small and enjoys excellent views of green islets offshore, though it drops straight off the coastal road so is hardly secluded. **Repulse Bay** is the most popular, partly because it contains a number of shops and restaurants, but also because of its **Tin Hau Temple**, which has a longevity bridge the crossing of which is said to add three days to your life. The backdrop to Repulse Bay is slightly bizarre, with an enormous, garish tower silhouetted against verdant hills, focused around the *The Repulse Bay* restaurant and shopping complex. South of Repulse Bay, you'll find **Middle Bay** and **South Bay**, fifteen and thirty minutes, respectively, farther along the coast. These offer more private but narrower beaches.

Stanley

Straddling the neck of Hong Kong's most southerly peninsula, **Stanley** is a residential town whose draws include a bustling tourist market, a clutch of expat-oriented restaurants, and Hong Kong's largest **Dragon-Boat Races**, held on the fifth day of the fifth month of the lunar calendar. Get here on **bus** #6, #66 or #260 from Central, #73 from Aberdeen or Repulse Bay, or green minibus #40 from Times Square in Causeway Bay.

Stanley is a tiny place – walk downhill from the bus stop and you'll fall into covered **Stanley Market**, which sells a mishmash of tourist souvenirs including clothes, embroideries and trinkets. Out the other side of the market is **Stanley Beach**, which, although not suitable for swimming, is lined by a row of romantic – if pricey – seafront restaurants. North along the shore, Stanley Plaza faces one of Hong Kong's oldest colonial buildings, two-storey **Murray House**, which was dismantled and removed from its original site in Central to make way for the Bank of China. Today, its elegant stone colonnades house stores, bars and restaurants, as well as the **Hong Kong Maritime Museum** (Tues–Sun 10am–6pm; $20), a small collection of photos, paintings and models relating to the sea. Just across the square from Murray House is yet another **Tin Hau Temple**, built in 1767, and worth a look for the blackened tiger skin spread-eagled on one wall, the remains of an animal bagged near here in 1942 – the last ever shot in Hong Kong.

South of the market down Wong Ma Kok Road, it's about a ten-minute walk to the pleasant **St Stephen's Beach**, the best in the area, accessible by steps down to the right immediately after a playing field. Beyond here is **Stanley Military Cemetery**, on Wong Ma Kok Road, containing the graves of many of those killed fighting the Japanese in World War II, and also the maximum-security Stanley Prison. The southern part of the peninsula is a closed military zone.

Moving on, take any of the above buses westwards, though to continue east you need to take the #14 or #314 bus to the Stanley–Shek O junction, and then bus #9 or minibus #16 to Shek O – tell the #14 or #314 driver that you're heading to Shek O and they'll put you off at the right place. The whole journey takes some thirty minutes.

Shek O

In the far southeast of the island, **Shek O** is Hong Kong's most remote settlement, with an almost Mediterranean flavour in its stone houses, narrow lanes and seafront location. There's a strong surf beating on the wide, white **beach**, which has a shady area of vine trellises at one end for barbecues and, during the week, is more or less deserted. Come for sunbathing and lunch at one of the cheap local restaurants. The surrounding headlands are also popular for **hiking**, especially the fearsome-sounding but straightforward, two-hour-long **Dragon's Back** trail – the HKTB can provide you with practical details.

You can't miss the beach – it's just 50m from the bus stop, beyond a small roundabout; nearby shops such as the Tung Lok Beachside Store sell beachwear, inflatable floats, plastic buckets and so on, and have storage lockers. Most of the other businesses in the village are welcoming and fairly inexpensive restaurants, mostly Vietnamese, Thai or both.

On Sunday afternoons (2.10–6.10pm), **bus** #309 runs hourly from Exchange Square in Central to Shek O; otherwise, first catch the MTR Island Line to **Shau Kei Wan MTR station** on Hong Kong's northeastern shore – from where you could detour to the Museum of Coastal Defence (see p.594) – and pick up bus #9 to Shek O. See the "Stanley" section on p.596 for details on how to get to there from Shek O.

Kowloon

A 4km-long strip of the mainland ceded to Britain in perpetuity in 1860 to add to their offshore island, **Kowloon** was accordingly developed with gusto and confidence. The skyline here has never matched Hong Kong Island's, thanks to Kowloon being in the flight path of the old airport at Kai Tak, though things could be changing: 2010 saw the completion of Hong Kong's tallest building, the 484m-high **International Commerce Centre** (ICC), atop Union Square and the Airport Express terminal in West Kowloon. With rocketing rents and dwindling space along the North Shore, perhaps ICC marks a shift in venue for Hong Kong's next wave of cutting-edge, harbourside architecture – though beyond its sheer height, ICC is just a large silver tower.

While Hong Kong Island has mountains and beaches to offset urban claustrophobia, Kowloon has just more shops, more restaurants and more hotels. Initially, it's hard to see how such an unmitigatedly built-up, commercial and intensely crowded place could possibly appeal to travellers. One reason is the staggering **view** across the harbour to Hong Kong Island's skyscrapers and peaks; another is the sheer density of shopping opportunities here – from high-end jewellery to cutting-edge electronic goods and outright tourist tack – especially in the couple of square kilometres at the tip of the peninsula that make up **Tsim Sha Tsui**. To the north, **Yau Ma Tei** and **Mong Kok** are less touristy – though no less crowded – districts teeming with soaring tenements and local **markets**, some of which sell modern daily necessities, others with a distinctly traditional Chinese twist.

These days, it's not so clear-cut where Kowloon really ends. The original "border" with the New Territories to the north was **Boundary Street**, though

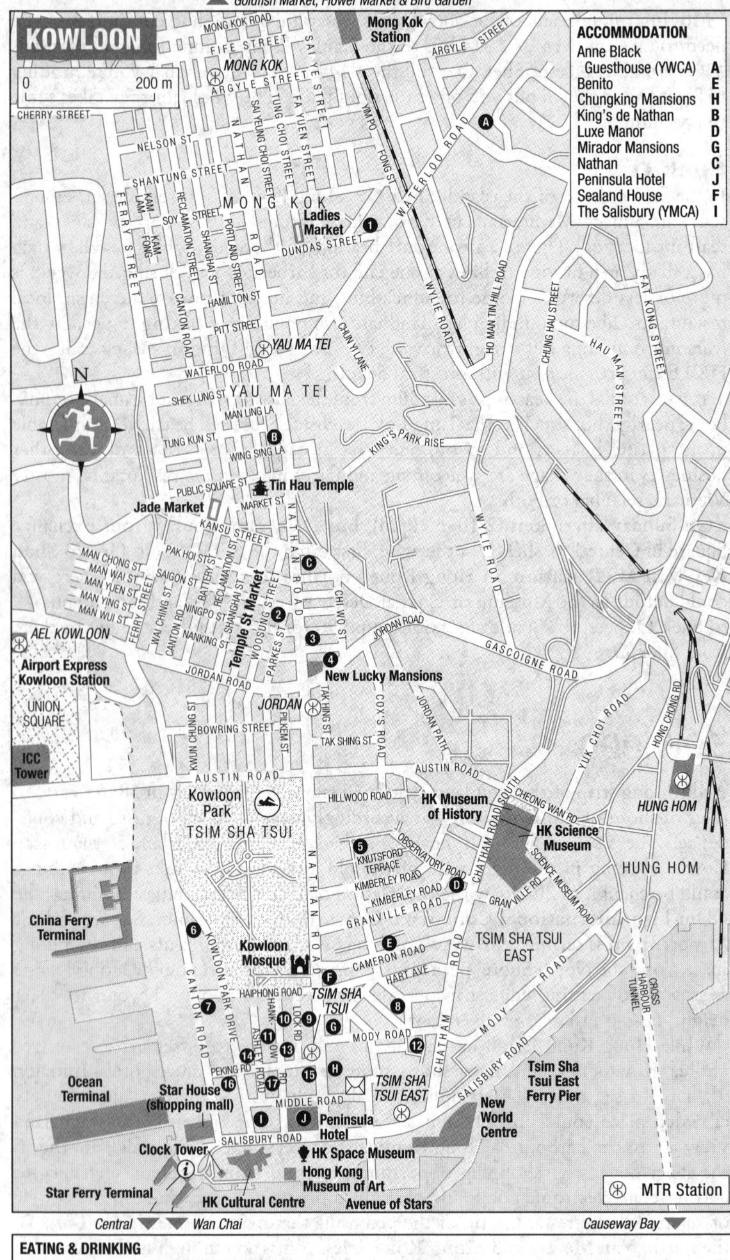

EATING & DRINKING

Aqua	16	Kakalok	11	Peninsula Hotel Lobby	I	Tao Heung	7
Bahama Mama's	5	Light Vegetarian	4	Sino Vegetarian	2	Tim Ho Wan	1
Chee Kee	9	Macau Restaurant	10	Spring Deer	12	TW Coffee Concept	13
Delaney's	15	Majesty Seafood	3	Stag's Head	8		
Felix	G	Ned Kelly's Last Stand	14	Sweet Dynasty	6		
Hing Fat	17						

now Kowloon district runs on for a further 3km or so, as the commercial emphasis shifts towards towering **residential estates** clustered around shopping plazas, parks and other amenities. A scattering of sights here includes one of Hong Kong's busiest temples, the **Wong Tai Sin**, and its prettiest, the **Chi Lin Nunnery** with its Tang-style architecture and beautiful traditional garden.

The two main ways to reach Kowloon are by the **Star Ferry** from Central to Tsim Sha Tsui, or along the **MTR's Tsuen Wan Line**, which runs from Central under the harbour and up through Kowloon, with stations dotted at regular intervals along Nathan Road.

Tsim Sha Tsui

The tourist heart of Hong Kong, **Tsim Sha Tsui** is an easy place to find your way around. The prime arrival point, the **Star Ferry Terminal**, is right on the south-western tip of the peninsula. East from here are a number of harbourside museums and galleries – not to mention outstanding views of Hong Kong Island. Hong Kong's most famous street, **Nathan Road**, runs north up through the middle of Tsim Sha Tsui, the streets either side alive with shops and shoppers at all hours of the day and night. In among all this brash commercial activity, **Kowloon Park** offers a bit of space to rest, surrounded by ornamental paving and shrubberies.

Along the harbour

Salisbury Road runs east from the Star Ferry Terminal, physically cutting off a strip of harbourside sights to the south from the rest of Tsim Sha Tsui – you can reach them on foot either from the ferry terminal, or via the pedestrian underpass off the end of Nathan Road.

Some 50m east of the Star Ferry Terminal, Tsim Sha Tsui's main antique is the **Clock Tower**, the only remaining piece of the Kowloon Railway Station, from where you could once take a train all the way back to Europe, via Mongolia and Russia. Today, it fronts the **Hong Kong Cultural Centre**, a drab, brown-tiled building, notable for its astonishing lack of windows over one of the most picturesque urban landscapes in the world – inside are concert halls, theatres and galleries. East again, the **Hong Kong Museum of Art** (Fri–Wed 10am–6pm; $10; Ⓦwww.lcsd.gov.hk/ce/Museum/Arts) has an excellent collection of Chinese calligraphy, paintings and other antiquities, all with informative English labelling; while the domed **Hong Kong Space Museum** (Mon & Wed–Fri 1–9pm, Sat & Sun 10am–9pm; $10; Ⓦhk.space.museum) houses user-friendly exhibition halls on astronomy and space exploration. There's also the **Space Theatre** planetarium here, which presents Omnimax shows for an additional fee ($24–32, concessions $16).

For **harbour views**, head down to the promenade that runs for around 500m east from the Clock Tower; it's especially good at night, when the skyscrapers across the water light up unashamedly in competing coloured, flashing neon. The eastern end of the promenade becomes the **Avenue of Stars**, a tribute to Hong Kong's film industry (the third largest in the world after India and the US). Along with actors' handprints pressed into the concrete, there's a large statue of martial-arts star **Bruce Lee**, the man who brought the local industry – and Chinese kung fu – to world attention in the 1970s.

Along Nathan Road

On the north side of Salisbury Road, the **Peninsula Hotel** – a colonial landmark worth a visit for afternoon tea, even if you can't afford to stay (see p.586) – sits on the corner with **Nathan Road**, which cuts through the heart of Kowloon. By no means a beautiful street, it nonetheless houses a staggeringly concentrated collection of electronics shops, tailors, jewellery stores and fashion boutiques, and is an essential place to experience the commercial spirit that really drives Hong Kong. Actually spending money here is not always such a good idea, however – for more details, see "Shopping", p.615. There's also a multicultural flavour provided by the dubious block of **Chungking Mansions**, the centre of Hong Kong's **budget accommodation** (see p.586) and an atmospheric shopping arcade where immigrants from the Indian subcontinent rub elbows with Western tourists, businessmen from central and southeastern Asia and African entrepreneurs.

A few hundred metres up past here on the west side of the road, **Kowloon Park** (daily 5am–midnight) is marked at its southeastern corner by the white-domed **Kowloon Mosque and Islamic Centre**, which caters to the substantial Muslim population of the area. The park itself provides welcome, green respite from the rest of Tsim Sha Tsui, though you can't see it from the street and have to climb steps up from Nathan Road. There's also an Olympic-size indoor and outdoor **swimming pool complex** (daily 8am–noon, 1.30–6pm & 7.30–10pm; $21), plus an aviary, sculpture walk, and **Kung Fu Corner** (up behind the mosque), where experts in various martial arts give demonstrations every Sunday between 2.30pm and 4.30pm.

East Kowloon

Around 700m east of Kowloon Park and across busy Chatham Road South, **East Kowloon** is home to a couple of informative museums, perhaps best saved for a wet day. The **Hong Kong Museum of History** (Mon & Wed–Sat 10am–6pm, Sun 10am–7pm; $10; ⓦhk.history.museum/index.php) features "the Hong Kong Story", a permanent history about the SAR's life and times, as well as numerous history-related, temporary exhibitions. Immediately south, the **Hong Kong Science Museum** (Mon–Wed & Fri 1–9pm, Sat & Sun 10am–9pm; $25; ⓦhk.science.museum) is of most fun for children, with a host of hands-on exhibits explaining the workings of everything from mobile phones to human perception.

Jordan to Mong Kok: Kowloon's markets

North of Tsim Sha Tsui's boundary on Jordan Road, the neighbourhoods of **Jordan**, **Yau Ma Tei** and **Mong Kok** offer more of a Chinese flavour, plus some interesting markets. Nathan Road continues to be the main artery, dotted with **MTR stations** that you'll probably end up using to avoid the incredible crowds that clog the streets after about 10am and make walking tedious.

Running north off Jordan Road and within easy range of Jordan MTR (take exit C2 and head west), **Temple Street** becomes a touristy but fun **night market** after 7pm every day. As well as shopping for cheap clothing, watches, DVDs and souvenirs, you can get your fortune told, eat some great seafood from street stalls, and sometimes listen in on impromptu performances of Chinese opera. A minute or two to the north of here is the local **Tin Hau Temple**, tucked away between Public Square Street and Market Street in a small, concreted park. Just west, under the Gascoigne Road flyover at the junction of Kansu and Battery streets, the **Jade Market** (daily 9am–6pm) has 450 stalls in two different sections, offering everything from souvenir trinkets to family heirlooms in jade, crystal, quartz and other stones.

Near Yau Ma Tei MTR and running north off Dundas Street, Tung Choi Street hosts a **Ladies Market** (daily noon–10.30pm), flogging piles of cheap clothes, jewellery, toys and bags. Parallel streets – the heart of **Mong Kok** district – are thick with shops specializing in computers, cameras and mobile phones, a more reliable place to buy these things than Tsim Sha Tsui. Push on north over Argyle Street – you're close to Mong Kok MTR here – and Tung Choi Street transforms into a **Goldfish Market** lined with shops stocking aquaria, corals, exotic fish and even some dubiously exotic breeds of snake, lizard and turtle.

Chinese cuisine

The principles of Chinese cuisine are based on a balance between the qualities of different ingredients. For the Chinese, this extends right down to considering the *yin* and *yang* attributes of various dishes, but is obvious even to foreigners in the use of contrasting textures and colour, designed to please the eye as well as the palate. Recipes and ingredients, however, are a response to more direct requirements. The chronic poverty of China's population is reflected in the traditionally scant quantity of meat used, while the need to minimize the use of firewood led to the invention of quick cooking techniques, such as stir-frying.

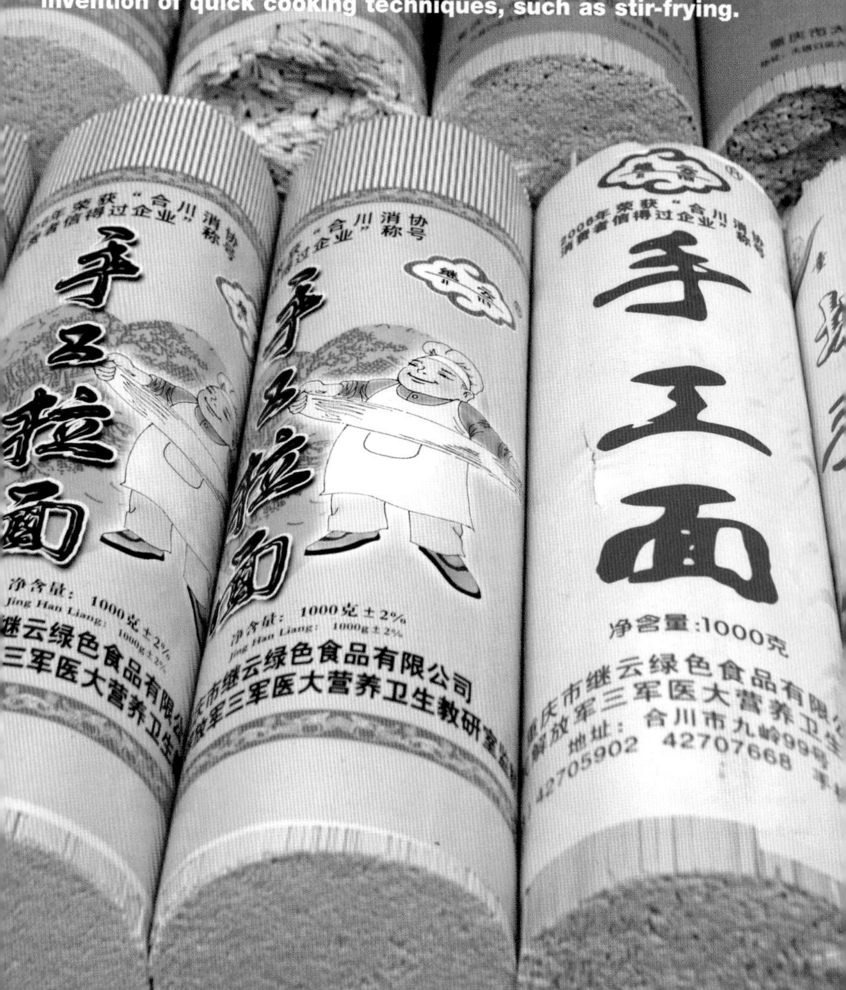

Chilli harvest, Qingha ▲

Rice soup with lotus root ▼

Taste

Taste in Chinese cuisine is sometimes something to be teased out of an ingredient, sometimes something to be suppressed. Sugar, soy sauce, rice wine and vinegar emphasize underlying fresh, sweet tastes; heavier flavours are moderated – or occasionally created – by **marinating** using **spices** such as chilli, pickled vegetables, ginger and garlic. Often, the object is to season without being too obvious, as any heavy-handedness could come across as an attempt to conceal a lack of **freshness**. This can be a major concern, especially in the south, where many restaurants keep live chickens, fish and seafood out front so diners can select the animal they want.

Texture

Texture is a crucial part of a dish – indeed, ingredients such as birds' nests and sea cucumber are only used to provide texture, being completely flavourless themselves. Texture can be a natural attribute – the softness of tofu, the crunchiness of bamboo shoots – although usually it's the result of a specific cooking method: deep-frying adds a layer of crispness to meats, while prolonged steaming or stewing renders fat and meat fibres butter-soft.

Regional cooking styles

Northern cookery was epitomized by the imperial court and so also became known as Mandarin or Beijing cooking. A solid diet of wheat and millet buns, noodles, pancakes and dumplings was accompanied by savoury tastes of dark soy sauce and bean paste, white cabbage, onions and garlic. The north's cooking was also influenced by the Mongols, who brought roast meats, and Muslims, who introduced a taste for mutton, beef and chicken. Combined with other exotic items, imperial kitchens turned these ingredients and cooking styles into sophisticated marvels such as **Beijing duck**. Mongolian hotpot is another northern speciality – raw meats and vegetables cooked in stock at the table.

Central coast provinces produce the **eastern style**, whose cooking delights in seasonal fresh seafood and river fish. Dried and salted ingredients also feature, pepping up rice noodles and dumplings. Based around Shanghai, eastern cuisine enjoys delicate forms and fresh, sweet flavours, though it's often oily.

Western China is dominated by the boisterous cooking of Sichuan and Hunan. Here, there's a heavy use of chillies and pungent, constructed flavours – vegetables are concealed with "fish-flavoured" sauce, and normally bland tofu is spiced enough to lift the top off your head. Yet there are still subtleties to enjoy in a cuisine that uses dried orange peel, aniseed, ginger and spring onions, and the cooking methods – dry-frying and smoking – are refreshingly unusual. Sichuan is also home of the now-ubiquitous – and chilli-laced – Sichuan hotpot (*huoguo*).

People from **southern China** are reknowned for eating anything: snake, dog and cane rat are some of the more unusual dishes, though fruit, vegetables, fish and shellfish are also consumed. Typically, the demand is for extremely fresh ingredients, quickly cooked and lightly seasoned, though the south is also home to that famous mainstay of Chinese restaurants overseas, sweet-and-sour sauce. The tradition of dim sum reached its pinnacle here, too, where a morning meal of tiny flavoured buns, filled dumplings and pancakes satisfies the Chinese liking for an assortment of small dishes.

▲ Beijing duck

▼ Hotpot

▼ Deep-fried scorpions

Rice dumplings wrapped in lotus leaf ▲

Food on display outside a restaurant, Dali ▼

Vegetarian food

Vegetarianism has been practised for almost two thousand years in China. Today, the cooking takes several forms: **plain vegetable dishes**, commonly served in ordinary restaurants; **imitation meat** dishes, which use gluten, bean curd and potato to mimic animal flesh, and often simply carry the name of the dish that inspired them, such as honey pork; and **Buddhist cooking**, which often avoids onions, ginger, garlic and other spices considered stimulating.

Sadly, vegetarians visiting China have limited options. The Chinese believe vegetables lack any fortifying properties, and strict vegetarian diets are unusual. There's also a stigma of poverty attached to not eating meat, and as a foreigner no one will understand why you don't want it when you could clearly afford it. To avoid being served anything of animal origin, tell your waiter you are a Buddhist (see p.1006) – though be aware cooking fat and stocks are often of animal origin.

Medicinal cooking

There's no boundary in Chinese cooking between food and medicine: in **Traditional Chinese Medicine** (TCM; see p.967) everything you consume is believed to affect your health. This means ordinary dishes can be regarded medicinally: chicken and beef are "warming" – they add *yang* energy – while seafood such as crab is *yin* or "cooling". Along with medicinal herbs, culinary spices such as garlic, chillies and tangerine peel have medicinal uses, too, which means – if you know what your ailment is in TCM terms – you can create dishes to restore your health. There are abundant medicinal cookery books but, sadly, very few restaurants in China specialize in the idea.

Further north again, over Prince Edward Road (Prince Edward MTR), it's a short walk east – past the top of Fa Yuen Street and its **discount clothing stores** – to the **Flower Market** (daily from 10am), in Flower Market Road. This is best on Sundays and in the run-up to Chinese New Year, when people come to buy narcissi, orange trees and plum blossom to decorate their apartments in order to bring good luck. Flower Market Road runs east to the **Bird Garden** (daily 7am–8pm), where hundreds of birds are on sale, along with intricately designed bamboo cages; there are also live crickets – food for the birds. Local men bring their own songbirds here for an airing, and the place gives a real glimpse into a traditional area of Chinese life – spiritually, a thousand miles from the rest of Kowloon.

North of Boundary Street

The 3km-deep area between Boundary Street and the steep Kowloon Hills – beyond which lie the New Territories – offers a mix of temples, more bargain shopping, some surprisingly ancient history and two unusual parks. With the exception of Kowloon Walled City Park, for which you'll need a bus, all are within twenty minutes of downtown Kowloon by MTR.

Sham Shui Po and the Han Tomb Museum

SHAM SHUI PO – reached via the Tsuen Wan MTR line – lies just 1km or so northwest of the Boundary Road/Nathan Road intersection. The district is jammed with **wholesale garment outlets**, which line central Cheung Sha Wan Road for a couple of blocks either side of Sham Shui Po MTR station. While not the height of fashion, if you're prepared to dig around there are some very good deals to be had. Parallel **Ap Liu Street** has an interesting **flea market** every day from about noon until 7pm; don't expect to find anything remotely valuable but it's a fun, untouristy place to browse.

From Sham Shui Po, ride the MTR one more stop to **Cheung Sha Wan MTR**, take exit A3, walk for five minutes along Tonkin Street, and you're outside the **Lei Cheng Uk Han Tomb Museum** (Mon–Wed, Fri & Sat 10am–1pm & 2–6pm, Sun 1–6pm; free). This is constructed over a 2000-year-old Han-dynasty tomb, which looks like a large brick oven and was uncovered in 1957. The tomb yielded a few bits of pottery but no evidence that it was ever used for a burial; its value lies more in the fact that it proves the long Han Chinese presence in the area.

Kowloon Walled City Park

Kowloon Walled City Park (daily 6.30am–6pm; free) is the site of a Qing-dynasty fortified garrison post whose soldiers refused to cede sovereignty to Britain when it took over the New Territories in 1898. The consequence was that for nearly a century it became a self-governing enclave of criminals and vagrants, off-limits to the authorities until they negotiated its closure and demolition in 1994. It's now an attractive spread of lawns, trees and traditional buildings, including the "city's" reconstructed *yamen* (courthouse building). Get here on **bus #1** from the Tsim Sha Tsui Star Ferry Pier (30min), which runs up Nathan Road, turns east along Boundary Street and then passes the park gates on Tung Tau Tsuen Road.

Wong Tai Sin, Chi Lin Nunnery and Nan Lian Gardens

Three sights northeast of Boundary Road can be easily tied together by using the **Kwun Tong MTR Line** from Yau Ma Tei. Aim first for Wong Tai Sin, site of the **Wong Tai Sin Temple** (daily 7am–5.30pm), a thriving complex dedicated to the mythical Yellow Immortal that's packed with more worshippers than any other in Hong Kong. Big, bright and colourful, it provides a good look at popular Chinese religion: vigorous kneeling, incense burning and the noisy rattling of joss sticks in canisters, as well as the presentation of food and drink to the deities. Large numbers of **fortune-tellers**, some of whom speak English, have stands to the right of the entrance and charge around $20 for palm-reading, about half that for a face-reading.

One stop further on at **Diamond Hill MTR** (exit C2 and follow the signs for 5min), the modern **Chi Lin Nunnery** (daily 9am–3.30pm; free) is an elegant wooden temple built without nails in the Tang style, just about the only example of this type of architecture in all China. Opposite, the tranquil and beautiful **Nan Lian Gardens** (daily 7am–9pm; free) continue the Tang theme in an exquisite reconstruction of a contemporary garden; there are contorted pine trees, artfully shaped hillocks, ornamental ponds populated by carp, wooden halls and brightly painted bridges and pavilions.

Moving on, buses from Diamond Hill run to Clear Water Bay or Sai Kung Town in the New Territories (see p.605).

The New Territories

Many people fly in and out of Hong Kong without even realizing that the SAR comprises anything more than the city itself. However, the **New Territories**, a 30km-deep swath between Kowloon and the Guangdong border, comes complete with country parks, beautiful coastlines, farming communities and craggy mountains – as well as booming **New Towns**, satellite settlements built from scratch in the last forty years to absorb the overflow from Hong Kong's burgeoning population. A whole series of designated **country parks** includes the unspoilt **Sai Kung Peninsula** to the east, offering excellent walking trails and secluded beaches. Less dedicated souls after birdlife should head northwest to the **Hong Kong Wetland Park**; elsewhere there's some architectural and cultural heritage to soak up around otherwise modern towns such as **Sha Tin**. For serious extended hikes, the **MacLehose Trail** runs for 100km across the New Territories; contact the **Country and Marine Parks** (Ⓦ www.afcd.gov.hk) for information on trails and conditions.

Travelling around the New Territories is straightforward. The Tsuen Wan MTR, East Rail and West Rail all run from the downtown past many of the sights, with frequent buses and minibuses available where needed.

The northwest

The **Hong Kong Wetland Park** is easily the main draw of the New Territories' northwest, offering a chance to see some genuinely wild wildlife – and how the Chinese like to organize nature. Also out this way there are good walks around **Shing Mun Reservoir** and up **Tai Mo Shan**, Hong Kong's highest peak; the walled village of **Kam Tin** provides a glimpse of old Hong Kong. Most of these require a mix of transport to reach, including the **West Rail Line** from Kowloon; see accounts for details.

Shing Mun Reservoir

Shing Mun Reservoir offers an easy few hours' walking, with the chance of seeing monkeys and other wildlife – choose a sunny day and take a packed lunch. The west side is wooded, with remains of an abandoned village and a few picnic areas, while the east side is more open with better views of the water. A clear, well-signposted circuit track runs around the lake, with a long, tiring extension possible up onto Tai Mo Shan (see below).

It takes about an hour to reach Shing Mun Reservoir from downtown. First ride the **Tsuen Wan MTR** to its terminus at Tsuen Wan; take exit B1 and then the pedestrian footbridge over Tsing Shan Road. Turn left along the road, then first right, first left onto **Shiu Wo Street**, from where **green minibus #82** (daily 6.45am–11.45pm; $3.90) runs to the reservoir.

Tai Mo Shan

Hong Kong's 957m apex, **Tai Mo Shan**, is nearly twice the height of The Peak on Hong Kong Island; people come up here on winter mornings hoping to see frost. The two-hour walk up the west face to the summit is steep but not difficult, following a sealed road most of the way past the **Sze Lok Yuen Youth Hostel** (Ⓣ2488 8188; dorm beds $100; bookings essential). Views from the top encompass Hong Kong Island, the Sai Kung Peninsula and Shenzhen's wall of skyscrapers, magnificent on a clear day. It's very exposed, however – bring a hat, water and sunscreen. Once at the top you can retrace your steps, or follow trails east down to Shing Mun Reservoir (allow two more hours).

For Tai Mo Shan catch the **West Rail Line** from Kowloon to **Tsuen Wan West Station**. Take exit D, turn left and walk 150m to the station where **bus #51** departs (daily 5.40am–10.50pm; $7.60). It's a fifteen-minute ride from here to the Tai Mo Shan Visitor Centre at the base of the mountain – tell the driver where you want to go. Note that bus #51 continues past Tai Mo Shan to Kam Tin (see below).

Kam Tin and Kat Hing Wai

Over on the far side of Tai Mo Shan, **KAM TIN** is the site of **Kat Hing Wai**, one of Hong Kong's last inhabited **walled settlements**. Dating back to the late seventeenth century when a clan named Tang settled here, the village ($3 donation to enter) still comprises thick, 6m-high walls and guard towers. Note the gates, too – confiscated by the British in the late nineteenth century, they were eventually found in Ireland and returned. Inside the walls, there's a wide lane running down the middle of the village, with tiny alleys leading off it. Old Hakka ladies in traditional hats pester visitors with cameras for more donations, and most of the buildings are modern, but the atmosphere is as different from downtown Hong Kong as you can imagine.

The quickest way here from downtown Hong Kong is on the **West Rail Line to Kam Sheung Road**; take exit B, cross the bridge over the storm-water canal, and follow signs for 250m. If you've arrived by **bus**, you'll be on the main road within two minutes' walk of Kat Hing Wai – just ask anyone to point the way. You can also catch **bus #64K** on from here via Kadoorie Farm and the Wishing Trees to Tai Po – see p.604 for more.

Hong Kong Wetland Park

Hong Kong Wetland Park (Wed–Mon 10am–5pm; Ⓦwww.wetlandpark.com; $30) covers 61 hectares of saltwater marsh up along the Chinese border, part of a larger system of lagoons known as the **Mai Po Marshes** that draws wintering wildfowl between November and February, and a host of migrating birds from August to October. The park itself is carefully landscaped to be just as attractive to human visitors, with paths, bridges, bird hides and an excellent visitor centre, and makes a great half-day out. Highlights include the mangrove boardwalk, where you can watch mudskippers and fiddler crabs scooting over the mud; huge lotus ponds (look for the occasional swimming snake); and the visitor centre's aquarium stocked with gharial crocodiles and fish. There's a branch of *Café de Coral* here, serving inexpensive lunches and drinks.

To reach the park, take the West Rail Line to **Tin Shui Wai**, then LRT (Light Rail) #705 or #706 to **Wetland Park Station**, from where the park is a signposted ten-minute walk past a surreal high-rise housing estate. The entire trip takes only around 1hr 15min from Tsim Sha Tsui.

The north

The **East Rail Line** runs due north for 30km from Kowloon through the New Territories to the border with mainland China. Along the way, **Sha Tin** and **Tai Po** each offer a mix of expected and esoteric attractions, and either could tie you up for most of a day. Alternatively, scenery and walks further up around **Plover Cove Country Park** will need a day in themselves.

Sha Tin

The booming New Town of **SHA TIN**, which spreads along either side of the Shing Mun River, is best known to Hong Kongers as the site of the territory's second **racecourse**. It's probably the most liveable New Town, with water out front and towering green mountains to the east, though it's a rather anonymous experience wandering the vast maze of air-conditioned shopping malls that fill the centre.

Hong Kong's **Heritage Museum** (Mon & Wed–Sat 10am–6pm, Sun 10am–7pm; $10; ⓦwww.heritagemuseum.gov.hk) is a well-signposted five-minute walk from **Che Kung Temple Station** on the Ma On Shan Line – ride the East Rail Line to Sha Tin, then change for one stop. Exhibits are similar to Tsim Sha Tsui's Musuem of History; one of the best covers life in the New Territories across the ages and features a reconstructed traditional fishing village, while another focuses on Cantonese Opera, with theatre mock-ups, plot accounts and photos of famous performers.

Across town, Sha Tin's eccentric **Ten Thousand Buddhas Monastery** (daily 9am–5pm; free) dates only to the 1960s, but is one of the most interesting temples in the New Territories. Signs from **Sha Tin station** lead past the entrance to Po Fook Ancestral Worship Halls to the temple path, which ascends a steep stairway flanked by five hundred gold-painted statues of Buddhist saints. The monastery comprises a garish collection of painted concrete statues and cheaply built halls, the main one of which houses some 13,000 miniature statues of Buddha. You can buy lunch here at the basic **vegetarian restaurant**.

Tai Po, the Wishing Trees and Kadoorie Farm

TAI PO is one of the New Territories' longest established towns, with an older centre surrounded by new housing estates. Get off the East Rail Line at **Tai Po Market** station, and follow signs for fifteen minutes via a covered walkway and the centre of town to the **Man Mo Temple** on Fu Shin Street. The temple is attractive, but the main action is in the busy market packing out surrounding lanes. Uphill from here at the end of On Fu Road, the **Hong Kong Railway Museum** (Mon & Wed–Sun 9am–5pm; free) occupies Tai Po's old Chinese-style station, built in 1913; model trains and photographs cover the construction of the original Kowloon-to-Canton Railway, with some old coaches and engines out back.

Back at Tai Po Market station, **bus #64K** (daily 5.40am–12.10am; $6.90) heads westwards past some excellent sights, especially if you have children in tow. The first are the **Lam Tsuen Wishing Trees**, around ten minutes along; people used to write wishes on red slips of paper and hurl them into the branches of these old fig trees, until the branches broke off under their accumulated weight – wishes are posted on nearby boards today.

Another twenty minutes brings you to the gates of **Kadoorie Farm** (daily 9.30am–5pm; $10; check opening hours – it's closed for even minor holidays – on ⓦwww.kfbg.org.hk or ⓣ2483 7200). This organic farm and wildlife sanctuary is terraced up steep slopes and offers walks, guided tours and close views of orphaned birds, wild boar, leopard cats and muntac deer – probably your only chance to see such elsusive creatures in Hong Kong.

Note that bus #64K continues past Kadoorie Farm **to Kam Tin** and Kat Hing Wai (see p.603).

Tai Mei Tuk and the Plover Cove Country Park

The coastline east from Tai Po fringes **Plover Cove Country Park**, which surrounds the massive Plover Cove Reservoir. There's a broad mix of outdoor activities here – everything from picnicking and playing under waterfalls to serious hiking – and the easy access means it gets very busy at weekends and holidays.

From Tai Po Market station, catch **bus #75K** (daily 5.30am–11.35pm; $4.70) to its terminus at the small village and service centre of **TAI MEI TUK**. There are a few low-key restaurants here, the *Bradbury Jockey Club Youth Hostel* (see p.587) and, just up the road, the **Country Park Visitors' Centre** (Sat & Sun 9.30am–4.30pm). From here it's about an hour's walk along the road, past barbecue sites overlooking the reservoir, to **Bride's Pool**, an attractively wooded picnic and camping site beside a shallow stream and waterfalls. Alternatively, it's a tough six- to eight-hour hike west up onto the serrated heights of **Pat Sin Leng**, the Eight Immortals' Ridge, to the village of **Hok Tau Wai**, from where you can catch **green minibus #52B** (daily 6am–8.20pm; $4.50) to Fan Ling on the East Rail Line. This is one of Hong Kong's best day hikes, for views at any rate; take plenty of water, sunscreen and a hat, and wear shoes with a good grip.

The east

The eastern part of the New Territories, around **Clear Water Bay** and the **Sai Kung Peninsula**, is where you'll find Hong Kong's prettiest beaches and walks. Things get busy at weekends, however – come during the week if possible. Sai Kung has plenty of good places to eat; elsewhere you'll need to bring a packed lunch. Though Clear Water Bay and Sai Kung are fairly close to each other, you'll need a whole day to do either place justice. The starting point for buses into both areas is **Diamond Hill Station** on the Kwun Tong MTR Line (see p.602).

Clear Water Bay

From Diamond Hill, catch **bus #91** (daily 6am–10.25pm; $6.10) for the forty-minute ride to **Clear Water Bay**. There are a couple of excellent, clean **beaches** at the penultimate stop, **Tai Au Mun**, or the Clear Water Bay terminus, though with no nearby shops or facilities. From the terminus, you can also catch **green minibus #16** south to the end of the road outside the members-only Clear Water Bay Golf and Country Club. From the car park, follow signposts and steps for 500m down to the wonderfully located **Tin Hau Temple** in **Joss House Bay**. As one of Hong Kong's few Tin Hau temples actually still commanding the sea, it's of immense significance: on the 23rd day of the third lunar month each year (Tin Hau's birthday) a colossal seaborne celebration takes place on fishing boats in the bay. A nearby **stone inscription**, dated to the Song dynasty and recording a visit by a government official, is the oldest such carving in Hong Kong.

Sai Kung Peninsula

Hong Kong's easternmost projection, the rugged **Sai Kung Peninsula** is a mass of jagged headlands, spiky peaks, vivid blue seascapes and tiny offshore islands. Most of the area is enclosed within **country parks**, with a range of picnic spots and walking trails around the coast and out to Hong Kong's finest beaches.

The main access point is little **SAI KUNG TOWN**, reached on **bus #92** from Diamond Hill MTR. While somewhat developed and with a large expat population, it's also a Chinese fishing town, the promenade packed with seafood restaurants and fishermen offering their wares. Shops sell swimming gear, sunscreen and bright inflatable floats; and there's a fruit market and supermarket if you're putting your own lunch together. The harbour is full of cruisers, small fishing boats and ad hoc ferries whose owners will offer rides out to various islands, the nearest and most popular of which is **Kiu Tsui Chau** (or Sharp Island), boasting a beach and a short hike to its highest point.

Buses depart Sai Kung Town for some good excursions. From the main open-air bus stop, **bus #94** (6am–9pm; $5.50) heads a few kilometres up the road to **Pak Tam Chung**, basically just some barbecue sites and a **visitor centre** offering hiking maps and information (Mon & Wed–Sun 9.30am–4.30pm), from where you can hike around **High Island Reservoir** in about six hours. If you're after a beach, though, catch **minibus #29R** (Mon–Sat 9.15am, 11.30am & 3.30pm; Sun 11 services 8.30am–4.30pm; $15) from outside *McDonald's* on Chan Man Street, Sai Kung Town to **Sai Wan Ting** – a pavilion at the end of a road. From here it's a ninety-minute walk, via beachside restaurant shacks at Sai Wan and Ham Ting Wan villages, to **Tai Long Wan**, a huge, empty stretch of golden sand. Take care in the water here, as there can be strong undercurrents. From here, follow trails inland again past a couple more villages and the track up Sharp Peak, to the main road at **Pak Tam Au**, from where you can catch bus #94 back to Sai Kung Town.

The Outlying Islands

Officially part of the New Territories, Hong Kong's 260-odd **Outlying Islands** make up twenty percent of the SAR's land area but contain just two percent of the population. As such, they offer visitors a delightful mix of seascape, low-key fishing villages and rural calm, with not much high-density development. The islands of **Lamma** and **Cheung Chau** are fairly small and easy to day-trip around, while **Lantau** has a far greater range of sights and might even demand a couple of visits. You can also make use of local **accommodation** (see p.588) and base yourself on any one of the three, or just hop over for an evening out at one of the many **fish restaurants**. The main point of departure for all three islands is the **Outlying Islands Ferry Pier** in Central; Lamma can also be reached by ferry from Aberdeen, while the **MTR** links a couple of places along Lantau's north coast.

Ferries to the islands

The following is a selection of the most useful island ferry services – full timetables can be picked up at the Outlying Islands Ferry Pier in Central. **Lamma ferries** are operated by HKKF (Ⓦwww.hkkf.com.hk), while those **to Cheung Chau** and **Lantau** are run by First Ferry (Ⓦwww.nwff.com.hk). Schedules differ slightly on Saturdays and Sundays; where available, fast ferries cost more than normal ones.

To Cheung Chau
From Outlying Islands Ferry Pier 24hr departures (at least every 30min 6.15am–11.45pm; 1hr; fast ferry 30min).

To Sok Kwu Wan, Lamma Island
From Outlying Islands Ferry Pier 11 daily 7.20am–10.30pm (50min; fast ferry 35min).

To Yung Shue Wan, Lamma Island
From Outlying Islands Ferry Pier at least hourly 6.30am–12.30am (40min; fast ferry 25min).
From Aberdeen 10 daily 6.30am–8.15pm (25min).

To Mui Wo (Silvermine Bay), Lantau Island
From Outlying Islands Ferry Pier at least hourly 5.55am–11.30pm (1hr).

Lamma

Lying just to the southwest of Aberdeen, Y-shaped **Lamma** is the third largest island in the SAR – though at only around 7km in length, it's still pleasantly small. The island is identifiable from afar thanks to its **power station**, whose chimneys are unfortunately obvious; and a new **wind turbine** on the island's northeastern headland. Lamma's population of five thousand live mostly in west-coast **Yung Shue Wan**, and the rest of the island is covered in open, hilly country, with walking trails out past a couple of beaches to **Sok Kwu Wan**, a tiny knot of **seafood restaurants** on the upper east coast.

A nice way to appreciate the island is to take a ferry to either Yung Shue Wan or Sok Kwu Wan, then walk to the other and catch the boat back from there.

Around the island

Yung Shue Wan is a pretty tree-shaded village with a large expat population, full of low-key modern buildings, which include several hotels, small stores and a **bank** with ATM. Of the **restaurants**, there are popular outdoor tables at the seafood-oriented *Man Fung*, between the ferry dock and the village; the *Sam Pan* does good *yum cha*; and the *Bookworm Café*, on the village main street, is a vegetarian place aimed at expats.

To walk to Sok Kwu Wan (1hr), follow the easy-to-find cement path that branches away from the shore past the grotty apartment buildings on the outskirts of the village, and you'll soon find yourself walking amid butterflies, long grass and trees. After about fifteen minutes you'll arrive at **Hung Shing Ye Beach**, a nice place if you stick to its northern half; stray a few metres to the south, though, and you'll find your horizon rapidly filling up with power station. The *Concerto Inn* is a decent place to dine here, where you can sit on the outdoor terrace and eat relatively inexpensive sandwiches, noodles and rice dishes.

Continue on for another forty minutes or so and you'll reach **Sok Kwu Wan**, which comprises a row of **seafood restaurants** built out over the water. The food and the atmosphere are good, and the restaurants are often full of large parties of locals enjoying lavish and noisy meals; some – like the popular *Rainbow Seafood* (Ⓣ2982 8100, Ⓦwww.rainbowrest.com.hk) – also operate **private boat services** for customers. If you're not taking a restaurant service, make sure you don't miss the last scheduled ferry back to Aberdeen at around 10pm, because there's nowhere to stay here – your only other option would be to hire a sampan back.

Cheung Chau

Another great place to spend a couple of hours strolling around and then have dinner, hourglass-shaped **Cheung Chau** covers just 2.5 square kilometres but is the most crowded of all the outer islands, with a population of 23,000. Historically, the island is one of the oldest settled parts of Hong Kong, being notorious as an eighteenth-century base for **pirates** who enjoyed waylaying the ships that ran between Guangzhou and Macau. Today, it still gives the impression of being an economically independent little unit, the main streets jam-packed with shops (including a **bank** with ATM), markets and more **seafood restaurants**. If you can, visit during the extraordinary **Tai Chiu (Bun) Festival** in April/May, when the island fills to critical mass with raucous martial-arts displays, dragon dances, and a competition to climb vast conical towers made of steamed buns.

From the ferry dock, turn left (north) up main-street **Pak She Praya Road** and you'll soon reach a 200-year-old **Pak Tai Temple**. Fishermen come to the temple to pray for protection, and beside the statue of Pak Tai, the God of the Sea, is an ancient iron sword, discovered by fishermen and supposedly symbolizing good luck.

Ahead from the ferry, through the town and across the island's narrow waist, scenic but crowded **Tung Wan Beach** is a 700m-long strip of sand, with various places to rent windsurfing gear, have a snack, or just laze on the sand. At the south end of the beach, *Warwick Hotel* is the most upmarket place to stay on the island, though there are also plenty of more modest guesthouses (see p.587).

Turn right (south) from the ferry and follow the harbour road past the popular *Hoi Lung Wong* **seafood restaurant** and small places specializing in sweet and sticky desserts, and it's a half-hour walk to Cheung Chau's **southern headland**. You can circumnavigate this via a bit of scrabbling up and down rocks and through bays; there's also a nice picnic pavilion with sea views, and the **Cheung Po Tsai Cave**, named after Cheung Chau's most famous pirate, who used to hide here in the nineteenth century – it's tightly set into the base of some large granite boulders, and you'll need a torch.

Lantau

Mountainous **Lantau** is twice as big as Hong Kong Island but far less developed, despite the proximity of the International Airport just off the north coast. More than half is a designated **country park** and remains fairly wild, with trails linking monasteries, old fishing villages and secluded beaches. There are some major sights here, however, notably **Hong Kong Disneyland** on the northeast coast; the western fishing village of **Tai O**; and **Po Lin Monastery**, with its mighty Big Buddha and wonderful **Ngong Ping 360** cable-car ride. Roads and buses link everything, so getting around isn't difficult, though hikers can also tackle the 70km **Lantau Trail** across the island – contact the Country Parks (Ⓦwww.afcd.gov.hk) for current information.

There are two ways to reach Lantau: by **ferry** from the Outlying Islands Ferry Pier to east-coast **Mui Wo** (Silvermine Bay); and on the **Tung Chung MTR Line**, which runs along the north coast to Disneyland and the town of **Tung Chung** – the latter terminus for the cable car, and close to the airport. Lantau is not necessarily somewhere to rush around, though to pack the island into one day you could arrive by ferry at Mui Wo, take buses across the island via a beach or two to Tai O and Po Lin, ride the cable car down to Tung Chung, and then catch the MTR back into town.

Mui Wo to Po Lin

MUI WO is just a clutch of restaurants grouped about the ferry pier, in front of which is a **bus stop** with departures around the rest of the island – though most of these only run every hour or so, so don't be in too much of a hurry. There's also a nice **beach** with a sprinkling of low-key hotels 500m to the north (see p.588), set in an attractive, curving, sandy bay.

The road west from Mui Wo passes along the southern shore, which is where Lantau's best beaches are located. **Cheung Sha Upper and Lower beaches** are the nicest: long, empty stretches of sand backed by a fringe of trees, with a couple of café-restaurants near the bus stops – buses #1, #2 and #4 all pass by. Beyond here, the road heads inland past the **Shek Pik Reservoir** – look north here and you'll glimpse the Big Buddha sitting up on the ridge – after which it divides: one fork and the #2 bus runs up to the Po Lin Monastery at Ngong Ping; the other and the #1 bus continues over to Tai O.

Located high up on the Ngong Ping Plateau, the **Po Lin Monastery** (daily 10am–6pm; free) is the largest temple in Hong Kong, though only established in 1927. A lively place of worship, the temple is overshadowed by the adjacent bronze **Tian Tan Buddha** (more often known as the Big Buddha), a 34m-high sculpture that depicts the Buddha sitting cross-legged in a lotus flower – climb the steps to the

Buddha's feet for views over the temple. Po Lin's **vegetarian restaurant** serves set meals (daily 11.30am–5pm; meal tickets from $60), with an attached cheaper canteen.

You can also stay the night nearby at the *S.G. Davis Youth Hostel* (see p.587), and then climb the 934m-high **Lantau Peak** – more properly known as Fung Wong Shan – which is a popular place to watch the sunrise. The steep, 2km trail from Po Lin to the summit takes about an hour to complete, and on a clear day views reach as far as Macau. You can pick up the Lantau Trail here and continue 5km (2hr 30min) east to the slightly lower **Tai Tung Shan**, or "Sunset Peak", from where it's a further five-hour hike to Mui Wo.

Moving on from Po Lin, bus #2 returns to Mui Wo, the #21 runs to Tai O, while the #23 goes to Tung Chung. A better way to reach Tung Chung, however, is on the **Ngong Ping 360 cable car** (Mon–Fri 10am–6pm, Sat & Sun 10am–6.30pm; $74 one-way, $107 return), a 5.7km ride that takes 25 minutes and provides fantastic panoramas of Lantau's steep north coast.

Tai O

Right on the far northwestern shore of Lantau, the fishing village of **TAI O** is home to two thousand people, and can be reached on bus #1 from Mui Wo, the #11 from Tung Chung or the #21 from Po Lin. There's plenty of interest in its old lanes, including shrines, temples and a quarter full of tin-roofed stilt-houses built over the mud flats. The main street is lined with stalls selling dried and live seafood, and there's also a tiny **museum** (9am–5pm; free), displaying everyday artefacts such as washboards, vases, a threshing machine and a cutlass.

The pick of the village's temples is **Hau Wong Miu** on Kat Hing Back Street, about two minutes' walk from the bridge. Built in 1699, it contains the local boat used in the annual Dragon-Boat Races (see p.618), some shark bones, a whale head found by Tai O fishermen and a carved roof-frieze displaying two roaring dragons.

The north coast: Hong Kong Disneyland and Tung Chung

The Tung Chung MTR Line can get you to two places along Lantau's north coast. Change at **Sunny Bay Station** for **Hong Kong Disneyland** (check Ⓦwww.hongkongdisneyland.com for times; $295), a tame place compared with their ten other franchises. It's split into four zones: **Main Street USA**, a recreated early twentieth-century mid-American shopping street (though the goods on sale are distinctly Chinese); **Adventureland**, home to Tarzan's treehouse and a jungle river cruise; **Tomorrowland**, whose excellent rides include a blacked-out roller coaster; and **Fantasyland**, populated by a host of Disney characters, and whose best feature is the PhilharMagic 4D film show.

At the end of the line, **TUNG CHUNG** is a burgeoning New Town near the airport. The only real reason to come here is for transport: there's the MTR; the **Ngong Ping 360 cable car** to Po Lin Monastery; and also a host of **buses**, including the #23 to Po Lin, the #3M to Mui Wo, and any service prefixed by "A" to the airport.

Eating, drinking and nightlife

Thanks to its cosmopolitan heritage and the importance attached to eating in Chinese culture, Hong Kong boasts a superb range of **restaurants**. The most prominent cooking style is local **Cantonese**, though you can also find places specializing in Chaozhou, Hakka, Beijing, Sichuanese and Shanghai food. International options include Western **fast-food** chains, curry houses, sushi bars,

Southeast Asian cuisine, hotel lunchtime buffets, pizzerias, vegetarian and South American. The choices below are a fraction of the total, with an emphasis on the less expensive end of the market. For up-to-date reviews, pick up copies of the **free weeklies** *BC* and *HK Magazine*, or check Ⓦwww.womguide.com and Ⓦwww.openrice.com/english/restaurant/index.htm.

Hong Kong's **pubs** and **bars** sometimes host **live music**, but the clutch of restaurant-, bar- and pub-crammed streets known as **Lan Kwai Fong** remains the heart of Hong Kong's party scene and drinking-culture nightlife. Despite its image as a cultural desert, **classical concerts** appear increasingly frequently at several venues, and there are a number of art, jazz and other **festivals** year-round (check the listings magazines detailed on p.581).

Popular English-language and regional films find their way to Hong Kong's **cinemas** soon after release, either shown in their original versions with Chinese subtitles, or dubbed into Cantonese. Some Chinese-language films are shown with English subtitles. There's also the two-week-long **Hong Kong International Film Festival**, held each March, with good Southeast Asian representation – see Ⓦwww.hkiff.org.hk for information.

Western breakfasts and snacks

For **Western breakfasts** of coffee, muffins and fry-ups try the places listed below, or café chains such as *Delifrance* and the ubiquitous *Pacific Coffee*. Bigger hotels also frequently offer fixed-price buffets with vast quantities of food. Most offer free wi-fi for customers. Unless otherwise stated, the places listed below are marked on the map on pp.576–577.

Café Habitu 8 Queen's Rd East, Wan Chai, Hong Kong Island. Small local chain striving to be an international café chain, but retaining a little more panache and style for the time being.

Flying Pan 9 Old Bailey St, Soho, Central, Hong Kong Island. Open around the clock for blow-out portions of toast, bacon, mushrooms, beans and eggs cooked however you want them, and served with juice and hot beverage of your choice. Their coffee isn't so great; otherwise an amazing experience.

TW Coffee Concept 19 Lock Rd, Tsim Sha Tsui, Kowloon; see map, p.598. Not only fine coffee, but also large set breakfasts of egg and toast, fried fillet of sole, or chicken steaks for under $30. Window bar for people-watching.

Dim sum

Dim sum is the classic Cantonese way to start the day – a selection of little dumplings and dishes eaten with tea. Many restaurants serve dim sum from early in the morning until mid-afternoon, when they switch over to more extensive menus, but the following places are particularly wellknown for their dim sum. It's an inexpensive way to eat if you stay away from more famous establishments – perhaps $50 per person on average – but get in early at the weekends when whole families pack out restaurants. Unless otherwise stated, the places listed below are marked on the map on pp.576–577.

Hak Ka Hut 21F, Lee Theatre Plaza, Causeway Bay Ⓣ2881 8578. Hakka and Chaozhou dim sum, meaning lots of clear-skinned *fun gwor* dumplings, stuffed bean curd, salt-baked chicken, *kourou* pork belly and baked turnip pastries.

Lok Cha Teahouse K.C. Lo Gallery, Hong Kong Park Ⓣ2801 7177. Vegetarian dim sum served in elegant teahouse, full of wooden screens and furniture. Atmospheric and with an excellent range of teas, but expensive: from $40/person for the tea, $20/dim sum serving. Bookings advised, especially at weekends. Daily 10am–10pm.

Luk Yu Tea House 24–26 Stanley St, just west of D'Aguilar St Ⓣ2523 5464. A snapshot from the 1930s, with old wooden furniture and ceiling fans, this self-consciously traditional dim sum restaurant is good but overrated, and the quality barely justifies the tourist-inflated prices. Upwards of $100/person.

Medicinal tea

All through downtown Hong Kong you'll see open-fronted shops with large brass urns set out on a counter, offering cups or bowls full of dark brown **medicinal tea** at around $5 a drink. The Cantonese name for this is *lo cha* or "cool tea", because in traditional Chinese medicine, tea is considered "cooling" to the body, though it can be served hot or cold. The teas are made from various ingredients and claim various benefits, but are almost always extremely bitter – ones to try include *ng fa cha* (five-flower tea) and *yat sei mei* (twenty-four-flavour tea). Two well-known medicinal tea-shops are the *Good Spring Company*, on Cochrane Street in Central; and *Lo Cha Da Yat Ga*, at the corner of Hennessy Road and Luard Road in Wan Chai – the latter is unusual for having all its brews named in English.

Majesty Seafood 3F, Prudential Centre, 216–228 Nathan Rd, Jordan ⓣ2723 2399; see map, p.598. First-rate beef balls, leek dumplings, *cha siu* puffs and egg custard tarts at this popular local venue – though surrounding tanks of rare reef fish awaiting their fate can be off-putting.

Metropol 4F, United Centre, 95 Queensway ⓣ2865 1988. Huge place that still uses trolleys to wheel the dim sum selection around – a dying sight in Hong Kong. Try the flaky *cha siu* pastries and crunchy prawn dumplings. Daily 8am–midnight.

Tao Heung 3F, Silvercord Complex, 30 Canton Rd (entrance on Haiphong Rd) ⓣ2375 9128; see map, p.598. Opens for dim sum daily at 7.30am; come early for a window seat facing Kowloon Park. No trolleys, but they have an English menu, and their selection is first rate and inexpensive.

Restaurants

The whole of **downtown Hong Kong** is thick with restaurants, and nowhere is a meal more than a few paces away. Cantonese places are ubiquitous, with the highest concentration of foreign cuisines in Central, Soho, Wan Chai and Tsim Sha Tsui. The scene is, however, notoriously fickle, with places continually opening and withering away. Outside the centre, there are several popular Western-oriented restaurants along Hong Kong Island's **south coast**, while the **Outlying Islands** are famous for their seafood restaurants (see island accounts for these).

The **cheapest meals** are found at local *cha chaan tengs* – literally "tea canteens" – and on the upper floor of indoor produce markets (also known as "wet markets"), where you can get a single-plate meal – wuntun noodle soup, or rice with roast pork – for around $30. City-wide versions of these places include *Fairwood*, *Café de Coral* and the above-average *Tsui Wah*, at 15–19 Wellington St, which serves great fishball soup and Hoinam Chicken (cooked in stock and served with rice). In a "proper" restaurant expect to pay upwards of $40 for a main dish, whatever the type of food being served – a full dinner won't cost less than $150 per person, with that figure climbing well above $700 in the plushest venues.

Restaurant opening hours are from around 11am to 3pm, and 6pm to late, though cheaper Chinese places open all day, winding down around 9pm. Don't worry too much about **tipping**: expensive restaurants add on a ten-percent service charge anyway, while in cheaper places it's customary to just leave the small change. Unless otherwise stated, the places listed below are marked on the map on pp.576–577.

Central

Chippy 51A Wellington St, entrance down the steps on Pottinger St. Last authentic British fish 'n' chip shop in Hong Kong; tiny sit-down counter serving great fries, though fish is sometimes a bit mushy. A large plate of battered cod and chips costs $85.

Habibi 112–114 Wellington St ⓣ2544 3886. Great Egyptian place with main restaurant (featuring weekend belly dancing) and a cheaper café. Food is filling, tasty and not too expensive – you can gorge yourself for $120.

Man Wah 25F, *Mandarin Oriental*, 5 Connaught Rd ☎2522 0111. Subtle and accomplished southern Chinese food at connoisseurs' prices, perhaps worth it if you want one, definitively excellent Cantonese meal – though the view sometimes outperforms the menu.

Nha Trang 88–90 Wellington St ☎2581 9992. First-rate Vietnamese food, whose crisp, clean and sharp flavours make a nice break from more muggy Chinese fare. The grilled prawn and pomelo salad, rice-skin rolls and lemongrass beef are excellent, and two can eat very well for $230.

Roof Garden Top floor at *The Fringe Club*, 2 Lower Albert Rd ☎2521 7251. Bar and buffet with rooftop tables, offering $65 vegetarian all-you-can-eat lunches, and evening tapas from $20. Drinks are cheaper here than in nearby Lan Kwai Fong, too.

Ser Wong Fun 30 Cochrane St (no English sign). Cantonese diner whose reputation rests on its snake soup, though it also does plenty of other straightforward dishes at low prices.

Tsim Chai Kee Noodle 98 Wellington St. No English sign, but easily located by the lunchtime queue tailing downhill; what makes it worth the wait and being jammed into the packed interior are the *wuntun* – jokingly known locally as "ping-pong wuntun" because of their huge size – served in soup for $16.

Yung Kee 32–40 Wellington St ☎2522 1624. An enormous place with bright lights, scurrying staff and seating for a thousand, this is one of Hong Kong's institutions. Their roast goose and pigeon are superb, and the dim sum is also good. Moderately expensive but highly recommended.

Soho

Fat Angelo's 49 Elgin St ☎2973 6808. Extremely popular, noisy Italian joint serving enormous pizzas for about $200 and a range of pasta dishes. Two people can happily share one dish, making a fairly inexpensive night out.

Ivan the Kozak 46–48 Cochrane St ☎2851 1193. Portions of chicken kiev, lamb stew, cabbage and potatoes are good value and tasty, but the highlight is donning a fur coat and walking into the huge freezer for a shot of vodka and a photo. About $200/person.

La Pampa 32 Staunton St ☎2868 6959. Argentinian restaurant that does what it does – barbecued steak, mainly – exceedingly well. You order by weight, it's grilled just how you want it, and served with nominal quantities of vegetables. Count on at least $350/person.

Wan Chai and Causeway Bay

Amici 2F, 50–52 Russel St (Times Square), Causeway Bay ☎2577 2477. The tiny entrance of this homey Italian restaurant is easy to miss. Best known for its superb pizzas.

Coyote 114–120 Lockhart Rd, Wan Chai. Lively Tex-Mex bar and grill with good barbecued ribs, full of tequila-quaffing patrons digging into plates of nachos and spicy pizzas. Around $100/person for a group.

Fook Lam Moon 35–45 Johnston Rd, Wan Chai ☎2866 0663. Very expensive Cantonese institution with astounding roast suckling pig, crispy-skinned chicken, abalone, and bird's-nest soup. Service is not good, however – unless you're famous in Hong Kong.

Green Willow Village 11F, World Trade Centre, Causeway Bay ☎2881 6669. Smart Shanghai restaurant featuring classic dishes such as soy-braised *dongpo* pork, lotus-leaf-wrapped pork, beggars' chicken (baked in mud) and braised stuffed duck. Mains upwards of $80.

Padang JP Plaza, 22–36 Patterson St, Causeway Bay ☎2881 5075. A bit overpriced, but very authentic-tasting Indonesian grilled fish, mutton soup and noodle dishes – the highlight, however, is their cake and durian-flavoured dessert selection.

R66 62F, Hopewell Centre, 183 Queen's Rd East, Wan Chai ☎2862 6166. Revolving restaurant rotating over Wan Chai, best visited for weekend buffet teas from 3–5pm ($98/person) or daily high tea ($158 for two) from 2.30–6pm. Don't expect the *Peninsula*'s quality.

Wing Wah 89 Hennessy Rd at Luard Rd, Wan Chai (there's no English sign). Known for its *wuntun*, this locally famous noodle house also does mostly inexpensive and unusual medicinal soups, beef tendon noodles, and shrimp paste on pomelo skins.

South Coast Hong Kong

See map, pp.590–591.

Boathouse 86–88 Stanley Main St, Stanley ☎2813 4467. Popular hangout, with waterfront views from the balcony of this stylish "Mediterranean" building. Food concentrates on fresh, unpretentiously cooked seafood. Booking essential.

Coco Thai Island Rd, Deepwater Bay, Hong Kong Island ☎2812 1826. Sit under umbrellas on the terrace, look out over the beach, sip drinks and stuff yourself on tasty Thai food: starters like beef salad or pomelo and prawn salad cost $80, while mains of curries or seafood are upwards of $150.

Happy Garden Vietnamese Thai Shek O. On the way from the main bus stop to the seafront. One of several laid-back places with outdoor tables, luridly coloured drinks, and excellent food – try the morning glory with *blechan* beef, or huge Thai fish cakes. Mains around $60.

Jumbo Floating Restaurant Aberdeen Harbour ⓣ2553 9111, ⓦwww.jumbokingdom.com. A Hong Kong institution, with several restaurants on three garishly decorated floors. While expensive and touristy, as a one-off trip it can also be a lot of fun. Mon–Sat 11am–11pm, Sun 7am–11pm.

Tsim Sha Tsui

See map, p.598.

Aqua 29F and Penthouse, 1 Peking Rd ⓣ3427 2288. Dark wooden floors and superlative harbour views through angled windows are the setting for consuming an unexpectedly successful blend of Italian and Japanese dishes. The atmosphere is informal, and the prices high. Reservations essential.

Chee Kee 52 Lock Rd ⓣ2368 2528. Bright Chinese diner serving unpretentious, good-quality *wuntun* and noodle soups, fried pork steak, crispy prawn rolls and fishballs. About $30/dish.

Felix 28F, *Peninsula Hotel* ⓣ2315 3188. The incredible views of Hong Kong Island (not least from the gents' glass-walled urinals) warrant a visit to this Philippe Starck-designed restaurant. The Eurasian menu averages over $600/person, but you can just come for one of their famous martinis.

Hing Fat 8–10 Ashley Rd, opposite *Ned Kelly's Last Stand*. Low prices and generous portions of simple, single-plate meals make this Cantonese canteen an excellent choice for a quick feed.

Kakalok Corner of Ashley Rd and Ichang St. Fast-food counter with the sole distinction of serving the cheapest fried noodles, rice and fish 'n' chips in Hong Kong. No seats, but Kowloon Park is 100m away.

Light Vegetarian 13 Jordan Rd ⓣ2384 2833. Comprehensive Chinese vegetarian menu, including taro fish, "bird's nest" basket filled with fried vegetables, pumpkin soup served in the shell, vegetarian duck and a big dim sum selection. Dishes from $35.

Macau Restaurant 25–27 Lock Rd. Inexpensive Macanese cooking with set meals from $25; packed out at lunchtime with local workers and office staff downing baked rice dishes, pork cutlets and curried crab.

Peninsula Hotel Lobby *Peninsula Hotel* ⓣ2366 6251. The set tea, served in the lobby from 2–7pm and accompanied by a string quartet, comes to around $185/person – a good way to get a glimpse of a more elegant, civilized and relaxed Hong Kong. Dress is smart-casual; no plastic or nylon footwear, no sportswear and no sleeveless shirts for men.

Sino Vegetarian 131–135 Parkes St, Yau Ma Tei ⓣ2771 2393. Vegetarian restaurant which doesn't simply rely on stodgy potato and tofu to mimic meat, but uses a range of dried Chinese vegetables too. Always tasty and unusual, and a photo-menu makes ordering easy. Mains around $55.

Spring Deer 42 Mody Rd ⓣ2366 4012. Faded Beijing restaurant that must have been grand when they last redecorated in the 1960s. The mid-range food – especially the steamed lamb and Beijing duck – is worth it, though.

Sweet Dynasty 100 Canton Rd. Noodles and rice dishes are tasty but expensive; best stick to the Southeast Asian-style desserts, featuring sago, tofu, mango, lotus seeds and red beans. The pomelo pudding in coconut milk is exceptional.

Tim Ho Wan Shop 8, 2–20 Kwong Wa St, Mong Kok, Kowloon ⓣ2332 2896. Crowds queue up from 10am–10pm to eat at this apparently insignificant place, hungry for their Michelin-star-rated lotus-leaf steamed rice, *cha siu* pastries, persimmon cakes and *fun gwor* dumplings. Booking essential, but you'll lose your reservation by being even a couple of minutes late. Around $40/person.

Curry houses in Chungking Mansions

It's not an attractive building, but Chungking Mansions on Nathan Road, Tsim Sha Tsui, is where you'll find some of Hong Kong's best-value curry houses, including:

Delhi Club 3F, Block C. A Nepali curry house par excellence, once you ignore the spartan surroundings and slap-down service. The ludicrously cheap set meal would feed an army.

Khyber Pass 7F, Block E. Consistently good Indian, Pakistani, Bangladeshi and Malay dishes; all *halal* and one of the best in Chungking Mansions.

Sher-E-Punjab 3F, Block B. Friendly service in clean surroundings, if slightly more expensive than some of its neighbours.

Taj Mahal Club 3F, Block B. Friendly place with excellent North Indian food. Good value if you avoid the relatively expensive drinks.

Bars, pubs and clubs

The most concentrated collection of bars is in the **Lan Kwai Fong** area on Hong Kong Island, perennially popular for late-night carousing, with drinkers spilling out onto the street. Other locations include the long-established, slightly sleazy expat scene around **Wan Chai**, and a scattering of options aimed at travellers in **Tsim Sha Tsui**.

Opening times are from 10am at the earliest and often extend well into the small hours. Some venues charge a $50–200 entrance fee on certain nights (generally Fri & Sat), though almost everywhere also offers daily **happy hours** at some point between 3 and 9pm – worth catching, as drinks are otherwise pricey. **Live music**, and sometimes even **raves**, can be found if you look hard, though they are unlikely to match what you're used to back home – for details, consult free *HK* or *Beats* magazines. The **gay scene**, while hardly prominent, is at least more active than in other Chinese cities, given that laws on homosexuality are more liberal here than on the mainland. Unless otherwise stated, the places listed below are marked on the map on pp.590–591.

Central

Agave's 33 D'Aguilar St, Lan Kwai Fong. Largest selection of tequilas in Hong Kong, so head here for frozen, fruit-flavoured margaritas.

Bit Point 31 D'Aguilar St, Lan Kwai Fong. German-themed bar, concentrating on meals until around 10pm, after which the bar starts selling industrial quantities of lager and schnapps as the jukebox blares.

C-Bar/Calafornia 30–32 D'Aguilar St, Lan Kwai Fong. Basement bar boasting an in-house DJ, VIP zones, velvet and fur decoration, heaped-up cushions and a ground-floor bar dishing out shorts and long drinks.

D26 26 D'Aguilar St, Lan Kwai Fong. Small, low-key bar; a good place for a warm-up drink or if you actually want a conversation with your companions.

Dublin Jack 17 Lan Kwai Fong. Lan Kwai Fong's biggest bar, serving draught Guinness, over a hundred different varieties of whiskey, big portions of Irish stew and chargrilled steaks; great views down over the street too. Daily noon–late; happy hour noon–8pm.

Fringe Club 2 Lower Albert Rd ⓦwww.hkfringeclub.com. Live acts, drinks, exhibitions and generally alternative culture in a rather bohemian hangout in the red-and-white Fringe building. One of the cheaper places, with a regular Happy Hour.

Le Jardin Wing Wah Lane. Almost impossible to find unless you already know it's there, this comfortable bar has a covered terrace and is usually quieter than alternatives in nearby Lan Kwai Fong.

Post '97 9 Lan Kwai Fong. A disco downstairs and a vaguely arty, bohemian atmosphere in the bar upstairs, with a strong gay presence on Fri nights. Serves fry-ups, sandwiches and all-day breakfasts.

Schnurrbart's 27 D'Aguilar St, Lan Kwai Fong. Long-standing German bar with herring and sausage snacks, and some of the best beer around. Serious headaches are available courtesy of the 25 different kinds of schnapps – try the butterscotch.

Wan Chai

Carnegie's 53–55 Lockhart Rd. Noise level means conversation here is only possible by flash cards, and once it's packed, hordes of punters, keen to party the night away, fight for dancing space on the bar. Regular live music.

Old China Hand 104 Lockhart Rd. Great food and atmosphere in this dark, barfly hangout, full of embittered, seedy expats acting the part.

The Pawn 62 Johnston Rd. Smart pub in restored old pawnbroker's building dating from 1888, with the facade and some old wooden fixtures still in place, plus a balcony overlooking the busy road. Extensive list of imported spirits, beers and wine, with pub-style fish and chips, ploughman's lunch and English breakfasts at $100–200.

Wanch 54 Jaffe Rd. A Hong Kong institution, this tiny bar has live music – usually folk and rock – every night. Also serves cheap chunky cheese-burgers and sandwiches. Mon–Sat 11am–2am, Sun noon–2am.

Tsim Sha Tsui

See map, p.598.

Bahama Mama's 4–5 Knutsford Terrace, just north of Kimberly Rd. A good atmosphere with a vibrant mix of nationalities, and plenty of space for pavement drinking. There's a beach-bar theme and outdoor terrace that prompts party-crowd antics. On club nights, there's a great range of mixed music.

Delaney's Basement, Mary Building, 71–77 Peking Rd. Friendly Irish pub with draught beers, including Guinness; features Irish folk music most nights.

Ned Kelly's Last Stand 11A Ashley Rd. Very popular, long-running venue, featuring a nightly performance from an excellent ragtime jazz band.

Stag's Head Hart Ave, Tsim Sha Tsui. Popular pub attracting expats and tourists alike; almost always has beer, spirit and wine promotions during happy hours.

Shopping

Many visitors come to Hong Kong to go **shopping**, drawn by the incredible range of goods packed into such a small area. While some things are good value for money – particularly **clothes, silk, jewellery, Chinese arts and crafts,** some **computer accessories** and **pirated software** – it's essential to research online prices for identical goods before buying, and to shop around. The farther you are from touristy Tsim Sha Tsui, the better value shopping becomes, and the less likely that you'll be **ripped off** by some scam.

Shops **open** daily; in downtown areas and shopping malls, 10am to 7pm or later is the norm. For more information, browse the HKTB's website (Ⓦwww.discoverhongkong.com), which includes information about shops listed under their Quality Tourism Services scheme.

Antiques, arts and crafts

Chinese collectors are too clued up to make it likely that you'll unearth bargain **antiques** in Hong Kong, but the quality is high and ranges from porcelain through to wooden screens and furniture, sculpture and embroidery. Hollywood Road (see p.589) is at the centre of the trade, a fun place to browse even if you don't intend to buy. "Antique" doesn't always mean more than 100 years old – ask to be sure. Hong Kong is also a reasonable place to pick up modern **arts and crafts,** with a couple of big chain stores dealing in Chinese products – prices are cheaper on the mainland, however. For **jade**, the Jade Market in Mong Kok (see p.600) is a good place to look, if you take everything the stallholders say with a pinch of salt. Some more general stores include:

Eu Yan Sang Ground Floor, 152–156 Queen's Rd, Central Ⓣ2544 3308, Ⓦwww.euyansang.com. One of the most famous medicine shops in town, founded in 1879, and now with branches right aross Southeast Asia. A source of teas, herbs and Chinese medicines, all carefully weighed and measured.

Karin Weber Gallery 20 Aberdeen St, Central Ⓣ2544 5004, Ⓦwww.karinwebergallery.com. Specializes in contemporary paintings from the mainland and Southeast Asia, plus antique Chinese furniture.

L&E 21F, Remex Centre, 42 Wong Chuk Hang Rd, east of Aberdeen Ⓣ2656 1220, Ⓦwww.lneco.com. Warehouse-sized store full of decorative porcelain and old Chinese furniture. Packing and shipping can be arranged.

Shoeni Art Gallery 27 Hollywood Rd Ⓣ2869 8802, Ⓦwww.schoeni.com.hk. Agents for modern Chinese artists such as Chen Yu, who combines Chinese images with Renaissance-era scenery.

Teresa Coleman 79 Wyndham St Ⓣ2526 2450, Ⓦwww.teresacoleman.com. One of Hong Kong's best-known dealers, with an international reputation for Chinese textiles. In addition, they have a good selection of pictures and prints.

Yue Hwa China Products 301–309 Nathan Rd, Jordan. Chinese medicines, clothing, sportswear, tea, books, spirits and every conceivable tourist knick-knack produced on the mainland.

Clothes

Clothes are good value in Hong Kong, particularly local fashion brand names such as Gordiano and Baleno, which have branches all over the city. Big-name foreign designer clothes are often more expensive than back home because of the cachet attached to foreign upmarket brands, but **sales** are worth checking out.

Another potentially cheap way to buy clothes (including designer clothes without the labels) is from **factory outlets**. These places open and close very quickly, so contact the HKTB for the latest information. Be sure to try things on before you buy – marked sizes mean nothing. For **markets** dealing in inexpensive clothes, try the Temple Street Night Market (p.600), Ladies Market (p.600) and stalls in lanes off **Ap Liu Street** in Kowloon (Sham Shui Po MTR).

If you just want to browse, good places to start include **Granville Road** in Tsim Sha Tsui, the **Pedder Building** on Pedder Street in Central and, just round the corner, **Wyndham** and **D'Aguilar streets**. Other places to look include:

Blanc De Chine 2F, Pedder Building, 12 Pedder St, Central. Elegant designs loosely based on traditional Chinese clothes, mostly in silk or cashmere.

Joyce Warehouse 21F, Horizon Plaza, Lee Nam Rd, Ap Lei Chau island, Aberdeen. Where the boutique sends last season's (or last month's) stuff that didn't sell, at discounts of up to eighty percent. Tues–Sat 10am–6pm.

Shanghai Tang Ground Floor, Pedder Building, 12 Pedder St, Central. A must-visit store, beautifully done up in 1930s Shanghai style. Specializes in new versions of traditional Chinese styles like the *cheongsam* split-sided dress, often in vibrant colours. They can also make to order. Expensive, even during sales.

Vivienne Tam Shop 209, Pacific Place, 88 Queensway, Admiralty; Shop 219, Times Square, 1 Matheson St, Causeway Bay; Shop G310–311, Harbour City, Tsim Sha Tsui. Funky shirts and dresses in David-Hockney-meets-Vivienne-Westwood style, often featuring Chairman Mao and other icons of the East.

Tailor-made clothes

Tailor-made clothes are a speciality of the Hong Kong tourist trade, and wherever you go in Tsim Sha Tsui you'll be accosted by Indian tailors offering this service. Sales pitches are hardcore and prices are relatively low, but not rock bottom; a man's cashmere suit, with a couple of shirts and ties, will cost upwards of $1500, more likely twice this. Don't commit yourself without knowing exactly what's included. Expect at least two or three fittings over several days if you want a good result. You'll need to pay about fifty percent of the price as deposit.

Johnson & Co 44 Hankow Rd, Kowloon. Does a lot of work for military and naval customers. Mostly male clientele.

Linva Tailor 38 Cochrane St, Central. Well-established ladies' tailor, popular with locals who want *cheongsams* for parties. They work a lot with embroidery.

Margaret Court Tailoress 8F, Winner Building, 27 D'Aguilar St, Lan Kwai Fong, Central. She has lots of local Western female clients, and a solid reputation for good work, although it doesn't come cheaply. A shirt costs around $500 plus fabric.

Pacific Custom Tailors 1F, 113 Pacific Place, 88 Queensway, Admiralty. Upmarket suits with a price to match, in one of Hong Kong's snazziest shopping malls.

Punjab House 5F, Suite C, Golden Crown Court, 66–70 Nathan Rd, Tsim Sha Tsui. Former favourite of the British Forces and Fire Fighters; good-quality male and female formal wear.

Sam's Tailors 94 Nathan Rd, Tsim Sha Tsui Ⓦwww.samstailor.biz. Probably the best-known tailor in Hong Kong, Sam is famous as much for his talent for self-publicity as for his clothes.

Electronic goods

With the advent of internet shopping, prices in Hong Kong for **electronic goods** such as cameras, MP3 players, mobile phones and computers are often no longer the bargain they once were. Add the difficulty of getting any sort of **warranty**, the possibility of being ripped off and the impossibility of getting a refund, and it's not usually worth the risks. If you do decide to buy, make sure you know exactly what you want, and the price you'd pay for it at home or online. Your best bet is when new models of products are about to be launched, as shops try to ditch their old stock before it becomes unsaleable to fashion-conscious locals. **Chain stores** such as Fortress are good places to get a base price, though you'll do better at the three warehouse-sized computer centres listed below. For **secondhand** mobile phones and household appliances, try **Ap Liu Street** in Sham Shui Po, Kowloon (exit A2 from Sham Shui Po MTR).

Pirated computer software is extremely cheap, though it's getting harder to find and if it doesn't work, don't expect a refund.

298 Computer Zone 298 Hennessy Rd, Wan Chai. Discounted computers and accessories, ranging from dodgy Chinese stuff to top-notch brands. You might also find pirated software here.

Golden Shopping Centre 156 Fuk Wah St, Sham Shui Po, Kowloon (Sham Shui Po MTR, exit D2). Lots of cheap computer goods.

Mong Kok Computer Centre Corner of Nelson St and Fa Yuen St, Mong Kok. More discounted goods; once also famous for pirated software, though this is much harder to find nowadays.

Malls and department stores

In summer, the air conditioning in Hong Kong's numerous, glossy shopping malls makes as good a reason as any to visit, and most have nice cafés to boot. Some of the best include **Times Square** (Causeway Bay MTR), **IFC Mall** (inside the International Finance Centre; Central MTR), **Lee Gardens** (Causeway Bay MTR) and **Festival Walk** (Kowloon Tong MTR). Department store chains include:

CRC Department Store Chiao Shang Building, 92 Queen's Rd, Central; Lok Sing Centre, 31 Yee Wo St, Causeway Bay. At the cheaper end of the spectrum, but a good supply of Chinese specialities such as medicines, foods, porcelain and handicrafts.

Lane Crawford Shop 126, Pacific Place, 88 Queensway, Admiralty and elsewhere. Hong Kong's oldest Western-style department store.

SOGO East Point Centre, 555 Hennessy Rd, Causeway Bay. The Japanese contingent. Immaculately presented goods inside one of the largest department stores in Hong Kong.

Wing On 26 Des Voeux Rd, Central (and other branches). Another long-established store, with branches throughout Hong Kong SAR. Standard, day-to-day goods rather than luxuries.

Jewellery

Hong Kongers love **jewellery**, and the city sports literally thousands of jewellers. Some offer pieces that look remarkably like the more popular designs of the famous international jewellery houses, but at much lower prices. As always, shop around, as different places may ask wildly different prices for the same design. The HKTB's free *Shopping Guide to Jewellery* is helpful for finding reputable stores.

Listings

Airlines Aeroflot, Suite 2918, 29F, Shui On Centre, 6–8 Harbour Rd, Wan Chai ☎2537 2611; Air Canada, Room 1608–12, Tower 1, New World Tower, 18 Queen's Rd, Central ☎2122 8124; Air India, Unit 4401, 44F Hopewell Centre, 183 Queens Rd East ☎2522 1176; Air New Zealand, Suite 1701, Jardine House, 1 Connaught Place, Central ☎2862 8192; British Airways, 24F, Jardine House, 1 Connaught Place, Central ☎3071 5083; Cathay Pacific, Suite 1808, 18F, Tower 6, The Gateway, Harbour City, 9 Canton Rd, Tsim Sha Tsui ☎2747 1577; China Eastern, Unit B, 31F, United Centre, 95 Queensway, Wan Chai ☎2861 1898; Dragonair, Suite 1808, 18F, The Gateway, Harbour City, 9 Canton Rd, Tsim Sha Tsui ☎3193 3888; Japan Airlines, 30F, Tower 6, The Gateway, Harbour City, 9 Canton Rd, Tsim Sha Tsui ☎2523 0081; KLM, Rm 2201–03, World Trade Centre, 280 Gloucester Rd, Causeway Bay ☎2808 2111; Malaysia Airlines, 1306 Princes Building, Chater Rd, Central ☎2521 2321; Qantas, 24F, Jardine House, 1 Connaught Place, Central ☎2822 9000; Singapore Airlines, 17F, United Centre, 95 Queensway, Admiralty ☎2520 2233; Thai International Airlines, 24F, United Centre, 95 Queensway, Admiralty ☎2876 6888; United Airlines, ☎2810 4888.

Banks and exchange Banks generally open Mon–Fri 9am–4.30pm, Sat 9am–12.30pm; almost all have ATMs capable of accepting foreign cards. Banks handling foreign exchange levy commissions on travellers' cheques. Licensed moneychangers, who open all hours including Sun, don't charge commission but usually give poor rates, so shop around and always establish the exact amount you will receive before handing any money over.

Bookshops The Swindon Book Company, 13–15 Lock Rd, Tsim Sha Tsui, is good for books on Hong Kong and China and for glossy art books. Dymock's, in many locations including the IFC Mall, Central, also has a good range of popular fiction and local interest. Cosmos Books, at 30 Johnston Rd, Wan Chai, and 96 Nathan Rd, Tsim Sha Tsui, offers a range of both English- and Chinese-language books on all topics.

Embassies and consulates Australia, 23F, Harbour Centre, 25 Harbour Rd, Wan Chai ⓣ2827 8881; Canada, 14F, 1 Exchange Square, Central ⓣ2847 7420; China, 7F, Lower Block, China Resources Building, 26 Harbour Rd, Wan Chai ⓣ3413 2424; India, 16F, United Centre, 95 Queensway, Admiralty ⓣ2528 4028; Ireland, Suite 1408, Two Pacific Place, 88 Queensway, Wan Chai ⓣ2527 4897; Japan, 46F, One Exchange Square, Central ⓣ2522 1184; Korea, 5F, Far East Finance Centre, 16 Harcourt Rd, Central ⓣ2529 4141; Malaysia, 24F, Malaysia Building, 50 Gloucester Rd, Wan Chai ⓣ2821 0800; New Zealand, 6501 Central Plaza, 18 Harbour Rd, Wan Chai ⓣ2525 5044; Philippines, 14F, United Centre, 95 Queensway, Admiralty ⓣ2823 8501; Singapore, 901–2 Tower 1, Admiralty Centre, Admiralty ⓣ2527 2212; South Africa, 2706 Great Eagle Centre, 23 Harbour Rd, Wan Chai ⓣ2577 3279; Thailand, 8F, Fairmont House, 8 Cotton Tree Drive, Central ⓣ2521 6481; UK, 1 Supreme Court Rd, Admiralty ⓣ2901 3000; US, 26 Garden Rd, Central ⓣ2523 9011; Vietnam, 15F, Great Smart Tower, 230 Wan Chai Rd, Wan Chai ⓣ2591 4517.

Festivals Festivals specific to Hong Kong include the Tin Hau Festival, in late April or May, in honour of the Goddess of the Sea. Large seaborne festivities take place, most notably at Joss House Bay on the Sai Kung Peninsula (see p.605). Another is the Tai Chiu Festival (known in English as the Bun Festival), held on Cheung Chau Island during May. The Tuen Ng (Dragon-Boat) Festival takes place in early June, with races in various places around the territory. Other Chinese festivals, such as New Year and Mid-Autumn, are celebrated in Hong Kong with as much, if not more, gusto than on the mainland.

Hospitals Government hospitals have 24hr casualty wards, where treatment is free. These include the Princess Margaret Hospital, Lai King Hill Rd, Lai Chi Kok, Kowloon ⓣ2990 1111; and the Queen Mary Hospital, Pokfulam Rd, Hong Kong Island ⓣ2855 3838. For an ambulance, dial ⓣ999.

Internet Café chains such as *Pacific Coffee* provide 15–30min free use, provided you purchase something from them; many offer free wi-fi for their customers. Hong Kong Library, opposite Victoria Park on Hong Kong Island, has free internet, though you have to wait for a terminal to become available, plus free wi-fi. There are also net bars in the lower two floors of Chungking Mansions, charging around $20/hour.

Laundry There are many laundries in Hong Kong where you pay by dry weight of clothes ($10–20/kilo) and then pick them up an hour or two later; ask at your accommodation for the nearest.

Left luggage There's an office in the departure lounge at the airport (daily 6.30am–1am), and at the Central and Kowloon stations for the Airport Express. There are also coin-operated lockers in the Hong Kong China Ferry Terminal in Tsim Sha Tsui. Costs are $20–80 depending on size of locker and time used. You can also negotiate to leave luggage at your guesthouse or hotel, but ensure you're happy with general security first.

Mail The general post office is at 2 Connaught Place, Central (Mon–Sat 8am–6pm, Sun 9am–2pm), facing Jardine House. Poste restante mail is delivered here (you can pick it up Mon–Sat 8am–6pm), unless specifically addressed to "Kowloon". The Kowloon main post office is at 10 Middle Rd, Tsim Sha Tsui. Both have shops that sell boxes, string and tape to pack any stuff you want to send home.

Police Crime hotline and taxi complaints ⓣ2527 7177. For general police enquiries, call ⓣ2860 2000.

Sport Every Easter, Hong Kong is host to an international Rugby Sevens tournament (information from Hong Kong Rugby Football Union ⓦwww.hkrugby.com). The following activities are also available in the territory: sailing (Hong Kong Yachting Association ⓦwww.sailing.org.hk); windsurfing (try the Windsurf Centre on Kwun Yam Wan Beach, Cheung Chau Island, for rentals and instruction); marathon running (the Hong Kong Marathon takes place in Feb; ⓦwww.hkmarathon.com). For tennis courts, contact the Hong Kong Tennis Association (ⓦwww.tennishk.org), whose website lists clubs, facilities and events.

Telephones All local calls are free, and you can usually use any phones in hotel lobbies and restaurants for no charge. Payphones cost $1 for five minutes. The cheapest way to make IDD calls is by buying a prepaid discount phone card for the country you want to call; there are heaps of stores selling them inside the Pedder Building on Queen's Rd in Central, and in Chungking Mansions in Tsim Sha Tsui. For directory enquiries in English, call ⓣ1081, and for emergency services, call ⓣ999.

Tours The HKTB runs a series of interesting theme tours – horse racing, harbour cruises, city sights and the like – best suited for those in a hurry; consult HKTB's brochures for details. Other tour operators include Star Ferry (ⓦwww.starferry.com.hk) for harbour cruises; Gray Line (ⓦwww.grayline.com.hk) for coach tours around the SAR; and Hong Kong Dolphinwatch (ⓦwww.hkdolphinwatch.com), who run boat trips out to see the renowned pink dolphins.

Travel agents Hong Kong is full of budget travel agents, all able to organize international flights as well as train tickets, tours, flights and visas to mainland China. These include Shoestring Travel Ltd, Flat A, 4F, Alpha House, 27–33 Nathan Rd, Tsim Tsa Shui (ⓣ2723 2306, ⓦwww.shoestringtravel.com.hk); Hong Kong Student Travel Ltd, Hang Lung Centre, Yee Wo St, Causeway Bay (ⓦen.hkst.com); and CTS, 4F, CTS House, 78–83 Connaught Rd, Central (ⓣ2789 5401, ⓦwww.ctshk.com), and 27–33 Nathan Rd (entrance on Peking Rd; ⓣ2315 7188). Cheaper hostels often have useful up-to-date information and contacts for budget travel as well.

Macau

Sixty kilometres west across the Pearl River Delta from Hong Kong lies the former Portuguese enclave of **MACAU**. Occupying a peninsula and a couple of islands of just thirty square kilometres in extent, Macau's unique atmosphere has been unmistakably shaped by a colonial past – predating Hong Kong's by nearly three hundred years – which has left old fortresses, Baroque churches, faded mansions, public squares, unusual food and Portuguese place names in its wake. But what draws in millions of big-spending tourists from Hong Kong, the mainland and neighbouring countries are Macau's **casinos**, the only place in China where they have been legalized. The income they generate – over five billion US dollars annually – now exceeds that of Las Vegas, and has funded a **construction boom** for themed resorts, roads and large-scale **land reclamation**.

Considering that costs are somewhat lower here than in Hong Kong, and the ease of travel between Shenzhen, Hong Kong and Macau, it's a great pity not to drop in on Macau if you are in the region. A day-trip from Hong Kong is possible (tens of thousands do it every weekend), though you really need a couple of nights to do the place justice.

The Macau **currency** is the pataca (abbreviated to "MOP$" in this book; also written as "M$" and "ptca"), which is worth fractionally less than the HK dollar. HK dollars (but not yuan) are freely accepted as currency in Macau, and a lot of visitors from Hong Kong don't bother changing money at all.

Some history

For more than a thousand years, all **trade** between China and the West had been indirectly carried out overland along the Silk Road through Central Asia. But from the fifteenth century onwards, seafaring European nations started making exploratory voyages around the globe, establishing garrisoned ports along the way and so creating new maritime trade routes over which they had direct control.

In 1557 – having already gained toeholds in India (Goa) and the Malay Peninsula (Malacca) – the **Portuguese** persuaded Chinese officials to rent them a strategically well-placed peninsula at the mouth of the Pearl River Delta, known as **Macao** (or "Aomen" in Mandarin). With their important trade links with Japan, as well as

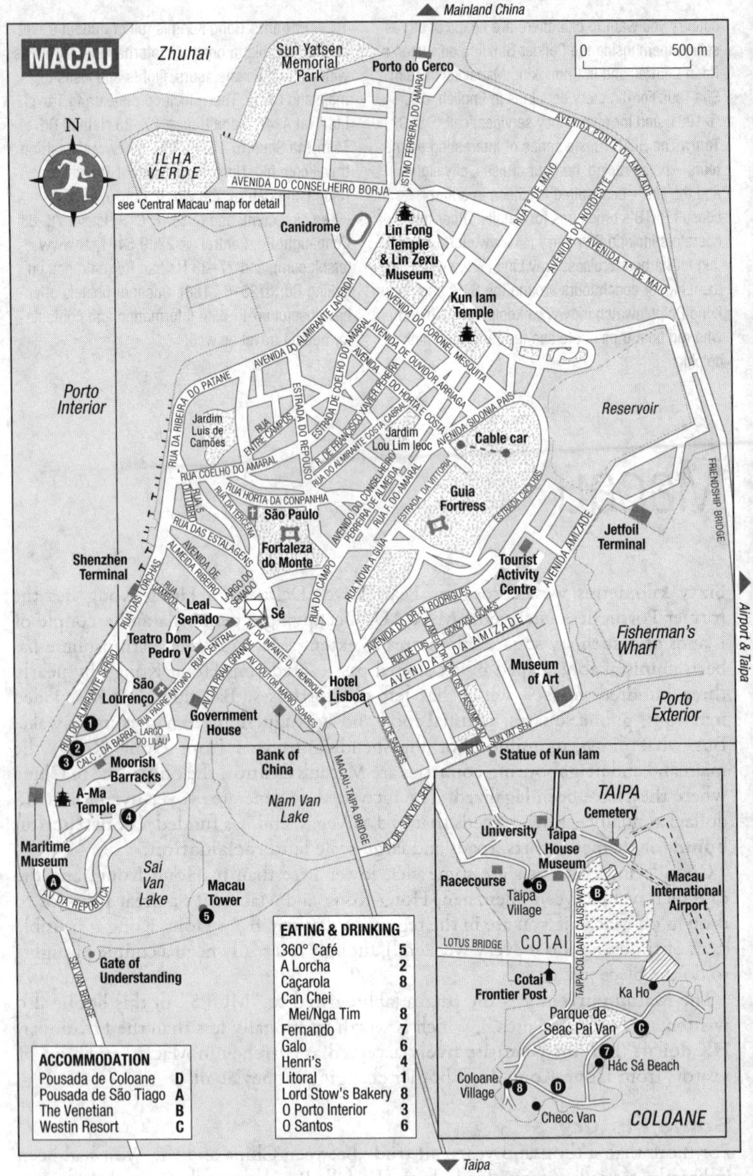

with India and Malaya, the Portuguese found themselves in the profitable position of being sole agents for merchants across a whole swath of East Asia. Given that the Chinese were forbidden from going abroad to trade themselves, and that other foreigners were not permitted to enter Chinese ports, their trade blossomed and Macau grew immensely wealthy. With the traders came **Christianity**, and among the luxurious homes and churches built during Macau's brief half-century of prosperity was the basilica of **São Paulo**, whose facade can still be seen today.

By the beginning of the seventeenth century, however, Macau's fortunes were waning alongside Portugal's decline as a maritime power. There was a brief respite when Macau became a base for European traders attempting to prise open the locked door of China during the eighteenth century, but following the British seizure of Hong Kong in 1841, Macau's status as a backwater was sealed. Despite the introduction of **licensed gambling** in 1847, as a means of securing some kind of income, virtually all trade was lost to Hong Kong.

As in Hong Kong, the twentieth century saw wave after wave of **immigrants** pouring into Macau to escape strife on the mainland – the territory's population today stands at 540,000 – but, unlike in Hong Kong, this growth was not accompanied by spectacular economic development. Indeed, when the Portuguese attempted unilaterally to hand Macau back to China during the 1960s and 1970s, they were rebuffed: the gambling, prostitution and organized crime that was Macau's lifeblood would only be an embarrassment to the Communist government if they had left it alone, yet cleaning it up would have proved too big a financial drain – after all, most of Macau's GDP and government revenue comes from gambling.

However, by the time China accepted the return of the colony – as the **Macau Special Administrative Region** (MSAR) – in 1999, the mainland had become both richer and more ideologically flexible. A pre-handover spree of violence by Triad gangs was dealt with, then the monopoly on casino licences – previously held by local billionaire **Dr Stanley Ho** – was ended in 2002, opening up this lucrative market to international competition. Response has been swift, and there are currently **33 casinos** in the territory, including the colossal *Venetian*, one of several US-owned properties. **Tourism** has increased alongside and the once-torpid economy is boiling, though an unforeseen embarrassment is that mainland officials have been accused of gambling away billions of yuan of public funds during holidays in the SAR. Meanwhile, Macau's **government** operates along the "One Country, Two Systems" principle, with very little dissent – the reality is that, even more than Hong Kong, Macau desperately needs the mainland for its continuing existence, as it has no resources of its own. To this end, some giant infrastructure projects – including a bridge to Hong Kong – are in the pipeline, as the SAR seeks to tie its economy closer to that of the booming Pearl River Delta area.

Arrival

Macau comprises several distinct parts. The largest and most densely settled area is the **peninsula**, bordering the Chinese mainland to the north, where the original city was located and where most of the historic sights and facilities remain. Off to the southeast and linked to the peninsula by bridges are **Taipa** and **Coloane**, once separate islands but now joined by a low-lying area of reclaimed land known as **Cotai**, which is being developed as a new entertainment strip. It's all very compact, and it's possible to get around much of Macau on foot, with public transport available for longer stretches.

All boats and helicopters from Hong Kong arrive at Macau's **Jetfoil Terminal** (Nova Terminal in Portuguese) on the east of the peninsula, from where **Avenida de Amizade** runs past a strip of casinos to **Avenida Almeida Ribeiro**, which cuts westwards through the historic quarter and budget-hotel area to the **Porto Interior** (Inner Harbour), where ferries from Shenzhen (Shekou) dock. City buses #3, #3A and #10A cover this entire route between the two ports.

Macau International Airport is on Taipa, from where buses #21 and #26 run to Avenida Almeida Ribeiro, or catch #AP1 to the Jetfoil Terminal. If you've walked in **from Zhuhai** Special Economic Zone on mainland China through the Porto do Cerco (Barrier Gate), take bus #AP1 to the Jetfoil Terminal, or #2, #3A, #5 or #18 to Avenida Almeida Ribeiro.

Getting to Macau and moving on

Visa regulations state currently that citizens of Britain, Ireland and most European countries can stay 90 days on arrival; those of Australia, New Zealand, Canada, South Africa, the US and several others can stay 30 days on arrival – check Ⓦwww.macautourism.gov.mo for the latest. In Hong Kong, the Macau Government Tourist Office is in the Shun Tak Centre (Hong Kong–Macau Ferry Terminal), 200 Connaught Rd, Central (Ⓣ2857 2287).

Ferries cross regularly to Macau from both Hong Kong and Shenzhen. **From Hong Kong**, First Ferry (Ⓦwww.nwff.com.hk) departs from the Hong Kong China Ferry Terminal on Canton Road, Tsim Sha Tsui, around twice an hour between 7am and midnight; Turbojet (Ⓦwww.turbojet.com.hk) runs between one and four times an hour, 6.40am to midnight, from the Hong Kong–Macau Ferry Terminal in the Shun Tak Centre, Central. Either service takes 55 minutes and costs about $140 one way, though discounts are often available. Usually you can buy a ticket immediately before departure, but at weekends and holidays – or if you're on a tight schedule – you should book the day before. Either way, turn up half an hour before sailing to clear customs. In Macau, both ferry services arrive and depart from the main Jetfoil Terminal. **From Shenzhen** (Shekou port), ferries depart six times daily between 8.45am and 7.30pm. Tickets cost ¥170 one way, and the journey takes around eighty minutes; you arrive in Macau at the Shenzhen Terminal, on Rua Das Lorchas.

Macau has **air** links to Taiwan, Bangkok, Kuala Lumpur, Manila, Seoul and Singapore, as well as an expanding range of Chinese cities including Beijing, Shanghai, Guangzhou, Xiamen and Kunming. There's also a **helicopter service** from the Hong Kong–Macau Ferry Terminal in Central – contact Sky Shuttle (Ⓦwww.skyshuttlehk.com).

By land, you can **walk** across the border (daily 7am–midnight) at the Porto do Cerco (Barrier Gate), into the Zhuhai Special Economic Zone. **By bus**, CTS (Rua de Nagasaki; Ⓣ2798 0877) run daily services to and from Macau and Hong Kong, Guangzhou, and Zhaoqing in Guangdong province for MOP$50–120, and can also organize two-month **Chinese visas** overnight.

Information

The **Macau Government Tourist Office**, or MGTO (tourist hotline Ⓣ2833 3000, Ⓦwww.macautourism.gov.mo) provides helpful leaflets on Macau's fortresses, museums, parks, churches, self-guided walks and outlying islands as well as a good city **map**. The main office is at Largo do Senado 9, with counters at the airport, the Jetfoil Terminal and the Zhuhai-border Porto do Cerco. All are open daily from 9am to 6pm.

In **Hong Kong**, MGTO have an office at the airport's arrivals hall, and in the Hong Kong–Macau Ferry Terminal, Room 336–337, Shun Tak Centre (daily 9am–10pm; Ⓣ2857 2287).

Transport

Macau's comprehensive **public bus** network charges a flat fare of MOP$3.20 on the peninsula, MOP$4.20 to Taipa, and MOP$5 to Coloane, except Hác Sá beach,

Macau phone numbers have no area codes. From outside the territory, dial the normal international access code + Ⓣ853 (country code) + the number. **To call Hong Kong from Macau**, dial Ⓣ01 + the number. To call Macau from mainland China, dial Ⓣ00 + 853 + the number.

which is MOP$6.40; you need the exact fare, as change is not given. Important interchanges include the Jetfoil Terminal; outside the *Hotel Lisboa*; Almeida Ribeiro; Barra (near the A-Ma Temple); and the Porto do Cerco. Useful routes are indicated where necessary in the text.

Taxis charge MOP$13 to hire – including surcharges, the one-way fare from downtown to Coloane's Hác Sá beach (the longest trip you can possibly make) costs about MOP$90.

Accommodation

Accommodation is a good deal in Macau: the money that would get you a dingy box in Hong Kong here provides a clean room with private shower and a window. Still, there are fewer real budget options and at weekends, holidays and during the Macau Grand Prix (third weekend in November), **prices** can more than double. Mid- and upper-range hotels often give discounted rates if you **book ahead**; while agents in Hong Kong such as the CTS offer good-value transport and accommodation **packages**.

The densest concentration and variety of hotels is found on the peninsula – especially in the vicinity of Avenida de Almirante Ribeiro – though Taipa, Cotai and Coloane also sport several upmarket resorts. Note that addresses in Macau are written with the number after the name of the street.

Western peninsula

Augusters Rua do Dr. Pedro Jose Lobo 24 ⓣ2871 3242, ⓦwww.augusters.de. Tidy, if elderly, dorms and double rooms in a central downtown block; all have a/c and shared facilities, including a kitchen. Dorms MOP$125, rooms ❸

East Asia Hotel Rua da Madeira 1 ⓣ2892 2433, ⓕ2892 2431. One of Macau's oldest hotels – a little shabby, but comfortable, with friendly staff and good views from some of the upstairs windows. ❸

Hotel Central Avenida de Almeida Ribeiro 26–28 ⓣ2837 3888. Hundreds of budget rooms on seven floors in this elderly, gloomy block just around the corner from the Largo do Senado. Lower-priced rooms are generally clean enough and good value, but ask to see a few. ❸

Ka Va Calcada de Sao Joao 5 ⓣ2832 3063. On the left as you head uphill from Rua da Sé to the Sé church. A good budget choice if you stick to the tidy rear rooms, though those facing the street are windowless and prone to damp. ❷

Ko Wah Rua da Felicidade 71 ⓣ2893 0755. Inexpensive hostel in one of Macau's most interesting quarters. Ride the lift from the cupboard-sized lobby to the second floor, where the rooms range from fairly modern to quite old; all are clean and en suite. ❸–❹

Man Va Travessa da Caldeira 30 ⓣ2838 8655, ⓕ2834 2179. Clean and well-designed rooms with spacious bathrooms, spotless carpets and helpful management, though no English spoken. Top value. ❹

Ole London Praça Ponte e Horta 4–6 ⓣ2893 7761, ⓕ2893 7790. Smart little boutique hotel with modern rooms and ADSL available. Cheapest rooms are windowless; best pay a little extra for one looking onto the square outside. ❹

San Va Rua da Felicidade 67 ⓣ8210 0193, ⓦwww.sanvahotel.com. Best budget deal in town, with no-frills but spotless rooms in an early 1900s building featuring wooden shutters,

Accommodation price codes

All the **accommodation** in this book has been graded according to price codes, which represent the cheapest double room available. Accommodation in **Macau** has been given codes from the categories below. Note that accommodation is generally cheaper on weekdays, unless stated otherwise.

❶ MOP$150 and under	❹ MOP$351–500	❼ MOP$1001–1500
❷ MOP$151–250	❺ MOP$501–750	❽ MOP$1501–2000
❸ MOP$251–350	❻ MOP$751–1000	❾ MOP$2001 and over

balconies over Rua da Felicidade and priceless atmosphere. Friendly management. ❶

Sun Sun Praça Ponte e Horta 14–16 ⓣ2893 9393, ⓦwww.bestwestern.com. Slightly sleazy area but the hotel is well managed, organized and gives midweek discounts. ❺

Universal Rua da Felicidade 73 ⓣ2857 3247. South of Almeida Ribeiro, this is an older, fairly large hotel, with a mix of tidy and spacious rooms. ❷

Southern and eastern peninsula

Hotel Lisboa Avenida de Lisboa 2–4 ⓣ2837 7666, HK reservations ⓣ800 969130, ⓦwww.hotelisboa.com. Once the most ostentatious building in Macau – but now overshadowed by the ludicrous *Grand Lisboa* opposite – tiled in orange and white and housing a casino, a shopping arcade and numerous restaurants. ❻–❼; check the website for current offers.

Metropole Hotel Avenida Praia Grande 493–501 ⓣ2838 8166, ⓕ2833 0890. A few hundred metres west of the *Lisboa*; well located and smartly fitted out, and you should find good deals on most discount booking websites. ❺

Pousada de São Tiago Avenida da República ⓣ2837 8111, ⓦwww.saotiago.com.mo. Constructed from a seventeenth-century fortress on the southern tip of the peninsula, with walled stairways lined by gushing streams, huge stone archways, and 12 luxurious suites. Nothing else like this in all China. ❾

Taipa, Cotai and Coloane

Pousada de Coloane Praia de Cheoc Van, Coloane ⓣ2888 2143, ⓦwww.hotelpcoloane.com.mo. Great scenery, if somewhat remote, situated by Cheoc Van beach on Coloane's far south shore. All rooms have balconies overlooking the beach, there's a swimming pool and an Italian restaurant. If you want a relaxing holiday experience, this is the place for it. ❺

Venetian Cotai ⓣ2883 7788, ⓦwww.venetianmacao.com. An incredible, full-scale replica of St Mark's Square in Venice (including canals with gondolas) fronts for a 3000-room resort, convention centre and casino complex: the convention space here alone is greater than the total available in Hong Kong. A sign of the wealth accruing in Macau – and where development is heading. ❼

Westin Resort Estrada de Hác Sá, Coloane ⓣ2887 1111, ⓦwww.starwoodhotels.com. At the far end of Hác Sá's fine beach, this is good for a quiet day or two, midweek, although it fills up with Hong Kong families at the weekend. Three restaurants and excellent sports facilities, including an eighteen-hole golf course, two pools and a jacuzzi. Often does good weekend special offers. D ❽

Macau peninsula

Sights on the **Macau peninsula** comprise the best of the narrow lanes, colonial buildings and cobbled squares which make Macau so much more charismatically historic than Hong Kong – though there is, of course, a strikingly modern district too, along Avenida da Amizade, where a string of casinos jostle for your attention. Everything is technically close enough to walk between, though it's likely you'll resort to buses or taxis to reach more distant attractions up along the Chinese border.

Largo do Senado

Macau's older core centres around **Largo do Senado**, a large cobbled square north off Avenida Almeida Ribeiro and surrounded by unmistakeably European-influenced buildings, with their stucco mouldings, colonnades and shuttered windows. At Largo do Senado's southern side – across Avenida Ribeira – stands the **Leal Senado** (Mon–Sat 1–7pm; free), generally considered the finest Portuguese building in the city. The interior courtyard sports walls decorated with wonderful blue-and-white Portuguese tiles, while up the staircase from the courtyard is the richly decorated **senate chamber**, still used by the municipal government of Macau. In the late sixteenth century, the entire citizenry of the colony would gather here to debate issues of importance, and the senate's title *leal* (loyal) was earned during the period when Spain occupied the Portuguese throne and Macau became the final stronghold of loyalists to the true king. Adjacent to the chamber is the wood-carved **public library**, whose collection includes a repository of fifteenth- and sixteenth-century books, which you can still see on the shelves; you're free to go in and browse.

Across the road at Largo do Senado's northern end, the honey-and-cream-coloured, seventeenth-century Baroque church, **São Domingos**, is adjoined by Macau's **Religious Museum**, containing a treasury of sacred art under a timbered roof.

São Paulo and Fortaleza do Monte

Continue north from **São Domingos** along the cobbled lane and you'll soon find yourself flanked by *pastellarias* (biscuit shops) and stores selling reproduction antique furniture. The lane then opens up, a broad stone staircase rising in front to the richly carved facade of **São Paulo**, Macau's most famous landmark. The original church, built in 1602 and hailed as the greatest Christian monument in East Asia, was – the facade aside – completely destroyed by fire in 1835. The former crypt and nave have become a small religious **museum**, detailing the building and design of the church, and holding the bones of the followers of St Francis Xavier (Mon & Wed–Sun 9am–6pm; free). You'll also notice a small temple huddled by the side of São Paulo and built into a fragment of the **old town walls**.

The tree-covered slope immediately east of São Paulo is crowned by another colonial relic, the seventeenth-century fortress **Fortaleza do Monte**. For some great views, take a stroll round the old ramparts, whose huge cannons repelled a Dutch attack in 1622, when a lucky shot blew up the Dutch magazine. Up here you'll also find the **Museo de Macau** (Tues–Sun 10am–6pm; MOP$15), whose excellent collection focuses on the SAR's traditions, culture and habits. Highlights include video shows, a mock-up of a traditional Macanese street, and depictions of local arts and crafts, complete with evocative soundtracks of local sellers' cries.

Jardim Luís de Camões

A few hundred metres northwest of São Paulo, Rua de Santo Antonio winds up at a small square, to the north of which is **Jardim Luís de Camões** (daily 6am–10pm; free), a shady park full of large trees and granite boulders covered in ferns. A grotto in the park was built in honour of the great sixteenth-century Portuguese poet, Luís de Camões, who is thought to have been banished here for part of his life. Immediately east of the square, though, is the real gem, the **Old Protestant Cemetery**, where all the non-Catholic traders, visitors, sailors and adventurers who happened to die in Macau were buried. The gravestones have been restored and are quite legible, recording the last testaments to these mainly British, American and German individuals who died far from home in the early part of the nineteenth century.

Jardim Lou Lim Ieoc and Guia Hill

About 1km northeast of the Fortaleza do Monte is another area worth walking around (buses #12 and #22 run up here from the *Hotel Lisboa*, along the Avenida do Conselheiro Ferreira de Almeida). At the junction with Estrada de Adolfo Loureiro, the first site you'll reach, screened off behind a high wall, is the scenic and calming **Jardim Lou Lim Ieoc** (daily 6am–9pm; free), a formal Chinese garden crowded with bamboos, pavilions, rocks and ancient trees arranged around a large pond.

East of here is **Guia Hill**, Macau's highest and steepest – if you don't want to walk up, catch a **cable car** (MOP$2 one way, MOP$3 return) from the **Botanical Garden** on Avenida de Sidonio Pais. The whole hilltop is one breezy park,

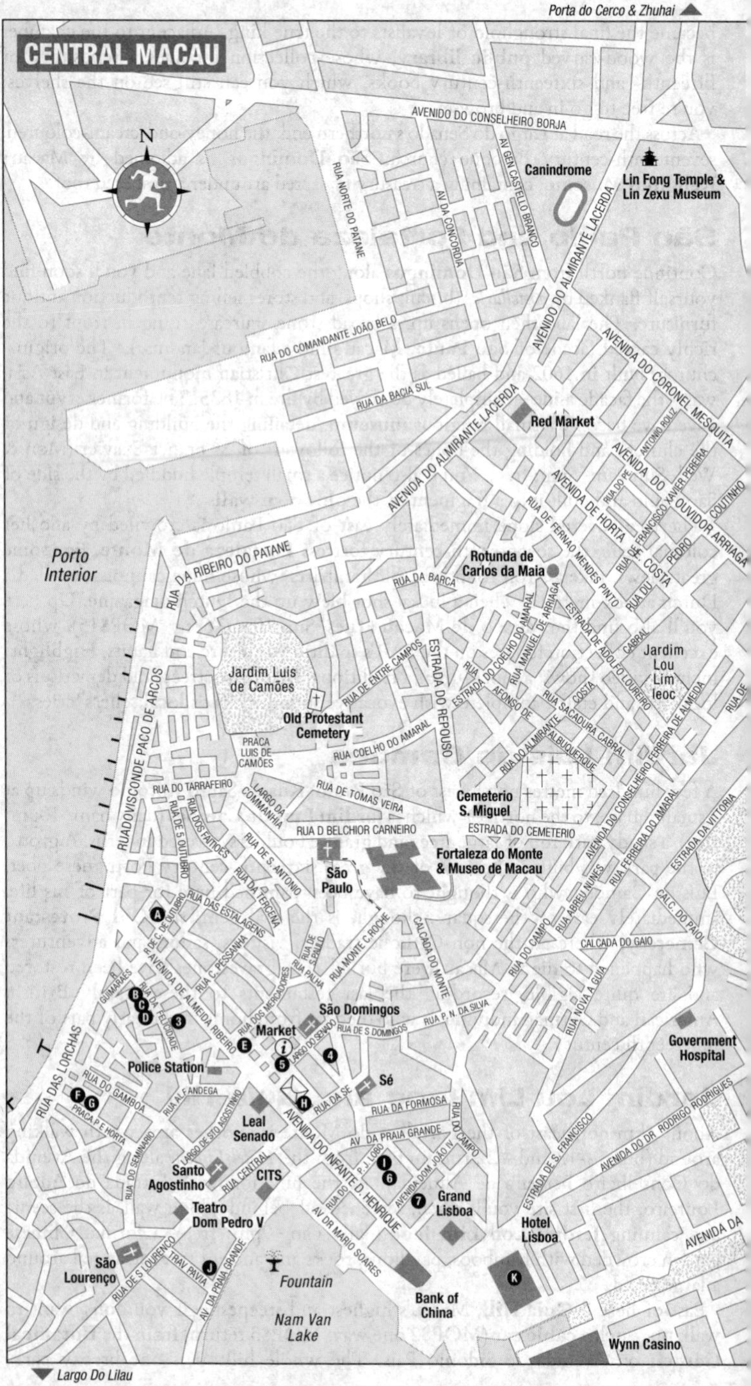

Porta do Cerco & Zhuhai

CENTRAL MACAU

N

Avenido do Conselheiro Borja
Av Gen Castello Branco
Av da Concordia
Rua Norte do Patane
Canindrome
Lin Fong Temple & Lin Zexu Museum
Avenido do Almirante Lacerda
Avenida do Coronel Mesquita
Rua do Comandante João Belo
Rua da Bacia Sul
Red Market
Avenida do Almirante Lacerda
Antonio Roliz
Avenida do Ouvidor Arriaga
Avenida de Horta
Rua do Pe.
Rua de Francisco Xavier Pereira
Coutinho
Rua de Fernao Mendes Pinto
Rua de H. Costa
Pedro
Rua du
Porto Interior
Rua da Ribeiro do Patane
Rua da Barca
Rotunda de Carlos da Maia
Rua Manuel de Arriaga
Estrada do Coelho do Amaral
Estrada de Adolfo Loureiro
Cabral
Jardim Lou Lim Ieoc
Rua de
Rua de Entre Campos
Estrada do Repouso
Rua Afonso de Albuquerque
Rua Sacadura Cabral
Costa
Rua do Almirante
Avenida do Conselheiro Ferreira de Almeida
Jardim Luis de Camões
Old Protestant Cemetery
Ruadoviscondo Paco de Arcos
Praca Luis de Camões
Rua Coelho do Amaral
Rua do Tarrafeiro
Largo da Commanhia
Rua de Tomas Veira
Cemeterio S. Miguel
Rua de 5 Outubro
Rua dos Faitoes
Rua D Belchior Carneiro
Estrada do Cemeterio
Rua Ferreira do Amaral
Estrada da Vittoria
Rua de S. Antonio
Rua da Tercena
São Paulo
Fortaleza do Monte & Museo de Macau
Rua Abreu Nunes
Rua das Estalagens
Rua de C. de Outubro
Rua do Campo
Calc. do Paiol
Calcada do Gaio
A
Rua de S. Paulo
Rua Monte C. Roche
Calcada do Monte
Rua C. Pessanha
Rua Palha
Rua Nova a Guia
R. Guimaraes
Avenida de Almeida Ribeiro
Rua dos Mercadores
B
C
D
Rua da Felicidade
3
São Domingos
Market
Rua de S Domingos
Rua P. N. da Silva
E
Largo do Senado
4
5
Government Hospital
Rua das Lorchas
Police Station
Rua do Gamboa
F
G
Praca P E Horta
Rua Alfandega
H
Rua da Se
Sé
Rua da Formosa
Avenida do Dr. Rodrigo Rodrigues
Rua do Seminario
Largo de Sto Agostinho
Leal Senado
Avenida do Infante D. Henrique
Av da Praia Grande
Rua do Campo
Estrada de S. Francisco
Santo Agostinho
Rua Central
CITS
P. J. Lobo
I
6
Avenida Dom João IV
Rua do
7
Grand Lisboa
Teatro Dom Pedro V
Av Dr Mario Soares
Hotel Lisboa
Avenida da
São Lourenço
Rua de S Lourenco
Trav Pavia
J
Av da Praia Grande
Fountain
K
Bank of China
Nam Van Lake
Wynn Casino

Largo Do Lilau

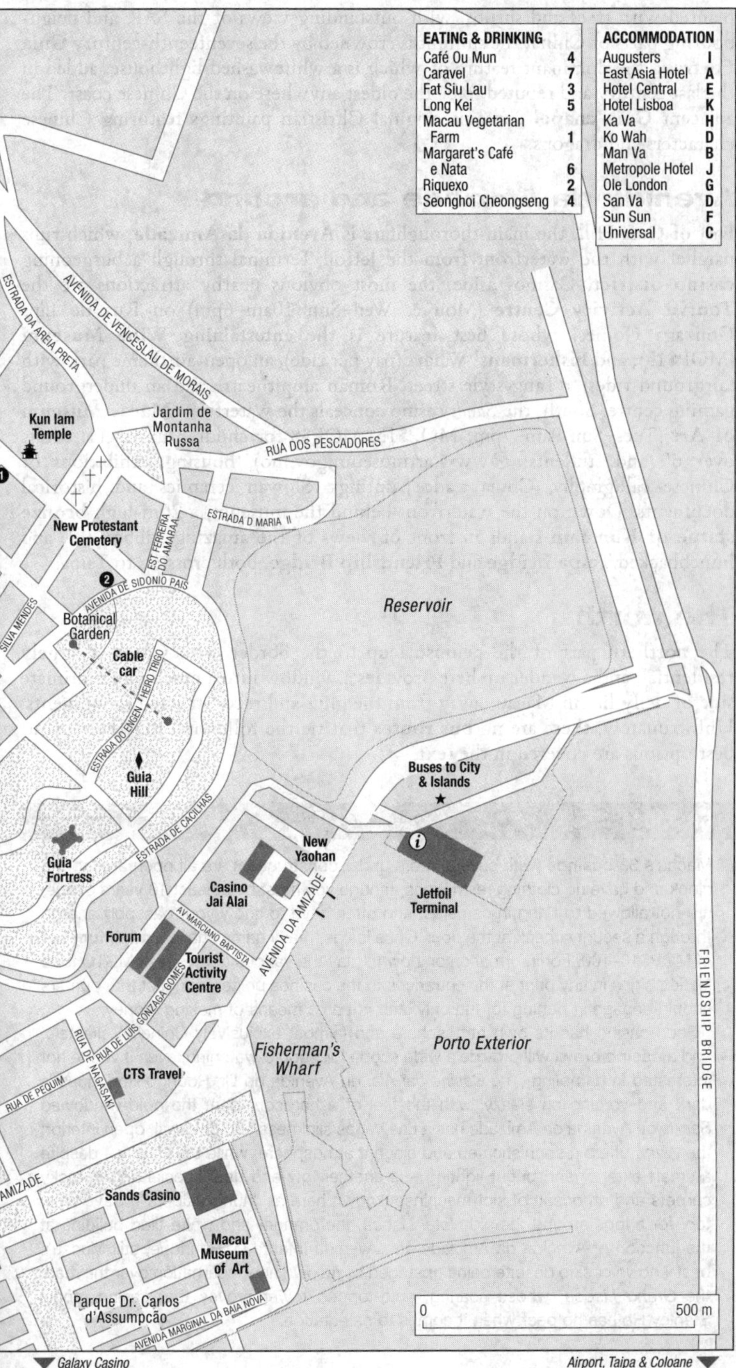
EATING & DRINKING
Café Ou Mun 4
Caravel 7
Fat Siu Lau 3
Long Kei 5
Macau Vegetarian Farm 1
Margaret's Café e Nata 6
Riquexo 2
Seonghoi Cheongseng 4
ACCOMMODATION
Augusters I
East Asia Hotel A
Hotel Central E
Hotel Lisboa K
Ka Va H
Ko Wah D
Man Va B
Metropole Hotel J
Ole London G
San Va D
Sun Sun F
Universal C
ESTRADA DA AREIA PRETA
AVENIDA DE VENCESLAU DE MORAIS
Kun Iam Temple
Jardim de Montanha Russa
RUA DOS PESCADORES
ESTRADA D MARIA II
New Protestant Cemetery
EST FERREIRA DO AMARAL
AVENIDA DE SIDONIO PAIS
SILVA MENDES
Botanical Garden
Cable car
ESTRADA DO ENGENHEIRO TRIGO
Guia Hill
Reservoir
Buses to City & Islands
Guia Fortress
ESTRADA DE CACILHAS
New Yaohan
Jetfoil Terminal
Casino Jai Alai
AVENIDA DA AMIZADE
AV MARCIANO BAPTISTA
Forum
Tourist Activity Centre
RUA DE LUIS GONZAGA GOMES
RUA DE NAGASAKI
RUA DE PEQUIM
CTS Travel
Fisherman's Wharf
Porto Exterior
FRIENDSHIP BRIDGE
AMIZADE
Sands Casino
Macau Museum of Art
Parque Dr. Carlos d'Assumpcão
AVENIDA MARGINAL DA BAIA NOVA
0
500 m
Galaxy Casino
Airport, Taipa & Coloane

planted with trees and shrubs, with outstanding views of the SAR and neighbouring parts of China; the summit is crowned by the seventeenth-century **Guia Fortress**, the dominant feature of which is a whitewashed lighthouse, added in the last century and reputed to be the oldest anywhere on the Chinese coast. The adjacent **Guia chapel** contains original Christian paintings featuring Chinese characters and dragons.

Avenida da Amizade and around

East of Guia Hill, the main thoroughfare is **Avenida da Amizade**, which runs parallel with the waterfront from the Jetfoil Terminal through a burgeoning **casino district**. Casinos aside, the most obvious nearby attractions are the **Tourist Activity Centre** (Mon & Wed–Sun 10am–6pm) on Rua de Luis Gonzaga Gomes, whose best feature is the entertaining **Wine Museum** (MOP$15); and **Fishermans' Wharf** (pay per ride), an open-air theme park with fairground rides, a Tang-style street, Roman ampitheatre and an underground gaming centre. South, the *Sands* casino conceals the waterfront **Macau Museum of Art** (Tues–Sun 9am–7pm; MOP$15, MOP$8 for children under 11, adults over 60 and students; Ⓦwww.artmuseum.gov.mo), housing exhibitions of Chinese calligraphy, China trade paintings, Shiwan ceramics and historical documents. Down on the waterfront behind the museum, a 20m-high **bronze statue of Kun Iam** stands in front of views of the amazing, ribbon-like and hunchbacked **Taipa Bridge** and **Friendship Bridge**, both crossing to Taipa.

The north

The northern part of the peninsula up to the border with China is largely residential, and a wander up here provides a window into a much more intimate side of daily life in Macau, away from the glitz and reconstructed monuments. Unfortunately, there are no **bus routes** that tie the following together – your best options are covered in the text.

Casinos

Macau's 33 **casinos** (with several more under construction) are all open around the clock and have no clothing restrictions, though you must be at least 18 years of age, are not allowed to bring in cameras, and often have to show your passport and go through a security check at the door. Once inside, many games have a **minimum bet** of MOP$10–100. For information on how to play the various games, ask MGTO for a leaflet; signs in tiny print at the entrances to the casinos politely suggest that punters should engage in betting for fun only, and not as a means of making money.

Each casino has its own atmosphere and (almost exclusively Chinese) clientele, and a **casino crawl** will provide a wide scope for people-watching, even if you're not interested in gambling. The *Casino Jai Alai* on Avenida do Dr. Rodrigo Rodrigues is dark and verging on sleazy, with the feel of a hardcore den; the gold-windowed *Sands* on Avenida da Amizade has a Las Vegas slickness and colossal, open interior; the *Wynn* offers a sophisticated and elegant atmosphere; while the *Galaxy* – despite a smart exterior and bright lighting – is another low-end deal specializing in tacky carpets and an ocean of slot machines (known here as "hungry tigers"). Save time, too, for a look around the old *Hotel Lisboa*, the orange- and white-tiled building at the junction of Avenida da Amizade and Avenida Infante D. Henrique, still Macau's best-known casino despite being upstaged by its own new incarnation over the road, the *Grand Lisboa*, whose soaring, gold-topped tower proves that casino mogul Stanley Ho has no peer when it comes to ostentation.

The Kun Iam Temple

On Avenida do Coronel Mesquita, which cuts the peninsula from east to west about 2km north of Almeida Ribeiro, is the enchanting **Kun Iam Temple** (daily 7am–6pm; free), accessible on bus #12 from the *Hotel Lisboa*. The complex of temples here, dedicated to the Goddess of Mercy, is around 400 years old, but the most interesting fact associated with the place is that here, in 1844, the United States and China signed their first treaty of trade and cooperation – though there are no monuments to the fact here. Inside the complex, shaded by banyan trees, are a number of small shrines, with the main temple hall approached via a flight of steps. Around the central statue of Kun Iam herself, to the rear, is a crowd of statues representing eighteen *arhats*, or Buddhist saints. The worshippers you'll see here shaking bamboo sticks in cylinders are trying to find out their fortunes.

The Red Market and Three Lamps District

A twenty-minute walk west from the Kun Iam Temple and near the intersection with Avenida de Horta e Costa and Avenida do Almirante Lacerda is the **Red Market**, an Art Deco affair designed in 1936 by local architect Jio Alberto Basto. Arranged over three levels, the market is a very down-to-earth venue for buying slabs of meat and frozen seafood for the dinner table, along with live chickens, pigeons, ducks, fish, frogs and turtles. Just south across Avenida de Horta e Costa, a warren of lanes chock-full of budget clothing stalls leads down to the blue-tiled Rotunda de Carlos da Maia, a roundabout marking the centre of the pedestrianized **Three Lamps District** or Sam Jan Dang. The whole area is a great place to browse and watch people bargaining for daily necessities.

To the border

North of the Red Market, Avenida do Almirante Lacerda passes Macau's **Canidrome** – Southeast Asia's only greyhound track, with races every Monday, Thursday, Saturday and Sunday from 7.45pm – and the **Lin Fung Temple**, whose main point of interest is its accompanying **Lin Zexu Museum** (Tues–Sun 9am–5pm; MOP$10), a monument to the man who destroyed British opium stocks in Guangzhou and so precipitated the first Opium War (see p.949). Another ten minutes' walk and you'll be facing the **Porto do Cerco**, or **Barrier Gate** (daily 7am–midnight), the nineteenth-century stuccoed archway marking the border with China. These days the old gate itself is redundant – people use the modern customs and immigration complex to one side. From here, bus #3 or #10 will get you back to Almeida Ribeiro and the *Hotel Lisboa*.

The south

The small but hilly tongue of land south of Largo do Senado is a tight web of lanes, with colonial mansions and their gardens looming up round every corner. A good walk through this area begins by following **Rua Central** south past the peppermint-coloured **Teatro Dom Pedro V**, built in 1873 and still staging occasional performances, despite its main function as the members-only *Clube Macao*. Opposite is the early nineteenth-century church of **Santo Agostinho**, whose pastel walls are decorated with delicate piped icing. Further down on Rua de São Lourenço, the square-towered **São Lourenço** is a wonderfully tropical nineteenth-century church, with a mildewed exterior framed by palms and fig trees.

Another few minutes south and you arrive at **Largo do Lilau**, a tiny, pretty square with a shady fig tree and **spring**, whose waters are said to impart longevity. This is the site of Macau's original residential area, and almost all buildings here are over a century old, including the heavy-walled **Mandarin's House**, just off to one side at 10 Traversa da Silva. You're now in the **Barra district**, and Rua Central has mutated into **Calçada da Barra**, which you follow downhill past more elderly buildings – including the strikingly crenellated, yellow and white **Moorish Barracks** – to the seafront on the southwestern side of the peninsula. The celebrated **A-Ma Temple** here may be as old as 600 years in parts, and certainly predates the arrival of the Portuguese on the peninsula. Dedicated to the goddess A-Ma (known in Hong Kong as Tin Hau), the temple is an attractive jumble of altars and little outhouses among the rocks.

Immediately across the road from here, the **Maritime Museum** (Mon & Wed–Fri 10am–5.30pm; MOP$10, MOP$5 at weekends) is excellently presented, covering old explorers, seafaring techniques, equipment, models and boats. A short walk south along the shore from the museum brings you to the very tip of the peninsula, which is today marked by the *Pousada de São Tiago*, a hotel built into the remains of the seventeenth-century Portuguese fortress, the **Fortaleza de Barra**. Enter the front door and you find yourself walking up a stone tunnel running with water – it's well worth climbing up to the *Pousada*'s veranda café for a drink overlooking the sea. The walk from here around the southern headland and back to the north again follows tree-lined Avenida da Republica, the old seafront promenade – today, its views take in **Sai Van Lake** and the 338m-high **Macau Tower** (daily 10am–9pm; various charges, up to MOP$70, depending on level of observation deck). At night, the waterfront promenade also offers Macau's version of Hong Kong's multicoloured harbourside skyline – except, of course, that here the financial institutions are casinos instead of banks.

Taipa, Cotai and Coloane

Macau's two islands, **Taipa** and **Coloane**, were originally dots of land supporting a few small fishing villages; now, joined by the rapidly developing strip of reclaimed land, **Cotai**, they look set to become part of a new entertainment district. Despite this, both retain quiet pockets of colonial architecture where you can just about imagine yourself in some European village, while Coloane also has a fine beach.

From Almeida Ribeiro, buses #11 and #33 go to Taipa Village; buses #21, #21A, #26 and #26A stop outside the *Hyatt Regency* on Taipa before going on to Coloane.

Taipa

Taipa, site of Macau International Airport, racecourse, sports stadium, university and residential "suburbs", at first seems too developed to warrant a special stop. However, tiny **Taipa Village** on the island's east side, with its old colonial promenade, makes a pleasant place for an extended lunch. The bus drops you off by a modern market, where the 100m-long **Rua da Cunha** (or "Food Street") leads down to the old covered **Feira do Carmo** market square, which is partly surrounded by a dragon wall and several restaurants (see p.632). On the far side of the square, turn right to more restaurants and a **Tin Hau Temple**, or left until you see a wavy set of tree-lined steps leading up to a small square and church above the old colonial promenade, **Avenida da Praia**. Five original, peppermint-green mansions with verandas here now form the **Taipa House Museum** (Tues–Sun 10am–6pm; MOP$10 allows entry to all five), which reveals details of early nineteenth-century domestic life for the resident Macanese families: high-ranking civil servants who were religious and well-to-do, but not enormously wealthy.

Cotai

A few years ago, views south from the museum took in mud flats, reeds and the sea; now this has all been filled in to form **Cotai district**, and the scene is as incongruous as you could imagine. Right ahead is the extraordinary **Venetian**, a full-scale reproduction of Venice's St Mark's Square housing the world's largest casino resort, with 850 gaming tables, 4100 slot machines and its own permanent Cirque de Soleil troupe. This is only the first of several similar projects, with **Macau Studio City** – combining a further resort and casino complex with film-production facilities – also set to open in the near future. Further reclamation means that Cotai's western side now bumps up against the Chinese mainland, with the **Cotai Frontier Post** (not yet open to pedestrians) making access easy for coachloads of holidaying mainlanders.

Coloane

Coloane comprises nine square kilometres of hilly parkland, more colonial fragments and some decent **beaches**, making it a pleasant place to spend a few hours. After crossing Cotai, buses pass the **Parque de Seac Pai Van** (Tues–Sun 9am–7pm; free), a large park with paths leading uphill to a white marble statue of the goddess A-Ma – at 19.99m high, it is the tallest in the world. A short way on, all buses stop at the roundabout in pretty **Coloane Village** on the western shore, overlooking mainland China just across the water and home to a fair number of expats; here, *Lord Stow's Bakery*, at the sea end of the square, offers irresistible **natas**, Portuguese egg tarts. To the north of the village are a few junk-building sheds, while the street leading south from the village roundabout, one block back from the shore, contains a couple of shops selling dried marine products and the unexpected yellow and white **St Francis Xavier Chapel**, where a relic of the saint's arm bone is venerated. A couple of hundred metres beyond this is the **Tam Kung Temple**, housing a metre-long whale bone carved into the shape of a ship.

Buses #21A, #26 or #26A from the village roundabout continue a final 3km farther round to **Hác Sá beach**. Tree-lined and stretching far off round the bay, Hác Sá is without doubt the best in Macau, despite the black colour of its volcanic sand, and has cafés, bars, showers and toilets as well as some fine restaurants nearby (see p.632). There's also a **sports and swimming pool complex** (Mon–Fri 9am–9pm, Sat & Sun until midnight; MOP$15) although it all gets pretty crowded at weekends. Otherwise, try the **Parque Natural da Barragem de Hác Sá**; a short hop from Hác Sá beach, this features barbecue pits, a kids' playground and maze, boating on a small reservoir, and various short trails in the hills (Tues–Fri 2–7pm, Sat & Sun 10am–7pm; MOP$10–40 for boat rental).

Eating, drinking and nightlife

Macanese cuisine fuses Chinese with Portuguese elements, further overlaid with tastes from Portugal's Indian and African colonies. Fresh bread, wine and coffee all feature, as well as an array of dishes ranging from *caldo verde* (vegetable soup) to *bacalhau* (dried salted cod). Macau's most interesting Portuguese colonial dish is probably **African chicken**, a concoction of Goan and East African influences, comprising chicken grilled with peppers and spices. Other things worth trying include Portuguese baked **custard tarts** (*natas*), served in many cafés; **almond biscuits**, formed in a wooden mould and baked in a charcoal oven, which can be bought by weight in many *pastellarias*, such as Koi Kei, around São Paulo and Rua da Felicidade; and sheets of pressed **roast meat**, also sold in *pastellarias*. Straightforward **Cantonese restaurants**, often serving dim sum for breakfast and lunch, are also plentiful, though you'll find wine on the menus even here. Cafés tend to **open** around 8.30am, while restaurant times are from about 11.30am to 2.30pm, and from 6pm until 10pm. **Prices** for the typically generous portions are low compared to Hong Kong, with bills even in smart venues rarely exceeding MOP$250 per person, though watch out for little extras such as water, bread and so forth, which can really add to the cost of a meal. A bottle of house red will set you back around MOP$120 in a restaurant.

Macau's **nightlife** is surprisingly flat, if you don't count the casinos – drinking is done in restaurants or in the handful of bars in the "Macau Lan Kwai Fong", located along the waterfront facing the Porto Exterior, and offering live music and street-side tables.

Cafés

Café Ou Mun Travessa de Sao Domingos 12, off Largo do Sendo. Fantastic breads, cakes and coffee, and light meals, very popular at lunchtime.

Caravel Avenida Dom João IV. Down an alley near the *Grand Lisboa*, this smart place serves top coffee, cakes and light meals through the day, and has a host of Portuguese expat regulars – who can get snotty about visitors taking "their" chairs.

Margaret's Café e Nata Rua Comandante Mata e Oliveira. Surrounded by gloomy apartment blocks, this is an excellent café with first-rate sandwiches and *natas*.

Restaurants

360° Café Level 60, Macau Tower ☎9888622. One of Macau's classiest places to dine, serving Indian and Macanese food in a revolving restaurant with unparalleled views. A good way not to bankrupt yourself is to opt for the set buffets at MOP$198 for lunch, and MOP$288 for supper.

A Lorcha Rua da Almirante Sérgio 289 ☎2831 3193. Genuine and excellent Spanish, Macanese and Portuguese food; the seafood rice or beer clams are outstanding.

Fat Siu Lau Rua da Felicidade 64 ☎2857 3585. A very popular, traditional old restaurant whose speciality is marinated roast pigeon, though they also do a great crab curry.

Henri's Avenida da República 4 ☎2855 6251. Order the grilled sardines or African chicken in the evening and kick back with a bottle of red at one of the pavement tables. Good food but tourist-inflated prices and irritating service.

Litoral Rua da Almirante Sérgio 261-A ☎2896 7878. Reputedly the best place for Macanese food in Macau, with excellent charcoal-grilled chicken, fish or steak; *feijoada*; and stewed chicken rice at MOP$100 or more a dish. Their mango pudding is the business, too. If you can't get in, nearby *O Porto Interior* or *A Lorcha* are almost as good.

Long Kei Largo do Senado 7B. A 100-year-old, traditional, but inexpensive and excellent Cantonese restaurant, on the left side as you face the square from Almeida Ribeiro.

Macau Vegetarian Farm Opposite the Kun Iam Temple, Avenida do Coronel Mesquita 11 (no English sign) ☎752824. Warehouse-sized, characterless restaurant offering good-quality Chinese vegetarian cuisine at MOP$30–50 a dish; no English translations, but lots of photos of the food on menus.

O Porto Interior Rua da Almirante Sérgio 259-B ☎2896 7770. Just by the A-Ma Temple, this features antique Chinese screens, superb old Macanese cuisine such as African chicken or grilled sardines, plus a splendid wine cellar.

Riquexo Avenida de Sidónio Pais 69-B. Self-service Portuguese canteen with no frills at all, though the food is hearty, and nearby office workers flock here for lunch. Menu changes daily but is likely to include *feijoada*, curry chicken, grilled lamb and *bacalhau* – at MOP$28–55 a serving.

Seonghoi Cheongseng Across from *Café Ou Mun* on Travessa de São Domingos (no English sign). Inexpensive – hence perpetually full – Shanghai stir-fry restaurant. Good for noodles, steamed buns and seafood dishes.

Taipa

Galo In the square at Rua da Cunha 45, Taipa Village ☎2882 7423. Cute, blue-shuttered place with low prices and family-run feel. The crab is good.

O Santos Rua da Cunha, Taipa Village ☎2882 7508. Huge helpings of seafood rice, pork and bean stew, rabbit, roast suckling pig and other Portuguese mainstays from MOP$85.

Coloane

Caçarola Rua das Gaivotas 8, Coloane Village ☎2888 2226. Welcoming and deservedly popular Portuguese restaurant with excellent daily specials, though becoming a little expensive. It's off the main village square.

Chan Chi Mei/Nga Tim Next to the St Francis Xavier Chapel, Coloane Village ☎2888 2086. A friendly Chinese place with outdoor tables under a colonnade, ideal for lunch or an evening drink; the best meals are crab or pork knuckle. Most mains under MOP$70.

Fernando Hác Sá beach, not far from the bus stop ⓣ2888 2531. A casual, cheerful atmosphere and great Portuguese food make it a favourite with expats. You might need a taxi to get home, though. Advance booking recommended, and a must at weekends.

Lord Stow's Bakery Coloane Village Square. The best baked custard tarts in Macau, said to be made to a secret recipe without animal fat. Buy take-aways from the bakery itself, or sit down for coffee and a light meal at their café around the corner.

Listings

Airlines Air Asia ⓦwww.airasia.com; Air Macau ⓦen.airmacau.com.mo; EVA Airways ⓣ2872 6865; Tiger Airways ⓦwww.tigerairways.com; Xiamen Airlines ⓣ2878 0663.

Banks and exchange Most banks have branches around the junction of Avenida Almeida Ribeiro and Avenida Praia Grande, where you'll also find plenty of attached ATMs. Banks generally open Mon–Fri from 9am until 4pm or 4.30pm, but close by lunchtime on Sat. There are also licensed moneychangers that exchange travellers' cheques (and that open seven days a week), including a 24hr one in the basement of the *Hotel Lisboa*, and one near the bottom of the steps leading up to São Paulo.

Bookshops The Portuguese Bookshop, Rua de São Domingos 18–22 (near São Domingos church), has a small English-language section with books on Macau's history, cooking and buildings.

Festivals The normal Chinese holidays are celebrated in Macau, plus some Catholic festivals introduced from Portugal, such as the annual Procession of Our Lady of Fatima from São Domingos church (May 13).

Hospitals There's a 24hr emergency department at the Centro Hospitalar Conde São Januário, Calçada Visconde São Januário ⓣ2831 3731; English is spoken.

Mail Macau's main post office is in Largo do Senado, on the east side (Mon–Fri 9am–6pm, Sat 9am–1pm); poste restante is delivered here. Small red booths all over the territory also dispense stamps from machines.

Police The main police station is at Avenida do Dr Rodrigo Rodrigues ⓣ2857 3333. For emergencies, call ⓣ999.

Telephones Local calls are free from private phones, MOP$1 from payphones. Cardphones work with CTM cards, issued by the Macau State Telecommunication Company, on sale in hotels or at the back of the main post office (open 24hr), where you can also make direct calls.

Travel agencies CITS, 5F, 315 Avenida da Praia Grande Avenida ⓣ2871 5454; CTS, Rua de Nagasaki ⓣ2870 6655, ⓕ2870 3789. Both can help organize flights, buses and accommodation, and visas for mainland China.

Travel details

Trains

Hong Kong to: Guangzhou (12 daily; 2–3hr); Lo Wu (East Rail Line, for Shenzhen; frequent; 50min).

Buses

Hong Kong to: Guangzhou (frequent; 3hr 30min); Shenzhen (frequent; 2hr); Shenzhen Airport (frequent; 2hr).

Macau to: Guangzhou (several daily; 4hr).

Ferries

Hong Kong to: Macau (frequent; 1hr); Shenzhen (12 daily; 45min).

Macau to: Hong Kong (frequent; 1hr); Shenzhen (six daily; 1hr).

Flights

Hong Kong is a major international gateway for flights both within Asia and beyond. You can also fly to every provincial capital and many major cities on the mainland, but you'll save a lot of money (and not lose much time) by picking up a flight over the border in Shenzhen. Macau offers international flights to and from Bangkok, Singapore, Kuala Lumpur and Taipei; plus internal services to Beijing, Shanghai and Xi'an.

CHAPTER 10 Highlights

✱ **Li River** Cruise between Guilin and Yangshuo through a forest of tall, weirdly contorted karst peaks. See p.642

✱ **Dong villages** Communities of wooden houses, bridges and drum towers pepper remote rural highlands along the Guangxi–Guizhou border. See p.651

✱ **Hua Shan** Another boat trip to see a whole cliffside of mysterious rock art flanking Guangxi's Zuo River. See p.659

✱ **Sisters' Meal Festival** Exuberant showpiece of Miao culture, featuring three days of dancing, bull fighting and dragon-boat racing. See p.670

✱ **Zhijin Caves** The largest, most spectacular of China's subterranean limestone caverns, full of creatively named rock formations. See p.678

✱ **Caohai** Spend a day punting around this beautiful lake, a haven for ducks and rare black-necked cranes. See p.678

▲ The Zhijin Caves, Guizhou

Guangxi and Guizhou

If there's one thing that defines the subtropical southwestern provinces of **Guangxi** and **Guizhou**, it's **limestone**: most of the rivers here are coloured a vivid blue-green by it; everywhere you look are weathered karst hills worn into poetic collections of tall, sharp peaks; and the ground beneath is riddled with extensive **caverns**, some flooded, others large enough to fit a cathedral inside.

Though something of a tourist phenomenon today, historically this topography has proved an immense barrier to communications and, being porous, created some of China's least arable land, with agriculture often confined to the small alluvial plains in between peaks. So poor that it wasn't worth the trouble of invading, for a long while the region was pretty well ignored by Han China, and evolved into a stronghold for **ethnic groups**. But a period of social stability during the early Qing dynasty caused a population explosion in eastern China and an expansion westwards by the Han. Some of the ethnic minorities kept their nominal identity but more or less integrated with the Chinese, while others resisted assimilation by occupying isolated highlands; but the new settlers put pressure on available resources, creating a hotbed of resentment against the government. This finally exploded in central Guangxi's **Taiping Uprising** of 1850 (see p.330), marking the start of a century of devastating civil conflict. Even today, while the minority groups have been enfranchised by the formation of several **autonomous prefectures**, industry and infrastructure remain underdeveloped and few of the cities – including **Nanning** and **Guiyang**, the provincial capitals – have much to offer except transport to more interesting locations.

Despite its bleak history, the region offers a huge range of diversions. The landscape is epitomized by the tall karst towers surrounding the city of **Guilin** in northeastern Guangxi, familiar to Chinese and Westerners alike through centuries of eulogistic poetry, paintings and photographs. Equally impressive are cave systems at **Longgong** and **Zhijin** in western Guizhou, while there's also the chance of close contact with ethnic groups, particularly the **Miao**, **Dong** and **Zhuang**, whose wooden villages, exuberant festivals, and traces of a prehistoric past are all worth indulging. It's also one of the few places in the country where you can be fairly sure of encountering rare wildlife: notably monkeys at **Chongzuo** in southwestern Guangxi; and cranes at **Caohai** in Guizhou's far west.

While **travel** out to all this can be time-consuming, a reasonable quantity of buses and trains means that remoteness is not the barrier it once was. **Language** is another matter, as many rural people speak only their own dialects or local versions of Mandarin, which can be virtually incomprehensible. With geography encompassing the South China Sea and some respectable mountains, **weather** is fairly localized, though you should expect hot, wet summers and surprisingly cold winters, especially up in the hills. April and May, and September and October, are probably the driest, most pleasant months to visit the region.

Guangxi

Guangxi (广西, *guǎngxī*) unfolds south from the cool highlands it shares with Guizhou to a tropical coast and border abutting Vietnam. Up in the northeast, the pick of the province's peak-and-paddy-field landscape is concentrated along the **Li River**, down which you can cruise between the city of **Guilin** and the travellers' haven of **Yangshuo**. Long famous and easily accessible, this has become a massive tourist draw, but remoter hills just a few hours north around **Longji** and **Sanjiang** are home to a mix of ethnic groups, whose architecture and way of life make for a fascinating trip up into Guizhou province, hopping between villages on public buses.

Diagonally across Guangxi, the tropically languid provincial capital **Nanning** has little of interest in itself but provides a base for exploring Guangxi's southwestern corner along the **open border with Vietnam**. Actually, since 1958 the

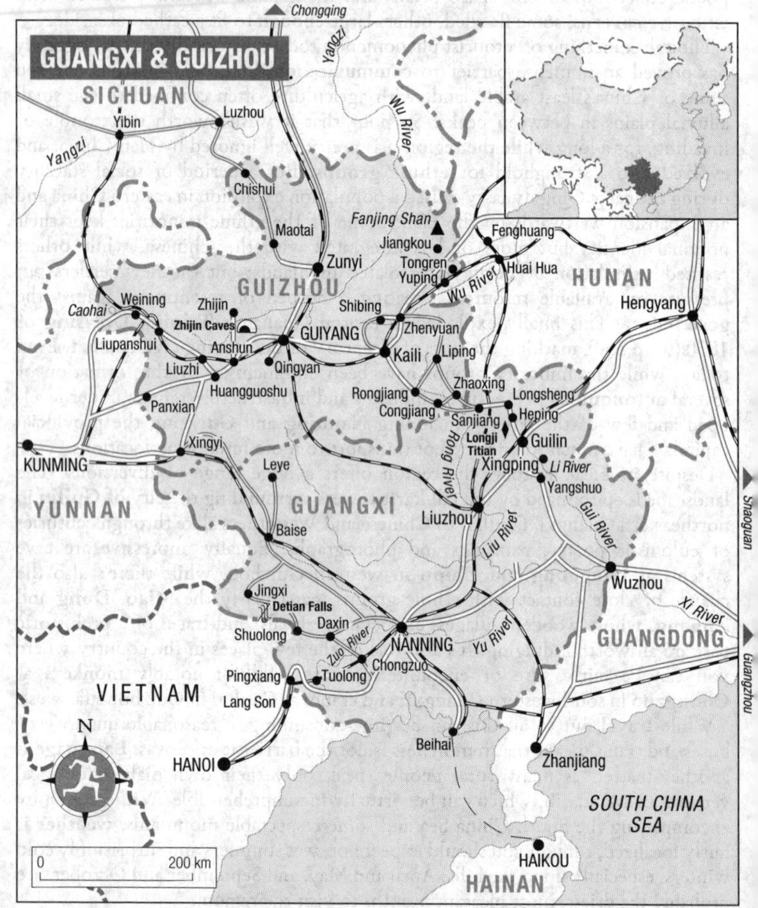

province has not been a province at all but the Guangxi Zhuang Autonomous Region, heartland of China's thirteen-million-strong Zhuang nationality. They constitute about a third of the regional population and, although largely assimilated into Chinese life today, there's enough archeological evidence to link them with a Bronze Age culture spread throughout Southeast Asia, including **prehistoric rock friezes** west of Nanning. Nearby are three other major draws: the **Detian Waterfall**, which actually pours over the Vietnamese border; massive limestone sinkholes at **Leye**; and **Chongzuo Ecology Park**, home of the critically endangered white-headed langur, a cliff-dwelling monkey. Down on the south coast, **Behai** sports some decent tropical beaches and offers transport to Hainan Island.

Though subject to fiercely hot, humid summers, Guangxi's **weather** can be deceptive – it actually snows in Guilin about once every ten years. Another thing of note is that the **Zhuang language**, instead of using pinyin, follows its own method of rendering Chinese characters into Roman text, so you'll see some unusual spelling on signs – "Minzu Dadao", for example, becomes "Minzcuzdadau".

Guilin

GUILIN (桂林, *guìlín*) has been famous since Tang times for its scenic location among a host of gnarled, 200m-high rocky hills on the **Li River**, down which you can **cruise** to the village of Yangshuo. The city rose from a rural backwater in 1372 when Emperor Hongwu decided to appoint **Zhou Shouqian**, a minor relative, to govern from here as the **Jinjiang Prince**, and this quasi-royal line ruled for fourteen generations, dying out in the 1650s when the entire city was razed in conflicts between Ming and Manchu forces. Guilin was later resurrected as de facto provincial capital until losing the position to Nanning in 1914; Sun Yatsen planned the Nationalists' "Northern Expedition" here in 1925; the Long Marchers were soundly trounced by Guomindang factions outside the city nine years later; and the war with Japan saw more than a million refugees hiding out here, until the city was occupied by the invaders – events harrowingly recounted in Amy Tan's *Joy Luck Club*. Wartime bombing spared the city's natural monuments but turned the centre into a shabby provincial shell, neatened up since the 1990s by plenty of well-designed landscaping, shady avenues and rocky parkland. Despite being prone to tourist-driven inflation and hard-sell irritations, the city is an attractive place to spend a day while organizing a cruise downstream.

Arrival

Central Guilin lies on the western bank of the Li River, with a handful of small, isolated peaks hemming in the perimeter and riverbanks. Parallel with the river and about 500m west, **Zhongshan Lu** is the main street, running north for 4km or so from the train station past a knot of accommodation and services, the long-distance bus station and on through the centre. The main roads which cross it are Nanhuan Lu, Ronghu Lu and adjoining Shanhu Lu, and Jiefang Lu, all of which stretch for at least 1km west across town from **Binjiang Lu**, the riverside promenade.

Liangjiang International Airport (桂林两江国际机场, *guìlín liǎng jiāng guójì jīchǎng*) is 30km west of the city, connected to the airlines office on Shanghai Lu by airport bus (every 30min 6.30am–9pm; ¥20) and taxi (about ¥85). The **train station** is centrally set at the back of a large square off Zhongshan Lu, within

Moving on from Guilin

Buses to Yangshuo (¥18) and Nanning leave the train station forecourt every few minutes through the day; watch out for bag-slashers and pickpockets who target foreigners. For anywhere else, head to the long-distance station: options include heading north to the rice terraces around Longji and on to Sanjiang and Guizhou province; east to the holy peaks at Heng Shan in Hunan; or southeast to Guangzhou. Bear in mind you're likely to get a much better seat here than if picking through services up at Yangshuo. **Flying** is similarly straightforward, with Guilin linked to cities right across the mainland, as well as to Hong Kong, Korea and Malaysia. The airport bus leaves the airlines office on Shanghai Lu every thirty minutes from 6.30am to 9pm, and costs ¥20.

Guilin also has good **rail links** to the rest of China, including direct services to Nanning, Shanghai, Xi'an, Beijing, Guangzhou, Chongqing and Kunming. If you book a few days in advance you should get what you want; the ticket office opens daily (7.30–11.30am, 12.30–2.30pm, 3–7pm, & 7.30–9.30pm), and queues are not too bad. **Agents** in both Guilin and Yangshuo can also sort things out, though they still need three days' notice and charge steep mark-ups for each ticket.

Details for arranging **Li River cruises** to Yangshuo are covered on p.642.

striking distance of accommodation and places of interest, with the **long-distance bus station** a couple of hundred metres further north. Buses from Yangshuo drop passengers in front of the train station. Most of Guilin's sights are close enough to walk to, others can be reached easily on public buses or taxi (¥7 to hire).

Accommodation

Guilin's **hotels** are mostly mid-range and upmarket, with the choice of **youth hostels** if you're after a budget bed. Competition is pretty stiff in town so always bargain at mid-range places, especially in winter, when discounted rates of fifty percent are not unusual. The nicest location is along the river, with lakeside options the next best thing. Everywhere will have a booking desk for cruises and local tours.

Backstreet Youth Hostel (后街国际青年旅馆, *hòujiē guójì qīngnián lǚguǎn*) 3 Renmin Lu, near the *Sheraton* ⓣ0773/2819936, ⓔguilinhostel@hotmail.com. Excellent location in the centre of town and close to the river, with café, internet and plain, comfortable doubles and triples – the one drawback being the persistent hawkers swarming outside. Dorms ¥30, rooms ❷

Eva Inn (四季春天酒店, *sìjì chūntiān jiǔdiàn*) 66 Binjiang Lu, close to the *Sheraton* ⓣ0773/2830666, ⓦevainn.com. Pleasant boutique-style place with smart, modern rooms and decent service. ❺

Fengyuan (丰源酒店, *fēngyuán jiǔdiàn*) 26 Zhongshan Zhong Lu, entrance on Yiren Lu ⓣ0773/2882306, ⓕ2827259. Just a clean, inner-city place with no outstanding features other than being reasonable value for money. ❸

Flowers Youth Hostel (花满国际青年旅馆, *huāmǎnguójì qīngnián lǚguǎn*) 6 Shangzhi Gang, Block 2, Zhongshan Lu ⓣ0773/3839625, ⓦwww.yhaguilin.com. A great option, hidden away behind the *Home Inn* opposite the train station: walk through a dreary alley to the back of the hotel, take the equally uninspiring stairs up a flight, and you'll find this warm, clean and friendly place, with a bar, café, internet, dorms and doubles. Dorms ¥30, rooms ❷

Guilin Riverside Hostel (桂林九龙别墅酒店, *guìlín jiǔlóng biéshù jiǔdiàn*) 5 Zhu Mu Xiang, Nanmen Qiao ⓣ0773/2580215, ⓦwww.guilin-hostel.com. A real gem, hidden down a quiet lane right in the town centre and set up like a European B&B. Very friendly and organized, so usually full. ❸

Home Inn Opposite the train station on Zhongshan Lu ⓣ0773/3877666, ⓕ3877555. Local representative of this budget hotel chain, offering good value for money – though cheaper rooms are windowless. Book in advance. ❸

Lijiang Waterfall (漓江大瀑布饭店, *líjiāng dàpùbù fàndiàn*) 1 Shanhu Lu ⓣ0773/2822881, ⓦwww.waterfallguilin.com. Huge tour-group and conference-delegate venue with all high-end frills. ⑨

Sheraton (大宇大饭店, *dàyǔ dàfàndiàn*) 15 Binjiang Lu ⓣ0773/2825588, ⓦwww.sheraton.com/guilin. One of the nicest hotels in town, with the best rooms overlooking the river and across to Seven Star Park, though you pay for the privilege. ⑨

The City

Look at a map and Guilin's **medieval city layout** is still clearly visible, defined by the river to the east, Gui Hu to the west, Nanhuan Lu to the south, and protected from the north by Diecai Shan. Separated by Zhongshan Lu, **Rong Hu** (榕湖, *róng hú*) and **Shan Hu** (杉湖, *shān hú*) are two tree-lined lakes that originally formed a moat surrounding the inner city walls – the last remnant of which is **Gu Nanmen** (古南门, *gǔ nánmén*) the tunnel-like Old South Gate on

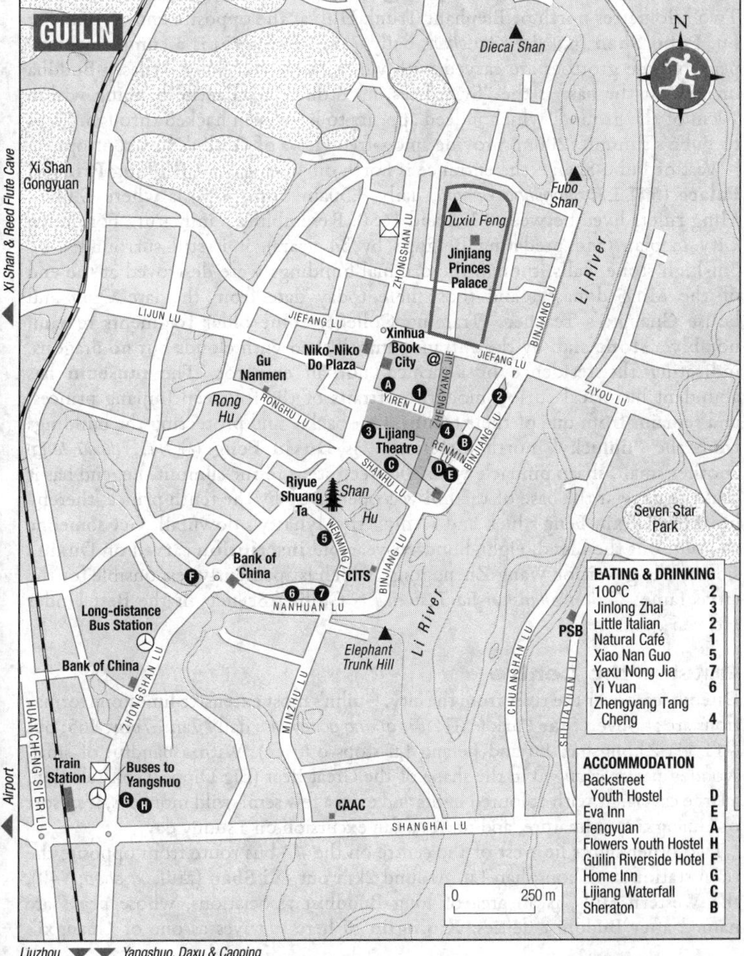

Ronghu Lu – and are now crossed by attractively hunchbacked stone bridges. Shan Hu is also overlooked by 40m-tall twin pagodas named **Riyue Shuang Ta** (日月双塔, *rìyuè shuāngtǎ*) one of which is painted gold, the other muted red and green, both attractively illuminated at night – you can climb to the top of both for ¥30.

Guilin's riverside promenade is Binjiang Lu, shaded from the summer sun by fig trees. Down at the southern end, these also strategically block views of **Elephant Trunk Hill** (象鼻山, *xiàngbí shān*; daily 6.30am–10pm; ¥40), said to be the fossilized body of a sick imperial baggage elephant who was cared for by locals. For once the name is not poetically obscure; the jutting cliff with an arched hole at the base really does resemble an elephant taking a drink from the river. There's an easy walk to a podgy pagoda on top, and, at river level, you can have your photo taken holding a parasol while you sit next to a cormorant on a brightly coloured bamboo raft.

Fubo Shan and the Jinjiang Princes' Palace

Two kilometres north of Elephant Trunk Hill, at the opposite end of Binjiang Lu, **Fubo Shan** (伏波山, *fúbō shān*; daily 7am–7pm; ¥15) is a complementary peak, whose grottoes are carved with worn Tang- and Song-dynasty Buddha images. At the base is the "Sword-testing Stone", a stalactite hanging within 10cm of the ground, which indeed appears to have been hacked through. Steps to Fubo's summit (200m) provide smog-free views of Guilin's low rooftops.

West of Fubo Shan – the entrance is north off Jiefang Lu – **Jinjiang Princes' Palace** (靖江王府, *jìngjiāng wángfǔ*; daily 8.30am–5pm; ¥70) is where Guilin's Ming rulers lived between 1372 and 1650. Resembling a miniature Forbidden City in plan (and predating Beijing's by 34 years), it is still surrounded by 5m-high stone walls, though the original buildings were destroyed at the end of the Ming dynasty, and those here today date from the late Qing and house Guangxi's Teachers' Training College. Some older fragments remain, notably a **stone slab** by the entrance embellished with clouds but no dragons, indicating the residence of a prince, not an emperor. The **museum** has abundant historical curios, modern portraits of the fourteen Jinjiang princes, and remains from one of their **tombs**. Out back – and protecting the buildings from the "unlucky" north direction – is **Duxiu Feng** (独秀峰, *dúxiù fēng*) another small, sharp pinnacle with 306 steep steps to the summit. Legend has it that the **cave** at the base of the hill was opened up by the tenth prince, thereby breaking Duxiu Feng's luck and seeding the dynasty's downfall. Get someone to point out the bland, eight-hundred-year-old **inscription** carved on Duxiu's side by the governor Wang Zhenggong, which is apparently responsible for the city's fame: *Guilin Shanshui Jia Tianxia* – "Guilin's Scenery is the Best Under Heaven".

Outside the centre

Directly east over the river from the city, Guilin's most extensive limestone formations are at **Seven Star Park** (七星公园, *qīxīng gōngyuán*; daily 7am–7pm; ¥65; bus #11 via Zhongshan Lu and Jiefang Lu stops outside). With a handful of small wooded peaks arranged in the shape of the Great Bear (Big Dipper) constellation, a large cavern lit with coloured lights and even a few semi-wild monkeys, it's a sort of Guangxi in miniature, and makes a fun excursion on a sunny day.

Two other sights lie west of the centre on the #3 bus route from opposite the train station on Zhongshan Lu. Around 2km out, **Xi Shan** (西山, *xī shān*; ¥40), the Western Hills, is an area of long Buddhist associations, whose peaks are named after Buddhist deities. **Xiqinglin Si** here survives as one of Guangxi's major Buddhist temples, filled with hundreds of exquisitely executed statues ranging from 10cm to more than 2m in height. There's also a regional **museum** in the park (daily 9am–noon & 2.30–5pm; free) – basically just a massive collection of ethnic clothing.

The #3 bus continues another 6km north to pass **Reed Flute Cave** (芦笛岩, *lúdí yán*; daily 8am–5.30pm; ¥60), a huge warren eaten into the south side of Guangming Shan which once provided a refuge from banditry and Japanese bombs. The caverns are not huge, but there are some interesting formations and a small underground lake, which makes for some nice reflections. You're meant to follow one of the tours that run every twenty minutes, but you can always linger inside and pick up a later group if you want to spend more time.

Eating

Guilin's **restaurants** are famous for serving rare game meats and, despite recent health scares, plenty of places still display live caged pheasants, cane rats, turtles, fish and snakes outside. Less confrontational options abound too, with everything from pizza to more standard Chinese fare available. The best concentrations of restaurants are along Nanhuan Lu, Wenming Lu, and Yiren Lu, and especially on pedestrianized **Zhengyang Jie**. For cheap stir-fries and one-dish meals, try canteens around the long-distance bus station.

Jinlong Zhai (金龙寨, *jīnlóng zhài*) 4F, corner of Zhongshan Lu and the adjacent plaza. Famous Guangxi chain specializing in local country dishes, such as roast fowl and fatty pork slices with taro. They also do Sichuanese staples and much lighter cold snacks. Mains around ¥30.

Little Italian Up past the *Sheraton* on Binjiang Lu. Small, friendly café (one of several nearby) with very good coffee, ginger and lemon tea, and light Western-style meals.

Natural Café (闻莺阁, *wényīng gé*) Yiren Lu. Eclectic "foreign" menu including spaghetti, borscht, pizza and Southeast Asian coconut curries from ¥25, and steaks for around ¥65.

Xiao Nan Guo (小南国菜馆, *xiǎonánguó càiguǎn*) 3 Wenming Lu. Big, bright, cheerful and very popular local-style restaurant, without your menu choices languishing in cages. There's no English menu, so non-Chinese-speakers will need to do a round of tables and point. Mains from ¥18.

Yaxu Nong Jia (雅叙农家菜馆, *yǎxù nóngjiā càiguǎn*) 159 Nanhuan Lu. One of several smart, "country-style" restaurants along this street, with staff dressed in peasant garb and captive wildlife outside awaiting your delectation. Good but pricey, with mains upwards of ¥50.

Yi Yuan (怡园饭店, *yíyuán fàndiàn*) 106 Nanhuan Lu. Sichuanese food served in comfortable surroundings and friendly, English-speaking staff make this a nice place to dine. Try the "mouth-watering" chicken, green beans with garlic, sugared walnuts, or garlic pork. Two or three can eat well for ¥35 each.

Zhengyang Tang Cheng (正阳汤城, *zhèngyáng tāngchéng*) Zhengyang Jie. Slow-simmered soups, plus Cantonese roast meats, sandpots and steamed greens. Not expensive at around ¥35/person, but their English menu is very sketchy – ask for the Chinese one.

Drinking and entertainment

For **drinking**, there's a knot of foreigner-oriented pubs along pedestrianized Zhengyang Jie, at the junction with Renmin Lu; the street also hosts a string of souvenir stalls and is a popular place to stroll in the evening, though expect to be relentlessly harassed by hawkers and women offering "massages". For **live music**, DJs and a bar, try *100°C* (百度酒吧100°C, *bǎidùjiǔba*). Alternatively, **Lijiang Theatre** (漓江剧院, *líjiāng jùyuàn*) holds daily performances of *Fantastic Guilin* (8pm; ¥150–220 depending on where you sit), a contemporary take on local ethnic dances, incorporating ballet, acrobatics and amazing visuals.

Listings

Airlines The airlines office (daily 9am–5pm; ⓣ0773/3890000) is on Shanghai Lu, with offices scattered all over the place. Hotel tour desks can also make bookings for you.

Banks and exchange There are several branches of the Bank of China with ATMs and foreign-exchange counters; the most useful lie between the bus and train stations on Zhongshan Lu, and on the corner of Zhongshan Lu and Nanhuan Lu.

Bookshops Xinhua Book City (新华书城, *xīnhuá shūchéng*) is south across from the Niko-Niko Do Plaza. Books in English – mostly translated Chinese classics – are on floor three.

Internet Several internet bars along Zhongshan Lu, and at the top end of pedestrianized Shazheng Yang Lu, charge ¥2/hour.

Mail The most convenient post office (daily 8am–7pm) is just north of the train station on Zhongshan Nan Lu, with mail services and poste restante downstairs.

PSB The visa extension department (Mon–Fri 9am–1pm & 3–5pm; ⓣ0773/5829930) is at 16 Shijiayuan Lu. Extensions usually take around 24hr.

Shopping Zhongshan Lu is lined with well-stocked department stores, the best of which is the Niko-Niko Do Plaza on the corner with Jiefang Lu. For local flavour, try osmanthus tea (*guicha*) or osmanthus wine (*guijiu*), both of which are quite pleasant (though some brands of wine are pretty rough). For souvenirs – mostly outright tack and ethnicky textiles – try your bargaining skills at the shops and stalls on Binjiang Lu and Zhengyang Jie, or the nightly street market spreading for about a block either side of Shanhu Bridge along Zhongshan Lu.

Travel agents Your hotel can sort out river cruises, book onward transport and organize day-trips to Longji Titian rice terraces (see p.650; ¥180/person includes return transport, entry and guide; you get around 5hr on site). For more of the same, CITS (ⓣ0773/2886393, ⓦwww.guilincits.com) are at 11 Binjiang Lu, with branches at many hotels.

The Li River, Xingping and Yangshuo

The **Li River** (漓江, *lí jiāng*) meanders south for 85km from Guilin through the finest scenery that this part of the country can provide, the shallow green water flanked by a procession of jutting karst peaks that have been carved by the elements into a host of bizarre shapes, every one of them with a name and associated legend. In between are pretty rural scenes of grazing water buffalo, farmers working their fields in conical hats, locals poling themselves along on half-submerged bamboo rafts and fishing with cormorants, and a couple of small villages with a scattering of old architecture; the densest concentration of peaks is grouped around the middle reaches between the villages of **Caoping** and **Xingping**.

A **cruise** through all this is, for some, the highlight of their trip to China, and it would be hard not to be won over by the scenery, which is at its best during the wet, humid months between May and September, when the landscape is at its lushest and the river runs deepest – a serious consideration, as the water can be so shallow in winter that vessels can't complete their journey. At the far end, the village of **Yangshuo** sits surrounded by more exquisite countryside, making it an attractive place to kick back for a couple of days and dig a little deeper into the region, though the village suffers from severe tourist overload during the peak season.

Cruising the Li River

The most popular **Li River cruises** take about four hours, cover the best stretches of scenery between Yangdi and Xingping and can be organized through the CITS or accommodation in Guilin (see p.642). The cheapest fares – around ¥250 – are on **Chinese cruise boats** from **Daxu wharf** (大圩码头, *dàxū mǎtóu*) and get you transport to the wharf, a one-way ferry ticket to Yangshuo and a filling meal.

Foreign cruise boats (¥350–500 depending on where you book) depart further downstream at Zhujiang wharf (竹江码头, *zhújiāng mătóu*) and include transport to the wharf, a one-way cruise, lunch, an English-speaking guide and a return bus from Yangshuo. Be aware that in winter the river often runs too low for vessels to make it down as far as Xingping, let alone Yangshuo, though you get charged the same amount and won't be told this beforehand.

Alternatively, you can also arrange **bamboo rafts** (¥100–150; 2hr) through the best of the scenery between **Yangdi wharf** (杨堤码头, *yángdī mătóu*) and Xingping. You get transport to the wharf and the cruise, but have to feed yourself and make your own way on from Xingping (which is not a problem; see below). There's no room on board for luggage, and you'll need appropriate clothing as the rafts give little protection from the elements. Operators in Yangshuo also offer a similar version of this trip for around ¥100.

Downstream to Xingping

Aside from a few minor peaks, the first place of interest on the Li is around 25km along at the dishevelled west bank town of **DAXU** (大圩, *dàxū*), which features a long, cobbled street, a few old wooden buildings, and a Ming-dynasty arched bridge. After this it's all rather flat until a grouping of peaks around **Wangfu Shi** (望夫石, *wàngfū shí*), an east bank outcrop said to be a wife who turned to stone while waiting for her travelling husband to return home. Not far on, **CAOPING** (草坪, *căopíng*) is around 40km from Guilin, marked by **Guan Yan** (冠岩, *guànyán*; ¥40), a tiara-shaped rise whose naturally hollowed interior forms a 12km-long cavern, garishly lit and complete with escalators and loudspeaker commentaries – access is from the shore (cruise boats don't pull in here).

South of here is the east bank settlement of **Yangdi** (杨堤, *yángdī*) and then you're into the best of the scenery, the hills suddenly tightly packed around the river. Pick of the peaks are **Eight Immortals Crossing the River** (八仙过江, *bāxiān guòjiāng*), and **Nine Horses Fresco Hill** (九马画山, *jiŭmă huàshān*), a 100m-high cliff on whose weathered face you can pick out some horsey patterns. Look into the water past here for **Yellow Cloth Shoal** (黄布滩, *huángbù tān*), a flat, submerged rock at one of the shallowest spots on the river.

Xingping

XINGPING (兴坪, *xīngpíng*), 70km from Guilin, is a small market town on the west bank of the river; tourism is in its infancy here but with a **rail station** due to open nearby in 2015 land prices have soared and developers are moving in. Mountains hem everything in and Xingping is somewhere you can enjoy doing very little, either hanging out among the wooden shops and restaurants along **Lao Jie** (老街, *lăo jiē*), an old lane back from the dock, or watching locals buying everything from fruit to carrypoles, medicinal herbs and bamboo chairs at the **market**, held on calendar dates ending in a 3, 6 or 9. For a fairly stiff **hike**, ask for directions to the ninety-minute trail over the hills to the tiny riverside village of **Yucun** (鱼村, *yúcūn*), though a far easier path leads upstream from the docks to the **¥20 Scenery** (20元背景图, *èrshí yuán bēijĭngtú*) – the landscape on the back of a twenty yuan note.

Accommodation includes *The Old Place YHA* (兴坪老地方国际青年旅, *xīngpíng lăo dìfang guójì qīngnián lǚshè*; ⓣ0773/8702887, ⓦwww.topxingping.com; dorms ¥30, rooms ❷) near the dock on main street Rongtan Lu; the fairly basic but clean *Integrity Hotel* (城信酒店, *chéngxìn jiŭdiàn*; ⓣ0773/8703699; ❶) further up on Rongtan Lu; or, if you want something more upmarket, *Xingping Our Inn* (宝熊庄, *băoxióng zhuāng*; ⓣ13659638096 or 15295923259, ⓦwww.ourinnxp.com; ❷), over the river at Dahebei village – check the website for details on how to get there. All offer **meals**, but the restaurants along Lao Jie are more atmospheric, even if their Western-Chinese menus are unadventurous – best is the *Old Neighbour* (老街坊餐吧, *lǎo jiēfang cānba*).

Moving on, **buses to Yangshuo** (¥7) leave through the day, while back on the water, the river broadens out for its final 20km stretch to Yangshuo's docks beneath Green Lotus Peak.

Yangshuo

Nestled 70km south of Guilin in the thick of China's most spectacular karst scenery, **YANGSHUO** (阳朔, *yángshuò*), meaning Bright Moon, rose to prominence during the mid-1980s, when foreign tourists on Li River cruises realized that the village made a great place to settle down and get on intimate terms with the river and its peaks. Yangshuo has grown considerably since then and, despite retaining an outdated reputation as a mellow haven among Western travellers, has become a rowdy draw for domestic tourists, with the majority of its bars, restaurants and shops catering to their tastes. It remains, however, an easy place to spend a few days: hills surround everything, village lanes swarm with activity, and there are restaurants and accommodation everywhere. You can rent a bike and spend a day zipping between hamlets, hike around or go **rock climbing** on nearby peaks, or study cooking or martial arts.

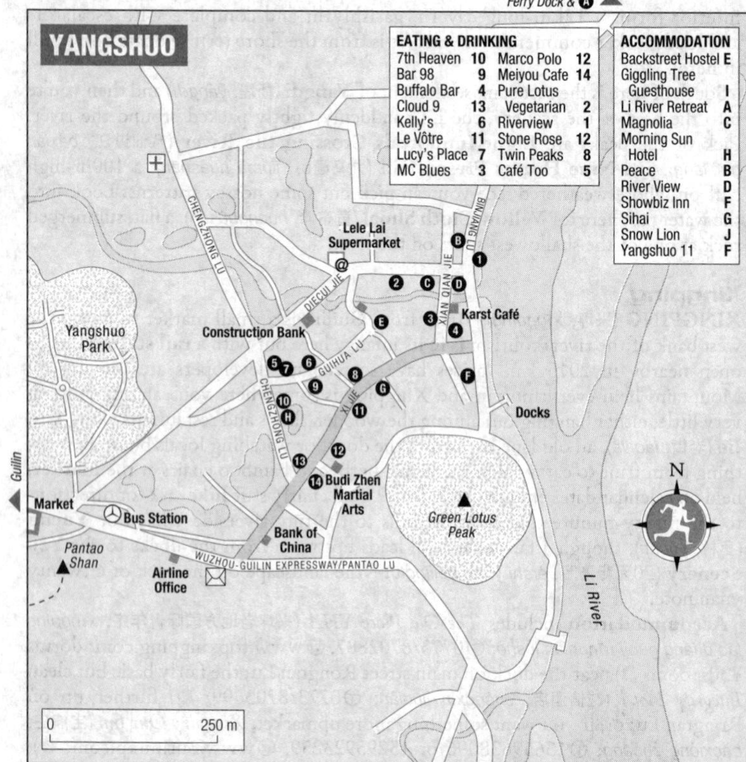

Arrival and information

Ferries arrive upstream from Yangshuo, where tourists face a 500m-long gauntlet of souvenir stalls on their way into the village. **Buses** terminate at the station along the highway (also known as Pantao Lu), off which Yangshuo's two main streets run northeast to the river; **Diecui Jie** extends from the bus station through the village centre, while east and parallel is flagstoned, vehicle-free **Xi Jie** (or West Street; 西街, *xījiē*), stretching down to the water past restaurants, bars, accommodation and shops.

There's a large quantity of **information** to be had in Yangshuo, either from the hotels – who all have tour desks – or foreigner-oriented cafés, most of which are located around central **Guihua Lu**. In addition, touts are everywhere, though they're relatively low-pressure and easy enough to brush off if you're not interested. Some cafés also offer book exchanges (the best being at *Café Too* on Chengzhong Lu) and all have **internet** access, usually free for customers. You can buy **maps** of the town, river and surrounding area at many shops.

Accommodation

Stiff competition means that Yangshuo's **accommodation prices** are good value: options range from basic dorm beds at ¥30 and comfy doubles from ¥100 in town, to relatively upmarket country retreats with river views in excess of ¥350 – worth the price if you want some quiet and scenic views. Rooms can vary greatly in quality though, even within individual establishments – Yangshuo's damp climate encourages mildew – so have a look at a few before choosing. Balconies, folksy furnishings and wooden floors are nice touches, locations near Xi Jie's nightclubs may not be if you want any sleep. Rates halve during the winter low season, when you'll want to check the availability of heating and hot water; in summer air conditioning is a must.

In Yangshuo

Backstreet Hostel (桂花街国际青年旅馆, *guìhuājiē guójì qīngnián lǚguǎn*) 60 Guihua Xiang ⓣ0773/8814077. Sister hostel to the one in Guilin, down a quiet lane, with good dorms and doubles. Dorm beds ¥30, rooms ❷

Magnolia (白玉兰酒店, *báiyùlán jiǔdiàn*) 7 Diecui Lu ⓣ0773/8819288, ⓕ8819218. Smart mid-range place with minimalist decor and huge rooms (though this and the tiling make it cold in winter); a popular choice with small group tours. ❺

Morning Sun Hotel (晨光酒店, *chéngguāng jiǔdiàn*) 4 Chengzhong Lu ⓣ0773/8813899, ⓦwww.morningsunhotel.com. One of a new block of low-rise budget hotels distant enough from Xi Jie's clamour for sleeping, but close enough not to lose your way home. Doubles with balcony ❹

Peace (和平客栈, *hépíng kèzhàn*) Xian Qian Jie ⓣ0773/8826262, ⓦwww.yangshuotour.org. One of the better deals in town: large rooms with a/c, bathroom and balconies in a quiet street just off Diecui Jie. ❷

River View (望江楼酒店, *wàngjiānglóu jiǔdiàn*) 11–15 Binjiang Lu ⓣ0773/8822688 (hotel) or 8829676 (hostel). They're a helpful bunch here and the location is good – at least it is after 4pm, when the tourist stalls outside have cleared off. Pricier rooms with balconies overlook the river across the road. Hostel beds ¥35, doubles in the hostel ❸, in the hotel ❹

Moving on from Yangshuo

Minibuses up the expressway to Guilin's train station (¥18) depart the bus station all day long, as do local services to Xingping (¥7) and other villages. Long-distance **buses** to Nanning, Guangzhou and elsewhere originate in Guilin, so if you're planning to take one go to Guilin first or put up with the worst berths – over the back wheel – as the bus will be full by the time it gets to Yangshuo. **Agents** can book long-distance bus tickets along with flights, taxis to Guilin airport (¥240, or sometimes a shared vehicle at ¥80/person) and train tickets from Guilin.

Showbiz Inn (秀界国际青年旅舍, *xiù jiè guójì qīngnián lǚ shè*) 4 Lianfeng Xiang ⓣ0773/8883123, ⓦwww.showbizinn.com. Terrible name for one of the best budget options in town; a clean, comfortable hostel tucked down an alley just metres from the river. Great views from their rooftop bar too. Dorm beds ¥30, rooms ❹

Sihai (四海饭店, *sìhǎi fàndiàn*) 73 Xi Jie ⓣ0773/8822013, ⓦwww.sihaihotel.com. About the only accommodation worth considering on Xi Jie, though showing its age; rooms at the back are insulated from neighbouring nightclubs. Dorm beds ¥30, doubles ❷

Yangshuo 11 (阳朔11青年客栈, *yángshuò shíyī qīngnián kèzhàn*) 11 Lianfeng Xiang ⓣ0773/6912228, ⓔyangshuo11hostel@hotmail.com. Similar option to nearby *Showbiz*, well-managed and helpful with tour information. Another good roof bar. Dorm beds ¥30, doubles ❷

Around Yangshuo

Giggling Tree Guesthouse Aishanmen village, about 5km south of Yangshuo along the Yulong River (see p.648) ⓣ0136/67866154, ⓦwww.gigglingtree.com. Converted stone farmhouse buildings now forming an attractive hotel and restaurant, with courtyard, tiled roofs and a beautiful mountain backdrop. ❹

Li River Retreat About 1.5km north of Yangshuo along the Li River ⓣ0773/8828950, ⓦwww.li-river-retreat.com. Upmarket affair in very pleasant riverside setting, with rooms decked out in Chinese antique chic. ❺

Snow Lion (雪狮岭度假饭店, *xuěshīlǐng dùjià fàndiàn*) Mushan village, about 2.5km south of Yangshuo ⓣ0773/8826689, ⓦwww.yangshuosnowlionresort.com. Fantastic food and scenery coupled with comfortable and airy rooms make this a great place for a break. ❺

The village

Yangshuo has few formal attractions – it was a simple country marketplace before tourists arrived – but there's still plenty to explore. West off Diecui Jie is **Yangshuo Park** (阳朔公园, *yángshuò gōngyuán*), a pleasant place in summer with its colourful formal garden and breezy vantages of town from pavilions lodged on the main rise. Squeezed between the highway and the river directly opposite is **Green Lotus Peak** (碧莲峰, *bìlián fēng*), the largest in the immediate area – there's a track to the top off the highway east of the post office, but it involves some scrambling. An easier path (leading to better views) ascends **Pantao Shan** (蟠桃山, *pāntáo shān*) from behind the market. Otherwise, just walk upstream from Yangshuo for a kilometre or two and take your pick of the rough trails that scale many other slopes to summits covered in tangled undergrowth and sharp, eroded rocks – again, be prepared for some scrambling, and for safety reasons don't go alone.

The presence of tourists hasn't entirely altered the daily routine of villagers, who spend hours inspecting and buying wares in the **produce market** (农贸市场, *nóngmào shìchǎng*). It's an interesting place to hang out, especially on market days (held on dates ending in a 3, 6 or 9). There's a good selection of game, fruit, nuts and mushrooms laid out on sheets in the street here – look out for rats and

Cormorant fishing

When you've had enough scenery for one day, do something unusual and spend an evening watching **cormorant fishing** (book through your hotel; ¥50 per person for a 90min trip). This involves heading out in a punt at dusk, closely following a tiny wooden fishing boat or bamboo raft from which a group of cormorants fish for their owner. Despite being turned into a tourist activity at Yangshuo, people still make their living from this age-old practice throughout central and southern China, raising young birds to dive into the water and swim back to the boat with full beaks. The birds are prevented from swallowing by rings or ties around their necks, but it's usual practice for the fisherman to slacken these off and let them eat every seventh fish – apparently, the cormorants refuse to work otherwise.

pheasants, fresh straw and needle mushrooms, and spiky water caltrops, which contain a kernel similar to a Brazil nut.

Xi Jie is Yangshuo's tourist drag, lined with shops selling a vast array of souvenirs. Trends change here all the time, but the current emphasis is towards clothes – from fake brand labels to Mao T-shirts, outdoor gear and even leatherwear – exorbitantly priced ethnic textiles, modern and traditional paintings, and a few stalls loaded with "new antiques". As always in China, check everything carefully before parting with your cash, don't forget to bargain – about a third of the asking price is recommended – and don't buy anything when tour boats from Guilin pull in unless you want to pay five times the going rate. In summer shops stay open late and at night the street is choked with crowds as they shop and orbit between the many restaurants and bars.

Yangshuo also offers a window into the more esoteric side of Chinese culture. For **martial arts**, the outstanding Budi Zhen school (Ⓣ1397/7350377, Ⓦbudizhen.net) is run by the irrepressible "Papa" Gao and his twin sons; or contact highly skilled *tai ji* practitioner Fu Nengbin (Ⓦwww.masterfu.net). The more peacefully inclined can check out **cookery classes** – contact Linda at *Cloud 9* restaurant.

Eating

Yangshuo's numerous **restaurants** and cafés are split between those along Xi Jie, which mainly cater to Chinese tourists seeking exotic Western food; and those along Chengzhong Lu and Guihua Lu, which serve backpacker staples and Chinese and Western fare to a largely foreign crowd. Both restaurants and cafés open early for Western breakfasts, and keep going well into the night; there are also plenty of inexpensive Chinese canteens and food stalls selling noodle soups and buns around the bus station.

7th Heaven Chengzhong Lu Ⓣ0773/8826101. Well-above-average Western and Chinese food in pleasant surroundings; the outdoor terrace by the bridge is a nice place to sit on a hot evening. Their bar is well stocked too. Around ¥40/person.

Cloud 9 Upstairs at the corner of Chengzhong Lu and Xi Jie Ⓣ0773/8813686. Seasonal country-style food, juicy and flavourful; locals recommend any one of their slow-simmered medicinal soups (which sell out early), rural specialities such as taro and pork stew, or Sichuanese classics like crispy-skinned chicken. Around ¥40/person.

Kelly's Guihua Lu. Friendly foreigners' café/restaurant, with Western food alongside good home-style Sichuan cooking – try their fiery hot boiled beef slices or cooling chicken salad.

Le Vôtre Xi Jie. Yangshuo's poshest dining, inside a Ming-era building complete with period furnishings. Food is French – snails, pâté, onion soup, steak *au poivre*, chocolate mousse – or Chinese seafood. Also, excellent coffee and croissants for breakfast. Expect to pay at least ¥50/person.

Lucy's Place Guihua Lu. Another foreign-friendly establishment with the usual mix of Chinese and Western meals, plus some of the best coffee in town.

MC Blues Xian Qian Jie. A long-running business catering to Western backpackers, serving toasted sandwiches, bamboo rats and vegetarian hotpots. Steer clear of their mushy beer-battered fish, though.

Meiyou Café Xi Jie. Founded during Yangshuo's early days, this warehouse-sized institution does pretty good Chinese staples at moderate prices; there are balcony tables but it's too busy for the atmosphere to be relaxing.

Pure Lotus Vegetarian 7 Diecui Lu. Attractive place with attractive food; not cheap but worth a slight splurge. The almond rolls, vegetables cooked with rose petals, steamed winter melon and "steak" with brandy sauce are all good. From ¥25/dish.

Riverview Overlooking the river at the end of Diecui Lu. The café-style food here is fine, but its romantic position as Yangshuo's only waterfront restaurant is the real attraction. Two can eat well for ¥80.

Twin Peaks Xi Jie. The nice cosy café downstairs serves good breakfasts; upstairs things get slightly smarter with window seats for people-watching and a more comprehensive menu – and they keep the after-dark music down to conversational levels.

Drinking and nightlife

Xi Jie has several **clubs and bars**, some of which host live music and all of which pump out raucous, high-decibel Chinese rock later on in the evenings; the current picks are the perennially heaving *Stone Rose* and slightly more sedate *Meiyou Café* and *Marco Polo*. For a quieter **pub-style** drink or meal, head to the *Buffalo Bar* on Xianqian Jie (Ⓦwww.yangshuo-buffalo-bar.com) or *Bar 98* on Guihua Lu, which has outdoor seating overlooking a stream and the cheapest spirits in town.

Yangshuo's major after-dark event however, is **Liu San Jie**, an open-air song, dance and light spectacular put together by renowned film director Zhang Yimou. Featuring a cast of 600 local cormorant fishermen, minority women, singing children and the like, the whole affair lasts an hour, costs ¥198–680 depending on your seat and takes place about 2km downstream from town – book through your accommodation.

Listings

Airlines The airline office (Ⓣ0773/8822111, Ⓦwww.cs-air.com) is just west of the post office on the highway. The nearest airport is Guilin's.
Bank There's a Bank of China with an ATM on Xi Jie (foreign currency transactions daily 9am–noon & 1–5pm), plus a Construction Bank ATM on Diecui Lu.
Internet Free at cafés if you have a meal too; otherwise, there's a big net bar above the Xinhua Bookstore and Lele Lai supermarket on Diecui Lu (¥3/hr).
Laundry On the highway near the post office; charges ¥10/kilo and uses dryers for same-day service.
Medical For acupuncture or Chinese massage, contact Dr Lily Li (Ⓣ13077632299, Ⓦwww.dr-lily-li.com) at 46 Guihua Lu. Therapeutic massages are relatively expensive at ¥80/hr, but – if pain is any indication of quality – might be the best you'll ever have; relaxation or foot massages are cheaper.
Post office On the highway (daily 8am–6pm).

Around Yangshuo

Getting to see the countryside around Yangshuo is easy enough, as the land between the hills is flat and perfect for **bicycles** – the highway end of Xi Jie is thick with rental touts if your accommodation can't help (¥20/day for a standard bike or ¥50 for a scooter up to 40km; plus at least ¥300 deposit). **Bike Asia**, above *Bar 98* on Guihua Lu (Ⓣ0773/8826521, Ⓦwww.bikeasia.com), are an extremely professional, competent operation who concentrate on trips around China but also organize local excursions. Cheaper **freelance touts** target foreigners' cafés, offering their services as guides for exploring villages – the relentlessly cheerful "Wendy" Li Yunzhao speaks good English and comes recommended (Ⓣ13197638186, Ⓔliyunzhaowendy@yahoo.com; ¥50/person/day).

To explore the **Li River**, accommodation can arrange bamboo raft trips between Xingping and Yangdi (2hr; ¥200) and full-day **kayak trips** (¥200); or in hot weather you can simply buy a **rubber tube** from shops along Diecui Jie and head down to the water for a splash – but leave it until the last ferries have departed upstream around 4pm.

The Yulong River

Paralleling the highway to Guilin, the **Yulong River** (玉龙河, *yùlóng hé*) west of Yangshuo offers a 12km walk or cycle between small hamlets, with a couple of old stone bridges and at least two older-style villages with a few antique buildings. The road from Yangshuo leaves the highway east of the bus station – you might have to ask for directions to **Chaoyang** (朝阳, *cháoyáng*), the first large settlement along the way – and follows the east side of the Yulong via **Xia Tangzhai** (下堂寨, *xiàtáng zhài*), the old villages of **Huang Tu** (黄土, *huáng tǔ*) and **Gu Cheng** (古城, *gǔ chéng*),

Climbing Yangshuo's peaks

Yangshuo is one of Asia's fastest-growing **rock-climbing** centres, with an estimated 70,000 pinnacles of up to 200m in height in the area. However, there are only about fifty established climbing routes, many of them under 30m in length – though those at Moon Hill are rated among the toughest in China – and, as most are within easy day-trips of Yangshuo, you won't need to plan any mighty expeditions (though camping out on site is fun).

The main **climbing season** lasts from October through to February, as the rest of the year can be uncomfortably hot or wet. There are several sources of local information along Xian Qian Jie in Yangshuo, notably China Climb at the *Lizard Lounge* (Ⓣ0773/8811033, Ⓦwww.chinaclimb.com) and the *Karst Café* (Ⓣ0773/8828482, Ⓦwww.karstclimber.com). The above places organize **equipment**, **instruction** and **guides**, and may have copies of *Rock Climbing in Yangshuo* by Paul Collis, which gives invaluable information on routes, access, local conditions and grades.

before rejoining the highway at **Baisha** (白沙, *báishā*), whose market runs on dates ending in a 1, 4 or 7 and where you can either cycle or catch a bus back to Yangshuo.

Staff on Li River cruise boats also offer a **tour** of the Yulong River area for ¥150 per person, which includes a bus out to an old village, a walk along the riverside and then a short raft trip where women dressed in minority garb encourage you to sing along to saucy folk tunes.

Moon Hill and caves

A slew of attractions line the highway southwest of Yangshuo. Most of these are mass-tourist developments, but a couple of cave systems and the justly renowned **Moon Hill** are worth a look, depending on your interests. If you don't want to cycle, catch one of the frequent departures from Yangshuo's bus station to **Gaotian town** (高田, *gāotián*) and ask the driver to put you off at the right spot.

Around 6km from Yangshuo, **Assembling Dragons Cave** (聚龙潭, *jù lóng tán*; 8.30am–5.30pm; ¥45) is a kilometre-long, flooded cavern full of impressive formations and slightly overdone festive lighting, which you explore by boat and on foot. **Water Cave** (龙门水岩, *lóngmén shŭiyán*; Ⓦwww.watercave.net; summer only; ¥150) is more of a natural theme park, with subterranean mud baths, waterfalls, hot springs, swimming holes and rock slides; come prepared to get wet, cold and very, very muddy. Tours last about three hours and depart from the ticket office on the highway, just short of Moon Hill.

Moon Hill (月亮山, *yuèliàng shān*; ¥15) lies on the highway 8km from town, named after a large crescent-shaped hole that pierces the peak. It takes an easy thirty minutes to ascend stone steps through bamboo and brambles to the summit where fairytale views take in the whole of the Li River valley, fields cut into uneven chequers by rice and vegetable plots, and Tolkienesque peaks framed through the hole.

Guilin to Guizhou

A hundred kilometres northwest of Guilin the road winds steeply through some fine stands of mountain bamboo, and enters the southern limit of a fascinating ethnic **autonomous region**. With a rich landscape of mountains and terraced fields as a backdrop – best perhaps at **Longji** – it's possible to hop on local transport and tour a rural corner of China that remains relatively unaffected by the modern world. Day-trips abound, but, with five days or so to spare, you can push right through the mountainous **Dong** heartlands northwest of **Sanjiang** into Guizhou province, a fabulous journey which takes you to the area around **Kaili**, similarly central to the Miao people (p.652). Before starting, note that there are **no banks** capable of cashing travellers' cheques between Guilin and Kaili.

Longji Titian

Around 90km north of Guilin, **Longji Titian** (龙脊梯田, *lóngjǐ tītián*; ¥50) – literally "Dragon's Spine Terraces" – is a range of steep-sided and closely packed hills, whose slopes have been carved out over centuries of farming to resemble the literal form of a contour map. Most of the people up here are Zhuang, but there are also communities of **Yao**, some of whom still hunt for a living. Tourism is well established, with the wooden villages of **Ping An** and **Dazhai** acting as comfortable bases for viewing the terraces or hiking around the hilltops.

Day-trips are offered by agents in Guilin (see p.642), but you'll get more by staying for a couple of nights and it's easy to reach here on local buses. **From Guilin**, there's one departure daily each to Ping An or Dazhai from the train station square (8.30am; 2–3hr; ¥50), or catch one of the regular buses to **Longsheng** (龙胜, *lóngshèng*) from the bus station. Tell the driver where you're heading and you should get dropped off at the main-road hamlet of **Heping** (和平, *hépíng*), where minibuses to Ping An or Dazhai depart when full. Coming **from Sanjiang**, aim first for Longsheng and then catch a direct minibuses (about ¥8) for the run to Ping An or Dazhai.

Leaving Ping An or Dazhai, check minibus departure times with your accommodation; there are single daily services direct to Guilin (¥50), or more regular departures through the day to Longsheng, for connections to Guilin or Sanjiang.

Ping An

PING AN (平安, *píng ān*) is a Zhuang village of wooden homes and cobbled paths squeezed into a steep fold between the terraces. You get dropped off in a car park below and walk up 500m of stone steps to the village, where you're faced with a glut of **accommodation**, all offering cosy rooms with or without en suite in "traditional-style" three-storey houses – look for something with a view. One of the first you reach is the *Countryside Café and Inn* (乡村咖啡店, *xiāngcūn kāfēidiàn*; ⓣ0773/7583020 or 15107837162, ⓔliyue_lu@hotmail.com; ❷); around in the second part of the village, both *Longying Fandian* (龙颖饭店, *lóngyǐng fàndiàn*; ⓣ0773/7583059, ⓦwww.longying88.com; ❸) and *Ping An Jiudian* (平安酒店, *píng ān jiǔdiàn*; ⓣ0773/7583198, ⓕ7583458; ❸) offer slightly better rooms and views. All accommodation serves **food** – Western staples and some good Chinese meals, including chicken grilled in bamboo tubes (竹筒鸡, *zhútǒng jī*).

Walks around Ping An include short climbs to lookouts at **Seven Stars** (七星, *qīxīng*) and **Nine Dragons and Five Tigers** (九龙五虎, *jiǔlóng wǔhǔ*), either of which give superlative views of the rice terraces. You can also **hike to Dazhai** in about five hours, via the attractive village of **Zhongliu** (中六, *zhōngliù*) – ask at accommodation for directions or a guide (about ¥50) as the path is not always clear.

Dazhai

DAZHAI (大寨, *dàzhài*) is a less touristy version of Ping An, reached along a separate road from Heping. Buses deliver to the main village at the bottom of a valley, with better views at hamlets such as **Tiantou** (田头, *tiántóu*), twenty minutes' walk up the hillside above – quite a hike with a heavy pack. At Tiantou, *Jintian Guesthouse* (金田酒店, *jīntián jiǔdiàn*; ⓣ0773/7585683, ⓦwww.ljjtjd.com; ❶) is typically friendly, tidy and clean, but there's better another half-hour's walk further up at *Jinmei Ge* (金美阁, *jīnměi gé*; ⓣ0773/7585638, or 13737377986; ❶), an incredibly welcoming place with good views and food, and well-positioned for the long circuit hike out to **Xi Shan** (西山, *xīshān*).

Sanjiang and Chengyang

Two hours west of Longsheng the road crosses a high stone bridge over the Rongshui River and lands you at small, dishevelled **SANJIANG** (三江, *sānjiāng*), capital of Sanjiang Dong Autonomous County. Most of the people here are **Dong**, renowned for their wooden houses, towers and bridges which dot the countryside hereabouts, most notably at **Chengyang** village to the north. Sanjiang's own unmissable **drum tower** rises 47m over the river; this one is modern, but similar towers were traditionally used as lookout posts in times of war, or social areas in times of peace.

Sanjiang's **long-distance bus station** lies south of the river in the newer part of town, with connections south as far as Guilin and north to Liping and Congjiang. **Local buses**, including to Chengyang and Zhaoxing, use the depot immediately north of the bridge in the older part of town. Sanjiang is also on the Huaihua–Liuzhou **rail line**, with services to Mayang in Hunan (for Fenghuang, see p.458); the train station is about 10km northwest of town with minibuses meeting arrivals and landing them immediately north of the bridge.

Places to stay north of the river include the budget *Department Store Hostel* (百货宾馆, *bǎihuò bīnguǎn*; dorm beds ¥35) – look for the English sign near the local bus station – the *Chengyang Qiao Binguan* (程阳桥宾馆, *chéngyáng qiáo bīnguǎn*; ⓣ0772/8613071; ❷), 100m west along the road; and, south of the river and about 100m back towards Longsheng from the long-distance station, the *Travellers' Home* (行旅之家, *xínglǚzhījiā*; ⓣ0772/8615584; ❷). For **food**, try the noodle and hotpot stalls north of the bridge, or your accommodation.

Chengyang

CHENGYANG (程阳, *chéngyáng*; ¥60), 18km north of Sanjiang on the Linxi River, is an attractive traditional Dong village reached over a covered **wind-and-rain bridge**, an all-wooden affair built in 1916. The village forms a collection of warped, two- and three-storeyed traditional **wooden houses** surrounding a square-sided drum tower, and makes a pleasantly rural place to spend a day, walking out to smaller hamlets with similar congregations of dark wood and cobbles, many with their own, less elaborate bridges and towers. Look for creaky black **water wheels** made from plaited bamboo, somehow managing to supply irrigation canals despite dribbling out most of their water in the process. For views over the whole region, return to Chengyang's main-road entrance and make the

short climb to two pavilions on the ridge above, offering vistas of dark, gloomy villages nestled among vivid green fields.

The last **bus back to Sanjiang** passes by around 5pm, but Chengyang is a better place to stay overnight, with plenty of **accommodation**. All the following offer rooms with or without en suite in folksy wooden houses: turn left over the bridge and it's 50m to *Dong Village Hotel* (ⓣ0772/8582421; ¥30/person); turn right to the village and you'll fall into either *Yang's Guesthouse* (程阳客栈, *chéngyáng kèzhàn*; ⓣ0772/8583126; ¥30/person) or the *Chengyang International Hostel* (程阳国际旅馆, *chéngyáng guójì lǚguǎn*; ⓣ0772/8582813; ¥30/person). All offer meals, can arrange bike rental and supply walking maps.

Into Guizhou: Sanjiang to Kaili

The road west of Sanjiang enters Guizhou and cuts through Dong territory and up to the Miao stronghold of **Kaili**, a 300km-long run of traditional villages, steeply terraced hillsides, vivid blue rivers and winding roads. Daily buses run from Sanjiang to **Zhaoxing** – itself a highlight – from where you can town-hop on to Kaili. Three days is a likely minimum for the trip, and it's not one that you'll get much out of by rushing in any case. Expect frugal facilities and food in villages, and cold, icy winters.

Zhaoxing

ZHAOXING (肇兴, *zhàoxīng*), around four hours by bus from Sanjiang, is a single-street Dong town set in a small valley, with a generous smattering of old buildings including five square-based **drum towers**, each differently styled and built by separate clans. Accompanying wind-and-rain bridges and theatre stages are decorated with fragments of mirrors and mouldings of actors and animals. Houses are hung with strings of drying radishes for sour hotpots, and the back lanes, teeming with roaming livestock, resound to the noise of freshly dyed cloth being pounded with wooden mallets to give it a shiny patina. Rice terraces and muddy tracks provide fine country walks, the best of which is 7km uphill through paddyfields to **Tang An** (堂安, *táng'ān*), another photogenic collection of wooden buildings.

Zhaoxing has many **places to stay**, from no-frills but comfy guesthouses such as the *Dong Village* (侗乡涉外旅馆, *dòngxiāng shèwài lǚguǎn*; ⓣ0855/6130188; ❶) and the very clued-up *Zhaoxing Fandian* (肇兴饭店, *zhàoxīng fàndiàn*; ⓣ0855/6130005; ❷), to the pricey but scenic *Zhaoxing Binguan* (肇兴宾馆, *zhàoxīng bīnguǎn*; ⓣ0855/6130800, ⓦwww.zgzhaoxing.cn; ❹). For **food**, there are a handful of open-fronted stir-fry restaurants along the main road, but – given the amount of dust stirred up by passing traffic – you might opt for an indoor venue such as the *Happy Farmer*; their home-made rice wine is pretty good too. **Moving on**, several buses run daily south to Sanjiang, and west to Congjiang.

Congjiang and Basha

CONGJIANG (从江, *cóngjiāng*) is a drab logging town on the Duliu River some two hours from Zhaoxing, with plenty of **accommodation** near the **bus station** on main street Jiangdong Nan Lu. *Wenguang Binguan* (文广宾馆, *wénguǎng bīnguǎn*; ⓣ0855/6418316; ❶) is old and tired but everything works and some rooms even have computers, while *Congjiang Ao Yue Jiudian* (从江奥悦酒店, *cóngjiāng aòyuè jiǔdiàn*; ⓣ0855/6411808; ❸) is the town's showpiece, with an air-conditioned lobby. There are precious few places to eat aside from stir-fry **canteens** around the station. **Moving on**, there are two buses to Zhaoxing daily, with more frequent departures to Rongjiang and Kaili.

The reason to stop in Congjiang is to make a side-trip to **BASHA** (岜沙, *bāshā*), a Miao hill village 8km southwest whose inhabitants grow a long topknot and wear traditionally embroidered clothes, heavy metal jewellery and pleated skirts as a matter of course, not just for festivals. Turn left out of Congjiang's bus station, walk 100m to the bridge, cross it and you'll find freelance **minibuses and motorbikes** hanging around on the left-hand corner; the ride to Basha costs ¥5–10. Basha is really a loose grouping of five separate wooden villages on a forested ridge, with cobbled lanes and paths off across the fields to explore. There are a few basic **places to stay** too, the pick of which is *Gufeng Zhai Qingnian Lüguan* (古风寨青年旅馆, *gǔfēngzhài qīngnián lǚguǎn*; ⓣ13885549720; beds ¥20, rooms ❶), a youth hostel with views and a small terraced garden.

Rongjiang and Zengchong

RONGJIANG (榕江, *róngjiāng*) is a comparitively large, modern town another two hours northwest across the mountains, and has a frenetic Sunday **market** where you can watch villagers bargaining the last mao out of a deal. There are plenty of decent, inexpensive places to stay here but none are authorized to take foreigners, and at present your sole option is the good but realtively pricey *Ronghe Dajiudian* (榕和大酒店, *rónghé dàjiǔdiàn*; ⓣ0855/6626599; ❸) about a ten-minute walk from the bus station on Xihuan Lu.

As at Congjiang, you're in Rongjiang to get out – this time 30km east to the isolated Dong village of **ZENGCHONG** (增冲, *zēngchōng*), which sports a four-hundred-year old drum tower. Access can be tricky; either catch one of the two daily buses to **Wangdong** (往洞, *wǎngdòng*) and then walk or hitch for the final 6km, or charter a minibus direct (about ¥250 for the return trip). Zengchong makes no concessions to the few tourists who drop in – it's an authentically poor, muddy, rickety place with a couple of tiny stores; Chinese-speakers can usually negotiate a homestay for the night.

From Rongjiang, several **buses** a day make the trip northwest via twisty roads and beautifully green mountains to Kaili (see p.669).

Nanning

Founded during the Yuan dynasty, **NANNING** (南宁, *nánníng*) was just a medium-sized market town until European traders opened a river route from neighbouring Guangdong in the early twentieth century, starting a period of rapid growth that saw the city supplanting Guilin as the provincial capital. Largely untouched by the civil war and Japanese invasion, it became a centre of supply and command first during the **Vietnam War**, and then a decade later when China and Vietnam came to blows in 1979. Following the resumption of cross-border traffic in the 1990s the city has capitalized on trade agreements with its neighbour, and today Nanning is a bright, easy-going place with a mild boom-town atmosphere and mix of leafy boulevards, modern architecture and a handful of narrow, colonial-era streets. There's good shopping, decent food, a **museum** strong on regional archeology, and both international and domestic transport connections – in particular, over the nearby **open border with Vietnam**.

Arrival and city transport

At over 10km across, with its downtown area concentrated on the northern bank of the **Yong Jiang River**, Nanning is a blandly user-friendly city, its streets hot and planted with exotic trees. Most of the city's accommodation and attractions are in the vicinity of **Chaoyang Lu**, Nanning's main shoping precinct, which runs for 2km south from the **train station**, through the city centre and down to the river.

Coming from almost anywhere **by bus** will probably see you winding up at **Langdong station** (琅东客运站, *lángdōng kèyùn zhàn*), 10km east of the centre on

Moving on from Nanning

The airlines **ticket office** (domestic bookings ⓣ0771/2416496, international bookings ⓣ0771/2428418, ⓦwww.travelsky.com) is up near the train station on Chaoyang Lu, and you can fly from Nanning to most cities in China. The airport bus (¥20) leaves hourly from this office and takes forty minutes; taxis congregate at the same place and charge ¥25/person (or ¥100 for the vehicle).

The biggest **bus station**, with departures for east and northern destinations including Beihai and Guilin, as well as Guiyang, is **Langdong station**, 10km to the east at the end of the number #6 bus route; allow 50 minutes. You can buy tickets for Langdong departures from booths at the corner of Chaoyang Lu and Hua Dong Lu; they also have timetables. For destinations around the southwestern border area such as Chongzuo, Ningming and Pingxiang, as well as Beihai and Guilin, and inter-provincial buses to Haikou, Guangzhou and Shenzhen, head 7km south to **Jiangnan station**, on the #31 bus route; allow 40 minutes. Jiangnan tickets and timetables can be obtained from a booth on Zhonghua Lu, about 500m west of the train station on the corner with Huaqiang Lu. Much closer in, the **Beida Transit Centre** is about 2km northwest of the train station, also on the #31 bus route, and is of most use for traffic to Daxin (for Detian Waterfall), Leye and Kunming.

Train destinations include Beihai, Guilin, Kunming, Beijing, Guangzhou, Shanghai, Chengdu and Wuhan, as well as Chongzuo, Tuolong and the Vietnamese border at Pingxiang. Ticket windows are open from 7am to 7pm; queues here can be tiring.

If you're heading **to Vietnam**, you'll need a **visa**: these are issued by the Vietnamese Consulate, 1F Investment Plaza, 109 Minzu Dadao (Mon–Fri 10am–3pm; ⓣ0771/5510561) and cost ¥380–580 depending on how fast you want them. Both *Lotusland* and *Nanning City Hostel* can also get them for you with no mark-up. **Buses** to Hanoi (8hr; ¥148), Haiphon (8hr; ¥158) and Yalong Bay (8hr; ¥168) depart several times daily from the **Nanning International Tourist Distribution Centre** (南宁国际旅游集散中心, *nánníng guójì lǚyóu jísàn zhōngxīn*) on You'an Nan Lu; you can also catch Hanoi buses from Langdong station. The direct **train to Hanoi** currently leaves at 6.45pm (12hr; sleeper ¥200–350); it stops for ages both sides of the border for passport checks and customs inspections. Finally, be **warned** that when crossing the border you should keep this book buried deep in your bags – customs officials have been confiscating them because the maps colour Taiwan in differently, which is taken to imply support for the island's separatist cause.

Minzu Dadao – a #6 bus will get you to Chaoyang Lu. Other arrival points include northeasterly **Jinqiao station** (金桥客运站, *jīnqiáo kèyùn zhàn*) on the #66 bus route to the train station; **Jiangnan station** (江南汽车站, *jiāngnán qìchēzhàn*), 7km south of Chaoyang Lu on the #31 bus; and the **Beida Transit Centre** (北大客运中心, *běidà kèyùn zhōngxīn*), 2km from the train station on the #31 bus route.

The **international airport** is 35km southwest of Nanning, with an **airport bus** (¥20) to the airlines office – taking a taxi costs around ¥100. In the city itself, a **taxi** costs ¥7 to hire.

Accommodation

There's plenty of good-value, central **accommodation** in Nanning for all budgets. Unusually for China, the train station area is by no means seedy or unpleasant.

Lotusland Hostel (荷逸居青年旅舍, *héyìjū qīngnián lǚshè*) 64 Shanghai Lu ⓣ0771/2432592, ⓔlotuslandhostel@163.com. Small grey-brick modern building hidden beside a tiny park; spotless inside, well-designed and furnished, and the manager can't do enough for you. Dorms ¥35, rooms ❷

Nanning (南宁饭店, *nánníng fàndiàn*) 38 Minsheng Lu ⓣ0771/2103888, ⓕ2103105. A very smart, upmarket business venue, right across from the city's newest shopping plaza. 8

Nanning City Hostel (南宁城市青年旅社, *nánníng chéngshì qīngnián lǚshè*) Apartment 1102, Building 12, Ou Jing Tingyuan 63-1, Minzu Dadao ⓣ15277717217, ⓦwww.nanningcityhostel.bravehost.com. Excellent-value dorms and doubles, plus large family rooms which come with balcony and spa bath. Located near the Provincial Museum, on #6 bus route between Langdong bus station and the train station – you'll need to download a map from their website to find it. Dorms ¥35, rooms 3

Wanxing Jiudian (万兴酒店, *wànxīng jiǔdiàn*) 47 Minzhu Lu ⓣ0771/2102888. Budget business hotel with two buildings, a block apart; the newer and far better wing is at this address. Smart, bright doubles 4

Yingbin (迎宾饭店, *yíngbīn fàndiàn*) 71Chaoyang Lu ⓣ0771/2116288. An unpretentious budget option close to the train station, taking up almost a whole block above fast-food canteens. Clean throughout, but some rooms are very basic – have a look at a few. 2

Yinhe (银河宾馆, *yínhé bīnguǎn*) 84–86 Chaoyang Lu ⓣ0771/2116688, ⓕ2420303. Two buildings 50m apart; the northernmost budget wing has spick-and-span dormitories and doubles, while the main hotel has more comfortable rooms with computers, though carpets are showing wear. Dorm beds ¥35, rooms 3

The City

To get the feel of Nanning's bustle, wander around the lanes west of Chaoyang Lu, crowded with fruit and hardware markets and warehouse-sized department stores packed to the rafters with clothes, fishing rods and coloured lighting. **Chaoyang Lu** itself is lined with modern shopping plazas; halfway along at the corner of

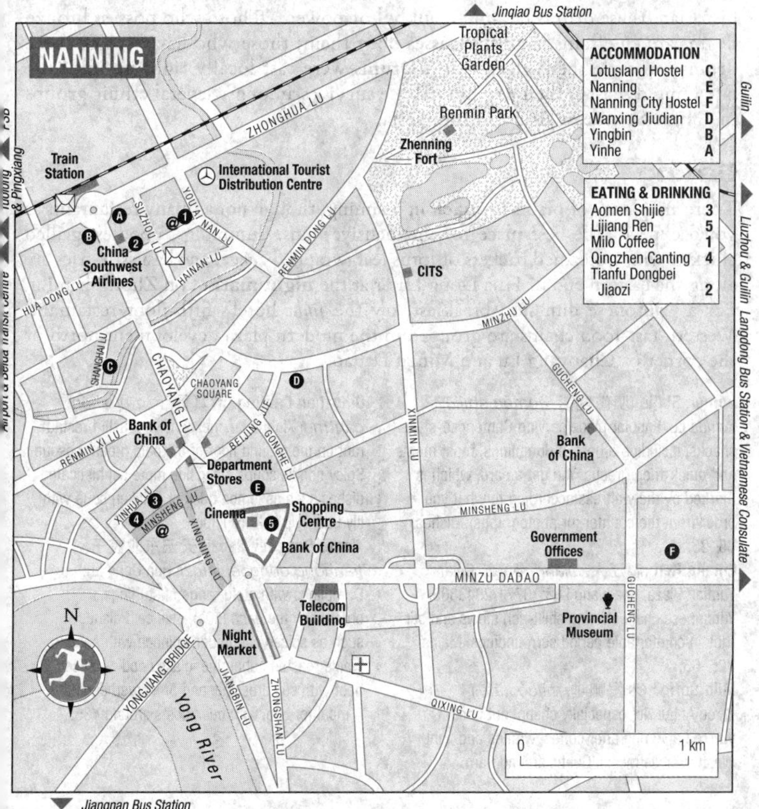

Renmin Dong Lu, **Chaoyang Square** (朝阳广场, *zhāoyáng guǎngchǎng*) is an area of tidy paving, park benches and shady trees, popular with early morning musicians, line dancers, and anyone after a breath of air. West from here and parallel with Chaoyang Lu, pedestrianized **Xingning Lu** and its offshoots sport the city's most attractive older facades, always near critical mass with shoppers orbiting between clothing stores.

For a bit of space head to **Renmin Park** (人民公园, *rénmín gōngyuán*) a couple of square kilometres of waters and woodland about a twenty-minute walk east of the train station on Renmin Dong Lu. On the western side, steps ascend to **Zhenning Fort** (古炮台, *gǔ pàotái*), a defensive structure built in 1917 to house a German naval cannon – a serious piece of firepower in such a commanding position, with clear views of the whole city.

The Provincial Museum

Nanning's well-presented **Provincial Museum** (省博物馆, *shěng bówùguǎn*; Tues–Sun 9am–5pm) on Gucheng Lu provides an insight into the **Baiyue culture**, which flourished in southern Guangxi from prehistoric times until the early Han dynasty; catch bus #6 from Chaoyang Lu. Aside from oddities like the neolithic "spades", found planted like rings of tombstones in several sites, the pick of the exhibits are **bronzes**: not just the usual bells, tripods and weapons, but also a wonderful duck-shaped lantern and several **storage drums** embossed with stylized images of rowers and birds. According to a Ming historian, these drums became a symbol of power: "Those who possess bronze drums are chieftains, and the masses obey them; those who have two or three drums can style themselves king". Drums were cast locally right up until the late Qing dynasty; their ceremonial use survives amongst several ethnic groups in China, Southeast Asia and Indonesia.

Eating

There are plenty of places to **snack** in Nanning, though not as many restaurants as you'd expect. The best place for inexpensive buns, dumplings, noodles, grilled chicken wings, steamed packets of lotus leaf-wrapped *zongzi* and basic stir-fries are along the eastern end of Hua Dong Lu or at the **night market** on Zhongshan Lu. For a Cantonese dim sum breakfast, try the *Jinhe* hotel's fifth-floor restaurant. Western fast-food chains are grouped in the modern plaza development north of the corner of Chaoyang Lu and Minzu Dadao.

Aomen Shijie (澳门食街, *àomén shíjiē*) Xinhua Lu. Popular place serving Cantonese-style snacks, including a host of dumplings, roast meats and quick-fried greens. You get a card, which is marked by the waitress according to what you order from the counter (or photographs). Dishes ¥5–25.

Lijiang Ren (漓江人, *líjiāng rén*) 2F Gelan Yuntian Plaza, Chaoyang Lu ⓣ0771/2843805. Yunnanese chain offering chilli-rich stews and stir-fries in comfortable period surroundings. Mains ¥25–65.

Milo Coffee (米罗咖啡, *mǐluó kāfēi*) 7 You Ai Lu. Not especially cheap, but good if you're hankering after coffee, waffles and light Western-style meals. Opens around 9am.

Qingzhen Canting (清真餐厅, *qīngzhēn cāntīng*) Xinhua Lu. Inexpensive Muslim restaurant on the ground floor of the pale green mosque. Spicy noodle soups alongside more sophisticated dishes such as lemon duck or chicken soup with lily buds. Up to ¥35/person.

Tianfu Dongbei Jiaozi (天宏东北饺子, *tiānhóng dōngběi jaǐozi*) Hua Dong Lu. Dumplings with a big range of stuffings, ordered by the *liang* (50g), plus cold dishes such as spiced cucumber, spinach with peanuts, whole roasted aubergine, glass noodles, sliced beef with soy dressing, and preserved eggs. A meal for two, with beer, costs around ¥35.

Listings

Banks and exchange The main Bank of China (foreign exchange Mon–Fri 8–11.30am & 2.30–5.30pm) is on Gucheng Lu, but there are smaller branches with ATMs all over town.
Hospital The City First Hospital (Shiyi Yiyuan) is southeast of the centre along Qixing Lu.
Internet There are net bars all over town charging ¥2/hr.
Mail The most central post office is on Suzhou Lu (daily 8am–7pm).
PSB The visa department (Mon–Thurs 9am–4.30pm, Fri 9am–noon; ⓣ0771/2891264 or 2891303) is 1.5km north of the train station, at 4 Xiuling Lu. Catch bus #14, #31, #71, #72, #84 or #85 and get off after the hospital.
Shopping Nanning is a great place to shop for clothes, either at the department stores full of good-quality, low-price attire along Chaoyang Lu or at the brand-label stores along Xingning Lu, such as Giordano, Baleno Meters/Bonwe and Yishion. The Nanning Antique Store, next to the Provincial Museum, has a touristy and expensive selection of teapots, chops, paintings and jade, set across two floors.

Detian and Leye

There are a couple of unusual natural attractions northwest of Nanning: **Detian Waterfall**, which actually straddles the **Vietnamese border**; and a mountainous area of giant sinkholes surrounding **Leye**. Both are accessible on public transport from Nanning, though you'll need an overnight trip or longer for either; Leye is perhaps best visited as a stop along the way into Yunnan.

Detian waterfall

Perched right on the Vietnamese border 150km from Nanning, **Detian waterfall** (德天瀑布, *détiān pùbù*) is worth the trip not just for the falls themselves – best in full flood during the summer rains – but also because it draws you into the Zhuang heartlands: a world of dark karst hills, grubby towns, water buffalo wallowing in green paddy fields, and Zhuang farmers in broad-sleeved pyjamas and conical hats.

During summer at least, there's one **direct bus daily** to Detian from Nanning's Langdong bus station at 8.30am (5hr; ¥50). Otherwise, catch a bus from the Beida Transit Centre to **Daxin** (大新, *dàxīn*; 3hr; ¥20), from where there are regular minibuses to **SHUOLONG** (硕龙, *shuòlóng*; 1hr; ¥8), a tiny marketplace and traffic nexus 15km short of the falls where you should be able to negotiate an onward ride. If you get stuck at Shuolong for the night, *Hongle Lüguan* (鸿乐旅馆, *hónglè lǚguǎn*; dorm beds ¥30, rooms ❶) at the marketplace is the best **place to stay**, with a couple of basic restaurants opposite.

The falls

Detian falls (¥80) form a delightful set of cataracts broader than their 30m height and framed by limestone peaks and fields. Paths lead down to the base past a series of pools and bamboo groves; at the bottom you can hire a **bamboo raft** and be punted over to straddle the mid-river borderline. The best part, however, is to follow the road along the top to its end in a field, where you'll find a **stone post** proclaiming the Sino-Vietnamese frontier in French and Chinese, along with a bizarre **border market** – a clutch of trestle tables laden with Vietnamese sweets, cigarettes and stamps in the middle of nowhere.

Accommodation options at the falls include *Detian Binguan* (德天 宾馆, *détiān bīnguǎn*; ⓣ0771/5595608), which offers clean, comfortable rooms (❸); and the upmarket ★ *Detian Shanzhuang Dajiudian* (德天山庄大酒店, *détiān shānzhuāng dàjiǔdiàn*; ⓣ0771/3773570; ❻), perched on a slope above the falls with stunning views across the river into Vietnam.

Leye

LEYE (乐业, *lèyè*) is a small town some 400km northwest of Nanning near the Guizhou border, set right on the edge of rugged landscape of huge **dolines**, or limestone sinkholes. The area is so remote that the largest of these, **Dashiwei Tiankeng**, was only explored for the first time during the 1980s. Tourism has barely started here, so if you like to explore away from the crowds, this is where to head.

Aim first for **BAISE** (百色, *bǎisè*), a large rail town 265km from Nanning on the Kunming line; there are nine trains a day (3hr; ¥45), or plenty of buses from Beida Transit Centre (3hr; ¥80). At Baise bus station – reached on bus #2 from the train station – pick up one of the regular buses to Leye (4hr; ¥30). The *Jindu Dajiudian* (金都大酒店, *jīndū dàjiǔdiàn*; ⓣ0776/2881180; ❸) at Baise bus station isn't in perfect condition, but makes a convenient place to stay.

Leye sits in a thin valley and comprises a 2km-long main street and a few adjacent lanes. The **new bus station** is right at the southern edge of town, from where you can catch a three-wheeler to the only **accommodation** accepting foreigners without a considerable struggle, the *Leye Fandian* (乐业饭店, *lèyè fàndiàn*; ⓣ0776/7928888; ❷). Stir-fry stalls around the central crossroads-cum-market offer the only cooked food in town, though there are a couple of small supermarkets. **Leaving**, buses return to Baise until 5.30pm.

Dashiwei Tiankeng

Dashiwei Tiankeng (大石围天坑, *dàshíwéi tiānkēng*; 8am–5pm; ¥70) is 15km west of Leye, reached by bus from Leye's old bus station (every other hour from 8am–4pm; ¥3). The bus winds up at the **park gates**, where you buy a ticket which includes a Chinese-speaking tour guide and transport around the park in an open-sided buggy. After stopping off at a few minor sinkholes you arrive at Dashiwei, which looks like – and probably is – a 1400m-high mountain which has collapsed in on itself, leaving a deep crater ringed by the jagged remnants of peaks. It takes a couple of hours to walk around the rim via interconnected stone staircases, with superlative views into the central sinkhole from the west ridge; sadly, you can't climb down inside. With some limestone caves thrown in on the return trip to the park gates, it's easy to spend four or five hours on site.

Nanning to Vietnam

The **Vietnamese border crossing** lies about 170km southwest of Nanning beyond the town of **Pingxiang**. Through trains and buses into Vietnam plough past without stopping, but a couple of offbeat attractions – namely rare monkeys at **Chongzuo Ecology Park** and **Hua Shan**'s prehistoric rock paintings – might tempt you to spend a couple of days in the region before crossing the border on foot. You can access the area by train or bus; see accounts for details.

Chongzuo Ecology Park

Chongzuo Ecology Park (崇左生态公园, *chóngzuǒ shēngtài gōngyuán*; ¥80), a small spread of limestone hills and flat valleys, was created to protect the endangered and endemic **white-headed langur** (白头叶猴, *baítóu yèhóu*) whose entire population numbers just 700 animals. The reserve is 15km southeast of **CHONGZUO** (崇左, *chóngzuǒ*), a small city around halfway down the rail line between Nanning and Pingxiang. It's easier, however, to get here **by bus** from Nanning's Jiangnan station (90min; ¥45) – ask the driver to drop you at the park gates. Alternatively, minibuses (¥5) run from Chongzuo's bus station past the park until late afternoon.

There are 250 monkeys in the reserve, and your chance of seeing some – albeit at a distance, as they spend much of their time bouncing around clifftops – is good. They form groups of around ten individuals, headed by a single adult male; the black-bodied adults have white heads and tail tips, and spend much of their time eating leaves (though they also like fruit and flowers). The babies, however, are golden all over, darkening during their first two years.

The park is fairly wild (cobras are common) and summers are exceedingly hot and wet. **Accommodation** is in the former army barracks (❸), and they provide ample Chinese meals at around ¥50 per person a day; there's also room to **camp**, if you have the gear, but pack a **torch** either way. Staff act as guides, with best viewing times at dawn and dusk.

Moving on, flag down a minibus from outside the park to Chongzuo, from where there are buses through the day back to Nanning, or on to Tuolong or Ningming (for Hua Shan), and Pingxiang.

Hua Shan and the Zuo River

Set in a beautifully isolated spot where tall karst peaks flank the **Zuo River** (左江, *zuŏjiāng*), waterfront cliffs at **Hua Shan** (花山, *huāshān*) are daubed with **rock art** associated with the prehistoric local culture. The access point is **TUOLONG** (驮龙, *tuólóng*), a single-street rail stop for the nearby town of **Ningming**: either catch the 7.40am Nanning–Pingxiang train (3hr; ¥26), or a bus from Nanning's Jiangnan station to Ningming, from where three-wheelers run 5km on to Tuolong (¥2).

Once at Tuolong, make your way to the **Tuolong Bridge Dock** (驮龙桥码头, *tuólóngqiáo mătóu*) – it's 200m from the train station – where you'll find sampan owners asking about ¥80 for the run upstream to Hua Shan; allow at least five hours for the return trip, including time to view the rock art. It's a placid journey up the Zuo, with buffalo wallowing in the shallows, people fishing from wooden rafts and tending family plots, and the banks thick with spindly-branched, red-flowering kapok trees. The boat docks just short of Hua Shan, where you pay the **entrance fee** (¥50) before walking along a track to the paintings. Nobody has worked out a definitive interpretation of the 1900 sharply posed figures, but they include drummers and dancers, dogs and cattle, a dragon-boat race, men with arms bent upwards, a "king" with a sword and just two women, long-haired and pregnant.

Heading on, there are two morning trains a day in each direction from Tuolong, so you'll probably need to catch a three-wheeler to **NINGMING** (宁明, *níngmíng*), a ghastly market town of cheap concrete construction drowned in exhaust fumes. Regular buses run from Ningming until around 4pm back to Nanning or on to Pingxiang – if you can't get out there are several cheap, nondescript places to stay around the bus station.

Pingxiang and the Friendship Pass

Surrounded by jutting karst hills, **PINGXIANG** (凭祥, *píngxiáng*) is a small trading town 15km from the Vietnamese border crossing. The **train station** lies about 3km outside town on the border road; the **bus station** is in the centre of town on the main street, Bei Da Lu. Gaggles of motor-rickshaws descend on new arrivals, the drivers engaging in Ben-Hur-like races down to the border – try for around ¥15.

You shouldn't really need to stay in Pingxiang, but almost every building within 100m of the bus station on Bei Da Lu offers **accommodation**: hostels ask ¥20–35 per person; while the *Jinxiangyu Dajiudian* (金祥玉大酒店, *jīnxiángyù dàjiŭdiàn*; ⓣ0771/8521303; ❷) is a typically clean, functional hotel. There's a huge produce **market** behind the bus station, a **Bank of China** on Bei Da Lu, and cheap places to eat everywhere. Heading **back to Nanning**, the train currently leaves at

3.20pm – stopping at Tuolong and Chongzuo – with buses running the same route between 7am and 7pm.

The **border crossing**, known here as **Friendship Pass** (友谊关, *yǒuyíguān*), is set in a natural gap through a series of steep cliffs; the Chinese side is marked by a French colonial Customs House built in 1914, a huge Chinese **gate tower** and a Ming-era defensive **stone wall**. Assuming you have a valid visa, entering Vietnam shouldn't be too complicated, though see the warning on p.33. The Vietnamese town on the far side is **Dong Dang**, where there's further transport 5km south to **Lang Son**, the railhead for Hanoi.

Beihai

BEIHAI (北海, *běihǎi*), a pleasant town on the Beibu Gulf, is Guangxi's sole seaport. A bland four-hour train ride southeast from Nanning, you're heading here either to catch the **ferry to Hainan Island**, or to sprawl on nearby **beaches** – though be warned that they're not all the Chinese tourist industry makes them out to be.

Arrival

Beihai's mesh of streets focuses on **Beibuwan Guangchang** (北部湾广场, *běibùwān guǎngchǎng*), a broad, paved public square at the intersection of Beibuwan Lu and Sichuan Lu. The **train station** is 3km southeast on the #2 bus route. **Buses** pull in either just east of the square at the **Transit Centre** (客运中心, *kèyùn zhōngxīn*), or 1km further east down Beibuwan Lu on the #3 bus route at the **bus station** (汽车总站, *qìchēzǒngzhàn*). **Hainan ferries** dock at **Beihai International Port** (北海国际客运港, *běihǎi guójì kèyùngǎng*), some 4km south of the square on Sichuan Lu; again, catch bus #3 to the town centre. **Taxis** cost ¥7 flagfall.

Accommodation

For **accommodation**, there's the quiet *Jinlong Binguan* (金龙宾馆, *jīnlóng bīnguǎn*; ⓣ0779/2211777; ❷), diagonally across from the Transit Centre at 40 Beibuwan Zhong Lu; the *Laolian Binguan* (劳联宾馆, *láolián bīnguǎn*; ⓣ0779/3080088; ❷), right next to the Transit Centre at 31 Beibuwan Zhong Lu, which offers spacious, clean rooms; and the smarter *Overseas Chinese Hotel* (北海华侨宾馆, *běihǎi huáqiáo bīnguǎn*; ⓣ0779/3081588; ❹), just south of the square at 55 Sichuan Nan Lu.

The Town

If you have some time to fill, head up to **Zhuhai Lu Lao Jie** (珠海路老街, *zhūhǎilù lǎojiē*), a pedestrianized "old street" north of the centre off Sichuan Lu, lined with mouldering colonial-era shop-houses whose deep colonnades provide shade and shelter from heavy tropical downpours. There are a few restaurants, bars and old shops, as well as some historic buildings, picked out by explanatory

Moving on from Beihai

Leaving Beihai, Hainan **ferries** depart at 1pm and 7pm (10hr; seats ¥120; basic private cabins ¥360/person); all toilets are shared, and hot water urns and a snack shop are the only sources of refreshment. There are also daily trains to **Nanning** (4hr; ¥38), and **buses** as far afield as Guilin, Nanning and Guangzhou.

plaques. Continue north up Sichuan Lu from here and you cross a bridge over **Waisha harbour**, packed with scores of wooden-hulled junks, to **Waisha Seafood Island** (外沙海鲜岛, *wàishā hǎixiān dǎo*), a good place to eat fresh grilled seafood in the evening.

Beihai's main stretch of sand is **Yin Tan** (银滩, *yín tān*), or Silver Beach, 6km south of the city centre down Sichuan Lu on the #3 bus route. Cross the bridge opposite the bus terminus and you're underneath coconut palms and within reach of sand, sea, showers and stalls offering trinkets and barbecued fish. It's all very clean, tidy and organized, but not desparately exciting, and the lack of decent accommodation in the area is a seriously missed opportunity.

Eating and drinking

For **food**, try the **night market snack stalls** east of Beibuwan Guangchang along Changqing Lu; and *Jinma Shicheng* (金马市城, *jīnmǎ shìchéng*), serving light meals from all over the country, in the basement of the He'an Shopping Centre between the Transit Centre and Beibuwan Guangchang. For Western **pub food** and ice-cold beer, head to *Tommy's Place* (汤米西餐厅, *tāngmǐ xīcàntīng*; ⓣ0779/2087020, ⓦwww.tommysplace.org), inside a blue-and-white building up at Waisha Seafood Island; a cab here from the centre should only cost the hire.

Guizhou

A traditional saying describes **Guizhou** (贵州, *guìzhōu*) as a land where there are "no three days without rain, no three hectares without a mountain, and no three coins in any pocket". This is pretty accurate: Guizhou records the highest rainfall in China and has a poverty ensured by more than eighty percent of its land being covered in untillable mountains or leached limestone soils. Chinese influence was established here around 100 BC, but it wasn't until the government began settling Han migrants in the province during the seventeenth century that the local **ethnic groups** began to fight back, resistance culminating in the **Miao Uprising** of 1854–73, which rivalled the contemporary Taiping insurrection in terms of chaos and bloodshed. Sixty years later the region still hadn't recovered: Red Army soldiers passing through Guizhou in the 1930s found people working naked in the fields and an economy based on opium, and it's only in the last decade that Guizhou's population has exceeded numbers prior to the uprising.

Still, ethnic identity and romantic landscapes have become marketable commodities in China, and Guizhou is beginning to capitalize on its two major assets. The province's most visible minority groups are the many branches of **Miao**, concentrated in the southeast around **Kaili**; and the **Bouyei**, who are based around the provincial capital, **Guiyang**, and the westerly town of **Anshun**. The Miao in particular indulge in a huge number of **festivals**, some of which attract tens of thousands of participants and are worth any effort to experience. As for **scenery**, there are spectacular **limestone caverns** at **Longgong** and **Zhijin**, both accessed from Anshun; impressive **waterfalls** at **Huangguoshu** – again near Anshun; and everywhere terraced hills, dotted with small villages. Naturalists will also want to clock up rare **black-necked cranes**, which winter along the northwestern border with Yunnan at **Caohai Lake**; and at least have a stab at seeing the reclusive **golden monkey**, which lives in the cloud forests atop Guizhou's single holy mountain, northeasterly **Fanjing Shan**.

While Guizhou's often shambolic towns are definitely not a high point of a trip to the region, Guiyang is comfortable enough, and conveniently central to the province. A couple of other places worth a visit in their own right are the historic northern city of **Zunyi**, which is steeped in Long March lore; and **Zhenyuan**, over on the eastern side of the province, which features some antique buildings squeezed along a beautiful stretch of river. Expect to spend more than usual on **accommodation**; there are still widespread restrictions on where foreigners are allowed to stay in Guizhou, sometimes limiting options to only one hotel per town.

Guiyang and around

GUIYANG (*guìyáng*) lies in a valley basin, encircled by a range of hills that hems in the city and concentrates its traffic pollution. Established as a capital during the Ming dynasty, modern Guiyang is a patchwork of elderly apartment blocks rubbing shoulders with glossy new high-rises and department stores, all intercut by a web of wide roads and flyovers. The effect may be downmarket and provincial – compounded by the cheap market stalls clogging the main streets every evening – but Guiyang is a friendly place, whose unexpected few antique buildings and a surprisingly wild park lend a bit of character. There's enough in here to fill a day in transit, and it's worth making an easy side-trip to the ancient garrison town of **Qingyan**.

Arrival and city transport

Central Guiyang comprises a concentrated couple of square kilometres around the narrow **Nanming River**, with the downtown area focused along Zhonghua Lu, which runs south through the centre into Zunyi Lu, crosses the river and continues for another kilometre before terminating at the **train station**. In the large square outside you'll find **taxis** (¥10), and a **city bus terminus** ahead to the east: #1,

Moving on from Guiyang

The main airlines office (☎0851/5977777) and separate China Southern (☎0851/5828429, ⓦwww.csair.com) are near each other on Zunyi Lu (both daily 8.30am–5.30pm). The **airport bus** leaves the main airlines office every thirty minutes between 8.30am and 7pm and costs ¥10.

Guiyang's **Jinyang bus station**, handling departures to everywhere outside the province and cities within, is 15km west of the city – catch bus #219 from outside the train station to get here. The **Tiyuguan bus station**, down near the train station on Jiefang Lu, has frequent, fast departures to Kaili, Zunyi and Anshun from dawn to dusk. Outside on Zunyi Lu, early-morning minibuses congregate offering **day-tours** of Longgong Caves and Huangguoshu waterfall.

Trains head east into central China and beyond via Kaili, Zhenyuan and Yuping (the jump-off point for Fanjing Shan); north to Zunyi and Chongqing; west to Kunming via Anshun and Liupanshui; and south into Guangxi. Buying tickets at the station is pretty easy, but you can also get them for a ¥5 mark-up at the **advance-purchase offices** (8.30am–noon & 1–4pm) outside the station and downtown on Fushui Lu; see the map opposite for locations.

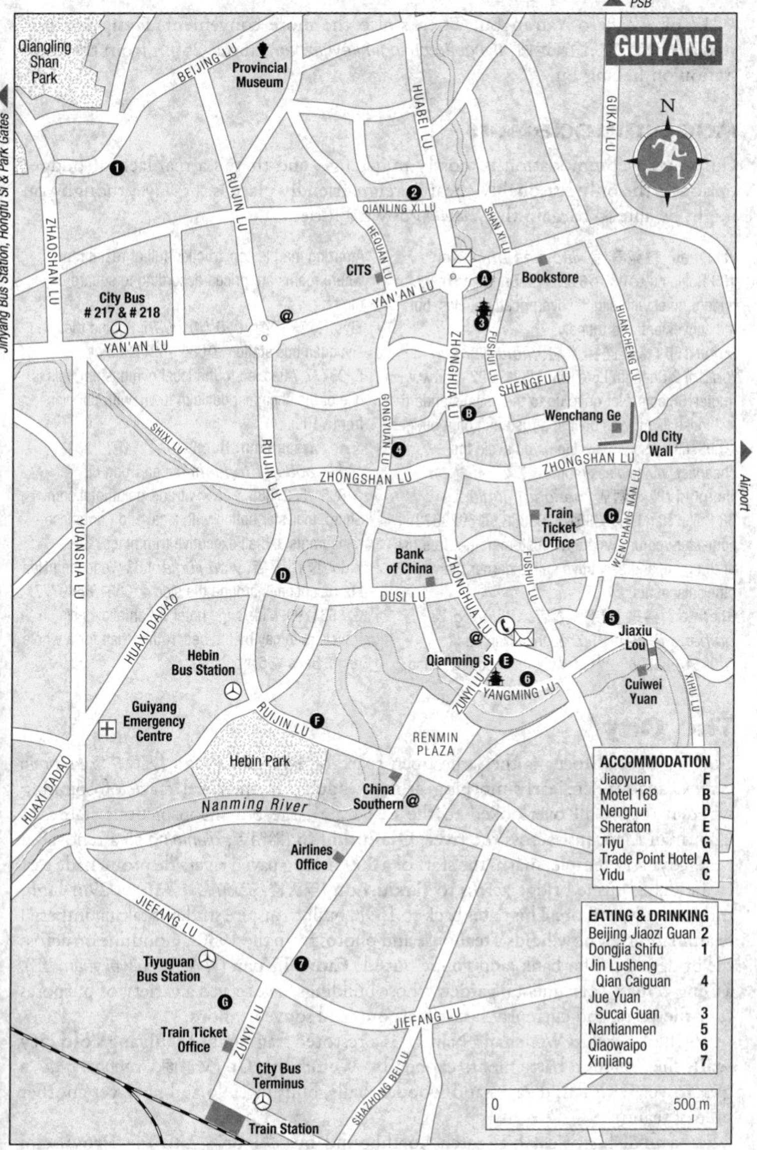

which goes along Zunyi Lu and Zhonghua Lu, turning west along Beijing Lu and back to the train station down Ruijin Lu; and bus #2, which does the same route in reverse, are the two best routes for getting you close to the hotels.

Guiyang's **airport** lies 15km east of town; it's ¥10 on the airport bus (every 30min) or a ¥60 for a taxi to the centre. Arriving by bus, you're most likely to end up at **Jinyang bus station** (金阳客车站, *jīnyáng kèchēzhàn*), a colossal new depot about 15km west of the city; from here, catch bus #219 to the train station or

#217 or #218 to Yan'an Lu. There's also the more convenient **Tiyuguan bus station** (体育馆长途客运站, *tǐyùguǎn chángtú kèyùnzhàn*), about 250m from the train station on Jiefang Lu.

Accommodation

Guiyang's accommodation is mostly mid-range, and there's a real lack of budget options – the only reasonably cheap foreign-friendly place is the *Tiyu*, though you might be able to bargain the *Jiaoyuan* down a little.

Jiaoyuan (教苑宾馆, *jiàoyuàn bīnguǎn*) 130 Ruijin Lu ⓣ0851/8129519. Bright, ordinary budget hotel with slightly overpriced doubles, but it's convenient and friendly. ❸

Motel 168 (莫泰连锁旅店, *mòtài liánsuǒ lǚdiàn*) 2 Shengfu Lu ⓣ0851/8217692, ⓦwww.motel168.com. Not quite up to the usual standard – it looks like it was built in a rush and on a budget – but still reasonable value if you avoid the cheapest, windowless rooms. ❹

Nenghui (能辉酒店, *nénghuī jiǔdiàn*) 38 Ruijin Nan Lu ⓣ0851/5898888, ⓕ6928622. Four-star venture where all customers get free use of the gym, and executive suites garner many other discounts. ❼

Sheraton (喜来登贵航酒店, *xǐláidēng guìháng jiǔdiàn*) 49 Zhonghua Nan Lu ⓣ0851/5888280, ⓦwww.sheraton.com/guiyang. Amazing marble construction full of restaurants, where rooms are priced according to square metreage. ❾

Tiyu (体育宾馆, *tǐyù bīnguǎn*) Behind the Tiyuguan bus station ⓣ0851/8277808 or 5798777. Attached to the local gymnasium, this is one of the cheapest deals in town, with doubles from ¥100. ❷

Trade Point Hotel (柏顿宾馆, *bódùn bīnguǎn*) Yan'an Dong Lu ⓣ0851/5827888, ⓦwww.trade-pointhotel.com. Sharp, four-star option with local and Cantonese restaurants and all executive trimmings. ❽

Yidu (逸都酒店, *yìdū jiǔdiàn*) 63 Wenchang Nan Lu; reception is around the side ⓣ0851/8649777, ⓕ8631799. Mid-range hotel which allows single travellers to pay by the bed, rather than for a whole room. Beds ¥65, doubles ❹

The City

Guiyang's social focus is the large open space of **Renmin Plaza** (人民广场, *rénmín guǎngchǎng*), where early-morning crowds indulge in the local craze of spinning wooden tops – all overlooked to the east by a large but inconspicuous statue of Chairman Mao. Just across the river, **Qianming Si** (黔明寺, *qiánmíng sì*) a renovated Ming-dynasty temple, marks the start of a 500m-long paved riverside promenade east to an arched stone bridge across to **Jiaxiu Lou** (甲秀楼, *jiǎxiù lóu*; ¥10), a 29m-high, three-storey pavilion. This dates back to 1598, built to inspire students taking imperial examinations; it now holds a teahouse and photos from the 1930s. Continue on across the bridge to the far bank, and you're outside **Cuiwei Yuan** (粹惟园, *cuìwéi yuán*; ¥2), a Qing-dynasty ornamental garden whose buildings have served a variety of purposes over the years, and currently house tearooms and souvenir shops.

North of here up Wenchang Nan Lu is a restored fragment of Guiyang's **old city wall**, the 7m-high battlements capped by **Wenchang Ge** (文昌阁, *wénchāng gé*) a gate tower with flared eaves and wooden halls, built in 1596 and now yet another breezy teahouse.

For a final historical hit, catch northbound bus #1 or #2 to the **Provincial Museum** (省博物馆, *shěng bówùguǎn*; Tues–Sun 9am–5pm), housed inside a grand 1950s building at 168 Beijing Lu; the entrance is on the left-hand side. The collection covers the entire province, and includes glazed Ming-dynasty tomb figurines from Zunyi, costumes and festival photos of Guizhou's many ethnic groups, ground opera masks from Anshun and a third-life-sized Han-dynasty bronze horse and carriage. Downstairs, the opposite wing of the building houses an antique-style **teahouse theatre**, showcasing Miao, Dong and Tujia song and dance routines nightly (8–9.30pm; ¥180).

Qianling Shan Park and Hongfu Si

About 1km west of the Provincial Museum, **Qianling Shan Park** (黔灵山公园, *qiánlíng shān gōngyuán*; ¥4) is a pleasant handful of hills right on the edge of town, thickly forested enough to harbour some colourful birdlife and noisy groups of monkeys. There's a series of ponds, bridges and ornamental undergrowth inside the entrance, but the highlight is **Hongfu Si** (弘福寺, *hóngfú sì*), an important Buddhist monastery up above – follow steps from the gates for thirty minutes to the top. You exit the woods into a courtyard containing the ornamental, 4m-high **Fahua Pagoda** and a screen showing Buddha being washed at birth by nine dragons. On the right is a **bell tower** with a five-hundred-year-old bell, while bearing left brings you to a new luohan hall inhabited by 500 glossy, chunky statues of Buddhist saints. The temple's main hall houses a 32-armed Guanyin, each palm displaying an eye, facing a rather benevolent-looking King of Hell.

Eating

With its predilection for dog meat (see below), chillies and sour soups, Guizhou's cuisine comes under the western Chinese cooking umbrella, though there's a wide variety of food available in town. Snack stalls are scattered through the centre; the block on Fushui Lu north of Zhongshan Lu has several long-established, inexpensive **duck canteens**, serving it crisp-fried in the local style. One local speciality is thin **crêpes** – called *siwawa*, or "silk dolls" (丝娃娃, *sīwáwa*) – which you fill from a selection of pickled and fresh vegetables to resemble an uncooked spring roll. The best places to try them lie just outside Qiangling Shan Park. **Hotpots** are a Guizhou institution offered everywhere, with tables centred round a bubbling pot of slightly sour, spicy stock, in which you cook your own food. **Dog** is eaten right across Guizhou, usually stir-fried with noodles, soya-braised or part of a hotpot. For **Western food**, there are dozens of **cafés** serving coffee and set meals of steak or burgers, and the *Trade Point Hotel* does a great buffet breakfast (7–10.30am; ¥81/person).

Beijing Jiaozi Guan (北京饺子馆, *běijīng jiǎoziguǎn*) Qianling Xi Lu. *Jiaozi* with a bewildering array of stuffings – coriander with pork and tofu with egg are good – along with side dishes such as marinated spare ribs, garlic cucumber and preserved eggs. You can bloat yourself for ¥20.

Dongjia Shifu (侗家食府, *dóngjiā shífǔ*) 242 Beijing Lu ⓣ0851/6507186. Dong minority theme restaurant with staff dressed in colourful garb. Though realistically the menu shouldn't stretch far beyond dog hotpot, noodles and sour soup, there's a good range of meat, fish and vegetable dishes – and a good deal of offal – and the place has some character. About ¥40/person for two.

Jin Lusheng Qian Caiguan (金芦笙黔菜馆, *jīn lúshēng qián càiguǎn*) 18 Gongyuan Lu ⓣ0851/5821388. Another ethnic theme restaurant, this time Miao. Downstairs is an inexpensive canteen with mostly noodle soups; head upstairs for more formal settings and a proper menu with pricey mains around ¥45.

Jue Yuan Sucai Guan (觉园素菜馆, *juéyuán sùcàiguǎn*) 51 Fushui Bei Lu. Downtown vegetarian restaurant attached to a small Buddhist temple. Along with fairly

Canine cuisine

Dog meat is widely appreciated not only in Guizhou, Guangxi and Guangdong, but also in culturally connected countries such as Indonesia, the Philippines and Vietnam. The meat is considered to be warming in cold weather and an aid to male virility. Chinese tourists to Guizhou generally make a point of trying a dog dish, but for Westerners, eating dog can be a touchy subject. Some find it almost akin to cannibalism, while others are discouraged by the way restaurants display bisected hindquarters in the window, or soaking in a bucket of water on the floor. If you're worried about being served dog by accident, 我不吃狗肉, *wǒ bùchī gǒuròu,* means "I don't eat dog".

inexpensive stir-fries, they also do elegant "Lion's Head" stewed rissoles, "Eight Treasure Duck" (stuffed with sweet beanpaste and sticky rice), "Lotus Fish" and Guizhou-style chicken – despite the names, all are made from meat substitutes. Photo menu and large portions. Dishes ¥20–65.

Nantianmen Chongqing Huoguo (南天门重庆火锅, *nántiānmén chóngqìng huǒguō*) Corner of Xihu Lu and Wenchang Nan Lu. Very popular, cavernous Sichuanese-style hotpot restaurant, with set selections starting at ¥35.

Qiaowaipo (巧外婆, *qiǎowàipó*) 6 Yangming Lu. Guizhou country cooking – lots of chillies, sour soups and pork stews – nicely served in a smart, modern establishment with views of the river. ¥45/person for two.

Xinjiang (新疆维吾尔天山餐厅, *xīnjiāng wéiwú'ěr tiānshān cāntīng*) Zunyi Lu, set back off the street north of Jiefang Lu. Lively, slightly seedy place offering Muslim grills, stews, noodles and breads from just a few yuan up to around ¥35 for *dapan ji*, a huge plate of spicy chicken.

Listings

Banks and exchange The main Bank of China (Mon–Fri 9–11.30am & 1.30–5pm) with an ATM is just west of Zhonghua Lu on Dusi Lu. There are other branches with ATMs at the eastern end of Yan'an Lu, and opposite the airline offices on Zunyi Lu.

Bookshops The Foreign Language Bookshop, on Yan'an Lu, is well stocked with classics, an eclectic range of children's books, maps of the city and province, and Chinese guidebooks on Guizhou.

Internet Two convenient places charging ¥2/hr are on Yan'an Lu, just east of Ruijin Lu; and opposite China Southern on Zunyi Lu.

Mail The main post office (daily 9am–6pm) is on the Huabei Lu/Yan'an Lu intersection.

PSB The visa department is at 5 Da Ying Rd (Mon–Fri 9am–noon & 1.30–5pm ⓣ0851/6797907).

Travel agents CITS (ⓣ0851/6901575, ⓕ6901660) are on 7F, Longquan Dasha, 1 Hequan Lu, near the corner with Yan'an Lu. The 25-storey yellow tower is easy to find, but the entrance is not, especially as there is no CITS sign outside – you have to cut around from Hequan Lu to a lift lobby at the back. Once there, you'll find the helpful staff speak English, French and German, and are a mine of information about the province. Ask for Jessica Xiao or Arnaud Xie.

Qingyan

The remains of a Ming-dynasty fortified town 30km south of Guiyang at **QINGYAN** (青岩, *qīngyán*) makes for an interesting few hours' excursion. Start by catching bus #201 from the **Hebin bus station** (河滨客运站, *hébīn kèyùnzhàn*) on Ruijin Lu to **Huaxi** (花溪, *huāxī*; 40min; ¥3); at Huaxi, cross the road and pick up a minibus to Qingyan (20min; ¥4).

On arrival, don't despair at the shabby main-road junction where the bus pulls up, but head west through the market into the **old town** (古镇, *gǔzhèn*), which was founded in 1373 as a military outpost during the first major Han incursions into the region. The best area is at the southern end, where a flagstoned street lined with low wooden shops leads to the **Baisui memorial arch** (百岁坊, *bǎisuì fāng*), decorated with crouching lions, and out through the town wall into the fields via the solid stone **south gate**. There are plenty of places to **snack** as you wander – deep-fried balls of tofu are a local speciality – and even an atmospheric **hotel**, the *Guzhen Kezhan* (ⓣ0851/3200031; ④), housed in an old guildhall next to the market. Transport connections back to Guiyang run until late afternoon.

Zunyi and the north

Northern Guizhou's mountainous reaches are famous for *baijiu* **distilleries**, with two interesting stops on the way up to Sichuan or Chongqing: the city of **Zunyi**, pivotal to modern Chinese history; and a wonderful spread of bamboo forests, waterfalls and red sandstone formations at **Chishui**. Zunyi is on the main road and rail routes, while Chishui lies off the beaten track, right up along the Sichuanese border in the northwestern corner of the province.

Zunyi

Some 170km north of Guiyang, **ZUNYI** (遵义, *zūnyì*) is surrounded by heavy industry, but the city centre contains a pleasant older quarter and hilly parkland. It was here that the Communist army arrived on their **Long March** in January 1935, in disarray after months on the run and having suffered two defeats in their attempts to join up with sympathetic forces in Hunan. Having captured the city by surprise, the leadership convened the **Zunyi Conference**, at which Mao Zedong supplanted Russian Comintern advisors as political head of the Communist Party. The Russians had modelled their strategies on urban-based uprisings, but Mao felt that China's revolution could only succeed by mobilizing the peasantry, and that the Communist forces should base themselves in the countryside to do this. His opinions carried the day, marking the Communists' first step towards Beijing. (For more on the Long March, see p.472.)

Arrival and orientation

Zunyi is awkwardly laid out around triangular **Fenghuang Shan** (凤凰山, *fènghuáng shān*): east of this hill, the **bus and train stations** are within 100m of each other in a grimy area on **Beijing Lu**; while the old town and revolutionary sites are 3km away via high street **Zhonghua Lu** on Fenghuang Shan's southwestern slopes.

Accommodation and eating

There's inexpensive **accommodation** up near the stations, which are surrounded by basic hostels (dorm beds ¥35) whose staff pounce on foreigners seen in the area. The bus station's own *Keyunzhan Binguan* (客运站宾馆, *kèyùnzhàn bīnguǎn*; ⓣ0852/8460000; ❶) isn't much more expensive, though its location makes it noisy; between the stations, the *Zunyi Tongda Dajiudian* (遵义通达大酒店, *zūnyì tōngdá dàjiǔdiàn*; ⓣ0852/3191188; ❷) combats this problem with some serious double-glazing, while *7 Days Inn* (7天连锁酒店, *qītiān laínsuǒ jiǔdiàn*; ⓣ0852/8702888; ❸), 250m away at 36 Beijing Lu, offers reliable, if ordinary, comforts. The station area has abundant places to get a bowl of noodles or plate of dumplings.

Revolutionary sites

The **Zunyi Conference Site** (遵义会议址, *zūnyì huìyìzhǐ*; daily 8.30am–5.30pm; free but passport required) sits southeast of Fenghuang Shan on bus routes #1, #3 or #4 from the train station via Beijing Lu. It occupies a block of the **old town** and adjacent lanes, with several 1930s grey-brick buildings restored and turned into museums. These include the grand **Zunyi Conference Museum** (遵义会议博物馆, *zūnyì huìyì bówùguǎn*) on Ziyin Lu, stocked with old photos, maps, heroic sculptures and a few period weapons captioned in Chinese; and the **Site of the Red Army Political Department** (红军总政治部旧址, *hóngjūn zǒngzhèngzhì bùjiùzhǐ*) in the grounds of a French Catholic Church behind, built in 1866 in an interesting compromise between Chinese and European Gothic styles. Strangely, the original Conference Hall is not even signposted – it's the locked, two-storey

Moving on from Zunyi

There are **buses** to Guiyang between 7am and 7pm (2hr 30min; ¥59); three morning buses to Chishui (¥60; 6hr) and trains through the day to Guiyang and Chongqing.

brick building on the right as you enter the Zunyi Conference Museum grounds. Just up the lane from here, 500m-long **Hongjun Jie** (红军街, *hóngjūn jīe*) has been turned into the inevitable pedestrianized "old street", full of souvenirs and local snack stalls.

North to Chishui and Sichuan

The rail line runs north of Zunyi to Chongqing, but there's also a 350km-long road northeast into Sichuan via Guizhou's second most impressive waterfalls at **Chishui**. Along the way, **Maotai town** (茅台, *máotái*) is the source of China's favourite brand of *baijiu* spirits, whose distinctive red-striped white porcelain bottle lurks on supermarket shelves and banquet tables between Guangzhou and Lhasa, though most Westerners find it a pretty rough tipple.

Chishui

CHISHUI (赤水, *chìshuǐ*) is a small riverside town on the Sichuanese border, among a forested spread of red sandstone formations: *chishui* means "red water" and during the summer rains the river runs a vivid ochre colour. The **forests** comprise verdant pockets of bamboos, 3m-high *spinulosa* tree ferns, gingers, orchids and moss-covered rocks, with the most accessible section 14km from town at **Sidong Gou** (四洞沟, *sìdòng gōu*). Minibuses (¥5) run through the day from Renmin Lu to the **park gates** (¥50), from where 6km of flagstoned paths follow either side of a small, bright-red river, up through thick bamboo forests past three big **waterfalls** – including one split by a large boulder – and several water curtains to walk behind, to the trail's end at 30m-high **Bailong Falls** (白龙瀑布, *báilóng pùbù*). The biggest waterfall, however, is 40km due south of Chishui where the Fengxi River steps out 72m at **Shizhang-dong Falls** (十丈洞瀑布, *shízhàngdòng pùbù*); buses run in summer, otherwise you'll need to hire a minibus for about ¥300.

Chishui is just 1km broad, with no real centre; the **bus station** is on Renmin Lu, which runs downhill for 700m to the river. Along the way there are damp and cheap rooms at the *Chishui Dajiudian* (赤水大酒店, *chìshuǐ dàjiǔdiàn*; Ⓣ0852/2821334; ❷), or damp and pricey ones east at 22 Nanzhen Jie at the *Zhongyue Dajiudian* (中悦大酒店, *zhōngyuè dàjiǔdiàn*; Ⓣ0852/2823888; ❹). Stalls and cheap diners down along the river wall are the best places to **eat**.

Leaving, three buses run daily to Zunyi (6hr) and one direct to Guiyang (9hr); if you're heading north into Sichuan, cross the river to tiny **Jiuzhi** (九支, *jiǔzhī*) and pick up one of the frequent minibuses to Luzhou (3hr; ¥20), from where you can head on to Yibin (see p.775).

Southeastern Guizhou

Southeastern Guizhou – known locally as **Qiandongnan** – forms a landscape of high hills cut by rivers and dotted with dark wooden houses with buffaloes plodding around rice terraces. Women working in the fields have babies strapped to their backs under brightly quilted pads, and their long braided hair is coiled into buns secured by silver hairpins and fluorescent plastic combs. They are **Miao**, and Qiandongnan is one of the best places in China to meet ethnic peoples on their own terms. Miao villages around the district capital, **Kaili**, are noted for their exuberant **festivals**, which though increasingly touristed have managed to retain their cultural integrity. Beyond Kaili, there's a scenic route southeast to the mountainous border with Guangxi province, where **Dong** hamlets sport their unique drum towers and bridges (see p.651); northeast lies the unusually attractive town of **Zhenyuan** and a tough ascent into **Fanjing Shan's** cloud forests. Kaili is connected by good road and rail links to Guiyang and neighbouring Hunan, with buses and minibuses providing regular services elsewhere.

Kaili

KAILI (凯里, *kǎilǐ*), 170km east of Guiyang, is a moderately industrialized, easy-going focus for China's 7.5 million **Miao ethnic minority**, though the town is more a service centre than a sight in its own right. The most interesting **market area** is along the eastern end of Ximen Jie, a narrow street packed with village-like stalls selling vegetables, trinkets, meat and even livestock. Dage Xiang heads uphill from here to **Dage Park** (大阁公园, *dàgé gōngyuán*), a wooded hilltop area with a granite **pagoda** where old men gather to smoke and decorate the trees with their caged songbirds. The town's only other diversion is the **museum** (¥10) at the far end of Zhaoshan Lu, two dusty floors of bright festival garments and silver jewellery, with more of the same on sale in the downstairs atrium.

Arrival and information

Kaili is oriented around the Beijing Lu–Zhaoshan Lu crossroads, known as **Dashizi** (大十子, *dàshízì*). The **train station** is 3km to the north, where taxis and buses #1 and #2 meet arrivals, while the **long-distance bus station** (长途客运站, *chángtú kèyùnzhàn*) is central on Wenhua Bei Lu.

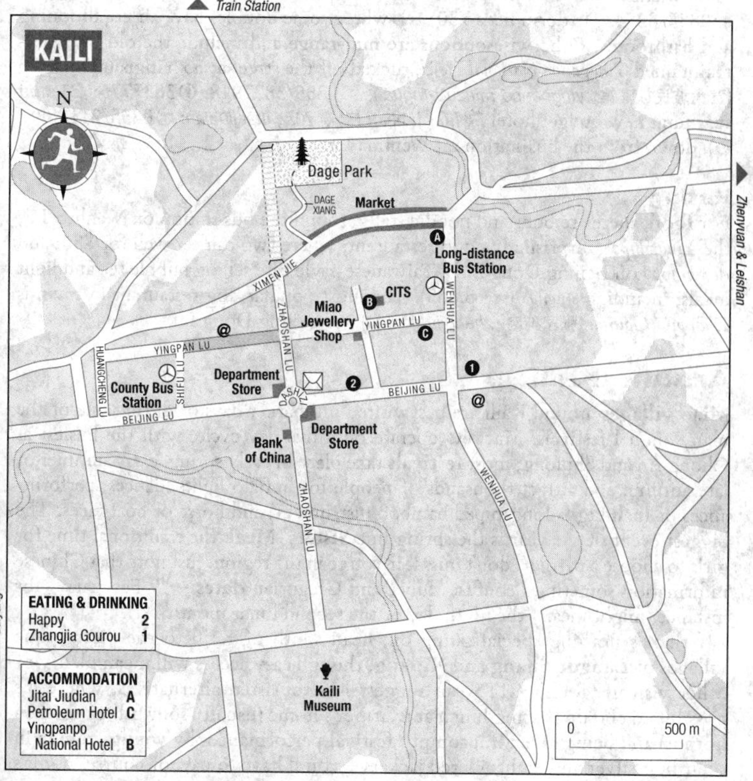

Moving on from Kaili

Kaili's main **bus station** has frequent departures through the day to Guiyang (¥55), Taijiang (¥15) and Rongjiang (¥65), with at least half a dozen each to Xijiang (¥15), Shidong (¥20), Huangping (¥17), Congjiang (¥90) and Zhenyuan (¥32). There are also a few daily to Zunyi and Anshun. The small **county bus station**, west across town on Shifu Lu, handles regular shuttles to Chong An (¥12) and Huangping (¥17), as well as a few buses to Guiyang. **Trains** run at intervals through the day to Guiyang (bus is quicker), and northeast to Zhenyuan, Yuping (for Fanjing Shan) and into Hunan.

For **information** about village festivals and market days, useful bilingual maps of Kaili and its environs, and to arrange guides, Kaili's **CITS** (Mon–Sat 8.30am–6pm; ⓣ0855/3818111, ⓦwww.toguizhou.com) are just left inside the gates at the *Yingpanpo Binguan* – manager and guide Wu Zeng Ou (ⓣ13985804487, ⓔzengouwu@hotmail.com, ⓦwww.crt118.com) knows the area backwards.

The main **Bank of China** and ATM is on Zhaoshan Lu (foreign exchange Mon–Fri 8.30–11am & 2–5pm) – the last branch until you reach Guilin in Guangxi province, if you're heading that way – and the **post office** is right on Dashizi.

Accommodation

The cheapest foreigner-friendly **accommodation** is near the bus station at the under-maintained *Petroleum Hotel* on Yingpan Lu (石油宾馆, *shíyóu bīnguǎn*; ⓣ0855/8234331; dorm beds ¥30; ❷), where some doubles have air conditioning and bathrooms. Otherwise options are mid-range and include the old but well-maintained *Yingpanpo National Hotel*, tucked off the street at 53 Yingpan Dong Lu (营盘坡民族宾馆, *yíngpánpō mínzú bīnguǎn;* ⓣ0855/3837918, ⓕ3837776; ❸), and sparkling new budget hotel *Jitai Jiudian* (吉泰酒店, *jítài jiǔdiàn*; ⓣ0855/2118888; ❸), down from the bus station on Wenhua Lu.

Eating

For **food**, there are buns and noodle stalls around the bus station on Wenhua Lu; the *Yingpanpo*'s surprisingly good restaurant, where two can eat well for ¥80; and the *Happy* on Beijing Dong Lu, a Taiwanese-style café selling bubble tea and light meals, including *siwawa* (see p.665). The most popular dog restaurant in town is *Zhangjia Gourou* (张家狗肉, *zhāngjiā gǒuròu*), on Beijing Dong Lu.

Around Kaili

Miao villages around Kaili are best visited on market days or during one of the many annual festivals. **Markets** operate on a five-day cycle, with the busiest at Chong An and Shidong; most **festivals** take place in early spring, early summer or late autumn and attract thousands of people for buffalo fights, dances, performances of **lusheng** (a long-piped bamboo instrument) and horse or boat races. The biggest event of the year is the springtime **Sisters' Meal**, the traditional time for girls to choose a partner: don't miss it if you're in the region. Just note that Chinese information sometimes confuses lunar and Gregorian **dates** – "9 February", for instance, might mean "the ninth day of the second lunar month".

If there's nothing special going on, head south of Kaili to the picturesque villages of **Langde Shang** and **Xijiang**, though easy access will mean plenty of other visitors. Kaili's CITS can suggest less touristed alternatives, where it's possible to end up sharing lunch at a farmer's home (usually sour fish or chicken hotpot) and being given impromptu festival performances by young women in their best silver and embroidered jackets – you'll have to pay, of course, but it's

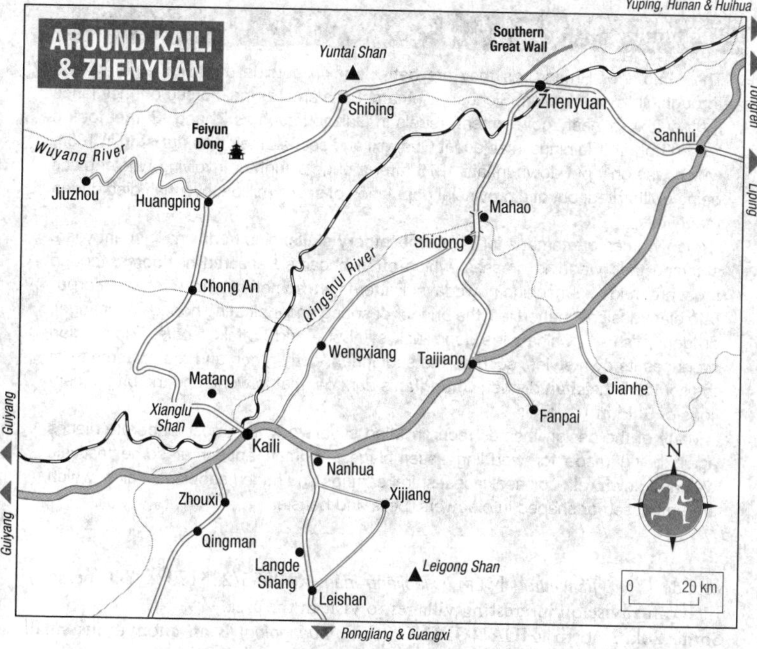

worth the price if you miss the real thing. Beware the hospitable Miao custom of encouraging guests to induldge in their very drinkable but potent **sticky rice wine**.

All the villages below are connected by at least daily bus services from Kaili, and also make possible stopovers on the way out of the region. Return transport can leave quite early, however, so be prepared to stay the night or hitch back if you leave things too late. There are **no banks** in any of the villages.

Matang, Chong An and Jiuzhou

Some interesting places **northwest of Kaili** can be tied together into a long day trip, or used as a stage in a roundabout journey to Zhenyuan (see p.673). **Buses** from either of Kaili's bus stations to Chong An (1hr 30min; ¥12) or Huangping (2hr; ¥17) can drop you off along the way.

First stop is **MATANG** (麻塘, *mátáng*), a village about 20km west of Kaili inhabited by **Geyi**, a group who, despite similarities with the Miao, insist on their individuality. Buses drop you off by a pink gateway on the main road, from where it's a twenty-minute walk to the village, an attractive place with many wooden buildings. Big groups get a welcome dance and there are always people selling embroideries and **batik**, a Geyi speciality.

Back on the main road, flag down northbound buses for the next 15km to **CHONG AN** (重安, *chóng ān*), a dishevelled riverside town with a few old wood-and-stone buildings and a superb **market** held every fifth day, where you'll be battered by diminutive Miao grandmothers as they shop or bring in clothes (everything from traditional pleated skirts to jeans) for dyeing in boiling vats of indigo. Two places offer very basic **accommodation**, both along Nan Jie, the old Kaili road: *Wenling Kezhan* (文灵客栈, *wénlíng kèzhàn*; ⓣ15085263831; ❷), in an old courtyard building down a side lane – look for a wooden gatetower; or the

The Miao

The **Miao** – or Hmong, as they are better known outside of China – are spread through Guizhou, Yunnan, Sichuan, Vietnam, Laos and Burma. Forced off their lands by the Qing-dynasty government, rebels in Guizhou such as **Zhang Xiumei** took a lesson from the Taipings in adjacent Guangxi and seeded their own **uprising** in 1854, which was only put down in late 1873 after a huge slaughter involving whole towns being obliterated; out of a provincial population of seven million, over half died during the revolt.

Miao women are famous for their **embroidery skills**: girls traditionally spent years stitching their wedding dresses, which often became treasured heirlooms, though most are made by machine nowadays. Patterns are sometimes abstract, or incorporate plant designs, butterflies (the bringer of spring and indicating hoped-for change), dragons, fish – a China-wide good luck symbol – and buffalo motifs. Each region produces its own styles, such as the sequinned, curly green and red patterns from the southerly **Leishan** district, **Chong'an**'s dark geometric work, and the bright, fiery lions of **Shidong**.

Many of the design themes recur in Miao **silverwork**, the most elaborate pieces again being made for wedding assemblages. Women appear at some festivals weighed down with coil necklaces, spiral earrings and huge headpieces, all of which are embossed or shaped into flowers, bells and beasts.

riverside *Xiao Jiangnan* (小江南, *xiǎojiāng nán*; ⓣ0855/2351208; ¥40/person), which can advise on interesting villages to visit in the area.

Some 20km north, **HUANGPING** (黄平, *huángpíng*) is an anonymous small town, from where frequent **minibuses to Jiuzhou** (40min; ¥5) depart from behind the main street fuel station. High up in the hills, **JIUZHOU** (旧洲, *jiùzhōu*) is a surprise: a substantial market town whose main street is lined with old buildings, some dating back three hundred years. Remains of a southern-style **Tianhou Temple** (天后宫, *tiānhòu gōng*), a European **Catholic Church** and a merchants' **guildhall** all point to a formerly cosmopolitan population, unexpected given the remote location. There's another big **market** here every four days; check dates with Kaili's CITS.

Back in Huangping, buses return to Kaili through the day; alternatively, you can head northeast of Huangping to **Shibing** (施秉, *shībǐng*; 1hr; ¥10) and then pick up buses **for Zhenyuan** (1hr; ¥15) until late afternoon.

Langde Shang and Xijiang

Langde Shang and Xijiang are two attractive Miao villages south of Kaili; both get busloads of day-trippers whipping through and you'll get a much better feel for the places once things have calmed down after 4pm or so.

For **LANGDE SHANG** (郎德上, *lángdé shàng*) catch one of the many **Leishan-bound** buses from Kaili's long-distance station and ask the driver to put you off at the right place (1hr; ¥10.5). Langde was a rebel base during the Miao Uprising and is still a tremendously photogenic collection of wooden houses, cobbles, fields and chickens set on a terraced hillside capped in pine trees, a twenty-minute walk from the main road. Plenty of silverwork is thrust at you as you wander, but get past this and the atmosphere is pretty genuine – locals might offer homestay accommodation for the night.

XIJIANG (西江, *xījiāng*) is an incredible collection of closely packed wooden houses built on river stone foundations, all ranged up the side of two adjacent hills about 90km southeast of Kaili. There are direct buses from Kaili (1hr 30min; ¥15); from Langde (or Rongjiang; see below), head for Leishan and pick up a bus from there. On arrival at Xijiang you pay the entry fee (¥60), and then you're free to wander the narrow, stepped, lanes through the village and onto the terraced fields above, where you could hike around for hours – views are tremendous. Xijiang has two basic **guesthouses** (❶) – the one above the post office, near where the buses pull up, is best – and a couple of early-closing shops selling rice noodles (boiled or fried). On market days, you can get transport back to Kaili or Leishan until dark; at other times, don't leave it this late, and confirm supposed departure times with bus drivers.

About 20km south of Langde and 35km southwest of Xijiang, **Leishan** (雷山, *léishān*) is a staging post for buses heading south over twisting mountain roads to **Rongjiang**, Guangxi and the fringes of the **Dong** regions. For more about the Dong, their architecture, and details of the trip.

Taijiang and Shidong

About 40km northeast of Kaili, **TAIJIANG** (台江, *táijiāng*) is a large, drab town where the first day of the annual **Sisters' Meal Festival** in Spring concludes with a riotous **dragon-lantern battle**. At other times skip it instead for market day at **SHIDONG** (施洞, *shīdòng*), a single-street market town on the banks of the **Qingshui River**, 60km northeast from Kaili along a different road (2hr 30min; ¥20). The market takes place out on the shingle, where jostling farmers sort though the selection of livestock, clothing, foodstuffs and modern silverwork and textiles. Shidong also hosts the second and third days of Sisters' Meal, featuring bullfights (head-to-head combat between rival buffaloes), dragon-boat races, communal dancing and mass consumption of rice wine. Shidong's only **accommodation** is at the very down-to-earth *Yingbin Zhaodaisuo* (迎宾招待所, *yíngbīn zhāodàisuǒ*; ⓣ0855/5359174; ❶) and *Luoping Zhaodaisuo* (罗萍招待所, *luópíng zhāodàisuǒ*; ⓣ0855/5359008; ❶), either side of the post office.

Leaving Shidong, there's fairly frequent transport back to Kaili until mid-afternoon on market days; **for Zhenyuan** (1hr; ¥12) you need to walk 1km north of town to the **vehicle bridge** over the river, where Kaili–Zhenyuan buses pass by between about 10am and 6pm.

Zhenyuan

ZHENYUAN (镇远, *zhènyuan*) was founded two thousand years ago, though today's town – occupying a straight, constricted valley 100km northeast of Kaili on the aquamarine **Wuyang River** – sprang up in the Ming dynasty to guard the trade route through to central China. The river runs westwards, with Zhenyuan's tall, antique-style houses piled together along both banks. The **train and bus stations** are next to each other about 3km west of town on the south side of the river – a taxi to the old town is ¥4.

Accommodation and eating

The **old town** (see below) has the pick of the **accommodation**: about 100m up Fuxing Xiang on the way to the Southern Great Wall, ★ *Quanjia Dayuan Kezhan* (全家大院客栈, *quánjiā dàyuàn kèzhàn*; ⓣ0855/5723999 or 15185636961; ❸) is a converted courtyard mansion, whose modern rooms an en suite and air

Moving on from Zhenyuan

There are half a dozen **buses** a day back southwest via Shidong to Kaili, and also east to Yuping (for Fanjing Shan) and **Tongren** (铜仁, *tóngrén*) for connections to Fenghuang in Hunan. **Trains** also run via Yuping to **Huaihua** (怀化, *huáihuà*) in Hunan, at the intersection of the Zhangjiajie–Sanjiang line.

condition; while on the main street, *Yongfurong Kezhan* (永福荣客栈, *yǒngfúróng kèzhàn*; ⓣ0855/5730888, ⓦwww.yongfurong.net; ❸) has river views and sits over a popular restaurant. For **cheaper rooms**, try the *Minju Binguan* (民居宾馆, *mínjū bīnguǎn*; ⓣ0855/5725488; ❷) near the *Yongfurong*, whose small, tidy, riverview doubles would be better without the attached karaoke bar; and *Xindaqiao Binguan* (新大桥宾馆, *xīn dàqiáo bīnguǎn*; ⓣ0855/3878777; ❷), by the new bridge.

The old town is lined with attractive **restaurants**, though food isn't memorable; in summer, it's more fun to head over the new bridge to the opposite bank and enjoy simple hotpots at alfresco tables with the rest of town.

The Town

On the north side of the river, **Tianhou Gong** (天后宫, *tiānhòu gōng*; ¥2) is a four-hundred-year-old complex at the west end of town founded by merchants from Guangdong or Fujian, with a balcony overhanging the street. Continuing east, you pass the **new bridge** (新大桥, *xīn dàqiáo*) and enter Zhenyuan's **old town** (古城, *gǔ chéng*), a kilometre of wood and stone buildings in the Qing style, backed up against stony cliffs.

In the old town main street, look for **Fuxing Xiang** (复兴巷, *fùxīng xiàng*), an alley marked by a small ornamental gateway, and follow it up through back lanes to where steps ascend in thirty minutes, via forest and a small temple, to a fragment of the thirteenth-century **Southern Great Wall** (南长城, *nán chángchéng*; ¥30). The wall, which runs eastwards to Fenghuang in Hunan (see p.458), is almost totally demolished, standing only 3m at its highest point, but there are superb views northeast into Hunan from the ridge.

Back in the old town, continue east down the main street and you'll reach a multiple-arch, solid stone **Ming-dynasty bridge** (祝圣桥, *zhùshèng qiáo*) over the river to sixteenth-century **Qinglong Dong** (青龙洞, *qīnglóng dòng*; 7.30am–6pm; ¥30), whose separate Taoist, Buddhist and Confucian halls appear to grow out of a cliff face, all dripping wet and hung with vines.

Fanjing Shan

Hidden away in Guizhou's remote northeastern corner, not far from the borders with Hunan, **Fanjing Shan** (梵净山, *fánjìng shān*) is covered in wild cloud forests inhabited by the engangered **golden monkeys** (金丝猴, *jīnsī hóu*), though with the entire population numbering only 400 adults, you'll be lucky to see them. This is not an easy trip: the mountain is sometimes isolated by landslides, and if you do make it through you'll find the ascent to the 2500m summit involves more than seven thousand stairs, which follow steep ridges with no regard for gradient. Take a torch and something warm for the top – it snows in winter – but don't bring up more than a day-pack.

The mountain is best reached via **Yuping** (玉屏, *yùpíng*), a stop on the Kaili–Zhenyuan–Hunan rail line where you'll find **buses** through the day to **Jiangkou** (江口, *jiāngkǒu*; 2hr). Here you change again for further frequent departures (1hr) to the park gates at **HEIWAN** (黑湾, *hēiwān*), a strangely despondent collection of food stalls and shops selling ponchos and walking sticks (both a good idea). Pay the **park entry fee** (¥50) and register at the **police station** here, then catch a minibus (¥40) for the 9km run to the start of Fanjing Shan's **steps**, which are numbered with red paint and carved inscriptions. Food and drink shacks provide sustenance until step 4500 and then there's nothing until the top. The forest – hung with vines and old man's beard and with a dwarf bamboo understorey – is vibrantly green and stiflingly humid in summer; allow five hours to reach the summit area, where **basic beds** (¥25) can be had at a concrete blockhouse just on the edge of the forest, or in a wooden bunkhouse attached to **Zhenguo Si** (镇国寺, *zhènguó sì*), a tiny, barely functional temple 100m further up in the open. Both provide cooked **meals**.

Give yourself a day to explore the summit area along the flagstoned **paths**, through a mix of open heath, woodland, rhododendron thickets and strangely piled rock formations such as **Mogu Shi** (蘑菇石, *mógū shí*), or "Mushroom Rocks".

Western Guizhou

Extending for 350km between Guiyang and the border with Yunnan province, **Western Guizhou** is a desperately poor region of beautiful mountainous country and depressingly functional mining towns. **Anshun** is a transit hub for visiting **Bouyei villages**, the tourist magnets of **Longgong Caves** and **Huangguoshu Falls** and the remoter, more spectacular **Zhijin Caves**.

All routes west from Anshun ultimately lead to Yunnan's capital, Kunming (see p.684), whether you travel by bus along one of the three highways or – more comfortably – take the train. The only place worth a special stopover along the way is the northwesterly wildfowl sanctuary of **Caohai** – being poled around this shallow lake on a sunny day is one of Guizhou's highlights. Transport is straightforward, though note that the west has **no banks** capable of changing travellers' cheques.

Anshun

Some 100km west of Guiyang, **ANSHUN** (安顺, *ānshùn*) was established as a garrisoned outpost in Ming times to keep an eye on the empire's unruly fringes. Today it's a healthy but rough-around-the-edges market town, whose modern facade vanishes the moment you leave the main roads and find yourself among muddy alleys running between tumbledown shacks and wobbly wooden houses.

The central crossroads is overlooked to the northwest by a hillock topped by **Bai Ta** (白塔, *báitǎ*) a short Ming-dynasty pagoda, with a park around the base containing some representative, restored antique buildings, including a long stone **church** with a Chinese-style bell tower. The other point of interest is **Wenhua Miao** (文化庙, *wénhuà miào*; ¥10), a Ming Confucian hall hidden away in the northeastern backstreets that, while somewhat neglected, has some superbly carved dragon pillars, which rival those at Qufu's Confucius Mansion (p.312).

Arrival and information

Anshun centres on **Xin Dashizi** (新大十子, *xīn dàshízì*), the large crossroads below Bai Ta; the **post office** and a **Bank of China** with an ATM are here too.

The **main bus station** (客车南站, *kèchē nánzhàn*), about 500m south of here on Zhonghua Nan Lu, handles traffic to Guiyang, Zhenning, Huangguoshu and Kunming; 200m west of Xin Dashizi on Ta Shan Xi Lu, the small **west bus station** (客车西站, *kèchē xīzhàn*) has further, frequent departures to Zhenning, Tianlong, Guiyang, Huangguoshu and Longgong. Finally, **Beimen bus station** (for Zhijin; 北门客车站, *běimén kèchēzhàn*) is a kilometre north of Xin Dashizi on Zhonghua Bei Lu. The **train station** (for everywhere between Guiyang and Kunming) is 1km south of town at the end of Zhonghua Nan Lu; catch **bus** #1 or #2 past the main bus station to Xin Dashizi and the west bus station.

Accommodation

Accommodation options for foreigners are limited. The cheapest place likely to take you is the *Tielu Jiudian* (铁路酒店, *tiělù jiǔdiàn*; ⓣ0853/3290555; ❷), immediately left out of the train station; otherwise there's the overpriced *Ruofei Binguan* (若飞宾馆, *ruòfēi bīnguǎn*; ⓣ0853/3520228; ❸), up from the main bus station at 43 Zhonghua Nan Lu; and the elderly and undistinguished *Xixiushan Binguan* (西秀山宾馆, *xīxiùshān bīnguǎn*; ⓣ0853/2211888; ❸), opposite at 63 Zhonghua Nan Lu.

Eating

There's inexpensive **food** at *Lanzhou Niurou Lamian* (兰州牛肉拉面, *lánzhōu niúròu lāmiàn*), a small Muslim place just north from the main bus station with a photo-menu on the wall and filling portions of spicy noodle and rice dishes; alternatively, the *Xixiushan Binguan* has a good **restaurant**, while *Gourou Wang* (狗肉王, *gǒuròu wáng*; ⓣ0853/3358991), 100m north of Xin Dashizi at 5 Ruofei Nan Lu, is where to try dog.

Around Anshun

The limestone countryside **around Anshun** is homeland to China's 2.5 million **Bouyei**, whose villages are built of split stone and roofed in large, irregularly laid slate tiles. Bouyei specialities include blue-and-white **batik work** and **ground opera** (地戏, *dìxì*) in which performers wear brightly painted wooden masks; though native to the region and overlaid with animistic rituals, the current forms are said to have been imported along with Han troops in the Ming dynasty, and are based on Chinese tales such as *The Three Kingdoms*. The Spring Festival period is a good time to see a performance, held in many **villages** around Anshun, including **Shitou Zhai** and **Tianlong**.

The area's key draws, however, are **Longgong Caves** and **Huangguoshu Falls**, which can be fitted into a day-trip from either here or Guiyang. The caves are flooded and romantically require boats for some of the route, but Huangguoshu – while impressive on a good day – doesn't quite live up to its reputation. Finally, the trip north to the splendid **Zhijin Caves** requires an overnight stop, though it's well worth the effort.

Tianlong

Some 30km east of Anshun off the Guiyang highway, **TIANLONG** (天龙屯, *tiānlóng tún*; ¥30) is an old stone settlement founded as a garrison town in the Ming dynasty whose inhabitants, though dressing in embroidered blue smocks like Bouyei, insist they are in fact descendents of the original Han settlers. Tour groups come for the ground opera shows at the **Dixi Performance Hall** (地戏堂, *dìxì táng*); otherwise a couple of twisting stone alleys and a nineteenth-century **church-school** built by French priests will keep you busy for an hour or so. Also worth a look is hilltop **Wulong Si** (伍龙寺, *wǔlóng sì*; ¥15), a fortress-like temple 3km east atop sheer-sided **Tiantai Shan** (天台山, *tiāntái shān*). This was founded by the traitorous Ming general **Wu Sangui**, who let the Qing armies through the Great Wall in 1644.

Buses to Tianlong theoretically depart Anshun's main bus station (30min; ¥8), but you almost always get left on the roadside well short of your destination – waiting minibuses charge ¥5. Heading on is no problem, however, with minibuses back to Anshun and east to **Pingba** (平坝, *píngbà*), for Guiyang traffic, until late afternoon.

Shitou Zhai

Six-hundred-year-old **SHITOU ZHAI** (石头寨, *shítóu zhài*) lies 30km southwest from Anshun off the Huangguoshu road; tell the driver, and Huangguoshu buses from the west station (40min; ¥8) will drop you at the junction, leaving a 2km walk along a quiet road to the **village gates** (¥40). Shitou Zhai comprises forty or so stone houses grouped around a rocky hillock, all surrounded by vegetable plots. You'll be offered batik jackets, and might witness the whole process, from drawing the designs in wax, to dyeing in indigo and boiling the wax away to leave a white pattern. You could also walk out to similar surrounding villages, none of which charges admission. To return, walk back to the main road and flag down buses to Huangguoshu, Anshun or **Zhenning** (镇宁, *zhènníng*).

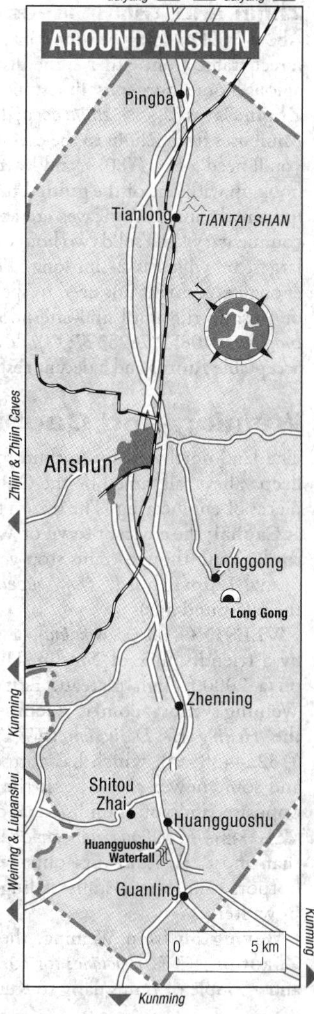

Longgong Caves

Longgong Caves (龙宫洞, *lónggōng dòng*) lie 28km from Anshun's west bus station (1hr; ¥5–10); you could be dropped at either **entrance** (¥120), which are about 5km apart.

From the nearer, western gate, you begin by being ferried down a river between willows and bamboo to a small knot of houses; walk through the arch, bear left, and it's 250m up some steps to **Guanyin Dong** (观音洞, *guānyīn dòng*), a broad cave filled with Buddhist statues. A seemingly minor path continues around the entrance but this is the one you want: it leads through a short cavern lit by coloured lights, then out around a hillside to **Jiujiu Tun** – site of an old guard post – and **Yulong Dong** (玉龙洞, *yùlóng dòng*), a large and spectacular cave system through which a guide will lead you (for free). Out the other side, a small river enters **Long Gong** (Dragon's Palace) itself, a two-stage boat ride through tall, flooded caverns picked out with florid lighting, exiting the caves into a broad pool at Longgong's eastern entrance.

Transport runs until late afternoon from the car park below to Huangguoshu and, less frequently, back to Anshun.

Huangguoshu Falls

Huangguoshu Falls (黄果树瀑布, *huángguǒshù pùbù*) lie 64km from Anshun's west or main bus stations (¥12), and about 30km from Longgong, along the Anshun–Yunnan highway. You get dropped off at little Huangguoshu township and walk down to the **entrance** (¥180); at 68m this may not quite rank as China's highest cataract, but in full flood it's the loudest, the thunder rolling way off into the distance. A staircase descends past plagues of souvenir stalls to the blue-green river below the falls; the most imposing view of Huangguoshu is off to the left where the full weight of its 81m span drops into the **Rhino Pool** – prepare yourself for a good soaking from the spray.

Moving on, buses return to Anshun and Guiyang through the day; if you're Yunnan-bound, first catch a minibus 7km west to the small town of **Guanling** (关岭, *guānlǐng*) and look for connections there.

Zhijin and Zhijin Caves

About 100km from Anshun (3hr) or 150km from Guiyang (4hr 30min) – there's direct traffic from either – the dismal country town of **ZHIJIN** (织金, *zhījīn*) sits among some gorgeous limestone pinnacles, beneath which are the astounding **Zhijin Caves** (织金洞, *zhījīn dòng*; daily 9am–5pm; ¥120), which lie 25km northeast. Minibuses from Zhijin to the caves (40min; ¥5) depart when full – if they don't fill, you'll need a taxi (¥80) – and leave you at the **visitors' centre** where you have to hook up with one of the **guided tours** that run whenever they have ten people. The immensely impressive caves are absolutely worth the money; tours with Chinese commentary last a solid two hours and wind through untold numbers of caverns, the largest of which is 240m long, 170m wide and 60m high. If you get here early enough you might not need to spend the night in Zhijin, as buses back to Guiyang or Anshun run until mid-afternoon; failing this, the *Jinye Binguan* (金叶宾馆, *jīnyè bīnguǎn*; ⓣ0857/7625327; ❷), downhill from the bus station near the market, has acceptable **rooms** and a decent **restaurant**.

Weining and Caohai

The land northwest of Anshun forms a tumultuous barrier of jagged peaks and deep valleys, all tamed by the Guiyang–Kunming road and rail line, both masterpieces of engineering. The reason to head up this way is to catch wintering birdlife at **Caohai**; the adjacent town of **Weining** can be reached directly from Anshun by road or rail (though trains stop very late in the day), but otherwise head first for dismal **Liupanshui** (六盘水, *liùpánshuǐ*) and pick up a minibus to Weining from there (around 3hr).

WEINING (威宁, *wēiníng*), a small, run-down shell of a place populated by a friendly mix of Muslim Hui, Yi and Dahua Miao, sits above the clouds on a 2000m-high plateau. Exit the bus station, turn right, and you'll find Weining's most comfy **accommodation** 100m beyond the crossroads at the *Heijing He Dajiudian* (黑颈鹤大酒店, *hēijǐnghè dàjiǔdiàn*; ⓣ0857/6229306, ⓕ6224438; ❸), which has a mix of older doubles with or without bathroom and some newer rooms; exit the station, turn left for 50m, and take the street opposite, and you'll find several cheaper options, such as *Juhongxuan Zhaodaisuo* (聚弘轩招待所, *jùhóngxuān zhāodàisuǒ*; ⓣ0857/6223480; ❶), which is cleaner than most. **Restaurants** outside the *Heijing He* do inexpensive stir-fries and hotpots, and street-stalls selling chilli-dusted potato kebabs are everywhere in winter.

Moving on from Weining, there are buses to Liupanshui, Anshun, Guiyang, **Zhaotong** (昭通, *zhāotōng*; for connections to Xichang in Sichuan) and Kunming; and a couple of trains daily to Kunming, Anshun and Guiyang.

Caohai

Immediately south of Weining – it's a ¥1.5 motor-rickshaw ride or a thirty-minute walk – **Caohai** (草海, *cǎohǎi*) the "Grass Lake", fills about a 5km-broad shallow basin, the core of a regional **nature reserve**. Wintering wildfowl shelter here in huge numbers, including 400 rare **black-necked cranes** (黑颈鹤, *hēijǐng hè*). Walk down to the lake and you'll be approached by touts wanting to take you out on a **boat trip**: you pay about ¥60 for a three-hour tour, being poled around in a four-person punt. The Chinese head first for a meal at the hamlet of **Longjia** (龙家, *lóngjiā*) on the far shore, famed for its food. On a sunny day, Caohai's overall tranquillity is a complete break with daily life in China; wintering cranes often hang out in the shallows near the shore and are not too hard to catch on camera.

Travel details

Trains

Anshun to: Guiyang (21 daily; 1hr 30min); Kunming (13 daily; 10hr); Liupanshui/Shuicheng (21 daily; 2hr).
Beihai to: Nanning (2 daily; 3hr 30min).
Guilin to: Beijing (4 daily; 28hr); Changsha (9 daily; 9hr); Guangzhou (2 daily; 11hr); Guiyang (1 daily; 12hr); Kunming (3 daily; 18hr); Nanning (16 daily; 6hr); Shanghai (4 daily; 24hr); Shenzhen (1 daily; 13hr).
Guiyang to: Anshun (21 daily; 1hr 30min); Beijing (4 daily; 30hr); Changsha (5 daily; 14hr); Chengdu (7 daily; 11–22hr); Chongqing (10 daily; 8–11hr); Guangzhou (5 daily; 21hr); Guilin (1 daily; 15hr); Huaihua (23 daily; 7hr); Kaili (23 daily; 3hr); Kunming (13 daily; 10–15hr); Liupanshui/Shuicheng (21 daily; 4hr); Shanghai (5 daily; 30hr); Yuping (23 daily; 6hr); Zhenyuan (17 daily; 5hr); Zunyi (16 daily; 3hr).
Kaili to: Changsha (5 daily; 10hr); Guiyang (23 daily; 3hr); Huaihua (23 daily; 4hr); Yuping (23 daily; 2hr 30min); Zhenyuan (17 daily; 1hr 30min).
Liupanshui to: Anshun (21 daily; 2hr); Guiyang (21 daily; 4hr); Kunming (17 daily; 8hr).
Nanning to: Beihai (2 daily; 3hr 20min); Beijing (2 daily; 28hr); Chengdu (daily; 32hr); Chongzuo (3 daily; 1hr 30min–3hr); Guangzhou (5 daily; 14hr); Guilin (16 daily; 6hr); Hanoi (1 daily; 12hr); Kunming (7 daily; 13hr); Pingxiang (3 daily; 3hr 30min–6hr); Tuolong/Ningming (2 daily; 3hr–4hr 30min).
Pingxiang to: Chongzuo (3 daily; 1hr 30min–2hr 30min); Nanning (2 daily; 3hr–4hr 30min); Tuolong/Ningming (2 daily; 45min).
Zhenyuan to: Guiyang (17 daily; 5hr); Huaihua (15 daily; 2hr 30min); Kaili (17 daily; 1hr 30min); Yuping (17 daily; 1hr).
Zunyi to: Chongqing (11 daily; 7hr); Guiyang (16 daily; 3hr).

Buses

Anshun to: Guiyang (2hr); Huangguoshu (1hr); Liupanshui (3hr); Longgong (1hr).
Beihai to: Nanning (3hr 30min); Shenzhen (10hr).
Congjiang to: Kaili (5hr); Rongjiang (2hr 30min); Zhaoxing (5hr).
Guilin to: Guangzhou (12hr); Hengyang (12hr); Longsheng (2hr); Nanning (6hr); Sanjiang (4hr); Yangshuo (1hr 15min).
Guiyang to: Anshun (2hr); Huangguoshu (3hr); Kaili (3hr); Kunming (19hr); Nanning (18hr); Rongjiang (8hr); Zunyi (2hr 30min).
Kaili to: Guiyang (2hr 30min); Rongjiang (5hr); Zhenyuan (4hr).
Liupanshui to: Anshun (3hr); Guiyang (4hr); Weining (3hr).
Nanning to: Beihai (3hr 30min); Chongzuo (1hr 30min); Guangzhou (18hr); Guilin (6hr); Ningming (4hr); Pingxiang (5hr); Yangshuo (6hr).
Pingxiang to: Chongzuo (5hr); Nanning (5hr); Ningming (1hr).
Sanjiang to: Chengyang (40min); Guilin (4hr); Longsheng (2hr); Zhaoxing (4hr).
Weining to: Anshun (5hr); Guiyang (7hr); Liupanshui (3hr).
Yangshuo to: Guilin (1hr 30min); Nanning (6hr).
Zhaoxing to: Congjiang (2hr); Rongjiang (5hr); Sanjiang (4hr).
Zunyi to: Chishui (6hr); Guiyang (2hr 30min).

Ferries

Beihai to: Haikou (2 daily; 10hr).

Flights

In addition to the domestic flights listed, there are international flights out of Guilin to Korea and Malaysia, and from Nanning to Vietnam.
Guilin to: Beijing (5 daily; 2hr 15min); Chengdu (2 daily; 1hr 20min); Guangzhou (8 daily; 50min); Guiyang (1 daily; 45min); Hong Kong (3 daily; 1hr); Kunming (2 daily; 1hr 20min); Shanghai (5 daily; 2hr); Shenzhen (4 daily; 1hr); Xi'an (6 daily; 1hr 30min).
Guiyang to: Beijing (8 daily; 2hr 30min); Chengdu (5 daily; 1hr); Guangzhou (4 daily; 1hr 30min); Guilin (1 daily; 50min); Kunming (3 daily; 55min); Nanning (2 daily; 1hr); Shanghai (8 daily; 2hr); Shenzhen (5 daily; 1hr 30min).
Nanning to: Beijing (6 daily; 3hr); Chengdu (3 daily; 1hr 30min); Chongqing (3 daily; 1hr 20min); Guangzhou (6 daily; 55min); Guiyang (2 daily; 1hr); Hanoi (4 weekly; 50min); Hong Kong (1 daily; 1hr); Kunming (2 daily; 1hr); Shanghai (6 daily; 2hr 15min); Shenzhen (6 daily; 55min); Xi'an (2 daily; 2hr).

CHAPTER 11

Highlights

* **Kunming's bars** Check out the laidback nightlife in one of China's most relaxed cities. See p.691

* **Yuanyang** Base yourself in this attractive town and visit nearby minority villages set in a landscape spectacularly sliced up by rice terraces. See p.696

* **Dali** An old town with an enjoyable, relaxed travellers' quarter, offering café society and lush scenery. See p.700

* **Cycling around Lijiang** Take yourself out of the touristy town centre and cycle around the well-preserved villages at the heart of the Naxi Kingdom. See p.713

* **Lugu Hu** Tranquil lakeside resort with matriarchal villages on a backroads route into Sichuan. See p.716

* **Tiger Leaping Gorge** Relax for a few days on the ridge of this dramatic gorge, trekking between farmstead homestays. See p.717

* **Meili Xue Shan** Dramatic jagged scenery along the northwestern border with Tibet. See p.723

* **Jungle trekking in Xishuangbanna** Explore a region populated by many different ethnic groups, each with their own distinctive dress and customs. See p.738

▲ Threshing rice, Yuanyang

11

Yunnan

Yunnan (云南, *yúnnán*) has always stood apart from the rest of China, set high on the southwestern frontiers of the empire, and shielded from the rest of the nation by the unruly, mountainous neighbours of Sichuan and Guizhou. Within this single province, unmatched in the complexity and scope of its history, landscape and peoples, you'll find a mix of geography, climates and nationalities that elsewhere on Earth takes entire continents to express.

The fairly flat, productive northeast of the province is home to the attractive capital, **Kunming**, whose mild climate earned Yunnan its name, meaning literally "south of the Clouds". A scattering of local sights extends southeast from the city towards the border with **Vietnam**.

Northwest of Kunming, the Yunnan plateau rises to serrated, snowbound peaks, extending north **to Tibet** and surrounding the ancient historic towns of **Dali** and **Lijiang**. The **Far West**, laid out along the ghost of old trade routes, has less of specific interest but allows gentle probing along the **border with Burma**. Yunnan's deep south comprises a further isolated stretch of the same frontier, which reaches down to the tropical forests and paddy fields of **Xishuangbanna**, a botanical, zoological and ethnic cornucopia abutting Burma and **Laos** – about as far from Han China as it's possible to be.

Dwelling in this stew of border markets, mountains, jungles, lakes, temples, modern political intrigue and remains of vanished kingdoms are 28 recognized **ethnic groups**, the greatest number in any province. Providing almost half the population and a prime reason to visit Yunnan in themselves, the indigenous list includes Dai and Bai, Wa, Lahu, Hani, Jingpo, Nu, Naxi and Lisu plus a host shared with other provinces (such as the Yi; see p.772) or adjoining nations. Each minority has its own spoken language, cuisine, distinctive form of dress for women, festivals and belief system, and with enough time you should be able to flesh out the superficial image of these groups laid on for the **tourist industry**. In recent years this has boomed out of all proportion to Yunnan's remote image, bringing batallions of tour buses, souvenir stalls and loudspeaker-toting guides from far and near; the upside for foreigners is an increasing number of resources geared to their needs, including backpacker cafés and companies offering cycling and trekking trips, ensuring that Yunnan is one of the easiest places to explore in China.

There are **international flights** into Kunming from Bangkok, Rangoon, Singapore and Vientiane, and to Jinghong – near the border with Burma and Laos – from Chiang Mai and Bangkok. Getting around can be time-consuming, thanks to Yunnan's sheer scale, but the state of country **buses and roads** is often surprisingly good; new expressways are springing up at a regular rate and it's an undeniable

achievement that some of the lesser routes exist at all. Yunnan's fairly limited **rail network** is due for expansion too, with recently completed services to Dali and Lijiang making these popular destinations more accessible than ever.

The **weather** is generally moderate throughout the year, though northern Yunnan has cold winters and heavy snow up around the Tibetan border, while the south is always warm, with a torrential wet season in summer.

Roads in the more remote areas are regularly closed during the rainy season, usually because of landslides and bad weather, but sometimes thanks to the army looking for illegal cross-border traffic in cars, timber, gems and **opiates**. Much of Asia's illegal drug production originates in Burma and is funnelled through China to overseas markets. Officially, the Yunnanese government is tough on the drugs trade, executing traffickers and forcibly rehabilitating addicts. All this means that there are military **checkpoints** on many rural roads, where you'll have to show passports.

Some history

According to the Han historian Sima Qian, the Chinese warrior prince **Zhuang Qiao** founded the pastoral **Dian Kingdom** in eastern Yunnan during the third century BC. The Dian were a slave society, who vividly recorded their daily life and ceremonies involving human sacrifice in sometimes gruesome **bronze**

models, which have been unearthed from their tombs. In 109 AD the kingdom was acknowledged by China: the emperor **Wu**, hoping to control the Southern Silk Road through to India, sent its ruler military aid and a golden seal. However, the collapse of the Han empire in 204 AD was followed by the dissolution of Dian into private statelets.

In the eighth century, an aspiring Yunnanese prince named **Piluoge**, favouring Dali for its location near trade routes beteen central and southeastern Asia, invited his rivals to dinner in the town, then set fire to the tent with them inside. Subsequently he established the **Nanzhao Kingdom** in Dali, which later expanded to include much of modern Burma, Thailand and Vietnam. In 937, the Bai warlord **Duan Siping** toppled the Nanzhao and set up a smaller **Dali Kingdom**, which survived until **Kublai Khan** and his Mongol hordes descended in 1252. Directly controlled by China for the first time, Yunnan served for a while as a remote dumping ground for political troublemakers, thereby escaping the population explosions, wars and migrations that plagued central China. However, the Mongol invasion had introduced a large **Muslim population** to the province, who, angered by their deteriorating status under the Chinese, staged the **Muslim Uprising** in 1856. Under the warlord **Du Wenxiu**, the rebellion laid waste to Kunming and founded an Islamic state in Dali before the Qing armies ended it with the wholesale massacre of Yunnan's Muslims in 1873, leaving a wasted Yunnan to local bandits and private armies for the following half-century.

Strangely, it was the **Japanese invasion** of China during the 1930s that sparked a resurgence of the province's fortunes. Blockaded into southwestern China, the **Guomindang government** initiated great programmes of rail-and-road building through the region, though they never really controlled Yunnan. The Communists didn't bring much joy either, and it's only recently that Yunnan has finally

Yunnanese food

Yunnanese food splits broadly into three cooking styles. In the **north**, the cold, pastoral lifestyle produces dried meats and – very unusually for China – **dairy products**, fused with a Muslim cuisine, a vestige of the thirteenth-century Mongolian invasion. Typical dishes include wind-cured ham (火腿, *huǒtuǐ*), sweetened, steamed and served with slices of bread; dried cheese or yoghurt wafers (乳扇, *rǔshān* or 乳饼, *rǔbǐng*); the local version of crisp-skinned duck (烧鸭,*shāoyā*), flavoured with Sichuan peppercorns – you'll see drum-shaped duck ovens outside many restaurants – and *shaguoyu* (沙锅鱼, *shāguō yú*), a tasty fish claypot.

Eastern Yunnan produces the most recognizably "Chinese" food. From here comes *qiguo* chicken (气锅鸡, *qìguōjī*) flavoured with medicinal herbs and stewed inside a specially shaped earthenware steamer, and **crossing-the-bridge noodles** (过桥米线, *guòqiáo mǐxiàn*), a sort of individualized hotpot eaten as a cheap snack all over the province; you pay by the size of the bowl. The curious name comes from a tale of a Qing scholar who retired every day to a lakeside pavilion to compose poetry. His wife, an understanding soul, used to cook him lunch, but the food always cooled as she carried it from their home over the bridge to where he studied – until she hit on the idea of keeping the heat in with a layer of oil on top of his soup.

Not surprisingly, Yunnan's **south** is strongly influenced by Burmese, Lao and Thai cooking methods, particularly in the use of such un-Chinese ingredients as lime juice, coconut, palm sugar, cloves and turmeric. Here you'll find a vast range of soups and stews, roughly recognizable as **curries**, displayed in aluminium pots outside fast-turnover restaurants, and oddities such as purple rice-flour pancakes sold at street markets. The south is also famous in China for producing good **coffee** and red *pu'er cha*, Yunnan's best **tea**.

benefited from its forced association with the rest of the country. Never agriculturally rich – only a tenth of the land is considered arable – the province looks to mineral resources, tourism and its potential as a future conduit between China and the much discussed, but as yet unformed, trading bloc of **Vietnam**, **Laos**, **Thailand** and **Burma**. Should these countries ever form an unrestricted economic alliance, the amount of trade passing through Yunnan would be immense, and highways, rail and air services have already been planned for the day the borders open freely.

Kunming and the southeast

All visitors to Yunnan find themselves at some point in **Kunming**, the province's comfortable capital and transport hub. The population of students and young foreign expats testifies to Kunming being perhaps China's most laidback large city and, while there's not really much to see here, an abundance of food and nightlife makes it a pleasant place to take stock for a couple of days. Heading southeast from Kunming towards the **Vietnamese border** brings you within striking distance of some scenic and ethnic distractions at **Yuanyang**, with old architecture and offbeat sights to slow you down around the country town of **Jianshui**.

Kunming and around

Basking 2000m above sea level in the fertile heart of the Yunnan plateau, **KUNMING** (昆明, *kūnmíng*) does its best to live up to its traditional nickname, the City of Eternal Spring. However, until recently it was considered a savage frontier settlement; the authorities only began to realize the city's promise when people exiled here during the Cultural Revolution refused offers to return home to eastern China, preferring Kunming's climate and more relaxed life. Today, its citizens remain mellow enough to mix typically Chinese garrulousness with introspective pleasures, such as quietly greeting the day with a stiff hit of Yunnanese tobacco from fat, brass-bound bamboo pipes. Other novelties – clean pavements enforced by on-the-spot fines, and an orderly traffic system – suggest that Kunming's four million or so residents enjoy a quality of life above that of most urban Chinese.

Once you've found your bearings in this largely modern city, the pick of the sights are extraordinary sculptures at westerly **Qiongzhu Si**, and the scenery along the nearby heights of Xi Shan, the **Western Hills**. Further afield, **Shilin**, the spectacular Stone Forest, is an enjoyable day-trip if you can accept the fairground atmosphere and the crowds dutifully tagging behind their cosmetically perfect tour guides.

Some history

Historically the domain of Yunnan's earliest inhabitants and first civilization, Kunming long profited from its position on the caravan roads through to Burma and Europe. It was visited in the thirteenth century by Marco Polo, who found the

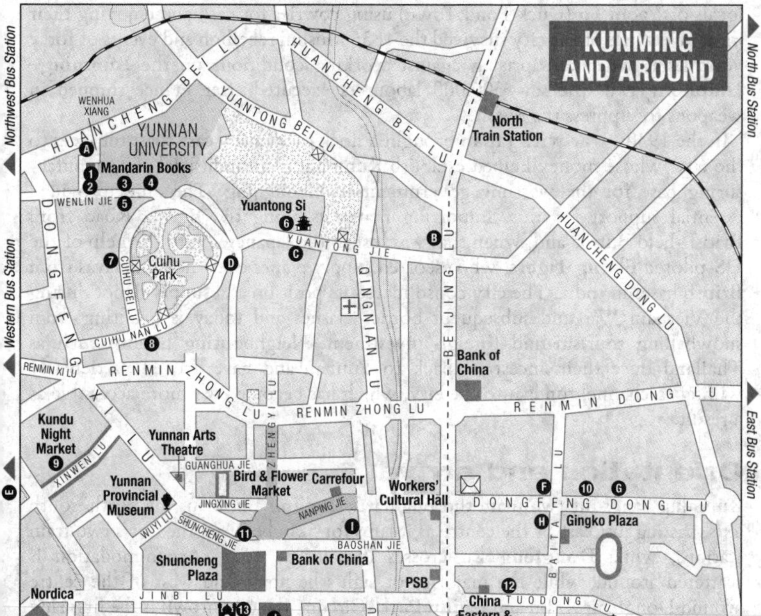

KUNMING AND AROUND

Northwest Bus Station
Western Bus Station
North Bus Station
East Bus Station
Airport & South Bus Station

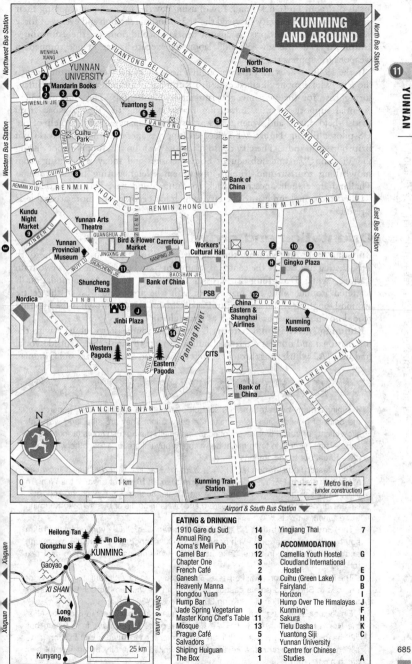

WENHUA XIANG
HUANCHENG BEI LU
YUANTONG BEI LU
YUNNAN UNIVERSITY
Mandarin Books
WENLIN JIE
DONGFENG XI LU
Yuantong Si
YUANTONG JIE
Cuihu Park
CUIHU BEI LU
CUIHU NAN LU
North Train Station
HUANCHENG DONG LU
QINGNIAN LU
BEIJING LU
Bank of China
RENMIN XI LU
RENMIN ZHONG LU
RENMIN DONG LU
ZHENGYI LU
Kundu Night Market
XINWEN LU
Yunnan Arts Theatre
GUANGHUA JIE
Bird & Flower Market
Carrefour
Workers' Cultural Hall
Yunnan Provincial Museum
JINGXING JIE
NANPING JIE
WUYI LU
SHUNCHENG JIE
BAOSHAN JIE
DONGFENG DONG LU
BAITA LU
Gingko Plaza
Shuncheng Plaza
Bank of China
PSB
Nordica
JINBI LU
TUODONG LU
China Eastern & Shanghai Airlines
Jinbi Plaza
Kunming Museum
HOUXIN JIE
XICHANG LU
Western Pagoda
DONGSI JIE
SHULIN JIE
Eastern Pagoda
Panlong River
CITS
CHUNCHENG LU
HUANCHENG NAN LU
WUJIN LU
Bank of China
N
0 1 km
Kunming Train Station
Metro line (under construction)

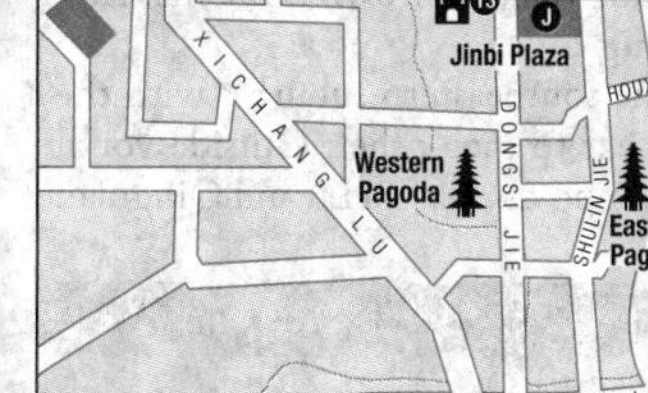

EATING & DRINKING

1910 Gare du Sud	14
Annual Ring	9
Aoma's Meili Pub	10
Camel Bar	12
Chapter One	3
French Café	2
Ganesh	4
Heavenly Manna	1
Hongdou Yuan	3
Hump Bar	J
Jade Spring Vegetarian	6
Master Kong Chef's Table	11
Mosque	13
Prague Café	5
Salvadors	1
Shiping Huiguan	8
The Box	1
Yingjiang Thai	7

ACCOMMODATION

Camellia Youth Hostel	G
Cloudland International Hostel	E
Cuihu (Green Lake)	D
Fairyland	B
Horizon	I
Hump Over The Himalayas	J
Kunming	F
Sakura	H
Tielu Dasha	K
Yuantong Siji	C
Yunnan University Centre for Chinese Studies	A

locals of **Yachi Fu** (Duck Pond Town) using cowries for cash and enjoying their meat raw. Little of the city survived the 1856 Muslim rebellion and events of forty years later, when an uprising against working conditions on the **Kunming–Haiphong rail line** saw 300,000 labourers executed after France shipped in weapons to suppress the revolt.

In the 1930s, **war with Japan** brought a flock of wealthy east coast refugees to the city, whose money helped establish Kunming as an industrial and manufacturing base for the wartime government in Chongqing. The allies provided essential support for this, importing materials along the Burma Road from British-held Burma and, when that was lost to the Japanese, with the help of the US-piloted **Flying Tigers**, who escorted supply planes over the Himalayas from British bases in India. The city consolidated its position as a supply depot during the Vietnam War and subsequent border clashes and today is profiting from snowballing tourism and foreign investment. Neighbouring nations such as Thailand trace their ancestries back to Yunnan and have proved particularly willing to channel funds into the city, which has become ever more accessible as a result.

Orientation and arrival

Kunming hangs off two main thoroughfares: **Beijing Lu** forms the north–south axis, passing just east of the centre as it runs for 5km between the city's two train stations, while **Dongfeng Lu** crosses it halfway along. Accommodation is scattered around, while the majority of sights lie north and west of the centre around Dongfeng Xi Lu and **Cuihu Park**. Circling the downtown is the first ring road, known for most of its length as **Huancheng Lu**.

Kunming International Airport is out in the southeastern suburbs, with the international and domestic terminal buildings next to each other. Outside you'll find **bus #A2** which runs through town via Tuodong Lu, Bai Ta Lu and Qingnian

Kunming's bus stations

Kunming's many **bus stations** are scattered around the city perimeter, generally at the point of the compass relevant to the destination. They are all a long way out: allow plenty of transit time, even in a cab, especially during rush hours (about 7–9am and 5–7pm). Agents in town might be willing to buy tickets for a fee, otherwise you'll have to get out to the stations yourself.

The **Western bus station** (西部汽车客运站, *xībù qìchē kèyùn zhàn*), also known as **Majie bus station** (马街客运站, *mă jiē kèyùn zhàn*), is 10km out towards the Western Hills. It deals with traffic to Xiaguan, Lijiang, Deqin, Shangri-La, Tengchong and Ruili. On arrival, catch bus #82 to the western end of Nanping Jie or bus #C72 to Kunming train station; a taxi is ¥30.

The **South bus station** (南部汽车客运站, *nánbù qìchē kèyùn zhàn*) is 15km southeast, past the airport, with departures to Xishuangbanna, Jianshui, Yuanyang and Luang Prabang in Laos. Take bus #C71 to Kunming Train Station, or a taxi for ¥45.

The **East bus station** (东部汽车客运站, *dōngbù qìchē kèyùn zhàn*), 10km out, is for services to Shilin and points east, plus Hekou on the Vietnam border. Bus #60 runs to Kunming train station via Bailong Lu; a taxi costs ¥30.

Finally, unless arriving from Panzhihua in Sichuan, you're unlikely to find yourself at the **North bus station** (北部汽车客运站, *běibù qìchē kèyùnzhàn*), from where bus #23 heads through town via both train stations; or the **Northwest bus station** (西北部汽车客运站, *xīběibù qìchē kèyùnzhàn*), not linked to the city by any useful bus; catch a cab (¥35).

Moving on from Kunming

For anyone catching a **domestic flight**, the China Eastern and Shanghai Airlines headquarters are on Tuodong Lu, but agents around town all offer the same fares. **Bus #A2** to the airport runs from the defunct North train station, via Qingnian Lu, Bai Ta Lu, Tuodong Lu and Chuncheng Lu; **bus #52** departs from westerly Dongfeng Xi Lu near Cuihu Park. A **taxi** from the centre costs a reasonable ¥35 and takes up to forty minutes, depending on traffic. When opened after 2013, metro line 6 should reach the airport too.

Kunming train station is two-tiered, with the ticket windows downstairs (5am–11pm) and departures upstairs. Inside Yunnan, there are direct trains to **Xiaguan** (for Dali) and **Lijiang** (quicker than the same journey by bus); heading into the rest of China, trains run north **to Chengdu** via Xichang in southern Sichuan, southeast via Xingyi **to Baise and Nanning** in Guangxi, and east to **Guizhou** and beyond. For **long-distance buses** from Kunming, see the box opposite.

Kunming is also the springboard for travel into Thailand, Laos, Vietnam and Burma, all of which maintain **consulates** in town; see p.692, for airline and consular information. For **Thailand**, there are flights to Bangkok from Kunming, and it's also possible to catch ferries from Jinghong in Xishuangbanna (see p.732). Many nationalities can stay visa-free in Thailand for 30 days if arriving at an airport, or 15 days arriving by land; if you need longer, head to Kunming's consulate for a visa. You can fly to **Vietnam** and **Laos** and there's also a daily direct bus (departs 7am; 30hr; ¥300) from Kunming's South bus station to Luang Prabang in Laos; for Vietnam, head first to Hekou (p.697) and cross the border on foot. Laos visas might again be avialable at the border depending on nationality; for Vietnam you'll need to get one in advance. For **Burma**, arrange both visas and obligatory tour package in Kunming before either flying direct to Yangon with China Eastern or crossing the border on foot near Ruili (see p.729).

Lu; alternatively, bus #52 terminates at the Dongfeng Xi Lu/Renmin Zhong Lu intersection near Cuihu Park. A **taxi** into town costs around ¥35.

Kunming train station is down at the southern end of Beijing Lu. Useful buses from here include #23 up Beijing Lu past the defunct North train station; and #59, which heads up Qingnian Lu to within striking distance of Yuantong Si and Cuihu Park. If you're immediately heading onwards, there's also bus #C71 to the South bus Station and buses #C72 or #80 to the Western bus station. For **Kunming's bus stations** themselves, see opposite.

City transport

Downtown Kunming is fairly compact and it's possible to walk everywhere, though **bicycles** (rented through accommodation) and **cabs** are probably the most convenient alternatives. You might resort to **city buses** (¥1–2) to reach some of the further-flung sights, but they're slow and not that useful around the centre. There's also a **metro** under construction, with the first lines opening around 2012 or 2013 – details are still vague, but extensive roadworks along Beijing Lu point to one line between the two train stations.

Accommodation

Kunming has abundant **accommodation**, mostly mid-range, scattered throughout the city centre.

Camellia Youth Hostel (茶花国际青年旅舍, *cháhuā guójì qīngnián lǚ shè*) 96 Dongfeng Dong Lu ⓣ0871/8374638, ⓦwww.kmcamelliahotel.com. Skip the tired mid-range hotel in the main building here for the youth hostel in a renovated wing out back;

there's a cheerful paint job, helpful staff and decent dorms, though doubles are overpriced. The tiny garden is a bonus. Take bus #2 or #23 from the main train station to Dongfeng Dong Lu, then any bus heading east for two stops. Dorms ¥35, rooms ❷

Cloudland International Hostel (大脚氏国际青年旅舍, *dàjiǎ shì guójì qīngnián lǚshè*) 23 Zhuantang Lu ⓣ0871/4103777. Hard to find, south off Xichang Lu near the Kundu Night Market, with the rooms in tiers around a self-contained courtyard. Good café and hiking info for Tiger Leaping Gorge and Meili Xue Shan. Can be noisy, depending on who is staying. Basic dorms ¥30, rooms ❸

Cuihu (翠湖宾馆, *cuìhú bīnguǎn*) 6 Cuihu Nan Lu ⓣ0871/5158888, ⓦwww.greenlakehotel.com. A long-established and good-value upmarket hotel in pleasant surroundings by Cuihu Park, with a fancy lobby complete with palm trees, and an excellent restaurant. Airport transfers can be arranged; all major credit cards are accepted. ❾

Fairyland (四季酒店鼓楼店, *sìjì jiǔdiàn gǔlóu diàn*) 716 Beijing Lu ⓣ0871/6285777. Budget business hotel, not in the smartest part of town but not far from Yuantong Si and Cuihu Park either; cheaper rooms are tiny, but pay a bit more and you get a modern, comfortable place to stay. Bus #23 stops nearby. ❸–❹

Horizon (天恒大酒店, *tiānhéng dàjiǔdiàn*) 432 Qingnian Lu ⓣ0871/3186666. Another overblown, multistarred place with a mountain of marble in the lobby and an overflow of cafés and restaurants – though smarter and better-placed than others. ❾

Hump Over The Himalayas (金马碧鸡坊金, *jīnmǎ bìjī fǎngjīn*), Jinbi Lu ⓣ0871/3640359, ⓦwww.thehumphostel.com. Three hundred police once raided this place to close it down but despite this wild reputation, today it's clean, organized and secure, with a comfy lounge-bar and rooftop terrace. The only downside is noise from surrounding nightclubs, but they'll give you earplugs if you ask. Dorms ¥35, doubles with en suite ❷

Kunming (昆明饭店, *kūnmíng fàndiàn*) 52 Dongfeng Dong Lu ⓣ0871/3162063, ⓦwww.kunminghotel.com.cn. A big, upmarket hotel with an absurd lobby, reasonable service, serviceable rooms and a restaurant specializing in dishes from Chaozhou in Guangdong province. ❽

Sakura (樱花酒店, *yīnghuā jiǔdiàn*) 29 Dongfeng Dong Lu ⓣ0871/3165888, ⓦwww.sakurahotel.cn. A tall, distinctive building with decent, mid-range rooms, though the lobby is rather poky. It's also home to a well-reputed Thai restaurant. Large discounts on the rack rate are sometimes available. ❽

Tielu Dasha (铁路大厦, *tiělù dàshà*) East side of Kunming train station square ⓣ0871/3511996 or 6123123. Tidy, clean, faultless en-suite doubles in a standard budget hotel; pricewise as cheap as they come – the only reason this isn't the best deal in the city is that you're too far from anywhere interesting. ❷

Yuantong Siji (圆通四季酒店, *yuántōng sìjì jiǔdiàn*) 88 Pingzhen Jie, diagonally across from Yuantong Si ⓣ0871/5150666, ⓕ5150966. Spanking new budget hotel, stylish, smart and modern – hence a bit more expensive than usual for the type. ❹

Yunnan University Centre for Chinese Studies (云南大学国际学术 教育交流中心, *yúnnán dàxué guójì xuéshù jiàoyù jiāoliú zhōngxīn*) Wenhua Xiang ⓣ0871/5033624, ⓕ5148513. Aimed at long-stay foreign students but open to anyone. It's opposite the university's west gate, in one of the nicest parts of town, with plenty of cafés and bars around. The old wing, to the south, is musty but has a garden and tiled patio; rooms in the bright new wing are a little more expensive. ❸

The City

Kunming's public focus is the huge square outside the grandiose **Workers' Cultural Hall** (工人文化宫, *gōngrén wénhuàgōng*) at the Beijing Lu/Dongfeng Lu crossroads, alive in the mornings with regimented crowds warming up on hip pivots and shuttlecock games. The city's true centre is west of here across the landscaped **Panlong River**, around the pedestrianized **Nanping Jie/Zhengyi Lu** intersection, a densely crowded shopping precinct packed with clothing and department stores.

Running west off Zhengyi Jie, **Jingxing Jie** leads into one of the more offbeat corners of the city, with Kunming's huge **bird and flower market** (花鸟市场, *huā niǎo shìchǎng*) convening there daily. At least at weekends, this is no run-of-the-mill mix of kittens and grotesque goldfish: multicoloured songbirds twitter and squawk to all sides, with reptiles, doormice, beetles and bunnies in cages beneath. There are **plants** here, too, along with **antique and curio** booths in the buildings between here and Shuncheng Lu, where you'll find coins and Cultural Revolution mementos, bamboo pipes and prayer rugs. The area is in redevelopment limbo at the moment, as the last of Kunming's old wooden shophouses are cleared away, but the market remains for now.

Yunnan Provincial Museum

About 500m west of the centre along Dongfeng Xi Lu the **Yunnan Provincial Museum** (云南省博物馆, *yúnnánshěng bówùguǎn*; daily 9am–5pm; free except special exhibitions) gives an insight into Yunnan's early Dian Kingdom. Best are the **bronzes** on the second floor, dating back more than two thousand years to the Warring States Period and excavated from tombs on the shores of Dian Chi, south of Kunming. The largest pieces include an ornamental plate of a tiger attacking an ox and a **coffin** in the shape of a bamboo house, but lids from **storage drums** used to hold cowries are the most impressive, decorated with dioramas of figurines fighting, sacrificing oxen and men and, rather more peacefully, posing with their families and farmyard animals outside their homes. A replica of the Chinese imperial **gold seal** given to the Dian king early in the second century implies that his aristocratic slave society had the tacit approval of the Han emperor.

Cuihu Park and Yuantong Si

Cuihu Park (翠湖公园, *cuìhú gōngyuán*; open from dawn until 10pm) is predominantly lake, a good place to join thousands of others exercising, singing, feeding wintering flocks of **gulls**, or just milling between the plum and magnolia gardens and over the maze of bridges. Main **entrances** are at the south, north and east of the park, and encircling Cuihu Lu is lined with restaurants and bars, which spill into adjacent **Wenlin Jie**, the best place in the city to look for a drink and a feed (see p.690). Immediately north of the park, the **Yunnan University** campus offers a glimpse of old Kunming, its partially overgrown 1920s exterior reached via a wide flight of stone steps.

East from Cuihu Park along Yuantong Jie, the Qing-vintage **Yuantong Si** (圆通寺, *yuántōng sì*; daily 9am–5.30pm; ¥6) has undergone major renovations to emerge as Kunming's brightest Buddhist temple. A bridge over the central pond crosses through an octagonal pavilion dedicated to a multi-armed Guanyin and white marble Sakyamuni, to the threshold of the **main hall**, where two huge central pillars wrapped in colourful, Manga-esque **dragons** support the ornate wooden ceiling. Faded frescoes on the back wall were painted in the thirteenth century, while the rear annexe houses a graceful gilded bronze Buddha flanked by peacocks, donated by the Thai government.

Kunming City Museum

The highlight of the **Kunming City Museum** (昆明市博物馆, *kūnmíngshì bówùguǎn*; Tues–Sun 9am–5pm; ¥15), east of Beijing Lu along Tuodong Lu, is the **Dali Sutra Pillar**. In its own room on the ground floor, it's a 6.5m-high, pagoda-like Song-dynasty sculpture, in pink sandstone; an octagonal base supports seven tiers covered in Buddha images, statues of fierce guardian gods standing on subjugated demons, and a mix of Tibetan and Chinese script, part of which is the Dharani Mantra. The rest is a dedication, identifying the pillar as having been raised by the Dali regent, **Yuan Douguang**, in memory of his general **Gao Ming**. The whole thing is topped by a ring of Buddhas carrying a ball – the universe – above them and the pillar is full of the energy that later seeped out of the mainstream of Chinese sculpture.

The other exhibits are a well-presented repeat of the Provincial Museum's collection. Enthusiasts of **bronze drums** can examine a range, from the oldest known example to relatively recent castings, to see how the decorations – sun and frog designs on top, long-plumed warriors in boats around the sides, tiger handles – became so stylized. There are cowrie-drum lids, too, and a host of other bronze pieces worth examining for nit-picking details of birds, animals and people. Other rooms contain five locally found **fossilized dinosaur skeletons** – including the bulky *Yunnanosaurus robustus*.

Two pagodas

Two large Tang-dynasty **pagodas**, each a solid thirteen storeys of whitewashed brick crowned with four jolly iron cockerels, rise a short walk south of the city centre. The **Eastern Pagoda** (东寺塔, *dōngsì tǎ*) on Shulin Jie sits in a little ornamental garden, while the **Western Pagoda** (西寺塔, *xīsì tǎ*) is a few minutes' walk away at the back of a flagstoned square on Dongsi Jie. You can't enter either, but the sight of these 1300-year-old towers surrounded by modern office blocks is striking.

Eating

Kunming is stacked with good places to eat, from street stalls and Western cafés to smart restaurants offering local cuisine. Back lanes off **Jinbi Lu** hold some great cheap places where you can battle with the locals over grilled cheese, hotpots, fried snacks rolled in chilli powder, loaves of excellent meat-stuffed soda bread, and rich duck and chicken casseroles. There's a string of inexpensive Muslim **duck restaurants** on Huashan Nan Lu, southeast of Cuihu Park, but by far the best place to look for a feed is around Cuihu Park itself, especially along **Wenlin Jie** and **Wenhua Xiang**. Indian, Chinese, Korean, Japanese, Thai and Western food can all be found here, as can a decent cup of coffee, in laidback surroundings.

1910 Gare du Sud (火车南站, *huǒchē nánzhàn*) 8 Houxin Jie ⓣ0871/3169486. Traditional Yunnan fare served in a former French colonial train station; there's a large balcony and courtyard and photos of colonial Kunming throughout. It's a popular place with trendy middle-class locals but nowhere near as expensive as you'd think from the smart-casual atmosphere, and two can eat very well for ¥100.

Annual Ring (年轮菜馆, *niánlún càiguǎn*) 144 Xinwen Lu, Kundu Night Market ⓣ0871/4114278. Spicy Yunnanese-Sichuanese blend of dishes, with fish as the speciality – choose yours fresh from the tank. No English spoken, but there's a photo menu. Mains about ¥35.

Aoma's Meili Pub (敖玛餐厅, *aómǎ cāntīng*) 60 Dongfeng Dong Lu. Set-meal steaks, pasta, pizzas and some local dishes, in an urbane and relaxed atmosphere. Packed with office workers at lunchtime. Mains upwards of ¥20.

French Café (兰白红咖啡, *lánbáihóng kāfēi*) Wenlin Jie. There's a large French contingent in Kunming, drawn perhaps by the colonial connection; this café, with its pastries, quiches and air of *hauteur*, must make them feel at home.

Heavenly Manna (吗哪, *manà*) 74 Wenhua Xiang ⓣ0871/5369399. Home-style Yunnanese dishes: inexpensive, varied, interesting and very spicy indeed. Setting is crowded, with no-frills low wooden tables and chairs; watch out for the low ceiling with protruding pipes upstairs.

Hongdou Yuan (红豆圆餐厅, *hóngdòuyuán cāntīng*) 142 Wenlin Jie. Branch of popular Sichuanese-Yunnanese chain, with an easy-to-follow photo menu. Not everything is spicy; they do excellent crisp-skinned duck with cut buns, cold-sliced pork, stewed spareibs and rice-coated pork slices. The fish looks good too. Mains ¥25–45.

Jade Spring Vegetarian (玉泉斋素食, *yùquánzhāi sùshí*) Near the Yuantong Si, Yuantong Jie. An excellent place, reasonably priced and with a picture menu. It serves a mix of straight vegetable and imitation-meat dishes – best of the latter are coconut-flavoured "spareribs" (bamboo shoots, celery and fried bean-curd skin), "chicken" and fungus rolls (dried bean curd), and "fish" (deep-fried mashed potato served in a rich garlic and vinegar sauce). Mains ¥25.

Master Kong Chef's Table (康师傅私房牛肉面, *kāng shīfu sīfáng niúròu miàn*) Nanping

Jie. Bright and slightly smart Taiwan-style noodle bar specializing in beef noodle soups from about ¥25. An easy, convenient place for a light lunch.

Mosque (清真寺餐厅, *qīngzhēnsì cāntīng*) Corner of Jinbi Lu and Dong Si Lu. Take the steps up from the shops at street level on Dong Si Lu to the mosque courtyard, where stalls serving all sorts of Chinese snacks for a few yuan each are arranged down one side. The restaurant beyond is more formal, with crisp-skinned chicken for ¥25.

Prague Café 40 Wenlin Jie. This offshoot of a successful Lijiang enterprise offers very strong coffee and a decent breakfast (¥22), as well as internet access and a book exchange. One of the better cafés in this locality, it's a good place to while away an afternoon.

Salvadors (沙尔瓦多咖啡馆, *shāěrwăduō kāfēiguăn*) 76 Wenhua Xiang. Expat-run and populated, and somewhere to get information and conversation from slightly jaded, in-the-know foreign residents. Well-stocked bar with pavement taking overflow, plus coffee and pub-style menu.

Shiping Huiguan (石屏会馆, *shípíng huì guăn*) 24 Zhonghe Xiang, Cuihu Nan Lu ⓣ0871/3627444. Tucked back off the street behind an ornamental archway and heavy stone wall, this elegantly restored courtyard restaurant is a great place to sample Yunnanese cuisine. It tends to get booked out by tour groups and wedding parties, so reservations are essential.

Yingjiang Thai (盈江傣味园, *yíngjiāng dăi wèi yuán*) 66 Cuihu Bei Lu ⓣ0871/5337889. Strongly Sinicized Thai food, though favourites like sweet pineapple rice, grilled fish, sour bamboo shoots and *laab* (spicy mince salad) are all pretty good. Count on ¥35/person in a group.

Drinking, nightlife and entertainment

Kunming is a great place to go out, with plenty of friendly, reasonably priced **bars and clubs** patronized by a mix of locals and foreigners. For information on the latest hotspots and up-and-coming entertainment and cultural events, check out **GoKunming** (ⓦwww.gokunming.com).

Jinbi Plaza on Jinbi Lu is a complex (or, after a few drinks, a maze) of inter-linked clubs such as *The Hump Bar* (驼峰酒吧, *tuófēng jiŭbā*) – stumble out of one and you fall straight into another. *The Camel Bar* (骆驼酒吧, *luòtuó jiŭbā*) at 4 Tuodong Lu is slightly more upmarket and polished, with a lively, predominantly Chinese clientele. Downstairs there's a dance floor, while the more laidback upstairs area is ideal for sitting over a coffee during the day. If you can't live without cheesy techno and flashing lights, head to the **Kundu Night Market** off Xinwen Lu, a clutch of bars and discos with late-night restaurants and nail bars and tattoo parlours in between. Everywhere's free to get in, but drinks cost at least ¥30.

For a more sedate atmosphere, head to the **Wenlin Jie** area and take your pick of the student-expat bars and pubs. *Chapter One* (ⓦwww.chapteronekunming.com), at 146 Wenlin Jie, is good for cheap Happy Hour drinks (5–8pm). At 156 Wenlin Jie, *Ganesh Bar & Restaurant* (印象阁, *yìnxiàng gé*) is a sports bar, more of a pub really, with good beer but terrible Indian food. *The Box* (老夫子, *lăo fūzĭ*; ⓦwww.saporeitalia.com.cn), at 69 Wenhua Xiang, is a perennial favourite and just about everyone ends up here at some point for Italian wine, a faceful of ice cream, or an argument.

Gigs, club nights and talks take place frequently at the Scandinavian-run **Nordica** (TCG诺地卡, *nuòdìkă*; ⓣ0871/4114692, ⓦwww.tcgnordica.com), 101 Xiba Lu, inside an old factory converted into a complex of galleries, cafés and studio spaces. Kunming attracts a lot of artists, and Nordica is a good place to find them and their work.

Listings

Airlines China Eastern and Shanghai Airlines share the main airline office building on Tuodong Lu (ⓣ0871/3164270 or 3138562; ⓦwww.travelsky.com). International airlines in Kunming include: Dragonair/Cathay Pacific, Room 1405-06, 14F, Kunming Hongta Mansion, 155 Beijing Lu (ⓣ400/8886628; Mon–Fri 9am–5pm); Laos Aviation, *Camellia Hotel*, 154 Dongfeng Dong Lu (ⓣ0871/3163000, ⓕ3125748; daily 9.30am–5pm); Thai Airways, *Jinjiang Hotel*, 98 Beijing Lu

(Ⓣ0871/3511515, Ⓔreservation.kmg@thaiairways.com.cn; Mon–Fri 9am–5.30pm); Vietnam Air, near the Vietnamese consulate, 2F, Tower C, *Kai Wah Plaza Hotel*, 157 Beijing Lu (Ⓣ0871/3515850, Ⓕ0871/3515852).

Banks and exchange The main branch of the Bank of China (Mon–Fri 9am–5.30pm) is at the corner of Beijing Lu and Renmin Dong Lu. There are smaller branches and ATMs all through the centre.

Bike rental The hostels all rent bikes for ¥3/hr.

Bookshops Kunming's best English-language bookshop – in fact one of the best in the country – is Mandarin Books at 52 Wenhua Xiang, near the university. It has many imported novels, obscure academic texts, guidebooks and much that is published in English in China, all of it fairly pricey.

Cinema The best in town, showing some films in English, is the Beijing-run Broadway Cinema, inside the Shuncheng Plaza between Shuncheng Jie and Jinbi Lu. There's an IMAX screen here too.

Consulates A new consular area has been established beyond the airport southeast of Kunming, and some of the following may relocate. Visas for these countries can also be obtained through travel agents. Note that at the time of writing, it was uncertain whether the Burmese consulate was dealing with Western travellers any more. Burma (Myanmar), Rooms B503 & A504, Long Yuan Jewelery Centre Building, 166 Weiyuan Jie, behind the giant Carrefour on Dongfeng Xi Lu (Ⓣ0871/3641268 or 3603477; Mon–Fri 8.30am–noon & 1–4.30pm, closed during Burmese public holidays); Laos, Foreign Consular Area, Guandu District, Kunluo Lu (Ⓣ0871/7335489; Mon–Fri 8.30–11.30am & 1.30–4.30pm; they take three working days to issue visas and charge according to the applicant's nationality); Thailand, in a building in front of the *Kunming* hotel on Dongfeng Dong Lu (Mon–Fri 9am–noon & 1–5pm; Ⓣ0871/3168916); Vietnam, 2F, *Jiahua Hotel*, 157 Beijing Lu (Ⓣ0871/3522669; Mon–Fri 9–11.30am; 30 day visas cost 400–¥600 depending on how quickly you want them).

Hospital Yunnan Province Red Cross hospital and emergency centre is on Qingnian Lu.

Internet Most accommodation and foreigner-friendly cafés have terminals and/or free wi-fi.

Mail The GPO is towards Kunming train station at 231 Beijing Lu (daily 8am–7pm).

Massage There are a few blind masseur studios around town, charging ¥30/hr for either feet or full body treatments – one is diagonally across from *The Box* bar on Wenhua Xiang.

PSB "Bureau Entry-Exit Certificates Service" – the visa extension office, in other words – is on Beijing Lu, just south of Shangyi Jie (Ⓣ0871/3017878; Mon–Fri 9–11.30am & 1–5pm). They speak good English but are fairly slow with visa extensions; expect five days.

Shopping Kunming's most upmarket department store is the Gingko Shopping Plaza on Baita Lu, full of inernational-brand clothing and accessory boutiques. For just about everything else, head to the centre: Nanping Jie and Zhengyi Lu are full of clothes stores; there's an antiques warehouse between Guanghua Lu and Jingxing Jie; the pet market area is full of souvenir stalls; and the huge Carrefour supermarket on Nanping Jie has a cache of imported Western foodstuffs, plus Yunnan ham sold in slices, chunks and entire hocks. Yunnan's famous *pu'er* tea, usually compressed into attractive "bricks" stamped with good-luck symbols, is sold almost everywhere.

Travel agents Travel agents abound in Kunming, with virtually every hotel offering at least one travel service able to organize visas and private tours around the city, and to Shilin, Dali, Lijiang and Xishuangbanna, and to obtain tickets for onwards travel. Expect to pay commissions of at least ¥20 for bus- or train-ticket reservations, though plane tickets shouldn't attract a mark-up. CITS (Ⓣ0871/3157499, Ⓕ0871/3157498; Mon–Sat 9am–6pm) are at 328 Beijing Lu, but are mostly concerned with organizing package tours. For flights and overland jeep trips to Lhasa in Tibet – if possible – visit Mister Chen (Rm 3116, *Camellia Hotel*, 154 Dongfeng Dong Lu; Ⓣ0871/3188114).

Heilong Tan and Jin Dian

Two pleasant temple parks can easily be visited from Kunming on public buses. Ten kilometres north of the centre on bus #9 from the North bus station, **Heilong Tan** (黑龙潭, *hēilóng tán*; daily 8am–6pm; ¥30) is set in a garden of ancient trees, full of plum blossoms in spring. The two Ming temple buildings are modest Taoist affairs dedicated to the Heavenly Emperor and other deities, while the pool itself is said to be inhabited by a dragon forced by the Immortal, Lu Dongbin, to provide a permanent source of water for the local people. It's also rumoured to be haunted by a patriotic Ming scholar who zealously drowned himself and his family as a gesture of defiance in the face of invading Qing armies; his tomb stands nearby.

The same distance to the northeast, on bus #71 from Beijing Lu north of Dongfeng Guangchang, or bus #76 from Heilong Tan, is **Jin Dian Park** (金殿公园, *jīndiàn gōngyuán*; daily 7.30am–6pm; ¥30). Steps head up through woodland to a cluster of pleasantly worn Qing-dynasty halls housing weapons used by the rebel general Wu Sangui in 1671, behind which is Jin Dian itself, a gilded **bronze temple** built as a replica of the one atop Wudang Shan in Hubei (see p.441). The woods here are full of fragrant camellias and weekend picnickers, and a tower on the hill behind encloses a large Ming bell from Kunming's demolished southern gates.

Avoid taking the cable car from the back of the park to the **1999 Horticultural Expo Site** – a monster rip-off at ¥100 for a walk through vast, drab squares of low-maintainance flower beds. The Chinese do excellent gardens, but this isn't one of them.

Qiongzhu Si

Up in the hills 10km west of Kunming, the tranquil temple of **Qiongzhu Si** (筇竹寺, *qióngzhú sì*; ¥6) features a fantastic array of over-the-top Buddhist sculptures. Yet unless you charter a taxi (¥35 each way on the meter, or around ¥100 return including waiting time), it's a time-consuming place to reach; catch bus #82 from the western end of Nanping Jie or bus #C72 from Kunming train station to the West bus station, and then bus #C61 (7am–7pm) to the temple; check with the driver because not all #C61 buses come here. Allow forty minutes for the cab ride, and twice this for the bus.

The temple, a dignified building with black and red woodwork standing on Yuan-dynasty foundations, has been restored continually through the ages. Late in the nineteenth century, the eminent Sichuanese sculptor **Li Guangxiu** and his five assistants were engaged to embellish the main halls with five hundred clay statues of *arhats*. This they accomplished with inspired gusto, spending ten years creating the comical and grotesquely distorted crew of monks, goblins, scribes, emperors and beggars that crowd the interior – some sit rapt with holy contemplation, others smirk, roar with hysterical mirth or snarl grimly as they ride a foaming sea alive with sea monsters. Unfortunately it all proved too absurd for Li's conservative contemporaries and this was his final commission.

Other courtyards at the temple are thick with **rhinoceros** motifs – the exact meaning is ambiguous, but it's always considered auspicious. There's also a good, if pricey, tea room and **vegetarian restaurant** here open at lunchtime.

Xi Shan: the Western Hills

Xi Shan (西山, *xī shān*), the well-wooded **Western Hills** 16km outside Kunming, are an easy place to spend a day out of doors, with cable cars and pleasant walking trails ascending a 2500m-high ridge for views over **Dian Chi** (滇池, *diānchí*), the broad lake southwest of town. Again, catch bus #82 from the western end of Nanping Jie or bus #C72 from Kunming train station to the Western bus station, then bus #6 (6.30am–8pm) from over the rail tracks to the **park gates** at **Gaoyao** (高峣, *gāoyáo*). It's free to enter the Xi Shan area, though you do need to pay to reach **Long Men**, the spectacular Dragon Gate.

It's over an hour's walk from the gate to the main sights, but take time to visit the atmospheric temples of **Huating Si** (华亭寺, *huátíng sì*) and **Taihua Si** (太华寺, *tàihuá sì*), the latter reached along a warped, flagstoned path through old-growth forest. Past here you come to two **cable car stations**: one crosses back towards town (¥40), the other climbs to the Long Men area (¥25). You can walk to Long Men too: just carry straight on along the road and it's about twenty minutes to the **ticket office** (¥40). Then it's up narrow flights of stone steps, past a group of minor temples, and into a series of chambers and narrow tunnels which exit at **Long Men** (龙门, *lóngmén*) itself, a narrow balcony and ornamented grotto on a sheer cliff overlooking the lake. It took the eighteenth-century monk **Wu Laiqing** and his successors more than seventy years to excavate the tunnels, which continue up to where another flight of steps climbs to further lookouts.

Shilin

Shilin (石林, *shílín*; daily 8.30am–6pm; ¥175), Yunnan's renowned **Stone Forest**, comprises an exposed bed of limestone spires weathered and split into intriguing clusters, 90km east of Kunming. Comfortable **day-trips** are run by every tour desk in Kunming, but there are also public buses (¥35) from the East bus station – make sure you get one to the **scenic area** (石林景区, *shílín jǐngqū*) and not to Shilin town.

Once at Shilin, it takes about an hour to cover slowly the main circuit through the pinnacles to **Sword Peak Pond**, an ornamental pool surrounded by particularly sharp ridges, which you can climb along a narrow track leading right up across the top of the forest. This is the most frequented part of the park, with large red characters incised into famous rocks, and ethnic **Sani**, a Yi subgroup, in unnaturally clean dresses strategically placed for photographers. This area can be intimidatingly crammed with Chinese tour groups, but the paths that head out towards the perimeter are much quieter, leading to smaller, separate stone groupings in the fields beyond where you could spend the whole day without seeing another visitor.

At the park gates, a mess of stalls and restaurants sell pretty good, reasonably priced **food** – roast duck, pheasant, pigeon or fish – as well as poor souvenir embroideries.

Southeastern Yunnan

The region southeast of Kunming is a nicely unpackaged corner of the province, and there are good reasons, besides the **Vietnamese border crossing** at Hekou, to head down this way. Amiable, old-fashioned **Jianshui** boasts a complement of Qing architecture, and an unusual attraction in nearby caves, while **Yuanyang** is the base for exploring the cultures and impressive terraced landscapes of the Hong He Valley. Jianshui and Yuanyang can be tied together in a trip to the border, or each are directly accessible by bus from Kunming.

If planning to cross the border, you must obtain a Vietnamese **visa** in advance.

Jianshui and Yanzi Dong

JIANSHUI (建水, *jiànshuǐ*), a country town 200km south of Kunming, has been an administrative centre for over a thousand years. There's a good feel to the place, buoyed by plenty of **old architecture** and a very casual approach to tourism, making for a pleasant overnight stop. While you're here, try to visit **Yanzi Dong**, some unusual limestone caverns out in the countryside nearby.

The Town

On arrival, head straight for Jianshui's scruffy **old town**, a web of lanes entered through the huge red gateway of **Chaoyang Lou** (朝阳楼, *cháoyáng lóu*), the

Ming-dynasty eastern gate tower. Past here, cobbled **Lin'an Lu** runs through the old town, lined with wooden-fronted shops; 200m along, turn right up equally antique **Hanlin Jie**, and you'll arrive shortly at the grand **Zhujia Huayuan**, the traditional Zhu Family Gardens (朱家花园, *zhūjiā huāyuán*; daily 9am–10pm; ¥60, or ¥133 for a joint ticket including the Confucian Academy and Yangzi Dong). It's a Chinese box of interlocking halls and courtyards, brightly painted and in good condition.

Back on Lin'an Lu, a few minutes' walk past more old shops brings you the entrance of Jianshui's venerable **Confucian Academy** (文庙, *wénmiào*; ¥60). Once in past the large lilly-pond out front, there are ornamental stone gateways and halls containing statues of the Great Sage and his more gifted followers, with worried parents bringing their offspring here to kowtow to this patron of learning before school exams in the summer. Although what survives here is in good condition, it's clear the academy has suffered very badly over the years.

Also off Lin'an Lu, little **Hongjing Jie** (红井街, *hóng jǐng jiē*) leads into a completely unrestored corner of town, past blocks of mud-brick mansions and a stack of ancient **wells**, many of which are clearly still used by locals.

Practicalities

The pick of Jianshui's **places to stay**, at least for atmosphere, is the *Zhu Family Gardens* (ⓣ0873/7667109; ❻) with its rooms full of imitation Qing furniture. Better value, however, can be had at the *Lin'an Inn* (临安客栈, *línān kèzhàn*; ⓣ0873/7655866, ⓔlinaninn@hotmail.com; ❷), just past the gardens on Hanlin Jie, a friendly, antique courtyard-style homestay; book in advance. Opposite, *Hongmantian Kezhan* (红满天客栈, *hóng mǎntiān kèzhàn*; ⓣ0873/3183818, mobile 13987333101; ❸–❹) is a newer place succesfully made over with folksy effects; rooms are huge. The **cheapest beds** in town are at drab hostels on Lin'an Lu near the Hanlin Jie intersection, such as the *Garden* (花园宾馆, *huāyuán bīnguǎn*; ❷).

For **food**, *Xiangman Lou* (香满楼, *xiāngmǎn lóu*) is one of a couple of wooden, old-style noodle houses along Hanlin Jie where you can get stir-fried staples at low cost. For something more unusual, head to the *Yangjia Huayuan Canting* (杨家花园餐厅, *yángjiā huāyuán cāntīng*) on Hongjing Jie; you'll probably need to ask directions. They serve excellent home-cooked meals in what remains of another courtyard mansion, with the ingredients on view for pointing to. Also look out around town for places offering **qiguo**, a casserole whose inverted funnel design simultaneously poaches meat and creates a soup.

Jianshui's **bus station** is a kilometre northeast of Chaoyang Lou in the bland modern town; **bus #15** or a **taxi** (¥4) from here can drop you off at the Lin'an Lu/Hanlin Jie intersection in the old town. There's a Construction Bank **ATM** taking foreign cards on Lin'an Lu.

Leaving Jianshui, there are regular buses to Kunming, and less frequent services to Hekou and Yuanyang – the latter a long trip on a direct, scenic but rough road.

Yanzi Dong

Yanzi Dong, the Swallows' Caves (燕子洞, *yànzidòng*; ¥40), lie about 30km from Jianshui in the forested Lu River valley. For the last few centuries people have come to see the tens of thousands of **swiftlets** who nest here – the noise of wheeling birds is deafening during the early summer. It's all an enjoyable Chinese-style tourist attraction, featuring wooden walkways, a few coloured lights and rock formations, and an **underground restaurant** selling bird's-nest cakes – swiftlet nests, constructed out of hardened bird spit, are an expensive delicacy for the Chinese. If you can, catch the **Bird Nest Festival** on August 8, the only day of the year that collecting the then-vacant nests is allowed – a very profitable and dangerous task for local Yi men, who scale the 60m-high cliffs as crowds look on.

Through **buses** (¥10) from Jianshui tend to drop you on the highway, which you then cross and get a lift the last 2km with waiting minibuses (¥5). A minibus or taxi from town right to the caves will cost ¥120 return, including waiting time.

The Hong He Valley and Yuanyang

Hong He, the **Red River**, starts life near Xiaguan in Yunnan's northwest and runs southeast across the province, entering Vietnam at Hekou and flowing through Hanoi before emptying its waters, laden with volcanic soil, into the Gulf of Tonkin. For much of its journey the river is straight, channelled by high mountain ranges into a series of fertile, steep-sided valleys. These have been **terraced** by resident **Hani**, whose mushroom-shaped adobe-and-thatch houses pepper the hills around **Yuanyang**. In spring and autumn thick mists blanket the area, muting the violent contrast between red soil and brilliant green paddy fields. Though the best time to see them is between March and May, when the paddies are full of water, they are spectacular at any time.

Yuanyang and Xinjie

The access point for viewing the terraces is **Yuanyang** (元阳, *yuányáng*), a district 80km south of Jianshui and 300km from Kunming. The name covers two settlements: the riverside township of **Nansha** (元阳南沙, *yuányáng nánshā*), terminus for Jianshui buses; and, where you actually want to base yourself, **XINJIE** (元阳新街镇, *yuányáng xīnjiēzhèn*), 30km uphill at the top of a high ridge. Xinjie is a small, untidy brick-and-concrete town which becomes a hive of activity on **market days** (every five days), when brightly dressed Hani, Miao, Yi and Yao women pour in from surrounding villages. Minibuses (¥10) shuttle between Nansha and Xinjie throughout the day. Along the pedestrian shopping street off the square, there's an Agricultural Bank **ATM** that takes apparently taking foreign cards, but don't count on it.

Moving on from Xinjie, there are three direct buses daily to Kunming's South bus station (5hr; ¥128), and a couple to Hekou. For Jianshui, you'll have to head downhill to Nansha first, and pick up transport from there (4hr; ¥33).

Accommodation and eating

Accommodation in Xinjie is plentiful. Immediately out of the bus station and left, *Chen Family Guesthouse* (陈家旅社, *chénjiā lǚshè*; ⓣ0873/5622343; beds ¥25, en suite with squat toilet ❶) is clean and basic, with some of the best views in town from their terrace. A couple more options in the same lane include the *Minzu Guesthouse* (民族旅社, *mínzu lǚshè*; ⓣ0873/5623618; ❶). The only place in town offering any real comforts is the *Yunti Hotel* (云梯大酒店, *yúntī dàjiǔdiàn*; ⓣ0873/5624858, ⓦyunti-hotel.cn; ❸) which can be found by heading downhill from the bus station, past the square where the main road goes through a short tunnel, and straight ahead up a flight of steps when the road bends left after the market.

There are at least three simple **restaurants** around Xinjie's main square, all serving Sichuanese food; *Chuan Yu Fandian* (川渝饭店, *chuān yú fàndiàn*) is perhaps the best, friendly and with a good menu.

Around Xinjie

Xinjie sits surrounded by pretty villages and deeply terraced hillsides, some within walking distance or a short drive on local transport; private minibuses ply popular routes from village to village for a few yuan per person (they display their destinations in their front windows). If you're pushed for time you'll probably need to hire a minibus; ¥250 for the vehicle should cover a day's exploration and get you around most of the sights. Try and catch at least one village **market**, where fruit and veg, daily necessities, wild honey, buffaloes and chickens are sold, and watch men discreetly gambling in the background. They run between villages on a rota, and peak around noon.

For **information** on where to go, how to get there and how much to pay, visit the World Vision-sponsored **Window on Yuanyang** (元阳之窗, *yuányáng zhī chuāng*; ⓣ0873/5623627) up the steps beside the *Yunti Hotel* (see opposite). They can organize minibus rental and tour guides, and have simple but useful **hiking maps** of the local area. One easy walk is a loop, via various hamlets, to the Hani village of **Jinzhuzhai** and **Longshuba**, a Yi settlement, which nestle quietly amid trees, giant bamboo and paddy fields.

There are several places from where you can view the famous **terraces**, each with an entry fee. A roadside viewing platform 18km northwest of town at **Mengping** (勐平, *mèngpíng*; ¥30), gives you the chance to be mobbed by Yi women selling postcards; **sunset** is the best time to visit. The southwestern road (¥60 covers all sights along it) will get you to viewpoints at **Bada** (坝达, *bàdá*; 16km from town) and the attractive farm village of **Duoyishu** (多依树, *duōyīshù*; 27km), where you can stay at the *Sunny Guesthouse* (阳光客栈, *yángguāng kèzhàn*; ⓣ15126399443; ❶) and catch the **sunrise** – the guesthouse is hard to find though, so give them a call first.

Hekou and the border

HEKOU (河口, *hékǒu*), 360km southeast of Kunming, is only worth a special visit if you're in transit between China and Vietnam – the border post is a few minutes' walk from the bus station. On the other side, **Lao Cai** has a huge game market, a few despondent hotels, and a **train station** 3km south that offers two services daily for the ten-hour run to Hanoi. Most travellers take a **bus** or motorbike-taxi (US$5) to the hill resort town of **Sa Pa**.

Arriving from Vietnam, head 50m up the main road and the bus station is on the left. Here you can catch fast buses to Kunming's East bus station (8hr; ¥139), or ordinary buses to Yuanyang and Jianshui. To **change money**, walk up the main street from the border, turn right after 200m, and you'll arrive at the Bank of China (daily 8am–5.30pm; foreign exchange closed Sun).

Northwestern Yunnan

Vigorously uplifted during the last fifty million years as the Indian subcontinent buckled up against China, **northwestern Yunnan** is a geologically unsettled region of subtropical forests, thin pasture, alpine lakes and shattered peaks painted crisply in blue, white and grey. **Xiaguan** is the regional hub, springboard for the route north via a string of old towns, once staging posts on the *chama dao*, the **trade routes** between China and Tibet, along which tea, salt and other goods were transported on horseback. The lakeshore town of **Dali** is the first, home to the Bai nationality and backed by a long mountain range; but picturesque **Lijiang**, a few hours up the road at the base of Yulong Xue Shan, pulls in the biggest crowds as the former capital of the **Naxi** kingdom. Hikers can organize themselves here for a two-day trek through **Tiger Leaping Gorge**, where a youthful Yangzi River cuts through the deepest chasm on Earth. Nearby is **Lugu Hu**, lakeside home to the matrilineal **Mosuo**, while north again is the Tibetan monastery town of **Shangri-La** (also more prosaically known as Zhongdian). By now you're barely in Yunnan, and a day's further travel will carry up to **Deqin**, where a spectacular string of peaks marks the Tibetan borderlands. Finally, northwest of Xiaguan, the **Nu Jiang Valley** is one of China's intriguing backwaters, with pristine jungle and isolated communities.

Xiaguan is just five hours from Kunming **by bus**, and from here there are at least regular, if not always speedy, services through the rest of the region. **Trains** link Kunming to Xiaguan (near Dali) and Lijiang, with talk of an extension to Shangri-La; and you can **fly** to Lijiang and Shangri-La. There are overland routes **into Sichuan** from Lijiang and Shangri-La too; but at the time of writing the **Tibet road** from Deqin, which follows the dramatic upper reaches of the Lancang River to Markam, then turns west towards Lhasa, was closed to foreigners. Ask agencies in Dali, Lijiang and Shangri-La about the latest situation.

If possible, it's probably best to head up this way in autumn: winters are extremely cold, and while early spring is often sunny, summers – though fairly mild – can also be very wet, leading to landslides. Also be aware that the border regions around Shangri-La and Deqin might be **closed off** during March, historically a time of political unrest in Tibet – see p.898.

Xiaguan and around

Some 380km west of Kunming underneath a string of mountain-top wind turbines, **Xiaguan** is a sprawling transport hub on the southern shore of Er Hai Lake, and you'll certainly end up here at some point, if only to change buses. Dali is barely an hour's ride up the lakeshore, but if you can resist its lure then both the holy mountain of **Jizu Shan** and **Weishan**, a small, unrestored market town to the south, are just about manageable as day-trips – though you'll get far more out of them by staying a night.

Xiaguan

XIAGUAN (下关, *xiàguān*), also confusingly known as **Dali Shi** (大理市, *dàlǐ shì*), is where most long-distance "Dali" transport actually terminates. The **train station** is in the east of town on Weishan Lu; city bus #8 to old Dali town stops right outside. Diagonally across the road, **Dali bus station** (大理汽车客运站, *dàlǐ qìchē kèyùn zhàn*) is of most use for Kunming and Binchuan (for Jizu Shan, see opposite); while a kilometre west on Xingcheng Lu, **Xingcheng express bus station** (兴盛高快客运站, *xīngshèng gāokuài kèyùn zhàn*) handles fast traffic to Kunming and points west, such as Baoshan and Tengchong; for old Dali town, turn right out of the bus station, walk to the main intersection, then turn right again and it's 150m to the #8 bus stop. There's also a **North bus station** (客运北站, *kèyùn běi zhàn*), 3km north of the centre on the Dali highway, with further buses to Kunming and regular departures for Lijiang and Shangri-La (Zhongdian) – again, the #8 bus stops right outside. The **airport** is 15km east, for which you'll need a taxi (¥60 to Dali old town).

With Dali so close, you won't need to spend the night in Xiaguan, and probably the only reason to come here aside from transport is to get a **China visa extension** from the helpful PSB (Mon–Fri 9–11.30am & 2–5pm; ⓣ0872/2142149). They're located north of town on the Xiaguan–Dali highway; get off the #8 bus at the Century Middle School stop (世纪中学, *shìjì zhōngxué*) – it's the building in front of you with a radio tower on the roof.

Jizu Shan

The holy mountain of **Jizu Shan** (鸡足山, *jīzú shān*; ¥60) lies about 90km northeast of Xiaguan, and is associated with Buddhism's Chan (Zen) sect. There are a handful of temples here, but perhaps the best thing about a visit is the scenery, especially views from the mountain's summit. On the trek up, you can ponder various unlikely explanations for Jizu Shan's odd name – it means "Chickenfoot Mountain".

To get here, catch one of the frequent buses from Xiaguan's Dali bus station to **Binchuan** (宾川, *bīnchuān*; 2hr; ¥25), then a minibus from the back of the station to Jizu Shan (¥13; 1hr 30min) – these leave when full, and run from around 8am until 4pm.

The road ends halfway up the mountain, in woodland between the simple **Shizhong Temple** (石钟寺, *shízhōng sì*) and larger **Wanshou Nunnery** (万寿庵, *wànshòu ān*). There's a knot of cheap **restaurants** off to one side here, whose owners also offer **beds** (❶). Follow the road up to a sharp kink, then take the unsigned path alongside the **horse pen** up the mountain. It's 3.5km on foot from here to the top, following steps through the forest and onto heathland; a kilometre along, there's also a **cable car** (¥40 one-way) to just below the summit. Walking, give yourself at least two hours to complete the ascent, which ends where the ninth-century **Lengyan Pagoda** (楞严塔, *lèngyán tǎ*) and accompanying **Jinding Si** (金顶寺, *jīndǐng sì*) – identical to Kunming's Jin Dian (see p.693) – rise splendidly against the skyline.

Weishan

WEISHAN (巍山, *wēishān*) is a charismatic old town 50km south of Xiaguan; now largely forgotten, it was the cradle of the Nanzhao kingdom and a prosperous stop on the tea-horse trade routes. Today it's a supply town for the local Bai, Muslim and – especially – **Yi** population; there's a huge **Yi market** every ten days just up the road at **Dian Nan** (甸南, *diànnán*), on the way down from Xiaguan. **Buses to Weishan** (1hr 30min; ¥13) depart Xiaguan's South bus station (客运南站, *kèyùn nán zhàn*) on Nanjian Lu; catch bus #4 from Dali, or a cab from other arrival points in Xiaguan.

The highway here runs down a long, low valley, where you get dropped at the **bus station** along Weishan's western edge. Turn left out of the bus station, then take any street left again and you'll soon be walking the cobbled lanes of the **old town**; there are few street signs, but the only thing you need to find anyway is **Gongchen Lou** (拱辰楼, *gǒngchén lóu*), a huge old gate tower marking the centre of town. Climb it and you'll see Weishan's pedestrianized main street, all lined with old wooden shops, running 500m south to smaller **Xinggong Lou** (星拱楼, *xīnggǒng lóu*), once a bell tower. Weishan's back lanes are full of markets and wobbly adobe houses, temples and pagodas, but the town's biggest appeal is the fact that nothing is geared to tourism, and people are just getting on with their lives. If you need action beyond people-watching, head 13km south to **Weibao Shan** (巍保山, *wēibǎo shān*), a Taoist holy mountain dotted with layered, Nanzhao-era pagodas.

Leaving, there are buses to Xiaguan every fifteen minutes, and three daily direct to Kunming (6hr; ¥110).

Accommodation and eating

Weishan's best **accommodation** is all central. Just east from Gongchen Lou at 59 Dongxin Jie, *Gucheng Kezhan* (古城客栈, *gǔchéng kèzhàn*; ⓣ0872/6122341; ❶) has basic beds with shared toilets in an old courtyard building, while nearby *Weishan Binguan* (巍山宾馆, *wēishān bīnguǎn*; ⓣ0872/6122655; ❶–❷) is more of a drab Chinese hotel, but with large en-suite rooms. The *Mengshe Stagehouse* (蒙舍驿站, *mēngshě yìzhàn*; ⓣ0872/6123338; ❷), 50m past Xinggong Lou at 9 Nanjie, is in a reconstructed old inn, though rooms are bland.

For **food**, head to **Xiaochi Jie** (小吃街, *xiǎochī jiē*) or "Snack Street", again near Gongchen Lou, which is lined with inexpensive restaurants.

Dali and around

A thirty-minute local bus ride north of Xiaguan, **DALI** draws swarms of holidaying middle-class urban Chinese seeking an "old China" experience, while foreign backpackers drift through a Westerner-friendly theme park of beer gardens and hippified cafés. It's not hard to see why people flock here: despite the tourist overkill along the main streets, Dali is pretty, interesting and relaxed, full of old houses and an indigenous **Bai** population rubbing shoulders with local Yi and Muslims. To the east lies the great lake, **Er Hai**, while the invitingly green valleys and clouded peaks of the **Cang Shan range** rear up behind town, the perfect setting for a few days' walking or relaxation. Some visitors, seduced by China's closest approximation to bohemia (and the local weed) forget to leave, and plenty of resident Westerners run businesses here.

There's also much more to Dali than its modern profile. Between the eighth and thirteenth centuries, the town was at the centre of the Nanzhao and Dali kingdoms, while in the mid-nineteenth century it briefly became capital of the state declared by **Du Wenxiu**, who led a Muslim rebellion against Chinese rule. Millions died in the revolt's suppression and Dali was devastated, never to recover its former political position. An earthquake destroyed the town in 1925, but it was rebuilt in its former style.

If you can, visit during the **Spring Fair**, held from the fifteenth day of the third lunar month (April or May). The event spans five hectic days of horse trading, wrestling, racing, dancing and singing, attracting thousands of people from all over the region to camp at the fairground just west of town. You'll probably have to follow suit, as beds in Dali will be in short supply. In addition, an impressive but frankly scary **Yi torch festival** is held on the 24th day of the sixth lunar month – flaming torches are paraded at night, and people even throw gunpowder at each other.

Orientation and arrival

Some 2km west of Er Hai and just below the slopes of Cang Shan, Dali's old town covers about four square kilometres, much of which is contained by remains of its Ming-dynasty walls. The main axis of its grid-like street plan is cobbled, pedestrianized **Fuxing Lu**, which runs between the old north and south gate towers. **Bo'ai Lu** runs parallel and to the west, while the centre hinges around **Huguo Lu** (whose pedestrianized western arm is known as **Yangren Jie**, or Foreigner's Street), cutting across both at right angles. Dali also sits between two wide **highways**: the one running alongside the western wall handles local traffic shuttling between Xiaguan and Shaping; while some lakeside buses, plus long-distance services between Xiaguan, Lijiang and points north, travel the eastern highway.

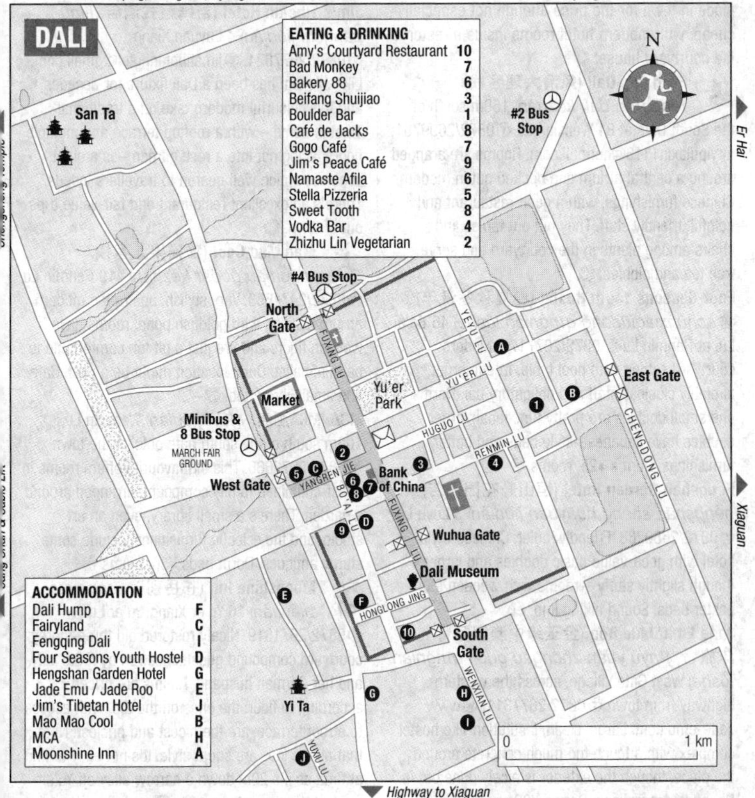

Arriving from Xiaguan, bus #8 comes up along eastern Chengdong Lu, turns west along Yu'er Lu, and terminates outside the West Gate; bus #4 runs up Bao'ai Lu before terminating by the North Gate. **From Lijiang**, Shangri-La and the north, you'll be dropped on the highway at the northeastern corner of town, from where you can catch bus #2 to Yu'er Lu. Dali doesn't have its own bus station so, **leaving**, book **long-distance bus tickets** through agents in town – who will also tell you where to pick buses up – or head down to the relevant stations in Xiaguan and sort things out yourself. Agents can also organize **train** and **plane** tickets.

Accommodation

Dali has plenty of good-value places to stay, though rates can double during local festivals. There's also more remote accommodation in the *Cang Shan* range at *Higherlander Inn* and the spartan Wuwei Si, and at Xizhou's upmarket *Linden Centre* – see p.706.

Dali Hump (大理驼峰青年旅舍, *dàlǐ tuófēng qīngnián lǚshě*) Honglong Jing ⓣ0872/2676933, ⓦwww.dalihump.com. Brand new sister to the Kunming operation, but already a major travellers' hangout. Two tiers of rooms around a broad courtyard, a bar, restaurant with communal seating arrangements and a laidback, hippyish vibe. Lots of musical activity in the evenings. Dorms ¥30, rooms ❷

Fairyland (连锁酒店, *liánsuǒ jiǔdiàn*) 31 Yangren Jie, west of Bo'ai Lu ⓣ0872/2680999. Probably the smartest place in town for the price, though not especially cheap, with modern hotel rooms inside a restored old courtyard house. ❹

Fengqing Dali (风清大理客栈, *fēngqīng dàlǐ kèzhàn*) 150m south of the South Gate at 81 Wenxian Lu ⓣ0872/2699761, ⓔyipulaxin1116@hotmail.com. Rooms are aranged around a central atrium and decked out in modern Chinese furnishings, with a good restaurant and helpful, friendly staff. They put out tables and chairs among plants in the courtyard and serve free tea and nibbles. ❸

Four Seasons Youth Hostel (春夏秋冬青年旅舍, *chūnxiàqiūdōng qīngnián lǚshè*) 46 Bo'ai Lu, at Renmin Lu ⓣ0872/2677177. Modern courtyard setting with pool table, free internet, aimiably clueless staff and obligatory bar. Dorms and small doubles are pretty functional; larger doubles have Japanese-style beds and better furnishings. Dorms ¥25, rooms ❷

Hengshan Garden Hotel (恒山升花园酒店, *héngshān shēng huāyuán jiǔdiàn*) 3 Luyu Lu ⓣ0872/2680288. Friendly, quiet, Chinese-style hotel with good-value basic doubles and larger – though slightly stuffy – rooms with wooden four-poster beds. Sound hiking info. ❷

Jade Emu/Jade Roo (金玉缘中澳国际青年旅舍, *jīnyù yuán zhōngào guójì qīngnián lǚshè*) West Gate Village, across the western highway from town ⓣ0872/2677311, ⓦwww.jade-emu.com. Large, clean, institution-like hostel complex with a touch too much concrete around the place, though the exterior is nicely done out in Bai-style decorations. Dorms ¥30, rooms ❷

Jim's Tibetan Hotel (吉姆藏式酒店, *jímǔ zāngshì jiǔdiàn*) 4 Luyuan Xiang ⓣ0872/2677824, ⓔjimstibetanhotel@gmail.com. Likeable Jim has been a Dali fixture for decades, and this colourful modern take on a traditional Tibetan home – with a rooftop terrace and multiple floors facing out into a rose garden – is a quiet, spacious option well geared to travellers' needs. There's an excellent restaurant and fair-value trips out of town. ❹

Mao Mao Cool (猫猫果儿客栈, *māomāo guǒér kèzhàn*) 419 Renmin Lu ⓣ0872/2474653. Very stylish, open-plan modern atrium building with goldfish pond; rooms have wooden floors and are just a bit too comfortable to be minimalist. Quiet location might be a plus. Café and small library too. ❷–❹

MCA (MCA酒店, *MCA jiǔdiàn*) Wenxian Lu, 100m south of the south gate outside the town ⓣ0872/2673666. This old favourite offers rooms in a self-contained family compound arranged around a garden. There's a small library, even an art studio, and the eclectic furnishings include some sturdy antiques. Dorm beds ¥30, rooms ❷

Moonshine Inn (苍岳别院, *cāngyuè biéyuàn*) 16 Yu'er Xiang, Yu'er Lu ⓣ0872/2671319. Nicely restored old three-storey courtyard compound guesthouse run by a Bai lady and her German husband. Rooms are priced according to floor: the ones on the top, with access to a roof terrace, are the nicest and priciest. Note that all the loos are squat style. It's not easy to find at first, as it's 20m down a narrow alley off Yu'er Lu; look for the red sign. ❷–❸

The Town

Get your bearings on top of Dali's old **South Gate** (南门, *nánmén*; ¥20), where you can study Xiaguan, Er Hai, the town and mountains from the comfort of a teahouse. Dali's antique **pagodas** stand as landmarks above the roof lines, **Yi Ta** due west, and the trinity of **San Ta** a few kilometres north. **Fuxing Lu**, choked with tour groups and souvenir stalls selling ethnic silverware and embroideries, runs north through the town: about 150m along, the heavy stone **Wuhua Gate** (五华楼, *wǔhuá lóu*) is a modern construction, similar in style to the South Gate. Past here, Fuxing Lu is crossed by **Renmin Lu** and **Yangren Jie**, which – along with parallel **Bo'ai Lu** – are where to find most of Dali's Westerner-friendly bars, cafés, masseurs, tour agents and trinket and clothing stalls. While browsing this area, you'll also be hounded by middle-aged Bai ladies hissing "ganja, ganja". Escape by detouring east down Renmin Lu to the splendid blue, multitiered Bai-style **Catholic Church** (天主教堂, *tiānzhǔjiào táng*) in an alley off to the south.

Beyond here, the mass-market crowds thin out considerably, and it's worth just wandering around Dali's cobbled residential back lanes. **Yu'er Park** (玉洱公园, *yù'ěr gōngyuán*; 6am–8pm) is a pleasant, if small, patch of trees; and Dali's northwestly **produce market** is worth a look too, especially when crowds of hawkers, farmers and shoppers descend for the weekly **market**. Finally, the

North Gate (北门, *běimén*) can again be climbed for views; Zhonghe Lu to the east is lined with little **marble factories**, turning out the grey-streaked sculptures for which Dali is famous.

Dali Museum

Down on Fuxing Lu near the South Gate, **Dali Museum** (大理博物馆, *dàlǐ bówùguǎn*; daily 8.30am–5pm; free) takes the form of a small Chinese palace with guardian stone lions and cannons in the courtyard. It was built for the Qing governor and appropriated as Du Wenxiu's "Forbidden City" during Du's insurrection. Historic relics include a strange bronze model of two circling dragons, jaws clenched around what might be a tree; a few Buddhist figurines from the Nanzhao period; and some lively statues of an orchestra and serving maids from a Ming noblewoman's tomb – a nice addition to the usual cases of snarling gods and warrior busts. The gardens outside are pleasant, planted with lantana and bougainvillea, with the mountains behind.

Yi Ta and San Ta

Built when the region was a major Buddhist centre, Dali's distinctively tall and elegant **pagodas** are still standing after a millennium of wars and earthquakes. Over the highway and uphill from Dali's southwestern corner is the solitary **Yi Ta** (一塔, *yītǎ*) a tenth-century tower surrounded by ancient trees. For the more ostentatious Three Pagodas, or **San Ta** (三塔, *sān tǎ*; daily 8am–7pm; ¥120, or ¥190 including the temple), catch bus #19 from outside the South Gate on Wenxian Lu, cycle, or walk for half an hour north along the highway. Built around 850, the 69m-tall, square-based **Qianxun tower** is a century older than the two smaller octagonal pagodas behind. As the structures are sealed, the stiff entrance fee gives access only to souvenir stalls around their base; if you've bought the full ticket, however, you can visit the artlessly huge and completely forgettable **Chongsheng Temple** (崇圣寺, *chóngshèng sì*) behind, built from scratch around 2005.

Eating and drinking

Chinese **restaurants** outside the south gate and around the intersections of Fuxing Lu with Renmin Lu and Huguo Lu offer steamers of dumplings and **Bai specialities** such as fish or tofu casseroles, snails and stir-fried mountain vegetables and fungi. On the whole, food at these places isn't great, despite fresh ingredients – though the home-made **plum wine** (梅酒, *méijiǔ*) is worth a try. Similar **Muslim** canteens display grilled kebabs and fresh bread, and are a sounder bet. For **cafés and bars** serving a mix of Western and Chinese staples, head to Renmin Lu's western end, along with adjacent Yangren Jie and Bo'ai Lu. Food aside, they make good places to meet other foreigners and swap news, use the **internet** (around ¥5/hr or free wi-fi) and get in touch with the latest martial-art, language or painting courses.

Dali's nightlife revolves around its **bars**. The best of these is the raucous *Bad Monkey* on Renmin Lu, run by a pair of English wide boys, who offer shepherds' pie, Lao and Belgian beer, and droll chat. There are plenty of smaller speakeasies further down, towards the east gate, such as the popular *Vodka Bar*. Alternatively, there are a stack of new places flanking the recently installed stream on **Honglong Jing**, with outdoor tables and lounge chairs – they're all identical, so suit yourself.

Amy's Courtyard Restaurant 2 Bo'ai Lu, just past the gate. One of the better places to try Bai fish head (or tofu) casseroles, cold cucumber salad and deep-fried goat's cheese with sugar. Around ¥25/person.

Bakery 88 88 Bo'ai Lu. German-run café with superb European cakes and breads to eat in or take away.

Beifang Shuijiao (北方水饺, *běifāng shuǐjiǎo*) Renmin Lu. Cheap, cheerful hole-in-the-wall specializing in northern Chinese *jiaozi*, with friendly, slow service.

Café de Jacks Bo'ai Lu. Large, cruisy, comfortable place to spend an afternoon over a coffee and chocolate cake, or dig into their selection of curries, pizzas and a few Bai dishes. The open fire makes it cosy on winter evenings.

Gogo Café Renmin Lu. Popular for spaghetti, pizzas, large breakfasts, fruit juices and good coffee. They also have a book exchange, free internet and can burn CDs. Like most restaurant-bars in the street, they stick tables outside during the summer.

Jim's Peace Café Bo'ai Lu. Restaurant underneath *Jim's Peace Guesthouse*, with comfy sofas, a well-stocked bar and a fine yak stew. Get four people together for a Tibetan banquet (¥30), cooked by the owner's mother.

Namaste Afila (亚菲拉印度菜, *yàfēilā yìndù cài*) Tucked into a small courtyard off Bo'ai Lu. A Moorish mud-brick-and-tiled courtyard, and a wide selection of mostly vegetarian Indian samosas, curries and thalis, make this a very attractive place to dine. There's a huge fireplace indoors for cooler weather. Stuff yourself for ¥50.

Stella Pizzeria Huguo Lu. The wood-fired clay oven delivers the best pizzas in town, and the laidback decor is appealing too, with lots of nooks and crannies for privacy.

Sweet Tooth 52 Bo'ai Lu. A polished and pristine café, run by deaf-and-dumb staff, with great cheesecake.

Zhizhu Lin Vegetarian (纸竹林素食苑, *zhǐ zhúlín sùshí yuàn*) Bo'ai Lu. Elegant courtyard teahouse and vegetarian restaurant, whose English menu explains the medicinal qualities of each dish. Imitation crispy duck and "boiled beef slices", along with aromatic lotus root, crunchy fungi and a good tea will set you back about ¥80.

Listings

Banks and exchange The Bank of China (foreign exchange daily 8am–7pm) is on Fuxing Lu, where you'll also find the only ATMs in town.

Bookshop There's a branch of Kunming's excellent English-language bookshop, Mandarin Books, on the western arm of Renmin Lu.

Internet There's a 24hr internet café (¥3/hr) at the top of Renmin Lu, near Bo'ai Lu, though most accommodation has terminals and free wi-fi.

Mail The post office (daily 8am–9pm) is is on Fuxing Lu, at Hugou Lu. Expect to have all parcels sent from here checked minutely for drugs.

Martial arts training Contact Wuwei Si (see p.706).

Around Dali

Lying either side of Dali, **Er Hai Lake** and the **Cang Shan Range** can keep you busy for a few days, though the lake itself is probably of less interest than the **villages** dotting its shore. Some of these also host **markets**, full of activity and local characters, where you can watch all manner of goods being traded and pick up local **tie-dyed cloth**.

Aside from local transport outlined below, **agents** in Dali – such as *Jim's Peace Café* or Michael's Travel (both on Bo'ai Lu) – can organize Er Hai boat trips (¥100/person), visits to a Bai home (¥50/person) and discounted tickets for the Cang Shan cableways. There are also a number of **specialist tour operators** based in Dali to help you get the most out of your trip: these include Climb Dali (Ⓣ0872/8871230, Ⓦwww.climbdali.com), based at the *Boulder Bar* at 393 Renmin Lu; Cycling Dali (Ⓣ0872/2671385), at 55 Bo'ai Lu; and Amiwa (Ⓦwww.amiwa-trek.com), a trekking company with Bai guides. For **outdoor gear**, try Active Traveller, next to *Jim's Peace Café* on Bo'ai Lu.

Cang Shan

Cang Shan (苍山, *cāng shān*; ¥30), the Green Mountains, are just that: a 50km-long range peaking between 2000m and 4000m, cloaked in thick forest and cloud – and, often well into spring, snow. Ascending the heights is easy thanks to two **cableways**, linked by a walking trail, or you can hike up.

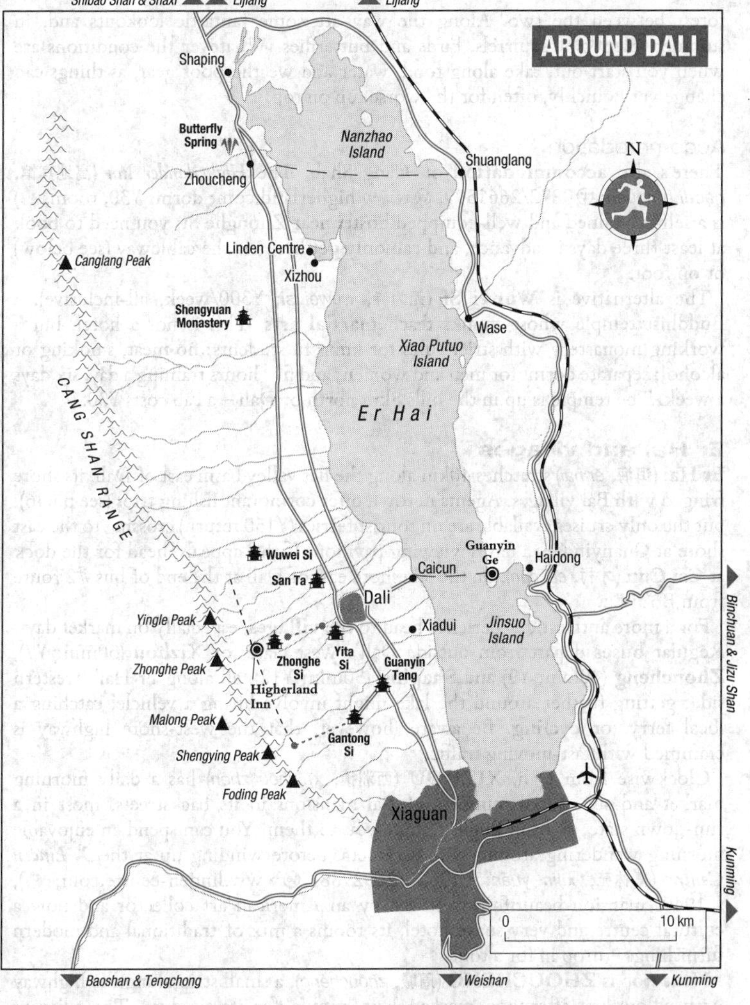

Cang Shan has two main **access points**. Catch bus #4 heading south down the highway west of Dali for 5km to the Guanyin Tang temple complex (观音堂, *guānyīn táng*), from where you can walk an hour uphill or catch a cab (¥10) to the cable car at **Gantong Si** (感通寺, *gǎntōng sì*; ¥50 one-way, ¥80 return). This offers a fantastic 25-minute ride over the treetops, with unsurpassed views of the lake, town and peaks along the way. The alternative is to catch a cab (¥10) 3km northwest to the **Zhonghe Si Cableway** (中和寺索道, *zhōnghé sì suǒdào*; ¥35 one-way, ¥50 return). This doesn't run on windy days, or if they don't think enough people are going to show – in which case you can **hike up** in about two hours. At the top is **Zhonghe Si** itself, a small temple, with more views and access to the *Higherland Inn* (see p.706).

A well-made, level, 13km-long **hiking track** connects the two upper cableway stations at Gantong Si and Zhonghe Si, allowing an easy 4hr walk through thick forest between the two. Along the way are some fantastic lookouts and, in summer, plenty of squirrels, birds and butterflies. Whatever the conditions are when you start out, take along food, water and weatherpoof gear, as things can change very quickly, often for the worse, up on top.

Accommodation

There's also **accommodation** on Cang Shan. The *Higherlander Inn* (高地宾馆, *gāodì bīnguen*; ⓣ0872/2661599, ⓦwww.higherland.com; dorms ¥30, rooms ❷) is a self-contained and well-equipped hostel near Zhonghe Si; you need to book at least three days in advance, and can only get here via the cableway (see below) or on foot.

The alternative is **Wuwei Si** (无为寺, *wúwéi sì*; ¥300/week, all-inclusive), a Buddhist temple whose monks teach **martial arts**. This is not a hotel, but a working monastery with strict rules for kung fu students: no meat, smoking or alcohol; separate dorms for men and women; and five hours training a day, six days a week. The temple is up in the hills 8km north of Dali – a cab costs ¥30.

Er Hai and villages

Er Hai (洱海, *ěr hǎi*) stretches 40km along the flat valley basin east of Dali, its shore fringed with Bai villages. Agents in town offer cormorant fishing trips (see p.646), but the only cruises available are on tourist ferries (¥150 return) crossing to the east shore at Guanyin Ge, a flashy viewing pavilion. If this appeals, head for the dock at **Cai Cun** (才村, *cái cūn*), on the lakeshore east of Dali at the end of bus #2 route from Bo'ai Lu.

For a more authentic experience head to the **villages**, especially on market days. Regular **buses** depart from outside Dali's West Gate for **Xizhou** (30min; ¥7), **Zhoucheng** (40min; ¥9) and **Shaping** (50min; ¥12), all along Er Hai's western side; getting further around the lake might involve hiring a vehicle, catching a local ferry, or **cycling**. Be aware, however, that the west-shore highway is crammed with fast-moving traffic.

Clockwise from Dali, **XIZHOU** (西洲镇, *xī zhōu zhèn*) has a daily morning market and substantial numbers of Bai mansions in its backstreets, most in a run-down state; signs in English guide you to them. You can spend an enjoyable morning wandering around with a camera, before winding up at the *Linden Centre* (喜林苑, *xǐlín yuàn*; ⓣ0872/2452988, ⓦwww.linden-centre.com; ❾), a 1940s mansion beautifully restored by an American art collector and now a cultural centre and very suave hotel, its rooms a mix of traditional and modern furnishings – drop in for a tour.

Next stop is **ZHOUCHENG** (周城, *zhōuchéng*), a small strip along the highway with a low-key afternoon market, best known for its tie-dyes. The adjacent **Butterfly Spring** (蝴蝶泉, *húdié quán*; ¥80) is an electric-blue pond haunted by clouds of butterflies when an overhanging acacia flowers in early summer. You can also catch a ferry to Shuanglang (1hr; around ¥40) from **Tauyuan dock** (桃源码头, *táoyuán mǎtóu*), just down off the main road; prices and schedules are by negotiation.

Overlooking the very top of the lake around 30km from Dali, **SHAPING** is worth a visit for its **Monday market**, when what seems like the entire regional population crowds on to the small hill behind town to trade. From here, public transport dries up as the road cuts around to Er Hai's east shore; there's a great Tuesday market at **SHUANGLANG** (双廊, *shuānglάng*) and another on dates ending in 5 or 0 at **WASE** (挖色, *wāsè*), about 15km south. From Wase, there are buses through the day to Xiaguan's Dali bus station.

Shaxi and Shibao Shan

SHAXI (沙系, *shāxī*; entry ¥30), 90km northwest of Dali, is a tiny rustic relic of the once busy **tea-horse trade route** between China and Tibet. Listed as an endangered site by the World Monuments Fund, much of the town has been sympathetically restored and has a lot to offer: **Xingjiao Temple** (兴教寺, *xīng jiāo sì*) was founded in 1415 and overlooks cobbled **Sifang** (四方, *sìfāng*), the main square; and there are stacks of muddy alleyways, old bridges and wood and stone mansions to admire. It's all very small and quiet, however; the best time to come is for the **Friday market** in Sideng (as Shaxi's centre is sometimes called), when Yi and Bai villagers descend from the remote hills roundabout.

Shaxi lies southwest of the Dali-Lijiang highway town of **Jianchuan** (剑川, *jiànchuān*): coming from the south, catch a Jianchuan bus and get off 10km short at the road junction settlement of **Diannan**, where Shaxi minibuses (¥8) wait; from the north, pick up the minibus (¥8) at Jianchuan itself.

Accommodation and eating

Despite its diminutive size, Shaxi has plenty of **accommodation**, all of it in converted old mansions. Right on Sifang, *Horse Pen 46* (马围客栈, *mǎwéi kèzhàn*; ⓣ0872/4722299, ⓦwww.horsepen46.com; dorms ¥35, rooms ❷) is a cute spot with English-speaking owners and good hiking information; *Laomadian Lodge* (沙系老马店, *shāxī laǒmǎdiàn*; ⓣ0872/4722666, ⓔlaomadian@gmail.com; ❺), also on Sifang, is in a class of its own, beautifully restored and with a superb restaurant; while *Tea and Horse Caravan Trail Inn* (古茶马客栈, *gǔ chámǎ kèzhàn*; ⓣ0872/4721051; dorms ¥40, rooms ❷) is another good choice, with modern doubles.

A handful of **cafés** and stir-fry kitchens can provide food through the day.

Shibao Shan

Shibao Shan (石宝山, *shíbǎo shān*; ¥50) forms a high, forested sandstone ridge scattered with small temples, a three-hour hike or a forty-minute taxi ride (¥150 return) from Shaxi. The main sight here is the Stone Bell Temple, **Shizhong Si** (石钟寺, *shízhōng sì*), a series of galleries of Tang-dynasty Buddhist figures carved into an overhang, with wooden awnings protecting the more exposed images. Some of the carvings depict Nanzhao kings, others show Buddha, Guanyin and other saints; many show a strong Indian influence. At the end is a carving of, as the sign tactfully phrases it, "female reproductive organs", and a further niche – generally closed off to view – decorated with graphically sexual frescoes.

Lijiang

LIJIANG (丽江, *lìjiāng*), capital of the **Naxi Kingdom**, nestles 150km north of Dali at foot of the inspiringly spiky and ice-bound massif of **Yulong Xue Shan**, the Jade Dragon Snow Mountain. Surrounded by green fields and pine forests, the town's winding cobbled lanes form a centuries-old maze, flanked by clean streams, weeping willows and rustic stone bridges. It is also, however, China's biggest **tourist black spot**, and while undeniably pretty, has become little more than a cultural theme park, and the template against which all "old towns" in China are being remodeled. Packs of visitors throng the streets, while the Naxi family homes that line them have been converted into rank after rank of guesthouses and souvenir shops, mostly run by Han Chinese posing in ethnic costumes. Despite this, it's easy to spend a couple of days in Lijiang, especially if you've been out in

The Naxi

The Naxi are descended from Tibetan nomads who settled the region before the tenth century, bringing with them a shamanistic religion known as **Dongba**. A blend of Tibetan Bon, animist and Taoist tendencies, Dongba's scriptures are written in the only hieroglyphic writing system still in use, with 1400 pictograms. The Naxi deity **Sanduo** is a warrior god depicted dressed in white, riding a white horse and wielding a white spear. Murals depicting him and other deities still decorate temples around Lijiang, and are a good excuse to explore nearby villages.

Strong **matriarchal** influences permeate Naxi society, particularly in the language. For example, nouns become weightier when the word female is added, so a female stone is a boulder, a male stone a pebble. Inheritance passes through the female line to the eldest daughter. Women do most of the work, and own most of the businesses; accordingly, the Naxi women's costume of caps, shawls and aprons is sturdy and practical, while retaining its symbolic meaning; the upper blue segment of the shawl represents night, a lower sheepskin band represents daylight, and those two circles around the shoulder depict the eyes of a frog deity. Naxi men often appear under-employed, though they have a reputation as good gardeners and musicians. You'll likely see a few falconers too. *Forgotten Kingdom*, by **Peter Goullart**, is an entertaining account of Lijiang and the Naxi during the 1930s; it's available at bookshops in town.

the wilds and need a good feed and a hot shower. Fairground atmosphere aside, there's also some genuine culture lurking around the town's fringes, and plenty of potential **excursions** into the countryside.

While there is no charge to enter Lijiang itself, you do have to buy an "Old Town Maintenance Fee" **ticket** (¥80; valid for a month) before you can visit specific sights in and around the town – though you still have to pay additional entry fees for these sights, where they exist.

Orientation and arrival

There are two parts to Lijiang: the **old town of Dayan** (大研古城, *dàyán gǔ chéng*) with all the quaint architecture, markets and pedestrianized streets; and the **new town**, a bland place of wide roads and low-rise boxes, which surrounds Dayan, mostly to the south and west. The old town's layout is virtually indescribable, but at its core is the central market square, **Sifang** (四方, *sìfāng*), and **Dong Dajie**, the road north from here to a wide, open area at the old town's border known as **Gucheng Kou** (古城口, *gǔchéng kǒu*). Beyond lies the new town and the crossroads at **Fuhui Lu** and **Xin Dajie**, the latter running a kilometre north to **Black Dragon Pool Park**.

Lijiang's **airport** is 20km southwest along the highway; airport buses (¥15) deliver to the **airline ticket office** (民航售票处, *mínháng shòupiàochù*), 1.5km west of the old town on Fuhui Lu – take bus #1 from here to Gucheng Kou; taxis charge ¥100. The **train station** is out in the country twenty minutes southeast of town at the end of the #13 bus route – catch this to Jinhong Lu, on the east side of Gucheng Kou. Lijiang's **main bus station** is down in the new town 3km south of Dayan from where bus #11 or #8 will get you to Gucheng Kou.

Information

Your best source of **information** is probably your accommodation or one of the Western cafés; the places around town calling themselves "Tourist Reception Centres" or similar only sell packaged tours. Look instead for booths labelled "Old Town Management Board Tourism Service Point", which give neutral

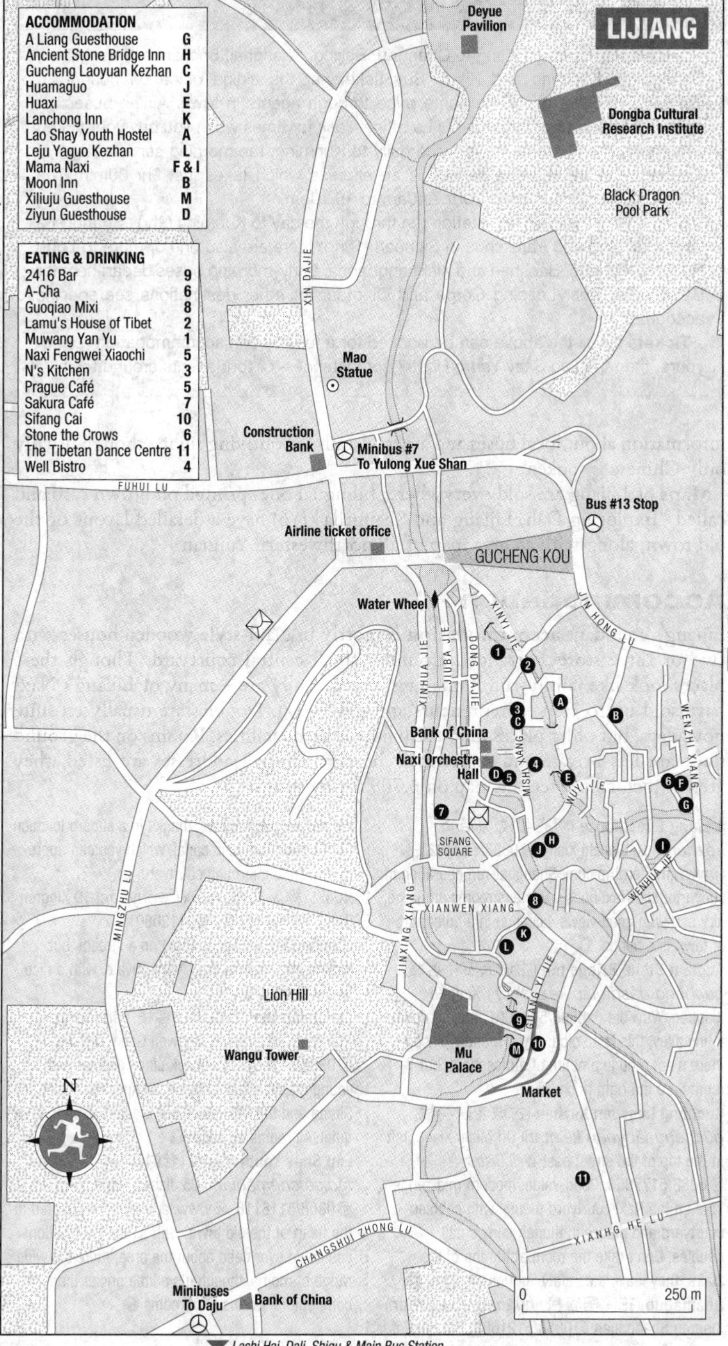
LIJIANG
ACCOMMODATION
A Liang Guesthouse G
Ancient Stone Bridge Inn H
Gucheng Laoyuan Kezhan C
Huamaguo J
Huaxi E
Lanchong Inn K
Lao Shay Youth Hostel A
Leju Yaguo Kezhan L
Mama Naxi F & I
Moon Inn B
Xiliuju Guesthouse M
Ziyun Guesthouse D
EATING & DRINKING
2416 Bar 9
A-Cha 6
Guoqiao Mixi 8
Lamu's House of Tibet 2
Muwang Yan Yu 1
Naxi Fengwei Xiaochi 5
N's Kitchen 3
Prague Café 5
Sakura Café 7
Sifang Cai 10
Stone the Crows 6
The Tibetan Dance Centre 11
Well Bistro 4
Baisha
Deyue Pavilion
Dongba Cultural Research Institute
Black Dragon Pool Park
XIN DAJIE
Mao Statue
Construction Bank
Minibus #7 To Yulong Xue Shan
FUHUI LU
Bus #13 Stop
Airline ticket office
GUCHENG KOU
Water Wheel
XINYI JIE
JIN HONG LU
Train Station
XINHUA JIE
JIUBA JIE
DONG DAJIE
WENZHI XIANG
Bank of China
Naxi Orchestra Hall
MISHI XIANG
WUYI JIE
SIFANG SQUARE
WENHUA JIE
XIANWEN XIANG
JINXING XIANG
MINGZHU LU
Lion Hill
GUANG YI JIE
Wangu Tower
Mu Palace
Market
N
XIANGHE LU
CHANGSHUI ZHONG LU
Minibuses To Daju
Bank of China
0 250 m
Lashi Hai, Dali, Shigu & Main Bus Station
Airline ticket office, Shuhe, Baisha, Airport & Daju

Moving on from Lijiang

There are **flights** from Lijiang to Chengdu, Beijing, Shanghai, Shenzhen, Guangzhou, Chongqing, Kunming and Xi'an. Buy tickets at the airline office on Fushui Lu (ⓣ0888/5399999), or for the same price through agents in town. Airline buses for each flight depart from the Fushui Lu office – ask for times when you buy your ticket.

At the moment, **trains** leave twice daily to Kunming; the morning service stops at Xiaguan, and the evening service is an express which takes just 9hr 30min. The station ticket office is open from 7.40am to 10.10pm.

Buses from the main bus station run through the day to Kunming (9hr) , Shangri-La (4hr), Dali (4hr) and Panzhihua in Sichuan (10hr); there are also one or more to Lugu Hu (8hr), Xichang, Baoshan and Xishuangbanna. Early-morning buses depart here for Baishui Tai, Tiger Leaping Gorge and Qiaotou; for other destinations see specific accounts.

Tickets for all the above can be booked for a fee through accommodation – if not yours, then the *Lao Shay Youth Hostel*, for instance – or tour agents around town.

information about local buses and access details for outlying sights, though usually only Chinese is spoken.

Maps of Lijiang are sold everywhere; bilingual ones printed on brown card and called "Exploring Dali, Lijiang and Shangrila" (¥6) have a detailed layout of the old town, along with an area map of all northwestern Yunnan.

Accommodation

Lijiang's abundant **accommodation** is mostly in Naxi-style wooden houses with two or three storeys arranged around a small central courtyard. Though these places look like family-run homestays, few actually are – many of Lijiang's Naxi have sold up to Han entrepreneurs and moved on. Doubles are usually en suite nowadays, but older places might still have shared facilities. Rooms on the ground floor are less private and sometimes cheaper. Though addresses are listed, they aren't much help – see the map on p.709 for locations.

A Liang Guesthouse (阿亮客栈, *āliàng kèzhàn*) 110 Wenzhi Xiang ⓣ0888/5129923, ⓦwww.moderntrip.com. Shanghai-run operation in converted old Naxi house; upstairs rooms are large, airy and with good views. Location in a quiet part of town is a bonus. ❸

Ancient Stone Bridge Inn (古城大石桥客栈, *gǔchéng dàshíqiáo kèzhàn*) 71 Xingren Xiaduan, Wuyi Jie ⓣ0888/5184001. Tucked down a tiny alley, this is an older-style, friendly place; there's not a huge amount of atmosphere, but rooms are the right price. ❷

Gucheng Laoyuan Kezhan (古城老院客栈, *gǔchéng lǎoyuàn kèzhàn*) Off Mishi Xiang, left at the top of the street past *Well Bistro* ⓣ0888/5177853. Good-value, modern mid-range take on the Naxi courtyard theme, with cobbled courtyard and pleasant, though fairly small, doubles. Don't take the room at the top of the stairs; they leave the safety light on all night. ❸

Huamaguo (花吗国客栈, *huāmaguó kèzhàn*) Xingren Shangduan ⓣ0888/5121688. The best of the newer guesthouses, thanks to a superb location right beside the main canal, which you can appreciate from a charming courtyard. ❸

Huaxi (桦溪文苑, *huàxī wényuàn*) 19 Xingren Duan, Wuyi Jie ⓣ0888/5112080, ⓔhuaxi828@163.com. Right on a stream, but tucked off the main drag. Very private, with a nice flower garden. ❹

Lanchong Inn (懒虫小住客栈, *lǎnchóng xiǎozhù kèzhàn*) 6 Xingwen Gang, Qiyi Jie ⓣ0888/5116515. Laidback place popular with young middle-class Chinese backpackers, close to Sifang and the Mu Palace but the lane itself is fairly quiet. All rooms en suite. ❸

Lao Shay Youth Hostel (老谢车马店, *lǎoxiè chēmǎdiàn*) 25 Jishan Xiang, Xinyi Jie ⓣ0888/5116118, ⓦwww.laoshay.com. Located at the heart of the old town, with all the information you could ever need about the area; there's a wide range of rooms, though it's a little pricier than its competitors. Dorms ¥30, rooms ❷

Leju Yaguo Kezhan (乐居雅国客栈, *lèjū yǎguó kèzhàn*) 13 Xinguan Xiang, Qiyi Jie ⓣ0888/8882266, ⓦwww.ljygkz.com. A real beauty, friendly and with a courtyard garden full of flowers. Rooms are smart and modern, and worth the higher-than-average price. ❹

Mama Naxi 78 Wenhua Jie, ⓣ0888/8881012; 70 Wenhua Jie ⓣ0888/5107713. The most popular backpacker guesthouse, thanks largely to its friendly management. All rooms, including three-bed dorms, are arranged around a courtyard. The second, larger, branch has an excellent restaurant offering communal meals cooked by the garrulous owner. Dorms ¥20, rooms ❷–❸

Moon Inn (新月阁, *xīnyuè gé*) 34 Xingren Xiang, Wuyi Jie ⓣ0888/5180520, ⓔmooninn@126.com. Large, quiet courtyard with chairs for lounging, and well-sized rooms. Popular with independent foreign travellers after some mid-range comforts. ❹

Xiliuju Guesthouse (溪留居客栈, *xīliújū kèzhàn*) 120 Zhongyi Xiang, Guangyi Jie ⓣ0888/5189667, ⓦwww.lijtaiwan.com. Cool, quiet budget choice, even if furnishings are verging towards standard Chinese hotel quality (worn). There's an open-air lobby to laze around in and watch passing street life. ❷

Ziyun Guesthouse (子云客栈, *zǐyún kèzhàn*) Around the back of the Naxi Orchestra Hall, off Xinyi Jie ⓣ0888/5124559. What makes this place memorable is that the staff are genuinely friendly, the rooms are tidy and simple, and prices are low. Small doubles with shared bathroom ❶, en-suite doubles ❷

The old town

It's not easy to navigate Dayan's crowded backstreets, but as there are few specific sights this hardly matters. Dong Dajie and adjacent lanes follow streams south to **Sifang**, formerly the main **marketplace**, a broad cobbled square sided with the inevitable souvenir shops selling silver jewellery, hand-woven cloth, *pu'er* tea and bright baubles. It's fun at dusk, when Naxi women gather for surprisingly authentic-feeling group dances, in which everyone is welcome to join. Heading south again takes you right into Dayan's maze, and eventually you'll find where Sifang's **market** has relocated; an acre of dried goods, fresh herbs, vegetables and fruit, jerked meat, pickles and Lijiang's famous copper and brass utensils. Clothing stalls towards the bottom of the market sell the handmade fleece jackets worn by Naxi women.

Closer to Sifang, the **Mu Palace** (木府, *mùfǔ*; daily 8.30am–5.30pm; ¥60) was home of the influential Mu family, the Qing-dynasty rulers of Lijiang, though they fell into decline in the nineteenth century. What was left of the mansion was destroyed during the terrible **earthquake** which flattened half the town in 1995, but the grounds – containing some ornamental pavilions and flower gardens – have been restored. You can walk through them and up onto pretty **Lion Hill** (狮子山, *shīzi shān*; ¥15), site of some ancient cypress trees and the **Wangu Tower** (万古楼, *wàngǔ lóu*), where you can look down over Dayan's sea of grey-tiled roofs.

Black Dragon Pool Park

Up on Lijiang's northern outskirts, **Black Dragon Pool Park** (黑龙潭公园, *hēilóngtán gōngyuán*; daily 7am–9pm; free with "Old Town Maintenance Fee" ticket) is a beautiful place to stroll. The sizeable, pale green pool here is known as **Yuquan** (Jade Spring) and, with the peaks of Yulong Xue Shan rising behind, the elegant mid-pool **Deyue Pavilion** is outrageously photogenic. In the early afternoon, you can watch traditionally garbed musicians performing **Naxi music** in the lakeside halls.

A path runs around the shore between a spread of trees and buildings, passing the cluster of compounds that comprise the **Dongba Cultural Research Institute** (东巴文化研究室, *dōngbā wénhuà yánjiūshì*). The word *dongba* relates to the Naxi shamans, about thirty of whom are still alive and kept busy here translating twenty

Naxi music and dancing

The **Naxi Orchestra** is an established part of Lijiang's tourist scene. Using antique instruments, the orchestra performs Song-dynasty tunes derived from the Taoist Dong Jin scriptures, a tradition said to have arrived in Lijiang with Kublai Khan, who donated half his court orchestra to the town after the Naxi chieftain helped his army cross the Yangzi. Banned from performing for many years, the orchestra regrouped after the Cultural Revolution under the guidance of **Xuan Ke**, though the deaths of many older musicians have reduced its repertoire. To counter this, the orchestra's scope has been broadened by including traditional **folk singing** in their performances.

The orchestra plays nightly in Lijiang in the well-marked hall on Dong Dajie (8pm; ¥120–160; some agents offer discounted tickets). The music is haunting, but Xuan Ke's commentaries are overlong; try to catch the orchestra practising in the afternoon in Black Dragon Pool Park, for free.

A little further north on Dong Dajie, another hall called the "Inheritance and Research Base of China" hosts a **song and dance troupe** who put on spirited nightly performances to a small audience (8–9.30pm; ¥80). Expect to be dragged on stage at the end. Similar audience participation is encouraged in the **nightly dances** that start around 7pm in Sifang Square.

thousand rolls of the old Naxi scriptures – *dongba jing* – for posterity. Further around, almost at the top end of the pool, is a group of halls imported in the 1970s from the site of what was once Lijiang's major temple, **Fuguo Si**. The finest of these is **Wufeng Lou** (五凤楼, *wǔfèng lóu*), a grand Ming-dynasty palace with a triple roof and interior walls embellished with reproductions of the murals at Baisha (see p.714).

Eating and drinking

Lijiang's plentiful **restaurants** serve a good range of Western and Chinese dishes. Local dishes include *baba*, a stodgy deep-fried flour patty stuffed with meat or cheese and honey; roast and steamed pork; Yunnan ham; chicken steamed in special *qiguo* casseroles; crossing-the-bridge noodles (see p.683); chicken steamed with local herbs; grilled fish; and wild plants such as fern tips. Mongolian-style **hotpots**, cooked at the table in a distinctive copper funnel-pot, are also a staple of Naxi home cooking. Foreigner-oriented **cafés** in the vicinity of Sifang all have wi-fi, book exchanges, melow music and set-price Western breakfasts. In winter, keep an eye open in the markets for the best **walnuts** in Yunnan, and bright orange **persimmons** growing on big, leafless trees around town – these have to be eaten very ripe and are an acquired taste. There's a **supermarket** near the Bank of China on Dong Dajie in the old town.

Parallel and west of Dong Dajie, narrow **Xinhua Jie** and **Jiuba Jie** are lined with barn-sized **nightclubs**, all sporting identical heavy wooden furniture, smoke machines, green-and-blue spots and dancers in fake-ethnic garb doing fake ethnic moves to high-decibel pop. *2416 Bar* at 19 Jinxing Gang, Guangyi Jie, advertises barbecues and bands every night. Across town, the eastern end of **Wuyi Jie** has smaller bars and pubs aimed at Westerners and Chinese backpackers; the best are *A-Cha* (阿茶酒吧, *ā chá jiǔbā*) at the intersection with Wenzhi Xiang, and *Stone the Crows* Irish bar, up on top; both have beer, spirits and small-scale live music.

Guoqiao Mixi (过桥米戏, *guòqiáo mǐxì*) 47 Guangmen Kou, Qiyi Jie. Cheerful place hung with red lanterns, right on the stream overlooking a little cascade; the name means "Crossing the Bridge Noodles" and, sure enough, this is the house speciality – ¥30 will fill you up. Many similar places nearby serve pizzas, casseroles or hotpots.

Lamu's House of Tibet 56 Xinyi Jie. Really tasty Western and Chinese staples, including filling breakfasts from 7am. One of the best places in town to pick up local cycling maps and the latest trekking information for Tiger Leaping Gorge.

Muwang Yan Yu (木王盐语, *mùwáng yán yǔ*) Xinyi Jie. One of several local streamside restaurants serving Naxi-inspired food; camphor-smoked duck, medicinal herb soups, vegetable hotpots and roast meats, plus some Cantonese dishes. Not cheap – expect ¥100/person – but the setting and good service makes it perhaps worth a splash.

N's Kitchen On Maicao Chang (卖草场, *màicăo chăng*), the old "Grass Market Square" where caravan owners would buy food for their horses. *N's* has, quite honestly, the best burgers you'll get in China, plus heaps of hiking and biking information, along with bike rental.

Naxi Fengwei Xiaochi (纳西风味小吃, *nàxī fēngwèi xiăochī*) Tucked just off the street past the *Prague Café*. Small, inexpensive courtyard canteen with run of Yunnan staples and snacks. Steer clear of the yak stew though – too much stew and precious little yak.

Prague Café Xinyi Jie. Scores highly for its location, excellent coffee, blueberry cake, DVD collection and menagerie of animals.

Sakura Café Off Sifang. Actually there are about five places with this name, all next to each other, and all claiming to be the first. All offer reasonably priced beers and coffees, Japanese and Korean food, and get lively in the evening.

Sifang Cai (私房菜, *sīfáng cài*) Near the Mu Palace and market on 84 Zhongyi Xiang. Naxi-style hotpots cooked by you at the table in copper funnel fondue pot; inexpensive and traditional local food.

The Tibetan Dance Centre 68–69 Guzuo Xiang, near the market Ⓦwww.thetibetandancecentre.org. Tibetan and vegetarian food, plus a nightly floor show of Tibetan dancing, starting at 9.30pm.

Well Bistro Mishi Xiang. This cosy place wins universal approval for its pasta, apple cake and chocolate brownies.

Listings

Banks The Bank of China, along with several ATMs, is in the old town, on Dong Dajie. There are more ATMs in the new town.

Internet All the foreigner-oriented cafés have internet access, and many have wi-fi.

Mail The post office (daily 8am–8pm) is in the old town, on Dong Dajie.

Massage There's a hard-fingered blind masseur (¥50/hr) on Guangyi Jie: head down Dong Dajie into Sifang, and Guangyi Jie is ahead and slightly to the left; the masseur is 75m along, up a staircase on the left-hand side. Perfect for strained muscles after a day out exploring the sights around Lijiang.

PSB For those wanting to extend their visa, note that the PSB have recently opened a new office in the south of Lijiang – ask your accommodation for the address.

Around Lijiang

Rich pickings surround Lijiang, with a stock of pleasant countryside, **temples** and villages on the lower slopes of **Yulong Xue Shan**, which rises about 18km north. Most of the following sights are within **bicycle range**; if your accommodation can't find you one to rent, try *N's Kitchen* (see above) who charge ¥10–30 per day, plus your passport or deposit. Aside from the transport listed below, go up to Gucheng Kou around Xin Dajie in the morning and you'll find **minibuses for rent** at ¥150 for a half-day; contact the reliable, Chinese-speaking Ms Mu Chou (mobile Ⓣ13908883404). For more ambitious schedules – including **long-distance trekking** – contact The Yak Traveller, at 188 Minzhu Lu (Ⓣ0888/5102666, Ⓦwww.theyaktraveller.com).

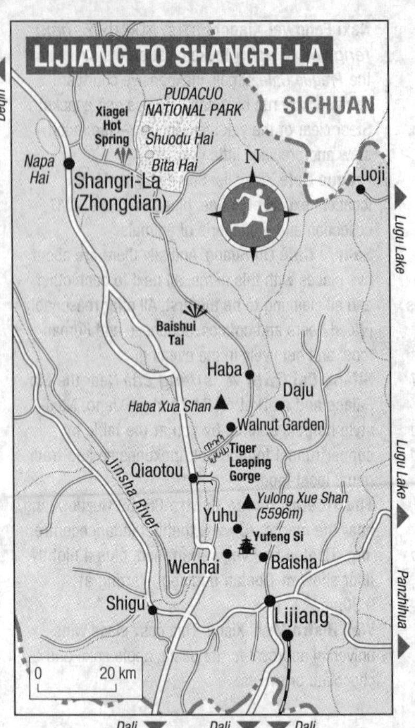

Shuhe and Lashi Hai

SHUHE (束河, *shùhé*), about 3km northwest of Lijiang via bus #11 from Fuhui Lu, is a missed opportunity: instead of being maintained as the small rural hamlet it was, it has been developed as a miniature carbon-copy of Lijiang, with the same mix of cafés, shops and restaurants set around recently installed streams and cobbles. There's a slightly more arty, bohemian feel to the place, but not enough to make it noticeably different from its larger neighbour.

On a completely different tack, **Lashi Hai** (拉市海, *lāshì hǎi*; ¥30; boating and horseriding about ¥90) is a seasonal wetlands area 10km west of Lijiang, with the pleasant, near-deserted Tibetan Buddhist complex **Zhiyun Si** (指云寺, *zhǐyún sì*; ¥15) on the far shore. The lake is best visited in winter, when hosts of migratory wildfowl pour in. At the time of writing, there were no buses to Lashi Hai but Lijiang's official information booths can arrange shared taxis for ¥10 per person each way.

Baisha to Yuhu

BAISHA (白沙, *báishā*), a small village about 10km north of Lijiang, is known for two things: the **Dabaoji Gong** temple complex (大宝积宫, *dàbǎojī gōng*; ¥30, plus the Lijiang Maintenance Fee ticket) with some fifteenth-century **murals** (白沙壁画, *báishā bìhuà*) – admittedly in sad condition; and **Doctor He**, a traditional Chinese physician whose knowledge of local medicinal herbs is second to none. Baisha comprises little more than a single main street and there's no trouble at all locating the sights (Doctor He's surgery is amply signed in several languages), or the excellent *Country Road Café* (Ⓣ15284480063; ❷), which supplies light meals, biking and hiking information, plus kung fu demonstrations and basic **homestay** accommodation. Baisha is also a staging post on the way to **Wenhai village** (see opposite).

You can reach Baisha from the old town via bus #11 south to the "Jinjia Shichang" stop (金甲市场, *jīnjiǎ shìchǎng*), then a shared minibus to Baisha for ¥5–10.

Yulong and Yuhu

YULONG (玉龙, *yùlóng*), a further 3km north of Baisha, is worth a quick pause to look at **Yufeng Si** (玉峰寺, *yùfēng sì*; ¥25, plus the Lijiang Maintenance Fee ticket), a small Tibetan temple set in a pine forest. It's not of great interest in itself, but the pair of ancient, intertwined **camellia trees** in the top terrace produce huge magenta flowers in spring, when the courtyard with its mosaic floor is a nice spot for peaceful contemplation.

Four kilometres beyond Yufeng Si, the tiny Naxi settlement of **YUHU** (玉湖村, *yùhú cūn*) is where the eccentric Austrian-American botanist-anthropologist **Joseph Rock** based himself from 1921 to 49, and where he wrote articles on the Naxi that appeared in *National Geographic* magazine. His old wooden **house** (洛克故居, *luòkè gùjū*; ¥15), now a simple museum to his memory with a few period photos, is on the main street and is visited daily by busloads of foreigners. Yuhu is otherwise little disturbed by tourism and, set in grassland on the slopes of Yulong Xue Shan, is an attractive place to stop over and do some hiking – again, Wenhai makes a good target. Down a back lane, *Nguluko Guest House* (Ⓣ0888/5131616 or 13988838431, Ⓔlilyhe9@gmail.com; ❷) provides simple but clean **accommodation** with meals and shared facilities, and can arrange hiking and horseriding tours.

Yulong Xue Shan and Wenhai

With a summit at 5596m, **Yulong Xue Shan** (¥80 entry, plus chairlift fees) can't be climbed without proper equipment, but you can take in alpine meadows, galciers and the peaks via three separate **chairlifts**. Reach the chairlift stations on **minibus #7** (¥15) from the northeastern corner of the Xin Dajie/Fuhui Lu intersection; the journey takes over an hour.

Yunsha Ping (云杉坪, *yúnshān píng*; chairlift ¥50) is a 3205m plateau with boardwalks leading out to grassland and fir trees, and views of the mountain's peaks rising above. Similar **Maoniu Ping** (牦牛坪, *máoniú píng*; ¥80) is higher at 3600m, with a temple; while the cable car at **Ganhaizi** (干海子, *gànhǎizǐ*; ¥160 one way) is an impressive 3km long and climbs to 4506m, where a short trail leads to a windswept viewing point over the **Yulong Glacier**. Ganhaizi is by far the most spectacular spot, and despite the altitude can get very crowded.

Alternatively, **WENHAI** (文海, *wénhǎi*) is a beautiful lakeside village in Yulong Xue Shan's foothills that's a three-hour trek from Baisha or Yuhu. **Xintuo Ecotourism** (Ⓣ13988826672, Ⓦwww.ecotourism.com.cn) charge ¥1000 for a five-day, four-night return trek to Wenhai from Lijiang, including all transport, guides, accommodation and food; contact them in advance about accommodation if you plan to visit independently.

Shigu

Seventy kilometres west of Lijiang on banks of the Yangzi River, **SHIGU** (Stone Drum; 石鼓, *shígǔ*) is a small place named after a tablet raised here in the sixteenth century by one of Lijiang's Mu clan to mark a particularly bloody victory over an invading army – whether a Tibetan or Chinese force depends on who is telling the story. The river makes its first major **bend** here, deflected sharply to the northeast towards Tiger Leaping Gorge, having flowed uninterrupted in a 1000km arc from its source away on the Tibet/Qinghai border; there are viewpoints along the waterfront. **Minibuses to Shigu** (¥10) run whenever full from Lijiang's bus station.

To Sichuan: Panzhihua and Lugu Hu

From Lijiang, there are **two routes into Sichuan**. The quickest begins by catching a bus 200km east to heavily industrialized **PANZHIHUA** (攀枝花, *pānzhīhuā*; 10hr; ¥80), a stop on the Kunming–Chengdu **rail line**. Buses set down right outside the train station: try and get on one of the evening trains, as Panzhihua is no place to stay for long. The train ride to Chengdu goes via Xichang and Emei Shan (see p.768), and takes a further 10–14 hours. There's a **hostel** (❷) opposite Panzhihua's train station, useful if you get stuck, and a daybreak bus back to Lijiang.

Lugu Hu

Much more fun is **Lugu Hu** (泸沽湖, *lúgū hú*; entry ¥80) a shallow, attractive lake bisected by the Sichuan border about 200km north of Lijiang. The people up here are **Mosuo**, who maintain **matrilineal traditions** such as *axia* marriage, where a woman takes several husbands. Women run the households and children are brought up by their mothers – men have no descendants or property rights. Glibly marketed as a "Girl Kingdom" to single Chinese men – who inevitably head back home disappointed – tourism has become well-established in recent years, but the lake remains a pleasant place to kick back for a couple of days before making the tiring journey to Xichang in southern Sichuan.

Lugu Hu is nine hours from Lijiang **by bus** (¥60), with stops at Luoshi and Lige (see below). There's also an **airport** under construction about two hours south of the lake at **Ninglang**; initial flights are scheduled to Kunming and Guangzhou.

Leaving, buses to Lijiang depart around 8am and you'll need to book your seat through accommodation the day before. Heading into Sichuan, there's morning traffic from Luguhu Zhen to **Xichang**, a town on the Kunming–Chengdu line (see p.772; 9hr; ¥97).

Towns and villages around Lugu Hu

Lugu Hu is 10km long and hourglass-shaped, with an attached inlet trailing east and settlements dotted around its shore. West-coast **LUOSHUI** (落水, *luòshuǐ*) is the largest, with cobbles, a central square, gift shops and a few facilities; but tiny **LIGE** (里格, *lǐgé*), further northwest, is set on an attractive bay with a better range of places to stay and eat. Past here and you're into Sichuan, where **LUGUHU ZHEN** (泸沽湖镇, *lúgūhú zhèn*) is the main town and **Wuzhiluo** (五指落, *wǔzhǐluò*) – a nearby string of houses along the shore – the nicest spot to settle down. Wherever you end up, **minibuses** shuttle between villages, **wooden canoes** can be hired out for trips across the lake, and accommodation can provide just about everything you'll need.

Accommodation and eating

The best **places to stay** are at **Lige**, where you'll find *Lao Shay Youth Hostel* (老谢车马店, *lǎoxiè chēmǎdiàn*; Ⓣ0888/5881555, Ⓦwww.laoshay.com; dorms ¥35, lakeview rooms ❷), sister to the one in Lijiang, the locally-owned *Lige Wan Kezhan* (里格湾客栈, *lǐgéwān kèzhàn*; Ⓣ0888/5823871; ❹), done up in Tibetan-Mosuo motifs, and *Lake View Romance* (印象传奇, *yìnxiàng chuánqí*; Ⓣ0888/5881050; ❸–❹), one of several new places jammed onto tiny Lige Island. At **Wuzhiluo**, *Wind's Guesthouse* (湖畔青年旅舍, *húpàn qīngnián lǚshè*; Ⓣ0888/5824284, Ⓔwind77777@163.com; beds ¥25, rooms ❷) fullfils all the usual backpacker needs and, with plenty of advance notice, can arrange ten-day **horse-treks to Yading** in Sichuan (see p.801).

Village **restaurants** lay on evening **barbecues** of grilled lake fish and whole suckling pigs, while *Lao Shay* and *Wind's* hostels serve pretty decent Chinese and Western staples – though come prepared for laidback service.

Tiger Leaping Gorge

Around 70km north of Lijiang, the Yangzi River channels violently through **Tiger Leaping Gorge** (虎跳峡, *hǔtiào xiá*; ¥80), the 3000m-deep rift between **Haba Xue Shan** to the north and Yulong Xue Shan to the south. The **hiking trail** through the gorge is one of the most accessible and satisfying in China, with dramatic scenery and – despite the 2500m-plus altitude – relatively straightforward walking. That said, you'll need to be fit, carrying full weatherproof gear, a torch and a first-aid pack, and to be stocked up with snacks and a water bottle. Solid boots are a plus but, as long as your shoes have a firm grip, not essential. **Weather** can be warm enough in summer to hike in a T-shirt, but don't count on it; winters are cold. **Accommodation** along the way is in guesthouses, so you won't need a tent. **Two days** is the minimum time needed for a hike; give yourself an extra day to make the most of the scenery.

Originally there were **two trails** through the gorge, but the former **Lower Path** has been surfaced to handle tour buses, and isn't suitable for hiking anymore – though it's useful if you're looking for a quick ride out at the end of your hike. The remaining **Upper Path** is the route described below. End points are at westerly **Qiaotou**, on the Lijiang to Shangri-La road, and easterly **Daju**, a small township on a back route to Lijiang. Most people hike from Qiaotou to the midpoint around **Walnut Garden** – which covers the best of the scenery – and then catch transport back to Qiaotou and thence on to Lijiang or Shangri-La; the advantage here is that you can leave heavy bags at Qiaotou. Alternatively, you can hike on from Walnut Garden to Daju, or – with a guide – north to Baishui Tai (see p.722). Before you arrive, try to pick up the home-made **maps** that float around cafés in Lijiang and Shangri-La.

There seem to be almost continual roadworks going on in the gorge, connected with ongoing construction of a **hydro dam** across the river. **Landslides** are a potentially lethal hazard, so do not hike in bad weather or during the June–September **rainy season**; there have also been a couple of knifepoint **muggings** of solo travellers in recent years. For current information, check Ⓦwww.tigerleapinggorge.com, run by *Sean's Guesthouse* in Walnut Garden.

Qiaotou to Walnut Garden

Buses from Lijiang (2hr) deliver to main-road **QIAOTOU** (桥头, *qiáotóu*), also known as **Hutiaoxia Zhen** (虎跳峡镇, *hǔtiàoxiá zhèn*), a knot of cafés and shops at the entrance to the gorge. Once across the bridge the vehicle road heads downhill, but past the **school** hikers need to start heading uphill – you'll be followed by **horse teams** offering to carry your bags. From here the going is steady until you reach the *Naxi Family Guesthouse* (纳西雅阁, *nàxī yǎgé*; ❶) at the start of the steep, twisting **Twenty-four Bends**. At the top of this you're about five hours into the hike at 2670m, near the *Tea Horse Guesthouse* (茶马客栈, *chámǎ kèzhàn*; ❶) and gifted with superb views.

From here the track levels out a bit before descending, via the *Halfway Guesthouse* at **Bendiwan village** (本地湾村, *běndìwān cūn*) and some waterfalls, to the vehicle road at *Tina's Guesthouse* (中峡国际青年旅舍, *zhōngxiá guóji qīngnián lǚshě*; Ⓣ0887/8202258, or 13988750111; dorms ¥35, rooms ❷). You've now been walking for around nine hours, with a further thirty-minute level track to **WALNUT GARDEN** (核桃园, *hétáo yuán*) and more accommodation at *Sean's Guesthouse* (山泉客栈, *shānquán kèzhàn*; Ⓣ0887/8202222, Ⓦwww.tigerleapinggorge.com; dorms ¥35, rooms ❷), a pleasantly low-key, friendly place with good meals, beer and warm beds. The alternative is *Woody's* (Ⓣ13988712705; ❶), whose unattractive building is still perfectly comfortable.

Sean's can arrange a **guide** for the popular two-day trek from Walnut Garden, via an overnight stop in **Haba village** (哈巴村, *hābācūn*), to **Baishui Tai**, which has charmless guesthouses and a bus on to **Shangri-La** (see below). You might prefer to tackle this trek southwards from Baishui Tai as an alternative route into Tiger Leaping Gorge – it heads downhill much of the time.

Walnut Garden to Daju

One option from Walnut Garden is simply to arrange a ride with minibuses **back to Qiaotou** along the vehicle road. Alternatively, it's a couple of hours eastwards, partly along the road, to the **New Ferry** over the Yangzi River. How much you'll pay depends on the whim of the ferryman, but don't expect to get off lightly – ¥40 or more per person is normal. From here, you've another hour's walk to the vehicle roadhead at **Xiahu Tiao** (下虎跳, *xiàhǔ tiào*), 7km from **DAJU** (大具, *dàjù*), where buses head south to Lijiang until about 1.30pm. If you're planning to start your Tiger Leaping Gorge trek here, **buses from Lijiang to Daju** depart first thing in the morning from the depot at the corner of Changshui Lu and Minzhu Lu, just outside the old town's southwestern edge.

Shangri-La and around

SHANGRI-LA, also known as **Zhongdian** (香格里拉/中甸, *xiānggélǐlā/zhōngdiàn*) – or **Gyalthang** in Tibetan – sits on a high plateau at the borderland between Yunnan, Sichuan and Tibet. When this former logging town was hit by a 1998 ban on deforestation, the provincial government renamed it Shangri-La after the Buddhist paradise of James Hilton's 1930s novel, *Lost Horizon*, to try to stimulate a tourist boom. They also spent a fortune turning the dismally poor Tibetan settlement here into what must be the newest "old town" in existence, complete with obligatory traditional houses, cobbled streets, religous monuments, cafés, guesthouses and bars; there are also less contrived attractions in the **monastery** just north of town and excellent possibilities for local **hiking** and horseriding. The altitude here is over 3000m, so take it easy if you've arrived from the lowlands, and be aware that's it's very chilly between October and March.

Arrival and information

Tiny **Shangri-La Airport** (香格里拉机场, *xiānggélǐlā jīchǎng*), also confusingly known as Deqing Airport, is 7km south; a taxi costs ¥25, or catch bus #6 to the **bus station**, in the far north of town at the intersection of Xiangbala Lu and

Moving on from Shangri-La

Flights leave Shangri-La to Lhasa (2 weekly; ¥1480) and Kunming (2 daily; ¥1180); but see the information below on entering Tibet. **Buses** head throughout the day to Lijiang, Dali and Kunming; there are three daily to Deqin; and one each to Haba (p.723), Xiangcheng in Sichuan, and Daocheng in Sichuan. Advance tickets are available 36 hours prior to departure at the bus station.

Travel to **Tibet** overland is difficult at the moment. Formerly, it was possible to arrange a **private jeep** from Shangri-La, via Deqin, right through to Lhasa. Contact agencies such as Khampa Caravan (see p.721) to arrange tours and for the latest on the situation.

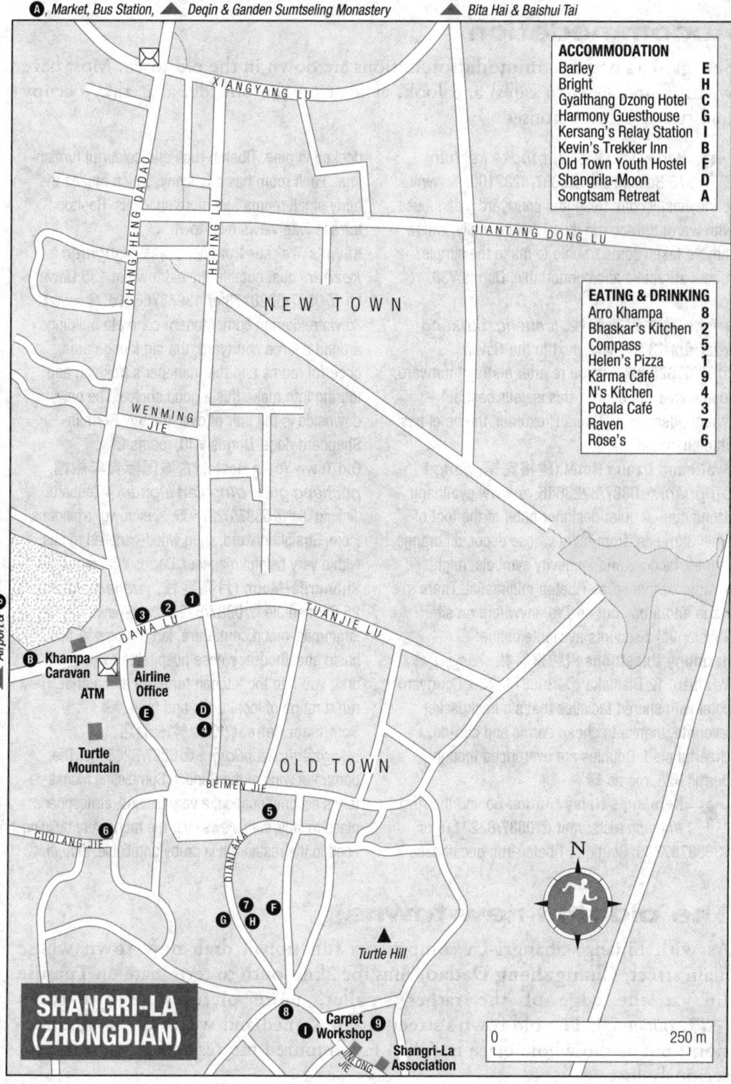

Kangding Lu. From here, bus #1 runs south to the old town's outskirts. There's talk of extending the Kunming–Dali–Lijiang **train line** to Shangri-La, but so far no dates are forthcoming. Incidentally, "Zhongdian" is the **name** you'll hear used most frequently; only the tourist industry favours "Shangri-La".

Shangri-La is small enough to walk everywhere, though some accommodation rent out **bikes** (¥20 plus passport) and **taxis** cost a fixed ¥6 within the town. There's a Construction Bank **ATM**, **post office** and **airline ticket office** (Ⓣ0887/8229555) just outside the old town at the small square on the junction of Changzheng Dadao and Tuanjie Lu, though the main branches for all these are up in the new town.

Accommodation

Shangri-La's best **accommodation** options are down in the old town. Most have wi-fi (if not, head to cafés) and look, at least on the outside, as if they occupy traditional Tibetan houses.

Barley (青稞客栈, *qīngkē kèzhàn*) 76 Beimen Jie ⓣ0887/8232100, ⓦwww.barleyhostel.com. Delightful courtyard guesthouse with warm terrace run by a Tibetan family, where they've taken some trouble to make the simple rooms attractive and comfortable. Dorms ¥30, rooms ❷

Bright (鲁生追康客栈, *lǔshēngzhuīkāng kèzhàn*) 13 Dianlaka next to the *Raven* ⓣ0887/8288687. If you're after a straightforward, roomy en-suite double, this is your best bet – though, despite a "Tibetan" exterior, the hotel has little character. ❷

Gyalthang Dzong Hotel (建格宾馆, *jiàngé bīnguǎn*) ⓣ0887/8223646, ⓦwww.gyalthangdzong.com. A quiet designer hotel at the foot of a hill 3km east from town whose decor, all orange drapes, lacquer and longevity symbols, might best be described as Tibetan minimalist. There's a spa and a bar, but no TVs anywhere on site. Substantial discounts available online. ❻

Harmony Guesthouse (融聚客栈, *róngjù kèzhàn*) 12 Dianlaka ⓣ13988747739. Courtyard hotel with shared facilities that's a backpacker favourite, thanks to cheap dorms and can-do, cheerful staff. Doubles are overpriced though. Dorms ¥25, rooms ❷

Kersang's Relay Station Behind the *Arro Khampa* restaurant ⓣ0887/8223118 or 13988797785. Boutique Tibetan-run guesthouse decked in pine, Tibetan rugs and colourful furnishings. Each room has a balcony, which makes the fairly small rooms feel more spacious. Rooftop terrace with views over town. ❸

Kevin's Trekker Inn (龙门客栈, *lóngmén kèzhàn*) Just outside the old town at 138 Dawa Lu ⓣ0887/8228178 or 13988766016, ⓦwww.kevintrekkerinn.com. Modern concrete buildings around a large courtyard; the big lounge area, cheerful rooms and the manager's trekking and touring info make this a good choice. The only downside is the pair of over-friendly German Shepherd dogs. Dorms ¥30, rooms ❷

Old Town Youth Hostel (古城国际青年旅馆, *gǔchéng guójì qīngnián lǚguǎn*) 4 Zoubarui, Jinlong Jie ⓣ0887/8227505, ⓔoldtowg_h@hotmail.com. Straightforward, snug wood-panelled rooms, with a very helpful manager. Dorms ¥25, rooms ❷

Shangrila-Moon (月亮客栈, *yuèliàng kèzhàn*) 25 Beimen Jie ⓣ0887/8225826, ⓦwww.shangrila-moon.com. Bare, large rooms in this basic guesthouse, whose hospitable owner will drag you into the kitchen for a tea and a chat. They run a range of local treks and tours. ❷

Songtsam Retreat (松赞林卡酒店, *sōngzànlínkǎ jiǔdiàn*) ⓣ0887/8285566. The upmarket wing of the Ganden Sumtseling Monastery's accommodation; a very tasteful, atmospheric place to stay, with views over the monastery building. Food in the restaurant is pretty unreliable, though. ❻

The old and new towns

As with Lijiang, Shangri-La comprises a functional, drab **new town** whose main street, **Changzheng Dadao**, runs for 2km south to terminate on **Tuanjie Lu**, at the edge of the rather smaller, more picturesque **old town** (古城, *gǔchéng*). The old town's streets are unsigned and weave off in all directions, but as the whole place is only a few hundred metres across you can't get seriously lost.

Shangri-La's old town is good for a couple of hours' wander, though there are no essential sights. The alleyways are lined with sturdy two-storey wooden Tibetan homes, all built with a great deal of skill and care; they look as though they'll stand for centuries, which you can't say about most contemporary Chinese buildings. Overlooking the old town, **Turtle Hill** is topped by a small temple and huge **golden prayer wheel**, apparently the largest in the world. Two businesses employing Tibetans and preserving locals crafts are the **Shangri-La Association** (ⓦwww.shangrilaassociation.org) at 31 Jinlong Jie, a cultural centre whose **Thangka painting studio** trains new artists; and a **carpet workshop** (ⓦwww.innerasiarugs.com) further up the street, producing gorgeous (and very expensive) handmade woollen rugs decorated with tigers and abstract motifs.

Despite a backdrop of scruffy concrete-and-tile buildings, there's also a bit of interest in the **new town**. Changzheng Dadao is lined with shops aimed at Tibetan customers, where you can buy everything from electric blenders for churning butter tea, to more carpets, horse saddles, copperware and fur-lined jackets and boots. The **market** (建塘农市场, *jiàntáng nóng shìchǎng*), about a block north of the post office, has more of the same along with big blocks of yak butter and other foodstuffs.

Shangri-La's star attraction is the splendid **Ganden Sumtseling Monastery** (松赞林寺, *sōngzànlín sì*; ¥85) just north of town; catch northbound bus #3 from Changzheng Dadao. Destroyed during the 1960s but later reactivated, it now houses four hundred Tibetan monks. Among butter sculptures and a forest of pillars, the freshly painted murals in the claustrophobic, windowless main hall are typically gruesome and colourful. Don't forget that, as in all Gelugpa-sect monasteries, you should walk **clockwise** around both the monastery and each hall.

Eating and drinking

As with accommodation, the old town has the pick of the eating opportunities; the cafés also have free wi-fi for customers. For **cheap Chinese staples**, there are a few hole-in-the-wall places on Tuanjie Lu serving noodles and dumplings. As there's no street lighting, mind those cobbles on the way home.

Arro Khampa (阿若康巴餐厅, *āruò kāngbā cāntīng*) South of the *Old Town Youth Hostel* ⓣ0887/8226442. Nepali, Indian and Tibetan cuisine served up in an atmosphere similar to – though without quite the panache – *Bhaskar's*. Expect to pay ¥60/person.

Bhaskar's Kitchen (巴斯卡厨房, *bāsīkǎ chúfáng*) Dawa Lu ⓣ0887/8881213. With charismatic Nepali owner-chef Bhaskar in control, this comfortable restaurant lives up to its claim to produce the "best curry in Shangri-La". Chicken or vegetarian thalis (¥38) are the business too.

Compass Just off the main square in the old town. Unashamedly Western food – pizza, burgers, spaghetti, sandwiches – served up in a sympathetic mock-Tibetan interior. Mains around ¥40.

Helen's Pizza Tuanjie Lu. Rated by nostalgic expats as whipping up the best pizza and calzone in all China – yours for only ¥38 – perhaps because they use imported olive oil, not yak butter.

Karma Café Almost unsigned behind an adobe wall in the back of town, at first sight the building looks run-down; inside, however, it's a beautifully restored old house serving outstanding yak steak and mashed potatoes for a bargain ¥48. Tibetan snacks and a set meal (¥60/person) will leave you bursting. Great place for quiet coffee too.

N's Kitchen Beimen Jie. This bright, modern and clean place is popular for Western breakfasts and great coffee, though it's just a little bit more expensive than its competitors. Pick up Napa Hai cycling maps here.

Potala Café Tuanjie Lu. This upstairs Tibetan teahouse serves up huge portions of Western, Tibetan and Chinese food, and hot chocolate made with the real thing, not powder. The ambience is pleasant, attracting a mix of Chinese tourists, grizzly locals and foreigners.

Raven (乌鸦酒吧, *wūyā jiǔbā*) 19 Dianlaka ⓣ0887/8289239. Friendly and atmospheric foreign-owned bar with pool table, beer and huge stock of spirits; the best place to get the lowdown on the local scene.

Rose's 15 Cuolang Jie. Tea, coffee and light meals in pleasant café surroundings.

Around Shangri-La

There is limitless **trekking** around Shangri-La, and a number of **specialist agents** can help you out with routes and guides. If you're planning anything major though, don't leave talking to them until you're in town – they'll need time to organize things. Cafés and hotels also provide information and can book you on **trips out** from Shangri-La – including the three-day hike via **Baishui** to **Tiger Leaping Gorge** (see p.717).

Tibetan-run Khampa Caravan on Dawa Lu (ⓣ0887/8288648, ⓦwww.khampacaravan.com) offer everything from easy day hikes and sorting out Tibet logistics to multiday treks to Lijiang or into Sichuan; one of their specialities is the demanding fourteen-day **kora circuit** around Meili Xue Shan (p.723). All their guides are local Tibetans, fluent in English. Foreign-owned Haiwei Trails (ⓣ0887/8289239, ⓦwww.haiweitrails.com), above the bar at the *Raven* (see p.721), also offer plenty of imaginative treks and **mountain-biking**, while Tibet specialists Kawa Gebo (ⓣ0887/8238828, ⓦwww.yaktraveler.com) are on the old town's main square. Another excellent option is Turtle Mountain (ⓣ0877/8233308, ⓦwww.turtlemountaingear.com), off Beimen Jie at 32 Gun Ma Lang, whose American owner, long resident in Shangri-La, has solid hiking and exploring information. They also stock a range of **camping supplies** and rent ski gear, snowboards, **motorbikes** (with breakdown support) and jeeps.

You can **cycle** from Shangri-La to a couple of the closer sights, but anywhere further will require a **vehicle** – either rented through Turtle Mountain (see above), or by heading down to the little square on Tuanjie Lu, at the edge of the old town, where minibus drivers will approach you and offer their services. The likely rate is ¥150–300 per day, depending on destination and bargaining skills.

Napa Hai and Xiagei Hot Springs

Napa Hai (纳帕海, *nàpà hǎi*; ¥40), 7km north of town, is a shallow, seasonal lake which attracts rare black-necked cranes in winter. Through the summer it's more of a pasture for yaks, thick with grass and flowers; there's a **Botanic Gardens** (¥20) and café just outside, where you can see blue poppies and orchids. Pick up a **cycling map** for Napa from *N's Kitchen* (see p.721) in Shangri-La.

Ten kilometres east of town, the **Xiagei Hot Springs** (下给温泉, *xiàgěi wēnquán*; ¥30) are attractively situated beside a river and below a cave. Eschew the claustrophobic private rooms and swim in the small public pool; a shop on site sells swimming trunks (¥20). There's also a walking trail, and you can arrange rafting on the river with any tour agency in town (¥200 for an afternoon).

Pudacuo National Park

Pudacuo National Park (普达措国家公园, *pǔdácuò guójiā gōngyuán*; ¥190 entry, including bus inside the park) covers a huge area some 25km east of Shangri-La past Xiagei, with **two lakes** within day-trip range. The first, **Shuodu Hai** (属都海, *shǔdōu hǎi*), is a renowned beauty spot that attracts plenty of tour buses. However, the day trippers don't seem to get much further than the restaurant and the huge shop in the car park that sells traditional medicines such as ginseng and dried ants. Turn right and follow the lakeshore for a pleasant, easy walk through old forest. Horses can carry you all the way around the lake for ¥80, which will take about two hours, or you can walk it in four.

Less visited **Bita Hai** (碧塔海, *bìtǎ hǎi*) is an attractive alpine lake set at an altitude of 3500m and surrounded by lush meadows and unspoilt forest. The best way to explore the place is to ask to be dropped at either of its two entrances, south or west, and then picked up at the other. Most visitors arrive at the south entrance, from where it's an easy walk down to the lake. Take a rowboat across (a negotiable ¥30/person) to the ferry quay, and you can then walk for around two hours along a well-marked trail to the west entrance. Horses can be rented at either entrance for ¥50 or so.

Baishui Tai

Around 60km southeast of Shangri-La on the north side of Haba Xue Shan from Tiger Leaping Gorge, **Baishui Tai** (白水台, *báishuǐ tái*) is a large, milky-white series of limestone terraces, built up over thousands of years as lime-rich water cascaded down a hillside. Plenty of less prosaic legends account for their formation too, and this is one of the holy sites of the Naxi. Wooden ladders allow in-depth exploration of the tiers, which glow orange at sunset. Until recently Baishu Tai was quite remote, but now a back road from Qiaotao, at the mouth of Tiger Leaping Gorge (see p.717), links it to Shangri-La. The village at the foot of the site, **Sanba** (三坝, *sānbà*) is busy transforming itself into a tourist town of guesthouses, all of which offer basic and fairly unattractive rooms.

The trip from Shangri-La only takes two hours, and Baishui Tai is also the start of a good two-day trek to **Walnut Garden** in Tiger Leaping Gorge (see p.717) via the pretty Haba valley and **HABA** village (哈巴乡, *hābā xiāng*) for which you'll need a **guide**, best arranged in Shangri-La. **Accommodation** is available in Haba at the welcoming *Haba Snow Mountain Guesthouse* (哈巴雪山招待所, *hābā xuěshān zhāodàisuǒ*; ❶), where not only is there a rudimentary shower, but the owner even serves coffee.

Deqin and Meili Xue Shan

DEQIN (德钦, *déqīn*) lies six hours north of Shangri-La across some permanently snowy ranges, only 80km from the Tibetan border. The town is no great shakes, but there are exciting opportunities for hiking around nearby **Meili Xue Shan**, whose thirteen peaks are of great religious significance to Tibetans. Be aware that a visit to the area should be taken seriously, despite the relatively well-worn trails: always carry food, water, a torch, first-aid kit, full weatherproof gear and good hiking shoes.

Deqin's most useful **accommodation** option is the *Trekker's Home* (旅行者之家, *lǚxíngzhě zhījiā*; Ⓣ0887/8413966; dorms ¥25); walk north from the bus station for 200m, turn left, and the hostel is on the right. The helpful owner has a lot of information on local treks. However, it's better to skip Deqin town altogether and instead head another 15km north to the Meili Xue Shan **viewing point** just below **Feilai Si** (飞来寺, *fēilái sì*) – it's about a ¥25 taxi ride. There used to be sublime vistas of the mountain here but, in a demonstration of extreme civic meanness, the local authorities have built a **wall**, forcing tourists to pay ¥60 to use an observation platform. It's still a nicer spot than town though, and **places to stay** include the friendly *Meili Guesthouse* (梅里客栈, *méilǐ kèzhàn*; Ⓣ0887/8416633 or 13988755717; dorm ¥25, rooms ❷) and *Meili Shanzhuang* (梅里山庄, *méilǐ shānzhuāng*; Ⓣ13988717636; dorms ¥25, rooms ❸). The best place to eat, the *Migrating Bird Café* (季侯鸟咖啡吧, *jìhóuniǎo kāfēiba*), also serves as an informal tourist agency and meeting point.

Meili Xue Shan

From the Feilai temple viewing point, it's a further ninety-minute drive to the **Meili Xue Shan reserve entrance** at pretty **Xidang village** (西当, *xīdāng*) – cabs charge about ¥200, or you can try hitching. The village sits above the Lancang Jiang (Mekong River), and there's a **guesthouse** here, *Nomad's* (Ⓣ15184990012, Ⓔnomad.china@hotmail.com; beds ¥35), offering meals and hiking information.

Two trails set off from the main entrance. There's talk of introducing a single entry ticket for the reserve, but at the moment you pay separately for each trail. The easiest heads east for the three-hour ascent to the **Mingyong glacier** (明永冰川, *míngyǒng bīngchuān*; ¥83) one of the world's lowest at 2700m, and advancing relatively quickly at 500m per year. The road is reasonably good for the area, and you'll find a fair few souvenir shops and guesthouses at the glacier viewing point.

Yubeng

A more interesting option is to head west from Xidang towards **Yubeng** (entry to area ¥85), though bear in mind this is a tough hike, not to be attempted alone or unprepared. Not far along are Xidang's **hot springs** (温泉, *wēnquán*), possibly the last hot water you'll see for a while. From here it's a gruelling four-hour ascent to the 3800m-high **Nazongla Pass**, followed by ninety minutes down a well-marked trail to **Upper Yubeng** (雨崩上村, *yǔbēng shàng cūn*), a Tibetan settlement of considerable charm. Though plenty of visitors stay here with local families (expect to pay ¥10/night, plus ¥10 for a meal), it's worth persevering to the even prettier **Lower Yubeng** (雨崩下村, *yǔbēng xià cūn*) – take the trail to the left as you come into Upper Yubeng and walk for thirty minutes, over a stream and then a bridge. At the end of Lower Yubeng, Aqinbu's *Shenbu Lodge* (神瀑客栈, *shénbào kèzhàn*; ⓣ0887/8411082; beds ¥20) is a handy base for further treks, on which the helpful owner can advise. The most popular trip from Lower Yubeng is the straightforward two-hour walk to the dramatic **Yubeng Shenpu** (雨崩神瀑, *yǔbēng shénpù*), a sacred waterfall, with bears, snow leopards and the highly endangered Yunnan golden monkey lurking in the nearby forests.

The Kawa Karpo kora

Meili Xue Shan's highest peak, unclimbed **Kawa Karpo** (6740m), is holy to Tibetans, who trek around its base every year to complete the **Kawa Karpo kora**, or pilgrimage circuit, three circumnavigations of which are said to guarantee a beneficial reincarnation. The circuit takes fourteen days or so, beginning in Deqin and ending in the village of Meili. If you plan to attempt it, be aware that the route **crosses the Tibetan border** and you need permits, as the police keep an eye on this area; you also definitely need a **guide** – you're above 4000m most of the time and people have died attempting the trek solo. Travel agencies in Shangri-La can make all arrangements for you.

The Nu Jiang valley

Far over on China's border with Burma, the **Nu Jiang** (怒江, *nùjiāng*), or **Salween River**, enters Yunnan from Tibet and flows south for over 500km through the province. To the east towers the Gaoligong mountain range, a huge rock wall that has kept this area an isolated backwater; the only connection with the rest of the province is the road **from Lushui**, which peters out in the far north of the valley. Unless you're a very hardy trekker with a local guide, the culmination of any trip here is the bus ride back down again, as there is no public road from the north end into Deqin.

However, there are some fascinating attractions in this, Yunnan's last true wilderness and part of the UNESCO World Heritage Site, **Three Parallel Rivers**. The river itself is narrow, fast, full of rapids and crisscrossed by precarious rope bridges, and the settlements clinging to the gorge's sides are highly picturesque. Most of the population are Tibetan, Lisu or Dulong, and there are a surprising number of Catholics, the result of French missionary work in the nineteenth century. Tourism is starting to make in-roads, with agencies based in Dali, Lijiang and Shangri-La offering **guided treks**, currently the best way to explore the area. While package tours organized from Dali and Lijiang are likely to access the river valley via Xiaguan, agencies in Shangri-La may be able to organize a trek west towards the far north of the area, depending on the time of year. Be wary trekking in winter and spring, however, when high rainfall makes landslides common.

Lushui and Fugong

Buses from Xiaguan or Baoshan can get you to **LUSHUI** (泸水县, *lúshuǐ xiàn*), formerly known as **Liuku** (六库, *liùkù*), the unexciting capital of Nu Jiang prefecture. There's not much to do except wander the streets, and nothing to buy unless you're interested in illegally logged Burmese teak or crossbows of dubious efficacy. This sleepy place is at its liveliest around December 20, when the Lisu hold the **Kuoshijie festival**, at which, besides singing and dancing, you'll see local men showing off by climbing poles barefoot using swords as steps.

Lushui straddles both sides of the Nu River, with the hotels and **bus station** on the east side. The cheapest **place to stay** is the dishevelled *Government Guesthouse* (政府招待所, *zhèngfǔ zhāodàisuǒ*; ⓣ0886/3622589; ❶) on Renmin Lu, north of the bus station. The *Post Office Hotel* (邮电宾馆, *yóudiàn bīnguǎn*; ⓣ0886/3620500; ❸), also on Renmin Lu, is better value, while the more upmarket *Nujiang Binguan* (怒江宾馆, *nùjiāng bīnguǎn*; ⓣ0886/3626888; ❹) on Chuancheng Lu, the street east and parallel to Renmin Lu, is overpriced. The **bank** and **post office** are on Renmin Lu. For **food**, try the covered night market just south of the intersection of Renmin Lu and Zhenxing Lu, where you'll see game from the surrounding forests as well as Yunnan staples.

Heading north from Lushui, you pass through some very scenic Lisu villages that cling to the steep sides of the gorge, and the river begins to reveal its fierce character, so it's a shame that the next big town, **FUGONG** (福贡, *fúgòng*), 123km from Lushui, is such a dump. Given its vistas of bleak concrete, it's basically a rest stop on the way to more interesting Gongshan; the *Fugong Binguan* (福贡宾馆, *fúgòng bīnguǎn*; ⓣ0886/3412900; ❷), opposite the bus station, is the best place to stay. Every five days there's a **market**, well attended by Lisu, Dulong and Nu people from nearby villages.

Gongshan, Bingzhong, Dimaluo and around

The **far north** of the Nu valley, being effectively a dead end, is Yunnan's most remote region, and with old forest, waterfalls and thatched-roofed villages, it's also one of the prettiest. But it's also very poor, and considerable degrees of malnutrition and alcoholism can be seen among the local minorities, who are nonetheless generally welcoming. Though tourism promises to be a lucrative new source of income, as yet there are fairly few facilities. Certainly it is not a good idea to venture too far alone, and a local guide is always advised for any ambitious walk.

First stop is the one-street town of **GONGSHAN** (贡山, *gòngshān*) around four hours' bus ride north of Fugong. You'll likely see plenty of Dulong people here: older women have tattooed faces, supposedly for beautification, though the practice seems to have started as a way to dissuade Tibetan slave-traders from kidnapping them. The *Bus Station Hostel* (贡山客运旅社, *gòngshān kèyùn lǚshè*; ⓣ0886/3511496; ❷) has hot water.

A bumpy two-hour journey north through dramatic gorge scenery brings you to **BINGZHONGLUO**, a little village at the end of the road, with a couple of basic guesthouses, the best of which is the *Chama Kezhan* (茶马客栈, *chámǎ kèzhàn*; ⓣ0886/3581277 or 13187499887; ❶). This is the best place to base yourself for treks. One popular walk, simple enough to do alone, is to **Dimaluo** (迪麻洛, *dímáluò*) a community of Catholic Tibetans. Board a bus heading south and get off at the footbridge that leads to **Pengdang** (捧当, *pěngdāng*), then cross the river and walk south until you reach a bridge and a dirt track, which you follow north to the village. The walk takes about two hours. At Dimaluo, there's accommodation and an intriguing **Catholic church** built in Tibetan style.

From Dimaluo, you'll need a guide for the stiff, two-day hike across the Nushan range to **Cizhong**, a village with another stone church in the parallel Lancang River valley; the locals even make their own red wine for communion, though Christianity has been laid on top of much older, animist beliefs. There is an irregular, fair-weather bus service south from Cizhong to **Weixi** (维西, *wéixī*; 6–10hr), from where you can catch a bus to Lijiang via Shigu (see p.715).

Yunnan's far west

Southwest of Xiaguan, **Yunnan's far west** bumps up against the **Burmese border**, an increasingly tropical area of mountain forests and broad valleys planted with rice and sugar cane, all cut by the deep watershed gorges of Southeast Asia's mighty **Mekong** and **Salween rivers** (in Chinese, the Lancang Jiang and Nu Jiang, respectively). Settlements here have large populations of Dai, Burmese and Jingpo, among others, and until recently mainstream China never had a great presence – indeed, at times it's still often unclear whether rules and regulations originate in Beijing or with the nearest officer in charge.

The main artery here, the underused **G56 Expressway**, roughly follows the route of the old **Burma Road**, built during WWII as a supply line between British-held Burma and Kunming, from where goods were shipped to China's wartime capital, Chongqing. Something of the road's original purpose survives today, with towns along the way, especially ethnically mixed **Ruili**, right on the Burmese frontier, still clearly benefitting from the cross-border traffic. With the exception of geologically unsettled **Tengchong**, however, sights out this way are few and – unless you're heading into Burma – the main point of visiting is simply to experience a fairly untouristed, if not actually remote, corner of the country.

Transport through the far west is by **bus**, though you can also **fly** to Baoshan, Tengchong and Mangshi. Some minor scuffles along the Burmese border in recent years, plus the area's perennial drug-trafficking problems, mean you might encounter **military checkpoints** in the region, where you have to show passports and wait while vehicles are checked for contraband. The **weather** is subtropically humid, especially during the **wet season** between May and October, when landslides frequently cut smaller roads.

Xiaguan to Ruili

Buses from Xiaguan can get you to the quirky border towns of **Wanding** and **Ruili** in a single day, but it's worth aiming first for pleasant **Tengchong**, an old market town surrounded by volcano cones and hot springs. Coming south from Lushui in the Nu Jiang valley (see p.725), aim first for **BAOSHAN** (保山, *bǎoshān*), a large grid of a town 150km from Xiaguan down the Ruili highway. Baoshan's huge bus station is on Jiulong Lu right at the southern end of town; the bus station's *Jiaotong Binguan* (交通宾馆, *jiāotōng bīnguǎn*; ⓣ0875/2122918; ❷), and justifiably three-starred *Landu Hotel* (兰都饭店, *lándū fàndiàn*; ⓣ0875/2121888; ❺), at 146 Baoxiu Xilu, are at opposite ends of the accommodation spectrum.

Tengchong and around

Some 90km west of Baoshan, **TENGCHONG** (腾冲, *téngchōng*) was once an important marketplace and administration post, now unfairly isolated and well off the new highway. The town's scruffy old core is surrounded by modern main roads and apartments, though numerous **earthquakes** have left Tengchong bereft of many historic monuments or tall buildings. The old stone gate tower, **Wenxing Lou** (文星楼, *wénxīng lóu*), survives on at the eastern end of central Fengshan Lu, and there's a big – though rather too organized – jade market known as **Yuquan Yuan** (玉泉园, *yùquán yuán*) at the northern edge of town; otherwise the main attraction is **Laifeng Shan Park** (来凤山公园, *láifēng shān gōngyuán*), several square kilometres of hilly woodland at the western end of Fengshan Lu. Paths ascend to **Laifeng Si**, a monastery-turned-museum, and a resurrected, thirteen-storey **pagoda** which will guide you to the park from town.

Arrival and information

Tengchong's kilometre-wide centre focuses around the **Fengshan Lu/ Guanghua Lu** crossroads, with newer bits of town all around the perimeter, especialy to the south. The **main bus station** (旅游客运站, *lǚyóu kèyùnzhàn*) is a kilometre south down Rehai Lu, handling traffic to Kunming, Xiaguan and Baoshan; while easterly **Tengchong bus station** (腾冲客运站, *téngchōng kèyùn zhàn*) on Dongfang Lu has frequent departures to Mangshi and Ruili between about 7am and 3pm.

There's a **Bank of China** with ATM, and a post office, at the Laifeng Shan Park end of Fengshan Lu. A **taxi** anywhere in town costs ¥5.

Accommodation and eating

For **accommodation**, *Tengchong Youth Hostel* (玉泉园青年旅舍, *yùquányuán qīngnián lǚshè*; ⓣ0875/5198677; dorms ¥40, rooms ❸) is in a spacious, new wooden building at the Yuquan Yuan jade market complex; English-speaking staff dispense local information, and the price includes breakfast. *Xintong Binguan* (鑫通宾馆, *xīntōng bīnguǎn*; ⓣ0875/5163199; ❷) on Dongfang Lu is an inexpensive, clean but basic Chinese option on five floors with no lifts, while Tenchong's plushest venue is the modern *Yudu Dajiudian* (玉都大酒店, *yùdōu dàjiǔdiàn*; ⓣ0875/5138666, ⓦwww.tcyuduhotel.com; ❺), again near the jade market on Tengyue Lu. There's also accommodation at **Heshun** (see below).

Places to **eat** lurk along Yingjiang Lu and Guanghua Lu, where evening stalls also sell charcoal-grilled chicken and fish.

Heshun

Five kilometres west of Tengchong – a shared minibus costs ¥2, a taxi ¥15 – **HESHUN** (和顺, *héshùn*) is a Qing-style village whose memorial gateways, ornamental gardens and thousand or more old stone houses are tightly packed within a whitewashed perimeter wall. **Entry** is free, but buying an ¥80 ticket allows you to enter various notable buildings in town. There's a **museum** here to the left of the entrance, full of saddles, swords and other paraphernalia from the old tea-horse trade days, along with ornamental ponds and encircling hills and paddyfields and, despite increasing commercialization, you could easily spend half a day wandering Heshun with a camera.

Many places offer **accommodation**, including *Lao Shay Youth Hostel* (老谢青年旅舍, *lǎoxiè qīngnián lǚshè*; ⓣ0875/5158398, ⓦwww.laoshay.com; dorms ¥30, rooms ❷) and *Zongbingfu Kezhan* (总兵府客栈, *zǒngbīngfǔ kèzhàn*; ⓣ0875/5150288; ❻) whose period rooms are housed in an old courtyard building.

Hot springs and volcanoes

Geological shuffles over the last fifty million years have opened up a couple of hotspots around Tengchong. The easiest to reach, the "Hot Sea", **Rehai** (热海, *rèhǎi*), is 11km southwest along the Ruili road, where the scalding **Liuhuang** and **Dagungguo** pools (each ¥30 entry; spa treatments up to ¥168) steam and bubble away, contained by incongruously neat stone paving and ornamental borders. Get there by minibus (¥5) from Huancheng Nan Lu, the southern ring road in Tengchong, at the junction with the Ruili road.

The nearest **volcano cones** are 25km north of Tengchong at **Mazhan Volcano Park** (马站火山公园, *mǎzhàn huǒshān gōngyuán*; ¥40); catch a minibus (¥10) from the small depot on Huoshan Lu, near Tengchong's youth hostel, to **Mazhan village** (马站, *mǎzhàn*) and then walk the last kilometre. Don't expect anything too spectacular; the volcanoes are long-dead and the cones worn to black rubble hills.

Mangshi

South of Baoshan, the highway makes a grand descent into the Nu Jiang Valley on the four-hour journey to **MANGSHI** (芒市, *mángshì*), also known as **Luxi** (潞西, *lùxī*). Set amid lush countryside, Mangshi has a reputation for excellent pineapples and silverwork, though the only reason you'd stop off here is to use the **airport**, 7km south, the closest one to the Burmese border at Ruili.

Incoming flights are met by taxis and minibuses to town, and also to Ruili – the latter journey should take under three hours, and cost ¥35. Most Mangshi vehicles will set down at the eastern end of main Tuanjie Dajie, either on the roundabout outside the **airline office** (daily 8.30am–5pm) or 1km west at the cluster of depots where **long-distance buses** and **minibuses** stop.

Should you find yourself stuck in town for the night, there are numerous cheap **guesthouses** around the bus station, while *De'an Jiudian* (德安酒店, *déān jiǔdiàn*; ⓣ0692/2211288 ❷), at 24 Kuoshi Lu, is a clean, basic hotel. Countless shacks serve buns and curries in almost every lane through the town.

Burmese glossary

Hello (polite)	*Min galaba jinbaya*	Pickled vegetables	*Lapatoh*
Thank you	*Jayzu tinbadé*	Rice	*Htamin*
I'd like to eat	*Htamin saa gyinbadé*	Sour sauce	*Achin*
		Spoon	*Zone*
Beef	*Améda*	Sticky rice (in a bamboo tube)	*Kauk nyaimn paung (tauk)*
Chicken	*Jeda*		
Curry	*Hin, tha*	Tea	*La pay-ee*
Cold drink	*A-ay*		
Crushed peanuts	*Nanthaung*	One	*Did*
		Two	*Nhid*
Dhal (split-pea soup)	*Pey hin pea*	Three	*Dhong*
		Four	*Lay*
Fish	*Nga*	Five	*Ngar*
Fish soup with banana stem and noodles	*Moh hin gha*	Six	*Chauk*
		Seven	*Khunik*
		Eight	*Chind*
Fork	*Khayan*	Nine	*Cho*
Milk	*Nwa nou*	Ten	*Desay*
Noodles	*Kaukswe*	Eleven	*Say did*

Wanding

Two hours south of Mangshi, the road crosses the **Long Jiang** (Shweli River), and then finally slaloms down the slopes of a narrow valley to the point where the shallow Wanding Stream separates Chinese **WANDING** (畹町, *wǎndīng*) from **Jiugu** over in Burma. Opened in 1938 as the purpose-built customs post for the Burma Road, Wanding has today been totally upstaged as a cross-border trade zone by nearby Ruili. The town is a sleepy hollow barely a kilometre long, and there's no reason to **stay** here; Ruili is just thirty minutes down the road and minibuses (¥10) shuttle between the two all day long.

Not that Wanding is uninteresting: the **Wanding Bridge crossing** is a marvel, decked in customs houses, smartly uniformed military, barriers, barbed wire, flags and signs everywhere prohibiting unauthorized passage. The bridge itself – though ridiculously short – is a sturdy concrete span, and there's even a prominent red line painted across the road on the Chinese side. But it's all a sham; walk 500m downstream and you'll find people rolling up their trousers and wading across a ford almost within sight of patrolling soldiers. Naturally everyone knows what's happening, but this arrangement spares authorities and locals endless official bother.

Unfortunately, **foreigners** wanting to cross will find the situation very different. Westerners can only enter Burma either by flying to Rangoon or, if wanting to cross the border overland, by joining an authorized tour and obtaining a permit available through agencies in Kunming (see p.692).

Ruili and around

Once the capital of the Mengmao Dai Kingdom, the frontier town of **RUILI** (瑞丽, *ruìlì*) revels in the possibilities of its proximity to Burma, 5km south over the Shweli River. So porous is the border between Jiegao in China and **Mu Se** on the Burmese side that locals quip, "Feed a chicken in China and you get an egg in Burma". This section of the border is still reckoned to be the main conduit for Burmese **drugs** entering China, and Ruili has one of the highest rates of drug addiction – and HIV/AIDS – in China.

Burmese, Pakistani and Bangladeshi nationals wander around in sarongs and thongs, clocks are often set to Rangoon time, and markets display foreign goods. Most Chinese in town are tourists, attracted by the chance to pick up cut-price trinkets and

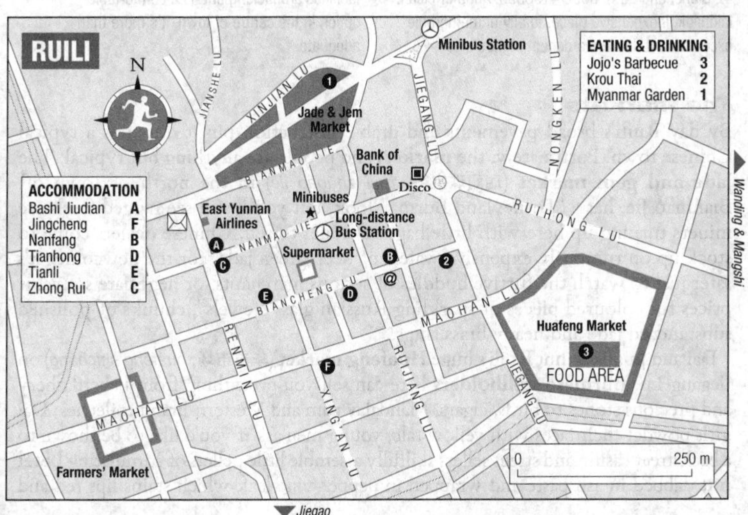

hop across the border to catch a Burmese transvestite show (see the pictures displayed in travel agency windows). The town's **markets** are fascinating; many foreign traders speak good English and make interesting company. Additionally, the surrounding countryside, studded with Dai villages and temples, is only a bike-ride away.

Arrival and information

Ruili's kilometre-long main street, **Nanmao Jie**, runs west from a tree-shaded roundabout, passing the Bank of China (foreign exchange Mon–Fri 9–11.30am & 2.30–4.30pm), and the **long-distance bus station**, before it crosses Renmin Lu. Turn north here and there's a **post office** 50m away on the corner of Xinjian Lu. Minibuses to Wanding and Mangshi depart from the minibus **station** opposite the north end of Jiegang Lu, and also the small depot opposite the bus station on Nanmao Jie. The long-distance station has at least daily services to everywhere along the highway between here and Kunming. Getting to and from Mangshi's **airport** costs ¥35 in a minibus or ¥50 per person in a taxi. East Yunnan Airlines, at 15 Renmin Lu (Ⓣ0692/4155700 or 4111111) usually offers discounted fares from Mangshi to Kunming and Guangzhou.

Accommodation

Ruili has enough **hotels** that there's a choice of good-value rooms right in the town centre, though there are no real budget bargains. You need air conditioning in summer.

Bashi Jiudian (巴石酒店, *bāshí jiǔdiàn*) At the Nanmao Jie/Renmin Lu intersection Ⓣ0692/4129088. Immediately recognizable for the Thai/Burmese trimmings at the front; it's a basic, spotless place favoured by gem dealers from over the border. Probably the cheapest proper hotel in town. ❶

Jingcheng (景成大酒店, *jǐngchéng dàjiǔdiàn*) Maohan Lu Ⓣ0692/4159666. A reliable starred pile with decent rooms, swimming pool, tennis court and gym. ❺

Nanfang (南方宾馆, *nánfāng bīnguǎn*) 42 Biancheng Lu Ⓣ0692/4156999. Another clean, laidback, inexpensive place, totally unmemorable except that it delivers a decent night's sleep. ❷

Tianhong (天宏宾馆, *tiānhóng bīnguǎn*) Behind the bus station at 83 Biancheng Lu Ⓣ0692/4101222. Cool, clean, absolutely ordinary Chinese hotel, with large tiled en suites. Some rooms come with computers. ❷

Tianli (天丽宾馆, *tiānlì bīnguǎn*) Biancheng Lu Ⓣ0692/4155188. Yet another simple, smart, clean option. ❷

Zhong Rui (钟瑞宾馆, *zhōngruì bīnguǎn*) 1 Nanmao Jie Ⓣ0692/4100556. Smart place with clean en-suite twins and doubles. Other facilities are lacking but as a comfortable option in the centre of town, it's more than adequate. ❸

The markets

By day Ruili's broad pavements and drab construction pin it down as a typical Chinese town. Fortunately, the **markets** and people are anything but typical. The **jade and gem market** (瑞丽珠宝街, *ruìlì zhūbǎo jiē*) in the north of town off Bianmao Jie, has a "Disneyland Burma" look, but you'll still see ragged freelance miners turning up here with little bags of stones to sell. Chinese dealers come to stock up on ruinously expensive wafers of deep green jade; for the newcomer it's safer just to watch the furtive huddles of serious merchants, or negotiate souvenir prices for coloured pieces of sparkling Russian glass "jewels", chunks of polished substandard jade and heavy brass rings.

Dai and Jingpo haunt Ruili's huge **Huafeng market** (华丰市场, *huáfēng shìchǎng*) on Jiegang Lu. **Burmese stallholders** here can sell you everything from haberdashery and precious stones to birds, cigars, Mandalay rum and Western-brand toiletries; Dai girls powder their faces with yellow talc, young men ask if you'd like to be shown to a backstreet casino and street sellers skilfully assemble little pellets of stimulating **betel nut** dabbed in ash paste and wrapped in pepper-vine leaf, which stains lips red and teeth black. It really comes alive at night when the stalls in a southeastern covered area start serving spicy Burmese barbecue and chilled Myanmar Beer.

For a more rough-and-ready shopping experience, try the morning **farmers' market** (综合农贸市场, *zōnghé nónghè shìchǎng*) at the western end of Maohan Lu, where you'll find not only meat, fish, fruit and vegetables, but also locally made wood and cane furniture as well as shoes, clothes and even roadside jewellers selling 'gold' rings and bracelets by the gram.

Eating and drinking

The real treat in Ruili is heading to the **covered food area** in Huafeng market, which has seating for several hundred diners and comes alive from about 8pm onwards, especially at weekends. *Jojo's Barbecue* is highly recommended, particularly the fish encrusted with tandooriesque, bright orange spices (look for the sign in English, though not much English is spoken, and not much Chinese either). The food is all laid out on show so ordering by pointing is simple, and you can wash it down with Myanmar Beer or any number of the fresh juices.

There's also **Thai food** around town. Best is the *Krou Thai Restaurant* (可傣饭店, *kě dǎi fàndiàn*) on Biancheng Lu, though the basic *Myanmar Garden*, up at the jade market, has outdoor seating and good Thai and Burmese snacks too. Plenty of places also sell freshly squeezed **fruit juices**, very refreshing on a hot day. For conventional **Chinese food**, head to the string of restaurants on Ruijiang Lu beside the long-distance bus station.

Around Ruili

Villages and Buddhist monuments dot the plains around Ruili, easy enough to explore either by asking your accommodation about renting a bicycle, or by **minibus** from the Nanmao Jie depot – just keep repeating the name of your destination and you'll be shepherded to the right vehicle. Most of the destinations below are only of mild interest in themselves, really just excuses to get out into Ruili's attractive countryside. For more about the Dai, see the Xishuangbanna section (p.734).

The quickest trip is virtually inside town. Hail a red taxi and you're ¥4 and five minutes from **Jiegao** (姐告, *jiěgào*), a huge trading estate on Ruili's southern outskirts, surrounded on all sides by Burma. You get dropped off right by the border crossing, among a vast grid of hotels, clubs and shops selling everything from vehicles to nautical compasses.

About 5km east of Ruili along the Wanding road is the two-hundred-year-old **Jiele Jin Ta** (姐勒金塔, *jiělè jīn tǎ*), a group of seventeen portly **Dai pagodas** painted gold and said to house several of Buddha's bones. In some open-air **hot springs** nearby, you can wash away various ailments. Further on in this direction, **Moli Rainsforest Scenic Area** (莫里雨林风景区, *mòlǐ yǔlín fēngjǐng qū*; ¥50) lies 5km north of the main road, about halfway between Ruili and Wanding, and features forest and a big waterfall. Hiring a minibus to take you there will cost ¥100, including waiting time, or you can walk from the main road.

Heading west, it's 5km to a small bridge near the region's largest Buddhist temple, the nicely decorated **Hansha Si** (喊沙寺, *hǎnshā sì*). Ten kilometres further on, the town of **JIEXIANG** (姐相, *jiěxiàng*) boasts the splendid Tang-era **Leizhuang Xiang** (雷奘相佛寺, *léizàngxīang fósì*), where the low square hall of a nunnery is dominated by a huge central pagoda and four corner towers, all in white. Another fine temple with typical Dai touches, such as "fiery" wooden eave decorations, **Denghannong Si** (等喊弄寺, *děnghǎnnòng sì*) is further west again. The current halls only date from the Qing dynasty, but Buddha is said to have stopped here once to preach.

Xishuangbanna

A tropical spread of rainforests, plantations and paddy fields nestled 750km southwest of Kunming along the Burmese and Laotian borders, **Xishuangbanna** (西双版纳, *xīshuāngbǎnnà*) has little in common with the rest of provincial China. Foremost of the region's many ethnic groups are the **Dai**, northern cousins to the Thais, whose distinctive temples, bulbous pagodas and saffron-robed clergy are a common sight down on the plains, particularly around **Jinghong**, Xishuangbanna's sleepy capital. The region's remaining 19,000 square kilometres of hills, farms and forest are split between the administrative townships of **Mengla** in the east and **Menghai** in the west, peppered with villages of Hani, Bulang, Jinuo, Wa and Lahu; remoter tribes are still animistic, and all have distinctive dress and customs. Cultural tourism aside, there are plenty of hiking trails and China's **open border with Laos** to explore.

Xishuangbanna's emphatically tropical **weather** divides into a dry stretch between November and May, when warm days, cool nights and dense morning mists are the norm; and the June–October **wet season**, featuring high heat and torrential daily rains. Given the climate, you'll need to take more than usual care of any cuts and abrasions, and to guard against mosquitoes (see p.60). The busiest time of the year here is mid-April, when thousands of tourists flood to Jinghong for the Dai **Water-splashing Festival**; hotels and flights will be booked solid for a week beforehand. **Getting around** Xishuangbanna is easy enough, with well-maintained roads connecting Jinghong to outlying

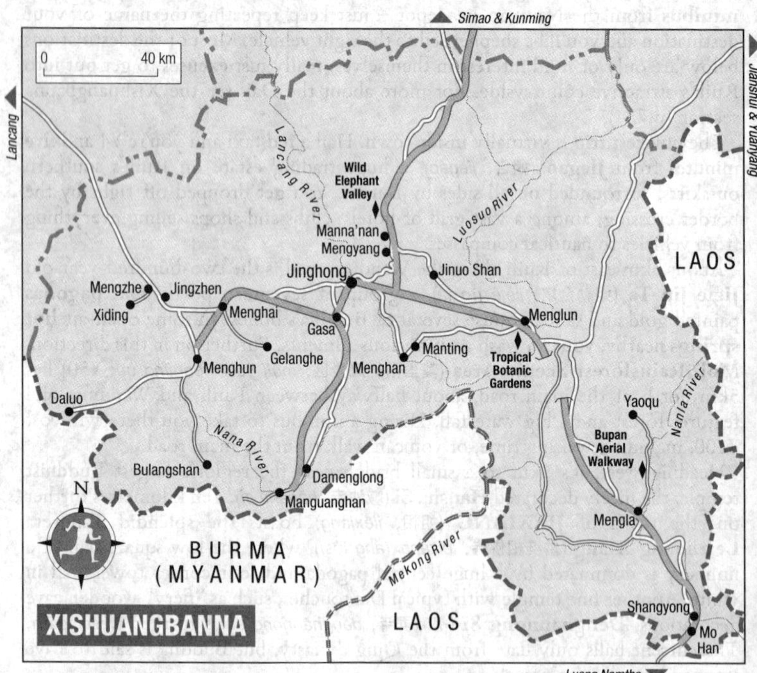

Getting to and from Xishuangbanna

Daily **flights** link Jinghong with Kunming, Xiaguan/Dali, Lijiang and a few cities elsewhere in China. There's also talk of Lao Air starting a service between Jinghong and Luang Prabang in northern **Laos**, while China Eastern fly once a week to **Bangkok** in Thailand. Buy onward tickets for all flights at China Eastern, 23 Minhang Lu (daily 8am–8pm; ⓣ0691/2126999), in Jinghong, or from agents around town who chalk up daily deals on blackboards outside.

Direct **buses to Jinghong** depart Kunming's South bus station (¥180–260; 10hr), Xiaguan/Dali (¥180; 18hr), Tengchong and Baoshan (¥220; 20hr), Ruili (¥300; 30hr) and Luang Namtha in **Laos** (US$12; 8hr). Coming from Yuanyang in southeast Yunnan, aim first for Jianshui (see p.694). Tickets to all these places are easily available through the relevant bus stations in Jinghong (see Jinghong "Arrival" on p.734).

Mekong ferries between Jinghong and Chiang Saen in northern Thailand take seven hours, leave Jinghong at 8am every other day (more or less), and cost ¥650. The ticket office (ⓣ0691/2211899) at the port is open from 8am to 5.30pm, or Jinghong's cafés can make bookings.

Remember to confirm **visa requirements** for Laos and Thailand before booking transport – the nearest consulates are in Kunming (see p.692).

districts. **Place names** can be confusing, though, as the words "meng-", designating a small town, or "man-", a village, prefix nearly every destination.

Some history

Historically, there was already a Dai state in Xishuangbanna two thousand years ago, important enough to send ambassadors to the Han court in 69 AD; it was subsequently incorporated into the Nanzhao and Dali kingdoms. A brief period of full independence ended with the Mongols' thirteenth-century conquest of Yunnan and the area's division into **twelve rice-growing districts** or *sipsawng pa na*, rendered as "Xishuangbanna" in Chinese. A fairly "hands-off" approach to Chinese rule ended in the 1950s, since when more contentious aspects of religion have been banned, extensive deforestation has occurred, and recent mass planting of **rubber** as a cash crop has changed the landscape. Many minority people feel that the government would really like them to behave like Han Chinese, except in regards to dress – since colourful traditional clothing attracts tourists – and it's certainly true that Xishuangbanna is a rather anaemic version of what lies across the border in Laos.

Jinghong

It was under the Dai warlord **Bazhen** that **JINGHONG** (景洪, *jǐnghóng*), Xishuangbanna's small and easy-going "Dawn Capital" (as it's called in Dai), first became a seat of power. Ever since Bazhen drove the Bulang and Hani tribes off these fertile central flatlands, and founded the independent kingdom of Cheli in 1180, Jinghong has been maintained as an administrative centre. There was a moment of excitement in the late nineteenth century when a battalion of British soldiers marched in during a foray from Burma, but they soon decided that Jinghong was too remote to be worth defending.

Today the grey edifices of Jinghong's contemporary Han architecture make a suitably colonial backdrop for the Dai women in bright sarongs and straw hats

The Dai

Although the Dai once spread as far north as the Yangzi Valley, they were driven south by the Mongol expansion in the thirteenth century. These days, they are found not only in southwest China but also throughout Thailand, Laos and Vietnam. Reputed as skilful farmers, they have always flourished in fertile river basins, growing rice, sugar cane, rubber trees and bananas. Accordingly, **Dai cuisine** is characterized by sweet flavours not found elsewhere in China – you'll encounter rice steamed inside bamboo or pineapple, for instance. Oddities such as fried moss and ant eggs appear on special occasions.

Dai women wear a sarong or long skirt, a bodice and a jacket, and keep their hair tied up and fixed with a comb, and often decorated with flowers. Married women wear silver wristbands. Dai men sport plenty of **tattoos**, usually across their chests and circling their wrists. Their homes are raised on stilts, with the livestock kept underneath. Some of the most distinctive and ornate Dai architecture is well decoration, as the Dai regard water as sacred. They're Buddhists, but like their compatriots in Southeast Asia follow the Thervada, or Lesser Wheel school, rather than the Mahayana school seen throughout the rest of China. When visiting Dai temples, it's important to **remove your shoes**, as the Dai consider feet to be the most unclean part of the body.

who meander along the gently simmering, palm-lined streets, and for the most part the city is an undemanding place to spend a couple of days investigating Dai culture. Aside from energetic excesses during the water-splashing festivities, you'll find the pace of life is set by the tropical heat – though the centre is often full of people, nobody bothers rushing anywhere. Once you've tried the local food and poked around the temples that encroach on the suburbs, there's plenty of transport into the rest of Xishuangbanna.

Arrival and city transport

Jinghong sits on the southwestern bank of the **Lancang River** (澜沧江, *láncāng jiāng*) which later winds downstream through Laos and Thailand as the Mekong. The city centre is around the intersection of **Mengle Dadao** and Xuanwei Dadao; the latter crosses east over the Lancang via the **Xishuangbanna suspension bridge** (西双版纳大桥, *xīshuāngbǎnnà dà qiáo*).

The **airport** lies about 10km southwest of the city; catch bus #1 to its terminus at the western extension of Mengla Lu, or it's a ten-minute, ¥25 taxi ride into the centre along an expressway. Long-distance buses – including those from Luang Namtha in Laos – wind up at the **Jinghong bus station** (景洪客运站, *jǐnghóng kèyùn zhàn*), on the northern arm of Mengle Dadao, though some Kunming services use the **South bus station** (客运南站, *kèyùn nán zhàn*), a kilometre south of town – catch bus #3 or a cab. Arriving from outlying villages in the region will either see you disembarking at the South bus station, or at the **Banna bus station** (版纳客运服务站, *bǎnnà kèyùn fúwù zhàn*), right in the centre on Minzu Lu. **Ferries from Thailand** dock on the far side of the river at Jinghong's **ferry port** (景洪港, *jǐnghóng gǎng*) – bus #2 from the road will get you into the north end of town.

Nowhere in Jinghong is more than a twenty-minute walk away, so **city buses** are only really necessary to reach outlying transit points; cabs charge ¥7 for anywhere in town. Watch out for **pickpockets** at the post office and bus stations.

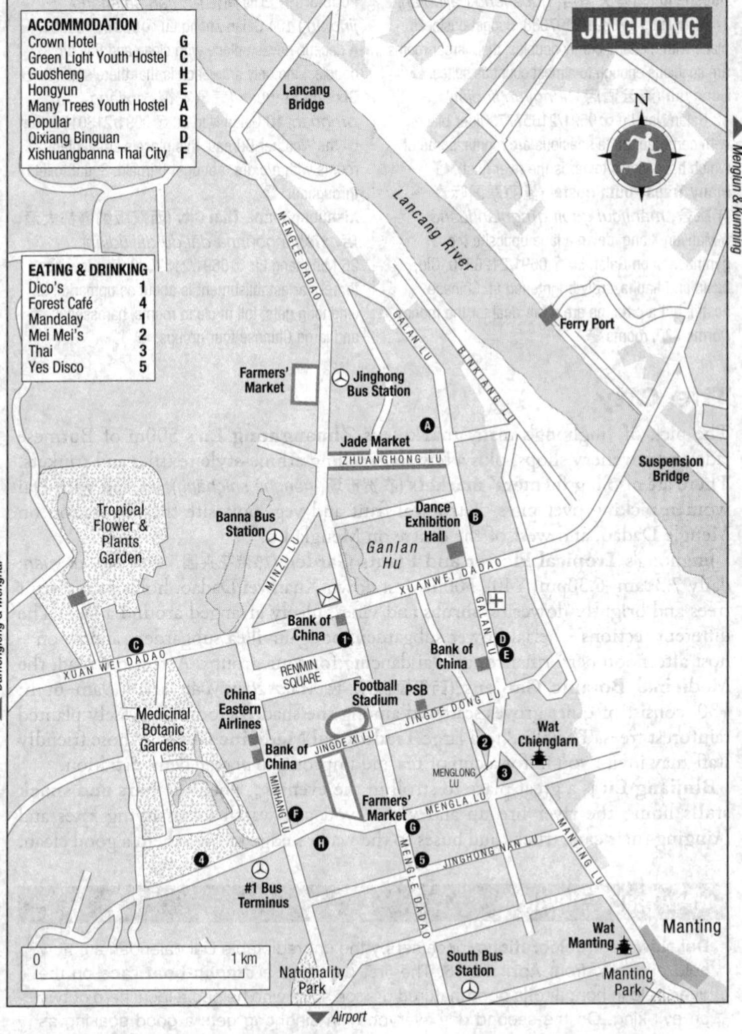

Accommodation

All but the smallest lodgings have restaurants and tour agencies, and some offer computers in the room for an extra ¥20 or so. You'll need air conditioning in summer. The two **hostels** can book tickets and rent bikes.

Crown Hotel (皇冠大酒店, *huángguān dàjiǔdiàn*) 70 Mengle Dadao ⓣ0691/2199883, ⓦwww.newtgh.com. One of a number of upmarket places grouped around the Mengle/Mengla intersection, all aimed at wealthy Chinese tourists. Unmemorable, but clean and comfortable. ❹

Green Light Youth Hostel (版纳绿光青年客栈, *bǎnnà lǜguāng qīngnián kèzhàn*) 93 Xuanwei Dadao ⓣ0691/2138365. This basic budget guesthouse, close to the botanical gardens in the grounds of the university, has dorms and twin rooms with 24hr solar-powered hot water. The a/c is extra. Dorms ¥25, rooms ❶

Guosheng (国盛大酒店, *guóshèng dàjiŭdiàn*) 14 Mengla Lu ☎0691/2197088. Budget business place with modern, comfy doubles; their larger rooms are spacious enough to almost count as suites. ❸

Hongyun (鸿云酒店, *hóngyún jiŭdiàn*) 12 Galan Nan Lu ☎0691/2165777. Older place with carpeted, quite spacious a/c rooms, some of which have views towards the river (just). ❷

Many Trees Youth Hostel (曼丽翠国际青年旅舍, *mànlìcuì guójì qīngnián lǚshě*) 5 Manyun Xiang, down a lane opposite the gymnasium on Galan Lu ☎0691/2126210. Old, basic and haphazardly brightened up Chinese hostel, but a/c rooms are a fair deal for the money. Dorms ¥30, rooms ❷

Popular (假日时尚酒店, *jiàrì shíshàng jiŭdiàn*) 104 Galan Zhong Lu ☎0691/2139001. A decent, newish place with clean and tidy a/c doubles; the only drawback is that there's no lift. ❷

Qixiang Binguan (气象宾馆, *qìxiàng bīnguăn*) 10 Galan Nan Lu ☎0691/2130188. Run by the Weather Bureau, this place's small tiled rooms with a/c are a budget bargain. Squat toilets throughout. ❶

Xishuangbanna Thai City (西双版纳傣都大酒店, *xīshāngbănnà dăi dū dàjiŭdiàn*) 26 Minghang Lu ☎0691/2137888. This low-key three-star establishment is about as upmarket as Jinghong gets, full of clean rooms, harassed staff and large Chinese tour groups. ❹

The City

The pick of Jinghong's many **markets** is **Zhuanghong Lu**'s 500m of Burmese jade and jewellery shops, plus a few stalls selling ethnic-style textiles and trinkets. There are also big **farmers' markets** (农贸市场, *nónghè shìchăng*), packed with Dai women picking over piles of tropical fruit and veg, opposite the bus station on Mengle Dadao, and west of the centre on Mengla Lu.

Jinghong's **Tropical Flower and Plants Garden** (热带花卉园, *rèdài huāhuì yuán*; daily 7.30am–6.30pm; ¥40), 500m west down Xuanwei Dadao, holds palms, fruit trees and brightly flowering shrubs and vines, nicely arranged around a lake. The different sections – aerial flower subgarden, bougainvillea subgarden, and so on – host afternoon performances of Dai dancing for tour groups. Across the road, the **Medicinal Botanic Gardens** (药用植物园, *yàoyòng zhíwùyuán*; daily 9am–6pm; ¥30) consist of quiet groves scattered among the shaded gloom of closely planted rainforest trees. They lead to a large **Traditional Medicine Clinic**, whose friendly staff may invite you in for a cup of tea and impromptu *qi gong* demonstration.

Binjiang Lu is a great place to stroll in the evening, when the **bars and snack stalls** lining the river fire up and where you can watch locals flying kites and bringing their cars, trucks and buses to the water's edge to give them a good clean.

New Year festivities

Dai New Year celebrations, once set by the unpredictable Dai calendar, are now held annually, from **April 13–16**. The first day sees a **dragon-boat race** on the river, held in honour of a good-natured dragon spirit who helped a local hero outwit an evil king. On the second day everybody in Jinghong gets a good soaking as **water-splashing** hysteria grips the town, and basinfuls are enthusiastically hurled over friends and strangers alike to wash away bad luck. Manting Park also hosts cockfighting and dancing all day. The finale includes **Diu Bao** (Throwing Pouches) games, where prospective couples fling small, triangular beanbags at each other to indicate their affection, and there's a mammoth **firework display**, when hundreds of bamboo tubes stuffed with gunpowder and good-luck gifts are rocketed out over the river. Nightly carousing and dancing – during which generous quantities of *lajiu*, the local firewater, are consumed – take place in the parks and public spaces. Look out for the **Peacock dance**, a fluid performance said to imitate the movements of the bird, bringer of good fortune in Dai lore, and the **Elephant-drum dance**, named after the instrument used to thump out the rhythm.

Manting

A kilometre southeast of the centre via Manting Lu, **Manting** (曼听, *mànting*) was once a separate village, now absorbed into Jinghong's lazy spread. Near the end of the road, **Wat Manting** (曼听佛寺, *màntīng fósì*) is Jinghong's main **Buddhist monastery** and the largest in all Xishuangbanna. Check out the very Dai gold trim, the guradian creatures at the gates, the glossy *jinghua* murals; and a giant ceremonial canoe in the monastery grounds. Traditionally, all Dai boys spend three years at temples like Wat Manting getting a grounding in Buddhism and learning to read and write.

Next to Wat Manting is the more secular **Manting Park** (曼听公园, *màntīng gōngyuán*; daily 7.30am–5.30pm; ¥40), where the royal slaves were formerly kept. A giant gold statue of former premier Zhou Enlai welcomes visitors to the park, tour groups are treated to water-splashing displays every afternoon, and there's also a large pen bursting with **peacocks**, which you can feed. Corners of the park are very pleasant, with paths crossing over one of the Lancang River's tiny tributaries to full-scale copies of Jingzhen's Bajiao Ting (see p.741) and a portly, Dai-style pagoda. The park hosts nightly **shows** (7.40–9.40pm; ¥160–280) featuring Dai dancing and mass water-splashings.

Eating, drinking and entertainment

Jinghong is the best place in Xishuangbanna to try **authentic Dai cooking**, either in restaurants or on the street. Formal menus often feature meat or fish courses flavoured with sour bamboo shoots or lemongrass, while oddities include **fried moss**, and **pineapple rice** for dessert – the fruit is hollowed out, stuffed with pineapple chunks and sweet glutinous rice, and steamed.

Tourist cafés are comparatively expensive places to eat, but aside from their Western-Dai menus they also hand out local information, rent bikes and arrange tours. The pick of these are the long-running *Mei Mei's* (Ⓣ0691/2161221, Ⓔzhanyanlan@hotmail.com) on Menglong Lu – one of a clutch of similar cafés – and the *Forest Café* (Ⓣ0691/8985122, Ⓦwww.forest-cafe.org) on Mengla Lu. Sarah at the *Forest Café*, in particular, is a mine of information about local treks. There's an inexpensive **Thai restaurant** opposite *Mei Mei's* – though it closes very early – and you can get cold fruit drinks and light Chinese, Western and Dai meals at *Mandalay* (耶待纳美餐厅, *yēdāinà měi cāntīng*), above the more visible *Dico's* on Mengle Dadao. There's also a small covered market at the top end of Manting Lu with nightly **barbecue stalls**.

Entertainment is unpredictable, but the best places to catch some ad-hoc music and minority dancing are in the evening at Ganlan Hu. For a more modern take on minority dances, try the *YES Disco* on Jinghong Nan Lu (open until 3am), which is packed every night with hard-drinking Dai kids. It's free to get in, and a beer costs ¥20. For a more sedate time head down to riverside Binjiang Lu, which has been developed into a **Nationality Snack Street** (民族食尚街, *mínzú shíshàng jiē*), a line of large, wooden restaurant-bars with loud – sometimes live – music on the promenade above the riverside, decked out in coloured fairy lights. It's a nice idea, but the establishments are all much the same and a drink costs at least ¥30.

Listings

Banks and exchange The main Bank of China (daily 8am–11.30am & 3–5.30pm) with ATM is at 29 Minhang Lu, at the junction with Jingde Lu. There are ATMs all around the centre.

Hospital The Provincial Hospital is at the lower end of Galan Lu.

Internet There are plenty of internet cafés along Manting Lu; foreigner cafés and some hotels have wi-fi.
Laundry Foreigner cafés offer the least expensive laundry services in town.
Mail and telecommunications The GPO (daily 8am–8pm), with poste restante and international telephones, is on the corner of Xuanwei Dadao and Mengle Dadao.
Massage Taiji Blind Massage (太极宣人按摩中心, *tàijí xuānrén ànmó zhōngxīn*) is just north of the Jingle Dong Lu/Mengle Dadao intersection, on the east side of the road. Go through the arch marked "Blind Massage" then immediately turn left up the staircase to the second floor. Full body ¥40, feet ¥50.
PSB 13 Jingde Lu (Mon–Fri 8–11.30am & 3–5.30pm; ⓣ0691/2130366) – look for the yellow English sign.
Shopping Jinghong's best supermarket is the Daxin Mart, underneath Renmin Square on Mengle Dadao; aside from daily necessities, you can buy cheese and small packets of Yunnan ham. For fresh fruit, including mangoes, coconuts, bananas, mangosteens and durian, head to either of the big produce markets on Mengle Dadao or Mengla Lu.

Exploring Xishuangbanna

Flowing down from the northwest, the Lancang River neatly cuts Xishuangbanna into two regions on either side of Jinghong. To the **east**, there's a choice of roads through highland forests or more cultivated flatlands to the botanic gardens at **Menglun**, down beyond which lies **Mengla**, and the open **Laotian border**. Head **west** and your options are split between the **Damenglong** and **Menghai** regions – with a more varied bag of ethnic groups and a border with **Burma**.

Any of the larger places can be visited on day-trips from Jinghong, but you won't see more than the superficial highlights unless you stop overnight. The towns are seldom attractive or interesting in themselves – though they host some good **markets** – so you'll need to get out to surrounding villages, small temples and the countryside to experience Xishuangbanna's better side. Be prepared for **basic accommodation** and generally bland, if plentiful, food. Many people are friendly and some villagers may offer meals and a bed for the night in return for a small consideration – or yank you enthusiastically into the middle of a festival, if you're lucky enough to stumble across one; elsewhere, locals are wary of strangers, so don't force your presence while looking around.

Xishuangbanna's towns are connected to Jinghong by **bus** from about 7am until late afternoon. Once out in the countryside, you'll be flagging down short-range minibuses between villages. **Cycling** is another possibility in the lowlands (Jinghong's cafés can rent you one) though Xishuangbanna's hill roads are steep, twisting and long. To get out to remoter villages, waterfalls and forest, with the chance of seeing some wildlife, it's best to take one of the **guided treks** offered by Jinghong's tourist cafés; the most experienced guide is Sarah at the *Forest Café* (ⓣ0691/8985122, ⓦwww.forest-cafe.org), though *Mei Mei's Café* (ⓣ0691/2161221, ⓔzhanyanlan@hotmail.com) also has good information. A recommended independent tour guide is Zhao Yao (English name "Joe"; ⓣ13769146987). Most trips include an overnight stay with a local host family and cost around ¥250 per person; prices fall as the number of people in your group goes up.

North and east

There's a small knot of attractions **north** of Jinghong, though the pick lies **east** towards the Lao border at the **Tropical Botanic Gardens** outside **Menglun**, which are just about worth an overnight stay. All traffic out this way departs from Jinghong's **Banna bus station**.

Mengyang and around

MENGYANG (勐养, *měngyǎng*), 30km north of Jinghong, is a market and transport stop surrounded by a host of **Huayao** villages. The Huayao ("Flower Belt") form one of three Dai subgroups, though they differ greatly from the lowland "Water Dai", who scorn them for their over-elaborate costumes – Huayao women wear turbans draped with thin silver chains – and the fact that they are not Buddhists. Though you'll see plenty of Huayao at Mengyang, the village considered most typical is about 10km further north along the main road at **MANNA'NAN** (曼那囡, *mànnànān*).

A further 8km beyond Manna'nan, the **Wild Elephant Valley** (版纳野象谷, *bǎnnà yěxiàng gǔ*; 8am–6.30pm; ¥80) is a chunk of rainforest based around the Sancha Stream. The main attractions for visitors are occasional sightings of **wild elephants**, though the jungle itself gets more interesting the further you venture along the overgrown, partially paved trails – you're sure to encounter elephant footprints, along with brightly coloured birds, butterflies and snakes. Give the **elephant displays** here a wide berth, however, unless you enjoy watching captive animals perform circus tricks while being jabbed with a spear.

Some 18km east of Mengyang, **JINUO SHAN** (基诺山, *jīnuò shān*), is home to the independently minded **Jinuo**. Jinuo women wear a distinctive white-peaked hood, while both sexes pierce their ears and sport tattoos. The **Jinuo Folk Culture Village** (基诺山民族山寨, *jīnuò shān mīnzú shān zhài*; ¥50) here is a bit touristy, but at any rate can give you a glimpse of Xishuangbanna's smallest ethnic group.

Menghan and Manting

MENGHAN (勐罕, *měnghǎn*), 30km southeast of Jinghong, is the main settlement of the fertile "Olive-shaped Flatland", as its alternative name, **Ganlanba** (橄榄坝, *gǎnlǎnbà*) translates. This is one of Xishuangbanna's three major agricultural areas, won by force of arms over the centuries and now vitally important to the Dai (the other two are west at Damenglong and Menghai). Menghan itself is pleasantly surrounded by paddy fields and low hills, with plenty of day walks and cycle rides – any place you stay will be able to help you rent a bike. One popular trip is to take a bike across the Mekong on the local ferry, and then head left for Dai villages. Just west of town, the **Xishuangbanna Dai Garden** (傣园, *dǎi yuán*; ¥100) offers a sanitized version of minority life and daily water-splashing festivals to visiting tour groups. You can stay here too, inside "Dai Family Homes" – or at any rate, a tourist industry vision of them – which also provide meals. Alternatively, the *Huaxin Binguan* (华鑫宾馆, *huáxīn bīnguǎn*; ⓣ0691/2411258; ❶), up on the main road, is a good deal. Aside from Jinghong, you can catch **buses to Menglun** until 2pm.

A couple of kilometres east at **MANTING** (曼听, *màntīng*), the excellent **Manting Buddhist Temple** (曼听佛寺, *màntīng fósì*) and **Dadu Pagoda** (大独塔, *dàdú tǎ*) are fine reconstructions of twelfth-century buildings destroyed during the 1960s. Paths lead further east from Manting along and across the river to more pagodas and villages, somewhere to spend a couple of days of easy exploration.

Menglun

MENGLUN (勐仑, *měnglún*), about 40km east of Menghan, comprises a dusty grid of streets overlooking the broad flow of the **Luosuo River**. There's no bus station, so vehicles pull up wherever convenient on the main road, usually among the restaurants and stores on the eastern side of town. Take the side street downhill through the all-day market, and within a couple of minutes you'll find yourself by a large pedestrian **suspension bridge** crossing to Menglun's superb **Tropical**

Botanic Gardens (热带植物园, *rèdài zhíwùyuán*; daily 7.30am–6.30pm; ¥80). These were carved out of the jungle in 1959, and are now divided up into shaded palm and bamboo groves, clusters of giant fig trees, lily ponds, vines and shrubs. There are plenty of birds and butterflies flitting about too – in all, an enjoyable mix of parkland and forgotten, overgrown corners. Look for Chinese visitors serenading the undistinguished-looking "Singing Plant", which is supposed to nod in time to music.

There's a very run-down **guesthouse** (❸) inside the gardens, with better rooms right by the suspension bridge in town at the *Chunlin Binguan* (春林宾馆, *chūnlín bīnguǎn*; ☎0691/8715681; ❶). To catch onward transport, head to the main road and flag down passing traffic.

Mengla and the Lao border

MENGLA (勐腊, *měnglà*), two hours southeast over the hills from Menglun via one of Xishuangbanna's largest surviving patches of rainforest, is a functional town, the last major settlement before the Lao border. Mengla's northern end has a proper **bus station**, with services to Menglun throughout the day, as well as to Jinghong. From here Mengla's main street, which holds the last **banks** before Laos, runs south for 1500m to the far end of town, and a **depot** for southbound vehicles. The *Post Office Hotel* (邮电宾馆, *yóudiàn bīnguǎn*; ☎0691/8128888; ❷), at 1 Mantala Lu, is typical of the town's accommodation, with plenty of other, cheaper options near the bus station, as well as a host of noodle shops and restaurants.

Mengla is a surprisingly pleasant place to do nothing much for a day, with a couple of nearby attractions: the bronze spire of **Manbeng Pagoda** (曼崩塔, *mànbēng tǎ*), 3km south of town, and the **Bupan aerial walkway** (补蚌望天树空中索道, *bǔbàng wàngtiānshù kōngzhōngsuǒdào*) 20km east, a very insecure-looking metal "sky bridge" running across the forest canopy. Otherwise, the Lao border is 60km south from Mengla's south bus station, via the small town of **SHANGYONG** (尚勇, *shàngyǒng*). This is home to Xishuangbanna's isolated **Miao** population, who arrived here during the 1970s after being chased out of Vietnam and Laos. Not much further on, **MO HAN** township (边贸站, *biānmào zhàn*) is just 6km from the laidback **border crossing**, which closes mid-afternoon.

Western Xishuangbanna

Western Xishuangbanna has a few more towns than the east, and also a few more untrodden areas up against the Burmese border (many of the treks run out of Jinghong's cafés come here) along with a handful of interesting **markets**. Again, most traffic departs from Jinghong's Banna bus station, with the exception of **buses to Damenglong**, which leave from the South bus station.

Into Laos

On the opposite side of the border from Mo Han lies the Laotian village of **Ban Boten**. Assuming you've already obtained a visa from the Laotian consulate in Kunming (see p.692), the border crossing itself should be free and uncomplicated. Yuan are accepted in Ban Boten, but there's nowhere to stay or change your Chinese currency for Laotian kip. The nearest banks and beds are a ¥10 truck ride away at the town of **Luang Namtha**, from where you can hitch out to the early-morning markets at Muong Sing to see local people in full tribal regalia. There's transport from Luang Namtha to **Nung Kie** via Muong Tai, and thence by boat down the Mekong to **Luang Phabang** (though you can also come the whole way from the border by road).

Damenglong

DAMENGLONG (大勐龙, *dàměnglóng*) – also known as **Menglong** – is a scruffy, busy crossroads town 55km southwest of Jinghong, with a big, all-day **Sunday market**. The disappointingly shoddy **Hei Ta** (黑塔, *hēi tǎ*), or Black Pagoda, is just south of the central crossroads and shouldn't be confused with **Bei Ta** (北塔, *běi tǎ*; ¥5), the North Pagoda, 2km north of town above the village of **Manfeilong** (曼飞龙, *mànfēilóng*). A long flight of stairs ascends to Bei Ta, which is adorned with fragments of evil-repelling mirrors and silver paint and is worshipped for the two **footprints** left by Sakyamuni in an alcove at the base. Bei Ta is also known as **Sun Ta** (笋塔, *sŭn tǎ*), or the Bamboo Shoot Pagoda, after its nine-spired design, which resembles an emerging cluster of bamboo tips.

Damenglong's best **place to stay** is the tidy *Jintai Binguan* (金泰宾馆, *jīntài bīnguǎn*; ⓣ0691/2740334; ❶), an eggshell-blue building down a backstreet towards the market. **Eating** options are street stalls or the Sichuanese place east from the crossroads, heading towards the highway.

Menghai

Western Xishuangbanna's principal town, **MENGHAI** (勐海, *měnghǎi*) is centrally placed on the highland plains 55km from Jinghong. A relatively organized assemblage of kilometre-long high street and back lanes, the town is little more than a stop on the way towards outlying Dai and Hani settlements, but has an important history. Menghai was once a **Hani** (Aini) settlement until, as elsewhere, the Hani were defeated in battle by the Dai and withdrew into the surrounding hills. They remain there today as Xishuangbanna's second-largest ethnic group and long-time cultivators of **pu'er tea**, the local red, slightly musty brew that's esteemed from Hong Kong to Tibet for its fat-reducing and generally invigorating properties.

The **bus station** – with buses to Jinghong and other centres, and minibuses to outlying villages – is at the eastern end of town. If you wind up in Menghai at mealtimes, head to the string of open-fronted Sichuanese **restaurants** across the intersection from the bus station.

Mengzhe and Xiding

Minibuses heading 20km west from Menghai can drop you at the bizarre **Jingzhen Octagonal Pavilion** (景真八角亭, *jĭngzhēn bājiăo tíng*; ¥20), built in the eighteenth century to quell an angry horde of wasps. This, along with **Manlei Buddhist Temple** (曼磊佛寺, *mànlěi fósì*; ¥20) 10km further on past **MENGZHE** (勐遮, *měngzhē*), are inferior copies of older buildings, but have important collections of Buddhist manuscripts written on fan-palm fibre. A better final target would be to catch transport 15km southwest from Mengzhe to the Hani village of **XIDING** (西定, *xīdìng*), whose busy Thursday **market** is one of the best in the region. You'll need to get here on Wednesday, as the market kicks off at dawn, and sleep over in one of Xiding's rudimentary guesthouses.

Menghun

The region south of Menghai is home to the **Akha**, a long-haired Hani subgroup; unmarried women have elaborate head ornaments while wives wear cloth caps decorated with silver beads and coins. You can meet them 25km southwest of Menghai at **MENGHUN**, whose excellent **Sunday market** starts at daybreak and continues until noon. Akha women arrive under their silver-beaded headdresses, Bulang wear heavy earrings and oversized black turbans, and remote hill-dwellers come in plain dress, carrying ancient rifles. Most common of all are the Dai, who buy rolls of home-made paper and sarongs. Take a look around Menghun itself, too, as there's a dilapidated nineteenth-century **monastery** with a pavilion built in the style of Jingzhen's octagonal effort, and a **pagoda** hidden in the bamboo groves on the hills behind town.

As at Xiding, it's a good idea to get here the night before, as then you'll already have seen plenty before the tour buses from Jinghong descend around 9am. The best **place to stay** is the basic *Dai Hotel* (傣家宾馆, *dǎijiā bīnguǎn*; ⓣ0691/5511209; ❶), signed in English near the post office.

Daluo and the Burmese border

At the end of the road 50km west of Menghun and served by two daily buses from Menghai, **DALUO** (打落镇, *dǎluò zhèn*) is set just in from the Burmese border. Here there's a multitrunked, giant **fig tree** whose descending mass of aerial roots form a "forest". There's a daily **border trade market**, timed for the arrival of Chinese package tours between 11am and 1pm. Chinese nationals can also get a two-hour visa for Burma, ostensibly to shop for jade; in fact, many are really going over to catch transvestite stage shows held for their benefit.

Travel details

Trains

Kunming to: Beijing (2 daily; 36–48hr); Chengdu (4 daily; 18–21hr); Chongqing (3 daily; 20hr); Guangzhou (2 daily; 23hr); Guiyang (5 daily; 12hr); Lijiang (2 daily; 9–12hr); Nanning (3 daily; 14hr); Shanghai (2 daily; 40hr); Xiaguan/Dali (3 daily; 8hr); Xi'an (3 daily; 36hr); Xichang (4 daily; 10hr).
Lijiang to: Dali (1 daily; 4hr); Kunming (2 daily; 9hr 30min–12hr).
Xiaguan/Dali to: Kunming (3 daily; 8hr); Lijiang (1 daily; 4hr).

Buses

Baoshan to: Jinghong (20hr); Kunming (8hr); Lijiang (8hr); Liushui (4hr); Mangshi (3hr); Ruili (4hr); Tengchong (3hr); Wanding (5hr); Xiaguan (3hr).
Dali to: Kunming (5hr 30min); Lijiang (3hr); Shangri-La (6hr); Shaping (1hr); Shaxi (3hr); Xiaguan (30min); Xizhou (30min); Zhoucheng (45min).
Daluo to: Menghai (2 daily; 2hr).
Deqin to: Shangri-La (6hr).
Hekou to: Jianshui (4hr); Kunming (7hr).
Jianshui to: Hekou (4hr); Jinghong (13hr); Kunming (3hr); Yuanyang (4hr).
Jinghong to: Baoshan (20hr); Damenglong (1hr 30min); Jianshui (13hr); Kunming (10hr); Menghai (1hr); Menghun (1hr 20min); Mengla (4hr); Menglun (2hr); Ruili (30hr); Xiaguan (18hr).
Kunming to: Baoshan (8hr); Hekou (7hr); Jianshui (3hr); Jinghong (10hr); Lijiang (10hr); Ruili (13hr); Shilin (3hr); Wanding (12hr); Weishan (7hr); Xiaguan (5hr); Yuanyang (5hr).
Lijiang to: Baoshan (8hr); Daju (3hr); Dali (3hr); Kunming (9hr); Lugu Hu (8hr); Qiaotou (2hr); Shangri-La (4hr); Shaxi (3hr); Shigu (2hr); Xiaguan (3hr 30min).
Ruili to: Baoshan (4hr); Jinghong (30hr); Kunming (13hr); Mangshi (2hr); Tengchong (6hr); Wanding (30min); Xiaguan (6hr).
Shangri-La to: Dali (6hr); Daocheng (5hr); Deqin (6hr); Lijiang (3hr); Litang (10hr); Xiaguan (6hr).
Tengchong to: Baoshan (3hr); Ruili (6hr); Xiaguan (6hr).
Xiaguan to: Baoshan (3hr); Binchuan (2hr); Dali (30min); Jinghong (18hr); Kunming (5hr); Lijiang (3hr 30min); Liushui (6hr); Mangshi (4hr); Ruili (6hr); Shangri-La (7hr); Tengchong (6hr); Wanding (5hr); Weishan (1hr 30min).
Yuanyang to: Jianshui (4hr); Kunming (5hr).

Ferries

Jinghong to: Chiang Saen (Thailand; 2 weekly; 7hr).

Flights

International flights from Kunming to: Bangkok, Calcutta, Kuala Lumpur, Phnom Penh, Singapore, Vientiane, Yangon; and from Jinghong to Bangkok.
Baoshan to: Kunming (4 daily; 1hr); Guangzhou (1 daily; 3hr 15min).
Dali (Xiaguan) to: Guangzhou (daily; 3hr 30min); Kunming (2 daily; 40min).
Jinghong to: Chengdu (1 daily; 3hr); Chongqing (1 daily; 3hr); Dali (1 daily; 50min); Kunming (21 daily; 55min); Lijiang (3 daily; 1hr); Shanghai (2 daily; 4hr).

Kunming to: Baoshan (4 daily; 1hr); Beijing (18 daily; 3hr 30min); Changsha (6 daily; 1hr 50min); Chengdu (11 daily; 1hr 25min); Chongqing (10 daily; 1hr); Dali (2 daily; 40min); Guangzhou (10 daily; 1hr 20min); Guilin (1 daily; 1hr 30min); Guiyang (5 daily; 1hr 10min); Hong Kong (3 daily; 2hr 45min); Jinghong (21 daily; 55min); Lhasa (6 weekly; 2hr 10min); Lijiang (14 daily, 40min); Mangshi (6 daily; 45min); Nanning (2 daily; 50min); Shanghai (13 daily; 2hr 30min); Shenzhen (7 daily; 2hr); Xi'an (5 daily; 1hr 40min).

Lijiang to: Beijing (1 daily; 5hr); Chengdu (4 daily; 1hr 10min); Chongqing (1 daily; 1hr 10min); Guangzhou (2 daily; 4hr); Jinghong (3 daily; 1hr); Kunming (14 daily; 40min); Shanghai (1 daily; 5hr); Shenzhen (1 daily; 4hr); Xi'an (6 weekly; 4hr).

Mangshi to: Guangzhou (1 daily; 4hr 40min); Kunming (6 daily; 50min).

Shangri-La to: Kunming (2 daily; 1hr).

CHAPTER 12 Highlights

* **Teahouses** A central feature of Sichuanese social life. See p.755
* **Chengdu Giant Panda Breeding Research Base** One of the few zoos in China where the animals are clearly happy, healthy and well cared for. See p.758
* **Huanglongxi** Crowded but enjoyably touristy village of Qing-dynasty shops and temples. See p.761
* **Dafo, Leshan** You will never forget the first time you see this gargantuan statue of the Buddha. See p.767
* **Emei Shan** A tough climb is rewarded with gorgeous scenery and monasteries that make atmospheric places to stay. See p.768
* **Dazu** China's most exquisite collection of Buddhist rock art, illustrating religious parables and cartoon-like scenes from daily life. See p.776
* **Cruising the Yangzi** Relax as your boat glides past the magnificent scenery of the towering Three Gorges. See p.784
* **Horse-trekking, Songpan** Get really out into the wild and give your feet – though not your seat – a rest. See p.789
* **Litang** Gritty Tibetan monastery town in the heart of Sichuan's wild west, where monks and cowboys tear around on motorbikes. See p.800

▲ Residents of the Chengdu Giant Panda Breeding Research Base

12

Sichuan and Chongqing

Ringed by mountains that, according to the Tang poet Li Bai, made the journey here "harder than the road to heaven", **Sichuan** (四川, *sìchuān*) and **Chongqing** (重庆, *chóngqìng*) stretch for more than 1000km across China's southwest. Administratively divided in 1997, when **Chongqing** was carved off the eastern end of Sichuan province, the region has long played the renegade, differing from the rest of China in everything from food to politics and inaccessible enough both to ignore central authority and to provide sanctuary for those fleeing it. Recent divisions aside, Sichuan and Chongqing share a common history, and the area splits more convincingly into very different geographic halves: a densely populated eastern plain, and a mountainous west, emphatically remote.

In the east, peaks surround one of the country's most densely settled areas, the fertile **Red Basin**, whose subtropical climate and rich soil conspire to produce endless green fields turning out three harvests a year. This bounty has created an air of easy affluence in **Chengdu**, Sichuan's relaxed capital, and the southern river towns of **Zigong** and **Yibin**. Elsewhere, visitors have the opportunity of joining pilgrims on **Emei Shan** in a hike up the holy mountain's forested slopes, or of sailing **down the Yangzi** from Chongqing, industrial powerhouse and terminus of one of the world's great river journeys. You'll also find that the influence of **Buddhism** has literally become part of the landscape, most notably at **Leshan**, where **Dafo**, a giant Buddha sculpted into riverside cliffs, provides one of the most evocative images of China; and farther east at **Dazu**, whose wooded hillsides conceal a marvellous procession of stone carvings.

In contrast, western Sichuan is dominated by densely buckled ranges overflowing from the heights of Tibet; this is a wild, thinly populated land of snowcapped peaks, where yaks roam the treeline and roads negotiate hair-raising gradients as they cross ridges or follow deep river valleys. Occupied but untamed by Han China, the west has its appeal in its **Tibetan heritage** – clearly visible in the many important **monasteries** – and raw, rugged alpine scenery. Travelling north towards Gansu takes you through ethnic Hui and Qiang heartlands past the vivid blue lakes and medieval battlements at **Songpan** and **Jiuzhaigou**, with the tranquil village of **Langmusi** the most remote of targets, right on the provincial border. Due west of Chengdu, the real wilds begin beyond **Kangding**, with the

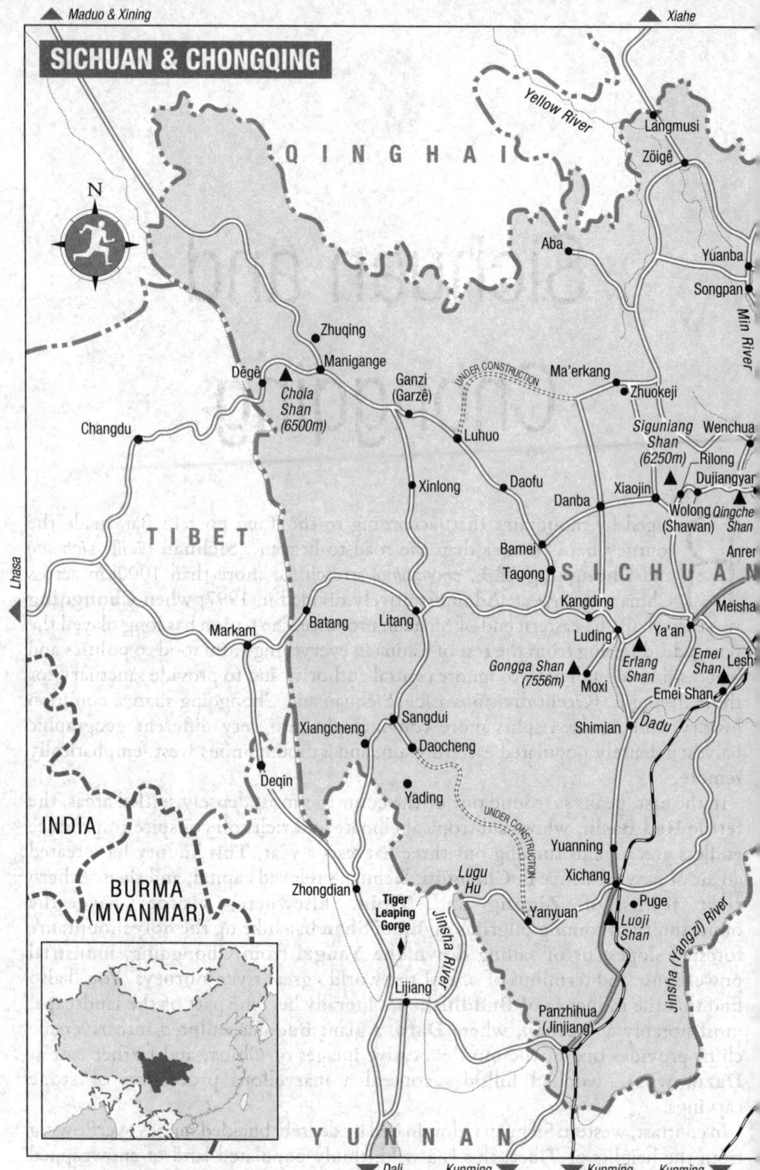

monastery towns of **Dêgê** and **Litang** the pick of destinations – not forgetting an exciting back-road **route to Yunnan**.

Getting around all this is fairly straightforward, though those heading westwards need to prepare for unpredictably long and uncomfortable journeys. **Rail lines** are restricted by geography and most people use the train only for travel

beyond regional borders; the most useful routes are the high-speed Chengdu–Chongqing link, and the Xi'an–Kunming line, which runs southwest from Chengdu via Emei Shan and Xichang. As for the **weather**, expect hot, humid summers and cold winters, with the north and west frequently buried under snow for three months of the year.

Eastern Sichuan and Chongqing

One of the most pleasant areas of China to explore randomly, eastern Sichuan is focused around **Chengdu**, the relaxed provincial capital. Famed not least for its fiery cuisine, the city offers a number of easy excursions to nearby sights, the most unusual of which is a two-thousand-year-old irrigation scheme at **Dujiangyan**. Northeast is the historically important **route to Shaanxi**, and also **Langzhong**,

Sichuanese cooking

Dominating the southwestern China cooking school, **Sichuanese cooking** is noted for its heavy use of **chilli**, which locals explain as a result of climate – according to Traditional Chinese Medicine, chillies dispel "wet" illnesses caused by Sichuan's seasonally damp or humid weather. You'll also find that chillies don't simply blast the taste buds, they stimulate them as well, and flavours here are far more complex than they might appear at the initial, eye-watering, mouthful.

Sichuan cuisine's defining taste is described as **mala** – "numb and hot" – created by the potent mix of chillies and **huajiao** (Sichuan pepper), with its soapy perfume and mouth-tingling afterbuzz. One classic *mala* dish is **mapo doufu**, bean curd and minced pork; others include **strange-flavoured chicken** (dressed with sesame paste, soy sauce, sugar and green onions mixed in with the chillies and *huajiao*), and the innocently named **boiled beef slices**, which actually packs more chillies per spoonful than almost any other Sichuanese dish.

A cooking technique unique to Sichuan is **dry-frying**, which involves deep frying to dehydrate the ingredients, followed by sautéeing in a sweet-salty sauce until the liquid has evaporated. **Dry-fried pork shreds**, where the slivers of pork end up dark, chewy and aromatic, is a classic example using meat; a vegetarian counterpart is **dry-fried green beans**, salty and rich with garlic.

Other more general dishes include **hot and sour soup**, flavoured with pepper and vinegar; **double-cooked pork**, where a piece of fatty meat is boiled, sliced thinly and then stir-fried with green chillies; **fish-flavoured pork** (whose "seafood" sauce is made from vinegar, soy sauce, sugar, ginger and sesame oil); **gongbao chicken**, the local version of stir-fried chicken and peanuts; **smoked duck**, a chilli-free cold dish, aromatic and juicy; and **crackling rice**, where a meat soup is poured over a sizzling bed of deep-fried rice crusts. There's also a great number of Sichuanese **snacks** – *xiaochi* – which some restaurants specialize in: green beans with ginger, pork with puréed garlic, cucumber with chilli-oil and sesame seeds, **dandan mian** ("carry-pole" noodles, named for the way in which street vendors used to carry them around), **tiger-skin peppers**, scorched then fried with salt and dark vinegar, **five-spiced meat** steamed in ground rice (served in the bamboo steamer), and a huge variety of sweet and savoury dumplings.

One Chongqing speciality now found all over Sichuan (and China) is **huoguo** (hotpot), a social dish eaten everywhere from streetside canteens to specialist restaurants. You get plates or skewers of meat, boiled eggs or vegetables, cooked – by you at the table – in a bubbling pot of stock liberally laced with chillies and cardamom pods. You then season the cooked food in oil spiced with MSG, salt and chilli powder. The effect is powerful, and during a cold winter you may well find that hotpots fast become your favourite food.

with its Qing-dynasty architecture; southwest, both road and rail run past Buddhist landmarks at **Emei Shan** and **Leshan** and down to the Yunnanese border via **Xichang**. Southeast of the capital, the historic towns of **Zigong** and **Yibin** offer access to picturesque bamboo forests. Further Buddhist sites surround the country town of **Dazu**, east of Chengdu; beyond, western China's largest city, **Chongqing**, marks the start of the **journey down the Yangzi** to Hubei province, with ferries exiting the region through the dramatic **Three Gorges**.

Some history

In prehistoric times, what is now eastern Sichuan and Chongqing was divided into the eastern **Ba** and western **Shu kingdoms**, which amalgamated during the Shang era (1600–1100 BC). Numerous sites across the region suggest the Ba-Shu was a slave society with highly developed metalworking skills and bizarre aesthetics. Agricultural innovations at the end of the third century BC opened up eastern Sichuan to intensive farming, and when the Qin armies stormed through, they found an economic base that financed their unification of China in 221 BC – as did Genghis Khan's forces almost 1500 years later. In between, the area became the Three Kingdoms state of **Shu** – a name by which Sichuan is still sometimes known – and later twice provided refuge for deposed emperors.

Otherwise too distant to play a central role in China's history, the region leapt to prominence in 1911, when government interference in local rail industries sparked the nationwide rebellions that toppled the Qing empire. The next four decades saw rival warlords fighting for control, though some stability came when the **Nationalist government** made Chongqing their capital after the Japanese invaded China in 1937. The province suffered badly during the Cultural Revolution – **Jung Chang**'s autobiography, *Wild Swans*, gives a first-hand account of the vicious arbitrariness of the times in Sichuan. Typically, it was the first province to reject Maoist ideals, when the Sichuan governor, Zhao Ziyang, allowed farmers to sell produce on the free market, spearheading the reforms of his fellow native Sichuanese, **Deng Xiaoping**. So effective were these reforms that by the 1990s Sichuan was competing vigorously with the east-coast economy, a situation for which Chongqing – the already heavily industrialized gateway river port between Sichuan and eastern China – claimed a large part of the credit; Chongqing's economic weight secured separate administrative status for the city and its surrounds. Meanwhile, development continues across the region, bringing all the problems of runaway growth: appalling industrial pollution, ecological devastation and an unbelievable scale of urban reconstruction.

Chengdu and around

Set on the western side of the Red Basin, **CHENGDU** (成都, *chéngdū*) is a determinedly modern city, full of traffic, high-rise department stores and residential blocks. But it's also a cheerful place: seasonal floral displays and ubiquitous **ginkgo trees** lend colour to its many excellent **parks**, rubbish is scrupulously collected, and the population is also nicely laidback, enjoying its **teahouse culture** at every opportunity and unfazed by this being interpreted as laziness by other Chinese.

Chengdu was styled **Brocade City** in Han times, when the urban elite were buried in elegantly decorated tombs, and its silk travelled west along the caravan routes as far as imperial Rome. A refuge for the eighth-century Tang emperor Xuan Zong after his army mutinied over his infatuation with the beautiful concubine Yang Guifei, the city later became a **printing** centre, producing the

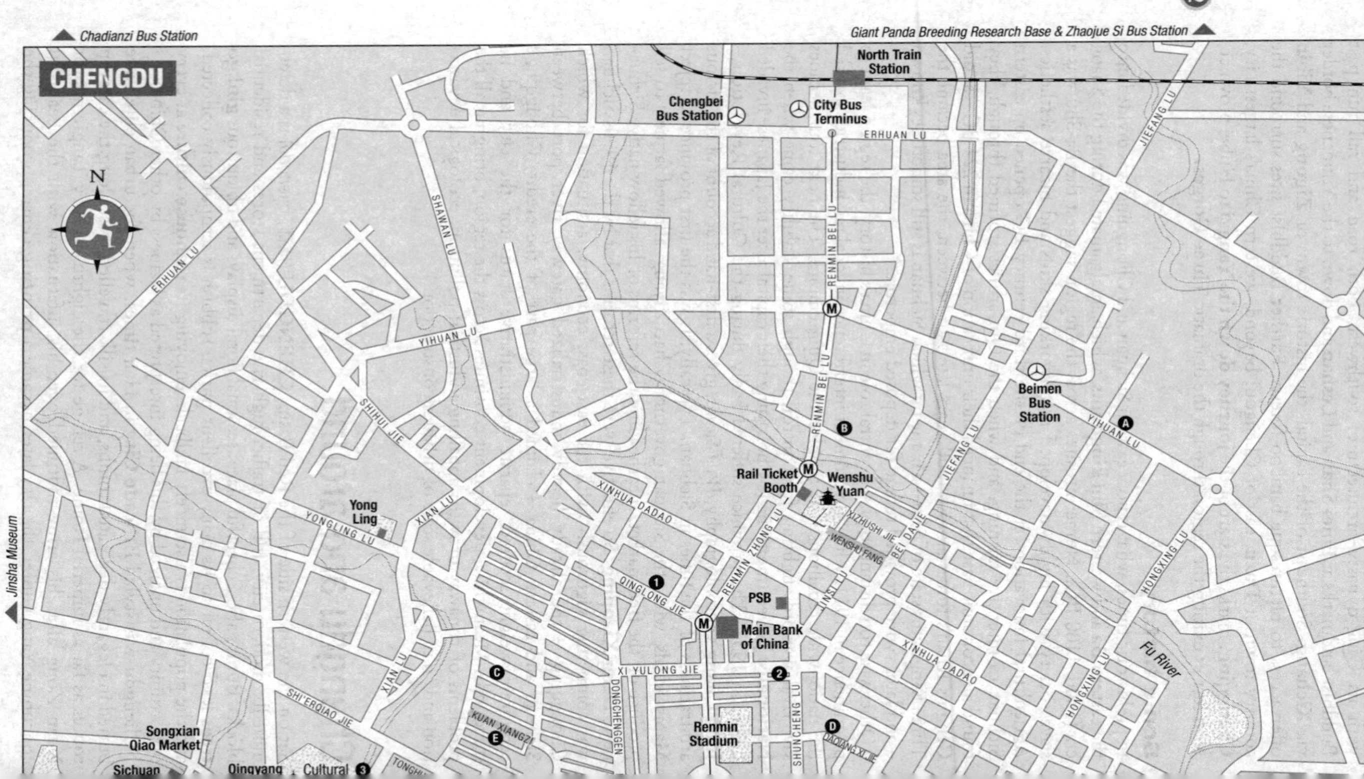
Chadianzi Bus Station
Giant Panda Breeding Research Base & Zhaojue Si Bus Station
CHENGDU
N
North Train Station
Chengbei Bus Station
City Bus Terminus
ERHUAN LU
JIEFANG LU
SHAWAN LU
RENMIN BEI LU
YIHUAN LU
Beimen Bus Station
A
B
SHIHUI JIE
Rail Ticket Booth
Wenshu Yuan
XINHUA DADAO
XIZHUSHI JIE
WENSHU FANG
BEI DAJIE
Yong Ling
YONGLING LU
XIAN LU
QINGLONG JIE
RENMIN ZHONG LU
PSB
JINSI LU
HONGXING LU
Main Bank of China
Fu River
XI YULONG JIE
DONGCHENGGEN
SHUNCHENG LU
DAQIANG XI JIE
C
D
E
KUAN XIANGZI
Renmin Stadium
SHI'ERQIAO JIE
Songxian Qiao Market
Sichuan
Qingyang
Cultural
TONGHUI
Jinsha Museum

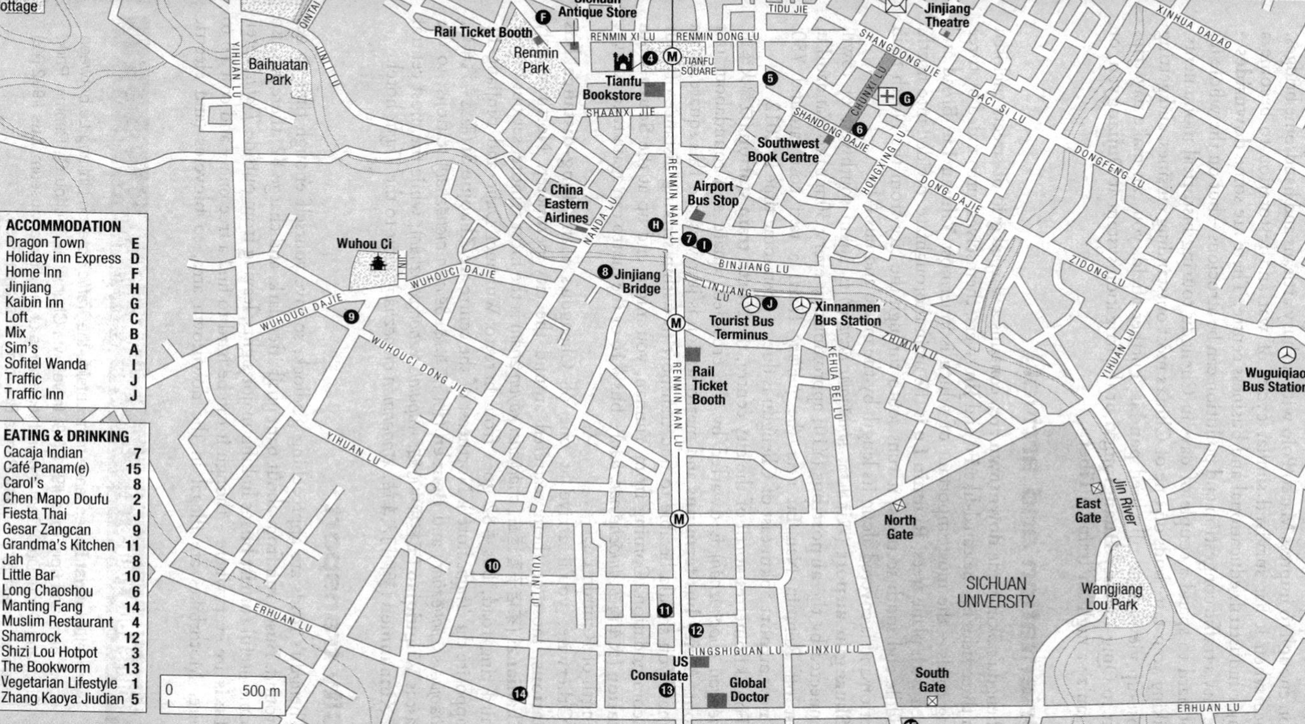
Cottage
Sichuan Antique Store
Rail Ticket Booth
Renmin Park
Baihuatan Park
Tianfu Bookstore
TIANFU SQUARE
RENMIN XI LU
RENMIN DONG LU
TIDU JIE
Jinjiang Theatre
XINHUA DADAO
SHANGDONG JIE
CHUNXI LU
SHAANXI JIE
SHANDONG DAJIE
Southwest Book Centre
DACI SI LU
DONGFENG LU
HONGXING LU
DONG DAJIE
QINTAI LU
JINLI LU
YIHUAN LU
China Eastern Airlines
NANDA LU
RENMIN NAN LU
Airport Bus Stop
BINJIANG LU
LINJIANG LU
ZIDONG LU
Wuhou Ci
WUHOUCI DAJIE
Jinjiang Bridge
Tourist Bus Terminus
Xinnanmen Bus Station
ZHIMIN LU
WUHOUCI DONG JIE
Rail Ticket Booth
KEHUA BEI LU
YIHUAN LU
Wuguiqiao Bus Station
North Gate
East Gate
Jin River
SICHUAN UNIVERSITY
Wangjiang Lou Park
YULIN LU
ERHUAN LU
LINGSHIGUAN LU
JINXIU LU
US Consulate
Global Doctor
South Gate
ERHUAN LU
0 500 m
Shuangliu Airport & South Train Station
ACCOMMODATION
Dragon Town E
Holiday inn Express D
Home Inn F
Jinjiang H
Kaibin Inn G
Loft C
Mix B
Sim's A
Sofitel Wanda I
Traffic J
Traffic Inn J
EATING & DRINKING
Cacaja Indian 7
Café Panam(e) 15
Carol's 8
Chen Mapo Doufu 2
Fiesta Thai J
Gesar Zangcan 9
Grandma's Kitchen 11
Jah 8
Little Bar 10
Long Chaoshou 6
Manting Fang 14
Muslim Restaurant 4
Shamrock 12
Shizi Lou Hotpot 3
The Bookworm 13
Vegetarian Lifestyle 1
Zhang Kaoya Jiudian 5

world's first paper money. Sacked by the Mongols in 1271, Chengdu recovered soon enough to impress Marco Polo with its busy artisans and handsome bridges, since when it has survived similar cycles of war and restoration to become a major industrial, educational and business centre. There are some **downsides** – the city's traffic congestion and pollution can be atrocious – but on the whole it's not hard to spend a couple of days in Chengdu touring historical monuments, spiking your taste buds on one of China's most outstanding cuisines, and getting close-up views of locally bred **pandas**. Further afield, you can make day-trips out to Qing-dynasty **Huanglongxi** or the irrigation system at **Dujiangyan**, or organize a flight or train **to Tibet**.

Orientation and arrival

Chengdu's 5km-wide **downtown** area contains a warped grid of streets enclosed on three sides by the canal-like **Fu** and **Jin** rivers, themselves surrounded by three ring roads – the most important of which is innermost **Yihuan Lu**. Broad and lined with plane trees, **Renmin Lu** is the main thoroughfare, divided into north, middle and south sections; it runs south through the city from the North train station and is covered along its length by the metro and bus #16.

Shuangliu airport (双流机场, *shuāngliú jīchǎng*) is 16km southwest of town, connected by the **airport bus** (¥10; approximately every 30min) to Yandao Lu, just off Renmin Nan Lu near the *Jinjiang Hotel*; a taxi costs around ¥50. A **new airport** 55km east of Chengdu is due to open some time in 2012.

Four kilometres north of the city centre, the **North train station** (成都火车站, *chéngdū huǒchēzhàn*) is dwarfed by the crowded square and roundabout out front. A **city bus terminus** and metro station is just west off this square, from where you should be able to find transport to within striking distance of your accommodation. Coming from Yunnan, you might end up at the **South train station** (火车南站, *huǒchē nánzhàn*) – bus #16 or the metro can again take you the length of Renmin Lu.

Otherwise, you'll arrive at one of Chengdu's many **long-distance bus stations**, most of them scattered around the city perimeter. Northwesterly **Chadianzi** (茶店子客运站, *chádiànzi kèyùn zhàn*) is the most remote, set out on the third ring road; bus #82 goes from here to Wuhouci Dajie and Binjiang Lu (opposite the *Traffic* hotel). Northeast of the centre are **Zhaojue Si** (照觉寺汽车站, *zhàojué sì qìchēzhàn*) and **Beimen** (北门汽车站, *běimén qìchēzhàn*) stations; to the east is **Wuguiqiao** (五桂桥中心站, *wǔguìqiáo zhōngxīnzhàn*); while the most central is **Xinnanmen** (新南门汽车站, *xīnnánmén qìchēzhàn*), next to the *Traffic* hotel.

City transport

Chengdu's roads are approaching gridlock, so give yourself enough time to get around. **Buses** run from about 6am until after dark, and charge ¥2; there are also some useful **tourist buses** linking major sights, leaving from outside *Traffic* hotel. **Taxis** are everywhere – though it can be hard to find a free one – and cost ¥6 to hire. Motorbikes are illegal in the downtown area, so **bicycles** (and electric

Tourist bus routes

Two useful **tourist buses** leave from outside the *Traffic* hotel on Linjiang Lu between about 8am and 6pm: **bus #901** (¥3) travels via Chunxi Lu, Wuhou Ci, Renmin Park, Qingyang Gong, Dufu Caotang and terminates at the Jinsha Museum; **bus #902** (¥2) heads northeast to the Giant Panda Breeding Research Base.

Moving on from Chengdu

Outbound **flights** connect Chengdu to major cities across China. The airport bus (7am–8pm; ¥10) leaves twice an hour from Yandao Lu, just off Renmin Nan Lu across from the *Jinjiang Hotel*; it takes half an hour and you should get to the airport with at least an hour to spare.

Flights **to Lhasa** cost about ¥1200, though the Tibet permit is an extra ¥400 and, at the time of writing, it was not possible to visit Tibet except as part of an organized tour (around ¥1000) – see the box on p.898.

By train

Chengdu is halfway along the Xi'an–Kunming **rail line**, and also connected to routes into Guizhou and central China through easterly Chongqing. You can reach Chongqing itself in just two hours aboard a D-class train, via the high-speed rail link. The rail **ticket office** is on the eastern side of the North train station square, but it's less hassle to buy tickets at the nearby Chengbei bus station (ticket window #9) or from various **booths** around town, which open from 8am to 8pm and charge a ¥5 fee per ticket: there's one at the north gate of Renmin Park; one halfway down Renmin Nan Lu; and another on Renmin Zhong Lu near the Wenshu Yuan. Hotel agents generally charge ¥40 or more per person.

Train tickets **to Lhasa** cost ¥700 hard sleeper, or ¥1000 soft sleeper; they can be hard to get hold of, so allow a few days. You need a Tibet permit (¥400 through an agent) before you can buy a ticket yourself though, again, visiting Tibet independently was not possible at the time of writing.

By bus

Though there is some overlap of services between Chengdu's many long-distance bus stations, they generally depart from the side of town relevant to the direction they're headed. Details for these and sights surrounding Chengdu are given in the related text as indicated.

Northeastern destinations are handled by the Zhaojue Si station (Jiangyou, Jianmen Guan and Guangyuan) and Beimen station (Langzhong). The **south** (Emei Shan and Leshan), as well as some **western** destinations – including **Jiuzhaigou, Kangding** and Ganzi – are covered from Xinnanmen station. Wuguiqiao is where to find transport for **eastern Sichuan and Chongqing**, including Chongqing, Yibin, Zigong, Gongxian and Dazu. Buses for most of **western Sichuan** – including Xiaojin, Songpan, Danba, Kangding, Ma'erkang, Jiuzhaigou and Zöige – depart from Chadianzi, usually first thing in the morning. If you don't fancy an early haul out to Chadianzi, stay overnight at Chandianzi's **bus-station hotel** (ⓣ028/87506615 or 87503312; dorms ¥30, rooms ❷).

mopeds) remain popular, with cycle lanes and guarded parking throughout the city – see p.760 for details on rentals.

Chengdu's first **metro line** opened in 2010, running north–south through the city; useful stops include the train stations, *Jianjiang Hotel* and Tianfu Square. It's open from 7am to 9pm and costs ¥2–4 depending on how many stations you travel from your starting point. It's hoped that the network, which will eventually comprise eight lines, will ease the city's chronic traffic congestion, but at the moment, ongoing metro construction is only making it worse.

Accommodation

Chengdu has a great number of **places to stay**, with a choice for every budget; the following are all central. Everywhere can make transport bookings, and **hostels** – as well as the *Traffic* hotel – also offer internet access, bike rental, travellers' noticeboards and good-value **tours** (see p.761). There's also accommodation at Chadianzi bus station for early-morning departures – see the box on p.753.

Hostels

Dragon Town (龙城宽巷子青年旅馆, *lóngchéng kuānxiàngzǐ qīngnián lǚguǎn*) 26 Kuan Xiangzi ⓣ028/86648408, ⓦwww.dragontown.com.cn. Atmospherically set in a reproduction period building in a quiet, old-style street. Staff are a bit slack, but otherwise this is a good budget choice. Dorms ¥35, rooms ❸

Loft (四号虎工厂青年旅馆, *sìhào hǔgōngchǎng qīngnián lǚguǎn*) 4 Tongren Lu, aka Xiangtong Xiang ⓣ028/86265770, ⓦwww.lofthostel.com. A very sharp operation in slickly converted 1980s warehouse, with a smart café and great second-floor venue offering pool table, video lounge and bar. But rooms are a little expensive for what you get. Dorms ¥40, rooms ❸

Mix 23 Xinghui Xi Lu ⓣ028/83222271, ⓦwww.mixhostel.com. Nasty tiled building on the outside but cosy and homely place once you're through the door. Fairly quiet residential district. Dorms ¥30, rooms ❷

Sim's (观华青年旅舍, *guānhuá qīngnián lǚshè*) North Section 4, 211 Yihuan Lu ⓣ028/83355322, ⓦwww.gogosc.com. A very friendly, roomy place, set around a garden. The owners and staff give the impression they can't do enough for you, and lay on heaps of information about travel in Sichuan. The only downside is the location – on a drab, busy stretch of the ring road – though also close to the train station and useful city buses. Dorm beds ¥30, rooms ❸

Traffic Inn (交通饭店, *jiāotōng fàndiàn*), behind the *Traffic* hotel at 77 Linjiang Lu, near Xinnanmen bus station ⓣ028/85450470, ⓦwww.redcliffinn.cn. Simple, clean, modern doubles and twins with or without bathroom, plus dorms (in the main hotel building). The *Highfly Café* here serves Western and Chinese staples. Dorms ¥25, rooms ❷

Hotels

Holiday inn Express (鼓楼快捷假日酒店, *gǔlóu kuàijié jiàrì jiǔdiàn*) 72 Daqiang Xi Jie ⓣ028/86785666, ⓦwww.hiexpress.com. Comfortable, modern and efficient – what you'd expect from this budget international chain. Prices rise considerably if there's a conference on in town. ❺

Home Inn (如家酒店, *rújiā jiǔdiàn*) 9 Shaocheng Lu ⓣ028/86253111. Right across from the north entrance to Renmin Park, this bright yellow building offers the dependable comforts associated with this chain – though prices are on the high side. ❹

Jinjiang (锦江宾馆, *jǐnjiāng bīnguǎn*) 80 Renmin Nan Lu ⓣ028/85506666, ⓦwww.jjhotel.com. Chengdu's original tourist hotel, now revamped with some panache to make the international grade and featuring smart rooms (from around ¥1200), bilingual staff, conference and business facilities, and a host of restaurants. ❾

Kaibin Inn (凯宾酒店盐市口店, *kǎi bīn jiǔdiàn yánshìkǒu diàn*), 1 Xiao Ke Jia Xiang ⓣ028/86672888, ⓔkaibinhotel@yahoo.com.cn. Hard to find the entrance – it's in a walkthrough between Chunxi Lu and Hongxing Lu – but this is another well-priced mid-range place, close to the shopping district. ❸

Sofitel Wanda (索菲特万达大饭店, *suǒfēitè wàndá dàfàndiàn*) 15 Binjiang Zhong Lu ⓣ028/66669999, ⓦwww.sofitel.com. Hard not to be impressed by the full-sized fan palms and acres of marble in the lobby. Restaurants, bars and a swimming pool are part of the package. ❾

Traffic (交通饭店, *jiāotōng fàndiàn*) 77 Linjiang Lu, near Xinnanmen bus station ⓣ028/85451017. Well-maintained stand-by, featuring spotless doubles with TV and shared or private bathroom. The attached *Traffic Inn* (see opposite) is their backpackers' wing. ❹

The City

Chengdu's centre is marked by **Tianfu Square** (天府广场, *tiānfǔ guǎngchǎng*) a huge space with dancing fountains, a subterranean metro stop and a white statue of Mao Zedong to the north. East of Tianfu, roads run through the heart of the city's commercial precinct, at the core of which is pedestrianized **Chunxi Lu**, full of clothes shops and upmarket department stores.

Just west of Tianfu Square, past the city's main **mosque**, is **Renmin Park** (人民公园, *rénmín gōngyuán*; free except during floral exhibitions), which offers an introduction to Chengdu's reputedly slack pace of life, comprising a few acres of trees, paved paths, ponds and ornamental gardens with seasonally varying

Teahouses

The Sichuanese have a reputation for being particularly garrulous, best experienced at one of the province's many **teahouses**. These hold much the same place in Sichuanese life as a local bar or pub does in the West; some are formal establishments with illuminated signs spelling out *chadian*, *chaguan* or *dachadian* (all meaning "teahouse"); others are just a humble spread of bamboo or plastic chairs in the corner of a park, a temple or indeed any available public space. Whatever the establishment, just sit down to have a waiter come over and ask you what sort of tea you'd like – the standard jasmine-scented variety costs around ¥5 a cup, up to ¥40 or more for a really fine brew. Most are served in the three-piece Sichuanese *gaiwancha*, a squat, handleless cup with lid and saucer. **Refills** are unlimited – either the waiter will give you a top-up on passing your table, or you'll be left with a flask of boiling water. In a country where it's usually difficult to find somewhere to relax in public, teahouses are very welcome: idlers can spend the whole day chatting, playing mahjong, reading or just staring into space, without anyone interrupting – except cruising masseurs and ear-wax removers.

displays. Near the north entrance there's an ever-busy **teahouse** shaded by wisteria (look for the large bronze teapot at the gate), and the tall **Monument to the Martyrs**, an obelisk commemorating the 1911 rail disputes that marked the beginning of the end for the Qing empire – hence the unusual motifs of trains and spanners. Otherwise, the park is just a good place to stroll; look for vendors with little burners and a slab of marble along the paths who execute skilful designs of Chinese zodiac animals in **toffee**; there's also a **canteen** next to the teahouse serving Sichuanese snacks. The park is crammed with martial-arts practitioners every morning.

After an uprising in Chengdu in 1789, a Manchu garrison was stationed in the city and built themselves a miniature version of Beijing's *hutongs* in the area north of Renmin Park along **Kuan Xiangzi** (宽巷子, *kuān xiàngzi*) and two adjacent lanes. The old streets and grey-brick houses here have been renovated and turned into a busy "antique" entertainment district, full of snack stalls, restaurants and crowds orbiting between them – all especially busy at night, when competing coloured lights are added to the mix.

Wenshu Yuan and around

Wenshu Yuan (文殊院, *wénshū yuàn*; daily 8am–5pm; ¥5), a bustling, atmospheric Chan (Zen) temple dedicated to **Wenshu**, the Buddhist incarnation of Wisdom, sits 1.5km north of Tianfu Square, just east off Renmin Zhong Lu. The temple's elegant single-storey halls are filled with motifs of **lions** – the symbol of Wenshu – such as the mural in the **fourth hall**, though this looks more like a shaggy, red-haired dog. If you bear east (right) immediately on entering the temple you'll encounter a narrow, eleven-storey **pagoda**. According to some, the gold-leafed object visible in the base includes the skull of **Xuanzang**, hero of *Journey to the West* (see p.864), though other temples in China also claim to own his mortal remains. Just past here under the ginkgo trees is a small open-air **teahouse** area, along with a fine **vegetarian restaurant** – both good reasons to visit Wenshu at lunchtime.

The **Wenshu Fang** (文殊坊, *wénshū fāng*) district east of Wenshu Yuan is another antique quarter of stone streets and brick and timber buildings. Though it's all very touristy, with shops selling fair-quality if pricey souvenirs, it's also quite atmospheric and there are some good places to eat local snacks – though check prices first.

Qingyang Gong and Sichuan Museum

Sited about 2km west of Renmin Park and reached on bus #901, **Qingyang Gong** (青羊宫, *qīngyáng gōng*; daily 8am–5pm; ¥10), or the Green Goat Temple, is dedicated to Taoism's mythical proponent, Laozi. The temple's unusual **Bagua Pavilion** is an eight-sided hall with supporting posts wreathed in golden dragons, which houses a statue of **Laozi** astride his buffalo. According to legend, Laozi lost interest in teaching and headed west into the sunset, first baffling posterity by saying that he could be found at the green goat market once his philosophy was understood – hence the temple's unusual name. The tale is again reflected at the main **Three Purities Hall**, where two **bronze goats** have been worn smooth by the caresses of luck-seekers. The right-hand "goat" is weird, being the simultaneous incarnation of all twelve zodiacal animals. For active entertainment head around the back of the next hall, where those after a blessing stumble with eyes shut and arms outstretched towards three large good-luck symbols painted on the bricks, hoping to make contact; onlookers laugh at their efforts before trying themselves.

The **Sichuan Museum** (四川博物馆, *sìchuān bówùguǎn*; Tues–Sun 9am–5pm; free), about 700m west of Qingyang Gong along Qingyang Shang Jie, provides a thorough – if unimaginatively presented – look at the province's recorded history. Spread over three floors, there is Han-dynasty pottery, antique bronzeware, ethnic embroideries and artefacts (including a collection of what are politely termed "double-bodied" statuettes from Tibet), shadow puppets and even examples of Chengdu's once-famous silk brocade. It's easy to spend an hour here, but save time for the livelier **Songxian Qiao curio market** (送仙桥古玩艺术城, *sòngxiānqiáo gǔwán yìshù chéng*) across the road.

Du Fu's Thatched Cottage

Vehicles jamming the forecourt carpark at **Du Fu's Thatched Cottage** (杜甫草堂, *dùfǔ cǎotáng*; daily 8am–6pm; ¥60), located 500m west of the Sichuan Museum on the #901 bus route, attests to the respect the Chinese hold for the Tang-dynasty poet **Du Fu**. His works record the upheavals of his sad and difficult life with compassion and humour, and are considered, along with the more romantic imagery of his contemporary Li Bai (see p.763), to comprise the epitome of Chinese poetry.

Three centuries after Du Fu's death in 770, a pleasant park was founded at the site of his cottage by fellow poet and admirer Wei Zhuang, and around 1800 it was expanded to its current layout of artfully arranged gardens, bamboo groves, pools, bridges and whitewashed halls. Besides antique and modern statues of Du Fu – depicted as sadly emaciated – there's a small, free **museum** illustrating his life.

Wuhou Ci

Wuhou Ci (武侯祠, *wǔhóu cí*; daily 8am–6pm; ¥60), southwest of the centre on Wuhouci Dajie (bus #1 from Renmin Nan Lu runs past, as does tourist bus #901), is a temple-like complex nominally dedicated to **Zhuge Liang**, the strategist of *The Three Kingdoms* fame. However, as his emperor **Liu Bei** is also buried here – or at least his head, at any rate – the whole site is really a big shrine to the Three Kingdoms era (see p.945).

The site dates to Liu Bei's funeral in 223, though most of the buildings are of early Qing design; as usual in Chengdu, everything is surrounded by gardens. To the left of the entrance, the **Three Kingdoms Culture Exhibition Hall** has contemporary sculptures, lacquered furniture, painted bricks showing daily life (picking mulberry leaves, herding camels, ploughing), and a few martial relics such as arrowheads and copper cavalry figurines. Elsewhere, halls and colonnaded galleries house brightly painted **statues** of the epic's heroes, notably a white-faced Liu Bei flanked by his oath-brothers Guan Yu and Zhang Fei; and Zhuge Liang (holding his feather fan) and his son and grandson. Over in the complex's northwestern corner, **Liu Bei's tomb** is a walled mound covered in trees and guarded by stone figures.

Jin Li and the Tibetan quarter

The lane immediately east of Wuhou Ci, **Jin Li** (锦里, *jǐn lǐ*) is yet another of Chengdu's new "old" streets: this one is more of an alley, about 300m long, and jammed with wooden-fronted shops selling snacks. It winds up at an open-air **theatre**, with performances of Sichuanese Opera nightly at 8pm and 9pm (see p.760) – buy tickets at the theatre's entrance.

The district south of Wuhou Ci forms Chengdu's **Tibetan quarter**, full of shops stocked to their roofs with heavy clothes, amber and turquoise jewellery, knives and prayer wheels, conches and other temple accessories – not to mention heavy-duty blenders capable of whipping up a gallon of butter tea in one go. None of this is for tourists; most customers are Tibetan monks, cowboys, and Khampa women with braided hair, all looking decidedly tall and robust next to the local Chinese.

Yong Ling

Northwest of the centre on Yongling Lu and the #46 bus route, **Yong Ling** (永陵博物馆, *yǒng líng bówùguǎn*; daily 8.30am–5pm; ¥20) is the tomb of **Wang Jian**, a member of the Imperial Guard under the Tang who broke away from the disintegrating dynasty and, in 907 AD, set himself up here as emperor of Shu. After Wang Jian's death in 918, his "fatuous and self-indulgent son" Wang Yan was unable to hold onto the kingdom, which the Tang empire reclaimed in 925. Tomb robbers stripped the site of artefacts centuries before it was excavated during the 1940s, but the brick-lined chambers retain Wang Jian's stone **sarcophagus platform**, richly carved with musicians and twelve very Central Asian-looking bodyguards, and a simply styled, placid **statue**.

Jinsha Museum

Around 5km west from the centre, at the terminus of the #901 tourist bus, the **Jinsha Museum** (金沙遗址博物馆, *jīnshā yízhǐ bówùguǎn*; daily 8am–6pm; ¥80) sits over the remains of one of western China's major prehistoric settlements. The museum, comprising two halls set among gardens, is fascinating but leaves plenty of unanswered questions as interpretation of the site – and the **Ba-Shu** culture that inhabited it – is still being pieced together.

The Chengdu region was already settled as early as 2700 BC, though its first cultural flowering came a thousand years later at Sanxingdui (see p.761), which itself went into a decline as the Jinsha settlement blossomed from 1200 to 600 BC. Covering five square kilometres in total, Jinsha has yielded house remains, tools and artefacts of all descriptions, thousands of graves, and scores of **sacrificial pits** filled with ornaments and animal bones, all dating back to the Shang dynasty. The **first hall** protects a collection of these pits, which were dug a couple of metres deep into the grey soil in a regular grid pattern; the glass-sided building is well lit, and wooden boardwalks allow a close look. The **second hall** houses dioramas of the site, plus the pick of the finds, including some beautifully coloured, transluscent jades, small statues of tigers and kneeling slaves with bound hands, and a thin, serrated **gold disc** interpreted as depicting the Sun God.

Pandas

Two animals share the name panda: the **giant panda**, black-eyed symbol of endangered species worldwide; and the unrelated, racoon-like **red panda**, to which the Nepalese name "panda" was originally applied in the West. The Chinese call the giant panda *da xiongmao*, meaning "big bear-cat".

News of giant pandas first reached Europe in the nineteenth century through the French zoologist and traveller **Père Armand David**, who came across a skin in China in 1869. They are decidedly odd creatures, bearlike, endowed with a carnivore's teeth and a digestive tract poorly adapted to their largely vegetarian diet. Though once widespread in southwestern China, they've probably never been very common, and today their endangered status is a result of human encroachment combined with the vagaries of their preferred food – **fountain bamboo** – which periodically flowers and dies off over huge areas, leaving the animals to make do with lesser shrubs and carrion, or starve. Half of Sichuan's panda habitat was lost to logging between 1974 and 1989, which, coupled with the results of a bamboo flowering during the 1980s, reduced the total wild population to just over a thousand animals, scattered through **reserves** in Sichuan, Yunnan and Guizhou.

The Giant Panda Breeding Research Base

Some 8km northeast of central Chengdu, the **Giant Panda Breeding Research Base** (大熊猫繁育研究基地, *dàxióngmāo fányù yánjiū jīdì*; daily 8am–6pm; ¥30) offers close-up views of both giant and arboreal red pandas. Perhaps uniquely for China, this zoo is a pleasant place, full of lawns for visitors and spacious pens for the animals, who are fed truckloads of fresh bamboo by concerned staff. If you feel flush, you can have a photo taken with an adult panda for ¥400, or cuddling a baby panda (subject to availability; ¥1000).

Tours to the base offered by hostels are convenient but expensive at ¥98 per person (including entry), though tourist bus #902 (¥2) from outside the *Traffic* hotel can take two hours to reach the base through Chengdu's traffic congestion. Try to get here early, as the pandas slump into a stupor after munching their way through piles of bamboo at around 10am.

Eating

Despite an understandable bias towards Sichuanese **restaurants**, there's quite a variety of food available in Chengdu. The best place to try **local snacks** are the canteen in Renmin Park and Jin Li "old" street. Western-style **cafés**, serving a run of coffee, pizzas, sandwiches, burgers, pasta and desserts, include *The Bookworm* (老书虫, *lǎo shūchóng*; ⓦ www.chengdubookworm.com) at 2–7 Yujie Dong Lu, off Renmin Nan Lu, a comfy expat haunt with well-stocked library and bar which also hosts regular events; the above-average *Grandma's Kitchen* (祖母的厨房, *zǔmǔ de chúfáng*) near the *Bookworm*; and the shabbily hip *Dave's Oasis* on Binjiang Lu, popular with backpackers. Inexpensive **hotpot** places are legion, and your accommodation can point you to the nearest; for vegetarian food, try Wenshu temple or *Vegetarian Lifestyle* (see below). Sichuanese cooking tastes especially good with **beer** – try locally brewed "Snow".

Cacaja Indian (印度菜菜, *yìndù cài cài*) 18 Binjiang Zhong Lu ⓣ028/86670399. Bollywood soundtracks and a cosy, orange-painted interior draped in saris and posters of deities. Curries, *bhajis*, fresh yoghurt *raitas*, *dal* and *biryanis*, and plenty of meat-free dishes for vegetarians. Need to book at weekends. Mains ¥18–40.

Chen Mapo Doufu (陈麻婆豆腐, *chén mápó dòufu*) Upstairs at 197 Xi Yulong Jie, not far from the PSB. Founded in 1862, this is the home of Grandma Chen's bean curd, where ¥20 buys a large bowl of tofu glowing with minced meat, chilli oil and *huajiao* sauce. They also do a good range of Sichuanese favourites.

Fiesta Thai (非常泰泰国风味餐厅, *fēichángtài tàiguó fēngwèi cāntīng*) Outside the *Traffic* hotel, Linjiang Lu. Silk-clad staff greet you in Thai, and the food, from green curry chicken, mother-in-law eggs (deep-fried boiled eggs), and pork and glass-noodle salad, through to coconut custard-filled pumpkin and other desserts, is faultless. Worth the ¥50/person price.

Gesar Zangcan Ximianqiao Heng Jie, near *Holly's Hostel*. One of many nearby Tibetan restaurants, authentic down to the DVDs of Tibetan pop, a cowboy clientele, and begging acolytes going round the tables. Expect butter tea in metal teapots, dumplings, fresh yoghurt, and fried, boiled or chopped yak; don't count on vegetables. Around ¥15/person.

Long Chaoshou (龙抄手饭店, *lóng chāoshǒu fàndiàn*) East of Chunxi Lu. A big, busy dumpling house renowned for its *chaoshou*, Sichuanese wuntun, and other local snacks. Eat in the downstairs canteen; the upper floors have the same food and terrible table service at ten times the price.

Manting Fang (满庭芳, *mǎnting fāng*) Erhuan Lu, at Yulin Lu ⓣ028/85177958. Classic Sichuanese dishes served in smart surroundings; try the mouthwatering chicken, rice-coated spareribs, dry-fried beans, tiger-skin chillies and *mapo* tofu. Fine flavours prove that Sichuanese cuisine can be about more than just chillies and oil. Count on ¥80/person in a group.

Muslim Restaurant (皇城寺大饭店, *huángchéngsì dà fàndiàn*) At the mosque on Xitu Jie. Catering to Chengdu's large Muslim population, this serves everything from *lamian* soup to meat-and-potato stew and upmarket Sichuanese dishes. Uyghurs stand outside grilling kebabs and bread, if you fancy a take-away.

Shizi Lou Hotpot (狮子楼火锅琴台店, *shīzi lóu huǒguō qíntái diàn*) 101 Qintai Lu, a "Chinatown" street between Renmin Park and Qingyang Gong. If you want to eat hotpot surrounded by smart gold-and-red glitz, and served by simpering waitstaff, this is where to come. You can choose white stock, red stock or a divided pot with both, then pay per plate of morsels to cook: ¥15–30 for straightforward veg and meat, up to several hundred yuan for rare fungi and game.

Vegetarian Lifestyle (枣子树铂金店, *zǎozǐshù bójīn diàn*) 3F Bojincheng Building, 27 Qinglong Jie, just west of the main Bank of China ⓣ028/86282848. Local branch of *Jujube Tree* Shanghai chain, serving excellent, imaginative vegetarian Chinese dishes in a minimalist-smart setting at about ¥45/person.

Zhang Kaoya Jiudian (张烤鸭酒店, *zhāng kǎoyā jiǔdiàn*) Qingnian Lu. With a tiny stairway entrance, this comprises a canteen downstairs with horrendous plastic decor and a nicer restaurant above, both serving an array of Sichuanese snacks and dishes; the real treat is the marinated roast duck in an aromatic stock. A plate of garlic cucumber or shredded white-radish soup balances the richness of the duck; a meal for two costs around ¥30.

Drinking, nightlife and entertainment

Chengdu has a solid **nightlife**, but venues open and close rapidly; the places listed below have been around a while and make good starting points, and you can check the latest in the **free magazine** *GoChengdoo* (ⓦwww.gochengdoo.com). As for **entertainment**, you should spend a couple of hours at the theatre, soaking up at least the atmosphere, if not the plots, of *chuanxi*, one of China's main **opera** styles. Don't overlook the *Bookworm*'s (see above) Friday night jazz sessions either.

Café Panam(e) (巴黎咖啡, *bālí kāfēi*) 143 Kehua Bei Lu, second floor balcony of a restaurant complex. A popular expat watering hole with half-litres of beer for ¥20, a pool table, DJs on Friday and bands some other nights.

Carol's & Jah Bar Situated next to each other near the river on Hongmen Jie, these both have beer and live music in equal quantities.

Little Bar (小酒吧玉林店, *xiǎo jiǔbā yùlín diàn*) 55 Yulin Xi Lu. Arty, vaguely bohemian place with regular live bands and good range of inexpensive beers and spirits – somewhere to chill out or hold a conversation rather than party. One of several bars in the Yulin district; they can also supply directions to their sister operation, the *New Little Bar*, which is better for live music featuring local bands.

Shamrock (三叶草西餐酒吧, *sānyè cǎo xīcān jiǔbā*) Renmin Nan Lu. This place has been going forever and still supplies loud, live music Wednesday and Sunday, with a DJ filling in Friday and Saturday.

Sichuan opera

Sichuan opera – known here as **chuanxi** – is a rustic variant on Beijing's, based on everyday events and local legends. Most pieces are performed in Sichuanese, a rhythmic dialect well suited to theatre, which allows for humour and clever wordplay to shine through. As well as the usual bright costumes, stylized action and glass-cracking vocals, *chuanxi* has two specialities: **fire-breathing** and **rapid face-changing**, where the performers – apparently simply by turning around or waving their arms across their faces – completely change their make-up.

Today, *chuanxi* has gone into a decline as a form of popular entertainment, and most locals are not much interested. There are several places to catch a show around town, however, catering to tourists with nightly **variety shows** featuring short opera scenes, fire-breathing and face-changing, comedy skits, puppetry, shadow-lantern play and storytelling. These are pretty enjoyable and you might even catch occasional full-length operas. Venues include **Shufeng Yayun** (蜀风雅韵, *shǔfēng yǎyùn*) in the **Cultural Park** (enter off Qintai Lu); the Ming-style open-air stage at the end of Jin Li, near **Wuhou Ci**; and the downtown **Jinjiang Theatre** (锦江川戏馆, *jǐnjiāng chuānxìguǎn*) in a lane north of Shangdong Jie. Seats cost ¥120–220, depending on the venue and row.

Listings

Airlines China Eastern is at the corner of Xia Nan Da Jie and Jinli Dong Lu (ⓣ028/86155233, ⓦwww.ce-air.com), though agents around town should be able to book flights at no mark-up.
Banks and exchange The main Bank of China (Mon–Fri 8.30am–5.30pm) is up on Renmin Zhong Lu. Many other branches and banks around town have ATMs accepting foreign cards.
Bike rental All hostels rent bikes for around ¥20/day, plus a ¥300 deposit.
Bookshops The Southwest Book Centre opposite the south end of Chunxi Lu, and the Tianfu Bookstore at the southwest corner of Tianfu Square, stock maps, guidebooks in Chinese, and English-language novels.
Camping supplies If you're heading to Tibet, western Sichuan or elsewhere in China's wilds, try the clutch of outdoor stores selling good-quality gear at competitive prices (compared to what you'd pay at home) on Yihuan Lu, just west of the intersection with Renmin Nan Lu.
Consulate US, 4 Lingshiguan Lu, Renmin Nan Lu (ⓣ028/85583992, ⓦchengdu.usembassy-china.org.cn).
Guides The best independent guide in Chengdu is Tray Lee (ⓣ0139/08035353, ⓔlee@rt98.com – he's not good at answering emails, though), who can often be found in Renmin Park. He speaks excellent English, knows Chengdu and Sichuan very well, and has been guiding foreigners around the province for twenty years. Another good option, especially for wildlife and ethnic adventure tours of Sichuan, Tibet and Qinghai, is Pepper Mountain (ⓦwww.peppermountains.com), run by a long-time resident Westerner.
Hospitals and medical centres People's No. 1 Hospital and Chengdu Municipal Chinese Medicine Research Institute, Chunxi Lu (ⓣ028/86667223). There's also the English-speaking Global Doctor, Ground Floor, Bangkok Garden, Erhuan Lu at Renmin Nan Lu (ⓣ028/85226058), 24hr emergency number (ⓣ0139/82256966, ⓦwww.globaldoctor.com.au).
Internet Hostels and the motels all have internet access; there's also a huge net bar above Xinnanmen bus station – enter from the river side, not the station.
Left luggage Accommodation will look after excess gear while you're off in the wilds for around ¥3/item/day.
Mail Chengdu's main post office (8am–6pm) is in a 1920s grey brick building on the corner of Shuwa Bei Yi Jie and Xinglong Jie, with an Express Mail centre opposite.
PSB The branch dealing with visa extensions and foreigners' problems (Mon–Fri 9am–noon & 1–5pm) is on Shuncheng Lu, just south of the intersection with Wenwu Lu on the west side of the street.
Shopping For clothing, head to Chunxi Lu, where all the Chinese designer brands (and a few Western ones) have stores. The Songxian Qiao curio market near Sichuan Museum is good for "Maomorabilia", wooden screens and all sorts of "new antiques". For genuine antique snuff bottles, jewellery, birdcages and porcelain, try the Sichuan Antique

Store, corner of Dongchenggen Lu and Renmin Xi Lu.

Travel agents and tours All hostels can make train and plane bookings, though they usually encourage you to buy your own bus tickets. They also all offer part- and multi-day tour packages – you don't have to be staying to make bookings. Two-hour Sichuan Opera trips cost ¥120; three hours at Chengdu's Giant Panda Breeding Research Base, including entry (¥98); a day-trip to Qingcheng Shan (¥120); four days at Jiuzhaigou and Huanglong (around ¥850). Hostels also arrange five-seater minibuses with a driver for the day to tour local sights (plus Leshan or Emei Shan) at ¥300–700 depending on distance. Most can also book you on Yangzi Ferry trips through the Three Gorges (see p.784). Tibet packages should come in below ¥2500 for flights, or ¥1800 for the train.

Around Chengdu

Chengdu's surrounding diversions are mostly ignored by visitors, lured or sated by grander prospects elsewhere. But the following all make worthy day-trips from the capital, and most can be used as first stops on longer routes. Just to the northeast, the **Sanxingdui Museum** is stuffed with inscrutable prehistoric bronzes, while unpretentious Qing architecture graces the picturesque market town of **Huanglongxi** southwest of Chengdu. Northwest, **Dujiangyan** sports a still-functional two-thousand-year-old irrigation scheme surrounded by wooded parkland, and nearby **Qingcheng Shan** is forested and peppered with Taoist shrines.

Sanxingdui Museum

In 1986, an archeological team, investigating what appeared to be a Shang-dynasty town 25km northeast of Chengdu, made an extraordinary discovery: a set of rectangular **sacrificial pits** containing a colossal trove of jade, ivory, gold and **bronze** artefacts, all of which had been deliberately broken up before burial. Subsequent excavation revealed a settlement that from 2700 BC is believed to have been a major centre for the shadowy **Ba-Shu culture**, until it was upstaged by Jinsha (see p.757) and abandoned around 800 BC.

All this is covered at the excellent **Sanxingdui Museum** (三星堆博物馆, *sānxīngduī bówùguǎn*; daily 8.30am–5pm; ¥80), with two main halls and English captions. The thousands of artefacts on display are both startling and nightmarish, the products of a very alien view of the world: a 2m-high bronze figure with a hook nose and oversized, grasping hands standing atop four elephants; metre-wide masks with obscene grins and eyes popping out on stalks; a 4m-high "spirit tree" entwined by a dragon with knives and human hands instead of limbs; and finely detailed bronzes, jade tools and pottery pieces.

To reach Sanxingdui, first catch a bus to **Guanghan** (广汉, *guǎnghàn*), 8km short of the site, from Chengdu's Zhaojue Si station (¥10; you can reach Zhaojue Si on city bus #1 or #45 from Renmin Nan Lu). From Guanghan's bus station, catch local bus #6 (¥1) to the museum.

Huanglongxi

HUANGLONGXI (黄龙溪古城, *huánglóng xī gǔchéng*), 40km south of Chengdu, is a riverside village with a half-dozen **Qing-dynasty streets**, all narrow, flagstoned and sided in rickety wooden shops. Tourism aside – and visitor numbers are frankly overwhelming at weekends or during holidays – it's a pretty place, also popular with old ladies coming to pray for grandchildren to Guanyin, to whom all the village's **temples** are dedicated.

Buses to Huanglongxi (¥8) leave Chengdu's Xinnanmen station half-hourly between 6.30am and 6pm. From the highway bus stop, it's 500m to the old village gate; take the left-hand lane, which is almost narrow enough to touch either side as you walk down the middle. All businesses are either shops selling irrelevant souvenirs or restaurants displaying **grindstones** for making one of Huanglongxi's specialities, douhua (soft bean curd). You soon reach the 500m-long main street; turn left for two tiny **nunneries** (one on the left, the other at the end of the street beside a beribboned banyan tree), both containing brightly painted statues of Guanyin, Puxian and Wenshu.

At the opposite end of town, larger **Gulong Si** (古龙寺, *gŭlóng sì*; ¥5) has two main halls with similar statuary in a wobbly state of repair. There's an ancient banyan supported by posts carved as dragons; the former **governor's court** with a dog-headed guillotine for executing criminals; and an unusually three-dimensional, fifty-armed Guanyin statue in the right-hand hall.

Wandering around will fill an hour, after which you'll want **lunch**; the river-front restaurants near the nunneries are best, serving *douhua*, fresh fish and crispy deep-fried prawns. You can also sit under willows at one of the outdoor **teahouses**, though at ¥20 (including tea) this is a bit of a rip-off.

Dujiangyan

DUJIANGYAN (都江堰, *dūjiāngyàn*) is a large town 60km northwest of Chengdu, where in 256 BC the provincial governor, **Li Bing**, set up the **Dujiangyan Irrigation Scheme** to harness the notoriously capricious Min River. Li used a central dam and artificial islands to split the Min into an inner flow for irrigation and an outer channel for flood control, and the scheme has been maintained ever since, the present system of dams, reservoirs and pumping stations irrigating 32,000 square kilometres – even though the project's flood-control aspects became redundant when the **Zipingpu Dam**, 9km upstream, began operation in 2006.

The scheme's **entrance** is at **Lidui Park** (离堆公园, *líduī gōngyuán*; daily 8am–6pm; ¥90), which encloses the original heart of the project. An ancient, 3m-high stone statue of Li Bing found on the riverbed in 1974 graces **Fulong Guan** (伏龙观, *fúlóng guān*), a 1600-year-old temple flanked with vertical nanmu trees, which sits right at the tip of the first channel. From here the path crosses to the midstream artificial islands, before arriving at the **Anlan Suspension Bridge**, which spans the width of the river. Crossing to the east side brings you to steps ascending to **Erwang Miao** (二王庙, *èrwáng miào*), an ornate Taoist hall dedicated to Li Bing and his son; look for a Qing mural showing a bird's-eye view of the whole scheme. Heading back, follow signs for the wooded **Songmao Road**, a fragment of the ancient route from Dujiangyan to Songpan, which passes through two stone gateways and the old **Town God's Temple** at the park exit on Xingful Lu, about 500m east of Lidui Park.

By far the easiest way to reach Dujiangyan is by **high-speed train** from Chengdu's North train station (9 services daily 7.15am–7.25pm; 50min; ¥15); the last train back departs Dujiangyan at 8.30pm. You can also catch buses, but they're very slow.

Qingcheng Shan

Covered in verdant forest and amazingly fresh after Chengdu's smog, **Qingcheng Shan** (青城山, *qīngchéng shān*; ¥90) is a smaller, easier version of Emei Shan. The mountain's many **Taoist shrines** are all set in courtyards with open-fronted halls, at the back of which are ornate, glassed-in cases containing painted statues of saints. Most have **restaurants**, and though the food isn't great, the mountain's gong **tea** is worth trying.

Again, you can get here by bus but it's much quicker taking the **train** that continues past Dujiangyan (see above) to the mountain. From the gates, the return walk to the 1200m summit takes around three hours, following stone steps through the forest; there's also a **cable car** (¥50 return). Pick of the shrines are **Ci Hang Dian**, dedicated to Ci Hang, the Taoist version of Guanyin; **Tianshi Dong**, a complex surrounding a small cave where Zhang Ling lived before his death at the age of 122; and **Shangqing Gong** (上青宫, *shàngqīng gōng*), whose attractions include gateway calligraphy by the Guomindang leader Chiang Kai-shek, shrines to the Three Purities and **accommodation** (❸, dorms ¥15). At the top is a six-storey **tower** containing a 12m-high golden statue of Laozi and his buffalo, with views from the balconies of back-sloping ridges and lower temples poking out of the forest.

Northeastern Sichuan

The fertile river valleys of **northeastern Sichuan** wind through awkwardly hilly, heavily farmed countryside, all abruptly terminated around 400km from Chengdu by severe escarpments marking the border with Shaanxi. Originally, the sole way through these ranges was provided by **Shudao**, the "Road to Sichuan" linking Chengdu with the former imperial capital Xi'an, along which culture and personalities flowed over the centuries. The region features in *The Three Kingdoms* lore; contains the hometowns of **Li Bai**, one of China's greatest poets, and the country's only empress, **Wu Zetian**; and was the escape route down which the Tang emperor Xuan Zong fled the An Lushan rebellion of 756 AD (see p.749). A Song-dynasty wooden structure and some death-defying martial monks survive at **Doutuan Shan**, while Shudao itself breaks out of the region through a sheer cleft in the ranges known as **Jianmenguan**, the Sword Pass.

The towns of primary interest along Shudao are **Jiangyou** and **Guangyuan**, the latter just 60km short of the Shaanxi border. Both are on the Chengdu–Xi'an **rail line**, and also on a fast expressway – you can get to Guangyuan in around four hours – covered by buses from Chengdu's Zhaojue Si station. Shudao can also serve as the first stage in a journey to **Jiuzhaigou** (see p.790); given the seemingly permanent roadworks underway on the Chengdu–Songpan highway (see p.788), it's sometimes the only viable route.

Well east from Shudao, a large grid of old streets at the pleasant riverside town of **Langzhong** is one of the few places in Sichuan where you can still see substantial areas of urban Qing-dynasty architecture – a welcome refuge from the country's frenzied demolition of its past. Fast **buses** to Langzhong from Chengdu depart Beimen station, northeast of the centre on the first ring road; you can also get here direct from Chongqing and Guangyuan.

Although there are plenty of **banks** with ATMs in the region, none can change travellers' cheques.

Jiangyou and Doutuan Shan

JIANGYOU (江油, *jiāngyóu*) is a pleasantly leafy town on the north bank of the Fu River some 170km from Chengdu, within sight of the steep line of hills slanting northeast towards the Shaanxi border. It's famed as the hometown of the Tang poet Li Bai, but what really justifies a visit is a side trip to quirky **Doutuan Shan**, whose monks perform some bizarre acrobatic stunts. Be aware, however, that the **2008 earthquake** (see p.788) destroyed almost all of Doutuan Shan's temples – you might find that there's little to see for the present.

Li Bai was born in a period when China's arts, stimulated by unparalleled contact with the outside world, reached their heights. He became China's most highly regarded romantic poet, his works masterpieces of Taoist, dream-like imagery, often clearly influenced by his notorious **drunkenness** – he drowned in the Yangzi in 762 AD, allegedly while trying to grasp the moon's reflection in the water. Bus

#9 from near Jiangyou's bus station on Taiping Lu heads 10km south to **Qinglian** township (青莲, *qīnglián*) above which, on a hill, sits **Li Bai's Former Residence** (李白故居, *lǐ bái gùjū*; 8am–5pm; ¥50). Rebuilt many times, the quiet Ming-era halls and courtyards are filled with statues and paintings illustrating his life, and a shrine to his ancestor, the Han-dynasty general Li Xin.

Doutuan Shan (窦团山, *dòutuán shān*; ¥67) is a little twin-peaked ridge famed for its martial arts and covered in historic temples, 26km northwest of Jiangyou. Extensive **reconstruction** in the wake of the earthquake should return the mountain's sights to their former glory by 2012. **Buses** to Doutuan Shan (¥18 return) depart from the little depot 150m west of Jiangyou's south bus station on Taiping Lu between 7am and 6pm; alternatively, catch a bus from the same place to **Wudu** (武都, *wǔdū*) and a Doutuan Shan bus from there.

Practicalities

Jiangyou's kilometre-wide centre is focused on the north–south Jiefang Lu and its intersections with Renmin Lu and Jinlun Lu; the little **Changming River** flows west of and parallel to Jiefang Lu through town. The **south bus station** is south of the centre on Taiping Lu; the **train station** is 5km to the east, from where city bus #2 will carry you to Taiping Lu.

There's **accommodation** next to the bus station on Taiping Lu at the excellent-value *Jinxin Binguan* (金鑫宾馆, *jīnxīn bīnguǎn*; Ⓣ0816/3277222; ❷), which also has a great **restaurant**; and over the road at the cheaper *Jindu Binguan* (金都宾馆, *jīndū bīnguǎn*; Ⓣ0816/3258133; ❷). The main **Bank of China** and ATM is in the centre on the Jiefang Lu/Jinlun Lu crossroads.

Leaving, buses to Chengdu, Guangyuan and Langzhong depart until late afternoon.

Jianmenguan

Jianmenguan (剑门关, *jiànménguān*; ¥100), the Sword Pass, commands a strategic position along Shudao as the only break through a tall line of hills 100km from Jiangyou and 50km from Guangyuan. Zhuge Liang's forces defended Shu from invasion here during the Three Kingdoms period, and in one spot the main path cuts through a crevice barely half a metre wide. **Buses** run here direct from Guangyuan (see below); coming from Jiangyou, you'll be dropped 14km short on the hard shoulder, and you'll have to walk down the sliproad for a kilometre to waiting minibuses (¥40 for the vehicle).

Jianmenguan forms a narrow slash in the surrounding 500m-high cliffs. The pass itself is marked by a heavy stone **gateway** and watchtower, around which progress is further slowed by the number of **restaurants** catering to tourists' needs. A **cable car** (¥40) heads up to a viewing area and tea terrace, or you can get here from the gateway by following Shudao's original route – a very narrow, steep, and slippery stone path along the base of the cliffs – for a couple of kilometres, after which you'll appreciate the sentiment behind Li Bai's poem, *Hard is the Road to Shu*. Back at the gateway, buses on **to Guangyuan** (¥10) pass by until late afternoon.

Guangyuan

GUANGYUAN (广元, *guǎngyuán*), on the Jialing River halfway between Chengdu and Xi'an, is an unattractive manufacturing town of use as a jumping-off point for **Jiuzhaigou** buses, but is also the birthplace of China's only acknowledged empress, the Tang-dynasty ruler **Wu Zetian** (see p.270). About 2km south along the river from the train station, Tang rock sculptures at **Huangze Si** (皇泽寺, *huángzé sì*; ¥25) offer a reappraisal of her reign after centuries of censure caused by her overturning of Confucian values, in which women had little status. Carvings here include portraits of Wu Zetian and an elegant, Indian-influenced sculpture of Guanyin.

Guangyuan's 2km-wide core, traversed by the main street, **Shumen Bei Lu**, is bounded by the Jialing River to the west, and the smaller Nan He River to the south. The **train station** and **main bus station** (客运中心, *kèyùn zhōngxīn*) share a huge square next to each other over the Jialing River, about 1.5km from the centre; buses #2 and #6 from here cross the bridge and run down Shumen Bei Lu. Alternatively, you might end up 2km south at the **Nanhe bus station** (南河汽车站, *nánhé qìchē zhàn*) on Shumen Nan Lu and the #6 bus route. A taxi anywhere shouldn't cost more than ¥7.

The train station square is surrounded by numerous **hostels** – touts will grab you – charging ¥30 a bed. More substantial options are available near the south bus station at the Shumen Bei Lu/Lizhou Lu crossroads, at hotels like the *Zhongyuan* (中源快睫88酒店, *zhōngyuán kuàijié bāshíbā jiǔdiàn*; ⓣ0839/3277888; ❷). For **meals**, hotpot stalls and restaurants fill the town's backstreets. The most convenient **Bank of China** with an ATM is at the corner of pedestrianized Shichang Jie and Bei Jie in the older part of town, west off Shumen Bei Lu.

Leaving, aside from trains to Chengdu and Xi'an, the main bus station has dawn departures for the 348km run **to Jiuzhaigou**, and services through the day to Xi'an and Langzhong. For Jianmenguan and all points south, buses go when full from the Nanhe station.

Langzhong

About 225km northeast of Chengdu, **LANGZHONG** (阆中, *lángzhōng*) is an unassuming town occupying a broad thumb of land around which the Jialing River loops on three sides. Yet Langzhong once played a pivotal role in provincial history, even becoming the **Sichuanese capital** for seventeen years at the start of the Qing. Notable people associated with the town include the Three Kingdoms general **Zhang Fei**, who is buried here, and **Luo Xiahong**, the Han-dynasty inventor of the Chinese calendar and armillary sphere. In addition, about a quarter of Langzhong comprises a protected **old town**, Sichuan's largest collection of antique architecture, whose streets, houses and temples provide a fascinating wander.

Arrival

Langzhong's main road, **Zhang Fei Dadao**, runs south for a couple of kilometres to the river, its midpoint marked by a large **equestrian statue** of Zhang Fei; a further block south from here, Tianshanggong Jie leads west to **Nei Dong Lu** and into the heart of the old town. Langzhong's **main bus station** (南部客运站, *nánbù kèyùn zhàn*) is 5km southeast on the highway, where you'll arrive from Chengdu; catch a city bus from the forecourt into town. The **Baba Si bus station**, in the north of town (巴巴寺汽车站, *bābā sì qìchēzhàn*) on Zhang Fei Dadao handles traffic to Guangyuan.

The Town

Langzhong's **old town** covers about a square kilometre southwest of the centre. Orient yourself near the river at **Huaguang Lou** (华光楼, *huáguāng lóu*; ¥15), a three-storey, 36m-high Tang-style gate tower on Dadong Jie, last reconstructed in 1867. From the top, there are views south over the river, north to the modern town, and down over the grey-tiled roofs and atriums of Langzhong's classical *siheyuan*, or **courtyard houses**. Many of these are open to the public (approx

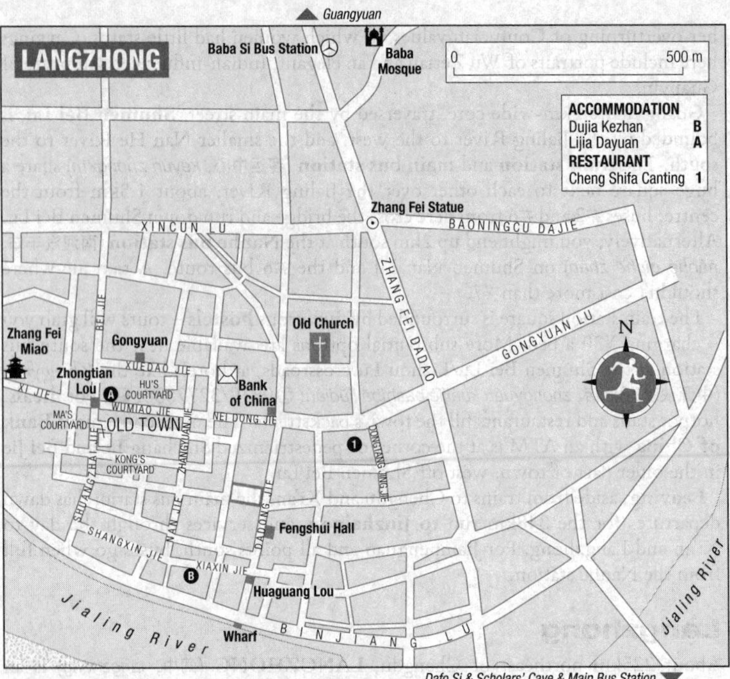

9am–6pm; ¥4–8) and house museums or even accommodation, but there's no need to see more than a couple to get the idea of a central hall divided up by wooden screens opening into a courtyard, decorated with potted flower gardens – check the map for locations. Aside from *siheyuan*, small industries survive alongside elderly canteens and teahouses, not to mention touristy shops selling antiques, locally produced Baoning vinegar and preserved Zhangfei beef.

An unusual target in the north of the old town is the seventeenth-century **Gongyuan** (贡院, *gòngyuàn*; ¥30), one of only two surviving imperial examination halls in China. Single-storey cells surround a long courtyard where prospective candidates lived and elaborated on their knowledge of the Confucian classics, on which the exams were based and according to which the country was governed. Langzhong's most popular sight, however, is the **Zhang Fei Miao** (张飞庙, *zhāngfēi miào*; ¥40), at the end of Xi Jie. This is a shrine to **Zhang Fei**, Liu Bei's foremost general during the Three Kingdoms period (see p.945), a ferocious man who was murdered in 221 AD by his own troops while campaigning at Langzhong. Four courtyards of Ming halls, full of painted statuary and interlocking roof brackets, lead through to the grassy mound of his **tomb**, in front of which a finally triumphant Zhang Fei sits between two demons who are holding his cringing assassins **Zhang Da** and **Fan Qiang** by the hair.

As well as the old town, it's worth heading east across the river below a prominent Ming-dynasty pagoda – catch a taxi for ¥7 – to **Scholars' Cave** (状元洞, *zhuàngyuán dòng*; ¥40), a peaceful grotto laid with ponds and willows where two students, both later court officials, studied in their youth. Behind here, **Dafo Si** (大佛寺, *dàfó sì*; ¥40) protects a 10m-high Buddha, which was carved into a rockface in Tang times and has survived more or less intact, along with thousands of smaller carvings and reliefs.

Accommodation and eating

Head to the old town for **accommodation**, where many places offer rooms inside antique buildings. Pick of the **hotels** is *Dujia Kezhan* (杜家客栈, *dùjiā kèzhàn*; ⓣ0817/6224436, ⓦwww.djkz.com.cn; ❸), in the south of the old town at 63 Xiaxin Jie; founded during the Tang dynasty it is, incredibly, still in business – though rooms now come with toilets and air conditioning. A similarly atmospheric option is the *Lijia Dayuan* (李家大院, *lǐjiā dàyuàn*; ⓣ0817/6236500; ❸), at 47 Wumiao Jie. You can also stay in any one of the family **hostels** scattered about, though you'll need some Chinese, if only to find them – look for flags with the characters for accommodation (住宿, *zhùsù*) or guesthouse (客栈, *kèzhàn*).

Decent **restaurants** are scarce in the old town; try *Cheng Shifa Canting* (城实发餐厅, *chéng shí fā cāntīng*), just east down narrow Dongtang Jing Jie, for a proper sit-down Sichuanese feed.

Southern Sichuan

Some 150km southwest of Chengdu lies the edge of the Red Basin and the foothills of mountain ranges that sprawl into Tibet and Yunnan. Fast-flowing rivers converge here at **Leshan**, where more than a thousand years ago sculptors created **Dafo**, a **giant Buddha** overlooking the waters, one of the world's most imposing religious monuments; an hour away, **Emei Shan** rises to more than 3000m, its forested slopes rich in scenery and temples. As Sichuan's most famous sights, Dafo and Emei Shan have become tourist black holes thanks to easy access – don't go near either during holidays, when crowds are so awful that the army is sometimes called in to sort out the chaos – but at other times they are well worth the effort.

Leshan's accommodation is poor, so Dafo is best tackled either going to or coming from Emei Shan, just an hour distant. If you're on your way down south to Yunnan, you might also want to break your journey at **Xichang**, a **Yi minority** town with a backroads route to **Lugu Hu**, right on the Yuannanese border. Emei and Dafo are best reached on buses, but it's easier to get to Xichang via the Chengdu–Emei Shan–Kunming rail line.

Leshan and Dafo

Set beside the wide convergence of the Qingyi, Min and Dadu rivers, 180km from Chengdu and 50km from Emei Shan, **LESHAN** (乐山, *lèshān*) is a spread-out market town with a modern northern fringe and older riverside core, a transit point for visiting **Dafo**, the Great Buddha, carved deep into a niche in the facing cliffs.

Leshan has at least three large bus stations, but you're most likely to arrive at the **transit centre** (乐山客运中心站, *lèshān kèyùn zhōngxīn zhàn*), several kilometres northwest of the sights on Baichang Xi Lu; buses #9 and #12 run from here to the **ferry terminals** on Binjiang Lu, while #3 will get you to Dafo's north entrance. A **taxi** to either shouldn't cost more than ¥12. Don't plan to stay at Leshan; the hotel situation is terrible and you're better off day-tripping from Emei or Chengdu. **Leaving**, the transit centre has regular connections to Chengdu, Emei Shan, Xichang, Zigong, Yibin and Chongqing.

Dafo

Impassive and gargantuan, **Dafo** (大佛, *dàfó*; daily: April–Sept 7.30am–6.30pm; Oct–March 8am–5.30pm; ¥90) peers out from under half-lidded eyes, oblivious

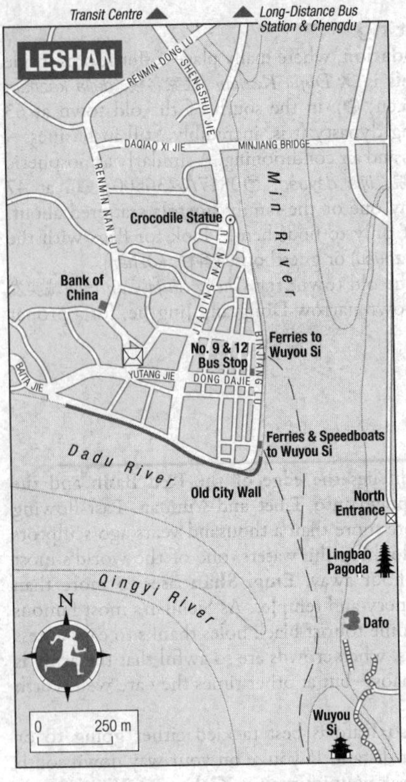

to the swarms of sightseers trying to photograph his bulk. In 713 AD the monk **Haitong** came up with the idea of filling in dangerous shoals below the sandstone cliffs of **Lingyun Shan** with rubble produced by carving out a giant Buddha image. The project took ninety years to complete and, once construction started, temples sprang up above the Buddha at Lingyun Shan and on adjacent **Wuyou Shan**. At 71m tall, Dafo is the world's largest Buddhist sculpture – his ears are 7m long, his eyes 10m wide, and around six people at once can stand on his big toenail – though statistics can't convey the initial sight of this squat icon, comfortably seated with his hands on his knees, looming over you.

The easiest route in is via the **north entrance** (大佛北门, *dàfó běimén*), from where you walk up to the crowded terrace around Dafo's ears; there's an insane-looking statue of Haitong here, and the one-way **staircase of nine turns** down to the Buddha's toes, after which you return to the top via the 500m-long **cliff road** cut into the rocks. From here you can press on to Maohao Mu, a set of Han-dynasty tombs, and then, via a covered bridge to **Wuyou Si** (乌优寺, *wūyōu sì*), a warm pink-walled monastery occupying the top of Wuyou Shan – don't miss the grotesque gallery of saints in the Luohan Hall. Downhill from here, **ferries** (¥70) can cart you back to the dock in Leshan town, via superb views of Dafo from the water. You could, of course, start by ferry from Leshan too; either way, give yourself a couple of hours to see everything.

Emei Shan

Thick forests and dozens of **temples**, all linked by exhausting flights of stone steps, have been pulling in pilgrims – and more recently, tourists – to **Emei Shan** (峨眉山, *éméi shān*) ever since the sixth-century visit of Bodhisattva **Puxian** and his six-tusked elephant (images of whom you'll see everywhere). Religion aside, the pristine natural environment is a major draw, and changes markedly through the year – lush, green and wet in the summer; brilliant with reds and yellows in autumn; white, clear and very cold in winter.

You can see something of the mountain in a single day, but three would allow you to experience more of the forests, spend a night or two in a temple, and perhaps assault **Wanfoding**, the highest of Emei's three peaks at 3099m. It's only worth climbing this high if the weather's good, however: for a richer bag of views,

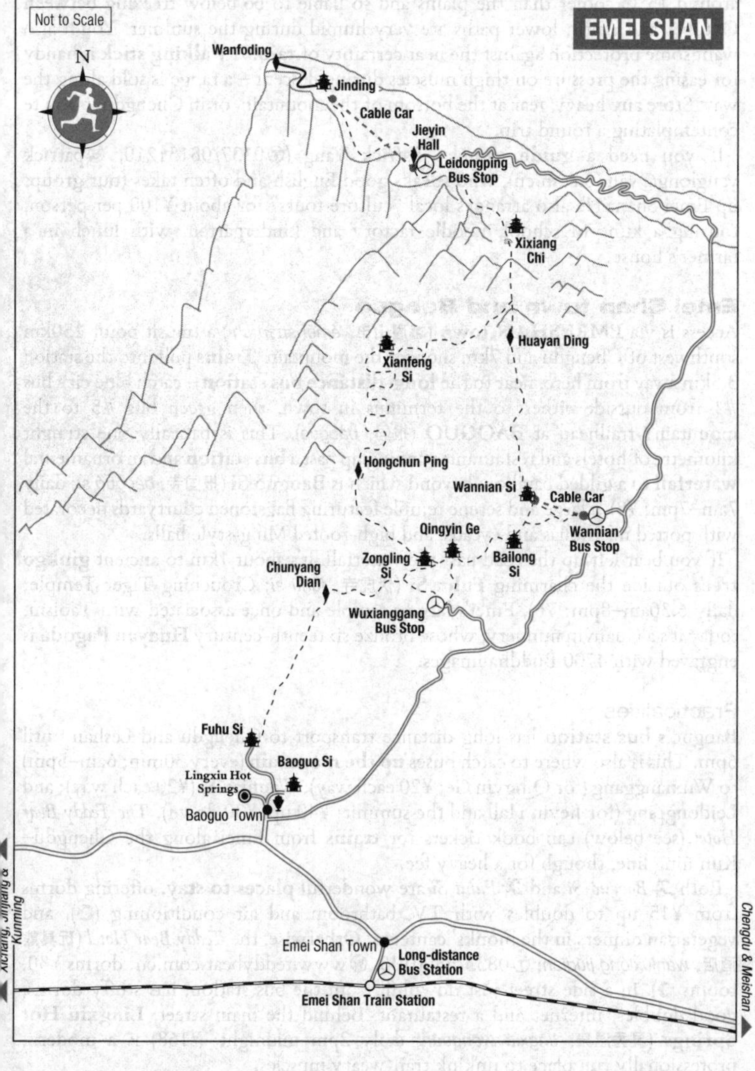

temples, streams and vegetation, you won't be disappointed with the lower paths.

There are some **hotels** on the mountain, but it can't be stressed enough that **temples** offer far more interesting lodgings, charging from ¥15 for a basic dorm bed to more than ¥150 for a double room with air conditioning and toilet. **Food** tends to be overpriced and ordinary; stir-fries and noodle soups are available either at roadside stalls or vegetarian temple restaurants.

Bring a **torch** in case you unexpectedly find yourself on a path after dark. **Footwear** needs to have a firm grip; in winter, when stone steps become dangerously icy, straw sandals and even iron cleats (sold for a few yuan and tied onto your soles) are an absolute necessity. Don't forget **warm clothing** for the top, which is around 15°C cooler than the plains and so liable to be below freezing between October and April; lower paths are very humid during the summer. You'll also want some protection against the near certainty of **rain**. A **walking stick** is handy for easing the pressure on thigh muscles during descent – a range is sold along the way. Store any heavy gear at the bottom of the mountain, or in Chengdu if you're contemplating a round trip.

If you need a **guide**, contact Patrick Yang (Ⓣ0137/08131210, Ⓔpatrickyanglong@yahoo.com.cn), who speaks good English and often takes tour groups up Emei Shan. He also arranges local "culture tours" for about ¥100 per person, touring a kung-fu school, noodle factory and kindergarten, with lunch in a farmer's house.

Emei Shan town and Baoguo

Access is via **EMEI SHAN town** (峨眉山市, *éméi shān shì*) a transit point 150km southwest of Chengdu and 7km short of the mountain. **Trains** pull into the station 3.5km away from here, near to the **long-distance bus station** – catch blue city bus #1 from outside either to the terminus in town, then green bus #5 to the mountain's trailhead at **BAOGUO** (报国, *bàoguó*). This is basically one straight kilometre of hotels and restaurants running up past a **bus station** and an ornamental **waterfall** to a gilded pavilion, beyond which is **Baoguo Si** (报国寺, *bàoguó sì*; daily 7am–7pm; ¥8), a large and serene temple featuring flagstoned courtyards decorated with potted magnolias and cycads, and high-roofed Ming-style halls.

If you bear left up the road past the waterfall, it's about 1km to ancient **ginkgo trees** outside the charming **Fuhu Si** (伏虎寺, *fúhǔ sì*; Crouching Tiger Temple; daily 6.30am–8pm; ¥6). Emei's largest temple and once associated with Taoism, today it's a Guanyin nunnery, whose bronze sixteenth-century **Huayan Pagoda** is engraved with 4700 Buddha images.

Practicalities

Baoguo's **bus station** has long-distance transport to Chengdu and Leshan until 6pm. This is also where to catch buses **up the mountain** (every 30min; 6am–5pm) to Wuxianggang (for Qingyin Ge; ¥20 each way); Wannian Si (¥20 each way); and Leidongping (for Jieyin Hall and the summit; ¥40 up, ¥30 down). *The Teddy Bear Hotel* (see below) can book tickets for **trains** from Emei along the Chengdu–Kunming line, though for a heavy fee.

Both *Baoguo Si* and *Fuhu Si* are wonderful **places to stay**, offering dorms from ¥15 up to doubles with TV, bathroom and air conditioning (❸), and vegetarian dinners in the monks' canteens. Otherwise, the *Teddy Bear Hotel* (玩具熊酒店, *wánjùxióng jiǔdiàn*; Ⓣ0833/5590135, Ⓦwww.teddybear.com.cn; dorms ¥30, rooms ❸), in a side street just downhill from the bus station, has stuffy dorms, good doubles, internet and a restaurant. Behind the main street, **Lingxiu Hot Springs** (灵秀温泉, *língxiù wēnquán*; daily 2pm–midnight; ¥168) is a modern, professionally run place to unkink trail-weary muscles.

The mountain

An ascent of Emei Shan can be tackled via two main **routes** from Baoguo: the 60km, three-day **long route**; and the 40km, two-day **short route**. Most people knock 15km or so off these by catching **buses** from Baoguo to alternative starting points near **Qingyin Ge** (Wuxianggang bus stop) or **Wannian Si**; leaving early enough, you could make it to the top in one day from either of these via the short route, descending the next day – though your legs will be like jelly afterwards. If you're really pushed for time, you could get up and down in a single day by catching a minibus between Baoguo Si and **Jieyin Hall** (Leidongping bus stop), located a cable-car ride from the summit, but this way you'll miss out on what makes Emei Shan such a special place. Once past the temples around Baoguo, you'll have to pay **Emei's entry fee** (¥150 for a ticket valid for three days; students and over-65s half-price; trails open daily 7am–6pm).

The long route

Following the **long route**, it's 5km from Fuhu Si to **Chunyang Dian** (纯阳殿, *chúnyáng diàn*), a nunnery founded in honour of the Taoist Immortal Lü Dongbin, spookily surrounded by mossy pine trees. A further 5km lands you at **Qingyin Ge** (清音阁, *qīngyīn gé*), a pavilion built deep in the forest where two streams converge and tumble through a small gorge down **Niuxin Shi** (牛心石, *niú xīnshí*), the ox-heart rock. It's a charming spot with a small **temple** (en-suite doubles ❸, dorms ¥15), though being also just a short walk from the Wuxianggang bus stop, it can also get quite busy with guests.

Qingyin Ge is just 3km from Wannian Si (see below), but to continue the long route, follow the path up past the left side of Qingyin; this takes you along a river bed and past a **monkey-watching area**, before starting to climb pretty steeply through a series of gorges. About 6km further on, **Hongchun Ping** (洪椿坪, *hóngchūn píng*; beds ¥40) is an eighteenth-century temple named after surrounding hongchun (toona) trees, and is about as far as you'd make it on the first day.

From here it's a very tough 15km of seemingly unending narrow stairs to **Xianfeng Si** (仙峰寺, *xiānfēng sì*; beds ¥40), a strangely unfriendly place, though well forested with pine and dove trees and planted with camellia and rhododendrons. The following 12.5km are slightly easier, heading partly downhill to a dragon-headed bridge, then up again to where the trail joins the north route near **Xixiang Chi** (see below), around 43km from Fuhu Si and two-thirds of the way to the summit.

The short route

Most people start their ascent by catching a bus from Baoguo to the Wannian Si bus stop at the start of Emei's **short route**. From here a 3km path or cable car (¥50) leads to **Wannian Si** (万年寺, *wànnián sì*; daily 7.30am–7pm; ¥6; dorms ¥20, rooms ❸), where a squat brick **pavilion** out back, built in 1601, houses a life-sized enamelled bronze **sculpture of Puxian**, riding a gilt lotus flower astride his great six-tusked white elephant – note the gold spots on the elephant's knees, which people rub for good luck.

From Wannian, a steady 14km hike through bamboo and pine groves should see you where the two routes converge just south of **Xixiang Chi** (洗象池, *xǐxiàng chí*; beds ¥20, rooms ❸). This eighteenth-century monastery sits on a ridge where Puxian's elephant stopped for a wash, and on cloudy days – being more or less open to the elements and prowled by monkeys – it's amazingly atmospheric, though somewhat run-down and frigid in winter. It's a popular place to rest up, however, so get in early to be sure of a bed.

On to the summit

Beyond Xixiang Chi the path gets easier, but you'll encounter gangs of aggressive **monkeys**; keep a good grip on your bags. The path continues for 9km past some ancient, gnarled rhododendrons to **Jieyin Hall** (接引殿, *jiēyǐn diàn*) where the 50km-long road from Baoguo, which has snaked its way round the back of the mountain, ends at **Leidongping bus stop** (雷洞坪车站, *léidòngpíng chēzhàn*) and a **cable car** to the summit (¥40 up, ¥30 down). The area is thick with minibus tour parties fired up for their one-day crack at the peak, and is also where to find buses back to Baoguo. **Hotels** around Jieyin are badly maintained and very expensive – they have been known to charge ¥200 for a mat on the floor – and you shouldn't plan to stay here.

Whether you take the cable car or spend the next couple of hours hoofing it, 3077m-high **Jinding** (金顶, *jīndǐng*), the Golden Summit, is most people's final stop. There are two temples: the friendly **Woyun Nunnery** (卧云庵, *wòyún ān*; dorms ¥30, rooms ④) and the oversized **Huazang Si** (华藏寺, *huázáng sì*; ④), crowned by a massive gilded statue of a multifaced Puxian on four elephants. Make an effort to catch the **sunrise**, which is marvellous on a good day, as it lights up the sea of clouds below the peak. In the afternoon, these clouds sometimes catch rainbow-like rings known as **Buddha's Halo**, which surround and move with your shadow, while in clear conditions you can even make out Gongga Shan (see p.795), 150km to the west.

Xichang and around

XICHANG (西昌, *xīchāng*), seven hours south from Emei Shan by train, is a surprisingly bustling place, focus for southwestern China's five-million-strong **Yi minority** – whose **torch festival** in August is one of the largest ethnic events in all Sichuan. Xichang is also a **satellite launching site** for China's Long March space programme, and a staging post for a couple of backroads trips into Yunnan, if the straightforward train ride to Kunming doesn't appeal.

In town itself, Xichang's partially walled **old town** is just northeast of the centre, a fifteen-minute walk north from Yuechang Plaza. The old quarter's streets form a cross, of which the southern extension, **Nan Jie**, is the most interesting, running 150m through a busy market and past rickety wooden teahouses to the heavy stone **south gate** and attached battlements.

The area around Xichang, known as **Liang Shan** (凉山, *liángshān*), the Cool Mountains, is heartland of the Yi community. Until the 1950s, the Yi here lived pretty much any way they wanted to, owning slaves, raiding the lowlands and conducting clan warfare. Ride bus #106 for 5km south to **Qionghai Hu** (邛海湖, *qiónghǎi hú*), a large lake where the **Museum of Liangshan Yi Slave Society** (凉山彝族奴隶社会博物馆, *liángshān yízúnúlì shèhuì bówùguǎn*) exhibits Yi festival clothing and household items, and books written in the Yi script – you'll also see this on official signs around town.

Practicalities

Xichang's centre forms a kilometre-wide wedge, with main street **Chang'an Dong Lu** running southwest, past the open space of **Yuecheng Plaza** and a China-Yi friendship **statue**, over the often dry Dong He River, and then down into the southern suburbs along **Sanchakou Lu**. The **train station** is in the western outskirts, from where bus #6 will get you to Chang'an Dong Lu; the **western bus station** (汽车西站, *qìchē xīzhàn*) is out this way too, handling traffic to Chengdu, Emei and Kangding in Western Sichuan (see p.787). Buses travelling the expressway to Panzhihua – where you can catch transport **to Lijiang** – and the rough road west to **Lugu Hu**, on the Yunnanese border, depart from the **south bus station** (汽车南站, *qìchē nánzhàn*), on Sanchakou Lu and the #14 bus route.

For **accommodation**, the *Ziwei Jiudian* (紫葳酒店, *zǐwēi jiǔdiàn*; ⓣ0834/3285888; ③) at 60 Chang'an Dong Lu, and the *Hotel Pretty* (ⓣ0834/2237777; ④), down near the main Bank of China at 79 Sancha Xi Lu, provide clean, modern budget hotel rooms; while the *Jinsha Binguan* (金沙宾馆, *jīnshā bīnguǎn*; ⓣ0834/3228169; ②) at 57 Chang'an Zhong Lu, is an older, quieter, cheaper place. Inexpensive **restaurants** are scattered through the old town. Xichang's **Bank of China** and ATM is over the bridge on Sancha Xi Lu, an extension of Chang'an Dong Lu.

Moving on, bus tickets are easily available at the stations. There's a **train ticket office** on Chang'an Dong Lu, just west of Shengli Lu, but be warned that Xichang is a tough place to get reserved berths – or even hard seats – from.

Southeastern Sichuan

Surrounding the fertile confluence of the Yangzi and Min rivers 250km from Chengdu, where Sichuan, Yunnan and Guizhou provinces meet, **southeastern Sichuan** has some intriguing attractions. The town of **Zigong** is a treat, with some well-preserved architecture, dinosaurs and salt mines, especially worth checking out during its Spring Festival lantern displays. Some 80km farther south, **Yibin** offers access to the aptly named **Shunan Bamboo Sea**.

Both Zigong and Yibin are easily accessible **by bus** from Chengdu, Chongqing and Leshan. An interesting way out of the region is by bus east to **Luzhou**, and then over to another bamboo forest at **Chishui** in Guizhou province (see p.668).

Zigong

ZIGONG (自贡, *zìgòng*) a thriving industrial centre, has long been an important source of **salt**, tapped for thousands of years from artesian basins below the city. In the fourth century, the Sichuanese were sinking 300m-deep boreholes here

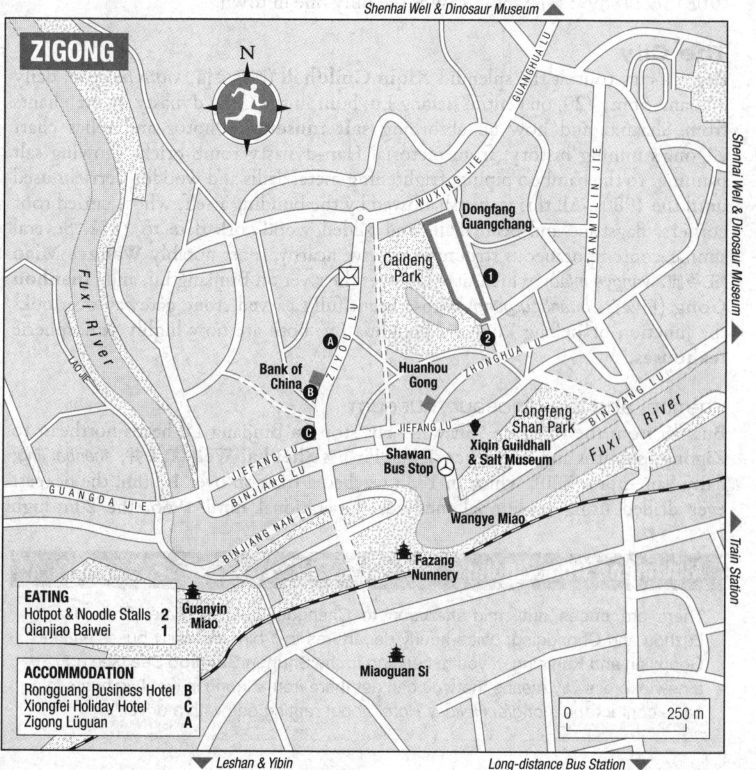

using bamboo-fibre cables attached to massive stone bits. By the 1600s, bamboo buckets were drawing brine from wells bored almost a kilometre beneath Zigong, centuries before European technology (which borrowed Chinese techniques) could reach this deep. **Natural gas**, a by-product of drilling, was used from the second century to boil brine in evaporation tanks, and now also powers Zigong's buses and taxis.

Arrival

Zigong's compact, hilly centre lies on the north side of the narrow **Fuxi River**. The **long-distance bus station** is about 2km south of town on Dangui Dajie; turn right out of the station and it's 100m to the city bus stop (#33 travels via the central "Shawan" bus stop, continuing to the bottom of Ziyou Lu). Taxis charge about ¥7. Zigong is on the Guangzhou–Chengdu rail line, with the **train station** 1.5km east of the river on Jiaotong Lu, from where bus #34 heads to the Shawan stop. There's no main street in town – all the roads surrounding **Caideng Park** are equally busy, with markets, shops and facilities spread around.

Accommodation

For bedrock **accommodation**, try the *Zigong Lüguan* (dorm beds ¥25, rooms ❷), on Ziyou Lu. Zigong's best mid-range option is the *Rongguang Business Hotel* at 25 Ziyou Lu (荣光商务酒店, *róngguāng shāngwù jiǔdiàn*; ⓣ0813/2117777; ❸), which has some tatty and some well-maintained rooms. A touch of luxury is provided by the smart *Xiongfei Holiday Hotel* at 193 Jiefang Lu (雄飞假日酒店, *xióngfēi jiàrì jiǔdiàn*; ⓣ0813/2118899; ❼), whose **café** is the only one in town.

The City

Begin a city tour at the splendid **Xiqin Guildhall** (西秦会馆, *xīqīn huìguǎn*; daily 8.30am–5pm; ¥20) on central Jiefang Lu, built in the Qing dynasty by merchants from Shaanxi and now an absorbing **salt museum**. Photos and relics chart Zigong's mining history, from pictorial Han-dynasty tomb bricks showing salt panning, to the bamboo piping, frightening metal drills and wooden derricks used until the 1980s. All this is overshadowed by the building itself, whose curled roof corners, flagstone-and-beam halls and gilded woodwork date to 1872. Several similar contemporaneous structures survive nearby, most notably **Wangye Miao** (王爷庙, *wángyé miào*), which sits high over the river on Binjiang Lu, and **Huanhou Gong** (桓侯宫, *huánhóu gōng*) whose beautifully carved stone gateway overlooks the junction of Jiefang Lu and Zhonghua Lu; both are now highly atmospheric **teahouses**.

Shenhai and the dinosaur museum

Bus #3 from the riverside "Shawan" bus stop on Binjiang Lu heads northeast to Zigong's suburbs and two other sights. First is **Shenhai Well** (燊海井, *shēnhǎi jǐng*; daily 9am–5pm; ¥20), which in 1835 reached a fraction over 1000m, the deepest ever drilled using traditional methods. Operational until 1966, the 20m-high

Moving on from Zigong

There are **buses** until mid-afternoon to Chengdu, Leshan, Emei Shan, Dazu, Luzhou and Chongqing; twice-hourly departures to Yibin; and daily buses each to Gongxian and Kunming. If you're heading to the **Shunan Bamboo Sea** (see p.776), a new expressway means that you can get there from Zigong in just two hours in a car – contact the *Xiongfei Holiday Hotel* about renting one with a driver.

wooden tripod minehead still overlooks the site, where you can inspect bamboo-fibre cables and the tiny well shaft itself, corked, reeking of gas, and barely 20cm across. Eight shallow vats in the building behind are evaporation pans, where the muddy brine is purified by mixing in tofu and skimming off the resultant scum as it rises, leaving a thick crust of pure salt when the liquid has been boiled off.

Back on the #3 bus, it's about 45 minutes from Binjiang Lu to the terminus at Zigong's **dinosaur museum** (恐龙博物馆, *kǒnglóng bówùguǎn*; daily 9am–5pm; ¥42), built over the site of excavations carried out during the 1980s. Near-perfect skeletal remains of dozens of Jurassic fish, amphibians and dinosaurs – including monumental thighbones, and Sichuan's own **Yangchuanosaurus**, a toothy, lightweight velociraptor – have been left partially excavated in situ, while others have been fully assembled for easy viewing, posed dramatically against painted backgrounds.

Eating

Zigong has an extraordinary density of **teahouses**, even for Sichuan; the most atmospheric are *Wangye Miao* and *Huanhou Gong*, with their century-old wood and stonework. Wuntun- and noodle-vendors surround the southern entrance to Caideng Park in a pedestrianized area known as **Dongfang Guangchang**, with light meals served up at *Xiao Ji* (小鸡饭店, *xiǎojī fàndiàn*), near the Rongguang. Meanwhile, *Qianjiao Baiwei* (千椒百味, *qiānjiāo bǎiwèi*) on Xinmin Jie is a hotpot restaurant upholding Zigong's reputation of serving the hottest food in Sichuan - the name means "A Thousand Chillies, a Hundred Flavours".

Yibin and around

A crowded, grubby port with a modern veneer, the city of **YIBIN** (宜宾, *yíbīn*) sits where the Jinsha and Min rivers combine to form the **Chang Jiang**, the main body of the Yangzi River. There's nothing to do here in between organizing transport to surrounding sights, though Yibin produces three substances known for wreaking havoc: enriched plutonium; Wuliangye *bai jiu*, China's second-favourite spirit; and *ranmian*, "burning noodles", whose chilli content has stripped many a stomach lining.

Yibin's kilometre-wide centre focuses on a central **crossroads**, from where Bei Dajie runs north, Minzhu Lu runs south into Nan Jie, Zhongshan Lu heads east, and Renmin Lu runs west. Another orientation point is **Daguan Lou**, an old bell tower just east off Minzhu Lu or south off Renmin Lu, though it's locked up. The **main bus station** (川高客运中心, *chuāngāo kèyùn zhōngxīn*) is a few kilometres north on the highway in from Zigong, though you could also end up at **Beimen bus station** (北门汽车客运站, *běimén qìchē kèyùnzhàn*), 250m northwest of the centre off **Zhenwu Lu**. The **Bank of China** (with ATM) and **post office** are next to each other at the bottom of Nan Jie.

Foreigner-friendly budget **accommodation** is scarce; best are the business-oriented *Jiudu Fandian* (酒都饭店, *jiǔdū fàndiàn*; Ⓣ0831/8188588; ❼) and decidely less upmarket *Tianhe* (天和宾馆, *tiānhé bīnguǎn*; Ⓣ0831/5166433; ❷), opposite each other in the east of town on Zhuanshu Jie. The *Jiudu* has a good **restaurant**; otherwise, the *Ranmian Fandian*, next to the crossroads on Renmin Lu, is typical of the town's canteens, where a bowl of cold *ranmian* noodles dressed in chopped nuts, coriander, vinegar and chillies is just ¥4.

Beimen and the main bus station handle **buses** to, among other places, Chongqing, Chengdu, Zigong and Luzhou (for connections to Chishui in Guizhou province). For the Shunan Bamboo Sea, catch city bus #4 from Nan Jie south over the river to **Nan'an bus station** (南岸汽车客运站, *nánàn qìchē kèyùn zhàn*).

The Shunan Bamboo Sea

Around 75km southeast of Yibin, the extraordinary **Shunan Bamboo Sea** (蜀南竹海国家公园, *shǔnán zhúhǎi guójiā gōngyuán*; ¥85) covers more than forty square kilometres of mountain slopes with feathery green tufts, and makes for a refreshing few days' rural escape. It's a relatively **expensive** one, however – if you want to see similar scenery at budget rates you're better off heading to Chishui in Guizhou province. The main problem is simply **getting around** within the park; bus services are unpredictable and you'll probably end up having to charter taxis for the day at ¥150–250.

Having said this, Shunan is a beautiful spot, if a bit spooky given the graceful 10m-high stems endlessly repeating into the distance. There's pleasure in just being driven around, but make sure you have at least one walk along any of the numerous paths – the trail paralleling the cable car is steep but superb, taking in a couple of waterfalls – and get a look down over the forest to see the bowed tips of bamboo ripple in waves as breezes sweep the slopes. The surreal atmosphere is enhanced by it being a favourite film location for martial-arts movies and TV series, so don't be too surprised if you encounter Song-dynasty warriors galloping along the roads.

Direct **buses to Shunan** from Yibin's Nan'an bus station are scarce and it's usually quicker to catch one of the many buses to **Changning** (长宁, *chángníng*; last bus at 7.30pm; ¥10), a small town 15km short of Shunan's main **West Gate**, which has bus connections to Chongqing, Chengdu and Luzhou, and minibuses into the park. These go to Shunan's two main settlements of **Wanling** (万岭, *wànlǐng*), 1.5km inside the gate, and **Wanli** (万里, *wànlǐ*), 20km inside, where you'll find plenty of **hotels** – the cheapest charge about ¥50 a bed, though most are mid-range (❺). Other places to stay are scattered in between; right at the park's centre, *Feicui Binguan* (翡翠宾馆, *fěicuì bīnguǎn*; Ⓣ0831/4970000, Ⓕ4970155; ❹) is a decent two-star option. **Food** in the park is universally good and not too expensive, with lots of fresh bamboo shoots and mushrooms.

As for **park transport**, stand by the road and wait for the next bus – they seem to run most frequently in the morning and afternoon, when locals are going to and from their villages – and don't be too surprised if drivers try to overcharge you. Otherwise, ask your accommodation to organize a motorbike-taxi or **minibus**.

Dazu

About 200km east of Chengdu and 100km west of Chongqing, **Dazu** is the base for viewing some fifty thousand Tang and Song dynasty **Buddhist cliff sculptures**, which are carved into caves and overhangs in the surrounding lush green hills – most notably at **Baoding Shan**, 16km to the northeast. What makes these carvings so special is not their scale – they cover very small areas compared with better-known sites at Luoyang or Dunhuang – but their quality, state of preservation, and variety of subject and style. Some are small, others huge, many are brightly painted and form comic-strip-like narratives, their characters portraying religious, moral and historical tales. While most are set fairly deeply into rockfaces or are protected by galleries, all can be viewed in natural light, and are connected by walkways and paths.

The Town

DAZU (大足, *dàzú*) is a small, quiet place whose centre forms a 700m-wide rectangle along the north bank of the mild Laixi River. The east side of the rectangle is Longzhong Lu, the north side Beihuan Zhong Lu, and the west side Bei Jie. The **bus**

station overlooks the river down at the southeast corner. Right next door, there's **accommodation** at the *Xingyuan Lüguan* (兴源旅馆, *xīngyuán lǚguǎn*; beds ¥35, rooms ❷) on Longxi Lu, or three-star comfort another 100m north up Longzhong Lu at the *Dazu Binguan* (大足宾馆, *dàzú bīnguǎn*; Ⓣ023/43721888, Ⓕ43722967; ❺), which is either packed with tour groups or empty. A further 500m up Longzhong Lu, the *Jinye Binguan* (金叶宾馆, *jīnyè bīnguǎn*; Ⓣ023/43775566; ❹) is a cosy alternative next to Dazu's tobacco factory. For **food**, cheap noodle and stir-fry places are all everywhere, with a string of inexpensive restaurants on Beihuan Zhong Lu, near the intersection with Bei Jie – *Panzhong Can* does great dry-fried green beans, double-cooked pork and stuffed aubergines.

Leaving, there are buses until early afternoon to Chengdu, Zigong, Yibin and Chongqing.

Baoding Shan

The carvings at **Baoding Shan** (宝顶山, *bǎodǐng shān*; daily 8.30am–6pm; ¥80) are exciting, comic and realistic by turns. The project was the life work of the monk **Zhao Zhifeng**, who raised the money and designed and oversaw the carving between 1179 and 1245, explaining the unusually cohesive nature of the ten thousand images depicted here. **Buses** (¥5) from Dazu's station leave twice an hour until around 4pm and take thirty minutes for the 16km run.

The bus drops you among a knot of souvenir stalls, with a path bearing right for a kilometre to the main site, **Dafowan**, whose 31 niches are naturally incorporated into the inner side of a broad, horseshoe-shaped gully. As every centimetre is carved with scenes illustrating Buddhist and Confucian moral tales, intercut with asides on daily life, you could spend a couple of hours walking the circuit here, though it's only around 700m long. Don't miss the fearsome 6m-high sculpture of a demon holding the segmented **Wheel of Predestination** (look for the faint relief near his ankles of a cat stalking a mouse); or the Dabei Pavilion, housing a magnificent gilded **Guanyin**, whose 1007 arms flicker out behind her like flames. The 20m-long **Reclining Buddha** features some realistic portraits of important donors, while the **Eighteen Layers of Hell** is a chamber-of-horrors scene interspersed with amusing cameos such as the Hen Wife and the Drunkard and his Mother. The final panel, illustrating the **Life of Liu Benzun**, a Tang-dynasty ascetic from Leshan, is a complete break from the rest, with the hermit surrounded by multifaced Tantric figures, showing a very Indian influence.

Chongqing and around

Based around a hilly, comma-shaped peninsula at the junction of the Yangzi and Jialing rivers, **CHONGQING** (重庆, *chóngqìng*) is southwestern China's dynamo, its largest city both in scale and population. Formerly part of Sichuan province and now the heavily industrialized core of **Chongqing Municipality**, which stretches 300km east to the Hubei border, the city is also a busy **port**, whose location 2400km upstream from Shanghai at the gateway between eastern and southwestern China has given Chongqing an enviable commercial acumen. While it's not such a bad spot to spend a day or two while arranging **Yangzi River cruises**, in many other respects the **Mountain City** (as locals refer to it) has little appeal. Overcrowded and fast-paced, the city is plagued by oppressive pollution, winter fogs and summer humidity. Nor is there much to illustrate Chongqing's history – as China's wartime capital, it was heavily bombed by the Japanese – though the nearby village of **Ciqi Kou** retains a glimmer of Qing times.

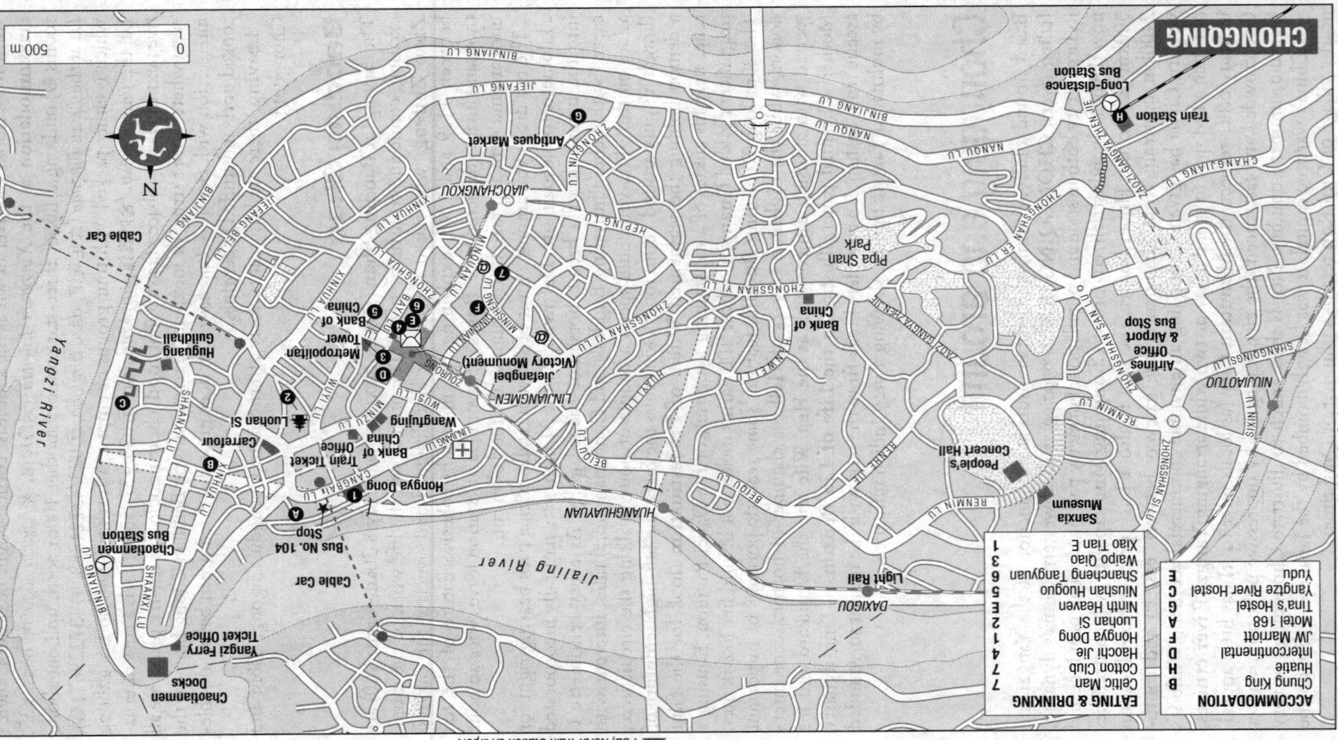
CHONGQING
ACCOMMODATION
Chung King B
Huatie H
Intercontinental D
JW Marriott F
Motel 168 A
Tina's Hostel G
Yangtze River Hostel C
Yudu E
EATING & DRINKING
Celtic Man 7
Cotton Club 7
Haochi Jie 4
Hongya Dong 1
Luohan Si 2
Ninth Heaven E
Niushan Huoguo 5
Shancheng Tangyuan 6
Waipo Qiao 3
Xiao Tian E 1
PSB, North Train Station & Airport
Stilwell Museum, Flying Tigers Museum & Ciqi Kou
Chaotianmen Docks
Yangzi Ferry Ticket Office
Chaotianmen Bus Station
Cable Car
Jialing River
Yangzi River
Bus No. 104 Stop
Hongya Dong
Train Ticket Office
Bank of China
Carrefour
Luohan Si
Wangfujing
Huguang Guildhall
Metropolitan Tower
Jiefangbei (Victory Monument)
LINJIANGMEN
JIAOCHANGKOU
Antiques Market
HUANGHUAYUAN
DAXIGOU
Light Rail
Sanxia Museum
People's Concert Hall
Pipa Shan Park
Airlines Office & Airport Bus Stop
NIUJIAOTUO
Train Station
Long-distance Bus Station
BINJIANG LU
SHAANXI LU
XINHUA LU
CANGBAI LU
LINJIANG LU
MINZU LU
WUSI LU
WUYI LU
ZOURONG
BAYI LU
ZHONGHUA LU
MINQUAN LU
MINSHENG LU
QINGNIAN LU
JIEFANG BEI LU
JIEFANG LU
HEPING LU
ZHONGXIN LU
BEIQU LU
HUAYI LI
JIANWEI LU
RENHE JIE
RENMIN LU
ZHONGSHAN YI LU
ZHONGSHAN ER LU
ZHONGSHAN SAN LU
ZHONGSHAN SI LU
ZAOZI GANGYA ZHEN JIE
SHANGQINGSI LU
SIXIN LU
CHANGJIANG LU
NANQU LU
N
0
500 m

Chongqing has been settled since around 1000 BC, with its current name, meaning "Double Celebration", bestowed by former resident **Zhaodun** on his becoming emperor in 1189. The city has a long tradition as a place of defiance against hostile powers, despite being ceded as a nineteenth-century **treaty port** to Britain and Japan. From 1242, Song forces held Mongol invaders at bay for 36 years at nearby **Hechuan**, during the longest continuous campaign on Chinese soil, and it was to Chongqing that the Guomindang government withdrew in 1937, having been driven out of Nanjing by the Japanese. The US military also had a toehold here under **General Stilwell**, who worked alongside the Nationalists until falling out with Chiang Kai-shek in 1944. Though still showing a few wartime scars, since the 1990s Chongqing has boomed; now over two million people rub elbows on the peninsula, with five times that number in the ever-expanding mantle of suburbs and industrial developments spreading away from the river.

Arrival and city transport

Chongqing centres on its 4km-long **peninsula**, whose downtown area surrounds the eastern **Jiefangbei** commercial district; **Chaotianmen docks**, where Yangzi ferries (see below) pull in, are just a short walk away at the eastern tip of the peninsula.

Moving on from Chongqing

Buses to Chengdu, Langzhong, Leshan, Emei Shan, Dazu, Zigong, Yibin, Changning (for the Shunan Bamboo Sea) and beyond depart through the day from Chongqing's main long-distance bus station; it's a crowded place, but buying tickets is easy enough.

Adjacent **Chongqing train station** has a single, overnight service to Chengdu (slower than the bus, but you save the price of a hotel room) and useful links through to Kunming, Guiyang, Xi'an, Beijing, Shanghai and beyond. The **North train station** has express trains to Chengdu (2hr; ¥100), by far the quickest way to get there. If you're heading to any towns along the Yangzi – to catch the hydrofoil between Wanzhou and Yichang for instance – you'll need the adjacent long-distance bus station. Note that you can buy **train tickets** for a ¥5 mark-up at the Yangzi Ferry Terminal, and also through a street-level booth in the building on the corner of Minzu and Wusi Lu.

By air, there are daily departures to Chengdu, Guiyang, Kunming and provincial capitals across China; buy tickets and catch the **airport bus** (6am–8.30pm; ¥15) at the airlines office on Zhongshan Lu.

Yangzi ferries

Public ferries and luxury cruise-boats through the Three Gorges to Yichang depart daily year-round from the **ferry terminal** at Chaotianmen's eastern tip. The main tourist season, when you might have trouble getting tickets for next-day departures, is May through to October.

Luxury cruisers cost upwards of ¥3000 per person and need to be booked through a reputable agent, preferably overseas, though you can also try out tour desks at upmarket hotels in Chongqing.

Buy tickets for **public ferries** either through an agent – such as accommodation in Xi'an, Chengdu or Chongqing – or at the ferry terminal at Chaotianmen (daily 8am–5pm), where electronic boards in Chinese show current timetables and prices. As a guide, ferry fares from Chongqing to Yichang cost approximately ¥850 per person for a double with bathroom, ¥540 for a bed in a quad, down to ¥150 for a bunk in a sixteen-berth dorm. Buy tickets for the **hydrofoil to Yichang** (6hr; ¥300) from the same places as public ferry tickets. The hydrofoil port is actually downstream at **Wanzhou** (see p.786), and buses to the port (3hr; ¥100) generally depart from Chongqing's North train station – ask when you buy your ticket.

The city's seething **main long-distance bus station** (重庆长途汽车站, *chóngqìng chángtú qìchēzhàn*) and **Chongqing train station** (重庆火车站, *chóngqìng huǒchēzhàn*) are on a complex traffic flow near river level at the western end of the peninsula. Bus #503, #120 or #68 will get you to **Chaotianmen bus station** (朝天门汽车站, *cháotiānmén qìchēzhàn*) at the peninsula's tip. Arriving at the **North train station** (重庆火车北站, *chóngqìng huǒchē běizhàn*), 5km from the peninsula – there's another long-distance bus station here too – catch bus #141 to Chaotianmen bus station, or, if it's finished, the light rail line to Jiefangbei. The **airport** is 30km west, with an airport bus (daily 6am–8.30pm; ¥15) running to Shangqing Si district, near the Sanxia Museum and light rail stations.

Chongqing's gradients and horrendous road interchanges mean that nobody uses bicycles. **City buses** (¥1–2) are comprehensive if slow, though there's also a nippy **light-rail network** (轻轨, *qīngguǐ*) handy for reaching several sights, with one line running along the north side of the peninsula and down to the city's southwest, and another handful under construction. Trains run every six minutes from 7am to 7pm and cost under ¥3 a ride, depending on distance; the stations can be very hard to find, though. **Taxis** cost ¥7 to hire and, while drivers aren't too unscrupulous, it won't hurt to be seen studying a map along the way.

Accommodation

Given that the ferry is the main reason to come to Chongqing, it makes sense to stay near the dock up in the peninsula's eastern end around Jiefangbei and Chaotianmen. There's little **budget accommodation**, however; most places are mid-range or upmarket – though everywhere discounts during the winter, when few tourists are in town.

Chung King (重庆饭店, *chóngqìng fàndiàn*) 41–43 Xinhua Lu ⓣ023/63916666, ⓦwww.chungkinghotel.cn. Renovated Art Deco building, though rooms are the standard urban Chinese model, albeit comfy enough. Tours groups tend to end up here. ❻

Huatie (华铁宾馆, *huátiě bīnguǎn*) Between the main bus and train stations ⓣ023/61603518. This is a well-run budget hotel managed by the railways, but the area is grotty. Dorm beds ¥35, rooms ❸

Intercontinental (重庆洲际酒店, *chóngqìng zhōujì jiǔdiàn*) 101 Minzu Lu ⓣ023/89066888, ⓦwww.intercontinental.com. Business hotel with good-sized rooms, coolly professional service, and a lobby café with piano and cream cakes. ❾

JW Marriott 77 Qingnian Lu ⓣ023/63888888, ⓦwww.marriot.com/ckgcn. Close to the centre, though the immediate streets are a little grotty. Nightclub complex over the road, city views from the *Manhattan Steakhouse* on the 39th floor, and the lobby café has weekly seafood buffets. ❽

Motel 168 (莫泰连锁旅店, *mòtài liánsuǒ lǚdiàn*) 52 Cangbai Lu ⓣ023/63849999, ⓦwww.motel168.com. The usual friendly deal with spacious rooms at bargain rates (if you call ahead), though rooms are subterranean and only the pricier ones have windows. ❹

Tina's Hostel (重庆老街客栈青年旅舍, *chóngqìng lǎojiē kèzhàn qīngnián lǚshè*) 149 Zhongxing Lu ⓣ023/86219188, ⓦwww.cqhostel.com. This place isn't easy to find, tucked down an alley near the antiques market, and it's in a shabby area, probably due for reclamation. Having said this, the hostel itself is in a nicely converted old building, the owner and staff are helpful and speak good English, and the food is above average. Dorms from ¥25, rooms ❸

Yangtze River Hostel (玺院国际青年旅舍, *xǐyuàn guójì qīngnián lǚshè*) 80 Changbin Lu ⓣ023/63104270, ⓦwww.chongqinghostels.com. Antique-style wood-and-grey-brick building, well located near the guildhall and within a short walk or bus ride of Chaotianmen docks and the main bus station. All the usual hostel facilities, with variable quality doubles. The staff are a bit vague, but helpful with information and tours. Dorms ¥30, rooms ❸

Yudu (渝都大酒店, *yúdū dàjiǔdiàn*) 168 Bayi Lu ⓣ023/63828888, ⓦwww.cqyuduhotel.com. Renovated older place and very comfortable; popular and a good deal out of season when you can get half the rack rate. ❻

The peninsula

During its Qing-dynasty heyday, the **peninsula** was Chongqing, an enormously rich port with mighty walls, temples, pagodas and public buildings. Not much of these times survive, largely thanks to Japanese saturation bombing during WWII, and the peninsula as a whole is shambolic – most development seems to be targeting Chongqing's newer, western suburbs – though it's being modernized to resemble a miniature Hong Kong, complete with skyscrapers, hills and a profit-hungry populace.

Jiefangbei and around

Isolated by a broad, paved pedestrian square and glassy modern tower blocks, **Jiefangbei** (解放碑, *jiěfàngbēi*) the Victory Monument – actually a clocktower – marks the peninsula's social and commercial heart. Northeast along Minzu Lu, **Luohan Si** (罗汉寺, *luóhàn sì*; daily 8am–6pm; ¥10) is named for its **luohan hall**, a maze of 524 life-sized, grotesque statues of Buddhist saints. The excellent **vegetarian restaurant** is open at lunchtime.

Across the road and around the corner from the temple, a **cable-car station** (嘉陵江索道, *jiālíng jiāng suǒdào*; ¥2.5) on Cangbai Lu offers rides high across the Jialing River to northern Chongqing; there's another cable car over the Yangzi (长江索道, *chángjiāng suǒdào*; ¥2.5) from Xinhua Lu. Views from either take in river traffic, trucks collecting landfill in low-season mud, and distant hills – merely faint grey silhouettes behind the haze. Across from the Cangbai Lu cable-car station, **Hongya Dong** (洪崖洞传统风貌区, *hóngyádòng chuántǒng fēngmào qū*) is a multilevel entertainment area with antique flourishes built into the cliffside facing the river; food stalls are probably its biggest attraction, though there are plenty of souvenir shops too.

To spy on more waterfront activity, head down to **Chaotianmen docks** (朝天门码头, *cháotiānmén mǎtóu*) a five-minute walk downhill from Luohan Si along Xinhua Lu. The paved **viewing area** on the high bank overlooking the tip of the peninsula makes a great perch to look down on **Yangzi ferries** and barges moored along the river.

Huguang Guildhall

The **Huguang Guildhall** (湖广会馆, *húguǎng huìguǎn*; daily 9am–6pm; ¥30; audio-guide ¥10 plus deposit), uphill in the back streets off Binjiang Lu, was built in 1759 as a hotel and meeting point for merchants from Jiangxi, Hunan and Hubei. Surrounded by a high, warm yellow wall, the complex comprises a dozen or more halls, atriums, ornate gateways and florid roof designs, now converted into a museum of Qing-dynasty trade. Cross the road in front and walk down to the river, and you pass through a surviving fragment of Chongqing's **old city wall**, via a heavy stone gateway and staircase.

The west end

The peninsula's west end is mostly a business district, but there are a couple of sights to visit, both close to the **Zengjiayan light-rail station** (曾家岩站, *zēngjiāyán zhàn*) – catch the train from **Linjiangmen station** (临江门站, *línjiāngmén zhàn*), just west of Jiefangbei. The mighty **Peoples' Concert Hall** (人民大礼堂, *rénmín dà lǐtáng*) on Renmin Lu was built in the 1950s along the lines of Beijing's Temple of Heaven, and accommodates four thousand opera-goers in the circular, green-tiled rotunda. Facing it across a porphyry-paved plaza, the **Sanxia Museum** (三峡博物馆, *sānxiá bówùguǎn*; daily 9am–5pm, last entry 4pm; free) commemorates Chongqing's regional history over four floors. Picks here include the Three Gorges Hall, with beautifully arranged dioramas of gorge scenery and a range of archeological finds; the Ba-Yu Hall, which covers everything from pre-human fossils to a marvellous array of Eastern Han tomb bricks; and the Li Chunli Hall, a donated collection of exquisite antique porcelain and paintings. You would, however, have to be very interested in period photos of Communist heroes to get much out of the "Anti Japanese Days (Savage Bombing in Chongqing)" Hall.

West along the Jialing River

Two worthwhile sights lie west of Chongqing's peninsula along a 12km strip of the Jialing River: the wartime US command centre at the **Stilwell Museum**, and antique streets at the one-time port town of **Ciqi Kou**. Both can be tied into a single trip using the light rail and city buses, but give yourself enough time – it can take well over an hour to get to Ciqi Kou from the centre.

The Stilwell and Flying Tigers museums

Just outside the peninsula on Jialingxin Lu, the **Stilwell Museum** (¥10) occupies the former home of General Joseph Stilwell, Chief Commander of the US forces' China, Burma and India operations from 1942 until 1944. Catch the light rail to **Fotuguan station** (佛图关站, *fótúguān zhàn*), then walk 250m downhill along the road to the museum.

Stilwell had served as a military attaché in China during the 1930s, and during the war had to coordinate the recapture of Burma and the re-establishment of overland supply lines into China from India. He was also caught up in keeping the shaky Nationalist-Communist alliance together, and his insistence that equal consideration be given to both the Guomindang and CCP caused him to fall out with Chiang Kai-shek. The modernist 1930s building has been decked out in period furniture, with informative photo displays charting Stilwell's career.

Opposite the entrance to the Stilwell Museum, the little **Flying Tigers Museum** (飞虎队展览馆, *fēihǔduì zhǎnlǎnguǎn*; March–Oct only; donation) is dedicated to the "American Volunteer Group of the Chinese Air Force", better known as the Flying Tigers, which formed under General Chennault in 1941 to protect supply flights over the "hump" of the Himalayas between Burma and China. There are maps and photos of pilots and their P-40 Tomahawk fighter planes painted with tigers' eyes and teeth, and the rear of the building has been turned into a pricey gallery selling contemporary Chinese paintings.

Ciqi Kou

Though well within the modern city's boundaries, **CIQI KOU** (磁器口, *cíqì kǒu*) a former porcelain production centre and port, incredibly retains a handful of flagstoned, one-hundred-year-old streets and wooden buildings. At weekends and holidays the place reaches critical mass with visitors; try to come mid-week. **Bus** #808 from the train-bus station, via the road below the Stilwell museum, or buses #215, #262 and #265 from Chaotianmen bus station, drop you outside the village gates. On your right, **Zhongjia Yuan** (¥4) is an old *siheyuan*, or courtyard house, worth a quick browse for its antique furniture, clothing and carvings in each room. Then you're into Ciqi Kou's crowded alleys and lanes, thronged with touristy crafts shops (selling embroideries and romantic paintings of Ciqi Kou), old-style teahouses featuring traditional music recitals, snack stalls and small restaurants. On sunny days, many people head down to the river, where there's a beach of sorts and thousands of deckchairs.

Eating and drinking

Chongqing's centre is alive with canteens and food stalls, and at meal times already busy side streets and markets become obstacle courses of plastic chairs, low tables and wok-wielding cooks. Local tastes lean towards Sichuanese *xiaochi*; a local speciality is the use of puréed raw garlic as a dressing, which only the Sichuanese could get away with. **Hotpot** is believed to have originated here, with the basic ingredients arriving on plates, not skewers, so the pots are divided up into compartments to prevent everyone's portions getting mixed up.

The restaurants below provide a good introduction to Chongqing's culinary potential; around Jiefangbei, **café** chains such as *Shangdao*, and a *KFC*, are your best bets for non-Sichuanese fare. Chongqing Beer is the local brew, served in squat, brown-glass bottles. For **nightlife**, head to the entertainment complex opposite the *JW Marriott* hotel, home to a stack of nightclubs, open from 9pm until late; the *Cotton Club* (面花酒乐吧, *miànhuā jiǔlè ba*) and *Celtic Man* pub, with live bands most nights, are the most popular.

Haochi Jie (好吃街小排档, *hǎochī jiē xiǎo páidǎng*) Bayi Lu. Bright, noisy restaurant serving steamers, small plates and bowlfuls of local snacks: cold spicy noodles, steamed spareribs, cold-dressed vegetables and the like. Point to displayed food or use the photo menu. Inexpensive except for beer.

Hongya Dong Cangbai Lu (see p.781). Level 4 of this cliffside development is a "food street", full of canteens serving snacks for a few yuan each, along with the *Xiao Tian E* (小天鹅火锅城, *xiǎotiāné huǒguō chéng*), rated as one of the best hotpot restaurants in Chongqing.

Luohan Si Luohan Si (see p.781). A comfy vegetarian temple restaurant serving everything from humble *douhua* (soft tofu served with a chilli relish), to imitation spareribs or smoked goose. The menu has pictures, and some staff speak English. You can eat well here for ¥30/person.

Ninth Heaven (九重天饭店, *jiǔchóngtiān fàndiàn*) 29F, *Yudu Hotel*. The Sichuanese food here is competent and tasty, if a little expensive – try the "rabbit threads" in cut buns and mountain mushrooms with cold bamboo shoots – but the bonus is that the restaurant revolves, with the city looking its best after dark. Count on ¥75/person.

Niushan Huoguo (牛山火锅, *niúshān huǒguō*) Wuyi Lu. Seemingly the last of the fast-and-furious hotpot shacks that once lined this street, where you bump elbows with your fellow diners while dipping skewers into boiling hot, chilli-laced oil. Inexpensive and unconcerned about hygiene.

Shancheng Tangyuan (山城汤圆, *shānchéng tāngyuán*) Literally a hole in the wall on the west side of Bayi Lu. Tiny shack famed city-wide for its glutinous rice dumplings at ¥3/serving.

Waipo Qiao (外婆桥, *wàipó qiáo*) 7F Metropolitan Tower, 68 Zourong Lu ☎023/63835988. On top of one of the city's swishest shopping malls, this excellent restaurant has three separate rooms, an inexpensive one for snacks, one for hotpot (with the ingredients floated past you in little boats) and a smart one for proper dining. They're all good and have bilingual photo menus.

Listings

Airlines The airlines office (daily 7.30am–6pm; ☎023/63862643 or 63602900) is on Zhongshan San Lu. An atmosphere of imminent closure hangs over the building, but for now it's where the airport buses arrive and depart from. You should be able to buy airline tickets through accommodation tour agents for the same price.

Banks and exchange The main Bank of China is in the centre of the peninsula on Zhongshan Yi Lu, though the Jiefangbei area is full of branches and ATMs.

Bookshops The huge Xinhua Bookstore just west of Jiefangbei on Zourong Lu has Chinese-language maps and guides on the first floor, and a small stock of English-language titles on the fourth floor.

Consulates Britain, Suite 2801, Metropolitan Tower, 68 Zourong Lu (☎023/63691500); Canada, Suite 1705, Metropolitan Tower, 68 Zourong Lu (☎023/63738007); Cambodia, Suite 1902, Building A, 9 Yanghe Lu, north of the river in Jiangbei District (☎023/63113666); Denmark, Suite 3101, Metropolitan Tower, 68 Zourong Lu (☎023/63810832).

Internet Free terminals at the hostels, plus most accommodation has wi-fi or ADSL sockets in rooms.

Mail There's a post office (daily 8.30am–9.30pm) in Jiefangbei behind all the mobile-phone sellers at 5 Minquan Lu.

PSB A long way north of the centre at 555 Huanglong Lu, Yubei District (☎023/63961916,

Ⓕ63961917), and its reputation for granting visa extensions is not good – best go elsewhere if possible.

Shopping The Metropolitan Tower at 68 Zourong Lu has smart international boutiques on the lower floors, an ice-rink on the 6th, and restaurants throughout; nearby Wangfujing has more of the same, plus a cinema. For all manner of food – including a few Western imports – head to Carrefour, just off Minzu Lu near Luohan Si. For a good browse through four floors of wooden screens, stone basins, Mao-era mementos, comics, pottery and ceramics, try the antiques market (收藏品市场, *shōuzáng pǐn shìchǎng*), inside what looks like an abandoned 1960s department store at 75 Zhongxin Lu.

The Yangzi River: Chongqing to Yichang

Rising in the mountains above Tibet, the **Yangzi** links together seven provinces as it sweeps 6400km across the country to spill its muddy waters into the East China Sea, making it the third-longest flow in the world. Appropriately, one of the Yangzi's Chinese names is **Chang Jiang**, the Long River, though above Yibin it's generally known as **Jinsha Jiang** (River of Golden Sands).

Although people have travelled along the Yangzi since recorded history, it was not, until recently, an easy route into Sichuan. The river's most dangerous stretch was the 200km-long **Three Gorges** (三峡, *sānxiá*) where the waters were squeezed between vertical limestone cliffs over fierce rapids, spread between **Baidicheng** and Yichang in Hubei province. Well into the twentieth century, nobody could negotiate this stretch of river alone; steamers couldn't pass at all, and small boats had to be hauled literally bit by bit through the rapids by teams of **trackers**, in a journey that could take several weeks, if the boat made it at all.

Cruising the Yangzi River

Chongqing is the departure point for the two-day cruise downriver through the **Three Gorges** to Yichang. There are two main **cruise options**, both of which run year-round: relatively inexpensive public ferries, which stop along the way to pick up passengers; and upmarket cruise ships, which only stop at tour sites. For **prices** from Chongqing to Yichang, along with practical information on buying both ferry and cruise-ship tickets, see p.779. You can also reach all the places covered here by **bus** from Chongqing, though roads get worse the further east you go.

Public ferries are crowded and noisy, with berths starting at **first class** – a double cabin with bathroom – and descending in varying permutations through triples and quads with shared toilets, to a bed in sixteen-person cabins; even first-class cabins are small and functional. **Timing** is important: try to avoid leaving Chongqing between 10am and noon, as you'll hit the first gorge too early and the third too late to see much. Not all ferries pull in at all ports, and schedules can change en route to compensate for delays, so it's possible that you'll miss some key sights. At each stop, departure times are announced in Chinese. **Meals** (buy tickets from the mid-deck office) are cheap, basic and only available for a short time at 7am, 10am and 6pm, though there's plenty available onshore at stops. Bring snacks, and in winter, **warm clothing**. Many tourists complain of unhelpful or plain useless tour guides, and of being harassed by ferry staff to buy expensive on-board tickets for observation decks when access is, in fact, free or much cheaper than advertised.

Alternatively, you could travel in style on a **cruise ship**. These vessels verge on five-star luxury, with comfortable cabins, glassed-in observation decks, games rooms and real restaurants. They're usually booked out by tour parties during peak season, though at other times you can often wrangle discounts and get a berth at short notice.

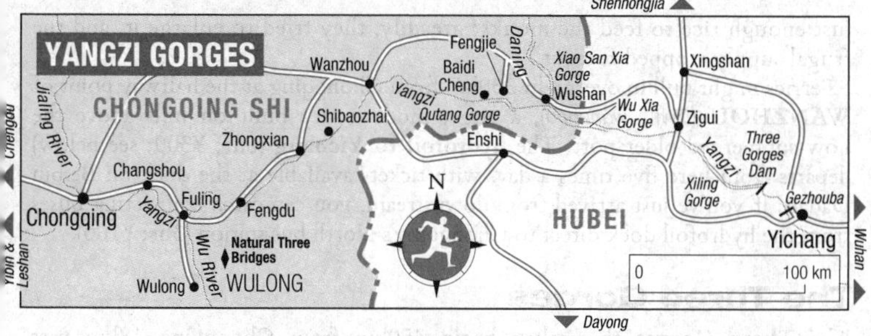

All this is very much academic today, however, as the new **Three Gorges Dam** above Yichang (see p.786) has raised water levels through the gorges by up to 175m, effectively turning the Chongqing–Yichang stretch into a huge lake and allowing **public ferries** and **cruise boats** easy access to the scenery. While rising waters have submerged some of the landscape – not to mention entire towns – many settlements have been rebuilt on higher ground, and many historical sites have been relocated or preserved one way or the other.

Chongqing to Wanzhou

The cruise's initial 250km, before the first of the Three Gorges begins at Baidicheng, takes in hilly farmland along the riverbanks, with the first likely stop 172km from Chongqing at south bank **FENGDU** (丰都, *fēngdū*) the "Ghost City". On the opposite side of the Yangzi, **Ming Shan Park** (名山公园, *míngshān gōngyuán*; ¥80) is a hillside covered in monuments to Tianzi, King of the Dead; the main temple here, **Tianzi Dian** (天子殿, *tiānzǐ diàn*), is crammed full of colourful demon statues and stern-faced judges of hell.

Wulong

Some 90km south of Fengdu along the Guizhou border, **Wulong** (武隆, *wǔlóng*) is a new national park enclosing a massive, rugged area of limestone sinkholes, caves and river systems. The access point is little **Wulong town** (武隆县, *wǔlóng xiàn*), on the Chongqing–Huai Hua rail line and long-distance bus routes from Fengdu. The *Hongfu Fandian* (宏福饭店, *hóngfú fàndiàn*; ⓣ023/64501666; ❹), on the corner of main street Wuxian Lu and Baiyang Lu, is overpriced but decent, and touts around the bus and train stations can lead you to cheaper places.

Buses from Wulong town's Baiyang Lu bus station run north into the national park through the day; the place to aim for at present is **Natural Three Bridges** (天生三桥, *tiānshēng sān qiáo*; daily 9am–6.30pm; bus from Wulong town ¥20; entry, including transport inside the park, ¥95), about 50 minutes away. Once inside the park, buses drop you off at a two-hour circuit walk through a system of colossal, collapsed tunnels and caves; the Tang-style buildings at the bottom of one sinkhole are sets from Zhang Yimou's period bodice-ripper *Curse of the Golden Flower*.

Zhongxian and Wanzhou

A further 70km along the Yangzi from Fengdu, **ZHONGXIAN** (中县, *zhōngxiàn*) is famous for **Shibaozhai** (石宝寨, *shíbǎozhài*), a 220m-high rocky buttress a few kilometres downstream. Grafted onto its side – and protected from new water levels by an embankment – is the twelve-storey, bright-red **Lanruo Dian** (兰若殿, *lánruò diàn*; ¥50), a pagoda built in 1819. The temple above dates to 1750, famed for a hole in its granary wall through which poured just enough rice to feed the monks; greedily, they tried to enlarge it, and the frugal supply stopped forever.

Ferries might pull in overnight 330km from Chongqing at the halfway point of **WANZHOU** (万州, *wànzhōu*), a large, modern city built on hills above the now-submerged older port. The **hydrofoil to Yichang** (6hr; ¥300; see below) departs from here five times a day, with tickets available at the dock on Beibin Dadao; if you've just arrived from downstream, you can catch connecting buses from the hydrofoil dock direct to Chongqing's North bus station (3hr; ¥100).

The Three Gorges

The **Three Gorges** themselves begin 450km from Chongqing 18km past **FENGJIE town** (奉节, *fèngjié*) at **Baidi Cheng** (白帝城, *báidì chéng*; ¥70), a fortified island strategically located right at the mouth of the first gorge. Baidi Cheng is closely associated with events of the *Romance of the Three Kingdoms* (see p.413); it was here in 265 AD that **Liu Bei** died after failing to avenge his sworn brother Guan Yu in the war against Wu. These events are recalled at the **Baidi temple** (白帝庙, *báidì miào*), where there's a tableau of Liu Bei on his deathbed, and paths up to lookout points into the gorge.

Beyond Baidicheng, the river pours through a narrow slash in the cliffs and into **Qutang Gorge** (瞿塘峡, *qútáng xiá*), the shortest at just 8km long, but also the narrowest and fiercest, its once-angry waters described by the Song poet Su Dongpo as "a thousand seas in one cup". The vertical cliffs, rising to a sharp peak on the north bank, are still impressive despite the new water levels.

On the far side of Qutang, **WUSHAN** (巫山, *wūshān*) marks a half-day detour north up the **Daning River** through the **Three Little Gorges** (小三峡, *xiǎo sānxiá*). This 33km excursion offers narrower, tighter and steeper scenery than along the Yangzi, particularly through the awesome **Longmen Gorge**. When you arrive in Wushan, make your way to the Xiao San Xia dock, where you pay ¥250 for a cruise up the Three Little Gorges in a modern, glass-topped canal boat.

Wu Gorge to Yichang

Wushan also sits at the mouth of 45km-long **Wu Gorge** (巫峡, *wū xiá*), where the goddess **Yao Ji** and her eleven sisters quelled some unruly river dragons and then turned themselves into mountains, thoughtfully positioned to help guide ships downriver. Out the other side and in Hubei province, **ZIGUI** (秭归, *zīguī*) was the birthplace of the poet **Qu Yuan**, whose suicide a couple of millennia ago is commemorated throughout China by dragon-boat races. Zigui is also where 76km-long **Xiling Gorge** (西陵峡, *xīlíng xiá*) begins. The Xiling stretch was once the most dangerous: Westerners passing through in the nineteenth century described the shoals as forming weirs across the river, the boat fended away from threatening rocks by trackers armed with iron-shod bamboo poles, as it rocked through into the sunless, narrow chasm. Nowadays vessels cruise through with ease, sailing on to a number of smaller gorges, some with splendid names – Sword and Book, Ox Liver and Horse Lung – suggested by the rock formations.

At the end, the monstrous **Three Gorges Dam** (三峡坝, *sānxiá bà*) at **Sandouping** is another possible stopover, with regular minibuses running tourists from the dock to the dam site (see p.437). Just downstream from here is the final port of call, **Yichang**. Aside from catching fast buses on from Yichang to Wuhan, or trains to Xi'an, you could also visit the **Shennongjia Forest Reserve** in Hubei's mountainous north – for details, see Chapter 7.

Western Sichuan

Sichuan's western half, extending north to Gansu, south to Yunnan and west to Tibet, is in every respect an exciting place to travel. The countryside couldn't be farther from the mild Chengdu plains, with the western highlands forming some of China's most imposing scenery – broad grasslands grazed by yaks and horses, ravens tumbling over snowbound gullies and passes, and unforgettable views of mountain ranges rising up against crisp blue skies.

Though larger towns throughout the west have to a certain extent been settled by Han and Hui (Muslims) – the latter spread between their major populations in adjoining provinces – historically the region was not part of Sichuan at all but was known as **Kham**, a set of small states covering what is now western Sichuan, plus the fringes of Qinghai and Yunnan. The Tibetans who live here, called the **Khampas**, speak their own dialect, and see themselves as distinct from Tibetans further west – it wasn't until the seventeenth century, during the aggressive rule of the **Fifth Dalai Lama**, Lobsang Gyatso (see p.893), that monasteries here were forcibly converted to the dominant Gelugpa sect and the people brought under Lhasa's thumb. The Khampas retain their tough, independent reputation today, and culturally the region remains emphatically Tibetan, containing not only some of the country's most important lamaseries, but also an overwhelmingly Tibetan population – indeed, statistically a far greater percentage than in Tibet proper. For details on Tibetan food, language and religious thought, see the relevant sections at the start of Chapter 14.

How you explore western Sichuan will depend on your long-term travel plans. If you're heading north out of the province **to Gansu**, you first want to aim for the walled town of **Songpan**, horse-trekking centre and base for excursions to the nearby scenic reserves of **Huanglong** and **Jiuzhaigou**. Beyond Songpan, the road continues north via the monastery town of **Langmusi**, and so over into Gansu province.

Sichuan's immense **far west** is accessed from the administrative capital **Kangding** – itself worth a stopover for easy access to the nearby **Hailuogou glacier** and **Tagong grasslands**, or as a springboard north to pretty **Danba** or the snowcapped peaks of **Siguniang Shan**. Alternatively, you can either weave northwest to Tibet via the monastery towns of **Ganzi** and **Dêgê**, with a faith-inducing mountain pass and Dêgê's **Scripture Printing Hall** as the pick of the sights along the way; or

Visiting monasteries

Among the draws of many towns in western Sichuan are their Tibetan Buddhist **monasteries**, most of which belong to the yellow-hat **Gelugpa sect** – though other sects are represented. Monasteries form huge medieval-looking complexes sprawling over hillsides, with a central core of large, red-walled, gold-roofed **temples** surrounded by a maze of smaller buildings housing monks and staff. Monasteries are **free to enter**, except where noted in the text; if there are no signs to the contrary, assume that **photography** is forbidden inside temples. **Monks** are generally friendly, encouraging you to explore, steering you firmly away from closed areas, and sometimes offering **food and accommodation** – though don't take these for granted. Most importantly, remember to orbit **clockwise** around both individual temples and the complex as a whole (the only exception to this rule being at the region's few Bon temples).

Dog warning

Western Sichuan's wild, open countryside makes for good hiking, but you need to beware of **dogs**. Some of these are just the scrawny mongrels that roam around all Tibetan settlements, including monasteries; carry a pocketful of stones and a good stick, and you should be fine. Guard dogs, however, you need to keep well clear of: you don't want an encounter with a Tibetan mastiff. These are kept chained up as a rule, but don't go near isolated houses or, especially, **nomad tents** without calling out so that people know you're there and will check that their dogs are secure.

head due west to the high-altitude monastic seat of **Litang**, from where you can continue down into Yunnan.

Travel in western Sichuan requires some stamina: journey times between towns are long, roads twist interminably, breakdowns are far from uncommon, and landslides, ice or heavy snow can block roads for days at a time. Almost all the region rises above 2500m – one pass exceeds 5000m – and you'll probably experience the effects of altitude (see p.60). You'll need to carry enough **cash** to see you through, as there are no banks capable of dealing with travellers' cheques. Be aware, too, that **bus fares** are high – sometimes double what you'd expect – and in places you might need to charter **minibuses** to get to your destination. **Horse-trekking** is a popular pastime in the region, too, with well-established operations at Songpan, Siguniang Shan, Tagong and Langmusi, and plenty of ad hoc opportunities elsewhere. As for the **seasons**, the area looks fantastic from spring through to autumn – though warm, weatherproof clothing is essential whatever the time of year. Also note that most of the region is **closed to foreigners through March**, anniversary of various uprisings in Tibet – Songpan and Jiuzhaigou will probably be open, but travel north to Gansu, or to Kangding and far western Sichuan, will probably be impossible.

To Songpan and Gansu

The 500km trip north from Chengdu via **Songpan** to the border with **Gansu** province hauls you through a region that's eminently Tibetan. The border village of **Langmusi** presents a vivid taste of monastic life, while the area's mountainous backdrop is enhanced by vivid blue waters at **Huanglong** and **Jiuzhaigou** reserves, both accessed from Songpan – just note that these are firmly on the Chinese tourist map, and are subject to severe visitor overload between spring and autumn. With this in mind, a few lesser-known reserves, rich in alpine grasslands, waterfalls and views, may be more appealing, and can be reached on **horseback** from Songpan.

In 2008, the area halfway between Chengdu and Songpan was hit by a terrible force-eight **earthquake** centred near the town of Wenchuan. Almost every building in the region was demolished, including all of Wenchuan; 80,000 people lost their lives; whole mountainsides collapsed, taking roads with them; and a panda breeding centre at **Wolong** was destroyed. Rebuilding towns and restoring infrastructure is going to take years, which for visitors means that journey times and routes through the region are unpredictable. At the time of writing, the direct road north from Chengdu was in a very bad state, taking anything between twelve and thirty-six hours to negotiate, and buses **from Chadianzi station** were making a very roundabout eleven-hour journey on good roads, northeast to **Pingwu** (平武, *píngwǔ*) then northwest via Jiuzhaigou to Songpan. This situation won't last for ever, but you might want to check to see whether your bus is going via Songpan or Jiuzhaigou.

Alternatively, **Jiuzhai airport**, 30km outside Songpan, has daily flights to and from Chengdu (at an extortionate ¥1200); a **rail line** to Songpan is also under construction, due for completion in 2013. **Tours** to Huanglong and Jiuzhaigou are offered by every travel agent in Sichuan, but avoid public holidays if you don't want to pay through the nose.

Songpan

SONGPAN (松潘, *sōngpān*) was founded 320km north of Chengdu in Qing times as a garrison town straddling both the Min River and the main road to Gansu. Strategically, it guards the neck of a valley, built up against a stony ridge to the west and surrounded on the remaining three sides by 8m-high stone **walls**. These have been partially restored, and you can walk between the north and east gates and above the south gate. Though increasingly a tourist town, Songpan's **shops**, stocked with handmade woollen blankets, fur-lined jackets, ornate knives, saddles, stirrups, bridles and all sorts of jewellery, cater primarily to local Tibetans and **Qiang**, another mountain-dwelling minority. In spring, Songpan – along with every town in western Sichuan – becomes a marketplace for bizarre **caterpillar fungus** (虫草, *chóng cǎo*) that grows in the mountains and is prized for use in Traditional Chinese Medicine. With luck, locals can find up to ten a day, worth here between ¥10 and ¥80 each (a fifth of their value in eastern China).

Songpan itself forms a small, easily navigated rectangle: the main road, partially pedestrianized, runs for about 750m from the **north gate** (北门, *běimén*) straight down to the **south gate** (南门, *nánmén*) – both mighty stone constructions topped with brightly painted wooden pavilions. Around two-thirds of the way down, covered **Gusong Bridge** (古松桥, *gǔsōng qiáo*) has a roof embellished with painted dragon, bear and flower carvings. Side roads head off to the **east gate** (东大门, *dōng dàmén*) – another monumental construction – and west into a small grid of market lanes surrounding the town's main **mosque** (古清真寺, *gǔ qīngzhēn sì*), an antique wooden affair painted in subdued yellows and greens, catering to the substantial Muslim population (there's another mosque north of town). Just outside the south gate is a **second gateway**, with what would originally have been a walled courtyard between the two, where caravans were inspected for dangerous goods before entering the city proper.

Arrival and information

Jiuzhai airport is 30km to the northeast, with transport waiting for Songpan, Huanglong and Jiuzhaigou. Songpan's **bus station** is about 250m outside the

Horse-trekking in Songpan

The reason to stop in Songpan is to spend a few days **horse-trekking** through the surrounding hills, which harbour hot springs and waterfalls, grassland plateaus, and permanently icy mountains. Shunjiang Horse Treks (☎0837/17231161 or 013909043513), on the main road between the bus station and the north gate, charge ¥220 a person per day, including everything except entry fees to reserves. Accommodation is in tents, and the guides are attentive, though prepare for extreme cold and tasteless food; some groups have bought and slaughtered a goat (¥400) to bolster rations. Note that the friendly veneer of the trekking company's managers disappears rapidly if they're presented with a complaint, so be sure to agree beforehand on exactly what your money is buying.

north gate, with daily departures to Chengdu, Jiuzhaigou, Ma'erkang, Pingwu, Zöigê and Xiahe. **For Langmusi**, Xiahe-bound buses might drop you off on the main road nearby, otherwise catch the 10am Zöigê bus, and with luck you'll just make the 2pm Zöigê-Langmusi service. If that fails, ask at *Emma's Kitchen* (Ⓣ0837/7231088, Ⓔemmachina@hotmail.com; see below), a foreigners' café, which can set up a shared taxi; it also has **internet** access and can provide **information** about local tours and bus times. There's a blind masseur next door to *Emma's* if you're stiff after a tour in the saddle.

Accommodation

Accommodation can be found at the bus station's serviceable *Jiaotong Binguan* (交通宾馆, *jiāotōng bīnguǎn*; Ⓣ0837/17231818; dorms ¥30, rooms ❷); opposite at *Guyun Kezhan* (古韵客栈, *gǔyùn kèzhàn*; Ⓣ0837/17231368; ❷), a Muslim homestay of wooden galleries around a central atrium; and at *Shunjiang Guesthouse* (顺江旅游客栈, *shùnjiāng lǚyóu kèzhàn*; Ⓣ0837/17231201; dorms ¥25, rooms ❷), next to their horse-trekking agency between the bus station and north gate. Songpan's **water** – hot or otherwise – flows at unpredictable times, ditto electricity, so use it when available. The Agricultural Bank of China, about 100m inside the north gate, has an **ATM** accepting credit cards.

Eating

Songpan's **places to eat** revolve around the numerous noodle joints between the north gate and the bus station; some 100m inside the north gate, the *Xingyue Lou* (星月楼, *xīngyuè lóu*) is a Muslim restaurant, serving delicious crisp-roast duck. South of the bus station, *Emma's Kitchen* (see above) serves tasty burgers or barley soup, among other options. *Maoniurou gan* (yak jerky) is sold in shops around town; you should also try *qingke jiu*, local **barley beer**.

Huanglong and Jiuzhaigou Scenic Reserve

Northeast of Songpan, the perpetually snow-clad Min Shan range encloses two separate valleys clothed in thick alpine forests and strung with hundreds of impossibly toned **blue lakes** – said to be the scattered shards of a mirror belonging to the Tibetan goddess **Semo**. Closest to Songpan, **Huanglong**, a string of lakes and small ponds in a calcified valley, is relatively small and can be walked around in a few hours; further north on a separate road, **Jiuzhaigou Scenic Reserve** is grander in every respect and requires a couple of days to see properly. Both are targets of intense tourism – don't come here expecting a quiet commune with nature, as each park clocks up over a million visitors annually.

Huanglong, in theory, can be reached from Songpan by getting a Pingwu-bound bus to drop you off en route (¥36), though in reality this might be impossible and you'll need to rent an eight-seater minibus-taxi (¥300–400). Coming back, Songpan buses pass Huanglong around 2pm or 3pm, and you'll need to be waiting on the roadside. Jiuzhaigou is covered by direct **buses** from Songpan and Chengdu, or from Jiangyou and Guangyuan via **Jiuzhaigou town** (九寨沟县, *jiǔzhàigōu xiàn*), 40km east of the reserve. There is also one bus daily each way between Jiuzhaigou and Huanglong.

Huanglong

Huanglong (黄龙, *huánglóng*; ¥200, plus optional ¥80 for the cable car) lies 60km northeast of Songpan via the **Xuebaoding Pass** below the red rocks of Hongxing Yan. Xuebaoding itself is the Min Shan range's highest peak, a 5588m-high white triangle visible to the east on clear days. On the far side, Huanglong reserve covers over a thousand square kilometres of rough terrain, though the accessible section that everyone comes to see is a 4km-long trough at an average altitude of 3000m, carved out by a now-vanished glacier. Limestone-rich waters flowing down the valley have left yellow calcified deposits between hundreds of shallow blue ponds, and their scaly appearance gives Huanglong – "Yellow Dragon" – its name.

An 8km circuit track on well-made boardwalks over the fragile formations – potentially tiring given the altitude – ascends east up the valley from the main-road **park gates**, through surprisingly thick deciduous woodland, pine forest and, finally, rhododendron thickets. Pick of the scenery includes the broad **Golden Flying Waterfall** and the kilometre-long calcified slope **Golden Sand on Earth**, where the shallow flow tinkles over innumerable ridges and pockmarks. Around 3km along, the small **Middle Temple** (中寺, *zhōng sì*) was once an important centre for **Bon**, Tibet's original religion; today, it seems inactive – even if signs do ask you to circuit to the right in the Bon manner. At the head of the valley, **Huanglong Gusi** (黄龙古寺, *huánglóng gŭsì*) is a slightly grander Qing building, featuring an atrium and two small Taoist halls, dedicated to the local guardian deity. Behind here, a 300m-long bowl is filled with multi-hued blue pools, contrasting brilliantly with the drab olive vegetation; the best views are from a small platform on the slopes above.

Huanglong's only **accommodation** is the upmarket *Huanglong Shanzhuang* (华龙山庄, *huálóng shānzhuāng*; Ⓣ0837/7249333, Ⓦwww.hlszhotel.com; ❻) at the park gates. Hotel aside, food is available at a single **canteen** near the Middle Temple. There are **toilets** all along the trail, along with posts offering free **oxygen** should you find things tough going.

Jiuzhaigou Kou

Around 100km from Songpan or Huanglong, **JIUZHAIGOU KOU** (九寨沟口, *jiŭzhàigōu kŏu*) is a kilometre-wide blob of services either side of the Jiuzhaigou Scenic Reserve park gates comprising accommodation, places to eat, and a **bus depot** with daily services to Chengdu, Ma'erkang, Lanzhou, Songpan, Jiangyou and Guangyuan (all depart 7am–8am; buy tickets in advance from the booth at the depot gates). If you need to get to or from Jiuzhaigou town, 40km east, **shared taxis** shuttle back and forth all day long, charging ¥10 per person.

Accommodation near the park entrance with 24-hour hot water includes the *Ziyou Youth Hostel* (自游国际青年旅舍, *zìyóu guójì qīngnián lǚshě*; Ⓣ0837/7764617; beds ¥35, rooms ❷) and *Grass Roots Hostel* (草根人家, *căogēn rénjiā*; Ⓣ0837/7764922; beds ¥35, rooms ❷), two carbon-copy youth hostels 250m west of the park gates; *MCA* (MCA国际乡村客栈, *MCA guójì xiāngcūn kèzhàn*; Ⓣ0837/7739818; beds ¥80, rooms ❺), more or less behind the bus station and east of the park gates alongside a stream; and the characterless, upmarket *Sheraton* (喜来登国际大酒店, *xĭláidēng guójì dàjiŭdiàn*; Ⓣ0837/7739988, Ⓦwww.starwoodhotels.com; ❾). Better than all these – though 13km west of the park – is *Zhuo Ma's* (Ⓣ013568783012, Ⓦwww.abuluzi.com; ¥180/person including all meals), a **Tibetan homestay** run by the welcoming Zhuo Ma. Call ahead and she'll pick you up from the park area.

For **eating**, the *Guibin Lou's* streamside restaurant is very pleasant, and there are dozens of Chinese places scattered about, but for local Tibetan food served in comfortable surroundings, head to *Abuluzi* (阿布氇孜风情藏餐吧, *ābùluzī fēngqíng zàng cānba*; Ⓣ13568783012), near *MCA* and the *Sheraton*, alongside the stream east of the reserve gates.

Jiuzhaigou Scenic Reserve

Jiuzhaigou Scenic Reserve (¥220/day; unlimited bus use around the park ¥90) was settled centuries ago by Tibetans, whose fenced villages gave Jiuzhaigou (Nine Stockades Gully) its name. Hemmed in by high, snowy peaks, the reserve's valleys form a south-orientated Y-shape, with **lakes** descending them in a series of broad steps, fringed in thick forests – spectacular in the autumn when the gold and red leaves contrast brilliantly with the water, or at the onset of winter in early December, when everything is dusted by snow. The park gets incredibly busy, though – the best you can do is to get in when the gates **open** at 7am and try to stay one step ahead of the hordes. Gates **close** at 5.30pm, and there is no accommodation inside the park. **Boardwalks** connect all the sights and some people plan to save on the bus fare by hiking everywhere, but given the distances involved – over 30km from the gates to the far end – this isn't a realistic option. You can, however, organize **three-day treks** through the adjacent Zharu Valley with Jiuzhaigou's **eco-tourism department** (¥1580, including entry fees, guides, food and all camping gear; ⓣ0837/7737811, ⓦwww.jiuzhai.com); the route circuits 4500m-high Zhayi Zhaga mountain.

It's 14km from the park gates at Jiuzhaigou Kou to the centre of the reserve around **Nuorilang**, a journey that passes a marshy complex of pools at the foot of imposing Dêgê Shan that forms the **Shuzheng lakes** (树正海, *shùzhèng hǎi*), the largest group in the reserve and cut part-way along by the 20m **Shuzheng Falls**.

At **Nuorilang** (诺日朗, *nuòrìlǎng*) you'll find a tourist **village** where you can don Tibetan garb and pose on horseback for photos; a **visitors' centre** with set lunches at around ¥60–80; and Jiuzhaigou's most famous cascades, the **Nuorilang Falls** (诺日朗瀑布, *nuòrìlǎng pùbù*). They look best from the road, framed by trees as water forks down over the strange, yellow crystalline rockfaces.

The road forks east and west at Nuorilang, with both forks around 18km long. The **eastern branch** first passes **Pearl Beach Falls** (珠滩瀑布, *zhūtān pùbù*), where a whole hillside has calcified into an ankle-deep cascade similar to Huanglong, but the main attraction here is the **Primeval Forest** (原始森林, *yuánshǐ sēnlín*), a dense and very atmospheric belt of ancient conifers right at the end of the road. There's less to see along the **western branch** from Nuorilang, but don't miss the stunning **Five-coloured Lake** (五彩池, *wǔcǎi chí*), which, for sheer intensity, if not scale, is unequalled in the park.

Zöigê, Langmusi and on to Gansu

Songpan sits just east of the vast, marshy **Aba grasslands**, which sprawl over the Sichuan, Gansu and Qinghai borders. Resting at around 3500m and draining into the headwaters of the Yellow River, the grasslands are home to nomadic herders and lots of **birdlife** – including black-necked cranes and golden eagles – and form a corridor between Sichuan and **Gansu** province. Buses from Songpan run north to the grassland town of **Zöigê** and over the border, with Tibetan monasteries at **Langmusi** offering a prime reason to stop off along the way.

Around 150km northwest of Songpan at the grasslands' northernmost edge, **ZÖIGÊ** (诺尔盖, *nuòěrgài*) is a tidy collection of markets and shops along Shuguang Lu and parallel Shangye Jie. The town's low-key **Daza monastery** (達扎寺, *dázā sì*) is worth a visit, but most people only spend time in Zöigê because they've missed the bus out.

For **accommodation**, the clean and quiet *Ruoliang Binguan* (若粮宾馆, *ruòliáng bīnguǎn*; ⓣ0837/2298081; ❷) and *Zangle Binguan* (藏乐宾馆, *zánglè bīnguǎn*; ⓣ0837/2298685; ❷) on Shangye Jie both advertise constant hot water; while the *Nuoergai Dajiudian* (诺尔盖大酒店, *nuòěrgài dàjiǔdiàn*; ⓣ0837/2291998; ❺) is the town's upmarket option. There are plenty of places to grab a simple meal, or you can just hang out at the *A-Lang* **teahouse** across from the post office on Shangye Jie. The **bus station** on Shuguang Lu has dawn departures for Songpan, Jiuzhaigou, Chengdu, Ma'erkang, Langmusi and Hezuo (in Gansu).

Chinese festivals

Whatever their origins, Chinese festivals are a time for family get-togethers and feasting. They're best experienced in the countryside – rural folk seem to observe them with more spirit than sophisticated city types – but wherever you are you're likely to enjoy dancing and a raucous sing-along, and you can generally bet on bright lights and pyrotechnics being involved somewhere. As well as the national events, every minority has its own celebrations, which are well worth seeking out. Just don't expect not to be invited to join in.

Burning fake money during Qingming ▲

Mid-Autumn Festival lanterns, Beijing ▼

Qingming

The **Qingming** festival, or **Mourning Day**, held on April 5 each year, is a time to honour the dead by freshening up graves and burning fake paper money and incense. Yet, as a springtime festival, it's also regarded as a time of renewal – a propitious time to plant trees and go on outings. Its bittersweet character is captured by Tang-dynasty poet Du Mu:

A drizzling rain falls like tears on the Mourning Day;
The mourner's heart is breaking on his way.
Where can a hostel be found to drown his sadness?
A cowherd points to Xing Hua village in the distance.

Mid-Autumn Festival

The **Mid-Autumn Festival** falls on the fifteenth day of the eighth lunar month, when the moon is at its fullest and brightest. It's a celebration of abundance and togetherness – sweet mooncakes are eaten, lanterns lit, and the introspective pleasure of moon-gazing indulged.

The Chinese say that the moon has a woman in it. Everyone knows a story about how she got there, though you'll rarely hear the same one twice. One of the more popular has it that she was the wife of the hero Hou Yi. The Mistress of Heaven gave Hou Yi an elixir that would allow him to join her in the sky. Not wishing to part with his wife, Chang'e, he refused to drink it, and gave it to his spouse for safekeeping. But villains heard about it and tried to steal it; to escape them, Chang'e drank it and found herself carried up to heaven. Now, she's trapped on the moon in the company (for no clear reason) of a rabbit; both are supposed to be visible as dark shadows on the moon's surface. Once a year, at the time of the Mid-Autumn Festival, she and Hou Yi are allowed to visit one another, meeting by means of a heavenly bridge – the Milky Way.

Chongyang

The ninth day of the ninth lunar month – usually in October – marks **Chongyang**, or the **Double Ninth Festival**. Traditionally, the number nine was thought to be *yang*, meaning masculine or positive, and that made the ninth of the ninth a dangerous and powerful day; to ward off bad luck, people head for the heights – you'll see plenty of day-trippers climbing towers and holy mountains. The less energetic can make do with eating cakes – cake (*gao*) being a homonym for "height" – with the best Chongyang cakes, of course, having nine layers. Good luck is further courted with plants associated with cleanliness; chrysanthemum wine is drunk and *zhuyu*, dogwood, carried or worn.

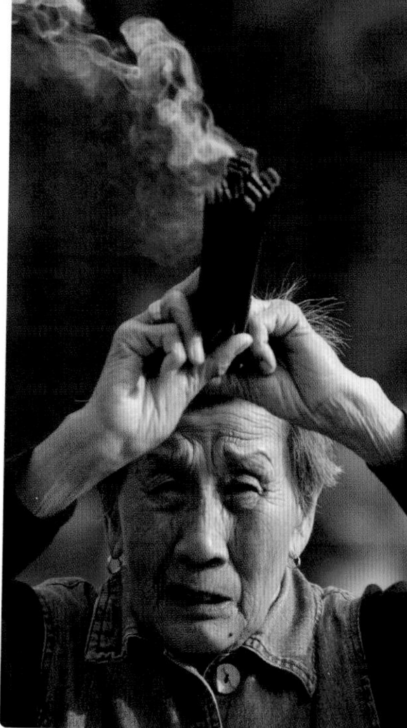

▲ Double Ninth Festival participant, Nanjing

▼ Dragon Boat races, Hong Kong

Dragon Boat Festival

Known in Chinese as *duanwu jie* or *chongwu*, "double fifth", after its date in the lunar calendar (some time in June), this festival commemorates the drowning suicide of the patriotic scholar-official Qu Yuan in 278 BC, and the unsuccessful race to save him in dragon boats. At least, this is the official version – some minority groups such as Guizhou's Miao people tell different stories about the festival's origin (such as battles against the Han Chinese).

Races take place across the country – the liveliest occur in Hong Kong – with teams of rowers powering long, narrow, and impressive-looking dragon-prowed vessels, after which much wine and *zongzi* rice packets are consumed in celebration.

Water Splashing Festival ▲

Midi Music Festival, Beijing ▲

Litang Horse Festival ▼

Five festivals to see

Though not as famous as Chinese New Year or the Mid-Autumn Festival, the following five local events offer a chance to see a more intimate side of traditional Chinese culture. Foreigners are rare sights at some, so don't expect to sit quietly on the sidelines – you'll probably be dragged in to participate at some point.

The Bai people of Dali hold the **Dali Spring Fair** (see p.700) every April. For once, locals outnumber the tourists as minority folk from surrounding villages flock into the town for five days of trading, singing and dancing.

Never mind those glorified wet T-shirt competitions put on for visiting tourists; the real Dai people's **Water Splashing Festival** (see p.736) is a riotous celebration – no one is going home dry. Get down to Jinghong in Xishuangbanna in April – and pack a towel.

Taijing plays host to the five-day Miao **Sisters' Meal Festival** (see p.673), held on the fifteenth day of the third lunar month (April/May). It's like a Brueghel painting come to life, with cockfighting, dragon dances, buffalo contests and, somewhere among the chaos, teenagers picking their partners.

For something completely different, check out the **Midi Music Festival** (see p.123) in May; since 1997 this has been China's Glastonbury, when all of Beijing's indie bands strut their stuff, for once, in daylight.

Only the Tibetans could mix gambling, drinking, horse racing and Buddhism. These equestrian events, all part of the **Tibetan Horse Racing Festival** (see p.801), are held all over Tibet, at different times of the year, but the biggest is in Litang at the beginning of August.

Langmusi

Just off the highway to Hezuo, 90km from Zöigê, you'll find the scruffy village of **LANGMUSI** (郎木寺, *lángmùsì*), whose surrounding forests, mountain scenery and **lamaseries** give an easy taster of Tibet. There's a direct **bus** from Zöigê, but coming from Hezuo you might get dropped at the main road intersection where jeeps wait to take you the 3km to the village itself (¥2–5). Either way, you end up on the single main street, with nearby **accommodation** at the *Langmusi Binguan* (郎木寺宾馆, *lángmùsì bīnguǎn*; ⓣ0941/6671086; beds ¥25, rooms ❸), which has hot water in the evening, a rooftop terrace and a very helpful manager, though you need to bargain doubles down; the tidy, basic *Nomad's Youth Hostel* (旅朋青年旅舍, *lǚpéng qīngnián lǚshè*; ⓣ0941/6671460; dorms ¥20); and the relatively smart *Dacang Langmu Binguan* (达仓朗木宾馆, *dácāng lǎngmù bīnguǎn*; ⓣ0941/6671338; beds ¥25, rooms ❸).

Langmusi's two small eighteenth-century **lamaseries** (¥25) sit at the western end of the village. Walk up the main street and bear right over a bridge, and the road leads uphill to **Saizu Gompa**, whose main hall's walls are covered in pictures of meditating Buddhas and where you might see monks debating in the courtyard outside. For **Gaerdi Gompa**, bear left along the main road and then aim for the temple buildings in the back lanes; this is the larger complex with several sizeable, tin-roofed halls, but seems almost totally deserted. There's immense **hiking** potential up to ridges and peaks beyond, but make sure you're equipped for dogs (see p.788) and changeable weather. To arrange longer guided hikes or **horse-trekking**, contact Langmusi Tibetan Horse Trekking (ⓣ0941/6671504, ⓦwww.langmusi.net), near the bus stop, a very organized operation whose one- to four-day trips take in nomad camps and mountain scenery – the website has current schedules and costs.

For **food**, there are several simple Muslim and Chinese restaurants along the main street, though foreigners tend to gravitate towards *Leisha's*, a traveller-style **café** where portions of Chinese-Tibetan-Muslim dishes are huge and tasty. There's also a **net bar** opposite the *Langmusi Binguan*, full of young, network-gaming monks, but **no banks** or anywhere to change money.

Leaving, buses assemble at dawn on the main street (ask at your accommodation the night before for times) for daily runs to Zöigê, and Xiahe and Hezuo in Gansu. If enough people show, you might also score a minibus ride later in the day to Zöigê, which would save time there in limbo between buses. Leisha's can help charter minibuses to Jiuzhaigou and elsewhere (about ¥800 for a five-seater).

Sichuan's far west

Sichuan's **far west** begins some six hours over the mountains from Chengdu at **Kangding**, the regional capital. Yet it's only after you leave Kangding, bound northwest to **Ganzi** and **Dêgê** or southwest to **Litang** and **Yunnan**, that you enter what, geographically and ethnically, may as well be Tibet. **Roads** beyond Kangding are rough in places – mostly due to landslides or roadworks – but on the whole, journeys are exhausting due to length rather than physical discomfort. What makes them worthwhile are your fellow passengers, mostly monks and wild-looking Khampa youths, who every time the bus crosses a mountain pass cheer wildly and throw handfuls of paper prayer flags out of the windows. **Buying bus tickets** is frustrating, however – expect to find flexible schedules, early departures, ticket offices open at unpredictable times and unhelpful station staff.

Even when Tibet is open to foreigners, it has never been easy to cross from Western Sichuan **into Tibet**; if you do manage to buy a ticket for the ride, you're likely to be hauled off the bus at the border and booted back the way you came. Coming the other way from inside Tibet, however, the authorities are hardly likely to send you back if you try to enter Sichuan here, though you may well be fined.

Kangding

KANGDING (康定, *kāngdìng*), 250km from Chengdu at the gateway to Sichuan's far west, is a crowded, artless collection of modern white-tiled blocks packed along the fast-flowing **Zheduo River**. Visually this is a very Chinese town, but the deep gorge that Kangding is set in is overlooked by chortens and the frosted peaks of **Daxue Shan** (the Great Snowy Mountains), and, whatever the maps might say, this is where Tibet really begins.

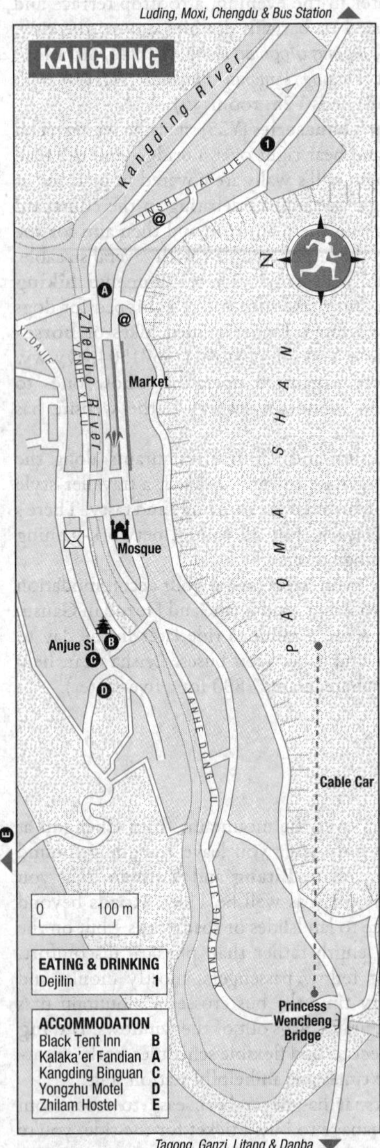

The town is the capital of huge **Ganzi prefecture** and bus schedules mean that a **stopover** here is likely, but with a couple of temples to check out and huge, communal evening dancing in the central square it's not the worst of fates. In addition, Kangding is a stepping stone for day-trips to the **Hailuogou Glacier Park**, which descends **Gongga Shan**, western China's highest peak.

Kangding's most central temple is **Anjue Si** (安觉寺, *ānjué sì*), just off Yanhe Xi Lu; a small affair, it was built in 1654 at the prompting of the Fifth Dalai Lama. Following the main road southwest out of town brings you to the short stone arch of the **Princess Wencheng Bridge** (文成公主桥, *wénchéng gōngzhǔ qiáo*); on the other side, a path runs uphill to **Nanfu Si** (南甫寺, *nánfǔ sì*), built here in 1639. Check out the murals of Buddha in all his incarnations here – with their typically Tibetan iconography of skulls, demons and fierce expressions, they paint a far less forgiving picture of Buddhism than the mainstream Chinese brand.

Kangding's **markets** – mostly selling clothing and household knick-knacks of all descriptions – surround the old town **spring** (水井子, *shuǐjǐngzi*) and a **mosque** off Yanhe Dong Lu. A lane opposite the mosque heads up to the entrance of pine-clad **Paoma Shan** (跑马山, *pǎomǎ shān*; ¥50) the mountain southeast of town, which hosts a **horse-race festival** in the middle of the fourth lunar month. It's a half-hour walk up stone steps to lookouts and the Roman-theatre-style racetrack, or you can catch a **cable car** (¥30 return) from near the Princess Wencheng Bridge.

Arrival and information

Kangding sits in a deep Y-shaped valley where the Zheduo River and a minor stream combine to form the Kangding River. The kilometre-long downtown area flanks the Zheduo River as it flows northeast into the Kangding, with the two main streets – **Yanhe Dong Lu** on the southern side, **Yanhe Xi Lu** on the northern – joined by four bridges. Yanhe Dong Lu continues southwest out of town towards Ganzi and Litang over the Princess Wencheng Bridge.

The **bus station** is a kilometre from town towards Chengdu, a ¥5 cab ride or twenty-minute walk to anywhere central. The station has departures until mid-afternoon to Chengdu and Danba, and early-morning runs to Xichang, Tagong, Ganzi, Dêgê, Litang, Xiangcheng and Daocheng. **Minibuses** touting for Danba, Tagong and Chengdu, and **taxis** to Luding, cruise the streets outside.

Accommodation and eating

Find **budget accommodation** at the basic *Black Tent Inn* (安觉寺黑包客栈, *ānjué sì hēibāo kèzhàn*; Ⓣ15808366530, beds ¥25) attached to Anjue Si; or just up the hill from here at the sparkling, clean *Yongzhu Motel* (拥珠驿栈, *yōngzhū yìzhàn*; Ⓣ0836/2832381; beds ¥40, rooms ❸). There's also the superb *Zhilam Hostel* (汇道客栈, *huìdào kèzhàn*; Ⓣ0836/2831100, Ⓦwww.zhilamhostel.com; beds ¥30, rooms ❹), a ten-minute uphill hike from town, or catch a cab for ¥7 or so. The *Kalaka'er Fandian* (卡拉卡尔饭店, *kălākăěr fàndiàn*; Ⓣ0836/2828888; ❻) on Yanhe Dong Lu, and elderly *Kangding Binguan* (康定宾馆, *kāngdìng bīnguǎn*; Ⓣ0836/2832077; ❺), near Anjue Si, are typical of Kangding's overpriced mid-range options.

For **eating**, Xinshi Qian Jie has heaps of cheap restaurants, along with the *Dejilin* (德吉林藏餐, *déjílín zàng cān*) one of several Tibetan diners with murals, butter tea, meat dumplings, yak stew and communal bench tables.

Luding, Moxi and Hailuogou Glacier Park

A fast road runs 100km from Kangding via Luding to the village of **Moxi**, at the Hailuogou Glacier Park gates; the journey takes two hours. Taxis outside Kangding bus station charge around ¥20 for a four-person cab to Luding, or ¥35 to Moxi.

Don't be surprised if you have to change vehicles an hour east of Kangding at the market town of **LUDING** (泸定, *lúdìng*). A few minutes here is enough to check out the attractive old **Luding Suspension Bridge** (泸定桥, *lúdìng qiáo*; ¥15) over the Dadu River, where 22 Communist soldiers climbed hand-over-hand across the chains and took Guomindang emplacements on the west bank during the Long March in 1935.

Moxi and Hailuogou

Hailuogou Glacier Park (海螺沟冰川公园, *hǎiluógōu bīngchuān gōngyuán*; entry ¥75, bus through park ¥60) encloses an alpine backdrop of deep valleys forested in pine and rhododendron, with the four **glaciers** in question descending **Gongga Shan** (贡嘎山, *gònggā shān*; **Minya Konka** in Tibetan). At 7556m, this is western China's highest point – a stunning sight on the rare mornings when the near-constant cloud cover and haze of wind-driven snow above the peak suddenly clear. Warm, weatherproof **clothing** is advisable whatever time of year you visit.

The **park entrance** is at **MOXI**, a group of hotels, restaurants and souvenir stalls centred around a crossroads where Luding and Kangding buses cluster. Downhill from the crossroads, it's 150m to Moxi's original single street of wooden shops and a small **Catholic church** built in the 1920s. Its colourful bell tower overlooks a European, box-like main building, its eaves pinched as a concession to local aesthetics. Top-notch **accommodation** is provided near the park gates by the *Mingzhu Huayuan Jiudian* (明珠花园酒店, *míngzhū huāyuán jiǔdiàn*; ⓣ0836/3266166; ❺), with cheaper options such as the *Milan Youth Hostel* (米兰青年旅舍, *mǐlán qīngnián lǚshè*; ⓣ0836/3266518; dorms ¥30, rooms ❷) near the church, and friendly *Hamu Hostel* (哈姆青年旅舍; *hāmǔ qīngnián lǚshè*; ⓣ15281572918; dorms ¥30, rooms ❷) where the road from Kangding enters town. **Eat** either at your accommodation or at any of the scores of stir-fry restaurants nearby.

A **road** runs 25km from the gates at Moxi to the main glacier. Most visitors take a **tour bus** from the park gates, though you can also hike, resting up at the three **camps** along the way at the 8-, 15- and 22-kilometre marks. These were once humble campsites, but each now hosts a large hotel (❺), with **hot springs** (¥65) on hand at the first two – camp 2, near where the thicker pine forests begin, is the nicest spot to stay within the park. From camp 3, it's 3.5km to the glacier, from where you can reach a **viewing platform** by cable car (¥150 return) or by simply hiking up along a small path; allow two hours. From the platform, the glacier is revealed as a tongue of blue-white ice scattered with boulders and streaked in crevasses edged in black gravel, with – if you're lucky – Gongga Shan's peak rising in the distance.

Danba, Ma'erkang and Siguniang Shan

Roads **north of Kangding** form a backroads route to Zôigê and Songpan, via a couple of sights well worth a visit in their own right. Around 120km from Kangding, **DANBA** (丹巴, *dānbā*) is a 2km-long service town for surrounding Tibetan hamlets; the **bus station** – with daily runs to Ma'erkang, Kangding and Ganzi, plus additional Kangding minibuses through the day – is at the west end, while minibuses to Xiaojin and Bamei (for connections to Tagong) leave from a depot at Danba's eastern side near the **Caihong bridge** (彩虹桥, *cǎihóng qiáo*). There's a hostel attached to the bus station (beds ¥30), but the *Zaxi Zhoukang Hostel* (扎西桌康游客之家, *zāxī zhuōkāng yóukè zhījiā*; ⓣ0836/3521806; beds ¥40), down by Caihong Bridge, has spotless rooms and can organize trips out to villages, though very little English is spoken. The restaurant opposite does a fantastic potato and sparerib stew (土豆排骨, *tǔdòu páigǔ*).

The most accessible of Danba's outlying Tibetan hamlets is **Jiaju** (甲居, *jiǎjū*; ¥30), just 7km up into the hills from town; a return minibus costs ¥80, including waiting time. Jiaju occupies a relatively flat terrace on an otherwise steep mountainside, all dotted with stone houses surrounded by their fields. Well-formed paths link clusters of farms, which you can spend a couple of hours exploring; some people offer **beds** for the night for ¥50 per person, including huge meals.

Xiaojin and Ma'erkang

About 60km east from Danba, **XIAOJIN** (小金, *xiǎojīn*) is a gritty transit town of tiled-box design laid out along hairpin bends above a deep gorge. Exit the bus station (which has morning services to Chengdu, Kangding and Ma'erkang), turn right and it's 150m to a small **minibus depot** for transport to Danba or Rilong; they leave when full and cost about ¥30 to either place. If you get stuck, stay next to the bus station at the *Dianhua Binguan* (ⓣ0837/2782888; ❷).

If you're heading on towards Songpan or Zöigê, you need first to aim for **MA'ERKANG** (马尔康, *mǎěrkāng*), a small administrative centre four hours north of Xiaojin. The **bus station** (with early departures to Chengdu, Xiaojin, Songpan, Zöigê and Danba) is about 3km east of town, connected by a local bus. There's standard **accommodation** next to the bus station at the *Yingbin Binguan* (迎宾宾馆, *yíngbīn bīnguǎn*; ❷), though it's lonely out here; and also in town at the riverside *Mingshan Binguan* (岷山宾馆, *mínshān bīnguǎn*; ⓣ0837/2822918; ❷).

Some 7km east (taxis charge ¥15), **Zhuokeji** (桌克基, *zhuōkèjī*) is a stone-built Tibetan village of twenty tightly packed houses with brightly coloured window frames and flower gardens overlooking barley fields; the village gates are guarded by a wooden cannon. On the hill opposite, the sheer, stark walls and watchtower of the unoccupied **Landlord's Fortress** (土司官寨, *tǔsī guānzhài*) offer a bleak contrast – the building was utilized by Mao during the Long March.

Siguniang Shan

Siguniang Shan (四姑娘山, *sìgūniang shān*) means "Four Girls Mountain", and this range does indeed include a row of **four peaks**, the highest of which touches 6250m and looks most poetic when lit by a low sun. The base for exploring the area is **RILONG** (日隆, *rìlōng*), a small and scruffy riverside tourist centre that hugs a bend in the road 60km east of Xiaojin.

Accommodation possibilities here include the very basic but friendly *Climbers and Travellers Hostel* (长坪山庄, *chángpíng shānzhuāng*; ⓣ0837/2791869 or 13684392478; beds ¥30), up at the bend, whose Chinese-speaking owner has extensive local climbing experience; or further downhill, the cosy ★ *Sunny Youth Hostel* (阳光青年旅舍, *yángguāng qīngnián lǚshè*; ⓣ0837/2791585, ⓦwww.yhachina.com; beds ¥30, rooms ❷) and adjacent, similar *Longyun Shanzhuang* (龙云山庄, *lóngyún shānzhuāng*; ⓣ0837/2791848 or 0138/82496631; rooms ❸). All can organize **rental** of horses, camping and climbing gear, and **guides** if wanted.

Leaving, minibuses to Xiaojin (¥30) shuttle around through the day; check to see whether the direct bus service east to Chengdu has resumed but don't count on it.

Rilong sits south of three valleys that run up below the snow-etched peaks; there are thick birch and pine forests draped in strings of "old man's beard", patches of meadow, and wildlife such as marmots, hares and plenty of birds. The closest valley to town is **Changping Gou** (长坪沟, *chángpíng gōu*; ¥70, plus ¥20 to use the bus), which starts 500m up along the river from the *Climbers and Travellers Hostel*. From the entrance, the road continues to **Lama Si** (喇嘛寺, *lǎmā sì*; 6.5km) before winding up at **Kushu Tan** (枯树滩, *kūshù tān*; another 3km); it's a 16km hike from here along the base of the four peaks to **Gou Wei** (沟尾, *gōu wěi*), literally the "Valley Tail". Come prepared for very changeable and potentially cold **weather**, even in summer.

Kangding to Ganzi and Dêgê

Northwest from Kangding, it's close on 600km across mountains and prairies to Tibet, and the main targets on the way are the people and monasteries around the highway towns of **Tagong**, **Ganzi** and **Dêgê**, the latter not far from the Tibetan border. The whole area hovers above 3500m, and the passes are considerably higher. **Buses** through the region run daily from Kangding via Tagong and take a full day to reach Ganzi, two for Dêgê.

The Tagong grasslands

Starting 110km northwest of Kangding, the **Tagong grasslands** (塔公草原, *tǎgōng cǎoyuán*) occupy a string of flat-bottomed valleys on a 3700m-high plateau, all surrounded by magnificent snowy peaks. Horseriding, hiking, and a temple at the Tibetan township of **TAGONG** (塔公, *tǎgōng*), are the attractions here; **buses** and minibuses connect the village daily with Kangding, Danba, Bamei and Ganzi and drop you off on the single street next to the temple square. You'll probably be grabbed on arrival by the owner of *Jya Drolma & Gayla's Guesthouse* (甲志玛大姐家, *jiāzhìmǎ dàjiějiā*; ⓣ0836/2866056; beds ¥25), whose hospitality and traditional Tibetan home – not to mention hot showers – are almost worth the trip in themselves; facing the temple, it's the building behind you on the left. Otherwise, also beside the temple, *Snowland Hostel* (雪域旅社, *xuěyù lǚshè*; ⓣ0836/2866098; beds ¥25) is next to *Sally's Kham Restaurant* (ⓣ13990454752, ⓔtagongsally@yahoo.com; often closed Nov–March), a foreigners' restaurant with Tibetan, Chinese and Western staples and plenty of helpful **information**. For **horse treks**, contact long-established Chyoger Treks (ⓣ0836/84493301, ⓦwww.definitelynomadic.com).

Tagong's focus is the modest **Tagong Si** (塔公寺, *tǎgōng sì*; ¥10), a complex built to honour Princess Wenchang but now busy with monks chatting on their mobile phones during morning prayers. The seventeenth-century main hall houses a sculpture of Sakyamuni as a youth, said to have been brought here by the princess in Tang times. Behind the monastery is **Fotalin**, a forest of a hundred 3m-high stupas, each built in memory of a monk. Follow the main road 500m past Tagong Si and you'll find the spectacular **golden stupa** (¥10), fully 20m tall and backed by snowy peaks, surrounded by a colonnade of prayer wheels – though according to the monks, this recent construction is less of a religious site than an excuse to collect tourist revenue.

The **grasslands** themselves begin at the golden stupa, a vast sprawl of pasture hemmed in by hillocks and peaks. Hiking and riding possibilities are legion: **Shedra Gompa**'s monastery and Buddhist college is only a couple of kilometres away; **Shamalong** village is two hours along a track from the stupa, and **Ani Gompa** is a valley nunnery with a sky-burial site some two hours' hike cross-country. Get full directions for these routes from *Sally's* – and beware of dogs.

Ganzi

GANZI (甘孜, *gānzī*) sits at 3500m in a broad, flat-bottomed river valley, with the long, serrated Que'er Shan range rising to the south. The dusty, noisy town owes its importance to the adjacent **Kandze monastery** (甘孜寺庙, *gānzī símiào*), founded by the Mongols after they invaded in 1642 and once the largest Gelugpa monastery in the Kham region. A bit empty today, it nevertheless remains an important cultural centre, especially for the teaching of religious dances and musical instruments.

Ganzi acts as transport and social focus, with blue trucks rumbling through at all hours, wild crowds cruising the streets, and markets throughout the back lanes; the kilometre-long main road is lined with shops selling knives, rugs, silverware, all sorts of jewellery, saddles, religious accessories, copper and tin kitchenware. The **monastery** is 2km north of town – follow Jiefang Lu uphill from the bus station – and for such an obvious structure the entrance is not easy to find, being hidden behind mud-brick homes among medieval backstreets. The recently renovated buildings are splendid, and just wandering around fills in time, though there's little specific to seek out aside from the **main hall** – covered in gold, murals and prayer flags, and with an incredible view of the valley and town from its roof. The large adobe walls below the monastery are remains of the Mazur and Khangsar **forts**, built by the Mongols after they took the region.

Back in Ganzi, the highway runs east–west as main **Chuanzang Lu**, the **crossroads** with north-oriented **Jiefang Lu** marking the town centre. The **bus station** is on the crossroads, with daily departures to Bâtâng, Kangding and Chengdu. Staff here are helpful enough with information but you might have to buy tickets on the bus. If you're aiming for **Litang** and want to avoid going all the way back to Kangding, there's also a morning bus south **to Xinlong** (新龙, *xīnlóng*), from where minibuses run to Litang if they get enough people (¥60–80 each, or about ¥300 for the whole van). Check with the Xinlong bus driver in Ganzi that the Xinlong–Litang stretch is open first, as it's barely more than a walking track in places, subject to wash-outs and landslides.

Ganzi's **accommodation** prospects are not outstanding, and the best bet is probably the *Golden Yak Hotel* (金牦牛宾馆, *jīn máoniú bīnguǎn*; Ⓣ0836/7525288, Ⓕ7525188; beds from ¥15, rooms ❸) inside the bus station compound, which has both dorms and comfy doubles. Otherwise, the *Chengxin Binguan* opposite (诚信宾馆, *chéngxìn bīnguǎn*; Ⓣ0836/7525289; dorms ¥30, rooms ❸) is typically functional. Almost every other business in town is a **restaurant**, though don't expect much beyond noodles and dumplings.

Dêgê

Eight hours from Ganzi via the crossroads town of **Manigange** (马尼干戈, *mănígàngē*) and scary, 5500m-high Chola Shan mountain pass, **DÊGÊ** (德格, *dégé*) initially appears to be no more than a small cluster of ageing concrete buildings squeezed into a narrow gorge. Dêgê was, however, once the most powerful Kham state, and the only one to resist the seventeenth-century Mongol invasion – hence the absence of Gelugpa-sect monasteries in the region. The **bus stop** is on the main road, just where Dêgê's single street crosses a stream and rises uphill to the monastery past shops, a **supermarket** and **internet bar** and dozens of stir-fry **restaurants**. The surly riverside *Dêgê Binguan* (雀儿山宾馆, *què ér shān bīnguǎn*; Ⓣ0836/8222167, Ⓕ8223997; dorms ¥25, rooms ❸) is the primary source of **beds**, with grubby dorms in an older wing and overpriced newer rooms in the main building; their comfortable tearoom, however, is a treat after the journey.

At the top of the main street is **Gongchen Gompa** (更庆寺庙, *gàngqìng sìmiào*), whose red-walled buildings form one of three hubs of Tibetan culture (the other two are Lhasa, and Xiahe in Gansu). The first building encountered is the famous **Bakong Scripture Printing Hall** (印经院, *yìnjīng yuàn*; ¥25; cameras forbidden), encircled by peregrinating pilgrims busy thumbing rosaries, who stick out their tongues in greeting if you join them. Built in 1729, the four-storey hall houses 290,000 **woodblocks** of Tibetan texts, stored in racks on the second floor like books in a library, and covering everything from scriptures to scientific treatises – some seventy percent of all Tibetan literary works. You can watch the **printing process** on the third floor: two printers sit facing each other, with the block in between on a sloping board; one printer inks the block with a pad and lays a fresh page over it; the other rubs a roller over the back of the page and then peels it off, placing it in a pile. Each page takes under six seconds to finish, and it's not unusual to watch ten pairs of printers going full pelt, turning out a hundred pages a minute between them.

Leaving, you'll need to buy Ganzi or Kangding tickets a day in advance; the main road bus-ticket booth opens at 7am and again at 2.30pm. There are also buses to Changdu (**Chamdo**) in Tibet – the border, marked by a youthful **Yangzi River** is about 15km west – if you want to try your luck with the border guards.

Kangding to Litang

From Kangding, it's 290km west to the monastery town of **Litang**, a major marketplace and transport hub from where you can head **southwest to Yunnan**. The Kangding–Litang road is a real treat, steadily rising to a mountain pass at 4700m. The pass opens onto undulating highlands, whose soft green slopes drop to forests far below – look for **marmots** on the ground and wedge-tailed **lammergeiers** (bearded vultures) circling far above. Just as you're wondering whether the road continues indefinitely, Litang appears below on a flat plain, ringed by mountains.

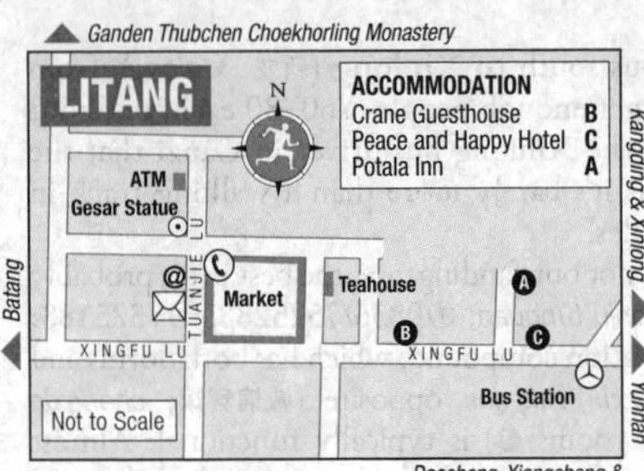

Litang

LITANG (理塘, *lǐtáng*) is a lively, outwardly gruff place with a large Tibetan population and an obvious Han presence in its businesses and army barracks. Wild West comparisons are inevitable – you'll soon get used to sharing the pavement with livestock, and watching monks and Khampa toughs with braided hair and boots tearing around the windy, dusty streets on ribboned motorbikes. It's also inescapably **high** – at 4014m above sea level, it actually beats Lhasa by over 300m – so don't be surprised if you find even gentle slopes strangely exhausting. As usual, the main distraction here is people-watching: the shops are packed with Tibetans bargaining for temple accessories, solar-power systems for tents and practical paraphernalia for daily use; meanwhile Muslim smiths are busy turning out the town's renowned knives and jewellery in backstreet shacks.

Arrival and information

Litang's main street is a 1.5km section of the highway known as **Xingfu Lu**, with the **bus station** at the eastern end. There are several buses daily to Kangding and at least one each to Xiangcheng and Daocheng, but the station staff probably won't sell you tickets and you may have to wait for the buses to turn up and see if seats are available. **Minibuses** and taxis to Daocheng, Xinlong (for Ganzi) and anywhere else they can get enough customers for hang around outside in the mornings. For **post**, **phones** and **internet**, head to Tuanjie Lu.

Accommodation and eating

The best budget **accommodation** options are across from the bus station on Xingfu Lu at the *Peace and Happy Hotel* (平安涉外旅馆, *píngān shèwài lǚguǎn*; ⓣ0836/5323861; beds ¥20), a friendly, grubby place with tiny rooms; or the efficient *Crane Guesthouse* (仙鸿宾馆, *xiānhóng bīnguǎn*; ⓣ0836/5323850; beds ¥20, ❸) 500m further west, with dorms at the front and doubles in the rear building. The tidy *Potala Inn* (布达拉大酒店, *bùdálā dàjiǔdiàn*; ⓣ0836/5322533; rooms ❸) is a Tibetan-run, Chinese-style place with spectacular views from its two front bedrooms.

Stir-fry **restaurants** run by migrants from Chengdu line the main street, some of which have English menus and all of which serve pretty much the same food.

Ganden Thubchen Choekhorling monastery

Litang's **Ganden Thubchen Choekhorling monastery** (理塘寺庙, *lǐtáng sìmiào*), founded in 1580 at the behest of the Third Dalai Lama, is today somewhat dilapidated but still populated by over a thousand monks. From the main crossroads in town, head north up Tuanjie Lu to the intersection, turn left, and follow the road – it's a fifteen-minute walk, or a ¥3 taxi ride. The complex is entirely encircled by a wall, the four main halls (two of them brand new) gleaming among an adobe township of monks' quarters. At the entrance is a large stupa and pile of brightly painted mani stones left by pilgrims for good luck, whose inscriptions have been carved to resemble yaks. The **upper temple** (Tsengyi Zhatsang) is the most interesting, its portico flanked by aggressively postured statues of guardians of the four directions, along with a typical, finely executed mural of a three-eyed demon wearing tiger skins and skulls, holding the Wheel Of Transmigration. Inside are

Litang's horse festival

Litang's week-long **horse festival** kicks off each August 1 on the plains outside town. Thousands of Tibetan horsemen from all over Kham descend to compete, decking their stocky steeds in bells and brightly decorated bridles and saddles. As well as the four daily **races**, the festival features amazing demonstrations of horsemanship, including acrobatics, plucking silk scarves off the ground, and shooting (guns and bows) – all performed at full tilt. In between, you'll see plenty of **dancing**, both religious (the dancers wearing grotesque wooden masks) and for fun, with both men and women gorgeously dressed in heavily embroidered long-sleeved smocks.

statues of Tsongkhapa and the Third Dalai Lama, along with photos of the current Dalai Lama and tenth Panchen Lama. Side gates in the wall allow you to hike up onto the hills behind the monastery, sharing the flower-filled pasture with yaks, or join pilgrims circuiting the walls to the **sky-burial ground** to the right of the main gates.

Litang to Yunnan

The road south of Litang runs, via the valley settlement of **Xiangcheng**, right down to Zhongdian in Yunnan, though it's worth detouring along the way to take in **Yading**, an alpine reserve accessed via **Daocheng**. Buses **to Shangri-la (Zhongdian) in Yunnan** (see p.718) originate in Daocheng and, though they pass through Xiangcheng en route, you'll have to be very lucky to find a free seat there.

Daocheng

DAOCHENG or **Dabpa** (稻城, *dàochéng*) is a small, touristy T-intersection of low buildings and shops, the road running in past the **bus station** to the junction. Turn left (north) and the road runs out into the countryside, degenerating into a track that winds up 5km later at some **hot springs** (茹布查卡温泉, *rúbù zhākǎ wēnquán*) set among a tiny village at the head of a valley. **Bathhouses** here ask ¥3 for a soak, and you can cross the valley and hike along a ridge back into town – tiring, given the 3500m altitude.

Otherwise, the main point of interest lies a 76km (2hr 30min ride south of Daocheng at **Yading** (亚丁, *yàdīng*; ¥150), a beautiful reserve of meadows, lakes and 6000m peaks. Everybody with a vehicle in Daocheng will offer to take you to the edge of the reserve at **Yading Cun** (also known as **Xianggelila**, or "Shangri-la") for about ¥50 a person; there's **accommodation** here at the *Kangba Hostel* (康吧旅馆, *kāngbā lǚguǎn*; ❷) with meals when the manager feels like it. You'll be glad to take extra food, water and sleeping bags. Some sights within the reserve can be reached by local bus, but ideally you'll be prepared to hike or travel on horseback.

Daocheng's best **accommodation** options are the warmly hospitable **Tibetan guesthouses** such as the *Seaburay* (喜波热, *xǐbōrè*; Ⓣ0836/5728668; ¥30/person; follow the English signs from near the bus station), where your ability to consume vast amounts of *tsampa*, dumplings and butter tea will be put to the test. Toilets are basic and you shower at the public bathhouse or, more enjoyably, at the hot springs. There's also the *Daocheng Youth Hostel* (稻城国际青年旅舍, *dàochéng guójì qīngnián lǚshě*; Ⓣ0836/5727772, Ⓔyourinn@gmail.com; beds ¥20, rooms ❸), though it's a little out of town over the Xingfu bridge; and the similar *Plateau Inn* (高原客栈, *gāoyuán kèzhàn*; Ⓣ0836/5728667, Ⓦwww.inoat.com; beds ¥30, rooms ❷) at 78 Gongga Lu, not far from the bus station; both have restaurants, bars and hot water.

Daily **buses** depart for Litang, Kangding, Xiangcheng and Shangri-la (Zhongdian) in Yunnan, all things being equal – but they often aren't. Note that the Shangri-la bus originates here, making it a better place to catch it than Xiangcheng (see below). Wherever you're headed, come to the ticket office around 2pm the day before and be prepared to fight for a place in the queue. You can also negotiate with **minibus** drivers outside for rides to Litang and Xiangcheng.

Xiangcheng and on to Yunnan

Some 200km from Litang or 160km from Daocheng, **XIANGCHENG** (乡城, *xiāngchéng*) is a functional few streets with the flat atmosphere of some long-abandoned outpost, but the small seventeenth-century **Chaktreng Gompa monastery** (桑披岭寺, *sāngpīlǐng sì*; ¥10; photos allowed) is highly unusual and well worth the 2km uphill hike from town. The three-storey temple has extraordinary decorations, including a portico carved with animals, murals of warrior demons squashing European-looking figures, and a sculpture of a multi-headed, many-limbed Samvara in primary blues and reds cavorting in Tantric postures. Among all this is an eerie seated statue of Tsongkhapa, wreathed in gold filigree and draped in silk scarves.

Xiangcheng's semi-derelict **bus station** is a walled compound dotted with rubble and excrement; the town's short main street stretches beyond. If the owner doesn't meet you, take the small steps uphill from inside the bus station and it's 50m to *Bamu Tibetan Guesthouse* (巴姆藏庄, *bāmǔ zàng zhuāng*; dorm beds ¥20, rooms ❶). This is Xiangcheng's highlight, a traditional three-storey Tibetan home decorated in murals, whose dormitory resembles the interior of a temple (the twin rooms are a bit poky, however). There are great views from the roof, and a basic outdoor shower and toilet – a torch is useful. Another decent option lies just outside the bus-station gates at the *Coffee Tea Hotel* (象泉宾馆, *xiàngquán bīnguǎn*; ⓣ0836/5826136; ❷), which also has a good **teahouse** and **bathhouse**.

There are usually daily buses to Litang, Daocheng and Zhongdian in Yunnan. You might be sold a ticket for Litang the day before departure at 2.30pm, but as Xiangcheng is only a brief stop on the Daocheng–Zhongdian run, you'll have to bargain with the driver for a seat to these destinations.

Travel details

Trains

Chengdu to: Beijing (3 daily; 25–30hr); Chongqing (20 daily; 2–6hr); Dujiangyan (9 daily; 50min); Emei (10 daily; 2–4hr); Guangyuan (many daily; 6–10hr); Guangzhou (4 daily; 30–40hr); Guiyang (7 daily; 18hr); Jiangyou (many daily; 2hr 30min); Kunming (5 daily; 19hr); Lhasa (1 daily; 44hr); Panzhihua (8 daily; 13hr); Qingcheng Shan (9 daily; 1hr 10min); Shanghai (4 daily; 36hr); Wuhan (7 daily; 17–23hr); Xi'an (9 daily; 12–20hr); Xichang (9 daily; 10hr).

Chongqing to: Beijing (2 daily; 24–40hr); Chengdu (20 daily; 2–6hr); Guangzhou (8 daily; 21–33hr); Guiyang (10 daily; 9–12hr); Shanghai (2 daily; 30–40hr); Wuhan (5 daily; 15–20hr); Xi'an (5 daily; 11hr).

Dujiangyan to: Chengdu (9 daily; 50min); Qingcheng Shan (9 daily; 20min).

Emei Shan to: Chengdu (10 daily; 2–4hr); Kunming (3 daily; 17hr); Panzhihua (8 daily; 11hr); Xichang (9 daily; 8hr).

Guangyuan to: Chengdu (many daily; 6–10hr); Xi'an (9 daily; 8–14hr).

Qingcheng Shan to: Chengdu (9 daily; 50min); Dujiangyan (9 daily; 20min).

Xichang to: Chengdu (9 daily; 10hr); Emei (9 daily; 8hr); Kunming (4 daily; 9hr); Panzhihua (10 daily; 3–6hr).

Buses

Changning to: Chengdu (10hr); Chongqing (6hr); Luzhou (3hr); Yibin (2hr).

Chengdu to: Chongqing (6hr); Daocheng (2 days); Dazu (4hr); Dujiangyan (2hr); Emei Shan (2hr 30min); Ganzi (2 days); Guanghan (1hr); Guangyuan (4hr); Huanglongxi (1hr); Jiangyou (2hr); Jiuzhaigou (10–12hr); Kangding (8hr); Langzhong (4hr 30min); Leshan (2hr 30min); Songpan (8hr); Xichang (8hr); Yibin (8hr); Zigong (6hr); Zöigê (14hr).
Chongqing to: Chengdu (6hr); Dazu (3hr); Langzhong (5hr); Yibin (3hr 30min); Zigong (1hr 30min).
Daocheng to: Litang (5hr); Shangri-la/Zhongdian (8–12hr); Xiangcheng (3hr).
Dazu to: Chengdu (4hr); Chongqing (3hr); Leshan (3hr); Yibin (4hr); Zigong (2hr).
Emei Shan to: Chengdu (2hr 30min); Leshan (1hr); Xichang (8hr).
Ganzi to: Chengdu (2 days); Dêgê (8hr); Kangding (12hr); Xinlong (3hr).
Guangyuan to: Chengdu (4hr); Jiangyou (2hr 30min); Jianmenguan (1hr); Jiuzhaigou Xian (8hr); Langzhong (4hr).
Jiangyou to: Chengdu (2hr); Doutuan Shan (1hr); Guangyuan (2hr 30min); Jianmenguan (1hr 30min); Jiuzhaigou Xian (8hr).
Kangding to: Chengdu (6–8hr); Danba (4hr); Daocheng (14hr); Daofu (9hr); Dêgê (2 days); Ganzi (12hr); Litang (9hr); Manigange (15hr); Tagong (3hr); Xichang (8hr).
Langzhong to: Chengdu (5hr); Chongqing (5hr); Guanyuan (4hr).
Leshan to: Chengdu (2hr 30min); Chongqing (5hr); Dazu (3hr); Emei (1hr); Xichang (8hr); Yibin (5hr); Zigong (2hr 30min).
Litang to: Daocheng (5hr); Kangding (9hr); Xiangcheng (5hr); Zhongdian (12hr).
Songpan to: Chengdu (8–12hr); Huanglong (2hr); Jiuzhaigou (2hr); Langmusi (4–6hr); Ma'erkang (10hr); Zöigê (4hr).
Xiangcheng to: Daocheng (3hr); Litang (5hr); Zhongdian (8hr).
Xichang to: Chengdu (8hr); Kangding (8hr); Kunming (24hr); Panzhihua (3hr).
Yibin to: Changning (1hr 30min); Chengdu (4hr); Chongqing (3hr 30min); Dazu (4hr); Gongxian (2hr 15min); Luzhou (3hr); Zigong (1hr 30min).
Zigong to: Chengdu (4hr); Chongqing (4hr); Dazu (2hr); Emei (3hr); Leshan (2hr 30min); Luzhou (5hr); Yibin (1hr 30min).

Ferries

Chongqing to: Wanzhou (daily; 12hr); Yichang (daily; 48hr).
Wanzhou hydrofoil to: Yichang (5 daily; 6hr).

Flights

Besides the domestic flights listed, there are flights from Chengdu to Amsterdam, Bangkok, Kathmandu, Narita, Tokyo and Singapore.
Chengdu to: Beijing (many daily; 2hr); Changsha (2 daily; 1hr 30min); Chongqing (1 daily; 45min); Guangzhou (many daily; 3hr); Guilin (1 daily; 1hr 20min); Guiyang (4 daily; 1hr); Hong Kong (3 daily; 2hr); Jiuzhaigou (4 daily; 45min); Kunming (15 daily; 90min); Lanzhou (3 daily; 1hr 20min); Lhasa (12 daily; 1hr 50min); Shanghai (many daily; 3hr 15min); Shenzhen (20 daily; 1hr 45min); Wuhan (3 daily; 1hr 20min); Wulumuqi (3 daily; 3hr 30min).
Chongqing to: Beijing (16 daily; 3hr); Chengdu (1 daily; 45min); Guangzhou (10 daily; 90min); Guilin (3 daily; 55min); Guiyang (2 daily; 1hr); Hong Kong (3 daily; 1hr 50min); Kunming (10 daily; 1hr 10min); Lhasa (1 daily; 2hr); Shanghai (many daily; 3hr); Shenzhen (9 daily; 2hr); Xi'an (4 daily; 1hr); Yichang (7 weekly; 1hr).
Jiuzhaigou to: Beijing (1 daily; 1hr 50min); Chengdu (4 daily; 1hr); Chongqing (4 weekly; 1hr); Xi'an (1 daily; 1hr 10min).

CHAPTER 13

Highlights

* **Labrang Monastery** The most imposing Lamaist monastery outside of Tibet, set in a beautiful mountain valley. See p.823
* **Qinghai Hu** China's largest salt lake is a magnet for birdwatchers and waterfowl, including the rare black-necked crane. See p.831
* **Jiayuguan Fort** Stronghold at the western end of the Great Wall, symbolically marking the end of China proper. See p.837
* **Mogao Caves** Huge collection of Buddhist grottoes and sculptures, carved into a desert gorge a millennium ago. See p.842
* **Turpan** Relax under grape trellises or investigate Muslim Uyghur culture and ancient Silk Road relics, such as the intriguing ruins of Jiaohe. See p.861
* **Kashgar's Sunday markets** Join crowds haggling for goats, carpets, knives and spices in China's most westerly and wild city. See p.874

▲ Emin Minaret, Turpan

13

The Northwest

The gigantic provinces of **Gansu**, **Qinghai** and **Xinjiang** spread across the whole of the Chinese northwest, an almost dizzying agglomeration of desert, grassland, raging rivers and colossal mountains. Despite the region's impressive size, which alone would form the **eighth largest country in the world**, it contains only four percent of China's population – quite a baffling statistic considering the region's staggering **ethnic variety**. Xinjiang is home to, and indeed an autonomous province for, a large population of **Uyghur**, a predominantly Muslim people who speak a language far more proximate to Turkish than Chinese. The province's deserts and mountains also harbour large communities of Kazakh, Krygyz and Tajik, making for the curious existence of occasional blond-haired, blue-eyed holders of a Chinese passport. Qinghai forms the northern edge of the Tibetan plateau; now that transport to Lhasa has been restricted and sanitized, the province is proving popular with those wishing to soak up a bit of "free" **Tibetan culture**. Over in Gansu, there are large communities of Mongolians and **Hui** Muslims, as well as lesser-known groups such as the Bao'an and Salar. Indeed, the Chinese of old thought the whole region was remote, subject to extremes of weather and populated by non-Chinese-speaking "barbarians" who were, quite literally, the peoples from beyond the pale – *sai wai ren*.

However, a **Chinese presence** in the area is not new. Imperial armies were already in control of virtually the whole northwest region by the time of the Han dynasty two thousand years ago, and since then Gansu and the eastern parts of Qinghai and Xinjiang have become Chinese almost to the core.

Today, the relatively unrestricted use of **local languages and religions** in these areas could be taken as a sign of China's desire to **nurture patriotism** in the minority peoples and regain some of the sympathy lost during disastrous repressions under communism and in previous eras. Furthermore, in economic terms, there is a clear transfer of wealth, in the form of industrial and agricultural aid, from the richer areas of eastern China to the poorer, outer fringes of the country. On the other hand, the degree of actual autonomy in the "autonomous" regions is strictly controlled, and relations between Han China and these more remote corners of the Republic remain fractious in places, most notably Xinjiang, recently subject to a substantial amount of inter-ethnic strife.

Organized tourism across the Northwest focuses on the **Silk Road**, a series of historic towns and ruins running from Xi'an in Shaanxi province, through Ningxia, Gansu and Xinjiang, and eventually into Central Asia. The Northwest also offers chances to enjoy the last great remaining **wildernesses** of China – the grasslands, mountains, lakes and deserts of the interior – far from the teeming population centres of the east. **Gansu**, the historical periphery of ancient China,

The Silk Road

The passes of Khunjerab and Torugut, linking China with western Asia – and, ultimately, with the whole of the Western world – have only in recent years reopened to a gradually increasing flow of cross-border traffic, mostly small-time traders. Yet a thousand years ago these were on crucial, well-trodden and incredibly long trade routes between eastern China and the Mediterranean. Starting from Chang'an (Xi'an), the **Silk Road** curved northwest through Gansu to the Yumen Pass, where it split. Leaving the protection of the Great Wall, travellers could follow one of two routes across the deserts of Lop Nor and Taklamakan, braving attacks from marauding bandits, to Kashgar. The **southern route** ran through Dunhuang, Lop Nor, Miran, Niya, Khotan and Yarkand; the **northern route** through Hami, Turpan, Kuqa and Aqsu. High in the Pamirs beyond Kashgar, the merchants traded their goods with the middlemen who carried them past the frontiers of China, either south to Kashmir, Bactria, Afghanistan and India, or north to Ferghana, Tashkent and Samarkand. Then, laden with Western goods, the Chinese merchants would turn back down the mountains for the 3000km journey home. **Oases** along the route inevitably prospered as staging posts and watering holes, becoming important and wealthy cities in their own right, with their own garrisons to protect the caravans. When Chinese domination periodically declined, many of these cities turned into self-sufficient city-states, or **khanates**. Today, many of these once powerful cities lie buried in the sands.

The foundations for this famous **road to the West**, which was to become one of the most important arteries of **trade and culture** in world history, were laid over two millennia ago. In the second century BC, nothing was known in China of the existence of people and lands beyond its borders, except by rumour. In 139 BC, the imperial court at Chang'an decided to despatch an emissary, a man called **Zhang Qiang**, to investigate the world to the west and to seek possible allies in the constant struggle against nomadic marauders from the north. Zhang set out with a party of a hundred men; thirteen years later he returned, with only two other members of his original expedition – and no alliances. But the news he brought nevertheless set Emperor Wu Di and his court aflame, including tales of Central Asia, Persia and even the Mediterranean world. Further **expeditions** were soon despatched, initially to purchase horses for military purposes, and from these beginnings trade soon developed.

By 100 BC a dozen immense caravans a year were heading into the desert. From the West came cucumbers, figs, chives, sesame, walnuts, grapes (and wine-making), wool, linen and ivory; from China, jade, porcelain, oranges, peaches, roses, chrysanthemums, cast iron, gunpowder, the crossbow, paper and printing, and **silk**. The silkworm had already been domesticated in China for hundreds of years, but in the West the means by which silk was manufactured remained a total mystery – people

is a rugged terrain of high peaks and desert spliced from east to west by the **Hexi Corridor**, historically the only road from China to the West, and still marked along its length by the Great Wall – terminating magnificently at the fortress of **Jiayuguan** – and a string of Silk Road towns culminating in **Dunhuang**, with its fabulous Buddhist cave art.

The Kunlun Mountains rise to the south of the Hexi Corridor and continue beyond to the high-altitude plateau stretching all the way to India. The ancient borderland between Tibet and China proper is **Qinghai**, perhaps the least-explored province in the whole of the Northwest, which has monasteries, mountains, the colossal lake of **Qinghai Hu** and, above all, a **route to Tibet** across one of the highest mountain ranges – and *the* highest train line – in the world. Originating in this province, too, are the Yellow and Yangzi rivers, the main transport arteries of China throughout recorded history.

believed it was combed from the leaves of trees. The Chinese took great pains to protect their monopoly, punishing any attempt to export silkworms with death. It was only many centuries later that sericulture finally began to spread west, when silkworm larvae were smuggled out of China in hollow walking sticks by Nestorian monks. The first time the **Romans** saw silk, snaking in the wind as the banners of their Parthian enemies, it filled them with terror and resulted in a humiliating rout. They determined to acquire it for themselves, and soon Roman society became obsessed with the fabric – by the first century AD it was coming west in such large quantities that the corresponding outflow of gold had begun to threaten the stability of the Roman economy.

As well as goods, the Silk Road carried new ideas in **art and religion**. Nestorian Christianity and Manichaeism trickled east across the mountains, but by far the most influential force was **Buddhism**. The first Buddhist missionaries appeared during the first century AD, crossing the High Pamirs from India, and their creed gained rapid acceptance among the nomads and oasis dwellers of what is now western China. By the fourth century, Buddhism had become the official religion of much of northern China, and by the eighth it was accepted throughout the empire. All along the road, monasteries, chapels, stupas and grottoes proliferated, often sponsored by wealthy traders. The remains of this early flowering of **Buddhist art** along the road are among the great attractions of the Northwest for modern-day travellers. Naturally, history has taken its toll – zealous Muslims, Western archeologists, Red Guards and the forces of nature have all played a destructive part – but some sites have survived intact, above all the cave art at **Mogao** outside Dunhuang.

The Silk Road continued to flourish for centuries, reaching its zenith under the Tang dynasty (618–907 AD) and bringing immense wealth to the Chinese nobility and merchants. But it remained a slow, dangerous and expensive route. Predatory tribes to the north and south harried the caravans despite garrisons and military escorts. Occasionally entire regions broke free of Chinese control, requiring years to be "re-pacified". The route was physically arduous, too, taking at least five months from Chang'an to Kashgar, and whole caravans could be lost in the deserts or in the high mountain passes.

There was a brief final flowering of trade in the thirteenth century, to which **Marco Polo** famously bore witness, when the whole Silk Road came temporarily under Mongol rule. But with the arrival of sericulture in Europe and the opening of sea routes between China and the West, the Silk Road had had its day. The road and its cities were slowly abandoned to the wind and the blowing sands.

Guarding the westernmost passes of the empire is **Xinjiang**, where China ends and another world – once known in the West as Chinese Turkestan – begins. Culturally and geographically, this vast, isolated region of searing deserts and snowy mountains, the most arduous and dreaded section of the Silk Road, is a part of Central Asia. Turkic Uyghurs outnumber Han Chinese, mosques stand in for temples and lamb kebabs replace steamed dumplings. Highlights of Xinjiang include the desert resort town of **Turpan** and, in the far west, fabled **Kashgar**, a city that until recently few Westerners had ever reached.

Travel can still be hard going, with **enormous distances** and an extremely **harsh continental climate**. **Winter** is particularly severe, with average temperatures as low as -15°C or -30°C in Qinghai and Xinjiang. Conversely, in **summer**, Turpan is China's hottest city, sometimes exceeding 40°C. Despite the wild, rugged terrain and the great expanses, however, facilities for tourists have

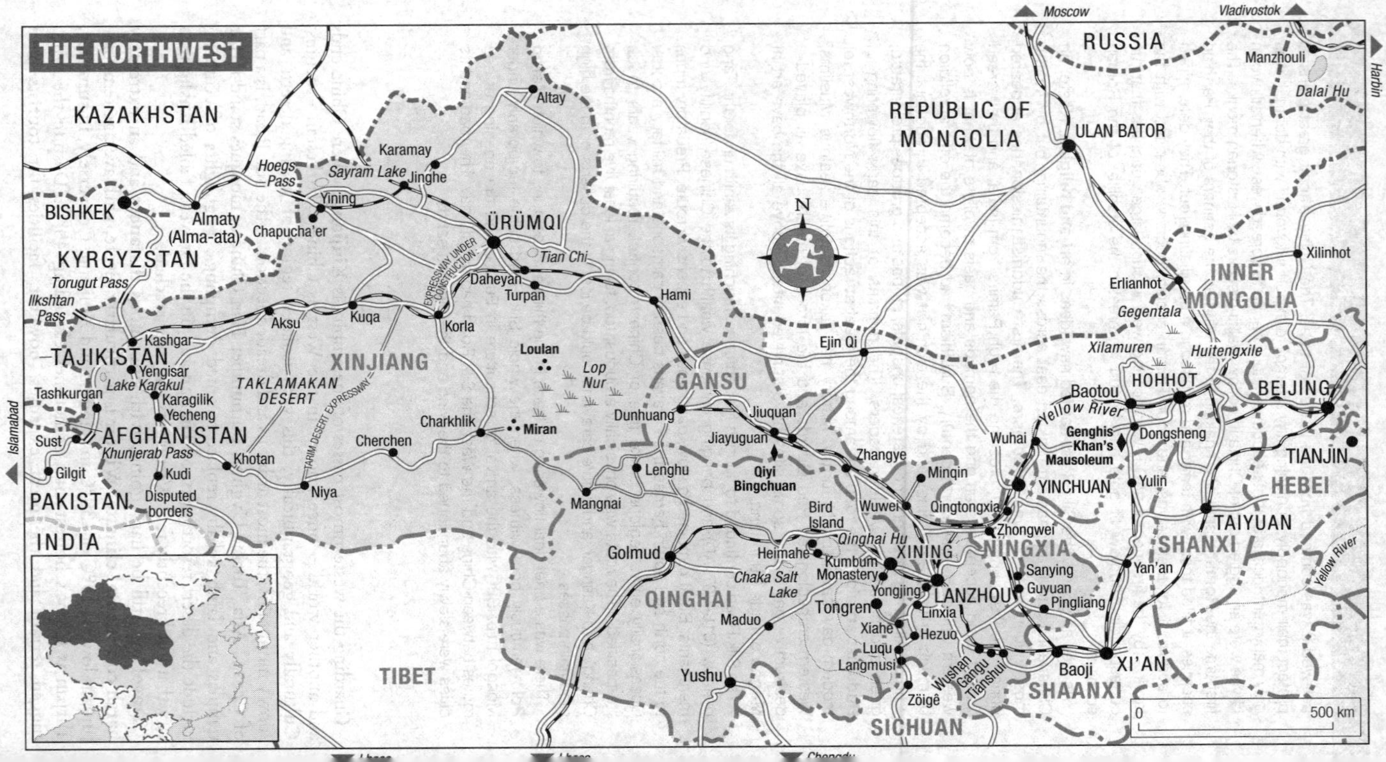

THE NORTHWEST

Moscow
Vladivostok
Harbin
Islamabad
Lhasa
Lhasa
Chengdu

RUSSIA
Manzhouli
Dalai Hu
REPUBLIC OF MONGOLIA
ULAN BATOR
KAZAKHSTAN
BISHKEK
Almaty (Alma-ata)
KYRGYZSTAN
Torugut Pass
Ilkshtan Pass
TAJIKISTAN
Tashkurgan
AFGHANISTAN
Khunjerab Pass
Sust
Gilgit
PAKISTAN
Disputed borders
INDIA
TIBET
Hoegs Pass
Sayram Lake
Karamay
Jinghe
Altay
Yining
Chapucha'er
ÜRÜMQI
EXPRESSWAY UNDER CONSTRUCTION
Tian Chi
Daheyan
Turpan
Hami
Kashgar
Yengisar
Lake Karakul
Karagilik
Yecheng
Aksu
Kuqa
Korla
XINJIANG
TAKLAMAKAN DESERT
TARIM DESERT EXPRESSWAY
Khotan
Kudi
Niya
Cherchen
Charkhlik
Loulan
Lop Nur
Miran
Mangnai
GANSU
Dunhuang
Jiuquan
Jiayuguan
Qiyi Bingchuan
Lenghu
Ejin Qi
Zhangye
Minqin
Wuwei
Golmud
QINGHAI
Bird Island
Qinghai Hu
Heimahe
Chaka Salt Lake
Kumbum Monastery
XINING
Yongjing
Tongren
Maduo
Yushu
Xiahe
Luqu
Langmusi
Zöigê
SICHUAN
LANZHOU
Linxia
Hezuo
Wushan
Gangu
Tianshui
Qingtongxia
Zhongwei
NINGXIA
Sanying
Guyuan
Pingliang
Baoji
XI'AN
SHAANXI
Wuhai
YINCHUAN
Genghis Khan's Mausoleum
Yellow River
Baotou
HOHHOT
Dongsheng
Yulin
Yan'an
INNER MONGOLIA
Erlianhot
Xilinhot
Gegentala
Xilamuren
Huitengxile
BEIJING
TIANJIN
HEBEI
TAIYUAN
SHANXI
Yellow River
0
500 km

developed considerably in recent years. In nearly all towns, hotels and restaurants now cater for a range of budgets – and in general, accommodation is a good deal cheaper here than in eastern China. Where rail lines have not been built, nearly everywhere is accessible by bus, and more and more towns by plane as well. Finally there is the possibility of **onward travel** to or from China's Central Asian neighbours – Kazakhstan, Kyrgyzstan and Pakistan can all be reached by road or rail from the provinces covered in this chapter.

Gansu and Qinghai

The gigantic, naturally splendid provinces of **Gansu** (甘肃, *gānsù*) and **Qinghai** (青海, *qīnghǎi*) sit side by side, far to the west of Beijing and the Chinese seaboard. Together they form an incredibly diverse expanse, from **colossal mountains** in the south to vast tracts of **desert land** in the northwest. On a map, these provinces would appear to be at the very centre of China, but this is only true in a geological sense. Traditionally, the Chinese have regarded Gansu, the "closer" of the pair, as marking the outer limit of Chinese cultural influence.

A harsh, barren land, subject to frequent droughts, **Gansu** has always been a better place for travelling through than settling down in. The province's geography is remarkable – from the great **Yellow River**, dense with silt, to the mountains and deserts of the **Hexi Corridor**, a 1000km route between mountain ranges that narrows at times to as little as 16km-wide bottlenecks. It's the Hexi Corridor that accounts for the curious dumbbell shape of the province: the Silk Road caravans funnelled this way, the Great Wall was built here and today's trains chug along here as well, on what was once the only link through Central Asia between China and the West. The towns along the Hexi Corridor are mere dots of life in the desert, sustained by irrigation using water from the mountains. Given that agriculture is barely sustainable here, central government has tried to import a certain amount of industry into the province, particularly in the east. The exploitation of mineral deposits, including oil and coal, was a tentative beginning, quickly followed by Mao's paranoid "Third Line" industrial development in the 1960s, when factories were built in remote areas to save them from possible Soviet attack. But still the population is relatively small – just 26 million – if of an extraordinary ethnic mix, with Hui, Kazakhs, Mongols and Tibetans all featuring prominently.

The province may be wild and remote by Chinese standards, but it has plenty of historical interest. The **Mogao Caves** at **Dunhuang** in the far west house the finest examples of Buddhist art in all China, and further Silk Road sights are scattered right along the length of the province, ranging from the country's largest reclining Buddha at **Zhangye** to the stunning Buddhist caves at **Bingling Si**, near Lanzhou, and **Maiji Shan**, near **Tianshui** in the far south. The Great Wall, snaking its way west, comes to a symbolic end at the great Ming fortress at **Jiayuguan**, and, in the southwest of the province, right on the edge of the Tibetan plateau, is the fascinating **Labrang Monastery** at the Tibetan town of **Xiahe**; from here, you can follow a loop route into Qinghai.

A huge, empty wilderness with a population of just 5.5 million, **Qinghai** is in many respects a part of Tibet, forming the northern section of the **Tibetan plateau** and owning a strong **minority presence** – as well as Tibetans and Hui, there are Salar, Tu, Mongol and Kazakh people all living here. Only the eastern part of the province around **Xining** has a long-established Han presence. With its lush green valleys and plentiful annual rainfall, this is also the only part of Qinghai where sustainable agriculture takes place. Close by is the splendid **Kumbum Monastery**, one of the four great Tibetan lamaseries, is located just outside Xining. The province has other attractions, too, chiefly as an unspoilt natural wilderness area incorporating the enormous **Qinghai Hu**, China's biggest lake, which offers opportunities for hikes and birdwatching. There are also possibilities for longer treks, rafting and mountaineering. Such activities are best arranged by local travel agents, who can sometimes do so with just a few days' notice.

Some history

During the Han dynasty (206 BC–220 AD), the first serious effort was made to expand into the western deserts, primarily as a means to ensure control over the Silk Road trade. Prefectures were established and, although **Gansu** did not officially become a Chinese province until the Mongolian Yuan dynasty (1279–1368), it is unquestionably a part of the Chinese heartland. At various stages over the last two thousand years Chinese control has extended well beyond here into Xinjiang. Nevertheless, right into the nineteenth century the primarily Muslim inhabitants of this province were considered little better than the "barbarian" Uyghurs of Xinjiang by central government; the great Muslim revolts of that period were ruthlessly quashed.

Geographically and culturally a part of the **Tibetan plateau**, **Qinghai** has for centuries been a frontier zone, contested between Han Chinese, Tibetans and Muslims who originally dwelt in its pastures and thin snatches of agricultural land. Significant Han migration didn't occur until the late nineteenth century, when it was encouraged by the Qing dynasty. However, effective Han political control was not established until 1949 when the Communists defeated **Ma Bufang**, a Hui warlord who had controlled the area since 1931. The area is still perceived by the Han Chinese as a frontier land for pioneers and prospectors, and, on a more sinister note, a dumping ground for criminals and political opponents to the regime. The number of inmates held in Qinghai **prison and labour camps**, including those released but who must remain in the province because they cannot regain residency rights in their home towns, is estimated at 400,000 – almost a tenth of the population.

Eastern Gansu

West of the border with Shaanxi, the first significant Silk Road city is **Tianshui**, with the spectacular **Maiji Shan** complex just a few kilometres to the southeast. Maiji Shan – literally "Wheatstack Mountain", a name derived from its shape – is the fourth-largest Buddhist cave complex in China, after Dunhuang, Datong and Luoyang. Set amid stunning wooded hills, the caves are easily accessed from Tianshui, which is about halfway along on the Lanzhou–Xi'an rail line. You will probably need to spend at least one night at Tianshui, the nearest transport hub to the caves, though in itself of limited interest to tourists. A little to the west of Tianshui, toward Lanzhou, are some more fascinating Silk Road relics, in and around the towns of **Gangu** and **Wushan**.

Tianshui

The area around **TIANSHUI** (天水, *tiānshuǐ*) was first settled back in Neolithic times, though today the city is an enormous industrial spread with two distinct centres, known as **Qincheng** (West Side) and **Beidao** (East Side), situated some 20km apart. Where you stay will probably be determined by whether you arrive at the Beidao train station or the Qincheng bus station. If your only interest is a trip to Maiji Shan and back, you should stay in Beidao, from where all the Maiji Shan minibuses depart, though this is the grottier of the two ends of town.

Gangu
Lanzhou
TIANSHUI (QINCHENG)
Yuquanguan Park
Yuquan Si
RENMIN XI LU
Long-distance Bus Station
Bank of China
PSB
MINZHU LU
CITS
Fuxi Miao
JIEFANG LU
ZHONGHUA LU
BUXING LU
HEZUO LU
YINGBIN LU
Ji River
0 1 km
N
Beidao & Maiji Shan

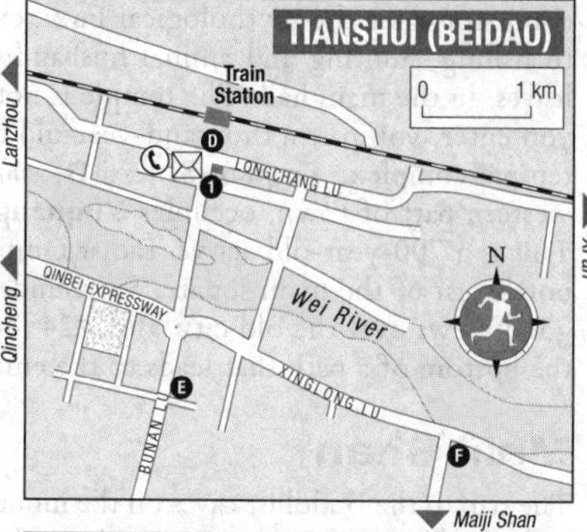

ACCOMMODATION			
Golden Sun Hotel	B	Yatai Hotel	F
Jianxin Hotel	A	Zhoulin Hotel	E
Maiji Hotel	D	**EATING & DRINKING**	
Tianshui Hotel	C	Tianhe	1

Arrival and information

All trains stop at the **train station** in Beidao. **Buses** usually use the long-distance station in Qincheng, or stop and start in front of the train station. **City transport** between the two centres is swift and efficient, with minibuses and bus #1 running between the two stations all day (6am–10pm; 30min; ¥2). A taxi between the two should cost around ¥20.

The Beidao **post office** is just southwest of the train station, the **Bank of China** just southeast. In Qincheng, the **Bank of China** head office is on Minzhu Lu; look for the twin lions outside. To make long-distance calls, use the main **post office** on Minzhu Lu. The Tianshui **CITS** (ⓣ0938/8287337) is on the northwest corner of the Hezuo Lu/Minzhu Lu intersection. English-speaking staff here can organize tours to Maiji Shan for a reasonable ¥200.

Accommodation and eating

There's adequate **accommodation** in both Beidao and Qincheng, but as there's little to detain you in town after a visit to Maiji Shan, you might consider getting a late train out. About the only decent place to get a **meal in Beidao** is at the *Tianhe* restaurant – head south from the station to the first crossroads, then turn left and it's on the corner. The staff are very friendly and the dishes great value for money. There's another good, cheap **restaurant in Qincheng**, opposite the *Jianxin* hotel.

Beidao

Maiji (麦积大酒店, *màijī dàjiǔdiàn*) Opposite the train station ⓣ0938/4920000, ⓕ4929320. Not a bad choice, with elderly furnished rooms and friendly staff. Dorm beds ¥40, rooms ❹

Yatai (亚太大酒店, *yàtài dàjiǔdiàn*) Xinglong Lu ⓣ0938/2727712. The lobby is a little pretentious given the fairly average rooms, but rates aren't expensive and, usefully, the place is on the minibus route to the caves. ❸

Zhoulin (舟林宾馆, *zhōulín bīnguǎn*) Bunan Lu ⓣ0938/2738118. Cheap and unattractive, but a good getaway from the crowds around the train station. Dorm beds ¥45, rooms ❷

Qincheng

Golden Sun (阳光饭店, *yángguāng fàndiàn*) On the pedestrianized Zhonghua Lu ⓣ0938/8277777. The most upmarket option in town, with a bar and a restaurant. The staff can speak English. A taxi from the nearby bus station costs ¥3. ❻

Jianxin (建新饭店, *jiànxīn fàndiàn*) 5min walk west of the bus station ⓣ0938/4985300. This aged hotel is a cheap and hospitable place. ❸

Tianshui (天水宾馆, *tiānshuǐ bīnguǎn*) Yingbin Lu ⓣ0938/8212611, ⓕ8213920. From the bus station, walk onto Minzhu Lu and catch bus #1, or any minibus, east to Yingbin Lu. You can also get here with bus #1 or minibuses from Beidao. One of the town's first hotels, and a bit frayed and pricey for what you get. ❺

The City

The only notable sights within Tianshui are in Qincheng. Best is **Fuxi Miao** (伏羲庙, *fúxī miào*; daily 8am–11pm; ¥30), a Ming-dynasty complex that commemorates the mythological Fuxi, credited with introducing the Chinese to fishing, hunting and animal husbandry – there is a statue of him, clad in leaves, in the main hall. The temple is notable for its beautiful cypress trees; as you enter, you pass a thousand-year-old tree on the right. Another interesting temple complex, **Yuquan Si** (玉泉寺, *yùquán sì*; daily 8am–7pm; ¥20), in the western part of town, occupies **Yuquanguan Park**, up above Renmin Xi Lu. This is a 700-year-old active Taoist temple, on a hill about ten minutes' walk northwest of the main square. Surrounded by attractive cypress trees, it offers good views over the old city. Bus #24 (¥0.5) from Fuxi Miao will take you to the bottom of a path that leads to the entrance.

Maiji Shan

The trip to the Buddhist caves on the mountain of **Maiji Shan** (麦积山, *màijī shān*) is the highlight of eastern Gansu. As is often the case with Buddhist cave sites in northwest China, the natural setting is spectacular: although the whole area is very hilly, the sheer, rocky cliffs of Maiji Shan, rising out of the forest, make this one hill a complete anomaly. The centrepiece of the statuary, the giant **16m-high Buddha** (complete with birds nesting in one of its nostrils), is visible from far away, hanging high up on the rock in conjunction with two smaller figures. The combination of rickety walkways on the cliff face with the beautiful wooded, mountain scenery opposite adds charm to the site.

The cliffs were split apart by an earthquake in the eighth century, leaving a total of 194 surviving **caves** on the eastern and western sections, dating from the northern Wei right through to the Qing. The wall paintings are fading due to rain erosion, but the statues are worth visiting. The western cliff caves are particularly well preserved, and date mainly from the fourth to the sixth century AD: Cave 133 is considered to be the finest, containing sculptures and engraved stones. You are free to explore on your own, climbing higher and higher up the narrow stairways on the sheer face of the mountain. The caves are all locked, though, and you often find yourself peering into half-lit caverns through wire grilles; for the non-specialist the view is probably adequate – at least some of the artwork and statuary shows up clearly. If you ask around at the site, you may be able to find an English-speaking guide to unlock the cave doors and explain the artwork. Another option is to arrange a guide with the Tianshui CITS before you set out.

Practicalities

Frequent **minibuses** run to the caves from the square outside Tianshui's train station (45min–1hr); the ride costs ¥5 each way, though foreigners are usually charged double. When you reach Maiji Shan (daily 8am–6pm), there is a fee of ¥70 or ¥80 per person – depending on whether you want the bus ride up the mountain – to enter the mountain area.

Gangu and Wushan

West of Tianshui, on the road and rail line to Lanzhou, are a couple of little-known but fascinating reminders of the Silk Road era. The prime attraction at **GANGU** (甘谷, *gāngǔ*), 65km west of Tianshui, reached by either train or bus, is **Daxiang Shan** (大像山, *dàxiàng shān*; ¥10). It gets its name – Giant Statue – from the hulking figure of an unusually moustached Sakyamuni Buddha that was carved out of a cliff during the Tang dynasty. The statue is more than 23m tall, and can be reached in about an hour by foot along a path leading uphill from the town, following a shrine-studded ridge all the way to the temple.

From **Wushan** (武山, *wǔ shān*), 45km west of Gangu, you can visit the **Water Curtain Grottoes** (水帘洞, *shuǐlián dòng*; ¥10), which contain a number of important relics, including the **Lashao Temple** (拉稍寺, *lāshāo sì*), as well as a Thousand Buddha Cave site. This extraordinary area is all the better preserved for being so inaccessible – the temple, set into a natural cave in a cliff, is not visible from the ground. Digging at the grottoes began during the Sixteen States period (304–439 AD) and continued through the dynasties. The Lashao Temple was built during the Northern Wei (386–534). There is a 40m-high statue of Sakyamuni on the mountain cliff, his feet surrounded by wild animals, including lions, deer and elephants. It is a design of the Hinayana branch of Buddhism – rarely found in Chinese cave art. The grottoes, about 30km north of Wushan, can only be reached along a dried-up riverbed; a new road is being built, but it's worth asking about the situation before heading out.

All **buses** – and all **trains** except for express services – running between Tianshui and Lanzhou stop at both Gangu and Wushan. It's also possible to visit Gangu as a day-trip from Tianshui; minibuses run from the Qincheng bus station in the morning. If you want to visit both Gangu and the grottoes in one day from Tianshui you have to rent a vehicle; to handle the rough road from Wushan, it is better to get a small minibus (¥600) rather than a taxi (¥250). It is a long, tiring excursion and might be simpler to stay a night at either Wushan or Gangu, perhaps as a stopover on the way between Tianshui and Lanzhou. Note that access to the Water Curtain Grottoes is dependent on the weather – you won't be able to use the riverbed if it has been wet recently.

Pingliang

An eight-hour bus journey away, the modern city of **PINGLIANG** (平凉, *píngliáng*) lies about 200km northeast of Tianshui. The surrounding area, a mountainous and beautiful part of Gansu province near the border with Ningxia, is little known to foreigners. The chief local attraction is **Kongtong Shan**, a one-time Taoist monastery that now integrates Buddhism into its practices. It is one of China's most venerated, perched precariously on a clifftop, with Guyuan in southern Ningxia a possible day-trip, two hours away by bus. The last bus to Guyuan is at 4pm, and there are trains leaving around midnight to Yinchuan and Xi'an.

Practicalities

Pingliang is accessible by **train**, but its station (2km northeast of the town centre) handles only a dozen or so services per day. If you arrive that way, the nearest **hotel** is the *Fenbu* (分部宾馆, *fēnbù bīnguǎn*; ⓣ0933/8623711; ❸, dorm beds ¥60), just south of the station, over the bridge and on the right. Continue down this road for 100m and you come to the **east bus station**, with sleeper buses to Xi'an (¥50) and Lanzhou (¥63) leaving every thirty minutes. The most convenient lodging from there is the well-maintained *Tianxing* (天兴宾馆, *tiānxīng bīnguǎn*;

Ⓣ0933/8713691; ❸, dorm beds ¥20); come out of the bus station, turn left over a bridge and it's about 200m down on the left. Continue down the road to a string of cheap **restaurants**; try the local *helao mian*, a noodle dish with vegetarian and meat choices (under ¥5). The plushest hotel in town is the *Pingliang* (平凉宾馆, *píngliáng bīnguǎn*; Ⓣ0933/8253361; ❹) on Xi Dajie – the rooms are spacious and spotless, and it's also a handy place to change foreign currencies. Bus #1 from the train station will get you there. The **west bus station** on the other side of town, also reached by bus #1, is busier, serving destinations including Beijing, Ürümqi, Yinchuan, Guyuan, Lanzhou and Tianshui.

Kongtong Shan

Kongtong Shan (崆峒山, *kōngtóng shān*) lies 15km west of Pingliang; around ¥30 by taxi, or ¥5 on one of the summer-only tourist buses from the west bus station. You'll be dropped at the bottom of the mountain, from where you then walk 4km up a winding road to the top, buying a ticket (¥60) on the way. Alternatively, a shuttle bus can save you the effort for ¥15. On arrival you're rewarded with spectacular views over an azure lake, the surrounding ribbed landscape dotted with Taoist temples. Maps of the area are available from kiosks at the top, and you're free to hike off in any direction – head up for the best buildings, or down toward the lake for the best scenery.

Your ¥60 ticket allows you to stay as long as you want, and it's certainly worth staying overnight if you want to avoid the day-tripping crowds; **accommodation** is available at the touristy *Kongtong Shanzhuang* (崆峒山庄, *kōngtóng shānzhuāng*; closed Nov–April; dorm beds ¥60, ❸) and at a primitive Taoist hostel, *Taihe Gong* (太和宫, *tàihé gōng*; dorm beds ¥20), in the resort site.

Lanzhou and around

Squeezed 1600m up into a narrow valley along the Yellow River, and stretching out pencil-thin for nearly 30km east to west, gritty **LANZHOU** (兰州, *lánzhōu*) is one of those cities in which few travellers choose to linger any longer than necessary. It sits at the head of the Hexi Corridor (see p.809), which means that almost everyone heading to Xinjiang from eastern China will have to pass by at some point. A great number of trains head straight on through, but given the distances a lot of travellers choose the break their journey here – they're usually back on the train before too long, thanks in no small part to the extraordinary level of **pollution**. The colossal assortment of factories and petroleum processing plants in and around the city, coupled with its location – hemmed in by large mountains – once earned it the unfortunate title of "World's Most Polluted City". Things are at least improving: in a 2007 survey, Lanzhou had dropped out of the Top Ten (but still qualified for a "special mention").

The city is at the least slowly becoming more attractive, especially with the tarting up of the **Yellow River**'s north bank. There are also a number of good day-trip possibilities, including the caves of **Bingling Si**, while Lanzhou forms the start or finish line for those doing the fascinating **Xiahe loop** (see p.819). Lastly, this is the best place in China in which to slurp down a bowl of **beef noodles** – a dish available all around the country, but at its best here.

Some history

On the map, Lanzhou appears to lie very much in the middle of China, though this is misleading. Culturally and politically, it remains remote from the great cities of eastern China, despite being both the provincial capital and the largest

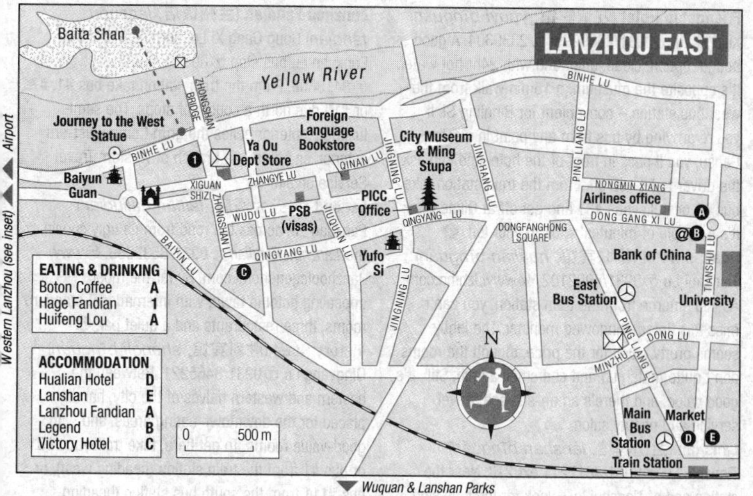

industrial centre in the Northwest. At the head of the Hexi Corridor, it was a vital stronghold along the Silk Road and was the principal crossing point of the mighty Yellow River. For centuries it has been a transportation hub, first for caravans, then shallow boats and now rail lines. Not until the Communist era, however, did it become a large population centre as well, in response to the city's burgeoning industry. Now the city has nearly three million people, the vast majority of them Han Chinese.

Arrival

Lanzhou's **airport** lies about 70km north of the city, at least a ninety-minute journey. Airport buses (¥30) terminate conveniently in the eastern part of the city, outside the CAAC office on Dong Gang Xi Lu.

As the main rail hub of northwest China, Lanzhou is an easy place to travel into or out of by train. Arriving this way, you will almost certainly be dropped off at the massive main **train station** in the far southeast of the city; some trains also stop at the **west train station**, more than a dozen kilometres away in a wretched part of town – a few bus routes head this way, or **taxi fares** start at ¥7 for 3km on the meter.

There are several **long-distance bus stations** in Lanzhou. Buses from **Xiahe** arrive at the **south bus station**; bus #111 outside can take you to Xiguan Shizi Lukou in the centre. Buses from the Hexi Corridor might wind up here too, or – along with traffic from everywhere else – terminate near the train station at the **main bus station** (well hidden off lower Ping Liang Lu) or at the larger **east bus station** 1km north. Schedules are in permanent flux, so ask at your hotel which station to use. At the time of writing, the south station was best for Xiahe, Linxia and the Hexi Corridor, the main and east stations best for Xining and eastern Gansu.

Accommodation

Most accommodation in Lanzhou is in the vicinity of the main **train station** – an inexpensive but grubby location. Unfortunately, there's next to nothing decent around the Yellow River, though the extensive riverbank redevelopment work should mean that something pops up in the near future.

Friendship Hotel (友谊宾馆, *yǒuyí bīnguǎn*) Xijin Xi Lu ⓣ0931/2689999, ⓕ2330304. A good budget option, clean, quiet and with 24hr hot water. It's opposite the museum, a 15min walk from the west bus station – convenient for Bingling Si. If you're arriving by bus from any point in western Gansu, you'll pass in front of the hotel and can ask the driver to let you off. From the train station take bus #1 or trolleybus #31 and get off at Qilihe Qiao; it's a couple of minutes' walk to your left. ❸

Hualian Hotel (华联宾馆, *huálián bīnguǎn*) Tianshui Lu ⓣ0931/4992102, ⓦwww.lzhlbg.com. As you emerge from the train station, you can't miss this tinted-windowed monster. The lobby seems pretty plush for the price, though the rooms don't quite match up and can smell a little. Still, it's good value, and there's an on-site spa, travel service and beauty salon. ❸

Lanshan (兰山宾馆, *lánshān bīnguǎn*) Tianshui Lu ⓣ0931/8617211 ext 218. Near the station end of Tianshui Lu – look for the blue sign. The interior is pretty basic, but rooms are cheap. ❶

Lanzhou Fandian (兰州饭店, *lánzhōu fàndiàn*) Dong Gang Xi Lu, northeast of the Panxuan Lu bus stop ⓣ0931/8416321, ⓕ8418608. From the train station take bus #1, #7 or #10 due north a couple of stops. The semi-luxurious interior belies the grim Communist-era exterior, and there's a branch of Western Travel Service on site. ❻

Legend (飞天大酒店, *fēitiān dàjiǔdiàn*) Panxuan Lu, across the road from its ugly cousin the *Lanzhou Fandian* ⓣ0931/8532888, ⓦwww.lanzhoulegendhotel.com. By far the most appealing hotel in town, with international-standard rooms, three restaurants and a quiet bar. ❼

Victory Hotel (胜利宾馆, *shènglì bīnguǎn*) Qingyang Lu ⓣ0931/8465221. Between the eastern and western halves of the city, handily placed for the downtown eating areas, and with good-value rooms. To get here, take trolleybus #31 or bus #1 from the train station (heading west), or bus #111 from the south bus station (heading northeast). ❺

The City

The best place to start a tour of Lanzhou is the main shopping district, roughly in the middle of the city in the blocks that lie to the north and east of Xiguan Shizi. There's a downtown feel to the place, with boutiques, Western music, fast food and smart department stores; the city's **Muslim quarter** and white-tiled mosque are also here, at the western end of Zhangye Lu.

The Yellow River and around

Immediately north, the city's greatest sight is the **Yellow River**, already flowing thick and fast, although it still has some 1500km to go before it finally reaches the sea at Qingdao. In summer, the water is a rich, muddy-brown colour, a legacy of the huge quantities of silt it picks up, and the fast flow helps to create a wind corridor through the city, which both moderates the climate and removes some of the worst effects of the pollution. At the time of writing, the north bank was being prettified, and it's possible to head just beyond to **Baita Shan Park** (白塔山公园, *báitǎ shān gōngyuán*; daily 6am–6pm; ¥5), ranged up a steep hillside with great views down over the river from stone terraces. A **cable car** (daily 9am–5pm; ¥30 return), a few minutes west of Zhongshan Lu on the south bank, can take you over the river to a viewpoint in the park among the hills. To go **boating** on the river itself, try the area just west of Zhongshan Bridge – a few motorboats run short scenic trips (¥20/10min; two-person minimum).

Binhe Lu, on the south bank, has a paved promenade from where you can watch the mud slide by, with large *Journey to the West* statues featuring Xuanzang, Monkey, Pigsy, Sandy and the horse (see p.864); across the road, **Baiyun Guan** (白云观, *báiyún guān*; daily 8am–8pm) is a small but cute Taoist temple that provides some respite from the hubbub.

Moving east from the central area takes you into the mainly modern part of the city, which has little to offer tourists. One possible exception, a few minutes southwest of Qingyang Lu, is the **Yufo Si** (玉佛寺, *yùfó sì*). The temple is interesting more for the poignancy of its location than anything else; with high-rise buildings looming on all sides, it looks as alien as a spaceship. Nearby, a few hundred metres west of **Dong Fanghong Square** on Qingyang Lu, is an impressive Ming-dynasty stupa, whose surrounding complex houses the **City Museum**, which opens irregularly for Chinese art exhibitions.

The Gansu Provincial Museum

The west of the city comprises a comparatively upmarket shopping and residential area strung out along Xijin Xi Lu; from the centre of town take bus #1, #6 or trolleybus #31. The one sight worth visiting here, the **Gansu Provincial Museum** (甘肃省博物馆, *gānsùshěng bówùguǎn*; Mon–Sat 9am–5.30pm; free), occupies a boxy Stalinist edifice opposite the *Youyi* hotel. It has an interesting collection, divided between natural resources of Gansu (including mammoth and dinosaur skeletons) and historical finds. There are some remarkable **ceramics** dating from the Neolithic age, as well as a huge collection of **wooden tablets and carvings** from the Han dynasty – priceless sources for studying the politics, culture and economy of the period. The bronze **Flying Horse of Wuwei**, two thousand years old and still with its accompanying procession of horses and chariots, is the highlight, however – note the stylish chariots for top officials with round seats and sunshades. The 14cm-tall horse, depicted with one front hoof stepping on the back of a flying swallow, was discovered in a Han-dynasty tomb in Wuwei in 1969.

Wuquan and Lanshan parks

In the hills bordering the south of the city lie **Wuquan** (五泉公园, *wǔquán gōngyuán*; daily 6.30am–6.30pm; ¥5) and **Lanshan parks** (兰山公园, *lánshān gōngyuán*; daily 6am–6pm; ¥5), just south of the terminus of bus #8 (which you can pick up anywhere on Jiuquan Lu in the centre of town). A nice place to wander with the locals on weekends, Wuquan Park (also known as "Five Springs Mountain Park") is full of mainly Qing pavilions, convoluted stairways twirling up the mountainside interspersed with teahouses, art-exhibition halls and ponds. One of the oldest buildings, the **Jingang Palace**, is Ming and contains a 5m-high bronze Buddha – though first cast in 1370, it was restored after being smashed into pieces in the late 1940s. From Wuquan Park, Lanshan Park can be reached by chair-lift (¥20) – it's about twenty minutes to the very top, from where you'll have superb views of the city, a full 600m down.

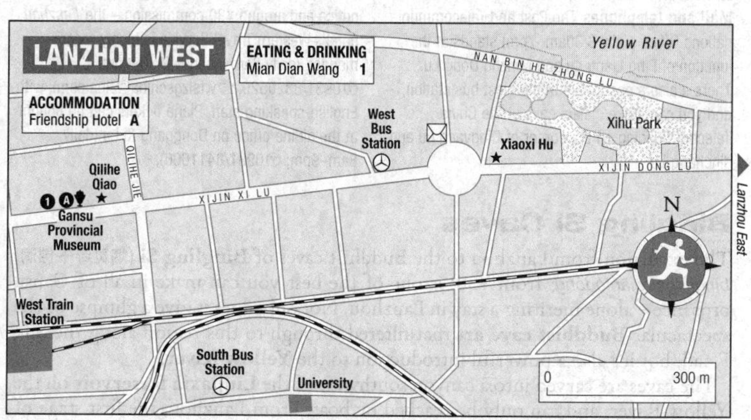

Eating and drinking

Lanzhou, famed around China for its **beef noodles** (牛肉面, *niúròumiàn*) and delicious summer fruits, has plenty of good places to eat. You can try the noodles even if you're not staying: the train station plaza is lined with such restaurants. Otherwise, Nongmin Xiang, north of *Lanzhou Fandian* off Tianshui Lu, is a good place to find inexpensive Chinese restaurants, as is the area around the west bus station, and there's a lively street food market behind the *Hualian Hotel*. The south bank of the Yellow River has a few overpriced "floating" fish restaurants, and lastly there are a few branches of *KFC*, including one at the entrance to the Zhong Ou Department Store and another on Dongfanghong Square.

Boton Coffee (伯顿餐厅, *bódùn cāntīng*) Tianshi Lu. The elegant Western-style interior of this café-cum-restaurant is a wonderful respite from the gritty city outside. Well-dressed waitresses float around delivering coffee (¥28 a pot) and snacks such as delicious pancakes, or larger meals like pizza or steak (around ¥40).

Hage Fandian (哈格饭店, *hāgé fàndiàn*) Opposite the post office on Zhongshan Lu. Small, family-run Muslim restaurant – best are the *shaguo* (vegetables or meat with noodles in clay pots) displayed outside the door.

Huifeng Lou (惠风楼, *huìfēng lóu*) In the *Lanzhou Fandian* compound, Dong Gang Xi Lu. Bright, busy mid-range place serving local delicacies. Try *jincheng niangpi* (spiced glass noodles) or *suancai fentiao* (noodles flavoured with pickled vegetables, chillies and aniseed).

Mian Dian Wang (面点王, *miàndiǎn wáng*) Xijin Xi Lu, west of the *Youyi* hotel. Cheap Chinese-style breakfasts of steamed or fried dumplings, rice porridge and bowls of soya milk with dough sticks.

Listings

Banks and exchange The main Bank of China (daily 8.30am–6pm) is on Tianshui Lu, just south of the *Lanzhou Legend*; foreign exchange is on the second floor. Other branches are scattered all over town.

Bookshops The Foreign Language Bookstore on Qinan Lu has a pitiful selection of novels in English.

Internet There are several internet bars around the train station, but most refuse to take foreigners without a Chinese ID card (ie, all travellers). One exception is a large second-floor room located just to the right of the *Hualian Hotel* entrance.

Mail and telephones The Post and Telecommunications Office (daily 8.30am–7pm) stands at the junction of Ping Liang Lu and Minzhu Dong Lu. There's also a post office at the west bus station, and you can make collect calls at the China Telecom Building on the corner of Qingyang Lu and Jinchang Lu.

PSB Visas can be extended at an office on Wudu Lu, a couple of hundred metres west of Jiuquan Lu.

Shopping Good things to buy in Lanzhou include army surplus clothes: winter coats, waistcoats, hats and boots are all locally produced, tough and cheap. They're made at the 3512 Leather and Garment factory at the west end of Yanchang Lu, north of the river, the largest factory of its kind in China. You can even visit and buy direct (bus #7 from the train station; get off at Caochang Jie).

Tickets and travel agents Plane and train tickets can be booked through travel agents with 36hr notice and around ¥30 commission – the *Lanzhou* hotel's Western Travel Service is highly recommended (daily 8am–noon & 2.30–6pm; ⓣ0931/8820529, ⓔwtslzgschina@sina.com), with English-speaking staff. Plane tickets can be bought at the airline office on Donggang Xi Lu (daily 8am–9pm; ⓣ0931/8411606).

Bingling Si Caves

The excursion from Lanzhou to the Buddhist caves of **Bingling Si** (炳灵寺千佛洞, *bǐnglíngsì qiānfódòng*; from ¥50) is one of the best you can make in all of Gansu province – alone meriting a stay in Lanzhou. Not only does it give a glimpse of the spectacular **Buddhist cave art** that filtered through to this region along the Silk Road, but it's also a powerful introduction to the **Yellow River**.

The caves are carved into a canyon southwest of the **Liujiaxia Reservoir** on the Yellow River, and can only be reached by boat. From Lanzhou, the first stage of the expedition is a two-hour bus ride through fertile fields to the massive **Liujiaxia Hydroelectric Dam**, a spectacular sight poised above the reservoir and surrounded by colourful mountains. At the dam you board a waiting ferry, which takes three hours to reach the caves and offers excellent views of fishermen busy at work and peasants cultivating wheat, sunflowers and rice on the dark, steep banks. During the trip, the ferry enters a tall **gorge** where the river froths and churns; you'll see sections of the bank being whipped away into the waters.

The ferry pulls in just below the Bingling Si Caves. Cut into sheer cliff, amid stunning scenery above a tributary of the river, the caves number 183 in all. They are among the earliest significant Buddhist monuments in China – started in the Western Jin and subsequently extended by the Northern Wei, the Tang, Song and Ming. The artwork at Bingling Si reached its peak under the Song and Ming dynasties, and though the wall paintings of this period have been virtually washed away, there remain a considerable number of small, exquisite carvings. Since their inaccessibility spared the caves the attentions of foreign "collectors" in the nineteenth century and the Red Guards in the twentieth, most of the cave sculpture is in good condition, and some impressive restoration work is in progress on the wall paintings. The centrepiece sculpture, approached along a dizzying network of stairs and ramps, is a huge 27m-high **seated Buddha** (cave 172), probably carved under the Tang; seeing this requires a special ¥300 ticket, available at the entrance or as part of a pre-booked tour.

Practicalities

The most convenient way to see the caves is on a pre-booked **day-trip** from Lanzhou (see travel agents in "Listings", opposite); solo travellers may have to hunt around in order to tag along with another group. For a maximum car-load of three passengers, an all-inclusive price (car, boat, entry ticket and insurance) usually comes to ¥400–500. The standard trip takes up to twelve hours, which includes less than two hours at the caves, but the scenery en route makes it worthwhile. If you want an in-depth guided tour, encompassing all the caves, it's worth asking about the possibility of a private trip.

Alternatively, you could consider travelling **independently** to the reservoir. From the west bus station, frequent **buses** (¥12) leave from 7am to Liujia Xia in **Yongjing** (永靖; *yǒngjìng*), 75km southwest of Lanzhou. At the bus stop there's an arch with a Chinese-only map; here, you can pick up a speedboat for a return trip (about 2–3hr one way; ¥80/person) or charter your own motorboat to the caves (around ¥400). On the way back you may need to stay the night in Yongjing, if the last public bus back to Lanzhou (around 5pm) leaves without you.

The Xiahe loop

The verdant, mountainous area to the south and southwest of Lanzhou, bordering Qinghai to the west and Sichuan to the south, is one of enormous scenic beauty, relatively untouched by the scars of industry and overpopulation. The people who live in the so-called **Xiahe loop** are few in number, but diverse in culture and ethnicity, with a very strong **Hui** and **Tibetan** presence in the towns of **Linxia** and **Xiahe,** respectively. Xiahe, in particular, is a delightful place to visit, housing one of the major Lamaist temples in China, and attracting monks and pilgrims from the whole Tibetan world. From Xiahe, you can loop back to Lanzhou via **Tongren** – itself home to a large Tibetan population – and Xining, both in **Qinghai** province, or even follow an adventurous route south into **Sichuan** province.

Travelling this loop is fairly straightforward, though the central section can be time-consuming. Regular **buses** connect Lanzhou to Linxia and Xining to Tongren, journeys that can also be made by **shared taxi** for a few extra yuan, money well spent for a trip lighter on the Chinese "triple-S" of spit, smoke and sunflower seeds. Few buses continue on the incredibly scenic road from Linxia to Xiahe, and there's just the one per day from Xiahe to Tongren. Again, shared taxis are an option, though the price will likely be too steep for those not travelling in a group of at least three. The **scenery** en route can be quite spectacular, especially in the upper reaches – think chiselled valley, isolated minority communities, and mountain goats in improbable locations.

Note that with the exception of Linxia, towns on this route are small affairs with few ATMs or exchange facilities – it's best to take enough **cash** to cover the entire trip.

From Lanzhou to Linxia

The road southeast from Lanzhou to Xiahe passes by first Yongjing and Liujiaxia, the jumping-off points for Bingling Si, before traversing **Dongxiang Autonomous County**. This route is absolutely jaw-dropping, racing along a **mountain ridge** for well over an hour, with picture-postcard valley views on both sides. The immediate horizon is punctuated from time to time with **mosques** – this area is home to the Dongxiang **minority people**, as well as other groups including the Hui, Bao'an and Salar (see box below, for more).

Such is the beauty of this trip that you may find yourself wanting to stop off along the way. There are a couple of ridge towns en route, their population almost entirely Muslim: you'll see very few men who aren't wearing skullcaps. Women additionally wear a square veil of fine lace, black if they are married and green if they are not. The largest ridge town goes by a few different names, but is generally referred to as **Dongxiang** (东乡, *dōngxiāng*). This makes for a fascinating stay, with its bustling livestock market (daily) particularly worth checking out.

Linxia

A three-hour bus journey from Lanzhou, **LINXIA** (临夏, *línxià*) is a very **Muslim** town, full of mosques, most of which have been restored since the depredations of the Cultural Revolution. However, Han Chinese influence is taking its toll, with factories and tower blocks sprouting up on the outskirts. There's not much to see, and the town is actually quite ugly; nevertheless, it's an interesting enough place to stroll around for a few hours if you plan to break up your journey from Lanzhou to Xiahe.

Ethnic minorities around Dongxiang

The **Dongxiang minority**, numbering nearly two hundred thousand, are Muslims with Mongol origins. These days, to outsiders at least, they are indistinguishable from the Hui except at certain celebrations when ancient Mongol customs re-emerge. Beyond the pilgrimage centre of Linxia, 60km from Lanzhou, the climb up to Xiahe takes three or four hours (but only two coming down again). The route passes through a zone of cultural overlap between ancient communities of Islamic and Buddhist peoples. A couple of China's lesser-known minorities – the **Bao'an** and the **Salar** – also live here. The Bao'an, who number barely eight thousand, are very similar to the Dongxiang people as they, too, are of Mongolian origins. The Salar are a Turkic-speaking people whose origins lie, it's thought, in Samarkand in Central Asia; they live primarily in Xunhua County in neighbouring Qinghai province.

Linxia's main street, which runs north–south through town, is called **Tuanjie Lu** in the north and **Jiefang Lu** in the south, with a large central square between the two. The main mosque, **Nanguan Mosque** (南关清真寺, *nánguān qīngzhēn sì*), is immediately south of the square; there's a Bank of China just to the south. There is no train station, though there are **two bus stations**. If you're arriving from the west (Xining or Tongren), you may be deposited at the smaller station in the far northwest of the city (known as the west bus station), from which you'll have to catch a cycle-rickshaw or a minivan (¥5) into town. There are plenty of cheap **hotels** dotted around Linxia; if you stay over, make sure to hit the pleasant **night market** (from around 6pm on), set around the central square. This is a good place to stuff yourself on heavy round bread rolls flavoured with curry powder; roast chicken and potatoes are also available, as well as noodles and soups. In addition, there are a couple of very pleasant **teahouses** on terraces overlooking the south side of the central square, where you can sit out and enjoy the night air.

Xiahe and around

A tiny, rural town tucked away 3000m up in the remote hills of southern Gansu, right on the edge of the Tibetan plateau, **XIAHE** (夏河, *xiàhé*) is unforgettable. This is a great place to experience a little Tibetan culture, while saving the price of a package tour to Lhasa. Xiahe is the most important Tibetan monastery town outside Tibet itself, and the **Labrang Monastery** is one of the six major centres of the Gelugpa, or Yellow Hat Sect (of the others, four are in Tibet and one, Kumbum Monastery, is just outside Xining in Qinghai province; see p.829). Tibetans from Tibet come here on pilgrimage in traditional dress (equipped with mittens, kneepads and even leather aprons to cushion themselves during their prostrations), and the constant flow of monks in bright purple, yellow and red, alongside semi-nomadic herdsmen wrapped in sheepskins, makes for an endlessly fascinating scene. As well as offering a glimpse into the lives of **Tibetan people**, Xiahe also offers visitors the rare chance to spend some time in open countryside, set as it is in a sunny, fresh valley surrounded by green hills.

The town is essentially built along a single street that stretches 3–4km along the north bank of the Daxia River, from the bus station in the east, through the Labrang Monastery in the middle, to the old Tibetan town and, finally, the *Labrang Hotel* in the west. The **eastern end** of town, predominantly Hui- and Han-populated, is the commercial and administrative section, with a couple of banks, a post office and plenty of shops and markets. The shops round here make interesting browsing, with lots of Tibetan religious objects for sale, including hand-printed sutras, prayer wheels, bells and jewellery. There's also riding equipment – saddles and bridles – for the nomads from the nearby grasslands who come striding into town, spurs jangling.

Beyond the monastery, at the **western end** of town, is the local Tibetan area. West of the bridge that carries all motorized traffic to the south side of the river, the road becomes a bumpy dirt track with homes built of mud and wood, and pigs and cows ambling around. There is one more religious building up here, the **Hongjiao Si**, or Temple of the Red Hat sect, whose monks, clad in red robes with a large white band, live in the shadow of their rich and more numerous Yellow Hat brethren.

Arrival and information

Nearly all travellers arrive by **bus** at the station at the far eastern end of town, which is served by frequent buses from Linxia and Hezuo; there are also a few to

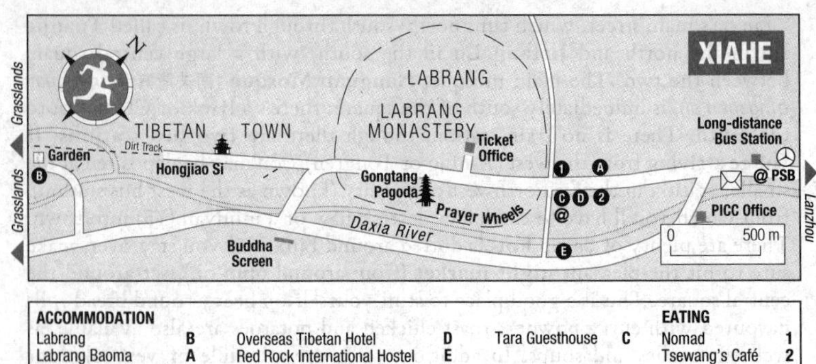

and from Lanzhou (though only one after 7.30am), and one morning departure for Tongren in Qinghai. For the route to Sichuan, take one of the two daily buses to Luqu and continue from there.

You can rent **bikes** from the *Overseas Tibetan* and *Labrang Baoma* hotels for ¥20 a day. There is no **Bank of China**, but the *Overseas Tibetan* can change cheques and cash (Euros and US dollars only), and some get lucky with the ATM at the **Construction Bank of China**.

A few agencies can arrange **tours** and onward travel, including *Tsewang's Cafe* (see p.824) and OT Travels (Ⓣ0941/7122642, Ⓔamdolosang@hotmail.com), which operates from the *Overseas Tibetan Hotel*.

Accommodation

The east end of town has plenty of comfy, Chinese-style hotels. However, it's more fun to try one of the charismatic Tibetan-owned **guesthouses** farther up the road, which attract a mixed clientele of pilgrims and budget travellers. All places listed are on Xiahe's single main road, unless otherwise stated.

Labrang (拉卜楞宾馆, *lābŭlèng bīnguăn*) In the fields to the west of the town Ⓣ0941/7121849. It's 4km from the bus station and nearly 1km from the next nearest building; from the station, a cycle-rickshaw shouldn't cost more than about ¥5. Accommodation ranges from simple three-bed dorms with bath to rather damp, concrete "Tibetan-style" cabins. Ring ahead if at all possible. Dorm beds ¥20, rooms ❻

Labrang Baoma (拉卜楞宝马宾馆, *lābŭlèng băomă bīnguăn*) In a courtyard opposite *Tsewang's Café* Ⓣ0941/7121078, Ⓦwww.labranghotel.com. Very popular hotel sporting traditionally decorated rooms, internet access, two small restaurants and 24hr hot water. Dorm beds ¥30, rooms ❸

Overseas Tibetan Hotel (华侨宾馆, *huáqiáo bīnguăn*) Ⓣ0941/7122642. A clean, well-maintained building offering private rooms pleasantly decorated in a vaguely Tibetan style, as well as a couple of cheap, stuffy dorms. Well staffed with English-speaking employees, plus a wide range of services. Rates include breakfast. Dorm beds ¥20, rooms ❹

Red Rock International Hostel (红石国际青年旅馆, *hóngshí guójì qīngnián lǚshè*) Ⓣ0941/7123698. South of the river and away from the hubbub of the main road, this new hostel centres on its lobby: with its alpine feel and wi-fi access, it makes a good place to meet fellow travellers (although the majority of guests are Chinese families). Communal showers are poor, but the rooms have been decorated with pleasing colours. Dorm beds ¥35, rooms ❸

Tara Guesthouse (才让卓玛旅舍, *cáiràng zhuómă lǚshè*) Ⓣ0941/7121274. The young Tibetan owners are a little odd (some say in a good way, others aren't so impressed) and the rooms can be shabby, but this is perfect for those on a tight budget. The 11pm curfew shouldn't matter too much – this is Xiahe, after all. Dorm beds from ¥10, rooms ❶

Labrang Monastery

Phenomenally beautiful and surrounded by mountains on all sides, **Labrang Monastery** (拉卜楞寺, *lābǔlèng sì*) sits just west of the town centre. There's no wall separating the town from the monastery – the two communities just merge together and the main road goes right through the middle of both. The only markers are the long lines of roofed **prayer wheels** stretching out to the right and left of the road, which together trace a near-complete circle around the monastery. To the south side in particular, along the north bank of the river, you can follow the prayer wheels almost to the other end of the monastery. It's mesmerizing to walk alongside the pilgrims (clockwise around the monastery), who turn each prayer wheel they pass.

The vast majority of the important **monastery buildings** are north of the main road. The buildings include six colleges, as well as temple halls, Jiemuyang residences and a mass of living quarters for the monks. The institutes, where monks study for degrees, are of Astronomy, Esoteric Buddhism, Law, Medicine and Theology (higher and lower). There are also schools for dance, music and painting. The **Gongtang Pagoda** (贡唐宝塔, *gòngtáng bǎotǎ*; daily 7am–11pm; ¥10), built in 1805, is the only major monastery building south of the main road – you pass it when following the prayer wheels. You can buy tickets from the lamas inside the pagoda if the outside ticket office is closed. It's worth climbing to the top for a spectacular view over the shining golden roofs of the monastery.

Some history

The monastery was founded in 1709 by a monk called E'Ang Zongzhe, who thereby became the first-generation Living Buddha, or **Jiemuyang**. Upon the death of each Jiemuyang, a new one is born, supposedly representing the reincarnation of the previous one. The present Jiemuyang, the sixth incarnation, is third in importance in the Tibetan Buddhist hierarchy after the Dalai Lama and Panchen Lama.

Although Labrang may seem a peaceful haven today, it has not always been so. In the 1920s, ferocious battles took place here between Muslim warlords and Tibetans, with atrocities being committed by both sides. With the Cultural Revolution came further disaster: persecution for the monks and the virtual destruction (and closure) of the monastery. It was not until 1980 that it reopened, and although it is flourishing once again, it is nevertheless a smaller place than before. For an idea of its original extent, see the painting in the Exhibition Hall, on the wall at the far end from the entrance. There are now around nine hundred registered lamas and two thousand unofficial monks, about half their former number.

Visiting the monastery

There is nothing to stop you, at any time of day or night, from wandering around the monastery site by yourself. You may even be allowed to walk into the temples – be sensitive and use your discretion, and move clockwise. On the other hand, given the bewildering wealth of architecture, art and statuary, it's a good idea to take a **guided tour** at some stage. This can be arranged at the ticket office – take the only sizeable turn off the north side of the road within the monastery area (the right if coming from the station). The hour-long tours (roughly at 10.15am and 3.15pm; ¥40) include entrance to five buildings and are led by English-speaking monks. You might also be approached by Tibetan students offering tours; settle a price (about ¥20) and route beforehand.

Labrang Monastery is the site of some spectacular **festivals** that, as with Chinese festivals, take place according to the lunar calendar. The largest is the **Monlam Festival**, three days after the Tibetan New Year (late Feb or early March). The opening of the festival is marked by the unfurling of a huge cloth adorned with a holy painting of the Buddha, measuring 20–30m, on the south side of the Daxia River. Processions, dances and the lighting of butter lamps take place on subsequent days.

Eating

Whether you want to eat Tibetan food or banana pancakes, the eastern part of town has plenty of **restaurants**. The friendly *Tsewang's Café*, above street level, between the *Gangjian* and *Overseas Tibetan* hotels, offers the "best pizzas in town"; the stream of glowing comments in the guestbook gives evidence in favour of this claim. The *Nomad Restaurant*, opposite the eastern entrance of the monastery, is also reliable, with rooftop views and an English menu. They serve good breakfasts and decent Western, Chinese and Tibetan food. There's plenty more of the *Nomad*'s ilk on the same stretch. The *Overseas Tibetan* also does decent set breakfasts for around ¥20 per person. For something more homely, try the tiny Hui noodle shop on the western side of the monastery; the grimy but atmospheric interior offers views of spinning prayer wheels.

Around Xiahe

Even without the monastery, Xiahe would be a delightful place to relax given its rural setting. There are a number of superb walks around town, including the **Upper Kora**, a pilgrim trail snaking through the peaks north of the monastery. Other hills around the valley offer excellent hiking opportunities, and the views down can be breathtaking. About 15km farther west up the valley, accessible by motor-rickshaw, are the **Sangke grasslands** (桑科草原, *sāngkē cǎoyuán*), a once-appealing slice of Tibetan life now utterly ruined by domestic tourism. It's not worth heading here, unless your version of Tibet includes neon signs, KTV and – heaven forfend – a casino. The **Gancha grasslands** (甘加草原, *gānjiā cǎoyuán*; ¥15), another 30km to the north, are vaster and less touristy, but harder to get to due to bad road conditions. A return trip by taxi costs around ¥200.

South to Sichuan

South of Xiahe the roads are narrow and traffic irregular; nevertheless, there is a route you can follow by public bus that leads ultimately to Chengdu in Sichuan province. It's a rough trip, requiring several stopovers in remote towns, but a fascinating one, through one of the most beautiful parts of China. Some of the villages en route, notably **Langmusi** just inside Sichuan (see p.793), are the most authentically **Tibetan** settlements most visitors are ever likely to see, given that it can be so hard to travel off the beaten track inside Tibet itself.

Hezuo

From Xiahe, the first stop is **HEZUO** (合作, *hézuò*), about 70km southeast. It's a trading post for Tibetan nomads, and you'll see some fairly wild-looking types in the town. Hezuo is centred on a crossroads with a sculpture of a Tibetan antelope in the middle, looking north. The **north bus station**, where you get off coming from Xiahe or Lanzhou, is on the northwest corner of the crossroads. Almost opposite, on the road leading north, is an adequate **hotel**, the *Gannan Binguan* (甘南宾馆, *gānnán bīnguǎn*; ⓣ0931/8213186; dorm beds ¥15, rooms ❶), kept very clean by its Muslim staff; look for the blue English sign. The Agricultural Bank, on the southwest corner, is the only place in town that will change **foreign currency**. Heading east from the crossroads is a fascinating little street, with a very good two-storey Muslim **restaurant** just a short way down on the right. Buses heading south leave from the **south bus station**; a taxi there from the north bus station will only cost a few yuan.

Hezuo also boasts one worthwhile attraction, the **Mila'erba Monastery** (米拉日巴佛楼阁, *mǐlā rìbā fólóugé*; ¥20, negotiable), in the north of the city. From the crossroads, head west for 500m then turn north for another 1.5km and you'll see it on the left – indeed, you can hardly miss the nine-storey central temple. The exterior may look stern and robust, but the interior is pure chocolate box, each room gaudy with paintings and sculpture. Provided you take your shoes off at the door, you are free to ascend every level. From the roof you can gaze at hills dotted with prayer flags.

South of Hezuo

Beyond Hezuo, the road runs **south to Sichuan** via **LUQU** (碌曲, *lùqǔ*), 80km from Hezuo and served by four to five buses daily from the south bus station. The countryside around Luqu is beautiful and easily accessible for hiking; a stroll up or down the river is likely to turn up one or two monasteries. In town you can **stay** at the *Nonghang Zhaodaisuo* (农行招待所, *nóngháng zhāodàisuǒ*; ⓣ0941/6621085; ❷); there's no English sign, but turn right out of the bus station and it's less than five minutes' walk. From Luqu, it's a further 80km south to charming **Langmusi**, just over the Sichuan border (see p.793).

West to Qinghai

To complete the Xiahe loop, head west into **Qinghai province** across a range of lofty mountains. There's one daily bus from Xiahe to the small town of **Tongren**; the views from this road are absolutely wonderful. Tongren has good connections to the Qinghai capital of Xining, though is well worth a night or two of your time.

Tongren

Just across the Qinghai border from Gansu, and approximately 180km south of Xining, is the autonomous Tibetan region of **Tongren** (同仁, *tóngrén*), its centre a small but growing city of the same name. Known as Repkong in Tibetan, this makes an excellent base for nearby sights, including **Wutun Si**, the source of Tibet's famed **thangka** paintings.

Buses arrive at a small riverside station on the eastern edge of town; there are plenty of services heading north to Xining, but the single departure to Xiahe leaves at 8am sharp. Zhongshan Lu, the road heading straight uphill from top of the station road, has everything you need if you're staying the night. These include a couple of **hotels**, best of which is the *Youzheng* (邮政宾馆, *yóuzhèng bīnguǎn*; ⓣ0973/8724555; ❸) at the very top of the road. On the opposite side of the road is *Repgong Teahouse*, which does small **meals** and, of course, good Tibetan tea. If you fancy a dance, there's even a club right next to the bus station: the *Sunday Super Shake Bar*, just as curious as its name might suggest and totally unused to foreign guests.

Wutun Si and Longwu Si

The superbly detailed pieces of Buddhist art known as *thangka* started life 8km northeast of town in the incredibly scenic village of **Wutun** (吾屯, *wútún*). They continue to be produced to this day in a number of artists' houses surrounding **Wutun Si** (吾屯寺, *wútún sì*), a temple split into upper (上, *shàng*) and lower (下, *xià*) sections that are about ten minutes from each other on foot. Small *thangka* can usually be acquired for around ¥300, while full-size versions – which take well over a month to make – will set you back over ten times that amount. The occasional minibus (¥2) comes here from Tongren, though it's far easier to take a cab (¥10). Some travellers choose to walk the whole way back to Tongren, but even if this sounds like too much work the dirt lanes of **Wutun village** are well worth a wander – basically, this is the Tibet people pay hundreds of dollars to see, an impoverished but happy collection of earth buildings with not a streetlight or mobile phone store in sight. You're almost certain to pick up a few young friends, Pied Piper style.

Closer to town is the Yuan-dynasty Tibetan lamasery **Longwu Si** (隆务寺, *lóngwù sì*; ¥10). Known as Gonchen Gompa in the local tongue, this has been around since the early fourteenth century, and offers an earthy atmosphere similar to what you'll find at Wutun Si. The temple is an easy walk from Zhongshan Lu – turn left at the T-junction at the top end of the road, and it'll appear on your left after 1km or so.

Mengda Nature Reserve

On the way to or from Tongren to Xining, it's worth making the detour to **Mengda Nature Reserve** (孟达自然保护区, *mèngdá zìrán bǎohùqū*; ¥45), an area of outstanding natural beauty. This part of the province, **Xunhua County**, is the homeland of the Salar people, a Muslim ethnic minority (see box, p.820). Its wet, mild climate is conducive to the prolific growth of trees and vegetation, and the woods here are full of wildflowers and inhabited by deer and foxes – the highlight of the place is the Heaven Lake, a sacred spot for the Salar. Hardly any foreign tourists come this way, but if you want to try, take a bus from Xining or Tongren to **Xunhua** (循化, *xúnhuà*), from where it's a short taxi ride to the reserve along a spectacular copper-coloured gorge; a return trip and a couple of hours at the site should run to about ¥70. Alternatively, you can sleep at the reserve (dorm beds ¥30), though it's advisable to bring along at least one day's food and water. If you get stuck in Xunhua, there are plenty of cheap hotels around the bus station.

Xining and around

The unassuming provincial capital of **Qinghai**, **XINING** (西宁, *xīníng*) contains few tourist sights and is usually regarded simply as a base from which to explore the nearby Tibetan **Kumbum monastery**, start a trip around Qinghai or head off on the superb **Xiahe loop** (see p.819). Nevertheless, as the only sizeable city in the province, Xining is an interesting place in its own right. Set in a rather extraordinary location, with imposing mountains rearing up right behind, the city has a cosy, reassuring feel. At a height of 2260m, on the outermost edge of the Tibetan plateau, Xining experiences pleasantly cool weather in summer and bitter cold in winter.

Although a centre of Han population, Xining is full of **minority nationalities**, in particular Hui and rather lost-looking Tibetans. It has quite an ancient history, having been settled probably as early as the Han dynasty. It even served as a stopover on a minor southern route of the Silk Road and has been a fairly important trading city for the Han since at least the sixteenth century. It became the provincial capital when Qinghai became a province proper in 1928. Today, connected by train to Lanzhou and other Chinese cities, Xining is a firmly established part of the network of Han China.

Arrival and information

Most of the city lies to the south of the river, though the **train station** lies immediately on the north bank, just across the bridge from the long-distance **bus station**. Xining's **airport** is 26km east of town; a bus (¥25) collects arrivals and drops them at the airline offices (daily 8.30am–noon & 2–5.30pm; ⓣ0971/8133333) on Bayi Lu, about 1500m southeast of the train station. CITS are at 156 Huanghe Lu (ⓣ0971/6133844).

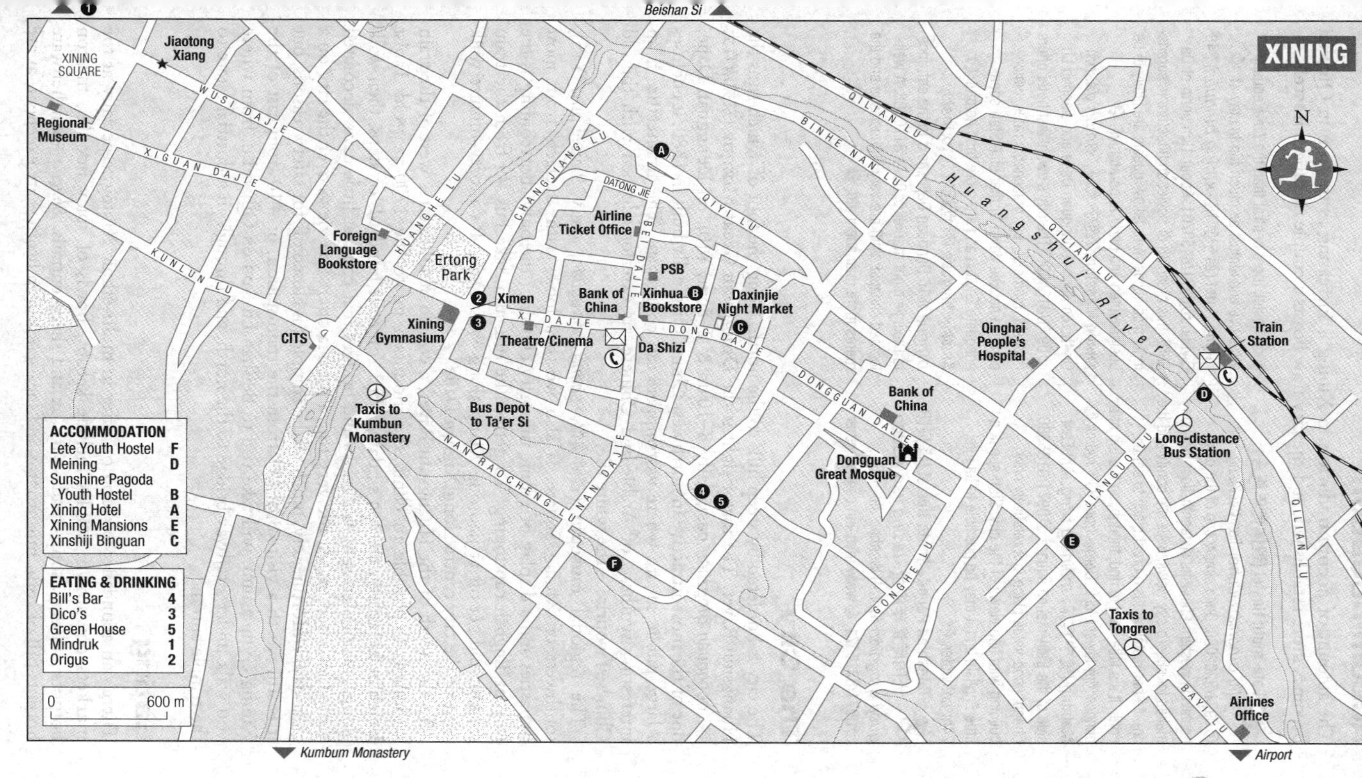
XINING
N
Beishan Si
Kumbum Monastery
Airport
1
Jiaotong Xiang
XINING SQUARE
Regional Museum
WUSI DAJIE
XIGUAN DAJIE
KUNLUN LU
HUANGHE LU
CHANGJIANG LU
DATONG JIE
QIYI LU
BEI DAJIE
XI DAJIE
DONG DAJIE
DONGGUAN DAJIE
NAN DAJIE
NAN RAOCHENG LU
GONGHE LU
JIANGUO LU
BAYI LU
QILIAN LU
BINHE NAN LU
Huangshui River
Foreign Language Bookstore
Ertong Park
Ximen
Xining Gymnasium
CITS
Theatre/Cinema
Airline Ticket Office
PSB
Bank of China
Xinhua Bookstore
Daxinjie Night Market
Da Shizi
Taxis to Kumbun Monastery
Bus Depot to Ta'er Si
Qinghai People's Hospital
Bank of China
Dongguan Great Mosque
Train Station
Long-distance Bus Station
Taxis to Tongren
Airlines Office
ACCOMMODATION
Lete Youth Hostel F
Meining D
Sunshine Pagoda Youth Hostel B
Xining Hotel A
Xining Mansions E
Xinshiji Binguan C
EATING & DRINKING
Bill's Bar 4
Dico's 3
Green House 5
Mindruk 1
Origus 2
0 600 m

Accommodation

The amount of **accommodation** in Xining is increasing as tourism in Qinghai becomes more established, and the city now boasts a couple of superb **hostels**.

Lete Youth Hostel (理体青年旅舍, *lǐtǐ qīngnián lǚshè*) Jian Cai Xiang ⓣ0971/8202080. Quite simply one of the best hostels in western China: its sixteenth-floor location makes for superb city views, beds are comfy and the on-site bar/restaurant is a great place to eat or drink. It's a little hard to find, though, on the top of a nondescript tower block. Dorms from ¥30, rooms ❸

Meining (美宁宾馆, *měiníng bīnguǎn*) East side of the train-station square ⓣ0971/8185380. Cheap, good-value place in a relatively new building with fine views of the city. Staff speak a little English, and it may be possible to haggle; 24hr hot water. ❸

Sunshine Pagoda Youth Hostel (塔顶阳光国际青年旅舍, *tādǐng yángguāng guójì qīngnián lǚshè*) Wenhua Jie ⓣ0971/8215571, ⓦwww.tdyg-inn.com. Another good hostel, more central than the *Lete*, equally attractive and almost as much fun to stay at. ❸

Xining Hotel (西宁宾馆, *xīníng bīnguǎn*) 348 Qiyi Lu ⓣ0971/8458701. About 1km north of Da Shizi, this monolith of Soviet architecture is surprisingly nice inside. Your fellow guests are likely to be businessmen and party apparatchiks. ❺

Xining Mansions (西宁大厦, *xīníng dàshà*) On the corner of Dongguan Dajie and Jianguo Lu ⓣ0971/8164800. The city's swankiest hotel offers fantastic rooms at very reasonable rates, which can be knocked down further still. Staff speak adequate English and are more than helpful. ❺

Xinshiji Binguan (新世纪宾馆, *xīnshìjì bīnguǎn*) 16 Donguan Dajie, next to the entrance to Daxinjie night market ⓣ0971/8176888. A well-located cheapie; staff are very enthusiastic and the rooms more than adequate. ❷

The City

The city is bordered by steep hills to the north, along the foot of which runs the Huangshui River. The major sight is the **Dongguan Great Mosque** (东关清真大寺, *dōngguān qīngzhēn dàsì*; daily 8–10am & 2–8pm; ¥10), on Dongguan Dajie, one of the most attractive in northwest China. Originally built in 1380, it encloses a large public square where worshippers can congregate. The architecture is an interesting synthesis of Arabic and Chinese, its exterior adorned with the old Chinese favourite – the white tile.

The regional **museum** (省博物馆, *shěng bówùguǎn*; daily 9am–5pm; ¥15), southwest of Xining Square, is also worth a look, with artefacts from most dynasties and a display of ethnic minority clothing; the only shortcoming is the lack of English captioning. To get to the museum, take bus #9 from the train station, and get off at Jiaotong Xiang along Wusi Dajie. It's a forty-minute walk west of the city centre along Xiguan Dajie.

To the north of the Huangshui River, a couple of kilometres west of the train station, it is possible to climb the mountain up to the 1700-year-old Taoist **Beishan Si** (北山寺, *běishān sì*; daily; ¥5). You scale hundreds of steps, then walk along a whole series of walkways and bridges that connect little caves decorated with Taoist designs. At the very top, a pagoda offers fine views over the city on a clear day. Unfortunately, much of the complex is closed off for safety reasons, but it is still worth a visit. Bus #11 from the train station, or #10 from east of the Xining Gymnasium, will take you to Beishan Lu Kou on Qilian Lu, from where you walk under a railway bridge to the north, and through an industrial estate to the temple entrance.

Eating

There's an abundance of food on offer in multi-ethnic Xining, especially at the **markets** downtown; staples include kebabs, bowls of spicy noodles, mutton hotpots and *zasui* soup, made with ox and sheep entrails. *Shaguo* – earthenware hotpots full of tofu, mushrooms and meat cooked in broth – are excellent, as are *jiaozi*, *hundun* soup and other basic dishes prepared on the spot. Alternatively, you can head to the excellent **Daxinjie night market**, one lane down from Dong Dajie, which turns into a fresh-food bonanza in the evenings. For Tibetan food head to *Mindruk*, run by a famous Tibetan singer; her main restaurant is just off Wusi Dajie, though you could ask directions to a better-looking – but almost impossible to find – secondary location nearby. If you're after Western food, head for *KFC*, *Origus* or *Dico's*, all on the Ximen intersection; best for **coffee** and cakes is the American-run *Green House*, off Nan Xiaojie, while *Bill's Bar* just down the road is a popular **drinking** hole.

Listings

Banks and exchange The main Bank of China is a huge building on Dongguan Dajie near the mosque, and it is only this branch that will change travellers' cheques.

Bookstore The Foreign Language bookstore, west of Ertong Park on Huanghe Lu, has a surprisingly good selection of English-language classics and Chinese works in translation.

Mail and telephones The main post office, where you can make IDD telephone calls, is on the southwest corner of Da Shizi; enter by climbing the raised pedestrian walkway. You'll find another office for making IDD calls a few minutes east of the train station, next to a smaller post office.

Travel agents For buying train or plane tickets, and for organizing trips to Qinghai Hu (see p.831) or more remote parts of Qinghai, the best by far is Tibetan Connections (Ⓦ www.tibetanconnections.com), which operates from the *Lete Youth Hostel*; also convenient is the Traffic Travel Service (Ⓣ 0971/8133928), based at the front of the long-distance bus station on Jianguo Lu – look for the red English sign.

Kumbum Monastery and beyond

About 25km southeast from Xining, **Kumbum Monastery** (塔尔寺, *tǎ'ěr sì*; daily 8.30am–4.30pm; ¥80 provides access to nine temples) is one of the most important monasteries outside Tibet. Although not as attractive as Labrang in Xiahe (see p.823), and often swamped by tourists, Kumbum is nevertheless a good introduction to Tibetan culture. As both the birthplace of Tsongkhapa, the founder of the **Yellow Hat Sect**, and the former home of the current Dalai Lama, the monastery attracts droves of pilgrims from Tibet, Qinghai and Mongolia, who present a startling picture with their rugged features, huge embroidered coats and chunky jewellery.

Aside from the hulking **military base** built right next to the monastery, the surrounding countryside is beautiful. The views stretch away to distant mountains, and you can ramble over hills of wheat, across pastures dotted with cattle and horses, and over ridges and passes dappled with wild flowers. Apart from the large numbers of Han Chinese tourists, the people you meet here will likely be Tibetan horsemen, workers in the fields who will offer an ear of roasted barley by way of hospitality, or pilgrims prostrating their way around the monastery walls.

The monastery

The monastery dates from 1560, when building was begun in honour of **Tsongkhapa**, founder of the reformist Yellow Hat Sect of Tibetan Buddhism, who was born on the Kumbum Monastery estates. Legend tells how, at Tsongkhapa's birth, drops of blood fell from his umbilical cord causing a tree with a thousand leaves to spring up; on each leaf was the face of the Buddha, and there was a Buddha image on the trunk (now preserved in one of the stupas). During his lifetime, Tsongkhapa's significance was subsequently borne out: his two major disciples were to become the two greatest living Buddhas, one the Dalai Lama, the other the Panchen Lama.

Set in the cleft of a valley, the **walled complex** is an imposing sight, an active place of worship for about six hundred monks as well as the constant succession of pilgrims. Ignore the furtive hawkers offering Dalai Lama pendants at the gate – possession of them is illegal.

The most attractive of the **temples** is perhaps the **Great Hall of Meditation** (temple 5 on your ticket), an enormous, very dimly lit prayer hall, colonnaded by dozens of carpeted pillars and hung with long silk tapestries (*thangkas*). Immediately adjacent to this is the **Great Hall of the Golden Roof**, with its gilded tiles, red-billed choughs nesting under the eaves, wall paintings of scenes from the Buddha's life and a brilliant silver stupa containing a statue of Tsongkhapa. The grooves on the wooden floor in front of the temple have been worn away by the hands of prostrating monks and pilgrims. This hall, built in 1560, is where the monastery began, on the site of the pipal tree that grew with its Buddha imprints. You will still see pilgrims studying fallen leaves here, apparently searching for the face of the Buddha.

Other noteworthy temples include the **Lesser Temple of the Golden Roof** (no. 1) and the **Hall of Butter Sculpture** (no. 7). The former is dedicated to animals, thought to manifest characteristics of certain deities – from the central courtyard you can see stuffed goats, cows and bears on the balcony, wrapped in scarves and flags. The Hall of Butter Sculpture contains a display of colourful painted yak-butter tableaux, depicting Tibetan and Buddhist legends. After touring the temples, you can climb the steep steps visible on one side of the monastery to get a general view over the temples and hills behind.

During the year, four major **festivals** are held at Kumbum, each fixed according to the lunar calendar. In January/February, at the end of the Chinese New Year festivities, there's a large ceremony centred around the lighting of yak-butter lamps. In April/May is the festival of Bathing Buddha, during which a giant *thangka* of Buddha is unfurled on a hillside facing the monastery. In July/August the birthday of Tsongkhapa is celebrated, and in September/October there's one more celebration commemorating the nirvana of Sakyamuni.

Practicalities

Buses from Xining to the monastery (¥5) depart from a depot on Xiguan Dajie near the roundabout for Kunlun Bridge. Minibuses run frequently from around 7.20am until late afternoon; private tour buses start rolling up at the monastery around 10am, after which the place gets crowded. **Shared taxis** from the roundabout on Kunlun Zhonglu should cost ¥6 for the same journey. The ride takes just over thirty minutes through summer scenery of wheat fields, green hills, lush woods and meadows of flowering yellow rape. On arrival, you may be dropped at the bus station 1km short of the monastery, or taken right up to the complex itself. From the bus station, it's a twenty-minute walk uphill past the trinket stalls and rug-sellers until you see the row of eight stupas at the monastery entrance. Returning to Xining, exit the monastery and grab a cab, or hang around on the street until the bus arrives.

Most visitors just come up to Kumbum for a few hours, but it is also possible to stay the night and appreciate the monastery in more peace. **Accommodation** is available at the sixteenth-century pilgrims' hostel *Kumbum Motel* (千佛塔, *qiānfó tă*; dorm beds ¥20) just inside the monastery entrance, whose basic facilities include an ancient balcony and peeling murals; it's often full. For something smarter, there's the large *Zongka Hotel* (宗喀宾馆, *zōngkā bīnguăn*; ⓣ0971/2236761; closed Dec–March; ❺) facing the monastery across a gully; the price includes a simple breakfast, but you should ask at the front desk for hot water. There are several places around serving simple **meals**.

Qutan Si

Another monastery, **Qutan Si** (瞿昙寺, *qútán sì*; ¥25), 85km to the east of Xining in Ledu County, is much less frequented by tourists than Kumbum – reason enough to hunt it down. Started in 1387 during the Ming dynasty, this was once among the most important Buddhist centres in China. Today, it is still impressive, with 51 rooms of murals, exceptionally fine examples of their type, illustrating the life story of Sakyamuni. You can reach the town of **Nianbo Zhen** (碾伯镇, *niǎnbó zhèn*) in Ledu County by local train or bus (¥10) from Kunlun Bridge in Xining. From Nianbo Zhen you should be able to find minibuses (¥20 one way) for the 67km-long ride to Qutan Si, or you could take a taxi there and back for about ¥200.

West of Xining

West of Xining, Qinghai for the most part comprises a great emptiness. The 3000m plateau is too high to support any farming, and population centres are almost nonexistent – the only people who traditionally have managed to eke out a living in this environment have been nomadic yak-herders. The real highlight of the area is the huge and virtually unspoilt saline lake of **Qinghai Hu**, the size of a small sea and home to thousands of birds. Beyond here, the solitary road and rail line wind their way slowly to **Golmud**, the only place of note for hundreds of kilometres, and then on to the Tibetan Plateau into Lhasa.

Qinghai Hu and around

Situated 150km west of Xining, high up on the Tibetan plateau, is the extraordinarily remote **Qinghai Hu** (青海湖, *qīnghǎi hú*; ¥100, includes the ferry trip). The lake is China's largest, occupying an area of more than 4500 square kilometres, and, at 3200m above sea level, its waters are profoundly cold and salty. They are nevertheless teeming with fish and populated by nesting seabirds, particularly at **Bird Island**, which has long been the main attraction of the lake for visitors. If you don't have time to stop here, you can at least admire the view while travelling between Golmud and Xining; it's well worth scheduling your journey to pass by during daylight hours. The train spends some hours running along the northern shore; by bus you'll skirt the southern shore instead.

Apart from a visit to Bird Island – which tends to be a rushed, hectic experience – you can also hike and camp in peaceful solitude around the lake. From the smooth, green, windy shores, grazed by yaks during the brief summer, the blue, icy waters stretch away as far as the eye can see. If you have a tent, and really want a wilderness experience in China, this may be the place to get it. Don't forget to bring warm clothes, sleeping bags and enough drinking water. To get to the lake, take any bus bound for Dulan or Wulan (both west of Xining) from Xining's long-distance bus station. Each route passes the lake – one possible place to get off is the **Qinghai Lake Tourist Centre**, where you can stay (❸, dorm beds ¥25) and enjoy boating, fishing and horseriding.

Bird Island

A tiny rocky outcrop, **Bird Island** (鸟岛, *niǎodǎo*) is situated at the far western side of the lake, and annually nested upon by literally thousands of birds. An immense variety of seasonal birds spend time here – gulls, cormorants, geese, swans and the rare **black-necked crane**. The main **birdwatching season** is from April to June, though the giant swans are best seen from November to February.

The optimal time to visit Bird Island is between June and August, when avian life is at its most active. The easiest way to get there is on a **day-trip** from Xining, and your best bet is to take an excursion with one of Xining's **travel services** (see p.829). Foreigners are charged ¥150 excluding food and **entrance fees** (¥78, including a tourist shuttle bus from the ticket office to the island). It's a very long day out, leaving at 7am and getting back at around 10pm – the island is pretty, for sure, but whether it's worth up to ten hours' driving is up for debate.

Visiting Bird Island **independently** is something of a challenge, but it's possible as a stopover between Xining and Golmud. Riding any bus between these two cities, make sure you get off at the right place by the lake – a grubby little Tibetan town called **Heimahe** (黑马和, *hēimǎhé*), about four hours from Xining, which has a shop and a basic hotel (❶). From here you'll have to hitch a ride from a passing tractor or car.

Chaka Salt Lake

Not far beyond Qinghai Hu is the **Chaka Salt Lake** (茶卡盐湖, *chákǎyán hú*; ¥70 including cruise), which has recently become something of a tourist attraction. It's a stunning place – from a distance the white gleaming salt crystals form a perfect mirror-like surface. At the site, you can ride a small freight train, visit a house of salt, walk on a 60km salt bridge – and take a hunk of the stuff home with you afterwards. To visit the lake **independently**, catch a bus heading to Dulan or Wulan from Xining's long-distance bus station and disembark at the small town of **Chaka Zhen** (茶卡镇, *chákǎ zhèn*), near the lake – the earliest bus leaves at 8am, and there's a hotel (❸) in Chaka Zhen if you get stuck. To return to Xining, flag down local buses to Heimahe, where there are more frequent buses back to Xining. Alternatively, you can visit the lake on a **tour** from Xining (see p.829 for some travel agencies), which will usually include a trip to Qinghai Hu.

Golmud

Nearly 3000m up on the Tibetan plateau, **GOLMUD** (格尔木, *gé'ěr mù*) is an incredibly isolated city, even by the standards of northwest China. An airport provides a link to Xining, but otherwise it lies at least nine hours away overland from the nearest sizeable population centre in Lhasa. In spite of this, it still manages to be the second-largest city in Qinghai, with around 130,000 residents, most of whom are Han Chinese and work at the local potash plants. Recently, the city has suffered somewhat since workers upped and left following the completion of the rail line to Lhasa; with buses to Tibet now a thing of the past for foreigners, few are bothering to stop in Golmud on their way. Geographically, Golmud is located close to the massive **Kunlun Mountains** to the south, and to the **Cai Erhan Salt Lake** to the north. Both are very scenic in parts, though they remain as yet virtually unexplored by foreign tourists.

Practicalities

Golmud's **train and bus stations** sit facing each other in the south of the city. The scene as you disembark here is bleak almost beyond belief: a vast empty square, with a statue of the Flying Horse of Wuwei and a plaque brashly proclaiming "Golmud: Top Tourist City of China". A **taxi** to anywhere in town costs ¥5.

Permits, tours and tickets to Tibet can be obtained at **CITS**, 60 Bayi Zhong Lu (Ⓣ0979/8412764), when it is staffed. As well as Tibet trips, CITS can arrange interesting local tours, in particular to **Cai Erhan Salt Lake**. There are **Bank of China** branches on Kunlun Lu, while 300m east of the junction along Chaidamu Lu is the **PSB** (Mon–Fri 8.30am–noon & 2.30–6pm) – look for the huge, white complex with a red/gold badge on top.

Yushu: after the quake

It was all looking so promising for **Yushu** (玉树, *yùshù*), an **autonomous Tibetan prefecture** perched 4000m above sea level at the far south of **Qinghai** province. The source of the famed Yellow River, this remote, mountainous area had started to establish itself on the backpacker trail, and for good reason: this extremely picturesque region proved a magnet for adventurous travellers seeking a Tibetan experience without having to pay through the nose for a sanitized, pre-packaged tour to Lhasa.

Then came the events of April 14, 2010, when a **7.1-magnitude earthquake** hit Yushu. The main tremor – and its devastating subsequent aftershocks – destroyed 85 percent of the houses in Gyegu, the county seat, and killed some 2700 people, a fair chunk of the tiny local population. The national authorities were quick to respond, having learned lessons from the far deadlier Wenchuan earthquake that struck Sichuan in 2008 (see p.788). Yushu had next to no medical facilities, which meant that everything had to be flown in – no mean feat, given the area's altitude and inaccessibility – and that those buried under earth or rubble had to be dug out, often by hand, in freezing conditions.

The area is slowly getting back on its feet, but is likely to remain off the travel radar for a while to come. However, after a necessary period of reconstruction, it's likely that Yushu will once again be winning the hearts of those lucky enough to visit. The *Lete Youth Hostel* in Xining (see p.828) made admirable fundraising efforts after the earthquake, and is as good a place as any to get up-to-date information about the area.

As you come out of the train station, immediately to your right is the convenient but scruffy *Golmud Mansion* (格尔木大厦, *gé'ěrmù dàshà*; Ⓣ0979/8450876; ④). A smarter option is *Qinggang Hotel* (青冈饭店, *qīnggāng fàndiàn*; Ⓣ0979/8456668, Ⓕ8456666; ⑤); a few minutes up Jiangyuan Lu from the long-distance bus station, it's the glassy building on the crossroads. The rooms are spacious and clean, though you'll have to call in advance as it is often fully booked.

The Hexi Corridor

For reasons of simple geography, travellers leaving or entering China to or from Central Asia and the West have always been channelled through the narrow strip of land that runs 1000km northwest of Lanzhou. With the foothills of the Tibetan plateau, in the form of the Qilian Shan range, soaring up to the south, and a merciless combination of waterless desert and mountain to the north, the road known as the **Hexi Corridor** offers the only feasible way through the physical obstacles that crowd in west of Lanzhou.

Historically, whoever controlled the corridor could operate a stranglehold on the fabulous riches of the Silk Road trade (see box, p.806). Inevitably the Chinese took an interest from the earliest times, and a certain amount of Great Wall-building was already taking place along the Hexi Corridor under Emperor Qin Shi Huang in the third century BC. Subsequently, the powerful Han dynasty succeeded in incorporating the region into their empire, though the influence of central government remained far from constant for many centuries afterwards, as Tibetans, Uyghurs and then Mongols vied for control. Not until the Mongol conquests of the thirteenth century did the corridor finally become a settled part of the Chinese empire, with the Ming consolidating the old Great Wall positions and building its magnificent last fort at **Jiayuguan**.

Two other cities along the corridor, **Wuwei** and **Zhangye**, offer convenient places to break the long journey from Lanzhou to Dunhuang, and have their own share of historic sights. All three cities lie on the same **train** line and have regular services.

Wuwei and around

Lying approximately halfway between Lanzhou and Zhangye is the small city of **WUWEI** (武威, *wǔwēi*). Gansu's most famous historic relic, the Han-dynasty **Flying Horse of Wuwei**, was discovered here in 1969 underneath the Leitai Si, a temple just north of town; it's now housed in the Lanzhou Museum (see p.817). The symbol of the horse, depicted in full gallop and stepping on the back of a swallow, can be seen everywhere in Wuwei.

Arrival and information

Wuwei's **train station** is 3km to the south, from where it costs a couple of yuan to take a minibus into the centre. All trains between Ürümqi and the east stop at Wuwei, and there's also a slow train to Zhongwei in Ningxia. It's easy to buy hard-seat tickets at the station – fine for the short hops to Lanzhou or Zhangye – but sleepers are best arranged through a travel agent. The **east bus station** lies just outside the old south gates, with the newer **west bus station** (the one for departures) just beyond.

The huge China Telecom building (daily 8am–6.30pm), where you can make long-distance phone calls, is immediately east of Wenhua Square, and across Bei Dajie is the **post office**. There's an unusually clean and friendly **internet café** to the southwest of the South Gate. The **Bank of China** is just east of the *Tianma* (Mon–Fri 8.30am–noon & 2.30–6pm). **CITS** (ⓣ0935/2267239), immediately outside the *Tianma*, can arrange train tickets (commission ¥15 for hard seat, ¥30 for sleeper), while the **PSB** office, which deals with visa extensions, is just a couple of minutes east of the *Liangzhou* – there's a small English sign outside the office.

Accommodation

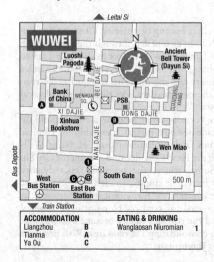

Good **accommodation** in Wuwei remains thin on the ground, but there are a few decent options. Just a few minutes west of the bus station is the very good value *Ya Ou* (亚欧宾馆, *yà'ōu bīnguǎn*; ⓣ0935/2265700; ❶). The *Liangzhou* on Dong Dajie (凉州宾馆, *liángzhōubīnguǎn*; ⓣ0935/2265999; ❹), a couple of minutes east of the central crossroads, has nice doubles with 24-hour hot water, and good off-peak discounts. The dull *Tianma*, west on Xi Dajie (天马宾馆, *tiānmǎ bīnguǎn*; ⓣ0935/2212356; ❸), is often packed with Japanese tourist groups. Ask for rooms on the eighth or ninth floor, which are cleaner and quieter.

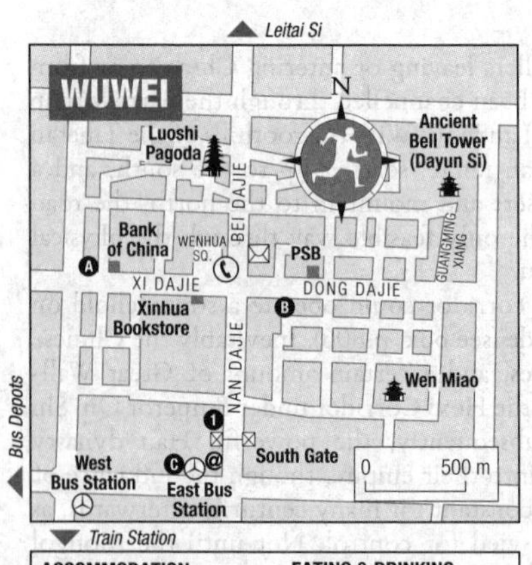

The City

Wenhua Square, in the centre of town, makes a good place to start exploring. It is interesting just to wander about the square on a warm day, where people assemble to play traditional musical instruments with snack and trinkets stands peppered around. There's a trace of the old city near the bus station on Nan Dajie, where the original **south gate** (南门, *nánmén*) has been impressively reconstructed. Heading north of the square, take the first major turn on the right and after ten minutes or so you'll arrive at the Ming-dynasty-built **Wen Miao** (文庙, *wénmiào*; daily 8am–6pm; ¥31), a delightful museum on the grounds of an old temple with large gardens full of oleanders and singing birds. The most captivating item in the museum is a stone stele with Chinese and Xixia language on both sides (see box, p.215).

About twenty minutes due north of here, through the last remains of the city's old adobe dwellings, the **Ancient Bell Tower** in **Dayun Si** (大云寺, *dàyúnsì*; daily 8am–6pm; ¥10) is worth a visit mostly for its grounds, where old men play mahjong or cards and drink tea under vine trellises and enormous hollyhocks. Occasional Taoist ceremonies are undertaken outside the main hall in the temple, depending upon local demand. A further twenty minutes' walk west brings you to Bei Dajie, near the 1600-year-old brick **Luoshi Pagoda** (罗什塔, *luóshí tǎ*) from where you can catch bus #2 a few kilometres or walk twenty minutes north to **Leitai Si** (擂台斯, *léitái sì*; daily 8am–6pm; ¥50). The temple, built high up on impressive mud ramparts, is surrounded by modern construction projects, but its grounds remain pleasantly calm and shady. Beneath the site, through a separate entrance, a Chinese-speaking tour guide will lead you to the famous **Han-dynasty tomb** where the Flying Horse statue was discovered. There's not much to see – a series of very low passageways, with a mock-up of the tomb contents at the back – but the 2000-year-old brickwork is still in perfect condition and amazingly modern in appearance. Ironically, the bronze Flying Horse, now a prized relic, remained in the tomb long after accompanying items of gold and silver had been stolen.

Eating

For **food**, there are numerous noodle houses around the bus station and on Nan Dajie north of the south gate, serving soups and mutton dishes heavily laced with chilli. Immediately left as you pass north under the South Gate, *Wanglaosan Niuroumian* (王老三牛肉面, *wánglǎosān niúròu miàn*) do a fantastic *chaomian* that serves up more or less like a huge spaghetti bolognese. The *Liangzhou* has a decent Chinese restaurant, and *Ya Ou*'s does passable one-person hotpots. There's also a *Dico's* just west of Renmin Square.

Zhangye and around

A medium-sized town, about 450km northwest of Lanzhou and 150km southeast of Jiayuguan on the edge of the Loess plateau, **ZHANGYE** (张掖, *zhāngyè*) has long been an important stopover for caravans and travellers on the Silk Road. Indeed, Marco Polo spent a whole year here. During the Ming period, Zhangye was an important garrison for soldiers guarding the **Great Wall**, and today the road from Wuwei to Zhangye is still a good place from which to view the Wall, visible for a large part of the way as a crumbling line of mud ramparts, a fascinating contrast to the restored sections elsewhere. Initially it runs to the north of the road, until, quite dramatically, the road cuts right through a hole in the Wall and continues on the other side.

Arrival and information

Zhangye's **train** station is some 7km away to the northeast; trains are met by waiting minibuses which take you into town for ¥1.5. You could also take a taxi (¥10). The so-called **main bus station** is south of the centre on Huancheng Nan

Lu, but most traffic goes through the newer and bigger **western bus station** about 1km west of Gulou off Xi Jie. There's also a smaller **eastern bus station** about 2km east of Gulou; a **Bank of China** (Mon–Fri 8.30am–6pm, Sat & Sun 9am–5pm), with ATM, and **CITS** (ⓣ0936/8243445) just north of the *Zhangye* hotel; and the mother of all **internet cafés** on the second floor of the building south of the *Jin Xin*. The **PSB** is on the fourth floor of a building on Qingnian Xi Jie, east of Mu Ta. Moving on, you can buy train tickets at the *Chengxin* or the rail office off Mingqing Jie; look for the Marco Polo statue – the office is to its southwest.

Accommodation

Hotels in Zhangye have enjoyed a boom in recent years, and there's a range of options available.

Chengxin Binguan (诚信宾馆, *chéngxìn bīnguǎn*) 18 Xianfu Jie ⓣ0936/8245800. Acceptable budget option with cheery staff, and a handy on-site travel service that will book train and bus tickets for a small fee. ❸

Huachen International (华晨国际大酒店, *huáchén guójì dàjiǔdiàn*) ⓣ0936/8257777, ⓔzyhcdh@public.lz.gs.cn. The most upmarket place in town; staff speak good English and rooms are good value. It's a few minutes east of the Daode Guan. ❻

Jin Xin (金鑫宾馆, *jīnxīn bīnguǎn*) ⓣ0936/8255058. Good-value option with clean, modern rooms and bathrooms of a standard you'll rarely see in this price range. Just northwest of the Drum Tower. ❸

The City

Although Zhangye is not especially attractive, there are a number of places that should fill at least a day of sightseeing. The centre of the town is marked, as in many Chinese towns, by a **Drum Tower** (古楼, *gŭlóu*) at the crossroads. The tower, built in 1507 during the Ming dynasty, has two tiers and houses a massive bronze bell. To the south, a central smoke-grimed hall at **Dafo Si** (大佛寺, *dàfó sì*; daily: summer 7.30am–6.30pm; winter 8am–6pm; ¥40) houses a 34m-long **reclining Buddha**, easily China's largest, whose calm expression and gentle form make a powerful impression. Immediately behind the Buddha are ten disciples and grotesque-looking luohans (saintly warriors) standing around in the gloom. Unusually, the hall itself, built in 1098 and restored in 1770, is almost entirely made of wood. In the same grounds the **Tu Ta** (土塔, *tŭtă*; same ticket) is a former Buddhist monastery. Now a local cultural centre, it features a single large stupa 20m in height and contrasts rather pleasingly with its neighbour.

On Xianfu Jie, a few hundred metres west of Dafo Si, looms the 31m-tall **Mu Ta** (木塔, *mùtă*; daily 8am–6pm; ¥5), built in the sixth century, before being burned down and then restored in 1925 … in brick. The octagonal tower is now home to a number of jackdaws. A few hundred metres south of here, and one block to the west, the **Xilai Si** (西来寺, *xīlái sì*) is a small Buddhist temple where you can see monks chanting at dusk and dawn.

Much farther away, about fifteen minutes' walk due east from the Drum Tower on the road to the train station, is a charming Taoist monastery, the **Daode Guan** (道德观, *dàodé guàn*). It's a small, dishevelled place of Ming origins, containing a tiny garden, some vine trellises and some well-maintained Taoist statues and wall paintings. Monks here are hospitable and seem completely detached from the modern world. Hidden in a jumble of narrow lanes on the north side of Dong Jie, the monastery can be hard to find among the neighbouring shops – look for the sign with gold characters on a blue background.

Eating

The northern end of Xianfu Jie leads onto Mingqing Jie – a mock Ming-dynasty **food street** with more restaurants than you can shake a chopstick at, serving noodle soups, kebabs, hotpots and the like. Several places here specialize in excellent *shuijiao*, stuffed with either vegetables, seafood, beef or more exotic meats, from about ¥10 a jin; you could also try the almost smart *Shibazhe Meishilin*, partway up the east side of the street, which serves an inexpensive range of casseroles, hotpots and local snacks.

Jiayuguan and beyond

One more cup of wine for our remaining happiness. There will be chilling parting dreams tonight.

Ninth-century poet on a leave-taking at Jiayuguan

To some Chinese, the very name **JIAYUGUAN** (嘉峪关, *jiāyù guān*) is synonymous with sorrow and ghastly remoteness. The last **fortress** of the Great Wall was built here by the Ming in 1372, over 5000km from the wall's easternmost point at Shanhaiguan, from which time the town made its living by supplying the needs of the fortress garrison. This was literally the final defence of the empire, the spot where China ended and beyond which lay a terrifying wilderness. The fort, just outside the town and perfectly restored, is one of the great sights of northwestern China, and there are also a number of other forts and beacons scattered around in the desert.

Apart from its main attraction, Jiayuguan is a bleak, lonely place. Despite this its inhabitants, on the whole, manage to be a cheerful bunch. Breaking the city's

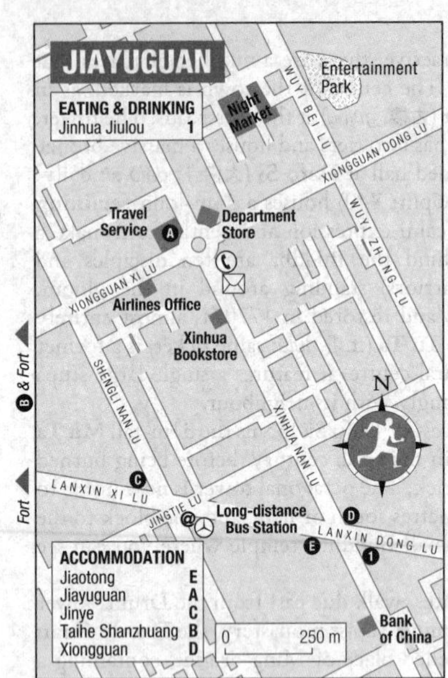

regular grid pattern, Lanxin Dong Lu slices through diagonally from east to west. The centre is a large traffic circle, overlooked by the *Jiayuguan* hotel and the post office; Xinhua Lu is the main street leading southeast from here. In the north of the town, the popular **Entertainment Park** (daily 8am–10pm) makes a good spot for an evening stroll among giant sculptures, pagodas, pleasure boats and dodgem cars. There's also an indoor swimming pool.

Arrival and information

Jiayuguan's **train station** is in the far southwest of the city and linked by bus or minibus #1 (¥1) to the centre. All trains running between Ürümqi and eastern China stop here. The **bus station** has a much more convenient location on Lanxin Dong Lu, about 1km south of the central roundabout. At the time of writing buses were no longer running from the **airport**, 10km from town; a taxi should cost ¥30, but you're more or less at the mercy of the drivers.

The **travel agents** in both the *Jiayuguan* and *Xiongguan* hotels can supply train tickets for a ¥30 commission and organize local tours. **Train tickets** out of Jiayuguan are hard to come by in peak season – you will almost certainly need the help of a travel service, and may need to resort to a more expensive soft sleeper if you want to get your head down. The airline office (daily 8.30am–6.30pm; ⓣ0937/6266677), opposite the *Jiayuguan* to the west, sells **flight tickets** to Lanzhou, Xi'an and Beijing. **Internet access** is available next to the bus station.

Accommodation

Accommodation in Jiayuguan is all fairly central if a little poor, though one cheap option is next to the fort itself.

Jiaotong (交通宾馆, *jiāotōng bīnguǎn*) ⓣ0937/6202260. This hotel has smart rooms that belie its modest exterior, plus hot water in the evenings from 8pm until late and generous discounts on weekdays. ❸

Jiayuguan (嘉峪关宾馆, *jiāyùguān bīnguǎn*) ⓣ0937/6226983, ⓕ6227174. The most upmarket option in town, right on the central roundabout and featuring a travel service. Standards have dropped, however, as its popularity with domestic tour groups has risen. ❻

Jinye (金叶宾馆, *jīnyè bīnguǎn*) ⓣ0937/6201333. Just north of the bus station, this small hotel offers clean and tidy rooms with 24hr hot water. ❹

Taihe Shanzhuang (泰和山庄, *tàihé shānzhuāng*) ⓣ0937/6396622. This cheap hotel is located inside the fort compound itself. This is, for some, already enough of a reason to stay, but decent rooms, low prices and tranquil surroundings make this a great pick for those who can bear to base themselves out of town. Staying here may also get you a free fort ticket – inspectors sometimes let hotel guests slip through. ❸

Xiongguan (雄关宾馆, *xióngguān bīnguǎn*) ⓣ0937/6201116. Slightly overpriced and with dubious plumbing, but this hotel is easy to find and has helpful staff, as well as a handy travel service on the third floor. ❹

The fort and beyond

The **fort** (城楼, *chénglóu*; daily 8.30am–5.30pm; ¥101, Nov–April ¥61) at the Jiayuguan Pass is the most important sight in the Hexi Corridor. Its location, between the permanently snowcapped Qilian Mountains to the north and the black Mazong (Horse's Mane) Mountains to the south, could not be more dramatic – or more strategically valuable. Everything that travelled between the deserts of Central Asia and the fertile lands of China – goods, traders, armies – had to file through this pass. The desolation of the landscape only adds to the melancholy: being forced to leave China altogether was a citizen's worst nightmare, and it was here that disgraced officials and condemned or fleeing criminals had to make their final, bitter farewells.

Some kind of fort may have occupied this site as early as the Han dynasty, but the surviving building is a Ming construction, completed in 1372. Sometimes referred to as the "Impregnable Defile under Heaven", it comprises an outer and an inner wall, the former more than 700m in circumference and about 10m high. At the east and the west of the inner wall stand symbolic gates, the Guanghua Men (Gate of Enlightenment) and the Rouyuan Men (Gate of Conciliation), respectively. Inside each are sloping walkways that lead to the top of the wall, enabling horses to climb up and patrol the turrets. In between the Gate of Enlightenment and the outer wall stand a pavilion, a temple and a somewhat haunting open-air theatre once used to entertain troops.

The entrance fee also covers the excellent **Great Wall Museum** (长城博物馆, *chángchéng bówùguǎn*; daily 9am–5pm), which reviews the history of the Wall from the Han to the last frenzied spurt of construction under the Ming. The highlights are photos and scale models of the Wall taken from points right across northern China, places that for the most part lie well away from tourist itineraries. In the past, travellers have found a couple of ways to avoid the fort's ticket price – the naughty one is to hunt down the rear entrance, while the more moral option is to stay at the *Taihe Shanzhuang* (see opposite), whose cheapest rooms cost barely more than the ticket price.

The so-called **Overhanging Wall** (悬壁长城, *xuánbì chángchéng*; daily 8am–7pm; ¥21), about 8km northwest of the fort, is a section of the Great Wall connecting the fort to the Mazong range, originally built in the sixteenth century and recently restored. The ramparts afford excellent views of the surrounding land; it was more atmospheric before they built a crassly environmentally insensitive tourist village nearby, but is still worth a visit so you can gaze out west and imagine what it was like when this place represented the end of China's civilized world.

The easiest way to reach both the fort and the Wall is to hire a **taxi** (around ¥100 for the whole trip). You can get to the fort by public transport in summer – take minibus #4 (¥1) from the roundabout outside the *Jiayuguan*. To **cycle** to the fort, follow Lanxin Xi Lu west from the bus station until you cross the bridge over the rail line. A blue sign pointing right indicates the way from here. It's about thirty minutes to the fort, another thirty to the Overhanging Wall and forty back into town.

Other desert sights

Several other desert attractions around Jiayuguan could be combined with a trip to the fort and the Wall. About 6km south of town are the ruins of the **First Beacon Tower** (第一墩, *dìyī dūn*; ¥21). Built on the Great Wall in the sixteenth century, the long-abandoned tower lies crumbling on a clifftop on the northern bank of the Taolai River at the foot of the Qilian Mountains. The desert also harbours a couple of unusual collections of ancient Chinese art. One is the **Underground Gallery** (新城魏晋墓, *xīnchéng wèijìnmù*; ¥31), about 20km northeast of Jiayuguan. Actually a burial site from the Wei and Jin periods, more than eighteen hundred years ago, the graves are brick-laid and contain vivid paintings depicting contemporary life on each brick. Not far beyond the fort, 9km northwest of Jiayuguan, are the **Heishan rock carvings** (黑山岩画, *hēishān yánhuà*). These look more like classic "cave man" art: a hundred or so pictures of hunting, horseriding and dancing, all dating back to the Warring States Period (476–221 BC), are etched into the cliffs of the Heishan Mountain. Visiting the First Beacon Tower and the two art sites in conjunction with a tour of the fort and Overhanging Wall takes a day and costs ¥200.

Finally, one stupendous but rather inaccessible natural sight is the **July 1st Glacier** (七一冰川, *qīyī bīngchuān*; ¥51), located 4300m up in the Qilian Mountains some 120km from Jiayuguan – remarkably close considering what a hot place Jiayuguan is in summer. A day-trip by taxi costs at least ¥500. Travel agents (see p.838) in town provide tours with an English guide for around ¥600. It's a long day, involving a three-hour drive, followed by five hours climbing up and down, and three hours driving back. The do-it-yourself option is to take a train to **Jingtieshan** (京铁山, *jīngtǐeshān*) then a taxi – around ¥140 return.

Eating

For food, the *Jiayuguan* **restaurant** serves bland Chinese breakfasts but better evening meals. Noodles and dumplings are available around the bus station and at the **night market** north of the *Jiayuguan* on the road to the Entertainment Park. If you want to sit down to standard Chinese food in a welcoming setting, try the excellent-value *Jinhua Jiulou* (金华酒楼, *jīnhuá jiǔlóu*), opposite the *Xiongguan*.

Dunhuang and the Mogao Caves

An oasis town surrounded by inhospitable desert, **DUNHUANG** (敦煌, *dūnhuáng*) has been a backpacker favourite for decades, with two main claims to fame. Colossal **sand dunes** – among the world's largest, some of them hundreds of metres in height – rise along its southern flank, while the nearby **Mogao Caves** boast a veritable encyclopedia of Chinese artwork on their walls. The town has become something of a desert resort for visiting the latter, with inexpensive hotels, lots of English-language menus in the restaurants and friendly people.

There's little to see in town bar the mediocre **Dunhuang City Museum** (敦煌市博物馆, *dūnhuángshì bówùguǎn*; April–Dec daily 8am–6pm; ¥10), which houses a few of the scrolls left behind after the depredations of the archeologist and adventurer Sir Aurel Stein (see box, p.844). Next to the museum, the **Dunhuang Theatre** (敦煌剧院, *dūnhuáng jùyuàn*) puts on hour-long regional cultural dance performances every night (May–Sept; ¥80–200). Come evening, the interesting **Shazhou night market** sells food (see p.842) and **souvenirs**, with no real pressure to buy. Coins, jade articles, Buddhas, Tibetan bells and horns, leather shadow puppets, scroll paintings and Chinese chops are all on sale.

Arrival and information

There are a few daily **trains from** Lanzhou, including one direct from Xi'an. Services from the west, however, have been patchy – the direct train from Ürümqi has been running off and on for years. If you're out of luck, you'll need to take a bus (¥20) or shared taxi (from ¥100 for the vehicle) from the station in Liuyuan (柳园, *liǔyuán*), about 120km to the north. It's best to book tickets from the booth on Mingshan Lu (or a travel agency, for a fee), as the train station is inconveniently located 12km to the east of town, right next to an **airport** that serves only Beijing,

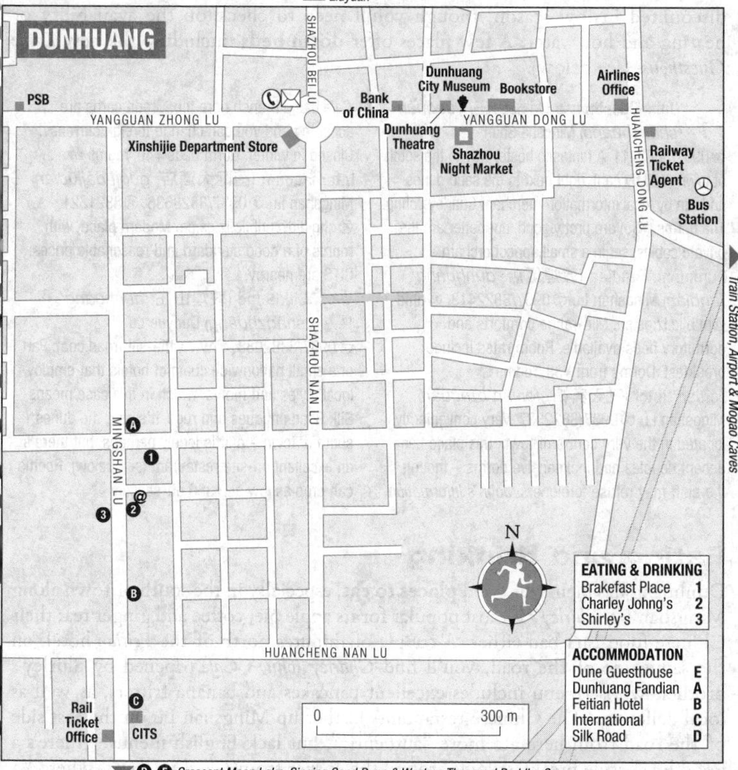

Xi'an, Lanzhou and Ürümqi; the airport bus (¥20) stops at the airline office (daily 8am–noon & 3–6pm; ⓣ0937/88222389) on Yangguan Dong Lu. The completion of the rail line means there's little need to use the new bus station on the eastern edge of the town centre; some of the roads heading out of Dunhuang remain in wretched condition in any case.

In addition to hotel **travel agents**, *Charley Johng's Café* (ⓔdhzhzh@public.lz.gs.cn) comes especially recommended for organizing transport and tours – especially an overnight **camel trip** into the dunes (¥300/person) – while *John's Information Café* in the *Feitian* hotel (ⓦwww.johncafe.net) is also worth checking out but gets poorer reviews. **CITS** are in the building next to the *International* hotel (ⓣ0937/8835529) – an English-speaking guide from here costs ¥150 for the day, while a car will set you back upwards of ¥500. Both of the **Bank of China** branches (Mon–Fri 8am–noon & 3–6.30pm), one on either side of the post office roundabout on Yangguan Lu, have **ATMs**. You can **rent bikes** from the two cafés mentioned above for ¥5 an hour. The same fee will get you a **taxi** ride to almost anywhere you want to go in the town centre – there are probably more cabs in Dunhuang than all other vehicles put together.

Accommodation

There's a glut of **accommodation** in Dunhuang, especially at the lower end of the market. Prices rise in peak season (July and Aug), and are considerably discounted in low season, though you'll need to check on the availability of heating and hot water. A few places offer **dorm beds**, including the new *Dune Guesthouse* (see below).

Dune Guesthouse (月泉山庄, *yuèquán shānzhuāng*) Mingsha Shan ⓣ0937/3882411. A fantastic hostel way to the south of town (¥10 by cab), right next to the sand dunes and run by local information merchant Charley Johng. The dorms (¥35) are pretty good, but better are the private cabins, set in a small apricot orchard. ③

Dunhuang Fandian (敦煌饭店, *dūnhuáng fàndiàn*) Mingshan Lu ⓣ0937/8822413, ⓔdhfd@public.lz.gs.cn. Mid-range comforts and dormitory beds available. Room rates include breakfast. Dorms from ¥30, rooms ⑥

Feitian Hotel (飞天宾馆, *fēitiān bīnguǎn*) Mingshan Lu ⓣ0937/8822337. Very conveniently located in the very centre of town, this place has decent doubles and inexpensive dorms – though the staff may refuse foreigners. *John's Information Café* has a branch here too. Credit cards are accepted and you can change foreign currency. Closed in winter. Dorm beds ¥40, rooms ⑥

International (国际大酒店, *guójì dàjiǔdiàn*) Mingshan Lu ⓣ0937/8828638, ⓕ8821821, ⓔdhgjdid@public.lz.gs.cn. Modern place, with rooms of a good standard and reasonable prices; CITS are nearby. ⑦

Silk Road (敦煌山庄, *dūnhuáng shānzhuāng*) Dunyue Lu ⓣ0937/8882088, ⓦwww.the-silk-road.com. Part of a small nationwide chain of hotels that employ local styles and motifs, which in this case means Silk Road antiques and rugs. It's near the dunes, south of town – a little lonely perhaps, but there's an excellent on-site restaurant (see below). Rooms can drop as low as ¥380 off-season. ⑧

Eating and drinking

Dunhuang has plenty of good **places to eat**, especially in the south of town along Mingshan Lu. *Shirley's* is most popular for its apple pie, coffee and ginger tea; their Chinese food isn't bad either. A couple of minutes north of the *Feitian* hotel, on the same side of the road, you'll find *Charley Johng's Café*, opened by Shirley's brother, whose menu includes excellent pancakes and banana fritters, as well as local delicacies. The Chinese restaurants farther up Mingshan Lu on the east side of the road from here are more "authentic", but lack English menus – there's a good local-style breakfast joint around the corner from *Charley Johng's*, where ¥5 will fill you up on dumplings, fried doughsticks and warm soy milk. The *Silk Road* hotel restaurant, atop the building, has stunning views of the sand dunes; ¥30 seems a small price to pay for a coffee or light meal while admiring the sunset. Nevertheless, the most atmospheric place to eat in the evening is the covered **Shazhou night market**. Inside, you can sit on deck chairs and drink *babao* (also known as "Eight Treasures Tea") containing various dry fruits and herbs (try the famous *liguang qing*, a local type of apricot), or have a full Muslim or Chinese meal.

The Mogao Caves

The **Mogao Caves** (莫高窟, *mògāo kū*), 25km southeast of Dunhuang, are one of the great archeological discovery stories of the East. The first-known **Buddhist temples** within the boundaries of the Chinese empire, supposedly established in 366 AD by a monk called Lie Zun, they were a centre of culture on the Silk Road right up until the fourteenth century, and contain religious artworks spanning a thousand years. Chinese Buddhism radiated out to the whole Han empire from these wild desert cliffs, and with it – gradually adapting to a Chinese context – came the artistic influences of Central Asia, India, Persia and the West.

Of the original thousand or more **caves**, over six hundred survive in recognizable form, but many are off-limits, either no longer considered to be of significant interest or else containing Tantric murals that the Chinese reckon are too sexually explicit for visitors. Of the thirty main caves open to the public, you are likely to manage only around fifteen in a single day.

Practicalities

Getting to the caves (daily 8.30–11.30am & 2.30–5.30pm; May–Sept; ¥180, Oct–April; ¥100) from Dunhuang is easy in summer. Step on to the street between eight and nine in the morning and you will instantly be accosted by **minibus** drivers, who charge ¥10 for the one-way fare; the trip takes about thirty minutes. Choose a minibus that is nearly full – they won't leave until the last seat is occupied. In winter, when transport is much less frequent, you can arrange a return trip with any taxi driver in town (half day around ¥80–100, full day ¥200).

The entrance fee to the caves includes an English-speaking guide and admission to the museum and Research and Exhibition Centre. You need an extremely expensive permit to take a **camera**, and all bags must be left at an office at the gate (¥2). If you're caught taking photos on the sly you'll be made to delete them or have your negatives confiscated and you will be subjected to a large fine. There are only ever twenty or thirty caves open at any one time to reduce wear and tear, and they are not lit, to avoid damage to the murals; your guide will have a **flashlight**, but you are advised to bring one of your own.

Guides are well informed, though their English is not always great, and they will follow a set route. The **museum** gives insight into all the caves and has a history in English of the site, plus more scrolls, nineteenth- and twentieth-century photos of Mogao, and reproductions of some of the plundered frescoes, now in Europe.

Before or after your tour, visit the **Research and Exhibition Centre** (石窟文物研究陈列中心, *shíkū wénwù yánjiū chénliè zhōngxīn*; daily 9am–5pm), the giant modern building opposite the car park. It holds replicas of eight caves – nos. 3, 45, 217, 220, 249, 275, 285 and 419 – but the big advantage here is that the lights are on, the colours are fresh and you can study the murals up close. The most impressive is the Bodhisattva statue of the one-thousand-hand and one-thousand-eye Guanyin – the original piece is no longer available for viewing due to the deteriorating conditions. A further cave is not from Mogao at all, but from the Yulin Caves (no. 25) in nearby Anxi County. Upstairs are a few surviving silk scrolls and manuscripts, and there's a film about the Mogao site.

Getting back to Dunhuang is simple in summer: go to the car park and wait for the next minibus; the last one leaves around 4pm. At other times you'll need to hire a taxi or prearrange transport.

The caves

What makes the caves so interesting is that you can trace the **development of Chinese art** over the centuries, from one dynasty to the next. Some grasp of the caves' history is essential to appreciate them properly, but be warned: restorations and replacements in the modern era have complicated the picture, and many of the statues, in particular, are not original. You may hear your guide blaming the ugly replacements on the Qing dynasty – in other words on the monk Wang Yuan Lu – but some of them are a good deal newer than that. The caves are all clearly labelled with numbers above the doors.

Northern Wei

The earliest caves were hewn out in the fourth and fifth centuries AD during the **Northern Wei** (386–581). The Turkic-speaking people known as the Tobas formed this dynasty, and as the centuries progressed there was constant friction between the forces of conservatism (who wanted to retain the ancient Toba customs) and those of change (who wanted to adapt Chinese customs).

The Wei caves are relatively small in size, and are often supported in the centre by a large column – a feature imported from India. A statue of the Buddha is usually central, surrounded in tiers on the walls by a **mass of tiny Buddhas** brilliantly

The Mogao cave treasures

The story of Mogao's development, then subsequent abandonment and rediscovery, is an intriguing one. Before the arrival of Buddhism from India, the Chinese – Taoist and Confucian – temple tradition had been mainly of buildings in wood, a material well adapted to most Chinese conditions. The idea of cave temples came to China from India, where poverty, lack of building materials and the intense heat had necessitated alternative methods.

The emergence of the complex of cave temples at **Mogao** dominated early Chinese Buddhism, as pilgrims, monks and scholars passing along the Silk Road settled and worked here, translating sutras, or holy texts. Merchants and nobles stopped too, endowing temples to ensure the success of their caravans or to benefit their souls, as they did in varying degrees all along the Silk Road. Huge numbers of **artists and craftsmen** were employed at Dunhuang, often lying on high scaffoldings in the dim light provided by oil lamps. The workers usually lived in tiny caves in the northern section of Mogao furnished with small brick beds and were paid a pittance – in one collection of Buddhist scriptures, archeologists discovered a bill of indenture signed by one sculptor for the sale of his son.

Under the Tang, which saw the establishment of Buddhism throughout the Chinese empire, the monastic community reached its peak, with more than a thousand cave temples in operation. Thereafter, however, as the new ocean-going trading links slowly supplanted the Silk Road, Mogao (and Dunhuang) became increasingly provincial. At some point in the fourteenth century, the caves were **sealed and abandoned**.

Although Mogao's existence remained known to a few Buddhist scholars, it was only in 1900 that a wandering monk, **Wang Yuan Lu**, stumbled upon them by accident and decided to begin the work of excavation. He at once realized their significance and made it his life's work to restore the site, excavating caves full of sand, touching up the murals, planting trees and gardens and building a guesthouse. This work he undertook with two acolytes and financed through begging expeditions.

The reconstructions might have gone on in relative obscurity were it not for the discovery of a bricked-up hidden chamber (cave 17), which Wang opened to reveal an enormous collection of **manuscripts**, **sutras** and **silk and paper paintings** – some 1000 years old and virtually undamaged. News of the cache soon reached the ears of the Dunhuang authorities, who, having appropriated a fair haul for themselves, decided to reseal them in the cave on the grounds that it would be too expensive to transport them. So it remained for a further seven years, until the arrival in 1907 of the Central

painted in black, white, blue, red and green. The statues are in fact made of terracotta: the soft rock inside the caves was not suited to detailed carving, so the craftsmen would first carve a rough outline of the figure, then build it up with clay.

The style of the murals in these caves shows a great deal of **foreign influence**. Faces have long noses and curly hair, and women are large-breasted. **Cave 101**, decorated towards the end of the fifth century, provides a good example: the Buddha, enclosed by attendant Bodhisattvas, is essentially a Western figure, recognizably Christ-like, reminiscent of Greek Byzantine frescoes. In **cave 257** the Buddha seems to be dressed in a toga, while no. **428** shows a notably Indian influence in both content (note the peacocks on the ceiling) and style. There are, however, also the beginnings of Chinese influence in the wavy, flower-like angels sometimes seen fluttering above.

Though originally designed as a focus of devotional contemplation, the murals gradually acquired a **narrative purpose** as well, and the paintings soon move towards a wider subject matter, their story sequences arranged in long horizontal

Asian explorer and scholar **Aurel Stein**. Stein, a Hungarian working for the British and the Indian Survey (in other words, a secret agent), had heard rumours of the caves and been offered items for sale. In good Howard Carter tradition, he persuaded Wang to reopen the chamber. This is how Stein later described what he saw:

> **The sight the small room disclosed was one to make my eyes open; heaped up in layers, but without any order, there appeared in the dim light of the priest's little lamp a solid mass of manuscript bundles rising to a height of nearly 10 feet and filling, as subsequent measurement showed, close on 500 cubic feet – an unparalleled archeological scoop.**

This was no understatement. Examining the manuscripts, Stein found original sutras brought from India by the Tang monk and traveller **Xuanzang**, along with other Buddhist texts written in Sanskrit, Sogdian, Tibetan, Runic-Turkic, Chinese, Uyghur and other languages unknown to the scholar. Amid the art finds, hardly less important were dozens of rare Tang-dynasty paintings on silk and paper – badly crushed but totally untouched by damp.

Eventually, Stein – donating the equivalent of £130 to Wang's restoration fund – left Mogao for England with some seven thousand manuscripts and five hundred paintings. Later in the year a Frenchman, Paul Pelliot, negotiated a similar deal, shipping six thousand manuscripts and many paintings back to Paris. And so, virtually overnight, and before the Beijing authorities could put a stop to it, the British Museum and the Louvre had acquired the core of their Chinese manuscript and painting collections. Not all the caves were looted, however; a fresh batch of 248 was only located in 2001, though the scrolls and artefacts they contained have yet to be fully assessed.

Today, fuelled perhaps by Greek claims on the Elgin marbles, the Chinese are pressing for the **return** of all paintings and manuscripts in foreign collections. It is hard to dispute the legitimacy of these claims, though it was only in 1961 that Mogao was declared a National Monument. Had the treasures not been removed, more would almost certainly have been lost in the chaotic years of the twentieth century. A large party of White Russians used the caves as a barracks in 1920, crawling their names over the frescoes. Fortunately, despite the massive loss in terms of manuscripts and scrolls, the artwork and statuary at the caves themselves are still fabulously preserved. The cave art was not damaged during the Cultural Revolution – protected, it is said, on a personal order from Premier Zhou Enlai.

strips. **Cave 135** (early sixth century) illustrates a *jataka* story – concerning a former life of Buddha – in which he gave his own body to feed a starving tigress, unable to succour her cubs. The narrative, read from right to left, is broken up by simple landscapes, a frequently used device. **Cave 254** shows the story of Buddha defeating Mara, or Illusion.

Artistic changes, and a shift towards a more distinctive Chinese style, began to appear at the end of the Northern Wei period, around the middle of the sixth century. One of the most strikingly Chinese of the Wei murals is in **cave 120N** and shows, above the devotional niches, a series of battle scenes, interesting for their total lack of perspective. All the figures are drawn as though seen straight on, regardless of their relative positions, a favourite device throughout the history of Chinese painting.

Sui

With the founding of the short-lived but dynamic **Sui dynasty** in 581, Western influences began to decline rapidly. The Chinese empire had been torn apart by civil wars, but now there followed a boom in Buddhism and Buddhist art. In the four decades up to the emergence of the Tang, more than seventy caves were carved at Mogao.

Structurally, they dispense with the central column, while artistically, they replace the bold, slightly crude Wei brushwork with intricate, flowing lines and an increasingly extravagant use of colour that includes gilding and washes of silver. In **cave 150**, for example, painted in the last year of the Sui, narrative has been discarded in favour of a repeated theme of throned Buddhas and Bodhisattvas. In terms of statuary, the Sui period also shows change, with the figures stiff and inflexible and dressed in Chinese robes. **Cave 427** contains some characteristic Sui figures – short legs, long bodies (indicating power and divinity) and big, square heads.

Tang

The **Tang-dynasty** artists (618–906), under whom the caves at Mogao reached their artistic zenith, drew from past traditions and real life. The classic Tang cave has a square floor, tapering roof and a niche for worship set into the back wall. The statuary includes **warriors** – a new theme – and all figures are carefully detailed, the Bodhisattvas in particular, with their pleats and folds clinging softly to undulating feminine figures.

Their **Buddhas** are famous for their sheer size: prominent examples can be found in **caves 96 and 130**. The astonishing 34m-high seated Buddha in cave 96 – dressed in the traditional dragon robe of the emperor – is thought by some to have been designed deliberately to remind pilgrims of the famous Tang empress Wu Zetian. Its counterpart in cave 130 is slightly smaller, but equally impressive – tours usually include one of the two. In **cave 148** there's yet another huge Buddha, this one reclining as though dead, and surrounded by disciples.

The **Tang paintings** range from huge murals depicting scenes from the sutras – now contained within one composition rather than the earlier cartoon-strip convention – to vivid paintings of individuals. One of the most popular and spectacular Tang mural themes was that of the *Visit of the Bodhisattva Manjusri to Vimalakirti*. **Cave 1** contains perhaps the utmost expression of this story. Vimalakirti, on the left, is attended by a great host of heavenly beings, eager to hear the discourse of the ailing old king. Above him the plane is tilted to take in a seemingly limitless landscape, with the Buddha surrounded by Bodhisattvas on an island in the middle. Another version can be seen in **cave 51E**, in a mural that is especially notable for the subtle shading of its portraiture, which includes a magnificently depicted Central Asian retinue. Other superb Tang murals include a very free, fluid landscape in **cave 70** and, perhaps most developed of all, **cave 139A**'s depiction of the *Western Paradise of the Amitabha Buddha*. This last is a supremely confident painting, working in elaborate displays of architecture and figures within a coherent whole. The theme is the Buddha's promise of paradise: the souls of the reborn rise from lotus flowers in the foreground, with heavenly scenes enclosing the Buddha above.

Later caves

Later work, executed by the **Five Dynasties**, **Song and Western Xia** (906–1227), shows little real progression from the Tang. Much, in any case, is simply restoration or repainting of existing murals. Song work is perhaps the most interesting, tending toward a heavy richness of colour, and with many of its figures displaying the features of minority races.

Toward the end of the Mongol **Yuan dynasty** (1260–1368), Mogao was abandoned, and the standard niche in the back wall of the caves gave way to a central altar, creating fresh and uncluttered space for murals. Tibetan-style Lamaist (or Tantric) figures were introduced, and occult diagrams (mandalas) became fashionable. The most interesting Yuan art is in **cave 465**, slightly set apart from the main body of grottoes. You could ask the guides if they will open this up for you, though they will probably only do so for a huge fee. In the fashion of Indian Buddhist painting, the murals include Tantric figures in the ultimate state of enlightenment, graphically represented by the state of sexual union.

Crescent Moon Lake and the Singing Sand Dune

A few kilometres to the south of town are the much-touted **Crescent Moon Lake** (月牙泉, *yuèyá quán*) and **Singing Sand Dune** (鸣沙山, *míngshā shān*), set amid the most impressive sand-dune scenery anywhere in China, with mounds 200–300m high. The sands reputedly make a humming noise in windy weather, hence the name. The Crescent Moon Lake is not much to look at, but is curious for its permanence, despite being surrounded by shifting sands – it was recorded in history at least two thousand years ago. A number of activities, including sand-tobogganing and paragliding, are on offer from the tops of the main dune. The paragliding is great fun and costs ¥30 – you get to try two or three times if your initial flight isn't successful. Tobogganing costs ¥10 and feels a little safer. Climbing the dune in the first place, however, is incredibly hot, exhausting work; you can ride up on a camel for ¥30 or use the wooden steps for ¥10.

In the summer heat the only sensible time to come is either by 8.30am or in the evening after 5pm. **Minibus #3** (daily 8am–10pm; ¥1–3/person) leaves from Mingshan Lu in Dunhuang and will drop you by the gate and **ticket office**. Otherwise you can walk here in about 45 minutes, or cycle in twenty – just head south out of town. Park your bike before the entrance, or pay ¥5 to put it in the bike park. A one-way taxi should cost ¥10 on the meter, but your driver may ask for more.

Admission to the dune is ¥120 in peak season, ¥80 otherwise; factor in also ¥10 for the bus from the gate to the dune, ¥10 for gaiters to prevent sand getting up your nether regions, and additional costs if you want to ascend the dune by steps or camel.

Other sights around Dunhuang

A number of other historical sites lie farther away from Dunhuang but within the scope of a day-trip. One is the **Western Thousand Buddha Caves** (西千佛洞, *xī qiānfódòng*; ¥30), 35km west, a site along the lines of Mogao, if incomparably smaller and less significant. If you are a real Buddhist art buff, talk to a travel service about visiting this place: in the past it was open to groups only, and individuals were turned away. A taxi for the return trip costs ¥80.

There are also two Han-dynasty gates, **Yumenguan** (玉门关, *yùmén guān*; ¥30) and **Yangguan** (阳关, *yángguān*; ¥40), which for periods of Chinese history marked the western border of China. They lie to the west of Dunhuang, 80km and 75km away respectively, and were originally joined together by a section of the Great Wall before being abandoned as long ago as the sixth century. Both sites are impressive for their historical resonance and total desolation as much as for anything else. The road to Yangguan is in good condition, but that to Yumenguan is relatively rough – to visit both gates by taxi would take all day and cost more than ¥300. One exciting option, however, is to visit them **by camel**; to see the two gates, and bits of the Han Great Wall (1km), takes around three to four days respectively or up to eight days for both, and in the mild months of the year – early or late summer – this can be an excellent expedition (from ¥300/day including food and tent accommodation; contact *Charley Johng's Café*, p.842, for more information).

Xinjiang

The **Uyghur autonomous region** of **Xinjiang** (新疆, *xīnjiāng*) is one of the most thrilling parts of China, an extraordinary terrain more than 3000km from any coast which, despite all the upheavals since the collapse of the Silk Road trade, still comprises the same old oasis settlements strung out along the ancient routes, many producing the silk and cotton for which they were famed in Roman times (see box, p.806).

Geographically, Xinjiang – literally "New Territories" – occupies an area slightly greater than Western Europe or Alaska, and yet its population is just 21 million. And with the Han population probably comprising more than fifty percent of the whole, Xinjiang is perhaps the least "Chinese" of all parts of the People's Republic. By far the largest minority in Xinjiang is the **Uyghur**, though there are also some dozen other Central Asian minority populations.

The land of Xinjiang is among the least hospitable in all China, covered for the most part by arid **desert and mountain** – the Tian Shan (Heavenly Mountain) range effectively bisects Xinjiang from west to east, with Kazakh

The Uyghur

The **Uyghur** are the easternmost branch of the extended family of **Turkic peoples** who inhabit most of Central Asia. Around nine million Uyghurs live in Xinjiang with another 300,000 in Kazakhstan. Despite centuries of domination by China and some racial mingling along the way, the Uyghur remain culturally distinct from the Han Chinese, and many Uyghurs look decidedly un-Chinese – stockily built, bearded, with brown hair and round eyes. Although originally Buddhists, the Uyghur have been **Muslim** for at least a thousand years and Islam remains the focus of their identity in the face of relentless Han penetration.

As the Uyghurs are for the most part unable to speak fluent Chinese and therefore unable to attend university or find well-paid work, their prospects for self-improvement within China are generally bleak. It is also true that many Han Chinese look down on the Uyghurs as unsophisticated ruffians, and are wary of their supposedly short tempers and love of knives. Perhaps as a consequence of this, Uyghurs seem at times to extend their mistrust of Han Chinese to all foreigners, tourists included. Nevertheless, gestures such as drinking tea with them, or trying a few words of their language, will help to break down the barriers, and invitations to Uyghur homes frequently follow.

Travellers' Uyghur

The **Uyghur language** is essentially an Eastern Turkish dialect, a branch of the Altaic languages from Central Asia (as well as Xinjiang, Uyghur is also spoken in parts of Kazakhstan, Kyrgyzstan and Uzbekistan). There are several dialects, of which the Central Uyghur (spoken from Ürümqi to Kashgar) is the most popular and hence given here, including commonly used alternatives. Unlike Chinese, Uyghur is not a tonal language. It involves eight vowels and 24 consonants and uses a slightly modified Arabic script. The only pronunciations you are likely to have difficulties with are **gh** and **kh**, but you can get away by rendering them as **g** and **k** with a light **h** at the end.

Hello	*Yahximusiz*	Please/Sorry	*Kequrung*
Goodbye/Cheers	*Hosh*	Yes	*He'e*
Thank you	*Rhamat sizge*	No	*Yakh*

and Mongol herdsmen living a partially nomadic existence on its fringes. The climate is not particularly hot in summer, and virtually Siberian from October through to March. To the south is the **Tarim Basin**, dominated by the scorching Taklamakan Desert, fiercely hot and dry in summer. Its sands cover countless forgotten cities, and another buried treasure – **oil**. Chinese estimates reckon that three times the proven US reserves of oil are under the Taklamakan alone, which is one reason that the government is firmly establishing a Han presence in the region.

Highlights of Xinjiang include the **Tian Shan** mountain pastures outside Ürümqi, where you can hike in rare solitude and stay beside Heaven Lake with Kazakhs in their yurts; but it is the old **Silk Road** that will attract most travellers. The most fascinating of the Silk Road oasis cities are **Turpan** and **Kashgar**. It is possible to follow not only the Northern Silk Road from Turpan to Kashgar via Aksu and Kuqa, but also the almost forgotten southern route via Khotan. The routes were established over two thousand years ago, but traffic reached its height during the Tang dynasty, when China's most famous Buddhist pilgrim, **Xuanzang**, used them on his seventeen-year voyage to India. There's still the possibility of continuing the Silk Road journey out beyond the borders of China itself – not only over the relatively well-established **Karakoram Highway** into Pakistan, but now also over the less well-known routes into Kazakhstan and Kyrgyzstan (see p.854).

Very	*Bek*	Hot	*Issikh*
What is your name?	*Ismingiz nime?*	Thirsty	*Ussitidighan*
My name is...	*Mening ismim...*	Hungry	*Ag khusakh*
How much is it?	*Bahasi khange?*	When?	*Vakhitta?*
OK	*Bolidu*	Now	*Emdi/hazir*
Good	*Yahxi*	Today	*Bugun*
Where is the...?	*...nede?*	Yesterday	*Tunogun*
toilet	*Hajethana*	Tomorrow	*Ete*
hospital	*Duhturhana*	Sunday	*Yekexembe*
temple	*Buthana*	Monday	*Doxembe*
tomb	*Khebre*	Tuesday	*Sixembe*
I don't have enough money	*Yenimda yeterlik pul yokh*	Wednesday	*Qarxembe*
		Thursday	*Peyxembe*
Please stop here	*Bu yerde tohtang*	Friday	*Jume*
This is delicious	*Temlik/lezzetlik*	Saturday	*Xembe*
Cold	*Soghukh*		

Numbers

1	*bir*	12	*on ikki*
2	*ikki*	etc	
3	*uq*	20	*yigrime*
4	*tort*	30	*ottuz*
5	*bash*	40	*khirkh*
6	*alte*	50	*ellik*
7	*yet'te*	60	*atmix*
8	*sekkiz*	70	*yetmix*
9	*tokh'khuz*	80	*seksen*
10	*on*	90	*tokhsen*
11	*on bir*	100	*yuz*

Some history

The region's history has been coloured by such personalities as Tamerlane, Genghis Khan, Attila the Hun, even Alexander the Great. More often, though, in counterpoint to the great movements of history, Xinjiang has been at the mercy of its isolation and the feudal warring between the rulers of its oasis kingdoms, or **khanates**.

The influence of China has been far from constant. The area – commonly referred to in the West as Eastern (or Chinese) Turkestan until 1949 – first passed under Han control in the second century BC, under Emperor Wu Di. But it was only during the **Tang dynasty** (650–850 AD) that this control amounted to more than a military presence. The Tang period for Xinjiang was something of a golden age, with the oases south of the Tian Shan largely populated by a mysterious but sophisticated Indo-European people, and the culture and Buddhist art of the oases at their zenith. Around the ninth century, however, came a change – the gradual rise to dominance of the **Uyghurs**, and their conversion to **Islam**.

Subsequent centuries saw the **conquests of the Mongols** under Genghis Khan and later, from the West, of Tamerlane. Both brought havoc and slaughter in their wake, though during the brief period of Mongol rule (1271–1368) the Silk Road trade was hugely facilitated by the fact that, for the first and only time in history, east and west Asia were under a single government.

After the fall of the Mongols and the final disappearance of the Silk Road, Xinjiang began to split into khanates and suffered a succession of religious and factional wars. Nonetheless, it was an independence of a kind, and Qing **reassertion** of Chinese domination in the eighteenth century was fiercely contested. A century later, in 1862, full-scale **Muslim rebellion** broke out, led by the ruler of Kashgaria, **Yakub Beg**, armed and supported by the British who were seeking influence in this buffer zone between India and Russia (for more on which, read Peter Hopkirk's excellent *The Great Game* – see p.984). Ultimately the revolt failed – Beg became a hated tyrant – and the region remained part of the Chinese empire.

At the beginning of the twentieth century, Xinjiang was still a Chinese backwater controlled by a succession of brutal warlords who acted virtually independently of the central government. The last one of these before World War II, **Sheng Shizai**, seemed momentarily to be a reforming force, instituting religious and ethnic freedoms, and establishing trade with the newly emergent Soviet Union. However, he ended by abandoning his moderate positions. Slamming the door on the Soviets and on leftist influences within Xinjiang itself in 1940, he began a reign of terror resulting in the deaths of more than two hundred thousand Communists, intellectuals, students and Muslim Nationalists.

The drive toward the defeat of the Guomindang in 1949 temporarily united the conflicting forces of Muslim nationalism and Chinese communism. After the Communist victory, however, there could be only one result. The principal Muslim Nationalist leaders were quietly murdered, allegedly killed in a plane

Xinjiang time

For travellers, the classic illustration of Xinjiang's remoteness from the rest of the country is in the fact that all parts of China set their clocks to Beijing time. The absurdity of this is at its most acute in Xinjiang, 3000–4000km distant from the capital – which means that in Kashgar, in the far west of the region, the summer sun rises at 9am or 10am and sets around midnight. Locally, there is such a thing as unofficial "**Xinjiang time**", a couple of hours behind Beijing time, which is used more frequently the further west you head towards Kashgar; when buying bus, train or plane tickets, you should be absolutely clear about which time is being used.

The 2009 riots

In July 2009, Ürümqi witnessed Xinjiang's worst-ever clashes between its **Uyghur** and **Han** populations, events that were to have serious repercussions across the entire province. Ironically, the trouble started on the opposite side of China in Guangdong province, where Uyghur workers at a factory in **Shaoguan** were accused of gang-raping two Han Chinese women. The allegations would, in time, prove to be unfounded, but the incident stirred tensions at the factory, whose workforce contained a mix of Han and Uyghur; at least two **Uyghurs were killed** by Han Chinese in assorted brawls. Back in Xinjiang, Uyghurs wondered why the authorities had failed to sufficiently protect the factory workers and why questions remained about the true number of dead. A **street protest** was organized in **Ürümqi** on 5 July – when the real trouble started.

The demonstrations began peacefully, but became violent within the day. The true cause is not clear – the official party line is that rioters began to attack police and destroy property in premeditated fashion, while the Uyghur claim that the police ignited the trouble by using excessive force. Fighting quickly spread throughout the city, with groups of Uyghur men attacking Han Chinese, and **vigilante mobs** biting back in reprisal. Such trouble went on for days, not just in Ürümqi but across the province; the main cities saw an influx of Uyghur men, though just as many were vanishing into the countryside for protection, including a fair number of **ethnic-Uyghur police** who were ordered to fire at their own people. Official sources put the number of dead at just under 200, the majority of them Han; Uyghur groups claim that the overall figure was much higher, and that hundreds of their own people's deaths had been covered up. Security was tightened across the region, and hundreds of Uyghur men were **arrested** in huge sweeps of the main cities; many were sentenced to death behind closed doors, and an unknown number have since been **executed**.

During the troubles, the use of **mobile phones** and the **internet** was suspended across the province, and hundreds of Xinjiang-based websites shut down. The phone restrictions were lifted in January 2010, and Xinjiang came back online the following May, signs that the province was finally shaking off the worst episode in its recent history.

crash, and the impetus towards a separate state was lost. The last Nationalist leader, a Kazakh named Osman, was executed in 1951.

Since 1949, the Chinese government has made strenuous attempts to stabilize the region by **settling Han Chinese** from the east, into Ürümqi in particular. The Uyghur population of Xinjiang slipped from ninety percent of the total in 1949 to below fifty percent in the 1980s, and is still on the way down, in spite of the minorities' exemption from the One Child Policy. Today, however, the Chinese government remains nervous about Xinjiang, especially given the enormous **economic potential** of the area, in terms of coal and now gold mining, oil exploration and tourism, plus its strategic value as a **nuclear test site**.

There have been outbursts of **Uyghur dissent** in the region; since the attacks of September 11, 2001, the Chinese government has equated Uyghur nationalism with global Islamic terrorism and indulged in its own "war on terror" by monitoring and arresting Uyghurs it claims are involved in separatist activities. These troubles came to the fore in the build-up to the Beijing Olympics in 2008. With China in the international spotlight, and apparently spurred on by the death of an Uyghur in police custody (as well as similar unrest in Tibet; see p.887), Uyghurs held **demonstrations** across the province, most prominently in Kashgar, Yining and Khoten; these occasionally bubbled up into more serious incidents, and there were numerous deaths and arrests over a period of months. Still, this was nothing compared to the **large-scale rioting** the following year in Ürümqi (see box, p.851). Tourist numbers have, understandably, taken a tumble, but the average traveller will notice little difference save for an increased security presence.

Ürümqi

Well connected by road, rail and plane to the rest of China, as well as a smattering of cities abroad, **ÜRÜMQI** (乌鲁木齐, *wūlŭmùqí*) forms the introduction to Xinjiang for many. Indeed, some of those on a tight schedule see this city and nothing else in the province, which is something of a mistake – the vast majority of the city's population of around two million are Han Chinese, and while you'll get to see Uyghur people and eat a bit of their food, you'll have a far more authentic experience elsewhere (even in Turpan, just a few hours away by bus; see p.861). Ürümqi means "Beautiful Pastures", yet the name hardly applies these days: this is a political, industrial and economic capital, and an extremely remote one, with scruffy streets and a generally glum atmosphere. Indeed, the only reason to stay here for anything more than a few days is if you're applying for Pakistani, Kazakh or Kyrgyz visas.

However, there are amusements to be had. The west of the city around **Renmin Park** can be pleasantly green in the summer, and the park itself is one of the best in China. In addition, the skyline to the east of town is dominated by the snowy massif of the **Tian Shan**; heading that way for three hours, the "Heavenly Lake" of **Tian Chi** is a welcome oasis. And for travellers arriving from western China or Central Asia, Ürümqi will be the first truly Chinese city on your route – modern Han culture can be just as interesting as that of the ancient Uyghurs. If you're heading the other way, there are still surprises in store as East meets West both in terms of geography and population. There are also lively bazaars and food markets, and a vibrant nightlife, its businesspeople, gold- and oil-miners lending the place a certain pioneering feel.

Some history

Under the name of **Dihua**, Ürümqi became the capital of Xinjiang in the late nineteenth century. During the first half of the twentieth century, the city was something of a battleground for feuding warlords – in 1916 Governor Yang Zengxin invited all his personal enemies to a dinner party here and had their heads cut off one by one during the course of the banquet. Later, shortly before the outbreak of World War II, **Soviet troops** entered the city to help quell a Muslim rebellion; they stayed until 1960. Ürümqi began to emerge from its extreme backwardness only with the completion of the Lanzhou–Ürümqi **rail line** in 1963. This more than anything helped to integrate the city, economically and psychologically, into the People's Republic. And with the opening of the Ürümqi–Almaty rail line in 1991, the final link in the long-heralded direct route from China through Central Asia to Europe was complete.

The story since then has been one of increased **Sinicization**, with Han Chinese moving to the city in their thousands. The murmurs of Uyghur discontent bubbled up in 1997 and again in 2008, but it was 2009 that saw the biggest episodes of **inter-ethnic strife** in the brief history of Xinjiang province (see box, p.851).

Arrival, information and city transport

Ürümqi's Diwopu International **Airport** is 15km northwest of the city; you can get into town on the CAAC airport bus (¥18), which delivers to various airline offices, or on the China Southern Airlines **shuttle bus**, which drops off at the

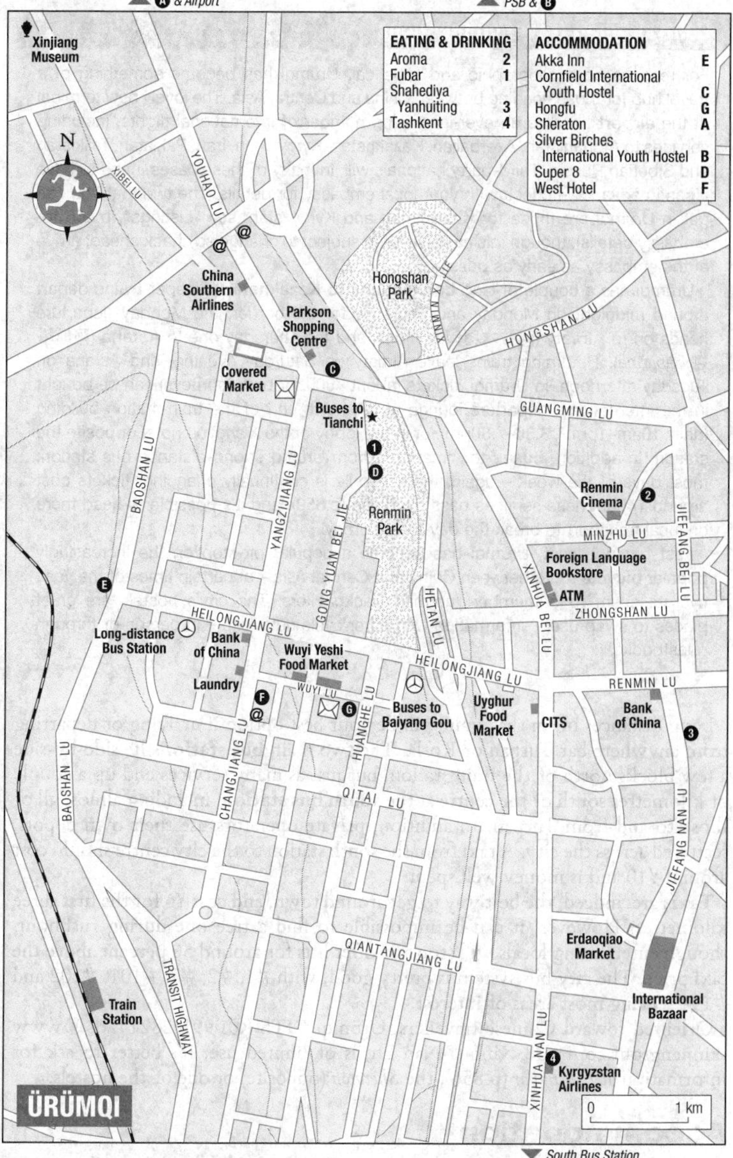

China Southern Airlines office on Youhao Lu (every 30min; ¥10). The airport has two terminals; the swish modern one is generally used for international flights (see box, p.854), though it also handles a few domestic services.

The **train station** – "Wulumuqi" on Chinese schedules – lies in the southwest of the city, with services arriving from as far afield as Beijing and Shanghai in the east, and Kashgar in the west, not to mention Almaty and Astana in Kazakhstan (see p.854).

Central Asian travel connections

For reasons both geographic and logistical, Ürümqi has become something of a travel hub for those heading between China and Central Asia. The lovely new terminal at the **airport** handles an ever-increasing number of international flights, including services to Afghanistan, Azerbaijan, Kazakhstan, Kyrgyzstan, Iran, Pakistan, Tajikistan and Siberian Russia. Third-party nationals will, in many of these cases, need to have **visas** in advance – check with your local embassy for details. The two that you can get in Ürümqi are those for Kazakhstan and Kyrgyzstan (see "Listings", p.856 for embassy details), though this has also been subject to change so check ahead; arrive at the embassy as early as possible.

Ürümqi has a couple of land **connections to Kazakhstan**. Sleeper **trains** depart around midnight on Monday and Thursday for the border; the Monday departure heads on to **Almaty** (阿拉木图, *ālā mùtú*), and the Thursday one to **Astana** (阿斯塔娜, *āsìtǎnà*). Returning trains leave Almaty on Saturday evening, and Astana on Tuesday afternoon. In Ürümqi, tickets (about ¥600 for both journeys) can be bought in the international departure lounge at the north end of the train-station building (daily 10am–1pm & 3.30–7.30pm), or in the lobby of the *Xiangyou* hotel opposite the station. In addition, **buses** to Almaty run from Ürümqi's long-distance bus station, most days of the week – again, the schedule is continually changing; tickets cost around ¥400. These services pass by Yining (p.859), and it's possible to head there on local transport to break the day-long journey.

Last but not least, Ürümqi has become a popular pit-stop on the increasingly popular **bicycle** route between China and Central Asia – at certain times of the year, cyclists seem to outnumber "normal" backpackers. The city's hostels are great places to swap useful information with other cycle nuts, either in person or through guestbooks.

Long distances mean that train will be your best option if arriving or departing from anywhere bar Turpan or Korla. The two main **bus stations** lie side-by-side a few blocks north of the train station, but just as many services end up a couple of kilometres south of the centre at the **south bus station**, including almost all of those to and from Turpan. In addition, private operators use their own depots, scattered across the city. A taxi from the south station to the city centre should cost around ¥10 and is money well spent.

Taxis are, indeed, the best way to get around town, and cost ¥6 for the first three kilometres. However, it can be impossible to find a free one during rushhour, though enterprising locals will stop and offer lifts for around 50 percent above the taxi price. The city bus system is pretty good, with #1, #2, #7, #101, #102 and #111 serving most areas of interest.

Oriented toward Chinese travellers, Ürümqi **CITS** (Ⓣ0991/2821426, Ⓦwww.xinjiangtour.com), 38 Xinhua Nan Lu, is of limited use. It's better to ask for information at the *Fubar* (p.856), the *Sheraton* (opposite) or one of the hostels.

Accommodation

Ürümqi's **accommodation** options are gratifyingly diverse, with lots of choice at both ends of the spectrum.

Akka Inn (家快捷酒店, *jiākuàijié jiǔdiàn*) 2 Baoshan Lu, near the north bus station Ⓣ0991/4557866. This imposing modern structure has grand vistas of Ürümqi and bright, up-to-date rooms. Discounts of more than 50 percent are often given. ❻

Cornfield International Youth Hostel (麦田国际青年旅舍, *màitián guójì qīngnián lǚshè*) Youhao Nan Lu Ⓣ0991/4591488. Passable hostel with good beds but indifferent staff – it's occasionally hard to tell who, if anyone, is on duty. Also known as the *Maitian*. Dorm beds from ¥40, rooms ❸

Hongfu (鸿福大饭店, *hóngfú dàjiǔdiàn*) 160 Wuyi Lu ⓣ0991/5881588. Get away from the major chains at this swanky, upper-class hotel, whose lobby features a small shopping centre and excellent restaurant. Rooms are very pretty, with curved floor-to-ceiling windows, thick carpets and quirky Xinjiangesque frills. ❽

Sheraton (喜来登酒店, *xǐláidēng jiǔdiàn*) 669 Youhao Bei Lu ⓣ0991/6999999, ⓦwww.sheraton.com. Excellent, modern hotel providing all the comfort you'd expect from the chain. Food, service standards and room quality are as good as you'll get in Xinjiang, and some rooms have tremendous mountain views. The only downside is a slightly out-of-the-way location on the airport road. ❾

Silver Birches International Youth Hostel (白桦林国际青年旅舍, *báihuálín guójì qīngnián lǚshè*) 186 Nanhu Nan Lu ⓣ0991/4881428. Like the *Cornfield*, this gets patchy reviews, but isn't a terribly bad place. The location isn't particularly convenient, but on the plus side it's quiet and relaxing. Dorm beds from ¥40, rooms ❸

Super 8 (速8酒店, *sùbā jiǔdiàn*) 140 Gong Yuan Bei Jie ⓣ0991/5590666, ⓦwww.super8.com.cn. Probably the most remote outpost of this chain of budget hotels, *Super 8* offers individually decorated rooms and suites, often at discounted rates. ❹

West Hotel (西部大酒店, *xībù dàjiǔdiàn*) 41 Changjiang Lu ⓣ0991/5566868. A long-time favourite with foreign visitors, this budget option has been newly renovated (ignore the still-grotty exterior), and its colourful rooms are excellent value for money. Those on the uppermost of the eighteen floors have predictably good views. ❹

The City

Ürümqi centres around the junction of Zhongshan Lu and Xinhua Lu, though visitors are more likely to find themselves gravitating toward the east of the city near **Renmin Park** (人民公园, *rénmín gōngyuán*; daily 8am–10.15pm; free). Almost every Chinese city boasts something similar, but this may well be the best in the land, a large expanse that numbers a boating pond and a funfair among its attractions, as well as scores of locals doing anything from practicising on musical instruments to group *tai ji*. Those travelling with children may be unwilling to unleash their progeny on the most rickety rides, but the sight of kids clay-painting, group-zorbing or racing around on hand-pedalled boats will have you wishing you were younger. Clearly visible on a hill to the north across Guangming Lu is **Hongshan Park** (红山公园, *hóngshān gōngyuán*; daily 7am–11pm; free), another lovely place with boating, pavilions and pagodas, and a steep hill to climb. At the cool, shady summit you can sit and have a drink while watching the locals clambering about over the rocks; on clear days the view over the rapidly changing city skyline, with desert and snowy mountains in the background, is impressive.

A must-see sight, the **Xinjiang Museum** (新疆博物馆, *xīnjiāng bówùguǎn*; daily 9.30am–7.30pm; ¥30, free on Sun), on Xibei Lu in the north of the city, focuses on the lives, culture and history of the peoples of the region along with a number of ancient, desiccated **corpses** retrieved from their desert burial sites. Among them is the so-called "Loulan Beauty", a woman with long fair hair, allegedly 3800 years old, recovered from the city of Loulan on the Southern Silk Road (p.881). Of a distinctly non-Chinese appearance, the Loulan Beauty has been taken to heart by some Uyghur nationalists as a symbol of the antiquity (and validity) of their claims for sovereignty over these lands; counterclaims of sorts are made by the museum, with some exhibits making it clear that Xinjiang is "together with the motherland forever". You can walk to the the museum from the city centre, or take bus #7 from Xinhua Bei Lu.

Eating and drinking

Ürümqi has a good variety of places to **eat**, whether you're after Uyghur specialities or Cantonese favourites, with a couple of exceptional food markets. For **drinking**, start at the *Fubar*, find some new friends and progress from there.

Shopping in Ürümqi

Consumerism has reached China's final frontier, and shopping in Ürümqi can be quite fun. Boutiques with pseudo-French and Italian names have been springing up along **Xinhua Bei Lu**, the main shopping street, but for a more local flavour head south of here, down **Jiefang Nan Lu**. The shops become steadily more Uyghur-oriented until you reach the **Erdaoqiao market**, a great place for souvenir shopping, selling knives, handmade musical instruments, jade, carpets, clothes and various ornate crafts (be prepared to bargain prices down to about one third of the initial cost). The **International Bazaar** complex opposite sells similar items at cheaper prices, in a more relaxed if less authentic atmosphere. A string of music shops here sell CDs of traditional **Uyghur music** (see box, p.863). To get a real feel for the area, try slipping down some of the alleyways off Jiefang Nan Lu, where you can find blacksmiths fashioning axes amidst a plethora of other traditional cottage industries.

Aroma Minzu Lu. Quality restaurant to the east of town serving excellent Maltese food. Maltese cuisine is somewhat akin to that of Italy and quite the treat in such a remote city; try the soup or pasta dishes. You'll be paying upward of ¥40/person.

Fubar (福吧, *fú bā*) 1 Gongyuan Bei Jie, Ⓦwww.fubarchina.com. Almost every traveller who passes through Ürümqi seems to end up here, and with good reason: it's a veritable oasis of travel information, wi-fi, beers, spirits and Western food, including great pizzas. Brave souls can try their signature "Stinger" cocktail, made with a scorpion tail and a sinful amount of alcohol.

Shahediya Yanhuiting (沙合迪亚宴会厅, *shāhédíyà yànhuìtīng*) 262 Jiefang Nan Lu Ⓣ0991/8872444. Locals flock to this traditional Uyghur restaurant with byzantine interior and nightly traditional song and dance shows. Ordering can be a problem with the lack of English and Chinese spoken.

Tashkent (塔什干餐厅, *tǎshígàn cāntīng*) 51 Xinhua Nan Lu Ⓣ0991/88557798. Uzbek restaurant in the heart of the Erdaoqiao market, serving up Uyghur and Central Asian food at reasonable prices. The borscht and grilled lamb chops are especially popular with locals.

Wuyi Yeshi (五一夜市, *wǔyī yèshì*) Wuyi Lu. This night food market launches an assault on the senses as crowds struggle through the fug of cooking smoke to gorge on cheap and plentiful delicacies from all over the country. Fires up daily from 8pm until late.

Listings

Airlines China Southern's office is at 576 Youhao Nan Lu (Ⓣ0991/2308788 or 2825368), and Siberian Airlines are just north of the *Ramada* hotel, 52 Changjiang Lu. Kyrgyzstan Airlines have been shifting around recently, and were last spotted on Xinhua Nan Lu – ask at your accommodation for details.

Banks and exchange The main Bank of China is at the junction of Renmin Lu and Jiefang Lu (Mon–Fri 9.30am–1.30pm & 4.30–7pm); its ATMs only accept charge cards. Any China Construction bank will take cards with Cirrus; try the one next to the Foreign Language Bookstore on Xinhua Bei Lu.

Bookshops The Foreign Language Bookstore (daily 9am–6pm) on Xinhua Bei Lu has English novels and a few Chinese classics In English on the third floor. Maps of Ürümuqi with English can also be found on the first floor.

Embassies Kazakhstan, 216 Kunming Lu (Ⓣ0991/3815796); Krygyzstan, 58 Hetan Lu (Ⓣ0991/5189980; closed Wed). Note that service at both of these embassies ranges from OKish to wretched – try not to make any firm travel plans until you have your visa in hand.

Mail and telephones The main post office (daily 10am–8pm) is west of the northern end of Renmin Park. For long-distance phone calls you can buy and use cards from the lobbies of upmarket hotels, post offices or *Fubar*.

Tian Chi and Baiyang Gou

Tian Chi (天池, *tiānchí*) means "Heaven Lake", and this unspoilt natural haven 110km east of Ürümqi – the starting point of Vikram Seth's book *From Heaven Lake* – almost lives up to its name, especially for travellers who have spent a long

time in the deserts of northwest China. At the cool, refreshing height of 2000m, the lake is surrounded by grassy meadows, steep, dense pine forests and jagged snow-covered peaks, including the mighty **Bogda Feng**, which soars to over 6000m. The nicest feature of the area is that you can wander at will (you are likely to see eagles flying overhead as you trek towards the far side of the lake); there are no restrictions on accommodation (most people stay in yurts, with the semi-nomadic Kazakh population), and there is virtually limitless hiking. You need only to watch the **weather** – bitterly cold in winter, the lake is really only accessible during the summer months, May to September.

The **Kazakhs**, who lead a semi-nomadic herding existence in these hills, are organized into communes, very loosely managed by the State, which in theory owns both their land and animals and lets them out on fifteen- or thirty-year "contracts". Their traditional livelihood is from sheep, selling lambs in spring if the winter spares them. But it's a hard, unpredictable business – the State sometimes has to bail them out if the winter is a disastrous one – and revenues come increasingly from tourism. As in Inner Mongolia, the Kazakhs have taken to performing at horse shows, mostly for tourists. The extra income from providing visitors with food and accommodation is also welcome.

If you have not pre-booked your accommodation, you can simply set off to find yourself a **yurt**. Staying in one is a well-established custom, and you'll soon find people eager to cater for you. Most tourists lodge by the near side of the lake, but you can climb right up into the remote valleys of the Tian Shan – choose the right-hand main road around the lake to several Kazakh catering points – or you can hire a guide and a horse for the trip (¥50–100/day), a service which young Kazakhs at the lakeside are happy to provide. Once up at the snowfields, the valleys are yours. Each is dotted with Kazakh yurts, and there's nearly always somewhere you can spend the night. One nice Kazakh stopover is **Dawanzi**, close to the lake's edge and about an hour's walk from the main camps as you approach the lake (look for the map on the way). If you come in May – considered the most beautiful time – you may get to try the alcoholic *kumiss*, fermented mare's milk, a rare delicacy. The rest of the year the Kazakhs make do with an infusion of dried snow lily and sheep's milk.

Practicalities

To get to the lake take a **bus** (9am–3pm; ¥50 return); tickets are available at booths around the northern entrance of Renmin Park. However, many of the private companies offering trips also sling in unwanted trips to jade markets and the like – no pressure to buy, but a bit of a waste of time. Going there **independently** by taking one of the hourly buses to **Fukang** (阜康, *fùkāng*) from Ürümqi's main bus station will avoid this, and give you time to stock up on food in this cute town on the way. From Fukang, it's ¥40 by taxi, or you can get a cab all the way from Ürümqi for ¥200. The journey takes around three hours, and the outward trip from Ürümqi is spectacular, initially taking you through flat desert, then climbing through green meadows, conifer forests and along a wild mountain river. However you come, you'll have to pay ¥35 for a minibus ride to the lake itself, unless you fancy walking the final 5km.

There's a ¥100 **entrance fee** to the lake area, which you pay just before arriving at the small lakeside **village**. This comprises a bus park, some shops and souvenir stands and a guesthouse – the only place to supply you with fresh water if you stay in the yurts with the Kazakhs. If you come by private transport, you are expected to pay an extra ¥10 parking fee when buying entrance tickets.

One way to avoid any anxieties around communication with the Kazakhs is to join a **pre-booked tour**, which will include yurt accommodation as well as transport between Ürümqi and the lake. Agents such as CITS in Ürümqi offer these, but they are relatively expensive and can be of dubious quality.

Baiyang Gou

Seventy-five kilometres south of Ürümqi spreads another natural paradise, the **Baiyang Gou** (白杨沟, *báiyáng gōu*) in the Nan Shan area of Tian Shan. Basically, it's another green valley with a stream and a waterfall, and a backdrop of fir trees and snowy peaks. The Kazakhs and Uzbeks like to summer here and, accordingly, there are opportunities for tourists to join them. There's a ¥10 entrance fee on the road leading to the area. Horseriding trips to the waterfall take about an hour and cost around ¥50 per person; you can also get here by **bus** (9.30am–4.30pm; 4 daily) from the depot well hidden in a lane off Heilongjiang Lu. Yurt accommodation is available on the pasture.

The Ili Valley

The pretty **Ili Valley** is centred around the city of **Yining**, just 60km east of the border with Kazakhstan and 400km northwest of Ürümqi. As it is right off the principal Silk Road routes, not many people make the detour to get here, but it's a worthwhile trip if you have the time, or are travelling to Kazakhstan. Ili is one of the three so-called **Kazakh Autonomous Prefectures** within Xinjiang (the other two are Karamay and Altai), which form a block along the northwest frontier. Despite the nominal Kazakh preponderance, the Uyghurs are the more dominant minority group in the city, and there have been occasional protests against Beijing's rule, with the area at the forefront of the troubles in 2008 (see p.851). Today, however, after years of Han migration, the "frontier" character of Yining is fast disappearing.

The **climate** in the valley is relatively cool and fresh even at the height of summer (and very chilly sometimes – make sure you have warm clothes whatever the time of year), and the views of the Tian Shan – from all routes into Yining, especially if you're coming up from Kuqa to the south – are fabulous. The road climbs the harsh, rocky landscape of the northern Taklamakan, then enters pure alpine scenery with marching forests of pine, azure skies and the glorious blue waters of **Big Dragon Lake**, before drifting into a vast grassland ringed by snowy peaks. Another draw, north of Yining, is the beautiful **Sayram Lake**, where you can find accommodation in Kazakh yurts.

Some history

The **history** of the Ili Valley is one of intermittent Chinese control. At the time of the Han dynasty, two thousand years ago, the area was occupied by the **Wusun kingdom**. The Wusun people, ancestors of today's Kazakhs, kept diplomatic relations with the Han court and were responsible for introducing them to the horse. By the eighth century, however, a Tang-dynasty army had taken control of the region for China – its value as a staging post for a newly developing branch of the Silk Road was too great a temptation. In the thirteenth and fourteenth centuries, the area was controlled first by Genghis Khan from the east, then Tamerlane from the west. This east–west tug of war has gone on ever since, with the Qing seizing the area in the eighteenth century, only for the Russians to march in, in 1871, under the cover of Yakub Beg's Xinjiang rebellion (see p.850). There remained a significant Russian presence in one form or another until 1949, and traces of this can still be seen in the architecture of Yining. During the 1960s there was a forced mass exodus of sixty thousand Kazakhs and Uyghurs to the USSR, an event that has left behind much bitterness.

Yining

Known to the Uyghurs as Ghulja, booming **YINING** (伊宁, *yīníng*) has changed almost unrecognizably from the remote backwater it once was. Nevertheless, it's a small place, pleasant for walking, and with an extraordinary amount of food for sale from street vendors. The centre of town isn't readily obvious – most of the action seems to be along **Jiefang Lu**, though the old city is centred around **Qingnian Park** to the southeast. The **Uyghur bazaars**, just south of the park, are well worth exploring.

Arrival and information

After a long wait, Yining was finally connected to the rest of China by rail in 2010. Two **trains** go to and from Ürümqi each day; along with a **flight** that does the same route, it's the easiest way to arrive. The road south to Kuqa was closed for years following a tunnel collapse right in the middle of the route, but was about to reopen at the time of writing. The **bus station** is in the northwest of the city, well concealed on Jiefang Lu, and has services to destinations across Xinjiang, as well as daily buses to Almaty (12hr; US$30) in Kazakhstan (get your visa in Ürümqi). Yining's airline office (ⓣ0999/8044000) is in the *Yilite* hotel, where there's also a helpful **travel service** (ⓣ0999/7829000).

Accommodation

Ili Hotel (伊犁宾馆, *yīlí bīnguǎn*) Yingbing Lu ⓣ0999/8023126, ⓕ8024964. Old-fashioned place in huge leafy grounds, with a number of buildings offering varying degrees of comfort and different prices – no. 4 has respectable, if small, doubles with bath. To reach the hotel from the bus station, take bus #1 heading east for three stops, cross the road and it's a few minutes' walk east along Yingbing Lu. ④

Yaxiya (亚细亚宾馆, *yàxìyà bīnguǎn*) Jiefang Lu ⓣ0999/8031800. There's no English sign, but you can recognize it from the Greek columns outside; the doubles with bath are clean and modern and breakfast is included in the price. Dorm beds ¥50, rooms ④

Yilite (伊力特大酒店, *yīlìtè dàjiǔdiàn*) On the crossroads just east of Qingnian Park ⓣ0999/7829000. A range of smart, sizeable rooms at reasonable prices. ⑤

Youdian (邮电宾馆, *yóudiàn bīnguǎn*) Jiefang Lu ⓣ0999/8223844. Mid-range doubles, slightly the worse for wear but not bad value. ③

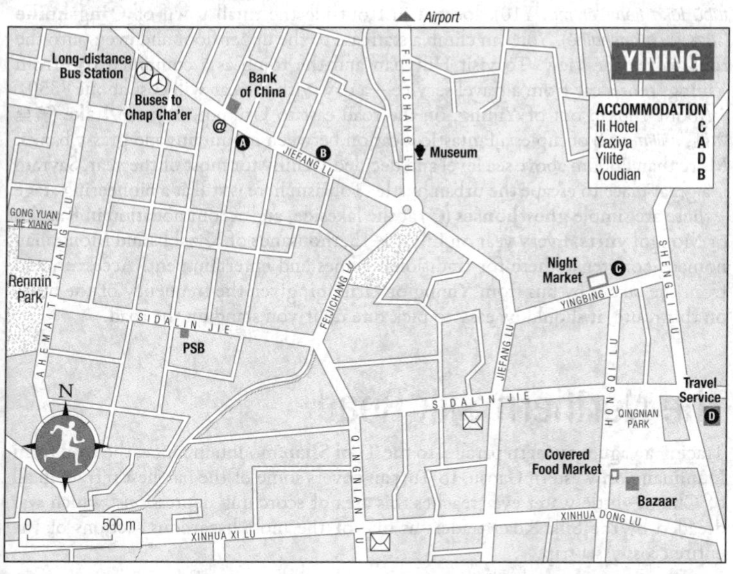

Eating and drinking

Street food is particularly good in Yining. Bundles of **food stalls** appear on the city streets as the sun sets, though this can depend on the weather. Immediately south of Qingnian Park is a covered **food market** where you can get food from all over China, including *baozi*, hotpots and grilled fish. You can also buy the excellent and locally made *kurut* – hard, dry little **cheeses** – from street vendors. Just outside the *Ili* hotel is a busy **Uyghur night market**. Roast chickens, *samsa*, kebabs and noodles are all available, along with the local **beer**, which is made with honey and sold in distinctive bottles with black rubber corks – it is advisable to imbibe no more than one of this sweet, sticky concoction. The Ili Valley is also famous for its **fruit**, so look out for apricots in June, and grapes and peaches in July.

As for **restaurants**, opposite the *Yaxiya* there is a nice unnamed Sichuan place where *tangcu liji*, a sweet-and-sour pork dish both filling and satisfying, is highly popular. The *Ili* has a pleasant Chinese restaurant and an expensive Western restaurant, while on Hongqi Lu opposite the hotel, leading down to Qingnian Park, there are lots of **outdoor restaurants** where a whole *dapan ji* will set you back around ¥40.

Around Yining

There are a couple of obscure and unusual destinations within a day of Yining, though at the time of writing you needed **permits** to visit many places out of town – these can be organized by more or less any tour agency in Xinjiang. About 20km south is the little town of **CHAPUCHA'ER** (察布查尔, *chábù chá'ěr*), home to the **Xibo** people, a tiny minority numbering just 28,000. Of Manchu descent, despatched to Xinjiang in 1764 as warriors to guard and colonize the area, the Xibo still zealously preserve their own language, script and other customs, including a prowess in archery that is of Olympic standard. Chapucha'er is just thirty minutes by bus from outside Yining's long-distance bus station. From the station buses also head to **HUIYUAN** (惠远, *huìyuǎn*), 30km west of Yining, a small but historic town with a three-storey **drum tower** (鼓楼, *gǔlóu*; ¥10) dating from the nineteenth century. Another 20km north of here is the pretty Persian-style tomb of fourteenth-century Muslim leader **Telug Timur** (吐虎鲁克铁木尔墓, *tǔhǔ lǔkè tiěmù'ěr mù*; ¥10), located just outside the small town of **Qingshuihe** (清水河, *qīngshuǐhé*). You can climb a staircase to the upper floor and even onto the roof to see the view. To visit Huiyuan and the tomb as a combined trip from Yining, rent a car from a travel service – a day with the car will cost about ¥350.

About 180km out of Yining, on the road east to Ürümqi, **Sayram Lake** (赛里木湖, *sàilǐmù hú*) occupies a fantastic location between mountains and grassy banks. More than 2000m above sea level and decidedly chilly for most of the year, Sayram is a great place to escape the urban hustle. Tourism here is still at a pioneering stage – there are simple **guesthouses** (❹) at the lakeside, and accommodation in Kazakh or Mongol **yurts**. Every year on July 13–15, thousands of Kazakhs and Mongolian nomads congregate here for traditional games and entertainment. Access to and from the lake is by bus from Yining or Ürümqi; given the frequency of the buses on this route, it should be easy to pick one up if you stand on the road.

The Northern Silk Road

Tracing a vague southern parallel to the **Tian Shan** mountain range, the road from Dunhuang, in western Gansu, to Turpan covers some of the harshest terrain in all of China – little water ever reaches this area of scorching depressions, which was dreaded by the Silk Road traders as one of the most hazardous sections of the entire cross-Asia trip.

The first major city you'll hit on crossing from Gansu is **Hami**. Known across China for its melons (and to readers of Marco Polo, evidently happy with being given "temporary wives" here), this is a bit of a nonentity, although there are hourly departures from its bus station into the Tian Shan mountains – after an hour or so, you'll be in the midst of superb alpine scenery, the valleys dotted with small tent communities. Next comes **Turpan**, famed for its grapes and for being the hottest city in the country; despite the heat it can be one of the most relaxing and enjoyable places in all China. The route then skirts along the Tarim Basin to the wealthy but dull town of **Korla**, though **Kuqa** just beyond is more deserving of a stopover, thanks to its traditional feel and the low-key Silk Road relics in the surrounding deserts. There's then a long journey to Kashgar, via Aksu – the scene of a major terrorist bombing in 2010.

The **road** is in fairly good condition all the way, though given the vast distances involved, it makes much more sense to travel by **train**. Note that east of Turpan (itself rather far from its attendant station), there are only a couple of services per day in either direction.

Turpan

The small oasis town of **TURPAN** (吐鲁番, *tǔlǔfān*) is an absolute must-see if you're in Xinjiang. Long a Silk Road outpost, it has been a favourite with adventurous travellers for some time, and before the travails of 2008 (see p.851) this little place had seen its stock rise considerably. Residents covered many streets and walkways with vine trellises, converting them into shady green tunnels (partly for the benefit of tourists), but have also managed to retain a relatively easy-going manner even in the heady economic climate of modern China.

The town is located in a depression 80m below sea level, which accounts for its extreme climate – well above 40°C in summer and well below freezing in winter. In summer the **dry heat** is so soporific that there is little call to do anything but sleep or sip cool drinks in outdoor cafés with other tourists or the friendly locals. To ease the consciences of the indolent there are a number of **ruined cities** and **Buddhist caves** worth visiting in the countryside around the city, testimony to its past role as an important Silk Road stopover. Rather surprisingly, despite its bone-dry surroundings, Turpan is an agricultural centre of note, famed across China for its **grapes**. Today, virtually every household in the town has a hand in the business, both in cultivating the vine, and in drying the grapes at the end of the season (a Grape Festival is held at the end of August).

Note that if you come out of season (Nov–March), Turpan is cold and uninspiring, with the vines cut back and most businesses closed – the surrounding sights, however, remain interesting, and at these times are almost devoid of other tourists.

Some history

Turpan is a largely **Uyghur-populated** area and, in Chinese terms, an obscure backwater, but it has not always been so. As early as the Han dynasty, the Turpan oasis was a crucial point along the Northern Silk Road, and the cities of **Jiaohe**, and later **Gaochang** (both of whose ruins can be visited from Turpan), were important and wealthy centres of power. On his way to India, Xuanzang spent more time than he had planned here, when the king virtually kidnapped him in order to have him preach to his subjects. This same king later turned his hand to robbing Silk Road traffic, and had his kingdom annexed by China in 640 as a result. From the ninth to the thirteenth century, a rich intellectual and artistic culture developed in Gaochang, resulting from a fusion between the original Indo-European inhabitants and the (pre-Islamic) Uyghurs. It was not until the fourteenth century that the Uyghurs of Turpan converted to Islam.

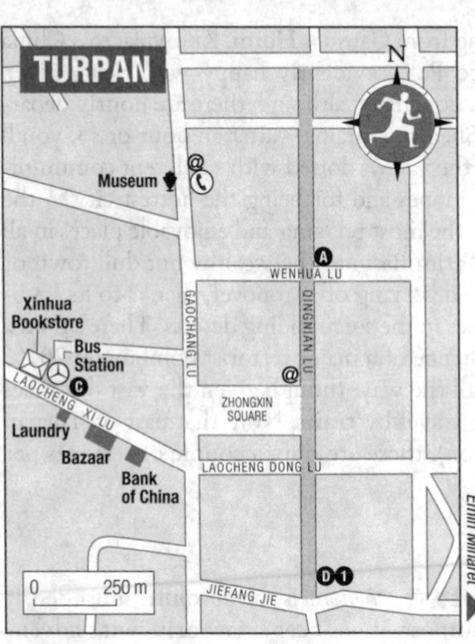

ACCOMMODATION		RESTAURANT	
Jiaohe Manor	B	John's Café	1
Jiaotong	C		
Turpan	D		
Xizhou Grand	A		

Arrival, information and town transport

The only way to arrive in downtown Turpan is by **bus**; most come from Ürümqi. From anywhere further than Korla or Hami you're going to want to arrive by **train**, though the station is inconveniently located 55km away at **Daheyan** (大河沿, *dàhéyán*; marked "Tulufan" on timetables) – from where it takes at least an hour to get into town by bus (summer 8am–11pm, winter 9am–8pm; ¥8). If you arrive after the buses have stopped, you can take advantage of the cheap hotels in Daheyan, or put on your bargaining hat and seek out a taxi.

Turpan has two **travel agents** that can help out with transport bookings for around ¥30 commission (including, in the absence of an airport at Turpan, flights out of Ürümqi), as well as local tours. CITS have a branch on the first floor of the *Jiaotong* (Ⓣ0995/8535809), and there's also the independent *John's Information Café* (Ⓦjohncafé.com) at the *Turpan* hotel. **Internet access** is available at a café on the corner of Qingnian Lu and the park. On Laocheng Wi Lu you will find a **Bank of China**, a laundry, and a Xinhua Bookstore across the road, which also serves as the **post office** (daily 9.30am–8pm).

Getting around Turpan is best done on foot, or – given the extreme summer heat – by bicycle (*John's Information Cafe* lends some out for ¥5/hr).

Accommodation

Turpan has a good range of **accommodation** available to foreigners, and everywhere, regardless of cost, has **air conditioning** – just make sure that yours is working when you check in.

Jiaohe Manor (交河庄园酒店, *jiāohé zhuāngyuán jiǔdiàn*) 9 Jiaohe Dado, 2km west of the centre of town Ⓣ0995/7685999. Built in the style of an old fort, this venture lies right in the heart of the old Uyghur district and all its vineyards. Rooms are as neat as you would expect in this range, with big reductions out of season. ❼

Jiaotong (交通宾馆, *jiāotōng bīnguǎn*) 230 Laocheng Xi Lu, at the bus station Ⓣ0995/8535809. Inexpensive, with grubby corridors that house surprisingly adequate rooms with 24hr hot water. ❸

Turpan (吐鲁番宾馆, *tǔlǔfān bīnguǎn*) South of Qingnian Lu Ⓣ0995/8568898, Ⓕ8569299. This hotel basically mops up almost all foreign visitors, and for good reason: rooms are cheap and perfectly adequate, they've got dorm beds, and there's a shady branch of *John's Café* out back. Dorms ¥50, rooms ❹

Xizhou Grand (西州, *xīzhōu dàjiǔdiàn*) 8 Qingnian Lu Ⓣ0995/8554000, Ⓕ8554068. The plushest place in the town centre, with comfortable, clean rooms and pleasant staff. ❺

The Town

For some travellers, the real draw of Turpan is its relaxing absence of sights. The downtown area doesn't amount to much, with most of the services near the bus

Uyghur music – muqam

Song and dance is at the core of Uyghur cultural identity and is commonly presented at all social gatherings. The most established form of Uyghur music, **muqam**, has developed since the sixth century into a unique collection of songs and instrumentals, quite separate from Arabic and Persian influence. A *muqam* must open with a flowing rhythm that complies with strict modal constraints, followed by a suite of pieces that tie into the opening. In the late sixteenth century scholars and folk musicians gathered to collate this music into a definitive collection of twelve *muqams*. The entire collection takes 24 hours to play and involves around fifteen traditional instruments such as the plucked mandolin-like *rawap*, metal-stringed sitar and large *dumbak* drums. Sadly, few people can play *muqam* nowadays, but recordings are popular and sold on CD and DVD throughout Xinjiang.

station on Laocheng Lu; pedestrianized Qingnian Lu is protected from the baking summer sun by vine trellises. There is a **museum** on Gaochang Xi Lu (吐鲁番博物馆, *tǔlǔfān bówùguǎn*; daily 10am–7.30pm; ¥20), with a smallish collection of dinosaur fossils as well as silk fragments, tools, manuscripts and preserved corpses recovered from the nearby Silk Road sites. Other than this, the **bazaars** off Laocheng Lu, almost opposite the bus station, are worth a casual look, though they are not comparable to anything in Kashgar. You'll find knives, clothes, hats and boots on sale, while the most distinctively local products include delicious sweet raisins, as well as walnuts and almonds.

One of the nicest ways to spend an evening after the heat of the day has passed is to **rent a donkey cart** and take a tour of the countryside south of town, a world of dusty tracks, vineyards, wheat fields, shady poplars, running streams and incredibly friendly people. You are unlikely to encounter many more tranquil rural settings than this. Donkey-cart drivers gather outside the *Turpan* hotel; two or three people will pay around ¥15 each for a tour lasting an hour or more.

Eating and drinking

Finding something good to **eat** is no easy task – there are plenty of so-so Chinese restaurants around, but few of note. Most atmospheric are probably the vine-covered ones lining the pedestrianized route ending at the *Turpan*. Sitting in solitude in the hotel's garden is *John's Café*, a relaxing venue with a range of Chinese and Western dishes, and a great place to drink beer in the evenings. Additionally, the Bazaar next to the Xinhua Bookstore is an excellent place to sample **Uyghur specialities** such as kebabs, *laghman* and dried and fresh fruits.

Around Turpan

Nearly all visitors to Turpan end up taking the customary **tour** of the historical and natural sights outside town. These are quite fun, as much for the chance to get out into the desert as for the sights in themselves, which usually include the two ancient cities of **Gaochang** and **Jiaohe**, the **Emin Minaret**, the **Karez irrigation site**, the **Bezeklik Caves** and **Astana Graves**. Sites are open daily, for most hours of daylight, but only Jiaohe is undisputably worth the cost – and, in fact, you can get good views of Gaocheng and the Emin Minaret without actually entering the sites.

The Emin Minaret is within **cycling** distance, and if you're a healthy sort then Jiaohe will be too. For sights further afield, you'll have to arrange a **shared taxi** or **minibus**, with prices dependent upon exactly what you wish to see; CITS is best for minibuses, and your accommodation can recommend a taxi driver. Be aware that, however you travel, you'll be in blistering heat for the whole of the day, so

Xuanzang and the *Journey to the West*

Trade goods were not the only things to travel along the Silk Road; it was along this route that **Buddhism** first arrived in China at some point in the first century AD. Cities along the way became bastions of the religion (which in part explains their abandonment and desecration following the introduction of Islam after 1000), and from early on, Chinese pilgrims visited India and brought back a varied bag of Buddhist teachings. The most famous was the Tang-dynasty monk **Xuanzang**, unique for the depth of his learning and the exhaustive quantity of material with which he returned after a seventeen-year journey from the then capital of China, Chang'an (Xi'an), to India.

Born near Luoyang in 602, Xuanzang favoured **Mahayana** Buddhism, which depicts the world as an illusion produced by our senses. Having studied in Luoyang, Chengdu and Chang'an, he became confused by often contradictory teachings, and in 629 he decided to visit India to study Buddhism at its source. China's new Tang rulers had forbidden foreign travel, so Xuanzang went without official permission, narrowly avoiding arrest in western Gansu. He almost died of thirst before reaching **Hami** and then **Turpan**, at the foot of the Flaming Mountains. Turpan's king detained him for a month to hear him preach but eventually provided a large retinue, money and passports for safe passage through other kingdoms. Xuanzang reached **Kuqa** unharmed, and spent two months waiting for the passes north over the Tian Shan to thaw – even so, a great number of his party died traversing the mountains. On the far side in modern Kyrgyzstan, Xuanzang's religious knowledge greatly impressed the Khan of the Western Turks, before he continued, via the great central Asian city of **Samarkand**, through modern-day Afghanistan, over the Hindu Kush and so down into **India**, arriving about a year after he set out. Xuanzang spent fifteen years in India visiting holy sites, including the Ganges and places from Buddha's life. He also studied Buddhism in major and esoteric forms, lectured, and entered debates – which he often won – with famous teachers on aspects of religious thought.

If he hoped to find ultimate clarity he was probably disappointed, as the interpretation of Buddhist lore in India was even more varied than in China. However, he did

sun cream, a hat, water bottle and sunglasses are essential. **Entry fees**, which are not included in the cost of a tour, range from ¥20 to ¥60 per site.

The Emin Minaret

You can walk to the eighteenth-century **Emin Minaret** (苏公塔, *sūgōng tǎ*; ¥30), 2km southeast of Turpan, by following Jiefang Jie east out of town for about thirty minutes. Unlike other Islamic architecture, the minaret is built to a very simple style – slightly bulging and potbellied – and erected from sun-dried brown bricks arranged in differing patterns. The tower tapers its way 40m skyward to a rounded tip, adjoining a mosque with a splendidly intricate latticework ceiling. You can see the complex without entering the site; otherwise you can ascend the tower to gain good views over the green oasis in the foreground and the distant snowy Tian Shan beyond.

Jiaohe

About 11km west of Turpan is the ruined city of **Jiaohe** (交河, *jiāohé*; ¥40; signposted in English), just about within cycling range on a hot day. Although Jiaohe was for large parts of its history under the control of Gaochang (see p.861), it became the regional administrative centre during the eighth century, and occupies a spectacular defensive setting on top of a 2km-long, steep-sided plateau carved out by the two halves of a forking river. What sets Jiaohe apart from all other ruined cities along the Silk Road is that although most of the buildings comprise little more than crumbling, windswept mud walls, so many survive, and of such a variety – gates, temples, public buildings, graveyards and ordinary dwellings – that Jiaohe's **street** manage to acquire a vast collection of Buddhist statues, relics and **texts**, and in 644 decided that it was his responsibility to return to China with this trove of knowledge. Given an **elephant** to carry his luggage by the powerful north Indian king Harsha, Xuanzang recrossed the Kush and turned east to travel over the Pamirs to **Tashkurgan** (near where the elephant unfortunately drowned) before heading up to **Kashgar** – then, as now, an outpost of the Chinese empire. From here he turned southeast to the silk and jade emporium of **Khotan**, whose king claimed Indian ancestry and where there were a hundred Buddhist monasteries. Xuanzang spent eight months here, waiting for replacements of Buddhist texts lost in northern India and a reply from the Tang emperor **Taizong**, to whom he had written requesting permission to re-enter China. When it came, permission was enthusiastic, and Xuanzang lost little time in returning to Chang'an via Niya, Miran, Loulan and **Dunhuang**, arriving in the Chinese capital in 645. He had left unknown, alone and almost as a fugitive; he returned to find tens of thousands of spectators crowding the road to Chang'an. The emperor became his patron, and he spent the last twenty years of his life translating part of the collection of Buddhist texts acquired on his travels.

Xuanzang wrote a biography, but highly coloured accounts of his travels also passed into folklore, becoming the subject of plays and the sixteenth-century novel *Journey to the West*, still a popular tale in China. In it, Xuanzang (known as **Tripitaka**) is depicted as terminally naïve, hopelessly dismayed by the various disasters that beset him. Fortunately, he's aided by the Bodhisattva of Mercy, **Guanyin**, who sends him spirits to protect him in his quest: the vague character of **Sandy**; the greedy and lecherous **Pigsy**; and **Sun Wu Kong**, the brilliant Monkey King. As many of the novel's episodes are similar, varying only in which particular demon has captured Tripitaka, the best parts are the lively exchanges between Pigsy and Monkey, as they endeavour to rescue their master. A good abridgement in English is Arthur Waley's *Monkey* – see "Books" on p.990 for a review.

plan is still evident; there's a real feeling of how great this city must have been. As with Gaochang, a Buddhist monastery marked the town centre, and its foundations – 50m on each side – can still be seen. Another feature is the presence of ancient wells still containing water. Make sure you walk to the far end of the site, where the base of a former tower, dated to around 360 AD, overlooks the river.

Karez

Returning from Jiaohe, minibus drivers usually drop you off at a dolled-up **Karez irrigation site** (坎儿井, *kǎn'ér jǐng*; ¥40), an intrinsically interesting place unfortunately turned into an ethnic theme park, complete with regular Uyghur dance shows, presumably to justify the entry fee. Karez irrigation taps natural underground channels carrying water from source – in this case glaciers at the base of the Tian Shan – to the point of use. Strategically dug wells then bring water to small surface channels that run around the streets of the town. Many ancient Silk Road cities relied on this system, including those much farther to the west, in areas such as modern Iran, and Karez systems are still in use throughout Xinjiang – there are plenty of opportunities to see them for free on the way to Kashgar.

The Bezeklik Caves

For sights any further than Jiaohe, you definitely need to take a minibus – they are too far to reach by bicycle. The first stop is usually the Bezeklik Caves, but on the way you'll pass the **Flaming Mountains**, made famous in the sixteenth-century Chinese novel *Journey to the West* (see p.864). It's not hard to see why the novel depicts these sandstone mountains as walls of flame, the red sandstone hillsides lined and creviced as though flickering with flame in the heat haze. The plains below are dotted with dozens of small "nodding donkey" **oil wells**, all tapping into Xinjiang's vast reserves.

The **Bezeklik Caves** (柏孜克里克石窟, *bózīkèlĭkè shíkū*; ¥30), in a valley among the Flaming Mountains some 50km northeast of Turpan, are disappointing, offering mere fragments of the former wealth of Buddhist cave art here, dating back to 640 AD. The location is nonetheless striking, with stark orange dunes behind and a deep river gorge fringed in green below, but most of the murals were cut out and removed to Berlin by Albert Von Le Coq at the beginning of the twentieth century, and the remainder painstakingly defaced by Muslim Red Guards during the 1960s. (A number of the murals removed by Le Coq were subsequently destroyed by the Allied bombing of Germany in World War II.) Outside the site you can ride **camels** along the Flaming Mountains for ¥80 per person. Just before the caves is a bizarre **theme park** (¥25), featuring giant sculptures of characters from *Journey to the West* – a very surreal sight springing up out of the desiccated landscape.

Astana Graves and Gaochang

South of the Bezeklik Caves, the **Astana Graves** (阿斯塔娜古墓区, *āsītănà gŭmùqū*; ¥20) mark the burial site of the imperial dead of Gaochang from the Tang dynasty. Unfortunately, the graves have had most of their interesting contents removed to museums in Ürümqi and Turpan, and little remains beyond a couple of preserved corpses and some murals. The adjacent ruins of **Gaochang** (高昌, *gāochāng*; ¥40) are somewhat more impressive, especially for their huge scale and despite having suffered from the ravages of both Western archeologists and the local population, who for centuries have been carting off bits of the city's 10m-high adobe walls to use as soil for their fields. You can walk, or take a donkey cart (¥20/person), from the entrance to the centre of the site, which is marked by a large square building, the remains of a monastery. Its outer walls are covered in niches, in each of which a Buddha was originally seated; just a few bare, broken traces of these Buddhas remain, along with their painted haloes. If you have time you can strike off on your own and listen to the hot wind whistling through the mud-brick walls.

Grape Valley and Aiding Lake

Thirteen kilometres north of Turpan, at the western end of the Flaming Mountains, is the so-called **Grape Valley** (葡萄沟, *pútáo gōu*; ¥60). There's very little point visiting out of season, but from mid-July to September it's a pleasant little refuge in the middle of a stark desert, covered in shady trellises bulging with fruit (which you have to pay for if you want to eat). Your ticket covers a Uyghur dance performance and a museum – you can find the locations of both on the map of the valley as you enter. This could be included on your minibus tour, or you could reach it on a very hot bicycle ride, but bear in mind that the scenery here is not much different from that of downtown Turpan.

Finally, about 50km south of Turpan, though not included on any tours, is the bleak but dramatic **Aiding Lake** (艾丁湖, *àidīng hú*). Located in a natural depression 154m below sea level, this is the second-lowest lake in the world after the Dead Sea, though you won't actually see any water here except in spring – the rest of the year the lake is a flat plain of dried salt deposits. The land around the lake is white with crusty salt and dotted with bright yellow-green pools of saturated water that feels like oil on the skin. Locals rub it over themselves enthusiastically, claiming that it's good for you. A car to the lake and back should cost around ¥180 – the road is very rough, and the (one-way) trip takes at least two hours. At the time of writing there was talk of turning the area into a resort of some kind with a whopping entry fee; ask at Turpan's **CITS** first. The area around the lake is very muddy, so don't take your best shoes.

Korla

There's been a settlement at **KORLA** (库尔勒, *kù'ěrlè*) since at least Tang times, and today the city is capital of the **Bayangol Mongol Autonomous Prefecture**, a vast region that encompasses the eastern side of the Taklamakan as well as better-watered areas around the city itself. Despite all this, Mongols are not much in evidence today, and Korla functions mostly as a base for companies tapping into the Taklamakan's **oil reserves**. It's also inescapable as a transport nexus: the rail line and roads from Ürümqi and Turpan converge here; the Northern Silk Road heads due west; and the Southern Silk Road curves down around the eastern side of the Taklamakan via Charkhlik. The town is also a terminus for buses shortcutting the Southern Silk Road by crossing diagonally southwest across the Taklamakan to Niya and Khotan.

There isn't anything aside from transport connections to justify a stopover, though the grey brickwork and red-tiled roof of the Ming-dynasty **Tiemen Guan** (铁门关, *tiěmén guān*; ¥6), the Iron Gateway, asserts Korla's age in the face of what is otherwise a relentlessly modern city – you'll see it from the bus to the north of town. In summer, locals spend their spare time 67km east at **Bosten Lake** (博斯腾湖, *bósīténg hú*; ¥30), a huge expanse of water where you can take a dip to cool off, rent a beach umbrella and kick back on the sand, admiring distant desert mountain ranges. A taxi return including two hours waiting costs around ¥300; you'll save a lot by taking a bus to **Yanqi Xian** (焉耆县, *yānqí xiàn*), then a one-way cab from there.

Korla's **centre** is only about 1km across, and you'll find everything you need on the main main street, Renmin Lu, including a range of hotels, plenty of restaurants and a Bank of China.

Kuqa and around

Pronounced "ku-cher" and known to the Chinese as "**Kuche**", **KUQA** (库车, *kùchē*) was once a cosmopolitan town full of Silk Road traders and travellers, the "land of jewels" in Xuanzang's journal. There's little evidence of past wealth; today, the small city is dusty and poor. It is effectively in two parts, the old to the west and the new to the east, cleaved in two by the Kuche River.

A good place to break the long journey to Kashgar, it does boast a long history and a largely Uyghur population. The fourth-century linguist and scholar **Kumarajiva**, one of the most famous of all Chinese Buddhists, came from here. Having travelled to Kashmir for his education, he later returned to China as a teacher and translator of Buddhist documents from Sanskrit into Chinese. It was in large measure thanks to him that Buddhism came to be so widely understood in China, and by the early Tang, Kuqa was a major **centre of Buddhism**. The fantastic wealth of the trade caravans subsidized giant monasteries here, and Xuanzang, passing through the city in the sixth century, reported the existence of two huge Buddha statues, 27m high, guarding its entrances. The city even had its own Indo-European language. With the arrival of Islam in the ninth century, however, this era finally began to draw to a close, and today only a few traces of Kuqa's ancient past remain.

Arrival and information

Flights connect Kuqa with Ürümqi; the New City is a very short taxi ride west of the **airport** (¥10). The **bus station** is in the far southeast of the New City, while the **train station** is 5km further south (¥5 in a taxi), seeing just a handful of services each day. You'd be mad to want to take a bus any further than Aksu to the west or Korla to the east, though the reopening of the tough road to Yining brings that city within reach.

For plane tickets out of Kuqa, and for **booking tours** of the sights outside the city, it's worth paying a call on the friendly Kuqa **CITS** (Mon–Sat 10am–1.30pm & 3.30–7.30pm; ⓣ0997/7136016, ⓕ7122524), in the upmarket *Qiuici Hotel* on

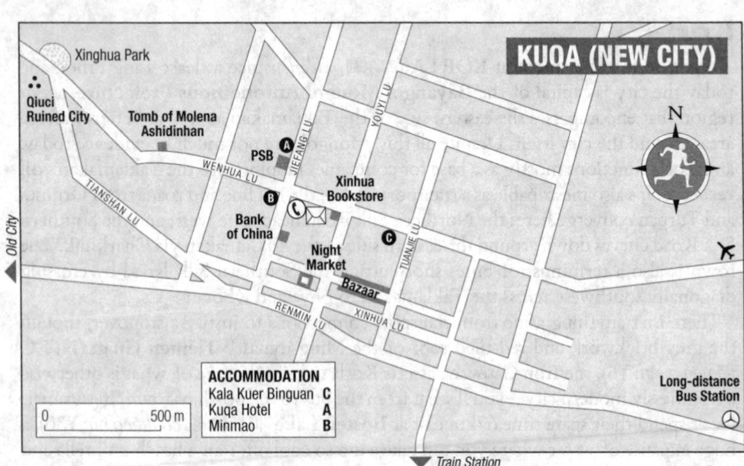

Tianshan Lu. For visa extensions, the **PSB** (Mon–Fri 9.30am–7.30pm) is on Jiefang Lu, five minutes' walk north of *Minmao* hotel. There's also a **Bank of China** (Mon–Fri 9.30am–8pm) south of here, and a **post office** on Wenhua Lu.

Accommodation

There are a couple of **hotels** right outside the bus station, but this is a rather distant corner of town to stay in. To reach the more central hotels, catch bus #2 from just in front of the station, heading west. Get off at the second stop and take the next road north, **Jiefang Lu**. Motor-rickshaws also run from the station, or it's around a twenty-minute walk.

Kala Kuer Binguan (卡拉库尔宾馆, *kālākù'ěr bīnguǎn*) One block east of the post office ☎0997/7122957. Clean and neat accommodation, with dorm beds available. Dorm beds ¥50, rooms ❸

Kuqa Hotel (库车宾馆, *kùchē bīnguǎn*) Jiefang Lu, north of the PSB ☎0997/7122901. The buildings have their own gardens, and the big and bright rooms have 24hr hot water. ❹

Minmao (民贸宾馆, *mínmào bīnguǎn*) On the southwest side of the intersection between Jiefang Lu and Wenhua Lu ☎0997/7122888. A convenient place to stay, with reasonably priced rooms, though the furniture has seen better days. ❸

The New City

The **New City**, largely Han-populated, contains all the facilities you'll need but has only a few sights of marginal interest. One is the remains of the ruined city of **Qiuci** (龟兹古城, *qiūcī gǔchéng*); this is the old name for Kuqa, and there's not much to see. If you follow Wenhua Xi Lu, the ruined city is about fifteen minutes' walk west of Wenhua Square, in the centre of the new town. Across the road from the old wall is the neglected **Xinghua Park** (杏花公园, *xìnghuā gōngyuán*; ¥3) – a peaceful place for a picnic. Slightly more exciting is the nearby **Tomb of Molena Ashidinhan** (莫拉纳俄什丁坟, *mòlānà'é shídīng fén*), a simple wooden shrine built in 1867 in honour of an Arab missionary who came to the city in the fourteenth century. It's on Wenhua Xi Lu, about fifteen minutes' walk west of the *Minmao* hotel. There's also a daily **bazaar** in the lane running east for several blocks from the Bank of China, north of and parallel with Xinhua Lu, containing Xinjiang's second-largest **goldsmiths' quarters** (after Kashgar).

The Old City

The **Old City**, largely Uyghur, is peppered with mosques and bazaars and has a Central Asian atmosphere – take any bus heading west along Renmin Lu, the main street on which the bus station is located, until you reach a bridge across the river (the Old City lies beyond the river).

Right by the bridge, the **bazaar** is the main venue for the highly enjoyable **Friday market**. Here, the Uyghur population are out in force, buying and selling leather jackets, carpets, knives, wooden boxes, goats and donkeys; cattle and sheep are traded on the riverbanks below. Beyond the bridge, you can soon lose yourself in the labyrinth of narrow streets and mud-brick houses. Right in the heart of this, approximately fifteen minutes northeast of the bridge, is the **Kuqa Mosque** (清真大寺, *qīngzhēnsì*; ¥20), built in 1923. Delightfully neat and compact, with an attractive green-tiled dome, this mosque is of wholly arabesque design, displaying none of the Chinese characteristics of mosques in more eastern parts of the country. Beyond the mosque, on Linji Lu, the town **museum** (库车博物馆, *kùchē bówùguǎn*; daily 9.30am–8.30pm; ¥15), houses interesting collections of Qiuci relics. From the bridge, rusty blue English signs direct you to the mosque and the museum along the main road, or you can hire a donkey cart for less than ¥1 per person per trip.

Eating and drinking

Near the New Town's market area around the Renmin Lu/Youyi Lu intersection are numerous **food stands** – hugely busy on Fridays – where you can tuck into delicious baked *kaobao*, *samsa*, bowls of *laghman* and Uyghur tea with great rough sticks and leaves floating in the cup. One thing definitely worth trying is the giant nan bread, served, unlike elsewhere in Xinjiang, thin and crispy and covered with onion, sesame and carrot. On Xinhua Lu, a little east of Jiefang Lu, is a busy, smoky **night market** full of the usual kebabs and roast chickens, as well as plenty of fresh fruit in season.

Around Kuqa

Around Kuqa, you can explore a whole series of ruined cities and Buddhist cave sites. The **Kizil Thousand Buddha Caves** (克孜尔千佛洞, *kèzī'ěr qiānfódòng*), 75km to the northwest of the city, were once a Central Asian treasure-trove, a mixture of Hellenistic, Indian and Persian styles with not even a suggestion of Chinese influence. Sadly, the caves suffered the ravages of the German archeologist and art thief **Albert Von Le Coq** (see p.866) who, at the beginning of the twentieth century, cut out and carried away many of the best frescoes. However, it is still an intriguing place to visit and even older than the more extensive Mogao Caves in Gansu. Your ticket (¥55) covers eight caves but you can pay extra to be guided round others, including no. 38, the "cave of musicians" – which has Bodhisattvas playing musical instruments on the ceiling.

Thirty kilometres north of Kuqa along a good paved road, the **Subashi Ancient Buddhist Complex** (苏巴什佛寺遗址, *sūbāshí fósì yízhǐ*), abandoned in the twelfth century, comprises fairly extensive ruins from east to west, intercepted by a river. The entrance fee is ¥15 to each side – the west parts of the ruins are more interesting and contain various pagodas and temples, and the remains of some wall paintings. The entire site looks very atmospheric with the bald, pink and black mountain ranges rising up behind. Along the way there, look for the **irrigation channels** carrying runoff from the mountains to villages.

To visit either of these sights, you'll need to rent a car (Kuqa CITS can arrange this – their day-trip tour to both Subashi and Kizil costs ¥400) or simply stop a taxi and start negotiating.

Kashgar

Some 1200m above sea level and almost as far west as you can possibly go in China, Uyghur-dominated **KASHGAR** (喀什, *kèshí*) has long been one of the most fascinating parts of the country. Its remoteness is palpable, as is a distinctively Central Asian air that makes it a visible bastion of old **Chinese Turkestan** – minarets pierce the horizon in their hundreds, and each evening the desert air is scented and blurred by the smoke of barbecued lamb. Set astride overland routes to Pakistan and Kyrgyzstan, the city is more than 4000km from Beijing, of which the thousand-plus kilometres from Ürümqi are for the most part sheer desert. Indeed, a large part of the excitement lies in the experience of reaching it – even the plane journey in is nothing short of spectacular. Yet Kashgar is a remarkably prosperous and pleasant place, despite being, in part, an essentially medieval city.

Part of this prosperity has come at a price. Han Chinese have relocated here in the thousands, and almost all of the old town has been ripped up, traditional housing and all, with residents moved to modern high-rises on the city limits; even more galling, some of the old areas are being preserved as tourist attractions, meaning that the Muslim population may soon have to pay to see their own culture. The locals are understandably angry: Kashgar is the focal point of the tense standoff between the Han and Uyghur peoples, as made painfully clear by the **security personnel** – both in uniform and undercover – ubiquitous around the city.

Combined with the enforced dilution of its distinctive culture, this inter-ethnic strife means that Kashgar, long a popular stop on the backpacker trail, is now on the wane as a tourist destination. It's hard not to feel sorry for the locals, whose generous hospitality lingers in the heart of many a traveller. Nonetheless, their city remains well worth a visit; despite Han migration, its population is still overwhelmingly Muslim, a fact you can hardly fail to notice with the great **Id Kah Mosque** dominating the central square, the Uyghur bazaars and teashops, the smell of grilled lamb and, above all, the faces of the Turkic people around you. If you can choose a time to be here, aim for the Uyghur Corban **festival** at the end of the Muslim month of Ramadan, which involves activities such as dancing and goat-tussling; something similar occurs exactly two months later. Whatever time of year you visit, don't miss Kashgar's **Sunday market**, for which half of Central Asia seems to converge on the city.

Some history

Kashgar's **strategic position** has determined its history. There was already a Chinese military governor here when Xuanzang passed through on his way back from India in 644. The city was Buddhist at the time, with hundreds of monasteries; Islam made inroads around 1000 and eventually became the state religion. More recently, the late nineteenth century saw Kashgar at the meeting point of three empires – **Chinese**, **Soviet and British**. Both Britain and the Soviet Union maintained consulates in Kashgar until 1949: the British with an eye to their interests across the frontier in India, the Soviets (so everyone assumed) with the long-term intention of absorbing Xinjiang into their Central Asian orbit. The conspiracies of this period are brilliantly evoked in Peter Fleming's *News from Tartary* (see p.987 for review) and Ella Maillart's *Forbidden Journey*. At the time of Fleming's visit in 1935, the city was in effect run by the Soviets, who had brought their rail line to within two days' worth of travel to Kashgar. During World War II, however, Kashgar swung back under Chinese control, and with the break in Sino-Soviet relations in the early 1960s, the Soviet border (and influence) firmly closed. In the wake of the break-up of the Soviet Union, however, it seemed that Kashgar would resume its status as one of the great travel crossroads of Asia, but this recovery sadly stalled after the conflict in

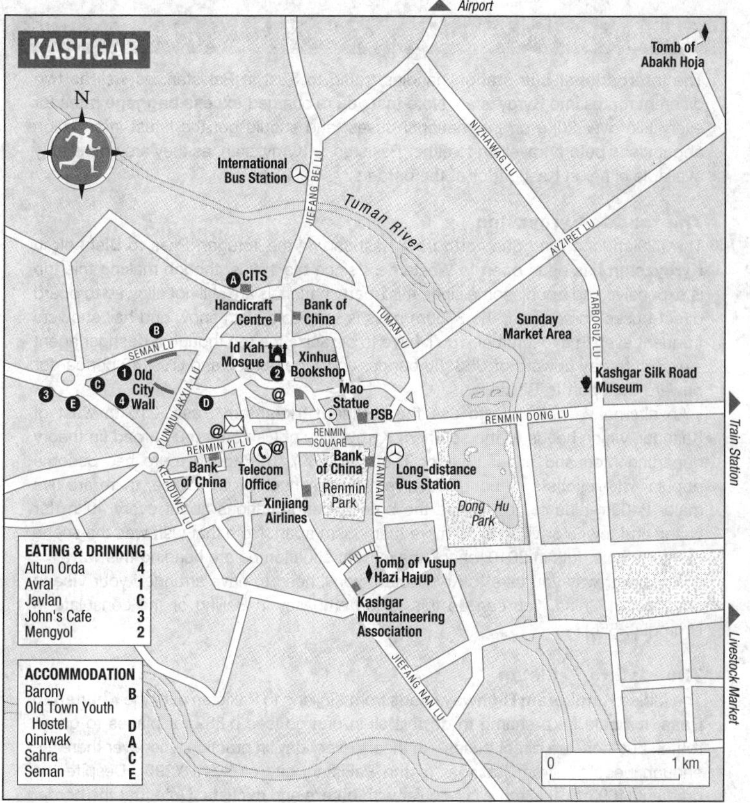

Afghanistan, then went into decline during the troubles of 2008 and 2009 (see p.851). The town is still experiencing something of a downturn, with neither traders nor tourists as plentiful as they once were.

Arrival and city transport

Kashgar's **airport** is 14km north of town; the airport bus (¥10) drives straight down Jiefang Lu to China Southern Airlines' Xinjiang office. It should be possible to take a taxi for ¥20, though drivers will doubtless ask for more. The journey between Ürümqi and Kashgar can be made by plane, which costs a little more but essentially buys you a day. The **train station** ("Kashi" on Chinese timetables) has just two services per day; it's 7km east of town, where minibuses and taxis, as well as bus #28 to the Id Kah Mosque, await new arrivals. Just east of the centre on Tiannan Lu is the main **long-distance bus station**, handling connections from most parts of Xinjiang, including Ürümqi, Kuqa, Korla, Yarkand and Khotan. The **international bus station**, on the #2 bus route, is the terminus for luxury buses from Ürümqi, as well as those from Tashkurgan, and for all international traffic (see box, p.872).

Taxis are cheap, ubiquitous and easy to hail, though most drivers prefer to agree a price rather than use the meter, which in many cases is unplugged or does not even exist. Even cheaper are the **moto-riders** who congregate around road

To Kyrgyzstan and Pakistan

The **international bus station** handles traffic to Sust in Pakistan, as well as two different routes into Kyrgyzstan. Note that you're charged **excess baggage** rates for every kilo over 20kg on international buses, and should get the latest information about **visas** before travelling to either Pakistan or Kyrgyzstan, as they are not reliably available either in Kashgar or at the borders.

The road to Kyrgyzstan

The 720km-long road due north from Kashgar via the Torugart Pass to **Bishkek** in **Kyrgyzstan** has been open to Westerners since the 1990s, though making this trip is expensive and troublesome since third-party nationals are still not allowed to board direct buses. In addition, the 3750m pass is very cold, with snow and hail showers frequent even in midsummer. You'll have to organize the trip though a Kashgar agent – expect to pay upward of US$180 per car up to the border, and US$140 per car for onward transport to Bishkek.

An alternative option is to use the southern **Irkeshtam Pass,** 210km west of Kashgar, which heads to the southern Kyrgyz city of Osh on a rough road (in theory departing Mon and either Wed or Thurs; US$50). This tough route has become popular with **cyclists**; although relatively flat for much of its course, there are five major 2400m-plus climbs before the border, petrol stations about every 40km for water, and towns or villages no more than 65km apart. Note that Osh was the scene of inter-ethnic riots in 2010; check the current situation before heading this way.

Whichever way you take to Krygyzstan, you'll need to have arranged your **visa** in advance; in China, you can do this at the embassy in Beijing or the consulate in Ürümqi (p.856).

The road to Pakistan

The fabled **Karakoram Highway** heads from Xinjiang to Pakistan over the **Khunerjab Pass**. It would be a shame to do this all in one go (see p.882 for places to go en route), but there are direct buses – in theory every day, in practice whenever there are enough people – from Kashgar to the Pakistani city of **Sust** (¥290). Despite the gradient (4693m), this route is popular with **bikers** and **cyclists**. Note that the border is open only from May 1 until some point in October (see p.882) and that third-party nationals will need to have organized their **visa**, only possible in China some 3500km away at the Beijing embassy.

junctions – it's now legal to use these, and a short trip will cost just ¥1–2. They rarely pester people for rides, but look interested and one will come over.

Accommodation

Kashgar's **accommodation** is surprisingly poor, something that – with its recent downturn – may not improve anytime soon.

Barony (邦臣酒店, *bāngchén jiǔdiàn*) 242 Seman Lu ⓣ0998/2586888, ⓦwww.barony txnhotels.com. Kashgar's swankiest establishment, with a gym, three restaurants and a small but well-tended garden. You can usually get them down to ¥600 or less. ❽

Old Town Youth Hostel (老城青年旅舍, *lǎochéng qīngnián lǚshè*) 233 Wusitangboyi Lu ⓣ0998/2823262, ⓦwww.kashgaroldcity.hostel.com. In the heart of the rapidly disintegrating old town (and therefore maybe not around for long in its present location), this hostel has decent rooms, helpful staff and a courtyard that's great for meeting other travellers. ❷

Qiniwak (其尼瓦克宾馆, *qíní wǎkè bīnguǎn*) 144 Seman Lu ⓣ0998/2982103, ⓕ2982299. Also known as the *Chini Bagh*, a popular place whose odd shape stands out near the Id Kah Mosque. Undergoing renovations at the time of writing, it has grand plans to become a five-star operation, and is likely to reopen at a higher price level. ❺

Sahra (色哈乐宾馆, *sèhālè bīnguǎn*) Seman Lu opposite the *Seman* ☎0998/2581122. A budget option with 24-hour hot water, a roof and beds. Popular with Pakistani traders, though it won't be to everyone's taste. ❷

Seman (色满宾馆, *sèmǎn bīnguǎn*) Seman Lu ☎0998/2822129. This rambling, nicely aged hotel is a popular choice, its cheap rooms augmented by *John's Café* just outside, the old Russian embassy out back, and a raft of useful tour agencies in the lobby. Dorms ¥40, rooms ❹

The City

For the time being, the **old town**, north of Renmin Lu, remains the focal point for foreign travellers. The main attractions are its ordinary streets – principally the bazaars, the restaurants, the teahouses and the people in them. These are, however, disappearing quickly, and you may even be asked to pay an **entrance fee** of ¥30 in some areas – refuse politely and head somewhere else (or back to the same place in the evening). Roads radiate out from the centre of the original Uyghur city, which is centred on **Id Kah Square**, with its clock tower and huge mosque.

A few hundred metres to the south of this old town is Kashgar's modern, commercial centre, whose main landmark is the absurdly colossal **statue of Mao Zedong** hailing a taxi on Renmin Dong Lu, a towering reminder of China's ultimate authority over the region. More interesting are a number of **mausoleums** to Uyghur heroes of the past, scattered around the fringes of the city and best reached by bus or bicycle.

Id Kah Square and around

The main historical sight in central Kashgar is the **Id Kah Mosque** (艾提尕尔清真寺, *àitígǎ'ěr qīngzhēnsì*), occupying the western side of Id Kah Square, off Jiefang Bei Lu. Originally built in 1442, it has been restored many times, most recently after the Cultural Revolution. It is one of the biggest mosques, and almost certainly the most active, in the country; you can even hear the call to prayer booming around the city centre – a rare sound in China. Although visitors are theoretically allowed in (there is a entrance fee of ¥20 to the grounds), Western tourists are sometimes shooed away by zealous worshippers – note that visitors of either sex should have their arms and legs fully covered when entering this (or any other) mosque. You certainly won't be admitted on Fridays, the main Muslim prayer day, when some ten thousand people crowd the mosque and square; the quietest time, when your presence will cause least disturbance, is probably early to mid-morning on any other day. Inside are pleasant courtyards and tree-lined gardens where worshippers assemble.

The main Uyghur bazaars are in the neighbouring streets; while you're in the area, keep an eye open for a couple of substantial fragments of Kashgar's **old city walls**, most easily viewed south of Seman Lu and west off Yunmulakxia Lu. And don't miss out on the **old consulates** either: the British had theirs behind the *Qiniwak* hotel, while the Russian headquarters survive as a nicely preserved period piece in the courtyard behind the *Seman* hotel.

The bazaars

The street heading northeast from Id Kah Square is the main **carpet** area. The region's best specimens are handmade in Khotan, but some good bargains can be had in the local bazaars. The rugs are relatively rough in quality and have geometric designs only, but the prices are about a third of the equivalent in Turkey. Bear in mind, of course, that not everyone is an expert, and there will be a few dubious traders looking to pocket your cash. Elvis Ablimit (see p.875) is an

Kashgar's Sunday market

Known in Uyghur as the **Yekshenba Bazaar**, or Sunday Bazaar (中细亚市场, *zhōngxìyà shìchǎng*), what was once the mother of all markets still attracts up to one hundred thousand villagers and nomads, all riding their donkey carts from the surrounding area and gathering in two sites to the east and the southeast of town. For the sheer scale of the occasion, it's the number-one sight in Kashgar, if not all Xinjiang. Considering the large numbers of minority peoples who come to trade here, all sporting their own particular headwear, it is also an anthropologist's delight. Knives, hats, pots, carpets, pans, fresh fruit and vegetables, clothes and boots and every kind of domestic and agricultural appliance – often handmade in wood and tin – are available, and some produce, such as Iranian saffron, has come a very long way to be sold here. The market goes on all day and into the early evening, and food and drink are widely available on and around the site.

Due to the traffic chaos it used to cause in the city centre every Sunday, the **livestock market** (and its thousands of animals) has been moved to an area a few kilometres south of town to **Ulagh Bazaar**, or **Yuanfang Shichang** in Chinese. Here you'll find traders haggling over everything from camels to cattle, while sheep turn a blind eye to the food stalls on the periphery.

To get to the Sunday market from Renmin Square, take bus #16 to its terminus; it heads on to Yekshenba Bazaar from there. From the Id Kah Mosque you can take a fascinating forty-minute walk through the old city with its adobe lanes full of traders, coppersmiths and blacksmiths; buses #7, #8 and #28 all follow the same route. A taxi from the centre of town will cost around ¥13.

antique carpet specialist and will be happy to help you should you wish to buy (Ⓣ13899136195). You can see people making them, along with musical instruments and jewellery, at the **Handicrafts Centre**, 200m north of Id Kah Square on Jiefang Lu. Kashgar **kilims**, produced by nomads, are highly sought after and almost impossible to find locally. If you really want one, again, contact Elvis Ablimit.

A small road east of Id Kah Square, parallel to Jiefang Lu, is good for Central Asian **hats**. As well as the green-and-white square-shaped variety so beloved by old Uyghur men, there are prayer caps, skullcaps, furry winter hats and plain workmen's caps. Following this lane south, turn right, where a large, semi-underground market occupies the space between the square and hat lane. Here you will find a large selection of **clothes**, carpets and **crockery**, as well as Uyghur nuts, sweets and spice stands, and the occasional blacksmith hammering at his trade. Further south down hat lane, you will come to a **woodcraft** area.

North of the square you'll find **jewellery** and high-quality ornate **knives**, produced in Yengisar. The lane directly south of Id Kah Mosque, heading due west, sells a mixture of hats, jewellery, large **chests** overlain with brightly coloured tin (purpose-built for carrying gifts for brides-to-be), and handmade **musical instruments**. The two-stringed *dutah* is the most common. The *tanber* is similar but has an even longer stem and a round bowl shaped like half a gourd, while the *rawupu* has five strings and a snakeskin drum.

In the southern part of the square is the Kashgar **night market**, while surrounding the Id Kah Mosque are a few **Uyghur teahouses** and small eating establishments, as well as daytime street food.

The outskirts

Kashgar's extant historic architecture chiefly comprises a number of mausoleums to famous Uyghur personages. The most central is the **Tomb of Yusup Hazi**

Hajup (哈撕哈吉南幕, *hāsīhā jí nánmù*; daily 10am–7pm; ¥30), the eleventh-century Uyghur poet and philosopher. The mausoleum, of handsome blue and white wall tiles, was slightly shoddily reconstructed in 1986, but is still worth seeing. It's about 1500m south of Renmin Lu, on Tiyu Lu, a small road located between Jiefang Nan Lu and Tiannan Lu – bus #8 down Jiefang Lu comes within striking distance.

A few kilometres east of the centre via the #10 bus, the **Kashgar Silk Road Museum** (喀什丝绸之路博物馆, *kāshí sīchóuzhīlù bówùguǎn*; daily 10am–8pm; ¥30), on Tarbogue Lu, holds an Iron Age **mummy** recovered from the nearby desert, still dressed in felt hat and fur-lined jacket, woollen trousers, leather boots and belt with herbs and knife attached. There are also examples of various ancient **scripts** found at Silk Road sites, including Indian-derived Kharosthi (from Khotan), along with the usual run of pottery, wooden and metal artefacts, some of which date back to 1000 BC.

The most impressive of all Kashgar's tombs is the **Tomb of Abakh Hoja** (阿巴克霍加麻扎, *abākè huòjiā mázhā*; daily 10am–7.30pm; ¥30), 8km northeast of the centre on bus #20 from Renmin Square, or forty minutes by bike through wheat fields and poplar woods. From downtown, head past the Sunday Market – the turning for the mausoleum is signposted in English after a few kilometres. A large, mosque-like building of blue and white tiles with a green dome and tiled minarets, it was constructed in the seventeenth century and is the resting place for a large number of people – the most famous being Abakh Hoja and his grand-daughter Ikparhan, who is known in Chinese as **Xiang Fei**, "Fragrant Concubine". Having led the Uyghurs in revolt against Beijing, she was subsequently captured and married to the Qing emperor Qian Long, and later ordered to commit suicide

Tours around Kashgar

One of the most convincing reasons to visit Kashgar is, a little paradoxically, the opportunity to get out of town. Distances can be huge, public transport non-existent and the weather unrelenting, so it's usually best to go through a **tour operator**. A number of these cluster in the lobby of the *Seman* hotel, which makes this the best place to bargain.

Among the tour programmes on offer – other than those to places nearby, detailed opposite – are **mountaineering expeditions**, trips to **Tibet**, day- to week-long **camel treks** across the Taklamakan desert, and visits to remote villages of minority peoples.

Abdul Wahab Tours ⓣ0998/2204012, ⓦwww.silkroadinn.com. Run by six friendly brothers and marshalled by Abdul himself, a real fountain of local knowledge. They can organize any trip imaginable, big or small, and in a number of languages including French, German and Russian.

CITS ⓣ0998/2984836, ⓔhjt56789@hotmail.com. This Chinese tourist staple has a branch inside the *Qiniwak*. Staff are friendly and speak English.

Elvis Ablimit ⓣ13899136195, ⓔElvisablimit@yahoo.com. A freelance operator providing camel safaris into the Taklamakan; his English is good, and he knows the surrounding terrain well, though this knowledge is surpassed by his expertise with antique carpets.

Kashgar Mountaineering Adventures ⓣ0998/2523660, ⓦwww.ksalpine.com. Inside the Kashgar Gymnasium on Jiefang Nan Lu, the helpful, English-speaking staff here can arrange private transport into Ali in Tibet, as well as a range of adventure activities including climbing and rafting trips. Contact them well in advance if you plan something ambitious, as most activities require some equipment and paperwork preparations.

by the emperor's jealous mother. In commemorating a local heroine and stirring anti-Qing propaganda in the cruelty she suffered, the story serves the convenient dual purpose of pleasing both the Uyghurs and the Han Chinese.

Accessible only by car, the **Moor Pagodas** (莫尔佛塔, *mò'ěr fótǎ*; ¥10) are at the **ancient city of Hanoi** on a rough road about 30km east of the city. The pagodas have been worn down to rough stumps about a dozen metres high, but the remains of the ruined Tang city walls of Hanoi make quite a dramatic scene in what is a virtual desert. To reach this place, you'll need to rent a car from a travel service, costing around ¥350 through the Mountaineering Association (see p.875), or deal directly with a taxi yourself – try for ¥60 return.

One "new" attraction is **Shipton's Arch** (天洞, *tiāndòng*), just over two hours' drive to the west of Kashgar; at a height of around 400m (just topping, say, the Empire State Building), this may be the tallest **natural rock arch** in the world. Though discovered long ago, its remoteness meant that it was only fully opened up to tourism in 2000. Even now you'll have to rent a four wheel drive and driver, which starts at around ¥800 all-in; this can usually be bargained down to around ¥600.

Eating and drinking

In contrast to its accommodation offerings, Kashgar has a slew of excellent **places to eat**. The best place to pick up **Uyghur food** is around Id Kah Square. Street vendors sell pilau, kebabs and cold spicy noodles; *laghman* is available almost everywhere.

Altun Orda This Uyghur place is perhaps the classiest restaurant in town, though there are some simple ¥10–20 dishes hidden away among the more expensive items on the picture menu. The ¥58 "tower kebab" is especially recommended, as is stepping outside to view the ornate barbecuing pit they use in its creation.

Avral If there's even one sweet tooth in your mouth, be sure to head to this inconspicuous café. The owners blew US$1000 on a special Arabic ice cream machine, and the results are rather dreamy: ¥7 will buy you a little bowlful of heaven. The menu is in Uyghur and Chinese only, but all bowls feature two scoops of berry-strewn vanilla, plus one of your choice; the chocolate (understood in English here) is a good fallback.

Javlan From a building whose exterior has been dolled up in faux-Uyghur style, this restaurant serves up Uyghur staples, mainly noodle-based, under a blanket of fake plastic leaves. Try the phenomenal saffron and rose tea.

John's Café Tucked away behind the *Seman* hotel, the original branch of this backpacker-friendly chain doles out Sino-Western food, coffees, juices and beer. A great place to relax over a book or to get travel advice (see p.873).

Mengyol Race up to this new fourth-floor venue overlooking the mosque to feast on Uyghur dumplings, pilaf or meat dishes; a range of teas (including one made with Iranian saffron) and juices are also available. Try to time your visit for sunset, when you'll hear the crying of the muezzin – sit mosque-side if at all possible.

Listings

Airline China Southern, 152 Seman Lu (daily: May–Oct 9am–8pm; Nov–April 10am–7.30pm; ⓣ0998/2985118).

Banks and exchange The main Bank of China, in the northeast corner of Renmin Square (daily: summer 9.30am–1.30pm & 4–7.30pm; winter 10am–2pm & 3.30–7pm), can change foreign currency. You may have to show proof of purchase for cashing travellers' cheques.

Bike rental By far the best, and most reliable, places to rent bikes are from the stall at the front gate of the *Qiniwak* and from the *Seman* hotel; both charge ¥30/day.

Bookshops Xinhua Bookshop is at 32 Jiefang Bei Lu, on the east side of the road and just north of the intersection with Renmin Lu.

Mail The post office is at 40 Renmin Xi Lu, a short walk west of Jiefang Lu (Mon–Sat 9.30am–8pm).

PSB Renmin Dong Lu (Mon–Fri 10.30am–2pm & 4–9.30pm), just opposite the Bank of China.

Telephones Direct-dial long-distance calls can be made from an office opposite the post office on Renmin Xi Lu, at China Telecom (daily 9.30am–8pm), or from the *Qiniwak* and *Seman* hotels. Both charge by the minute.

The Southern Silk Road

Originally, the **Southern Silk Road** split off from the northern route at Kashgar, skirted the southern rim of the **Taklamakan** before crossing to **Charkhlik** on the desert's eastern edge, then rejoined the northern route near Dunhuang in Gansu province (p.840). In modern times this path has fallen into obscurity, with distances huge and punishing, towns dusty and forlorn, and transport connections sparse. Of the two branches, however, this is actually the older and historically more important. The most famous Silk Road travellers used it, including the Chinese Buddhist pilgrims Fa Xian and Xuanzang (see p.864), as well as Marco Polo, and, in the 1930s, the British journalist and adventurer Peter Fleming. The ancient settlements along the way were oases in the desert, kept alive by streams flowing down from the snowy peaks of the Kunlun Shan, which constitute the outer rim of the Tibetan plateau to the south.

Following the remains of this southern route opens up the prospect of travelling overland from Kashgar to Turpan one way, and returning another, thus circumnavigating the entire Taklamakan Desert. The road from Kashgar runs for 1400km to the town of Charkhlik, from where it's still a fair way back to Turpan, or a hellish mountain journey to Qinghai. The ancient city of **Khotan** is the pick of places to get off the bus and explore; it's also linked to Korla via the splendid 522km-long **Tarim Desert Expressway**, one of the longest desert roads in the world.

Kashgar to Khotan

The first 500km of the Southern Silk Road runs southeast from Kashgar to Khotan through a dusty wasteland interspersed with dunes, camels, mountain ranges and sudden patches of greenery marking irrigated settlements.

Yengisar

First up, a mere 70km from Kashgar, is the town of **YENGISAR** (英吉沙, *yīngjí shā*), which has for centuries been supplying the Uyghur people with handcrafted knives. Most of the knives on sale in Xinjiang these days are factory-made, but at this **knife factory** (小刀厂, *xiǎodāochǎng*), a few craftsmen still ply their old skills, inlaying handles with horn or silver alloy. Some of the more decorative examples take nearly a fortnight to forge.

Yarkand

The town of **YARKAND** (莎车, *shāchē*), another 125km southwest, has been a strategically important staging post for at least the last thousand years; now that Kashgar is becoming ever more developed and sanitized, this may be the best place to soak up the character of Muslim Xinjiang and old-time Central Asia. The best thing to do here is simply wander the northeastern backstreets, a warren of muddy lanes lined with willows and crowded by donkey carts, artisans' quarters, bazaars and traditional adobe homes with wooden-framed balconies. You'll find the town's major sights here too, close together on a road running north off Laocheng Lu: the **old fort** is opposite the **Altunluq mosque** (阿勒屯清真寺, *ālètún qīngzhēnsì*) and **Amannisahan tomb** (阿曼尼莎汗纪念陵, *āmànìshāhàn jìniànlíng*; ¥10), flanked by two narrow towers. The mosque is off limits to non-Muslims, but the tomb, built for Amannisahan, the wife of a sixteenth-century khan, is a beautiful white- and blue-tiled affair; Amannisahan was also the most influential contributor to *muqam* music (see box, p.863). The adjacent **cemetery** contains the mausoleums of several of Yarkand's former rulers, including Amannisahan's husband, and is also crowded with more ordinary cylindrical Muslim tombs and ancient trees. Sundays are the best time to visit Yarkand, when a huge rustic **market** along the same lines as the more famous one in Kashgar is held in the main bazaar behind the fort – though this area is pretty good most days.

Practicalities

The town centres on a crossroads, from where Xincheng Lu runs west through the Han-dominated part of town towards Kashgar, while Laocheng Lu runs east into the older, Uyghur quarters. The **bus station**, with frequent departures through the day to Kashgar and Khotan, is south off Xincheng Lu. You can find the **Bank of China**, **post office** and **China Telecom** around the crossroads. A decent **hotel** that accepts foreigners – almost no places here do – is the *Shache Binguan* (莎车宾馆, *shāchē bīnguǎn*; ⓣ0998/8512365; ❹), a ten-minute walk west along Xincheng Lu from the crossroads. The best place to **eat** is the *Meraj Restaurant* (米热吉快餐, *mǐrèjí kuàicān*), on the northeast corner of the crossroads. Extremely popular with local Uyghurs, they serve stuffed nan bread and all kinds of noodle dishes; the delicacy here is pigeon meat.

Karagilik

Sixty kilometres further on is **KARAGILIK** (叶城, *yèchéng*), a kind of giant Uyghur highway service station, with flashing lights, fires, bubbling cauldrons, overhead awnings and great hunks of mutton hanging from meat hooks. **Accommodation** is available just outside the bus station at the basic *Jiaotong* (交通宾馆, *jiāotōng bīnguǎn*; ⓣ0998/7285540; ❸, dorm beds ¥50), but this is extremely unappealing; the only other place in town that accepts foreigners is the *K2 Hotel* (乔戈里峰宾馆, *qiáogēlǐfēng bīnguǎn*; ⓣ0998/7485000; ❸), similar in price but much nicer. Every Wednesday there's a fantastic **market** about 1km out of town toward Khotan. A lot more earthy and colourful than the Kashgar Sunday market, it's well worth your time.

The road divides at Karagilik, with one fork running southwest into **Tibet**; this used to be a prime target for those attempting to sneak to Ali in the back of a truck, but security these days makes that unadvisable – you'll have to arrange a tour in Kashgar (see p.875).

Khotan and around

Predominantly Uyghur, **KHOTAN** (和田, *hétián*) has for centuries enjoyed countrywide fame for its **carpets**, **silk** and **white jade**. A bleak and dusty grid of wide streets, the town is pretty ordinary, but the people are hospitable, and there's ample opportunity to see traditional weaving and the like.

Arrival and information

Khotan's **airport** lies 10km southwest of town; you can reach the centre either by taxi (¥20) or by the airport bus that meets incoming flights. The **bus station** is on the south end of Taibei Xi Lu, north of the city, with six daily services to Korla and Ürümqi via the Taklamakan Desert, and to everywhere else along the Southern Silk Road between Kashgar and Cherchen. Other useful bus routes include Yining and Turpan in the east of Xinjiang. Taxis charge ¥5 to any hotel.

You can buy flight tickets at the airline **office**, 14 Wulumuqi Lu (daily 10am–8.30pm; ⓣ0903/2518999), a few minutes north of the *Hetian Binguan*. South from here, your visa can be extended at the **PSB** (Mon–Fri 10am–2pm & 3.30–7.30pm). All hotels have **travel services** for booking plane and bus tickets and arranging **tours**. Local excursions with a guide, taking in the carpet and silk factories, should set you back ¥50–100, and it's possible to organize lengthier jeep or camel trips around the region, using routes not necessarily covered by public transport. Expect to pay ¥300 per day for a jeep, ¥100 for a camel; camping gear is around ¥50 per person, and a guide will cost ¥100 a day. If your hotel can't help,

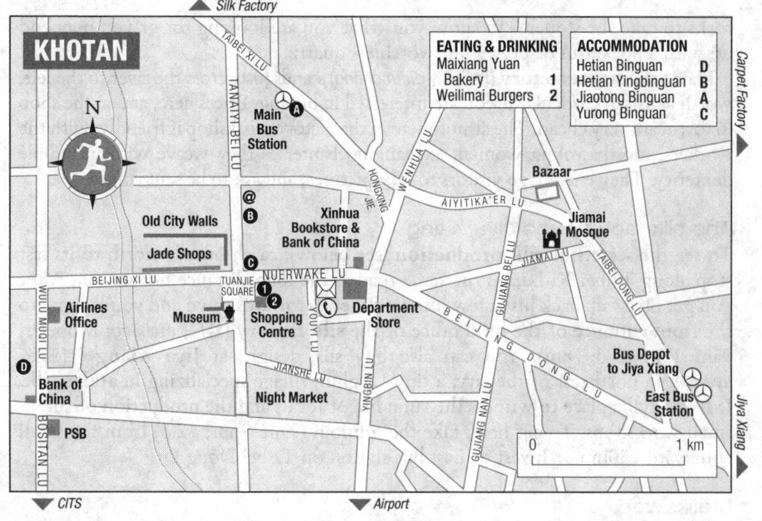

try **CITS** (ⓣ0903/2516090), inconveniently located on the third floor of a building at the end of Bositan Lu.

Accommodation

Right beside the bus-station entrance, the *Jiaotong* (交通宾馆, *jiāotōng bīnguǎn*; ⓣ0903/2032700; ③) is the cleanest of several **hotels** in the station area, though that's not saying much; more central options include the rather gloomy but friendly *Hetian Yingbinguan* (和田迎宾馆, *hétián yíngbīnguǎn*; ⓣ0903/2022824; ④ including breakfast), and the genial, unpretentious *Yurong Binguan* (玉融宾馆, *yùróng bīnguǎn*; ⓣ0903/7829666; ④), more or less on Tuanjie Square. Finally, the *Hetian Binguan* in the southwest of the city on Wulumuqi Nan Lu (和田宾馆, *hétián bīnguǎn*; ⓣ0903/2029999; ⑤ including breakfast) is comfortable and good value, despite the slightly aged furniture.

The Town

Khotan centres on **Tuanjie Square**, from where the city is partitioned by Beijing Lu (running east–west) and Tanaiyi Lu (north–south). The crenellated **old city walls** still dot along the west side of Tanaiyi Bei Lu, east of the river – surrounded by fences in a vain effort to protect them from development. The giant sculpture in the middle of the square shows Chairman Mao shaking hands with a local Uyghur old man, an actual person who went to Beijing to congratulate the Communist party on its victory in the 1950s – the symbol still serves its function, though the hostility of the local Uyghurs towards Han Chinese is no secret.

Khotan's fascinating **bazaar** takes place every Friday and Sunday. Silk, carpets, leather jackets, fruit and spices are all on sale, with innumerable blacksmiths, tinsmiths, goldsmiths and carpenters hard at work among the stalls. The bazaar stretches across the whole of the northeast part of town; the easiest way to reach it is to head east along Aiyitika'er Lu, off Wenhua Lu near the centre. Follow the stalls south toward Jiamai Lu, along which you can see a pretty Jiamai mosque.

About 4km to the east of town, following Beijing Dong Lu, is the **Jade Dragon Kashgar River** (玉龙喀什河, *yùlóng kāshíhé*), which still yields the odd stone for casual searchers. The river flows through a wide, stony plain; it's easy to get down here and forage, but you'll need to find one of the locals – who come with garden forks to rake the stones – to show you what you are looking for or you may end up with a pocketful of pretty but worthless quartz.

The town **carpet factory** (地毯厂, *dìtǎn chǎng*) stands just across the river to the left, worth a visit in particular if you are interested in buying. Prices here, and in the shop in town, are very cheap. The atmosphere in the factory workshop is friendly, with the workers, mostly young women, exchanging banter as they weave with incredible dexterity. They encourage visitors to take pictures, and ask to be sent copies.

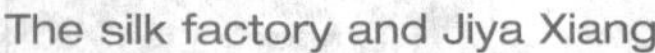

The silk factory and Jiya Xiang

To see the secrets of **silk production** (see below), catch bus #1 north to its last stop along Taibei Xi Lu, on the same road as the long-distance bus station. After you get off, walk back just a few hundred metres towards town and you'll come to the front entrance of the head office of the **silk factory** (丝厂, *sīchǎng*; Mon–Fri 9am–1pm & 3–7pm). You can also buy silk designs at **Jiya Xiang** (吉亚乡, *jíyà xiāng*), northeast of the city, a tiny Uyghur village specializing in **atalas silk**. It is an idyllic place to witness the rural life of locals and the production of silk in small workshops. To get here, take the minibus (9am–9pm; ¥2.5) from the small courtyard 150m northwest of East bus station on Taibei Dong Lu.

Melikawat

Silk Road specialists should visit the ruined city of **Melikawat** (米力克瓦特古城, *mǐlìkèwǎtè gǔchéng*; ¥20, plus ¥5 to take photos), out in the desert 30km to the south of town beside the Jade Dragon Kashgar River. This city, formerly an important Buddhist centre on the Silk Road, was abandoned well over a thousand years ago, and the arrival of Islam in the region did nothing to aid its preservation. The site is a fragmentary collection of crumbling walls set among the dunes and tamarisk bushes, thousands of wind-polished pot shards littering the ground – you might find odd bits of glass or wood poking out of the ruins. To visit, contact a travel service (see p.878) or flag down a taxi and start some hard bargaining; ¥100 is a reasonable price for the return trip.

Eating

Eating in Khotan is pretty straightforward, with Muslim restaurants everywhere you look; perhaps most interesting for visitors is the Uyghur street food on offer just south of Tuanjie Square. The *Maixiang Yuan Bakery* on the northeast corner of

Silky secrets in Khotan

One of Khotan's best assets is the chance to see **silk** being made – not just the showy nonsense laid on for tour groups throughout the land, but the whole process from grub to garment. At the **silk factory** (see above), you'll be able to see the last stages: the initial unpicking of the cocoons, the twisting together of the strands to form a thread (ten strands for each silk thread), the winding of the thread onto reels and finally the weaving and dyeing. The women here have it hard compared to their sisters in the carpet factory: the noise in the workshops is quite loud, and they stand all day long.

To see the nurturing of the **silkworms** themselves – only possible in summer – you'll need to explore some of the nearby country lanes in Jiya Xiang (see above) or in the vicinity of the silk factory. If you are able to explain your purpose to people (a drawing of a silkworm might do the trick), they will take you to see silkworms munching away on rattan trays of fresh, cleaned mulberry leaves in cool, dark sheds. Eventually each worm should spin itself a cocoon of pure silk; each cocoon comprises a single strand about 1km in length. The farmers sell the cocoons to the factory, but hatching and rearing of silkworms is unreliable work, and for most farmers it's a sideline.

Tuanjie Square is a great place if you miss **Western food**, as is *Weilimai Burgers* a few doors south.

From Khotan to Korla

The cities of Khotan and Korla (p.867) – respectively on the Northern and Southern silk routes – can be linked in three different ways. The most painless option is to take the new **cross-desert highway** from Khotan to **Aksu** (阿克苏; *ākèsū*) on the Northern Silk Route, from where you'll at least have the option of continuing on by train; the 440km journey across the desert takes just five or six hours, since there's precious little chance of a traffic jam. There's another such highway several hundred kilometres to the east of Khotan, its southern terminus the town of **Niya**; this is longer at 522km, and will save you a little time if you're heading directly to Korla, Turpan or Ürümqi. Both roads cross the **Taklamakan desert**, and will give you a close-up of why the Uyghurs call this the "Sea of Death". Unfortunately, most buses coming either way make the crossing at night, so you don't get a view of the impressive irrigation grid that provides water for shrubs to protect the road from the ever-shifting desert sands. For a dustier, rougher, more rewarding trip to Korla, you'll want to catch a bus east from Khotan, continuing on the **Southern Silk Road**.

Niya and Cherchen

On the way to **NIYA** (民丰, *mínfēng*), 300km east of Khotan, you'll pass through some of the most vividly empty landscapes you will ever see, a formless expanse of sky and desert merging at a vague, dusty yellow horizon. The town has a pleasant frontier atmosphere, and you can stay at the simple *Xiyu Binguan* (西域宾馆, *xīyù bīnguǎn*; ❷, dorm beds ¥40), 50m north of Niya's bus station. Niya comes alive every evening, when long-distance buses converge and the main street becomes one long, chaotic strip of kebab, bread and noodle vendors.

The next settlement of any size is **CHERCHEN** (且末, *qiěmò*), another 300km along and another small, surprisingly modern town famed for the frequency of its sandstorms (especially in April). There are **ruins** about 10km to the northwest at **Qiemo Gucheng** (且末古城, *qiěmò gǔchéng*), dated to at least 2000 years old. A taxi here and back shouldn't cost more than ¥40, though the entrance fee, depending upon how well your driver knows the site staff, will range from ¥15 to ¥300.

Charkhlik

Next stop is **CHARKHLIK** (若羌, *ruòqiāng*), a further 360km from Cherchen – buses don't ply this route every day. A small, busy place, Charkhlik is most notable for being the jumping-off point for treks by camel or jeep out to two little-known ruined cities of Silk Road vintage. **Accommodation** is available at the primitive *Jiaotong Binguan* (交通宾馆; *jiāotōng bīnguǎn*; ❸, dorm beds ¥30) just north of the bus station.

The first ruined city, **Miran** (米兰古城, *mǐlán gǔchéng*; ¥160) – subject of Christa Paula's book *Voyage to Miran* – is relatively accessible, approximately 75km northeast of Charkhlik; a far more ambitious trip would be to **Loulan** (楼兰古城, *loúlán gǔchéng*), 250km from town on the western edge of Lop Nor. Loulan's very existence had been completely forgotten until the Swedish explorer **Sven Anders Hedin** rediscovered the site, which had been buried in sand, in the early twentieth century; it wasn't until the 1980s that the first Chinese archeological surveys were undertaken, during which distinctively un-Chinese mummified remains, including the "**Loulan Beauty**", were found (see p.855). Entrance fees vary greatly, so contact a tour operator before heading this way; note, too, that local authorities seem intent on making a trip here a rather touristy experience.

From Charkhlik, it's one final long push across the desert to **Korla** (p.867). Some of the few travellers who make it this far even choose to head off across the mountains to **Golmud** (p.832) in **Qinghai province**, a rough trip taking two or three days.

The Karakoram Highway

For centuries the **Khunjerab Pass**, some 400km south of Kashgar, was the key Silk Road crossing point between the Chinese world and the Indian subcontinent – and thence to the whole of the Western world. Today the 4700m pass still marks the frontier between China and **Pakistan**, but, while crossing the mountains used to be a highly perilous journey undertaken on horse, camel or foot, modern engineering has blasted a highway right through the pass, opening the route to a seasonal stream of trucks and buses. The entire 1300km route from Kashgar over the mountains to Rawalpindi in northern Pakistan is known as the **Karakoram Highway** (中巴公路, *zhōngbā gōnglù*). The trip is still not without its perils, but it's hard to think of a more exciting route into or out of China. If the highway is closed for any reason, note that you can also **fly** direct from Ürümqi to Islamabad.

En route from Kashgar, travellers have to spend a night in **Tashkurgan** on the Chinese side, before crossing over the pass to the Pakistani town of **Sust**. There is also the option of camping out for a night or two by the wintry but beautiful **Lake Karakul**, in the lee of glaciers. The road over the pass is open from the beginning of May until the end of October each year, though it can close without notice when the weather is bad, for days at a time, even in summer. The journey from Kashgar to Rawalpindi/Islamabad, or vice versa, takes a minimum of four days if there are no hold-ups. Most travellers need a **visa to enter Pakistan**; at the time of writing, you'll need to arrange this in your home country – neither Beijing nor Ürümqi supplies the service.

Lake Karakul

Southwest of Kashgar, the road soon leaves the valley, with its mud-brick buildings and irrigated wheat and rice plantations, behind. Climbing through river gorges strewn with giant boulders, it creeps into a land of treeless, bare dunes of sand and gravel, interspersed with pastures scattered with grazing yaks and camels. The sudden appearance of **Lake Karakul** (喀拉湖, *kālā hú*; ¥50) by the roadside, some 200km out of Kashgar, is dramatic. Right under the feet of the Pamir Mountains and the magnificent 7546m Mount Muztagata, whose vast snowy flanks have been split open by colossal glaciers, the waters of the lake are luminous blue.

Practicalities

Transport to the lake is simple. From the Kashgar international bus station there are two daily **buses** (¥50; May–Oct), leaving at 10am and 4pm. From Tashkurgan you can take the Kashgar bus and get off at the lake. Leaving the lake requires slightly more ingenuity – for either direction you will need to flag down the passing buses or taxis, which may involve standing assertively in the middle of the road; taxis back to Kashgar cost a minimum of ¥100 per person.

The opportunities for **hiking** over the surrounding green pasture remain extensive, though authorities have tightened controls over routes and slapped a ¥280 fee on hikers. Those willing to persist should take a tent and warm clothing; at 3800m, the weather can be extremely cold even in summer, with snow showers normal well into June. It's possible to walk round the lake in a day, in which case you will almost certainly encounter some friendly **Kyrgyz yurt dwellers** on the way. Otherwise, if you are without your own tent, you can stay at a rather dull and not particularly enticing **tour-group yurt site** just off the road, with its own decent restaurant and friendly local attendants. This costs about ¥90 per head (based on four people in a yurt), plus ¥70 per person per day for all meals. There are very rudimentary washing and toilet facilities, and fresh drinking water originates from the lake, hence swimming is forbidden.

Tashkurgan

The last town before the border, **TASHKURGAN** (塔什库尔干, *tăshí kù'ĕrgān*) lies 280km southeast of Kashgar, and about 220km north of the Pakistani town of **Sust** (苏斯特, *sūsī tè*). Its primary importance for travellers is as a staging post between the two towns, and all travellers passing through, in either direction, must stay the night here. It's a tiny place, comprising a couple of tree-lined streets, with the bus station and several budget hotels in the northwestern part of town.

The native population is mainly **Tajik**, but there are also groups of melancholy Han Chinese, thousands of miles from home, as well as intrepid Pakistanis setting up shop outside their country – plus a minor entertainment industry involving sex and alcohol for Pakistani tourists. Few visitors bother to stop longer than necessary, but you could pleasantly rest up here for 24 hours or so. Worth a look, especially at sunset, is the six-hundred-year-old, crumbling, mud-brick **Stone City** (石头城; *shítou chéng*; ¥10, negotiable). If you clamber to the top, the scenes of snowy mountains running parallel on both flanks, and woods and wetland dotted around, are more than picturesque. To reach it, walk east from the bus station right to the end of town passing the *Pamir* hotel, then strike off a few hundred metres to the left.

Arrival and information

Tashkurgan is small enough to be navigated on foot, and the **bus station** is right in the middle of things. The **PSB office** is diagonally opposite the post office just to the southeast, while an Agricultural Bank of China (Mon–Fri 10.30am–2pm & 4–7pm) lies 300m to the south of the station. Cash (and sometimes travellers' cheques) can be changed here at official exchange rates. If arriving from Pakistan, you can easily change your rupees with the locally resident Pakistanis if the banks are closed. If you plan to get off at Lake Karakul (see opposite) en route to Kashgar, you may be asked to pay the full Kashgar fare anyway. The alternative to catching buses is to **hitch a ride** on a truck; these often cruise around town in the evening looking for prospective customers to Kashgar (or Karakul) for the day after. You'll pay, but it will be cheaper than travelling by bus.

Accommodation and eating

At the **bus station**, the *Jiaotong Hotel* (交通宾馆, *jiāotōng bīnguăn*; April–Nov; ⓣ0998/3421192; ❹, dorm beds in triples ¥20) is a simple **place to stay**; 24-hour hot water is available in the double rooms. Alternatively, you can try the primitive *Ice Mountain* (冰山旅店, *bīngshān lǚdiàn*; ❸, dorm beds ¥15). As you exit the bus station, turn right and walk 100m to the east along Hongqilapu Lu; it's across the road. The *Pamir* at the east end of the same road is much more upmarket (帕米尔宾馆, *pàmĭ'ĕr bīnguăn*; April–Oct; ⓣ0998/3421085; ❹), with high ceilings and eclectic decor. Hot water is available all day, though you may need to double-check with the friendly staff. The plentiful **beer** in Tashkurgan often comes as a relief to travellers arriving from Pakistan. For **food**, your best bet is to try one of the many Chinese restaurants.

On to Pakistan

Whichever direction you're travelling in, bring **warm clothing** and plenty of **snacks and water** on your Karakoram journey. Travellers heading to Pakistan do not need to buy onward bus tickets – the ticket from Kashgar covers the whole route right through to Sust – but Western tourists should be aware that they'll need to have arranged a Pakistani **visa** beforehand in their home country (though it's worth checking the current state of play at their Beijing embassy; Ⓦwww.pakembassy.cn). Stamp in hand, the **entry and exit formalities** are dealt with a few hundred metres south from the bank, and are straightforward to the point of being lax. Note that **cyclists** are not allowed to ride their bikes through the pass, but have to bus it between Tashkurgan and Sust. As for **Sust**, there's plenty of accommodation to go around, as well as places in which to change yuan for rupees.

The Khunjerab Pass

Khunjerab means "River of Blood" in the local Tadjik language – which may refer to the rusty colour of local rivers, or to the long traditions of banditry in these areas. The trip across the border at the **Khunjerab Pass** (红其拉浦口岸, *hóngqí lāpŭ kŏu'àn*) is not a totally risk-free affair – people are killed almost every year by falling rocks on the highway and you should be aware that if your bus departs in rainy weather, you can almost certainly expect mud slides.

From Tashkurgan, the road climbs into a vast, bright plain, grazed by yaks and camels, with the mountains, clad in snow mantles hundreds of metres thick, pressing in all around. Emerging onto the **top of the pass**, you're greeted by a clear, silent, windswept space of frozen streams, protruding glaciers and glimpses of green pasture under the sunshine. The only creature that lives here is the chubby ginger Himalayan marmot; a kind of large squirrel or woodchuck, easily spotted from the bus. At these heights (the pass lies at some 4800m) a lot of travellers experience some form of **altitude sickness**, though most people will feel little more than faintly feverish or nauseous. The journey time between Tashkurgan and the small town of **Sust**, where Pakistani customs and immigration take place, takes about seven hours. Travellers in both directions have to spend a night here, and accommodation is plentiful. From Sust there are direct daily buses to Gilgit, from where frequent buses cover the sixteen-hour route to **Rawalpindi** and **Islamabad**.

Travel details

Trains

Times given are for the fastest possible connections; there are usually slower services available at a slightly cheaper price.

Dunhuang to: Lanzhou (3 daily; 15hr); Ürümqi (daily; 15hr); Xi'an (daily; 23hr).

Golmud to: Lhasa (5 daily; 13hr 30min); Xining (10 daily; 9hr).

Guyuan to: Lanzhou (daily; 10hr); Yinchuan (5 daily; 6hr 20min); Zhongwei (7 daily; 3hr 20min).

Jiayuguan to: Daheyan (14 daily; 10hr 20min); Lanzhou (regular; 7hr); Tianshui (13 daily; 12hr); Ürümqi (14 daily; 12hr); Wuwei (regular; 4hr 30min); Zhangye (regular; 2hr).

Kashgar to: Korla (2 daily; 13hr 20min); Kuqa (2 daily; 8hr 40min); Ürümqi (2 daily; 24hr 30min).

Korla to: Daheyan (6 daily; 9hr); Kashgar (2 daily; 13hr 20min); Kuqa (4 daily; 4hr 20min); Ürümqi (4 daily; 11hr).

Lanzhou to: Beijing (6 daily; 19hr); Chengdu (4 daily; 18hr); Daheyan (13 daily; 18hr 30min); Hohhot (3 daily; 17hr); Guangzhou (2 daily; 29hr); Guyuan (daily; 10hr); Jiayuguan (regular; 7hr); Lhasa (6 daily; 27hr); Shanghai (5 daily; 22hr); Tianshui (regular; 3hr 45min); Ürümqi (13 daily; 20hr); Wuwei (regular; 2hr 30min); Xi'an (regular; 7hr 30min); Xining (regular; 2hr); Yinchuan (4 daily; 8hr); Zhangye (regular; 5hr); Zhongwei (5 daily; 5hr 30min).

Tianshui to: Jiayuguan (13 daily; 12hr); Lanzhou (regular; 3hr 45min); Ürümqi (11 daily; 24hr); Wuwei (14 daily; 7hr); Zhangye (14 daily; 9hr 30min).

Turpan (aka **Daheyan**) to: Jiayuguan (14 daily; 10hr 20min); Korla (6 daily; 9hr); Lanzhou (13 daily; 18hr 30min); Ürümqi (regular; 2hr).

Ürümqi to: Almaty (Kazakhstan; weekly; 33hr); Astana (Kazakhstan; weekly; 40hr); Beijing (daily; 42hr); Chengdu (daily; 49hr); Daheyan (regular; 2hr); Jiayuguan (14 daily; 12hr); Kashgar (2 daily; 24hr 30min); Korla (4 daily; 11hr); Lanzhou (13 daily; 20hr); Shanghai (daily; 45hr); Tianshui (11 daily; 24hr); Xi'an (10 daily; 29hr).
Wuwei to: Daheyan (16 daily; 15hr); Jiayuguan (regular; 4hr 30min); Lanzhou (regular; 2hr 30min); Zhangye (regular; 2hr).
Xining to: Beijing (2 daily; 21hr); Golmud (10 daily; 9hr); Lanzhou (regular; 2hr); Lhasa (8 daily; 23hr); Shanghai (2 daily; 25hr); Xi'an (10 daily; 10hr).
Zhangye to: Daheyan (16 daily; 13hr); Jiayuguan (regular; 2hr); Lanzhou (regular; 5hr); Wuwei (regular; 2hr).

Buses

Dunhuang to: Golmud (10hr); Jiayuguan (5hr); Lanzhou (17hr); Wuwei (15hr); Zhangye (13hr).
Golmud to: Dunhuang (10hr); Xining (16hr).
Guyuan to: Lanzhou (7hr); Pingliang (2hr); Sanying (40min); Tianshui (6hr); Xi'an (7hr); Yinchuan (4hr 30min).
Jiayuguan to: Dunhuang (5hr); Zhangye (5hr).
Kashgar to: Khotan (11hr); Korla (30hr); Kuqa (20hr); Lake Karakul (6hr); Sust (36hr); Tashkurgan (8hr); Yarkand (2hr 30min); Yecheng (4hr).
Khotan to: Kashgar (11hr); Korla (17hr); Niya (5hr); Cherchen (12hr); Ürümqi (22hr); Yarkand (5hr).
Korla to: Kashgar (30hr); Khotan (17hr); Kuqa (12hr); Turpan (10hr); Ürümqi (5hr).
Kuqa to: Aksu (12hr); Korla (10hr); Turpan (14hr); Ürümqi (12hr); Yining (24hr).
Lanzhou to: Guyuan (7hr); Hezuo (5hr); Linxia (2hr); Tianshui (5hr); Wuwei (5hr); Xiahe (5hr); Xining (3hr); Zhangye (10hr).
Linxia to: Lanzhou (3hr); Tianshui (9hr); Wuwei (9hr); Xiahe (5hr); Xining (11hr).
Pingliang to: Guyuan (2hr); Lanzhou (5hr); Xi'an (5hr).
Tianshui to: Guyuan (daily; 10hr); Lanzhou (8hr); Linxia (9hr); Pingliang (6hr); Wushan (5hr); Xi'an (9hr).
Turpan to: Hami (6hr 30min); Korla (10hr); Kuqa (12hr); Ürümqi (3hr).
Ürümqi to: Almaty (Kazakhstan; 36hr); Kashgar (35hr); Khotan (22hr); Korla (10hr); Kuqa (15hr); Turpan (3hr); Yining (15hr).
Wuwei to: Dunhuang (14hr 30min); Lanzhou (4hr); Minqin (1hr 30min); Zhangye (4hr).
Xiahe to: Hezuo (2hr); Lanzhou (5hr); Linxia (4hr); Tongren (4hr).
Xining to: Golmud (16hr); Lanzhou (5hr); Linxia (11hr); Maduo (24hr); Tongren (8hr); Zhangye (24hr).
Yecheng to: Kashgar (4hr); Khotan (2hr 30min); Ürümqi (24hr).
Yining to: Almaty (Kazakhstan; 12hr); Ürümqi (13hr).
Zhangye to: Dunhuang (8hr); Jiayuguan (5hr); Lanzhou (10hr); Wuwei (6hr).

Flights

Besides the domestic services listed below, there are international flights linking Ürümqi with Almaty, Astana, Bishkek, Dushanbe, Irkutsk, Islamabad, Moscow, Novosibirsk, Osh, Seoul and Tehran.
Dunhuang to: Beijing (daily; 3hr); Lanzhou (1–2 daily; 1hr 30min); Ürümqi (1–2 daily; 1hr 30min); Xi'an (2–3 daily; 2hr 30min).
Jiayuguan to: Lanzhou (daily; 1hr 10min); Xian (daily; 2hr).
Kashgar to: Ürümqi (7 daily; 1hr 30min).
Khotan to: Ürümqi (4–5 daily; 1hr 45min).
Korla to: Ürümqi (9 daily; 1hr).
Kuqa to: Ürümqi (2 daily; 1hr 40min).
Lanzhou to: Beijing (9 daily; 2hr); Chengdu (3 daily; 1hr); Chongqing (4 weekly; 1hr 40min); Dunhuang (1–2 daily; 1hr 30min); Guangzhou (4 daily; 3hr); Jiayuguan (daily; 1hr 20min); Kunming (1–2 daily; 2hr); Shanghai (5 daily; 2hr 30min); Ürümqi (5–7 daily; 2hr 30min); Xi'an (5 daily; 1hr); Yinchuan (daily; 50min).
Ürümqi to: Beijing (regular; 3hr 30min); Chengdu (9 daily; 3hr 20min); Chongqing (8 daily; 3hr 30min); Dunhuang (1–2 daily; 1hr 30min); Guangzhou (3 daily; 4hr 40min); Kashgar (7 daily; 1hr 20min); Khotan (4–5 daily; 1hr 45min); Korla (9 daily; 1hr); Lanzhou (5–7 daily; 2hr 30min); Shanghai (7 daily; 4hr); Xi'an (5 daily; 2hr 45min); Xining (3 daily; 2hr 20min); Yinchuan (3 daily; 3hr); Yining (8 daily; 2hr).
Xining to: Beijing (6 daily; 2hr 10min); Chengdu (2 daily; 1hr 20min); Guangzhou (2 daily; 3hr); Shanghai (3 daily; 2hr 40min); Ürümqi (3 daily; 2hr 20min); Xi'an (3 daily; 3hr).
Yining to: Ürümqi (8 daily; 2hr).

CHAPTER 14

Highlights

* **The Jokhang, Lhasa** Shrouded in juniper smoke and surrounded by prostrating pilgrims, it's hard not to be affected by this, one of the world's most venerated sites. See p.909

* **Samye** Remote walled town encapsulating Tibet's first Buddhist monastery. See p.920

* **Namtso Lake** A dream image of Tibet, lies bright as a jewel beneath muscular peaks. See p.926

* **The Friendship Highway** This undulating road connecting Lhasa and Nepal cuts through some of the region's best and certainly most accessible sights. See p.935

* **Mount Everest Base Camp** Breathe deep and gaze up at the jagged, snow-blown peak of the world's highest mountain. See p.937

* **Mount Kailash** The world's holiest mountain, its very remoteness an intrinsic part of its appeal. See p.940

▲ A woman turns prayer wheels at Jokhang temple, Lhasa

14

Tibet

Tibet (Bod to Tibetans, Xizang to the Chinese; 西藏, *xīzàng*), the "Roof of the World", has exerted a magnetic pull over travellers for centuries. The scenery is awe-inspiring, the religious devotion overwhelming, and the Tibetan people welcoming and wonderful. Scratch below the surface, however, and it is all too apparent that Tibet's past has been tragic, its present painful and the future bleak. Tibet today is a sad, subjugated colony of China. While foreign visitors are perhaps more worldly than to expect a romantic Shangri-la, there is no doubt that many are shocked by the heavy military presence and authoritarian restrictions, both reinforced following protests in 2007–08. The growing civilian Chinese presence, and construction of apartments and factories alongside traditional Tibetan rural homes and monasteries, are further causes of disquiet, but all this doesn't mean you should stay away. Many people, the Dalai Lama included, believe travellers should visit Tibet to learn all they can of the country and its people.

In reaching Tibet, you'll have entered one of the most isolated parts of the world. The massive **Tibetan plateau**, at an average height of 4500m above sea level, is guarded on all sides by towering **mountain ranges**: the Himalayas separate Tibet from India, Nepal and Bhutan to the south, the Karakoram from Pakistan to the west, and the Kunlun from Xinjiang to the north. To the east, dividing Tibet from Sichuan and Yunnan, an extensive series of subsidiary ranges covers almost a thousand kilometres. The plateau is also birthplace to some of the greatest **rivers** of Asia, with the Yangzi, Mekong, Yellow and Salween rising in the east, and the

Travel restrictions in Tibet

Following riots across the Tibetan region in 2008, foreigners have not been able to travel overland into Tibet, nor to travel independently after arrival. All visitors must be booked on **fixed-itinerary guided tours** and must stick to the itinerary – you are not allowed to stay on after the tour ends. The situation, as always, is flexible: travellers have occasionally made it through to Tibet on their own (usually in winter, when the security forces let their guard down a bit), while you're unlikely to be allowed into Tibet at all in March, always a time of unrest. How long these restrictions will last are anyone's guess; contact one of the more established agencies (see p.900) to arrange tours and to get the latest on the situation. Despite this, **basic public transport information** is included in some of the accounts below, in the hopes that independent travel may one day again be possible. However, all foreigners would be **advised against** attempting these routes without first establishing whether they are currently allowed to do so.

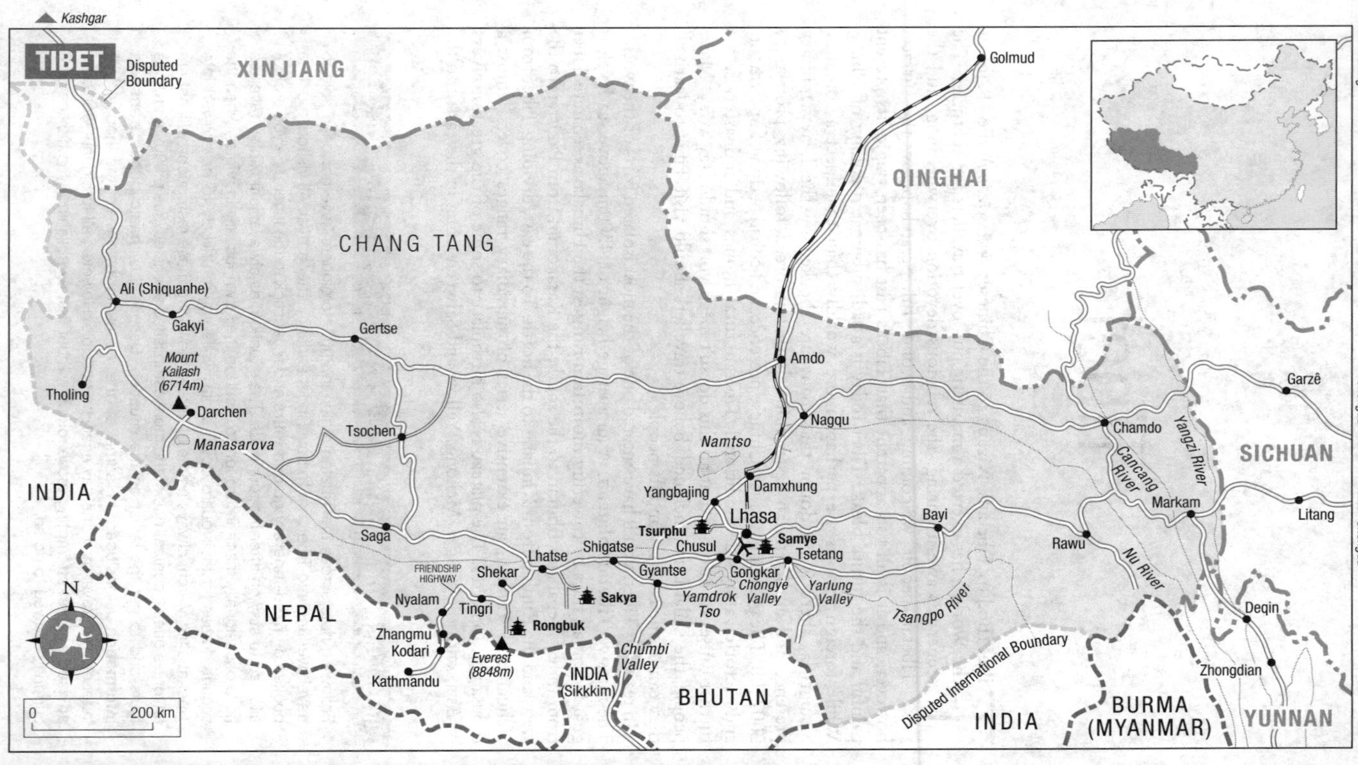
TIBET
Kashgar
Disputed Boundary
XINJIANG
QINGHAI
CHANG TANG
Golmud
Xining
Ali (Shiquanhe)
Gakyi
Gertse
Amdo
Mount Kailash (6714m)
Tholing
Darchen
Manasarova
Tsochen
Nagqu
Namtso
Damxhung
Yangbajing
Lhasa
Tsurphu
Samye
Chusul
Tsetang
Gongkar
Chongye Valley
Yarlung Valley
Shigatse
Gyantse
Lhatse
Saga
Sakya
Yamdrok Tso
FRIENDSHIP HIGHWAY
Shekar
Tingri
Nyalam
Rongbuk
Zhangmu
Kodari
Everest (8848m)
Kathmandu
Chumbi Valley
INDIA (Sikkkim)
BHUTAN
INDIA
NEPAL
Bayi
Rawu
Tsangpo River
Nu River
Disputed International Boundary
Chamdo
Cancang River
Yangzi River
Markam
Garzê
Chengdu
SICHUAN
Litang
Deqin
Zhongdian
YUNNAN
BURMA (MYANMAR)
N
0 200 km

Indus, Brahmaputra, Sutlej and some feeder rivers of the Ganges in the west, near Mount Kailash.

Tibet's isolation has long stirred the imagination of the West, yet until a British expedition under the command of Colonel Francis Younghusband invaded in 1904, only a trickle of bold eccentrics, adventurers and Jesuit missionaries had succeeded in getting close to Lhasa, and then only at serious risk to their lives – it was Tibetan policy to repel all influence from the outside world. So great was the uncertainty about the geographical nature of the country even 150 years ago, that the British in India despatched carefully trained spies, known as pundits, to walk the length and breadth of the country, counting their footsteps with rosaries and mapping as they went. When Younghusband's expeditionary force finally reached Lhasa, they were, perhaps inevitably, disappointed. One journalist accompanying them wrote:

> If one approached within a league of Lhasa, saw the glittering domes of the Potala and turned back without entering the precincts one might still imagine an enchanted city. It was in fact an unsanitary slum. In the pitted streets pools of rainwater and piles of refuse were everywhere: the houses were mean and filthy, the stench pervasive. Pigs and ravens competed for nameless delicacies in open sewers.

Since the Chinese **invasion** in 1950 (China prefers the term "liberation", to which you'll see endless Communist-erected monuments), Tibet has become increasingly accessible, with approaches eased by plane links, paved roads and the controversial Qinghai–Lhasa railway. Each new route has accelerated heavy, government-sponsored migration into the region, and although it is impossible to know how many Chinese now live here – like so much else, population data is strongly disputed – it is likely they outnumber ethnic Tibetans. The situation is most marked in the cities, where the greatest opportunities exist: not only are the numbers of Han and other Chinese growing all the time, but they are also increasingly economically dominant – a situation further exacerbated by the rail line.

Today's **Tibetan Autonomous Region** (TAR), though covering a massive 1.2 million square kilometres, is but a shadow of the former Tibetan lands. The old area, sometimes referred to as Greater Tibet, was carved up by the Chinese following their invasion, when the Amdo and Kham regions were absorbed into Qinghai, Sichuan, Gansu and Yunnan provinces. The TAR consists only of the West and Central (U-Tsang) regions of Greater Tibet and divides into four geographical areas. The northern and largest portion is the almost uninhabited **Chang Tang**, a rocky desert at an average altitude of 4000m, where winter temperatures can fall to minus 44°C. South of this is the **mountainous grazing area**, land that cannot support settled agriculture, inhabited by the wide-ranging nomadic people with their herds of yaks, sheep and goats. **Eastern Tibet**, occupying around a quarter of the TAR, is heavily forested. The relatively temperate **southern valleys**, sandwiched between the nomad areas and the Himalayas along the southern border, are the most hospitable for human habitation. As such, this is the most populated area and where visitors spend the majority of their time, particularly in the extensive valley system of the Tsangpo River (Brahmaputra) and its tributaries.

Lhasa, **Shigatse** and **Gyantse** offer the most accessible **monasteries** and **temples** – the Jokhang, Tashilunpo and the Kumbum, respectively – and are also tourist-friendly cities with the biggest range of facilities in the region. The **Potala Palace** in Lhasa remains an enduring image of Tibet in the Western mind and should on no account be missed, plus there are plenty of smaller sights in the city to keep anyone busy for several days. Farther afield, the **Yarlung** and **Chongye**

valleys to the southeast boast temples and ancient monuments, and the ancient walled monastery of **Samye** is easily combined with these. The route between Zhangmu on the Nepalese border and Lhasa is well established, although by no means overcrowded, and trips can be made to the huge Mongolian-style monastery at **Sakya** and to **Everest Base Camp**.

Whatever your destination, any trip to Tibet faces obstacles. As part of their Beijing Olympic bid, the Chinese government promised increased freedom for

Tibetan Buddhism

There is little ceremony attached to **visiting Buddhist temples**, which are generally welcoming places. Most temples are open in the mornings (9am–noon), when pilgrims do the rounds, and usually again after lunch (around 2pm or 3pm, until 5pm). Smaller places may well be locked, but ask for the caretaker and the chances are you'll be let in. There is no need to remove your shoes, but when walking inside the chapels or around the complex or building, you should proceed **clockwise**, and you shouldn't eat, drink or smoke inside. It is polite to ask before taking photographs, which isn't always allowed, and if it is, you may be charged for the privilege. The Chinese authorities take the **entrance fees** collected from tourists, so if you want to give to the institution itself, leave an offering on an altar or pay the photography charge.

The range of **offerings** devout Tibetans make to their gods is enormous. It includes juniper smoke sent skyward in incense burners, prayer flags printed with prayers erected on rooftops and mountains, tiny papers printed with religious images (*lungda*) and cast to the wind on bridges and passes, white scarves (*katag*) presented to statues and lamas, butter to keep lamps burning on altars, repetitious mantras invoking the gods and the spinning of prayer wheels that have printed prayers rolled up inside. The idea of each is to gain merit in this life and hence affect karma. If you want to take part, watch what other people do and copy them; nobody is at all precious about religion in Tibet. Giving **alms to beggars** is another way of gaining merit, and most large Tibetan temples have a horde of beggars who survive on charity from pilgrims. Whether or not you give money is up to you, but if you do it's wise to give a few small denomination notes or so, the same amount as Tibetans.

Tibetan Buddhism is divided into several schools that have different philosophical emphases rather than fundamental differences. The **Nyingma**, the Old Order, traces its origins back to Guru Rinpoche, Padmasambhava, who brought Buddhism to Tibet. The **Kagyupa**, **Sakya** and **Kadampa** all developed during the eleventh-century revival of Buddhism, while the now-dominant **Gelugpa** (Virtuous School) was founded by Tsongkhapa (1357–1419) and numbers the Dalai Lama and Panchen Lama among its adherents. Virtually all monasteries and temples are aligned to one or other of the schools, but, apart from an abundance of statues of revered lamas of that particular school, you'll spot little difference between the temples. Tibetan people are pretty eclectic and will worship in temples that they feel are particularly sacred and seek blessings from lamas they feel are endowed with special powers, regardless of the school they belong to.

Gods and goddesses

Tibetan Buddhism has an overwhelming number of **gods and goddesses**, and each deity in turn has different manifestations or forms. For example, there are 21 forms of the favourite goddess Tara, and even the most straightforward image has both a Sanskrit and Tibetan name. Below are some of the most common you will encounter:

Amitayus (Tsepame) and **Vijaya** (Namgyelma), often placed with White Tara to form the Three Gods of Longevity.

Tibetans and for foreigners visiting the region, but a confluence of events – the unfurling of a Tibetan flag at Everest Base Camp by some American students in 2007, mass protests and rioting by Tibetans in spring 2008 – ended those dreams. Extremely **strict travel regulations** are now in effect now (see p.887). Travel to the region is likely to be expensive: the restrictions both limit movement and push up the amount foreign tourists have to spend, creating economic pressure for them to stay in place. **Tibetan organizations** abroad ask that visitors try, wherever

Avalokiteshvara (Chenresi in Tibetan, Guanyin in Chinese temples), patron god of Tibet, with many forms, most noticeably with eleven faces and a thousand arms.

Maitreya (Jampa), the Buddha of the Future.

Manjusri (Jampelyang), the God of Wisdom.

Padmasambhava, with eight manifestations, most apparent as Guru Rinpoche. You may see him with his consorts, Yeshe Tsogyel and Mandarava.

Sakyamuni, Buddha of the Present.

Tara (Dolma), Goddess of Compassion. Green Tara is associated with protection and White Tara with long life.

Festivals

Festival dates are calculated using the Tibetan lunar calendar and thus correspond to different dates on the Western calendar each year. There is a list of festival dates in the Western calendar at ⓦwww.kalachakranet.org/ta_tibetan_calendar.html.

February/March

Driving out of evil spirits. Twenty-ninth day of the twelfth lunar month, the last day of the year.

Losar, Tibetan New Year. First day of the first lunar month.

Monlam, Great Prayer Festival, Lhasa. Eighth day of the first lunar month.

Butter Lamp Festival, on the final day of Monlam. Fifteenth day of the first lunar month.

May/June

Birth of Buddha. Seventh day of the fourth lunar month.

Saga Dawa (Buddha's Enlightenment). Fifteenth day of the fourth lunar month.

Gyantse Horse Festival. Fifteenth day of the fourth lunar month.

July

Tashilunpo Festival, Shigatse. Fifteenth day of the fifth lunar month.

July/August

Buddha's First Sermon. Fourth day of the sixth lunar month.

Drepung Festival. Thirtieth day of the sixth lunar month.

August/September

Shotun (Yoghurt Festival), Lhasa. First to the seventh day of the seventh lunar month.

Bathing Festival, Lhasa. Twenty-seventh day of the seventh lunar month.

September

Damxhung Horse Festival. Thirtieth day of the seventh lunar month.

September/October

Harvest Festival. First to the seventh day of the eighth lunar month.

November

Lhabab (Buddha's descent from heaven). Twenty-second day of the ninth lunar month.

November/December

Palden Lhamo Festival, Lhasa. Fifteenth day of the tenth lunar month.

possible, to buy from Tibetans and to hire Tibetan guides. At all times, you should avoid putting Tibetans – and yourself – at risk by bringing up **politically sensitive issues**. You can go home, Tibetans have to live here. Emails are another area where you should be careful – the Chinese authorities monitor emails more strictly here than in the rest of the Republic – so, again, avoid sensitive topics and mentioning people by name. Sensitive websites, including any suggesting support for Tibetan independence or the Dalai Lama, are of course blocked in China.

However, it's important to remember that there are two sides to every story. The pre-Chinese Tibetan administration was a xenophobic religious dictatorship, feudal in nature, that stifled economic progress and tolerated slavery. The people who had the most to lose in Tibet when the Chinese arrived, the monied and the ruling classes, were the same people that fled to India and never returned. What they left behind was a working class so uneducated the people didn't even know they had been existing in a state of serfdom.

Economic development brought by the Chinese, as well as things like running water, electricity and health care, mean Tibetan people have a chance to make a better life for themselves and ironically, strengthen their culture. Meanwhile, the Han and other ethnic Chinese groups migrating into Tibet are not demons. Most are people trying to make a life for themselves and their families, and they may have little knowledge or understanding of the wider political implications of their presence – as with Taiwan and Xinjiang, all Chinese are taught almost from birth that Tibet is an "inalienable part of China", and to suggest otherwise is heresy.

Some history

According to legend, the **earliest Tibetans** came from the union of the ogress, Sinmo, and a monkey, reincarnation of the god Chenresi, on the mountain of Gangpo Ri near Tsetang. Ethnographers, however, think it likely the Tibetans are descended from the nomadic Qiang, who roamed eastern Central Asia, to the northwest of China, several thousand years ago. The first Tibetan king, Nyatri Tsenpo, believed to have come to earth via a magical "sky-cord", was the first of a long lineage of 27 kings who ruled in a pre-Buddhist era when the indigenous, shamanistic **Bon religion** held sway throughout the land. Each of the **early kings** held power over a small area, the geographical isolation of Tibet making outside contact difficult. Nevertheless, it is apparent that as early as the seventh century there was considerable cultural exchange between Tibet and its neighbours. Pens, ink, silks, jewels and probably tea reached Tibet from China in the seventh century, and for many centuries Tibet looked to India for religious teaching.

It was in the time of **King Songtsen Gampo**, the 33rd ruler in the dynasty, born in 617 AD, that expansionism began. Songtsen Gampo's twenty-year rule saw the unification of the country and the aggressive spread of his empire from northern India to China. To placate their assertive neighbour, China and Nepal each offered Songtsen Gampo a wife: in 632, he married Princess Bhrikuti (also known as Tritsun) of Nepal, and in 641 Princess Wencheng arrived from the Tang court, sent by her father, Emperor Taizong. They both brought their **Buddhist faith** and magnificent statues of the Buddha, which are now the centrepieces of Ramoche temple and the Jokhang in Lhasa. Songtsen Gampo himself embraced the Buddhist faith and established Buddhist temples throughout the country, although the indigenous Bon faith remained the religion of the ordinary people. Following his death in 650, his descendants strengthened the kingdom politically, and in 763, Tibetan armies even took the Chinese capital Chang'an (modern Xi'an). Trisong Detsen (742–797), another champion of the new faith, invited two Indian Buddhist teachers to Tibet: Shantarakshita and the charismatic and flamboyant **Padmasambhava**. The latter, who was also known as Guru Rinpoche, is regarded as responsible for overcoming the resistance of the Bon religion and ensuring the spread of Buddhism within Tibet. Although he is closely associated with the Nyingma school of Buddhism, you'll spot his image somewhere in most temples.

In 838, the infamous **Langdarma** came to the throne, having assassinated his brother. A fervent supporter of Bon, he set about annihilating the Buddhist faith. Temples and monasteries were destroyed, monks forced to flee and the previously unified Tibet broke up into a number of small principalities. A Buddhist revival involving monastery construction, the translation of scriptures into Tibetan and the establishment of several of the schools of Tibetan Buddhism was spearheaded by the arrival of **Atisha** (982–1054), the most famous Indian scholar of the time. Politically, the country was not united, but the various independent principalities lived largely in harmony and there was little contact with China.

Absorbed in domestic events, the Tibetans had largely neglected the outside world, where the Muslim surge across India in the twelfth and thirteenth centuries resulted in the destruction of the great Buddhist centres of teaching to which the Tibetans had looked for generations. And to the north and east of Tibet, the **Mongol leader** Genghis Khan was beginning his assault on China. In 1207, Genghis Khan sent envoys to Tibet demanding submission, which was given without a fight, and the territory was largely ignored until Genghis Khan's grandson, Godan, sent raiding parties deep into the country. Hearing from his troops about the spirituality of the Tibetan lamas, Godan invited the head of the Sakya order, Sakya Pandita, to his court. In exchange for peace, Sakya Pandita again offered Tibetan submission and was created regent of Tibet at the Mongolian court, making the Sakya lamas the effective rulers of Tibet under the patronage of the emperor. This lasted through the generations, with Godan's son **Kublai Khan** deeply impressed by Sakya Pandita's nephew, Phagpa.

When the Chinese Ming dynasty overcame the Mongols in the fourteenth century, Tibet began a long period of independence, which ended in 1642 with the Mongols intervening directly in support of the Fifth Dalai Lama, Lobsang Gyatso (1617–82), of the **Gelugpa order**. Often referred to as **"the Great Fifth"**, he united the country under Gelugpa rule and within fifteen years, largely neglected by Mongol rulers, established authority from Kham to Kailash – the first time that one religious and political leader had united and ruled the country. He invited scholars to Tibet, restored and expanded religious institutions and began work on the Potala in Lhasa.

One disadvantage of the **reincarnation system** of succession (in which a newborn child is identified as the next manifestation of the dead lama) is that an unstable period of fifteen or twenty years inevitably follows a death while the next reincarnation grows up. Initially, the death of the Fifth Dalai Lama in 1682 was concealed by his regent, Sangye Gyatso, who raised the Sixth Dalai Lama to adulthood while claiming the Fifth Dalai Lama had entered a period of solitary meditation. The following two centuries saw no strong leadership from the Dalai Lamas, and there were repeated incursions by Mongolian factions. The most influential figures in Tibet at this time were the regents and representatives of the Manchu rulers in China, the ambans. During the **nineteenth century**, Tibet became increasingly isolationist, fearing Russian plans to expand their empire south and British plans to expand theirs north. Afraid of being caught in the middle, Tibet simply banned foreigners from their land. But at their borders, Tibetans continued trading with Indians, and in 1904, their one-sided trading arrangements exasperated the British, who determined to forge a fair treaty on the subject. The Tibetans refused to negotiate, so an expeditionary force was sent in

1904 under Colonel Younghusband. Meeting with obfuscation and hostility from Tibet's rulers, the invaders marched further and further into Tibet, and fought a couple of dispiriting battles against peasant soldiers armed with scythes and charms of invulnerability – gifts from their lamas, who stood at the back yelling encouragement. Patching up their poor opponents in improvised field hospitals along the way, the British marched up to Gyantse through the Chumbi Valley and eventually on to Lhasa. A series of British representatives in Lhasa forged good relationships with Tibet and became a window on the outside world.

The **Thirteenth Dalai Lama**, Tubten Gyatso (1876–1933), was an insightful and capable leader who realized that Tibet's political position needed urgent clarification, but he had a difficult rule, fleeing into exile twice, and was much occupied with border fighting against the Chinese and tensions with conservatives inside the country. Following his death, the **Fourteenth Dalai Lama** was identified in Amdo in 1938 and was still a young man when world events began to close in on Tibet. The British left India in 1947, withdrawing their representative from Lhasa. In 1949, the Communists, under Mao Zedong, created the People's Republic of China and the following year declared their intention "to liberate the oppressed and exploited Tibetans and reunite them with the great motherland". This probably had as much to do with Tibetan Khampa tribesmen attacking the bedraggled Red Army on the Long March as with Chinese notions of irredentism. In October 1950, the People's Liberation Army invaded the Kham region of eastern Tibet before proceeding to Lhasa the following year. Under considerable duress, Tibet signed a seventeen-point treaty in 1951, allowing for the "peaceful integration of Tibet".

The Chinese era

Initially, the Chinese offered goodwill and modernization. Tibet had made little headway into the twentieth century; there were few roads, no electricity, and glass windows, steel girders and concrete were all recent introductions. Hygiene and healthcare were patchy, and lay education was unavailable. While some Tibetans viewed modernization as necessary, the opposition was stiff, as many within the religious hierarchy saw changes within the country and overtures to the outside world as a threat to their influence. Throughout the 1950s, an underground resistance operated, which flared into a public confrontation in March 1959, fuelled by mounting distrust and hostility – refugees from eastern Tibet fled to Lhasa and told of the brutality of Chinese rule, including the sexual humiliation of monks and nuns, arbitrary executions and even crucifixions. In Lhasa, the Chinese invited the Dalai Lama to a theatrical performance at the Chinese military HQ. It was popularly perceived as a ploy to kidnap him, and huge numbers of Tibetans mounted demonstrations and surrounded the Norbulingka where the Dalai Lama was staying. On the night of March 17, the Dalai Lama and his entourage escaped, heading into **exile** in India where they were later joined (and still are today) by tens of thousands of refugees.

Meanwhile, the **uprising in Lhasa** was ferociously suppressed – the Chinese killed 87,000 people between March 1959 and September 1960. From that point on, all pretence of goodwill vanished, and a huge military force moved in, with a Chinese bureaucracy replacing Tibetan institutions. Temples and monasteries were destroyed, and Chinese **agricultural policies** proved particularly disastrous. During the years of the Great Leap Forward (1959–60), it is estimated that ten percent of Tibetans starved, and it wasn't until the early 1980s that the food situation in Tibet began to improve. Harrowing accounts tell of parents mixing their own blood with hot water and *tsampa* to feed their children.

In September 1965, the U-Tsang and western areas of Tibet officially became the **Xizang Autonomous Region** of the People's Republic of China, but more significant was the **Cultural Revolution** (1966–76), during which mass eradication of religious monuments and practices took place under the orders of the Red Guards, many of them young Tibetans. In 1959, there were 2700 monasteries and temples in Tibet; by 1978, there were just eight monasteries and fewer than a thousand monks and nuns in the TAR. Liberalization followed Mao's death in 1976, leading to a period of relative openness and peace in the early 1980s when monasteries were rebuilt, religion revived and tourism introduced. However, by the end of the decade, martial law was again in place – thanks to China's current leader, Hu Jintao – following riots in Lhasa in 1988–89. In the early 1990s, foreigners were allowed back into the region, and as the decade progressed it appeared the Chinese government was keen to exploit Tibet's potential for tourism. Assurances given in the build-up to the 2008 Beijing Olympics also indicated an eagerness to move away from the hardline authoritarian stance in the region, which was proving a source of diplomatic friction. In the event, riots and protests in Tibet, as well as Sichuan, Gansu and Qinghai, meant a return to sealed borders and all-but martial law. Though exact numbers of political prisoners are unknown, around 1000 Tibetans are still unaccounted for following the crackdown in response to pre-Olympic protests, and dissent of any kind is dealt with more harshly now than ever.

Meanwhile, the profile of the **Tibetan Government in Exile**, led by the Dalai Lama, is again on the wane following a peak in the early 1990s when it was fashionable for the likes of Richard Gere and Steven Seagal (who claims to be the reincarnation of a great lama) to be seen shaking hands with His Holiness. Based in Dharamsala in northern India, the organization represents some 130,000 Tibetan refugees, 100,000 of whom are in India.

In the face of China's growing economic power, the world community has evaded making a stand on Tibet, leaders now even dodging meetings with the Dalai Lama to avoid recriminations from Beijing. For his part, the Dalai Lama, known to the Tibetans as Gyalwa Rinpoche and regarded as the earthly incarnation of the god Chenresi, has never faltered from advocating a peaceful solution for Tibet, a stance that led to his being awarded the 1989 Nobel Peace Prize. Relations between the Dalai Lama and Beijing, which had thawed leading to serious discussion of him being allowed to visit Tibet, were again stymied in the run-up to the Olympics. Chinese officials publicly blamed the Dalai Lama and his "clique" for violent protests and branded him "a wolf in monk's clothing" and "a devil with the face of a human but the heart of a beast". It can only be assumed that such rabid name-calling plays out better with Chinese audiences than the international community.

In the meantime, several thousand Tibetans every year make the one-month trek to India, an arduous and dangerous journey over the mountains. Pilgrims have been picked off by Chinese snipers as they crossed the Himalayas – an incident in 2006 caused international outcry when it was captured on film by a team of mountaineers – though increasingly those who escape stay only for a few years before heading back home.

For the Tibetans who remain, the reality of life in Tibet is harsh. Per capita annual income in rural areas is less than £1 per day and adult literacy across Tibet less than fifty percent. It is estimated that China subsidized the TAR between 1952 and 1998 to the tune of ¥40 billion – yet Tibetans are among the poorest people in China and have the lowest life expectancy in the country. As Tibet provides the Chinese with land for their exploding population along with a wealth of yet-to-be exploited natural resources, the influx of more educated and better-skilled Chinese settlers, with considerably more financial resources, threatens to swamp the Tibetan population, culture and economy. However, the largest threat to the Tibetan way of life – and the biggest promise of modernization, and therefore rising living standards – comes from the **Qinghai–Lhasa railway line** built at a cost of US$4 billion. It makes little economic sense in the short term but is proof to foreign investors of China's commitment to improving the infrastructure to facilitate mining operations – uranium and copper are in particular abundance in the region. It aids the immigrant Han population, who consume huge quantities of expensively imported food – the Tibetans, in contrast, are largely self-sufficient. The line also allows for the swift and large-scale movement of troops and military hardware into Tibet.

The project was hugely ambitious, with more than 1200km of new track being built by 11,000 migrant workers (few of them Tibetan), much of it at an altitude of over 4000m and on permafrost, with more than 30km of tunnels. It was claimed the train carriages were to be pressurized, like an aircraft, to avoid passengers suffering the discomforts of altitude sickness during their journey; however, open windows in toilets, and splitting headaches and nausea during the journey, suggest this was more hype than reality.

If you're interested in doing some background **reading** on Tibet (see p.985), it's best to begin at home before you leave, as much that would be considered essential reading by Western audiences is simply not allowed or available in China – this

Travellers' Tibetan

Although most tour guides are now conversant in several languages, including English, most Tibetans speak only their native tongue, with perhaps a smattering of Mandarin. A few words of Tibetan are not only greeted enthusiastically, but are nigh-on essential if you manage to get off the beaten track or go trekking.

Tibetan belongs to the small Tibeto-Burmese group of languages and has no similarity at all to Mandarin or Hindi, despite what Chinese texts say. Tibetan script was developed in the seventh century and has thirty consonants and five vowels, which are placed either beside, above or below other letters when written down. There are obvious inaccuracies when trying to render this into the Roman alphabet, and the situation is further complicated by the many dialects across the region; the Lhasa dialect is used in the vocabulary below. Word order is back-to-front relative to English, and verbs are placed at the ends of sentences – "this noodle soup is delicious" becomes "tukpa dee shimbo doo", literally "noodle soup this delicious is". The only sound you are likely to have trouble with is "**ng**" at the beginning of words – it is pronounced as in "sa**ng**".

Basic phrases

Hello	*tashi delay*
Goodbye, to someone staying	*kalay shu*
Goodbye, to someone going	*kalay pay*
Thank you	*tuk too jay*
Sorry	*gonda*
Please	*coochee*
How are you?	*kusu debo yinbay?* or *kam sangbo dugay?*
I'm ...	*nga...*
Fine	*debo yin*
Cold	*kya*
Hungry	*throko-doe*
Thirsty	*ka gom*
Tired	*galay ka*
I don't understand	*nga ha ko ma-song*
What is your name?	*kayranggi mingla karay ray?*
My name is...	*ngeye mingla...sa*
Where are you from?	*kayrang kanay ray?*
I'm from...	*nga ... nay yin*
Britain	*Injee*
Australia	*Otaleeya*
America	*Amerika*
How old are you?	*kayrang lo katsay ray?*
I'm...	*nga lo ... yin*

includes almost all guide books (including this one), with their bourgeois imperialist references to Tibetan independence.

But beware: **searches** of luggage do take place – particularly at the Nepal–Tibet border at Zhangmu – where any literature deemed unpatriotic to China, anything remotely resembling a Tibetan flag and anything containing images of the Dalai Lama (though, with all pictures of him banned, it's worth pondering how the guards looking for the pictures know what he looks like), will be confiscated.

Tibet practicalities

The **best time to visit** Tibet is from April to October, outside the coldest months. June to September is the wettest period, when blocked roads and swollen rivers can make travel difficult, but the countryside will be at its greenest. However, health considerations should be taken seriously at any time of the year, and even in relatively balmy Lhasa, temperatures fall below freezing on a regular basis. In winter, as long as you come fully prepared for the cold (most hotels have no

Where are you going?	*kaba drogee yin?*
I'm going to...	*nga ... la drogee yin*
Where is the...?	*...kaba doo?*
hospital	*menkang*
monastery	*gompa*
temple/chapel	*lhakhang*
restaurant	*sakang*
convent	*ani gompa*
caretaker	*konyer*
Is there...?	*... doo gay?*
hot water	*chu tsa-bo*
a candle	*yangla*
I don't have...	*nga ... mindoo*
Is this OK/ can I do this?	*deegee rebay?*
It's (not) OK	*deegee (ma)ray*
(Not) Good	*yaggo (min)doo*
This is delicious	*dee shimbo doo*
Do you want ...?	*kayrang... gobay?*
I want tea	*nga cha go*
I don't want this	*dee me-go*
What is this/that?	*dee/day karray ray?*
How much is this?	*gong kadso ray?*
When?	*kadoo?*
Now	*danta*
Today	*dering*
Yesterday	*kezang*
Tomorrow	*sangnyee*
Monday	*sa dowa*
Tuesday	*sa mingma*
Wednesday	*sa lagba*
Thursday	*sa purbur*
Friday	*sa pasang*
Saturday	*sa pemba*
Sunday	*sa nima*

Numbers

1	*chee*
2	*nyee*
3	*soom*
4	*zhee*
5	*nga*
6	*droo*
7	*doon*
8	*gyay*
9	*goo*
10	*chew*
11	*chew chee*
12	*chew nyee*
20	*nyi shoo*
21	*nyi shoo chee etc*
30	*soom chew*
40	*shib chew*
50	*ngab chew*
60	*drook chew*
70	*doon chew*
80	*gyay chew*
90	*goop chew*
100	*gya*
200	*nyee gya*
1000	*dong*

heating) and possible delays due to snow-covered passes, the lack of tourists and the preoccupation of the security forces with staying warm can make for a pleasant trip.

Chinese authorities are much pricklier around **festival times** (see p.891) and the week before and after certain historically significant dates, when they'll be much more likely to **clamp down** on unregulated travel and demand permits for inspection. Dates to bear in mind include March 5 and 10 (the anniversaries of uprisings in 1959, 1988, 1989 and 2008), July 6 (the Dalai Lama's birthday), September 27 and October 1 (the anniversaries of protests in 1987), and December 10 (International Human Rights Day, and the anniversary of the Dalai Lama's Nobel Peace Prize).

Getting there

At time of writing, entry permits and restrictions on the movement of foreigners within Tibet stood at almost North Korean levels (see p.887). To enter Tibet travellers must have a **Tibet Travel Permit** listing their full itinerary. These permits are only issued to registered travel agencies for their clients once they have booked a tour. In short, all travel in Tibet outside of Lhasa must be booked before arrival, and all travellers must employ a driver and guide for each day of their stay. Anyone overstaying beyond the date of their travel permit faces fines and deportation from the region. The agency that applies for the permit on your behalf may also face stiff penalties, so your guides will also be anxious for you to stick to the leaving dates set out on the permit. Though officially carrying no cost, agencies arranging for travel permits will likely charge a significant handling fee for the service. You are free, however, to arrange your own transport into and out of the region, though realistically this will almost certainly be either by train or plane.

Bear in mind that regulations have shifted fairly regularly in the past, so its best to check up on the latest requirements (and possible loopholes) before forking out for a tour.

By air

Domestic flights operate daily to Lhasa from Chengdu (¥1300), and there are also services from Beijing (¥2000), and from Shangri-La (¥2500) and Kunming (¥2000) in Yunnan (prices quoted are economy one-way). The easiest and cheapest option is to fly from Chengdu, where plenty of tour operators, most of them grouped around the *Traffic Hotel*, offer tickets, tours and permits.

It is also possible to fly in to Lhasa from **Kathmandu** in Nepal, but you will need to ensure you have a Chinese visa and Tibet Travel Permit before attempting the journey. As permits can now be emailed for you to print out, you are not limited to booking your tour in Nepal, and, as long as you can arrange payment, any of the China- or Tibet-based agencies will be able to meet you off the plane in Lhasa.

By land

At the time of writing the **train line** was the only viable overland option for foreigners, regulations barring independent transport on buses from places like Golmud, or Kathmandu via Kodari (in Nepal) then Zhangmu (in Tibet).

To get a Chinese visa in **Nepal** and secure the necessary Tibet Travel Permit, you will have to be booked on an organized tour. This can be done through travel companies in Kathmandu, or you may be able to find a Tibet-based agency who, after finishing one tour from Lhasa to Zhangmu, might be keen to pick a group up at the border and run the tour in the opposite direction on their way back. Visas issued in **Kathmandu** are often only valid for three weeks, so if you plan on crossing from Nepal into Tibet, it's worth getting your Chinese visa elsewhere before entering Nepal. Expect to pay around US$600 for an organized seven-day

Getting to Tibet on the Qinghai–Lhasa railway

The **Golmud–Lhasa section** of the **Qinghai–Lhasa Railway** is the world's longest (1956km) and highest plateau railway, peaking at heights of over 5000m during the fourteen-and-a-half-hour journey (¥160). Since its opening, ahead of schedule, in June 2006, the rail link has proved increasingly popular, and the once-hectic bus station at Golmud is now a depressing shell of a place, with only the occasional passenger and disinterested staff. However, many travellers are using Golmud as their departure point by train due to ease of ticket purchase.

Passengers who had hoped to be protected from the effects of altitude by the much-vaunted "**pressurized carriages**" will be disappointed – with toilet windows left open and some passengers experiencing altitude sickness, the carriages are not all they're cracked up to be, though they are comfortable. The journey itself, however, provides fantastic vistas of the plateau, with herds of yaks and fascinating glimpses of human life that exists – against the odds – in this thinly oxygenated environment.

There are numerous **departure points to Lhasa**, in addition to Golmud: Beijing (¥813); Chengdu (¥712); Chongqing (¥754); Guangzhou (¥1000); Lanzhou (¥552); Shanghai (¥850); and Xining (¥523). Prices quoted are for a single in a hard-sleeper berth. Tickets to Lhasa go on sale ten days before departure, and demand is high, particularly during the summer when sleeper tickets are incredibly hard to come by, even on the day of release. Mysteriously, travel agencies don't seem to have the same problems and can usually supply any tickets you need, but often with a mark-up of several hundred per cent.

Hard-seat tickets are easier to secure yourself, but with a forty-hour journey time between Beijing and Lhasa this is not for the faint of heart (or tender of bottom), though, with everybody crammed in like sardines, it is an unavoidable way of making plenty of new friends.

Tickets out of Lhasa are far easier to secure, and hard or soft sleepers can be bought at the Tibet Tourism Office on Luobulingka Lu, at the station itself, or from any of the travel agencies.

overland trip to Lhasa, or around US$400 for a three-day trip – but make sure you are clear on exactly what is and isn't included in terms of accommodation, food and entry tickets. One agency that will group individual travellers together is Nature Trail Trekking at Durbar Marg in Kathmandu (Ⓣ977 1470 1925, Ⓦwww.allnepal.com), which charges US$650 for an eight-day overland tour to Lhasa. The best advice is to spend some time in Kathmandu to get a feel for the current situation and check out your options. Beware of your guides offering money-changing services, citing a dearth of options in Tibet. This is untrue, and once you're in Tibet you'll find plenty places to change cash at more competitive rates.

Getting around

One benefit of the new regulations is that getting around is considerably more straightforward than before – now you just get in a jeep and go where your tour guide takes you. That said, **Foreigners' Travel Permits** (around ¥150 depending on which areas they cover, but likely to be included in the travel agency's tour fee – and your guide will handle all the admin) are still issued by the PSB, giving permission to visit specified places within specified time limits – they were becoming increasingly irrelevant and were even due to be scrapped altogether until the rather ill-judged and poorly executed protest at Everest Base Camp by some Americans in spring 2007. The most popular place for guides to apply is at the office in Shigatse, which can issue permits for travel along the Friendship Highway, up to Everest and also to Mount Kailash. There are plenty of areas, however, where a permit will not be given under any circumstances, such as the highly militarized Chumbi Valley. The status of other areas seems to change from one day to the next. Penalties for being caught somewhere without a permit can be fairly heavy: travellers have faced big fines, been harangued at length, and forced to write "confessions".

Arranging tours

Independent travel in Tibet is virtually impossible for foreign visitors, and the only option for travelling outside Lhasa is to book a **guided tour** – including a private tour vehicle, driver and guide – through an agency before you arrive.

While it may be tempting to try to sidestep the regulations, foreign travellers frequently have permits checked on arrival at train and bus stations within Tibet and at Lhasa airport, many hotels will not let foreigners stay unless they present a valid permit, and permits are required to be shown again when visiting the Potala Palace and other tourist sights. Add the regular checkpoints along roads outside Lhasa and it would take a serious, concerted effort and a massive slice of luck for a permitless traveller to get very far.

Despite the huge number of travel agencies in Chengdu, Xining, Golmud and Lhasa, all claiming to offer a unique service, the fact is most operate through CITS or FIT in Lhasa, hiring drivers and tour guides who are registered with the Lhasa authorities and work as freelancers. This makes it incredibly hard to recommend one single agency or tour company, and can make a mockery of the idea that you get what you pay for.

That you are forced to book from outside the region, preventing you from meeting the tour guide or seeing the vehicle before signing up, means it pays to be circumspect – try to get a recommendation from a fellow traveller if possible, and go through your itinerary with a fine-tooth comb working out exactly what is covered and what you will have to pay extra for. Getting a group of five together to fill a **jeep** will ensure the per person cost is as low as it can be, though if you are on your own or part of a couple, most agencies will be able to match you up with a group which still has spaces that need filling.

The **most popular tour** follows the Friendship Highway up to the Nepalese border, and includes three days in Lhasa and five on the road taking in Gyantse, Shigatse and Everest Base Camp. It costs around ¥4000 per person, not including accommodation.

As you have to book a driver, guide and vehicle anyway, there is no reason to simply stick to the tours offered – you can draw up your own itinerary and negotiate costs with the agency. Expect to pay around ¥1300 per day to hire a Land Cruiser. For driver and guide fees it is best to haggle prices as low as you can with the agency and tip heavily at the end of the tour to ensure the money goes where you want it to.

Many groups supporting Tibetans recommend that travellers insist on Tibetan guides and drivers as a way of supporting the indigenous economy, though in reality this can be hard to enforce.

Some established agencies are:

Budget Tibet Tour Ⓦwww.budgettibettour.com

CITS Ⓦwww.tibettravel.org

FIT Ⓣ0086 891 6320200, Ⓔttbfitsonam@hotmail.com

Khampa Caravan Ⓦwww.khampacaravan.com

Tibet Culture Tour Ⓦwww.tibetculturetour.com

Tibet Nakqu International Travel Service Ⓣ0086 891 6328851, Ⓔnamgyal_tenzin@hotmail.com

Wind Horse Ⓦwww.windhorsetour.com

In the event of a misunderstanding, you may wish to complain to the Tour Service Inspection Office of Lhasa's Tibet Tourism Bureau, 208 Luobulingka Lu (Ⓣ0891/6333476 or 6334193).

The **public transport system** in Tibet, such as it is, consists of large public **buses** and smaller, nippier **minibuses**. In-town use of public transport by foreigners is generally tolerated, though probably only in Lhasa might it be actually necessary for getting around. Intercity travel by bus is not permitted, and even if you can find someone willing to sell you a ticket and a driver happy to take you, you are unlikely to make your destination without running into a checkpoint of some kind, where you will be fined and ordered to leave Tibet. Nevertheless, **basic public transport information** is included in the following sections in the hopes that independent travel may one day again be possible. All foreigners would be advised against attempting these routes without first establishing whether they are currently allowed to do so.

Long-distance cycling is not technically illegal, but even cyclists have to hire a guide, jeep and driver while they are on the road. Authorities (and the tour agency) will do their best to make sure you stay in hotels, even if you come equipped with camping and warm-weather gear. To be fair, having a backup team can prove helpful – though most of the traditional route from Kathmandu to Lhasa is level and the road in decent condition, dogs and weather can be a hazard, and there are five 5000m passes to contend with. The route is covered by a few cycle tour companies, such as the UK-based Exodus (Ⓣ0870/240 5550, Ⓦwww.exodus.co.uk) and HMB Tours in Kathmandu (Ⓣ977 1470 0437, Ⓦwww.bikingnepal.com), or you can negotiate with any of the Lhasa-based tour companies on prices for your required chaperone.

A free, Chinese-only map of Lhasa can be purchased from most hotels and restaurants, while English maps can be purchased at hotels and newsstands for around ¥10. For an alternative view of the city, the *On This Spot Lhasa Map*, published by the International Campaign for Tibet, includes the notorious Drapchi Prison, security facilities and army bases – needless to say, you shouldn't take it there with you.

Health

Tibet poses particular health hazards to travellers. Almost every visitor is affected by **altitude sickness**, as most of Tibet is over 3000m, with plenty of passes over 5000m. For your first two or three days, rest as much as possible and drink plenty of water. You can buy oxygen canisters in most hotel receptions (¥20), though whether they're much use is debatable. A few painkillers should help to relieve any aches and pains and headaches, but more serious problems can develop; see Basics, p.60, for more details. The prescription drug Diamox can help, but is no substitute for descent – altitude sickness can be fatal and it's not worth taking the risk. Trekkers and climbers need also to be particularly aware of the dangers of **hypothermia**.

Travellers to Tibet should seriously consider **rabies immunization** before they travel. The dogs are very aggressive, bites are common and, if you get bitten, Kathmandu is the nearest place stocking rabies serum. A significant number of travellers to Tibet also suffer from **giardiasis**, an unpleasant and debilitating intestinal complaint, although there is some controversy over whether it is endemic to the region or brought in from outside. The treatment is Tinadozol or Flagyl, neither or which is reliably available in Lhasa; bring a course along with you if you're planning an ambitious or lengthy trip. They can both be purchased cheaply and easily in big cities within China.

Clothing

Despite the plateau's altitude and the perennially snow-capped mountains, not everywhere in Tibet is constantly beset by ice and freezing temperatures. In summer, Lhasa and the valleys across the region reach temperatures well into the 20s. During the day T-shirt and shorts are perfectly adequate, though a hat and serious sun cream are advisable to fend off the UV rays (be aware that long trousers are required for entry into most temples, and hats should be removed once inside). Summer evenings and nighttimes can be chilly, and a jumper is the minimum requirement. Everest Base Camp can fall below zero even in the summer – thermals, winter jacket, gloves and woolly hat are all recommended whatever the time of year. All hotels, including the guesthouse tents at Everest, supply their own bedding, but bringing your own winter sleeping bag is not a bad idea for hygiene as well as thermal considerations, especially if you're planning on hostelling. Don't worry if you don't want to lug your full winter wardrobe around until you get to Tibet; there is a good supply of cheap anoraks, winter jackets and general hiking and camping gear in Lhasa, most of it reasonable quality fakes imported from Nepal.

Accommodation

Despite the requirement to book a tour, regulations do not stipulate that accommodation reservations are made in advance. As a result many tour agencies do not include accommodation or food, as a way of reducing their headline price – so you will at least have some freedom to choose where you stay. In most Tibetan towns, simple **guesthouses** offer accommodation to foreigners, pilgrims and truck drivers. You can expect the basic dormitory experience, with bedding (of variable cleanliness) provided. The communal toilets are often pit latrines and there are few washing facilities, although most places have bowls. Hot water in vacuum flasks, for drinks and washing, can be found everywhere.

There is a greater choice in the main tourist centres of Lhasa, Shigatse, Gyantse, Tsetang and Zhangmu, where hotels provide comfortable rooms with attached bathrooms and at least some hours of hot water. In the administrative centres of Lhasa and Shigatse, foreigners are allowed to stay at **mid-range hotels**, with rooms of a similar quality and, typically, reasonable value for money.

If you are trekking, you can **camp**, although many trekkers find accommodation in village houses or with nomadic yak-herders. You should not expect them to feed you, and should pay ¥20 or so per night.

Eating, drinking and nightlife

The traditional **Tibetan diet** – constrained by what little will grow at over 4000m – consists in large part of **butter tea**, a unique mixture of yak butter, tea and salt, all churned into a blend that many Westerners find undrinkable, but which Tibetans consume in huge quantities. Into this is stirred **tsampa**, roasted barley flour, to make dough with the consistency of raw pastry and a not unpleasant nutty flavour. Yak meat, yoghurt and cheese (often dried into bite-sized cubes to preserve it) and sometimes a soup of a few vegetables supplement this. **Thukpa** (pronounced "tukpa") is a noodle soup with a few bits and pieces of whatever is available thrown in. If you're lucky, you'll find **momos**, tiny steamed or fried dough parcels containing meat or vegetables (a *thri momo* is a solid dough parcel without a filling). The local **brew**, Lhasa Beer, is widely available – and very drinkable.

Lhasa

Situated in a wide, mountain-fringed valley on the north bank of the Kyichu River, **LHASA** (拉萨, *lāsà*; Ground of the Gods), at 3700m, is a sprawling modern Chinese city with a population of around 200,000. An important settlement for well over a thousand years, it was originally called Rasa, but was renamed by King Songtsen Gampo in the seventh century when he moved his capital here from the Yarlung Valley. Following the collapse of the Yarlung dynasty two centuries later, power dispersed among local chieftains, and the city lost its pre-eminence. It was not until the seventeenth century, with the installation of the Fifth Dalai Lama as ruler by the Mongolian emperor, Gushri Khan, that Lhasa once again became the seat of government. It continues now as the capital of the TAR, and while glorious sights from earlier times are spread throughout the area, it is this third period of growth, following the Chinese invasion, which has given the city its most obvious features – wide boulevards and concrete-and-glass blocks. Despite the passing of sixty years, Lhasa is still clearly a city under occupation, with armed soldiers standing sentry on street corners and rooftops, and constant patrols throughout the city.

There are plenty of sights in and around Lhasa to keep most visitors occupied for at least a week (even if most tours cram them into a few days): the **Potala**, **Jokhang** and the **Barkhor** district are not to be missed, and at least one trip to an outlying monastery is a must. It's also worth taking time to see some of the smaller, less showy temples and simply to absorb the atmosphere of the "Forbidden City", which large numbers of explorers died in vain efforts to reach just over a hundred years ago.

Offering tourists better **facilities**, with more choice of accommodation, restaurants and shopping than anywhere else in Tibet, Lhasa makes for a relatively pain-free introduction to the region. But, whatever its comforts, the city is just one face of Tibet – 88 percent of the population lives in the countryside.

Orientation

The **central areas** of Lhasa are along and between three main roads that run east–west, parallel to and north of the Kyichu River: Chingdol Lu, Beijing Lu and Lingkuo Lu. Lhasa is at its most sprawling to the west, where there is very little countryside between the outskirts of the city and the monastery of Drepung, 8km west of town, and north, where the city virtually merges into the Sera monastery complex, 4km distant. So far, the river has prevented a spread south, while to the east the city peters out within a few kilometres. The Potala Palace, on Beijing Zhong Lu, is the major landmark visible throughout the city and, together with the Tibetan enclave around the Jokhang temple (known as the Barkhor), forms the centre of interest for most visitors. The Golden Yaks Statue, at the junction of Beijing Zhong Lu and Luobulingka Lu in the west of the city, erected in 1991 to celebrate the fortieth anniversary of the "liberation" of Tibet, is another useful landmark.

Arrival

Arriving **by air**, you'll land at Lhasa airport at Gongkhar, a hefty 93km to the southeast of the city. CAAC buses (¥25) bring you to the CAAC office on Nyangrain Lu in less than two hours, while foreigners coming on tours will usually be met by guides with transport. Arriving in Lhasa by bus, the main bus station, west of the centre, is at the junction of Chingdol Zhong Lu and Minzu Lu. From here, either take a taxi into town (¥10), or use the #2 minibus (¥2), which will take you most of the way (see "City transport", below). The enormous new **train station** is about 3km from the centre of Lhasa; catching a taxi costs ¥10 from the station to the town, but ¥20 in the opposite direction from the town to the station. Alternatively, hop on buses #105 or #89, which will ferry you in either direction for ¥1.

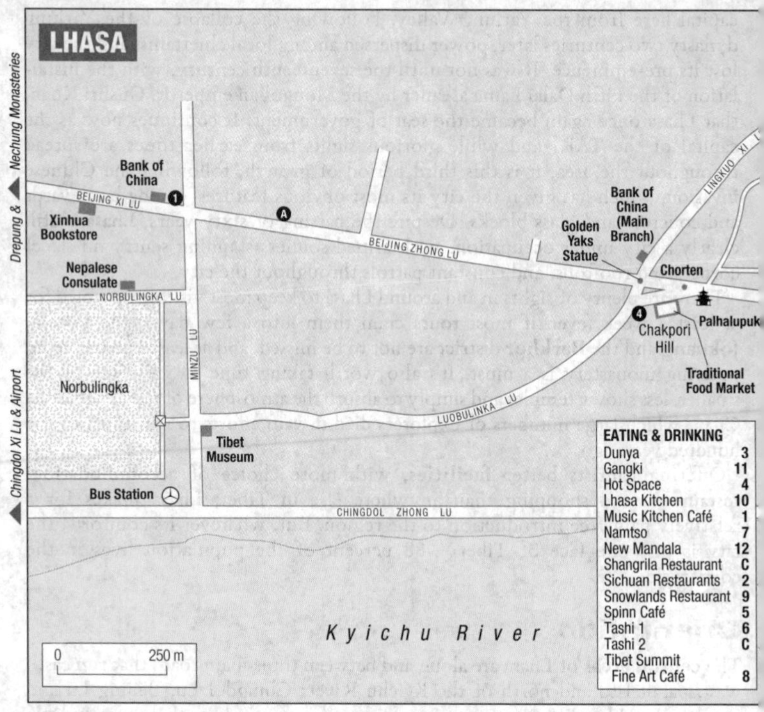

City transport

The easiest way to get around the city and its environs is by **minibus** (daily 7am–10pm; ¥1–2 flat fare) or on a **cycle-rickshaw**; you'll have to haggle a little for the latter, which should run around ¥4–5 for most trips. There are plenty of taxis, which have a ¥10 basic rate that should cover most destinations in town. **Bike rental** is available at several places along Beijing Lu and, though actual rental is cheap – ¥20–40 per day – deposits are ¥800–1000. Apart from the altitude, there are few problems with cycling in Lhasa; main roads are wide and have designated cycle lanes, and there are traffic lights and traffic police at the main junctions

Useful minibus routes

#2 West from the small minibus stand opposite the cinema on Yuthok Lu, north up Kharnga Dong Lu and then west along the front of the Potala Palace. Some head west on Beijing Zhong Lu and Beijing Xi Lu and then turn south at the *Lhasa Hotel*, past the Norbulingka, while others follow the old road, Yuan Lin Lu, to the Norbulingka. All pass the bus station and then head west out of the city on Chingdol Xi Lu.

#3 From Beijing Dong Lu at the junction with Dosengge Lu, then loops north at Nyangrain Lu, west along Lingkouo Bei Lu, down to the Golden Yaks Statue, then east along Beijing Zhong Lu and Beijing Xi Lu past the *Lhasa Hotel* and out to Drepung and Nechung monasteries.

#5 From the stand opposite the cinema on Yuthok Lu, north up Dosengge Lu, then west along Beijing Dong Lu and north up Nyangrain Lu to Sera Monastery.

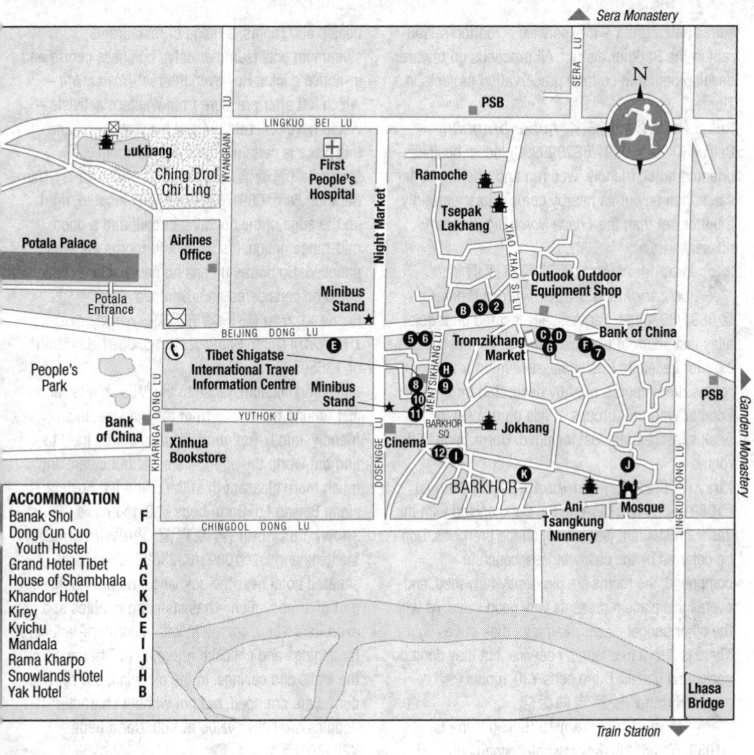

to control the flow. The main danger comes from cycle-rickshaws, which tend to ignore both of these.

Accommodation

Whether you are looking for **budget** or **luxury** accommodation, the area around the **Barkhor** is the place to stay. Mid-range hotels are springing up west of the centre, and with the sustained cranking up of investment in China, big Western names are likely to soon re-enter the market (*Holiday Inn* withdrew in 1997 under pressure from rights groups). However comfortable, they simply cannot compete with the atmosphere of the labyrinthine old town.

Banak Shol (八朗学旅馆, *bālángxué lǚguǎn*) Beijing Dong Lu ⓣ0891/6323829. Once clean and homely, this place has gone downhill, crossing the line from appealingly chaotic to just worn out; the staff are lazy, the facilities shoddy, but it is popular with Chinese backpackers. There's a range of rooms with and without bath, but beware the rooms at the front, which can be noisy. One significant advantage, however, is the free laundry service. ❶–❸

Dong Cun Cuo Youth Hostel (正昌东措国际青年旅馆, *zhèng chāng dōng cuò guójìqīngnián lǚguǎn*)10 Beijing Dong Lu ⓣ0891/6273388 ext 8888. Well-liked, well-located, spacious establishment, with six-bed dorms, that's clean and well run, with a Korean restaurant attached. Dorm beds ¥25, rooms ❶–❷

Grand Hotel Tibet (西藏国际大酒店, *xīzàng guójì dàjiǔdiàn*) 67 Beijing Zhong Lu ⓣ0891/6816666. Shiny and fair value, with good facilities and a surplus-to-requirements oxygen bar. Big discounts on standard doubles outside the Oct and May national holidays. ❺

House of Shambhala (香巴拉宫, *xiāng bālāgōng*) 7 Jiri Erxiang ⓣ0891/6326533, ⓦwww.houseofshambhala.com. Newly built in traditional Tibetan style, this boutique hotel, run by the nonprofit Shambhala organization, offers stylish suites and a great – if expensive – rooftop restaurant in the Barkhor district. All proceeds go towards development and cultural preservation projects in Tibet. ❽

Hubei Hotel (湖北宾馆, *húběi bīnguǎn*) Beijing Xi Lu ⓣ0891/6820999. Chinese, business-oriented hotel, friendly, well run and offering better value than any of its nearby competitors; certainly a better bet than the *Lhasa Hotel*. Big discounts off-season. ❺

Khandor Hotel (西藏康卓渡假村, *xīzàngkāngzhuódùjiàcūn*) Bakhor ⓣ0891/6378444. Fantastically located on a quiet alley just south of the Jokhang, the nondescript exterior belies its traditional-style interior with rooms running off a brightly decorated atrium. Popular with tour groups, it fills up quickly in peak season. Breakfast included. Dorm beds ¥50, rooms ❸

Kirey (吉日宾馆, *jírìbīnguǎn*) Beijing Dong Lu ⓣ0891/6323462. Close to the Barkhor, and with the *Tashi 2* restaurant (see p.913) on the premises. Don't be deterred by the characterless, concrete compound; the rooms are pleasantly furnished, and overall this place represents very good value. As with the other budget places, staff take their duties lightly. There is also a free laundry service, but they don't do socks and undies. Dorm beds ¥30, rooms ❷

Kyichu (拉萨吉曲饭店, *lāsàjíqūfàndiàn*) 19 Beijing Dong Lu ⓣ0891/6338824, ⓦwww.hotelkyichu.com. Centrally located, good value, with friendly Tibetan staff, this is one of the best mid-range choices, with practical, large and not over-decorated rooms. Rates are negotiable. ❸

Lhasa Hotel (拉萨饭店, *lāsàfàndiàn*) Minzu Lu ⓣ0891/66832221, ⓕ6834117. Formerly the *Holiday Inn* (as a sign outside informs you), this used to be Lhasa's most luxurious hotel and still boasts 460 rooms, a range of restaurants, swimming pool (summer only), business centre and in-house doctor. However, the real *Holiday Inn* – which left after pressure from Western activists – would never tolerate present lax standards, and this place is certainly not value for money. ❼

Mandala (满斋酒店, *mǎnzhāi jiǔdiàn*) 31 Nan Barkhor Jie ⓣ0891/6324783. Well located, right on the edge of the Jokhang circuit, and a good mid-range option. It's quiet, and rooms are wood-panelled. No dorms means no backpackers, which could be considered an advantage. ❹

Rama Kharpo (热玛嘎布宾馆, *rèmǎgābù bīnguǎn*) Ongto Shingka Lam ⓣ0891/6346963 or 13659505918, ⓦwww.lhasabarkhor.com. Close to the Muslim quarter, just around the corner from the mosque, this friendly, family-run guesthouse is a little hard to find but worth the effort. It's basic but clean, and much more pleasant than the crammed hostels along Beijing Lu. Dorm beds ¥30, rooms ❷–❸

Snowlands Hotel (雪域宾馆, *xuěyùbīnguǎn*) Mentsikhang Lu ⓣ0891/6323687. Lively, well-situated hotel near the Jokhang. The new wing – part of a renovation – has standard doubles at an exorbitant ¥350, complete with nightmare-inducing furnishings and childlike attempts at Tibetan art on the walls and ceilings. In the old wing, the six-bed dorms are cramped, but not without character; doubles are better value at ¥80. Dorm beds ¥25–30, rooms ❷–❻

Yak Hotel (亚宾馆, *yàbīnguǎn*) 100 Beijing Dong Lu ⓣ0891/6323496. Following a massive overhaul, this hotel is no longer the budget favourite it once was. Dorms have been rebranded as "common" rooms, while doubles offer greater comforts – TV, tea-making facilities, private bathrooms – but come with some rather ugly, over-engineered, Chinese-style furniture. Dorm beds ¥30–40, rooms ❺

The City

With ascendant Chinese modernity and ancient Tibetan traditions set side by side, Lhasa is a vibrant, fast-changing city that throws up some bizarre paradoxes – witness the pilgrims on their rounds of prostrations passing the ATM machines of the Bank of China, or groups of Tibetan teenagers breakdancing in the alleys around the Barkhor. Construction sites abound, but it is still easy to get around to all the major monuments, many of which are within walking distance of the two central landmarks, the **Potala Palace** and **Jokhang**.

The Potala Palace

Perched 130m above Lhasa atop Marpo Ri (Red Mountain), and named after India's Riwo Potala – holy mountain of the god Chenresi – the **Potala Palace** (布达拉宫, *bùdálāgōng*; daily 8.30am–6pm, last entry 3.30pm; Nov–April ¥100, May–Oct ¥200) is dazzling inside and out, an enduring landmark of the city of Lhasa. As you revel in the views from the roof, gaze at the glittering array of gold and jewels and wend your way from chapel to chapel, you'll rub shoulders with excited and awestruck pilgrims from all over ethnic Tibet, making offerings at each of the altars. But be aware that, beyond the areas approved for tourists and pilgrims, the Potala is a shadow of its former self: most of the rooms are off limits, part of a UNESCO World Heritage grant was spent on a CCTV system and the caretaker monks are not allowed to wear their robes. And don't tackle the Potala on your first day at altitude – the palace is a long climb, and even the Tibetans huff and puff on the way up; you'll enjoy it more once you've acclimatized.

Rising thirteen dramatic storeys and consisting of over a thousand rooms, the palace complex took a workforce of at least seven thousand builders and fifteen hundred artists and craftsmen over fifty years to complete. The main mass of the Potala is the **White Palace** (Potrange Karpo), while the building rising from its centre is the **Red Palace** (Potrang Marpo). Built for several purposes, the Potala served as administrative centre, seat of government, monastery, fortress and the home of all the Dalai Lamas from the Fifth to the Fourteenth, although from the end of the eighteenth century, when the Norbulingka was built as the Summer Palace, they stayed here only in winter. It was King Songtsen Gampo who built the first palace on this site in the seventh century, though invaders later destroyed it. Today's White Palace (1645–48) was built during the reign of the Fifth Dalai Lama, who took up residence in 1649, while the Red Palace, begun at the same time, was completed in 1693. Both survived the Cultural Revolution relatively unscathed; apparently Zhou Enlai ordered their protection.

Tickets have to be bought one or two days in advance, foreign tourists must be accompanied by a guide and a visit will almost certainly be part of any tour to Tibet, with the travel agency supplying tickets as part of the package. A major downside of this is that registered tour groups are limited to just an hour inside; some visitors have reported being able to buy their own time-unlimited tickets the day before, but with only 2300 tickets issued per day – and 1600 of these reserved for tour groups – you'll need to get to the ticket office early and be prepared for disappointment. Morning is certainly the best time to visit, when the place bustles with excited pilgrims. Photography is banned inside, and neither, bizarrely, are you supposed to take pictures of the fabulous views from the roof. Snapping away in the palace's courtyards is tolerated, however.

Into the palace

The palace is central enough to be reached on foot; otherwise, a taxi will cost ¥10 from virtually anywhere in the city, and the #2 minibus passes the front gate. The tour goup entrance is on the western side of the huge compound, and after a permit check and bag x-ray you'll find yourself standing in the grounds of the Dalai Lama's winter home. Follow the path up to the inner courtyard of the White Palace, the **Deyang Shar**, flanked by monks' rooms and stores and with the **Quarters of the Dalai Lama** at its eastern end. The opulently carved and painted **Official Reception Hall** beyond is dominated by the bulk of the high throne and hung with fabulous brocade and *thangkas* (embroidered or painted religious scrolls), with a small doorway leading into the private quarters of the Fourteenth Dalai Lama next door. There's a small audience chamber, a chapel, a hallway and finally the bedroom, with an extremely well-painted mural of Tsongkhapa, founder of the Gelugpa school to which the Dalai Lama belongs, over the bed. On the other side of the Official Reception Hall are the private quarters of the previous Dalai Lamas, but these are closed to the public.

Stairs lead from the inner courtyard up into the **Red Palace** and continue straight to the roof, for fabulous views across Lhasa. You can then descend a floor at a time to tour the palace, moving clockwise all the way. The first room on the

upper floor is the **Maitreya Chapel**, its huge number of fabulously ornate statues setting the tone for the remainder of the chapels. It's dominated by a seated statue of Maitreya, made at the time of the Eighth Dalai Lama and said to contain the brain of Atisha, the eleventh-century Indian scholar responsible for a Buddhist revival in Tibet (see p.893). On the far left of the Dalai Lama's throne is a statue of the Fifth Dalai Lama, commissioned soon after his death and supposedly containing some of his hair.

The Red Palace is the final resting place of the Fifth to Thirteenth Dalai Lamas, except for the Sixth, who died on his way to China and is said to be buried near Qinghai Hu in Qinghai province. However, not all the tombs are open. Although they vary in size, all are jewel-encrusted golden chortens (traditional multi-tiered Tibetan Buddhist monuments that usually contain sacred objects), supporting tier upon tier of fantastic engravings; encased deep within are the bodies, preserved in dry salt. You should at least be able to see either the Tomb of the Thirteenth Dalai Lama or of the Eighth Dalai Lama on the upper floor.

Considered the oldest and holiest shrines in the Potala, the **Lokeshvara Chapel**, on the upper floor, and the **Practice Chamber of the Dharma King**, directly below on the upper middle floor, date back to Songtsen Gampo's original construction, and are the focus of all Potala pilgrims. It's easy to miss the Practice Chamber, entered from a small corridor from the balcony. King Songtsen Gampo supposedly meditated in this dark, dingy room now dominated by statues of the king and his ministers, Tonmi Sambhota and Gawa. At the base of the main pillar is a stove, apparently used by Songtsen Gampo himself.

Although you pass through the **lower middle floor**, the chapels here are all closed and the remainder of the open rooms are on the lower floor leading off the large, many-columned Assembly Hall. The highlight down here is the grand **Chapel of the Dalai Lamas' Tombs**, containing the awesome golden chorten of the Fifth Dalai Lama, which is three storeys high and made from 3700kg of gold. To the left and right are smaller chortens with the remains of the Tenth and Twelfth Dalai Lamas, and the chortens on either side of these main ones are believed to contain relics of Buddha himself. Visitors leave by a door behind the altar in the **Chapel of the Holy Born**, from where the path winds down the west side of the hill to the western gate.

Around the Potala Palace

The area around the Potala Palace offers plenty of enjoyable sights. Opposite the front of the palace, on the south side of Beijing Dong Lu, **People's Park** is a mini Tian'anmen Square, built in an effort to reinforce China's claim to the region; there is a Chinese flag and a monument celebrating Tibet's "liberation". Farther west along Beijing Dong Lu, the new chorten in the middle of the road marks the site of the old West Gate to the city. South of here, **Chakpori Hill** – topped by a radio transmitter – once provided a scenic view of the Potala Palace, but is now closed off; the best you can do is pay ¥2 and ascend to a balcony just across the road from the chorten.

From just east of the public toilets at the chorten, a path leads a couple of hundred metres to the fabulously atmospheric **Palhalupuk Temple** (¥20), built around an ancient cave. You'll spot the far less interesting ochre-and-maroon **Neten Temple** on the cliff first; Palhalupuk is the smaller, white building below. Entered from an ante-chapel, the cave, about five square metres, was King Songtsen Gampo's retreat in the seventh century and is lined with rock carvings, many of which date from that time. The most important altar is in front of the huge rock pillar that supports the roof, the main image being of Sakyamuni, flanked by his chief disciples. At the far right-hand corner stands a jewel- and *katag*-bedecked statue of Pelden Lhamo, the fierce protective deity of Tibet, on a tiny altar. The back wall has been left untouched, and it's said that the jewels of Songtsen Gampo's Nepalese wife, Princess Bhrikuti, are hidden behind. The temple isn't on most tour group itineraries so it's a bit less hectic than others, and the caretaker and monks will be pleased to see you.

Unfortunately, the main area of **rock carvings** on **Chakpori Hill**, numbering around five thousand and supposedly representing the visions seen by King Songtsen Gampo during his meditation, is out of bounds, but modern-day carvers can be seen at work along the path to the Palhalupuk Temple – the speed and intricacy of their work is absolutely mind-boggling.

North of the Potala Palace

Around the other side of the Potala Palace is the park of **Ching Drol Chi Ling** (free), which has fine views of the north facade of the Potala and sports a large area of trees plus two boating lakes (formed by the removal of earth during the construction of the palace). On an island in the westernmost of the two lakes is the small, pleasant Lukhang, or **Dragon King Temple** (禄康, *lùkāng*; daily 8am–5pm; ¥10), built by the Sixth Dalai Lama in honour of the naga king for use as a retreat. Legend tells of a pact between the builder of the Potala and the king of the **nagas**, subterranean creatures who resemble dragons – the earth could be used as long as a chapel was built in their honour. The temple is famed for the very old and detailed murals on the middle and top floors, but you'll need a torch if you want to study them in detail – the protective wire in front doesn't help. The top-floor pictures showing the stages of human life, the journey of the soul after death, and various legends, are somewhat esoteric, but the middle-floor murals, depicting the construction of the great monasteries of Sera and Drepung among others, are far more comprehensible.

The Jokhang

The **Jokhang** (大昭寺, *dàzhāosì*; daily 8am–6pm; ¥85) – sometimes called Tshuglakhang (Cathedral), and the holiest temple in the Tibetan Buddhist world – can be somewhat unprepossessing from afar, but get closer and you'll be swept up by the anticipation of the pilgrims and the almost palpable air of veneration. Inside, you're in for one of the most unforgettable experiences in Tibet; some visitors end up returning day after day.

King Songtsen Gampo built the Jokhang in the seventh century to house the **dowry** brought by his Nepalese bride, Princess Bhrikuti, including the statue known as the Akshobhya Buddha. This later changed places with the Jowo Sakyamuni statue from Princess Wencheng's dowry, which was initially installed in Ramoche temple (see p.912), and which is now regarded as Tibet's most sacred object. The **site** of the temple was decided by Princess Wencheng after consulting astrological charts, and confirmed by the king following a vision while meditating. However, construction was fraught with problems. Another vision revealed to the king and his queens was that beneath the land of Tibet lay a huge, sleeping demoness with her head in the east, feet to the west and heart beneath Lhasa. Only by building monasteries at suitable points to pin her to the earth, could construction of the Jokhang succeed. The king embarked on a scheme to construct twelve demon-suppressing temples: four around Lhasa, which included Trandruk (see p.923), to pin her at hips and shoulders; a set of four farther away, to pin her at elbows and knees; and four even more distant, to pin her hands and feet. When these were finished, construction of the Jokhang began.

The Jokhang stands 1km or so east of the Potala Palace, in the centre of the only remaining Tibetan enclave in the city, the **Barkhor** (八角街, *bājiaǒjiē*) area, a maze of cobbled alleyways between Beijing Dong Lu and Chingdol Dong Lu. If you're coming from the western side of town, the #2 or #3 minibus may come into Barkhor Square or – more likely – drop you about five minutes' walk away on Dosengge Lu or Beijing Dong Lu.

Pilgrims go in at the front, but the **foreign visitors' entrance** is further to your left as you look at the building. The best time to visit is in the morning, when most pilgrims do the rounds.

Inside the temple

The **main entrance** to the Jokhang is from **Barkhor Square** (八角街广场, *bājiaŏjiēguăngchăng*), which is to the west of the temple and full of stalls selling prayer flags, white scarves (*katag*), incense and all manner of religious souvenirs. Two bulbous incense burners in front of the temple send out juniper smoke as an offering to the gods, and the two walled enclosures here contain three ancient engraved pillars. The tallest is inscribed with the Tibetan-Chinese agreement of 821 AD and reads: "Tibet and China shall abide by the frontiers of which they are now in occupation. All to the east is the country of Great China; and all to the west is, without question, the country of Great Tibet. Henceforth on neither side shall there be waging of war or seizing of territory".

In front of the huge temple doors, a constant crowd of pilgrims prostrate themselves – you can hear the clack of the wooden protectors on their hands and the hiss as the wood moves along the flagstones when they lie flat on the ground. Head round the southern side to the visitors' entrance to enter the main courtyard, where ceremonies and their preparations take place. Rows of tiny butter lamps burn on shelves along the far wall, and it's a bustling scene as monks make butter statues and dough offerings and tend the lamps. Through a corridor in the north wall, with small chapels to left and right, you pass into the inner area of the temple. The central section, **Kyilkhor Thil**, houses statues galore, six of them considered particularly important. The most dramatic are the 6m-high Padmasambhava on the left, which dates from 1955, and the half-seated figure of Maitreya, the Buddha of the Future, to the right.

Devout pilgrims turn left to move clockwise and enter each chapel in turn to pray and make offerings. They don't hang around, though; stand still to admire the statues and you'll get trampled in the rush. Some of the wooden door frames and columns are original – the door frame of the Chapel of Chenresi, in the north, and the columns in front of the Chapel of Jowo Sakyamuni, in the east, were created by Niwari craftsmen from Nepal during the temple's early years. As with all temples in Tibet, it's often difficult to know exactly what you are looking at. Some of the statues are original, others were damaged during the Cultural Revolution and have been restored either slightly or extensively, and others are replicas; in any event, all are held in deep reverence by the pilgrims.

It's easy to feel overwhelmed in the crush, but if you manage only one chapel it should be the **Chapel of Jowo Sakyamuni** in the middle of the eastern, back wall of the temple. The 1.5m-high Sakyamuni is depicted at twelve years of age, with a sublimely beautiful golden face. Draped in heavy brocade and jewels, this is the most deeply venerated statue in Tibet. Although the Jokhang was originally built to house the statue, the Jowo Sakyamuni first stood in the temple of Ramoche until rumours of a Tang invasion late in the seventh century led to its removal to a hiding place in the Jokhang. During the reign of Trisong Detsen, the Bon opponents of Buddhism removed the statue and buried it, but it was found and sent out of Lhasa for safety. The statue was again buried during King Langdarma's attempt to annihilate Buddhism, but eventually returned to the Jokhang. Although there is a rumour that the original was destroyed in the eighteenth century by Mongol invaders, neither it nor the chapel was harmed during the

Cultural Revolution, and the statue is widely regarded as the original. Monks here keep the butter lamps topped up while the pilgrims move around the altar, bowing their heads to Jowo Sakyamuni's right leg and then his left.

By the time you reach the **upper floor**, you'll probably be punch-drunk; fortunately perhaps, there is less to detain you up here, although most of the chapels are now open after restoration. Of most interest is the **Chapel of Songtsen Gampo**, directly above the main entrance in the west wall and featuring a large statue of the king flanked by his two queens. Continue up the stairs in the southwest corner of the chapel to one fierce and one peaceful image of **Pelden Lhamo**, who is regarded as the protective deity of Tibet and is particularly popular with pilgrims.

From the temple **roof**, the views over Barkhor Square, into the temple courtyard and as far as the Potala Palace in the distance, are wonderful, and the golden statues even more impressive. You can get up to the roof using any of a number of staircases, located just to the right of the main entrance, in the far southeast corner of the temple itself or at the far end of the side courtyard to the right of the main entrance.

The Barkhor

Traditionally, pilgrims to Lhasa circled the city on two clockwise routes: an outer circuit called the Lingkhor, now vanished under two-lane highways and rebuilding, and the shorter **Barkhor** (八角街, *bājiaǒjiē*) circuit through the alleyways a short distance from the Jokhang walls. This maze of picturesque streets, a world away from the rest of Lhasa, has survived. It's now lined with the stalls of an outdoor market selling all manner of goods – saddles and stirrups, Chinese army gear, *thangkas*, jewellery, blankets, DVDs, carpets, tin trunks and pictures of lamas, to mention a fraction only. The many trinkets and "antiques" are, of course, fakes, made in Nepal, but the pilgrims are an amazing sight: statuesque Khampa men with their traditional knives and red-braided hair, decorated with huge chunks of turquoise; Amdo women dripping jewels with their hair in 108 plaits; and old ladies spinning their tiny prayer wheels and intoning mantras. The Barkhor circuit is most atmospheric in the early hours of the morning, before the sun has risen and stallholders have set up. That's when a feeling of devotion is prevalent, as the constant mumble of prayer and shuffle of prostrations emanate from the shadows cast by the lambent pre-dawn light.

The whole Barkhor area is worth exploring – with its huge wooden doors set in long, white walls and leading into hidden courtyards – but try not to miss **Tromzikhang market** to the north of the Jokhang; take the main alleyway into the Barkhor that leads off Beijing Dong Lu just east of Ramoche Lu and it's just down on your left. The two-storey modern building is a bit soulless, but nowhere else in the world can you see (or smell) so much yak butter in one place.

Rubbing up against the Jokhang's back wall, though easily missed behind the market stalls, are a further three temples hidden along the narrow, and fantastically preserved, **Sela Da Guoxiang** (色拉达果巷, *sèlādáguǒxiàng*). The first temple, closest to the Barkhor, houses a single giant prayer wheel – you'll hear the ringing of its bell before you see it – eagerly turned by a devoted scrum.

One other sight to seek out here is the **Ani Tsangkung Nunnery** (¥30) to the southeast of the Jokhang; you'll probably need to ask the way. With over a hundred nuns in residence, several of whom speak good English, there is a lively but devout atmosphere, especially around prayer time at 11am. A fabulous Chenresi in a glass case dominates the main chapel. From the back of the chapel, facing the main door, you can head right, round the outside, to visit the long, narrow room containing King Songtsen Gampo's meditation chamber in a pit at the end. Supposedly, his meditation altered the course of the Kyichu River when it looked likely to flood the construction of the Jokhang.

Ramoche

The three-storey, robust **Ramoche temple** (小昭寺, *xiǎozhāosì*; daily 9am–4.30pm; ¥30, plus up to ¥50/chapel for photographs) is small but intriguing, and second only in importance to the Jokhang. A short walk north of the Barkhor, on Xiao Zhaosi Lu between Beijing Dong Lu and Lingkuo Bei Lu, it was built in the seventh century by Songtsen Gampo's Chinese wife, Princess Wencheng, to house the Jowo Sakyamuni statue that she brought to Tibet. The statue later ended up in the Jokhang and was replaced by the Akshobhya Buddha, a representation of Sakyamuni at the age of 8. This much-revered statue was broken in two during the Cultural Revolution, with one part taken to China and narrowly saved from being melted down, while the other was later discovered on a factory scrapheap in Tibet. The statue in position today in the main shrine, the Tsangkhang at the back of the temple, is likely to be a copy.

While you're in the area, call in on the tiny **Tsepak Lakhang** to the south of Ramoche. The little entrance is just beside a huge incense burner, and, once inside, you pass along a small alley lined with a row of prayer wheels. There are two small chapels in this hugely popular temple, and the 55 friendly monks in residence chant their daily prayers around noon. You can walk the small circuit around the walls of Tsepak Lakhang, where the murals have been newly painted.

Norbulingka and the Tibet Museum

Situated in the west of town, on the route of the #2 minibus, **Norbulingka** (罗布林卡, *luóbùlínkǎ*; Jewel Park), the Summer Palace of the Dalai Lamas (daily 9am–6.30pm; ¥60), is not in the top league of Lhasa sights, but is worth a look if you've time on your hands and don't object to the steep entrance fee. However, if you're in Lhasa during the festivals of the Worship of the Buddha (July) or during Shotun, the Yoghurt Festival (Aug/Sept), when crowds flock here for picnics and to see masked dances and traditional opera, you should definitely make the trip. The park has been used as a recreation area by the Dalai Lamas since the time of the Seventh incarnation. The first palace to be built on site was the **Palace of the Eighth Dalai Lama**, constructed towards the end of the eighteenth century, and the closest to the entrance. This palace became the official summer residence to which all Dalai Lamas moved, with due ceremony, on the eighteenth day of the third lunar month.

Other buildings open to the public are the **Palace of the Thirteenth Dalai Lama** in the far northwest corner – beyond the appalling zoo – and, the highlight of the visit, the **New Summer Palace**, built in 1956 by the Fourteenth Dalai Lama; it was from here that he fled Lhasa in 1959. Visitors pass through the audience chamber, via an anteroom, to the meditation chamber, on to his bedroom and then into the reception hall dominated by a fabulously carved golden throne, before passing through to the quarters of the Dalai Lama's mother. Western plumbing and a radio sit beside fabulous *thangkas* and religious murals. It's all very sad and amazingly atmospheric, the forlorn rooms bringing home the reality of exile.

Opposite the Norbulingka, the **Tibet Museum** (西藏博物馆, *xīzàngbówùguǎn*; Tues–Sun, 10am–6pm; ¥35) offers curiosities to anyone who's had enough of religious iconography; there are some fascinating *thangkas* illustrating theories from Tibetan medicine, as well as stuffed Tibetan wildlife, Neolithic tools and the like. Its primary purpose, however, is propaganda, so it's best to take the captions with a pinch of salt.

Eating

Besides the vast number of **restaurants** in Lhasa, there are noodle places near Tromzikhang market, and bakeries outside the mosque in Barkhor selling nan breads. For **trekking food** try one of the supermarkets at the west end of Lingkuo Bei Lu – thanks to Lhasa's large military presence army rations of tinned beef and high-calorie energy bars crop up on many shelves. There is also a traditional **food market** – complete with live produce, as well as fruit, vegetables, tins and an impressive array of spices – just west of the chorten. For a more civilized picnic, both the *Dunya* and *New Mandala* turn out excellent lunchboxes.

Dunya Beijing Dong Lu ⓦwww.dunyarestaurant.com. Dutch-run and very civilized, but not particularly Tibetan. A diverse range of specials, good Western, Indian and Nepali food, and even half-decent Australian wine. Expect to pay around ¥60 a head. The tasty breakfast buffet is ¥25. The upstairs bar is one of the liveliest in the east end of Lhasa.

Gangki Corner of Mentsikhang Lu and Barkhor Square. This rooftop place is good value and has great views of the Jokhang. Very popular with Tibetans and often extremely busy. Main dishes cost ¥10–30; Tibetan tea and *tsampa* are also available. No toilets.

Hot Space (麻辣空间, *málàkōngjiān*) Luobulinka Lu/Beijing Dong Lu. An enormous hotpot restaurant just west of the chorten, this is in no way traditional, but their spicy broth is guaranteed to warm you up if the Tibetan chill is biting.

Lhasa Kitchen (拉萨厨房, *lāsàchúfáng*) Mentsikhang Lu, opposite the *Snowlands Hotel*. Ignore the terrible service, and focus instead on the excellent Tibetan cuisine: soup with *shaphali* (meat and vegetable patties) followed by *deysee* (rice, raisins and yoghurt), for example. Popular with tour groups – if you want to see your food in less than an hour get your order in before they do.

Namtso (纳木错餐厅, *nàmùcuòcāngtīng*) In the Banak Shol, Beijing Dong Lu. This excellent eatery serves a set breakfast of sausage or bacon, plus eggs, toast, hash browns and tomatoes for ¥25. Other crowd-pleasers include the vegetable gratin, spinach patties and spaghetti bolognese.

New Mandala (新满斋餐厅, *xīnmǎnzhāicāntīng*) On the southwest corner of Barkhor Square, and not to be confused with the restaurant next to the *Mandala* hotel, this two-level affair specializes in Nepali and Indian cuisine. The main draw is the rooftop seating area with a great view of the Jokhang and attendant military on the building opposite. The *saag aloo* is fantastic, as is the ginger tea.

Shangrila Restaurant (香格里拉餐厅, *xiānggélǐlācāntīng*) In the courtyard of the *Kirey*. Pleasant Tibetan furnishings, with a large menu, though the food is designed not to tax the palate of any of the tour groups who invade en masse every evening to watch Tibetan singing and dancing (7pm).

Sichuan restaurants Beijing Dong Lu. Perhaps it's preferable to go Tibetan, but it has to be admitted that their Chinese counterparts make tastier food – the three little places here do inexpensive and delicious Sichuan food and hotpots.

Snowlands Restaurant (雪域餐厅, *xuěyùcāntīng*) Mentsikhang Lu. Tour group-friendly, long-established eatery with bland curries and standard Western and Tibetan dishes.

Spinn Café (风转, *fēngzhǔan*) Qingu Xiang, Beijing Donglu ⓦwww.cafespin.com. Run by two cycling-mad expats – Kong from Hong Kong and Oat from Thailand – this is a nice enough place for a decent cup of coffee, the owners are a fount of knowledge and their website is regularly updated with the latest travel situation.

Tashi 1 and 2 Corner of Beijing Dong Lu and Mentsikhang Lu; in the *Kirey* hotel. Sister restaurants – *Tashi 2* is the rather more atmospheric of the two – that form the mainstay for budget travellers in Lhasa. Both offer the same small and inexpensive menu.

Tibet Summit Fine Art Café (顶蜂美艺术咖啡店, *dǐngfēngmeǐyìshùkāfeīdiàn*) 1 Danjielin Lu, off Zangyi Lu. American-owned venture aiming to promote the arts in Tibet by serving up what are arguably the best cakes and coffee in the city amidst overpriced works by local artists.

Drinking and entertainment

To the west of town there's a scattering of **bars** aimed at the well-off Chinese. Best here is the *Music Kitchen Café*, but there's no need to head out so far; drinking holes have sprung up far more centrally, including several opposite *Dunya* on Beijing Lu, and the alley running west from Mentsikhang Lu by the *Lhasa Kitchen* is ideal for bar hopping.

Sadly, there's not much chance to see traditional **Tibetan music**, **dance** or **opera**, unless you're here during a festival. There are occasional shows put on for tourists; ask in your hotel, check for notices in the *Lhasa* or *Tibet* hotels, or look in on the *Shangrila Restaurant* (see p.913).

The **cinema** on Yuthok Lu at the junction with Dosengge Lu sometimes has films from the West, but check whether they've been dubbed into Chinese before you bother.

Shopping

A major tourist activity in Lhasa is **shopping**. The main area for browsing is the **Barkhor**, where the better stuff is in the shops behind the stalls, but they're much more expensive than vendors outside. The vendors on the street outside the *Lhasa Hotel* have essentially the same range, but in smaller quantities, and they start off at even higher prices. A string of gift shops on Mentsikhang Lu sells jewellery, handmade paper and the like.

The search for **postcards** can be frustrating and expensive, as sets on offer at the main sights are generally pricey; those at the post office and the Xinhua Bookstores are the best value.

Finally, if you feel like doing some shopping *for* rather than *from* Tibetans, buy notebooks and pens to donate to an orphanage and give them to Neema at the *Snowlands Restaurant*. Alternatively, turn up at the orphanage itself, at 42 Beijing Xi Lu.

Books

While plenty of books have been written about Tibet, much that would be considered essential reading by Western audiences is simply not allowed or available in China – this includes almost all guide books (including this one. So while several decent coffee-table books of photographs are available from Xinhua bookstores, Tibet is pretty much the worst place you could possibly go to find books about Tibet. If you're interested in doing some background reading on the current situation and the country's history, begin at home; the book reviews on p.985 in Contexts should provide a good starting point.

For a Tibetan **novel** you can get hold of in Tibet, look for *The Secret Tale of Tesur House*, sold in the *Banak Shol* and the shop at the *Pentoc Hotel*. The first fiction translated from Tibetan into English, it's not a bad read, with a plot centred on gory murders and business intrigue. It's full of fascinating descriptions of Tibetan life and customs – the kind of minutiae that you won't find described elsewhere.

Carpets and paintings

If it's **carpets** you're after, visit **Khawachen**, at 103 Chingdol Xi Lu (Mon–Sat 9am–6.30pm; ⓣ0891/6333255, ⓦwww.innerasiarugs.com), on the route of the #2 minibus. This government-affiliated and US-financed organization offers the best selection in Lhasa and the chance to watch them being produced; they can also arrange to ship the merchandise home for you. Available in muted, traditional designs, plus some with a modern slant, the carpets range in size and price – from tens of dollars to well over a thousand. The **Lhasa Carpet Factory**, out of town on Chingdol Dong Lu (Mon–Fri 9am–1pm & 3.30–6pm, Sat 9am–1pm; ⓣ0891/6323447), is a bigger operation, where you can watch huge carpets being woven; an extensive range of traditional and modern patterns is available here, and shipping can be arranged. In town, the Shambhala carpet shop on Jiri Erxiang (right out of the *Kirey* and first right) has a selection of on-site crafted rugs and carpets which again can be shipped back home for you after purchase.

Tibetan **thangkas** (religious scrolls) and religious and secular paintings would appear to be obvious souvenirs, but many are of poor quality – best to spend some time browsing before you buy. The least expensive *thangkas* have a printed religious picture in the middle, while the better quality, higher-priced ones have a hand-painted image. Look carefully, though, at the quality of the painting itself: the best ones have finely drawn and highly detailed backgrounds, while the less skilled artists leave larger areas of the canvas blank, with less meticulously painted details. The asking prices are high – bargain hard. An excellent range of good-quality, hand-painted *thangkas* is available at the Tibet Traditional Art Gallery, just a shop, despite the name, next door to the Ramoche – expect prices to start at ¥3000.

Clothes

There are plenty of tailors in town, both Chinese and Tibetan, who can make traditional Tibetan or Western **clothes**; look on Beijing Dong Lu west of the *Yak Hotel*. A huge range of materials, from light, summer-weight stuff, to heavier, warmer textiles, is available. Prices depend on the material, but light jackets start at around ¥100, while skirts, trousers or a floor-length Tibetan woman's dress (*chuba*) cost ¥80 and up. Many places have samples made up and you can simply shop around until you find the style and material you want. From first measuring to collecting the finished item, usually takes 24 hours.

Trekking equipment

For rucksacks, sleeping bags and serious **hiking gear**, check out Outlook Outdoor Equipment on Beijing Dong Lu, opposite the *Kirey* (Ⓦwww.ontheway.com.cn). Export-quality Chinese sleeping bags cost anywhere from ¥80 to ¥600, while equipment is also available to rent, including tents,

Trekking Tibet

For the experienced hiker, Tibet offers plenty of enticing **trekking routes** – though you will need to negotiate for a guide and a travel agency to endorse your travel permit and accompany you for the entire duration of the trek. The popular Ganden–Samye trek (see box, p.920) has the advantages that both the start and finish points are relatively accessible from Lhasa and that it takes only three to four days. Also worth considering are treks to the cave hermitage of **Drak Yerpa** from Lhasa (allow a full day and be prepared to camp), and the five-day trek from Tingri to **Everest Base Camp** via Rongbuk. More challenging options include: the sixteen-day mammoth trek to the **Kangshung** face of Everest, exploring the valleys east of the mountain (the trip to second base camp and beyond on the mountain itself should only be tackled by experienced climbers); the 24-day circumnavigation of **Namtso Lake**, including the arduous exploration of the Shang Valley to the southwest; and the great thirty-day circuit from Lhatse to **Lake Dangra** up on the Chang Tang plateau.

Spring (April–June) and autumn (Sept–Nov) are the best **seasons** in which to trek, though cold-weather threats such as hypothermia and frostbite should be taken seriously even in these months. While trekking is possible at any time in the valleys, high altitudes become virtually impossible in the winter; anyone contemplating trekking at this time should be sure to check information about the terrain and likely conditions. During the wettest months (June–Sept), rivers are in flood, and crossing them can be difficult, even impossible. Once you start trekking, you get off the beaten track extremely quickly, and there is no infrastructure to support trekkers and no rescue service; you therefore need to be fit, acclimatized, self-reliant and prepared to do some research before you go. There are two essential books: *Tibet Handbook: a Pilgrimage Guide* by Victor Chan (Moon), and *Trekking in Tibet* by Gary McCue (Cordee), which is especially good for shorter day-treks that anyone can do without all the gear.

rucksacks, Karrimats and stoves. Nikko Outdoor Commodities on Mentsikhan Lu also has a good selection of gear at some of the best prices in town, with very helpful English-speaking staff.

Listings

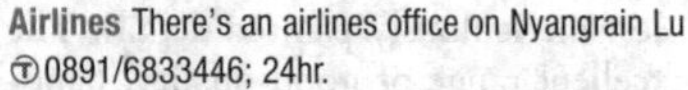

Airlines There's an airlines office on Nyangrain Lu ☎0891/6833446; 24hr.
Banks and exchange There are several branches of the Bank of China around town, but the main one is on Lingkuo Bei Lu, north of the Golden Yaks Statue (Mon–Fri 9am–1pm & 3.30–6pm). The branch on Beijing Dong Lu is conveniently located close to the Banak Shol (Mon–Fri 9.30am–6pm, Sat & Sun 11am–3pm).
Bike rental The *Snowlands* and *Pentoc* offer a small range of clunky bikes for rent at ¥30 a day. Bike shops on Beijing Dong Lu offer better bikes, often at better rates, but large deposits are required.
Consulates The Nepalese Consulate, 13 Norbulingka Lu (Mon–Fri 10am–noon; ☎0891/6830609), has a next-day visa service, for which you'll need to submit one passport photograph. You can get single-entry visas at Kodari (at the Zhagmu border, see p.939), but payment there has to be in US dollars.
Hospital First People's Hospital, Lingkuo Bei Lu (Mon–Fri 10am–12.30pm & 4–6pm; at weekends, emergencies only). It's better to go in the morning when more staff are available, and you'll need to take a Chinese translator.
Internet Cybercafés are not hard to find in Lhasa. The most convenient are next to the *Dong Cun Cuo Youth Hostel*, in the *Shangrila* bar, and in the *Bank Shol*, all on Beijing Dong Lu.
Mail and telephones The main post office is on Beijing Dong Lu, just east of the Potala Palace (daily 9am–8pm). Poste restante and international customs (Mon–Fri 9.30am–1pm & 3.30–6pm) is the counter facing you on the far left as you enter. Mail to be collected here should be addressed Poste Restante, Main Post Office, Lhasa, Tibet, China. Check both the book that lists mail received at the office and ask to see new mail. There's a charge of ¥1.5/item received. EMS collection is in the post office across the road from the Potala Palace.
Pharmacies Most are along Yuthok Lu around the junction with Dosengge Lu. There is a pharmacy specializing in Tibetan medicine on the north side of Barkhor Square. Again, you'll need a translator.
PSB Lingkuo Bei Lu and also Beijing Dong Lu (both Mon–Fri 9.30am–1pm & 3.30–7pm). While PSB offices should be the place to go for factual information about closed and open areas, the information is rarely reliable and frequently inconsistent from one office to the next. The office on Beijing Dong Lu is larger and handles permits and visa extensions.
Tour agencies These are all over town and offer much the same services, but the official agency, FIT, in the courtyards of the *Banak Shol* and opposite the *Snowlands Hotel,* is sometimes able to offer trips the others cannot.

Around Lhasa

Not only is Lhasa awash with enough sights to keep even the most energetic visitor busy for days, but also the major monasteries of **Sera**, **Drepung**, **Nechung** and **Ganden** are easily accessible from the city as half-day or day-trips. Indeed, Sera and Drepung have virtually been gobbled up in the urban sprawl that now characterizes Lhasa, while the trip to Ganden is a good chance to get out into the countryside. Morning visits to any of them are likely to be in the company of parties of devout pilgrims who'll scurry around the temples making their offerings before heading on to the next target. Follow on behind them and you'll visit all the main buildings; don't worry too much if you aren't sure what you are looking at – most of the pilgrims haven't a clue either. The monasteries are generally peaceful and atmospheric places where nobody minds you ambling at will, and sooner or later you're bound to come across some monks who want to practise their English. Nearby, the walled, combined village and monastery of **Samye** is the most ancient in Tibet, and a lively and interesting place to spend a day or two.

Sera Monastery

Sera Monastery (色拉寺, *sèlāsī*; Mon–Sat 9am–4pm; ¥50), 4km north of central Lhasa, will be included on most tour itineraries, but given that it is now well within with the city limits, an independent trip out by public transport is perfectly feasible; just take a **#5 minibus** from the southern end of Nyangrain Lu, or from the small minibus stand opposite the cinema on Yuthok Lu. A taxi will cost around ¥10–15. You'll either be dropped on the road, about 500m outside the white-walled monastery compound, or be taken along the track to the entrance. To get transport back, it's better to walk back out to the road. The last minibuses leave just after the end of the debating at about 5pm. Alternatively, you can cycle there – it's surprisingly close.

Founded in 1419 by Sakya Yeshe, one of the main disciples of Tsongkhapa, founder of the Gelugpa order, Sera is situated below a hermitage where the great man spent many years in retreat. Spared during the Cultural Revolution, the buildings are in good repair, although there is always a fair amount of ongoing building work. Pilgrims proceed on a clockwise circuit, visiting the three main **colleges** – Sera Me, Sera Ngag-Pa and Sera Je – and the main assembly hall, Tsokchen. All are constructed with chapels leading off a central hall and more chapels on an upper floor. They're great places to linger and watch the pilgrims rushing about their devotions. However, if you just want to catch the flavour of the most dramatic buildings, head straight up the hill from the main entrance.

Life in the great monasteries

Fifty years ago, there were still six great, functioning **Gelugpa monasteries**: Sera, Drepung and Ganden near Lhasa, plus Tashilunpo in Shigatse (see p.932), Labrang (see p.823) and Kumbum (see p.829). They each operated on a similar system to cope with the huge numbers of monks that were drawn to these major institutions from all over Tibet. In their heyday, Sera and Ganden had five thousand residents each and Drepung (possibly the largest monastery the world has ever known) had between eight and ten thousand.

Each monastery was divided into colleges, **dratsang**, which differed from each other in the type of studies undertaken. Each college was under the management of an abbot (*khenpo*), and a monk responsible for discipline (*ge-kor*). Attached to each college were a number of houses or *khangsten*, where the monks lived during their time at the monastery. Usually, these houses catered for students from different geographical regions, and admission to the monastery was controlled by the heads of the houses to whom aspirant monks would apply. Each college had its own assembly hall and chapels, but there was also a main assembly hall where the entire community could gather.

Not every member of the community spent their time in scholarly pursuits. Communities the size of these took huge amounts of organization, and the largest monasteries also maintained large estates worked by serfs. About half the monks might be engaged in academic study while the other half worked at administration, the supervision of the estate work and the day-to-day running of what was essentially a small town.

The most obvious feature of these **monasteries today** is their emptiness; hundreds of monks now rattle around in massive compounds built for thousands. Such has been the fate of religious establishments under the Chinese and the flow of lamas into exile that there are now questions about the quality of the Buddhist education available at the monasteries inside Tibet. Monks and nuns need to be vetted and receive Chinese-government approval before they can join a monastery or convent, and although there are persistent rumours of tourists being informed on by monks, it's also apparent that both monks and nuns have been, and continue to be, at the forefront of open political opposition to the Chinese inside Tibet.

After a couple of hundred metres, you'll reach the **Tsokchen**, Sera's largest building, built in 1710. The hall is supported by over a hundred columns, and it's here, between statues of the Fifth and Thirteenth Dalai Lamas, that you'll find the main statue of Sakya Yeshe, the founder of the monastery. The Sakya Yeshe statue is a reproduction of the original one in Sera Ngag-Pa college. When there were plans to move the original to the Tsokchen, the story goes that the statue itself said that it wished to stay in the college, so a copy was made.

At the top of the path, the walled and shady **debating courtyard** is definitely worth a visit at 3.30pm, when the monks assemble in small animated groups to practise their highly stylized debating skills, involving much posturing, clapping and stamping. They're used to visitors – indeed, it's hard not to feel the whole circus is put on for tourists – and there seems to be no problem about taking photographs.

To the left of the courtyard, the college of **Sera Je** is the best to visit if you manage only one. Its spacious assembly hall is hung with fine *thangkas*, but the focus for pilgrims here is the Hayagriva Chapel (Hayagriva or Tamdrin, "the Horse-Headed One", is the protective deity of Sera), reached via an entrance in the left-hand wall.

If you're feeling energetic, take the path up the hillside, from behind the Tsokchen (follow the telegraph wires) to **Choding Khang** (Tsongkhapa's Hermitage), which is a reconstruction of the original – his meditation cave is a bit farther up. There are splendid views over Lhasa from here.

Drepung and Nechung monasteries

Once the largest monastery in the world, **Drepung Monastery** was an immediate success, and a year after opening, there were already two thousand monks in residence, and ten thousand by the time of the Fifth Dalai Lama (1617–82). To reach Drepung, 8km west of Lhasa, catch the **#3 minibus** from the stand at the junction of Dossenge Lu and Beijing Dong Lu. It may drop you on the main road (¥2), leaving you with a thirty-minute walk, or carry on up the hill to the entrance of the massive, walled monastery (¥3). Minibuses come back to Lhasa infrequently from the monastery itself, and it's better to walk down the hill to Nechung and then out to the main road to pick up transport there. Easily combined with a trip to Drepung is the eerie **Nechung Monastery**, less than 1km southeast via a well-trodden path.

Drepung Monastery

Drepung Monastery (哲蚌寺, *zhébàngsì*; daily 9am–6pm, chapels closed noon–3pm; ¥50) was founded in 1416 by Jamyang Choje, a leading disciple of Tsongkhapa. Although it has been sacked three times – in 1618 by the king of Tsang, in 1635 by the Mongols, and in the early eighteenth century by the Dzungars – there was relatively little damage during the Cultural Revolution.

Drepung is a huge place, and it's easy to attempt to see everything and get overloaded. One thing to make sure to do is to go up on to the **roofs** – the views across the Kyichu Valley are splendid – and it's definitely worth spending a bit of time just wandering the alleyways, through courtyards, and past ancient doorways.

The easiest way to find your way around is to follow the clockwise pilgrim circuit. This leads left from the entrance up to the grand and imposing **Ganden Palace**, built in 1530 by the Second Dalai Lama, and home to the Dalai Lamas until the Fifth incarnation moved to the Potala Palace. The private quarters of the Dalai Lama are behind the balcony at the top right-hand side of the building, but there's little to see inside.

The next stop is the **Tsokchen**, the main assembly hall, its entrance via a small door on the left-hand side, facing the building. Its roof supported by over 180 solid wooden columns, the hall is the highlight of Drepung, a space of awesome size and scale. The *thangkas* and brocade hangings add to the incredible ambience, with dust motes highlighted by the rays of the sun slanting down from the high windows. The main chapel at the rear of the hall is the **Buddha of the Three Ages Chapel**, the most impressive in Drepung, with statues crammed together in such profusion the mind reels. The central figures are Sakyamuni with his two main disciples, Shariputra and Maudgalyayana.

There are two upper storeys, both definitely worth a visit. On the next floor up, the **Maitreya Chapel** contains the head and shoulders of a massive statue of Maitreya at a young age, commissioned by Tsongkhapa himself, while the **Tara Chapel** contains a version of the Kanjur, sacred Buddhist scriptures, dating from the time of the Fifth Dalai Lama. In the middle of the volumes, which are loose leaves stored between wooden planks and wrapped in brocade, sits a statue of Prajnaparamita, the Mother of Buddhas; the amulet on her lap is said to contain a tooth of Tsongkhapa's. Of the three chapels on the top floor, the highlight is the stunning statue of the head of Maitreya, boasting exquisite gold ornamentation.

Behind the Tsokchen, there's a tiny **Manjusri Temple**, obligatory for the pilgrims who make offerings to the image of the Bodhisattva of Wisdom, carved out of a large rock. The remainder of the circuit is taken up with the **Ngag-Pa College**, to the northwest of the Tsokchen, and **Loseling**, **Gomang** and **Deyang colleges** to the southeast. They all have items of interest – the stuffed goat at the entrance to the Protector Chapel on the upper storey of Loseling, the cosy Deyang, and the wonderful array of statues in the central chapel of Gomang – but don't feel too bad if you've had enough by now. The main steps of the Tsokchen, looking across the huge courtyard in front of the building, are a good place to sit and admire the view and watch the comings and goings of the other visitors.

Nechung Monastery

Nechung Monastery (乃琼寺, *nǎiqióngsì*; daily 9am–6pm, chapels closed noon–3pm; ¥10) was, until 1959, the seat of the **state oracle of Tibet**. By means of complex ritual and chanting, an oracle enters a trance and becomes the mouthpiece of a god, in this case Dorje Drakden, the chief minister of the main spiritual protector of Tibet, Pehar Gyalpo; no important decisions are made by the Dalai Lama or government without reference to Drakden. The original shrine on the site was built in the twelfth century, and the Fifth Dalai Lama built the temple later. It was much damaged during the Cultural Revolution, but restoration work is now proceeding quickly. The state oracle fled Tibet in the footsteps of the Dalai Lama in 1959, having questioned Dorje Drakden himself as to what he should do. He died in 1985 in Dharamsala, but a successor has been identified there.

Nechung's spookiness begins outside. The beggars are abject, and the villagers seem sullen. Inside you are confronted by a panoply of gore – the doors are decorated with images of flayed human skins and the murals in the courtyard depict torture by devils and people drowning in a sea of blood. In the chapels, unusually subdued supplicants are more likely to offer booze than apples. Bloodshot eyes sunk into the sockets of grinning skulls seem to follow you around.

Upstairs, the main room is the audience chamber, where the Dalai Lama would come to consult the oracle. The inner chapel is dedicated to Tsongkhapa, whose statue is between those of his two main disciples, Gyeltsab Je and Khedrup Je. In the only chapel at roof level is the statue of Padmasambhava that, though it dates from the early 1980s, is gloriously bedecked in old Chinese brocade. It's worth the climb up, if only to escape the air of sinister corruption below.

Try to visit on the 8th, 15th or 30th days of the Tibetan lunar month, when the faithful seek special favour.

Ganden Monastery

Farther than the other main temples, **Ganden Monastery** (甘丹寺, *gāndānsì*; daily 9am–4pm; ¥45) is 45km east of Lhasa, the final 6km of the journey along a winding track off the Lhasa–Sichuan Highway. It is also the most dramatically situated, high up on the Gokpori Ridge with excellent views over the surrounding countryside. There is a **pilgrim bus**, which leaves Lhasa daily at 6.30am from the west side of Barkhor Square (3–4hr; ¥20) and returns at 2pm, though, of course, foreigners are currently banned from this.

Founded by Tsongkhapa himself in 1410 on a site associated with King Songtsen Gampo and his queens, the main hall was not completed until 1417, two years before Tsongkhapa died after announcing his disciple, Gyeltsab Je, as the new **Ganden Tripa**, the leader of the Gelugpa order. The appointment is not based on reincarnation but on particular academic qualifications. The Chinese have always particularly targeted Ganden, possibly because it is the main seat of the Dalai Lama's order, and what you see today is all reconstruction.

While it is possible, as always, to follow the pilgrims through the various buildings on their circuit, the highlight is the imposing **Serdung Lhakhang**, on the left side as you follow the main path north from the car park. This temple contains a huge gold and silver chorten. The original contained the body of Tsongkhapa, who was said to have changed into a 16-year-old youth when he died. The body was embalmed and placed in the chorten and, when the Red Guards broke it open during the Cultural Revolution, they supposedly found the body perfectly preserved, with the hair and fingernails still growing. Only a few pieces of skull survived the destruction and they are in the reconstructed chorten. Up the hill and to the right, the **Sertrikhang** houses the golden throne of Tsongkhapa and all later Ganden Tripas; the bag on the throne contains the yellow hat of the present Dalai Lama.

Be sure to allow time to walk the **Ganden kora**, the path around the monastery. The views are startling, and it takes about an hour to follow round. There is a basic guesthouse at the monastery, used mostly by people heading off on the Ganden–Samye trek (see box below).

Samye

A visit to **SAMYE**, on the north bank of the Tsangpo River, is a highlight of Tibet. A unique monastery and walled village rolled into one, it's situated in wonderful scenery and, however you arrive, the journey is splendid. You can

The Ganden–Samye trek

Though popular, the **Ganden–Samye trek** is no less serious or demanding than other treks. The route, which takes four days to complete, crosses the mountains that divide the **Kyichu Valley** from that of the Tsangpo and travels through high mountain passes and alpine pasture to the dry, almost desert-like countryside around Samye. The trek goes by **Hebu** village (three hours south of Ganden and a good place to hire yaks and guides) and involves camping out or sleeping in caves or nomad encampments, long climbs to the Jooker La and Sukhe La passes, and some deep-river wading.

climb the sacred Hepo Ri to the east of the complex for excellent views (1hr); it was here that Padmasambhava is said to have subdued the local spirits and won them over to Buddhism.

The monastery

Tibet's first monastery, **Samye** (桑木耶寺, *sāngmùyēsì*) was founded in the eighth century during King Trisong Detsen's reign, with the help of the Indian masters Padmasambhava and Shantarakshita, whom he had invited to Tibet to help spread the Buddhist faith. The first Tibetan Buddhist monks were ordained here after examination and are referred to as the "Seven Examined Men". Over the years, Samye has been associated with several of the schools of Tibetan Buddhism – Padmasambhava's involvement in the founding of the monastery makes it important in the Nyingma school, and later it was taken over by the Sakya and Gelugpa traditions. Nowadays, followers of all traditions worship here, and Samye is a popular destination for Tibetan pilgrims, some of whom travel for weeks to reach it.

The design of the extensive monastery complex, several hundred metres in diameter, is of a giant **mandala**, a representation of the Buddhist universe, styled after the Indian temple of Odantapuri in Bihar. The main temple, the **utse**, represents Buddha's palace on the summit of Mount Meru, the mythical mountain at the centre of the Buddhist universe. The four continents in the vast ocean around Mount Meru are represented by the *lingshi* temples, a couple of hundred metres away at the cardinal points, each flanked by two smaller temples, *lingtren*, representing islands in the ocean. The *utse* is surrounded by four giant chortens, each several storeys high, at the corners, and there are *nyima* (sun) and *dawa* (moon) temples to the north and south, respectively. A renovated enclosing wall, topped by 1008 tiny chortens with gates at the cardinal points, flanks the whole complex. This sounds hugely ordered, but the reality is far more confusing and fun. Samye has suffered much damage and restoration over the years; today, you'll find the temples dotted among houses, barns and animal pens, with only a few of the original 108 buildings on the site remaining in their entirety.

The utse

A grand, six-story construction, the **utse** (daily 9am–12.30pm & 3–5pm; ¥40) needs a couple of hours to be seen thoroughly. Be sure to take a torch as there are some good murals tucked away in shadowy corners.

The main assembly hall dominates the first floor, with fine, old mandalas on the high ceiling. On either side of the entrance to the adjoining main chapel are statues of historical figures associated with the monastery. Those on the left include Shantarakshita, Padmasambhava (said to be a good likeness of him), Trisong Detsen and Songtsen Gampo. The impressive main chapel, **Jowo Khang**, is reached through three tall doorways and is home to a Sakyamuni statue showing Buddha at the age of 38. To the left of the assembly hall a small temple, **Chenresi Lhakhang**, houses a gorgeous statue of Chenresi with an eye meticulously painted on the palm of each of his thousand hands – if you look at nothing else in Samye, search this out. To the right is the **Gonkhang**, a protector chapel, with all the statues heavily and dramatically draped. Most of the deities here were established as the demons of the Bon religion and were adopted by Buddhism as the fierce protectors – the chapel is an eerie place, imbued with centuries' worth of fear.

Although the first floor is the most striking, the upper storeys are also worth a look. The **second floor** is an open roof area, where monks and local people carry out the craftwork needed for the temple. The highlight of the **third floor** is the **Quarters of the Dalai Lama**, consisting of a small anteroom, a throne room and a bedroom. A securely barred, glass-fronted case in the bedroom is stuffed full of fantastic relics, including Padmasambhava's hair and walking stick, a Tara statue that is reputed to speak, and the skull of the Indian master Shantarakshita. The Tibetan pilgrims take this room very seriously, and the crush of bodies may mean you can't linger as long as you would like. From the **fourth floor** up, you'll see only recent reconstruction, but the views from the balconies are extensive.

The surrounding buildings

The rest of the buildings in the complex are in varying stages of renovation. Unashamedly modern, the four coloured **chortens** are each slightly different, and visitors love or hate them. There are internal stairs and tiny interior chapels, but generally they are more dramatic from a distance. It's difficult to locate the outer temples accurately, and many are still awaiting renovation – some serve as barns and stables, others show the effects of the Cultural Revolution. The most finely worked murals in Samye are in **Mani Lhakhang**, now a chapel in a house compound in the northwest of the complex, but the occupants are happy for visitors to look around.

Practicalities

The Lhasa–Tsetang road runs along the south bank of the Tsangpo and is served by public transport from both ends. To reach the monastery, you'll need to cross the river via the **Samye ferry**, 33km from Tsetang and 150km from Lhasa. Ferries leave when full and are more frequent in the morning, but run until mid-afternoon. The crossing (¥10) is highly picturesque and takes an hour or more as the boats wind their way among the sandbanks inhabited by Brahmini ducks, grebes and plovers. On the other side, tractors (45min; ¥5) and trucks (30min; ¥3) ply the bumpy 8km to Samye through rolling, deforested sand dunes, newly planted here and there with willows. If you want to make life easier for yourself, you can take the bus from Barkhor Square (¥40); it leaves between 6am and 8am, returning at 2pm. The small, white-painted chortens carved out of the hillside about halfway along mark the place where King Trisong Detsen met Padmasambhava when he came to Samye in the eighth century. **Leaving**, a very useful truck departs from the front of the *utse* each morning at 8am to connect with the ferry and a Lhasa-bound bus on the other side of the river. In addition, local tractors and trucks run until mid-afternoon, but you may well have to wait at the ferry and on the other side of the river for connections.

The only **place to stay** at Samye is the guesthouse next to the *utse*, which provides comfortable, cheap dorm accommodation (❶, dorm beds ¥20). The monastery **restaurant** is just north of the *utse*, but a tastier option is the newer establishment opposite the east reception office near the east gate.

Tsetang and around

The town of **Tsetang**, southeast of Lhasa and just south of the Tsangpo River, and the nearby valleys of **Yarlung** and **Chongye**, are steeped in ancient history. Legend claims the first Tibetans originated on the slopes of Gongpo Ri to the east of Tsetang, and that the Yarlung Valley was where the first king of Tibet descended from the heavens to earth upon a sky-cord. This king then fathered the first royal dynasty, many members of which are buried in the nearby **Chongye Valley**. The Yarlung Valley was also where, in the fourth century, the first Buddhist scriptures fell from the sky upon the first king's palace at Yumbulakhang.

Tsetang is the base for a trip to **Lhamo Lhatso**, a sacred lake 115km to the northeast, where it's reputed that visions appearing on the surface of the water contain prophecies. Regents searching for the next incarnations of high lamas come here for clues, and Dalai Lamas have traditionally visited for hints about the future. From the nearest town, Gyatsa, it's a five-hour walk up to the lake, so you'll have to negotiate with your guide whether to camp or make the long return journey in a single day.

Tsetang

There is little to recommend an extended stay in the town of **TSETANG** (泽当, *zédāng*), administrative centre of Lhoka province, a region stretching from the Tsangpo down to the Bhutan border. However, Tsetang is largely unavoidable as a base for explorations of the area.

Heading south from the main traffic intersection along Naidong Lu, take a narrow left turn through the small, bustling market into the **Tibetan area** of town, a typical jumble of walled compounds swarming with unwelcoming dogs and children scrapping in the dust. The first – and largest – monastery you'll come to is **Ganden Chukorlin** (¥45), now bright and gleaming from restoration, having been used as a storeroom for many years. It was founded in the mid-eighteenth century on the site of an earlier monastery, and there are good views of the Tibetan quarter from the roof. At the nearby fourteenth-century **Narchu Monastery**, restoration is less complete, but it's worth stopping by for the three unusual, brown-painted Sakyamuni statues on the altar. A little farther up the hill, the **Sanarsensky Nunnery** was one of the first of its kind in Tibet. It was founded in the fourteenth century in the Sakya tradition, later becoming a Gelugpa establishment.

Practicalities

Daily public **buses** leave Lhasa between 6am and 8am from Barkhor Square and run as far as the Samye ferry point (4hr). You'll then need to pick up another bus or a minibus for the remaining 33km on to Tsetang – it's a bit hit-and-miss, but you shouldn't have to wait more than an hour or so. Alternatively, direct **minibuses** leave the main bus station in Lhasa for Tsetang from 8am onwards (3hr). Tsetang's bus station is about 500m west of the main traffic intersection in town.

Unfortunately, **accommodation** in Tsetang is neither particularly good nor cheap (typically costing over ¥500 for a double room). Turn right at the intersection on to Naidong Lu past the post office and numerous restaurants and you'll come to the only comparatively inexpensive hotel that will take foreigners, the *Postal House* (➍), though with dingy rooms and sullied corridors, it's far from a bargain. Continue down the road to clean and modern, if rather pricey, *Tsetang Hotel* (☎0893/21899; ➑). Naidong Lu itself is lined with **bars** and **restaurants**.

The Yarlung Valley

Though the **Yarlung Valley** (雅鲁鲁流域, *yǎlǔlǔliúyù*) is renowned as the seat of the first Tibetan kings, these days it is the dramatically sited and picturesque Yumbulakhang, the first Tibetan palace, which draws visitors to the area.

Trandruk Monastery

The small but significant **Trandruk Monastery** (昌珠寺, *chāngzhūsì*; ¥70), 7km south of Tsetang, is a grand and imposing structure. One of the earliest Buddhist temples in Tibet, Trandruk was built in the seventh century during the reign of King Songtsen Gampo and is one of the twelve Demon-Suppressing Temples (see p.909) – Trandruk anchors the demoness's left shoulder to the earth. Legend tells how the site chosen for Trandruk was covered by a large lake containing a five-headed dragon. King Songtsen Gampo emerged from a period of meditation with such power that he was able to summon a supernatural falcon to defeat the dragon and drink up all the water of the lake, leaving the earth ready for Trandruk (meaning Falcon-Dragon). Damaged during the Bon reaction against Buddhism in the ninth century, and again by Dzungar invaders in the eighteenth century, the temple then suffered the loss of many highly prized religious relics and objects following the Chinese invasion. Its remaining glory is the **Pearl Thangka**, an image of King Songtsen Gampo's wife, Princess Wencheng, as the White Tara, created from thousands of tiny pearls meticulously sewn onto a pink background. This is in the central chapel upstairs, which also houses an original statue of Padmasambhava at the age of 8.

Yumbulakhang

From afar, the fortress temple of **Yumbulakhang** (雍布拉康, *yōngbùlākāng*; ¥70), 12km south of Tsetang, appears dwarfed by the scale of the Yarlung Valley. But once you get close and make the thirty-minute climb up the spur on which it is perched, the drama of the position and the airiness of the site are apparent. Widely regarded as the work of the first king of Tibet, Nyatri Tsenpo, when he arrived in Yarlung, the original Yumbulakhang would have been over two thousand years old and the oldest building in Tibet when it was almost totally destroyed during the Cultural Revolution. The present building is a 1982 reconstruction in two parts, with a small, two-storey chapel and an 11m-high tower. The lower floor of the chapel is dedicated to the early Tibetan kings: Nyatri Tsenpo is to the left and Songtsen Gampo to the right of the central Buddha statue. The delightful and unusual upper-storey chapel, with Chenresi as the central image, is built on a balcony. Some of the modern murals up here show legendary events in Tibetan history; look out on the left for Nyatri Tsenpo and for the Buddhist scriptures descending from heaven. The energetic can ascend by ladders almost to the top of the tower where King Nyatri Tsenpo supposedly meditated. The deep, slit windows at knee level mean the views aren't that wonderful, however; for the best scenery, take a walk up to the ridge behind the temple.

The Chongye Valley

From Tsetang it's a bumpy 27km south along unsurfaced roads through the attractive Chongye Valley to the village of **CHONGYE** (阱结, *jǐngyiē*), a sleepy little place but expanding with plenty of new buildings. There are a couple of restaurants and a basic guesthouse here, which you'll need to ask to find. On the way, you'll pass the **Tangboche Monastery**. However, the target for most visitors, the **Tombs of the Kings**, is around a kilometre farther south from Chongye. The entire valley is an agricultural development area and the patchwork of fields is interspersed with irrigation work. Be warned, though, that there's no public transport out here from Tsetang, and very little traffic either.

Tangboche Monastery

On the east side of the valley, about 20km southeast of Tsetang, **Tangboche Monastery** sits at the base of the hill and is somewhat difficult to spot among the village houses. Founded in the eleventh century, it was said to have hosted the great Tsongkhapa, originator of the Gelugpa tradition, three centuries later. Take a torch so you can really appreciate the most interesting features – genuine old murals, commissioned in 1915 by the Thirteenth Dalai Lama, are too numerous to list. Look out in particular for Pelden Lhamo on the left as you enter, and, on the right-hand wall, Padmasambhava, Trisong Detsen and Shantarakshita. The artistry and detail of subject and background make an interesting comparison with some of the more modern painting you'll see in Tibet. A couple of hundred metres up the hill is the **hermitage** where the scholar **Atisha** spent some time in the eleventh century. It's small, recently renovated and, not surprisingly, dominated by rather lurid images of the Indian master.

The Tombs of the Kings

One kilometre south of Chongye, the **Tombs of the Kings** are scattered over a vast area on and around the slopes of Mura Ri. Some are huge, up to 200m in length and 30m high. The body of each king was buried along with statues, precious objects and, some sources suggest, live servants. Some of the greatest kings of the Yarlung dynasty were interred here, although there is disagreement over the precise number of tombs – some sources claim it's 21, but far fewer are visible, and there is uncertainty about which tomb belongs to which king.

For the best view of the entire area, climb the largest tomb, **Bangso Marpo** (Red Tomb), belonging to **Songtsen Gampo**, just beside the road that heads south along the valley; it's easily identifiable by the chapel on the top. Songtsen Gampo, supposedly embalmed and incarcerated in a silver coffin, was entombed with huge numbers of precious gems, gifts from neighbouring countries (India sent a golden suit of armour), his own jewelled robes and objects of religious significance, all of which were looted long ago. The cosy chapel (¥10), originally built in the twelfth century, has central statues of Songtsen Gampo, his wives and principal ministers, Gar and Thonmi Sambhota.

Looking east from this viewpoint, the large tomb straight ahead belongs to Songtsen Gampo's grandson, **Mangsong Mangtsen** (646–676), who became king at the age of 4. The tomb some distance to the left is that of **Tri Ralpachan** (805–836), and the nearby enclosure contains an ancient pillar that records the events of his reign and is constructed on top of a stone turtle symbolizing the foundation of the universe. Originally, every tomb had one of these pillars on top, but the others have long since disappeared.

The ruins of **Chingwa Tagste Dzong**, perched high on the mountainside to the west, give an idea of the scale of the fortress and capital of the early Yarlung kings before Songtsen Gampo moved to Lhasa. To the left, the monastery of **Riwo Dechen** is visible, and a rough road means you can drive to within ten minutes' walk of this thriving Gelugpa community of around eighty monks. Originally founded in the fifteenth century, it was later expanded by the Seventh Dalai Lama and restored in the mid-1980s. There are three main chapels, the central one dominated by a large Tsongkhapa figure.

Tsurphu and Namtso

One of the most rewarding and popular trips in Tibet is to **Namtso Lake**, around 230km northwest of Lhasa, taking in **Tsurphu Monastery** on the way. This can be done on a two-night/three-day jaunt from Lhasa by jeep.

Tsurphu Monastery

Some 70km or so northeast of Lhasa, **Tsurphu Monastery** (楚布寺, *chŭbùsī*; daily 9am–1pm; ¥45), set at an altitude of 4480m, is a couple hours' jeep ride or a **pilgrims' bus** (daily between 7am and 8am; ¥25) away from the western end of Barkhor Square. The monastery is the seat of the **Karmapa Lama**, though it's a seat that's pretty cold these days as the present incumbent, the Seventeenth, Urgyen Trinley Dorge, fled to India in 1999. Identified in 1992 at the age of 7, Urgyen is the second holiest Tibetan after the Dalai Lama and seems charismatic and able; he's regarded by many in the government in exile as a natural successor for the role of leader when the Dalai Lama dies.

Founded in the twelfth century by Dusun Khenyapa, the Karmapa order is a branch of the Kagyupa tradition, where members are known as the **Black Hats** after the Second Karmapa was presented with one by Kublai Khan. Most powerful during the fifteenth century, when they were close to the ruling families of the time, they were eventually eclipsed in 1642 when the Fifth Dalai Lama and the Gelugpa order, aided by the Mongol army, gained the ascendancy. The Karmapa were the first order to institute the system of reincarnated lamas, tulkus, a tradition later adopted by the Gelugpa school.

Tsurphu is still undergoing reconstruction after being damaged in the years after the Chinese invasion. The solid **Zhiwa Tratsang** has a splendidly ornate gold roof and houses the main assembly hall, dominated by statues of Sakyamuni and a chorten containing the relics of the Sixteenth Karmapa Lama, who played a major part in establishing the order overseas and died in Chicago in 1981. The murals here depict the successive Karmapa lamas. The festival of **Saga Dawa**, on the 15th day of the fourth lunar month, usually in May or June, is especially fine at Tsurphu, as the massive new *thangka*, completed in recent years, is displayed at this time.

A visit to the monastery can be exhausting, as it's at a considerably higher altitude than Lhasa. In addition, the clockwise path, the **kora**, climbs steeply up the hill behind the monastery from the left of the temple complex and circles around high above and behind the monastery before descending on the right. The views are great and the truly fit can even clamber to the top of the ridge, but you need to allow two to three hours for the walk.

There's little reason to stay at Tsurphu unless you're trekking in the area, although there is a basic monastery **guesthouse** (❶) – you'll need to take your own sleeping bag, food and candles.

Damxhung and Namtso

If you're heading up to Namtso, you'll need to continue on the main highway past the Yangbajing turning for another 80km to **DAMXHUNG** (当雄, *dāngxióng*; 4360m), a bleak truck-stop town. The road is good, and the awesome Nyanchen Tanglha mountain range to the north is dramatically topped by the peak of Nyanchen Tanglha itself (7117m). Minibuses bound for these two places leave Lhasa from just east of the *Yak Hotel* around 7am each morning (3–4hr; ¥30). The turning north to Namtso is about halfway through the town, where a large concrete bridge crosses the river towards the mountains.

For **accommodation** in Damxhung, there are several unmemorable places, including the noisy and basic *Tang Shung Shey* (❶), opposite the new petrol station at the far end of town. In front stands the cavernous but atmospheric Muslim **restaurant**, *Ching Jeng*, an inexpensive change from yak meat and Nepalese curry, and there are plenty of Chinese spots around.

Namtso

Set at 4700m and frozen over from November to May, **Namtso** (纳木错, *nàmùcuò*; Sky Lake) is 70km long and 30km wide, the second largest saltwater lake in China (only Qinghai Hu is bigger; see p.831). The scenery comes straight from a dream image of Tibet, with snowcapped mountains towering behind the massive lake and yaks grazing on the plains around nomadic herders' tents.

From Damxhung, it takes around two hours to pass through the Nyanchen Tanglha mountain range at Lhachen La (5150m) and descend to **Namtso Qu**, the district centre numbering just a couple of houses at the eastern end of the lake. Here you'll be charged an entrance fee of ¥85. The target of most visitors is **Tashi Dor Monastery**, considerably farther west (a hefty 42km from Lhachen La), tucked away behind two massive red rocks on a promontory jutting into the lake. At Tashi Dor (¥10), a small Nyingma monastery is built around a cave, and there's a dirt-floored **guesthouse** (❶) between the monastery and lake. It's a glorious site, but facilities are limited – bring your own food and torches. Although some bedding is provided, you'll be more comfortable in your own sleeping bag, and your own stove and fuel would be an advantage. You can walk around the rock at the end of the promontory and also climb to the top for even more startling views. For true devotees, a circuit of the lake can be attempted, though this takes twenty days and involves camping on the way.

The old southern road and Gyantse

The road west from Lhasa divides at the Chusul Bridge and most vehicles follow the paved Friendship Highway along the course of the Yarlung Tsangpo to Shigatse. However, there is an alternative route, the longer but extremely picturesque **old southern road** that heads southwest to the shores of **Yamdrok Tso**, before turning west to **Gyantse** and then northwest to Shigatse – it is this route that most tour groups follow. Expect around six or seven hours' driving time from Lhasa to Gyantse in a good jeep, but day-trips to Yamdrok Tso from Lhasa are feasible.

Yamdrok Tso

From Chusul Bridge, on the western outskirts of Lhasa, the southern road climbs steeply up to the Kampa La Pass (4794m); at the top, a car park offers stunning views of the turquoise waters of the sacred **Yamdrok Tso** (羊卓雍错, *yángzhuóyōngcuò*), the third largest lake in Tibet. It's a good place to take a picture, and there are plenty of Tibetans armed with baby goats, yaks and Tibetan Mastiffs – dogs traditionally used by nomads to fend off wolves – who will be only too happy to pose with you, for a small fee. It is said that if the lake ever dries up then Tibet itself will no longer support life – a tale of heightened importance now that Yamdrok Tso, which has no inflowing rivers to help keep it topped up, is powering a controversial hydroelectric scheme. From the pass, the road descends to Yamtso village before skirting the northern and western shores amid wild scenery dotted with a few tiny hamlets, yaks by the lakeside and small boats on the water.

On the western side of the lake, 57km beyond the Kampa La Pass, the dusty village of **Nakartse** (4500m) is the birthplace of the mother of the Great Fifth Dalai Lama. There is basic **accommodation** in the village, but few tours overnight here, preferring to push on to Gyantse or Shigatse – though most do stop for lunch. There are several Chinese **restaurants**, but the favourite with visitors is the **Tibetan restaurant** with tables in a tiny courtyard, hidden away in the middle of the village, where you can eat rice with potato and meat curry (they fish out the meat for vegetarians) under the watchful eyes of local dogs. Jeep drivers usually come here; otherwise, look for the tourist vehicles parked outside.

Yamdrok Tso has many picturesque islands and inlets visible from the road, and there's a seven-day **circular trek** from Nakartse exploring the major promontory into the lake. The climb up from Nakartse to the glacier-topped **Karo La Pass** (5045m) is long and dramatic, with towering peaks on either side as the road heads south and then west toward apparently impenetrable rock faces. From the pass, the road descends gradually, via the mineral mines at Chewang, and the stunning reservoir at the **Simila Pass** (4717m) to the broad, fertile and densely farmed **Nyang Chu Valley** leading to Gyantse.

Gyantse

On the eastern banks of the Nyang Chu at the base of a natural amphitheatre of rocky ridges, **GYANTSE** (江孜, *jiāngzī*) is an attractive, relaxed town, offering the splendid sights of the **Gyantse Kumbum** – famous among scholars of Tibetan art throughout the world – and the old Gyantse Dzong. Despite the rapidly expanding Chinese section of town, it has retained a pleasant, laidback air. It lies 263km from Lhasa on the old southern road and 90km southeast of Shigatse.

Little is known about the history of any settlement at Gyantse before the fourteenth century, when it emerged as the capital of a small kingdom ruled by a lineage of princes claiming descent from the legendary Tibetan folk hero, King Gesar of Ling. Hailing originally from northeast Tibet, they allied themselves to the powerful Sakya order. Also at this time, Gyantse operated as a staging post in the **wool trade** between Tibet and India, thanks to its position between Lhasa and Shigatse. By the mid-fifteenth century, the Gyantse Dzong, Pelkor Chode Monastery and the Kumbum had been built, although decline followed as other local families increased their influence.

Gyantse rose to prominence again in 1904 when Younghusband's British expedition, equipped with modern firearms, approached the town via the trade route from Sikkim, routed 1500 Tibetans – killing over half of them – and then marched on Gyantse. In July 1904, the British took the Dzong with four casualties while three hundred Tibetans were killed. From here the British marched on to Lhasa. As part of the ensuing agreement between Tibet and Britain, a British Trade Agency was established in Gyantse and as relations between Tibet and the British in India thawed, the trade route from Calcutta up through Sikkim and on to Gyantse became an effective one.

The Town

The best way to get your bearings is to stand at the main traffic intersection, where, in lieu of a bus station, minibuses drop you off. Heading northeast from here takes you past the cheaper hotels and to the square at the base of the Gyantse Dzong, where Baiju Lu leads off west to the Gyantse Kumbum.

The original **Gyantse Dzong** (江孜古堡, *jiāngzīgŭbaŏ*; daily 7am–7pm; ¥60) dates from the mid-fourteenth century, though the damage caused by the British in 1904 means a lot of what you see is a reconstruction. Having climbed up to the fort, visitors are allowed into the **Meeting Hall**, which houses a waxworks tableau, and the **Anti-British Imperialist Museum**, where weapons, used by the defenders against the British, are on display. Climb higher and you reach the upper and lower chapels of the **Sampal Norbuling Monastery**. A few of the murals in the upper chapel probably date from the early fifteenth century, but most of the other artefacts are modern. The best views are from the top of the tallest tower in the north of the complex. You'll need to climb some very rickety ladders, but the scenery is well worth it.

Gyantse Kumbum and Pelkor Chode Monastery

At the northern edge of town, the rather barren monastic compound that now contains Pelkor Chode Monastery and the glorious **Gyantse Kumbum** (江孜千佛塔, *jiāngzīqiānfótă*; daily 9am–8pm; ¥40, additional up to ¥20/chapel for photographs) was once home to religious colleges and temples belonging to three schools of Tibetan Buddhism: the Gelugpa, Sakya and Bu (the last of these is a small order whose main centre is at Zhalu; see p.930).

Constructed around 1440 by Rabten Kunsang, the Gyantse prince most responsible for the town's fine buildings, the Gyantse Kumbum is a remarkable building, a huge chorten crowned with a golden dome and umbrella, with chapels bristling with statuary and smothered with paintings at each level. It's a style unique to Tibetan architecture and, while several such buildings have survived, Gyantse is the best preserved (despite some damage in the 1960s) and most accessible. The word kumbum means "a hundred thousand images" – which is probably an overestimate, but not by much. Many of the statues have needed extensive renovation, and most of the murals are very old – take a torch if you want a good look.

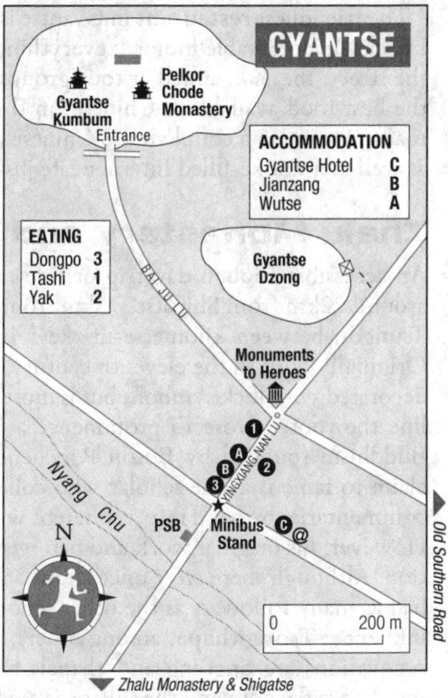

The structure has eight levels, decreasing in size as you ascend; most of the chapels within, except those on the uppermost floors, are open. With almost seventy chapels on the first four levels alone, there's plenty to see. The highlights, with the densest, most lavish decoration, include the two-storey chapels at the cardinal points on the first and third levels and the four chapels on the fifth level. The views of the town and surrounding area get better the higher you go, and some of the outside stucco work is especially fine. At the sixth level, you'll emerge onto an open platform, level with the eyes of the chorten that look in each direction.

The other main building in the compound is **Pelkor Chode Monastery**, built by Rabten Kunsang some twenty years earlier than the Kumbum and used for worship by monks from all the surrounding monasteries. Today, the main assembly hall contains two thrones, one for the Dalai Lama and one for the main Sakya Lama. The glitter and gold and the sunlight and flickering butter lamps in the chapels make a fine contrast to the gloom of much of the Kumbum. The main chapel, **Tsangkhang**, is at the back of the assembly hall and has a statue of Sakyamuni flanked by deities amid some impressive wood carvings – look for the two peacocks perched on a beam. The second floor of the monastery contains five chapels, and the top level just one, **Shalyekhang** (Peak of the Celestial Mansion), with some very impressive, 2m-wide mandalas.

Practicalities

Minibuses operate between the bus station in Shigatse and the main traffic intersection in Gyantse from around 8am to 4pm daily.

Accommodation options are all within easy walking distance; north of the main crossroads on Yingxiong Nan Lu, the *Jianzang* (建藏饭店, *jiànzàngfàndiàn*; ⓣ0892/8173720) and the *A Wutse* (乌孜饭店, *wūzīfàndiàn*; ⓣ0892/8172909) are the two best budget options. Both are built around old courtyards, and offer dorms (❶) and rooms (❸–❺) as well as food and laundry services. The tour-group favourite *Gyantse Hotel* (江孜饭店, *jiāngzīfàndiàn*; ⓣ0892/8172222; ❺), east of the main crossroads, is the most comfortable place in town, with a spacious, Tibetan-style lobby and 24-hour hot water and satellite TV.

The friendliest **restaurant** in Gyantse is the *Tashi*, just north of the Wutse, which knocks up acceptable momos; everything here is ¥20–30. On the opposite side of the street, the *Yak*, aimed at tour groups, does decent Nepalese curries. As usual, the best food available is Chinese; in this case at the *Dongpo*, on the main crossroads. There are a couple more Chinese restaurants just west of the *Gyantse Hotel*, as well as a smoke-filled internet café just to the east.

Zhalu Monastery and Gyankhor Lhakhang

An accessible enough day-trip or side-trip, **Zhalu Monastery** (夏鲁寺, *xiàlǔsì*) is around 22km from Shigatse, 75km from Gyantse and 4km south of the village of Tsungdu between kilometre-markers 18 and 19 on the Gyantse–Shigatse road. Originally built in the eleventh century, Zhalu has a finely colonnaded courtyard decorated with luck symbols, but is most remarkable for the green-glazed tiles that line the roof. It rose to prominence as the seat of the Bu tradition of Tibetan Buddhism founded by Buton Rinchendrub in the fourteenth century. Buton's claim to fame is as the scholar who collected, organized and copied the Tengyur commentaries by hand into a coherent whole, comprising 227 thick volumes in all. However, his original work and pen were destroyed during the Cultural Revolution. Although there were once about 3500 monks living here, the tradition never had as many followers as the other schools. It did, however, have a fair degree of influence: **Tsongkhapa**, among others, was inspired by Buton's teachings. Major renovations are ongoing and chapels have been closed and rearranged, but the monks are friendly and the village is a quiet and pleasant place. For the energetic, it's a one- to two-hour walk up in the hills southwest of Zhalu to the hermitage of **Riphuk**, where Atisha (see p.893) is supposed to have meditated. You'll need directions or a guide from Zhalu, as you can't see it from the monastery.

About 1km north of Zhalu, **Gyankor Lhakhang** dates from 997. Sakya Pandita, who established the relationship between the Mongol Khans and the Sakya hierarchy in the thirteenth century (see p.893), was ordained here as a monk, and the stone bowl over which he shaved his head prior to ordination is in the courtyard. Just inside the entrance is a conch shell, said to date from the time of Buton Rinchendrub and reputedly able to sound without human assistance.

Shigatse

Traditionally the home of the Panchen Lamas – historically religious and political rivals to the Dalai Lamas – Tibet's second city, **SHIGATSE** (日喀则, *rìkāzé*), is often only used by travellers as an overnight stop on the way to or from Lhasa. One day is long enough to see the two main sights, **Tashilunpo Monastery** and **Shigatse Dzong**, but if you're not pressed for time it's worth spending at least an extra night here simply to do everything at a more leisurely pace, take in the market, wander the attractive, tree-lined streets and absorb the atmosphere.

Arrival

From Lhasa, public **buses** run to Shigatse from the bus station (¥65), and there are also **minibuses** (¥40) from Beijing Dong Lu, just east of the *Yak Hotel*. Public buses terminate at the bus station on Shanghai Lu, returning to Lhasa from here early in the morning (8am & 9am). Minibuses to and from Gyantse run until around 4pm. **Taxis** are ¥10 for any destination in town, or it's about a twenty-minute walk from the bus station to the *Tenzin Hotel*. By private jeep, Gyantse to Shigatse will take around three hours, while Lhasa to Shigatse will take seven hours at least.

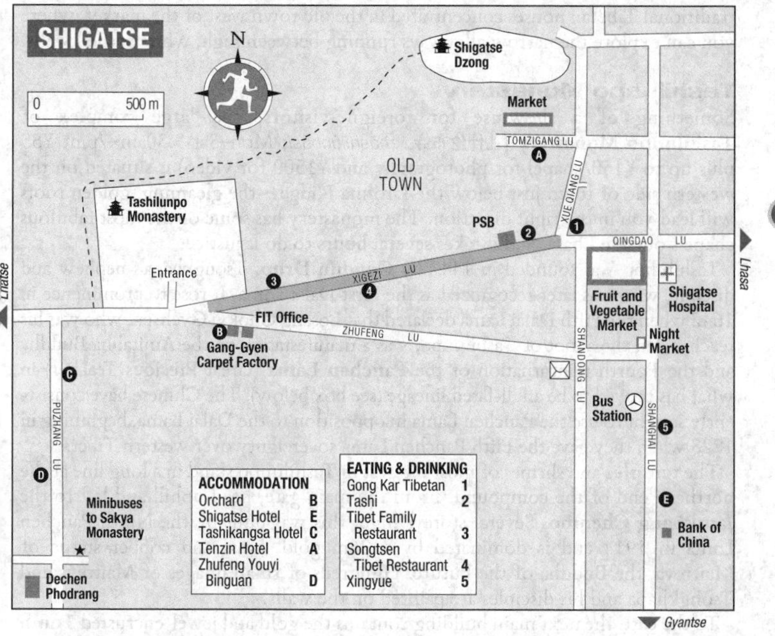

Accommodation

Orchard Hotel (刚坚宾馆, *gāngjiānbīnguǎn*) Zhufeng Lu ⓣ0892/8820234.The *Orchard* has possibly the plushest dorms in China for ¥40, as well as decent mid-range rooms. ❸

Shigatse Hotel (日喀则饭店, *rìkāzéfàndiàn*) 13 Shanghai Zhonglu ⓣ0892/8822525. Tour-group hotel, a bit out of the way, and it's rather cavernous if there aren't plenty of people around. There's the choice of taking heavily decorated "Tibetan-style" rooms over the cookie-cutter Chinese options. Discounts often given. ❻

Tashikangsa Hotel (扎西康萨宾馆, *zhāxīkāngsàbīnguǎn*) Puzhang Lu ⓣ0892/8822124. Close to the Tashilunpo Monastery, this place has one main reason to stay here: the bargain basement dorm rooms that go for just ¥20/bed. There are no showers, but the toilets do flush, and it's a great place to rub shoulders with pilgrims from all over Tibet. ❷

Tenzin Hotel (旦增宾馆, *dànzēngbīnguǎn*) Opposite the market on Bangchelling ⓣ0892/8822018. A long-standing travellers' haunt, though renovation has removed its ramshackle charm; it now looks like everywhere else and charges twice as much. Six-bed dorms are ¥35. ❸

Zhufeng Youyi Binguan (珠峰友谊宾馆, *zhūfēngyoǔyìbīnguǎn*) Puzhang Lu ⓣ0892/8821929. Slightly upmarket facilities in what is billed as the highest-altitude hotel in Shigatse, but it's a bit out of town. ❹

The City

Although the city is fairly spread out, about 2km from end to end, most of the sights and the facilities that you'll need are in or near the north–south corridor around Shanghai Lu and Shandong Lu, extending north along Xue Qiang Lu to the market and Dzong. The main exception is **Tashilunpo Monastery**, which is a bit of a hike west. Shigatse offers an adequate range of accommodation, a variety of shops and some pleasant restaurants, and the dramatic **Drolma Ridge** rising up on the northern side of town helps you get your bearings easily. The pace of life here is unhurried, but there's a buzz provided by the huge numbers of Tibetan pilgrims and foreign visitors. Although most of the city is modern, you'll find the traditional Tibetan houses concentrated in the old town west of the market, where you can explore the narrow alleyways running between high, whitewashed walls.

Tashilunpo Monastery

Something of a showcase for foreign visitors, the large complex of **Tashilunpo Monastery** (扎什伦布寺, *zhāshílúnbùsì*; Mon–Sat 9.30am–7pm; ¥55 plus up to ¥150/chapel for photography and ¥1500 for video) is situated on the western side of town just below the Drolma Ridge – the gleaming, golden roofs will lead you in the right direction. The monastery has some of the most fabulous chapels outside Lhasa, and it takes several hours to do it justice.

Tashilunpo was founded in 1447 by **Gendun Drup**, Tsongkhapa's nephew and disciple, who was later recognized as the First Dalai Lama. It rose to prominence in 1642 when the Fifth Dalai Lama declared that Losang Chokyi Gyeltsen, who was his teacher and the abbot of Tashilunpo, was a manifestation of the Amitabha Buddha and the Fourth reincarnation of the **Panchen Lama** (Great Precious Teacher) in what has proved to be an ill-fated lineage (see box below). The Chinese have consistently sought to use the Panchen Lama in opposition to the Dalai Lama, beginning in 1728 when they gave the Fifth Panchen Lama sovereignty over western Tibet.

The **temples** and shrines of most interest in Tashilunpo stand in a long line at the northern end of the compound. From the main gate, head uphill and left to the **Jamkhang Chenmo**. Several storeys high, this was built by the Ninth Panchen Lama in 1914 and is dominated by a 26m gold, brass and copper statue of Maitreya, the Buddha of the Future. Hundreds of small images of Maitreya and Tsongkhapa and his disciples are painted on the walls.

To the east, the next main building contains the gold and jewel-encrusted **Tomb of the Tenth Panchen Lama**, which was consecrated in 1994 and cost US$8

The Panchen Lama controversy

The life of the **Tenth Panchen Lama** (1938–89) was a tragic one. Identified at 11 years of age by the Nationalists in 1949 in Xining, without approval from Lhasa, he fell into Communist hands and was for many years the highest-profile collaborator of the People's Republic of China. His stance changed in 1959 when he openly referred to the Dalai Lama as the true ruler of Tibet. In 1961, in Beijing, the Panchen Lama informed Mao of the appalling conditions in Tibet and pleaded for aid, religious freedom and an end to the huge numbers of arrests. Mao assured the Panchen Lama these would be granted, but nothing changed. Instructed to give a speech condemning the Dalai Lama, he refused and was prevented from speaking in public until the 1964 Monlam Great Prayer Festival in Lhasa. With an audience of ten thousand people, he again ignored instructions and spoke in the Dalai Lama's support, ending with the words, "Long live the Dalai Lama". He was immediately placed under house arrest, and the Chinese instituted a campaign to "Thoroughly Smash the Panchen Reactionary Clique". The Panchen Lama's trial in August 1964 lasted seventeen days, following which he vanished into prison for fourteen years, where he was tortured and attempted suicide. He was released in 1978, two years after the death of Zhou Enlai, and the Chinese used him as evidence that there was a thawing of their hard-line attitude towards Tibet. He never again criticized the Chinese in public, and in private he argued that Tibetan culture must survive at all costs, even if it meant giving up claims for independence. Some Tibetans saw this as a sellout; others worshipped him as a hero when he returned on visits to Tibet. He died in 1989; the Chinese say from a heart attack, others say he was poisoned.

The search for the **Eleventh Panchen Lama** was always likely to be fraught. The central issue is whether the Dalai Lama or the Chinese government have the right to million. Near the top is a small window cut into a tiny niche, containing his picture. The next building, the **Palace of the Panchen Lamas**, built in the eighteenth century, is closed to the public, but the long building in front houses a series of small, first-floor chapels. The Yulo Drolma Lhakhang, farthest to the right, is worth a look and contains 21 small statues showing each of the 21 manifestations of Tara, the most popular goddess in Tibet.

To the east again, the **Tomb of the Fourth Panchen Lama** contains his 11m-high chorten, with statues of Amitayus, White Tara and Vijaya, the so-called Three Gods of Longevity, in front. His entire body was supposedly interred in the chorten in a standing position, together with an ancient manuscript and *thangkas* sent by the second Manchu emperor. Next comes the **Kelsang Lhakhang**, the largest, most intricate and confusing building in Tashilunpo, in front of the Tomb of the Fifth Panchen Lama. The Lhakhang consists of a courtyard, the fifteenth-century assembly hall and a whole maze of small chapels, often interconnecting, in the surrounding buildings. The flagged **courtyard** is the setting for all the major temple festivals; the surrounding three-level colonnaded cloisters are covered with murals, many recently renovated. The huge throne of the Panchen Lama and the hanging *thangkas*, depicting all his incarnations, dominate the **assembly hall**. If you've got the energy, it's worth trying to find the **Thongwa Donden Lhakhang**, one of the most sacred chapels in the complex, containing burial chortens, including that of the founder of Tashilunpo, the First Dalai Lama, Gendun Drup, as well as early Panchen Lamas and abbots of Tashilunpo.

Spare an hour or so to walk the 3km **kora**, the pilgrim circuit, which follows a clockwise path around the outside walls of the monastery. Turn right on the main road as you exit the monastery and continue around the walls; a stick is useful, as

determine the identity of the next incarnation. Stuck in the middle was the abbot of Tashilunpo, Chadrel Rinpoche, who initially led the search according to the normal pattern, with reports of "unusual" children checked out by high-ranking monks. On January 25, 1995, the Dalai Lama decided that Gendun Choekyi Nyima, the son of a doctor, was the reincarnation, but – concerned for the child's safety – he hesitated about a public announcement. The search committee headed by Chadrel Rinpoche supported the same child.

However, the Chinese decreed that the selection should take place by the drawing of lots from the Golden Urn, an eighteenth-century gold vase, one of a pair used by the Qing emperor Qianlong to resolve disputes in his lands. Chadrel Rinpoche argued against its use. In May, the Dalai Lama, concerned about the delay of an announcement from China, publicly recognized Gendun Choekyi Nyima, and the following day Chadrel Rinpoche was arrested while trying to return to Tibet from Beijing. Within days, Gendun Choekyi Nyima and his family were taken from their home by the authorities, put on a plane and disappeared. The Chinese will only admit they are holding them "for protection". Fifty Communist Party officials then moved into Tashilunpo to identify monks still loyal to the Dalai Lama and his choice of Panchen Lama. In July, riot police quelled an open revolt by the monks. By the end of 1995, they had re-established enough control to hold the Golden Urn ceremony in the Jokhang in Lhasa, where an elderly monk drew out the name of a boy, Gyaincain Norbu. He was enthroned at Tashilunpo and taken to Beijing for publicity appearances. A decade and a half later, the whereabouts of Gendun Choekyi Nyima and his family are still unknown.

some of the dogs are aggressive. The highlight of the walk is the view of the glorious golden roofs from above the top wall. The massive, white-painted wall at the top northeast corner is where the 40m, giant, appliquéd *thangka* is displayed annually at the festival on the fifteenth day of the fifth lunar month (usually in July). At this point, instead of returning downhill to the main road, you can follow the track that continues on around the hillside above the Tibetan part of town and leads eventually to the old Shigatse Dzong.

Shigatse Dzong

Shigatse Dzong (日喀则宗, *rìkāzézōng*), undergoing extensive renovation at the time of writing, was built in the seventeenth century by Karma Phuntso Namgyel when he was king of the Tsang region and held sway over much of the country. It's thought that its design was used as the basis for the later construction of the Potala Palace in Lhasa. The structure was initially ruined by the Dzungars in 1717, and further damage took place in the 1950s. The main reason to climb up is for the fantastic views.

The market and the Tibet Gang-Gyen Carpet Factory

The **market**, opposite the *Tenzin Hotel*, is worth a browse for souvenirs, jewellery, fake antiques and religious objects (if not for its most obvious product, whole dead sheep), and the scale of the place is a bit easier to manage than Lhasa's Barkhor. You'll need to brush up on your bargaining skills and be patient – the stallholders are used to hit-and-run tourists, so the first asking price can be sky-high.

If you're interested in carpets, drop into the **Tibet Gang-Gyen Carpet Factory** (刚坚地毯厂, *gāngjiāndìtǎnchǎng*; Mon–Fri 9am–12.30pm & 2.30–7pm) on Zhufeng Lu, a few minutes' walk from the entrance of Tashilunpo. Their carpets are made from ninety-percent sheep's wool and ten-percent cotton, and you can watch the whole process, from the winding of the wool through to the weaving and finishing. They have a good range of traditional and modern designs, ranging in price from tens of dollars to hundreds, and can also arrange shipping.

Eating and drinking

There's no shortage of **restaurants** in Shigatse, including several aimed at the steady flow of Western tourists. The Nepalese chefs at *A Tashi*, on pedestrianized Xigezi Lu, whip up great Chinese, Tibetan and Nepalese standards, as do those at *Songtsen Tibetan Restaurant* further west on the opposite side of the road. These are where all the tour groups are herded to, so can be a little pricey (¥30 and up). On Qingdao Lu, the *A Gong Kar* Tibetan restaurant has fabulously painted pillars outside and comfortable sofas within. Adventurous carnivores can try yak's heart salad, pig's trotters and ears here, although there are also more mainstream meat and vegetable dishes (¥12–20). Upmarket Chinese food can be had at the *Xingyue*, north of the *Shigatse Hotel*. There's a small **night market** on the corner of Zhufeng Lu and Shanghai Lu, where you can sit on sofas on the pavement and eat spicy kebabs and nourishing bowls of noodles. If you're getting a **picnic** together, visit the **fruit and vegetable market** off Shandong Lu.

Listings

Banks and exchange The Bank of China (Mon–Sat 10am–4pm), just beyond the *Shigatse Hotel*, cashes travellers' cheques and gives advances on visa cards. If you're heading west, stock up here on local currency, as there are no more facilities until Zhangmu.

Hospital The Shigatse hospital on Shanghai Lu has a first-aid post (daily 10am–12.30pm & 4–6pm) – take a Chinese translator with you.

Internet There are a couple of internet cafés just south of the post office and also opposite the *Shigatse Hotel*.

Post office Corner of Shandong Lu and Zhufeng Lu (daily 9am–7pm). You can send international letters and faxes, but not parcels, and they don't stock postcards – go to the *Shigatse Hotel* for those.
Tourist office Shigatse's PSB, on Xigezi Lu (Mon–Fri 9.30am–1pm & 3.30–7pm), is used to dealing with tour groups and is where permits for Everest (¥50) are issued – at the moment such formalities will most likely be handled by your tour guide.

The Friendship Highway

From Shigatse, the **Friendship Highway** west to Zhangmu on the Nepalese border is now surfaced all the way to the border. The only public buses in this direction are the Shigatse to Sakya, Lhatse and Tingri services. From the broad plain around Shigatse, the road gradually climbs to the pass of Tsuo La (4500m) before the steep descent to the Sakya Bridge and the turn-off to Sakya village. If you have time, a detour off the Friendship Highway to **Sakya** is worthwhile; the valleys are picturesque, the villages retain the rhythm of their rural life and Sakya Monastery is a dramatic sight, unlike anything you'll encounter elsewhere in Tibet. Further south, the side-trip to **Mount Everest Base Camp** is a once-in-a-lifetime experience.

Sakya

The small but rapidly growing village of **SAKYA** (萨迦, *sàjiā*), set in the midst of an attractive plain, straddles the small Trum River and is highly significant as the centre of the Sakya school of Tibetan Buddhism. The main reason to visit is to see the remaining monastery, a unique, Mongol-style construction dramatically visible from far away. The village around is now a burgeoning Chinese community, full of ugly concrete, and has been corrupted by tourism; children everywhere will try to sell you quartz, fossils or, sometimes, just rocks, and food is expensive.

Sakya Monastery

Originally, there were two monasteries at the present-day **Sakya Monastery** (萨迦寺, *sàjiāsi*; Mon–Sat 9am–6pm; ¥45, photographs inside ¥25/chapel): the imposing, Mongol-style structure of the **Southern Monastery** that most visitors come to see today, and the **Northern Monastery** across the river, which was a more typical monastic complex containing 108 chapels. The latter was completely destroyed during the Cultural Revolution and has been largely replaced by housing. Prior to the Chinese occupation, there were around five hundred monks in the two monasteries; there are now about a hundred. The Northern Monastery was founded in 1073 by Kong Chogyal Pho, a member of the Khon family, whose son, Kunga Nyingpo, did much to establish Sakya as an important religious centre. He married and had four sons; three became monks, but the fourth remained a layman and continued the family line. The Sakya order has remained something of a family affair, and, while the monks take vows of celibacy, their lay brothers ensure the leadership remains with their kin. One of the early leaders was a grandson of Kunga Nyingpo, known as Sakya Pandita. He began the most illustrious era of the order in the thirteenth century when he journeyed to the court of the Mongol emperor, Godan Khan, and established the Sakya lamas as religious advisers to subsequent emperors and effective rulers of Tibet. This state of affairs lasted until the overthrow of the Mongols in 1354.

The Southern Monastery

The entrance to the **Southern Monastery** (萨迦南寺, *sàjiānánsi*) is in its east wall. On the way there, note the unusual decoration of houses in the area – grey, with white and red vertical stripes; this dates back to a time when it denoted their taxable status within the Sakya principality.

A massive fortress, the Southern Monastery was built in the thirteenth century on the orders of **Phagpa**, nephew of Sakya Pandita. The five main temples in the complex are surrounded by a huge wall with turrets at each corner. On the left of the entrance is the tall, spacious chapel on the second floor of the **Puntsok Palace**, the traditional home of one of the two main Sakya lamas, who now lives in the US. It is lined with statues – White Tara is nearest to the door and Sakya Pandita farther along the same wall. The central figure of Kunga Nyingpo, the founder of the Northern Monastery, shows him as an old man. The chortens contain the remains of early Sakya lamas. As you move clockwise around the courtyard, the next chapel is the Phurkhang, with statues of Sakyamuni to the left and Manjusri to the right of Sakya Pandita. The whole temple is stuffed with thousands of small statues and editions of sacred texts with murals on the back wall.

Facing the entrance to the courtyard, the **Great Assembly Hall** is an imposing chapel, with walls 3.5m thick. Its roof is supported by forty solid wooden columns, one of which was said to be a personal gift from Kublai Khan and carried by hand from China; another was supposedly fetched from India on the back of a tiger, a third brought in the horns of a yak and yet another is said to weep the black blood of the naga water spirit that lived in the tree used for the column. The chapel is overwhelmingly full of brocade hangings, fine statues, butter lamps, thrones, murals and holy books. The grandest statues, of Buddha, are against a golden, carved background, and contain the remains of previous Sakya lamas.

Next along, the **Silver Chorten Chapel** houses eleven chortens, with more in the chapel behind. Completing the circuit, the **Drolma Lhakhang** is on the second floor of the building to the right of the entrance. This is the residence of the other principal Sakya lama, the **Sakya Trizin**, currently residing in India (Ⓦwww.hhthesakyatrizin.org), where he has established his seat in exile in Rajpur. Be sure to take time to walk around the top of the walls for fine views, both into the monastery and over the surrounding area.

Practicalities

Situated 150km southwest of Shigatse, Sakya is an easy side-trip off the Friendship Highway if you've got your own transport; most tours call in here on the way to Everest before overnighting at Lhatse. Public **buses** run here from Shigatse on weekdays (see p.930), returning from Sakya at 11am the next morning; it's a surprisingly slow trip – allow six hours or more each way. If you want to continue from Sakya to Lhatse, get the bus to drop you at the Friendship Highway turn-off, which it reaches around 1pm. The bus from Shigatse to Lhatse passes here about 1.30pm, so you shouldn't have to wait for long.

Few tour groups stop over in Sakya, but **accommodation** is available. Turn right out of the bus station entrance – avoiding the miserable **guesthouses** right nearby – and walk straight ahead for 150m to the *Tibetan Hotel* (❷), opposite the north wall of the monastery; it is marginally better.

Sakya to Mount Everest

Just 24km west of Sakya Bridge, the truck-stop town of **Lhatse** (拉孜, *lāzī*; 4050m) sits alongside the Friendship Highway and has plenty of restaurants and basic accommodation. There's little to detain you, but most bus drivers stop here, and it's where many tour groups spend the night. Top billing in town goes to the Chinese-run *Shanghai Hotel* (上海大酒店, *shànghǎidàjiǔdiàn*; Ⓣ0892/8323678, Ⓦwww.lazihotel.com; ❹), which dominates the central square;

far more popular is the *Tibetan Farmer's Adventure Hostel* (西藏拉孜农民娱乐旅馆, *xīzànglāzīnóngmínyúlèlǔguǎn*; ⓣ0892/8322858; ❸) at the western end of town, which proudly proclaims itself "Tibet's first hotel by peasants". Try to get one of the new, decidedly unpeasant-like en-suite rooms at the back of the compound. Both hotels have restaurants, and there are numerous places – Sichuan, especially – to eat along the main drag. Another 6km west from Lhatse, the road divides: the Friendship Highway continues to the left, and the route to the far west of Tibet heads right.

Sticking on the Friendship Highway, allow about four hours in a good jeep up over the Lhakpa La Pass (5220m) to **New Tingri** (新定日, *xīndìngrì*; also known as *Shekar*). Almost entirely constructed from concrete blocks, it's not the nicest place, but it holds the ticket office for entry to the Mount Everest area (¥180/person) and represents the last chance to stock up on provisions before the mountain.

There's a checkpoint on the highway about 5km further on where some visitors have reported guards being particularly assiduous in confiscating printed material specifically about Tibet (books on China that include Tibet seem to be fine). Just 7km west of this checkpoint, the small turning to **Rongbuk Monastery** and on up to **Mount Everest Base Camp** is on the south side of the road. It's a long, windy, spellbinding 90km to Rongbuk and worth every tortured minute of the three-hour drive.

The road zigzags steeply up to the **Pang La Pass** (5150m), from where the glory of the Everest region is laid out before you – the earlier you go in the day the better the views, as it clouds over later. There's a lookout spot with a plan to help you identify individual peaks such as Cho Oyu (8153m), Lhotse (8501m) and Makalu (8463m), as well as the mighty Mount Everest (8848m; Chomolungma in Tibetan, Zhumulangma in Chinese). From here the road descends into a network of fertile valleys with small villages in a patchwork of fields. You'll gradually start climbing again and pass through Peruche (19km from Pang La), Passum (10km further), where there is **accommodation** just beside the road at the *Passumpembah Teahouse* (❶), and Chodzom (another 12km), before the scenery becomes rockier and starker and you eventually reach Rongbuk Monastery, 22km farther on.

Rongbuk Monastery and Everest Base Camp

Rongbuk Monastery (¥25) – at 4980m, the highest in the world – was founded in 1902 by the Nyingma Lama, Ngawang Tenzin Norbu, although a hardy community of nuns had used meditation huts on the site for about two hundred years before this. The chapels themselves are of limited interest; Padmasambhava is in pride of place and the new murals are attractive, but the position of the monastery, perched on the side of the Rongbuk Valley leading straight towards the north face of Everest, is stunning. Just to sit outside and watch the play of light on the face of the mountain is the experience of a lifetime.

It's possible to camp near the monastery, and there are also two guesthouses offering **accommodation** (❷–❸), one a concrete monstrosity, the other a collection of smaller, more traditional buildings directly across the road from the monastery. There's a small monastery shop selling mostly leftovers from mountaineering expeditions and also a basic, but expensive restaurant.

Carry on a couple of kilometres and you'll come to a large horseshoe of tents pitched around what is presumably the world's highest car park. Each of the tents claims the status of a guesthouse – including at least one *Hotel California* – offering dormitory accommodation (¥40) and with a stove in the centre of each they provide relatively comfortable lodgings for the single night most people stay. Basic, overpriced food is also available for around ¥20–30 per dish, and in the corner of the car park is a post office from where you can send Everest-stamped postcards.

Everest Base Camp (珠峰大本营, *zhūfēngdàběnyíng*; 5150m) is another 4km due south. There's a bus (¥20), but the walk alongside the river through the boulder-strewn landscape and past a small monastery on the cliff is glorious and the route fairly flat. Base camp is often a bit of a surprise, especially during the climbing seasons (March–May, Sept & Oct), when you'll find a colourful and untidy tent city festooned with Calor gas bottles and satellite dishes, though at other times of year it's almost completely deserted, save for a perpetual detachment of Chinese troops keeping an eye out for potential "trouble".

Don't be surprised if you suffer with the **altitude** here – breathlessness and headaches are the norm. However well you were acclimatized in Lhasa, base camp is around 1500m higher, so be sensible and don't contemplate a trip here immediately after arrival up on the Tibetan plateau.

To the Nepalese border

From the Rongbuk and Mount Everest Base Camp turning on the Friendship Highway, it's a fast 50km south to **TINGRI** (定日, *dìngrì*; 4342m). The road is good, and you should allow about an hour in a jeep. A convenient stop on the final day's drive to Zhangmu, Tingri has some good restaurants – the *Snowland Hotel* at the western end of town is particularly popular with tour groups – and excellent views south towards Everest. To get the best of these, climb up to the old fort that stands sentinel over the main part of the village.

The road west of Tingri is good and lined with ruins of buildings destroyed in an eighteenth-century Gurkha incursion from Nepal. The road climbs gradually for 85km to the double-topped **Lalung La Pass** (5050m), from where the views of the Himalayas are breathtaking, especially looking west to the great slab of Shishapangma (8013m). The descent from the pass is steep and startling as the road drops off the edge of the Tibetan plateau and heads down the gorge of the Po Chu River. Vegetation appears, and it becomes noticeably warmer as you near Nyalam, around four hours' drive by jeep from Tingri.

Milarepa's Cave

Although difficult to spot if you're coming from the north, **Milarepa's Cave** (10km north of Nyalam) is worth a halt – look out for a white chorten, to the left of the road on the edge of the gorge. Milarepa (1040–1123) was a much-revered Tibetan mystic who led an ascetic, itinerant life in caves and was loved for his religious songs. The Kagyu order of Tibetan Buddhism was founded by his followers, and the impressions in the walls and roof are believed to have been made by Milarepa himself. A temple has been built around the cave, the main statue being of Padmasambhava. Perched on the side of the Matsang Zangpo River gorge, **Nyalam** (3750m) is a small village with several Chinese restaurants and a variety of basic accommodation, although there is little to recommend staying the night here rather than continuing to Zhangmu.

Zhangmu

The steep descent through the Himalayas continues and the bare mountain scrub gives way to sudden greenery, trees and almost unbelievably beautiful alpine scenery with rivers cascading down both sides of the sheer valley. Here, **ZHANGMU** (樟木, *zhāngmù*; 2300m), a Chinese-Tibetan-Nepalese hybrid clings gamely to the mountainside, a collection of guesthouses, restaurants, construction sites, shops, brothels and offices. It's a great place, with a Wild-West-comes-to-Asia atmosphere, although good-quality **accommodation** is limited. With hot running water and sanitation still something of a novelty in Zhangmu, the best place to stay is whichever guesthouse has been most recently renovated. At the time of writing

Entering Nepal

The **border posts** (both open daily 9.30am–5pm Chinese time) on the Chinese and Nepalese side, at **Kodari** (1770m), are separated by the short "Friendship Bridge", about 7km further downhill from Zhangmu. It can be extremely busy with tour groups and local traders crossing back and forth so it's best to get here early – baggage checks on leaving and entering Tibet on this route are noted for their rigour, which can add to the time spent queuing. The **Nepalese Immigration** post is a couple of hundred metres over the bridge on the left. You can only get single-entry visas here, and you have to pay in US dollars and produce a passport photograph (see p.916 for details of Nepali visas available in Lhasa). Don't forget to put your watch back (2hr 15min) when you cross into Nepal.

To head to **Kathmandu**, either take the express bus direct or the cheaper local service to Barabise and then change for Kathmandu. Alternatively, there are taxis in Kodari, or you can negotiate for space in a tourist bus that has just dropped its group at the border – bargain hard and you'll end up paying Rs400–600 (US$13 or so) per person for the four-hour trip.

this was the *Sunny Youth Hostel* (阳光渴栈, *yángguāngkězhàn*; ⓣ13386510058; ❸), near the bottom end of town, though it is not a registered youth hostel. Across the road the *JinXin* (金鑫宾馆, *jīnxīnbīnguǎn*; ⓣ0892/8743299; ❸) has en-suite rooms and is popular with tour groups, as is the *Tibet Sherpa Hotel* (厦尔巴酒店, *shàěrbājiǔdiàn*; ⓣ0892/8742098; ❸), further downhill on a sharp bend in the road. The *Sherpa* has a good restaurant, though there are plenty of places to choose from, most serving fantastic Nepalese curry.

The **PSB** is up at the top of town close to the **Bank of China** (both Mon–Fri 10am–1pm & 3.30–6.30pm, Sat 10am–2pm). Even if you produce exchange certificates, they'll refuse to change Chinese money into either Nepalese or other hard currency.

There's a thriving black market for money changing and you will no doubt be endlessly approached with offers, but rates are bad and you shouldn't have any trouble changing Chinese currency once in Nepal.

Western Tibet

Travellers in Lhasa spend huge amounts of time and energy plotting and planning trips to the highlights of **western Tibet**: Mount Kailash (冈仁波齐峰, *gāngrénbōqífēng*), Lake Manasarova (玛旁雍错, *mǎpángyōngcuò*) and, less popular but just as enticing, the remains of the tenth-century Guge kingdom, its capital at Tsaparang and main monastery at Tholing. However, this is no guarantee of reaching any of these destinations – regulations change frequently and weather can be a factor – and it can be dangerous. Access to **Mount Kailash** generally isn't a problem – you just need to find a tour agency running the trip. Cost is likely to be the largest obstacle as tours to Kailash generally take at least two weeks.

The **southern route** passes through Saga, Dongpa and Horpa, a stunningly picturesque journey, parallel to the Himalayas, but with rivers that become swollen and passes that get blocked by snow. This route is most reliable from May through to the beginning of July, and again in October and November, although luck plays a big part. The distance is around 1400km from Lhasa to Mount Kailash. The alternative **northern route** via Tsochen, Gertse and Gakyi is longer; Lhasa to Ali (Shiquanhe) is over 1700km and then it's another 300km or so southeast to Mount Kailash. It is also less scenic, but more reliable. Many tours plan to go on one route and return on the other – expect at least a week travelling time on either.

Mount Kailash and around

Top of most itineraries is **Mount Kailash** (6714m), Gang Rinpoche to the Tibetans, the sacred mountain at the centre of the universe for Buddhists, Hindus and Jains. Access is via **DARCHEN**, where there's a guesthouse used as a base by visiting pilgrims. The 58km tour around the mountain takes around three days; you might consider hiring a porter and/or yak (from about ¥45/day each) as it's a tough walk and you need to carry all your gear, including a stove, fuel and food. On the first day you should aim to reach **Drirapuk Monastery**; on the second day you climb over the Dolma La Pass (5636m) to **Zutrulpuk Monastery**; and the third day you arrive back in Darchen.

After the exertions of Mount Kailash, most tours head south 30km to **Manasarova Lake** (Mapham Tso), the holiest lake in Asia for Hindus and Tibetan Buddhists alike. For the energetic, it's a four-day, 90km trek to get around the lake, but plenty of travellers just relax by the lakeside for a day or two.

The third major pilgrimage site in Western Tibet is **Tirthapuri Hot Springs**, which are closely associated with Padmasambhava; they're situated about 80km northwest of Mount Kailash and accessible by road. Pilgrims immerse themselves in the pools, visit the monastery containing his footprint and the cave that he used, and dig for small, pearl-like stones that are believed to have healing properties.

The only remains of the tenth-century kingdom of **Guge**, where Buddhism survived while eclipsed in other parts of Tibet, are the main monastery of **Tholing**, 278km from Ali, and the old capital of **Tsaparang**, 26km west of Tholing. Both are famous for their extensive ruins, some of which are around 1000 years old, and there are many well-preserved murals, but it's all even less accessible than Mount Kailash and Lake Manasarova.

The major town in the area, **ALI** (also known as Shiquanhe), is a modern Chinese-style settlement at the confluence of the Indus and Gar rivers. The only official foreigners' **accommodation** is the overpriced *Ali Hotel* (❸), west of the main crossroads.

Travel details

Buses

Gyantse to: Shigatse (frequent minibuses; 2hr).
Lhasa to: Damxhung (daily minibus; 3–4hr); Ganden (daily pilgrim bus; 3hr); Golmud (daily bus; 30hr); Samye ferry crossing (daily bus; 4hr); Shigatse (daily bus; 8hr; frequent minibuses; 9hr); Tsetang (frequent minibuses; 3hr); Tsurphu (daily pilgrim bus; 2–3hr); Xining (daily bus; 40hr).
Sakya to: Shigatse (daily; 7hr).
Shigatse to: Gyantse (frequent minibuses; 2hr); Lhasa (daily bus; 8hr; frequent minibuses; 9hr); Lhatse (daily bus; 4hr);Sakya (daily bus; 5hr); Tingri (daily bus; 10hr).
Tsetang to: Lhasa (frequent minibuses; 3hr).

Trains

Lhasa to: Beijing (daily; 47hr); Changsha (every other day; 48hr); Chengdu (every other day; 43hr); Chongqing (daily; 43hr); Golmud (4 daily; 13hr); Guangzhou (every other day; 58hr); Lanzhou (3 daily; 24–27hr); Shijiazhuang (daily; 44hr); Xian (2 daily; 34hr); Xining (4 daily; 24 hr).

Flights

Lhasa to: Beijing (daily; 4hr 30min); Chengdu (daily; 2hr); Chongqing (4 weekly; 2hr); Kathmandu (March–Oct 2 weekly; 1hr).

Contexts

Contexts

History

As modern archeology gradually confirms ancient records of China's earliest times, it seems that, however far back you go, Chinese history is essentially the saga of the country's autocratic **dynasties**. Although this generalized view is inevitable in the brief account below, bear in mind that, while the concept of being Chinese has been around for over two thousand years, the closer you look, the less "China" seems to exist as an entity – right from the start, **regionalism** played an important role. And while concentrating on the great events, it's easy to forget that life for the ordinary people wavered between periods of stability, when writers, poets and artisans were at their most creative, and dire times of heavy taxation, war and famine. While the Cultural Revolution, ingrained corruption and clampdowns on political dissent may not be a good track record for the People's Republic, it's also true that since the 1980s – only yesterday in China's immense timescale – the quality of life for ordinary citizens has vastly improved.

Prehistory and the Three Dynasties

Chinese legends relate that the creator, **Pan Ku**, was born from the egg of chaos and grew to fill the space between Yin, the earth, and Yang, the heavens. When he died his body became the soil, rivers and rain, and his eyes became the sun and moon, while his parasites transformed into human beings. A pantheon of semi-divine rulers known as the **Five Sovereigns** followed, inventing fire, the calendar, agriculture, silk-breeding and marriage. Later a famous triumvirate included **Yao the Benevolent** who abdicated in favour of **Shu**. Shu toiled in the sun until his skin turned black and then he abdicated in favour of **Yu the Great**, the tamer of floods. **Yu** was said to be the founder of China's first dynasty, the **Xia**, which was reputed to have lasted 439 years until its last degenerate and corrupt king was overthrown by the **Shang** dynasty. The Shang was in turn succeeded by the **Zhou**, whose written court histories put an end to this legendary era. Together, the Xia, Shang and Zhou are generally known as the **Three Dynasties**.

As far as archeology is concerned, **homo erectus** remains indicate that China was already broadly occupied by human ancestors well before modern mankind began to emerge 200,000 years ago. Excavations of more recent Stone Age sites show that agricultural communities based around the fertile Yellow River and Yangzi basins, such as **Banpo** in Shaanxi and **Homudu** in Zhejiang, were producing pottery and silk by 5000 BC. It was along the Yellow River, too, that solid evidence of the bronze-working Three Dynasties first came to light, with the discovery of a series of large rammed-earth palaces at **Erlitou** near Luoyang, now believed to have been the Xia capital in 2000 BC.

Little is known about the Xia, though their territory apparently encompassed Shaanxi, Henan and Hebei. The events of the subsequent Shang dynasty, however, were first documented just before the time of Christ by the historian **Sima Qian**. Shang society, based over much the same area as its predecessors and lasting from roughly 1750 BC to 1040 BC, had a king, a class system and a skilled **bronze technology** which permeated beyond the borders into Sichuan, and which produced the splendid vessels found in today's museums. Excavations on the site of Yin, the Shang capital, have found tombs stuffed with weapons, jade ornaments, traces of silk and sacrificial victims – indicating belief in **ancestor worship** and an afterlife. The Shang also practised divination by incising questions onto tortoiseshell or bone and then heating them to study the way in which the material cracked around the words. These **oracle bones** provide China's **earliest written records**, covering topics as diverse as rainfall, dreams and ancestral curses.

Around 1040 BC a northern tribe, the **Zhou**, overthrew the Shang, expanded their kingdom west of the Yellow River into Shaanxi and set up a capital at Xi'an. Adopting many Shang customs, the Zhou also introduced the doctrine of the **Mandate of Heaven**, a belief justifying successful rebellion by declaring that heaven grants ruling authority to leaders who are strong and wise, and takes it from those who aren't – a concept that remains integral to the Chinese political perspective. The Zhou consequently styled themselves "Sons of Heaven" and ruled through a hierarchy of vassal lords, whose growing independence led to the gradual dissolution of the Zhou kingdom from around 600 BC.

The decline of the Zhou dynasty

Driven to a new capital at Luoyang, later Zhou rulers exercised only a symbolic role; real power was fought over by some two hundred city states and kingdoms during the four hundred years known as the **Spring and Autumn** and the **Warring States** periods. This time of violence was also an era of vitality and change, with the rise of the ethics of **Confucianism** and **Taoism** (see p.962 & p.963). As the warring states rubbed up against one another, agriculture and irrigation, trade, transport and diplomacy were all galvanized; iron was first smelted for weapons and tools, and great discoveries were made in medicine, astronomy and mathematics. Three hundred years of war and annexation reduced the competitors to seven states, whose territories, collectively known as Zhong Guo, the **Middle Kingdom**, had now expanded west into Sichuan, south to Hunan and north to the Mongolian border.

The Qin dynasty

The Warring States Period came to an end in 221 BC, when the **Qin** armies overran the last opposition and united China as a single centralized state for the first time, introducing systems of currency and writing that were to last two millennia. The rule of China's first emperor, **Qin Shi Huang**, was absolute and harsh, his advisers favouring the philosophy of **Legalism** – the idea that mankind is inherently bad, and needs to be kept in line by draconian punishments. Ancient literature and historical records were destroyed to wipe out any ideas that conflicted with his own, and peasants were forced off their land to work as labourers on massive construction projects, including his tomb outside Xi'an (guarded by the famous **Terracotta Army**) and an early version of the **Great Wall**. Determined to rule the entire known world, Huang gradually pushed his armies beyond the Middle Kingdom, expanding Chinese rule, if not absolute control, west and southeast. When he died in 210 BC – ironically, during a search for mythical herbs of immortality – the provinces rose in revolt, and his heirs soon proved to lack the personal authority that had held his empire together.

The Han dynasty

In 206 BC the rebel warlord **Liu Bang** took Xi'an and founded the **Han dynasty**. Lasting some four hundred years and larger at its height than contemporary imperial Rome, the Han was the first great **Chinese** empire, one that experienced a flowering of culture and a major impetus to push out frontiers and open them to trade, people and new ideas. In doing so it defined the national identity to such an extent that the main body of the Chinese people still style themselves "**Han Chinese**".

While Liu Bang maintained the Qin model of local government, to prevent others from repeating his own military takeover, he strengthened his position by handing out large chunks of land to his relatives. This secured a period of stability, with effective taxation financing a growing civil service and the construction of a huge and cosmopolitan capital, **Chang'an**, at today's Xi'an. Growing revenue also refuelled the expansionist policies of a subsequent ruler, **Wu**. From 135 to 90 BC he extended his lines of defence well into Xinjiang and Yunnan, opening up the Silk Road for trade in tea, spices and silk with India, west Asia and Rome. At home Wu stressed the Confucian model for his growing civil service, beginning a two-thousand-year institution of Confucianism in government offices.

By 9 AD, however, the empire's resources and supply lines were stretched to breaking point. Increased taxation led to unrest, and the ruling house was split by political intrigue. Following fifteen years of civil war, the dynasty re-formed as the **Eastern Han** at a new capital, Luoyang, where the classical tradition was reimposed under Emperor **Liu Xiu**. But the Han had passed their peak, and were unable to stem the civil strife caused by local authorities setting themselves up as semi-independent rulers. Despite everything, Confucianism's ideology of a centralized universal order had crystallized imperial authority; and **Buddhism**, introduced into the country from India, began to enrich life and thought, especially in the fine arts and literature, while itself being absorbed and changed by native beliefs.

The Three Kingdoms to the Sui

Nearly four hundred years separate the collapse of the Han in about 220 AD from the return of unity under the Sui in 589. However, although China was under a single government for only about fifty years of that time, the idea of a unified empire was never forgotten.

From 200 AD the three states of **Wei**, **Wu** and **Shu** struggled for supremacy in a protracted and complicated war (later immortalized in the saga *Romance of the Three Kingdoms*; see p.993) that ruined central China and encouraged mass migrations southwards. The following centuries saw China's regionalism becoming entrenched: the **Southern Empire** suffered weak and short-lived dynasties, but nevertheless saw prosperity and economic growth, with the capital at **Nanjing** becoming a thriving trading and cultural centre. Meanwhile, with the borders unprotected, the north was invaded in 386 by the **Tobas**, who established the northern **Wei dynasty** after their aristocracy adopted Chinese manners and customs – a pattern of assimilation that was to recur with other invaders. At their first capital, **Datong**, the **Tobas** created a wonderful series of Buddhist carvings, but in 534 their empire fell apart.

The period was a dark age of war, violence and genocide, but it was also a richly formative one, and when the dust had settled a very different society had emerged. For much of this time, many areas produced sufficient **food surpluses** to support a rich and leisured ruling class in the cities and the countryside, as well as large armies and burgeoning Buddhist communities. So culture developed, literature flourished, and calligraphy and sculpture – especially Buddhist carvings, all enriched by Indian and Central Asian elements – reached unsurpassed levels.

The Sui

After grabbing power from his regent in 581, general **Yang Jian** unified the fragmented northern states and then went on to conquer southern China by land and sea, founding the **Sui dynasty**. The Sui get short shrift in historical surveys, but – though they were soon eclipsed by their successors, the Tang – two of the dynasty's three emperors could claim considerable achievements. Until his death in 604, Yang Jian (Emperor **Wen)** was an active ruler who took the best from the past and built on it. He simplified and strengthened the bureaucracy, brought in a new legal code, recentralized civil and military authority and made tax collection more efficient. Near Xi'an his architects designed a new capital, **Da Xing Cheng** (City of Great Prosperity), with an outer wall over 35km round – the largest city in the world at that time.

Following Wen's death in 604, **Yang Di** elbowed his elder brother out to become emperor. Yang improved administration, encouraged a revival of Confucian learning and promoted a strong foreign policy. Universally, he is portrayed as a proverbially "Evil Emperor", thanks to the use of forced labour to complete engineering projects. Half the total workforce of 5,500,000 died during the construction of the 2000km **Grand Canal**, built to transport produce from the southern Yangzi to his capital at Xi'an. Yang was assassinated in 618 after popular hatred inspired a military revolt led by General **Li Yuan**.

Medieval China: Tang to Song

The seventh century marks the beginning of the medieval period of Chinese history. This was the age in which Chinese culture reached its peak, a time of experimentation in literature, art, music and agriculture, and one which unified seemingly incompatible elements.

Having changed his name to **Gao Zu**, Li Yuan consolidated his new **Tang dynasty** by spending the rest of his eight-year reign eliminating rivals. Under his son **Tai Zong**, Tang China broadened its horizons: the Turkic peoples of the Northwest were crushed, the Tibetans brought to heel and relations established with Byzantium. China kept open house for traders and travellers of all races and creeds, who settled in the mercantile cities of Yangzhou and Guangzhou, bringing with them their religions, especially **Islam**, and influencing the arts, cookery, fashion and entertainment. Chinese goods flowed out to India, Persia, the Near East and many other countries, and China's language and religion gained currency in Japan and Korea. At home, **Buddhism** remained the all-pervading foreign influence, with Chinese pilgrims travelling widely in India. The best known of these, **Xuanzang** (see p.845), set off in 629 and returned after sixteen years in India with a mass of Buddhist sutras, adding greatly to China's storehouse of knowledge.

As the population of Xi'an swelled to over a million, the city became one of the world's great cultural centres, at the heart of a centralized and powerful state. Within a decade after Tai Zong's death in 649, his short-lived son **Gao Zong** and China's only empress, **Wu Zetian**, had expanded the Tang empire's direct influence from Korea to Iran, and south into Vietnam. Though widely unpopular, Wu Zetian was a great patron of Buddhism, commissioning the famous Longmen carvings outside Luoyang; she also created a civil service selected on merit rather than birth. Her successor, **Xuan Zong**, began well in 712, but his later infatuation with the beautiful concubine **Yang Guifei** led to the **An Lushan rebellion** of 755, his flight to Sichuan and Yang's ignominious death at the hands of his mutinying army. Xuan Zong's son, **Su Zong**, enlisted the help of Tibetan and Uyghur forces and recaptured Xi'an from the rebels; but though the court was re-established, it had lost its authority, and real power was once again shifting to the provinces.

The following two hundred years saw the country split into regional political and military alliances. From 907 to 960, all the successive **Five Dynasties** were too short-lived to be effective. China's northern defences were permanently weakened, while her economic dependence on the south increased and the dispersal of power brought social changes. The traditional elite whose fortunes were tied to the dynasty gave way to a military and merchant class who bought land to acquire status, alongside a professional ruling class selected by examination. In the south, the **Ten Kingdoms** (some existing side by side) managed to retain what was left of the Tang civilization, their greater stability and economic prosperity sustaining a relatively high cultural level.

Eventually, in 960, a disaffected army in the north put a successful general, **Song Tai Zu**, on the throne. His new ruling house, known as the **Northern Song**, made its capital at **Kaifeng** in the Yellow River basin, well placed at the head of the Grand Canal for transport to supply its million people with grain from the south. By skilled politicking rather than military might, the new dynasty consolidated authority over surrounding petty kingdoms and re-established civilian primacy. However, northern China was occupied by the **Jin** in 1115, who pushed the imperial court south to **Hangzhou** where, guarded by the Yangzi River, their culture continued to flourish from 1126 as the **Southern Song**. Developments during their 150-year dynasty included gunpowder, the magnetic compass, fine porcelain and moveable type printing. In due course, however, the Song preoccupation with art and sophistication saw their military might decline and led them to underrate their aggressive "barbarian" neighbours, whose own expansionist policies culminated in the thirteenth-century **Mongol Invasion**.

The Yuan dynasty

In fact, Mongolian influence had first penetrated China in the eleventh century, when the Song emperors paid tribute to separate Mongolian states to keep their armies from invading. These individual fiefdoms were unified by **Genghis Khan** in 1206 to form an immensely powerful army, which swiftly embarked upon the conquest of northern China. Despite Chinese resistance and Mongol infighting, the **Yuan dynasty** was on the Chinese throne by 1271, with **Kublai Khan**, Genghis Khan's grandson, at the head of an empire that stretched way beyond the borders of China. The Yuan emperors' central control from their capital at Khanbalik – modern **Beijing** – boosted China's economy and helped repair five centuries of civil war. China was thrown wide open to foreign travellers, traders and missionaries; Arabs and Venetians were to be found in Chinese ports, and a Russian came top of the Imperial Civil Service exam of 1341. The Grand Canal was extended from Beijing to Hangzhou, while in Beijing the **Palace of All Tranquillities** was built inside a new city wall, later known as the **Forbidden City**. Descriptions of much of this were brought back to Europe by **Marco Polo**, who recorded his impressions of Yuan lifestyle and treasures after he'd lived in Beijing for several years and served in the government of Kublai Khan.

The Yuan only retained control over all China until 1368. Their power was ultimately sapped by the combination of becoming too Chinese for their northern brethren to tolerate, and too aloof from the Chinese to assimilate. After northern tribes had rebelled, and famine and disastrous floods brought a series of uprisings in China, a monk-turned-bandit leader from the south, **Zhu Yuanzhang**, seized the throne from the last boy emperor of the Yuan in 1368.

The Ming dynasty

Taking the name **Hong Wu,** Zhu Yuanzhang proclaimed himself the first emperor of the **Ming dynasty**, with Nanjing as his capital. Zhu's influences on China's history were far-reaching. His extreme despotism culminated in two appalling purges in which thousands of civil servants and literati died, and he initiated a course of **isolationism** from the outside world which lasted throughout the Ming and Qing eras. Consequently, Chinese culture became inward-looking, and the benefits of trade and connections with foreign powers were lost. Nowhere is this more apparent than in the Ming construction of the current Great Wall, a grandiose but futile attempt to stem the invasion of northern tribes into China, built in the fifteenth century as military might and diplomacy began to break down.

Yet the period also produced fine artistic accomplishments, particularly **porcelain** from the imperial kilns at Jingdezhen, which became famous worldwide. Nor were the Ming rulers entirely isolationist. During the reign of **Yongle**, Zhu's 26th son, the imperial navy (commanded by the Muslim eunuch, Admiral **Zheng He**) ranged right across the Indian Ocean as far as the east coast of Africa on a fact-finding mission. But stagnation set in after Yongle's death in 1424, and the maritime missions were cancelled as being incompatible with Confucian values, which held contempt for foreigners. Thus the initiative for world trade and exploration passed into the hands of the Europeans, with the great period of world voyages by Columbus, Magellan and Vasco da Gama. In 1514, **Portuguese** vessels appeared in the Pearl River at the southern port of Guangzhou (Canton), and though they were swiftly expelled, Portugal was allowed to colonize nearby **Macau** in 1557. Although all dealings with foreigners were officially despised by the imperial court, trade flourished as Chinese merchants and officials were eager to milk the profits.

In later years, a succession of less-able Ming rulers allowed power to slip into the hands of the seventy thousand inner court officials, who used it not to run the empire but in intriguing among the "eunuch bureaucracy". By the early seventeenth century, frontier defences had fallen into decay, and the **Manchu tribes** in the north were already across the Great Wall. A series of peasant and military uprisings against the Ming began in 1627, and when rebel forces led by **Li Zicheng** managed to break into the capital in 1644, the last Ming emperor fled from his palace and hanged himself – an ignoble end to a three-hundred-year-old dynasty.

The Qing dynasty

The Manchus weren't slow to turn internal dissent to their advantage. Sweeping down on Beijing, they threw out Li Zicheng's army, claimed the capital as their own and founded the **Qing dynasty**. It took a further twenty years for the Manchus to capture the south of the country, but on its capitulation China was once again under foreign rule. Like the Mongol Yuan dynasty before them, the Qing initially did little to assimilate domestic culture, ruling as separate overlords. Manchu became the official language, the Chinese were obliged to wear the Manchu **pigtail**, and intermarriage between a Manchu and a Chinese was strictly forbidden. Under the Qing dynasty the distant areas of Inner and Outer Mongolia, Tibet and Turkestan were fully incorporated into the Chinese empire, uniting the Chinese world to a greater extent than during the Tang period.

Soon, however, the Manchus proved themselves susceptible to Chinese culture, and ultimately they became deeply influenced by it. Three outstanding early Qing emperors also brought an infusion of new blood and vigour to government. **Kangxi**, who began his 61-year reign in 1654 at the age of six, was a great patron of the arts, blotting countless scrolls of famous calligraphy and paintings with his seals as evidence that he had seen them. He assiduously cultivated his image as the Son of Heaven by making royal progresses throughout the country and by his personal style of leadership. His fourth son, the Emperor **Yungzheng** (1678–1735), ruled over what is considered one of the most efficient and least corrupt administrations ever enjoyed by China. This was inherited by **Qianlong** (1711–99), whose reign saw China's frontiers widely extended and the economy stimulated by peace and prosperity. In 1750 the nation was perhaps at its apex, one of the strongest, wealthiest and most powerful countries in the world.

During the latter half of the eighteenth century, however, economic problems began to increase. Settled society had produced a **population explosion**, putting pressure on food resources and causing a land shortage. This in turn saw trouble flaring as migrants from central China tried to settle the remoter western provinces, dispossessing the original inhabitants. Meanwhile, expanding European nations were looking for financial opportunities. From around 1660, Portuguese traders in Guangzhou had been joined by British merchants shopping for tea, silk and porcelain, and during the eighteenth century the British **East India Company** moved in, eager for a monopoly. Convinced of their own superiority, however, China's immensely rich and powerful rulers had no desire to deal directly with foreigners. When **Lord Macartney** arrived in 1793 to propose a political and trade treaty between Britain and China, he found that the emperor totally rejected any idea of alliance with one who, according to Chinese ideas, was a subordinate.

The Opium Wars and the Taiping Uprising

Foiled in their attempts at official negotiations with the Qing court, the East India Company decided to take matters into their own hands and create a clandestine market in China for Western goods. Instead of silver, they began to pay for tea and silk with **opium**, cheaply imported from India. As demand escalated during the early nineteenth century, China's trade surplus became a deficit, as silver drained out of the country to pay for the drug. The emperor intervened in 1840 by ordering the confiscation and destruction of over twenty thousand chests of opium – the start of the first **Opium War**. After two years of British gunboats shelling coastal ports, the Chinese were forced to sign the **Treaty of Nanking**, whose humiliating terms included a huge indemnity, the opening up of new ports to foreign trade, and the **cession of Hong Kong**.

To be conquered by foreigners was a crushing blow for the Chinese, who now suffered major internal **rebellions** inspired by anti-Manchu feeling and economic hardship – themselves fuelled by rising taxes to pay off China's war indemnity. While serious unrest occurred in Guizhou and Yunnan, the most widespread revolt was the **Taiping Uprising**, which stormed through central China in the 1850s to occupy much of the rich Yangzi Valley. Having captured Nanjing as their "Heavenly Capital", the Taipings began to make military forays towards Beijing, and European powers decided to step in, worried that the Taiping's anti-foreign government might take control of the country. With their support, Qing troops defeated the Taipings in 1864, leaving twenty million people dead and five provinces in ruins.

It was during the uprising that the **Empress Dowager Wu Cixi** first took control of the country, ruling from behind various emperors from 1861 until 1908. Ignorant, vain and certain that reform would weaken the Qings' grasp on power, she pursued a deep conservatism at a time when China needed desperately to overhaul its political and economic structure. Her stance saw increased foreign ownership of industry, rising Christian missionary activity that undermined traditional society, and the disintegration of China's **colonial empire**. France took the former vassal states of Laos, Cambodia and Vietnam in 1883–85; Britain gained Burma; and **Tibet**, which had nominally been under China's control since Tang times, began to assert its independence. Even worse, a failed military foray into Korea in 1894 saw China lose control of **Taiwan** to Japan, while a Russian-built rail line into the northeast effectively gave Russia control of Manchuria.

The Boxer Movement – the end of imperial China

By the 1890s China was dissolving into chaos, and popular resentment against the authorities who had allowed the country to be humiliated by foreigners finally crystallized into the **Boxer Rebellion**. The Boxers suffered an initial defeat at the hands of Cixi's troops in 1899, but Cixi's government then decided that the Boxer army might in fact make a useful tool, and set them loose to slaughter missionaries and Christian converts. During the summer of 1900 the Boxers took control of Beijing, besieging the foreign legation compound, though they were routed when an international relief force arrived on August 14. In the massacre, looting and confusion which followed, Cixi and the emperor disguised themselves as peasants and fled to Xi'an in a cart, leaving her ministers to negotiate a peace.

Though they clung feebly on for another decade, this was the end of the Qing, and internal movements to dismantle the dynastic system and build a new China proliferated. The most influential of these was the **Tong Meng Hui** society, founded in 1905 in Japan by the exile **Sun Yatsen**, a doctor from a wealthy Guangdong family. Cixi died three years later, and, in 1911, opposition to the construction of railways by foreigners drew events to a head in Wuchang, Hubei province, igniting a popular uprising which finally toppled the dynasty. As two thousand years of dynastic succession ended, Sun Yatsen returned to China to take the lead in the provisional **Republican Government** at Nanjing.

From republic to communism

Almost immediately the new republic was in trouble. Though a **parliament** was duly elected in 1913, the reality was that northern China was controlled by the former leader of the Imperial Army, **Yuan Shikai** (who had forced the abdication of the last emperor, **Pu Yi**). Sun Yatsen, faced with a choice between probable civil war and relinquishing his presidency at the head of the newly formed

Nationalist People's Party, the **Guomindang**, stepped down. Yuan promptly dismissed the government, forced Sun into renewed exile, and attempted to establish a new dynasty. But his plans were stalled by his generals, who wanted private fiefdoms of their own, and Yuan's sudden death in 1916 marked the last time in 34 years that China would be united under a single authority. As civil war erupted, Sun Yatsen returned once more, this time to found a southern Guomindang government.

Thus divided, China was unable to stem the increasingly bold territorial incursions made by Japan and other colonial powers as a result of **World War I**. Siding with the Allies, Japan had claimed the German port of Qingdao and all German shipping and industry in the Shangdong Peninsula on the outbreak of war, and in 1915 presented China with **Twenty-One Demands**, many of which Yuan Shikai, under threat of a Japanese invasion, was forced to accept. After the war, hopes that the 1919 **Treaty of Versailles** would end Japanese aggression (as well as the unequal treaties and foreign concessions) were dashed when the Western powers, who had already signed secret pacts with Japan, confirmed Japan's rights in China. This ignited what became known as the **May 4 Movement**, the first in a series of anti-foreign demonstrations and riots.

The rise of the CCP

As a reflection of these events, the **Chinese Communist Party** (CCP) was formed in Shanghai in 1921, its leadership including the young **Mao Zedong** and **Zhou Enlai**. Though the CCP initially listened to its Russian advisers and supported the Guomindang in its military campaigns against the northern warlords, this alliance began to look shaky after Sun Yatsen died in 1925. He was succeeded by his brother-in-law and military chief **Chiang Kai-shek** (better known in China as Jiang Jieshe), a nationalist who had no time for the CCP or its plans to end China's class divisions. In 1927, Communist elements in Shanghai organized a general strike against Chiang, seizing the military arsenal and arming workers. Industry bosses and foreign owners quickly financed a militia for Chiang, which massacred around five thousand workers and Communists, including much of the original Communist hierarchy. Chiang was declared head of a national government in 1928.

Those Communists who had escaped Chiang's purge regrouped in remote areas across the country, principally at **Jinggang Shan** in Jiangxi province, under the leadership of Mao Zedong.

Mao Zedong, the Red Army and the Long March

Son of a well-off Hunanese farmer, **Mao** believed social reform lay in the hands of the peasants who, despite the overthrow of the emperors, still had few rights and no power base. Drawing upon the analyses of Karl Marx, Mao recognized the parallels between nineteenth-century Europe and twentieth-century China, and argued that a mass armed rising was the only way the old order could be replaced.

After events in Shanghai, Mao organized the first peasant-worker army in Changsha, in what was later to be called the **Autumn Harvest Uprising**. Moving with other Communist forces to the Hunan-Jiangxi border in 1927, the **Red Army** of peasants, miners and Guomindang deserters achieved unexpected successes against the Nationalist troops sent against them until **Li Lisan**, the overall Communist leader, ordered Mao out of his mountain base to attack the cities. After the ensuing open assaults against the vastly superior Guomindang forces proved disastrous, Chiang Kai-shek mobilized half a million troops, and encircled Jinggang Shan with a ring of concrete block-houses and barbed-wire entanglements.

Forced to choose between fight or flight, in October 1934 Mao organized eighty thousand troops in an epic 9500km retreat which became known as the **Long March**. By the time they reached safety in **Yan'an** in Shaanxi province a year later, the Communists had lost three-quarters of their followers to the rigours of the trip, but had also started their path towards victory: Mao had become undisputed leader of the CCP at the **Zunyi Conference**, severing the Party from its Russian advisers.

Japanese invasion and the United Front

Meanwhile, **Japan** had taken over Chinese Manchuria in 1933 and installed Pu Yi (last emperor of the Qing dynasty) as puppet leader. The Japanese were obviously preparing to invade eastern China, and Mao wrote to Chiang Kai-shek advocating an end to civil war and a **United Front** against the threat. Chiang's response was to move his Manchurian armies, under **Zhang Xueliang**, down to finish off the Reds in Shaanxi. Zhang, however, saw an alliance as the only way to evict the Japanese from his homeland, and so secretly entered into an agreement with the Communist forces. On December 12, 1936, Chiang was kidnapped by his own troops in what became known as the **Xi'an Incident**. With Zhou Enlai as a mediator, he reluctantly signed his assent to the United Front on Christmas Day. Briefly, the parties were united, though both sides knew that the alliance would last only as long as the Japanese threat.

Full-scale war broke out in July 1937 when the Japanese attacked Beijing. Inadequately armed or trained, the GMD were forced west and south. By the end of the year, the Japanese had taken most of eastern China between Beijing and Guangzhou. With a capital-in-occupation at Nanjing, the Japanese concentrated their efforts on routing the GMD, leaving a vacuum in the north that was filled by the Communists, establishing what amounted to stable government of a hundred million people across the North China Plain.

The outbreak of war in Europe in September 1939 soon had repercussions in China. Nazi Germany stopped supplying the weaponry upon which the GMD relied, while the bombing of Pearl Harbor two years later put an end to all military aid from the United States to Japan. With the country's heavy industry in Japanese hands, China's United Front government, having withdrawn to **Chongqing** in Sichuan province, became dependent on supplies flown over the Himalayas by the Americans and British. Chiang's true allegiances were never far below the surface, however, and after he failed to distribute the arms among the Red Army in 1941, the United Front effectively collapsed.

The end of the war and the Guomindang

By the time the two atom bombs ended the Japanese empire and World War II in 1945, the Red Army was close on a million strong, with a widespread following throughout the country; Communism in China was established. It was not, however, that secure. Predictably enough, the US sided with Chiang Kai-shek and the GMD; more surprisingly, so did the Soviet Union – Stalin believed that with American aid, the GMD would easily destroy the CCP. All the same, **peace negotiations** between the Nationalist and Communist sides were brokered by the US in Chongqing, where Chiang refused to admit the CCP into government, knowing that its policies were uncontrollable while the Red Army still existed. For their part, it was evident to the CCP that without an army, they were nothing. The talks ended in stalemate.

However, buoyed by popular support in the wake of Chiang's mishandling of the economy, in 1948 the Communists' newly named **People's Liberation Army**

(PLA) rose against the GMD, decisively trouncing them that winter at the massive battle of **Huai Hai** in Anhui province. With Shanghai about to fall before the PLA in early 1949, Chiang Kai-shek packed the country's entire gold reserves into a plane and took off for **Taiwan** to form the **Republic of China**. Here he was to remain until his death in 1975, forlornly waiting to liberate the mainland with the two million troops and refugees who later joined him. Mopping-up operations against mainland pockets of GMD resistance would continue for several years, but in October 1949 Mao was able to proclaim the formation of the **People's Republic of China** in Beijing. The world's most populous nation was now Communist.

The People's Republic under Mao

With the country laid waste by over a century of economic mismanagement and war, massive problems faced the new republic. Though Russia offered its support, the US refused to recognize Mao's government, siding with Chiang Kai-shek. China's infrastructure, industries and agriculture were wrecked, and there were no monetary reserves. By the mid-1950s, however, all industry had been nationalized and output was back at prewar levels, while, for the first time in Chinese history, land was handed over to the peasants as their own. A million former landlords were executed, while others were enrolled in "**criticism and self-criticism**" classes, a traumatic re-education designed to prevent elitism or bourgeois deviancy from contaminating the revolutionary spirit.

With all the difficulties on the home front, the government could well have done without the distraction of the **Korean War**. After Communist North Korea invaded the south in 1950, US forces intervened on behalf of the south and, despite warnings from Zhou Enlai, continued through to Chinese territory. China declared war in June, and sent a million troops to push the Americans back to the 38th parallel and force peace negotiations. As a boost for the morale of the new nation, the campaign could not have been better timed. Meanwhile, China's far western borders were seen to be threatened by an uprising in **Tibet**, and Chinese troops were sent there in 1951, swiftly occupying the entire country and instituting de facto Chinese rule. Eight years later, a failed coup against the occupation by Tibetan monks saw a massive clampdown on religion, and the flight of the **Dalai Lama** and his followers to Nepal.

The Hundred Flowers campaign and the Great Leap Forward

By 1956 China's economy was healthy, but there were signs that the euphoria driving the country was slowing. Mao – whose principles held that constant struggle was part of existence, and thus that acceptance of the status quo was in itself a bad thing – felt that both government and industry needed to be prodded back into gear. In 1957 he decided to loosen restrictions on public expression, and following the slogan "Let a hundred flowers bloom, and a hundred schools of thought contend", intellectuals were encouraged to voice their complaints. The plan backfired: instead of picking on inefficient officials as Mao had hoped, the **Hundred Flowers** campaign resulted in attacks on the Communist system itself. As Mao was never one to take personal criticism lightly, those who had spoken out found themselves victims of an **anti-rightist** campaign, confined to jail or undergoing heavy bouts of self-criticism. From this point on, intellectuals as a group were mistrusted and scrutinized.

Agriculture and industry were next to receive a shake-up. In August 1958 it was announced that all farmland was to be pooled into 24,000 self-governing **communes**, with the aim of turning small-scale farming units into hyper-efficient agricultural areas. Industry was to be fired into activity by the co-option of seasonally employed workers, who would construct heavy industrial plants, dig canals and drain marshes. Propaganda campaigns promised eternal well-being in return for initial austerity; in a single **Great Leap Forward**, China would match British industrial output in ten years.

From the outset, the Great Leap Forward was a disaster. Having been given their land, the peasants now found themselves losing it once more, and were not eager to work in huge units. This, combined with the problem of ill-trained commune management, led to a slump in agricultural and industrial production. In the face of a stream of ridiculous **quotas** supplied by Beijing – one campaign required that all communes must produce certain quantities of steel, regardless of the availability of raw materials – no one had time to tend the fields. The 1959 and 1960 harvests both failed, and millions starved. As if this wasn't enough, a thaw in US-USSR relations in 1960 saw the Soviet Union stopping all aid to China.

With the economy in tatters, the commune policy was abandoned, but the incident had ruined Mao's reputation and set members of the Communist Party Central Committee against his policies. One critic was **Deng Xiaoping**, who had diffused the effects of commune policy by creating a limited free-market economy among the country's traders. Behind this doctrine of material incentives for workers was a large bureaucracy over which Mao held little political sway.

The Cultural Revolution

Mao sought to regain his authority. Using a campaign created by Communist Party Vice-Chairman **Lin Biao**, he began in 1964 to orchestrate the youth of China against his moderate opponents in what became known as the **Great Proletarian Cultural Revolution**. Under Mao's guidance, the movement spread in 1966 to Beijing University, where the students organized themselves into a political militia – the **Red Guard** – and within weeks were moving out onto the streets.

The enemies of the Red Guard were the **Four Olds**: old ideas, old culture, old customs and old habits. Brandishing copies of the *Quotations of Chairman Mao Zedong* (the famous **Little Red Book**), the Red Guard attacked anything redolent of capitalism, the West or the Soviet Union. Academics were assaulted, books were burned, temples and ancient monuments desecrated. Shops selling anything remotely Western were destroyed along with the gardens of the "decadent bourgeoisie". As under the commune system, quotas were set, this time for unearthing and turning in the "Rightists", "Revisionists" and "Capitalist Roaders" corrupting Communist society. Officials who failed to fill their quotas were likely to fall victim themselves, as were those who failed to destroy property or denounce others enthusiastically enough. Offenders were paraded through the streets wearing placards carrying humiliating slogans; tens of thousands were ostracized, imprisoned, beaten to death or driven to suicide. On August 5, 1966, Mao proclaimed that reactionaries had reached the highest levels of the CCP: Deng Xiaoping and his followers were dismissed from their posts and imprisoned, condemned to wait on tables at a Party canteen, or given menial jobs.

Meanwhile, the violence was getting completely out of control, with Red Guard factions attacking foreign embassies and even turning on each other. In August

1967 Mao ordered the arrest of several Red Guard leaders and the surrender of all weapons to the army, but was too late to stop nationwide street fighting, which was halted only after the military stormed the Guard's university strongholds. To clear them out of the way, millions of Red Guards were rounded up and shipped off into the countryside, ostensibly to reinforce the Communist message among the rural community.

Ping-pong diplomacy and the rise of the radicals

The US, its foreign policy determined by business and political interests that stood to gain from the collapse of Communism, had continued to support Chiang Kai-shek's Guomindang in the postwar period, while also stirring up paranoia over the possibility of a Sino-Soviet pact (despite the split between Khrushchev and Mao in 1960). After China exploded its first **atomic bomb** in 1964, however, and joined the league of nuclear powers not automatically friendly to Washington, the US began to tread a more pragmatic path. In 1970, envoy Henry Kissinger opened communications between the two countries, cultural and sporting links were formed (the latter gave rise to the phrase "**ping-pong diplomacy**"), and in 1971 the People's Republic became the official representative at the UN of the nation called China, invalidating claims of Chiang Kai-shek for Taiwan. The following year US president **Richard Nixon** was walking on the Great Wall and holding talks with Mao, trade restrictions were lifted and China began commerce with the West. The "bamboo curtain" had parted, and the damage caused by the Cultural Revolution began slowly to be repaired.

This new attitude of realistic reform derived from the moderate wing of the Communist Party, headed by Premier Zhou Enlai – seen as a voice of reason – and his protégé Deng Xiaoping, now in control of the day-to-day running of the Communist Party Central Committee. Zhou's tact had given him a charmed political existence which for fifty years kept him at Mao's side despite policy disagreements; several holy sites were apparently saved from the Red Guards at Zhou's order. But with Zhou's death early in 1976, the reform movement immediately succumbed to the **Gang of Four**, who, led by Mao's third wife **Jiang Qing**, had become the radical mouthpiece of an increasingly absent Mao. In early April, at the time of the **Qing Ming** festival commemorating the dead, the Heroes Monument in Beijing's Tian'anmen Square was filled with wreaths in memory of Zhou. On April 5 radicals removed the wreaths and moderate supporters flooded into the square in protest; a riot broke out and hundreds were attacked and arrested. The obvious scapegoat for what became known as the **Tian'anmen Incident**, Deng Xiaoping, was publicly discredited and thrown out of office for a second time.

The death of Mao

In July 1976 a catastrophic **earthquake** centred on Hebei province killed half a million people. The Chinese hold that natural disasters always foreshadow great events, and no one was too surprised when Mao himself died on September 9. Deprived of their figurehead, and with memories of the Cultural Revolution clear in everyone's mind, his supporters in the Party lost ground to the Right. Just a month after Mao's death, Jiang Qing and the other members of the Gang of Four were arrested. Deng returned to the political scene for the third time and was granted a string of positions that included Vice-Chairman of the Communist Party, Vice-Premier and Chief of Staff to the PLA; titles aside, he was now running the country. The move away from Mao's policies was rapid: in 1978 anti-Maoist **dissidents** were allowed to display wall posters in Beijing and elsewhere, and by 1980 Deng and the moderates were secure enough to sanction officially a cautious condemnation of Mao's actions. His ubiquitous portraits and statues began to come down, and his cult was gradually undermined.

"One Party" capitalism

Under **Deng Xiaoping**, China became unrecognizable from the days when Western thought was automatically suspect and the Red Guards enforced ideological purity. Deng's legacy was the "open door" policy, which brought about new social freedoms as well as a huge rise in the trappings of Westernization, especially in the cities. The impetus for such sweeping changes was economic. Deng's statement, "I don't care whether the cat is black or white as long as it catches mice", illustrates the pragmatic approach that he took to the economy, one which has guided policy ever since. Deng **decentralized production**, allowing more rational decision-making based on local conditions, and the production and allocation of goods according to market forces; factories now contracted with each other instead of with the state. In agriculture, the collective economy was replaced, and farming households, after meeting government targets, were allowed to sell their surpluses on the free market. On the coast, **Special Economic Zones** (SEZs) were set up, where foreign investment was encouraged and Western management practices, such as the firing of unsatisfactory workers, were cautiously introduced.

Economic reform did not precipitate **political reform**, and was really a way of staving it off, with the Party hoping that allowing the populace the right to get rich would halt demands for political rights. However, dissatisfaction with corruption, rising inflation, low wages and the lack of freedom was vividly expressed in the demonstrations in **Tian'anmen Square** in 1989. These started as a mourning service for former Party General Secretary **Hu Yaobang**, who had been too liberal for Deng's liking and was dismissed in 1987; by mid-May there were nearly a million students, workers and even Party cadets around the square, demanding free speech and an end to corruption. On May 20, **martial law** was declared, and by the beginning of June, 350,000 troops were massed around Beijing. In the early hours of June 4 they moved in, crushing barriers with tanks and firing into the crowds, killing hundreds or possibly thousands of the demonstrators. Discussion of the event is still contentious in China – particularly as the issues the students identified have not been dealt with – but the Party's moral authority has been greatly reduced.

China in the twenty-first century

The spectacular **growth** of the Chinese economy was among the great success stories of the twentieth century and will be one of the most important factors in defining the character of the twenty-first. For a quarter of a century, China's GDP has grown at an average rate of nine percent per year, and it came quickly out of the global recession in 2010; that year it overtook Japan to become the world's second largest economy. China is now the world's main producer of coal and steel and, among other things, makes two thirds of the world's shoes, DVD players and photocopiers. Chinese production and US consumption together form the engines for global growth. But China is also a massive consumer; in 2004, for instance, the nation bought almost half of the world's cement. Some predict that the Chinese economy will overtake that of the US by 2040. The speed of this is

How China is governed

Since 1949 the Chinese state has been controlled by the **Communist Party**, which brooks no dissent or rival, and which, with 66 million members, is the biggest political party in the world. It has a pyramid structure resting on millions of local organizations, and whose apex is formed by a Politburo of 24 members controlled by a nine-man standing committee. The Party's workings are opaque; personal relations count more than job titles, and a leader's influence rests on the relations he builds with superiors and protégé, with retired party elders often retaining a great deal of influence. Towards the end of his life, for example, Deng Xiaoping was virtually running the country when his only official title was head of a bridge club. The country's head of state is its president, while the head of government is the premier. Politburo members are supposedly chosen by the three thousand delegates of the National People's Congress, officially a parliament though it in fact serves largely as a rubber stamp for Politburo decisions. In recent years, though, it has displayed a modicum of independence, for instance delaying an unpopular fuel tax in 1999.

The Party owes its success, of course, to the **military**, and links with the PLA remain close, though the army has lost power since Jiang Zemin stripped its huge business empire in the 1990s. There is no PLA representative on the standing committee, but the military has a strong influence on policy issues, particularly over Taiwan and relations with the US, and generally maintains a hard line.

The law in China is a mix of legislation based on party priorities and new statutes to haul the economy into line with those of major foreign investors. The National People's Congress is responsible for drafting laws covering taxation and human rights, among other subjects. In other areas, the State Council and local governments can legislate. Even after laws have been passed there is no guarantee they will be respected; provincial governments and state-owned enterprises view court decisions as negotiable, and for the party and the state, the rule of law is not allowed to supersede its own interests.

astonishing: in the 1970s the "three big buys" – consumer goods to which families could realistically aspire – were a bicycle, a watch and a radio; in the 1980s they were a washing machine, a TV and a refrigerator; and the urban Chinese today can aspire to the same material comforts as their Western counterparts. No wonder the country comes across as confident and ambitious.

Under **Jiang Zemin**, who took power in 1993, and then under his protégé **Hu Jintao**, who took over in 2002, China continued its course of controlled liberalization. In its pursuit of a "socialist market economy with Chinese characteristics", the state continued to retreat from whole areas of life. Mechanisms of control such as the household registration and work-unit systems have largely been abandoned. The private sector now accounts for almost half of the economy, and foreign-funded ventures represent more than half the country's exports.

Today, "scientific development" and "harmonious society" are the catchphrases coming from the Politburo technocrats. In practise that means both heavy handed political control and a genuine effort to deal with social problems. Alarmed at growing income inequality, efforts have been made to shift society away from unbridled capitalism towards a more socially responsible model of development.

Stumbling blocks

Behind the talk of a wonder economy there are **problems**. Even now, more than half of China's citizens live on less than a dollar a day. Prosperity has been delivered unevenly – the east coast cities have benefited most – **inflation** is rising, and there's little in the way of medical care or subsidized education for either urban or rural poor. One of the more visible results of rising living costs (exacerbated by increased agricultural mechanization) has been the **mass migration** of the working class from the country to the cities, where most remain unemployed or are hired by the day as labourers.

Fifteen million new jobs need to be created every year just to keep up with population growth. Bubbles are forming in property and the steel market. Power generation and water supplies are running up against capacity constraints. The banking system is inefficient, with US$500 billion of bad loans. Only a high domestic savings rate and uncontrolled exploitation of natural resources make China's growth possible, and neither is sustainable.

Short-term gain has become the overriding factor in Chinese planning, with the result that the future is mortgaged for present wealth. Too little thought is given to the environmental effects of modernization, and China now boasts eight of the top ten most **polluted cities** in the world. As success is largely dependent on *guanxi* (connections), the potential for **corruption** is enormous – indeed, graft is thought to be slicing at least a percentage point off growth figures. As in the past, a desperately poor peasantry is at the mercy of corrupt cadres who enrich themselves by setting and purloining local taxes.

Perhaps China's biggest problem is its massive **population** (1.3 billion in 2007), which could put unbearable pressure on resources if it continues to rise. Under the **one-child policy**, which began in 1979, couples who have a second

Human rights

Despite magnificent progress on the economic level, the Chinese state continues to be one of the world's worst regimes for human rights abuses – despite many of those rights being enshrined in its own constitution.

The Communist Party ... tolerates no dissent, permits no rivals and ... locks up anyone perceived as a challenge, be they journalists, lawyers, bloggers, whistleblowers, petitioners or followers of religious cults such as Falun Gong. The highest profile incarcerated dissident is Nobel prize winner **Liu Xiaobo**, whose crime was to write "Charter 08", a document calling for political reform; he is now serving an eleven-year sentence. Other activists currently in prison include Doctor Gao Yaojie, who exposed how blood collectors were spreading AIDS; Zhao Lianhai, who lobbied for compensation for the families whose babies were harmed by tainted baby milk; and Chen Guancheng, who campaigned against forced sterilizations. There are many more, and observers say that the situation for activists has worsened in recent years.

China has no independent judiciary, rule of law or due process, and around half a million people are currently enduring detention without charge or trial. Torture and execution remain commonplace. But the country's most serious human rights abuses are being perpetrated in **Tibet**, where dissent is ruthlessly suppressed and Tibetan culture is being swamped by Han migration. In 1995, when the exiled Dalai Lama selected a new Panchen Lama following the death of the previous one, the boy he chose, Gedhun Choekyi Nyima, was arrested, along with his family; he remains the world's youngest political prisoner. It is common for Tibetans to receive long sentences of hard labour not just for criticizing the regime (Dhondup Wangchen is serving six years for his short film, *Leaving Fear Behind*) but also for singing songs about freedom or owning a picture of the Dalai Lama.

In 2008 a group of Tibetans fleeing to Nepal were fired on by border guards at the Nangpa Pass; they shot a teenage nun, Kelsang Namtso, in the back then left her to die in the snow. What is unusual about this incident is not that it occurred – exiles say that sort of thing happens all the time – but that it was filmed by Western climbers. You can see the footage on YouTube (search for "Murder in the Snow").

child face a cut in wages and restricted access to health care and housing. The policy has been most successful in the cities, but given the heavy preference for male children, female infanticide and the selling of girls as brides are not unusual, while there is a growing trend for kidnapping male children for ransom or, again, sale.

Despite all the gleaming high-rises, little progress has been made on the hallmarks of genuine modernity – investment in education, the rule of law, the freedom of the press and executive accountability. Every year, there are widespread demonstrations by industrial workers who are out of work or owed back pay, by villagers protesting at pollution or corruption, and by homeowners protesting at enforced demolitions. Such actions represent possibly the biggest internal threat to the state. The blame, as well as the credit for creating and managing an economic boom, lies squarely with the Communist Party; designed to change society, it is now incapable of adapting to it. That's fine, as long as economic growth continues apace. But without the safety valves provided by transparency and democracy, if the economy falters, China's political stability is far from assured.

China and the world

Historically, being surrounded by "barbarians" and inhospitable terrain has led China towards **insularity**. Accordingly, the government's tactic during China's stellar period of economic development has been not to intervene on the world stage. But its explosive expansion is now forcing engagement, and the country is coming under scrutiny as never before. As the world's biggest emitter of greenhouse gases, it is under increasing international pressure to start cleaning up its act. China's skewed **business environment** – lax enforcement of intellectual property and business laws, bullying of foreign companies in favour of local competition, unfair regulatory barriers and an artificially low currency – is now attracting plenty of criticism from its trading partners.

In order to fuel growth, China needs to look elsewhere for raw materials: in Africa, the Pacific and Southeast Asia, China has become the new **resource colonizer**, striking deals with all comers, including nations shunned by the West such as Zimbabwe and Sudan. How China handles its growing influence will determine whether east Asia remains stable enough to continue to prosper, or tumbles back into conflict and rivalry. China's willingness to bind itself to global rules, such as those of the World Trade Organization, has been a welcome way to assimilate it, but an authoritarian, anti-democratic China will never be easy for its neighbours to live with, and Chinese primacy in the Pacific is contested by both Japan and the US.

China's antipathy towards **Japan** stems from Japan's perceived failure to be properly contrite over its crimes in World War II, ongoing territorial disputes over some insignificant islands, and simple rivalry; every year some trivial issue becomes a flashpoint for anti-Japanese demonstrations. These are awkward for the government: patriotic demonstrations in the last century were often the precursor to pro-democracy unrest, but at the same time the Party would rather not crack down on expressions of nationalism, as such fervour is whipped up by the Party to justify its existence and right to rule.

China today embraces the outside world as never before; witness the passion with which the English language is studied and the fascination with foreign mores, goods, even football teams. Both China and the world have much to gain from Chinese openness. It would be a shame for both should political shakiness lead to a retreat from that.

Chronology

4800 BC ▸ First evidence of **human settlement**. **Banpo** in the Yellow River basin build Bronze Age town of **Erlitou** in Henan. **Yin** in Anyang boasts a rich and developed culture.

21C–16C BC ▸ **Xia dynasty**.

16C–11C BC ▸ **Shang dynasty**. First extant writing in China.

11C–771 BC ▸ **Zhou dynasty**. Concept of **Mandate of Heaven** introduced.

770 BC–476 BC ▸ **Spring and Autumn** period. Kong Fuzi or **Confucius** (c. 500 BC) teaches a philosophy of adherence to ritual and propriety.

457 BC–221 BC ▸ **Warring States** period. The **Great Wall** "completed".

221 BC–207 BC ▸ **Qin dynasty**. Emperor **Qin Shi Huang** founds first centralized empire. **Terracotta Army** guard Qin's tomb.

206 BC–220 AD ▸ **Han dynasty**. Han emperors bring stability and great advances in trade; leave **Han tombs** near Xi'an. **Confucianism** and **Buddhism** ascendant. **Silk Road** opens up first trade with Central Asia.

220–280 ▸ **Three Kingdoms** period; influence of Buddhist **India** and **Central Asia** enlivens a Dark Age.

265–420 ▸ **Jin dynasty**. Northern barbarians absorbed into Chinese culture.

420–581 ▸ **Southern dynasties and Northern dynasties**: rapid succession of short-lived dynasties brings disunity. Earliest **Longmen caves** near Luoyang.

581–618 ▸ **Sui dynasty**. Centralization and growth under **Wen Di**. Extension and strengthening of **Great Wall**; digging of **Grand Canal**.

618–907 ▸ **Tang dynasty**. Arts and literature reach their most developed stage. **Great Buddha** at Leshan completed.

907–960 ▸ **Five dynasties**. Decline of culture and the northern defences. **Cliff sculptures** of Dazu.

960–1271 ▸ **Song dynasties**. Consolidation of the lesser kingdoms.

1271–1368 ▸ **Yuan dynasty**. **Genghis Khan** invades. Trade with Europe develops under **Kublai Khan**. **Forbidden City** built. **Marco Polo** visits China 1273–92.

1368–1644 ▸ **Ming dynasty**. Imperial investigative fleet under **Admiral Zheng He** reaches Africa. Later isolationist policies restrict contact with rest of world.

1644 ▸ **Qing dynasty** begins. **Manchus** gain control over China and extend its boundaries.

Mid- to late 17C ▸ **Potala Palace** in Lhasa rebuilt by Fifth Dalai Lama.

Late 18C ▸ **East India Company** monopolizes trade with Britain. **Summer Palace** in Beijing completed.

1839–62 ▸ **Opium Wars**. As part of the surrender settlement, **Hong Kong** is ceded to Britain.

1851–64 ▸ **Taiping Uprising**. Conservative policies of Dowager Empress **Cixi** allow foreign powers to take control of China's industry.

1899 ▸ **Boxer Rebellion**.

1911 ▸ **End of imperial China**. **Sun Yatsen** becomes leader of the **Republic**.

1921 ▸ **Chinese Communist Party** founded in Beijing.

1927 ▸ **Chiang Kai-shek** orders massacre of Communists in Shanghai. **Mao Zedong** organizes first peasant-worker army.

1932 ▸ Japan invades **Manchuria**.

1936–41 ▸ The Nationalist **Guomindang** and the **People's Liberation Army form the United Front** against the Japanese.

1945 ▸ Surrender of Japan. **Civil war** between the Guomindang and the People's Liberation Army.

1949 ▸ Communist takeover. Chiang Kai-shek flees to **Taiwan**. The newly proclaimed **People's Republic of China** supports North Korea in the **Korean War**.

1957 ▸ The **Hundred Flowers** campaign unsuccessfully attempts liberalization.

1958 ▸ Agricultural and industrial reform in the shape of the **commune system** and the **Great Leap Forward**. Widespread famine results.

1964 ▸ China explodes its first atomic weapon.

1966–68 ▸ In the **Cultural Revolution**, Red Guards purge anti-Maoist elements along with "ideologically unsound" art and architecture.

1971 ▸ People's Republic replaces Taiwan at the **United Nations**.

1972 ▸ **US president Nixon** visits Beijing.

1976 ▸ The **Tian'anmen Incident** reveals public support for moderate **Deng Xiaoping**. **Mao Zedong dies**, and the **Gang of Four** are arrested shortly afterwards.

1977 ▸ Deng Xiaoping rises to become **Party Chairman**.

1980 ▸ Beginning of the "open door" policy.

1981 ▸ Trial of the **Gang of Four**.

1989 ▸ Suppression of the democracy movement in **Tian'anmen Square**.

1992 ▸ Major **cabinet reshuffle** puts Deng's men in power.

1995 ▸ Death of Chen Yun, last of the hardline Maoists in the Politburo. Work begins on the **Three Gorges Dam**.

1997 ▸ **Hong Kong** returns to the mainland. Death of **Deng Xiaoping**.

1999 ▸ **Macau** returns to the mainland. Persecution of **Falun Gong** begins.

2001 ▸ China admitted to the **World Trade Organization**.

2002 ▸ **Hu Jintao** becomes President.

2003 ▸ China puts a man into space.

2004 ▸ **SARS** epidemic; China's population reaches 1.3 billion.

2006 ▸ The **Three Gorges Dam** is finished, and the new railway line to **Tibet** opens.

2008 ▸ The lavish **Beijing Olympic Games**, at which China topped the medals table, served to cement China's status as the new major global power.

2010 ▸ World Expo held in Shanghai; just over 73 million visitors attend.

Chinese beliefs

The resilience of ancient beliefs in China, and the ability of the Chinese people to absorb new streams of thought and eventually to dominate them, has been demonstrated repeatedly over the centuries. That said, any visitor to modern China will find few obvious indications of the traditional beliefs that have underpinned the country's civilization for three thousand years. Certainly, the remains of religious buildings litter the cities and the countryside, yet they appear sadly incongruous amid the furious pace of change all around. The restored temples – now "cultural relics" – are garish and evoke few mysteries.

This apparent lack of religion is hardly surprising, however: for decades, the old beliefs have been derided by the authorities as feudal **superstition**, and the oldest and most firmly rooted of them all, Confucianism, has been criticized and repudiated for nearly a century. Yet in actual fact, the outward manifestations of the ancient beliefs are not essential: the traditions are expressed more clearly in how the Chinese think and act than in the symbols and rituals of overt worship.

The Three Teachings

The product of the oldest continuous civilization on earth, **Chinese religion** actually comprises a number of disparate and sometimes contradictory elements. At the heart of it lie **three basic philosophies**: Confucianism, Taoism and Buddhism. The way in which a harmonious balance has been created among these three is expressed in the often quoted maxim *san jiao fa yi* – "Three Teachings Flow into One".

Confucianism

China's oldest and greatest philosopher, Kong Zi, known in the West by his Latinized name **Confucius**, was in his lifetime an obscure and unsuccessful scholar. Born in 551 BC, during the so-called Warring States Period, he lived in an

Superstitions

Though the Chinese are not generally religious in the conventional sense, they are often very **superstitious**. You'll see evidence of this everywhere you go, especially in the form of wordplay. Thus the Chinese expression for "let luck come", *fudao*, happens to sound similar to "upside-down luck"; hence the inverted *fu* character pasted up outside homes and businesses at Spring Festival, encouraging good fortune to arrive on the premises. Other **lucky symbols** include peaches and cranes (for longevity), fish (prosperity), mandarin ducks (marital fidelity), dragons (male power), phoenixes (female power) and bats (happiness).

Colours are also important. **Red**, the colour of fire, and **gold**, the colour of money, are auspicious, and used extensively for decorations, packaging, weddings and festive occasions. **White** traditionally represents death or mourning, though traditional Western wedding dresses are becoming increasingly popular. **Yellow** is the colour of heaven, hence the yellow roof tiles used on temples; yellow clothing was formerly reserved for the emperor alone.

age of petty kingdoms where life was blighted by constant conflict. Confucius taught the simple message that society could be improved if individuals behaved properly. Harking back to an earlier, mythic age of peace and social virtues, he preached adherence to **ritual and propriety** as the supreme answer to the horrifying disorder of the world as he found it. No one paid much attention while he was alive; after his death, however, his writings were collected as the **Analects**, and this book became the most influential and fundamental of Chinese philosophies.

Never a religion in the sense of postulating a higher deity, Confucianism is rather a set of **moral and social values** designed to bring the ways of citizens and governments into harmony with each other. Through proper training in the scholarly classics and rigid adherence to the rules of propriety, including ancestor-worship, the superior man could attain a level of moral righteousness that would, in turn, assure a stable and righteous social order. As a political theory, Confucianism called for the "**wisest sage**", the one whose moral sense was most refined, to be ruler. A good ruler who exemplified the **five Confucian virtues** – benevolence, righteousness, propriety, wisdom and trustworthiness – would bring society naturally to order. As Confucius said:

> **Just as the ruler genuinely desires the good, the people will be good. The virtue of the ruler may be compared to the wind and that of the common people to the grass. The grass under the force of the wind cannot but bend.**

Instead of God, **five hierarchical relationships** are the prerequisites for a well-ordered society; given proper performance of the duties entailed in these, society should be "at ease with itself". The five relationships outline a structure of duty and obedience to authority: ruler to ruled, son to father, younger brother to older, wife to husband, and – the only relationship between equals – friend to friend. In practice, adherence to the unbending hierarchy of these relationships, as well as to the precepts of filial piety, has been used to justify totalitarian rule throughout Chinese history. The supreme virtue of the well-cultivated man and woman was always **obedience**.

During the time of the Han dynasty (206 BC–220 AD), Confucianism became institutionalized as a **system of government** that was to prevail for two thousand years. With it, and with the notion of the scholar-official as the ideal administrator, came the notorious Chinese **bureaucracy**. Men would study half their lives in order to pass examinations on Confucian thought and attain a government commission. Right until the start of the twentieth century, power was wielded through a bureaucracy steeped in the rites and rituals written five hundred years before Christ.

The Confucian ideal ruler, of course, never quite emerged (the emperor was not expected to sit the exams), and the scholar-officials often deteriorated into corrupt bureaucrats and exploitative landlords. Today, its rituals are no longer practiced and its ideas have no currency. However, just as Protestantism is seen as having provided the underpinning to the advance of the West, so Confucianism, with its emphasis on order, harmony and co-operation, has been regarded as providing the ideological foundations for the recent successes of Asian culture.

Taoism

Taoism is the study and pursuit of the ineffable "Way", as outlined in the fundamental text, the **Daodejing** (often written as *Tao Te Ching*) or "The Way of Power". This obscure and mystical text comprises a compilation of the wise sayings of the semi-mythical hermit **Lao Zi**, a contemporary of Confucius. The

Daodejing was not compiled until at least three centuries after his death.

The *Tao* is never really defined – indeed by its very nature it is undefinable. To the despair of the rationalist, the first lines of the *Daodejing* read:

The Tao that can be told
is not the eternal Tao.
The name that can be named
is not the eternal name.

In essence, however, it might be thought of as the underlying principle and source of all being, the bond that unites man and nature. Its central principle, **Wu Wei**, can crudely be translated as "no action", though it is probably better understood as "no action which runs contrary to nature". Whereas Confucianism is concerned with repairing social order and social relationships, Taoism is interested in the relationship of the individual with the natural universe.

Taoism's second major text is a book of parables written by one ideal practitioner of the Way, **Zhuang Zi**, another semi-mythical figure. In the famous butterfly parable, Zhuang Zi examines the many faces of reality:

Once upon a time Zhuang Zi dreamed he was a butterfly. A butterfly flying around and enjoying itself. It did not know it was Zhuang Zi again. We do not know whether it was Zhuang Zi dreaming that he was a butterfly, or a butterfly dreaming he was Zhuang Zi.

In its affirmation of the irrational and natural sources of life, Taoism has provided Chinese culture with a balance to the rigid social mores of Confucianism. In traditional China it was said that the perfect lifestyle was to be Confucian during the day – a righteous and firm administrator, upholding the virtues of the gentleman ruler – and a Taoist when relaxing. If Confucianism preaches duty to family and to society, Taoism champions the sublimity of withdrawal, non-committedness and "dropping out". The **art and literature** of China have been greatly enriched by Taoism's notions of contemplation, detachment and freedom from social entanglement, and the Tao has become embedded in the Chinese soul as a doctrine of yielding to the inevitable forces of nature.

Buddhism

The first organized religion to penetrate China, **Buddhism** enjoyed a glorious, if brief, period of ascendancy under the Tang dynasty (618–907 AD). In the eighth

Getting around a Chinese temple

Whether Buddhist or Taoist, Chinese temples share the same broad **features**. Like cities, they **face south** and are surrounded by walls. Gates are sealed by **heavy doors**, guarded by paintings or statues of warrior deities to chase away evil. Further protection is ensured by a **spirit wall** that blocks direct entry; although easy enough for the living to walk around, this foils spirits, who are unable to turn corners. Once inside, you'll find a succession of **halls** arranged in ornamental courtyards. In case evil influences should manage to get in, the area nearest the entrance contains the least important rooms or buildings, while those of greater significance – living quarters or main temple halls – are set deeper inside the complex.

One way to tell **Buddhist** and **Taoist** temples apart is by the colour of the **supporting pillars** – Buddhists use bright red, while Taoists favour black. **Animal carvings** are more popular with Taoists, who use decorative good-luck and longevity symbols such as bats and cranes; some Taoist halls also have distinctive raised octagonal cupolas sporting the black-and-white *yin-yang* symbol.

century there were over 300,000 Buddhist monks in China. This time saw the creation of much of the country's **great religious art** – above all the cave shrines at **Luoyang** (Henan), **Datong** (Shaanxi) and **Dunhuang** (Gansu), where thousands of carvings of the Buddha and paintings of holy figures attest to the powerful influence of Indian art and religion.

Gradually, though, Buddhism was submerged into the native belief system. Most contemporary schools of Indian Buddhism taught that life on earth was essentially one of suffering, an endless cycle in which people were born, grew old and died, only to be born again in other bodies; the goal was to break out of this by attaining nirvana, which could be done by losing all desire for things of the world. This essentially individualistic doctrine was not likely to appeal to the regimented Chinese, however, and so it was the relatively small **Mahayana School** of Buddhism that came to dominate Chinese thinking. The Mahayana taught that perfection for the individual was not possible without perfection for all – and that those who had already attained enlightenment would remain active in the world as **Bodhisattvas**, to help others along the path. In time Bodhisattvas came to be ascribed miraculous powers, and were prayed to in a manner remarkably similar to conventional Confucian ancestor-worship. The mainstream of Chinese Buddhism came to be more about maintaining harmonious relations with Bodhisattvas than about attaining nirvana.

Another entirely new sect of Buddhism also arose in China through contact with Taoism. Known in China as **Chan** (and in Japan as Zen) Buddhism, it offered a less extreme path to enlightenment. For a Chan Buddhist, it was not necessary to become a monk or a recluse in order to achieve nirvana – instead this ultimate state of being could be reached through life in accord with, and in contemplation of, the Way.

In short, the Chinese managed to marry Buddhism to their pre-existing belief structures with very little difficulty. This was facilitated by the general absence of dogma within Buddhist thought. Like the Chinese, the **Tibetans**, too, found themselves able to adapt the new belief system to their old religion, **Bon** (see p.791), rather than simply replacing it. Over the centuries, they established their own schools of Buddhism, often referred to as Lamaist Buddhism or **Lamaism**, which differ from the Chinese versions in minor respects. The now dominant **Gelugpa** (or Yellow Hat) school, of which the Dalai and Panchen Lamas are members, dates back to the teachings of Tsongkhapa (1357–1419). For more on Buddhism in Tibet, see p.890 & p.891.

Minority faiths and popular beliefs

Though Buddhism was the only foreign religion to leave a substantial mark on China, it was not the only one to enter China via the Silk Road. Both **Islam** and **Christianity** also trickled into the country this way, and to this day a significant minority of Chinese, numbering in the tens of millions, are Muslim. Unlike much of the rest of Asia, however, China did not yield wholesale to the tide of Islam, and thoroughly rejected it as a political doctrine.

When Jesuit missionaries first arrived in China in the sixteenth and seventeenth centuries, they were astounded and dismayed by the Chinese **flexibility of belief**. One frustrated Jesuit put it thus: "In China, the educated believe nothing and the uneducated believe everything". For those versed in the classics of Confucianism, Taoism and Buddhism, the normal belief was a healthy and tolerant scepticism.

For the great majority of illiterate peasants, however, **popular religion** offered a plethora of ghosts, spirits, gods and ancestors who ruled over a capricious nature and protected humanity. If Christian missionaries handed out rice, perhaps Christ too deserved a place alongside them. In popular Buddhism the hope was to reach the "Pure Land", a kind of heaven for believers ruled over by a female deity known as the Mother Ruler. Popular Taoism shared this feminine deity, but its concerns were rather with the sorcerers, alchemists and martial-arts aficionados who sought solutions to the riddle of immortality; you may see some of these figures depicted in Taoist temples.

Modern China

During the twentieth century, confronted by the superior military and technical power of the West, the Chinese have striven to break free from the shackles of superstition. Since the imperial examinations were abolished at the start of the twentieth century, Chinese intellectuals have been searching for a modern yet essentially Chinese philosophy. The **Cultural Revolution** can be seen as the culmination of these efforts to repudiate the past. Hundreds of thousands of temples, ancestral halls and religious objects were defaced and destroyed. Monasteries were burnt to the ground, and their monks imprisoned. The classics of literature and philosophy – the "residue of the reactionary feudal past" – were burned. In 1974, towards the end of the Cultural Revolution, a campaign was launched to "criticize Lin Biao and Confucius", pairing the general with the sage to imply that both were equally reactionary in their opposition to the government.

Yet the very fact that Confucius could still be held up as an object for derision in 1974 reveals the tenacity of traditional beliefs. With the Cultural Revolution now long gone, they are once again being accepted as an essential part of the cultural tradition that binds the Chinese people together. Despite a lifetime of commitment to the Marxist revolution, the older generation are comforted and strengthened by their knowledge of the national heritage, while the young are rediscovering the classics, the forbidden fruit of their school days. The welcome result is that Chinese temples of all descriptions are once more prosperous, busy places, teeming with people who have come to ask for grandchildren or simply for money. The atmosphere may not seem devout or religious, but then perhaps it never did.

Traditional Chinese Medicine

As an agricultural society, the Chinese have long been aware of the importance of the **balance** of natural, elemental forces: too much heat causes drought; too much rain, floods; while the correct measure of both encourages farmers' crops to grow. The ancient Chinese saw heaven, earth and humankind existing as an integral whole, such that if people lived in harmony with heaven and earth, then their collective health would be good. The medical treatise *Huang Di Neijing*, attributed to the semi-mythical Yellow Emperor (2500 BC), mentions the importance of spiritual balance, acupuncture and herbal medicine in treating illnesses, and attests to the venerable age of China's medical beliefs – it may well be a compilation of even earlier texts. Acupuncture was certainly in use by the Han period, as tombs in Hebei dated to 113 BC have yielded acupuncture needles made of gold and silver.

The belief in universal balance is known as **Dao** (or Tao) – literally "the Way". As an extension of Daoist principles, life is seen as consisting of opposites – man and woman, sun and moon, right and left, giving and receiving – whereby all things exist as a result of their interaction with their opposites. This is expressed in the black-and-white Daoist diagram which shows two interacting opposites, the **yin** ("female", passive energy) and the **yang** ("male", active energy). At the core of Traditional Chinese Medicine lies the belief that in order for a body to be healthy, its opposites must also be in a state of dynamic balance; there is a constant fluctuation, for example, between the body's heat, depending on its level of activity and the weather, and the amount of water needed to keep the body at the correct temperature. An excess of water in the system creates oedema, too little creates dehydration; too much heat will cause a temperature, and too little cause chills. Chinese medicine therefore views the body as an integrated whole, so that in sickness, the whole body – rather than just the "ill" part of it – requires treatment.

Qi and acupuncture

An underlying feature of Chinese medical philosophy, **qi** (or *chi*) is the energy of life: in the same way that electricity powers a light bulb, *qi*, so the theory goes, enables us to move, see and speak. *Qi* is said to flow along the body's network of **meridians**, or energy pathways, linking the surface tissues to specific internal **organs** that act as *qi* reservoirs; the twelve major meridians are named after the organ to which they are connected. The meridians are further classed as *yin* or *yang* depending on whether they are exposed or protected. In the limbs, for instance, the channels of the outer sides are *yang*, and important for resisting disease, while the channels of the inner sides are *yin*, and more involved with nourishing the body.

Mental and physical tensions, poor diet, anger or depression, even adverse weather, are said to inhibit *qi* flow, causing illness. Needles inserted (and then rotated as necessary) in the body's **acupuncture points**, most of which lie on meridians and so are connected to internal organs, reinforce or reduce the *qi* flow along a meridian, in turn influencing the activities of the organs. When the *qi* is balanced and flowing smoothly once more, good health is regained; acupuncture is specifically used to combat inflammation, to regenerate damaged tissue and to improve the functional power of internal organs.

That said, despite the growing acceptance of acupuncture in the West, there remains no good evidence for its efficacy. Studies have found that patients treated by acupuncturists had the same recovery rate as patients poked with needles at random positions. Sceptics argue that the act of sticking needles in the body produces pain-killing endorphins, which, combined with the placebo effect, aids recovery.

Herbal medicine

In the 2200 years since the semi-mythical Xia king **Shennong** compiled his classic work on **medicinal herbs**, a vast amount of experience has been gained to help perfect their clinical use. Approximately seven thousand herbs, derived from roots, leaves, twigs and fruit, are today commonly used in Chinese medicine, with another thousand or so of animal or mineral origin (still nonetheless classified as "herbs"). Each is first processed by cleaning, soaking, slicing, drying or roasting, or even stir-frying with wine, ginger or vinegar, to influence its effects; the brew is then boiled down and drunk as a tea (typically very bitter and earthy tasting).

Herbs are used to prevent or combat a wide variety of diseases. Some are used to treat the underlying cause of the complaint, others to treat symptoms and help strengthen the body's own immune system, in turn helping it to combat the problem. An everyday example is in the treatment of flu: the herbal formula would include a "cold action" herb to reduce the fever, a herb to induce sweating and thus clear the body-ache, a purgative to clear the virus from the system, and a tonic herb to replenish the immune system. In all treatments, the patient is re-examined each week, and as the condition improves the herbal formula is changed accordingly.

Just as Western aspirin is derived from willow bark, many Chinese drugs have been developed from herbs. One example is the anti-malarial herb *qinghaosu*, or artemisinin, which has proved effective in treating chloroquine-resistant strains of malaria with minimal side effects.

Art

Chinese art objects have had a difficult modern history: in the nineteenth century many were acquired by Westerners; then the greatest collections were taken by the Nationalists to Taiwan, where they are now in the National Palace Museum; many more art objects were destroyed during the Cultural Revolution. Yet what remains is still an astonishing wealth of treasures.

Pottery, bronzes and sculpture

The earliest Chinese objects date back to the Neolithic farmers of the **Yangshao** culture – **pottery** vessels painted with geometric designs. The decoration is from the shoulders of the pots upwards, as what has survived is mostly from graves and was designed to be seen from above when the pots were placed round the dead. From the same period come decorated clay heads, and pendants and ornaments of polished stone or jade – a simplified sitting bird in polished jade is a very early example of the Chinese tradition of animal sculpture. Rather later is the Neolithic **Longshan** pottery – black, thin and fine, wheel-turned and often highly polished, with elegant, sharply defined shapes.

The subsequent era, from around 1500 BC, is dominated by **Shang and Zhou bronze vessels** that were used for preparing and serving food and wine, and for ceremonies and sacrifices. One of the most common shapes is the *ding*, a three- or four-legged vessel that harks back to the Neolithic pots used for cooking over open fires. Casting methods were highly sophisticated, using moulds, while design was firm and assured and decoration often stylized and linear, featuring geometric and animal motifs, as well as grinning masks of humans and fabulous beasts. There are some naturalistic animal forms among the vessels, too – fierce tigers, solid elephants and surly rhinoceroses. Other bronze finds include weapons, decorated horse harnesses and sets of bells used in ritual music.

Later, under the **Zhou**, the style of the bronzes becomes more varied and rich: some animal vessels are fantastically shaped and extravagantly decorated; others are simplified natural forms; others again seem to be depicting not so much a fierce tiger, for example, as utter ferocity itself. You'll also see from the Shang and Zhou small objects – ornaments, ritual pieces and jewellery pendants – bearing highly simplified but vivid forms of tortoises, salamanders and flying birds. Some painted clay funeral figures and a few carved wooden figures also survive from the end of this period.

Although the Shang produced a few small sculpted human figures and animals in marble, **sculptures** and works in stone begin to be found in great quantities in **Han-dynasty** tombs. The decorated bricks and tiles, the bas-reliefs and the terracotta figurines of acrobats, horsemen and ladies-in-waiting placed in the tombs to serve the dead, even the massive stone men and beasts set to guard the Spirit Way leading to the tomb, are all lifelike and reflect concern with everyday activities and material possessions. The scale models of houses with people looking out of the windows and of farmyards with their animals have a spontaneous gaiety and vigour; some of the watchdogs are the most realistic of all.

It was the advent of **Buddhism** that encouraged stone carving on a large scale in the round, using mallet and chisel. **Religious sculpture** was introduced from India; in the fourth-century caves at **Datong** (see p.234), and the earlier caves at **Longmen**, near Luoyang (see p.277), the Indian influence is most strongly felt in the stylized Buddhas and attendants. Sometimes of huge size, these have an aloof grace and a rhythmic quality in their flowing robes, but also a smooth, bland and static quality. Not until the **Tang** do you get the full flowering of a native Chinese style, where the figures are rounder, with movement, and the positions, expressions and clothes are more natural and realistic. Some of the best examples are to be seen at **Dunhuang** (see p.840) and in the later caves at Longmen. The **Song** continued to carve religious figures, and at **Dazu** in Sichuan (see p.776), you'll find good examples of a decorative style that had broadened its subject matter to include animals, ordinary people and scenes of everyday life; the treatment is down-to-earth, individual, even comic. As the Dazu carvings are well preserved, they can still be seen painted, as they were meant to be. In later years, less statuary was produced until the **Ming** with their taste for massive tomb sculptures. You can see the best of these in **Nanjing** and **Beijing**.

Ceramics

From Neolithic painted pottery onwards, China developed excellent **ceramics**, a pre-eminence recognized even in the English language, which took the word "china" to mean fine-quality ceramic ware. In some of the early wares you can see the influence of shapes derived from bronzes, but soon the rise of regional potteries using different materials, and the development of special types for different uses, led to an enormous variety of shapes, textures and colours. This was really noticeable in the **Tang dynasty**, when an increase in the production of pottery for daily use was stimulated by the spread of tea drinking, and by the restriction of the use of valuable copper and bronze to coinage. The Tang also saw major technical advances; the production of true **porcelain** was finally achieved, and Tang potters became skilled in the delicate art of polychrome glazing. You can see evidence of this in the *san cai* (three-colour) statuettes of horses and camels, jugglers, traders, polo players, grooms and court ladies, which have come in great numbers from imperial tombs, and which reflect in vivid, often humorous, detail and still-brilliant colours so many aspects of the life of the time.

The **Song** dynasty witnessed a refinement of ceramic techniques and of regional specialization. The keynote was simplicity and quiet elegance, in both colour and form. There was a preference for using **single pure colours**, and for incized wares made to resemble damask cloth. In the museums you'll see the famous green celadons, the thin white porcelain *ding* ware and the pale grey-green *ju* ware reserved for imperial use. The Mongol **Yuan** dynasty, in the early fourteenth century, enriched Chinese tradition with outside influences – notably the introduction of **cobalt blue underglaze**, early examples of the blue and white porcelain that was to become so famous.

The **Ming** saw the flowering of great potteries under imperial patronage, especially **Jingdezhen**. Taste moved away from Song simplicity and returned to the liking for the vivid, almost gaudy colour previously displayed by the Tang – deep **red**, **yellow** and **orange** glazes, with a developing taste for pictorial representation. From the seventeenth century onwards, Chinese export wares flowed in great quantity and variety to the West to satisfy a growing demand for chinoiserie, and the efforts of the Chinese artists to follow what they saw as the tastes and techniques of the West produced a style of its own. The early **Qing** created delicate enamel wares and *famille rose* and *verte*. So precise were the craftsmen that some porcelain includes the instructions for the pattern in the glaze.

You can visit potteries such as at **Jingdezhen** in Jiangxi province, where both early wares and modern trends are on display. Not so long ago they were turning out thousands of figurines of Mao and Lu Xun sitting in armchairs; now the emphasis is on table lamp bases, Laughing Buddhas and the like.

Painting and calligraphy

While China's famous ceramics were made by craftsmen who remained anonymous, **painting and calligraphy** pieces were produced by famous scholars, officials and poets. It has been said that the four great treasures of Chinese painting are the brush, the ink, the inkstone and the paper or silk. The earliest **brush** to have been found dates from about 400 BC, and is made out of animal hairs glued to a hollow bamboo tube. **Ink** was made from pine soot, mixed with glue and hardened into a stick that would be rubbed with water on a slate **inkstone**. The first known painting on silk was found in a **Han** tomb; records show that a great deal of such painting was created, but in 190 AD the vast imperial collection was destroyed in a civil war, when soldiers used the silk to make tents and knapsacks. All we know of Han painting comes from decorated tiles, lacquer, painted pottery and a few painted tombs, enough to show a great sense of movement and energy. The British Museum holds a scroll in ink and colour on silk from around 400 AD, attributed to **Gu Kaizhi** and entitled *Admonitions of the Instructress to Court Ladies*, and it's known that the theory of painting was already being discussed by then, as the treatise *The Six Principles of Painting* dates from about 500 AD.

The **Sui-Tang** period, with a powerful stable empire and a brilliant court, was the perfect moment for painting to develop. A great tradition of **figure painting** grew up, especially of court subjects – portraits and pictures of the emperor receiving envoys, and of court ladies, can be seen in Beijing. Although only a few of these survived, the walls of Tang tombs, such as those near Xi'an, are rich in vivid frescoes that provide a realistic portrayal of court life. Wang Wei in the mid-eighth century was an early exponent of monochrome **landscape painting**, but the great flowering of landscape painting came with the **Song dynasty**. An academy was set up under imperial patronage, and different schools of painting emerged which analysed the natural world with great concentration and intensity; their style has set a mark on Chinese landscape painting ever since. There was also lively **figure painting**, as epitomized by a famous horizontal scroll in Beijing that depicts the Qing Ming River Festival. The Southern Song preferred a more intimate style, and such subjects as flowers, birds and still life grew in popularity.

Under the **Mongols**, many officials found themselves unwanted or unwilling to serve the alien Yuan dynasty, and preferred to retire and paint. This produced the **"literati" school**, in which many painters harked back to the styles of the tenth century. One great master, **Ni Can**, also devoted himself, among many others, to the ink paintings of bamboo that became important at this time. In this school, of which many examples remain extant, the highest skills of techniques and composition were applied to the simplest of subjects, such as plum flowers. Both ink painting as well as more conventional media continued to be employed by painters during the next three or more centuries. From the **Yuan** onwards, a tremendous quantity of paintings has survived. The **Ming dynasty** saw a great interest in collecting the works of previous ages, and a willingness by painters to be influenced by tradition. There are plenty of examples of bamboo and plum blossom, and bird and flower paintings being brought to a high decorative pitch, as well as schools of landscape painting firmly rooted in traditional techniques. The arrival of the Manchu **Qing dynasty** did not disrupt the continuity of Chinese painting, but the art became wide open to many influences. It included the Italian **Castiglione** (Lang Shi-ning in Chinese) who specialized in horses, dogs and flowers under imperial patronage; the Four Wangs who reinterpreted Song and Yuan styles in an orthodox manner; and individualists such as the Eight Eccentrics of Yangzhou and certain Buddhist monks who objected to derivative art and sought a more distinctive approach to subject and style.

Contemporary art

Contemporary art is both flourishing and highly accessible in China. There are hundreds of private galleries and every major city has an arts centre, often an old factory converted into studios and exhibition spaces – 798 in Beijing and 50 Moganshan Lu in Shanghai are the biggest examples, but it's also worth noting Nordica in Kunming and OCT in Shenzhen, among others. Fairs such as the Shanghai Biennale and Guangzhou's triennial have become enormous events. Chinese art is seen as hot by investors, and there's plenty of money sloshing around; it helps that art is less easy to counterfeit than other cultural forms, and, because "meaning" in art can be nebulous, trickier for the government to censor.

However, the first crop of modern Chinese artists, who emerged in the 1990s, worked in obscurity with, it seemed, no prospects of exhibition. They banded together for survival in artists' villages, most famously at the **Yuanmingyuan Artists Community** outside Beijing. The artists here developed a school of painting that expressed their individualism and their sceptical, often ironic and sometimes jaundiced view of contemporary China; this was, of course, the generation that had seen its dreams of change shot down at Tian'anmen Square. Nurtured by curator **Li Xianting**, known as the "Godfather of Chinese art", as well as sympathetic foreign collectors, they built the foundations of the art scene as it is today. The most famous of these so-called "cynical realists" is **Fang Lijun**, whose paintings of disembodied bald heads against desolate landscapes are now some of the most characteristic images of modern Chinese art. Look out too for **Yue Minjun**'s paintings of the Tian'anmen massacre that reference Goya, **Yang Shaobin**'s slickly painted sinister figures, and the bitingly satirical caricatures of **Wang Yinsong** and **Song Yonghong**.

Artists such as **Wang Guangyi** developed another school of distinctly Chinese contemporary art, "political pop". Here, a mocking twist is given to the iconography of the Cultural Revolution in order to critique a society that has become brashly commercial; Red Guards are shown waving iPods instead of Little Red Books and so on. Of late this has become rather a hackneyed genre, though every artist seems to go through a phase of it, and it's enthusiastically collected in the West.

Although it's hard to pick out trends amid such a ferment of activity, artists these days are not surprisingly preoccupied with documenting the destruction of the Chinese urban landscape and the gut-wrenching changes that have accompanied modernization. As spaces for viewing art have grown, artists have diversified into new media such as **performance and video**; exciting new faces to look out for include **Cui Xiuwen**, whose videos of women in a toilet at a karaoke bar are shocking and memorable, and **Xu Zhen**, whose video *Rainbow* shows his back turning red from unseen slaps. **Documentary photography** is also popular; among its finest exponents is **Yang Fudong**, notable for his wistful images of city life. **Wu Gaozhong** first drew attention for a performance piece in which he climbed into the belly of a slaughtered cow, but his recent work, involving giant props implanted with boar hair, is more subtle, and has a creepy beauty. And it's always worth looking out for a show curated by *enfant terrible* **Gu Zhenqing**, who has a reputation for gleefully pushing the limits.

Calligraphy

Calligraphy – the word is derived from the Greek for "beautiful writing" – was crystallized into a high art form in China, where the use of the brush saw the development of handwriting of various styles, valued on a par with painting. Of the various different scripts, the **seal script** is the archaic form found on oracle bones; the **lishu** is the clerical style and was used in inscriptions on stone; the **kaishu** is the regular style closest to the modern printed form; and the cursive **cao shu** (grass script) is the most individual handwritten style. Emperors, poets and scholars over centuries have left examples of their calligraphy cut into stone at beauty spots, on mountains and in grottoes, tombs and temples all over China; you can see some early examples in the caves at Longmen (see p.277). At one stage during the Tang dynasty, calligraphy was so highly prized that it was the yardstick for the selection of high officials.

Other arts

Jade and lacquerware have also been constantly in use in China since earliest times. In Chinese eyes, **jade**, in white and shades of green or brown, is the most precious of stones. It was used to make the earliest ritual objects, such as the flat disc **Pi**, symbol of Heaven, which was found in Shang and Zhou graves. Jade was also used as a mark of rank and for ornament, in its most striking form in the jade burial suits to be seen in the country's museums.

Lacquer, made from the sap of the lac tree, is also found as early as the Zhou. Many layers of the stuff were painted on a wood or cloth base that was then carved and inlaid with gold, silver or tortoiseshell, or often most delicately painted. Numerous examples of painted lacquer boxes and baskets survive from the Han, and, as with jade, the use of this material has continued ever since.

Music

The casual visitor to China could be forgiven for thinking that the only traditional style of music to compete with bland pop is that of the kitsch folk troupes to be heard in hotels and concert halls. But an earthy **traditional music** still abounds throughout the countryside; it can be heard at weddings, funerals, temple fairs and New Year celebrations – and even downtown in teahouses. A very different, edgier sound can be heard in certain smoky city bars – the new **Chinese rock**, with its energetic expressions of urban angst.

Traditional music

Han music (like Irish music) is **heterophonic** – the musicians play differently decorated versions of a single melodic line. Percussion plays a major role, both in instrumental ensembles and as accompaniment to opera, narrative-singing, ritual music and dance.

Chinese musical roots date back millennia – archeological finds include a magnificent set of 65 bronze bells from the fifth century BC – and its forms can be directly traced to the Tang dynasty.

But in the turbulent years after 1911, some intriguing **urban forms** sprang up from the meeting of East and West, such as the wonderfully sleazy Cantonese music of the 1920s and 1930s. As the movie industry developed, people in Shanghai, colonial Canton (Guangzhou) and nearby Hong Kong threw themselves into the craze for Western-style dance halls, fusing the local traditional music with jazz, and adding saxophone, violin and xylophone to Chinese instruments such as the *gaohu* (high-pitched fiddle) and the *yangqin* (dulcimer). Composers **Lü Wencheng** and **Qiu Hechou** (Yau Hokchau), the violinist **Yin Zizhong** (Yi Tzuchung), and **He Dasha** ("Thicko He"), guitarist and singer of clown roles in Cantonese opera, made many wonderful commercial 78s during this period. While these musicians kept their roots in Cantonese music, the more Westernized (and even more popular) compositions of **Li Jinhui** and his star singer **Zhou Xuan** subsequently earned severe disapproval from Maoist critics as decadent and pornographic.

New "**revolutionary**" music, composed from the 1930s onwards, was generally march-like and optimistic, while in the wake of the Communist victory of 1949, the whole ethos of traditional music was challenged. Anything "feudal" or "superstitious" – which included a lot of traditional folk customs and music – was severely restricted, while Chinese melodies were "cleaned up" with the addition of rudimentary harmonies and bass lines. The Communist anthem **"The East is Red"**, which began life as a folksong from the northern Shaanxi province (from where Mao's revolution also sprang), is symptomatic. Its local colour was ironed out as it was turned into a conventionally harmonized hymn-like tune. It was later adopted as the unofficial anthem of the Cultural Revolution, during which time musical life was driven underground, with only eight model operas and ballets permitted on stage.

The **conservatoire style** of **guoyue** (national music) was an artificial attempt to create a pan-Chinese style for the concert hall, with composed arrangements in a style akin to Western light music. There are still many conservatoire-style chamber groups – typically including *erhu* (fiddle), *dizi* (flute), *pipa* (lute) and *zheng* (zither) – playing evocatively titled pieces, some of which are newly composed. While the plaintive pieces for solo *erhu* by musicians such as **Liu Tianhua** and the blind beggar **Abing** (also a Daoist priest), or atmospheric tweetings on the *dizi*, have been much recorded by *guoyue* virtuosos like **Min Huifen** or **Lu Chunling** respectively, there is much more to Chinese music than this. Folk music has a life of its own, and tends to follow the Confucian ideals of moderation and harmony, in which showy virtuosity is out of place.

The *qin* and solo traditions

The genuine solo traditions date back to the scholar-literati of imperial times, and live on in the conservatoires today, in pieces for the *pipa*, *zheng* and *qin*.

The **qin** (also known as *guqin*) is the most exalted of these instruments. A seven-string plucked zither, it is the most delicate and contemplative instrument in the Chinese palette. It's also the most accessible, producing expressive slides and ethereal harmonics. Modern traditions of the **pipa** (lute) and **zheng** (zither) derive from regional styles, transmitted from master to pupil, although "national" repertoires developed during the twentieth century. For the *zheng*, the northern styles of Henan and Shandong, and the southern Chaozhou and Hakka schools, are best known. The *pipa*, on the other hand, has thrived in the Shanghai region. It makes riveting listening, with its contrast between intimate "civil" pieces and the startlingly modern-sounding martial style of traditional pieces such as "Ambush from All Sides" (*Shimian maifu*), with its frenetic percussive evocation of the sounds of battle.

The north: blowers and drummers

Classical traditions derived from the elite of imperial times live on today in **folk ensembles**, which are generally found in the north of the country. The most exciting examples are to be heard at **weddings** and **funerals**.

These occasions usually feature raucous **shawm** (a ubiquitous instrument in China, rather like a crude clarinet) and percussion groups called **chuigushou** – "blowers and drummers". While wedding bands naturally tend to use more jolly music, funerals may also feature lively pieces to entertain the guests. The blowers and drummers play not only lengthy and solemn suites but also the latest pop hits and theme tunes from TV and films. They milk the audience by sustaining notes, using circular breathing, playing even while dismantling and reassembling their *shawms*, or by balancing plates on sticks on the end of their instruments while playing.

Mentioned as far back as the tenth century BC, the **sheng** ranks among the oldest Chinese instruments. It comprises a group of bamboo pipes of different lengths bound in a circle and set in a wooden or metal base into which the player blows. Frequently used for ceremonial music, it adds an incisive rhythmic bite. Long and deafening strings of firecrackers are another inescapable part of village ceremony. Some processions are led by a Western-style brass band with a *shawm*-and-percussion group behind, competing in volume, oblivious of key. In northern villages, apart from the blowers and drummers, ritual **shengguan** ensembles are also common, with their exquisite combination of mouth organs and oboes, as well as darting flutes and the shimmering halo of the *yunluo* gong-frame, accompanied by percussion. Apart from this haunting melodic music, they perform some spectacular ritual percussion – the intricate arm movements of the cymbal players almost resemble martial arts.

Around Xi'an, groups performing similar wind and percussion music, misleadingly dubbed **Xi'an Drum Music** (**Xi'an guyue**), are active for temple festivals not only in the villages but also in the towns, especially in the sixth moon, around

July. If you remember the tough *shawm* bands and haunting folksong of Chen Kaige's film *Yellow Earth*, or the harsh falsetto narrative in Zhang Yimou's *The Story of Qiuju*, go for the real thing among the barren hills of northern Shaanxi. This area is home to fantastic folk singers, local opera (such as the Qinqiang and Meihu styles), puppeteers, *shawm* bands and folk ritual specialists. Even *yangge* dancing, which in the towns is often a geriatric form of conga dancing, has a wild power here, again accompanied by *shawms* and percussion.

The south: silk and bamboo

In southeast China, the best-known instrumental music is that of **sizhu** ("silk and bamboo") ensembles, using flutes (of bamboo) and plucked and bowed strings (until recently of silk). More mellifluous than the outdoor wind bands of the north, these provide perhaps the most accessible Chinese folk music.

The most famous of the many regional styles is that of **Shanghai**, where enthusiasts get together in the afternoons, sit round a table and take it in turns to play a set with Chinese fiddles, flutes and banjos. You can't help thinking of an Irish session, with Chinese tea replacing Guinness. The most celebrated meeting place is the teahouse in the **Chenghuang Miao** (see p.388), a picturesque two-storey structure on an island in the old quarter, where there are Monday-afternoon gatherings. The contrasting textures of plucked, bowed and blown sounds are part of the attraction of this music, each offering individual decorations to the gradually unfolding melody. Many pieces consist of successive decorations of a theme, beginning with the most ornate and accelerating as the decorations are gradually stripped down to a fast and bare final statement of the theme itself. Above the chinking of tea bowls and subdued chatter of the teahouse, enjoy the gradual unravelling of a piece like "Sanliu", or feel the exhilarating dash to the finish of "Xingjie", with its breathless syncopations.

Amateur *sizhu* clubs can be found throughout the lower Yangzi area, including the cities of Nanjing and Hangzhou. Although this music is secular and recreational in its urban form, the *sizhu* instrumentation originated in ritual ensembles and is still so used in the villages and temples of southern Jiangsu. In fact, amateur ritual associations exist all over southern China, as far afield as Yunnan, punctuating their ceremonies with sedate music reminiscent of the Shanghai teahouses, albeit often featuring the *yunluo* gong-frame of northern China.

Another fantastic area for folk music is the coastal region of **southern Fujian**, notably the delightful cities of Quanzhou and Xiamen. Here you can find not only opera, ritual music and puppetry, but the haunting **nanguan ballads**. Popular all along the coast of southern Fujian, as in Taiwan across the strait, *nanguan* features a female singer accompanied by end-blown flute and plucked and bowed lutes. The ancient texts depict the sorrows of love, particularly of women, while the music is mostly stately and the delivery restrained yet anguished.

Still further south, the coastal regions of **Chaozhou** and **Shantou**, and the **Hakka** area (inland around Meixian and Dabu), also boast celebrated string ensembles that feature a high-pitched *erxian* (bowed fiddle) and *zheng* (plucked zither), as well as large and imposing ceremonial percussion bands, sometimes accompanied by shrill flutes.

The temples

All over China, particularly on the great religious mountains such as **Wutai Shan**, **Tai Shan**, **Qingcheng Shan**, **Wudang Shan** and **Putuo Shan**, temples are not just historical monuments but living sites of worship. Morning and evening services are held daily, and larger rituals on special occasions. The priests mainly perform vocal liturgy accompanied by percussion. They intone sung hymns with long melismas, alternating with chanted sections accompanied by the relentless and hypnotic beat of the woodblock.

Melodic instrumental music tends to be added when priests perform rituals outside the temples. These styles are more earthy and accessible even to ears unaccustomed to Chinese music. The Daoist priests from the Xuanmiao Guan in **Suzhou**, for example, perform wonderfully mellifluous pieces for silk-and-bamboo instruments, gutsy blasts on the *shawm*, music for spectacularly long trumpets, and a whole battery of percussion.

Opera and other vocal music

Chinese musical drama dates back at least two thousand years, and became overwhelmingly popular with both the elite and common people from the Yuan dynasty onwards. Of the several hundred types of regional opera, **Beijing Opera**, a rather late hybrid form dating from the eighteenth century, is the most widely known – now heard throughout China, it's the closest thing to a "national" theatre. The rigorous training the form demands – and the heavy hand of ideology that saw it as the most important of "the people's arts" – is graphically displayed in Chen Kaige's film *Farewell My Concubine*. Many librettos now performed date back to the seventeenth century and describe the intrigues of emperors and gods, as well as love stories and comedy. Northern "**clapper operas**" (*bangzi xi*), named after the high-pitched woodblock that insistently runs through them, are earthy in flavour – for example, the "Qinqiang" of Shaanxi province. **Sichuan opera** is remarkable for its female chorus. **Ritual masked opera** may be performed in the countryside of Yunnan, Anhui and Guizhou. Chaozhou and Fujian also have beautiful ancient styles of opera: **Pingju** and **Huangmei Xi** are genteel in style, while **Cantonese opera** is funkier. If you're looking for more music and less acrobatics, try to seek out the classical but now rare **Kunqu**, often accompanied by the sweet-toned *qudi* flute. There are also some beautiful **puppet operas**, often performed for ritual events; Quanzhou in Fujian boasts a celebrated marionette troupe, and other likely areas include northern Shaanxi and the Tangshan and Laoting areas of eastern Hebei.

While Chinese opera makes a great visual spectacle, musically it is frankly an acquired taste, resembling to the uninitiated the din of cats fighting in a blazing firework factory. The singing style is tense, guttural and high-pitched, while the music is dominated by the bowed string accompaniment of the *jinghu*, a sort of sawn-off *erhu*. It also features plucked lutes, flutes and – for transitional points – a piercing *shawm*. The action is driven by percussion, with drum and clappers leading an ensemble of gongs and cymbals in an assortment of set patterns. Professional opera troupes exist in the major towns, but rural opera performances, which are given for temple fairs and even weddings, tend to be livelier. Even in Beijing you may come across groups of old folk meeting in parks to go through their favourite Beijing Opera excerpts.

Narrative-singing also features long classical stories. You may find a teahouse full of old people following these story-songs avidly, particularly in Sichuan, where one popular style is accompanied by the *yangqin* (dulcimer). In Beijing, or more often in Tianjin, amateurs sing through traditional *jingyun dagu* ballads, accompanied by drum and *sanxian* banjo. In Suzhou, *pingtan*, also accompanied by a plucked lute, is a beautiful genre. Found in Beijing and elsewhere, *xiangsheng* is a comic dialogue with a know-all and a straight man, though its subtle parodies of traditional opera may elude the outsider.

Chinese rock

Although often connected to the Hong Kong/Taiwanese entertainment industry, China's indigenous **rock** is a different beast, one which has its traditions in passionate and fiery protest, and which still possesses a cultural and political self-awareness. The rock scene was nonexistent in China until the mid-1980s, when foreign students on cultural exchange brought tapes of their favourite rock and pop music (and their own electric guitars) to the Chinese mainland, and shared them with their fellow students. Their music quickly caught the imagination of Chinese university youth and the urban vanguard.

Chinese **protest-rock** really began with singer-trumpeter-guitarist Cui Jian, who was influenced by the Taiwanese singer **Teresa Teng** (known to the Chinese by her original name, Deng Lijun; 1953–95). Teng's singing style can be directly traced to Zhou Xuan and 1930s Shanghai. Probably the most popular Chinese singer of her time, her recordings were circulated in China on the black market from the late 1970s onwards, when such music was officially banned.

A Beijinger born of parents of Korean descent, **Cui Jian** studied the trumpet at an early age, trained as a classical musician and joined the Beijing Symphony Orchestra in 1981. After being introduced to Anglo-American rock in the mid-1980s, however, he forged an independent path and his gritty voice became the primary reference point of Chinese rock. His love song "Nothing To My Name" became an anthem of the democracy movement, evoking a memorable complaint from General Wang Zhen, a veteran of the Long March: "What do you mean, you have nothing to your name? You've got the Communist Party, haven't you?"

Notable **1980s bands** that followed in Cui Jian's wake include Black Panther (*Hei Bao*) and Tang Dynasty, though their long hair and leathers were perhaps more influential than their soft rock. They were followed by Cobra, China's first all-female rock band, folk-rocker Zhang Chu, bad boy He Yong, Compass, Overload, and Breathing, among others. Unsigned, these bands would perform for very little money as part of vaudeville shows, until 1990, when China's first domestic full-scale rock concert took place. Six bands, including Tang Dynasty and Cobra, played at the Beijing Exhibition Centre Arena and were immediately signed by Japanese and Taiwanese labels, who then brought their music to the mainstream. They paved the way for homegrown labels such as Modern Sky, Scream, New Bees Records and Badhead, which now specialize in Chinese rock, hip-hop and alternative music.

The rock scene these days is healthy, with hundreds of bands, though it does centre heavily on **Beijing**. For visitors, it's well worth exploring, and surprisingly accessible, as most bands sing at least half of their songs in English. Acts to look out for include Sex Pistols wannabes Joyside, who recently toured America; folk punk showmen Top Floor Circus; long running ska punk outfit Brain Failure; and Joy Divisionistas, the Retros. For dance and electronica you can't beat Queen Sea Big Shark, while Car Sick Cars are the indie shoegazers to catch. To fully immerse yourself in the scene, visit Beijing's annual three-day **Midi Festival** in July. For free downloads, check out Ⓦwww.yuyintang.com.

Stephen Jones & Joanna Lee,
with additional contributions from Simon Lewis

Film

Film came early to China. The first moving picture was exhibited in 1896 at a "teahouse variety show" in Shanghai, where the country's first cinema was built just twelve years later. By the 1930s, cinema was playing an important role in the cultural life of Shanghai, though the huge number of resident foreigners ensured a largely Western diet of films. Nevertheless, local Chinese films were also being made, mainly by the so-called **May Fourth intellectuals** (middle-class liberals inspired by the uprising of May 4, 1919), who wanted to modernize China along Western lines. Naturally, Western influence on these films was strong, and they have little to do with the highly stylized, formal world of traditional performance arts such as Beijing Opera or shadow-puppet theatre. Early film showings often employed a "storyteller", who sat near the screen reading out the titles for the benefit of those who could not read.

The Shanghai studios

Of the handful of important **studios** in Shanghai operating in the 1920s and 1930s, the most famous was the **Mingxing**, whose films were left-leaning and anti-imperialist. *Sister Flower* (1933) tells the story of twin sisters separated at birth, one of whom ends up a city girl living in Shanghai, while the other remains a poor villager. Another film from the same year, *Spring Silk Worm*, portrays economic decline and hardship in Zhejiang province, and levels the finger of accusation at Japanese imperialism. Finally, *The Goddess* (1934), from the **Lianhua** studio, depicts the struggle of a prostitute to have her son educated. The improbably glamorous prostitute was played by China's own Garbo, the languorous Ruan Lingyu. Despite the liberal pretensions of these films, it was inevitable – given that audiences comprised a tiny elite – that they would later be derided by the Communists as bourgeois.

When the **Japanese occupied** Shanghai in 1937, "subversive" studios such as the Mingxing and Lianhua were immediately closed, and much of the film-making talent fled into the interior. The experience of war put film-makers in touch with their potential future audiences, the Chinese masses. China's great wartime epic, **Spring River Flows East** (1947–48), was the cinematic result of this experience. The story spans the duration of the anti-Japanese war – and the ensuing civil war – through the lives of a single family torn apart by the conflict. The heroine, living in poverty, contrasts with her husband, who has abandoned his wife for a decadent existence in Shanghai. Traumatized by a decade of war, the Chinese who saw this film appreciated it as an authentic account of the sufferings through which the nation had lived. Over 750,000 people saw the film at its release, a remarkable figure given that the country was still at war.

Communism and the cinema

The story of Chinese film-making under the **Communists** really dates back to 1938, when Mao Zedong and his fellow Long Marchers set up their base in **Yan'an**. No world could have been further removed from the glamour of Shanghai than this dusty, poverty-stricken town, but it was the ideal location for the film-makers of the future People's Republic to learn their skills. Talent escaping through Japanese lines trickled through in search of employment, among them the actress **Jiang Qing**, later to become Mao's wife and self-appointed empress of Chinese culture. One thing upon which all the leading Communists in Yan'an were agreed was the importance of film as a **centralizing medium**, which could be used to unify the culture of the nation after the war had been won.

The immediate consequence of the Communist victory in 1949 was that the showing of foreign films was curtailed, and the private Shanghai studios wound down. A **Film Guidance committee** was set up to decide upon film output for the entire nation. The first major socialist epic, **Bridge**, appeared in 1949, depicting the mass mobilization of workers rushing enthusiastically to construct a bridge in record time. Although predictably dull in terms of character and plot, the cast still contained a number of prewar Shanghai actors to divert audiences. At the end of the film the entire cast gathers to shout "Long live Chairman Mao!", a scene that was to be re-enacted time and again in the coming years.

A year after *Bridge*, one of the very last non-government Shanghai studio films appeared, **The Life of Wu Xun**, a huge project that had started well before 1949, and, surprisingly, was allowed to run to completion. Its subject was the famous nineteenth-century entrepreneur, Wu Xun, who started out as a beggar and rose to enormous riches, whereupon he set out on his lifetime's ambition to educate the peasantry. Despite the addition of a narrator's voice at the end of the film, pointing out that it was revolution and not education that peasants needed, the film was a disaster for the Shanghai film industry. Mao wrote a damning critique of it for idolizing a "Qing landlord", and a campaign was launched against the legacy of the entire Shanghai film world – studios, actors, critics and audiences alike.

The remains of the May Fourth movement struggled on. The consolation for the old guard was that newer generations of Chinese film-makers had not yet solved the problem of how to portray life in the contemporary era. The 1952 screen adaptation of Lao She's short story *Dragon's Beard Ditch*, for example, was supposed to contrast the miserable pre-1949 life of a poor district of Beijing with the prosperous life that was being lived under the Communists. The only problem, as audiences could immediately see, was that the supposedly miserable pre-1949 scenes actually looked a good deal more heart-warming than the later ones.

Nevertheless, the Communists did achieve some of their original targets during the **1950s**. The promotion of a universal culture and language was one of them. All characters in all films – from Tibetans to Mongolians to Cantonese – were depicted as speaking in flawless **Mandarin Chinese**. Above all, there was an explosion in audiences, from around 47 million tickets sold in 1949, to 600 million in 1956, to over 4 billion in 1959. The latter figure should be understood in the context of the madness surrounding the Great Leap Forward, a time of crazed overproduction in all fields, film included. Film studios sprouted in every town in China, though with a catastrophic loss of quality – a typical studio in Jiangxi province comprised one man, his bicycle and an antique stills camera. The colossal output of that year included uninspiring titles such as *Loving the Factory as One's Home*.

The conspicuous failure of the Great Leap Forward did, however, bring certain short-lived advantages to the film industry. While Mao was forced temporarily into the political sidelines during the late 1950s, the cultural bureaucrats signalled that in addition to "revolutionary realism", a certain degree of "**revolutionary romanticism**" was to be encouraged. Chinese themes and subjects, as opposed to pure Marxism, were looked upon with more favour. A slight blossoming occurred, with improbable films such as *Lin Zexu* (1959), which covered the life of the great Qing-dynasty official who stood up to the British at the time of the Opium Wars.

There was even a tentative branching out into comedy, with the film *What's Eating You?* based on the relatively un-socialist antics of a Suzhou waiter. Unusually, the film featured local dialects, as well as a faintly detectable parody of the government's campaign to encourage greater sacrifices by promoting the mythical hero worker Lei Feng.

The Cultural Revolution

Sadly, this bright period came to a swift end in 1966 with the **Cultural Revolution**. No interesting work was made in China for nearly fifteen years – indeed, no film was produced anywhere in the whole country between 1966 and 1970. The few films that did subsequently appear before Mao's death were made under the personal supervision of Jiang Qing, and all were on the revolutionary model, a kind of ballet with flag waving. Attendance at these dreadful films was virtually **compulsory** for people who did not wish to be denounced for a lack of revolutionary zeal. Ironically, Jiang Qing herself was a big fan of Hollywood productions, which she would watch in secret.

Recovery from the trauma of the Cultural Revolution was bound to take time, but the years 1979 and 1980 saw a small crop of films attempting to assess the horror through which the country had just lived. The best known, *The Legend of Tianyun Mountain*, made in Shanghai in 1980, featured two men, one of whom had denounced the other for "Rightism" in 1958. The subsequent story is one of guilt, love, emotions and human relationships, all subjects that had been banned during the Cultural Revolution. Understandably, the film was an enormous popular success, though before audiences had time to get too carried away, a subsequent film, *Unrequited Love* (1981), was officially criticized for blurring too many issues.

Modern cinema

In **1984** the Chinese film industry was suddenly brought to international attention for the first time by the arrival of the so-called **"fifth generation"** of Chinese film-makers. That year, director **Chen Kaige** and his cameraman **Zhang Yimou**, both graduates from the first post-Cultural Revolution class (1982) of the Beijing Film School, made the superb art-house film **Yellow Earth**. The story of *Yellow Earth* is a minor feature; the interest is in the images and the colours. Still shots predominate, recalling traditional Chinese scroll painting, with giant landscapes framed by hills and the distant Yellow River. The film was not particularly well received in China, either by audiences, who expected something more modern, or by the authorities, who expected something more optimistic. Nevertheless, it set the pattern for a series of increasingly overseas-funded (and overseas-watched) films comprising stunning images of a "traditional" China, irritating the censors at home and delighting audiences abroad.

Chen Kaige's protégé Zhang Yimou was soon stealing a march on his former boss with his first film **Red Sorghum** (1987), set in a remote wine-producing village of northern China at the time of the Japanese invasion. This film was not only beautiful, and reassuringly patriotic, but it also introduced the world to **Gong Li**, the actress who was to become China's first international heart-throb. The fact that Gong Li and Zhang Yimou were soon to be lovers added to the general media interest in their work, both in China and abroad. They worked together on a string of hits, including *Judou*, *The Story of Qiu Ju*, *Raise the Red Lantern*, *Shanghai Triad* and *To Live*. None of these could be described as art-house in the way that *Yellow Earth* had been, and the potent mix of Gong Li's sexuality with exotic, mysterious locations in 1930s China was clearly targeted at Western rather than Chinese audiences. Chinese like to point out that the figure-hugging Chinese dresses regularly worn by Gong Li are entirely unlike the period costume they purport to represent.

One of Zhang Yimou's most powerful films, **To Live** (1994), follows the fortunes of a family from "liberation" to the Great Leap Forward and the Cultural Revolution. The essence of the story is that life cannot be lived to prescription. Its power lies in the fact that it is a very real reflection of the experience of millions of Chinese people. Similarly, Chen Kaige's superb **Farewell My Concubine** (1994) incorporates the whole span of modern Chinese history, and although the main protagonist – a homosexual Chinese opera singer – is hardly typical of modern China, the tears aroused by the film are wept for the country as a whole.

Zhang Yimou has since been warmly embraced by the authorities and his films have got worse. His most recent Hollywood-friendly martial-arts spectaculars **Hero** (2002), **The House of Flying Daggers** (2004) and **Curse of the Golden Flower** (2007) are commercial successes, and beautifully shot, but they are shallow and soulless.

Contemporary realism

The best Chinese films of the modern age are those that have turned their back on the frigid perfection on offer from Zhang Yimou and are raw, gritty reflections of Chinese life. Inevitably, the fifth generation was followed by a sixth, which produced **underground movies**, generally shot in black-and-white, depicting what they consider to be the true story of contemporary China – ugly cities, cold flats, broken and depressed people. One of these, **Beijing Bastards** (1993), had a role for rock singer and rebel **Cui Jian**, who is depicted drinking, swearing and playing the guitar.

Many of the finest modern movies turn a baleful eye on the recent past. **Lei Feng is Gone** (1997) is based on the true story of the man who accidentally killed the iconic hero of Maoist China, the soldier Lei Feng. The potent personal story also works as a metaphor for the state of the nation. **In the Heat of the Sun** (1995), directed by Jiang Wen, chronicles the antics of a Beijing street gang in the 1970s. Written by Wang Shuo, the bad boy of contemporary Chinese literature, it displays his characteristic irreverence and earthy humour. Jiang Wen's next film, **Devils at the Doorstep** (2000) goes a little further back, and its eye is even more jaundiced. Set during the anti-Japanese war, it's a black farce concerning a group of peasants who get a couple of hostages dumped on their farm by the local Communists. Unwilling to execute them or release them, they decide to try and return them to the Japanese in return for food.

Many films are simply too controversial for domestic release, but if they garner attention abroad they then become available at home as illegal DVDs. The most notable film to become popular in this way is **Xiao Wu** (1997), the intimate portrayal of a pickpocket whose life is falling apart, directed by **Jia Zhangke**. Jia's other films revisit similar territory, depicting moral wastelands and loss; **The World** (2004) is set in a world culture theme park in Beijing, where the workers squabble and fail to communicate against a backdrop of tiny replicas of the world's famous monuments; the protagonists of **Still Life** (2007) search for people who have gone missing in the mass displacements caused by the Three Gorges Dam project; and **24 City** (2009) is set in a factory that's closing down.

But the best of the banned genre is **Blind Shaft** (2003), directed by Yang Li, about two coal miners who kill colleagues, make it look like an accident, then collect the mine owner's hush money. As well as a telling indictment of runaway capitalism, it's a great piece of film noir. The follow up, **Blind Mountain** (2007), is about a young girl who is kidnapped and sold as a bride, and again combines social critique with a sharp crime story.

Similar in its clever combination of genre and uncompromising realism is **Ke Ke Xi Li** (Chuan Lu; 2004), a hard-boiled true story about a volunteer gang fighting against ruthless antelope poachers on the high Tibetan plateau. It was filmed using non-professional local actors and has the feel of a western, but is entirely unsentimental. More non-professional actors and grand scenery were used to great effect in Wang Quan'an's documentary-style **Tuya's Marriage** (2006), the story of a Mongolian herdswomen's search for a new husband, which won first prize at the 2007 Berlin Film Festival. Like much good contemporary Chinese art of all genres, its subject is people struggling to cope with vast social change.

Hong Kong

The movies that have the least difficulty with the Chinese censors are those produced in **Hong Kong**, the world's third-largest movie producer, behind India and the US. Its popular appeal is made easier by the content: generally easy-to-digest romances, comedies or high-speed action, with little interest in deeper meanings or the outside world – and certainly not in politics.

World interest in Hong Kong's film industry dates back to 1970s martial-arts legend **Bruce Lee**. Although Lee was better known overseas for the Hollywood-financed *Enter the Dragon* (1973), the success in Hong Kong of his earlier films *Fist of Fury* and *The Big Boss* launched a domestic **kung-fu movie boom**, off the back of which sprung **Jackie Chan** and a much-needed element of slapstick comedy – best seen in Chan's early works, such as *Drunken Master* (1978). As the genre faltered in the 1980s, directors mixed in a supernatural aspect, pioneered by **Tsui Hark** in *Zu: Warriors from the Magic Mountain* (1983) and *Chinese Ghost Story* (1987). The kung-fu genre has been recently revived by director **Stephen Chow**, whose *Shaolin Soccer* (2001) and *Kung Fu Hustle* (2004) sport uniquely surreal humour and visuals.

Martial arts remain an inevitable component of Hong Kong's modern **action movies** and **police thrillers**. This genre can largely be attributed to **John Woo**'s influential hits *A Better Tomorrow* (1986) and *Hard Boiled* (1992), which feature Chow Yun Fat shooting his way through relentless scenes of orchestrated violence. Woo's many imitators have mostly succeeded only in making pointless, bloody movies whose plots inevitably conclude with the massacre of the entire cast, though recent efforts such as *Infernal Affairs* (2002; remade in the US as *The Departed* in 2006) at least add a little depth to the heroes' moody characters.

At present, Hong Kong's only director interested in anything but light entertainment is **Wong Karwai**, whose early works such as *Chungking Express* (1994) and *Fallen Angels* (1995) depict Hong Kong as a crowded, disjointed city where people, though forced together, seem unable to communicate. His more recent films have added a European sense of style, which worked in the sensuous *In the Mood for Love* (2000) but overwhelmed the plot in the obscure, self-referential *2046* (2004).

Books

The last few years have seen a glut of excellent writing coming out of China, from Western commentators' views on current economic and social upheavals, to translated journalism and popular novels, and often eccentric expat memoirs.

Classics aside, few of the titles below are available in China (though you might get lucky in Hong Kong), so it's best to locate them before your trip; the publishers are listed throughout. Titles marked 🏃 are particularly recommended.

History

Patricia Ebrey *Cambridge Illustrated History of China* (Cambridge University Press, UK). An up-to-date, easy-going historical overview, excellently illustrated and clearly written.

Peter Fleming *The Siege at Peking* (Oxford University Press, UK). An account of the events that led up to June 20, 1900, when the foreign legations in Beijing were attacked by the Boxers and Chinese imperial troops. The 55-day siege marked a watershed in China's relations with the rest of the world.

Jacques Gernet *Daily Life in China on the Eve of the Mongol Invasion 1250–1276* (Allen and Unwin, UK; Stanford University Press, US). Based on assorted Chinese sources, this is a fascinating survey of southern China under the Song, focusing on the capital, Hangzhou, then the largest and richest city in the world. Gernet also deals with the daily lives of a cross-section of society, from peasant to leisured gentry, covering everything from cookery to death.

🏃 **Larry Gonick** *The Cartoon History of the Universe vols II and III* (W. W. Norton, US). A masterwork setting world history in cartoon format, full of verve, great visuals and awful puns, but also accurate – the bibliography shows how much research has gone into this manic project. About the only textbook that seriously attempts to set Chinese history in a world context.

🏃 **Peter Hopkirk** *Foreign Devils on the Silk Road* and *The Great Game* (Oxford University Press, UK). *Foreign Devils* is the story of the machinations of the various international booty-hunters who operated in Turkestan and the Gobi Desert during the early twentieth century – essential for an appreciation of China's northwest regions. *The Great Game* is a hugely entertaining account of the nineteenth-century struggle between Britain and Russia for control of Central Asia. In tracing the roots of the Chinese occupations of Tibet and Xinjiang, and also detailing the invariable consequences for foreign powers who meddle with Afghanistan, it's also disturbingly topical.

Ann Paludan *Chronicle of the Chinese Emperors* (Thames and Hudson, UK). Lively stories on the lives of all 157 of those strangest of characters, the Chinese emperors. Well illustrated and a good starting point for getting to grips with Chinese history.

Sima Qian *Historical Records* aka *Records of the Historian* (Oxford Paperbacks, UK; Columbia University Press, US). Written by the Han-dynasty court historian, *Records* is a masterpiece, using contemporary court documents and oral tradition to illuminate key characters – everyone from emperors to famous con men – from Chinese history up to that point. Although long discredited, Sima Qian's accounts have now been partially corroborated by recent archeology.

Edgar Snow *Red Star Over China* (Penguin, UK; Grove Press, US). The definitive first-hand account of the early days of Mao and the Communist "bandits", written in 1936 after Snow, an American journalist, wriggled through the Guomindang blockade and spent months at the Red base in Yan'an.

Jonathan Spence *The Gate of Heavenly Peace* (Penguin, UK & US), *The Search for Modern China* (W. W. Norton, US). The first of these traces the history of twentieth-century China through the eyes of the men and women caught up in it – writers, revolutionaries, poets and politicians – and is among the best books for getting to grips with China's complex modern history. Though quite hard for a straight-through read, *The Search for Modern China* is authoritative and probably the best overall history of China available.

Susan Whitfield *Life Along the Silk Road* (John Murray, UK). Using archeological remains and historical sources, Whitfield creates ten fictional characters to illustrate life in northwestern China during its tenth-century Buddhist heyday.

Tibet

John Avedon *In Exile From the Land of Snows* (HarperCollins, UK; Perennial, US). A detailed and moving account of modern Tibetan history, covering both those who remained in the country and those who fled into exile. Required reading for anyone contemplating a trip.

Edmund Candler *The Unveiling of Lhasa* (Earnshaw Books, Hong Kong). China was not the first country to invade Tibet: in 1905, a British military expedition marched on Lhasa, using modern machine guns against the peasant armies sent to stop them. Candler, a journalist embedded with the expedition, paints an honest and ultimately disillusioned picture of the events, which were to ultimately open the country up to colonization.

Victor Chan *Tibet Handbook: a Pilgrimage Guide* (Avalon Travel, US). A hugely detailed guide to Tibet's pilgrimage sites and treks, and how to reach them. Absolutely essential if you're considering a trek.

Graham Coleman (ed) *A Handbook of Tibetan Culture: a Guide to Tibetan Centres and Resources Throughout the World* (Shambhala, UK). The subtitle says it all; the book exhaustively documents cultural organizations, teaching centres and libraries across the globe that have a Tibetan focus. It also includes biographies of major Tibetan lamas, brief histories of the major schools of Tibetan Buddhism and an illustrated glossary.

Jonathan Green *Murder in the High Himalaya* (Public Affairs, US). In 2008 a Romanian mountain climber filmed border guards shooting down fleeing Tibetans in cold blood. This sad but gripping telling of the story gives equal weight to both refugees and climbers in one of the few good reads to come out of the tragedy of modern Tibet.

Heinrich Harrer *Seven Years in Tibet* (Flamingo, UK; Jeremy P. Tarcher, US). A classic account of a remarkable journey to reach Lhasa and of the years there prior to the Chinese invasion, when Harrer was tutor to the Fourteenth Dalai Lama.

Isabel Hilton *The Search for the Panchen Lama* (Penguin, UK & US). The whole sorry story of the search for the Eleventh Panchen Lama, and how the Tibetans' choice ended up as the world's youngest political prisoner.

Peter Hopkirk *Trespassers on the Roof of the World: the Race for Lhasa* (Oxford University Press, UK). Around the start of the twentieth century, imperial Britain, with the help of a remarkable band of pundits and wallahs from the Indian Survey, was discreetly charting every nook of the most inaccessible part of the earth, the High Tibetan plateau. Peter Hopkirk researched his subject thoroughly and came up with a highly readable account of this fascinating backwater of history.

Thubten Jigme and Colin Turnbull *Tibet, Its History, Religion and People* (Penguin, UK & US). The best account around of the traditional everyday lives of the Tibetan people, co-authored by the brother of the Fourteenth Dalai Lama.

Culture and society

Ian Buruma *Bad Elements* (Orion, UK; Random House, US). Interviews with dissident exiles abroad tell an (inevitably anti-government) story of modern China.

Jasper Becker *The Chinese* (John Murray, UK). An incisive portrait of modern China at both government and individual level by one of the great Sinologists. Becker draws intriguing parallels between modern rulers and ancient emperors. His latest book, *The City of Heavenly Tranquility*, is an excellent look at Beijing's history, and a condemnation of its rapid destruction.

David Bonavia *The Chinese: a Portrait* (Penguin, UK & US). A highly readable introduction to contemporary China, focusing on the human aspects as a balance to the socio-political trends.

Gordon Chang *The Coming Collapse of China* (Arrow, UK; Random House, US). A detailed and well-informed overview of what's wrong with contemporary Chinese society by an influential prophet of doom, though his thesis, that a popular revolution will eventually destroy the Communist Party, is overstretched; they've been saying this for years and it hasn't happened yet.

Leslie T. Chang *Factory Girls* (Picador, US). This tells the personal stories of a couple of migrant workers, giving the story of wrenching change and development in modern China a human face. Good for general readers.

Chen Guidi and Wu Chuntao *Will the Boat Sink the Water?* (Public Affairs, UK). Modern China was founded to improve the lot of its peasant majority, but the journalist authors show how – and how badly – the country's officials are failing them. Banned in China, it has since sold ten million copies on the black market.

Tim Glissold *Mr China* (Constable and Robinson, UK). The well-told and eye-opening story of how the author went to China to make a fortune and lost US$400 million. A great first-person account of the eccentric Chinese business environment, and a must for anyone thinking of investing there.

Alexandra Harney *The China Price* (Penguin Press, UK & US). This powerful exposé of the true environmental and social costs of manufacturing in China makes a compelling, if uncomfortable, read, especially for anyone thinking of outsourcing production.

Duncan Hewitt *Getting Rich First* (Chatto and Windus, UK). Written by a long-term foreign resident and journalist, this excellent book moves beyond commonplace Western views of China – all dynastic history,

Cultural Revolution and economic boom – with an informed look at the major social themes shaping the nation.

Jen Lin-Liu *Serve the People* (Mariner, US) Equal parts travelogue and cook book, which tries to understand the Chinese by heading in through the stomach. Light, witty and entertaining.

Joe Studwell *The China Dream* (Profile, UK; Grove Press, US). Mandatory reading for foreign businesspeople in China, this is a cautionary tale, written in layman's terms, debunking the myth that there's easy money to be made from China's vast markets. A great read for anyone interested in business, economics or human greed.

Robert Temple *The Genius of China* (Andre Deutsch, UK; Inner Traditions, US). Derived from Joseph Needham's epic work *Science and Civilization in China*, this thoroughly illustrated compendium covers hundreds of important Chinese inventions through the ages – though the text does labour over how little credit the West gives China's creative talent.

Xinran *The Good Women of China* (Chatto and Windus, UK; Anchor, US). Tales of the struggles of Chinese women; their stories are heart-warming though the editor, a Beijing journalist, seems smug and self-obsessed.

Lin Yutang *My Country and My People*. An expatriate Chinese scholar writes for Western audiences in the 1930s about what it means to be Chinese. Obviously dated in parts, but overall remarkably fresh and accessible.

Zhang Xinxin and Sang Ye *Chinese Lives* (Penguin, UK; Pan Macmillan, US). This Studs Terkel-like series of first-person narratives from interviews with a broad range of Chinese people is both readable and informative, full of fascinating details of day-to-day existence that you won't read anywhere else.

Travel writing

Charles Blackmore *The Worst Desert on Earth* (John Murray, UK; Trafalgar Square, US). Sergeant-Majorly account of an arduous and possibly unique trip across the Taklamakan Desert in northwest China.

Mildred Cable with Francesca French *The Gobi Desert* (Virago Press, UK; Beacon Press, US). Cable and French were missionaries with the China Inland Mission in the early part of the twentieth century. *The Gobi Desert* is a poetic description of their life and travels in Gansu and Xinjiang, without the sanctimonious and patronizing tone adopted by some of their contemporary missionaries.

Austin Coates *Myself a Mandarin* (Oxford UP East Asia, UK). Despite dated views and the changing times, this humorous account of the author's time as a Hong Kong magistrate during the 1950s still rings true.

Rachel DeWoskin *Foreign Babes in Beijing* (Granta, UK). Wry, witty snapshot of 1990s Beijing as a place of untested, unexpected opportunities: the author arrives to manage a PR firm and ends up as a bohemian soap-opera star.

Peter Fleming *One's Company: a Journey to China* (Pimlico, UK) and *News from Tartary* (Birlinn, UK; Tarcher, US). The former is an amusing account of a journey through Russia and Manchuria to China in the 1930s. En route, Peter Fleming (brother of Ian) encounters a wild assortment of Chinese and Japanese officials, and the puppet emperor Henry Pu Yi himself. *News from*

Tartary records an epic journey of 5600km across the roof of the world to Kashmir in 1935.

Peter Hessler *River Town – Two Years on the Yangtze* (John Murray, UK; Perennial, US). One of the best of the mini-genre "how I taught English for a couple of years in China and survived". The book accepts China's positive aspects and avoids cynicism when dealing with social problems and contradictions. His other books, *Oracle Bones* and *Country Driving*, are informative if unfocused travelogues based on interviews.

Somerset Maugham *On a Chinese Screen* (Vintage, UK; Arno Press, US). Brief, sometimes humorous, and often biting sketches of the European missionaries, diplomats and businessmen whom Maugham encountered in China between 1919 and 1921; worth reading for background detail.

Matthew Polly *American Shaolin* (Little, Brown). A stereotypical weakling, Polly dropped out of a US college to spend two years studying kung fu at the legendary Shaolin temple. Not just the macho romp you'd expect, the book is self-deprecating, funny and steers clear of cultural cringe.

Marco Polo *The Travels* (Penguin, UK & US). Said to have inspired Columbus, *The Travels* is a fantastic read, full of amazing details picked up during Polo's 26 years of wandering in Asia between Venice and the court of Kublai Khan. It's not, however, a coherent history, having been ghost-written by a novelist from Marco's notes.

Vikram Seth *From Heaven Lake: Travels through Sinkiang and Tibet* (Phoenix, UK; Random House, US). A student for two years at Nanjing University, Seth set out in 1982 to return home to Delhi via Tibet and Nepal. This account of how he hitched his way through four provinces – Xinjiang, Gansu, Qinghai and Tibet – is in the finest tradition of the early travel books.

Colin Thubron *Behind the Wall* (Vintage, UK; HarperCollins, US). A thoughtful and superbly poetic description of an extensive journey through China just after it opened up in the early 1980s. The single best piece of travel writing to have come out of modern China.

Guides and reference books

Kit Chow and Ione Kramer *All the Tea in China* (Sinolingua, UK; China Books, US). Everything you need to know about Chinese teas, from variations in growing and processing techniques to a rundown of fifty of the most famous brews. Good fun and nicely illustrated.

Mackinnon, Showler and Phillipps *A Field Guide to the Birds of China* (Oxford University Press, UK). By far the best book on the subject, with over 1300 species illustrated (mostly in colour), plus outline text descriptions and distribution maps.

Jessica Rawson *Ancient China: Art and Archaeology* (Icon, UK & US). By an oriental antiquities specialist at the British Museum, this scholarly introduction to Chinese art puts the subject in historical context. Beginning in Neolithic times, the book explores the technology and social organization that shaped its development up to the Han dynasty.

George Schaller *Wildlife of the Tibetan Steppe* (University of Chicago Press, US). Reference book on the mammals – especially the rare Tibetan antelope – that inhabit the inhospitable Chang Tang region, by a zoologist who has spent over thirty years studying China's wildlife.

Karen Smith *Nine Lives: Birth of Avant-Garde Art in New China* (Scalo, US). Explores the development of the Chinese contemporary art scene through dense studies of nine of its founders and key players.

Mary Tregear *Chinese Art* (Thames and Hudson, UK & US). An authoritative, clearly written and well-illustrated summary of the main strands in Chinese art from Neolithic times, through the Bronze Age and up to the twentieth century.

Cookery

Fuchsia Dunlop *Sichuan Cookery* (Penguin, UK; W. W. Norton, US). The best available English-language cookbook on Chinese cuisine, from a talented writer who spent three years honing her skills at a Chengdu cookery school. Dishes smell, look and taste exactly as you find them in Sichuan.

Hsiang Ju Lin and Tsuifeng Lin *Chinese Gastronomy* (Tuttle, US). A classic work, relatively short on recipes but strong on cooking methods and philosophy – essential reading for anyone serious about learning the finer details of Chinese cooking. Wavers in and out of print, sometimes under different titles; look for Lin as the author name.

Kenneth Lo *Chinese Food* (Faber and Faber, US). Good general-purpose cookbook covering a wide range of methods and styles, from Westernized dishes to regional specialities.

Wei Chuan Cultural Education Foundation *Vegetarian Cooking* and *Chinese Dim Sum* (Wei Chuan, Taiwan). Two in a series of excellent, easy-to-follow cookbooks published by the Taiwanese Wei Chuan cooking school; simplified versions of classic dishes that produce good results. Not available in China, but easy enough to find in major bookstores in the West.

Religion and philosophy

Asiapac series (Asiapac Books, Singapore). These entertaining titles, available in Hong Kong and Beijing, present ancient Chinese philosophy in comic-book format, making it accessible without losing its complexity. They are all well written and well drawn. Particularly good are the *Book of Zen*, a collection of stories and parables, and the *Sayings of Confucius*.

Kenneth Chen *Buddhism in China* (Princeton University Press, US). Very helpful for tracing the origin of Buddhist thought in China, the development of its many different schools and the four-way traffic of influence between India, Tibet, Japan and China.

Chuang Tzu *The Book of Chuang Tzu* (Penguin, UK & US). Wonderful Taoist parables, written in antiquity by a philosopher who clearly had a keen sense of humour and a delight in life's very inexplicability.

Confucius *The Analects* (Penguin, UK & US). Good modern translation of this classic text, a collection of Confucius's teachings focusing on morality and the state.

Lao Zi *Tao Te Ching* (Penguin, UK & US). The collection of mystical thoughts and philosophical speculation that form the basis of Taoist philosophy.

Arthur Waley *Three Ways of Thought in Ancient China* (Routledge-Curzon UK; Stanford University Press US). Translated extracts from the writings of three of the early philosophers – Zhuang Zi, Mencius and Han Feizi. A useful introduction.

Biographies and autobiographies

Anchee Min *Red Azalea* (Orion, UK; Berkley, US). Half-autobiography, half-novel, this beautifully written book is an unusually personal and highly romantic account of surviving the Cultural Revolution.

Dalai Lama *Freedom in Exile* (Abacus, UK; HarperCollins, US). The autobiography of the charismatic, Nobel Prize-winning Fourteenth Dalai Lama.

Richard Evans *Deng Xiaoping* (Penguin, UK & US). The basic handbook if you want to understand the motives and inspirations that lay behind one of the most influential men in modern China.

Jung Chang *Wild Swans* (Perennial, UK; Touchstone, US). Enormously popular in the West, this three-generation family saga was banned in China for its honest account of the horrors of life in turbulent twentieth-century China. As well as being a good read, it serves as an excellent introduction to modern Chinese history.

Ma Jian *Red Dust* (Vintage, UK; Anchor, US). Facing arrest for spiritual pollution, writer and artist Ma Jian fled Beijing to travel around China's remotest corners in the 1980s, often in extreme poverty. This picaresque tale of China in the first phase of its opening up is told in lively prose and offers the kind of insights only an alienated insider could garner. Another work, *The Noodle Maker*, is a satirical novel about a propagandist and a professional blood donor. An early travelogue, *Stick out Your Tongue,* set in a gritty and unromanticized Tibet, has also been translated into English.

John Man *Genghis Khan* (Bantam, UK). Lively and readable biography of the illiterate nomad who built the biggest empire the world has ever seen, intercut with Man's travels to Mongolia and China to find his tomb.

Naisingoro Pu Yi *From Emperor to Citizen* (FLP). The autobiography of the young boy who was born into the Qing imperial family and chosen by the Japanese to become the puppet emperor of the state of Manchukuo in 1931.

Philip Short *Mao: a Life* (John Murray, UK; Owl Books, US). Despite its length, an extremely readable account of Mao and his times – even if the Great Helmsman's ideologies are becoming ever less relevant in contemporary China.

Hugh Trevor-Roper *Hermit of Peking: the Hidden Life of Sir Edmund Backhouse* (Eland, UK). Sparked by Backhouse's thoroughly obscene memoirs, *Hermit of Peking* uses external sources in an attempt to uncover the facts behind the extraordinarily convoluted life of Edmund Backhouse – Chinese scholar, eccentric recluse and phenomenal liar – who lived in Beijing from the late nineteenth century until his death in 1944.

Marina Warner *The Dragon Empress* (Vintage, UK; Atheneum, US). An exploration of the life of Cixi, one of only two women rulers of China, that lays bare the complex personality whose conservatism, passion for power, vanity and greed had such a great impact on the events that culminated in the collapse of the imperial ruling house and the founding of the republic.

Literature

Modern writing

JG Ballard *Empire of the Sun* (Harper Perennial, UK; Simon and Schuster, US). This, the best literary evocation of old Shanghai, is a compelling tale of how the gilded life of expat Shanghai collapsed into chaos with the onset of war, based on the author's own experience growing up in a Japanese internment camp. It was made into a pretty decent film by Steven Spielberg.

Pearl S. Buck *The Good Earth* (Simon and Schuster, UK; Washington Square Press, US). The best story from a writer who grew up in China during the early twentieth century, *The Good Earth* follows the fortunes of the peasant Wang Lung from his wedding day to his dotage, as he struggles to hold onto his land for his family through a series of political upheavals.

Louis Cha *The Book and the Sword* (Oxford). Northwestern China becomes a battleground for secret societies, evil henchmen, Muslim warlords and sword-wielding Taoists as a quest to save a valuable copy of the Quran uncovers a secret that threatens to topple the Qing emperor. Written in the 1950s by China's foremost martial-arts novelist, it has inspired numerous films and TV shows.

Chen Yuanbin *The Story of Qiuju* (Panda Books, China). A collection of four tales, of which the title story, about a peasant woman pushing for justice after her husband is assaulted by the village chief, was made into a film by award-winning director Zhang Yimou.

Chun Sue *Beijing Doll* (Abacus Books, UK; Riverhead Books, US). A rambling *roman à clef* about a confused teenage girl who has unsatisfactory sexual encounters with preening rock and rollers – it has to be said, if it wasn't China it wouldn't be interesting.

Robert Van Gulik *The Judge Dee Mysteries* (Perennial, UK; University of Chicago Press, US). Sherlock Holmes-style detective stories set in the Tang dynasty and starring the wily Judge Dee, who gets tough on crime as detective, judge and jury. Recommended are *The Red Pavilion*, *Murder in Canton* and *The Chinese Nail Murders*. Fun, informative and unusual.

Guo Xiaolu *The Village of Stone* (Chatto and Windus, UK). A sensitive study of a woman reflecting on her life as a modern metropolitan citizen, and her tough country childhood. Her later *A Chinese English Dictionary for Lovers*, concerning a Chinese girl's journey of self-discovery when she comes to London, is a bright, lively book, daringly written in Chinglish.

James Hilton *Lost Horizon* (Summersdale, UK; Pocket, US). The classic 1930s novel of longevity in a secret Tibetan valley, which gave the world – and the Chinese tourist industry – the myth of Shangri-la.

Lao She *Rickshaw Boy* (FLP). Lao She was driven to suicide during the Cultural Revolution for his belief that all politics were inherently unjust. The story is a haunting account of a young rickshaw-puller in pre-1949 Beijing.

Lu Xun *The True Story of Ah Q* (FLP). Widely read in China today, Lu Xun is regarded as the father of modern Chinese writing. *Ah Q* is one of his best tales, short, allegorical and cynical, about a simpleton who is swept up in the 1911 revolution.

Mian Mian *Candy* (Back Bay Books, US). This louche tale of self-destruction, drugs, sex and navel-gazing garnered its colourful Shanghai authoress a reputation as China's foremost literary wild child – it helped, of course, that it was banned.

Mo Yan *The Garlic Ballads* (Penguin, UK & US). A hard-hitting novel of rural life by one of China's greatest modern writers, banned in China.

Qian Zhongshu *Fortress Besieged* (Penguin, UK). Scathing satire, set in the 1930s, about a failed student who uses a fake degree to win a teaching post and a wife. Now highly influential, it was banned for years in both mainland China and Taiwan.

Qiu Xiaolong *When Red Is Black, A Loyal Character Dancer, A Case of Two Cities, The Mao Case*. Procedural detective stories set in Shanghai, featuring the poetry-loving Inspector Chen. Though sometimes Qiu seems more interested in examining society and morals than in weaving a mystery, his stories of corrupt officials, sharp operators and compromised cops are some of the best evocations of modern China in contemporary English-language fiction.

Neal Stephenson *The Diamond Age* (Penguin). An ambitious, flawed but brilliant science fiction novel set in China, in "Nu-Chusan" – a re-imagining of Shanghai's concession era in the age of nano-technology.

Wang Shuo *Playing for Thrills* (Penguin, UK & US) and *Please Don't Call Me Human* (No Exit Press, UK; Oldcastle, US). Wang Shuo writes in colourful Beijing dialect about the city's wide boys and chancers. *Playing for Thrills* is fairly representative – a mystery story whose boorish narrator spends most of his time drinking, gambling and chasing girls. *Please Don't Call Me Human* is a satire of modern China as a place where greed is everything, as the Party turns a dignified martial artist into a vacuous dancer in order to win an Olympic gold medal.

Wei Hui *Shanghai Baby* (Constable and Robinson, UK; Washington Square Press, US). Salacious chick-lit about a Chinese girl who can't decide between her Western lover and her drug-addled Chinese boyfriend (though her real love seems to be for designer labels). Notable for the Chinese authorities' attempts to ban it and for spawning a genre in modern Chinese writing, the urban girl's saucy confessional.

Classics

Asiapac series (Asiapac Books, Singapore). Chinese classics and folk tales entertainingly rendered into cartoon format. Titles include *Journey to the West*, *Tales of Laozhai* and *Chinese Eunuchs*.

Cyril Birch (ed) *Anthology of Chinese Literature* (Avalon Travel, US). Two volumes that cover three thousand years of poetry, philosophy, drama, biography and prose fiction, with interesting variations of translation.

Cao Xueqing and Gao E *Dream of Red Mansions/Story of the Stone* (FLP; Penguin, UK & US). This intricate eighteenth-century tale of manners follows the fortunes of the Jia clan through the emotionally charged adolescent lives of Jia Baoyu and his two girl cousins, Lin Daiyu and Xue Baochai. The full translation fills five paperbacks, but there's also a much simplified English version available in China.

Li Bai and Du Fu *Li Po and Tu Fu* (Penguin, UK & US). Fine translations of China's greatest Tang-dynasty poets, with a detailed introduction that puts them in context. Li Bai was a drunken spiritualist, Du Fu a sharp-eyed realist, and their surprisingly accessible and complementary works form an apex of Chinese literature.

Luo Guanzhong *Romance of the Three Kingdoms* (FLP China). Despite being written 1200 years after the events it portrays, this tale vividly evokes the battles, political schemings and myths surrounding China's turbulent Three Kingdoms period. One of the world's great historical novels.

Pu Songling *Strange Tales from a Chinese Studio* (Penguin, UK & US). Born during the early Qing dynasty, Pu Songling spent his life amassing these contemporary folk tales, which range from the almost believable to downright weird stories of spirits, ghosts and demons.

Shi Nai'an and Luo Guanzhong *Outlaws of the Marsh* aka *The Water Margin* (FLP China). A heavy dose of popular legend as a group of Robin Hood-like outlaws takes on the government in feudal times. Wildly uneven, and hard to read right through, but some amazing characters and set pieces.

Sun Zi *The Art of War* (Penguin, UK; Running Press, US). "Lure them with the prospect of gain, then take them by confusion". This classic on strategy and warfare, told in pithy maxims, is as relevant today as when it was written around 500 BC. A favourite with the modern business community.

Wu Cheng'en *Journey to the West* (FLP China). Absurd, lively rendering of the Buddhist monk Xuanzang's pilgrimage to India to collect sacred scriptures, aided by Sandy, Pigsy and the irrepressible Sun Wu Kong, the monkey king. Arthur Waley's version, *Monkey* (Penguin, UK), retains the spirit of the tale while shortening the hundred-chapter opus to paperback length.

Language

Language

Chinese

As the **most widely spoken** language on earth, Chinese can hardly be overlooked. Chinese is, strictly speaking, a series of **dialects** spoken by the dominant ethnic group within China, the Han. Indeed, the term most commonly used by the Chinese themselves to refer to the language is **hanyu**, meaning "Han-language", though *zhongyu*, *zhongwen* and *zhongguohua* are frequently used as well. However, non-Han peoples such as Uyghurs and Tibetans speak languages which have little or nothing to do with Chinese.

The dialects of *hanyu* are diverse, having about as much in common as, say, German and English. The better-known and most distinct dialects include those spoken around China's coastal fringes, such as **Shanghainese** (*shanghai hua*), **Fujianese** (*minnan hua*) and **Cantonese** (*guangdong hua* or *yueyu*). Cantonese and Fujianese are themselves languages of worldwide significance, being the dialects spoken by the people of Hong Kong and among Overseas Chinese communities, particularly those in Southeast Asia.

What enables Chinese from different parts of the country to converse is **Mandarin Chinese**. Historically based on the language of Han officialdom in the Beijing area, Mandarin has been promoted over the past hundred years or so to be the official, unifying language of the Chinese people. It is known in mainland China as **putonghua** – "common language". As the language of education, government and the media, Mandarin is understood to a greater or lesser extent by the vast majority of Han Chinese, and by many non-Han as well.

Another element tying the various dialects together is the Chinese **script**. No matter how different two dialects may sound when spoken, once they are written down in the form of Chinese characters they become mutually comprehensible again, as the different dialects use the same written characters.

From the point of view of foreigners, the main distinguishing characteristic of Chinese is that it is a **tonal** language: in order to pronounce a word correctly, it is necessary to know not only its sound but also its correct tone. Accuracy in **pronunciation** is particularly important in Chinese, for which an understanding of the **pinyin** phonetic system is vital (see p.998).

Chinese characters

There are tens of thousands of **Chinese characters**, though the vast majority are obsolete – you need about 2500 to read a newspaper, and even educated Chinese are unlikely to know more than ten thousand. The characters themselves are **pictograms**, each representing a **concept** rather than a specific pronunciation. Chinese speakers have to memorize the sounds of individual characters, and the meanings attached to them.

Although to untrained eyes many Chinese characters seem impossibly complex, there is a logic behind their structure which helps in their memorization. Firstly, each character is written using an exact number of brush (or pen) **strokes**: thus the character for "mouth", which forms a square, is always written using only three strokes: first the left side, then the top and right side together, and finally the base. Secondly, characters can very broadly be broken up into two components, which often also exist as characters in their own right: a **main** part, which frequently gives a clue as to the pronunciation; and a **radical**, which usually appears on the left side of the character and which vaguely categorizes the meaning. As an example, the character for "mother" is made up of the character for "horse" (to which it sounds similar), combined with a radical which means "female". In some cases, the connection between the pictogram and its meaning is obvious – the character *mu*, wood, resembles a tree – though others require some lateral thinking or have become so abstract or complex that the meaning is hidden.

Given the time and difficulty involved in **learning characters**, and the negative impact this has had on the general level of literacy, in 1954 a couple of thousand of the most common characters were **simplified**, making them easier to learn and quicker to write. These simplified characters were adopted in mainland China and Singapore, but Hong Kong and Taiwan continue to use the older, traditional forms.

Grammar

Chinese **grammar** is relatively simple. There is no need to conjugate verbs, decline nouns or make adjectives agree – being attached to immutable Chinese characters, Chinese words simply cannot have different "endings". Instead, context and fairly rigid rules about word order are relied on to make those distinctions of time, number and gender that Indo-European languages are so concerned with. Instead of cumbersome tenses, the Chinese make use of words such as "yesterday" or "tomorrow"; instead of plural endings they simply state how many things there are, or use quantifier words equivalent to "some" or "many".

For English-speakers, **Chinese word order** follows the familiar subject-verb-object pattern, and you'll find that by simply stringing words together you'll be producing fairly grammatical Chinese. Just note that adjectives, as well as all qualifying and describing phrases, precede nouns.

Pronunciation and pinyin

Back in the 1950s it was hoped eventually to replace Chinese characters with a regular alphabet of Roman letters, and to this end the **pinyin** system was devised. Basically, pinyin is a way of using the Roman alphabet (except the letter "v") to write out the sounds of Mandarin Chinese, with Mandarin's four tones represented by **accents** above each syllable. Other dialects of Chinese, such as Cantonese – having nine tones – cannot be written in pinyin.

The aim of replacing Chinese characters with pinyin was abandoned long ago, but in the meantime pinyin has one very important function, that of helping foreigners to pronounce Chinese words. However, in pinyin the letters do not all have the sounds you would expect, and you'll need to spend an hour or two learning these. You'll often see pinyin in China, on street signs and shop displays, but only well-educated locals know the system well. Occasionally, you will come across **other systems** of rendering Mandarin into Roman letters, such as **Wade-Giles**, which writes Mao Zedong as Mao Tse-tung. These forms are no longer used in mainland China, but you may see them in Western books about China.

The Chinese terms in this book have been given both in characters and in pinyin; the pronunciation guide below is your first step to making yourself comprehensible. Don't get overly paranoid about your tones: with the help of context, intelligent listeners should be able to work out what you are trying to say. If you're just uttering a single word, however, for example a place name – without a context – you need to hit exactly the right tone, otherwise don't be surprised if nobody understands you.

The tones

There are **four tones** in Mandarin Chinese, and every syllable of every word is characterized by one of them, except for a few syllables which are considered toneless. This emphasis on tones does not make Chinese a particularly musical language – English, for example, uses all of the tones of Chinese and many more. The difference is that English uses tone for effect – exclaiming, questioning, listing, rebuking and so on. In English, to change the tone is to change the mood or the emphasis; in Chinese, to change the tone is to change the word itself.

First or "High" *ā ē ī ō ū*. In English this level tone is used when mimicking robotic or very boring, flat voices.

Second or "Rising" *á é í ó ú*. Used in English when asking a question showing surprise, for example "eh?".

Third or "Falling-rising" *ǎ ě ǐ ǒ ǔ* . Used in English when echoing someone's words with a measure of incredulity. For example, "John's dead." "De-ad?!".

Fourth or "Falling" *à è ì ò ù*. Often used in English when counting in a brusque manner – "One! Two! Three! Four!".

Toneless A few syllables do not have a tone accent. These are pronounced without emphasis, such as in the English **up**on.

Note that if there are two consecutive characters with the third tone, the first character is pronounced as though it carries the second tone.

Consonants

Most consonants are pronounced in a similar way to their English equivalents, with the following exceptions:

c as in ha**ts**

g is hard as in **g**od (except when preceded by "n", when it sounds like sa**ng**)

q as in **ch**eese

x has no direct equivalent in English, but you can make the sound by sliding from an "s" sound to a "sh" sound and stopping midway between the two

z as in su**ds**

zh as in fud**ge**

Vowels and diphthongs

As in most languages, the vowel sounds are rather harder to quantify than the consonants. The examples here give a rough description of the sound of each vowel followed by related combination sounds.

a usually somewhere between f**a**r and m**a**n

ai as in **eye**

ao as in c**ow**

e usually as in f**ur**

ei as in g**ay**

en is an unstressed sound as at the end of hyph**en**

eng as in s**ung**

er as in **fur** (ie with a stressed "r")

i usually as in **tea**, except in *zi*, *ci*, *si*, *ri*, *zhi*, *chi* and *shi*, when it is a short clipped sound like the American military "**sir**"

ia as in **yak**

ian as in **yen**

ie as in **yeah**

o as in **bore**

ou as in **show**

ü as in the German ü (make an "ee" sound and glide slowly into an "oo"; at the mid-point between the two sounds you should hit the ü sound)

u usually as in **fool** except where *u* follows *j*, *q*, *x* or *y*, when it is always pronounced **ü**

ua as in **suave**

uai as in **why**

ue as though contracting "you" and "air" together, **you'air**

ui as in **way**

uo as in **wore**

Useful words and phrases

Chinese put their **family names first** followed by their given names, the reverse of Western convention. The vast majority of Chinese family names comprise a single character, while given names are either one or two characters long. So a man known as Zhang Dawei has the family name of Zhang, and the given name of Dawei.

When asked for their name, the Chinese tend to provide either just their family name, or their whole name. In **formal situations**, you might come across the terms "Mr" (*xiansheng*), "Mrs" (*taitai*, though this is being replaced by the more neutral term *airen*) or "Miss" (*xiaojie*), which are attached after the family name: for example, Mr Zhang is *zhang xiansheng*. In more casual encounters, people use familiar terms such as "old" (*lao*) or "young" (*xiao*) attached in front of the family name, though "old" or "young" are more relative terms of status than indications of actual age in this case: Mr Zhang's friend might call him "Lao Zhang", for instance.

Basics

I	我	*wǒ*
You (singular)	你	*nǐ*
He	他	*tā*
She	她	*tā*
We	我们	*wǒmén*
You (plural)	你们	*nǐmén*
They	他们	*tāmén*
I want...	我要	*wǒ yào...*
No, I don't want...	我不要...	*wǒ bú yào...*
Is it possible...?	可不可以...?	*kěbùkěyǐ...?*
It is (not) possible.	(不)可以	*(bù) kěyǐ*
Is there any/Have you got any...?	有没有...?	*yǒuméi yǒu...?*
There is/I have	有	*yǒu*
There isn't/I haven't	没有	*méiyǒu*
Please help me	请帮我忙	*qǐng bāng wǒ máng*
Mr...	...先生	*xiānshēng*
Mrs...	...太太	*tàitài*
Miss...	...小姐	*xiǎojiě*

Communicating

I don't speak Chinese	我不会说中文	*wǒ bú huì shuō zhōngwén*
My Chinese is terrible	我的中文很差	*wǒ de zhōngwén hěn chà*
Can you speak English?	你会说英语吗?	*nǐ huì shuō yīngyǔ ma?*
Can you get someone who speaks English?	请给我找一个会说英语的人	*qǐng gěi wǒ zhǎo yí ge huì shuō yīngyǔ de rén?*
Please speak slowly	请说得慢一点	*qǐng shuōde màn yìdiǎn*
Please say that again	请再说一遍	*qǐng zài shuō yí biàn*
I understand	我听得懂	*wǒ tīngdedǒng*
I don't understand	我听不懂	*wǒ tīngbùdǒng*
I can't read Chinese characters	我看不懂汉字	*wǒ kànbùdong hànzì*
What does this mean?	这是什么意思?	*zhè shì shénme yìsì?*
How do you pronounce this character?	这个字怎么念?	*zhè ge zì zěnme niàn?*

Greetings and basic courtesies

Hello/How do you do?	你好	*nǐ hǎo?*
How are you?	你好吗?	*nǐ hǎo ma?*
I'm fine	我很好	*wǒ hěn hǎo*
Thank you	谢谢	*xièxie*
Don't mention it/You're welcome	不客气	*búkèqì*
Sorry to bother you...	麻烦你	*máfan nǐ*
Sorry/I apologize	对不起	*duìbùqǐ*
It's not important/No problem	没关系	*méi guānxi*
Goodbye	再见	*zài jiàn*
Chitchat	聊天	*liáotiān*
What country are you from?	你是哪个国家的?	*nǐ shì nǎ ge guójiā de?*
Britain	英国	*yīngguó*
Ireland	爱尔兰	*ài'ěrlán*
America	美国	*měiguó*
Canada	加拿大	*jiā'nádà*
Australia	澳大利亚	*àodàlìyà*
New Zealand	新西兰	*xīnxīlán*
China	中国	*zhōngguó*
Outside China	外国	*wàiguó*
What's your name?	你叫什么名字?	*nǐ jiào shěnme míngzi?*
My name is...	我叫...	*wǒ jiào...*
Are you married?	你结婚了吗?	*nǐ jiéhūn le ma?*
I am (not) married	我(没有)结婚(了)	*wǒ (méiyǒu) jiéhūn (le)*
Have you got (children)?	你有没有孩子?	*nǐ yǒu méiyǒu háizi?*
Do you like...?	你喜不喜欢...?	*nǐ xǐ bùxǐhuān...?*
I (don't) like...	我不喜欢...	*wǒ (bù) xǐhuān...*
What's your job?	你干什么工作?	*nǐ gàn shénme gōngzuò?*
I'm a foreign student	我是留学生	*wǒ shì liúxuéshēng*
I'm a teacher	我是老师	*wǒ shì laǒshī*
I work in a company	我在一个公司工作	*wǒ zài yí ge gōngsī gōngzuò*
I don't work	我不工作	*wǒ bù gōngzuò*

Clean/dirty	干净/脏	*gānjìng/zāng*
Hot/cold	热/冷	*rè/lěng*
Fast/slow	快/慢	*kuài/màn*
Pretty	漂亮	*piàoliàng*
Interesting	有意思	*yǒuyìsi*

Numbers

Zero	零	*líng*
One	一	*yī*
Two	二/两	*èr/liǎng**
Three	三	*sān*
Four	四	*sì*
Five	五	*wǔ*
Six	六	*liù*
Seven	七	*qī*
Eight	八	*bā*
Nine	九	*jiǔ*
Ten	十	*shí*
Eleven	十一	*shíyī*
Twelve	十二	*shíèr*
Twenty	二十	*èrshí*
Twenty-one	二十一	*èrshíyī*
One hundred	一百	*yībǎi*
Two hundred	二百	*èrbǎi*
One thousand	一千	*yīqiān*
Ten thousand	一万	*yīwàn*
One hundred thousand	十万	*shíwàn*
One million	一百万	*yībǎiwàn*

**liǎng* is used when enumerating, for example "two people" is *liǎng ge rén*. *èr* is used when counting.

Time

Now	现在	*xiànzài*
Today	今天	*jīntiān*
(In the) morning	早上	*zǎoshàng*
(In the) afternoon	下午	*xiàwǔ*
(In the) evening	晚上	*wǎnshàng*
Tomorrow	明天	*míngtiān*
The day after tomorrow	后天	*hòutiān*
Yesterday	昨天	*zuótiān*
Week/month/year	星期/月/年	*xīngqī/yuè/nián*
Monday	星期一	*xīngqī yī*
Tuesday	星期二	*xīngqī èr*
Wednesday	星期三	*xīngqī sān*
Thursday	星期四	*xīngqī sì*
Friday	星期五	*xīngqī wǔ*
Saturday	星期六	*xīngqī liù*

Sunday	星期天	*xīngqī tiān*
What's the time?	几点了?	*jǐdiǎn le?*
10 o'clock	十点钟	*shídiǎn zhōng*
10.20	十点二十	*shídiǎn èrshí*
10.30	十点半	*shídiǎn bàn*

Travelling and getting about town

North	北	*běi*
South	南	*nán*
East	东	*dōng*
West	西	*xī*
Airport	机场	*jīchǎng*
Ferry dock	船码头	*chuánmǎtóu*
Left-luggage office	寄存处	*jìcún chù*
Ticket office	售票处	*shòupiào chù*
Ticket	票	*piào*
Can you buy me a ticket to…?	可不可以给我买到…的票?	*kěbùkěyǐ gěi wǒ mǎi dào de piào?*
I want to go to…	我想到…去	*wǒ xiǎng dào qù*
I want to leave at (8 o'clock)	我想(八点钟)离开	*wǒ xiǎng (bā diǎn zhōng) líkāi*
When does it leave?	什么时候出发?	*shénme shíhòu chūfā?*
When does it arrive?	什么时候到?	*shénme shíhòu dào?*
How long does it take?	路上得多长时间?	*lùshàng děi duōcháng shíjiān?*
CAAC	中国民航	*zhōngguó mínháng*
CITS	中国国际旅行社	*zhōngguó guójì lǚxíngshè*
Train	火车	*huǒchē*
(Main) Train station	主要火车站	*(zhǔyào) huǒchēzhàn*
Bus	公共汽车	*gōnggòng qìchē*
Bus station	汽车站	*qìchēzhàn*
Long-distance bus station	长途汽车站	*chángtú qìchēzhàn*
Express train/bus	特快车	*tèkuài chē*
Fast train/bus	快车	*kuài chē*
Ordinary train/bus	普通车	*pǔtōng chē*
Minibus	小车	*xiǎo chē*
Sleeper bus	卧铺车	*wòpù chē*
Lower bunk	下铺	*xiàpù*
Middle bunk	中铺	*zhōngpù*
Upper bunk	上铺	*shàngpù*
Hard seat	硬座	*yìngzuò*
Soft seat	软座	*ruǎnzuò*
Hard sleeper	硬卧	*yìngwò*
Soft sleeper	软卧	*ruǎnwò*
Soft-seat waiting room	软卧候车室	*ruǎnwò hòuchēshì*
Timetable	时间表	*shíjiān biǎo*
Upgrade ticket	补票	*bǔpiào*
Unreserved ticket	无座	*wúzuò*
Returned ticket window	退票	*tuìpiào*
Platform	站台	*zhàntái*

Getting about town

Map	地图	*dìtú*
Where is…?	……在哪里?	*zài nǎlǐ?*
Go straight on	往前走	*wǎng qián zǒu*
Turn right	往右拐	*wǎng yòu guǎi*
Turn left	往左拐	*wǎng zuǒ guǎi*
Taxi	出租车	*chūzū chē*
Please use the meter	请打开记价器	*qǐng dǎkāi jìjiàqì*
Underground/Subway station	地铁站	*dìtiě zhàn*
Bicycle	自行车	*zìxíngchē*
I want to rent a bicycle	我想租自行车	*wǒ xiǎng zū zìxíngchē*
How much is it per hour?	一个小时得多少钱?	*yí gè xiǎoshí děi duōshǎo qián?*
Bus	公共汽车	*gōnggòngqìchē*
Which bus goes to…?	几路车到...去?	*jǐ lù chē dào…qù?*
Number (10) bus	(十)路车	*(shí) lù chē*
Does this bus go to…?	这车到...去吗?	*zhè chē dào…qù ma?*
When is the next bus?	下一班车几点开?	*xià yì bān chē jǐ diǎn kāi?*
The first bus	头班车	*tóubān chē*
The last bus	末班车	*mòbān chē*
Please tell me where to get off	请告诉我在哪里下车	*qǐng gàosù wǒ zài nǎlǐ xià chē*
Museum	博物馆	*bówùguǎn*
Temple	寺院	*sìyuàn*
Church	教堂	*jiàotáng*
Mosque	清真寺	*qīngzhēn sì*
Toilet (men's)	男厕所	*nán cèsuǒ*
Toilet (women's)	女厕所	*nǚ cèsuǒ*

Accommodation

Accommodation	住宿	*zhùsù*
Hotel (upmarket)	宾馆	*bīnguǎn*
Hotel (downmarket)	招待所，旅馆	*zhāodàisuǒ, lǚguǎn*
Hostel	旅社	*lǚshè*
Foreigners' guesthouse (at a university)	外国专家楼	*wàiguó zhuānjiā lóu*
Is it possible to stay here?	能不能住在这里?	*néng bù néng zhù zài zhèlǐ ?*
Can I have a look at the room?	能不能看一下房间？	*néng bù néng kàn yíxià fángjiān?*
I want the cheapest bed you've got	我要你最便宜的床位	*wǒ yào nǐ zuì piányi de chuángwèi*
Single room	单人房	*dānrénfáng*
Twin room	双人房	*shuāngrénfáng*
Three-bed room	三人房	*sānrénfáng*
Dormitory	多人房	*duōrénfáng*
Suite	套房	*tàofáng*
(Large) bed	(大)床	*(dà) chuáng*
Passport	护照	*hùzhào*
Deposit	押金	*yājīn*

Key	钥匙	*yàoshi*
I want to change my room	我想换一个房间	*wǒ xiǎng huàn yí ge fángjiān*
Laundry (the action)	洗衣服	*xǐyīfu*
Laundry (the place)	洗衣店	*xǐyīdiàn*
Washing powder	洗衣粉	*xǐyīfěn*

Shopping, money and banks, and the police

How much is it?	这是多少钱?	*zhè shì duōshǎo qián?*
That's too expensive	太贵了	*tài guì le*
Have you got anything cheaper?	有没有便宜一点的?	*yǒu méiyǒu piányi yìdiǎn de?*
Department store	百货商店	*bǎihuò shāngdiàn*
Market	市场	*shìchǎng*
¥1 (RMB)	一块(人民币)	*yí kuài (rénmínbì)*
US$1	一块美金	*yí kuài měijīn*
£1	一个英磅	*yí gè yīngbàng*
HK$1	一块港币	*yí kuài gǎngbì*
Change money	换钱	*huàn qián*
Bank of China	中国银行	*zhōngguó yínháng*
Travellers' cheques	旅行支票	*lǚxíngzhīpiào*
PSB	公安局	*gōng'ān jú*

Communications

Post office	邮电局	*yóudiànjú*
Envelope	信封	*xìnfēng*
Stamp	邮票	*yóupiào*
Airmail	航空信	*hángkōngxìn*
Surface mail	平信	*píngxìn*
Telephone	电话	*diànhuà*
International telephone call	国际电话	*guójì diànhuà*
Reverse charges/collect call	对方付钱电话	*duìfāngfùqián diànhuà*
Fax	传真	*chuánzhēn*
Telephone card	电话卡	*diànhuàkǎ*
I want to make a telephone call to (Britain)	我想给(英国)打电话	*wǒ xiǎng gěi (yīngguó) dǎ diànhuà*
I want to send a fax to (US)	我想给(美国)发一个传真	*wǒ xiǎng gěi (měiguó) fā yí ge chuánzhēn*
Can I receive a fax here?	能不能在这里收传真?	*néng bù néng zài zhèlǐ shōu chuánzhēn?*
Internet café	网吧	*wǎngbā*

Health

Hospital	医院	*yīyuàn*
Pharmacy	药店	*yàodiàn*
Medicine	药	*yào*
Chinese medicine	中药	*zhōngyào*
Diarrhoea	腹泻	*fùxiè*
Vomit	呕吐	*ǒutù*
Fever	发烧	*fāshāo*

I'm ill	我生病了	*wǒ shēngbìng le*
I've got flu	我感冒了	*wǒ gǎnmào le*
I'm (not) allergic to	我对…(不)过敏	*wǒ duì…(bù) guòmǐn*
Antibiotics	抗生素	*kàngshēngsù*
Condom	避孕套	*bìyùntào*
Mosquito coil	蚊香	*wénxiāng*
Mosquito netting	蚊帐纱	*wénzhàngshā*

A food and drink glossary

The following lists should help out in deciphering the characters on a Chinese menu – if they're written clearly. If you know what you're after, try sifting through the staples and cooking methods to create your order, or sample one of the everyday or regional suggestions, many of which are available all over the country. Don't forget to tailor your demands to the capabilities of where you're ordering, however – a street cook with a wok isn't going to be able to whip up anything more complicated than a basic stir-fry. Note that some items, such as seafood and *jiaozi*, are ordered by weight.

General

Restaurant	餐厅	*cāntīng*
House speciality	拿手好菜	*náshǒuhaǒcài*
How much is that?	多少钱?	*duōshǎo qián?*
I don't eat (meat)	我不吃(肉)	*wǒ bù chī (ròu)*
I'm Buddhist/I'm vegetarian	我是佛教徒/我只吃素	*wǒ shì fójiàotú/wǒ zhǐ chī sù*
I would like...	我想要....	*wǒ xiǎng yào...*
Local dishes	地方菜	*dìfāng cài*
Snacks	小吃	*xiǎochī*
Menu/set menu/English menu	菜单/套餐/英文菜单	*càidān/tàocān/yīngwén càidān*
Small portion	少量	*shǎoliàng*
Chopsticks	筷子	*kuàizi*
Knife and fork	刀叉	*dāochā*
Spoon	勺子	*sháozi*
Waiter/waitress	服务员/小姐	*fúwùyuán/xiǎojiě*
Bill/cheque	买单	*mǎidān*
Cook these ingredients together	一快儿做	*yíkuàir zuò*
Not spicy/no chilli please	请不要辣椒	*qǐng búyào làjiāo*
Only a little spice/chilli	一点辣椒	*yìdiǎn làjiāo*
500 grams	斤	*jīn*
1 kilo	公斤	*gōngjīn*

Drinks

Beer	啤酒	*píjiǔ*
Sweet fizzy drink	汽水	*qìshuǐ*
Coffee	咖啡	*kāfēi*
Milk	牛奶	*niúnǎi*

(Mineral) water	(矿泉)水	*(kuàngquán) shuǐ*
Wine	葡萄酒	*pútáojiǔ*
Spirits	白酒	*báijiǔ*
Soya milk	豆浆	*dòujiāng*
Yoghurt	酸奶	*suānnǎi*

Teas

Tea	茶	*chá*
Black tea	红茶	*hóng chá*
Chrysanthemum	菊花茶	*júhuā chá*
Green tea	绿茶	*lǜ chá*
Iron Buddha	铁观音	*tiěguānyīn*
Jasmine	茉莉花茶	*mòlìhuā chá*
Pu'er	普洱茶	*pǔ'ěr chá*

Staple foods

Aubergine	茄子	*qiézi*
Bamboo shoots	笋尖	*sǔnjiān*
Bean sprouts	豆芽	*dòuyá*
Beans	豆	*dòu*
Beef	牛肉	*niúròu*
Bitter gourd	葫芦	*húlu*
Black bean sauce	黑豆豉	*hēidòuchǐ*
Bread	面包	*miànbāo*
Buns (filled)	包子	*bāozi*
Buns (plain)	馒头	*mántou*
Carrot	胡萝卜	*húluóbo*
Cashew nuts	腰果	*yāoguǒ*
Cauliflower	菜花	*càihuā*
Chicken	鸡	*jī*
Chilli	辣椒	*làjiāo*
Chocolate	巧克力	*qiǎokèlì*
Coriander (leaves)	香菜	*xiāngcài*
Crab	蟹	*xiè*
Cucumber	黄瓜	*huángguā*
Duck	鸭	*yā*
Eel	鳝鱼	*shànyú*
Eggs (fried)	煎鸡蛋	*jiānjīdàn*
Fish	鱼	*yú*
Fried dough stick	油条	*yóutiáo*
Garlic	大蒜	*dàsuàn*
Ginger	姜	*jiāng*
Green pepper (capsicum)	青椒	*qīngjiāo*
Green vegetables	绿叶素菜	*lǜ yè*
Jiaozi (ravioli, steamed or boiled)	饺子	*jiǎozi*
Lamb	羊肉	*yángròu*
Lotus root	莲心	*liánxīn*
MSG	味精	*wèijīng*

Mushrooms	磨菇	*mógu*
Noodles	面条	*miàntiáo*
Omelette	摊鸡蛋	*tānjīdàn*
Onions	洋葱	*yángcōng*
Oyster sauce	蚝油	*háoyóu*
Pancake	摊饼	*tānbǐng*
Peanut	花生	*huāshēng*
Pork	猪肉	*zhūròu*
Potato (stir-fried)	(炒)土豆	*(chǎo) tǔdòu*
Prawns	虾	*xiā*
Preserved egg	皮蛋	*pídàn*
Rice, boiled	白饭	*báifàn*
Rice, fried	炒饭	*chǎofàn*
Rice noodles	河粉	*héfěn*
Rice porridge (aka "congee")	粥	*zhōu*
Salt	盐	*yán*
Sesame oil	芝麻油	*zhīma yóu*
Sichuan pepper	四川辣椒	*sìchuān làjiāo*
Snails	蜗牛	*wōniú*
Snake	蛇肉	*shéròu*
Soup	汤	*tāng*
Soy sauce	酱油	*jiàngyóu*
Squid	鱿鱼	*yóuyú*
Sugar	糖	*táng*
Tofu	豆腐	*dòufu*
Tomato	蕃茄	*fānqié*
Vinegar	醋	*cù*
Water chestnuts	马蹄	*mǎtí*
White radish	白萝卜	*báiluóbo*
Yam	芋头	*yùtóu*

Cooking methods

Boiled	煮	*zhǔ*
Casseroled (see also "Claypot" opposite)	焙	*bèi*
Deep-fried	油煎	*yóujiān*
Fried	炒	*chǎo*
Poached	白煮	*báizhǔ*
Red-cooked (stewed in soy sauce)	红烧	*hóngshāo*
Roast	烤	*kǎo*
Steamed	蒸	*zhēng*
Stir-fried	清炒	*qīngchǎo*

Everyday dishes

Braised duck with vegetables	炖鸭素菜	*dùnyā sùcài*
Cabbage rolls (stuffed with meat or vegetables)	卷心菜	*juǎnxīn cài*

Chicken and sweetcorn soup	玉米鸡丝汤	*yùmǐ jīsī tāng*
Chicken with bamboo shoots and babycorn	笋尖嫩玉米炒鸡片	*sǔnjiān nènyùmǐ chǎojīpiàn*
Chicken with cashew nuts	腰果鸡片	*yāoguǒ jīpiàn*
Claypot/sandpot (casserole)	沙锅	*shāguō*
Crispy aromatic duck	香酥鸭	*xiāngsūyā*
Egg flower soup with tomato	蕃茄蛋汤	*fānqié dàn tāng*
Egg-fried rice	蛋炒饭	*dànchǎofàn*
Fish-ball soup with white radish	萝卜鱼蛋汤	*luóbo yúdàn tāng*
Fish casserole	焙鱼	*bèiyú*
Fried shredded pork with garlic and chilli	大蒜辣椒炒肉片	*dàsuàn làjiāo chǎoròupiàn*
Hotpot	火锅	*huǒguō*
Kebab	串肉	*chuànròu*
Noodle soup	汤面	*tāngmiàn*
Pork and mustard greens	芥末肉片	*jièmò ròupiàn*
Pork and water chestnut	马蹄猪肉	*mǎtí zhūròu*
Pork and white radish pie	白萝卜肉馅饼	*báiluóbo ròuxiànbǐng*
Prawn with garlic sauce	大蒜炒虾	*dàsuàn chǎoxiā*
"Pulled" noodles	拉面	*lāmiàn*
Roast duck	烤鸭	*kǎoyā*
Scrambled egg with pork on rice	滑蛋猪肉饭	*huádàn zhūròufàn*
Sliced pork with yellow bean sauce	黄豆肉片	*huángdòu ròupiàn*
Squid with green pepper and black beans	豆豉青椒炒鱿鱼	*dòuchǐ qīngjiāo chǎoyóuyú*
Steamed eel with black beans	豆豉蒸鳝	*dòuchǐ zhēngshàn*
Steamed rice packets wrapped in lotus leaves	荷叶蒸饭	*héyè zhēngfàn*
Stewed pork belly with vegetables	回锅肉	*huíguōròu*
Stir-fried chicken and bamboo shoots	笋尖炒鸡片	*sǔnjiān chǎojīpiàn*
Stuffed bean-curd soup	豆腐汤	*dòufutāng*
Stuffed bean curd with aubergine and green pepper	茄子青椒煲	*qiézi qīngjiāobāo*
Sweet-and-sour spareribs	糖醋排骨	*tángcù páigǔ*
Sweet bean paste pancakes	赤豆摊饼	*chìdòu tānbǐng*
White radish soup	白萝卜汤	*báiluóbo tāng*
Wuntun soup	馄饨汤	*húntun tāng*

Vegetables and eggs

Aubergine with chilli and garlic sauce	大蒜辣椒炒茄子	*dàsuàn làjiāo chǎoqiézi*
Aubergine with sesame sauce	拌茄子片	*bànqiézipiàn*
Bean curd and spinach soup	菠菜豆腐汤	*bōcài dòufu tāng*
Bean-curd slivers	豆腐花	*dòufuhuā*
Bean curd with chestnuts	马蹄豆腐	*mǎtí dòufu*

Braised mountain fungus	炖香菇	*dùnxiānggū*
Egg fried with tomatoes	蕃茄炒蛋	*fānqié chǎodàn*
Fried bean curd with vegetables	豆腐素菜	*dòufu sùcài*
Fried bean sprouts	炒豆芽	*chǎodòuyá*
Monks' vegetarian dish (stir-fry of mixed vegetables and fungi)	罗汉斋	*luóhànzhāi*
Pressed bean curd with cabbage	卷心菜豆腐	*juǎnxīncài dòufu*
Spicy braised aubergine	香茄子条	*xiāngqiézitiáo*
Stir-fried bamboo shoots	炒冬笋	*chǎodōngsǔn*
Stir-fried mushrooms	炒鲜菇	*chǎoxiān'gū*
Vegetable soup	素菜汤	*sùcài tāng*

Regional dishes

Northern

Aromatic fried lamb	炒羊肉	*chǎoyángròu*
Beijing (Peking) duck	北京烤鸭	*běijīng kǎoyā*
Fish with ham and vegetables	火腿素菜鱼片	*huǒtuǐ sùcài yúpiàn*
Fried prawn balls	炒虾球	*chǎoxiāqiú*
Lion's head (pork rissoles casseroled with greens)	狮子头	*shīzitóu*
Mongolian hotpot	蒙古火锅	*ménggǔ huǒguō*
Red-cooked lamb	红烧羊肉	*hóngshāo yángròu*

Eastern

Beggars' chicken (baked)	叫花鸡	*jiàohuājī*
Brine duck	盐水鸭	*yánshuǐ yā*
Crab soup	蟹肉汤	*xièròu tāng*
Dongpo pork casserole (steamed in wine)	东坡焙肉	*dōngpō bèiròu*
Drunken prawns	醉虾	*zuìxiā*
Five flower pork (steamed in lotus leaves)	五花肉	*wǔhuāròu*
Fried crab with eggs	蟹肉鸡蛋	*xièròu jīdàn*
Pearl balls (rice-grain-coated, steamed rissoles)	珍珠球	*zhēnzhūqiú*
Shaoxing chicken	绍兴鸡	*shàoxīng jī*
Soup dumplings (steamed, containing jellied stock)	汤包	*tāngbāo*
Steamed sea bass	清蒸鲈鱼	*qīngzhēnglúyú*
Stuffed green peppers	馅青椒	*xiànqīngjiāo*
West Lake fish (braised in a sour sauce)	西湖醋鱼	*xīhúcùyú*
"White-cut" beef (spiced and steamed)	白切牛肉	*báiqiē niúròu*
Yangzhou fried rice	杨州炒饭	*yángzhōu chǎofàn*

Sichuan and western China

Boiled beef slices (spicy)	水煮牛肉	*shuǐzhǔ niúròu*
Carry-pole noodles (with a chilli-vinegar-sesame sauce)	担担面	*dàndànmiàn*
Crackling-rice with pork	爆米肉片	*bàomǐ ròupiàn*
Crossing-the-bridge noodles	过桥面	*guòqiáomiàn*
Deep-fried green beans with garlic	大蒜刀豆	*dàsuàn dāodòu*
Dong'an chicken (poached in spicy sauce)	东安鸡子	*dōng'ān jīzǐ*
Doubled-cooked pork	回锅肉	*huíguōròu*
Dried yoghurt wafers	乳饼	*rǔbǐng*
Dry-fried pork shreds	油炸肉丝	*yóuzhá ròusī*
Fish-flavoured aubergine	鱼香茄子	*yúxiāng qiézi*
Gongbao chicken (with chillies and peanuts)	宫保鸡丁	*gōngbǎo jīdīng*
Green pepper with spring onion and black bean sauce	豆豉青椒	*dòuchǐ qīngjiāo*
Hot and sour soup (flavoured with vinegar and white pepper)	酸辣汤	*suānlà tāng*
Hot-spiced bean curd	麻婆豆腐	*mápódòufu*
Rice-flour balls, stuffed with sweet paste	汤圆	*tāngyuán*
Smoked duck	熏鸭	*xūnyā*
Strange flavoured chicken (with sesame-garlic-chilli)	怪味鸡	*guàiwèijī*
Stuffed aubergine slices	馅茄子	*xiànqiézi*
Tangerine chicken	桔子鸡	*júzijī*
"Tiger-skin" peppers (pan-fried with salt)	虎皮炒椒	*hǔpí chǎojiāo*
Wind-cured ham	火腿	*huǒtuǐ*

Southern Chinese/Cantonese

Baked crab with chilli and black beans	辣椒豆豉焙蟹	*làjiāo dòuchǐ bèixiè*
Barbecued pork ("char siew")	叉烧	*chāshāo*
Casseroled bean curd stuffed with pork mince	豆腐煲	*dòufubǎo*
Claypot rice with sweet sausage	香肠饭	*xiāngchángfàn*
Crisp-skinned pork on rice	脆皮肉饭	*cuìpíròufàn*
Fish-head casserole	焙鱼头	*bèiyútóu*
Fish steamed with ginger and spring onion	清蒸鱼	*qīngzhēngyú*
Fried chicken with yam	芋头炒鸡片	*yùtóu chǎojīpiàn*
Honey-roast pork	叉烧	*chāshāo*
Kale in oyster sauce	蚝油白菜	*háoyóu báicài*
Lemon chicken	柠檬鸡	*níngméngjī*
Litchi (lychee) pork	荔枝肉片	*lìzhīròupiàn*

Salt-baked chicken	盐鸡	*yánjī*
White fungus and wolfberry soup (sweet)	枸杞炖银耳	*gǒuqǐ dùnyín'ěr*

Dim sum

Dim sum	点心	*diǎnxīn*
Barbecued pork bun	叉烧包	*chāshāo bāo*
Crab and prawn dumpling	蟹肉虾饺	*xièròu xiājiǎo*
Custard tart	蛋挞	*dàntà*
Doughnut	炸面饼圈	*zhá miànbǐngquān*
Fried taro and mince dumpling	蕃薯糊饺	*fānshǔ hújiǎo*
Lotus paste bun	莲蓉糕	*liánrónggāo*
Moon cake (sweet bean paste in flaky pastry)	月饼	*yuèbǐng*
Paper-wrapped prawns	纸包虾	*zhǐbāoxiā*
Pork and prawn dumpling	烧麦	*shāomài*
Prawn crackers	虾片	*xiāpiàn*
Prawn dumpling	虾饺	*xiājiǎo*
Prawn paste on fried toast	芝麻虾	*zhīmaxiā*
Shanghai fried meat and vegetable dumpling ("potstickers")	锅贴	*guōtiē*
Spring roll	春卷	*chūnjuǎn*
Steamed spareribs and chilli	排骨	*páigǔ*
Stuffed rice-flour roll	肠粉	*chángfěn*
Stuffed green peppers with black bean sauce	豆豉馅青椒	*dòuchǐ xiànqīngjiāo*
Sweet sesame balls	芝麻球	*zhīma qiú*
Turnip-paste patty	萝卜糕	*luóbo gāo*

Fruit

Fruit	水果	*shuǐguǒ*
Apple	苹果	*píngguǒ*
Banana	香蕉	*xiāngjiāo*
Durian	榴莲	*liúlián*
Grape	葡萄	*pútáo*
Honeydew melon	哈密瓜	*hāmì guā*
Longan	龙眼	*lóngyǎn*
Lychee	荔枝	*lìzhī*
Mandarin orange	橘子	*júzi*
Mango	芒果	*mángguǒ*
Orange	橙子	*chéngzi*
Peach	桃子	*táozi*
Pear	梨	*lí*
Persimmon	柿子	*shìzi*
Plum	李子	*lǐzi*
Pomegranate	石榴	*shíliu*
Pomelo	柚子	*yòuzi*
Watermelon	西瓜	*xīguā*

Glossary

Arhat Buddhist saint.

Bei North.

Binguan Hotel; generally a large one, for tourists.

Bodhisattva A follower of Buddhism who has attained enlightenment, but has chosen to stay on earth to teach rather than enter nirvana; Buddhist god or goddess.

Boxers The name given to an anti-foreign organization which originated in Shandong in 1898 (see p.115 & p.950).

Chorten Tibetan stupa.

CITS China International Travel Service. Tourist organization primarily interested in selling tours, though they can help with obtaining train tickets.

CTS China Travel Service. Tourist organization similar to CITS.

Concession Part of a town or city ceded to a foreign power in the nineteenth century.

Cultural Revolution Ten-year period beginning in 1966 and characterized by destruction, persecution and fanatical devotion to Mao (see p.954).

Dagoba Another name for a stupa.

Dong East.

Dougong Large, carved wooden brackets, a common feature of temple design.

Fandian Restaurant or hotel.

Fen Smallest denomination of Chinese currency – there are one hundred fen to the yuan.

Feng Peak.

Feng shui A system of geomancy used to determine the positioning of buildings.

Gang of Four Mao's widow and her supporters who were put on trial immediately after Mao's death for their role in the Cultural Revolution, for which they were convenient scapegoats.

Ge Pavilion.

Gong Palace; usually indicates a Taoist temple.

Guan Pass; in temple names, usually denotes a Taoist shrine.

Guanxi Literally "connections": the reciprocal favours inherent in the process of official appointments and transactions.

Guanyin The ubiquitous Buddhist Goddess of Mercy, the most popular Bodhisattva in China.

Gulou Drum tower; traditionally marking the centre of a town.

Guomindang (GMD) The Nationalist Peoples' Party. Under Chiang Kai-shek, the GMD fought Communist forces for 25 years before being defeated and moving to Taiwan in 1949, where it remains a major political party.

Hai Sea.

Han Chinese The main body of the Chinese people, as distinct from other ethnic groups such as Uyghur, Miao, Hui or Tibetan.

He River.

Hu Lake.

Hui Muslim minority, mainly based in Gansu and Ningxia. Visually they are often indistinguishable from Han Chinese.

Hutong A narrow alleyway.

I Ching The Book of Changes, an ancient handbook for divination that includes some of the fundamental concepts of Chinese thought, such as the duality *yin* and *yang*.

Inkstones Decoratively carved blocks traditionally used by artists and calligraphers as a palette for mixing ink powder with water.

Jiang River.

Jiao (or **mao**) Ten fen.

Jiaozi Crescent-shaped, ravioli-like dumpling, usually served fried by the plateful for breakfast.

Jie Street.

Kang A raised wooden platform in a Chinese home, heated by the stove, on which the residents eat and sleep.

Kazakh A minority, mostly nomadic, in Xinjiang.

Lamian "Pulled noodles", a Muslim speciality usually served in a spicy soup.

Legalism In the Chinese context, a belief that humans are intrinsically bad and that strict laws are need to rein in their behaviour.

Ling Tomb.

Little Red Book A selection of "Quotations from Chairman Mao Zedong", produced in 1966 as a philosophical treatise for Red Guards during the Cultural Revolution.

Long March The Communists' 9500km tactical retreat in 1934–35 from Guomindang troops.

Lu Street.

Luohan Buddhist disciple.

Mandala Mystic diagram which forms an important part of Buddhist iconography, especially in Tibet.

Mantou Steamed bread bun (literally "bald head").

Men Gate/door.

Miao Temple, usually Confucian.

Middle Kingdom A literal translation of the Chinese words for China.

Nan South.

PLA The People's Liberation Army.

PSB Public Security Bureau, the branch of China's police force which deals directly with foreigners.

Pagoda Tower with distinctively tapering structure, often associated with pseudo-science of *feng shui*.

Pinyin The official system of transliterating Chinese script into Roman characters.

Putonghua Mandarin Chinese; literally "Common Language".

Qianfodong Literally, "Thousand Buddha Cave", the name given to any Buddhist cave site along the Chinese section of the Silk Road.

Qiao Bridge.

RMB Renminbi. Another name for Chinese currency literally meaning "the people's money".

Red Guards The unruly factional forces unleashed by Mao during the Cultural Revolution to find and destroy brutally any "reactionaries" among the populace.

Renmin The people.

SEZ Special Economic Zone. A region in which state controls on production have been loosened and Western techniques of economic management are experimented with.

Sakyamuni Name given to future incarnation of Buddha.

Shan Mountain.

Shi City or municipality.

Shui Water.

Shuijiao Similar to *jiaozi* but boiled or served in a thin soup.

Si Temple, usually Buddhist.

Siheyuan Traditional courtyard house.

Spirit wall Wall behind the main gateway to a house, designed to thwart evil spirits, which, it was believed, could move only in straight lines.

Spirit Way The straight road leading to a tomb, lined with guardian figures.

Stele Freestanding stone tablet carved with text.

Stupa Multi-tiered tower associated with Buddhist temples that usually contains sacred objects.

Sutra Buddhist texts, often illustrative doctrines arranged in prayer form.

Ta Tower or pagoda.

Tian Heaven or the sky.

Taiping Uprising Peasant rebellion against Qing rule during the mid-nineteenth century.

Uyghur Substantial minority of Turkic people, living mainly in Xinjiang.

Waiguoren Foreigner.

Xi West.

Yuan China's unit of currency. Also a courtyard or garden (and the name of the Mongol dynasty).

Yurt Round, felt tent used by nomads. Also known as *ger*.

Zhan Station.

Zhao Temple; term used mainly in Inner Mongolia.

Zhong Middle; China is referred to as *zhongguo*, the Middle Kingdom.

Zhonglou Bell tower, usually twinned with a Gulou.

Zhou Place or region.

Small print and Index

A Rough Guide to Rough Guides

Published in 1982, the first Rough Guide – to Greece – was a student scheme that became a publishing phenomenon. Mark Ellingham, a recent graduate in English from Bristol University, had been travelling in Greece the previous summer and couldn't find the right guidebook. With a small group of friends he wrote his own guide, combining a highly contemporary, journalistic style with a thoroughly practical approach to travellers' needs.

The immediate success of the book spawned a series that rapidly covered dozens of destinations. And, in addition to impecunious backpackers, Rough Guides soon acquired a much broader and older readership that relished the guides' wit and inquisitiveness as much as their enthusiastic, critical approach and value-for-money ethos.

These days, Rough Guides include recommendations from shoestring to luxury and cover more than 200 destinations around the globe, including almost every country in the Americas and Europe, more than half of Africa and most of Asia and Australasia. Our ever-growing team of authors and photographers is spread all over the world, particularly in Europe, the US and Australia.

In the early 1990s, Rough Guides branched out of travel, with the publication of Rough Guides to World Music, Classical Music and the Internet. All three have become benchmark titles in their fields, spearheading the publication of a wide range of books under the Rough Guide name.

Including the travel series, Rough Guides now number more than 350 titles, covering: phrasebooks, waterproof maps, music guides from Opera to Heavy Metal, reference works as diverse as Conspiracy Theories and Shakespeare, and popular culture books from iPods to Poker. Rough Guides also produce a series of more than 120 World Music CDs in partnership with World Music Network.

Visit www.roughguides.com to see our latest publications.

Rough Guide credits

Text editors: Harry Wilson, Andrew Rosenberg
Layout: Pradeep Thapliyal
Cartography: Rajesh Chhibber
Picture editor: Natascha Sturny
Production: Rebecca Short
Proofreaders: Samantha Cook, Grace Pai
Cover design: Nicole Newman, Dan May, Jess Carter
Photographer: Tim Draper
Editorial: **London** Andy Turner, Keith Drew, Edward Aves, Alice Park, Lucy White, Jo Kirby, James Smart, Natasha Foges, James Rice, Emma Beatson, Emma Gibbs, Kathryn Lane, Monica Woods, Mani Ramaswamy, Lucy Cowie, Alison Roberts, Lara Kavanagh, Eleanor Aldridge, Ian Blenkinsop, Charlotte Melville, Joe Staines, Matthew Milton, Tracy Hopkins; **Delhi** Madhavi Singh, Jalpreen Kaur Chhatwal, Jubbi Francis
Design & Pictures: **London** Scott Stickland, Dan May, Diana Jarvis, Mark Thomas, Nicole Newman, Sarah Cummins; **Delhi** Umesh Aggarwal, Ajay Verma, Jessica Subramanian, Ankur Guha, Sachin Tanwar, Anita Singh, Nikhil Agarwal, Sachin Gupta
Production: Liz Cherry, Louise Minihane, Erika Pepe
Cartography: London Ed Wright, Katie Lloyd-Jones; **Delhi** Ashutosh Bharti, Rajesh Mishra, Animesh Pathak, Jasbir Sandhu, Swati Handoo, Deshpal Dabas, Lokamata Sahu
Marketing, Publicity & roughguides.com: Liz Statham
Digital Travel Publisher: Peter Buckley
Reference Director: Andrew Lockett
Operations Coordinator: Becky Doyle
Operations Assistant: Johanna Wurm
Publishing Director (Travel): Clare Currie
Commercial Manager: Gino Magnotta
Managing Director: John Duhigg

Publishing information

This sixth edition published June 2011 by
Rough Guides Ltd,
80 Strand, London WC2R 0RL
11, Community Centre, Panchsheel Park, New Delhi 110017, India

Distributed by the Penguin Group

Penguin Books Ltd,
80 Strand, London WC2R 0RL

Penguin Group (USA)
375 Hudson Street, NY 10014, USA

Penguin Group (Australia)
250 Camberwell Road, Camberwell, Victoria 3124, Australia

Penguin Group (NZ)
67 Apollo Drive, Mairangi Bay, Auckland 1310, New Zealand

Rough Guides is represented in Canada by Tourmaline Editions Inc. 662 King Street West, Suite 304, Toronto, Ontario M5V 1M7

Cover concept by Peter Dyer.

Typeset in Bembo and Helvetica to an original design by Henry Iles.

Printed in Italy by L.E.G.O. S.p.A, Lavis (TN)

1032pp includes index
A catalogue record for this book is available from the British Library
ISBN: 978-1-84836-660-2

1 3 5 7 9 8 6 4 2

Help us update

We've gone to a lot of effort to ensure that the sixth edition of **The Rough Guide to China** is accurate and up-to-date. However, things change – places get "discovered", opening hours are notoriously fickle, restaurants and rooms raise prices or lower standards. If you feel we've got it wrong or left something out, we'd like to know, and if you can remember the address, the price, the hours, the phone number, so much the better.

Please send your comments with the subject line "**Rough Guide China Update**" to ⓔmail@uk.roughguides.com. We'll credit all contributions and send a copy of the next edition (or any other Rough Guide if you prefer) for the very best emails.

Find more travel information, connect with fellow travellers and book your trip on ⓦwww.roughguides.com

Acknowledgements

David Leffman For Narrell, with love. Immense thanks to the following for information, company, conversation and hand-to-hand combat: Kirsten Allen, Heather Bacon, Dr Sarah Bexell, Terry Bolger and Noi, Chicory, Kim Dallas, Dwight, Kieran Fitzgerald, John Gardener, Peter Goff, Michelle Haynes, Chris Horton and Matthew, Jay, Mr Jiang, Joe and Jo, Hope Justman, Emily King, Phillip Kenny, Li Guirong, Li Laoshi, Jacob Lotinga, Faraz Maani, Daniel McCrohan, Darren Novac, Catherine Platt, Rui Xi, Damien Ryan, Amanda Schmidt, Christine Shives, Xiao Shusheng, CS Tang,"Rainbow" Zhu.

Simon Lewis Many thanks to Noe, Du, Craig and Shen Ye, Summer, Ling Ling, Penny, Mark and Tim.

Mark South Thanks to: David Niven, Forbidden City FC, Babi, Sarah, Hsuan-Fen, Simons Lewis and Farnham, Martin, David and all in the press team at the British Red Cross.

Martin Zatko Covered eleven provinces for this guide, and as such feels obliged to apportion most of his gratitude to China's ever-improving trains, as well as Shannon and Jah Ying for pointing out how easy it was to buy plane tickets online. Big shouts out to Irmuun Demberel and the rest of the GTI crew in Beijing, as well as Caroline Tan, Jessica Tou and Nick Bonner. Sorry to the largely Scottish crew in Dunhuang for falling asleep during the World Cup Final, and thanks to Simon Cockerell (cheese on toast), weathergirl Halla (sausage rolls) and sister Nicole (Crouchie chameleon) for making the Germany game so memorable.

Readers' letters

Thanks to all the readers who have taken the time to write in with comments and suggestions (and apologies if we've inadvertently omitted or misspelt anyone's name):

Allan Dreyer Andersen, Richard Conviser, Dennis Conway, Brian Goodness, Carole Grant, Helen Kennedy, Ralph Leitloff, Patsilla Li, Jacob Lotinga, Tristan & Michele McDonald, Kristel Ouwehand, Philip Plowden, Nigel Roese, David Thomas, Clive Walker, Nina Weymann-Schulz, Yeo Whui-Mei.

Photo credits

All photos © Rough Guides except the following:

Introduction

Yao girl, rice terraces © Keren Su/China Span/Corbis
Lion sculpture © Yang Liu/Corbis
Potala Palace © Natalie Tepper/Corbis
Lijiang © Angelo Cavalli/Corbis
Miao girls © Michele Burgess/Alamy
Golden monkeys © Jeremy Woodhouse/Getty
Incense, Emeni Shan © Mosafer/Alamy
Man with horse © Angelo Cavalli/Robert Harding/Corbis
Calligrapher © Andrea Pistolesi/Image Bank/Getty

Things not to miss

01 Li River scenery © Steven Vidler/Eurasia Press/Corbis
02 Bird-watching, Cao Hai © Panorama Stock/Robert Harding
03 Mount Everest © Bjorn Svensson/Robert Harding
04 Terracotta Army © Danny Lehman/Corbis
05 Jiayuguan © Jose Fuste Raga/Corbis
06 Sisters' Meal Festival © Huang Xiaohai/Xinhua/Xinhua Press/Corbis
07 Lijiang © Dang Ngo/ZUMA Press/Axiom
08 Silk Road © Bob Krist/Corbis
09 Yellow River © Aldo Pavan/Superstock
10 Labrang Monastery © Jose Fuste Raga/Corbis
11 The Jokhang © Teh Eng Koon/AFP
12 Beijing duck © Keren Su/China Span
13 Harbin Ice Festival © Iain Masterton/Alamy
14 Confucius Temple © TAO Images Ltd/Alamy
15 Yangzi cruise © Andrew McConnell
17 Changbai Shan © JTB Photo/Superstock
18 Dim sum © Tim Hall/Axiom
19 Temple of Universal Happiness © Steven Vidler/Corbis
20 Great Buddha © JTB Photo/Alamy
21 Sichuan teahouse © Reinhard Krause/Reuters/Corbis
22 Meili Xue Shan © Liu Liqun/Corbis
24 Mogao Caves © Art Archive/Superstock
25 Tiger Leaping Gorge © BambooSIL/Purestock/Superstock
26 Hong Kong © Karen Trist
27 Kashgar Sunday market © Keren Su/Corbis
28 Minority villages © Wong Adam/Redlink/Corbis
29 Hanging Temple © Gardel Bertrand/Hemis/Axiom
30 Tai Shan © Bruno Perousse/Photolibrary

Chinese festivals colour section

Masked dancer © Jason Lee/Corbis
Burning money © Michael Reynolds/Corbis
Mid-Autumn Festival © Jason Lee/Reuters/Corbis
Double Ninth Festival © Sean Yong/Corbis
Dragon Boat Festival © Ed Jones/Getty
Water Splashing Festival © Lu Chuanquan/Corbis
Midi Festival © Chien-Min Chung/In Pictures/Corbis
Litang Horse Festival © Craig Lovell/Corbis

Chinese cuisine colour section

Rice noodle packages © Danita Delimont Creative/Alamy
Chillies © Reuters/Corbis
Rice soup © LOOK GmbH/Alamy
Beijing duck © Aurora Photos/Alamy
Scorpions © Tim Graham/Alamy
Rice dumplings © Tsang Jackie/Redlink/Corbis
Food display © Christian Kober/Robert Harding

Chinese architecture colour section

Temple of Heaven © View Stock/Alamy
Wudang Shan © Ryan Pyle/Corbis
Foshan Ancestral Temple © Panorama Media Ltd/Alamy
Bridge © Seux Paule/Superstock
Hakka homes © Christian Kober/Superstock
China Pavillion © Redlink/Corbis
CCTV building © View Stock/Alamy

Black and whites

p.142 Chengde © Franck Guiziou/Hemis/Corbis
p.168 Dandong © Qi Wanpeng/Xinhua Press
p.204 Pingyao © JBT Photo/Photolibrary
p.294 Suzhou © Christian Kober/Robert Harding/Corbis
p.410 Pottery © Christian Kober/Robert Harding/Corbis
p.476 Hakka home © Li Luan Han/Redlink/Corbis
p.634 Zhijin Caves © An Qi/Alamy
p.680 Men in rice paddy © Dave Stamboulis/age fotostock/Robert Harding
p.744 Pandas © Alfred Cheng Jin/Reuters/Corbis
p.804 Turpan mosque © Tibor Bognar/Corbis
p.886 Jokhang prayer wheels © Yang Liu/Corbis

Index

Map entries are in colour.

The following abbreviations are used throughout this index:

AH Anhui	**HEB** Hebel	**QH** Qinghal
BJ Beijing	**HEN** Henan	**SAX** Shaanxi
CQ Chongqing	**HN** Hainan	**SC** Sichuan
DB Dongbei	**HUB** Hubei	**SD** Shandong
FJ Fujian	**HUN** Hunan	**SX** Shanxi
GD Guangdong	**IM** Inner Mongolia	**T** Tibet
GS Gansu	**JS** Jiangsu	**XJ** Xinjiang
GX Guangxi	**JX** Jiangxi	**YN** Yunnan
GZ Guizhou	**NX** Ningxia	**ZJ** Zhejiang

C

D

E

F

G

H

I

J

K

L

M

N

O

P

T

Map symbols

maps are listed in the full index using coloured text

International boundary
Provincial boundary
Chapter boundary
Disputed boundary
Expressway
Major road
Minor road
Pedestrianized road
Steps
Tunnel
Path
Railway
Metro station & line
Monorail
Funicular railway
Cable car
Ferry route
Waterway & dam
Canal
Wall
River
Gate
Bridge
Mountain range
Mountain peak
Cliffs
Gorge/cutting
Marshland
Waterfall
Spring
Tree
Caves
Swimming pool

Viewpoint
Point of interest
Arch
Statue
Public gardens
Airport
Bus station/depot
Minibus stand/bus stop
Embassy/consulate
Hospital
Internet access
Telecom office
Information office
Post office
Hotel
Restaurant
Skiing area
Museum
Ruins
Tower
Monument
Border-crossing post
Temple/monastery
Pagoda
Mosque
Stupa
Building
Church/cathedral
Market
Stadium
Park
Beach
Cemetery